LAROUSSE

DICTIONNAIRE
DE POCHE

**FRANÇAIS
ANGLAIS**

**ANGLAIS
FRANÇAIS**

Sara . T

LAROUSSE

21, rue du Montparnasse 75283 Paris Cedex 06

© **Larousse/VUEF, 2002**
21, rue du Montparnasse
75283 Paris Cedex 06, France

ISBN 2-03-540060-0
Larousse/VUEF, Paris
Distributeur exclusif au Québec : Messageries ADP, 1751 Richardson, Montréal (Québec)

ISBN 2-03-542010-5
Sales: Houghton Mifflin Company, Boston
Library of Congress CIP Data
has been applied for.

LAROUSSE

POCKET
DICTIONARY

**FRENCH
ENGLISH**

**ENGLISH
FRENCH**

LAROUSSE

21, rue du Montparnasse 75283 Paris Cedex 06

Sommaire

Sommaire	IV
Au lecteur	V
Liste des abréviations	VI-IX
Phonétique	X
Conjugaisons françaises	XI-XV
Conjugaisons anglaises	XVI-XVII
Comment utiliser le dictionnaire	XVII
Dictionnaire Français-Anglais	
Dictionnaire Anglais-Français	

Contents

Contents	IV
Preface	V
List of abbreviations	VI-IX
Phonetics	X
Irregular French verbs	XI-XV
Irregular English verbs	XVI-XVII
How to use the dictionary	XXII
French-English dictionary	
English-French dictionary	

TRADEMARKS
Words considered to be trademarks have been designated in this dictionary by the symbol ®. However, neither the presence nor the absence of such designation should be regarded as affecting the legal status of any trademark.

NOMS DE MARQUE
Les noms de marque sont désignés dans ce dictionnaire par le symbole ®. Néanmoins, ni ce symbole ni son absence éventuelle ne peuvent être considérés comme susceptibles d'avoir une incidence quelconque sur le statut légal d'une marque.

Au lecteur

Ce DICTIONNAIRE LAROUSSE français-anglais, anglais-français est un ouvrage spécialement conçu pour ceux qui apprennent l'anglais.

Avec 55 000 mots et expressions et 80 000 traductions, il couvre l'ensemble de l'anglais contemporain.

Par le traitement clair et détaillé du vocabulaire général, les exemples de constructions grammaticales, les tournures idiomatiques, les indications de sens soulignant la traduction appropriée, le DICTIONNAIRE LAROUSSE français-anglais, anglais-français permet de s'exprimer sans hésiter et sans faire de contresens.

Offrir un outil pratique et pédagogique à tous ceux qui apprennent l'anglais, tel est le but que nous nous sommes fixé avec le DICTIONNAIRE LAROUSSE français-anglais, anglais-français.

L'Éditeur

To our readers

This DICTIONARY has been designed as a reliable and user-friendly tool for use in all language situations. It provides accurate and up-to-date information on written and spoken French and English as they are used today.

Its 55,000 words and phrases and 80,000 translations give you access to French texts of all types. The dictionary aims to be as comprehensive as possible in a book of this size, and includes many proper names and abbreviations, as well as a selection of the most common terms from computing, business and current affairs.

Carefully constructed entries and a clear page design help you to find the translation that you are looking for fast. Examples (from basic constructions and common phrases to idioms) have been included to help put a word in context and give a clear picture of how it is used.

The publisher

Abbreviations

Abréviations

abbreviation	*abbr/abr*	abréviation
adjective	*adj*	adjectif
administration, administrative	ADMIN	administration
adverb	*adv*	adverbe
aeronautics, aviation	AERON/AÉRON	aéronautique
agriculture, farming	AGR(IC)	agriculture
American English	*Am*	anglais américain
anatomy	ANAT	anatomie
archaeology	ARCHAEOL/ ARCHÉOL	archéologie
architecture	ARCHIT	architecture
slang	*arg*	argot
article	*art*	article
astrology	ASTROL	astrologie
astronomy	ASTRON	astronomie
automobile, cars	AUT(OM)	automobile
auxiliary	*aux*	auxiliaire
before noun	*avant n*	avant le nom
– indicates that the translation is always used directly before the noun which it modifies		– appliqué à la traduction d'un adjectif français, indique l'emploi d'un nom anglais avec valeur d'adjectif ; souligne aussi les cas où la traduction d'un adjectif est nécessairement antéposée
Belgian French	*Belg*	belgicisme
biology	BIOL	biologie
botany	BOT	botanique
British English	*Br*	anglais britannique
Canadian English/French	*Can*	canadianisme
chemistry	CHEM/CHIM	chimie
cinema, film-making	CIN(EMA)	cinéma
commerce, business	COMM	commerce
compound	*comp*	nom anglais utilisé en apposition
comparative	*compar*	comparatif
computers, computer science	COMPUT	informatique
conjunction	*conj*	conjonction
construction, building trade	CONSTR	construction, bâtiment
continuous	*cont*	progressif
sewing	COUT	couture
culinary, cooking	CULIN	cuisine, art culinaire
definite	*def/déf*	défini
demonstrative	*dem*	démonstratif
ecology	ÉCOL	écologie
economics	ECON/ÉCON	économie
electricity	ELEC/ÉLECTR	électricité
electronics	ELECTRON/ ÉLECTRON	électronique
especially	*esp*	particulièrement
exclamation	*excl*	interjection

feminine	*f*	féminin
informal	*fam*	familier
figurative	*fig*	figuré
finance, financial	FIN	finances
formal	*fml*	soutenu
soccer	FTBL	football
inseparable	*fus*	non séparable

— shows that a phrasal verb is "fused", i.e. inseparable, e.g. **look after**, e.g. *I looked after him* but not *I looked him after*

— indique qu'un verbe anglais à particule (« phrasal verb ») ne peut pas être séparé de sa particule, par exemple, *I looked after him* et non *I looked him after*

generally, in most cases	*gen/gén*	généralement
geography, geographical	GEOGR/GÉOGR	géographie
geology, geological	GEOL/GÉOL	géologie
geometry	GEOM/GÉOM	géométrie
grammar	GRAM(M)	grammaire
Swiss French	*Helv*	helvétisme
history	HIST	histoire
humorous	*hum*	humoristique
industry	IND	industrie
indefinite	*indef/indéf*	indéfini
informal	*inf*	familier
infinitive	*infin*	infinitif
computers, computer science	INFORM	informatique
exclamation	*interj*	interjection
interrogative	*interr*	interrogatif
invariable	*inv*	invariable
ironic	*iro/iron*	ironique
juridical, legal	JUR	juridique
linguistics	LING	linguistique
literal	*lit/litt*	littéral
phrase(s)	*loc*	locution(s)
adjectival phrase	*loc adj*	locution adjectivale
adverbial phrase	*loc adv*	locution adverbiale
conjunctive phrase	*loc conj*	locution conjonctive
prepositional phrase	*loc prép*	locution prépositionnelle

— adjectives, adverbs and prepositions consisting of more than one word, e.g. **d'affilée**, **par dépit**

— adjectifs, adverbes et prépositions composés de plusieurs mots, **d'affilée, par dépit**, par exemple

masculine	*m*	masculin
mathematics	MATH(S)	mathématiques
medicine	MED/MÉD	médecine
weather, meteorology	METEOR/MÉTÉOR	météorologie
military	MIL	domaine militaire
music	MUS	musique
mythology	MYTH	mythologie
noun	*n*	nom
nautical, maritime	NAUT/NAVIG	navigation
numeral	*num*	numéral
oneself	*o.s.*	

pejorative	*pej/péj*	péjoratif
personal	*pers*	personnel
pharmacology, pharmaceutics	PHARM	pharmacologie
philosophy	PHILO	philosophie
photography	PHOT	photographie
phrase(s)	*phr*	locution(s)
physics	PHYS	physique
plural	*pl*	pluriel
politics	POL(IT)	politique
possessive	*poss*	possessif
past participle	*pp*	participe passé
present participle	*ppr*	participe présent
preposition	*prep/prép*	préposition
pronoun	*pron*	pronom
psychology, psychiatry	PSYCH(OL)	psychologie
past tense	*pt*	passé
	qqch	quelque chose
	qqn	quelqu'un
registered trademark	®	nom déposé
railways	RAIL	rail
relative	*rel*	relatif
religion	RELIG	religion
someone, somebody	*sb*	
school	SCH/SCOL	scolarité
Scottish English	*Scot*	anglais écossais
separable	*sep*	séparable
– shows that a phrasal verb is separable, e.g. **let in, help out**: *I let her in, he helped me out*		– indique qu'un verbe anglais à post-position (« phrasal verb ») peut être séparé de sa particule, par exemple *I let her in, he helped me out*
singular	*sg*	singulier
slang	*sl*	argot
sociology	SOCIOL	sociologie
formal	*sout*	soutenu
stock exchange	ST EX	Bourse
something	*sthg*	
subject	*subj/suj*	sujet
superlative	*superl*	superlatif
technology, technical	TECH(NOL)	domaine technique et technologique
telecommunications	TELEC/TÉLÉCOM	télécommunications
very informal	*tfam*	très familier
television	TV/TÉLÉ	télévision
printing, typography	TYPO	typographie
uncountable noun	*U*	substantif non comptable
– i.e. an English noun which is never used in the plural or with "a" or "an"; used when the French word is or can be a plural, e.g. **applause** *n* (*U*) applaudissements *mpl*, **battement** *nm* beat, beating (*U*)		– désigne en anglais les noms qui ne sont jamais utilisés au pluriel, lorsque le terme français est un pluriel, ou peut être mis au pluriel, par exemple **applause** *n* (*U*) applaudissements *mpl*, **battement** *nm* beat, beating (*U*)

university	UNIV	université
usually	*usu*	habituellement
link verb followed by a predicative adjective or noun	*v attr*	verbe suivi d'un attribut
verb	*vb/v*	verbe
veterinary science	VETER	médecine vétérinaire
intransitive verb	*vi*	verbe intransitif
impersonal verb	*v impers*	verbe impersonnel
very informal	*v inf*	très familier
pronominal verb	*vp*	verbe pronominal
transitive verb	*vt*	verbe transitif
vulgar	*vulg*	vulgaire
zoology	ZOOL	zoologie
cultural equivalent	≃	équivalence culturelle
introduces a new part of speech within an entry	◇	introduit une nouvelle catégorie grammaticale dans une entrée
introduces a sub-entry, such as a plural form with its own specific meaning or a set phrase containing the headword (e.g. a phrasal verb or adverbial phrase)	◆	introduit une sous-entrée, par exemple une forme plurielle ayant un sens propre, ou une locution (locution adverbiale, verbe pronominal, etc.)

The symbol ['] has been used to represent the French "h aspiré", e.g. **hachis** ['aʃi].

Le symbole ['] représente le « h aspiré » français, e.g. **hachis** ['aʃi].

The symbol ['] indicates that the following syllable carries primary stress and the symbol [ˌ] that the following syllable carries secondary stress.

Les symboles ['] et [ˌ] indiquent respectivement un accent primaire et un accent secondaire sur la syllabe suivante.

The symbol [ʳ] in English phonetics indicates that the final "r" is pronounced only when followed by a word beginning with a vowel. Note that it is nearly always pronounced in American English.

Le symbole [ʳ] indique que le « r » final d'un mot anglais ne se prononce que lorsqu'il forme une liaison avec la voyelle du mot suivant ; le « r » final est presque toujours prononcé en anglais américain.

A phonetic transcription has been given where appropriate after every French headword (the main word which starts an entry). All one-word English headwords similarly have phonetics. For English compound headwords, whether hyphenated or of two or more words, phonetics are given for any element which does not appear elsewhere in the dictionary as a headword in its own right.

Une transcription phonétique – quand elle a été jugée nécessaire – suit chaque libellé (terme-vedette de l'entrée) français, ainsi que chaque libellé anglais écrit en un seul mot. Pour les mots composés anglais (avec ou sans trait d'union, et composés de deux éléments ou plus), la phonétique est présente pour ceux des éléments qui n'apparaissent pas dans le dictionnaire en tant que libellé à part entière.

Phonetic Transcription Transcription Phonétique

English Vowels

[ɪ]   pit, big, rid
[e]   pet, tend
[æ]   pat, bag, mad
[ʌ]   putt, cut
[ɒ]   pot, log
[ʊ]   put, full
[ə]   mother, suppose
[iː]   bean, weed
[ɑː]   barn, car, laugh
[ɔː]   born, lawn
[uː]   loop, loose
[ɜː]   burn, learn, bird

English Diphthongs

[eɪ]   bay, late, great
[aɪ]   buy, light, aisle
[ɔɪ]   boy , foil
[əʊ]   no, road, blow
[aʊ]   now, shout, town
[ɪə]   peer, fierce, idea
[eə]   pair, bear, share
[ʊə]   poor, sure, tour

Voyelles françaises

[i]   fille, île
[e]   pays, année
[ɛ]   bec, aime
[a]   lac, papillon
[ɑ]   tas, âme
[o]   drôle, aube
[ɔ]   botte, automne
[u]   outil, goût
[y]   usage, lune
[ø]   aveu, jeu
[œ]   peuple, bœuf
[ə]   le, je

Nasales françaises

[ɛ̃]   limbe, main
[ɑ̃]   champ, ennui
[ɔ̃]   ongle, mon
[œ̃]   parfum, brun

Semi-vowels

you, spaniel
wet, why, twin

Semi-voyelles

[j]   yeux, lieu
[w]   ouest, oui
[ɥ]   lui, nuit

Consonants

pop, people
bottle, bib
train, tip
dog, did
come, kitchen
gag, great
chain, wretched
jig, fridge
fib, physical
vine, livid
think, fifth
this, with
seal, peace
zip, his
sheep, machine
usual, measure
how, perhaps
metal, comb
night, dinner
sung, parking

little, help
right, carry

Consonnes

[p]   prendre, grippe
[b]   bateau, rosbif
[t]   théâtre, temps
[d]   dalle, ronde
[k]   coq, quatre
[g]   garder, épilogue
[tʃ]
[dʒ]
[f]   physique, fort
[v]   voir, rive
[θ]
[ð]
[s]   cela, savant
[z]   fraise, zéro
[ʃ]   charrue, schéma
[ʒ]   rouge, jabot
[h]
[m]   mât, drame
[n]   nager, trône
[ŋ]
[ɲ]   agneau, peigner
[l]   halle, lit
[r]   arracher, sabrebend

Conjugaisons françaises

1. **avoir** : ind prés ai, as, a, avons, avez, ont ; imparfait avais, avais, avait, avions aviez, avaient ; ind fut aurai, auras, aura, aurons, aurez, auront ; subj prés que j'aie, que tu aies, qu'il ait, que nous ayons, que vous ayez, qu'ils aient ; imp aie, ayons ; pprés ayant ; pp eu

2. **être** : ind prés suis, es, est, sommes, êtes, sont ; imparfait étais, étais, était, étions, étiez, étaient ; ind fut serai, seras, sera, serons, serez, seront ; subj prés que je sois, que tu sois, qu'il soit, que nous soyons, que vous soyez, qu'ils soient ; imp sois, soyons ; pprés étant ; pp été

3. **chanter** : ind prés chante, chantes, chante, chantons, chantez, chantent ; imparfait chantais, chantais chantait, chantions, chantiez, chantaient ; ind fut chanterai, chanteras, chantera, chanterons, chanterez, chanteront ; subj prés que je chante, que tu chantes, qu'il chante, que nous chantions, que vous chantiez, qu'ils chantent ; imp chante, chantons ; pprés chantant ; pp chanté

4. **baisser** : ind prés baisse, baissons ; imparfait baissais ; ind fut baisserai ; subj prés que je baisse ; imp baisse, baissons ; pprés baissant ; pp baissé

5. **pleurer** : ind prés pleure, pleurons ; imparfait pleurais ; ind fut pleurerai ; subj prés que je pleure ; imp pleure, pleurons ; pprés pleurant ; pp pleuré

6. **jouer** : ind prés joue, jouons ; imparfait jouais ; ind fut jouerai ; subj prés que je joue ; imp joue, jouons ; pprés jouant ; pp joué

7. **saluer** : ind prés salue; saluons ; imparfait saluais ; ind fut saluerai ; subj prés que je salue ; imp salue, saluons ; pprés saluant ; pp salué

8. **arguer** : ind prés argue, arguons imparfait arguais ; ind fut arguerai ; subj prés que j'argue ; imp argue, arguons ; pprés arguant ; pp argué

9. **copier** : ind prés copie, copions ; imparfait copiais ; ind fut copierai ; subj prés que je copie ; imp copie, copions ; pprés copiant ; pp copié

10. **prier** : ind prés prie, prions ; imparfait priais ; ind fut prierai ; subj prés que je prie ; imp prie, prions ; pprés priant ; pp prié

11. **payer** : ind prés paie, payons, paient ; imparfait payais ; ind fut paierai ; subj prés que je paie ; imp paie, payons ; pprés payant ; pp payé

12. **grasseyer** : ind prés grasseye, grasseyons ; imparfait grasseyais ; ind fut grasseyerai ; subj prés que je grasseye ; imp grasseye, grasseyons ; pprés grasseyant ; pp grasseyé

13. **ployer** : ind prés ploie, ployons, ploient ; imparfait ployais ; ind fut ploierai ; subj prés que je ploie ; imp ploie, ployons ; pprés ployant ; pp ployé

14. **essuyer** : ind prés essuie, essuyons, essuient ; imparfait essuyais ; ind fut essuirai ; subj prés que j'essuie, que nous essuyions ; imp essuie, essuyons ; pprés essuyant ; pp essuyé

15. **créer** : ind prés crée, créons ; Imparfait créais ; ind fut créerai ; subj prés que je crée ; imp crée, créons ; pprés créant ; pp créé

16. **avancer** : ind prés avance, avançons, avancent ; imparfait avançais ; ind fut avancerai ; subj prés que j'avance ; imp avance, avançons , pprés avançant ; pp avancé

17. **manger** : ind prés mange, mangeons ; imparfait mangeais ; ind fut mangerai ; subj prés que je mange ; imp mange, mangeons ; pprés mangeant ; pp mangé

18. **céder** : ind prés cède, cédons, cèdent ; imparfait cédais ; ind fut céderai ; subj prés que je cède ; imp cède, cédons ; pprés cédant ; pp cédé

19. **semer** : ind prés sème, semons sèment ; imparfait semais ; ind fut sèmerai ; subj pres que je sème ; imp sème, semons ; pprés semant ; pp semé

20. **rapiécer** : ind prés rapièce, rapiéçons, rapiècent ; imparfait rapiéçais ; ind fut rapiécerai ; subj prés que je rapièce ; imp rapièce, rapiéçons ; pprés rapiéçant ; pp rapiécé

21. acquiescer : ind prés acquiesce, acquiesçons, acquiescent ; imparfait acquiesçais ; ind fut acquiescerai ; subj prés que j'acquiesce ; imp acquiesce, acquiesçons ; pprés acquiesçant; pp acquiescé

22. siéger : ind prés siège, siégeons, siègent ; imparfait siégeais ; ind fut siégerai ; subj prés que je siège ; imp siège, siégeons ; pprés siégeant; pp siégé

23. déneiger : ind prés déneige, déneigeons ; imparfait déneigeais ; ind fut déneigerai ; subj prés que je déneige ; imp déneige, déneigeons ; pprés déneigeant; pp déneigé

24. appeler : ind prés appelle, appelons, appellent ; imparfait appelais ; ind fut appellerai ; subj prés que j'appelle ; imp appelle, appelons ; pprés appelant ; pp appelé

25. peler : ind prés pèle, pelons, pèlent ; imparfait pelais ; ind fut pèlerai ; subj prés que je pèle ; imp pèle, pelons ; pprés pelant ; pp pelé

26. interpeller : ind prés interpelle, interpellons ; imparfait interpellais ; ind fut interpellerai ; subj prés que j'interpelle ; imp interpelle, interpellons ; pprés interpellant ; pp interpellé

27. jeter : ind prés jette, jetons, jettent; imparfait jetais ; ind fut jetterai ; subj prés que je jette ; imp jette, jetons ; pprés jetant ; pp jeté

28. acheter : ind prés achète, achetons, achètent ; imparfait achetais ; ind fut achèterai ; subj prés que j'achète ; imp achète, achetons ; pprés achetant ; pp acheté

29. dépecer : ind prés dépèce, dépeçons, dépècent ; imparfait dépeçais ; ind fut dépècerai ; subj prés que je dépèce ; imp dépèce, dépeçons ; pprés dépeçant; pp dépecé

30. envoyer : ind prés envoie, envoyons, envoient ; imparfait envoyais ; ind fut enverrai ; subj prés que j'envoie ; imp envoie, envoyons ; pprés envoyant; pp envoyé

31. aller : ind prés vais, allons, vont ; imparfait allais ; ind fut irai ; subj prés que j'aille ; imp va, allons ; pprés allant ; pp allé

32. finir : ind prés finis, finis, finit, finissons, finissez, finissent ; imparfait finissais, finissais, finissait, finissions, finissiez, finissaient; ind fut finirai, finiras, finira, finirons, finirez, finiront ; subj prés que je finisse, que tu finisses, qu'il finisse, que nous finissions, que vous finissiez, qu'ils finissent ; imp finis, finissons ; pprés finissant; pp fini

33. haïr : ind prés je hais, haïssons ; imparfait haïssais ; ind fut haïrai ; subj prés que je haïsse ; imp hais, haïssons ; pprés haïssant ; pp haï

34. ouvrir : ind prés ouvre, ouvrons ; imparfait ouvrais ; ind fut ouvrirai ; subj prés que j'ouvre ; imp ouvre, ouvrons ; pprés ouvrant ; pp ouvert

35. fuir : ind prés fuis, fuyons, fuient ; imparfait fuyais ; ind fut fuirai ; subj prés que je fuie ; imp fuis, fuyons ; pprés fuyant ; pp fui

36. dormir : ind prés dors, dormons ; imparfait dormais ; ind fut dormirai; subj prés que je dorme ; imp dors, dormons ; pprés dormant; pp dormi

37. mentir : ind prés mens, mentons ; imparfait mentais ; ind fut mentirai; subj prés que je mente ; imp mentais ; pprés mentant ; pp menti

38. servir : ind prés sers, servons ; imparfait servais ; ind fut servirai ; subj prés que je serve ; imp sers, servons ; pprés servant; pp servi

39. acquérir : ind prés acquiers, acquérons, acquièrent ; imparfait acquérais ; ind fut acquerrai ; subj prés que j'acquière ; imp acquiers, acquérons ; pprés acquérant ; pp acquis

40 venir : ind prés viens, venons, viennent ; imparfait venais ; ind fut viendrai ; subj prés que je vienne ; imp viens, venons ; pprés venant ; pp venu

41. cueillir : ind prés cueille, cueillons ; imparfait cueillais ; ind fut cueillerai; subj prés que je cueille ; imp cueille, cueillons ; pprés cueillant ; pp cueilli

42. mourir : ind prés meurs, mourons, meurent ; imparfait mourais ; ind fut mourrai ; subj prés que je meure ; imp meurs, mourons ; pprés mourant; pp mort

43. partir : ind prés pars, partons ;
imparfait partais ; ind fut partirai ;
subj prés que je parte ; imp pars,
partons ; pprés partant ; pp parti

44. revêtir : ind prés revêts, revêtons ;
imparfait revêtais ; ind fut revêtirai ;
subj prés que je revête ; imp revêts,
revêtons ; pprés revêtant ; pp revêtu

45. courir : ind prés cours, courons ;
imparfait courais ; ind fut courrai ;
subj prés que je coure ; imp cours,
courons ; pprés courant; pp couru

46. faillir : ind prés faillis, faillissons ;
imparfait faillissais ; ind fut faillirai ;
subj prés que je faillisse ; pprés
faillissant ; pp failli

47. défaillir : ind prés défaille,
défaillons ; imparfait défaillais ;
ind fut défaillirai ; subj prés que je
défaille ; imp défaille, défaillons ;
pprés défaillant ; pp défailli

48. bouillir : ind prés bous, bouillons ;
imparfait bouillais ; ind fut bouillirai ;
subj prés que je bouille ; imp bous,
bouillons ; pprés bouillant ; pp bouilli

49. gésir : ind prés gis, gisons ; imparfait
gisais ; pprés gisant

50. saillir : ind prés il saille, ils saillent ;
imparfait il saillait ; ind fut il saillera ;
subj prés qu'il saille, qu'ils saillent ;
pprés saillant ; pp sailli

51. ouïr : ind prés ouïs, ouïssons ; imparfait ouïssais ; ind fut ouïrai ; subj prés
que j'ouïsse ; imp ouïs, ouïssons ;
pprés oyant ; pp ouï

52. recevoir : ind prés reçois, recevons,
reçoivent ; imparfait recevais ; ind fut
recevrai ; subj prés que je reçoive ;
imp reçois, recevons ; pprés recevant ;
pp reçu

53. devoir : ind prés dois, devons,
doivent ; imparfait devais ; ind fut
devrai ; subj prés que je doive ; pprés
devant ; pp dû

54. mouvoir : ind prés meus, mouvons,
meuvent ; imparfait mouvais ;
ind fut mouvrai ; subj prés meuve,
mouvions, meuvent ; imp meus,
mouvons ; pprés mouvant; pp mû

55. émouvoir : ind prés émeus, émouvons, émeuvent ; imparfait émouvais ;
ind fut émouvrai ; subj prés que
j'émeuve ; imp émeus, émouvons ;
pprés émouvant ; pp ému

56. promouvoir : ind prés promeus,
promouvons, promeuvent ; imparfait
promouvais ; ind fut promouvrai ;
subj prés que je promeuve ;
imp promeus, promouvons ;
pprés promouvant ; pp promu

57. vouloir : ind prés veux, voulons,
veulent ; imparfait voulais ; ind fut
voudrai ; subj prés que je veuille,
que nous voulions, qu'ils veuillent ;
imp veuille, veuillons ; pprés voulant ;
pp voulu

58. pouvoir : ind prés peux, pouvons,
peuvent ; imparfait pouvais ;
ind fut pourrai ; subj prés que je
puisse ; pprés pouvant ; pp pu

59. savoir : ind prés sais, savons ;
imparfait savais ; ind fut saurai ;
subj prés que je sache ; imp sache,
sachons ; pprés sachant ; pp su

60. valoir : ind prés vaux, valons ;
imparfait valais ; ind fut vaudrai ;
subj prés que je vaille ; imp vaux,
valons ; pprés valant ; pp valu

61. prévaloir : ind prés prévaux,
prévalons ; imparfait prévalais ;
nd fut prévaudrai ; subj prés que je
prévale ; imp prévaux, prévalons ;
pprés prévalant ; pp prévalu

62. voir : ind prés vois, voyons, voient ;
imparfait voyais ; ind fut verrai ;
subj prés que je voie ; imp vois,
voyons ; pprés voyant ; pp vu

63. prévoir : ind prés prévois,
prévoyons, prévoient ; imparfait
prévoyais ; ind fut prévoirai ; subj
prés que je prévoie ; imp prévois,
prévoyons ; pprés prévoyant ;
pp prévu

64. pourvoir : ind prés pourvois,
pourvoyons, pourvoient ; imparfait
pourvoyais ; ind fut pourvoirai ;
subj prés que je pourvoie ;
imp pourvois, pourvoyons ;
pprés pourvoyant ; pp pourvu

65. asseoir : ind prés assieds, asseyons,
assoient ; imparfait asseyais ;
ind fut assiérai ; subj prés que
j'asseye ; imp assieds, asseyons ;
pprés asseyant ; pp assis

66. surseoir : ind prés sursois, sur-
soyons, sursoient ; imparfait sur-
soyais ; ind fut surseoirai ; subj prés
que je surseoie ; imp sursois, sur-
soyons ; pprés sursoyant ; pp sursis

67. seoir : ind prés il sied, ils siéent ;
imparfait il seyait ; ind fut il siéra ;
subj prés qu'il siée, qu'ils siéent ;
pprés seyant

68. pleuvoir : ind prés il pleut ; imparfait
il pleuvait ; ind fut il pleuvra ; subj
prés qu'il pleuve ; pprés pleuvant ; pp
plu

69. falloir : ind prés il faut ; imparfait il
fallait ; ind fut il faudra ; subj prés
qu'il faille ; pp fallu

70. échoir : ind prés il échoit, ils
échoient ; imparfait il échoyait ; ind
fut il échoira ; subj prés qu'il échoie ;
pprés échéant ; pp échu

71. déchoir : ind prés déchois,
déchoyons, déchoient ; ind fut
déchoirai ; subj prés que je déchoie,
qu'ils déchoient ; pp déchu

72. choir : ind prés je chois, ils choient ;
ind fut choirai ; pp chu

73. vendre : ind prés vends, vends,
vend, vendons, vendez, vendent ;
imparfait vendais, vendais, vendait,
vendions, vendiez, vendaient ; ind
fut vendrai, vendras, vendra, ven-
drons, vendrez, vendront ; subj prés
que je vende, que tu vendes, qu'il
vende, que nous vendions, que vous
vendiez, qu'ils vendent ; imp vends,
vendons ; pprés vendant ; pp vendu

74. répandre : ind prés répands, répandons ; imparfait répandais ; ind fut
répandrai; subj prés que je répande ;
imp répands, répandons ; pprés
répandant ; pp répandu

75. répondre : ind prés réponds, répondons ; imparfait répondais ; ind fut
répondrai ; subj prés que je réponde ;
imp réponds, répondons; pprés
répondant ; pp répondu

76. mordre : ind prés mors, mordons ;
imparfait mordais ; ind fut mordrai ;
subj prés que je morde ; imp mors,
mordons ; pprés mordant ;
pp mordu

77. perdre : ind prés perds, perdons ;
imparfait perdais ; ind fut perdrai ;
subj prés que je perde ; imp perds,
perdons ; pprés perdant; pp perdu

78. rompre : ind prés romps, rompons ;
imparfait rompais ; ind fut romprai ;
subj prés que je rompe ; imp romps,
rompons ; pprés rompant ; pp rompu

79. prendre : ind prés prends, prenons,
prennent ; imparfait prenais ; ind fut
prendrai ; subj prés que je prenne ;
imp prends, prenons ; pprés prenant ;
pp pris

80. craindre : ind prés crains, craignons ;
imparfait craignais ;
ind fut craindrai ; subj prés que je
craigne ; imp crains, craignons ; pprés
craignant ; pp craint

81. peindre : ind prés peins, peignons ;
imparfait peignais ;
ind fut peindrai ; subj prés que je
peigne ; imp peins, peignons ;
pprés peignant ; pp peint

82. joindre : ind prés joins, joignons ;
imparfait joignais ; ind fut joindrai ;
subj prés que je joigne ; imp joins,
joignons ; pprés joignant ; pp joint

83. battre : ind prés bats, battons ;
imparfait battais ; ind fut battrai ; subj
prés que je batte ; imp bats, battons ;
pprés battant ; pp battu

84. mettre : ind prés mets, mettons ;
imparfait mettais ; ind fut mettrai ;
subj prés que je mette ; imp mets,
mettons ; pprés mettant; pp mis

85. moudre : ind prés mouds, moulons ;
imparfait moulais ;
ind fut moudrai; subj prés que je
moule ; imp mouds, moulons ; pprés
moulant; pp moulu

86. coudre : ind prés couds, cousons ;
imparfait cousait ; ind fut coudrai ;
subj prés que je couse ; imp couds,
cousons ; pprés cousant ; pp cousu

87. absoudre : ind prés absous,
absolvons ; imparfait absolvais ;
ind fut absoudrai ; subj prés que j'absolve ; imp absous, absolvons ; pprés
absolvant ; pp absous

88. résoudre : ind prés résous,
résolvons ; imparfait résolvais ;
ind fut résoudrai ; subj prés que je
résolve ; imp résous, résolvons ;
pprés résolvant; pp résolu

89. suivre : ind prés suis, suivons ;
imparfait suivais ; ind fut suivrai ;
subj prés que je suive ; imp suis, suivons ; pprés suivant ; pp suivi

90. vivre : ind prés vis, vivons ; imparfait
vivais ; ind fut vivrai ; subj prés que je
vive, que nous vivions ; imp vis,
vivons ; pprés vivant ; pp vécu

91. paraître : ind prés parais, paraissons ; imparfait paraissais ; ind fut paraîtrai ; subj prés que je paraisse ; imp parais, paraissons ; pprés paraissant ; pp paru

92. naître : ind prés nais, naissons ; imparfait naissais ; ind fut naîtrai ; subj prés que je naisse ; imp nais, naissons ; pprés naissant ; pp né

93. croître : ind prés croîs, croissons ; imparfait croissait ; ind fut croîtrai ; subj prés que je croisse ; imp croîs, croissons ; pprés croissant ; pp crû

94. accroître : ind prés accrois, accroissons ; imparfait accroissait ; ind fut accroîtrai ; subj prés que j'accroisse ; imp accrois, accroissons ; pprés accroissant ; pp accru

95. rire : ind prés ris, rions ; imparfait riais ; ind fut rirai ; subj prés que je rie ; imp ris, rions ; pprés riant ; pp ri

96. conclure : ind prés conclus, concluons ; imparfait concluais ; ind fut conclurai ; subj prés que je conclue ; imp conclus, concluons ; pprés concluant ; pp conclu

97. nuire : ind prés nuis, nuisons ; imparfait nuisais ; ind fut nuirai ; subj prés que je nuise ; imp nuis, nuisons ; pprés nuisant ; pp nui

98. conduire : ind prés conduis, conduisons ; imparfait conduisais ; ind fut conduirai ; subj prés que je conduise ; imp conduis, conduisons ; pprés conduisant ; pp conduit

99. écrire : ind prés écris, écrivons ; imparfait écrivais ; ind fut écrirai ; subj prés que j'écrive ; imp écris, écrivons ; pprés écrivant ; pp écrit

100. suffire : ind prés suffis, suffisons ; imparfait suffisais ; ind fut suffirai ; subj prés que je suffise ; pprés suffisant ; pp suffi

101. confire : ind prés confis, confisons ; imparfait confisais ; ind fut confirai ; subj prés que je confise ; imp confis, confisons ; pprés confisant ; pp confit

102. dire : ind prés dis, disons ; imparfait disais ; ind fut dirai ; subj prés que je dise ; imp dis, disons ; pprés disant ; pp dit

103. contredire : ind prés contredis, contredisons ; imparfait contredisais ; ind fut contredirai ; subj prés que je contredise ; imp contredis, contredisons ; pprés contredisant ; pp contredit

104. maudire : ind prés maudis, maudissons ; imparfait maudissais ; ind fut maudirai ; subj prés que je maudisse ; imp maudis, maudissons ; pprés maudissant ; pp maudit

105. bruire : ind prés bruis ; imparfait bruyais ; ind fut bruirai ; pp bruit

106. lire : ind prés lis, lisons ; imparfait lisais ; ind fut lirai ; subj prés que je lise, que nous lisions ; imp lis, lisons ; pprés lisant ; pp lu

107. croire : ind prés crois, croyons, croient ; imparfait croyais ; ind fut croirai ; subj prés que je croie ; imp crois, croyons ; pprés croyant ; pp cru

108. boire : ind prés bois, buvons, boivent ; imparfait buvais ; ind fut boirai ; subj prés que je boive ; imp bois, buvons ; pprés buvant ; pp bu

109. faire : ind prés fais, faisons, font ; imparfait faisais ; ind fut ferai, subj prés que je fasse ; imp fais, faisons, faites ; pprés faisant ; pp fait

110. plaire : ind prés plais, plaisons ; imparfait plaisais ; ind fut plairai ; subj prés que je plaise ; imp plais, plaisons ; pprés plaisant ; pp plu

111. taire : ind prés tais, taisons ; imparfait taisais ; ind fut tairai ; subj prés que je taise ; imp tais, taisons ; pprés taisant ; pp tu

112. extraire : ind prés extrais, extrayons, extraient ; imparfait extrayais ; ind fut extrairai ; subj prés que j'extraie ; imp extrais, extrayons ; pprés extrayant ; pp extrait

113. clore : ind prés clos, closons ; ind fut clorai ; subj prés que je close ; imp clos ; pprés closant ; pp clos

114. vaincre : ind prés vaincs, vainquons ; imparfait vainquais ; ind fut vaincrai ; subj prés que je vainque ; imp vaincs, vainquons ; pprés vainquant ; pp vaincu

115. frire : ind prés fris ; ind fut frirai ; imp fris ; pp frit

116. foutre : ind prés fous, foutons ; imparfait foutais ; ind fut foutrai ; subj prés que je foute ; imp fous, foutons ; pprés foutant ; pp foutu

Verbes Irréguliers

Première catégorie

Le prétérit et le participe passé de ces verbes ont la même forme. En voici
quelques-uns parmi les plus fréquents :

bend	→	bent	bind	→	bound
bleed	→	bled	breed	→	bred
bring	→	brought	build	→	built
burn[1]	→	burnt	buy	→	bought
catch	→	caught	cling	→	clung
creep	→	crept	deal	→	dealt
dig	→	dug	dream[1]	→	dreamt
dwell[1]	→	dwelt	feed	→	fed
feel	→	felt	fight	→	fought
find	→	found	flee	→	fled
fling	→	flung	foretell	→	foretold
grind	→	ground	have	→	had
hear	→	heard	hold	→	held
keep	→	kept	kneel[1]	→	knelt
lay	→	laid	lead	→	led
lean[1]	→	leant	leap[1]	→	leapt
learn[1]	→	learnt	leave	→	left
lend	→	lent	light[1]	→	lit
lose	→	lost	make	→	made
mean	→	meant	meet	→	met
pay	→	paid	read	→	read
say	→	said	seek	→	sought
sell	→	sold	send	→	sent
shoot	→	shot	sit	→	sat
sleep	→	slept	slide	→	slid
sling	→	slung	smell[1]	→	smelt
speed	→	sped	spell[1]	→	spelt
spend[1]	→	spent	spill[1]	→	spilt
spit	→	spat	spoil[1]	→	spoilt
stand	→	stood	stick	→	stuck
sting	→	stung	strike	→	struck
sweep	→	swept	swing	→	swung
teach	→	taught	tell	→	told
think	→	thought	understand	→	understood
weep	→	wept	win	→	won
wind	→	wound	withhold	→	withheld
wring	→	wrung			

Première catégorie :
En anglais américain, les
verbes suivis du chiffre[1]
peuvent avoir des formes
régulières en **-ed** (**burned,
spoiled** ...)

Deuxième catégorie :
1 **Ate** (prétérit de **eat**) se prononce [et] en anglais
   britannique et [eɪt] en anglais américain.
2 En anglais américain, une des formes du participe
   passé de **get** est **gotten**.
3 Ces verbes peuvent avoir des formes régulières
   dans certains sens (**show, showed, showed**).

Deuxième catégorie

Le prétérit et le participe passé ont des formes différentes. Voici une liste non exhaustive de ces verbes :

Base v.	Prétérit	Part. Passé	Base v.	Prétérit	Part. Passé
be	was	been	bear	bore	borne
beat	beat	beaten	become	became	become
begin	began	begun	bite	bit	bitten
blow	blew	blown	break	broke	broken
choose	chose	chosen	come	came	come
do	did	done	draw	drew	drawn
drink	drank	drunk	drive	drove	driven
eat	ate[1]	eaten	fall	fell	fallen
fly	flew	flown	forbid	forbade	forbidden
forego	forewent	foregone	foresee	foresaw	foreseen
forget	forgot	forgotten	forgive	forgave	forgiven
freeze	froze	frozen	get	got	got[2]
give	gave	given	go	went	gone
grow	grew	grown	hang[3]	hung	hung
hide	hid	hidden	know	knew	known
lie	lay	lain	mistake	mistook	mistaken
mow[3]	mowed	mown	ride	rode	ridden
ring	rang	rung	rise	rose	risen
run	ran	run	see	saw	seen
shake	shook	shaken	shine[3]	shone	shone
show[3]	showed	shown	shrink	shrank/shrunk	shrunk
sing	sang	sung	sink	sank	sunk
speak	spoke	spoken	spin	span/spun	spun
spring	sprang	sprung	steal	stole	stolen
stink	stank/stunk	stunk	stride	strode	stridden
swear	swore	sworn	swell[3]	swelled	swollen
swim	swam	swum	take	took	taken
tear	tore	torn	throw	threw	thrown
tread	trod	trodden	wake[3]	woke	woken
wear	wore	worn	weave	wove	woven
withdraw	withdrew	withdrawn	write	wrote	written

Troisième catégorie

Ces verbes, d'une seule syllabe, se terminent par **-d** ou **-t** et ont une même forme pour la base verbale, le prétérit et le participe passé :

bet	hit	set
bid	hurt	shut
burst	let	slit
cast (*also* forecast)	put	split
cost	quit	spread
cut	rid	thrust

Comment utiliser le dictionnaire ?

Comment trouver le mot ou l'expression que l'on recherche ?

Il faut d'abord se poser plusieurs questions :
- S'agit-il d'un mot isolé, d'un mot à trait d'union ou d'une abréviation ?
- S'agit-il d'un nom composé ?
- S'agit-il d'une expression ou d'une locution ?
- S'agit-il d'un verbe pronominal ?
- S'agit-il d'un verbe à particules anglais ?
- S'agit-il d'une forme irrégulière ?

Mots isolés, mots à trait d'union et abréviations

En règle générale, on trouve le mot recherché à la place qui lui correspond dans l'ordre alphabétique.

Les entrées commençant par une *majuscule* apparaissent après celles qui s'écrivent de la même façon mais commencent par une minuscule. Si le mot avec majuscule et le mot avec minuscule sont liés du point de vue du sens, on trouvera la version avec majuscule sous son équivalent avec minuscule, après un losange noir (◆). Il s'agit d'un type de « sous-entrée » (voir plus bas).

> **réunion** [reynjɔ̃] *nf* - **1.** [séance] meeting - **2.** [jonction] union, merging.
>
> **Réunion** [reunjɔ̃] *nf* : **(l'île de) la ~** Réunion.

> **congress** ['kɒŋgres] *n* [meeting] congrès *m.* ◆ **Congress** *n Am* POL le Congrès.

Dans certains cas, l'entrée est suivie d'un chiffre en *exposant*. Ceci veut dire que, juste avant ou juste après, figure une autre entrée, elle aussi suivie d'un chiffre, qui s'écrit de la

> **tear**[1] [tɪəʳ] *n* larme *f.*
>
> **tear**[2] [teəʳ] (*pt* **tore**, *pp* **torn**) *vt* [rip] déchirer.

même façon mais a un sens ou une prononciation totalement différents.

Ce sont ce que l'on appelle des homographes. Il faut s'assurer que l'on ne se trompe pas d'entrée. Faisons donc bien attention à la catégorie grammaticale et à la prononciation. Dans l'exemple ci-dessus, les deux mots « tear » n'ont pas la même phonétique ; il faut par ailleurs se demander si l'on recherche un nom (n) ou un verbe transitif (vt).

Les mots comportant un *trait d'union,* un *point* ou une *apostrophe* viennent après ceux qui s'écrivent de la même façon mais sans aucun de ces signes.

> **second hand** ['sekənd-] *n* [of clock] trotteuse *f.*
>
> **second-hand** ['sekənd-] *adj* [goods, shop] d'occasion.

Les entrées portant un *accent* se trouvent après celles qui s'écrivent de la même façon mais sans accent.

> **ou** [u] *conj* [indique une alternative, une approximation] or.
> **où** [u] *pron rel* [spatial] where.

Certains mots sont traités en sous-entrée, précédés d'un losange noir (◆). Il s'agit notamment, comme on l'a vu plus haut, de formes avec majuscule sous la forme équivalente sans majuscule, ou bien de noms placés sous un adjectif.

> **animal, e, aux** [animal, o] *adj* - **1.** [propre à l'animal] animal *(avant n)* - **2.** [instinctif] instinctive. ◆ **animal** *nm* [bête] animal.

Si l'on cherche un nom qui, au *pluriel*, a un sens différent de celui du singulier (comme *glass/glasses* en anglais), c'est sous la forme au singulier qu'on le trouvera : le mot au pluriel y figure en sous-entrée.

> **glass** [glɑːs] ◇ *n* - **1.** [gen] verre *m* - **2.** *(U)* [glassware] verrerie *f*. ◇ *comp* [bottle, jar] en OR de verre ; [door, partition] vitré(e). ◆ **glasses** *npl* [spectacles] lunettes *fpl*.

Certains noms apparaissent directement au pluriel dans la liste alphabétique, soit parce qu'ils n'existent pas au singulier, soit parce que ce dernier est rare (*scissors* en anglais, *abats* en français).

Noms composés

Un nom composé est une expression dotée d'une signification globale, mais constituée de plusieurs mots (p. ex. *homme d'affaires* ou *joint venture*). Dans la partie français-anglais, on trouve ces composés dans le dictionnaire à l'entrée correspondant au premier élément. Ainsi, *homme d'affaires* sera sous *homme*. Au sein d'une entrée, les différents noms composés sont classés par ordre alphabétique, sans tenir compte de la préposition médiane ; dans l'entrée *café*, par exemple, *café au lait* vient après *café glacé* et *café en grains*.

Certains composés français dont le sens est éloigné du mot d'entrée figurent dans l'article après un losange noir (◆).

> **fuseau, x** [fyzo] *nm* - **1.** [outil] spindle - **2.** [pantalon] ski-pants *(pl)*. ◆ **fuseau horaire** *nm* time zone.

Du côté anglais, les noms composés apparaissent comme des entrées à part entière.

Il existe aussi des composés dont les deux éléments sont séparés par un trait d'union. Ils figurent dans le dictionnaire en entrée, par exemple *train-spotter* ou *time-sharing*.

> **blood donor** *n* donneur *m*, -euse *f* de sang.
> **bloodshot** ['blʌdʃɒt] *adj* [eyes] injecté(e) de sang.

Expressions et locutions

Par « expression » on entend un groupe de mots qui se mani-
festent toujours dans le même ordre et qui ont un sens global
(*prendre part à qqch*, *to do sb credit*). C'est notamment
le cas des expressions figurées et idiomatiques, ainsi que des
proverbes (*avoir un chat dans la gorge*, *to pull sb's leg*).

Toutes les expressions sont à chercher sous le premier nom dont elles se com-
posent (*prendre part à qqch* sous *part*, *to do sb credit* sous *credit*). S'il n'y
a pas de nom dans l'expression, on cherchera sous le verbe.

Certaines expressions très figées
ayant une valeur grammaticale globale (locutions) sont traitées en
sous-entrée sous le premier élément
signifiant, précédées du symbole ➤,

part [par] *nf* [de gâteau] portion ; [de bonheur, d'héritage] share ; [partie] **part.**
➤ **d'autre part** *loc adv* besides, moreover.

de façon à mettre en relief la différence de sens et de fonction grammaticale
entre la locution et l'entrée à laquelle elle se rattache.

Verbes pronominaux

La plupart des verbes pronominaux
sont placés en sous-entrée sous la
forme principale qui leur correspond
après le symbole ➤.

cacher [3] [kaʃe] *vt* - **1.** [gén] to hide ; **je ne
vous cache pas que ...** to be honest, ...
- **2.** [vue] to mask. ➤ **se cacher** *vp* : **se
~ (de qqn)** to hide (from sb).

Verbes à particules anglais

Les verbes à particules anglais figurent en sous-entrée sous la forme
principale du verbe.

get [get] (*Br pt & pp* got, *Am pt* got, *pp*
gotten) *vt* [cause to do] : **to ~ sb to do sthg**
faire faire qqch à qqn. ➤ **get along** *vi*
- **1.** [manage] se débrouiller - **2.** [progress]
avancer, faire des progrès - **3.** [have a good
relationship] s'entendre. ➤ **get up** ◇ *vi*
se lever. ◇ *vt fus* [petition, demonstration]
organiser.

Formes irrégulières

Les formes irrégulières des noms,
adjectifs et verbes sont données en
entrée dans le dictionnaire.

belle [bɛl] *adj & nf* ➤ beau.

En outre, une liste des verbes irré-
guliers anglais avec leurs différentes
formes figure en annexe.

went [went] *pt* ▷ **go**.

Comment trouver la bonne traduction anglaise

Une fois que l'on aura localisé en français le mot ou l'expression recherchés, il apparaîtra peut-être qu'il existe plusieurs
traductions possibles. Qu'à cela ne tienne, on trouvera dans
le dictionnaire tous les éléments nécessaires pour identifier la
bonne traduction.

Comment fonctionne une entrée de
dictionnaire ? Examinons l'entrée
sauter.

Les losanges blancs (◇) introduisent
une catégorie grammaticale lorsqu'un même mot peut en avoir plusieurs - ici, *vi* (verbe intransitif) puis
vt (verbe transitif). Voir la liste des
abréviations p. VII-X.

sauter [3] [sote] ◇ *vi* - **1.** [bondir] to
jump, to leap ; ~ **à la corde** to skip ; ~ **de
joie** *fig* to jump for joy ; ~ **au cou de qqn** *fig*
to throw one's arms around sb - **2.** [explo-
ser] to blow up ; [fusible] to blow - **3.** [être
projeté - bouchon] to fly out ; [- serrure] to
burst off ; [- bouton] to fly off - **4.** *fam* [em-
ployé] to get the sack. ◇ *vt* - **1.** [fossé, obs-
tacle] to jump ou leap over - **2.** *fig* [page, re-
pas] to skip.

Chaque catégorie grammaticale est
alors divisée en catégories de sens, introduites par des chiffres en gras (-**1.**, -**2.**),
lorsque le mot a plusieurs sens. Des indicateurs entre crochets ([bondir]) per-
mettent d'identifier le sens recherché.

Imaginons que l'on veuille traduire *tu as sauté une page.*

La phrase à traduire comporte un verbe dont nous savons qu'il peut être soit
intransitif, soit transitif ; ici, c'est le verbe transitif qui nous intéresse (◇ vt)
puisqu'il y a un complément d'objet dans la phrase.

Examinons le sens du verbe : le contexte étant celui d'un livre, c'est dans la
catégorie -**2.** que l'on trouvera la traduction souhaitée, qui est *to skip*.

Examinons à présent l'entrée *page*.

La catégorie grammaticale qui nous
intéresse est la première ◇ nf:
« page » en tant que substantif
féminin. Ensuite, c'est sous la première division sémantique, suivie de

page [paʒ] ◇ *nf* - **1.** [feuillet] page ;
~ **blanche** blank page ; **mettre en ~s** TYPO to
make up (into pages) ; ~ **d'accueil** INFORM
home page - **2.** *loc* : **être à la ~** to be up-to-
date. ◇ *nm* page (boy).

l'indicateur [feuillet], que l'on trouvera la bonne traduction : *page*.

Il ne reste plus qu'à combiner les mots trouvés pour traduire la phrase, en
mettant bien sûr le verbe *to skip* au temps et à la forme voulus : *you have
skipped a page.*

How to use the dictionary

Finding the word or phrase you are seeking

First you can ask yourself some basic questions:
- Is it a single word, a hyphenated word or an abbreviation?
- Is it a compound noun?
- Is it a phrase or an idiom?
- Is it a phrasal verb?
- Is it a reflexive verb?
- Is it an irregular form?

Single words, hyphenated words and abbreviations

As a general rule, you will find the word you are seeking in its alphabetical order in the dictionary. If you wish to translate a French word into English, look in the French-English section. If you seek the meaning of an English term, look in the English-French section.

Words in **bold type** that begin an article are known as "entries". Words that are written with an *initial capital letter* appear as separate entries and are placed after words spelled the same way but beginning with a small letter.

> **china** ['tʃaɪnə] *n* porcelaine *f*.
> **China** ['tʃaɪnə] *n* Chine *f*.

Words with a *hyphen*, a *full stop* or an *apostrophe* come after those spelled the same way but without any of these punctuation marks.

> **am** [æm] ▷ be.
> **a.m.** (*abbr of* **ante meridiem**) : at 3 ~ à 3h (du matin).

French *accented words* come after entries spelled in the same way but unaccented.

> **ou** [u] *conj* [indique une alternative, une approximation] or.
> **où** [u] *pron rel* [spatial] where.

Some entries are followed by a *superscript number*. These are homographs: words that are spelled in the same way but that have distinct meanings or pronunciations. You must be careful to identify correctly the entry you need.

> **mine**[1] [maɪn] *poss pron* le mien (la mienne), les miens (les miennes) (*pl*) ; **that money is ~** cet argent est à moi ...
> **mine**[2] [maɪn] ◇ *n* mine *f*. ◇ *vt* - **1.** [coal, gold] extraire ...

On the French-English side of the dictionary, you will find certain words preceded by a black diamond (◆) and called "subentries". The

> **animal, e, aux** [animal, o] *adj* - **1.** [propre à l'animal] animal (*avant n*) - **2.** [instinctif] instinctive. ◆ **animal** *nm* [bête] animal.

main entry has a masculine and a feminine form; the subentry has only one of these forms.

If you are looking for a noun which in the plural has its own distinct meaning, you will find it under the singular form as a subentry.

> **glass** [glɑːs] ⬦ *n* - **1.** [gen] verre *m* - **2.** *(U)* [glassware] verrerie *f.* ⬦ *comp* [bottle, jar] en OR de verre ; [door, partition] vitré(e). ◆ **glasses** *npl* [spectacles] lunettes *fpl.*

Some plural nouns appear as headwords when they are never or rarely used in the singular, e.g. *sneakers* in English or *abats* in French.

Irregular plurals appear as entries with cross-references to the headword in the singular.

> **man** [mæn] (*pl* **men** [men]) *n* homme *m.*
> **men** [men] *pl* ⊳ **man.**

Compound nouns

A compound noun is a word or expression which has a single meaning but is made up of more than one word, e.g. *gardien de but*. When a French compound noun is made up of several words separated by spaces, you will find it in the dictionary under the first element of the compound (e.g. *gardien de but* under *gardien*).

Some English compound nouns such as kiss of life or virtual reality are presented as separate entries in their alphabetical order in the dictionary.

Phrases and idioms

On the French-English side of the dictionary, phrases and idioms are to be found under the first noun element of the phrase. If there is no noun, you should look under the adjective or else under the verb. On the English-French side, look for the most important word; e.g. in *to fancy doing sthg*, *to take a fancy to* or *fancy that!*, the most important word is *fancy*.

> **fancy** ['fænsɪ] ... ⬦ *n* [desire, liking] envie *f*, lubie *f* ; **to take a ~ to sb** se prendre d'affection pour qqn ; **to take a ~ to sthg** se mettre à aimer qqch ; ... ⬦ *vt* - **1.** *inf* [want] avoir envie de ; **to ~ doing sthg** avoir envie de faire qqch - **2.** *inf* [like] : **I ~ her** elle me plaît - **3.** [imagine] : **~ that!** ça alors!

Some very fixed phrases such as bien entendu or at home appear under the most important element as subentries after the black diamond (◆).

English phrasal verbs

English phrasal verbs (e.g. *to put off*, *to fork out*) are entered under the main form as subentries.

> **fork** [fɔːk] ⬦ *n* - **1.** [for eating] fourchette *f* - **2.** [for gardening] fourche *f* - **3.** [in road] bifurcation *f* ; [of river] embranchement *m.* ⬦ *vi* bifurquer. ◆ **fork out** *inf* ⬦ *vt fus* allonger, débourser. ⬦ *vi* : **to ~ out (for)** casquer (pour).

French reflexive verbs

French reflexive verbs are entered under the main form after the symbol ➡.

rappeler [24] [raple] *vt* - **1.** [gén] to call back ... ➡ **se rappeler** *vp* to remember.

Irregular English verbs

If you are unsure of the infinitive of a verb, refer to pages XII-XIII.

caught [kɔːt] *pt* & *pp* ➪ **catch**.

Irregular forms also appear in the dictionary as entries that are cross-referenced to the main form.

Finding the right translation

Once you have found the word or phrase you are seeking, you will have to identify the right translation. Some entries may have only one translation, but others may be subdivided into different grammatical categories and these in turn may be subdivided into different sense categories. If a word has more than one part of speech, each grammatical category is separated and indicated by a white diamond (◇).

Let us say that you want to translate the sentence *he has skipped a page*.

You must first decide what part of speech *skip* is in this instance. It is a verb with a direct object and therefore you must look for the translation under the transitive verb category, marked "vt" (see pages VII-X for the list of abbreviations). To further reassure you that this is the right category, you will find the noun "page" along with other nouns that are used typically with the verb *skip* in square brackets before the translation. So the translation you need here is *sauter*.

skip [skɪp] ◇ *n* - **1.** [jump] petit saut *m* - **2.** *Br* [container] benne *f.* ◇ *vt* [page, class, meal] sauter. ◇ *vi* - **1.** [gen] sauter, sautiller - **2.** *Br* [over rope] sauter à la corde.

Now look at the word *page*.

Again you must decide what part of speech the word is. Here it is a noun. You will notice that the noun category is divided again into several senses. When a word has several meanings within one part of speech, these are separated into numbered categories. To choose the right numbered category, you must use the information provided in the brackets to pinpoint the exact meaning of the word in its context.

page [peɪdʒ] ◇ *n* - **1.** [of book] page *f* - **2.** [sheet of paper] feuille *f.* ◇ *vt* [in airport] appeler au micro.

In this case, we may assume that it is a page in a book rather than a single sheet of paper so the correct translation is *page*. After the translation you will notice the letter "f" in italics, indicating that the French noun is feminine.

You can translate the sentence, once you have conjugated the verb (see conjugation tables on pages XII-XIII), as: *il a sauté une page*.

a¹, A [a] *nm inv* a, A ; **de A à Z** from beginning to end. **➡ A**

a² ⬦ L▷ **avoir**. ⬦ *(abr de* **are**) a.

à [a] *prép (contraction de à + le =* **au**, *contraction de à + les =* **aux**) **- 1.** [introduisant un complément d'objet indirect] to ; **parler à qqn** to speak to sb ; **donner qqch à qqn** to give sthg to sb, to give sb sthg **- 2.** [introduisant un complément de lieu - situation] at, in ; [- direction] to ; **être à la maison/au bureau** to be at home/at the office ; **il habite à Paris/à la campagne** he lives in Paris/in the country ; **aller à Paris/à la campagne/au Pérou** to go to Paris/to the country/to Peru ; **un voyage à Londres/aux Seychelles** a journey to London/to the Seychelles **- 3.** [introduisant un complément de temps] : **à onze heures** at eleven o'clock ; **au mois de février** in the month of February ; **à lundi!** see you (on) Monday! ; **à plus tard!** see you later! ; **de huit à dix heures** from eight to ten o'clock ; **se situer à une heure/à 10 kilomètres de l'aéroport** to be situated an hour/10 kilometres (away) from the airport **- 4.** [introduisant un complément de manière, de moyen] : **à haute voix** out loud, aloud ; **rire aux éclats** to roar with laughter ; **agir à son gré** to do as one pleases ; **acheter à crédit** to buy on credit ; **à pied/cheval** on foot/horseback **- 5.** [indiquant une caractéristique] with ; **une fille aux cheveux longs** a girl with long hair ; **l'homme à l'imperméable** the man with the raincoat **- 6.** [introduisant un chiffre] : **ils sont venus à dix** ten of them came ; **un livre à 10 euros** a 10-euro book, a book costing 10 euros ; **la vitesse est limitée à 50 km à l'heure** the speed limit is 50 km per ou an hour ; **un groupe de 10 à 12 personnes** a group of 10 to 12 people, a group of between 10 and 12 people ; **deux à deux** two by two **- 7.** [marque l'appartenance] : **c'est à moi/toi/lui/elle** it's mine/yours/his/hers ; **ce vélo est à ma sœur** this bike is my sister's ou belongs to my sister ; **une amie à moi** a friend of mine **- 8.** [introduit le but] : **coupe à champagne** champagne goblet ; **le courrier à poster** the mail to be posted ; **appartement à vendre/louer** flat for sale/to let.

AB *(abr de* **assez bien**) *fair grade (as assessment of schoolwork).*

abaisser [4] [abese] *vt* **- 1.** [rideau, voile] to lower ; [levier, manette] to push ou pull down **- 2.** [diminuer] to reduce, to lower. **➡ s'abaisser** *vp* **- 1.** [descendre - rideau] to fall, to come down ; [- terrain] to fall away **- 2.** [s'humilier] to demean o.s. ; **s'~ à faire qqch** to lower o.s. to do sthg.

abandon [abɑ̃dɔ̃] *nm* **- 1.** [désertion, délaissement] desertion ; **à l'~** [jardin, maison] neglected, in a state of neglect **- 2.** [renonciation] abandoning, giving up **- 3.** [nonchalance, confiance] abandon.

abandonner [3] [abɑ̃dɔne] *vt* **- 1.** [quitter - femme, enfants] to abandon, to desert ; [- voiture, propriété] to abandon **- 2.** [renoncer à] to give up, to abandon **- 3.** [se retirer de - course, concours] to withdraw from **- 4.** [céder] : **~ qqch à qqn** to leave sthg to sb, to leave sb sthg.

abasourdi, e [abazurdi] *adj* stunned.

abat-jour [abaʒur] *nm inv* lampshade.

abats [aba] *nmpl* [d'animal] offal *(U)* ; [de volaille] giblets.

abattement [abatmɑ̃] *nm* **- 1.** [faiblesse physique] weakness **- 2.** [désespoir] dejection **- 3.** [déduction] reduction ; **~ fiscal** tax allowance.

abattis [abati] *nmpl* giblets.

abattoir [abatwar] *nm* abattoir, slaughterhouse.

abattre [83] [abatr] *vt* **- 1.** [faire tomber - mur] to knock down ; [- arbre] to cut down, to fell ; [- avion] to bring down **- 2.** [tuer - gén] to kill ; [- dans un abattoir] to slaughter **- 3.** [épuiser] to wear out ; [démoraliser] to demoralize.

abbaye [abei] *nf* abbey.

abbé [abe] *nm* - **1.** [prêtre] priest - **2.** [de couvent] abbot.

abc [abese] *nm* basics *(pl)*.

abcès [apsɛ] *nm* abscess.

abdiquer [3] [abdike] ◇ *vt* [renoncer à] to renounce. ◇ *vi* [roi] to abdicate.

abdomen [abdɔmɛn] *nm* abdomen.

abeille [abɛj] *nf* bee.

aberrant, e [aberɑ̃, ɑ̃t] *adj* absurd.

abîme [abim] *nm* abyss, gulf.

abîmer [3] [abime] *vt* [détériorer - objet] to damage ; [- partie du corps, vue] to ruin. ◆ **s'abîmer** *vp* [gén] to be damaged ; [fruits] to go bad.

abject, e [abʒɛkt] *adj* despicable, contemptible.

aboiement [abwamɑ̃] *nm* bark, barking *(U)*.

abolir [32] [abɔlir] *vt* to abolish.

abominable [abɔminabl] *adj* appalling, awful.

abondance [abɔ̃dɑ̃s] *nf* - **1.** [profusion] abundance - **2.** [opulence] affluence.

abondant, e [abɔ̃dɑ̃, ɑ̃t] *adj* [gén] plentiful ; [végétation, chevelure] luxuriant ; [pluie] heavy.

abonder [3] [abɔ̃de] *vi* to abound, to be abundant ; ~ **en qqch** to be rich in sthg ; ~ **dans le sens de qqn** to be entirely of sb's opinion.

abonné, e [abɔne] *nm, f* - **1.** [à un journal, à une chaîne de télé] subscriber ; [à un théâtre] season-ticket holder - **2.** [à un service public] consumer.

abonnement [abɔnmɑ̃] *nm* - **1.** [à un journal, à une chaîne de télé] subscription ; [à un théâtre] season ticket - **2.** [au téléphone] rental ; [au gaz, à l'électricité] standing charge.

abonner [3] [abɔne] ◆ **s'abonner** *vp* : **s'~ à qqch** [journal, chaîne de télé] to take out a subscription to sthg ; [service public] to get connected to sthg ; [théâtre] to buy a season ticket for sthg.

abord [abɔr] *nm* : **être d'un ~ facile/difficile** to be very/not very approachable. ◆ **abords** *nmpl* [gén] surrounding area *(sg)* ; [de ville] outskirts. ◆ **d'abord** *loc adv* - **1.** [en premier lieu] first - **2.** [avant tout] : **(tout) d'~** first (of all), in the first place.

abordable [abɔrdabl] *adj* [lieu] accessible ; [personne] approachable ; [de prix modéré] affordable.

aborder [3] [abɔrde] ◇ *vi* to land. ◇ *vt* - **1.** [personne, lieu] to approach - **2.** [question] to tackle.

aborigène [abɔriʒɛn] *adj* aboriginal. ◆ **Aborigène** *nmf* (Australian) aborigine.

abouti, e [abuti] *adj* [projet, démarche] successful.

aboutir [32] [abutir] *vi* - **1.** [chemin] : ~ **à/dans** to end at/in - **2.** [négociation] to be successful ; ~ **à qqch** to result in sthg.

aboyer [13] [abwaje] *vi* to bark.

abrasif, ive [abrazif, iv] *adj* abrasive.

abrégé, e [abreʒe] *adj* abridged.

abréger [22] [abreʒe] *vt* [visite, réunion] to cut short ; [discours] to shorten ; [mot] to abbreviate.

abreuvoir [abrœvwar] *nm* [lieu] watering place ; [installation] drinking trough.

abréviation [abrevjasjɔ̃] *nf* abbreviation.

abri [abri] *nm* shelter ; **à l'~ de** sheltered from ; *fig* safe from ; ~ **de jardin** garden shed.

abricot [abriko] *nm & adj inv* apricot.

abricotier [abrikɔtje] *nm* apricot tree.

abriter [3] [abrite] *vt* - **1.** [protéger] : ~ **qqn/qqch (de)** to shelter sb/sthg (from) - **2.** [héberger] to accommodate. ◆ **s'abriter** *vp* : **s'~ (de)** to shelter (from).

abroger [17] [abrɔʒe] *vt* to repeal.

abrupt, e [abrypt] *adj* - **1.** [raide] steep - **2.** [rude] abrupt, brusque.

abruti, e [abryti] *fam nm, f* moron.

abrutir [32] [abrytir] *vt* - **1.** [abêtir] : ~ **qqn** to deaden sb's mind - **2.** [accabler] : ~ **qqn de travail** to work sb silly.

abrutissant, e [abrytisɑ̃, ɑ̃t] *adj* - **1.** [bruit, travail] stupefying - **2.** [jeu, feuilleton] moronic.

absence [apsɑ̃s] *nf* - **1.** [de personne] absence - **2.** [carence] lack.

absent, e [apsɑ̃, ɑ̃t] ◇ *adj* - **1.** [personne] : ~ **(de)** [gén] away (from) ; [pour maladie] absent (from) - **2.** [regard, air] vacant, absent - **3.** [manquant] lacking. ◇ *nm, f* absentee.

absenter [3] [apsɑ̃te] ◆ **s'absenter** *vp* : **s'~ (de la pièce)** to leave (the room).

absinthe [apsɛ̃t] *nf* [plante] wormwood ; [boisson] absinth.

absolu, e [apsɔly] *adj* [gén] absolute ; [décision, jugement] uncompromising.

absolument [apsɔlymɑ̃] *adv* absolutely.

absorbant, e [apsɔrbɑ̃, ɑ̃t] *adj* - **1.** [matière] absorbent - **2.** [occupation] absorbing.

absorber [3] [apsɔrbe] *vt* - **1.** [gén] to absorb - **2.** [manger] to take.

abstenir [40] [apstənir] ◆ **s'abstenir** *vp*

- 1. [ne rien faire] : **s'~ (de qqch/de faire qqch)** to refrain (from sthg/from doing sthg) **- 2.** [ne pas voter] to abstain.

abstention [apstɑ̃sjɔ̃] *nf* abstention.

abstentionnisme [apstɑ̃sjɔnism] *nm* abstaining.

abstinence [apstinɑ̃s] *nf* abstinence.

abstraction [apstraksjɔ̃] *nf* abstraction ; **faire ~ de** to disregard.

abstrait, e [apstrɛ, ɛt] *adj* abstract.

absurde [apsyrd] *adj* absurd.

absurdité [apsyrdite] *nf* absurdity ; **dire des ~s** to talk nonsense (U).

abus [aby] *nm* abuse ; **~ de confiance** breach of trust ; **~ de pouvoir** abuse of power.

abuser [3] [abyze] *vi* **- 1.** [dépasser les bornes] to go too far **- 2.** [user] : **~ de** [autorité, pouvoir] to overstep the bounds of ; **~ de ses forces** to overexert o.s.

abusif, ive [abyzif, iv] *adj* **- 1.** [excessif] excessive **- 2.** [fautif] improper.

acabit [akabi] *nm* : **du même ~** *péj* of the same type.

acacia [akasja] *nm* acacia.

académicien, enne [akademisjɛ̃, ɛn] *nm, f* academician ; [de l'Académie française] member of the French Academy.

académie [akademi] *nf* **- 1.** SCOL & UNIV ~ regional education authority Br, ≃ school district Am **- 2.** [institut] academy ; **l'Académie française** the French Academy (*learned society of leading men and women of letters*).

acajou [akaʒu] *nm & adj inv* mahogany.

acariâtre [akarjɑtr] *adj* bad-tempered, cantankerous.

acarien [akarjɛ̃] *nm* [gén] acarid ; [de poussière] dust mite.

accablant, e [akablɑ̃, ɑ̃t] *adj* **- 1.** [soleil, chaleur] oppressive **- 2.** [preuve, témoignage] overwhelming.

accabler [3] [akable] *vt* **- 1.** [surcharger] : **~ qqn de** [travail] to overwhelm sb with ; **~ qqn d'injures** to shower sb with abuse **- 2.** [accuser] to condemn.

accalmie [akalmi] *nf litt & fig* lull.

accéder [18] [aksede] ◆ **accéder à** *vt* **- 1.** [pénétrer dans] to reach, to get to **- 2.** [parvenir à] to attain **- 3.** [consentir à] to comply with.

accélérateur [akseleratœr] *nm* accelerator.

accélération [akselerasjɔ̃] *nf* [de voiture, machine] acceleration ; [de projet] speeding up.

accélérer [18] [akselere] ◇ *vt* to acceler-

ate, to speed up. ◇ *vi* AUTOM to accelerate.

accent [aksɑ̃] *nm* **- 1.** [gén] accent ; **~ aigu/grave/circonflexe** acute/grave/circumflex (accent) **- 2.** [intonation] tone ; **mettre l'~ sur** to stress, to emphasize.

accentuation [aksɑ̃tɥasjɔ̃] *nf* [à l'écrit] accenting ; [en parlant] stress.

accentuer [7] [aksɑ̃tɥe] *vt* **- 1.** [insister sur, souligner] to emphasize, to accentuate **- 2.** [intensifier] to intensify **- 3.** [à l'écrit] to put the accent on ; [en parlant] to stress. ◆ **s'accentuer** *vp* to become more pronounced.

acceptable [akseptabl] *adj* satisfactory, acceptable.

acceptation [akseptasjɔ̃] *nf* acceptance.

accepter [4] [aksepte] *vt* to accept ; **~ de faire qqch** to agree to do sthg ; **~ que** (+ *subjonctif*) : **~ que qqn fasse qqch** to agree to sb doing sthg ; **je n'accepte pas qu'il me parle ainsi** I won't have him talking to me like that.

acception [aksepsjɔ̃] *nf* sense.

accès [aksɛ] *nm* **- 1.** [entrée] entry ; **avoir/donner ~ à** to have/to give access to ; **'~ interdit'** 'no entry' **- 2.** [voie d'entrée] entrance **- 3.** [crise] bout ; **~ de colère** fit of anger.

accessible [aksesibl] *adj* [lieu, livre] accessible ; [personne] approachable ; [prix, équipement] affordable.

accession [aksesjɔ̃] *nf* : **~ à** [trône, présidence] accession to ; [indépendance] attainment of.

accessoire [akseswar] ◇ *nm* **- 1.** [gén] accessory **- 2.** [de théâtre, cinéma] prop. ◇ *adj* secondary.

accident [aksidɑ̃] *nm* accident ; **par ~** by chance, by accident ; **~ de la route/de voiture/du travail** road/car/industrial accident.

accidenté, e [aksidɑ̃te] ◇ *adj* **- 1.** [terrain, surface] uneven **- 2.** [voiture] damaged ◇ *nm, f* (*gén pl*) : **~ de la route** accident victim.

accidentel, elle [aksidɑ̃tɛl] *adj* accidental.

acclamation [aklamasjɔ̃] *nf* (*gén pl*) cheers (*pl*), cheering (U).

acclamer [3] [aklame] *vt* to cheer.

acclimatation [aklimatasjɔ̃] *nf* acclimatization.

acclimater [3] [aklimate] *vt* to acclimatize ; *fig* to introduce. ◆ **s'acclimater** *vp* : **s'~ à** to become acclimatized to.

accolade [akɔlad] *nf* - 1. TYPO brace - 2. [embrassade] embrace.

accommodant, e [akɔmɔdɑ̃, ɑ̃t] *adj* obliging.

accommodement [akɔmɔdmɑ̃] *nm* compromise.

accommoder [3] [akɔmɔde] *vt* CULIN to prepare.

accompagnateur, trice [akɔ̃paɲatœr, tris] *nm, f* - 1. MUS accompanist - 2. [guide] guide.

accompagnement [akɔ̃paɲmɑ̃] *nm* MUS accompaniment.

accompagner [3] [akɔ̃paɲe] *vt* - 1. [personne] to go with, to accompany - 2. [agrémenter] : ~ **qqch de** to accompany sthg with - 3. MUS to accompany.

accompli, e [akɔ̃pli] *adj* accomplished.

accomplir [32] [akɔ̃plir] *vt* to carry out. ◆ **s'accomplir** *vp* to come about.

accomplissement [akɔ̃plismɑ̃] *nm* [d'apprentissage] completion ; [de travail] fulfilment.

accord [akɔr] *nm* - 1. [gén & LING] agreement - 2.MUS chord - 3. [acceptation] approval ; **donner son ~ à qqch** to approve sthg. ◆ **d'accord** ◇ *loc adv* OK, all right. ◇ *loc adj* : **être d'~ (avec)** to agree (with) ; **tomber** OU **se mettre d'~** to come to an agreement, to agree.

accordéon [akɔrdeɔ̃] *nm* accordion.

accorder [3] [akɔrde] *vt* - 1. [donner] : ~ **qqch à qqn** to grant sb sthg - 2. [attribuer] : ~ **qqch à qqch** to accord sthg to sthg ; ~ **de l'importance à** to attach importance to - 3. [harmoniser] to match - 4. GRAM : ~ **qqch avec qqch** to make sthg agree with sthg - 5. MUS to tune. ◆ **s'accorder** *vp* - 1. [gén] : **s'~ (pour faire qqch)** to agree (to do sthg) ; **s'~ à faire qqch** to be unanimous in doing sthg - 2. [être assorti] to match - 3. GRAM to agree.

accoster [3] [akɔste] ◇ *vt* - 1. NAVIG to come alongside - 2. [personne] to accost. ◇ *vi* NAVIG to dock.

accotement [akɔtmɑ̃] *nm* [de route] shoulder ; ~ **non stabilisé** soft verge *Br*, soft shoulder *Am*.

accouchement [akuʃmɑ̃] *nm* childbirth ; ~ **sans douleur** natural childbirth.

accoucher [3] [akuʃe] *vi* : ~ **(de)** to give birth (to).

accouder [3] [akude] ◆ **s'accouder** *vp* to lean on one's elbows ; **s'~ à** to lean one's elbows on.

accoudoir [akudwar] *nm* armrest.

accouplement [akupləmɑ̃] *nm* mating, coupling.

accourir [45] [akurir] *vi* to run up, to rush up.

accouru, e [akury] *pp* ▷ **accourir**.

accoutré, e [akutre] *adj péj* : **être bizarrement ~** to be oddly got up.

accoutrement [akutrəmɑ̃] *nm péj* getup.

accoutumer [3] [akutyme] *vt* : ~ **qqn à qqn/qqch** to get sb used to sb/sthg ; ~ **qqn à faire qqch** to get sb used to doing sthg. ◆ **s'accoutumer** *vp* : **s'~ à qqn/qqch** to get used to sb/sthg ; **s'~ à faire qqch** to get used to doing sthg.

accréditer [3] [akredite] *vt* [rumeur] to substantiate ; ~ **qqn auprès de** to accredit sb to.

accro [akro] *fam* ◇ *adj* : ~ **à** hooked on. ◇ *nmf* : **c'est une ~ de la planche** she's a windsurfing freak.

accroc [akro] *nm* - 1. [déchirure] tear - 2. [incident] hitch.

accrochage [akrɔʃaʒ] *nm* - 1. [accident] collision - 2. *fam* [dispute] row.

accroche [akrɔʃ] *nf* COMM catch line.

accrocher [3] [akrɔʃe] *vt* - 1. [suspendre] : ~ **qqch (à)** to hang sthg up (on) - 2. [déchirer] : ~ **qqch (à)** to catch sthg (on) - 3. [attacher] : ~ **qqch (à)** to hitch sthg (to). ◆ **s'accrocher** *vp* - 1. [s'agripper] : **s'~ (à)** to hang on (to) ; **s'~ à qqn** *fig* to cling to sb - 2. *fam* [se disputer] to row, to have a row - 3. *fam* [persévérer] to stick at it.

accroissement [akrwasmɑ̃] *nm* increase, growth.

accroître [94] [akrwatr] *vt* to increase. ◆ **s'accroître** *vp* to increase, to grow.

accroupir [32] [akrupir] ◆ **s'accroupir** *vp* to squat.

accru, e [akry] *pp* ▷ **accroître**.

accueil [akœj] *nm* - 1. [lieu] reception - 2. [action] welcome, reception.

accueillant, e [akœjɑ̃, ɑ̃t] *adj* welcoming, friendly.

accueillir [41] [akœjir] *vt* - 1. [gén] to welcome - 2. [loger] to accommodate.

accumulateur [akymylatœr] *nm* accumulator, battery.

accumulation [akymylasjɔ̃] *nf* accumulation.

accumuler [3] [akymyle] *vt* to accumulate ; *fig* to store up. ◆ **s'accumuler** *vp* to pile up.

accusateur, trice [akyzatœr, tris] ◇ *adj* accusing. ◇ *nm, f* accuser.

accusation [akyzasjɔ̃] *nf* - 1. [reproche]

accusation - **2.** JUR charge ; **mettre en ~ to indict** ; **l'~** the prosecution.

accusé, e [akyze] *nm, f* accused, defendant. ◆ **accusé de réception** *nm* acknowledgement (of receipt).

accuser [3] [akyze] *vt-* **1.** [porter une accusation contre] : **~ qqn (de qqch)** to accuse sb (of sthg) - **2.** JUR : **~ qqn de qqch** to charge sb with sthg.

acerbe [asɛrb] *adj* acerbic.

acéré, e [asere] *adj* sharp.

achalandé, e [aʃalɑ̃de] *adj* [en marchandises] : **bien ~** well-stocked.

acharné, e [aʃarne] *adj* [combat] fierce ; [travail] unremitting.

acharnement [aʃarnəmɑ̃] *nm* relentlessness.

acharner [3] [aʃarne] ◆ **s'acharner** *vp* - **1.** [combattre] : **s'~ contre** OU **après** OU **sur qqn** [ennemi, victime] to hound sb ; [suj : malheur] to dog sb - **2.** [s'obstiner] : **s'~ (à faire qqch)** to persist (in doing sthg).

achat [aʃa] *nm* purchase ; **faire des ~s** to go shopping.

acheminer [3] [aʃmine] *vt* to dispatch. ◆ **s'acheminer** *vp* ; **s'~ vers** [lieu, désastre] to head for ; [solution, paix] to move towards *Br* OU toward *Am*.

acheter [28] [aʃte] *vt litt & fig* to buy ; **~ qqch à** OU **pour qqn** to buy sthg for sb, to buy sb sthg.

acheteur, euse [aʃtœr, øz] *nm, f* buyer, purchaser.

achevé, e [aʃve] *adj sout* : **d'un ridicule ~** utterly ridiculous.

achèvement [aʃɛvmɑ̃] *nm* completion.

achever [19] [aʃve] *vt* - **1.** [terminer] to complete, to finish (off) - **2.** [tuer, accabler] to finish off. ◆ **s'achever** *vp* to end, to come to an end.

achoppement [aʃɔpmɑ̃] ▷ **pierre.**

acide [asid] ◇ *adj* - **1.** [saveur] sour - **2.** [propos] sharp, acid - **3.** CHIM acid. ◇ *nm* CHIM acid.

acidité [asidite] *nf* **1.** CHIM acidity - **2.** [saveur] sourness - **3.** [de propos] sharpness.

acidulé, e [asidyle] *adj* slightly acid ; ▷ **bonbon.**

acier [asje] *nm* steel ; **~ inoxydable** stainless steel.

aciérie [asjeri] *nf* steelworks *(sg)*.

acné [akne] *nf* acne.

acolyte [akɔlit] *nm péj* henchman.

acompte [akɔ̃t] *nm* deposit.

à-côté [akote] *(pl* à-côtés) *nm* - **1.** [point accessoire] side issue - **2.** [gain d'appoint] extra.

à-coup [aku] *(pl* à-coups) *nm* jerk ; **par ~s** in fits and starts.

acoustique [akustik] *nf* - **1.** [science] acoustics *(U)* - **2.** [d'une salle] acoustics *(pl)*.

acquéreur [akerœr] *nm* buyer.

acquérir [39] [akerir] *vt* [gén] to acquire.

acquiescement [akjɛsmɑ̃] *nm* approval.

acquiescer [21] [akjese] *vi* to acquiesce ; **~ à** to agree to.

acquis, e [aki, iz] ◇ *pp* ▷ **acquérir.** ◇ *adj* - **1.** [caractère] acquired - **2.** [droit, avantage] established. ◆ **acquis** *nmpl* [connaissances] knowledge *(U)*.

acquisition [akizisjɔ̃] *nf* acquisition.

acquit [aki] *nm* receipt ; **pour ~** COMM received ; **faire qqch par ~ de conscience** *fig* to do sthg to set one's mind at rest.

acquittement [akitmɑ̃] *nm* - **1.** [d'obligation] settlement - **2.** JUR acquittal.

acquitter [3] [akite] *vt* - **1.** JUR to acquit - **2.** [régler] to pay - **3.** [libérer] : **~ qqn de** to release sb from.

âcre [akr] *adj* - **1.** [saveur] bitter - **2.** [fumée] acrid.

acrobate [akrɔbat] *nmf* acrobat.

acrobatie [akrɔbasi] *nf* acrobatics *(U)*.

acrylique [akrilik] *adj* & *nm* acrylic.

acte [akt] *nm* - **1.** [action] act, action ; **faire ~ d'autorité** to exercise one's authority ; **faire ~ de candidature** to submit an application - **2.** THÉÂTRE act - **3.** JUR deed ; **d'accusation** charge ; **~ de naissance/de mariage** birth/marriage certificate ; **~ de vente** bill of sale - **4.** RELIG certificate - **5.** *loc* : **faire ~ de présence** to put in an appearance ; **prendre ~ de** to note, to take note of. ◆ **actes** *nmpl* [de colloque] proceedings.

acteur, trice [aktœr, tris] *nm, f* actor (*f* actress).

actif, ive [aktif, iv] *adj* [gén] active ; **la population active** the working population. ◆ **actif** *nm* - **1.** FIN assets *(pl)* - **2.** *loc* : **avoir qqch à son ~** to have sthg to one's credit.

action [aksjɔ̃] *nf* - **1.** [gén] action ; **sous l'~ de** under the action of - **2.** [acte] action, act ; **bonne/mauvaise ~** good/bad deed - **3.** JUR action, lawsuit - **4.** FIN share.

actionnaire [aksjɔnɛr] *nmf* FIN shareholder.

actionner [3] [aksjɔne] *vt* to work, to activate.

activement [aktivmɑ̃] *adv* actively.

activer [3] [aktive] *vt* to speed up. ◆ **s'activer** *vp* to bustle about.

activiste [aktivist] *adj* & *nmf* activist.

activité [aktivite] *nf* [gén] activity ; en ~ [volcan] active.

actualisation [aktɥalizasjɔ̃] *nf* [d'un texte] updating.

actualiser [3] [aktɥalize] *vt* to bring up to date.

actualité [aktɥalite] *nf* - **1.** [d'un sujet] topicality - **2.** [événements] : **l'~ sportive/ politique/littéraire** the current sports/ political/literary scene. ◆ **actualités** *nfpl* : **les ~s** the news *(sg).*

actuel, elle [aktɥɛl] *adj* [contemporain, présent] current, present ; **à l'heure ~le** at the present time.

actuellement [aktɥɛlmɑ̃] *adv* at present, currently.

acuité [akɥite] *nf* acuteness.

acupuncture, acuponcture [akypɔ̃ktyr] *nf* acupuncture.

adage [adaʒ] *nm* adage, saying.

adaptateur, trice [adaptatœr, tris] *nm, f* adapter. ◆ **adaptateur** *nm* ÉLECTR adapter.

adaptation [adaptasjɔ̃] *nf* adaptation.

adapter [3] [adapte] *vt* - **1.** [gén] to adapt - **2.** [fixer] to fit. ◆ **s'adapter** *vp* : **s'~ (à)** to adapt (to).

additif [aditif] *nm* - **1.** [supplément] rider, additional clause - **2.** [substance] additive.

addition [adisjɔ̃] *nf* - **1.** [ajout, calcul] addition - **2.** [note] bill *Br*, check *Am*.

additionner [3] [adisjɔne] *vt* - **1.** [mélanger] : **~ une poudre d'eau** to add water to a powder - **2.** [chiffres] to add up.

adepte [adɛpt] *nmf* follower.

adéquat, e [adekwa, at] *adj* suitable, appropriate.

adhérence [aderɑ̃s] *nf* [de pneu] grip.

adhérent, e [aderɑ̃, ɑ̃t] *nm, f* : **~ (de)** member (of).

adhérer [18] [adere] *vi* - **1.** [coller] to stick, to adhere ; **~ à** [se fixer sur] to stick ou adhere to ; [être d'accord avec] *fig* to support, to adhere to - **2.** [être membre] : **~ à** to become a member of, to join.

adhésif, ive [adezif, iv] *adj* sticky, adhesive. ◆ **adhésif** *nm* adhesive.

adhésion [adezjɔ̃] *nf* - **1.** [à une idée] : **~ (à)** support (for) - **2.** [à un parti] : **~ (à)** membership (of).

adieu [adjø] <> *interj* goodbye!, farewell! ; **dire ~ à qqch** *fig* to say goodbye to sthg. <> *nm (gén pl)* farewell ; **faire ses ~x à qqn** to say one's farewells to sb.

adipeux, euse [adipø, øz] *adj* [tissu] adipose ; [personne] fat.

adjectif [adʒɛktif] *nm* GRAM adjective.

adjoint, e [adʒwɛ̃, ɛ̃t] <> *adj* deputy *(avant n)*, assistant *(avant n).* <> *nm, f* deputy, assistant ; **~ au maire** deputy mayor.

adjonction [adʒɔ̃ksjɔ̃] *nf* addition.

adjudant [adʒydɑ̃] *nm* [dans la marine] warrant officer.

adjuger [17] [adʒyʒe] *vt* : **~ qqch (à qqn)** [aux enchères] to auction sthg (to sb) ; [décerner] to award sthg (to sb) ; **adjugé!** sold!

admettre [84] [admɛtr] *vt* - **1.** [tolérer, accepter] to allow, to accept - **2.** [autoriser] to allow - **3.** [accueillir, reconnaître] to admit.

administrateur, trice [administratœr, tris] *nm, f* - **1.** [gérant] administrator ; **~ judiciaire** receiver - **2.** [de conseil d'administration] director.

administratif, ive [administratif, iv] *adj* administrative.

administration [administrasjɔ̃] *nf* - **1.** [service public] : **l'Administration** ≃ the Civil Service - **2.** [gestion] administration.

administrer [3] [administre] *vt* - **1.** [gérer] to manage, to administer - **2.** [médicament, sacrement] to administer.

admirable [admirabl] *adj* - **1.** [personne, comportement] admirable - **2.** [paysage, spectacle] wonderful.

admiratif, ive [admiratif, iv] *adj* admiring.

admiration [admirasjɔ̃] *nf* admiration.

admirer [3] [admire] *vt* to admire.

admis, e [admi, iz] *pp* ▷ **admettre.**

admissible [admisibl] *adj* - **1.** [attitude] acceptable - **2.** SCOL eligible.

admission [admisjɔ̃] *nf* admission.

ADN *(abr de* **acide désoxyribonucléique)** *nm* DNA.

ado [ado] *(abr de* **adolescent)** *nmf fam* teenager.

adolescence [adɔlesɑ̃s] *nf* adolescence.

adolescent, e [adɔlesɑ̃, ɑ̃t] *nm, f* adolescent, teenager.

adonner [3] [adɔne] ◆ **s'adonner** *vp* : **s'~ à** [sport, activité] to devote o.s. to ; [vice] to take to.

adopter [3] [adɔpte] *vt* - **1.** [gén] to adopt - **2.** [loi] to pass.

adoptif, ive [adɔptif, iv] *adj* [famille] adoptive ; [pays, enfant] adopted.

adoption [adɔpsjɔ̃] *nf* adoption ; **d'~** [pays, ville] adopted ; [famille] adoptive.

adorable [adɔrabl] *adj* adorable, delightful.

adoration [adɔrasjɔ̃] *nf* - **1.** [amour] adoration - **2.** RELIG worship.

adorer [3] [adɔre] vt - **1.** [personne, chose] to adore - **2.** RELIG to worship.

adosser [3] [adose] vt : ~ qqch à qqch to place sthg against sthg. ◆ **s'adosser** vp : **s'~ à** OU **contre qqch** to lean against sthg.

adoucir [32] [adusir] vt - **1.** [gén] to soften - **2.** [chagrin, peine] to ease, to soothe. ◆ **s'adoucir** vp - **1.** [temps] to become OU get milder - **2.** [personne] to mellow.

adoucissant, e [adusisɑ̃, ɑ̃t] adj soothing. ◆ **adoucissant** nm softener.

adoucisseur [adusisœr] nm : ~ **d'eau** water softener.

adresse [adres] nf - **1.** [gén & INFORM] address ; ~ **électronique** e-mail address - **2.** [habileté] skill.

adresser [4] [adrese] vt - **1.** [faire parvenir] : ~ **qqch à qqn** to address sthg to sb - **2.** [envoyer] : ~ **qqn à qqn** to refer sb to sb. ◆ **s'adresser** vp : **s'~ à** [parler à] to speak to ; [être destiné à] to be aimed at, to be intended for.

Adriatique [adriatik] nf : **l'~** the Adriatic.

adroit, e [adrwa, at] adj skilful.

aduler [3] [adyle] vt to adulate.

adulte [adylt] nmf & adj adult.

adultère [adylter] <> nm [acte] adultery. <> adj adulterous.

advenir [40] [advənir] v impers to happen ; **qu'advient-il de ...?** what is happening to ...? ; **qu'est-il advenu de ...?** what has happened to ou become of ...?

advenu [advəny] pp L ➤ advenir.

adverbe [adverb] nm adverb.

adversaire [adverser] nmf adversary, opponent.

adverse [advers] adj [opposé] opposing ; **l'~ parti.**

adversité [adversite] nf adversity.

aération [aerasjɔ̃] nf [circulation d'air] ventilation ; [action] airing.

aéré, e [aere] adj - **1.** [pièce] well-ventilated ; **mal ~** stuffy - **2.** fig [présentation] well-spaced.

aérer [18] [aere] vt - **1.** [pièce, chose] to air - **2.** fig [présentation, mise en page] to lighten.

aérien, enne [aerjɛ̃, ɛn] adj - **1.** [câble] overhead (avant n) - **2.** [transports, attaque] air (avant n) ; **compagnie ~ne** airline (company).

aérobic [aerɔbik] nm aerobics (U).

aérodrome [aerɔdrom] nm aerodrome.

aérodynamique [aerɔdinamik] adj streamlined, aerodynamic.

aérogare [aerɔgar] nf - **1.** [aéroport] airport - **2.** [gare] air terminal.

aéroglisseur [aerɔglisœr] nm hovercraft.

aérogramme [aerɔgram] nm aerogramme.

aéronautique [aerɔnotik] nf aeronautics (U).

aéronaval, e, als [aerɔnaval] adj air and sea (avant n).

aérophagie [aerɔfaʒi] nf abdominal wind.

aéroport [aerɔpɔr] nm airport.

aéroporté, e [aerɔpɔrte] adj airborne.

aérosol [aerɔsɔl] nm & adj inv aerosol.

aérospatial, e, aux [aerɔspasjal, o] adj aerospace (avant n). ◆ **aérospatiale** nf aerospace industry.

affable [afabl] adj - **1.** [personne] affable, agreeable - **2.** [parole] kind.

affaiblir [32] [afeblir] vt litt & fig to weaken. ◆ **s'affaiblir** vp litt & fig to weaken, to become weaker.

affaire [afer] nf - **1.** [question] matter - **2.** [situation, polémique] affair - **3.** [marché] deal ; **faire une ~** to get a bargain ou a good deal - **4.** [entreprise] business - **5.** [procès] case - **6.** loc : **avoir ~ à qqn** to deal with sb , **vous aurez ~ à moi!** you'll have me to deal with! ; **faire l'~** to do nicely. ◆ **affaires** nfpl - **1.** COMM business (U) - **2.** [objets personnels] things, belongings - **3.** [activités] affairs ; **les Affaires étrangères** = the Foreign Office (sg).

affairé, e [afere] adj busy.

affairer [4] [afere] ◆ **s'affairer** vp to bustle about.

affairisme [aferism] nm racketeering.

affaisser [4] [afese] ◆ **s'affaisser** vp - **1.** [se creuser] to subside, to sink - **2.** [tomber] to collapse.

affaler [3] [afale] ◆ **s'affaler** vp to collapse.

affamé, e [afame] adj starving.

affecter [4] [afekte] vt - **1.** [consacrer] : ~ **qqch à** to allocate sthg to - **2.** [nommer] : ~ **qqn à** to appoint sb to - **3.** [feindre] to feign - **4.** [émouvoir] to affect, to move.

affectif, ive [afektif, iv] adj emotional.

affection [afeksjɔ̃] nf - **1.** [sentiment] affection ; **avoir de l'~ pour** to be fond of - **2.** [maladie] complaint.

affectionner [3] [afeksjɔne] vt to be fond of.

affectueusement [afektɥøzmɑ̃] adv affectionately.

affectueux, euse [afektɥø, øz] adj affectionate.

affichage [afiʃaʒ] *nm* - **1.** [d'un poster, d'un avis] putting up, displaying - **2.** ÉLECTRON : ~ **à cristaux liquides** LCD, liquid crystal display ; ~ **numérique** digital display.

affiche [afiʃ] *nf* [gén] poster ; [officielle] notice.

afficher [3] [afiʃe] *vt* - **1.** [liste, poster] to put up ; [vente, réglementation] to put up a notice about - **2.** [laisser transparaître] to display, to exhibit.

affilée [afile] ◆ **d'affilée** *loc adv* : **trois jours d'~** three days running.

affiler [3] [afile] *vt* to sharpen.

affiner [3] [afine] *vt litt & fig* to refine.

affinité [afinite] *nf* affinity.

affirmatif, ive [afirmatif, iv] *adj* - **1.** [réponse] affirmative - **2.** [personne] positive. ◆ **affirmative** *nf* : **dans l'affirmative** if yes, if the answer is yes ; **répondre par l'affirmative** to reply in the affirmative.

affirmation [afirmasjɔ̃] *nf* assertion.

affirmer [3] [afirme] *vt* - **1.** [certifier] to maintain, to claim - **2.** [exprimer] to assert.

affliction [afliksjɔ̃] *nf* affliction.

affligeant, e [afliʒɑ̃, ɑ̃t] *adj* - **1.** [désolant] saddening, distressing - **2.** [lamentable] appalling.

affliger [17] [afliʒe] *vt sout* - **1.** [attrister] to sadden, to distress - **2.** [de défaut, de maladie] : **être affligé de** to be afflicted with.

affluence [aflyɑ̃s] *nf* crowd, crowds (*pl*).

affluent [aflyɑ̃] *nm* tributary.

affluer [3] [aflye] *vi* - **1.** [choses] to pour in, to flood in - **2.** [personnes] to flock in - **3.** [sang] : ~ **(à)** to rush (to).

afflux [afly] *nm* - **1.** [de liquide, dons, capitaux] flow - **2.** [de personnes] flood.

affolement [afɔlmɑ̃] *nm* panic.

affoler [3] [afɔle] *vt* [inquiéter] to terrify. ◆ **s'affoler** *vp* [paniquer] to panic.

affranchir [32] [afrɑ̃ʃir] *vt* - **1.** [lettre - avec timbre] to stamp ; [- à la machine] to frank - **2.** [esclave] to set free, to liberate.

affreux, euse [afrø, øz] *adj* - **1.** [repoussant] horrible - **2.** [effrayant] terrifying - **3.** [détestable] awful, dreadful.

affriolant, e [afrijolɑ̃, ɑ̃t] *adj* enticing.

affront [afrɔ̃] *nm* insult, affront.

affrontement [afrɔ̃tmɑ̃] *nm* confrontation.

affronter [3] [afrɔ̃te] *vt* to confront.

affubler [3] [afyble] *vt péj* : **être affublé de** to be got up in.

affût [afy] *nm* : **être à l'~ (de)** to be lying in wait (for) ; *fig* to be on the lookout (for).

affûter [3] [afyte] *vt* to sharpen.

Afghanistan [afganistɑ̃] *nm* : **l'~** Afghanistan.

afin [afɛ̃] ◆ **afin de** *loc prép* in order to. ◆ **afin que** *loc conj* (+ *subjonctif*) so that.

a fortiori [aforsjori] *adv* all the more.

africain, e [afrikɛ̃, ɛn] *adj* African. ◆ **Africain, e** *nm, f* African.

Afrique [afrik] *nf* : **l'~** Africa ; **l'~ du Nord** North Africa ; **l'~ du Sud** South Africa.

agacer [16] [agase] *vt* to irritate.

âge [aʒ] *nm* age ; **quel ~ as-tu?** how old are you? ; **prendre de l'~** to age ; **l'~ adulte** adulthood ; **l'~ ingrat** the awkward ou difficult age ; ~ **d'or** golden age ; **le troisième ~** [personnes] the over-sixties.

âgé, e [aʒe] *adj* old, elderly ; **être ~ de 20 ans** to be 20 years old ou of age ; **un enfant ~ de 3 ans** a 3-year-old child.

agence [aʒɑ̃s] *nf* agency ; ~ **immobilière** estate agent's *Br*, real estate agent's *Am* ; ~ **matrimoniale** marriage bureau ; **Agence nationale pour l'emploi** ≃ job centre ; ~ **de publicité** advertising agency ; ~ **de voyages** travel agent's, travel agency.

agencer [16] [aʒɑ̃se] *vt* to arrange ; *fig* to put together.

agenda [aʒɛ̃da] *nm* diary.

agenouiller [3] [aʒnuje] ◆ **s'agenouiller** *vp* to kneel.

agent [aʒɑ̃] *nm* agent ; ~ **de change** stockbroker ; ~ **de police** police officer ; ~ **secret** secret agent.

agglomération [aglɔmerasjɔ̃] *nf* [ville] conurbation.

aggloméré [aglɔmere] *nm* chipboard.

agglomérer [18] [aglɔmere] *vt* to mix together.

agglutiner [3] [aglytine] *vt* to stick together. ◆ **s'agglutiner** *vp* [foule] to gather, to congregate.

aggraver [3] [agrave] *vt* to make worse. ◆ **s'aggraver** *vp* to get worse, to worsen.

agile [aʒil] *adj* agile, nimble.

agilité [aʒilite] *nf litt & fig* agility.

agios [aʒjo] *nmpl* FIN bank charges.

agir [32] [aʒir] *vi* - **1.** [faire, être efficace] to act - **2.** [se comporter] to behave - **3.** [influer] : ~ **sur** to have an effect on. ◆ **s'agir** *v impers* : **il s'agit de ...** it's a matter of ... ; **de quoi s'agit-il?** what's it about?

agissements [aʒismɑ̃] *nmpl péj* schemes, intrigues.

agitateur, trice [aʒitatœr, tris] *nm, f* POLIT agitator.

agitation [aʒitasjɔ̃] *nf* agitation ; [politique, sociale] unrest.

agité, e [aʒite] *adj* - **1.** [gén] restless ; [enfant, classe] restless, fidgety ; [journée, atmosphère] hectic - **2.** [mer] rough.

agiter [3] [aʒite] *vt* - **1.** [remuer - flacon, objet] to shake ; [- drapeau, bras] to wave - **2.** [énerver] to perturb. ◆ **s'agiter** *vp* [personne] to move about, to fidget ; [mer] to stir ; [population] to get restless.

agneau [aɲo] *nm* - **1.** [animal, viande] lamb - **2.** [cuir] lambskin.

agonie [agɔni] *nf* [de personne] mortal agony ; *fig* death throes *(pl)*.

agoniser [3] [agɔnize] *vi* [personne] to be dying ; *fig* to be on its last legs.

agrafe [agraf] *nf* - **1.** [de bureau] staple - **2.** MÉD clip.

agrafer [3] [agrafe] *vt* [attacher] to fasten.

agrafeuse [agraføz] *nf* stapler.

agrandir [32] [agrãdir] *vt* - **1.** [élargir - gén & PHOT] to enlarge ; [- rue, écart] to widen - **2.** *fig* [développer] to expand. ◆ **s'agrandir** *vp* **1.** [s'étendre] to grow - **2.** *fig* [se développer] to expand.

agrandissement [agrãdismã] *nm* - **1.** [gén & PHOT] enlargement - **2.** *fig* [développement] expansion.

agréable [agreabl] *adj* pleasant, nice.

agréé, e [agree] *adj* [concessionnaire, appareil] authorized

agréer [15] [agree] *vt sout* - **1.** [accepter] : **veuillez ~ mes salutations distinguées** ou **l'expression de mes sentiments distingués** yours faithfully - **2.** [convenir] : **~ à qqn** to suit ou please sb.

agrégation [agregasjɔ̃] *nf* competitive examination for secondary school and university teachers.

agrégé, e [agreʒe] *nm, f* holder of the agrégation.

agrément [agremã] *nm* - **1.** [caractère agréable] attractiveness - **2.** [approbation] consent, approval.

agrès [agrɛ] *nmpl* SPORT gym apparatus *(U)*.

agresser [4] [agrese] *vt* **1.** [suj : personne] to attack - **2.** *fig* [suj : bruit, pollution] to assault.

agresseur [agresœr] *nm* attacker.

agressif, ive [agresif, iv] *adj* aggressive.

agression [agresjɔ̃] *nf* attack ; MIL & PSYCHOL aggression.

agricole [agrikɔl] *adj* agricultural.

agriculteur, trice [agrikyltœr, tris] *nm, f* farmer.

agriculture [agrikyltyr] *nf* agriculture, farming.

agripper [3] [agripe] *vt* - **1.** [personne] to cling ou hang on to - **2.** [objet] to grip, to clutch.

agroalimentaire [agroalimãtɛr] *<> adj* : **industrie ~** food-processing industry ; **les produits ~s** processed foods ou foodstuffs. *<> nm* : **l'~** the food processing industry.

agronomie [agrɔnɔmi] *nf* agronomy.

agrume [agrym] *nm* citrus fruit.

aguets [agɛ] ◆ **aux aguets** *loc adv* : **être/rester aux ~** to be ou keep on the lookout.

ahuri, e [ayri] *adj* : **être ~ (par qqch)** to be taken aback (by sthg).

ahurissant, e [ayrisã, ãt] *adj* astounding.

ai ⊏> avoir.

aide [ɛd] *nf* - **1.** [gén] help ; **appeler (qqn) à l'~** to call (to sb) for help ; **venir en ~ à qqn** to come to sb's aid, to help sb ; **~ ménagère** home help - **2.** [secours financier] aid ; **~ sociale** social security *Br*, welfare *Am*. ◆ **à l'aide de** *loc prép* with the help ou aid of.

aide-mémoire [ɛdmemwar] *nm inv* aidemémoire, [pour examen] revision notes *(pl)*.

aider [4] [ede] *vt* to help ; **~ qqn à faire qqch** to help sb to do sthg ; **~ à faire qqch** to help to do sthg. ◆ **s'aider** *vp* - **1.** [s'assister mutuellement] to help each other - **2.** [avoir recours] : **s'~ de** to use, to make use of.

aide-soignant, e [ɛdswaɲã, ãt] *nm, f* nursing auxiliary *Br*, nurse's aide *Am*.

aie, aies *etc* ⊏> avoir.

aïe [aj] *interj* [exprime la douleur] ow!, ouch!

aïeul, e [ajœl] *nm, f sout* grandparent, grandfather (*f* grandmother).

aïeux [ajø] *nmpl* ancestors.

aigle [ɛgl] *nm* eagle.

aigre [ɛgr] *adj* - **1.** [gén] sour - **2.** [propos] harsh.

aigre-doux, aigre-douce [ɛgrədu, ɛgrədus] *adj* - **1.** CULIN sweet-and-sour - **2.** [propos] bittersweet.

aigrelet, ette [ɛgrəlɛ, ɛt] *adj* - **1.** [vin] vinegary - **2.** [voix] sharpish.

aigreur [ɛgrœr] *nf* - **1.** [d'un aliment] sourness - **2.** [d'un propos] harshness. ◆ **aigreurs d'estomac** *nfpl* heartburn *(U)*.

aigri, e [ɛgri] *adj* embittered.

aigu, uë [egy] *adj* - **1.** [son] high-pitched - **2.** [objet, lame] sharp ; [angle] acute

- **3.** [douleur] sharp, acute - **4.** [intelligence, sens] acute, keen. ➤ **aigu** *nm* high note.

aiguillage [egɥijaʒ] *nm* [RAIL - manœuvre] shunting *Br*, switching *Am* ; [- dispositif] points *(pl) Br*, switch *Am*.

aiguille [egɥij] *nf* - **1.** [gén] needle ; ~ à tricoter knitting needle ; ~ de pin pine needle - **2.** [de pendule] hand.

aiguiller [3] [egɥije] *vt* - **1.** RAIL to shunt *Br*, to switch *Am* - **2.** [personne, conversation] to steer, to direct.

aiguilleur [egɥijœr] *nm* - **1.** RAIL pointsman *Br*, switchman *Am* - **2.** AÉRON : ~ du ciel air traffic controller.

aiguiser [3] [egize] *vt litt & fig* to sharpen.

ail [aj] *(pl* ails *ou* aulx [o]) *nm* garlic *(U)* ; ~ des bois *Can* wild leek.

aile [ɛl] *nf* [gén] wing.

aileron [ɛlrɔ̃] *nm* - **1.** [de requin] fin - **2.** [d'avion] aileron.

ailier [elje] *nm* winger.

aille, ailles *etc* ➣ aller.

ailleurs [ajœr] *adv* elsewhere, somewhere *Br* ou someplace *Am* else ; nulle part ~ nowhere *Br* ou no-place *Am* else ; partout ~ everywhere *Br* ou everyplace *Am* else. ➤ **d'ailleurs** *loc adv* moreover, besides. ➤ **par ailleurs** *loc adv* moreover.

aimable [ɛmabl] *adj* kind, nice.

aimablement [ɛmabləmɑ̃] *adv* kindly.

aimant¹, e [ɛmɑ̃, ɑ̃t] *adj* loving.

aimant² [ɛmɑ̃] *nm* magnet.

aimer [4] [eme] *vt* - **1.** [gén] to like ; ~ bien qqch/qqn to like sthg/sb, to be fond of sthg/sb ; ~ bien faire qqch to (really) like doing sthg ; ~ **(à)** faire qqch to like to do sthg, to like doing sthg ; j'aime à croire que ... I like to think that ... ; elle aime qu'on l'appelle par son surnom she likes being called by her nickname ; je n'aime pas que tu rentres seule le soir I don't like you coming home alone at night ; j'aimerais **(bien)** que tu viennes avec moi I'd like you to come with me ; j'aimerais bien une autre tasse de café I wouldn't mind another cup of coffee ; ~ mieux qqch to prefer sthg ; ~ mieux faire qqch to prefer doing ou to do sthg - **2.** [d'amour] to love. ➤ **s'aimer** *vp (emploi réciproque)* to love each other ; s'~ bien to like each other.

aine [ɛn] *nf* groin.

aîné, e [ene] <> *adj* [plus âgé] elder, older ; [le plus âgé] eldest, oldest. <> *nm, f* [plus âgé] older ou elder child, older ou eldest son/daughter ; [le plus âgé] oldest ou eldest child, oldest ou eldest son/daughter ; elle est mon ~e de deux ans she is two years older than me.

aînesse [ɛnɛs] ➣ droit.

ainsi [ɛ̃si] *adv* - **1.** [manière] in this way, like this - **2.** [valeur conclusive] thus ; et ~ de suite and so on, and so forth ; pour ~ dire so to speak. ➤ **ainsi que** *loc conj* [et] as well as.

air [ɛr] *nm* - **1.** [gén] air ; en plein ~ (out) in the open air, outside ; en l'~ [projet] (up) in the air ; *fig* [paroles] empty ; ~ conditionné air-conditioning - **2.** [apparence, mine] air, look ; il a l'~ triste he looks sad ; il a l'~ de bouder it looks as if he's sulking ; il a l'~ de faire beau it looks like being a nice day - **3.** MUS tune.

Airbag® [ɛrbag] *nm* airbag.

aire [ɛr] *nf* [gén] area ; ~ d'atterrissage landing strip ; ~ de jeu playground ; ~ de repos lay-by ; ~ de stationnement parking area.

aisance [ɛzɑ̃s] *nf* - **1.** [facilité] ease - **2.** [richesse] : il vit dans l'~ he has an affluent lifestyle.

aise [ɛz] *nf sout* pleasure ; être à l'~ ou à son ~ [confortable] to feel comfortable ; [financièrement] to be comfortably off ; mettez-vous à l'~ make yourself comfortable ; mettre qqn mal à l'~ to make sb feel ill at ease ou uneasy. ➤ **aises** *nfpl* : aimer ses ~s to like one's (home) comforts ; prendre ses ~s to make o.s. comfortable.

aisé, e [eze] *adj* - **1.** [facile] easy - **2.** [riche] well-off.

aisselle [ɛsɛl] *nf* armpit.

ajourner [3] [aʒurne] *vt* - **1.** [reporter - décision etc] to postpone ; [- réunion, procès] to adjourn - **2.** [candidat] to refer.

ajout [aʒu] *nm* addition.

ajouter [3] [aʒute] *vt* to add ; ~ foi à qqch *sout* to give credence to sthg. ➤ **s'ajouter** *vp* : s'~ à qqch to be in addition to sthg.

ajuster [3] [aʒyste] *vt* - **1.** [monter] : ~ qqch **(à)** to fit sthg (to) - **2.** [régler] to adjust - **3.** [vêtement] to alter - **4.** [tir, coup] to aim. ➤ **s'ajuster** *vp* to be adaptable.

alarme [alarm] *nf* alarm ; donner l'~ to give ou raise the alarm.

alarmer [3] [alarme] *vt* to alarm. ➤ **s'alarmer** *vp* to get ou become alarmed.

albanais, e [albanɛ, ɛz] *adj* Albanian. ➤ **albanais** *nm* [langue] Albanian. ➤ **Albanais, e** *nm, f* Albanian.

Albanie [albani] *nf* : l'~ Albania.

albâtre [albatr] *nm* alabaster.

albatros [albatros] *nm* albatross.

albinos [albinos] *nmf & adj inv* albino.

album [albɔm] *nm* album ; **~ (de) photo** photo album.

alchimiste [alʃimist] *nmf* alchemist.

alcool [alkɔl] *nm* alcohol ; **~ à brûler** methylated spirits *(pl)* ; **~ à 90 degrés** surgical spirit.

alcoolique [alkɔlik] *nmf & adj* alcoholic.

alcoolisé, e [alkɔlize] *adj* alcoholic.

alcoolisme [alkɔlism] *nm* alcoholism.

Alc(o)otest® [alkɔtɛst] *nm* ≃ Breathalyser®.

alcôve [alkov] *nf* recess.

aléatoire [aleatwar] *adj* - **1.** [avenir] uncertain - **2.** [choix] random.

alentour [alɑ̃tur] *adv* around, round about. **◆ alentours** *nmpl* surroundings ; **aux ~s de** [spatial] in the vicinity of ; [temporel] around.

alerte [alɛrt] ◇ *adj* - **1.** [personne, esprit] agile, alert - **2.** [style, pas] lively. ◇ *nf* alarm, alert ; **donner l'~** to sound ou give the alert ; **~ à la bombe** bomb scare.

alerter [3] [alɛrte] *vt* to warn, to alert.

algèbre [alʒɛbr] *nf* algebra.

Alger [alʒe] *n* Algiers.

Algérie [alʒeri] *nf* : **l'~** Algeria.

algérien, enne [alʒerjɛ̃, ɛn] *adj* Algerian. **◆ Algérien, enne** *nm, f* Algerian.

algue [alg] *nf* seaweed *(U)*.

alibi [alibi] *nm* alibi.

aliénation [aljenasjɔ̃] *nf* alienation ; **~ mentale** insanity.

aliéné, e [aljene] ◇ *adj* - **1.** MÉD insane - **2.** JUR alienated. ◇ *nm, f* MÉD insane person.

aliéner [18] [aljene] *vt* to alienate.

alignement [aliɲmɑ̃] *nm* alignment, lining up.

aligner [3] [aliɲe] *vt* - **1.** [disposer en ligne] to line up, to align - **2.** [adapter] : **~ qqch sur** to align sthg with, to bring sthg into line with. **◆ s'aligner** *vp* to line up ; **s'~ sur** POLIT to align o.s. with.

aliment [alimɑ̃] *nm* [nourriture] food *(U)*.

alimentaire [alimɑ̃tɛr] *adj* - **1.** [gén] food *(avant n)* ; **c'est juste un travail ~** I'm doing this job just for the money - **2.** JUR maintenance *(avant n)*.

alimentation [alimɑ̃tasjɔ̃] *nf* - **1.** [nourriture] diet ; **magasin d'~** food store - **2.** [approvisionnement] : **~ (en)** supply ou supplying *(U)* (of).

alimenter [3] [alimɑ̃te] *vt* - **1.** [nourrir] to feed - **2.** [approvisionner] : **~ qqch en** to supply sthg with.

alinéa [alinea] *nm* - **1.** [retrait de ligne] indent - **2.** [dans un document officiel] paragraph.

aliter [3] [alite] *vt* : **être alité** to be bedridden. **◆ s'aliter** *vp* to take to one's bed.

allaitement [alɛtmɑ̃] *nm* [d'enfant] breast-feeding ; [d'animal] suckling.

allaiter [4] [alete] *vt* [enfant] to breast-feed ; [animal] to suckle.

allé, e [ale] *pp* ▷ aller.

alléchant, e [aleʃɑ̃, ɑ̃t] *adj* mouthwatering, tempting.

allécher [18] [aleʃe] *vt* : **il a été alléché par l'odeur/la perspective** the smell/prospect made his mouth water.

allée [ale] *nf* - **1.** [dans un jardin] path ; [dans une ville] avenue - **2.** [trajet] : **~s et venues** comings and goings - **3.** *Can* GOLF fairway.

allégé, e [aleʒe] *adj* [régime, produit] low-fat.

alléger [22] [aleʒe] *vt* - **1.** [fardeau] to lighten - **2.** [douleur] to soothe.

allégorie [alegɔri] *nf* allegory.

allègre [alɛgr] *adj* - **1.** [ton] cheerful - **2.** [démarche] jaunty.

allégresse [alegrɛs] *nf* elation.

alléguer [18] [alege] *vt* : **~ une excuse** to put forward an excuse ; **~ que** to plead (that).

Allemagne [alman] *nf* : **l'~** Germany ; **l'(ex-)~ de l'Est** (former) East Germany ; **l'(ex-)~ de l'Ouest** (former) West Germany.

allemand, e [almɑ̃, ɑ̃d] *adj* German. **◆ allemand** *nm* [langue] German. **◆ Allemand, e** *nm, f* German ; **un Allemand de l'Est/l'Ouest** an East/a West German.

aller [31] [ale] ◇ *nm* - **1.** [trajet] outward journey - **2.** [billet] single ticket *Br*, oneway ticket *Am*. ◇ *vi* - **1.** [gén] to go ; **allez!** come on! ; **vas-y!** go on! ; **allons-y!, on y va!** let's go!, off we go! - **2.** (+ infinitif) : **~ faire qqch** to go and do sthg ; **~ chercher les enfants à l'école** to go and fetch the children from school ; **~ travailler/se promener** to go to work/for a walk - **3.** [indiquant un état] : **comment vas-tu?** how are you? ; **je vais bien** I'm very well, I'm fine ; **comment ça va?** — **ça va** [santé] how are you? — fine ou all right ; [situation] how are things? — fine ou all right ; **~ mieux** to be better - **4.** [convenir] : **ce type de clou ne va pas pour ce travail** this kind of nail won't do ou isn't suitable for this job ; **~ avec** to go with ; **~ à qqn** to suit sb ; [suj : vêtement, taille] to fit sb ; **ces couleurs ne vont pas ensemble** these colours don't go well together - **5.** loc : **cela va de soi, cela va sans dire** that goes without saying ; **il en va de ... comme ...** the same goes for ... as ... ; **il en va de même pour lui** the same goes for him. ◇ v aux (+ infinitif) [exprime le futur proche] to be going to, will ; **je vais arriver en retard** I'm going to arrive late, I'll arrive late ; **nous allons bientôt avoir fini** we'll soon have finished. ➡ **s'en aller** vp - **1.** [partir] to go, to be off ; **allez-vous-en!** go away! - **2.** [disparaître] to go away.

allergie [alɛrʒi] nf allergy.

allergique [alɛrʒik] adj : ~ (à) allergic (to).

aller-retour [alerətur] nm return (ticket).

alliage [aljaʒ] nm alloy.

alliance [aljɑ̃s] nf - **1.** [union - stratégique] alliance ; [- par le mariage] union, marriage ; **cousin par ~** cousin by marriage - **2.** [bague] wedding ring.

allié, e [alje] ◇ adj : ~ (à) allied (to). ◇ nm, f ally. ➡ **Alliés** nmpl : **les Alliés** the Allies.

allier [9] [alje] vt [associer] to combine. ➡ **s'allier** vp to become allies ; **s'~ qqn** to win sb over as an ally ; **s'~ à qqn** to ally with sb.

alligator [aligatɔr] nm alligator.

allô [alo] interj hello!

allocation [alɔkasjɔ̃] nf - **1.** [attribution] allocation - **2.** [aide financière] : **~ chômage** unemployment benefit (U) Br ou compensation (U) Am ; **~ logement** housing benefit (U) Br, rent subsidy (U) Am ; **~s familiales** child benefit (U) Br, welfare (U) Am.

allocution [alɔkysjɔ̃] nf short speech.

allongé, e [alɔ̃ʒe] adj - **1.** [position] : **être ~** to be lying down ou stretched out - **2.** [forme] elongated.

allonger [17] [alɔ̃ʒe] vt - **1.** [gén] to lengthen, to make longer - **2.** [jambe, bras] to stretch (out) - **3.** [personne] to lay down. ➡ **s'allonger** vp - **1.** [gén] to get longer - **2.** [se coucher] to lie down.

allopathique [alɔpatik] adj allopathic.

allumage [alymaʒ] nm - **1.** [de feu] lighting - **2.** [d'appareil électrique] switching ou turning on - **3.** [de moteur] ignition.

allume-cigares [alymsigar] nm inv cigar lighter.

allume-gaz [alymgaz] nm inv gas lighter.

allumer [3] [alyme] vt - **1.** [lampe, radio, télévision] to turn ou switch on ; **allume dans la cuisine** turn the kitchen light on - **2.** [gaz] to light ; [cigarette] to light (up) - **3.** fam [personne] to turn on.

allumette [alymɛt] nf match.

allumeuse [alymøz] nf fam péj tease.

allure [alyr] nf - **1.** [vitesse] speed ; **à toute ~ at top** ou **full speed** - **2.** [prestance] presence ; **avoir de l'~** to have style - **3.** [apparence générale] appearance.

allusion [alyzjɔ̃] nf allusion ; **faire ~ à** to refer ou allude to.

almanach [almana] nm almanac.

aloi [alwa] nm : **de bon ~** [mesure] of real worth ; **de mauvais ~** [gaîté] not genuine ; [plaisanterie] in bad taste.

alors [alɔr] adv - **1.** [jadis] then, at that time - **2.** [à ce moment-là] then - **3.** [exprimant la conséquence] then, so ; **et ~, qu'est-ce qui s'est passé?** so what happened? ; **il va se mettre en colère — et ~?** he'll be angry — so what? - **4.** [emploi expressif] well (then) ; **~, qu'est-ce qu'on fait?** well, what are we doing? ; **ça ~!** well fancy that! ➡ **alors que** loc conj - **1.** [exprimant le temps] while, when - **2.** [exprimant l'opposition] even though ; **elle est sortie ~ que c'était interdit** she went out even though it was forbidden ; **ils aiment le café ~ que nous, nous buvons du thé** they like coffee whereas we drink tea.

alouette [alwɛt] nf lark.

alourdir [32] [alurdir] vt - **1.** [gén] to weigh down, to make heavy - **2.** fig [impôts] to increase.

aloyau [alwajo] nm sirloin.

Alpes [alp] nfpl : **les ~** the Alps.

alphabet [alfabɛ] nm alphabet.

alphabétique [alfabetik] adj alphabetical.

alphabétiser [3] [alfabetize] vt : **~ qqn** to teach sb (how) to read and write ; **~ un pays** to eliminate illiteracy from a country.

alpin, e [alpɛ̃, in] adj alpine.

alpinisme [alpinism] nm mountaineering.

alpiniste [alpinist] nmf mountaineer.

Alsace [alzas] nf : **l'~** Alsace.

altérer [18] [altere] vt - **1.** [détériorer] to spoil - **2.** [santé] to harm, to affect ; [vérité, récit] to distort. ➡ **s'altérer** vp - **1.** [matière - métal] to deteriorate ; [- aliment] to go off, to spoil - **2.** [santé] to deteriorate.

alternance [altɛrnɑ̃s] nf - **1.** [succession] alternation ; **en ~** alternately - **2.** POLIT change of government party.

alternatif, ive [altɛrnatif, iv] adj - **1.** [périodique] alternating - **2.** [parallèle] alternative. ➡ **alternative** nf alternative.

alternativement [altɛrnativmɑ̃] adv alternately.

alterner [3] [altɛrne] vi [se succéder] : **~ (avec)** to alternate (with).

altier, ère [altje, ɛr] adj haughty.

altitude [altityd] *nf* altitude, height ; **en ~** at (high) altitude.

alto [alto] *nm* [MUS - voix] alto ; [- instrument] viola.

alu [aly] *fam* <> *nm* [métal] aluminium *Br*, aluminum *Am* ; [papier] aluminium *Br* ou aluminum *Am* foil, tinfoil. <> *adj* : **papier ~** aluminium *Br* ou aluminum *Am* foil, tinfoil.

aluminium [alyminjɔm] *nm* aluminium *Br*, aluminum *Am*.

alvéole [alveɔl] *nf* - **1.** [cavité] cavity - **2.** [de ruche, poumon] alveolus.

amabilité [amabilite] *nf* kindness ; **avoir l'~ de faire qqch** to be so kind as to do sthg.

amadouer [6] [amadwe] *vt* [adoucir] to tame, to pacify ; [persuader] to coax.

amaigrir [32] [amegrir] *vt* to make thin ou thinner.

amaigrissant, e [amegrisã, ãt] *adj* slimming *(avant n) Br*, reducing *(avant n) Am*.

amaigrissement [amegrismã] *nm* loss of weight.

amalgame [amalgam] *nm* - **1.** TECHNOL amalgam - **2.** [de styles] mixture - **3.** [d'idées, de notions] : **il ne faut pas faire l'~ entre ces deux questions** the two issues must not be confused.

amalgamer [3] [amalgame] *vt* to combine.

amande [amãd] *nf* almond.

amandier [amãdje] *nm* almond tree.

amant [amã] *nm* lover.

amarre [amar] *nf* rope, cable.

amarrer [3] [amare] *vt* - **1.** NAVIG to moor - **2.** [fixer] to tie down.

amas [ama] *nm* pile.

amasser [3] [amase] *vt* - **1.** [objets] to pile up - **2.** [argent] to accumulate.

amateur [amatœr] *nm* - **1.** [connaisseur - d'art, de bon café] : **~ de** lover of - **2.** [non-professionnel] amateur ; **faire qqch en ~** to do sthg as a hobby - **3.** *péj* [dilettante] amateur.

amazone [amazon] *nf* horsewoman ; **monter en ~** to ride sidesaddle.

Amazonie [amazoni] *nf* : **l'~** the Amazon (Basin).

amazonien, enne [amazonjẽ, ɛn] *adj* Amazonian ; **la forêt ~ne** the Amazon rain forest.

ambassade [ãbasad] *nf* embassy.

ambassadeur, drice [ãbasadœr, dris] *nm, f* ambassador.

ambiance [ãbjãs] *nf* atmosphere.

ambiant, e [ãbjã, ãt] *adj* : **température ~e** room temperature.

ambidextre [ãbidɛkstr] *adj* ambidextrous.

ambigu, uë [ãbigy] *adj* ambiguous.

ambiguïté [ãbiguite] *nf* ambiguity.

ambitieux, euse [ãbisjø, øz] *adj* ambitious.

ambition [ãbisjõ] *nf* - **1.** *péj* [arrivisme] ambitiousness - **2.** [désir] ambition ; **avoir l'~ de faire qqch** to have an ambition to do sthg.

ambivalent, e [ãbivalã, ãt] *adj* ambivalent.

ambre [ãbr] *nm* - **1.** [couleur] amber - **2.** [matière] : **~ (gris)** ambergris.

ambré, e [ãbre] *adj* [couleur] amber.

ambulance [ãbylãs] *nf* ambulance.

ambulant, e [ãbylã, ãt] *adj* travelling *(avant n)*.

âme [am] *nf* - **1.** [gén] soul ; **avoir une ~ de comédien** to be a born actor ; **~ sœur** soulmate - **2.** [caractère] spirit, soul.

amélioration [ameljorasjõ] *nf* improvement.

améliorer [3] [ameljore] *vt* to improve. **s'améliorer** *vp* to improve.

amen [amɛn] *adv* amen.

aménagement [amenaʒmã] *nm* - **1.** [de lieu] fitting out - **2.** [de programme] planning, organizing.

aménager [17] [amenaʒe] *vt* - **1.** [pièce] to fit out - **2.** [programme] to plan, to organize.

amende [amãd] *nf* fine.

amendement [amãdmã] *nm* POLIT amendment.

amender [3] [amãde] *vt* - **1.** POLIT to amend - **2.** AGRIC to enrich. **s'amender** *vp* to mend one's ways.

amener [19] [amne] *vt* - **1.** [mener] to bring - **2.** [inciter] : **~ qqn à faire qqch** [suj : circonstances] to lead sb to do sthg ; [suj : personne] to get sb to do sthg - **3.** [occasionner, préparer] to bring about.

amenuiser [3] [amənɥize] *vt* - **1.** [rendre plus petit] : **ses cheveux amenuisent son visage** her hair makes her face look thinner - **2.** [réduire] to diminish, to reduce. **s'amenuiser** *vp* to dwindle, to diminish.

amer, ère [amer] *adj* bitter.

américain, e [amerikẽ, ɛn] *adj* American. **américain** *nm* [langue] American English. **Américain, e** *nm, f* American.

américanisme [amerikanism] *nm* Americanism.

Amérique [amerik] *nf* : **l'~** America ; **l'~ centrale** Central America ; **l'~ du Nord**

North America ; **l'~ du Sud** South America ; **l'~ latine** Latin America.

amertume [amɛrtym] *nf* bitterness.

améthyste [ametist] *nf* amethyst.

ameublement [amœbləmã] *nm* [meubles] furniture ; [action de meubler] furnishing.

ami, e [ami] ⬦ *adj* friendly. ⬦ *nm, f* - **1.** [camarade] friend ; **petit ~** boyfriend ; **petite ~e** girlfriend - **2.** [partisan] supporter, friend.

amiable [amjabl] *adj* [accord] friendly, informal. ⬦ **à l'amiable** *loc adv* & *loc adj* out of court.

amiante [amjãt] *nm* asbestos.

amibe [amib] *nf* amoeba.

amical, e, aux [amikal, o] *adj* friendly. ⬦ **amicale** *nf* association, club *(for people with a shared interest).*

amicalement [amikalmã] *adv* - **1.** [de façon amicale] amicably, in a friendly way - **2.** [dans une lettre] yours (ever), (with) best wishes.

amidon [amidõ] *nm* starch.

amidonner [3] [amidɔne] *vt* to starch.

amincissant, e [amɛ̃sisã, ãt] *adj* slimming.

amiral, aux [amiral, o] *nm* admiral.

amitié [amitje] *nf* - **1.** [affection] affection ; **prendre qqn en ~** to befriend sb - **2.** [rapports amicaux] friendship ; **faire ses ~s à qqn** to give sb one's good *ou* best wishes.

ammoniac, aque [amɔnjak] *adj* CHIM ammoniac. ⬦ **ammoniac** *nm* ammonia. ⬦ **ammoniaque** *nf* ammonia (water).

amnésie [amnezi] *nf* amnesia.

amniocentèse [amnjɔsɛ̃tɛz] *nf* amniocentesis.

amnistie [amnisti] *nf* amnesty.

amnistier [9] [amnistje] *vt* to amnesty.

amoindrir [32] [amwɛ̃drir] *vt* to diminish.

amonceler [24] [amõsle] *vt* to accumulate.

amont [amõ] *nm* upstream (water) ; **en ~ de** [rivière] upriver *ou* upstream from ; *fig* prior to.

amoral, e, aux [amɔral, o] *adj* - **1.** [qui ignore la morale] amoral - **2.** [débauché] immoral.

amorce [amɔrs] *nf* - **1.** [d'explosif] priming ; [de cartouche, d'obus] cap - **2.** PÊCHE bait - **3.** *fig* [commencement] beginnings *(pl)*, germ.

amorcer [16] [amɔrse] *vt* - **1.** [explosif] to prime - **2.** PÊCHE to bait - **3.** *fig* [commencer] to begin, to initiate.

amorphe [amɔrf] *adj* [personne] lifeless.

amortir [32] [amɔrtir] *vt* - **1.** [atténuer - choc] to absorb ; [- bruit] to deaden, to muffle - **2.** [dette] to pay off - **3.** [achat] to write off.

amour [amur] *nm* [gén] love ; **faire l'~** to make love. ⬦ **amours** *nfpl* [vie sentimentale] love-life.

amoureux, euse [amurø, øz] ⬦ *adj* - **1.** [personne] in love ; **être/tomber ~ (de)** to be/fall in love (with) - **2.** [regard, geste] loving. ⬦ *nm, f* - **1.** [prétendant] suitor - **2.** [passionné] : **~ de** lover of ; **un ~ de la nature** a nature lover.

amour-propre [amurprɔpr] *nm* pride, self-respect.

amovible [amɔvibl] *adj* [déplaçable] detachable, removable.

ampère [ɑ̃pɛr] *nm* amp, ampere.

amphétamine [ɑ̃fetamin] *nf* amphetamine.

amphi [ɑ̃fi] *nm fam* lecture hall *ou* theatre ; **cours en ~** lecture.

amphibie [ɑ̃fibi] *adj* amphibious.

amphithéâtre [ɑ̃fiteatr] *nm* - **1.** HIST amphitheatre - **2.** [d'université] lecture hall *ou* theatre.

ample [ɑ̃pl] *adj* - **1.** [vêtement - gén] loose-fitting ; [- jupe] full - **2.** [projet] extensive ; **pour de plus ~s informations** for further details - **3.** [geste] broad, sweeping.

amplement [ɑ̃pləmã] *adv* [largement] fully, amply.

ampleur [ɑ̃plœr] *nf* - **1.** [de vêtement] fullness - **2.** [d'événement, de dégâts] extent.

ampli [ɑ̃pli] *nm* amp.

amplificateur, trice [ɑ̃plifikatœr, tris] *adj* ÉLECTR amplifying ; **un phénomène ~ de la croissance** *fig* a phenomenon which increases growth. ⬦ **amplificateur** *nm* - **1.** [gén] amplifier - **2.** PHOT enlarger.

amplifier [9] [ɑ̃plifje] *vt* - **1.** [mouvement, son] to amplify ; [image] to magnify, to enlarge - **2.** [scandale] to increase ; [événement, problème] to highlight.

amplitude [ɑ̃plityd] *nf* - **1.** [de geste] fullness - **2.** [d'onde] amplitude - **3.** [de température] range.

ampoule [ɑ̃pul] *nf* - **1.** [de lampe] bulb - **2.** [sur la peau] blister - **3.** [médicament] ampoule, phial.

amputation [ɑ̃pytasjõ] *nf* MÉD amputation.

amputer [3] [ɑ̃pyte] *vt* MÉD to amputate ; *fig* [couper] to cut (back *ou* down) ; **son article a été amputé d'un tiers** his article was cut by a third.

amulette [amylɛt] *nf* amulet.

amusant, e [amyzɑ̃, ɑ̃t] *adj* [drôle] funny ; [distrayant] amusing ; **c'est très ~** it's great fun.

amuse-gueule [amyzgœl] *nm inv fam* cocktail snack, (party) nibble.

amusement [amyzmɑ̃] *nm* amusement *(U)*.

amuser [3] [amyze] *vt* to amuse, to entertain. ◆ **s'amuser** *vp* to have fun, to have a good time ; **s'~ à faire qqch** to amuse o.s. (by) doing sth.

amygdale [amidal] *nf* tonsil.

an [ɑ̃] *nm* year ; **avoir sept ~s** to be seven (years old) ; **en l'~ 2000** in the year 2000 ; **le nouvel ~** the New Year.

anabolisant [anabɔlizɑ̃] *nm* anabolic steroid.

anachronique [anakrɔnik] *adj* anachronistic.

anagramme [anagram] *nf* anagram.

anal, e, aux [anal, o] *adj* anal.

analgésique [analʒezik] *nm & adj* analgesic.

anallergique [analɛrʒik] *adj* hypoallergenic.

analogie [analɔʒi] *nf* analogy.

analogique [analɔʒik] *adj* analogue *Br*, analog *Am*.

analogue [analɔg] *adj* analogous, comparable.

analphabète [analfabɛt] *nmf & adj* illiterate.

analyse [analiz] *nf* - **1.** [étude] analysis - **2.** CHIM & MÉD test, analysis - **3.** [psychanalyse] analysis *(U)*.

analyser [3] [analize] *vt* - **1.** [étudier, psychanalyser] to analyse *Br*, to analyze *Am* - **2.** CHIM & MÉD to test, to analyse *Br*, to analyze *Am*.

analyste [analist] *nmf* analyst.

analyste-programmeur, euse [analistprɔgramœr, øz] *nm, f* systems analyst.

analytique [analitik] *adj* analytical.

ananas [anana(s)] *nm* pineapple.

anarchie [anarʃi] *nf* - **1.** POLIT anarchy - **2.** [désordre] chaos, anarchy.

anarchique [anarʃik] *adj* anarchic.

anarchiste [anarʃist] *nmf & adj* anarchist.

anatomie [anatɔmi] *nf* anatomy.

anatomique [anatɔmik] *adj* anatomical.

ancestral, e, aux [ɑ̃sestral, o] *adj* ancestral.

ancêtre [ɑ̃sɛtr] *nmf* [aïeul] ancestor ; *fig* [forme première] forerunner, ancestor ; *fig* [initiateur] father (*f* mother).

anchois [ɑ̃ʃwa] *nm* anchovy.

ancien, enne [ɑ̃sjɛ̃, ɛn] *adj* - **1.** [gén] old - **2.** *(avant n)* [précédent] former, old - **3.** [qui a de l'ancienneté] senior - **4.** [du passé] ancient.

anciennement [ɑ̃sjɛnmɑ̃] *adv* formerly, previously.

ancienneté [ɑ̃sjɛnte] *nf* - **1.** [d'une tradition] oldness - **2.** [d'un employé] seniority.

ancre [ɑ̃kr] *nf* NAVIG anchor ; **jeter l'~** to drop anchor ; **lever l'~** to weigh anchor ; *fam* [partir] to make tracks.

ancrer [3] [ɑ̃kre] *vt* [bateau] to anchor ; *fig* [idée, habitude] to root.

Andes [ɑ̃d] *nfpl* : **les ~** the Andes.

Andorre [ɑ̃dɔr] *nf* : **(la principauté d')~** (the principality of) Andorra.

andouille [ɑ̃duj] *nf* - **1.** [charcuterie] *type of sausage made of chitterlings (pig's intestines eaten cold)* - **2.** *fam* [imbécile] prat, twit.

âne [an] *nm* - **1.** ZOOL ass, donkey - **2.** *fam* [imbécile] ass.

anéantir [32] [aneɑ̃tir] *vt* - **1.** [détruire] to annihilate ; *fig* to ruin, to wreck - **2.** [démoraliser] to crush, to overwhelm.

anecdote [anɛkdɔt] *nf* anecdote.

anecdotique [anɛkdɔtik] *adj* anecdotal.

anémie [anemi] *nf* MÉD anaemia *Br*, anemia *Am* ; *fig* enfeeblement.

anémié, e [anemje] *adj* anaemic *Br*, anemic *Am*.

anémique [anemik] *adj* anaemic *Br*, anemic *Am*.

anémone [anemɔn] *nf* anemone.

ânerie [anri] *nf fam* [parole, acte] : **dire/ faire une ~** to say/do something stupid.

ânesse [anɛs] *nf* she-ass, she-donkey.

anesthésie [anɛstezi] *nf* anaesthesia *Br*, anesthesia *Am* ; **~ locale** local anaesthetic *Br* ou anesthetic *Am* ; **~ générale** general anaesthetic *Br* ou anesthetic *Am*.

anesthésier [9] [anɛstezje] *vt* to anaesthetize *Br*, to anesthetize *Am*.

anesthésique [anɛstezik] *nm & adj* anaesthetic *Br*, anesthetic *Am*.

anesthésiste [anɛstezist] *nmf* anaesthetist *Br*, anesthetist *Am*.

anfractuosité [ɑ̃fraktɥozite] *nf* crevice.

ange [ɑ̃ʒ] *nm* angel ; **~ gardien** guardian angel ; **être aux ~s** *fig* to be in one's seventh heaven.

angélique [ɑ̃ʒelik] *adj* angelic.

angélus [ɑ̃ʒelys] *nm* [sonnerie] angelus (bell).

angine [ɑ̃ʒin] *nf* [pharyngite] pharyngitis ; [amygdalite] tonsillitis.

anglais, e [ɑ̃glɛ, ɛz] *adj* English. ◆ **anglais** *nm* [langue] English. ◆ **Anglais, e** *nm, f* Englishman (*f* Englishwoman) ; **les Anglais** the English. ◆ **anglaises** *nfpl* ringlets.

angle [ɑ̃gl] *nm* - **1.** [coin] corner - **2.** MATHS angle ; ~ **droit/aigu/obtus** right/acute/obtuse angle.

Angleterre [ɑ̃glətɛr] *nf* : l' ~ England.

anglican, e [ɑ̃glikɑ̃, an] *adj & nm, f* Anglican.

anglophone [ɑ̃glɔfɔn] <> *nmf* English-speaker. <> *adj* English-speaking, anglophone.

anglo-saxon, onne [ɑ̃glosaksɔ̃, ɔn] *adj* Anglo-Saxon. ◆ **anglo-saxon** *nm* [langue] Anglo-Saxon, Old English. ◆ **Anglo-Saxon, onne** *nm, f* Anglo-Saxon.

angoisse [ɑ̃gwas] *nf* anguish.

angoisser [3] [ɑ̃gwase] *vt* [effrayer] to cause anxiety to. ◆ **s'angoisser** *vp* - **1.** [être anxieux] to be overcome with anxiety - **2.** *fam* [s'inquiéter] to fret.

anguille [ɑ̃gij] *nf* eel.

anguleux, euse [ɑ̃gylø, øz] *adj* angular.

anicroche [anikrɔʃ] *nf* hitch.

animal, e, aux [animal, o] *adj* - **1.** [propre à l'animal] animal (*avant n*) - **2.** [instinctif] instinctive. ◆ **animal** *nm* [bête] animal ; ~ **sauvage/domestique** wild/domestic animal.

animateur, trice [animatœr, tris] *nm, f* - **1.** RADIO & TÉLÉ presenter - **2.** [socioculturel, sportif] activities organizer.

animation [animasjɔ̃] *nf* - **1.** [de rue] activity, life ; [de conversation, visage] animation - **2.** [activités] activities (*pl*) - **3.** CIN animation.

animé, e [anime] *adj* [rue] lively ; [conversation, visage] animated ; [objet] animate.

animer [3] [anime] *vt* - **1.** [mettre de l'entrain dans] to animate, to liven up - **2.** [présenter] to present - **3.** [organiser des activités pour] to organize activities for. ◆ **s'animer** *vp* - **1.** [visage] to light up - **2.** [rue] to come to life, to liven up.

animosité [animozite] *nf* animosity.

anis [ani(s)] *nm* BOT anise ; CULIN aniseed.

ankylosé, e [ɑ̃kiloze] *adj* [paralysé] stiff ; [engourdi] numb.

annales [anal] *nfpl* - **1.** [d'examen] past papers - **2.** [chronique annuelle] chronicle (*sg*), annals.

anneau, x [ano] *nm* - **1.** [gén] ring - **2.** [maillon] link.

année [ane] *nf* year ; **souhaiter la bonne ~ à qqn** to wish sb a Happy New Year ; ~ **bissextile** leap year ; ~**-lumière** light year ; ~ **scolaire** school year.

annexe [anɛks] <> *nf* - **1.** [de dossier] appendix, annexe - **2.** [de bâtiment] annexe. <> *adj* related, associated.

annexer [4] [anɛkse] *vt* - **1.** [incorporer] : ~ **qqch (à qqch)** to append OU annex sthg (to sthg) - **2.** [pays] to annex.

annexion [anɛksjɔ̃] *nf* annexation.

annihiler [3] [aniile] *vt* [réduire à néant] to destroy, to wreck.

anniversaire [anivɛrsɛr] <> *nm* [de mariage, mort, événement] anniversary ; [de naissance] birthday ; **bon** OU **joyeux ~!** happy birthday! <> *adj* anniversary (*avant n*).

annonce [anɔ̃s] *nf* - **1.** [déclaration] announcement ; *fig* sign, indication - **2.** [texte] advertisement ; **petite ~** classified advertisement, small ad.

annoncer [16] [anɔ̃se] *vt* - **1.** [faire savoir] to announce - **2.** [prédire] to predict.

annonciateur, trice [anɔ̃sjatœr, tris] *adj* : ~ **de qqch** heralding sthg.

annoter [3] [anɔte] *vt* to annotate.

annuaire [anɥɛr] *nm* annual, yearbook ; ~ **téléphonique** telephone directory, phone book.

annuel, elle [anɥɛl] *adj* - **1.** [tous les ans] annual, yearly - **2.** [d'une année] annual.

annuité [anɥite] *nf* - **1.** [paiement] annual payment, annual instalment *Br* OU installment *Am* - **2.** [année de service] year (of service).

annulaire [anɥlɛr] *nm* ring finger.

annulation [anylasjɔ̃] *nf* - **1.** [de rendez-vous, réservation] cancellation - **2.** [de mariage] annulment.

annuler [3] [anyle] *vt* - **1.** [rendez-vous, réservation] to cancel - **2.** [mariage] to annul. ◆ **s'annuler** *vp* to cancel each other out.

anoblir [32] [anɔblir] *vt* to ennoble.

anodin, e [anɔdɛ̃, in] *adj* - **1.** [blessure] minor - **2.** [propos] harmless - **3.** [détail, personne] insignificant.

anomalie [anɔmali] *nf* anomaly.

ânon [anɔ̃] *nm* young donkey OU ass.

ânonner [3] [anɔne] *vt & vi* to recite in a drone.

anonymat [anɔnima] *nm* anonymity.

anonyme [anɔnim] *adj* anonymous.

anorak [anɔrak] *nm* anorak.

anorexie [anɔrɛksi] *nf* anorexia.

anormal, e, aux [anɔrmal, o] ◇ *adj*
- **1.** [inhabituel] abnormal, not normal
- **2.** [intolérable, injuste] wrong, not right
- **3.** [arriéré] (mentally) subnormal. ◇ *nm, f*
mental defective.

ANPE (*abr de* **Agence nationale pour l'emploi**) *nf French national employment agency,* ≃
job centre *Br.*

anse [ɑ̃s] *nf* - **1.** [d'ustensile] handle
- **2.** GÉOGR cove.

antagoniste [ɑ̃tagɔnist] *adj* antagonistic.

antan [ɑ̃tɑ̃] ◆ **d'antan** *loc adj littéraire* of
old, of yesteryear.

antarctique [ɑ̃tarktik] *adj* Antarctic ; **le
cercle polaire ~** the Antarctic Circle.
◆ **Antarctique** *nm* - **1.** [continent] : **l'~**
Antarctica - **2.** [océan] : **l'~** the Antarctic
(Ocean).

antécédent [ɑ̃tesedɑ̃] *nm* (*gén pl*) [passé]
history (*sg*).

antenne [ɑ̃tɛn] *nf* - **1.** [d'insecte] antenna,
feeler - **2.** [de télévision, de radio] aerial *Br*,
antenna ; **~ parabolique** dish aerial ou antenna *Am*, satellite dish - **3.** [succursale]
branch, office.

antérieur, e [ɑ̃terjœr] *adj* - **1.** [dans le
temps] earlier, previous ; **~ à** previous ou
prior to - **2.** [dans l'espace] front (*avant n*).

antérieurement [ɑ̃terjœrmɑ̃] *adv* earlier, previously ; **~ à** prior to.

anthologie [ɑ̃tɔlɔʒi] *nf* anthology.

anthracite [ɑ̃trasit] ◇ *nm* anthracite.
◇ *adj inv* charcoal grey *Br* ou gray *Am*.

anthrax® [ɑ̃traks] *nm fam* MED anthrax.

anthropologie [ɑ̃trɔpɔlɔʒi] *nf* anthropology.

anthropophage [ɑ̃trɔpɔfaʒ] *nmf* cannibal.

antialcoolique [ɑ̃tialkɔlik] *adj* : **ligue ~**
temperance league.

antibiotique [ɑ̃tibjɔtik] *nm & adj* antibiotic.

antibrouillard [ɑ̃tibrujar] *nm & adj inv* :
(phare ou **feu) ~** fog lamp *Br*, foglight *Am*.

antichambre [ɑ̃tiʃɑ̃br] *nf* antechamber ;
faire ~ *fig* to wait patiently (*to see somebody*).

anticipation [ɑ̃tisipasjɔ̃] *nf* LITTÉRATURE :
roman d'~ science fiction novel.

anticipé, e [ɑ̃tisipe] *adj* early.

anticiper [ɑ̃tisipe] ◇ *vt* to anticipate.
◇ *vi* : **~ (sur qqch)** to anticipate (sthg).

anticonformiste [ɑ̃tikɔ̃fɔrmist] *adj &
nmf* non-conformist.

anticorps [ɑ̃tikɔr] *nm* antibody.

anticyclone [ɑ̃tisiklon] *nm* anticyclone.

antidater [3] [ɑ̃tidate] *vt* to backdate.

antidémarrage [ɑ̃tidemaraʒ] *adj inv* :
système ~ immobilizer.

antidépresseur [ɑ̃tidepresœr] *nm &
adj m* antidepressant.

antidopage [ɑ̃tidɔpaʒ], **antidoping**
[ɑ̃tidɔpiŋ] *adj inv* : **contrôle ~** dope test,
drugs test.

antidote [ɑ̃tidɔt] *nm* antidote.

antigel [ɑ̃tiʒɛl] *nm inv & adj inv* antifreeze.

antillais, e [ɑ̃tije, ɛz] *adj* West Indian.
◆ **Antillais, e** *nm, f* West Indian.

Antilles [ɑ̃tij] *nfpl* : **les ~** the West Indies.

antilope [ɑ̃tilɔp] *nf* antelope.

antimilitariste [ɑ̃timilitarist] *nmf & adj*
antimilitarist.

antimite [ɑ̃timit] *adj inv* : **boule ~** mothball.

antipathie [ɑ̃tipati] *nf* antipathy, hostility.

antipathique [ɑ̃tipatik] *adj* unpleasant ;
elle m'est ~ I dislike her, I don't like her.

antipelliculaire [ɑ̃tipelikylɛr] *adj* :
shampooing ~ anti-dandruff shampoo.

antiquaire [ɑ̃tikɛr] *nmf* antique dealer.

antique [ɑ̃tik] *adj* - **1.** [de l'antiquité - civilisation] ancient ; [- vase, objet] antique
- **2.** [vieux] antiquated, ancient.

antiquité [ɑ̃tikite] *nf* - **1.** [époque] : **l'Antiquité** antiquity - **2.** [objet] antique.

antirabique [ɑ̃tirabik] *adj* : **vaccin ~** rabies vaccine.

antiraciste [ɑ̃tirasist] *adj & nmf* antiracist.

antirides [ɑ̃tirid] *adj inv* anti-wrinkle.

antirouille [ɑ̃tiruj] *adj inv* [traitement]
rust (*avant n*) ; [revêtement, peinture] rustproof.

antisèche [ɑ̃tisɛʃ] *nf arg scol* crib *Br*, cheat
sheet *Am*.

antisémite [ɑ̃tisemit] ◇ *nmf* anti-Semite. ◇ *adj* anti-Semitic.

antiseptique [ɑ̃tisɛptik] *nm & adj* antiseptic.

antisismique [ɑ̃tisismik] *adj* earthquakeproof.

antithèse [ɑ̃titɛz] *nf* antithesis.

antiviral, aux [ɑ̃tiviral, o] *nm* antivirus.

antivol [ɑ̃tivɔl] *nm inv* anti-theft device.

antre [ɑ̃tr] *nm* den, lair.

anus [anys] *nm* anus.

anxiété [ɑ̃ksjete] *nf* anxiety.

anxieux, euse [ɑ̃ksjø, øz] ◇ *adj* anxious, worried ; **être ~ de qqch** to be worried ou anxious about sthg ; **être ~ de faire**

qqch to be anxious to do sthg. ◇ *nm, f* worrier.

aorte [aɔrt] *nf* aorta.

août [u(t)] *nm* August ; *voir aussi* **septembre.**

apaisement [apɛzmɑ̃] *nm* - **1.** [moral] comfort - **2.** [de douleur] alleviation - **3.** [de tension, de crise] calming.

apaiser [4] [apeze] *vt* - **1.** [personne] to calm down, to pacify - **2.** [conscience] to salve ; [douleur] to soothe ; [soif] to slake, to quench ; [faim] to assuage. ◆ **s'apaiser** *vp* - **1.** [personne] to calm down - **2.** [besoin] to be assuaged ; [tempête] to subside, to abate ; [douleur] to die down ; [scrupules] to be allayed.

apanage [apanaʒ] *nm sout* privilege ; **être l'~ de qqn/qqch** to be the prerogative of sb/sthg.

aparté [aparte] *nm* - **1.** THÉÂTRE aside - **2.** [conversation] private conversation ; **prendre qqn en ~** to take sb aside.

apartheid [apartɛd] *nm* apartheid.

apathie [apati] *nf* apathy.

apathique [apatik] *adj* apathetic.

apatride [apatrid] *nmf* stateless person.

apercevoir [52] [apɛrsəvwar] *vt* [voir] to see, to catch sight of. ◆ **s'apercevoir** *vp* : **s'~ de qqch** to notice sthg ; **s'~ que** to notice (that).

aperçu, e [apɛrsy] *pp* ▷ **apercevoir.** ◆ **aperçu** *nm* general idea.

apéritif, ive [aperitif, iv] *adj* which whets the appetite. ◆ **apéritif** *nm* aperitif ; **prendre l'~** to have an aperitif, to have drinks *(before a meal).*

apesanteur [apəzɑ̃tœr] *nf* weightlessness.

à-peu-près [apøprɛ] *nm inv* approximation.

aphone [afɔn] *adj* voiceless.

aphrodisiaque [afrɔdizjak] *nm & adj* aphrodisiac.

aphte [aft] *nm* mouth ulcer.

apiculteur, trice [apikyltœr, tris] *nm, f* beekeeper.

apitoyer [13] [apitwaje] *vt* to move to pity. ◆ **s'apitoyer** *vp* to feel pity ; **s'~ sur** to feel sorry for.

ap. J.-C. *(abr de* **après Jésus-Christ)** AD.

aplanir [32] [aplanir] *vt* - **1.** [aplatir] to level - **2.** *fig* [difficulté, obstacle] to smooth away, to iron out.

aplatir [32] [aplatir] *vt* [gén] to flatten ; [couture] to press flat ; [cheveux] to smooth down.

aplomb [aplɔ̃] *nm* - **1.** [stabilité] balance - **2.** [audace] nerve, cheek. ◆ **d'aplomb** *loc adv* steady.

apocalypse [apɔkalips] *nf* apocalypse.

apogée [apɔʒe] *nm* ASTRON apogee ; *fig* peak.

apolitique [apɔlitik] *adj* apolitical, unpolitical.

apologie [apɔlɔʒi] *nf* justification, apology.

apoplexie [apɔplɛksi] *nf* apoplexy.

apostrophe [apɔstrɔf] *nf* [signe graphique] apostrophe.

apostropher [3] [apɔstrɔfe] *vt* : **~ qqn** to speak rudely to sb.

apothéose [apɔteoz] *nf* - **1.** [consécration] great honour *Br* ou honor *Am* - **2.** [point culminant - d'un spectacle] grand finale ; [- d'une carrière] crowning glory.

apôtre [apotr] *nm* apostle, disciple.

apparaître [91] [aparɛtr] ◇ *vi* - **1.** [gén] to appear - **2.** [se dévoiler] to come to light. ◇ *v impers* : **il apparaît que** it seems ou appears that.

apparat [apara] *nm* pomp ; **d'~** [dîner, habit] ceremonial.

appareil [aparɛj] *nm* - **1.** [gén] device ; [électrique] appliance - **2.** [téléphone] phone, telephone ; **qui est à l'~?** who's speaking? - **3.** [avion] aircraft. ◆ **appareil digestif** *nm* digestive system. ◆ **appareil photo** *nm* camera ; **~ photo numérique** digital camera.

appareillage [aparɛjaʒ] *nm* - **1.** [équipement] equipment - **2.** NAVIG getting under way.

appareiller [4] [apareje] ◇ *vt* [assortir] to match up. ◇ *vi* NAVIG to get under way.

apparemment [aparamɑ̃] *adv* apparently.

apparence [aparɑ̃s] *nf* appearance. ◆ **en apparence** *loc adv* seemingly, apparently.

apparent, e [aparɑ̃, ɑ̃t] *adj* - **1.** [superficiel, illusoire] apparent - **2.** [visible] visible.

apparenté, e [aparɑ̃te] *adj* : **~ à** [personne] related to ; *fig* [ressemblant] similar to.

appariteur [aparitœr] *nm* porter *(in university).*

apparition [aparisjɔ̃] *nf* - **1.** [gén] appearance - **2.** [vision - RELIG] vision ; [- de fantôme] apparition.

appart [apart] *(abr de* **appartement)** *nm fam* flat *Br*, apartment *Am*.

appartement [apartəmɑ̃] *nm* flat *Br*, apartment *Am*.

appartenir [40] [apartənir] *vi* - **1.** [être la propriété de] : **~ à qqn** to belong to sb

- **2.** [faire partie de] **: ~ à qqch** to belong to sthg, to be a member of sthg ; **il ne m'appartient pas de faire ...** *fig & sout* it's not up to me to do ...

appartenu [apartəny] *pp inv* ⊳ **appartenir.**

apparu, e [apary] *pp* ⊳ **apparaître.**

appâter [3] [apate] *vt litt & fig* to lure.

appauvrir [32] [apovrir] *vt* to impoverish. ➧ **s'appauvrir** *vp* to grow poorer, to become impoverished.

appel [apɛl] *nm* - **1.** [gén] call ; **faire ~ à qqn** to appeal to sb ; **faire ~ à qqch** [nécessiter] to call for sthg ; [avoir recours à] to call on sthg ; **~ (téléphonique)** (phone) call - **2.** JUR appeal ; **faire ~** JUR to appeal ; **sans ~** final - **3.** [pour vérifier - gén] roll-call ; [- SCOL] registration - **4.** COMM : **~ d'offre** invitation to tender - **5.** [signe] : **faire un ~ de phares** to flash one's headlights.

appelé [aple] *nm* conscript.

appeler [24] [aple] *vt* - **1.** [gén] to call - **2.** [téléphoner] to ring, to call - **3.** [exiger] to call for. ➧ **s'appeler** *vp* - **1.** [se nommer] to be called ; **comment cela s'appelle? what is it called?** ; **il s'appelle Patrick** his name is Patrick, he's called Patrick - **2.** [se téléphoner] : **on s'appelle demain?** shall we talk tomorrow?

appendice [apɛ̃dis] *nm* appendix.

appendicite [apɛ̃disit] *nf* appendicitis.

appentis [apɑ̃ti] *nm* lean-to.

appesantir [32] [apəzɑ̃tir] *vt* [démarche] to slow down. ➧ **s'appesantir** *vp* - **1.** [s'alourdir] to become heavy - **2.** [insister] : **s'~ sur qqch** to dwell on sthg.

appétissant, e [apetisɑ̃, ɑ̃t] *adj* [nourriture] appetizing.

appétit [apeti] *nm* appetite ; **bon ~!** enjoy your meal!

applaudir [32] [aplodir] ◇ *vt* to applaud. ◇ *vi* to clap, to applaud ; **~ à qqch** *fig* to applaud sthg ; **~ à tout rompre** *fig* to bring the house down.

applaudissements [aplodismɑ̃] *nmpl* applause (U), clapping (U).

applicable [aplikabl] *adj* : **~ à** applicable (to).

application [aplikasjɔ̃] *nf* [gén & INFORM] application.

applique [aplik] *nf* wall lamp.

appliquer [3] [aplike] *vt* [gén] to apply ; [loi] to enforce. ➧ **s'appliquer** *vp* - **1.** [s'étaler, se poser] : **cette peinture s'applique facilement** this paint goes on easily - **2.** [se concentrer] : **s'~ (à faire qqch)** to apply o.s. (to doing sthg).

appoint [apwɛ̃] *nm* - **1.** [monnaie] change ; **faire l'~** to give the right money - **2.** [aide] help, support ; **d'~** [salaire, chauffage] extra ; **lit d'~** spare bed.

appointements [apwɛ̃tmɑ̃] *nmpl* salary *(sg).*

apport [apɔr] *nm* - **1.** [gén & FIN] contribution - **2.** [de chaleur] input.

apporter [3] [apɔrte] *vt* - **1.** [gén] to bring ; **ça m'a beaucoup apporté** *fig* I got a lot from it - **2.** [raison, preuve] to provide, to give - **3.** [mettre - soin] to exercise ; [- attention] to give.

apposer [3] [apoze] *vt* - **1.** [affiche] to put up - **2.** [signature] to append.

apposition [apozisjɔ̃] *nf* GRAM apposition.

appréciable [apresjabl] *adj* - **1.** [notable] appreciable - **2.** [précieux] : **un grand jardin, c'est ~!** I/we really appreciate having a big garden.

appréciation [apresjasjɔ̃] *nf* - **1.** [de valeur] valuation ; [de distance, poids] estimation - **2.** [jugement] judgment - **3.** SCOL assessment.

apprécier [9] [apresje] *vt* - **1.** [gén] to appreciate - **2.** [évaluer] to estimate, to assess.

appréhender [3] [apreɑ̃de] *vt* - **1.** [arrêter] to arrest - **2.** [craindre] : **~ qqch/de faire qqch** to dread sthg/doing sthg.

appréhension [apreɑ̃sjɔ̃] *nf* apprehension.

apprendre [79] [aprɑ̃dr] *vt* - **1.** [étudier] to learn ; **~ à faire qqch** to learn (how) to do sthg - **2.** [enseigner] to teach ; **~ qqch à qqn** to teach sb sthg ; **~ à qqn à faire qqch** to teach sb (how) to do sthg - **3.** [nouvelle] to hear of, to learn ; **~ que** to hear that, to learn that ; **~ qqch à qqn** to tell sb of sthg.

apprenti, e [aprɑ̃ti] *nm, f* [élève] apprentice ; *fig* beginner.

apprentissage [aprɑ̃tisaʒ] *nm* - **1.** [de métier] apprenticeship - **2.** [formation] learning.

apprêter [4] [aprete] *vt* to prepare. ➧ **s'apprêter** *vp* - **1.** [être sur le point] : **s'~ à faire qqch** to get ready to do sthg - **2.** [s'habiller] : **s'~ pour qqch** to dress up for sthg.

appris, e [apri, iz] *pp* ⊳ **apprendre.**

apprivoiser [3] [aprivwaze] *vt* to tame.

approbateur, trice [aprobatœr, tris] *adj* approving.

approbation [aprobasjɔ̃] *nf* approval.

approchant, e [aprofɑ̃, ɑ̃t] *adj* similar.

approche [aprof] *nf* [arrivée] approach ; **à l'~ des fêtes** as the Christmas holidays draw near ; **il a pressé le pas à l'~ de la maison** he quickened his step as he approached the house.

approcher [3] [aprɔʃe] ◇ *vt* - **1.** [mettre plus près] to move near, to bring near ; **~ qqch de qqn/qqch** to move sthg near (to) sb/sthg - **2.** [aborder] to go up to, to approach. ◇ *vi* to approach, to go/come near ; **approchez!** come nearer! ; **n'approchez pas!** keep ou stay away! ; **~ de** [moment, fin] to approach. ◆ **s'approcher** *vp* to come/go near, to approach ; **s'~ de qqn/qqch** to approach sb/sthg.

approfondir [32] [aprɔfɔ̃dir] *vt* - **1.** [creuser] to make deeper - **2.** [développer] to go further into.

approprié, e [aproprije] *adj* : **~ (à)** appropriate (to).

approprier [10] [aproprije] *vt* - **1.** [adapter] to adapt - **2.** *Belg* to clean. ◆ **s'approprier** *vp* [s'adjuger] to appropriate.

approuver [3] [apruve] *vt* [gén] to approve of.

approvisionnement [aprɔvizjɔnmɑ̃] *nm* supplies *(pl)*, stocks *(pl)*.

approvisionner [3] [aprɔvizjɔne] *vt* - **1.** [compte en banque] to pay money into - **2.** [magasin, pays] to supply.

approximatif, ive [aprɔksimatif, iv] *adj* approximate, rough.

approximation [aprɔksimasjɔ̃] *nf* approximation.

approximativement [aprɔksimativmɑ̃] *adv* approximately, roughly.

appt *abr de* appartement.

appui [apɥi] *nm* [soutien] support.

appui-tête [apɥitɛt] *(pl* appuis-tête) *nm* headrest.

appuyer [14] [apɥije] ◇ *vt* - **1.** [poser] : **~ qqch sur/contre qqch** to lean sthg on/against sthg, to rest sthg on/against sthg - **2.** [presser] : **~ qqch sur/contre** to press sthg on/against - **3.** *fig* [soutenir] to support. ◇ *vi* - **1.** [reposer] : **~ sur** to lean ou rest on - **2.** [presser] to push ; **~ sur** [bouton] to press - **3.** *fig* [insister] : **~ sur** to stress - **4.** [se diriger] : **~ sur la** ou **à droite** to bear right. ◆ **s'appuyer** *vp* - **1.** [se tenir] : **s'~ contre/sur** to lean against/on, to rest against/on - **2.** [se baser] : **s'~ sur** to rely on.

âpre [apr] *adj* - **1.** [goût, discussion, combat] bitter - **2.** [ton, épreuve, critique] harsh - **3.** [concurrence] fierce.

après [aprɛ] ◇ *prép* - **1.** [gén] after ; **~ avoir mangé, ils ...** after having eaten ou after they had eaten, they ... ; **~ cela** after that ; **~ quoi** after which - **2.** [indiquant l'attirance, l'attachement, l'hostilité] : **soupirer**

~ qqn to yearn for sb ; **aboyer ~ qqn** to bark at sb. ◇ *adv* - **1.** [temps] afterwards ; **un mois ~** one month later ; **le mois d'~** the following ou next month - **2.** [lieu, dans un ordre, dans un rang] : **la rue d'~** the next street ; **c'est ma sœur qui vient ~** my sister's next. ◆ **après coup** *loc adv* afterwards, after the event. ◆ **après que** *loc conj* (+ *indicatif*) after ; **je le verrai ~ qu'il aura fini** I'll see him after ou when he's finished ; **~ qu'ils eurent dîné, ...** after dinner ou after they had dined, ... ◆ **après tout** *loc adv* after all. ◆ **d'après** *loc prép* according to ; **d'~ moi** in my opinion ; **d'~ lui** according to him. ◆ **et après** *loc adv* (*employée interrogativement*) - **1.** [questionnement sur la suite] and then what? - **2.** [exprime l'indifférence] so what?

après-demain [apredmɛ̃] *adv* the day after tomorrow.

après-guerre [apregɛr] *nm* post-war years *(pl)* ; **d'~** post-war.

après-midi [apremidi] *nm inv* ou *nf inv* afternoon.

après-rasage [aprerazaʒ] *nm* & *adj inv* aftershave.

après-ski [apreski] *nm* [chaussure] snow-boot.

après-soleil [apresɔlej] *adj inv* after-sun (*avant n*).

après-vente [aprevɑ̃t] ▷ **service**.

à-propos [apropo] *nm inv* [de remarque] aptness ; **faire preuve d'~** to show presence of mind.

apte [apt] *adj* : **~ à qqch/à faire qqch** capable of sthg/of doing sthg ; **~ (au service)** MIL fit (for service).

aquagym [akwaʒim] *nf* aquarobics *(U)*.

aquarelle [akwarɛl] *nf* watercolour.

aquarium [akwarjɔm] *nm* aquarium.

aquatique [akwatik] *adj* [plante, animal] aquatic ; [milieu, paysage] watery, marshy.

aqueduc [akdyk] *nm* aqueduct.

aqueux, euse [akø, øz] *adj* watery.

aquilin [akilɛ̃] ▷ **nez**.

arabe [arab] ◇ *adj* [peuple] Arab ; [désert] Arabian. ◇ *nm* [langue] Arabic. ◆ **Arabe** *nmf* Arab.

arabesque [arabɛsk] *nf* - **1.** [ornement] arabesque - **2.** [ligne sinueuse] flourish.

Arabie [arabi] *nf* : **l'~** Arabia ; **l'~ Saoudite** Saudi Arabia.

arabophone [arabɔfɔn] ◇ *adj* Arabic-speaking. ◇ *nmf* Arabic speaker.

arachide [araʃid] *nf* - **1.** [plante] groundnut - **2.** [graine] peanut, groundnut.

araignée [arɛɲe] *nf* spider. ➡ **araignée de mer** *nf* spider crab.

arbalète [arbalɛt] *nf* crossbow.

arbitrage [arbitraʒ] *nm* - **1.** [SPORT - gén] refereeing ; [- au tennis, cricket] umpiring - **2.** JUR arbitration.

arbitraire [arbitrɛr] *adj* arbitrary.

arbitre [arbitr] *nm* - **1.** [SPORT - gén] referee ; [- au tennis, cricket] umpire - **2.** [conciliateur] arbitrator.

arbitrer [3] [arbitre] *vt* - **1.** [SPORT - gén] to referee ; [- au tennis, cricket] to umpire - **2.** [conflit] to arbitrate.

arbre [arbr] *nm* - **1.** BOT & *fig* tree ; **~ généalogique** family tree - **2.** [axe] shaft.

arbrisseau, x [arbriso] *nm* shrub.

arbuste [arbyst] *nm* shrub.

arc [ark] *nm* - **1.** [arme] bow - **2.** [courbe] arc ; **~ de cercle** arc of a circle - **3.** ARCHIT arch.

arcade [arkad] *nf* - **1.** ARCHIT arch ; **~s** arcade *(sg)* - **2.** ANAT : **~ sourcilière** arch of the eyebrows.

arc-bouter [3] [arkbute] ➡ **s'arc-bouter** *vp* to brace o.s.

arceau, x [arso] *nm* - **1.** ARCHIT arch - **2.** [objet métallique] hoop.

arc-en-ciel [arkɑ̃sjɛl] (*pl* arcs-en-ciel) *nm* rainbow.

archaïque [arkaik] *adj* archaic.

arche [arʃ] *nf* ARCHIT arch.

archéologie [arkeɔlɔʒi] *nf* archaeology.

archéologique [arkeɔlɔʒik] *adj* archaeological.

archéologue [arkeɔlɔg] *nmf* archaeologist.

archet [arʃɛ] *nm* MUS bow.

archevêque [arʃəvɛk] *nm* archbishop.

archipel [arʃipɛl] *nm* archipelago.

architecte [arʃitɛkt] *nmf* architect.

architecture [arʃitɛktyr] *nf* architecture ; *fig* structure.

archives [arʃiv] *nfpl* [de bureau] records ; [de musée] archives.

archiviste [arʃivist] *nmf* archivist.

arctique [arktik] *adj* Arctic ; **le cercle polaire ~** the Arctic Circle. ➡ **Arctique** *nm* : **l'~** the Arctic.

ardemment [ardamɑ̃] *adv* fervently, passionately.

ardent, e [ardɑ̃, ɑ̃t] *adj* - **1.** [soleil] blazing - **2.** [soif, fièvre] raging ; [passion] burning.

ardeur [ardœr] *nf* - **1.** [vigueur] fervour, enthusiasm - **2.** [chaleur] blazing heat.

ardoise [ardwaz] *nf* slate.

ardu, e [ardy] *adj* [travail] arduous ; [problème] difficult.

are [ar] *nm 100 square metres.*

arène [arɛn] *nf* arena. ➡ **arènes** *nfpl* [romaines] amphitheatre *(sg)* ; [pour corridas] bullring *(sg)*.

arête [arɛt] *nf* - **1.** [de poisson] bone - **2.** [du nez] bridge.

argent [arʒɑ̃] *nm* - **1.** [métal, couleur] silver - **2.** [monnaie] money ; **~ liquide** (ready) cash ; **~ de poche** pocket money.

argenté, e [arʒɑ̃te] *adj* silvery, silver.

argenterie [arʒɑ̃tri] *nf* silverware.

Argentine [arʒɑ̃tin] *nf* : **l'~** Argentina.

argile [arʒil] *nf* clay.

argileux, euse [arʒilø, øz] *adj* clayey.

argot [argo] *nm* slang.

argotique [argɔtik] *adj* slang (*avant n*), slangy.

argument [argymɑ̃] *nm* argument.

argumentation [argymɑ̃tasjɔ̃] *nf* argumentation.

argus [argys] *nm* : **coté à l'~** *rated in the guide to secondhand car prices.*

aride [arid] *adj litt* & *fig* arid ; [travail] thankless.

aristocrate [aristɔkrat] *nmf* aristocrat.

aristocratie [aristɔkrasi] *nf* aristocracy.

arithmétique [aritmetik] *nf* arithmetic.

armateur [armatœr] *nm* ship owner

armature [armatyr] *nf* - **1.** CONSTR & *fig* framework - **2.** [de parapluie] frame ; [de soutien-gorge] underwiring.

arme [arm] *nf litt* & *fig* weapon ; **~ blanche** blade ; **~ à feu** firearm. ➡ **armes** *nfpl* - **1.** [armée] : **les ~s** the army - **2.** [blason] coat of arms *(sg)* - **3.** *loc* : **partir avec ~s et bagages** to leave taking everything.

armée [arme] *nf* army ; **l'~ de l'air** the air force ; **l'~ de terre** the army. ➡ **Armée du salut** *nf* : **l'Armée du salut** the Salvation Army

armement [armamɑ̃] *nm* [MIL - de personne] arming ; [- de pays] armament ; [- ensemble d'armes] arms (*pl*) ; **la course aux ~s** the arms race.

Arménie [armeni] *nf* : **l'~** Armenia.

armer [3] [arme] *vt* - **1.** [pourvoir en armes] to arm ; **être armé pour qqch/pour faire qqch** *fig* [préparé] to be equipped for sthg/to do sthg - **2.** [fusil] to cock - **3.** [appareil photo] to wind on - **4.** [navire] to fit out.

armistice [armistis] *nm* armistice.

armoire [armwar] *nf* [gén] cupboard *Br*, closet *Am* ; [garde-robe] wardrobe ; **c'est**

une **~ à glace!** *fam fig* he's built like a tank! ; **~ à pharmacie** medicine cabinet.

armoiries [armwari] *nfpl* coat of arms *(sg)*.

armure [armyr] *nf* armour *Br*, armor *Am*.

armurier [armyrje] *nm* [d'armes à feu] gunsmith ; [d'armes blanches] armourer.

arnaque [arnak] *nf fam* rip-off.

arnaquer [3] [arnake] *vt fam* to do *Br*, to swindle ; **se faire ~** to be had.

aromate [arɔmat] *nm* [épice] spice ; [fine herbe] herb.

arôme [arom] *nm* **- 1.** [gén] aroma ; [de fleur, parfum] fragrance **- 2.** [goût] flavour.

arpège [arpɛʒ] *nm* arpeggio.

arpenter [3] [arpɑ̃te] *vt* [marcher] to pace up and down.

arqué, e [arke] *adj* **- 1.** [objet] curved **- 2.** [jambe] bow *(avant n)*, bandy ; [nez] hooked ; [sourcil] arched.

arr. *abr de* arrondissement.

arrache-pied [araʃpje] **◆ d'arrache-pied** *loc adv* : **travailler d'~** to work away furiously.

arracher [3] [araʃe] *vt* **- 1.** [extraire - plante] to pull up ou out ; [- dent] to extract **- 2.** [déchirer - page] to tear off ou out ; [- chemise, bras] to tear off **- 3.** [prendre] : **~ qqch à qqn** to snatch sthg from sb ; [susciter] to wring sthg from sb **- 4.** [soustraire] : **~ qqn à** [milieu, lieu] to drag sb away from ; [lit, sommeil] to drag sb from ; [habitude, torpeur] to force sb out of.

arrangeant, e [arɑ̃ʒɑ̃, ɑ̃t] *adj* obliging.

arrangement [arɑ̃ʒmɑ̃] *nm* **- 1.** [gén] arrangement **- 2.** [accord] agreement, arrangement.

arranger [17] [arɑ̃ʒe] *vt* **- 1.** [gén] to arrange **- 2.** [convenir à] to suit **- 3.** [régler] to settle **- 4.** [améliorer] to sort out **- 5.** [réparer] to fix. **◆ s'arranger** *vp* to come to an agreement ; **s'~ pour faire qqch** to manage to do sthg ; **arrangez-vous pour être là à cinq heures** make sure you're there at five o'clock ; **cela va s'~** things will work out.

arrdt. *abr de* arrondissement.

arrestation [arɛstasjɔ̃] *nf* arrest ; **être en état d'~** to be under arrest.

arrêt [arɛ] *nm* **- 1.** [d'un mouvement] stopping ; **à l'~** [véhicule] stationary ; [machine] (switched) off ; **tomber en ~ devant qqch** to stop dead in front of sthg **- 2.** [interruption] interruption ; **sans ~** [sans interruption] non-stop ; [sans relâche] constantly, continually ; **être en ~ maladie** to be on sick leave ; **~ maladie** ou **de travail** doctor's certificate ; **~ du travail** stoppage **- 3.** [station] : **~ (d'autobus)** (bus) stop **- 4.** JUR decision, judgment.

arrêté [arete] *nm* ADMIN order, decree.

arrêter [4] [arete] **◇** *vt* **- 1.** [gén] to stop **- 2.** [cesser] : **~ de faire qqch** to stop doing sthg ; **~ de fumer** to stop smoking **- 3.** [voleur] to arrest. **◇** *vi* to stop. **◆ s'arrêter** *vp* to stop ; **s'~ à qqch : il ne s'arrête pas à ces détails** he's not going to dwell on these details ; **s'~ de faire** to stop doing.

arrhes [ar] *nfpl* deposit *(sg)*.

arrière [arjɛr] **◇** *adj inv* back, rear ; **roue ~** rear ou back wheel ; **marche ~** reverse gear. **◇** *nm* **- 1.** [partie postérieure] back ; **à l'~** at the back *Br*, in back *Am* **- 2.** SPORT back. **◆ en arrière** *loc adv* **- 1.** [dans la direction opposée] back, backwards ; **faire un pas en ~** to take a step back ou backwards **- 2.** [derrière, à la traîne] behind ; **rester en ~** to lag behind.

arriéré, e [arjere] *adj* [mentalité, pays] backward. **◆ arriéré** *nm* arrears *(pl)*.

arrière-boutique [arjɛrbutik] *(pl* arrière-boutiques) *nf* back shop.

arrière-garde [arjɛrgard] *(pl* arrière-gardes) *nf* rearguard.

arrière-goût [arjɛrgu] *(pl* arrière-goûts) *nm* aftertaste.

arrière-grand-mère [arjɛrgrɑ̃mɛr] *(pl* arrière-grands-mères) *nf* great-grand-mother.

arrière-grand-père [arjɛrgrɑ̃pɛr] *(pl* arrière-grands-pères) *nm* great-grand-father.

arrière-pays [arjɛrpei] *nm inv* hinterland.

arrière-pensée [arjɛrpɑ̃se] *(pl* arrière-pensées) *nf* [raison intéressée] ulterior motive.

arrière-plan [arjɛrplɑ̃] *(pl* arrière-plans) *nm* background.

arrière-saison [arjɛrsɛzɔ̃] *(pl* arrière-saisons) *nf* late autumn.

arrière-train [arjɛrtrɛ̃] *(pl* arrière-trains) *nm* hindquarters *(pl)*.

arrimer [3] [arime] *vt* **- 1.** [attacher] to secure **- 2.** NAVIG to stow.

arrivage [arivaʒ] *nm* [de marchandises] consignment, delivery.

arrivée [arive] *nf* **- 1.** [venue] arrival **- 2.** TECHNOL inlet.

arriver [3] [arive] **◇** *vi* **- 1.** [venir] to arrive ; **j'arrive!** (I'm) coming! ; **~ à Paris** to arrive in ou reach Paris ; **l'eau m'arrivait aux genoux** the water came up to my knees **- 2.** [parvenir] : **~ à faire qqch** to manage to do sthg, to succeed in doing sthg ; **il n'arrive pas à faire ses devoirs** he can't do his homework. ◇ v impers to happen ; il **arrive que** (+ subjonctif) : **il arrive qu'il soit en retard** he is sometimes late ; **il arrive à tout le monde de se décourager** we all get fed up sometimes ; **il arrive à tout le monde de se tromper** anyone can make a mistake ; **il lui arrive d'oublier quel jour on est** he sometimes forgets what day it is ; **quoi qu'il arrive** whatever happens.

arrivisme [arivism] nm péj ambition.

arrobas, arobas [arɔbas] nf [dans une adresse électronique] at.

arrogance [arɔgɑ̃s] nf arrogance.

arrogant, e [arɔgɑ̃, ɑ̃t] adj arrogant.

arroger [17] [arɔʒe] ◆ **s'arroger** vp : **s'~ le droit de faire qqch** to take it upon o.s. to do sthg.

arrondi [arɔ̃di] nm [de jupe] hemline.

arrondir [32] [arɔ̃dir] vt - **1.** [forme] to make round - **2.** [chiffre - au-dessus] to round up ; [- en dessous] to round down.

arrondissement [arɔ̃dismɑ̃] nm ADMIN arrondissement (administrative division of a département or city).

arroser [3] [aroze] vt - **1.** [jardin] to water, to spray - **2.** fam [célébrer] to celebrate.

arrosoir [arozwar] nm watering can.

arsenal, aux [arsənal, o] nm - **1.** [de navires] naval dockyard - **2.** [d'armes] arsenal.

arsenic [arsənik] nm arsenic.

art [ar] nm art ; **le septième ~** cinema ; **s et métiers** state-funded institution offering vocational courses by correspondence or evening classes.

art. abr de **article**.

Arte [arte] n Franco-German cultural television channel.

artère [arter] nf - **1.** ANAT artery - **2.** [rue] arterial road.

artériel, elle [arterjɛl] adj arterial.

artériosclérose [arterjoskleroz] nf arteriosclerosis.

arthrite [artrit] nf arthritis.

arthrose [artroz] nf osteoarthritis.

artichaut [artiʃo] nm artichoke.

article [artikl] nm - **1.** [gén] article ; **~ de fond** feature - **2.** loc : **à l'~ de la mort** at death's door.

articulation [artikylasjɔ̃] nf - **1.** ANAT & TECHNOL joint - **2.** [prononciation] articulation.

articuler [3] [artikyle] vt - **1.** [prononcer] to articulate - **2.** ANAT & TECHNOL to articulate, to joint.

artifice [artifis] nm - **1.** [moyen astucieux] clever device ou trick - **2.** [tromperie] trick.

artificiel, elle [artifisjɛl] adj artificial.

artillerie [artijri] nf MIL artillery.

artisan, e [artizɑ̃, an] nm, f craftsman (f craftswoman).

artisanal, e, aux [artizanal, o] adj craft (avant n).

artisanat [artizana] nm [métier] craft ; [classe] craftsmen.

artiste [artist] nmf - **1.** [créateur] artist ; **~ peintre** painter - **2.** [interprète] performer.

artistique [artistik] adj artistic.

as¹ [a] ▷ avoir.

as² [as] nm - **1.** [carte] ace - **2.** [champion] star, ace.

ascendant, e [asɑ̃dɑ̃, ɑ̃t] adj rising. ◆ **ascendant** nm - **1.** [influence] influence, power - **2.** ASTROL ascendant.

ascenseur [asɑ̃sœr] nm lift Br, elevator Am.

ascension [asɑ̃sjɔ̃] nf - **1.** [de montagne] ascent - **2.** [progression] rise. ◆ **Ascension** nf : **l'Ascension** Ascension (Day).

ascète [asɛt] nmf ascetic.

asiatique [azjatik] adj - **1.** [de l'Asie en général] Asian - **2.** [d'Extrême-Orient] oriental. ◆ **Asiatique** nmf Asian.

Asie [azi] nf : **l'~** Asia ; **l'~ du Sud-Est** Southeast Asia.

asile [azil] nm - **1.** [refuge] refuge - **2.** POLIT : **demander/accorder l'~ politique** to seek/to grant political asylum - **3.** vieilli [psychiatrique] asylum.

asocial, e, aux [asɔsjal, o] ◇ adj antisocial. ◇ nm, f social misfit.

aspect [aspɛ] nm - **1.** [apparence] appearance ; **d'~ agréable** nice-looking - **2.** [angle & LING] aspect.

asperge [aspɛrʒ] nf [légume] asparagus.

asperger [17] [aspɛrʒe] vt : **~ qqch de qqch** to spray sthg with sthg ; **~ qqn de qqch** [arroser] to spray sb with sthg ; [éclabousser] to splash sb with sthg.

aspérité [asperite] nf [du sol] bump.

asphalte [asfalt] nm asphalt.

asphyxier [9] [asfiksje] vt - **1.** MÉD to asphyxiate, to suffocate - **2.** fig [économie] to paralyse Br, to paralyze Am.

aspic [aspik] nm [vipère] asp.

aspirant, e [aspirɑ̃, ɑ̃t] adj : **hotte ~e** cooker hood Br, cooker range Am ; **pompe ~e** suction pump. ◆ **aspirant** nm [armée] ≃ officer cadet ; [marine] ≃ midshipman.

aspirateur [aspiratœr] nm Hoover® Br, vacuum cleaner ; **passer l'~** to do the vacuuming ou hoovering.

aspiration [aspirasjɔ̃] nf - **1.** [souffle] inhalation - **2.** TECHNOL suction. ➡ **aspirations** *nfpl* aspirations.

aspirer [3] [aspire] *vt* - **1.** [air] to inhale ; [liquide] to suck up - **2.** TECHNOL to suck up, to draw up - **3.** [désirer] : **~ à qqch/à faire qqch** to aspire to sthg/to do sthg.

aspirine [aspirin] *nf* aspirin.

assagir [32] [asaʒir] *vt* to quieten down.

assaillant, e [asajā, āt] *nm, f* assailant, attacker.

assaillir [47] [asajir] *vt* to attack, to assault ; **~ qqn de qqch** *fig* to assail ou bombard sb with sthg.

assainir [32] [asenir] *vt* - **1.** [logement] to clean up - **2.** [eau] to purify - **3.** ÉCON to rectify, to stabilize.

assaisonnement [asɛzɔnmā] *nm* [sauce] dressing ; [condiments] seasoning.

assaisonner [3] [asɛzɔne] *vt* [salade] to dress ; [viande, plat] to season.

assassin, e [asasē, in] *adj* provocative. ➡ **assassin** *nm* [gén] murderer ; POLIT assassin.

assassinat [asasina] *nm* [gén] murder ; POLIT assassination.

assassiner [3] [asasine] *vt* [tuer - gén] to murder ; [- POLIT] to assassinate.

assaut [aso] *nm* [attaque] assault, attack ; **prendre d'~** [lieu] to storm ; [personne] to attack.

assécher [18] [aseʃe] *vt* to drain.

ASSEDIC, Assedic [asedik] (*abr de* **Association pour l'emploi dans l'industrie et le commerce**) *nfpl* French unemployment insurance scheme ; **toucher les ~** to get unemployment benefit Br ou welfare Am.

assemblage [asāblaʒ] *nm* [gén] assembly.

assemblée [asāble] *nf* - **1.** [réunion] meeting - **2.** [public] gathering - **3.** ADMIN & POLIT assembly ; **l'Assemblée nationale** *lower house of the French parliament*.

assembler [asāble] *vt* - **1.** [monter] to put together - **2.** [réunir - objets] to gather (together) - **3.** [personnes - gén] to bring together, to assemble. ➡ **s'assembler** *vp* to gather.

assener [19] [asəne], **asséner** [18] [asene] *vt* : **~ un coup à qqn** [frapper] to strike sb, to deal sb a blow.

assentiment [asātimā] *nm* assent.

asseoir [65] [aswar] <> *vt* - **1.** [sur un siège] to put - **2.** [fondations] to lay - **3.** *fig* [réputation] to establish. <> *vi* : **faire ~ qqn** to seat sb, to ask sb to take a seat. ➡ **s'asseoir** *vp* to sit (down).

assermenté, e [asɛrmāte] *adj* [fonctionnaire, expert] sworn.

assertion [asɛrsjɔ̃] *nf* assertion.

assesseur [asesœr] *nm* assessor.

assez [ase] *adv* - **1.** [suffisamment] enough ; **~ grand pour qqch/pour faire qqch** big enough for sthg/to do sthg ; **~ de** enough ; **~ de lait/chaises** enough milk/chairs ; **en avoir ~ de qqn/qqch** to have had enough of sb/sthg, to be fed up with sb/sthg - **2.** [plutôt] quite, rather.

assidu, e [asidy] *adj* - **1.** [élève] diligent - **2.** [travail] painstaking - **3.** [empressé] : **~ (auprès de qqn)** attentive (to sb).

assiduité [asiduite] *nf* - **1.** [zèle] diligence - **2.** [fréquence] : **avec ~** regularly. ➡ **assiduités** *nfpl péj & sout* attentions.

assiéger [22] [asjeʒe] *vt litt & fig* to besiege.

assiette [asjɛt] *nf* - **1.** [vaisselle] plate ; **~ creuse** ou **à soupe** soup plate ; **~ à dessert** dessert plate ; **~ plate** dinner plate - **2.** [d'impôt] base - **3.** CULIN : **~ anglaise** assorted cold meats (*pl*) Br, cold cuts (*pl*) Am.

assigner [3] [asiɲe] *vt* JUR : **~ qqn en justice** to issue a writ against sb.

assimiler [3] [asimile] *vt* - **1.** [aliment, connaissances] to assimilate - **2.** [confondre] : **~ qqch (à qqch)** to liken sthg (to sthg) ; **~ qqn à qqn** to compare sb to ou with sb.

assis, e [asi, iz] <> *pp* ⊳ **asseoir**. <> *adj* sitting, seated ; **place ~e** seat. ➡ **assise** *nf* [base] seat, seating. ➡ **assises** *nfpl* - **1.** JUR : **(cour d')~es** Crown Court Br, Circuit court Am - **2.** [congrès] conference (*sg*).

assistance [asistās] *nf* - **1.** [aide] assistance ; **l'Assistance publique** *French authority which manages the social services and state-owned hospitals* - **2.** [auditoire] audience.

assistant, e [asistā, āt] *nm, f* - **1.** [auxiliaire] assistant ; **~e sociale** social worker - **2.** UNIV assistant lecturer.

assister [3] [asiste] <> *vi* : **~ à qqch** to be at sthg, to attend sthg. <> *vt* to assist.

association [asɔsjasjɔ̃] *nf* - **1.** [gén] association - **2.** [union] society, association ; **~ sportive** sports club - **3.** COMM partnership.

associé, e [asɔsje] <> *adj* associated. <> *nm, f* - **1.** [collaborateur] associate - **2.** [actionnaire] partner.

associer [9] [asɔsje] *vt* - **1.** [personnes] to bring together - **2.** [idées] to associate - **3.** [faire participer] : **~ qqn à qqch** [inclure] to bring sb in on sthg ; [prendre pour partenaire] to make sb a partner in sthg. ➡ **s'associer** *vp* - **1.** [prendre part] : **s'~ à**

qqch [participer] to join ou participate in sthg ; [partager] to share sthg - **2.** [collaborer] : **s'~ à** ou **avec qqn** to join forces with sb.

assoiffé, e [aswafe] *adj* thirsty ; ~ **de pouvoir** *fig* power-hungry.

assombrir [32] [asɔbrir] *vt* - **1.** [plonger dans l'obscurité] to darken - **2.** *fig* [attrister] to cast a shadow over. **◆ s'assombrir** *vp* - **1.** [devenir sombre] to grow dark - **2.** *fig* [s'attrister] to darken.

assommer [3] [asɔme] *vt* - **1.** [frapper] to knock out - **2.** [ennuyer] to bore stiff.

Assomption [asɔpsjɔ] *nf* : **l'~** the Assumption.

assorti, e [asɔrti] *adj* [accordé] : **bien ~** well-matched ; **mal ~** ill-matched ; **une cravate ~e au costume** a tie which matches the suit.

assortiment [asɔrtimã] *nm* assortment, selection.

assortir [32] [asɔrtir] *vt* [objets] : **~ qqch à qqch** to match sthg to ou with sthg.

assoupi, e [asupi] *adj* [endormi] dozing.

assouplir [32] [asuplir] *vt* sout [enfant] to send to sleep. **◆ s'assouplir** *vp* [s'endormir] to doze off.

assouplir [32] [asuplir] *vt* - **1.** [corps] to make supple - **2.** [matière] to soften - **3.** [règlement] to relax.

assourdir [32] [asurdir] *vt* - **1.** [rendre sourd] to deafen - **2.** [amortir] to deaden, to muffle.

assouvir [32] [asuvir] *vt* to satisfy.

assujettir [32] [asyʒetir] *vt* - **1.** [peuple] to subjugate - **2.** [soumettre] : **~ qqn à qqch** to subject sb to sthg.

assumer [3] [asyme] *vt* - **1.** [fonction - exercer] to carry out - **2.** [risque, responsabilité] to accept - **3.** [condition] to come to terms with - **4.** [frais] to meet.

assurance [asyrãs] *nf* - **1.** [gén] assurance - **2.** [contrat] insurance ; **~ maladie** health insurance ; **~ tous risques** AUTOM comprehensive insurance ; **~-vie** life assurance.

assuré, e [asyre] *nm, f* policy holder ; **~ social** National Insurance contributor *Br*, Social Security contributor *Am*.

assurément [asyremã] *adv* sout certainly.

assurer [3] [asyre] *vt* - **1.** [promettre] : **~ à qqn que** to assure sb (that) ; **~ qqn de qqch** to assure sb of sthg - **2.** [permanence, liaison] to provide - **3.** [voiture] to insure. **◆ s'assurer** *vp* - **1.** [vérifier] : **s'~ que** to make sure (that) ; **s'~ de qqch** to ensure sthg, to make sure of sthg - **2.** COMM : **s'~ (contre qqch)** to insure o.s. (against sthg) - **3.** [obtenir] : **s'~ qqch** to secure sthg.

astérisque [asterisk] *nm* asterisk.

asthme [asm] *nm* MÉD asthma.

asticot [astiko] *nm* maggot.

astiquer [3] [astike] *vt* to polish.

astre [astr] *nm* star.

astreignant, e [astreɲã, ãt] *adj* demanding.

astreindre [81] [astrɛdr] *vt* : **~ qqn à qqch** to subject sb to sthg ; **~ qqn à faire qqch** to compel sb to do sthg.

astreint, e [astrɛ, ɛt] *pp* ▷ **astreindre**.

astringent, e [astrɛʒã, ãt] *adj* astringent.

astrologie [astrɔlɔʒi] *nf* astrology.

astrologue [astrɔlɔg] *nm* astrologer.

astronaute [astronot] *nmf* astronaut.

astronautique [astronotik] *nf* astronautics (*U*).

astronomie [astrɔnɔmi] *nf* astronomy.

astronomique [astrɔnɔmik] *adj* astronomical.

astuce [astys] *nf* - **1.** [ruse] (clever) trick - **2.** [ingéniosité] shrewdness (*U*).

astucieux, euse [astysjø, øz] *adj* - **1.** [idée] clever - **2.** [personne] shrewd.

asymétrique [asimetrik] *adj* asymmetric, asymmetrical.

atelier [atəlje] *nm* - **1.** [d'artisan] workshop - **2.** [de peintre] studio.

athée [ate] <> *nmf* atheist. <> *adj* atheistic.

Athènes [atɛn] *n* Athens.

athlète [atlɛt] *nmf* athlete.

athlétisme [atletism] *nm* athletics (*U*).

atlantique [atlãtik] *adj* Atlantic. **◆ Atlantique** *nm* : **l'Atlantique** the Atlantic (Ocean).

atlas [atlas] *nm* atlas.

atmosphère [atmɔsfɛr] *nf* atmosphere.

atome [atom] *nm* atom.

atomique [atɔmik] *adj* - **1.** [gén] nuclear - **2.** CHIM & PHYS atomic.

atomiseur [atɔmizœr] *nm* spray.

atone [atɔn] *adj* [inexpressif] lifeless.

atout [atu] *nm* - **1.** [carte] trump ; **~ cœur/pique/trèfle/carreau** hearts/spades/clubs/diamonds are trumps - **2.** *fig* [ressource] asset, advantage.

âtre [atr] *nm* littéraire hearth.

atroce [atrɔs] *adj* - **1.** [crime] atrocious, dreadful - **2.** [souffrance] horrific, atrocious.

atrocité [atrɔsite] *nf* - **1.** [horreur] atrocity - **2.** [calomnie] insult.

atrophier [9] [atrɔfje] **◆ s'atrophier** *vp* to atrophy.

attabler [3] [atable] ➦ **s'attabler** *vp* to sit down (at the table).

attachant, e [ataʃɑ̃, ɑ̃t] *adj* lovable.

attache [ataʃ] *nf* [lien] fastening. ➦ **attaches** *nfpl* links, connections.

attaché, e [ataʃe] *nm, f* attaché ; ~ **de presse** [diplomatique] press attaché ; [d'organisme, d'entreprise] press officer.

attaché-case [ataʃekɛz] (*pl* **attachés-cases**) *nm* attaché case.

attachement [ataʃmɑ̃] *nm* attachment.

attacher [3] [ataʃe] ◇ *vt* - 1. [lier] : ~ **qqch (à)** to fasten ou tie sthg (to) - 2. [paquet] to tie up - 3. [lacet] to do up ; [ceinture de sécurité] to fasten. ◇ *vi* CULIN : ~ **(à)** to stick (to). ➦ **s'attacher** *vp* - 1. [émotionnellement] : **s'~ à qqn/qqch** to become attached to sb/sthg - 2. [se fermer] to fasten ; **s'~ avec** ou **par qqch** to do up ou fasten with sthg - 3. [s'appliquer] : **s'~ à qqch/à faire qqch** to devote o.s. to sthg/to doing sthg, to apply o.s. to sthg/to doing sthg.

attaquant, e [atakɑ̃, ɑ̃t] *nm, f* attacker.

attaque [atak] *nf* [gén & MÉD] attack ; *fig* : ~ **contre qqn/qqch** attack on sb/sthg.

attaquer [3] [atake] *vt* - 1. [gén] to attack - 2. [JUR - personne] to take to court ; [- jugement] to contest - 3. *fam* [plat] to tuck into. ➦ **s'attaquer** *vp* - 1. [combattre] : **s'~ à qqn** to attack sb - 2. *fig* : **s'~ à qqch** [tâche] to tackle sthg.

attardé, e [atarde] *adj* - 1. [idées] outdated - 2. [passants] late - 3. [enfant] backward.

attarder [3] [atarde] ➦ **s'attarder** *vp* : **s'~ sur qqch** to dwell on sthg ; **s'~ à faire qqch** to stay on to do sthg, to stay behind to do sthg.

atteindre [8] [atɛ̃dr] *vt* - 1. [gén] to reach - 2. [toucher] to hit - 3. [affecter] to affect.

atteint, e [atɛ̃, ɛ̃t] ◇ *pp* ⊳ **atteindre**. ◇ *adj* [malade] : **être ~ de** to be suffering from. ➦ **atteinte** *nf* - 1. [préjudice] : **porter ~e à** to undermine ; **hors d'~e** [hors de portée] out of reach ; [inattaquable] beyond reach - 2. [effet] effect.

attelage [atlaʒ] *nm* [chevaux] team.

atteler [24] [atle] *vt* [animaux, véhicules] to hitch up ; [wagons] to couple.

attelle [atɛl] *nf* splint.

attenant, e [atnɑ̃, ɑ̃t] *adj* : ~ **(à qqch)** adjoining (sthg).

attendre [73] [atɑ̃dr] ◇ *vt* - 1. [gén] to wait for ; **le déjeuner nous attend** lunch is ready ; ~ **que** (+ *subjonctif*) : ~ **que la pluie s'arrête** to wait for the rain to stop ; **faire ~ qqn** [personne] to keep sb waiting - 2. [espérer] : ~ **qqch (de qqn/qqch)** to expect sthg

(from sb/sthg) - 3. [suj : surprise, épreuve] to be in store for. ◇ *vi* to wait ; **attends!** hang on! ➦ **s'attendre** *vp* : **s'~ à** to expect. ➦ **en attendant** *loc adv* - 1. [pendant ce temps] meanwhile, in the meantime - 2. [quand même] all the same.

attendrir [32] [atɑ̃drir] *vt* - 1. [viande] to tenderize - 2. [personne] to move. ➦ **s'attendrir** *vp* : **s'~ (sur qqn/qqch)** to be moved (by sb/sthg).

attendrissant, e [atɑ̃drisɑ̃, ɑ̃t] *adj* moving, touching.

attendu, e [atɑ̃dy] *pp* ⊳ **attendre**. ➦ **attendu que** *loc conj* since, considering that.

attentat [atɑ̃ta] *nm* attack ; ~ **à la bombe** bomb attack, bombing.

attente [atɑ̃t] *nf* - 1. [station] wait ; **en ~** in abeyance - 2. [espoir] expectation ; **répondre aux ~s de qqn** to live up to sb's expectations.

attenter [3] [atɑ̃te] *vi* : ~ **à** [liberté, droit] to violate ; ~ **à ses jours** to attempt suicide ; ~ **à la vie de qqn** to make an attempt on sb's life.

attentif, ive [atɑ̃tif, iv] *adj* [auditoire] : ~ **(à qqch)** attentive (to sthg).

attention [atɑ̃sjɔ̃] ◇ *nf* attention ; **à l'~ de** for the attention of ; **faire ~ à** [prudence] to be careful of ; [concentration] to pay attention to. ◇ *interj* watch out!, be careful!

attentionné, e [atɑ̃sjɔne] *adj* thoughtful.

attentivement [atɑ̃tivmɑ̃] *adv* attentively, carefully.

atténuer [7] [atenɥe] *vt* [douleur] to ease ; [propos, ton] to tone down ; [lumière] to dim, to subdue ; [bruit] to quieten. ➦ **s'atténuer** *vp* [lumière] to dim, to fade ; [bruit] to fade ; [douleur] to ease.

atterrer [4] [atere] *vt* to stagger.

atterrir [32] [aterir] *vi* to land ; ~ **dans qqch** *fig* to land up in sthg.

atterrissage [aterisaʒ] *nm* landing.

attestation [atɛstasjɔ̃] *nf* [certificat] certificate.

attester [3] [atɛste] *vt* - 1. [confirmer] to vouch for, to testify to - 2. [certifier] to attest.

attirail [atiraj] *nm fam* [équipement] gear.

attirance [atirɑ̃s] *nf* attraction.

attirant, e [atirɑ̃, ɑ̃t] *adj* attractive.

attirer [3] [atire] *vt* - 1. [gén] to attract - 2. [amener vers soi] : ~ **qqn à/vers soi** to draw sb to/towards one - 3. [provoquer] : ~ **des ennuis à qqn** to cause trouble for sb.

s'attirer *vp* : s'~ qqch to bring sthg on o.s.

attiser [3] [atize] *vt* - 1. [feu] to poke - 2. *fig* [haine] to stir up.

attitré, e [atitre] *adj* - 1. [habituel] usual - 2. [titulaire - fournisseur] by appointment ; [- représentant] accredited.

attitude [atityd] *nf* - 1. [comportement, approche] attitude - 2. [posture] posture.

attouchement [atuʃmã] *nm* caress.

attractif, ive [atraktif, iv] *adj* - 1. [force] magnetic - 2. [prix] attractive.

attraction [atraksjɔ̃] *nf* - 1. [gén] attraction - 2. [force] : ~ magnétique magnetic force. **attractions** *nfpl* - 1. [jeux] amusements - 2. [spectacle] attractions.

attrait [atrɛ] *nm* - 1. [séduction] appeal - 2. [intérêt] attraction.

attrape-nigaud [atrapnigo] (*pl* attrape-nigauds) *nm* con.

attraper [3] [atrape] *vt* - 1. [gén] to catch - 2. *fam* [gronder] to tell off - 3. *fam* [tromper] to take in.

attrayant, e [atrɛjã, ɑ̃t] *adj* attractive.

attribuer [7] [atribɥe] *vt* - 1. [tâche, part] : qqch à qqn to assign ou allocate sthg to sb, to assign ou allocate sb sthg ; [privilège] to grant sthg to sb, to grant sb sthg ; [récompense] to award sthg to sb, to award sb sthg - 2. [faute] : ~ qqch à qqn to attribute sthg to sb, to put sthg down to sb. **s'attribuer** *vp* - 1. [s'approprier] to appropriate (for o.s.) - 2. [revendiquer] to claim (for o.s.).

attribut [atriby] *nm* - 1. [gén] attribute - 2. GRAM complement.

attribution [atribysjɔ̃] *nf* - 1. [de prix] awarding, award - 2. [de part, tâche] allocation, assignment - 3. [d'avantage] bestowing. **attributions** *nfpl* [fonctions] duties.

attrister [3] [atriste] *vt* to sadden. **s'attrister** *vp* to be saddened.

attroupement [atrupmã] *nm* crowd.

attrouper [3] [atrupe] **s'attrouper** *vp* to form a crowd, to gather.

au [o] ⊏⊐ à.

aubade [obad] *nf* dawn serenade.

aubaine [obɛn] *nf* piece of good fortune.

aube [ob] *nf* [aurore] dawn, daybreak ; à l'~ at dawn.

aubépine [obepin] *nf* hawthorn.

auberge [obɛrʒ] *nf* [hôtel] inn ; ~ de jeunesse youth hostel.

aubergine [obɛrʒin] *nf* - 1. BOT aubergine *Br*, eggplant *Am* - 2. *péj* [contractuelle] traffic warden *Br*, meter maid *Am*.

aubergiste [obɛrʒist] *nmf* innkeeper.

auburn [obœrn] *adj inv* auburn.

aucun, e [okœ, yn] ⟨⟩ *adj* - 1. [sens négatif] : ne ... ~ no ; il n'y a ~e voiture dans la rue there aren't any cars in the street, there are no cars in the street ; sans faire ~ bruit without making a sound - 2. [sens positif] any ; il lit plus qu'~ autre enfant he reads more than any other child. ⟨⟩ *pron* - 1. [sens négatif] none ; ~ des enfants none of the children ; ~ d'entre nous none of us ; ~ (des deux) neither (of them) - 2. [sens positif] : plus qu'~ de nous more than any of us.

aucunement [okynmã] *adv* not at all, in no way.

audace [odas] *nf* - 1. [hardiesse] daring, boldness - 2. [insolence] audacity - 3. [innovation] daring innovation.

audacieux, euse [odasjø, øz] *adj* - 1. [projet] daring, bold - 2. [personne, geste] bold.

au-dedans [odədã] *loc adv* inside. **au-dedans de** *loc prép* inside.

au-dehors [odəɔr] *loc adv* outside. **au-dehors de** *loc prép* outside.

au-delà [odəla] ⟨⟩ *loc adv* - 1. [plus loin] beyond - 2. [davantage, plus] more ⟨⟩ *nm* : l'~ the hereafter, the afterlife. **au-delà de** *loc prép* beyond.

au-dessous [odəsu] *loc adv* below, underneath. **au-dessous de** *loc prép* below, under.

au-dessus [odəsy] *loc adv* above. **au-dessus de** *loc prép* above, over.

au-devant [odəvã] *loc adv* ahead. **au-devant de** *loc prép* : aller ~ de to go to meet, aller ~ du danger to court danger.

audible [odibl] *adj* audible.

audience [odjãs] *nf* - 1. [public, entretien] audience - 2. JUR hearing.

Audimat® [odimat] *nm* audience rating.

audionumérique [odjonymerik] *adj* digital audio.

audiovisuel, elle [odjovizɥɛl] *adj* audiovisual. **audiovisuel** *nm* TV and radio.

audit [odit] *nm* audit.

auditeur, trice [oditœr, tris] *nm, f* listener. **auditeur** *nm* - 1. UNIV : ~ libre *person allowed to attend lectures without being registered*, auditor *Am* - 2. FIN auditor.

audition [odisjɔ̃] *nf* - 1. [fait d'entendre] hearing - 2. JUR examination - 3. THÉÂTRE audition - 4. MUS recital.

auditionner [3] [odisjone] *vt & vi* to audition.

auditoire [oditwar] *nm* [public] audience.

auditorium [oditɔrjɔm] *nm* [de concert] auditorium ; [d'enregistrement] studio.

auge [oʒ] *nf* [pour animaux] trough.

augmentation [ogmɑ̃tasjɔ̃] *nf* : ~ (de) increase (in) ; ~ (de salaire) rise (in salary).

augmenter [3] [ogmɑ̃te] <> *vt* to increase ; [prix, salaire] to raise ; [personne] to give a rise to *Br*, to give a raise to *Am*. <> *vi* to increase, to rise ; **le froid augmente** it's getting colder ; **la douleur augmente** the pain is getting worse.

augure [ogyr] *nm* [présage] omen ; **être de bon/mauvais** ~ to be a good/bad sign.

aujourd'hui [oʒurdɥi] *adv* today.

aulx ▷ **ail**.

aumône [omon] *nf* : **faire l'**~ **à qqn** to give alms to sb.

auparavant [oparavɑ̃] *adv* **- 1.** [tout d'abord] first (of all) **- 2.** [avant] before, previously.

auprès [oprɛ] ◆ **auprès de** *loc prép* **- 1.** [à côté de] beside, next to **- 2.** [comparé à] compared with **- 3.** [en s'adressant à] to.

auquel [okɛl] ▷ **lequel**.

aurai, auras *etc* ▷ **avoir**.

auréole [oreɔl] *nf* **- 1.** ASTRON & RELIG halo **- 2.** [trace] ring.

auriculaire [orikylɛr] *nm* little finger.

aurore [orɔr] *nf* dawn.

ausculter [3] [oskylte] *vt* MÉD to sound.

auspice [ospis] *nm* (*gén pl*) sign, auspice ; **sous les** ~**s de qqn** under the auspices of sb.

aussi [osi] *adv* **- 1.** [pareillement, en plus] also, too ; **moi** ~ me too ; **j'y vais** ~ I'm going too *ou* as well **- 2.** [dans une comparaison] : ~ ... **que** as ... as ; **il n'est pas** ~ **intelligent que son frère** he's not as clever as his brother ; **je n'ai jamais rien vu d'**~ **beau** I've never seen anything so beautiful ; ~ **incroyable que cela paraisse** incredible though *ou* as it may seem. ◆ **(tout) aussi bien** *loc adv* just as easily, just as well ; **j'aurais pu (tout)** ~ **bien refuser** I could just as easily have said no. ◆ **aussi bien ... que** *loc conj* as well ... as ; **tu le sais** ~ **bien que moi** you know as well as I do.

aussitôt [osito] *adv* immediately. ◆ **aussitôt que** *loc conj* as soon as.

austère [ostɛr] *adj* **- 1.** [personne, vie] austere **- 2.** [vêtement] severe ; [paysage] harsh.

austérité [osterite] *nf* **- 1.** [de personne, vie] austerity **- 2.** [de vêtement] severeness ; [de paysage] harshness.

austral, e [ostral] (*pl* **australs** *ou* **austraux** [ostro]) *adj* southern.

Australie [ostrali] *nf* : **l'**~ Australia.

australien, enne [ostraljɛ̃, ɛn] *adj* Australian. ◆ **Australien, -enne** *nm, f* Australian.

autant [otɑ̃] *adv* **- 1.** [comparatif] : ~ **que** as much as ; **ce livre coûte** ~ **que l'autre** this book costs as much as the other one ; ~ **de** (... **que**) [quantité] as much (... as) ; [nombre] as many (... as) ; **il a dépensé** ~ **d'argent que moi** he spent as much money as I did ; **il y a** ~ **de femmes que d'hommes** there are as many women as men **- 2.** [à un tel point, en si grande quantité] so much ; [en si grand nombre] so many ; ~ **de patience** so much patience ; ~ **de gens** so many people ; **il ne peut pas en être** ~ he can't say the same ; **en faire** ~ to do likewise **- 3.** [il vaut mieux] : ~ **dire la vérité** we/you *etc* may as well tell the truth. ◆ **autant que** *loc conj* : **(pour)** ~ **que je sache** as far as I know. ◆ **d'autant** *loc adv* accordingly, in proportion. ◆ **d'autant mieux** *loc adv* all the better ; **d'**~ **mieux que** all the better since. ◆ **d'autant que** *loc conj* : **d'**~ **(plus) que** all the more so since ; **d'**~ **moins que** all the less so since. ◆ **pour autant** *loc adv* for all that.

autel [otɛl] *nm* altar.

auteur [otœr] *nm* **- 1.** [d'œuvre] author **- 2.** [responsable] perpetrator.

authentique [otɑ̃tik] *adj* authentic, genuine.

autiste [otist] *adj* autistic.

auto [oto] *nf* car.

autobiographie [otɔbjɔgrafi] *nf* autobiography.

autobronzant, e [otɔbrɔ̃zɑ̃, ɑ̃t] *adj* self-tanning.

autobus [otɔbys] *nm* bus.

autocar [otɔkar] *nm* coach.

autochtone [otɔktɔn] *nmf & adj* native.

autocollant, e [otɔkɔlɑ̃, ɑ̃t] *adj* self-adhesive, sticky. ◆ **autocollant** *nm* sticker.

autocouchettes [otɔkuʃɛt] *adj inv* : **train** ~ ≃ Motorail® train.

autocritique [otɔkritik] *nf* self-criticism.

autocuiseur [otɔkɥizœr] *nm* pressure cooker.

autodéfense [otɔdefɑ̃s] *nf* self-defence *Br*, self-defense *Am*.

autodétruire [98] [otɔdetrɥir] ◆ **s'autodétruire** *vp* **- 1.** [machine] to self-destruct **- 2.** [personne] to destroy o.s.

autodidacte [otɔdidakt] *nmf* self-taught person.

auto-école [otɔekɔl] (*pl* **auto-écoles**) *nf* driving school.

autofinancement [otɔfinɑ̃smɑ̃] *nm* self-financing.

autofocus [otɔfɔkys] *nm & adj inv* auto-focus.

autogestion [otɔʒɛstjɔ̃] *nf* workers' control.

autographe [otɔgraf] *nm* autograph.

automate [otɔmat] *nm* [robot] automaton.

automatique [otɔmatik] <> *nm* - **1.** [pistolet] automatic - **2.** TÉLÉCOM ≃ direct dialling. <> *adj* automatic.

automatisation [otɔmatizasjɔ̃] *nf* automation.

automatisme [otɔmatism] *nm* - **1.** [de machine] automatic operation - **2.** [réflexe] automatic reaction, automatism.

automédication [otɔmedikasjɔ̃] *nf* self-medication.

automne [otɔn] *nm* autumn, fall *Am* ; **en ~** in the autumn, in the fall *Am*.

automobile [otɔmɔbil] <> *nf* car, automobile *Am*. <> *adj* [industrie, accessoires] car *(avant n)*, automobile *(avant n) Am* ; [véhicule] motor *(avant n)*.

automobiliste [otɔmɔbilist] *nmf* driver, motorist *Br*.

autonettoyant, e [otɔnɛtwajɑ̃, ɑt] *adj* self-cleaning.

autonome [otɔnɔm] *adj* - **1.** [gén] autonomous, independent - **2.** [appareil] self-contained.

autonomie [otɔnɔmi] *nf* - **1.** [indépendance] autonomy, independence - **2.** AUTOM & AVIAT range - **3.** POLIT autonomy, self-government.

autonomiste [otɔnɔmist] *nmf & adj* separatist.

autoportrait [otɔpɔrtrɛ] *nm* self-portrait.

autopsie [otɔpsi] *nf* post-mortem, autopsy.

autoradio [otɔradjo] *nm* car radio.

autorail [otɔraj] *nm* railcar.

autorisation [otɔrizasjɔ̃] *nf* - **1.** [permission] permission, authorization ; **avoir l'~ de faire qqch** to be allowed to do sthg - **2.** [attestation] pass, permit.

autorisé, e [otɔrize] *adj* [personne] in authority ; **milieux ~s** official circles.

autoriser [3] [otɔrize] *vt* to authorize, to permit ; **~ qqn à faire qqch** [permission] to give sb permission to do sthg ; [possibilité] to permit ou allow sb to do sthg.

autoritaire [otɔritɛr] *adj* authoritarian.

autorité [otɔrite] *nf* authority ; **faire ~** [ouvrage] to be authoritative ; [personne] to be an authority.

autoroute [otɔrut] *nf* motorway *Br*, high-way *Am*, freeway *Am* ; **~ de l'information** INFORM information highway ou super-highway.

auto-stop [otɔstɔp] *nm* hitchhiking.

auto-stoppeur, euse [otɔstɔpœr, øz] *(mpl* auto-stoppeurs, *fpl* auto-stoppeuses) *nm, f* hitchhiker, hitcher.

autour [otur] *adv* round, around. **autour de** *loc prép* - **1.** [sens spatial] round, around - **2.** [sens temporel] about, around.

autre [otr] <> *adj indéf* - **1.** [distinct, différent] other, different ; **je préfère une ~ marque de café** I prefer another ou a different brand of coffee ; **l'un et l'~ projets** both projects ; **~ chose** something else - **2.** [supplémentaire] other ; **tu veux une ~ tasse de café?** would you like another cup of coffee? - **3.** [qui reste] other, remaining ; **les ~s passagers ont été rapatriés en autobus** the other ou remaining passengers were bussed home. <> *pron indéf* : **l'~** the other (one) ; **un ~** another (one) ; **les ~s** [personnes] the others ; [objets] the others, the other ones ; **l'un à côté de l'~** side by side ; **d'une semaine à l'~** from one week to the next ; **aucun ~, nul ~, personne d'~** no one else, nobody else ; **quelqu'un d'~** somebody else, someone else ; **rien d'~** nothing else ; **l'un et l'~ sont venus** they both came, both of them came ; **l'un ou l'~ ira** one or other (of them) will go ; **ni l'un ni l'~ n'est venu** neither (of them) came.

autrefois [otrəfwa] *adv* in the past, formerly.

autrement [otrəmɑ̃] *adv* - **1.** [différemment] otherwise, differently ; **je n'ai pas pu faire ~ que d'y aller** I had no choice but to go ; **~ dit** in other words - **2.** [sinon] other-wise.

Autriche [otriʃ] *nf* : **l'~** Austria.

autrichien, enne [otriʃjɛ̃, ɛn] *adj* Austrian. **Autrichien, enne** *nm, f* Austrian.

autruche [otryʃ] *nf* ostrich.

autrui [otrɥi] *pron* others, other people.

auvent [ovɑ̃] *nm* canopy.

aux [o] ⊳ **à**.

auxiliaire [oksiljɛr] <> *nmf* [assistant] assistant. <> *nm* GRAM auxiliary (verb). <> *adj* - **1.** [secondaire] auxiliary - **2.** ADMIN assistant *(avant n)*.

auxquels, auxquelles [okɛl] ⊳ **lequel**.

av. *abr de* avenue.

avachi, e [avaʃi] *adj* - **1.** [gén] misshapen - **2.** [personne] listless ; **il était ~ dans un fauteuil** he was slumped in an armchair.

aval, als [aval] *nm* backing (U), endorsement. ◆ **en aval** *loc adv litt & fig* downstream.

avalanche [avalɑ̃ʃ] *nf litt & fig* avalanche.

avaler [3] [avale] *vt* - **1.** [gén] to swallow - **2.** *fig* [supporter] to take ; **dur à ~** difficult to swallow.

avance [avɑ̃s] *nf* - **1.** [progression, somme d'argent] advance - **2.** [distance, temps] lead ; **le train a dix minutes d'~** the train is ten minutes early ; **le train a une ~ de dix minutes sur l'horaire** the train is running ten minutes ahead of schedule ; **prendre de l'~ (dans qqch)** to get ahead (in sthg). ◆ **avances** *nfpl* : **faire des ~s à qqn** to make advances towards sb. ◆ **à l'avance** *loc adv* in advance. ◆ **d'avance** *loc adv* in advance. ◆ **en avance** *loc adv* : **être en ~** to be early ; **être en ~ sur qqch** to be ahead of sthg. ◆ **par avance** *loc adv* in advance.

avancement [avɑ̃smɑ̃] *nm* - **1.** [développement] progress - **2.** [promotion] promotion.

avancer [16] [avɑ̃se] ◇ *vt* - **1.** [objet, tête] to move forward ; [date, départ] to bring forward ; [main] to hold out - **2.** [projet, travail] to advance - **3.** [montre, horloge] to put forward - **4.** [argent] : **~ qqch à qqn** to advance sb sthg. ◇ *vi* - **1.** [approcher] to move forward - **2.** [progresser] to advance ; **~ dans qqch** to make progress in sthg - **3.** [faire saillie] : **~ (dans/sur)** to jut out (into/over) ; to project (into/over) - **4.** [montre, horloge] : **ma montre avance de dix minutes** my watch is ten minutes fast - **5.** [servir] : **ça n'avance à rien** that won't get us/you anywhere. ◆ **s'avancer** *vp* - **1.** [s'approcher] to move forward ; **s'~ vers qqn/qqch** to move towards *Br* ou toward *Am* sb/sthg - **2.** [s'engager] to commit o.s.

avant [avɑ̃] ◇ *prép* before. ◇ *adv* before ; **quelques jours ~** a few days earlier ou before ; **tu connais le cinéma? ma maison se situe un peu ~** do you know the cinema? my house is just this side of it. ◇ *adj inv* front ; **les roues ~** the front wheels. ◇ *nm* - **1.** [partie antérieure] front - **2.** SPORT forward. ◆ **avant de** *loc prép* : **~ de faire qqch** before doing sthg ; **~ de partir** before leaving. ◆ **avant que** *loc conj (+ subjonctif)* : **je dois te parler ~ que tu partes** I must speak to you before you leave. ◆ **avant tout** *loc adv* above all ; **sa carrière passe ~ tout** his career comes first. ◆ **en avant** *loc adv* forward, forwards.

avantage [avɑ̃taʒ] *nm* [gén & TENNIS] advantage ; **se montrer à son ~** to look one's best.

avantager [17] [avɑ̃taʒe] *vt* - **1.** [favoriser] to favour *Br*, to favor *Am* - **2.** [mettre en valeur] to flatter.

avantageux, euse [avɑ̃taʒø, øz] *adj* - **1.** [profitable] profitable, lucrative - **2.** [flatteur] flattering.

avant-bras [avɑ̃bra] *nm inv* forearm.

avant-centre [avɑ̃sɑ̃tr] (*pl* **avants-centres**) *nm* centre *Br* ou center *Am* forward.

avant-coureur [avɑ̃kurœr] ▷ **signe**.

avant-dernier, ère [avɑ̃dɛrnje, ɛr] (*mpl* **avant-derniers**, *fpl* **avant-dernières**) *adj* second to last, penultimate.

avant-garde [avɑ̃gard] (*pl* **avant-gardes**) *nf* - **1.** MIL vanguard - **2.** [idées] avant-garde.

avant-goût [avɑ̃gu] (*pl* **avant-goûts**) *nm* foretaste.

avant-hier [avɑ̃tjɛr] *adv* the day before yesterday.

avant-première [avɑ̃prəmjɛr] (*pl* **avant-premières**) *nf* preview.

avant-projet [avɑ̃prɔʒe] (*pl* **avant-projets**) *nm* draft.

avant-propos [avɑ̃prɔpo] *nm inv* foreword.

avant-veille [avɑ̃vɛj] (*pl* **avant-veilles**) *nf* : **l'~** two days earlier.

avare [avar] ◇ *nmf* miser. ◇ *adj* miserly ; **être ~ de qqch** *fig* to be sparing with sthg.

avarice [avaris] *nf* avarice.

avarie [avari] *nf* damage *(U)*.

avarié, e [avarje] *adj* rotting, bad.

avatar [avatar] *nm* [transformation] metamorphosis. ◆ **avatars** *nmpl* [mésaventures] misfortunes.

avec [avɛk] ◇ *prép* - **1.** [gén] with ; **~ respect** with respect, respectfully ; **c'est fait ~ du cuir** it's made from leather ; **et ~ ça?**, **et ~ ceci?** *fam* [dans un magasin] anything else? - **2.** [vis-à-vis de] to, towards *Br*, toward *Am*. ◇ *adv fam* with it/him *etc* ; **tiens mon sac, je ne peux pas courir ~!** hold my bag, I can't run with it!

Ave (Maria) [ave(marja)] *nm inv* Hail Mary.

avenant, e [avnɑ̃, ɑ̃t] *adj* pleasant. ◆ **avenant** *nm* JUR additional clause. ◆ **à l'avenant** *loc adv* in the same vein.

avènement [avɛnmɑ̃] *nm* - **1.** [d'un roi] accession - **2.** *fig* [début] advent.

avenir [avnir] *nm* future ; **avoir de l'~** to have a future ; **d'~** [profession, concept] with a future, with prospects. ◆ **à l'avenir** *loc adv* in future.

Avent [avɑ̃] *nm* : **l'~** Advent.

aventure [avɑ̃tyʀ] *nf* - **1.** [gén] adventure - **2.** [liaison amoureuse] affair.

aventurer [3] [avɑ̃tyʀe] *vt* [risquer] to risk. ➤ **s'aventurer** *vp* to venture (out) ; **s'~ à faire qqch** *fig* to venture to do sthg.

aventureux, euse [avɑ̃tyʀø, øz] *adj* - **1.** [personne, vie] adventurous - **2.** [projet] risky.

aventurier, ère [avɑ̃tyʀje, ɛʀ] *nm, f* adventurer.

avenu [avny] *adj m* : **nul et non ~** JUR null and void.

avenue [avny] *nf* avenue.

avérer [18] [aveʀe] ➤ **s'avérer** *vp* : **il s'est avéré (être) à la hauteur** he proved (to be) up to it ; **il s'est avéré (être) un musicien accompli** he proved to be an accomplished musician.

averse [avɛʀs] *nf* downpour ; **~ de neige** snowflurry.

averti, e [avɛʀti] *adj* - **1.** [expérimenté] experienced - **2.** [initié] : **~ (de)** informed OU well-informed (about).

avertir [32] [avɛʀtiʀ] *vt* - **1.** [mettre en garde] to **warn** - **2.** [prévenir] to inform ; **avertissez-moi dès que possible** let me know as soon as possible.

avertissement [avɛʀtismɑ̃] *nm* - **1.** [gén] warning - **2.** [avis] notice, notification.

avertisseur, euse [avɛʀtisœʀ, øz] *nm* - **1.** [Klaxon] horn - **2.** [d'incendie] alarm.

aveu, x [avø] *nm* confession.

aveugle [avœgl] <> *nmf* blind person ; **les ~s** the blind. <> *adj litt & fig* blind.

aveuglement [avœgləmɑ̃] *nm* blindness.

aveuglément [avœglemɑ̃] *adv* blindly.

aveugler [5] [avœgle] *vt litt & fig* [priver de la vue] to blind.

aveuglette [avœglɛt] ➤ **à l'aveuglette** *loc adv* : **marcher à l'~** to grope one's way ; **avancer à l'~** *fig* to be in the dark.

aviateur, trice [avjatœʀ, tʀis] *nm, f* aviator.

aviation [avjasjɔ̃] *nf* - **1.** [transport aérien] aviation - **2.** MIL airforce.

avide [avid] *adj* - **1.** [vorace, cupide] greedy - **2.** [désireux] : **~ (de qqch/de faire qqch)** eager (for sthg/to do sthg).

avidité [avidite] *nf* - **1.** [voracité, cupidité] greed - **2.** [passion] eagerness.

avilir [32] [aviliʀ] *vt* [personne] to degrade. ➤ **s'avilir** *vp* - **1.** [personne] to demean o.s. - **2.** [monnaie, marchandise] to depreciate.

aviné, e [avine] *adj* - **1.** [personne] inebriated - **2.** [haleine] smelling of alcohol.

avion [avjɔ̃] *nm* plane, aeroplane, air-

plane *Am* ; **en ~** by plane, by air ; **par ~** [courrier] airmail ; **~ à réaction** jet (plane).

aviron [aviʀɔ̃] *nm* - **1.** [rame] oar - **2.** SPORT : **l'~** rowing.

avis [avi] *nm* - **1.** [opinion] opinion ; **changer d'~** to change one's mind ; **être d'~ que** to think that, to be of the opinion that ; **à mon ~** in my opinion - **2.** [conseil] advice *(U)* - **3.** [notification] notification, notice ; **sauf ~ contraire** unless otherwise informed.

avisé, e [avize] *adj* [sensé] sensible ; **être bien/mal ~ de faire qqch** to be well-advised/ill-advised to do sthg.

aviser [3] [avize] <> *vt* [informer] : **~ qqn de qqch** to inform sb of sthg. <> *vi* to reassess the situation. ➤ **s'aviser** *vp* - **1.** *sout* [s'apercevoir] : **s'~ de qqch** to notice sthg - **2.** [oser] : **s'~ de faire qqch** to take it into one's head to do sthg ; **ne t'avise pas de répondre!** don't you dare answer me back!

av. J.-C. (*abr de* avant Jésus-Christ) BC.

avocat, e [avɔka, at] *nm, f* JUR barrister *Br*, attorney-at-law *Am* ; **~ de la défense** counsel for the defence *Br*, defense counsel *Am* ; **~ général** ≃ counsel for the prosecution *Br*, prosecuting attorney *Am*. ➤ **avocat** *nm* [fruit] avocado.

avoine [avwan] *nf* oats *(pl)*.

avoir [1] [avwaʀ] <> *nm* - **1.** [biens] assets *(pl)* - **2.** [document] credit note. <> *v aux* to have ; **j'ai fini** I have finished ; **il a attendu pendant deux heures** he waited for two hours. <> *vt* - **1.** [posséder] to have (got) ; **il a deux enfants/les cheveux bruns** he has a **deux enfants/les cheveux bruns** he has a grand jardin the house has (got) a large garden - **2.** [être âgé de] : **il a 20 ans** he is 20 (years old) ; **il a deux ans de plus que son frère** he is two years older than his brother - **3.** [obtenir] to get - **4.** [éprouver] to have ; **~ du chagrin** to feel sorrowful ; **~ de la sympathie pour qqn** to have a liking for sb ; *voir aussi* **faim** ; *voir aussi* **peur** ; *voir aussi* **soif** *etc* - **5.** *loc* : **se faire ~** *fam* to be had OU conned ; **en ~ assez (de qqch/de faire qqch)** to have had enough (of sthg/of doing sthg) ; **j'en ai pour cinq minutes** it'll take me five minutes ; **en ~ après qqn** to have (got) it in for sb. ➤ **avoir à** *vi + prép* [devoir] : **~ à faire qqch** to have to do sthg ; **tu n'avais pas à lui parler sur ce ton** you had no need to speak to him like that, you shouldn't have spoken to him like that ; **tu n'avais qu'à me demander** you only had to ask me ; **tu n'as qu'à y aller toi-même** just go (there) yourself, why don't you just go (there) yourself? ➤ **il y a** *v impers* - **1.** [présentatif] there is/are ; **il y a un pro-**

blème there's a problem ; **il y a des problèmes** there are (some) problems ; **qu'est-ce qu'il y a?** what's the matter?, what is it? ; **il n'y a qu'à en finir** we'll/you'll *etc* just have to have done (with it) - **2.** [temporel] : **il y a trois ans** three years ago ; **il y a longtemps de cela** that was a long time ago ; **il y a longtemps qu'il est parti** he left a long time ago.

avoisinant, e [avwazinɑ̃, ɑ̃t] *adj* - **1.** [lieu, maison] neighbouring *Br*, neighboring *Am* - **2.** [sens, couleur] similar.

avortement [avɔrtəmɑ̃] *nm* MÉD abortion.

avorter [3] [avɔrte] *vi* - **1.** MÉD : **(se faire) ~** to have an abortion - **2.** [échouer] to fail.

avorton [avɔrtɔ̃] *nm péj* [nabot] runt.

avouer [6] [avwe] *vt* - **1.** [confesser] to confess (to) - **2.** [reconnaître] to admit.

avril [avril] *nm* April ; *voir aussi* **septembre**.

axe [aks] *nm* - **1.** GÉOM & PHYS axis - **2.** [de roue] axle - **3.** [prolongement] : **dans l'~ de** directly in line with.

axer [3] [akse] *vt* : **~ qqch sur qqch** to centre *Br* ou center *Am* sthg on sthg ; **~ qqch autour de qqch** to centre *Br* ou center *Am* sthg around sthg.

axiome [aksjom] *nm* axiom.

ayant [ɛjɑ̃] *ppr* ⮕ **avoir**.

azalée [azale] *nf* azalea.

azimut [azimyt] ⮕ **tous azimuts** *loc adj* [défense, offensive] all-out.

azote [azɔt] *nm* nitrogen.

azur [azyr] *nm littéraire* - **1.** [couleur] azure - **2.** [ciel] skies *(pl)*.

b, B [be] *nm inv* b, B. ⮕ **B** *(abr de* **bien**) good grade *(as assessment on schoolwork)*, ≃ B.

BA *(abr de* **bonne action**) *nf fam* good deed.

babiller [3] [babije] *vi* to babble.

babines [babin] *nfpl* chops.

bâbord [babɔr] *nm* port ; **à ~** to port, on the port side.

babouin [babwɛ̃] *nm* baboon.

baby-sitter [bebisitœr] *(pl* **baby-sitters**) *nmf* baby-sitter.

baby-sitting [bebisitiŋ] *nm* baby-sitting ; **faire du ~** to baby-sit.

bac [bak] *nm* - **1.** = **baccalauréat** - **2.** [bateau] ferry - **3.** [de réfrigérateur] : **~ à glace** ice tray ; **~ à légumes** vegetable drawer.

baccalauréat [bakalɔrea] *nm* school-leaving examinations leading to university entrance qualification.

bâche [baʃ] *nf* [toile] tarpaulin.

bachelier, ère [baʃəlje, ɛr] *nm, f* holder of the baccalauréat.

bacille [basil] *nm* bacillus.

bâcler [3] [bakle] *vt* to botch.

bactérie [bakteri] *nf* bacterium.

badaud, e [bado, od] *nm, f* gawper.

badge [badʒ] *nm* badge.

badigeonner [3] [badiʒɔne] *vt* [mur] to whitewash.

badiner [3] [badine] *vi sout* to joke ; **ne pas ~ avec qqch** not to treat sthg lightly.

badminton [badmintɔn] *nm* badminton.

baffe [baf] *nf fam* slap.

baffle [bafl] *nm* speaker.

bafouiller [3] [bafuje] *vi & vt* to mumble.

bâfrer [3] [bafre] *fam vi* to guzzle.

bagage [bagaʒ] *nm* - **1.** *(gén pl)* [valises, sacs] luggage *(U)*, baggage *(U)* ; **faire ses ~s** to pack ; **~s à main** hand luggage - **2.** [connaissances] (fund of) knowledge ; **~ intellectuel/culturel** intellectual/cultural baggage.

bagagiste [bagaʒist] *nmf* [chargement des avions] baggage handler ; [à l'hôtel etc] porter ; [fabricant] travel goods manufacturer.

bagarre [bagar] *nf* brawl, fight.

bagarrer [3] [bagare] *vi* to fight. ⮕ **se bagarrer** *vp* to fight.

bagatelle [bagatɛl] *nf* - **1.** [objet] trinket - **2.** [somme d'argent] : **acheter qqch pour une ~** to buy sthg for next to nothing ; **la ~ de X euros** *iron* a mere X euros - **3.** [chose futile] trifle.

bagnard [baɲar] *nm* convict.

bagne [baɲ] *nm* [prison] labour *Br* ou labor *Am* camp.

bagnole [baɲɔl] *nf fam* car.

bague [bag] *nf* - **1.** [bijou, anneau] ring ; **~ de fiançailles** engagement ring - **2.** TECH : **~ de serrage** clip.

baguer [3] [bage] *vt* [oiseau, arbre] to ring.

baguette [bagɛt] *nf* - **1.** [pain] French stick - **2.** [petit bâton] stick ; **~ magique** magic wand ; **~ de tambour** drumstick ; **mener qqn à la ~** to rule sb with a rod of iron - **3.** [pour manger] chopstick - **4.** [de chef d'orchestre] baton.

bahut [bay] *nm* - **1.** [buffet] sideboard - **2.** *arg scol* [lycée] secondary school.

baie [bɛ] *nf* - **1.** [fruit] berry - **2.** GÉOGR bay - **3.** [fenêtre] : **~ vitrée** picture window.

baignade [bɛɲad] *nf* [action] bathing *(U)* *Br*, swimming *(U)* ; **'~ interdite'** 'no bathing/swimming'.

baigner [4] [beɲe] ◇ *vt* - **1.** [donner un bain à] to bath - **2.** [tremper, remplir] to bathe ; **baigné de soleil** bathed in sunlight. ◇ *vi* : **~ dans son sang** to lie in a pool of blood ; **les tomates baignaient dans l'huile** the tomatoes were swimming in oil. ➤ **se baigner** *vp* - **1.** [dans la mer] to go swimming, to swim - **2.** [dans une baignoire] to have a bath.

baigneur, euse [bɛɲœr, øz] *nm, f* bather *Br*, swimmer. ➤ **baigneur** *nm* [poupée] baby doll.

baignoire [bɛɲwar] *nf* bath.

bail [baj] *(pl* **baux** [bo]*) nm* JUR lease.

bâillement [bajmã] *nm* yawning *(U)*, yawn.

bâiller [3] [baje] *vi* - **1.** [personne] to yawn - **2.** [vêtement] to gape.

bailleur, eresse [bajœr, bajrɛs] *nm, f* lessor ; **~ de fonds** backer.

bâillon [bajɔ̃] *nm* gag.

bâillonner [3] [bajɔne] *vt* to gag.

bain [bɛ̃] *nm* - **1.** [gén] bath ; **prendre un ~** to have ou take a bath ; **~ moussant** foaming bath oil ; **~ à remous** spa bath, whirlpool bath ; **~s-douches** public baths - **2.** [dans mer, piscine] swim ; **~ de mer** sea bathing *Br* ou swimming - **3.** *loc* : **prendre un ~ de soleil** to sunbathe.

bain-marie [bɛ̃mari] *(pl* **bains-marie***) nm* : **au ~** in a bain-marie.

baïonnette [bajɔnɛt] *nf* - **1.** [arme] bayonet - **2.** ÉLECTR bayonet fitting.

baiser [4] [beze] *nm* kiss.

baisse [bɛs] *nf* [gén] : **~ (de)** drop (in), fall (in) ; **en ~** falling ; **la tendance est à la ~** there is a downward trend.

baisser [4] [bese] ◇ *vt* [gén] to lower ; [radio] to turn down. ◇ *vi* - **1.** [descendre] to go down ; **le jour baisse** it's getting dark - **2.** [santé, vue] to fail - **3.** [prix] to fall. ➤ **se baisser** *vp* to bend down.

bajoues [baʒu] *nfpl* jowls.

bal [bal] *nm* ball ; **~ masqué/costumé** masked/fancy-dress ball ; **~ populaire** ou **musette** *popular old-fashioned dance accompanied by accordion.*

balade [balad] *nf fam* stroll.

balader [3] [balade] *vt* - **1.** *fam* [traîner avec soi] to trail around - **2.** [emmener en prome-

nade] to take for a walk. ➤ **se balader** *vp fam* [se promener - à pied] to go for a walk ; [- en voiture] to go for a drive.

baladeur, euse [baladœr, øz] *adj* wandering. ➤ **baladeur** *nm* personal stereo.

balafre [balafr] *nf* - **1.** [blessure] gash - **2.** [cicatrice] scar.

balafré, e [balafre] *adj* scarred.

balai [balɛ] *nm* - **1.** [de nettoyage] broom, brush - **2.** *fam* [an] : **il a 50 ~s** he's 50 years old.

balai-brosse [balɛbrɔs] *nm* (long-handled) scrubbing *Br* ou scrub *Am* brush.

balance [balãs] *nf* - **1.** [instrument] scales *(pl)* - **2.** COMM & POLIT balance. ➤ **Balance** *nf* ASTROL Libra.

balancer [16] [balãse] *vt* - **1.** [bouger] to swing - **2.** *fam* [lancer] to chuck - **3.** *fam* [jeter] to chuck out. ➤ **se balancer** *vp* - **1.** [sur une chaise] to rock backwards and forwards - **2.** [sur une balançoire] to swing - **3.** *fam* : **se ~ de qqch** not to give a damn about sthg.

balancier [balãsje] *nm* - **1.** [de pendule] pendulum - **2.** [de funambule] pole.

balançoire [balãswar] *nf* [suspendue] swing ; [bascule] see-saw.

balayage [balɛjaʒ] *nm* [gén] sweeping ; TECHNOL scanning.

balayer [11] [balɛje] *vt* - **1.** [nettoyer] to sweep - **2.** [chasser] to sweep away - **3.** [suj : radar] to scan ; [suj : projecteurs] to sweep (across).

balayette [balɛjɛt] *nf* small brush.

balayeur, euse [balɛjœr, øz] *nm, f* roadsweeper *Br*, streetsweeper *Am*. ➤ **balayeuse** *nf* [machine] roadsweeper.

balbutier [9] [balbysje] ◇ *vi* [bafouiller] to stammer. ◇ *vt* [bafouiller] to stammer (out).

balcon [balkɔ̃] *nm* - **1.** [de maison terrasse] balcony ; [- balustrade] parapet - **2.** [de théâtre, de cinéma] circle.

balconnet [balkɔnɛ] *nm* : **soutien-gorge à ~** half-cup bra.

baldaquin [baldakɛ̃] *nm* ▷ lit.

baleine [balɛn] *nf* - **1.** [mammifère] whale - **2.** [de corset] whalebone - **3.** [de parapluie] rib.

balise [baliz] *nf* - **1.** NAVIG marker (buoy) - **2.** AÉRON runway light - **3.** AUTOM road sign - **4.** INFORM tag.

baliser [3] [balize] *vt* to mark out.

balivernes [balivɛrn] *nfpl* nonsense *(U)*.

Balkans [balkã] *nmpl* : **les ~** the Balkans.

ballade [balad] *nf* ballad.

ballant, e [balɑ̃, ɑ̃t] *adj* : **les bras ~s** arms dangling.

ballast [balast] *nm* - **1.** [chemin de fer] ballast - **2.** NAVIG ballast tank.

balle [bal] *nf* - **1.** [d'arme à feu] bullet ; **~ perdue** stray bullet - **2.** [de jeu] ball - **3.** [de marchandises] bale.

ballerine [balʁin] *nf* - **1.** [danseuse] ballerina - **2.** [chaussure] ballet shoe.

ballet [balɛ] *nm* [gén] ballet ; *fig* [activité intense] to-ing and fro-ing.

ballon [balɔ̃] *nm* - **1.** JEU & SPORT ball ; **~ de football** football - **2.** [montgolfière, de fête] balloon.

ballonné, e [balɔne] *adj* : **avoir le ventre ~, être ~** to be bloated.

ballot [balo] *nm* - **1.** [de marchandises] bundle - **2.** *vieilli* [imbécile] twit.

ballottage [balɔtaʒ] *nm* POLIT second ballot ; **en ~** standing for a second ballot.

ballotter [3] [balɔte] ◇ *vt* to toss about. ◇ *vi* [chose] to roll around.

ballottine [balɔtin] *nf* : **~ de foie gras** *type of galantine made with foie gras.*

ball-trap [baltʁap] *nm* clay pigeon shooting.

balluchon = baluchon.

balnéaire [balneɛʁ] *adj* : **station ~** seaside resort.

balourd, e [baluʁ, uʁd] *adj* clumsy.

balte [balt] *adj* Baltic. ◆ **Balte** *nmf* native of the Baltic states.

Baltique [baltik] *nf* : **la ~** the Baltic (Sea).

baluchon, balluchon [balyʃɔ̃] *nm* bundle ; **faire son ~** *fam* to pack one's bags (and leave).

balustrade [balystʁad] *nf* - **1.** [de terrasse] balustrade - **2.** [rambarde] guardrail.

bambin [bɑ̃bɛ̃] *nm* kiddie.

bambou [bɑ̃bu] *nm* [plante] bamboo.

ban [bɑ̃] *nm* - **1.** [de mariage] : **publier** OU **afficher les ~s** to publish OU display the banns - **2.** *loc* : **être/mettre qqn au ~ de la société** to be outlawed/to outlaw sb (from society) ; **le ~ et l'arrière-~** the whole lot of them.

banal, e, als [banal] *adj* commonplace, banal.

banaliser [3] [banalize] *vt* : **voiture banalisée** unmarked police car.

banalité [banalite] *nf* - **1.** [caractère banal] banality - **2.** [cliché] commonplace.

banane [banan] *nf* - **1.** [fruit] banana - **2.** [sac] bum-bag - **3.** [coiffure] quiff.

bananier, ère [bananje, ɛʁ] *adj* banana

(avant n). ◆ **bananier** *nm* - **1.** [arbre] banana tree - **2.** [cargo] banana boat.

banc [bɑ̃] *nm* [siège] bench ; **le ~ des accusés** JUR the dock ; **~ d'essai** test-bed ; **être au ~ d'essai** *fig* to be at the test stage ; **~ de sable** sandbank.

bancaire [bɑ̃kɛʁ] *adj* bank *(avant n)*, banking *(avant n)*.

bancal, e, als [bɑ̃kal] *adj* - **1.** [meuble] wobbly - **2.** [théorie, idée] unsound.

bandage [bɑ̃daʒ] *nm* [de blessé] bandage.

bande [bɑ̃d] *nf* - **1.** [de tissu, de papier] strip ; **~ dessinée** comic strip - **2.** [bandage] bandage ; **~ Velpeau®** crepe bandage - **3.** [de billard] cushion ; **par la ~** *fig* by a roundabout route - **4.** [groupe] band ; **en ~** in a group - **5.** [pellicule de film] film - **6.** [d'enregistrement] tape ; **~ magnétique** (magnetic) tape ; **~ originale** CIN original soundtrack ; **~ vidéo** video (tape) - **7.** [voie] : **~ d'arrêt d'urgence** hard shoulder - **8.** RADIO : **~ de fréquence** waveband - **9.** NAVIG : **donner de la ~** to list.

bande-annonce [bɑ̃danɔ̃s] *nf* trailer.

bandeau, x [bɑ̃do] *nm* - **1.** [sur les yeux] blindfold - **2.** [dans les cheveux] headband.

bandelette [bɑ̃dlɛt] *nf* strip (of cloth).

bander [3] [bɑ̃de] ◇ *vt* - **1.** MÉD to bandage ; **~ les yeux de qqn** to blindfold sb - **2.** [arc] to draw back - **3.** [muscle] to flex. ◇ *vi vulg* to have a hard-on.

banderole [bɑ̃dʁɔl] *nf* streamer.

bande-son [bɑ̃dsɔ̃] *(pl* **bandes-son)** *nf* soundtrack.

bandit [bɑ̃di] *nm* [voleur] bandit.

banditisme [bɑ̃ditism] *nm* serious crime.

bandoulière [bɑ̃duljɛʁ] *nf* bandolier ; **en ~** across the shoulder.

banlieue [bɑ̃ljø] *nf* suburbs *(pl)*.

banlieusard, e [bɑ̃ljøzaʁ, aʁd] *nm, f* *person living in the suburbs.*

bannière [banjɛʁ] *nf* [étendard] banner.

bannir [32] [baniʁ] *vt* : **~ qqn/qqch (de)** to banish sb/sthg (from).

banque [bɑ̃k] *nf* - **1.** [activité] banking - **2.** [établissement, au jeu] bank ; **Banque centrale européenne** European Central Bank - **3.** INFORM : **~ de données** data bank - **4.** MÉD : **~ d'organes/du sang/du sperme** organ/blood/sperm bank.

banqueroute [bɑ̃kʁut] *nf* bankruptcy ; **faire ~** to go bankrupt.

banquet [bɑ̃kɛ] *nm* (celebration) dinner ; [de gala] banquet.

banquette [bɑ̃kɛt] *nf* seat.

banquier, ère [bɑ̃kje, ɛʁ] *nm, f* banker.

banquise [bɑ̃kiz] *nf* ice field.

baptême [batɛm] *nm* - **1.** RELIG baptism, christening - **2.** [première fois] : **~ de l'air** maiden flight.

baptiser [3] [batize] *vt* to baptize, to christen.

baquet [bakɛ] *nm* [cuve] tub.

bar [bar] *nm* - **1.** [café, unité de pression] bar - **2.** [poisson] bass.

baraque [barak] *nf* - **1.** [cabane] hut - **2.** *fam* [maison] house - **3.** [de forain] stall, stand.

baraqué, e [barake] *adj fam* well-built.

baraquement [barakmɑ̃] *nm* camp *(of huts for refugees, workers etc)*.

baratin [baratɛ̃] *nm fam* smooth talk ; **faire du ~ à qqn** to sweet-talk sb.

baratiner [3] [baratine] *fam* ⟨⟩ *vt* [femme] to chat up ; [client] to give one's sales pitch to. ⟨⟩ *vi* to be a smooth talker.

barbare [barbar] ⟨⟩ *nm* barbarian. ⟨⟩ *adj* - **1.** *péj* [non civilisé] barbarous - **2.** [cruel] barbaric.

barbe [barb] *nf* beard ; **se laisser pousser la ~** to grow a beard ; **~ à papa** candy floss *Br*, cotton candy *Am* ; **quelle** ou **la ~!** *fam* what a drag!

barbelé, e [barbəle] *adj* barbed. ◆ **barbelé** *nm* barbed wire *(U)*.

barbiche [barbiʃ] *nf* goatee (beard).

barbiturique [barbityrik] *nm* barbiturate.

barboter [3] [barbɔte] *vi* to paddle.

barboteuse [barbɔtøz] *nf* romper-suit.

barbouillé, e [barbuje] *adj* : **être ~, avoir l'estomac ~** to feel sick.

barbouiller [3] [barbuje] *vt* [salir] ; **~ qqch (de)** to smear sthg (with).

barbu, e [barby] *adj* bearded. ◆ **barbu** *nm* bearded man.

bardé, e [barde] *adj* : **il est ~ de diplômes** he's got heaps of diplomas.

barder [3] [barde] ⟨⟩ *vt* CULIN to bard. ⟨⟩ *vi fam* : **ça va ~** there'll be trouble.

barème [barɛm] *nm* [de référence] table ; [de salaires] scale.

baril [baril] *nm* barrel.

bariolé, e [barjɔle] *adj* multicoloured *Br*, multicolored *Am*.

barjo(t) [barʒo] *adj inv fam* nuts.

barmaid [barmɛd] *nf* barmaid.

barman [barman] *(pl* barmans *ou* barmen [barmɛn]) *nm* barman.

baromètre [barɔmɛtr] *nm* barometer.

baron, onne [barɔ̃, ɔn] *nm, f* baron *(f* baroness).

baroque [barɔk] *adj* - **1.** [style] baroque - **2.** [bizarre] weird.

barque [bark] *nf* small boat.

barquette [barkɛt] *nf* - **1.** [tartelette] pastry boat - **2.** [récipient - de fruits] punnet ; [- de crème glacée] tub.

barrage [baraʒ] *nm* - **1.** [de rue] roadblock - **2.** CONSTR dam.

barre [bar] *nf* - **1.** [gén & JUR] bar ; **~ fixe** GYM high bar ; **~ des témoins** JUR witness box *Br* ou stand *Am* - **2.** NAVIG helm - **3.** [trait] stroke - **4.** INFORM : **~ d'espacement** space bar.

barreau, x [baro] *nm* bar ; **le ~** JUR the Bar.

barrer [3] [bare] *vt* - **1.** [rue, route] to block - **2.** [mot, phrase] to cross out - **3.** [bateau] to steer. ◆ **se barrer** *vp fam* to clear off.

barrette [barɛt] *nf* [pince à cheveux] (hair) slide *Br*, barrette *Am*.

barreur, euse [barœr, øz] *nm, f* NAVIG helmsman ; [à l'aviron] cox.

barricade [barikad] *nf* barricade.

barrière [barjɛr] *nf litt & fig* barrier.

barrique [barik] *nf* barrel.

baryton [baritɔ̃] *nm* baritone.

bas, basse [ba, baz *devant nm commençant par voyelle ou h muet,* bas] *adj* - **1.** [gén] low - **2.** *péj* [vil] base, low - **3.** MUS bass. ◆ **bas** ⟨⟩ *nm* - **1.** [partie inférieure] bottom, lower part ; **avoir/connaître des hauts et des ~** to have/go through ups and downs - **2.** [vêtement] stocking ; **~ de laine** woollen *Br* ou woolen *Am* stocking ; *fig* nest egg. ⟨⟩ *adv* low ; **à ~ ...!** down with ...! ; **parler ~** to speak in a low voice, to speak softly ; **mettre ~** [animal] to give birth. ◆ **en bas** *loc adv* at the bottom ; [dans une maison] downstairs. ◆ **en bas de** *loc prép* at the bottom of ; **attendre qqn en ~ de chez lui** to wait for sb downstairs. ◆ **bas de gamme** ⟨⟩ *adj* downmarket. ⟨⟩ *nm* bottom of the range.

basalte [bazalt] *nm* basalt.

basané, e [bazane] *adj* tanned.

bas-côté [bakote] *nm* [de route] verge.

bascule [baskyl] *nf* [balançoire] seesaw.

basculer [3] [baskyle] ⟨⟩ *vi* to fall over, to overbalance ; [benne] to tip up ; **~ dans qqch** *fig* to tip over into sthg. ⟨⟩ *vt* to tip up, to tilt.

base [baz] *nf* - **1.** [partie inférieure] base - **2.** [principe fondamental] basis ; **à ~ de** based on ; **de ~** basic ; **une boisson à ~ d'orange** an orange-based drink ; **sur la ~ de** on the basis of - **3.** INFORM : **~ de données** database.

baser [3] [baze] *vt* to base. ◆ **se baser**

vp : **sur quoi vous basez-vous pour affirmer cela?** what are you basing this statement on?

bas-fond [baf3] *nm* [de l'océan] shallow. ➤ **bas-fonds** *nmpl fig* - **1.** [de la société] dregs - **2.** [quartiers pauvres] slums.

basilic [bazilik] *nm* [plante] basil.

basilique [bazilik] *nf* basilica.

basique [bazik] *adj* basic.

basket [baskɛt] ⟨⟩ *nm* = **basket-ball**. ⟨⟩ *nf* [chaussure] trainer *Br*, sneaker *Am* ; **lâche-moi les ~s!** *fam fig* get off my back!

basket-ball [baskɛtbol] *nm* basketball.

basque [bask] ⟨⟩ *adj* Basque ; **le Pays ~** the Basque country. ⟨⟩ *nm* [langue] Basque. ⟨⟩ *nf* [vêtement] tail *(of coat)* ; **être toujours pendu aux ~s de qqn** *fam fig* to be always tagging along after sb. ➤ **Basque** *nmf* Basque.

bas-relief [barəljɛf] *nm* bas-relief.

basse [bas] ⟨⟩ *adj* ⊏ **bas**. ⟨⟩ *nf* MUS bass.

basse-cour [baskur] *nf* - **1.** [volaille] poultry - **2.** [partie de ferme] farmyard.

bassement [basmɑ̃] *adv* despicably.

basset [basɛ] *nm* basset hound.

bassin [basɛ̃] *nm* - **1.** [cuvette] bowl - **2.** [pièce d'eau] (ornamental) pond - **3.** [de piscine] : **petit/grand ~** children's/main pool - **4.** ANAT pelvis - **5.** GÉOL basin ; **~ houiller** coalfield ; **le Bassin parisien** the Paris basin.

bassine [basin] *nf* bowl, basin.

bassiste [basist] *nmf* bass player.

basson [bas3] *nm* [instrument] bassoon ; [personne] bassoonist.

bastide [bastid] *nf* traditional farmhouse or country house in southern France ; walled town (in south-west France).

bastingage [bastɛ̃gaʒ] *nm* (ship's) rail.

bastion [bastjɔ̃] *nm litt & fig* bastion.

baston [bastɔ̃] *nf tfam* punch-up.

bas-ventre [bavɑ̃tr] *nm* lower abdomen.

bataille [bataj] *nf* - **1.** MIL battle - **2.** [bagarre] fight - **3.** [jeu de cartes] ≃ beggar-my-neighbour - **4.** *loc* : **en ~** [cheveux] dishevelled *Br*, disheveled *Am*.

bataillon [batajɔ̃] *nm* MIL battalion ; *fig* horde.

bâtard, e [batar, ard] ⟨⟩ *adj* - **1.** [enfant] illegitimate - **2.** *péj* [style, solution] hybrid. ⟨⟩ *nm, f* illegitimate child. ➤ **bâtard** *nm* - **1.** [pain] short loaf of bread - **2.** [chien] mongrel.

batavia [batavja] *nf* Webb lettuce.

bateau, x [bato] *nm* - **1.** [embarcation - gén] boat ; [- plus grand] ship ; **~ à voile/moteur** sailing/motor boat ; **~ de pêche** fishing boat ; **mener qqn en ~** *fig* to take sb for a ride - **2.** [de trottoir] driveway entrance (low kerb) - **3.** (en apposition inv) [sujet, thème] well-worn ; **c'est ~!** it's the same old stuff!

bateau-mouche [batomuʃ] *(pl* bateaux-mouches) *nm* riverboat *(on the Seine)*.

bâti, e [bati] *adj* - **1.** [terrain] developed - **2.** [personne] : **bien ~** well-built. ➤ **bâti** *nm* - **1.** COUTURE tacking - **2.** CONSTR frame, framework.

batifoler [3] [batifɔle] *vi* to frolic.

bâtiment [batimɑ̃] *nm* - **1.** [édifice] building - **2.** IND : **le ~** the building trade - **3.** NAVIG ship, vessel.

bâtir [32] [batir] *vt* - **1.** CONSTR to build - **2.** *fig* [réputation, fortune] to build (up) ; [théorie, phrase] to construct - **3.** COUTURE to tack.

bâtisse [batis] *nf souvent péj* house.

bâton [batɔ̃] *nm* - **1.** [gén] stick ; **~ de ski** ski pole - **2.** *fam* fig 10,000 francs - **3.** *loc* : **mettre des ~s dans les roues à qqn** to put a spoke in sb's wheel ; **à ~s rompus** [conversation] rambling ; **parler à ~s rompus** to talk of this and that.

bâtonnet [batɔnɛ] *nm* rod.

batracien [batrasjɛ̃] *nm* amphibian.

battage [bataʒ] *nm* : **~ (publicitaire OU médiatique)** (media) hype.

battant, e [batɑ̃, ɑ̃t] ⟨⟩ *adj* : **sous une pluie ~e** in the pouring OU driving rain ; **le cœur ~** with beating heart. ⟨⟩ *nm, f* fighter. ➤ **battant** *nm* - **1.** [de porte] door *(of double doors)* ; [de fenêtre] half *(of double window)* - **2.** [de cloche] clapper.

battement [batmɑ̃] *nm* - **1.** [mouvement - d'ailes] flap, beating *(U)* ; [- de cœur, pouls] beat, beating *(U)* ; [- de cils, paupières] flutter, fluttering *(U)* - **2.** [intervalle de temps] break ; **une heure de ~** an hour free.

batterie [batri] *nf* - **1.** ÉLECTR & MIL battery ; **recharger ses ~s** *fig* to recharge one's batteries - **2.** [attirail] : **~ de cuisine** kitchen utensils *(pl)* - **3.** MUS drums *(pl)* - **4.** [série] : **une ~ de** a string of.

batteur [batœr] *nm* - **1.** MUS drummer - **2.** CULIN beater, whisk - **3.** [SPORT - de cricket] batsman ; [- de base-ball] batter.

battre [83] [batr] ⟨⟩ *vt* - **1.** [gén] to beat ; **~ en neige** [blancs d'œufs] to beat until stiff - **2.** [cartes] to shuffle. ⟨⟩ *vi* [gén] to beat ; **~ des cils** to blink ; **~ des mains** to clap (one's hands). ➤ **se battre** *vp* to fight ; **se ~ contre qqn** to fight sb.

battu, e [baty] ⟨⟩ *pp* ⊏ **battre**. ⟨⟩ *adj* - **1.** [tassé] hard-packed ; **jouer sur terre ~e**

TENNIS to play on clay - **2.** [fatigué] : **avoir les yeux ~s** to have shadows under one's eyes. ◆ **battue** *nf* - **1.** [chasse] beat - **2.** [chasse à l'homme] manhunt.

baume [bom] *nm litt & fig* balm ; **mettre du ~ au cœur de qqn** to comfort sb.

baux ▷ **bail.**

bavard, e [bavar, ard] ◇ *adj* talkative. ◇ *nm, f* chatterbox ; *péj* gossip.

bavardage [bavardaʒ] *nm* - **1.** [papotage] chattering - **2.** (*gén pl*) [raconter] gossip (*U*).

bavarder [3] [bavarde] *vi* to chatter ; *péj* to gossip.

bave [bav] *nf* - **1.** [salive] dribble - **2.** [d'animal] slaver - **3.** [de limace] slime.

baver [3] [bave] *vi* - **1.** [personne] to dribble - **2.** [animal] to slaver - **3.** [limace] to leave a trail - **4.** [stylo] to leak - **5.** *loc* : **en ~** *fam* to have a hard ou rough time of it.

bavette [bavɛt] *nf* - **1.** [bavoir, de tablier] bib - **2.** [viande] flank - **3.** *loc* : **tailler une ~ (avec qqn)** *fam* to have a chinwag (with sb).

baveux, euse [bavø, øz] *adj* - **1.** [bébé] dribbling - **2.** [omelette] runny

bavoir [bavwar] *nm* bib.

bavure [bavyr] *nf* - **1.** [tache] smudge - **2.** [erreur] blunder.

bayer [3] [baje] *vi* : **~ aux corneilles** to stand gazing into space.

bazar [bazar] *nm* - **1.** [boutique] general store - **2.** *fam* [désordre] jumble, clutter.

bazarder [3] [bazarde] *vt fam* to chuck out, to get rid of.

BCBG (*abr de* **bon chic bon genre**) *nmf & adj* term used to describe an upper-class lifestyle reflected especially in expensive and conservative clothes.

BCE (*abr de* **Banque centrale européenne**) *nf* ECB.

bcp *abr de* **beaucoup.**

bd *abr de* **boulevard.**

BD, bédé [bede] (*abr de* **bande dessinée**) *nf* : **une ~** a comic strip.

béant, e [beã, ãt] *adj* [plaie, gouffre] gaping ; [yeux] wide open.

béat, e [bea, at] *adj* [heureux] blissful.

beau, belle, beaux [bo, bɛl] *adj* (**bel** [bɛl] *devant voyelle ou h muet*) - **1.** [joli - femme] beautiful, good-looking ; [- homme] handsome, good-looking ; [- chose] beautiful - **2.** [temps] fine, good - **3.** (*toujours avant le nom*) [important] fine, excellent ; **une belle somme** a tidy sum (of money) - **4.** *iron* [mauvais] : **une belle grippe** a nasty dose of the flu ; **un ~ travail** a fine piece of work - **5.** (*sens intensif*) : **un ~ jour** one fine day

- **6.** *loc* : **elle a ~ jeu de dire ça** it's easy ou all very well for her to say that. ◆ **beau** ◇ *adv* : **il fait ~** the weather is good ou fine ; **j'ai ~ essayer ...** however hard I try ..., try as I may ... ; **j'ai ~ dire ...** whatever I say ... ◇ *nm* : **être au ~ fixe** to be set fair ; **avoir le moral au ~ fixe** *fig* to have a sunny disposition ; **faire le ~** [chien] to sit up and beg. ◆ **belle** *nf* - **1.** [femme] lady friend - **2.** [dans un jeu] decider. ◆ **de plus belle** *loc adv* more than ever.

Beaubourg [bobur] *n* name commonly used to refer to the Pompidou Centre.

beaucoup [boku] ◇ *adv* - **1.** [un grand nombre] : **~ de** a lot of, many ; **il y en a ~** there are many ou a lot (of them) - **2.** [une grande quantité] : **~ de** a lot of ; **~ d'énergie** a lot of energy ; **il n'a pas ~ de temps** he hasn't a lot of ou much time ; **il n'en a pas ~** he doesn't have much ou a lot (of it) - **3.** (*modifiant un verbe*) a lot ; **il boit ~** he drinks a lot ; **c'est ~ dire** that's saying a lot - **4.** (*modifiant un adjectif comparatif*) much, a lot ; **c'est ~ mieux** it's much ou a lot better ; **~ trop vite** much too quickly. ◇ *pron inv* many ; **nous sommes ~ à penser que ...** many of us think that ... ◆ **de beaucoup** *loc adv* by far.

beauf [bof] *nm* - **1.** *péj* stereotype of average French man with narrow views - **2.** *fam* [beau-frère] brother-in-law.

beau-fils [bofis] *nm* - **1.** [gendre] son-in-law - **2.** [de remariage] stepson.

beau-frère [bofrɛr] *nm* brother-in-law.

beau-père [boper] *nm* - **1.** [père du conjoint] father-in-law - **2.** [de remariage] stepfather.

beauté [bote] *nf* beauty ; **de toute ~** absolutely beautiful ; **en ~** [magnifiquement] in great style.

beaux-arts [bozar] *nmpl* fine art (*sg*). ◆ **Beaux-Arts** *nmpl* : **les Beaux-Arts** French national art school.

beaux-parents [boparã] *nmpl* - **1.** [de l'homme] husband's parents, in-laws - **2.** [de la femme] wife's parents, in-laws.

bébé [bebe] *nm* baby.

bébé-éprouvette [bebeepruvɛt] (*pl* **bébés-éprouvette**) *nm* test-tube baby.

bébête [bebɛt] *adj* silly.

bec [bɛk] *nm* - **1.** [d'oiseau] beak - **2.** [d'instrument de musique] mouthpiece - **3.** [de casserole etc] lip ; **~ de gaz** gaslamp (*in street*) ; **~ verseur** spout - **4.** *fam* [bouche] mouth ; **ouvrir le ~** to open one's mouth ; **clouer le ~ à qqn** to shut sb up.

bécane [bekan] *nf fam* - **1.** [moto, vélo] bike - **2.** [ordinateur etc] machine.

bécasse [bekas] *nf* - **1.** [oiseau] woodcock - **2.** *fam* [femme sotte] silly goose.

bec-de-lièvre [bɛkdəljɛvr] (*pl* becs-de-lièvre) *nm* harelip.

bêche [bɛʃ] *nf* spade.

bêcher [4] [beʃe] *vt* to dig.

bécoter [3] [bekɔte] *vt fam* to snog *Br* ou smooch with. ⇌ **se bécoter** *vp* to snog *Br*, to smooch.

becquée [beke] *nf* : donner la ~ à to feed.

becqueter, béqueter [27] [bɛkte] *vt* to peck at.

bedaine [bədɛn] *nf* potbelly.

bédé = BD.

bedonnant, e [bədɔnɑ̃, ɑ̃t] *adj* pot-bellied.

bée [be] *adj* : bouche ~ open-mouthed.

bégayer [11] [begeje] ⬦ *vi* to have a stutter ou stammer. ⬦ *vt* to stammer (out).

bégonia [begɔnja] *nm* begonia.

bègue [bɛg] ⬦ *adj* : être ~ to have a stutter ou stammer. ⬦ *nmf* stutterer, stammerer.

béguin [begɛ̃] *nm fam* : avoir le ~ pour qqn to have a crush on sb.

beige [bɛʒ] *adj & nm* beige.

beignet [bɛɲɛ] *nm* fritter.

bel [bɛl] ⊳ **beau**.

bêler [4] [bele] *vi* to bleat.

belette [bəlɛt] *nf* weasel.

belge [bɛlʒ] *adj* Belgian. ⇌ **Belge** *nmf* Belgian.

Belgique [bɛlʒik] *nf* : la ~ Belgium.

bélier [belje] *nm* - **1.** [animal] ram - **2.** [poutre] battering ram. ⇌ **Bélier** *nm* ASTROL Aries.

belladone [beladɔn] *nf* deadly nightshade.

belle [bɛl] *adj & nf* ⊳ **beau**.

belle-famille [bɛlfamij] *nf* - **1.** [de l'homme] husband's family, in-laws (*pl*) - **2.** [de la femme] wife's family, in-laws (*pl*).

belle-fille [bɛlfij] *nf* - **1.** [épouse du fils] daughter-in-law - **2.** [de remariage] stepdaughter.

belle-mère [bɛlmɛr] *nf* - **1.** [mère du conjoint] mother-in-law - **2.** [de remariage] stepmother.

belle-sœur [bɛlsœr] *nf* sister-in-law.

belligérant, e [beliʒerɑ̃, ɑ̃t] *adj & nm, f* belligerent.

belliqueux, euse [belikø, øz] *adj* [peuple] warlike ; [humeur, tempérament] aggressive.

belvédère [bɛlveder] *nm* - **1.** [construction] belvedere - **2.** [terrasse] viewpoint.

bémol [bemɔl] *adj & nm* MUS flat.

bénédiction [benediksjɔ̃] *nf* blessing.

bénéfice [benefis] *nm* - **1.** [avantage] advantage, benefit ; au ~ de in aid of - **2.** [profit] profit.

bénéficiaire [benefisjɛr] ⬦ *nmf* [gén] beneficiary ; [de chèque] payee. ⬦ *adj* [marge] profit (*avant n*) ; [résultat, société] profit-making.

bénéficier [9] [benefisje] *vi* : ~ de [profiter de] to benefit from ; [jouir de] to have, to enjoy ; [obtenir] to have, to get.

bénéfique [benefik] *adj* beneficial.

Bénélux [benelyks] *nm* : le ~ Benelux.

benêt [bənɛ] *nm* clod.

bénévole [benevɔl] ⬦ *adj* voluntary. ⬦ *nmf* volunteer, voluntary worker.

bénin, igne [benɛ̃, iɲ] *adj* [maladie, accident] minor ; [tumeur] benign.

bénir [32] [benir] *vt* - **1.** [gén] to bless - **2.** [se réjouir de] to thank God for.

bénitier [benitje] *nm* holy water font.

benjamin, e [bɛ̃ʒamɛ̃, in] *nm, f* [de famille] youngest child ; [de groupe] youngest member.

benne [bɛn] *nf* - **1.** [de camion] tipper - **2.** [de téléphérique] car - **3.** [pour déchets] skip.

benzine [bɛ̃zin] *nf* benzine.

béotien, enne [beɔsjɛ̃, ɛn] *nm, f* philistine.

BEP, Bep (*abr de* brevet d'études professionnelles) *nm* school-leaver's diploma (*taken at age 18*).

BEPC, Bepc (*abr de* brevet d'études du premier cycle) *nm* former school certificate (*taken at age 16*).

béquille [bekij] *nf* - **1.** [pour marcher] crutch - **2.** [d'un deux-roues] stand.

berceau, x [bɛrso] *nm* cradle.

bercer [16] [bɛrse] *vt* [bébé, bateau] to rock.

berceuse [bɛrsøz] *nf* - **1.** [chanson] lullaby - **2.** *Can* [fauteuil] rocking chair.

béret [berɛ] *nm* beret.

berge [bɛrʒ] *nf* - **1.** [bord] bank - **2.** *fam* [an] : il a plus de 50 ~s he's over 50.

berger, ère [bɛrʒe, ɛr] *nm, f* shepherd (*f* shepherdess). ⇌ **berger allemand** *nm* alsatian *Br*, German shepherd.

bergerie [bɛrʒəri] *nf* sheepfold.

Berlin [bɛrlɛ̃] *n* Berlin.

berline [bɛrlin] *nf* saloon (car) *Br*, sedan *Am*.

berlingot [bɛrlɛ̃go] *nm* - **1.** [de lait] carton - **2.** [bonbon] boiled sweet.

berlue [bɛrly] *nf* : **j'ai la ~!** I must be seeing things!

bermuda [bɛrmyda] *nm* bermuda shorts *(pl)*.

berne [bɛrn] *nf* : **en ~** ≃ at half-mast.

berner [3] [bɛrne] *vt* to fool.

besogne [bəzɔɲ] *nf* job, work *(U)*.

besoin [bəzwɛ̃] *nm* need ; **avoir ~ de qqch/de faire qqch** to need sthg/to do sthg ; **au ~** if necessary, if need ou needs be. ◆ **besoins** *nmpl* - **1.** [exigences] needs - **2.** *loc* : **faire ses ~s** to relieve o.s.

bestial, e, aux [bɛstjal, o] *adj* bestial, brutish.

bestiole [bɛstjɔl] *nf* (little) creature.

bétail [betaj] *nm* cattle *(pl)*.

bête [bɛt] ◇ *nf* [animal] animal ; [insecte] insect ; **~ de somme** beast of burden. ◇ *adj* [stupide] stupid.

bêtise [betiz] *nf* - **1.** [stupidité] stupidity - **2.** [action, remarque] stupid thing ; **faire/dire une ~** to do/say something stupid.

béton [betɔ̃] *nm* [matériau] concrete ; **~ armé** reinforced concrete.

bétonnière [betɔnjɛr] *nf* cement mixer.

betterave [bɛtrav] *nf* beetroot *Br*, beet *Am* ; **~ sucrière** ou **à sucre** sugar beet.

beugler [5] [bøgle] *vi* [bovin] to moo, to low.

beurre [bœr] *nm* [aliment] butter.

beurrer [5] [bœre] *vt* to butter.

beurrier [bœrje] *nm* butter dish.

beuverie [bœvri] *nf* drinking session.

bévue [bevy] *nf* blunder.

Beyrouth [berut] *n* Beirut.

biais [bjɛ] *nm* - **1.** [ligne oblique] slant ; **en** ou **de ~** [de travers] at an angle ; *fig* indirectly - **2.** COUTURE bias - **3.** [moyen détourné] expedient ; **par le ~ de** by means of.

biaiser [4] [bjeze] *vi fig* to dodge the issue.

bibelot [biblo] *nm* trinket, curio.

biberon [bibrɔ̃] *nm* baby's bottle.

bible [bibl] *nf* bible.

bibliographie [biblijɔgrafi] *nf* bibliography.

bibliophile [biblijɔfil] *nmf* book lover.

bibliothécaire [biblijɔtekɛr] *nmf* librarian.

bibliothèque [biblijɔtɛk] *nf* - **1.** [meuble] bookcase - **2.** [édifice, collection] library ; **la Bibliothèque nationale de France** the French national library.

biblique [biblik] *adj* biblical.

bicarbonate [bikarbɔnat] *nm* : **~ (de soude)** bicarbonate of soda.

biceps [bisɛps] *nm* biceps.

biche [biʃ] *nf* ZOOL hind, doe.

bicolore [bikɔlɔr] *adj* two-coloured *Br*, two-colored *Am*.

bicoque [bikɔk] *nf péj* house.

bicorne [bikɔrn] *nm* cocked hat.

bicyclette [bisiklɛt] *nf* bicycle ; **rouler à ~** to cycle.

bide [bid] *nm fam* - **1.** [ventre] belly - **2.** [échec] flop.

bidet [bidɛ] *nm* - **1.** [sanitaire] bidet - **2.** *hum* [cheval] nag.

bidon [bidɔ̃] *nm* - **1.** [récipient] can - **2.** *fam* [ventre] belly - **3.** *(en apposition inv) fam* [faux] phoney *Br*, phony *Am*.

bidonville [bidɔ̃vil] *nm* shantytown.

bielle [bjɛl] *nf* connecting rod.

bien [bjɛ̃] *(compar & superl* **mieux**) ◇ *adj inv* - **1.** [satisfaisant] good ; **il est ~ comme prof** he's a good teacher ; **il est ~, ce bureau** this is a good office - **2.** [en bonne santé] well ; **je ne me sens pas ~** I don't feel well - **3.** [joli] good-looking ; **tu ne trouves pas qu'elle est ~ comme ça?** don't you think she looks good ou nice like that? - **4.** [à l'aise] comfortable - **5.** [convenable] respectable. ◇ *nm* - **1.** [sens moral] : **le ~ et le mal** good and evil - **2.** [intérêt] good ; **je te dis ça pour ton ~** I'm telling you this for your own good - **3.** [richesse, propriété] property, possession ; **~s de consommation** consumer goods - **4.** *loc* : **faire du ~ à qqn** to do sb good ; **dire du ~ de qqn/qqch** to speak well of sb/sthg ; **mener à ~** to bring to fruition, to complete. ◇ *adv* - **1.** [de manière satisfaisante] well ; **on mange ~ ici** the food's good here ; **il ne s'est pas ~ conduit** he didn't behave well ; **tu as ~ fait** you did the right thing ; **tu ferais ~ d'y aller** you would be wise to go ; **c'est ~ fait!** it serves him/her *etc* right! - **2.** [sens intensif] quite, really ; **~ souvent** quite often ; **en es-tu ~ sûr?** are you quite sure (about it)? ; **j'espère ~ que ...** I do hope that ... ; **on a ~ ri** we had a good laugh ; **il y a ~ trois heures que j'attends** I've been waiting for at least three hours ; **c'est ~ aimable à vous** it's very kind ou good of you - **3.** [renforçant un comparatif] : **il est parti ~ plus tard** he left much later ; **on était ~ moins riches** we were a lot worse off ou poorer - **4.** [servant à conclure ou à introduire] : **~, je t'écoute** well, I'm listening - **5.** [en effet] : **c'est ~ lui** it really IS him ; **c'est ~ ce que je disais** that's just what I said. ◇ *interj* : **eh ~!** oh well! ; **eh ~, qu'en penses-tu?** well, what do you think? ➤ **biens** *nmpl* property *(U).* ➤ **bien de, bien des** *loc adj* : ~ **des gens sont venus** quite a lot of people came ; ~ **des fois** many times ; **il a ~ de la chance** he's very OU really lucky ; **il a eu ~ de la peine à me convaincre** he had quite a lot of trouble convincing me. ➤ **bien entendu** *loc adv* of course. ➤ **bien que** *conj* (+ *subjonctif*) although, though. ➤ **bien sûr** *loc adv* of course, certainly.

bien-aimé, e [bjɛ̃neme] (*mpl* **bien-aimés**, *fpl* **bien-aimées**) *adj & nm, f* beloved.

bien-être [bjɛ̃nɛtr] *nm inv* [physique] wellbeing.

bienfaisance [bjɛ̃fəzɑ̃s] *nf* charity.

bienfaisant, e [bjɛ̃fəzɑ̃, ɑ̃t] *adj* beneficial.

bienfait [bjɛ̃fɛ] *nm* - **1.** [effet bénéfique] benefit - **2.** [faveur] kindness.

bienfaiteur, trice [bjɛ̃fɛtœr, tris] *nm, f* benefactor.

bien-fondé [bjɛ̃fɔ̃de] (*pl* **bien-fondés**) *nm* validity.

bienheureux, euse [bjɛ̃nœrø, øz] *adj* - **1.** RELIG blessed - **2.** [heureux] happy.

bientôt [bjɛ̃to] *adv* soon ; **à ~!** see you soon!

bienveillance [bjɛ̃vejɑ̃s] *nf* kindness.

bienveillant, e [bjɛ̃vejɑ̃, ɑ̃t] *adj* kindly.

bienvenu, e [bjɛ̃vny] <> *adj* [qui arrive à propos] welcome. <> *nm, f* : **être le ~/la ~e** to be welcome ; **soyez le ~!** welcome! ➤ **bienvenue** *nf* welcome ; **souhaiter la ~e à qqn** to welcome sb.

bière [bjɛr] *nf* - **1.** [boisson] beer ; ~ **blonde** lager ; ~ **brune** brown ale ; ~ **pression** draught *Br* OU draft *Am* beer - **2.** [cercueil] coffin.

bifidus [bifidys] *nm* bifidus ; **yaourt au ~ bio** yogurt, yogurt containing bifidus.

bifteck [biftɛk] *nm* steak.

bifurcation [bifyrkasjɔ̃] *nf* [embranchement] fork ; *fig* new direction.

bifurquer [3] [bifyrke] *vi* - **1.** [route, voie ferrée] to fork - **2.** [voiture] to turn off - **3.** *fig* [personne] to branch off.

bigamie [bigami] *nf* bigamy.

bigoudi [bigudi] *nm* curler.

bijou, x [biʒu] *nm* - **1.** [joyau] jewel - **2.** *fig* [chef-d'œuvre] gem.

bijouterie [biʒutri] *nf* [magasin] jeweller's *Br* OU jeweler's *Am* (shop).

bijoutier, ère [biʒutje, ɛr] *nm, f* jeweller *Br*, jeweler *Am*.

Bikini® [bikini] *nm* bikini.

bilan [bilɑ̃] *nm* - **1.** FIN balance sheet ; **déposer son ~** to declare bankruptcy - **2.** [état

d'une situation] state of affairs ; **faire le ~ (de)** to take stock (of) ; ~ **de santé** checkup.

bilatéral, e, aux [bilateral, o] *adj* - **1.** [stationnement] on both sides (of the road) - **2.** [contrat, accord] bilateral.

bile [bil] *nf* bile ; **se faire de la ~** *fam* to worry.

biliaire [biljɛr] *adj* biliary ; **calcul ~** gallstone ; **vésicule ~** gall bladder.

bilingue [bilɛ̃g] *adj* bilingual.

billard [bijar] *nm* - **1.** [jeu] billiards *(U)* - **2.** [table de jeu] billiard table.

bille [bij] *nf* - **1.** [d'enfant] marble - **2.** [de bois] block of wood.

billet [bijɛ] *nm* - **1.** [lettre] note - **2.** [argent] : ~ **(de banque)** (bank) note ; **un ~ de 100 euros** a 100-euro note - **3.** [ticket] ticket ; ~ **de train/d'avion** train/plane ticket ; ~ **de loterie** lottery ticket.

billetterie [bijɛtri] *nf* - **1.** [à l'aéroport] ticket desk ; [à la gare] booking office OU hall - **2.** BANQUE cash dispenser.

billion [biljɔ̃] *nm* billion *Br*, trillion *Am*.

bimensuel, elle [bimɑ̃sɥɛl] *adj* fortnightly *Br*, twice monthly. ➤ **bimensuel** *nm* fortnightly review *Br*, semimonthly *Am*.

bimoteur [bimɔtœr] *nm* twin-engined plane.

binaire [binɛr] *adj* binary.

biner [3] [bine] *vt* to hoe.

binocle [binɔkl] *nm* pince-nez. ➤ **binocles** *nmpl fam vieilli* specs.

bio [bjo] *adj inv* natural ; **aliments ~** wholefood, health food.

biocarburant [bjɔkarbyrɑ̃] *nm* biofuel.

biochimie [bjɔʃimi] *nf* biochemistry.

biodégradable [bjɔdegradabl] *adj* biodegradable.

biographie [bjɔgrafi] *nf* biography.

biologie [bjɔlɔʒi] *nf* biology.

biologique [bjɔlɔʒik] *adj* - **1.** SCIENCE biological - **2.** [naturel] organic.

biopsie [bjɔpsi] *nf* biopsy.

biorythme [bjɔritm] *nm* biorhythm.

bip [bip] *nm* - **1.** [signal] tone, beep ; **parlez après le ~ (sonore)** please speak after the beep OU tone - **2.** [appareil] bleeper.

biréacteur [bireaktœr] *nm* twin-engined jet.

bis¹, e [bi, biz] *adj* greyish-brown ; **pain ~** brown bread.

bis² [bis] *adv* - **1.** [dans adresse] : **5 ~ 5a** - **2.** [à la fin d'un spectacle] encore.

bisannuel, elle [bizanɥɛl] *adj* biennial.

biscornu, e [biskɔrny] *adj* - **1.** [difforme] irregularly shaped - **2.** [bizarre] weird.

biscotte [biskɔt] *nf toasted bread sold in packets and often eaten for breakfast.*

biscuit [biskɥi] *nm* - **1.** [sec] biscuit *Br*, cookie *Am* ; [salé] cracker - **2.** [gâteau] sponge.

bise [biz] *nf* - **1.** [vent] north wind - **2.** *fam* [baiser] kiss ; **grosses ~s** love and kisses.

biseau, x [bizo] *nm* bevel ; **en ~** bevelled *Br*, beleved *Am*.

bison [bizɔ̃] *nm* bison.

bisou [bizu] *nm fam* kiss.

bissextile [bisɛkstil] ▷ **année.**

bistouri [bisturi] *nm* lancet.

bistrot, bistro [bistro] *nm fam* cafe, bar.

bit [bit] *nm* INFORM bit.

bivouac [bivwak] *nm* bivouac.

bivouaquer [3] [bivwake] *vi* to bivouac.

bizarre [bizar] *adj* strange, odd.

bizutage [bizytaʒ] *nm practical jokes played on new arrivals in a school or college.*

black-out [blakawt] *nm* blackout.

blafard, e [blafar, ard] *adj* pale.

blague [blag] *nf* [plaisanterie] joke.

blaguer [3] [blage] *fam vi* to joke.

blagueur, euse [blagœr, øz] *fam* ◇ *adj* jokey. ◇ *nm, f* joker.

blaireau, x [blɛro] *nm* - **1.** [animal] badger - **2.** [de rasage] shaving brush.

blâme [blɑm] *nm* - **1.** [désapprobation] disapproval - **2.** [sanction] reprimand.

blâmer [3] [blɑme] *vt* - **1.** [désapprouver] to blame - **2.** [sanctionner] to reprimand.

blanc, blanche [blɑ̃, blɑ̃ʃ] *adj* - **1.** [gén] white - **2.** [non écrit] blank - **3.** [pâle] pale. ◆ **blanc** *nm* - **1.** [couleur] white - **2.** [personne] white (man) - **3.** [linge de maison] : **le ~** the (household) linen - **4.** [sur page] blank (space) ; **en ~** [chèque] blank - **5.** [de volaille] white meat - **6.** [vin] white (wine) - **7.** *loc* : **chauffé à ~** white-hot. ◆ **blanche** *nf* - **1.** [personne] white (woman) - **2.** MUS minim. ◆ **blanc d'œuf** *nm* egg white.

blancheur [blɑ̃ʃœr] *nf* whiteness.

blanchir [32] [blɑ̃ʃir] ◇ *vt* - **1.** [mur] to whitewash - **2.** [linge, argent] to launder - **3.** [légumes] to blanch - **4.** [sucre] to refine ; [papier, tissu] to bleach. ◇ *vi* : **~ (de)** to go white (with).

blanchissage [blɑ̃ʃisaʒ] *nm* [de linge] laundering.

blanchisserie [blɑ̃ʃisri] *nf* laundry.

blasé, e [blaze] *adj* blasé.

blason [blazɔ̃] *nm* coat of arms.

blasphème [blasfɛm] *nm* blasphemy.

blasphémer [18] [blasfeme] *vt & vi* to blaspheme.

blatte [blat] *nf* cockroach.

blazer [blazɛr] *nm* blazer.

blé [ble] *nm* - **1.** [céréale] wheat, corn - **2.** *fam* [argent] dough.

blême [blɛm] *adj* : **~ (de)** pale (with).

blennorragie [blenɔraʒi] *nf* gonorrhoea.

blessant, e [blɛsɑ̃, ɑ̃t] *adj* hurtful.

blessé, e [blese] *nm, f* wounded ou injured person.

blesser [4] [blese] *vt* - **1.** [physiquement - accidentellement] to injure, to hurt ; [- par arme] to wound ; **ses chaussures lui blessent les pieds** his shoes make his feet sore - **2.** [moralement] to hurt. ◆ **se blesser** *vp* to injure o.s., to hurt o.s.

blessure [blesyr] *nf litt & fig* wound.

blet, blette [blɛ, blɛt] *adj* overripe.

bleu, e [blø] *adj* - **1.** [couleur] blue - **2.** [viande] very rare. ◆ **bleu** *nm* - **1.** [couleur] blue - **2.** [meurtrissure] bruise - **3.** *fam* [novice - à l'armée] raw recruit ; [- à l'université] freshman, fresher *Br* - **4.** [fromage] blue cheese - **5.** [vêtement] : **~ de travail** overalls *(pl).*

bleuet [bløɛ] *nm* cornflower ; *Can* [fruit] blueberry.

bleuir [32] [bløir] *vt & vi* to turn blue.

bleuté, e [bløte] *adj* bluish.

blindé, e [blɛ̃de] *adj* [véhicule] armoured *Br*, armored *Am* ; [porte, coffre] armour-plated *Br*, armor-plated *Am*. ◆ **blindé** *nm* armoured *Br* ou armored *Am* car.

blinder [3] [blɛ̃de] *vt* [véhicule] to armour *Br*, to armor *Am* ; [porte, coffre] to armour-plate *Br*, to armor-plate *Am*.

blizzard [blizar] *nm* blizzard.

bloc [blɔk] *nm* - **1.** [gén] block ; **en ~** wholesale - **2.** [assemblage] unit ; **~ d'alimentation** INFORM power pack ; **~ opératoire** operating theatre ; **~ sanitaire** toilet block.

blocage [blɔkaʒ] *nm* - **1.** ÉCON freeze, freezing *(U)* - **2.** [de roue] locking - **3.** PSYCHOL [mental] block.

blockhaus [blɔkos] *nm* blockhouse.

bloc-notes [blɔknɔt] *nm* notepad.

blocus [blɔkys] *nm* blockade.

blond, e [blɔ̃, blɔ̃d] ◇ *adj* fair, blond. ◇ *nm, f* fair-haired ou blond man (f fair-haired) ou blonde woman. ◆ **blond** *nm* : **~ cendré/vénitien/platine** ash/strawberry/platinum blond. ◆ **blonde** *nf* - **1.** [cigarette] Virginia cigarette - **2.** [bière] lager.

blondeur [blɔ̃dœr] *nf* blondness, fairness.

bloquer [3] [blɔke] *vt* - **1.** [porte, freins] to

jam ; [roues] to lock - **2.** [route, chemin] to block ; [personne] : **être bloqué** to be stuck - **3.** [prix, salaires, crédit] to freeze - **4.** PSYCHOL : **être bloqué** to have a (mental) block. ◂▸ **se bloquer** *vp* [se coincer] to jam.

blottir [32] [blɔtir] ◂▸ **se blottir** *vp* : se ~ (contre) to snuggle up (to).

blouse [bluz] *nf* [de travail, d'écolier] smock.

blouson [bluzɔ̃] *nm* bomber jacket, blouson.

blue-jean [bludʒin] (*pl* **blue-jeans** [bludʒins]) *nm* jeans (*pl*).

blues [bluz] *nm inv* blues.

bluffer [3] [blœfe] *fam vi & vt* to bluff.

blush [blœʃ] *nm* blusher.

BNF *nf abr de* **Bibliothèque nationale de France**.

boa [bɔa] *nm* boa.

bobard [bɔbar] *nm fam* fib.

bobine [bɔbin] *nf* - **1.** [cylindre] reel, spool - **2.** ÉLECTR coil.

bobsleigh [bɔbslɛg] *nm* bobsleigh.

bocage [bɔkaʒ] *nm* GÉOGR bocage.

bocal, aux [bɔkal, o] *nm* jar.

body-building [bɔdibildiŋ] *nm* : **le ~ body building** (*U*).

bœuf [bœf, pl bø] *nm* - **1.** [animal] ox - **2.** [viande] beef ; **~ bourguignon** *beef stew in a red-wine sauce.*

bof [bɔf] *interj fam* [exprime le mépris] so what? ; [exprime la lassitude] I don't really care.

bogue [bɔg], **bug** [bʌg] *nm* INFORM bug ; **le ~ de l'an 2000** the millennium bug.

bohème [bɔɛm] *adj* bohemian.

bohémien, enne [bɔemjɛ̃, ɛn] *nm, f* - **1.** [tsigane] gipsy - **2.** [non-conformiste] bohemian.

boire [108] [bwar] ◇ *vt* - **1.** [s'abreuver] to drink - **2.** [absorber] to soak up, to absorb. ◇ *vi* to drink.

bois [bwa] ◇ *nm* wood ; **en ~** wooden. ◇ *nmpl* - **1.** MUS woodwind (*U*) - **2.** [cornes] antlers.

boisé, e [bwaze] *adj* wooded.

boiserie [bwazri] *nf* panelling (*U*) *Br*, paneling (*U*) *Am*.

boisson [bwasɔ̃] *nf* [breuvage] drink.

boîte [bwat] *nf* - **1.** [récipient] box ; **en ~ tinned, canned ; ~ de conserve** tin *Br*, can ; **~ aux lettres** [pour la réception] letterbox ; [pour l'envoi] postbox *Br*, mailbox *Am* ; **~ à musique** music box *Br*, music box *Am* ; **~ postale** post office box - **2.**

AUTOM : ~ **à gants** glove compartment ; ~ **de vitesses** gearbox - **3.** INFORM : ~ **aux lettres électronique** electronic mailbox ; ~ **vocale** voice mail - **4.** *fam* [entreprise] company, firm ; [lycée] school - **5.** *fam* [discothèque] : ~ **(de nuit)** nightclub, club.

boiter [3] [bwate] *vi* [personne] to limp.

boiteux, euse [bwatø, øz] *adj* - **1.** [personne] lame - **2.** [meuble] wobbly - **3.** *fig* [raisonnement] shaky.

boîtier [bwatje] *nm* - **1.** [boîte] case - **2.** TECHNOL casing.

bol [bɔl] *nm* - **1.** [récipient] bowl - **2.** [contenu] bowl, bowlful - **3.** *loc* : **prendre un ~ d'air** to get some fresh air.

bolet [bɔlɛ] *nm* boletus.

bolide [bɔlid] *nm* [véhicule] racing *Br* ou race *Am* car.

Bolivie [bɔlivi] *nf* : **la ~** Bolivia.

bombance [bɔ̃bɑ̃s] *nf* : **faire ~** *fam* to have a feast.

bombardement [bɔ̃bardəmɑ̃] *nm* bombardment, bombing (*U*).

bombarder [3] [bɔ̃barde] *vt* - **1.** MIL to bomb - **2.** [assaillir] : ~ **qqn/qqch de** to bombard sb/sthg with.

bombardier [bɔ̃bardje] *nm* - **1.** [avion] bomber - **2.** [aviateur] bombardier.

bombe [bɔ̃b] *nf* - **1.** [projectile] bomb ; *fig* bombshell ; ~ **atomique** atomic bomb ; ~ **à retardement** time bomb - **2.** [casquette] riding hat - **3.** [atomiseur] spray, aerosol.

bombé, e [bɔ̃be] *adj* bulging, rounded.

bon, bonne [bɔ̃, bɔn] (*compar & superl* **meilleur**) *adj* - **1.** [gén] good - **2.** [généreux] good, kind - **3.** [utilisable - billet, carte] valid - **4.** [correct] right - **5.** [dans l'expression d'un souhait] : **bonne année!** Happy New Year! ; **bonne chance!** good luck! ; **bonnes vacances!** have a nice holiday! - **6.** *loc* : **être ~ pour qqch/pour faire qqch** *fam* to be fit for sthg/for doing sthg ; **tu es ~ pour une contravention** you'll end up with ou you'll get a parking ticket ; ~ **à savoir** that's worth knowing. ◂▸ **bon** ◇ *adv* : **il fait ~** the weather's fine, it's fine ; **sentir ~** to smell good ; **tenir ~** to stand firm. ◇ *interj* - **1.** [marque de satisfaction] good! - **2.** [marque de surprise] : **ah ~!** really? ◇ *nm* - **1.** [constatant un droit] voucher ; ~ **de commande** order form ; ~ **du Trésor** FIN Treasury bill ou bond - **2.** (*gén pl*) [personne] : **les ~s et les méchants** good people and wicked people. ◂▸ **pour de bon** *loc adv* seriously, really.

bonbon [bɔ̃bɔ̃] *nm* - **1.** [friandise] sweet *Br*, piece of candy *Am* - **2.** *Belg* [gâteau] biscuit.

bonbonne [bɔ̃bɔn] *nf* demijohn.

bonbonnière [bɔ̃bɔnjɛr] *nf* [boîte] sweet-box *Br*, candy box *Am*.

bond [bɔ̃] *nm* [d'animal, de personne] leap, bound ; [de balle] bounce ; **faire un ~** to leap (forward).

bonde [bɔ̃d] *nf* - **1.** [d'évier] plug - **2.** [trou] bunghole - **3.** [bouchon] bung.

bondé, e [bɔ̃de] *adj* packed.

bondir [32] [bɔ̃dir] *vi* - **1.** [sauter] to leap, to bound ; **~ sur qqn/qqch** to pounce on sb/ sthg - **2.** [s'élancer] to leap forward.

bonheur [bɔnœr] *nm* - **1.** [félicité] happiness - **2.** [chance] (good) luck, good fortune ; **par ~** happily, fortunately ; **porter ~** to be lucky, to bring good luck.

bonhomme [bɔnɔm] (*pl* bonshommes [bɔ̃zɔm]) *nm* - **1.** *fam péj* [homme] fellow - **2.** [représentation] man ; **~ de neige** snowman.

bonification [bɔnifikasjɔ̃] *nf* - **1.** [de terre, de vin] improvement - **2.** SPORT bonus points *(pl)*.

bonjour [bɔ̃ʒur] *nm* hello ; [avant midi] good morning ; [après midi] good afternoon.

bonne [bɔn] <> *nf* maid. <> *adj* ⊳ **bon**.

bonnet [bɔnɛ] *nm* - **1.** [coiffure] (woolly) hat ; **~ de bain** swimming cap - **2.** [de soutien-gorge] cup.

bonneterie [bɔnɛtri] *nf* [commerce] hosiery (business ou trade).

bonsoir [bɔ̃swar] *nm* [en arrivant] hello, good evening ; [en partant] goodbye, good evening ; [en se couchant] good night.

bonté [bɔ̃te] *nf* - **1.** [qualité] goodness, kindness ; **avoir la ~ de faire qqch** *sout* to be so good ou kind as to do sthg - **2.** *(gén pl)* [acte] act of kindness.

bonus [bɔnys] *nm* [prime d'assurance] no-claims bonus.

bord [bɔr] *nm* - **1.** [de table, de vêtement] edge ; [de verre, de chapeau] rim ; **à ras ~s** to the brim - **2.** [de rivière] bank ; [de lac] edge, shore ; **au ~ de la mer** at the seaside - **3.** [de bois, jardin] edge ; [de route] edge, side - **4.** [d'un moyen de transport] : **passer par-dessus ~** to fall overboard. ◆ **à bord de** *loc prép* : **à ~ de qqch** on board sthg. ◆ **au bord de** *loc prép* at the edge of ; *fig* on the verge of.

bordeaux [bɔrdo] <> *nm* - **1.** [vin] Bordeaux - **2.** [couleur] claret. <> *adj inv* claret.

bordel [bɔrdɛl] *nm vulg* - **1.** [maison close] brothel - **2.** [désordre] shambles *(sg)*.

border [3] [bɔrde] *vt* - **1.** [vêtement] : **~ qqch de** to edge sthg with - **2.** [être en bordure de] to line - **3.** [couverture, personne] to tuck in.

bordereau, x [bɔrdəro] *nm* - **1.** [liste] schedule - **2.** [facture] invoice - **3.** [relevé] slip.

bordure [bɔrdyr] *nf* - **1.** [bord] edge ; **en ~ de** on the edge of - **2.** [de fleurs] border.

borgne [bɔrɲ] *adj* [personne] one-eyed.

borne [bɔrn] *nf* - **1.** [marque] boundary marker - **2.** [limite] limit, bounds *(pl)* ; **dépasser les ~s** to go too far ; **sans ~s** boundless - **3.** *fam* [kilomètre] kilometre *Br*, kilometer *Am*.

borné, e [bɔrne] *adj* [personne] narrow-minded ; [esprit] narrow.

borner [3] [bɔrne] *vt* [terrain] to limit ; [projet, ambition] to limit, to restrict. ◆ **se borner** *vp* : **se ~ à qqch/à faire qqch** [suj : personne] to confine o.s. to sthg/to doing sthg.

bosniaque [bɔsnjak] *adj* Bosnian. ◆ **Bosniaque** *nmf* Bosnian.

Bosnie [bɔsni] *nf* : **la ~** Bosnia.

bosquet [bɔskɛ] *nm* copse.

bosse [bɔs] *nf* - **1.** [sur tête, sur route] bump - **2.** [de bossu, chameau] hump.

bosser [8] [bɔse] *vi fam* to work hard.

bossu, e [bɔsy] <> *adj* hunchbacked. <> *nm, f* hunchback.

bot [bo] <> **pied.**

botanique [bɔtanik] <> *adj* botanical. <> *nf* : **la ~** botany.

botte [bɔt] *nf* - **1.** [chaussure] boot - **2.** [de légumes] bunch - **3.** [en escrime] thrust, lunge.

botter [3] [bɔte] *vt* - **1.** [chausser] : **être botté de cuir** to be wearing leather boots - **2.** *fam* [donner un coup de pied à] to boot - **3.** *fam vieilli* [plaire à] : **ça me botte** I dig it.

bottier [bɔtje] *nm* [de bottes] bootmaker, [de chaussures] shoemaker.

Bottin® [bɔtɛ̃] *nm* phone book.

bottine [bɔtin] *nf* (ankle) boot.

bouc [buk] *nm* - **1.** [animal] (billy) goat ; **~ émissaire** *fig* scapegoat - **2.** [barbe] goatee.

boucan [bukɑ̃] *nm fam* row, racket.

bouche [buʃ] *nf* [gén] mouth ; **~ d'incendie** fire hydrant ; **~ de métro** metro entrance ou exit.

bouché, e [buʃe] *adj* - **1.** [en bouteille] bottled - **2.** *fam* [personne] dumb, thick *Br*.

bouche-à-bouche [buʃabuʃ] *nm inv* : **faire du ~ à qqn** to give sb mouth-to-mouth resuscitation.

bouchée [buʃe] *nf* mouthful.

boucher[1] [3] [buʃe] *vt* - **1.** [fermer - bouteille] to cork ; [- trou] to fill (in ou up) - **2.** [passage, vue] to block.

boucher², **ère** [buʃe, ɛr] *nm, f* butcher.

boucherie [buʃri] *nf* - **1.** [magasin] butcher's (shop) - **2.** *fig* [carnage] slaughter.

bouche-trou [buʃtru] (*pl* bouche-trous) *nm* - **1.** [personne] : **servir de ~ to** make up (the) numbers - **2.** [objet] stopgap.

bouchon [buʃɔ̃] *nm* - **1.** [pour obturer - gén] top ; [- de réservoir] cap ; [- de bouteille] cork - **2.** [de canne à pêche] float - **3.** [embouteillage] traffic jam.

boucle [bukl] *nf* - **1.** [de ceinture, soulier] buckle - **2.** [bijou] : ~ **d'oreille** earring - **3.** [de cheveux] curl - **4.** [de fleuve, d'avion & INFORM] loop.

bouclé, e [bukle] *adj* [cheveux] curly ; [personne] curly-haired.

boucler [3] [bukle] *vt* - **1.** [attacher] to buckle ; [ceinture de sécurité] to fasten - **2.** [fermer] to shut - **3.** *fam* [enfermer - voleur] to lock up ; [- malade] to shut away - **4.** [encercler] to seal off - **5.** [terminer] to finish.

bouclier [buklije] *nm litt & fig* shield.

bouddhiste [budist] *nmf & adj* Buddhist.

bouder [3] [bude] ⋄ *vi* to sulk. ⋄ *vt* [chose] to dislike ; [personne] to shun ; **elle me boude depuis que je lui ai fait faux-bond** she has cold-shouldered me ever since I let her down.

boudeur, euse [budœr, øz] *adj* sulky.

boudin [budɛ̃] *nm* CULIN blood pudding.

boue [bu] *nf* mud.

bouée [bwe] *nf* - **1.** [balise] buoy - **2.** [pour flotter] rubber ring ; ~ **de sauvetage** lifebelt.

boueux, euse [buø, øz] *adj* muddy.

bouffe [buf] *nf fam* grub.

bouffée [bufe] *nf* - **1.** [de fumée] puff ; [de parfum] whiff ; [d'air] breath - **2.** [accès] surge ; ~**s délirantes** mad fits.

bouffer [3] [bufe] *vt fam* [manger] to eat.

bouffi, e [bufi] *adj* : ~ **(de)** swollen (with).

bouffon, onne [bufɔ̃, ɔn] *adj* farcical.
◆ **bouffon** *nm* - **1.** HIST jester - **2.** [pitre] clown.

bouge [buʒ] *nm péj* - **1.** [taudis] hovel - **2.** [café] dive.

bougeoir [buʒwar] *nm* candlestick.

bougeotte [buʒɔt] *nf* : **avoir la ~** to have itchy feet.

bouger [17] [buʒe] ⋄ *vt* [déplacer] to move. ⋄ *vi* - **1.** [remuer] to move - **2.** [changer] to change - **3.** [s'agiter] : **ça bouge partout dans le monde** there is unrest all over the world.

bougie [buʒi] *nf* - **1.** [chandelle] candle - **2.** [de moteur] spark plug, sparking plug.

bougon, onne [bugɔ̃, ɔn] *adj* grumpy.

bougonner [3] [bugɔne] *vt & vi* to grumble.

bouillant, e [bujɑ̃, ɑ̃t] *adj* - **1.** [qui bout] boiling - **2.** [très chaud] boiling hot.

bouillie [buji] *nf* baby's cereal ; **réduire en ~** [légumes] to puree ; [personne] to reduce to a pulp.

bouillir [48] [bujir] *vi* [aliments] to boil ; **faire ~** to boil.

bouilloire [bujwar] *nf* kettle.

bouillon [bujɔ̃] *nm* - **1.** [soupe] stock - **2.** [bouillonnement] bubble ; **faire bouillir à gros ~s** to bring to a rolling boil.

bouillonner [3] [bujɔne] *vi* - **1.** [liquide] to bubble - **2.** [torrent] to foam - **3.** *fig* [personne] to seethe.

bouillotte [bujɔt] *nf* hot-water bottle.

boul. *abr de* **boulevard**.

boulanger, ère [bulɑ̃ʒe, ɛr] *nm, f* baker.

boulangerie [bulɑ̃ʒri] *nf* - **1.** [magasin] baker's (shop) - **2.** [commerce] bakery trade.

boule [bul] *nf* [gén] ball ; [de loto] counter ; [de pétanque] bowl ; ~ **de neige** snowball.
◆ **boules** *nfpl* [jeux] *game played on bare ground with steel bowls.*

bouleau, x [bulo] *nm* silver birch.

bouledogue [buldɔg] *nm* bulldog.

boulet [bulɛ] *nm* - **1.** [munition] : ~ **de canon** cannonball - **2.** [de forçat] ball and chain - **3.** *fig* [fardeau] millstone (round one's neck).

boulette [bulɛt] *nf* - **1.** [petite boule] pellet - **2.** [de viande] meatball.

boulevard [bulvar] *nm* - **1.** [rue] boulevard - **2.** THÉÂTRE light comedy *(U)*.

bouleversant, e [bulvɛrsɑ̃, ɑ̃t] *adj* distressing.

bouleversement [bulvɛrsəmɑ̃] *nm* disruption.

bouleverser [3] [bulvɛrse] *vt* - **1.** [objets] to turn upside down - **2.** [modifier] to disrupt - **3.** [émouvoir] to distress.

boulier [bulje] *nm* abacus.

boulimie [bulimi] *nf* bulimia.

boulon [bulɔ̃] *nm* bolt.

boulonner [3] [bulɔne] ⋄ *vt* to bolt. ⋄ *vi fam* to slog (away).

boulot [bulo] *nm fam* - **1.** [travail] work - **2.** [emploi] job.

boum [bum] *nf fam vieilli* party.

bouquet [bukɛ] *nm* - **1.** [de fleurs - gén] bunch (of flowers) - **2.** [de vin] bouquet - **3.** [de feu d'artifice] crowning piece

- **4.** TÉLÉ : ~ **de programmes** multi-channel package.

bouquin [bukɛ̃] *nm fam* book.

bouquiner [3] [bukine] *vi & vt fam* to read.

bouquiniste [bukinist] *nmf* secondhand bookseller.

bourbier [burbje] *nm* [lieu] quagmire, mire ; *fig* mess.

bourde [burd] *nf fam* [erreur] blunder.

bourdon [burdɔ̃] *nm* [insecte] bumblebee.

bourdonnement [burdɔnmɑ̃] *nm* [d'insecte, de voix, de moteur] buzz *(U)*.

bourdonner [3] [burdɔne] *vi* - **1.** [insecte, machine, voix] to buzz - **2.** [oreille] to ring.

bourgeois, e [burʒwa, az] ◇ *adj* - **1.** [valeur] middle-class - **2.** [cuisine] plain - **3.** *péj* [personne] bourgeois. ◇ *nm, f* bourgeois.

bourgeoisie [burʒwazi] *nf* ≃ middle classes *(pl)*.

bourgeon [burʒɔ̃] *nm* bud.

bourgeonner [3] [burʒɔne] *vi* to bud.

Bourgogne [burgɔɲ] *nf* : **la ~** Burgundy.

bourlinguer [3] [burlɛ̃ge] *vi fam* [voyager] to bum around the world.

bourrade [burad] *nf* thump.

bourrage [buraʒ] *nm* [de coussin] stuffing.
➤ **bourrage de crâne** *nm* - **1.** [bachotage] swotting - **2.** [propagande] brainwashing.

bourrasque [burask] *nf* gust of wind.

bourratif, ive [buratif, iv] *adj* stodgy.

bourreau, x [buro] *nm* HIST executioner.

bourrelet [burlɛ] *nm* [de graisse] roll of fat.

bourrer [3] [bure] *vt* - **1.** [remplir - coussin] to stuff ; [- sac, armoire] ; **~ qqch (de)** to cram sthg full (with) - **2.** *fam* [gaver] : **~ qqn (de)** to stuff sb (with).

bourrique [burik] *nf* - **1.** [ânesse] she-ass - **2.** *fam* [personne] pigheaded person.

bourru, e [bury] *adj* [peu aimable] surly.

bourse [burs] *nf* - **1.** [porte-monnaie] purse - **2.** [d'études] grant. ➤ **Bourse** *nf* [marché] stock exchange, stock market ; **la Bourse de Paris** the Paris Stock Exchange ; **jouer en Bourse** to speculate on the stock exchange ou stock market ; **Bourse de commerce** commodity market.

boursier, ère [bursje, ɛr] *adj* - **1.** [élève] on a grant - **2.** FIN stock-exchange, stock-market *(avant n)*.

boursouflé, e [bursufle] *adj* [enflé] swollen.

bousculade [buskylad] *nf* - **1.** [cohue] crush - **2.** [agitation] rush.

bousculer [3] [buskyle] *vt* - **1.** [faire tomber] to knock over - **2.** [presser] to rush - **3.** [modifier] to overturn.

bouse [buz] *nf* : **~ de vache** cow dung.

bousiller [3] [buzije] *vt fam* [abîmer] to ruin, to knacker *Br*.

boussole [busɔl] *nf* compass.

bout [bu] *nm* - **1.** [extrémité, fin] end ; **au ~ de** [temps] after ; [espace] at the end of ; **d'un ~ à l'autre** [de ville etc] from one end to the other ; [de livre] from beginning to end - **2.** [morceau] bit - **3.** *loc* : **être à ~** to be exhausted ; **à ~ portant** at point-blank range ; **pousser qqn à ~** to drive sb to distraction ; **venir à ~ de** [personne] to get the better of ; [difficulté] to overcome.

boutade [butad] *nf* [plaisanterie] jest.

boute-en-train [butɑ̃trɛ̃] *nm inv* live wire ; **il était le ~ de la soirée** he was the life and soul of the party.

bouteille [butɛj] *nf* bottle.

boutique [butik] *nf* [gén] shop ; [de mode] boutique.

bouton [butɔ̃] *nm* - **1.** COUTURE button ; **~ de manchette** cuff link - **2.** [sur la peau] spot - **3.** [de porte] knob - **4.** [commutateur] switch - **5.** [bourgeon] bud.

bouton-d'or [butɔ̃dɔr] *(pl* boutons-d'or*)* *nm* buttercup.

boutonner [3] [butɔne] *vt* to button (up).

boutonneux, euse [butɔnø, øz] *adj* spotty.

boutonnière [butɔnjɛr] *nf* [de vêtement] buttonhole.

bouton-pression [butɔ̃presjɔ̃] *(pl* boutons-pression*)* *nm* press-stud *Br*, snap fastener *Am*.

bouture [butyr] *nf* cutting.

bovin, e [bɔvɛ̃, in] *adj* bovine. ➤ **bovins** *nmpl* cattle.

bowling [buliŋ] *nm* - **1.** [jeu] bowling - **2.** [lieu] bowling alley.

box [bɔks] *(pl* boxes*)* *nm* - **1.** [d'écurie] loose box - **2.** [compartiment] cubicle ; **le ~ des accusés** the dock - **3.** [parking] lock-up garage.

boxe [bɔks] *nf* boxing.

boxer¹ [3] [bɔkse] ◇ *vi* to box. ◇ *vt fam* to thump.

boxer² [bɔksɛr] *nm* [chien] boxer.

boxeur [bɔksœr] *nm* SPORT boxer.

boyau, x [bwajo] *nm* - **1.** [chambre à air] inner tube - **2.** [corde] catgut - **3.** [galerie] narrow gallery. ➤ **boyaux** *nmpl* [intestins] guts.

boycotter [3] [bɔjkɔte] *vt* to boycott.

BP *(abr de* boîte postale*)* *nf* PO Box.

bracelet [braslɛ] *nm* - **1.** [bijou] bracelet - **2.** [de montre] strap.

bracelet-montre [braslɛmɔ̃tr] *nm* wristwatch.

braconner [3] [brakɔne] *vi* to go poaching, to poach.

braconnier [brakɔnje] *nm* poacher.

brader [3] [brade] *vt* [solder] to sell off ; [vendre à bas prix] to sell for next to nothing.

braderie [bradri] *nf* clearance sale.

braguette [bragɛt] *nf* flies *(pl)*.

braille [braj] *nm* Braille.

brailler [3] [braje] *vi* to bawl.

braire [112] [brer] *vi* [âne] to bray.

braise [brez] *nf* embers *(pl)*.

bramer [3] [brame] *vi* [cerf] to bell.

brancard [brɑ̃kar] *nm* - 1. [civière] stretcher - 2. [de charrette] shaft.

brancardier, ère [brɑ̃kardje, ɛr] *nm, f* stretcher-bearer.

branchage [brɑ̃ʃaʒ] *nm* branches *(pl)*.

branche [brɑ̃ʃ] *nf* - 1. [gén] branch - 2. [de lunettes] arm.

branché, e [brɑ̃ʃe] *adj* - 1. ÉLECTR plugged in, connected - 2. *fam* [à la mode] trendy.

branchement [brɑ̃ʃmɑ̃] *nm* [raccordement] connection, plugging in.

brancher [3] [brɑ̃ʃe] *vt* - 1. [raccorder & INFORM] to connect ; **~ qqch sur** ÉLECTR to plug sthg into - 2. *fam* [orienter] to steer ; **~ qqn sur qqch** to start sb off on sthg - 3. *fam* [plaire] to appeal to.

branchies [brɑ̃ʃi] *nfpl* [de poisson] gills.

brandir [32] [brɑ̃dir] *vt* to wave.

branlant, e [brɑ̃lɑ̃, ɑ̃t] *adj* [escalier, mur] shaky ; [meuble, dent] wobbly.

branle-bas [brɑ̃lba] *nm inv* pandemonium *(U)*.

braquage [brakaʒ] *nm* - 1. AUTOM lock - 2. [attaque] holdup.

braquer [3] [brake] <> *vt* - 1. [diriger] : **~ qqch sur** [arme] to aim sthg at ; [télescope] [regard] to fix sthg on - 2. *fam* [attaquer] to hold up. <> *vi* to turn (the wheel). ◆ **se braquer** *vp* [personne] to take a stand.

bras [bra] *nm* - 1. [gén] arm ; **~ droit** right-hand man *ou* woman ; **~ de fer** [jeu] arm wrestling ; *fig* trial of strength ; **avoir le ~ long** [avoir de l'influence] to have pull - 2. [de cours d'eau] branch ; **~ de mer** arm of the sea.

brasier [brazje] *nm* [incendie] blaze, inferno.

bras-le-corps [bralkɔr] ◆ **à bras-le-corps** *loc adv* bodily.

brassage [brasaʒ] *nm* - 1. [de bière] brewing - 2. *fig* [mélange] mixing.

brassard [brasar] *nm* armband.

brasse [bras] *nf* [nage] breaststroke ; **~ papillon** butterfly (stroke).

brassée [brase] *nf* armful.

brasser [3] [brase] *vt* - 1. [bière] to brew - 2. [mélanger] to mix - 3. *fig* [manier] to handle.

brasserie [brasri] *nf* - 1. [usine] brewery - 2. [café-restaurant] brasserie.

brasseur, euse [brasœr, øz] *nm, f* [de bière] brewer.

brassière [brasjɛr] *nf* - 1. [de bébé] (baby's) vest *Br ou* undershirt *Am* - 2. *Can* [soutien-gorge] bra.

bravade [bravad] *nf* : **par ~** out of bravado.

brave [brav] <> *adj* - 1. *(après n)* [courageux] brave - 2. *(avant n)* [honnête] decent - 3. [naïf et gentil] nice. <> *nmf* : **mon ~** my good man.

braver [3] [brave] *vt* - 1. [parents, règlement] to defy - 2. [mépriser] to brave.

bravo [bravo] *interj* bravo! ◆ **bravos** *nmpl* cheers.

bravoure [bravur] *nf* bravery.

break [brɛk] *nm* - 1. [voiture] estate (car) *Br*, station wagon *Am* - 2. [pause] break.

brebis [brəbi] *nf* ewe ; **~ galeuse** black sheep.

brèche [brɛʃ] *nf* - 1. [de mur] gap - 2. MIL breach.

bredouiller [3] [brəduje] *vi* to stammer.

bref, brève [brɛf, brɛv] *adj* - 1. [gén] short, brief ; **soyez ~ !** make it brief! - 2. LING short. ◆ **bref** *adv* in short, in a word. ◆ **brève** *nf* PRESSE brief news item.

brelan [brəlɑ̃] *nm* : **un ~** three of a kind ; **un ~ de valets** three jacks.

Brésil [brezil] *nm* : **le ~** Brazil.

Bretagne [brətaɲ] *nf* : **la ~** Brittany.

bretelle [brətɛl] *nf* - 1. [d'autoroute] access road, slip road *Br* - 2. [de pantalon] : **~s** braces *Br*, suspenders *Am* - 3. [de bustier] strap.

breuvage [brœvaʒ] *nm* [boisson] beverage.

brève ▷ bref.

brevet [brəvɛ] *nm* - 1. [certificat] certificate ; **~ de secouriste** first-aid certificate - 2. [diplôme] diploma ; **~ des collèges** *school certificate taken after four years of secondary education* - 3. [d'invention] patent.

breveter [27] [brəvte] *vt* to patent.

bréviaire [brevjɛr] *nm* breviary.

bribe [brib] *nf* [fragment] scrap, bit ; *fig* snippet ; **~s de conversation** snatches of conversation.

bric [brik] ◆ **de bric et de broc** *loc adv* any old how.

bric-à-brac [brikabrak] *nm inv* bric-a-brac.

bricolage [brikɔlaʒ] *nm* - **1.** [travaux] do-it-yourself, DIY - **2.** [réparation provisoire] patching up.

bricole [brikɔl] *nf* - **1.** [babiole] trinket - **2.** [chose insignifiante] trivial matter.

bricoler [3] [brikɔle] ◇ *vi* to do odd jobs (around the house). ◇ *vt* - **1.** [réparer] to fix, to mend - **2.** [fabriquer] to make, to knock up *Br.*

bricoleur, euse [brikɔlœr, øz] *nm, f* home handyman (*f* handywoman).

bride [brid] *nf* - **1.** [de cheval] bridle - **2.** [de chapeau] string - **3.** COUTURE bride, bar - **4.** TECHNOL flange.

bridé [bride] ▷ œil.

brider [3] [bride] *vt* [cheval] to bridle ; *fig* to rein (in).

bridge [bridʒ] *nm* bridge.

briefer [3] [brife] *vt* to brief.

briefing [brifiŋ] *nm* briefing.

brièvement [brijɛvmɑ̃] *adv* briefly.

brièveté [brijɛvte] *nf* brevity, briefness.

brigade [brigad] *nf* - **1.** [d'ouvriers, de soldats] brigade - **2.** [détachement] squad ; **~ volante** flying squad.

brigand [brigɑ̃] *nm* [bandit] bandit.

brillamment [brijamɑ̃] *adv* [gén] brilliantly ; [réussir un examen] with flying colours.

brillant, e [brijɑ̃, ɑ̃t] *adj* - **1.** [qui brille - gén] sparkling ; [- cheveux] glossy ; [- yeux] bright - **2.** [remarquable] brilliant. ◆ **brillant** *nm* [diamant] brilliant.

briller [3] [brije] *vi* to shine.

brimer [3] [brime] *vt* to victimize, to bully.

brin [brɛ̃] *nm* - **1.** [tige] twig ; **~ d'herbe** blade of grass - **2.** [fil] strand - **3.** [petite quantité] : **un ~ (de)** a bit (of) ; **faire un ~ de toilette** to have a quick wash.

brindille [brɛ̃dij] *nf* twig.

bringuebaler, brinquebaler [3] [brɛ̃gbale] *vi* [voiture] to jolt along.

brio [brijo] *nm* [talent] : **avec ~** brilliantly.

brioche [brijɔʃ] *nf* - **1.** [pâtisserie] brioche - **2.** *fam* [ventre] paunch.

brioché, e [brijɔʃe] *adj* [pain] brioche-style.

brique [brik] *nf* - **1.** [pierre] brick - **2.** [emballage] carton - **3.** *fam* [argent] *10,000 francs*.

briquer [3] [brike] *vt* to scrub.

briquet [brikɛ] *nm* (cigarette) lighter.

brisant [brizɑ̃] *nm* [écueil] reef. ◆ **brisants** *nmpl* [récif] breakers.

brise [briz] *nf* breeze.

brise-glace(s) [brizglas] *nm inv* [navire] icebreaker.

brise-lames [brizlam] *nm inv* breakwater.

briser [3] [brize] *vt* - **1.** [gén] to break - **2.** *fig* [carrière] to ruin ; [conversation] to break off ; [espérances] to shatter. ◆ **se briser** *vp* - **1.** [gén] to break - **2.** *fig* [espoir] to be dashed ; [efforts] to be thwarted.

briseur, euse [brizœr, øz] *nm, f* : **~ de grève** strike-breaker.

britannique [britanik] *adj* British. ◆ **Britannique** *nmf* British person, Briton ; **les Britanniques** the British.

broc [bro] *nm* jug.

brocante [brokɑ̃t] *nf* - **1.** [commerce] secondhand trade - **2.** [objets] secondhand goods (*pl*).

brocanteur, euse [brokɑ̃tœr, øz] *nm, f* dealer in secondhand goods.

broche [brɔʃ] *nf* - **1.** [bijou] brooch - **2.** CULIN spit ; **cuire à la ~** to spit-roast - **3.** ÉLECTR & MÉD pin.

broché, e [brɔʃe] *adj* - **1.** [tissu] brocade (*avant n*), brocaded - **2.** TYPO : **livre ~** paperback (book).

brochet [brɔʃɛ] *nm* pike.

brochette [brɔʃɛt] *nf* - **1.** [ustensile] skewer - **2.** [plat] kebab - **3.** *fam fig* [groupe] string, row.

brochure [brɔʃyr] *nf* [imprimé] brochure, booklet.

broder [3] [brɔde] *vt & vi* to embroider.

broderie [brɔdri] *nf* - **1.** [art] embroidery - **2.** [ouvrage] (piece of) embroidery.

bromure [brɔmyr] *nm* bromide.

bronche [brɔ̃ʃ] *nf* bronchus ; **j'ai des problèmes de ~s** I've got chest problems.

broncher [3] [brɔ̃ʃe] *vi* : **sans ~** without complaining, uncomplainingly.

bronchite [brɔ̃ʃit] *nf* bronchitis (*U*).

bronzage [brɔ̃zaʒ] *nm* [de peau] tan, suntan.

bronze [brɔ̃z] *nm* bronze.

bronzé, e [brɔ̃ze] *adj* tanned, suntanned.

bronzer [3] [brɔ̃ze] *vi* [peau] to tan ; [personne] to get a tan.

brosse [brɔs] *nf* brush ; **~ à cheveux** hairbrush ; **~ à dents** toothbrush ; **avoir les cheveux en ~** to have a crew cut.

brosser [3] [brɔse] *vt* - **1.** [habits, cheveux] to brush - **2.** [paysage, portrait] to paint. ◆ **se brosser** *vp* : **se ~ les cheveux/les dents** to brush one's hair/teeth.

brouette [bruɛt] *nf* wheelbarrow.

brouhaha [bruaa] *nm* hubbub.

brouillard [brujar] *nm* [léger] mist ; [dense] fog ; ~ **givrant** freezing fog ; **être dans le** ~ *fig* to be lost.

brouille [bruj] *nf* quarrel.

brouillé, e [bruje] *adj* - **1.** [fâché] : **être** ~ **avec qqn** to be on bad terms with sb ; **être** ~ **avec qqch** *fig* to be hopeless ou useless at sthg - **2.** [teint] muddy - **3.** ▷ **œuf.**

brouiller [3] [bruje] *vt* - **1.** [désunir] to set at odds, to put on bad terms - **2.** [vue] to blur - **3.** RADIO - accidentellement] to cause interference to ; [- délibérément] to jam - **4.** [rendre confus] to muddle (up). ◆ **se brouiller** *vp* - **1.** [se fâcher] to fall out ; **se** ~ **avec qqn (pour qqch)** to fall out with sb (over sthg) - **2.** [se troubler] to become blurred - **3.** MÉTÉOR to cloud over.

brouillon, onne [brujɔ̃, ɔn] *adj* careless, untidy. ◆ **brouillon** *nm* rough copy, draft.

broussaille [brusaj] *nf* : **les** ~**s** the undergrowth ; **en** ~ *fig* [cheveux] untidy ; [sourcils] bushy.

brousse [brus] *nf* GÉOGR scrubland, bush.

brouter [3] [brute] ◇ *vt* to graze on. ◇ *vi* - **1.** [animal] to graze - **2.** TECHNOL to judder.

broutille [brutij] *nf* trifle.

broyer [13] [brwaje] *vt* to grind, to crush.

bru [bry] *nf* sout daughter-in-law.

brugnon [bryɲɔ̃] *nm* nectarine.

bruine [bruin] *nf* drizzle.

bruissement [bruismɑ̃] *nm* [de feuilles, d'étoffe] rustle, rustling (U) ; [d'eau] murmur, murmuring (U).

bruit [bruji] *nm* - **1.** [son] noise, sound ; ~ **de fond** background noise - **2.** [vacarme & TECHNOL] noise ; **faire du** ~ to make a noise ; **sans** ~ silently, noiselessly - **3.** [rumeur] rumour *Br*, rumor *Am* - **4.** [retentissement] fuss ; **faire du** ~ to cause a stir.

bruitage [brɥitaʒ] *nm* sound-effects (*pl*).

brûlant, e [brylɑ̃, ɑ̃t] *adj* - **1.** [gén] burning (hot) ; [liquide] boiling (hot) ; [plat] piping hot - **2.** *fig* [amour, question] burning.

brûle-pourpoint [brylpurpwɛ̃] ◆ **à brûle-pourpoint** *loc adv* point-blank, straight out.

brûler [3] [bryle] ◇ *vt* - **1.** [gén] to burn ; [suj : eau bouillante] to scald ; **la fumée me brûle les yeux** the smoke is making my eyes sting - **2.** [feu rouge] to drive through ; [étape] to miss out, to skip. ◇ *vi* - **1.** [gén] to burn ; [maison, forêt] to be on fire - **2.** [être brûlant] to be burning (hot) ; **se** ~ *fig* to be consumed with ; ~ **de faire qqch** to be longing ou dying to do sthg ; ~ **de fièvre**

to be running a high temperature. ◆ **se brûler** *vp* to burn o.s.

brûlure [brylyr] *nf* - **1.** [lésion] burn ; ~ **au premier/troisième degré** first-degree/third-degree burn - **2.** [sensation] burning (sensation) ; **avoir des** ~**s d'estomac** to have heartburn.

brume [brym] *nf* mist.

brumeux, euse [brymø, øz] *adj* misty ; *fig* hazy.

brun, e [brœ̃, bryn] ◇ *adj* brown ; [cheveux] dark. ◇ *nm, f* dark-haired man (*f* woman). ◆ **brun** *nm* [couleur] brown. ◆ **brune** *nf* - **1.** [cigarette] *cigarette made of dark tobacco* - **2.** [bière] brown ale.

brunir [32] [brynir] *vi* [personne] to get a tan ; [peau] to tan.

Brushing® [brœʃiŋ] *nm* : **faire un** ~ **à qqn** to give sb a blow-dry, to blow-dry sb's hair.

brusque [brysk] *adj* abrupt.

brusquement [bryskəmɑ̃] *adv* abruptly.

brusquer [3] [bryske] *vt* to rush ; [élève] to push.

brusquerie [bryskəri] *nf* abruptness.

brut, e [bryt] *adj* - **1.** [pierre précieuse, bois] rough ; [sucre] unrefined ; [métal, soie] raw ; [champagne] extra dry ; **(pétrole)** ~ crude (oil) - **2.** *fig* [fait, idées] crude, raw - **3.** ÉCON gross. ◆ **brute** *nf* brute.

brutal, e, aux [brytal, o] *adj* - **1.** [violent] violent, brutal - **2.** [soudain] sudden - **3.** [manière] blunt.

brutaliser [3] [brytalize] *vt* to mistreat.

brutalité [brytalite] *nf* - **1.** [violence] violence, brutality - **2.** [caractère soudain] suddenness.

Bruxelles [bry(k)sɛl] *n* Brussels.

bruyamment [brɥijamɑ̃] *adv* noisily.

bruyant, e [brɥijɑ̃, ɑ̃t] *adj* noisy.

bruyère [bryjɛr] *nf* [plante] heather.

BT *nm* (*abr de* **brevet de technicien**) *vocational training certificate (taken at age 18)*.

BTP (*abr de* **bâtiment et travaux publics**) *nmpl building and public works sector*.

BTS (*abr de* **brevet de technicien supérieur**) *nm advanced vocational training certificate (taken at the end of a 2-year higher education course)*.

bu, e [by] *pp* ▷ **boire.**

buanderie [bɥɑ̃dri] *nf* laundry.

buccal, e, aux [bykal, o] *adj* buccal.

bûche [byʃ] *nf* [bois] log ; ~ **de Noël** Yule log ; **prendre** ou **ramasser une** ~ *fam* to fall flat on one's face.

bûcher¹ [byʃe] *nm* - **1.** [supplice] : **le** ~ the stake - **2.** [funéraire] pyre.

bûcher² [3] [byʃe] ◇ *vi* to swot. ◇ *vt* to swot up.

bûcheron, onne [byʃrɔ̃, ɔn] *nm, f* forestry worker.

bûcheur, euse [byʃœr, øz] ◇ *adj* hardworking. ◇ *nm, f* *fam* swot *Br*, grind *Am*.

bucolique [bykɔlik] *adj* pastoral.

budget [bydʒɛ] *nm* budget.

budgétaire [bydʒetɛr] *adj* budgetary ; année ~ financial *Br* ou fiscal *Am* year.

buée [bɥe] *nf* [sur vitre] condensation.

buffet [byfɛ] *nm* - **1.** [meuble] sideboard - **2.** [repas] buffet - **3.** [café-restaurant] : ~ de gare station buffet.

buffle [byfl] *nm* [animal] buffalo.

bug [bʌg] *nm* = bogue.

buis [bɥi] *nm* box(wood).

buisson [bɥisɔ̃] *nm* bush.

buissonnière [bɥisɔnjɛr] ▷ ~ école.

bulbe [bylb] *nm* bulb.

bulgare [bylgar] *adj* Bulgarian. ◆ **bulgare** *nm* [langue] Bulgarian. ◆ **Bulgare** *nmf* Bulgarian.

Bulgarie [bylgari] *nf* : la ~ Bulgaria.

bulldozer [byldozɛr] *nm* bulldozer.

bulle [byl] *nf* - **1.** [gén] bubble ; ~ de savon soap bubble - **2.** [de bande dessinée] speech balloon.

bulletin [byltɛ̃] *nm* - **1.** [communiqué] bulletin ; ~ de la météo weather forecast ; ~ de santé medical bulletin - **2.** [imprimé] form ; ~ de vote ballot paper - **3.** SCOL. report - **4.** [certificat] certificate ; ~ de salaire ou de paye pay slip.

bulletin-réponse [byltɛ̃repɔ̃s] (*pl* bulletins-réponse) *nm* reply form.

buraliste [byralist] *nmf* [d'un bureau de tabac] tobacconist.

bureau, x [byro] *nm* - **1.** [gén] office ; ~ d'aide sociale social security office ; ~ de change bureau de change ; ~ d'études design office ; ~ de poste post office ; ~ de tabac tobacconist's ; ~ de vote polling station - **2.** [meuble] desk.

bureaucrate [byrokrat] *nmf* bureaucrat.

bureaucratie [byrokrasi] *nf* bureaucracy.

bureautique [byrotik] *nf* office automation.

burette [byrɛt] *nf* [de mécanicien] oilcan.

burin [byrɛ̃] *nm* [outil] chisel.

buriné, e [byrine] *adj* engraved ; [visage, traits] lined.

burlesque [byrlɛsk] *adj* - **1.** [comique] funny - **2.** [ridicule] ludicrous, absurd - **3.** THÉÂTRE burlesque.

bus [bys] *nm* bus.

busqué [byske] ▷ nez.

buste [byst] *nm* [torse] chest ; [poitrine de femme, sculpture] bust.

bustier [bystje] *nm* [corsage] strapless top ; [soutien-gorge] longline bra.

but [byt] *nm* - **1.** [point visé] target - **2.** [objectif] goal, aim, purpose ; errer sans ~ to wander aimlessly ; il touche au ~ he's nearly there ; à ~ non lucratif JUR non-profit-making *Br*, non-profit *Am* ; aller droit au ~ to go straight to the point ; dans le ~ de faire qqch with the aim ou intention of doing sthg - **3.** SPORT goal ; marquer un ~ to score a goal - **4.** *loc* : de ~ en blanc point-blank, straight out.

butane [bytan] *nm* : (gaz) ~ butane ; [domestique] Calor gas® *Br*, butane.

buté, e [byte] *adj* stubborn.

buter [3] [byte] ◇ *vi* [se heurter] : ~ sur/contre qqch to stumble on/over sthg, to trip on/over sthg. ◇ *vt* *tfam* [tuer] to do in, to bump off. ◆ **se buter** *vp* to dig one's heels in ; se ~ contre *fig* to refuse to listen to.

butin [bytɛ̃] *nm* [de guerre] booty ; [de vol] loot ; [de recherche] finds (*pl*).

butiner [3] [bytine] *vi* to collect nectar.

butte [byt] *nf* [colline] mound, rise ; être en ~ à *fig* to be exposed to.

buvard [byvar] *nm* [papier] blotting-paper ; [sous-main] blotter.

buvette [byvɛt] *nf* [café] refreshment room, buffet.

buveur, euse [byvœr, øz] *nm, f* drinker.

c¹, C [se] *nm inv* c, C. ◆ **C** (*abr de* celsius, centigrade) C.

c² *abr de* centime.

c' ▷ ce.

CA *nm abr de* chiffre d'affaires.

ça [sa] *pron dém* - **1.** [désignant un objet - éloigné] that ; [- proche] this - **2.** [sujet indéterminé] it, that ; comment ~ va? how are you?, how are things? ; ~ ira comme ~ that will be fine ; ~ y est that's it ; c'est ~ that's right - **3.** [renforcement expressif] : où ~? where? ; qui ~? who?

çà [sa] *adv* : ~ et là here and there.

caban [kabã] *nm* reefer (jacket).

cabane [kaban] *nf* [abri] cabin, hut ; [remise] shed ; ~ **à lapins** hutch.

cabanon [kabanõ] *nm* - **1.** [à la campagne] cottage - **2.** [sur la plage] chalet - **3.** [cellule] padded cell - **4.** [de rangement] shed.

cabaret [kabaʀɛ] *nm* cabaret.

cabas [kaba] *nm* shopping-bag.

cabillaud [kabijo] *nm* (fresh) cod.

cabine [kabin] *nf* - **1.** [de navire, d'avion, de véhicule] cabin - **2.** [compartiment, petit local] cubicle ; ~ **d'essayage** fitting room ; ~ **téléphonique** phone box.

cabinet [kabinɛ] *nm* - **1.** [pièce] : ~ **de toilette** ≃ bathroom - **2.** [local professionnel] office ; ~ **dentaire/médical** dentist's/doctor's surgery *Br*, dentist's/doctor's office *Am* - **3.** [de ministre] advisers *(pl)*. ◆ **cabinets** *nmpl* toilet *(sg)*.

câble [kabl] *nm* cable ; **télévision par** ~ cable television.

câblé, e [kable] *adj* TÉLÉ equipped with cable TV.

cabosser [3] [kabɔse] *vt* to dent.

cabotage [kabɔtaʒ] *nm* coastal navigation.

caboteur [kabɔtœʀ] *nm* [navire] coaster.

cabrer [3] [kabʀe] ◆ **se cabrer** *vp* - **1.** [cheval] to rear (up) ; [avion] to climb steeply - **2.** *fig* [personne] to take offence *Br* ou offense *Am*.

cabri [kabʀi] *nm* kid.

cabriole [kabʀijɔl] *nf* [bond] caper ; [pirouette] somersault.

cabriolet [kabʀijɔlɛ] *nm* convertible.

CAC, Cac [kak] *(abr de* **Compagnie des agents de change)** *nf* : **l'indice ~~40** *the French stock exchange shares index.*

caca [kaka] *nm fam* pooh ; **faire** ~ to do a pooh ; ~ **d'oie** greeny-yellow.

cacahouète, cacahuète [kakawɛt] *nf* peanut.

cacao [kakao] *nm* - **1.** [poudre] cocoa (powder) - **2.** [boisson] cocoa.

cachalot [kaʃalo] *nm* sperm whale.

cache [kaʃ] ◇ *nf* [cachette] hiding place. ◇ *nm* [masque] card *(for masking text etc)*.

cache-cache [kaʃkaʃ] *nm inv* : **jouer à** ~ to play hide and seek.

cachemire [kaʃmiʀ] *nm* - **1.** [laine] cashmere - **2.** [dessin] paisley.

cache-nez [kaʃne] *nm inv* scarf.

cache-pot [kaʃpo] *nm inv* flowerpot-holder.

cacher [3] [kaʃe] *vt* - **1.** [gén] to hide ; **je ne vous cache pas que ...** to be honest, ...

- **2.** [vue] to mask. ◆ **se cacher** *vp* : **se** ~ **(de qqn)** to hide (from sb).

cachet [kaʃɛ] *nm* - **1.** [comprimé] tablet, pill - **2.** [marque] postmark - **3.** [style] style, character ; **avoir du** ~ to have character - **4.** [rétribution] fee.

cacheter [27] [kaʃte] *vt* to seal.

cachette [kaʃɛt] *nf* hiding place ; **en** ~ secretly.

cachot [kaʃo] *nm* [cellule] cell.

cachotterie [kaʃɔtʀi] *nf* little secret ; **faire des ~s (à qqn)** to hide things (from sb).

cachottier, ère [kaʃɔtje, ɛʀ] *nm, f* secretive person.

cactus [kaktys] *nm* cactus.

c.-à-d. *(abr de* **c'est-à-dire)** i.e.

cadastre [kadastʀ] *nm* [registre] ≃ land register ; [service] ≃ land registry, ≃ land office *Am*.

cadavérique [kadaveʀik] *adj* deathly.

cadavre [kadavʀ] *nm* corpse, (dead) body.

Caddie® [kadi] *nm* [chariot] trolley.

cadeau, x [kado] ◇ *nm* present, gift ; **faire** ~ **de qqch à qqn** to give sthg to sb (as a present). ◇ *adj inv* : **idée** ~ gift idea.

cadenas [kadna] *nm* padlock.

cadenasser [3] [kadnase] *vt* to padlock.

cadence [kadãs] *nf* - **1.** [rythme musical] rhythm ; **en** ~ in time - **2.** [de travail] rate.

cadencé, e [kadãse] *adj* rhythmical.

cadet, ette [kadɛ, ɛt] *nm, f* - **1.** [de deux enfants] younger ; [de plusieurs enfants] youngest ; **il est mon** ~ **de deux ans** he's two years younger than me - **2.** SPORT junior.

cadran [kadʀã] *nm* dial ; ~ **solaire** sundial.

cadre [kadʀ] *nm* - **1.** [de tableau, de porte] frame - **2.** [contexte] context - **3.** [décor, milieu] surroundings *(pl)* - **4.** [responsable] : ~ **moyen/supérieur** middle/senior manager - **5.** [sur formulaire] box.

cadrer [3] [kadʀe] ◇ *vi* to agree, to tally. ◇ *vt* CIN, PHOT & TÉLÉ to frame.

caduc, caduque [kadyk] *adj* - **1.** [feuille] deciduous - **2.** [qui n'est plus valide] obsolete.

cafard [kafaʀ] *nm* - **1.** [insecte] cockroach - **2.** *fig* [mélancolie] : **avoir le** ~ to feel low ou down.

café [kafe] *nm* - **1.** [plante, boisson] coffee ; ~ **crème** *coffee with frothy milk* ; ~ **en grains** coffee beans ; ~ **au lait** white coffee *(with hot milk)* ; ~ **moulu** ground coffee ; ~ **noir** black coffee ; ~ **en poudre** ou **soluble** instant coffee - **2.** [lieu] bar, café.

caféine [kafein] *nf* caffeine.

cafétéria [kafeterja] *nf* cafeteria.

café-théâtre [kafeteatr] *nm* ≃ cabaret.

cafetière [kaftjɛr] *nf* - **1.** [récipient] coffee-pot - **2.** [électrique] coffee-maker ; [italienne] percolator.

cafouiller [3] [kafuje] *vi fam* - **1.** [s'embrouiller] to get into a mess - **2.** [moteur] to misfire ; TÉLÉ to be on the blink.

cage [kaʒ] *nf* - **1.** [pour animaux] cage - **2.** [dans une maison] : **~ d'escalier** stairwell - **3.** ANAT : **~ thoracique** rib cage.

cageot [kaʒo] *nm* [caisse] crate.

cagibi [kaʒibi] *nm* boxroom *Br*, storage room *Am*.

cagneux, euse [kaɲø, øz] *adj* : **avoir les genoux ~** to be knock-kneed.

cagnotte [kaɲɔt] *nf* - **1.** [caisse commune] kitty - **2.** [économies] savings *(pl)*.

cagoule [kagul] *nf* - **1.** [passe-montagne] balaclava - **2.** [de voleur, de pénitent] hood.

cahier [kaje] *nm* - **1.** [de notes] exercise book, notebook ; **~ de brouillon** rough book ; **~ de textes** homework book - **2.** COMM : **~ des charges** specification.

cahin-caha [kaɛ̃kaa] *adv* : **aller ~** to be jogging along.

cahot [kao] *nm* bump, jolt.

cahoter [3] [kaote] *vi* to jolt around.

cahute [kayt] *nf* shack.

caille [kaj] *nf* quail.

caillé, e [kaje] *adj* [lait] curdled ; [sang] clotted.

caillot [kajo] *nm* clot.

caillou, x [kaju] *nm* - **1.** [pierre] stone, pebble - **2.** *fam* [crâne] head.

caillouteux, euse [kajutø, øz] *adj* stony.

caïman [kaimɑ̃] *nm* cayman.

Caire [kɛr] *n* : **Le ~** Cairo.

caisse [kɛs] *nf* - **1.** [boîte] crate, box ; **~ à outils** toolbox - **2.** TECHNOL case - **3.** [guichet] cash desk, till ; [de supermarché] checkout, till ; **~ enregistreuse** cash register - **4.** [recette] takings *(pl)* - **5.** [organisme] : **~ d'allocation** ≃ social security office ; **~ d'épargne** [fonds] savings fund ; [établissement] savings bank ; **~ de retraite** pension fund.

caissier, ère [kesje, ɛr] *nm, f* cashier.

caisson [kesɔ̃] *nm* - **1.** MIL & TECHNOL caisson - **2.** ARCHIT coffer.

cajoler [3] [kaʒɔle] *vt* to make a fuss of, to cuddle.

cajou [kaʒu] ▷ **noix**.

cake [kɛk] *nm* fruit-cake.

cal¹ [kal] *nm* callus.

cal² (*abr de* **calorie**) cal.

calamar [kalamar], **calmar** [kalmar] *nm* squid.

calamité [kalamite] *nf* disaster.

calandre [kalɑ̃dr] *nf* - **1.** [de voiture] radiator grille - **2.** [machine] calender.

calanque [kalɑ̃k] *nf* rocky inlet.

calcaire [kalkɛr] ◇ *adj* [eau] hard ; [sol] chalky ; [roche] limestone *(avant n)*. ◇ *nm* limestone.

calciner [3] [kalsine] *vt* to burn to a cinder.

calcium [kalsjɔm] *nm* calcium.

calcul [kalkyl] *nm* - **1.** [opération] : **le ~** arithmetic ; **~ mental** mental arithmetic - **2.** [compte] calculation - **3.** *fig* [plan] plan - **4.** MÉD : **~ (rénal)** kidney stone.

calculateur, trice [kalkylatœr, tris] *adj péj* calculating. ◆ **calculateur** *nm* computer. ◆ **calculatrice** *nf* calculator.

calculer [3] [kalkyle] ◇ *vt* - **1.** [déterminer] to calculate, to work out - **2.** [prévoir] to plan ; **mal/bien ~ qqch** to judge sthg badly/well. ◇ *vi péj* [dépenser avec parcimonie] to count the pennies.

calculette [kalkylɛt] *nf* pocket calculator.

cale [kal] *nf* - **1.** [de navire] hold ; **~ sèche** dry dock - **2.** [pour immobiliser] wedge.

calé, e [kale] *adj fam* [personne] clever, brainy ; **être ~ en** to be good at.

calèche [kalɛʃ] *nf* (horse-drawn) carriage.

caleçon [kalsɔ̃] *nm* - **1.** [sous-vêtement masculin] boxer shorts *(pl)*, pair of boxer shorts - **2.** [vêtement féminin] leggings *(pl)*, pair of leggings.

calembour [kalɑ̃bur] *nm* pun, play on words.

calendrier [kalɑ̃drije] *nm* - **1.** [système, agenda, d'un festival] calendar - **2.** [emploi du temps] timetable - **3.** [d'un voyage] schedule.

cale-pied [kalpje] *(pl* cale-pieds*)* *nm* toe-clip.

calepin [kalpɛ̃] *nm* notebook.

caler [3] [kale] ◇ *vt* - **1.** [avec cale] to wedge - **2.** [stabiliser, appuyer] to prop up - **3.** *fam* [remplir] : **ça cale (l'estomac)** it's filling. ◇ *vi* - **1.** [moteur, véhicule] to stall - **2.** *fam* [personne] to give up.

calfeutrer [3] [kalføtre] *vt* to draughtproof. ◆ **se calfeutrer** *vp* to shut o.s. up ou away.

calibre [kalibr] *nm* - **1.** [de tuyau] diameter, bore ; [de fusil] calibre ; [de fruit, d'œuf] size - **2.** *fam fig* [envergure] calibre.

calibrer [3] [kalibre] *vt* - **1.** [machine, fusil] to calibrate - **2.** [fruit, œuf] to grade.

Californie [kalifɔrni] *nf* : **la ~** California.

califourchon [kalifurʃɔ̃] ◆ **à califourchon** *loc adv* astride ; **être (assis) à ~ sur** qqch to sit astride sthg.

câlin, e [kalɛ̃, in] *adj* affectionate. ◆ **câlin** *nm* cuddle.

câliner [3] [kaline] *vt* to cuddle.

calleux, euse [kalø, øz] *adj* calloused.

call-girl [kɔlgœrl] *(pl* **call-girls)** *nf* call girl.

calligraphie [kaligrafi] *nf* calligraphy.

calmant, e [kalmã, ãt] *adj* soothing. ◆ **calmant** *nm* [pour la douleur] painkiller ; [pour l'anxiété] tranquillizer, sedative.

calmar ⊳ calamar.

calme [kalm] ◇ *adj* quiet, calm. ◇ *nm* - **1.** [gén] calm, calmness - **2.** [absence de bruit] peace (and quiet).

calmer [3] [kalme] *vt* - **1.** [apaiser] to calm (down) - **2.** [réduire - douleur] to soothe ; [- inquiétude] to allay. ◆ **se calmer** *vp* - **1.** [s'apaiser - personne, discussion] to calm down ; [- tempête] to abate ; [- mer] to become calm - **2.** [diminuer - douleur] to ease ; [- fièvre, inquiétude, désir] to subside.

calomnie [kalɔmni] *nf* [écrits] libel ; [paroles] slander.

calorie [kalɔri] *nf* calorie.

calorique [kalɔrik] *adj* calorific.

calot [kalo] *nm* [bille] (large) marble.

calotte [kalɔt] *nf* - **1.** [bonnet] skullcap - **2.** GÉOGR : **~ glaciaire** ice cap.

calque [kalk] *nm* - **1.** [dessin] tracing - **2.** [papier] : **(papier) ~** tracing paper - **3.** *fig* [imitation] (exact) copy.

calquer [3] [kalke] *vt* - **1.** [carte] to trace - **2.** [imiter] to copy exactly ; **~ qqch sur** qqch to model sthg on sthg.

calvaire [kalvɛr] *nm* - **1.** [croix] wayside cross - **2.** *fig* [épreuve] ordeal.

calvitie [kalvisi] *nf* baldness.

camaïeu [kamajø] *nm* monochrome.

camarade [kamarad] *nmf* - **1.** [compagnon, ami] friend ; **~ de classe** classmate ; **~ d'école** schoolfriend - **2.** POLIT comrade.

camaraderie [kamaradri] *nf* - **1.** [familiarité, entente] friendship - **2.** [solidarité] comradeship, camaraderie.

Cambodge [kɑ̃bɔdʒ] *nm* : **le ~** Cambodia.

cambouis [kɑ̃bwi] *nm* dirty grease.

cambré, e [kɑ̃bre] *adj* arched.

cambriolage [kɑ̃brijɔlaʒ] *nm* burglary.

cambrioler [3] [kɑ̃brijɔle] *vt* to burgle *Br*, to burglarize *Am*.

cambrioleur, euse [kɑ̃brijɔlœr, øz] *nm, f* burglar.

camée [kame] *nm* cameo.

caméléon [kameleɔ̃] *nm litt & fig* chameleon.

camélia [kamelja] *nm* camellia.

camelote [kamlɔt] *nf* [marchandise de mauvaise qualité] junk, rubbish *Br*.

caméra [kamera] *nf* - **1.** CIN & TÉLÉ camera - **2.** [d'amateur] cinecamera.

cameraman [kameraman] *(pl* **cameramen** [kameramɛn], **cameramans)** *nm* cameraman.

Cameroun [kamrun] *nm* : **le ~** Cameroon.

Caméscope® [kameskɔp] *nm* camcorder.

camion [kamjɔ̃] *nm* lorry *Br*, truck *Am* ; **~ de déménagement** removal van *Br*, moving van *Am*.

camion-citerne [kamjɔ̃sitɛrn] *nm* tanker *Br*, tanker truck *Am*.

camionnage [kamjɔnaʒ] *nm* road haulage *Br*, trucking *Am*.

camionnette [kamjɔnɛt] *nf* van.

camionneur [kamjɔnœr] *nm* - **1.** [conducteur] lorry-driver *Br*, truck-driver *Am* - **2.** [entrepreneur] road haulier *Br*, trucker *Am*.

camisole [kamizɔl] ◆ **camisole de force** *nf* straitjacket.

camouflage [kamuflaʒ] *nm* [déguisement] camouflage ; *fig* [dissimulation] concealment.

camoufler [3] [kamufle] *vt* [déguiser] to camouflage ; *fig* [dissimuler] to conceal, to cover up.

camp [kɑ̃] *nm* - **1.** [gén] camp ; **~ de concentration** concentration camp - **2.** SPORT half (of the field) - **3.** [parti] side.

campagnard, e [kɑ̃paɲar, ard] *adj* - **1.** [de la campagne] country *(avant n)* - **2.** [rustique] rustic.

campagne [kɑ̃paɲ] *nf* - **1.** [régions rurales] country ; **à la ~** in the country - **2.** MIL, POLIT & PUBLICITÉ campaign ; **faire ~ pour/ contre** to campaign for/against ; **~ d'affichage** poster campaign ; **~ électorale** election campaign ; **~ de presse** press campaign ; **~ publicitaire** advertising campaign ; **~ de vente** sales campaign.

campement [kɑ̃pmã] *nm* camp, encampment.

camper [3] [kɑ̃pe] ◇ *vi* to camp. ◇ *vt* - **1.** [poser solidement] to place firmly - **2.** *fig* [esquisser] to portray.

campeur, euse [kɑ̃pœr, øz] *nm, f* camper.

camphre [kɑ̃fr] *nm* camphor.

camping [kɑ̃piŋ] *nm* - **1.** [activité] camping ; **faire du ~** to go camping - **2.** [terrain] campsite.

Canada [kanada] *nm* : le ~ Canada.

canadien, enne [kanadjɛ̃, ɛn] *adj* Canadian. ➤ **canadienne** *nf* [veste] sheepskin jacket. ➤ **Canadien, enne** *nm, f* Canadian.

canaille [kanaj] <> *adj* - **1.** [coquin] roguish - **2.** [vulgaire] crude. <> *nf* - **1.** [scélérat] scoundrel - **2.** *hum* [coquin] little devil.

canal, aux [kanal, o] *nm* - **1.** [gén] channel ; par le ~ de qqn *fig* [par l'entremise de] through sb - **2.** [voie d'eau] canal - **3.** ANAT canal, duct. ➤ **Canal** *nm* : Canal+ *French TV pay channel.*

canalisation [kanalizasjɔ̃] *nf* [conduit] pipe.

canaliser [3] [kanalize] *vt* - **1.** [cours d'eau] to canalize - **2.** *fig* [orienter] to channel.

canapé [kanape] *nm* [siège] sofa.

canapé-lit [kanapeli] *nm* sofa bed.

canaque, kanak [kanak] *adj* Kanak. ➤ **Canaque** *nmf* Kanak.

canard [kanar] *nm* - **1.** [oiseau] duck - **2.** [fausse note] wrong note - **3.** *fam* [journal] rag.

canari [kanari] *nm* canary.

cancan [kɑ̃kɑ̃] *nm* - **1.** [ragot] piece of gossip - **2.** [danse] cancan.

cancer [kɑ̃sɛr] *nm* MÉD cancer. ➤ **Cancer** *nm* ASTROL Cancer.

cancéreux, euse [kɑ̃serø, øz] <> *adj* - **1.** [personne] suffering from cancer - **2.** [tumeur] cancerous. <> *nm, f* [personne] cancer sufferer.

cancérigène [kɑ̃seriʒɛn] *adj* carcinogenic.

cancre [kɑ̃kr] *nm fam* dunce.

cancrelat [kɑ̃krəla] *nm* cockroach.

candélabre [kɑ̃delabr] *nm* candelabra.

candeur [kɑ̃dœr] *nf* ingenuousness.

candi [kɑ̃di] *adj* : sucre ~ (sugar) candy.

candidat, e [kɑ̃dida, at] *nm, f* : ~ (à) candidate (for).

candidature [kɑ̃didatyr] *nf* - **1.** [à un poste] application ; poser sa ~ pour qqch to apply for sthg - **2.** [à une élection] candidature.

candide [kɑ̃did] *adj* ingenuous.

cane [kan] *nf* (female) duck.

caneton [kantɔ̃] *nm* (male) duckling.

canette [kanɛt] *nf* - **1.** [de fil] spool - **2.** [petite cane] (female) duckling - **3.** [de boisson - bouteille] bottle ; [- boîte] can.

canevas [kanva] *nm* COUTURE canvas.

caniche [kaniʃ] *nm* poodle.

canicule [kanikyl] *nf* heatwave.

canif [kanif] *nm* penknife.

canin, e [kanɛ̃, in] *adj* canine ; exposition ~e dog show. ➤ **canine** *nf* canine (tooth).

caniveau, x [kanivo] *nm* gutter.

canne [kan] *nf* - **1.** [bâton] walking stick ; ~ à pêche fishing rod - **2.** *fam* [jambe] pin. ➤ **canne à sucre** *nf* sugar cane.

cannelle [kanɛl] *nf* [aromate] cinnamon.

cannelure [kanlyr] *nf* [de colonne] flute.

cannibale [kanibal] *nmf & adj* cannibal.

canoë [kanɔe] *nm* canoe.

canoë-kayak [kanɔekajak] *nm* kayak.

canon [kanɔ̃] *nm* - **1.** [arme] gun - **2.** [tube d'arme] barrel - **3.** MUS : chanter en ~ to sing in canon - **4.** [norme & RELIG] canon.

canoniser [3] [kanɔnize] *vt* to canonize.

canot [kano] *nm* dinghy ; ~ pneumatique inflatable dinghy ; ~ de sauvetage lifeboat.

cantatrice [kɑ̃tatris] *nf* prima donna.

cantine [kɑ̃tin] *nf* - **1.** [réfectoire] canteen - **2.** [malle] trunk.

cantique [kɑ̃tik] *nm* hymn.

canton [kɑ̃tɔ̃] *nm* - **1.** [en France] ≈ district - **2.** [en Suisse] canton.

cantonade [kɑ̃tɔnad] ➤ **à la cantonade** *loc adv* : parler à la ~ to speak to everyone (in general).

cantonais, e [kɑ̃tɔnɛ, ɛz] *adj* Cantonese ; riz ~ egg fried rice. ➤ **cantonais** *nm* [langue] Cantonese.

cantonner [3] [kɑ̃tɔne] *vt* - **1.** MIL to quarter, to billet *Br* - **2.** [maintenir] to confine ; ~ qqn à OU dans to confine sb to.

cantonnier [kɑ̃tɔnje] *nm* roadman.

canular [kanylar] *nm fam* hoax.

canyon, cañon [kanjon, kanjɔ̃] *nm* canyon.

canyoning [kanɔniŋ] *nm* canyoning.

caoutchouc [kautʃu] *nm* - **1.** [substance] rubber - **2.** [plante] rubber plant.

caoutchouteux, euse [kautʃutø, øz] *adj* rubbery.

cap [kap] *nm* - **1.** GÉOGR cape ; le ~ de Bonne-Espérance the Cape of Good Hope ; le ~ Horn Cape Horn ; passer le ~ de qqch *fig* to get through sthg ; passer le ~ de la quarantaine *fig* to turn forty - **2.** [direction] course ; changer de ~ to change course ; mettre le ~ sur to head for. ➤ **Cap** *nm* : Le Cap Cape Town.

CAP (*abr de* certificat d'aptitude professionnelle) *nm vocational training certificate* (*taken at secondary school*).

capable [kapabl] *adj* - **1.** [apte] : ~ (de qqch/de faire qqch) capable (of sthg/of doing sthg) - **2.** [à même] **: ~ de faire qqch** likely to do sthg.

capacité [kapasite] *nf* - **1.** [de récipient] capacity - **2.** [de personne] ability - **3.** UNIV **: ~ en droit** [diplôme] *qualifying certificate in law gained by examination after 2 years' study.*

cape [kap] *nf* [vêtement] cloak **; rire sous ~** *fig* to laugh up one's sleeve.

CAPES, Capes [kapɛs] (*abr de* **certificat d'aptitude au professorat de l'enseignement du second degré**) *nm secondary school teaching certificate.*

capharnaüm [kafarnaɔm] *nm* mess.

capillaire [kapilɛr] <> *adj* - **1.** [lotion] hair (*avant n*) - **2.** ANAT & BOT capillary. <> *nm* - **1.** BOT maidenhair fern - **2.** ANAT capillary.

capillarité [kapilarite] *nf* PHYS capillarity.

capitaine [kapitɛn] *nm* captain.

capitainerie [kapitɛnri] *nf* harbour Br ou harbor Am master's office.

capital, e, aux [kapital, o] *adj* - **1.** [décision, événement] major - **2.** JUR capital. ➤ **capital** *nm* FIN capital **; ~ santé** *fig* reserves (*pl*) of health **; ~ social** authorized ou share capital. ➤ **capitale** *nf* [ville, lettre] capital. ➤ **capitaux** *nmpl* capital (*U*).

capitaliser [3] [kapitalize] <> *vt* FIN to capitalize **;** *fig* to accumulate. <> *vi* to save.

capitalisme [kapitalism] *nm* capitalism.

capitaliste [kapitalist] *nmf* & *adj* capitalist.

capiteux, euse [kapitø, øz] *adj* [vin] intoxicating **;** [parfum] heady.

capitonné, e [kapitɔne] *adj* padded.

capituler [3] [kapityle] *vi* to surrender **; ~ devant qqn/qqch** to surrender to sb/sthg.

caporal, aux [kapɔral, o] *nm* - **1.** MIL lance corporal - **2.** [tabac] caporal.

capot [kapo] *nm* - **1.** [de voiture] bonnet Br, hood Am - **2.** [de machine] (protective) cover.

capote [kapɔt] *nf* - **1.** [de voiture] hood Br, top Am - **2.** fam [préservatif] **: ~ (anglaise)** condom.

câpre [kapr] *nf* caper.

caprice [kapris] *nm* whim.

capricieux, euse [kaprisjø, øz] <> *adj* [changeant] capricious **;** [coléreux] temperamental. <> *nm, f* temperamental person.

capricorne [kaprikɔrn] *nm* ZOOL capricorn beetle. ➤ **Capricorne** *nm* ASTROL Capricorn.

capsule [kapsyl] *nf* - **1.** [de bouteille] cap - **2.** ASTRON, BOT & MÉD capsule.

capter [3] [kapte] *vt* - **1.** [recevoir sur émetteur] to pick up - **2.** [source, rivière] to har-

ness - **3.** *fig* [attention, confiance] to gain, to win.

captif, ive [kaptif, iv] <> *adj* captive. <> *nm, f* prisoner.

captivant, e [kaptivɑ̃, ɑ̃t] *adj* [livre, film] enthralling **;** [personne] captivating.

captiver [3] [kaptive] *vt* to captivate.

captivité [kaptivite] *nf* captivity.

capture [kaptyr] *nf* - **1.** [action] capture - **2.** [prise] catch.

capturer [3] [kaptyre] *vt* to catch, to capture.

capuche [kapyʃ] *nf* (detachable) hood.

capuchon [kapyʃɔ̃] *nm* - **1.** [bonnet - d'imperméable] hood - **2.** [bouchon] cap, top.

capucine [kapysin] *nf* [fleur] nasturtium.

caquet [kakɛ] *nm péj* [bavardage] **: rabattre le ~ à** ou **de qqn** to shut sb up.

caqueter [27] [kakte] *vi* - **1.** [poule] to cackle - **2.** *péj* [personne] to chatter.

car¹ [kar] *nm* coach Br, bus Am.

car² [kar] *conj* because, for.

carabine [karabin] *nf* rifle.

caractère [karaktɛr] *nm* [gén] character **; avoir du ~** to have character **; avoir mauvais ~** to be bad-tempered **; en petits/gros ~s** in small/large print **; ~s d'imprimerie** block capitals.

caractériel, elle [karakterjɛl] *adj* [troubles] emotional **;** [personne] emotionally disturbed.

caractérisé, e [karakterize] *adj* [net] clear.

caractériser [3] [karakterize] *vt* to be characteristic of. ➤ **se caractériser** *vp* **: se ~ par qqch** to be characterized by sthg.

caractéristique [karakteristik] <> *nf* characteristic, feature. <> *adj* **: ~ (de)** characteristic (of).

carafe [karaf] *nf* [pour vin; eau] carafe **;** [pour alcool] decanter.

caraïbe [karaib] *adj* Caribbean. ➤ **Caraïbes** [karaib] *nfpl* **: les ~s** the Caribbean.

carambolage [karɑ̃bɔlaʒ] *nm* pile-up.

caramel [karamɛl] *nm* - **1.** CULIN caramel - **2.** [bonbon - dur] toffee, caramel **;** [- mou] fudge.

carapace [karapas] *nf* shell **;** *fig* protection, shield.

carapater [3] [karapate] ➤ **se carapater** *vp fam* to scarper, to hop it.

carat [kara] *nm* carat **; or à 9 ~s** 9-carat gold.

caravane [karavan] *nf* [de camping, de désert] caravan.

caravaning [karavaniŋ] *nm* caravanning.

carbone [karbɔn] *nm* carbon ; **(papier)** ~ carbon paper.

carbonique [karbɔnik] *adj* : **gaz** ~ carbon dioxide ; **neige** ~ dry ice.

carboniser [3] [karbɔnize] *vt* to burn to a cinder.

carburant [karbyrɑ̃] *nm* fuel.

carburateur [karbyratœr] *nm* carburettor *Br*, carburetor *Am*.

carcan [karkɑ̃] *nm* HIST iron collar ; *fig* yoke.

carcasse [karkas] *nf* - **1.** [d'animal] carcass - **2.** [de bâtiment, navire] framework - **3.** [de véhicule] shell.

cardiaque [kardjak] *adj* cardiac ; **être** ~ to have a heart condition ; **crise** ~ heart attack.

cardigan [kardigɑ̃] *nm* cardigan.

cardinal, e, aux [kardinal, o] *adj* cardinal. ◆ **cardinal** *nm* - **1.** RELIG cardinal - **2.** [nombre] cardinal number.

cardiologue [kardjɔlɔg] *nmf* heart specialist, cardiologist.

cardio-vasculaire [kardjovaskylɛr] (*pl* cardio-vasculaires) *adj* cardiovascular.

Carême [karɛm] *nm* : **le** ~ Lent.

carence [karɑ̃s] *nf* [manque] : ~ **(en)** deficiency (in).

carène [karɛn] *nf* NAVIG hull.

caressant, e [karesɑ̃, ɑ̃t] *adj* affectionate.

caresse [karɛs] *nf* caress.

caresser [4] [karese] *vt* - **1.** [personne] to caress ; [animal, objet] to stroke - **2.** *fig* [espoir] to cherish.

cargaison [kargɛzɔ̃] *nf* TRANSPORT cargo.

cargo [kargo] *nm* - **1.** [navire] freighter - **2.** [avion] cargo plane.

caricature [karikatyr] *nf* - **1.** [gén] caricature - **2.** *péj* [personne] sight.

carie [kari] *nf* MÉD caries.

carillon [karijɔ̃] *nm* - **1.** [cloches] bells (*pl*) - **2.** [d'horloge, de porte] chime.

carlingue [karlɛ̃g] *nf* - **1.** [d'avion] cabin - **2.** [de navire] keelson.

carmin [karmɛ̃] *adj inv* crimson.

carnage [karnaʒ] *nm* slaughter, carnage.

carnassier [karnasje] *nm* carnivore.

carnaval [karnaval] *nm* carnival.

carnet [karnɛ] *nm* - **1.** [petit cahier] notebook ; ~ **d'adresses** address book ; ~ **de notes** SCOL report card - **2.** [bloc de feuilles] book ; ~ **de chèques** cheque book *Br*, checkbook *Am* ; ~ **de tickets** book of tickets.

carnivore [karnivɔr] ◇ *adj* carnivorous. ◇ *nm* carnivore.

carotte [karɔt] *nf* carrot.

carpe [karp] *nf* carp.

carpette [karpɛt] *nf* - **1.** [petit tapis] rug - **2.** *fam péj* [personne] doormat.

carquois [karkwa] *nm* quiver.

carré, e [kare] *adj* [gén] square ; **20 mètres** ~**s** 20 square metres. ◆ **carré** *nm* - **1.** [quadrilatère] square ; **élever un nombre au** ~ MATHS to square a number ; ~ **blanc** TV *white square in the corner of the screen indicating that a television programme is not recommended for children* - **2.** CARTES : **un** ~ **d'as** four aces - **3.** [petit terrain] patch, plot.

carreau, x [karo] *nm* - **1.** [carrelage] tile - **2.** [vitre] window pane - **3.** [motif carré] check ; **à** ~**x** [tissu] checked ; [papier] squared - **4.** CARTES diamond.

carrefour [karfur] *nm* [de routes, de la vie] crossroads (*sg*).

carrelage [karlaʒ] *nm* [surface] tiles (*pl*).

carrément [karemɑ̃] *adv* - **1.** [franchement] bluntly - **2.** [complètement] completely, quite - **3.** [sans hésiter] straight.

carrière [karjɛr] *nf* - **1.** [profession] career ; **faire** ~ **dans qqch** to make a career (for o.s.) in sthg - **2.** [gisement] quarry.

carriériste [karjerist] *nmf péj* careerist.

carriole [karjɔl] *nf* - **1.** [petite charrette] cart - **2.** *Can* [traîneau] sleigh.

carrossable [karɔsabl] *adj* suitable for vehicles.

carrosse [karɔs] *nm* (horse-drawn) coach.

carrosserie [karɔsri] *nf* [de voiture] bodywork, body.

carrossier [karɔsje] *nm* coachbuilder.

carrure [karyr] *nf* [de personne] build ; *fig* stature.

cartable [kartabl] *nm* schoolbag.

carte [kart] *nf* - **1.** [gén] card ; ~ **d'abonnement** season ticket ; ~ **bancaire** cash card *Br* ; ~ **de crédit** credit card ; ~ **d'étudiant** student card ; ~ **graphique** INFORM graphics board ; ~ **à gratter** scratch card ; ~ **grise** ≃ logbook *Br*, ≃ car registration papers *Am* ; ~ **d'identité** identity card ; ~ **à mémoire** memory card ; **Carte Orange** season ticket *(for use on public transport in Paris)* ; ~ **postale** postcard ; ~ **à puce** smart card ; ~ **de séjour** residence permit ; ~ **son** INFORM sound card ; **Carte Vermeil** *card entitling senior citizens to reduced rates in cinemas, on public transport etc* ; ~ **de visite** visiting card *Br*, calling card *Am* ; **donner** ~ **blanche à qqn** *fig* to give sb a free hand - **2.** [de jeu] : ~ **(à jouer)** (playing) card - **3.** GÉOGR map ; ~ **d'état-major** ≃ Ordnance Survey map *Br*, ≃ Geological Survey map *Am* ; ~ **routière** road map

- **4.** [au restaurant] menu ; **à la ~** [menu] à la carte ; [horaires] flexible ; **~ des vins** wine list.

cartilage [kartilaʒ] *nm* cartilage.

cartomancien, enne [kartɔmɑ̃sjɛ̃, ɛn] *nm, f* fortune-teller *(using cards)*.

carton [kartɔ̃] *nm* - **1.** [matière] cardboard - **2.** [emballage] cardboard box ; **~ à dessin** portfolio.

cartonné, e [kartɔne] *adj* [livre] hardback.

carton-pâte [kartɔ̃pat] *nm* pasteboard.

cartouche [kartuʃ] *nf* - **1.** [gén & INFORM] cartridge - **2.** [de cigarettes] carton.

cas [ka] *nm* case ; **au ~ où** in case ; **en aucun ~** under no circumstances ; **en tout ~** in any case, anyway ; **en ~ de** in case of ; **en ~ de besoin** if need be ; **le ~ échéant** if the need arises, if need be ; **~ de conscience** matter of conscience ; **~ social** person with social problems.

casanier, ère [kazanje, ɛr] *adj & nm, f* stay-at-home.

casaque [kazak] *nf* - **1.** [veste] overblouse - **2.** HIPPISME blouse.

cascade [kaskad] *nf* - **1.** [chute d'eau] waterfall ; *fig* stream, torrent - **2.** CIN stunt.

cascadeur, euse [kaskadœr, øz] *nm, f* CIN stuntman (*f* stuntwoman).

cascher = **kas(c)her**.

case [kaz] *nf* - **1.** [habitation] hut - **2.** [de boîte, tiroir] compartment ; [d'échiquier] square ; [sur un formulaire] box.

caser [3] [kaze] *vt* - **1.** *fam* [trouver un emploi pour] to get a job for - **2.** *fam* [marier] to marry off - **3.** [placer] to put. ◆ **se caser** *vp fam* - **1.** [trouver un emploi] to get (o.s.) a job - **2.** [se marier] to get hitched.

caserne [kazɛrn] *nf* barracks.

cash [kaʃ] *nm* cash ; **payer ~** to pay (in) cash.

casier [kazje] *nm* - **1.** [compartiment] compartment ; [pour le courrier] pigeonhole - **2.** [meuble - à bouteilles] rack ; [- à courrier] set of pigeonholes - **3.** PÊCHE lobster pot. ◆ **casier judiciaire** *nm* police record ; **~ judiciaire vierge** clean (police) record.

casino [kazino] *nm* casino.

casque [kask] *nm* - **1.** [de protection] helmet - **2.** [à écouteurs] headphones (*pl*). ◆ **Casques bleus** *nmpl* : **les Casques bleus** the UN peace-keeping force.

casquette [kaskɛt] *nf* cap.

cassant, e [kasɑ̃, ɑ̃t] *adj* - **1.** [fragile - verre] fragile ; [- cheveux] brittle - **2.** [dur] brusque.

cassation [kasasjɔ̃] ▷ **cour.**

casse [kas] ◇ *nf* - **1.** *fam* [violence] aggro - **2.** [de voitures] scrapyard. ◇ *nm fam* [cambriolage] break-in.

casse-cou [kasku] *nmf inv* [personne] daredevil.

casse-croûte [kaskrut] *nm inv* snack.

casse-noisettes [kasnwazɛt], **casse-noix** [kasnwa] *nm inv* nutcrackers (*pl*).

casse-pieds [kaspje] ◇ *adj inv fam* annoying. ◇ *nmf inv* pain (in the neck).

casser [3] [kase] ◇ *vt* - **1.** [briser] to break - **2.** JUR to quash. ◇ **les prix** to slash prices. ◇ *vi* to break. ◆ **se casser** *vp* - **1.** [se briser] to break - **2.** [membre] : **se ~ un bras** to break one's arm.

casserole [kasrɔl] *nf* [ustensile] saucepan.

casse-tête [kastɛt] *nm inv* - **1.** *fig* [problème] headache - **2.** [jeu] puzzle.

cassette [kasɛt] *nf* - **1.** [coffret] casket - **2.** [de musique, vidéo] cassette.

cassis [kasis] *nm* - **1.** [fruit] blackcurrant ; [arbuste] blackcurrant bush ; [liqueur] blackcurrant liqueur - **2.** [sur la route] dip.

cassure [kasyr] *nf* break.

caste [kast] *nf* caste.

casting [kastiŋ] *nm* [acteurs] cast ; [sélection] casting ; **aller à un ~** to go to an audition.

castor [kastɔr] *nm* beaver.

castrer [3] [kastre] *vt* to castrate ; [chat] to neuter ; [chatte] to spay.

cataclysme [kataklism] *nm* cataclysm.

catadioptre [katadjɔptr], **Cataphote®** [katafɔt] *nm* - **1.** [sur la route] cat's eye *Br*, highway reflector *Am* - **2.** [de véhicule] reflector.

catalogue [katalɔg] *nm* catalogue *Br*, catalog *Am*.

cataloguer [3] [katalɔge] *vt* - **1.** [classer] to catalogue *Br*, to catalog *Am* - **2.** *péj* [juger] to label.

catalyseur [katalizœr] *nm* CHIM & *fig* catalyst.

catalytique [katalitik] ▷ **pot.**

catamaran [katamarɑ̃] *nm* [voilier] catamaran.

Cataphote® = **catadioptre**.

cataplasme [kataplasm] *nm* poultice.

catapulter [3] [katapylte] *vt* to catapult.

cataracte [katarakt] *nf* cataract.

catarrhe [katar] *nm* catarrh.

catastrophe [katastrɔf] *nf* disaster, catastrophe.

catastrophé, e [katastrɔfe] *adj* shocked, upset.

catastrophique [katastrɔfik] *adj* disastrous, catastrophic.

catch [katʃ] *nm* wrestling.

catéchisme [kateʃism] *nm* catechism.

catégorie [kategɔri] *nf* [gén] category ; [de personnel] grade ; [de viande, fruits] quality ; ~ **socio-professionnelle** ÉCON socio-economic group.

catégorique [kategɔrik] *adj* categorical.

cathédrale [katedral] *nf* cathedral.

cathodique [katɔdik] ▷ tube.

catholicisme [katɔlisism] *nm* Catholicism.

catholique [katɔlik] *adj* Catholic.

catimini [katimini] ◆ **en catimini** *loc adv* secretly.

cauchemar [koʃmar] *nm litt & fig* nightmare.

cauchemardesque [koʃmardɛsk] *adj* nightmarish.

cause [koz] *nf* - **1.** [gén] cause ; **à ~ de** because of ; **pour ~ de** on account of, because of - **2.** JUR case - **3.** *loc* : **être en ~** [intérêts] to be at stake ; [honnêteté] to be in doubt ou in question ; **remettre en ~** to challenge, to question.

causer [3] [koze] ◇ *vt* : **~ qqch à qqn** to cause sb sthg. ◇ *vi* [bavarder] : **~ (de)** to chat (about).

causerie [kozri] *nf* talk.

caustique [kostik] *adj & nm* caustic.

cautériser [3] [koterize] *vt* to cauterize.

caution [kosjɔ̃] *nf* - **1.** [somme d'argent] guarantee - **2.** [personne] guarantor ; **se porter ~ pour qqn** to act as guarantor for sb.

cautionner [3] [kosjone] *vt* - **1.** [se porter garant de] to guarantee - **2.** *fig* [appuyer] to support, to back.

cavalcade [kavalkad] *nf* - **1.** [de cavaliers] cavalcade - **2.** [d'enfants] stampede.

cavalerie [kavalri] *nf* MIL cavalry.

cavalier, ère [kavalje, ɛr] *nm, f* - **1.** [à cheval] rider - **2.** [partenaire] partner. ◆ **cavalier** *nm* [aux échecs] knight.

cavalièrement [kavaljɛrmɑ̃] *adv* in an offhand manner.

cave [kav] ◇ *nf* - **1.** [sous-sol] cellar - **2.** [de vins] (wine) cellar. ◇ *adj* [joues] hollow ; [yeux] sunken.

caveau, x [kavo] *nm* - **1.** [petite cave] small cellar - **2.** [sépulture] vault.

caverne [kavɛrn] *nf* cave.

caviar [kavjar] *nm* caviar.

cavité [kavite] *nf* cavity.

CB (*abr de* **citizen's band, canaux banalisés**) *nf* CB.

cc *abr de* **charges comprises**.

CCP (*abr de* **compte chèque postal, compte courant postal**) *nm* post office account, ≃ Giro *Br*.

CD *nm* (*abr de* **compact disc**) CD.

CDD *nm abr de* **contrat à durée déterminée**.

CDI *nm* - **1.** (*abr de* **centre de documentation et d'information**) *school library* - **2.** *abr de* **contrat à durée indéterminée**.

ce [sə] ◇ *adj dém* (**cet** [sɛt] *devant voyelle ou h muet*, *f* **cette** [sɛt], *pl* **ces** [se]) [proche] this, these *(pl)* ; [éloigné] that, those *(pl)* ; **~ mois, ~ mois-ci** this month ; **cette année, cette année-là** that year. ◇ *pron dém* (**c'** *devant voyelle*) **c'est** it is, it's ; **~ sont** they are, they're ; **c'est mon bureau** this is my office, it's my office ; **~ sont mes enfants** these are my children, they're my children ; **c'est à Paris** it's in Paris ; **qui est-~?** who is it? ; **~ qui, ~ que** what ; **ils ont eu ~ qui leur revenait** they got what they deserved ..., **~ qui est étonnant** ..., which is surprising ; **vous savez bien ~ à quoi je pense** you know exactly what I'm thinking about ; **faites donc ~ pour quoi on vous paie** do what you're paid to do.

CE ◇ *nm* - **1.** *abr de* **comité d'entreprise** - **2.** (*abr de* **cours élémentaire**) : **~1** *second year of primary school* ; **~2** *third year of primary school*. ◇ *nf* (*abr de* **Communauté européenne**) EC.

ceci [səsi] *pron dém* this ; **à ~ près que** with the exception that, except that.

cécité [sesite] *nf* blindness.

céder [18] [sede] ◇ *vt* - **1.** [donner] to give up ; **'cédez le passage'** 'give way' *Br*, 'yield' *Am* - **2.** [revendre] to sell. ◇ *vi* - **1.** [personne] : **~ (à)** to give in (to), to yield (to) - **2.** [chaise, plancher] to give way.

CEDEX, Cedex [sedɛks] (*abr de* **courrier d'entreprise à distribution exceptionnelle**) *nm accelerated postal service for bulk users*.

cédille [sedij] *nf* cedilla.

cèdre [sedr] *nm* cedar.

CEE (*abr de* **Communauté économique européenne**) *nf* EEC.

CEI (*abr de* **Communauté d'États Indépendants**) *nf* CIS.

ceinture [sɛ̃tyr] *nf* - **1.** [gén] belt ; **~ de sécurité** safety ou seat belt - **2.** ANAT waist.

ceinturon [sɛ̃tyrɔ̃] *nm* belt.

cela [səla] *pron dém* that ; **~ ne vous regarde pas** it's ou that's none of your business ; **il y a des années de ~** that was many years ago ; **c'est ~** that's right ; **~ dit** ... having said that ... ; **malgré ~** in spite of that, nevertheless.

célèbre [selɛbr] *adj* famous.

célébrer [18] [selebre] *vt* - **1.** [gén] to celebrate - **2.** [faire la louange de] to praise.

célébrité [selebrite] *nf* - **1.** [renommée] fame - **2.** [personne] celebrity.

céleri [sɛlri] *nm* celery.

céleste [selɛst] *adj* heavenly.

célibat [seliba] *nm* celibacy.

célibataire [selibatɛr] ◇ *adj* single, unmarried ; **père** OU **mère ~** single parent. ◇ *nmf* single person, single man (*f* woman).

celle ▷ celui.

celle-ci ▷ celui-ci.

celle-là ▷ celui-là.

celles ▷ celui.

celles-ci ▷ celui-ci.

celles-là ▷ celui-là.

cellier [selje] *nm* storeroom.

Cellophane® [selɔfan] *nf* Cellophane®.

cellulaire [selylɛr] *adj* - **1.** BIOL & TÉLÉCOM cellular - **2.** [destiné aux prisonniers] : **régime ~** solitary confinement ; **voiture ~** prison van.

cellule [selyl] *nf* - **1.** [gén & INFORM] cell - **2.** [groupe] unit.

cellulite [selylit] *nf* cellulite.

celte [sɛlt] *adj* Celtic. ◆ **Celte** *nmf* Celt.

celui [səlɥi] (*f* **celle** [sɛl], *mpl* **ceux** [sø], *fpl* **celles** [sɛl]) *pron dém* - **1.** [suivi d'un complément prépositionnel] the one ; **celle de devant** the one in front ; **ceux d'entre vous qui ...** those of you who ... - **2.** [suivi d'un pronom relatif] : **~ qui** [objet] the one which OU that ; [personne] the one who ; **c'est celle qui te va le mieux** that's the one which OU that suits you best ; **~ que vous voyez** the one (which OU that) you can see, the one whom you can see ; **ceux que je connais** those I know.

celui-ci [səlɥisi] (*f* **celle-ci** [sɛlsi], *mpl* **ceux-ci** [søsi], *fpl* **celles-ci** [sɛlsi]) *pron dém* this one, these ones (*pl*).

celui-là [səlɥila] (*f* **celle-là** [sɛlla], *mpl* **ceux-là** [søla], *fpl* **celles-là** [sɛlla]) *pron dém* that one, those ones (*pl*) ; **~ ... celui-ci** the former ... the latter.

cendre [sɑ̃dr] *nf* ash.

cendré, e [sɑ̃dre] *adj* [chevelure] : **blond ~** ash blond.

cendrier [sɑ̃drije] *nm* - **1.** [de fumeur] ashtray - **2.** [de poêle] ashpan.

cène [sɛn] *nf* (Holy) Communion. ◆ **Cène** *nf* : **la Cène** the Last Supper.

censé, e [sɑ̃se] *adj* : **être ~ faire qqch** to be supposed to do sthg.

censeur [sɑ̃sœr] *nm* - **1.** SCOL ≃ deputy head *Br*, ≃ vice-principal *Am* - **2.** CIN & PRESSE censor.

censure [sɑ̃syr] *nf* - **1.** [presse & CIN - contrôle] censorship ; [- censeurs] censors (*pl*) - **2.** POLIT censure - **3.** PSYCHOL censor.

censurer [3] [sɑ̃syre] *vt* - **1.** CIN, PRESSE & PSYCHOL to censor - **2.** [juger] to censure.

cent [sɑ̃] ◇ *adj num* one hundred, a hundred. ◇ *nm* - **1.** [nombre] a hundred ; *voir aussi* **six** - **2.** [mesure de proportion] : **pour ~** percent.

centaine [sɑ̃tɛn] *nf* - **1.** [cent unités] hundred - **2.** [un grand nombre] : **une ~ de** about a hundred ; **des ~s (de)** hundreds (of) ; **plusieurs ~s de** several hundred ; **par ~s** in hundreds.

centenaire [sɑ̃tnɛr] ◇ *adj* hundred-year-old (*avant n*) ; **être ~** to be a hundred years old. ◇ *nmf* centenarian. ◇ *nm* [anniversaire] centenary *Br*, centennial *Am*.

centiare [sɑ̃tjar] *nm* square metre *Br* OU meter *Am*.

centième [sɑ̃tjɛm] *adj num, nm* OU *nmf* hundredth ; *voir aussi* **sixième**.

centigrade [sɑ̃tigrad] ▷ degré.

centilitre [sɑ̃tilitr] *nm* centilitre *Br*, centiliter *Am*.

centime [sɑ̃tim] *nm* centime.

centimètre [sɑ̃timɛtr] *nm* - **1.** [mesure] centimetre *Br*, centimeter *Am* - **2.** [ruban, règle] tape measure.

central, e, aux [sɑ̃tral, o] *adj* central. ◆ **central** *nm* [de réseau] : **~ téléphonique** telephone exchange. ◆ **centrale** *nf* - **1.** [usine] power plant OU station ; **~e hydroélectrique** hydroelectric power station ; **~e nucléaire** nuclear power plant OU station - **2.** COMM : **~e d'achat** buying group.

centraliser [3] [sɑ̃tralize] *vt* to centralize.

centre [sɑ̃tr] *nm* [gén] centre *Br*, center *Am* ; **~ aéré** outdoor centre *Br* OU center *Am* ; **~ d'appels** call centre *Br* OU center *Am* ; **~ commercial** shopping centre *Br* OU mall *Am* ; **~ culturel** arts centre *Br* OU center *Am* ; **~ de gravité** centre *Br* OU center *Am* of gravity ; **~ nerveux** nerve centre *Br* OU center *Am*.

centrer [3] [sɑ̃tre] *vt* to centre *Br*, to center *Am*.

centre-ville [sɑ̃trəvil] *nm* city centre *Br* OU center *Am*, town centre *Br* OU center *Am*.

centrifuge [sɑ̃trify3] ▷ force.

centrifugeuse [sɑ̃trify3øz] *nf* - **1.** TECHNOL centrifuge - **2.** CULIN juice extractor.

centuple [sɑ̃typl] *nm* : **être le ~ de qqch** to be a hundred times sthg ; **au ~** a hundredfold.

cep [sɛp] *nm* stock.

cèpe [sɛp] *nm* cep.

cependant [səpɑ̃dɑ̃] *conj* however, yet.

céramique [seramik] *nf* [matière, objet] ceramic.

cerceau, x [sɛrso] *nm* hoop.

cercle [sɛrkl] *nm* circle ; **~ vicieux** vicious circle.

cercueil [sɛrkœj] *nm* coffin.

céréale [sereal] *nf* cereal.

cérémonial, als [seremɔnjal] *nm* ceremonial.

cérémonie [seremɔni] *nf* ceremony.

cérémonieux, euse [seremɔnjø, øz] *adj* ceremonious.

cerf [sɛr] *nm* stag.

cerf-volant [sɛrvɔlɑ̃] *nm* [jouet] kite.

cerise [səriz] <> *nf* cherry. <> *adj inv* cherry.

cerisier [sərizje] *nm* [arbre] cherry (tree) ; [bois] cherry (wood).

cerne [sɛrn] *nm* ring.

cerné [sɛrne] *⊳* œil.

cerner [sɛrne] *vt* - **1.** [encercler] to surround - **2.** *fig* [sujet] to define.

certain, e [sɛrtɛ̃, ɛn] <> *adj* certain ; **être ~ de qqch** to be certain ou sure of sthg ; **je suis pourtant ~ d'avoir mis mes clés là** but I'm certain ou sure I left my keys there. <> *adj indéf (avant n)* certain ; **il a un ~ talent** he has some talent ou a certain talent ; **un ~ temps** for a while ; **avoir un ~ âge** to be getting on, to be past one's prime ; **c'est un monsieur d'un ~ âge** he's getting on a bit ; **un ~ M. Lebrun** a Mr Lebrun. **◆ certains** *(fpl* certaines*) pron indéf pl* some.

certainement [sɛrtɛnmɑ̃] *adv* [probablement] most probably, most likely ; [bien sûr] certainly.

certes [sɛrt] *adv* of course.

certificat [sɛrtifika] *nm* [attestation, diplôme] certificate ; **~ médical** medical certificate.

certifié, e [sɛrtifje] *adj* : **professeur ~** qualified teacher.

certifier [9] [sɛrtifje] *vt* - **1.** [assurer] : **~ qqch à qqn** to assure sb of sthg - **2.** [authentifier] to certify.

certitude [sɛrtityd] *nf* certainty.

cerveau, x [sɛrvo] *nm* brain.

cervelle [sɛrvɛl] *nf* - **1.** ANAT brain - **2.** [facultés mentales, aliment] brains *(pl)*.

cervical, e, aux [sɛrvikal, o] *adj* cervical.

ces *⊳* ce.

CES *nm* - **1.** (*abr de* **collège d'enseignement secondaire**) *former secondary school* - **2.** *abr de* **Contrat emploi-solidarité**.

césarienne [sezarjɛn] *nf* caesarean (section).

cesse [sɛs] *nf* : **n'avoir de ~ que** (+ *subjonctif*) *sout* not to rest until. **◆ sans cesse** *loc adv* continually, constantly.

cesser [4] [sese] <> *vi* to stop, to cease. <> *vt* to stop ; **~ de faire qqch** to stop doing sthg.

cessez-le-feu [seselfø] *nm inv* cease-fire.

cession [sesjɔ̃] *nf* transfer.

c'est-à-dire [sɛtadir] *conj* - **1.** [en d'autres termes] : **~ (que)** that is (to say) - **2.** [introduit une restriction, précision, réponse] : **~ que** well ..., actually ...

cet *⊳* ce.

cétacé [setase] *nm* cetacean.

cette *⊳* ce.

ceux *⊳* celui.

ceux-ci *⊳* celui-ci.

ceux-là *⊳* celui-là.

cf. (*abr de* confer) cf.

CFC (*abr de* chlorofluorocarbone) *nm* CFC.

chacal [ʃakal] *nm* jackal.

chacun, e [ʃakœ̃, yn] *pron indéf* each (one) ; [tout le monde] everyone, everybody ; **~ de nous/de vous/d'eux** each of us/you/them ; **~ pour soi** every man for himself ; **tout un ~** every one of us/them.

chagrin, e [ʃagrɛ̃, in] *adj* [personne] grieving ; [caractère, humeur] morose. **◆ chagrin** *nm* grief ; **avoir du ~** to grieve.

chagriner [3] [ʃagrine] *vt* - **1.** [peiner] to grieve, to distress - **2.** [contrarier] to upset.

chahut [ʃay] *nm* uproar.

chahuter [3] [ʃayte] <> *vi* to cause an uproar. <> *vt* - **1.** [importuner - professeur] to rag, to tease ; [- orateur] to heckle - **2.** [bousculer] to jostle.

chaîne [ʃɛn] *nf* - **1.** [gén] chain ; **~ de montagnes** mountain range - **2.** IND : **~ de fabrication/de montage** production/assembly line ; **travail à la ~** production-line work ; **produire qqch à la ~** to mass-produce sthg - **3.** TÉLÉ channel ; **~ à péage** pay TV channel ; **~ de télévision** television channel, TV channel ; **~ thématique** specialized channel - **4.** [appareil] stereo (system) ; **~ hi-fi** hi-fi system. **◆ chaînes** *nfpl fig* chains, bonds.

chaînon [ʃɛnɔ̃] *nm litt & fig* link.

chair [ʃɛr] *nf* flesh ; **avoir la ~ de poule** to have goose pimples OU gooseflesh, to have goosebumps *Am*.

chaire [ʃɛr] *nf* - **1.** [estrade - de prédicateur] pulpit ; [- de professeur] rostrum - **2.** UNIV chair.

chaise [ʃɛz] *nf* chair ; **~ longue** deckchair.

châle [ʃal] *nm* shawl.

chalet [ʃalɛ] *nm* - **1.** [de montagne] chalet - **2.** *Can* [maison de campagne] (holiday) cottage.

chaleur [ʃalœr] *nf* heat ; [agréable] warmth.

chaleureux, euse [ʃalœrø, øz] *adj* warm.

challenge [ʃalɑ̃ʒ] *nm* - **1.** SPORT tournament - **2.** *fig* [défi] challenge.

chaloupe [ʃalup] *nf* rowing boat *Br*, rowboat *Am*.

chalumeau [ʃalymo] *nm* TECHNOL blowlamp *Br*, blowtorch *Am*.

chalutier [ʃalytje] *nm* [bateau] trawler.

chamailler [3] [ʃamaje] ◆ **sechamailler** *vp fam* to squabble.

chambranle [ʃɑ̃brɑ̃l] *nm* [de porte, fenêtre] frame ; [de cheminée] mantelpiece.

chambre [ʃɑ̃br] *nf* - **1.** [où l'on dort] : **~ (à coucher)** bedroom ; **~ à un lit, ~ pour une personne** single room ; **~ pour deux personnes** double room ; **~ à deux lits** twin-bedded room ; **~ d'amis** spare room ; **~ d'hôte** bed and breakfast - **2.** [local] room ; **~ forte** strongroom ; **~ froide** cold store ; **~ noire** darkroom - **3.** JUR division ; **~ d'accusation** court of criminal appeal - **4.** POLIT chamber, house ; **Chambre des députés** ≃ House of Commons *Br*, ≃ House of Representatives *Am* - **5.** TECHNOL chamber ; **~ à air** [de pneu] inner tube.

chambrer [3] [ʃɑ̃bre] *vt* - **1.** [vin] to bring to room temperature - **2.** *fam* [se moquer] : **~ qqn** to pull sb's leg, to wind sb up *Br*.

chameau, x [ʃamo] *nm* [mammifère] camel.

chamois [ʃamwa] *nm* chamois ; [peau] chamois (leather).

champ [ʃɑ̃] *nm* - **1.** [gén & INFORM] field ; **~ de bataille** battlefield ; **~ de courses** racecourse - **2.** [étendue] area.

champagne [ʃɑ̃paɲ] *nm* champagne.

champêtre [ʃɑ̃pɛtr] *adj* rural.

champignon [ʃɑ̃piɲɔ̃] *nm* - **1.** BOT & MÉD fungus - **2.** [comestible] mushroom ; **~ vénéneux** toadstool.

champion, onne [ʃɑ̃pjɔ̃, ɔn] ◇ *nm, f* champion. ◇ *adj fam* brilliant.

championnat [ʃɑ̃pjɔna] *nm* championship.

chance [ʃɑ̃s] *nf* - **1.** [bonheur] luck (U) ; **avoir de la ~** to be lucky ; **ne pas avoir de ~** to be unlucky ; **porter ~** to bring good luck - **2.** [probabilité, possibilité] chance, opportunity ; **avoir des ~s de faire qqch** to have a chance of doing sthg.

chanceler [24] [ʃɑ̃sle] *vi* [personne, gouvernement] to totter ; [meuble] to wobble.

chancelier [ʃɑ̃səlje] *nm* - **1.** [premier ministre] chancellor - **2.** [de consulat, d'ambassade] secretary.

chanceux, euse [ʃɑ̃sø, øz] *adj* lucky.

chandail [ʃɑ̃daj] *nm* [thick] sweater.

Chandeleur [ʃɑ̃dlœr] *nf* Candlemas.

chandelier [ʃɑ̃dəlje] *nm* [pour une bougie] candlestick ; [à plusieurs branches] candelabra.

chandelle [ʃɑ̃dɛl] *nf* [bougie] candle.

change [ʃɑ̃ʒ] *nm* - **1.** [troc & FIN] exchange - **2.** [couche de bébé] disposable nappy *Br*, diaper *Am*.

changeant, e [ʃɑ̃ʒɑ̃, ɑ̃t] *adj* - **1.** [temps, humeur] changeable - **2.** [reflet] shimmering.

changement [ʃɑ̃ʒmɑ̃] *nm* change.

changer [17] [ʃɑ̃ʒe] ◇ *vt* - **1.** [gén] to change ; **~ qqch contre** to change OU exchange sthg for ; **~ qqn en** to change sb into ; **~ des euros en dollars** to change euros into dollars, to exchange euros for dollars - **2.** [modifier] to change, to alter ; **ça me/te changera** that will be a (nice) change for me/you. ◇ *vi* - **1.** [gén] to change ; **~ de train (à)** to change trains (at) ; **~ d'avis** to change one's mind ; **ça changera!** that'll make a change! ; **~ de direction** to change direction ; **~ de place (avec qqn)** to change places (with sb) ; **pour ~** for a change - **2.** [modifier] to change, to alter ; **~ de comportement** to alter one's behaviour *Br* OU behavior *Am*.

chanson [ʃɑ̃sɔ̃] *nf* song ; **c'est toujours la même ~** *fig* it's the same old story.

chansonnier, ère [ʃɑ̃sɔnje, ɛr] *nm, f* cabaret singer-songwriter.

chant [ʃɑ̃] *nm* - **1.** [chanson] song, singing (U) ; [sacré] hymn - **2.** [art] singing.

chantage [ʃɑ̃taʒ] *nm litt & fig* blackmail ; **faire du ~** to use OU resort to blackmail ; **faire du ~ à qqn** to blackmail sb.

chanter [3] [ʃɑ̃te] ◇ *vt* - **1.** [chanson] to sing - **2.** *littéraire* [célébrer] to sing OU tell of ; **~ les louanges de qqn** to sing sb's praises. ◇ *vi* - **1.** [gén] to sing - **2.** *loc* : **faire ~ qqn** to blackmail sb ; **si ça vous chante!** *fam* if you feel like OU fancy it!

chanteur, euse [ʃɑ̃tœr, øz] *nm, f* singer.

chantier [ʃɑ̃tje] *nm* - **1.** CONSTR (building) site ; [sur la route] roadworks *(pl)* ; **~ naval** shipyard, dockyard - **2.** *fig* [désordre] shambles *(sg)*, mess.

Chantilly [ʃɑ̃tiji] *nf* : **(crème) ~** *stiffly whipped cream sweetened and flavoured.*

chantonner [3] [ʃɑ̃tɔne] *vt & vi* to hum.

chanvre [ʃɑ̃vr] *nm* hemp.

chaos [kao] *nm* chaos.

chap. *(abr de* **chapitre)** ch.

chaparder [3] [ʃaparde] *vt* to steal.

chapeau, x [ʃapo] *nm* - **1.** [coiffure] hat - **2.** PRESSE introductory paragraph.

chapeauter [3] [ʃapote] *vt* [service] to head ; [personnes] to supervise.

chapelet [ʃaplɛ] *nm* - **1.** RELIG rosary - **2.** *fig* [d'injures] string, torrent.

chapelle [ʃapɛl] *nf* [petite église] chapel ; [partie d'église] choir.

chapelure [ʃaplyr] *nf* (dried) bread-crumbs *(pl)*.

chapiteau [ʃapito] *nm* [de cirque] big top.

chapitre [ʃapitr] *nm* [de livre & RELIG] chapter.

chaque [ʃak] *adj indéf* each, every ; **~ personne** each person, everyone ; **j'ai payé ces livres 100 euros ~** I paid 100 euros each for these books.

char [ʃar] *nm* - **1.** MIL : **~ (d'assaut)** tank - **2.** [de carnaval] float - **3.** *Can* [voiture] car.

charabia [ʃarabja] *nm* gibberish.

charade [ʃarad] *nf* charade.

charbon [ʃarbɔ̃] *nm* [combustible] coal ; **~ de bois** charcoal.

charcuter [3] [ʃarkyte] *vt fam péj* to butcher.

charcuterie [ʃarkytri] *nf* - **1.** [magasin] pork butcher's - **2.** [produits] pork meat products.

charcutier, ère [ʃarkytje, ɛr] *nm, f* [commerçant] pork butcher.

chardon [ʃardɔ̃] *nm* [plante] thistle.

charge [ʃarʒ] *nf* - **1.** [fardeau] load - **2.** [fonction] office - **3.** [responsabilité] responsibility ; **être à la ~ de** [personne] to be dependent on ; **les travaux sont à la ~ du propriétaire** the owner is liable for the cost of the work ; **prendre qqch en ~** [payer] to pay (for) sthg ; [s'occuper de] to take charge of sthg ; **prendre qqn en ~** to take charge of sb - **4.** ÉLECTR, JUR & MIL charge. ◆ **charges** *nfpl* - **1.** [d'appartement] service charge - **2.** ÉCON expenses, costs ; **~s sociales** ≃ employer's contributions.

chargé, e [ʃarʒe] ◇ *adj* - **1.** [véhicule, personne] : **~ (de)** loaded (with) - **2.** [responsable] : **~ (de)** responsible (for) - **3.** [occupé] full, busy. ◇ *nm, f* : **~ d'affaires** chargé d'affaires ; **~ de mission** head of mission.

chargement [ʃarʒəmɑ̃] *nm* - **1.** [action] loading - **2.** [marchandises] load.

charger [17] [ʃarʒe] *vt* - **1.** [gén & INFORM] to load - **2.** ÉLECTR, JUR & MIL to charge - **3.** [donner une mission à] : **~ qqn de faire qqch** to put sb in charge of doing sthg. ◆ **se charger** *vp* : **se ~ de qqn/qqch** to take care of sb/sthg, to take charge of sb/ sthg ; **se ~ de faire qqch** to undertake to do sthg.

chargeur [ʃarʒœr] *nm* - **1.** ÉLECTR charger - **2.** [d'arme] magazine.

chariot [ʃarjo] *nm* - **1.** [charrette] handcart - **2.** [à bagages, dans un hôpital] trolley *Br*, wagon *Am* - **3.** [de machine à écrire] carriage.

charisme [karism] *nm* charisma.

charitable [ʃaritabl] *adj* charitable ; [conseil] friendly.

charité [ʃarite] *nf* - **1.** [aumône & RELIG] charity - **2.** [bonté] kindness.

charlatan [ʃarlatɑ̃] *nm péj* charlatan.

charmant, e [ʃarmɑ̃, ɑ̃t] *adj* charming.

charme [ʃarm] *nm* - **1.** [séduction] charm - **2.** [enchantement] spell - **3.** [arbre] ironwood, hornbeam.

charmer [3] [ʃarme] *vt* to charm ; **être charmé de faire qqch** to be delighted to do sthg.

charmeur, euse [ʃarmœr, øz] ◇ *adj* charming. ◇ *nm, f* charmer ; **~ de serpents** snake charmer.

charnel, elle [ʃarnɛl] *adj* carnal.

charnier [ʃarnje] *nm* mass grave.

charnière [ʃarnjɛr] ◇ *nf* hinge ; *fig* turning point. ◇ *adj* [période] transitional.

charnu, e [ʃarny] *adj* fleshy.

charogne [ʃarɔɲ] *nf* [d'animal] carrion *(U)*.

charpente [ʃarpɑ̃t] *nf* - **1.** [de bâtiment, de roman] framework - **2.** [ossature] frame.

charpentier [ʃarpɑ̃tje] *nm* carpenter.

charretier, ère [ʃartje, ɛr] *nm, f* carter.

charrette [ʃarɛt] *nf* cart.

charrier [9] [ʃarje] ◇ *vt* - **1.** to carry - **2.** *fam* [se moquer de] : **~ qqn** to take sb for a ride. ◇ *vi fam* [exagérer] to go too far.

charrue [ʃary] *nf* plough *Br*, plow *Am*.

charte [ʃart] *nf* charter.

charter [ʃartɛr] *nm* chartered plane.

chartreuse [ʃartrøz] *nf* - **1.** RELIG Carthusian monastery - **2.** [liqueur] Chartreuse.

chas [ʃa] *nm* eye (*of needle*).

chasse [ʃas] *nf* - 1. [action] hunting ; ~ à courre hunting (*on horseback with hounds*) - 2. [période] : la ~ est ouverte/fermée it's the open/close season - 3. [domaine] : ~ gardée private hunting ou shooting preserve ; *fig* preserve - 4. [poursuite] chase ; faire la ~ à qqn/qqch *fig* to hunt (for) sb/sthg, to hunt sb/sthg down ; prendre qqn/qqch en ~ to give chase to sb/sthg - 5. [des cabinets] : ~ (d'eau) flush ; tirer la ~ to flush the toilet.

chassé-croisé [ʃasekwaze] *nm* toing and froing.

chasse-neige [ʃasnɛʒ] *nm inv* snowplough *Br*, snowplow *Am*.

chasser [3] [ʃase] *vt* - 1. [animal] to hunt - 2. [faire partir - personne] to drive ou chase away ; [- odeur, souci] to dispel.

chasseur, euse [ʃasœr, øz] *nm, f* hunter.
➤ **chasseur** *nm* - 1. [d'hôtel] page, messenger - 2. MIL : ~ alpin *soldier specially trained for operations in mountainous terrain* - 3. [avion] fighter.

châssis [ʃasi] *nm* - 1. [de fenêtre, de porte, de machine] frame - 2. [de véhicule] chassis.

chaste [ʃast] *adj* chaste.

chasteté [ʃastəte] *nf* chastity.

chasuble [ʃazybl] *nf* chasuble.

chat, chatte [ʃa, ʃat] *nm, f* cat.

châtaigne [ʃatɛɲ] *nf* - 1. [fruit] chestnut - 2. *fam* [coup] clout.

châtaignier [ʃatɛɲe] *nm* [arbre] chestnut (tree) ; [bois] chestnut.

châtain [ʃatɛ̃] *adj & nm* chestnut, chestnut-brown.

château, x [ʃato] *nm* - 1. [forteresse] : ~ (fort) castle - 2. [résidence - seigneuriale] mansion ; [- de monarque, d'évêque] palace ; ~ de sable sandcastle ; les ~x de la Loire the Châteaux of the Loire - 3. [réservoir] : ~ d'eau water tower.

châtiment [ʃatimɑ̃] *nm* punishment.

chaton [ʃatɔ̃] *nm* - 1. [petit chat] kitten - 2. BOT catkin.

chatouiller [3] [ʃatuje] *vt* - 1. [faire des chatouilles à] to tickle - 2. *fig* [titiller] to titillate.

chatoyant, e [ʃatwajɑ̃, ɑ̃t] *adj* [reflet, étoffe] shimmering ; [bijou] sparkling.

châtrer [3] [ʃatre] *vt* to castrate ; [chat] to neuter ; [chatte] to spay.

chatte ➲ chat.

chaud, e [ʃo, ʃod] *adj* - 1. [gén] warm ; [de température très élevée, sensuel] hot - 2. *fig* [enthousiaste] : être ~ pour qqch/pour faire qqch to be keen on sthg/on doing sthg.

➤ **chaud** ◇ *adv* : avoir ~ to be warm ou hot ; il fait ~ it's warm ou hot ; manger ~ to have something hot (to eat). ◇ *nm* heat ; rester au ~ to stay in the warm.

chaudement [ʃodmɑ̃] *adv* warmly.

chaudière [ʃodjɛr] *nf* boiler.

chaudron [ʃodrɔ̃] *nm* cauldron.

chauffage [ʃofaʒ] *nm* [appareil] heating (system) ; ~ central central heating.

chauffant, e [ʃofɑ̃, ɑ̃t] *adj* heating ; plaque ~e hotplate.

chauffard [ʃofar] *nm péj* reckless driver.

chauffe-eau [ʃofo] *nm inv* water-heater.

chauffer [3] [ʃofe] ◇ *vt* [rendre chaud] to heat (up). ◇ *vi* - 1. [devenir chaud] to heat up - 2. [moteur] to overheat - 3. *fam* [barder] : ça va ~ there's going to be trouble.

chauffeur [ʃofœr] *nm* AUTOM driver.

chaume [ʃom] *nm* [paille] thatch.

chaumière [ʃomjɛr] *nf* cottage.

chaussée [ʃose] *nf* road, roadway ; '~ déformée' 'uneven road surface'.

chausse-pied [ʃospje] (*pl* chausse-pieds) *nm* shoehorn.

chausser [3] [ʃose] ◇ *vt* [chaussures, lunettes, skis] to put on. ◇ *vi* : du 39 to take size 39 (shoes). ➤ **se chausser** *vp* to put one's shoes on.

chaussette [ʃosɛt] *nf* sock.

chausson [ʃosɔ̃] *nm* - 1. [pantoufle] slipper - 2. [de danse] ballet shoe - 3. [de bébé] bootee - 4. CULIN turnover ; ~ aux pommes apple turnover.

chaussure [ʃosyr] *nf* - 1. [soulier] shoe ; ~ basse low-heeled shoe, flat shoe ; ~ de marche [de randonnée] hiking ou walking boot ; [confortable] walking shoe ; ~ à scratch shoe with Velcro® fastenings ; ~ de ski ski boot - 2. [industrie] footwear industry.

chauve [ʃov] *adj* [sans cheveux] bald.

chauve-souris [ʃovsuri] *nf* bat.

chauvin, e [ʃovɛ̃, in] *adj* chauvinistic.

chaux [ʃo] *nf* lime ; blanchi à la ~ whitewashed.

chavirer [3] [ʃavire] *vi* - 1. [bateau] to capsize - 2. *fig* [tourner] to spin.

chef [ʃɛf] *nm* - 1. [d'un groupe] head, leader ; [au travail] boss ; en ~ in chief ; ~ d'entreprise company head ; ~ d'État head of state ; ~ de famille head of the family ; ~ de file POLIT (party) leader ; ~ de gare stationmaster ; ~ d'orchestre conductor ; ~ de rayon departmental manager ou supervisor ; ~ de service ADMIN departmental manager - 2. [cuisinier] chef. ➤ **chef d'accusation** *nm* charge, count.

chef-d'œuvre [ʃɛdœvr] (*pl* **chefs-d'œuvre**) *nm* masterpiece.

chef-lieu [ʃɛfljø] *nm* ≃ county town *Br*, county seat *Am*.

cheik [ʃɛk] *nm* sheikh.

chemin [ʃəmɛ̃] *nm* - **1.** [voie] path ; ~ vicinal byroad, minor road - **2.** [parcours] way ; *fig* road ; **en** ~ on the way. ◆ **chemin de fer** *nm* railway *Br*, railroad *Am*.

cheminée [ʃəmine] *nf* - **1.** [foyer] fireplace - **2.** [conduit d'usine] chimney - **3.** [encadrement] mantelpiece - **4.** [de paquebot, locomotive] funnel.

cheminement [ʃəminmɑ̃] *nm* [progression] advance ; *fig* [d'idée] development.

cheminer [3] [ʃəmine] *vi* [avancer] to make one's way ; *fig* [idée] to develop.

cheminot [ʃəmino] *nm* railwayman *Br*, railroad man *Am*.

chemise [ʃəmiz] *nf* - **1.** [d'homme] shirt ; ~ **de nuit** [de femme] nightdress - **2.** [dossier] folder.

chemisette [ʃəmizɛt] *nf* [d'homme] short-sleeved shirt ; [de femme] short-sleeved blouse.

chemisier [ʃəmizje] *nm* [vêtement] blouse.

chenal, aux [ʃənal, o] *nm* [canal] channel.

chêne [ʃɛn] *nm* [arbre] oak (tree) ; [bois] oak.

chenet [ʃənɛ] *nm* firedog.

chenil [ʃənil] *nm* [pour chiens] kennel.

chenille [ʃənij] *nf* - **1.** [insecte] caterpillar - **2.** [courroie] caterpillar track.

chèque [ʃɛk] *nm* cheque *Br*, check *Am* ; **faire un** ~ to write a cheque *Br* ou check *Am* ; **toucher un** ~ to cash a cheque *Br* ou check *Am* ; ~ **(bancaire)** (bank) cheque *Br* ou check *Am* ; ~ **barré** crossed cheque *Br* ou check *Am* ; ~ **postal** post office cheque *Br* ou check *Am* ; ~ **sans provision** bad cheque *Br* ou check *Am* ; ~ **de voyage** traveller's cheque *Br*, traveler's check *Am*.

chèque-cadeau [ʃɛkkado] *nm* gift token.

chèque-repas [ʃɛkrəpa] (*pl* **chèques-repas**), **chèque-restaurant** [ʃɛkrɛstɔrɑ̃] (*pl* **chèques-restaurant**) *nm* luncheon voucher.

chéquier [ʃekje] *nm* chequebook *Br*, checkbook *Am*.

cher, chère [ʃɛr] <> *adj* - **1.** [aimé] : ~ **(à qqn)** dear (to sb) ; **Cher Monsieur** [au début d'une lettre] Dear Sir ; **Chère Madame** [au début d'une lettre] Dear Madam - **2.** [produit, vie, commerçant] expensive. <> *nm, f hum* : **mon** ~ dear. ◆ **cher** *adv* : **valoir** ~, **coûter** ~ to be expensive, to cost a lot ; **payer** ~ to pay a lot ; **je l'ai payé** ~ *litt & fig*

it cost me a lot. ◆ **chère** *nf* : **aimer la bonne chère** *sout* to like to eat well.

chercher [3] [ʃɛrʃe] <> *vt* - **1.** [gén] to look for - **2.** [prendre] : **aller/venir** ~ **qqn** [à un rendez-vous] to (go/come and) meet sb ; [en voiture] to (go/come and) pick sb up ; **aller/venir** ~ **qqch** to (go/come and) get sthg. <> *vi* : **à faire qqch** to try to do sthg.

chercheur, euse [ʃɛrʃœr, øz] *nm, f* [scientifique] researcher.

chéri, e [ʃeri] <> *adj* dear. <> *nm, f* darling.

chérir [32] [ʃerir] *vt* [personne] to love dearly ; [chose, idée] to cherish.

chétif, ive [ʃetif, iv] *adj* [malingre] sickly, weak.

cheval, aux [ʃəval, o] *nm* - **1.** [animal] horse ; **à** ~ on horseback ; **être à** ~ **sur qqch** [être assis] to be sitting astride sthg ; *fig* [sièges] to straddle sthg ; *fig* [tenir à] to be a stickler for sthg ; ~ **d'arçons** horse (*in gymnastics*) - **2.** [équitation] riding, horse-riding ; **faire du** ~ to ride - **3.** AUTOM : ~, ~**-vapeur** horsepower.

chevalerie [ʃəvalri] *nf* - **1.** [qualité] chivalry - **2.** HIST knighthood.

chevalet [ʃəvalɛ] *nm* [de peintre] easel.

chevalier [ʃəvalje] *nm* knight.

chevalière [ʃəvaljɛr] *nf* [bague] signet ring.

chevauchée [ʃəvoʃe] *nf* [course] ride, horse-ride.

chevaucher [3] [ʃəvoʃe] *vt* [être assis] to sit on ou be astride. ◆ **se chevaucher** *vp* to overlap.

chevelu, e [ʃəvly] *adj* hairy.

chevelure [ʃəvlyr] *nf* [cheveux] hair.

chevet [ʃəvɛ] *nm* head (*of bed*) ; **être au** ~ **de qqn** to be at sb's bedside.

cheveu, x [ʃəvø] *nm* [chevelure] hair ; **se faire couper les** ~**x** to have one's hair cut.

cheville [ʃəvij] *nf* - **1.** ANAT ankle - **2.** [pour fixer une vis] Rawlplug®.

chèvre [ʃɛvr] <> *nf* [animal] goat. <> *nm* [fromage] goat's cheese.

chevreau, x [ʃəvro] *nm* kid.

chèvrefeuille [ʃɛvrəfœj] *nm* honeysuckle.

chevreuil [ʃəvrœj] *nm* - **1.** [animal] roe deer - **2.** CULIN venison.

chevronné, e [ʃəvrɔne] *adj* [expérimenté] experienced.

chevrotant, e [ʃəvrɔtɑ̃, ɑ̃t] *adj* tremulous.

chevrotine [ʃəvrɔtin] *nf* buckshot.

chewing-gum [ʃwiŋgɔm] (*pl* **chewing-gums**) *nm* chewing gum *(U)*.

chez [ʃe] *prép* - **1.** [dans la maison de] : **il est ~ lui** he's at home ; **il rentre ~ lui** he's going home ; **être ~ le coiffeur/médecin** to be at the hairdresser's/doctor's ; **aller ~ le coiffeur/médecin** to go to the hairdresser's/doctor's ; **il va venir ~ nous** he is going to come to our place ou house ; **il habite ~ nous** he lives with us - **2.** [en ce qui concerne] : **~ les jeunes** among young people ; **~ les Anglais** in England - **3.** [dans les œuvres de] : **~ Proust** in (the works of) Proust - **4.** [dans le caractère de] : **ce que j'apprécie ~ lui, c'est sa gentillesse** what I like about him is his kindness.

chez-soi [ʃeswa] *nm inv* home, place of one's own.

chic [ʃik] ◇ *adj (inv en genre)* - **1.** [élégant] smart, chic - **2.** *vieilli* [serviable] nice. ◇ *nm* style. ◇ *interj* : **~ (alors)!** great!

chicorée [ʃikɔre] *nf* [salade] endive ; [à café] chicory.

chien [ʃjɛ̃] *nm* - **1.** [animal] dog ; **~ de chasse** [d'arrêt] gundog ; **~ de garde** guard dog - **2.** [d'arme] hammer - **3.** *loc* : **avoir un mal de ~ à faire qqch** to have a lot of trouble doing sthg ; **en ~ de fusil** curled up.

chiendent [ʃjɛ̃dɑ̃] *nm* couch grass.

chien-loup [ʃjɛ̃lu] *nm* Alsatian (dog).

chienne [ʃjɛn] *nf* (female) dog, bitch.

chiffe [ʃif] *nf* : **c'est une ~ molle** he's spineless, he's a weed.

chiffon [ʃifɔ̃] *nm* [linge] rag.

chiffonné, e [ʃifɔne] *adj* [visage, mine] worn.

chiffre [ʃifr] *nm* - **1.** [caractère] figure, number ; **~ arabe/romain** Arabic/Roman numeral - **2.** [montant] sum ; **~ d'affaires** COMM turnover *Br*, net revenue *Am* ; **~ rond** round number ; **~ de ventes** sales figures *(pl)*.

chiffrer [3] [ʃifre] ◇ *vt* - **1.** [évaluer] to calculate, to assess - **2.** [coder] to encode. ◇ *vi fam* to mount up.

chignole [ʃiɲɔl] *nf* drill.

chignon [ʃiɲɔ̃] *nm* bun *(in hair)* ; **se crêper le ~** *fig* to scratch each other's eyes out.

Chili [ʃili] *nm* : **le ~** Chile.

chimère [ʃimɛr] *nf* - **1.** MYTH chimera - **2.** [illusion] illusion, dream.

chimie [ʃimi] *nf* chemistry.

chimiothérapie [ʃimjɔterapi] *nf* chemotherapy.

chimique [ʃimik] *adj* chemical.

chimiste [ʃimist] *nmf* chemist.

chimpanzé [ʃɛ̃pɑ̃ze] *nm* chimpanzee.

Chine [ʃin] *nf* : **la ~** China.

chiné, e [ʃine] *adj* mottled.

chiner [3] [ʃine] *vi* to look for bargains.

chinois, e [ʃinwa, az] *adj* Chinese. ◆ **chinois** *nm* - **1.** [langue] Chinese - **2.** [passoire] conical sieve. ◆ **Chinois, e** *nm, f* Chinese person ; **les Chinois** the Chinese.

chiot [ʃjo] *nm* puppy.

chipie [ʃipi] *nf* vixen *péj*.

chips [ʃips] *nfpl* : **(pommes) ~** (potato) crisps *Br*, (potato) chips *Am*.

chiquenaude [ʃiknod] *nf* flick.

chiquer [3] [ʃike] ◇ *vt* to chew. ◇ *vi* to chew tobacco.

chirurgical, e, aux [ʃiryrʒikal, o] *adj* surgical.

chirurgie [ʃiryrʒi] *nf* surgery.

chirurgien [ʃiryrʒjɛ̃] *nm* surgeon.

chiure [ʃjyr] *nf* : **~ (de mouche)** flyspecks *(pl)*.

chlore [klɔr] *nm* chlorine.

chloroforme [klɔrɔfɔrm] *nm* chloroform.

chlorophylle [klɔrɔfil] *nf* chlorophyll.

choc [ʃɔk] *nm* - **1.** [heurt, coup] impact - **2.** [conflit] clash - **3.** [émotion] shock - **4.** *(en apposition)* : **images-~s** shock pictures ; **prix-~** amazing bargain.

chocolat [ʃɔkɔla] ◇ *nm* chocolate ; **~ au lait/noir** milk/plain chocolate ; **~ à croquer** cooking/eating chocolate. ◇ *adj inv* chocolate (brown).

chœur [kœr] *nm* - **1.** [chorale] choir ; [d'opéra] *fig* chorus ; **en ~** *fig* all together - **2.** [d'église] choir, chancel.

choisi, e [ʃwazi] *adj* selected ; [termes, langage] carefully chosen.

choisir [32] [ʃwazir] ◇ *vt* : **~ (de faire qqch)** to choose (to do sthg). ◇ *vi* to choose.

choix [ʃwa] *nm* - **1.** [gén] choice ; **le livre de ton ~** any book you like ; **au ~** as you prefer ; **avoir le ~** to have the choice - **2.** [qualité] : **de premier ~** grade ou class one ; **articles de second ~** seconds.

choléra [kɔlera] *nm* cholera.

cholestérol [kɔlesterɔl] *nm* cholesterol.

chômage [ʃomaʒ] *nm* unemployment ; **en ~, au ~** unemployed ; **être mis au ~ technique** to be laid off.

chômeur, euse [ʃomœr, øz] *nm, f* : **les ~s** the unemployed.

chope [ʃɔp] *nf* tankard.

choper [3] [ʃɔpe] *vt fam* - **1.** [voler, arrêter] to nick *Br*, to pinch - **2.** [attraper] to catch.

choquant, e [ʃɔkɑ̃, ɑ̃t] *adj* shocking.

choquer [3] [ʃɔke] *vt* - **1.** [scandaliser] to shock - **2.** [traumatiser] to shake (up).

choral, e, als ou **aux** [kɔral, o] *adj* choral.
➡ **chorale** *nf* [groupe] choir.

chorégraphie [kɔregrafi] *nf* choreography.

choriste [kɔrist] *nmf* chorister.

chose [ʃoz] *nf* thing ; **c'est (bien) peu de ~** it's nothing really ; **c'est la moindre des ~s** it's the least I/we can do ; **de deux ~s l'une** (it's got to be) one thing or the other ; **parler de ~s et d'autres** to talk of this and that.

chou, x [ʃu] ◇ *nm* - **1.** [légume] cabbage - **2.** [pâtisserie] choux bun. ◇ *adj inv* sweet, cute.

chouchou, oute [ʃuʃu, ut] *nm, f* favourite ; [élève] teacher's pet.

choucroute [ʃukrut] *nf* sauerkraut.

chouette [ʃwɛt] ◇ *nf* [oiseau] owl. ◇ *adj fam* great. ◇ *interj* : **~ (alors)!** great!

chou-fleur [ʃuflœr] *nm* cauliflower.

choyer [13] [ʃwaje] *vt sout* to pamper.

chrétien, enne [kretjɛ̃, ɛn] *adj & nm, f* Christian.

chrétienté [kretjete] *nf* Christendom.

Christ [krist] *nm* Christ.

christianisme [kristjanism] *nm* Christianity.

chrome [krom] *nm* CHIM chromium.

chromé, e [krome] *adj* chrome-plated ; **acier ~** chrome steel.

chromosome [krɔmɔzom] *nm* chromosome.

chronique [krɔnik] ◇ *nf* - **1.** [annales] chronicle - **2.** PRESSE : **~ sportive** sports section. ◇ *adj* chronic.

chronologie [krɔnɔlɔʒi] *nf* chronology.

chronologique [krɔnɔlɔʒik] *adj* chronological.

chronomètre [krɔnɔmɛtr] *nm* SPORT stopwatch.

chronométrer [18] [krɔnɔmetre] *vt* to time.

chrysalide [krizalid] *nf* chrysalis.

chrysanthème [krizɑtɛm] *nm* chrysanthemum.

chuchotement [ʃyʃɔtmɑ̃] *nm* whisper.

chuchoter [3] [ʃyʃɔte] *vt & vi* to whisper.

chut [ʃyt] *interj* sh!, hush!

chute [ʃyt] *nf* - **1.** [gén] fall ; **~ d'eau** waterfall ; **~ de neige** snowfall ; **la ~ du mur de Berlin** the fall of the Berlin Wall - **2.** [de tissu] scrap.

ci [si] *adv (après n)* : **ce livre-~** this book ; **ces jours-~** these days.

ci-après [siaprɛ] *adv* below.

cible [sibl] *nf litt & fig* target.

cicatrice [sikatris] *nf* scar.

cicatriser [3] [sikatrize] *vt litt & fig* to heal.

ci-contre [sikɔ̃tr] *adv* opposite.

ci-dessous [sidəsu] *adv* below.

ci-dessus [sidəsy] *adv* above.

cidre [sidr] *nm* cider.

ciel (*pl sens 1* **ciels** [sjɛl], *pl sens 2* **cieux** [sjø]) *nm* - **1.** [firmament] sky ; **à ~ ouvert** open-air - **2.** [paradis, providence] heaven.
➡ **cieux** *nmpl* heaven (*sg*).

cierge [sjɛrʒ] *nm* RELIG (votive) candle.

cigale [sigal] *nf* cicada.

cigare [sigar] *nm* cigar.

cigarette [sigarɛt] *nf* cigarette.

ci-gît [siʒi] *adv* here lies.

cigogne [sigɔɲ] *nf* stork.

ci-inclus, e [siɛkly, yz] *adj* enclosed. ➡
ci-inclus *adv* enclosed.

ci-joint, e [siʒwɛ̃, ɛ̃t] *adj* enclosed. ➡
ci-joint *adv* : **veuillez trouver ~ ...** please find enclosed

cil [sil] *nm* ANAT eyelash, lash.

ciller [3] [sije] *vi* to blink (one's eyes).

cime [sim] *nf* [d'arbre, de montagne] top ; *fig* height.

ciment [simɑ̃] *nm* cement.

cimenter [3] [simɑ̃te] *vt* to cement.

cimetière [simtjɛr] *nm* cemetery.

ciné [sine] *nm fam* cinema.

cinéaste [sineast] *nmf* film-maker.

ciné-club [sineklœb] (*pl* **ciné-clubs**) *nm* film club.

cinéma [sinema] *nm* - **1.** [salle, industrie] cinema - **2.** [art] cinema, film ; **un acteur de ~** a film star.

cinémathèque [sinematɛk] *nf* film archive.

cinématographique [sinematɔgrafik] *adj* cinematographic.

cinéphile [sinefil] *nmf* film buff.

cinglé, e [sɛ̃gle] *fam adj* nuts, nutty.

cingler [3] [sɛ̃gle] *vt* to lash.

cinq [sɛ̃k] ◇ *adj num* five. ◇ *nm* five ; *voir aussi* **six**.

cinquantaine [sɛ̃kɑ̃tɛn] *nf* - **1.** [nombre] : **une ~ de** about fifty - **2.** [âge] : **avoir la ~** to be in one's fifties.

cinquante [sɛ̃kɑ̃t] *adj num & nm* fifty ; *voir aussi* **six**.

cinquantième [sɛ̃kɑ̃tjɛm] *adj num, nm* ou *nmf* fiftieth ; *voir aussi* **sixième**.

cinquième [sɛ̃kjɛm] ◇ *adj num, nm* ou

nmf fifth. $\diamondsuit$ *nf* SCOL $\simeq$ second year ou form *Br*, $\simeq$ seventh grade *Am* ; *voir aussi* **sixième**.

cintre [sɛtr] *nm* [pour vêtements] coat hanger.

cintré, e [sɛtre] *adj* COUTURE waisted.

cirage [siraʒ] *nm* [produit] shoe polish.

circoncision [sirkɔ̃sizjɔ̃] *nf* circumcision.

circonférence [sirkɔ̃ferɑ̃s] *nf* - **1.** GÉOM circumference - **2.** [pourtour] boundary.

circonflexe [sirkɔ̃flɛks] $\triangleright$ **accent**.

circonscription [sirkɔ̃skripsjɔ̃] *nf* district.

circonscrire [99] [sirkɔ̃skrir] *vt* - **1.** [incendie, épidémie] to contain - **2.** *fig* [sujet] to define.

circonspect, e [sirkɔ̃spɛ, ɛkt] *adj* cautious.

circonstance [sirkɔ̃stɑ̃s] *nf* - **1.** [occasion] occasion - **2.** *(gén pl)* [contexte, conjoncture] circumstance ; **~s atténuantes** JUR mitigating circumstances.

circonstancié, e [sirkɔ̃stɑ̃sje] *adj* detailed.

circonstanciel, elle [sirkɔ̃stɑ̃sjɛl] *adj* GRAM adverbial.

circuit [sirkɥi] *nm* - **1.** [chemin] route - **2.** [parcours touristique] tour - **3.** SPORT & TECHNOL circuit ; **en ~ fermé** [en boucle] closed-circuit *(avant n)* ; *fig* within a limited circle.

circulaire [sirkylɛr] *nf* & *adj* circular.

circulation [sirkylasjɔ̃] *nf* - **1.** [mouvement] circulation ; **mettre en ~** to circulate ; **~ (du sang)** circulation - **2.** [trafic] traffic.

circuler [3] [sirkyle] *vi* - **1.** [sang, air, argent] to circulate ; **faire ~ qqch** to circulate sthg - **2.** [aller et venir] to move (along) ; **on circule mal en ville** the traffic is bad in town - **3.** [train, bus] to run - **4.** *fig* [rumeur, nouvelle] to spread.

cire [sir] *nf* - **1.** [matière] wax - **2.** [encaustique] polish.

ciré, e [sire] *adj* - **1.** [parquet] polished - **2.** $\triangleright$ **toile**. $\blacklozenge$ **ciré** *nm* oilskin.

cirer [3] [sire] *vt* - **1.** to polish - **2.** *loc fam* : **j'en ai rien à ~** I don't give a damn.

cirque [sirk] *nm* - **1.** [gén] circus - **2.** GÉOL cirque - **3.** *fam fig* [désordre, chahut] chaos *(U)*.

cirrhose [siroz] *nf* cirrhosis *(U)*.

cisaille [sizaj] *nf* shears *(pl)*.

cisailler [3] [sizaje] *vt* [métal] to cut ; [branches] to prune.

ciseau, x [sizo] *nm* chisel. $\blacklozenge$ **ciseaux** *nmpl* scissors.

ciseler [25] [sizle] *vt* - **1.** [pierre, métal] to chisel - **2.** [bijou] to engrave.

Cisjordanie [sizʒɔrdani] *nf* : **la ~** the West Bank.

citadelle [sitadɛl] *nf litt* & *fig* citadel.

citadin, e [sitadɛ̃, in] $\diamondsuit$ *adj* city *(avant n)*, urban. $\diamondsuit$ *nm, f* city dweller.

citation [sitasjɔ̃] *nf* - **1.** JUR summons *(sg)* - **2.** [extrait] quote, quotation.

cité [site] *nf* - **1.** [ville] city - **2.** [lotissement] housing estate *Br* ou project *Am* ; **~ universitaire** halls *(pl)* of residence.

citer [3] [site] *vt* - **1.** [exemple, propos, auteur] to quote - **2.** JUR [convoquer] to summon - **3.** MIL : **être cité à l'ordre du jour** to be mentioned in dispatches.

citerne [sitɛrn] *nf* - **1.** [d'eau] water tank - **2.** [cuve] tank.

cité U [sitey] *nf fam abr de* **cité universitaire**.

citoyen, enne [sitwajɛ̃, ɛn] *nm, f* citizen.

citoyenneté [sitwajɛnte] *nf* citizenship.

citron [sitrɔ̃] *nm* lemon ; **~ pressé** fresh lemon juice ; **~ vert** lime.

citronnade [sitrɔnad] *nf* (still) lemonade.

citronnier [sitrɔnje] *nm* lemon tree.

citrouille [sitruj] *nf* pumpkin.

civet [sivɛ] *nm* stew ; **~ de lièvre** jugged hare.

civière [sivjɛr] *nf* stretcher.

civil, e [sivil] $\diamondsuit$ *adj* - **1.** [gén] civil - **2.** [non militaire] civilian. $\diamondsuit$ *nm, f* civilian ; **dans le ~** in civilian life ; **policier en ~** plain-clothes policeman *(f* policewoman) ; **soldat en ~** soldier in civilian clothes.

civilement [sivilmɑ̃] *adv* : **se marier ~** to get married at a registry office.

civilisation [sivilizasjɔ̃] *nf* civilization.

civilisé, e [sivilize] *adj* civilized.

civiliser [3] [sivilize] *vt* to civilize.

civique [sivik] *adj* civic ; **instruction ~** civics *(U)*.

civisme [sivism] *nm* sense of civic responsibility.

cl *(abr de* **centilitre***)* cl.

clair, e [klɛr] *adj* - **1.** [gén] clear ; **c'est ~ et net** there's no two ways about it - **2.** [lumineux] bright - **3.** [pâle - couleur, teint] light ; [- tissu, cheveux] light-coloured *Br*, light-colored *Am*. $\blacklozenge$ **clair** $\diamondsuit$ *adv* : **voir ~ (dans qqch)** *fig* to have a clear understanding (of sthg). $\diamondsuit$ *nm* : **mettre** ou **tirer qqch au ~** to shed light upon sthg. $\blacklozenge$ **clair de lune** *(pl* **clairs de lune***) nm* moonlight *(U)*. $\blacklozenge$ **en clair** *loc adv* TÉLÉ unscrambled *(esp of a private TV channel)*.

clairement [klɛrmɑ̃] *adv* clearly.

claire-voie [klɛrvwa] ➭ **à claire-voie** *loc adv* openwork *(avant n)*.

clairière [klɛrjɛr] *nf* clearing.

clairon [klɛrɔ̃] *nm* bugle.

claironner [3] [klɛrɔne] *vt fig* [crier] : **~ qqch** to shout sthg from the rooftops.

clairsemé, e [klɛrsəme] *adj* [cheveux] thin ; [arbres] scattered ; [population] sparse.

clairvoyant, e [klɛrvwajɑ̃, ɑ̃t] *adj* perceptive.

clamer [3] [klame] *vt* to proclaim.

clameur [klamœr] *nf* clamour *Br*, clamor *Am*.

clan [klɑ̃] *nm* clan.

clandestin, e [klɑ̃dɛstɛ̃, in] ➭ *adj* [journal, commerce] clandestine ; [activité] covert. ➭ *nm, f* [étranger] illegal immigrant ou alien ; [voyageur] stowaway.

clapier [klapje] *nm* [à lapins] hutch.

clapoter [3] [klapɔte] *vi* [vagues] to lap.

claquage [klakaʒ] *nm* MÉD strain ; **se faire un ~** to pull ou to strain a muscle.

claque [klak] *nf* **- 1.** [gifle] slap **- 2.** THÉÂTRE claque.

claquer [3] [klake] ➭ *vt* **- 1.** [fermer] to slam **- 2.** : **faire ~** [langue] to click ; [doigts] to snap ; [fouet] to crack **- 3.** *fam* [gifler] to slap **- 4.** *fam* [dépenser] to blow. ➭ *vi* [porte, volet] to bang.

claquettes [klakɛt] *nfpl* [danse] tap dancing *(U)*.

clarifier [9] [klarifje] *vt litt & fig* to clarify.

clarinette [klarinɛt] *nf* [instrument] clarinet

clarté [klarte] *nf* **- 1.** [lumière] brightness **- 2.** [netteté] clarity.

classe [klɑs] *nf* **1.** [gén] class ; **~ touriste** economy class **- 2.** SCOL : **aller en ~** to go to school ; **~ de neige** skiing trip *(with school)* ; **~ verte** field trip *(with school)* **- 3.** MIL rank **- 4.** *loc* : **faire ses ~s** MIL to do one's training.

classé, e [klase] *adj* [monument] listed.

classement [klasmɑ̃] *nm* **- 1.** [rangement] filing **- 2.** [classification] classification **- 3.** [rang SCOL] position ; [- SPORT] placing **- 4.** [liste - SCOL] class list ; [- SPORT] final placings *(pl)*.

classer [3] [klase] *vt* **- 1.** [ranger] to file **- 2.** [plantes, animaux] to classify **- 3.** [cataloguer] : **~ qqn (parmi)** to label sb (as) **- 4.** [attribuer un rang à] to rank. ➭ **se classer** *vp* to be classed, to rank ; **se ~ troisième** to come third.

classeur [klasœr] *nm* **- 1.** [meuble] filing cabinet **- 2.** [d'écolier] ring binder.

classification [klasifikasjɔ̃] *nf* classification.

classique [klasik] ➭ *nm* **- 1.** [auteur] classical author **- 2.** [œuvre] classic. ➭ *adj* **- 1.** ART & MUS classical **- 2.** [sobre] classic **- 3.** [habituel] classic ; **ça, c'est l'histoire ~!** it's the usual story!

clause [kloz] *nf* clause.

claustrophobie [klostrɔfɔbi] *nf* claustrophobia.

clavecin [klavsɛ̃] *nm* harpsichord.

clavicule [klavikyl] *nf* collarbone.

clavier [klavje] *nm* keyboard.

clé, clef [kle] ➭ *nf* **- 1.** [gén] key ; **la ~ du mystère** the key to the mystery ; **mettre qqn/qqch sous ~** to lock sb/sthg up ; **~ de contact** AUTOM ignition key **- 2.** [outil] : **~ anglaise** ou **à molette** adjustable spanner *Br* ou wrench *Am*, monkey wrench **- 3.** MUS [signe] clef ; **~ de sol/fa** treble/bass clef. ➭ *adj* : **industrie/rôle ~** key industry/role. ➭ **clé de voûte** *nf litt & fig* keystone.

clément, e [klemɑ̃, ɑ̃t] *adj* **- 1.** [indulgent] lenient **- 2.** *fig* [température] mild.

clémentine [klemɑ̃tin] *nf* clementine.

cleptomane = kleptomane.

clerc [klɛr] *nm* [assistant] clerk.

clergé [klɛrʒe] *nm* clergy.

Clic-Clac® [klikklak] *nm* pull-out sofa bed.

cliché [kliʃe] *nm* **- 1.** PHOT negative **- 2.** [banalité] cliché.

client, e [klijɑ̃, ɑ̃t] *nm, f* **- 1.** [de notaire, d'agence] client ; [de médecin] patient **- 2.** [acheteur] customer **- 3.** [habitué] regular (customer).

clientèle [klijɑ̃tɛl] *nf* **- 1.** [ensemble des clients] customers *(pl)* ; [de profession libérale] clientele **- 2.** [fait d'être client] custom : **accorder sa ~ à** to give one's custom to.

cligner [3] [kliɲe] *vi* : **~ de l'œil** to wink ; **~ des yeux** to blink.

clignotant, e [kliɲɔtɑ̃, ɑ̃t] *adj* [lumière] flickering. ➭ **clignotant** *nm* AUTOM indicator.

clignoter [3] [kliɲɔte] *vi* **- 1.** [yeux] to blink **- 2.** [lumière] to flicker.

climat [klima] *nm litt & fig* climate.

climatisation [klimatizasjɔ̃] *nf* air-conditioning.

climatisé, e [klimatize] *adj* air-conditioned.

clin [klɛ̃] ➭ **clin d'œil** *nm* : **faire un ~ d'œil (à)** to wink (at) ; **en un ~ d'œil** in a flash.

clinique [klinik] ➭ *nf* clinic. ➭ *adj* clinical.

clip [klip] *nm* - **1.** [vidéo] pop video - **2.** [boucle d'oreilles] clip-on earring.

cliquer [3] [klike] *vi* INFORM to click.

cliqueter [27] [klikte] *vi* - **1.** [pièces, clés, chaînes] to jingle, to jangle - **2.** [verres] to clink.

clivage [kliva3] *nm fig* [division] division.

clochard, e [kloʃar, ard] *nm, f* tramp.

cloche [kloʃ] ◇ *nf* - **1.** [d'église] bell - **2.** *fam* [idiot] idiot, clot *Br.* ◇ *adj fam* : **ce qu'elle peut être ~, celle-là!** she can be a right idiot!

cloche-pied [kloʃpje] ➧ **à cloche-pied** *loc adv* hopping ; **sauter à ~** to hop.

clocher [kloʃe] *nm* [d'église] church tower.

clochette [kloʃɛt] *nf* - **1.** [petite cloche] (little) bell - **2.** [de fleur] bell.

clodo [klodo] *nmf fam* tramp.

cloison [klwazɔ̃] *nf* [mur] partition.

cloisonner [3] [klwazɔne] *vt* [pièce, maison] to partition (off) ; *fig* to compartmentalize.

cloître [klwatr] *nm* cloister.

clopiner [3] [klɔpine] *vi* to hobble along.

cloporte [klɔpɔrt] *nm* woodlouse.

cloque [klɔk] *nf* blister.

clore [113] [klɔr] *vt* to close ; [négociations] to conclude.

clos, e [klo, kloz] ◇ *pp* ➩ **clore.** ◇ *adj* closed.

clôture [klotyr] *nf* - **1.** [haie] hedge ; [de fil de fer] fence - **2.** [fermeture] closing, closure - **3.** [fin] end, conclusion.

clôturer [3] [klotyre] *vt* - **1.** [terrain] to enclose - **2.** [négociation] to close, to conclude.

clou [klu] *nm* - **1.** [pointe] nail ; **~ de girofle** CULIN clove - **2.** [attraction] highlight.

clouer [3] [klue] *vt* [fixer - couvercle, planche] to nail (down) ; [- tableau, caisse] to nail (up) ; *fig* [immobiliser] : **rester cloué sur place** to be rooted to the spot.

clouté, e [klute] *adj* [vêtement] studded.

clown [klun] *nm* clown ; **faire le ~** to clown around, to act the fool.

club [klœb] *nm* club.

cm (*abr de* **centimètre**) cm.

CM *nm* (*abr de* **cours moyen**) : **~1** *fourth year of primary school* ; **~2** *fifth year of primary school.*

CNAM [knam] (*abr de* **Conservatoire national des arts et métiers**) *nm science and technology school in Paris.*

CNRS (*abr de* **Centre national de la recherche scientifique**) *nm national scientific research organization.*

coaguler [3] [kɔagyle] *vi* - **1.** [sang] to clot - **2.** [lait] to curdle.

coalition [kɔalisjɔ̃] *nf* coalition.

coasser [3] [kɔase] *vi* [grenouille] to croak.

cobaye [kɔbaj] *nm litt & fig* guinea pig.

cobra [kɔbra] *nm* cobra.

Coca® [kɔka] *nm* [boisson] Coke®.

cocaïne [kɔkain] *nf* cocaine.

cocaïnomane [kokainɔman] *nmf* cocaine addict.

cocarde [kɔkard] *nf* - **1.** [insigne] roundel - **2.** [distinction] rosette.

cocardier, ère [kɔkardje, ɛr] *adj* [chauvin] jingoistic.

cocasse [kɔkas] *adj* funny.

coccinelle [kɔksinɛl] *nf* - **1.** [insecte] ladybird *Br*, ladybug *Am* - **2.** [voiture] Beetle.

coccyx [kɔksis] *nm* coccyx.

cocher¹ [kɔʃe] *nm* coachman.

cocher² [3] [kɔʃe] *vt* to tick (off) *Br*, to check (off) *Am*.

cochon, onne [kɔʃɔ̃, ɔn] ◇ *adj* dirty, smutty. ◇ *nm, f fam péj* pig ; **un tour de ~** a dirty trick. ➧ **cochon** *nm* pig.

cochonnerie [kɔʃɔnri] *nf fam* - **1.** [nourriture] muck (*U*) - **2.** [chose] rubbish (*U*) - **3.** [saleté] mess (*U*) - **4.** [obscénité] dirty joke, smut (*U*).

cochonnet [kɔʃɔnɛ] *nm* JEU jack.

cocktail [kɔktɛl] *nm* - **1.** [réception] cocktail party - **2.** [boisson] cocktail - **3.** *fig* [mélange] mixture.

coco [kɔko] *nm* - **1.** ➩ **noix** - **2.** *péj* [communiste] commie.

cocon [kɔkɔ̃] *nm* ZOOL & *fig* cocoon.

cocorico [kɔkɔriko] *nm* [du coq] cock-a-doodle-doo.

cocotier [kɔkɔtje] *nm* coconut tree.

cocotte [kɔkɔt] *nf* - **1.** [marmite] casserole (dish) - **2.** [poule] hen - **3.** *péj* [courtisane] tart.

Cocotte-Minute® [kɔkɔtminyt] *nf* pressure cooker.

cocu, e [kɔky] *nm, f & adj fam* cuckold.

code [kɔd] *nm* - **1.** [gén] code ; **~ barres** bar code ; **~ pénal** penal code ; **~ postal** postcode *Br*, zip code *Am* ; **~ de la route** highway code ; **~ secret** [pour carte de crédit] PIN number - **2.** [phares] dipped headlights (*pl*).

coder [3] [kɔde] *vt* to code.

coefficient [kɔefisjɑ̃] *nm* coefficient.

coéquipier, ère [kɔekipje, ɛr] *nm, f* teammate.

cœur [kœr] *nm* heart ; **au ~ de l'hiver** in the depths of winter ; **au ~ de l'été** at the height of summer ; **au ~ du conflit** at the height of the conflict ; **de bon ~** willingly ; **de tout son ~** with all one's heart ; **apprendre par ~** to learn by heart ; **avoir bon ~** to be kind-hearted ; **avoir mal au ~** to feel sick ; **s'en donner à ~ joie** [prendre beaucoup de plaisir] to have a whale of a time ; **manquer de ~, ne pas avoir de ~** to be heartless ; **soulever le ~ à qqn** to make sb feel sick.

coexister [3] [kɔɛgziste] *vi* to coexist.

coffre [kɔfr] *nm* - **1.** [meuble] chest - **2.** [de voiture] boot *Br*, trunk *Am* - **3.** [coffre-fort] safe.

coffre-fort [kɔfrəfɔr] *nm* safe.

coffret [kɔfrɛ] *nm* - **1.** [petit coffre] casket ; **~ à bijoux** jewellery *Br* ou jewelry *Am* box - **2.** [de disques] boxed set.

cogner [3] [kɔɲe] *vi* - **1.** [heurter] to bang - **2.** *fam* [donner des coups] to hit - **3.** [soleil] to beat down. ◆ **se cogner** *vp* [se heurter] to bump o.s. ; **se ~ à** ou **contre qqch** to bump into sthg ; **se ~ la tête/le genou** to hit one's head/knee.

cohabiter [3] [kɔabite] *vi* - **1.** [habiter ensemble] to live together - **2.** POLIT to cohabit.

cohérence [kɔerɑ̃s] *nf* consistency, coherence.

cohérent, e [kɔerɑ̃, ɑ̃t] *adj* - **1.** [logique] consistent, coherent - **2.** [unifié] coherent.

cohésion [kɔezjɔ̃] *nf* cohesion.

cohorte [kɔɔrt] *nf* [groupe] troop.

cohue [kɔy] *nf* - **1.** [foule] crowd - **2.** [bousculade] crush.

coi, coite [kwa, kwat] *adj* : **rester ~** *sout* to remain silent.

coiffe [kwaf] *nf* headdress.

coiffé, e [kwafe] *adj* : **être bien/mal ~** to have tidy/untidy hair ; **être ~ d'une casquette** to be wearing a cap.

coiffer [3] [kwafe] *vt* - **1.** [mettre sur la tête] : **~ qqn de qqch** to put sthg on sb's head - **2.** [les cheveux] : **~ qqn** to do sb's hair. ◆ **se coiffer** *vp* - **1.** [les cheveux] to do one's hair - **2.** [mettre sur sa tête] : **se ~ de** to wear, to put on.

coiffeur, euse [kwafœr, øz] *nm, f* hairdresser. ◆ **coiffeuse** *nf* [meuble] dressing table.

coiffure [kwafyr] *nf* - **1.** [chapeau] hat - **2.** [cheveux] hairstyle.

coin [kwɛ̃] *nm* - **1.** [angle] corner ; **au ~ du feu** by the fireside - **2.** [parcelle, endroit] place, spot ; **dans le ~** in the area ; **un ~ de ciel bleu** a patch of blue sky ; **~ cuisine** kitchen area ; **le petit ~** *fam* the little boys'/girls' room - **3.** [outil] wedge.

coincer [16] [kwɛ̃se] *vt* - **1.** [bloquer] to jam - **2.** *fam* [prendre] to nab ; *fig* to catch out - **3.** [acculer] to corner, to trap.

coïncidence [kɔɛ̃sidɑ̃s] *nf* coincidence.

coïncider [3] [kɔɛ̃side] *vi* to coincide.

coing [kwɛ̃] *nm* [fruit] quince.

coït [kɔit] *nm* coitus.

col [kɔl] *nm* - **1.** [de vêtement] collar ; **~ roulé** polo neck *Br*, turtleneck *Am* - **2.** [partie étroite] neck - **3.** ANAT : **~ du fémur** neck of the thighbone ou femur ; **~ de l'utérus** cervix, neck of the womb - **4.** GÉOGR pass.

coléoptère [kɔleɔptɛr] *nm* beetle.

colère [kɔlɛr] *nf* - **1.** [irritation] anger ; **être/se mettre en ~** to be/get angry ; **accès d'humeur** fit of anger ou rage ; **piquer une ~** to fly into a rage.

coléreux, euse [kɔlerø, øz], **colérique** [kɔlerik] *adj* - **1.** [tempérament] fiery ; [personne] quick-tempered.

colimaçon [kɔlimasɔ̃] ◆ **en colimaçon** *loc adv* spiral.

colique [kɔlik] *nf* - **1.** (*gén pl*) [douleur] colic (*U*) - **2.** [diarrhée] diarrhoea.

colis [kɔli] *nm* parcel.

collaborateur, trice [kɔlaboratœr, tris] *nm, f* - **1.** [employé] colleague - **2.** HIST collaborator.

collaboration [kɔlaborasjɔ̃] *nf* collaboration.

collaborer [3] [kɔlabɔre] *vi* - **1.** [coopérer, sous l'Occupation] to collaborate - **2.** [participer] : **~ à** to contribute to.

collant, e [kɔlɑ̃, ɑ̃t] *adj* - **1.** [substance] sticky - **2.** *fam* [personne] clinging, cloying. ◆ **collant** *nm* tights (*pl*) *Br*, panty hose (*pl*) *Am*

colle [kɔl] *nf* - **1.** [substance] glue - **2.** [question] poser - **3.** [SCOL - interrogation] test ; [- retenue] detention.

collecte [kɔlɛkt] *nf* collection.

collectif, ive [kɔlɛktif, iv] *adj* - **1.** [responsabilité, travail] collective - **2.** [billet, voyage] group (*avant n*). ◆ **collectif** *nm* - **1.** [équipe] team - **2.** LING collective noun - **3.** FIN : **~ budgétaire** collection of budgetary measures.

collection [kɔlɛksjɔ̃] *nf* - **1.** [d'objets, de livres, de vêtements] collection ; **faire la ~ de** to collect - **2.** COMM line.

collectionner [3] [kɔlɛksjɔne] *vt litt & fig* to collect.

collectionneur, euse [kɔlɛksjɔnœr, øz] *nm, f* collector.

collectivité [kɔlɛktivite] *nf* community ; **les ~s locales** ADMIN the local communities.

collège [kɔlɛʒ] *nm* - **1.** SCOL ≃ secondary school - **2.** [de personnes] college.

collégien, enne [kɔleʒjɛ̃, ɛn] *nm, f* schoolboy (*f* schoolgirl).

collègue [kɔlɛg] *nmf* colleague.

coller [3] [kɔle] ◇ *vt* - **1.** [fixer - affiche] to stick (up) ; [- timbre] to stick - **2.** [appuyer] to press - **3.** INFORM to paste - **4.** *fam* [mettre] to stick, to dump - **5.** SCOL to give (a) detention to, to keep behind. ◇ *vi* - **1.** [adhérer] to stick - **2.** [être adapté] : **~ à qqch** [vêtement] to cling to sthg, *fig* to fit in with sthg, to adhere to sthg. ◆ **se coller** *vp* [se plaquer] : **se ~ contre qqn/qqch** to press o.s. against sb/sthg.

collerette [kɔlrɛt] *nf* [de vêtement] ruff.

collet [kɔlɛ] *nm* - **1.** [de vêtement] collar ; **être ~ monté** [affecté, guindé] to be strait-laced - **2.** [piège] snare.

collier [kɔlje] *nm* - **1.** [bijou] necklace - **2.** [d'animal] collar - **3.** [barbe] *fringe of beard along the jawline.*

colline [kɔlin] *nf* hill.

collision [kɔlizjɔ̃] *nf* [choc] collision, crash ; **entrer en ~ avec** to collide with.

colloque [kɔlɔk] *nm* colloquium.

colmater [3] [kɔlmate] *vt* - **1.** [fuite] to plug, to seal off - **2.** [brèche] to fill, to seal.

colo [kɔlo] *nf fam* children's holiday camp *Br*, summer camp *Am*.

colombe [kɔlɔ̃b] *nf* dove.

Colombie [kɔlɔ̃bi] *nf* : **la ~** Colombia.

colon [kɔlɔ̃] *nm* settler.

côlon [kolɔ̃] *nm* colon.

colonel [kɔlɔnɛl] *nm* colonel.

colonial, e, aux [kɔlɔnjal, o] *adj* colonial.

colonialisme [kɔlɔnjalism] *nm* colonialism.

colonie [kɔlɔni] *nf* - **1.** [territoire] colony - **2.** [d'expatriés] community ; **~ de vacances** holiday *Br* ou summer camp *Am*.

colonisation [kɔlɔnizasjɔ̃] *nf* colonization.

coloniser [3] [kɔlɔnize] *vt litt & fig* to colonize.

colonne [kɔlɔn] *nf* column. ◆ **colonne vertébrale** *nf* spine, spinal column.

colorant, e [kɔlɔrɑ̃, ɑ̃t] *adj* colouring *Br*, coloring *Am*. ◆ **colorant** *nm* colouring *Br*, coloring *Am*.

colorer [3] [kɔlɔre] *vt* [teindre] to colour *Br*, to color *Am*.

colorier [9] [kɔlɔrje] *vt* to colour in *Br*, to color in *Am*.

coloris [kɔlɔri] *nm* shade.

colorisation [kɔlɔrizasjɔ̃] *nf* CIN colourization *Br*, colorization *Am*.

coloriser [3] [kɔlɔrize] *vt* CIN to colourize *Br*, to colorize *Am*.

colossal, e, aux [kɔlɔsal, o] *adj* colossal, huge.

colporter [3] [kɔlpɔrte] *vt* [marchandise] to hawk ; [information] to spread.

coma [kɔma] *nm* coma ; **être dans le ~** to be in a coma.

comateux, euse [kɔmatø, øz] *adj* comatose.

combat [kɔ̃ba] *nm* - **1.** [bataille] battle, fight - **2.** *fig* [lutte] struggle - **3.** SPORT fight.

combatif, ive [kɔ̃batif, iv] *adj* [humeur] fighting *(avant n)* ; [troupes] willing to fight.

combattant, e [kɔ̃batɑ̃, ɑ̃t] *nm, f* [en guerre] combatant ; [dans bagarre] fighter ; **ancien ~** veteran.

combattre [83] [kɔ̃batr] ◇ *vt litt & fig* to fight (against). ◇ *vi* to fight.

combattu, e [kɔ̃baty] *pp* ▷ **combattre**.

combien [kɔ̃bjɛ̃] ◇ *conj* how much ; **~ de** [nombre] how many ; [quantité] how much ; **~ de temps?** how long? ; **ça fait ~?** [prix] how much is that? ; [longueur, hauteur etc] how long/high *etc* is it? ◇ *adv* how (much). ◇ *nm inv* : **le ~ sommes-nous?** what date is it? ; **tous les ~?** how often?

combinaison [kɔ̃binɛzɔ̃] *nf* - **1.** [d'éléments] combination - **2.** [de femme] slip - **3.** [vêtement - de mécanicien] boiler suit *Br*, overalls *(pl) Br*, overall *Am* ; [- de ski] ski suit - **4.** [de coffre] combination.

combine [kɔ̃bin] *nf fam* trick.

combiné [kɔ̃bine] *nm* receiver.

combiner [3] [kɔ̃bine] *vt* - **1.** [arranger] to combine - **2.** [organiser] to devise. ◆ **se combiner** *vp* to turn out.

comble [kɔ̃bl] ◇ *nm* height ; **c'est un ou le ~!** that beats everything! ◇ *adj* packed. ◆ **combles** *nmpl* attic *(sg)*, loft *(sg)*.

combler [3] [kɔ̃ble] *vt* - **1.** [gâter] : **~ qqn de** to shower sb with - **2.** [boucher] to fill in - **3.** [déficit] to make good ; [lacune] to fill.

combustible [kɔ̃bystibl] ◇ *nm* fuel. ◇ *adj* combustible.

combustion [kɔ̃bystjɔ̃] *nf* combustion.

comédie [kɔmedi] *nf* - **1.** CIN & THÉÂTRE comedy ; **~ musicale** musical - **2.** [complication] palaver.

comédien, enne [kɔmedjɛ̃, ɛn] *nm, f* [acteur] actor (*f* actress) ; *fig* & *péj* sham.

comestible [kɔmɛstibl] *adj* edible.

comète [kɔmɛt] *nf* comet.

comique [kɔmik] ◇ *nm* THÉÂTRE comic

actor. ⬦ *adj* - **1.** [style] comic - **2.** [drôle] comical, funny.

comité [kɔmite] *nm* committee ; ~ **d'entreprise** works council *(also organizing leisure activities)*.

commandant [kɔmɑ̃dɑ̃] *nm* commander.

commande [kɔmɑ̃d] *nf* - **1.** [de marchandises] order ; **passer une** ~ to place an order ; **sur** ~ to order ; **disponible sur** ~ available on request - **2.** TECHNOL control - **3.** INFORM command ; ~ **numérique** digital control.

commander [3] [kɔmɑ̃de] ⬦ *vt* - **1.** MIL to command - **2.** [contrôler] to operate, to control - **3.** COMM to order. ⬦ *vi* to be in charge ; ~ **à qqn de faire qqch** to order sb to do sthg.

commanditer [3] [kɔmɑ̃dite] *vt* - **1.** [entreprise] to finance - **2.** [meurtre] to put up the money for.

commando [kɔmɑ̃do] *nm* commando (unit).

comme [kɔm] ⬦ *conj* - **1.** [introduisant une comparaison] like ; **il sera médecin** ~ **son père** he'll become a doctor (just) like his father - **2.** [exprimant la manière] as ; **fais** ~ **il te plaira** do as you wish , ~ **prévu/convenu** as planned/agreed ; ~ **bon vous semble** as you think best ; ~ **ci** ~ **ça** *fam* so-so - **3.** [tel que] like, such as ; **les arbres** ~ **le marronnier** trees such as ou like the chestnut - **4.** [en tant que] as - **5.** [ainsi que] : **les filles** ~ **les garçons iront jouer au foot** both girls and boys will play football ; **l'un** ~ **l'autre sont très gentils** the one is as kind as the other, they are equally kind - **6.** [introduisant une cause] as, since ; ~ **il pleuvait nous sommes rentrés** as it was raining we went back. ⬦ *adv* [marquant l'intensité] how ; ~ **tu as grandi!** how you've grown! ; ~ **c'est difficile!** it's so difficult! ; **regarde** ~ **il nage bien!** (just) look what a good swimmer he is!, (just) look how well he swims!

commémoration [kɔmemɔrasjɔ̃] *nf* commemoration.

commémorer [3] [kɔmemɔre] *vt* to commemorate.

commencement [kɔmɑ̃smɑ̃] *nm* beginning, start.

commencer [16] [kɔmɑ̃se] ⬦ *vt* [entreprendre] to begin, to start ; [être au début de] to begin. ⬦ *vi* to start, to begin ; ~ **à faire qqch** to begin ou start to do sthg, to begin ou start doing sthg ; ~ **par faire qqch** to begin ou start by doing sthg.

comment [kɔmɑ̃] ⬦ *adv* how ; **comment? what?** ; ~ **ça va?** how are you? ; ~ **cela?** how come? ⬦ *nm inv* ⬦ **pourquoi**.

commentaire [kɔmɑ̃tɛr] *nm* - **1.** [explication] commentary - **2.** [observation] comment.

commentateur, trice [kɔmɑ̃tatœr, tris] *nm, f* RADIO & TÉLÉ commentator.

commenter [3] [kɔmɑ̃te] *vt* to comment on.

commérage [kɔmeraʒ] *nm péj* gossip (U).

commerçant, e [kɔmɛrsɑ̃, ɑ̃t] ⬦ *adj* [rue] shopping *(avant n)* ; [quartier] commercial ; [personne] business-minded. ⬦ *nm, f* shopkeeper.

commerce [kɔmɛrs] *nm* - **1.** [achat et vente] commerce, trade ; ~ **de gros/détail** wholesale/retail trade ; ~ **électronique** electronic commerce, e-commerce ; ~ **extérieur** foreign trade - **2.** [magasin] business ; **le petit** ~ small shopkeepers *(pl)*.

commercial, e, aux [kɔmɛrsjal, o] ⬦ *adj* [entreprise, valeur] commercial ; [politique] trade *(avant n)*. ⬦ *nm, f* marketing man *(f* woman).

commercialiser [3] [kɔmɛrsjalize] *vt* to market.

commère [kɔmɛr] *nf péj* gossip.

commettre [84] [kɔmetr] *vt* to commit.

commis, e [kɔmi, iz] *pp* ⬦ **commettre**.
⬦ **commis** *nm* assistant ; ~ **voyageur** commercial traveller *Br* ou traveler *Am*.

commisération [kɔmizerasjɔ̃] *nf sout* commiseration.

commissaire [kɔmisɛr] *nm* commissioner ; ~ **de police** (police) superintendent *Br*, (police) captain *Am*.

commissaire-priseur [kɔmisɛrprizœr] *nm* auctioneer.

commissariat [kɔmisarja] *nm* ; ~ **de police** police station.

commission [kɔmisjɔ̃] *nf* - **1.** [délégation] commission, committee - **2.** [message] message - **3.** [rémunération] commission.
⬦ **commissions** *nfpl* shopping (U) ; **faire les** ~**s** to do the shopping.

commissure [kɔmisyr] *nf* : **la** ~ **des lèvres** the corner of the mouth.

commode [kɔmɔd] ⬦ *nf* chest of drawers. ⬦ *adj* - **1.** [pratique - système] convenient ; [- outil] handy - **2.** [aimable] : **pas** ~ awkward.

commodité [kɔmɔdite] *nf* convenience.

commotion [kɔmosjɔ̃] *nf* MÉD shock ; ~ **cérébrale** concussion.

commun, e [kɔmœ̃, yn] *adj* - **1.** [gén] common ; [décision, effort] joint ; [salle, jardin] shared ; **avoir qqch en** ~ to have sthg in common ; **faire qqch en** ~ to do sthg together - **2.** [courant] usual, common. ◆ **commune** *nf* town.

communal, e, aux [kɔmynal, o] *adj* [école] local ; [bâtiments] council *(avant n)*.

communauté [kɔmynote] *nf* - **1.** [groupe] community - **2.** [de sentiments, d'idées] identity - **3.** POL : **la Communauté européenne** the European Community.

commune ⊳ **commun.**

communément [kɔmynemɑ̃] *adv* commonly.

communiant, e [kɔmynjɑ̃, ɑ̃t] *nm, f* communicant ; **premier ~** *child taking first communion.*

communication [kɔmynikasjɔ̃] *nf* - **1.** [gén] communication - **2.** TÉLÉCOM : **~ (téléphonique)** (phone) call ; **être en ~ avec qqn** to be talking to sb ; **obtenir la ~** to get through ; **recevoir/prendre une ~** to receive/take a (phone) call ; **~ interurbaine** long-distance (phone) call.

communier [9] [kɔmynje] *vi* RELIG to take communion.

communion [kɔmynjɔ̃] *nf* RELIG communion.

communiqué [kɔmynike] *nm* communiqué ; **~ de presse** press release.

communiquer [3] [kɔmynike] *vt* : **~ qqch à** [information, sentiment] to pass on ou communicate sthg to ; [chaleur] to transmit sthg to.

communisme [kɔmynism] *nm* communism.

communiste [kɔmynist] *nmf & adj* communist.

commutateur [kɔmytatœr] *nm* switch.

compact, e [kɔ̃pakt] *adj* - **1.** [épais, dense] dense - **2.** [petit] compact. ◆ **compact** *nm* [disque laser] compact disc, CD.

compagne ⊳ **compagnon.**

compagnie [kɔ̃paɲi] *nf* - **1.** [gén & COMM] company ; **tenir ~ à qqn** to keep sb company ; **en ~ de** in the company of - **2.** [assemblée] gathering.

compagnon [kɔ̃paɲɔ̃], **compagne** [kɔ̃paɲ] *nm, f* companion. ◆ **compagnon** *nm* HIST journeyman.

comparable [kɔ̃parabl] *adj* comparable.

comparaison [kɔ̃parɛzɔ̃] *nf* [parallèle] comparison ; **en ~ de, par ~ avec** compared with, in ou by comparison with.

comparaître [91] [kɔ̃parɛtr] *vi* JUR : **~ (devant)** to appear (before).

comparatif, ive [kɔ̃paratif, iv] *adj* comparative.

comparé, e [kɔ̃pare] *adj* comparative ; [mérites] relative.

comparer [3] [kɔ̃pare] *vt* - **1.** [confronter] : **~ (avec)** to compare (with) - **2.** [assimiler] : **~ qqch à** to compare ou liken sthg to.

comparse [kɔ̃pars] *nmf péj* stooge.

compartiment [kɔ̃partimɑ̃] *nm* compartment.

comparu, e [kɔ̃pary] *pp* ⊳ **comparaître.**

comparution [kɔ̃parysjɔ̃] *nf* JUR appearance.

compas [kɔ̃pa] *nm* - **1.** [de dessin] pair of compasses, compasses *(pl)* - **2.** NAVIG compass.

compassion [kɔ̃pasjɔ̃] *nf sout* compassion.

compatible [kɔ̃patibl] *adj* : **~ (avec)** compatible (with).

compatir [32] [kɔ̃patir] *vi* : **~ (à)** to sympathize (with).

compatriote [kɔ̃patrijɔt] *nmf* compatriot, fellow countryman (*f* countrywoman).

compensation [kɔ̃pɑ̃sasjɔ̃] *nf* [dédommagement] compensation.

compensé, e [kɔ̃pɑ̃se] *adj* built-up.

compenser [3] [kɔ̃pɑ̃se] *vt* to compensate ou make up for.

compétence [kɔ̃petɑ̃s] *nf* - **1.** [qualification] skill, ability - **2.** JUR competence ; **cela n'entre pas dans mes ~s** that's outside my scope.

compétent, e [kɔ̃petɑ̃, ɑ̃t] *adj* - **1.** [capable] capable, competent - **2.** ADMIN & JUR competent ; **les autorités ~es** the relevant authorities.

compétitif, ive [kɔ̃petitif, iv] *adj* competitive.

compétition [kɔ̃petisjɔ̃] *nf* competition ; **faire de la ~** to go in for competitive sport.

compil [kɔ̃pil] *nf fam* compilation album.

complainte [kɔ̃plɛ̃t] *nf* lament.

complaisant, e [kɔ̃plɛzɑ̃, ɑ̃t] *adj* - **1.** [aimable] obliging, kind - **2.** [indulgent] indulgent.

complément [kɔ̃plemɑ̃] *nm* - **1.** [gén & GRAM] complement - **2.** [reste] remainder.

complémentaire [kɔ̃plemɑ̃tɛr] *adj* - **1.** [supplémentaire] supplementary - **2.** [caractères, couleurs] complementary.

complet, ète [kɔ̃plɛ, ɛt] *adj* - **1.** [gén] complete - **2.** [plein] full. ◆ **complet(-veston)** *nm* suit.

complètement [kɔ̃plɛtmɑ̃] *adv* - **1.** [vraiment] absolutely, totally - **2.** [entièrement] completely.

compléter [18] [kɔ̃plete] *vt* [gén] to complete, to complement ; [somme d'argent] to make up.

complexe [kɔ̃plɛks] <> *nm* - **1.** PSYCHOL complex ; ~ **d'infériorité/de supériorité** inferiority/superiority complex - **2.** [ensemble] complex ; ~ **multisalle** multiplex (cinema). <> *adj* complex, complicated.

complexé, e [kɔ̃plɛkse] *adj* hung up, mixed up.

complexifier [kɔ̃plɛksifje] *vt* to make (more) complex.

complexité [kɔ̃plɛksite] *nf* complexity.

complication [kɔ̃plikasjɔ̃] *nf* intricacy, complexity. ◆ **complications** *nfpl* complications.

complice [kɔ̃plis] <> *nmf* accomplice. <> *adj* [sourire, regard, air] knowing.

complicité [kɔ̃plisite] *nf* complicity.

compliment [kɔ̃plimã] *nm* compliment.

complimenter [3] [kɔ̃plimɑ̃te] *vt* to compliment.

compliqué, e [kɔ̃plike] *adj* [problème] complex, complicated ; [personne] complicated.

compliquer [3] [kɔ̃plike] *vt* to complicate.

complot [kɔ̃plo] *nm* plot.

comploter [3] [kɔ̃plɔte] *vt & vi litt & fig* to plot.

comportement [kɔ̃pɔrtəmã] *nm* behaviour *Br*, behavior *Am*.

comportemental, e, aux [kɔ̃pɔrtəmãtal, o] *adj* behavioural *Br*, behavioral *Am*.

comporter [3] [kɔ̃pɔrte] *vt* - **1.** [contenir] to include, to contain - **2.** [être composé de] to consist of, to be made up of. ◆ **se comporter** *vp* to behave.

composant, e [kɔ̃pozã, ãt] *adj* constituent, component. ◆ **composant** *nm* component. ◆ **composante** *nf* component.

composé, e [kɔ̃poze] *adj* compound. ◆ **composé** *nm* - **1.** [mélange] combination - **2.** CHIM & LING compound.

composer [3] [kɔ̃poze] <> *vt* - **1.** [constituer] to make up, to form - **2.** [créer - musique] to compose, to write - **3.** [numéro de téléphone] to dial ; [code] to key in. <> *vi* to compromise. ◆ **se composer** *vp* [être constitué] : **se ~ de** to be composed of, to be made up of.

composite [kɔ̃pozit] *adj* - **1.** [disparate - mobilier] assorted, of various types ; [- foule] heterogeneous - **2.** [matériau] composite.

compositeur, trice [kɔ̃pozitœr, tris] *nm, f* - **1.** MUS composer - **2.** TYPO typesetter.

composition [kɔ̃pozisjɔ̃] *nf* - **1.** [gén]

composition ; [de roman] writing, composition - **2.** SCOL test - **3.** [caractère] : **être de bonne ~** to be good-natured.

composter [3] [kɔ̃pɔste] *vt* [ticket, billet] to date-stamp.

compote [kɔ̃pɔt] *nf* compote ; ~ **de pommes** stewed apple, apple sauce.

compréhensible [kɔ̃preãsibl] *adj* [texte, parole] comprehensible ; *fig* [réaction] understandable.

compréhensif, ive [kɔ̃preãsif, iv] *adj* understanding.

compréhension [kɔ̃preãsjɔ̃] *nf* - **1.** [de texte] comprehension, understanding - **2.** [indulgence] understanding.

comprendre [79] [kɔ̃prãdr] *vt* - **1.** [gén] to understand ; **je comprends! I see! ; se faire ~** to make o.s. understood ; **mal ~** to misunderstand - **2.** [comporter] to comprise, to consist of - **3.** [inclure] to include.

compresse [kɔ̃prɛs] *nf* compress.

compresseur [kɔ̃presœr] ▷ rouleau.

compression [kɔ̃presjɔ̃] *nf* [de gaz] compression ; *fig* cutback, reduction.

comprimé, e [kɔ̃prime] *adj* compressed. ◆ **comprimé** *nm* tablet ; ~ **effervescent** effervescent tablet.

comprimer [3] [kɔ̃prime] *vt* - **1.** [gaz, vapeur] to compress - **2.** [personnes] : **être comprimés dans** to be packed into.

compris, e [kɔ̃pri, iz] <> *pp* ▷ comprendre. <> *adj* - **1.** [situé] lying, contained - **2.** [inclus] : **charges (non) ~es** (not) including bills, bills (not) included ; **tout ~** all inclusive, all in ; **y ~** including.

compromettre [84] [kɔ̃prɔmɛtr] *vt* to compromise.

compromis, e [kɔ̃prɔmi, iz] *pp* ▷ compromettre. ◆ **compromis** *nm* compromise.

compromission [kɔ̃prɔmisjɔ̃] *nf péj* base action.

comptabilité [kɔ̃tabilite] *nf* [comptes] accounts (*pl*) ; [service] : **la ~** accounts, the accounts department.

comptable [kɔ̃tabl] *nmf* accountant.

comptant [kɔ̃tã] *adv* : **payer** ou **régler ~** to pay cash. ◆ **au comptant** *loc adv* : **payer au ~** to pay cash.

compte [kɔ̃t] *nm* - **1.** [action] count, counting (*U*) ; [total] number ; **faire le ~ (de)** countdown ; ~ **à rebours** countdown - **2.** BANQUE, COMM & COMPTABILITÉ account ; **ouvrir un ~** to open an account ; ~ **bancaire** ou **en banque** bank account ; ~ **courant** current account, checking account *Am* ; ~ **créditeur** account in credit ;

~ **débiteur** overdrawn account ; ~ **de dépôt** deposit account ; ~ **d'épargne** savings account ; ~ **d'exploitation** operating account ; ~ **postal** post office account - **3.** *loc* : **avoir son** ~ to have had enough ; **être/se mettre à son** ~ to be/become self-employed ; **prendre qqch en** ~, **tenir** ~ **de qqch** to take sthg into account ; **se rendre** ~ **de qqch** to realize sthg ; **s'en tirer à bon** ~ to get off lightly ; **tout** ~ **fait** all things considered. ◆ **comptes** *nmpl* accounts ; **faire ses ~s** to do one's accounts.

compte-chèques, compte chèques [kɔ̃tʃɛk] *nm* current account, checking account *Am*.

compte-gouttes [kɔ̃tgut] *nm inv* dropper.

compter [3] [kɔ̃te] <> *vt* - **1.** [dénombrer] to count - **2.** [avoir l'intention de] : ~ **faire qqch** to intend to do sthg, to plan to do sthg. <> *vi* - **1.** [calculer] to count - **2.** [être important] to count, to matter ; ~ **pour** to count for - **3.** : ~ **sur** [se fier à] to rely ou count on. ◆ **sans compter que** *loc conj* besides which.

compte rendu, compte-rendu [kɔ̃trɑ̃dy] *nm* report, account.

compteur [kɔ̃tœr] *nm* meter.

comptine [kɔ̃tin] *nf* nursery rhyme.

comptoir [kɔ̃twar] *nm* - **1.** [de bar] bar ; [de magasin] counter - **2.** HIST trading post - **3.** *Helv* [foire] trade fair.

compulser [3] [kɔ̃pylse] *vt* to consult.

comte [kɔ̃t] *nm* count.

comtesse [kɔ̃tɛs] *nf* countess.

con, conne [kɔ̃, kɔn] *tfam* <> *adj* bloody *Br* ou damned stupid. <> *nm, f* stupid bastard (*f* bitch).

concave [kɔ̃kav] *adj* concave.

concéder [18] [kɔ̃sede] *vt* : ~ **qqch à** [droit, terrain] to grant sthg to ; [point, victoire] to concede sthg to ; ~ **que** to admit (that), to concede (that).

concentration [kɔ̃sɑ̃trasjɔ̃] *nf* concentration.

concentré, e [kɔ̃sɑ̃tre] *adj* - **1.** [gén] concentrated - **2.** [personne] : **elle était très ~e** she was concentrating hard - **3.** ⊳ **lait.** ◆ **concentré** *nm* concentrate ; ~ **de tomates** CULIN tomato purée.

concentrer [3] [kɔ̃sɑ̃tre] *vt* to concentrate. ◆ **se concentrer** *vp* - **1.** [se rassembler] to be concentrated - **2.** [personne] to concentrate.

concentrique [kɔ̃sɑ̃trik] *adj* concentric.

concept [kɔ̃sɛpt] *nm* concept.

conception [kɔ̃sɛpsjɔ̃] *nf* - **1.** [gén] conception - **2.** [d'un produit, d'une campagne] design, designing (*U*).

concernant [kɔ̃sɛrnɑ̃] *prép* regarding, concerning.

concerner [3] [kɔ̃sɛrne] *vt* to concern ; **être/se sentir concerné par qqch** to be/feel concerned by sthg ; **en ce qui me concerne** as far as I'm concerned.

concert [kɔ̃sɛr] *nm* MUS concert.

concertation [kɔ̃sɛrtasjɔ̃] *nf* consultation.

concerter [3] [kɔ̃sɛrte] *vt* [organiser] to devise (jointly). ◆ **se concerter** *vp* to consult (each other).

concerto [kɔ̃sɛrto] *nm* concerto.

concession [kɔ̃sesjɔ̃] *nf* - **1.** [compromis & GRAM] concession - **2.** [autorisation] rights (*pl*), concession.

concessionnaire [kɔ̃sesjɔnɛr] *nmf* - **1.** [automobile] (car) dealer - **2.** [qui possède une franchise] franchise holder.

concevable [kɔ̃səvabl] *adj* conceivable.

concevoir [52] [kɔ̃səvwar] *vt* - **1.** [enfant, projet] to conceive - **2.** [comprendre] to conceive of ; **je ne peux pas** ~ **comment/pourquoi** I cannot conceive how/why.

concierge [kɔ̃sjɛrʒ] *nmf* caretaker, concierge.

conciliation [kɔ̃siljasjɔ̃] *nf* - **1.** [règlement d'un conflit] reconciliation, reconciling - **2.** [accord & JUR] reconciliation.

concilier [9] [kɔ̃silje] *vt* [mettre d'accord, allier] to reconcile ; ~ **qqch et** ou **avec qqch** to reconcile sthg with sthg.

concis, e [kɔ̃si, iz] *adj* [style, discours] concise ; [personne] terse.

concision [kɔ̃sizjɔ̃] *nf* conciseness, concision.

concitoyen, enne [kɔ̃sitwajɛ̃, ɛn] *nm, f* fellow citizen.

conclu, e [kɔ̃kly] *pp* ⊳ **conclure.**

concluant, e [kɔ̃klyɑ̃, ɑ̃t] *adj* [convaincant] conclusive.

conclure [96] [kɔ̃klyr] <> *vt* to conclude ; **en** ~ **que** to deduce (that). <> *vi* : **les experts ont conclu à la folie** the experts concluded he/she was mad.

conclusion [kɔ̃klyzjɔ̃] *nf* - **1.** [gén] conclusion - **2.** [partie finale] close.

concombre [kɔ̃kɔ̃br] *nm* cucumber.

concordance [kɔ̃kɔrdɑ̃s] *nf* [conformité] agreement ; ~ **des temps** GRAM sequence of tenses.

concorder [3] [kɔ̃kɔrde] *vi* - **1.** [coïncider] to agree, to coincide - **2.** [être en accord] : ~ **(avec)** to be in accordance (with).

concourir [45] [kɔ̃kurir] *vi* - **1.** [contri-

confetti

buer] : ~ **à** to work towards *Br* ou toward
Am - **2.** [participer à un concours] to compete.

concours [kɔ̃kur] *nm* - **1.** [examen] competitive examination - **2.** [compétition]
competition, contest - **3.** [coïncidence] :
~ **de circonstances** combination of circumstances.

concret, ète [kɔ̃krɛ, ɛt] *adj* concrete.

concrétiser [3] [kɔ̃kretize] *vt* [projet] to
give shape to ; [rêve, espoir] to give solid
form to. ◆ **se concrétiser** *vp* [projet] to
take shape ; [rêve, espoir] to materialize.

conçu, e [kɔ̃sy] *pp* ▷ **concevoir.**

concubinage [kɔ̃kybinaʒ] *nm* living together, cohabitation.

concupiscent, e [kɔ̃kypisɑ̃, ɑ̃t] *adj* concupiscent.

concurremment [kɔ̃kyramɑ̃] *adv* jointly.

concurrence [kɔ̃kyrɑ̃s] *nf* - **1.** [rivalité] rivalry - **2.** ÉCON competition.

concurrent, e [kɔ̃kyrɑ̃, ɑ̃t] ◇ *adj* rival,
competing. ◇ *nm, f* competitor.

concurrentiel, elle [kɔ̃kyrɑ̃sjɛl] *adj*
competitive.

condamnation [kɔ̃danasjɔ̃] *nf* - **1.** JUR
sentence - **2.** [dénonciation] condemna-
tion.

condamné, e [kɔ̃dane] *nm, f* convict,
prisoner.

condamner [3] [kɔ̃dane] *vt* - **1.** JUR : ~ **qqn
(à)** to sentence sb (to) ; ~ **qqn à une amende**
to fine sb - **2.** *fig* [obliger] : ~ **qqn à qqch**
to condemn sb to sthg **3.** [malade] : **être
condamné** to be terminally ill - **4.** [interdire]
to forbid - **5.** [blâmer] to condemn - **6.** [fer-
mer] to fill in, to block up.

condensation [kɔ̃dɑ̃sasjɔ̃] *nf* condensation.

condensé [kɔ̃dɑ̃se] ◇ *nm* summary.
◇ *adj* ▷ **lait.**

condenser [3] [kɔ̃dɑ̃se] *vt* to condense.

condescendant, e [kɔ̃desɑ̃dɑ̃, ɑ̃t] *adj*
condescending.

condiment [kɔ̃dimɑ̃] *nm* condiment.

condisciple [kɔ̃disipl] *nmf* fellow student.

condition [kɔ̃disjɔ̃] *nf* - **1.** [gén] condition ; **se mettre en** ~ [physiquement] to get
into shape - **2.** [place sociale] station ; **la
~ des ouvriers** the workers' lot. ◆ **conditions** *nfpl* - **1.** [circonstances] conditions ;
~**s de vie** living conditions - **2.** [de paiement]
terms. ◆ **à condition de** *loc prép* providing ou provided (that). ◆ **à condition
que** *loc conj* (+ *subjonctif*) providing ou provided (that). ◆ **sans conditions** ◇ *loc adj*
unconditional. ◇ *loc adv* unconditionally.

conditionné, e [kɔ̃disjɔne] *adj* - **1.** [em-
ballé] : ~ **sous vide** vacuum-packed - **2.** ▷
air.

conditionnel, elle [kɔ̃disjɔnɛl] *adj* conditional. ◆ **conditionnel** *nm* GRAM conditional.

conditionnement [kɔ̃disjɔnmɑ̃] *nm*
- **1.** [action d'emballer] packaging, packing
- **2.** [emballage] package - **3.** PSYCHOL &
TECHNOL conditioning.

conditionner [3] [kɔ̃disjɔne] *vt* - **1.** [déter-
miner] to govern - **2.** PSYCHOL & TECHNOL to
condition - **3.** [emballer] to pack.

condoléances [kɔ̃dɔleɑ̃s] *nfpl* condolences.

conducteur, trice [kɔ̃dyktœr, tris] ◇
adj conductive. ◇ *nm, f* [de véhicule]
driver. ◆ **conducteur** *nm* ÉLECTR conductor.

conduire [98] [kɔ̃dɥir] ◇ *vt* - **1.** [voiture,
personne] to drive - **2.** [transmettre] to conduct - **3.** *fig* [diriger] to manage - **4.** *fig* [à la
ruine, au désespoir] : ~ **qqn à qqch** to drive
sb to sthg. ◇ *vi* - **1.** AUTOM to drive
- **2.** [mener] : ~ **à** to lead to. ◆ **se conduire**
vp to behave.

conduit, e [kɔ̃dɥi, it] *pp* ▷ **conduire.**
◆ **conduit** *nm* - **1.** [tuyau] conduit, pipe
- **2.** ANAT duct, canal. ◆ **conduite** *nf*
- **1.** [pilotage d'un véhicule] driving ; ~**e à
droite/gauche** right-hand/left-hand drive
- **2.** [comportement] behaviour (*U*) *Br*, behavior (*U*) *Am* - **3.** [canalisation] : ~**e de gaz/
d'eau** gas/water main, gas/water pipe.

cône [kon] *nm* GÉOM cone.

confection [kɔ̃fɛksjɔ̃] *nf* - **1.** [réalisation]
making - **2.** [industrie] clothing industry.

confectionner [3] [kɔ̃fɛksjɔne] *vt* to
make.

confédération [kɔ̃federasjɔ̃] *nf* - **1.**
[d'états] confederacy - **2.** [d'associations]
confederation.

conférence [kɔ̃ferɑ̃s] *nf* - **1.** [exposé] lecture - **2.** [réunion] conference ; ~ **de presse**
press conference.

conférencier, ère [kɔ̃ferɑ̃sje, ɛr] *nm, f*
lecturer.

conférer [18] [kɔ̃fere] *vt* [accorder] :
~ **qqch à qqn** to confer sthg on sb.

confesser [4] [kɔ̃fese] *vt* - **1.** [avouer] to
confess - **2.** RELIG : ~ **qqn** to hear sb's confession. ◆ **se confesser** *vp* to go to confession.

confession [kɔ̃fesjɔ̃] *nf* confession.

confessionnal, aux [kɔ̃fesjɔnal, o] *nm*
confessional.

confetti [kɔ̃feti] *nm* confetti (*U*).

confiance [kɔ̃fjɑ̃s] *nf* confidence ; avoir ~ en to have confidence ou faith in ; avoir ~ en soi to be self-confident ; en toute ~ with complete confidence ; de ~ trustworthy ; faire ~ à qqn/qqch to trust sb/sthg.

confiant, e [kɔ̃fjɑ̃, ɑ̃t] *adj* [sans méfiance] trusting.

confidence [kɔ̃fidɑ̃s] *nf* confidence.

confident, e [kɔ̃fidɑ̃, ɑ̃t] *nm, f* confidant (*f* confidante).

confidentiel, elle [kɔ̃fidɑ̃sjɛl] *adj* confidential.

confier [9] [kɔ̃fje] *vt* - **1.** [donner] : ~ qqn/qqch à qqn to entrust sb/sthg to sb - **2.** [dire] : ~ qqch à qqn to confide sthg to sb. ◆ **se confier** *vp* : se ~ à qqn to confide in sb.

confiné, e [kɔ̃fine] *adj* - **1.** [air] stale ; [atmosphère] enclosed - **2.** [enfermé] shut away.

confins [kɔ̃fɛ̃] *nmpl* : aux ~ de on the borders of.

confirmation [kɔ̃firmasjɔ̃] *nf* confirmation.

confirmer [3] [kɔ̃firme] *vt* [certifier] to confirm. ◆ **se confirmer** *vp* to be confirmed.

confiscation [kɔ̃fiskasjɔ̃] *nf* confiscation.

confiserie [kɔ̃fizri] *nf* - **1.** [magasin] sweet shop *Br*, candy store *Am*, confectioner's - **2.** [sucreries] sweets *(pl) Br*, candy *(U) Am*, confectionery *(U)*.

confiseur, euse [kɔ̃fizœr, øz] *nm, f* confectioner.

confisquer [3] [kɔ̃fiske] *vt* to confiscate.

confiture [kɔ̃fityr] *nf* jam.

conflit [kɔ̃fli] *nm* - **1.** [situation tendue] clash, conflict - **2.** [entre États] conflict.

confondre [75] [kɔ̃fɔ̃dr] *vt* - **1.** [ne pas distinguer] to confuse - **2.** [accusé] to confound - **3.** [stupéfier] to astound.

confondu, e [kɔ̃fɔ̃dy] *pp* ▷ confondre.

conformation [kɔ̃fɔrmasjɔ̃] *nf* structure.

conforme [kɔ̃fɔrm] *adj* : ~ à in accordance with.

conformément [kɔ̃fɔrmemɑ̃] ◆ **conformément à** *loc prép* in accordance with.

conformer [3] [kɔ̃fɔrme] *vt* : ~ qqch à to shape sthg according to. ◆ **se conformer** *vp* : se ~ à [s'adapter] to conform to ; [obéir] to comply with.

conformiste [kɔ̃fɔrmist] ◇ *nmf* conformist. ◇ *adj* - **1.** [traditionaliste] conformist - **2.** [Anglican] Anglican.

conformité [kɔ̃fɔrmite] *nf* [accord] : être en ~ avec to be in accordance with.

confort [kɔ̃fɔr] *nm* comfort ; tout ~ with all mod cons *Br*, with all modern conveniences *Am*.

confortable [kɔ̃fɔrtabl] *adj* comfortable.

confrère, consœur [kɔ̃frɛr, kɔ̃sœr] *nm, f* colleague.

confrontation [kɔ̃frɔ̃tasjɔ̃] *nf* [face à face] confrontation.

confronter [3] [kɔ̃frɔ̃te] *vt* [mettre face à face] to confront ; *fig* : être confronté à to be confronted ou faced with.

confus, e [kɔ̃fy, yz] *adj* - **1.** [indistinct, embrouillé] confused - **2.** [gêné] embarrassed.

confusion [kɔ̃fyzjɔ̃] *nf* - **1.** [gén] confusion - **2.** [embarras] confusion, embarrassment.

congé [kɔ̃ʒe] *nm* - **1.** [arrêt de travail] leave *(U)* ; ~ (de) maladie sick leave ; ~ de maternité maternity leave - **2.** [vacances] holiday *Br*, vacation *Am* ; en ~ on holiday ; ~s payés paid holiday *(U)* ou holidays ou leave *(U) Br*, paid vacation *Am* ; une journée/semaine de ~ a day/week off - **3.** [renvoi] notice ; donner son ~ à qqn to give sb his/her notice ; prendre ~ (de qqn) *sout* to take one's leave (of sb).

congédier [9] [kɔ̃ʒedje] *vt* to dismiss.

congé-formation [kɔ̃ʒefɔrmasjɔ̃] *(pl* congés-formation) *nm* training leave.

congélateur [kɔ̃ʒelatœr] *nm* freezer.

congeler [25] [kɔ̃ʒle] *vt* to freeze.

congénital, e, aux [kɔ̃ʒenital, o] *adj* congenital.

congère [kɔ̃ʒɛr] *nf* snowdrift.

congestion [kɔ̃ʒɛstjɔ̃] *nf* congestion ; ~ pulmonaire pulmonary congestion.

Congo [kɔ̃go] *nm* [pays] : le ~ the Congo ; la République démocratique du ~ the Democratic Republic of Congo ; [fleuve] : le ~ the Congo.

congratuler [3] [kɔ̃gratyle] *vt* to congratulate.

congrégation [kɔ̃gregasjɔ̃] *nf* congregation.

congrès [kɔ̃grɛ] *nm* [colloque] assembly.

conifère [kɔnifɛr] *nm* conifer.

conjecture [kɔ̃ʒɛktyr] *nf* conjecture.

conjecturer [3] [kɔ̃ʒɛktyre] *vt & vi* to conjecture.

conjoint, e [kɔ̃ʒwɛ̃, ɛ̃t] ◇ *adj* joint. ◇ *nm, f* spouse.

conjonction [kɔ̃ʒɔ̃ksjɔ̃] *nf* conjunction.

conjonctivite [kɔ̃ʒɔ̃ktivit] *nf* conjunctivitis *(U)*.

conjoncture [kɔ̃ʒɔ̃ktyr] *nf* ÉCON situation, circumstances *(pl)*.

conjugaison [kɔ̃ʒygɛzɔ̃] nf - **1.** [union] uniting - **2.** GRAM conjugation.

conjugal, e, aux [kɔ̃ʒygal, o] adj conjugal.

conjuguer [3] [kɔ̃ʒyge] vt - **1.** [unir] to combine - **2.** GRAM to conjugate.

conjuration [kɔ̃ʒyrasjɔ̃] nf - **1.** [conspiration] conspiracy - **2.** [exorcisme] exorcism.

connaissance [kɔnɛsɑ̃s] nf - **1.** [savoir] knowledge (U) ; **à ma ~** to (the best of) my knowledge ; **en ~ de cause** with full knowledge of the facts ; **prendre ~ de qqch** to study sthg, to examine sthg - **2.** [personne] acquaintance ; **faire ~ (avec qqn)** to become acquainted (with sb) ; **faire la ~ de** to meet - **3.** [conscience] : **perdre/reprendre ~** to lose/regain consciousness.

connaisseur, euse [kɔnɛsœr, øz] <> adj expert (avant n). <> nm, f connoisseur.

connaître [91] [kɔnɛtr] vt - **1.** [gén] to know ; **~ qqn de nom/de vue** to know sb by name/sight - **2.** [éprouver] to experience. <> **se connaître** vp - **1.** : **s'y ~ en** [être expert] to know about ; **il s'y connaît** he knows what he's talking about/doing - **2.** [soi-même] to know o.s. - **3.** [se rencontrer] to meet (each other) ; **ils se connaissent** they've met each other.

connecter [4] [kɔnɛkte] vt to connect.

connexion [kɔnɛksjɔ̃] nf connection.

connu, e [kɔny] <> pp ▷ connaître. <> adj [célèbre] well-known, famous.

conquérant, e [kɔ̃kerɑ̃, ɑ̃t] <> adj conquering. <> nm, f conqueror.

conquérir [39] [kɔ̃kerir] vt to conquer.

conquête [kɔ̃kɛt] nf conquest.

conquis, e [kɔ̃ki, iz] pp ▷ conquérir.

consacrer [3] [kɔ̃sakre] vt - **1.** RELIG to consecrate - **2.** [employer] : **~ qqch à** to devote sthg to. <> **se consacrer** vp : **se ~ à** to dedicate o.s. to, to devote o.s. to.

conscience [kɔ̃sjɑ̃s] nf - **1.** [connaissance & PSYCHOL] consciousness ; **avoir ~ de qqch** to be aware of sthg - **2.** [morale] conscience ; **bonne/mauvaise ~** clear/guilty conscience ; **~ professionnelle** professional integrity, conscientiousness.

consciencieux, euse [kɔ̃sjɑ̃sjø, øz] adj conscientious.

conscient, e [kɔ̃sjɑ̃, ɑ̃t] adj conscious ; **être ~ de qqch** [connaître] to be conscious of sthg.

conscription [kɔ̃skripsjɔ̃] nf conscription, draft Am.

conscrit [kɔ̃skri] nm conscript, recruit, draftee Am.

consécration [kɔ̃sekrasjɔ̃] nf - **1.** [reconnaissance] recognition ; [de droit, coutume] establishment - **2.** RELIG consecration.

consécutif, ive [kɔ̃sekytif, iv] adj - **1.** [successif & GRAM] consecutive - **2.** [résultant] : **~ à** resulting from.

conseil [kɔ̃sɛj] nm - **1.** [avis] piece of advice, advice (U) ; **donner un ~ ou des ~s (à qqn)** to give (sb) advice - **2.** [personne] : **~ (en)** consultant (in) - **3.** [assemblée] council ; **~ d'administration** board of directors ; **~ de classe** staff meeting ; **~ de discipline** disciplinary committee.

conseiller¹ [4] [kɔ̃seje] <> vt - **1.** [recommander] to advise ; **~ qqch à qqn** to recommend sthg to sb - **2.** [guider] to advise, to counsel. <> vi [donner un conseil] : **~ à qqn de faire qqch** to advise sb to do sthg.

conseiller², ère [kɔ̃seje, ɛr] nm, f - **1.** [guide] counsellor Br, counselor Am - **2.** [d'un conseil] councillor Br, councilor Am ; **~ municipal** town councillor Br, city councilman (f councilwoman) Am.

consensuel, elle [kɔ̃sɑ̃sɥɛl] adj : **politique ~le** consensus politics.

consentement [kɔ̃sɑ̃tmɑ̃] nm consent.

consentir [87] [kɔ̃sɑ̃tir] vi : **~ à qqch** to consent to sthg.

conséquence [kɔ̃sekɑ̃s] nf consequence, result ; **ne pas tirer à ~** to be of no consequence.

conséquent, e [kɔ̃sekɑ̃, ɑ̃t] adj - **1.** [cohérent] consistent - **2.** [important] sizeable, considerable. ◆ **par conséquent** loc adv therefore, consequently.

conservateur, trice [kɔ̃sɛrvatœr, tris] <> adj conservative. <> nm, f - **1.** POLIT conservative - **2.** [administrateur] curator. ◆ **conservateur** nm preservative.

conservation [kɔ̃sɛrvasjɔ̃] nf - **1.** [état, entretien] preservation - **2.** [d'aliment] preserving.

conservatoire [kɔ̃sɛrvatwar] nm academy ; **~ de musique** music college.

conserve [kɔ̃sɛrv] nf tinned Br ou canned food ; **en ~** [en boîte] tinned, canned ; [en bocal] preserved, bottled.

conserver [3] [kɔ̃sɛrve] vt - **1.** [garder, entretenir] to keep - **2.** [entreposer - en boîte] to can ; [- en bocal] to bottle.

considérable [kɔ̃siderabl] adj considerable.

considération [kɔ̃siderasjɔ̃] nf - **1.** [réflexion, motivation] consideration ; **prendre qqch en ~** to take sthg into consideration - **2.** [estime] respect.

considérer [18] [kɔ̃sidere] vt to consider ; **tout bien considéré** all things considered.

consigne [kɔ̃siɲ] nf - **1.** (gén pl) [instruction] instructions *(pl)* - **2.** [entrepôt de bagages] left-luggage office *Br*, checkroom *Am*, baggage room *Am* ; ~ **automatique** left-luggage lockers *(pl) Br* - **3.** [somme d'argent] deposit.

consigné, e [kɔ̃siɲe] *adj* returnable.

consistance [kɔ̃sistɑ̃s] *nf* [solidité] consistency ; *fig* substance.

consistant, e [kɔ̃sistɑ̃, ɑ̃t] *adj* - **1.** [épais] thick - **2.** [nourrissant] substantial - **3.** [fondé] sound.

consister [3] [kɔ̃siste] *vi* : ~ **en** to consist of ; ~ **à faire qqch** to consist in doing sthg.

consœur ⊳ **confrère.**

consolation [kɔ̃sɔlasjɔ̃] *nf* consolation.

console [kɔ̃sɔl] *nf* - **1.** [table] console (table) - **2.** INFORM : ~ **de jeux** games console ; ~ **de visualisation** VDU, visual display unit.

consoler [3] [kɔ̃sɔle] *vt* [réconforter] : ~ **qqn (de qqch)** to comfort sb (in sthg).

consolider [3] [kɔ̃sɔlide] *vt litt & fig* to strengthen.

consommateur, trice [kɔ̃sɔmatœr, tris] *nm, f* [acheteur] consumer ; [d'un bar] customer.

consommation [kɔ̃sɔmasjɔ̃] *nf* - **1.** [utilisation] consumption ; **faire une grande** ou **grosse ~ de** to use (up) a lot of - **2.** [boisson] drink.

consommé, e [kɔ̃sɔme] *adj sout* consummate. ◆ **consommé** *nm* consommé.

consommer [3] [kɔ̃sɔme] ⟷ *vt* - **1.** [utiliser] to use (up) - **2.** [manger] to eat - **3.** [énergie] to consume, to use. ⟷ *vi* - **1.** [boire] to drink - **2.** [voiture] : **cette voiture consomme beaucoup** this car uses a lot of fuel.

consonance [kɔ̃sɔnɑ̃s] *nf* consonance.

consonne [kɔ̃sɔn] *nf* consonant.

conspirateur, trice [kɔ̃spiratœr, tris] *nm, f* conspirator.

conspiration [kɔ̃spirasjɔ̃] *nf* conspiracy.

conspirer [3] [kɔ̃spire] ⟷ *vt* [comploter] to plot. ⟷ *vi* to conspire.

constamment [kɔ̃stamɑ̃] *adv* constantly.

constant, e [kɔ̃stɑ̃, ɑ̃t] *adj* constant.

constat [kɔ̃sta] *nm* - **1.** [procès-verbal] report - **2.** [constatation] established fact.

constatation [kɔ̃statasjɔ̃] *nf* - **1.** [révélation] observation - **2.** [fait retenu] finding.

constater [3] [kɔ̃state] *vt* - **1.** [se rendre compte de] to see, to note - **2.** [consigner - fait, infraction] to record ; [- décès, authenticité] to certify.

constellation [kɔ̃stelasjɔ̃] *nf* ASTRON constellation.

consternation [kɔ̃sternasjɔ̃] *nf* dismay.

consterner [3] [kɔ̃sterne] *vt* to dismay.

constipation [kɔ̃stipasjɔ̃] *nf* constipation.

constipé, e [kɔ̃stipe] *adj* - **1.** MÉD constipated - **2.** *fam fig* [manière, air] ill at ease.

constituer [7] [kɔ̃stitɥe] *vt* - **1.** [élaborer] to set up - **2.** [composer] to make up - **3.** [représenter] to constitute.

constitution [kɔ̃stitysjɔ̃] *nf* - **1.** [création] setting up - **2.** [de pays, de corps] constitution.

constructeur [kɔ̃stryktœr] *nm* - **1.** [fabricant] manufacturer ; [de navire] shipbuilder - **2.** [bâtisseur] builder.

construction [kɔ̃stryksjɔ̃] *nf* - **1.** IND building, construction ; ~ **navale** shipbuilding - **2.** [édifice] structure, building - **3.** GRAM & *fig* construction.

construire [98] [kɔ̃strɥir] *vt* - **1.** [bâtir, fabriquer] to build - **2.** [théorie, phrase] to construct.

construit, e [kɔ̃strɥi, it] *pp* ⊳ **construire.**

consulat [kɔ̃syla] *nm* [résidence] consulate.

consultation [kɔ̃syltasjɔ̃] *nf* - **1.** [d'ouvrage] : **de ~ aisée** easy to use - **2.** MÉD & POLIT consultation.

consulter [3] [kɔ̃sylte] ⟷ *vt* - **1.** [compulser] to consult - **2.** [interroger, demander conseil à] to consult, to ask - **3.** [spécialiste] to consult, to see. ⟷ *vi* [médecin] to take ou hold surgery ; [avocat] to be available for consultation. ◆ **se consulter** *vp* to confer.

contact [kɔ̃takt] *nm* - **1.** [gén] contact ; **le ~ du marbre est froid** marble is cold to the touch ; **prendre ~ avec** to make contact with ; **rester en ~ (avec)** to stay in touch (with) ; **au ~ de** on contact with - **2.** AUTOM ignition ; **mettre/couper le ~** to switch on/off the ignition.

contacter [3] [kɔ̃takte] *vt* to contact.

contagieux, euse [kɔ̃taʒjø, øz] *adj* MÉD contagious ; *fig* infectious.

contagion [kɔ̃taʒjɔ̃] *nf* MÉD contagion ; *fig* infectiousness.

contaminer [3] [kɔ̃tamine] *vt* [infecter] to contaminate ; *fig* to contaminate, to infect.

conte [kɔ̃t] *nm* story ; ~ **de fées** fairy tale.

contemplation [kɔ̃tɑ̃plasjɔ̃] *nf* contemplation.

contempler [3] [kɔ̃tɑ̃ple] *vt* to contemplate.

contemporain, e [kɔ̃tɑ̃pɔrɛ̃, ɛn] *nm, f* contemporary.

contenance [kɔ̃tnɑ̃s] *nf* - **1.** [capacité volumique] capacity - **2.** [attitude] : **se donner une ~** to give an impression of composure ; **perdre ~** to lose one's composure.

contenir [40] [kɔ̃tnir] *vt* to contain, to hold, to take. ◆ **se contenir** *vp* to contain o.s., to control o.s.

content, e [kɔ̃tɑ̃, ɑ̃t] *adj* [satisfait] : **~ (de qqn/qqch)** happy (with sb/sthg), content (with sb/sthg) ; **~ de faire qqch** happy to do sthg.

contentement [kɔ̃tɑ̃tmɑ̃] *nm* satisfaction.

contenter [3] [kɔ̃tɑ̃te] *vt* to satisfy. ◆ **se contenter** *vp* : **se ~ de qqch/de faire qqch** to content o.s. with sthg/with doing sthg.

contentieux [kɔ̃tɑ̃sjø] *nm* [litige] dispute ; [service] legal department.

contenu, e [kɔ̃tny] *pp* ▷ **contenir**. ◆ **contenu** *nm* - **1.** [de récipient] contents *(pl)* - **2.** [de texte, discours] content.

conter [3] [kɔ̃te] *vt* to tell.

contestable [kɔ̃tɛstabl] *adj* questionable.

contestation [kɔ̃tɛstasjɔ̃] *nf* - **1.** [protestation] protest, dispute - **2.** POLIT : **la ~** anti-establishment activity.

conteste [kɔ̃tɛst] ◆ **sans conteste** *loc adv* unquestionably.

contester [3] [kɔ̃tɛste] ◇ *vt* to dispute, to contest. ◇ *vi* to protest.

conteur, euse [kɔ̃tœr, øz] *nm, f* storyteller.

contexte [kɔ̃tɛkst] *nm* context.

contigu, uë [kɔ̃tigy] *adj* : **(à)** adjacent (to).

continent [kɔ̃tinɑ̃] *nm* continent.

continental, e, aux [kɔ̃tinɑ̃tal, o] *adj* continental.

contingence [kɔ̃tɛ̃ʒɑ̃s] *nf (gén pl)* contingency.

contingent [kɔ̃tɛ̃ʒɑ̃] *nm* - **1.** MIL national service conscripts *(pl)*, draft *Am* - **2.** COMM quota.

continu, e [kɔ̃tiny] *adj* continuous.

continuation [kɔ̃tinɥasjɔ̃] *nf* continuation.

continuel, elle [kɔ̃tinɥɛl] *adj* - **1.** [continu] continuous - **2.** [répété] continual.

continuellement [kɔ̃tinɥɛlmɑ̃] *adv* continually.

continuer [7] [kɔ̃tinɥe] ◇ *vt* [poursuivre] to carry on with, to continue (with). ◇ *vi* to continue, to go on ; **~ à** ou **de faire qqch** to continue to do ou doing sthg.

continuité [kɔ̃tinɥite] *nf* continuity.

contorsionner [3] [kɔ̃tɔrsjɔne] ◆ **se contorsionner** *vp* to contort (o.s.), to writhe.

contour [kɔ̃tur] *nm* - **1.** [limite] outline - **2.** *(gén pl)* [courbe] bend.

contourner [3] [kɔ̃turne] *vt litt & fig* to bypass, to get round.

contraceptif, ive [kɔ̃trasɛptif, iv] *adj* contraceptive. ◆ **contraceptif** *nm* contraceptive.

contraception [kɔ̃trasɛpsjɔ̃] *nf* contraception.

contracter [3] [kɔ̃trakte] *vt* - **1.** [muscle] to contract, to tense ; [visage] to contort - **2.** [maladie] to contract, to catch - **3.** [engagement] to contract ; [assurance] to take out.

contraction [kɔ̃traksjɔ̃] *nf* contraction ; [état de muscle] tenseness.

contractuel, elle [kɔ̃traktɥɛl] *nm, f* traffic warden *Br*.

contradiction [kɔ̃tradiksjɔ̃] *nf* contradiction.

contradictoire [kɔ̃tradiktwar] *adj* contradictory ; **débat ~** open debate.

contraignant, e [kɔ̃trɛɲɑ̃, ɑ̃t] *adj* restricting.

contraindre [80] [kɔ̃trɛ̃dr] *vt* : **~ qqn à faire qqch** to compel ou force sb to do sthg ; **être contraint de faire qqch** to be compelled ou forced to do sthg.

contraire [kɔ̃trɛr] ◇ *nm* : **le ~** the opposite ; **je n'ai jamais dit le ~** I have never denied it. ◇ *adj* opposite ; **~ à** [non conforme à] contrary to ; [nuisible à] harmful to, damaging to. ◆ **au contraire** *loc adv* on the contrary. ◆ **au contraire de** *loc prép* unlike.

contrairement [kɔ̃trɛrmɑ̃] ◆ **contrairement à** *loc prép* contrary to.

contrarier [9] [kɔ̃trarje] *vt* - **1.** [contrecarrer] to thwart, to frustrate - **2.** [irriter] to annoy.

contrariété [kɔ̃trarjete] *nf* annoyance.

contraste [kɔ̃trast] *nm* contrast.

contraster [3] [kɔ̃traste] *vt & vi* to contrast.

contrat [kɔ̃tra] *nm* contract, agreement ; **~ d'apprentissage** apprenticeship contract ; **~ à durée déterminée/indéterminée** fixed-term/permanent contract ; **Contrat emploi-solidarité** *government-sponsored contract for the unemployed involving professional training.*

contravention [kɔ̃travɑ̃sjɔ̃] *nf* [amende] fine ; **~ pour stationnement interdit** parking ticket ; **dresser une ~ à qqn** to fine sb.

contre [kɔ̃tr] ⟨⟩ *prép* - **1.** [juxtaposition, opposition] **against** - **2.** [proportion, comparaison] : **élu à 15 voix ~ 9** elected by 15 votes to 9 - **3.** [échange] (in exchange) for. ⟨⟩ *adv* [juxtaposition] : **prends la rampe et appuie-toi ~** take hold of the rail and lean against it. ◆ **par contre** *loc adv* on the other hand.

contre-attaque [kɔ̃tratak] (*pl* **contre-attaques**) *nf* counterattack.

contrebalancer [16] [kɔ̃trəbalɑ̃se] *vt* to counterbalance, to offset.

contrebande [kɔ̃trəbɑ̃d] *nf* [activité] smuggling ; [marchandises] contraband.

contrebandier, ère [kɔ̃trəbɑ̃dje, ɛr] *nm, f* smuggler.

contrebas [kɔ̃trəba] ◆ **en contrebas** *loc adv* (down) below.

contrebasse [kɔ̃trəbas] *nf* [instrument] (double) bass.

contrecarrer [3] [kɔ̃trəkare] *vt* to thwart, to frustrate.

contrecœur [kɔ̃trəkœr] ◆ **à contrecœur** *loc adv* grudgingly.

contrecoup [kɔ̃trəku] *nm* consequence.

contre-courant [kɔ̃trəkurɑ̃] ◆ **à contre-courant** *loc adv* against the current.

contredire [103] [kɔ̃trədir] *vt* to contradict. ◆ **se contredire** *vp* - **1.** (*emploi réciproque*) to contradict (each other) - **2.** (*emploi réfléchi*) to contradict o.s.

contredit, e [kɔ̃trədi, it] *pp* ▷ **contredire**.

contrée [kɔ̃tre] *nf* [pays] land ; [région] region.

contre-espionnage [kɔ̃trɛspjɔnaʒ] *nm* counterespionage.

contre-exemple [kɔ̃trɛgzɑ̃pl] (*pl* **contre-exemples**) *nm* example to the contrary.

contre-expertise [kɔ̃trɛkspɛrtiz] (*pl* **contre-expertises**) *nf* second (expert) opinion.

contrefaçon [kɔ̃trəfasɔ̃] *nf* [activité] counterfeiting ; [produit] forgery.

contrefaire [109] [kɔ̃trəfɛr] *vt* - **1.** [signature, monnaie] to counterfeit, to forge - **2.** [voix] to disguise.

contrefort [kɔ̃trəfɔr] *nm* - **1.** [pilier] buttress - **2.** [de chaussure] back. ◆ **contreforts** *nmpl* foothills.

contre-indication [kɔ̃trɛ̃dikasjɔ̃] (*pl* **contre-indications**) *nf* contraindication.

contre-jour [kɔ̃trəʒur] ◆ **à contre-jour** *loc adv* against the light.

contremaître, esse [kɔ̃trəmɛtr, ɛs] *nm, f* foreman (*f* forewoman).

contremarque [kɔ̃trəmark] *nf* [pour sortir d'un spectacle] pass-out ticket.

contre-offensive [kɔ̃trɔfɑ̃siv] (*pl* **contre-offensives**) *nf* counteroffensive.

contre-ordre = contrordre.

contrepartie [kɔ̃trəparti] *nf* - **1.** [compensation] compensation - **2.** [contraire] opposing view. ◆ **en contrepartie** *loc adv* in return.

contre-performance [kɔ̃trəpɛrfɔrmɑ̃s] (*pl* **contre-performances**) *nf* disappointing performance.

contrepèterie [kɔ̃trəpɛtri] *nf* spoonerism.

contre-pied [kɔ̃trəpje] *nm* : **prendre le ~ de** to do the opposite of.

contreplaqué, contre-plaqué [kɔ̃trəplake] *nm* plywood.

contrepoids [kɔ̃trəpwa] *nm litt & fig* counterbalance, counterweight.

contre-pouvoir [kɔ̃trəpuvwar] (*pl* **contre-pouvoirs**) *nm* counterbalance.

contrer [3] [kɔ̃tre] *vt* - **1.** [s'opposer à] to counter - **2.** CARTES to double.

contresens [kɔ̃trəsɑ̃s] *nm* - **1.** [erreur - de traduction] mistranslation ; [- d'interprétation] misinterpretation - **2.** [absurdité] nonsense (*U*). ◆ **à contresens** *loc adv litt & fig* the wrong way.

contresigner [3] [kɔ̃trəsiɲe] *vt* to countersign.

contretemps [kɔ̃trətɑ̃] *nm* hitch, mishap. ◆ **à contretemps** *loc adv* MUS out of time ; *fig* at the wrong moment.

contrevenir [40] [kɔ̃trəvnir] *vi* : **~ à** to contravene, to infringe.

contribuable [kɔ̃tribɥabl] *nmf* taxpayer.

contribuer [7] [kɔ̃tribɥe] *vi* : **~ à** to contribute to OU towards.

contribution [kɔ̃tribysjɔ̃] *nf* : **- (à)** contribution (to) ; **mettre qqn à ~** to call on sb's services. ◆ **contributions** *nfpl* taxes ; **~s directes/indirectes** direct/indirect taxation.

contrit, e [kɔ̃tri, it] *adj* contrite.

contrôle [kɔ̃trol] *nm* - **1.** [vérification - de déclaration] check, checking (*U*) ; [- de documents, billets] inspection ; **~ d'identité** identity check - **2.** [maîtrise, commande] control ; **perdre le ~ de qqch** to lose control of sthg ; **~ des naissances** birth control ; **~ des prix** price control - **3.** SCOL test.

contrôler [3] [kɔ̃trole] *vt* - **1.** [vérifier - documents, billets] to inspect ; [- déclaration] to check ; [- connaissances] to test - **2.** [maîtriser, diriger] to control - **3.** TECHNOL to monitor, to control.

contrôleur, euse [kɔ̃trolœr, øz] *nm, f* [de train] ticket inspector ; [d'autobus] (bus) conductor (*f* conductress) ; ~ **aérien** air traffic controller.

contrordre, contre-ordre (*pl* contre-ordres) [kɔ̃trɔrdr] *nm* countermand ; **sauf** ~ unless otherwise instructed.

controverse [kɔ̃trɔvɛrs] *nf* controversy.

controversé, e [kɔ̃trɔvɛrse] *adj* [personne, décision] controversial.

contumace [kɔ̃tymas] *nf* JUR : **condamné par** ~ sentenced in absentia.

contusion [kɔ̃tyzjɔ̃] *nf* bruise, contusion.

convaincant, e [kɔ̃vɛ̃kɑ̃, ɑ̃t] *adj* convincing.

convaincre [114] [kɔ̃vɛ̃kr] *vt* - **1.** [persuader] : ~ **qqn (de qqch)** to convince sb (of sthg) ; ~ **qqn (de faire qqch)** to persuade sb (to do sthg) - **2.** JUR : ~ **qqn de** to find sb guilty of, to convict sb of.

convaincu, e [kɔ̃vɛ̃ky] <> *pp* ⊳ **convaincre**. <> *adj* [partisan] committed ; **d'un ton** ~, **d'un air** ~ with conviction.

convainquant [kɔ̃vɛ̃kɑ̃] *ppr* ⊳ **convaincre**.

convalescence [kɔ̃valesɑ̃s] *nf* convalescence ; **être en** ~ to be convalescing ou recovering.

convalescent, e [kɔ̃valesɑ̃, ɑ̃t] *adj* & *nm, f* convalescent.

convenable [kɔ̃vnabl] *adj* - **1.** [manières, comportement] polite ; [tenue, personne] decent, respectable - **2.** [acceptable] adequate, acceptable.

convenance [kɔ̃vnɑ̃s] *nf* : **à ma/votre** ~ to my/your convenience. ◆ **convenances** *nfpl* proprietes.

convenir [40] [kɔ̃vnir] *vi* - **1.** [décider] : ~ **de qqch/de faire qqch** to agree on sthg/to do sthg - **2.** [plaire] : ~ **à qqn** to suit sb, to be convenient for sb - **3.** [être approprié] : ~ **à** ou **pour** to be suitable for - **4.** *sout* [admettre] : ~ **de qqch** to admit to sthg ; ~ **que** to admit (that).

convention [kɔ̃vɑ̃sjɔ̃] *nf* - **1.** [règle, assemblée] convention - **2.** [accord] agreement ; ~ **collective** collective agreement.

conventionné, e [kɔ̃vɑ̃sjɔne] *adj* ≈ National Health (*avant n*) Br.

conventionnel, elle [kɔ̃vɑ̃sjɔnɛl] *adj* conventional.

convenu, e [kɔ̃vny] <> *pp* ⊳ **convenir**. <> *adj* [décidé] : **comme** ~ as agreed.

convergent, e [kɔ̃vɛrʒɑ̃, ɑ̃t] *adj* convergent.

converger [17] [kɔ̃vɛrʒe] *vi* : ~ **(vers)** to converge (on).

conversation [kɔ̃vɛrsasjɔ̃] *nf* conversation.

converser [3] [kɔ̃vɛrse] *vi* *sout* : ~ **(avec)** to converse (with).

conversion [kɔ̃vɛrsjɔ̃] *nf* [gén] : ~ **(à/en)** conversion (to/into).

convertible [kɔ̃vɛrtibl] *nm* [canapé-lit] sofa bed.

convertir [32] [kɔ̃vɛrtir] *vt* : ~ **qqn (à)** to convert sb (to) ; ~ **qqch (en)** to convert sthg (into). ◆ **se convertir** *vp* : **se** ~ **(à)** to be converted (to).

convexe [kɔ̃vɛks] *adj* convex.

conviction [kɔ̃viksjɔ̃] *nf* conviction.

convier [9] [kɔ̃vje] *vt* : ~ **qqn à** to invite sb to.

convive [kɔ̃viv] *nmf* guest (*at a meal*).

convivial, e, aux [kɔ̃vivjal, o] *adj* - **1.** [réunion] convivial - **2.** INFORM user-friendly.

convocation [kɔ̃vɔkasjɔ̃] *nf* [avis écrit] summons (*sg*), notification to attend.

convoi [kɔ̃vwa] *nm* - **1.** [de véhicules] convoy - **2.** [train] train.

convoiter [3] [kɔ̃vwate] *vt* to covet.

convoitise [kɔ̃vwatiz] *nf* covetousness.

convoquer [3] [kɔ̃vɔke] *vt* - **1.** [assemblée] to convene - **2.** [pour un entretien] to invite - **3.** [subalterne, témoin] to summon - **4.** [à un examen] : ~ **qqn** to ask sb to attend.

convoyer [13] [kɔ̃vwaje] *vt* to escort.

convoyeur, euse [kɔ̃vwajœr, øz] *nm, f* escort ; ~ **de fonds** security guard.

convulsion [kɔ̃vylsjɔ̃] *nf* convulsion.

coopération [kɔɔperasjɔ̃] *nf* - **1.** [collaboration] cooperation - **2.** [aide] : **la** ~ ≈ overseas development.

coopérer [18] [kɔɔpere] *vi* : ~ **(à)** to cooperate (in).

coordination [kɔɔrdinasjɔ̃] *nf* coordination.

coordonnée [kɔɔrdɔne] *nf* - **1.** LING coordinate clause - **2.** MATHS coordinate. ◆ **coordonnées** *nfpl* - **1.** GÉOGR coordinates - **2.** [adresse] address and phone number, details.

coordonner [3] [kɔɔrdɔne] *vt* to coordinate.

copain, ine [kɔpɛ̃, in] <> *adj* matey ; **être très** ~**s** to be great pals. <> *nm, f* [ami] friend, mate ; [petit ami] boyfriend (*f* girlfriend).

copeau, x [kɔpo] *nm* [de bois] (wood) shaving.

Copenhague [kɔpɛnag] *n* Copenhagen.

copie [kɔpi] *nf* - **1.** [double, reproduction]

copy - 2. [SCOL - de devoir] fair copy ; [- d'examen] paper, script.

copier [9] [kɔpje] <> vt [gén & INFORM] to copy. <> vi : ~ **sur qqn** to copy from sb.

copieux, euse [kɔpjø, øz] adj copious.

copilote [kɔpilɔt] nmf copilot.

copine ▷ copain.

coproduction [kɔprɔdyksjɔ̃] nf coproduction.

copropriété [kɔprɔprijete] nf co-ownership, joint ownership.

coq [kɔk] nm cock, cockerel ; ~ **au vin** chicken cooked with red wine, bacon, mushrooms and shallots ; **sauter** ou **passer du ~ à l'âne** to jump from one subject to another.

coque [kɔk] nf - 1. [de noix] shell - 2. [de navire] hull.

coquelicot [kɔkliko] nm poppy.

coqueluche [kɔklyʃ] nf whooping cough.

coquet, ette [kɔkɛ, ɛt] adj - 1. [vêtements] smart, stylish ; [ville, jeune fille] pretty - 2. (avant n) hum [important] : **la ~te somme de 100 livres** the tidy sum of £100. ❧ **coquette** nf flirt.

coquetier [kɔktje] nm eggcup.

coquetterie [kɔkɛtri] nf [désir de plaire] coquettishness.

coquillage [kɔkijaʒ] nm - 1. [mollusque] shellfish - 2. [coquille] shell.

coquille [kɔkij] nf - 1. [de mollusque, noix, œuf] shell ; ~ **de noix** [embarcation] cockleshell - 2. TYPO misprint.

coquillettes [kɔkijɛt] nfpl pasta shells.

coquin, e [kɔkɛ̃, in] <> adj [sous-vêtement] sexy, naughty ; [regard, histoire] saucy. <> nm, f rascal.

cor [kɔr] nm - 1. [instrument] horn - 2. [au pied] corn. ❧ **à cor et à cri** loc adv : **réclamer qqch à ~ et à cri** to clamour Br ou clamor Am for sthg.

corail, aux [kɔraj, o] nm - 1. [gén] coral - 2. RAIL : **train ~** ≃ express train.

Coran [kɔrɑ̃] nm : **le ~** the Koran.

corbeau, x [kɔrbo] nm - 1. [oiseau] crow - 2. [délateur] writer of poison-pen letters.

corbeille [kɔrbɛj] nf - 1. [panier] basket ; ~ **à papier** waste paper basket - 2. THÉÂTRE (dress) circle - 3. [de Bourse] stockbrokers' enclosure (at Paris Stock Exchange).

corbillard [kɔrbijar] nm hearse.

cordage [kɔrdaʒ] nm - 1. [de bateau] rigging (U) - 2. [de raquette] strings (pl).

corde [kɔrd] nf - 1. [filin] rope ; ~ **à linge** washing ou clothes line ; ~ **à sauter** skipping rope - 2. [d'instrument, arc] string

- 3. ANAT : ~**s vocales** vocal cords - 4. HIPPISME rails (pl) ; ATHLÉTISME inside (lane).

cordée [kɔrde] nf ALPINISME roped party (of mountaineers).

cordial, e, aux [kɔrdjal, o] adj warm, cordial.

cordon [kɔrdɔ̃] nm string, cord ; ~ **ombilical** umbilical cord ; ~ **de police** police cordon.

cordon-bleu [kɔrdɔ̃blø] nm cordon bleu cook.

cordonnerie [kɔrdɔnri] nf [magasin] shoe repairer's, cobbler's.

cordonnier, ère [kɔrdɔnje, ɛr] nm, f shoe repairer, cobbler.

Corée [kɔre] nf Korea.

coriace [kɔrjas] adj litt & fig tough.

cormoran [kɔrmɔrɑ̃] nm cormorant.

corne [kɔrn] nf - 1. [gén] horn ; [de cerf] antler - 2. [callosité] hard skin (U), callus.

cornée [kɔrne] nf cornea.

corneille [kɔrnɛj] nf crow.

cornemuse [kɔrnəmyz] nf bagpipes (pl).

corner[1] [3] [kɔrne] vt [page] to turn down the corner of.

corner[2] [kɔrnɛr] nm FOOTBALL corner (kick).

cornet [kɔrnɛ] nm - 1. [d'aliment] cornet, cone - 2. [de jeu] (dice) shaker.

corniaud, corniot [kɔrnjo] nm - 1. [chien] mongrel - 2. fam [imbécile] twit.

corniche [kɔrniʃ] nf - 1. [route] cliff road - 2. [moulure] cornice.

cornichon [kɔrniʃɔ̃] nm - 1. [condiment] gherkin - 2. fam [imbécile] twit.

corniot = corniaud.

Cornouailles [kɔrnwaj] nf : **la ~** Cornwall.

corollaire [kɔrɔlɛr] nm corollary.

corolle [kɔrɔl] nf corolla.

coron [kɔrɔ̃] nm [village] mining village.

corporation [kɔrpɔrasjɔ̃] nf corporate body.

corporel, elle [kɔrpɔrɛl] adj [physique - besoin] bodily ; [- châtiment] corporal.

corps [kɔr] nm - 1. [gén] body - 2. [groupe] : ~ **d'armée** (army) corps ; ~ **enseignant** [profession] teaching profession ; [d'école] teaching staff.

corpulent, e [kɔrpylɑ̃, ɑ̃t] adj corpulent, stout.

correct, e [kɔrɛkt] adj - 1. [exact] correct, right - 2. [honnête] correct, proper - 3. [acceptable] decent ; [travail] fair.

correcteur, trice [kɔrɛktœr, tris] <> adj

corrective. <> *nm, f* - **1.** [d'examen] examiner, marker *Br*, grader *Am* - **2.** TYPO proofreader. ◆ **correcteur orthographique** *nm* spell-checker.

correction [kɔrɛksjɔ̃] *nf* - **1.** [d'erreur] correction - **2.** [punition] punishment - **3.** TYPO proofreading - **4.** [notation] marking - **5.** [bienséance] propriety.

corrélation [kɔrelasjɔ̃] *nf* correlation.

correspondance [kɔrɛspɔ̃dɑ̃s] *nf* - **1.** [gén] correspondence ; **cours par ~** correspondence course - **2.** TRANSPORT connection ; **assurer la ~ avec** to connect with.

correspondant, e [kɔrɛspɔ̃dɑ̃, ɑ̃t] <> *adj* corresponding. <> *nm, f* - **1.** [par lettres] penfriend, correspondent - **2.** [par téléphone] : **je vous passe votre ~** I'll put you through - **3.** PRESSE correspondent.

correspondre [75] [kɔrɛspɔ̃dr] *vi* - **1.** [être conforme] : **~ à** to correspond to - **2.** [par lettres] : **~ avec** to correspond with.

corridor [kɔridɔr] *nm* corridor.

corrigé [kɔriʒe] *nm* correct version.

corriger [17] [kɔriʒe] *vt* - **1.** TYPO to correct, to proofread - **2.** [noter] to mark - **3.** [guérir] : **~ qqn de** to cure sb of - **4.** [punir] to give a good hiding to. ◆ **se corriger** *vp* [d'un défaut] : **se ~ de** to cure o.s. of.

corroborer [3] [kɔrɔbɔre] *vt* to corroborate.

corroder [3] [kɔrɔde] *vt* [ronger] to corrode ; *fig* to erode.

corrompre [78] [kɔrɔ̃pr] *vt* - **1.** [soudoyer] to bribe - **2.** [dépraver] to corrupt.

corrosion [kɔrozjɔ̃] *nf* corrosion.

corruption [kɔrypsjɔ̃] *nf* - **1.** [subornation] bribery - **2.** [dépravation] corruption.

corsage [kɔrsaʒ] *nm* - **1.** [chemisier] blouse - **2.** [de robe] bodice.

corsaire [kɔrsɛr] *nm* - **1.** [navire, marin] corsair, privateer - **2.** [pantalon] pedal-pushers *(pl)*.

corse [kɔrs] <> *adj* Corsican. <> *nm* [langue] Corsican. ◆ **Corse** <> *nmf* Corsican. <> *nf* : **la Corse** Corsica.

corsé, e [kɔrse] *adj* [café] strong ; [vin] full-bodied ; [plat, histoire] spicy.

corset [kɔrsɛ] *nm* corset.

cortège [kɔrtɛʒ] *nm* procession.

corvée [kɔrve] *nf* - **1.** MIL fatigue (duty) - **2.** [activité pénible] chore.

cosmétique [kɔsmetik] *nm & adj* cosmetic.

cosmique [kɔsmik] *adj* cosmic.

cosmonaute [kɔsmɔnot] *nmf* cosmonaut.

cosmopolite [kɔsmɔpɔlit] *adj* cosmopolitan.

cosmos [kɔsmos] *nm* - **1.** [univers] cosmos - **2.** [espace] outer space.

cossu, e [kɔsy] *adj* [maison] opulent.

Costa Rica [kɔstarika] *nm* : **le ~** Costa Rica.

costaud (*f inv* ou **e**) [kɔsto, od] *adj* sturdily built.

costume [kɔstym] *nm* - **1.** [folklorique, de théâtre] costume - **2.** [vêtement d'homme] suit.

costumé, e [kɔstyme] *adj* fancy-dress *(avant n)*.

costumier, ère [kɔstymje, ɛr] *nm, f* THÉÂTRE wardrobe master (*f* mistress).

cotation [kɔtasjɔ̃] *nf* FIN quotation.

cote [kɔt] *nf* - **1.** [marque de classement] classification mark ; [marque numérale] serial number - **2.** FIN quotation - **3.** [popularité] rating - **4.** [niveau] level ; **~ d'alerte** [de cours d'eau] danger level ; *fig* crisis point.

côte [kot] *nf* - **1.** ANAT & BOT [de bœuf] rib ; [de porc, mouton, agneau] chop ; **~ à ~** side by side - **2.** [pente] hill - **3.** [littoral] coast ; **la Côte d'Azur** the French Riviera.

côté [kote] *nm* - **1.** [gén] side ; **être couché sur le ~** to be lying on one's side ; **être aux ~s de qqn** *fig* to be by sb's side ; **d'un ~ ..., de l'autre ~ ...** on the one hand ..., on the other hand ... ; **et ~ finances, ça va?** *fam* how are things moneywise? - **2.** [endroit, direction] direction, way ; **de quel ~ est-il parti?** which way did he go? ; **de l'autre ~ de** on the other side ; **de tous ~s** from all directions ; **du ~ de** [près de] near ; [direction] towards *Br*, toward *Am* ; [provenance] from. ◆ **à côté** *loc adv* - **1.** [lieu - gén] nearby ; [- dans la maison adjacente] next door - **2.** [cible] : **tirer à ~** to shoot wide (of the target). ◆ **à côté de** *loc prép* - **1.** [proximité] beside, next to - **2.** [en comparaison avec] beside, compared to - **3.** [en dehors de] : **être à ~ du sujet** to be off the point. ◆ **de côté** *loc adv* - **1.** [se placer, marcher] sideways - **2.** [en réserve] aside.

coteau, x [kɔto] *nm* - **1.** [colline] hill - **2.** [versant] slope.

Côte-d'Ivoire [kotdivwar] *nf* : **la ~** the Ivory Coast.

côtelé, e [kotle] *adj* ribbed ; **velours ~** corduroy.

côtelette [kotlɛt] *nf* [de porc, mouton, d'agneau] chop ; [de veau] cutlet.

coter [3] [kɔte] *vt* - **1.** [marquer, noter] to mark - **2.** FIN to quote.

côtier, ère [kotje, ɛr] *adj* coastal.

cotisation [kɔtizasjɔ̃] *nf* [à club, parti] subscription ; [à la Sécurité sociale] contribution.

cotiser [3] [kɔtize] *vi* [à un club, un parti] to subscribe ; [à la Sécurité sociale] to contribute. ◆ **se cotiser** *vp* to club together.

coton [kɔtɔ̃] *nm* cotton ; ~ **(hydrophile)** cotton wool.

Coton-Tige® [kɔtɔ̃tiʒ] *nm* cotton bud *Br*, Q-tip® *Am*.

côtoyer [13] [kotwaje] *vt fig* [fréquenter] to mix with.

cou [ku] *nm* [de personne, bouteille] neck.

couchant [kuʃɑ̃] ◇ *adj* ▷ **soleil**. ◇ *nm* west.

couche [kuʃ] *nf* - **1.** [de peinture, de vernis] coat, layer ; [de poussière] film, layer - **2.** [épaisseur] layer ; ~ **d'ozone** ozone layer - **3.** [de bébé] nappy *Br*, diaper *Am* - **4.** [classe sociale] stratum. ◆ **fausse couche** *nf* miscarriage.

couché, e [kuʃe] *adj* : **être ~** [étendu] to be lying down ; [au lit] to be in bed.

couche-culotte [kuʃkylɔt] *nf* disposable nappy *Br* ou diaper *Am*.

coucher[1] [3] [kuʃe] ◇ *vt* - **1.** [enfant] to put to bed - **2.** [objet, blessé] to lay down. ◇ *vi* - **1.** [passer la nuit] to spend the night - **2.** *fam* [avoir des rapports sexuels] : ~ **avec** to sleep with. ◆ **se coucher** *vp* - **1.** [s'allonger] to lie down - **2.** [se mettre au lit] to go to bed - **3.** [astre] to set.

coucher[2] [kuʃe] *nm* [d'astre] setting ; **au ~ du soleil** at sunset.

couchette [kuʃɛt] *nf* - **1.** [de train] couchette - **2.** [de navire] berth.

coucou [kuku] ◇ *nm* - **1.** [oiseau] cuckoo - **2.** [pendule] cuckoo clock - **3.** *péj* [avion] crate. ◇ *interj* peekaboo!

coude [kud] *nm* - **1.** [de personne, de vêtement] elbow - **2.** [courbe] bend.

cou-de-pied [kudpje] (*pl* **cous-de-pied**) *nm* instep.

coudre [86] [kudr] *vt* [bouton] to sew on.

couette [kwɛt] *nf* - **1.** [édredon] duvet - **2.** [coiffure] bunches (*pl*).

couffin [kufɛ̃] *nm* [berceau] Moses basket.

couille [kuj] *nf* (*gén pl*) *vulg* ball.

couiner [3] [kwine] *vi* - **1.** [animal] to squeal - **2.** [pleurnicher] to whine.

coulée [kule] *nf* - **1.** [de matière liquide] : ~ **de lave** lava flow ; ~ **de boue** mudslide - **2.** [de métal] casting.

couler [3] [kule] ◇ *vi* - **1.** [liquide] to flow ; **faire ~ un bain** to run a bath - **2.** [beurre, fromage, nez] to run - **3.** [navire,

entreprise] to sink. ◇ *vt* - **1.** [navire] to sink - **2.** [métal, bronze] to cast.

couleur [kulœr] ◇ *nf* - **1.** [teinte, caractère] colour *Br*, color *Am* - **2.** [linge] coloureds (*pl*) *Br*, coloreds (*pl*) *Am* - **3.** CARTES suit. ◇ *adj inv* [télévision, pellicule] colour (*avant n*) *Br*, color (*avant n*) *Am*.

couleuvre [kulœvr] *nf* grass snake.

coulisse [kulis] *nf* [glissière] : **fenêtre/ porte à ~** sliding window/door. ◆ **coulisses** *nfpl* THÉÂTRE wings.

coulisser [3] [kulise] *vi* to slide.

couloir [kulwar] *nm* - **1.** [corridor] corridor - **2.** GÉOGR gully - **3.** SPORT & TRANSPORT lane.

coup [ku] *nm* - **1.** [choc - physique, moral] blow ; ~ **de couteau** stab (*with a knife*) ; **un ~ dur** *fig* a heavy blow ; **donner un ~ de fouet à qqn** *fig* to give sb a shot in the arm ; ~ **de grâce** *litt* & *fig* coup de grâce, death-blow ; ~ **de pied** kick ; ~ **de poing** punch - **2.** [action nuisible] trick - **3.** [SPORT - au tennis] stroke ; [- en boxe] blow, punch ; [- au football] kick - **4.** [d'éponge, de chiffon] wipe ; **un ~ de crayon** a pencil stroke - **5.** [bruit] noise ; ~ **de feu** shot, gunshot ; ~ **de tonnerre** thunderclap - **6.** [action spectaculaire] : ~ **d'État** coup (d'état) ; ~ **de théâtre** *fig* dramatic turn of events - **7.** *fam* [fois] time - **8.** *loc* : **boire un ~** to have a drink ; **donner un ~ de main à qqn** to give sb a helping hand ; **jeter un ~ d'œil à** to glance at ; **tenir le ~** to hold out ; **valoir le ~** to be well worth it. ◆ **coup de fil** *nm* phone call. ◆ **coup de foudre** *nm* love at first sight. ◆ **coup du lapin** *nm* AUTOM whiplash (*U*). ◆ **coup de soleil** *nm* sunburn (*U*). ◆ **coup de téléphone** *nm* phone call ; **donner** ou **passer un ~ de téléphone à qqn** to telephone ou phone sb. ◆ **coup de vent** *nm* gust of wind ; **partir en ~ de vent** to rush off. ◆ **à coup sûr** *loc adv* definitely. ◆ **du coup** *loc adv* as a result. ◆ **coup sur coup** *loc adv* one after the other. ◆ **du premier coup** *loc adv* first time, at the first attempt. ◆ **sous le coup de** *loc prép* - **1.** [sous l'action de] : **tomber sous le ~ de la loi** to be a statutory offence *Br* ou offense *Am* - **2.** [sous l'effet de] in the grip of. ◆ **tout à coup** *loc adv* suddenly.

coupable [kupabl] ◇ *adj* - **1.** [personne, pensée] guilty - **2.** [action, dessein] culpable, reprehensible ; [négligence, oubli] sinful. ◇ *nmf* guilty person (*pl*).

coupant, e [kupɑ̃, ɑ̃t] *adj* - **1.** [tranchant] cutting - **2.** *fig* [sec] sharp.

coupe [kup] *nf* - **1.** [verre] glass - **2.** [à fruits] dish - **3.** SPORT cup - **4.** [de vêtement, aux cartes] cut - **5.** [plan, surface] (cross) section - **6.** [réduction] cut, cutback.

coupé, e [kupe] *adj* : **bien/mal ~** well/badly cut.

coupe-ongles [kupɔ̃gl] *nm inv* nail clippers.

coupe-papier [kuppapje] (*pl inv* ou **coupe-papiers**) *nm* paper knife.

couper [3] [kupe] ⬦ *vt* - **1.** [gén & INFORM] to cut - **2.** [arbre] to cut down - **3.** [pain] to slice ; [rôti] to carve - **4.** [envie, appétit] to take away - **5.** [vin] to dilute - **6.** [CARTES - avec atout] to trump ; [- paquet] to cut - **7.** [interrompre, trancher] to cut off - **8.** [traverser] to cut across. ⬦ *vi* [gén] to cut. ➡ **se couper** *vp* - **1.** [se blesser] to cut o.s. - **2.** [se croiser] to cross - **3.** [s'isoler] : **se ~ de** to cut o.s. off from.

couper-coller *nm inv* INFORM : **faire un ~** to cut and paste.

couperet [kupʀɛ] *nm* - **1.** [de boucher] cleaver - **2.** [de guillotine] blade.

couperosé, e [kupʀoze] *adj* blotchy.

couple [kupl] *nm* [de personnes] couple ; [d'animaux] pair.

coupler [3] [kuple] *vt* [objets] to couple.

couplet [kuplɛ] *nm* verse.

coupole [kupɔl] *nf* ARCHIT dome, cupola.

coupon [kupɔ̃] *nm* - **1.** [d'étoffe] remnant - **2.** [billet] ticket.

coupon-réponse [kupɔ̃ʀepɔ̃s] (*pl* **coupons-réponse**) *nm* reply coupon.

coupure [kupyʀ] *nf* - **1.** [gén] cut ; [billet de banque] : **petite ~** small denomination note ; **~ de courant** ÉLECTR power cut ; INFORM blackout - **2.** *fig* [rupture] break.

cour [kuʀ] *nf* - **1.** [espace] courtyard - **2.** [du roi, tribunal] court ; *fig & hum* following ; **Cour de cassation** Court of Appeal ; **~ martiale** court-martial.

courage [kuʀaʒ] *nm* courage ; **bon ~!** good luck! ; **je n'ai pas le ~ de faire mes devoirs** I can't bring myself to do my homework.

courageux, euse [kuʀaʒø, øz] *adj* - **1.** [brave] brave - **2.** [audacieux] bold.

couramment [kuʀamɑ̃] *adv* - **1.** [parler une langue] fluently - **2.** [communément] commonly.

courant, e [kuʀɑ̃, ɑ̃t] *adj* - **1.** [habituel] everyday *(avant n)* - **2.** [en cours] present. ➡ **courant** *nm* - **1.** [marin, atmosphérique, électrique] current ; **~ d'air** draught *Br*, draft *Am* - **2.** [d'idées] current - **3.** [laps de temps] : **dans le ~ du mois/de l'année** in the course of the month/the year. ➡ **au courant** *loc adv* : **être au ~** to know (about it) ; **mettre**

qqn **au ~ (de)** to tell sb (about) ; **tenir** qqn **au ~ (de)** to keep sb informed (about) ; **se mettre/se tenir au ~ (de)** to get/keep up to date (with).

courbature [kuʀbatyʀ] *nf* ache.

courbaturé, e [kuʀbatyʀe] *adj* aching.

courbe [kuʀb] ⬦ *nf* curve ; **~ de niveau** [sur une carte] contour (line). ⬦ *adj* curved.

courber [3] [kuʀbe] ⬦ *vt* - **1.** [tige] to bend - **2.** [tête] to bow. ⬦ *vi* to bow. ➡ **se courber** *vp* - **1.** [chose] to bend - **2.** [personne] to bow, to bend down.

courbette [kuʀbɛt] *nf* [révérence] bow ; **faire des ~s** *fig* to bow and scrape.

coureur, euse [kuʀœʀ, øz] *nm, f* SPORT runner ; **~ cycliste** racing cyclist.

courge [kuʀʒ] *nf* - **1.** [légume] marrow *Br*, squash *Am* - **2.** *fam* [imbécile] dimwit.

courgette [kuʀʒɛt] *nf* courgette *Br*, zucchini *Am*.

courir [45] [kuʀiʀ] ⬦ *vi* - **1.** [aller rapidement] to run - **2.** SPORT to race - **3.** [se précipiter, rivière] to rush - **4.** [se propager] : **le bruit court que ...** rumour *Br* ou rumor *Am* has it that ... ; **faire ~ un bruit** to spread a rumour *Br* ou rumor *Am*. ⬦ *vt* - **1.** SPORT to run in - **2.** [parcourir] to roam (through) - **3.** [fréquenter bals, musées] to do the rounds of.

couronne [kuʀɔn] *nf* - **1.** [ornement, autorité] crown - **2.** [de fleurs] wreath - **3.** [monnaie - de Suède, d'Islande] krona ; [- du Danemark, de Norvège] krone ; [- de la République tchèque] crown.

couronnement [kuʀɔnmɑ̃] *nm* - **1.** [de monarque] coronation - **2.** *fig* [apogée] crowning achievement.

couronner [3] [kuʀɔne] *vt* - **1.** [monarque] to crown - **2.** [récompenser] to give a prize to.

courre [kuʀ] ➡ **chasse**.

courrier [kuʀje] *nm* mail, letters *(pl)* ; **~ du cœur** agony column.

courroie [kuʀwa] *nf* TECHNOL belt ; [attache] strap ; **~ de transmission** driving belt ; **~ de ventilateur** fanbelt.

courroucer [16] [kuʀuse] *vt littéraire* to anger.

cours [kuʀ] *nm* - **1.** [écoulement] flow ; **~ d'eau** waterway ; **donner** ou **laisser libre ~ à** *fig* to give free rein to - **2.** [déroulement] course ; **au ~ de** during, in the course of ; **en ~** [année, dossier] current ; [affaires] in hand ; **en ~ de route** on the way - **3.** FIN price ; **avoir ~** [monnaie] to be legal tender - **4.** [leçon] class, lesson ; **donner des ~ (à** qqn**)** to teach (sb) - **5.** [classe] : **~ élémen-**

taire *years two and three of primary school* ; ~ **moyen** *last two years of primary school* ; ~ **préparatoire** ≃ first-year infants *Br*, ≃ nursery school *Am*.

course [kurs] *nf* - **1.** [action] running *(U)* ; **au pas de ~** at a run - **2.** [compétition] race - **3.** [en taxi] journey - **4.** [mouvement] flight, course - **5.** [commission] errand ; **faire des ~s** to go shopping.

coursier, ère [kursje, ɛr] *nm, f* messenger.

court, e [kur, kurt] *adj* short. ◆ **court** ◇ *adv* : **être à ~ d'argent/d'idées/d'arguments** to be short of money/ideas/arguments ; **prendre qqn de ~** to catch sb unawares ; **tourner ~** to stop suddenly. ◇ *nm* : **~ de tennis** tennis court.

court-bouillon [kurbujɔ̃] *nm* court-bouillon.

court-circuit [kursirkɥi] *nm* short circuit.

courtier, ère [kurtje, ɛr] *nm, f* broker.

courtisan, e [kurtizɑ̃, an] *nm, f* - **1.** HIST courtier - **2.** [flatteur] sycophant. ◆ **courtisane** *nf* courtesan.

courtiser [3] [kurtize] *vt* - **1.** [femme] to woo, to court - **2.** *péj* [flatter] to flatter.

court-métrage [kurmetraʒ] *nm* short (film).

courtois, e [kurtwa, az] *adj* courteous.

courtoisie [kurtwazi] *nf* courtesy.

couru, e [kury] ◇ *pp* ▷ **courir**. ◇ *adj* popular.

couscous [kuskus] *nm* couscous, *traditional North African dish of semolina served with a spicy stew of meat and vegetables*.

cousin, e [kuzɛ̃, in] *nm, f* cousin ; ~ **germain** first cousin.

coussin [kusɛ̃] *nm* [de siège] cushion.

cousu, e [kuzy] *pp* ▷ **coudre**.

coût [ku] *nm* cost.

coûtant [kutɑ̃] ▷ **prix**.

couteau, x [kuto] *nm* - **1.** [gén] knife ; ~ **à cran d'arrêt** flick knife - **2.** [coquillage] razor shell *Br*, razor clam *Am*.

coûter [3] [kute] ◇ *vi* - **1.** [valoir] to cost ; **ça coûte combien ?** how much is it ? ; ~ **cher à qqn** to cost sb a lot ; *fig* to cost sb dear *ou* dearly - **2.** *fig* [être pénible] to be difficult. ◇ *vt fig* to cost. ◆ **coûte que coûte** *loc adv* at all costs.

coûteux, euse [kutø, øz] *adj* costly, expensive.

coutume [kutym] *nf* [gén & JUR] custom.

couture [kutyr] *nf* - **1.** [action] sewing - **2.** [points] seam - **3.** [activité] dressmaking ; **haute ~** designer fashion.

couturier, ère [kutyrje, ɛr] *nm, f* couturier.

couvée [kuve] *nf* [d'œufs] clutch ; [de poussins] brood.

couvent [kuvɑ̃] *nm* [de sœurs] convent ; [de moines] monastery.

couver [3] [kuve] ◇ *vt* - **1.** [œufs] to sit on - **2.** [dorloter] to mollycoddle - **3.** [maladie] to be sickening for. ◇ *vi* [poule] to brood ; *fig* [complot] to hatch.

couvercle [kuvɛrkl] *nm* [de casserole, boîte] lid, cover.

couvert, e [kuvɛr, ɛrt] ◇ *pp* ▷ **couvrir**. ◇ *adj* - **1.** [submergé] covered ; ~ **de** covered with - **2.** [habillé] dressed ; **être bien ~** to be well wrapped up - **3.** [nuageux] overcast. ◆ **couvert** *nm* - **1.** [abri] : **se mettre à ~** to take shelter - **2.** [place à table] place (setting) ; **mettre** *ou* **dresser le ~** to set *ou* lay the table. ◆ **couverts** *nmpl* cutlery *(U)*.

couverture [kuvɛrtyr] *nf* - **1.** [gén] cover - **2.** [de lit] blanket ; ~ **chauffante** electric blanket - **3.** [toit] roofing *(U)*.

couveuse [kuvøz] *nf* - **1.** [poule] sitting hen - **2.** [machine] incubator.

couvre-chef [kuvrəʃɛf] *(pl* **couvre-chefs)** *nm hum* hat.

couvre-feu [kuvrəfø] *(pl* **couvre-feux)** *nm* curfew.

couvreur [kuvrœr] *nm* roofer.

couvrir [34] [kuvrir] *vt* - **1.** [gén] to cover ; ~ **qqn/qqch de** *litt & fig* to cover sb/sthg with - **2.** [protéger] to shield. ◆ **se couvrir** *vp* - **1.** [se vêtir] to wrap up - **2.** [se recouvrir] : **se ~ de feuilles/de fleurs** to come into leaf/blossom - **3.** [ciel] to cloud over - **4.** [se protéger] to cover o.s.

covoiturage [kɔvwatyraʒ] *nm* car sharing ; **pratiquer le ~** to belong to a car pool.

CP *nm abr de* **cours préparatoire**.

CQFD *(abr de* **ce qu'il fallait démontrer)** QED.

crabe [krab] *nm* crab.

crachat [kraʃa] *nm* spit *(U)*.

cracher [3] [kraʃe] ◇ *vi* - **1.** [personne] to spit - **2.** *fam* [dédaigner] : **ne pas ~ sur qqch** not to turn one's nose up at sthg. ◇ *vt* [sang] to spit (up) ; [lave, injures] to spit (out).

crachin [kraʃɛ̃] *nm* drizzle.

crachoir [kraʃwar] *nm* spittoon.

craie [krɛ] *nf* chalk.

craindre [80] [krɛ̃dr] *vt* - **1.** [redouter] to fear, to be afraid of ; ~ **de faire qqch** to be afraid of doing sthg ; **je crains d'avoir oublié mes papiers** I'm afraid I've forgotten my papers ; ~ **que** (+ *subjonctif*) to be afraid (that) ; **je crains qu'il oublie** OU **n'oublie** I'm afraid he may forget - **2.** [être sensible à] to be susceptible to.

craint, e [krɛ̃, ɛ̃t] *pp* ▷ **craindre.**

crainte [krɛ̃t] *nf* fear ; **de ~ de faire qqch** for fear of doing sthg ; **de ~ que** (+ *subjonctif*) for fear that ; **il a fui de ~ qu'on ne le voie** he fled for fear that he might be seen OU for fear of being seen.

craintif, ive [krɛ̃tif, iv] *adj* timid.

cramoisi, e [kramwazi] *adj* crimson.

crampe [krɑ̃p] *nf* cramp.

crampon [krɑ̃pɔ̃] *nm* [crochet - gén] clamp ; [- pour alpinisme] crampon.

cramponner [3] [krɑ̃pɔne] ◆ **se cramponner** *vp* [s'agripper] to hang on ; **se ~ à qqn/qqch** *litt & fig* to cling to sb/sthg.

cran [krɑ̃] *nm* - **1.** [entaille, degré] notch, cut - **2.** (U) [audace] guts (pl).

crâne [kran] *nm* skull.

crâner [3] [krane] *vi fam* to show off.

crânien, enne [kranjɛ̃, ɛn] *adj* : **boîte ~ne** skull ; **traumatisme ~** head injury.

crapaud [krapo] *nm* toad.

crapule [krapyl] *nf* scum (U).

craquelure [kraklyr] *nf* crack.

craquement [krakmɑ̃] *nm* crack, cracking (U).

craquer [3] [krake] ◇ *vi* - **1.** [produire un bruit] to crack ; [plancher, chaussure] to creak - **2.** [se déchirer] to split - **3.** [s'effondrer - personne] to crack up - **4.** [être séduit par] : **~ pour** to fall for. ◇ *vt* [allumette] to strike.

crasse [kras] *nf* - **1.** [saleté] dirt, filth - **2.** *fam* [mauvais tour] dirty trick.

crasseux, euse [krasø, øz] *adj* filthy.

cratère [krater] *nm* crater.

cravache [kravaʃ] *nf* riding crop.

cravate [kravat] *nf* tie.

crawl [krol] *nm* crawl.

crayon [krɛjɔ̃] *nm* - **1.** [gén] pencil ; **~ à bille** ballpoint (pen) ; **~ de couleur** crayon - **2.** TECHNOL pen ; **~ optique** light pen.

créancier, ère [kreɑ̃sje, ɛr] *nm, f* creditor.

créateur, trice [kreatœr, tris] ◇ *adj* creative. ◇ *nm, f* creator. ◆ **Créateur** *nm* : **le Créateur** the Creator.

créatif, ive [kreatif, iv] *adj* creative.

création [kreasjɔ̃] *nf* creation.

créativité [kreativite] *nf* creativity.

créature [kreatyr] *nf* creature.

crécelle [kresɛl] *nf* rattle.

crèche [krɛʃ] *nf* - **1.** [de Noël] crib - **2.** [garderie] crèche.

crédible [kredibl] *adj* credible.

crédit [kredi] *nm* - **1.** [gén] credit ; **faire ~ à qqn** to give sb credit ; **acheter/vendre qqch à ~** to buy/sell sthg on credit ; **~ municipal** pawnshop - **2.** *fig & sout* influence.

crédit-bail [kredibaj] (*pl* **crédits-bails**) *nm* leasing.

créditeur, trice [kreditœr, tris] ◇ *adj* in credit. ◇ *nm, f* creditor.

crédule [kredyl] *adj* credulous.

crédulité [kredylite] *nf* credulity.

créer [15] [kree] *vt* - **1.** RELIG [inventer] to create - **2.** [fonder] to found, to start up.

crémaillère [kremajɛr] *nf* - **1.** [de cheminée] trammel ; **pendre la ~** *fig* to have a housewarming (party) - **2.** TECHNOL rack.

crémation [kremasjɔ̃] *nf* cremation.

crématoire [krematwar] ▷ **four.**

crème [krɛm] ◇ *nf* [gén] cream ; **~ fouettée/fraîche/glacée** whipped/fresh/ice cream ; **~ anglaise** custard ; **~ hydratante** moisturizer. ◇ *adj inv* cream.

crémerie [kremri] *nf* dairy.

crémier, ère [kremje, ɛr] *nm, f* dairyman (*f* dairywoman).

créneau, x [kreno] *nm* - **1.** [de fortification] crenel - **2.** [pour se garer] : **faire un ~** to reverse into a parking space - **3.** [de marché] niche - **4.** [horaire] window, gap.

créole [kreɔl] *adj & nm* creole.

crêpe [krɛp] ◇ *nf* CULIN pancake. ◇ *nm* [tissu] crepe.

crêperie [krɛpri] *nf* pancake restaurant.

crépi [krepi] *nm* roughcast.

crépir [32] [krepir] *vt* to roughcast.

crépiter [3] [krepite] *vi* [feu, flammes] to crackle ; [pluie] to patter.

crépon [krepɔ̃] ◇ *adj* ▷ **papier.** ◇ *nm* seersucker.

crépu, e [krepy] *adj* frizzy.

crépuscule [krepyskyl] *nm* [du jour] dusk, twilight ; *fig* twilight.

crescendo [kreʃɛndo, kreʃɛdo] ◇ *adv* crescendo ; **aller ~** *fig* [bruit] to get OU grow louder and louder. ◇ *nm inv* MUS & *fig* crescendo.

cresson [kresɔ̃] *nm* watercress.

Crète [krɛt] *nf* : **la ~** Crete.

crête [krɛt] *nf* - **1.** [de coq] comb - **2.** [de montagne, vague, oiseau] crest.

crétin, e [kretɛ̃, in] *fam* ◇ *adj* cretinous, idiotic. ◇ *nm, f* cretin, idiot.

creuser [3] [krøze] *vt* - **1.** [trou] to dig

- **2.** [objet] to hollow out - **3.** *fig* [approfondir] to go into deeply.

creux, creuse [krø, krøz] *adj* - **1.** [vide, concave] hollow - **2.** [période - d'activité réduite] slack ; [- à tarif réduit] off-peak - **3.** [paroles] empty. ◆ **creux** *nm* - **1.** [concavité] hollow - **2.** [période] lull.

crevaison [krəvɛzɔ̃] *nf* puncture.

crevant, e [krəvɑ̃, ɑ̃t] *adj fam* [fatigant] exhausting, knackering *Br*.

crevasse [krəvas] *nf* [de mur] crevice, crack ; [de glacier] crevasse ; [sur la main] crack.

crevé, e [krəve] *adj* - **1.** [pneu] burst, punctured - **2.** *fam* [fatigué] dead, shattered *Br*.

crève-cœur [krɛvkœr] *nm inv* heartbreak.

crever [19] [krəve] ◇ *vi* - **1.** [éclater] to burst - **2.** *tfam* [mourir] to die ; ~ de *fig* [jalousie, orgueil] to be bursting with. ◇ *vt* - **1.** [percer] to burst - **2.** *fam* [épuiser] to wear out.

crevette [krəvɛt] *nf* : ~ **(grise)** shrimp ; ~ **(rose)** prawn.

cri [kri] *nm* - **1.** [de personne] cry, shout ; [perçant] scream ; [d'animal] cry ; **pousser un ~** to cry (out), to shout ; **pousser un ~ de douleur** to cry out in pain - **2.** [appel] cry ; **le dernier ~** *fig* the latest thing.

criant, e [krijɑ̃, ɑ̃t] *adj* [injustice] blatant.

criard, e [krijar, ard] *adj* - **1.** [voix] strident, piercing - **2.** [couleur] loud.

crible [kribl] *nm* [instrument] sieve ; **passer qqch au ~** *fig* to examine sthg closely.

criblé, e [krible] *adj* riddled ; **être ~ de dettes** to be up to one's eyes in debt.

cric [krik] *nm* jack.

cricket [krikɛt] *nm* cricket.

crier [10] [krije] ◇ *vi* - **1.** [pousser un cri] to shout (out), to yell - **2.** [parler fort] to shout - **3.** [protester] : ~ **contre** ou **après qqn** to nag sb, to go on at sb. ◇ *vt* to shout (out).

crime [krim] *nm* - **1.** [délit] crime - **2.** [meurtre] murder ; **~s contre l'humanité** crime against humanity.

criminalité [kriminalite] *nf* crime.

criminel, elle [kriminɛl] ◇ *adj* criminal. ◇ *nm, f* criminal ; ~ **de guerre** war criminal.

crin [krɛ̃] *nm* [d'animal] hair.

crinière [krinjɛr] *nf* mane.

crique [krik] *nf* creek.

criquet [krikɛ] *nm* locust ; [sauterelle] grasshopper.

crise [kriz] *nf* - **1.** MÉD attack ; ~ **cardiaque** heart attack ; ~ **de foie** bilious attack

- **2.** [accès] fit ; ~ **de nerfs** attack of nerves - **3.** [phase critique] crisis.

crispation [krispasjɔ̃] *nf* - **1.** [contraction] contraction - **2.** [agacement] irritation.

crispé, e [krispe] *adj* tense, on edge.

crisper [3] [krispe] *vt* - **1.** [contracter - visage] to tense ; [- poing] to clench - **2.** [agacer] to irritate. ◆ **se crisper** *vp* - **1.** [se contracter] to tense (up) - **2.** [s'irriter] to get irritated.

crisser [3] [krise] *vi* [pneu] to screech ; [étoffe] to rustle.

cristal, aux [kristal, o] *nm* crystal ; ~ **de roche** quartz.

cristallin, e [kristalɛ̃, in] *adj* - **1.** [limpide] crystal clear, crystalline - **2.** [roche] crystalline. ◆ **cristallin** *nm* crystalline lens.

critère [kritɛr] *nm* criterion.

critique [kritik] ◇ *adj* critical. ◇ *nmf* critic. ◇ *nf* criticism.

critiquer [3] [kritike] *vt* to criticize.

croasser [3] [krɔase] *vi* to croak, to caw.

croate [krɔat] *adj* Croat, Croatian. ◆ **Croate** *nmf* Croat, Croatian.

Croatie [krɔasi] *nf* : **la ~** Croatia.

croc [kro] *nm* [de chien] fang.

croche [krɔʃ] *nf* quaver *Br*, eighth (note) *Am*.

croche-pied [krɔʃpje] (*pl* **croche-pieds**) *nm* : **faire un ~ à qqn** to trip sb up.

crochet [krɔʃɛ] *nm* - **1.** [de métal] hook ; **vivre aux ~s de qqn** to live off sb *fig* - **2.** TRICOT crochet hook - **3.** TYPO square bracket - **4.** BOXE : ~ **du gauche/du droit** left/right hook.

crochu, e [krɔʃy] *adj* [doigts] claw-like ; [nez] hooked.

crocodile [krɔkɔdil] *nm* crocodile.

croire [107] [krwar] ◇ *vt* - **1.** [chose, personne] to believe - **2.** [penser] to think ; **tu crois?** do you think so? ; **il le croyait parti** he thought you'd left ; ~ **que** to think (that). ◇ *vi* : ~ **à** to believe in ; ~ **en** to believe in, to have faith in.

croisade [krwazad] *nf* HIST & *fig* crusade.

croisé, e [krwaze] *adj* [veste] double-breasted. ◆ **croisé** *nm* HIST crusader.

croisement [krwazmɑ̃] *nm* - **1.** [intersection] junction, intersection - **2.** BIOL cross-breeding.

croiser [3] [krwaze] ◇ *vt* - **1.** [jambes] to cross ; [bras] to fold - **2.** [passer à côté de] to pass - **3.** [chemin] to cross, to cut across - **4.** [métisser] to interbreed. ◇ *vi* NAVIG to cruise. ◆ **se croiser** *vp* [chemins] to cross, to intersect ; [personnes] to pass ; [lettres] to cross ; [regards] to meet.

croisière [krwazjɛr] *nf* cruise.

croisillon [krwazijɔ̃] *nm* : **à ~s** lattice *(avant n)*.

croissance [krwasɑ̃s] *nf* growth, development ; **~ économique** economic growth OU development.

croissant, e [krwasɑ̃, ɑ̃t] *adj* increasing, growing. ◆ **croissant** *nm* - **1.** [de lune] crescent - **2.** CULIN croissant.

croître [93] [krwatr] *vi* - **1.** [grandir] to grow - **2.** [augmenter] to increase.

croix [krwa] *nf* cross ; **en ~** in the shape of a cross ; **~ gammée** swastika.

Croix-Rouge [krwaruʒ] *nf* : **la ~** the Red Cross.

croquant, e [krɔkɑ̃, ɑ̃t] *adj* crisp, crunchy.

croque-mitaine [krɔkmitɛn] (*pl* **croque-mitaines**) *nm* bogeyman.

croque-monsieur [krɔkməsjø] *nm inv* toasted cheese and ham sandwich.

croque-mort [krɔkmɔr] (*pl* **croque-morts**) *nm fam* undertaker.

croquer [3] [krɔke] ◇ *vt* - **1.** [manger] to crunch - **2.** [dessiner] to sketch. ◇ *vi* to be crunchy.

croquette [krɔkɛt] *nf* croquette.

croquis [krɔki] *nm* sketch.

cross [krɔs] *nm* [exercice] cross-country (running) ; [course] cross-country race.

crotte [krɔt] *nf* [de lapin etc] droppings (*pl*) ; [de chien] dirt.

crottin [krɔtɛ̃] *nm* [de cheval] (horse) manure.

crouler [3] [krule] *vi* to crumble ; **~ sous** *litt & fig* to collapse under.

croupe [krup] *nf* rump ; **monter en ~** to ride pillion.

croupier [krupje] *nm* croupier.

croupir [32] [krupir] *vi litt & fig* to stagnate.

croustillant, e [krustijɑ̃, ɑ̃t] *adj* [croquant - pain] crusty ; [- biscuit] crunchy.

croûte [krut] *nf* - **1.** [du pain, terrestre] crust - **2.** [de fromage] rind - **3.** [de plaie] scab - **4.** *fam péj* [tableau] daub.

croûton [krutɔ̃] *nm* - **1.** [bout du pain] crust - **2.** [pain frit] crouton - **3.** *fam péj* [personne] fuddy-duddy.

croyance [krwajɑ̃s] *nf* belief.

croyant, e [krwajɑ̃, ɑ̃t] ◇ *adj* : **être ~** to be a believer. ◇ *nm, f* believer.

CRS (*abr de* **Compagnie républicaine de sécurité**) *nm* member of the French riot police.

cru, e [kry] ◇ *pp* ▷ **croire**. ◇ *adj* - **1.** [non cuit] raw - **2.** [violent] harsh - **3.** [di-

rect] blunt - **4.** [grivois] crude. ◆ **cru** *nm* [vin] vintage, wine ; [vignoble] vineyard ; **du ~** *fig* local ; **de son propre ~** of one's own devising.

crû [kry] *pp* ▷ **croître**.

cruauté [kryote] *nf* cruelty.

cruche [kryʃ] *nf* - **1.** [objet] jug - **2.** *fam péj* [personne niaise] twit.

crucial, e, aux [krysjal, o] *adj* crucial.

crucifix [krysifi] *nm* crucifix.

crudité [krydite] *nf* crudeness. ◆ **crudités** *nfpl* crudités.

crue [kry] *nf* rise in the water level.

cruel, elle [kryɛl] *adj* cruel.

crustacé [krystase] *nm* shellfish, crustacean ; **~s** shellfish *(U)*.

crypter [kripte] *vt* to encrypt ; **chaîne cryptée** encrypted channel.

Cuba [kyba] *n* Cuba.

cubain, aine [kybɛ̃, ɛn] *adj* Cuban. ◆ **Cubain, aine** *nm, f* Cuban.

cube [kyb] *nm* cube ; **4 au ~ = 64** 4 cubed is 64 ; **mètre ~** cubic metre *Br* OU meter *Am*.

cueillette [kœjɛt] *nf* picking, harvesting.

cueilli, e [kœji] *pp* ▷ **cueillir**.

cueillir [41] [kœjir] *vt* [fruits, fleurs] to pick.

cuillère, cuiller [kɥijɛr] *nf* spoon ; **~ à café** coffee spoon ; CULIN teaspoon ; **~ à dessert** dessertspoon ; **~ à soupe** soup spoon ; CULIN tablespoon ; **petite ~** teaspoon.

cuillerée [kɥijere] *nf* spoonful ; **~ à café** CULIN teaspoonful ; **~ à soupe** CULIN tablespoonful.

cuir [kɥir] *nm* leather ; [non tanné] hide ; **~ chevelu** ANAT scalp.

cuirasse [kɥiras] *nf* [de chevalier] breastplate ; *fig* armour *Br*, armor *Am*.

cuirassé [kɥirase] *nm* battleship.

cuire [98] [kɥir] ◇ *vt* [viande, œuf] to cook ; [tarte, gâteau] to bake. ◇ *vi* - **1.** [viande, œuf] to cook ; [tarte, gâteau] to bake ; **faire ~ qqch** to cook/bake sthg - **2.** *fig* [personne] to roast, to be boiling.

cuisine [kɥizin] *nf* - **1.** [pièce] kitchen - **2.** [art] cooking, cookery ; **faire la ~** to do the cooking, to cook.

cuisiné, e [kɥizine] *adj* : **plat ~** ready-cooked meal.

cuisiner [3] [kɥizine] ◇ *vt* - **1.** [aliment] to cook - **2.** *fam* [personne] to grill. ◇ *vi* to cook ; **bien/mal ~** to be a good/bad cook.

cuisinier, ère [kɥizinje, ɛr] *nm, f* cook. ◆ **cuisinière** *nf* cooker *Br*, stove *Am* ; **cuisinière électrique/à gaz** electric/gas cooker *Br* OU stove *Am*.

cuisse [kɥis] *nf* - **1.** ANAT thigh - **2.** CULIN leg.

cuisson [kɥisɔ̃] *nf* cooking.

cuit, e [kɥi, kɥit] ◇ *pp* ▷ **cuire.** ◇ *adj* : **bien ~** [steak] well-done.

cuivre [kɥivr] *nm* [métal] : **~ (rouge)** copper ; **~ jaune** brass. ◆ **cuivres** *nmpl* : **les ~s** MUS the brass.

cuivré, e [kɥivre] *adj* [couleur, reflet] coppery ; [teint] bronzed.

cul [ky] *nm* - **1.** *tfam* [postérieur] bum - **2.** [de bouteille] bottom.

culbute [kylbyt] *nf* - **1.** [saut] somersault - **2.** [chute] tumble, fall.

cul-de-sac [kydsak] (*pl* **culs-de-sac**) *nm* dead end.

culinaire [kyliner] *adj* culinary.

culminant [kylminã] ▷ **point.**

culot [kylo] *nm* - **1.** *fam* [toupet] cheek, nerve ; **avoir du ~** to have a lot of nerve - **2.** [de cartouche, ampoule] cap.

culotte [kylɔt] *nf* [sous-vêtement féminin] knickers (*pl*), panties (*pl*), pair of knickers ou panties.

culotté, e [kylɔte] *adj* [effronté] : **elle est ~e** she's got a nerve.

culpabilité [kylpabilite] *nf* guilt.

culte [kylt] *nm* - **1.** [vénération, amour] worship - **2.** [religion] religion.

cultivateur, trice [kyltivatœr, tris] *nm, f* farmer.

cultivé, e [kyltive] *adj* [personne] educated, cultured.

cultiver [3] [kyltive] *vt* - **1.** [terre, goût, relation] to cultivate - **2.** [plante] to grow.

culture [kyltyr] *nf* - **1.** AGRIC cultivation, farming ; **les ~s** cultivated land - **2.** [savoir] culture, knowledge ; **~ physique** physical training - **3.** [civilisation] culture.

culturel, elle [kyltyrɛl] *adj* cultural.

culturisme [kyltyrism] *nm* bodybuilding.

cumin [kymɛ̃] *nm* cumin.

cumuler [3] [kymyle] *vt* [fonctions, titres] to hold simultaneously ; [salaires] to draw simultaneously.

cupide [kypid] *adj* greedy.

cure [kyr] *nf* (course of) treatment ; **faire une ~ de fruits** to go on a fruit-based diet ; **~ de désintoxication** [d'alcool] drying-out treatment ; [de drogue] detoxication treatment ; **~ de sommeil** sleep therapy ; **faire une ~ thermale** to take the waters.

curé [kyre] *nm* parish priest.

cure-dents [kyrdã] *nm inv* toothpick.

curer [3] [kyre] *vt* to clean out.

curieux, euse [kyrjø, øz] ◇ *adj* - **1.** [intéressé] curious ; **~ de qqch/de faire qqch** curious about sthg/to do sthg - **2.** [indiscret] inquisitive - **3.** [étrange] strange, curious. ◇ *nm, f* busybody.

curiosité [kyrjozite] *nf* curiosity.

curriculum vitae [kyrikylɔmvite] *nm inv* curriculum vitae *Br*, résumé *Am*.

curry [kyri], **carry** [kari], **cari** [kari] *nm* - **1.** [épice] curry powder - **2.** [plat] curry.

curseur [kyrsœr] *nm* cursor.

cutané, e [kytane] *adj* cutaneous, skin (*avant n*).

cutiréaction, cuti-réaction (*pl* **cuti-réactions**) [kytireaksjɔ̃] *nf* skin test.

cuve [kyv] *nf* - **1.** [citerne] tank - **2.** [à vin] vat.

cuvée [kyve] *nf* [récolte] vintage.

cuvette [kyvɛt] *nf* - **1.** [récipient] basin, bowl - **2.** [de lavabo] basin ; [de W.-C.] bowl - **3.** GÉOGR basin.

CV *nm* - **1.** (*abr de* **curriculum vitae**) CV *Br*, résumé *Am* - **2.** (*abr de* **cheval-vapeur**) hp ; [puissance fiscale] *classification for scaling of car tax.*

cyanure [sjanyr] *nm* cyanide.

cybercafé [siberkafe] *nm* cybercafé, internet café.

cybercommerce [siberkɔmers] *nm* e-commerce.

cyberespace [siberespas], **cybermonde** [sibermɔ̃d] *nm* cyberspace.

cybernaute [sibernot] *nm* (net) surfer, cybersurfer, cybernaut.

cyclable [siklabl] ▷ **piste.**

cycle [sikl] *nm* cycle ; **premier ~** UNIV ≃ first and second year ; SCOL middle school *Br*, junior high school *Am* ; **second ~** UNIV ≃ final year *Br*, ≃ senior year *Am* ; SCOL upper school *Br*, high school *Am* ; **troisième ~** UNIV ≃ postgraduate year ou years.

cyclique [siklik] *adj* cyclic, cyclical.

cyclisme [siklism] *nm* cycling.

cycliste [siklist] *nmf* cyclist.

cyclone [siklon] *nm* cyclone.

cygne [siɲ] *nm* swan.

cylindre [silɛ̃dr] *nm* - **1.** AUTOM & GÉOM cylinder - **2.** [rouleau] roller.

cymbale [sɛ̃bal] *nf* cymbal.

cynique [sinik] *adj* cynical.

cynisme [sinism] *nm* cynicism.

cyprès [siprɛ] *nm* cypress.

cyrillique [sirilik] *adj* Cyrillic.

d, D [de] *nm inv* d, D.

d' ⊳ de.

d'abord [dabɔr] ⊳ abord.

d'accord [dakɔr] *loc adv* : **d'accord!** all right!, OK! ; **être ~ avec** to agree with.

dactylo [daktilo] *nf* [personne] typist ; [procédé] typing.

dactylographier [9] [daktilɔgrafje] *vt* to type.

dada [dada] *nm* - **1.** [cheval] gee-gee - **2.** *fam* [occupation] hobby - **3.** *fam* [idée] hobby-horse - **4.** ART Dadaism.

dahlia [dalja] *nm* dahlia.

daigner [4] [deɲe] *vi* to deign.

daim [dɛ̃] *nm* - **1.** [animal] fallow deer - **2.** [peau] suede.

dallage [dalaʒ] *nm* [action] paving ; [dalles] pavement.

dalle [dal] *nf* [de pierre] slab ; [de lino] tile.

dalmatien, enne [dalmasjɛ̃, ɛn] *nm, f* dalmatian.

daltonien, enne [daltɔnjɛ̃, ɛn] *adj* colour-blind *Br*, color-blind *Am*.

dame [dam] *nf* - **1.** [femme] lady - **2.** CARTES & ÉCHECS queen. ◆ **dames** *nfpl* draughts *Br*, checkers *Am*.

damier [damje] *nm* - **1.** [de jeu] draughtboard *Br*, checkerboard *Am* - **2.** [motif] : **à ~** checked.

damné, e [dane] *adj fam* damned.

damner [3] [dane] *vt* to damn.

dancing [dɑ̃siŋ] *nm* dance hall.

dandiner [3] [dɑ̃dine] ◆ **se dandiner** *vp* to waddle.

Danemark [danmark] *nm* : **le ~** Denmark.

danger [dɑ̃ʒe] *nm* danger ; **en ~** in danger ; **courir un ~** to run a risk.

dangereux, euse [dɑ̃ʒrø, øz] *adj* dangerous.

danois, e [danwa, az] *adj* Danish. ◆ **danois** *nm* - **1.** [langue] Danish - **2.** [chien] Great Dane. ◆ **Danois, e** *nm, f* Dane.

dans [dɑ̃] *prép* - **1.** [dans le temps] in ; **je reviens ~ un mois** I'll be back in a month *ou* in a month's time - **2.** [dans l'espace] in ; **~ une boîte** in *ou* inside a box - **3.** [avec mouvement] into ; **entrer ~ une chambre** to come into a room, to enter a room - **4.** [indiquant un état, une manière] in ; **vivre ~ la misère** to live in poverty ; **il est ~ le commerce** he's in business - **5.** [environ] : **~ les ... about ... ; ça coûte ~ les 30 euros** it costs about 30 euros.

dansant, e [dɑ̃sɑ̃, ɑ̃t] *adj litt & fig* dancing ; **soirée ~e** dance ; **thé ~** tea dance.

danse [dɑ̃s] *nf* - **1.** [art] dancing - **2.** [musique] dance.

danser [3] [dɑ̃se] ◇ *vi* - **1.** [personne] to dance - **2.** [bateau] to bob ; [flammes] to flicker. ◇ *vt* to dance.

danseur, euse [dɑ̃sœr, øz] *nm, f* dancer.

dard [dar] *nm* [d'animal] sting.

date [dat] *nf* - **1.** [jour+mois+année] date ; **~ de naissance** date of birth - **2.** [moment] event.

dater [3] [date] ◇ *vt* to date. ◇ *vi* - **1.** [marquer] to be *ou* mark a milestone - **2.** *fam* [être démodé] to be dated. ◆ **à dater de** *loc prép* as of *ou* from.

datte [dat] *nf* date.

dattier [datje] *nm* date palm.

dauphin [dofɛ̃] *nm* - **1.** [mammifère] dolphin - **2.** HIST heir apparent.

daurade [dɔrad] *nf* sea bream.

davantage [davɑ̃taʒ] *adv* - **1.** [plus] more ; **~ de** more - **2.** [plus longtemps] (any) longer.

de [də] *(contraction de de + le = du* [dy]*, de + les = des* [de]*)* ◇ *prép* - **1.** [provenance] from ; **revenir ~ Paris** to come back *ou* return from Paris ; **il est sorti ~ la maison** he left the house, he went out of the house - **2.** [avec à] : **~ ... à** from ... to ; **~ Paris à Tokyo** from Paris to Tokyo ; **~ dix heures à midi** from ten o'clock to *ou* till midday ; **il y avait ~ quinze à vingt mille spectateurs** there were between fifteen and twenty thousand spectators - **3.** [appartenance] of ; **la porte du salon** the door of the sitting room, the sitting room door ; **le frère ~ Pierre** Pierre's brother - **4.** [indique la détermination, la qualité] : **un verre d'eau** a glass of water ; **un peignoir ~ soie** a silk dressing gown ; **un appartement ~ 60 m²** a flat 60 metres square ; **un bébé ~ trois jours** a three-day-old baby ; **une ville ~ 500 000 habitants** a town with *ou* of 500,000 inhabitants ; **le train ~ 9 h 30** the 9.30 train. ◇ *article partitif* - **1.** [dans une phrase affirmative] some ; **je voudrais du vin/du lait** I'd like (some) wine/(some) milk ; **boire ~ l'eau** to drink (some) water ; **acheter des légumes** to buy some vegetables - **2.** [dans une interrogation ou une négation] any ; **ils n'ont pas d'enfants** they don't have any children, they have no children ; **avez-**

vous du pain? do you have any bread?, have you got any bread? ; **voulez-vous du thé?** would you like some tea?

dé [de] *nm* - **1.** [à jouer] dice, die - **2.** COUTURE : ~ **(à coudre)** thimble.

DEA (*abr de* **diplôme d'études approfondies**) *nm* postgraduate diploma.

dealer[1] [dile] *vt* to deal.

dealer[2] [dilœr] *nm fam* dealer.

déambuler [3] [deãbyle] *vi* to stroll (around).

débâcle [debakl] *nf* [débandade] rout ; *fig* collapse.

déballer [3] [debale] *vt* to unpack ; *fam fig* to pour out.

débandade [debãdad] *nf* dispersal.

débarbouiller [3] [debarbuje] *vt* : ~ **qqn** to wash sb's face. ➡ **se débarbouiller** *vp* to wash one's face.

débarcadère [debarkadɛr] *nm* landing stage.

débardeur [debardœr] *nm* - **1.** [ouvrier] docker - **2.** [vêtement] slipover.

débarquement [debarkəmã] *nm* [de marchandises] unloading.

débarquer [3] [debarke] ◇ *vt* [marchandises] to unload ; [passagers & MIL] to land. ◇ *vi* - **1.** [d'un bateau] to disembark - **2.** MIL to land - **3.** *fam* [arriver à l'improviste] to turn up ; *fig* to know nothing.

débarras [debara] *nm* junk room ; **bon ~!** *fig* good riddance!

débarrasser [3] [debarase] *vt* - **1.** [pièce] to clear up ; [table] to clear - **2.** [ôter] : ~ **qqn de qqch** to take sthg from sb. ➡ **se débarrasser** *vp* : **se ~ de** to get rid of.

débat [deba] *nm* debate.

débattre [83] [debatr] *vt* to debate, to discuss. ➡ **se débattre** *vp* to struggle.

débattu, e [debaty] *pp* ▷ **débattre**.

débauche [deboʃ] *nf* debauchery.

débaucher [3] [deboʃe] *vt* - **1.** [corrompre] to debauch, to corrupt - **2.** [licencier] to make redundant.

débile [debil] ◇ *nmf* - **1.** [attardé] retarded person ; ~ **mental** mentally retarded person - **2.** *fam* [idiot] moron. ◇ *adj fam* stupid.

débit [debi] *nm* - **1.** [de marchandises] (retail) sale - **2.** [magasin] : ~ **de boissons** bar ; ~ **de tabac** tobacconist's *Br*, tobacco shop *Am* - **3.** [coupe] sawing up, cutting up - **4.** [de liquide] (rate of) flow - **5.** [élocution] delivery - **6.** FIN debit ; **avoir un ~ de 100 euros** to be 100 euros overdrawn.

débiter [3] [debite] *vt* - **1.** [marchandises] to sell - **2.** [arbre] to saw up ; [viande] to cut

up - **3.** [suj : robinet] to have a flow of - **4.** *fam fig* [prononcer] to spout - **5.** FIN to debit.

débiteur, trice [debitœr, tris] ◇ *adj* - **1.** [personne] debtor *(avant n)* - **2.** FIN debit *(avant n)*, in the red. ◇ *nm, f* debtor.

déblayer [11] [debleje] *vt* [dégager] to clear ; ~ **le terrain** *fig* to clear the ground.

débloquer[3] [deblɔke]◇*vt*- **1.**[machine] to get going again - **2.** [crédit] to release - **3.** [compte, salaires, prix] to unfreeze. ◇ *vi fam* to talk rubbish.

déboires [debwar] *nmpl* - **1.** [déceptions] disappointments - **2.** [échecs] setbacks - **3.** [ennuis] trouble *(U)*, problems.

déboiser [3] [debwaze] *vt* [région] to deforest ; [terrain] to clear (of trees).

déboîter [3] [debwate] ◇ *vt* - **1.** [objet] to dislodge - **2.** [membre] to dislocate. ◇ *vi* AUTOM to pull out. ➡ **se déboîter** *vp* - **1.** [se démonter] to come apart ; [porte] to come off its hinges - **2.** [membre] to dislocate.

débonnaire [debɔnɛr] *adj* good-natured, easy-going.

déborder [3] [debɔrde] *vi* [fleuve, liquide] to overflow ; *fig* to flood ; ~ **de** [vie, joie] to be bubbling with.

débouché [debuʃe] *nm* - **1.** [issue] end - **2.** *(gén pl)* COMM outlet - **3.** [de carrière] prospect, opening.

déboucher[3] [debuʃe] ◇*vt*- **1.**[bouteille] to open - **2.** [conduite, nez] to unblock. ◇ *vi* : ~ **sur** [arriver] to open out into ; *fig* to lead to, to achieve.

débourser [3] [deburse] *vt* to pay out.

debout [dəbu] *adv* - **1.** [gén] : **être ~** [sur ses pieds] to be standing (up) ; [réveillé] to be up ; [objet] to be standing up ou upright ; **mettre qqch ~** to stand sthg up ; **se mettre ~** to stand up ; **debout!** get up!, on your feet! - **2.** *loc* : **tenir ~** [bâtiment] to remain standing ; [argument] to stand up ; **il ne tient pas ~** he's asleep on his feet.

déboutonner [3] [debutɔne] *vt* to unbutton, to undo.

débraillé, e [debraje] *adj* dishevelled *Br*, disheveled *Am*.

débrayage [debrɛjaʒ] *nm* [arrêt de travail] stoppage.

débrayer [11] [debreje] *vi* AUTOM to disengage the clutch, to declutch.

débris [debri] ◇ *nm* piece, fragment. ◇ *nmpl* [restes] leftovers.

débrouillard, e [debrujar, ard] *fam adj* resourceful.

débrouiller [3] [debruje] *vt* - **1.** [démêler]

to untangle - **2.** *fig* [résoudre] to unravel, to solve. ◆ **se débrouiller** *vp* : se ~ (pour faire qqch) to manage (to do sthg) ; se ~ en anglais/math to get by in English/maths ; débrouille-toi! you'll have to sort it out (by) yourself!

débroussailler [3] [debrusaje] *vt* [terrain] to clear ; *fig* to do the groundwork for.

début [deby] *nm* beginning, start ; au ~ at the start ou beginning ; au ~ de at the beginning of ; dès le ~ (right) from the start.

débutant, e [debytɑ̃, ɑ̃t] *nm, f* beginner.

débuter [3] [debyte] *vi* - **1.** [commencer] : ~ (par) to begin (with), to start (with) - **2.** [faire ses débuts] to start out.

déca [deka] *nm fam* decaff.

deçà [dəsa] ◆ **en deçà de** *loc prép* - **1.** [de ce côté-ci de] on this side of - **2.** [en dessous de] short of.

décacheter [27] [dekaʃte] *vt* to open.

décadence [dekadɑ̃s] *nf* - **1.** [déclin] decline - **2.** [débauche] decadence.

décadent, e [dekadɑ̃, ɑ̃t] *adj* decadent.

décaféiné, e [dekafeine] *adj* decaffeinated. ◆ **décaféiné** *nm* decaffeinated coffee.

décalage [dekalaʒ] *nm* gap ; *fig* gulf, discrepancy ; ~ horaire [entre zones] time difference ; [après un vol] jet lag.

décaler [3] [dekale] *vt* - **1.** [dans le temps - avancer] to bring forward ; [- retarder] to put back - **2.** [dans l'espace] to move, to shift.

décalquer [3] [dekalke] *vt* to trace.

décamper [3] [dekɑ̃pe] *vi fam* to clear off.

décapant, e [dekapɑ̃, ɑ̃t] *adj* - **1.** [nettoyant] stripping - **2.** *fig* [incisif] cutting, caustic. ◆ **décapant** *nm* (paint) stripper.

décaper [3] [dekape] *vt* to strip, to sand.

décapiter [3] [dekapite] *vt* - **1.** [personne - volontairement] to behead ; [- accidentellement] to decapitate - **2.** [arbre] to cut the top off - **3.** *fig* [organisation, parti] to remove the leader ou leaders of.

décapotable [dekapɔtabl] *nf & adj* convertible.

décapsuler [3] [dekapsyle] *vt* to take the top off, to open.

décapsuleur [dekapsylœr] *nm* bottle opener.

décédé, e [desede] *adj* deceased.

décéder [18] [desede] *vi* to die.

déceler [25] [desle] *vt* [repérer] to detect.

décembre [desɑ̃br] *nm* December ; *voir aussi* **septembre**.

décemment [desamɑ̃] *adv* - **1.** [convena-

blement] properly - **2.** [raisonnablement] reasonably.

décence [desɑ̃s] *nf* decency.

décennie [deseni] *nf* decade.

décent, e [desɑ̃, ɑ̃t] *adj* decent.

décentralisation [desɑ̃tralizasjɔ̃] *nf* decentralization.

décentrer [3] [desɑ̃tre] *vt* to move off-centre *Br* ou off-center *Am*.

déception [desɛpsjɔ̃] *nf* disappointment.

décerner [3] [deserne] *vt* : ~ qqch à to award sthg to.

décès [desɛ] *nm* death.

décevant, e [desəvɑ̃, ɑ̃t] *adj* disappointing.

décevoir [52] [desəvwar] *vt* to disappoint.

déchaîné, e [deʃene] *adj* - **1.** [vent, mer] stormy, wild - **2.** [personne] wild.

déchaîner [4] [deʃene] *vt* [passion] to unleash ; [rires] to cause an outburst of. ◆ **se déchaîner** *vp* - **1.** [éléments naturels] to erupt - **2.** [personne] to fly into a rage.

déchanter [3] [deʃɑ̃te] *vi* to become disillusioned.

décharge [deʃarʒ] *nf* - **1.** JUR discharge - **2.** ÉLECTR discharge ; ~ électrique electric *Br* ou electrical *Am* shock - **3.** [dépotoir] rubbish tip ou dump *Br*, garbage dump *Am*.

déchargement [deʃarʒəmɑ̃] *nm* unloading.

décharger [17] [deʃarʒe] *vt* - **1.** [véhicule, marchandises] to unload - **2.** [arme - tirer] to fire, to discharge ; [- enlever la charge de] to unload - **3.** [soulager - cœur] to unburden ; [- conscience] to salve ; [- colère] to vent - **4.** [libérer] : qqn de to release sb from.

décharné, e [deʃarne] *adj* [maigre] emaciated.

déchausser [3] [deʃose] *vt* : ~ qqn to take sb's shoes off. ◆ **se déchausser** *vp* - **1.** [personne] to take one's shoes off - **2.** [dent] to come loose.

déchéance [deʃeɑ̃s] *nf* [déclin] degeneration, decline.

déchet [deʃɛ] *nm* [de matériau] scrap. ◆ **déchets** *nmpl* refuse (*U*), waste (*U*).

déchiffrer [3] [deʃifre] *vt* - **1.** [inscription, hiéroglyphes] to decipher ; [énigme] to unravel - **2.** MUS to sight-read.

déchiqueter [27] [deʃikte] *vt* to tear to shreds.

déchirant, e [deʃirɑ̃, ɑ̃t] *adj* heartrending.

déchirement [deʃirmɑ̃] *nm* [souffrance morale] heartbreak, distress.

déchirer [3] [defire] *vt* [papier, tissu] to tear up, to rip up. ➠ **se déchirer** *vp* - **1.** [personnes] to tear each other apart - **2.** [matériau, muscle] to tear.

déchirure [defiryr] *nf* tear ; *fig* wrench ; ~ **musculaire** MÉD torn muscle.

déchu, e [defy] *adj* - **1.** [homme, ange] fallen ; [souverain] deposed - **2.** JUR : **être ~ de** to be deprived of.

décibel [desibɛl] *nm* decibel.

décidé, e [deside] *adj* - **1.** [résolu] determined - **2.** [arrêté] settled.

décidément [desidemɑ̃] *adv* really.

décider [3] [deside] *vt* - **1.** [prendre une décision] : ~ **(de faire qqch)** to decide (to do sthg) - **2.** [convaincre] : ~ **qqn à faire qqch** to persuade sb to do sthg. ➠ **se décider** *vp* - **1.** [personne] : **se ~ (à faire qqch)** to make up one's mind (to do sthg) - **2.** [choisir] : **se ~ pour** to decide on, to settle on.

décilitre [desilitr] *nm* decilitre.

décimal, e, aux [desimal, o] *adj* decimal. ➠ **décimale** *nf* decimal.

décimer [3] [desime] *vt* to decimate.

décimètre [desimɛtr] *nm* - **1.** [dixième de mètre] decimetre - **2.** [règle] ruler ; **double ~ ≃** foot rule.

décisif, ive [desizif, iv] *adj* decisive.

décision [desizjɔ̃] *nf* decision.

décisionnaire [desizjɔnɛr] *nmf* decision-maker.

déclamer [3] [deklame] *vt* to declaim.

déclaration [deklarasjɔ̃] *nf* - **1.** [orale] declaration, announcement - **2.** [écrite] report, declaration ; [d'assurance] claim ; ~ **de naissance/de décès** registration of birth/death ; ~ **d'impôts** tax return ; ~ **de revenus** statement of income.

déclarer [3] [deklare] *vt* - **1.** [annoncer] to declare - **2.** [signaler] to report ; **rien à ~** nothing to declare ; ~ **une naissance** to register a birth. ➠ **se déclarer** *vp* - **1.** [se prononcer] : **se ~ pour/contre qqch** to come out in favour of/against sthg - **2.** [se manifester] to break out.

déclenchement [deklɑ̃ʃmɑ̃] *nm* [de mécanisme] activating, setting off ; *fig* launching.

déclencher [3] [deklɑ̃ʃe] *vt* [mécanisme] to activate, to set off ; *fig* to launch. ➠ **se déclencher** *vp* [mécanisme] to go off, to be activated ; *fig* to be triggered off.

déclic [deklik] *nm* - **1.** [mécanisme] trigger - **2.** [bruit] click.

déclin [deklɛ̃] *nm* - **1.** [de civilisation, population, santé] decline - **2.** [fin] close.

déclinaison [deklinɛzɔ̃] *nf* GRAM declension.

décliner [3] [dekline] ◇ *vi* [santé, population, popularité] to decline. ◇ *vt* - **1.** [offre, honneur] to decline - **2.** GRAM to decline ; *fig* [gamme de produits] to develop.

décoder [3] [dekɔde] *vt* to decode.

décoiffer [3] [dekwafe] *vt* [cheveux] to mess up.

décoincer [16] [dekwɛ̃se] *vt* - **1.** [chose] to loosen ; [mécanisme] to unjam - **2.** *fam* [personne] to loosen up.

décollage [dekɔlaʒ] *nm litt & fig* takeoff.

décoller [3] [dekɔle] ◇ *vt* [étiquette, timbre] to unstick ; [papier peint] to strip (off). ◇ *vi litt & fig* to take off.

décolleté, e [dekɔlte] *adj* [vêtement] low-cut. ➠ **décolleté** *nm* - **1.** [de personne] neck and shoulders *(pl)* - **2.** [de vêtement] neckline, neck.

décolonisation [dekɔlɔnizasjɔ̃] *nf* decolonization.

décolorer [3] [dekɔlɔre] *vt* [par décolorant] to bleach, to lighten ; [par usure] to fade.

décombres [dekɔ̃br] *nmpl* debris (U).

décommander [3] [dekɔmɑ̃de] *vt* to cancel.

décomposé, e [dekɔ̃poze] *adj* - **1.** [pourri] decomposed - **2.** [visage] haggard ; [personne] in shock.

décomposer [3] [dekɔ̃poze] *vt* [gén] : ~ **(en)** to break down (into). ➠ **se décomposer** *vp* - **1.** [se putréfier] to rot, to decompose - **2.** [se diviser] : **se ~ en** to be broken down into.

décomposition [dekɔ̃pozisjɔ̃] *nf* - **1.** [putréfaction] decomposition - **2.** *fig* [analyse] breaking down, analysis.

décompresser [4] [dekɔ̃prese] ◇ *vt* TECHNOL to decompress. ◇ *vi* to unwind.

décompression [dekɔ̃presjɔ̃] *nf* decompression.

décompte [dekɔ̃t] *nm* [calcul] breakdown (of an amount).

déconcentrer [3] [dekɔ̃sɑ̃tre] *vt* [distraire] to distract. ➠ **se déconcentrer** *vp* to be distracted.

déconcerter [3] [dekɔ̃sɛrte] *vt* to disconcert.

déconfiture [dekɔ̃fityr] *nf* collapse, ruin.

décongeler [25] [dekɔ̃ʒle] *vt* to defrost.

décongestionner [3] [dekɔ̃ʒɛstjɔne] *vt* to relieve congestion in.

déconnecter [4] [dekɔnɛkte] *vt* to disconnect.

déconseillé, e [dekɔ̃seje] *adj* : **c'est fortement ~** it's extremely inadvisable.

déconseiller [4] [dekɔ̃seje] *vt* : ~ qqch à qqn to advise sb against sthg ; ~ à qqn de faire qqch to advise sb against doing sthg.

déconsidérer [18] [dekɔ̃sidere] *vt* to discredit.

décontaminer [3] [dekɔ̃tamine] *vt* to decontaminate.

décontenancer [16] [dekɔ̃tnɑ̃se] *vt* to put out.

décontracté, e [dekɔ̃trakte] *adj* - 1. [muscle] relaxed - 2. [détendu] casual, laid-back.

décontracter [3] [dekɔ̃trakte] *vt* to relax. ◆ **se décontracter** *vp* to relax.

décor [dekɔr] *nm* - 1. [cadre] scenery - 2. THÉÂTRE scenery *(U)* ; CIN sets *(pl)*, décor.

décorateur, trice [dekɔratœr, tris] *nm, f* CIN & THÉÂTRE designer ; ~ d'intérieur interior decorator.

décoratif, ive [dekɔratif, iv] *adj* decorative.

décoration [dekɔrasjɔ̃] *nf* decoration.

décorer [3] [dekɔre] *vt* to decorate.

décortiquer [3] [dekɔrtike] *vt* [noix] to shell ; [graine] to husk ; *fig* to analyse *Br* ou analyze *Am* in minute detail.

découcher [3] [dekuʃe] *vi* to stay out all night.

découdre [86] [dekudr] *vt* COUTURE to unpick.

découler [3] [dekule] *vi* : ~ de to follow from.

découpage [dekupaʒ] *nm* - 1. [action] cutting out ; [résultat] paper cutout - 2. ADMIN : ~ (électoral) division into constituencies.

découper [3] [dekupe] *vt* - 1. [couper] to cut up - 2. *fig* [diviser] to cut out.

découpure [dekupyr] *nf* [bord] indentations *(pl)*, jagged outline.

découragement [dekuraʒmɑ̃] *nm* discouragement.

décourager [17] [dekuraʒe] *vt* to discourage ; ~ qqn de qqch to put sb off sthg ; ~ qqn de faire qqch to discourage sb from doing sthg. ◆ **se décourager** *vp* to lose heart.

décousu, e [dekuzy] ◇ *pp* ▷ découdre. ◇ *adj fig* [conversation] disjointed.

découvert, e [dekuver, ert] ◇ *pp* ▷ découvrir. ◇ *adj* [tête] bare ; [terrain] exposed. ◆ **découvert** *nm* BANQUE overdraft ; être à ~ (de 1 000 euros) to be (1,000 euros) overdrawn. ◆ **découverte** *nf* discovery ; aller à la ~ de to explore.

découvrir [34] [dekuvrir] *vt* - 1. [trouver, surprendre] to discover - 2. [ôter ce qui couvre, mettre à jour] to uncover.

décrasser [3] [dekrase] *vt* to scrub.

décret [dekrɛ] *nm* decree.

décréter [18] [dekrete] *vt* [décider] : ~ que to decide that.

décrire [99] [dekrir] *vt* to describe.

décrit, e [dekri, it] *pp* ▷ décrire.

décrocher [3] [dekrɔʃe] ◇ *vt* - 1. [enlever] to take down - 2. [téléphone] to pick up - 3. *fam* [obtenir] to land. ◇ *vi fam* [abandonner] to drop out.

décroître [94] [dekrwatr] *vi* to decrease, to diminish ; [jours] to get shorter.

décrypter [3] [dekripte] *vt* to decipher.

déçu, e [desy] ◇ *pp* ▷ décevoir. ◇ *adj* disappointed.

déculotter [3] [dekylɔte] *vt* : ~ qqn to take sb's trousers off.

dédaigner [4] [dedɛɲe] *vt* - 1. [mépriser - personne] to despise ; [- conseils, injures] to scorn - 2. [refuser] : ~ de faire qqch *sout* to disdain to do sthg ; ne pas ~ qqch/de faire qqch not to be above sthg/above doing sthg.

dédaigneux, euse [dedɛɲø, øz] *adj* disdainful.

dédain [dedɛ̃] *nm* disdain, contempt.

dédale [dedal] *nm litt & fig* maze.

dedans [dədɑ̃] *adv & nm* inside. ◆ **de dedans** *loc adv* from inside, from within. ◆ **en dedans** *loc adv* inside, within. ◆ **en dedans de** *loc prép* inside, within ; *voir aussi* là-dedans.

dédicace [dedikas] *nf* dedication.

dédicacer [16] [dedikase] *vt* : ~ qqch (à qqn) to sign ou autograph sthg (for sb).

dédier [9] [dedje] *vt* : ~ qqch (à qqn/à qqch) to dedicate sthg (to sb/to sthg).

dédire [103] [dedir] ◆ **se dédire** *vp sout* to go back on one's word.

dédommagement [dedɔmaʒmɑ̃] *nm* compensation.

dédommager [17] [dedɔmaʒe] *vt* - 1. [indemniser] to compensate - 2. *fig* [remercier] to repay.

dédouaner [3] [dedwane] *vt* [marchandises] to clear through customs.

dédoubler [3] [deduble] *vt* to halve, to split ; [fil] to separate.

déduction [dedyksjɔ̃] *nf* deduction.

déduire [98] [dedɥir] *vt* : ~ qqch (de) [ôter] to deduct sthg (from) ; [conclure] to deduce sthg (from).

déduit, e [dedɥi, it] *pp* ▷ déduire.

déesse [deɛs] *nf* goddess.

défaillance [defajãs] *nf* - **1.** [incapacité - de machine] failure ; [- de personne, organisation] weakness - **2.** [malaise] blackout, fainting fit.

défaillant, e [defajã, ãt] *adj* [faible] failing.

défaillir [47] [defajir] *vi* [s'évanouir] to faint.

défaire [109] [defɛr] *vt* [détacher] to undo ; [valise] to unpack ; [lit] to strip. ◆ **se défaire** *vp* - **1.** [ne pas tenir] to come undone - **2.** *sout* [se séparer] : **se ~ de** to get rid of.

défait, e [defɛ, ɛt] ⬦ *pp* ▷ **défaire**. ⬦ *adj fig* [épuisé] haggard. ◆ **défaite** *nf* defeat.

défaitiste [defetist] *nmf & adj* defeatist.

défaut [defo] *nm* - **1.** [imperfection - gén] flaw ; [- de personne] fault, shortcoming ; **~ de fabrication** manufacturing fault - **2.** [manque] lack ; **à ~ de** for lack ou want of ; **l'eau fait (cruellement) ~** there is a serious water shortage.

défaveur [defavœr] *nf* disfavour *Br*, disfavor *Am* ; **être en ~** to be out of favour *Br* ou favor *Am* ; **tomber en ~** to fall out of favour *Br* ou favor *Am*.

défavorable [defavɔrabl] *adj* unfavourable *Br*, unfavorable *Am*.

défavorisé, e [defavɔrize] *adj* disadvantaged, underprivileged.

défavoriser [3] [defavɔrize] *vt* to handicap, to penalize.

défection [defɛksjɔ̃] *nf* - **1.** [absence] absence - **2.** [abandon] defection.

défectueux, euse [defɛktɥø, øz] *adj* faulty, defective.

défendeur, eresse [defãdœr, rɛs] *nm, f* defendant.

défendre [73] [defãdr] *vt* - **1.** [personne, opinion, client] to defend - **2.** [interdire] to forbid ; **~ qqch à qqn** to forbid sb sthg ; **~ à qqn de faire qqch** to forbid sb to do sthg ; **~ que qqn fasse qqch** to forbid sb to do sthg. ◆ **se défendre** *vp* - **1.** [se battre, se justifier] to defend o.s. - **2.** [nier] : **se ~ de faire qqch** to deny doing sthg - **3.** [thèse] to stand up.

défendu, e [defãdy] ⬦ *pp* ▷ **défendre**. ⬦ *adj* : **'il est ~ de jouer au ballon'** 'no ball games'.

défense [defãs] *nf* - **1.** [d'éléphant] tusk - **2.** [interdiction] prohibition, ban ; **'~ de fumer/de stationner/d'entrer'** 'no smoking/parking/entry' ; **'~ d'afficher'** 'stick no bills' - **3.** [protection] defence *Br*, defense *Am* ; **prendre la ~ de** to stand up for ;

légitime ~ JUR self-defence *Br*, self-defense *Am*.

défenseur [defãsœr] *nm* [partisan] champion.

défensif, ive [defãsif, iv] *adj* defensive. ◆ **défensive** *nf* : **être sur la défensive** to be on the defensive.

déférence [deferãs] *nf* deference.

déferlement [defɛrləmã] *nm* [de vagues] breaking ; *fig* surge, upsurge.

déferler [3] [defɛrle] *vi* [vagues] to break ; *fig* to surge.

défi [defi] *nm* challenge.

défiance [defjãs] *nf* distrust, mistrust.

déficience [defisjãs] *nf* deficiency.

déficit [defisit] *nm* FIN deficit ; **être en ~** to be in deficit.

déficitaire [defisitɛr] *adj* in deficit.

défier [9] [defje] *vt* [braver] : **~ qqn de faire qqch** to defy sb to do sthg.

défigurer [3] [defigyre] *vt* - **1.** [blesser] to disfigure - **2.** [enlaidir] to deface.

défilé [defile] *nm* - **1.** [parade] parade - **2.** [couloir] defile, narrow pass.

défiler [3] [defile] *vi* - **1.** [dans une parade] to march past - **2.** [se succéder] to pass. ◆ **se défiler** *vp fam* to back out.

défini, e [defini] *adj* - **1.** [précis] clear, precise - **2.** GRAM definite.

définir [32] [definir] *vt* to define.

définitif, ive [definitif, iv] *adj* definitive, final. ◆ **en définitive** *loc adv* in the end.

définition [definisjɔ̃] *nf* definition.

définitivement [definitivmã] *adv* for good, permanently.

défiscaliser [3] [defiskalize] *vt* to exempt from taxation.

déflationniste [deflasjɔnist] *adj* deflationary, deflationist.

défoncer [16] [defɔ̃se] *vt* [caisse, porte] to smash in ; [route] to break up ; [mur] to smash down ; [chaise] to break.

déformation [defɔrmasjɔ̃] *nf* - **1.** [d'objet, de théorie] distortion - **2.** MÉD deformity ; **~ professionnelle** *mental conditioning caused by one's job*.

déformer [3] [defɔrme] *vt* to distort. ◆ **se déformer** *vp* [changer de forme] to be distorted, to be deformed ; [se courber] to bend.

défouler [3] [defule] *vt fam* to unwind. ◆ **se défouler** *vp fam* to let off steam, to unwind.

défricher [3] [defriʃe] *vt* [terrain] to clear ; *fig* [question] to do the groundwork for.

défunt, e [defœ̃, œ̃t] ⟷ *adj* [décédé] late. ⟷ *nm, f* deceased.

dégagé, e [degaʒe] *adj* **- 1.** [ciel, vue] clear ; [partie du corps] bare **- 2.** [désinvolte] casual, airy **- 3.** [libre] **:** ~ **de** free from.

dégager [17] [degaʒe] ⟷ *vt* **- 1.** [odeur] to produce, to give off **- 2.** [délivrer - blessé] to free, to extricate **- 3.** [bénéfice] to show **- 4.** [pièce] to clear **- 5.** [libérer] **:** ~ **qqn de** to release sb from. ⟷ *vi fam* [partir] to clear off. ◆ **se dégager** *vp* **- 1.** [se délivrer] **: se** ~ **de qqch** to free o.s. from sthg ; *fig* to get out of sthg **- 2.** [émaner] to be given off **- 3.** [émerger] to emerge.

dégarnir [32] [degarnir] *vt* to strip, to clear. ◆ **se dégarnir** *vp* [vitrine] to be cleared ; [arbre] to lose its leaves ; **sa tête se dégarnit, il se dégarnit** he's going bald.

dégât [dega] *nm littéraire & fig* damage (*U*) ; **faire des ~s** to cause damage.

dégel [deʒɛl] *nm* [fonte des glaces] thaw.

dégeler [25] [deʒle] ⟷ *vt* [produit surgelé] to thaw. ⟷ *vi* to thaw.

dégénéré, e [deʒenere] *adj & nm, f* degenerate.

dégénérer [18] [deʒenere] *vi* to degenerate ; ~ **en** to degenerate into.

dégivrer [3] [deʒivre] *vt* [pare-brise] to de-ice ; [réfrigérateur] to defrost.

dégonfler [3] [degɔ̃fle] ⟷ *vt* to deflate, to let down. ⟷ *vi* to go down. ◆ **se dégonfler** *vp* **- 1.** [objet] to go down **- 2.** *fam* [personne] to chicken out.

dégouliner [3] [deguline] *vi* to trickle.

dégourdi, e [degurdi] *adj* clever.

dégourdir [32] [degurdir] *vt* **- 1.** [membres - ankylosés] to restore the circulation to **- 2.** *fig* [déniaiser] **: qqn** to teach sb a thing or two. ◆ **se dégourdir** *vp* **- 1.** [membres] **: se** ~ **les jambes** to stretch one's legs **- 2.** *fig* [acquérir de l'aisance] to learn a thing or two.

dégoût [degu] *nm* disgust, distaste.

dégoûtant, e [degutɑ̃, ɑ̃t] *adj* **- 1.** [sale] filthy, disgusting **- 2.** [révoltant, grossier] disgusting.

dégoûter [3] [degute] *vt* to disgust.

dégoutter [3] [degute] *vi* **:** ~ **(de qqch)** to drip (with sthg).

dégradé, e [degrade] *adj* [couleur] shading off. ◆ **dégradé** *nm* gradation ; **un** ~ **de bleu** a blue shading. ◆ **en dégradé** *loc adv* [cheveux] layered.

dégrader [3] [degrade] *vt* **- 1.** [officier] to degrade **- 2.** [abîmer -] to damage **- 3.** *fig* [avilir] to degrade, to debase. ◆ **se dé-**

grader *vp* **- 1.** [bâtiment, santé] to deteriorate **- 2.** *fig* [personne] to degrade o.s.

dégrafer [3] [degrafe] *vt* to undo, to unfasten.

dégraissage [degresaʒ] *nm* **- 1.** [de vêtement] dry-cleaning **- 2.** [de personnel] trimming, cutting back.

degré [dəgre] *nm* [gén] degree ; **~s centigrades** OU **Celsius** degrees centigrade OU Celsius ; **prendre qqn/qqch au premier** ~ to take sb/sthg at face value.

dégressif, ive [degresif, iv] *adj* **: tarif** ~ decreasing price scale.

dégringoler [3] [degrɛ̃gɔle] *fam vi* [tomber] to tumble ; *fig* to crash.

déguenillé, e [degənije] *adj* ragged.

déguerpir [32] [degerpir] *vi* to clear off.

dégueulasse [degœlas] *tfam* ⟷ *adj* **- 1.** [très sale, grossier] filthy **- 2.** [très mauvais - plat] disgusting ; [- temps] lousy. ⟷ *nmf* scum (*U*).

dégueuler [5] [degœle] *vi fam* to throw up.

déguisement [degizmɑ̃] *nm* disguise ; [pour bal masqué] fancy dress.

déguiser [3] [degize] *vt* to disguise. ◆ **se déguiser** *vp* **: se** ~ **en** [pour tromper] to disguise o.s. as ; [pour s'amuser] to dress up as.

dégustation [degystasjɔ̃] *nf* tasting, sampling ; ~ **de vin** wine tasting.

déguster [3] [degyste] ⟷ *vt* [savourer] to taste, to sample. ⟷ *vi fam* [subir] **: il va ~!** he'll be for it!

déhancher [3] [deɑ̃ʃe] ◆ **se déhancher** *vp* [en marchant] to swing one's hips ; [en restant immobile] to put all one's weight on one leg.

dehors [dəɔr] ⟷ *adv* outside ; **aller** ~ to go outside ; **dormir** ~ to sleep out of doors, to sleep out ; **jeter** OU **mettre qqn** ~ to throw sb out. ⟷ *nm* outside. ⟷ *nmpl* **: les** ~ [les apparences] appearances. ◆ **en dehors** *loc adv* outside, outwards *Br*, outward *Am*. ◆ **en dehors de** *loc prép* [excepté] apart from.

déjà [deʒa] *adv* **- 1.** [dès cet instant] already **- 2.** [précédemment] already, before **- 3.** [au fait] **: quel est ton nom ~?** what did you say your name was? **- 4.** [renforce une affirmation] **: ce n'est ~ pas si mal** that's not bad at all.

déjeuner [5] [deʒœne] ⟷ *vi* **- 1.** [le matin] to have breakfast **- 2.** [à midi] to have lunch. ⟷ *nm* **- 1.** [repas de midi] lunch **- 2.** *Can* [dîner] dinner.

déjouer [6] [deʒwe] *vt* to frustrate ; ~ **la**

surveillance de qqn to elude sb's surveillance.

delà [dəla] ▷ au-delà.

délabré, e [delabre] *adj* ruined.

délacer [16] [delase] *vt* to unlace, to undo.

délai [delɛ] *nm* - **1.** [temps accordé] period ; **sans ~** immediately, without delay ; **~ de livraison** delivery time, lead time - **2.** [sursis] extension (of deadline).

délaisser [4] [delese] *vt* - **1.** [abandonner] to leave - **2.** [négliger] to neglect.

délassement [delasmā] *nm* relaxation.

délasser [3] [delase] *vt* to refresh. ◆ **se délasser** *vp* to relax.

délation [delasjɔ̃] *nf* informing.

délavé, e [delave] *adj* faded.

délayer [11] [deleje] *vt* [diluer] : **~ qqch dans qqch** to mix sthg with sthg.

délecter [4] [delɛkte] ◆ **se délecter** *vp* : **se ~ de qqch/à faire qqch** to delight in sthg/in doing sthg.

délégation [delegasjɔ̃] *nf* delegation ; **agir par ~** to be delegated to act.

délégué, e [delege] ◇ *adj* [personne] delegated. ◇ *nm, f* [représentant] : **~ (à)** delegate (to).

déléguer [18] [delege] *vt* : **~ qqn (à qqch)** to delegate sb (to sthg).

délester [3] [delɛste] *vt* - **1.** [circulation routière] to set up a diversion on, to divert - **2.** *fig & hum* [voler] : **~ qqn de qqch** to relieve sb of sthg.

délibération [deliberasjɔ̃] *nf* deliberation.

délibéré, e [delibere] *adj* - **1.** [intentionnel] deliberate - **2.** [résolu] determined.

délibérer [18] [delibere] *vi* : **~ (de ou sur)** to deliberate (on ou over).

délicat, e [delika, at] *adj* - **1.** [gén] delicate - **2.** [exigeant] fussy, difficult.

délicatement [delikatmā] *adv* delicately.

délicatesse [delikatɛs] *nf* - **1.** [gén] delicacy - **2.** [tact] delicacy, tact.

délice [delis] *nm* delight.

délicieux, euse [delisjø, øz] *adj* - **1.** [savoureux] delicious - **2.** [agréable] delightful.

délié, e [delje] *adj* [doigts] nimble.

délier [9] [delje] *vt* to untie.

délimiter [3] [delimite] *vt* [frontière] to fix ; *fig* [question, domaine] to define, to demarcate.

délinquance [delɛ̃kãs] *nf* delinquency.

délinquant, e [delɛ̃kã, ãt] *nm, f* delinquent.

délirant, e [delirã, ãt] *adj* - **1.** MÉD deliri-ous - **2.** [extravagant] frenzied - **3.** *fam* [extraordinaire] crazy.

délire [delir] *nm* MÉD delirium ; **en ~** *fig* frenzied.

délirer [3] [delire] *vi* MÉD to be ou become delirious ; *fam fig* to rave.

délit [deli] *nm* crime, offence *Br*, offense *Am* ; **en flagrant ~** red-handed, in the act.

délivrance [delivrãs] *nf* - **1.** [libération] freeing, release - **2.** [soulagement] relief - **3.** [accouchement] delivery.

délivrer [3] [delivre] *vt* - **1.** [prisonnier] to free, to release - **2.** [pays] to deliver, to free ; **~ de** to free from ; *fig* to relieve from - **3.** [remettre] : **~ qqch (à qqn)** to issue sthg (to sb) - **4.** [marchandise] to deliver.

déloger [17] [delɔʒe] *vt* : **~ (de)** to dislodge (from).

déloyal, e, aux [delwajal, o] *adj* - **1.** [infidèle] disloyal - **2.** [malhonnête] unfair.

delta [dɛlta] *nm* delta.

deltaplane, delta-plane (*pl* delta-planes) [dɛltaplan] *nm* hang glider.

déluge [delyʒ] *nm* - **1.** RELIG : **le Déluge** the Flood - **2.** [pluie] downpour, deluge ; **un ~ de** *fig* a flood of.

déluré, e [delyre] *adj* [malin] quick-witted ; *péj* [dévergondé] saucy.

démagogie [demagɔʒi] *nf* pandering to public opinion, demagogy.

demain [dəmɛ̃] ◇ *adv* - **1.** [le jour suivant] tomorrow ; **~ matin** tomorrow morning - **2.** *fig* [plus tard] in the future. ◇ *nm* tomorrow ; **à ~ !** see you tomorrow!

demande [dəmãd] *nf* - **1.** [souhait] request - **2.** [démarche] proposal ; **~ en mariage** proposal of marriage - **3.** [candidature] application ; **~ d'emploi** job application ; **'~s d'emploi'** 'situations wanted' - **4.** ÉCON demand.

demandé, e [dəmãde] *adj* in demand.

demander [3] [dəmãde] ◇ *vt* - **1.** [réclamer, s'enquérir] to ask for ; **~ qqch à qqn** to ask sb for sthg - **2.** [appeler] to call ; **on vous demande à la réception/au téléphone** you're wanted at reception/on the telephone - **3.** [désirer] to ask, to want ; **je ne demande pas mieux** I'd be only too pleased (to), I'd love to - **4.** [exiger] : **tu m'en demandes trop** you're asking too much of me - **5.** [nécessiter] to require. ◇ *vi* - **1.** [réclamer] : **~ à qqn de faire qqch** to ask sb to do sthg ; **ne ~ qu'à ...** to be ready to ... - **2.** [nécessiter] : **ce projet demande à être étudié** this project requires investigation ou needs investigating. ◆ **se demander** *vp* : **se ~ (si)** to wonder (if ou whether).

demandeur, euse [dəmɑ̃dœr, øz] *nm, f* [solliciteur] : ~ **d'asile** asylum-seeker ; ~ **d'emploi** job-seeker.

démangeaison [demɑ̃ʒɛzɔ̃] *nf* [irritation] itch, itching (U) ; *fam fig* urge.

démanger [17] [demɑ̃ʒe] *vi* [gratter] to itch ; **ça me démange de ...** *fig* I'm itching ou dying to ...

démanteler [25] [demɑ̃tle] *vt* [construction] to demolish ; *fig* to break up.

démaquillant, e [demakijɑ̃, ɑ̃t] *adj* make-up-removing *(avant n)*. ➡ **démaquillant** *nm* make-up remover.

démaquiller [3] [demakije] *vt* to remove make-up from. ➡ **se démaquiller** *vp* to remove one's make-up.

démarche [demarʃ] *nf* - **1.** [manière de marcher] gait, walk - **2.** [raisonnement] approach, method - **3.** [requête] step ; **faire les ~s pour faire qqch** to take the necessary steps to do sthg.

démarcheur, euse [demarʃœr, øz] *nm, f* [représentant] door-to-door salesman *(f* saleswoman*)*.

démarquer [3] [demarke] *vt* - **1.** [solder] to mark down - **2.** SPORT not to mark. ➡ **se démarquer** *vp* - **1.** SPORT to shake off one's marker - **2.** *fig* [se distinguer] : **se ~ (de)** to distinguish o.s. (from).

démarrage [demaraʒ] *nm* starting, start ; ~ **en côte** hill start.

démarrer [3] [demare] <> *vi* - **1.** [véhicule] to start (up) ; [conducteur] to drive off - **2.** *fig* [affaire, projet] to get off the ground. <> *vt* - **1.** [véhicule] to start (up) - **2.** *fam fig* [commencer] ; ~ **qqch** to get sthg going.

démarreur [demarœr] *nm* starter.

démasquer [3] [demaske] *vt* - **1.** [personne] to unmask - **2.** *fig* [complot, plan] to unveil.

démêlant, e [demelɑ̃, ɑ̃t] *adj* conditioning *(avant n)*. ➡ **démêlant** *nm* conditioner.

démêlé [demele] *nm* quarrel ; **avoir des ~s avec la justice** to get into trouble with the law.

démêler [4] [demele] *vt* [cheveux, fil] to untangle ; *fig* to unravel. ➡ **se démêler** *vp* : **se ~ de** *fig* to extricate o.s. from.

déménagement [demenaʒmɑ̃] *nm* removal.

déménager [17] [demenaʒe] <> *vt* to move. <> *vi* to move (house).

déménageur [demenaʒœr] *nm* removal man *Br*, mover *Am*.

démence [demɑ̃s] *nf* MÉD dementia ; [bêtise] madness.

démener [19] [demne] ➡ **se démener** *vp litt & fig* to struggle.

dément, e [demɑ̃, ɑ̃t] <> *adj* MÉD demented ; *fam* [extraordinaire, extravagant] crazy. <> *nm, f* demented person.

démenti [demɑ̃ti] *nm* denial.

démentiel, elle [demɑ̃sjɛl] *adj* MÉD demented ; *fam* [incroyable] crazy.

démentir [37] [demɑ̃tir] *vt* - **1.** [réfuter] to deny - **2.** [contredire] to contradict.

démesure [deməzyr] *nf* excess, immoderation.

démettre [84] [demetr] *vt* - **1.** MÉD to put out (of joint) - **2.** [congédier] : ~ **qqn de** to dismiss sb from. ➡ **se démettre** *vp* - **1.** MÉD : **se ~ l'épaule** to put one's shoulder out (of joint) - **2.** [démissionner] : **se ~ de ses fonctions** to resign.

demeurant [dəmœrɑ̃] ➡ **au demeurant** *loc adv* all things considered.

demeure [dəmœr] *nf sout* [domicile, habitation] residence. ➡ **à demeure** *loc adv* permanently.

demeuré, e [dəmœre] <> *adj* simple, half-witted. <> *nm, f* half-wit.

demeurer [5] [dəmœre] *vi* - **1.** *(aux : avoir)* [habiter] to live - **2.** *(aux : être)* [rester] to remain.

demi, e [dəmi] *adj* half ; **un kilo et ~** one and a half kilos ; **il est une heure et ~e** it's half past one ; **à ~** half ; **dormir à ~** to be nearly asleep ; **ouvrir à ~** to half-open ; **faire les choses à ~** to do things by halves. ➡ **demi** *nm* - **1.** [bière] beer, ≈ half-pint *Br* - **2.** FOOTBALL midfielder. ➡ **demie** *nf* : **à la ~e** on the half-hour.

demi-cercle [dəmiserkl] *(pl* demi-cercles*) nm* semicircle.

demi-douzaine [dəmiduzɛn] *(pl* demi-douzaines*) nf* half-dozen ; **une ~ (de)** half a dozen.

demi-finale [dəmifinal] *(pl* demi-finales*) nf* semifinal.

demi-frère [dəmifrɛr] *(pl* demi-frères*) nm* half-brother.

demi-gros [dəmigro] *nm* : **(commerce de) ~** cash and carry.

demi-heure [dəmijœr] *(pl* demi-heures*) nf* half an hour, half-hour.

demi-journée [dəmiʒurne] *(pl* demi-journées*) nf* half a day, half-day.

démilitariser [3] [demilitarize] *vt* to demilitarize.

demi-litre [dəmilitr] *(pl* demi-litres*) nm* half a litre *Br* ou liter *Am*, half-litre *Br*, half-liter *Am*.

demi-mesure [dəmiməzyr] *(pl* demi-me-

sures) *nf* - 1. [quantité] half a measure - 2. [compromis] half-measure.

demi-mot [dəmimo] ◆ **à demi-mot** *loc adv* : **comprendre à ~** to understand without things having to be spelled out.

déminer [3] [demine] *vt* to clear of mines.

demi-pension [dəmipɑ̃sjɔ̃] *(pl* **demi-pensions)** *nf* - 1. [d'hôtel] half-board - 2. [d'école] : **être en ~** to take school dinners *(pl).*

démis, e [demi, iz] *pp* ▷ **démettre.**

demi-sœur [dəmisœr] *(pl* **demi-sœurs)** *nf* half-sister.

démission [demisjɔ̃] *nf* resignation.

démissionner [3] [demisjɔne] *vi* [d'un emploi] to resign ; *fig* to give up.

demi-tarif [dəmitarif] *(pl* **demi-tarifs)** ◇ *adj* half-price. ◇ *nm* - 1. [tarification] half-fare - 2. [billet] half-price ticket.

demi-tour [dəmitur] *(pl* **demi-tours)** *nm* [gén] half-turn ; MIL about-turn ; **faire ~** to turn back.

démocrate [demɔkrat] *nmf* democrat.

démocratie [demɔkrasi] *nf* democracy.

démocratique [demɔkratik] *adj* democratic.

démocratiser [3] [demɔkratize] *vt* to democratize.

démodé, e [demɔde] *adj* old-fashioned.

démographique [demɔgrafik] *adj* demographic.

demoiselle [dəmwazɛl] *nf* [jeune fille] maid ; **~ d'honneur** bridesmaid.

démolir [32] [demɔlir] *vt* [gén] to demolish.

démolition [demɔlisjɔ̃] *nf* demolition.

démon [demɔ̃] *nm* [diable, personne] devil, demon ; **le ~** RELIG the Devil.

démoniaque [demɔnjak] *adj* [diabolique] diabolical.

démonstratif, ive [demɔ̃stratif, iv] *adj* [personne & GRAM] demonstrative. ◆ **démonstratif** *nm* GRAM demonstrative.

démonstration [demɔ̃strasjɔ̃] *nf* [gén] demonstration.

démonter [3] [demɔ̃te] *vt* - 1. [appareil] to dismantle, to take apart - 2. [troubler] : **~ qqn** to put sb out. ◆ **se démonter** *vp* *fam* to be put out.

démontrer [3] [demɔ̃tre] *vt* - 1. [prouver] to prove, to demonstrate - 2. [témoigner de] to show, to demonstrate.

démoralisant, e [demɔralizɑ̃, ɑ̃t] *adj* demoralizing.

démoraliser [3] [demɔralize] *vt* to de-moralize. ◆ **se démoraliser** *vp* to lose heart.

démordre [76] [demɔrdr] *vt* : **ne pas ~ de** to stick to.

démotiver [3] [demɔtive] *vt* to demotivate.

démouler [3] [demule] *vt* to turn out of a mould, to remove from a mould.

démunir [32] [demynir] *vt* to deprive. ◆ **se démunir** *vp* : **se ~ de** to part with.

dénaturer [3] [denatyre] *vt* - 1. [goût] to impair, to mar - 2. TECHNOL to denature - 3. [déformer] to distort.

dénégation [denegasjɔ̃] *nf* denial.

dénicher [3] [deniʃe] *vt* *fig* - 1. [personne] to flush out - 2. *fam* [objet] to unearth.

dénigrer [3] [denigre] *vt* to denigrate, to run down.

dénivelé [denivle] *nm* difference in level ou height.

dénivellation [denivɛlasjɔ̃] *nf* - 1. [différence de niveau] difference in height ou level - 2. [pente] slope.

dénombrer [3] [denɔ̃bre] *vt* [compter] to count ; [énumérer] to enumerate.

dénominateur [denɔminatœr] *nm* denominator.

dénomination [denɔminasjɔ̃] *nf* name.

dénommé, e [denɔme] *adj* : **un ~ Robert** someone by the name of Robert.

dénoncer [16] [denɔ̃se] *vt* - 1. [gén] to denounce ; **~ qqn à qqn** to denounce sb to sb, to inform on sb - 2. *fig* [trahir] to betray.

dénonciation [denɔ̃sjasjɔ̃] *nf* denunciation.

dénoter [3] [denɔte] *vt* to show, to indicate.

dénouement [denumɑ̃] *nm* - 1. [issue] outcome - 2. [d'un film, d'un livre] denouement.

dénouer [6] [denwe] *vt* [nœud] to untie, to undo ; *fig* to unravel.

dénoyauter [3] [denwajote] *vt* [fruit] to stone.

denrée [dɑ̃re] *nf* [produit] produce *(U)* ; **~s alimentaires** foodstuffs.

dense [dɑ̃s] *adj* - 1. [gén] dense - 2. [style] condensed.

densité [dɑ̃site] *nf* density.

dent [dɑ̃] *nf* - 1. [de personne, d'objet] tooth ; **faire ses ~s** to cut one's teeth, to teethe ; **~ de lait/de sagesse** milk/wisdom tooth - 2. GÉOGR peak.

dentaire [dɑ̃ter] *adj* dental.

dentelé, e [dɑ̃tle] *adj* serrated, jagged.

dentelle [dɑ̃tɛl] *nf* lace *(U)*.

dentier [dɑ̃tje] *nm* [dents] dentures *(pl)*.

dentifrice [dɑ̃tifris] *nm* toothpaste.

dentiste [dɑ̃tist] *nmf* dentist.

dentition [dɑ̃tisjɔ̃] *nf* teeth *(pl)*, dentition.

dénuder [3] [denyde] *vt* to leave bare ; [fil électrique] to strip.

dénué, e [denɥe] *adj sout* : ~ **de** devoid of.

dénuement [denymɑ̃] *nm* destitution *(U)*.

déodorant, e [deɔdɔrɑ̃, ɑ̃t] *adj* deodorant. ◆ **déodorant** *nm* deodorant.

déontologie [deɔ̃tɔlɔʒi] *nf* professional ethics *(pl)*.

dépannage [depanaʒ] *nm* repair ; **service de ~** AUT breakdown service.

dépanner [3] [depane] *vt* - **1.** [réparer] to repair, to fix - **2.** *fam* [aider] to bail out.

dépanneur, euse [depanœr, øz] *nm, f* repairman (*f* repairwoman). ◆ **dépanneuse** *nf* [véhicule] (breakdown) recovery vehicle.

dépareillé, e [depareje] *adj* [ensemble] non-matching ; [paire] odd.

départ [depar] *nm* - **1.** [de personne] departure, leaving ; [de véhicule] departure ; **les grands ~s** the holiday exodus *(sg)* - **2.** SPORT & *fig* start. ◆ **au départ** *loc adv* to start with.

départager [17] [departaʒe] *vt* - **1.** [concurrents, opinions] to decide between - **2.** [séparer] to separate.

département [departɑmɑ̃] *nm* - **1.** [territoire] *territorial and administrative division of France* - **2.** [service] department.

départemental, e, aux [departɑmɑtal, o] *adj of* a French *département*. ◆ **départementale** *nf* secondary road, ≃ B road *Br*.

dépassé, e [depase] *adj* - **1.** [périmé] old-fashioned - **2.** *fam* [déconcerté] : ~ **par** overwhelmed by.

dépassement [depasmɑ̃] *nm* [en voiture] overtaking.

dépasser [3] [depase] ⬦ *vt* - **1.** [doubler] to overtake - **2.** [être plus grand que] to be taller than - **3.** [excéder] to exceed, to be more than - **4.** [durer plus longtemps que] : ~ **une heure** to go on for more than an hour - **5.** [aller au-delà de] to exceed - **6.** [franchir] to pass. ⬦ *vi* : ~ **(de)** to stick out (from).

dépayser [3] [depeize] *vt* - **1.** [désorienter] to disorientate *Br*, to disorient *Am* - **2.** [changer agréablement] to make a change of scene for.

dépecer [29] [depəse] *vt* - **1.** [découper] to chop up - **2.** [déchiqueter] to tear apart.

dépêche [depɛʃ] *nf* dispatch.

dépêcher [4] [depeʃe] *vt sout* [envoyer] to dispatch. ◆ **se dépêcher** *vp* to hurry up ; **se ~ de faire qqch** to hurry to do sthg.

dépeindre [81] [depɛ̃dr] *vt* to depict, to describe.

dépeint, e [depɛ̃, ɛ̃t] *pp* ▷ **dépeindre**.

dépendance [depɑ̃dɑ̃s] *nf* - **1.** [de personne] dependence ; **être sous la ~ de** to be dependent on - **2.** [à la drogue] dependency - **3.** [de bâtiment] outbuilding.

dépendre [73] [depɑ̃dr] *vt* - **1.** [être soumis] : ~ **de** to depend on ; **ça dépend** it depends - **2.** [appartenir] : ~ **de** to belong to.

dépens [depɑ̃] *nmpl* JUR costs ; **aux ~ de qqn** at sb's expense ; **je l'ai appris à mes ~** I learned that to my cost.

dépense [depɑ̃s] *nf* - **1.** [frais] expense - **2.** FIN & *fig* expenditure *(U)* ; **les ~s publiques** public spending *(U)*.

dépenser [3] [depɑ̃se] *vt* - **1.** [argent] to spend - **2.** *fig* [énergie] to expend. ◆ **se dépenser** *vp litt & fig* to exert o.s.

dépensier, ère [depɑ̃sje, ɛr] *adj* extravagant.

déperdition [deperdisjɔ̃] *nf* loss.

dépérir [32] [deperir] *vi* - **1.** [personne] to waste away - **2.** [santé, affaire] to decline - **3.** [plante] to wither.

dépeupler [5] [depœple] *vt* - **1.** [pays] to depopulate - **2.** [étang, rivière, forêt] to drive the wildlife from.

déphasé, e [defaze] *adj* ÉLECTR out of phase ; *fam fig* out of touch.

dépilatoire [depilatwar] *adj* . **crème ~** depilatory cream.

dépistage [depistaʒ] *nm* [de maladie] screening ; **~ du SIDA** AIDS testing.

dépister [3] [depiste] *vt* - **1.** [gibier, voleur] to track down - **2.** [maladie] to screen for.

dépit [depi] *nm* pique, spite. ◆ **en dépit de** *loc prép* in spite of.

déplacé, e [deplase] *adj* - **1.** [propos, attitude, présence] out of place - **2.** [personne] displaced.

déplacement [deplasmɑ̃] *nm* - **1.** [d'objet] moving - **2.** [voyage] travelling *(U) Br*, traveling *(U) Am*.

déplacer [16] [deplase] *vt* - **1.** [objet] to move, to shift ; *fig* [problème] to shift the emphasis of - **2.** [muter] to transfer. ◆ **se déplacer** *vp* - **1.** [se mouvoir - animal] to move (around) ; [- personne] to walk - **2.** [voyager] to travel - **3.** MÉD : **se ~ une vertèbre** to slip a disc *Br* ou disk *Am*.

déplaire [110] [depler] *vt* - **1.** [ne pas

plaire] : **cela me déplaît** I don't like it - **2.** [irriter] to displease.

déplaisant, e [deplɛzɑ̃, ɑ̃t] *adj sout* unpleasant.

dépliant [deplijɑ̃] *nm* leaflet ; ~ **touristique** tourist brochure.

déplier [10] [deplije] *vt* to unfold.

déploiement [deplwamɑ̃] *nm* - **1.** MIL deployment - **2.** [d'ailes] spreading - **3.** *fig* [d'efforts] display.

déplorer [3] [deplɔre] *vt* [regretter] to deplore.

déployer [13] [deplwaje] *vt* - **1.** [déplier - gén] to unfold ; [- plan, journal] to open ; [ailes] to spread - **2.** MIL to deploy - **3.** [mettre en œuvre] to expend.

déplu [deply] *pp* ⮞ **déplaire**.

déportation [depɔrtasjɔ̃] *nf* - **1.** [exil] deportation - **2.** [internement] transportation to a concentration camp.

déporté, e [depɔrte] *nm, f* - **1.** [exilé] deportee - **2.** [interné] prisoner *(in a concentration camp)*.

déporter [3] [depɔrte] *vt* - **1.** [dévier] to carry off course - **2.** [exiler] to deport - **3.** [interner] to send to a concentration camp.

déposé, e [depoze] *adj* : **marque ~e** registered trademark ; **modèle ~** patented design.

déposer [3] [depoze] ◇ *vt* - **1.** [poser] to put down - **2.** [personne, paquet] to drop - **3.** [argent, sédiment] to deposit - **4.** JUR to file ; ~ **son bilan** FIN to go into liquidation - **5.** [monarque] to depose. ◇ *vi* JUR to testify, to give evidence. ⮞ **se déposer** *vp* to settle.

dépositaire [depozitɛr] *nmf* - **1.** COMM agent - **2.** [d'objet] bailee ; ~ **de** *fig* person entrusted with.

déposition [depozisjɔ̃] *nf* deposition.

déposséder [18] [deposede] *vt* : ~ **qqn de** to dispossess sb of.

dépôt [depo] *nm* - **1.** [d'objet, d'argent, de sédiment] deposit, depositing *(U)* ; **verser un ~ (de garantie)** to put down a deposit ; ~ **d'ordures** (rubbish) dump *Br*, garbage dump *Am* - **2.** ADMIN registration ; ~ **légal** copyright registration - **3.** [garage] depot - **4.** [entrepôt] store, warehouse - **5.** [prison] ≃ police cells *(pl)*.

dépotoir [depɔtwar] *nm* [décharge] (rubbish) dump *Br*, garbage dump *Am* ; *fam fig* dump,.tip.

dépouille [depuj] *nf* - **1.** [peau] hide, skin - **2.** [humaine] remains *(pl)*.

dépouillement [depujmɑ̃] *nm* [sobriété] austerity, sobriety.

dépouiller [3] [depuje] *vt* - **1.** [priver] : ~ **qqn (de)** to strip sb (of) - **2.** [examiner] to peruse ; ~ **un scrutin** to count the votes.

dépourvu, e [depurvy] *adj* : ~ **de** without, lacking in. ⮞ **au dépourvu** *loc adv* : **prendre qqn au ~** to catch sb unawares.

dépoussiérer [18] [depusjere] *vt* to dust (off).

dépravé, e [deprave] ◇ *adj* depraved. ◇ *nm, f* degenerate.

dépréciation [depresjasjɔ̃] *nf* depreciation.

déprécier [9] [depresje] *vt* - **1.** [marchandise] to reduce the value of - **2.** [œuvre] to disparage. ⮞ **se déprécier** *vp* - **1.** [marchandise] to depreciate - **2.** [personne] to put o.s. down.

dépressif, ive [depresif, iv] *adj* depressive.

dépression [depresjɔ̃] *nf* depression ; ~ **nerveuse** nervous breakdown.

déprimant, e [deprimɑ̃, ɑ̃t] *adj* depressing.

déprime [deprim] *nf fam* : **faire une ~** to be (feeling) down.

déprimé, e [deprime] *adj* depressed.

déprimer [3] [deprime] ◇ *vt* to depress. ◇ *vi fam* to be (feeling) down.

déprogrammer [3] [deprɔgrame] *vt* to remove from the schedule ; TÉLÉ to take off the air.

dépuceler [24] [depysle] *vt fam* : ~ **qqn** to take sb's virginity.

depuis [dəpɥi] ◇ *prép* - **1.** [à partir d'une date ou d'un moment précis] since ; **je ne l'ai pas vu ~ son mariage** I haven't seen him since he got married ; **il est parti ~ hier** he's been away since yesterday ; ~ **le début jusqu'à la fin** from beginning to end - **2.** [exprimant une durée] for ; **il est malade ~ une semaine** he has been ill for a week ; ~ **10 ans/longtemps** for 10 years/a long time ; ~ **toujours** always - **3.** [dans l'espace] from ; ~ **la route, on pouvait voir la mer** you could see the sea from the road. ◇ *adv* since (then) ; ~**, nous ne l'avons pas revu** we haven't seen him since (then). ⮞ **depuis que** *loc conj* since ; **je ne l'ai pas revu ~ qu'il s'est marié** I haven't seen him since he got married.

député [depyte] *nm* [au parlement] member of parliament *Br*, representative *Am*.

déraciner [3] [derasine] *vt litt & fig* to uproot.

déraillement [derajmɑ̃] *nm* derailment.

dérailler [3] [deraje] *vi* - **1.** [train] to leave the rails, to be derailed - **2.** *fam fig* [mécanisme] to go on the blink - **3.** *fam fig* [personne] to go to pieces.

dérailleur [derajœr] *nm* [de bicyclette] derailleur.

déraisonnable [derɛzɔnabl] *adj* unreasonable.

dérangement [derãʒmã] *nm* trouble ; **en ~** out of order.

déranger [17] [derãʒe] ◇ *vt* - **1.** [personne] to disturb, to bother ; **ça vous dérange si je fume?** do you mind if I smoke? - **2.** [plan] to disrupt - **3.** [maison, pièce] to disarrange, to make untidy. ◇ *vi* to be disturbing. ◆ **se déranger** *vp* - **1.** [se déplacer] to move - **2.** [se gêner] to put o.s. out.

dérapage [derapaʒ] *nm* [glissement] skid ; *fig* excess.

déraper [3] [derape] *vi* [glisser] to skid ; *fig* to get out of hand.

déréglementer [3] [deregləmãte] *vt* to deregulate.

dérégler [18] [deregle] *vt* [mécanisme] to put out of order ; *fig* to upset. ◆ **se dérégler** *vp* [mécanisme] to go wrong ; *fig* to be upset ou unsettled.

dérider [3] [deride] *vt fig* : **~ qqn** to cheer sb up.

dérision [derizjõ] *nf* derision ; **tourner qqch en ~** to hold sthg up to ridicule.

dérisoire [derizwar] *adj* derisory.

dérivatif, ive [derivatif, iv] *adj* derivative. ◆ **dérivatif** *nm* distraction.

dérive [deriv] *nf* [mouvement] drift, drifting *(U)* ; **aller** ou **partir à la ~** *fig* to fall apart.

dérivé [derive] *nm* derivative.

dériver [3] [derive] ◇ *vt* [détourner] to divert. ◇ *vi* - **1.** [aller à la dérive] to drift - **2.** *fig* [découler] : **~ de** to derive from.

dermatologie [dɛrmatɔlɔʒi] *nf* dermatology.

dermatologue [dɛrmatɔlɔg] *nmf* dermatologist.

dernier, ère [dɛrnje, ɛr] ◇ *adj* - **1.** [gén] last ; **l'année dernière** last year - **2.** [ultime] last, final - **3.** [plus récent] latest. ◇ *nm, f* last ; **ce ~** the latter. ◆ **en dernier** *loc adv* last.

dernièrement [dɛrnjɛrmã] *adv* recently, lately.

dernier-né, dernière-née [dɛrnjene, dɛrnjɛrne] *nm, f* [bébé] youngest (child).

dérobade [derɔbad] *nf* evasion, shirking *(U)*.

dérobé, e [derɔbe] *adj* - **1.** [volé] stolen

- **2.** [caché] hidden. ◆ **à la dérobée** *loc adv* surreptitiously.

dérober [3] [derɔbe] *vt sout* to steal. ◆ **se dérober** *vp* - **1.** [se soustraire] : **se ~ à qqch** to shirk sthg - **2.** [s'effondrer] to give way.

dérogation [derɔgasjõ] *nf* [action] dispensation ; [résultat] exception.

déroulement [derulmã] *nm* - **1.** [de bobine] unwinding - **2.** *fig* [d'événement] development.

dérouler [3] [derule] *vt* [fil] to unwind ; [papier, tissu] to unroll. ◆ **se dérouler** *vp* to take place.

déroute [derut] *nf* MIL rout ; *fig* collapse.

dérouter [3] [derute] *vt* - **1.** [déconcerter] to disconcert, to put out - **2.** [dévier] to divert.

derrière [dɛrjɛr] ◇ *prép & adv* behind. ◇ *nm* - **1.** [partie arrière] back ; **la porte de ~** the back door - **2.** [partie du corps] bottom, behind.

des [de] ◇ *art indéf* ➤ **un.** ◇ *prép* ➤ **de.**

dès [dɛ] *prép* from ; **~ son arrivée** the minute he arrives/arrived, as soon as he arrives/arrived ; **~ l'enfance** since childhood ; **~ 1900** as far back as 1900, as early as 1900 ; **~ maintenant** from now on ; **~ demain** starting ou from tomorrow. ◆ **dès que** *loc conj* as soon as.

désabusé, e [dezabyze] *adj* disillusioned.

désaccord [dezakɔr] *nm* disagreement.

désaccordé, e [dezakɔrde] *adj* out of tune.

désaffecté, e [dezafɛkte] *adj* disused.

désaffection [dezafɛksjõ] *nf* disaffection.

désagréable [dezagreabl] *adj* unpleasant.

désagréger [22] [dezagreʒe] *vt* to break up. ◆ **se désagréger** *vp* to break up.

désagrément [dezagremã] *nm* annoyance.

désaltérant, e [dezalterã, ãt] *adj* thirst-quenching.

désaltérer [18] [dezaltere] ◆ **se désaltérer** *vp* to quench one's thirst.

désamorcer [16] [dezamɔrse] *vt* [arme] to remove the primer from ; [bombe] to defuse ; *fig* [complot] to nip in the bud.

désappointer [3] [dezapwɛte] *vt* to disappoint.

désapprobation [dezaprɔbasjõ] *nf* disapproval.

désapprouver [3] [dezapruve] ◇ *vt* to disapprove of. ◇ *vi* to be disapproving.

désarmement [dezarməmã] *nm* disarmament.

désarmer [3] [dezarme] *vt* to disarm ; [fusil] to unload.

désarroi [dezarwa] *nm* confusion.

désastre [dezastr] *nm* disaster.

désastreux, euse [dezastrø, øz] *adj* disastrous.

désavantage [dezavãtaʒ] *nm* disadvantage.

désavantager [17] [dezavãtaʒe] *vt* to disadvantage.

désavantageux, euse [dezavãtaʒø, øz] *adj* unfavourable *Br*, unfavorable *Am*.

désavouer [6] [dezavwe] *vt* to disown.

désaxé, e [dezakse] ◇ *adj* [mentalement] disordered, unhinged. ◇ *nm, f* unhinged person.

descendance [desãdãs] *nf* [progéniture] descendants *(pl)*.

descendant, e [desãdã, ãt] *nm, f* [héritier] descendant.

descendre [73] [desãdr] ◇ *vt (aux : avoir)* - **1.** [escalier, pente] to go/come down ; ~ **la rue en courant** to run down the street - **2.** [rideau, tableau] to lower - **3.** [apporter] to bring/take down - **4.** *fam* [personne, avion] to shoot down. ◇ *vi (aux : être)* - **1.** [gén] to go/come down ; [température, niveau] to fall - **2.** [passager] to get off ; ~ **d'un bus** to get off a bus ; ~ **d'une voiture** to get out of a car - **3.** [être issu] : ~ **de** to be descended from - **4.** [marée] to go out.

descendu, e [desãdy] *pp* ▷ **descendre**.

descente [desãt] *nf* - **1.** [action] descent - **2.** [pente] downhill slope ou stretch - **3.** [irruption] raid - **4.** [tapis] : ~ **de lit** bedside rug.

descriptif, ive [dɛskriptif, iv] *adj* descriptive. ◆ **descriptif** *nm* [de lieu] particulars *(pl)* ; [d'appareil] specification.

description [dɛskripsjɔ̃] *nf* description.

désemparé, e [dezãpare] *adj* [personne] helpless ; [avion, navire] disabled.

désendettement [dezãdɛtmã] *nm* degearing, debt reduction.

désenfler [3] [dezãfle] *vi* to go down, to become less swollen.

désensibiliser [3] [desãsibilize] *vt* to desensitize.

déséquilibre [dezekilibr] *nm* imbalance.

déséquilibré, e [dezekilibre] *nm, f* unbalanced person.

déséquilibrer [3] [dezekilibre] *vt* - **1.** [physiquement] : ~ **qqn** to throw sb off balance - **2.** [perturber] to unbalance.

désert, e [dezɛr, ɛrt] *adj* [désertique - île]

desert *(avant n)* ; [peu fréquenté] deserted. ◆ **désert** *nm* desert.

déserter [3] [dezɛrte] *vt & vi* to desert.

déserteur [dezɛrtœr] *nm* MIL deserter ; *fig & péj* traitor.

désertion [dezɛrsjɔ̃] *nf* desertion.

désertique [dezɛrtik] *adj* desert *(avant n)*.

désespéré, e [dezɛspere] *adj* - **1.** [regard] desperate - **2.** [situation] hopeless.

désespérément [dezɛsperemã] *adv* - **1.** [sans espoir] hopelessly - **2.** [avec acharnement] desperately.

désespérer [18] [dezɛspere] ◇ *vt* - **1.** [décourager] : ~ **qqn** to drive sb to despair - **2.** [perdre espoir] : ~ **que qqch arrive** to give up hope of sthg happening. ◇ *vi* : ~ **(de)** to despair (of). ◆ **se désespérer** *vp* to despair.

désespoir [dezɛspwar] *nm* despair ; **en** ~ **de cause** as a last resort.

déshabillé [dezabije] *nm* negligee.

déshabiller [3] [dezabije] *vt* to undress. ◆ **se déshabiller** *vp* to undress, to get undressed.

désherbant, e [dezɛrbã, ãt] *adj* weedkilling. ◆ **désherbant** *nm* weedkiller.

déshérité, e [dezerite] ◇ *adj* - **1.** [privé d'héritage] disinherited - **2.** [pauvre] deprived. ◇ *nm, f* [pauvre] deprived person.

déshériter [3] [dezerite] *vt* to disinherit.

déshonneur [dezɔnœr] *nm* disgrace.

déshonorer [3] [dezɔnɔre] *vt* to disgrace, to bring disgrace on.

déshydrater [3] [dezidrate] *vt* to dehydrate. ◆ **se déshydrater** *vp* to become dehydrated.

désigner [3] [dezine] *vt* - **1.** [choisir] to appoint - **2.** [signaler] to point out - **3.** [nommer] to designate.

désillusion [dezilyzjɔ̃] *nf* disillusion.

désincarné, e [dezɛ̃karne] *adj* - **1.** RELIG disembodied - **2.** [éthéré] unearthly.

désinfectant, e [dezɛ̃fɛktã, ãt] *adj* disinfectant. ◆ **désinfectant** *nm* disinfectant.

désinfecter [4] [dezɛ̃fɛkte] *vt* to disinfect.

désinflation [dezɛ̃flasjɔ̃] *nf* disinflation.

désintégrer [18] [dezɛ̃tegre] *vt* to break up. ◆ **se désintégrer** *vp* to disintegrate, to break up.

désintéressé, e [dezɛ̃terese] *adj* disinterested.

désintéresser [4] [dezɛ̃terese] ◆ **se désintéresser** *vp* : **se** ~ **de** to lose interest in.

désintoxication [dezɛ̃tɔksikasjɔ̃] *nf* detoxification.

désinvolte [dezɛ̃vɔlt] *adj* - **1.** [à l'aise] casual - **2.** *péj* [sans-gêne] offhand.

désinvolture [dezɛ̃vɔltyr] *nf* - **1.** [légèreté] casualness - **2.** *péj* [sans-gêne] offhandedness.

désir [dezir] *nm* - **1.** [souhait] desire, wish - **2.** [charnel] desire.

désirable [dezirabl] *adj* desirable.

désirer [3] [dezire] *vt* - **1.** *sout* [chose] : ~ faire qqch to wish to do sthg ; **vous désirez?** [dans un magasin] can I help you? ; [dans un café] what can I get you? - **2.** [sexuellement] to desire.

désistement [dezistəmɑ̃] *nm* : ~ **(de)** withdrawal (from).

désister [3] [deziste] ◆ **se désister** *vp* [se retirer] to withdraw, to stand down.

désobéir [32] [dezɔbeir] *vi* : ~ **(à qqn)** to disobey (sb).

désobéissant, e [dezɔbeisɑ̃, ɑ̃t] *adj* disobedient.

désobligeant, e [dezɔbliʒɑ̃, ɑ̃t] *adj* *sout* offensive.

désodorisant, e [dezodɔrizɑ̃, ɑ̃t] *adj* deodorant. ◆ **désodorisant** *nm* air freshener.

désœuvré, e [dezœvre] *adj* idle.

désolation [dezɔlasjɔ̃] *nf* - **1.** [destruction] desolation - **2.** *sout* [affliction] distress.

désolé, e [dezɔle] *adj* - **1.** [ravagé] desolate - **2.** [contrarié] very sorry.

désoler [3] [dezɔle] *vt* - **1.** [affliger] to sadden - **2.** [contrarier] to upset, to make sorry. ◆ **se désoler** *vp* [être contrarié] to be upset.

désolidariser [3] [desɔlidarize] *vt* - **1.** [choses] : ~ qqch **(de)** to disengage ou disconnect sthg (from) - **2.** [personnes] to estrange. ◆ **se désolidariser** *vp* : se ~ de to dissociate o.s. from.

désopilant, e [dezɔpilɑ̃, ɑ̃t] *adj* hilarious.

désordonné, e [dezɔrdɔne] *adj* [maison, personne] untidy ; *fig* [vie] disorganized.

désordre [dezɔrdr] *nm* - **1.** [fouillis] untidiness ; *en* ~ untidy - **2.** [agitation] disturbances *(pl)*, disorder *(U)*.

désorganiser [3] [dezɔrganize] *vt* to disrupt.

désorienté, e [dezɔrjɑ̃te] *adj* disoriented, disorientated.

désormais [dezɔrmɛ] *adv* from now on, in future.

désosser [3] [dezɔse] *vt* to bone.

despote [dɛspɔt] *nm* [chef d'État] despot ; *fig & péj* tyrant.

despotisme [dɛspɔtism] *nm* [gouvernement] despotism ; *fig & péj* tyranny.

desquels, desquelles [dekɛl] ➪ **lequel.**

DESS *(abr de* diplôme d'études supérieures spécialisées*) nm postgraduate diploma.*

dessécher [18] [deseʃe] *vt* [peau] to dry (out) ; *fig* [cœur] to harden. ◆ **se dessécher** *vp* [peau, terre] to dry out ; [plante] to wither ; *fig* to harden.

desserrer [4] [desere] *vt* to loosen ; [poing, dents] to unclench ; [frein] to release.

dessert [desɛr] *nm* dessert.

desserte [desɛrt] *nf* - **1.** TRANSPORT (transport) service - **2.** [meuble] sideboard.

desservir [38] [desɛrvir] *vt* - **1.** TRANSPORT to serve - **2.** [table] to clear - **3.** [désavantager] to do a disservice to.

dessin [desɛ̃] *nm* - **1.** [graphique] drawing ; ~ animé cartoon *(film)* ; ~ humoristique cartoon *(drawing)* - **2.** *fig* [contour] outline.

dessinateur, trice [desinatœr, tris] *nm, f* artist, draughtsman *(f* draughtswoman*) Br,* draftsman *(f* draftswoman*) Am.*

dessiner [3] [desine] ◇ *vt* [représenter] to draw ; *fig* to outline. ◇ *vi* to draw.

dessous [dəsu] ◇ *adv* underneath ◇ *nm* [partie inférieure gén] underside ; [- d'un tissu] wrong side. ◇ *nmpl* [sous-vêtements féminins] underwear *(U).* ◆ **en dessous** *loc adv* underneath ; [plus bas] below ; **ils habitent l'appartement d'en ~** they live in the flat below ou downstairs.

dessous-de-plat [dəsudpla] *nm inv* tablemat

dessus [dəsy] ◇ *adv* on top ; **faites attention à ne pas marcher ~** be careful not to walk on it. ◇ *nm* - **1.** [partie supérieure] top - **2.** [étage supérieur] upstairs ; **les voisins du ~** the upstairs neighbours - **3.** *loc* : **avoir le ~** to have the upper hand ; **reprendre le ~** to get over it. ◆ **en dessus** *loc adv* on top.

dessus-de-lit [dəsydli] *nm inv* bedspread.

déstabiliser [3] [destabilize] *vt* to destabilize.

destin [dɛstɛ̃] *nm* fate.

destinataire [dɛstinatɛr] *nmf* addressee.

destination [dɛstinasjɔ̃] *nf* - **1.** [direction] destination ; **un avion à ~ de Paris** a plane to ou for Paris - **2.** [rôle] purpose.

destinée [dɛstine] *nf* destiny.

destiner [3] [dɛstine] *vt* - **1.** [consacrer] : ~ qqch à to intend sthg for, to mean sthg for - **2.** [vouer] : ~ qqn à qqch/à faire qqch [à un métier] to destine sb for sthg/to do sthg ; [sort] to mark sb out for sthg/to do sthg.

destituer [7] [dɛstitɥe] vt to dismiss.

destructeur, trice [dɛstryktœr, tris] <> adj destructive. <> nm, f destroyer.

destruction [dɛstryksjɔ̃] nf destruction.

désuet, ète [dezɥɛ, ɛt] adj [expression, coutume] obsolete ; [style, tableau] outmoded.

désuni, e [dezyni] adj divided.

détachable [detaʃabl] adj detachable, removable.

détachant, e [detaʃɑ̃, ɑ̃t] adj stain-removing. ← **détachant** nm stain remover.

détaché, e [detaʃe] adj detached.

détachement [detaʃmɑ̃] nm - 1. [d'esprit] detachment - 2. [de fonctionnaire] secondment - 3. MIL detachment.

détacher [3] [detaʃe] vt - 1. [enlever] : ~ qqch (de) [objet] to detach sthg (from) ; fig to free sthg (from) - 2. [nettoyer] to remove stains from, to clean - 3. [délier] to undo ; [cheveux] to untie - 4. ADMIN : ~ qqn auprès de to second sb to. ← **se détacher** vp - 1. [tomber] : se ~ (de) to come off ; fig to free o.s. (from) - 2. [se défaire] to come undone - 3. [ressortir] : se ~ sur to stand out on - 4. [se désintéresser] : se ~ de qqn to drift apart from sb.

détail [detaj] nm - 1. [précision] detail - 2. COMM : le ~ retail. ← **au détail** loc adj & loc adv retail. ← **en détail** loc adv in detail.

détaillant, e [detajɑ̃, ɑ̃t] nm, f retailer.

détaillé, e [detaje] adj detailed.

détailler [3] [detaje] vt - 1. [expliquer] to give details of - 2. [vendre] to retail.

détaler [3] [detale] vi - 1. [personne] to clear out - 2. [animal] to bolt.

détartrant, e [detartrɑ̃, ɑ̃t] adj descaling. ← **détartrant** nm descaling agent.

détaxe [detaks] nf : ~ (sur) [suppression] removal of tax (from) ; [réduction] reduction in tax (on).

détecter [4] [detɛkte] vt to detect.

détecteur, trice [detɛktœr, tris] adj detecting, detector (avant n). ← **détecteur** nm detector.

détection [detɛksjɔ̃] nf detection.

détective [detɛktiv] nm detective ; ~ privé private detective.

déteindre [81] [detɛ̃dr] vi to fade.

déteint, e [detɛ̃, ɛ̃t] pp ⊳ déteindre.

dételer [24] [detle] vt [cheval] to unharness.

détendre [73] [detɑ̃dr] vt - 1. [corde] to loosen, to slacken ; fig to ease - 2. [personne] to relax. ← **se détendre** vp - 1. [se relâcher] to slacken ; fig [situation] to ease ; [atmosphère] to become more relaxed - 2. [se reposer] to relax.

détendu, e [detɑ̃dy] <> pp ⊳ détendre. <> adj - 1. [corde] loose, slack - 2. [personne] relaxed.

détenir [40] [detnir] vt - 1. [objet] to have, to hold - 2. [personne] to detain, to hold.

détente [detɑ̃t] nf - 1. [de ressort] release - 2. [d'une arme] trigger - 3. [repos] relaxation - 4. POLIT détente.

détenteur, trice [detɑ̃tœr, tris] nm, f [d'objet, de secret] possessor ; [de prix, record] holder.

détention [detɑ̃sjɔ̃] nf - 1. [possession] possession - 2. [emprisonnement] detention.

détenu, e [detny] <> pp ⊳ détenir. <> adj detained. <> nm, f prisoner.

détergent, e [detɛrʒɑ̃, ɑ̃t] adj detergent (avant n). ← **détergent** nm detergent.

détérioration [deterjɔrasjɔ̃] nf [de bâtiment] deterioration ; [de situation] worsening.

détériorer [3] [deterjɔre] vt - 1. [abîmer] to damage - 2. [altérer] to ruin. ← **se détériorer** vp - 1. [bâtiment] to deteriorate ; [situation] to worsen - 2. [s'altérer] to be spoiled.

déterminant, e [detɛrminɑ̃, ɑ̃t] adj decisive, determining. ← **déterminant** nm LING determiner.

détermination [detɛrminasjɔ̃] nf [résolution] decision.

déterminé, e [detɛrmine] adj - 1. [quantité] given (avant n) - 2. [expression] determined.

déterminer [3] [detɛrmine] vt - 1. [préciser] to determine, to specify - 2. [provoquer] to bring about.

déterrer [4] [detere] vt to dig up.

détestable [detɛstabl] adj dreadful.

détester [3] [detɛste] vt to detest.

détonateur [detɔnatœr] nm TECHNOL detonator ; fig trigger.

détoner [3] [detɔne] vi to detonate.

détonner [3] [detɔne] vi MUS to be out of tune ; [couleur] to clash ; [personne] to be out of place.

détour [detur] nm - 1. [crochet] detour - 2. [méandre] bend ; fig directly.

détourné, e [deturne] adj [dévié] indirect ; fig roundabout (avant n).

détournement [deturnəmɑ̃] nm diversion ; ~ **d'avion** hijacking ; ~ **de fonds** embezzlement ; ~ **de mineur** corruption of a minor.

détourner [3] [deturne] *vt* - **1.** [dévier - gén] to divert ; [- avion] to hijack - **2.** [écarter] : ~ **qqn de** to distract sb from, to divert sb from - **3.** [la tête, les yeux] to turn away - **4.** [argent] to embezzle. ◆ **se détourner** *vp* to turn away ; **se ~ de** *fig* to move away from.

détraquer [3] [detrake] *vt fam* [dérégler] to break ; *fig* to upset. ◆ **se détraquer** *vp fam* [se dérégler] to go wrong ; *fig* to become unsettled.

détresse [detrɛs] *nf* distress.

détriment [detrimã] ◆ **au détriment de** *loc prép* to the detriment of.

détritus [detrity(s)] *nm* detritus.

détroit [detrwa] *nm* strait ; **le ~ de Bering** the Bering Strait ; **le ~ de Gibraltar** the Strait of Gibraltar.

détromper [3] [detrɔ̃pe] *vt* to disabuse.

détrôner [3] [detrone] *vt* [souverain] to dethrone ; *fig* to oust.

détruire [98] [detrɥir] *vt* - **1.** [démolir, éliminer] to destroy - **2.** *fig* [anéantir] to ruin.

détruit, e [detrɥi, it] *pp* ▷ **détruire**.

dette [dɛt] *nf* debt.

DEUG, Deug [dœg] (*abr de* **diplôme d'études universitaires générales**) *nm university diploma taken after two years of arts courses.*

deuil [dœj] *nm* [douleur, mort] bereavement ; [vêtements, période] mourning *(U)* ; **porter le ~** to be in ou wear mourning.

DEUST, Deust [dœst] (*abr de* **diplôme d'études universitaires scientifiques et techniques**) *nm university diploma taken after two years of science courses ; voir aussi* **DEUG**.

deux [dø] ◇ *adj num* two ; **ses ~ fils** both his sons, his two sons ; **tous les ~ jours** every other day, every two days, every second day. ◇ *nm* two ; **les ~** both ; **par ~** in pairs ; *voir aussi* **six**.

deuxième [døzjɛm] *adj num, nm* ou *nmf* second ; *voir aussi* **sixième**.

deux-pièces [døpjɛs] *nm inv* - **1.** [appartement] two-room flat *Br* ou apartment *Am* - **2.** [bikini] two piece (swimming costume).

deux-points [døpwɛ̃] *nm inv* colon.

deux-roues [døru] *nm inv* two-wheeled vehicle.

dévaler [3] [devale] *vt* to run down.

dévaliser [3] [devalize] *vt* [cambrioler - maison] to ransack ; [- personne] to rob ; *fig* to strip bare.

dévaloriser [3] [devalɔrize] *vt* - **1.** [mon-

naie] to devalue - **2.** [personne] to run ou put down. ◆ **se dévaloriser** *vp* - **1.** [monnaie] to fall in value - **2.** [personne] *fig* to run ou put o.s. down.

dévaluation [devalɥasjɔ̃] *nf* devaluation.

dévaluer [7] [devalɥe] *vt* to devalue. ◆ **se dévaluer** *vp* to devalue.

devancer [16] [dəvãse] *vt* - **1.** [précéder] to arrive before - **2.** [anticiper] to anticipate.

devant [dəvã] ◇ *prép* - **1.** [en face de] in front of - **2.** [en avant de] ahead of, in front of ; **aller droit ~ soi** to go straight ahead ou on - **3.** [en présence de, face à] in the face of. ◇ *adv* - **1.** [en face] in front - **2.** [en avant] in front, ahead. ◇ *nm* front ; **prendre les ~s** to make the first move, to take the initiative. ◆ **de devant** *loc adj* [pattes, roues] front *(avant n)*.

devanture [dəvãtyr] *nf* shop window.

dévaster [3] [devaste] *vt* to devastate.

développement [devlɔpmã] *nm* - **1.** [gén] development - **2.** PHOT developing.

développer [3] [devlɔpe] *vt* to develop ; [industrie, commerce] to expand. ◆ **se développer** *vp* - **1.** [s'épanouir] to spread - **2.** ÉCON to grow, to expand.

devenir [40] [dəvnir] *vi* to become ; **que devenez-vous?** *fig* how are you doing?

devenu, e [dəvny] *pp* ▷ **devenir**.

dévergondé, e [devergɔ̃de] ◇ *adj* shameless, wild. ◇ *nm, f* shameless person.

déverser [3] [devɛrse] *vt* - **1.** [liquide] to pour out - **2.** [ordures] to tip (out) - **3.** *fig* [injures] to pour out.

déviation [devjasjɔ̃] *nf* - **1.** [gén] deviation - **2.** [d'itinéraire] diversion.

dévier [9] [devje] ◇ *vi* ~ **de** to deviate from. ◇ *vt* to divert.

devin, devineresse [dəvɛ̃, dəvinrɛs] *nm, f* : **je ne suis pas ~!** I'm not psychic!

deviner [3] [dəvine] *vt* to guess.

devinette [dəvinɛt] *nf* riddle.

devis [dəvi] *nm* estimate ; **faire un ~** to (give an) estimate.

dévisager [17] [devizaʒe] *vt* to stare at.

devise [dəviz] *nf* - **1.** [formule] motto - **2.** [monnaie] currency. ◆ **devises** *nfpl* [argent] currency *(U)*.

dévisser [3] [devise] ◇ *vt* to unscrew. ◇ *vi* ALPINISME to fall (off).

dévoiler [3] [devwale] *vt* to unveil ; *fig* to reveal.

devoir [53] [dəvwar] ◇ *nm* - **1.** [obligation] duty - **2.** SCOL homework *(U)* ; **faire ses ~s** to do one's homework. ◇ *vt* - **1.** [argent, respect] : ~ **qqch (à qqn)** to owe (sb) sth - **2.** [marque l'obligation] : ~ **faire qqch** to have to do sthg ; **je dois partir à l'heure ce soir** I have to ou must leave on time tonight ; **tu devrais faire attention** you should be ou ought to be careful ; **il n'aurait pas dû mentir** he shouldn't have lied, he ought not to have lied - **3.** [marque la probabilité] : **il doit faire chaud là-bas** it must be hot over there ; **il a dû oublier** he must have forgotten - **4.** [marque le futur, l'intention] : ~ **faire qqch** to be (due) to do sthg, to be going to do sthg ; **elle doit arriver à 6 heures** she's due to arrive at 6 o'clock ; **je dois voir mes parents ce week-end** I'm seeing ou going to see my parents this weekend - **5.** [être destiné à] : **il devait mourir trois ans plus tard** he was to die three years later ; **cela devait arriver** it had to happen, it was bound to happen. ◆ **se devoir** vp : **se ~ de faire qqch** to be duty-bound to do sthg ; **comme il se doit** as is proper.

dévolu, e [devɔly] adj sout : ~ **à** allotted to. ◆ **dévolu** nm : **jeter son ~ sur** to set one's sights on.

dévorer [3] [devɔre] vt to devour.

dévotion [devɔsjɔ̃] nf devotion ; **avec ~** [prier] devoutly ; [soigner, aimer] devotedly.

dévoué, e [devwe] adj devoted.

dévouement [devumɑ̃] nm devotion.

dévouer [6] [devwe] ◆ **se dévouer** vp - **1.** [se consacrer] : **se ~ à** to devote o.s. to - **2.** fig [se sacrifier] : **se ~ pour qqch/pour faire qqch** to sacrifice o.s. for sthg/to do sthg.

dévoyé, e [devwaje] adj & nm, f delinquent.

devrai, devras etc ⟾ **devoir.**

dextérité [dɛksterite] nf dexterity, skill.

diabète [djabɛt] nm diabetes (U).

diabétique [djabetik] nmf & adj diabetic.

diable [djabl] nm devil.

diabolique [djabɔlik] adj diabolical.

diabolo [djabɔlo] nm [boisson] fruit cordial and lemonade ; ~ **menthe** mint (cordial) and lemonade.

diadème [djadɛm] nm diadem.

diagnostic [djagnɔstik] nm MÉD & fig diagnosis.

diagnostiquer [3] [djagnɔstike] vt MÉD & fig to diagnose.

diagonale [djagɔnal] nf diagonal.

dialecte [djalɛkt] nm dialect.

dialogue [djalɔg] nm discussion.

dialoguer [3] [djalɔge] vi - **1.** [converser] to converse - **2.** INFORM to interact.

diamant [djamɑ̃] nm [pierre] diamond.

diamètre [djamɛtr] nm diameter.

diapason [djapazɔ̃] nm [instrument] tuning fork.

diapositive [djapozitiv] nf slide.

diarrhée [djare] nf diarrhoea.

dictateur [diktatœr] nm dictator.

dictature [diktatyr] nf dictatorship.

dictée [dikte] nf dictation.

dicter [3] [dikte] vt to dictate.

diction [diksjɔ̃] nf diction.

dictionnaire [diksjɔner] nm dictionary.

dicton [diktɔ̃] nm saying, dictum.

dièse [djɛz] ⟷ adj sharp ; **do/fa ~** C/F sharp. ⟷ nm sharp.

diesel [djezɛl] adj inv diesel.

diète [djɛt] nf diet ; [jeûne] to be fasting.

diététicien, enne [djetetisjɛ̃, ɛn] nm, f dietician.

diététique [djetetik] ⟷ nf dietetics (U). ⟷ adj [considération, raison] dietary ; [produit, magasin] health (avant n).

dieu, x [djø] nm god. ◆ **Dieu** nm God ; **mon Dieu!** my God!

diffamation [difamasjɔ̃] nf [écrite] libel ; [orale] slander.

différé, e [difere] adj recorded. ◆ **différé** nm : **en ~** TÉLÉ recorded ; INFORM off-line.

différence [diferɑ̃s] nf difference.

différencier [9] [diferɑ̃sje] vt : ~ **qqch de qqch** to differentiate sthg from sthg. ◆ **se différencier** vp : **se ~ de** to be different from.

différend [diferɑ̃] nm [désaccord] difference of opinion.

différent, e [diferɑ̃, ɑ̃t] adj : ~ **(de)** different (from).

différer [18] [difere] ⟷ vt [retarder] to postpone. ⟷ vi : ~ **de** to differ from, to be different from.

difficile [difisil] adj difficult.

difficilement [difisilmɑ̃] adv with difficulty.

difficulté [difikylte] nf - **1.** [complexité, peine] difficulty - **2.** [obstacle] problem.

difforme [difɔrm] adj deformed.

diffuser [3] [difyze] vt - **1.** [lumière] to diffuse - **2.** [émission] to broadcast - **3.** [livres] to distribute.

diffuseur [difyzœr] nm - **1.** [appareil] diffuser - **2.** [de livres] distributor.

diffusion [difyzjɔ̃] nf - **1.** [d'émission, d'onde] broadcast - **2.** [de livres] distribution.

digérer [18] [diʒere] ◇ *vi* to digest. ◇ *vt* - **1.** [repas, connaissance] to digest - **2.** *fam fig* [désagrément] to put up with.

digestif, ive [diʒestif, iv] *adj* digestive. ◆ **digestif** *nm* liqueur.

digestion [diʒestjɔ̃] *nf* digestion.

digital, e, aux [diʒital, o] *adj* - **1.** TECHNOL digital - **2.** ▷ **empreinte**.

digne [diɲ] *adj* - **1.** [honorable] dignified - **2.** [méritant] : ~ **de** worthy of.

dignité [diɲite] *nf* dignity.

digression [digresjɔ̃] *nf* digression.

digue [dig] *nf* dike.

dilapider [3] [dilapide] *vt* to squander.

dilater [3] [dilate] *vt* to dilate.

dilemme [dilɛm] *nm* dilemma.

diligence [diliʒɑ̃s] *nf* HIST & *sout* diligence.

diluant [dilɥɑ̃] *nm* thinner.

diluer [7] [dilɥe] *vt* to dilute.

diluvien, enne [dilyvjɛ̃, ɛn] *adj* torrential.

dimanche [dimɑ̃ʃ] *nm* Sunday.

dimension [dimɑ̃sjɔ̃] *nf* - **1.** [mesure] dimension - **2.** [taille] dimensions (*pl*), size - **3.** *fig* [importance] magnitude.

diminuer [7] [diminɥe] ◇ *vt* [réduire] to diminish, to reduce. ◇ *vi* [intensité] to diminish, to decrease.

diminutif, ive [diminytif, iv] *adj* diminutive. ◆ **diminutif** *nm* diminutive.

diminution [diminysjɔ̃] *nf* diminution.

dinde [dɛ̃d] *nf* - **1.** [animal] turkey - **2.** *péj* [femme] stupid woman.

dindon [dɛ̃dɔ̃] *nm* turkey ; **être le ~ de la farce** *fig* to be made a fool of.

dîner [3] [dine] ◇ *vi* to dine. ◇ *nm* dinner.

dingue [dɛ̃g] *fam* ◇ *adj* - **1.** [personne] crazy - **2.** [histoire] incredible. ◇ *nmf* loony.

dinosaure [dinozɔr] *nm* dinosaur.

diplomate [diplɔmat] ◇ *nmf* [ambassadeur] diplomat. ◇ *adj* diplomatic.

diplomatie [diplɔmasi] *nf* diplomacy.

diplomatique [diplɔmatik] *adj* diplomatic.

diplôme [diplom] *nm* diploma.

diplômé, e [diplome] ◇ *adj* : **être ~ de/en** to be a graduate of/in. ◇ *nm, f* graduate.

dire [102] [dir] *vt* : ~ **qqch (à qqn)** [parole] to say sthg (to sb) ; [vérité, mensonge, secret] to tell (sb) sthg ; ~ **à qqn de faire qqch** to tell sb to do sthg ; **il m'a dit que ...** he told me (that) ... ; **c'est vite dit** *fam* that's

easy (for you/him *etc*) to say ; **c'est beaucoup ~** that's saying a lot ; **la ville proprement dite** the actual town ; ~ **du bien/du mal (de)** to speak well/ill (of) ; **que dirais-tu de ...?** what would you say to ...? ; **qu'en dis-tu?** what do you think (of it)? ; **on dirait que ...** it looks as if ... ; **on dirait de la soie** it looks like silk, you'd think it was silk ; **et ~ que je n'étais pas là!** and to think I wasn't there! ; **ça ne me dit rien** [pas envie] I don't fancy that ; [jamais entendu] I've never heard of it. ◆ **se dire** *vp* - **1.** [penser] to think (to o.s.) - **2.** [s'employer] : **ça ne se dit pas** [par décence] you mustn't say that ; [par usage] people don't say that, nobody says that - **3.** [se traduire] : **'chat' se dit 'gato' en espagnol** the Spanish for 'cat' is 'gato'. ◆ **cela dit** *loc adv* having said that. ◆ **dis donc** *loc adv fam* so ; [au fait] by the way ; [à qqn qui exagère] look here! ◆ **pour ainsi dire** *loc adv* so to speak. ◆ **à vrai dire** *loc adv* to tell the truth.

direct, e [dirɛkt] *adj* direct. ◆ **direct** *nm* - **1.** BOXE jab - **2.** [train] direct train - **3.** RADIO & TÉLÉ : **le ~** live transmission (*U*) ; **en ~** live.

directement [dirɛktəmɑ̃] *adv* directly.

directeur, trice [dirɛktœr, tris] ◇ *adj* - **1.** [dirigeant] leading ; **comité ~** steering committee - **2.** [central] guiding. ◇ *nm, f* director, manager ; ~ **général** general manager, managing director *Br*, chief executive officer *Am*.

direction [dirɛksjɔ̃] *nf* - **1.** [gestion, ensemble des cadres] management ; **sous la ~ de** under the management of - **2.** [orientation] direction ; **en** ou **dans la ~ de** in the direction of - **3.** AUTOM steering.

directive [dirɛktiv] *nf* directive.

directrice ▷ **directeur.**

dirigeable [diriʒabl] *nm* : (**ballon**) ~ airship.

dirigeant, e [diriʒɑ̃, ɑ̃t] ◇ *adj* ruling. ◇ *nm, f* [de pays] leader ; [d'entreprise] manager.

diriger [17] [diriʒe] *vt* - **1.** [mener - entreprise] to run, to manage ; [- orchestre] to conduct ; [- film, acteurs] to direct ; [- recherches, projet] to supervise - **2.** [conduire] to steer - **3.** [orienter] : ~ **qqch sur** to aim sthg at ; ~ **qqch vers** to aim sthg towards *Br* ou toward *Am*. ◆ **se diriger** *vp* : **se ~ vers** to go towards *Br* ou toward *Am*, to head towards *Br* ou toward *Am*.

discernement [disɛrnəmɑ̃] *nm* [jugement] discernment.

discerner [3] [disɛrne] *vt* - **1.** [distinguer] : ~ **qqch de** to distinguish sthg from - **2.** [deviner] to discern.

disciple [disipl] *nmf* disciple.

disciplinaire [disipliner] *adj* disciplinary.

discipline [disiplin] *nf* discipline.

discipliner [3] [discipline] *vt* [personne] to discipline ; [cheveux] to control.

disco [disko] *nm* disco (music).

discontinu, e [diskɔ̃tiny] *adj* [ligne] broken ; [bruit, effort] intermittent.

discordant, e [diskɔrdɑ̃, ɑ̃t] *adj* discordant.

discorde [diskɔrd] *nf* discord.

discothèque [diskɔtɛk] *nf* - **1.** [boîte de nuit] night club - **2.** [de prêt] record library.

discourir [45] [diskurir] *vi* to talk at length.

discours [diskur] *nm* [allocution] speech.

discréditer [3] [diskredite] *vt* to discredit.

discret, ète [diskrɛ, ɛt] *adj* [gén] discreet ; [réservé] reserved.

discrètement [diskrɛtmɑ̃] *adv* discreetly.

discrétion [diskresjɔ̃] *nf* [réserve, tact, silence] discretion.

discrimination [diskriminasjɔ̃] *nf* discrimination ; **sans ~** indiscriminately.

discriminatoire [diskriminatwar] *adj* discriminatory.

disculper [3] [diskylpe] *vt* to exonerate. ➡ **se disculper** *vp* to exonerate o.s.

discussion [diskysjɔ̃] *nf* - **1.** [conversation, examen] discussion - **2.** [contestation, altercation] argument.

discutable [diskytabl] *adj* [contestable] questionable.

discuter [3] [diskyte] ◇ *vt* - **1.** [débattre] : **~ (de) qqch** to discuss sthg - **2.** [contester] to dispute. ◇ *vi* - **1.** [parlementer] to discuss - **2.** [converser] to talk - **3.** [contester] to argue.

diseur, euse [dizœr, øz] *nm, f* : **~ de bonne aventure** fortune-teller.

disgracieux, euse [disgrasjø, øz] *adj* - **1.** [sans grâce] awkward, graceless - **2.** [laid] plain.

disjoncter [disʒɔ̃kte] *vi* - **1.** ÉLECTR to short-circuit - **2.** *fam* [perdre la tête] to flip, to crack up.

disjoncteur [disʒɔ̃ktœr] *nm* trip switch, circuit breaker.

disloquer [3] [disbke] *vt* - **1.** MÉD to dislocate - **2.** [machine, empire] to dismantle. ➡ **se disloquer** *vp* [machine] to fall apart ou to pieces ; *fig* [empire] to break up.

disparaître [91] [disparɛtr] *vi* - **1.** [gén] to disappear, to vanish ; **faire ~** [personne] to get rid of ; [obstacle] to remove - **2.** [mourir] to die.

disparité [disparite] *nf* [différence - d'éléments] disparity ; [- de couleurs] mismatch.

disparition [disparisjɔ̃] *nf* - **1.** [gén] disappearance ; [d'espèce] extinction ; **en voie de ~** endangered - **2.** [mort] passing.

disparu, e [dispary] ◇ *pp* ▷ **disparaître**. ◇ *nm, f* dead person, deceased.

dispatcher [3] [dispatʃe] *vt* to dispatch, to despatch.

dispensaire [dispɑ̃sɛr] *nm* community clinic *Br*, free clinic *Am*.

dispense [dispɑ̃s] *nf* [exemption] exemption.

dispenser [3] [dispɑ̃se] *vt* - **1.** [distribuer] to dispense - **2.** [exempter] : **~ qqn de qqch** [corvée] to excuse sb sthg, to let sb off sthg ; **je te dispense de tes réflexions!** *fig* spare us the comments!, keep your comments to yourself!

disperser [3] [disperse] *vt* to scatter (about ou around) ; [collection, brume, foule] to break up ; *fig* [efforts, forces] to dissipate, to waste. ➡ **se disperser** *vp* - **1.** [feuilles, cendres] to scatter ; [brume, foule] to break up, to clear - **2.** [personne] to take on too much at once, to spread o.s. too thin.

dispersion [dispersjɔ̃] *nf* scattering ; [de collection, brume, foule] breaking up ; *fig* [d'efforts, de forces] waste, squandering.

disponibilité [disponibilite] *nf* - **1.** [de choses] availability - **2.** [de fonctionnaire] leave of absence - **3.** [d'esprit] alertness, receptiveness.

disponible [disponibl] *adj* [place, personne] available, free.

disposé, e [dispoze] *adj* : **être ~ à faire qqch** to be prepared ou willing to do sthg ; **être bien ~ envers qqn** to be well-disposed towards *Br* ou toward *Am* sb.

disposer [3] [dispoze] ◇ *vt* [arranger] to arrange. ◇ *vi* : **~ de** [moyens, argent] to have available (to one), to have at one's disposal ; [chose] to have the use of ; [temps] to have free ou available.

dispositif [dispozitif] *nm* [mécanisme] device, mechanism.

disposition [dispozisjɔ̃] *nf* - **1.** [arrangement] arrangement - **2.** [disponibilité] : **à la ~ de** at the disposal of, available to. ➡ **dispositions** *nfpl* - **1.** [mesures] arrangements, measures - **2.** [dons] : **avoir des ~s pour** to have a gift for.

disproportionné, e [disproporsjone] *adj* out of proportion.

dispute [dispyt] *nf* argument, quarrel.

disputer [3] [dispyte] *vt* - **1.** [SPORT - course] to run ; [- match] to play - **2.** [lutter pour] to fight for. ◆ **se disputer** *vp* - **1.** [se quereller] to quarrel, to fight - **2.** [lutter pour] to fight over ou for.

disquaire [disker] *nm* record dealer.

disqualifier [9] [diskalifje] *vt* to disqualify.

disque [disk] *nm* - **1.** MUS record ; [vidéo] video disc ; ~ **compact** ou **laser** compact disc - **2.** ANAT disc *Br*, disk *Am* - **3.** INFORM disk ; ~ **dur** hard disk - **4.** SPORT discus.

disquette [disket] *nf* diskette, floppy disk ; ~ **système** system diskette.

dissection [diseksjɔ̃] *nf* dissection.

dissemblable [disãblabl] *adj* dissimilar.

disséminer [3] [disemine] *vt* [graines, maisons] to scatter, to spread (out) ; *fig* [idées] to disseminate, to spread.

disséquer [18] [diseke] *vt litt & fig* to dissect.

dissertation [disertasjɔ̃] *nf* essay.

dissident, e [disidɑ̃, ɑ̃t] *adj & nm, f* dissident.

dissimulation [disimylasjɔ̃] *nf* - **1.** [hypocrisie] duplicity - **2.** [de la vérité] concealment.

dissimuler [3] [disimyle] *vt* to conceal. ◆ **se dissimuler** *vp* - **1.** [se cacher] to conceal o.s., to hide - **2.** [refuser de voir] : **se ~ qqch** to close one's eyes to sthg.

dissipation [disipasjɔ̃] *nf* - **1.** [dispersion] dispersal, breaking up ; *fig* [de malentendu] clearing up ; [de craintes] dispelling - **2.** [in discipline] indiscipline, misbehaviour *Br*, misbehavior *Am*

dissiper [3] [disipe] *vt* - **1.** [chasser] to break up, to clear ; *fig* to dispel - **2.** [distraire] to lead astray. ◆ **se dissiper** *vp* - **1.** [brouillard, fumée] to clear - **2.** [élève] to misbehave - **3.** *fig* [malaise, fatigue] to go away ; [doute] to be dispelled.

dissocier [9] [disɔsje] *vt* [séparer] to separate, to distinguish.

dissolution [disɔlysjɔ̃] *nf* - **1.** JUR dissolution - **2.** [mélange] dissolving - **3.** *sout* [débauche] dissipation.

dissolvant, e [disɔlvɑ̃, ɑ̃t] *adj* solvent. ◆ **dissolvant** *nm* [solvant] solvent ; [pour vernis à ongles] nail varnish remover.

dissoudre [87] [disudr] *vt* : **(faire) ~** to dissolve. ◆ **se dissoudre** *vp* [substance] to dissolve.

dissous, oute [disu, ut] *pp* ▷ dissoudre.

dissuader [3] [disɥade] *vt* to dissuade.

dissuasion [disɥazjɔ̃] *nf* dissuasion ; **force de ~** deterrent (effect).

distance [distɑ̃s] *nf* - **1.** [éloignement] distance ; **à ~** at a distance ; [télécommander] by remote control ; **à une ~ de 300 mètres** 300 metres away - **2.** [intervalle] interval - **3.** [écart] gap.

distancer [16] [distɑ̃se] *vt* to outstrip.

distant, e [distɑ̃, ɑ̃t] *adj* - **1.** [éloigné] : **une ville ~e de 10 km** a town 10 km away ; **des villes ~es de 10 km** towns 10 km apart - **2.** [froid] distant.

distendre [73] [distɑ̃dr] *vt* [ressort, corde] to stretch ; [abdomen] to distend. ◆ **se distendre** *vp* to distend.

distendu, e [distɑ̃dy] *pp* ▷ distendre.

distiller [3] [distile] *vt* [alcool] to distil *Br*, to distill *Am* ; [pétrole] to refine ; [miel] to secrete ; *fig & littéraire* to exude.

distinct, e [distɛ̃, ɛ̃kt] *adj* distinct.

distinctement [distɛ̃ktəmɑ̃] *adv* distinctly, clearly.

distinctif, ive [distɛ̃ktif, iv] *adj* distinctive.

distinction [distɛ̃ksjɔ̃] *nf* distinction.

distingué, e [distɛ̃ge] *adj* distinguished.

distinguer [3] [distɛ̃ge] *vt* - **1.** [différencier] to tell apart, to distinguish - **2.** [percevoir] to make out, to distinguish - **3.** [rendre différent] : ~ **de** to distinguish from, to set apart from. ◆ **se distinguer** *vp* - **1.** [se différencier] : **se ~ (de)** to stand out (from) - **2.** [s'illustrer] to distinguish o.s.

distraction [distraksjɔ̃] *nf* - **1.** [inattention] inattention, absent-mindedness - **2.** [passe-temps] leisure activity.

distraire [112] [distrer] *vt* - **1.** [déranger] to distract - **2.** [divertir] to amuse, to entertain. ◆ **se distraire** *vp* to amuse o.s.

distrait, e [distrɛ, ɛt] ◇ *pp* ▷ distraire. ◇ *adj* absent-minded.

distribuer [7] [distribɥe] *vt* to distribute ; [courrier] to deliver ; [ordres] to give out ; [cartes] to deal ; [coups, sourires] to dispense.

distributeur, trice [distribytœr, tris] *nm, f* distributor. ◆ **distributeur** *nm* - **1.** AUTOM & COMM distributor - **2.** [machine] : ~ **(automatique) de billets** BANQUE cash machine, cash dispenser ; TRANSPORT ticket machine ; ~ **de boissons** drinks machine.

distribution [distribysjɔ̃] *nf* - **1.** [répartition, diffusion, disposition] distribution ; ~ **des prix** SCOL prize-giving - **2.** CIN & THÉÂTRE cast.

dit, dite [di, dit] ◇ *pp* ▷ dire. ◇ *adj*

- **1.** [appelé] known as - **2.** JUR said, above - **3.** [fixé] : **à l'heure ~e** at the appointed time.

divagation [divagasjɔ̃] *nf* wandering.

divaguer [3] [divage] *vi* to ramble.

divan [divɑ̃] *nm* divan *(seat)*.

divergence [divɛrʒɑ̃s] *nf* divergence, difference ; [d'opinions] difference.

diverger [17] [divɛrʒe] *vi* to diverge ; [opinions] to differ.

divers, e [divɛr, ɛrs] *adj* - **1.** [différent] different, various - **2.** [disparate] diverse - **3.** *(avant n)* [plusieurs] various, several.

diversifier [9] [diversifje] *vt* to vary, to diversify. ➤ **se diversifier** *vp* to diversify.

diversion [divɛrsjɔ̃] *nf* diversion.

diversité [divɛrsite] *nf* diversity.

divertir [32] [divɛrtir] *vt* [distraire] to entertain, to amuse. ➤ **se divertir** *vp* to amuse o.s., to entertain o.s.

divertissement [divɛrtismɑ̃] *nm* [passetemps] form of relaxation.

divin, e [divɛ̃, in] *adj* divine.

divinité [divinite] *nf* divinity.

diviser [3] [divize] *vt* - **1.** [gén] to divide, to split up - **2.** MATHS to divide ; **8 par 4** to divide 8 by 4.

division [divizjɔ̃] *nf* division.

divorce [divɔrs] *nm* - **1.** JUR divorce - **2.** *fig* [divergence] gulf, separation.

divorcé, e [divɔrse] ◇ *adj* divorced. ◇ *nm, f* divorcee, divorced person.

divorcer [16] [divɔrse] *vi* to divorce.

divulguer [3] [divylge] *vt* to divulge.

dix [dis] *adj num* & *nm* ten ; *voir aussi* **six**.

dix-huit [dizɥit] *adj num* & *nm* eighteen ; *voir aussi* **six**.

dix-huitième [dizɥitjɛm] *adj num, nm* OU *nmf* eighteenth ; *voir aussi* **sixième**.

dixième [dizjɛm] *adj num, nm* OU *nmf* tenth ; *voir aussi* **sixième**.

dix-neuf [diznœf] *adj num* & *nm* nineteen ; *voir aussi* **six**.

dix-neuvième [diznœvjɛm] *adj num, nm* OU *nmf* nineteenth ; *voir aussi* **sixième**.

dix-sept [disɛt] *adj num* & *nm* seventeen ; *voir aussi* **six**.

dix-septième [disɛtjɛm] *adj num, nm* OU *nmf* seventeenth ; *voir aussi* **sixième**.

dizaine [dizɛn] *nf* - **1.** MATHS ten - **2.** [environ dix] : **une ~ de** about ten ; **par ~s** [en grand nombre] in their dozens.

DM *(abr de* **deutsche Mark**) DM.

do [do] *nm inv* MUS C ; [chanté] doh.

doc [dɔk] *(abr de* **documentation**) *nf* literature, brochures *(pl)*.

doc. *(abr de* **document**) doc.

docile [dɔsil] *adj* [obéissant] docile.

dock [dɔk] *nm* - **1.** [bassin] dock - **2.** [hangar] warehouse.

docker [dɔkɛr] *nm* docker.

docteur [dɔktœr] *nm* - **1.** [médecin] doctor - **2.** UNIV : **~ ès lettres/sciences** ≃ PhD.

doctorat [dɔktɔra] *nm* [grade] doctorate.

doctrine [dɔktrin] *nf* doctrine.

document [dɔkymɑ̃] *nm* document.

documentaire [dɔkymɑ̃tɛr] *nm & adj* documentary.

documentaliste [dɔkymɑ̃talist] *nmf* [d'archives] archivist ; PRESSE & TÉLÉ researcher.

documentation [dɔkymɑ̃tasjɔ̃] *nf* - **1.** [travail] research - **2.** [documents] paperwork, papers *(pl)* - **3.** [brochures] documentation.

documenter [3] [dɔkymɑ̃te] *vt* to document. ➤ **se documenter** *vp* to do some research.

dodo [dodo] *nm fam* beddy-byes ; **faire ~** to sleep.

dodu, e [dody] *adj fam* [enfant, joue, bras] chubby ; [animal] plump.

dogme [dɔgm] *nm* dogma.

dogue [dɔg] *nm* mastiff.

doigt [dwa] *nm* finger ; **un ~ de** (just) a drop OU finger of ; **montrer qqch du ~** to point at sthg ; **~ de pied** toe.

dois ⊳ **devoir**.

doive ⊳ **devoir**.

dollar [dɔlar] *nm* dollar.

domaine [dɔmɛn] *nm* - **1.** [propriété] estate - **2.** [secteur, champ d'activité] field, domain.

dôme [dom] *nm* - **1.** ARCHIT dome - **2.** GÉOGR rounded peak.

domestique [dɔmɛstik] ◇ *nmf* (domestic) servant. ◇ *adj* family *(avant n)* ; [travaux] household *(avant n)*.

domestiquer [3] [dɔmɛstike] *vt* - **1.** [animal] to domesticate - **2.** [éléments naturels] to harness.

domicile [dɔmisil] *nm* [gén] (place of) residence ; **travailler à ~** to work from OU at home ; **ils livrent à ~** they do deliveries.

dominant, e [dɔminɑ̃, ɑ̃t] *adj* [qui prévaut] dominant. ➤ **dominante** *nf* dominant feature.

domination [dɔminasjɔ̃] *nf* - **1.** [autorité] domination, dominion - **2.** [influence] influence.

dominer [3] [dɔmine] ◇ *vt* - **1.** [surplomber, avoir de l'autorité sur] to dominate - **2.** [surpasser] to outclass - **3.** [maîtriser] to control, to master - **4.** *fig* [connaître] to master. ◇ *vi* - **1.** [régner] to dominate, to be dominant - **2.** [prédominer] to predominate - **3.** [triompher] to be on top, to hold sway. ◆ **se dominer** *vp* to control o.s.

Dominique [dɔminik] *nf* : **la ~** Dominica.

domino [dɔmino] *nm* domino.

dommage [dɔmaʒ] *nm* - **1.** [préjudice] harm *(U)* ; **~s et intérêts, ~s-intérêts** damages ; **quel ~!** what a shame! ; **c'est ~ que** (+ *subjonctif*) it's a pity ou shame (that) - **2.** [dégâts] damage *(U)*.

dompter [3] [dɔ̃te] *vt* - **1.** [animal, fauve] to tame - **2.** *fig* [maîtriser] to overcome, to control.

dompteur, euse [dɔ̃tœr, øz] *nm, f* [de fauves] tamer.

DOM-TOM [dɔmtɔm] *(abr de* **départements d'outre-mer/territoires d'outre-mer)** *nmpl French overseas départements and territories.*

don [dɔ̃] *nm* - **1.** [cadeau] gift - **2.** [aptitude] knack.

donateur, trice [dɔnatœr, tris] *nm, f* donor.

donation [dɔnasjɔ̃] *nf* settlement.

donc [dɔ̃k] *conj* so ; **je disais ~** ... so as I was saying ... ; **allons ~!** come on! ; **tais-toi ~!** will you be quiet!

donjon [dɔ̃ʒɔ̃] *nm* keep.

donné, e [dɔne] *adj* given ; **étant ~ que** given that, considering (that). ◆ **donnée** *nf* - **1.** INFORM & MATHS datum, piece of data ; **~es numériques** numerical data - **2.** [élément] fact, particular.

donner [3] [dɔne] ◇ *vt* - **1.** [gén] to give ; [se débarrasser de] to give away ; **~ qqch à qqn** to give sb sthg, to give sthg to sb ; **~ qqch à faire à qqn** to give sb sthg to do, to give sthg to sb to do ; **~ sa voiture à réparer** to leave one's car to be repaired ; **quel âge lui donnes-tu?** how old do you think he/she is? - **2.** [occasionner] to give, to cause. ◇ *vi* - **1.** [s'ouvrir] : **~ sur** to look out onto - **2.** [produire] to produce, to yield.

donneur, euse [dɔnœr, øz] *nm, f* - **1.** MÉD donor - **2.** CARTES dealer.

dont [dɔ̃] *pron rel* - **1.** [complément de verbe ou d'adjectif] : **la personne ~ tu parles** the person you're speaking about, the person about whom you are speaking ; **l'accident ~ il est responsable** the accident for which he is responsible ; **c'est quelqu'un ~ on dit le plus grand bien** he's someone about whom people speak highly *(la traduction varie selon la préposition anglaise utilisée avec le verbe ou l'adjectif)* - **2.** [complément de nom

ou de pronom - relatif à l'objet] of which, whose ; [- relatif à personne] whose ; **la boîte ~ le couvercle est jaune** the box whose lid is yellow, the box with the yellow lid ; **c'est quelqu'un ~ j'apprécie l'honnêteté** he's someone whose honesty I appreciate ; **celui ~ les parents sont divorcés** the one whose parents are divorced - **3.** [indiquant la partie d'un tout] : **plusieurs personnes ont téléphoné, ~ ton frère** several people phoned, one of which was your brother ou and among them was your brother.

dopage [dɔpaʒ] *nm* doping.

doper [3] [dɔpe] *vt* to dope. ◆ **se doper** *vp* to take stimulants.

dorade [dɔrad] = **daurade**.

doré, e [dɔre] *adj* - **1.** [couvert de dorure] gilded, gilt - **2.** [couleur] golden.

dorénavant [dɔrenavɑ̃] *adv* from now on, in future.

dorer [3] [dɔre] *vt* - **1.** [couvrir d'or] to gild - **2.** [peau] to tan - **3.** CULIN to glaze.

dorloter [3] [dɔrlɔte] *vt* to pamper, to cosset.

dormir [36] [dɔrmir] *vi* - **1.** [sommeiller] to sleep - **2.** [rester inactif - personne] to slack, to stand around (doing nothing) ; [- capitaux] to lie idle.

dortoir [dɔrtwar] *nm* dormitory.

dos [do] *nm* back ; **de ~** from behind ; **'voir au ~'** 'see over' ; **~ crawlé** backstroke.

DOS, Dos [dɔs] *(abr de* **Disk Operating System)** *nm* DOS.

dosage [dozaʒ] *nm* [de médicament] dose ; [d'ingrédient] amount.

dos-d'âne [dodan] *nm* bump.

dose [doz] *nf* - **1.** [quantité de médicament] dose - **2.** [quantité] share ; **forcer la ~** *fam fig* to overdo it ; **une (bonne) ~ de bêtise** *fam fig* a lot of silliness.

doser [3] [doze] *vt* [médicament, ingrédient] to measure out ; *fig* to weigh up.

dossard [dɔsar] *nm* number *(on competitor's back)*.

dossier [dɔsje] *nm* - **1.** [de fauteuil] back - **2.** [documents] file, dossier - **3.** [classeur] file, folder - **4.** *fig* [question] question.

dot [dɔt] *nf* dowry.

doter [3] [dɔte] *vt* [pourvoir] : **~ de** [talent] to endow with ; [machine] to equip with.

douane [dwan] *nf* - **1.** [service, lieu] customs *(pl)* ; **passer la ~** to go through customs - **2.** [taxe] (import) duty.

douanier, ère [dwanje, ɛr] ◇ *adj* customs *(avant n)*. ◇ *nm, f* customs officer.

doublage [dublaʒ] *nm* - **1.** [renforcement] lining - **2.** [de film] dubbing - **3.** [d'acteur] understudying.

double [dubl] <> *adj* double. <> *adv* double. <> *nm* - **1.** [quantité] : **le ~ double** - **2.** [copie] copy ; **en ~** in duplicate - **3.** TENNIS **doubles** *(pl)*.

doublé [duble] *nm* [réussite double] double.

doublement [dubləmã] *adv* doubly.

doubler [3] [duble] <> *vt* - **1.** [multiplier] to double - **2.** [plier] to (fold) double - **3.** [renforcer] : **~ (de)** to line (with) - **4.** [dépasser] to overtake - **5.** [film, acteur] to dub - **6.** [augmenter] to double. <> *vi* - **1.** [véhicule] to overtake - **2.** [augmenter] to double.

doublure [dublyr] *nf* - **1.** [renforcement] lining - **2.** CIN stand-in.

douce ⊳ **doux**.

doucement [dusmã] *adv* - **1.** [descendre] carefully ; [frapper] gently - **2.** [traiter] gently ; [parler] softly.

douceur [dusœr] *nf* - **1.** [de saveur, parfum] sweetness - **2.** [d'éclairage, de peau, de musique] softness - **3.** [de climat] mildness - **4.** [de caractère] gentleness. ◆ **douceurs** *nfpl* [friandises] sweets.

douche [duʃ] *nf* - **1.** [appareil, action] shower - **2.** *fam fig* [déception] letdown.

doucher [3] [duʃe] *vt* - **1.** [donner une douche à] : **~ qqn** to give sb a shower - **2.** *fam fig* [décevoir] to let down. ◆ **se doucher** *vp* to take ou have a shower, to shower.

doué, e [dwe] *adj* talented ; **être ~ pour** to have a gift for.

douillet, ette [dujɛ, ɛt] <> *adj* - **1.** [confortable] snug, cosy - **2.** [sensible] soft. <> *nm, f* wimp.

douleur [dulœr] *nf litt & fig* pain.

douloureux, euse [dulurø, øz] *adj* - **1.** [physiquement] painful - **2.** [moralement] distressing - **3.** [regard, air] sorrowful.

doute [dut] *nm* doubt. ◆ **sans doute** *loc adv* no doubt ; **sans aucun ~** without (a) doubt.

douter [3] [dute] <> *vt* [ne pas croire] : **~ que** (+ *subjonctif*) to doubt (that). <> *vi* [ne pas avoir confiance] : **~ de qqn/de qqch** to doubt sb/sthg, to have doubts about sb/sthg ; **j'en doute** I doubt it. ◆ **se douter** *vp* : **se ~ de qqch** to suspect sthg ; **je m'en doutais** I thought so.

douteux, euse [dutø, øz] *adj* - **1.** [incertain] doubtful - **2.** [contestable] questionable - **3.** *péj* [mœurs] dubious ; [vêtements, personne] dubious-looking.

Douvres [duvr] *n* Dover.

doux, douce [du, dus] *adj* - **1.** [éclairage, peau, musique] soft - **2.** [saveur, parfum] sweet - **3.** [climat, condiment] mild - **4.** [pente, regard, caractère] gentle.

douzaine [duzɛn] *nf* - **1.** [douze] dozen - **2.** [environ douze] : **une ~ de** about twelve.

douze [duz] *adj num & nm* twelve ; *voir aussi* **six**.

douzième [duzjɛm] *adj num, nm* OU *nmf* twelfth ; *voir aussi* **sixième**.

doyen, enne [dwajɛ, ɛn] *nm, f* [le plus ancien] most senior member.

Dr (*abr de* **Docteur**) Dr.

draconien, enne [drakɔnjɛ, ɛn] *adj* draconian.

dragée [draʒe] *nf* - **1.** [confiserie] sugared almond - **2.** [comprimé] pill.

dragon [dragɔ] *nm* - **1.** [monstre, personne autoritaire] dragon - **2.** [soldat] dragoon.

draguer [3] [drage] *vt* - **1.** [nettoyer] to dredge - **2.** *fam* [personne] to chat up, to get off with.

dragueur, euse [dragœr, øz] *nm, f fam* [homme] womanizer ; **quelle dragueuse!** she's always chasing after men!

drainage [drɛnaʒ] *nm* draining.

drainer [4] [drene] *vt* - **1.** [terrain, plaie] to drain - **2.** *fig* [attirer] to drain off.

dramatique [dramatik] <> *nf* play. <> *adj* - **1.** THÉÂTRE dramatic - **2.** [grave] tragic.

dramatiser [3] [dramatize] *vt* [exagérer] to dramatize.

drame [dram] *nm* - **1.** [catastrophe] tragedy ; **faire un ~ de qqch** *fig* to make a drama of sthg - **2.** LITTÉRATURE drama.

drap [dra] *nm* - **1.** [de lit] sheet - **2.** [tissu] woollen *Br* OU woolen *Am* cloth.

drapeau, x [drapo] *nm* flag ; **être sous les ~x** *fig* to be doing military service.

draper [3] [drape] *vt* to drape.

draperie [drapri] *nf* [tenture] drapery.

dresser [4] [drese] *vt* - **1.** [lever] to raise - **2.** [faire tenir] to put up - **3.** *sout* [construire] to erect - **4.** [acte, liste, carte] to draw up ; [procès-verbal] to make out - **5.** [dompter] to train - **6.** *fig* [opposer] : **~ qqn contre qqn** to set sb against sb. ◆ **se dresser** *vp* - **1.** [se lever] to stand up - **2.** [s'élever] to rise (up) ; *fig* to stand ; **se ~ contre qqch** to rise up against sthg.

dresseur, euse [dresœr, øz] *nm, f* trainer.

dribbler [3] [drible] SPORT <> *vi* to dribble. <> *vt* : **~ qqn** to dribble past sb.

drogue [drɔg] *nf* [stupéfiant] *fig* drug ; **la ~** drugs *(pl)*.

drogué, e [drɔge] ◇ *adj* drugged. ◇ *nm, f* drug addict.

droguer [3] [drɔge] *vt* [victime] to drug. ➡ **se droguer** *vp* [de stupéfiants] to take drugs.

droguerie [drɔgri] *nf* hardware shop.

droguiste [drɔgist] *nmf* : **chez le ~** at the hardware shop.

droit, e [drwa, drwat] *adj* - **1.** [du côté droit] right - **2.** [rectiligne, vertical, honnête] straight. ➡ **droit** ◇ *adv* straight ; **tout ~** straight ahead. ◇ *nm* - **1.** JUR law - **2.** [prérogative] right ; **avoir ~ à** to be entitled to ; **avoir le ~ de faire qqch** to be allowed to do sthg ; **être en ~ de faire qqch** to have a right to do sthg ; **~ d'aînesse** birthright ; **~ de vote** right to vote ; **~s de l'homme** human rights. ➡ **droite** *nf* - **1.** [gén] right, right-hand side ; **à ~e** on the right ; **à ~e de** to the right of - **2.** POLIT : **la ~e** the right (wing) ; **de ~e** right-wing.

droitier, ère [drwatje, ɛr] ◇ *adj* right-handed. ◇ *nm, f* right-handed person, right-hander.

drôle [drol] *adj* - **1.** [amusant] funny - **2.** **~ de** [bizarre] funny ; *fam* [remarquable] amazing.

dromadaire [drɔmadɛr] *nm* dromedary.

dru, e [dry] *adj* thick.

ds *abr de* **dans**.

du ◇ de.

dû, due [dy] ◇ *pp* ◇ **devoir.** ◇ *adj* due, owing. ➡ **dû** *nm* due.

Dublin [dyblɛ̃] *n* Dublin.

duc [dyk] *nm* duke.

duchesse [dyʃɛs] *nf* duchess.

duel [dɥɛl] *nm* duel.

dûment [dymɑ̃] *adv* duly.

dune [dyn] *nf* dune.

duo [dɥo] *nm* - **1.** MUS duet - **2.** [couple] duo.

dupe [dyp] ◇ *nf* dupe. ◇ *adj* gullible.

duper [3] [dype] *vt sout* to dupe, to take sb in.

duplex [dyplɛks] *nm* - **1.** [appartement] split-level flat, maisonette *Br*, duplex *Am* - **2.** RADIO & TÉLÉ link-up.

duplicata [dyplikata] *nm inv* duplicate.

dupliquer [3] [dyplike] *vt* [document] to duplicate.

duquel [dykɛl] ◇ **lequel.**

dur, e [dyr] ◇ *adj* - **1.** [matière, personne, travail] hard ; [carton] stiff - **2.** [viande] tough - **3.** [climat, punition, loi] harsh. ◇ *nm, f fam* : **~ (à cuire)** tough nut. ➡ **dur** *adv* hard.

durable [dyrabl] *adj* lasting.

durant [dyrɑ̃] *prép* - **1.** [pendant] for - **2.** [au cours de] during.

durcir [32] [dyrsir] ◇ *vt litt & fig* to harden. ◇ *vi* to harden, to become hard.

durée [dyre] *nf* length.

durement [dyrmɑ̃] *adv* - **1.** [violemment] hard, vigorously - **2.** [péniblement] severely - **3.** [méchamment] harshly.

durer [3] [dyre] *vi* to last.

dureté [dyrte] *nf* - **1.** [de matériau, de l'eau] hardness - **2.** [d'époque, de climat, de personne] harshness - **3.** [de punition] severity.

dus, dut *etc* ◇ **devoir.**

DUT (*abr de* **diplôme universitaire de technologie**) *nm university diploma in technology.*

duvet [dyvɛ] *nm* - **1.** [plumes, poils fins] down - **2.** [sac de couchage] sleeping bag.

DVD-ROM [dvdrɔm] (*abr de* **Digital Video ou Versatile Disc Read Only Memory**) *nm* DVD-ROM.

dynamique [dinamik] *adj* dynamic.

dynamisme [dynamism] *nm* dynamism.

dynamite [dinamit] *nf* dynamite.

dynastie [dinasti] *nf* dynasty.

dyslexique [dislɛksik] *adj* dyslexic.

e, E [ə] *nm inv* e, E. ➡ **E** (*abr de* **est**) E

eau, x [o] *nf* water ; **~ douce/salée/de mer** fresh/salt/sea water ; **~ gazeuse/plate** fizzy/still water ; **~ courante** running water ; **~ minérale** mineral water ; **~ oxygénée** hydrogen peroxide ; **~ de toilette** toilet water ; **les ~x territoriales** territorial waters ; **tomber à l'~** *fig* to fall through.

eau-de-vie [odvi] (*pl* **eaux-de-vie**) *nf* brandy.

ébahi, e [ebai] *adj* staggered, astounded.

ébattre [83] [ebatr] ➡ **s'ébattre** *vp littéraire* to frolic.

ébauche [eboʃ] *nf* [esquisse] sketch ; *fig* outline ; **l'~ d'un sourire** the ghost of a smile.

ébaucher [3] [eboʃe] *vt* - **1.** [esquisser] to rough out - **2.** *fig* [commencer] : **~ un geste** to start to make a gesture.

ébène [ebɛn] *nf* ebony.

ébéniste [ebenist] *nm* cabinet-maker.

éberlué, e [ebɛrlɥe] *adj* flabbergasted.

éblouir [32] [ebluir] *vt* to dazzle.

éblouissement [ebluismã] *nm* - **1.** [aveuglement] glare, dazzle - **2.** [vertige] dizziness - **3.** [émerveillement] amazement.

éborgner [3] [ebɔrɲe] *vt* : ~ **qqn** to put sb's eye out.

éboueur [ebwœr] *nm* dustman *Br*, garbage collector *Am*.

ébouillanter [3] [ebujãte] *vt* to scald.

éboulement [ebulmã] *nm* caving in, fall.

éboulis [ebuli] *nm* mass of fallen rocks.

ébouriffer [3] [eburife] *vt* [cheveux] to ruffle.

ébranler [3] [ebrãle] *vt* - **1.** [bâtiment, opinion] to shake - **2.** [gouvernement, nerfs] to weaken. ➡ **s'ébranler** *vp* [train] to move off.

ébrécher [18] [ebreʃe] *vt* [assiette, verre] to chip ; *fam fig* to break into.

ébriété [ebrijete] *nf* drunkenness.

ébrouer [3] [ebrue] ➡ **s'ébrouer** *vp* [animal] to shake o.s.

ébruiter [3] [ebrɥite] *vt* to spread.

ébullition [ebylisjɔ̃] *nf* - **1.** [de liquide] boiling point - **2.** [effervescence] : **en ~** *fig* in a state of agitation.

écaille [ekaj] *nf* - **1.** [de poisson, reptile] scale ; [de tortue] shell - **2.** [de plâtre, peinture, vernis] flake - **3.** [matière] tortoiseshell ; **en ~** [lunettes] horn-rimmed.

écailler [3] [ekaje] *vt* - **1.** [poisson] to scale - **2.** [huîtres] to open. ➡ **s'écailler** *vp* to flake ou peel off.

écarlate [ekarlat] *adj* & *nf* scarlet.

écarquiller [3] [ekarkije] *vt* : ~ **les yeux** to stare wide-eyed.

écart [ekar] *nm* - **1.** [espace] space - **2.** [temps] gap - **3.** [différence] difference - **4.** [déviation] : **faire un ~** [personne] to step aside ; [cheval] to shy ; **être à l'~** to be in the background.

écarteler [25] [ekartəle] *vt* *fig* to tear apart.

écartement [ekartəmã] *nm* : ~ **entre** space between.

écarter [3] [ekarte] *vt* - **1.** [bras, jambes] to open, to spread ; ~ **qqch de** to move sthg away from - **2.** [obstacle, danger] to brush aside - **3.** [foule, rideaux] to push aside ; [solution] to dismiss ; ~ **qqn de** to exclude sb from. ➡ **s'écarter** *vp* - **1.** [se séparer] to part - **2.** [se détourner] : **s'~ de** to deviate from.

ecchymose [ekimoz] *nf* bruise.

ecclésiastique [eklezjastik] ◇ *nm* clergyman. ◇ *adj* ecclesiastical.

écervelé, e [esɛrvəle] ◇ *adj* scatty, scatterbrained. ◇ *nm, f* scatterbrain.

échafaud [eʃafo] *nm* scaffold.

échafaudage [eʃafodaʒ] *nm* - **1.** CONSTR scaffolding - **2.** [amas] pile.

échalote [eʃalɔt] *nf* shallot.

échancrure [eʃãkryr] *nf* - **1.** [de robe] low neckline - **2.** [de côte] indentation.

échange [eʃãʒ] *nm* [de choses] exchange ; **en ~ (de)** in exchange (for).

échanger [17] [eʃãʒe] *vt* - **1.** [troquer] to swap, to exchange - **2.** [marchandise] : ~ **qqch (contre)** to change sthg (for) - **3.** [communiquer] to exchange.

échangisme [eʃãʒism] *nm* [de partenaires sexuels] partner-swapping.

échantillon [eʃãtijɔ̃] *nm* [de produit, de population] sample ; *fig* example.

échappatoire [eʃapatwar] *nf* way out.

échappement [eʃapmã] *nm* AUTOM exhaust ▷ **pot**.

échapper [3] [eʃape] *vi* - **1.** : ~ **à** [personne, situation] to escape from ; [danger, mort] to escape ; [suj : détail, parole, sens] to escape - **2.** [glisser] : **laisser** ~ to let slip. ➡ **s'échapper** *vp* : **s'~ (de)** to escape (from).

écharde [eʃard] *nf* splinter.

écharpe [eʃarp] *nf* scarf ; **en ~** in a sling.

écharper [3] [eʃarpe] *vt* to rip to pieces ou shreds.

échasse [eʃas] *nf* [de berger, oiseau] stilt.

échassier [eʃasje] *nm* wader.

échauffement [eʃofmã] *nm* SPORT warm-up.

échauffer [3] [eʃofe] *vt* - **1.** [chauffer] to overheat - **2.** [exciter] to excite - **3.** [énerver] to irritate. ➡ **s'échauffer** *vp* - **1.** SPORT to warm up - **2.** *fig* [s'animer] to become heated.

échéance [eʃeãs] *nf* - **1.** [délai] expiry ; **à longue** ~ in the long term - **2.** [date] payment date ; **arriver à ~** to fall due.

échéant [eʃeã] *adj* : **le cas** ~ if necessary, if need be.

échec [eʃɛk] *nm* - **1.** [insuccès] failure ; **être en situation d'~ scolaire** to have learning difficulties - **2.** JEU : ~ **et mat** checkmate. ➡ **échecs** *nmpl* chess (U).

échelle [eʃɛl] *nf* - **1.** [objet] ladder - **2.** [ordre de grandeur] scale.

échelon [eʃlɔ̃] *nm* - **1.** [barreau] rung - **2.** *fig* [niveau] level.

échelonner [3] [eʃlɔne] *vt* [espacer] to spread out.

échevelé, e [eʃəvle] *adj* **- 1.** [ébouriffé] dishevelled *Br*, disheveled *Am* **- 2.** [frénétique] wild.

échine [eʃin] *nf* ANAT spine.

échiquier [eʃikje] *nm* JEU chessboard.

écho [eko] *nm* echo.

échographie [ekɔgrafi] *nf* [examen] ultrasound (scan).

échoir [70] [eʃwar] *vi* **- 1.** [être dévolu] : ~ à to fall to **- 2.** [expirer] to fall due.

échoppe [eʃɔp] *nf* stall.

échouer [6] [eʃwe] *vi* [ne pas réussir] to fail ; ~ à un examen to fail an exam. ➡ **s'échouer** *vp* [navire] to run aground.

échu, e [eʃy] *pp* ⊳ échoir.

éclabousser [3] [eklabuse] *vt* **- 1.** [suj : liquide] to spatter **- 2.** *fig* [compromettre] to compromise.

éclair [eklɛr] ◇ *nm* **- 1.** [de lumière] flash of lightning - **2.** *fig* [instant] : ~ de flash of. ◇ *adj inv* : visite ~ flying visit, guerre ~ blitzkrieg.

éclairage [eklɛraʒ] *nm* **- 1.** [lumière] lighting - **2.** *fig* [point de vue] light.

éclaircie [eklɛrsi] *nf* bright interval, sunny spell.

éclaircir [32] [eklɛrsir] *vt* **- 1.** [rendre plus clair] to lighten **- 2.** [rendre moins épais] to thin **- 3.** *fig* [clarifier] to clarify. ➡ **s'éclaircir** *vp* **- 1.** [devenir plus clair] to clear **- 2.** [devenir moins épais] to thin **- 3.** [se clarifier] to become clearer.

éclaircissement [eklɛrsismɑ̃] *nm* [explication] explanation.

éclairer [4] [eklere] *vt* **- 1.** [de lumière] to light up **- 2.** [expliquer] to clarify. ➡ **s'éclairer** *vp* **- 1.** [personne] to light one's way **- 2.** [regard, visage] to light up **- 3.** [rue, ville] to light up.

éclaireur [eklɛrœr] *nm* scout.

éclat [ekla] *nm* **- 1.** [de verre, d'os] splinter ; [de pierre] chip **- 2.** [de lumière] brilliance **- 3.** [de couleur] vividness **- 4.** [beauté] radiance **- 5.** [faste] splendour *Br*, splendor *Am* **- 6.** [bruit] burst ; ~ de rire burst of laughter ; ~s de voix shouts ; faire un ~ to cause a scandal **- 7.** *loc* : rire aux ~s to roar ou shriek with laughter.

éclater [3] [eklate] *vi* **- 1.** [exploser - pneu] to burst ; [- verre] to shatter ; [- obus] to explode ; faire ~ [ballon] to burst ; [bombe] to explode ; [pétard] to let off **- 2.** [incendie, rires] to break out **- 3.** [joie] to shine ; laisser ~ to give vent to **- 4.** *fig* [nouvelles, scandale] to break. ➡ **s'éclater** *vp fam* to have a great time.

éclectique [eklɛktik] *adj* eclectic.

éclipse [eklips] *nf* ASTRON eclipse ; ~ de lune/soleil eclipse of the moon/sun.

éclipser [3] [eklipse] *vt* to eclipse. ➡ **s'éclipser** *vp* **- 1.** ASTRON to go into eclipse **- 2.** *fam* [s'esquiver] to slip away.

éclopé, e [eklɔpe] ◇ *adj* lame. ◇ *nm, f* lame person.

éclore [113] [eklɔr] *vi* [s'ouvrir - fleur] to open out, to blossom ; [- œuf] to hatch.

éclos, e [eklo, oz] *pp* ⊳ éclore.

écluse [eklyz] *nf* lock.

écœurant, e [ekœrɑ̃, ɑ̃t] *adj* **- 1.** [gén] disgusting **- 2.** [démoralisant] sickening.

écœurer [5] [ekœre] *vt* **- 1.** [dégoûter] to sicken, to disgust **- 2.** *fig* [indigner] to sicken **- 3.** [décourager] to discourage.

école [ekɔl] *nf* **- 1.** [gén] school ; ~ maternelle nursery school ; ~ normale ≃ teacher training college *Br*, ≃ teachers college *Am* ; École normale supérieure *grande école for secondary and university teachers* ; ~ primaire/secondaire primary/secondary school *Br*, grade/high school *Am* ; grande ~ *specialist training establishment, entered by competitive exam and highly prestigious* ; faire l'~ buissonnière to play truant *Br* ou hooky *Am* ; faire ~ to be accepted **- 2.** [éducation] schooling ; l'~ privée private education.

écolier, ère [ekɔlje, ɛr] *nm, f* [élève] pupil.

écolo [ekɔlo] *nmf fam* ecologist ; les ~s the Greens.

écologie [ekɔlɔʒi] *nf* ecology.

écologiste [ekɔlɔʒist] *nmf* ecologist.

écomusée [ekɔmyze] *nm* museum of the environment.

éconduire [98] [ekɔ̃dɥir] *vt* [repousser - demande] to dismiss ; [- visiteur, soupirant] to show to the door.

économe [ekɔnɔm] ◇ *nmf* bursar. ◇ *adj* careful, thrifty.

économie [ekɔnɔmi] *nf* **1.** [science] economics (*U*) **- 2.** POLIT economy ; ~ de marché market economy **- 3.** [parcimonie] economy, thrift **- 4.** (*gén pl*) [pécule] savings (*pl*) ; faire des ~s to save up **- 5.** (*gén pl*) : ~s d'échelle economies of scale.

économique [ekɔnɔmik] *adj* **- 1.** ÉCON economic **- 2.** [avantageux] economical.

économiser [3] [ekɔnɔmize] *vt litt & fig* to save.

économiste [ekɔnɔmist] *nmf* economist.

écoper [3] [ekɔpe] *vt* **- 1.** NAVIG to bale out **- 2.** *fam* [sanction] : ~ (de) qqch to get sthg.

écoproduit [ekɔprɔdɥi] *nm* green product.

écorce [ekɔrs] *nf* - **1.** [d'arbre] bark - **2.** [d'agrume] peel - **3.** GÉOL crust.

écorcher [3] [ekɔrʃe] *vt* - **1.** [lapin] to skin - **2.** [bras, jambe] to scratch - **3.** *fig* [langue, nom] to mispronounce.

écorchure [ekɔrʃyr] *nf* graze, scratch.

écorecharge [ekɔrəʃarʒ] *nf* ecorefill.

écossais, e [ekɔsɛ, ɛz] *adj* - **1.** [de l'Écosse] Scottish ; [whisky] Scotch - **2.** [tissu] tartan. ⬥ **écossais** *nm* [langue] Scots. ⬥ **Écossais, e** *nm, f* Scot, Scotsman (*f* Scotswoman).

Écosse [ekɔs] *nf* : l'~ Scotland.

écosser [3] [ekɔse] *vt* to shell.

écosystème [ekɔsistɛm] *nm* ecosystem.

écotourisme [ekɔturism] *nm* ecotourism.

écouler [3] [ekule] *vt* to sell. ⬥ **s'écouler** *vp* - **1.** [eau] to flow - **2.** [personnes] to flow out - **3.** [temps] to pass.

écourter [3] [ekurte] *vt* to shorten.

écouter [3] [ekute] *vt* to listen to.

écouteur [ekutœr] *nm* [de téléphone] earpiece. ⬥ **écouteurs** *nmpl* [de radio] headphones.

écoutille [ekutij] *nf* hatchway.

écran [ekrã] *nm* - **1.** CIN & INFORM screen ; le petit ~ television ; ~ **tactile** tactile screen touch - **2.** [de protection] shield.

écrasant, e [ekrazã, ãt] *adj fig* [accablant] overwhelming.

écraser [3] [ekraze] *vt* - **1.** [comprimer - cigarette] to stub out ; [- pied] to tread on ; [- insecte, raisin] to crush - **2.** [accabler] : ~ **qqn (de)** to burden sb (with) - **3.** [vaincre] to crush - **4.** [renverser] to run over. ⬥ **s'écraser** *vp* [avion, automobile] : s'~ **(contre)** to crash (into).

écrémer [18] [ekreme] *vt* [lait] to skim.

écrevisse [ekrəvis] *nf* crayfish.

écrier [10] [ekrije] ⬥ **s'écrier** *vp* to cry out.

écrin [ekrɛ̃] *nm* case.

écrire [99] [ekrir] *vt* - **1.** [phrase, livre] to write - **2.** [orthographier] to spell. ⬥ **s'écrire** *vp* [s'épeler] to be spelled.

écrit, e [ekri, it] ◇ *pp* ▷ **écrire**. ◇ *adj* written. ⬥ **écrit** *nm* - **1.** [ouvrage] writing - **2.** [examen] written exam - **3.** [document] piece of writing. ⬥ **par écrit** *loc adv* in writing.

écriteau, x [ekrito] *nm* notice.

écriture [ekrityr] *nf* - **1.** [gén] writing - **2.** (*gén pl*) COMM [comptes] books (*pl*).

écrivain [ekrivɛ̃] *nm* writer, author.

écrou [ekru] *nm* TECHNOL nut.

écrouer [3] [ekrue] *vt* to imprison.

écrouler [3] [ekrule] ⬥ **s'écrouler** *vp litt & fig* to collapse.

écru, e [ekry] *adj* [naturel] unbleached.

ECU [eky] (*abr de* European Currency Unit) *nm* ECU.

écu [eky] *nm* - **1.** [bouclier, armoiries] shield - **2.** [monnaie ancienne] crown - **3.** = ECU.

écueil [ekœj] *nm* - **1.** [rocher] reef - **2.** *fig* [obstacle] stumbling block.

écuelle [ekɥɛl] *nf* [objet] bowl.

éculé, e [ekyle] *adj* - **1.** [chaussure] down-at-heel - **2.** *fig* [plaisanterie] hackneyed.

écume [ekym] *nf* [mousse, bave] foam.

écumoire [ekymwar] *nf* skimmer.

écureuil [ekyrœj] *nm* squirrel.

écurie [ekyri] *nf* - **1.** [pour chevaux & SPORT] stable - **2.** *fig* [local sale] pigsty.

écusson [ekysɔ̃] *nm* - **1.** [d'armoiries] coat-of-arms - **2.** MIL badge.

écuyer, ère [ekɥije, ɛr] *nm, f* [de cirque] rider. ⬥ **écuyer** *nm* [de chevalier] squire.

eczéma [ɛgzema] *nm* eczema.

édenté, e [edãte] *adj* toothless.

EDF, Edf (*abr de* Électricité de France) *nf French national electricity company.*

édifice [edifis] *nm* - **1.** [construction] building - **2.** *fig* [institution] : l'~ **social** the fabric of society.

édifier [9] [edifje] *vt* - **1.** [ville, église] to build - **2.** *fig* [théorie] to construct - **3.** [personne] to edify ; *iron* to enlighten.

Édimbourg [edɛ̃bur] *n* Edinburgh.

éditer [3] [edite] *vt* to publish.

éditeur, trice [editœr, tris] *nm, f* publisher.

édition [edisjɔ̃] *nf* - **1.** [profession] publishing - **2.** [de journal, livre] edition ; ~ **électronique** electronic publishing.

éditorial, aux [editɔrjal, o] *nm* leader, editorial.

édredon [edrədɔ̃] *nm* eiderdown.

éducateur, trice [edykatœr, tris] *nm, f* teacher ; ~ **spécialisé** *teacher of children with special educational needs.*

éducatif, ive [edykatif, iv] *adj* educational.

éducation [edykasjɔ̃] *nf* - **1.** [apprentissage] education ; l'**Éducation nationale** ≃ the Department for Education *Br*, ≃ the Department of Education *Am* - **2.** [parentale] upbringing - **3.** [savoir-vivre] breeding.

édulcorant [edylkɔrã] *nm* : ~ **(de synthèse)** (artificial) sweetener.

édulcorer [3] [edylkɔre] vt - **1.** sout [tisane] to sweeten - **2.** fig [propos] to tone down.

éduquer [3] [edyke] vt [enfant] to bring up ; [élève] to educate.

effacé, e [efase] adj - **1.** [teinte] faded - **2.** [modeste-rôle] unobtrusive ; [-personne] self-effacing.

effacer [16] [efase] vt - **1.** [mot] to erase, to rub out ; INFORM to delete - **2.** [souvenir] to erase - **3.** [réussite] to eclipse. ➤ **s'effacer** vp - **1.** [s'estomper] to fade (away) - **2.** sout [s'écarter] to move aside - **3.** fig [s'incliner] to give way.

effarant, e [efarã, ãt] adj frightening.

effarer [3] [efare] vt to frighten, to scare.

effaroucher [3] [efaruʃe] vt - **1.** [effrayer] to scare off - **2.** [intimider] to overawe.

effectif, ive [efɛktif, iv] adj - **1.** [remède] effective - **2.** [aide] positive. ➤ **effectif** nm - **1.** MIL strength - **2.** [de groupe] total number.

effectivement [efɛktivmã] adv - **1.** [réellement] effectively - **2.** [confirmation] in fact.

effectuer [7] [efɛktɥe] vt [réaliser - manœuvre] to carry out ; [- trajet, paiement] to make.

efféminé, e [efemine] adj effeminate.

effervescent, e [efɛrvesã, ãt] adj [boisson] effervescent ; fig [pays] in turmoil.

effet [efɛ] nm - **1.** [gén] effect ; **sous l'~ de** under the effects of ; **~ de serre** greenhouse effect - **2.** [impression recherchée] impression - **3.** COMM [titre] bill. ➤ **en effet** loc adv in fact, indeed.

effeuiller [5] [efœje] vt [arbre] to remove the leaves from ; [fleur] to remove the petals from.

efficace [efikas] adj - **1.** [remède, mesure] effective - **2.** [personne, machine] efficient.

effigie [efiʒi] nf effigy.

effiler [3] [efile] vt - **1.** [tissu] to fray - **2.** [lame] to sharpen - **3.** [cheveux] to thin.

effilocher [3] [efiloʃe] vt to fray. ➤ **s'effilocher** vp to fray.

efflanqué, e [eflãke] adj emaciated.

effleurer [5] [eflœre] vt - **1.** [visage, bras] to brush (against) - **2.** fig [problème, thème] to touch on - **3.** fig [suj : pensée, idée] : **~ qqn** to cross sb's mind.

effluve [eflyv] nm exhalation ; fig [d'enfance, du passé] breath.

effondrement [efɔ̃drəmã] nm collapse.

effondrer [3] [efɔ̃dre] ➤ **s'effondrer** vp litt & fig to collapse.

efforcer [16] [eforse] ➤ **s'efforcer** vp : **s'~ de faire qqch** to make an effort to do sthg.

effort [efɔr] nm - **1.** [de personne] effort - **2.** TECHNOL stress.

effraction [efraksjɔ̃] nf breaking in ; **entrer par ~ dans** to break into.

effrayer [11] [efreje] vt to frighten, to scare.

effréné, e [efrene] adj [course] frantic.

effriter [3] [efrite] vt to cause to crumble. ➤ **s'effriter** vp [mur] to crumble.

effroi [efrwa] nm fear, dread.

effronté, e [efrɔ̃te] ◇ adj insolent. ◇ nm, f insolent person.

effronterie [efrɔ̃tri] nf insolence.

effroyable [efrwajabl] adj - **1.** [catastrophe, misère] appalling - **2.** [laideur] hideous.

effusion [efyzjɔ̃] nf - **1.** [de liquide] effusion - **2.** [de sentiments] effusiveness.

égal, e, aux [egal, o] ◇ adj - **1.** [équivalent] equal - **2.** [régulier] even. ◇ nm, f equal.

également [egalmã] adv - **1.** [avec égalité] equally - **2.** [aussi] as well, too.

égaler [3] [egale] vt - **1.** MATHS to equal - **2.** [beauté] to match, to compare with.

égaliser [3] [egalize] ◇ vt [haie, cheveux] to trim. ◇ vi SPORT to equalize Br, to tie Am.

égalitaire [egaliter] adj egalitarian.

égalité [egalite] nf - **1.** [gén] equality - **2.** [d'humeur] evenness - **3.** SPORT : **être à ~** to be level.

égard [egar] nm consideration ; **à cet ~** in this respect. ➤ **à l'égard de** loc prép with regard to, towards Br, toward Am.

égarement [egarmã] nm - **1.** [de jeunesse] wildness - **2.** [de raisonnement] aberration.

égarer [3] [egare] vt - **1.** [objet] to mislay, to lose - **2.** [personne] to mislead - **3.** fig & sout [suj : passion] to lead astray. ➤ **s'égarer** vp - **1.** [lettre] to get lost, to go astray ; [personne] to get lost, to lose one's way - **2.** fig & sout [personne] to stray from the point.

égayer [11] [egeje] vt - **1.** [personne] to cheer up - **2.** [pièce] to brighten up.

égide [eʒid] nf protection ; **sous l'~ de** littéraire under the aegis of.

église [egliz] nf church. ➤ **Église** nf : **l'Église** the Church.

égocentrique [egɔsãtrik] adj self-centred, egocentric.

égoïsme [egɔism] nm selfishness, egoism.

égoïste [egɔist] <> *nmf* selfish person. <> *adj* selfish, egoistic.

égorger [17] [egɔrʒe] *vt* [animal, personne] to cut the throat of.

égosiller [3] [egozije] **s'égosiller** *vp fam* - **1.** [crier] to bawl, to shout - **2.** [chanter] to sing one's head off.

égout [egu] *nm* sewer.

égoutter [3] [egute] *vt* - **1.** [vaisselle] to leave to drain - **2.** [légumes, fromage] to drain. **s'égoutter** *vp* to drip, to drain.

égouttoir [egutwar] *nm* - **1.** [à légumes] colander, strainer - **2.** [à vaisselle] rack *(for washing-up)*.

égratigner [3] [egratiɲe] *vt* to scratch ; *fig* to have a go ou dig at. **s'égratigner** *vp* : **s'~ la main** to scratch one's hand.

égratignure [egratiɲyr] *nf* scratch, graze ; *fig* dig.

égrener [19] [egrəne] *vt* - **1.** [détacher les grains de - épi, cosse] to shell ; [- grappe] to pick grapes from - **2.** [chapelet] to tell - **3.** *fig* [marquer] to mark.

égrillard, e [egrijar, ard] *adj* ribald, bawdy.

Égypte [eʒipt] *nf* : **l'~** Egypt.

égyptien, enne [eʒipsjẽ, ɛn] *adj* Egyptian. **égyptien** *nm* [langue] Egyptian. **Égyptien, enne** *nm, f* Egyptian.

égyptologie [eʒiptɔlɔʒi] *nf* Egyptology.

eh [e] *interj* hey! ; **~ bien** well.

éhonté, e [eɔ̃te] *adj* shameless.

Eiffel [efel] *n* : **la tour ~** the Eiffel Tower.

éjaculation [eʒakylasjɔ̃] *nf* ejaculation.

éjectable [eʒɛktabl] *adj* : **siège ~** ejector seat.

éjecter [4] [eʒɛkte] *vt* - **1.** [douille] to eject - **2.** *fam* [personne] to kick out.

élaboration [elabɔrasjɔ̃] *nf* [de plan, système] working out, development.

élaboré, e [elabɔre] *adj* elaborate.

élaborer [3] [elabɔre] *vt* [plan, système] to work out, to develop.

élaguer [3] [elage] *vt litt & fig* to prune.

élan [elɑ̃] *nm* - **1.** ZOOL elk - **2.** SPORT run-up ; *Can* GOLF swing ; **prendre son ~** to take a run-up, to gather speed - **3.** *fig* [de joie] outburst.

élancé, e [elɑ̃se] *adj* slender.

élancer [16] [elɑ̃se] *vi* MÉD to give shooting pains. **s'élancer** *vp* - **1.** [se précipiter] to rush, to dash - **2.** SPORT to take a run-up - **3.** *fig* [s'envoler] to soar.

élargir [32] [elarʒir] *vt* to widen ; [vêtement] to let out ; *fig* to expand. **s'élar-**

gir *vp* [s'agrandir] to widen ; [vêtement] to stretch ; *fig* to expand.

élasticité [elastisite] *nf* PHYS elasticity.

élastique [elastik] <> *nm* - **1.** [pour attacher] elastic band - **2.** [matière] elastic. <> *adj* - **1.** PHYS elastic - **2.** [corps] flexible - **3.** *fig* [conscience] accommodating.

électeur, trice [elɛktœr, tris] *nm, f* voter, elector.

élection [elɛksjɔ̃] *nf* [vote] election ; **~ présidentielle** presidential election ; **~s municipales** local elections.

électoral, e, aux [elɛktɔral, o] *adj* electoral ; [campagne, réunion] election *(avant n)*.

électricien, enne [elɛktrisjẽ, ɛn] *nm, f* electrician.

électricité [elɛktrisite] *nf* electricity.

électrifier [9] [elɛktrifje] *vt* to electrify.

électrique [elɛktrik] *adj litt & fig* electric.

électroaimant [elɛktrɔɛmɑ̃] *nm* electromagnet.

électrocardiogramme [elɛktrɔkardjɔgram] *nm* electrocardiogram.

électrochoc [elɛktrɔʃɔk] *nm* electroshock therapy.

électrocuter [3] [elɛktrɔkyte] *vt* to electrocute.

électrode [elɛktrɔd] *nf* electrode.

électroencéphalogramme [elɛktrɔãsefalɔgram] *nm* electroencephalogram.

électrogène [elɛktrɔʒɛn] *adj* : **groupe ~** generating unit.

électrolyse [elɛktrɔliz] *nf* electrolysis.

électromagnétique [elɛktrɔmaɲetik] *adj* electromagnetic.

électroménager [elɛktrɔmenaʒe] *nm* household electrical appliances *(pl)*.

électron [elɛktrɔ̃] *nm* electron.

électronicien, enne [elɛktrɔnisjẽ, ɛn] *nm, f* electronics specialist.

électronique [elɛktrɔnik] <> *nf* SCIENCE electronics *(U)*. <> *adj* electronic ; [microscope] electron *(avant n)*.

électrophone [elɛktrɔfɔn] *nm* record player.

élégance [elegɑ̃s] *nf* [de personne, style] elegance.

élégant, e [elegɑ̃, ɑ̃t] *adj* - **1.** [personne, style] elegant - **2.** [délicat - solution, procédé] elegant ; [- comportement] generous.

élément [elemɑ̃] *nm* - **1.** [gén] element ; **être dans son ~** to be in one's element - **2.** [de machine] component.

élémentaire [elemɑ̃tɛr] *adj* - **1.** [gén] elementary - **2.** [installation, besoin] basic.

éléphant [elefɑ̃] *nm* elephant.

élevage [ɛlvaʒ] *nm* breeding, rearing ; [installation] farm.

élévateur, trice [elevatœr, tris] *adj* elevator *(avant n)*.

élevé, e [ɛlve] *adj* - **1.** [haut] high - **2.** *fig* [sentiment, âme] noble - **3.** [enfant] : **bien/mal ~** well/badly brought up.

élève [elɛv] *nmf* [écolier, disciple] pupil.

élever [19] [ɛlve] *vt* - **1.** [gén] to raise - **2.** [statue] to put up, to erect - **3.** [à un rang supérieur] to elevate - **4.** [esprit] to improve - **5.** [enfant] to bring up - **6.** [poulets] to rear, to breed. ➡ **s'élever** *vp* - **1.** [gén] to rise - **2.** [montant] : **s'~ à** to add up to - **3.** [protester] : **s'~ contre qqn/qqch** to protest against sb/sthg.

éleveur, euse [ɛlvœr, øz] *nm, f* breeder.

elfe [ɛlf] *nm* elf.

éligible [eliʒibl] *adj* eligible.

élimé, e [elime] *adj* threadbare.

élimination [eliminasjɔ̃] *nf* elimination.

éliminatoire [eliminatwar] ⬦ *nf (gén pl)* SPORT qualifying heat ou round. ⬦ *adj* qualifying *(avant n)*.

éliminer [3] [elimine] *vt* to eliminate.

élire [106] [elir] *vt* to elect.

élite [elit] *nf* elite ; **d'~** choice, select.

élitiste [elitist] *nmf & adj* elitist.

elle [ɛl] *pron pers* - **1.** [sujet - personne] she ; [- animal] it, she ; [- chose] it ⬦ [complément - personne] her ; [- animal] it, her ; [- chose] it ➡ **elles** *pron pers pl* - **1.** [sujet] they - **2.** [complément] them. ➡ **elle-même** *pron pers* [personne] herself ; [animal] itself, herself ; [chose] itself. ➡ **elles-mêmes** *pron pers pl* themselves.

ellipse [elips] *nf* - **1.** GÉOM ellipse - **2.** LING ellipsis.

élocution [elɔkysjɔ̃] *nf* delivery ; **défaut d'~** speech defect.

éloge [elɔʒ] *nm* [louange] praise ; **faire l'~ de qqn/qqch** [louer] to speak highly of sb/sthg ; **couvrir qqn d'~s** to shower sb with praise.

élogieux, euse [elɔʒjø, øz] *adj* laudatory.

éloignement [elwaɲmɑ̃] *nm* - **1.** [mise à l'écart] removal - **2.** [séparation] absence - **3.** [dans l'espace, le temps] distance.

éloigner [3] [elwaɲe] *vt* - **1.** [écarter] to move away ; **~ qqch de** to move sthg away from - **2.** [détourner] to turn away - **3.** [chasser] to dismiss. ➡ **s'éloigner** *vp* - **1.** [partir] to move ou go away - **2.** *fig* [du sujet] to

stray from the point - **3.** [se détacher] to distance o.s.

éloquence [elɔkɑ̃s] *nf* [d'orateur, d'expression] eloquence.

éloquent, e [elɔkɑ̃, ɑ̃t] *adj* - **1.** [avocat, silence] eloquent - **2.** [données] significant.

élu, e [ely] ⬦ *pp* ⊳ **élire**. ⬦ *adj* POLIT elected. ⬦ *nm, f* - **1.** POLIT elected representative - **2.** RELIG chosen one ; **l'~ de son cœur** *hum ou sout* one's heart's desire.

élucider [3] [elyside] *vt* to clear up.

éluder [3] [elyde] *vt* to evade.

Élysée [elize] *nm* : **l'~** *the official residence of the French President and, by extension, the President himself.*

émacié, e [emasje] *adj littéraire* emaciated.

émail, aux [emaj, emo] *nm* enamel ; **en ~** enamel, enamelled *Br*, enameled *Am*.

e-mail [imɛl] *(pl* **e-mails***) nm* e-mail, E-mail.

émanation [emanasjɔ̃] *nf* emanation ; **être l'~ de** *fig* to emanate from.

émanciper [3] [emɑ̃sipe] *vt* to emancipate. ➡ **s'émanciper** *vp* - **1.** [se libérer] to become free ou liberated - **2.** *fam* [se dévergonder] to become emancipated.

émaner [3] [emane] *vi* : **~ de** to emanate from.

émarger [17] [emarʒe] *vt* [signer] to sign.

émasculer [3] [emaskyle] *vt* to emasculate.

emballage [ɑ̃balaʒ] *nm* packaging.

emballer [3] [ɑ̃bale] *vt* - **1.** [objet] to pack (up), to wrap (up) - **2.** *fam* [plaire à] to thrill. ➡ **s'emballer** *vp* - **1.** [moteur] to race - **2.** [cheval] to bolt - **3.** *fam* [personne - s'enthousiasmer] to get carried away ; [- s'emporter] to lose one's temper.

embarcadère [ɑ̃barkadɛr] *nm* landing stage.

embarcation [ɑ̃barkasjɔ̃] *nf* small boat.

embardée [ɑ̃barde] *nf* swerve ; **faire une ~** to swerve.

embargo [ɑ̃bargo] *nm* embargo.

embarquement [ɑ̃barkəmɑ̃] *nm* - **1.** [de marchandises] loading - **2.** [de passagers] boarding.

embarquer [3] [ɑ̃barke] ⬦ *vt* - **1.** [marchandises] to load - **2.** [passagers] to (take on) board - **3.** *fam* [arrêter] to pick up - **4.** *fam fig* [engager] : **~ qqn dans** to involve sb in - **5.** *fam* [emmener] to cart off. ⬦ *vi* : **~ (pour)** to sail (for). ➡ **s'embarquer** *vp* - **1.** [sur un bateau] to (set) sail - **2.** *fam fig* [s'engager] : **s'~ dans** to get involved in.

embarras [ɑ̃bara] *nm* - **1.** [incertitude]

(state of) uncertainty ; **avoir l'~ du choix** to be spoilt for choice - **2.** [situation difficile] predicament ; **être dans l'~** to be in a predicament ; **mettre qqn dans l'~** to place sb in an awkward position ; **tirer qqn d'~** to get sb out of a tight spot - **3.** [gêne] embarrassment - **4.** [souci] difficulty, worry.

embarrassé, e [ɑ̃barase] *adj* - **1.** [encombré - pièce, bureau] cluttered ; **avoir les mains ~es** to have one's hands full - **2.** [gêné] embarrassed - **3.** [confus] confused.

embarrasser [3] [ɑ̃barase] *vt* - **1.** [encombrer - pièce] to clutter up ; [- personne] to hamper - **2.** [gêner] to put in an awkward position. ◆ **s'embarrasser** *vp* [se charger] : **s'~ de qqch** to burden o.s. with sthg ; *fig* to bother about sthg.

embauche [ɑ̃boʃ] *nf*, **embauchage** [ɑ̃boʃaʒ] *nm* hiring, employment.

embaucher [3] [ɑ̃boʃe] *vt* - **1.** [employer] to employ, to take on - **2.** *fam* [occuper] : **je t'embauche!** I need your help!

embaumer [3] [ɑ̃bome] ⟨⟩ *vt* - **1.** [cadavre] to embalm - **2.** [parfumer] to scent. ⟨⟩ *vi* to be fragrant.

embellir [32] [ɑ̃belir] ⟨⟩ *vt* - **1.** [agrémenter] to brighten up - **2.** *fig* [enjoliver] to embellish. ⟨⟩ *vi* [devenir plus beau] to become more attractive ; *fig & hum* to grow, to increase.

embêtant, e [ɑ̃betɑ̃, ɑ̃t] *adj fam* annoying.

embêtement [ɑ̃betmɑ̃] *nm fam* trouble.

embêter [4] [ɑ̃bete] *vt fam* [contrarier, importuner] to annoy. ◆ **s'embêter** *vp fam* [s'ennuyer] to be bored.

emblée [ɑ̃ble] ◆ **d'emblée** *loc adv* right away.

emblème [ɑ̃blɛm] *nm* emblem.

emboîter [3] [ɑ̃bwate] *vt* : **~ qqch dans qqch** to fit sthg into sthg. ◆ **s'emboîter** *vp* to fit together.

embonpoint [ɑ̃bɔ̃pwɛ̃] *nm* stoutness.

embouché, e [ɑ̃buʃe] *adj fam* : **mal ~** foulmouthed.

embouchure [ɑ̃buʃyr] *nf* [de fleuve] mouth.

embourber [3] [ɑ̃burbe] ◆ **s'embourber** *vp* [s'enliser] to get stuck in the mud ; *fig* to get bogged down.

embourgeoiser [3] [ɑ̃burʒwaze] *vt* [personne] to instil *Br* ou instill *Am* middle-class values in ; [quartier] to gentrify. ◆ **s'embourgeoiser** *vp* [personne] to adopt middle-class values ; [quartier] to become gentrified.

embout [ɑ̃bu] *nm* [protection] tip ; [extrémité d'un tube] nozzle.

embouteillage [ɑ̃butɛjaʒ] *nm* [circulation] traffic jam.

emboutir [32] [ɑ̃butir] *vt* - **1.** *fam* [voiture] to crash into - **2.** TECHNOL to stamp.

embranchement [ɑ̃brɑ̃ʃmɑ̃] *nm* - **1.** [carrefour] junction - **2.** [division] branching (out) ; *fig* branch.

embraser [3] [ɑ̃braze] *vt* [incendier, éclairer] to set ablaze ; *fig* [d'amour] to (set on) fire, to inflame. ◆ **s'embraser** *vp* [prendre feu, s'éclairer] to be ablaze ; *fig & littéraire* to be inflamed.

embrassade [ɑ̃brasad] *nf* embrace.

embrasser [3] [ɑ̃brase] *vt* - **1.** [donner un baiser à] to kiss - **2.** [étreindre] to embrace - **3.** *fig* [du regard] to take in. ◆ **s'embrasser** *vp* to kiss (each other).

embrasure [ɑ̃brazyr] *nf* : **dans l'~ de la fenêtre** in the window.

embrayage [ɑ̃brɛjaʒ] *nm* [mécanisme] clutch.

embrayer [11] [ɑ̃breje] *vi* AUTOM to engage the clutch.

embrocher [3] [ɑ̃brɔʃe] *vt* to skewer.

embrouillamini [ɑ̃brujamini] *nm fam* muddle.

embrouiller [3] [ɑ̃bruje] *vt* - **1.** [mélanger] to mix (up), to muddle (up) - **2.** *fig* [compliquer] to confuse.

embruns [ɑ̃brœ̃] *nmpl* spray *(U)*.

embryon [ɑ̃brijɔ̃] *nm litt & fig* embryo.

embûche [ɑ̃byʃ] *nf* pitfall.

embuer [7] [ɑ̃bɥe] *vt* - **1.** [de vapeur] to steam up - **2.** [de larmes] to mist (over).

embuscade [ɑ̃byskad] *nf* ambush.

éméché, e [emeʃe] *adj fam* merry, tipsy.

émeraude [emrod] *nf* emerald.

émerger [17] [emerʒe] *vi* - **1.** [gén] to emerge - **2.** NAVIG & *fig* to surface.

émeri [emri] *nm* : **papier** ou **toile ~** emery paper.

émérite [emerit] *adj* distinguished, eminent.

émerveiller [4] [emɛrveje] *vt* to fill with wonder.

émetteur, trice [emetœr, tris] *adj* transmitting ; **poste ~** transmitter. ◆ **émetteur** *nm* [appareil] transmitter.

émettre [84] [emɛtr] *vt* - **1.** [produire] to emit - **2.** [diffuser] to transmit, to broadcast - **3.** [mettre en circulation] to issue - **4.** [exprimer] to express.

émeute [emøt] *nf* riot.

émietter [4] [emjete] *vt* - **1.** [du pain] to crumble - **2.** [morceler] to divide up.

émigrant, e [emigrã, ãt] *adj & nm, f* emigrant.

émigré, e [emigre] <> *adj* migrant. <> *nm, f* emigrant.

émigrer [3] [emigre] *vi* - **1.** [personnes] to emigrate - **2.** [animaux] to migrate.

émincé, e [emẽse] *adj* sliced thinly. ➤ **émincé** *nm thin slices of meat served in a sauce.*

éminemment [eminamã] *adv* eminently.

éminence [eminãs] *nf* hill.

éminent, e [eminã, ãt] *adj* eminent, distinguished.

émir [emir] *nm* emir.

émirat [emira] *nm* emirate. ➤ **Émirat** *nm* : **les Émirats arabes unis** the United Arab Emirates.

émis, e [emi, iz] *pp* ⊏ **émettre.**

émissaire [emiser] <> *nm* [envoyé] emissary, envoy. <> *adj* ⊏ **bouc.**

émission [emisjõ] *nf* - **1.** [de gaz, de son etc] emission - **2.** [RADIO & TÉLÉ - transmission] transmission, broadcasting ; [- programme] programme *Br*, program *Am* - **3.** [mise en circulation] issue.

emmagasiner [3] [amagazine] *vt* - **1.** [stocker] to store - **2.** *fig* [accumuler] to store up.

emmailloter [3] [amajɔte] *vt* to wrap up.

emmanchure [ãmãʃyr] *nf* armhole.

emmêler [4] [ãmele] *vt* - **1.** [fils] to tangle up - **2.** *fig* [idées] to muddle up, to confuse ➤ **s'emmêler** *vp* - **1.** [fils] to get into a tangle - **2.** *fig* [personne] to get mixed up.

emménagement [ãmenaʒmã] *nm* moving in.

emménager [17] [ãmenaʒe] *vi* to move in.

emmener [19] [ãmne] *vt* to take.

emmerder [3] [ãmerde] *vt tfam* to piss off. ➤ **s'emmerder** *vp tfam* [s'embêter] to be bored stiff.

emmitoufler [3] [ãmitufle] *vt* to wrap up. ➤ **s'emmitoufler** *vp* to wrap o.s. up.

émoi [emwa] *nm* - **1.** *sout* [agitation] agitation, commotion ; **en ~** in turmoil - **2.** [émotion] emotion.

émotif, ive [emɔtif, iv] *adj* emotional.

émotion [emosjõ] *nf* - **1.** [sentiment] emotion - **2.** [peur] fright, shock.

émotionnel, elle [emosjɔnel] *adj* emotional.

émousser [3] [emuse] *vt litt & fig* to blunt.

émouvant, e [emuvã, ãt] *adj* moving.

émouvoir [55] [emuvwar] *vt* - **1.** [troubler] to disturb, to upset - **2.** [susciter la sympathie de] to move, to touch. ➤ **s'émouvoir** *vp* to show emotion, to be upset.

empailler [3] [ãpaje] *vt* - **1.** [animal] to stuff - **2.** [chaise] to upholster (with straw).

empaler [3] [ãpale] *vt* to impale.

empaqueter [27] [ãpakte] *vt* to pack (up), to wrap (up).

empâter [3] [ãpate] *vt* - **1.** [visage, traits] to fatten out - **2.** [bouche, langue] to coat, to fur up. ➤ **s'empâter** *vp* to put on weight.

empêchement [ãpɛʃmã] *nm* obstacle ; **j'ai un ~** something has come up.

empêcher [4] [ãpeʃe] *vt* to prevent ; **~ qqn/qqch de faire qqch** to prevent sb/sthg from doing sthg ; **~ que qqn (ne) fasse qqch** to prevent sb from doing sthg ; **(il) n'empêche que** nevertheless, all the same.

empereur [ãprœr] *nm* emperor.

empesé, e [ãpəze] *adj* - **1.** [linge] starched - **2.** *fig* [style] stiff.

empester [3] [ãpeste] *vi* to stink.

empêtrer [4] [ãpetre] *vt* : **être empêtré dans** to be tangled up in. ➤ **s'empêtrer** *vp* : **s'~ (dans)** to get tangled up (in).

emphase [ãfaz] *nf péj* pomposity.

empiéter [18] [ãpjete] *vi* : **~ sur** to encroach on.

empiffrer [3] [ãpifre] ➤ **s'empiffrer** *vp fam* to stuff o.s.

empiler [3] [ãpile] *vt* [entasser] to pile up, to stack up.

empire [ãpir] *nm* - **1.** HIST & *fig* empire - **2.** *sout* [contrôle] influence.

empirer [3] [ãpire] *vi & vt* to worsen.

empirique [ãpirik] *adj* empirical.

emplacement [ãplasmã] *nm* [gén] site, location ; [dans un camping] place.

emplette [ãplet] *nf* (gén pl) purchase.

emplir [32] [ãplir] *vt sout* : **~ (de)** to fill (with). ➤ **s'emplir** *vp* : **s'~ (de)** to fill (with).

emploi [ãplwa] *nm* - **1.** [utilisation] use ; **~ du temps** timetable ; **mode d'~** instructions (pl) (for use) - **2.** [travail] job.

employé, e [ãplwaje] *nm, f* employee ; **~ de bureau** office employee ou worker.

employer [13] [ãplwaje] *vt* - **1.** [utiliser] to use - **2.** [salarier] to employ.

employeur, euse [ãplwajœr, øz] *nm, f* employer.

empocher [3] [ãpɔʃe] *vt fam* to pocket.

empoignade [ãpwaɲad] *nf* row.

empoigner [3] [ãpwaɲe] *vt* [saisir] to grasp. ➤ **s'empoigner** *vp fig* to come to blows.

empoisonnement [ɑ̃pwazɔnmɑ̃] *nm* [intoxication] poisoning.

empoisonner [3] [ɑ̃pwazɔne] *vt* - **1.** [gén] to poison - **2.** *fam* [ennuyer] to annoy, to bug.

emporté, e [ɑ̃pɔrte] *adj* short-tempered.

emportement [ɑ̃pɔrtəmɑ̃] *nm* anger.

emporter [3] [ɑ̃pɔrte] *vt* - **1.** [emmener] to take (away) ; **à** - [plats] to take away, to go *Am* - **2.** [entraîner] to carry along - **3.** [arracher] to tear off, to blow off - **4.** [faire mourir] to carry off - **5.** [surpasser] : **l'~ sur** to get the better of. ◆ **s'emporter** *vp* to get angry, to lose one's temper.

empoté, e [ɑ̃pɔte] *fam* ◇ *adj* clumsy. ◇ *nm, f* clumsy person.

empreinte [ɑ̃prɛ̃t] *nf* [trace] print ; *fig* mark, trace ; **~s digitales** fingerprints.

empressement [ɑ̃prɛsmɑ̃] *nm* - **1.** [zèle] attentiveness - **2.** [enthousiasme] eagerness.

empresser [4] [ɑ̃prese] ◆ **s'empresser** *vp* : **s'~ de faire qqch** to hurry to do sthg ; **s'~ auprès de qqn** to be attentive to sb.

emprise [ɑ̃priz] *nf* [ascendant] influence.

emprisonnement [ɑ̃prizɔnmɑ̃] *nm* imprisonment.

emprisonner [3] [ɑ̃prizɔne] *vt* [voleur] to imprison.

emprunt [ɑ̃prœ̃] *nm* - **1.** FIN loan - **2.** LING & *fig* borrowing.

emprunté, e [ɑ̃prœ̃te] *adj* awkward, self-conscious.

emprunter [3] [ɑ̃prœ̃te] *vt* - **1.** [gén] to borrow ; **~ qqch à** to borrow sthg from - **2.** [route] to take.

ému, e [emy] ◇ *pp* ▷ **émouvoir**. ◇ *adj* [personne] moved, touched ; [regard, sourire] emotional.

émulation [emylasjɔ̃] *nf* - **1.** [concurrence] rivalry - **2.** [imitation] emulation.

émule [emyl] *nmf* - **1.** [imitateur] emulator - **2.** [concurrent] rival.

émulsion [emylsjɔ̃] *nf* emulsion.

en [ɑ̃] ◇ *prép* - **1.** [temps] in ; **~ 1994** in 1994 ; **~ hiver/septembre** in winter/September - **2.** [lieu] in ; [direction] to ; **habiter ~ Sicile/ville** to live in Sicily/town ; **aller ~ Sicile/ville** to go to Sicily/town - **3.** [matière] made of ; **c'est ~ métal** it's (made of) metal ; **une théière ~ argent** a silver teapot - **4.** [état, forme, manière] : **les arbres sont ~ fleurs** the trees are in blossom ; **du sucre ~ morceaux** sugar cubes ; **du lait ~ poudre** powdered milk ; **je la préfère ~ vert** I prefer it in green ; **agir ~ traître** to behave treacherously ; **je l'ai eu ~ ca-**deau I was given it as a present ; **dire qqch ~ anglais** to say sthg in English ; **~ vacances** on holiday - **5.** [moyen] by ; **~ avion/bateau/train** by plane/boat/train - **6.** [mesure] in ; **vous l'avez ~ 38?** do you have it in a 38? ; **compter ~ dollars** to calculate in dollars - **7.** [devant un participe présent] : **~ arrivant à Paris** on arriving in Paris, as he/she *etc* arrived in Paris ; **~ faisant un effort** by making an effort ; **~ mangeant** while eating ; **elle répondit ~ souriant** she replied with a smile. ◇ *pron adv* - **1.** [complément de verbe, de nom, d'adjectif] : **il s'~ est souvenu** he remembered it ; **nous ~ avons déjà parlé** we've already spoken about it ; **je m'~ porte garant** I'll vouch for it - **2.** [avec un indéfini, exprimant une quantité] : **j'ai du chocolat, tu ~ veux?** I've got some chocolate, do you want some? ; **tu ~ as?** have you got any?, do you have any? ; **il y ~ a plusieurs** there are several (of them) - **3.** [provenance] from there.

ENA, Ena [ena] (*abr de* **École nationale d'administration**) *nf prestigious grande école training future government officials.*

encadrement [ɑ̃kadrəmɑ̃] *nm* - **1.** [de tableau, porte] frame - **2.** [dans une entreprise] managerial staff ; [à l'armée] officers *(pl)* ; [à l'école] staff - **3.** [du crédit] restriction.

encadrer [3] [ɑ̃kadre] *vt* - **1.** [photo, visage] to frame - **2.** [employés] to supervise ; [soldats] to be in command of ; [élèves] to teach.

encaissé, e [ɑ̃kese] *adj* [vallée] deep and narrow ; [rivière] steep-banked.

encaisser [4] [ɑ̃kese] *vt* - **1.** [argent, coups, insultes] to take - **2.** [chèque] to cash.

encart [ɑ̃kar] *nm* insert.

encastrer [3] [ɑ̃kastre] *vt* to fit. ◆ **s'encastrer** *vp* to fit (exactly).

encaustique [ɑ̃kɔstik] *nf* [cire] polish.

enceinte [ɑ̃sɛ̃t] ◇ *adj f* pregnant ; **~ de 4 mois** 4 months pregnant. ◇ *nf* - **1.** [muraille] wall - **2.** [espace] : **dans l'~ de** within (the confines of) - **3.** [baffle] : **~ (acoustique)** speaker.

encens [ɑ̃sɑ̃] *nm* incense.

encenser [3] [ɑ̃sɑ̃se] *vt* - **1.** [brûler de l'encens dans] to burn incense in - **2.** *fig* [louer] to flatter.

encensoir [ɑ̃sɑ̃swar] *nm* censer.

encercler [3] [ɑ̃sɛrkle] *vt* - **1.** [cerner, environner] to surround - **2.** [entourer] to circle.

enchaînement [ɑ̃ʃɛnmɑ̃] *nm* - **1.** [succession] series - **2.** [liaison] link.

enchaîner [4] [ɑ̃ʃene] ◇ *vt* - **1.** [attacher] to chain up - **2.** *fig* [asservir] to enslave - **3.** [coordonner] to link. ◇ *vi* : **~ (sur)** to move on (to). **s'enchaîner** *vp* [se suivre] to follow on from each other.

enchanté, e [ɑ̃ʃɑ̃te] *adj* - **1.** [ravi] delighted ; ~ **de faire votre connaissance** pleased to meet you - **2.** [ensorcelé] enchanted.

enchantement [ɑ̃ʃɑ̃tmɑ̃] *nm* - **1.** [sortilège] magic spell ; **comme par ~** as if by magic - **2.** *sout* [ravissement] delight - **3.** [merveille] wonder.

enchanter [3] [ɑ̃ʃɑ̃te] *vt* - **1.** [ensorceler, charmer] to enchant - **2.** [ravir] to delight.

enchâsser [3] [ɑ̃ʃase] *vt* - **1.** [encastrer] to fit - **2.** [sertir] to set.

enchère [ɑ̃ʃɛr] *nf* bid ; **vendre qqch aux ~s** to sell sthg at ou by auction.

enchevêtrer [4] [ɑ̃ʃəvetre] *vt* [emmêler] to tangle up ; *fig* to muddle, to confuse.

enclave [ɑ̃klav] *nf* enclave.

enclencher [3] [ɑ̃klɑ̃ʃe] *vt* [mécanisme] to engage. **s'enclencher** *vp* - **1.** TECHNOL to engage - **2.** *fig* [commencer] to begin.

enclin, e [ɑ̃klɛ̃, in] *adj* : ~ **à qqch/à faire qqch** inclined to sthg/to do sthg.

enclore [113] [ɑ̃klɔr] *vt* to fence in, to enclose.

enclos, e [ɑ̃klo, oz] *pp* ▷ enclore. **enclos** *nm* enclosure.

enclume [ɑ̃klym] *nf* anvil.

encoche [ɑ̃kɔʃ] *nf* notch.

encoignure [ɑ̃kwaɲyr, ɑ̃kɔɲyr] *nf* [coin] corner.

encolure [ɑ̃kɔlyr] *nf* neck.

encombrant, e [ɑ̃kɔ̃brɑ̃, ɑ̃t] *adj* cumbersome ; *fig* [personne] undesirable.

encombre [ɑ̃kɔ̃br] **sans encombre** *loc adv* without a hitch.

encombré, e [ɑ̃kɔ̃bre] *adj* [lieu] busy, congested ; *fig* saturated.

encombrement [ɑ̃kɔ̃brəmɑ̃] *nm* - **1.** [d'une pièce] clutter - **2.** [d'un objet] overall dimensions *(pl)* - **3.** [embouteillage] traffic jam - **4.** INFORM footprint.

encombrer [3] [ɑ̃kɔ̃bre] *vt* to clutter (up).

encontre [ɑ̃kɔ̃tr] **à l'encontre de** *loc prép* : **aller à l'~ de** to go against, to oppose.

encore [ɑ̃kɔr] *adv* - **1.** [toujours] still ; ~ **un mois** one more month ; **pas ~** not yet ; **elle ne travaille pas ~** she's not working yet - **2.** [de nouveau] again ; **il m'a ~ menti** he's lied to me again ; **quoi ~?** what now? ; **l'ascenseur est en panne - ~!** the lift's out of order - not again! ; ~ **de la glace?** some more ice cream? ; ~ **une fois** once more, once again - **3.** [marque le renforcement] even ; ~ **mieux/pire** even better/worse. **et encore** *loc adv* : **j'ai eu le temps de**

prendre un sandwich, et ~! I had time for a sandwich, but only just!. ~ **si encore** *loc adv* if only. ~ **encore que** *loc conj* (+ *subjonctif*) although.

encouragement [ɑ̃kuraʒmɑ̃] *nm* [parole] (word of) encouragement.

encourager [17] [ɑ̃kuraʒe] *vt* to encourage ; ~ **qqn à faire qqch** to encourage sb to do sthg.

encourir [45] [ɑ̃kurir] *vt sout* to incur.

encouru, e [ɑ̃kury] *pp* ▷ encourir.

encrasser [3] [ɑ̃krase] *vt* - **1.** TECHNOL to clog up - **2.** *fam* [salir] to make dirty ou filthy. **s'encrasser** *vp* - **1.** TECHNOL to clog up - **2.** *fam* [se salir] to get dirty ou filthy.

encre [ɑ̃kr] *nf* ink.

encrer [3] [ɑ̃kre] *vt* to ink.

encrier [ɑ̃krije] *nm* inkwell.

encroûter [3] [ɑ̃krute] **s'encroûter** *vp fam* to get into a rut ; **s'~ dans ses habitudes** to become set in one's ways.

encyclopédie [ɑ̃siklɔpedi] *nf* encyclopedia.

encyclopédique [ɑ̃siklɔpedik] *adj* encyclopedic.

endémique [ɑ̃demik] *adj* endemic.

endetter [4] [ɑ̃dete] **s'endetter** *vp* to get into debt.

endeuiller [5] [ɑ̃dœje] *vt* to plunge into mourning.

endiablé, e [ɑ̃djable] *adj* [frénétique] frantic, frenzied.

endiguer [3] [ɑ̃dige] *vt* - **1.** [fleuve] to dam - **2.** *fig* [réprimer] to stem.

endimanché, e [ɑ̃dimɑ̃ʃe] *adj* in one's Sunday best.

endive [ɑ̃div] *nf* chicory (U).

endoctriner [3] [ɑ̃dɔktrine] *vt* to indoctrinate.

endommager [17] [ɑ̃dɔmaʒe] *vt* to damage.

endormi, e [ɑ̃dɔrmi] *adj* - **1.** [personne] sleeping, asleep - **2.** *fig* [village] sleepy ; [jambe] numb ; [passion] dormant ; *fam* [apathique] sluggish.

endormir [36] [ɑ̃dɔrmir] *vt* - **1.** [assoupir, ennuyer] to send to sleep - **2.** [anesthésier - patient] to anaesthetize *Br*, anesthetize *Am* ; [- douleur] to ease - **3.** *fig* [tromper] to allay. **s'endormir** *vp* [s'assoupir] to fall asleep.

endosser [3] [ɑ̃dose] *vt* - **1.** [vêtement] to put on - **2.** FIN & JUR to endorse ; ~ **un chèque** to endorse a cheque *Br* ou check *Am* - **3.** *fig* [responsabilité] to take on.

endroit [ɑ̃drwa] *nm* - **1.** [lieu, point] place ;

à quel ~? where? **- 2.** [passage] part **- 3.** [côté] right side ; **à l'~** the right way round.

enduire [98] [ɑ̃dɥir] *vt* : **~ qqch (de)** to coat sthg (with).

enduit, e [ɑ̃dɥi, it] *pp* ▷ **enduire**. ◆ **enduit** *nm* coating.

endurance [ɑ̃dyrɑ̃s] *nf* endurance.

endurcir [32] [ɑ̃dyrsir] *vt* to harden. ◆ **s'endurcir** *vp* : **s'~ à** to become hardened to.

endurer [3] [ɑ̃dyre] *vt* to endure.

énergétique [enɛrʒetik] *adj* **- 1.** [ressource] energy *(avant n)* **- 2.** [aliment] energy-giving.

énergie [enɛrʒi] *nf* energy ; **~ renouvelable** renewable energy.

énergique [enɛrʒik] *adj* [gén] energetic ; [remède] powerful ; [mesure] drastic.

énergumène [enɛrɡymɛn] *nmf* rowdy character.

énerver [3] [enɛrve] *vt* to irritate, to annoy. ◆ **s'énerver** *vp* [être irrité] to get annoyed ; [être excité] to get worked up ou excited.

enfance [ɑ̃fɑ̃s] *nf* **- 1.** [âge] childhood **- 2.** [enfants] children *(pl)* **- 3.** *fig* [débuts] infancy ; [de civilisation, de l'humanité] dawn.

enfant [ɑ̃fɑ̃] *nmf* [gén] child ; **attendre un ~** to be expecting a baby. ◆ **bon enfant** *loc adj* good-natured.

enfanter [3] [ɑ̃fɑ̃te] *vt littéraire* to give birth to.

enfantillage [ɑ̃fɑ̃tijaʒ] *nm* childishness *(U)*.

enfantin, e [ɑ̃fɑ̃tɛ̃, in] *adj* **- 1.** [propre à l'enfance] childlike ; *péj* childish ; [jeu, chanson] children's *(avant n)* **- 2.** [facile] childishly simple.

enfer [ɑ̃fɛr] *nm* RELIG & *fig* hell. ◆ **Enfers** *nmpl* : **les Enfers** the Underworld *(sg)*.

enfermer [3] [ɑ̃fɛrme] *vt* [séquestrer, ranger] to shut away. ◆ **s'enfermer** *vp* to shut o.s. away ou up ; **s'~ dans** *fig* to retreat into.

enfilade [ɑ̃filad] *nf* row.

enfiler [3] [ɑ̃file] *vt* **- 1.** [aiguille, sur un fil] to thread **- 2.** [vêtements] to slip on.

enfin [ɑ̃fɛ̃] *adv* **- 1.** [en dernier lieu] finally, at last ; [dans une liste] lastly **- 2.** [avant une récapitulation] in a word, in short **- 3.** [introduit une rectification] that is, well **- 4.** [introduit une concession] anyway.

enflammer [3] [ɑ̃flame] *vt* **- 1.** [bois] to set fire to **- 2.** *fig* [exalter] to inflame. ◆ **s'enflammer** *vp* **- 1.** [bois] to catch fire **- 2.** *fig* [s'exalter] to flare up.

enflé, e [ɑ̃fle] *adj* [style] turgid.

enfler [3] [ɑ̃fle] *vi* to swell (up).

enfoncer [16] [ɑ̃fɔ̃se] *vt* **- 1.** [faire pénétrer] to drive in ; **~ qqch dans qqch** to drive sthg into sthg **- 2.** [enfouir] : **~ ses mains dans ses poches** to thrust one's hands into one's pockets **- 3.** [défoncer] to break down. ◆ **s'enfoncer** *vp* **- 1.** : **s'~ dans** [eau, boue] to sink into ; [bois, ville] to disappear into **- 2.** [céder] to give way.

enfouir [32] [ɑ̃fwir] *vt* **- 1.** [cacher] to hide **- 2.** [ensevelir] to bury.

enfourcher [3] [ɑ̃furʃe] *vt* to get on, to mount.

enfourner [3] [ɑ̃furne] *vt* **- 1.** [pain] to put in the oven **- 2.** *fam* [avaler] to gobble up.

enfreindre [81] [ɑ̃frɛ̃dr] *vt* to infringe.

enfreint, e [ɑ̃frɛ̃, ɛ̃t] *pp* ▷ **enfreindre**.

enfuir [35] [ɑ̃fɥir] ◆ **s'enfuir** *vp* [fuir] to run away.

enfumer [3] [ɑ̃fyme] *vt* to fill with smoke.

engagé, e [ɑ̃gaʒe] *adj* committed.

engageant, e [ɑ̃gaʒɑ̃, ɑ̃t] *adj* engaging.

engagement [ɑ̃gaʒmɑ̃] *nm* **- 1.** [promesse] commitment **- 2.** JUR contract **- 3.** [MIL - de soldats] enlistment ; [- combat] engagement **- 4.** FOOTBALL & RUGBY kick-off.

engager [17] [ɑ̃gaʒe] *vt* **- 1.** [lier] to commit **- 2.** [embaucher] to take on, to engage **- 3.** [faire entrer] : **~ qqch dans** to insert sthg into **- 4.** [commencer] to start **- 5.** [impliquer] to involve **- 6.** [encourager] : **~ qqn à faire qqch** to urge sb to do sthg. ◆ **s'engager** *vp* **- 1.** [promettre] : **s'~ à qqch/à faire qqch** to commit o.s. to sthg/to doing sthg **- 2.** MIL : **s'~ (dans)** to enlist (in) **- 3.** [pénétrer] : **s'~ dans** to enter.

engelure [ɑ̃ʒlyr] *nf* chilblain.

engendrer [3] [ɑ̃ʒɑ̃dre] *vt* **- 1.** *littéraire* to father **- 2.** *fig* [produire] to cause, to give rise to ; [sentiment] to engender.

engin [ɑ̃ʒɛ̃] *nm* **- 1.** [machine] machine **- 2.** MIL missile **- 3.** *fam péj* [objet] thing.

englober [3] [ɑ̃glɔbe] *vt* to include.

engloutir [32] [ɑ̃glutir] *vt* **- 1.** [dévorer] to gobble up **- 2.** [faire disparaître] to engulf **- 3.** *fig* [dilapider] to squander.

engorger [17] [ɑ̃gɔrʒe] *vt* **- 1.** [obstruer] to block, to obstruct **- 2.** MÉD to engorge. ◆ **s'engorger** *vp* to become blocked.

engouement [ɑ̃gumɑ̃] *nm* [enthousiasme] infatuation.

engouffrer [3] [ɑ̃gufre] *vt fam* [dévorer] to wolf down. ◆ **s'engouffrer** *vp* : **s'~ dans** to rush into.

engourdi, e [ɑ̃gurdi] *adj* numb ; *fig* dull.

engourdir [32] [ãgurdir] *vt* to numb ; *fig* to dull. ➦ **s'engourdir** *vp* to go numb.

engrais [ãgrɛ] *nm* fertilizer.

engraisser [4] [ãgrese] ⬦ *vt* - **1.** [animal] to fatten - **2.** [terre] to fertilize. ⬦ *vi* to put on weight.

engrenage [ãgrənaʒ] *nm* - **1.** TECHNOL gears *(pl)* - **2.** *fig* [circonstances] : **être pris dans l'~** to be caught up in the system.

engueulade [ãgœlad] *nf fam* bawling out.

engueuler [5] [ãgœle] *vt fam* : **~ qqn** to bawl sb out. ➦ **s'engueuler** *vp fam* to have a row, to have a slanging match *Br*.

enhardir [32] [ãardir] *vt* to make bold. ➦ **s'enhardir** *vp* to pluck up one's courage.

énième [enjɛm] *adj fam* : **la ~ fois** the nth time.

énigmatique [enigmatik] *adj* enigmatic.

énigme [enigm] *nf* - **1.** [mystère] enigma - **2.** [jeu] riddle.

enivrant, e [ãnivrã, ãt] *adj litt & fig* intoxicating.

enivrer [3] [ãnivre] *vt litt* to get drunk ; *fig* to intoxicate. ➦ **s'enivrer** *vp* : **s'~ (de)** to get drunk (on) ; *fig* to become intoxicated (with).

enjambée [ãʒãbe] *nf* stride.

enjamber [3] [ãʒãbe] *vt* - **1.** [obstacle] to step over - **2.** [cours d'eau] to straddle

enjeu, x [ãʒø] *nm* [mise] stake ; **quel est l'~ ici?** *fig* what's at stake here?

enjoindre [82] [ãʒwɛ̃dr] *vt littéraire* : **~ à qqn de faire qqch** to enjoin sb to do sthg.

enjoint [ãʒwɛ̃] *pp inv* ➢ **enjoindre**.

enjôler [3] [ãʒole] *vt* to coax.

enjoliver [3] [ãʒolive] *vt* to embellish.

enjoliveur [ãʒolivœr] *nm* [de roue] hubcap ; [de calandre] badge.

enjoué, e [ãʒwe] *adj* cheerful.

enlacer [16] [ãlase] *vt* [prendre dans ses bras] to embrace, to hug. ➦ **s'enlacer** *vp* [s'embrasser] to embrace, to hug.

enlaidir [32] [ãledir] ⬦ *vt* to make ugly ⬦ *vi* to become ugly.

enlèvement [ãlɛvmã] *nm* - **1.** [action d'enlever] removal - **2.** [rapt] abduction.

enlever [19] [ãlve] *vt* - **1.** [gén] to remove ; [vêtement] to take off - **2.** [prendre] : **~ qqch à qqn** to take sthg away from sb - **3.** [kidnapper] to abduct.

enliser [3] [ãlize] ➦ **s'enliser** *vp* - **1.** [s'embourber] to sink, to get stuck - **2.** *fig* [piétiner] : **s'~ dans qqch** to get bogged down in sthg.

enluminure [ãlyminyr] *nf* illumination.

enneigé, e [ãneʒe] *adj* snow-covered.

ennemi, e [ɛnmi] ⬦ *adj* enemy *(avant n)*. ⬦ *nm, f* enemy.

ennui [ãnɥi] *nm* - **1.** [lassitude] boredom - **2.** [contrariété] annoyance ; **l'~, c'est que ...** the annoying thing is that ... - **3.** [problème] trouble *(U)* ; **avoir des ~s** to have problems.

ennuyer [14] [ãnɥije] *vt* - **1.** [agacer, contrarier] to annoy ; **cela t'ennuierait de venir me chercher?** would you mind picking me up? - **2.** [lasser] to bore - **3.** [inquiéter] to bother. ➦ **s'ennuyer** *vp* - **1.** [se morfondre] to be bored - **2.** [déplorer l'absence] : **s'~ de qqn/qqch** to miss sb/sthg.

ennuyeux, euse [ãnɥijø, øz] *adj* - **1.** [lassant] boring - **2.** [contrariant] annoying.

énoncé [enɔ̃se] *nm* [libellé] wording.

énoncer [16] [enɔ̃se] *vt* - **1.** [libeller] to word - **2.** [exposer] to expound ; [théorème] to set forth.

énorme [enɔrm] *adj* - **1.** *litt & fig* [immense] enormous - **2.** *fam fig* [incroyable] far-fetched.

énormément [enɔrmemã] *adv* enormously ; **~ de** a great deal of.

enquête [ãkɛt] *nf* - **1.** [de police, recherches] investigation - **2.** [sondage] survey.

enquêter [4] [ãkete] *vi* - **1.** [police, chercheur] to investigate - **2.** [sonder] to conduct a survey.

enragé, e [ãraʒe] *adj* - **1.** [chien] rabid, with rabies - **2.** *fig* [invétéré] keen.

enrager [17] [ãraʒe] *vi* to be furious ; **faire ~ qqn** to infuriate sb.

enrayer [11] [ãreje] *vt* - **1.** [épidémie] to check, to stop - **2.** [mécanisme] to jam. ➦ **s'enrayer** *vp* [mécanisme] to jam.

enregistrement [ãrəʒistrəmã] *nm* - **1.** [de son, d'images, d'informations] recording - **2.** [inscription] registration - **3.** [à l'aéroport] check-in ; **~ des bagages** baggage registration.

enregistrer [3] [ãrəʒistre] *vt* - **1.** [son, images, informations] to record - **2.** INFORM to store - **3.** [inscrire] to register - **4.** [à l'aéroport] to check in - **5.** *fam* [mémoriser] to make a mental note of.

enrhumé, e [ãryme] *adj* : **je suis ~** I have a cold.

enrhumer [3] [ãryme] ➦ **s'enrhumer** *vp* to catch (a) cold.

enrichir [32] [ãriʃir] *vt* - **1.** [financièrement] to make rich - **2.** [terre] *fig* to enrich. ➦ **s'enrichir** *vp* - **1.** [financièrement] to grow rich - **2.** [sol] *fig* to become enriched.

enrobé, e [ɑ̃ʀɔbe] *adj* **- 1.** [recouvert] : **~ de** coated with **- 2.** *fam* [grassouillet] plump.

enrober [3] [ɑ̃ʀɔbe] *vt* [recouvrir] : **~ qqch de** to coat sthg with. ➡ **s'enrober** *vp* to put on weight.

enrôler [3] [ɑ̃ʀole] *vt* to enrol *Br*, to enroll *Am* ; MIL to enlist. ➡ **s'enrôler** *vp* to enrol *Br*, to enroll *Am* ; MIL to enlist.

enroué, e [ɑ̃ʀwe] *adj* hoarse.

enrouler [3] [ɑ̃ʀule] *vt* to roll up ; **~ qqch autour de qqch** to wind sthg round sthg. ➡ **s'enrouler** *vp* **- 1.** [entourer] : **s'~ sur** OU **autour de qqch** to wind around sthg **- 2.** [se pelotonner] : **s'~ dans qqch** to wrap o.s. up in sthg.

ensabler [3] [ɑ̃sable] *vt* to silt up. ➡ **s'ensabler** *vp* to silt up.

enseignant, e [ɑ̃sɛɲɑ̃, ɑ̃t] ◇ *adj* teaching *(avant n)*. ◇ *nm, f* teacher.

enseigne [ɑ̃sɛɲ] *nf* **- 1.** [de commerce] sign **- 2.** [drapeau, soldat] ensign.

enseignement [ɑ̃sɛɲmɑ̃] *nm* **- 1.** [gén] teaching ; **~ primaire/secondaire** primary/secondary education **- 2.** [leçon] lesson.

enseigner [4] [ɑ̃sɛɲe] *vt litt & fig* to teach ; **~ qqch à qqn** to teach sb sthg, to teach sthg to sb.

ensemble [ɑ̃sɑ̃bl] ◇ *adv* together ; **aller ~** to go together. ◇ *nm* **- 1.** [totalité] whole ; **idée d'~** general idea ; **dans l'~** on the whole **- 2.** [harmonie] unity **- 3.** [vêtement] outfit **- 4.** [série] collection **- 5.** MATHS set **- 6.** MUS ensemble.

ensemencer [16] [ɑ̃səmɑ̃se] *vt* **- 1.** [terre] to sow **- 2.** [rivière] to stock.

enserrer [4] [ɑ̃sere] *vt* [entourer] to encircle ; *fig* to imprison.

ensevelir [32] [ɑ̃səvliʀ] *vt litt & fig* to bury.

ensoleillé, e [ɑ̃sɔleje] *adj* sunny.

ensoleillement [ɑ̃sɔlejmɑ̃] *nm* sunshine.

ensommeillé, e [ɑ̃sɔmeje] *adj* sleepy.

ensorceler [24] [ɑ̃sɔʀsəle] *vt* to bewitch.

ensuite [ɑ̃sɥit] *adv* **- 1.** [après, plus tard] after, afterwards, later **- 2.** [puis] then, next, after that ; **et ~?** what then?, what next?

ensuivre [89] [ɑ̃sɥivʀ] ➡ **s'ensuivre** *vp* to follow ; **il s'ensuit que** it follows that.

entaille [ɑ̃taj] *nf* cut.

entailler [3] [ɑ̃taje] *vt* to cut.

entamer [3] [ɑ̃tame] *vt* **- 1.** [gâteau, fromage] to start (on) ; [bouteille, conserve] to start, to open **- 2.** [capital] to dip into **- 3.** [cuir, réputation] to damage **- 4.** [courage] to shake.

entartrer [3] [ɑ̃taʀtʀe] *vt* to fur up. ➡ **s'entartrer** *vp* to fur up.

entasser [3] [ɑ̃tase] *vt* **- 1.** [accumuler, mul-tiplier] to pile up **- 2.** [serrer] to squeeze. ➡ **s'entasser** *vp* **- 1.** [objets] to pile up **- 2.** [personnes] : **s'~ dans** to squeeze into.

entendement [ɑ̃tɑ̃dmɑ̃] *nm* understanding.

entendre [73] [ɑ̃tɑ̃dʀ] *vt* **- 1.** [percevoir, écouter] to hear ; **~ parler de qqch** to hear of OU about sthg **- 2.** *sout* [comprendre] to understand ; **laisser ~ que** to imply that **- 3.** *sout* [vouloir] : **~ faire qqch** to intend to do sthg **- 4.** [vouloir dire] to mean. ➡ **s'entendre** *vp* **- 1.** [sympathiser] : **s'~ avec qqn** to get on with sb **- 2.** [s'accorder] to agree.

entendu, e [ɑ̃tɑ̃dy] ◇ *pp* ➡ entendre. ◇ *adj* **- 1.** [compris] agreed, understood **- 2.** [complice] knowing.

entente [ɑ̃tɑ̃t] *nf* **- 1.** [harmonie] understanding **- 2.** [accord] agreement.

entériner [3] [ɑ̃teʀine] *vt* to ratify.

enterrement [ɑ̃tɛʀmɑ̃] *nm* burial.

enterrer [4] [ɑ̃tere] *vt litt & fig* to bury ; **~ sa vie de garçon** to have a stag party.

en-tête [ɑ̃tɛt] *(pl* **en-têtes)** *nm* heading.

entêté, e [ɑ̃tete] *adj* stubborn.

entêter [4] [ɑ̃tete] ➡ **s'entêter** *vp* to persist ; **s'~ à faire qqch** to persist in doing sthg.

enthousiasme [ɑ̃tuzjasm] *nm* enthusiasm.

enthousiasmer [3] [ɑ̃tuzjasme] *vt* to fill with enthusiasm. ➡ **s'enthousiasmer** *vp* : **s'~ pour** to be enthusiastic about.

enticher [3] [ɑ̃tiʃe] ➡ **s'enticher** *vp* : **s'~ de qqn/qqch** to become obsessed with sb/sthg.

entier, ère [ɑ̃tje, ɛʀ] *adj* whole, entire. ➡ **en entier** *loc adv* in its/their entirety.

entièrement [ɑ̃tjɛʀmɑ̃] *adv* **- 1.** [complètement] fully **- 2.** [pleinement] wholly, entirely.

entité [ɑ̃tite] *nf* entity.

entonner [3] [ɑ̃tɔne] *vt* [chant] to strike up.

entonnoir [ɑ̃tɔnwaʀ] *nm* **- 1.** [instrument] funnel **- 2.** [cavité] crater.

entorse [ɑ̃tɔʀs] *nf* MÉD sprain ; **se faire une ~ à la cheville/au poignet** to sprain one's ankle/wrist.

entortiller [3] [ɑ̃tɔʀtije] *vt* **- 1.** [entrelacer] to twist **- 2.** [envelopper] : **~ qqch autour de qqch** to wrap sthg round sthg **- 3.** *fam fig* [personne] to sweet-talk.

entourage [ɑ̃tuʀaʒ] *nm* [milieu] entourage.

entourer [3] [ɑ̃tuʀe] *vt* **- 1.** [enclore, encercler] : ~ **(de)** to surround (with) - **2.** *fig* [soutenir] to rally round.

entourloupette [ɑ̃turlupɛt] *nf fam* dirty trick.

entournure [ɑ̃turnyr] *nf* : **être gêné aux ~s** *fig* [financièrement] to feel the pinch ; [être mal à l'aise] to feel awkward.

entracte [ɑ̃trakt] *nm* interval ; *fig* interlude.

entraide [ɑ̃trɛd] *nf* mutual assistance.

entrailles [ɑ̃traj] *nfpl* - **1.** [intestins] entrails - **2.** *sout* [profondeurs] depths.

entrain [ɑ̃trɛ̃] *nm* drive.

entraînement [ɑ̃trɛnmɑ̃] *nm* [préparation] practice ; SPORT training.

entraîner [4] [ɑ̃trene] *vt* - **1.** TECHNOL to drive - **2.** [tirer] to pull - **3.** [susciter] to lead to - **4.** SPORT to coach - **5.** [emmener] to take along - **6.** [séduire] to influence ; ~ **qqn à faire qqch** to talk sb into sthg. ◆ **s'entraîner** *vp* to practise ; SPORT to train ; **s'~ à faire qqch** to practise doing sthg.

entraîneur, euse [ɑ̃trenœr, øz] *nm, f* trainer, coach.

entrave [ɑ̃trav] *nf* hobble ; *fig* obstruction.

entraver [3] [ɑ̃trave] *vt* to hobble ; *fig* to hinder.

entre [ɑ̃tr] *prép* - **1.** [gén] between ; ~ **nous** between you and me, between ourselves - **2.** [parmi] among ; **l'un d'~ nous ira** one of us will go ; **généralement ils restent ~ eux** they tend to keep themselves to themselves ; **ils se battent ~ eux** they're fighting among ou amongst themselves. ◆ **entre autres** *loc prép* : **~ autres (choses)** among other things.

entrebâiller [3] [ɑ̃trəbaje] *vt* to open slightly.

entrechoquer [3] [ɑ̃trəʃɔke] *vt* to bang together. ◆ **s'entrechoquer** *vp* to bang into each other.

entrecôte [ɑ̃trəkot] *nf* entrecôte.

entrecouper [3] [ɑ̃trəkupe] *vt* to intersperse.

entrecroiser [3] [ɑ̃trəkrwaze] *vt* to interlace. ◆ **s'entrecroiser** *vp* to intersect.

entrée [ɑ̃tre] *nf* - **1.** [arrivée, accès] entry, entrance ; **'~ interdite'** 'no admittance' ; **'~ libre'** [dans un musée] 'admission free' ; [dans une boutique] 'browsers welcome' - **2.** [porte] entrance - **3.** [vestibule] (entrance) hall - **4.** [billet] ticket - **5.** [plat] starter, first course.

entrefaites [ɑ̃trəfɛt] *nfpl* : **sur ces ~** just at that moment.

entrefilet [ɑ̃trəfilɛ] *nm* paragraph.

entrejambe, entre-jambes [ɑ̃trəʒɑ̃b] *nm* crotch.

entrelacer [16] [ɑ̃trəlase] *vt* to intertwine.

entrelarder [3] [ɑ̃trəlarde] *vt* - **1.** CULIN to lard - **2.** *fam fig* [discours] : ~ **de** to lace with.

entremêler [4] [ɑ̃trəmele] *vt* to mix ; ~ **de** to mix with.

entremets [ɑ̃trəmɛ] *nm* dessert.

entremettre [84] [ɑ̃trəmɛtr] ◆ **s'entremettre** *vp* : **s'~ (dans)** to mediate (in).

entremise [ɑ̃trəmiz] *nf* intervention ; **par l'~ de** through.

entrepont [ɑ̃trəpɔ̃] *nm* steerage.

entreposer [3] [ɑ̃trəpoze] *vt* to store.

entrepôt [ɑ̃trəpo] *nm* warehouse.

entreprendre [79] [ɑ̃trəprɑ̃dr] *vt* to undertake ; [commencer] to start ; ~ **de faire qqch** to undertake to do sthg.

entrepreneur, euse [ɑ̃trəprənœr, øz] *nm, f* [de services & CONSTR] contractor.

entrepris, e [ɑ̃trəpri, iz] *pp* ▷ **entreprendre**.

entreprise [ɑ̃trəpriz] *nf* - **1.** [travail, initiative] enterprise - **2.** [société] company.

entrer [3] [ɑ̃tre] ◇ *vi (aux : être)* - **1.** [pénétrer] to enter, to go in, to come in ; ~ **dans** [gén] to enter ; [pièce] to go/come into ; [bain, voiture] to get into ; *fig* [sujet] to go into ; ~ **par** to go in ou enter by ; **faire ~ qqn** to show sb in ; **faire ~ qqch** to bring sthg in - **2.** [faire partie] : ~ **dans** to go into, to be part of - **3.** [être admis, devenir membre] : ~ **à** [club, parti] to join ; ~ **dans** [les affaires, l'enseignement] to go into ; [la police, l'armée] to join ; ~ **à l'université** to enter university ; ~ **à l'hôpital** to go into hospital. ◇ *vt (aux : avoir)* - **1.** [gén] to bring in - **2.** INFORM to enter, to input.

entresol [ɑ̃trəsɔl] *nm* mezzanine.

entre-temps [ɑ̃trətɑ̃] *adv* meanwhile.

entretenir [40] [ɑ̃trətnir] *vt* - **1.** [faire durer] to keep alive - **2.** [cultiver] to maintain - **3.** [soigner] to look after - **4.** [personne, famille] to support - **5.** [parler à] : ~ **qqn de qqch** to speak to sb about sthg. ◆ **s'entretenir** *vp* [se parler] : **s'~ (de)** to talk (about).

entretien [ɑ̃trətjɛ̃] *nm* - **1.** [de voiture, jardin] maintenance, upkeep - **2.** [conversation] discussion ; [colloque] debate.

entre-tuer [7] [ɑ̃trətɥe] ◆ **s'entre-tuer** *vp* to kill each other.

entrevoir [62] [ɑ̃trəvwar] *vt* - **1.** [distinguer] to make out - **2.** [voir rapidement] to see briefly - **3.** *fig* [deviner] to glimpse.

entrevu, e [ɑ̃trəvy] *pp* ▷ **entrevoir**.

entrevue [ɑ̃trəvy] *nf* meeting.

entrouvert, e [ɑ̃truvɛr, ɛrt] ◇ *pp* ▷ entrouvrir. ◇ *adj* half-open.

entrouvrir [34] [ɑ̃truvrir] *vt* to open partly. ◆ **s'entrouvrir** *vp* to open partly.

énumération [enymerasjɔ̃] *nf* enumeration.

énumérer [18] [enymere] *vt* to enumerate.

env. (*abr de* **environ**) approx.

envahir [32] [ɑ̃vair] *vt* - **1.** [gén & MIL] to invade - **2.** *fig* [suj : sommeil, doute] to overcome - **3.** *fig* [déranger] to intrude on.

envahissant, e [ɑ̃vaisɑ̃, ɑ̃t] *adj* - **1.** [herbes] invasive - **2.** [personne] intrusive.

envahisseur [ɑ̃vaisœr] *nm* invader.

enveloppe [ɑ̃vlɔp] *nf* - **1.** [de lettre] envelope - **2.** [d'emballage] covering - **3.** [membrane] membrane ; [de graine] husk.

envelopper [3] [ɑ̃vlɔpe] *vt* - **1.** [emballer] to wrap (up) - **2.** [suj : brouillard] to envelop - **3.** [déguiser] to mask. ◆ **s'envelopper** *vp* : **s'~ dans** to wrap o.s. up in.

envenimer [3] [ɑ̃vnime] *vt* - **1.** [blessure] to infect - **2.** *fig* [querelle] to poison. ◆ **s'envenimer** *vp* - **1.** [s'infecter] to become infected - **2.** *fig* [se détériorer] to become poisoned.

envergure [ɑ̃vergyr] *nf* - **1.** [largeur] span ; [d'oiseau, d'avion] wingspan - **2.** *fig* [qualité] calibre - **3.** *fig* [importance] scope ; **prendre de l'~** to expand.

envers[1] [ɑ̃vɛr] *prép* towards *Br*, toward *Am*.

envers[2] [ɑ̃vɛr] *nm* - **1.** [de tissu] wrong side ; [de feuillet etc] back ; [de médaille] reverse - **2.** [face cachée] other side. ◆ **à l'envers** *loc adv* [vêtement] inside out ; [portrait, feuille] upside down ; *fig* the wrong way.

envi [ɑ̃vi] ◆ **à l'envi** *loc adv littéraire* trying to outdo each other.

envie [ɑ̃vi] *nf* - **1.** [désir] desire ; **avoir ~ de qqch/de faire qqch** to feel like sthg/like doing sthg, to want sthg/to do sthg - **2.** [convoitise] envy ; **ce tailleur me fait ~** I'd love to buy that suit.

envier [9] [ɑ̃vje] *vt* to envy.

envieux, euse [ɑ̃vjø, øz] ◇ *adj* envious. ◇ *nm, f* envious person ; **faire des ~** to make other people envious.

environ [ɑ̃virɔ̃] *adv* [à peu près] about.

environnement [ɑ̃virɔnmɑ̃] *nm* environment.

environnemental, e, aux [ɑ̃virɔnmɑ̃tal, o] *adj* environmental.

environs [ɑ̃virɔ̃] *nmpl* (surrounding) area

(*sg*) ; **aux ~ de** [lieu] near ; [époque] round about, around.

envisager [17] [ɑ̃vizaʒe] *vt* to consider ; **~ de faire qqch** to be considering doing sthg.

envoi [ɑ̃vwa] *nm* - **1.** [action] sending, dispatch - **2.** [colis] parcel.

envol [ɑ̃vɔl] *nm* takeoff.

envolée [ɑ̃vɔle] *nf* - **1.** [d'oiseaux] *fig* flight - **2.** [augmentation] : **l'~ du dollar** the rapid rise in the value of the dollar.

envoler [3] [ɑ̃vɔle] ◆ **s'envoler** *vp* - **1.** [oiseau] to fly away - **2.** [avion] to take off - **3.** [disparaître] to disappear into thin air.

envoûter [3] [ɑ̃vute] *vt* to bewitch.

envoyé, e [ɑ̃vwaje] ◇ *adj* : **bien ~** well-aimed. ◇ *nm, f* envoy.

envoyer [30] [ɑ̃vwaje] *vt* to send ; **~ qqch à qqn** [expédier] to send sb sthg, to send sthg to sb ; [jeter] to throw sb sthg, to throw sthg to sb ; **~ qqn faire qqch** to send sb to do sthg ; **~ chercher qqn/qqch** to send for sb/sthg.

épagneul [epaɲœl] *nm* spaniel.

épais, aisse [epɛ, ɛs] *adj* - **1.** [large, dense] thick - **2.** [grossier] crude.

épaisseur [epɛsœr] *nf* - **1.** [largeur, densité] thickness - **2.** *fig* [consistance] depth.

épaissir [32] [epesir] *vt & vi* to thicken. ◆ **s'épaissir** *vp* - **1.** [liquide] to thicken - **2.** *fig* [mystère] to deepen.

épanchement [epɑ̃ʃmɑ̃] *nm* - **1.** [effusion] outpouring - **2.** MÉD effusion.

épancher [3] [epɑ̃ʃe] *vt* to pour out. ◆ **s'épancher** *vp* [se confier] to pour one's heart out.

épanoui, e [epanwi] *adj* - **1.** [fleur] in full bloom - **2.** [expression] radiant - **3.** [corps] fully formed ; **aux formes ~es** well-rounded.

épanouir [32] [epanwir] *vt* [personne] to make happy. ◆ **s'épanouir** *vp* - **1.** [fleur] to open - **2.** [visage] to light up - **3.** [corps] to fill out - **4.** [personnalité] to blossom.

épanouissement [epanwismɑ̃] *nm* - **1.** [de fleur] blooming, opening - **2.** [de visage] brightening - **3.** [de corps] filling out - **4.** [de personnalité] flowering.

épargnant, e [eparɲɑ̃, ɑ̃t] *nm, f* saver.

épargne [eparɲ] *nf* - **1.** [action, vertu] saving - **2.** [somme] savings (*pl*) ; **~ logement** savings account (*to buy property*).

épargner [3] [eparɲe] *vt* - **1.** [gén] to spare ; **~ qqch à qqn** to spare sb sthg - **2.** [économiser] to save.

éparpiller [3] [eparpije] *vt* - **1.** [choses,

personnes] to scatter - **2.** *fig* [forces] to dissipate. **s'éparpiller** *vp* - **1.** [se disperser] to scatter - **2.** *fig* [perdre son temps] to lack focus.

épars, e [epar, ars] *adj sout* [objets] scattered ; [végétation, cheveux] sparse.

épatant, e [epatã, ãt] *adj fam* great.

épaté, e [epate] *adj* - **1.** [nez] flat - **2.** *fam* [étonné] amazed.

épaule [epol] *nf* shoulder.

épauler [3] [epole] *vt* to support, to back up.

épaulette [epolɛt] *nf* - **1.** MIL epaulet - **2.** [rembourrage] shoulder pad.

épave [epav] *nf* wreck.

épée [epe] *nf* sword.

épeler [24] [eple] *vt* to spell.

éperdu, e [eperdy] *adj* [sentiment] passionate ; ~ **de** [personne] overcome with.

éperon [eprɔ̃] *nm* [de cavalier, de montagne] spur ; [de navire] ram.

éperonner [3] [eprɔne] *vt* to spur on.

épervier [epɛrvje] *nm* sparrowhawk.

éphèbe [elɛb] *nm hum* Adonis.

éphémère [efemɛr] <> *adj* [bref] ephemeral, fleeting. <> *nm* ZOOL mayfly.

éphéméride [efemerid] *nf* tear-off calendar.

épi [epi] *nm* - **1.** [de céréale] ear - **2.** [cheveux] tuft.

épice [epis] *nf* spice.

épicé, e [epise] *adj* spicy.

épicéa [episea] *nm* spruce.

épicer [16] [epise] *vt* [plat] to spice.

épicerie [episri] *nf* - **1.** [magasin] grocer's (shop) - **2.** [denrées] groceries *(pl)*.

épicier, ère [episje, ɛr] *nm, f* grocer.

épidémie [epidemi] *nf* epidemic.

épiderme [epidɛrm] *nm* epidermis.

épier [9] [epje] *vt* - **1.** [espionner] to spy on - **2.** [observer] to look for.

épilation [epilasjɔ̃] *nf* hair removal.

épilepsie [epilɛpsi] *nf* epilepsy.

épiler [3] [epile] *vt* [jambes] to remove hair from ; [sourcils] to pluck. **s'épiler** *vp* . **s'~ les jambes** to remove the hair from one's legs ; [à la cire] to wax one's legs ; **s'~ les sourcils** to pluck one's eyebrows.

épilogue [epilɔg] *nm* - **1.** [de roman] epilogue *Br*, epilog *Am* - **2.** [d'affaire] outcome.

épinards [epinar] *nmpl* spinach *(U)*.

épine [epin] *nf* [piquant - de rosier] thorn ; [- de hérisson] spine.

épineux, euse [epinø, øz] *adj* thorny.

épingle [epɛ̃gl] *nf* [instrument] pin.

épingler [3] [epɛ̃gle] *vt* - **1.** [fixer] to pin (up) - **2.** *fam fig* [arrêter] to nab, to nick *Br*.

épinière [epinjɛr] ▷ **moelle**.

Épiphanie [epifani] *nf* Epiphany.

épique [epik] *adj* epic.

épiscopal, e, aux [episkɔpal, o] *adj* episcopal.

épisode [epizɔd] *nm* episode.

épisodique [epizɔdik] *adj* - **1.** [occasionnel] occasional - **2.** [secondaire] minor.

épistolaire [epistɔlɛr] *adj* - **1.** [échange] of letters ; **être en relations ~s avec qqn** to be in (regular) correspondence with sb - **2.** [roman] epistolary.

épitaphe [epitaf] *nf* epitaph.

épithète [epitɛt] <> *nf* - **1.** GRAM attribute - **2.** [qualificatif] term. <> *adj* attributive.

épître [epitr] *nf* epistle.

éploré, e [eplɔre] *adj* [personne] in tears ; [visage, air] tearful.

épluche-légumes [eplyʃlegym] *nm inv* potato peeler.

éplucher [3] [eplyʃe] *vt* - **1.** [légumes] to peel - **2.** [textes] to dissect ; [comptes] to scrutinize.

épluchure [eplyʃyr] *nf* peelings *(pl)*.

éponge [epɔ̃ʒ] *nf* sponge.

éponger [17] [epɔ̃ʒe] *vt* - **1.** [liquide, déficit] to mop up - **2.** [visage] to mop, to wipe.

épopée [epɔpe] *nf* epic.

époque [epɔk] *nf* - **1.** [de l'année] time - **2.** [de l'histoire] period.

épouiller [3] [epuje] *vt* to delouse.

époumoner [3] [epumɔne] **s'époumoner** *vp* to shout o.s. hoarse.

épouse ▷ **époux**.

épouser [3] [epuze] *vt* - **1.** [personne] to marry - **2.** [forme] to hug - **3.** *fig* [idée, principe] to espouse.

épousseter [27] [epuste] *vt* to dust.

époustouflant, e [epustuflã, ãt] *adj fam* amazing.

épouvantable [epuvãtabl] *adj* dreadful.

épouvantail [epuvãtaj] *nm* [à moineaux] scarecrow ; *fig* bogeyman.

épouvanter [3] [epuvãte] *vt* to terrify.

époux, épouse [epu, epuz] *nm, f* spouse.

éprendre [79] [eprãdr] **s'éprendre** *vp sout* : **s'~ de** to fall in love with.

épreuve [eprœv] *nf* - **1.** [essai, examen] test ; **à l'~ du feu** fireproof ; **à l'~ des balles** bullet-proof ; **~ de force** *fig* trial of strength - **2.** [malheur] ordeal - **3.** SPORT event - **4.** TYPO proof - **5.** PHOT print.

épris, e [epri, iz] <> *pp* ▷ **éprendre**. <> *adj sout* : **~ de** in love with.

éprouver [3] [epʁuve] vt - **1.** [tester] to test - **2.** [ressentir] to feel - **3.** [faire souffrir] to distress ; **être éprouvé par** to be afflicted by - **4.** [difficultés, problèmes] to experience. nf PE.

éprouvette [epʁuvɛt] nf - **1.** [tube à essai] test tube - **2.** [échantillon] sample.

EPS (abr de **éducation physique et sportive**) nf PE.

épuisé, e [epɥize] adj - **1.** [personne, corps] exhausted - **2.** [marchandise] sold out, out of stock ; [livre] out of print.

épuisement [epɥizmɑ̃] nm exhaustion.

épuiser [3] [epɥize] vt to exhaust.

épuisette [epɥizɛt] nf landing net.

épurer [3] [epyʁe] vt - **1.** [eau, huile] to purify - **2.** POLIT to purge.

équarrir [32] [ekaʁiʁ] vt - **1.** [animal] to cut up - **2.** [poutre] to square - **3.** fig [personne] : **mal équarri** rough, crude.

équateur [ekwatœʁ] nm equator.

Équateur [ekwatœʁ] nm : **l'~** Ecuador.

équation [ekwasjɔ̃] nf equation.

équatorial, e, aux [ekwatɔʁjal, o] adj equatorial.

équerre [ekɛʁ] nf [instrument] set square ; [en T] T-square.

équestre [ekɛstʁ] adj equestrian.

équilatéral, e, aux [ekɥilateʁal, o] adj equilateral.

équilibre [ekilibʁ] nm - **1.** [gén] balance - **2.** [psychique] stability.

équilibré, e [ekilibʁe] adj - **1.** [personne] well-balanced - **2.** [vie] stable - **3.** ARCHIT : **aux proportions ~es** well-proportioned.

équilibrer [3] [ekilibʁe] vt to balance. ◆ **s'équilibrer** vp to balance each other out.

équilibriste [ekilibʁist] nmf tightrope walker.

équipage [ekipaʒ] nm crew.

équipe [ekip] nf team.

équipé, e [ekipe] adj : **cuisine ~e** fitted kitchen.

équipement [ekipmɑ̃] nm - **1.** [matériel] equipment - **2.** [aménagement] facilities (pl) ; **~s sportifs/scolaires** sports/educational facilities.

équiper [3] [ekipe] vt - **1.** [navire, armée] to equip - **2.** [personne, local] to equip, to fit out ; **~ qqn/qqch de** to equip sb/sthg with, to fit sb/sthg out with. ◆ **s'équiper** vp : **s'~ (de)** to equip o.s. (with).

équipier, ère [ekipje, ɛʁ] nm, f team member.

équitable [ekitabl] adj fair.

équitation [ekitasjɔ̃] nf riding, horse-riding.

équité [ekite] nf fairness.

équivalent, e [ekivalɑ̃, ɑ̃t] adj equivalent. ◆ **équivalent** nm equivalent.

équivaloir [60] [ekivalwaʁ] vi : **~ à** to be equivalent to.

équivoque [ekivɔk] ◇ adj - **1.** [ambigu] ambiguous - **2.** [mystérieux] dubious. ◇ nf ambiguity ; **sans ~** unequivocal (adj), unequivocally (adv).

érable [eʁabl] nm maple.

éradiquer [3] [eʁadike] vt to eradicate.

érafler [3] [eʁafle] vt - **1.** [peau] to scratch - **2.** [mur, voiture] to scrape.

éraflure [eʁaflyʁ] nf - **1.** [de peau] scratch - **2.** [de mur, voiture] scrape.

éraillé, e [eʁaje] adj [voix] hoarse.

ère [ɛʁ] nf era.

érection [eʁɛksjɔ̃] nf erection.

éreintant, e [eʁɛ̃tɑ̃, ɑ̃t] adj exhausting.

éreinter [3] [eʁɛ̃te] vt - **1.** [fatiguer] to exhaust - **2.** [critiquer] to pull to pieces.

ergonomique [ɛʁgɔnɔmik] adj ergonomic.

ériger [17] [eʁiʒe] vt - **1.** [monument] to erect - **2.** [tribunal] to set up - **3.** fig [transformer] : **~ qqn en** to set sb up as.

ermite [ɛʁmit] nm hermit.

éroder [3] [eʁɔde] vt to erode.

érogène [eʁɔʒɛn] adj erogenous.

érosion [eʁozjɔ̃] nf erosion.

érotique [eʁɔtik] adj erotic.

érotisme [eʁɔtism] nm eroticism.

errance [eʁɑ̃s] nf wandering.

erratum [eʁatɔm] (pl **errata** [eʁata]) nm erratum.

errer [4] [eʁe] vi to wander.

erreur [eʁœʁ] nf mistake ; **par ~** by mistake.

erroné, e [eʁɔne] adj sout wrong.

ersatz [ɛʁzats] nm inv ersatz.

éructer [3] [eʁykte] vi to belch.

érudit, e [eʁydi, it] ◇ adj erudite, learned. ◇ nm, f learned person.

éruption [eʁypsjɔ̃] nf - **1.** MÉD rash - **2.** [de volcan] eruption.

es ▷ **être**.

ès [ɛs] prép of (in certain titles) ; **docteur ~ lettres** ≃ PhD, doctor of philosophy.

escabeau, x [ɛskabo] nm - **1.** [échelle] stepladder - **2.** vieilli [tabouret] stool.

escadre [ɛskadʁ] nf - **1.** [navires] fleet - **2.** [avions] wing.

escadrille [ɛskadrij] nf - **1.** [navires] flotilla - **2.** [avions] flight.

escadron [ɛskadrɔ̃] nm squadron.

escalade [ɛskalad] nf - **1.** [de montagne, grille] climbing - **2.** [des prix, de violence] escalation.

escalader [3] [ɛskalade] vt to climb.

escale [ɛskal] nf- **1.** [lieu - pour navire] port of call ; [- pour avion] stopover - **2.** [arrêt - de navire] call ; [- d'avion] stopover, stop ; **faire ~ à** [navire] to put in at, to call at ; [avion] to stop over at.

escalier [ɛskalje] nm stairs (pl) ; **descendre/monter l'~** to go downstairs/upstairs ; **~ roulant** ou **mécanique** escalator.

escalope [ɛskalɔp] nf escalope.

escamotable [ɛskamɔtabl] adj - **1.** [train d'atterrissage] retractable ; [antenne] telescopic - **2.** [table] folding.

escamoter [3] [ɛskamɔte] vt - **1.** [faire disparaître] to make disappear - **2.** [voler] to lift - **3.** [rentrer] to retract - **4.** [phrase, mot] to swallow - **5.** [éluder - question] to evade ; [- objection] to get round.

escapade [ɛskapad] nf - **1.** [voyage] outing - **2.** [fugue] escapade.

escargot [ɛskargo] nm snail.

escarmouche [ɛskarmuʃ] nf skirmish.

escarpé, e [ɛskarpe] adj steep.

escarpement [ɛskarpəmɑ̃] nm - **1.** [de pente] steep slope - **2.** GÉOGR escarpment.

escarpin [ɛskarpɛ̃] nm court shoe Br, pump Am.

escarre [ɛskar] nf bedsore, pressure sore.

escient [ɛsjɑ̃] nm : **à bon ~** advisedly ; **à mauvais ~** ill-advisedly.

esclaffer [3] [ɛsklafe] ◆ **s'esclaffer** vp to burst out laughing.

esclandre [ɛsklɑ̃dr] nm sout scene.

esclavage [ɛsklavaʒ] nm slavery.

esclave [ɛsklav] <> nmf slave. <> adj : **être ~ de** to be a slave to.

escompte [ɛskɔ̃t] nm discount.

escompter [3] [ɛskɔ̃te] vt - **1.** [prévoir] to count on - **2.** FIN to discount.

escorte [ɛskɔrt] nf escort.

escorter [3] [ɛskɔrte] vt to escort.

escouade [ɛskwad] nf squad.

escrime [ɛskrim] nf fencing.

escrimer [3] [ɛskrime] ◆ **s'escrimer** vp : **s'~ à faire qqch** to work (away) at doing sthg.

escroc [ɛskro] nm swindler.

escroquer [3] [ɛskrɔke] vt to swindle ; **~ qqch à qqn** to swindle sb out of sthg.

escroquerie [ɛskrɔkri] nf swindle, swindling (U).

eskimo, Eskimo ⊳ esquimau.

espace [ɛspas] nm space ; **~ vert** green space, green area.

espacer [16] [ɛspase] vt - **1.** [dans l'espace] to space out - **2.** [dans le temps - visites] to space out ; [- paiements] to spread out.

espadon [ɛspadɔ̃] nm [poisson] swordfish.

espadrille [ɛspadrij] nf espadrille.

Espagne [ɛspaɲ] nf : **l'~** Spain.

espagnol, e [ɛspaɲɔl] adj Spanish. ◆ **espagnol** nm [langue] Spanish. ◆ **Espagnol, e** nm, f Spaniard ; **les Espagnols** the Spanish.

espèce [ɛspɛs] nf - **1.** BIOL, BOT & ZOOL species - **2.** [sorte] kind, sort ; **~ d'idiot!** you stupid fool! ◆ **espèces** nfpl cash ; **payer en ~s** to pay (in) cash.

espérance [ɛsperɑ̃s] nf hope ; **~ de vie** life expectancy.

espérer [18] [ɛspere] <> vt to hope for ; **~ que** to hope (that) ; **~ faire qqch** to hope to do sthg. <> vi to hope ; **~ en qqn/qqch** to trust in sb/sthg.

espiègle [ɛspjɛgl] adj mischievous.

espion, onne [ɛspjɔ̃, ɔn] nm, f spy.

espionnage [ɛspjɔnaʒ] nm spying ; **~ industriel** industrial espionage.

espionner [3] [ɛspjɔne] vt to spy on.

esplanade [ɛsplanad] nf esplanade.

espoir [ɛspwar] nm hope.

esprit [ɛspri] nm - **1.** [entendement, personne, pensée] mind ; **reprendre ses ~s** to recover - **2.** [attitude] spirit ; **~ de compétition** competitive spirit ; **~ critique** critical acumen - **3.** [humour] wit - **4.** [fantôme] esprit, ghost.

esquif [ɛskif] nm littéraire skiff.

esquimau, aude, aux, eskimo, aude [ɛskimo, od] adj Eskimo. ◆ **Esquimau** nm, f, **Eskimo** nmf Eskimo (beware : the term 'Esquimau', like its English equivalent, is often considered offensive in North America. The term 'Inuit' is preferred).

esquinter [3] [ɛskɛ̃te] vt fam - **1.** [abîmer] to ruin - **2.** [critiquer] to slate Br, to pan. ◆ **s'esquinter** vp : **s'~ à faire qqch** to kill o.s. doing sthg.

esquiver [3] [ɛskive] vt to dodge. ◆ **s'esquiver** vp to slip away.

essai [ɛse] nm - **1.** [vérification] test, testing (U) ; **à l'~** on trial - **2.** [tentative] attempt - **3.** RUGBY try.

essaim [ɛsɛ̃] nm litt & fig swarm.

essayage [ɛsɛjaʒ] nm fitting.

essayer [11] [eseje] vt to try ; ~ **de faire qqch** to try to do sthg.

essence [esɑ̃s] nf - **1.** [fondement, de plante] essence ; **par ~** sout in essence - **2.** [carburant] petrol Br, gas Am - **3.** [d'arbre] species.

essentiel, elle [esɑ̃sjɛl] adj - **1.** [indispensable] essential - **2.** [fondamental] basic. ➤ **essentiel** nm - **1.** [point] : **l'~** [le principal] the essential ou main thing ; [objets] the essentials (pl) - **2.** [quantité] : **l'~ de** the main ou greater part of.

essentiellement [esɑ̃sjɛlmɑ̃] adv - **1.** [avant tout] above all - **2.** [par essence] essentially.

esseulé, e [esœle] adj littéraire forsaken.

essieu, x [esjø] nm axle.

essor [esɔr] nm flight, expansion, boom ; **prendre son ~** to take flight ; fig to take off.

essorer [3] [esɔre] vt [à la main, à rouleaux] to wring out ; [à la machine] to spin-dry ; [salade] to spin, to dry.

essoreuse [esɔrøz] nf [à rouleaux] mangle ; [électrique] spin-dryer ; [à salade] salad spinner.

essouffler [3] [esufle] vt to make breathless. ➤ **s'essouffler** vp to be breathless ou out of breath ; fig to run out of steam.

essuie-glace [esɥiɡlas] (pl essuie-glaces) nm windscreen wiper Br, windshield wiper Am.

essuie-mains [esɥimɛ̃] nm inv hand towel.

essuie-tout [esɥitu] nm inv kitchen roll.

essuyer [14] [esɥije] vt - **1.** [sécher] to dry - **2.** [nettoyer] to wipe - **3.** fig [subir] to suffer. ➤ **s'essuyer** vp to dry o.s.

est¹ [est] ⟨⟩ nm east ; **un vent d'~** an easterly wind ; **à l'~** in the east ; **à l'~ (de)** to the east (of). ⟨⟩ adj inv [gén] east ; [province, région] eastern.

est² [e] ⟩ **être**.

estafette [estafɛt] nf dispatch-rider ; MIL liaison officer.

estafilade [estafilad] nf slash, gash.

est-allemand, e [estalmɑ̃, ɑ̃d] adj East German.

estampe [estɑ̃p] nf print.

estampille [estɑ̃pij] nf stamp.

est-ce que [ɛskə] adv interr : **est-ce qu'il fait beau?** is the weather good? ; **~ vous aimez l'accordéon?** do you like the accordion? ; **où ~ tu es?** where are you?

esthète [ɛstɛt] nmf aesthete.

esthétique [ɛstetik] adj - **1.** [relatif à la beauté] aesthetic - **2.** [harmonieux] attractive.

estimation [ɛstimasjɔ̃] nf estimate, estimation.

estime [ɛstim] nf respect, esteem.

estimer [3] [ɛstime] vt - **1.** [expertiser] to value - **2.** [évaluer] to estimate ; **j'estime la durée du voyage à 2 heures** I reckon the journey time is 2 hours - **3.** [respecter] to respect - **4.** [penser] : **~ que** to feel (that).

estival, e, aux [ɛstival, o] adj summer (avant n).

estivant, e [ɛstivɑ̃, ɑ̃t] nm, f (summer) holiday-maker Br ou vacationer Am.

estomac [ɛstɔma] nm ANAT stomach.

estomper [3] [ɛstɔ̃pe] vt to blur ; fig [douleur] to lessen. ➤ **s'estomper** vp to become blurred ; fig [douleur] to lessen.

Estonie [ɛstɔni] nf : **l'~** Estonia.

estrade [ɛstrad] nf dais.

estragon [ɛstraɡɔ̃] nm tarragon.

estropié, e [ɛstrɔpje] ⟨⟩ adj crippled. ⟨⟩ nm, f cripple.

estuaire [ɛstɥɛr] nm estuary.

esturgeon [ɛstyrʒɔ̃] nm sturgeon.

et [e] conj - **1.** [gén] and ; **~ moi?** what about me? - **2.** [dans les fractions et les nombres composés] : **vingt ~ un** twenty-one ; **il y a deux ans ~ demi** two and a half years ago ; **à deux heures ~ demie** at half past two.

ét. (abr de étage) fl.

ETA (abr de Euskadi ta Askatasuna) nf ETA.

étable [etabl] nf cowshed.

établi [etabli] nm workbench.

établir [32] [etablir] vt - **1.** [gén] to establish ; [record] to set - **2.** [dresser] to draw up. ➤ **s'établir** vp - **1.** [s'installer] to settle - **2.** [s'instaurer] to become established.

établissement [etablismɑ̃] nm establishment ; **~ hospitalier** hospital ; **~ scolaire** educational establishment.

étage [etaʒ] nm - **1.** [de bâtiment] floor, storey Br, story Am ; **à l'~** upstairs ; **un immeuble à quatre ~s** a four-storey Br ou four-story Am block of flats ; **au premier ~** on the first floor Br, on the second floor Am - **2.** [de fusée] stage.

étagère [etaʒɛr] nf - **1.** [rayon] shelf - **2.** [meuble] shelves (pl), set of shelves.

étain [etɛ̃] nm [métal] tin ; [alliage] pewter.

étais, était etc ⟩ **être**.

étal [etal] (pl s ou étaux [eto]) nm - **1.** [éventaire] stall - **2.** [de boucher] butcher's block.

étalage [etalaʒ] nm - **1.** [action, ensemble d'objets] display ; **faire ~ de** fig to flaunt - **2.** [devanture] window display.

étalagiste [etalaʒist] nmf - **1.** [décorateur] window-dresser - **2.** [vendeur] stall-holder.

étaler [3] [etale] *vt* - **1.** [exposer] to display - **2.** [étendre] to spread out - **3.** [dans le temps] to stagger - **4.** [mettre une couche de] to spread - **5.** [exhiber] to parade. ◆ **s'étaler** *vp* - **1.** [s'étendre] to spread - **2.** [dans le temps] : **s'~ (sur)** to be spread (over) - **3.** *fam* [tomber] to come a cropper *Br*, to fall flat on one's face.

étalon [etalɔ̃] *nm* - **1.** [cheval] stallion - **2.** [mesure] standard.

étamine [etamin] *nf* [de fleur] stamen.

étanche [etɑ̃ʃ] *adj* watertight ; [montre] waterproof.

étancher [3] [etɑ̃ʃe] *vt* - **1.** [sang, larmes] to stem (the flow of) - **2.** [assouvir] to quench.

étang [etɑ̃] *nm* pond.

étant *ppr* ▷ être.

étape [etap] *nf* - **1.** [gén] stage - **2.** [halte] stop ; **faire ~ à** to break one's journey at.

état [eta] *nm* - **1.** [manière d'être] state ; **être en ~/hors d'~ de faire qqch** to be in a/ in no fit state to do sthg ; **en bon/mauvais ~** in good/poor condition ; **en marche** in working order ; **~ d'âme** mood ; **~ d'esprit** state of mind ; **~ de santé** (state of) health ; **être dans tous ses ~s** *fig* to be in a state - **2.** [métier, statut] status ; **~ civil** ADMIN ≃ marital status - **3.** [inventaire - gén] inventory ; [- de dépenses] statement ; **~ des lieux** *inventory and inspection of rented property*. ◆ **État** *nm* [nation] state ; **l'État** the State ; **État membre** member state.

état-major [etamaʒɔr] *nm* - **1.** ADMIN & MIL staff ; [de parti] leadership - **2.** [lieu] headquarters *(pl)*.

États-Unis [etazyni] *nmpl* : **les ~ (d'Amérique)** the United States (of America).

étau [eto] *nm* vice.

étayer [11] [eteje] *vt* to prop up ; *fig* to back up.

etc. (*abr de* et cætera) etc.

été [ete] ◇ *pp inv* ▷ être. ◇ *nm* summer ; **en ~** in (the) summer.

éteindre [81] [etɛ̃dr] *vt* [incendie, bougie, cigarette] to put out ; [radio, chauffage, lampe] to turn off, to switch off. ◆ **s'éteindre** *vp* - **1.** [feu, lampe] to go out - **2.** [bruit, souvenir] to fade (away) - **3.** *fig & littéraire* [personne] to pass away - **4.** [race] to die out.

étendard [etɑ̃dar] *nm* standard.

étendre [73] [etɑ̃dr] *vt* - **1.** [déployer] to stretch ; [journal, linge] to spread (out) - **2.** [coucher] to lay - **3.** [appliquer] to spread - **4.** [accroître] to extend - **5.** [diluer] to dilute ; [sauce] to thin. ◆ **s'étendre** *vp* - **1.** [se coucher] to lie down - **2.** [s'étaler au loin] : **s'~ (de/jusqu'à)** to stretch (from/as

far as) - **3.** [croître] to spread - **4.** [s'attarder] : **s'~ sur** to elaborate on.

étendu, e [etɑ̃dy] ◇ *pp* ▷ étendre. ◇ *adj* - **1.** [bras, main] outstretched - **2.** [plaine, connaissances] extensive. ◆ **étendue** *nf* - **1.** [surface] area, expanse - **2.** [durée] length - **3.** [importance] extent - **4.** MUS range.

éternel, elle [etɛrnɛl] *adj* eternal ; **ce ne sera pas ~** this won't last for ever.

éterniser [3] [etɛrnize] *vt* [prolonger] to drag out. ◆ **s'éterniser** *vp* - **1.** [se prolonger] to drag out - **2.** *fam* [rester] to stay for ever.

éternité [etɛrnite] *nf* eternity.

éternuer [7] [etɛrnɥe] *vi* to sneeze.

êtes ▷ être.

étêter [4] [etete] *vt* to cut the head off.

éther [etɛr] *nm* ether.

Éthiopie [etjɔpi] *nf* : **l'~** Ethiopia.

éthique [etik] ◇ *nf* ethics (*U or pl*). ◇ *adj* ethical.

ethnie [etni] *nf* ethnic group.

ethnique [etnik] *adj* ethnic.

ethnologie [etnɔlɔʒi] *nf* ethnology.

éthylisme [etilism] *nm* alcoholism.

éliez, étions *etc* ▷ être.

étincelant, e [etɛ̃slɑ̃, ɑ̃t] *adj* sparkling.

étinceler [24] [etɛ̃sle] *vi* to sparkle.

étincelle [etɛ̃sɛl] *nf* spark.

étioler [3] [etjɔle] ◆ **s'étioler** *vp* [plante] to wilt ; [personne] to weaken ; [mémoire] to go.

étiqueter [27] [etikte] *vt litt & fig* to label.

étiquette [etikɛt] *nf* - **1.** [marque] *fig* label - **2.** [protocole] etiquette.

étirer [3] [etire] *vt* to stretch ◆ **s'étirer** *vp* to stretch.

étoffe [etɔf] *nf* fabric, material.

étoile [etwal] *nf* star ; **~ filante** shooting star ; **à la belle ~** *fig* under the stars. ◆ **étoile de mer** *nf* starfish.

étoilé, e [etwale] *adj* - **1.** [ciel, nuit] starry ; **la bannière ~e** the Star-Spangled Banner - **2.** [vitre, pare-brise] shattered.

étole [etɔl] *nf* stole.

étonnant, e [etɔnɑ̃, ɑ̃t] *adj* astonishing.

étonnement [etɔnmɑ̃] *nm* astonishment, surprise.

étonner [3] [etɔne] *vt* to surprise, to astonish. ◆ **s'étonner** *vp* : **s'~ (de)** to be surprised (by) ; **s'~ que** (*+ subjonctif*) to be surprised (that).

étouffant, e [etufɑ̃, ɑ̃t] *adj* stifling.

étouffée [etufe] ◆ **à l'étouffée** *loc adv* steamed ; [viande] braised.

étouffer [3] [etufe] ⟨⟩ *vt* - **1.** [gén] to stifle - **2.** [asphyxier] to suffocate - **3.** [feu] to smother - **4.** [scandale, révolte] to suppress. ⟨⟩ *vi* to suffocate. ➡ **s'étouffer** *vp* [s'étrangler] to choke.

étourderie [eturdəri] *nf* - **1.** [distraction] thoughtlessness - **2.** [bévue] careless mistake ; [acte irréfléchi] thoughtless act.

étourdi, e [eturdi] ⟨⟩ *adj* scatterbrained. ⟨⟩ *nm, f* scatterbrain.

étourdir [32] [eturdir] *vt* [assommer] to daze.

étourdissement [eturdismã] *nm* dizzy spell.

étourneau, x [eturno] *nm* starling.

étrange [etrãʒ] *adj* strange.

étranger, ère [etrãʒe, ɛr] ⟨⟩ *adj* - **1.** [gén] foreign - **2.** [différent, isolé] unknown, unfamiliar ; **être ~ à qqn** to be unknown to sb ; **être ~ à qqch** to have no connection with sthg ; **se sentir ~** to feel like an outsider. ⟨⟩ *nm, f* - **1.** [de nationalité différente] foreigner - **2.** [inconnu] stranger - **3.** [exclu] outsider. ➡ **étranger** *nm* : **à l'~** abroad.

étrangeté [etrãʒte] *nf* strangeness.

étranglement [etrãɡləmã] *nm* - **1.** [strangulation] strangulation - **2.** [rétrécissement] constriction.

étrangler [3] [etrãgle] *vt* - **1.** [gén] to choke - **2.** [stranguler] to strangle - **3.** [réprimer] to stifle - **4.** [serrer] to constrict. ➡ **s'étrangler** *vp* [s'étouffer] to choke.

étrave [etrav] *nf* stem.

être [2] [ɛtr] ⟨⟩ *nm* being ; **les ~s vivants/ humains** living/human beings. ⟨⟩ *v aux* - **1.** [pour les temps composés] to have/to be ; **il est parti hier** he left yesterday ; **il est déjà arrivé** he has already arrived ; **il est né en 1952** he was born in 1952 - **2.** [pour le passif] to be ; **la maison a été vendue** the house has been ou was sold. ⟨⟩ *v attr* - **1.** [état] to be ; **la maison est blanche** the house is white ; **il est médecin** he's a doctor ; **sois sage!** be good! - **2.** [possession] : **~ à qqn** to be sb's, to belong to sb ; **c'est à vous, cette voiture?** is this your car?, is this car yours? ; **cette maison est à lui/eux** this house is his/theirs, this is his/their house. ⟨⟩ *v impers* - **1.** [exprimant le temps] : **quelle heure est-il?** what time is it?, what's the time? ; **il est dix heures dix** it's ten past ten *Br*, it's ten after ten *Am* - **2.** [suivi d'un adjectif] : **il est ... it is ... ; il est inutile de** it's useless to ; **il serait bon de/que** it would be good to/if, it would be a good idea to/if. ⟨⟩ *vi* - **1.** [exister] to be ; **n'~ plus** *sout* [être décédé] to be no more - **2.** [indique une situation, un état] to be ; **il est à Paris** he's in Paris ; **nous sommes au printemps/en été** it's spring/summer - **3.** [indiquant une origine] : **il est de Paris** he's from Paris. ➡ **être à** *v + prép* - **1.** [indiquant une obligation] : **c'est à vérifier** it needs to be checked ; **c'est à voir** that remains to be seen - **2.** [indiquant une continuité] : **il est toujours à ne rien faire** he never does a thing.

étreindre [81] [etrɛ̃dr] *vt* - **1.** [embrasser] to hug, to embrace - **2.** *fig* [tenailler] to grip, to clutch. ➡ **s'étreindre** *vp* to embrace each other.

étreinte [etrɛ̃t] *nf* - **1.** [enlacement] embrace - **2.** [pression] stranglehold.

étrenner [4] [etrene] *vt* to use for the first time.

étrennes [etrɛn] *nfpl* Christmas box *(sg)*.

étrier [etrije] *nm* stirrup.

étriller [3] [etrije] *vt* - **1.** [cheval] to curry - **2.** [personne] to wipe the floor with ; [film] to tear to pieces.

étriper [3] [etripe] *vt* - **1.** [animal] to disembowel - **2.** *fam fig* [tuer] to murder. ➡ **s'étriper** *vp fam* to tear each other to pieces.

étriqué, e [etrike] *adj* - **1.** [vêtement] tight ; [appartement] cramped - **2.** [esprit] narrow.

étroit, e [etrwa, at] *adj* - **1.** [gén] narrow - **2.** [intime] close - **3.** [serré] tight. ➡ **à l'étroit** *loc adj* : **être à l'~** to be cramped.

étroitesse [etrwatɛs] *nf* narrowness.

étude [etyd] *nf* - **1.** [gén] study ; **à l'~** under consideration ; **~ de marché** market research *(U)* - **2.** [de notaire - local] office ; [- charge] practice - **3.** MUS étude. ➡ **études** *nfpl* studies ; **faire des ~s** to study.

étudiant, e [etydjã, ãt] *nm, f* student.

étudié, e [etydje] *adj* studied.

étudier [9] [etydje] *vt* to study.

étui [etɥi] *nm* case ; **~ à cigarettes/ lunettes** cigarette/glasses case.

étuve [etyv] *nf* - **1.** [local] steam room ; *fig* oven - **2.** [appareil] sterilizer.

étuvée [etyve] ➡ **à l'étuvée** *loc adv* braised.

étymologie [etimɔlɔʒi] *nf* etymology.

eu, e [y] *pp* ⟨⟩ avoir.

E-U, E-U A (*abr de* États-Unis (d'Amérique)) *nmpl* US, USA.

eucalyptus [økaliptys] *nm* eucalyptus.

euh [ø] *interj* er.

eunuque [ønyk] *nm* eunuch.

euphémisme [øfemism] *nm* euphemism.

euphorie [øfɔri] *nf* euphoria.

euphorisant, e [øfɔrizɑ̃, ɑ̃t] *adj* exhilarating. ➡ **euphorisant** *nm* antidepressant.

eurent ⊳ avoir.

euro [ørɔ] *nm* euro ; **zone ~** euro zone, euro area.

eurodéputé [ørɔdepyte] *nm* Euro MP.

eurodevise [ørɔdəviz] *nf* Eurocurrency.

Europe [ørɔp] *nf* : l'~ Europe.

européen, enne [ørɔpeɛ̃, ɛn] *adj* European. ➡ **Européen, enne** *nm, f* European.

eus, eut *etc* ⊳ avoir.

eût ⊳ avoir.

euthanasie [øtanazi] *nf* euthanasia.

eux [ø] *pron pers* - **1.** [sujet] they ; **ce sont ~ qui me l'ont dit** they're the ones who told me - **2.** [complément] them. ➡ **eux-mêmes** *pron pers* themselves.

évacuer [7] [evakɥe] *vt* - **1.** [gén] to evacuate - **2.** [liquide] to drain.

évadé, e [evade] *nm, f* escaped prisoner.

évader [3] [evade] ➡ **s'évader** *vp* : **s'~ (de)** to escape (from).

évaluation [evalɥasjɔ̃] *nf* [action] valuation ; [résultat] estimate.

évaluer [7] [evalɥe] *vt* [distance] to estimate ; [tableau] to value ; [risque] to assess.

évangélique [evɑ̃ʒelik] *adj* evangelical.

évangéliser [3] [evɑ̃ʒelize] *vt* to evangelize.

évangile [evɑ̃ʒil] *nm* gospel.

évanouir [32] [evanwir] ➡ **s'évanouir** *vp* - **1.** [défaillir] to faint - **2.** [disparaître] to fade.

évanouissement [evanwismɑ̃] *nm* [syncope] fainting fit.

évaporer [3] [evapɔre] ➡ **s'évaporer** *vp* to evaporate.

évasé, e [evaze] *adj* flared.

évasif, ive [evazif, iv] *adj* evasive.

évasion [evazjɔ̃] *nf* escape.

évêché [eveʃe] *nm* [territoire] diocese ; [résidence] bishop's palace.

éveil [evɛj] *nm* awakening ; **en ~** on the alert.

éveillé, e [eveje] *adj* - **1.** [qui ne dort pas] wide awake - **2.** [vif, alerte] alert.

éveiller [4] [eveje] *vt* to arouse ; [intelligence, dormeur] to awaken. ➡ **s'éveiller** *vp* - **1.** [dormeur] to wake, to awaken - **2.** [curiosité] to be aroused - **3.** [esprit, intelligence] to be awakened - **4.** [s'ouvrir] : **s'~ à qqch** to discover sthg.

événement [evɛnmɑ̃] *nm* event.

événementiel, elle [evɛnmɑ̃sjɛl] *adj* [histoire] factual.

éventail [evɑ̃taj] *nm* - **1.** [objet] fan ; **en ~** fan-shaped - **2.** [choix] range.

éventaire [evɑ̃tɛr] *nm* - **1.** [étalage] stall, stand - **2.** [corbeille] tray.

éventer [3] [evɑ̃te] *vt* - **1.** [rafraîchir] to fan - **2.** [divulguer] to give away. ➡ **s'éventer** *vp* - **1.** [se rafraîchir] to fan o.s. - **2.** [parfum, vin] to go stale.

éventrer [3] [evɑ̃tre] *vt* - **1.** [étriper] to disembowel - **2.** [fendre] to rip open.

éventualité [evɑ̃tɥalite] *nf* - **1.** [possibilité] possibility - **2.** [circonstance] eventuality ; **dans l'~ de** in the event of.

éventuel, elle [evɑ̃tɥɛl] *adj* possible.

éventuellement [evɑ̃tɥɛlmɑ̃] *adv* possibly.

évêque [evɛk] *nm* bishop.

évertuer [7] [evɛrtɥe] ➡ **s'évertuer** *vp* : **s'~ à faire qqch** to strive to do sthg.

évidemment [evidamɑ̃] *adv* obviously.

évidence [evidɑ̃s] *nf* [caractère] evidence ; [fait] obvious fact ; **mettre en ~** to emphasize, to highlight.

évident, e [evidɑ̃, ɑ̃t] *adj* obvious.

évider [3] [evide] *vt* to hollow out.

évier [evje] *nm* sink.

évincer [16] [evɛ̃se] *vt* : **~ qqn (de)** to oust sb (from).

éviter [3] [evite] *vt* - **1.** [esquiver] to avoid - **2.** [s'abstenir] : **~ de faire qqch** to avoid doing sthg - **3.** [épargner] : **~ qqch à qqn** to save sb sthg.

évocateur, trice [evɔkatœr, tris] *adj* [geste, regard] meaningful.

évocation [evɔkasjɔ̃] *nf* evocation.

évolué, e [evɔlɥe] *adj* - **1.** [développé] developed - **2.** [libéral, progressiste] broadminded.

évoluer [7] [evɔlɥe] *vi* - **1.** [changer] to evolve ; [personne] to change - **2.** [se mouvoir] to move about.

évolution [evɔlysjɔ̃] *nf* - **1.** [transformation] development - **2.** BIOL evolution - **3.** MÉD progress.

évoquer [3] [evɔke] *vt* - **1.** [souvenir] to evoke - **2.** [problème] to refer to - **3.** [esprits, démons] to call up.

exacerber [3] [ɛgzaserbe] *vt* to heighten.

exact, e [ɛgzakt] *adj* - **1.** [calcul] correct - **2.** [récit, copie] exact - **3.** [ponctuel] punctual.

exactement [ɛgzaktəmɑ̃] *adv* exactly.

exaction [ɛgzaksjɔ̃] *nf* extortion.

exactitude [ɛgzaktityd] *nf* - **1.** [de calcul,

montre] accuracy - **2.** [ponctualité] punctuality.

ex æquo [ɛgzeko] ◇ *adj inv & nmf inv* equal. ◇ *adv* equal ; **troisième ~** third equal.

exagération [ɛgzaʒerasjɔ̃] *nf* exaggeration.

exagéré, e [ɛgzaʒere] *adj* exaggerated.

exagérer [18] [ɛgzaʒere] *vt & vi* to exaggerate.

exalté, e [ɛgzalte] ◇ *adj* [sentiment] elated ; [tempérament] over-excited ; [imagination] vivid. ◇ *nm, f* fanatic.

exalter [3] [ɛgzalte] *vt* to excite. ► **s'exalter** *vp* to get carried away.

examen [ɛgzamɛ̃] *nm* examination ; SCOL exam, examination ; **~ médical** medical (examination) ; **mise en ~** JUR indictment.

examinateur, trice [ɛgzaminatœr, tris] *nm, f* examiner.

examiner [3] [ɛgzamine] *vt* to examine.

exaspération [ɛgzasperasjɔ̃] *nf* exasperation.

exaspérer [18] [ɛgzaspere] *vt* to exasperate.

exaucer [16] [ɛgzose] *vt* to grant ; **~ qqn** to answer sb's prayers.

excédent [ɛksedɑ̃] *nm* surplus ; **en ~** surplus *(avant n)*.

excéder [18] [ɛksede] *vt* - **1.** [gén] to exceed - **2.** [exaspérer] to exasperate.

excellence [ɛkselɑ̃s] *nf* excellence ; **par ~** par excellence.

excellent, e [ɛkselɑ̃, ɑ̃t] *adj* excellent.

exceller [4] [ɛksele] *vi* : **~ en** OU **dans qqch** to excel at OU in sthg ; **~ à faire qqch** to excel at doing sthg.

excentré, e [ɛksɑ̃tre] *adj* : **c'est très ~** it's quite a long way out.

excentrique [ɛksɑ̃trik] ◇ *nmf* eccentric. ◇ *adj* - **1.** [gén] eccentric - **2.** [quartier] outlying.

excepté, e [ɛksɛpte] *adj* : **tous sont venus, lui ~** everyone came except (for) him. ► **excepté** *prép* apart from, except.

exception [ɛksɛpsjɔ̃] *nf* exception ; **à l'~ de** except for.

exceptionnel, elle [ɛksɛpsjɔnɛl] *adj* exceptional.

excès [ɛksɛ] ◇ *nm* excess ; **~ de zèle** overzealousness. ◇ *nmpl* excesses.

excessif, ive [ɛksesif, iv] *adj* - **1.** [démesuré] excessive - **2.** [extrême] extreme.

excitant, e [ɛksitɑ̃, ɑ̃t] *adj* [stimulant, passionnant] exciting. ► **excitant** *nm* stimulant.

excitation [ɛksitasjɔ̃] *nf* - **1.** [énervement] excitement - **2.** [stimulation] encouragement - **3.** MÉD stimulation.

excité, e [ɛksite] ◇ *adj* [énervé] excited. ◇ *nm, f* hothead.

exciter [3] [ɛksite] *vt* - **1.** [gén] to excite - **2.** [inciter] : **~ qqn (à qqch/à faire qqch)** to incite sb (to sthg/to do sthg) - **3.** MÉD to stimulate.

exclamation [ɛksklamasjɔ̃] *nf* exclamation.

exclamer [3] [ɛksklame] ► **s'exclamer** *vp* : **s'~ (devant)** to exclaim (at OU over).

exclu, e [ɛkskly] ◇ *pp* ▷ **exclure**. ◇ *adj* excluded. ◇ *nm, f* outsider.

exclure [96] [ɛksklyr] *vt* to exclude ; [expulser] to expel.

exclusion [ɛksklyzjɔ̃] *nf* expulsion ; **à l'~ de** to the exclusion of.

exclusivement [ɛksklyzivmɑ̃] *adv* - **1.** [uniquement] exclusively - **2.** [non inclus] exclusive.

exclusivité [ɛksklyzivite] *nf* - **1.** COMM exclusive rights *(pl)* - **2.** CIN sole screening rights *(pl)* ; **en ~** exclusively - **3.** [de sentiment] exclusiveness.

excommunier [9] [ɛkskɔmynje] *vt* to excommunicate.

excrément [ɛkskremɑ̃] *nm* (gén pl) excrement *(U)*.

excroissance [ɛkskrwasɑ̃s] *nf* excrescence.

excursion [ɛkskyrsjɔ̃] *nf* excursion.

excursionniste [ɛkskyrsjɔnist] *nmf* daytripper *Br*, vacationer *Am*.

excuse [ɛkskyz] *nf* excuse.

excuser [3] [ɛkskyze] *vt* to excuse ; **excusez-moi** [pour réparer] I'm sorry ; [pour demander] excuse me. ► **s'excuser** *vp* [demander pardon] to apologize ; **s'~ de qqch/de faire qqch** to apologize for sthg/for doing sthg.

exécrable [ɛgzekrabl] *adj* atrocious.

exécrer [18] [ɛgzekre] *vt* to loathe.

exécutant, e [ɛgzekytɑ̃, ɑ̃t] *nm, f* - **1.** [personne] underling - **2.** MUS performer.

exécuter [3] [ɛgzekyte] *vt* - **1.** [réaliser] to carry out ; [tableau] to paint - **2.** MUS to play, to perform - **3.** [mettre à mort] to execute. ► **s'exécuter** *vp* to comply.

exécutif, ive [ɛgzekytif, iv] *adj* executive. ► **exécutif** *nm* : **l'~** the executive.

exécution [ɛgzekysjɔ̃] *nf* - **1.** [réalisation] carrying out ; [de tableau] painting - **2.** MUS performance - **3.** [mise à mort] execution.

exemplaire [ɛgzɑ̃plɛr] <> *nm* copy. <> *adj* exemplary.

exemple [ɛgzɑ̃pl] *nm* example ; par ~ for example, for instance.

exempté, e [ɛgzɑ̃te] *adj* : ~ (de) exempt (from).

exercer [16] [ɛgzɛrse] *vt* - **1.** [entraîner, mettre en usage] to exercise ; [autorité, influence] to exert - **2.** [métier] to carry on ; [médecine] to practise. ◆ **s'exercer** *vp* - **1.** [s'entraîner] to practise ; **s'~ à qqch/à faire qqch** to practise sthg/doing sthg - **2.** [se manifester] : **s'~ (sur** ou **contre)** to be exerted (on).

exercice [ɛgzɛrsis] *nm* - **1.** [gén] exercise - **2.** [entraînement] practice - **3.** [de métier, fonction] carrying out ; **en ~** in office.

exhaler [3] [ɛgzale] *vt littéraire* - **1.** [odeur] to give off - **2.** [plainte, soupir] to utter. ◆ **s'exhaler** *vp* - **1.** [odeur] to rise - **2.** [plainte, soupir] : **s'~ de** to rise from.

exhaustif, ive [ɛgzostif, iv] *adj* exhaustive.

exhiber [3] [ɛgzibe] *vt* [présenter] to show ; [faire étalage de] to show off. ◆ **s'exhiber** *vp* to make an exhibition of o.s.

exhibitionniste [ɛgzibisjɔnist] *nmf* exhibitionist.

exhorter [3] [ɛgzɔrte] *vt* : ~ **qqn à qqch/à faire qqch** to urge sb to sthg/to do sthg.

exhumer [3] [ɛgzyme] *vt* to exhume ; *fig* to unearth, to dig up.

exigeant, e [ɛgziʒɑ̃, ɑ̃t] *adj* demanding.

exigence [ɛgziʒɑ̃s] *nf* [demande] demand.

exiger [17] [ɛgziʒe] *vt* - **1.** [demander] to demand ; ~ **que** (+ *subjonctif*) to demand that ; ~ **qqch de qqn** to demand sthg from sb - **2.** [nécessiter] to require.

exigible [ɛgziʒibl] *adj* payable.

exigu, ë [ɛgzigy] *adj* cramped.

exil [ɛgzil] *nm* exile ; **en ~** exiled.

exilé, e [ɛgzile] *nm, f* exile.

exiler [3] [ɛgzile] *vt* to exile. ◆ **s'exiler** *vp* - **1.** POLIT to go into exile - **2.** *fig* [partir] to go into seclusion.

existence [ɛgzistɑ̃s] *nf* existence.

exister [3] [ɛgziste] <> *vi* to exist. <> *v impers* : **il existe** [il y a] there is/are.

exode [ɛgzɔd] *nm* exodus.

exonération [ɛgzɔnerasjɔ̃] *nf* exemption ; ~ **d'impôts** tax exemption.

exorbitant, e [ɛgzɔrbitɑ̃, ɑ̃t] *adj* exorbitant.

exorbité, e [ɛgzɔrbite] ⊳ **œil.**

exorciser [3] [ɛgzɔrsize] *vt* to exorcize.

exotique [ɛgzɔtik] *adj* exotic.

exotisme [ɛgzɔtism] *nm* exoticism.

expansif, ive [ɛkspɑ̃sif, iv] *adj* expansive.

expansion [ɛkspɑ̃sjɔ̃] *nf* expansion.

expansionniste [ɛkspɑ̃sjɔnist] *nmf* & *adj* expansionist.

expatrié, e [ɛkspatrije] *adj* & *nm, f* expatriate.

expatrier [10] [ɛkspatrije] *vt* to expatriate. ◆ **s'expatrier** *vp* to leave one's country.

expédier [9] [ɛkspedje] *vt* - **1.** [lettre, marchandise] to send, to dispatch - **2.** [personne] to get rid of ; [question] to dispose of - **3.** [travail] to dash off.

expéditeur, trice [ɛkspeditœr, tris] *nm, f* sender.

expéditif, ive [ɛkspeditif, iv] *adj* quick, expeditious.

expédition [ɛkspedisjɔ̃] *nf* - **1.** [envoi] sending - **2.** [voyage, campagne militaire] expedition.

expérience [ɛksperjɑ̃s] *nf* - **1.** [pratique] experience ; **avoir de l'~** to have experience, to be experienced - **2.** [essai] experiment.

expérimental, e, aux [ɛksperimɑ̃tal, o] *adj* experimental.

expérimenté, e [ɛksperimɑ̃te] *adj* experienced.

expert, e [ɛkspɛr, ɛrt] *adj* expert. ◆ **expert** *nm* expert.

expert-comptable [ɛkspɛrkɔ̃tabl] *nm* chartered accountant *Br*, certified public accountant *Am*.

expertise [ɛkspɛrtiz] *nf* - **1.** [examen] expert appraisal ; [estimation] (expert) valuation - **2.** [compétence] expertise.

expertiser [3] [ɛkspɛrtize] *vt* to value ; [dégâts] to assess.

expier [9] [ɛkspje] *vt* to pay for.

expiration [ɛkspirasjɔ̃] *nf* - **1.** [d'air] exhalation - **2.** [de contrat] expiry.

expirer [3] [ɛkspire] <> *vt* to breathe out. <> *vi* [contrat] to expire.

explicatif, ive [ɛksplikatif, iv] *adj* explanatory.

explication [ɛksplikasjɔ̃] *nf* explanation ; ~ **de texte** (literary) criticism.

explicite [ɛksplisit] *adj* explicit.

expliciter [3] [ɛksplisite] *vt* to make explicit.

expliquer [3] [ɛksplike] *vt* - **1.** [gén] to explain - **2.** [texte] to criticize. ◆ **s'expliquer** *vp* - **1.** [se justifier] to explain o.s.

- **2.** [comprendre] to understand - **3.** [discuter] to have it out - **4.** [devenir compréhensible] to be explained.

exploit [εksplwa] *nm* exploit, feat ; *iron* [maladresse] achievement.

exploitant, e [εksplwatɑ̃, ɑ̃t] *nm, f* farmer.

exploitation [εksplwatasjɔ̃] *nf* - **1.** [mise en valeur] running ; [de mine] working - **2.** [entreprise] operation, concern ; ~ **agricole** farm - **3.** [d'une personne] exploitation.

exploiter [3] [εksplwate] *vt* - **1.** [gén] to exploit - **2.** [entreprise] to operate, to run.

explorateur, trice [εksplɔratœr, tris] *nm, f* explorer.

explorer [3] [εksplɔre] *vt* to explore.

exploser [3] [εksploze] *vi* to explode.

explosif, ive [εksplozif, iv] *adj* explosive. ◆ **explosif** *nm* explosive.

explosion [εksplozjɔ̃] *nf* explosion ; [de colère, joie] outburst.

expo [εkspo] *nf fam* exhibition.

exportateur, trice [εkspɔrtatœr, tris] ◇ *adj* exporting. ◇ *nm, f* exporter.

exportation [εkspɔrtasjɔ̃] *nf* export.

exporter [3] [εkspɔrte] *vt* to export.

exposé, e [εkspoze] *adj* - **1.** [orienté] : **bien** ~ facing the sun - **2.** [vulnérable] exposed. ◆ **exposé** *nm* account ; SCOL talk.

exposer [3] [εkspoze] *vt* - **1.** [orienter, mettre en danger] to expose - **2.** [présenter -] to display ; [- tableaux] to show, to exhibit - **3.** [expliquer] to explain, to set out. ◆ **s'exposer** *vp* : **s'**~ **à qqch** to expose o.s. to sthg.

exposition [εkspozisjɔ̃] *nf* - **1.** [présentation] exhibition - **2.** [orientation] aspect.

exprès¹, esse [εksprεs] *adj* [formel] formal, express. ◆ **exprès** *adj inv* [urgent] express.

exprès² [εksprε] *adv* on purpose ; **faire** ~ **de faire qqch** to do sthg deliberately OU on purpose.

express [εksprεs] ◇ *nm inv* - **1.** [train] express - **2.** [café] espresso. ◇ *adj inv* express.

expressément [εkspresemɑ̃] *adv* expressly.

expressif, ive [εkspresif, iv] *adj* expressive.

expression [εkspresjɔ̃] *nf* expression.

exprimer [3] [εksprime] *vt* [pensées, sentiments] to express. ◆ **s'exprimer** *vp* to express o.s.

expropriation [εksprɔprijasjɔ̃] *nf* expropriation.

exproprier [10] [εksprɔprije] *vt* to expropriate.

expulser [3] [εkspylse] *vt* : ~ **(de)** to expel (from) ; [locataire] to evict (from).

expulsion [εkspylsjɔ̃] *nf* expulsion ; [de locataire] eviction.

expurger [17] [εkspyrʒe] *vt* to expurgate.

exquis, e [εkski, iz] *adj* - **1.** [délicieux] exquisite - **2.** [distingué, agréable] delightful.

exsangue [εksɑ̃g] *adj* [blême] deathly pale.

extase [εkstaz] *nf* ecstasy.

extasier [9] [εkstazje] ◆ **s'extasier** *vp* : **s'**~ **devant** to go into ecstasies over.

extensible [εkstɑ̃sibl] *adj* stretchable.

extension [εkstɑ̃sjɔ̃] *nf* - **1.** [étirement] stretching - **2.** [élargissement] extension ; **par** ~ by extension.

exténuer [7] [εkstenɥe] *vt* to exhaust.

extérieur, e [εksterjœr] *adj* - **1.** [au dehors] outside ; [étranger] external ; [apparent] outward - **2.** ÉCON & POLIT foreign. ◆ **extérieur** *nm* [dehors] outside ; [de maison] exterior ; **à l'**~ **de qqch** outside sthg.

extérieurement [εksterjœrmɑ̃] *adv* - **1.** [à l'extérieur] on the outside, externally - **2.** [en apparence] outwardly.

extérioriser [3] [εksterjɔrize] *vt* to show.

exterminer [3] [εkstεrmine] *vt* to exterminate.

externat [εkstεrna] *nm* - **1.** SCOL day school - **2.** MÉD *non-resident medical studentship*.

externe [εkstεrn] ◇ *nmf* - **1.** SCOL day pupil - **2.** MÉD *non-resident medical student*, ≃ extern *Am*. ◇ *adj* outer, external.

extincteur [εkstɛ̃ktœr] *nm* (fire) extinguisher.

extinction [εkstɛ̃ksjɔ̃] *nf* - **1.** [action d'éteindre] putting out, extinguishing - **2.** *fig* [disparition] extinction ; ~ **de voix** loss of one's voice.

extirper [3] [εkstirpe] *vt* : ~ **(de)** [épine, réponse, secret] to drag (out of).

extorquer [3] [εkstɔrke] *vt* : ~ **qqch à qqn** to extort sthg from sb.

extra [εkstra] ◇ *nm inv* - **1.** [employé] extra help (U) - **2.** [chose inhabituelle] (special) treat. ◇ *adj inv* - **1.** [de qualité] top-quality - **2.** *fam* [génial] great, fantastic.

extraction [εkstraksjɔ̃] *nf* extraction.

extrader [3] [εkstrade] *vt* to extradite.

extraire [112] [εkstrεr] *vt* : ~ **(de)** to extract (from).

extrait, e [εkstrε, εt] *pp* ▷ **extraire**.

extrait *nm* extract ; ~ **de naissancè** birth certificate.

extraordinaire [ɛkstraɔrdinɛr] *adj* extraordinary.

extrapoler [3] [ɛkstrapɔle] *vt* & *vi* to extrapolate.

extraterrestre [ɛkstraterɛstr] *nmf* & *adj* extraterrestrial.

extravagance [ɛkstravagɑ̃s] *nf* extravagance.

extravagant, e [ɛkstravagɑ̃, ɑ̃t] *adj* extravagant ; [idée, propos] wild.

extraverti, e [ɛkstravɛrti] *nm, f* & *adj* extrovert.

extrême [ɛkstrɛm] ◇ *nm* extreme ; **d'un** ~ **à l'autre** from one extreme to the other. ◇ *adj* extreme ; [limite] furthest ; **les sports ~s** extreme sports.

extrêmement [ɛkstrɛmmɑ̃] *adv* extremely.

extrême-onction [ɛkstrɛmɔ̃ksjɔ̃] *nf* last rites *(pl)*, extreme unction.

Extrême-Orient [ɛkstrɛmɔrjɑ̃] *nm* : l'~ the Far East.

extrémiste [ɛkstremist] *nmf* & *adj* extremist.

extrémité [ɛkstremite] *nf* - 1. [bout] end - 2. [situation critique] straights *(pl)*.

exubérant, e [ɛgzyberɑ̃, ɑ̃t] *adj* - 1. [personne] exuberant - 2. [végétation] luxuriant.

exulter [3] [ɛgzylte] *vi* to exult.

f, F [ɛf] *nm inv* f, F ; **F3** three-room flat *Br* ou apartment *Am*. ◆ **F - 1.** (*abr de* **Fahrenheit**) F - 2. (*abr de* franc) F, Fr.

fa [fa] *nm inv* F ; [chanté] fa.

fable [fabl] *nf* fable.

fabricant, e [fabrikɑ̃, ɑ̃t] *nm, f* manufacturer.

fabrication [fabrikasjɔ̃] *nf* manufacture, manufacturing.

fabrique [fabrik] *nf* [usine] factory.

fabriquer [3] [fabrike] *vt* - 1. [confectionner] to manufacture, to make - 2. *fam* [faire] : **qu'est-ce que tu fabriques?** what are you up to? - 3. [inventer] to fabricate.

fabulation [fabylasjɔ̃] *nf* fabrication.

fabuleux, euse [fabylø, øz] *adj* fabulous.

fac [fak] *nf fam* college, uni *Br*.

façade [fasad] *nf litt* & *fig* facade.

face [fas] *nf* - 1. [visage] face - 2. [côté] side ; **faire** ~ **à qqch** [maison] to face sthg, to be opposite sthg ; *fig* [affronter] to face up to sthg ; **de** ~ from the front ; **en** ~ **de qqn/ qqch** opposite sb/sthg.

face-à-face [fasafas] *nm inv* debate.

facétie [fasesi] *nf* practical joke.

facette [fasɛt] *nf litt* & *fig* facet.

fâché, e [faʃe] *adj* - 1. [en colère] angry ; [contrarié] annoyed - 2. [brouillé] on bad terms.

fâcher [3] [faʃe] *vt* [mettre en colère] to anger, to make angry ; [contrarier] to annoy, to make annoyed. ◆ **se fâcher** *vp* - 1. [se mettre en colère] : **se** ~ **(contre qqn)** to get angry (with sb) - 2. [se brouiller] : **se** ~ **(avec qqn)** to fall out (with sb).

fâcheux, euse [faʃø, øz] *adj* unfortunate.

facile [fasil] *adj* - 1. [aisé] easy ; ~ **à faire/ prononcer** easy to do/pronounce - 2. [peu subtil] facile - 3. [complaisant] easy-going.

facilement [fasilmɑ̃] *adv* easily.

facilité [fasilite] *nf* - 1. [de tâche, problème] easiness - 2. [capacité] ease - 3. [dispositions] aptitude - 4. COMM : ~**s de paiement** easy (payment) terms.

faciliter [3] [fasilite] *vt* to make easier.

façon [fasɔ̃] *nf* - 1. [manière] way - 2. [travail] work ; COUTURE making-up - 3. [imitation] : ~ **cuir** imitation leather. ◆ **de façon à** *loc prép* so as to. ◆ **de façon que** (+ *subjonctif*) *loc conj* so that. ◆ **de toute façon** *loc adv* anyway, in any case.

fac-similé [faksimile] (*pl* **fac-similés**) *nm* facsimile.

facteur, trice [faktœr, tris] *nm, f* [des postes] postman (*f* postwoman) *Br*, mailman (*f* mailwoman) *Am*. ◆ **facteur** *nm* [élément & MATHS] factor.

factice [faktis] *adj* artificial.

faction [faksjɔ̃] *nf* - 1. [groupe] faction - 2. MIL : **être en** ou **de** ~ to be on guard (duty) ou on sentry duty.

facture [faktyr] *nf* - 1. COMM invoice ; [de gaz, d'électricité] bill - 2. ART technique.

facturer [3] [faktyre] *vt* COMM to invoice.

facturette [faktyrɛt] *nf fam* credit card slip.

facultatif, ive [fakyltatif, iv] *adj* optional.

faculté [fakylte] *nf* - 1. [don & UNIV] faculty ; ~ **de lettres/de droit/de médecine** Faculty of Arts/Law/Medicine - 2. [possibilité] freedom - **3.** [pouvoir] power. ➧ **facultés** *nfpl* (mental) faculties.

fadaises [fadɛz] *nfpl* drivel *(U)*.

fade [fad] *adj* - **1.** [sans saveur] bland - **2.** [sans intérêt] insipid.

fagot [fago] *nm* bundle of sticks.

faible [fɛbl] ◇ *adj* - **1.** [gén] weak ; **être ~ en maths** to be not very good at maths - **2.** [petit - montant, proportion] small ; [- revenu] low - **3.** [lueur, bruit] faint. ◇ *nmf* weak person ; **~ d'esprit** feeble-minded person. ◇ *nm* weakness.

faiblement [fɛbləmɑ̃] *adv* - **1.** [mollement] weakly, feebly - **2.** [imperceptiblement] faintly - **3.** [peu] slightly.

faiblesse [fɛblɛs] *nf* - **1.** [gén] weakness - **2.** [petitesse] smallness.

faiblir [32] [feblir] *vi* - **1.** [personne, monnaie] to weaken - **2.** [forces] to diminish, to fail - **3.** [tempête, vent] to die down.

faïence [fajɑ̃s] *nf* earthenware.

faignant, e = fainéant.

faille [faj] ◇ ▭ falloir. ◇ *nf* - **1.** GÉOL fault - **2.** [défaut] flaw.

faillible [fajibl] *adj* fallible.

faillir [46] [fajir] *vi* - **1.** [manquer] : **~ à** [promesse] not to keep ; [devoir] not to do - **2.** [être sur le point de] : **~ faire qqch** to nearly OU almost do sthg.

faillite [fajit] *nf* FIN bankruptcy ; **faire ~** to go bankrupt ; **en ~** bankrupt.

faim [fɛ̃] *nf* hunger ; **avoir ~** to be hungry.

fainéant, e [feneɑ̃, ɑ̃t], **feignant, e**, **faignant, e** [fɛɲɑ̃, ɑ̃t] ◇ *adj* lazy, idle. ◇ *nm, f* lazybones.

faire [109] [fer] ◇ *vt* - **1.** [fabriquer, préparer] to make ; **~ une tarte/du café/un film** to make a tart/coffee/a film ; **~ qqch de qqch** [transformer] to make sthg into sthg ; **~ qqch de qqn** *fig* to make sthg of sb ; **il veut en ~ un avocat** he wants him to be a lawyer, he wants to make a lawyer of him - **2.** [s'occuper à, entreprendre] to do ; **qu'est-ce qu'il fait dans la vie?** what does he do (for a living)? ; **que fais-tu dimanche?** what are you doing on Sunday? - **3.** [étudier] to do ; **~ de l'anglais/des maths/du droit** to do English/maths/law - **4.** [sport, musique] to play ; **~ du football/de la clarinette** to play football/the clarinet - **5.** [effectuer] to do ; **~ le ménage** to do the housework ; **~ la cuisine** to cook, to do the cooking ; **~ la lessive** to do the washing - **6.** [occasionner] : **~ de la peine à qqn** to hurt sb ; **~ du mal à** to harm ; **~ du bruit** to make a noise ; **ça ne fait rien** it doesn't matter - **7.** [imiter] : **~ le sourd/l'innocent** to act deaf/(the) innocent - **8.** [calcul, me-

sure] : **un et un font deux** one and one are OU make two ; **ça fait combien (de kilomètres) jusqu'à la mer?** how far is it to the sea? ; **la table fait 2 mètres de long** the table is 2 metres *Br* OU meters *Am* long ; **~ du 38** to take a size 38 - **9.** [coûter] to be, to cost ; **ça vous fait 10 euros en tout** that'll be 10 euros altogether - **10.** [dire] : **«tiens», fit-elle** "really", she said - **11.** : **ne ~ que** [faire sans cesse] to do nothing but ; **elle ne fait que bavarder** she does nothing but gossip, she's always gossiping ; **je ne fais que passer** I've just popped in. ◇ *vi* [agir] to do, to act ; **fais vite!** hurry up! ; **que ~?** what is to be done? ; **tu ferais bien d'aller voir ce qui se passe** you ought to OU you'd better go and see what's happening ; **~ comme chez soi** to make o.s. at home. ◇ *v attr* [avoir l'air] to look ; **~ démodé/joli** to look old-fashioned/pretty ; **ça fait jeune** it makes you look young. ◇ *v substitut* to do ; **je lui ai dit de prendre une échelle mais il ne l'a pas fait** I told him to use a ladder but he didn't ; **faites!** please do! ◇ *v impers* - **1.** [climat, temps] : **il fait beau/froid** it's fine/cold ; **il fait 20 degrés** it's 20 degrees ; **il fait jour/nuit** it's light/dark - **2.** [exprime la durée, la distance] : **ça fait six mois que je ne l'ai pas vu** it's six months since I last saw him ; **ça fait six mois que je fais du portugais** I've been going to Portuguese classes for six months ; **ça fait 30 kilomètres qu'on roule sans phares** we've been driving without lights for 30 kilometres. ◇ *v auxiliaire* - **1.** [à l'actif] to make ; **~ démarrer une voiture** to start a car ; **~ tomber qqch** to make sthg fall ; **l'aspirine fait baisser la fièvre** aspirin brings down the temperature ; **~ travailler qqn** to make sb work ; **~ traverser la rue à un aveugle** to help a blind man cross the road - **2.** [au passif] : **~ faire qqch (par qqn)** to have sthg done (by sb) ; **~ réparer sa voiture/nettoyer ses vitres** to have one's car repaired/one's windows cleaned. ➧ **se faire** *vp* - **1.** [avoir lieu] to take place - **2.** [être convenable] : **ça ne se fait pas (de faire qqch)** it's not done (to do sthg) - **3.** [devenir] : **se ~** *(+ adjectif)* to get, to become ; **il se fait tard** it's getting late ; **se ~ beau** to make o.s. beautiful - **4.** [causer] *(+ nom)* : **se ~ mal** to hurt o.s. ; **se ~ des amis** to make friends ; **se ~ une idée sur qqch** to get some idea about sthg - **5.** *(+ infinitif)* : **se ~ écraser** to get run over ; **se ~ opérer** to have an operation ; **se ~ aider (par qqn)** to get help (from sb) ; **se ~ faire un costume** to have a suit made (for o.s.) - **6.** *loc* : **comment se fait-il que ...?** how is it that ...?, how come ...? ; **s'en ~** to worry ; **ne vous en**

faites pas! don't worry! ~ **se faire à** vp + prép to get used to.

faire-part [fɛrpar] nm inv announcement.

fais, fait etc ⊏ faire.

faisable [fəzabl] adj feasible.

faisan, e [fəzɑ̃, an] nm, f pheasant.

faisandé, e [fəzɑ̃de] adj CULIN high.

faisceau, x [fɛso] nm [rayon] beam.

faisons ⊏ faire.

fait, faite [fɛ, fɛt] ◇ pp ⊏ faire. ◇ adj - **1.** [fabriqué] made ; **il n'est pas ~ pour mener cette vie** he's not cut out for this kind of life - **2.** [physique] : **bien ~** well-built - **3.** [fromage] ripe - **4.** loc : **c'est bien ~ pour lui** (it) serves him right ; **c'en est ~ de nous** we're done for. ~ **fait** nm - **1.** [acte] act ; **mettre qqn devant le ~ accompli** to present sb with a fait accompli ; **prendre qqn sur le ~** to catch sb in the act ; **~s et gestes** doings, actions - **2.** [événement] event ; **~s divers** news in brief - **3.** [réalité] fact. ~ **au fait** loc adv by the way. ~ **en fait** loc adv in (actual) fact. ~ **en fait de** loc prép by way of. ~ **du fait de** loc prép because of.

faîte [fɛt] nm - **1.** [de toit] ridge - **2.** [d'arbre] top - **3.** fig [sommet] pinnacle.

faites ⊏ faire.

fait-tout (pl inv), **faitout** (pl faitouts) [fɛtu] nm stewpan.

fakir [fakir] nm fakir.

falaise [falɛz] nf cliff.

fallacieux, euse [falasjø, øz] adj - **1.** [promesse] false - **2.** [argument] fallacious.

falloir [69] [falwar] v impers . **il me faut du temps** I need (some) time ; **il faut que tu partes** you must go ou leave, you'll have to go ou leave ; **il faut toujours qu'elle intervienne!** she always has to interfere! ; **il faut faire attention** we/you etc must be careful, we'll/you'll etc have to be careful ; **s'il le faut** if necessary. ~ **s'en falloir** v impers : **il s'en faut de peu pour qu'il puisse acheter cette maison** he can almost afford to buy the house ; **il s'en faut de 20 cm pour que l'armoire tienne dans le coin** the cupboard is 20 cm too big to fit into the corner ; **il s'en faut de beaucoup pour qu'il ait l'examen** it'll take a lot for him to pass the exam ; **peu s'en est fallu qu'il démissionne** he very nearly resigned, he came close to resigning.

fallu [faly] pp inv ⊏ falloir.

falot, e [falo, ɔt] adj dull.

falsifier [9] [falsifje] vt [document, signature, faits] to falsify.

famé, e [fame] adj : **mal ~** with a (bad) reputation.

famélique [famelik] adj half-starved.

fameux, euse [famø, øz] adj - **1.** [célèbre] famous - **2.** fam [remarquable] great.

familial, e, aux [familjal, o] adj family (avant n).

familiariser [3] [familjarize] vt : **~ qqn avec** to familiarize sb with.

familiarité [familjarite] nf familiarity. ~ **familiarités** nfpl liberties.

familier, ère [familje, ɛr] adj familiar. ~ **familier** nm regular (customer).

famille [famij] nf family ; [ensemble des parents] relatives, relations ; **~ d'accueil** [lors d'un séjour linguistique] host family ; [pour enfant en difficulté] foster home.

famine [famin] nf famine.

fan [fan] nmf fam fan.

fanal, aux [fanal, o] nm - **1.** [de phare] beacon - **2.** [lanterne] lantern.

fanatique [fanatik] ◇ nmf fanatic. ◇ adj fanatical.

fanatisme [fanatism] nm fanaticism.

faner [3] [fane] ◇ vt [altérer] to fade. ◇ vi - **1.** [fleur] to wither - **2.** [beauté, couleur] to fade. ~ **se faner** vp - **1.** [fleur] to wither - **2.** [beauté, couleur] to fade.

fanfare [fɑ̃far] nf - **1.** [orchestre] brass band - **2.** [musique] fanfare.

fanfaron, onne [fɑ̃farɔ̃, ɔn] ◇ adj boastful. ◇ nm, f braggart.

fange [fɑ̃ʒ] nf littéraire mire.

fanion [fanjɔ̃] nm pennant.

fantaisie [fɑ̃tezi] ◇ nf - **1.** [caprice] whim - **2.** (U) [goût] fancy - **3.** [imagination] imagination. ◇ adj inv : **chapeau ~** fancy hat ; **bijoux ~** fake jewellery Br ou jewelry Am.

fantaisiste [fɑ̃tezist] ◇ nmf entertainer. ◇ adj [bizarre] fanciful.

fantasme [fɑ̃tasm] nm fantasy.

fantasque [fɑ̃task] adj - **1.** [personne] whimsical - **2.** [humeur] capricious.

fantassin [fɑ̃tasɛ̃] nm infantryman.

fantastique [fɑ̃tastik] ◇ adj fantastic. ◇ nm : **le ~** the fantastic.

fantoche [fɑ̃tɔʃ] ◇ adj puppet (avant n). ◇ nm puppet.

fantôme [fɑ̃tom] ◇ nm ghost. ◇ adj [inexistant] phantom.

faon [fɑ̃] nm fawn.

farandole [farɑ̃dɔl] nf farandole.

farce [fars] nf - **1.** CULIN stuffing - **2.** [blague] (practical) joke ; **~s et attrapes** jokes and novelties.

farceur, euse [faʀsœʀ, øz] *nm, f* (practical) joker.

farcir [32] [faʀsiʀ] *vt* - **1.** CULIN to stuff - **2.** [remplir] : ~ **qqch de** to stuff ou cram sthg with.

fard [faʀ] *nm* make-up.

fardeau, x [faʀdo] *nm* [poids] load ; *fig* burden.

farder [3] [faʀde] *vt* [maquiller] to make up. ✦ **se farder** *vp* to make o.s. up, to put on one's make-up.

farfelu, e [faʀfəly] *fam* ◇ *adj* weird. ◇ *nm, f* weirdo.

farfouiller [3] [faʀfuje] *vi fam* to rummage.

farine [faʀin] *nf* flour.

farouche [faʀuʃ] *adj* - **1.** [animal] wild, not tame ; [personne] shy, withdrawn - **2.** [sentiment] fierce.

fart [faʀ(t)] *nm* (ski) wax.

fascicule [fasikyl] *nm* part, instalment *Br*, installment *Am*.

fascination [fasinasjɔ̃] *nf* fascination.

fasciner [3] [fasine] *vt* to fascinate.

fascisme [faʃism] *nm* fascism.

fasse, fassions *etc* ⊳ **faire**.

faste [fast] ◇ *nm* splendour *Br*, splendor *Am*. ◇ *adj* [favorable] lucky.

fastidieux, euse [fastidjø, øz] *adj* boring.

fastueux, euse [fastɥø, øz] *adj* luxurious.

fatal, e [fatal] *adj* - **1.** [mortel, funeste] fatal - **2.** [inévitable] inevitable.

fataliste [fatalist] *adj* fatalistic.

fatalité [fatalite] *nf* - **1.** [destin] fate - **2.** [inéluctabilité] inevitability.

fatigant, e [fatigɑ̃, ɑ̃t] *adj* - **1.** [épuisant] tiring - **2.** [ennuyeux] tiresome.

fatiguant [fatigɑ̃] *ppr* ⊳ **fatiguer**.

fatigue [fatig] *nf* tiredness.

fatigué, e [fatige] *adj* tired ; [cœur, yeux] strained.

fatiguer [3] [fatige] ◇ *vt* - **1.** [épuiser, affecter] to tire ; [cœur, yeux] to strain - **2.** [ennuyer] to wear out. ◇ *vi* - **1.** [personne] to grow tired - **2.** [moteur] to strain. ✦ **se fatiguer** *vp* to get tired ; **se ~ de qqch** to get tired of sthg ; **se ~ à faire qqch** to wear o.s. out doing sthg.

fatras [fatʀa] *nm* jumble.

faubourg [fobuʀ] *nm* suburb.

fauché, e [foʃe] *adj fam* broke, hard-up.

faucher [3] [foʃe] *vt* - **1.** [couper - herbe, blé] to cut - **2.** *fam* [voler] : ~ **qqch à qqn** to

pinch sthg from sb - **3.** [piéton] to run over - **4.** *fig* [suj : mort, maladie] to cut down.

faucille [fosij] *nf* sickle.

faucon [fokɔ̃] *nm* hawk.

faudra ⊳ **falloir**.

faufiler [3] [fofile] *vt* to tack, to baste. ✦ **se faufiler** *vp* : **se ~ dans** to slip into ; **se ~ entre** to thread one's way between.

faune [fon] ◇ *nf* - **1.** [animaux] fauna - **2.** *péj* [personnes] : **la ~ qui fréquente ce bar** the sort of people who hang round that bar. ◇ *nm* MYTH faun.

faussaire [fosɛʀ] *nmf* forger.

faussement [fosmɑ̃] *adv* - **1.** [à tort] wrongly - **2.** [prétendument] falsely.

fausser [3] [fose] *vt* - **1.** [déformer] to bend - **2.** [rendre faux] to distort.

fausseté [foste] *nf* - **1.** [hypocrisie] duplicity - **2.** [de jugement, d'idée] falsity.

faut ⊳ **falloir**.

faute [fot] *nf* - **1.** [erreur] mistake, error ; ~ **de frappe** [à la machine à écrire] typing error ; [à l'ordinateur] keying error ; ~ **d'orthographe** spelling mistake - **2.** [méfait, infraction] offence *Br*, offense *Am* ; **prendre qqn en ~** to catch sb out ; ~ **professionnelle** professional misdemeanour *Br* misdemeanor *Am* - **3.** TENNIS fault ; FOOTBALL foul - **4.** [responsabilité] fault ; **de ma/ta** *etc* ~ my/your *etc* fault ; **par la ~ de qqn** because of sb. ✦ **faute de** *loc prép* for want ou lack of ; ~ **de mieux** for want ou lack of anything better. ✦ **sans faute** *loc adv* without fail.

fauteuil [fotœj] *nm* - **1.** [siège] armchair ; ~ **roulant** wheelchair - **2.** [de théâtre] seat - **3.** [de président] chair ; [d'académicien] seat.

fautif, ive [fotif, iv] ◇ *adj* - **1.** [coupable] guilty - **2.** [défectueux] faulty. ◇ *nm, f* guilty party.

fauve [fov] ◇ *nm* - **1.** [animal] big cat - **2.** [couleur] fawn - **3.** ART Fauve. ◇ *adj* - **1.** [animal] wild - **2.** [cuir, cheveux] tawny - **3.** ART Fauvist.

fauvette [fovɛt] *nf* warbler.

faux, fausse [fo, fos] *adj* - **1.** [incorrect] wrong - **2.** [postiche, mensonger, hypocrite] false ; ~ **témoignage** JUR perjury - **3.** [monnaie, papiers] forged, fake ; [bijou, marbre] imitation, fake - **4.** [injustifié] : **fausse alerte** false alarm ; **c'est un ~ problème** that's not an issue (here). ✦ **faux** ◇ *nm* [document, tableau] forgery, fake. ◇ *nf* scythe. ◇ *adv* : **chanter/jouer** ~ MUS to sing/play out of tune ; **sonner** ~ *fig* not to ring true.

faux-filet, faux filet [fofile] *nm* sirloin.

faux-fuyant [fofɥijɑ̃] *nm* excuse.

faux-monnayeur [fomɔnɛjœr] *nm* counterfeiter.

faux-sens [fosɑ̃s] *nm inv* mistranslation.

faveur [favœr] *nf* favour *Br*, favor *Am*.
➤ **à la faveur de** *loc prép* thanks to.
➤ **en faveur de** *loc prép* in favour *Br* ou favor *Am* of.

favorable [favɔrabl] *adj* : ~ (à) favourable *Br* ou favorable *Am* (to).

favori, ite [favɔri, it] *adj & nm, f* favourite *Br*, favorite *Am*.

favoriser [3] [favɔrize] *vt* - **1.** [avantager] to favour *Br*, to favor *Am* - **2.** [contribuer à] to promote.

fax [faks] *nm* fax.

faxer [3] [fakse] *vt* to fax.

fayot [fajo] *nm fam* [personne] creep, crawler.

fébrile [febril] *adj* feverish.

fécond, e [fekɔ̃, ɔ̃d] *adj* - **1.** [femelle, terre, esprit] fertile - **2.** [écrivain] prolific.

fécondation [fekɔ̃dasjɔ̃] *nf* fertilization ; ~ in vitro in vitro fertilization.

féconder [3] [fekɔ̃de] *vt* - **1.** [ovule] to fertilize - **2.** [femme, femelle] to impregnate.

fécondité [fekɔ̃dite] *nf* - **1.** [gén] fertility - **2.** [d'écrivain] productiveness.

fécule [fekyl] *nf* starch.

féculent, e [fekylɑ̃, ɑ̃t] *adj* starchy.
➤ **féculent** *nm* starchy food.

fédéral, e, aux [federal, o] *adj* federal.

fédération [federasjɔ̃] *nf* federation.

fée [fe] *nf* fairy.

féerique [fe(e)rik] *adj* [enchanteur] enchanting.

feignant, e = fainéant.

feindre [81] [fɛ̃dr] <> *vt* to feign ; ~ de faire qqch to pretend to do sthg. <> *vi* to pretend.

feint, e [fɛ̃, fɛ̃t] *pp* ⊏ feindre.

feinte [fɛ̃t] *nf* - **1.** [ruse] ruse - **2.** FOOTBALL dummy ; BOXE feint.

fêlé, e [fele] *adj* - **1.** [assiette] cracked - **2.** *fam* [personne] cracked, loony.

fêler [4] [fele] *vt* to crack.

félicitations [felisitasjɔ̃] *nfpl* congratulations.

féliciter [3] [felisite] *vt* to congratulate.
➤ **se féliciter** *vp* : se ~ de to congratulate o.s. on.

félin, e [felɛ̃, in] *adj* feline. ➤ **félin** *nm* big cat.

fêlure [felyr] *nf* crack.

femelle [fəmɛl] *nf & adj* female.

féminin, e [feminɛ̃, in] *adj* - **1.** [gén] femi-

nine - **2.** [revue, équipe] women's *(avant n)*.
➤ **féminin** *nm* GRAM feminine.

féminisme [feminism] *nm* feminism.

féminité [feminite] *nf* femininity.

femme [fam] *nf* - **1.** [personne de sexe féminin] woman ; ~ **de chambre** chambermaid ; ~ **de ménage** cleaning woman - **2.** [épouse] wife.

fémur [femyr] *nm* femur.

fendre [73] [fɑ̃dr] *vt* - **1.** [bois] to split - **2.** [foule, flots] to cut through. ➤ **se fendre** *vp* [se crevasser] to crack.

fendu, e [fɑ̃dy] *pp* ⊏ fendre.

fenêtre [fənɛtr] *nf* [gén & INFORM] window.

fenouil [fənuj] *nm* fennel.

fente [fɑ̃t] *nf* - **1.** [fissure] crack - **2.** [interstice, de vêtement] slit.

féodal, e, aux [feɔdal, o] *adj* feudal.

féodalité [feɔdalite] *nf* feudalism.

fer [fɛr] *nm* iron ; ~ **à cheval** horseshoe ; ~ **forgé** wrought iron ; ~ **à repasser** iron ; ~ **à souder** soldering iron.

feral, feras *etc* ⊏ faire.

fer-blanc [fɛrblɑ̃] *nm* tinplate, tin.

ferblanterie [fɛrblɑ̃tri] *nf* - **1.** [commerce] tin industry - **2.** [ustensiles] tinware.

férié, e [ferje] *adj* ⊏ jour.

férir [ferir] *vt* : sans coup ~ without meeting any resistance ou obstacle.

ferme¹ [fɛrm] *nf* farm.

ferme² [fɛrm] <> *adj* firm ; **être ~ sur ses jambes** to be steady on one's feet. <> *adv* - **1.** [beaucoup] a lot - **2.** [définitivement] : acheter/vendre ~ to make a firm purchase/sale.

fermement [fɛrməmɑ̃] *adv* firmly.

ferment [fɛrmɑ̃] *nm* - **1.** [levure] ferment - **2.** *fig* [germe] seed, seeds *(pl)*.

fermentation [fɛrmɑ̃tasjɔ̃] *nf* CHIM fermentation ; *fig* ferment.

fermer [3] [fɛrme] <> *vt* - **1.** [porte, tiroir, yeux] to close, to shut ; [rideaux] to close, to draw ; [store] to pull down ; [enveloppe] to seal - **2.** [bloquer] to close ; ~ **son esprit à qqch** to close one's mind to sthg - **3.** [gaz, lumière] to turn off - **4.** [vêtement] to do up - **5.** [entreprise] to close down - **6.** [interdire] : ~ **qqch à qqn** to close sthg to sb. <> *vi* - **1.** [gén] to shut, to close - **2.** [vêtement] to do up - **3.** [entreprise] to close down. ➤ **se fermer** *vp* - **1.** [porte] to close, to shut - **2.** [plaie] to close up - **3.** [vêtement] to do up.

fermeté [fɛrməte] *nf* firmness.

fermeture [fɛrmətyr] *nf* - **1.** [de porte]

closing - **2.** [de vêtement, sac] fastening ;
~ **Éclair®** zip *Br*, zipper *Am* - **3.** [d'établissement - temporaire] closing ; [- définitive]
closure ; ~ **hebdomadaire/annuelle** week-
ly/annual closing.

fermier, ère [fɛrmje, ɛr] *nm, f* farmer.

fermoir [fɛrmwar] *nm* clasp.

féroce [feʀɔs] *adj* [animal, appétit] ferocious ; [personne, désir] fierce.

ferraille [fɛraj] *nf* - **1.** [vieux fer] scrap iron
(U) ; **bon à mettre à la** ~ fit for the scrap
heap - **2.** *fam* [monnaie] loose change.

ferronnerie [fɛrɔnri] *nf* - **1.** [objet, métier]
ironwork *(U)* - **2.** [atelier] ironworks *(sg)*.

ferroviaire [feʀɔvjɛr] *adj* rail *(avant n)*.

ferry-boat [feʀibot] *(pl* ferry-boats*) nm*
ferry.

fertile [fɛrtil] *adj litt & fig* fertile ; ~ **en** *fig*
filled with, full of.

fertiliser [3] [fɛrtilize] *vt* to fertilize.

fertilité [fɛrtilite] *nf* fertility.

féru, e [fery] *adj sout* [passionné] : **être**
~ **de qqch** to have a passion for sthg.

fervent, e [fɛrvɑ̃, ɑ̃t] *adj* [chrétien] fervent ; [amoureux, démocrate] ardent.

ferveur [fɛrvœr] *nf* [dévotion] fervour *Br*,
fervor *Am*.

fesse [fɛs] *nf* buttock.

fessée [fese] *nf* spanking, smack (on the
bottom).

festin [fɛstɛ̃] *nm* banquet, feast.

festival, als [fɛstival] *nm* festival.

festivités [fɛstivite] *nfpl* festivities.

feston [fɛstɔ̃] *nm* - **1.** ARCHIT festoon
- **2.** COUTURE scallop.

festoyer [13] [fɛstwaje] *vi* to feast.

fêtard, e [fetar, ard] *nm, f* fun-loving person.

fête [fɛt] *nf* - **1.** [congé] holiday ; **les ~s (de
fin d'année)** the Christmas holidays ; ~ **nationale** national holiday - **2.** [réunion, ré-
ception] celebration - **3.** [kermesse] fair ;
~ **foraine** funfair - **4.** [jour de célébration - de
personne] saint's day ; [- de saint] feast
(day) - **5.** [soirée] party - **6.** *loc* : **faire ~ à qqn**
to make a fuss of sb ; **faire la ~** to have a
good time.

fêter [4] [fete] *vt* [événement] to celebrate ;
[personne] to have a party for.

fétiche [fetiʃ] *nm* - **1.** [objet de culte] fetish
- **2.** [mascotte] mascot.

fétichisme [fetiʃism] *nm* [culte, perver-
sion] fetishism.

fétide [fetid] *adj* fetid.

fétu [fety] *nm* : ~ **(de paille)** wisp (of
straw).

feu¹, e [fø] *adj* : ~ **M. X** the late Mr X ;
~ **mon mari** my late husband.

feu², x [fø] *nm* - **1.** [flamme, incendie] fire ;
au ~! fire! ; **en** ~ *litt & fig* on fire ; **avez-vous
du** ~? have you got a light? ; **faire** ~ MIL to
fire ; **mettre le** ~ **à qqch** to set fire to sthg,
to set sthg on fire ; **prendre** ~ to catch fire ;
~ **de camp** camp fire ; ~ **de cheminée** chimney fire ; ~ **follet** will-o'-the-wisp - **2.** [si-
gnal] light ; ~ **rouge/vert** red/green light ;
~**x de croisement** dipped headlights ; ~**x de
position** sidelights ; ~**x de route** headlights
on full beam - **3.** CULIN ring *Br*, burner *Am* ;
à ~ **doux/vif** on a low/high flame ; **à petit** ~
gently - **4.** CIN & THÉÂTRE light *(U)*. ◆ **feu
d'artifice** *nm* firework.

feuillage [fœjaʒ] *nm* foliage.

feuille [fœj] *nf* - **1.** [d'arbre] leaf ; ~ **morte**
dead leaf ; ~ **de vigne** BOT vine leaf
- **2.** [page] sheet ; ~ **de papier** sheet of paper
- **3.** [document] form ; ~ **de soins** *claim form
for reimbursement of medical expenses*.

feuillet [fœjɛ] *nm* page.

feuilleté, e [fœjte] *adj* - **1.** CULIN : **pâte ~e**
puff pastry - **2.** GÉOL foliated.

feuilleter [27] [fœjte] *vt* to flick through.

feuilleton [fœjtɔ̃] *nm* serial.

feutre [føtr] *nm* - **1.** [étoffe] felt - **2.** [cha-
peau] felt hat - **3.** [crayon] felt-tip pen.

feutré, e [føtre] *adj* - **1.** [garni de feutre]
trimmed with felt ; [qui a l'aspect du feutre]
felted - **2.** [bruit, cri] muffled.

feutrine [føtrin] *nf* lightweight felt.

fève [fɛv] *nf* broad bean.

février [fevrije] *nm* February ; *voir aussi*
septembre.

fg *abr de* **faubourg**.

fi [fi] *interj* : **faire** ~ **de** to scorn.

fiable [fjabl] *adj* reliable.

fiacre [fjakr] *nm* hackney carriage.

fiançailles [fjɑ̃saj] *nfpl* engagement *(sg)*.

fiancé, e [fjɑ̃se] *nm, f* fiancé *(f* fiancée*)*.

fiancer [16] [fjɑ̃se] ◆ **se fiancer** *vp* : se
~ **(avec)** to get engaged (to).

fibre [fibr] *nf* ANAT, BIOL & TECHNOL fibre
Br, fiber *Am* ; ~ **de verre** fibreglass *Br* ou
fiberglass *Am*, glass fibre *Br*.

ficelé, e [fisle] *adj fam* dressed.

ficeler [24] [fisle] *vt* [lier] to tie up.

ficelle [fisɛl] *nf* - **1.** [fil] string - **2.** [pain] *thin
French stick* - **3.** *(gén pl)* [truc] trick.

fiche [fiʃ] *nf* - **1.** [document] card ; ~ **de
paie** pay slip - **2.** ÉLECTR & TECHNOL pin.

ficher [3] [fiʃe] *(pp vt sens 1 & 2* fiché, *pp vt
sens 3 & 4* fichu*) vt* - **1.** [enfoncer] : ~ **qqch
dans** to stick sthg into - **2.** [inscrire] to put

on file - **3.** *fam* [faire] : **qu'est-ce qu'il fiche?** what's he doing? - **4.** *fam* [mettre] to put ; **~ qqch par terre** *fig* to mess ou muck sthg up. ◆ **se ficher** *vp* - **1.** [s'enfoncer - suj : clou, pique] : **se ~ dans** to go into - **2.** *fam* [se moquer] : **se ~ de** to make fun of - **3.** *fam* [ne pas tenir compte] : **se ~ de** not to give a damn about.

fichier [fiʃje] *nm* file.

fichu, e [fiʃy] *adj* - **1.** *fam* [cassé, fini] done for - **2.** *(avant n)* [désagréable] nasty - **3.** *loc* : **être mal ~** *fam* [personne] to feel rotten ; [objet] to be badly made ; **il n'est même pas ~ de faire son lit** *fam* he can't even make his own bed. ◆ **fichu** *nm* scarf.

fictif, ive [fiktif, iv] *adj* - **1.** [imaginaire] imaginary - **2.** [faux] false.

fiction [fiksjɔ̃] *nf* - **1.** LITTÉRATURE fiction - **2.** [monde imaginaire] dream world.

fidèle [fidɛl] ◇ *nmf* - **1.** RELIG believer - **2.** [adepte] fan. ◇ *adj* - **1.** [loyal, exact, semblable] : **~ (à)** faithful (to) ; **~ à la réalité** accurate - **2.** [habitué] regular. ◆ **fidèlement** *adv* faithfully.

fidéliser [3] [fidelize] *vt* to attract and keep.

fidélité [fidelite] *nf* faithfulness.

fief [fjɛf] *nm* fief ; *fig* stronghold.

fiel [fjɛl] *nm* *litt* & *fig* gall.

fier¹, fière [fjɛr] *adj* - **1.** [gén] proud ; **~ de qqn/qqch** proud of sb/sthg ; **~ de faire qqch** proud to be doing sthg - **2.** [noble] noble.

fier² [9] [fje] ◆ **se fier** *vp* : **se ~ à** to trust, to rely on.

fierté [fjɛrte] *nf* - **1.** [satisfaction, dignité] pride - **2.** [arrogance] arrogance.

fièvre [fjɛvr] *nf* - **1.** MÉD fever ; **avoir 40 de ~** to have a temperature of 105 (degrees) - **2.** *fig* [excitation] excitement.

fiévreux, euse [fjevrø, øz] *adj* *litt* & *fig* feverish.

fig. *abr de* figure.

figer [17] [fiʒe] *vt* to paralyse *Br*, to paralyze *Am*. ◆ **se figer** *vp* - **1.** [s'immobiliser] to freeze - **2.** [se solidifier] to congeal.

fignoler [3] [fiɲɔle] *vt* to put the finishing touches to.

figue [fig] *nf* fig.

figuier [figje] *nm* fig-tree.

figurant, e [figyrɑ̃, ɑ̃t] *nm, f* extra.

figuratif, ive [figyratif, iv] *adj* figurative.

figure [figyr] *nf* - **1.** [gén] figure ; **faire ~ de** to look like - **2.** [visage] face.

figuré, e [figyre] *adj* [sens] figurative. ◆ **figuré** *nm* : **au ~** in the figurative sense.

figurer [3] [figyre] ◇ *vt* to represent. ◇ *vi* : **~ dans/parmi** to figure in/among.

figurine [figyrin] *nf* figurine.

fil [fil] *nm* - **1.** [brin] thread ; **~ à plomb** plumb line ; **perdre le ~ (de qqch)** *fig* to lose the thread (of sthg) - **2.** [câble] wire ; **~ de fer** wire - **3.** [cours] course ; **au ~ de** in the course of - **4.** [tissu] linen - **5.** [tranchant] edge.

filament [filamɑ̃] *nm* - **1.** ANAT & ÉLECTR filament - **2.** [végétal] fibre *Br*, fiber *Am* - **3.** [de colle, bave] thread.

filandreux, euse [filɑ̃drø, øz] *adj* [viande] stringy.

filasse [filas] ◇ *nf* tow. ◇ *adj inv* flaxen.

filature [filatyr] *nf* - **1.** [usine] mill ; [fabrication] spinning - **2.** [poursuite] tailing.

file [fil] *nf* line ; **à la ~** in a line ; **se garer en double ~** to double-park ; **~ d'attente** queue *Br*, line *Am*.

filer [3] [file] ◇ *vt* - **1.** [soie, coton] to spin - **2.** [personne] to tail - **3.** *fam* [donner] : **~ qqch à qqn** to slip sthg to sb, to slip sb sthg. ◇ *vi* - **1.** [bas] to ladder *Br*, to run *Am* - **2.** [aller vite - temps, véhicule] to fly (by) - **3.** *fam* [partir] to dash off - **4.** *loc* : **~ doux** to behave nicely.

filet [filɛ] *nm* - **1.** [à mailles] net ; **~ de pêche** fishing net ; **~ à provisions** string bag - **2.** CULIN fillet *Br*, filet *Am* ; **~ de sole** fillet *Br* ou filet *Am* of sole - **3.** [de liquide] drop, dash ; [de lumière] shaft.

filial, e, aux [filjal, o] *adj* filial. ◆ **filiale** *nf* FCON subsidiary.

filiation [filjasjɔ̃] *nf* [lien de parenté] line.

filière [filjɛr] *nf* - **1.** [voie] : **suivre la ~** [professionnelle] to work one's way up ; **suivre la ~ hiérarchique** to go through the right channels - **2.** [réseau] network.

filiforme [filiform] *adj* skinny.

filigrane [filigran] *nm* [dessin] watermark ; **en ~** *fig* between the lines.

filin [filɛ̃] *nm* rope.

fille [fij] *nf* - **1.** [enfant] daughter - **2.** [femme] girl ; **jeune ~** girl ; **~ mère** *péj* single mother ; **vieille ~** *péj* spinster.

fillette [fijɛt] *nf* little girl.

filleul, e [fijœl] *nm, f* godchild.

film [film] *nm* - **1.** [gén] film ; **~ catastrophe** disaster movie ; **~ d'épouvante** horror film ; **~ policier** detective film - **2.** *fig* [déroulement] course.

filmer [3] [filme] *vt* to film.

filmographie [filmɔgrafi] *nf* filmography, films *(pl)*.

filon [filɔ̃] *nm* - **1.** [de mine] vein - **2.** *fam* *fig* [possibilité] cushy number.

fils [fis] *nm* son ; ~ **de famille** boy from a privileged background.

filtrant, e [filtrã, ãt] *adj* [verre] tinted.

filtre [filtr] *nm* filter ; ~ **à café** coffee filter.

filtrer [3] [filtre] <> *vt* to filter ; *fig* to screen. <> *vi* to filter ; *fig* to filter through.

fin, fine [fẽ, fin] <> *adj* - **1.** [gén] fine - **2.** [partie du corps] slender ; [couche, papier] thin - **3.** [subtil] shrewd - **4.** [ouïe, vue] keen. <> *adv* finely ; ~ **prêt** quite ready. ➤ **fin** *nf* end ; ~ **mars** at the end of March ; **mettre ~ à** to put a stop to ; **prendre ~** to come to an end ; **tirer** ou **toucher à sa ~** to draw to a close ; **arriver** ou **parvenir à ses ~s** to achieve one's ends ou aims. ➤ **fin de série** *nf* oddment. ➤ **à la fin** *loc adv* : **tu vas m'écouter, à la ~?** will you listen to me? ➤ **à la fin de** *loc prép* at the end of. ➤ **sans fin** *loc adj* endless.

final, e [final] (*pl* **finals** ou **finaux** [fino]) *adj* final. ➤ **finale** *nf* SPORT final.

finalement [finalmã] *adv* finally.

finaliste [finalist] *nmf & adj* finalist.

finalité [finalite] *nf sout* [fonction] purpose.

finance [finãs] *nf* finance. ➤ **finances** *nfpl* finances.

financer [16] [finãse] *vt* to finance, to fund.

financier, ère [finãsje, ɛr] *adj* financial. ➤ **financier** *nm* financier.

finaud, e [fino, od] *adj* wily, crafty.

finesse [fines] *nf* - **1.** [gén] fineness - **2.** [minceur] slenderness - **3.** [perspicacité] shrewdness - **4.** [subtilité] subtlety.

fini, e [fini] *adj* - **1.** *péj* [fieffé] : **un crétin ~** a complete idiot - **2.** *fam* [usé, diminué] finished - **3.** [limité] finite. ➤ **fini** *nm* [d'objet] finish.

finir [32] [finir] <> *vt* - **1.** [gén] to finish, to end - **2.** [vider] to empty. <> *vi* - **1.** [gén] to finish, to end ; ~ **par faire qqch** to do sthg eventually ; **tu vas ~ par tomber!** you're going to fall! ; **mal ~** to end badly - **2.** [arrêter] : **~ de faire qqch** to stop doing sthg ; **en ~ (avec)** to finish (with).

finition [finisjõ] *nf* [d'objet] finish.

finlandais, e [fẽlãdɛ, ɛz] *adj* Finnish. ➤ **Finlandais, e** *nm, f* Finn.

Finlande [fẽlãd] *nf* : **la ~** Finland.

finnois, e [finwa, az] *adj* Finnish. ➤ **finnois** *nm* [langue] Finnish. ➤ **Finnois, e** *nm, f* Finn.

fiole [fjɔl] *nf* flask.

fioriture [fjɔrityr] *nf* flourish.

fioul = fuel.

firmament [firmamã] *nm* firmament.

firme [firm] *nf* firm.

fis, fit *etc* ⊳ **faire.**

fisc [fisk] *nm* ≃ Inland Revenue *Br*, ≃ Internal Revenue *Am*.

fiscal, e, aux [fiskal, o] *adj* tax *(avant n)*, fiscal.

fiscalité [fiskalite] *nf* tax system.

fissure [fisyr] *nf litt & fig* crack.

fissurer [3] [fisyre] *vt* [fendre] to crack ; *fig* to split. ➤ **se fissurer** *vp* to crack.

fiston [fistõ] *nm fam* son.

FIV [fiv] (*abr de* **fécondation in vitro**) *nf* IVF.

fixation [fiksasjõ] *nf* - **1.** [action de fixer] fixing - **2.** [attache] fastening, fastener ; [de ski] binding - **3.** PSYCHOL fixation.

fixe [fiks] *adj* fixed ; [encre] permanent. ➤ **fixe** *nm* fixed salary.

fixement [fiksəmã] *adv* fixedly.

fixer [3] [fikse] *vt* - **1.** [gén] to fix ; [règle] to set ; ~ **son choix sur** to decide on - **2.** [monter] to hang - **3.** [regarder] to stare at - **4.** [renseigner] : ~ **qqn sur qqch** to put sb in the picture about sthg ; **être fixé sur qqch** to know all about sthg. ➤ **se fixer** *vp* to settle ; **se ~ sur** [suj : choix, personne] to settle on ; [suj : regard] to rest on.

fjord [fjɔrd] *nm* fjord.

flacon [flakõ] *nm* small bottle ; ~ **à parfum** perfume bottle.

flageller [4] [flaʒele] *vt* [fouetter] to flagellate.

flageoler [3] [flaʒɔle] *vi* to tremble.

flageolet [flaʒɔlɛ] *nm* - **1.** [haricot] flageolet bean - **2.** MUS flageolet.

flagrant, e [flagrã, ãt] *adj* flagrant ⊳ **délit.**

flair [flɛr] *nm* sense of smell.

flairer [4] [flɛre] *vt* to sniff, to smell ; *fig* to scent.

flamand, e [flamã, ãd] *adj* Flemish. ➤ **flamand** *nm* [langue] Flemish. ➤ **Flamand, e** *nm, f* Flemish person, Fleming.

flamant [flamã] *nm* flamingo ; ~ **rose** pink flamingo.

flambeau, x [flãbo] *nm* torch ; *fig* flame.

flamber [3] [flãbe] <> *vi* - **1.** [brûler] to blaze - **2.** *fam* JEU to play for high stakes. <> *vt* - **1.** [crêpe] to flambé - **2.** [volaille] to singe.

flamboyant, e [flãbwajã, ãt] *adj* - **1.** [ciel, regard] blazing ; [couleur] flaming - **2.** ARCHIT flamboyant.

flamboyer [13] [flãbwaje] *vi* to blaze.

flamme [flam] *nf* flame ; *fig* fervour *Br*, fervor *Am*, fire.

flan [flɑ̃] nm baked custard.

flanc [flɑ̃] nm [de personne, navire, montagne] side ; [d'animal, d'armée] flank.

flancher [3] [flɑ̃ʃe] vi fam to give up.

flanelle [flanɛl] nf flannel.

flâner [3] [flane] vi [se promener] to stroll.

flanquer [3] [flɑ̃ke] vt - **1.** fam [jeter] : ~ **qqch par terre** to fling sthg to the ground ; ~ **qqn dehors** to chuck ou fling sb out - **2.** fam [donner] : ~ **une gifle à qqn** to clout sb round the ear ; ~ **la frousse à qqn** to put the wind up sb - **3.** [accompagner] : **être flanqué de** to be flanked by.

flapi, e [flapi] adj fam dead beat.

flaque [flak] nf pool.

flash [flaʃ] nm - **1.** PHOT flash - **2.** RADIO & TÉLÉ : ~ **(d'information)** newsflash ; ~ **de publicité** commercial.

flash-back [flaʃbak] (pl inv ou **flash-backs**) nm CIN flashback.

flasher [3] [flaʃe] vi fam : ~ **sur qqn/qqch** to be turned on by sb/sthg.

flasque [flask] <> nf flask. <> adj flabby, limp.

flatter [3] [flate] vt - **1.** [louer] to flatter - **2.** [caresser] to stroke. ◆ **se flatter** vp to flatter o.s. ; **je me flatte de le convaincre** I flatter myself that I can convince him ; **se ~ de faire qqch** to pride o.s. on doing sthg.

flatterie [flatri] nf flattery.

flatteur, euse [flatœr, øz] <> adj flattering. <> nm, f flatterer.

fléau, x [fleo] nm - **1.** litt & fig [calamité] scourge - **2.** [instrument] flail.

flèche [flɛʃ] nf - **1.** [gén] arrow - **2.** [d'église] spire - **3.** fig [critique] shaft.

fléchette [fleʃet] nf dart. ◆ **fléchettes** nfpl darts (sg).

fléchir [32] [fleʃir] <> vt to bend, to flex ; fig to sway. <> vi to bend ; fig to weaken.

fléchissement [fleʃismɑ̃] nm flexing, bending ; fig weakening.

flegmatique [flegmatik] adj phlegmatic.

flegme [flegm] nm composure.

flemmard, e [flemar, ard] fam <> adj lazy. <> nm, f lazybones (sg).

flemme [flem] nf fam laziness ; **j'ai la ~ (de sortir)** I can't be bothered (to go out).

flétrir [32] [fletrir] vt [fleur, visage] to wither. ◆ **se flétrir** vp to wither.

fleur [flœr] nf BOT & fig flower ; **en ~, en ~s** [arbre] in flower, in blossom ; **à ~s** [motif] flowered.

fleuret [flœrɛ] nm foil.

fleuri, e [flœri] adj - **1.** [jardin, pré] in flower ; [vase] of flowers ; [tissu] flowered ;

[table, appartement] decorated with flowers - **2.** fig [style] flowery.

fleurir [32] [flœrir] <> vi to blossom ; fig to flourish. <> vt [maison] to decorate with flowers ; [tombe] to lay flowers on.

fleuriste [flœrist] nmf florist.

fleuron [flœrɔ̃] nm fig jewel.

fleuve [flœv] nm - **1.** [cours d'eau] river - **2.** (en apposition) [interminable] lengthy, interminable.

flexible [flɛksibl] adj flexible.

flexion [flɛksjɔ̃] nf - **1.** [de genou, de poutre] bending - **2.** LING inflexion.

flibustier [flibystje] nm buccaneer.

flic [flik] nm fam cop.

flinguer [3] [flɛ̃ge] vt fam to gun down. ◆ **se flinguer** vp fam to blow one's brains out.

flipper [flipœr] nm pin-ball machine.

flirter [3] [flœrte] vi : ~ **(avec qqn)** to flirt (with sb) ; ~ **avec qqch** fig to flirt with sthg.

flocon [flɔkɔ̃] nm flake ; ~ **de neige** snowflake.

flonflon [flɔ̃flɔ̃] nm (gén pl) blare.

flop [flɔp] nm [échec] flop, failure.

floraison [flɔrezɔ̃] nf litt & fig flowering, blossoming.

floral, e, aux [flɔral, o] adj floral.

flore [flɔr] nf flora.

Floride [flɔrid] nf : **la ~** Florida.

florissant, e [flɔrisɑ̃, ɑ̃t] adj [santé] blooming ; [économie] flourishing.

flot [flo] nm flood, stream ; **être à ~** [navire] to be afloat ; fig to be back to normal. ◆ **flots** nmpl littéraire waves.

flottaison [flɔtɛzɔ̃] nf floating.

flottant, e [flɔtɑ̃, ɑ̃t] adj - **1.** [gén] floating ; [esprit] irresolute - **2.** [robe] loose-fitting.

flotte [flɔt] nf - **1.** AÉRON & NAVIG fleet - **2.** fam [eau] water - **3.** fam [pluie] rain.

flottement [flɔtmɑ̃] nm - **1.** [indécision] hesitation, wavering - **2.** [de monnaie] floating.

flotter [3] [flɔte] <> vi - **1.** [sur l'eau] to float - **2.** [drapeau] to flap ; [brume, odeur] to drift - **3.** [dans un vêtement] : **tu flottes dedans** it's baggy on you. <> v impers fam : **il flotte** it's raining.

flotteur [flɔtœr] nm [de ligne de pêche, d'hydravion] float ; [de chasse d'eau] ballcock.

flou, e [flu] adj - **1.** [couleur, coiffure] soft - **2.** [photo] blurred, fuzzy - **3.** [pensée] vague, woolly. ◆ **flou** nm [de photo] fuzziness ; [de décision] vagueness.

flouer [3] [flue] *vt fam* to do, to swindle.

fluctuer [3] [flyktɥe] *vi* to fluctuate.

fluet, ette [flyɛ, ɛt] *adj* [personne] thin, slender ; [voix] thin.

fluide [flɥid] <> *nm* - 1. [matière] fluid - 2. *fig* [pouvoir] (occult) power. <> *adj* [matière] fluid ; [circulation] flowing freely.

fluidifier [9] [flɥidifje] *vt* [trafic] to improve the flow of.

fluidité [flɥidite] *nf* [gén] fluidity ; [de circulation] easy flow.

fluor [flyɔr] *nm* fluorine.

fluorescent, e [flyɔresɑ̃, ɑ̃t] *adj* fluorescent.

flûte [flyt] <> *nf* - 1. MUS flute - 2. [verre] flute (glass). <> *interj fam* bother!

flûtiste [flytist] *nmf* flautist *Br*, flutist *Am*.

fluvial, e, aux [flyvjal, o] *adj* [eaux, pêche] river *(avant n)* ; [alluvions] fluvial.

flux [fly] *nm* - 1. [écoulement] flow - 2. [marée] flood tide - 3. PHYS flux.

fluxion [flyksjɔ̃] *nf* inflammation.

FM *(abr de* frequency modulation) *nf* FM.

FMI *(abr de* Fonds monétaire international) *nm* IMF.

FN *(abr de* Front national) *nm extreme right-wing French political party.*

foc [fɔk] *nm* jib.

focal, e, aux [fɔkal, o] *adj* focal.

fœtal, e, aux [fetal, o] *adj* foetal.

fœtus [fetys] *nm* foetus.

foi [fwa] *nf* - 1. RELIG faith - 2. [confiance] trust ; **avoir ~ en qqn/qqch** to trust sb/sthg, to have faith in sb/sthg - 3. *loc* : **être de bonne/mauvaise ~** to be in good/bad faith.

foie [fwa] *nm* ANAT & CULIN liver.

foin [fwɛ̃] *nm* hay.

foire [fwar] *nf* - 1. [fête] funfair - 2. [exposition, salon] trade fair.

fois [fwa] *nf* time ; **une ~** once ; **deux ~** twice ; **trois/quatre ~** three/four times ; **deux ~ plus long** twice as long ; **neuf ~ sur dix** nine times out of ten ; **deux ~ trois** two times three ; **cette ~** this time ; **il était une ~ ...** once upon a time there was ... ; **une (bonne) ~ pour toutes** once and for all. ➜ **à la fois** *loc adv* at the same time, at once. ➜ **des fois** *loc adv* [parfois] sometimes ; **non, mais des ~!** *fam* look here! ➜ **si des fois** *loc conj fam* if ever. ➜ **une fois que** *loc conj* once.

foison [fwazɔ̃] ➜ **à foison** *loc adv* in abundance.

foisonner [3] [fwazɔne] *vi* to abound.

folâtre [fɔlatr] *adj* playful.

folâtrer [3] [fɔlatre] *vi* to romp (about).

folie [fɔli] *nf litt & fig* madness.

folklore [fɔlklɔr] *nm* [de pays] folklore.

folklorique [fɔlklɔrik] *adj* - 1. [danse] folk - 2. *fig* [situation, personne] bizarre, quaint.

folle ⊳ **fou.**

follement [fɔlmɑ̃] *adv* madly, wildly.

follet [fɔlɛ] ⊳ **feu.**

fomenter [3] [fɔmɑ̃te] *vt* to foment.

foncé, e [fɔ̃se] *adj* dark.

foncer [16] [fɔ̃se] *vi* - 1. [teinte] to darken - 2. [se ruer] : **~ sur** to rush at - 3. *fam* [se dépêcher] to get a move on.

foncier, ère [fɔ̃sje, ɛr] *adj* - 1. [impôt] land *(avant n)* ; **propriétaire ~** landowner - 2. [fondamental] basic, fundamental.

foncièrement [fɔ̃sjɛrmɑ̃] *adv* basically.

fonction [fɔ̃ksjɔ̃] *nf* - 1. [gén] function ; **faire ~ de** to act as - 2. [profession] post ; **entrer en ~** to take up one's post ou duties. ➜ **en fonction de** *loc prép* according to.

fonctionnaire [fɔ̃ksjɔnɛr] *nmf* [de l'État] state employee ; [dans l'administration] civil servant ; **haut ~** senior civil servant.

fonctionnel, elle [fɔ̃ksjɔnɛl] *adj* functional.

fonctionnement [fɔ̃ksjɔnmɑ̃] *nm* working, functioning.

fonctionner [3] [fɔ̃ksjɔne] *vi* to work, to function.

fond [fɔ̃] *nm* - 1. [de récipient, puits, mer] bottom ; [de pièce] back ; **sans ~** bottomless - 2. [substance] heart, root ; **le ~ de ma pensée** what I really think ; **le ~ et la forme** content and form - 3. [arrière-plan] background. ➜ **fond de teint** *nm* foundation. ➜ **à fond** *loc adv* - 1. [entièrement] thoroughly ; **se donner à ~** to give one's all - 2. [très vite] at top speed. ➜ **au fond, dans le fond** *loc adv* basically. ➜ **au fond de** *loc prép* : **au ~ de moi-même/lui-même** *etc* at heart, deep down.

fondamental, e, aux [fɔ̃damɑ̃tal, o] *adj* fundamental.

fondant, e [fɔ̃dɑ̃, ɑ̃t] *adj* [neige, glace] melting ; [aliment] which melts in the mouth.

fondateur, trice [fɔ̃datœr, tris] *nm, f* founder.

fondation [fɔ̃dasjɔ̃] *nf* foundation. ➜ **fondations** *nfpl* CONSTR foundations.

fondé, e [fɔ̃de] *adj* [craintes, reproches] justified, well-founded ; **non ~** unfounded. ➜ **fondé de pouvoir** *nm* authorized representative.

fondement [fɔ̃dmɑ̃] *nm* [base, motif] foundation ; **sans ~** groundless, without foundation.

fonder [3] [fɔ̃de] *vt* - **1.** [créer] to found - **2.** [baser] : ~ **qqch sur** to base sthg on ; ~ **de grands espoirs sur qqn** to pin one's hopes on sb. ◆ **se fonder** *vp* : **se ~ sur** [suj : personne] to base o.s. on ; [suj : argument] to be based on.

fonderie [fɔ̃dri] *nf* [usine] foundry.

fondre [75] [fɔ̃dr] ◇ *vt* - **1.** [beurre, neige] to melt ; [sucre, sel] to dissolve ; [métal] to melt down - **2.** [mouler] to cast - **3.** [mêler] to blend. ◇ *vi* - **1.** [beurre, neige] to melt ; [sucre, sel] to dissolve ; *fig* to melt away - **2.** [maigrir] to lose weight - **3.** [se ruer] : ~ **sur** to swoop down on.

fonds [fɔ̃] ◇ *nm* - **1.** [ressources] fund ; **le Fonds monétaire international** the International Monetary Fund - **2.** [bien immobilier] : ~ **(de commerce)** business. ◇ *nmpl* funds.

fondu, e [fɔ̃dy] *pp* ▷ **fondre.** ◆ **fondue** *nf* fondue.

font ▷ **faire.**

fontaine [fɔ̃tɛn] *nf* [naturelle] spring ; [publique] fountain.

fonte [fɔ̃t] *nf* - **1.** [de glace, beurre] melting ; [de métal] melting down - **2.** [alliage] cast iron.

foot [fut] = **football.**

football [futbol] *nm* football *Br*, soccer.

footballeur, euse [futbolœr, øz] *nm, f* footballer *Br*, soccer player.

footing [futiŋ] *nm* jogging.

for [fɔr] *nm* : **dans son ~ intérieur** in his/her heart of hearts.

forage [fɔraʒ] *nm* drilling.

forain, e [fɔrɛ̃, ɛn] *adj* ▷ **fête.** ◆ **forain** *nm* stallholder.

forçat [fɔrsa] *nm* convict.

force [fɔrs] *nf* - **1.** [vigueur] strength ; **c'est ce qui fait sa ~** that's where his strength lies - **2.** [violence, puissance, MIL & PHYS] force ; **faire faire qqch à qqn de ~** to force sb to do sthg ; **avoir ~ de loi** to have force of law ; **obtenir qqch par la ~** to obtain sthg by force ; ~ **centrifuge** PHYS centrifugal force. ◆ **forces** *nfpl* [physique] strength *(sg)* ; **de toutes ses ~s** with all his/her strength. ◆ **à force de** *loc prép* by dint of.

forcément [fɔrsemɑ̃] *adv* inevitably.

forcené, e [fɔrsəne] *nm, f* maniac.

forceps [fɔrsɛps] *nm* forceps *(pl)*.

forcer [16] [fɔrse] ◇ *vt* - **1.** [gén] to force ; ~ **qqn à qqch/à faire qqch** to force sb into sthg/to do sthg - **2.** [admiration, respect] to compel, to command - **3.** [talent, voix] to strain. ◇ *vi* : **ça ne sert à rien de ~, ça ne**

passe pas there's no point in forcing it, it won't go through ; ~ **sur qqch** to overdo sthg. ◆ **se forcer** *vp* [s'obliger] : **se ~ à faire qqch** to force o.s. to do sthg.

forcir [32] [fɔrsir] *vi* to put on weight.

forer [3] [fɔre] *vt* to drill.

forestier, ère [fɔrɛstje, ɛr] *adj* forest *(avant n).*

forêt [fɔrɛ] *nf* forest.

forfait [fɔrfɛ] *nm* - **1.** [prix fixe] fixed price - **2.** SPORT : **déclarer ~** [abandonner] to withdraw ; *fig* to give up - **3.** *littéraire* [crime] heinous crime.

forfaitaire [fɔrfɛtɛr] *adj* inclusive.

forge [fɔrʒ] *nf* forge.

forger [17] [fɔrʒe] *vt* - **1.** [métal] to forge - **2.** *fig* [caractère] to form.

forgeron [fɔrʒərɔ̃] *nm* blacksmith.

formaliser [3] [fɔrmalize] *vt* to formalize. ◆ **se formaliser** *vp* : **se ~ (de)** to take offence *Br* ou offense *Am* (at).

formalisme [fɔrmalism] *nm* formality.

formaliste [fɔrmalist] ◇ *nmf* formalist. ◇ *adj* [milieu] conventional ; [personne] : **être ~** to be a stickler for the rules.

formalité [fɔrmalite] *nf* formality.

format [fɔrma] *nm* [dimension] size.

formatage [fɔrmataʒ] *nm* INFORM formatting.

formater [3] [fɔrmate] *vt* INFORM to format.

formateur, trice [fɔrmatœr, tris] ◇ *adj* formative. ◇ *nm, f* trainer.

formation [fɔrmasjɔ̃] *nf* - **1.** [gén] formation - **2.** [apprentissage] training.

forme [fɔrm] *nf* - **1.** [aspect] shape, form ; **en ~ de** in the shape of - **2.** [état] form ; **être en (pleine) ~** to be in (great) shape, to be on (top) form. ◆ **formes** *nfpl* figure *(sg).*

formel, elle [fɔrmɛl] *adj* - **1.** [définitif, ferme] positive, definite - **2.** [poli] formal.

former [3] [fɔrme] *vt* - **1.** [gén] to form - **2.** [personnel, élèves] to train - **3.** [goût, sensibilité] to develop. ◆ **se former** *vp* - **1.** [se constituer] to form - **2.** [s'instruire] to train o.s.

Formica® [fɔrmika] *nm inv* Formica®.

formidable [fɔrmidabl] *adj* - **1.** [épatant] great, tremendous - **2.** [incroyable] incredible.

formol [fɔrmɔl] *nm* formalin.

formulaire [fɔrmylɛr] *nm* form ; **remplir un ~** to fill in a form.

formule [fɔrmyl] *nf* - **1.** [expression] expression ; ~ **de politesse** [orale] polite phrase ; [épistolaire] letter ending - **2.** CHIM

& MATHS formula - **3.** [méthode] way, method.

formuler [3] [fɔrmyle] *vt* to formulate, to express.

fort, e [fɔr, fɔrt] ⟨⟩ *adj* - **1.** [gén] strong ; **et le plus ~, c'est que …** and the most amazing thing about it is … ; **c'est plus ~ que moi** I can't help it - **2.** [corpulent] heavy, big - **3.** [doué] gifted ; **être ~ en qqch** to be good at sthg - **4.** [puissant - voix] loud ; [- vent, lumière, accent] strong - **5.** [considérable] large ; **il y a de ~es chances qu'il gagne** there's a good chance he'll win. ⟨⟩ *adv* - **1.** [frapper, battre] hard ; [sonner, parler] loud, loudly - **2.** *sout* [très] very. ⟨⟩ *nm* - **1.** [château] fort - **2.** [spécialité] **: ce n'est pas mon ~** it's not my forte ou strong point.

forteresse [fɔrtərɛs] *nf* fortress.

fortifiant, e [fɔrtifjɑ̃, ɑ̃t] *adj* fortifying. ➤ **fortifiant** *nm* tonic.

fortification [fɔrtifikasjɔ̃] *nf* fortification.

fortifier [9] [fɔrtifje] *vt* [personne, ville] to fortify ; **~ qqn dans qqch** *fig* to strengthen sb in sthg.

fortuit, e [fɔrtɥi, it] *adj* chance *(avant n)*, fortuitous.

fortune [fɔrtyn] *nf* - **1.** [richesse] fortune - **2.** [hasard] luck, fortune.

fortuné, e [fɔrtyne] *adj* - **1.** [riche] wealthy - **2.** [chanceux] fortunate, lucky.

forum [fɔrɔm] *nm* forum.

fosse [fos] *nf* - **1.** [trou] pit - **2.** [tombe] grave.

fossé [fose] *nm* ditch ; *fig* gap.

fossette [fosɛt] *nf* dimple.

fossile [fosil] *nm* - **1.** [de plante, d'animal] fossil - **2.** *fig & péj* [personne] fossil, fogy.

fossoyeur, euse [foswajœr, øz] *nm, f* gravedigger.

fou, folle [fu, fɔl] ⟨⟩ *adj* (**fol** *devant voyelle ou h muet*) mad, insane ; [prodigieux] tremendous. ⟨⟩ *nm, f* madman (*f* madwoman).

foudre [fudr] *nf* lightning.

foudroyant, e [fudrwajɑ̃, ɑ̃t] *adj* - **1.** [progrès, vitesse] lightning *(avant n)* ; [succès] stunning - **2.** [nouvelle] devastating ; [regard] withering.

foudroyer [13] [fudrwaje] *vt* - **1.** [suj : foudre] to strike ; **l'arbre a été foudroyé** the tree was struck by lightning - **2.** *fig* [abattre] to strike down, to kill ; **~ qqn du regard** to glare at sb.

fouet [fwɛ] *nm* - **1.** [en cuir] whip - **2.** CULIN whisk.

fouetter [4] [fwete] *vt* - **1.** [gén] to whip ; [suj : pluie] to lash (against) - **2.** [stimuler] to stimulate.

fougère [fuʒɛr] *nf* fern.

fougue [fug] *nf* ardour *Br*, ardor *Am*.

fougueux, euse [fugø, øz] *adj* ardent, spirited.

fouille [fuj] *nf* - **1.** [de personne, maison] search - **2.** [du sol] dig, excavation.

fouiller [3] [fuje] ⟨⟩ *vt* - **1.** [gén] to search - **2.** *fig* [approfondir] to examine closely. ⟨⟩ *vi* **: ~ dans** to go through.

fouillis [fuji] *nm* jumble, muddle.

fouine [fwin] *nf* stone-marten.

fouiner [3] [fwine] *vi* to ferret about.

foulard [fular] *nm* scarf.

foule [ful] *nf* [de gens] crowd.

foulée [fule] *nf* [de coureur] stride.

fouler [3] [fule] *vt* [raisin] to press ; [sol] to walk on. ➤ **se fouler** *vp* MÉD **: se ~ le poignet/la cheville** to sprain one's wrist/ankle.

foulure [fulyr] *nf* sprain.

four [fur] *nm* - **1.** [de cuisson] oven ; **~ électrique/à micro-ondes** electric/microwave oven ; **~ crématoire** HIST oven - **2.** THÉÂTRE flop.

fourbe [furb] *adj* treacherous, deceitful.

fourbu, e [furby] *adj* tired out, exhausted.

fourche [furʃ] *nf* - **1.** [outil] pitchfork - **2.** [de vélo, route] fork - **3.** *Belg* SCOL free period.

fourchette [furʃɛt] *nf* - **1.** [couvert] fork - **2.** [écart] range, bracket.

fourgon [furgɔ̃] *nm* - **1.** [camionnette] van ; **~ cellulaire** police van *Br*, patrol wagon *Am* - **2.** [ferroviaire] **: ~ à bestiaux** cattle truck ; **~ postal** mail van.

fourgonnette [furgɔnɛt] *nf* small van.

fourmi [furmi] *nf* [insecte] ant ; *fig* hard worker.

fourmilière [furmiljɛr] *nf* anthill.

fourmiller [3] [furmije] *vi* [pulluler] to swarm ; **~ de** *fig* to be swarming with.

fournaise [furnɛz] *nf* furnace.

fourneau, x [furno] *nm* - **1.** [cuisinière, poêle] stove - **2.** [de fonderie] furnace.

fournée [furne] *nf* batch.

fourni, e [furni] *adj* [barbe, cheveux] thick.

fournil [furnil] *nm* bakery.

fournir [32] [furnir] *vt* - **1.** [procurer] **: ~ qqch à qqn** to supply ou provide sb with sthg - **2.** [produire] **: ~ un effort** to make an effort - **3.** [approvisionner] : **~ qqn (en)** to supply sb (with).

fournisseur, euse [furnisœr, øz] *nm, f* supplier.

fourniture [furnityr] *nf* supply, supplying *(U).* ◆ **fournitures** *nfpl* : **~s de bureau** office supplies ; **~s scolaires** school supplies.

fourrage [furaʒ] *nm* fodder.

fourré [fure] *nm* thicket.

fourreau, x [furo] *nm* - **1.** [d'épée] sheath ; [de parapluie] cover - **2.** [robe] sheath dress.

fourrer [3] [fure] *vt* - **1.** CULIN to stuff, to fill - **2.** *fam* [mettre] : **~ qqch (dans)** to stuff sthg (into). ◆ **se fourrer** *vp* : **se ~ une idée dans la tête** to get an idea into one's head ; **je ne savais plus où me ~** I didn't know where to put myself.

fourre-tout [furtu] *nm inv* - **1.** [pièce] lumber room *Br*, junk room *Am* - **2.** [sac] hold-all.

fourreur [furœr] *nm* furrier.

fourrière [furjɛr] *nf* pound.

fourrure [furyr] *nf* fur.

fourvoyer [13] [furvwaje] ◆ **se fourvoyer** *vp sout* [s'égarer] to lose one's way ; [se tromper] to go off on the wrong track.

foutre [116] [futr] *vt tfam* - **1.** [mettre] to shove, to stick ; **~ qqn dehors** OU **à la porte** to chuck sb out - **2.** [donner] : **~ la trouille à qqn** to put the wind up sb ; **il lui a foutu une baffe** he thumped him one - **3.** [faire] to do ; **ne rien ~ de la journée** to do damn all all day ; **j'en ai rien à ~** I don't give a toss. ◆ **se foutre** *vp tfam* - **1.** [se mettre] : **se ~ dans** [situation] to get o.s. into - **2.** [se moquer] : **se ~ de (la gueule de) qqn** to laugh at sb, to take the mickey out of sb *Br* - **3.** [ne pas s'intéresser] : **je m'en fous** I don't give a damn about it.

foyer [fwaje] *nm* - **1.** [maison] home - **2.** [résidence] home, hostel - **3.** [point central] centre *Br*, center *Am* - **4.** [de lunettes] focus ; **verres à double ~** bifocals.

fracas [fraka] *nm* roar.

fracasser [3] [frakase] *vt* to smash, to shatter.

fraction [traksjɔ̃] *nf* fraction.

fractionner [3] [fraksjone] *vt* to divide (up), to split up.

fracture [fraktyr] *nf* MÉD fracture.

fracturer [3] [fraktyre] *vt* - **1.** MÉD to fracture - **2.** [coffre, serrure] to break open.

fragile [fraʒil] *adj* [gén] fragile ; [peau, santé] delicate.

fragiliser [3] [fraʒilize] *vt* to weaken.

fragilité [fraʒilite] *nf* fragility.

fragment [fragmã] *nm* - **1.** [morceau] fragment - **2.** [extrait - d'œuvre] extract ; [- de conversation] snatch.

fragmenter [3] [fragmãte] *vt* to fragment, to break up.

fraîche ⊳ **frais.**

fraîcheur [freʃœr] *nf* - **1.** [d'air, d'accueil] coolness - **2.** [de teint, d'aliment] freshness.

frais, fraîche [frɛ, freʃ] *adj* - **1.** [air, accueil] cool ; **boisson fraîche** cold drink - **2.** [récent - trace] fresh ; [- encre] wet - **3.** [teint] fresh, clear. ◆ **frais** ⊳ *nm* : **mettre qqch au ~** to put sthg in a cool place. ⊳ *nmpl* [dépenses] expenses, costs ; **aux ~ de la maison** at the company's expense ; **faire des ~** to spend a lot of money ; **rentrer dans ses ~** to cover one's expenses ; **~ fixes** fixed costs. ⊳ *adv* : **il fait ~** it's cool.

fraise [frɛz] *nf* - **1.** [fruit] strawberry - **2.** [de dentiste] drill ; [de menuisier] bit.

fraiser [4] [freze] *vt* to countersink.

fraiseuse [frezøz] *nf* milling machine.

fraisier [frezje] *nm* - **1.** [plante] strawberry plant - **2.** [gâteau] strawberry sponge.

framboise [frãbwaz] *nf* - **1.** [fruit] raspberry - **2.** [liqueur] raspberry liqueur.

franc, franche [frã, frãʃ] *adj* - **1.** [sincère] frank - **2.** [net] clear, definite. ◆ **franc** *nm* franc.

français, e [frãsɛ, ɛz] *adj* French. ◆ **français** *nm* [langue] French. ◆ **Français, e** *nm, f* Frenchman (f Frenchwoman) ; **les Français** the French.

France [frãs] *nf* : **la ~ France** ; **~ 2, ~ 3** TÉLÉ *French state-owned television channels.*

franche ⊳ **franc.**

franchement [frãʃmã] *adv* - **1.** [sincèrement] frankly - **2.** [nettement] clearly - **3.** [tout à fait] completely, downright.

franchir [32] [frãʃir] *vt* - **1.** [obstacle] to get over - **2.** [porte] to go through ; [seuil] to cross - **3.** [distance] to cover.

franchise [frãʃiz] *nf* - **1.** [sincérité] frankness - **2.** COMM franchise - **3.** [d'assurance] excess - **4.** [détaxe] exemption.

francilien, enne [frãsiljɛ̃, ɛn] *adj* of OU from the Île-de-France. ◆ **Francilien, enne** *nm, f* inhabitant of the Île-de-France.

franciscain, e [frãsiskɛ̃, ɛn] *adj & nm, f* Franciscan.

franciser [3] [frãsize] *vt* to frenchify.

franc-jeu [frãʒø] *nm* : **jouer ~** to play fair.

franc-maçon, onne [frãmasɔ̃, ɔn] *(mpl francs-maçons, fpl franc-maçonnes) adj* masonic. ← **franc-maçon** nm freemason.

franc-maçonnerie [frãmasɔnri] nf freemasonry (U).

franco [frãko] adv COMM : ~ de port carriage paid.

francophone [frãkɔfɔn] <> adj French-speaking. <> nmf French speaker.

francophonie [frãkɔfɔni] nf : la ~ French-speaking nations (pl).

franc-parler [frãparle] nm : avoir son ~ to speak one's mind.

franc-tireur [frãtirœr] nm MIL irregular.

frange [frãʒ] nf fringe.

frangipane [frãʒipan] nf almond paste.

franglais [frãgle] nm Franglais.

franquette [frãket] ← à la bonne **franquette** loc adv informally, without any ceremony.

frappant, e [frapã, ãt] adj striking.

frapper [3] [frape] <> vt - **1.** [gén] to strike - **2.** [boisson] to chill. <> vi to knock.

frasques [frask] nfpl pranks, escapades.

fraternel, elle [fraternel] adj fraternal, brotherly.

fraterniser [3] [fraternize] vi to fraternize.

fraternité [fraternite] nf brotherhood.

fratricide [fratrisid] nmf fratricide.

fraude [frod] nf fraud.

frauder [3] [frode] vt & vi to cheat.

frauduleux, euse [frodylø, øz] adj fraudulent.

frayer [11] [freje] ← se frayer vp : se ~ un chemin (à travers une foule) to force one's way through (a crowd).

frayeur [frejœr] nf fright, fear.

fredaines [frəden] nfpl pranks.

fredonner [3] [frədɔne] vt & vi to hum.

freezer [frizœr] nm freezer compartment.

frégate [fregat] nf [bateau] frigate.

frein [frɛ̃] nm - **1.** AUTOM brake ; ~ à main handbrake - **2.** fig [obstacle] brake, check.

freinage [frenaʒ] nm braking.

freiner [4] [frene] <> vt - **1.** [mouvement, véhicule] to slow down ; [inflation, dépenses] to curb - **2.** [personne] to restrain. <> vi to brake.

frelaté, e [frəlate] adj [vin] adulterated ; fig corrupt.

frêle [frel] adj [enfant, voix] frail.

frelon [frəlɔ̃] nm hornet.

frémir [32] [fremir] vi - **1.** [corps, personne] to tremble - **2.** [eau] to simmer.

frémissement [fremismã] nm - **1.** [de corps, personne] shiver, trembling (U) - **2.** [d'eau] simmering.

frêne [fren] nm ash.

frénésie [frenezi] nf frenzy.

frénétique [frenetik] adj frenzied.

fréquemment [frekamã] adv frequently.

fréquence [frekãs] nf frequency.

fréquent, e [frekã, ãt] adj frequent.

fréquentation [frekãtasjɔ̃] nf - **1.** [d'endroit] frequenting - **2.** [de personne] association. ← **fréquentations** nfpl company (U).

fréquenté, e [frekãte] adj : très ~ busy ; c'est très bien/mal ~ the right/wrong sort of people go there.

fréquenter [3] [frekãte] vt - **1.** [endroit] to frequent - **2.** [personne] to associate with ; [petit ami] to go out with, to see.

frère [frer] <> nm brother. <> adj [parti, pays] sister (avant n).

fresque [fresk] nf fresco.

fret [fre] nm freight.

frétiller [3] [fretije] vi [poisson, personne] to wriggle.

fretin [frətɛ̃] nm : le menu ~ the small fry.

friable [frijabl] adj crumbly.

friand, e [frijã, ãd] adj : être ~ de to be partial to.

friandise [frijãdiz] nf delicacy.

fric [frik] nm fam cash.

friche [friʃ] nf fallow land ; en ~ fallow.

friction [friksjɔ̃] nf - **1.** [massage] massage - **2.** fig [désaccord] friction.

frictionner [3] [friksjɔne] vt to rub.

Frigidaire® [friʒider] nm fridge, refrigerator.

frigide [friʒid] adj frigid.

frigo [frigo] nm fam fridge.

frigorifié, e [frigɔrifje] adj fam frozen.

frileux, euse [frilø, øz] adj - **1.** [craignant le froid] sensitive to the cold - **2.** [prudent] unadventurous.

frimas [frima] nm littéraire foggy winter weather.

frimer [3] [frime] vi fam [bluffer] to pretend ; [se mettre en valeur] to show off.

frimousse [frimus] nf fam dear little face.

fringale [frɛ̃gal] nf fam : avoir la ~ to be starving.

fringant, e [frɛ̃gã, ãt] adj high-spirited.

fripe [frip] nf : les ~s secondhand clothes.

fripon, onne [fripɔ̃, ɔn] <> nm, f fam vieilli rogue, rascal. <> adj mischievous, cheeky.

fripouille [fripuj] *nf fam* scoundrel ; **petite ~** little devil.

frire [115] [frir] ◇ *vt* to fry. ◇ *vi* to fry.

frise [friz] *nf* ARCHIT frieze.

frisé, e [frize] *adj* [cheveux] curly ; [personne] curly-haired.

friser [3] [frize] ◇ *vt* - **1**. [cheveux] to curl - **2**. *fig* [ressembler à] to border on. ◇ *vi* to curl.

frisquet [friske] *adj m* : **il fait ~** it's chilly.

frisson [frisɔ̃] *nm* [gén] shiver ; [de dégoût] shudder.

frissonner [3] [frisɔne] *vi* - **1**. [trembler] to shiver ; [de dégoût] to shudder - **2**. [s'agiter - eau] to ripple ; [- feuillage] to tremble.

frit, e [fri, frit] *pp* ▷ **frire**.

frite [frit] *nf* chip *Br*, (French) fry *Am*.

friteuse [fritøz] *nf* deep fat fryer.

friture [frityr] *nf* - **1**. [poisson] fried fish - **2**. *fam* RADIO crackle.

frivole [frivɔl] *adj* frivolous.

frivolité [frivɔlite] *nf* frivolity.

froid, froide [frwa, frwad] *adj litt & fig* cold ; **rester ~** to be unmoved. ◆ **froid** ◇ *nm* - **1**. [température] cold ; **prendre ~** to catch (a) cold - **2**. [tension] coolness. ◇ *adv* : **il fait ~** it's cold ; **avoir ~** to be cold.

froidement [frwadmɑ̃] *adv* - **1**. [accueillir] coldly - **2**. [écouter, parler] coolly - **3**. [tuer] cold-bloodedly.

froisser [3] [frwase] *vt* - **1**. [tissu, papier] to crumple, to crease - **2**. *fig* [offenser] to offend. ◆ **se froisser** *vp* **1**. [tissu] to crumple, to crease **2**. MÉD : **se ~ un muscle** to strain a muscle - **3**. [se vexer] to take offence *Br* ou offense *Am*.

frôler [3] [frole] *vt* to brush against ; *fig* to have a brush with, to come close to.

fromage [frɔmaʒ] *nm* cheese ; **~ de brebis** sheep's milk ; **~ de chèvre** goat's cheese.

fromager, ère [frɔmaʒe, ɛr] *nm, f* [fabricant] cheesemaker.

fromagerie [frɔmaʒri] *nf* cheese shop.

froment [frɔmɑ̃] *nm* wheat.

froncer [16] [frɔ̃se] *vt* - **1**. COUTURE to gather - **2**. [plisser] : **~ les sourcils** to frown.

frondaison [frɔ̃dezɔ̃] *nf* - **1**. [phénomène] foliation - **2**. [feuillage] foliage.

fronde [frɔ̃d] *nf* - **1**. [arme] sling ; [jouet] catapult *Br*, slingshot *Am* - **2**. [révolte] rebellion.

front [frɔ̃] *nm* - **1**. ANAT forehead - **2**. *fig* [audace] cheek - **3**. [avant] front ; [de bâtiment] front, façade ; **~ de mer** (sea) front - **4**. MÉTÉOR, MIL & POLIT front.

frontal, e, aux [frɔ̃tal, o] *adj* - **1**. ANAT frontal - **2**. [collision, attaque] head-on.

frontalier, ère [frɔ̃talje, ɛr] ◇ *adj* frontier (avant n) ; **travailleur ~** person who lives on one side of the border and works on the other. ◇ *nm, f* inhabitant of border area.

frontière [frɔ̃tjer] ◇ *adj* border (avant n). ◇ *nf* frontier, border ; *fig* frontier.

fronton [frɔ̃tɔ̃] *nm* ARCHIT pediment.

frottement [frɔtmɑ̃] *nm* - **1**. [action] rubbing - **2**. [contact, difficulté] friction.

frotter [3] [frɔte] ◇ *vt* to rub ; [parquet] to scrub. ◇ *vi* to rub, to scrape.

frottis [frɔti] *nm* smear.

fructifier [9] [fryktifje] *vi* - **1**. [investissement] to give ou yield a profit - **2**. [terre] to be productive - **3**. [arbre, idée] to bear fruit.

fructueux, euse [fryktɥø, øz] *adj* fruitful, profitable.

frugal, e, aux [frygal, o] *adj* frugal.

fruit [frɥi] *nm litt & fig* fruit (U) ; **~s de mer** seafood (U).

fruité, e [frɥite] *adj* fruity.

fruitier, ère [frɥitje, ɛr] ◇ *adj* [arbre] fruit (avant n). ◇ *nm, f* fruiterer.

fruste [fryst] *adj* uncouth.

frustration [frystraasjɔ̃] *nf* frustration.

frustrer [8] [frystre] *vt* - **1**. [priver] : **~ qqn de** to deprive sb of - **2**. [décevoir] to frustrate.

fuchsia [fyʃja] *nm* fuchsia.

fuel, fioul [fjul] *nm* - **1**. [de chauffage] fuel - **2**. [carburant] fuel oil.

fugace [fygas] *adj* fleeting.

fugitif, ive [fyʒitif, iv] ◇ *adj* fleeting. ◇ *nm, f* fugitive.

fugue [fyg] *nf* - **1**. [de personne] flight ; **faire une ~** to run away - **2**. MUS fugue.

fui [fɥi] *pp inv* ▷ **fuir**.

fuir [35] [fɥir] ◇ *vi* - **1**. [détaler] to flee - **2**. [tuyau] to leak - **3**. *fig* [s'écouler] to fly by. ◇ *vt* [éviter] to avoid, to shun.

fuite [fɥit] *nf* - **1**. [de personne] escape, flight - **2**. [écoulement, d'information] leak.

fulgurant, e [fylgyrɑ̃, ɑ̃t] *adj* - **1**. [découverte] dazzling - **2**. [vitesse] lightning (avant n) - **3**. [douleur] searing.

fulminer [3] [fylmine] *vi* [personne] : **~ (contre)** to fulminate (against).

fumé, e [fyme] *adj* - **1**. CULIN smoked - **2**. [verres] tinted.

fumée [fyme] *nf* [de combustion] smoke.

fumer [3] [fyme] ◇ *vi* - **1**. [personne, cheminée] to smoke - **2**. [bouilloire, plat] to steam. ◇ *vt* - **1**. [cigarette, aliment] to smoke - **2**. AGRIC to spread manure on.

fumeur, euse [fymœr, øz] *nm, f* smoker.

fumier [fymje] *nm* AGRIC dung, manure.

fumiste [fymist] *nmf péj* skiver *Br*, shirker.

fumisterie [fymistəri] *nf fam* skiving *Br*, shirking.

fumoir [fymwar] *nm* - **1.** [pour aliments] smokehouse - **2.** [pièce] smoking room.

funambule [fynãbyl] *nmf* tightrope walker.

funèbre [fynɛbr] *adj* - **1.** [de funérailles] funeral *(avant n)* - **2.** [lugubre] funereal ; [sentiments] dismal.

funérailles [fyneraj] *nfpl* funeral *(sg)*.

funéraire [fynerɛr] *adj* funeral *(avant n)*.

funeste [fynɛst] *adj* - **1.** [accident] fatal - **2.** [initiative, erreur] disastrous - **3.** [présage] of doom.

funiculaire [fynikylɛr] *nm* funicular railway.

fur [fyr] ◆ **au fur et à mesure** *loc adv* as I/you *etc* go along ; **au ~ et à mesure des besoins** as (and when) needed. ◆ **au fur et à mesure que** *loc conj* as (and when).

furet [fyrɛ] *nm* [animal] ferret.

fureter [28] [fyrte] *vi* [fouiller] to ferret around.

fureur [fyrœr] *nf* [colère] fury.

furibond, e [fyribɔ̃, ɔ̃d] *adj* furious.

furie [fyri] *nf* - **1.** [colère, agitation] fury ; **en ~** [personne] infuriated ; [éléments] raging - **2.** *fig* [femme] shrew.

furieux, euse [fyrjø, øz] *adj* - **1.** [personne] furious - **2.** [énorme] tremendous.

furoncle [fyrɔ̃kl] *nm* boil.

furtif, ive [fyrtif, iv] *adj* furtive.

fus, fut *etc* ⊳ être.

fusain [fyzɛ̃] *nm* - **1.** [crayon] charcoal - **2.** [dessin] charcoal drawing.

fuseau, x [fyzo] *nm* - **1.** [outil] spindle - **2.** [pantalon] ski-pants *(pl)*. ◆ **fuseau horaire** *nm* time zone.

fusée [fyze] *nf* [pièce d'artifice & AÉRON] rocket.

fuselage [fyzlaʒ] *nm* fuselage.

fuselé, e [fyzle] *adj* [doigts] tapering ; [jambes] slender.

fuser [3] [fyze] *vi* [cri, rire] to burst forth ou out.

fusible [fyzibl] *nm* fuse.

fusil [fyzi] *nm* [arme] gun.

fusillade [fyzijad] *nf* [combat] gunfire *(U)*, fusillade.

fusiller [3] [fyzije] *vt* [exécuter] to shoot.

fusion [fyzjɔ̃] *nf* - **1.** [gén] fusion - **2.** [fonte] smelting - **3.** ÉCON & POLIT merger.

fusionner [3] [fyzjɔne] *vt* & *vi* to merge.

fustiger [17] [fystiʒe] *vt* to castigate.

fut ⊳ être.

fût [fy] *nm* - **1.** [d'arbre] trunk - **2.** [tonneau] barrel, cask - **3.** [d'arme] stock - **4.** [de colonne] shaft.

futaie [fytɛ] *nf* wood.

futile [fytil] *adj* - **1.** [insignifiant] futile - **2.** [frivole] frivolous.

futur, e [fytyr] ⇔ *adj* future *(avant n)*. ⇔ *nm, f* [fiancé] intended. ◆ **futur** *nm* future.

futuriste [fytyrist] *adj* futuristic.

fuyant, e [fɥijã, ãt] *adj* - **1.** [perspective, front] receding *(avant n)* - **2.** [regard] evasive.

fuyard, e [fɥijar, ard] *nm, f* runaway.

G

g, G [ʒe] *nm inv* g, G.

gabardine [gabardin] *nf* gabardine.

gabarit [gabari] *nm* [dimension] size.

Gabon [gabɔ̃] *nm* : **le ~** Gabon.

gâcher [3] [gaʃe] *vt* - **1.** [gaspiller] to waste - **2.** [gâter] to spoil - **3.** CONSTR to mix.

gâchette [gaʃɛt] *nf* trigger.

gâchis [gaʃi] *nm* [gaspillage] waste *(U)*.

gadget [gadʒɛt] *nm* gadget.

gadoue [gadu] *nf fam* [boue] mud ; [engrais] sludge.

gaélique [gaelik] ⇔ *adj* Gaelic. ⇔ *nm* Gaelic.

gaffe [gaf] *nf* - **1.** *fam* [maladresse] clanger - **2.** [outil] boat hook.

gaffer [3] [gafe] *vi fam* to put one's foot in it.

gag [gag] *nm* gag.

gage [gaʒ] *nm* - **1.** [dépôt] pledge ; **mettre qqch en ~** to pawn sthg - **2.** [assurance, preuve] proof - **3.** [dans jeu] forfeit.

gager [17] [gaʒe] *vt* : **~ que** to bet (that).

gageure [gaʒyr] *nf* challenge.

gagnant, e [gaɲã, ãt] ⇔ *adj* winning *(avant n)*. ⇔ *nm, f* winner.

gagne-pain [gaɲpɛ̃] *nm inv* livelihood.

gagner [3] [gaɲe] ⇔ *vt* - **1.** [salaire, argent, repos] to earn - **2.** [course, prix, affection] to win - **3.** [obtenir, économiser] to gain ; **~ du**

temps/de la place to gain time/space - **4.** [atteindre] to reach ; [suj : - feu, engourdissement] to spread to ; [- sommeil, froid] to overcome. ◇ *vi* - **1.** [être vainqueur] to win - **2.** [bénéficier] to gain ; ~ **à faire qqch** to be better off doing sthg ; **qu'est-ce que j'y gagne ?** what do I get out of it ? - **3.** [s'améliorer] : ~ **en** to increase in.

gai, e [ge] *adj* - **1.** [joyeux] cheerful, happy - **2.** [vif, plaisant] bright.

gaieté [gete] *nf* - **1.** [joie] cheerfulness - **2.** [vivacité] brightness.

gaillard, e [gajar, ard] ◇ *adj* - **1.** [alerte] sprightly, spry - **2.** [licencieux] ribald. ◇ *nm, f* strapping individual.

gain [gɛ̃] *nm* - **1.** [profit] gain, profit - **2.** [succès] winning - **3.** [économie] saving. ◆ **gains** *nmpl* earnings.

gaine [gɛn] *nf* - **1.** [étui, enveloppe] sheath - **2.** [sous-vêtement] girdle, corset.

gainer [4] [gene] *vt* to sheathe.

gala [gala] *nm* gala, reception.

galant, e [galɑ̃, ɑ̃t] *adj* - **1.** [courtois] gallant - **2.** [amoureux] flirtatious. ◆ **galant** *nm* admirer.

galanterie [galɑ̃tri] *nf* - **1.** [courtoisie] gallantry, politeness - **2.** [flatterie] compliment.

galaxie [galaksi] *nf* galaxy.

galbe [galb] *nm* curve.

gale [gal] *nf* MÉD scabies (U).

galère [galɛr] *nf* NAVIG galley ; **quelle ~!** *fig* what a hassle!, what a drag!

galérer [18] [galere] *vi fam* to have a hard time.

galerie [galri] *nf* - **1.** [gén] gallery ; ~ **marchande** ou **commerciale** shopping arcade - **2.** THÉÂTRE circle - **3.** [porte-bagages] roof rack

galet [galɛ] *nm* - **1.** [caillou] pebble - **2.** TECHNOL wheel, roller.

galette [galɛt] *nf* CULIN pancake (made from buckwheat flour).

galipette [galipɛt] *nf fam* somersault.

Galles [gal] ⊳ **pays**.

gallicisme [galisism] *nm* [expression] French idiom ; [dans une langue étrangère] gallicism.

gallois, e [galwa, az] *adj* Welsh. ◆ **gallois** *nm* [langue] Welsh. ◆ **Gallois, e** *nm, f* Welshman (f Welshwoman) ; **les Gallois** the Welsh.

galon [galɔ̃] *nm* - **1.** COUTURE braid (U) - **2.** MIL stripe.

galop [galo] *nm* [allure] gallop ; **au ~** [cheval] at a gallop ; *fig* at the double.

galoper [3] [galɔpe] *vi* - **1.** [cheval] to gallop - **2.** [personne] to run about - **3.** [imagination] to run riot.

galopin [galɔpɛ̃] *nm fam* brat.

galvaniser [3] [galvanize] *vt litt & fig* to galvanize.

galvauder [3] [galvode] *vt* [ternir] to tarnish.

gambader [3] [gɑ̃bade] *vi* [sautiller] to leap about ; [agneau] to gambol.

gamelle [gamɛl] *nf* [plat] mess tin *Br*, kit *Am*.

gamin, e [gamɛ̃, in] ◇ *adj* [puéril] childish. ◇ *nm, f fam* [enfant] kid.

gamme [gam] *nf* - **1.** [série] range ; ~ **de produits** product range - **2.** MUS scale.

ganglion [gɑ̃glijɔ̃] *nm* ganglion.

gangrène [gɑ̃grɛn] *nf* gangrene ; *fig* corruption, canker.

gangue [gɑ̃g] *nf* - **1.** [de minerai] gangue - **2.** *fig* [carcan] straitjacket.

gant [gɑ̃] *nm* glove ; ~ **de toilette** face cloth, flannel *Br*.

garage [garaʒ] *nm* garage.

garagiste [garaʒist] *nmf* [propriétaire] garage owner ; [réparateur] garage mechanic.

garant, e [garɑ̃, ɑ̃t] *nm, f* [responsable] guarantor ; **se porter ~ de** to vouch for. ◆ **garant** *nm* [garantie] guarantee.

garantie [garɑ̃ti] *nf* [gén] guarantee.

garantir [32] [garɑ̃tir] *vt* - **1.** [assurer & COMM] to guarantee ; ~ **à qqn que** to assure ou guarantee sb that - **2.** [protéger] : ~ **qqch (de)** to protect sthg (from).

garçon [garsɔ̃] *nm* - **1.** [enfant] boy - **2.** [célibataire] : **vieux** ~ confirmed bachelor - **3.** [serveur] : ~ **(de café)** waiter.

garçonnet [garsɔnɛ] *nm* little boy

garçonnière [garsɔnjɛr] *nf* bachelor flat *Br* ou apartment *Am*.

garde [gard] ◇ *nf* - **1.** [surveillance] protection - **2.** [veille] : **pharmacie de ~** duty chemist - **3.** MIL guard ; **monter la ~** to go on guard - **4.** *loc* : **être/se tenir sur ses ~s** to be/stay on one's guard ; **mettre qqn en ~ contre qqch** to put sb on their guard about sthg ; **mise en ~** warning ◇ *nmf* keeper ; ~ **du corps** bodyguard ; ~ **d'enfants** childminder.

garde-à-vous [gardavu] *nm inv* attention ; **se mettre au ~** to stand to attention.

garde-boue [gardəbu] *nm inv* mudguard *Br*, fender *Am*.

garde-chasse [gardəʃas] (*pl* **gardes-chasse** ou **gardes-chasses**) *nm* gamekeeper.

garde-fou [gardəfu] (*pl* **garde-fous**) *nm* railing, parapet.

158

garde-malade [gardəmalad] (*pl* **gardes-malades**) *nmf* nurse.

garde-manger [gardəmɑ̃ʒe] *nm inv* [pièce] pantry, larder ; [armoire] meat safe *Br*, cooler *Am*.

garde-pêche [gardəpɛʃ] (*pl* **gardes-pêche**) *nm* [personne] water bailiff *Br*, fishwarden *Am*.

garder [3] [garde] *vt* - **1.** [gén] to keep ; [vêtement] to keep on - **2.** [surveiller] to mind, to look after ; [défendre] to guard - **3.** [protéger] : **~ qqn de qqch** to save sb from sthg. **◆ se garder** *vp* - **1.** [se conserver] to keep - **2.** [se méfier] : **se ~ de qqn/qqch** to beware of sb/sthg - **3.** [s'abstenir] : **se ~ de faire qqch** to take care not to do sthg.

garderie [gardəri] *nf* crèche *Br*, day nursery *Br*, day-care center *Am*.

garde-robe [gardərɔb] (*pl* **garde-robes**) *nf* wardrobe.

gardien, enne [gardjɛ̃, ɛn] *nm, f* - **1.** [surveillant] guard, keeper ; **~ de but** goalkeeper ; **~ de nuit** night watchman - **2.** *fig* [défenseur] protector, guardian - **3.** [agent] : **~ de la paix** policeman.

gare¹ [gar] *nf* station ; **~ routière** [de marchandises] road haulage depot ; [pour passagers] bus station.

gare² [gar] *interj* [attention] watch out! ; **~ aux voleurs** watch out for pickpockets.

garer [3] [gare] *vt* - **1.** [ranger] to park - **2.** [mettre à l'abri] to put in a safe place. **◆ se garer** *vp* - **1.** [stationner] to park - **2.** [se ranger] to pull over.

gargariser [3] [gargarize] **◆ se gargariser** *vp* - **1.** [se rincer] to gargle - **2.** *péj* [se délecter] : **se ~ de** to delight ou revel in.

gargouiller [3] [garguje] *vi* - **1.** [eau] to gurgle - **2.** [intestins] to rumble.

garnement [garnəmɑ̃] *nm* rascal, pest.

garni [garni] *nm vieilli* furnished accommodation (*U*) *Br* ou accommodations (*pl*) *Am*.

garnir [32] [garnir] *vt* - **1.** [équiper] to fit out, to furnish - **2.** [remplir] to fill - **3.** [orner] : **~ qqch de** to decorate sthg with ; COUTURE to trim sthg with.

garnison [garnizɔ̃] *nf* garrison.

garniture [garnityr] *nf* - **1.** [ornement] trimming ; [de lit] bed linen - **2.** [CULIN - pour accompagner] garnish *Br*, fixings (*pl*) *Am* ; [- pour remplir] filling.

garrigue [garig] *nf* scrub.

garrot [garo] *nm* - **1.** [de cheval] withers (*pl*) - **2.** MÉD tourniquet.

gars [ga] *nm fam* - **1.** [garçon, homme] lad - **2.** [type] guy, bloke *Br*.

gas-oil [gazɔjl, gazwal], **gazole** [gazɔl] *nm* diesel oil.

gaspillage [gaspijaʒ] *nm* waste.

gaspiller [3] [gaspije] *vt* to waste.

gastrique [gastrik] *adj* gastric.

gastro-entérite [gastroɑ̃terit] (*pl* **gastro-entérites**) *nf* gastroenteritis (*U*).

gastronome [gastrɔnɔm] *nmf* gourmet.

gastronomie [gastrɔnɔmi] *nf* gastronomy.

gâteau, x [gato] *nm* cake ; **~ sec** biscuit *Br*, cookie *Am*.

gâter [3] [gate] *vt* - **1.** [gén] to spoil ; [vacances, affaires] to ruin, to spoil - **2.** *iron* [combler] to be too good to ; **on est gâté!** just marvellous! **◆ se gâter** *vp* - **1.** [temps] to change for the worse - **2.** [situation] to take a turn for the worse.

gâteux, euse [gato, øz] *adj* senile.

gauche [goʃ] ◇ *nf* - **1.** [côté] left, left-hand side ; **à ~ (de)** on the left (of) - **2.** POLIT : **la ~** the left (wing) ; **de ~** left-wing. ◇ *adj* - **1.** [côté] left - **2.** [personne] clumsy.

gaucher, ère [goʃe, ɛr] ◇ *adj* left-handed. ◇ *nm, f* left-handed person.

gauchiste [goʃist] *nmf* leftist.

gaufre [gofr] *nf* waffle.

gaufrer [3] [gofre] *vt* to emboss.

gaufrette [gofrɛt] *nf* wafer.

gaule [gol] *nf* - **1.** [perche] pole - **2.** [canne à pêche] fishing rod.

gauler [3] [gole] *vt* to bring ou shake down.

gaulliste [golist] *nmf & adj* Gaullist.

gaulois, e [golwa, az] *adj* [de Gaule] Gallic. **◆ Gaulois, e** *nm, f* Gaul.

gaver [3] [gave] *vt* - **1.** [animal] to force-feed - **2.** [personne] : **~ qqn de** to feed sb full of.

gay [gɛ] *adj inv & nm* gay.

gaz [gaz] *nm inv* gas.

gaze [gaz] *nf* gauze.

gazelle [gazɛl] *nf* gazelle.

gazer [3] [gaze] *vt* to gas.

gazette [gazɛt] *nf* newspaper, gazette.

gazeux, euse [gazø, øz] *adj* - **1.** CHIM gaseous - **2.** [boisson] fizzy.

gazoduc [gazɔdyk] *nm* gas pipeline.

gazole = **gas-oil**.

gazon [gazɔ̃] *nm* [herbe] grass ; [terrain] lawn.

gazouiller [3] [gazuje] *vi* - **1.** [oiseau] to chirp, to twitter - **2.** [bébé] to gurgle.

GB, G-B (*abr de* **Grande-Bretagne**) *nf* GB.

gd *abr de* **grand**.

GDF, Gdf (*abr de* **Gaz de France**) *French national gas company.*

geai [ʒɛ] *nm* jay.

géant, e [ʒeɑ̃, ɑ̃t] <> *adj* gigantic, giant. <> *nm, f* giant.

geindre [81] [ʒɛ̃dr] *vi* - **1.** [gémir] to moan - **2.** *fam* [pleurnicher] to whine.

gel [ʒɛl] *nm* - **1.** MÉTÉOR frost - **2.** [d'eau] freezing - **3.** [cosmétique] gel.

gélatine [ʒelatin] *nf* gelatine.

gelée [ʒəle] *nf* - **1.** MÉTÉOR frost - **2.** CULIN jelly.

geler [25] [ʒəle] *vt & vi* - **1.** [gén] to freeze - **2.** [projet] to halt.

gélule [ʒelyl] *nf* capsule.

Gémeaux [ʒemo] *nmpl* ASTROL Gemini.

gémir [32] [ʒemir] *vi* - **1.** [gén] to moan - **2.** [par déception] to groan.

gémissement [ʒemismɑ̃] *nm* - **1.** [gén] moan ; [du vent] moaning *(U)* - **2.** [de déception] groan.

gemme [ʒɛm] *nf* gem, precious stone.

gênant, e [ʒenɑ̃, ɑ̃t] *adj* - **1.** [encombrant] in the way - **2.** [embarrassant] awkward, embarrassing - **3.** [énervant] : **être ~** to be a nuisance.

gencive [ʒɑ̃siv] *nf* gum.

gendarme [ʒɑ̃darm] *nm* policeman.

gendarmerie [ʒɑ̃darməri] *nf* - **1.** [corps] police force - **2.** [lieu] police station.

gendre [ʒɑ̃dr] *nm* son-in-law.

gène [ʒɛn] *nm* gene.

gêne [ʒɛn] *nf* - **1.** [physique] difficulty - **2.** [psychologique] embarrassment - **3.** [financière] difficulty.

généalogie [ʒenealɔʒi] *nf* genealogy.

généalogique [ʒenealɔʒik] *adj* genealogical ; **arbre ~** family tree.

gêner [4] [ʒene] *vt* - **1.** [physiquement - gén] to be too tight for ; [- suj : chaussures] to pinch - **2.** [moralement] to embarrass - **3.** [incommoder] to bother - **4.** [encombrer] to hamper.

général, e, aux [ʒeneral, o] *adj* general ; **en ~** generally, in general ; **répétition ~e** dress rehearsal. ◆ **général** *nm* MIL general. ◆ **générale** *nf* THÉÂTRE dress rehearsal.

généralement [ʒeneralmɑ̃] *adv* generally.

généralisation [ʒeneralizasjɔ̃] *nf* generalization.

généraliser [3] [ʒeneralize] *vt & vi* to generalize. ◆ **se généraliser** *vp* to become general ou widespread.

généraliste [ʒeneralist] <> *nmf* GP *Br*, family doctor. <> *adj* general.

généralité [ʒeneralite] *nf* - **1.** [idée] generality - **2.** [universalité] general nature. ◆ **généralités** *nfpl* generalities.

générateur, trice [ʒeneratœr, tris] *adj* generating. ◆ **générateur** *nm* TECHNOL generator.

génération [ʒenerasjɔ̃] *nf* generation.

générer [18] [ʒenere] *vt* to generate.

généreux, euse [ʒenerø, øz] *adj* generous ; [terre] fertile.

générique [ʒenerik] <> *adj* generic ; **médicament ~** MÉD generic drug. <> *nm* - **1.** CIN & TÉLÉ credits *(pl)* - **2.** MÉD generic drug.

générosité [ʒenerozite] *nf* generosity.

genèse [ʒənɛz] *nf* [création] genesis. ◆ **Genèse** *nf* BIBLE Genesis.

genêt [ʒənɛ] *nm* broom.

génétique [ʒenetik] <> *adj* genetic. <> *nf* genetics *(U)*.

Genève [ʒənɛv] *n* Geneva.

génial, e, aux [ʒenjal, o] *adj* - **1.** [personne] of genius - **2.** [idée, invention] inspired - **3.** *fam* [formidable] : **c'est ~!** that's great!, that's terrific!

génie [ʒeni] *nm* - **1.** [personne, aptitude] genius - **2.** MYTH spirit, genie - **3.** TECHNOL engineering ; **le ~** MIL ≃ the Royal Engineers *Br*, ≃ the (Army) Corps of Engineers *Am*.

genièvre [ʒənjɛvr] *nm* juniper.

génisse [ʒenis] *nf* heifer.

génital, e, aux [ʒenital, o] *adj* genital.

génitif [ʒenitif] *nm* genitive (case).

génocide [ʒenɔsid] *nm* genocide.

genou, x [ʒənu] *nm* knee ; **à ~x** on one's knees, kneeling.

genouillère [ʒənujɛr] *nf* - **1.** [bandage] knee bandage - **2.** SPORT kneepad.

genre [ʒɑ̃r] *nm* - **1.** [type] type, kind - **2.** LITTÉRATURE genre - **3.** [style de personne] style - **4.** GRAM gender.

gens [ʒɑ̃] *nmpl* people.

gentiane [ʒɑ̃sjan] *nf* gentian.

gentil, ille [ʒɑ̃ti, ij] *adj* - **1.** [agréable] nice - **2.** [aimable] kind, nice.

gentillesse [ʒɑ̃tijɛs] *nf* kindness.

gentiment [ʒɑ̃timɑ̃] *adv* - **1.** [sagement] nicely - **2.** [aimablement] kindly, nicely - **3.** *Helv* [tranquillement] calmly, quietly.

génuflexion [ʒenyflɛksjɔ̃] *nf* genuflexion.

géographie [ʒeɔgrafi] *nf* geography.

geôlier, ère [ʒolje, ɛr] *nm, f* gaoler.

géologie [ʒeɔlɔʒi] *nf* geology.

géologue [ʒeɔlɔg] *nmf* geologist.

géomètre [ʒeɔmɛtr] *nmf* - **1.** [spécialiste] geometer, geometrician - **2.** [technicien] surveyor.

géométrie [ʒeɔmetri] *nf* geometry.

gérance [ʒerɑ̃s] *nf* management.

géranium [ʒeranjɔm] *nm* geranium.

gérant, e [ʒerɑ̃, ɑ̃t] *nm, f* manager.

gerbe [ʒɛrb] *nf* - **1.** [de blé] sheaf ; [de fleurs] spray - **2.** [d'étincelles, d'eau] shower.

gercé, e [ʒɛrse] *adj* chapped.

gérer [18] [ʒere] *vt* to manage.

gériatrie [ʒerjatri] *nf* geriatrics *(U)*.

germain, e [ʒɛrmɛ̃, ɛn] ⊳ **cousin**.

germanique [ʒɛrmanik] *adj* Germanic.

germe [ʒɛrm] *nm* - **1.** BOT & MÉD germ ; [de pomme de terre] eye - **2.** *fig* [origine] seed, cause.

germer [3] [ʒɛrme] *vi* to germinate.

gésier [ʒezje] *nm* gizzard.

gésir [49] [ʒezir] *vi littéraire* to lie.

gestation [ʒɛstasjɔ̃] *nf* gestation.

geste [ʒɛst] *nm* - **1.** [mouvement] gesture - **2.** [acte] act, deed.

gesticuler [3] [ʒɛstikyle] *vi* to gesticulate.

gestion [ʒɛstjɔ̃] *nf* management ; JUR administration ; ~ **de fichiers** INFORM file management.

Ghana [gana] *nm* : **le ~** Ghana.

ghetto [gɛto] *nm litt & fig* ghetto.

gibet [ʒibɛ] *nm* gallows *(sg)*, gibbet.

gibier [ʒibje] *nm* game ; *fig* [personne] prey.

giboulée [ʒibule] *nf* sudden shower.

gicler [3] [ʒikle] *vi* to squirt, to spurt.

gifle [ʒifl] *nf* slap.

gifler [3] [ʒifle] *vt* to slap ; *fig* [suj : vent, pluie] to whip, to lash.

gigantesque [ʒigɑ̃tɛsk] *adj* gigantic.

gigolo [ʒigɔlo] *nm* gigolo.

gigot [ʒigo] *nm* CULIN leg.

gigoter [3] [ʒigɔte] *vi* to squirm, to wriggle.

gilet [ʒilɛ] *nm* - **1.** [cardigan] cardigan - **2.** [sans manches] waistcoat *Br*, vest *Am*.

gin [dʒin] *nm* gin.

gingembre [ʒɛ̃ʒɑ̃br] *nm* ginger.

girafe [ʒiraf] *nf* giraffe.

giratoire [ʒiratwar] *adj* gyrating ; **sens ~** roundabout *Br*, traffic circle *Am*.

girofle [ʒirɔfl] ⊳ **clou**.

girouette [ʒirwɛt] *nf* weathercock.

gisement [ʒizmɑ̃] *nm* deposit.

gît ⊳ **gésir**.

gitan, e [ʒitɑ̃, an] *adj* Gipsy *(avant n)*. ➧ **Gitan, e** *nm, f* Gipsy.

gîte [ʒit] *nm* - **1.** [logement] : **~ (rural)** gîte, self-catering accommodation in the country - **2.** [du bœuf] shin *Br*, shank *Am*.

givre [ʒivr] *nm* frost.

glabre [glabr] *adj* hairless.

glace [glas] *nf* - **1.** [eau congelée] ice - **2.** [crème glacée] ice cream - **3.** [vitre -] pane ; [- de voiture] window - **4.** [miroir] mirror.

glacé, e [glase] *adj* - **1.** [gelé] frozen - **2.** [très froid] freezing - **3.** *fig* [hostile] cold - **4.** [dessert] iced ; [viande] glazed ; [fruit] glacé.

glacer [16] [glase] *vt* - **1.** [geler, paralyser] to chill - **2.** [étoffe, papier] to glaze - **3.** [gâteau] to ice *Br*, to frost *Am*.

glacial, e, aux [glasjal, o] *adj litt & fig* icy.

glacier [glasje] *nm* - **1.** GÉOGR glacier - **2.** [marchand] ice cream seller *ou* man.

glaçon [glasɔ̃] *nm* - **1.** [dans boisson] ice cube - **2.** [sur toit] icicle - **3.** *fam fig* [personne] iceberg.

glaïeul [glajœl] *nm* gladiolus.

glaire [glɛr] *nf* MÉD phlegm.

glaise [glɛz] *nf* clay.

glaive [glɛv] *nm* sword.

gland [glɑ̃] *nm* - **1.** [de chêne] acorn - **2.** [ornement] tassel - **3.** ANAT glans.

glande [glɑ̃d] *nf* gland.

glaner [3] [glane] *vt* to glean.

glapir [32] [glapir] *vi* to yelp, to yap.

glas [gla] *nm* knell.

glauque [glok] *adj* - **1.** [couleur] blueygreen - **2.** *fam* [lugubre] gloomy - **3.** *fam* [sordide] sordid.

glissade [glisad] *nf* slip.

glissant, e [glisɑ̃, ɑ̃t] *adj* slippery.

glissement [glismɑ̃] *nm* - **1.** [action de glisser] gliding, sliding - **2.** *fig* [électoral] swing, shift.

glisser [3] [glise] ◇ *vi* - **1.** [se déplacer] : **~ (sur)** to glide (over), to slide (over) - **2.** [déraper] : **~ (sur)** to slip (on) - **3.** *fig* [passer rapidement] : **~ sur** to skate over - **4.** [surface] to be slippery - **5.** [progresser] to slip ; **~ dans** to slip into, to slide into ; **~ vers** to slip towards *Br ou* toward *Am*, to slide towards *Br ou* toward *Am*. ◇ *vt* to slip ; **~ un regard à qqn** *fig* to give sb a sidelong glance. ➧ **se glisser** *vp* to slip ; **se ~ dans**

[lit] to slip ou slide into ; *fig* to slip ou creep into.

glissière [glisjɛr] *nf* runner.

global, e, aux [glɔbal, o] *adj* global.

globalement [glɔbalmɑ̃] *adv* on the whole.

globe [glɔb] *nm* - **1.** [sphère, terre] globe - **2.** [de verre] glass cover.

globule [glɔbyl] *nm* corpuscle, blood cell ; ~ blanc/rouge white/red corpuscle.

globuleux [glɔbylø] ▭ œil.

gloire [glwar] *nf* - **1.** [renommée] glory ; [de vedette] fame, stardom - **2.** [mérite] credit.

glorieux, euse [glɔrjø, øz] *adj* [mort, combat] glorious ; [héros, soldat] renowned.

glossaire [glɔsɛr] *nm* glossary.

glousser [3] [gluse] *vi* - **1.** [poule] to cluck - **2.** *fam* [personne] to chortle, to chuckle.

glouton, onne [glutɔ̃, ɔn] ◇ *adj* greedy. ◇ *nm, f* glutton.

glu [gly] *nf* [colle] glue.

gluant, e [glyɑ̃, ɑt] *adj* sticky.

glucide [glysid] *nm* glucide.

glycémie [glisemi] *nf* glycaemia.

glycine [glisin] *nf* wisteria.

go [go] ◆ **tout de go** *loc adv* straight.

GO (*abr de* **grandes ondes**) *nfpl* LW.

goal [gol] *nm* goalkeeper.

gobelet [gɔblɛ] *nm* beaker, tumbler.

gober [3] [gɔbe] *vt* - **1.** [avaler] to gulp down - **2.** *fam* [croire] to swallow.

godet [gɔdɛ] *nm* - **1.** [récipient] jar, pot - **2.** COUTURE flare.

godiller [3] [gɔdije] *vi* - **1.** [rameur] to scull - **2.** [skieur] to wedeln.

goéland [gɔelɑ̃] *nm* gull, seagull.

goélette [gɔelɛt] *nf* schooner.

goguenard, e [gɔgnar, ard] *adj* mocking.

goinfre [gwɛ̃fr] *nmf fam* pig.

goitre [gwatr] *nm* goitre.

golf [gɔlf] *nm* [sport] golf ; [terrain] golf course.

golfe [gɔlf] *nm* gulf, bay ; **le ~ de Gascogne** the Bay of Biscay ; **le ~ Persique** the (Persian) Gulf.

gomme [gɔm] *nf* - **1.** [substance, bonbon] gum - **2.** [pour effacer] rubber *Br*, eraser.

gommer [3] [gɔme] *vt* to rub out, to erase ; *fig* to erase.

gond [gɔ̃] *nm* hinge.

gondole [gɔ̃dɔl] *nf* gondola.

gondoler [3] [gɔ̃dɔle] *vi* [bois] to warp ; [carton] to curl.

gonfler [3] [gɔ̃fle] ◇ *vt* - **1.** [ballon, pneu] to blow up, to inflate ; [rivière, poitrine, yeux] to swell ; [joues] to blow out - **2.** *fig* [grossir] to exaggerate. ◇ *vi* to swell.

gonflette [gɔ̃flɛt] *nf fam* : **faire de la ~** to pump iron.

gong [gɔ̃g] *nm* gong.

gorge [gɔrʒ] *nf* - **1.** [gosier, cou] throat - **2.** (*gén pl*) [vallée] gorge.

gorgée [gɔrʒe] *nf* mouthful.

gorger [17] [gɔrʒe] *vt* : ~ **qqn de qqch** [gaver] to stuff sb with sthg ; [combler] to heap sthg on sb ; ~ **qqch de** to fill sthg with.

gorille [gɔrij] *nm* [animal] gorilla.

gosier [gozje] *nm* throat, gullet.

gosse [gɔs] *nmf fam* kid.

gothique [gɔtik] *adj* - **1.** ARCHIT Gothic - **2.** TYPO : **écriture ~** Gothic script.

gouache [gwaʃ] *nf* gouache.

goudron [gudrɔ̃] *nm* tar.

goudronner [3] [gudrɔne] *vt* to tar.

gouffre [gufr] *nm* abyss.

goujat [guʒa] *nm* boor.

goulet [gulɛ] *nm* narrows (*pl*).

goulot [gulo] *nm* neck.

goulu, e [guly] *adj* greedy, gluttonous.

goupillon [gupijɔ̃] *nm* - **1.** RELIG [holy water] sprinkler - **2.** [à bouteille] bottle brush.

gourd, e [gur, gurd] *adj* numb.

gourde [gurd] ◇ *nf* - **1.** [récipient] flask, water bottle - **2.** *fam* [personne] clot *Br*. ◇ *adj fam* thick.

gourdin [gurdɛ̃] *nm* club.

gourmand, e [gurmɑ̃, ɑ̃d] ◇ *adj* greedy. ◇ *nm, f* glutton.

gourmandise [gurmɑ̃diz] *nf* - **1.** [caractère] greed, greediness - **2.** [sucrerie] sweet thing.

gourmette [gurmɛt] *nf* chain bracelet.

gousse [gus] *nf* pod ; ~ **d'ail** clove of garlic.

goût [gu] *nm* taste ; **de mauvais ~** tasteless, in bad taste ; **chacun ses ~s, à chacun son ~** each to his own.

goûter [3] [gute] ◇ *vt* - **1.** [déguster] to taste - **2.** [savourer] to enjoy. ◇ *vi* to have an afternoon snack ; ~ **à** to taste. ◇ *nm afternoon snack for children, typically consisting of bread, butter, chocolate and a drink.*

goutte [gut] *nf* - **1.** [de pluie, d'eau] drop - **2.** MÉD [maladie] gout. ◆ **gouttes** *nfpl* MÉD drops.

goutte-à-goutte [gutagut] *nm inv* (intravenous) drip *Br*, IV *Am*.

gouttelette [gutlɛt] *nf* droplet.

gouttière [gutjɛr] *nf* - **1.** [CONSTR - hori-

zontale] gutter ; [- verticale] drainpipe
- **2.** MÉD splint.

gouvernail [guvɛrnaj] *nm* rudder.

gouvernante [guvɛrnɑ̃t] *nf* - **1.** [d'enfants] governess - **2.** [de maison] housekeeper.

gouvernement [guvɛrnəmɑ̃] *nm* government.

gouverner [3] [guvɛrne] *vt* to govern.

gouverneur [guvɛrnœr] *nm* governor.

grâce [gras] *nf* - **1.** [charme] grace ; **de bonne ~** with good grace, willingly ; **de mauvaise ~** with bad grace, reluctantly - **2.** [faveur] favour *Br*, favor *Am* - **3.** [miséricorde] mercy. ◆ **grâce à** *loc prép* thanks to.

gracier [9] [grasje] *vt* to pardon.

gracieusement [grasjøzmɑ̃] *adv* - **1.** [avec grâce] graciously - **2.** [gratuitement] free (of charge).

gracieux, euse [grasjø, øz] *adj* - **1.** [charmant] graceful - **2.** [gratuit] free.

gradation [gradasjɔ̃] *nf* gradation.

grade [grad] *nm* [échelon] rank ; [universitaire] qualification.

gradé, e [grade] ◇ *adj* non-commissioned. ◇ *nm, f* non-commissioned officer, NCO.

gradin [gradɛ̃] *nm* [de stade, de théâtre] tier ; [de terrain] terrace.

graduation [graduasjɔ̃] *nf* graduation.

graduel, elle [graduɛl] *adj* gradual ; [difficultés] increasing.

graduer [7] [gradue] *vt* - **1.** [récipient, règle] to graduate - **2.** *fig* [effort, travail] to increase gradually.

graffiti [grafiti] *nm inv* graffiti *(U)*.

grain [grɛ̃] *nm* - **1.** [gén] grain ; [de moutarde] seed ; [de café] bean ; **~ de raisin** grape - **2.** [point] : **~ de beauté** mole, beauty spot - **3.** [averse] squall.

graine [grɛn] *nf* BOT seed.

graisse [grɛs] *nf* - **1.** ANAT & CULIN fat - **2.** [pour lubrifier] grease.

graisser [4] [grɛse] *vt* - **1.** [machine] to grease, to lubricate - **2.** [vêtements] to get grease on.

grammaire [gramɛr] *nf* grammar.

grammatical, e, aux [gramatikal, o] *adj* grammatical.

gramme [gram] *nm* gram, gramme.

grand, e [grɑ̃, grɑ̃d] ◇ *adj* - **1.** [en hauteur] tall ; [en dimensions] big, large ; [en quantité, nombre] large, great ; **un ~ nombre de** a large ou great number of ; **en ~** [dimension] full-size - **2.** [âgé] grown-up ; **les ~es personnes** grown-ups ; **~ frère** big ou

older brother - **3.** [important, remarquable] great ; **un ~ homme** a great man - **4.** [intense] : **un ~ blessé/brûlé** a person with serious wounds/burns ; **un ~ buveur/fumeur** a heavy drinker/smoker. ◇ *nm, f (gén pl)* - **1.** [personnage] great man *(f* woman) ; **c'est l'un des ~s de l'électroménager** he's one of the big names in electrical appliances - **2.** [enfant] older ou bigger boy *(f* girl).

grand-angle [grɑ̃tɑ̃gl] *nm* wide-angle lens.

grand-chose [grɑ̃ʃoz] ◆ **pas grand-chose** *pron indéf* not much.

Grande-Bretagne [grɑ̃dbrətaɲ] *nf* : **la ~** Great Britain.

grandeur [grɑ̃dœr] *nf* - **1.** [taille] size - **2.** [apogée] *fig* greatness ; **~ d'âme** *fig* magnanimity.

grandir [32] [grɑ̃dir] ◇ *vt* : **~ qqn** [suj : chaussures] to make sb look taller ; *fig* to increase sb's standing. ◇ *vi* [personne, plante] to grow ; [obscurité, bruit] to increase, to grow.

grand-mère [grɑ̃mɛr] *nf* grandmother ; *fam fig* old biddy.

grand-père [grɑ̃pɛr] *nm* grandfather ; *fam fig* old geezer.

grands-parents [grɑ̃parɑ̃] *nmpl* grandparents.

grange [grɑ̃ʒ] *nf* barn.

granit(e) [granit] *nm* granite.

granulé, e [granyle] *adj* [surface] granular. ◆ **granulé** *nm* tablet.

granuleux, euse [granylø, øz] *adj* granular.

graphique [grafik] ◇ *nm* diagram ; [graphe] graph. ◇ *adj* graphic.

graphisme [grafism] *nm* - **1.** [écriture] handwriting - **2.** ART style of drawing.

graphologie [grafɔlɔʒi] *nf* graphology.

grappe [grap] *nf* - **1.** [de fruits] bunch ; [de fleurs] stem - **2.** *fig* [de gens] knot.

grappiller [3] [grapije] *vt litt & fig* to gather, to pick up.

grappin [grapɛ̃] *nm* [ancre] grapnel.

gras, grasse [gra, gras] *adj* - **1.** [personne, animal] fat - **2.** [plat, aliment] fatty ; **matières grasses** fats - **3.** [cheveux, mains] greasy - **4.** [sol] clayey ; [crayon] soft - **5.** *fig* [rire] throaty ; [toux] phlegmy. ◆ **gras** ◇ *nm* - **1.** [du jambon] fat - **2.** TYPO bold (type). ◇ *adv* : **manger ~** to eat fatty foods.

grassement [grasmɑ̃] *adv* - **1.** [rire] coarsely - **2.** [payer] a lot.

gratifier [9] [gratifje] *vt* - **1.** [accorder] : **~ qqn de qqch** to present sb with sthg, to present sthg to sb ; *fig* to reward sb with sthg - **2.** [stimuler] to gratify.

gratin [gratɛ̃] *nm* - **1.** CULIN *dish sprinkled with breadcrumbs or cheese and browned* ; ~ **dauphinois** *sliced potatoes baked with cream and browned on top* - **2.** *fam fig* [haute société] upper crust.

gratiné, e [gratine] *adj* - **1.** CULIN *sprinkled with breadcrumbs or cheese and browned* - **2.** *fam fig* [ardu] stiff.

gratis [gratis] *adv* free.

gratitude [gratityd] *nf* : ~ **(envers)** gratitude (to ou towards).

gratte-ciel [gratsjɛl] *nm inv* skyscraper.

grattement [gratmɑ̃] *nm* scratching.

gratter [3] [grate] <> *vt* [gén] to scratch ; [pour enlever] to scrape off. <> *vi* - **1.** [démanger] to itch, to be itchy - **2.** *fam* [écrire] to scribble - **3.** [frapper] : ~ **à la porte** to tap at the door - **4.** *fam* [travailler] to slave, to slog. ◆ **se gratter** *vp* to scratch.

gratuit, e [gratɥi, it] *adj* - **1.** [entrée] free - **2.** [violence] gratuitous.

gratuitement [gratɥitmɑ̃] *adv* - **1.** [sans payer] free, for nothing - **2.** [sans raison] gratuitously.

gravats [grava] *nmpl* rubble *(U)*.

grave [grav] <> *adj* - **1.** [attitude, faute, maladie] serious, grave ; **ce n'est pas** ~ [ce n'est rien] don't worry about it - **2.** [voix] deep - **3.** LING : **accent** ~ grave accent. <> *nm (gén pl)* MUS low register.

gravement [gravmɑ̃] *adv* gravely, seriously.

graver [3] [grave] *vt* - **1.** [gén] to engrave - **2.** [bois] to carve - **3.** [disque] to cut.

gravier [gravje] *nm* gravel *(U)*.

gravillon [gravijɔ̃] *nm* fine gravel *(U)*.

gravir [32] [gravir] *vt* to climb.

gravité [gravite] *nf* - **1.** [importance] seriousness, gravity - **2.** PHYS gravity.

graviter [3] [gravite] *vi* - **1.** [astre] to revolve - **2.** *fig* [évoluer] to gravitate.

gravure [gravyr] *nf* - **1.** [technique] : ~ **(sur)** engraving (on) - **2.** [reproduction] print ; [dans livre] plate.

gré [gre] *nm* - **1.** [goût] : **à mon/son** ~ for my/his taste, for my/his liking - **2.** [volonté] : **bon** ~ **mal** ~ willy nilly ; **de** ~ **ou de force** *fig* whether you/they *etc* like it or not ; **de mon/son plein** ~ of my/his own free will.

grec, grecque [grɛk] *adj* Greek. ◆ **grec** *nm* [langue] Greek. ◆ **Grec, Grecque** *nm, f* Greek.

Grèce [grɛs] *nf* : **la** ~ Greece.

gréement [gremɑ̃] *nm* rigging.

greffe [grɛf] *nf* - **1.** MÉD transplant ; [de peau] graft - **2.** BOT graft.

greffer [4] [grefe] *vt* - **1.** MÉD to transplant ; [peau] to graft ; ~ **un rein/un cœur à qqn** to give sb a kidney/heart transplant - **2.** BOT to graft. ◆ **se greffer** *vp* : **se** ~ **sur qqch** to be added to sthg.

greffier [grefje] *nm* clerk of the court.

grégaire [greger] *adj* gregarious.

grêle [grɛl] <> *nf* hail. <> *adj* - **1.** [jambes] spindly - **2.** [son] shrill.

grêler [4] [grele] *v impers* to hail ; **il grêle** it's hailing.

grêlon [grɛlɔ̃] *nm* hailstone.

grelot [grəlo] *nm* bell.

grelotter [3] [grəlɔte] *vi* : ~ **(de)** to shiver (with).

grenade [grənad] *nf* - **1.** [fruit] pomegranate - **2.** MIL grenade.

grenat [grəna] *adj inv* dark red.

grenier [grənje] *nm* - **1.** [de maison] attic - **2.** [à foin] loft.

grenouille [grənuj] *nf* frog.

grès [grɛ] *nm* - **1.** [roche] sandstone - **2.** [poterie] stoneware.

grésiller [3] [grezije] *vi* - **1.** [friture] to sizzle ; [feu] to crackle - **2.** [radio] to crackle.

grève [grɛv] *nf* - **1.** [arrêt du travail] strike ; **être en** ~ to be on strike ; **faire** ~ to strike, to go on strike - **2.** [rivage] shore.

grever [19] [grəve] *vt* to burden ; [budget] to put a strain on.

gréviste [grevist] *nmf* striker.

gribouiller [3] [gribuje] *vt & vi* - **1.** [écrire] to scrawl - **2.** [dessiner] to doodle.

grief [grijɛf] *nm* grievance ; **faire** ~ **de qqch à qqn** to hold sthg against sb.

grièvement [grijɛvmɑ̃] *adv* seriously.

griffe [grif] *nf* - **1.** [d'animal] claw - **2.** *Belg* [éraflure] scratch.

griffer [3] [grife] *vt* [suj : chat etc] to claw.

grignoter [3] [griɲɔte] <> *vt* - **1.** [manger] to nibble - **2.** *fam fig* [réduire - capital] to eat away (at) - **3.** *fam fig* [gagner - avantage] to gain. <> *vi* - **1.** [manger] to nibble - **2.** *fam fig* [prendre] : ~ **sur** to nibble away at.

gril [gril] *nm* grill.

grillade [grijad] *nf* CULIN grilled meat.

grillage [grijaʒ] *nm* - **1.** [de porte, de fenêtre] wire netting - **2.** [clôture] wire fence.

grille [grij] *nf* - **1.** [portail] gate - **2.** [d'orifice, de guichet] grille ; [de fenêtre] bars *(pl)* - **3.** [de mots croisés, de loto] grid - **4.** [tableau] table.

grille-pain [grijpɛ̃] *nm inv* toaster.

griller [3] [grije] <> *vt* - **1.** [viande] to grill

Br, to broil *Am* ; [pain] to toast ; [café, marrons] to roast **- 2.** *fig* [au soleil - personne] to burn ; [- végétation] to shrivel **- 3.** *fam fig* [dépasser - concurrents] to outstrip ; **~ un feu rouge** to jump the lights **- 4.** *fig* [compromettre] to ruin. ◇ *vi* **- 1.** [viande] to grill *Br,* to broil *Am* **- 2.** [ampoule] to blow.

grillon [grijɔ̃] *nm* [insecte] cricket.

grimace [grimas] *nf* grimace.

grimer [3] [grime] *vt* CIN & THÉÂTRE to make up.

grimper [3] [grɛ̃pe] ◇ *vt* to climb. ◇ *vi* to climb ; **~ à un arbre/une échelle** to climb a tree/a ladder.

grincement [grɛ̃smɑ̃] *nm* [de charnière] squeaking ; [de porte, plancher] creaking.

grincer [16] [grɛ̃se] *vi* [charnière] to squeak ; [porte, plancher] to creak.

grincheux, euse [grɛ̃ʃø, øz] ◇ *adj* grumpy. ◇ *nm, f* moaner, grumbler.

grippe [grip] *nf* MÉD flu *(U).*

grippé, e [gripe] *adj* [malade] **: être ~ to** have flu.

gripper [3] [gripe] *vi* **- 1.** [mécanisme] to jam **- 2.** *fig* [processus] to stall.

gris, e [gri, griz] *adj* **- 1.** [couleur] grey *Br,* gray *Am* **- 2.** *fig* [morne] dismal **- 3.** [saoul] tipsy. ◆ **gris** *nm* [couleur] grey *Br,* gray *Am.*

grisaille [grizaj] *nf* **- 1.** [de ciel] greyness *Br,* grayness *Am* **- 2.** *fig* [de vie] dullness.

grisant, e [grizɑ̃, ɑ̃t] *adj* intoxicating.

griser [3] [grize] *vt* to intoxicate.

grisonner [3] [grizɔne] *vi* to turn grey *Br* ou gray *Am.*

grisou [grizu] *nm* firedamp.

grive [griv] *nf* thrush.

grivois, e [grivwa, az] *adj* ribald.

Groenland [grɔɛnlɑ̃d] *nm* **: le ~** Greenland.

grog [grɔg] *nm* (hot) toddy.

grognement [grɔɲmɑ̃] *nm* **- 1.** [son] grunt ; [d'ours, de chien] growl **- 2.** [protestation] grumble.

grogner [3] [grɔɲe] *vi* **- 1.** [émettre un son] to grunt ; [ours, chien] to growl **- 2.** [protester] to grumble.

groin [grwɛ̃] *nm* snout.

grommeler [24] [grɔmle] *vt & vi* to mutter.

grondement [grɔ̃dmɑ̃] *nm* [d'animal] growl ; [de tonnerre, de train] rumble ; [de torrent] roar.

gronder [3] [grɔ̃de] ◇ *vi* [animal] to growl ; [tonnerre] to rumble. ◇ *vt* to scold.

gros, grosse [gro, gros] *adj (gén avant n)* **- 1.** [gén] large, big ; *péj* big **- 2.** *(avant ou après n)* [corpulent] fat **- 3.** [grossier] coarse **- 4.** [fort, sonore] loud **- 5.** [important, grave - ennuis] serious ; [- dépense] major. ◆ **gros** ◇ *adv* [beaucoup] a lot. ◇ *nm* [partie] **: le (plus) ~ (de qqch)** the main part (of sthg). ◆ **en gros** *loc adv & loc adj* **- 1.** COMM wholesale **- 2.** [en grands caractères] in large letters **- 3.** [grosso modo] roughly.

groseille [grozɛj] *nf* currant.

grosse [gros] *adj* ⊏ **gros.**

grossesse [grosɛs] *nf* pregnancy.

grosseur [grosœr] *nf* **- 1.** [dimension, taille] size **- 2.** MÉD lump.

grossier, ère [grosje, ɛr] *adj* **- 1.** [matière] coarse **- 2.** [sommaire] rough **- 3.** [insolent] rude **- 4.** [vulgaire] crude **- 5.** [erreur] crass.

grossièrement [grosjɛrmɑ̃] *adv* **- 1.** [sommairement] roughly **- 2.** [vulgairement] crudely.

grossir [32] [grosir] ◇ *vi* **- 1.** [prendre du poids] to put on weight **- 2.** [augmenter] to grow **- 3.** [s'intensifier] to increase. ◇ *vt* **- 1.** [suj : microscope, verre] to magnify **- 2.** [suj : vêtement] : **~ qqn** to make sb look fatter **- 3.** [exagérer] to exaggerate.

grossiste [grosist] *nmf* wholesaler.

grosso modo [grosomɔdo] *adv* roughly.

grotte [grɔt] *nf* cave.

grouiller [3] [gruje] *vi* **: ~ (de)** to swarm (with).

groupe [grup] *nm* group ; **~ armé** armed group. ◆ **groupe sanguin** *nm* blood group.

groupement [grupmɑ̃] *nm* **- 1.** [action] grouping **- 2.** [groupe] group.

grouper [3] [grupe] *vt* to group. ◆ **se grouper** *vp* to come together.

grue [gry] *nf* TECHNOL & ZOOL crane.

grumeau, x [grymo] *nm* lump.

grunge [grʌnʒ] *adj* grunge *(modif).*

Guadeloupe [gwadlup] *nf* **: la ~** Guadeloupe.

Guatemala [gwatemala] *nm* **: le ~** Guatemala.

gué [ge] *nm* ford ; **traverser à ~** to ford.

guenilles [gənij] *nfpl* rags.

guenon [gənɔ̃] *nf* female monkey.

guépard [gepar] *nm* cheetah.

guêpe [gɛp] *nf* wasp.

guêpier [gepje] *nm* wasp's nest ; *fig* hornet's nest.

guère [gɛr] *adv* [peu] hardly ; **ne** (+ *verbe*)

~ [peu] hardly ; **il ne l'aime ~** he doesn't like him/her very much.

guéridon [geridɔ̃] *nm* pedestal table.

guérilla [gerija] *nf* guerrilla warfare.

guérir [32] [gerir] ◇ *vt* to cure ; **~ qqn de** *litt & fig* to cure sb of. ◇ *vi* to recover, to get better.

guérison [gerizɔ̃] *nf* - **1.** [de malade] recovery - **2.** [de maladie] cure.

guerre [gɛr] *nf* - **1.** MIL & *fig* war ; **faire la ~ à un pays** to make ou wage war on a country ; **Première/Seconde Guerre mondiale** First/Second World War - **2.** [technique] warfare *(U)*.

guerrier, ère [gɛrje, ɛr] *adj* - **1.** [de guerre] war *(avant n)* - **2.** [peuple] warlike. ◆ **guerrier** *nm* warrior.

guet-apens [gɛtapɑ̃] *nm* ambush ; *fig* trap.

guêtre [gɛtr] *nf* gaiter.

guetter [4] [gete] *vt* - **1.** [épier] to lie in wait for - **2.** [attendre] to be on the look-out for, to watch for - **3.** [menacer] to threaten.

gueule [gœl] *nf* - **1.** [d'animal, ouverture] mouth - **2.** *tfam* [bouche de l'homme] gob *Br*, yap *Am* - **3.** *fam* [visage] face.

gueuleton [gœltɔ̃] *nm fam* blowout.

gui [gi] *nm* mistletoe.

guichet [giʃɛ] *nm* counter ; [de gare, de théâtre] ticket office.

guide [gid] *nm* - **1.** [gén] guide - **2.** [livre] guidebook.

guider [3] [gide] *vt* to guide.

guidon [gidɔ̃] *nm* handlebars *(pl)*.

guignol [giɲɔl] *nm* - **1.** [marionnette] glove puppet - **2.** [théâtre] ≃ Punch and Judy show.

guillemet [gijmɛ] *nm* inverted comma, quotation mark.

guilleret, ette [gijrɛ, ɛt] *adj* perky.

guillotine [gijɔtin] *nf* - **1.** [instrument] guillotine - **2.** [de fenêtre] sash.

guindé, e [gɛ̃de] *adj* stiff.

Guinée [gine] *nf* : **la ~** Guinea.

guirlande [girlɑ̃d] *nf* - **1.** [de fleurs] garland - **2.** [de papier] chain ; [de Noël] tinsel *(U)*.

guise [giz] *nf* : **à ma ~** as I please ou like ; **en ~ de** by way of.

guitare [gitar] *nf* guitar.

guitariste [gitarist] *nmf* guitarist.

guttural, e, aux [gytyral, o] *adj* guttural.

Guyane [gɥijan] *nf* : **la ~** French Guiana.

gymnastique [ʒimnastik] *nf* SPORT & *fig* gymnastics *(U)* ; **faire de la ~** to do keep-fit exercises.

gynécologie [ʒinekɔlɔʒi] *nf* gynaecology *Br*, gynecology *Am*.

gynécologue [ʒinekɔlɔg] *nmf* gynaecologist *Br*, gynecologist *Am*.

h¹, H [aʃ] *nm inv* h, H.

h² (*abr de* **heure**) hr.

ha (*abr de* **hectare**) ha.

hab. *abr de* **habitant.**

habile [abil] *adj* skilful ; [démarche] clever.

habileté [abilte] *nf* skill.

habiller [3] [abije] *vt* - **1.** [vêtir] : **~ qqn (de)** to dress sb (in) - **2.** [recouvrir] to cover. ◆ **s'habiller** *vp* - **1.** [se vêtir] to dress, to get dressed - **2.** [se vêtir élégamment] to dress up.

habit [abi] *nm* - **1.** [costume] suit - **2.** RELIG habit. ◆ **habits** *nmpl* [vêtements] clothes.

habitacle [abitakl] *nm* [d'avion] cockpit ; [de voiture] passenger compartment.

habitant, e [abitɑ̃, ɑ̃t] *nm, f* - **1.** [de pays] inhabitant - **2.** [d'immeuble] occupant - **3.** *Can* [paysan] farmer.

habitation [abitasjɔ̃] *nf* - **1.** [fait d'habiter] housing - **2.** [résidence] house, home.

habiter [3] [abite] ◇ *vt* [résider] to live in. ◇ *vi* to live ; **~ à** to live in.

habitude [abityd] *nf* [façon de faire] habit ; **avoir l'~ de faire qqch** to be in the habit of doing sthg ; **d'~** usually.

habituel, elle [abityɛl] *adj* [coutumier] usual, customary.

habituer [7] [abitye] *vt* : **~ qqn à qqch/à faire qqch** to get sb used to sthg/to doing sthg. ◆ **s'habituer** *vp* : **s'~ à qqch/à faire qqch** to get used to sthg/to doing sthg.

hache [ˈaʃ] *nf* axe *Br*, ax *Am*.

hacher [3] [ˈaʃe] *vt* - **1.** [couper - gén] to chop finely ; [- viande] to mince *Br*, to grind *Am* - **2.** [entrecouper] to interrupt.

hachisch = **haschisch.**

hachoir [ˈaʃwar] *nm* - **1.** [couteau] chopper - **2.** [appareil] mincer *Br*, grinder *Am* - **3.** [planche] chopping-board.

hachure [ˈaʃyr] *nf* hatching.

hagard, e [ˈagar, ard] *adj* haggard.

haie [ˈɛ] nf - **1.** [d'arbustes] hedge - **2.** [de personnes] row ; [de soldats, d'agents de police] line - **3.** SPORT hurdle.

haillons [ˈajɔ] nmpl rags.

haine [ˈɛn] nf hatred.

haïr [33] [ˈair] vt to hate.

Haïti [aiti] n Haiti.

hâle [ˈal] nm tan.

hâlé, e [ˈale] adj tanned.

haleine [alɛn] nf breath.

haleter [28] [ˈalte] vi to pant.

hall [ˈol] nm - **1.** [vestibule, entrée] foyer, lobby - **2.** [salle publique] concourse.

halle [ˈal] nf covered market.

hallucination [alysinasjɔ] nf hallucination.

halo [ˈalo] nm [cercle lumineux] halo.

halogène [alɔʒɛn] nm & adj halogen.

halte [ˈalt] <> nf stop. <> interj stop!

haltère [altɛr] nm dumbbell.

haltérophilie [alterɔfili] nf weightlifting.

hamac [ˈamak] nm hammock.

hamburger [ˈɑburgœr] nm hamburger.

hameau, x [ˈamo] nm hamlet.

hameçon [amsɔ] nm fish-hook.

hamster [ˈamstɛr] nm hamster.

hanche [ˈɑʃ] nf hip.

handball [ˈɑdbal] nm handball.

handicap [ˈɑdikap] nm handicap.

handicapé, e [ˈɑdikape] <> adj handicapped. <> nm, f handicapped person.

handicaper [3] [ˈɑdikape] vt to handicap.

hangar [ˈɑgar] nm shed ; AÉRON hangar.

hanneton [ˈantɔ] nm cockchafer.

hanter [3] [ˈɑte] vt to haunt.

hantise [ˈɑtiz] nf obsession.

happer [3] [ˈape] vt [attraper] to snap up.

haranguer [3] [ˈarɑge] vt to harangue.

haras [ˈara] nm stud (farm).

harassant, e [ˈarasɑ, ɑt] adj exhausting.

harceler [25] [ˈarsəle] vt - **1.** [relancer] to harass - **2.** MIL to harry - **3.** [importuner] : ~ qqn (de) to pester sb (with).

hardes [ˈard] nfpl old clothes.

hardi, e [ˈardi] adj bold, daring.

hareng [ˈarɑ] nm herring.

hargne [ˈarɲ] nf spite (U), bad temper.

haricot [ˈariko] nm bean ; ~s verts/blancs/rouges green/haricot/kidney beans.

harmonica [armɔnika] nm harmonica, mouth organ.

harmonie [armɔni] nf - **1.** [gén] harmony - **2.** [de visage] symmetry.

harmonieux, euse [armɔnjø, øz] adj - **1.** [gén] harmonious - **2.** [voix] melodious - **3.** [traits, silhouette] regular.

harmoniser [3] [armɔnize] vt MUS & fig to harmonize ; [salaires] to bring into line.

harnacher [3] [ˈarnaʃe] vt [cheval] to harness.

harnais [ˈarnɛ] nm - **1.** [de cheval, de parachutiste] harness - **2.** TECHNOL train.

harpe [ˈarp] nf harp.

harpon [ˈarpɔ] nm harpoon.

harponner [3] [ˈarpɔne] vt - **1.** [poisson] to harpoon - **2.** fam [personne] to waylay.

hasard [ˈazar] nm chance ; **au ~** at random ; **par ~** by accident, by chance.

hasarder [3] [ˈazarde] vt - **1.** [tenter] to venture - **2.** [risquer] to hazard. <> **se hasarder** vp : **se ~ à faire qqch** to risk doing sthg.

haschisch, haschich, hachisch [ˈaʃiʃ] nm hashish.

hâte [ˈat] nf haste.

hâter [3] [ˈate] vt - **1.** [activer] to hasten - **2.** [avancer] to bring forward. <> **se hâter** vp to hurry ; **se ~ de faire qqch** to hurry to do sthg.

hausse [ˈos] nf [augmentation] rise, increase.

hausser [3] [ˈose] vt to raise.

haut, e [o, ot] adj - **1.** [gén] high ; **~ de 20 m** 20 m high - **2.** [classe sociale, pays, région] upper - **3.** [responsable] senior. <> **haut** <> adv - **1.** [gén] high ; [placé] highly - **2.** [fort] loudly. <> nm - **1.** [hauteur] height ; **faire 2 m de ~** to be 2 m high ou in height - **2.** [sommet, vêtement] top - **3.** loc : **avoir** ou **connaître des ~s et des bas** to have one's ups and downs. <> **de haut** loc adv [avec dédain] haughtily ; **le prendre de ~** to react haughtily. <> **de haut en bas** loc adv from top to bottom. <> **du haut de** loc prép from the top of. <> **en haut de** loc prép at the top of.

hautain, e [ˈotɛ, ɛn] adj haughty.

hautbois [ˈobwa] nm oboe.

haut de gamme [odgam] <> adj upmarket ; **une chaîne ~** a state-of-the-art hi-fi system. <> nm top of the range.

haute-fidélité [otfidelite] nf high fidelity, hi-fi.

hautement [ˈotmɑ] adv highly.

hauteur [ˈotœr] nf height ; **à ~ d'épaule** at shoulder level ou height.

haut-fourneau [ˈofurno] nm blast furnace.

haut-parleur [ˈoparlœr] (pl **haut-parleurs**) nm loudspeaker.

havre [ˈavr] *nm* [refuge] haven.

Haye [ˈɛ] *n* : **La ~** the Hague.

hayon [ˈajɔ̃] *nm* hatchback.

hebdomadaire [ɛbdɔmadɛr] *nm & adj* weekly.

hébergement [ebɛrʒəmɑ̃] *nm* accommodation *Br*, accommodations *(pl) Am*.

héberger [17] [ebɛrʒe] *vt* - 1. [loger] to put up - 2. [suj : hôtel] to take in.

hébété, e [ebete] *adj* dazed.

hébraïque [ebraik] *adj* Hebrew.

hébreu, x [ebrø] *adj* Hebrew. ➡ **hébreu** *nm* [langue] Hebrew. ➡ **Hébreu, x** *nm* Hebrew.

hécatombe [ekatɔ̃b] *nf litt & fig* slaughter.

hectare [ɛktar] *nm* hectare.

hectolitre [ɛktɔlitr] *nm* hectolitre.

hégémonie [eʒemɔni] *nf* hegemony.

hein [ˈɛ̃] *interj fam* eh?, what? ; **tu m'en veux, ~?** you're cross with me, aren't you?

hélas [elas] *interj* unfortunately, alas.

héler [18] [ele] *vt sout* to hail.

hélice [elis] *nf* - 1. [d'avion, de bateau] propeller - 2. MATHS helix.

hélicoptère [elikɔptɛr] *nm* helicopter.

héliport [elipɔr] *nm* heliport.

hélium [eljɔm] *nm* helium.

Helsinki [ˈɛlsiŋki] *n* Helsinki.

hématome [ematom] *nm* MÉD haematoma.

hémicycle [emisikl] *nm* POLIT : **l'~** the Assemblée Nationale.

hémisphère [emisfɛr] *nm* hemisphere.

hémophile [emɔfil] ◇ *nmf* haemophiliac. ◇ *adj* haemophilic.

hémorragie [emɔraʒi] *nf* - 1. MÉD haemorrhage - 2. *fig* [perte, fuite] loss.

hémorroïdes [emɔrɔid] *nfpl* haemorrhoids, piles.

hennir [32] [ˈenir] *vi* to neigh, to whinny.

hépatite [epatit] *nf* MÉD hepatitis.

herbe [ɛrb] *nf* - 1. BOT grass - 2. CULIN & MÉD herb - 3. *fam* [marijuana] grass.

herbicide [ɛrbisid] *nm* weedkiller, herbicide.

herboriste [ɛrbɔrist] *nmf* herbalist.

héréditaire [ereditɛr] *adj* hereditary.

hérédité [eredite] *nf* [génétique] heredity.

hérésie [erezi] *nf* heresy.

hérisson [erisɔ̃] *nm* ZOOL hedgehog.

héritage [eritaʒ] *nm* - 1. [de biens] inheritance - 2. [culturel] heritage.

hériter [3] [erite] ◇ *vi* to inherit ; **~ de**

qqch to inherit sthg. ◇ *vt* : **~ qqch de qqn** *litt & fig* to inherit sthg from sb.

héritier, ère [eritje, ɛr] *nm, f* heir (*f* heiress).

hermétique [ermetik] *adj* - 1. [étanche] hermetic - 2. [incompréhensible] inaccessible, impossible to understand - 3. [impénétrable] impenetrable.

hermine [ermin] *nf* - 1. [animal] stoat - 2. [fourrure] ermine.

hernie [ˈerni] *nf* hernia.

héroïne [erɔin] *nf* - 1. [personne] heroine - 2. [drogue] heroin.

héroïque [erɔik] *adj* heroic.

héroïsme [erɔism] *nm* heroism.

héron [ˈerɔ̃] *nm* heron.

héros [ˈero] *nm* hero.

hertz [ˈɛrts] *nm inv* hertz.

hésitant, e [ezitɑ̃, ɑ̃t] *adj* hesitant.

hésitation [ezitasjɔ̃] *nf* hesitation.

hésiter [3] [ezite] *vi* to hesitate ; **~ entre/sur** to hesitate between/over ; **~ à faire qqch** to hesitate to do sthg.

hétéroclite [eterɔklit] *adj* motley.

hétérogène [eterɔʒɛn] *adj* heterogeneous.

hétérosexuel, elle [eterɔsɛksɥɛl] *adj & nm, f* heterosexual.

hêtre [ˈɛtr] *nm* beech.

heure [ˈœr] *nf* - 1. [unité de temps] hour ; **250 km à l'~** 250 km per ou an hour ; **faire des ~s supplémentaires** to work overtime - 2. [moment du jour] time ; **il est deux ~s** it's two o'clock ; **quelle ~ est-il?** what time is it? ; **être à l'~** to be on time ; **à quelle ~?** when?, (at) what time? ; **~ de pointe** rush hour ; **~s de bureau** office hours - 3. SCOL class, period - 4. *loc* : **c'est l'~ (de faire qqch)** it's time (to do sthg) ; **de bonne ~** early.

heureusement [œrøzmɑ̃] *adv* [par chance] luckily, fortunately.

heureux, euse [œrø, øz] *adj* - 1. [gén] happy ; [favorable] fortunate ; **être ~ de faire qqch** to be happy to do sthg - 2. [réussi] successful, happy.

heurt [ˈœr] *nm* - 1. [choc] collision, impact - 2. [désaccord] clash.

heurter [3] [ˈœrte] *vt* - 1. [rentrer dans - gén] to hit ; [- suj : personne] to bump into - 2. [offenser - personne, sensibilité] to offend - 3. [bon sens, convenances] to go against. ➡ **se heurter** *vp* - 1. [gén] : **se ~ (contre)** to collide (with) - 2. [rencontrer] : **se ~ à qqch** to come up against sthg.

hexagonal, e, aux [ɛgzagɔnal, o] *adj* - 1. GÉOM hexagonal - 2. [français] French.

hexagone [ɛgzagɔn] *nm* GÉOM hexagon.

Hexagone *nm* : **l'Hexagone** (metropolitan) France.

hiatus [jatys] *nm inv* hiatus.

hiberner [3] [ibɛrne] *vi* to hibernate.

hibou, x ['ibu] *nm* owl.

hideux, euse ['idø, øz] *adj* hideous.

hier [ijɛr] *adv* yesterday.

hiérarchie ['jerarʃi] *nf* hierarchy.

hiéroglyphe [jeroglif] *nm* hieroglyph, hieroglyphic.

hilare [ilar] *adj* beaming.

hilarité [ilarite] *nf* hilarity.

Himalaya [imalaja] *nm* : **l'~** the Himalayas *(pl)*.

hindou, e [ẽdu] *adj* Hindu. **Hindou, e** *nm, f* Hindu.

hippie, hippy ['ipi] *(pl* **hippies)** *nmf & adj* hippy.

hippique [ipik] *adj* horse *(avant n)*.

hippodrome [ipodrom] *nm* race-course.

hippopotame [ipopotam] *nm* hippopotamus.

hirondelle [irõdɛl] *nf* swallow.

hirsute [irsyt] *adj* [chevelure, barbe] shaggy.

hispanique [ispanik] *adj* [gén] Hispanic.

hisser [3] ['ise] *vt* - **1.** [voile, drapeau] to hoist - **2.** [charge] to heave, to haul. **se hisser** *vp* - **1.** [grimper] : **se ~ (sur)** to heave ou haul o.s. up (onto) - **2.** *fig* [s'élever] : **se ~ à** to pull o.s. up to.

histoire [istwar] *nf* - **1.** [science] history ; **~ naturelle** natural history - **2.** [récit, mensonge] story - **3.** [aventure] funny ou strange thing - **4.** *(gén pl)* [ennui] trouble *(U)*.

historique [istorik] *adj* - **1.** [roman, recherches] historical - **2.** [monument, événement] historic.

hit-parade ['itparad] *(pl* **hit-parades)** *nm* : **le ~** the charts *(pl)*.

hiver [ivɛr] *nm* winter ; **en ~** in (the) winter.

HLM *(abr de* habitation à loyer modéré) *nm* OU *nf low-rent, state-owned housing*, ≃ council house/flat *Br*, ≃ public housing unit *Am*.

hobby ['ɔbi] *(pl* **hobbies)** *nm* hobby.

hocher [3] ['ɔʃe] *vt* : **~ la tête** [affirmativement] to nod (one's head) ; [négativement] to shake one's head.

hochet ['ɔʃɛ] *nm* rattle.

hockey ['ɔkɛ] *nm* hockey ; **~ sur glace** ice hockey *Br*, hockey *Am*.

holding ['ɔldiŋ] *nm* OU *nf* holding company.

hold-up ['ɔldœp] *nm inv* hold-up.

hollandais, e ['ɔlãdɛ, ɛz] *adj* Dutch. **hollandais** *nm* [langue] Dutch. **Hollandais, e** *nm, f* Dutchman (*f* Dutchwoman).

Hollande ['ɔlãd] *nf* : **la ~** Holland.

holocauste [ɔlɔkost] *nm* holocaust.

homard ['ɔmar] *nm* lobster.

homéopathie [ɔmeopati] *nf* homeopathy.

homicide [ɔmisid] *nm* [meurtre] murder.

hommage [ɔmaʒ] *nm* [témoignage d'estime] tribute ; **rendre ~ à qqn/qqch** to pay tribute to sb/sthg.

homme [ɔm] *nm* man ; **~ d'affaires** businessman ; **~ d'État** statesman ; **~ politique** politician.

homme-grenouille [ɔmgrənuj] *nm* frogman.

homogène [ɔmɔʒɛn] *adj* homogeneous.

homologue [ɔmɔlɔg] *nm* counterpart, opposite number.

homonyme [ɔmɔnim] *nm* - **1.** LING homonym - **2.** [personne, ville] namesake.

homosexualité [ɔmɔsɛksɥalite] *nf* homosexuality.

homosexuel, elle [ɔmɔsɛksɥɛl] *adj & nm, f* homosexual.

Honduras ['õdyras] *nm* : **le ~** Honduras.

Hongrie ['õgri] *nf* : **la ~** Hungary.

hongrois, e ['õgrwa, az] *adj* Hungarian. **hongrois** *nm* [langue] Hungarian. **Hongrois, e** *nm, f* Hungarian.

honnête [ɔnɛt] *adj* - **1.** [intègre] honest - **2.** [correct] honourable *Br*, honorable *Am* - **3.** [convenable - travail, résultat] reasonable.

honnêtement [ɔnɛtmã] *adv* - **1.** [de façon intègre, franchement] honestly - **2.** [correctement] honourably *Br*, honorably *Am*.

honnêteté [ɔnɛtte] *nf* honesty.

honneur [ɔnœr] *nm* honour *Br*, honor *Am* ; **faire ~ à qqn/qqch** to be a credit to sb/to sthg ; **faire ~ à un repas** *fig* to do justice to a meal.

honorable [ɔnɔrabl] *adj* - **1.** [digne] honourable *Br*, honorable *Am* - **2.** [convenable] respectable.

honoraire [ɔnɔrɛr] *adj* honorary. **honoraires** *nmpl* fee *(sg)*, fees.

honorer [3] [ɔnɔre] *vt* - **1.** [faire honneur à] to be a credit to - **2.** [payer] to honour *Br*, to honor *Am*.

honte ['õt] *nf* [sentiment] shame ; **avoir ~ de qqn/qqch** to be ashamed of sb/sthg ; **avoir ~ de faire qqch** to be ashamed of doing sthg.

honteux, euse ['ɔ̃tø, øz] *adj* shameful ; [personne] ashamed.

hooligan, houligan ['uligan] *nm* hooligan.

hôpital, aux [ɔpital, o] *nm* hospital.

hoquet ['ɔkɛ] *nm* hiccup.

horaire [ɔrɛr] ◇ *nm* - **1.** [de départ, d'arrivée] timetable - **2.** [de travail] hours *(pl)* (of work). ◇ *adj* hourly.

horizon [ɔrizɔ̃] *nm* - **1.** [ligne, perspective] horizon - **2.** [panorama] view.

horizontal, e, aux [ɔrizɔ̃tal, o] *adj* horizontal. ➡ **horizontale** *nf* MATHS horizontal.

horloge [ɔrlɔʒ] *nf* clock.

hormis ['ɔrmi] *prép* save.

hormone [ɔrmɔn] *nf* hormone.

horodateur [ɔrɔdatœr] *nm* [à l'usine] clock ; [au parking] ticket machine.

horoscope [ɔrɔskɔp] *nm* horoscope.

horreur [ɔrœr] *nf* horror ; **avoir ~ de qqn/qqch** to hate sb/sthg ; **avoir ~ de faire qqch** to hate doing sthg ; **quelle ~!** how dreadful!, how awful!

horrible [ɔribl] *adj* - **1.** [affreux] horrible - **2.** *fig* [terrible] terrible, dreadful.

horrifier [9] [ɔrifje] *vt* to horrify.

horripiler [3] [ɔripile] *vt* to exasperate.

hors ['ɔr] *prép* ▷ **pair, service**. ➡ **hors de** *loc prép* outside.

hors-bord ['ɔrbɔr] *nm inv* speedboat.

hors-d'œuvre ['ɔrdœvr] *nm inv* hors d'oeuvre, starter.

hors-jeu ['ɔrʒø] *nm inv & adj inv* offside.

hors-la-loi ['ɔrlalwa] *nm inv* outlaw.

hors-piste ['ɔrpist] *nm inv* off-piste skiing.

hortensia [ɔrtɑ̃sja] *nm* hydrangea.

horticulture [ɔrtikyltyr] *nf* horticulture.

hospice [ɔspis] *nm* home.

hospitalier, ère [ɔspitalje, ɛr] *adj* - **1.** [accueillant] hospitable - **2.** [relatif aux hôpitaux] hospital *(avant n)*.

hospitaliser [3] [ɔspitalize] *vt* to hospitalize.

hospitalité [ɔspitalite] *nf* hospitality.

hostie [ɔsti] *nf* host.

hostile [ɔstil] *adj* : **~ (à)** hostile (to).

hostilité [ɔstilite] *nf* hostility. ➡ **hostilités** *nfpl* hostilities.

hôte, hôtesse [ot, otɛs] *nm, f* host (*f* hostess) ; **hôtesse de l'air** air hostess. ➡ **hôte** *nm* [invité] guest.

hôtel [otɛl] *nm* - **1.** [d'hébergement] hotel - **2.** [établissement public] public building ;

~ de ville town hall - **3.** [demeure] : **~ (particulier)** (private) mansion.

hot line ['ɔtlain] *(pl* **hot lines***)* *nf* hot line.

hotte ['ɔt] *nf* - **1.** [panier] basket - **2.** [d'aération] hood.

houblon ['ublɔ̃] *nm* - **1.** BOT hop - **2.** [de la bière] hops *(pl)*.

houille ['uj] *nf* coal.

houiller, ère ['uje, ɛr] *adj* coal *(avant n)*. ➡ **houillère** *nf* coalmine.

houle ['ul] *nf* swell.

houlette ['ulɛt] *nf sout* : **sous la ~ de qqn** under the guidance of sb.

houppe ['up] *nf* - **1.** [à poudre] powder puff - **2.** [de cheveux] tuft.

hourra, hurrah ['ura] *interj* hurrah!

house [aws], **house music** [awsmjuzik] *nf* house (music).

houspiller [3] ['uspije] *vt* to tell off.

housse ['us] *nf* cover.

houx ['u] *nm* holly.

HS *(abr de* **hors service***) adj* out of order ; **je suis ~** *fam* I'm completely washed out.

hublot ['yblo] *nm* [de bateau] porthole.

huer [7] ['ɥe] *vt* [siffler] to boo.

huile [ɥil] *nf* - **1.** [gen] oil ; **~ d'arachide/d'olive** groundnut/olive oil - **2.** [peinture] oil painting - **3.** *fam* [personnalité] bigwig.

huis [ɥi] *nm littéraire* door ; **à ~ clos** JUR in camera.

huissier [ɥisje] *nm* - **1.** [appariteur] usher - **2.** JUR bailiff.

huit ['ɥit] ◇ *adj num* eight. ◇ *nm* eight ; **lundi en ~** a week on Monday *Br*, Monday week *Br*, a week from Monday *Am* ; *voir aussi* **six**.

huitième ['ɥitjɛm] ◇ *adj num & nmf* eighth. ◇ *nm* eighth ; **le ~ de finale** *round before the quarterfinal*. ◇ *nf* SCOL ≃ second year ou form *(at junior school) Br*, ≃ fourth grade *Am* ; *voir aussi* **sixième**.

huître [ɥitr] *nf* oyster.

humain, e [ymɛ̃, ɛn] *adj* - **1.** [gén] human - **2.** [sensible] humane. ➡ **humain** *nm* [être humain] human (being).

humanitaire [ymaniter] ◇ *adj* humanitarian. ◇ *nm* : **l' ~** humanitarian ou relief work.

humanité [ymanite] *nf* humanity. ➡ **humanités** *nfpl Belg* humanities.

humble [œbl] *adj* humble.

humecter [4] [ymɛkte] *vt* to moisten.

humer [3] ['yme] *vt* to smell.

humérus [ymerys] *nm* humerus.

humeur [ymœr] *nf* - **1.** [disposition] mood ; **être de bonne/mauvaise ~** to be in

a good/bad mood - **2.** [caractère] nature
- **3.** *sout* [irritation] temper.

humide [ymid] *adj* [air, climat] humid ;
[terre, herbe, mur] wet, damp ; [saison]
rainy ; [front, yeux] moist.

humidité [ymidite] *nf* [de climat, d'air] humidity ; [de terre, mur] dampness.

humiliation [ymiljasjɔ̃] *nf* humiliation.

humilier [9] [ymilje] *vt* to humiliate.
➤ **s'humilier** *vp* : **s'~ devant qqn** to
grovel to sb.

humilité [ymilite] *nf* humility.

humoristique [ymɔristik] *adj* humorous.

humour [ymur] *nm* humour *Br*, humor
Am.

humus [ymys] *nm* humus.

huppé, e [‘ype] *adj* - **1.** *fam* [société]
upper-crust - **2.** [oiseau] crested.

hurlement [‘yrləmã] *nm* howl.

hurler [3] [‘yrle] *vi* [gén] to howl.

hurrah = hourra.

hutte [‘yt] *nf* hut.

hybride [ibrid] *nm & adj* hybrid.

hydratant, e [idratã, ãt] *adj* moisturiz-
ing.

hydrater [3] [idrate] *vt* - **1.** CHIM to hydrate - **2.** [peau] to moisturize.

hydraulique [idrolik] *adj* hydraulic.

hydravion [idravjɔ̃] *nm* seaplane, hydroplane.

hydrocarbure [idrɔkarbyr] *nm* hydrocar-
bon.

hydrocution [idrɔkysjɔ̃] *nf* immersion
syncope.

hydroélectrique [idrɔelɛktrik] *adj*
hydroelectric.

hydrogène [idrɔʒɛn] *nm* hydrogen.

hydroglisseur [idrɔglisœr] *nm* jetfoil,
hydroplane.

hydrophile [idrɔfil] *adj* ▷ coton.

hyène [jɛn] *nf* hyena.

hygiène [iʒjɛn] *nf* hygiene.

hygiénique [iʒjenik] *adj* - **1.** [sanitaire]
hygienic - **2.** [bon pour la santé] healthy.

hymne [imn] *nm* hymn ; **~ national** national anthem.

hypermarché [ipɛrmarʃe] *nm* hypermarket.

hypermétrope [ipɛrmetrɔp] ◇ *nmf*
longsighted person. ◇ *adj* longsighted.

hypertension [ipɛrtãsjɔ̃] *nf* high blood
pressure, hypertension.

hypertrophié [ipɛrtrɔfje] *adj* hyper-
trophic ; *fig* exaggerated.

hypnotiser [3] [ipnɔtize] *vt* to hypnotize ;
fig to mesmerize.

hypoallergénique [ipɔalɛrʒenik] *adj*
hypoallergenic.

hypocondriaque [ipɔkɔ̃drijak] *nmf &
adj* hypochondriac.

hypocrisie [ipɔkrizi] *nf* hypocrisy.

hypocrite [ipɔkrit] ◇ *nmf* hypocrite.
◇ *adj* hypocritical.

hypoglycémie [ipɔglisemi] *nf* hypogly-
caemia.

hypotension [ipɔtãsjɔ̃] *nf* low blood
pressure.

hypothèque [ipɔtɛk] *nf* mortgage.

hypothèse [ipɔtɛz] *nf* hypothesis.

hystérie [isteri] *nf* hysteria.

hystérique [isterik] *adj* hysterical.

i, I [i] *nm inv* i, I ; **mettre les points sur les i**
to dot the i's and cross the t's.

ibérique [iberik] *adj* : **la péninsule ~** the
Iberian Peninsula.

iceberg [ajsbɛrg] *nm* iceberg.

ici [isi] *adv* - **1.** [lieu] here ; **par ~** [direction]
this way ; [alentour] around here
- **2.** [temps] now ; **d'~ (à) une semaine** in a
week's time, a week fron now ; **d'~ là** by
then.

icône [ikon] *nf* INFORM & RELIG icon.

idéal, e [ideal] (*pl* idéals ou idéaux [ideo])
adj ideal. ➤ **idéal** *nm* ideal.

idéaliste [idealist] ◇ *nmf* idealist. ◇ *adj*
idealistic.

idée [ide] *nf* idea ; **à l'~ de/que** at the idea
of/that ; **se faire des ~s** to imagine things ;
cela ne m'est jamais venu à l'~ it never oc-
curred to me.

identification [idãtifikasjɔ̃] *nf* : **~ (à)**
identification (with).

identifier [9] [idãtifje] *vt* to identify.
➤ **s'identifier** *vp* : **s'~ à qqn/qqch** to
identify with sb/sthg.

identique [idãtik] *adj* : **~ (à)** identical (to).

identité [idãtite] *nf* identity.

idéologie [ideɔlɔʒi] *nf* ideology.

idiomatique [idjɔmatik] *adj* idiomatic.

idiot, e [idjo, ɔt] <> *adj* idiotic ; MÉD idiot *(avant n).* <> *nm, f* idiot.

idiotie [idjɔsi] *nf* - **1.** [stupidité] idiocy - **2.** [action, parole] idiotic thing.

idolâtrer [3] [idɔlatre] *vt* to idolize.

idole [idɔl] *nf* idol.

idylle [idil] *nf* [amour] romance.

idyllique [idilik] *adj* [idéal] idyllic.

if [if] *nm* yew.

igloo, iglou [iglu] *nm* igloo.

ignare [iɲar] <> *nmf* ignoramus. <> *adj* ignorant.

ignoble [iɲɔbl] *adj* - **1.** [abject] base - **2.** [hideux] vile.

ignominie [iɲɔmini] *nf* - **1.** [état] disgrace - **2.** [action] disgraceful act.

ignorance [iɲɔrɑ̃s] *nf* ignorance.

ignorant, e [iɲɔrɑ̃, ɑ̃t] <> *adj* ignorant. <> *nm, f* ignoramus.

ignorer [3] [iɲɔre] *vt* - **1.** [ne pas savoir] not to know, to be unaware of - **2.** [ne pas tenir compte de] to ignore - **3.** [ne pas connaître] to have no experience of.

il [il] *pron pers* - **1.** [sujet - personne] he ; [- animal] it, he ; [- chose] it - **2.** [sujet d'un verbe impersonnel] it ; **~ pleut** it's raining. ➡ **ils** *pron pers pl* they.

île [il] *nf* island ; **les ~s Anglo-Normandes** the Channel Islands ; **les ~s Baléares** the Balearic Islands ; **les ~s Britanniques** the British Isles ; **les ~s Canaries** the Canary Islands ; **les ~s Malouines** the Falkland Islands ; **l'~ Maurice** Mauritius.

illégal, e, aux [ilegal, o] *adj* illegal.

illégalité [ilegalite] *nf* [fait d'être illégal] illegality.

illégitime [ileʒitim] *adj* - **1.** [enfant] illegitimate ; [union] unlawful - **2.** [non justifié] unwarranted.

illettré, e [iletre] *adj & nm, f* illiterate.

illicite [ilisit] *adj* illicit.

illimité, e [ilimite] *adj* - **1.** [sans limites] unlimited - **2.** [indéterminé] indefinite.

illisible [ilizibl] *adj* - **1.** [indéchiffrable] illegible - **2.** [incompréhensible & INFORM] unreadable.

illogique [ilɔʒik] *adj* illogical.

illumination [ilyminasjɔ̃] *nf* - **1.** [éclairage] lighting - **2.** [idée soudaine] inspiration.

illuminer [3] [ilymine] *vt* to light up ; [bâtiment, rue] to illuminate. ➡ **s'illuminer** *vp* : **s'~ de joie** to light up with joy.

illusion [ilyzjɔ̃] *nf* illusion.

illusoire [ilyzwar] *adj* illusory.

illustration [ilystrasjɔ̃] *nf* illustration.

illustre [ilystr] *adj* illustrious.

illustré, e [ilystre] *adj* illustrated. ➡ **illustré** *nm* illustrated magazine.

illustrer [3] [ilystre] *vt* - **1.** [gén] to illustrate - **2.** [rendre célèbre] to make famous. ➡ **s'illustrer** *vp* to distinguish o.s.

îlot [ilo] *nm* - **1.** [île] small island, islet - **2.** *fig* [de résistance] pocket.

ils ⊳ il.

image [imaʒ] *nf* - **1.** [vision mentale, comparaison, ressemblance] image - **2.** [dessin] picture.

imaginaire [imaʒinɛr] *adj* imaginary.

imagination [imaʒinasjɔ̃] *nf* imagination ; **avoir de l'~** to be imaginative.

imaginer [3] [imaʒine] *vt* - **1.** [supposer, croire] to imagine - **2.** [trouver] to think of. ➡ **s'imaginer** *vp* - **1.** [se voir] to see o.s. - **2.** [croire] to imagine.

imam [imam] *nm* imam.

imbattable [ɛ̃batabl] *adj* unbeatable.

imbécile [ɛ̃besil] *nmf* imbecile.

imberbe [ɛ̃bɛrb] *adj* beardless.

imbiber [3] [ɛ̃bibe] *vt* : **~ qqch de qqch** to soak sthg with ou in sthg.

imbriqué, e [ɛ̃brike] *adj* overlapping.

imbroglio [ɛ̃brɔljo] *nm* imbroglio.

imbu, e [ɛ̃by] *adj* : **être ~ de** to be full of.

imbuvable [ɛ̃byvabl] *adj* - **1.** [eau] undrinkable - **2.** *fam* [personne] unbearable.

imitateur, trice [imitatœr, tris] *nm, f* - **1.** [comique] impersonator - **2.** *péj* [copieur] imitator.

imitation [imitasjɔ̃] *nf* imitation.

imiter [3] [imite] *vt* - **1.** [s'inspirer de, contrefaire] to imitate - **2.** [reproduire l'aspect de] to look (just) like.

immaculé, e [imakyle] *adj* immaculate.

immangeable [ɛ̃mɑ̃ʒabl] *adj* inedible.

immanquable [ɛ̃mɑ̃kabl] *adj* impossible to miss ; [sort, échec] inevitable.

immatriculation [imatrikylasjɔ̃] *nf* registration.

immédiat, e [imedja, at] *adj* immediate.

immédiatement [imedjatmɑ̃] *adv* immediately.

immense [imɑ̃s] *adj* immense.

immerger [17] [imɛrʒe] *vt* to submerge. ➡ **s'immerger** *vp* to submerge o.s.

immérité, e [imerite] *adj* undeserved.

immeuble [imœbl] *nm* building.

immigration [imigrasjɔ̃] *nf* immigration.

immigré, e [imigre] *adj & nm, f* immigrant.

immigrer [3] [imigre] *vi* to immigrate.

imminent, e [iminɑ̃, ɑ̃t] *adj* imminent.

immiscer [16] [imise] ◆ **s'immiscer**
vp : **s'~ dans** to interfere in ou with.

immobile [imɔbil] *adj* - **1.** [personne, vi-
sage] motionless - **2.** [mécanisme] fixed,
stationary - **3.** *fig* [figé] immovable.

immobilier, ère [imɔbilje, ɛr] *adj* : biens
~s property *(U) Br*, real estate *(U) Am*.

immobiliser [3] [imɔbilize] *vt* to immobilize. ◆ **s'immobiliser** *vp* to stop.

immobilité [imɔbilite] *nf* immobility ;
[de paysage, de lac] stillness.

immodéré, e [imɔdere] *adj* inordinate.

immoler [3] [imɔle] *vt* to sacrifice ; RELIG
to immolate. ◆ **s'immoler** *vp* to immolate o.s.

immonde [imɔ̃d] *adj* - **1.** [sale] foul - **2.** [ab-
ject] vile.

immondices [imɔ̃dis] *nfpl* waste *(U)*, refuse *(U)*.

immoral, e, aux [imɔral, o] *adj* immoral.

immortaliser [3] [imɔrtalize] *vt* to immortalize.

immortel, elle [imɔrtɛl] *adj* immortal.
◆ **Immortel, elle** *nm, f fam* member of the
Académie française.

immuable [imɥabl] *adj* - **1.** [éternel - loi]
immutable - **2.** [constant] unchanging.

immuniser [3] [imynize] *vt* - **1.** [vacciner]
to immunize - **2.** *fig* [garantir] : **~ qqn contre
qqch** to make sb immune to sthg.

immunité [imynite] *nf* immunity.

impact [ɛ̃pakt] *nm* impact ; **avoir de l'~ sur**
to have an impact on.

impair, e [ɛ̃pɛr] *adj* odd. ◆ **impair** *nm*
[faux-pas] gaffe.

imparable [ɛ̃parabl] *adj* - **1.** [coup] unstoppable - **2.** [argument] unanswerable.

impardonnable [ɛ̃pardɔnabl] *adj* unforgivable.

imparfait, e [ɛ̃parfɛ, ɛt] *adj* - **1.** [défec-
tueux] imperfect - **2.** [inachevé] incomplete.
◆ **imparfait** *nm* GRAM imperfect (tense).

impartial, e, aux [ɛ̃parsjal, o] *adj* impartial.

impartir [32] [ɛ̃partir] *vt* : **~ qqch à qqn** *littéraire* [délai, droit] to grant sthg to sb.

impasse [ɛ̃pas] *nf* - **1.** [rue] dead end - **2.** *fig*
[difficulté] impasse, deadlock.

impassible [ɛ̃pasibl] *adj* impassive.

impatience [ɛ̃pasjɑ̃s] *nf* impatience.

impatient, e [ɛ̃pasjɑ̃, ɑ̃t] *adj* impatient.

impatienter [3] [ɛ̃pasjɑ̃te] *vt* to annoy.
◆ **s'impatienter** *vp* : **s'~ (de/contre)** to
get impatient (at/with).

impayé, e [ɛ̃peje] *adj* unpaid, outstand-

ing. ◆ **impayé** *nm* outstanding payment.

impeccable [ɛ̃pekabl] *adj* - **1.** [parfait] impeccable, faultless - **2.** [propre] spotless,
immaculate.

impénétrable [ɛ̃penetrabl] *adj* impenetrable.

impénitent, e [ɛ̃penitɑ̃, ɑ̃t] *adj* unre-
pentant.

impensable [ɛ̃pɑ̃sabl] *adj* unthinkable.

impératif, ive [ɛ̃peratif, iv] *adj* - **1.** [ton,
air] imperious - **2.** [besoin] imperative, essential. ◆ **impératif** *nm* GRAM imperative.

impératrice [ɛ̃peratris] *nf* empress.

imperceptible [ɛ̃persɛptibl] *adj* imperceptible.

imperfection [ɛ̃pɛrfɛksjɔ̃] *nf* imperfection.

impérialisme [ɛ̃perjalism] *nm* POLIT im-
perialism ; *fig* dominance.

impérieux, euse [ɛ̃perjø, øz] *adj* - **1.** [ton,
air] imperious - **2.** [nécessité] urgent.

impérissable [ɛ̃perisabl] *adj* undying.

imperméabiliser [3] [ɛ̃pɛrmeabilize] *vt*
to waterproof.

imperméable [ɛ̃pɛrmeabl] <> *adj* waterproof ; **~ à** [étanche] impermeable to ; *fig*
impervious ou immune to. <> *nm* raincoat.

impersonnel, elle [ɛ̃pɛrsɔnɛl] *adj* impersonal.

impertinence [ɛ̃pɛrtinɑ̃s] *nf* impertinence *(U)*.

impertinent, e [ɛ̃pɛrtinɑ̃, ɑ̃t] <> *adj* impertinent. <> *nm, f* impertinent person.

imperturbable [ɛ̃pɛrtyrbabl] *adj* imperturbable.

impétueux, euse [ɛ̃petɥø, øz] *adj* [per-
sonne, caractère] impetuous.

impie [ɛ̃pi] *littéraire & vieilli adj* impious.

impitoyable [ɛ̃pitwajabl] *adj* merciless,
pitiless.

implacable [ɛ̃plakabl] *adj* implacable.

implanter [3] [ɛ̃plɑ̃te] *vt* - **1.** [entreprise,
système] to establish - **2.** *fig* [préjugé] to implant. ◆ **s'implanter** *vp* [entreprise] to
set up ; [coutume] to become established.

implication [ɛ̃plikasjɔ̃] *nf* - **1.** [participa-
tion] : **~ (dans)** involvement (in) - **2.** *(gén pl)*
[conséquence] implication.

implicite [ɛ̃plisit] *adj* implicit.

impliquer [3] [ɛ̃plike] *vt* - **1.** [comprome-
ttre] : **~ qqn dans** to implicate sb in - **2.** [re-
quérir, entraîner] to imply. ◆ **s'impli-**

quer *vp* : **s'~ dans** *fam* to become involved in.

implorer [3] [ɛplɔre] *vt* to beseech.

implosion [ɛplozjɔ̃] *nf* implosion.

impoli, e [ɛpɔli] *adj* rude, impolite.

impopulaire [ɛpɔpylɛr] *adj* unpopular.

importance [ɛpɔrtɑ̃s] *nf* - **1.** [gén] importance ; [de problème, montant] magnitude - **2.** [de dommages] extent - **3.** [de ville] size.

important, e [ɛpɔrtɑ̃, ɑ̃t] *adj* - **1.** [personnage, découverte, rôle] important ; [événement, changement] important, significant - **2.** [quantité, collection, somme] considerable, sizeable ; [dommages] extensive.

importation [ɛpɔrtasjɔ̃] *nf* COMM & *fig* import.

importer [3] [ɛpɔrte] ◇ *vt* to import. ◇ *v impers* : **~ (à)** to matter (to) ; **il importe de/que** it is important to/that ; **qu'importe!, peu importe!** it doesn't matter! ; **n'importe qui** anyone (at all) ; **n'importe quoi** anything (at all) ; **n'importe où** anywhere (at all) ; **n'importe quand** at any time (at all).

import-export [ɛpɔrɛkspɔr] *nm* import-export.

importuner [3] [ɛpɔrtyne] *vt* to irk.

imposable [ɛpozabl] *adj* taxable.

imposant, e [ɛpozɑ̃, ɑ̃t] *adj* imposing.

imposé, e [ɛpoze] *adj* - **1.** [contribuable] taxed - **2.** SPORT [figure] compulsory.

imposer [3] [ɛpoze] *vt* - **1.** [gén] : **~ qqch/ qqn à qqn** to impose sthg/sb on sb - **2.** [impressionner] : **en ~ à qqn** to impress sb - **3.** [taxer] to tax. ◆ **s'imposer** *vp* - **1.** [être nécessaire] to be essential ou imperative - **2.** [forcer le respect] to stand out - **3.** [avoir pour règle] : **s'~ de faire qqch** to make it a rule to do sthg.

impossibilité [ɛpɔsibilite] *nf* impossibility ; **être dans l'~ de faire qqch** to find it impossible ou to be unable to do sthg.

impossible [ɛpɔsibl] ◇ *adj* impossible. ◇ *nm* : **tenter l'~** to attempt the impossible.

imposteur [ɛpɔstœr] *nm* impostor.

impôt [ɛpo] *nm* tax ; **~s locaux** council tax *Br*, local tax *Am* ; **~ sur le revenu** income tax.

impotent, e [ɛpɔtɑ̃, ɑ̃t] *adj* disabled.

impraticable [ɛpratikabl] *adj* - **1.** [inapplicable] impracticable - **2.** [inaccessible] impassable.

imprécis, e [ɛpresi, iz] *adj* imprecise.

imprégner [18] [ɛpreɲe] *vt* [imbiber] : **~ qqch de qqch** to soak sthg in sthg ; **~ qqn de qqch** *fig* to fill sb with sthg. ◆ **s'im-**

prégner *vp* : **s'~ de qqch** [s'imbiber] to soak sthg up ; *fig* to soak sthg up, to steep o.s. in sthg.

imprenable [ɛprənabl] *adj* - **1.** [forteresse] impregnable - **2.** [vue] unimpeded.

imprésario, impresario [ɛpresarjo] *nm* impresario.

impression [ɛpresjɔ̃] *nf* - **1.** [gén] impression ; **avoir l'~ que** to have the impression ou feeling that - **2.** [de livre, tissu] printing - **3.** PHOT print.

impressionner [3] [ɛpresjɔne] *vt* - **1.** [frapper] to impress - **2.** [choquer] to shock, to upset - **3.** [intimider] to frighten - **4.** PHOT expose.

impressionniste [ɛpresjɔnist] *nmf* & *adj* impressionist.

imprévisible [ɛprevizibl] *adj* unforeseeable.

imprévu, e [ɛprevy] *adj* unforeseen. ◆ **imprévu** *nm* unforeseen situation.

imprimante [ɛprimɑ̃t] *nf* printer.

imprimé, e [ɛprime] *adj* printed. ◆ **imprimé** *nm* - **1.** POSTES printed matter *(U)* - **2.** [formulaire] printed form - **3.** [tissu] print.

imprimer [3] [ɛprime] *vt* - **1.** [texte, tissu] to print - **2.** [mouvement] to impart - **3.** [marque, empreinte] to leave.

imprimerie [ɛprimri] *nf* - **1.** [technique] printing - **2.** [usine] printing works *(sg)*.

improbable [ɛprɔbabl] *adj* improbable.

improductif, ive [ɛprɔdyktif, iv] *adj* unproductive.

impromptu, e [ɛprɔ̃pty] *adj* impromptu.

impropre [ɛprɔpr] *adj* - **1.** GRAM incorrect - **2.** [inadapté] : **~ à** unfit for.

improviser [3] [ɛprɔvize] *vt* to improvise. ◆ **s'improviser** *vp* - **1.** [s'organiser] to be improvised - **2.** [devenir] : **s'~ metteur en scène** to act as director.

improviste [ɛprɔvist] ◆ **à l'improviste** *loc adv* unexpectedly, without warning.

imprudence [ɛprydɑ̃s] *nf* - **1.** [de personne, d'acte] rashness - **2.** [acte] rash act.

imprudent, e [ɛprydɑ̃, ɑ̃t] ◇ *adj* rash. ◇ *nm, f* rash person.

impubère [ɛpybɛr] *adj* [avant la puberté] pre-pubescent.

impudent, e [ɛpydɑ̃, ɑ̃t] ◇ *adj* impudent. ◇ *nm, f* impudent person.

impudique [ɛpydik] *adj* shameless.

impuissant, e [ɛpɥisɑ̃, ɑ̃t] *adj* - **1.** [incapable] : **~ (à faire qqch)** powerless (to do sthg) - **2.** [homme, fureur] impotent. ◆ **impuissant** *nm* impotent man.

impulsif, ive [ɛ̃pylsif, iv] ⟸ *adj* impulsive. ⟸ *nm, f* impulsive person.

impulsion [ɛ̃pylsjɔ̃] *nf* - **1.** [poussée, essor] impetus - **2.** [instinct] impulse, instinct - **3.** *fig* : **sous l'~ de qqn** [influence] at the prompting ou instigation of sb ; **sous l'~ de qqch** [effet] impelled by sthg.

impunément [ɛ̃pynemɑ̃] *adv* with impunity.

impunité [ɛ̃pynite] *nf* impunity ; **en toute ~** with impunity.

impur, e [ɛ̃pyr] *adj* impure.

impureté [ɛ̃pyrte] *nf* impurity.

imputer [3] [ɛ̃pyte] *vt* : **~ qqch à qqn/à qqch** to attribute sthg to sb/to sthg ; **~ qqch à qqch** FIN to charge sthg to sthg.

imputrescible [ɛ̃pytresibl] *adj* [bois] rot-proof ; [déchets] non-degradable.

inabordable [inabɔrdabl] *adj* - **1.** [prix] prohibitive - **2.** GÉOGR inaccessible *(by boat)* - **3.** [personne] unapproachable.

inacceptable [inaksɛptabl] *adj* unacceptable.

inaccessible [inaksesibl] *adj* [destination, domaine, personne] inaccessible ; [objectif, poste] unattainable ; **~ à** [sentiment] impervious to.

inaccoutumé, e [inakutyme] *adj* unaccustomed.

inachevé, e [inaʃve] *adj* unfinished, uncompleted.

inactif, ive [inaktif, iv] *adj* - **1.** [sans occupation, non utilisé] idle - **2.** [sans effet] ineffective - **3.** [sans emploi] non-working.

inaction [inaksjɔ̃] *nf* inaction.

inadapté, e [inadapte] *adj* - **1.** [non adapté] : **~ (à)** unsuitable (for), unsuited (to) - **2.** [asocial] maladjusted.

inadmissible [inadmisibl] *adj* [conduite] unacceptable.

inadvertance [inadvɛrtɑ̃s] *nf* *littéraire* oversight ; **par ~** inadvertently.

inaliénable [inaljenabl] *adj* inalienable.

inaltérable [inalterabl] *adj* - **1.** [matériau] stable - **2.** [sentiment] unfailing.

inamovible [inamɔvibl] *adj* fixed.

inanimé, e [inanime] *adj* - **1.** [sans vie] inanimate - **2.** [inerte, évanoui] senseless.

inanition [inanisjɔ̃] *nf* : **tomber/mourir d'~** to faint with/die of hunger.

inaperçu, e [inapɛrsy] *adj* unnoticed.

inappréciable [inapresjabl] *adj* [précieux] invaluable.

inapprochable [inaprɔʃabl] *adj* : **il est vraiment ~ en ce moment** you can't say anything to him at the moment.

inapte [inapt] *adj* - **1.** [incapable] : **~ à qqch/à faire qqch** incapable of sthg/of doing sthg - **2.** MIL unfit.

inattaquable [inatakabl] *adj* - **1.** [imprenable] impregnable - **2.** [irréprochable] irreproachable, beyond reproach - **3.** [irréfutable] irrefutable.

inattendu, e [inatɑ̃dy] *adj* unexpected.

inattention [inatɑ̃sjɔ̃] *nf* inattention ; **faute d'~** careless mistake.

inaudible [inodibl] *adj* [impossible à entendre] inaudible.

inauguration [inogyrasjɔ̃] *nf* [cérémonie] inauguration, opening (ceremony).

inaugurer [3] [inogyre] *vt* - **1.** [monument] to unveil ; [installation, route] to open ; [procédé, édifice] to inaugurate - **2.** [époque] to usher in.

inavouable [inavwabl] *adj* unmentionable.

incalculable [ɛ̃kalkylabl] *adj* incalculable.

incandescence [ɛ̃kɑ̃desɑ̃s] *nf* incandescence.

incantation [ɛ̃kɑ̃tasjɔ̃] *nf* incantation.

incapable [ɛ̃kapabl] ⟸ *nmf* [raté] incompetent. ⟸ *adj* : **~ de faire qqch** [inapte à] incapable of doing sthg ; [dans l'impossibilité de] unable to do sthg.

incapacité [ɛ̃kapasite] *nf* - **1.** [impossibilité] : **~ à** ou **de faire qqch** inability to do sthg - **2.** [invalidité] disability.

incarcération [ɛ̃karserasjɔ̃] *nf* incarceration.

incarner [3] [ɛ̃karne] *vt* - **1.** [personnifier] to be the incarnation of - **2.** CIN & THÉÂTRE to play.

incartade [ɛ̃kartad] *nf* misdemeanour *Br*, misdemeanor *Am*.

incassable [ɛ̃kasabl] *adj* unbreakable.

incendie [ɛ̃sɑ̃di] *nm* fire ; *fig* flames *(pl)*.

incendier [9] [ɛ̃sɑ̃dje] *vt* [mettre le feu à] to set alight, to set fire to.

incertain, e [ɛ̃sɛrtɛ̃, ɛn] *adj* - **1.** [gén] uncertain ; [temps] unsettled - **2.** [vague - lumière] dim ; [- contour] blurred.

incertitude [ɛ̃sɛrtityd] *nf* uncertainty.

incessamment [ɛ̃sesamɑ̃] *adv* at any moment, any moment now.

incessant, e [ɛ̃sesɑ̃, ɑ̃t] *adj* incessant.

inceste [ɛ̃sɛst] *nm* incest.

inchangé, e [ɛ̃ʃɑ̃ʒe] *adj* unchanged.

incidence [ɛ̃sidɑ̃s] *nf* [conséquence] effect, impact *(U)*.

incident, e [ɛ̃sidɑ̃, ɑ̃t] *adj* [accessoire] incidental. **➤ incident** *nm* [gén] incident ; [ennui] hitch.

incinérer [18] [ɛ̃sinere] *vt* - **1.** [corps] to cremate - **2.** [ordures] to incinerate.

inciser [3] [ɛ̃size] *vt* to incise, to make an incision in.

incisif, ive [ɛ̃sizif, iv] *adj* incisive. **➤ incisive** *nf* incisor.

inciter [3] [ɛ̃site] *vt* - **1.** [provoquer] : ~ **qqn à qqch/à faire qqch** to incite sb to sthg/to do sthg - **2.** [encourager] : ~ **qqn à faire qqch** to encourage sb to do sthg.

inclassable [ɛ̃klasabl] *adj* unclassifiable.

inclinable [ɛ̃klinabl] *adj* reclinable, reclining.

inclinaison [ɛ̃klinɛzɔ̃] *nf* - **1.** [pente] incline - **2.** [de tête, chapeau] angle, tilt.

incliner [3] [ɛ̃kline] *vt* [pencher] to tilt, to lean. **➤ s'incliner** *vp* - **1.** [se pencher] to tilt, to lean - **2.** [céder] : **s'~ (devant)** to give in (to), to yield (to).

inclure [96] [ɛ̃klyr] *vt* [mettre dedans] : ~ **qqch dans qqch** to include sthg in sthg ; [joindre] to enclose sthg with sthg.

inclus, e [ɛ̃kly, yz] ⋄ *pp* ⊳ **inclure**. ⋄ *adj* - **1.** [compris - taxe, frais] included ; [joint - lettre] enclosed ; **jusqu'à la page 10 ~e** up to and including page 10 **2.** MATHS : **etre ~ dans** to be a subset of.

incoercible [ɛ̃koɛrsibl] *adj* sout uncontrollable.

incognito [ɛ̃kɔɲito] *adv* incognito.

incohérent, e [ɛ̃kɔerɑ̃, ɑ̃t] *adj* [paroles] incoherent ; [actes] inconsistent.

incollable [ɛ̃kɔlabl] *adj* - **1.** [riz] nonstick - **2.** *fam* [imbattable] unbeatable.

incolore [ɛ̃kɔlɔr] *adj* colourless *Br*, colorless *Am*.

incomber [3] [ɛ̃kɔbe] *vi* : ~ **à qqn** to be sb's responsibility ; **il incombe à qqn de faire qqch** *(emploi impersonnel)* it falls to sb ou it is incumbent on sb to do sthg.

incommensurable [ɛ̃kɔmɑ̃syrabl] *adj* [immense] immeasurable.

incommoder [3] [ɛ̃kɔmɔde] *vt* sout to trouble.

incomparable [ɛ̃kɔparabl] *adj* - **1.** [différent] not comparable - **2.** [sans pareil] incomparable.

incompatible [ɛ̃kɔpatibl] *adj* incompatible.

incompétent, e [ɛ̃kɔpetɑ̃, ɑ̃t] *adj* [incapable] incompetent.

incomplet, ète [ɛ̃kɔplɛ, ɛt] *adj* incomplete.

incompréhensible [ɛ̃kɔpreɑ̃sibl] *adj* incomprehensible.

incompris, e [ɛ̃kɔpri, iz] ⋄ *adj* misunderstood, not appreciated. ⋄ *nm, f* misunderstood person.

inconcevable [ɛ̃kɔsvabl] *adj* unimaginable.

inconciliable [ɛ̃kɔsiljabl] *adj* irreconcilable.

inconditionnel, elle [ɛ̃kɔdisjɔnɛl] ⋄ *adj* - **1.** [total] unconditional - **2.** [fervent] ardent. ⋄ *nm, f* ardent supporter ou admirer.

inconfortable [ɛ̃kɔfɔrtabl] *adj* uncomfortable.

incongru, e [ɛ̃kɔgry] *adj* - **1.** [malséant] unseemly, inappropriate - **2.** [bizarre] incongruous.

inconnu, e [ɛ̃kɔny] ⋄ *adj* unknown. ⋄ *nm, f* stranger. **➤ inconnue** *nf* - **1.** MATHS unknown - **2.** [variable] unknown (factor).

inconsciemment [ɛ̃kɔsjamɑ̃] *adv* - **1.** [sans en avoir conscience] unconsciously, unwittingly - **2.** [à la légère] thoughtlessly.

inconscient, e [ɛ̃kɔsjɑ̃, ɑ̃t] *adj* - **1.** [évanoui, machinal] unconscious - **2.** [irresponsable] thoughtless. **➤ inconscient** *nm* : **l'~** the unconscious.

inconsidéré, e [ɛ̃kɔsidere] *adj* ill-considered, thoughtless.

inconsistant, e [ɛ̃kɔsistɑ̃, ɑ̃t] *adj* - **1.** [aliment] thin, watery - **2.** [caractère] frivolous.

inconsolable [ɛ̃kɔsɔlabl] *adj* inconsolable.

incontestable [ɛ̃kɔtɛstabl] *adj* unquestionable, indisputable.

incontinent, e [ɛ̃kɔtinɑ̃, ɑ̃t] *adj* MÉD incontinent.

incontournable [ɛ̃kɔturnabl] *adj* unavoidable.

inconvenant, e [ɛ̃kɔvnɑ̃, ɑ̃t] *adj* improper, unseemly.

inconvénient [ɛ̃kɔvenjɑ̃] *nm* - **1.** [obstacle] problem - **2.** [désavantage] disadvantage, drawback - **3.** [risque] risk.

incorporé, e [ɛ̃kɔrpɔre] *adj* [intégré] built-in.

incorporer [3] [ɛ̃kɔrpɔre] *vt* - **1.** [gén] to incorporate ; ~ **qqch dans** to incorporate sthg into ; ~ **qqch à** CULIN to mix ou blend sthg into - **2.** MIL to enlist.

incorrect, e [ɛ̃kɔrɛkt] *adj* - **1.** [faux] incorrect - **2.** [inconvenant] inappropriate ; [impoli] rude - **3.** [déloyal] unfair ; **être ~ avec qqn** to treat sb unfairly.

incorrection [ɛ̃kɔrɛksjɔ̃] *nf* - **1.** [impolitesse] impropriety - **2.** [de langage] grammatical mistake - **3.** [malhonnêteté] dishonesty.

incorrigible [ɛ̃kɔriʒibl] *adj* incorrigible.

incorruptible [ɛ̃kɔryptibl] *adj* incorruptible.

incrédule [ɛ̃kredyl] *adj* - **1.** [sceptique] incredulous, sceptical *Br*, skeptical *Am* - **2.** RELIG unbelieving.

increvable [ɛ̃krəvabl] *adj* - **1.** [ballon, pneu] puncture-proof - **2.** *fam fig* [personne] tireless ; [machine] that will withstand rough treatment.

incriminer [3] [ɛ̃krimine] *vt* - **1.** [personne] to incriminate - **2.** [conduite] to condemn.

incroyable [ɛ̃krwajabl] *adj* incredible, unbelievable.

incroyant, e [ɛ̃krwajɑ̃, ɑ̃t] *nm, f* unbeliever.

incruster [3] [ɛ̃kryste] *vt* - **1.** [insérer] : ~ qqch dans qqch to inlay sthg into sthg - **2.** [décorer] : ~ qqch de qqch to inlay sthg with sthg - **3.** [couvrir d'un dépôt] to fur up.
➤ **s'incruster** *vp* [s'insérer] : **s'~ dans qqch** to become embedded in sthg.

incubation [ɛ̃kybasjɔ̃] *nf* [d'œuf, de maladie] incubation ; *fig* hatching.

inculpation [ɛ̃kylpasjɔ̃] *nf* charge.

inculper [3] [ɛ̃kylpe] *vt* to charge ; ~ qqn de to charge sb with.

inculquer [3] [ɛ̃kylke] *vt* : ~ qqch à qqn to instil *Br* ou instill *Am* sthg in sb.

inculte [ɛ̃kylt] *adj* - **1.** [terre] uncultivated - **2.** *péj* [personne] uneducated.

incurable [ɛ̃kyrabl] *adj* incurable.

incursion [ɛ̃kyrsjɔ̃] *nf* incursion, foray.

Inde [ɛ̃d] *nf* : l'~ India.

indécent, e [ɛ̃desɑ̃, ɑ̃t] *adj* - **1.** [impudique] indecent - **2.** [immoral] scandalous.

indéchiffrable [ɛ̃deʃifrabl] *adj* - **1.** [texte, écriture] indecipherable - **2.** *fig* [regard] inscrutable, impenetrable.

indécis, e [ɛ̃desi, iz] <> *adj* - **1.** [personne - sur le moment] undecided ; [- de nature] indecisive - **2.** [sourire] vague. <> *nm, f* indecisive person.

indécision [ɛ̃desizjɔ̃] *nf* indecision ; [perpétuelle] indecisiveness.

indécrottable [ɛ̃dekrɔtabl] *adj fam* - **1.** [borné] incredibly dumb - **2.** [incorrigible] hopeless.

indéfendable [ɛ̃defɑ̃dabl] *adj* indefensible.

indéfini, e [ɛ̃defini] *adj* [quantité, pronom] indefinite.

indéfinissable [ɛ̃definisabl] *adj* indefinable.

indéformable [ɛ̃defɔrmabl] *adj* that retains its shape.

indélébile [ɛ̃delebil] *adj* indelible.

indélicat, e [ɛ̃delika, at] *adj* - **1.** [mufle] indelicate - **2.** [malhonnête] dishonest.

indemne [ɛ̃dɛmn] *adj* unscathed, unharmed.

indemniser [3] [ɛ̃dɛmnize] *vt* : ~ qqn de qqch [perte, préjudice] to compensate sb for sthg ; [frais] to reimburse sb for sthg.

indemnité [ɛ̃dɛmnite] *nf* - **1.** [de perte, préjudice] compensation - **2.** [de frais] allowance.

indémodable [ɛ̃demodabl] *adj* : ce style est ~ this style doesn't date.

indéniable [ɛ̃denjabl] *adj* undeniable.

indépendance [ɛ̃depɑ̃dɑ̃s] *nf* independence.

indépendant, e [ɛ̃depɑ̃dɑ̃, ɑ̃t] *adj* - **1.** [gén] independent ; [entrée] separate ; ~ **de ma volonté** beyond my control - **2.** [travailleur] self-employed.

indéracinable [ɛ̃derasinabl] *adj* [arbre] impossible to uproot ; *fig* ineradicable.

indescriptible [ɛ̃dɛskriptibl] *adj* indescribable.

indestructible [ɛ̃dɛstryktibl] *adj* indestructible.

indéterminé, e [ɛ̃detɛrmine] *adj* - **1.** [indéfini] indeterminate, indefinite - **2.** [vague] vague - **3.** [personne] undecided.

index [ɛ̃dɛks] *nm* - **1.** [doigt] index finger - **2.** [aiguille] pointer, needle - **3.** [registre] index.

indexer [4] [ɛ̃dɛkse] *vt* - **1.** ÉCON : ~ qqch sur qqch to index sthg to sthg - **2.** [livre] to index.

indicateur, trice [ɛ̃dikatœr, tris] *adj* : poteau ~ signpost ; panneau ~ road sign.
➤ **indicateur** *nm* - **1.** [guide] directory, guide ; ~ des chemins de fer railway *Br* ou railroad *Am* timetable - **2.** TECHNOL gauge - **3.** ÉCON indicator - **4.** [de police] informer.

indicatif, ive [ɛ̃dikatif, iv] *adj* indicative.
➤ **indicatif** *nm* - **1.** RADIO & TÉLÉ signature tune - **2.** [code] : ~ (téléphonique) dialling code *Br*, dial code *Am* - **3.** GRAM : l'~ the indicative.

indication [ɛ̃dikasjɔ̃] *nf* - **1.** [mention] indication - **2.** [renseignement] information (*U*) - **3.** [directive] instruction ; THÉÂTRE direction ; sauf ~ contraire unless otherwise instructed.

indice [ɛ̃dis] *nm* - **1.** [signe] sign - **2.** [dans une enquête] clue - **3.** [taux] rating ; ~ du coût de la vie ÉCON cost-of-living index - **4.** MATHS index.

indicible [ɛ̃disibl] adj inexpressible.
indien, enne [ɛ̃djɛ̃, ɛn] adj - 1. [d'Inde]
Indian - 2. [d'Amérique] American Indian,
Native American. ◆ **Indien, enne** nm, f
- 1. [d'Inde] Indian - 2. [d'Amérique] American Indian, Native American.
indifféremment [ɛ̃diferamɑ̃] adv indif-
ferently.
indifférent, e [ɛ̃diferɑ̃, ɑ̃t] <> adj [gén] :
~ à indifferent to. <> nm, f unconcerned
person.
indigence [ɛ̃diʒɑ̃s] nf poverty.
indigène [ɛ̃diʒɛn] <> nmf native. <> adj
[peuple] native ; [faune, flore] indigenous.
indigent, e [ɛ̃diʒɑ̃, ɑ̃t] <> adj [pauvre]
destitute, poverty-stricken ; fig [intellec-
tuellement] impoverished. <> nm, f poor
person ; les ~s the poor, the destitute.
indigeste [ɛ̃diʒɛst] adj indigestible.
indigestion [ɛ̃diʒɛstjɔ̃] nf - 1. [alimen-
taire] indigestion - 2. fig [saturation] surfeit.
indignation [ɛ̃diɲasjɔ̃] nf indignation.
indigné, e [ɛ̃diɲe] adj indignant.
indigner [3] [ɛ̃diɲe] vt to make indignant.
◆ **s'indigner** vp : s'~ de ou contre qqch
to get indignant about sthg.
indigo [ɛ̃digo] <> nm indigo. <> adj inv
indigo (blue).
indiquer [3] [ɛ̃dike] vt - 1. [désigner] to indicate, to point out - 2. [afficher, montrer - suj : carte, pendule, aiguille] to show,
to indicate - 3. [recommander] : ~ qqn/qqch
à qqn to tell sb of sb/sthg, to suggest sb/
sthg to sb - 4. [dire, renseigner sur] to tell ;
pourriez-vous m'~ l'heure? could you tell
me the time? - 5. [fixer - heure, date, lieu] to
name, to indicate.
indirect, e [ɛ̃dirɛkt] adj [gén] indirect ;
[itinéraire] roundabout.
indiscipliné, e [ɛ̃disipline] adj - 1 [éco-
lier, esprit] undisciplined, unruly - 2. fig
[mèches de cheveux] unmanageable.
indiscret, ète [ɛ̃diskrɛ, ɛt] <> adj indiscreet ; [curieux] inquisitive. <> nm, f indiscreet person.
indiscrétion [ɛ̃diskresjɔ̃] nf indiscretion ;
[curiosité] curiosity.
indiscutable [ɛ̃diskytabl] adj unquestionable, indisputable.
indispensable [ɛ̃dispɑ̃sabl] adj indispensable, essential ; ~ à indispensable to, essential to ; il est ~ de faire qqch it is essential ou vital to do sthg.
indisponible [ɛ̃dispɔnibl] adj unavailable.
indisposer [3] [ɛ̃dispoze] vt sout [rendre
malade] to indispose.

indistinct, e [ɛ̃distɛ̃(kt), ɛ̃kt] adj indistinct ; [souvenir] hazy.
individu [ɛ̃dividy] nm individual.
individuel, elle [ɛ̃dividɥɛl] adj individual.
indivisible [ɛ̃divizibl] adj indivisible.
Indochine [ɛ̃dɔʃin] nf : l'~ Indochina.
indolent, e [ɛ̃dɔlɑ̃, ɑ̃t] adj - 1. [personne]
indolent, lethargic - 2. [geste, regard] languid.
indolore [ɛ̃dɔlɔr] adj painless.
indomptable [ɛ̃dɔ̃tabl] adj - 1. [animal]
untamable - 2. [personne] indomitable.
Indonésie [ɛ̃dɔnezi] nf : l'~ Indonesia.
indu, e [ɛ̃dy] adj [heure] ungodly, unearthly.
indubitable [ɛ̃dybitabl] adj indubitable,
undoubted ; il est ~ que it is indisputable
ou beyond doubt that.
induire [98] [ɛ̃dɥir] vt to induce ; ~ qqn à
faire qqch to induce sb to do sthg ; ~ qqn
en erreur to mislead sb ; en ~ que to infer
ou gather that.
induit, e [ɛ̃dɥi, ɥit] <> pp ▷ induire.
<> adj - 1. [consécutif] resulting - 2. ÉLECTR
induced.
indulgence [ɛ̃dylʒɑ̃s] nf [de juge] leni-
ency ; [de parent] indulgence.
indulgent, e [ɛ̃dylʒɑ̃, ɑ̃t] adj [juge] lenient ; [parent] indulgent.
indûment [ɛ̃dymɑ̃] adv unduly.
industrialisé, e [ɛ̃dystrijalize] adj industrialized ; pays ~ industrialized country.
industrialiser [3] [ɛ̃dystrijalize] vt to in-
dustrialize. ◆ **s'industrialiser** vp to become industrialized.
industrie [ɛ̃dystri] nf industry.
industriel, elle [ɛ̃dystrijɛl] adj industrial. ◆ **industriel** nm industrialist.
inébranlable [inebrɑ̃labl] adj - 1. [roc]
solid, immovable - 2. fig [conviction] un-
shakeable.
inédit, e [inedi, it] adj - 1. [texte] unpub-
lished - 2. [trouvaille] novel, original.
ineffable [inefabl] adj ineffable.
ineffaçable [inefasabl] adj indelible.
inefficace [inefikas] adj - 1. [personne,
machine] inefficient - 2. [solution, remède,
mesure] ineffective.
inefficacité [inefikasite] nf - 1. [de personne, machine] inefficiency - 2. [de solution, remède, mesure] ineffectiveness.
inégal, e, aux [inegal, o] adj - 1. [diffé-
rent, disproportionné] unequal - 2. [irrégu-
lier] uneven - 3. [changeant] changeable ;
[artiste, travail] erratic.

inégalé, e [inegale] *adj* unequalled *Br*, unequaled *Am*.

inégalité [inegalite] *nf* - **1.** [injustice, disproportion] inequality - **2.** [différence] difference, disparity - **3.** [irrégularité] unevenness - **4.** [d'humeur] changeability.

inélégant, e [inelegã, ãt] *adj* - **1.** [dans l'habillement] inelegant - **2.** *fig* [indélicat] discourteous.

inéligible [inelizibl] *adj* ineligible.

inéluctable [inelyktabl] *adj* inescapable.

inénarrable [inenarabl] *adj* very funny.

inepte [inɛpt] *adj* inept.

ineptie [inɛpsi] *nf* - **1.** [bêtise] ineptitude - **2.** [chose idiote] nonsense *(U)*.

inépuisable [inepɥizabl] *adj* inexhaustible.

inerte [inɛrt] *adj* - **1.** [corps, membre] lifeless - **2.** [personne] passive, inert - **3.** PHYS inert.

inertie [inɛrsi] *nf* - **1.** [manque de réaction] apathy, inertia - **2.** PHYS inertia.

inespéré, e [inɛspere] *adj* unexpected, unhoped-for.

inesthétique [inɛstetik] *adj* unaesthetic.

inestimable [inɛstimabl] *adj* : **d'une valeur ~** priceless ; *fig* invaluable.

inévitable [inevitabl] *adj* [obstacle] unavoidable ; [conséquence] inevitable.

inexact, e [inɛgza(kt), akt] *adj* - **1.** [faux, incomplet] inaccurate, inexact - **2.** [en retard] unpunctual.

inexactitude [inɛgzaktityd] *nf* [erreur, imprécision] inaccuracy.

inexcusable [inɛkskyzabl] *adj* unforgivable, inexcusable.

inexistant, e [inɛgzistã, ãt] *adj* nonexistent.

inexorable [inɛgzɔrabl] *adj* inexorable.

inexpérience [inɛksperjãs] *nf* lack of experience, inexperience.

inexplicable [inɛksplikabl] *adj* inexplicable, unexplainable.

inexpliqué, e [inɛksplike] *adj* unexplained.

inexpressif, ive [inɛkspresif, iv] *adj* inexpressive.

inexprimable [inɛksprimabl] *adj* inexpressible.

inextensible [inɛkstãsibl] *adj* - **1.** [matériau] unstretchable - **2.** [étoffe] non-stretch.

in extremis [inɛkstremis] *adv* at the last minute.

inextricable [inɛkstrikabl] *adj* - **1.** [fouillis] inextricable - **2.** *fig* [affaire, mystère] that cannot be unravelled.

infaillible [ɛ̃fajibl] *adj* [personne, méthode] infallible ; [instinct] unerring.

infâme [ɛ̃fam] *adj* - **1.** [ignoble] despicable - **2.** *hum ou littéraire* [dégoûtant] vile.

infanterie [ɛ̃fãtri] *nf* infantry.

infanticide [ɛ̃fãtisid] ⋄ *nmf* infanticide, child-killer. ⋄ *adj* infanticidal.

infantile [ɛ̃fãtil] *adj* - **1.** [maladie] childhood *(avant n)* - **2.** [médecine] for children - **3.** [comportement] infantile.

infarctus [ɛ̃farktys] *nm* infarction, infarct ; **~ du myocarde** coronary thrombosis, myocardial infarction.

infatigable [ɛ̃fatigabl] *adj* - **1.** [personne] tireless - **2.** [attitude] untiring.

infect, e [ɛ̃fɛkt] *adj* [dégoûtant] vile.

infecter [4] [ɛ̃fɛkte] *vt* - **1.** [eau] to contaminate - **2.** [plaie] to infect - **3.** [empoisonner] to poison. ◆ **s'infecter** *vp* to become infected, to turn septic.

infectieux, euse [ɛ̃fɛksjø, øz] *adj* infectious.

infection [ɛ̃fɛksjɔ̃] *nf* - **1.** MÉD infection - **2.** *fig & péj* [puanteur] stench.

inférer [18] [ɛ̃fere] *vt littéraire* : **~ qqch de qqch** to infer sthg from sthg.

inférieur, e [ɛ̃ferjœr] ⋄ *adj* - **1.** [qui est en bas] lower - **2.** [dans une hiérarchie] inferior ; **~ à** [qualité] inferior to ; [quantité] less than. ⋄ *nm, f* inferior.

infériorité [ɛ̃ferjɔrite] *nf* inferiority.

infernal, e, aux [ɛ̃fɛrnal, o] *adj* - **1.** [personne] fiendish - **2.** *fig* [bruit, chaleur, rythme] infernal ; [vision] diabolical.

infester [3] [ɛ̃fɛste] *vt* to infest ; **être infesté de** [rats, moustiques] to be infested with ; [touristes] to be overrun by.

infidèle [ɛ̃fidɛl] *adj* - **1.** [mari, femme, ami] : **~ (à)** unfaithful (to) - **2.** [traducteur, historien] inaccurate.

infidélité [ɛ̃fidelite] *nf* [trahison] infidelity.

infiltration [ɛ̃filtrasjɔ̃] *nf* infiltration.

infiltrer [3] [ɛ̃filtre] *vt* to infiltrate. ◆ **s'infiltrer** *vp* - **1.** [pluie, lumière] **s'~ par/dans** to filter through/into - **2.** [hommes, idées] to infiltrate.

infime [ɛ̃fim] *adj* minute, infinitesimal.

infini, e [ɛ̃fini] *adj* - **1.** [sans bornes] infinite, boundless - **2.** MATHS, PHILO & RELIG infinite - **3.** *fig* [interminable] endless, interminable. ◆ **infini** *nm* infinity. ◆ **à l'infini** *loc adv* - **1.** MATHS to infinity - **2.** [discourir] ad infinitum, endlessly.

infiniment [ɛ̃finimã] *adv* extremely, immensely.

infinité [ɛ̃finite] *nf* infinity, infinite number.

infinitif, ive [ɛ̃finitif, iv] *adj* infinitive.
➤ **infinitif** *nm* infinitive.

infirme [ɛ̃firm] <> *adj* [handicapé] disabled ; [avec l'âge] infirm. <> *nmf* disabled person.

infirmer [3] [ɛ̃firme] *vt* - **1.** [démentir] to invalidate - **2.** JUR to annul.

infirmerie [ɛ̃firməri] *nf* infirmary.

infirmier, ère [ɛ̃firmje, ɛr] *nm, f* nurse.

infirmité [ɛ̃firmite] *nf* [handicap] disability ; [de vieillesse] infirmity.

inflammable [ɛ̃flamabl] *adj* inflammable, flammable.

inflammation [ɛ̃flamasjɔ̃] *nf* inflammation.

inflation [ɛ̃flasjɔ̃] *nf* ÉCON inflation ; *fig* increase.

inflationniste [ɛ̃flasjɔnist] *adj & nmf* inflationist.

infléchir [9] [ɛ̃fleʃir] *vt* *fig* [politique] to modify.

inflexible [ɛ̃flɛksibl] *adj* inflexible.

inflexion [ɛ̃flɛksjɔ̃] *nf* - **1.** [de tête] nod - **2.** [de voix] inflection.

infliger [17] [ɛ̃fliʒe] *vt* : **~ qqch à qqn** to inflict sthg on sb ; [amende] to impose sthg on sb.

influençable [ɛ̃flyɑ̃sabl] *adj* easily influenced.

influence [ɛ̃flyɑ̃s] *nf* influence ; [de médicament] effect.

influencer [16] [ɛ̃flyɑ̃se] *vt* to influence.

influer [3] [ɛ̃flye] *vi* : **~ sur qqch** to influence sthg, to have an effect on sthg.

Infographie® [ɛ̃fɔgrafi] *nf* computer graphics (U).

informaticien, enne [ɛ̃fɔrmatisjɛ̃, ɛn] *nm, f* computer scientist.

information [ɛ̃fɔrmasjɔ̃] *nf* - **1.** [renseignement] piece of information - **2.** [renseignements & INFORM] information (U) - **3.** [nouvelle] piece of news. ➤ **informations** *nfpl* MÉDIA news (sg).

informatique [ɛ̃fɔrmatik] <> *nf* - **1.** [technique] computers - **2.** [science] computer science. <> *adj* data-processing (avant n), computer (avant n).

informatiser [3] [ɛ̃fɔrmatize] *vt* to computerize.

informe [ɛ̃fɔrm] *adj* [masse, vêtement, silhouette] shapeless.

informel, elle [ɛ̃fɔrmɛl] *adj* informal.

informer [3] [ɛ̃fɔrme] *vt* to inform ; **~ qqn sur** ou **de qqch** to inform sb about sthg.

➤ **s'informer** *vp* to inform o.s. ; **s'~ de qqch** to ask about sthg ; **s'~ sur qqch** to find out about sthg.

infortune [ɛ̃fɔrtyn] *nf* misfortune.

infos [ɛ̃fo] (abr de **informations**) *nfpl fam* : **les ~** the news (sg).

infraction [ɛ̃fraksjɔ̃] *nf* offence ; **être en ~** to be in breach of the law.

infranchissable [ɛ̃frɑ̃ʃisabl] *adj* insurmountable.

infrarouge [ɛ̃fraruʒ] *nm & adj* infrared.

infrastructure [ɛ̃frastryktyr] *nf* infrastructure.

infroissable [ɛ̃frwasabl] *adj* crease-resistant.

infructueux, euse [ɛ̃fryktɥø, øz] *adj* fruitless.

infuser [3] [ɛ̃fyze] *vi* [tisane] to infuse ; [thé] to brew.

infusion [ɛ̃fyzjɔ̃] *nf* infusion.

ingénier [9] [ɛ̃ʒenje] ➤ **s'ingénier** *vp* : **s'~ à faire qqch** to try hard to do sthg.

ingénieur [ɛ̃ʒenjœr] *nm* engineer.

ingénieux, euse [ɛ̃ʒenjø, øz] *adj* ingenious.

ingéniosité [ɛ̃ʒenjozite] *nf* ingenuity.

ingénu, e [ɛ̃ʒeny] *adj* littéraire [candide] artless ; *hum & péj* [trop candide] naïve.

ingérable [ɛ̃ʒerabl] *adj* unmanageable.

ingérer [18] [ɛ̃ʒere] *vt* to ingest. ➤ **s'ingérer** *vp* : **s'~ dans** to interfere in.

ingrat, e [ɛ̃gra, at] <> *adj* - **1.** [personne] ungrateful - **2.** [métier] thankless, unrewarding - **3.** [sol] barren - **4.** [physique] unattractive. <> *nm, f* ungrateful wretch.

ingratitude [ɛ̃gratityd] *nf* ingratitude.

ingrédient [ɛ̃gredjɑ̃] *nm* ingredient.

inguérissable [ɛ̃gerisabl] *adj* incurable.

ingurgiter [3] [ɛ̃gyrʒite] *vt* - **1.** [avaler] to swallow - **2.** *fig* [connaissances] to absorb.

inhabitable [inabitabl] *adj* uninhabitable.

inhabité, e [inabite] *adj* uninhabited.

inhabituel, elle [inabitɥɛl] *adj* unusual.

inhalateur, trice [inalatœr, tris] *adj* : **appareil ~** inhaler. ➤ **inhalateur** *nm* inhaler.

inhalation [inalasjɔ̃] *nf* inhalation.

inhérent, e [inerɑ̃, ɑ̃t] *adj* : **~ à** inherent in.

inhibition [inibisjɔ̃] *nf* inhibition.

inhospitalier, ère [inɔspitalje, ɛr] *adj* inhospitable.

inhumain, e [inymɛ̃, ɛn] *adj* inhuman.

inhumation [inymasjɔ̃] *nf* burial.

inhumer [3] [inyme] *vt* to bury.

inimaginable [inimaʒinabl] *adj* incredible, unimaginable.

inimitable [inimitabl] *adj* inimitable.

ininflammable [inɛ̃flamabl] *adj* nonflammable.

inintelligible [inɛ̃teliʒibl] *adj* unintelligible.

inintéressant, e [inɛ̃teresɑ̃, ɑ̃t] *adj* uninteresting.

ininterrompu, e [inɛ̃terɔ̃py] *adj* [file, vacarme] uninterrupted ; [ligne, suite] unbroken ; [travail, effort] continuous.

inique [inik] *adj* iniquitous.

initial, e, aux [inisjal, o] *adj* [lettre] initial. ➡ **initiale** *nf* initial.

initiateur, trice [inisjatœr, tris] *nm, f* - 1. [maître] initiator - 2. [précurseur] innovator.

initiation [inisjasjɔ̃] *nf* : ~ (à) [discipline] introduction (to) ; [rituel] initiation (into).

initiative [inisjativ] *nf* initiative ; **prendre l'~ de qqch/de faire qqch** to take the initiative for sthg/in doing sthg.

initié, e [inisje] ⬦ *adj* initiated. ⬦ *nm, f* initiate.

initier [9] [inisje] *vt* : ~ **qqn à** to initiate sb into.

injecté, e [ɛ̃ʒɛkte] *adj* : **yeux ~s de sang** bloodshot eyes.

injecter [4] [ɛ̃ʒɛkte] *vt* to inject.

injection [ɛ̃ʒɛksjɔ̃] *nf* injection.

injoignable [ɛ̃ʒwaɲabl] *adj* : **j'ai essayé de lui téléphoner mais il est ~** I tried to phone him but I couldn't get through to him OU reach him OU get hold of him.

injonction [ɛ̃ʒɔ̃ksjɔ̃] *nf* injunction.

injure [ɛ̃ʒyr] *nf* insult.

injurier [9] [ɛ̃ʒyrje] *vt* to insult.

injurieux, euse [ɛ̃ʒyrjø, øz] *adj* abusive, insulting.

injuste [ɛ̃ʒyst] *adj* unjust, unfair.

injustice [ɛ̃ʒystis] *nf* injustice.

inlassable [ɛ̃lasabl] *adj* tireless.

inlassablement [ɛ̃lasabləmɑ̃] *adv* tirelessly.

inné, e [ine] *adj* innate.

innocence [inɔsɑ̃s] *nf* innocence.

innocent, e [inɔsɑ̃, ɑ̃t] ⬦ *adj* innocent. ⬦ *nm, f* - 1. JUR innocent person - 2. [inoffensif, candide] innocent - 3. *vieilli* [idiot] simpleton.

innocenter [3] [inɔsɑ̃te] *vt* - 1. JUR to clear - 2. *fig* [excuser] to justify.

innombrable [inɔ̃brabl] *adj* innumerable ; [foule] vast.

innover [3] [inɔve] *vi* to innovate.

inobservation [inɔpsɛrvasjɔ̃] *nf* inobservance.

inoccupé, e [inɔkype] *adj* [lieu] empty, unoccupied.

inoculer [3] [inɔkyle] *vt* MÉD : ~ **qqch à qqn** [volontairement] to inoculate sb with sthg ; [accidentellement] to infect sb with sthg.

inodore [inɔdɔr] *adj* odourless *Br*, odorless *Am*.

inoffensif, ive [inɔfɑ̃sif, iv] *adj* harmless.

inondation [inɔ̃dasjɔ̃] *nf* - 1. [action] flooding - 2. [résultat] flood.

inonder [3] [inɔ̃de] *vt* to flood ; ~ **de** *fig* to flood with.

inopérable [inɔperabl] *adj* inoperable.

inopérant, e [inɔperɑ̃, ɑ̃t] *adj* ineffective.

inopiné, e [inɔpine] *adj* unexpected.

inopportun, e [inɔpɔrtœ̃, yn] *adj* inopportune.

inoubliable [inublijabl] *adj* unforgettable.

inouï, e [inwi] *adj* incredible, extraordinary.

Inox® [inɔks] *nm inv & adj inv* stainless steel.

inoxydable [inɔksidabl] *adj* stainless ; [casserole] stainless steel *(avant n)*.

inqualifiable [ɛ̃kalifjabl] *adj* unspeakable.

inquiet, ète [ɛ̃kjɛ, ɛt] *adj* - 1. [gén] anxious - 2. [tourmenté] feverish

inquiéter [18] [ɛ̃kjete] *vt* - 1. [donner du souci à] to worry - 2. [déranger] to disturb. ➡ **s'inquiéter** *vp* - 1. [s'alarmer] to be worried - 2. [se préoccuper] : **s'~ de** [s'enquérir de] to enquire about ; [se soucier de] to worry about.

inquiétude [ɛ̃kjetyd] *nf* anxiety, worry.

inquisiteur, trice [ɛ̃kizitœr, tris] *adj* prying.

insaisissable [ɛ̃sezisabl] *adj* - 1. [personne] elusive - 2. *fig* [nuance] imperceptible.

insalubre [ɛ̃salybr] *adj* unhealthy.

insatiable [ɛ̃sasjabl] *adj* insatiable.

insatisfait, e [ɛ̃satisfɛ, ɛt] ⬦ *adj* [personne] dissatisfied. ⬦ *nm, f* malcontent.

inscription [ɛ̃skripsjɔ̃] *nf* - 1. [action, écrit] inscription - 2. [enregistrement] enrolment *Br*, enrollment *Am*, registration.

inscrire [99] [ɛ̃skrir] *vt* - 1. [écrire] to write down ; [graver] to inscribe - 2. [personne] : ~ **qqn à qqch** to enrol *Br* OU enroll *Am* sb for sthg, to register sb for sthg ; ~ **qqn sur qqch** to put sb's name down on sthg - 3. SPORT

[but] to score. **s'inscrire** *vp* [personne] : **s'~ à qqch** to enrol *Br* ou enroll *Am* for sthg, to register for sthg ; **s'~ sur qqch** to put one's name down on sthg.

inscrit, e [ɛ̃skri, it] <> *pp* ▷ inscrire. <> *adj* [sur liste] registered ; **être ~ sur une liste** to have one's name on a list. <> *nm, f* registered person.

insecte [ɛ̃sɛkt] *nm* insect.

insecticide [ɛ̃sɛktisid] *nm & adj* insecticide.

insécurité [ɛ̃sekyrite] *nf* insecurity.

insémination [ɛ̃seminasjɔ̃] *nf* insemination ; **~ artificielle** artificial insemination.

insensé, e [ɛ̃sɑ̃se] *adj* - 1. [déraisonnable] insane - 2. [incroyable, excentrique] extraordinary.

insensibiliser [3] [ɛ̃sɑ̃sibilize] *vt* to anaesthetize *Br*, to anesthetize *Am* ; **~ qqn (à)** *fig* to make sb insensitive (to).

insensible [ɛ̃sɑ̃sibl] *adj* - 1. [gén] : **~ (à)** insensitive (to) - 2. [imperceptible] imperceptible.

insensiblement [ɛ̃sɑ̃sibləmɑ̃] *adv* imperceptibly.

inséparable [ɛ̃separabl] *adj* : **~ (de)** inseparable (from).

insérer [18] [ɛ̃sere] *vt* to insert ; **~ une annonce dans un journal** to put an advertisement in a newspaper. **s'insérer** *vp* [s'intégrer] : **s'~ dans** to fit into.

insidieux, euse [ɛ̃sidjø, øz] *adj* insidious.

insigne [ɛ̃siɲ] <> *nm* badge. <> *adj* - 1. *littéraire* [honneur] distinguished - 2. *hum* [maladresse] remarkable.

insignifiant, e [ɛ̃siɲifjɑ̃, ɑ̃t] *adj* insignificant.

insinuation [ɛ̃sinɥasjɔ̃] *nf* insinuation, innuendo.

insinuer [7] [ɛ̃sinɥe] *vt* to insinuate, to imply. **s'insinuer** *vp* : **s'~ dans** [eau, humidité, odeur] to seep into ; *fig* [personne] to insinuate o.s. into.

insipide [ɛ̃sipid] *adj* [aliment] insipid, tasteless ; *fig* insipid.

insistance [ɛ̃sistɑ̃s] *nf* insistence.

insister [3] [ɛ̃siste] *vi* to insist ; **~ sur** to insist on ; **~ pour faire qqch** to insist on doing sthg.

insolation [ɛ̃sɔlasjɔ̃] *nf* [malaise] sunstroke *(U)*.

insolence [ɛ̃sɔlɑ̃s] *nf* insolence *(U)*.

insolent, e [ɛ̃sɔlɑ̃, ɑ̃t] <> *adj* - 1. [personne, acte] insolent - 2. [joie, succès] unashamed, blatant. <> *nm, f* insolent person.

insolite [ɛ̃sɔlit] *adj* unusual.

insoluble [ɛ̃sɔlybl] *adj* insoluble *Br*, insolvable *Am*.

insolvable [ɛ̃sɔlvabl] *adj* insolvent.

insomnie [ɛ̃sɔmni] *nf* insomnia *(U)*.

insondable [ɛ̃sɔ̃dabl] *adj* [gouffre, mystère] unfathomable ; [bêtise] abysmal.

insonoriser [3] [ɛ̃sɔnɔrize] *vt* to soundproof.

insouciance [ɛ̃susjɑ̃s] *nf* [légèreté] carefree attitude.

insouciant, e [ɛ̃susjɑ̃, ɑ̃t] *adj* [sans-souci] carefree.

insoumis, e [ɛ̃sumi, iz] *adj* - 1. [caractère] rebellious - 2. [peuple] unsubjugated - 3. [soldat] deserting.

insoumission [ɛ̃sumisjɔ̃] *nf* - 1. [caractère rebelle] rebelliousness - 2. MIL desertion.

insoupçonné, e [ɛ̃supsɔne] *adj* unsuspected.

insoutenable [ɛ̃sutnabl] *adj* - 1. [rythme] unsustainable - 2. [scène, violence] unbearable - 3. [théorie] untenable.

inspecter [4] [ɛ̃spɛkte] *vt* to inspect.

inspecteur, trice [ɛ̃spɛktœr, tris] *nm, f* inspector.

inspection [ɛ̃spɛksjɔ̃] *nf* - 1. [contrôle] inspection - 2. [fonction] inspectorate.

inspiration [ɛ̃spirasjɔ̃] *nf* - 1. [gén] inspiration ; [idée] bright idea, brainwave ; **avoir de l'~** to be inspired - 2. [d'air] breathing in.

inspiré, e [ɛ̃spire] *adj* inspired.

inspirer [3] [ɛ̃spire] *vt* - 1. [gén] to inspire ; **~ qqch à qqn** to inspire sb with sthg - 2. [air] to breathe in, to inhale. **s'inspirer** *vp* [prendre modèle sur] : **s'~ de qqn/qqch** to be inspired by sb/sthg.

instable [ɛ̃stabl] *adj* - 1. [gén] unstable - 2. [vie, temps] unsettled.

installation [ɛ̃stalasjɔ̃] *nf* - 1. [de gaz, eau, électricité] installation - 2. [de personne - comme médecin, artisan] setting up ; [- dans appartement] settling in - 3. *(gén pl)* [équipement] **installations** *(pl)*, fittings *(pl)* ; [usine] plant *(U)* ; [de loisirs] facilities *(pl)* ; **~ électrique** wiring.

installer [3] [ɛ̃stale] *vt* - 1. [gaz, eau, électricité] to install *Br*, to instal *Am*, to put in - 2. [appartement] to fit out - 3. [rideaux, étagères] to put up ; [meubles] to put in - 4. [personne] : **~ qqn** to get sb settled, to install *Br* ou instal *Am* sb. **s'installer** *vp* - 1. [comme médecin, artisan etc] to set (o.s.) up - 2. [emménager] to settle in ; **s'~ chez qqn** to move in with sb - 3. [dans fauteuil] to settle down - **4.** *fig* [maladie, routine] to set in.

instamment [ɛ̃stamɑ̃] *adv* insistently.

instance [ɛ̃stɑ̃s] *nf* - **1.** [autorité] authority - **2.** JUR proceedings *(pl)* - **3.** [insistance] entreaties *(pl)*. ◆ **en instance** *loc adj* pending. ◆ **en instance de** *loc adv* on the point of.

instant [ɛ̃stɑ̃] *nm* instant ; **à l'~** [il y a peu de temps] a moment ago ; [immédiatement] this minute ; **à tout ~** [en permanence] at all times ; [d'un moment à l'autre] at any moment ; **pour l'~** for the moment.

instantané, e [ɛ̃stɑ̃tane] *adj* - **1.** [immédiat] instantaneous - **2.** [soluble] instant. ◆ **instantané** *nm* snapshot.

instar [ɛ̃star] ◆ **à l'instar de** *loc prép* following the example of.

instaurer [3] [ɛ̃stɔre] *vt* [instituer] to establish ; *fig* [peur, confiance] to instil *Br*, to instill *Am*.

instigateur, trice [ɛ̃stigatœr, tris] *nm, f* instigator.

instigation [ɛ̃stigasjɔ̃] *nf* instigation. ◆ **à l'instigation de, sur l'instigation de** *loc prép* at the instigation of.

instinct [ɛ̃stɛ̃] *nm* instinct.

instinctif, ive [ɛ̃stɛ̃ktif, iv] ◇ *adj* instinctive. ◇ *nm, f* instinctive person.

instituer [7] [ɛ̃stitɥe] *vt* - **1.** [pratique] to institute - **2.** JUR [personne] to appoint.

institut [ɛ̃stity] *nm* - **1.** [gén] institute ; **l'~ Pasteur** *important medical research centre* - **2.** [de soins] : **~ de beauté** beauty salon.

instituteur, trice [ɛ̃stitytœr, tris] *nm, f* primary school teacher *Br*, grade school teacher *Am*.

institution [ɛ̃stitysjɔ̃] *nf* - **1.** [gén] institution - **2.** [école privée] private school. ◆ **institutions** *nfpl* POLIT institutions.

instructif, ive [ɛ̃stryktif, iv] *adj* instructive, educational.

instruction [ɛ̃stryksjɔ̃] *nf* - **1.** [enseignement, savoir] education - **2.** [formation] training - **3.** [directive] order - **4.** JUR (pretrial) investigation. ◆ **instructions** *nfpl* instructions.

instruit, e [ɛ̃strɥi, it] *adj* educated.

instrument [ɛ̃strymɑ̃] *nm* instrument ; **~ de musique** musical instrument.

insu [ɛ̃sy] ◆ **à l'insu de** *loc prép* : **à l'~ de qqn** without sb knowing ; **ils ont tout organisé à mon ~** they organized it all without my knowing.

insubmersible [ɛ̃sybmɛrsibl] *adj* unsinkable.

insubordination [ɛ̃sybɔrdinasjɔ̃] *nf* insubordination.

insuccès [ɛ̃syksɛ] *nm* failure.

insuffisance [ɛ̃syfizɑ̃s] *nf* - **1.** [manque] insufficiency - **2.** MÉD deficiency. ◆ **insuffisances** *nfpl* [faiblesses] shortcomings.

insuffisant, e [ɛ̃syfizɑ̃, ɑ̃t] *adj* - **1.** [en quantité] insufficient - **2.** [en qualité] inadequate, unsatisfactory.

insuffler [3] [ɛ̃syfle] *vt* - **1.** [air] to blow - **2.** *fig* [sentiment] : **~ qqch à qqn** to inspire sb with sthg.

insulaire [ɛ̃sylɛr] ◇ *nmf* islander. ◇ *adj* GÉOGR island *(avant n)*.

insuline [ɛ̃sylin] *nf* insulin.

insulte [ɛ̃sylt] *nf* insult.

insulter [3] [ɛ̃sylte] *vt* to insult.

insupportable [ɛ̃sypɔrtabl] *adj* unbearable.

insurgé, e [ɛ̃syrʒe] *adj & nm, f* insurgent, rebel.

insurger [17] [ɛ̃syrʒe] ◆ **s'insurger** *vp* to rebel, to revolt ; **s'~ contre qqch** to protest against sthg.

insurmontable [ɛ̃syrmɔ̃tabl] *adj* [difficulté] insurmountable ; [dégoût] uncontrollable.

insurrection [ɛ̃syrɛksjɔ̃] *nf* insurrection.

intact, e [ɛ̃takt] *adj* intact.

intangible [ɛ̃tɑ̃ʒibl] *adj* - **1.** *littéraire* [impalpable] intangible - **2.** [sacré] inviolable.

intarissable [ɛ̃tarisabl] *adj* inexhaustible ; **il est ~** he could go on talking for ever.

intégral, e, aux [ɛ̃tegral, o] *adj* - **1.** [paiement] in full ; [texte] unabridged, complete - **2.** MATHS : **calcul ~** integral calculus.

intégralement [ɛ̃tegralmɑ̃] *adv* fully, in full.

intégrant, e [ɛ̃tegrɑ̃, ɑ̃t] ▷ **parti**.

intègre [ɛ̃tɛgr] *adj* honest, of integrity.

intégré, e [ɛ̃tegre] *adj* [élément] built-in.

intégrer [18] [ɛ̃tegre] *vt* [assimiler] : **~ (à ou dans)** to integrate (into). ◆ **s'intégrer** *vp* - **1.** [s'incorporer] : **s'~ dans ou à** to fit into - **2.** [s'adapter] to integrate.

intégrisme [ɛ̃tegrism] *nm* fundamentalism.

intégrité [ɛ̃tegrite] *nf* - **1.** [totalité] entirety - **2.** [honnêteté] integrity.

intellectuel, elle [ɛ̃telɛktɥɛl] *adj & nm, f* intellectual.

intelligence [ɛ̃teliʒɑ̃s] *nf* - **1.** [facultés mentales] intelligence ; **~ artificielle** artificial intelligence - **2.** [compréhension, complicité] understanding.

intelligent, e [ɛ̃teliʒɑ̃, ɑ̃t] *adj* intelligent.

intelligible [ɛ̃teliʒibl] *adj* - **1.** [voix] clear - **2.** [concept, texte] intelligible.

intello [ɛ̃telo] *adj inv* & *nmf péj* highbrow.

intempéries [ɛ̃tɑ̃peri] *nfpl* bad weather *(U)*.

intempestif, ive [ɛ̃tɑ̃pɛstif, iv] *adj* untimely.

intenable [ɛ̃tənabl] *adj* - **1.** [chaleur, personne] unbearable - **2.** [position] untenable, indefensible.

intendance [ɛ̃tɑ̃dɑ̃s] *nf* - **1.** MIL commissariat ; SCOL & UNIV bursar's office - **2.** *fig* [questions matérielles] housekeeping.

intendant, e [ɛ̃tɑ̃dɑ̃, ɑ̃t] *nm, f* - **1.** SCOL & UNIV bursar - **2.** [de manoir] steward. ◆ **intendant** *nm* MIL quartermaster.

intense [ɛ̃tɑ̃s] *adj* [gén] intense.

intensif, ive [ɛ̃tɑ̃sif, iv] *adj* intensive.

intensité [ɛ̃tɑ̃site] *nf* intensity.

intenter [3] [ɛ̃tɑ̃te] *vt* JUR : **~ qqch contre** ou **à qqn** to bring sthg against sb.

intention [ɛ̃tɑ̃sjɔ̃] *nf* intention ; **avoir l'~ de faire qqch** to intend to do sthg. ◆ **à l'intention de** *loc prép* for.

intentionné, e [ɛ̃tɑ̃sjɔne] *adj* : **bien ~** well-meaning ; **mal ~** ill-disposed.

intentionnel, elle [ɛ̃tɑ̃sjɔnɛl] *adj* intentional.

interactif, ive [ɛ̃teraktif, iv] *adj* interactive.

intercalaire [ɛ̃terkalɛr] ◇ *nm* insert. ◇ *adj* : **feuillet ~** insert.

intercaler [3] [ɛ̃terkale] *vt* : **~ qqch dans qqch** [feuillet, citation] to insert sthg in sthg ; [dans le temps] to fit sthg into sthg.

intercéder [18] [ɛ̃tersede] *vi* : **~ pour** ou **en faveur de qqn auprès de qqn** to intercede with sb on behalf of sb.

intercepter [4] [ɛ̃tersɛpte] *vt* - **1.** [lettre, ballon] to intercept - **2.** [chaleur] to block.

interchangeable [ɛ̃terʃɑ̃ʒabl] *adj* interchangeable.

interclasse [ɛ̃terklas] *nm* break.

interdiction [ɛ̃terdiksjɔ̃] *nf* - **1.** [défense] : **'~ de stationner'** 'strictly no parking' - **2.** [prohibition, suspension] : **~ (de)** ban (on), banning (of) ; **~ de séjour** order banning released prisoner from living in certain areas.

interdire [103] [ɛ̃terdir] *vt* - **1.** [prohiber] : **~ qqch à qqn** to forbid sb sthg ; **~ à qqn de faire qqch** to forbid sb to do sthg - **2.** [empêcher] to prevent ; **~ à qqn de faire qqch** to prevent sb from doing sthg - **3.** [bloquer] to block.

interdit, e [ɛ̃terdi, it] ◇ *pp* ▷ **interdire**. ◇ *adj* - **1.** [défendu] forbidden ; **'film ~ aux moins de 18 ans'** ≃ (18) ; **il est ~ de**

fumer you're not allowed to smoke - **2.** [ébahi] : **rester ~** to be stunned - **3.** [privé] : **être ~ de chéquier** to have had one's chequebook *Br* ou checkbook *Am* facilities withdrawn ; **~ de séjour** banned from entering the country.

intéressant, e [ɛ̃teresɑ̃, ɑ̃t] *adj* - **1.** [captivant] interesting - **2.** [avantageux] advantageous, good.

intéressé, e [ɛ̃terese] *adj* [concerné] concerned, involved ; *péj* [motivé] self-interested.

intéresser [4] [ɛ̃terese] *vt* - **1.** [captiver] to interest ; **~ qqn à qqch** to interest sb in sthg - **2.** COMM [faire participer] : **~ les employés (aux bénéfices)** to give one's employees a share in the profits ; **~ qqn dans son commerce** to give sb a financial interest in one's business - **3.** [concerner] to concern. ◆ **s'intéresser** *vp* : **s'~ à qqn/qqch** to take an interest in sb/sthg, to be interested in sb/sthg.

intérêt [ɛ̃terɛ] *nm* - **1.** [gén] interest ; **~ pour** interest in ; **avoir ~ à faire qqch** to be well advised to do sthg - **2.** [importance] significance. ◆ **intérêts** *nmpl* - **1.** FIN interest *(sg)* - **2.** COMM : **avoir des ~s dans** to have a stake in.

interface [ɛ̃terfas] *nf* INFORM interface ; **~ graphique** graphic interface.

interférer [18] [ɛ̃terfere] *vi* - **1.** PHYS to interfere - **2.** *fig* [s'immiscer] : **~ dans qqch** to interfere in sthg.

intérieur, e [ɛ̃terjœr] *adj* - **1.** [gén] inner - **2.** [de pays] domestic. ◆ **intérieur** *nm* - **1.** [gén] inside ; **de l'~** from the inside ; **à l'~ (de qqch)** inside (sthg) - **2.** [de pays] interior.

intérim [ɛ̃terim] *nm* - **1.** [période] interim period ; **par ~** acting - **2.** [travail temporaire] temporary ou casual work ; [dans un bureau] temping.

intérimaire [ɛ̃terimɛr] ◇ *adj* - **1.** [ministre, directeur] acting *(avant n)* - **2.** [employé, fonctions] temporary. ◇ *nmf* [employé] temp.

intérioriser [3] [ɛ̃terjɔrize] *vt* to internalize.

interjection [ɛ̃terʒɛksjɔ̃] *nf* LING interjection.

interligne [ɛ̃terliɲ] *nm* (line) spacing.

interlocuteur, trice [ɛ̃terlɔkytœr, tris] *nm, f* - **1.** [dans conversation] speaker ; **mon ~** the person to whom I am/was speaking - **2.** [dans négociation] negotiator.

interloquer [3] [ɛ̃terlɔke] *vt* to disconcert.

interlude [ɛ̃terlyd] *nm* interlude.

intermède [ɛ̃tɛrmɛd] *nm* interlude.

intermédiaire [ɛ̃tɛrmedjɛr] ◇ *nm* intermediary, go-between ; **par l'~ de qqn/qqch** through sb/sthg. ◇ *adj* intermediate.

interminable [ɛ̃tɛrminabl] *adj* never-ending, interminable.

intermittence [ɛ̃tɛrmitɑ̃s] *nf* [discontinuité] : **par ~** intermittently, off and on.

intermittent, e [ɛ̃tɛrmitɑ̃, ɑ̃t] *adj* intermittent.

internat [ɛ̃tɛrna] *nm* [SCOL - établissement] boarding school ; [- système] boarding.

international, e, aux [ɛ̃tɛrnasjɔnal, o] *adj* international.

internaute [ɛ̃tɛrnot] *nmf* INFORM (net) surfer, cybersurfer, cybernaut.

interne [ɛ̃tɛrn] ◇ *nmf* **- 1.** [élève] boarder **- 2.** MÉD & UNIV houseman *Br*, intern *Am*. ◇ *adj* **- 1.** ANAT internal ; [oreille] inner **- 2.** [du pays] domestic.

interner [3] [ɛ̃tɛrne] *vt* **- 1.** MÉD to commit *(to psychiatric hospital)* **- 2.** POLIT to intern.

Internet, internet [ɛ̃tɛrnɛt] *nm* : **(l')~** (the) internet, (the) Internet.

interpeller [26] [ɛ̃tɛrpəle] *vt* **- 1.** [apostropher] to call ou shout out to **- 2.** [interroger] to take in for questioning.

Interphone® [ɛ̃tɛrfɔn] *nm* intercom ; [d'un immeuble] entry phone.

interposer [3] [ɛ̃tɛrpoze] *vt* to interpose. ◆ **s'interposer** *vp* : **s'~ entre qqn et qqn** to intervene ou come between sb and sb.

interprète [ɛ̃tɛrprɛt] *nmf* **- 1.** [gén] interpreter **- 2.** CIN, MUS & THÉÂTRE performer.

interpréter [18] [ɛ̃tɛrprete] *vt* to interpret.

interrogateur, trice [ɛ̃tɛrɔgatœr, tris] *adj* inquiring *(avant n)*.

interrogatif, ive [ɛ̃tɛrɔgatif, iv] *adj* GRAM interrogative.

interrogation [ɛ̃tɛrɔgasjɔ̃] *nf* **- 1.** [de prisonnier] interrogation ; [de témoin] questioning **- 2.** [question] question **- 3.** SCOL test.

interrogatoire [ɛ̃tɛrɔgatwar] *nm* **- 1.** [de police, juge] questioning **- 2.** [procès-verbal] statement.

interrogeable [ɛ̃tɛrɔʒabl] *adj* : **répondeur ~ à distance** answerphone with remote playback facility.

interroger [17] [ɛ̃tɛrɔʒe] *vt* **- 1.** [questionner] to question ; [accusé, base de données] to interrogate ; **~ qqn (sur qqch)** to question sb (about sthg) **- 2.** [faits, conscience] to examine. ◆ **s'interroger** *vp* : **s'~ sur** to wonder about.

interrompre [78] [ɛ̃tɛrɔ̃pr] *vt* to interrupt. ◆ **s'interrompre** *vp* to stop.

interrompu, e [ɛ̃tɛrɔ̃py] *pp* ▷ interrompre.

interrupteur [ɛ̃tɛryptœr] *nm* switch.

interruption [ɛ̃tɛrypsjɔ̃] *nf* **- 1.** [arrêt] break **- 2.** [action] interruption.

intersection [ɛ̃tɛrsɛksjɔ̃] *nf* intersection.

interstice [ɛ̃tɛrstis] *nm* chink, crack.

interurbain, e [ɛ̃tɛryrbɛ̃, ɛn] *adj* long-distance. ◆ **interurbain** *nm* : **l'~** the long-distance telephone service.

intervalle [ɛ̃tɛrval] *nm* **- 1.** [spatial] space, gap **- 2.** [temporel] interval, period (of time) ; **à 6 jours d'~** after 6 days **- 3.** MUS interval.

intervenant, e [ɛ̃tɛrvənɑ̃, ɑ̃t] *nm, f* [orateur] speaker.

intervenir [40] [ɛ̃tɛrvənir] *vi* **- 1.** [personne] to intervene ; **~ auprès de qqn** to intervene with sb ; **~ dans qqch** to intervene in sthg ; **faire ~ qqn** to bring ou call in sb **- 2.** [événement] to take place.

intervention [ɛ̃tɛrvɑ̃sjɔ̃] *nf* **- 1.** [gén] intervention **- 2.** MÉD operation ; **subir une ~ chirurgicale** to have an operation, to have surgery **- 3.** [discours] speech.

intervenu, e [ɛ̃tɛrvəny] *pp* ▷ intervenir.

intervertir [32] [ɛ̃tɛrvɛrtir] *vt* to reverse, to invert.

interview [ɛ̃tɛrvju] *nf* interview.

interviewer [3] [ɛ̃tɛrvjuve] *vt* to interview.

intestin [ɛ̃tɛstɛ̃] *nm* intestine.

intestinal, e, aux [ɛ̃tɛstinal, o] *adj* intestinal.

intime [ɛ̃tim] ◇ *nmf* close friend. ◇ *adj* [gén] intimate ; [vie, journal] private.

intimider [3] [ɛ̃timide] *vt* to intimidate.

intimité [ɛ̃timite] *nf* **- 1.** [secret] depths *(pl)* **- 2.** [familiarité, confort] intimacy **- 3.** [vie privée] privacy.

intitulé [ɛ̃tityle] *nm* [titre] title ; [de paragraphe] heading.

intituler [3] [ɛ̃tityle] *vt* to call, to entitle. ◆ **s'intituler** *vp* [ouvrage] to be called ou entitled.

intolérable [ɛ̃tɔlerabl] *adj* intolerable.

intolérance [ɛ̃tɔlerɑ̃s] *nf* [religieuse, politique] intolerance.

intolérant, e [ɛ̃tɔlerɑ̃, ɑ̃t] *adj* intolerant.

intonation [ɛ̃tɔnasjɔ̃] *nf* intonation.

intouchable [ɛ̃tuʃabl] *nmf* & *adj* untouchable.

intoxication [ɛ̃tɔksikasjɔ̃] *nf* **- 1.** [empoisonnement] poisoning - 2. *fig* [propagande] brainwashing.

intoxiquer [3] [ɛtɔksike] *vt* : ~ qqn par [empoisonner] to poison sb with ; *fig* to indoctrinate sb with.

intraduisible [ɛtradɥizibl] *adj* [texte] untranslatable.

intraitable [ɛtrɛtabl] *adj* : ~ (sur) inflexible (about).

intransigeant, e [ɛtrɑ̃ziʒɑ̃, ɑ̃t] *adj* intransigent.

intransitif, ive [ɛtrɑ̃zitif, iv] *adj* intransitive.

intransportable [ɛtrɑ̃spɔrtabl] *adj* : il est ~ he/it cannot be moved.

intraveineux, euse [ɛtravɛnø, øz] *adj* intravenous.

intrépide [ɛtrepid] *adj* bold, intrepid.

intrigue [ɛtrig] *nf* - 1. [manœuvre] intrigue - 2. CIN, LITTÉRATURE & THÉÂTRE plot.

intriguer [3] [ɛtrige] ◇ *vt* to intrigue. ◇ *vi* to scheme, to intrigue.

introduction [ɛtrɔdyksjɔ̃] *nf* - 1. [gén] : ~ (à) introduction (to) - 2. [insertion] insertion.

introduire [98] [ɛtrɔdɥir] *vt* - 1. [gén] to introduce - 2. [faire entrer] to show in - 3. [insérer] to insert. ◆ **s'introduire** *vp* - 1. [pénétrer] to enter ; s'~ dans une maison [cambrioleur] to get into ou enter a house - 2. [s'implanter] to be introduced.

introduit, e [ɛtrɔdɥi, it] *pp* ⮑ introduire.

introspection [ɛtrɔspɛksjɔ̃] *nf* introspection.

introuvable [ɛtruvabl] *adj* nowhere ou no-place *Am* to be found.

introverti, e [ɛtrɔvɛrti] ◇ *adj* introverted. ◇ *nm, f* introvert.

intrus, e [ɛtry, yz] *nm, f* intruder.

intrusion [ɛtryzjɔ̃] *nf* - 1. [gén & GÉOL] intrusion - 2. [ingérence] interference.

intuitif, ive [ɛtɥitif, iv] *adj* intuitive.

intuition [ɛtɥisjɔ̃] *nf* intuition.

inusable [inyzabl] *adj* hardwearing.

inusité, e [inyzite] *adj* unusual, uncommon.

inutile [inytil] *adj* [objet, personne] useless ; [effort, démarche] pointless.

inutilisable [inytilizabl] *adj* unusable.

inutilité [inytilite] *nf* [de personne, d'objet] uselessness ; [de démarche, d'effort] pointlessness.

invaincu, e [ɛ̃vɛ̃ky] *adj* SPORT unbeaten.

invalide [ɛ̃valid] ◇ *nmf* disabled person ; ~ du travail industrially disabled person. ◇ *adj* disabled.

invalidité [ɛ̃validite] *nf* - 1. JUR invalidity - 2. MÉD disability.

invariable [ɛ̃varjabl] *adj* - 1. [immuable] unchanging - 2. GRAM invariable.

invasion [ɛ̃vazjɔ̃] *nf* invasion.

invendable [ɛ̃vɑ̃dabl] *adj* unsaleable, unsellable.

invendu, e [ɛ̃vɑ̃dy] *adj* unsold. ◆ **invendu** *(gén pl) nm* remainder.

inventaire [ɛ̃vɑ̃tɛr] *nm* - 1. [gén] inventory - 2. [COMM - activité] stocktaking *Br*, inventory *Am* ; [- liste] list.

inventer [3] [ɛ̃vɑ̃te] *vt* to invent.

inventeur [ɛ̃vɑ̃tœr] *nm* [de machine] inventor.

invention [ɛ̃vɑ̃sjɔ̃] *nf* - 1. [découverte, mensonge] invention - 2. [imagination] inventiveness.

inventorier [9] [ɛ̃vɑ̃tɔrje] *vt* to make an inventory of.

Inverse [ɛ̃vɛrs] ◇ *nm* opposite, reverse. ◇ *adj* 1. [sens] opposite ; [ordre] reverse ; en sens ~ (de) in the opposite direction (to) - 2. [rapport] inverse.

Inversement [ɛ̃vɛrsəmɑ̃] *adv* - 1. MATHS inversely - 2. [au contraire] on the other hand - 3. [vice versa] vice versa.

inverser [3] [ɛ̃vɛrse] *vt* to reverse.

invertébré, e [ɛ̃vɛrtebre] *adj* invertebrate. ◆ **invertébré** *nm* invertebrate.

investigation [ɛ̃vɛstigasjɔ̃] *nf* investigation.

investir [32] [ɛ̃vɛstir] *vt* to invest.

investissement [ɛ̃vɛstismɑ̃] *nm* investment.

investisseur, euse [ɛ̃vɛstisœr, øz] *nm, f* investor.

investiture [ɛ̃vɛstityr] *nf* investiture.

invétéré, e [ɛ̃vetere] *adj péj* inveterate.

invincible [ɛ̃vɛ̃sibl] *adj* [gén] invincible ; [difficulté] insurmountable ; [charme] irresistible.

inviolable [ɛ̃vjɔlabl] *adj* - 1. JUR inviolable - 2. [coffre] impregnable.

invisible [ɛ̃vizibl] *adj* invisible.

invitation [ɛ̃vitasjɔ̃] *nf* : ~ (à) invitation (to) ; sur ~ by invitation.

invité, e [ɛ̃vite] ◇ *adj* [hôte] invited ; [professeur, conférencier] guest *(avant n)*. ◇ *nm, f* guest.

inviter [3] [ɛ̃vite] *vt* to invite ; ~ qqn à faire qqch to invite sb to do sthg ; *fig* [suj : chose] to be an invitation to sb to do sthg ; je vous invite! it's my treat!

in vitro [invitro] ⊏▷ fécondation.

invivable [ɛ̃vivabl] *adj* unbearable.

involontaire [ɛ̃vɔlɔ̃tɛr] *adj* [acte] involuntary.

invoquer [3] [ɛ̃vɔke] *vt* - **1.** [alléguer] to put forward - **2.** [citer, appeler à l'aide] to invoke ; [paix] to call for.

invraisemblable [ɛ̃vrɛsɑ̃blabl] *adj* - **1.** [incroyable] unlikely, improbable - **2.** [extravagant] incredible.

invulnérable [ɛ̃vylnerabl] *adj* invulnerable.

iode [jɔd] *nm* iodine.

ion [jɔ̃] *nm* ion.

IRA [ira] (*abr de* **Irish Republican Army**) *nf* IRA.

irai, iras *etc* ⊏▷ aller.

Irak, Iraq [irak] *nm* : **l'~** Iraq.

irakien, enne, iraquien, enne [irakjɛ̃, ɛn] *adj* Iraqi. ➼ **Irakien, enne, Iraquien, enne** *nm, f* Iraqi.

Iran [irɑ̃] *nm* : **l'~** Iran.

iranien, enne [iranjɛ̃, ɛn] *adj* Iranian. ➼ **iranien** *nm* [langue] Iranian. ➼ **Iranien, enne** *nm, f* Iranian.

Iraq = Irak.

iraquien = irakien.

irascible [irasibl] *adj* irascible.

iris [iris] *nm* ANAT & BOT iris.

irisé, e [irize] *adj* iridescent.

irlandais, e [irlɑ̃dɛ, ɛz] *adj* Irish. ➼ **irlandais** *nm* [langue] Irish. ➼ **Irlandais, e** *nm, f* Irishman (*f* Irishwoman).

Irlande [irlɑ̃d] *nf* : **l'~** Ireland ; **l'~ du Nord/Sud** Northern/Southern Ireland.

ironie [irɔni] *nf* irony.

ironique [irɔnik] *adj* ironic.

ironiser [3] [irɔnize] *vi* to speak ironically.

irradier [9] [iradje] ◇ *vi* to radiate. ◇ *vt* to irradiate.

irraisonné, e [irɛzɔne] *adj* irrational.

irrationnel, elle [irasjɔnɛl] *adj* irrational.

irréalisable [irealizabl] *adj* unrealizable.

irrécupérable [irekyperabl] *adj* - **1.** [irrécouvrable] irretrievable - **2.** [irréparable] beyond repair - **3.** *fam* [personne] beyond hope.

irrécusable [irekyzabl] *adj* unimpeachable.

irréductible [iredyktibl] ◇ *nmf* diehard. ◇ *adj* - **1.** CHIM, MATHS & MÉD irreducible - **2.** *fig* [volonté] indomitable ; [personne] implacable ; [communiste] diehard (*avant n*).

irréel, elle [ireɛl] *adj* unreal.

irréfléchi, e [irefleʃi] *adj* unthinking.

irréfutable [irefytabl] *adj* irrefutable.

irrégularité [iregylarite] *nf* - **1.** [gén] irregularity - **2.** [de terrain, performance] unevenness.

irrégulier, ère [iregylje, ɛr] *adj* - **1.** [gén] irregular - **2.** [terrain, surface] uneven, irregular - **3.** [employé, athlète] erratic.

irrémédiable [iremedjabl] *adj* [irréparable] irreparable.

irremplaçable [irɑ̃plasabl] *adj* irreplaceable.

irréparable [ireparabl] *adj* - **1.** [objet] beyond repair - **2.** *fig* [perte, erreur] irreparable.

irrépressible [irepresibl] *adj* irrepressible.

irréprochable [ireprɔʃabl] *adj* irreproachable.

irrésistible [irezistibl] *adj* - **1.** [tentation, femme] irresistible - **2.** [amusant] entertaining.

irrésolu, e [irezɔly] *adj* - **1.** [indécis] irresolute - **2.** [sans solution] unresolved.

irrespirable [irɛspirabl] *adj* - **1.** [air] unbreathable - **2.** *fig* [oppressant] oppressive.

irresponsable [irɛspɔ̃sabl] ◇ *nmf* irresponsible person. ◇ *adj* irresponsible.

irréversible [irevɛrsibl] *adj* irreversible.

irrévocable [irevɔkabl] *adj* irrevocable.

irrigation [irigasjɔ̃] *nf* irrigation.

irriguer [3] [irige] *vt* to irrigate.

irritable [iritabl] *adj* irritable.

irritation [iritasjɔ̃] *nf* irritation.

irriter [3] [irite] *vt* - **1.** [exaspérer] to irritate, to annoy - **2.** MÉD to irritate. ➼ **s'irriter** *vp* to get irritated ; **s'~ contre qqn/de qqch** to get irritated with sb/at sthg.

irruption [irypsjɔ̃] *nf* - **1.** [invasion] invasion - **2.** [entrée brusque] irruption.

islam [islam] *nm* Islam.

islamique [islamik] *adj* Islamic.

islandais, e [islɑ̃dɛ, ɛz] *adj* Icelandic. ➼ **islandais** *nm* [langue] Icelandic. ➼ **Islandais, e** *nm, f* Icelander.

Islande [islɑ̃d] *nf* : **l'~** Iceland.

isocèle [izɔsɛl] *adj* isoceles.

isolant, e [izɔlɑ̃, ɑ̃t] *adj* insulating. ➼ **isolant** *nm* insulator, insulating material.

isolation [izɔlasjɔ̃] *nf* insulation.

isolé, e [izɔle] *adj* isolated.

isoler [3] [izɔle] *vt* - **1.** [séparer] to isolate - **2.** CONSTR & ÉLECTR to insulate ; **~ qqch du froid** to insulate sthg (against the cold) ; **~ qqch du bruit** to soundproof sthg.

s'isoler *vp* : s'~ **(de)** to isolate o.s. (from).

isoloir [izɔlwar] *nm* polling booth.

isotherme [izɔtɛrm] *adj* isothermal.

Israël [israɛl] *n* Israel.

israélien, enne [israeljɛ̃, ɛn] *adj* Israeli. ➤ **Israélien, enne** *nm, f* Israeli.

israélite [israelit] *adj* Jewish. ➤ **Israélite** *nmf* Jew.

issu, e [isy] *adj* : être ~ de [résulter de] to emerge ou stem from ; [personne] to come from. ➤ **issue** *nf* - **1.** [sortie] exit ; ~e de secours emergency exit - **2.** *fig* [solution] way out, solution - **3.** [terme] outcome.

isthme [ism] *nm* isthmus.

Italie [itali] *nf* : l'~ Italy.

italien, enne [italjɛ̃, ɛn] *adj* Italian. ➤ **italien** *nm* [langue] Italian. ➤ **Italien, enne** *nm, f* Italian.

italique [italik] *nm* TYPO italics *(pl)* ; **en ~** in italics.

itinéraire [itinerɛr] *nm* itinerary, route.

itinérant, e [itinerã, ãt] *adj* [spectacle, troupe] itinerant.

IUT *(abr de* **Institut universitaire de technologie)** *nm* = technical college.

IVG *(abr de* **interruption volontaire de grossesse)** *nf* abortion.

ivoire [ivwar] *nm* ivory.

ivre [ivr] *adj* drunk.

ivresse [ivrɛs] *nf* drunkenness ; [extase] rapture.

ivrogne [ivrɔɲ] *nmf* drunkard.

j, J [ʒi] *nm inv* j, J.

j' ➢ **je.**

jabot [ʒabo] *nm* - **1.** [d'oiseau] crop - **2.** [de chemise] frill.

jacasser [3] [ʒakase] *vi péj* to chatter, to jabber.

jacinthe [ʒasɛ̃t] *nf* hyacinth.

Jacuzzi® [ʒakuzi] *nm* Jacuzzi®.

jade [ʒad] *nm* jade.

jadis [ʒadis] *adv* formerly, in former times.

jaguar [ʒagwar] *nm* jaguar.

jaillir [32] [ʒajir] *vi* - **1.** [liquide] to gush ;

[flammes] to leap - **2.** [cri] to ring out - **3.** [personne] to spring out.

jais [ʒɛ] *nm* jet.

jalon [ʒalɔ̃] *nm* marker pole.

jalonner [3] [ʒalɔne] *vt* to mark (out).

jalousie [ʒaluzi] *nf* - **1.** [envie] jealousy - **2.** [store] blind.

jaloux, ouse [ʒalu, uz] *adj* : ~ **(de)** jealous (of).

Jamaïque [ʒamaik] *nf* : la ~ Jamaica.

jamais [ʒamɛ] *adv* - **1.** [sens négatif] never ; ne ... ~, ~ ne never ; je ne reviendrai ~, ~ je ne reviendrai I'll never come back ; (ne) ... ~ plus, plus ~ **(ne)** never again ; je ne viendrai ~ plus, plus ~ je ne viendrai I'll never come here again - **2.** [sens positif] : plus que ~ more than ever ; il est plus triste que ~ he's sadder than ever ; si ~ tu le vois if you should happen to see him, should you happen to see him. ➤ **à jamais** *loc adv* for ever.

jambe [ʒãb] *nf* leg.

jambières [ʒãbjɛr] *nfpl* [de football] shin pads ; [de cricket] pads.

jambon [ʒãbɔ̃] *nm* ham ; **blanc** ham ; un ~ beurre *fam* a ham sandwich.

jante [ʒãt] *nf* (wheel) rim.

janvier [ʒãvje] *nm* January ; *voir aussi* **septembre.**

Japon [ʒapɔ̃] *nm* : le ~ Japan.

japonais, e [ʒapɔnɛ, ɛz] *adj* Japanese. ➤ **japonais** *nm* [langue] Japanese. ➤ **Japonais, e** *nm, f* Japanese (person) ; les Japonais the Japanese.

japper [3] [ʒape] *vi* to yap.

jaquette [ʒakɛt] *nf* - **1.** [vêtement] jacket - **2.** [de livre] (dust) jacket.

jardin [ʒardɛ̃] *nm* garden ; ~ public park.

jardinage [ʒardinaʒ] *nm* gardening.

jardinier, ère [ʒardinje, ɛr] *nm, f* gardener. ➤ **jardinière** *nf* [bac à fleurs] window box.

jargon [ʒargɔ̃] *nm* - **1.** [langage spécialisé] jargon - **2.** *fam* [charabia] gibberish.

jarret [ʒarɛ] *nm* - **1.** ANAT back of the knee - **2.** CULIN knuckle of veal.

jarretelle [ʒartɛl] *nf* suspender *Br*, garter *Am*.

jarretière [ʒartjɛr] *nf* garter.

jars [ʒar] *nm* gander.

jaser [3] [ʒaze] *vi* [bavarder] to gossip.

jasmin [ʒasmɛ̃] *nm* jasmine.

jatte [ʒat] *nf* bowl.

jauge [ʒoʒ] *nf* [instrument] gauge.

jauger [17] [ʒoʒe] *vt* to gauge.

jaunâtre [ʒonatr] *adj* yellowish.

jaune [ʒon] ◇ *nm* [couleur] yellow. ◇ *adj* yellow. ◆ **jaune d'œuf** *nm* (egg) yolk.

jaunir [32] [ʒonir] *vt & vi* to turn yellow.

jaunisse [ʒonis] *nf* MÉD jaundice.

java [ʒava] *nf type of popular dance.*

Javel [ʒavɛl] *nf* : eau de ~ bleach.

javelot [ʒavlo] *nm* javelin.

jazz [dʒaz] *nm* jazz.

J.-C. (*abr de* Jésus-Christ) J.C.

je [ʒə], **j'** *(devant voyelle et h muet)* pron pers I.

jean [dʒin], **jeans** [dʒins] *nm* jeans *(pl)*, pair of jeans.

Jeep® [dʒip] *nf* Jeep®.

jérémiades [ʒeremjad] *nfpl* moaning (U), whining (U).

jerrycan, jerricane [ʒerikan] *nm* jerry can.

jersey [ʒɛrzɛ] *nm* jersey.

jésuite [ʒezɥit] *nm* Jesuit.

Jésus-Christ [ʒezykri] *nm* Jesus Christ.

jet¹ [ʒɛ] *nm* - **1.** [action de jeter] throw - **2.** [de liquide] jet.

jet² [dʒɛt] *nm* [avion] jet.

jetable [ʒətabl] *adj* disposable.

jeté, e [ʒəte] *pp* ▷ jeter.

jetée [ʒəte] *nf* jetty.

jeter [27] [ʒəte] *vt* to throw ; [se débarrasser de] to throw away ; ~ **qqch à qqn** [lancer] to throw sthg to sb, to throw sb sthg ; [pour faire mal] to throw sthg at sb. ◆ **se jeter** *vp* : **se ~ sur** to pounce on ; **se ~ dans** [suj : rivière] to flow into.

jeton [ʒətɔ̃] *nm* [de jeu] counter ; [de téléphone] token.

jeu, x [ʒø] *nm* - **1.** [divertissement] play (U), playing (U) ; ~ **de mots** play on words, pun - **2.** [régi par des règles] game ; **mettre un joueur hors ~** to put a player offside ; ~ **de société** parlour *Br* OU parlor *Am* game - **3.** [d'argent] : **le ~** gambling - **4.** [d'échecs, de clés] set ; ~ **de cartes** pack of cards - **5.** [manière de jouer - MUS] playing ; [- THÉÂTRE] acting ; [- SPORT] game - **6.** TECHNOL play - **7.** *loc* : **cacher son ~** to play one's cards close to one's chest. ◆ **Jeux Olympiques** *nmpl* : **les Jeux Olympiques** the Olympic Games.

jeudi [ʒødi] *nm* Thursday.

jeun [ʒœ̃] ◆ **à jeun** *loc adv* on an empty stomach.

jeune [ʒœn] ◇ *adj* young ; [style, apparence] youthful ; ~ **homme/femme** young man/woman. ◇ *nm* young person ; **les ~s** young people.

jeûne [ʒøn] *nm* fast.

jeunesse [ʒœnɛs] *nf* - **1.** [âge] youth ; [de style, apparence] youthfulness - **2.** [jeunes gens] young people *(pl)*.

jingle [dʒingəl] *nm* jingle.

JO *nmpl* (*abr de* Jeux Olympiques) Olympic Games.

joaillier, ère [ʒɔaje, ɛr] *nm, f* jeweller *Br*, jeweler *Am*.

job [dʒɔb] *nm fam* job.

jockey [ʒɔkɛ] *nm* jockey.

jogging [dʒɔgiŋ] *nm* - **1.** [activité] jogging - **2.** [vêtement] tracksuit, jogging suit.

joie [ʒwa] *nf* joy.

joindre [82] [ʒwɛ̃dr] *vt* - **1.** [rapprocher] to join ; [mains] to put together - **2.** [ajouter] : ~ **qqch (à)** to attach sthg (to) ; [adjoindre] to enclose sthg (with) - **3.** [par téléphone] to contact, to reach. ◆ **se joindre** *vp* : **se ~ à qqn** to join sb ; **se ~ à qqch** to join in sthg.

joint, e [ʒwɛ̃, ɛ̃t] *pp* ▷ joindre. ◆ **joint** *nm* - **1.** [d'étanchéité] seal - **2.** *fam* [drogue] joint.

joker [ʒɔkɛr] *nm* joker.

joli, e [ʒɔli] *adj* - **1.** [femme, chose] pretty, attractive - **2.** [somme, situation] nice.

joliment [ʒɔlimɑ̃] *adv* - **1.** [bien] prettily, attractively ; *iron* nicely - **2.** *fam* [beaucoup] really.

jonc [ʒɔ̃] *nm* rush, bulrush.

joncher [3] [ʒɔ̃ʃe] *vt* to strew ; **être jonché de** to be strewn with.

jonction [ʒɔ̃ksjɔ̃] *nf* [de routes] junction.

jongler [3] [ʒɔ̃gle] *vi* to juggle.

jongleur, euse [ʒɔ̃glœr, øz] *nm, f* juggler.

jonquille [ʒɔ̃kij] *nf* daffodil.

Jordanie [ʒɔrdani] *nf* : **la ~** Jordan.

joue [ʒu] *nf* cheek ; **tenir** OU **mettre qqn en ~** *fig* to take aim at sb.

jouer [6] [ʒwe] ◇ *vi* - **1.** [gén] to play ; ~ **avec qqn/qqch** to play with sb/sthg ; ~ **à qqch** [jeu, sport] to play sthg ; ~ **de** MUS to play ; **à toi de ~!** (it's) your turn! ; *fig* your move! - **2.** CIN & THÉÂTRE to act - **3.** [parier] to gamble. ◇ *vt* - **1.** [carte, partie] to play - **2.** [somme d'argent] to bet, to wager ; *fig* to gamble with - **3.** [THÉÂTRE - personnage, rôle] to play ; [- pièce] to put on, to perform - **4.** [avoir à l'affiche] to show - **5.** MUS to perform, to play.

jouet [ʒwɛ] *nm* toy.

joueur, euse [ʒwœr, øz] *nm, f* - **1.** SPORT player ; ~ **de football** footballer, football player - **2.** [au casino] gambler.

joufflu, e [ʒufly] *adj* [personne] chubby-cheeked.

joug [ʒu] *nm* yoke.

jouir [32] [ʒwir] *vi* - **1.** [profiter] : ~ **de** to enjoy - **2.** [sexuellement] to have an orgasm.

jouissance [ʒwisɑ̃s] *nf* - **1.** JUR [d'un bien] use - **2.** [sexuelle] orgasm.

joujou, x [ʒuʒu] *nm* toy.

jour [ʒur] *nm* - **1.** [unité de temps] day ; **huit ~s** a week ; **quinze ~s** a fortnight *Br*, two weeks ; **de ~ en ~** day by day ; **~ après ~** day after day ; **au ~ le ~** from day to day ; ~ **et nuit** night and day ; **le ~ de l'an** New Year's Day ; ~ **chômé** public holiday ; ~ **de congé** day off ; ~ **férié** public holiday ; ~ **ouvrable** working day - **2.** [lumière] daylight ; **de ~** in the daytime, by day - **3.** *loc* : **mettre qqch à ~** to update sthg, to bring sthg up to date ; **de nos ~s** these days, nowadays.

journal, aux [ʒurnal, o] *nm* - **1.** [publication] newspaper, paper - **2.** TÉLÉ : ~ **télévisé** television news - **3.** [écrit] : ~ **(intime)** diary, journal.

journalier, ère [ʒurnalje, ɛr] *adj* daily.

journalisme [ʒurnalism] *nm* journalism.

journaliste [ʒurnalist] *nmf* journalist, reporter.

journée [ʒurne] *nf* day.

joute [ʒut] *nf* joust ; *fig* duel.

jovial, e, aux [ʒɔvjal, o] *adj* jovial, jolly.

joyau, x [ʒwajo] *nm* jewel.

joyeux, euse [ʒwajø, øz] *adj* joyful, happy ; **~ Noël!** Merry Christmas!

jubilé [ʒybile] *nm* jubilee.

jubiler [3] [ʒybile] *vi fam* to be jubilant.

jucher [3] [ʒyʃe] *vt* : ~ **qqn sur qqch** to perch sb on sthg.

judaïque [ʒydaik] *adj* [loi] Judaic ; [tradition, religion] Jewish.

judaïsme [ʒydaism] *nm* Judaism.

judas [ʒyda] *nm* [ouverture] peephole.

judéo-chrétien, enne [ʒydeokretjɛ̃, ɛn] (*mpl* **judéo-chrétiens**, *fpl* **judéo-chrétiennes**) *adj* Judaeo-Christian.

judiciaire [ʒydisjɛr] *adj* judicial.

judicieux, euse [ʒydisjø, øz] *adj* judicious.

judo [ʒydo] *nm* judo.

juge [ʒyʒ] *nm* judge ; ~ **d'instruction** examining magistrate.

jugé [ʒyʒe] ◆ **au jugé** *loc adv* by guesswork ; **tirer au ~** to fire blind.

jugement [ʒyʒmɑ̃] *nm* judgment ; **prononcer un ~** to pass sentence.

jugeote [ʒyʒɔt] *nf fam* common sense.

juger [17] [ʒyʒe] ◇ *vt* to judge ; [accusé] to try ; ~ **que** to judge (that), to consider (that) ; ~ **qqn/qqch inutile** to consider sb/sthg useless. ◇ *vi* to judge ; ~ **de qqch** to judge sthg ; **si j'en juge d'après mon expérience** judging from my experience ; **jugez de ma surprise!** imagine my surprise!

juif, ive [ʒɥif, iv] *adj* Jewish. ◆ **Juif, ive** *nm, f* Jew.

juillet [ʒɥijɛ] *nm* July ; **la fête du 14 Juillet** *national holiday to mark the anniversary of the storming of the Bastille* ; *voir aussi* **septembre**.

juin [ʒɥɛ̃] *nm* June ; *voir aussi* **septembre**.

juke-box [dʒukbɔks] *nm inv* jukebox.

jumeau, elle, x [ʒymo, ɛl, o] ◇ *adj* twin (*avant n*). ◇ *nm, f* twin. ◆ **jumelles** *nfpl* OPTIQUE binoculars.

jumelé, e [ʒymle] *adj* [villes] twinned ; [maisons] semidetached.

jumeler [24] [ʒymle] *vt* to twin.

jumelle ▷ **jumeau**.

jument [ʒymɑ̃] *nf* mare.

jungle [ʒœ̃gl] *nf* jungle.

junior [ʒynjɔr] *adj & nmf* SPORT junior.

junte [ʒœ̃t] *nf* junta.

jupe [ʒyp] *nf* skirt.

jupe-culotte [ʒypkylɔt] *nf* culottes (*pl*).

jupon [ʒypɔ̃] *nm* petticoat, slip.

juré [ʒyre] *nm* JUR juror.

jurer [3] [ʒyre] ◇ *vt* : ~ **qqch à qqn** to swear ou pledge sthg to sb ; ~ **(à qqn) que ...** to swear (to sb) that ... ; ~ **de faire qqch** to swear ou vow to do sthg ; **je vous jure!** *fam* honestly! ◇ *vi* - **1.** [blasphémer] to swear, to curse - **2.** [ne pas aller ensemble] : ~ **(avec)** to clash (with). ◆ **se jurer** *vp* : **se ~ de faire qqch** to swear ou vow to do sthg.

juridiction [ʒyridiksjɔ̃] *nf* jurisdiction.

juridique [ʒyridik] *adj* legal.

jurisprudence [ʒyrisprydɑ̃s] *nf* jurisprudence.

juriste [ʒyrist] *nmf* lawyer.

juron [ʒyrɔ̃] *nm* swearword, oath.

jury [ʒyri] *nm* - **1.** JUR jury - **2.** [SCOL - d'examen] examining board ; [- de concours] admissions board.

jus [ʒy] *nm* - **1.** [de fruits, légumes] juice - **2.** [de viande] gravy.

jusque, jusqu' [ʒysk(ə)] ◆ **jusqu'à** *loc prép* - **1.** [sens temporel] until, till ; **jusqu'à nouvel ordre** until further notice ; **jusqu'à présent** up until now, so far - **2.** [sens spatial] as far as ; **jusqu'au bout** to the end - **3.** [même] even. ◆ **jusqu'à ce que** *loc conj* until, till. ◆ **jusqu'en** *loc prép* up until. ◆ **jusqu'ici** *loc adv* [lieu] up to here ; [temps] up until now, so far. ◆ **jusquelà** *loc adv* [lieu] up to there ; [temps] up until then.

justaucorps [ʒystɔkɔr] *nm* [maillot] leotard.

juste [ʒyst] ⟨⟩ *adj* - **1.** [équitable] fair - **2.** [exact] right, correct - **3.** [trop petit] tight. ⟨⟩ *adv* - **1.** [bien] correctly, right - **2.** [exactement, seulement] just.

justement [ʒystəmã] *adv* - **1.** [avec raison] rightly - **2.** [précisément] exactly, precisely.

justesse [ʒystɛs] *nf* [de remarque] aptness ; [de raisonnement] soundness. ➤ **de justesse** *loc adv* only just.

justice [ʒystis] *nf* - **1.** JUR justice ; **passer en ~ to stand trial - 2.** [équité] fairness.

justicier, ère [ʒystisje, ɛr] *nm, f* righter of wrongs.

justifiable [ʒystifjabl] *adj* justifiable.

justificatif, ive [ʒystifikatif, iv] *adj* supporting. ➤ **justificatif** *nm* written proof *(U)*.

justification [ʒystifikasjɔ̃] *nf* justification.

justifier [9] [ʒystifje] *vt* [gén] to justify. ➤ **se justifier** *vp* to justify o.s.

jute [ʒyt] *nm* jute.

juteux, euse [ʒytø, øz] *adj* juicy.

juvénile [ʒyvenil] *adj* youthful.

juxtaposer [3] [ʒykstapoze] *vt* to juxtapose, to place side by side.

K

k, K [ka] *nm inv* k, K.

K7 [kasɛt] *(abr de* **cassette)** *nf* cassette.

kaki [kaki] ⟨⟩ *nm* - **1.** [couleur] khaki - **2.** [fruit] persimmon. ⟨⟩ *adj inv* khaki.

kaléidoscope [kaleidɔskɔp] *nm* kaleidoscope.

kamikaze [kamikaz] *nm* kamikaze pilot.

kanak = **canaque**.

kangourou [kãguru] *nm* kangaroo.

karaoké [karaɔke] *nm* karaoke.

karaté [karate] *nm* karate.

karting [kartiŋ] *nm* go-karting.

kas(c)her [kaʃɛr], **cascher** *adj inv* kosher.

kayak [kajak] *nm* kayak.

Kenya [kenja] *nm* : **le ~** Kenya.

képi [kepi] *nm* kepi.

kératine [keratin] *nf* keratin.

kermesse [kɛrmɛs] *nf* - **1.** [foire] fair - **2.** [fête de bienfaisance] fête.

kérosène [kerɔzɛn] *nm* kerosene.

ketchup [kɛtʃœp] *nm* ketchup.

keuf [kœf] *nm fam* cop.

keum [kœm] *nm fam* guy, bloke.

kg *(abr de* **kilogramme)** kg.

kibboutz [kibuts] *nm inv* kibbutz.

kidnapper [3] [kidnape] *vt* to kidnap.

kidnappeur, euse [kidnapœr, øz] *nm, f* kidnapper.

kilo [kilo] *nm* kilo.

kilogramme [kilɔgram] *nm* kilogram.

kilométrage [kilɔmetraʒ] *nm* - **1.** [de voiture] ≃ mileage - **2.** [distance] distance.

kilomètre [kilɔmɛtr] *nm* kilometre *Br*, kilometer *Am*.

kilo-octet [kilɔɔkte] *nm* INFORM kilobyte.

kilowatt [kilɔwat] *nm* kilowatt.

kilt [kilt] *nm* kilt.

kimono [kimɔno] *nm* kimono.

kinésithérapeute [kineziterapøt] *nmf* physiotherapist.

kiosque [kjɔsk] *nm* - **1.** [de vente] kiosk - **2.** [pavillon] pavilion.

kir [kir] *nm apéritif made with white wine and blackcurrant liqueur.*

kirsch [kirʃ] *nm* cherry brandy.

kitchenette [kitʃənɛt] *nf* kitchenette.

kitsch [kitʃ] *adj inv* kitsch.

kiwi [kiwi] *nm* - **1.** [oiseau] kiwi - **2.** [fruit] kiwi, kiwi fruit *(U)*.

Klaxon® [klaksɔ̃] *nm* horn.

klaxonner [3] [klaksɔne] *vi* to hoot.

kleptomane, cleptomane [klɛptɔman] *nmf* kleptomaniac.

km *(abr de* **kilomètre)** km.

km/h *(abr de* **kilomètre par heure)** kph.

Ko *(abr de* **kilo-octet)** K.

K.-O. [kao] *nm* : **mettre qqn ~ to knock sb out.**

Koweït [kɔwɛt] *nm* [pays, ville] Kuwait ; **le ~** Kuwait.

krach [krak] *nm* crash ; **~ boursier** stock market crash.

kung-fu [kuŋfu] *nm* kung fu.

kurde [kyrd] ⟨⟩ *adj* Kurdish. ⟨⟩ *nm* [langue] Kurdish. ➤ **Kurde** *nmf* Kurd.

kyrielle [kirjɛl] *nf fam* stream ; [d'enfants] horde.

kyste [kist] *nm* cyst.

l, L [ɛl] ◇ *nm inv* l, L. ◇ (*abr de* litre) l.

l' ▷ le.

la¹ [la] *art déf & pron déf* ▷ le.

la² [la] *nm inv* MUS A ; [chanté] la.

là [la] *adv* - 1. [lieu] there ; **à 3 kilomètres de** ~ 3 kilometres from there ; **passe par ~** go that way ; **c'est ~ que je travaille** that's where I work ; **je suis ~** I'm here - 2. [temps] then ; **à quelques jours de ~** a few days later, a few days after - 3. [avec une proposition relative] : **~ où** [lieu] where ; [temps] when.

là-bas [laba] *adv* (over) there.

label [label] *nm* - 1. [étiquette] : **~ de qualité** label guaranteeing quality - 2. [commerce] label, brand name.

labeur [labœr] *nm sout* labour *Br*, labor *Am*.

labo [labo] (*abr de* laboratoire) *nm fam* lab.

laborantin, e [labɔrɑ̃tɛ̃, in] *nm, f* laboratory assistant.

laboratoire [labɔratwar] *nm* laboratory.

laborieux, euse [labɔrjø, øz] *adj* [difficile] laborious.

labourer [3] [labure] *vt* - 1. AGRIC to plough *Br*, to plow *Am* - 2. *fig* [creuser] to make a gash in.

laboureur [laburœr] *nm* ploughman.

labyrinthe [labirɛ̃t] *nm* labyrinth.

lac [lak] *nm* lake ; **les Grands Lacs** the Great Lakes ; **le Léman Lake** Geneva.

lacer [16] [lase] *vt* to tie.

lacérer [18] [lasere] *vt* - 1. [déchirer] to shred - 2. [blesser, griffer] to slash.

lacet [lasɛ] *nm* - 1. [cordon] lace - 2. [de route] bend - 3. [piège] snare.

lâche [laʃ] ◇ *nmf* coward. ◇ *adj* - 1. [nœud] loose - 2. [personne, comportement] cowardly.

lâcher [3] [laʃe] ◇ *vt* - 1. [libérer - bras, objet] to let go of ; [- animal] to let go, to release - 2. [émettre - son, mot] to let out, to come out with - 3. [desserrer] to loosen - 4. [laisser tomber] : **~ qqch** to drop sthg. ◇ *vi* to give way.

lâcheté [laʃte] *nf* - 1. [couardise] cowardice - 2. [acte] cowardly act.

lacis [lasi] *nm* [labyrinthe] maze.

laconique [lakɔnik] *adj* laconic.

lacrymogène [lakrimɔʒɛn] *adj* tear (*avant n*).

lacune [lakyn] *nf* [manque] gap.

lacustre [lakystr] *adj* [faune, plante] lake (*avant n*) ; [cité, village] on stilts.

lad [lad] *nm* stable lad.

là-dedans [ladədɑ̃] *adv* inside, in there ; **il y a quelque chose qui m'intrigue ~** there's something in that which intrigues me.

là-dessous [ladsu] *adv* underneath, under there ; *fig* behind that.

là-dessus [ladsy] *adv* on that ; **~, il partit** at that point ou with that, he left ; **je suis d'accord ~** I agree about that.

ladite ▷ ledit.

lagon [lagɔ̃] *nm*, **lagune** [lagyn] *nf* lagoon.

là-haut [lao] *adv* up there.

laïc, laïque [laik] ◇ *adj* lay (*avant n*) ; [juridiction] civil (*avant n*) ; [école] state (*avant n*). ◇ *nm, f* layman (*f* laywoman).

laid, e [lɛ, lɛd] *adj* - 1. [esthétiquement] ugly - 2. [moralement] wicked.

laideron [lɛdrɔ̃] *nm* ugly woman.

laideur [lɛdœr] *nf* - 1. [physique] ugliness - 2. [morale] wickedness.

lainage [lɛnaʒ] *nm* [étoffe] woollen *Br* ou woolen *Am* material ; [vêtement] woolly, woollen *Br* ou woolen *Am* garment.

laine [lɛn] *nf* wool ; **~ polaire** polar fleece.

laineux, euse [lɛnø, øz] *adj* woolly.

laïque = laïc.

laisse [lɛs] *nf* [corde] lead, leash ; **tenir en ~** [chien] to keep on a lead ou leash.

laisser [4] [lese] ◇ *v aux* (+ *infinitif*) : **~ qqn faire qqch** to let sb do sthg ; **laisse le faire** leave him alone, don't interfere ; **~ tomber qqch** *litt & fig* to drop sthg, **laisse tomber!** *fam* drop it! ◇ *vt* - 1. [gén] to leave ; **~ qqn/ qqch à qqn** [confier] to leave sb/sthg with sb - 2. [céder] : **~ qqch à qqn** to let sb have sthg. ◆ **se laisser** *vp* : **se ~ faire** to let o.s. be persuaded ; **se ~ aller** to relax ; [dans son apparence] to let o.s. go ; **se ~ aller à qqch** to indulge in sthg.

laisser-aller [leseale] *nm inv* carelessness.

laissez-passer [lesepase] *nm inv* pass.

lait [lɛ] *nm* - 1. [gén] milk ; **~ entier/écrémé** whole/skimmed milk ; **~ concentré** ou **condensé** [sucré] condensed milk ; [non sucré] evaporated milk - 2. [cosmétique] : **~ démaquillant** cleansing milk ou lotion.

laitage [lɛtaʒ] *nm* dairy product.

laiterie [lɛtri] *nf* dairy.

laitier, ère [lɛtje, ɛr] ◇ *adj* dairy (*avant n*). ◇ *nm, f* milkman (*f* milkwoman).

laiton [lɛtɔ̃] *nm* brass.

laitue [lety] *nf* lettuce.

laïus [lajys] *nm* long speech.

lambeau, x [lãbo] *nm* [morceau] shred.

lambris [lãbri] *nm* panelling *Br*, paneling *Am*.

lame [lam] *nf* - 1. [fer] blade ; ~ **de rasoir** razor blade - 2. [lamelle] strip - 3. [vague] wave.

lamé, e [lame] *adj* lamé. ◆ **lamé** *nm* lamé.

lamelle [lamɛl] *nf* - 1. [de champignon] gill - 2. [tranche] thin slice - 3. [de verre] slide.

lamentable [lamãtabl] *adj* - 1. [résultats, sort] appalling - 2. [ton] plaintive.

lamentation [lamãtasjɔ̃] *nf* - 1. [plainte] lamentation - 2. *(gén pl)* [jérémiade] moaning *(U)*.

lamenter [3] [lamãte] ◆ **se lamenter** *vp* to complain.

laminer [3] [lamine] *vt* IND to laminate ; *fig* [personne, revenus] to eat away at.

lampadaire [lãpadɛr] *nm* [d'intérieur] standard lamp *Br*, floor lamp *Am* ; [de rue] street lamp *ou* light.

lampe [lãp] *nf* lamp, light ; ~ **de chevet** bedside lamp ; ~ **halogène** halogen light ; ~ **de poche** torch *Br*, flashlight *Am*.

lampion [lãpjɔ̃] *nm* Chinese lantern.

lance [lãs] *nf* - 1. [arme] spear - 2. [de tuyau] nozzle ; ~ **d'incendie** fire hose.

lance-flammes [lãsflam] *nm inv* flame-thrower.

lancement [lãsmã] *nm* [d'entreprise, produit, navire] launching.

lance-pierres [lãspjɛr] *nm inv* catapult.

lancer [16] [lãse] ◇ *vt* - 1. [pierre, javelot] to throw ; ~ **qqch sur qqn** to throw sthg at sb - 2. [fusée, produit, style] to launch - 3. [émettre] to give off ; [cri] to let out ; [injures] to hurl ; [ultimatum] to issue - 4. [moteur] to start up - 5. [INFORM - programme] to start ; [- système] to boot (up) - 6. *fig* [sur un sujet] : ~ **qqn sur qqch** to get sb started on sthg. ◇ *nm* - 1. PÊCHE casting - 2. SPORT throwing ; ~ **du poids** shotput. ◆ **se lancer** *vp* - 1. [débuter] to make a name for o.s - 2. [s'engager] : **se** ~ **dans** [dépenses, explication, lecture] to embark on.

lancinant, e [lãsinã, ãt] *adj* - 1. [douleur] shooting - 2. *fig* [obsédant] haunting - 3. [monotone] insistent.

landau [lãdo] *nm* [d'enfant] pram.

lande [lãd] *nf* moor.

langage [lãgaʒ] *nm* language.

lange [lãʒ] *nm* nappy *Br*, diaper *Am*.

langer [17] [lãʒe] *vt* to change.

langoureux, euse [lãgurø, øz] *adj* languorous.

langouste [lãgust] *nf* crayfish.

langoustine [lãgustin] *nf* langoustine.

langue [lãg] *nf* - 1. ANAT & *fig* tongue - 2. LING language ; ~ **maternelle** mother tongue ; ~ **morte/vivante** dead/modern language.

languette [lãgɛt] *nf* tongue.

langueur [lãgœr] *nf* - 1. [dépérissement, mélancolie] languor - 2. [apathie] apathy.

languir [32] [lãgir] *vi* - 1. [dépérir] : ~ **(de)** to languish (with) - 2. *sout* [attendre] to wait ; **faire** ~ **qqn** to keep sb waiting.

lanière [lanjɛr] *nf* strip.

lanterne [lãtɛrn] *nf* - 1. [éclairage] lantern - 2. [phare] light.

Laos [laos] *nm* : **le** ~ Laos.

laper [3] [lape] *vt* & *vi* to lap.

lapider [3] [lapide] *vt* [tuer] to stone.

lapin, e [lapɛ̃, in] *nm, f* CULIN & ZOOL rabbit. ◆ **lapin** *nm* [fourrure] rabbit fur.

Laponie [laponi] *nf* : **la** ~ Lapland.

laps [laps] *nm* : **(dans) un** ~ **de temps** (in) a while.

lapsus [lapsys] *nm* slip (of the tongue/pen).

laquais [lakɛ] *nm* lackey.

laque [lak] *nf* - 1. [vernis, peinture] lacquer - 2. [pour cheveux] hair spray, lacquer.

laqué, e [lake] *adj* lacquered.

laquelle ▷ **lequel**.

larbin [larbɛ̃] *nm* - 1. [domestique] servant - 2. [personne servile] yes-man.

larcin [larsɛ̃] *nm* - 1. [vol] larceny, theft - 2. [butin] spoils *(pl)*.

lard [lar] *nm* - 1. [graisse de porc] lard - 2. [viande] bacon.

lardon [lardɔ̃] *nm* - 1. CULIN *cube or strip of bacon* - 2. *fam* [enfant] kid.

large [larʒ] ◇ *adj* - 1. [étendu, grand] wide ; ~ **de 5 mètres** 5 metres wide - 2. [important, considérable] large, big - 3. [esprit, sourire] broad - 4. [généreux - personne] generous. ◇ *nm* - 1. [largeur] : **5 mètres de** ~ 5 metres wide - 2. [mer] : **le** ~ the open sea ; **au** ~ **de la côte française** off the French coast.

largement [larʒəmã] *adv* - 1. [diffuser, répandre] widely ; **la porte était** ~ **ouverte** the door was wide open - 2. [donner, payer] generously ; [dépasser] considerably ; [récompenser] amply ; **avoir** ~ **le temps** to have plenty of time - 3. [au moins] easily.

largeur [larʒœr] *nf* - 1. [d'avenue, de cercle] width - 2. *fig* [d'idées, d'esprit] breadth.

larguer [3] [large] *vt* - 1. [voile] to unfurl

- **2.** [bombe, parachutiste] to drop - **3.** *fam fig* [abandonner] to chuck.

larme [larm] *nf* [pleur] tear ; **être en ~s** to be in tears.

larmoyant, e [larmwajɑ̃, ɑ̃t] *adj* - **1.** [yeux, personne] tearful - **2.** *péj* [histoire] tearjerking.

larron [larɔ̃] *nm vieilli* [voleur] thief.

larve [larv] *nf* - **1.** ZOOL larva - **2.** *péj* [personne] wimp.

laryngite [larɛ̃ʒit] *nf* laryngitis *(U).*

larynx [larɛ̃ks] *nm* larynx.

las, lasse [la, las] *adj littéraire* [fatigué] weary.

lascif, ive [lasif, iv] *adj* lascivious.

laser [lazɛr] <> *nm* laser. <> *adj inv* laser *(avant n).*

lasser [3] [lase] *vt sout* [personne] to weary ; [patience] to try. ◆ **se lasser** *vp* to weary.

lassitude [lasityd] *nf* lassitude.

lasso [laso] *nm* lasso.

latent, e [latɑ̃, ɑ̃t] *adj* latent.

latéral, e, aux [lateral, o] *adj* lateral.

latex [latɛks] *nm inv* latex.

latin, e [latɛ̃, in] *adj* Latin. ◆ **latin** *nm* [langue] Latin.

latiniste [latinist] *nmf* [spécialiste] Latinist ; [étudiant] Latin student.

latino-américain, e [latinoamerikɛ̃, ɛn] *(mpl* **latino-américains**, *fpl* **latino-américaines)** *adj* Latin-American, Hispanic.

latitude [latityd] *nf litt & fig* latitude.

latrines [latrin] *nfpl* latrines.

latte [lat] *nf* lath, slat.

lauréat, e [lɔrea, at] *nm, f* prizewinner, winner.

laurier [lɔrje] *nm* BOT laurel.

lavable [lavabl] *adj* washable.

lavabo [lavabo] *nm* - **1.** [cuvette] basin - **2.** *(gén pl)* [local] toilet.

lavage [lavaʒ] *nm* washing.

lavande [lavɑ̃d] *nf* BOT lavender.

lave [lav] *nf* lava.

lave-glace [lavglas] *(pl* **lave-glaces)** *nm* windscreen washer *Br,* windshield washer *Am.*

lave-linge [lavlɛ̃ʒ] *nm inv* washing machine.

laver [3] [lave] *vt* - **1.** [nettoyer] to wash - **2.** *fig* [disculper] : **~ qqn de qqch** to clear sb of sthg. ◆ **se laver** *vp* [se nettoyer] to wash o.s., to have a wash ; **se ~ les mains/les cheveux** to wash one's hands/hair.

laverie [lavri] *nf* [commerce] laundry ; **~ automatique** launderette.

lavette [lavɛt] *nf* - **1.** [brosse] washing-up brush ; [en tissu] dishcloth - **2.** *fam* [homme] drip.

laveur, euse [lavœr, øz] *nm, f* washer ; **~ de carreaux** window cleaner *(person).*

lave-vaisselle [lavvesɛl] *nm inv* dishwasher.

lavoir [lavwar] *nm* [lieu] laundry.

laxatif, ive [laksatif, iv] *adj* laxative. ◆ **laxatif** *nm* laxative.

laxisme [laksism] *nm* laxity.

laxiste [laksist] *adj* lax.

layette [lɛjɛt] *nf* layette.

le [lə], **l'** *(devant voyelle ou h muet) (f* **la** [la], *pl* **les** [le]) <> *art déf* - **1.** [gén] the ; **~ lac** the lake ; **la fenêtre** the window ; **l'homme** the man ; **les enfants** the children - **2.** [devant les noms abstraits] : **l'amour** love ; **la liberté** freedom ; **la vieillesse** old age - **3.** [temps] : **~ 15 janvier 1993** 15th January 1993 ; **je suis arrivé ~ 15 janvier 1993** I arrived on the 15th of January 1993 ; **~ lundi** [habituellement] on Mondays ; [jour précis] on (the) Monday - **4.** [distributif] **per,** *a ;* **2 euros ~ mètre** 2 euros per metre *Br* ou meter *Am,* 2 euros a metre *Br* ou meter *Am.* <> *pron pers* - **1.** [personne] him *(f* her), [chose] it, *pl* them ; [animal] it, him *(f* her), *pl* them ; **je ~/la/les connais bien** I know him/her/them well ; **tu dois avoir la clé, donne-la moi** you must have the key, give it to me - **2.** [représente une proposition] : **je ~ sais bien** I know, I'm well aware (of it) ; **je te l'avais bien dit!** I told you so!

LEA *(abr de* **langues étrangères appliquées)** *nfpl* applied modern languages.

leader [lidœr] *nm* [de parti, course] leader.

leadership [lidœrʃip] *nm* leadership.

lécher [18] [leʃe] *vt* - **1.** [passer la langue sur, effleurer] to lick ; [suj : vague] to wash against - **2.** *fam* [fignoler] to polish (up).

lèche-vitrines [lɛʃvitrin] *nm inv* window-shopping ; **faire du ~** to go window-shopping.

leçon [ləsɔ̃] *nf* - **1.** [gén] lesson ; **~s de conduite** driving lessons ; **~s particulières** private lessons ou classes - **2.** [conseil] advice *(U) ;* **faire la ~ à qqn** to lecture sb.

lecteur, trice [lɛktœr, tris] *nm, f* - **1.** [de livres] reader - **2.** UNIV foreign language assistant. ◆ **lecteur** *nm* - **1.** [gén] head ; **~ de cassettes/CD** cassette/CD player - **2.** INFORM reader.

lecture [lɛktyr] *nf* reading.

ledit, ladite [lədi, ladit] *(mpl* **lesdits** [ledi], *fpl* **lesdites** [ledit]) *adj* the said, the aforementioned.

légal, e, aux [legal, o] *adj* legal.

légalement [legalmã] *adv* legally.

légaliser [3] [legalize] *vt* [rendre légal] to legalize.

légalité [legalite] *nf* - 1. [de contrat, d'acte] legality, lawfulness - 2. [loi] law.

légataire [legatɛr] *nmf* legatee.

légendaire [leʒãdɛr] *adj* legendary.

légende [leʒãd] *nf* - 1. [fable] legend - 2. [de carte, de schéma] key.

léger, ère [leʒe, ɛr] *adj* - 1. [objet, étoffe, repas] light - 2. [bruit, différence, odeur] slight - 3. [alcool, tabac] low-strength - 4. [femme] flighty - 5. [insouciant - ton] light-hearted ; [- conduite] thoughtless.
◆ **à la légère** *loc adv* lightly, thoughtlessly.

légèrement [leʒɛrmã] *adv* - 1. [s'habiller, poser] lightly - 2. [agir] thoughtlessly - 3. [blesser, remuer] slightly.

légèreté [leʒɛrte] *nf* - 1. [d'objet, de repas, de punition] lightness - 2. [de style] gracefulness - 3. [de conduite] thoughtlessness - 4. [de personne] flightiness.

légiférer [18] [leʒifere] *vi* to legislate.

légion [leʒjɔ̃] *nf* MIL legion.

légionnaire [leʒjɔnɛr] *nm* legionary.

législatif, ive [leʒislatif, iv] *adj* legislative. ◆ **législatives** *nfpl* : **les législatives** the legislative elections, ≃ the general election *(sg)* Br.

législation [leʒislasjɔ̃] *nf* legislation.

légiste [leʒist] *adj* - 1. [juriste] jurist - 2. ▷ **médecin**.

légitime [leʒitim] *adj* legitimate.

légitimer [3] [leʒitime] *vt* - 1. [reconnaître] to recognize ; [enfant] to legitimize - 2. [justifier] to justify.

legs [lɛg] *nm* legacy.

léguer [18] [lege] *vt* : ~ **qqch à qqn** JUR to bequeath sthg to sb ; *fig* to pass sthg on to sb.

légume [legym] *nm* vegetable.

leitmotiv [lajtmɔtif, lɛtmɔtif] *nm* leitmotif.

Léman [lemã] ▷ **lac**.

lendemain [lãdmɛ̃] *nm* [jour] day after ; **le ~ matin** the next morning ; **au ~ de** after, in the days following.

lénifiant, e [lenifjã, ãt] *adj litt & fig* soothing.

lent, e [lã, lãt] *adj* slow.

lente [lãt] *nf* nit.

lentement [lãtmã] *adv* slowly.

lenteur [lãtœr] *nf* slowness *(U)*.

lentille [lãtij] *nf* - 1. BOT & CULIN lentil - 2. [d'optique] lens ; **~s de contact** contact lenses.

léopard [leɔpar] *nm* leopard.

lèpre [lɛpr] *nf* MÉD leprosy.

lequel [ləkɛl] (*f* **laquelle** [lakɛl], *mpl* **lesquels** [lekɛl], *fpl* **lesquelles** [lekɛl]) (*contraction de à + lequel* = **auquel**, *de + lequel* = **duquel**, *à + lesquels/lesquelles* = **auxquels/auxquelles**, *de + lesquels/lesquelles* = **desquels/desquelles**) ◇ *pron rel* - 1. [complément - personne] whom ; [- chose] which - 2. [sujet - personne] who ; [- chose] which. ◇ *pron interr* : **lequel?** which (one)?

les ▷ **le**.

lesbienne [lɛsbjɛn] *nf* lesbian.

lesdits, lesdites ▷ **ledit**.

léser [18] [leze] *vt* [frustrer] to wrong.

lésiner [3] [lezine] *vi* to skimp ; **ne pas ~ sur** not to skimp on.

lésion [lezjɔ̃] *nf* lesion.

lesquels, lesquelles ▷ **lequel**.

lessive [lɛsiv] *nf* - 1. [nettoyage, linge] washing - 2. [produit] washing powder.

lest [lɛst] *nm* ballast.

leste [lɛst] *adj* - 1. [agile] nimble, agile - 2. [licencieux] crude.

lester [3] [lɛste] *vt* [garnir de lest] to ballast.

léthargie [letarʒi] *nf litt & fig* lethargy.

Lettonie [lɛtɔni] *nf* : **la ~** Latvia.

lettre [lɛtr] *nf* - 1. [gén] letter ; **en toutes ~s** in words, in full - 2. [sens des mots] : **à la ~** to the letter. ◆ **lettres** *nfpl* - 1. [culture littéraire] letters ; **~s classiques** classics ; **~s modernes** French language and literature.

leucémie [løsemi] *nf* leukemia.

leucocyte [løkɔsit] *nm* leucocyte.

leur [lœr] *pron pers inv* (to) them ; **je voudrais ~ parler** I'd like to speak to them ; **je ~ ai donné la lettre** I gave them the letter, I gave the letter to them. ◆ **leur** (*pl* **leurs**) *adj poss* their ; **c'est ~ tour** it's their turn ; **~s enfants** their children. ◆ **le leur** (*f* **la leur**, *pl* **les leurs**) *pron poss* theirs ; **il faudra qu'ils y mettent du ~** they've got to pull their weight.

leurrer [5] [lœre] *vt* to deceive. ◆ **se leurrer** *vp* to deceive o.s.

levain [ləvɛ̃] *nm* CULIN : **pain au ~/sans ~** leavened/unleavened bread.

levant [ləvã] ◇ *nm* east. ◇ *adj* ▷ **soleil**.

lever [19] [ləve] ◇ *vt* - 1. [objet, blocus, interdiction] to lift - 2. [main, tête, armée] to raise - 3. [scellés, difficulté] to remove - 4. [séance] to close, to end - 5. [impôts, courrier] to collect - **6.** [enfant, malade] : ~ **qqn** to get sb up. ◇ *vi* - **1.** [plante] to come up - **2.** [pâte] to rise. ◇ *nm* - **1.** [d'astre] rising, rise ; ~ **du jour** daybreak ; ~ **du soleil** sunrise - **2.** [de personne] : **il est toujours de mauvaise humeur au** ~ he's always in a bad mood when he gets up. ➡ **se lever** *vp* - **1.** [personne] to get up, to rise ; [vent] to get up - **2.** [soleil, lune] to rise ; [jour] to break - **3.** [temps] to clear.

lève-tard [lɛvtar] *nmf inv* late riser.

lève-tôt [lɛvto] *nmf inv* early riser.

levier [ləvje] *nm litt & fig* lever ; ~ **de vitesses** gear lever *Br*, gear shift *Am*.

lévitation [levitasjɔ̃] *nf* levitation.

lèvre [lɛvr] *nf* ANAT lip ; [de vulve] labium.

lévrier, levrette [levrije, ləvrɛt] *nm, f* greyhound.

levure [ləvyr] *nf* yeast ; ~ **chimique** baking powder.

lexicographie [lɛksikɔgrafi] *nf* lexicography.

lexique [lɛksik] *nm* - **1.** [dictionnaire] glossary - **2.** [vocabulaire] vocabulary.

lézard [lezar] *nm* [animal] lizard.

lézarder [3] [lezarde] ◇ *vt* to crack. ◇ *vi fam* [paresser] to bask. ➡ **se lézarder** *vp* to crack.

liaison [ljɛzɔ̃] *nf* - **1.** [jonction, enchaînement] connection - **2.** CULIN & LING liaison - **3.** [contact, relation] contact ; **avoir une** ~ to have an affair - **4.** TRANSPORT link.

liane [ljan] *nf* creeper.

liant, e [ljɑ̃, ɑ̃t] *adj* sociable. ➡ **liant** *nm* [substance] binder.

liasse [ljas] *nf* bundle ; [de billets de banque] wad.

Liban [libɑ̃] *nm* : **le** ~ Lebanon.

libanais, e [libanɛ, ɛz] *adj* Lebanese. ➡ **Libanais, e** *nm, f* Lebanese (person) ; **les Libanais** the Lebanese.

libeller [4] [libele] *vt* - **1.** [chèque] to make out - **2.** [lettre] to word.

libellule [libelyl] *nf* dragonfly.

libéral, e, aux [liberal, o] ◇ *adj* [attitude, idée, parti] liberal. ◇ *nm, f* POLIT liberal.

libéraliser [3] [liberalize] *vt* to liberalize.

libéralisme [liberalism] *nm* liberalism.

libération [liberasjɔ̃] *nf* - **1.** [de prisonnier] release, freeing - **2.** [de pays, de la femme] liberation - **3.** [d'énergie] release.

libérer [18] [libere] *vt* - **1.** [prisonnier, fonds] to release, to free - **2.** [pays, la femme] to liberate ; ~ **qqn de qqch** to free sb from sthg - **3.** [passage] to clear - **4.** [énergie] to release - **5.** [instincts, passions] to give free rein to. ➡ **se libérer** *vp* - **1.** [se rendre disponible] to get away - **2.** [se dégager] : **se**

~ **de** [lien] to free o.s. from ; [engagement] to get out of.

liberté [libɛrte] *nf* - **1.** [gén] freedom ; **en** ~ free ; **parler en toute** ~ to speak freely ; **vivre en** ~ to live in freedom ; ~ **d'expression** freedom of expression ; ~ **d'opinion** freedom of thought - **2.** JUR release - **3.** [loisir] free time.

libertin, e [libɛrtɛ̃, in] *nm, f* libertine.

libidineux, euse [libidinø, øz] *adj* lecherous.

libido [libido] *nf* libido.

libraire [librɛr] *nmf* bookseller.

librairie [libreri] *nf* [magasin] bookshop *Br*, bookstore *Am*.

libre [libr] *adj* - **1.** [gén] free ; ~ **de qqch** free from sthg ; **être** ~ **de faire qqch** to be free to do sthg - **2.** [école, secteur] private - **3.** [passage] clear.

libre-échange [librefɑ̃ʒ] *nm* free trade (U).

librement [librəmɑ̃] *adv* freely.

libre-service [librəsɛrvis] *nm* [magasin] self-service store *ou* shop ; [restaurant] self-service restaurant.

Libye [libi] *nf* : **la** ~ Libya.

libyen, enne [libjɛ̃, ɛn] *adj* Libyan. ➡ **Libyen, enne** *nm, f* Libyan.

licence [lisɑ̃s] *nf* - **1.** [permis] permit ; COMM licence - **2.** UNIV (first) degree ; ~ **ès lettres/en droit** ≃ Bachelor of Arts/Law degree - **3.** *littéraire* [liberté] licence.

licencié, e [lisɑ̃sje] ◇ *adj* UNIV graduate (*avant n*). ◇ *nm, f* - **1.** UNIV graduate - **2.** [titulaire d'un permis] permit holder ; COMM licence-holder.

licenciement [lisɑ̃simɑ̃] *nm* dismissal ; [économique] layoff, redundancy *Br*.

licencier [9] [lisɑ̃sje] *vt* to dismiss ; [pour cause économique] to lay off, to make redundant *Br*.

lichen [likɛn] *nm* lichen.

licite [lisit] *adj* lawful, legal.

licorne [likɔrn] *nf* unicorn.

lie [li] *nf* [dépôt] dregs *(pl)*, sediment.

lié, e [lje] *adj* - **1.** [mains] bound - **2.** [amis] : **être très** ~ **aver** to be great friends with.

Liechtenstein [liʃtɛnʃtajn] *nm* : **le** Liechtenstein.

lie-de-vin [lidəvɛ̃] *adj inv* burgundy, wine-coloured *Br*, wine-colored *Am*.

liège [ljɛʒ] *nm* cork.

lien [ljɛ̃] *nm* - **1.** [sangle] bond - **2.** [relation, affinité] bond, tie ; **avoir des** ~**s de parenté avec** to be related to - **3.** *fig* [enchaînement] connection, link.

lier [9] [lje] *vt* - **1.** [attacher] to tie (up) ; ~ **qqn/qqch à** to tie sb/sthg to - **2.** [suj : contrat, promesse] to bind ; ~ **qqn/qqch par** to bind sb/sthg by - **3.** [relier par la logique] to link, to connect ; ~ **qqch à** to link sthg to, to connect sthg with - **4.** [commencer] : ~ **connaissance/conversation avec** to strike up an acquaintance/a conversation with - **5.** [suj : sentiment, intérêt] to unite - **6.** CULIN to thicken. ➡ **se lier** *vp* [s'attacher] : **se ~ (d'amitié) avec qqn** to make friends with sb.

lierre [ljɛr] *nm* ivy.

liesse [ljɛs] *nf* jubilation.

lieu, x [ljø] *nm* - **1.** [endroit] place ; **en ~ sûr** in a safe place ; ~ **de naissance** birthplace - **2.** *loc* : **avoir ~** to take place. ➡ **lieux** *nmpl* - **1.** [scène] scene *(sg)*, spot *(sg)* ; **sur les ~x (d'un crime/d'un accident)** at the scene (of a crime/an accident) - **2.** [domicile] premises. ➡ **lieu commun** *nm* commonplace. ➡ **au lieu de** *loc prép* : **au ~ de qqch/de faire qqch** instead of sthg/of doing sthg. ➡ **en dernier lieu** *loc adv* lastly. ➡ **en premier lieu** *loc adv* in the first place.

lieu-dit [ljødi] *(pl* lieux-dits) *nm* locality, place.

lieue [ljø] *nf* league.

lieutenant [ljøtnɑ̃] *nm* lieutenant.

lièvre [ljɛvr] *nm* hare.

lifter [3] [lifte] *vt* TENNIS to spin, to put a spin on.

lifting [liftiŋ] *nm* face-lift.

ligament [ligamɑ̃] *nm* ligament.

ligaturer [3] [ligatyre] *vt* MÉD to ligature, to ligate.

ligne [liɲ] *nf* - **1.** [gén] line ; **à la ~** new line OU paragraph ; **en ~** [personnes] in a line ; INFORM on line ; **restez en ~!** TÉLÉCOM who's speaking OU calling? ; ~ **de départ/d'arrivée** starting/finishing line ; ~ **aérienne** airline ; ~ **de commande** INFORM command line ; ~ **de conduite** line of conduct ; ~ **directrice** guideline ; **~s de la main** lines of the hand ; **les grandes ~s** TRANSPORT the main lines - **2.** [forme - de voiture, meuble] lines *(pl)* - **3.** [silhouette] : **garder la ~** to keep one's figure ; **surveiller sa ~** to watch one's waistline - **4.** [de pêche] fishing line ; **pêcher à la ~** to go angling - **5.** *loc* : **dans les grandes ~s** in outline ; **entrer en ~ de compte** to be taken into account.

lignée [liɲe] *nf* [famille] descendants *(pl)* ; **dans la ~ de** *fig* [d'écrivains, d'artistes] in the tradition of.

ligoter [3] [ligɔte] *vt* - **1.** [attacher] to tie up ; ~ **qqn à qqch** to tie sb to sthg - **2.** *fig* [entraver] to bind.

ligue [lig] *nf* league.

liguer [3] [lige] ➡ **se liguer** *vp* to form a league ; **se ~ contre** to conspire against.

lilas [lila] *nm & adj inv* lilac.

limace [limas] *nf* ZOOL slug.

limaille [limaj] *nf* filings *(pl)*.

limande [limɑ̃d] *nf* dab.

lime [lim] *nf* - **1.** [outil] file ; ~ **à ongles** nail file - **2.** BOT lime.

limer [3] [lime] *vt* [ongles] to file ; [aspérités] to file down ; [barreau] to file through.

limier [limje] *nm* - **1.** [chien] bloodhound - **2.** [détective] sleuth.

liminaire [liminɛr] *adj* introductory.

limitation [limitasjɔ̃] *nf* limitation ; [de naissances] control ; ~ **de vitesse** speed limit.

limite [limit] ⬦ *nf* - **1.** [gén] limit ; **à la ~** [au pire] at worst ; **à la ~, j'accepterais de le voir** if pushed, I'd agree to see him - **2.** [terme, échéance] deadline ; ~ **d'âge** age limit. ⬦ *adj* [extrême] maximum *(avant n)* ; **cas ~** borderline case ; **date ~** deadline ; **date ~ de vente/consommation** sell-by/use-by date.

limiter [3] [limite] *vt* - **1.** [borner] to border, to bound - **2.** [restreindre] to limit. ➡ **se limiter** *vp* - **1.** [se restreindre] : **se ~ à qqch/à faire qqch** to limit o.s. to sthg/to doing sthg - **2.** [se borner] : **se ~ à** to be limited to.

limitrophe [limitrɔf] *adj* - **1.** [frontalier] border *(avant n)* ; **être ~ de** to border on - **2.** [voisin] adjacent.

limoger [17] [limɔʒe] *vt* to dismiss.

limon [limɔ̃] *nm* GÉOL alluvium, silt.

limonade [limɔnad] *nf* lemonade.

limpide [lɛ̃pid] *adj* - **1.** [eau] limpid - **2.** [ciel, regard] clear - **3.** [explication, style] clear, lucid.

lin [lɛ̃] *nm* - **1.** BOT flax - **2.** [tissu] linen.

linceul [lɛ̃sœl] *nm* shroud.

linéaire [lineɛr] *adj* [mesure, perspective] linear.

linge [lɛ̃ʒ] *nm* - **1.** [lessive] washing - **2.** [de lit, de table] linen - **3.** [sous-vêtements] underwear - **4.** [morceau de tissu] cloth.

lingerie [lɛ̃ʒri] *nf* - **1.** [local] linen room - **2.** [sous-vêtements] lingerie.

lingot [lɛ̃go] *nm* ingot.

linguistique [lɛ̃gɥistik] ⬦ *nf* linguistics *(U)*. ⬦ *adj* linguistic.

linoléum [linɔleɔm] *nm* lino, linoleum.

lion, lionne [ljɔ̃, ljɔn] *nm, f* lion *(f* lioness). ➡ **Lion** *nm* ASTROL Leo.

lionceau, x [ljɔ̃so] *nm* lion cub.

lipide [lipid] *nm* lipid.

liquéfier [9] [likefje] *vt* to liquefy. ➡ **se**

liquéfier *vp* - 1. [matière] to liquefy - 2. *fig* [personne] to turn to jelly.

liqueur [likœr] *nf* liqueur.

liquidation [likidasjɔ̃] *nf* - 1. [de compte & BOURSE] settlement - 2. [de société, stock] liquidation.

liquide [likid] <> *nm* - 1. [substance] liquid - 2. [argent] cash ; **en ~** in cash. <> *adj* [corps & LING] liquid.

liquider [3] [likide] *vt* - 1. [compte & BOURSE] to settle - 2. [société, stock] to liquidate - 3. *arg crime* [témoin] to liquidate, to eliminate ; *fig* [problème] to eliminate, to get rid of.

liquidité [likidite] *nf* liquidity. ◆ **liquidités** *nfpl* liquid assets.

liquoreux, euse [likɔrø, øz] *adj* syrupy.

lire¹ [106] [lir] *vt* to read ; **lu et approuvé** read and approved.

lire² [lir] *nf* lira.

lis, lys [lis] *nm* lily.

Lisbonne [lizbɔn] *n* Lisbon.

liseré [lizre], **liséré** [lizere] *nm* - 1. [ruban] binding - 2. [bande] border, edging.

liseron [lizrɔ̃] *nm* bindweed.

liseuse [lizøz] *nf* - 1. [vêtement] bedjacket - 2. [lampe] reading light.

lisible [lizibl] *adj* [écriture] legible.

lisière [lizjɛr] *nf* [limite] edge.

lisse [lis] *adj* [surface, peau] smooth.

lisser [3] [lise] *vt* - 1. [papier, vêtements] to smooth (out) - 2. [moustache, cheveux] to smooth (down) - 3. [plumes] to preen.

liste [list] *nf* list ; **~ d'attente** waiting list ; **~ électorale** electoral roll ; **~ de mariage** wedding present list ; **être sur la ~ rouge** to be ex-directory.

lister [3] [liste] *vt* to list.

listing [listiŋ] *nm* listing.

lit [li] *nm* [gén] bed ; **faire son ~** to make one's bed ; **garder le ~** to stay in bed ; **se mettre au ~** to go to bed ; **~ à baldaquin** four-poster bed ; **~ de camp** camp bed.

litanie [litani] *nf* litany.

literie [litri] *nf* bedding.

lithographie [litɔgrafi] *nf* - 1. [procédé] lithography - 2. [image] lithograph.

litière [litjɛr] *nf* litter.

litige [litiʒ] *nm* - 1. JUR lawsuit - 2. [désaccord] dispute.

litigieux, euse [litiʒjø, øz] *adj* - 1. JUR litigious - 2. [douteux] disputed.

litre [litr] *nm* - 1. [mesure, quantité] litre *Br*, liter *Am* - 2. [récipient] litre *Br* ou liter *Am* bottle.

littéraire [literɛr] *adj* literary.

littéral, e, aux [literal, o] *adj* - 1. [gén] literal - 2. [écrit] written.

littérature [literatyr] *nf* [gén] literature.

littoral, e, aux [litɔral, o] *adj* coastal. ◆ **littoral** *nm* coast, coastline.

Lituanie [lityani] *nf* : **la ~** Lithuania.

liturgie [lityrʒi] *nf* liturgy.

livide [livid] *adj* [blême] pallid.

livraison [livrɛzɔ̃] *nf* [de marchandise] delivery ; **~ à domicile** home delivery.

livre [livr] <> *nm* [gén] book ; **~ de cuisine** cookery book ; **~ électronique** e-book ; **~ d'images** picture book ; **~ d'or** visitors' book ; **~ de poche** paperback. <> *nf* pound ; **~ sterling** pound sterling.

livrée [livre] *nf* [uniforme] livery.

livrer [3] [livre] *vt* - 1. COMM to deliver ; **~ qqch à qqn** [achat] to deliver sthg to sb ; *fig* [secret] to reveal ou give away sthg to sb - 2. [coupable, complice] : **~ qqn à qqn** to hand sb over to sb - 3. [abandonner] : **~ qqch à qqch** to give sthg over to sthg ; **~ qqn à lui-même** to leave sb to his own devices. ◆ **se livrer** *vp* - 1. [se rendre] : **se ~ à** [police, ennemi] to give o.s. up to - 2. [se confier] : **se ~ à** [ami] to open up to, to confide in - 3. [se consacrer] : **se ~ à** [occupation] to devote o.s. to ; [excès] to indulge in.

livret [livrɛ] *nm* - 1. [carnet] booklet ; **~ de caisse d'épargne** passbook, bankbook ; **~ de famille** *official family record book, given by registrar to newlyweds* ; **~ scolaire** ≃ school report - 2. [catalogue] catalogue *Br*, catalog *Am* - 3. MUS book, libretto.

livreur, euse [livrœr, øz] *nm, f* delivery man (*f* woman).

lobby [lɔbi] (*pl* **lobbies**) *nm* lobby.

lobe [lɔb] *nm* ANAT & BOT lobe.

lober [3] [lɔbe] *vt* to lob.

local, e, aux [lɔkal, o] *adj* local ; [douleur] localized. ◆ **local** *nm* room, premises (*pl*). ◆ **locaux** *nmpl* premises, offices.

localiser [3] [lɔkalize] *vt* - 1. [avion, bruit] to locate - 2. [épidémie, conflit, produit multimédia] to localize.

localité [lɔkalite] *nf* (small) town.

locataire [lɔkatɛr] *nmf* tenant.

location [lɔkasjɔ̃] *nf* - 1. [de propriété - par propriétaire] letting *Br*, renting *Am* ; [- par locataire] renting ; [de machine] leasing ; **~ de voitures/vélos** car/bicycle hire *Br*, car/bicycle rent *Am* - 2. [bail] lease - 3. [maison, appartement] rented property - 4. [réservation] booking.

location-vente [lɔkasjɔ̃vɑ̃t] *nf* ≃ hire purchase *Br*, ≃ installment plan *Am*.

locomotion [lɔkɔmɔsjɔ̃] *nf* locomotion.

locomotive [lɔkɔmɔtiv] *nf* - **1.** [machine] locomotive - **2.** *fig* [leader] moving force.

locution [lɔkysjɔ̃] *nf* expression, phrase.

loft [lɔft] *nm* (converted) loft.

logarithme [lɔgaritm] *nm* logarithm.

loge [lɔʒ] *nf* - **1.** [de concierge, de francs-maçons] lodge - **2.** [d'acteur] dressing room.

logement [lɔʒmɑ̃] *nm* - **1.** [hébergement] accommodation *Br*, accommodations *(pl) Am* - **2.** [appartement] flat *Br*, apartment *Am* ; ~ **de fonction** company flat *Br* OU apartment *Am*.

loger [17] [lɔʒe] <> *vi* [habiter] to live. <> *vt* - **1.** [amis, invités] to put up - **2.** [suj : hôtel, maison] to accommodate, to take. **se loger** *vp* - **1.** [trouver un logement] to find accommodation *Br* OU accommodations *Am* - **2.** [se placer - ballon, balle] : **se ~ dans** to lodge in, to stick in.

logeur, euse [lɔʒœr, øz] *nm, f* landlord (*f* landlady).

logiciel [lɔʒisjɛl] *nm* software (*U*) ; ~ **intégré** integrated software.

logique [lɔʒik] <> *nf* logic. <> *adj* logical.

logiquement [lɔʒikmɑ̃] *adv* logically.

logis [lɔʒi] *nm* abode.

logistique [lɔʒistik] *nf* logistics (*pl*).

logo [lɔgo] *nm* logo.

loi [lwa] *nf* [gén] law.

loin [lwɛ̃] *adv* - **1.** [dans l'espace] far ; **plus ~** further - **2.** [dans le temps - passé] a long time ago ; [- futur] a long way off. **au loin** *loc adv* in the distance, far off. **de loin** *loc adv* [depuis une grande distance] from a distance ; **de plus ~** from further away. **loin de** *loc prép* - **1.** [gén] far from ; ~ **de là!** *fig* far from it! - **2.** [dans le temps] : **il n'est pas ~ de 9 h** it's nearly 9 o'clock, it's not far off 9 o'clock.

lointain, e [lwɛ̃tɛ̃, ɛn] *adj* [pays, avenir, parent] distant.

loir [lwar] *nm* dormouse.

loisir [lwazir] *nm* - **1.** [temps libre] leisure - **2.** (*gén pl*) [distractions] leisure activities (*pl*).

londonien, enne [lɔ̃dɔnjɛ̃, ɛn] *adj* London (*avant n*). **Londonien, enne** *nm, f* Londoner.

Londres [lɔ̃dr] *n* London.

long, longue [lɔ̃, lɔ̃g] *adj* - **1.** [gén] long - **2.** [lent] slow ; **être ~ à faire qqch** to take a long time doing sthg. **long** <> *nm* [longueur] : **4 mètres de ~** 4 metres long OU in length ; **de ~ en large** up and down, to and fro ; **en ~ et en large** in great detail ; **(tout) le ~ de** [espace] all along ; **tout au ~ de** [année, carrière] throughout. <> *adv* [beaucoup] : **en savoir ~ sur qqch** to know a

lot about sthg. **à la longue** *loc adv* in the end.

longe [lɔ̃ʒ] *nf* [courroie] halter.

longer [17] [lɔ̃ʒe] *vt* - **1.** [border] to go along OU alongside - **2.** [marcher le long de] to walk along ; [raser] to stay close to, to hug.

longévité [lɔ̃ʒevite] *nf* longevity.

longiligne [lɔ̃ʒiliɲ] *adj* long-limbed.

longitude [lɔ̃ʒityd] *nf* longitude.

longtemps [lɔ̃tɑ̃] *adv* (for) a long time ; **depuis ~** (for) a long time ; **il y a ~ que ...** it's been a long time since ... ; **il y a ~ qu'il est là** he's been here a long time ; **mettre ~ à faire qqch** to take a long time to do sthg.

longue ▷ **long**.

longuement [lɔ̃gmɑ̃] *adv* - **1.** [longtemps] for a long time - **2.** [en détail] at length.

longueur [lɔ̃gœr] *nf* length ; **faire 5 mètres de ~** to be 5 metres long ; **disposer qqch en ~** to put sthg lengthways ; **à ~ de journée/temps** the entire day/time ; **à ~ d'année** all year long ; **~ d'onde** wavelength. **longueurs** *nfpl* [de film, de livre] boring parts.

longue-vue [lɔ̃gvy] *nf* telescope.

look [luk] *nm* look ; **avoir un ~** to have a style.

looping [lupiŋ] *nm* loop the loop.

lopin [lɔpɛ̃] *nm* : ~ **(de terre)** patch OU plot of land.

loquace [lɔkas] *adj* loquacious.

loque [lɔk] *nf* - **1.** [lambeau] rag - **2.** *fig* [personne] wreck.

loquet [lɔkɛ] *nm* latch.

lorgner [3] [lɔrɲe] *vt fam* - **1.** [observer] to eye - **2.** [guigner] to have one's eye on.

lors [lɔr] *adv* : **depuis ~** since that time ; **~ de** at the time of.

lorsque [lɔrsk(ə)] *conj* when.

losange [lɔzɑ̃ʒ] *nm* lozenge.

lot [lo] *nm* - **1.** [part] share ; [de terre] plot - **2.** [stock] batch - **3.** [prix] prize - **4.** *fig* [destin] fate, lot.

loterie [lɔtri] *nf* lottery.

loti, e [lɔti] *adj* : **être bien/mal ~** to be well/badly off.

lotion [lɔsjɔ̃] *nf* lotion.

lotir [32] [lɔtir] *vt* to divide up.

lotissement [lɔtismɑ̃] *nm* [terrain] plot.

loto [lɔto] *nm* - **1.** [jeu de société] lotto - **2.** [loterie] *popular national lottery*.

lotte [lɔt] *nf* monkfish.

lotus [lɔtys] *nm* lotus.

louange [lwɑ̃ʒ] *nf* praise.

louche[1] [luʃ] *nf* ladle.

louche² [luʃ] *adj fam* [personne, histoire] suspicious.

loucher [3] [luʃe] *vi* - **1.** [être atteint de strabisme] to squint - **2.** *fam fig* [lorgner] : **~ sur** to have one's eye on.

louer [6] [lwe] *vt* - **1.** [glorifier] to praise - **2.** [donner en location] to rent (out) ; **à -** for rent - **3.** [prendre en location] to rent - **4.** [réserver] to book. ◆ **se louer** *vp sout* [se féliciter] : **se ~ de qqch/de faire qqch** to be very pleased with sthg/about doing sthg.

loufoque [lufɔk] *fam adj* nuts, crazy.

loup [lu] *nm* - **1.** [carnassier] wolf - **2.** [poisson] bass - **3.** [masque] mask.

loupe [lup] *nf* [optique] magnifying glass.

louper [3] [lupe] *vt fam* [travail] to make a mess of ; [train] to miss.

loup-garou [lugaru] (*pl* **loups-garous**) *nm* werewolf.

lourd, e [lur, lurd] *adj* - **1.** [gén] heavy ; **~ de** *fig* full of - **2.** [tâche] difficult ; [faute] serious - **3.** [maladroit] clumsy, heavy-handed - **4.** MÉTÉOR close. ◆ **lourd** *adv* : **peser ~** to be heavy, to weigh a lot ; **il n'en fait pas ~** *fam* he doesn't do much.

loutre [lutr] *nf* otter.

louve [luv] *nf* she-wolf.

louveteau, x [luvto] *nm* - **1.** ZOOL wolf cub - **2.** [scout] cub.

louvoyer [13] [luvwaje] *vi* - **1.** NAVIG to tack - **2.** *fig* [tergiverser] to beat about the bush.

Louvre [luvr] *n* : **le ~** the Louvre (museum).

lover [3] [lɔve] ◆ **se lover** *vp* [serpent] to coil up.

loyal, e, aux [lwajal, o] *adj* - **1.** [fidèle] loyal - **2.** [honnête] fair.

loyauté [lwajote] *nf* - **1.** [fidélité] loyalty - **2.** [honnêteté] fairness.

loyer [lwaje] *nm* rent.

LP (*abr de* **lycée professionnel**) *nm* secondary school for vocational training.

lu, e [ly] *pp* ▷ **lire¹**.

lubie [lybi] *nf fam* whim.

lubrifier [9] [lybrifje] *vt* to lubricate.

lubrique [lybrik] *adj* lewd.

lucarne [lykarn] *nf* - **1.** [fenêtre] skylight - **2.** FOOTBALL top corner of the net.

lucide [lysid] *adj* lucid.

lucidité [lysidite] *nf* lucidity.

lucratif, ive [lykratif, iv] *adj* lucrative.

ludique [lydik] *adj* play (*avant n*).

ludo-éducatif [lydoedykatif] *nm* edutainment.

ludothèque [lydɔtɛk] *nf* toy library.

lueur [lɥœr] *nf* - **1.** [de bougie, d'étoile]

light ; **à la ~ de** by the light of - **2.** *fig* [de colère] gleam ; [de raison] spark ; **~ d'espoir** glimmer of hope.

luge [lyʒ] *nf* toboggan.

lugubre [lygybr] *adj* lugubrious.

lui¹ [lɥi] *pp inv* ▷ **luire**.

lui² [lɥi] *pron pers* - **1.** [complément d'objet indirect - homme] (to) him ; [- femme] (to) her ; [- animal, chose] (to) it ; **je ~ ai parlé** I've spoken to him/to her ; **il ~ a serré la main** he shook his/her hand - **2.** [sujet, en renforcement de "il"] he - **3.** [objet, après préposition, comparatif - personne] him ; [- animal, chose] it ; **sans ~** without him ; **je vais chez ~** I'm going to his place ; **elle est plus jeune que ~** she's younger than him ou than he is - **4.** [remplaçant 'soi' en fonction de pronom réfléchi - personne] himself ; [- animal, chose] itself ; **il est content de ~** he's pleased with himself. ◆ **lui-même** *pron pers* [personne] himself ; [animal, chose] itself.

luire [97] [lɥir] *vi* [soleil, métal] to shine ; *fig* [espoir] to glow, to glimmer.

luisant, e [lɥizɑ̃, ɑ̃t] *adj* gleaming.

lumière [lymjɛr] *nf* [éclairage] *fig* light.

lumineux, euse [lyminø, øz] *adj* - **1.** [couleur, cadran] luminous - **2.** *fig* [visage] radiant ; [idée] brilliant - **3.** [explication] clear.

luminosité [lyminozite] *nf* - **1.** [du regard, ciel] radiance - **2.** SCIENCE luminosity.

lump [lœ̃p] *nm* : **œufs de ~** lumpfish roe.

lunaire [lynɛr] *adj* - **1.** ASTRON lunar - **2.** *fig* [visage] moon (*avant n*) ; [paysage] lunar.

lunatique [lynatik] *adj* temperamental.

lunch [lœ̃ʃ] *nm* buffet lunch.

lundi [lœ̃di] *nm* Monday.

lune [lyn] *nf* ASTRON moon ; **pleine ~** full moon ; **~ de miel** *fig* honeymoon.

lunette [lynɛt] *nf* ASTRON telescope. ◆ **lunettes** *nfpl* glasses ; **~s de soleil** sunglasses.

lurette [lyrɛt] *nf* : **il y a belle ~ que ...** *fam* it's been ages since ...

luron, onne [lyrɔ̃, ɔn] *nm, f fam* : **un joyeux ~** a bit of a lad.

lustre [lystr] *nm* - **1.** [luminaire] chandelier - **2.** [éclat] sheen, shine ; *fig* reputation.

lustrer [3] [lystre] *vt* - **1.** [faire briller] to make shine - **2.** [user] to wear.

luth [lyt] *nm* lute.

lutin, e [lytɛ̃, in] *adj* mischievous. ◆ **lutin** *nm* imp.

lutte [lyt] *nf* - **1.** [combat] fight, struggle ; **la ~ des classes** the class struggle - **2.** SPORT wrestling.

lutter [3] [lyte] *vi* to fight, to struggle ; ~ **contre** to fight (against).

lutteur, euse [lytœr, øz] *nm, f* SPORT wrestler ; *fig* fighter.

luxation [lyksasjɔ̃] *nf* dislocation.

luxe [lyks] *nm* luxury ; **de ~** luxury.

Luxembourg [lyksɑ̃bur] *nm* [pays] : **le ~** Luxembourg.

luxueux, euse [lyksɥø, øz] *adj* luxurious.

luxure [lyksyr] *nf* lust.

luzerne [lyzɛrn] *nf* lucerne, alfalfa.

lycée [lise] *nm* ≃ secondary school *Br*, ≃ high school *Am* ; **~ technique/ professionnel** ≃ technical/training college.

lycéen, enne [liseɛ̃, ɛn] *nm, f* secondary school pupil *Br*, high school pupil *Am*.

lymphatique [lɛ̃fatik] *adj* **- 1.** MÉD lymphatic **- 2.** *fig* [apathique] sluggish.

lyncher [3] [lɛ̃ʃe] *vt* to lynch.

lynx [lɛ̃ks] *nm* lynx.

Lyon [ljɔ̃] *n* Lyons.

lyre [lir] *nf* lyre.

lyrique [lirik] *adj* [poésie] *fig* lyrical ; [drame, chanteur, poète] lyric.

lys = lis.

m, M [ɛm] <> *nm inv* m, M. <> (*abr de* **mètre**) m. ◆ **M - 1.** (*abr de* **Monsieur**) Mr **- 2.** (*abr de* **million**) M.

m' ▷ me.

ma ▷ mon.

macabre [makabr] *adj* macabre.

macadam [makadam] *nm* [revêtement] macadam ; [route] road.

macaron [makarɔ̃] *nm* **- 1.** [pâtisserie] macaroon **- 2.** [autocollant] sticker.

macaronis [makarɔni] *nmpl* CULIN macaroni *(U)*.

macédoine [masedwan] *nf* CULIN : **~ de fruits** fruit salad.

macérer [18] [masere] <> *vt* to steep. <> *vi* **- 1.** [mariner] to steep ; **faire ~** to steep **- 2.** *fig & péj* [personne] to wallow.

mâche [maʃ] *nf* lamb's lettuce.

mâcher [3] [maʃe] *vt* [mastiquer] to chew.

machiavélique [makjavelik] *adj* Machiavellian.

machin [maʃɛ̃] *nm fam* [chose] thing, thingumajig.

Machin, e [maʃɛ̃, in] *nm, f fam* what's his name (*f* what's her name).

machinal, e, aux [maʃinal, o] *adj* mechanical.

machination [maʃinasjɔ̃] *nf* machination.

machine [maʃin] *nf* **- 1.** TECHNOL machine ; **~ à coudre** sewing machine ; **~ à écrire** typewriter ; **~ à laver** washing machine **- 2.** [organisation] machinery *(U)* **- 3.** NAVIG engine.

machine-outil [maʃinuti] *nf* machine tool.

machiniste [maʃinist] *nm* **- 1.** CIN & THÉÂTRE scene shifter **- 2.** TRANSPORT driver.

macho [matʃo] *péj nm* macho man.

mâchoire [maʃwar] *nf* jaw.

mâchonner [3] [maʃɔne] *vt* [mâcher, mordiller] to chew.

maçon [masɔ̃] *nm* mason.

maçonnerie [masɔnri] *nf* [travaux] building ; [construction] masonry ; [francmaçonnerie] freemasonry.

macramé [makrame] *nm* macramé.

macrobiotique [makrɔbjɔtik] *nf* macrobiotics *(U)*.

maculer [3] [makyle] *vt* to stain.

madame [madam] (*pl* **mesdames** [medam]) *nf* [titre] : **~ X** Mrs X ; **bonjour ~!** good morning! ; [dans hôtel, restaurant] good morning, madam! ; **bonjour mesdames!** good morning (ladies)! ; **Madame le Ministre n'est pas là** the Minister is out.

mademoiselle [madmwazɛl] (*pl* **mesdemoiselles** [medmwazɛl]) *nf* [titre] : **~ X** Miss X ; **bonjour ~!** good morning! ; [à l'école, dans hôtel] good morning, miss! ; **bonjour mesdemoiselles!** good morning (ladies)!

madone [madɔn] *nf* ART & RELIG Madonna.

Madrid [madrid] *n* Madrid.

madrier [madrije] *nm* beam.

maf(f)ia [mafja] *nf* Mafia.

magasin [magazɛ̃] *nm* **- 1.** [boutique] shop *Br*, store *Am* ; **grand ~** department store ; **faire les ~s** *fig* to go round the shops *Br* ou stores *Am* **- 2.** [d'arme, d'appareil photo] magazine.

magazine [magazin] *nm* magazine.

mage [maʒ] *nm* : **les Rois ~s** the Three Wise Men.

Maghreb [magrɛb] *nm* : **le ~** the Maghreb.

maghrébin, e [magrebɛ̃, in] *adj* North African. ◆ **Maghrébin, e** *nm, f* North African.

magicien, enne [maʒisjɛ̃, ɛn] *nm, f* magician.

magie [maʒi] *nf* magic.

magique [maʒik] *adj* - **1.** [occulte] magic - **2.** [merveilleux] magical.

magistral, e, aux [maʒistral, o] *adj* - **1.** [œuvre, habileté] masterly - **2.** [dispute, fessée] enormous - **3.** [attitude, ton] authoritative.

magistrat [maʒistra] *nm* magistrate.

magistrature [maʒistratyr] *nf* magistracy, magistrature.

magma [magma] *nm* - **1.** GÉOL magma - **2.** *fig* [mélange] muddle.

magnanime [maɲanim] *adj* magnanimous.

magnat [maɲa] *nm* magnate, tycoon.

magnésium [maɲezjɔm] *nm* magnesium.

magnétique [maɲetik] *adj* magnetic.

magnétisme [maɲetism] *nm* PHYS [fascination] magnetism.

magnéto(phone) [maɲeto(fɔn)] *nm* tape recorder.

magnétoscope [maɲetɔskɔp] *nm* videorecorder.

magnificence [maɲifisɑ̃s] *nf* magnificence.

magnifique [maɲifik] *adj* magnificent.

magnum [magnɔm] *nm* magnum.

magot [mago] *nm fam* tidy sum, packet.

mai [mɛ] *nm* May ; **le premier ~** May Day.

maigre [mɛgr] *adj* - **1.** [tres mince] thin **2.** [aliment] low-fat ; [viande] lean - **3.** [peu important] meagre *Br*, meager *Am* ; [végétation] sparse.

maigreur [mɛgrœr] *nf* thinness.

maigrir [32] [megrir] *vi* to lose weight.

mailing [melin] *nm* mailing, mailshot.

maille [maj] *nf* - **1.** [de tricot] stitch - **2.** [de filet] mesh.

maillet [majɛ] *nm* mallet.

maillon [majɔ̃] *nm* link.

maillot [majo] *nm* [de sport] shirt, jersey ; **~ de bain** swimsuit ; **~ de corps** vest *Br*, undershirt *Am*.

main [mɛ̃] *nf* hand ; **à la ~** by hand ; **attaque à ~ armée** armed attack ; **donner la ~ à qqn** to take sb's hand ; **haut les ~s!** hands up!

main-d'œuvre [mɛ̃dœvr] *nf* labour *Br*, labor *Am*, workforce.

mainmise [mɛ̃miz] *nf* seizure.

maint, e [mɛ̃, mɛ̃t] *adj littéraire* many a ; **~s** many ; **~es fois** time and time again.

maintenance [mɛ̃tnɑ̃s] *nf* maintenance.

maintenant [mɛ̃tnɑ̃] *adv* now. ◆ **maintenant que** *loc prép* now that.

maintenir [40] [mɛ̃tnir] *vt* - **1.** [soutenir] to support ; **~ qqn à distance** to keep sb away - **2.** [garder, conserver] to maintain - **3.** [affirmer] : **~ que** to maintain (that). ◆ **se maintenir** *vp* - **1.** [durer] to last - **2.** [rester] to remain.

maintenu, e [mɛ̃tny] *pp* ▷ **maintenir.**

maintien [mɛ̃tjɛ̃] *nm* - **1.** [conservation] maintenance ; [de tradition] upholding - **2.** [tenue] posture.

maire [mɛr] *nm* mayor.

mairie [meri] *nf* - **1.** [bâtiment] town hall *Br*, city hall *Am* - **2.** [administration] town council *Br*, city hall *Am*.

mais [mɛ] ◇ *conj* but ; **~ non!** of course not! ; **~ alors, tu l'as vu ou non?** so did you see him or not? ; **il a pleuré, ~ pleuré!** he cried, and how! ; **non ~ ça ne va pas!** that's just not on! ◇ *adv* but ; **vous êtes prêts? - ~ bien sûr!** are you ready? - but of course! ◇ *nm* : **il y a un ~** there's a hitch ou a snag ; **il n'y a pas de ~** (there are) no buts.

maïs [mais] *nm* maize *Br*, corn *Am*.

maison [mɛzɔ̃] *nf* - **1.** [habitation, lignée & ASTROL] house ; **~ individuelle** detached house - **2.** [foyer] home ; [famille] family ; **à la ~** [au domicile] at home - **3.** COMM company - **4.** [institut] : **~ d'arrêt** prison ; **~ de la culture** arts centre *Br* ou center *Am* ; **~ de retraite** old people's home - **5.** *(en apposition)* [artisanal] homemade ; [dans restaurant - vin] house *(avant n).*

Maison-Blanche [mɛzɔ̃blɑ̃ʃ] *nf* : **la ~** the White House.

maisonnée [mɛzɔne] *nf* household.

maisonnette [mɛzɔnɛt] *nf* small house.

maître, esse [mɛtr, mɛtrɛs] *nm, f* - **1.** [professeur] teacher ; **~ chanteur** blackmailer ; **~ de conférences** UNIV ≃ senior lecturer ; **~ d'école** schoolteacher ; **~ nageur** swimming instructor - **2.** [modèle, artiste] *fig* master - **3.** [dirigeant] ruler ; [d'animal] master (*f* mistress) ; **~ d'hôtel** head waiter ; **être ~ de soi** to be in control of oneself, to have self-control - **4.** *(en apposition)* [principal] main, principal. ◆ **Maître** *nm form of address for lawyers.* ◆ **maîtresse** *nf* [amie] mistress.

maître-assistant, e [mɛtrasistɑ̃, ɑ̃t] *nm, f* ≃ lecturer *Br*, ≃ assistant professor *Am*.

maîtresse ▷ **maître.**

maîtrise [mɛtriz] *nf* - **1.** [sang-froid, domination] control - **2.** [connaissance] mastery, command ; [habileté] skill - **3.** UNIV ≃ master's degree.

maîtriser [3] [metrize] *vt* - **1.** [animal, forcené] to subdue - **2.** [émotion, réaction] to control, to master - **3.** [incendie] to bring under control. ◆ **se maîtriser** *vp* to control o.s.

majesté [maʒɛste] *nf* majesty. ◆ **Majesté** *nf* : Sa Majesté His/Her Majesty.

majestueux, euse [maʒɛstɥø, øz] *adj* majestic.

majeur, e [maʒœr] *adj* - **1.** [gén] major - **2.** [personne] of age. ◆ **majeur** *nm* middle finger.

major [maʒɔr] *nm* - **1.** MIL ≃ adjudant - **2.** SCOL : ~ **(de promotion)** first in ou top of one's year group.

majordome [maʒɔrdɔm] *nm* majordomo.

majorer [3] [maʒɔre] *vt* to increase.

majorette [maʒɔrɛt] *nf* majorette.

majoritaire [maʒɔritɛr] *adj* majority *(avant n)* ; **être ~** to be in the majority.

majorité [maʒɔrite] *nf* majority ; **en (grande) ~** in the majority ; **~ absolue/relative** POLIT absolute/relative majority.

majuscule [maʒyskyl] ◇ *nf* capital (letter). ◇ *adj* capital *(avant n)*.

mal, maux [mal, mo] *nm* - **1.** [ce qui est contraire à la morale] evil - **2.** [souffrance physique] pain ; **avoir ~ au bras** to have a sore arm ; **avoir ~ au cœur** to feel sick ; **avoir ~ au dos** to have backache ; **avoir ~ à la gorge** to have a sore throat ; **avoir le ~ de mer** to be seasick ; **avoir ~ aux dents/à la tête** to have toothache/a headache ; **avoir ~ au ventre** to have (a) stomachache ; **faire ~ à qqn** to hurt sb ; **ça fait ~** it hurts ; **se faire ~** to hurt o.s. - **3.** [difficulté] difficulty - **4.** [douleur morale] pain, suffering *(U)* ; **être en ~ de qqch** to long for sthg ; **faire du ~ (à qqn)** to hurt (sb). ◆ **mal** *adv* - **1.** [malade] ill ; **aller ~** not to be well ; **se sentir ~** to feel ill ; **être au plus ~** to be extremely ill - **2.** [respirer] with difficulty - **3.** [informé, se conduire] badly ; **~ prendre qqch** to take sthg badly ; **~ tourner** to go wrong - **4.** *loc* : **pas ~** not bad *(adj)*, not badly *(adv)* ; **pas ~ de** quite a lot of.

malade [malad] ◇ *nmf* invalid, sick person ; **~ mental** mentally ill person. ◇ *adj* - **1.** [souffrant - personne] ill, sick ; [- organe] bad ; **tomber ~** to fall ill ou sick - **2.** *fam* [fou] crazy.

maladie [maladi] *nf* - **1.** MÉD illness ; **~ d'Alzheimer** Alzheimer's disease ; **~ de Creutzfeldt-Jakob** Creutzfeldt-Jakob disease ; **~ de Parkinson** Parkinson's disease ;

~ de la vache folle mad cow disease - **2.** [passion, manie] mania.

maladresse [maladrɛs] *nf* - **1.** [inhabileté] clumsiness - **2.** [bévue] blunder.

maladroit, e [maladrwa, at] *adj* clumsy.

malaise [malɛz] *nm* - **1.** [indisposition] discomfort - **2.** [trouble] unease *(U)*.

malaisé, e [maleze] *adj* difficult.

Malaisie [malɛzi] *nf* : la ~ Malaya.

malappris, e [malapri, iz] *nm, f* lout.

malaria [malarja] *nf* malaria.

malaxer [3] [malakse] *vt* to knead.

malchance [malʃɑ̃s] *nf* bad luck *(U)*.

malchanceux, euse [malʃɑ̃sø, øz] ◇ *adj* unlucky. ◇ *nm, f* unlucky person.

malcommode [malkɔmɔd] *adj* inconvenient ; [meuble] impractical.

mâle [mal] ◇ *adj* - **1.** [enfant, animal, hormone] male - **2.** [voix, assurance] manly - **3.** ÉLECTR male. ◇ *nm* male.

malédiction [malediksjɔ̃] *nf* curse.

maléfique [malefik] *adj* sout evil.

malencontreux, euse [malɑ̃kɔ̃trø, øz] *adj* [hasard, rencontre] unfortunate.

malentendant, e [malɑ̃tɑ̃dɑ̃, ɑ̃t] *nm, f* person who is hard of hearing.

malentendu [malɑ̃tɑ̃dy] *nm* misunderstanding.

malfaçon [malfasɔ̃] *nf* defect.

malfaiteur [malfɛtœr] *nm* criminal.

malfamé, e, mal famé, e [malfame] *adj* disreputable.

malformation [malfɔrmasjɔ̃] *nf* malformation.

malfrat [malfra] *nm fam* crook.

malgré [malgre] *prép* in spite of ; **~ tout** [quoi qu'il arrive] in spite of everything ; [pourtant] even so, yet. ◆ **malgré que** *loc conj* (+ *subjonctif*) *fam* although, in spite of the fact that.

malhabile [malabil] *adj* clumsy.

malheur [malœr] *nm* misfortune ; **par ~** unfortunately ; **porter ~ à qqn** to bring sb bad luck.

malheureusement [malœrøzmɑ̃] *adv* unfortunately.

malheureux, euse [malœrø, øz] ◇ *adj* - **1.** [triste] unhappy - **2.** [désastreux, regrettable] unfortunate - **3.** [malchanceux] unlucky - **4.** *(avant n)* [sans valeur] pathetic, miserable. ◇ *nm, f* - **1.** [infortuné] poor soul - **2.** [indigent] poor person.

malhonnête [malɔnɛt] ◇ *nmf* dishonest person. ◇ *adj* - **1.** [personne, affaire] dishonest - **2.** *hum* [proposition, propos] indecent.

malhonnêteté [malɔnɛtte] *nf* - **1.** [de personne] dishonesty - **2.** [action] dishonest action.

Mali [mali] *nm* : le ~ Mali.

malice [malis] *nf* mischief.

malicieux, euse [malisjø, øz] *adj* mischievous.

malin, igne [malẽ, iɲ] <> *adj* - **1.** [rusé] crafty, cunning ; [regard, sourire] knowing - **2.** [méchant] malicious, spiteful - **3.** MÉD malignant. <> *nm, f* cunning ou crafty person.

malingre [malẽgr] *adj* sickly.

malle [mal] *nf* [coffre] trunk ; [de voiture] boot *Br*, trunk *Am*.

malléable [maleabl] *adj* malleable.

mallette [malɛt] *nf* briefcase.

mal-logé, e [mallɔʒe] (*mpl* mal-logés, *fpl* mal-logées) *nm, f person living in poor accommodation.*

malmener [19] [malmǝne] *vt* [brutaliser] to handle roughly, to ill-treat.

malnutrition [malnytrisjɔ̃] *nf* malnutrition.

malodorant, e [malɔdɔrɑ̃, ɑ̃t] *adj* smelly.

malotru, e [malɔtry] *nm, f lout.*

malpoli, e [malpɔli] *nm, f* rude person.

malpropre [malprɔpr] *adj* [sale] dirty.

malsain, e [malsẽ, ɛn] *adj* unhealthy.

malt [malt] *nm* - **1.** [céréale] malt - **2.** [whisky] malt (whisky).

Malte [malt] *n* Malta.

maltraiter [4] [maltrete] *vt* to ill-treat ; [en paroles] to attack, to run down.

malus [malys] *nm increase in car insurance charges, due to loss of no-claims bonus.*

malveillant, e [malvɛjɑ̃, ɑ̃t] *adj* spiteful.

malversation [malversasjɔ̃] *nf* embezzlement.

malvoyant, e [malvwajɑ̃, ɑ̃t] *nm, f person who is partially sighted.*

maman [mamɑ̃] *nf* mummy.

mamelle [mamɛl] *nf* teat ; [de vache] udder.

mamelon [mamlɔ̃] *nm* [du sein] nipple.

mamie, mamy [mami] *nf* granny, grandma.

mammifère [mamifɛr] *nm* mammal.

mammouth [mamut] *nm* mammoth.

mamy = mamie.

management [manadʒmɛnt] *nm* management.

manager [manadʒɛr] *nm* manager.

manche [mɑ̃ʃ] <> *nf* - **1.** [de vêtement] sleeve ; ~s courtes/longues short/long sleeves - **2.** [de jeu] round, game ; TENNIS set. <> *nm* - **1.** [d'outil] handle ; ~ à balai broomstick ; [d'avion] joystick - **2.** MUS neck.

Manche [mɑ̃ʃ] *nf* [mer] : la ~ the English Channel.

manchette [mɑ̃ʃɛt] *nf* - **1.** [de chemise] cuff - **2.** [de journal] headline - **3.** [coup] forearm blow.

manchon [mɑ̃ʃɔ̃] *nm* - **1.** [en fourrure] muff - **2.** TECHNOL casing, sleeve.

manchot, ote [mɑ̃ʃo, ɔt] <> *adj* one-armed. <> *nm, f* one-armed person. ◆ **manchot** *nm* penguin.

mandarine [mɑ̃darin] *nf* mandarin (orange).

mandat [mɑ̃da] *nm* - **1.** [pouvoir, fonction] mandate - **2.** JUR warrant ; ~ de perquisition search warrant - **3.** [titre postal] money order ; ~ postal postal order *Br*, money order *Am*.

mandataire [mɑ̃datɛr] *nmf* proxy, representative.

mandibule [mɑ̃dibyl] *nf* mandible.

mandoline [mɑ̃dɔlin] *nf* mandolin.

manège [manɛʒ] *nm* - **1.** [attraction] merry-go round, roundabout *Br*, carousel *Am* - **2.** [de chevaux - lieu] riding school - **3.** [manœuvre] scheme, game.

manette [manɛt] *nf* lever.

manganèse [mɑ̃ganɛz] *nm* manganese.

mangeable [mɑ̃ʒabl] *adj* edible.

mangeoire [mɑ̃ʒwar] *nf* manger.

manger [17] [mɑ̃ʒe] <> *vt* - **1.** [nourriture] to eat - **2.** [fortune] to get through, to squander. <> *vi* to eat.

mangue [mɑ̃g] *nf* mango.

maniable [manjabl] *adj* [instrument] manageable.

maniaque [manjak] <> *nmf* - **1.** [méticuleux] fusspot - **2.** [fou] maniac. <> *adj* - **1.** [méticuleux] fussy - **2.** [fou] maniacal.

manie [mani] *nf* - **1.** [habitude] funny habit ; avoir la ~ de qqch/de faire qqch to have a mania for sthg/for doing sthg - **2.** [obsession] mania.

maniement [manimɑ̃] *nm* handling.

manier [9] [manje] *vt* [manipuler, utiliser] to handle ; *fig* [ironie, mots] to handle skilfully.

manière [manjɛr] *nf* [méthode] manner, way ; de toute ~ at any rate ; d'une ~ générale generally speaking. ◆ **manières** *nfpl* manners. ◆ **de manière à** *loc conj* (in order) to ; de ~ à ce que (+ *subjonctif*) so that.

◆ **de manière que** *loc conj (+ subjonctif)* in such a way that.

maniéré, e [manjere] *adj* affected.

manif [manif] *nf fam* demo.

manifestant, e [manifɛstɑ̃, ɑ̃t] *nm, f* demonstrator.

manifestation [manifɛstasjɔ̃] *nf* - **1.** [témoignage] expression - **2.** [mouvement collectif] demonstration - **3.** [apparition - de maladie] appearance.

manifester [3] [manifɛste] ◇ *vt* to show, to express. ◇ *vi* to demonstrate.
◆ **se manifester** *vp* - **1.** [apparaître] to show ou manifest itself - **2.** [se montrer] to turn up, to appear.

manigancer [16] [manigɑ̃se] *vt fam* to plot.

manioc [manjɔk] *nm* manioc.

manipuler [3] [manipyle] *vt* - **1.** [colis, appareil] to handle - **2.** [statistiques, résultats] to falsify, to rig - **3.** *péj* [personne] to manipulate.

manivelle [manivɛl] *nf* crank.

manne [man] *nf* RELIG manna ; *fig & littéraire* godsend.

mannequin [mankɛ̃] *nm* - **1.** [forme humaine] model, dummy - **2.** [personne] model, mannequin.

manœuvre [manœvr] ◇ *nf* - **1.** [d'appareil, de véhicule] driving, handling - **2.** MIL manoeuvre *Br*, maneuver *Am*, exercise - **3.** [machination] ploy, scheme. ◇ *nm* labourer *Br*, laborer *Am*.

manœuvrer [5] [manœvre] ◇ *vi* to manoeuvre *Br*, to maneuver *Am*. ◇ *vt* - **1.** [faire fonctionner] to operate, to work ; [voiture] to manoeuvre *Br*, to maneuver *Am* - **2.** [influencer] to manipulate.

manoir [manwar] *nm* manor, country house.

manquant, e [mɑ̃kɑ̃, ɑ̃t] *adj* missing.

manque [mɑ̃k] *nm* - **1.** [pénurie] lack, shortage ; **par ~ de** for want of - **2.** [de toxicomane] withdrawal symptoms *(pl)* - **3.** [lacune] gap.

manqué, e [mɑ̃ke] *adj* [raté] failed ; [rendez-vous] missed.

manquer [3] [mɑ̃ke] ◇ *vi* - **1.** [faire défaut] to be lacking, to be missing ; **l'argent/le temps me manque** I don't have enough money/time ; **tu me manques** I miss you - **2.** [être absent] : **~ (à)** to be absent (from), to be missing (from) - **3.** [échouer] to fail - **4.** [ne pas avoir assez] : **~ de qqch** to lack sthg, to be short of sthg - **5.** [faillir] : **il a manqué de se noyer** he nearly ou almost drowned ; **ne manquez pas de lui dire** don't forget to tell him ; **je n'y manquerai**

pas I certainly will, I'll definitely do it - **6.** [ne pas respecter] : **~ à** [devoir] to fail in ; **~ à sa parole** to break one's word. ◇ *vt* - **1.** [gén] to miss - **2.** [échouer à] to bungle, to botch. ◇ *v impers* : **il manque quelqu'un** somebody is missing ; **il me manque 3 euros** I'm 3 euros short.

mansarde [mɑ̃sard] *nf* attic.

mansardé, e [mɑ̃sarde] *adj* attic *(avant n)*.

mansuétude [mɑ̃sɥetyd] *nf littéraire* indulgence.

mante [mɑ̃t] *nf* HIST mantle. ◆ **mante religieuse** *nf* praying mantis.

manteau, x [mɑ̃to] *nm* [vêtement] coat.

manucure [manykyr] *nmf* manicurist.

manuel, elle [manɥɛl] *adj* manual.
◆ **manuel** *nm* manual.

manufacture [manyfaktyr] *nf* [fabrique] factory.

manuscrit, e [manyskri, it] *adj* handwritten. ◆ **manuscrit** *nm* manuscript.

manutention [manytɑ̃sjɔ̃] *nf* handling.

manutentionnaire [manytɑ̃sjɔnɛr] *nmf* packer.

mappemonde [mapmɔ̃d] *nf* - **1.** [carte] map of the world - **2.** [sphère] globe.

maquereau, elle, x [makro, ɛl, o] *nm, f fam* pimp (*f* madam). ◆ **maquereau** *nm* mackerel.

maquette [makɛt] *nf* - **1.** [ébauche] paste-up - **2.** [modèle réduit] model.

maquillage [makijaʒ] *nm* [action, produits] make-up.

maquiller [3] [makije] *vt* - **1.** [farder] to make up - **2.** [fausser - gén] to disguise ; [- passeport] to falsify ; [- chiffres] to doctor. ◆ **se maquiller** *vp* to make up, to put on one's make-up.

maquis [maki] *nm* - **1.** [végétation] scrub, brush - **2.** HIST Maquis.

marabout [marabu] *nm* - **1.** ZOOL marabou - **2.** [guérisseur] marabout.

maraîcher, ère [mareʃe, ɛr] ◇ *adj* market garden *(avant n) Br*, truck farming *(avant n) Am*. ◇ *nm, f* market gardener *Br*, truck farmer *Am*.

marais [marɛ] *nm* [marécage] marsh, swamp ; **~ salant** saltpan.

marasme [marasm] *nm* [récession] stagnation.

marathon [maratɔ̃] *nm* marathon.

marâtre [maratr] *nf vieilli* - **1.** [mauvaise mère] bad mother - **2.** [belle-mère] stepmother.

maraude [marod] *nf*, **maraudage** [marodaʒ] *nm* pilfering.

marbre [marbr] *nm* [roche, objet] marble.

marc [mar] *nm* - **1.** [eau-de-vie] *spirit distilled from grape residue* - **2.** [de fruits] residue ; [de thé] leaves ; ~ **de café** grounds *(pl)*.

marcassin [markasɛ̃] *nm* young wild boar.

marchand, e [marʃɑ̃, ɑ̃d] <> *adj* [valeur] market *(avant n)* ; [prix] trade *(avant n)*. <> *nm, f* [commerçant] merchant ; [détaillant] shopkeeper *Br*, storekeeper *Am* ; ~ **de journaux** newsagent *Br*, newsdealer *Am*.

marchander [3] [marʃɑ̃de] <> *vt* - **1.** [prix] to haggle over - **2.** [appui] to begrudge. <> *vi* to bargain, to haggle.

marchandise [marʃɑ̃diz] *nf* merchandise (U), goods *(pl)*.

marche [marʃ] *nf* - **1.** [d'escalier] step - **2.** [activité, sport] walking ; ~ **à pied** walking ; ~ **à suivre** *fig* correct procedure - **3.** [promenade] walk - **4.** MUS march - **5.** [déplacement - du temps, d'astre] course ; **assis dans le sens de la ~** [en train] sitting facing the engine ; **en ~ arrière** in reverse ; **faire ~ arrière** to reverse ; *fig* to backpedal, to backtrack - **6.** [fonctionnement] running, working ; **en ~** running ; **se mettre en ~** to start (up).

marché [marʃe] *nm* - **1.** [gén] market ; **faire son ~** to go shopping, to do one's shopping ; **le ~ du travail** the labour *Br* ou labor *Am* market ; ~ **noir** black market ; ~ **aux puces** flea market - **2.** [contrat] bargain, deal ; **(à) bon ~** cheap. <> **Marché commun** *nm* : **le Marché commun** the Common Market.

marchepied [marʃəpje] *nm* [de train] step ; [escabeau] steps *(pl) Br*, stepladder ; *fig* stepping-stone.

marcher [3] [marʃe] *vi* - **1.** [aller à pied] to walk - **2.** [poser le pied] to step - **3.** [fonctionner, tourner] to work ; **son affaire marche bien** his business is doing well - **4.** *fam* [accepter] to agree - **5.** *loc* : **faire ~ qqn** *fam* to take sb for a ride.

mardi [mardi] *nm* Tuesday ; ~ **gras** Shrove Tuesday ; *voir aussi* **samedi**.

mare [mar] *nf* pool.

marécage [mareka3] *nm* marsh, bog.

marécageux, euse [mareka3ø, øz] *adj* [terrain] marshy, boggy.

maréchal, aux [mareʃal, o] *nm* marshal.

marée [mare] *nf* - **1.** [de la mer] tide ; **(à) ~ haute/basse** (at) high/low tide - **2.** *fig* [de personnes] wave, surge. <> **marée noire** *nf* oil slick.

marelle [marɛl] *nf* hopscotch.

margarine [margarin] *nf* margarine.

marge [mar3] *nf* - **1.** [espace] margin ; **vivre en ~ de la société** *fig* to live on the fringes of society - **2.** [latitude] leeway ; ~ **d'erreur** margin of error - **3.** COMM margin ; ~ **commerciale** gross margin.

margelle [mar3ɛl] *nf* coping.

marginal, e, aux [mar3inal, o] <> *adj* - **1.** [gén] marginal - **2.** [groupe] dropout *(avant n)*. <> *nm, f* dropout.

marguerite [margərit] *nf* - **1.** BOT daisy - **2.** [d'imprimante] daisy wheel.

mari [mari] *nm* husband.

mariage [marja3] *nm* - **1.** [union, institution] marriage - **2.** [cérémonie] wedding ; ~ **civil/religieux** civil/church wedding - **3.** *fig* [de choses] blend.

Marianne [marjan] *n personification of the French Republic.*

marié, e [marje] <> *adj* married. <> *nm, f* groom, bridegroom *(f* bride).

marier [9] [marje] *vt* - **1.** [personne] to marry - **2.** *fig* [couleurs] to blend. <> **se marier** *vp* - **1.** [personnes] to get married ; **se ~ avec qqn** to marry sb - **2.** *fig* [couleurs] to blend.

marihuana [mariɪwana], **marijuana** [mari3yana] *nf* marijuana.

marin, e [marɛ̃, in] *adj* - **1.** [de la mer] sea *(avant n)* ; [faune, biologie] marine - **2.** NAVIG [carte, mille] nautical. <> **marin** *nm* - **1.** [navigateur] seafarer - **2.** [matelot] sailor ; ~ **pêcheur** deep-sea fisherman. <> **marine** <> *nf* - **1.** [navigation] seamanship, navigation - **2.** [navires] navy ; ~ **marchande** merchant navy *Br* ou marine *Am* ; ~ **nationale** navy. <> *nm* - **1.** MIL marine - **2.** [couleur] navy (blue). <> *adj inv* navy.

mariner [3] [marine] <> *vt* to marinate. <> *vi* - **1.** [aliment] to marinate ; **faire ~ qqch** to marinate sthg - **2.** *fam fig* [attendre] to hang around ; **faire ~ qqn** to let sb stew.

marinier [marinje] *nm* bargee *Br*, bargeman *Am*.

marionnette [marjɔnɛt] *nf* puppet.

marital, e, aux [marital, o] *adj* : **autorisation ~e** husband's permission.

maritime [maritim] *adj* [navigation] maritime ; [ville] coastal.

mark [mark] *nm* [monnaie] mark.

marketing [marketiŋ] *nm* marketing ; ~ **téléphonique** telemarketing.

marmaille [marmaj] *nf fam* brood (of kids).

marmelade [marməlad] *nf* stewed fruit.

marmite [marmit] *nf* [casserole] pot.

marmonner [3] [marmɔne] *vt & vi* to mutter, to mumble.

marmot [marmo] *nm fam* kid.

marmotte [marmɔt] *nf* marmot.

Maroc [marɔk] *nm* : le ~ Morocco.

marocain, e [marɔkɛ̃, ɛn] *adj* Moroccan.
➦ **Marocain, e** *nm, f* Moroccan.

maroquinerie [marɔkinri] *nf* [magasin] leather-goods shop *Br* ou store *Am*.

marotte [marɔt] *nf* [dada] craze.

marquant, e [markɑ̃, ɑ̃t] *adj* outstanding.

marque [mark] *nf* - **1.** [signe, trace] mark ; *fig* stamp, mark - **2.** [label, fabricant] make, brand ; **de ~** designer *(avant n)* ; *fig* important ; **~ déposée** registered trademark - **3.** SPORT score ; **à vos ~s, prêts, partez!** on your marks, get set, go!, ready, steady, go! - **4.** [témoignage] sign, token.

marqué, e [marke] *adj* - **1.** [net] marked, pronounced - **2.** [personne, visage] marked.

marquer [3] [marke] ◇ *vt* - **1.** [gén] to mark - **2.** *fam* [écrire] to write down, to note down - **3.** [indiquer, manifester] to show - **4.** [SPORT - but, point] to score ; [- joueur] to mark. ◇ *vi* - **1.** [événement, expérience] to leave its mark - **2.** SPORT to score.

marqueur [markœr] *nm* [crayon] marker (pen).

marquis, e [marki, iz] *nm, f* marquis (*f* marchioness).

marraine [marɛn] *nf* - **1.** [de filleul] godmother - **2.** [de navire] christener.

marrant, e [marɑ̃, ɑ̃t] *adj fam* funny.

marre [mar] *adv* : **en avoir ~ (de)** *fam* to be fed up (with).

marrer [3] [mare] ➦ **se marrer** *vp fam* to split one's sides.

marron, onne [marɔ̃, ɔn] *adj péj* [médecin] quack *(avant n)* ; [avocat] crooked.
➦ **marron** ◇ *nm* - **1.** [fruit] chestnut - **2.** [couleur] brown. ◇ *adj inv* brown.

marronnier [marɔnje] *nm* chestnut tree.

mars [mars] *nm* March ; *voir aussi* **septembre**.

Marseille [marsɛj] *n* Marseilles.

marsouin [marswɛ̃] *nm* porpoise.

marteau, x [marto] ◇ *nm* - **1.** [gén] hammer ; **~ piqueur**, **~ pneumatique** pneumatic drill - **2.** [heurtoir] knocker. ◇ *adj fam* barmy.

marteler [25] [martəle] *vt* - **1.** [pieu] to hammer ; [table, porte] to hammer on, to pound - **2.** [phrase] to rap out.

martial, e, aux [marsjal, o] *adj* martial.

martien, enne [marsjɛ̃, ɛn] *adj & nm, f* Martian.

martinet [martinɛ] *nm* - **1.** ZOOL swift - **2.** [fouet] whip.

martingale [martɛ̃gal] *nf* - **1.** [de vêtement] half-belt - **2.** JEU winning system.

Martini® [martini] *nm* Martini®.

Martinique [martinik] *nf* : **la ~** Martinique.

martyr, e [martir] ◇ *adj* martyred. ◇ *nm, f* martyr. ➦ **martyre** *nm* martyrdom.

martyriser [3] [martirize] *vt* to torment.

marxisme [marksism] *nm* Marxism.

mascarade [maskarad] *nf* [mise en scène] masquerade.

mascotte [maskɔt] *nf* mascot.

masculin, e [maskylɛ̃, in] *adj* [apparence & GRAM] masculine ; [métier, population, sexe] male. ➦ **masculin** *nm* GRAM masculine.

maso [mazo] *fam* ◇ *nm* masochist. ◇ *adj* masochistic.

masochisme [mazɔʃism] *nm* masochism.

masque [mask] *nm* - **1.** [gén] mask ; **~ à gaz** gas mask - **2.** *fig* [façade] front, façade.

masquer [3] [maske] *vt* - **1.** [vérité, crime, problème] to conceal - **2.** [maison, visage] to conceal, to hide.

massacre [masakr] *nm litt & fig* massacre.

massacrer [3] [masakre] *vt* to massacre ; [voiture] to smash up.

massage [masaʒ] *nm* massage.

masse [mas] *nf* - **1.** [de pierre] block ; [d'eau] volume - **2.** [grande quantité] : **une ~ de masses** *(pl)* ou loads *(pl)* of - **3.** PHYS mass - **4.** ÉLECTR earth *Br*, ground *Am* - **5.** [maillet] sledgehammer. ➦ **en masse** *loc adv* [venir] en masse, all together ; *fam* [acheter] in bulk.

masser [3] [mase] *vt* - **1.** [assembler] to assemble - **2.** [frotter] to massage. ➦ **se masser** *vp* - **1.** [s'assembler] to assemble, to gather - **2.** [se frotter] : **se ~ le bras** to massage one's arm.

masseur, euse [masœr, øz] *nm, f* [personne] masseur (*f* masseuse).

massicot [masiko] *nm* guillotine.

massif, ive [masif, iv] *adj* - **1.** [monument, personne, dose] massive - **2.** [or, chêne] solid. ➦ **massif** *nm* - **1.** [de plantes] clump - **2.** [de montagnes] massif.

massue [masy] *nf* club.

mastic [mastik] *nm* mastic, putty.

mastiquer [3] [mastike] *vt* [mâcher] to chew.

masturber [3] [mastyrbe] ➦ **se masturber** *vp* to masturbate.

masure [mazyr] *nf* hovel.

mat, e [mat] *adj* - **1.** [peinture, surface] matt *Br*, matte *Am* - **2.** [peau, personne] dusky - **3.** [bruit, son] dull - **4.** [aux échecs] checkmated. **➤ mat** *nm* checkmate.

mât [ma] *nm* - **1.** NAVIG mast - **2.** [poteau] pole, post.

match [matʃ] (*pl* **matches** ou **matchs**) *nm* match ; **(faire)** ~ **nul** (to) draw ; ~ **aller/ retour** first/second leg.

matelas [matla] *nm inv* [de lit] mattress ; ~ **pneumatique** airbed.

matelot [matlo] *nm* sailor.

mater [3] [mate] *vt* - **1.** [soumettre, neutraliser] to subdue - **2.** *fam* [regarder] to eye up.

matérialiser [3] [materjalize] **➤ se matérialiser** *vp* [aspirations] to be realized.

matérialiste [materjalist] ◇ *nmf* materialist. ◇ *adj* materialistic.

matériau, x [materjo] *nm* material. **➤ matériaux** *nmpl* CONSTR material *(U)*, materials.

matériel, elle [materjɛl] *adj* - **1.** [être, substance] material, physical ; [confort, avantage, aide] material - **2.** [considération] practical. **➤ matériel** *nm* - **1.** [gén] equipment *(U)* - **2.** INFORM hardware *(U)*.

maternel, elle [matɛrnɛl] *adj* maternal ; [langue] mother *(avant n)*. **➤ maternelle** *nf* nursery school.

maternité [maternite] *nf* - **1.** [qualité] maternity, motherhood - **2.** [hôpital] maternity hospital.

mathématicien, enne [matematisjɛ̃, ɛn] *nm, f* mathematician.

mathématique [matematik] *adj* mathematical. **➤ mathématiques** *nfpl* mathematics *(U)*.

maths [mat] *nfpl fam* maths *Br*, math *Am*.

matière [matjɛr] *nf* - **1.** [substance] matter ; ~**s grasses** fats ; ~ **grise** grey *Br* ou gray *Am* matter - **2.** [matériau] material ; ~**s premières** raw materials - **3.** [discipline, sujet] subject ; **en ~ de sport/littérature** as far as sport/literature is concerned.

matin [matɛ̃] *nm* morning ; **le ~** in the morning ; **ce ~** this morning ; **à trois heures du ~** at 3 o'clock in the morning ; **du ~ au soir** *fig* from dawn to dusk.

matinal, e, aux [matinal, o] *adj* - **1.** [gymnastique, émission] morning *(avant n)* - **2.** [personne] : **être ~** to be an early riser.

matinée [matine] *nf* - **1.** [matin] morning ; **faire la grasse ~** to have a lie in - **2.** [spectacle] matinée, afternoon performance.

matou [matu] *nm* tom, tomcat.

matraque [matrak] *nf* truncheon.

matraquer [3] [matrake] *vt* - **1.** [frapper] to

beat, to club - **2.** *fig* [intoxiquer] to bombard.

matriarcat [matrijarka] *nm* matriarchy.

matrice [matris] *nf* - **1.** [moule] mould - **2.** MATHS matrix - **3.** ANAT womb.

matricule [matrikyl] *nm* : **(numéro)** ~ number.

matrimonial, e, aux [matrimɔnjal, o] *adj* matrimonial.

matrone [matron] *nf péj* old bag.

mature [matyr] *adj* mature.

mâture [matyr] *nf* masts *(pl)*.

maturité [matyrite] *nf* maturity ; [de fruit] ripeness.

maudire [104] [modir] *vt* to curse.

maudit, e [modi, it] ◇ *pp* ➭ **maudire**. ◇ *adj* - **1.** [réprouvé] accursed - **2.** *(avant n)* [exécrable] damned.

maugréer [15] [mogree] ◇ *vt* to mutter. ◇ *vi* : ~ **(contre)** to grumble (about).

Maurice [moris] ➭ **île**.

mausolée [mozole] *nm* mausoleum.

maussade [mosad] *adj* - **1.** [personne, air] sullen - **2.** [temps] gloomy.

mauvais, e [movɛ, ɛz] *adj* - **1.** [gén] bad - **2.** [moment, numéro, réponse] wrong - **3.** [mer] rough - **4.** [personne, regard] nasty. **➤ mauvais** *adv* : **il fait ~** the weather is bad ; **sentir ~** to smell bad.

mauve [mov] *nm & adj* mauve.

mauviette [movjɛt] *nf fam* - **1.** [physiquement] weakling - **2.** [moralement] coward, wimp.

maux [mo] ➭ **mal**.

max [maks] (*abr de* **maximum**) *nm fam* : **un ~ de fric** loads of money.

max. (*abr de* **maximum**) max.

maxillaire [maksilɛr] *nm* jawbone.

maxime [maksim] *nf* maxim.

maximum [maksimɔm] (*pl* **maxima** [maksima]) ◇ *nm* maximum ; **le ~ de personnes** the greatest (possible) number of people ; **au ~** at the most. ◇ *adj* maximum.

maya [maja] *adj* Mayan. **➤ Maya** *nmf* : **les Mayas** the Maya.

mayonnaise [majɔnɛz] *nf* mayonnaise.

mazout [mazut] *nm* fuel oil.

me [mə], **m'** *(devant voyelle ou h muet)* *pron pers* - **1.** [complément d'objet direct] me - **2.** [complément d'objet indirect] (to) me - **3.** [réfléchi] myself - **4.** [avec un présentatif] : ~ **voici** here I am.

méandre [meɑ̃dr] *nm* [de rivière] meander, bend. **➤ méandres** *nmpl* [détours sinueux] meanderings *(pl)*.

mec [mɛk] *nm fam* guy, bloke.

mécanicien, enne [mekanisjɛ̃, ɛn] *nm, f*
- **1.** [de garage] mechanic - **2.** [conducteur de train] train driver *Br*, engineer *Am*.

mécanique [mekanik] ◇ *nf* - **1.** TECHNOL mechanical engineering - **2.** MATHS & PHYS mechanics *(U)* - **3.** [mécanisme] mechanism. ◇ *adj* mechanical.

mécanisme [mekanism] *nm* mechanism.

mécène [mesɛn] *nm* patron.

méchamment [meʃamɑ̃] *adv* [cruellement] nastily.

méchanceté [meʃɑ̃ste] *nf* - **1.** [attitude] nastiness - **2.** *fam* [rosserie] nasty thing.

méchant, e [meʃɑ̃, ɑ̃t] ◇ *adj* - **1.** [malveillant, cruel] nasty, wicked ; [animal] vicious - **2.** [désobéissant] naughty. ◇ *nm, f* [en langage enfantin] baddy.

mèche [meʃ] *nf* - **1.** [de bougie] wick - **2.** [de cheveux] lock - **3.** [de bombe] fuse.

méchoui [meʃwi] *nm* whole roast sheep.

méconnaissable [mekɔnɛsabl] *adj* unrecognizable.

méconnu, e [mekɔny] *adj* unrecognized.

mécontent, e [mekɔ̃tɑ̃, ɑ̃t] ◇ *adj* unhappy. ◇ *nm, f* malcontent.

mécontenter [3] [mekɔ̃tɑ̃te] *vt* to displease.

Mecque [mɛk] *n* : **La** ~ Mecca.

mécréant, e [mekreɑ̃, ɑ̃t] *nm, f* nonbeliever.

médaille [medaj] *nf* - **1.** [pièce, décoration] medal - **2.** [bijou] medallion - **3.** [de chien] identification disc *Br* ou disk *Am*, tag.

médaillon [medajɔ̃] *nm* - **1.** [bijou] locket - **2.** ART & CULIN medallion.

médecin [medsɛ̃] *nm* doctor ; ~ **conventionné** ≃ National Health doctor *Br* ; ~ **de famille** family doctor, GP *Br* ; ~ **de garde** doctor on duty, duty doctor ; ~ **généraliste** general practitioner, GP *Br* ; ~ **légiste** forensic scientist *Br*, medical examiner *Am* ; **votre ~ traitant** your (usual) doctor ; **Médecins du monde, Médecins sans frontières** *organizations providing medical aid to victims of war and disasters, especially in the Third World.*

médecine [medsin] *nf* medicine.

Medef [medɛf] *(abr de* **Mouvement des entreprises de France)** *nm national council of French employers,* ≃ CBI.

média [medja] *nm* : **les ~s** the (mass) media.

médian, e [medjɑ̃, an] *adj* median.
◆ **médiane** *nf* median.

médiateur, trice [medjatœr, tris] ◇ *adj* mediating *(avant n).* ◇ *nm, f* mediator ; [dans un conflit de travail] arbitrator.

◆ **médiateur** *nm* ADMIN ombudsman.
◆ **médiatrice** *nf* median.

médiathèque [medjatɛk] *nf* media library.

médiatique [medjatik] *adj* media *(avant n).*

médiatiser [3] [medjatize] *vt péj* to turn into a media event.

médical, e, aux [medikal, o] *adj* medical.

médicament [medikamɑ̃] *nm* medicine, drug.

médicinal, e, aux [medisinal, o] *adj* medicinal.

médico-légal, e, aux [medikɔlegal, o] *adj* forensic.

médiéval, e, aux [medjeval, o] *adj* medieval.

médiocre [medjɔkr] *adj* mediocre.

médiocrité [medjɔkrite] *nf* mediocrity.

médire [103] [medir] *vi* to gossip ; ~ **de qqn** to speak ill of sb.

médisant, e [medizɑ̃, ɑ̃t] *adj* slanderous.

méditation [meditasjɔ̃] *nf* meditation.

méditer [3] [medite] ◇ *vt* [projeter] to plan ; ~ **de faire qqch** to plan to do sthg. ◇ *vi* : ~ **(sur)** to meditate (on).

Méditerranée [mediterane] *nf* : **la** ~ the Mediterranean (Sea).

méditerranéen, enne [mediteraneɛ̃, ɛn] *adj* Mediterranean. ◆ **Méditerranéen, enne** *nm, f* person from the Mediterranean.

médium [medjɔm] *nm* [personne] medium.

médius [medjys] *nm* middle finger.

méduse [medyz] *nf* jellyfish.

méduser [3] [medyze] *vt* to dumbfound.

méfait [mefɛ] *nm* misdemeanour *Br*, misdemeanor *Am*, misdeed. ◆ **méfaits** *nmpl* [du temps] ravages.

méfiance [mefjɑ̃s] *nf* suspicion, distrust.

méfiant, e [mefjɑ̃, ɑ̃t] *adj* suspicious, distrustful.

méfier [9] [mefje] ◆ **se méfier** *vp* to be wary ou careful ; **se ~ de qqn/qqch** to distrust sb/sthg.

mégalo [megalo] *nmf & adj fam* megalomaniac.

mégalomane [megalɔman] *nmf & adj* megalomaniac.

mégalomanie [megalɔmani] *nf* megalomania.

méga-octet [megaɔktɛ] *nm* megabyte.

mégapole [megapɔl] *nf* megalopolis, megacity.

mégarde [megard] ◆ **par mégarde** *loc adv* by mistake.

mégère [meʒɛr] *nf péj* shrew.

mégot [mego] *nm fam* fag-end *Br*, butt *Am*.

meilleur, e [mɛjœr] ◇ *adj (compar)* better ; *(superl)* best. ◇ *nm, f* best. ◆ **meilleur** ◇ *nm* : **le ~** the best. ◇ *adv* better.

mélancolie [melɑ̃kɔli] *nf* melancholy.

mélancolique [melɑ̃kɔlik] *adj* melancholy.

mélange [melɑ̃ʒ] *nm* - **1.** [action] mixing - **2.** [mixture] mixture.

mélanger [17] [melɑ̃ʒe] *vt* - **1.** [mettre ensemble] to mix - **2.** [déranger] to mix up, to muddle up. ◆ **se mélanger** *vp* - **1.** [se mêler] to mix - **2.** [se brouiller] to get mixed up.

mêlée [mele] *nf* - **1.** [combat] fray - **2.** RUGBY scrum.

mêler [4] [mele] *vt* - **1.** [mélanger] to mix - **2.** [déranger] to muddle up, to mix up - **3.** [impliquer] : **~ qqn à qqch** to involve sb in sthg. ◆ **se mêler** *vp* - **1.** [se joindre] : **se ~ à** [groupe] to join - **2.** [s'ingérer] : **se ~ de qqch** to get mixed up in sthg ; **mêlez-vous de ce qui vous regarde!** mind your own business!

mélèze [melɛz] *nm* larch.

mélo [melo] *nm fam* melodrama.

mélodie [melɔdi] *nf* melody.

mélodieux, euse [melɔdjø, øz] *adj* melodious, tuneful.

mélodrame [melɔdram] *nm* melodrama.

mélomane [melɔman] ◇ *nmf* music lover. ◇ *adj* music-loving.

melon [məlɔ̃] *nm* - **1.** [fruit] melon - **2.** [chapeau] bowler (hat).

membrane [mɑ̃brɑn] *nf* membrane.

membre [mɑ̃br] ◇ *nm* - **1.** [du corps] limb - **2.** [personne, pays, partie] member. ◇ *adj* member *(avant n)*.

mémé = **mémère**.

même [mɛm] ◇ *adj indéf* - **1.** [indique une identité ou une ressemblance] same ; **il a le ~ âge que moi** he's the same age as me - **2.** [sert à souligner] : **ce sont ses paroles ~s** those are his very words ; **elle est la bonté ~** she's kindness itself. ◇ *pron indéf* : **le/la ~** the same one ; **ce sont toujours les ~s qui gagnent** it's always the same people who win. ◇ *adv* even ; **il n'est ~ pas diplômé** he isn't even qualified. ◆ **de même** *loc adv* similarly, likewise ; **il en va de ~ pour lui** the same goes for him. ◆ **de même que** *loc conj* just as. ◆ **tout de même** *loc adv* all the same. ◆ **à même** *loc prép* : **s'asseoir à ~ le sol** to sit on the bare

ground. ◆ **à même de** *loc prép* : **être à ~ de faire qqch** to be able to do sthg, to be in a position to do sthg. ◆ **même si** *loc conj* even if.

mémento [memɛ̃to] *nm* - **1.** [agenda] pocket diary - **2.** [ouvrage] notes *(title of school textbook)*.

mémère [memɛr], **mémé** [meme] *nf fam* - **1.** [grand-mère] granny - **2.** *péj* [vieille femme] old biddy.

mémoire [memwar] ◇ *nf* [gén & INFORM] memory ; **de ~** from memory ; **avoir bonne/mauvaise ~** to have a good/bad memory ; **mettre en ~** INFORM to store ; **~ tampon** INFORM buffer ; **~ vive** INFORM random access memory ; **à la ~ de** in memory of. ◇ *nm* UNIV dissertation, paper. ◆ **mémoires** *nmpl* memoirs.

mémorable [memɔrabl] *adj* memorable.

mémorial, aux [memɔrjal, o] *nm* [monument] memorial.

mémorisable [memɔrizabl] *adj* INFORM storable.

menaçant, e [mənasɑ̃, ɑ̃t] *adj* threatening.

menace [mənas] *nf* : **~ (pour)** threat (to).

menacer [16] [mənase] ◇ *vt* to threaten ; **~ de faire qqch** to threaten to do sthg, **~ qqn de qqch** to threaten sb with sthg. ◇ *vi* : **la pluie menace** it looks like rain.

ménage [menaʒ] *nm* - **1.** [nettoyage] housework *(U)* ; **faire le ~** to do the housework - **2.** [couple] couple - **3.** ÉCON household.

ménagement [menaʒmɑ̃] *nm* [égards] consideration ; **sans ~** brutally.

ménager¹, ère [menaʒe, ɛr] *adj* household *(avant n)*, domestic. ◆ **ménagère** *nf* - **1.** [femme] housewife - **2.** [de couverts] canteen.

ménager² [17] [menaʒe] *vt* - **1.** [bien traiter] to treat gently - **2.** [économiser - réserves] to use sparingly ; [- argent, temps] to use carefully ; **~ ses forces** to conserve one's strength ; **~ sa santé** to take care of one's health - **3.** [préparer - surprise] to prepare. ◆ **se ménager** *vp* to take care of o.s., to look after o.s.

ménagerie [menaʒri] *nf* menagerie.

mendiant, e [mɑ̃djɑ̃, ɑ̃t] *nm, f* beggar.

mendier [9] [mɑ̃dje] ◇ *vt* [argent] to beg for. ◇ *vi* to beg.

mener [19] [məne] ◇ *vt* - **1.** [emmener] to take - **2.** [diriger - débat, enquête] to conduct ; [- affaires] to manage, to run ; **~ qqch à bonne fin** ou **à bien** to see sthg through, to bring sthg to a successful conclusion - **3.** [être en tête de] to lead. ◇ *vi* to lead.

meneur, euse [mənœr, øz] *nm, f* [chef] ringleader ; ~ **d'hommes** born leader.

menhir [menir] *nm* standing stone.

méningite [menɛ̃ʒit] *nf* meningitis (U).

ménisque [menisk] *nm* meniscus.

ménopause [menɔpoz] *nf* menopause.

menotte [mənɔt] *nf* [main] little hand.
   ◆ **menottes** *nfpl* handcuffs ; **passer les ~s à qqn** to handcuff sb.

mensonge [mɑ̃sɔ̃ʒ] *nm* [propos] lie.

mensonger, ère [mɑ̃sɔ̃ʒe, ɛr] *adj* false.

menstruel, elle [mɑ̃stryɛl] *adj* menstrual.

mensualiser [3] [mɑ̃sɥalize] *vt* to pay monthly.

mensualité [mɑ̃sɥalite] *nf* - 1. [traite] monthly instalment *Br* ou installment *Am* - 2. [salaire] (monthly) salary.

mensuel, elle [mɑ̃sɥɛl] *adj* monthly.
   ◆ **mensuel** *nm* monthly (magazine).

mensuration [mɑ̃syrasjɔ̃] *nf* measuring.
   ◆ **mensurations** *nfpl* measurements.

mental, e, aux [mɑ̃tal, o] *adj* mental.

mentalité [mɑ̃talite] *nf* mentality.

menteur, euse [mɑ̃tœr, øz] *nm, f* liar.

menthe [mɑ̃t] *nf* mint.

menti [mɑ̃ti] *pp inv* ▷ **mentir**.

mention [mɑ̃sjɔ̃] *nf* - 1. [citation] mention - 2. [note] note ; **'rayer la ~ inutile'** 'delete as appropriate' - 3. UNIV : **avec ~** with distinction.

mentionner [3] [mɑ̃sjɔne] *vt* to mention.

mentir [37] [mɑ̃tir] *vi* : ~ **(à)** to lie (to).

menton [mɑ̃tɔ̃] *nm* chin.

menu, e [məny] *adj* [très petit] tiny ; [mince] thin. ◆ **menu** *nm* [gén & INFORM] menu ; [repas à prix fixe] set menu ; ~ **déroulant** INFORM pull-down menu ; ~ **gastronomique/touristique** gourmet/tourist menu.

menuiserie [mənɥizri] *nf* - 1. [métier] joinery, carpentry - 2. [atelier] joinery (workshop).

menuisier [mənɥizje] *nm* joiner, carpenter.

méprendre [79] [meprɑ̃dr] ◆ **se méprendre** *vp littéraire* : **se ~ sur** to be mistaken about.

mépris, e [mepri, iz] *pp* ▷ **méprendre**.
   ◆ **mépris** *nm* - 1. [dédain] : ~ **(pour)** contempt (for), scorn (for) - 2. [indifférence] : ~ **de** disregard for. ◆ **au mépris de** *loc prép* regardless of.

méprisable [meprizabl] *adj* contemptible, despicable.

méprisant, e [meprizɑ̃, ɑ̃t] *adj* contemptuous, scornful.

mépriser [3] [meprize] *vt* to despise ; [danger, offre] to scorn.

mer [mɛr] *nf* sea ; **en ~** at sea ; **prendre la ~** to put to sea ; **haute** ou **pleine ~** open sea ; **la ~ d'Irlande** the Irish Sea ; **la ~ Morte** the Dead Sea ; **la ~ Noire** the Black Sea ; **la ~ du Nord** the North Sea.

mercantile [mɛrkɑ̃til] *adj péj* mercenary.

mercenaire [mɛrsənɛr] *nm & adj* mercenary.

mercerie [mɛrsəri] *nf* - 1. [articles] haberdashery *Br*, notions *(pl) Am* - 2. [boutique] haberdasher's shop *Br*, notions store *Am*.

merci [mɛrsi] ◇ *interj* thank you!, thanks! ; ~ **beaucoup!** thank you very much! ◇ *nm* : ~ **(de** ou **pour)** thank you (for) ; **dire ~ à qqn** to thank sb, to say thank you to sb. ◇ *nf* mercy ; **être à la ~ de** to be at the mercy of.

mercier, ère [mɛrsje, ɛr] *nm, f* haberdasher *Br*, notions dealer *Am*.

mercredi [mɛrkrədi] *nm* Wednesday ; *voir aussi* **samedi**.

mercure [mɛrkyr] *nm* mercury.

merde [mɛrd] *tfam nf* shit.

mère [mɛr] *nf* mother ; ~ **de famille** mother.

merguez [mɛrgez] *nf inv* North African spiced sausage.

méridien, enne [meridjɛ̃, ɛn] *adj* [ligne] meridian. ◆ **méridien** *nm* meridian.

méridional, e, aux [meridjɔnal, o] *adj* southern ; [du sud de la France] Southern (French).

meringue [mərɛ̃g] *nf* meringue.

merisier [mərizje] *nm* - 1. [arbre] wild cherry (tree) - 2. [bois] cherry.

mérite [merit] *nm* merit.

mériter [3] [merite] *vt* - 1. [être digne de, encourir] to deserve - 2. [valoir] to be worth, to merit.

merlan [mɛrlɑ̃] *nm* whiting.

merle [mɛrl] *nm* blackbird.

merveille [mɛrvej] *nf* marvel, wonder ; **à ~** marvellously *Br*, marvelously *Am*, wonderfully.

merveilleux, euse [mɛrvejø, øz] *adj* - 1. [remarquable, prodigieux] marvellous *Br*, marvelous *Am*, wonderful - 2. [magique] magic, magical. ◆ **merveilleux** *nm* : **le ~** the supernatural.

mes ▷ **mon**.

mésalliance [mezaljɑ̃s] *nf* unsuitable marriage, misalliance.

mésange [mezɑ̃ʒ] *nf* ZOOL tit.

mésaventure [mezavɑ̃tyr] *nf* misfortune.

mesdames ⬅ **madame**.

mesdemoiselles ⬅ **mademoiselle**.

mésentente [mezɑ̃tɑ̃t] *nf* disagreement.

mesquin, e [mɛskɛ̃, in] *adj* mean, petty.

mesquinerie [mɛskinri] *nf* [étroitesse d'esprit] meanness, pettiness.

mess [mɛs] *nm* mess.

message [mesaʒ] *nm* message ; **laisser un ~ à qqn** to leave a message for sb.

messager, ère [mesaʒe, ɛr] *nm, f* messenger.

messagerie [mesaʒri] *nf* **- 1.** *(gén pl)* [transport de marchandises] freight *(U)* **- 2.** INFORM : **~ électronique** electronic mail.

messe [mɛs] *nf* mass ; **aller à la ~** to go to mass.

messie [mesi] *nm* Messiah ; *fig* saviour *Br*, savior *Am*.

messieurs ⬅ **monsieur**.

mesure [məzyr] *nf* **- 1.** [disposition, acte] measure, step ; **prendre des ~s** to take measures ou steps **2.** [évaluation, dimension] measurement ; **prendre les ~s de qqn/qqch** to measure sb/sthg **3.** [étalon, récipient] measure **- 4.** MUS time, tempo **- 5.** [modération] moderation **- 6.** *loc* : **dans la ~ du possible** as far as possible ; **être en ~ de** to be in a position to. ➡ **à la mesure de** *loc prép* worthy of. ➡ **à mesure que** *loc conj* as. ➡ **outre mesure** *loc adv* excessively. ➡ **sur mesure** *loc adj* custommade ; [costume] made-to-measure.

mesurer [3] [məzyre] *vt* **- 1.** [gén] to measure ; **elle mesure 1,50 m** she's 5 feet tall ; **la table mesure 1,50 m** the table is 5 feet long **- 2.** [risques, portée, ampleur] to weigh up ; **~ ses paroles** to weigh one's words, ➡ **se mesurer** *vp* : **se ~ avec** ou **à qqn** to pit o.s. against sb.

métabolisme [metabɔlism] *nm* metabolism.

métal, aux [metal, o] *nm* metal.

métallique [metalik] *adj* **- 1.** [en métal] metal *(avant n)* **- 2.** [éclat, son] metallic.

métallurgie [metalyrʒi] *nf* **- 1.** [industrie] metallurgical industry **- 2.** [technique] metallurgy.

métamorphose [metamɔrfoz] *nf* metamorphosis.

métaphore [metafɔr] *nf* metaphor.

métaphysique [metafizik] ◇ *nf* metaphysics *(U).* ◇ *adj* metaphysical.

métayer, ère [meteje, metɛjer] *nm, f* tenant farmer.

météo [meteo] *nf* **- 1.** [bulletin] weather

forecast **- 2.** [service] ≃ Met Office *Br*, ≃ National Weather Service *Am*.

météore [meteɔr] *nm* meteor.

météorite [meteɔrit] *nm* OU *nf* meteorite.

météorologie [meteɔrɔlɔʒi] *nf* SCIENCE meteorology.

météorologique [meteɔrɔlɔʒik] *adj* meteorological, weather *(avant n).*

méthane [metan] *nm* methane.

méthode [metɔd] *nf* **- 1.** [gén] method **- 2.** [ouvrage - gén] manual ; [- de lecture, de langue] primer.

méthodologie [metɔdɔlɔʒi] *nf* methodology.

méticuleux, euse [metikylø, øz] *adj* meticulous.

métier [metje] *nm* [profession - manuelle] occupation, trade ; [- intellectuelle] occupation, profession ; **il est du ~** he's in the same trade ou same line of work ; **avoir du ~** to have experience.

métis, isse [metis] *nm, f* half-caste. ➡ **métis** *nm* [tissu] cotton-linen mix.

métrage [metraʒ] *nm* **- 1.** [mesure] measurement, measuring **- 2.** [COUTURE - coupon] length **- 3.** CIN footage ; **long ~** feature film ; **court ~** short (film).

mètre [mɛtr] *nm* **- 1.** LITTÉRATURE & MATHS metre *Br*, meter *Am* ; **~ carré** square metre *Br* ou meter *Am* ; **~ cube** cubic metre *Br* ou meter *Am* **- 2.** [instrument] rule.

métro [metro] *nm* underground *Br*, subway *Am*.

métronome [metronɔm] *nm* metronome.

métropole [metrɔpɔl] *nf* **- 1.** [ville] metropolis **- 2.** [pays] home country.

métropolitain, e [metrɔpɔlitɛ̃, ɛn] *adj* métropolitain, **la France** ou metropolitan ou mainland France.

mets [mɛ] *nm* CULIN dish.

metteur [metœr] *nm* : **~ en scène** THÉÂTRE producer ; CIN director.

mettre [84] [mɛtr] *vt* **- 1.** [placer] to put ; **~ de l'eau à bouillir** to put some water on to boil **- 2.** [revêtir] to put on ; **mets ta robe noire** put your black dress on ; **je ne mets plus ma robe noire** I don't wear my black dress any more **- 3.** [consacrer - temps] to take ; [- argent] to spend ; **~ longtemps à faire qqch** to take a long time to do sthg **- 4.** [allumer - radio, chauffage] to put on, to switch on **- 5.** [installer] to put in ; **faire ~ l'électricité** to have electricity put in ; **faire ~ de la moquette** to have a carpet put down ou fitted **- 6.** [inscrire] to put (down). ➡ **se mettre** *vp* **- 1.** [se placer] : **où est-ce**

que ça se met? where does this go? ; se ~ au lit to get into bed ; se ~ à côté de qqn to sit/stand near to sb - 2. [devenir] : se ~ en colère to get angry - 3. [commencer] : se ~ à qqch/à faire qqch to start sthg/doing sthg - 4. [revêtir] : to put on ; je n'ai rien à me ~ I haven't got a thing to wear.

meuble [mœbl] <> nm piece of furniture ; ~s furniture (U). <> adj - 1. [terre, sol] easily worked - 2. JUR movable.

meublé, e [mœble] adj furnished. ➡ **meublé** nm furnished room/flat Br, furnished apartment Am.

meubler [5] [mœble] vt - 1. [pièce, maison] to furnish - 2. fig [occuper] : ~ qqch (de) to fill sthg (with). ➡ **se meubler** vp to furnish one's home.

meuf [mœf] nf fam woman.

meugler [5] [møgle] vi to moo.

meule [møl] nf - 1. [à moudre] millstone - 2. [à aiguiser] grindstone - 3. [de fromage] round - 4. AGRIC stack ; ~ de foin haystack.

meunier, ère [mønje, εr] nm, f miller (f miller's wife).

meurtre [mœrtr] nm murder.

meurtrier, ère [mœrtrije, εr] <> adj [épidémie, arme] deadly ; [fureur] murderous ; [combat] bloody. <> nm, f murderer.

meurtrir [32] [mœrtrir] vt - 1. [contusionner] to bruise - 2. fig [blesser] to wound.

meurtrissure [mœrtrisyr] nf [marque] bruise.

meute [møt] nf pack.

mexicain, e [mεksikε̃, εn] adj Mexican. ➡ **Mexicain, e** nm, f Mexican.

Mexique [mεksik] nm : le ~ Mexico.

mezzanine [mεdzanin] nf mezzanine.

mezzo-soprano [mεdzosoprano] (pl mezzo-sopranos) nm mezzo-soprano.

mi [mi] nm inv E ; [chanté] mi.

mi- [mi] <> adj inv half ; à la ~juin in mid-June. <> adv half-.

miasme [mjasm] nm (gén pl) putrid ou foul smell.

miaulement [mjolmɑ̃] nm miaowing Br, meowing Am.

miauler [3] [mjole] vi to miaow Br, to meow Am.

mi-bas [miba] nm inv knee-sock.

mi-carême [mikarεm] nf feast day on third Thursday in Lent.

mi-chemin [miʃmε̃] ➡ **à mi-chemin** loc adv halfway (there).

mi-clos, e [miklo, oz] adj half-closed.

micro [mikro] <> nm - 1. [microphone]

mike - 2. [micro-ordinateur] micro. <> nf microcomputing.

microbe [mikrɔb] nm - 1. MÉD microbe, germ - 2. péj [avorton] (little) runt.

microclimat [mikroklima] nm microclimate.

microcosme [mikrokɔsm] nm microcosm.

microfiche [mikrofiʃ] nf microfiche.

microfilm [mikrofilm] nm microfilm.

micro-ondes [mikroɔ̃d] nfpl microwaves ; four à ~ microwave (oven).

micro-ordinateur [mikroɔrdinatœr] (pl micro-ordinateurs) nm micro, microcomputer.

microphone [mikrofɔn] nm microphone.

microprocesseur [mikroprosesœr] nm microprocessor.

microscope [mikroskɔp] nm microscope.

midi [midi] nm - 1. [période du déjeuner] lunchtime - 2. [heure] midday, noon - 3. [sud] south. ➡ **Midi** nm : le Midi the South of France.

mie [mi] nf [de pain] soft part, inside.

miel [mjεl] nm honey.

mielleux, euse [mjεlø, øz] adj [personne] unctuous ; [paroles, air] honeyed.

mien [mjε̃] ➡ **le mien** (f la mienne [lamjεn], mpl les miens [lemjε̃], fpl les miennes [lemjεn]) pron poss mine.

miette [mjεt] nf - 1. [de pain] crumb, breadcrumb - 2. (gén pl) [débris] shreds (pl).

mieux [mjø] <> adv - 1. [comparatif] : ~ (que) better (than) ; il pourrait ~ faire he could do better ; il va ~ he's better ; faire ~ de faire qqch to do better to do sthg ; vous feriez ~ de vous taire you would do better to keep quiet - 2. [superlatif] best ; il est le ~ payé du service he's the best ou highest paid member of the department ; le ~ qu'il peut as best he can. <> adj better. <> nm - 1. (sans déterminant) : j'espérais ~ I was hoping for something better - 2. (avec déterminant) best ; il y a un ou du ~ there's been an improvement ; faire de son ~ to do one's best. ➡ **au mieux** loc adv at best. ➡ **pour le mieux** loc adv for the best. ➡ **de mieux en mieux** loc adv better and better.

mièvre [mjεvr] adj insipid.

mignon, onne [miɲɔ̃, ɔn] <> adj - 1. [charmant] sweet, cute - 2. [gentil] nice. <> nm, f darling, sweetheart.

migraine [migrεn] nf headache ; MÉD migraine.

migrant, e [migrɑ̃, ɑ̃t] nm, f migrant.

migrateur, trice [migratœr, tris] *adj* migratory.

migration [migrasjɔ̃] *nf* migration.

mijoter [3] [miʒɔte] ◇ *vt fam* [tramer] to cook up. ◇ *vi* CULIN to simmer.

mi-journée [miʒurne] *nf* : **les informations de la ~** the lunchtime news.

mil [mij] *nm* millet.

milan [milɑ̃] *nm* kite *(bird)*.

milice [milis] *nf* militia.

milicien, enne [milisjɛ̃, ɛn] *nm, f* militiaman *(f* militiawoman).

milieu, x [miljø] *nm* - **1.** [centre] middle ; **au ~ de** [au centre de] in the middle of ; [parmi] among, surrounded by - **2.** [stade intermédiaire] middle course - **3.** BIOL & SOCIOL environment ; **~ familial** family background - **4.** [pègre] : **le ~ the** underworld - **5.** FOOTBALL : **~ de terrain** midfielder, midfield player.

militaire [militɛr] ◇ *nm* soldier ; **~ de carrière** professional soldier. ◇ *adj* military.

militant, e [militɑ̃, ɑ̃t] *adj & nm, f* militant.

militer [3] [milite] *vi* to be active ; **~ pour** to militate in favour *Br* ou favor *Am* of ; **~ contre** to militate against.

mille [mil] ◇ *nm inv* - **1.** [unité] a ou one thousand - **2.** [de cible] : **dans le ~** on target - **3.** NAVIG : **~ marin** nautical mile - **4.** *Can* [distance] mile. ◇ *adj inv* thousand ; **c'est ~ fois trop** it's far too much ; **je lui ai dit ~ fois** I've told him/her a thousand times ; *voir aussi* **six**.

mille-feuille [milfœj] *(pl* **mille-feuilles)** *nm* ≃ vanilla slice *Br*, ≃ napoleon *Am*.

millénaire [milenɛr] ◇ *nm* millennium, thousand years *(pl)*. ◇ *adj* thousand-year-old *(avant n)*.

mille-pattes [milpat] *nm inv* centipede, millipede.

millésime [milezim] *nm* - **1.** [de pièce] date - **2.** [de vin] vintage, year.

millésimé, e [milezime] *adj* [vin] vintage *(avant n)*.

millet [mijɛ] *nm* millet.

milliard [miljar] *nm* thousand million *Br*, billion *Am* ; **par ~s** *fig* in (their) millions.

milliardaire [miljardɛr] *nmf* multimillionaire *Br*, billionaire *Am*.

millième [miljɛm] *adj, nm* ou *nmf* thousandth ; *voir aussi* **sixième**.

millier [milje] *nm* thousand ; **un ~ d'euros** about a thousand euros ; **un ~ de personnes** about a thousand people ; **par ~s** in (their) thousands.

milligramme [miligram] *nm* milligram, milligramme.

millilitre [mililitr] *nm* millilitre *Br*, milliliter *Am*.

millimètre [milimɛtr] *nm* millimetre *Br*, millimeter *Am*.

million [miljɔ̃] *nm* million ; **un ~ d'euros** a million euros.

millionnaire [miljɔnɛr] *nmf* millionaire.

mime [mim] *nm* mime.

mimer [3] [mime] *vt* - **1.** [exprimer sans parler] to mime - **2.** [imiter] to mimic.

mimétisme [mimetism] *nm* mimicry.

mimique [mimik] *nf* - **1.** [grimace] face - **2.** [geste] sign language *(U)*.

mimosa [mimɔza] *nm* mimosa.

min. *(abr de* **minimum)** min.

minable [minabl] *adj fam* - **1.** [misérable] seedy, shabby - **2.** [médiocre] pathetic.

minaret [minarɛ] *nm* minaret.

minauder [3] [minode] *vi* to simper.

mince [mɛ̃s] *adj* - **1.** [maigre - gén] thin ; [- personne, taille] slender, slim - **2.** *fig* [faible] small, meagre *Br*, meager *Am*.

minceur [mɛ̃sœr] *nf* - **1.** [gén] thinness ; [de personne] slenderness, slimness - **2.** *fig* [insuffisance] meagreness *Br*, meagerness *Am*.

mincir [32] [mɛ̃sir] *vi* to get thinner ou slimmer.

mine [min] *nf* - **1.** [expression] look ; **avoir bonne/mauvaise ~** to look well/ill - **2.** [apparence] appearance - **3.** [gisement] *fig* mine ; [exploitation] mining ; **~ de charbon** coalmine - **4.** [explosif] mine - **5.** [de crayon] lead.

miner [3] [mine] *vt* - **1.** MIL to mine - **2.** [ronger] to undermine, to wear away ; *fig* to wear down.

minéral [mineral] *nm* ore.

minéral, e, aux [mineral, o] *adj* - **1.** CHIM inorganic - **2.** [eau, source] mineral *(avant n)*. ➔ **minéral** *nm* mineral.

minéralogie [mineralɔʒi] *nf* mineralogy.

minéralogique [mineralɔʒik] *adj* - **1.** AUTOM : **plaque ~** numberplate *Br*, license plate *Am* - **2.** GÉOL mineralogical.

minet, ette [minɛ, ɛt] *nm, f fam* - **1.** [chat] pussy cat, pussy - **2.** [personne] trendy.

mineur, e [minœr] ◇ *adj* minor. ◇ *nm, f* JUR minor. ➔ **mineur** *nm* [ouvrier] miner ; **~ de fond** face worker.

miniature [minjatyr] ◇ *nf* miniature. ◇ *adj* miniature.

miniaturiser [3] [minjatyrize] *vt* to miniaturize.

minibus [minibys] *nm* minibus.

minichaîne [miniʃɛn] *nf* portable hi-fi.

minier, ère [minje, εr] *adj* mining *(avant n)*.

minijupe [miniʒyp] *nf* miniskirt.

minimal, e, aux [minimal, o] *adj* minimum.

minimalisme [minimalism] *nm* minimalism.

minime [minim] <> *nmf* SPORT ≈ junior. <> *adj* minimal.

minimiser [3] [minimize] *vt* to minimize.

minimum [minimɔm] (*pl* **minimums** ou **minima** [minima]) <> *nm* [gén & MATHS] minimum ; **au** ~ at least ; **le strict** ~ the bare minimum. <> *adj* minimum.

ministère [ministεr] *nm* - 1. [département] ministry *Br*, department - 2. [cabinet] government - 3. RELIG ministry.

ministériel, elle [ministerjεl] *adj* [du ministère] departmental, ministerial *Br*.

ministre [ministr] *nm* secretary, minister *Br* ; ~ **d'État** secretary of state, cabinet minister *Br* ; **premier** ~ prime minister.

Minitel® [minitεl] *nm teletext system run by the French national telephone company, providing an information and communication network.*

minitéliste [minitelist] *nmf* Minitel® user.

minois [minwa] *nm* sweet (little) face.

minoritaire [minɔritεr] *adj* minority *(avant n)* ; **être** ~ to be in the minority.

minorité [minɔrite] *nf* minority ; **en** ~ in the minority.

minuit [minɥi] *nm* midnight.

minuscule [minyskyl] <> *nf* [lettre] small letter. <> *adj* - 1. [lettre] small - 2. [très petit] tiny, minuscule.

minute [minyt] <> *nf* minute ; **dans une** ~ in a minute ; **d'une** ~ **à l'autre** in next to no time. <> *interj fam* hang on (a minute)!

minuter [3] [minyte] *vt* [chronométrer] to time (precisely).

minuterie [minytri] *nf* [d'éclairage] time switch, timer.

minuteur [minytœr] *nm* timer.

minutie [minysi] *nf* [soin] meticulousness ; [précision] attention to detail ; **avec** ~ [avec soin] meticulously ; [dans le détail] in minute detail.

minutieux, euse [minysjø, øz] *adj* [méticuleux] meticulous ; [détaillé] minutely detailed ; **un travail** ~ a job requiring great attention to detail.

mioche [mjɔʃ] *nmf fam* kiddy.

mirabelle [mirabεl] *nf* - 1. [fruit] mirabelle (plum) - 2. [alcool] plum brandy.

miracle [mirakl] *nm* miracle ; **par** ~ by some ou a miracle, miraculously.

miraculeux, euse [mirakylø, øz] *adj* miraculous.

mirador [miradɔr] *nm* MIL watchtower.

mirage [miraʒ] *nm* mirage.

mire [mir] *nf* - 1. TÉLÉ test card - 2. [visée] : **ligne de** ~ line of sight.

mirifique [mirifik] *adj* fabulous.

mirobolant, e [mirɔbɔlɑ̃, ɑ̃t] *adj* fabulous, fantastic.

miroir [mirwar] *nm* mirror.

miroiter [3] [mirwate] *vi* to sparkle, to gleam ; **faire** ~ **qqch à qqn** to hold out the prospect of sthg to sb.

mis, mise [mi, miz] *pp* ▷ **mettre**.

misanthrope [mizɑ̃trɔp] <> *nmf* misanthropist, misanthrope. <> *adj* misanthropic.

mise [miz] *nf* - 1. [action] putting ; ~ **à jour** updating ; ~ **en page** making up, composing ; ~ **au point** PHOT focusing ; TECHNOL adjustment ; *fig* clarification ; ~ **en scène** production - 2. [d'argent] stake.

miser [3] [mize] <> *vt* to bet. <> *vi* : ~ **sur** to bet on ; *fig* to count on.

misérable [mizerabl] *adj* - 1. [pauvre] poor, wretched - 2. [sans valeur] paltry, miserable.

misère [mizεr] *nf* - 1. [indigence] poverty - 2. [infortune] misery - 3. *fig* [bagatelle] trifle.

miséricorde [mizerikɔrd] *nf* [clémence] mercy.

misogyne [mizɔʒin] *adj* misogynous.

misogynie [mizɔʒini] *nf* misogyny.

missel [misεl] *nm* missal.

missile [misil] *nm* missile.

mission [misjɔ̃] *nf* mission ; **en** ~ on a mission.

missionnaire [misjɔnεr] *nmf* missionary.

missive [misiv] *nf* letter.

mistral [mistral] *nm strong cold wind that blows down the Rhône Valley and through Southern France.*

mitaine [mitεn] *nf* fingerless glove.

mite [mit] *nf* (clothes) moth.

mité, e [mite] *adj* moth-eaten.

mi-temps [mitɑ̃] <> *nf inv* [SPORT - période] half ; [- pause] half-time. <> *nm* part-time work. ◆ **à mi-temps** *loc adj* & *loc adv* part-time.

miteux, euse [mitø, øz] *fam adj* seedy, dingy.

mitigé, e [mitiʒe] *adj* - 1. [tempéré] lukewarm - 2. *fam* [mélangé] mixed.

mitonner [3] [mitɔne] <> *vt* - 1. [faire cuire]

to simmer - **2.** [préparer avec soin] to prepare lovingly. ◇ *vi* CULIN to simmer.

mitoyen, enne [mitwajɛ̃, ɛn] *adj* [commun] common ; [attenant] adjoining ; **mur ~** party wall.

mitrailler [3] [mitraje] *vt* - **1.** MIL to machinegun - **2.** *fam* [photographier] to click away at - **3.** *fig* [assaillir] **: ~ qqn (de)** to bombard sb (with).

mitraillette [mitrajɛt] *nf* submachine gun.

mitrailleuse [mitrajøz] *nf* machinegun.

mitre [mitr] *nf* [d'évêque] mitre *Br*, miter *Am*.

mi-voix [mivwa] ◆ **à mi-voix** *loc adv* in a low voice.

mixage [miksaʒ] *nm* CIN & RADIO (sound) mixing.

mixer¹, mixeur [miksœr] *nm* (food) mixer.

mixer² [3] [mikse] *vt* to mix.

mixte [mikst] *adj* mixed.

mixture [mikstyr] *nf* - **1.** CHIM & CULIN mixture - **2.** *péj* [mélange] concoction.

MJC *(abr de* **maison des jeunes et de la culture)** *nf youth and cultural centre*

ml *(abr de* **millilitre)** ml.

Mlle *(abr de* **Mademoiselle)** Miss.

mm *(abr de* **millimètre)** mm.

MM *(abr de* **Messieurs)** Messrs.

Mme *(abr de* **Madame)** Mrs.

mnémotechnique [mnemɔtɛknik] *adj* mnemonic.

Mo *(abr de* **méga-octet)** MB.

mobile [mɔbil] ◇ *nm* - **1.** [objet] mobile - **2.** [motivation] motive. ◇ *adj* **1.** [gén] movable, mobile ; [partie, pièce] moving - **2.** [population, main d'œuvre] mobile.

mobilier, ère [mɔbilje, ɛr] *adj* JUR movable. ◆ **mobilier** *nm* furniture.

mobilisation [mɔbilizasjɔ̃] *nf* mobilization.

mobiliser [3] [mɔbilize] *vt* - **1.** [gén] to mobilize - **2.** [moralement] to rally. ◆ **se mobiliser** *vp* to mobilize, to rally.

mobilité [mɔbilite] *nf* mobility.

Mobylette® [mɔbilɛt] *nf* moped.

mocassin [mɔkasɛ̃] *nm* moccasin.

moche [mɔʃ] *adj fam* - **1.** [laid] ugly - **2.** [triste, méprisable] lousy, rotten.

modalité [mɔdalite] *nf* [convention] form ; **~s de paiement** methods of payment.

mode [mɔd] ◇ *nf* - **1.** [gén] fashion ; **à la ~** in fashion, fashionable - **2.** [coutume] custom, style ; **à la ~ de** in the style of. ◇ *nm*

- **1.** [manière] mode, form ; **~ de vie** way of life - **2.** [méthode] method ; **~ d'emploi** instructions (for use) - **3.** GRAM mood - **4.** MUS mode.

modèle [mɔdɛl] *nm* - **1.** [gén] model ; **sur le ~ de** on the model of ; **~ déposé** patented design - **2.** *(en apposition)* [exemplaire] model *(avant n)*.

modeler [25] [mɔdle] *vt* to shape ; **~ qqch sur qqch** *fig* to model sthg on sthg.

modélisme [mɔdelism] *nm* modelling *(of scale models)*.

modération [mɔderasjɔ̃] *nf* moderation.

modéré, e [mɔdere] *adj* & *nm, f* moderate.

modérer [18] [mɔdere] *vt* to moderate. ◆ **se modérer** *vp* to restrain o.s., to control o.s.

moderne [mɔdɛrn] *adj* modern ; [mathématiques] new.

moderniser [3] [mɔdɛrnize] *vt* to modernize. ◆ **se moderniser** *vp* to become (more) modern.

modeste [mɔdɛst] *adj* modest ; [origine] humble.

modestie [mɔdɛsti] *nf* modesty ; **fausse ~** false modesty.

modification [mɔdifikasjɔ̃] *nf* alteration, modification.

modifier [9] [mɔdifje] *vt* to alter, to modify. ◆ **se modifier** *vp* to alter.

modique [mɔdik] *adj* modest.

modiste [mɔdist] *nf* milliner.

modulation [mɔdylasjɔ̃] *nf* modulation.

module [mɔdyl] *nm* module.

moduler [3] [mɔdyle] *vt* - **1.** [air] to warble - **2.** [structure] to adjust.

moelle [mwal] *nf* ANAT marrow. ◆ **moelle épinière** *nf* spinal cord.

moelleux, euse [mwalø, øz] *adj* - **1.** [canapé, tapis] soft - **2.** [fromage, vin] mellow.

moellon [mwalɔ̃] *nm* rubble stone.

mœurs [mœr(s)] *nfpl* - **1.** [morale] morals - **2.** [coutumes] customs, habits - **3.** ZOOL behaviour *(U) Br*, behavior *(U) Am*.

mohair [mɔɛr] *nm* mohair.

moi [mwa] *pron pers* - **1.** [objet, après préposition, comparatif] me ; **aide-~** help me ; **il me l'a dit, à ~** he told ME ; **c'est pour ~** it's for me ; **plus âgé que ~** older than me ou than I (am) - **2.** [sujet] I ; **~ non plus, je n'en sais rien** I don't know anything about it either ; **qui est là? - (c'est) ~** who's there? - it's me ; **je l'ai vu hier - ~ aussi** I saw him yesterday - me too ; **c'est ~ qui lui ai dit de venir** I was the one who told him to come. ◆ **moi-même** *pron pers* myself.

moignon [mwaɲɔ̃] *nm* stump.

moindre [mwɛ̃dr] <> *adj superl* : **le/la ~** the least ; *(avec négation)* the least ou slightest ; **les ~s détails** the smallest details ; **sans la ~ difficulté** without the slightest problem ; **c'est la ~ des choses** it's the least I/you *etc* could do. <> *adj compar* less ; [prix] lower ; **à un ~ degré** to a lesser extent.

moine [mwan] *nm* monk.

moineau, x [mwano] *nm* sparrow.

moins [mwɛ̃] <> *adv* **- 1.** [quantité] less ; **~ de lais (than)** ; **~ de lait** less milk ; **~ de gens** fewer people ; **~ de dix** less than ten ; **il est un peu ~ de 10 heures** it's nearly 10 o'clock **- 2.** [comparatif] : **~ (que)** less (than) ; **il est ~ vieux que ton frère** he's not as old as your brother, he's younger than your brother ; **bien ~ grand que** much smaller than ; **~ il mange, ~ il travaille** the less he eats, the less he works **- 3.** [superlatif] : **le ~** (the) least ; **le ~ riche des hommes** the poorest man ; **c'est lui qui travaille le ~** he works (the) least ; **le ~ possible** as little as possible. <> *prép* **- 1.** [gén] minus ; **dix ~ huit font deux** ten minus eight is two, ten take away eight is two ; **il fait ~ vingt** it's twenty below, it's minus twenty **- 2.** [servant à indiquer l'heure] : **il est 3 heures ~ le quart** it's quarter to 3 ; **il est ~ dix** it's ten to. <> *nm* **- 1.** [signe] minus (sign) **- 2.** *loc* : **le ~ qu'on puisse dire, c'est que ...** it's an understatement to say ... ◆ **à moins de** *loc prép* : **à ~ de battre le record** unless I/you *etc* beat the record. ◆ **à moins que** *loc conj* (+ *subjonctif*) unless. ◆ **au moins** *loc adv* at least. ◆ **de moins en moins** *loc adv* less and less. ◆ **du moins** *loc adv* at least. ◆ **en moins** *loc adv* : **il a une dent en ~** he's missing ou minus a tooth ; **c'était le paradis, les anges en ~** it was heaven, minus the angels. ◆ **pour le moins** *loc adv* at the (very) least. ◆ **tout au moins** *loc adv* at (the very) least.

moiré, e [mware] *adj* **- 1.** [tissu] watered **- 2.** *littéraire* [reflet] shimmering.

mois [mwa] *nm* [laps de temps] month.

moisi, e [mwazi] *adj* mouldy *Br*, moldy *Am*. ◆ **moisi** *nm* mould *Br*, mold *Am*.

moisir [32] [mwazir] *vi* **- 1.** [pourrir] to go mouldy *Br* ou moldy *Am* **- 2.** *fig* [personne] to rot.

moisissure [mwazisyr] *nf* mould *Br*, mold *Am*.

moisson [mwasɔ̃] *nf* **- 1.** [récolte] harvest ; **faire la ~** ou **les ~s** to harvest, to bring in the harvest **- 2.** *fig* [d'idées, de projets] wealth.

moissonner [3] [mwasɔne] *vt* to harvest, to gather (in) ; *fig* to collect, to gather.

moissonneuse-batteuse [mwasɔnøzbatøz] *nf* combine (harvester).

moite [mwat] *adj* [peau, mains] moist, sweaty ; [atmosphère] muggy.

moiteur [mwatœr] *nf* [de peau, mains] moistness ; [d'atmosphère] mugginess.

moitié [mwatje] *nf* [gén] half ; **à ~ vide** half-empty ; **faire qqch à ~** to half-do sthg ; **la ~ du temps** half the time ; **à la ~ de qqch** halfway through sthg.

moka [mɔka] *nm* **- 1.** [café] mocha (coffee) **- 2.** [gâteau] coffee cake.

mol ▷ **mou.**

molaire [mɔlɛr] *nf* molar.

molécule [mɔlekyl] *nf* molecule.

molester [3] [mɔlɛste] *vt* to manhandle.

molle ▷ **mou.**

mollement [mɔlmɑ̃] *adv* **- 1.** [faiblement] weakly, feebly **- 2.** *littéraire* [paresseusement] sluggishly, lethargically.

mollesse [mɔlɛs] *nf* **- 1.** [de chose] softness **- 2.** [de personne] lethargy.

mollet [mɔlɛ] <> *nm* calf. <> *adj* ▷ **œuf.**

mollir [32] [mɔlir] *vi* **- 1.** [physiquement, moralement] to give way **- 2.** [vent] to drop, to die down.

mollusque [mɔlysk] *nm* ZOOL mollusc.

molosse [mɔlɔs] *nm* **- 1.** [chien] *large ferocious dog* **- 2.** *fig & péj* [personne] hulking great brute ou fellow.

môme [mom] *fam nmf* [enfant] kid, youngster.

moment [mɔmɑ̃] *nm* **- 1.** [gén] moment ; **au ~ de l'accident** at the time of the accident, when the accident happened ; **au ~ de partir** just as we/you *etc* were leaving ; **au ~ où** just as ; **dans un ~** in a moment ; **d'un ~ à l'autre, à tout ~** (at) any moment, any moment now ; **à un ~ donné** at a given moment ; **par ~s** at times, now and then ; **en ce ~** at the moment ; **pour le ~** for the moment **- 2.** [durée] (short) time ; **passer un mauvais ~** to have a bad time **- 3.** [occasion] time ; **ce n'est pas le ~ (de faire qqch)** this is not the time (to do sthg). ◆ **du moment que** *loc prép* since, as.

momentané, e [mɔmɑ̃tane] *adj* temporary.

momie [mɔmi] *nf* mummy.

mon [mɔ̃] (*f* **ma** [ma], *pl* **mes** [me]) *adj poss* my.

monacal, e, aux [mɔnakal, o] *adj* monastic.

Monaco [mɔnako] *n* : **(la principauté de) ~** (the principality of) Monaco.

monarchie [mɔnarʃi] *nf* monarchy ;

~ **absolue/constitutionnelle** absolute/constitutional monarchy.

monarque [mɔnark] *nm* monarch.

monastère [mɔnastɛr] *nm* monastery.

monceau, x [mɔ̃so] *nm* [tas] heap.

mondain, e [mɔ̃dɛ̃, ɛn] *adj* - **1.** [chronique, journaliste] society *(avant n)* - **2.** *péj* [futile] frivolous, superficial.

mondanités [mɔ̃danite] *nfpl* - **1.** [événements] society life *(U)* - **2.** [paroles] small talk *(U)* ; [comportements] formalities.

monde [mɔ̃d] *nm* - **1.** [gén] world ; **le/la plus ... au ~, le/la plus ... du ~** the most ... in the world ; **pour rien au ~** not for the world, not for all the tea in China ; **mettre un enfant au ~** to bring a child into the world ; **venir au ~** to come into the world - **2.** [gens] people *(pl)* ; **beaucoup/peu de ~** a lot of/not many people ; **tout le ~** everyone, everybody - **3.** *loc* : **c'est un ~!** that's really the limit! ; **se faire un ~ de qqch** to make too much of sthg ; **noir de ~** packed with people.

mondial, e, aux [mɔ̃djal, o] *adj* world *(avant n)*.

mondialement [mɔ̃djalmɑ̃] *adv* throughout ou all over the world.

mondialisation *nf* globalization.

monétaire [mɔnetɛr] *adj* monetary.

Mongolie [mɔ̃gɔli] *nf* : **la ~** Mongolia.

mongolien, enne [mɔ̃gɔljɛ̃, ɛn] *nm, f* Mongol.

moniteur, trice [mɔnitœr, tris] *nm, f* - **1.** [enseignant] instructor, coach ; **~ d'auto-école** driving instructor - **2.** [de colonie de vacances] supervisor, leader. ◆ **moniteur** *nm* [appareil & INFORM] monitor.

monnaie [mɔnɛ] *nf* - **1.** [moyen de paiement] money - **2.** [de pays] currency ; **~ unique** single currency - **3.** [pièces] change ; **avoir de la ~** to have change ; **avoir la ~** to have the change ; **faire (de) la ~** to get (some) change.

monnayer [11] [mɔneje] *vt* - **1.** [biens] to convert into cash - **2.** *fig* [silence] to buy.

monochrome [mɔnɔkrom] *adj* monochrome, monochromatic.

monocle [mɔnɔkl] *nm* monocle.

monocoque [mɔnɔkɔk] *nm & adj* [bateau] monohull.

monocorde [mɔnɔkɔrd] *adj* [monotone] monotonous.

monogramme [mɔnɔgram] *nm* monogram.

monolingue [mɔnɔlɛ̃g] *adj* monolingual.

monologue [mɔnɔlɔg] *nm* - **1.** THÉÂTRE soliloquy - **2.** [discours individuel] monologue.

monologuer [3] [mɔnɔlɔge] *vi* - **1.** THÉÂTRE to soliloquize - **2.** *fig & péj* [parler] to talk away.

monoparental, e, aux [mɔnɔparɑ̃tal, o] *adj* single-parent *(avant n)*.

monoplace [mɔnɔplas] *adj* single-seater *(avant n)*.

monopole [mɔnɔpɔl] *nm* monopoly ; **avoir le ~ de qqch** *litt & fig* to have a monopoly of ou on sthg ; **~ d'État** state monopoly.

monopoliser [3] [mɔnɔpɔlize] *vt* to monopolize.

monoski [mɔnɔski] *nm* - **1.** [objet] monoski - **2.** SPORT monoskiing.

monospace [mɔnɔspas] *nm* people carrier *Br*, minivan *Am*.

monosyllabe [mɔnɔsilab] <> *nm* monosyllable. <> *adj* monosyllabic.

monotone [mɔnɔtɔn] *adj* monotonous.

monotonie [mɔnɔtɔni] *nf* monotony.

monseigneur [mɔ̃sɛɲœr] *(pl* **messeigneurs** [mesɛɲœr]) *nm* [titre - d'évêque, de duc] His Grace ; [- de cardinal] His Eminence ; [- de prince] His (Royal) Highness.

monsieur [məsjø] *(pl* **messieurs** [mesjø]) *nm* - **1.** [titre] : **~ X** Mr X ; **bonjour ~** good morning ; [dans hôtel, restaurant] good morning, sir ; **bonjour messieurs** good morning (gentlemen) ; **messieurs dames** ladies and gentlemen ; **Monsieur le Ministre n'est pas là** the Minister is out - **2.** [homme quelconque] gentleman.

monstre [mɔ̃str] *nm* - **1.** [gén] monster - **2.** *(en apposition)* *fam* [énorme] colossal.

monstrueux, euse [mɔ̃stryø, øz] *adj* - **1.** [gén] monstrous - **2.** *fig* [erreur] terrible.

monstruosité [mɔ̃stryozite] *nf* monstrosity.

mont [mɔ̃] *nm* GÉOGR Mount ; **le ~ Blanc** Mont Blanc ; **le ~ Cervin** the Matterhorn.

montage [mɔ̃taʒ] *nm* - **1.** [assemblage] assembly ; [de bijou] setting - **2.** PHOT photomontage - **3.** CIN editing.

montagnard, e [mɔ̃taɲar, ard] *nm, f* mountain dweller.

montagne [mɔ̃taɲ] *nf* - **1.** [gén] mountain ; **les ~s Rocheuses** the Rocky Mountains - **2.** [région] : **la ~** the mountains *(pl)* ; **à la ~** in the mountains ; **en haute ~** at high altitudes. ◆ **montagnes russes** *nfpl* big dipper *(sg)*, roller coaster *(sg)*.

montagneux, euse [mɔ̃taɲø, øz] *adj* mountainous.

montant, e [mɔ̃tɑ̃, ɑ̃t] *adj* [mouvement]

rising. ◆ **montant** *nm* - **1.** [pièce verticale] upright - **2.** [somme] total (amount).

mont-de-piété [mɔ̃dpjete] (*pl* **monts-de-piété**) *nm* pawnshop.

monte-charge [mɔ̃tʃarʒ] *nm inv* goods lift *Br*, service elevator *Am*.

montée [mɔ̃te] *nf* - **1.** [de montagne] climb, ascent - **2.** [de prix] rise - **3.** [relief] slope, gradient.

monte-plats [mɔ̃tpla] *nm inv* dumbwaiter.

monter [3] [mɔ̃te] ◇ *vi (aux : être)* - **1.** [personne] to come/go up ; [température, niveau] to rise ; [route, avion] to climb ; ~ **sur qqch** to climb onto sthg - **2.** [passager] to get on ; ~ **dans un bus** to get on a bus ; ~ **dans une voiture** to get into a car - **3.** [cavalier] to ride ; ~ **à cheval** to ride - **4.** [marée] to go/come in. ◇ *vt (aux : avoir)* - **1.** [escalier, côte] to climb, to come/go up ; ~ **la rue en courant** to run up the street - **2.** [chauffage, son] to turn up - **3.** [valise] to take/bring up - **4.** [meuble] to assemble ; COUTURE to assemble, to put ou sew together ; [tente] to put up - **5.** [cheval] to mount - **6.** THÉÂTRE to put on - **7.** [société, club] to set up - **8.** CULIN to beat, to whisk (up). ◆ **se monter** *vp* - **1.** [s'assembler] : **se ~ facilement** to be easy to assemble - **2.** [atteindre] : **se ~ à** to amount to, to add up to.

monteur, euse [mɔ̃tœr, øz] *nm, f* - **1.** TECHNOL fitter - **2.** CIN editor.

monticule [mɔ̃tikyl] *nm* mound.

montre [mɔ̃tr] *nf* watch ; ~ **à quartz** quartz watch ; ~ **en main** to the minute, exactly ; **contre la** ~ [sport] time-trialling ; [épreuve] time trial ; **une course contre la** ~ *fig* a race against time.

montre-bracelet [mɔ̃trabraslɛ] *nf* wristwatch.

montrer [3] [mɔ̃tre] *vt* - **1.** [gén] to show ; ~ **qqch à qqn** to show sb sthg, to show sthg to sb - **2.** [désigner] to show, to point out ; ~ **qqch du doigt** to point at ou to sthg. ◆ **se montrer** *vp* - **1.** [se faire voir] to appear - **2.** *fig* [se présenter] to show o.s. - **3.** *fig* [se révéler] to prove (to be).

monture [mɔ̃tyr] *nf* - **1.** [animal] mount - **2.** [de lunettes] frame.

monument [mɔnymɑ̃] *nm* [gén] : ~ **(à)** monument (to) ; ~ **aux morts** war memorial.

monumental, e, aux [mɔnymɑ̃tal, o] *adj* monumental.

moquer [3] [mɔke] ◆ **se moquer** *vp* : **se ~ de** [plaisanter sur] to make fun of, to laugh at ; [ne pas se soucier de] not to give a damn about.

moquerie [mɔkri] *nf* mockery *(U)*, jibe.

moquette [mɔkɛt] *nf* (fitted) carpet.

moqueur, euse [mɔkœr, øz] *adj* mocking.

moral, e, aux [mɔral, o] *adj* moral. ◆ **moral** *nm* - **1.** [mental] : **au ~ comme au physique** mentally as well as physically - **2.** [état d'esprit] morale, spirits *(pl)* ; **avoir/ne pas avoir le ~** to be in good/bad spirits ; **remonter le ~ à qqn** to cheer sb up. ◆ **morale** *nf* - **1.** [science] moral philosophy, morals *(pl)* - **2.** [règle] morality - **3.** [mœurs] morals *(pl)* - **4.** [leçon] moral ; **faire la ~e à qqn** to preach to ou lecture sb.

moralisateur, trice [mɔralizatœr, tris] ◇ *adj* moralizing. ◇ *nm, f* moralizer.

moraliste [mɔralist] *nmf* moralist.

moralité [mɔralite] *nf* - **1.** [gén] morality - **2.** [enseignement] morals.

moratoire [mɔratwar] *nm* moratorium.

morbide [mɔrbid] *adj* morbid.

morceau, x [mɔrso] *nm* - **1.** [gén] piece - **2.** [de poème, de film] passage.

morceler [24] [mɔrsəle] *vt* to break up, to split up.

mordant, e [mɔrdɑ̃, ɑ̃t] *adj* biting. ◆ **mordant** *nm* [vivacité] keenness, bite.

mordiller [3] [mɔrdije] *vt* to nibble.

mordoré, e [mɔrdɔre] *adj* bronze.

mordre [76] [mɔrdr] ◇ *vt* [blesser] to bite. ◇ *vi* - **1.** [saisir avec les dents] : ~ **à** to bite - **2.** [croquer] : ~ **dans qqch** to bite into sthg - **3.** SPORT : ~ **sur la ligne** to step over the line.

mordu, e [mɔrdy] ◇ *pp* ▷ **mordre**. ◇ *adj* [amoureux] hooked. ◇ *nm, f* : ~ **de foot/ski** *etc* football/ski *etc* addict.

morfondre [75] [mɔrfɔ̃dr] ◆ **se morfondre** *vp* to mope.

morgue [mɔrg] *nf* - **1.** [attitude] pride - **2.** [lieu] morgue.

moribond, e [mɔribɔ̃, ɔ̃d] ◇ *adj* dying. ◇ *nm, f* dying person.

morille [mɔrij] *nf* morel.

morne [mɔrn] *adj* [personne, visage] gloomy ; [paysage, temps, ville] dismal, dreary.

morose [mɔroz] *adj* gloomy.

morphine [mɔrfin] *nf* morphine.

morphologie [mɔrfɔlɔʒi] *nf* morphology.

mors [mɔr] *nm* bit.

morse [mɔrs] *nm* - **1.** ZOOL walrus - **2.** [code] Morse (code).

morsure [mɔrsyr] *nf* bite.

mort, e [mɔr, mɔrt] ◇ *pp* ▷ **mourir**.

◇ *adj* dead ; ~ **de fatigue** *fig* dead tired ; ~ **de peur** *fig* frightened to death. ◇ *nm, f* - **1.** [cadavre] corpse, dead body - **2.** [défunt] dead person. ◆ **mort** ◇ *nm* - **1.** [victime] fatality - **2.** CARTES dummy. ◇ *nf litt & fig* death ; **de** ~ [silence] deathly ; **condamner qqn à** ~ JUR to sentence sb to death ; **se donner la** ~ to take one's own life, to commit suicide.

mortadelle [mɔrtadɛl] *nf* mortadella.

mortalité [mɔrtalite] *nf* mortality, death rate.

mort-aux-rats [mɔrora] *nf inv* rat poison.

Morte ⊳ mer.

mortel, elle [mɔrtɛl] ◇ *adj* - **1.** [humain] mortal - **2.** [accident, maladie] fatal - **3.** *fig* [ennuyeux] deadly (dull). ◇ *nm, f* mortal.

morte-saison [mɔrtsɛzɔ̃] *nf* slack season, off-season.

mortier [mɔrtje] *nm* mortar.

mortification [mɔrtifikasjɔ̃] *nf* mortification.

mort-né, e [mɔrne] (*mpl* **mort-nés**, *fpl* **mort-nées**) *adj* [enfant] still-born.

mortuaire [mɔrtɥɛr] *adj* funeral (*avant n*).

morue [mɔry] *nf* ZOOL cod.

mosaïque [mɔzaik] *nf litt & fig* mosaic.

Moscou [mɔsku] *n* Moscow.

mosquée [mɔske] *nf* mosque.

mot [mo] *nm* - **1.** [gén] word ; **gros ~** swearword ; ~ **de passe** password ; **~s croisés** crossword (puzzle) (*sg*) - **2.** [message] note, message.

motard [mɔtar] *nm* - **1.** [motocycliste] motorcyclist - **2.** [policier] motorcycle policeman.

motel [mɔtɛl] *nm* motel.

moteur, trice [mɔtœr, tris] *adj* [force, énergie] driving (*avant n*) ; **à quatre roues motrices** AUTOM with four-wheel drive. ◆ **moteur** *nm* TECHNOL motor, engine ; *fig* driving force ; ~ **de recherche** INFORM search engine.

motif [mɔtif] *nm* - **1.** [raison] motive, grounds (*pl*) - **2.** [dessin, impression] motif.

motion [mɔsjɔ̃] *nf* POLIT motion ; ~ **de censure** motion of censure.

motiver [3] [mɔtive] *vt* - **1.** [stimuler] to motivate - **2.** [justifier] to justify.

moto [mɔto] *nf* motorbike.

motocross [mɔtokrɔs] *nm* motocross.

motoculteur [mɔtɔkyltœr] *nm* ≃ Rotavator®.

motocyclette [mɔtɔsiklɛt] *nf* motorcycle, motorbike.

motocycliste [mɔtɔsiklist] *nmf* motorcyclist.

motorisé, e [mɔtɔrize] *adj* motorized.

motrice ⊳ moteur.

motricité [mɔtrisite] *nf* motor functions (*pl*).

motte [mɔt] *nf* : ~ **(de terre)** clod, lump of earth ; ~ **de beurre** slab of butter.

mou, molle [mu, mɔl] *adj* (**mol** *devant voyelle ou h muet*) - **1.** [gén] soft - **2.** [faible] weak - **3.** [résistance, protestation] half-hearted - **4.** *fam* [de caractère] wet, wimpy. ◆ **mou** *nm* - **1.** [de corde] : **avoir du ~** to be slack - **2.** [abats] lungs (*pl*).

mouchard, e [muʃar, ard] *nm, f fam* [personne] sneak. ◆ **mouchard** *nm fam* [dans camion, train] spy in the cab.

mouche [muʃ] *nf* - **1.** ZOOL fly - **2.** [accessoire féminin] beauty spot.

moucher [3] [muʃe] *vt* - **1.** [nez] to wipe ; ~ **un enfant** to wipe a child's nose - **2.** [chandelle] to snuff out - **3.** *fam fig* [personne] : ~ **qqn** to put sb in his/her place. ◆ **se moucher** *vp* to blow ou wipe one's nose.

moucheron [muʃrɔ̃] *nm* [insecte] gnat.

moucheté, e [muʃte] *adj* - **1.** [laine] flecked - **2.** [animal] spotted, speckled.

mouchoir [muʃwar] *nm* handkerchief.

moudre [85] [mudr] *vt* to grind.

moue [mu] *nf* pout ; **faire la** ~ to pull a face.

mouette [mwɛt] *nf* seagull.

moufle [mufl] *nf* mitten.

mouflon [muflɔ̃] *nm* wild sheep.

mouillage [mujaʒ] *nm* [NAVIG - emplacement] anchorage, moorings (*pl*).

mouillé, e [muje] *adj* wet.

mouiller [3] [muje] *vt* - **1.** [personne, objet] to wet ; **se faire** ~ to get wet ou soaked - **2.** NAVIG : ~ **l'ancre** to drop anchor - **3.** *fam fig* [compromettre] to involve. ◆ **se mouiller** *vp* - **1.** [se tremper] to get wet - **2.** *fam fig* [prendre des risques] to stick one's neck out.

moulage [mulaʒ] *nm* - **1.** [action] moulding *Br*, molding *Am*, casting - **2.** [objet] cast.

moule [mul] ◇ *nm* mould *Br*, mold *Am* ; ~ **à gâteau** cake tin *Br* ou pan *Am* ; ~ **à tarte** flan dish. ◇ *nf* ZOOL mussel.

mouler [3] [mule] *vt* - **1.** [objet] to mould *Br*, to mold *Am* - **2.** [forme] to make a cast of.

moulin [mulɛ̃] *nm* mill ; ~ **à café** coffee mill ; ~ **à paroles** *fig* chatterbox.

moulinet [mulinɛ] *nm* - **1.** PÊCHE reel

- **2.** [mouvement] : **faire des ~s** to whirl one's arms around.

Moulinette® [mulinɛt] *nf* food mill.

moulu, e [muly] *adj* [en poudre] ground.

moulure [mulyr] *nf* moulding.

mourant, e [murɑ̃, ɑ̃t] <> *adj* - **1.** [moribond] dying - **2.** *fig* [voix] faint. <> *nm, f* dying person.

mourir [42] [murir] *vi* - **1.** [personne] to die ; **s'ennuyer à ~** to be bored to death - **2.** [feu] to die down.

mousquetaire [muskətɛr] *nm* musketeer.

moussant, e [musɑ̃, ɑ̃t] *adj* foaming.

mousse [mus] <> *nf* - **1.** BOT moss - **2.** [substance] foam ; **~ à raser** shaving foam - **3.** CULIN mousse - **4.** [matière plastique] foam rubber. <> *nm* NAVIG cabin boy.

mousseline [muslin] *nf* muslin.

mousser [3] [muse] *vi* to foam, to lather.

mousseux, euse [musø, øz] *adj* - **1.** [shampooing] foaming, frothy - **2.** [vin, cidre] sparkling. ◆ **mousseux** *nm* sparkling wine.

mousson [musɔ̃] *nf* monsoon.

moussu, e [musy] *adj* mossy, moss-covered.

moustache [mustaʃ] *nf* moustache *Br*, mustache *Am*. ◆ **moustaches** *nfpl* [d'animal] whiskers.

moustachu, e [mustaʃy] *adj* with a moustache *Br* ou mustache *Am*.

moustiquaire [mustikɛr] *nf* mosquito net.

moustique [mustik] *nm* mosquito.

moutarde [mutard] *nf* mustard.

mouton [mutɔ̃] *nm* - **1.** ZOOL & *fig* sheep - **2.** [viande] mutton - **3.** *fam* [poussière] piece of fluff, fluff (*U*).

mouture [mutyr] *nf* - **1.** [de céréales, de café] grinding - **2.** [de thème, d'œuvre] rehash.

mouvance [muvɑ̃s] *nf* [domaine] sphere of influence.

mouvant, e [muvɑ̃, ɑ̃t] *adj* - **1.** [terrain] unstable - **2.** [situation] uncertain.

mouvement [muvmɑ̃] *nm* - **1.** [gén] movement ; **en ~** on the move - **2.** [de colère, d'indignation] burst, fit.

mouvementé, e [muvmɑ̃te] *adj* - **1.** [terrain] rough - **2.** [réunion, soirée] eventful.

mouvoir [54] [muvwar] *vt* to move. ◆ **se mouvoir** *vp* to move.

moyen, enne [mwajɛ̃, ɛn] *adj* - **1.** [intermédiaire] medium - **2.** [médiocre, courant] average. ◆ **moyen** *nm* means (*sg*), way ; **~ de communication** means of communi-

cation ; **~ de locomotion** OU **transport** means of transport. ◆ **moyenne** *nf* average ; **en moyenne** on average ; **la moyenne d'âge** the average age. ◆ **moyens** *nmpl* - **1.** [ressources] means ; **avoir les ~s** to be comfortably off - **2.** [capacités] powers, ability ; **faire qqch par ses propres ~s** to do sthg on one's own. ◆ **au moyen de** *loc prép* by means of.

Moyen Âge [mwajɛnaʒ] *nm* : **le ~** the Middle Ages (*pl*).

Moyen-Orient [mwajɛnɔrjɑ̃] *nm* : **le ~** the Middle East.

MST *nf* - **1.** (*abr de* **maladie sexuellement transmissible**) STD - **2.** (*abr de* **maîtrise de sciences et techniques**) *masters degree in science and technology*.

mû, mue [my] *pp* ▷ **mouvoir**.

mue [my] *nf* - **1.** [de pelage] moulting - **2.** [de serpent] skin, slough - **3.** [de voix] breaking.

muer [7] [mɥe] *vi* - **1.** [mammifère] to moult - **2.** [serpent] to slough its skin - **3.** [voix] to break ; [jeune homme] : **il mue** his voice is breaking.

muet, muette [mɥɛ, ɛt] <> *adj* - **1.** MÉD dumb - **2.** [silencieux] silent ; **~ d'admiration/d'étonnement** speechless with admiration/surprise - **3.** LING silent, mute. <> *nm, f* mute, dumb person. ◆ **muet** *nm* : **le ~** CIN silent films (*pl*).

muezzin [mɥedzin] *nm* muezzin.

mufle [myfl] *nm* - **1.** [d'animal] muzzle, snout - **2.** *fig* [goujat] lout.

muflerie [myfləri] *nf* loutishness.

mugir [32] [myʒir] *vi* - **1.** [vache] to moo - **2.** [vent, sirène] to howl.

muguet [myɡɛ] *nm* - **1.** [fleur] lily of the valley - **2.** MÉD thrush.

mule [myl] *nf* mule.

mulet [mylɛ] *nm* - **1.** [âne] mule - **2.** [poisson] mullet.

mulot [mylo] *nm* field mouse.

multicolore [myltikɔlɔr] *adj* multicoloured.

multifonction [myltifɔ̃ksjɔ̃] *adj inv* multifunction.

multilatéral, e, aux [myltilateral, o] *adj* multilateral.

multinational, e, aux [myltinasjɔnal, o] *adj* multinational. ◆ **multinationale** *nf* multinational (company).

multiple [myltipl] <> *nm* multiple. <> *adj* - **1.** [nombreux] multiple, numerous - **2.** [divers] many, various.

multiplication [myltiplikasjɔ̃] *nf* multiplication.

multiplier [10] [myltiplije] vt - **1.** [accroître] to increase - **2.** MATHS to multiply ; **X multiplié par Y égale Z** X multiplied by ou times Y equals Z. ➤ **se multiplier** vp to multiply.

multiracial, e, aux [myltirasjal, o] adj multiracial.

multirisque [myltirisk] adj comprehensive.

multitude [myltityd] nf : ~ **(de)** multitude (of).

municipal, e, aux [mynisipal, o] adj municipal. ➤ **municipales** nfpl : **les ~es** the local government elections.

municipalité [mynisipalite] nf - **1.** [commune] municipality - **2.** [conseil] town council.

munir [32] [mynir] vt : ~ **qqn/qqch de** to equip sb/sthg with. ➤ **se munir** vp : **se ~ de** to equip o.s. with.

munitions [mynisjɔ̃] nfpl ammunition (U), munitions.

muqueuse [mykøz] nf mucous membrane.

mur [myr] nm - **1.** [gén] wall - **2.** fig [obstacle] barrier, brick wall ; ~ **du son** AÉRON sound barrier.

mûr, mûre [myr] adj ripe ; [personne] mature. ➤ **mûre** nf - **1.** [de mûrier] mulberry - **2.** [de ronce] blackberry, bramble.

muraille [myraj] nf wall.

murène [myrɛn] nf moray eel.

murer [3] [myre] vt - **1.** [boucher] to wall up, to block up - **2.** [enfermer] to wall in. ➤ **se murer** vp to shut o.s. up ou away ; **se ~ dans** fig to retreat into.

muret [myrɛ] nm low wall.

mûrier [myrje] nm - **1.** [arbre] mulberry tree - **2.** [ronce] blackberry bush, bramble bush.

mûrir [32] [myrir] vi - **1.** [fruits, légumes] to ripen - **2.** fig [idée, projet] to develop - **3.** [personne] to mature.

murmure [myrmyr] nm murmur.

murmurer [3] [myrmyre] vt & vi to murmur.

musaraigne [myzarɛɲ] nf shrew.

musarder [3] [myzarde] vi fam to dawdle.

muscade [myskad] nf nutmeg.

muscat [myska] nm - **1.** [raisin] muscat grape - **2.** [vin] sweet wine.

muscle [myskl] nm muscle.

musclé, e [myskle] adj - **1.** [personne] muscular - **2.** fig [mesure, décision] forceful.

muscler [3] [myskle] vt : ~ **son corps** to build up one's muscles. ➤ **se muscler** vp to build up one's muscles.

musculation [myskylasjɔ̃] nf : **faire de la ~** to do muscle-building exercises.

muse [myz] nf muse.

museau, x [myzo] nm - **1.** [d'animal] muzzle, snout - **2.** fam [de personne] face.

musée [myze] nm museum ; [d'art] art gallery.

museler [24] [myzle] vt litt & fig to muzzle.

muselière [myzəljɛr] nf muzzle.

musette [myzɛt] nf haversack ; [d'écolier] satchel.

musical, e, aux [myzikal, o] adj - **1.** [son] musical - **2.** [émission, critique] music (avant n).

music-hall [myzikol] (pl music-halls) nm music-hall.

musicien, enne [myzisjɛ̃, ɛn] ◇ adj musical. ◇ nm, f musician.

musique [myzik] nf music ; ~ **de chambre** chamber music ; ~ **de film** film Br ou movie Am score.

musulman, e [myzylmɑ̃, an] adj & nm, f Muslim.

mutant, e [mytɑ̃, ɑ̃t] adj & nm, f mutant.

mutation [mytasjɔ̃] nf - **1.** BIOL mutation - **2.** fig [changement] transformation - **3.** [de fonctionnaire] transfer.

muter [3] [myte] vt to transfer.

mutilation [mytilasjɔ̃] nf mutilation.

mutilé, e [mytile] nm, f disabled person.

mutiler [3] [mytile] vt to mutilate ; **il a été mutilé du bras droit** he lost his right arm.

mutin, e [mytɛ̃, in] adj littéraire impish. ➤ **mutin** nm rebel ; MIL & NAVIG mutineer.

mutinerie [mytinri] nf rebellion ; MIL & NAVIG mutiny.

mutisme [mytism] nm silence.

mutualité [mytɥalite] nf [assurance] mutual insurance.

mutuel, elle [mytɥɛl] adj mutual. ➤ **mutuelle** nf mutual insurance company.

mycose [mikoz] nf mycosis, fungal infection.

myocarde [mjɔkard] nm myocardium.

myopathie [mjɔpati] nf myopathy.

myope [mjɔp] ◇ nmf shortsighted person. ◇ adj shortsighted, myopic.

myopie [mjɔpi] nf shortsightedness, myopia.

myosotis [mjozɔtis] nm forget-me-not.

myrtille [mirtij] *nf* bilberry *Br*, blueberry *Am*.

mystère [mistɛr] *nm* [gén] mystery.

mystérieux, euse [misterjø, øz] *adj* mysterious.

mysticisme [mistisism] *nm* mysticism.

mystification [mistifikasjɔ̃] *nf* [tromperie] hoax, practical joke.

mystifier [9] [mistifje] *vt* [duper] to take in.

mystique [mistik] ⟨⟩ *nmf* mystic. ⟨⟩ *adj* mystic, mystical.

mythe [mit] *nm* myth.

mythique [mitik] *adj* mythical.

mythologie [mitɔlɔʒi] *nf* mythology.

mythomane [mitɔman] *nmf* pathological liar.

n, N [ɛn] *nm inv* [lettre] n, N. ◆ **N** (*abr de* **nord**) N.

n' ⟹ **ne**.

nacelle [nasɛl] *nf* [de montgolfière] basket.

nacre [nakr] *nf* mother-of-pearl.

nage [naʒ] *nf* - **1.** [natation] swimming ; **traverser à la ~** to swim across - **2.** *loc* : **en ~** bathed in sweat.

nageoire [naʒwar] *nf* fin.

nager [17] [naʒe] *vi* - **1.** [se baigner] to swim - **2.** [flotter] to float - **3.** *fig* [dans vêtement] : **~ dans** to be lost in ; **~ dans la joie** to be incredibly happy.

nageur, euse [naʒœr, øz] *nm, f* swimmer.

naguère [nagɛr] *adv littéraire* a short time ago.

naïf, naïve [naif, iv] *adj* - **1.** [ingénu, art] naive - **2.** *péj* [crédule] gullible.

nain, e [nɛ̃, nɛn] ⟨⟩ *adj* dwarf (*avant n*). ⟨⟩ *nm, f* dwarf.

naissance [nɛsɑ̃s] *nf* - **1.** [de personne] birth ; **donner ~ à** to give birth to ; **le contrôle des ~s** birth control - **2.** [endroit] source ; [du cou] nape - **3.** *fig* [de science, nation] birth ; **donner ~ à** to give rise to.

naissant, e [nɛsɑ̃, ɑ̃t] *adj* - **1.** [brise] rising ; [jour] dawning - **2.** [barbe] incipient.

naître [92] [nɛtr] *vi* - **1.** [enfant] to be born ;

elle est née en **1965** she was born in 1965 - **2.** [espoir] to spring up ; **~ de** to arise from ; **faire ~ qqch** to give rise to sthg.

naïveté [naivte] *nf* - **1.** [candeur] innocence - **2.** *péj* [crédulité] gullibility.

nana [nana] *nf fam* [jeune fille] girl.

nanti, e [nɑ̃ti] *nm, f* wealthy person.

nantir [32] [nɑ̃tir] *vt littéraire* : **~ qqn de** to provide sb with.

nappe [nap] *nf* - **1.** [de table] tablecloth, cloth - **2.** *fig* [étendue - gén] sheet ; [- de brouillard] blanket - **3.** [couche] layer.

napper [3] [nape] *vt* CULIN to coat.

napperon [naprɔ̃] *nm* tablemat.

narcisse [narsis] *nm* BOT narcissus.

narcissisme [narsisism] *nm* narcissism.

narcotique [narkɔtik] *nm & adj* narcotic.

narguer [3] [narge] *vt* [danger] to flout ; [personne] to scorn, to scoff at.

narine [narin] *nf* nostril.

narquois, e [narkwa, az] *adj* sardonic.

narrateur, trice [naratœr, tris] *nm, f* narrator.

narrer [3] [nare] *vt littéraire* to narrate.

nasal, e, aux [nazal, o] *adj* nasal.

naseau, x [nazo] *nm* nostril.

nasillard, e [nazijar, ard] *adj* nasal.

nasse [nas] *nf* keep net.

natal, e, als [natal] *adj* [d'origine] native.

natalité [natalite] *nf* birth rate.

natation [natasjɔ̃] *nf* swimming ; **faire de la ~** to swim.

natif, ive [natif, iv] ⟨⟩ *adj* [originaire] : **~ de** native of. ⟨⟩ *nm, f* native.

nation [nasjɔ̃] *nf* nation. ◆ **Nations unies** *nfpl* : **les Nations unies** the United Nations.

national, e, aux [nasjɔnal, o] *adj* national. ◆ **nationale** *nf* : (route) **~e** ≃ A road *Br*, ≃ state highway *Am*.

nationaliser [3] [nasjɔnalize] *vt* to nationalize.

nationalisme [nasjɔnalism] *nm* nationalism.

nationalité [nasjɔnalite] *nf* nationality ; **de ~ française** of French nationality.

nativité [nativite] *nf* nativity.

natte [nat] *nf* - **1.** [tresse] plait - **2.** [tapis] mat.

naturaliser [3] [natyralize] *vt* - **1.** [personne, plante] to naturalize - **2.** [empailler] to stuff.

naturaliste [natyralist] ⟨⟩ *nmf* - **1.** LITTÉRATURE & ZOOL naturalist - **2.** [empailleur] taxidermist. ⟨⟩ *adj* naturalistic.

nature [natyr] <> *nf* nature. <> *adj inv* - **1.** [simple] plain - **2.** *fam* [spontané] natural.

naturel, elle [natyrɛl] *adj* natural. ➥ **naturel** *nm* - **1.** [tempérament] nature ; **être d'un ~ affable/sensible** *etc* to be affable/sensitive *etc* by nature - **2.** [aisance, spontanéité] naturalness.

naturellement [natyrɛlmɑ̃] *adv* - **1.** [gén] naturally - **2.** [logiquement] rationally.

naturiste [natyrist] *nmf* naturist.

naufrage [nofraʒ] *nm* - **1.** [navire] shipwreck ; **faire ~** to be wrecked - **2.** *fig* [effondrement] collapse.

naufragé, e [nofraʒe] <> *adj* shipwrecked. <> *nm, f* shipwrecked person.

nauséabond, e [nozeabɔ̃, ɔ̃d] *adj* nauseating.

nausée [noze] *nf* - **1.** MÉD nausea ; **avoir la ~** to feel nauseous OU sick - **2.** [dégoût] disgust.

nautique [notik] *adj* nautical ; [ski, sport] water *(avant n)*.

naval, e, als [naval] *adj* naval.

navet [navɛ] *nm* - **1.** BOT turnip - **2.** *fam péj* [œuvre] load of rubbish.

navette [navɛt] *nf* shuttle ; **~ spatiale** AÉRON space shuttle ; **faire la ~** to shuttle.

navigable [navigabl] *adj* navigable.

navigateur, trice [navigatœr, tris] *nm, f* navigator. ➥ **navigateur** *nm* INFORM browser.

navigation [navigasjɔ̃] *nf* navigation ; COMM shipping.

naviguer [3] [navige] *vi* - **1.** [voguer] to sail - **2.** [piloter] to navigate - **3.** INFORM to browse.

navire [navir] *nm* ship.

navrant, e [navrɑ̃, ɑ̃t] *adj* - **1.** [triste] upsetting, distressing - **2.** [regrettable, mauvais] unfortunate.

navrer [3] [navre] *vt* to upset ; **être navré de qqch/de faire qqch** to be sorry about sthg/to do sthg.

nazi, e [nazi] *nm, f* Nazi.

nazisme [nazism] *nm* Nazism.

NB *(abr de* **Nota Bene)** NB.

NDLR *(abr de* **note de la rédaction)** editor's note.

NDT *(abr de* **note du traducteur)** translator's note.

ne [nə], **n'** *(devant voyelle ou h muet) adv* - **1.** [négation] ⊏▷ **pas²**, **plus**, **rien** *etc* - **2.** [négation implicite] : **il se porte mieux que je ~ (le) croyais** he's in better health than I thought (he would be) - **3.** [avec verbes ou expressions marquant le doute, la

crainte etc] : **je crains qu'il n'oublie** I'm afraid he'll forget ; **j'ai peur qu'il n'en parle** I'm frightened he'll talk about it.

né, e [ne] *adj* born ; **~ en 1965** born in 1965 ; **~ le 17 juin** born on the 17th June ; **Mme X, ~e Y** Mrs X née Y.

néanmoins [neɑ̃mwɛ̃] *adv* nevertheless.

néant [neɑ̃] *nm* - **1.** [absence de valeur] worthlessness - **2.** [absence d'existence] nothingness ; **réduire à ~** to reduce to nothing.

nébuleux, euse [nebylø, øz] *adj* - **1.** [ciel] cloudy - **2.** [idée, projet] nebulous. ➥ **nébuleuse** *nf* ASTRON nebula.

nécessaire [neseser] <> *adj* necessary ; **~ à** necessary for ; **il est ~ de faire qqch** it is necessary to do sthg ; **il est ~ que** *(+ subjonctif)* : **il est ~ qu'elle vienne** she must come. <> *nm* - **1.** [biens] necessities *(pl)* ; **le strict ~** the bare essentials *(pl)* - **2.** [mesures] : **faire le ~** to do the necessary - **3.** [trousse] bag.

nécessité [nesesite] *nf* [obligation, situation] necessity ; **être dans la ~ de faire qqch** to have no choice OU alternative but to do sthg.

nécessiter [3] [nesesite] *vt* to necessitate.

nécrologique [nekrolɔʒik] *adj* obituary *(avant n)*.

nectar [nektar] *nm* nectar.

nectarine [nektarin] *nf* nectarine.

néerlandais, e [neerlɑ̃de, ɛz] *adj* Dutch. ➥ **néerlandais** *nm* [langue] Dutch. ➥ **Néerlandais, e** *nm, f* Dutchman *(f* Dutchwoman)* ; **les Néerlandais** the Dutch.

nef [nef] *nf* - **1.** [d'église] nave - **2.** *littéraire* [bateau] vessel.

néfaste [nefast] *adj* - **1.** [jour, événement] fateful - **2.** [influence] harmful.

négatif, ive [negatif, iv] *adj* negative. ➥ **négatif** *nm* PHOT negative. ➥ **négative** *nf* : **répondre par la négative** to reply in the negative.

négation [negasjɔ̃] *nf* - **1.** [rejet] denial - **2.** GRAM negative.

négligé, e [negliʒe] *adj* - **1.** [travail, tenue] untidy - **2.** [ami, jardin] neglected.

négligeable [negliʒabl] *adj* negligible.

négligemment [negliʒamɑ̃] *adv* - **1.** [sans soin] carelessly - **2.** [avec indifférence] casually.

négligence [negliʒɑ̃s] *nf* - **1.** [laisser-aller] carelessness - **2.** [omission] negligence ; **par ~** out of negligence.

négligent, e [negliʒɑ̃, ɑ̃t] *adj* - **1.** [sans soin] careless - **2.** [indifférent] casual.

négliger [17] [negliʒe] *vt* - **1.** [ami, jardin]

to neglect ; **~ de faire qqch** to fail to do sthg - **2.** [avertissement] to ignore. ◆ **se négliger** *vp* to neglect o.s.

négoce [negɔs] *nm* business.

négociant, e [negɔsjɑ̃, ɑ̃t] *nm, f* dealer.

négociateur, trice [negɔsjatœr, tris] *nm, f* negotiator.

négociation [negɔsjasjɔ̃] *nf* negotiation ; **~s de paix** peace negotiations.

négocier [9] [negɔsje] *vt* to negotiate.

nègre, négresse [nɛgr, negrɛs] *nm, f* negro (*f* negress) *(beware : the terms 'nègre' and 'négresse' are considered racist)*. ◆ **nègre** ◇ *nm fam* ghost writer. ◇ *adj* negro *(avant n) (beware : the term 'nègre' is considered racist)*.

neige [nɛʒ] *nf* [flocons] snow.

neiger [23] [neʒe] *v impers* : **il neige** it is snowing.

neigeux, euse [nɛʒø, øz] *adj* snowy.

nénuphar [nenyfar] *nm* water-lily.

néologisme [neɔlɔʒism] *nm* neologism.

néon [neɔ̃] *nm* - **1.** [gaz] neon - **2.** [enseigne] neon light.

néophyte [neɔfit] *nmf* novice.

néo-zélandais, e [neozelɑ̃dɛ, ɛz] *(mpl inv, fpl* **néo-zélandaises**) *adj* New Zealand *(avant n)*. ◆ **Néo-Zélandais, e** *nm, f* New Zealander.

Népal [nepal] *nm* : **le ~** Nepal.

nerf [nɛr] *nm* - **1.** ANAT nerve - **2.** *fig* [vigueur] spirit.

nerveux, euse [nɛrvø, øz] *adj* - **1.** [gén] nervous - **2.** [viande] stringy - **3.** [style] vigorous ; [voiture] nippy.

nervosité [nɛrvozite] *nf* nervousness.

nervure [nɛrvyr] *nf* [de feuille, d'aile] vein.

n'est-ce pas [nɛspa] *adv* : **vous me croyez, ~?** you believe me, don't you? ; **c'est délicieux, ~?** it's delicious, isn't it? ; **~ que vous vous êtes bien amusés?** you enjoyed yourselves, didn't you?

net, nette [nɛt] *adj* - **1.** [écriture, image, idée] clear - **2.** [propre, rangé] clean, neat - **3.** COMM & FIN net ; **~ d'impôt** tax-free *Br*, tax-exempt *Am* - **4.** [visible, manifeste] definite, distinct. ◆ **net** *adv* [sur le coup] on the spot ; **s'arrêter ~** to stop dead ; **se casser ~** to break clean off.

Net [nɛt] *nm fam* : **le ~** the Net, the net ; **surfer sur le ~** to surf the Net.

nettement [nɛtmɑ̃] *adv* - **1.** [clairement] clearly - **2.** [incontestablement] definitely ; **~ plus/moins** much more/less.

netteté [nɛtte] *nf* clearness.

nettoyage [netwajaʒ] *nm* [de vêtement] cleaning ; **~ à sec** dry cleaning.

nettoyer [13] [netwaje] *vt* - **1.** [gén] to clean - **2.** [grenier] to clear out.

neuf¹, neuve [nœf, nœv] *adj* new. ◆ **neuf** *nm* : **vêtu de ~** wearing new clothes ; **quoi de ~?** what's new? ; **rien de ~** nothing new.

neuf² [nœf] *adj num* & *nm* nine ; *voir aussi* **six**.

neurasthénique [nørastenik] *nmf* & *adj* depressive.

neurologie [nørɔlɔʒi] *nf* neurology.

neutraliser [3] [nøtralize] *vt* to neutralize.

neutralité [nøtralite] *nf* neutrality.

neutre [nøtr] ◇ *nm* LING neuter. ◇ *adj* - **1.** [gén] neutral - **2.** LING neuter.

neutron [nøtrɔ̃] *nm* neutron.

neuve ➭ **neuf¹**.

neuvième [nœvjɛm] *adj num, nm* OU *nmf* ninth ; *voir aussi* **sixième**.

névé [neve] *nm* snowbank.

neveu [nəvø] *nm* nephew.

névralgie [nevralʒi] *nf* MÉD neuralgia.

névrose [nevroz] *nf* neurosis.

névrosé, e [nevroze] *adj* & *nm, f* neurotic.

nez [ne] *nm* nose ; **saigner du ~** to have a nosebleed ; **~ aquilin** aquiline nose ; **~ busqué** hooked nose ; **~ à ~** face to face.

ni [ni] *conj* : **sans pull ~ écharpe** without a sweater or a scarf ; **je ne peux ~ ne veux venir** I neither can nor want to come. ◆ **ni ... ni** *loc corrélative* neither ... nor ; **~ lui ~ moi** neither of us ; **~ l'un ~ l'autre n'a parlé** neither of them spoke ; **je ne les aime ~ l'un ~ l'autre** I don't like either of them.

niais, e [njɛ, njɛz] ◇ *adj* silly, foolish. ◇ *nm, f* fool.

Nicaragua [nikaragwa] *nm* : **le ~** Nicaragua.

niche [niʃ] *nf* - **1.** [de chien] kennel - **2.** [de statue] niche.

nicher [3] [niʃe] *vi* [oiseaux] to nest.

nickel [nikɛl] ◇ *nm* nickel. ◇ *adj inv fam* spotless, spick and span.

nicotine [nikɔtin] *nf* nicotine.

nid [ni] *nm* nest.

nièce [njɛs] *nf* niece.

nier [9] [nje] *vt* to deny.

nigaud, e [nigo, od] *nm, f* simpleton.

Niger [niʒɛr] *nm* - **1.** [fleuve] : **le ~** the River Niger - **2.** [État] : **le ~** Niger.

Nigeria [niʒerja] *nm* : **le ~** Nigeria.

Nil [nil] *nm* : **le ~** the Nile.

n'importe ▷ importer.

nippon, one [nipɔ̃, ɔn] *adj* Japanese. ◆ **Nippon, one** *nm, f* Japanese (person) ; **les Nippons** the Japanese.

nirvana [nirvana] *nm* nirvana.

nitrate [nitrat] *nm* nitrate.

nitroglycérine [nitrɔgliserin] *nf* nitroglycerine.

niveau, x [nivo] *nm* [gén] level ; **de même ~** *fig* of the same standard ; **au-dessus du ~ de la mer** above sea level ; **~ de vie** standard of living ; **au ~ de** at the level of ; *fig* [en ce qui concerne] as regards.

niveler [24] [nivle] *vt* to level ; *fig* to level out.

noble [nɔbl] ◇ *nmf* nobleman (*f* noblewoman). ◇ *adj* noble.

noblesse [nɔblɛs] *nf* nobility.

noce [nɔs] *nf* - 1. [mariage] wedding - 2. [invités] wedding party. ◆ **noces** *nfpl* wedding (*sg*) ; **~s d'or/d'argent** golden/silver wedding (anniversary).

nocif, ive [nɔsif, iv] *adj* [produit, gaz] noxious.

noctambule [nɔktɑ̃byl] *nmf* night bird

nocturne [nɔktyrn] ◇ *nm* ou *nf* [d'un magasin] late opening. ◇ *adj* - 1. [émission, attaque] night (*avant n*) - 2. [animal] nocturnal.

Noël [nɔɛl] *nm* Christmas ; **joyeux ~!** happy ou merry Christmas!

nœud [nø] *nm* - 1. [de fil, de bois] knot ; **double ~** double knot - 2. NAVIG knot ; **filer à X ~s** NAVIG to do X knots - 3. [de l'action, du problème] crux - 4. [ornement] bow ; **~ de cravate** knot (*in one's tie*) ; **~ papillon** bow tie - 5. ANAT, ASTRON, ÉLECTR & RAIL node.

noir, e [nwar] *adj* - 1. [gén] black ; **~ de** [poussière, suie] black with - 2. [pièce, couloir] dark. ◆ **Noir, e** *nm, f* black. ◆ **noir** *nm* - 1. [couleur] black ; **~ sur blanc** *fig* in black and white - 2. [obscurité] dark - 3. *loc* : **acheter qqch au ~** to buy sthg on the black market ; **travail au ~** moonlighting. ◆ **noire** *nf* crotchet *Br*, quarter note *Am*.

noirâtre [nwaratr] *adj* blackish.

noirceur [nwarsœr] *nf fig* [méchanceté] wickedness.

noircir [32] [nwarsir] ◇ *vi* to darken. ◇ *vt litt* & *fig* to blacken.

Noire ▷ mer.

noisetier [nwaztje] *nm* hazel tree.

noisette [nwazɛt] *nf* [fruit] hazelnut.

noix [nwa] *nf* - 1. [fruit] walnut ; **~ de cajou** cashew (nut) ; **~ de coco** coconut ; **~ de**

muscade nutmeg - 2. *loc* : **à la ~** *fam* dreadful.

nom [nɔ̃] *nm* - 1. [gén] name ; **au ~ de** in the name of ; **~ déposé** trade name ; **~ de famille** surname ; **~ de jeune fille** maiden name - 2. [prénom] (first) name - 3. GRAM noun ; **~ propre/commun** proper/common noun.

nomade [nɔmad] ◇ *nmf* nomad. ◇ *adj* nomadic.

nombre [nɔ̃br] *nm* number ; **~ pair/impair** even/odd number.

nombreux, euse [nɔ̃brø, øz] *adj* - 1. [famille, foule] large - 2. [erreurs, occasions] numerous ; **peu ~** few.

nombril [nɔ̃bril] *nm* navel ; **il se prend pour le ~ du monde** he thinks the world revolves around him.

nominal, e, aux [nɔminal, o] *adj* - 1. [liste] of names - 2. [valeur, autorité] nominal - 3. GRAM noun (*avant n*).

nomination [nɔminasjɔ̃] *nf* nomination, appointment.

nommé, e [nɔme] *adj* - 1. [désigné] named - 2. [choisi] appointed.

nommément [nɔmemɑ̃] *adv* [citer] by name

nommer [3] [nɔme] *vt* - 1. [appeler] to name, to call - 2. [qualifier] to call - 3. [promouvoir] to appoint, to nominate - 4. [dénoncer, mentionner] to name. ◆ **se nommer** *vp* - 1. [s'appeler] to be called - 2. [se désigner] to give one's name.

non [nɔ̃] ◇ *adv* - 1. [réponse négative] no - 2. [se rapportant à une phrase précédente] not ; **moi ~** not me ; **moi ~ plus** (and) neither am/do *etc* I - 3. [sert à demander une confirmation] ; **c'est une bonne idée, ~?** it's a good idea, isn't it? - 4. [modifie un adjectif ou un adverbe] not ; **~ loin d'ici** not far from here ; **une difficulté ~ négligeable** a not inconsiderable problem. ◇ *nm inv* no. ◆ **non (pas) que ... mais** *loc corrélative* not that ... but.

nonagénaire [nɔnaʒener] *nmf* & *adj* nonagenarian.

non-agression [nɔnagresjɔ̃] *nf* non-aggression.

nonante [nɔnɑ̃t] *adj num Belg* & *Helv* ninety.

nonchalance [nɔ̃ʃalɑ̃s] *nf* nonchalance, casualness.

non-fumeur, euse [nɔ̃fymœr, øz] *nm, f* non-smoker.

non-lieu [nɔ̃ljø] (*pl* **non-lieux**) *nm* JUR dismissal through lack of evidence ; **rendre un ~** to dismiss a case for lack of evidence.

nonne [nɔn] *nf* nun.

non-sens [nɔ̃sɑ̃s] *nm inv* - **1.** [absurdité] nonsense - **2.** [contresens] meaningless word.

non-violence [nɔ̃vjɔlɑ̃s] *nf* non-violence.

non-voyant, e [nɔ̃vwajɑ̃, ɑ̃t] *nm, f* visually handicapped.

nord [nɔr] <> *nm* north ; **un vent du ~** a northerly wind ; **au ~** in the north ; **au ~ (de)** to the north (of) ; **le grand Nord** the frozen North. <> *adj inv* north ; [province, région] northern.

nord-africain, e [nɔrafrikɛ̃, ɛn] (*mpl* **nord-africains,** *fpl* **nord-africaines**) *adj* North African. ➡ **Nord-Africain, e** *nm, f* North African.

nord-américain, e [nɔramerikɛ̃, ɛn] (*mpl* **nord-américains,** *fpl* **nord-américaines**) *adj* North American. ➡ **Nord-Américain, e** *nm, f* North American.

nord-est [nɔrɛst] *nm & adj inv* northeast.

nordique [nɔrdik] *adj* Nordic, Scandinavian. ➡ **Nordique** *nmf* - **1.** [Scandinave] Scandinavian - **2.** *Can* North Canadian.

nord-ouest [nɔrwɛst] *nm & adj inv* north-west.

normal, e, aux [nɔrmal, o] *adj* normal. ➡ **normale** *nf* [moyenne] : **la ~e** the norm.

normalement [nɔrmalmɑ̃] *adv* normally, usually ; **~ il devrait déjà être arrivé** he should have arrived by now.

normalien, enne [nɔrmaljɛ̃, ɛn] *nm, f* - **1.** [élève d'une école normale] student at teacher training college *Br* ou teachers college *Am* - **2.** [ancien élève de l'École normale supérieure] graduate of the École normale supérieure.

normaliser [3] [nɔrmalize] *vt* - **1.** [situation] to normalize - **2.** [produit] to standardize.

normand, e [nɔrmɑ̃, ɑ̃d] *adj* Norman. ➡ **Normand, e** *nm, f* Norman.

Normandie [nɔrmɑ̃di] *nf* : **la ~** Normandy.

norme [nɔrm] *nf* - **1.** [gén] standard, norm - **2.** [critère] criterion.

Norvège [nɔrvɛʒ] *nf* : **la ~** Norway.

norvégien, enne [nɔrveʒjɛ̃, ɛn] *adj* Norwegian. ➡ **norvégien** *nm* [langue] Norwegian. ➡ **Norvégien, enne** *nm, f* Norwegian.

nos ▷ notre.

nostalgie [nɔstalʒi] *nf* nostalgia.

nostalgique [nɔstalʒik] *adj* nostalgic.

notable [nɔtabl] <> *adj* noteworthy, notable. <> *nm* notable.

notaire [nɔtɛr] *nm* ≃ solicitor *Br*, ≃ lawyer.

notamment [nɔtamɑ̃] *adv* in particular.

note [nɔt] *nf* - **1.** [gén & MUS] note ; **prendre des ~s** to take notes - **2.** SCOL & UNIV mark, grade *Am* ; **avoir une bonne/mauvaise ~** to have a good/bad mark - **3.** [facture] bill.

noter [3] [nɔte] *vt* - **1.** [écrire] to note down - **2.** [constater] to note, to notice - **3.** SCOL & UNIV to mark, to grade *Am*.

notice [nɔtis] *nf* instructions (*pl*).

notifier [9] [nɔtifje] *vt* : **~ qqch à qqn** to notify sb of sthg.

notion [nɔsjɔ̃] *nf* - **1.** [conscience, concept] notion, concept - **2.** (*gén pl*) [rudiment] smattering (*U*).

notoire [nɔtwar] *adj* [fait] well-known ; [criminel] notorious.

notre [nɔtr] (*pl* **nos** [no]) *adj poss* our.

nôtre [nɔtr] ➡ **le nôtre** (*f* **la nôtre,** *pl* **les nôtres**) *pron poss* ours ; **les ~s** our family (*sg*) ; **serez-vous des ~s demain?** will you be joining us tomorrow?

nouer [6] [nwe] *vt* - **1.** [corde, lacet] to tie ; [bouquet] to tie up - **2.** *fig* [gorge, estomac] to knot. ➡ **se nouer** *vp* - **1.** [gorge] to tighten up - **2.** [intrigue] to start.

noueux, euse [nwø, øz] *adj* [bois] knotty ; [mains] gnarled.

nougat [nuga] *nm* nougat.

nouille [nuj] *nf fam péj* idiot. ➡ **nouilles** *nfpl* [pâtes] pasta (*U*), noodles (*pl*).

nourrice [nuris] *nf* [garde d'enfants] nanny, child-minder ; [qui allaite] wet nurse.

nourrir [32] [nurir] *vt* - **1.** [gén] to feed - **2.** [sentiment, projet] to nurture. ➡ **se nourrir** *vp* to eat ; **se ~ de qqch** *litt & fig* to live on sthg.

nourrissant, e [nurisɑ̃, ɑ̃t] *adj* nutritious, nourishing.

nourrisson [nurisɔ̃] *nm* infant.

nourriture [nurityr] *nf* food.

nous [nu] *pron pers* - **1.** [sujet] we - **2.** [objet] us. ➡ **nous-mêmes** *pron pers* ourselves.

nouveau, elle, x [nuvo, ɛl, o] (*nouvel devant voyelle et h muet*) <> *adj* new ; **~x mariés** newlyweds. <> *nm, f* new boy (*f* new girl). ➡ **nouveau** *nm* : **il y a du ~** there's something new. ➡ **nouvelle** *nf* - **1.** [information] (piece of) news (*U*) - **2.** [court récit] short story. ➡ **nouvelles** *nfpl* news ; **les nouvelles** MÉDIA the news (*sg*) ; **il a donné de ses nouvelles** I/we *etc* have heard from him. ➡ **à nouveau** *loc adv* - **1.** [encore] again - **2.** [de manière différente] afresh, anew. ➞ **de nouveau** *loc adv* again.

nouveau-né, e [nuvone] (*mpl* **nouveau-nés**, *fpl* **nouveau-nées**) *nm, f* newborn baby.

nouveauté [nuvote] *nf* - **1.** [actualité] novelty - **2.** [innovation] something new - **3.** [ouvrage] new book/film *etc*.

nouvel, nouvelle ⊏➞ nouveau.

Nouvelle-Calédonie [nuvɛlkaledɔni] *nf* : la ~ New Caledonia.

Nouvelle-Guinée [nuvɛlgine] *nf* : la ~ New Guinea.

Nouvelle-Zélande [nuvɛlzelɑ̃d] *nf* : la ~ New Zealand.

novateur, trice [nɔvatœr, tris] ⟨⟩ *adj* innovative. ⟨⟩ *nm, f* innovator.

novembre [nɔvɑ̃br] *nm* November ; *voir aussi* **septembre**.

novice [nɔvis] ⟨⟩ *nmf* novice. ⟨⟩ *adj* inexperienced.

noyade [nwajad] *nf* drowning.

noyau, x [nwajo] *nm* - **1.** [de fruit] stone, pit - **2.** ASTRON, BIOL & PHYS nucleus - **3.** *fig* [d'amis] group, circle ; [d'opposants, de résistants] cell ; ~ **dur** hard core - **4.** *fig* [centre] core.

noyauter [3] [nwajote] *vt* to infiltrate.

noyé, e [nwaje] ⟨⟩ *adj* - **1.** [personne] drowned - **2.** [inondé] flooded ; **yeux ~s de larmes** eyes swimming with tears. ⟨⟩ *nm, f* drowned person.

noyer [13] [nwaje] *vt* - **1.** [animal, personne] to drown - **2.** [terre, moteur] to flood - **3.** [estomper, diluer] to swamp ; [contours] to blur. ➞ **se noyer** *vp* - **1.** [personne] to drown - **2.** *fig* [se perdre] : **se ~ dans** to become bogged down in.

N/Réf (*abr de* **Notre référence**) O/Ref.

nu, e [ny] *adj* - **1.** [personne] naked - **2.** [paysage, fil électrique] bare - **3.** [style, vérité] plain. ➞ **nu** *nm* nude ; **à ~** stripped, bare ; **mettre à ~** to strip bare.

nuage [nɥaʒ] *nm* - **1.** [gén] cloud - **2.** [petite quantité] : **un ~ de lait** a drop of milk.

nuageux, euse [nɥaʒø, øz] *adj* - **1.** [temps, ciel] cloudy - **2.** *fig* [esprit] hazy.

nuance [nɥɑ̃s] *nf* [de couleur] shade ; [de son, de sens] nuance.

nubile [nybil] *adj* nubile.

nucléaire [nykleɛr] ⟨⟩ *nm* nuclear energy. ⟨⟩ *adj* nuclear.

nudisme [nydism] *nm* nudism, naturism.

nudité [nydite] *nf* - **1.** [de personne] nudity, nakedness - **2.** [de lieu, style] bareness.

nuée [nɥe] *nf* - **1.** [multitude] : **une ~ de** a horde of - **2.** *littéraire* [nuage] cloud.

nues [ny] *nfpl* : **tomber des ~** to be completely taken aback.

nui [nɥi] *pp inv* ⊏➞ nuire.

nuire [97] [nɥir] *vi* : ~ **à** to harm, to injure.

nuisance [nɥizɑ̃s] *nf* nuisance (U), harm (U).

nuisette [nɥizɛt] *nf* short nightgown, babydoll nightgown.

nuisible [nɥizibl] *adj* harmful.

nuit [nɥi] *nf* - **1.** [laps de temps] night ; **cette ~** [la nuit dernière] last night ; [la nuit prochaine] tonight ; **de ~** at night ; **bateau/vol de ~** night ferry/flight ; **~ blanche** sleepless night - **2.** [obscurité] darkness, night ; **il fait ~** it's dark.

nuitée [nɥite] *nf* overnight stay.

nul, nulle [nyl] ⟨⟩ *adj indéf (avant n) littéraire* no. ⟨⟩ *adj (après n)* - **1.** [égal à zéro] nil - **2.** [sans valeur] useless, hopeless ; **être ~ en maths** to be hopeless *ou* useless at maths - **3.** [sans résultat] : **match ~** draw. ⟨⟩ *nm, f péj* nonentity. ⟨⟩ *pron indéf sout* no one, nobody. ➞ **nulle part** *loc adv* nowhere *Br*, no-place *Am*.

nullement [nylmɑ̃] *adv* by no means.

nullité [nylite] *nf* - **1.** [médiocrité] incompetence - **2.** JUR invalidity, nullity.

numéraire [nymerɛr] *nm* cash.

numération [nymerasjɔ̃] *nf* MÉD : ~ **globulaire** blood count.

numérique [nymerik] *adj* - **1.** [gén] numerical - **2.** INFORM digital.

numéro [nymero] *nm* - **1.** [gén] number ; **composer** *ou* **faire un ~** to dial a number ; **faire un faux ~** to dial a wrong number ; **~ minéralogique** *ou* **d'immatriculation** registration *Br ou* license *Am* number ; **~ de téléphone** telephone number ; **~ vert** ≃ freefone number - **2.** [de spectacle] act, turn - **3.** *fam* [personne] : **quel ~!** what a character!

numéroter [3] [nymerɔte] *vt* to number.

nu-pieds [nypje] *nm inv* [sandale] sandal.

nuptial, e, aux [nypsjal, o] *adj* nuptial.

nuque [nyk] *nf* nape.

nurse [nœrs] *nf* children's nurse, nanny.

nursery [nœrsəri] (*pl* **nurseries**) *nf* - **1.** [dans un hôpital] nursery - **2.** [dans un lieu public] parent-and-baby clinic.

nutritif, ive [nytritif, iv] *adj* nutritious.

nutritionniste [nytrisjɔnist] *nmf* nutritionist, dietician.

Nylon® [nilɔ̃] *nm* nylon.

nymphe [nɛ̃f] *nf* nymph.

nymphomane [nɛ̃fɔman] *nf & adj* nymphomaniac.

o, O [o] *nm inv* [lettre] o, O. ➤ **O** (*abr de* Ouest) W.

ô [o] *interj* oh!, O!

oasis [ɔazis] *nf* - 1. [dans désert] oasis - 2. *fig* [de calme] haven, oasis.

obéir [32] [ɔbeir] *vi* - 1. [personne] : ~ à qqn/qqch to obey sb/sthg - 2. [freins] to respond.

obéissant, e [ɔbeisɑ̃, ɑ̃t] *adj* obedient.

obélisque [ɔbelisk] *nm* obelisk.

obèse [ɔbɛz] *adj* obese.

obésité [ɔbezite] *nf* obesity.

objecteur [ɔbʒɛktœr] *nm* objector ; ~ de conscience conscientious objector.

objectif, ive [ɔbʒɛktif, iv] *adj* objective. ➤ **objectif** *nm* - 1. PHOT lens - 2. [but, cible] objective, target.

objection [ɔbʒɛksjɔ̃] *nf* objection ; **faire** ~ à to object to.

objectivité [ɔbʒɛktivite] *nf* objectivity.

objet [ɔbʒɛ] *nm* - 1. [chose] object ; ~ **d'art** objet d'art ; ~ **de valeur** valuable ; ~**s trouvés** lost property office *Br*, lost and found (office) *Am* - 2. [sujet] subject.

obligation [ɔbligasjɔ̃] *nf* - 1. [gén] obligation ; **être dans l'~ de faire qqch** to be obliged to do sthg - 2. FIN bond, debenture.

obligatoire [ɔbligatwar] *adj* - 1. [imposé] compulsory, obligatory - 2. *fam* [inéluctable] inevitable.

obligeance [ɔbliʒɑ̃s] *nf sout* obligingness ; **avoir l'~ de faire qqch** to be good ou kind enough to do sthg.

obliger [17] [ɔbliʒe] *vt* - 1. [forcer] : ~ **qqn à qqch** to impose sthg on sb ; ~ **qqn à faire qqch** to force sb to do sthg ; **être obligé de faire qqch** to be obliged to do sthg - 2. [rendre service à] to oblige. ➤ **s'obliger** *vp* : **s'~ à qqch** to impose sthg on o.s. ; **s'~ à faire qqch** to force o.s. to do sthg.

oblique [ɔblik] *adj* oblique.

obliquer [3] [ɔblike] *vi* to turn off.

oblitérer [18] [ɔblitere] *vt* - 1. [tamponner] to cancel - 2. MÉD to obstruct - 3. [effacer] to obliterate.

obnubiler [3] [ɔbnybile] *vt* to obsess ; **être obnubilé par** to be obsessed with ou by.

obole [ɔbɔl] *nf* small contribution.

obscène [ɔpsɛn] *adj* obscene.

obscénité [ɔpsenite] *nf* obscenity.

obscur, e [ɔpskyr] *adj* - 1. [sombre] dark - 2. [confus] vague - 3. [inconnu, douteux] obscure.

obscurantisme [ɔpskyrɑ̃tism] *nm* obscurantism.

obscurcir [32] [ɔpskyrsir] *vt* - 1. [assombrir] to darken - 2. [embrouiller] to confuse. ➤ **s'obscurcir** *vp* - 1. [s'assombrir] to grow dark - 2. [s'embrouiller] to become confused.

obscurité [ɔpskyrite] *nf* [nuit] darkness.

obsédé, e [ɔpsede] ◇ *adj* obsessed. ◇ *nm, f* obsessive.

obséder [18] [ɔpsede] *vt* to obsess, to haunt.

obsèques [ɔpsɛk] *nfpl* funeral *(sg)*.

obséquieux, euse [ɔpsekjø, øz] *adj* obsequious.

observateur, trice [ɔpsɛrvatœr, tris] ◇ *adj* observant. ◇ *nm, f* observer.

observation [ɔpsɛrvasjɔ̃] *nf* - 1. [gén] observation ; **être en ~** MÉD to be under observation - 2. [critique] remark.

observatoire [ɔpsɛrvatwar] *nm* - 1. ASTRON observatory - 2. [lieu de surveillance] observation post.

observer [3] [ɔpsɛrve] *vt* - 1. [regarder, remarquer, respecter] to observe - 2. [épier] to watch - 3. [constater] : ~ **que** to note that ; **faire ~ qqch à qqn** to point sthg out to sb.

obsession [ɔpsesjɔ̃] *nf* obsession.

obsolète [ɔpsɔlɛt] *adj* obsolete.

obstacle [ɔpstakl] *nm* - 1. [entrave] obstacle - 2. *fig* [difficulté] hindrance ; **faire ~ à qqch/qqn** to hinder sthg/sb.

obstétrique [ɔpstetrik] *nf* obstetrics *(U)*.

obstination [ɔpstinasjɔ̃] *nf* stubbornness, obstinacy.

obstiné, e [ɔpstine] *adj* - 1. [entêté] stubborn, obstinate - 2. [acharné] dogged.

obstiner [3] [ɔpstine] ➤ **s'obstiner** *vp* to insist ; **s'~ à faire qqch** to persist stubbornly in doing sthg ; **s'~ dans qqch** to cling stubbornly to sthg.

obstruction [ɔpstryksjɔ̃] *nf* - 1. MÉD obstruction, blockage - 2. POLIT & SPORT obstruction.

obstruer [3] [ɔpstrye] *vt* to block, to obstruct. ➤ **s'obstruer** *vp* to become blocked.

obtempérer [18] [ɔptɑ̃pere] *vi* : ~ **à** to comply with.

obtenir [40] [ɔptənir] *vt* to get, to obtain ; ~ **qqch de qqn** to get sthg from sb ; ~ **qqch à** ou **pour qqn** to obtain sthg for sb.

obtention [ɔptɑ̃sjɔ̃] *nf* obtaining.

obtenu, e [ɔptəny] *pp* ⊳ **obtenir**.

obturer [3] [ɔptyre] *vt* to close, to seal ; [dent] to fill.

obtus, e [ɔpty, yz] *adj* obtuse.

obus [ɔby] *nm* shell.

OC (*abr de* **ondes courtes**) SW.

occasion [ɔkazjɔ̃] *nf* - **1.** [possibilité, chance] opportunity, chance ; **saisir l'~ (de faire qqch)** to seize ou grab the chance (to do sthg) ; **rater une ~ (de faire qqch)** to miss a chance (to do sthg) ; **à l'~** some time ; [de temps en temps] sometimes, on occasion ; **à la première ~** at the first opportunity - **2.** [circonstance] occasion ; **à l'~ de** on the occasion of - **3.** [bonne affaire] bargain. ◆ **d'occasion** *loc adv* & *loc adj* second-hand.

occasionnel, elle [ɔkazjɔnɛl] *adj* [irrégulier - visite, problème] occasional ; [- travail] casual.

occasionner [3] [ɔkazjɔne] *vt* to cause.

occident [ɔksidɑ̃] *nm* west. ◆ **Occident** *nm* : **l'Occident** the West.

occidental, e, aux [ɔksidɑtal, o] *adj* western. ◆ **Occidental, e, aux** *nm, f* Westerner.

occlusion [ɔklyzjɔ̃] *nf* - **1.** MED blockage, obstruction - **2.** LING & CHIM occlusion.

occulte [ɔkylt] *adj* occult.

occulter [3] [ɔkylte] *vt* [sentiments] to conceal.

occupation [ɔkypasjɔ̃] *nf* - **1.** [activité] occupation, job - **2.** MIL occupation.

occupé, e [ɔkype] *adj* - **1.** [personne] busy ; **être ~ à qqch** to be busy with sthg - **2.** [appartement, zone] occupied - **3.** [place] taken ; [toilettes] engaged ; **c'est ~** [téléphone] it's engaged *Br* ou busy *Am*.

occuper [3] [ɔkype] *vt* - **1.** [gén] to occupy - **2.** [espace] to take up - **3.** [fonction, poste] to hold - **4.** [main-d'œuvre] to employ. ◆ **s'occuper** *vp* - **1.** [s'activer] to keep o.s. busy ; **s'~ à qqch/à faire qqch** to be busy with sthg/doing sthg - **2.** : **s'~ de qqch** [se charger de] to take care of sthg, to deal with sthg ; [s'intéresser à] to take an interest in, to be interested in ; **occupez-vous de vos affaires!** mind your own business! - **3.** [prendre soin] : **s'~ de qqn** to take care of sb, to look after sb.

occurrence [ɔkyrɑ̃s] *nf* - **1.** [circonstance] : **en l'~** in this case - **2.** LING occurrence.

OCDE (*abr de* **Organisation de coopération et de développement économique**) *nf* OECD.

océan [ɔseɑ̃] *nm* ocean ; **l'~ Antarctique** the Antarctic Ocean ; **l'~ Arctique** the Arctic Ocean ; **l'~ Atlantique** the Atlantic Ocean ; **l'~ Indien** the Indian Ocean ; **l'~ Pacifique** the Pacific Ocean.

Océanie [ɔseani] *nf* : **l'~** Oceania.

océanique [ɔseanik] *adj* ocean (*avant n*).

océanographie [ɔseanɔgrafi] *nf* oceanography.

ocre [ɔkr] *adj inv* & *nf* ochre *Br*, ocher *Am*.

octante [ɔktɑ̃t] *adj num Belg* & *Helv* eighty.

octave [ɔktav] *nf* octave.

octet [ɔktɛ] *nm* INFORM byte.

octobre [ɔktɔbr] *nm* October ; *voir aussi* **septembre**.

octogénaire [ɔktɔʒenɛr] *nmf* & *adj* octogenarian.

octroyer [13] [ɔktrwaje] *vt* : **~ qqch à qqn** to grant sb sthg, to grant sthg to sb. ◆ **s'octroyer** *vp* to grant o.s., to treat o.s. to.

oculaire [ɔkylɛr] ◇ *nm* eyepiece. ◇ *adj* ocular, eye (*avant n*) ; **témoin ~** eyewitness.

oculiste [ɔkylist] *nmf* ophthalmologist.

ode [ɔd] *nf* ode.

odeur [ɔdœr] *nf* smell.

odieux, euse [ɔdjø, øz] *adj* - **1.** [crime] odious, abominable - **2.** [personne, attitude] unbearable, obnoxious.

odorant, e [ɔdɔrɑ̃, ɑ̃t] *adj* sweet-smelling, fragrant.

odorat [ɔdɔra] *nm* (sense of) smell.

œdème [edɛm] *nm* oedema.

œil [œj] (*pl* **yeux** [jø]) *nm* - **1.** [gén] eye ; **yeux bridés/exorbités/globuleux** slanting/bulging/protuding eyes ; **avoir les yeux cernés** to have bags under one's eyes ; **baisser/lever les yeux** to look down/up, to lower/raise one's eyes ; **à l'~ nu** to the naked eye ; **à vue d'~** visibly - **2.** *loc* : **avoir qqch/qqn à l'~** to have one's eye on sthg/sb ; **n'avoir pas froid aux yeux** not to be afraid of anything, to have plenty of nerve ; **mon ~!** *fam* like hell! ; **cela saute aux yeux** it's obvious.

œillade [œjad] *nf* wink ; **lancer une ~ à qqn** to wink at sb.

œillère [œjɛr] *nf* eyebath. ◆ **œillères** *nfpl* blinkers *Br*, blinders *Am*.

œillet [œjɛ] *nm* - **1.** [fleur] carnation - **2.** [de chaussure] eyelet.

œnologue [enɔlɔg] *nmf* wine expert.

œsophage [ezɔfaʒ] *nm* oesophagus *Br*, esophagus *Am*.

œstrogène [ɛstrɔʒɛn] *nm* oestrogen *Br*, estrogen *Am*.

œuf [œf] *nm* egg ; **~ à la coque/au plat/poché** boiled/fried/poached egg ; **~ mollet/dur** soft-boiled/hard-boiled egg ; **~s brouillés** scrambled eggs.

œuvre [œvr] *nf* - **1.** [travail] work ; **être à l'~** to be working OU at work ; **se mettre à l'~** to get down to work ; **mettre qqch en ~** to make use of sthg ; [loi, accord, projet] to implement sthg - **2.** [artistique] work ; [ensemble de la production d'un artiste] works *(pl)* ; **~ d'art** work of art ; [organisation] charity ; **~ de bienfaisance** charity, charitable organization.

off [ɔf] *adj inv* CIN [voix, son] off.

offense [ɔfɑ̃s] *nf* - **1.** [insulte] insult - **2.** RELIG trespass.

offenser [3] [ɔfɑ̃se] *vt* - **1.** [personne] to offend - **2.** [bon goût] to offend against. ➡ **s'offenser** *vp* : **s'~ de** to take offence BR OU offense AM at, to be offended by.

offensif, ive [ɔfɑ̃sif, iv] *adj* offensive. ➡ **offensive** *nf* - **1.** MIL offensive ; **passer à l'offensive** to go on the offensive ; **prendre l'offensive** to take the offensive - **2.** *fig* [du froid] (sudden) onset.

offert, e [ɔfɛr, ɛrt] *pp* ▷ **offrir**.

office [ɔfis] *nm* - **1.** [bureau] office, agency ; **~ du tourisme** tourist office - **2.** [fonction] : **faire ~ de** to act as ; **remplir son ~** to do its job, to fulfil its function - **3.** RELIG service. ➡ **d'office** *loc adv* automatically, as a matter of course ; **commis d'~** officially appointed.

officialiser [3] [ɔfisjalize] *vt* to make official.

officiel, elle [ɔfisjɛl] *adj & nm, f* official.

officier[1] [9] [ɔfisje] *vi* to officiate.

officier[2] [ɔfisje] *nm* officer.

officieux, euse [ɔfisjø, øz] *adj* unofficial.

offrande [ɔfrɑ̃d] *nf* - **1.** [don] offering - **2.** RELIG offertory.

offre [ɔfr] *nf* - **1.** [proposition] offer ; [aux enchères] bid ; [pour contrat] tender ; **'~s d'emploi** 'situations vacant', ' vacancies' ; **~ d'essai** trial offer ; **~ de lancement** introductory offer ; **~ publique d'achat** takeover bid - **2.** ÉCON supply ; **la loi de l'~ et de la demande** the law of supply and demand.

offrir [34] [ɔfrir] *vt* - **1.** [faire cadeau] : **~ qqch à qqn** to give sb sthg, to give sthg to sb - **2.** [proposer] : **~ qqch à qqn** to offer sb sthg OU sthg to sb - **3.** [présenter] to offer, to present ; **son visage n'offrait rien d'accueillant** his/her face showed no sign of welcome. ➡ **s'offrir** *vp* - **1.** [croisière, livre] to treat o.s. to - **2.** [se présenter] to present itself - **3.** [se proposer] to offer one's services, to offer o.s.

offusquer [3] [ɔfyske] *vt* to offend. ➡ **s'offusquer** *vp* : **s'~ (de)** to take offence BR OU offense AM at.

ogive [ɔʒiv] *nf* - **1.** ARCHIT ogive - **2.** MIL [d'obus] head ; [de fusée] nosecone ; **~ nucléaire** nuclear warhead.

OGM (*abr de* **organisme génétiquement modifié**) *nm* GMO.

ogre, ogresse [ɔgr, ɔgrɛs] *nm, f* ogre (*f* ogress).

oh [o] *interj* oh! ; **~ la la!** dear oh dear!

ohé [ɔe] *interj* hey!

oie [wa] *nf* goose.

oignon [ɔɲɔ̃] *nm* - **1.** [plante] onion - **2.** [bulbe] bulb - **3.** MÉD bunion.

oiseau, x [wazo] *nm* - **1.** ZOOL bird ; **~ de proie** bird of prey - **2.** *fam péj* [individu] character.

oisif, ive [wazif, iv] ◇ *adj* idle. ◇ *nm, f* man of leisure (*f* woman of leisure).

oisillon [wazijɔ̃] *nm* fledgling.

oisiveté [wazivte] *nf* idleness.

O.K. [ɔke] *interj fam* okay.

oléoduc [ɔleɔdyk] *nm* (oil) pipeline.

olfactif, ive [ɔlfaktif, iv] *adj* olfactory.

olive [ɔliv] *nf* olive.

olivier [ɔlivje] *nm* [arbre] olive tree ; [bois] olive wood.

OLP (*abr de* **Organisation de libération de la Palestine**) *nf* PLO.

olympique [ɔlɛ̃pik] *adj* Olympic (*avant n*).

ombilical, e, aux [ɔ̃bilikal, o] *adj* umbilical.

ombrage [ɔ̃braʒ] *nm* shade.

ombragé, e [ɔ̃braʒe] *adj* shady.

ombrageux, euse [ɔ̃braʒø, øz] *adj* - **1.** [personne] touchy, prickly - **2.** [cheval] nervous, skittish.

ombre [ɔ̃br] *nf* - **1.** [zone sombre] shade ; **à l'~ de** [arbre] in the shade of ; [maison] in the shade of ; **laisser qqch dans l'~** *fig* to deliberately ignore sthg ; **vivre dans l'~** *fig* to live in obscurity - **2.** [forme, fantôme] shadow - **3.** [trace] hint.

ombrelle [ɔ̃brɛl] *nf* parasol.

OMC (*abr de* **Organisation mondiale du commerce**) *nf* WTO.

omelette [ɔmlɛt] *nf* omelette.

omettre [84] [ɔmɛtr] *vt* to omit ; **~ de faire qqch** to omit to do sthg.

omis, e [ɔmi, iz] *pp* ▷ **omettre**.

omission [ɔmisjɔ̃] *nf* omission ; **par ~** by omission.

omnibus [ɔmnibys] *nm* stopping OU local train.

231

omniprésent, e [ɔmniprezɑ̃, ɑ̃t] *adj* omniprésent.

omnisports [ɔmnispɔr] *adj inv* sports *(avant n).*

omnivore [ɔmnivɔr] ◇ *nm* omnivore. ◇ *adj* omnivorous.

omoplate [ɔmɔplat] *nf* [os] shoulder blade ; [épaule] shoulder.

OMS (*abr de* **Organisation mondiale de la santé**) *nf* WHO.

on [ɔ̃] *pron pers indéf* - **1.** [indéterminé] you, one ; ~ **n'a pas le droit de fumer ici** you're not allowed ou one isn't allowed to smoke here, smoking isn't allowed here - **2.** [les gens, l'espèce humaine] they, people ; ~ **vit de plus en plus vieux en Europe** people in Europe are living longer and longer - **3.** [quelqu'un] someone ; ~ **vous a appelé au téléphone ce matin** there was a telephone call for you this morning - **4.** *fam* [nous] we ; ~ **s'en va** we're off, we're going.

oncle [ɔ̃kl] *nm* uncle.

onctueux, euse [ɔ̃ktɥø, øz] *adj* smooth.

onde [ɔ̃d] *nf* PHYS wave. ◆ **ondes** *nfpl* [radio] air *(sg).*

ondée [ɔ̃de] *nf* shower (of rain).

ondoyer [13] [ɔ̃dwaje] *vi* to ripple.

ondulation [ɔ̃dylasjɔ̃] *nf* - **1.** [mouvement] rippling ; [de sol, terrain] undulation - **2.** [de coiffure] wave.

onduler [3] [ɔ̃dyle] *vi* [drapeau] to ripple, to wave ; [cheveux] to be wavy ; [route] to undulate.

onéreux, euse [ɔnerø, øz] *adj* costly.

ongle [ɔ̃gl] *nm* - **1.** [de personne] fingernail, nail ; **se ronger les** ~ to bite one's nails - **2.** [d'animal] claw.

onglet [ɔ̃glɛ] *nm* - **1.** [de reliure] tab - **2.** [de lame] thumbnail groove - **3.** CULIN top skirt.

onguent [ɔ̃gɑ̃] *nm* ointment.

onomatopée [ɔnɔmatɔpe] *nf* onomatopoeia.

ont ▷ avoir.

ONU, Onu [ɔny] (*abr de* **Organisation des Nations unies**) *nf* UN, UNO.

onyx [ɔniks] *nm* onyx.

onze [ɔ̃z] ◇ *adj num* eleven. ◇ *nm* [chiffre & SPORT] eleven ; *voir aussi* **six.**

onzième [ɔ̃zjɛm] *adj num, nm* OU *nmf* eleventh ; *voir aussi* **sixième.**

OPA (*abr de* **offre publique d'achat**) *nf* takeover bid.

opacité [ɔpasite] *nf* opacity.

opale [ɔpal] *nf & adj inv* opal.

opaline [ɔpalin] *nf* opaline.

opaque [ɔpak] *adj* : ~ **(à)** opaque (to).

OPEP, Opep [ɔpɛp] (*abr de* **Organisation des pays exportateurs de pétrole**) *nf* OPEC.

opéra [ɔpera] *nm* - **1.** MUS opera - **2.** [théâtre] opera house.

opéra-comique [ɔperakɔmik] *nm* light opera.

opérateur, trice [ɔperatœr, tris] *nm, f* operator.

opération [ɔperasjɔ̃] *nf* - **1.** [gén] operation - **2.** COMM deal, transaction.

opérationnel, elle [ɔperasjɔnɛl] *adj* operational.

opérer [18] [ɔpere] ◇ *vt* - **1.** MÉD to operate on - **2.** [exécuter] to carry out, to implement ; [choix, tri] to make. ◇ *vi* [agir] to take effect ; [personne] to operate, to proceed. ◆ **s'opérer** *vp* to come about, to take place.

opérette [ɔperɛt] *nf* operetta.

ophtalmologiste [ɔftalmɔlɔʒist] *nmf* ophthalmologist.

Opinel® [ɔpinɛl] *nm folding knife used especially for outdoor activities, scouting etc.*

opiniâtre [ɔpinjɑtr] *adj* - **1.** [caractère, personne] stubborn, obstinate - **2.** [effort] dogged ; [travail] unrelenting ; [fièvre, toux] persistent.

opinion [ɔpinjɔ̃] *nf* opinion ; **avoir (une) bonne/mauvaise** ~ **de** to have a good/bad opinion of ; **l'~ publique** public opinion.

opium [ɔpjɔm] *nm* opium.

opportun, e [ɔpɔrtœ̃, yn] *adj* opportune, timely.

opportuniste [ɔpɔrtynist] ◇ *nmf* opportunist. ◇ *adj* opportunistic.

opportunité [ɔpɔrtynite] *nf* - **1.** [à-propos] opportuneness, timeliness - **2.** [occasion] opportunity.

opposant, e [ɔpozɑ̃, ɑ̃t] ◇ *adj* opposing. ◇ *nm, f* : ~ **(à)** opponent (of).

opposé, e [ɔpoze] *adj* - **1.** [direction, côté, angle] opposite - **2.** [intérêts, opinions] conflicting ; [forces] opposing - **3.** [hostile] : ~ **à** opposed to. ◆ **opposé** *nm* : **l'~** the opposite ; **à l'~ de** in the opposite direction from ; *fig* unlike, contrary to.

opposer [3] [ɔpoze] *vt* - **1.** [mettre en opposition - choses, notions] : ~ **qqch (à)** to contrast sthg (with) - **2.** [mettre en présence - personnes, armées] to oppose ; ~ **deux équipes** to bring two teams together ; ~ **qqn à qqn** to pit ou set sb against sb - **3.** [refus, protestation, objection] to put forward - **4.** [diviser] to divide. ◆ **s'opposer** *vp* - **1.** [contraster] to contrast - **2.** [entrer en conflit] to clash - **3. : s'~ à** [se dresser contre] to oppose, to be opposed to ; **s'~ à ce que qqn fasse qqch** to be opposed to sb's doing sthg.

opposition [ɔpozisjɔ̃] *nf* - **1.** [gén] opposition ; **faire ~ à** [décision, mariage] to oppose ; [chèque] to stop ; **entrer en ~ avec** to come into conflict with - **2.** JUR **: ~ (à)** objection (to) - **3.** [contraste] contrast ; **par ~ à** in contrast with, as opposed to.

oppresser [4] [ɔprese] *vt* - **1.** [étouffer] to suffocate, to stifle - **2.** *fig* [tourmenter] to oppress.

oppresseur [ɔpresœr] *nm* oppressor.

oppressif, ive [ɔpresif, iv] *adj* oppressive.

oppression [ɔpresjɔ̃] *nf* - **1.** [asservissement] oppression - **2.** [malaise] tightness of the chest.

opprimé, e [ɔprime] <> *adj* oppressed. <> *nm, f* oppressed person.

opprimer [3] [ɔprime] *vt* - **1.** [asservir] to oppress - **2.** [étouffer] to stifle.

opter [3] [ɔpte] *vi* **: ~ pour** to opt for.

opticien, enne [ɔptisjɛ̃, ɛn] *nm, f* optician.

optimal, e, aux [ɔptimal, o] *adj* optimal.

optimiste [ɔptimist] <> *nmf* optimist. <> *adj* optimistic.

option [ɔpsjɔ̃] *nf* - **1.** [gén] option ; **prendre une ~ sur** FIN to take (out) an option on - **2.** [accessoire] optional extra.

optionnel, elle [ɔpsjɔnɛl] *adj* optional.

optique [ɔptik] <> *nf* - **1.** [science, technique] optics *(U)* - **2.** [perspective] viewpoint. <> *adj* [nerf] optic ; [verre] optical.

opulence [ɔpylɑ̃s] *nf* - **1.** [richesse] opulence - **2.** [ampleur] fullness, ampleness.

opulent, e [ɔpylɑ̃, ɑ̃t] *adj* - **1.** [riche] rich - **2.** [gros] ample.

or¹ [ɔr] *nm* - **1.** [métal, couleur] gold ; **en ~** [objet] gold *(avant n)* ; **une occasion en ~** a golden opportunity ; **une affaire en ~** [achat] an excellent bargain ; [commerce] a lucrative line of business ; **j'ai une femme en ~** I've a wonderful wife ; **~ massif** solid gold - **2.** [dorure] gilding.

or² [ɔr] *conj* [au début d'une phrase] now ; [pour introduire un contraste] well, but.

oracle [ɔrakl] *nm* oracle.

orage [ɔraʒ] *nm* [tempête] storm.

orageux, euse [ɔraʒø, øz] *adj* stormy.

oraison [ɔrɛzɔ̃] *nf* prayer ; **~ funèbre** funeral oration.

oral, e, aux [ɔral, o] *adj* oral. ◆ **oral** *nm* oral (examination) ; **~ de rattrapage** *oral examination taken after failing written exams.*

oralement [ɔralmɑ̃] *adv* orally.

orange [ɔrɑ̃ʒ] <> *nf* orange. <> *nm & adj inv* [couleur] orange.

orangé, e [ɔrɑ̃ʒe] *adj* orangey.

orangeade [ɔrɑ̃ʒad] *nf* orange squash.

oranger [ɔrɑ̃ʒe] *nm* orange tree.

orang-outan, orang-outang [ɔrɑ̃utɑ̃] *nm* orangutan.

orateur, trice [ɔratœr, tris] *nm, f* - **1.** [conférencier] speaker - **2.** [personne éloquente] orator.

orbital, e, aux [ɔrbital, o] *adj* [mouvement] orbital ; [station] orbiting.

orbite [ɔrbit] *nf* - **1.** ANAT (eye) socket - **2.** ASTRON & *fig* orbit ; **mettre sur ~** AÉRON to put into orbit ; *fig* to launch.

orchestre [ɔrkɛstr] *nm* - **1.** MUS orchestra - **2.** CIN & THÉÂTRE stalls *(pl)* *Br*, orchestra *Am* ; **fauteuil d'~** seat in the stalls *Br*, orchestra seat *Am*.

orchestrer [3] [ɔrkɛstre] *vt litt & fig* to orchestrate.

orchidée [ɔrkide] *nf* orchid.

ordinaire [ɔrdinɛr] <> *adj* - **1.** [usuel, standard] ordinary, normal - **2.** *péj* [commun] ordinary, common. <> *nm* - **1.** [moyenne] **: l'~** the ordinary - **2.** [alimentation] usual diet. ◆ **d'ordinaire** *loc adv* normally, usually.

ordinal, e, aux [ɔrdinal, o] *adj* ordinal. ◆ **ordinal, aux** *nm* ordinal (number).

ordinateur [ɔrdinatœr] *nm* computer ; **~ individuel** personal computer, PC ; **~ de poche** palmtop.

ordonnance [ɔrdɔnɑ̃s] <> *nf* - **1.** MÉD prescription - **2.** [de gouvernement, juge] order. <> *nm* OU *nf* MIL orderly.

ordonné, e [ɔrdɔne] *adj* [maison, élève] tidy.

ordonner [3] [ɔrdɔne] *vt* - **1.** [ranger] to organize, to put in order - **2.** [enjoindre] to order, to tell ; **~ à qqn de faire qqch** to order sb to do sthg - **3.** RELIG to ordain - **4.** MATHS to arrange in order. ◆ **s'ordonner** *vp* to be arranged OU put in order.

ordre [ɔrdr] *nm* - **1.** [gén, MIL & RELIG] order ; **par ~ alphabétique/chronologique/ décroissant** in alphabetical/chronological/ descending order ; **donner un ~ à qqn** to give sb an order ; **être aux ~s de qqn** to be at sb's disposal ; **jusqu'à nouvel ~** until further notice ; **l'~ public** law and order - **2.** [bonne organisation] tidiness, orderliness ; **en ~** orderly, tidy ; **mettre en ~** to put in order, to tidy (up) - **3.** [catégorie] **: de premier ~** first-rate ; **de second ~** second-rate ; **d'~ privé/pratique** of a private/practical nature ; **pouvez-vous me donner un ~ de**

grandeur? can you give me some idea of the size/amount *etc*? **- 4.** [corporation] professional association ; **l'Ordre des médecins** ≈ the British Medical Association *Br*, ≈ the American Medical Association *Am* **- 5.** FIN : **à l'~ de** payable to. ◆ **ordre du jour** *nm* **- 1.** [de réunion] agenda ; **à l'~ du jour** [de réunion] on the agenda ; *fig* topical **- 2.** MIL order of the day.

ordure [ɔrdyr] *nf* **- 1.** *fig* [grossièreté] filth *(U)* **- 2.** *péj* [personne] scum *(U)*, bastard. ◆ **ordures** *nfpl* [déchets] rubbish *(U) Br*, garbage *(U) Am*.

ordurier, ère [ɔrdyrje, ɛr] *adj* filthy, obscene.

orée [ɔre] *nf* edge.

oreille [ɔrɛj] *nf* **- 1.** ANAT ear **- 2.** [ouïe] hearing **- 3.** [de fauteuil, écrou] wing ; [de marmite, tasse] handle.

oreiller [ɔrɛje] *nm* pillow.

oreillette [ɔrɛjɛt] *nf* **- 1.** [du cœur] auricle **- 2.** [de casquette] earflap.

oreillons [ɔrɛjɔ̃] *nmpl* mumps *(sg)*.

ores [ɔr] ◆ **d'ores et déjà** *loc adv* from now on.

orfèvre [ɔrfɛvr] *nm* goldsmith ; [d'argent] silversmith.

orfèvrerie [ɔrfɛvrəri] *nf* **- 1.** [art] goldsmith's art ; [d'argent] silversmith's art **- 2.** [commerce] goldsmith's trade ; [d'argent] silversmith's trade.

organe [ɔrgan] *nm* **- 1.** ANAT organ **- 2.** [institution] organ, body **- 3.** *fig* [porte-parole] representative.

organigramme [ɔrganigram] *nm* **- 1.** [hiérarchique] organization chart **- 2.** INFORM flow chart.

organique [ɔrganik] *adj* organic.

organisateur, trice [ɔrganizatœr, tris] ◇ *adj* organizing *(avant n)*. ◇ *nm, f* organizer.

organisation [ɔrganizasjɔ̃] *nf* organization ; **Organisation mondiale du commerce** World Trade Organization.

organisé, e [ɔrganize] *adj* organized.

organiser [3] [ɔrganize] *vt* to organize. ◆ **s'organiser** *vp* **- 1.** [personne] to be ou get organized **- 2.** [prendre forme] to take shape.

organisme [ɔrganism] *nm* **- 1.** BIOL & ZOOL organism ; **~ génétiquement modifié** genetically modified organism **- 2.** [institution] body, organization.

organiste [ɔrganist] *nmf* organist.

orgasme [ɔrgasm] *nm* orgasm.

orge [ɔrʒ] *nf* barley.

orgie [ɔrʒi] *nf* orgy.

orgue [ɔrg] *nm* organ.

orgueil [ɔrgœj] *nm* pride.

orgueilleux, euse [ɔrgœjø, øz] ◇ *adj* proud. ◇ *nm, f* proud person.

orient [ɔrjɑ̃] *nm* east. ◆ **Orient** *nm* : **l'Orient** the Orient, the East.

oriental, e, aux [ɔrjɑ̃tal, o] *adj* [région, frontière] eastern ; [d'Extrême-Orient] oriental.

orientation [ɔrjɑ̃tasjɔ̃] *nf* **- 1.** [direction] orientation ; **avoir le sens de l'~** to have a good sense of direction **- 2.** SCOL career **- 3.** [de maison] aspect **- 4.** *fig* [de politique, recherche] direction, trend.

orienté, e [ɔrjɑ̃te] *adj* [tendancieux] biased.

orienter [3] [ɔrjɑ̃te] *vt* **- 1.** [disposer] to position **- 2.** [voyageur, élève, recherches] to guide, to direct. ◆ **s'orienter** *vp* **- 1.** [se repérer] to find ou get one's bearings **- 2.** *fig* [se diriger] : **s'~ vers** to move towards *Br* ou toward *Am*.

orifice [ɔrifis] *nm* orifice.

originaire [ɔriʒinɛr] *adj* **- 1.** [natif] : **être ~ de** to originate from ; [personne] to be a native of **- 2.** [premier] original.

original, e, aux [ɔriʒinal, o] ◇ *adj* **- 1.** [premier, inédit] original **- 2.** [singulier] eccentric. ◇ *nm, f* [personne] (outlandish) character. ◆ **original, aux** *nm* [œuvre, document] original.

originalité [ɔriʒinalite] *nf* **- 1.** [nouveauté] originality ; [caractéristique] original feature **- 2.** [excentricité] eccentricity.

origine [ɔriʒin] *nf* **- 1.** [gén] origin ; **d'~** [originel] original ; [de départ] of origin ; **pays d'~** country of origin ; **d'~ anglaise** of English origin ; **à l'~** originally **- 2.** [souche] origins *(pl)* **- 3.** [provenance] source.

ORL *nmf (abr de* **oto-rhino-laryngologiste)** ENT specialist.

orme [ɔrm] *nm* elm.

ornement [ɔrnəmɑ̃] *nm* **- 1.** [gén & MUS] ornament ; **d'~** [plante, arbre] ornamental **- 2.** ARCHIT embellishment.

orner [3] [ɔrne] *vt* **- 1.** [décorer] : **~ (de)** to decorate (with) **- 2.** [agrémenter] to adorn.

ornière [ɔrnjɛr] *nf* rut.

ornithologie [ɔrnitɔlɔʒi] *nf* ornithology.

orphelin, e [ɔrfəlɛ̃, in] ◇ *adj* orphan *(avant n)*, orphaned. ◇ *nm, f* orphan.

orphelinat [ɔrfəlina] *nm* orphanage.

orteil [ɔrtɛj] *nm* toe.

orthodontiste [ɔrtɔdɔ̃tist] *nmf* orthodontist.

orthodoxe [ɔrtɔdɔks] ◇ *adj* **- 1.** RELIG

Orthodox - 2. [conformiste] orthodox. ◇ nmf RELIG Orthodox Christian.

orthographe [ɔrtɔgraf] nf spelling.

orthopédiste [ɔrtɔpedist] nmf orthopaedist.

orthophoniste [ɔrtɔfɔnist] nmf speech therapist.

ortie [ɔrti] nf nettle.

os [ɔs, pl o] nm - 1. [gén] bone ; ~ à moelle marrowbone - 2. fam fig [difficulté] snag, hitch.

oscillation [ɔsilasjɔ̃] nf oscillation ; [de navire] rocking.

osciller [3] [ɔsile] vi - 1. [se balancer] to swing ; [navire] to rock - 2. [vaciller, hésiter] to waver.

osé, e [oze] adj daring, audacious.

oseille [ozɛj] nf BOT sorrel.

oser [3] [oze] vt to dare ; ~ faire qqch to dare (to) do sthg.

osier [ozje] nm - 1. BOT osier - 2. [fibre] wicker.

Oslo [ɔslo] n Oslo.

ossature [ɔsatyr] nf - 1. ANAT skeleton - 2. fig [structure] framework.

ossements [ɔsmã] nmpl bones.

osseux, euse [ɔsø, øz] adj - 1. ANAT & MÉD bone (avant n) - 2. [maigre] bony.

ossuaire [ɔsɥɛr] nm ossuary.

ostensible [ɔstɑ̃sibl] adj conspicuous.

ostentation [ɔstɑ̃tasjɔ̃] nf ostentation.

ostéopathe [ɔsteɔpat] nmf osteopath.

otage [ɔtaʒ] nm hostage ; prendre qqn en ~ to take sb hostage.

OTAN, Otan [ɔtɑ̃] (abr de Organisation du traité de l'Atlantique Nord) nf NATO.

otarie [ɔtari] nf sea lion.

ôter [3] [ote] vt - 1. [enlever] to take off - 2. [soustraire] to take away - 3. [retirer, prendre] : ~ qqch à qqn to take sthg away from sb.

otite [ɔtit] nf ear infection.

oto-rhino-laryngologie [ɔtɔrinɔlarɛ̃gɔlɔʒi] nf ear, nose and throat medicine, ENT.

ou [u] conj - 1. [indique une alternative, une approximation] or - 2. [sinon] : ~ (bien) or (else). ◆ ou (bien) ... ou (bien) loc corrélative either ... or ; ~ c'est elle, ~ c'est moi! it's either her or me!

où [u] ◇ pron rel - 1. [spatial] where ; le village ~ j'habite the village where I live, the village I live in ; pose-le là ~ tu l'as trouvé put it back where you found it ; partout ~ vous irez wherever you go - 2. [temporel] that ; le jour ~ je suis venu the day (that) I

came. ◇ adv where ; je vais ~ je veux I go where I please ; ~ que vous alliez wherever you go. ◇ adv interr where? ; ~ vas-tu? where are you going? ; dites-moi ~ il est allé tell me where he's gone. ◆ d'où loc adv [conséquence] hence.

ouaté, e [wate] adj - 1. [garni d'ouate] cotton wool Br (avant n), cotton Am (avant n) ; [vêtement] quilted - 2. fig [feutré] muffled.

oubli [ubli] nm - 1. [acte d'oublier] forgetting - 2. [négligence] omission ; [étourderie] oversight - 3. [général] oblivion ; tomber dans l'~ to sink into oblivion.

oublier [10] [ublije] vt to forget ; [laisser quelque part] to leave behind ; ~ de faire qqch to forget to do sthg.

oubliettes [ublijɛt] nfpl dungeon (sg).

ouest [wɛst] ◇ nm west ; un vent d'~ a westerly wind ; à l'~ in the west ; à l'~ (de) to the west (of). ◇ adj inv [gén] west ; [province, région] western.

ouest-allemand, e [wɛstalmã, ãd] adj West German.

ouf [uf] interj phew!

Ouganda [ugãda] nm : l'~ Uganda.

oui [wi] ◇ adv yes ; tu viens? - ~ are you coming? - yes (I am) ; tu viens, ~ ou non? are you coming or not?, are you coming or aren't you? ; je crois que ~ I think so ; faire signe que ~ to nod ; mais ~, bien sûr que ~ yes, of course. ◇ nm inv yes ; pour un ~ pour un non for no apparent reason.

ouï-dire [widir] nm inv : par ~ by ou from hearsay.

ouïe [wi] nf hearing ; avoir l'~ fine to have excellent hearing. ◆ ouïes nfpl [de poisson] gills.

ouragan [uragã] nm MÉTÉOR hurricane.

ourlet [urlɛ] nm COUTURE hem.

ours [urs] nm bear ; ~ (en peluche) teddy (bear) ; ~ polaire polar bear.

ourse [urs] nf she-bear.

oursin [ursɛ̃] nm sea urchin.

ourson [ursɔ̃] nm bear cub.

outil [uti] nm tool.

outillage [utijaʒ] nm [équipement] tools (pl), equipment.

outrage [utraʒ] nm - 1. sout [insulte] insult - 2. JUR : ~ à la pudeur indecent behaviour (U) Br ou behavior (U) Am.

outrager [17] [utraʒe] vt [offenser] to insult.

outrance [utrãs] nf excess ; à ~ excessively.

outrancier, ère [utrãsje, ɛr] adj extravagant.

outre[1] [utr] nf wineskin.

outre² [utr] ◇ *prép* besides, as well as. ◇ *adv* : **passer ~** to go on, to proceed further. ◆ **en outre** *loc adv* moreover, besides.

outre-Atlantique [utratlɑ̃tik] *loc adv* across the Atlantic.

outre-Manche [utrəmɑ̃ʃ] *loc adv* across the Channel.

outremer [utrəmɛr] ◇ *nm* [pierre] lapis lazuli ; [couleur] ultramarine. ◇ *adj inv* ultramarine.

outre-mer [utrəmɛr] *loc adv* overseas.

outrepasser [3] [utrəpase] *vt* to exceed.

outrer [3] [utre] *vt* [personne] to outrage.

outre-Rhin [utrərɛ̃] *loc adv* across the Rhine.

outsider [awtsajdœr] *nm* outsider.

ouvert, e [uver, ɛrt] ◇ *pp* ▷ **ouvrir**. ◇ *adj* - **1.** [gén] open ; **grand ~** wide open - **2.** [robinet] on, running.

ouvertement [uvɛrtəmɑ̃] *adv* openly.

ouverture [uvɛrtyr] *nf* - **1.** [gén] opening ; [d'hostilités] outbreak ; **~ d'esprit** open-mindedness - **2.** MUS overture - **3.** PHOT aperture. ◆ **ouvertures** *nfpl* [propositions] overtures.

ouvrable [uvrabl] *adj* working ; **heures ~s** hours of business.

ouvrage [uvraʒ] *nm* - **1.** [travail] work *(U)*, task ; **se mettre à l'~** to start work - **2.** [objet produit] (piece of) work ; COUTURE work *(U)* - **3.** [livre, écrit] work ; **~ de référence** reference work.

ouvré, e [uvre] *adj* : **jour ~** working day.

ouvre-boîtes [uvrəbwat] *nm inv* tin opener *Br*, can opener.

ouvre-bouteilles [uvrəbutɛj] *nm inv* bottle opener.

ouvreuse [uvrøz] *nf* usherette.

ouvrier, ère [uvrije, ɛr] ◇ *adj* [quartier, enfance] working-class ; [conflit] industrial ; [questions, statut] labour *(avant n) Br*, labor *(avant n) Am* ; **classe ouvrière** working class. ◇ *nm, f* worker ; **~ agricole** farm worker ; **~ qualifié** skilled worker ; **~ spécialisé** semi-skilled worker.

ouvrir [34] [uvrir] ◇ *vt* - **1.** [gén] to open - **2.** [chemin, voie] to open up - **3.** [gaz] to turn on. ◇ *vi* to open ; **~ sur qqch** to open onto sthg. ◆ **s'ouvrir** *vp* - **1.** [porte, fleur] to open - **2.** [route, perspectives] to open up - **3.** [personne] : **s'~ (à qqn)** to confide (in sb), to open up (to sb) - **4.** [se blesser] : **s'~ le genou** to cut one's knee open ; **s'~ les veines** to slash ou cut one's wrists.

ovaire [ɔver] *nm* ovary.

ovale [ɔval] *adj & nm* oval.

ovation [ɔvasjɔ̃] *nf* ovation ; **faire une ~ à qqn** to give sb an ovation.

overdose [ɔvœrdoz] *nf* overdose.

ovin, e [ɔvɛ̃, in] *adj* ovine. ◆ **ovin** *nm* sheep.

OVNI, Ovni [ɔvni] *(abr de* objet volant non identifié) *nm* UFO.

oxydation [ɔksidasjɔ̃] *nf* oxidation, oxidization.

oxyde [ɔksid] *nm* oxide.

oxyder [3] [ɔkside] *vt* to oxidize.

oxygène [ɔksiʒɛn] *nm* oxygen.

oxygéné, e [ɔksiʒene] *adj* CHIM oxygenated ▷ **eau**.

ozone [ozon] *nm* ozone.

P

p¹, P [pe] *nm inv* p, P.

p² - **1.** *(abr de* page) p - **2.** *abr de* **pièce**.

pacemaker [pɛsmekœr] *nm* pacemaker.

pachyderme [paʃidɛrm] *nm* elephant ; **les ~s** (the) pachyderms.

pacifier [9] [pasifje] *vt* to pacify.

pacifique [pasifik] *adj* peaceful.

Pacifique [pasifik] *nm* : **le ~** the Pacific (Ocean).

pacifiste [pasifist] *nmf & adj* pacifist.

pack [pak] *nm* pack.

pacotille [pakɔtij] *nf* shoddy goods *(pl)*, rubbish ; **de ~** cheap.

PACS [paks] *(abr de* Pacte civil de solidarité) *nm* Civil Solidarity Pact, *civil contract conferring marital rights on the contrating parties*.

pacte [pakt] *nm* pact.

pactiser [3] [paktize] *vi* : **~ avec** [faire un pacte avec] to make a pact with ; [transiger avec] to come to terms with.

pactole [paktɔl] *nm* gold mine *fig*.

pagaie [pagɛ] *nf* paddle.

pagaille, pagaye, pagaïe [pagaj] *nf fam* mess.

pagayer [11] [pageje] *vi* to paddle.

page [paʒ] ◇ *nf* - **1.** [feuillet] page ; **~ blanche** blank page ; **mettre en ~s** TYPO to make up (into pages) ; **~ d'accueil** INFORM home page - **2.** *loc* : **être à la ~** to be up-to-date. ◇ *nm* page (boy).

pagne [paɲ] *nm* loincloth.

pagode [pagɔd] *nf* pagoda.

paie, paye [pɛ] *nf* pay (U), wages (*pl*).

paiement, payement [pɛmɑ̃] *nm* payment.

païen, ïenne [pajɛ̃, ɛn] *adj & nm, f* pagan, heathen.

paillard, e [pajar, ard] *adj* bawdy.

paillasse [pajas] *nf* - **1.** [matelas] straw mattress - **2.** [d'évier] draining board.

paillasson [pajasɔ̃] *nm* [tapis] doormat.

paille [paj] *nf* - **1.** BOT straw - **2.** [pour boire] straw. ◆ **paille de fer** *nf* steel wool.

pailleté, e [pajte] *adj* sequined.

paillette [pajɛt] *nf* (*gén pl*) - **1.** [sur vêtements] sequin, spangle - **2.** [d'or] grain of gold dust - **3.** [de lessive, savon] flake ; **savon en ~s** soap flakes (*pl*).

pain [pɛ̃] *nm* - **1.** [aliment] bread ; **un ~** a loaf ; **petit ~** (bread) roll ; **~ de campagne** ≃ farmhouse loaf ; **~ complet** wholemeal bread ; **~ d'épice** ≃ gingerbread ; **~ de mie** sandwich loaf - **2.** [de savon, cire] bar.

pair, e [pɛr] *adj* even. ◆ **pair** *nm* peer. ◆ **paire** *nf* pair ; **une ~e de** [lunettes, ciseaux, chaussures] a pair of. ◆ **au pair** *loc adv* for board and lodging, for one's keep ; **jeune fille au ~** au pair (girl). ◆ **de pair** *loc adv* : **aller de ~ avec** to go hand in hand with.

paisible [pɛzibl] *adj* peaceful.

paître [91] [pɛtr] *vi* to graze.

paix [pɛ] *nf* peace ; **en ~** [en harmonie] at peace ; [tranquillement] in peace ; **avoir la ~** to have peace and quiet ; **faire la ~ avec qqn** to make peace with sb.

Pakistan [pakistɑ̃] *nm* : **le ~** Pakistan.

palace [palas] *nm* luxury hotel.

palais [palɛ] *nm* - **1.** [château] palace - **2.** [grand édifice] centre *Br*, center *Am* ; **~ de justice** JUR law courts (*pl*) ; **le Grand Palais** the Grand Palais ; **le Petit Palais** the Petit Palais - **3.** ANAT palate.

palan [palɑ̃] *nm* block and tackle, hoist.

pale [pal] *nf* [de rame, d'hélice] blade.

pâle [pal] *adj* pale.

paléontologie [paleɔ̃tɔlɔʒi] *nf* paleontology.

Palestine [palɛstin] *nf* : **la ~** Palestine.

palet [palɛ] *nm* HOCKEY puck.

palette [palɛt] *nf* [de peintre] palette.

pâleur [palœr] *nf* [de visage] pallor.

palier [palje] *nm* - **1.** [d'escalier] landing - **2.** [étape] level - **3.** TECHNOL bearing.

pâlir [32] [palir] *vi* [couleur, lumière] to fade ; [personne] to turn ou go pale.

palissade [palisad] *nf* [clôture] fence ; [de verdure] hedge.

palliatif, ive [paljatif, iv] *adj* palliative. ◆ **palliatif** *nm* - **1.** MÉD palliative - **2.** *fig* stopgap measure.

pallier [9] [palje] *vt* to make up for.

palmarès [palmarɛs] *nm* - **1.** [de lauréats] list of (medal) winners ; SCOL list of prizewinners - **2.** [de succès] record (of achievements).

palme [palm] *nf* - **1.** [de palmier] palm-leaf - **2.** [de nageur] flipper - **3.** [décoration, distinction] : **avec ~** MIL ≃ with bar.

palmé, e [palme] *adj* - **1.** BOT palmate - **2.** ZOOL web-footed ; [patte] webbed.

palmeraie [palmərɛ] *nf* palm grove.

palmier [palmje] *nm* BOT palm tree.

palmipède [palmipɛd] *nm* web-footed bird.

palombe [palɔ̃b] *nf* woodpigeon.

pâlot, otte [palo, ɔt] *adj* pale, sickly-looking.

palourde [palurd] *nf* clam.

palper [3] [palpe] *vt* [toucher] to feel, to finger ; MÉD to palpate.

palpitant, e [palpitɑ̃, ɑ̃t] *adj* exciting, thrilling.

palpitation [palpitasjɔ̃] *nf* palpitation.

palpiter [3] [palpite] *vi* [paupières] to flutter ; [cœur] to pound.

paludisme [palydism] *nm* malaria.

pâmer [3] [pame] ◆ **se pâmer** *vp littéraire* [s'évanouir] to swoon (away).

pamphlet [pɑ̃flɛ] *nm* satirical tract.

pamplemousse [pɑ̃pləmus] *nm* grapefruit.

pan [pɑ̃] ◇ *nm* - **1.** [de vêtement] tail - **2.** [d'affiche] piece, bit ; **~ de mur** section of wall. ◇ *interj* bang!

panache [panaʃ] *nm* - **1.** [de plumes, fumée] plume - **2.** [éclat] panache.

panaché, e [panaʃe] *adj* - **1.** [de plusieurs couleurs] multicoloured *Br*, multicolored *Am* - **2.** [mélangé] mixed. ◆ **panaché** *nm* shandy.

Panama [panama] *nm* [pays] : **le ~** Panama.

panaris [panari] *nm* whitlow.

pancarte [pɑ̃kart] *nf* - **1.** [de manifestant] placard - **2.** [de signalisation] sign.

pancréas [pɑ̃kreas] *nm* pancreas.

pané, e [pane] *adj* breaded, in breadcrumbs.

panier [panje] *nm* basket ; **~ à provisions** shopping basket ; **mettre au ~** *fig* to throw out.

panini [panini] (*pl* **paninis**) *nm* panini.

panique [panik] <> *nf* panic. <> *adj* panicky ; **être pris d'une peur ~** to be panic-stricken.

paniquer [3] [panike] *vt & vi* to panic.

panne [pan] *nf* [arrêt] breakdown ; **tomber en ~** to break down ; **~ de courant** ou **d'électricité** power failure ; **tomber en ~ d'essence** ou **en ~ sèche** to run out of petrol *Br* ou gas *Am*.

panneau, x [pano] *nm* - **1.** [pancarte] sign ; **~ indicateur** signpost ; **~ publicitaire** (advertising) hoarding *Br*, billboard *Am* ; **~ de signalisation** road sign - **2.** [élément] panel.

panoplie [panɔpli] *nf* - **1.** [jouet] outfit - **2.** *fig* [de mesures] package.

panorama [panɔrama] *nm* [vue] view, panorama ; *fig* overview.

panse [pɑ̃s] *nf* - **1.** [d'estomac] first stomach, rumen - **2.** *fam* [gros ventre] belly, paunch - **3.** [partie arrondie] bulge.

pansement [pɑ̃smɑ̃] *nm* dressing, bandage ; **~ (adhésif)** (sticking) plaster *Br*, Band-Aid® *Am*.

panser [3] [pɑ̃se] *vt* - **1.** [plaie] to dress, to bandage ; [jambe] to put a dressing on, to bandage ; [avec pansement adhésif] to put a plaster *Br* ou Band-Aid® *Am* on - **2.** [cheval] to groom.

pantalon [pɑ̃talɔ̃] *nm* trousers *(pl) Br*, pants *(pl) Am*, pair of trousers *Br* ou pants *Am*.

pantelant, e [pɑ̃tlɑ̃, ɑ̃t] *adj* panting, gasping.

panthère [pɑ̃tɛr] *nf* panther.

pantin [pɑ̃tɛ̃] *nm* - **1.** [jouet] jumping jack - **2.** *péj* [personne] puppet.

pantomime [pɑ̃tɔmim] *nf* [art, pièce] mime.

pantoufle [pɑ̃tufl] *nf* slipper.

PAO (*abr de* **publication assistée par ordinateur**) *nf* DTP.

paon [pɑ̃] *nm* peacock.

papa [papa] *nm* dad, daddy.

papauté [papote] *nf* papacy.

pape [pap] *nm* RELIG pope.

paperasse [papras] *nf péj* - **1.** [papier sans importance] bumf *(U) Br*, papers *(pl)* - **2.** [papiers administratifs] paperwork *(U)*.

papeterie [papetri] *nf* [magasin] stationer's ; [fabrique] paper mill.

papetier, ère [papətje, ɛr] *nm, f* [commerçant] stationer ; [fabricant] paper manufacturer.

papier [papje] *nm* [matière, écrit] paper ; **~ alu** ou **aluminium** aluminium *Br* ou aluminum *Am* foil, tinfoil ; **~ carbone** carbon

paper ; **~ crépon** crêpe paper ; **~ d'emballage** wrapping paper ; **~ à en-tête** headed notepaper ; **~ hygiénique** ou **toilette** toilet paper ; **~ à lettres** writing paper, notepaper ; **~ peint** wallpaper ; **~ de verre** glasspaper, sandpaper. **papiers** *nmpl* : **~s (d'identité)** (identity) papers.

papier-calque [papjekalk] (*pl* **papiers-calque**) *nm* tracing paper.

papille [papij] *nf* : **~s gustatives** taste buds.

papillon [papijɔ̃] *nm* - **1.** ZOOL butterfly - **2.** [écrou] wing nut - **3.** [nage] butterfly (stroke).

papillonner [3] [papijɔne] *vi* to flit about ou around.

papillote [papijɔt] *nf* - **1.** [de bonbon] sweet paper ou wrapper *Br*, candy paper *Am* - **2.** [de cheveux] curl paper.

papilloter [3] [papijɔte] *vi* [lumière] to twinkle ; [yeux] to blink.

papoter [3] [papɔte] *vi fam* to chatter.

paprika [paprika] *nm* paprika.

paquebot [pakbo] *nm* liner.

pâquerette [pakrɛt] *nf* daisy.

Pâques [pɑk] *nfpl* Easter *(sg)* ; **joyeuses Pâques** Happy Easter.

paquet [pakɛ] *nm* - **1.** [colis] parcel - **2.** [emballage] packet ; **~-cadeau** gift-wrapped parcel.

paquetage [pakta3] *nm* MIL kit.

par [par] *prép* - **1.** [spatial] through, by (way of) ; **passer ~ la Suède et le Danemark** to go via Sweden and Denmark ; **regarder ~ la fenêtre** to look out of the window ; **~ endroits** in places ; **~ ici/là** this/that way ; **mon cousin habite ~ ici** my cousin lives round here - **2.** [temporel] on ; **~ un beau jour d'été** on a lovely summer's day ; **~ le passé** in the past - **3.** [moyen, manière, cause] by ; **~ bateau/train/avion** by boat/train/plane ; **~ pitié** out of ou from pity ; **~ accident** by accident, by chance - **4.** [introduit le complément d'agent] by ; **faire faire qqch ~ qqn** to have sthg done by sb - **5.** [sens distributif] per, a ; **une heure ~ jour** one hour a ou per day ; **deux ~ deux** two at a time ; **marcher deux ~ deux** to walk in twos. **par-ci par-là** *loc adv* here and there.

para [para] (*abr de* **parachutiste**) *nm* para.

parabole [parabɔl] *nf* - **1.** [récit] parable - **2.** MATHS parabola.

parabolique [parabɔlik] *adj* parabolic.

paracétamol [19] [parasetamɔl] *nm* paracetamol.

parachever [19] [paraʃve] *vt* to put the finishing touches to.

parachute [paraʃyt] *nm* parachute ; ~ **ascensionnel** parachute *(for parascending)*.

parachutiste [paraʃytist] *nmf* parachutist ; MIL. paratrooper.

parade [parad] *nf* - **1.** [spectacle] parade - **2.** [défense] parry ; *fig* riposte.

paradis [paradi] *nm* paradise.

paradoxal, e, aux [paradɔksal, o] *adj* paradoxical.

paradoxe [paradɔks] *nm* paradox.

parafe, paraphe [paraf] *nm* initials *(pl)*.

parafer, parapher [3] [parafe] *vt* to initial.

paraffine [parafin] *nf* paraffin *Br*, kerosene *Am* ; [solide] paraffin wax.

parages [paraʒ] *nmpl* : **être** OU **se trouver dans les ~** *fig* to be in the area OU vicinity.

paragraphe [paragraf] *nm* paragraph.

Paraguay [paragwɛ] *nm* : **le ~** Paraguay.

paraître [91] [parɛtr] ◇ *v attr* to look, to seem, to appear. ◇ *vi* - **1.** [se montrer] to appear - **2.** [être publié] to come out, to be published. ◇ *v impers* : **il paraît/paraîtrait que** it appears/would appear that.

parallèle [paralɛl] ◇ *nm* parallel ; **établir un ~ entre** *fig* to draw a parallel between. ◇ *nf* parallel (line). ◇ *adj* - **1.** [action, en maths] parallel - **2.** [marché] unofficial ; [médecine, énergie] alternative.

parallélisme [paralelism] *nm* parallelism ; [de roues] alignment.

paralyser [3] [paralize] *vt* to paralyse.

paralysie [paralizi] *nf* paralysis.

paramédical, e, aux [paramedikal, o] *adj* paramedical.

paramètre [parametr] *nm* parameter.

paranoïa [paranɔja] *nf* paranoia.

paranoïaque [paranɔjak] ◇ *adj* paranoid. ◇ *nmf* paranoiac.

parapente [parapɑ̃t] *nm* paragliding ; **faire du ~** to go paragliding.

parapet [parapɛ] *nm* parapet.

paraphe = **parafe**.

parapher = **parafer**.

paraphrase [parafraz] *nf* paraphrase.

paraplégique [parapleʒik] *nmf* & *adj* paraplegic.

parapluie [paraplɥi] *nm* umbrella.

parasite [parazit] ◇ *nm* parasite. ◇ *adj* parasitic. ◆ **parasites** *nmpl* RADIO & TÉLÉ interference *(U)*.

parasol [parasɔl] *nm* parasol, sunshade.

paratonnerre [paratɔnɛr] *nm* lightning conductor *Br* OU rod *Am*.

paravent [paravɑ̃] *nm* screen.

parc [park] *nm* - **1.** [jardin] park ; [de château] grounds *(pl)* ; ~ **d'attractions** amusement park ; ~ **de loisirs** ≃ leisure park ; ~ **national** national park ; ~ **à thème** ≃ theme park - **2.** [pour l'élevage] pen - **3.** [de bébé] playpen - **4.** [de voitures] fleet ; **le ~ automobile** the number of cars on the roads.

parcelle [parsɛl] *nf* - **1.** [petite partie] fragment, particle - **2.** [terrain] parcel of land.

parce que [parsk(ə)] *loc conj* because.

parchemin [parʃəmɛ̃] *nm* parchment.

parcimonie [parsimɔni] *nf* parsimoniousness ; **avec ~** sparingly, parsimoniously.

parcimonieux, euse [parsimɔnjø, øz] *adj* parsimonious.

parcmètre [parkmɛtr] *nm* parking meter.

parcourir [45] [parkurir] *vt* - **1.** [région, route] to cover - **2.** [journal, dossier] to skim OU glance through, to scan.

parcours [parkur] *nm* - **1.** [trajet, voyage] journey ; [itinéraire] route ; ~ **santé** trail *in the countryside where signs encourage people to do exercises for their health* - **2.** GOLF [terrain] course ; [trajet] round.

parcouru, e [parkury] *pp* ⊳ **parcourir**.

par-delà [pardəla] *prép* beyond.

par-derrière [pardɛrjɛr] *adv* - **1.** [par le côté arrière] round the back - **2.** [en cachette] behind one's back.

par-dessous [pardəsu] *prép* & *adv* under, underneath.

pardessus [pardəsy] *nm inv* overcoat.

par-dessus [pardəsy] ◇ *prép* over, over the top of ; ~ **tout** above all. ◇ *adv* over, over the top.

par-devant [pardəvɑ̃] ◇ *prép* in front of. ◇ *adv* in front.

pardi [pardi] *interj fam* of course!

pardon [pardɔ̃] ◇ *nm* forgiveness ; **demander ~** to say (one is) sorry. ◇ *interj* [excuses] (I'm) sorry! ; [pour attirer l'attention] excuse me! ; **pardon?** (I beg your) pardon? *Br*, pardon me? *Am*.

pardonner [3] [pardɔne] ◇ *vt* to forgive ; ~ **qqch à qqn** to forgive sb for sthg ; ~ **à qqn d'avoir fait qqch** to forgive sb for doing sthg. ◇ *vi* : **ce genre d'erreur ne pardonne pas** this kind of mistake is fatal.

paré, e [pare] *adj* [prêt] ready.

pare-balles [parbal] *adj inv* bullet-proof.

pare-brise [parbriz] *nm inv* windscreen *Br*, windshield *Am*.

pare-chocs [parʃɔk] *nm inv* bumper.

pareil, eille [parɛj] *adj* - **1.** [semblable] : ~ **(à)** similar (to) - **2.** [tel] such ; **un ~ film**

such a film, a film like this ; **de ~s films** such films, films like these. ➤ **pareil** *adv fam* the same (way).

parent, e [parɑ̃, ɑ̃t] ◇ *adj* : **~ (de)** related (to). ◇ *nm, f* relative, relation. ➤ **parents** *nmpl* [père et mère] parents, mother and father.

parenté [parɑ̃te] *nf* [lien, affinité] relationship.

parenthèse [parɑ̃tεz] *nf* - **1.** [digression] digression, parenthesis - **2.** TYPO bracket, parenthesis ; **entre ~s** in brackets ; *fig* incidentally, by the way ; **ouvrir/fermer la ~** to open/close brackets.

parer [3] [pare] ◇ *vt* - **1.** *sout* [orner] to adorn - **2.** [vêtir] : **~ qqn de qqch** to dress sb up in sthg, to deck sb out in sthg ; *fig* to attribute sthg to sb - **3.** [contrer] to ward off, to parry. ◇ *vi* : **~ à** [faire face à] to deal with ; [pourvoir à] to prepare for ; **~ au plus pressé** to see to what is most urgent. ➤ **se parer** *vp* to dress up, to put on all one's finery.

pare-soleil [parsɔlεj] *nm inv* sun visor.

paresse [parεs] *nf* - **1.** [fainéantise] laziness, idleness - **2.** MÉD sluggishness.

paresser [4] [parese] *vi* to laze about ou around.

paresseux, euse [parεsø, øz] ◇ *adj* - **1.** [fainéant] lazy - **2.** MÉD sluggish. ◇ *nm, f* [personne] lazy ou idle person. ➤ **paresseux** *nm* [animal] sloth.

parfaire [109] [parfεr] *vt* to complete, to perfect.

parfait, e [parfε, εt] *adj* perfect. ➤ **parfait** *nm* GRAM perfect (tense).

parfaitement [parfεtmɑ̃] *adv* - **1.** [admirablement, très] perfectly - **2.** [marque l'assentiment] absolutely.

parfois [parfwa] *adv* sometimes.

parfum [parfœ̃] *nm* - **1.** [de fleur] scent, fragrance - **2.** [à base d'essences] perfume, scent - **3.** [de glace] flavour.

parfumé, e [parfyme] *adj* - **1.** [fleur] fragrant - **2.** [mouchoir] perfumed - **3.** [femme] : **elle est trop ~e** she's wearing too much perfume.

parfumer [3] [parfyme] *vt* - **1.** [suj : fleurs] to perfume - **2.** [mouchoir] to perfume, to scent - **3.** CULIN to flavour. ➤ **se parfumer** *vp* to put perfume on.

parfumerie [parfymri] *nf* perfumery.

pari [pari] *nm* - **1.** [entre personnes] bet - **2.** [jeu] betting (U).

paria [parja] *nm* pariah.

parier [9] [parje] *vt* : **~ (sur)** to bet (on).

parieur [parjœr] *nm* punter.

Paris [pari] *n* Paris.

parisien, enne [parizjε̃, εn] *adj* [vie, société] Parisian ; [métro, banlieue, région] Paris *(avant n)*. ➤ **Parisien, enne** *nm, f* Parisian.

paritaire [paritεr] *adj* : **commission ~** joint commission *(with both sides equally represented)*.

parité [parite] *nf* parity.

parjure [parʒyr] ◇ *nmf* [personne] perjurer. ◇ *nm* [faux serment] perjury.

parjurer [3] [parʒyre] ➤ **se parjurer** *vp* to perjure o.s.

parka [parka] *nm* OU *nf* parka.

parking [parkiŋ] *nm* [parc] car park *Br*, parking lot *Am*.

parlant, e [parlɑ̃, ɑ̃t] *adj* - **1.** [qui parle] : **le cinéma ~** talking pictures ; **l'horloge ~e** TÉLÉCOM the speaking clock - **2.** *fig* [chiffres, données] eloquent ; [portrait] vivid.

parlement [parləmɑ̃] *nm* parliament ; **le Parlement européen** the European Parliament.

parlementaire [parləmɑ̃tεr] ◇ *nmf* [député] member of parliament ; [négociateur] negotiator. ◇ *adj* parliamentary.

parlementer [3] [parləmɑ̃te] *vi* - **1.** [négocier] to negotiate, to parley - **2.** [parler longtemps] to talk at length.

parler [3] [parle] ◇ *vi* - **1.** [gén] to talk, to speak ; **~ à/avec qqn** to speak to/with sb ; **~ de qqch à qqn** to talk to/with sb about sthg ; **~ de qqn/qqch** to talk ou speak about sb/sthg ; **~ de faire qqch** to talk about doing sthg ; **~ en français** to speak in French ; **sans ~ de** apart from, not to mention ; **à proprement ~** strictly speaking ; **tu parles!** *fam* you can say that again! ; **n'en parlons plus** we'll say no more about it - **2.** [avouer] to talk. ◇ *vt* [langue] to speak ; **~ (le) français** to speak French.

parloir [parlwar] *nm* parlour *Br*, parlor *Am*.

parmi [parmi] *prép* among.

parodie [parɔdi] *nf* parody.

parodier [9] [parɔdje] *vt* to parody.

paroi [parwa] *nf* - **1.** [mur] wall ; [cloison] partition ; **~ rocheuse** rock face - **2.** [de récipient] inner side.

paroisse [parwas] *nf* parish.

paroissial, e, aux [parwasjal, o] *adj* parish *(avant n)*.

paroissien, enne [parwasjε̃, εn] *nm, f* parishioner.

parole [parɔl] *nf* - **1.** [faculté de parler] : **la ~** speech - **2.** [propos, discours] : **adresser la**

~ **à qqn** to speak to sb ; **couper la ~ à qqn** to cut sb off ; **prendre la ~** to speak - 3. [promesse, mot] word ; **tenir ~** to keep one's word ; **donner sa ~ d'honneur** to give one's word of honour *Br* ou honor *Am*. ◆ **paroles** *nfpl* MUS words, lyrics.

paroxysme [parɔksism] *nm* height.

parquer [3] [parke] *vt* - 1. [animaux] to pen in ou up - 2. [prisonniers] to shut up ou in - 3. [voiture] to park.

parquet [parkɛ] *nm* - 1. [plancher] parquet floor - 2. JUR ≃ Crown Prosecution Service *Br*, ≃ District Attorney's office *Am*.

parqueter [27] [parkəte] *vt* to lay a parquet floor in.

parrain [parɛ̃] *nm* - 1. [d'enfant] godfather - 2. [de festival, sportif] sponsor.

parrainer [4] [parɛne] *vt* to sponsor, to back.

parricide [parisid] *nm* [crime] parricide.

parsemer [19] [parsəme] *vt* : ~ **(de)** to strew (with).

part [par] *nf* - 1. [de gâteau] portion ; [de bonheur, d'héritage] share ; [partie] part - 2. [participation] : **prendre ~ à qqch** to take part in sthg - 3. *loc* : **de la ~ de** from ; [appeler, remercier] on behalf of ; **c'est de la ~ de qui?** [au téléphone] who's speaking ou calling? ; **dites-lui de ma ~ que ...** tell him from me that ... ; **ce serait bien aimable de votre ~** it would be very kind of you ; **pour ma ~** as far as I'm concerned ; **faire ~ à qqn de qqch** to inform sb of sthg. ◆ **à part** ◇ *loc adv* aside, separately. ◇ *loc adj* exceptional. ◇ *loc prép* apart from. ◆ **autre part** *loc adv* somewhere *Br* ou someplace *Am* else. ◆ **d'autre part** *loc adv* besides, moreover. ◆ **de part et d'autre** *loc adv* on both sides. ◆ **d'une part ..., d'autre part** *loc corrélative* on the one hand ..., on the other hand. ◆ **quelque part** *loc adv* somewhere *Br*, someplace *Am*.

part. *abr de* **particulier**.

partage [partaʒ] *nm* [action] sharing (out).

partager [17] [partaʒe] *vt* - 1. [morceler] to divide (up) ; **être partagé** *fig* to be divided - 2. [mettre en commun] : ~ **qqch avec qqn** to share sthg with sb. ◆ **se partager** *vp* - 1. [se diviser] to be divided - 2. [partager son temps] to divide one's time - 3. [se répartir] : **se ~ qqch** to share sthg between themselves/ourselves *etc*.

partance [partɑ̃s] *nf* : **en ~** outward bound ; **en ~ pour** bound for.

partant, e [partɑ̃, ɑ̃t] *adj* : **être ~ pour** to be ready for. ◆ **partant** *nm* starter.

partenaire [partənɛr] *nmf* partner.

partenariat [partənarja] *nm* partnership.

parterre [partɛr] *nm* - 1. [de fleurs] (flower) bed - 2. THÉÂTRE stalls *(pl) Br*, orchestra *Am*.

parti, e [parti] ◇ *pp* ▷ **partir**. ◇ *adj fam* [ivre] tipsy. ◆ **parti** *nm* - 1. POLIT party - 2. [choix, décision] course of action ; **prendre ~** to make up one's mind ; **prendre le ~ de faire qqch** to make up one's mind to do sthg ; **en prendre son ~** to be resigned ; **être de ~ pris** to be prejudiced ou biased ; **tirer ~ de** to make (good) use of - 3. [personne à marier] match. ◆ **partie** *nf* - 1. [élément, portion] part ; **en grande ~e** largely ; **en majeure ~e** for the most part ; **faire ~e (intégrante) de qqch** to be (an integral) part of sthg - 2. [domaine d'activité] field, subject - 3. SPORT game - 4. JUR party ; **la ~e adverse** the opposing party - 5. *loc* : **prendre qqn à ~e** to attack sb. ◆ **en partie** *loc adv* partly, in part.

partial, e, aux [parsjal, o] *adj* biased.

partialité [parsjalite] *nf* partiality, bias.

participant, e [partisipɑ̃, ɑ̃t] ◇ *adj* participating. ◇ *nm, f* - 1. [à réunion] participant - 2. SPORT competitor - 3. [à concours] entrant.

participation [partisipasjɔ̃] *nf* - 1. [collaboration] participation - 2. ÉCON interest ; **~ aux bénéfices** profit-sharing.

participe [partisip] *nm* participle ; **~ passé/présent** past/present participle.

participer [3] [partisipe] *vi* : ~ **à** [réunion, concours] to take part in ; [frais] to contribute to ; [bénéfices] to share in.

particularité [partikylarite] *nf* distinctive feature.

particule [partikyl] *nf* - 1. [gén & LING] particle - 2. [nobiliaire] nobiliary particle.

particulier, ère [partikylje, ɛr] *adj* - 1. [personnel, privé] private - 2. [spécial] particular, special ; [propre] peculiar, characteristic ; **~ à** peculiar to, characteristic of - 3. [remarquable] unusual, exceptional ; **cas ~** special case - 4. [assez bizarre] peculiar. ◆ **particulier** *nm* [personne] private individual.

particulièrement [partikyljɛrmɑ̃] *adv* particularly ; **tout ~** especially.

partie ▷ **parti**.

partiel, elle [parsjɛl] *adj* partial. ◆ **partiel** *nm* UNIV ≃ end-of-term exam.

partir [43] [partir] *vi* - 1. [personne] to go, to leave ; **~ à** to go to ; **~ pour** to leave for ; **~ de** [bureau] to leave ; [aéroport, gare] to leave from ; [hypothèse, route] to start from ; [date] to run from - 2. [voiture] to start - 3. [coup de feu] to go off ; [bouchon]

to pop - **4.** [tache] to come out, to go. ◆ **à partir de** *loc prép* from.

partisan, e [partizɑ̃, an] *adj* [partial] partisan ; **être ~ de** to be in favour *Br* ou favor *Am* of. ◆ **partisan** *nm* [adepte] supporter, advocate.

partition [partisjɔ̃] *nf* - **1.** [séparation] partition - **2.** MUS score.

partout [partu] *adv* everywhere ; **un peu ~** all over, everywhere.

paru, e [pary] *pp* ▷ **paraître**.

parure [paryr] *nf* (matching) set.

parution [parysjɔ̃] *nf* publication.

parvenir [40] [parvənir] *vi* : **~ à faire qqch** to manage to do sthg ; **faire ~ qqch à qqn** to send sthg to sb.

parvenu, e [parvəny] ◇ *pp* ▷ **parvenir**. ◇ *nm, f* *péj* parvenu, upstart.

pas¹ [pa] *nm* - **1.** [gén] step ; **allonger le ~** to quicken one's pace ; **revenir sur ses ~** to retrace one's steps ; **~ à ~** step by step ; **à ~ de loup** *fig* stealthily ; **à ~ feutrés** *fig* with muffled footsteps - **2.** TECHNOL thread - **3.** *loc* : **c'est à deux ~ (d'ici)** it's very near (here) ; **faire les cent ~** to pace up and down ; **faire un faux ~** to slip ; *fig* to make a faux pas ; **faire le premier ~** to make the first move ; **franchir** ou **sauter le ~** to take the plunge ; **(rouler) au ~** (to move) at a snail's pace ; **sur le ~ de la porte** on the doorstep ; **tirer qqn d'un mauvais ~** to get sb out of a tight spot.

pas² [pa] *adv* - **1.** [avec ne] not ; **elle ne vient ~** she's not ou she isn't coming ; **elle n'a ~ mangé** she hasn't eaten ; **je ne le connais ~** I don't know him ; **il n'y a ~ de vin** there's no wine, there isn't any wine ; **je préférerais ne ~ le rencontrer** I would prefer not to meet him, I would rather not meet him - **2.** [sans ne] not ; **l'as-tu vu ou ~ ?** have you seen him or not ?, **il est très satisfait, moi ~** he's very pleased, but I'm not ; **~ encore** not yet ; **~ du tout** not at all - **3.** [avec pron indéf] : **~ un** [aucun] none, not one ; **~ un d'eux n'est venu** none of them ou not one of them came.

pascal, e [paskal] (*pl* **pascals** ou **pascaux** [pasko]) *adj* Easter (avant n). ◆ **pascal** *nm* - **1.** INFORM Pascal - **2.** PHYS pascal.

passable [pasabl] *adj* passable, fair.

passage [pasaʒ] *nm* - **1.** [action - de passer] going past ; [- de traverser] crossing ; **être de ~** to be passing through - **2.** [endroit] passage, way ; '**~ interdit**' 'no entry' ; **~ clouté** ou **pour piétons** pedestrian crossing ; **~ à niveau** level crossing *Br*, grade crossing *Am* ; **~ protégé** priority given to traffic

on the main road ; **~ souterrain** underpass *Br*, subway *Am* - **3.** [extrait] excerpt.

passager, ère [pasaʒe, ɛr] ◇ *adj* [bonheur] fleeting, short-lived. ◇ *nm, f* passenger.

passant, e [pasɑ̃, ɑ̃t] ◇ *adj* busy. ◇ *nm, f* passer-by. ◆ **passant** *nm* [de ceinture] (belt) loop.

passe [pas] ◇ *nm* passkey. ◇ *nf* - **1.** [au sport] pass - **2.** NAVIG channel.

passé, e [pase] *adj* - **1.** [qui n'est plus] past ; [précédent] : **la semaine ~e** last week ; **au cours de la semaine ~e** in the last week ; **il est trois heures ~es** it's gone three *Br*, it's after three - **2.** [fané] faded. ◆ **passé** *nm* past ; **~ composé** perfect tense ; **~ simple** past historic. ◇ *prép* after.

passe-droit [pasdrwa] (*pl* **passe-droits**) *nm* privilege.

passe-montagne [pasmɔ̃taɲ] (*pl* **passe-montagnes**) *nm* Balaclava (helmet).

passe-partout [paspartu] *nm inv* - **1.** [clé] passkey - **2.** (en apposition) [tenue] all-purpose ; [phrase] stock (avant n).

passeport [paspɔr] *nm* passport.

passer [3] [pase] ◇ *vi* (aux : être) - **1.** [se frayer un chemin] to pass, to get past - **2.** [défiler] to go by ou past - **3.** [aller] to go ; **~ à** ou **au travers** ou **par** to pass through ; **~ chez qqn** to call on sb, to drop in on sb ; **~ devant** [bâtiment] to pass ; [juge] to come before ; **en passant** in passing - **4.** [venir - facteur] to come, to call - **5.** SCOL to pass, to be admitted ; **~ dans la classe supérieure** to move up, to be moved up (a class) - **6.** [être accepté] to be accepted - **7.** [fermer les yeux] : **~ sur qqch** to pass over sthg - **8.** [temps] to pass, to go by - **9.** [disparaître - souvenir, couleur] to fade ; [- douleur] to pass, to go away - **10.** CIN, TÉLÉ & THÉÂTRE to be on ; **~ à la radio/télévision** to be on the radio/television - **11.** CARTES to pass - **12.** [devenir] : **~ président/directeur** to become president/director, to be appointed president/director - **13.** *loc* : **~ inaperçu** to pass ou go unnoticed ; **passons ...** let's move on ... ; **~ pour** to be regarded as ; **se faire ~ pour qqn** to pass o.s. off as sb ; **il y est passé** *fam* [mort] he kicked the bucket. ◇ *vt* (aux : avoir) - **1.** [franchir - frontière, rivière] to cross ; [- douane] to go through - **2.** [soirée, vacances] to spend - **3.** [sauter - ligne, tour] to miss - **4.** [défauts] : **~ qqch à qqn** to overlook sthg in sb - **5.** [faire aller - bras] to pass, to put - **6.** [filtrer - huile] to strain ; [- café] to filter - **7.** [film, disque] to put on - **8.** [vêtement] to slip on - **9.** [vitesses] to change ; **~ la** ou **en troisième** to

change into third (gear) - **10.** [donner] :
~ **qqch à qqn** to pass sb sthg ; MÉD to give
sb sthg - **11.** [accord] : ~ **un contrat avec
qqn** to have an agreement with sb
- **12.** SCOL & UNIV [examen] to sit, to take
- **13.** [au téléphone] : **je vous passe Mme Ledoux** [transmettre] I'll put you through to
Mme Ledoux ; [donner l'écouteur à] I'll
hand you Mme Ledoux. ◆ **se passer** *vp*
- **1.** [événement] to happen, to take place ;
comment ça s'est passé? how did it go? ;
ça ne se passera pas comme ça! I'm not
putting up with that! - **2.** [s'enduire - crème]
to put on - **3.** [s'abstenir] : **se ~ de qqch/de
faire qqch** to do without sthg/doing sthg.

passerelle [pasʀɛl] *nf* - **1.** [pont] footbridge - **2.** [passage mobile] gangway.

passe-temps [pastɑ̃] *nm inv* pastime.

passif, ive [pasif, iv] *adj* passive.
◆ **passif** *nm* - **1.** GRAM passive - **2.** FIN liabilities *(pl)*.

passion [pasjɔ̃] *nf* passion ; **avoir la ~ de
qqch** to have a passion for sthg.

passionnant, e [pasjɔnɑ̃, ɑ̃t] *adj* exciting, fascinating.

passionné, e [pasjɔne] *adj* - **1.** [per-
sonne] passionate - **2.** [récit, débat] impas-
sioned. ◇ *nm, f* passionate person ; ~ **de
ski/d'échecs** *etc* skiing/chess *etc* fanatic.

passionnel, elle [pasjɔnɛl] *adj* [crime] of
passion.

passionner [3] [pasjɔne] *vt* [personne] to
grip, to fascinate. ◆ **se passionner** *vp* :
se ~ pour to have a passion for.

passivité [pasivite] *nf* passivity.

passoire [paswar] *nf* [à liquide] sieve ; [à
légumes] colander.

pastel [pastɛl] ◇ *nm* pastel. ◇ *adj inv*
[couleur] pastel *(avant n)*.

pastèque [pastɛk] *nf* watermelon.

pasteur [pastœr] *nm* - **1.** *littéraire* [berger]
shepherd - **2.** RELIG pastor, minister.

pasteuriser [3] [pastœrize] *vt* to pasteurize.

pastille [pastij] *nf* [bonbon] pastille, lozenge.

pastis [pastis] *nm aniseed-flavoured aperitif.*

patate [patat] *nf* - **1.** *fam* [pomme de terre]
spud - **2.** *fam* [imbécile] fathead.

patauger [17] [patoʒe] *vi* [barboter] to
splash about.

patch [patʃ] *nm* MÉD patch.

pâte [pat] *nf* - **1.** [à tarte] pastry ; [à pain]
dough ; ~ **brisée** shortcrust pastry ; ~ **feuilletée** puff pastry ; ~ **à frire** batter ; ~ **à pain**
bread dough - **2.** [mélange] paste ;
~ **d'amandes** almond paste ; ~ **de fruits** *jelly*

made from fruit paste ; ~ **à modeler** modelling
clay. ◆ **pâtes** *nfpl* pasta *(sg)*.

pâté [pate] *nm* - **1.** CULIN pâté ; ~ **de campagne** farmhouse pâté ; ~ **en croûte** *pâté
baked in a pastry case* ; ~ **de foie** liver pâté
- **2.** [tache] ink blot - **3.** [bloc] : ~ **de maisons**
block (of houses).

patelin [patlɛ̃] *nm fam* village, place.

patente [patɑ̃t] *nf* licence fee *(for traders
and professionals)*.

patère [patɛr] *nf* [portemanteau] coat
hook.

paternalisme [patɛrnalism] *nm* paternal-
ism.

paternel, elle [patɛrnɛl] *adj* [devoir, au-
torité] paternal ; [amour, ton] fatherly.

paternité [patɛrnite] *nf* paternity, father-
hood ; *fig* authorship, paternity.

pâteux, euse [patø, øz] *adj* [aliment]
doughy ; [encre] thick.

pathétique [patetik] *adj* moving, pathetic.

pathologie [patɔlɔʒi] *nf* pathology.

patibulaire [patibylɛr] *adj péj* sinister.

patience [pasjɑ̃s] *nf* - **1.** [gén] patience
- **2.** [jeu de cartes] patience *Br*, solitaire *Am*.

patient, e [pasjɑ̃, ɑ̃t] ◇ *adj* patient.
◇ *nm, f* MÉD patient.

patienter [3] [pasjɑ̃te] *vi* to wait.

patin [patɛ̃] *nm* SPORT skate ; ~ **à glace/à
roulettes** ice/roller skate ; **faire du ~ à
glace/à roulettes** to go ice-/roller-skating.

patinage [patinaʒ] *nm* SPORT skating ;
~ **artistique/de vitesse** figure/speed skating.

patiner [3] [patine] ◇ *vi* - **1.** SPORT to
skate - **2.** [véhicule] to skid. ◇ *vt* [objet] to
give a patina to ; [avec vernis] to varnish.
◆ **se patiner** *vp* to take on a patina.

patineur, euse [patinœr, øz] *nm, f*
skater.

patinoire [patinwar] *nf* ice ou skating
rink.

pâtisserie [patisri] *nf* - **1.** [gâteau] pastry
- **2.** [art, métier] pastry-making - **3.** [com-
merce] ≃ cake shop.

pâtissier, ère [patisje, ɛr] ◇ *adj* : **crème
pâtissière** confectioner's custard. ◇ *nm, f*
pastrycook.

patois [patwa] *nm* patois.

patriarche [patrijarʃ] *nm* patriarch.

patrie [patri] *nf* country, homeland.

patrimoine [patrimwan] *nm* [familial] inheritance ; [collectif] heritage.

patriote [patrijɔt] *nmf* patriot.

patriotique [patrijɔtik] *adj* patriotic.

patron, onne [patrɔ̃, ɔn] *nm, f* - **1.** [d'entreprise] head - **2.** [chef] boss - **3.** RELIG patron saint. **patron** *nm* [modèle] pattern.

patronage [patrɔnaʒ] *nm* - **1.** [protection] patronage ; [de saint] protection - **2.** [organisation] youth club.

patronal, e, aux [patrɔnal, o] *adj* [organisation, intérêts] employers' *(avant n)*.

patronat [patrɔna] *nm* employers.

patronyme [patrɔnim] *nm* patronymic.

patrouille [patruj] *nf* patrol.

patte [pat] *nf* - **1.** [d'animal] paw ; [d'oiseau] foot - **2.** *fam* [jambe] leg ; [pied] foot ; [main] hand, paw - **3.** [favori] sideburn.

pâturage [patyraʒ] *nm* [lieu] pasture land.

pâture [patyr] *nf* [nourriture] food, fodder ; *fig* intellectual nourishment.

paume [pom] *nf* - **1.** [de main] palm - **2.** SPORT real tennis.

paumé, e [pome] *fam* ◇ *adj* lost. ◇ *nm, f* down and out.

paumer [3] [pome] *fam vt* to lose. **se paumer** *vp* to get lost.

paupière [popjɛr] *nf* eyelid.

pause [poz] *nf* - **1.** [arrêt] break ; **~-cafe** coffee-break - **2.** MUS pause.

pauvre [povr] ◇ *nmf* poor person. ◇ *adj* poor ; **~ en** low in.

pauvreté [povrəte] *nf* poverty.

pavaner [3] [pavane] **se pavaner** *vp* to strut.

pavé, e [pave] *adj* cobbled. **pavé** *nm* - **1.** [chaussée] : **être sur le ~** *fig* to be out on the streets ; **battre le ~** *fig* to walk the streets - **2.** [de pierre] cobblestone, paving stone - **3.** *fam* [livre] tome - **4.** INFORM **~ numérique** numeric keypad.

pavillon [pavijɔ̃] *nm* - **1.** [bâtiment] detached house - **2.** [de trompette] bell - **3.** [d'oreille] pinna, auricle - **4.** [drapeau] flag.

pavot [pavo] *nm* poppy.

payant, e [pɛjɑ̃, ɑ̃t] *adj* - **1.** [hôte] paying *(avant n)* - **2.** [spectacle] with an admission charge - **3.** *fam* [affaire] profitable.

paye = paie².

payement = paiement.

payer [11] [peje] ◇ *vt* - **1.** [gén] to pay ; [achat] to pay for ; **~ qqch à qqn** to buy sthg for sb, to buy sb sthg ; to treat sb to sthg - **2.** [expier - crime, faute] to pay for. ◇ *vi* : **~ (pour)** to pay (for).

pays [pei] *nm* - **1.** [gén] country - **2.** [région, province] region. **pays de Galles** *nm* : **le ~ de Galles** Wales.

paysage [peizaʒ] *nm* - **1.** [site, vue] landscape, scenery - **2.** [tableau] landscape.

paysagiste [peizaʒist] *nmf* - **1.** [peintre] landscape artist - **2.** [concepteur de parcs] landscape gardener.

paysan, anne [peizɑ̃, an] ◇ *adj* [vie, coutume] country *(avant n)*, rural ; [organisation, revendication] farmers' *(avant n)* ; *péj* peasant *(avant n)*. ◇ *nm, f* - **1.** [agriculteur] (small) farmer - **2.** *péj* [rustre] peasant.

Pays-Bas [peiba] *nmpl* : **les ~** the Netherlands.

PC *nm* - **1.** (abr de **Parti communiste**) Communist Party - **2.** (abr de **personal computer**) PC - **3.** (abr de **Petite Ceinture**) bus following the inner ring road in Paris.

PCV (abr de **à percevoir**) *nm* reverse charge call.

P-DG (abr de **président-directeur général**) *nm* Chairman and Managing Director *Br*, Chairman and President *Am*.

péage [peaʒ] *nm* toll.

peau [po] *nf* - **1.** [gén] skin ; **~ d'orange** orange peel ; MÉD ≃ cellulite - **2.** [cuir] hide, leather (U).

peaufiner [3] [pofine] *vt fig* [travail] to polish up.

péché [peʃe] *nm* sin.

pêche [pɛʃ] *nf* - **1.** [fruit] peach - **2.** [activité] fishing ; [poissons] catch ; **aller à la ~** to go fishing.

pécher [18] [peʃe] *vi* to sin.

pêcher¹ [4] [peʃe] *vt* - **1.** [poisson] to catch - **2.** *fam* [trouver] to dig up.

pêcher² [peʃe] *nm* peach tree.

pécheur, eresse [peʃœr, peʃrɛs] ◇ *adj* sinful. ◇ *nm, f* sinner.

pêcheur, euse [pɛʃœr, øz] *nm, f* fisherman (f fisherwoman).

pectoral, e, aux [pɛktɔral, o] *adj* [sirop] cough *(avant n)*. **pectoraux** *nmpl* pectorals.

pécuniaire [pekynjɛr] *adj* financial.

pédagogie [pedagɔʒi] *nf* - **1.** [science] education, pedagogy - **2.** [qualité] teaching ability.

pédagogue [pedagɔg] ◇ *nmf* teacher. ◇ *adj* : **être ~** to be a good teacher.

pédale [pedal] *nf* [gén] pedal.

pédaler [3] [pedale] *vi* [à bicyclette] to pedal.

Pédalo® [pedalo] *nm* pedal boat.

pédant, e [pedɑ̃, ɑ̃t] *adj* pedantic.

pédéraste [pederast] *nm* homosexual, pederast.

pédiatre [pedjatr] *nmf* pediatrician.

pédiatrie [pedjatri] *nf* pediatrics (U).

pédicure [pedikyr] *nmf* chiropodist.

peigne [pɛɲ] *nm* - **1.** [démêloir, barrette] comb - **2.** [de tissage] card.

peigner [4] [peɲe] *vt* - **1.** [cheveux] to comb - **2.** [fibres] to card. ◆ **se peigner** *vp* to comb one's hair.

peignoir [pɛɲwar] *nm* dressing gown *Br*, robe *Am*, bathrobe *Am*.

peindre [81] [pɛ̃dr] *vt* to paint ; *fig* [décrire] to depict.

peine [pɛn] *nf* - **1.** [châtiment] punishment, penalty ; JUR sentence ; **sous ~ de qqch** on pain of sthg ; **~ capitale** OU **de mort** capital punishment ; **death sentence** - **2.** [chagrin] sorrow, sadness (U) ; **faire de la ~ à qqn** to upset sb, to distress sb - **3.** [effort] trouble ; **ça ne vaut pas** OU **ce n'est pas la ~** it's not worth it - **4.** [difficulté] difficulty ; **avoir de la ~ à faire qqch** to have difficulty OU trouble doing sthg ; **à grand-~** with great difficulty ; **sans ~** without difficulty, easily. ◆ **à peine** *loc adv* scarcely, hardly ; **à ~ ... que** hardly ... than ; **c'est à ~ si on se parle** we hardly speak (to each other).

peint, e [pɛ̃, pɛ̃t] *pp* ⊳ peindre.

peintre [pɛ̃tr] *nm* painter.

peinture [pɛ̃tyr] *nf* - **1.** [gén] painting - **2.** [produit] paint ; **'~ fraîche'** 'wet paint'.

péjoratif, ive [peʒɔratif, iv] *adj* pejorative.

Pékin [pekɛ̃] *n* Peking, Beijing.

pékinois, e [pekinwa, az] *adj* of/from Peking. ◆ **pékinois** *nm* - **1.** [langue] Mandarin - **2.** [chien] pekinese. ◆ **Pékinois, e** *nm, f* native OU inhabitant of Peking.

pelage [pəlaʒ] *nm* coat, fur.

pêle-mêle [pɛlmɛl] *adv* pell-mell.

peler [25] [pəle] *vt & vi* to peel.

pèlerin [pɛlrɛ̃] *nm* pilgrim.

pèlerinage [pɛlrinaʒ] *nm* - **1.** [voyage] pilgrimage - **2.** [lieu] place of pilgrimage.

pélican [pelikɑ̃] *nm* pelican.

pelle [pɛl] *nf* - **1.** [instrument] shovel - **2.** [machine] digger.

pelleter [27] [pɛlte] *vt* to shovel.

pellicule [pelikyl] *nf* film. ◆ **pellicules** *nfpl* dandruff (U).

pelote [pəlɔt] *nf* [de laine, ficelle] ball.

peloter [3] [pəlɔte] *vt fam* to paw.

peloton [pləɔtɔ̃] *nm* - **1.** [de soldats] squad ; **~ d'exécution** firing squad - **2.** [de concurrents] pack.

pelotonner [3] [pəlɔtɔne] ◆ **se pelotonner** *vp* to curl up.

pelouse [pəluz] *nf* - **1.** [de jardin] lawn - **2.** [de champ de courses] public enclosure - **3.** FOOTBALL & RUGBY field.

peluche [pəlyʃ] *nf* - **1.** [jouet] soft toy, stuffed animal - **2.** [d'étoffe] piece of fluff.

pelure [pəlyr] *nf* [fruit] peel.

pénal, e, aux [penal, o] *adj* penal.

pénaliser [3] [penalize] *vt* to penalize.

penalty [penalti] (*pl* **penaltys** OU **penalties**) *nm* penalty.

penaud, e [pəno, od] *adj* sheepish.

penchant [pɑ̃ʃɑ̃] *nm* - **1.** [inclination] tendency - **2.** [sympathie] : **~ pour** liking OU fondness for.

pencher [3] [pɑ̃ʃe] ◇ *vi* to lean ; **~ vers** *fig* to incline towards *Br* OU toward *Am* ; **~ pour** to incline in favour *Br* OU favor *Am* of. ◇ *vt* to bend. ◆ **se pencher** *vp* [s'incliner] to lean over ; [se baisser] to bend down ; **se ~ sur qqn/qqch** to lean over sb/sthg.

pendaison [pɑ̃dɛzɔ̃] *nf* hanging.

pendant¹, e [pɑ̃dɑ̃, ɑ̃t] *adj* [bras] hanging, dangling. ◆ **pendant** *nm* - **1.** [bijou] : **~ d'oreilles** (drop) earring - **2.** [de paire] counterpart.

pendant² [pɑ̃dɑ̃] *prép* during. ◆ **pendant que** *loc conj* while, whilst ; **~ que j'y suis, ...** while I'm at it, ...

pendentif [pɑ̃dɑ̃tif] *nm* pendant.

penderie [pɑ̃dri] *nf* wardrobe.

pendre [73] [pɑ̃dr] ◇ *vi* - **1.** [être fixé en haut] : **~ (à)** to hang (from) - **2.** [descendre trop bas] to hang down. ◇ *vt* - **1.** [rideaux, tableau] to hang (up), to put up - **2.** [personne] to hang. ◆ **se pendre** *vp* [se suicider] to hang o.s.

pendule [pɑ̃dyl] ◇ *nm* pendulum. ◇ *nf* clock.

pénétrer [18] [penetre] ◇ *vi* to enter. ◇ *vt* [mur, vêtement] to penetrate.

pénible [penibl] *adj* - **1.** [travail] laborious - **2.** [nouvelle, maladie] painful - **3.** *fam* [personne] tiresome.

péniche [peniʃ] *nf* barge.

pénicilline [penisilin] *nf* penicillin.

péninsule [penɛ̃syl] *nf* peninsula.

pénis [penis] *nm* penis.

pénitence [penitɑ̃s] *nf* - **1.** [repentir] penitence - **2.** [peine, punition] penance.

pénitencier [penitɑ̃sje] *nm* prison, penitentiary *Am*.

pénombre [penɔ̃br] *nf* half-light.

pense-bête [pɑ̃sbɛt] (*pl* **pense-bêtes**) *nm* reminder.

pensée [pɑ̃se] *nf* - **1.** [idée, faculté] thought - **2.** [esprit] mind, thoughts (*pl*) - **3.** [doctrine] thought, thinking - **4.** BOT pansy.

penser [3] [pɑ̃se] <> *vi* to think ; ~ **à qqn/qqch** [avoir à l'esprit] to think of sb/sthg, to think about sb/sthg ; [se rappeler] to remember sb/sthg ; ~ **à faire qqch** [avoir à l'esprit] to think of doing sthg ; [se rappeler] to remember to do sthg ; **qu'est-ce que tu en penses?** what do you think (of it)? ; **faire ~ à qqn/qqch** to make one think of sb/sthg ; **faire ~ à qqn à faire qqch** to remind sb to do sthg. <> *vt* to think ; **je pense que oui** I think so ; **je pense que non** I don't think so ; ~ **faire qqch** to be planning to do sthg.

pensif, ive [pɑ̃sif, iv] *adj* pensive, thoughtful.

pension [pɑ̃sjɔ̃] *nf* - **1.** [allocation] pension ; ~ **alimentaire** [dans un divorce] alimony - **2.** [hébergement] board and lodgings ; ~ **complète** full board ; **demi-~** half board - **3.** [hôtel] guesthouse ; ~ **de famille** guesthouse, boarding house - **4.** [prix de l'hébergement] = rent, keep - **5.** [internat] boarding school ; **être en ~** to be a boarder ou at boarding school.

pensionnaire [pɑ̃sjɔner] *nmf* - **1.** [élève] boarder - **2.** [hôte payant] lodger.

pensionnat [pɑ̃sjɔna] *nm* [internat] boarding school.

pentagone [pɛ̃tagon] *nm* pentagon.

pente [pɑ̃t] *nf* slope ; **en ~** sloping, inclined.

pentecôte [pɑ̃tkot] *nf* [juive] Pentecost ; [chrétienne] Whitsun.

pénurie [penyri] *nf* shortage.

pépier [9] [pepje] *vi* to chirp.

pépin [pepɛ̃] *nm* - **1.** [graine] pip - **2.** *fam* [ennui] hitch - **3.** *fam* [parapluie] umbrella, brolly *Br*.

pépinière [pepinjer] *nf* tree nursery ; *fig* [école, établissement] nursery.

pépite [pepit] *nf* nugget.

perçant, e [pɛrsɑ̃, ɑ̃t] *adj* - **1.** [regard, son] piercing - **2.** [froid] bitter, biting.

percepteur [pɛrseptœr] *nm* tax collector.

perception [pɛrsepsjɔ̃] *nf* - **1.** [d'impôts] collection - **2.** [bureau] tax office - **3.** [sensation] perception.

percer [16] [pɛrse] <> *vt* - **1.** [mur, roche] to make a hole in ; [coffre-fort] to crack - **2.** [trou] to make ; [avec perceuse] to drill - **3.** [silence, oreille] to pierce - **4.** [foule] to make one's way through - **5.** *fig* [mystère] to penetrate. <> *vi* - **1.** [soleil] to break through - **2.** [abcès] to burst ; **avoir une dent qui perce** to be cutting a tooth - **3.** [réussir] to make a name for o.s., to break through.

perceuse [pɛrsøz] *nf* drill.

percevoir [52] [pɛrsəvwar] *vt* - **1.** [intention, nuance] to perceive - **2.** [retraite, indemnité] to receive - **3.** [impôts] to collect.

perche [pɛrʃ] *nf* - **1.** [poisson] perch - **2.** [de bois, métal] pole.

percher [3] [pɛrʃe] <> *vi* [oiseau] to perch. <> *vt* to perch. • **se percher** *vp* to perch.

perchoir [pɛrʃwar] *nm* perch.

percolateur [pɛrkɔlatœr] *nm* percolator.

perçu, e [pɛrsy] *pp* ▷ percevoir.

percussion [pɛrkysjɔ̃] *nf* percussion.

percutant, e [pɛrkytɑ̃, ɑ̃t] *adj* - **1.** [obus] explosive - **2.** *fig* [argument] forceful.

percuter [3] [pɛrkyte] <> *vt* to strike, to smash into. <> *vi* to explode.

perdant, e [pɛrdɑ̃, ɑ̃t] <> *adj* losing. <> *nm, f* loser.

perdre [77] [pɛrdr] <> *vt* - **1.** [gén] to lose - **2.** [temps] to waste ; [occasion] to miss, to waste - **3.** [suj : bonté, propos] to be the ruin of. <> *vi* to lose. • **se perdre** *vp* - **1.** [coutume] to die out, to become lost - **2.** [personne] to get lost, to lose one's way

perdrix [pɛrdri] *nf* partridge.

perdu, e [pɛrdy] <> *pp* ▷ perdre. <> *adj* - **1.** [égaré] lost - **2.** [endroit] out-of-the-way - **3.** [balle] stray - **4.** [emballage] non-returnable - **5.** [temps, occasion] wasted - **6.** [malade] dying - **7.** [récolte, robe] spoilt, ruined.

père [pɛr] *nm* [gén] father ; ~ **de famille** father. • **père Noël** *nm* : **le ~** Noël Father Christmas, Santa Claus.

péremptoire [perɑ̃ptwar] *adj* peremptory.

perfection [pɛrfɛksjɔ̃] *nf* [qualité] perfection.

perfectionner [3] [pɛrfɛksjɔne] *vt* to perfect. • **se perfectionner** *vp* to improve.

perfide [pɛrfid] *adj* perfidious.

perforer [3] [pɛrfɔre] *vt* to perforate.

performance [pɛrfɔrmɑ̃s] *nf* performance.

performant, e [pɛrfɔrmɑ̃, ɑ̃t] *adj* - **1.** [personne] efficient - **2.** [machine] high-performance *(avant n)*.

perfusion [pɛrfyzjɔ̃] *nf* perfusion.

péridurale [peridyral] *nf* epidural.

péril [peril] *nm* peril.

périlleux, euse [perijø, øz] *adj* perilous, dangerous.

périmé, e [perime] *adj* out-of-date ; *fig* [idées] outdated.

périmètre [perimɛtr] *nm* - **1.** [contour] perimeter - **2.** [contenu] area.

période [perjɔd] *nf* period.

périodique [perjɔdik] <> *nm* periodical. <> *adj* periodic.

péripétie [peripesi] *nf* event.

périphérie [periferi] *nf* - **1.** [de ville] outskirts *(pl)* - **2.** [bord] periphery ; [de cercle] circumference.

périphérique [periferik] <> *nm* - **1.** [route] ring road *Br*, beltway *Am* - **2.** INFORM peripheral device. <> *adj* peripheral.

périphrase [perifraz] *nf* periphrasis.

périple [peripl] *nm* - **1.** NAVIG voyage - **2.** [voyage] trip.

périr [32] [perir] *vi* to perish.

périssable [perisabl] *adj* - **1.** [denrée] perishable - **2.** *littéraire* [sentiment] transient.

perle [pɛrl] *nf* - **1.** [de nacre] pearl - **2.** [de bois, verre] bead - **3.** [personne] gem.

permanence [pɛrmanɑ̃s] *nf* - **1.** [continuité] permanence ; **en ~** constantly - **2.** [service] : **être de ~** to be on duty - **3.** SCOL : **(salle de)** study room.

permanent, e [pɛrmanɑ̃, ɑ̃t] *adj* permanent ; [cinéma] with continuous showings ; [comité] standing *(avant n)*. ◆ **permanente** *nf* perm.

permettre [84] [pɛrmɛtr] *vt* to permit, to allow ; **~ à qqn de faire qqch** to permit ou allow sb to do sthg. ◆ **se permettre** *vp* : **se ~ qqch** to allow o.s sthg ; [avoir les moyens de] to be able to afford sthg ; **se ~ de faire qqch** to take the liberty of doing sthg.

permis, e [pɛrmi, iz] *pp* ▷ **permettre**. ◆ **permis** *nm* licence *Br*, license *Am*, permit ; **~ de conduire** driving licence *Br*, driver's license *Am* ; **~ de construire** planning permission *Br*, building permit *Am* ; **~ de travail** work permit.

permission [pɛrmisjɔ̃] *nf* - **1.** [autorisation] permission - **2.** MIL leave.

permuter [3] [pɛrmyte] <> *vt* to change round ; [mots, figures] to transpose. <> *vi* to change, to switch.

pérorer [3] [perɔre] *vi péj* to hold forth.

Pérou [peru] *nm* : **le ~** Peru.

perpendiculaire [pɛrpɑ̃dikylɛr] <> *nf* perpendicular. <> *adj* : **~ (à)** perpendicular (to).

perpétrer [18] [pɛrpetre] *vt* to perpetrate.

perpétuel, elle [pɛrpetɥɛl] *adj* - **1.** [fréquent, continu] perpetual - **2.** [rente] life *(avant n)* ; [secrétaire] permanent.

perpétuer [7] [pɛrpetɥe] *vt* to perpetuate. ◆ **se perpétuer** *vp* to continue ; [espèce] to perpetuate itself.

perpétuité [pɛrpetɥite] *nf* perpetuity ; **à ~ for life** ; **être condamné à ~** to be sentenced to life imprisonment.

perplexe [pɛrplɛks] *adj* perplexed.

perquisition [pɛrkizisjɔ̃] *nf* search.

perron [pɛrɔ̃] *nm* steps *(pl)* (at entrance to building).

perroquet [pɛrɔkɛ] *nm* [animal] parrot.

perruche [peryʃ] *nf* budgerigar.

perruque [peryk] *nf* wig.

persan, e [pɛrsɑ̃, an] *adj* Persian. ◆ **persan** *nm* [chat] Persian (cat).

persécuter [3] [pɛrsekyte] *vt* - **1.** [martyriser] to persecute - **2.** [harceler] to harass.

persécution [pɛrsekysjɔ̃] *nf* persecution.

persévérant, e [pɛrseverɑ̃, ɑ̃t] *adj* persevering.

persévérer [18] [pɛrsevere] *vi* : **~ (dans)** to persevere (in).

persienne [pɛrsjɛn] *nf* shutter.

persifler [3] [pɛrsifle] *vt littéraire* to mock.

persil [pɛrsi] *nm* parsley.

Persique [pɛrsik] ▷ **golfe**.

persistant, e [pɛrsistɑ̃, ɑ̃t] *adj* persistent ; **arbre à feuillage ~** evergreen (tree).

persister [3] [pɛrsiste] *vi* to persist ; **~ à faire qqch** to persist in doing sthg.

personnage [pɛrsɔnaʒ] *nm* - **1.** THÉÂTRE character ; ART figure - **2.** [personnalité] image.

personnalité [pɛrsɔnalite] *nf* - **1.** [gén] personality - **2.** JUR status.

personne [pɛrsɔn] <> *nf* person ; **~s** people ; **en ~** in person, personally ; **~ âgée** elderly person. <> *pron indéf* - **1.** [quelqu'un] anybody, anyone - **2.** [aucune personne] nobody, no one ; **~ ne viendra** nobody will come ; **il n'y a jamais ~** there's never anybody there, nobody is ever there.

personnel, elle [pɛrsɔnɛl] *adj* - **1.** [gén] personal - **2.** [égoïste] self-centred. ◆ **personnel** *nm* staff, personnel.

personnellement [pɛrsɔnɛlmɑ̃] *adv* personally.

personnifier [9] [pɛrsɔnifje] *vt* to personify.

perspective [pɛrspɛktiv] *nf* - **1.** ART [point de vue] perspective - **2.** [panorama] view - **3.** [éventualité] prospect.

perspicace [pɛrspikas] *adj* perspicacious.

persuader [3] [pɛrsɥade] *vt* : **~ qqn de qqch/de faire qqch** to persuade sb of sthg/ to do sthg, to convince sb of sthg/to do sthg.

persuasif, ive [pɛrsɥazif, iv] *adj* persuasive.

persuasion [pɛrsɥazjɔ̃] *nf* persuasion.

perte [pɛrt] *nf* - **1.** [gén] loss - **2.** [gaspillage - de temps] waste - **3.** [ruine, déchéance] ruin. ◆ **pertes** *nfpl* [morts] losses. ◆ **à perte de vue** *loc adv* as far as the eye can see.

pertinent, e [pɛrtinɑ̃, ɑ̃t] *adj* pertinent, relevant.

perturber [3] [pɛrtyrbe] *vt* - **1.** [gén] to disrupt ; **~ l'ordre public** to disturb the peace - **2.** PSYCHOL to disturb.

pervenche [pɛrvɑ̃ʃ] *nf* - **1.** BOT periwinkle - **2.** *fam* [contractuelle] traffic warden *Br*, meter maid *Am*.

pervers, e [pɛrver, ɛrs] ◇ *adj* - **1.** [vicieux] perverted - **2.** [effet] unwanted. ◇ *nm, f* pervert.

perversion [pɛrvɛrsjɔ̃] *nf* perversion.

perversité [pɛrvɛrsite] *nf* perversity.

pervertir [32] [pɛrvɛrtir] *vt* to pervert.

pesamment [pəzamɑ̃] *adv* heavily.

pesant, e [pəzɑ̃, ɑ̃t] *adj* - **1.** [lourd] heavy - **2.** [style, architecture] ponderous.

pesanteur [pəzɑ̃tœr] *nf* - **1.** PHYS gravity - **2.** [lourdeur] heaviness.

pesée [pəze] *nf* [opération] weighing.

pèse-personne [pɛzpɛrsɔn] (*pl inv ou* **pèse-personnes**) *nm* scales (*pl*).

peser [19] [pəze] ◇ *vt* to weigh. ◇ *vi* - **1.** [avoir un certain poids] to weigh - **2.** [être lourd] to be heavy - **3.** [appuyer] : **~ sur qqch** to press (down) on sthg.

peseta [pezeta] *nf* peseta.

pessimisme [pesimism] *nm* pessimism.

pessimiste [pesimist] ◇ *nmf* pessimist. ◇ *adj* pessimistic.

peste [pɛst] *nf* - **1.** MÉD plague - **2.** [personne] pest.

pestiféré, e [pestifere] ◇ *adj* plague-stricken ◇ *nm, f* plague victim.

pestilentiel, elle [pestilɑ̃sjɛl] *adj* pestilential.

pet [pɛ] *nm fam* fart.

pétale [petal] *nm* petal.

pétanque [petɑ̃k] *nf* ≃ bowls (*U*).

pétarader [3] [petarade] *vi* to backfire.

pétard [petar] *nm* - **1.** [petit explosif] banger *Br*, firecracker - **2.** *fam* [revolver] gun - **3.** *fam* [haschich] joint.

péter [18] [pete] ◇ *vi* - **1.** *tfam* [personne] to fart - **2.** *fam* [câble, élastique] to snap. ◇ *vt fam* to bust.

pétiller [3] [petije] *vi* - **1.** [vin, eau] to sparkle, to bubble - **2.** [feu] to crackle - **3.** *fig* [yeux] to sparkle.

petit, e [pəti, it] ◇ *adj* - **1.** [de taille, jeune] small, little ; **~ frère** little *ou* younger brother ; **~e sœur** little *ou* younger sister - **2.** [voyage, visite] short, little - **3.** [faible, infime - somme d'argent] small ; [- bruit] faint, slight ; **c'est une ~e nature** he/she is slightly built - **4.** [de peu d'importance, de peu de valeur] minor - **5.** [médiocre, mesquin] petty - **6.** [de rang modeste - commerçant, propriétaire, pays] small ; [- fonctionnaire] minor. ◇ *nm, f* [enfant] little one, child ; **bonjour, mon ~/ma ~e** good morning, my dear ; **pauvre ~!** poor little thing! ; **la classe des ~s** SCOL the infant class. ◇ *nm* [jeune animal] young (*U*) ; **faire des ~s** to have puppies/kittens *etc.* ◆ **petit à petit** *loc adv* little by little, gradually.

petit déjeuner [p(ə)tideʒœne] *nm* breakfast.

petite-fille [p(ə)titfij] *nf* granddaughter.

petitement [p(ə)titmɑ̃] *adv* - **1.** [chichement - vivre] poorly - **2.** [mesquinement] pettily.

petitesse [p(ə)tites] *nf* - **1.** [de personne, de revenu] smallness - **2.** [d'esprit] pettiness.

petit-fils [p(ə)titfis] *nm* grandson.

petit-four [p(ə)tifur] *nm* petit four.

pétition [petisjɔ̃] *nf* petition.

petit-lait [p(ə)tile] *nm* whey.

petit-nègre [p(ə)tinegr] *nm inv fam* pidgin French.

petits-enfants [p(ə)tizɑ̃fɑ̃] *nmpl* grandchildren.

petit-suisse [p(ə)tisɥis] *nm* fresh soft cheese, eaten with sugar.

pétrifier [9] [petrifje] *vt litt & fig* to petrify.

pétrin [petrɛ̃] *nm* - **1.** [de boulanger] kneading machine - **2.** *fam* [embarras] pickle ; **se fourrer/être dans le ~** to get into/to be in a pickle.

pétrir [32] [petrir] *vt* [pâte, muscle] to knead.

pétrole [petrɔl] *nm* oil, petroleum.

pétrolier, ère [petrɔlje, ɛr] *adj* oil (*avant n*), petroleum (*avant n*). ◆ **pétrolier** *nm* [navire] oil tanker.

pétrolifère [petrɔlifɛr] *adj* oil-bearing.

pétulant, e [petylɑ̃, ɑ̃t] *adj* exuberant.

peu [pø] ◇ *adv* - **1.** (*avec verbe, adjectif, adverbe*) : **il a ~ dormi** he didn't sleep much, he slept little ; **~ souvent** not very often, rarely ; **très ~** very little - **2.** : **~ de** (*+ nom sg*) little, not much ; (*+ nom pl*) few, not many ; **il a ~ de travail** he hasn't got much work, he has little work ; **il reste ~ de jours** there aren't many days left ; **~ de gens le con-**

naissent few ou not many know him. ◇ *nm* - **1.** [petite quantité] : **le ~ de** (+ *nom sg*) the little ; (+ *nom pl*) the few - **2.** : **un ~ a** little, a bit ; **je le connais un ~** I know him slightly ou a little ; **un (tout) petit ~** a little bit ; **elle est un ~ sotte** she's a bit stupid ; **un ~ de** a little ; **un ~ de vin/patience** a little wine/patience. ➡ **avant peu** *loc adv* soon, before long. ➡ **depuis peu** *loc adv* recently. ➡ **peu à peu** *loc adv* gradually, little by little. ➡ **pour peu que** (+ *subjonctif*) *loc conj* if ever, if only. ➡ **pour un peu** *loc adv* nearly, almost. ➡ **si peu que** (+ *subjonctif*) *loc conj* however little. ➡ **sous peu** *loc adv* soon, shortly.

peuplade [pœplad] *nf* tribe.

peuple [pœpl] *nm* - **1.** [gén] people ; **le ~** the (common) people - **2.** *fam* [multitude] : **quel ~!** what a crowd!

peuplement [pœpləmɑ̃] *nm* - **1.** [action] populating - **2.** [population] population.

peupler [5] [pœple] *vt* - **1.** [pourvoir d'habitants - région] to populate ; [- bois, étang] to stock - **2.** [habiter, occuper] to inhabit - **3.** *fig* [remplir] to fill. ➡ **se peupler** *vp* - **1.** [région] to become populated - **2.** [rue, salle] to be filled.

peuplier [pøplije] *nm* poplar.

peur [pœr] *nf* fear ; **avoir ~ de qqn/qqch** to be afraid of sb/sthg ; **avoir ~ de faire qqch** to be afraid of doing sthg ; **avoir ~ que** (+ *subjonctif*) to be afraid that ; **j'ai ~ qu'il ne vienne pas** I'm afraid he won't come ; **faire ~ à qqn** to frighten sb ; **par** ou **de ~ de qqch** for fear of sthg ; **par** ou **de ~ de faire qqch** for fear of doing sthg.

peureux, euse [pœrø, øz] ◇ *adj* fearful, timid. ◇ *nm, f* fearful ou timid person.

peut ▷ **pouvoir**.

peut-être [pøtɛtr] *adv* perhaps, maybe ; **~ qu'ils ne viendront pas, ils ne viendront ~ pas** perhaps ou maybe they won't come.

peux ▷ **pouvoir**.

phalange [falɑ̃ʒ] *nf* ANAT phalanx.

phallocrate [falɔkrat] *nm* male chauvinist.

phallus [falys] *nm* phallus.

pharaon [faraɔ̃] *nm* pharaoh.

phare [far] ◇ *nm* - **1.** [tour] lighthouse - **2.** AUTOM headlight ; **~ antibrouillard** fog lamp. ◇ *adj* landmark (*avant n*) ; **une industrie ~** a flagship ou pioneering industry.

pharmaceutique [farmasøtik] *adj* pharmaceutical.

pharmacie [farmasi] *nf* - **1.** [science] pharmacology - **2.** [magasin] chemist's *Br*, drugstore *Am* - **3.** [meuble] : **(armoire à) ~** medicine cupboard.

pharmacien, enne [farmasjɛ̃, ɛn] *nm, f* chemist *Br*, druggist *Am*.

pharynx [farɛ̃ks] *nm* pharynx.

phase [faz] *nf* phase ; **être en ~ avec qqn** to be on the same wavelength as sb.

phénoménal, e, aux [fenɔmenal, o] *adj* phenomenal.

phénomène [fenɔmɛn] *nm* - **1.** [fait] phenomenon - **2.** [être anormal] freak - **3.** *fam* [excentrique] character.

philanthropie [filɑ̃trɔpi] *nf* philanthropy.

philatélie [filateli] *nf* philately, stamp-collecting.

philharmonique [filarmɔnik] *adj* philharmonic.

Philippines [filipin] *nfpl* : **les ~** the Philippines.

philologie [filɔlɔʒi] *nf* philology.

philosophe [filɔzɔf] ◇ *nmf* philosopher. ◇ *adj* philosophical.

philosophie [filɔzɔfi] *nf* philosophy.

phobie [fɔbi] *nf* phobia.

phonétique [fɔnetik] ◇ *nf* phonetics (*U*). ◇ *adj* phonetic.

phonographe [fɔnɔgraf] *nm vieilli* gramophone *Br*, phonograph *Am*.

phoque [fɔk] *nm* seal.

phosphate [fɔsfat] *nm* phosphate.

phosphore [fɔsfɔr] *nm* phosphorus.

phosphorescent, e [fɔsfɔresɑ̃, ɑ̃t] *adj* phosphorescent.

photo [fɔto] ◇ *nf* - **1.** [technique] photography - **2.** [image] photo, picture ; **prendre qqn en ~** to take a photo of sb ; **~ d'identité** passport photo ; **~ couleur** colour *Br* ou color *Am* photo ; **y'a pas ~** *fam* there's no comparison. ◇ *adj inv* : **appareil ~** camera.

photocomposition [fɔtokɔ̃pozisjɔ̃] *nf* filmsetting *Br*, photocomposition *Am*.

photocopie [fɔtokɔpi] *nf* - **1.** [procédé] photocopying - **2.** [document] photocopy.

photocopier [9] [fɔtokɔpje] *vt* to photocopy.

photocopieur [fɔtokɔpjœr] *nm*, **photocopieuse** [fɔtokɔpjøz] *nf* photocopier.

photoélectrique [fɔtoelɛktrik] *adj* photoelectric.

photogénique [fɔtoʒenik] *adj* photogenic.

photographe [fɔtograf] *nmf* - **1.** [artiste, technicien] photographer - **2.** [commerçant] camera dealer.

photographie [fɔtografi] *nf* - **1.** [technique] photography - **2.** [cliché] photograph.

photographier [9] [fɔtɔgrafje] *vt* to photograph.

Photomaton® [fɔtɔmatɔ̃] *nm* photo booth.

photoreportage [fɔtɔrəpɔrtaʒ] *nm* PRESSE report *(consisting mainly of photographs)*.

phrase [fraz] *nf* - **1.** LING sentence ; ~ **toute faite** stock phrase - **2.** MUS phrase.

physicien, enne [fizisjɛ̃, ɛn] *nm, f* physicist.

physiologie [fizjɔlɔʒi] *nf* physiology.

physiologique [fizjɔlɔʒik] *adj* physiological.

physionomie [fizjɔnɔmi] *nf* - **1.** [faciès] face - **2.** [apparence] physiognomy.

physionomiste [fizjɔnɔmist] *adj* : **être ~** to have a good memory for faces.

physique [fizik] <> *adj* physical. <> *nf* SCIENCE physics *(U).* <> *nm* - **1.** [constitution] physical well-being - **2.** [apparence] physique.

physiquement [fizikmɑ̃] *adv* physically.

piaffer [3] [pjafe] *vi* - **1.** [cheval] to paw the ground - **2.** [personne] to fidget.

piailler [3] [pjaje] *vi* **1.** [oiseaux] to cheep - **2.** [enfant] to squawk.

pianiste [pjanist] *nmf* pianist.

piano [pjano] <> *nm* piano. <> *adv* - **1.** MUS piano - **2.** [doucement] gently.

pianoter [3] [pjanɔte] *vi* - **1.** [jouer du piano] to plunk away (on the piano) - **2.** [sur table] to drum one's fingers.

piaule [pjol] *nf fam* [hébergement] place ; [chambre] room.

PIB *(abr de* **produit intérieur brut)** *nm* GDP.

pic [pik] *nm* - **1.** [outil] pick, pickaxe *Br*, pickax *Am* - **2.** [montagne] peak - **3.** [oiseau] woodpecker - **4.** *fig* [maximum] ~ **d'audience** top (audience) ratings ; **on a observé des ~s de pollution** pollution levels reached a peak, pollution levels peaked. ◆ **à pic** *loc adv* - **1.** [verticalement] vertically ; **couler à ~** to sink like a stone - **2.** *fam fig* [à point nommé] just at the right moment.

pichenette [piʃnɛt] *nf* flick (of the finger).

pichet [piʃɛ] *nm* jug.

pickpocket [pikpɔkɛt] *nm* pickpocket.

picorer [3] [pikɔre] *vi & vt* to peck.

picotement [pikɔtmɑ̃] *nm* prickling *(U)*, prickle.

pie [pi] <> *nf* - **1.** [oiseau] magpie - **2.** *fig & péj* [bavard] chatterbox. <> *adj inv* [cheval] piebald.

pièce [pjɛs] *nf* - **1.** [élément] piece ; [de moteur] part ; ~ **de collection** collector's item ;

~ **détachée** spare part - **2.** [unité] : **deux euros** ~ deux euros each OU apiece ; **acheter/vendre qqch à la** ~ to buy/sell sthg singly, to buy/sell sthg separately ; **travailler à la** ~ to do piece work - **3.** [document] document, paper ; ~ **d'identité** identification papers *(pl)* ; ~ **justificative** written proof *(U)*, supporting document - **4.** [œuvre littéraire ou musicale] piece ; ~ **(de théâtre)** play - **5.** [argent] : ~ **(de monnaie)** coin - **6.** [de maison] room - **7.** COUTURE patch.

pied [pje] *nm* - **1.** [gén] foot ; **à** ~ on foot ; **avoir** ~ to be able to touch the bottom ; **perdre** ~ *litt & fig* to be out of one's depth ; **être/marcher ~s nus** OU **nu-~s** to be/to go barefoot ; ~ **bot** [handicap] clubfoot - **2.** [base - de montagne, table] foot ; [- de verre] stem ; [- de lampe] base - **3.** [plant - de tomate] stalk ; [- de vigne] stock - **4.** *loc* : **être sur** ~ to be (back) on one's feet, to be up and about ; **faire du** ~ **à** to play footsie with ; **mettre qqch sur** ~ to get sthg on its feet, to get sthg off the ground ; **je n'ai jamais mis les ~s chez lui** I've never set foot in his house ; **au ~ de la lettre** literally, to the letter. ◆ **en pied** *loc adj* [portrait] full-length.

pied-de-biche [pjedbiʃ] *(pl* **pieds-de-biche)** *nm* [outil] nail claw.

piédestal, aux [pjedɛstal, o] *nm* pedestal.

pied-noir [pjenwar] *nmf French settler in Algeria.*

piège [pjɛʒ] *nm litt & fig* trap.

piéger [22] [pjeʒe] *vt* - **1.** [animal, personne] to trap - **2.** [colis, véhicule] to booby-trap.

piercing [piːrsiŋ] *nm* body piercing.

pierraille [pjeraj] *nf* loose stones *(pl)*.

pierre [pjɛr] *nf* stone ; ~ **d'achoppement** *fig* stumbling block ; ~ **précieuse** precious stone.

pierreries [pjɛrri] *nfpl* precious stones, jewels.

piété [pjete] *nf* piety.

piétiner [3] [pjetine] <> *vi* - **1.** [trépigner] to stamp (one's feet) - **2.** *fig* [ne pas avancer] to make no progress, to be at a standstill. <> *vt* [personne, parterre] to trample.

piéton, onne [pjetɔ̃, ɔn] <> *nm, f* pedestrian. <> *adj* pedestrian *(avant n)*.

piétonnier, ère [pjetɔnje, ɛr] *adj* pedestrian *(avant n)*.

piètre [pjɛtr] *adj* poor.

pieu, x [pjø] *nm* - **1.** [poteau] post, stake - **2.** *fam* [lit] pit *Br*, sack *Am*.

pieuvre [pjœvr] *nf* octopus ; *fig & péj* leech.

pieux, pieuse [pjø, pjøz] *adj* [personne, livre] pious.

pif [pif] *nm fam* conk, hooter *Br* ; **au ~** *fig* by guesswork.

pigeon [piʒɔ̃] *nm* - **1.** [oiseau] pigeon - **2.** *fam péj* [personne] sucker.

pigeonnier [piʒɔnje] *nm* [pour pigeons] pigeon loft, dovecote.

pigment [pigmɑ̃] *nm* pigment.

pignon [piɲɔ̃] *nm* - **1.** [de mur] gable - **2.** [d'engrenage] gearwheel - **3.** [de pomme de pin] pine kernel.

pile [pil] <> *nf* - **1.** [de livres, journaux] pile - **2.** ÉLECTR battery - **3.** [de pièce] : **~ ou face** heads or tails. <> *adv fam* on the dot ; **tomber/arriver ~** to come/to arrive at just the right time.

piler [3] [pile] <> *vt* [amandes] to crush, to grind. <> *vi fam* AUTOM to jam on the brakes.

pileux, euse [pilø, øz] *adj* hairy *(avant n)* ; **système ~** hair.

pilier [pilje] *nm* - **1.** [de construction] pillar - **2.** *fig* [soutien] mainstay, pillar - **3.** RUGBY prop (forward).

pillard, e [pijar, ard] *nm, f* looter.

piller [3] [pije] *vt* - **1.** [ville, biens] to loot - **2.** *fig* [ouvrage, auteur] to plagiarize.

pilon [pilɔ̃] *nm* - **1.** [instrument] pestle - **2.** [de poulet] drumstick - **3.** [jambe de bois] wooden leg.

pilonner [3] [pilɔne] *vt* to pound.

pilori [pilɔri] *nm* pillory ; **mettre** OU **clouer qqn au ~** *fig* to pillory sb.

pilotage [pilɔtaʒ] *nm* piloting ; **~ automatique** automatic piloting.

pilote [pilɔt] <> *nm* [d'avion] pilot ; [de voiture] driver ; **~ automatique** autopilot ; **~ de chasse** fighter pilot ; **~ de course** racing *Br* OU race *Am* driver ; **~ d'essai** test pilot ; **~ de ligne** airline pilot. <> *adj* pilot *(avant n)*, experimental.

piloter [3] [pilɔte] *vt* - **1.** [avion] to pilot ; [voiture] to drive - **2.** [personne] to show around.

pilotis [pilɔti] *nm* pile.

pilule [pilyl] *nf* pill ; **prendre la ~** to be on the pill.

piment [pimɑ̃] *nm* - **1.** [plante] pepper, capsicum ; **~ rouge** chilli pepper, hot red pepper - **2.** *fig* [piquant] spice.

pimpant, e [pɛ̃pɑ̃, ɑ̃t] *adj* smart.

pin [pɛ̃] *nm* pine ; **~ parasol** umbrella pine ; **~ sylvestre** Scots pine.

pin's [pinz] *nm inv* badge.

pince [pɛ̃s] *nf* - **1.** [grande] pliers *(pl)* - **2.** [petite] : **~ (à épiler)** tweezers *(pl)* ; **~ à**

linge clothes peg *Br*, clothespin *Am* - **3.** [de crabe] pincer - **4.** COUTURE dart.

pinceau, x [pɛ̃so] *nm* [pour peindre] brush.

pincée [pɛ̃se] *nf* pinch.

pincer [16] [pɛ̃se] <> *vt* - **1.** [serrer] to pinch ; MUS to pluck ; [lèvres] to purse - **2.** *fam fig* [arrêter] to nick *Br*, to catch - **3.** [suj : froid] to nip. <> *vi fam* [faire froid] : **ça pince!** it's a bit nippy!

pincettes [pɛ̃sɛt] *nfpl* [ustensile] tongs.

pingouin [pɛ̃gwɛ̃] *nm* penguin.

ping-pong [piɲpɔ̃g] *nm* ping pong, table tennis.

pinson [pɛ̃sɔ̃] *nm* chaffinch.

pintade [pɛ̃tad] *nf* guinea fowl.

pin-up [pinœp] *nf inv* pinup (girl).

pioche [pjɔʃ] *nf* - **1.** [outil] pick - **2.** JEU pile.

piocher [3] [pjɔʃe] <> *vt* - **1.** [terre] to dig - **2.** JEU to take - **3.** *fig* [choisir] to pick at random. <> *vi* - **1.** [creuser] to dig - **2.** JEU to pick up ; **~ dans** [tas] to delve into ; [économies] to dip into.

pion, pionne [pjɔ̃, pjɔn] *nm, f fam* SCOL supervisor *(often a student who does this as a part-time job)*. ◆ **pion** *nm* [aux échecs] pawn ; [aux dames] piece ; **n'être qu'un ~** *fig* to be just a pawn in the game.

pionnier, ère [pjɔnje, ɛr] *nm, f* pioneer.

pipe [pip] *nf* pipe.

pipeline, pipe-line [pajplajn, piplin] *(pl* **pipe-lines)** *nm* pipeline.

pipi [pipi] *nm fam* wee ; **faire ~** to have a wee.

piquant, e [pikɑ̃, ɑ̃t] *adj* - **1.** [barbe, feuille] prickly - **2.** [sauce] spicy, hot. ◆ **piquant** *nm* - **1.** [d'animal] spine ; [de végétal] thorn, prickle - **2.** *fig* [d'histoire] spice.

pique [pik] <> *nf* - **1.** [arme] pike - **2.** *fig* [mot blessant] barbed comment. <> *nm* [aux cartes] spade.

pique-assiette [pikasjɛt] *(pl inv* OU **pique-assiettes)** *nmf péj* sponger.

pique-nique [piknik] *(pl* **pique-niques)** *nm* picnic.

piquer [3] [pike] <> *vt* - **1.** [suj : guêpe, méduse] to sting ; [suj : serpent, moustique] to bite - **2.** [avec pointe] to prick - **3.** MÉD to give an injection to - **4.** [animal] to put down - **5.** [fleur] : **~ qqch dans** to stick sthg into - **6.** [suj : tissu, barbe] to prickle - **7.** [suj : fumée, froid] to sting - **8.** COUTURE to sew, to machine - **9.** *fam* [voler] to pinch - **10.** *fig* [curiosité] to excite, to arouse - **11.** *fam* [voleur, escroc] to nick *Br*, to catch. <> *vi* - **1.** [ronce] to prick ; [ortie] to sting - **2.** [guêpe, méduse] to sting ; [serpent, moustique]

to bite - **3.** [épice] to burn - **4.** *fam* [voler] :
~ **(dans)** to pinch (from) - **5.** [avion] to dive.

piquet [pikɛ] *nm* [pieu] peg, stake. ◆ **piquet de grève** *nm* picket.

piqûre [pikyr] *nf* - **1.** [de guêpe, de méduse] sting ; [de serpent, de moustique] bite - **2.** [d'ortie] sting - **3.** [injection] jab *Br*, shot.

piratage [pirataʒ] *nm* piracy ; INFORM hacking.

pirate [pirat] ◇ *nm* [corsaire] pirate ; ~ **de l'air** hijacker, skyjacker. ◇ *adj* pirate *(avant n)*.

pire [pir] ◇ *adj* - **1.** [comparatif relatif] worse - **2.** [superlatif] : **le/la ~** the worst. ◇ *nm* : **le ~ (de)** the worst (of).

pirogue [pirɔg] *nf* dugout canoe.

pirouette [pirwɛt] *nf* - **1.** [saut] pirouette - **2.** *fig* [faux-fuyant] prevarication, evasive answer.

pis [pi] ◇ *adj littéraire* [pire] worse. ◇ *adv* worse ; **de mal en ~** from bad to worse. ◇ *nm* udder.

pis-aller [pizale] *nm inv* last resort.

pisciculture [pisikyltyr] *nf* fish farming.

piscine [pisin] *nf* swimming pool ; ~ **couverte/découverte** indoor/open-air swimming pool.

pissenlit [pisɑ̃li] *nm* dandelion.

pisser [3] [pise] *fam* ◇ *vt* - **1.** [suj : personne] : ~ **du sang** to pass blood - **2.** [suj : plaie] : **son genou pissait le sang** blood was gushing from his knee. ◇ *vi* to pee, to piss.

pissotière [pisɔtjɛr] *nf fam* public urinal.

pistache [pistaʃ] *nf* [fruit] pistachio (nut).

piste [pist] *nf* - **1.** [trace] trail - **2.** [zone aménagée] : ~ **d'atterrissage** runway ; ~ **cyclable** cycle track ; ~ **de danse** dance floor ; ~ **de ski** ski run - **3.** [chemin] path, track - **4.** [d'enregistrement] track.

pistil [pistil] *nm* pistil.

pistolet [pistɔlɛ] *nm* - **1.** [arme] pistol, gun - **2.** [à peinture] spray gun.

piston [pistɔ̃] *nm* - **1.** [de moteur] piston - **2.** MUS [d'instrument] valve - **3.** *fig* [appui] string-pulling.

pistonner [3] [pistɔne] *vt* to pull strings for ; **se faire ~** to have strings pulled for one.

pitance [pitɑ̃s] *nf péj & vieilli* sustenance.

pitbull, pit-bull [pitbul] *(pl* pit-bulls) *nm* pitbull (terrier).

piteux, euse [pitø, øz] *adj* piteous.

pitié [pitje] *nf* pity ; **avoir ~ de qqn** to have pity on sb, to pity sb.

piton [pitɔ̃] *nm* - **1.** [clou] piton - **2.** [pic] peak.

pitoyable [pitwajabl] *adj* pitiful.

pitre [pitr] *nm* clown.

pitrerie [pitrəri] *nf* tomfoolery.

pittoresque [pitɔrɛsk] *adj* - **1.** [région] picturesque - **2.** [détail] colourful *Br*, colorful *Am*, vivid.

pivot [pivo] *nm* - **1.** [de machine, au basket] pivot - **2.** [de dent] post - **3.** [centre] *fig* mainspring.

pivoter [3] [pivɔte] *vi* to pivot ; [porte] to revolve.

pizza [pidza] *nf* pizza.

Pl., pl. *abr de* place.

placage [plakaʒ] *nm* [de bois] veneer.

placard [plakar] *nm* - **1.** [armoire] cupboard - **2.** [affiche] poster, notice.

placarder [3] [plakarde] *vt* [affiche] to put up, to stick up ; [mur] to placard, to stick a notice on.

place [plas] *nf* - **1.** [espace] space, room ; **prendre de la ~** to take up (a lot of) space ; **faire ~ à** [amour, haine] to give way to - **2.** [emplacement, position] position ; **changer qqch de ~** to put sthg in a different place, to move sthg ; **prendre la ~ de qqn** to take sb's place ; **à la ~ de qqn** instead of sb, in sb's place ; **à ta ~** if I were you, in your place - **3.** [siège] seat ; ~ **assise** seat - **4.** [rang] place - **5.** [de ville] square - **6.** [emploi] position, job - **7.** MIL [de garnison] garrison (town) ; ~ **forte** fortified town.

placement [plasmɑ̃] *nm* - **1.** [d'argent] investment - **2.** [d'employé] placing.

placenta [plasɛ̃ta] *nm* ANAT placenta.

placer [16] [plase] *vt* - **1.** [gén] to put, to place ; [invités, spectateurs] to seat - **2.** [mot, anecdote] to put in, to get in - **3.** [argent] to invest. ◆ **se placer** *vp* - **1.** [prendre place - debout] to stand ; [- assis] to sit (down) - **2.** *fig* [dans une situation] to put o.s. - **3.** [se classer] to come, to be.

placide [plasid] *adj* placid.

plafond [plafɔ̃] *nm litt & fig* ceiling ; **faux ~** false ceiling.

plafonner [3] [plafɔne] *vi* [prix, élève] to peak ; [avion] to reach its ceiling.

plage [plaʒ] *nf* - **1.** [de sable] beach - **2.** [d'ombre, de prix] band ; *fig* [de temps] slot - **3.** [de disque] track - **4.** [dans une voiture] : ~ **arrière** back shelf.

plagiat [plaʒja] *nm* plagiarism.

plagier [9] [plaʒje] *vt* to plagiarize.

plaider [4] [plede] JUR ◇ *vt* to plead. ◇ *vi* to plead ; ~ **contre qqn** to plead against sb ; ~ **pour qqn** JUR to plead for sb ; [justifier] to plead sb's cause.

plaidoirie [plɛdwaRi] *nf*, **plaidoyer** [plɛdwaje] *nm* JUR speech for the defence *Br* OU defense *Am* ; *fig* plea.

plaie [plɛ] *nf* - **1.** *litt & fig* wound - **2.** *fam* [personne] pest.

plaindre [80] [plɛ̃dR] *vt* to pity. ◆ **se plaindre** *vp* to complain.

plaine [plɛn] *nf* plain.

plain-pied [plɛ̃pje] ◆ **de plain-pied** *loc adv* - **1.** [pièce] on one floor ; **de ~ avec** *litt & fig* on a level with - **2.** *fig* [directement] straight.

plaint, e [plɛ̃, plɛ̃t] *pp* ▷ **plaindre**.

plainte [plɛ̃t] *nf* - **1.** [gémissement] moan, groan ; *fig & litt* [du vent] moan - **2.** [doléance & JUR] complaint ; **porter ~** to lodge a complaint ; **~ contre X** ≃ complaint against person or persons unknown.

plaintif, ive [plɛ̃tif, iv] *adj* plaintive.

plaire [110] [plɛR] *vi* to be liked ; **il me plaît** I like him ; **ça te plairait d'aller au cinéma?** would you like to go to the cinema? ; **s'il vous/te plaît** please.

plaisance [plɛzɑ̃s] ◆ **de plaisance** *loc adj* pleasure *(avant n)* ; **navigation de ~** sailing ; **port de ~** marina.

plaisancier, ère [plɛzɑ̃sje, ɛR] *nm, f* (amateur) sailor.

plaisant, e [plɛzɑ̃, ɑ̃t] *adj* pleasant.

plaisanter [3] [plɛzɑ̃te] *vi* to joke ; **tu plaisantes?** you must be joking!

plaisanterie [plɛzɑ̃tRi] *nf* joke ; **c'est une ~?** *iron* you must be joking!

plaisantin [plɛzɑ̃tɛ̃] *nm* joker.

plaisir [plɛziR] *nm* pleasure ; **les ~s de la vie** life's pleasures ; **avoir du/prendre ~ à faire qqch** to have/to take pleasure in doing sthg ; **faire ~ à qqn** to please sb ; **avec ~** with pleasure ; **j'ai le ~ de vous annoncer que ...** I have the (great) pleasure of announcing that ...

plan¹, e [plɑ̃, plan] *adj* level, flat.

plan² [plɑ̃] *nm* - **1.** [dessin - de ville] map ; [- de maison] plan - **2.** [projet] plan ; **faire des ~s** to make plans ; **avoir son ~** to have something in mind - **3.** [domaine] : **sur tous les ~s** in all respects ; **sur le ~ affectif** emotionally ; **sur le ~ familial** as far as the family is concerned - **4.** [surface] : **~ d'eau** lake ; **~ de travail** work surface, worktop - **5.** GÉOM plane - **6.** CINÉMA take ; **gros ~** close-up. ◆ **plan social** *nm* redundancy scheme OU plan. ◆ **à l'arrière-plan** *loc adv* in the background. ◆ **au premier plan** *loc adv* [dans l'espace] in the foreground. ◆ **en plan** *loc adv* : **laisser qqn**

en ~ to leave sb stranded, to abandon sb ; **il a tout laissé en ~** he dropped everything. ◆ **sur le même plan** *loc adj* on the same level.

planche [plɑ̃ʃ] *nf* - **1.** [en bois] plank ; **~ à dessin** drawing board ; **~ à repasser** ironing board ; **~ à voile** [planche] sailboard ; [sport] windsurfing ; **faire la ~** *fig* to float - **2.** [d'illustration] plate.

plancher [plɑ̃ʃe] *nm* - **1.** [de maison, de voiture] floor - **2.** *fig* [limite] floor, lower limit.

plancton [plɑ̃ktɔ̃] *nm* plankton.

planer [3] [plane] *vi* - **1.** [avion, oiseau] to glide - **2.** [nuage, fumée, brouillard] to float - **3.** *fig* [danger] : **~ sur qqn** to hang over sb - **4.** *fam* [personne] to be out of touch with reality.

planétaire [planetɛR] *adj* - **1.** ASTRON planetary - **2.** [mondial] world *(avant n)*.

planétarium [planetaRjɔm] *nm* planetarium.

planète [planɛt] *nf* planet.

planeur [planœR] *nm* glider.

planification [planifikasjɔ̃] *nf* ÉCON planning.

planisphère [planisfɛR] *nm* map of the world, planisphere.

planning [planiŋ] *nm* - **1.** [de fabrication] workflow schedule - **2.** [agenda personnel] schedule ; **~ familial** [contrôle] family planning ; [organisme] family planning clinic.

planque [plɑ̃k] *nf fam* - **1.** [cachette] hideout - **2.** *fig* [situation, travail] cushy number.

plant [plɑ̃] *nm* [plante] seedling.

plantaire [plɑ̃tɛR] *adj* plantar.

plantation [plɑ̃tasjɔ̃] *nf* - **1.** [exploitation - d'arbres, de coton, de café] plantation ; [- de légumes] patch - **2.** [action] planting.

plante [plɑ̃t] *nf* - **1.** BOT plant ; **~ verte** OU **d'appartement** OU **d'intérieur** house OU pot plant - **2.** ANAT sole.

planter [3] [plɑ̃te] ◇ *vt* - **1.** [arbre, terrain] to plant - **2.** [clou] to hammer in, to drive in ; [pieu] to drive in ; [couteau, griffes] to stick in - **3.** [tente] to pitch - **4.** *fam fig* [laisser tomber] to dump - **5.** *fig* [chapeau] to stick ; [baiser] to plant ; **~ son regard dans celui de qqn** to look sb right in the eyes. ◇ *vi* INFORM *fam* to crash.

plantureux, euse [plɑ̃tyRø, øz] *adj* - **1.** [repas] lavish - **2.** [femme] buxom.

plaque [plak] *nf* - **1.** [de métal, de verre, de verglas] sheet ; [de marbre] slab ; **~ chauffante** OU **de cuisson** hotplate ; **~ de chocolat** bar of chocolate - **2.** [gravée] plaque ;

~ d'immatriculation OU **minéralogique** number plate Br, license plate Am - **3.** [insigne] badge - **4.** [sur la peau] patch - **5.** [dentaire] plaque.

plaqué, e [plake] adj [métal] plated ; ~ or/ argent gold-/silver-plated. ◆ **plaqué** nm [métal] : **du ~ or/argent** gold/silver plate.

plaquer [3] [plake] vt - **1.** [métal] to plate - **2.** [bois] to veneer - **3.** [aplatir] to flatten ; **~ qqn contre qqch** to pin sb against sthg ; **~ qqch contre qqch** to stick sthg onto sthg - **4.** RUGBY to tackle - **5.** MUS [accord] to play - **6.** fam [travail, personne] to chuck.

plaquette [plaket] nf - **1.** [de métal] plaque ; [de marbre] tablet - **2.** [de chocolat] bar ; [de beurre] pat - **3.** [de comprimés] packet, strip - **4.** (gén pl) BIOL platelet - **5.** AUTOM : **~ de frein** brake pad.

plasma [plasma] nm plasma.

plastique [plastik] adj & nm plastic.

plastiquer [3] [plastike] vt to blow up (with plastic explosives).

plat, e [pla, plat] adj - **1.** [gén] flat - **2.** [eau] still. ◆ **plat** nm - **1.** [partie plate] flat - **2.** [récipient] dish - **3.** [mets] course ; **~ cuisiné** ready-cooked meal ou dish ; **~ du jour** today's special ; **~ préparé** ready meal ; **~ de résistance** main course - **4.** [plongeon] belly-flop. ◆ **à plat** loc adv - **1.** [horizontalement, dégonflé] flat - **2.** fam [épuisé] exhausted.

platane [platan] nm plane tree.

plateau [plato] nm - **1.** [de cuisine] tray ; **~ de/à fromages** cheese board - **2.** [de balance] pan - **3.** GÉOGR & fig plateau - **4.** THÉÂTRE stage ; CIN & TÉLÉ set - **5.** [de vélo] chain wheel.

plateau-repas [platorapa] nm tray (of food).

plate-bande [platbɑ̃d] nf flower bed.

plate-forme [platform] nf [gén] platform ; **~ de forage** drilling platform.

platine [platin] ◇ adj inv platinum. ◇ nm [métal] platinum. ◇ nf [de tournedisque] deck ; **~ laser** compact disc player.

platonique [platonik] adj [amour, amitié] platonic.

plâtras [platra] nm [gravats] rubble.

plâtre [platr] nm - **1.** CONSTR & MÉD plaster - **2.** [sculpture] plaster cast - **3.** péj [fromage] : **c'est du vrai ~** it's like sawdust.

plâtrer [3] [platre] vt - **1.** [mur] to plaster - **2.** MÉD to put in plaster.

plausible [plozibl] adj plausible.

play-back [plɛbak] nm inv miming ; **chanter en ~** to mime.

play-boy [plɛbɔj] (pl **play-boys**) nm playboy.

plébiscite [plebisit] nm plebiscite.

plein, e [plɛ̃, plɛn] adj - **1.** [rempli, complet] full ; **c'est la ~e forme** I am/they are etc in top form ; **en ~e nuit** in the middle of the night ; **en ~ air** in the open air - **2.** [non creux] solid - **3.** [femelle] pregnant. ◆ **plein** ◇ adv fam : **il a de l'encre ~ les doigts** he has ink all over his fingers ; **en ~ dans/sur qqch** right in/on sthg. ◇ nm [de réservoir] full tank ; **le ~, s'il vous plaît** fill her up please ; **faire le ~** to fill up.

plein-temps [plɛ̃tɑ̃] nm full-time job.

plénitude [plenityd] nf fullness.

pléonasme [pleonasm] nm pleonasm.

pleurer [5] [plœre] ◇ vi - **1.** [larmoyer] to cry ; **~ de joie** to weep for joy, to cry with joy - **2.** péj [se plaindre] to whinge - **3.** [se lamenter] : **~ sur** to lament. ◇ vt to mourn.

pleurnicher [3] [plœrniʃe] vi to whine, to whinge.

pleurs [plœr] nmpl : **être en ~** to be in tears.

pleuvoir [68] [pløvwar] v impers litt & fig to rain ; **il pleut** it is raining.

Plexiglas® [plɛksiglas] nm Plexiglass®.

plexus [plɛksys] nm plexus ; **~ solaire** solar plexus.

pli [pli] nm - **1.** [de tissu] pleat ; [de pantalon] crease ; **faux ~** crease - **2.** [du front] line ; [du cou] fold - **3.** [lettre] letter ; [enveloppe] envelope ; **sous ~ séparé** under separate cover - **4.** CARTES trick - **5.** GÉOL fold.

pliant, e [plijɑ̃, ɑ̃t] adj folding (avant n).

plier [10] [plije] ◇ vt - **1.** [papier, tissu] to fold - **2.** [vêtement, vélo] to fold (up) - **3.** [branche, bras] to bend. ◇ vi - **1.** [se courber] to bend - **2.** fig [céder] to bow. ◆ **se plier** vp - **1.** [être pliable] to fold (up) - **2.** fig [se soumettre] : **se ~ à qqch** to bow to sthg.

plinthe [plɛ̃t] nf plinth.

plissé, e [plise] adj - **1.** [jupe] pleated - **2.** [peau] wrinkled.

plissement [plismɑ̃] nm - **1.** [de front] creasing ; [d'yeux] screwing up - **2.** GÉOL fold.

plisser [3] [plise] ◇ vt - **1.** COUTURE to pleat - **2.** [front] to crease ; [lèvres] to pucker ; [yeux] to screw up. ◇ vi [étoffe] to crease.

plomb [plɔ̃] nm - **1.** [métal, de vitrail] lead - **2.** [de chasse] shot - **3.** ÉLECTR fuse ; **les ~s ont sauté** a fuse has blown ou gone - **4.** [de pêche] sinker.

plombage [plɔ̃baʒ] nm [de dent] filling.

plomber [3] [plɔ̃be] *vt* - **1.** [ligne] to weight (with lead) - **2.** [dent] to fill.

plombier [plɔ̃bje] *nm* plumber.

plonge [plɔ̃ʒ] *nf fam* dishwashing ; **faire la ~** to wash dishes.

plongeant, e [plɔ̃ʒɑ̃, ɑ̃t] *adj* - **1.** [vue] from above - **2.** [décolleté] plunging.

plongée [plɔ̃ʒe] *nf* [immersion] diving ; **~ sous-marine** scuba diving.

plongeoir [plɔ̃ʒwar] *nm* diving board.

plongeon [plɔ̃ʒɔ̃] *nm* [dans l'eau, au football] dive.

plonger [17] [plɔ̃ʒe] ◇ *vt* - **1.** [immerger, enfoncer] to plunge ; **~ la tête sous l'eau** to put one's head under the water - **2.** *fig* [précipiter] : **~ qqn dans qqch** to throw sb into sthg ; **~ une pièce dans l'obscurité** to plunge a room into darkness. ◇ *vi* [dans l'eau, gardien de but] to dive. ◆ **se plonger** *vp* - **1.** [s'immerger] to submerge - **2.** *fig* [s'absorber] : **se ~ dans qqch** to immerse o.s. in sthg.

plongeur, euse [plɔ̃ʒœr, øz] *nm, f* - **1.** [dans l'eau] diver - **2.** [dans restaurant] dishwasher.

ployer [13] [plwaje] *vt & vi litt & fig* to bend.

plu [ply] ◇ *pp inv* ▷ **plaire.** ◇ *pp inv* ▷ **pleuvoir.**

pluie [plɥi] *nf* - **1.** [averse] rain *(U)* ; **sous la ~** in the rain ; **une ~ battante** driving rain ; **une ~ fine** drizzle - **2.** *fig* [grande quantité] : **une ~ de** a shower of.

plume [plym] *nf* - **1.** [d'oiseau] feather - **2.** [pour écrire - d'oiseau] quill pen ; [- de stylo] nib.

plumeau, x [plymo] *nm* feather duster.

plumer [3] [plyme] *vt* - **1.** [volaille] to pluck - **2.** *fam fig & péj* [personne] to fleece.

plumier [plymje] *nm* pencil box.

plupart [plypar] *nf* : **la ~ de** most of, the majority of ; **la ~ du temps** most of the time, mostly ; **pour la ~** mostly, for the most part.

pluriel, elle [plyrjɛl] *adj* - **1.** GRAM plural - **2.** [société] pluralist. ◆ **pluriel** *nm* plural ; **au ~** in the plural.

plus [ply(s)] ◇ *adv* - **1.** [quantité] more ; **je ne peux vous en dire ~** I can't tell you anything more ; **beaucoup ~ de** *(+ nom sg)* a lot more, much more ; *(+ nom pl)* a lot more, many more ; **un peu ~ de** *(+ nom sg)* a little more ; *(+ nom pl)* a few more ; **il y a (un peu) ~ de 15 ans** (a little) more than 15 years ago ; **~ j'y pense, ~ je me dis que ...** the more I think about it, the more I'm sure ... - **2.** [comparaison] more ; **c'est ~ court par là** it's shorter that way ; **viens ~ souvent** come more often ; **c'est un peu ~ loin** it's a (little) bit further ; **~ jeune (que)** younger (than) ; **c'est ~ simple qu'on ne le croit** it's simpler than you think - **3.** [superlatif] : **le ~** the most ; **c'est lui qui travaille le ~** he's the hardest worker, he's the one who works (the) hardest ; **un de ses tableaux les ~ connus** one of his best-known paintings ; **le ~ souvent** the most often ; **le ~ loin** the furthest ; **le ~ vite possible** as quickly as possible - **4.** [négation] no more ; **~ un mot!** not another word! ; **ne ... ~** no longer, no more ; **il ne vient ~ me voir** he doesn't come to see me any more, he no longer comes to see me ; **je n'y vais ~ du tout** I don't go there any more. ◇ *nm* - **1.** [signe] plus (sign) - **2.** *fig* [atout] plus. ◇ *prép* plus ; **trois ~ trois font six** three plus three is six, three and three are six. ◆ **au plus** *loc adv* at the most ; **tout au ~** at the very most. ◆ **de plus** *loc adv* - **1.** [en supplément, en trop] more ; **elle a cinq ans de ~ que moi** she's five years older than me - **2.** [en outre] furthermore, what's more. ◆ **de plus en plus** *loc adv* more and more. ◆ **de plus en plus de** *loc prép* more and more. ◆ **en plus** *loc adv* - **1.** [en supplément] extra - **2.** [d'ailleurs] moreover, what's more. ◆ **en plus de** *loc prép* in addition to. ◆ **ni plus ni moins** *loc adv* no more no less. ◆ **plus ou moins** *loc adv* more or less. ◆ **sans plus** *loc adv* : **elle est gentille, sans ~** she's nice, but no more than that.

plusieurs [plyzjœr] *adj indéf pl & pron indéf mfpl* several.

plus-que-parfait [plyskəparfɛ] *nm* GRAM pluperfect.

plus-value [plyvaly] *nf* - **1.** [d'investissement] appreciation - **2.** [excédent] surplus - **3.** [bénéfice] profit.

plutôt [plyto] *adv* rather ; **~ que de faire qqch** instead of doing sthg, rather than doing ou do sthg.

pluvieux, euse [plyvjø, øz] *adj* rainy.

PME (*abr de* **petite et moyenne entreprise**) *nf* SME.

PMI *nf* (*abr de* **petite et moyenne industrie**) small industrial firm.

PMU (*abr de* **Pari mutuel urbain**) *nm system for betting on horses.*

PNB (*abr de* **produit national brut**) *nm* GNP.

pneu [pnø] *nm* [de véhicule] tyre *Br*, tire *Am* ; **~ arrière** rear tyre *Br* ou tire *Am* ; **~-neige** winter tyre *Br* ou tire *Am*.

pneumatique [pnømatik] ◇ *nf* PHYS pneumatics *(U)*. ◇ *adj* - **1.** [fonctionnant à l'air] pneumatic - **2.** [gonflé à l'air] inflatable.

pneumonie [pnømɔni] *nf* pneumonia.

PO (*abr de* **petites ondes**) MW.

poche [pɔʃ] *nf* - **1.** [de vêtement, de sac, d'air] pocket ; **de ~** pocket (*avant n*) - **2.** [sac, sous les yeux] bag ; **faire des ~s** [vêtement] to bag.

pocher [3] [pɔʃe] *vt* - **1.** CULIN to poach - **2.** [blesser] : **~ l'œil à qqn** to give sb a black eye.

pochette [pɔʃɛt] *nf* - **1.** [enveloppe] envelope ; [d'allumettes] book ; [de photos] packet - **2.** [de disque] sleeve - **3.** [mouchoir] (pocket) handkerchief.

pochoir [pɔʃwar] *nm* stencil.

podium [pɔdjɔm] *nm* podium.

poêle [pwal] ⋄ *nf* pan ; **~ à frire** frying pan. ⋄ *nm* stove.

poème [pɔɛm] *nm* poem.

poésie [pɔezi] *nf* - **1.** [genre, émotion] poetry - **2.** [pièce écrite] poem.

poète [pɔɛt] *nm* - **1.** [écrivain] poet - **2.** *fig & hum* [rêveur] dreamer.

pogrom(e) [pɔgrɔm] *nm* pogrom.

poids [pwa] *nm* - **1.** [gén] weight ; **quel ~ fait-il?** how heavy is it/he? ; **perdre/ prendre du ~** to lose/gain weight ; **vendre au ~** to sell by weight ; **lourd** BOXE heavyweight ; [camion] heavy goods vehicle ; **de ~** [argument] weighty - **2.** SPORT [lancer] shot.

poignant, e [pwaɲɑ̃, ɑ̃t] *adj* poignant.

poignard [pwaɲar] *nm* dagger.

poignée [pwaɲe] *nf* - **1.** [quantité, petit nombre] handful - **2.** [manche] handle. ◆ **poignée de main** *nf* handshake.

poignet [pwaɲɛ] *nm* - **1.** ANAT wrist - **2.** [de vêtement] cuff.

poil [pwal] *nm* - **1.** [du corps] hair - **2.** [d'animal] hair, coat - **3.** [de pinceau] bristle ; [de tapis] strand - **4.** *fam* [peu] : **il s'en est fallu d'un ~ que je réussisse** I came within a hair's breadth of succeeding.

poilu, e [pwaly] *adj* hairy.

poinçon [pwɛ̃sɔ̃] *nm* - **1.** [outil] awl - **2.** [marque] hallmark.

poinçonner [3] [pwɛ̃sɔne] *vt* - **1.** [bijou] to hallmark - **2.** [billet, tôle] to punch.

poing [pwɛ̃] *nm* fist.

point [pwɛ̃] ⋄ *nm* - **1.** COUTURE & TRICOT stitch ; **~s de suture** MÉD stitches - **2.** [de ponctuation] : **~ (final)** full stop *Br*, period *Am* ; **~ d'interrogation/d'exclamation** question/exclamation mark ; **~s de suspension** suspension points - **3.** [petite tache] : **~ noir** [sur la peau] blackhead ; *fig* [problème] problem - **4.** [endroit] spot, point ; *fig* point ; **~ d'appui** [support] something to lean on ; **~ culminant** [en montagne] summit ; *fig* climax ; **de ~ de repère** [temporel] reference point ; [spatial] landmark ; **~ de vente** point of sale, sale outlet ; **~ de vue** [panorama] viewpoint ; *fig* [opinion, aspect] point of view ; **avoir un ~ commun avec qqn** to have something in common with sb - **5.** [degré] point ; **au ~ que, à tel ~ que** to such an extent that ; **je ne pensais pas que cela le vexerait à ce ~** I didn't think it would make him so cross ; **être ... au ~ de faire qqch** to be so ... as to do sthg - **6.** *fig* [position] position - **7.** [réglage] : **mettre au ~** [machine] to adjust ; [idée, projet] to finalize ; **à ~** [cuisson] just right ; **à ~ (nommé)** just in time - **8.** [question, détail] point, detail ; **~ faible** weak point - **9.** [score] point - **10.** [douleur] pain ; **~ de côté** stitch - **11.** [début] : **être sur le ~ de faire qqch** to be on the point of doing sthg, to be about to do sthg - **12.** AUTOM : **au ~ mort** in neutral - **13.** GÉOGR : **~s cardinaux** points of the compass. ⋄ *adv vieilli* : **ne ~** not (at all).

pointe [pwɛ̃t] *nf* - **1.** [extrémité] point ; [de nez] tip ; **se hausser sur la ~ des pieds** to stand on tiptoe ; **en ~** pointed ; **tailler en ~** to taper ; **se terminer en ~** to taper ; **~ d'asperge** asparagus tip - **2.** [clou] tack - **3.** [sommet] peak, summit ; **à la ~ de** *fig* at the peak of ; **à la ~ de la technique** at the forefront ou leading edge of technology - **4.** *fig* [trait d'esprit] witticism - **5.** *fig* [petite quantité] : **une ~ de** a touch of. ◆ **pointes** *nfpl* DANSE points ; **faire des** ou **les ~s** to dance on one's points. ◆ **de pointe** *loc adj* - **1.** [vitesse] maximum, top - **2.** [industrie, secteur] leading ; [technique] latest.

pointer [3] [pwɛ̃te] ⋄ *vt* - **1.** [cocher] to tick (off) - **2.** [employés - à l'entrée] to check in ; [- à la sortie] to check out - **3.** [diriger] : **~ qqch vers** to point sthg towards *Br* ou toward *Am* ; **~ qqch sur** to point sthg at. ⋄ *vi* - **1.** [à l'usine - à l'entrée] to clock in ; [- à la sortie] to clock out - **2.** [à la pétanque] to get as close to the jack as possible - **3.** [jour] to break.

pointillé [pwɛ̃tije] *nm* - **1.** [ligne] dotted line ; **en ~** [ligne] dotted - **2.** [perforations] perforations *(pl)*.

pointilleux, euse [pwɛ̃tijø, øz] *adj* : **~ (sur)** particular (about).

pointu, e [pwɛ̃ty] *adj* - **1.** [objet] pointed - **2.** [voix, ton] sharp - **3.** [étude, formation] specialized.

pointure [pwɛ̃tyr] *nf* (shoe) size.

point-virgule [pwɛ̃virgyl] *nm* semicolon.

poire [pwar] *nf* - **1.** [fruit] pear - **2.** MÉD : **~ à**

injections syringe - **3.** *fam* [visage] face - **4.** *fam* [naïf] dope.

poireau, x [pwaro] *nm* leek.

poirier [pwarje] *nm* pear tree.

pois [pwa] *nm* - **1.** BOT pea ; ~ **chiche** chickpea ; **petits** ~ garden peas, petits pois ; ~ **de senteur** sweet pea - **2.** *fig* [motif] dot, spot ; **à** ~ spotted, polka-dot.

poison [pwazɔ̃] ◇ *nm* [substance] poison. ◇ *nmf fam fig* [personne] drag, pain ; [enfant] brat.

poisse [pwas] *nf fam* bad luck ; **porter la** ~ to be bad luck.

poisseux, euse [pwasø, øz] *adj* sticky.

poisson [pwasɔ̃] *nm* fish ; ~ **d'avril** [farce] April fool ; [en papier] *paper fish pinned to someone's back as a prank on April Fools' Day* ; ~ **rouge** goldfish. ◆ **Poissons** *nmpl* ASTROL Pisces *(sg)*.

poissonnerie [pwasɔnri] *nf* [boutique] fish shop, fishmonger's (shop).

poissonnier, ère [pwasɔnje, ɛr] *nm, f* fishmonger.

poitrine [pwatrin] *nf* [thorax] chest ; [de femme] chest, bust.

poivre [pwavr] *nm* pepper ; ~ **blanc** white pepper ; ~ **gris**, ~ **noir** black pepper.

poivrier [pwavrije] *nm*, **poivrière** [pwavrijɛr] *nf* pepper pot *Br*, pepperbox *Am*.

poivron [pwavrɔ̃] *nm* pepper, capsicum ; ~ **rouge/vert** red/green pepper.

poker [pɔkɛr] *nm* poker.

polaire [pɔlɛr] *adj* polar.

polar [pɔlar] *nm fam* thriller, whodunnit.

Polaroïd® [pɔlarɔid] *nm* Polaroid®.

polder [pɔldɛr] *nm* polder.

pôle [pol] *nm* pole ; ~ **Nord/Sud** North/ South Pole.

polémique [pɔlemik] ◇ *nf* controversy. ◇ *adj* [style, ton] polemical.

poli, e [pɔli] *adj* - **1.** [personne] polite - **2.** [surface] polished.

police [pɔlis] *nf* - **1.** [force de l'ordre] police ; **être de** OU **dans la** ~ to be in the police ; ~ **secours** *emergency service provided by the police* - **2.** [contrat] policy ; ~ **d'assurance** insurance policy.

polichinelle [pɔliʃinɛl] *nm* [personnage] Punch ; **secret de** ~ *fig* open secret.

policier, ère [pɔlisje, ɛr] *adj* - **1.** [de la police] police *(avant n)* - **2.** [film, roman] detective *(avant n)*. ◆ **policier** *nm* police officer.

poliomyélite [pɔljɔmjelit] *nf* poliomyelitis.

polir [32] [pɔlir] *vt* to polish.

polisson, onne [pɔlisɔ̃, ɔn] ◇ *adj* - **1.** [chanson, propos] lewd, suggestive - **2.** [enfant] naughty. ◇ *nm, f* [enfant] naughty child.

politesse [pɔlitɛs] *nf* - **1.** [courtoisie] politeness - **2.** [action] polite action.

politicien, enne [pɔlitisjɛ̃, ɛn] ◇ *adj péj* politicking, politically unscrupulous. ◇ *nm, f* politician, politico.

politique [pɔlitik] ◇ *nf* - **1.** [de gouvernement, de personne] policy - **2.** [affaires publiques] politics *(U)*. ◇ *adj* - **1.** [pouvoir, théorie] political ; **homme** ~ politician - **2.** *littéraire* [choix, réponse] politic.

politiser [3] [pɔlitize] *vt* to politicize.

pollen [pɔlɛn] *nm* pollen.

polluer [7] [pɔlɥe] *vt* to pollute.

pollution [pɔlysjɔ̃] *nf* pollution.

polo [pɔlo] *nm* - **1.** [sport] polo - **2.** [chemise] polo shirt.

Pologne [pɔlɔɲ] *nf* : **la** ~ Poland.

polonais, e [pɔlɔnɛ, ɛz] *adj* Polish. ◆ **polonais** *nm* [langue] Polish. ◆ **Polonais, e** *nm, f* Pole.

poltron, onne [pɔltrɔ̃, ɔn] ◇ *nm, f* coward. ◇ *adj* cowardly.

polychrome [pɔlikrom] *adj* polychrome, polychromatic.

polyclinique [pɔliklinik] *nf* general hospital.

polycopié, e [pɔlikɔpje] *adj* duplicate *(avant n)*. ◆ **polycopié** *nm* duplicated lecture notes *(pl)*.

polyester [pɔliɛstɛr] *nm* polyester.

polygame [pɔligam] *adj* polygamous.

polyglotte [pɔliglɔt] *nmf & adj* polyglot.

polygone [pɔligɔn] *nm* MATHS polygon.

Polynésie [pɔlinezi] *nf* : **la** ~ Polynesia.

polystyrène [pɔlistirɛn] *nm* polystyrene.

polytechnicien, enne [pɔlitɛknisjɛ̃, ɛn] *nm, f* student or ex-student of the École Polytechnique.

Polytechnique [pɔlitɛknik] *n* : **l'École** ~ *prestigious engineering college*.

polyvalent, e [pɔlivalɑ̃, ɑ̃t] *adj* - **1.** [salle] multi-purpose - **2.** [personne] versatile.

pommade [pɔmad] *nf* [médicament] ointment.

pomme [pɔm] *nf* - **1.** [fruit] apple ; ~ **de pin** pine OU fir cone - **2.** [pomme de terre] : ~**s allumettes** *very thin chips* ; ~**s frites** chips *Br*, (French) fries *Am* ; ~**s vapeur** steamed potatoes. ◆ **pomme d'Adam** *nf* Adam's apple.

pomme de terre [pɔmdətɛr] *nf* potato.

pommette [pɔmɛt] *nf* cheekbone.

pommier [pɔmje] *nm* apple tree.

pompe [pɔ̃p] *nf* - **1.** [appareil] pump ; **~ à essence** petrol pump *Br*, gas pump *Am* - **2.** [magnificence] pomp, ceremony - **3.** *fam* [chaussure] shoe. ➤ **pompes funèbres** *nfpl* undertaker's *(sg)*, funeral director's *(sg) Br*, mortician's *(sg) Am*.

pomper [3] [pɔ̃pe] *vt* [eau, air] to pump.

pompeux, euse [pɔ̃pø, øz] *adj* pompous.

pompier [pɔ̃pje] *nm* fireman *Br*, fire fighter *Am*.

pompiste [pɔ̃pist] *nmf* petrol *Br* ou gas *Am* pump attendant.

pompon [pɔ̃pɔ̃] *nm* pompom.

pomponner [3] [pɔ̃pɔne] ➤ **se pomponner** *vp* to get dressed up.

ponce [pɔ̃s] *adj* : **pierre ~** pumice (stone).

poncer [16] [pɔ̃se] *vt* [bois] to sand (down).

ponceuse [pɔ̃søz] *nf* sander, sanding machine.

ponction [pɔ̃ksjɔ̃] *nf* - **1.** [MÉD - lombaire] puncture ; [- pulmonaire] tapping - **2.** *fig* [prélèvement] withdrawal.

ponctualité [pɔ̃ktɥalite] *nf* punctuality.

ponctuation [pɔ̃ktɥasjɔ̃] *nf* punctuation.

ponctuel, elle [pɔ̃ktɥɛl] *adj* - **1.** [action] specific, selective - **2.** [personne] punctual.

ponctuer [7] [pɔ̃ktɥe] *vt* to punctuate ; **~ qqch de qqch** *fig* to punctuate sthg with sthg.

pondéré, e [pɔ̃dere] *adj* - **1.** [personne] level-headed - **2.** ÉCON weighted.

pondre [75] [pɔ̃dr] *vt* - **1.** [œufs] to lay - **2.** *fam fig* [projet, texte] to produce.

pondu, e [pɔ̃dy] *pp* ▷ **pondre**.

poney [pɔnɛ] *nm* pony.

pont [pɔ̃] *nm* - **1.** CONSTR bridge ; **~s et chaussées** ADMIN ≈ highways department - **2.** [lien] link, connection ; **~ aérien** airlift - **3.** [congé] *day off granted by an employer to fill the gap between a national holiday and a weekend* - **4.** [de navire] deck.

ponte [pɔ̃t] ⋄ *nf* [action] laying ; [œufs] clutch. ⋄ *nm fam* [autorité] big shot.

pont-levis [pɔ̃lvi] *nm* drawbridge.

ponton [pɔ̃tɔ̃] *nm* [plate-forme] pontoon.

pop [pɔp] ⋄ *nm* pop. ⋄ *adj* pop (avant n).

pop-corn [pɔpkɔrn] *nm inv* popcorn (U).

populace [pɔpylas] *nf péj* mob.

populaire [pɔpylɛr] *adj* - **1.** [du peuple - volonté] popular, of the people ; [- quartier] working-class ; [- art, chanson] folk - **2.** [personne] popular.

populariser [3] [pɔpylarize] *vt* to popularize.

popularité [pɔpylarite] *nf* popularity.

population [pɔpylasjɔ̃] *nf* population ; **~ active** working population.

porc [pɔr] *nm* - **1.** [animal] pig, hog *Am* - **2.** *fig & péj* [personne] pig, swine - **3.** [viande] pork - **4.** [peau] pigskin.

porcelaine [pɔrsəlɛn] *nf* - **1.** [matière] china, porcelain - **2.** [objet] piece of china ou porcelain.

porc-épic [pɔrkepik] *nm* porcupine.

porche [pɔrʃ] *nm* porch.

porcherie [pɔrʃəri] *nf litt & fig* pigsty.

porcin, e [pɔrsɛ̃, in] *adj* - **1.** [élevage] pig (avant n) - **2.** *fig & péj* [yeux] piggy.

pore [pɔr] *nm* pore.

poreux, euse [pɔrø, øz] *adj* porous.

pornographie [pɔrnɔgrafi] *nf* pornography.

port [pɔr] *nm* - **1.** [lieu] port ; **~ de commerce/pêche** commercial/fishing port - **2.** [fait de porter sur soi - d'objet] carrying ; [- de vêtement, décoration] wearing ; **~ d'armes** carrying of weapons - **3.** [transport] carriage ; **franco de ~** carriage paid.

portable [pɔrtabl] ⋄ *nm* TV portable ; INFORM laptop, portable ; [téléphone] mobile. ⋄ *adj* - **1.** [vêtement] wearable - **2.** [ordinateur, machine à écrire] portable, laptop.

portail [pɔrtaj] *nm* portal.

portant, e [pɔrtɑ̃, ɑ̃t] *adj* : **être bien/mal ~** to be in good/poor health.

portatif, ive [pɔrtatif, iv] *adj* portable.

porte [pɔrt] *nf* - **1.** [de maison, voiture] door ; **mettre qqn à la ~** to throw sb out ; **~ d'entrée** front door - **2.** AÉRON & SKI [de ville] gate - **3.** *fig* [de région] gateway.

porte-à-faux [pɔrtafo] *nm inv* [roche] overhang ; CONSTR cantilever ; **en ~** overhanging ; CONSTR cantilevered ; *fig* in a delicate situation.

porte-à-porte [pɔrtapɔrt] *nm inv* : **faire du ~** to sell from door to door.

porte-avions [pɔrtavjɔ̃] *nm inv* aircraft carrier.

porte-bagages [pɔrtbagaʒ] *nm inv* luggage rack ; [de voiture] roof rack.

porte-bonheur [pɔrtbɔnœr] *nm inv* lucky charm.

porte-clefs, porte-clés [pɔrtəkle] *nm inv* keyring.

porte-documents [pɔrtdɔkymɑ̃] *nm inv* attaché ou document case.

portée [pɔrte] *nf* - **1.** [de missile] range ; **à ~ de** within range of ; **à ~ de main** within reach ; **à ~ de voix** within earshot ; **à ~ de vue** in sight ; **à la ~ de qqn** *fig* within sb's reach - **2.** [d'événement] impact, significance - **3.** MUS stave, staff - **4.** [de femelle] litter.

porte-fenêtre [pɔrtfənɛtr] *nf* French window ou door *Am*.

portefeuille [pɔrtəfœj] *nm* - **1.** [pour billets] wallet - **2.** FIN & POLIT portfolio.

porte-jarretelles [pɔrtʒartɛl] *nm inv* suspender belt *Br*, garter belt *Am*.

portemanteau, x [pɔrtmɑ̃to] *nm* [au mur] coat-rack ; [sur pied] coat stand.

porte-monnaie [pɔrtmɔnɛ] *nm inv* purse.

porte-parole [pɔrtparɔl] *nm inv* spokesman (*f* spokeswoman).

porter [3] [pɔrte] ◇ *vt* - **1.** [gén] to carry - **2.** [vêtement, lunettes, montre] to wear ; [barbe] to have - **3.** [nom, date, inscription] to bear - **4.** [inscrire] to put down, to write down ; **porté disparu** reported missing. ◇ *vi* - **1.** [remarque] to strike home - **2.** [voix, tir] to carry. ◆ **se porter** ◇ *vp* [se sentir] : **se ~ bien/mal** to be well/unwell. ◇ *v attr* : **se ~ garant de qqch** to guarantee sthg, to vouch for sthg ; **se ~ candidat à** to stand for election in *Br*, to run for *Am*.

porte-savon [pɔrtsavɔ̃] (*pl inv* ou **portesavons**) *nm* soap dish.

porte-serviettes [pɔrtsɛrvjɛt] *nm inv* towel rail.

porteur, euse [pɔrtœr, øz] ◇ *adj* : **marché ~** COMM growth market ; **mère porteuse** surrogate mother ; **mur ~** loadbearing wall. ◇ *nm, f* - **1.** [de message, nouvelle] bringer, bearer - **2.** [de bagages] porter - **3.** [détenteur - de papiers, d'actions] holder ; [- de chèque] bearer - **4.** [de maladie] carrier.

portier [pɔrtje] *nm* commissionaire.

portière [pɔrtjɛr] *nf* [de voiture, train] door.

portillon [pɔrtijɔ̃] *nm* barrier, gate.

portion [pɔrsjɔ̃] *nf* [de gâteau] portion, helping.

portique [pɔrtik] *nm* - **1.** ARCHIT portico - **2.** SPORT crossbeam *(for hanging apparatus)*.

porto [pɔrto] *nm* port.

Porto Rico [pɔrtoriko], **Puerto Rico** [pwɛrtoriko] *n* Puerto Rico.

portrait [pɔrtrɛ] *nm* portrait ; PHOT photograph ; **faire le ~ de qqn** *fig* to describe sb.

portraitiste [pɔrtretist] *nmf* portrait painter.

portrait-robot [pɔrtrɛrɔbo] *nm* Photofit® picture, Identikit® picture.

portuaire [pɔrtɥɛr] *adj* port *(avant n)*, harbour *(avant n) Br*, harbor *(avant n) Am*.

portugais, e [pɔrtygɛ, ɛz] *adj* Portuguese. ◆ **portugais** *nm* [langue] Portuguese. ◆ **Portugais, e** *nm, f* Portuguese (person) ; **les Portugais** the Portuguese.

Portugal [pɔrtygal] *nm* : **le ~** Portugal.

pose [poz] *nf* - **1.** [de pierre, moquette] laying ; [de papier peint, rideaux] hanging - **2.** [position] pose - **3.** PHOT exposure.

posé, e [poze] *adj* sober, steady.

poser [3] [poze] ◇ *vt* - **1.** [mettre] to put down ; **qqch sur qqch** to put sthg on sthg - **2.** [installer - rideaux, papier peint] to hang ; [- étagère] to put up ; [- moquette, carrelage] to lay - **3.** [donner à résoudre - problème, difficulté] to pose ; **une question** to ask a question ; **~ sa candidature** to apply ; [- POLIT] to stand for election. ◇ *vi* to pose. ◆ **se poser** *vp* - **1.** [oiseau, avion] to land ; *fig* [choix, regard] : **se ~ sur** to fall on - **2.** [question, problème] to arise, to come up.

positif, ive [pozitif, iv] *adj* positive.

position [pozisjɔ̃] *nf* position ; **prendre ~** *fig* to take up a position, to take a stand.

posologie [pozolɔʒi] *nf* dosage.

posséder [18] [pɔsede] *vt* - **1.** [détenir - voiture, maison] to possess, to own ; [- diplôme] to have ; [- capacités, connaissances] to possess, to have - **2.** [langue, art] to have mastered - **3.** *fam* [personne] to have.

possesseur [pɔsesœr] *nm* - **1.** [de bien] possessor, owner - **2.** [de secret, diplôme] holder.

possessif, ive [pɔsesif, iv] *adj* possessive. ◆ **possessif** *nm* GRAM possessive.

possession [pɔsesjɔ̃] *nf* [gén] possession ; **être en ma/ta** *etc* **~** to be in my/your *etc* possession.

possibilité [pɔsibilite] *nf* - **1.** [gén] possibility - **2.** [moyen] chance, opportunity.

possible [pɔsibl] ◇ *adj* possible ; **c'est/ce n'est pas ~** that's possible/impossible ; **dès que** ou **aussitôt que ~** as soon as possible. ◇ *nm* : **faire tout son ~** to do one's utmost, to do everything possible ; **dans la mesure du ~** as far as possible.

postal, e, aux [pɔstal, o] *adj* postal.

poste [pɔst] ◇ *nf* - **1.** [service] post *Br*, mail *Am* ; **envoyer/recevoir qqch par la ~** to send/receive sthg by post - **2.** [bureau] post office ; **~ restante** poste restante *Br*, general delivery *Am*. ◇ *nm* - **1.** [emplacement] post ; **~ de police** police station - **2.** [emploi] position, post - **3.** [appareil] : **~ de radio** radio ; ~ **de télévision** television (set) - **4.** TÉLÉCOM extension.

poster[1] [pɔstɛr] *nm* poster.

poster[2] [3] [pɔste] *vt* - **1.** [lettre] to post *Br*, to mail *Am* - **2.** [sentinelle] to post. ◆ **se poster** *vp* to position o.s., to station o.s.

postérieur, e [pɔsterjœr] *adj* - **1.** [date] later, subsequent - **2.** [membre] hind *(avant n)*, back *(avant n)*. ◆ **postérieur** *nm hum* posterior.

posteriori [pɔsterjɔri] ◆ **a posteriori** *loc adv* a posteriori.

postérité [pɔsterite] *nf* [générations à venir] posterity.

posthume [pɔstym] *adj* posthumous.

postiche [pɔstiʃ] *adj* false.

postier, ère [pɔstje, ɛr] *nm, f* post-office worker.

postillonner [3] [pɔstijɔne] *vi* to splutter.

Post-it® [pɔstit] *nm inv* Post-it®, Post-it® note.

post-scriptum [pɔstskriptɔm] *nm inv* postscript.

postulant, e [pɔstylɑ̃, ɑ̃t] *nm, f* [pour emploi] applicant.

postuler [3] [pɔstyle] *vt* - **1.** [emploi] to apply for - **2.** PHILO to postulate.

posture [pɔstyr] *nf* posture ; **être** OU **se trouver en mauvaise ~** *fig* to be in a difficult position.

pot [po] *nm* - **1.** [récipient] pot, jar ; [à eau, à lait] jug ; ~ **de chambre** chamber pot ; ~ **de fleurs** flowerpot - **2.** AUTOM : ~ **catalytique** catalytic convertor ; ~ **d'échappement** exhaust (pipe) ; [silencieux] silencer *Br*, muffler *Am* - **3.** *fam* [boisson] drink ; **faire un ~** to have a drinks party.

potable [pɔtabl] *adj* - **1.** [liquide] drinkable ; **eau ~** drinking water - **2.** *fam* [travail] acceptable.

potage [pɔtaʒ] *nm* soup.

potager, ère [pɔtaʒe, ɛr] *adj* : **jardin ~** vegetable garden ; **plante potagère** vegetable. ◆ **potager** *nm* kitchen OU vegetable garden.

potasser [3] [pɔtase] *vt fam* [cours] to swot up *Br*, to bone up on *Am* ; [examen] to swot up for *Br*, to bone up for *Am*.

potassium [pɔtasjɔm] *nm* potassium.

pot-au-feu [pɔtofø] *nm inv* - **1.** [plat] boiled beef with vegetables - **2.** [viande] ≃ piece of stewing steak *Br* OU stewbeef *Am*.

pot-de-vin [podvɛ̃] *(pl* pots-de-vin*) nm* bribe.

pote [pɔt] *nm fam* mate *Br*, buddy *Am*.

poteau, x [pɔto] *nm* post ; ~ **de but** goal-

post ; ~ **indicateur** signpost ; ~ **télégraphique** telegraph pole.

potelé, e [pɔtle] *adj* plump, chubby.

potence [pɔtɑ̃s] *nf* - **1.** CONSTR bracket - **2.** [de pendaison] gallows *(sg)*.

potentiel, elle [pɔtɑ̃sjɛl] *adj* potential. ◆ **potentiel** *nm* potential.

poterie [pɔtri] *nf* - **1.** [art] pottery - **2.** [objet] piece of pottery.

potiche [pɔtiʃ] *nf* [vase] vase.

potier, ère [pɔtje, ɛr] *nm, f* potter.

potin [pɔtɛ̃] *nm fam* [bruit] din. ◆ **potins** *nmpl fam* [ragots] gossip *(U)*.

potion [pɔsjɔ̃] *nf* potion.

potiron [pɔtirɔ̃] *nm* pumpkin.

pot-pourri [popuri] *nm* potpourri.

pou, x [pu] *nm* louse.

poubelle [pubɛl] *nf* dustbin *Br*, trashcan *Am*.

pouce [pus] *nm* - **1.** [de main] thumb ; [de pied] big toe - **2.** [mesure] inch.

poudre [pudr] *nf* powder ; **prendre la ~ d'escampette** to make off.

poudreux, euse [pudrø, øz] *adj* powdery. ◆ **poudreuse** *nf* powder (snow).

poudrier [pudrije] *nm* [boîte] powder compact.

poudrière [pudrijɛr] *nf* powder magazine ; *fig* powder keg.

pouf [puf] ◇ *nm* pouffe. ◇ *interj* thud !

pouffer [3] [pufe] *vi* : ~ **(de rire)** to snigger.

pouilleux, euse [pujø, øz] *adj* - **1.** [personne, animal] flea-ridden - **2.** [endroit] squalid.

poulailler [pulaje] *nm* - **1.** [de ferme] henhouse - **2.** *fam* THÉÂTRE gods *(sg)*.

poulain [pulɛ̃] *nm* foal ; *fig* protégé.

poule [pul] *nf* - **1.** ZOOL hen - **2.** *fam péj* [femme] bird *Br*, broad *Am* - **3.** SPORT [compétition] round robin ; RUGBY [groupe] pool.

poulet [pulɛ] *nm* - **1.** ZOOL chicken ; ~ **fermier** free-range chicken - **2.** *fam* [policier] cop.

pouliche [puliʃ] *nf* filly.

poulie [puli] *nf* pulley.

poulpe [pulp] *nm* octopus.

pouls [pu] *nm* pulse.

poumon [pumɔ̃] *nm* lung.

poupe [pup] *nf* stern.

poupée [pupe] *nf* [jouet] doll.

poupon [pupɔ̃] *nm* - **1.** [bébé] little baby - **2.** [jouet] baby doll.

pouponnière [puponjɛr] *nf* nursery.

pour [pur] ◇ *prép* - **1.** [gén] for - **2.** (+ infinitif) : ~ **faire** in order to do, (so as) to do ; **je**

suis venu ~ vous voir I've come to see you ; ~ m'avoir aidé for having helped me, for helping me - **3.** [indique un rapport] for ; avancé ~ son âge advanced for his/her age ; ~ moi for my part, as far as I'm concerned ; ~ ce qui est de as regards, with regard to. <> *adv* : je suis ~ I'm (all) for it. <> *nm* : le ~ et le contre the pros and cons *(pl)*. **◆ pour que** *loc conj (+ subjonctif)* so that, in order that.

pourboire [purbwar] *nm* tip.

pourcentage [pursãtaʒ] *nm* percentage.

pourparlers [purparle] *nmpl* talks.

pourpre [purpr] *nm & adj* crimson.

pourquoi [purkwa] <> *adv* why ? ~ pas? why not? ; c'est ~ ... that's why ... <> *nm inv* : le ~ (de) the reason (for).

pourri, e [puri] *adj* - **1.** [fruit] rotten - **2.** [personne, milieu] corrupt - **3.** [enfant] spoiled rotten, ruined.

pourrir [32] [purir] <> *vt* - **1.** [matière, aliment] to rot, to spoil - **2.** [enfant] to ruin, to spoil rotten. <> *vi* [matière] to rot ; [fruit, aliment] to go rotten ou bad.

pourriture [purityr] *nf* - **1.** [d'aliment] rot - **2.** *fig* [de personne, de milieu] corruption - **3.** *injurieux* [personne] bastard.

poursuite [pursɥit] *nf* - **1.** [de personne] chase - **2.** [d'argent, de vérité] pursuit - **3.** [de négociations] continuation. **◆ poursuites** *nfpl* JUR (legal) proceedings.

poursuivi, e [pursɥivi] *pp* ▷ **poursuivre**.

poursuivre [89] [pursɥivr] <> *vt* - **1.** [voleur] to pursue, to chase ; [gibier] to hunt - **2.** [rêve, vengeance] to pursue - **3.** [enquête, travail] to carry on with, to continue - **4.** JUR [criminel] to prosecute ; [voisin] to sue. <> *vi* to go on, to carry on.

pourtant [purtã] *adv* nevertheless, even so.

pourtour [purtur] *nm* perimeter.

pourvoi [purvwa] *nm* JUR appeal.

pourvoir [64] [purvwar] <> *vt* : ~ qqn de to provide sb with ; ~ qqch de to equip ou fit sthg with. <> *vi* : ~ à to provide for.

pourvu, e [purvy] *pp* ▷ **pourvoir**. **◆ pourvu que** (+ *subjonctif*) *loc conj* - **1.** [condition] providing, provided (that) - **2.** [souhait] let's hope (that).

pousse [pus] *nf* - **1.** [croissance] growth - **2.** [bourgeon] shoot.

poussé, e [puse] *adj* - **1.** [travail] meticulous - **2.** [moteur] souped-up.

pousse-café [puskafe] *nm inv fam* liqueur.

poussée [puse] *nf* - **1.** [pression] pressure - **2.** [coup] push - **3.** [de fièvre, inflation] rise.

pousse-pousse [puspus] *nm inv* - **1.** [voiture] rickshaw - **2.** *Helv* [poussette] push-chair.

pousser [3] [puse] <> *vt* - **1.** [personne, objet] to push - **2.** [moteur, voiture] to drive hard - **3.** [recherches, études] to carry on, to continue - **4.** [cri, soupir] to give - **5.** [inciter] : ~ qqn à faire qqch to urge sb to do sthg - **6.** [au crime, au suicide] : ~ qqn à to drive sb to. <> *vi* - **1.** [exercer une pression] to push - **2.** [croître] to grow - **3.** *fam* [exagérer] to overdo it. **◆ se pousser** *vp* to move up.

poussette [pusɛt] *nf* pushchair *Br*, stroller *Am*.

poussière [pusjɛr] *nf* [gén] dust.

poussiéreux, euse [pusjerø, øz] *adj* - **1.** [meuble] dusty - **2.** *fig* [organisation] old-fashioned.

poussif, ive [pusif, iv] *adj fam* wheezy.

poussin [pusɛ̃] *nm* - **1.** ZOOL chick - **2.** SPORT under-11.

poutre [putr] *nf* beam.

poutrelle [putrɛl] *nf* girder.

pouvoir [58] [puvwar] <> *nm* - **1.** [gén] power ; ~ d'achat purchasing power ; les ~s publics the authorities - **2.** JUR proxy, power of attorney. <> *vt* - **1.** [avoir la possibilité de, parvenir à] : ~ faire qqch to be able to do sthg ; je ne peux pas venir ce soir I can't come tonight ; pouvez-vous ...? can you ...?, could you ...? ; je n'en peux plus [exaspéré] I'm at the end of my tether ; [fatigué] I'm exhausted ; je/tu n'y peux rien there's nothing I/you can do about it ; tu aurais pu me le dire! you might have ou could have told me! - **2.** [avoir la permission de] : je peux prendre la voiture? can I borrow the car? ; aucun élève ne peut partir no pupil may leave - **3.** [indiquant l'éventualité] : il peut pleuvoir it may rain ; vous pourriez rater votre train you could ou might miss your train. **◆ se pouvoir** *v impers* : il se peut que je me trompe I may be mistaken ; cela se peut/pourrait bien that's quite possible.

pragmatique [pragmatik] *adj* pragmatic.

Prague [prag] *n* Prague.

prairie [preri] *nf* meadow ; [aux États-Unis] prairie.

praline [pralin] *nf* - **1.** [amande] sugared almond - **2.** *Belg* [chocolat] chocolate.

praticable [pratikabl] *adj* - **1.** [route] passable - **2.** [plan] feasible, practicable.

praticien, enne [pratisjɛ̃, ɛn] *nm, f* practitioner ; MÉD medical practitioner.

pratiquant, e [pratikã, ãt] *adj* practising.

pratique [pratik] <> *nf* - **1.** [expérience] practical experience - **2.** [usage] practice ; **mettre qqch en ~** to put sthg into practice. <> *adj* practical ; [gadget, outil] handy.

pratiquement [pratikmã] *adv* - **1.** [en fait] in practice - **2.** [quasiment] practically.

pratiquer [3] [pratike] <> *vt* - **1.** [métier] to practise *Br*, to practice *Am* ; [sport] to do ; [jeu de ballon] to play ; [méthode] to apply - **2.** [ouverture] to make. <> *vi* RELIG to be a practising Christian/Jew/Muslim *etc*.

pré [pre] *nm* meadow.

préalable [prealabl] <> *adj* prior, previous. <> *nm* precondition. ◆ **au préalable** *loc adv* first, beforehand.

préambule [preãbyl] *nm* - **1.** [introduction, propos] preamble ; **sans ~** immediately - **2.** [prélude] : **~ de** prelude to.

préau, x [preo] *nm* [d'école] (covered) play area.

préavis [preavi] *nm inv* advance notice ou warning.

précaire [preker] *adj* [incertain] precarious.

précaution [prekosjõ] *nf* - **1.** [prévoyance] precaution ; **par ~** as a precaution ; **prendre des ~s** to take precautions - **2.** [prudence] caution.

précédent, e [presedã, ãt] *adj* previous. ◆ **précédent** *nm* precedent ; **sans ~** unprecedented.

précéder [18] [presede] *vt* - **1.** [dans le temps - gén] to precede ; [- suj : personne] to arrive before - **2.** [marcher devant] to go in front of - **3.** *fig* [devancer] to get ahead of.

précepte [presept] *nm* precept.

précepteur, trice [preseptœr, tris] *nm, f* (private) tutor.

prêcher [4] [prefe] *vt & vi* to preach.

précieux, euse [presjø, øz] *adj* - **1.** [pierre, métal] precious ; [objet] valuable ; [collaborateur] invaluable, valued - **2.** *péj* [style] precious, affected.

précipice [presipis] *nm* precipice.

précipitation [presipitasjõ] *nf* - **1.** [hâte] haste - **2.** CHIM precipitation. ◆ **précipitations** *nfpl* MÉTÉOR precipitation *(U)*.

précipiter [3] [presipite] *vt* - **1.** [objet, personne] to throw, to hurl ; **~ qqn/qqch du haut de** to throw sb/sthg off, to hurl sb/sthg off - **2.** [départ] to hasten. ◆ **se précipiter** *vp* - **1.** [se jeter] to throw o.s., to hurl o.s. - **2.** [s'élancer] : **se ~ (vers qqn)** to rush ou hurry (towards sb) - **3.** [s'accélérer - gén]

to speed up ; [- choses, événements] to move faster.

précis, e [presi, iz] *adj* - **1.** [exact] precise, accurate - **2.** [fixé] definite, precise. ◆ **précis** *nm* handbook.

précisément [presizemã] *adv* precisely, exactly.

préciser [3] [presize] *vt* - **1.** [heure, lieu] to specify - **2.** [pensée] to clarify. ◆ **se préciser** *vp* to become clear.

précision [presizjõ] *nf* - **1.** [de style, d'explication] precision - **2.** [détail] detail.

précoce [prekɔs] *adj* - **1.** [plante, fruit] early - **2.** [enfant] precocious.

préconçu, e [prekõsy] *adj* preconceived.

préconiser [3] [prekɔnize] *vt* to recommend ; **~ de faire qqch** to recommend doing sthg.

précurseur [prekyrsœr] <> *nm* precursor, forerunner. <> *adj* precursory.

prédateur, trice [predatœr, tris] *adj* predatory. ◆ **prédateur** *nm* predator.

prédécesseur [predesesœr] *nm* predecessor.

prédestiner [3] [predestine] *vt* to predestine ; **être prédestiné à qqch/à faire qqch** to be predestined for sthg/to do sthg.

prédicateur, trice [predikatœr, tris] *nm, f* preacher.

prédiction [prediksjõ] *nf* prediction.

prédilection [predileksjõ] *nf* partiality, ; **avoir une ~ pour** to have a partiality ou liking for.

prédire [103] [predir] *vt* to predict.

prédit, e [predi, it] *pp* ▷ **prédire**.

prédominer [3] [predomine] *vt* to predominate.

préfabriqué, e [prefabrike] *adj* - **1.** [maison] prefabricated - **2.** [accusation, sourire] false. ◆ **préfabriqué** *nm* prefabricated material.

préface [prefas] *nf* preface.

préfecture [prefektyr] *nf* prefecture.

préférable [preferabl] *adj* preferable.

préféré, e [prefere] *adj & nm, f* favourite *Br*, favorite *Am*.

préférence [preferãs] *nf* preference ; **de ~** preferably.

préférentiel, elle [preferãsjɛl] *adj* preferential.

préférer [18] [prefere] *vt* : **~ qqn/qqch (à)** to prefer sb/sthg (to) ; **je préfère rentrer** I would rather go home, I would prefer to go home ; **je préfère ça!** I like that better!, I prefer that!

préfet [prefɛ] *nm* prefect.

préfixe [prefiks] *nm* prefix.

préhistoire [preistwar] *nf* prehistory.

préinscription [preẽskripsjɔ̃] *nf* pre-registration.

préjudice [preʒydis] *nm* harm *(U)*, detriment *(U)* ; **porter ~ à qqn** to harm sb.

préjugé [preʒyʒe] *nm* : **~ (contre)** prejudice (against).

prélasser [3] [prelase] ◆ **se prélasser** *vp* to lounge.

prélat [prela] *nm* prelate.

prélavage [prelavaʒ] *nm* pre-wash.

prélèvement [prelɛvmɑ̃] *nm* - **1.** MÉD removal ; [de sang] sample - **2.** FIN deduction ; **~ automatique** direct debit ; **~ mensuel** monthly standing order ; **~s obligatoires** tax and social security contributions.

prélever [19] [prelve] *vt* - **1.** FIN : **~ de l'argent (sur)** to deduct money (from) - **2.** MÉD to remove ; **~ du sang** to take a blood sample.

préliminaire [preliminɛr] *adj* preliminary. ◆ **préliminaires** *nmpl* - **1.** [de paix] preliminary talks - **2.** [de discours] preliminaries.

prématuré, e [prematyre] ◇ *adj* premature. ◇ *nm, f* premature baby.

préméditation [premeditasjɔ̃] *nf* premeditation ; **avec ~** [meurtre] premeditated ; [agir] with premeditation.

premier, ère [prəmje, ɛr] ◇ *adj* - **1.** [gén] first ; [étage] first *Br*, second *Am* - **2.** [qualité] top - **3.** [état] original. ◇ *nm, f* first ; **jeune ~** CIN leading man. ◆ **première** *nf* - **1.** CIN première ; THÉÂTRE première, first night - **2.** [exploit] first - **3.** [première classe] first class - **4.** SCOL ≃ lower sixth year ou form *Br*, ≃ eleventh grade *Am* - **5.** AUTOM first (gear). ◆ **premier de l'an** *nm* : **le ~ de l'an** New Year's Day. ◆ **en premier** *loc adv* first, firstly.

premièrement [prəmjɛrmɑ̃] *adv* first, firstly.

prémonition [premɔnisjɔ̃] *nf* premonition.

prémunir [32] [premynir] *vt* : **~ qqn (contre)** to protect sb (against). ◆ **se prémunir** *vp* to protect o.s. ; **se ~ contre qqch** to guard against sthg.

prénatal, e [prenatal] (*pl* **prénatals** ou **prénataux** [prenato]) *adj* antenatal ; [allocation] maternity *(avant n)*.

prendre [79] [prɑ̃dr] ◇ *vt* - **1.** [gén] to take - **2.** [enlever] to take (away) ; **~ qqch à qqn** to take sthg from sb - **3.** [aller chercher - objet] to get, to fetch ; [- personne] to pick up - **4.** [repas, boisson] to have ; **vous prendrez quelque chose?** would you like

something to eat/drink? - **5.** [voleur] to catch ; **se faire ~** to get caught - **6.** [responsabilité] to take (on) - **7.** [aborder - personne] to handle ; [- problème] to tackle - **8.** [réserver] to book ; [louer] to rent, to take ; [acheter] to buy - **9.** [poids] to gain, to put on. ◇ *vi* - **1.** [ciment, sauce] to set - **2.** [plante, greffe] to take ; [mode] to catch on - **3.** [feu] to catch - **4.** [se diriger] : **~ à droite** to turn right. ◆ **se prendre** *vp* - **1.** [se considérer] : **pour qui se prend-il?** who does he think he is? - **2.** *loc* : **s'en ~ à qqn** [physiquement] to set about sb ; [verbalement] to take it out on sb ; **je sais comment m'y ~** I know how to do it ou go about it.

prénom [prenɔ̃] *nm* first name.

prénommer [3] [prenɔme] *vt* to name, to call. ◆ **se prénommer** *vp* to be called.

prénuptial, e, aux [prenypsjal, o] *adj* premarital.

préoccupation [preɔkypasjɔ̃] *nf* preoccupation.

préoccuper [3] [preɔkype] *vt* to preoccupy. ◆ **se préoccuper** *vp* : **se ~ de qqch** to be worried about sthg.

préparatifs [preparatif] *nmpl* preparations.

préparation [preparasjɔ̃] *nf* preparation.

préparer [3] [prepare] *vt* - **1.** [gén] to prepare ; [plat, repas] to cook, to prepare ; **~ qqn à qqch** to prepare sb for sthg - **2.** [réserver] : **~ qqch à qqn** to have sthg in store for sb - **3.** [congrès] to organize. ◆ **se préparer** *vp* - **1.** [personne] : **se ~ à qqch/à faire qqch** to prepare for sthg/to do sthg - **2.** [tempête] to be brewing.

prépondérant, e [prepɔ̃derɑ̃, ɑ̃t] *adj* dominating.

préposé, e [prepoze] *nm, f* (minor) official ; [de vestiaire] attendant ; [facteur] postman (*f* postwoman) *Br*, mailman (*f* mailwoman) *Am* ; **~ à qqch** person in charge of sthg.

préposition [prepozisjɔ̃] *nf* preposition.

préretraite [prerətrɛt] *nf* early retirement ; [allocation] early retirement pension.

prérogative [prerɔgativ] *nf* prerogative.

près [prɛ] *adv* near, close. ◆ **de près** *loc adv* closely ; **regarder qqch de ~** to watch sthg closely. ◆ **près de** *loc prép* - **1.** [dans l'espace] near, close to - **2.** [dans le temps] close to - **3.** [presque] nearly, almost. ◆ **à peu près** *loc adv* more or less, just about ; **il est à peu ~ cinq heures** it's about five o'clock. ◆ **à ceci près que, à cela près que** *loc conj* except that, apart from the fact that. ◆ **à ... près** *loc adv* : **à dix centimè-**

tres ~ to within ten centimetres ; **il n'en est pas à un ou deux jours** ~ a day or two more or less won't make any difference.

présage [preza3] *nm* omen.

présager [17] [preza3e] *vt* - **1.** [annoncer] to portend - **2.** [prévoir] to predict.

presbytère [presbiter] *nm* presbytery.

presbytie [presbisi] *nf* longsightedness *Br*, farsightedness *Am*.

prescription [preskripsjɔ̃] *nf* - **1.** MÉD prescription - **2.** JUR limitation.

prescrire [99] [preskrir] *vt* - **1.** [mesures, conditions] to lay down, to stipulate - **2.** MÉD to prescribe.

prescrit, e [preskri, it] *pp* ⊏> prescrire.

préséance [preseɑ̃s] *nf* precedence.

présélection [preseleksjɔ̃] *nf* preselection ; [pour concours] making a list of finalists, short-listing *Br*.

présence [prezɑ̃s] *nf* - **1.** [gén] presence ; **en ~ face to face** ; **en ~ de** in the presence of - **2.** [compagnie] company *(U)* - **3.** [assiduité] attendance ; **feuille de ~** attendance sheet.
◆ **présence d'esprit** *nf* presence of mind.

présent, e [prezɑ̃, ɑ̃t] *adj* [gén] present ; **le ouvrage this law** , **la ~e loi this law** , **avoir qqch à l'esprit** to remember sthg.
◆ **présent** *nm* - **1.** [gén] present ; **à ~** at present ; **à ~ que** now that ; **jusqu'à ~** up to now, so far ; **dès à ~** right away - **2.** GRAM : **le ~** the present tense.

présentable [prezɑ̃tabl] *adj* [d'aspect] presentable.

présentateur, trice [prezɑ̃tatœr, tris] *nm, f* presenter.

présentation [prezɑ̃tasjɔ̃] *nf* - **1.** [de personne] : **faire les ~s** to make the introductions - **2.** [aspect extérieur] appearance - **3.** [de papiers, de produit, de film] presentation - **4.** [de magazine] layout.

présenter [3] [prezɑ̃te] *vt* - **1.** [gén] to present ; [projet] to present, to submit - **2.** [invité] to introduce - **3.** [condoléances, félicitations, avantages] to offer ; [hommages] to pay ; **~ qqch à qqn** to offer sb sthg.
◆ **se présenter** *vp* - **1.** [se faire connaître] : **se ~ (à)** to introduce o.s. (to) - **2.** [être candidat] : **se ~ à** [élection] to stand in *Br*, to run in *Am* ; [examen] to sit *Br*, to take - **3.** [paraître] to appear - **4.** [occasion, situation] to arise, to present itself - **5.** [affaire, contrat] : **se ~ bien/mal** to look good/bad.

présentoir [prezɑ̃twar] *nm* display stand.

préservatif [prezervatif] *nm* condom.

préserver [3] [prezerve] *vt* to preserve.
◆ **se préserver** *vp* : **se ~ de** to protect o.s. from.

présidence [prezidɑ̃s] *nf* - **1.** [de groupe] chairmanship - **2.** [d'État] presidency.

président, e [prezidɑ̃, ɑ̃t] *nm, f* - **1.** [d'assemblée] chairman (*f* chairwoman) - **2.** [d'État] president ; **~ de la République** President (of the Republic) of France - **3.** JUR [de tribunal] presiding judge ; [de jury] foreman (*f* forewoman).

présider [3] [prezide] <> *vt* - **1.** [réunion] to chair - **2.** [banquet, dîner] to preside over.
<> *vi* : **~ à** to be in charge of ; *fig* to govern, to preside at.

présomption [prezɔ̃psjɔ̃] *nf* - **1.** [hypothèse] presumption - **2.** JUR presumption.

présomptueux, euse [prezɔ̃ptɥø, øz] *adj* presumptuous.

presque [presk] *adv* almost, nearly ; **~ rien** next to nothing, scarcely anything ; **~ jamais** hardly ever.

presqu'île [preskil] *nf* peninsula.

pressant, e [presɑ̃, ɑ̃t] *adj* pressing.

presse [pres] *nf* press.

pressé, e [prese] *adj* - **1.** [travail] urgent - **2.** [personne] : **être ~** to be in a hurry - **3.** [citron, orange] freshly squeezed.

pressentiment [presɑ̃timɑ̃] *nm* premonition.

pressentir [37] [presɑ̃tir] *vt* [événement] to have a premonition of.

presse-papiers [prespapje] *nm inv* paperweight.

presser [4] [prese] *vt* - **1.** [écraser - olives] to press ; [- citron, orange] to squeeze - **2.** [bouton] to press, to push - **3.** *sout* [harceler] : **~ qqn de faire qqch** to press sb to do sthg - **4.** [accélérer] to speed up ; **le pas** to speed up, to walk faster. ◆ **se presser** *vp* - **1.** [se dépêcher] to hurry (up) - **2.** [s'agglutiner] ; **se ~ (autour de)** to crowd (around) - **3.** [se serrer] to huddle.

pressing [presiŋ] *nm* [établissement] dry cleaner's.

pression [presjɔ̃] *nf* - **1.** [gén] pressure ; **exercer une ~ sur qqch** to exert pressure on sthg ; **sous ~** [liquide] *fig* under pressure ; [cabine] pressurized - **2.** [sur vêtement] press stud *Br*, popper *Br*, snap fastener *Am* - **3.** [bière] draught *Br ou* draft *Am* beer.

pressoir [preswar] *nm* - **1.** [machine] press - **2.** [lieu] press house.

pressurer [3] [presyre] *vt* - **1.** [objet] to press, to squeeze - **2.** *fig* [contribuable] to squeeze.

prestance [prestɑ̃s] *nf* bearing ; **avoir de la ~** to have presence.

prestataire [prestater] *nmf* - **1.** [bénéficiaire] person in receipt of benefit, claimant - 2. [fournisseur] provider ; ~ **de service** service provider.

prestation [prɛstasjɔ̃] *nf* - 1. [allocation] benefit ; ~ **en nature** payment in kind - 2. [de comédien] performance.

preste [prɛst] *adj littéraire* nimble.

prestidigitateur, trice [prɛstidiʒitatœr, tris] *nm, f* conjurer.

prestige [prɛstiʒ] *nm* prestige.

prestigieux, euse [prɛstiʒjø, øz] *adj* [réputé] prestigious.

présumer [3] [prezyme] ⇔ *vt* to presume, to assume ; **être présumé coupable/ innocent** to be presumed guilty/innocent. ⇔ *vi* : ~ **de qqch** to overestimate sthg.

prêt, e [prɛ, prɛt] *adj* ready ; ~ **à qqch/à faire qqch** ready for sthg/to do sthg ; **~s? partez!** SPORT get set, go!, ready, steady, go! ➤ **prêt** *nm* [action] lending *(U)* ; [somme] loan.

prêt-à-porter [prɛtaporte] *(pl* **prêts-à-porter)** *nm* ready-to-wear clothing *(U)*.

prétendant [pretɑ̃dɑ̃] *nm* - 1. [au trône] pretender - 2. [amoureux] suitor.

prétendre [73] [pretɑ̃dr] *vt* - 1. [affecter] : ~ **faire qqch** to claim to do sthg - 2. [affirmer] : ~ **que** to claim (that), to maintain (that).

prétendu, e [pretɑ̃dy] ⇔ *pp* ⇨ prétendre. ⇔ *adj (avant n)* so-called.

prête-nom [prɛtnɔ̃] *(pl* **prête-noms)** *nm* front man.

prétentieux, euse [pretɑ̃sjø, øz] *adj* pretentious.

prétention [pretɑ̃sjɔ̃] *nf* - 1. [suffisance] pretentiousness - 2. [ambition] pretension, ambition ; **avoir la ~ de faire qqch** to claim ou pretend to do sthg.

prêter [4] [prete] *vt* - 1. [fournir] : ~ **qqch (à qqn)** [objet, argent] to lend (sb) sthg ; *fig* [concours, appui] to lend (sb) sthg, to give (sb) sthg - 2. [attribuer] : ~ **qqch à qqn** to attribute sthg to sb. ➤ **se prêter** *vp* : **se ~ à** [participer à] to go along with ; [convenir à] to fit, to suit.

prétérit [preterit] *nm* preterite.

prêteur, euse [prɛtœr, øz] *nm, f* : ~ **sur gages** pawnbroker.

prétexte [pretɛkst] *nm* pretext, excuse ; **sous ~ de faire qqch/que** on the pretext of doing sthg/that, under the pretext of doing sthg/that ; **sous aucun ~** on no account.

prétexter [4] [pretɛkste] *vt* to give as an excuse.

prêtre [prɛtr] *nm* priest.

preuve [prœv] *nf* - 1. [gén] proof - 2. JUR evidence - 3. [témoignage] sign, token ;

faire ~ **de qqch** to show sthg ; **faire ses ~s** to prove o.s./itself.

prévaloir [61] [prevalwar] *vi* [dominer] : ~ **(sur)** to prevail (over). ➤ **se prévaloir** *vp* : **se ~ de** to boast about.

prévalu [prevaly] *pp inv* ⇨ prévaloir.

prévenance [prevnɑ̃s] *nf* [attitude] thoughtfulness, consideration.

prévenant, e [prevnɑ̃, ɑ̃t] *adj* considerate, attentive.

prévenir [40] [prevnir] *vt* - 1. [employé, élève] : ~ **qqn (de)** to warn sb (about) - 2. [police] to inform - 3. [désirs] to anticipate - 4. [maladie] to prevent.

préventif, ive [prevɑ̃tif, iv] *adj* - 1. [mesure, médecine] preventive - 2. JUR : **être en détention préventive** to be on remand.

prévention [prevɑ̃sjɔ̃] *nf* - 1. [protection] : ~ **(contre)** prevention (of) ; ~ **routière** road safety (measures) - 2. JUR remand.

prévenu, e [prevny] ⇔ *pp* ⇨ prévenir. ⇔ *nm, f* accused, defendant.

prévision [previzjɔ̃] *nf* forecast, prediction ; [de coûts] estimate ; ÉCON forecast ; **les ~s météorologiques** the weather forecast. ➤ **en prévision de** *loc prép* in anticipation of.

prévoir [63] [prevwar] *vt* - 1. [s'attendre à] to expect - 2. [prédire] to predict - 3. [anticiper] to foresee, to anticipate - 4. [programmer] to plan ; **comme prévu** as planned, according to plan.

prévoyant, e [prevwajɑ̃, ɑ̃t] *adj* provident.

prévu, e [prevy] *pp* ⇨ prévoir.

prier [10] [prije] ⇔ *vt* - 1. RELIG to pray to - 2. [implorer] to beg ; **(ne pas) se faire ~ (pour faire qqch)** (not) to need to be persuaded (to do sthg) ; **je vous en prie** [de grâce] please, I beg you ; [de rien] don't mention it, not at all - 3. *sout* [demander] : ~ **qqn de faire qqch** to request sb to do sthg. ⇔ *vi* RELIG to pray.

prière [prijɛr] *nf* - 1. [RELIG - recueillement] prayer *(U)*, praying *(U)* ; [- formule] prayer - 2. *littéraire* [demande] entreaty ; ~ **de frapper avant d'entrer** please knock before entering.

primaire [primɛr] *adj* - 1. [premier] : **études ~s** primary education *(U)* - 2. *péj* [primitif] limited.

prime [prim] ⇔ *nf* - 1. [d'employé] bonus ; ~ **d'intéressement** profit-related bonus - 2. [allocation - de déménagement, de transport] allowance ; [- à l'exportation] incentive - 3. [d'assurance] premium. ⇔ *adj* - 1. [premier] : **de ~ abord** at first glance ; **de**

~ **jeunesse** in the first flush of youth - **2.** MATHS prime.

primer [3] [prime] ⬦ *vi* to take precedence, to come first. ⬦ *vt* - **1.** [être supérieur à] to take precedence over - **2.** [récompenser] to award a prize to ; **le film a été primé au festival** the film won an award at the festival.

primeur [primœr] *nf* immediacy ; **avoir la ~ de qqch** to be the first to hear sthg. ◆ **primeurs** *nfpl* early produce *(U)*.

primevère [primvɛr] *nf* primrose.

primitif, ive [primitif, iv] ⬦ *adj* - **1.** [gén] primitive - **2.** [aspect] original. ⬦ *nm, f* primitive.

primordial, e, aux [primɔrdjal, o] *adj* essential.

prince [prɛs] *nm* prince.

princesse [prɛsɛs] *nf* princess.

princier, ère [prɛsje, ɛr] *adj* princely.

principal, e, aux [prɛsipal, o] ⬦ *adj* [gén] main, principal. ⬦ *nm, f* - **1.** [important] : **le ~** the main thing - **2.** SCOL headmaster (*f* headmistress) *Br*, principal *Am*

principalement [prɛsipalmɑ̃] *adv* mainly, principally.

principauté [prɛsipote] *nf* principality.

principe [prɛsip] *nm* principle ; **par ~** on principle. ◆ **en principe** *loc adv* theoretically, in principle.

printanier, ère [prɛtanje, ɛr] *adj* [temps] spring-like.

printemps [prɛtɑ̃] *nm* - **1.** [saison] spring - **2.** *fam* [année] : **avoir 20 ~** to be 20.

priori [prijɔri] ◆ **a priori** ⬦ *loc adv* in principle. ⬦ *nm inv* initial reaction.

prioritaire [prijɔritɛr] *adj* - **1.** [industrie, mesure] priority *(avant n)* - **2.** AUTOM with right of way.

priorité [prijɔrite] *nf* - **1.** [importance primordiale] priority ; **en ~** first - **2.** AUTOM right of way ; **~ à droite** give way to the right.

pris, e [pri, priz] ⬦ *pp* ▷ **prendre**. ⬦ *adj* - **1.** [place] taken ; [personne] busy ; [mains] full - **2.** [nez] blocked ; [gorge] sore. ◆ **prise** *nf* - **1.** [sur barre, sur branche] grip, hold ; **lâcher ~e** to let go ; *fig* to give up - **2.** [action de prendre - de ville] seizure, capture ; **~e en charge** [par Sécurité sociale] (guaranteed) reimbursement ; **~e d'otages** hostage taking ; **~e de sang** blood test ; **~e de vue** shot ; **~e de vue** ou **vues** [action] filming, shooting - **3.** [à la pêche] haul - **4.** ÉLECTR : **~e (de courant)** [mâle] plug ; [femelle] socket - **5.** [de judo] hold.

prisme [prism] *nm* prism.

prison [prizɔ̃] *nf* - **1.** [établissement] prison - **2.** [réclusion] imprisonment.

prisonnier, ère [prizɔnje, ɛr] ⬦ *nm, f* prisoner ; **faire qqn ~** to take sb prisoner, to capture sb. ⬦ *adj* imprisoned ; *fig* trapped.

privation [privasjɔ̃] *nf* deprivation. ◆ **privations** *nfpl* privations, hardships.

privatisation [privatizasjɔ̃] *nf* privatization.

privatiser [3] [privatize] *vt* to privatize.

privé, e [prive] *adj* private. ◆ **privé** *nm* - **1.** ÉCON private sector - **2.** [détective] private eye - **3.** [intimité] : **en ~** in private ; **dans le ~** in private life.

priver [3] [prive] *vt* : **~ qqn (de)** to deprive sb (of).

privilège [privilɛ3] *nm* privilege.

privilégié, e [privile3je] ⬦ *adj* - **1.** [personne] privileged - **2.** [climat, site] favoured *Br*, favored *Am*. ⬦ *nm, f* privileged person.

prix [pri] *nm* - **1.** [coût] price ; **à** ou **au ~ coûtant** at cost (price) ; **~ d'achat** purchase price ; **à aucun ~** on no account ; **à ~ fixe** set-price *(avant n)* ; **hors de ~** too expensive ; **à moitié ~** at half price ; **à tout ~** at all costs ; **~ net** (price) ; **~ de revient** cost price ; **y mettre le ~** to pay a lot - **2.** [importance] value - **3.** [récompense] prize.

probabilité [prɔbabilite] *nf* - **1.** [chance] probability - **2.** [vraisemblance] probability, likelihood ; **selon toute ~** in all probability.

probable [prɔbabl] *adj* probable, likely.

probablement [prɔbabləmɑ̃] *adv* probably.

probant, e [prɔbɑ̃, ɑ̃t] *adj* convincing, conclusive.

probité [prɔbite] *nf* integrity.

problème [prɔblɛm] *nm* problem ; **sans ~!**, **(il n'y a) pas de ~!** *fam* no problem! ; **ça ne lui pose aucun ~** *hum* that doesn't worry him/her.

procédé [prɔsede] *nm* - **1.** [méthode] process - **2.** [conduite] behaviour *(U)* *Br*, behavior *(U)* *Am*.

procéder [18] [prɔsede] *vi* - **1.** [agir] to proceed - **2.** [exécuter] : **~ à qqch** to set about sthg.

procédure [prɔsedyr] *nf* procedure ; [démarche] proceedings *(pl)*.

procès [prɔsɛ] *nm* JUR trial ; **intenter un ~ à qqn** to sue sb.

processeur [prɔsesœr] *nm* processor.

procession [prɔsesjɔ̃] *nf* procession.

processus [prɔsesys] *nm* process.

procès-verbal [prɔsɛverbal] *nm* - **1.** [contravention - gén] ticket ; [pour stationnement interdit] parking ticket - **2.** [compterendu] minutes.

prochain, e [prɔʃɛ̃, ɛn] *adj* - **1.** [suivant] next ; **à la ~e!** *fam* see you! - **2.** [imminent] impending. ◆ **prochain** *nm littéraire* [semblable] fellow man.

prochainement [prɔʃɛnmɑ̃] *adv* soon, shortly.

proche [prɔʃ] *adj* - **1.** [dans l'espace] near ; **~ de** near, close to ; [semblable à] very similar to, closely related to - **2.** [dans le temps] imminent, near ; **dans un ~ avenir** in the immediate future - **3.** [ami, parent] close. ◆ **proches** *nmpl* : **les ~s** close friends and relatives *(sg)*. ◆ **de proche en proche** *loc adv sout* gradually.

Proche-Orient [prɔʃɔrjɑ̃] *nm* : **le ~** the Near East.

proclamation [prɔklamasjɔ̃] *nf* proclamation.

proclamer [3] [prɔklame] *vt* to proclaim, to declare.

procréer [15] [prɔkree] *vt littéraire* to procreate.

procuration [prɔkyrasjɔ̃] *nf* proxy ; **par ~** by proxy.

procurer [3] [prɔkyre] *vt* : **~ qqch à qqn** [suj : personne] to obtain sthg for sb ; [suj : chose] to give ou bring sb sthg. ◆ **se procurer** *vp* : **se ~ qqch** to obtain sthg.

procureur [prɔkyrœr] *nm* : **Procureur de la République** ≃ Attorney General.

prodige [prɔdiʒ] *nm* - **1.** [miracle] miracle - **2.** [tour de force] marvel, wonder - **3.** [génie] prodigy.

prodigieux, euse [prɔdiʒjø, øz] *adj* fantastic, incredible.

prodigue [prɔdig] *adj* [dépensier] extravagant.

prodiguer [3] [prɔdige] *vt littéraire* [soins, amitié] : **~ qqch (à)** to lavish sthg (on).

producteur, trice [prɔdyktœr, tris] ◇ *nm, f* - **1.** [gén] producer - **2.** AGRIC producer, grower. ◇ *adj* : **~ de pétrole** oil-producing *(avant n)*.

productif, ive [prɔdyktif, iv] *adj* productive.

production [prɔdyksjɔ̃] *nf* - **1.** [gén] production ; **la ~ littéraire d'un pays** the literature of a country - **2.** [producteurs] producers *(pl)*.

productivité [prɔdyktivite] *nf* productivity.

produire [98] [prɔdɥir] *vt* - **1.** [gén] to produce - **2.** [provoquer] to cause. ◆ **se produire** *vp* - **1.** [arriver] to occur, to take place - **2.** [acteur, chanteur] to appear.

produit, e [prɔdɥi, it] *pp* ▷ **produire**. ◆ **produit** *nm* [gén] product ; **~s alimentaires** foodstuffs, foods ; **~ de beauté** cosmetic, beauty product ; **~s chimiques** chemicals ; **~s d'entretien** cleaning products ; **~ financier** financial product ; **~ de grande consommation** mass consumption product.

proéminent, e [prɔeminɑ̃, ɑ̃t] *adj* prominent.

profane [prɔfan] ◇ *nmf* - **1.** [non religieux] non-believer - **2.** [novice] layman. ◇ *adj* - **1.** [laïc] secular - **2.** [ignorant] ignorant.

profaner [3] [prɔfane] *vt* - **1.** [église] to desecrate - **2.** *fig* [mémoire] to defile.

proférer [18] [prɔfere] *vt* to utter.

professeur [prɔfesœr] *nm* [gén] teacher ; [dans l'enseignement supérieur] lecturer ; [titulaire] professor.

profession [prɔfesjɔ̃] *nf* - **1.** [métier] occupation ; **sans ~** unemployed ; **~ libérale** profession ; [corps de métier - libéral] profession ; [- manuel] trade.

professionnel, elle [prɔfesjɔnɛl] ◇ *adj* - **1.** [gén] professional - **2.** [école] technical ; [enseignement] vocational. ◇ *nm, f* professional.

professorat [prɔfesɔra] *nm* teaching.

profil [prɔfil] *nm* - **1.** [de personne, d'emploi] profile ; [de bâtiment] outline ; **de ~** [visage, corps] in profile ; [objet] from the side - **2.** [coupe] section.

profiler [3] [prɔfile] *vt* to shape. ◆ **se profiler** *vp* - **1.** [bâtiment, arbre] to stand out - **2.** [solution] to emerge.

profit [prɔfi] *nm* - **1.** [avantage] benefit ; **au ~ de** in aid of ; **tirer ~ de** to profit from, to benefit from - **2.** [gain] profit.

profitable [prɔfitabl] *adj* profitable ; **être ~ à qqn** to benefit sb, to be beneficial to sb.

profiter [3] [prɔfite] *vi* [tirer avantage] : **~ de** [vacances] to benefit from ; [personne] to take advantage of ; **~ de qqch pour faire qqch** to take advantage of sthg to do sthg ; **en ~** to make the most of it.

profond, e [prɔfɔ̃, ɔ̃d] *adj* - **1.** [gén] deep - **2.** [pensée] deep, profound.

profondément [prɔfɔ̃demɑ̃] *adv* - **1.** [enfoui] deep - **2.** [intensément - aimer, intéresser] deeply ; [- dormir] soundly ; **être ~ endormi** to be fast asleep - **3.** [extrêmement - convaincu, ému] deeply, profoundly ; [- différent] profoundly.

profondeur [prɔfɔ̃dœr] *nf* depth ; **en ~** in depth.

profusion [prɔfyzjɔ̃] *nf* : **une ~ de** a profusion of ; **à ~** in abundance, in profusion.

progéniture [prɔʒenityr] *nf* offspring.

programmable [prɔgramabl] *adj* programmable.

programmateur, trice [prɔgramatœr, tris] *nm, f* programme *Br* ou program *Am* planner. ➡ **programmateur** *nm* automatic control unit.

programmation [prɔgramasjɔ̃] *nf* - **1.** INFORM programming - **2.** RADIO & TÉLÉ programme *Br* ou program *Am* planning.

programme [prɔgram] *nm* - **1.** [gén] programme *Br*, program *Am* - **2.** INFORM program - **3.** [planning] schedule - **4.** SCOL syllabus.

programmer [3] [prɔgrame] *vt* - **1.** [organiser] to plan - **2.** RADIO & TÉLÉ to schedule - **3.** INFORM to program.

programmeur, euse [prɔgramœr, øz] *nm, f* INFORM (computer) programmer.

progrès [prɔgrɛ] *nm* progress *(U)* ; **faire des ~** to make progress.

progresser [4] [prɔgrese] *vi* - **1.** [avancer] to progress, to advance - **2.** [maladie] to spread - **3.** [élève] to make progress.

progressif, ive [prɔgresif, iv] *adj* progressive ; [difficulté] increasing.

progression [prɔgresjɔ̃] *nf* - **1.** [avancée] advance - **2.** [de maladie, du nationalisme] spread.

prohiber [3] [prɔibe] *vt* to ban, to prohibit.

proie [prwa] *nf* prey ; **être la ~ de qqch** *fig* to be the victim of sthg ; **etre en ~ à** [sentiment] to be prey to.

projecteur [prɔʒɛktœr] *nm* - **1.** [de lumière] floodlight ; THÉÂTRE spotlight - **2.** [d'images] projector.

projectile [prɔʒɛktil] *nm* missile.

projection [prɔʒɛksjɔ̃] *nf* - **1.** [gén] projection - **2.** [jet] throwing.

projectionniste [prɔʒɛksjɔnist] *nmf* projectionist.

projet [prɔʒɛ] *nm* - **1.** [perspective] plan - **2.** [étude, ébauche] draft ; **~ de loi** bill.

projeter [27] [prɔʃte] *vt* - **1.** [envisager] to plan ; **~ de faire qqch** to plan to do sthg - **2.** [missile, pierre] to throw - **3.** [film, diapositives] to show.

prolétaire [prɔletɛr] *nmf* & *adj* proletarian.

prolétariat [prɔletarja] *nm* proletariat.

proliférer [18] [prɔlifere] *vi* to proliferate.

prolifique [prɔlifik] *adj* prolific.

prologue [prɔlɔg] *nm* prologue.

prolongation [prɔlɔ̃gasjɔ̃] *nf* [extension] extension, prolongation. ➡ **prolongations** *nfpl* SPORT extra time *(U)*.

prolongement [prɔlɔ̃gmɑ̃] *nm* [de mur, quai] extension ; **être dans le ~ de** to be a continuation of. ➡ **prolongements** *nmpl* [conséquences] repercussions.

prolonger [17] [prɔlɔ̃ʒe] *vt* - **1.** [dans le temps] : **~ qqch (de)** to prolong sthg (by) - **2.** [dans l'espace] : **~ qqch (de)** to extend sthg (by).

promenade [prɔmnad] *nf* - **1.** [balade] walk, stroll ; *fig* trip, excursion ; **~ en voiture** drive ; **~ à vélo** (bike) ride ; **faire une ~** to go for a walk - **2.** [lieu] promenade.

promener [19] [prɔmne] *vt* - **1.** [personne] to take out (for a walk) ; [en voiture] to take for a drive - **2.** *fig* [regard, doigts] : **~ qqch sur** to run sthg over. ➡ **se promener** *vp* to go for a walk.

promesse [prɔmɛs] *nf* - **1.** [serment] promise ; **tenir sa ~** to keep one's promise - **2.** [engagement] undertaking ; **~ d'achat/de vente** JUR agreement to purchase/to sell - **3.** *fig* [espérance] : **être plein de ~s** to be very promising.

prometteur, euse [prɔmetœr, øz] *adj* promising.

promettre [84] [prɔmɛtr] ⬥ *vt* to promise ; **~ qqch à qqn** to promise sb sthg ; **~ de faire qqch** to promise to do sthg ; **~ à qqn que** to promise sb that. ⬥ *vi* to be promising ; **ça promet!** *iron* that bodes well!

promis, e [prɔmi, iz] ⬥ *pp* ▷ promettre. ⬥ *adj* promised. ⬥ *nm, f hum* intended.

promiscuité [prɔmiskɥite] *nf* overcrowding ; **~ sexuelle** (sexual) promiscuity.

promontoire [prɔmɔ̃twar] *nm* promontory.

promoteur, trice [prɔmɔtœr, tris] *nm, f* - **1.** [novateur] instigator - **2.** [constructeur] property developer.

promotion [prɔmɔsjɔ̃] *nf* - **1.** [gén] promotion ; **en ~** [produit] on special offer - **2.** MIL & SCOL year.

promouvoir [56] [prɔmuvwar] *vt* to promote.

prompt, e [prɔ̃, prɔ̃t] *adj sout* : **~ (à faire qqch)** swift (to do sthg).

promu, e [prɔmy] *pp* ▷ promouvoir.

promulguer [3] [prɔmylge] *vt* to promulgate.

prôner [3] [prone] *vt sout* to advocate.

pronom [prɔnɔ̃] *nm* pronoun.

pronominal, e, aux [prɔnɔminal, o] *adj* pronominal.

prononcé, e [prɔnɔ̃se] *adj* marked.

prononcer [16] [prɔnɔ̃se] *vt* - **1.** JUR & LING

to·pronounce - **2**. [dire] to utter. ◆ **se prononcer** *vp* - **1**. [se dire] to be pronounced - **2**. [trancher - assemblée] to decide, to reach a decision ; [- magistrat] to deliver a verdict ; **se ~ sur** to give one's opinion of.

prononciation [prɔnɔ̃sjasjɔ̃] *nf* - **1**. LING pronunciation - **2**. JUR pronouncement.

pronostic [prɔnɔstik] *nm* - **1**. (*gén pl*) [prévision] forecast - **2**. MÉD prognosis.

propagande [prɔpagɑ̃d] *nf* - **1**. [endoctrinement] propaganda - **2**. *fig & hum* [publicité] **: faire de la ~ pour qqch** to plug sthg.

propager [17] [prɔpaʒe] *vt* to spread. ◆ **se propager** *vp* to spread ; BIOL to be propagated ; PHYS to propagate.

propane [prɔpan] *nm* propane.

prophète, prophétesse [prɔfɛt, prɔfetɛs] *nm, f* prophet (*f* prophetess).

prophétie [prɔfesi] *nf* prophecy.

prophétiser [3] [prɔfetize] *vt* to prophesy.

propice [prɔpis] *adj* favourable *Br*, favorable *Am*.

proportion [prɔpɔrsjɔ̃] *nf* proportion ; **toutes ~s gardées** relatively speaking.

proportionné, e [prɔpɔrsjɔne] *adj* : **bien/mal ~** well-/badly-proportioned.

proportionnel, elle [prɔpɔrsjɔnɛl] *adj* : **~ (à)** proportional (to). ◆ **proportionnelle** *nf* : **la ~le** proportional representation.

propos [prɔpo] ◇ *nm* - **1**. [discours] talk - **2**. [but] intention ; **c'est à quel ~?** what is it about? ; **hors de ~** at the wrong time. ◇ *nmpl* [paroles] talk (*U*), words. ◆ **à propos** *loc adv* - **1**. [opportunément] at (just) the right time - **2**. [au fait] by the way. ◆ **à propos de** *loc prép* about.

proposer [3] [prɔpoze] *vt* - **1**. [offrir] to offer, to propose ; **~ qqch à qqn** to offer sb sthg, to offer sthg to sb ; **~ à qqn de faire qqch** to offer to do sthg for sb - **2**. [suggérer] to suggest, to propose ; **~ de faire qqch** to suggest ou propose doing sthg - **3**. [loi, candidat] to propose.

proposition [prɔpozisjɔ̃] *nf* - **1**. [offre] offer, proposal - **2**. [suggestion] suggestion, proposal - **3**. GRAM clause.

propre [prɔpr] ◇ *adj* - **1**. [nettoyé] clean - **2**. [soigné] neat, tidy - **3**. [éduqué - enfant] toilet-trained ; [- animal] house-trained *Br*, housebroken *Am* - **4**. [personnel] own - **5**. [particulier] : **~ à** peculiar to - **6**. [de nature] : **~ à faire qqch** capable of doing sthg. ◇ *nm* [propreté] cleanness, cleanliness ; **recopier qqch au ~** to make a fair copy of

sthg, to copy sthg up. ◆ **au propre** *loc adv* LING literally.

proprement [prɔprəmɑ̃] *adv* - **1**. [convenablement - habillé] neatly, tidily ; [- se tenir] correctly - **2**. [véritablement] completely ; **à ~ parler** strictly ou properly speaking ; **l'événement ~ dit** the event itself, the actual event.

propreté [prɔprəte] *nf* cleanness, cleanliness.

propriétaire [prɔprijetɛr] *nmf* - **1**. [possesseur] owner ; **~ terrien** landowner - **2**. [dans l'immobilier] landlord.

propriété [prɔprijete] *nf* - **1**. [gén] property ; **~ privée** private property - **2**. [droit] ownership - **3**. [terres] property (*U*) - **4**. [convenance] suitability.

propulser [3] [prɔpylse] *vt litt & fig* to propel. ◆ **se propulser** *vp* to move forward, to propel o.s. forward ou along ; *fig* to shoot.

prorata [prɔrata] ◆ **au prorata de** *loc prép* in proportion to.

prosaïque [prɔzaik] *adj* prosaic, mundane.

proscrit, e [prɔskri, it] *adj* [interdit] banned, prohibited.

prose [proz] *nf* prose ; **en ~** in prose.

prospecter [4] [prɔspɛkte] *vt* - **1**. [pays, région] to prospect - **2**. COMM to canvass.

prospection [prɔspɛksjɔ̃] *nf* - **1**. [de ressources] prospecting - **2**. COMM canvassing.

prospectus [prɔspɛktys] *nm* (advertising) leaflet.

prospérer [18] [prɔspere] *vi* to prosper, to thrive ; [plante, insecte] to thrive.

prospérité [prɔsperite] *nf* - **1**. [richesse] prosperity - **2**. [bien-être] well-being.

prostate [prɔstat] *nf* prostate (gland).

prosterner [3] [prɔstɛrne] ◆ **se prosterner** *vp* to bow down ; **se ~ devant** to bow down before ; *fig* to kowtow to.

prostituée [prɔstitɥe] *nf* prostitute.

prostituer [7] [prɔstitɥe] ◆ **se prostituer** *vp* to prostitute o.s.

prostitution [prɔstitysjɔ̃] *nf* prostitution.

prostré, e [prɔstre] *adj* prostrate.

protagoniste [prɔtagɔnist] *nmf* protagonist, hero (*f* heroine).

protecteur, trice [prɔtɛktœr, tris] ◇ *adj* protective. ◇ *nm, f* - **1**. [défenseur] protector - **2**. [des arts] patron - **3**. [souteneur] pimp.

protection [prɔtɛksjɔ̃] *nf* - **1**. [défense] protection ; **prendre qqn sous sa ~** to take sb under one's wing - **2.** [des arts] patronage.

protectionnisme [prɔtɛksjɔnism] *nm* protectionism.

protégé, e [prɔteʒe] <> *adj* protected. <> *nm, f* protégé.

protège-cahier [prɔtɛʒkaje] (*pl* protège-cahiers) *nm* exercise book cover.

protéger [22] [prɔteʒe] *vt* [gén] to protect.

protéine [prɔtein] *nf* protein.

protestant, e [prɔtɛstɑ̃, ɑ̃t] *adj & nm, f* Protestant.

protestation [prɔtɛstasjɔ̃] *nf* [contestation] protest.

protester [3] [prɔtɛste] *vi* to protest ; ~ **contre qqch** to protest against sthg, to protest sthg *Am*.

prothèse [prɔtɛz] *nf* prosthesis ; ~ **dentaire** dentures *(pl)*, false teeth *(pl)*.

protide [prɔtid] *nm* protein.

protocolaire [prɔtɔkɔlɛr] *adj* [poli] conforming to etiquette.

protocole [prɔtɔkɔl] *nm* protocol.

proton [prɔtɔ̃] *nm* proton.

prototype [prɔtɔtip] *nm* prototype.

protubérance [prɔtyberɑ̃s] *nf* bulge, protuberance.

proue [pru] *nf* bows *(pl)*, prow.

prouesse [prues] *nf* feat.

prouver [3] [pruve] *vt* - **1.** [établir] to prove - **2.** [montrer] to demonstrate, to show.

provenance [prɔvnɑ̃s] *nf* origin ; **en ~ de** from.

provençal, e, aux [prɔvɑ̃sal, o] *adj* - **1.** [de Provence] of/from Provence - **2.** CULIN with *tomatoes, garlic and onions.* ◆ **provençal** *nm* [langue] Provençal.

Provence [prɔvɑ̃s] *nf* : **la ~** Provence.

provenir [40] [prɔvnir] *vi* : ~ **de** to come from ; *fig* to be due to, to be caused by.

proverbe [prɔvɛrb] *nm* proverb.

proverbial, e, aux [prɔvɛrbjal, o] *adj* proverbial.

providence [prɔvidɑ̃s] *nf* providence.

providentiel, elle [prɔvidɑ̃sjɛl] *adj* providential.

province [prɔvɛ̃s] *nf* - **1.** [gén] province - **2.** [campagne] provinces *(pl)*.

provincial, e, aux [prɔvɛ̃sjal, o] *adj & nm, f* provincial.

proviseur [prɔvizœr] *nm* ≃ head *Br*, ≃ headteacher *Br*, ≃ headmaster (*f* headmistress) *Br*, ≃ principal *Am*.

provision [prɔvizjɔ̃] *nf* - **1.** [réserve] stock, supply - **2.** FIN retainer ⊳ **chèque**. ◆ **provisions** *nfpl* provisions.

provisoire [prɔvizwar] <> *adj* temporary ; JUR provisional. <> *nm* : **ce n'est que du ~** it's only a temporary arrangement.

provocant, e [prɔvɔkɑ̃, ɑ̃t] *adj* provocative.

provocation [prɔvɔkasjɔ̃] *nf* provocation.

provoquer [3] [prɔvɔke] *vt* - **1.** [entraîner] to cause - **2.** [personne] to provoke.

proxénète [prɔksenɛt] *nm* pimp.

proximité [prɔksimite] *nf* [de lieu] proximity, nearness ; **à ~ de** near.

prude [pryd] *adj* prudish.

prudence [prydɑ̃s] *nf* care, caution.

prudent, e [prydɑ̃, ɑ̃t] *adj* careful, cautious.

prune [pryn] *nf* plum.

pruneau, x [pryno] *nm* [fruit] prune.

prunelle [prynɛl] *nf* ANAT pupil.

prunier [prynje] *nm* plum tree.

PS¹ (*abr de* **Parti socialiste**) *nm* French socialist party.

PS², P-S (*abr de* **post-scriptum**) *nm* PS.

psalmodier [9] [psalmɔdje] <> *vt* to chant ; *fig & péj* to drone. <> *vi* to drone.

psaume [psom] *nm* psalm.

pseudonyme [psødɔnim] *nm* pseudonym.

psy [psi] *fam nmf* (*abr de* **psychiatre**) shrink.

psychanalyse [psikanaliz] *nf* psychoanalysis.

psychanalyste [psikanalist] *nmf* psychoanalyst, analyst.

psychédélique [psikedelik] *adj* psychedelic.

psychiatre [psikjatr] *nmf* psychiatrist.

psychiatrie [psikjatri] *nf* psychiatry.

psychique [psiʃik] *adj* psychic ; [maladie] psychosomatic.

psychologie [psikɔlɔʒi] *nf* psychology.

psychologique [psikɔlɔʒik] *adj* psychological.

psychologue [psikɔlɔg] <> *nmf* psychologist. <> *adj* psychological.

psychose [psikoz] *nf* - **1.** MÉD psychosis - **2.** [crainte] obsessive fear.

psychosomatique [psikɔsɔmatik] *adj* psychosomatic.

psychothérapie [psikɔterapi] *nf* psychotherapy.

Pte - **1.** *abr de* **porte** - **2.** *abr de* **pointe**.

PTT (*abr de* **Postes, télécommunications et télédiffusion**) *nfpl* former French post office and telecommunications network.

pu [py] *pp* ⊳ **pouvoir**.

puant, e [pɥɑ̃, ɑ̃t] *adj* - **1.** [fétide] smelly, stinking - **2.** *fam fig* [personne] bumptious, full of oneself.

puanteur [pɥɑ̃tœr] *nf* stink, stench.

pub¹ [pyb] *nf fam* ad, advert *Br* ; [métier] advertising.

pub² [pœb] *nm* pub.

pubère [pybɛr] *adj* pubescent.

puberté [pybɛrte] *nf* puberty.

pubis [pybis] *nm* [zone] pubis.

public, ique [pyblik] *adj* public. ◆ **public** *nm* - **1.** [auditoire] audience ; **en ~** in public - **2.** [population] public.

publication [pyblikasjɔ̃] *nf* publication.

publicitaire [pyblisitɛr] *adj* [campagne] advertising *(avant n)* ; [vente, film] promotional.

publicité [pyblisite] *nf* - **1.** [domaine] advertising ; **~ comparative** comparative advertising ; **~ mensongère** misleading advertising, deceptive advertising - **2.** [réclame] advertisement, advert - **3.** [autour d'une affaire] publicity *(U)*.

publier [10] [pyblije] *vt* [livre] to publish ; [communiqué] to issue, to release.

publireportage [pyblirəpɔrtaʒ] *nm* free write-up *Br*, reading notice *Am*.

puce [pys] *nf* - **1.** [insecte] flea - **2.** INFORM (silicon) chip - **3.** *fig* [terme affectueux] pet, love.

puceau, elle, x [pyso, ɛl, o] *nm, f & adj fam* virgin.

pudeur [pydœr] *nf* - **1.** [physique] modesty, decency - **2.** [morale] restraint.

pudibond, e [pydibɔ̃, ɔ̃d] *adj* prudish, prim and proper.

pudique [pydik] *adj* - **1.** [physiquement] modest, decent - **2.** [moralement] restrained.

puer [7] [pɥe] <> *vi* to stink ; **ça pue ici!** it stinks in here! <> *vt* to reek of, to stink of.

puéricultrice [pɥerikyltris] *nf* nursery nurse.

puériculture [pɥerikyltyr] *nf* childcare.

puéril, e [pɥeril] *adj* childish.

Puerto Rico = Porto Rico.

pugilat [pyʒila] *nm* fight.

puis [pɥi] *adv* then ; **et ~** [d'ailleurs] and moreover ou besides.

puiser [3] [pɥize] *vt* [liquide] to draw ; **~ qqch dans qqch** *fig* to draw ou take sthg from sthg.

puisque [pɥiskə] *conj* [gén] since.

puissance [pɥisɑ̃s] *nf* power. ◆ **en puissance** *loc adj* potential.

puissant, e [pɥisɑ̃, ɑ̃t] *adj* powerful. ◆ **puissant** *nm* : **les ~s** the powerful.

puisse, puisses *etc* ⊳ **pouvoir**.

puits [pɥi] *nm* - **1.** [d'eau] well - **2.** [de gisement] shaft ; **~ de pétrole** oil well.

pull [pyl], **pull-over** [pylɔvɛr] *(pl* **pull-overs)** *nm* jumper *Br*, sweater.

pulluler [3] [pylyle] *vi* to swarm.

pulmonaire [pylmɔnɛr] *adj* lung *(avant n)*, pulmonary.

pulpe [pylp] *nf* pulp.

pulsation [pylsasjɔ̃] *nf* beat, beating *(U)*.

pulsion [pylsjɔ̃] *nf* impulse.

pulvérisation [pylverizasjɔ̃] *nf* - **1.** [d'insecticide] spraying - **2.** MÉD spray ; [traitement] spraying.

pulvériser [3] [pylverize] *vt* - **1.** [projeter] to spray - **2.** [détruire] to pulverize ; *fig* to smash.

puma [pyma] *nm* puma.

punaise [pynɛz] *nf* - **1.** [insecte] bug - **2.** [clou] drawing pin *Br*, thumbtack *Am*.

punch [pɔ̃ʃ] *nm* punch.

puni, e [pyni] *adj* punished.

punir [32] [pynir] *vt* : **~ qqn (de)** to punish sb (with).

punition [pynisjɔ̃] *nf* punishment.

pupille [pypij] <> *nf* ANAT pupil. <> *nmf* [orphelin] ward ; **~ de l'État** ≃ child in care ; **~ de la Nation** war orphan *(in care)*.

pupitre [pypitr] *nm* - **1.** [d'orateur] lectern ; MUS stand - **2.** TECHNOL console - **3.** [d'écolier] desk.

pur, e [pyr] *adj* - **1.** [gén] pure - **2.** *fig* [absolu] pure, sheer ; **~ et simple** pure and simple - **3.** *fig & littéraire* [intention] honourable *Br*, honorable *Am* - **4.** [lignes] pure, clean.

purée [pyre] *nf* purée ; **~ de pommes de terre** mashed potatoes *(pl)*.

purement [pyrmɑ̃] *adv* purely ; **~ et simplement** purely and simply.

pureté [pyrte] *nf* - **1.** [gén] purity - **2.** [de sculpture, de diamant] perfection - **3.** [d'intention] honourableness.

purgatoire [pyrgatwar] *nm* purgatory.

purge [pyrʒ] *nf* - **1.** MÉD & POLIT purge - **2.** [de radiateur] bleeding.

purger [17] [pyrʒe] *vt* - **1.** MÉD & POLIT to purge - **2.** [radiateur] to bleed - **3.** [peine] to serve.

purifier [9] [pyrifje] *vt* to purify.

purin [pyrɛ̃] *nm* slurry.

puritain, e [pyritɛ̃, ɛn] <> *adj* [pudibond] puritanical. <> *nm, f* - **1.** [prude] puritan - **2.** RELIG Puritan.

puritanisme [pyritanism] *nm* puritanism ; RELIG Puritanism.

pur-sang [pyrsɑ̃] *nm inv* thoroughbred.

purulent, e [pyrylɑ̃, ɑ̃t] *adj* purulent.

pus [py] *nm* pus.

pusillanime [pyzilanim] *adj* pusillanimous.

putain [pytɛ̃] *nf vulg* - **1.** *péj* [prostituée] whore - **2.** *fig* [pour exprimer le mécontentement] : **(ce) ~ de ...** this/that sodding ... *Br*, this/that goddam ... *Am*.

putréfier [9] [pytrefje] ◆ **se putréfier** *vp* to putrefy, to rot.

putsch [putʃ] *nm* uprising, coup.

puzzle [pœzl] *nm* jigsaw (puzzle).

P-V *nm abr de* **procès-verbal**.

pyjama [piʒama] *nm* pyjamas *(pl)*.

pylône [pilon] *nm* pylon.

pyramide [piramid] *nf* pyramid.

Pyrénées [pirene] *nfpl* : **les ~** the Pyrenees.

Pyrex® [pirɛks] *nm* Pyrex®.

pyromane [piroman] *nmf* arsonist ; MÉD pyromaniac.

python [pitɔ̃] *nm* python.

q, Q [ky] *nm inv* [lettre] q, Q.

QCM (*abr de* **questionnaire à choix multiple**) *nm* multiple choice questionnaire.

QG (*abr de* **quartier général**) *nm* HQ.

QI (*abr de* **quotient intellectuel**) *nm* IQ.

qqch (*abr de* **quelque chose**) sthg.

qqn (*abr de* **quelqu'un**) s.o., sb.

qu' ➭ **que**.

quadragénaire [kwadraʒenɛr] *nmf* forty year old.

quadrilatère [kwadrilatɛr] *nm* quadrilateral.

quadrillage [kadrijaʒ] *nm* - **1.** [de papier, de tissu] criss-cross pattern - **2.** [policier] combing.

quadriller [3] [kadrije] *vt* - **1.** [papier] to mark with squares - **2.** [ville - suj : rues] to criss-cross ; [- suj : police] to comb.

quadrimoteur [kwadrimɔtœr] *nm* four-engined plane.

quadrupède [k(w)adrypɛd] *nm & adj* quadruped.

quadruplés, ées [k(w)adryple] *nm, f pl* quadruplets, quads.

quai [kɛ] *nm* - **1.** [de gare] platform - **2.** [de port] quay, wharf - **3.** [de rivière] embankment.

qualificatif, ive [kalifikatif, iv] *adj* qualifying. ◆ **qualificatif** *nm* term.

qualification [kalifikasjɔ̃] *nf* [gén] qualification.

qualifier [9] [kalifje] *vt* - **1.** [gén] to qualify ; **être qualifié pour qqch/pour faire qqch** to be qualified for sthg/to do sthg - **2.** [caractériser] : **qqn/qqch de qqch** to describe sb/sthg as sthg, to call sb/sthg sthg. ◆ **se qualifier** *vp* to qualify.

qualitatif, ive [kalitatif, iv] *adj* qualitative.

qualité [kalite] *nf* - **1.** [gén] quality ; **de bonne/mauvaise ~** of good/poor quality - **2.** [condition] position, capacity.

quand [kɑ̃] ◇ *conj* [lorsque, alors que] when ; **~ tu le verras, demande-lui de me téléphoner** when you see him, ask him to phone me. ◇ *adv interr* when ; **~ arriveras-tu?** when will you arrive? ; **jusqu'à ~ restez-vous?** how long are you staying for? ◆ **quand même** ◇ *loc adv* all the same ; **je pense qu'il ne viendra pas, mais je l'inviterai ~ même** I don't think he'll come but I'll invite him all the same ; **tu pourrais faire attention ~ même!** you might at least be careful! ◇ *interj* : **~ même, à son âge!** really, at his/her age! ◆ **quand bien même** *loc conj sout* even though, even if.

quant [kɑ̃] ◆ **quant à** *loc prép* as for.

quantifier [9] [kɑ̃tifje] *vt* to quantify.

quantitatif, ive [kɑ̃titatif, iv] *adj* quantitative.

quantité [kɑ̃tite] *nf* - **1.** [mesure] quantity, amount - **2.** [abondance] : **(une) ~ de** a great many, a lot of ; **en ~** in large numbers ; **des exemplaires en ~** a large number of copies.

quarantaine [karɑ̃tɛn] *nf* - **1.** [nombre] : **une ~ de** about forty - **2.** [âge] : **avoir la ~** to be in one's forties - **3.** [isolement] quarantine.

quarante [karɑ̃t] *adj num & nm* forty ; *voir aussi* **six**.

quarantième [karɑ̃tjɛm] *adj num, nm* OU *nmf* fortieth ; *voir aussi* **sixième**.

quart [kar] *nm* - **1.** [fraction] quarter ; **deux heures moins le ~** (a) quarter to two, (a) quarter of two *Am* ; **deux heures et ~ (a) quarter past two, (a) quarter after two** *Am* ; **il est moins le ~** it's (a) quarter to ; **un ~ de a** quarter of - **2.** NAVIG watch - **3.** : **~ de finale** quarter final.

quartier [kartje] *nm* - **1.** [de ville] area, district ; **le ~ latin** the Latin quarter - **2.** [de fruit] piece ; [de viande] quarter - **3.** [héraldique, de lune] quarter - **4.** *(gén pl)* MIL quarters *(pl)* ; **~ général** headquarters *(pl)*.

quart-monde [karmɔ̃d] *(pl* **quarts-mondes)** *nm* : **le ~** the Fourth World.

quartz [kwarts] *nm* quartz ; **montre à ~** quartz watch.

quasi [kazi] *adv* almost, nearly.

quasi- [kazi] *préfixe* near ; **~collision** near collision.

quasiment [kazimɑ̃] *adv fam* almost, nearly.

quatorze [katɔrz] *adj num & nm* fourteen ; *voir aussi* **six.**

quatorzième [katɔrzjɛm] *adj num, nm* OU *nmf* fourteenth ; *voir aussi* **sixième.**

quatrain [katrɛ̃] *nm* quatrain.

quatre [katr] <> *adj num* four ; **monter l'escalier ~ à ~** to take the stairs four at a time ; **se mettre en ~ pour qqn** to bend over backwards for sb. <> *nm* four ; *voir aussi* **six.**

quatre-vingt = **quatre-vingts.**

quatre-vingt-dix [katrəvɛ̃dis] *adj num & nm* ninety ; *voir aussi* **six.**

quatre-vingt-dixième [katrəvɛ̃dizjɛm] *adj num, nm* OU *nmf* ninetieth ; *voir aussi* **sixième.**

quatre-vingtième [katrəvɛ̃tjɛm] *adj num, nm* OU *nmf* eightieth ; *voir aussi* **sixième.**

quatre-vingts, quatre-vingt [katrəvɛ̃] *adj num & nm* eighty ; *voir aussi* **six.**

quatrième [katrijɛm] <> *adj num, nm* OU *nmf* fourth ; *voir aussi* **sixième.** <> *nf* SCOL ≃ third year OU form *Br*, ≃ eighth grade *Am*.

quatuor [kwatɥɔr] *nm* quartet.

que [k(ə)] <> *conj* - **1.** [introduit une subordonnée] that ; **il a dit qu'il viendrait** he said (that) he'd come ; **il veut ~ tu viennes** he wants you to come - **2.** [introduit une hypothèse] whether ; **~ vous le vouliez ou non** whether you like it or not - **3.** [reprend une autre conjonction] : **s'il fait beau et que nous avons le temps ...** if the weather is good and we have time ... - **4.** [indique un ordre, un souhait] : **qu'il entre!** let him come in! ; **~ tout le monde sorte!** every-

body out! - **5.** [après un présentatif] : **voilà/voici ~ ça recommence!** here we go again! - **6.** [comparatif - après moins, plus] than ; [- après autant, aussi, même] as ; **plus jeune ~ moi** younger than I (am) OU than me ; **elle a la même robe ~ moi** she has the same dress as I do OU as me - **7.** [seulement] : **ne ... ~** only ; **je n'ai qu'une sœur** I've only got one sister. <> *pron rel* [chose, animal] which, that ; [personne] whom, that ; **la femme ~ j'aime** the woman (whom OU that) I love ; **le livre qu'il m'a prêté** the book (which OU that) he lent me. <> *pron interr* what ; **~ savez-vous au juste?** what exactly do you know? ; **~ faire?** what can I/we/one do? ; **je me demande ~ faire** I wonder what I should do. <> *adv excl* : **qu'elle est belle!** how beautiful she is! ; **~ de monde!** what a lot of people! ◆ **c'est que** *loc conj* it's because ; **si je vais me coucher, c'est ~ j'ai sommeil** if I'm going to bed, it's because I'm tired. ◆ **qu'est-ce que** *pron interr* what ; **qu'est-ce ~ tu veux encore?** what else do you want? ◆ **qu'est-ce qui** *pron interr* what ; **qu'est-ce qui se passe?** what's going on?

Québec [kebɛk] *nm* [province] : **le ~** Quebec.

québécois, e [kebekwa, az] *adj* Quebec *(avant n).* ◆ **québécois** *nm* [langue] Quebec French. ◆ **Québécois, e** *nm, f* Quebecker, Québécois.

quel [kɛl] *(f* **quelle,** *mpl* **quels,** *fpl* **quelles)** <> *adj interr* [personne] which ; [chose] what, which ; **~ homme?** which man? ; **~ livre voulez-vous?** what OU which book do you want? ; **de ~ côté es-tu?** what OU which side are you on? ; **je ne sais ~s ses projets** I don't know what his plans are ; **quelle heure est-il?** what time is it?, what's the time?. <> *adj excl* : **~ idiot!** what an idiot! ; **quelle honte!** the shame of it! <> *adj indéf* : **~ que** (+ subjonctif) [chose, animal] whatever ; [personne] whoever ; **il se baigne, ~ que soit le temps** he goes swimming whatever the weather ; **il refuse de voir les nouveaux arrivants, ~s qu'ils soient** he refuses to see new arrivals, whoever they may be. <> *pron interr* which (one) ; **de vous trois, ~ est le plus jeune?** which (one) of you three is the youngest?

quelconque [kɛlkɔ̃k] *adj* - **1.** [n'importe lequel] any ; **donner un prétexte ~** to give any old excuse ; **si pour une raison ~ ...** if for any reason ... ; **une ~ observation** some remark or other - **2.** *(après n) péj* [banal] ordinary, mediocre.

quelque [kɛlk(ə)] <> *adj indéf* some ; **à**

~ **distance de là** some way away (from there) ; **j'ai ~s lettres à écrire** I have some ou a few letters to write ; **vous n'avez pas ~s livres à me montrer?** don't you have any books to show me? ; **les ~s fois où j'étais absent** the few times I wasn't there ; **les ~s 30 euros qu'il m'a prêtés** the 30 euros or so (that) he lent me ; ~ **route que je prenne** whatever route I take ; ~ **peu** somewhat, rather. ◇ *adv* [environ] about ; **30 euros et ~** some ou about 30 euros ; **il est midi et ~** *fam* it's just after midday.

quelque chose [kɛlkəʃoz] *pron indéf* something ; **de différent** something different ; ~ **d'autre** something else ; **tu veux boire ~?** do you want something ou anything to drink? ; **apporter un petit ~ à qqn** to give sb a little something ; **c'est ~!** [ton admiratif] it's really something! ; **cela m'a fait ~** I really felt it.

quelquefois [kɛlkəfwa] *adv* sometimes, occasionally.

quelque part [kɛlkəpar] *adv* somewhere *Br*, someplace *Am* ; **l'as-tu vu ~?** did you see him anywhere *Br* ou anyplace *Am*?, have you seen him anywhere *Br* ou anyplace *Am*?

quelques-uns, quelques-unes [kɛlkəzœ̃, yn] *pron indéf* some, a few.

quelqu'un [kɛlkœ̃] *pron indéf m* someone, somebody ; **c'est ~ d'ouvert/d'intelligent** he's/she's a frank/an intelligent person.

quémander [3] [kemɑ̃de] *vt* to beg for ; ~ **qqch à qqn** to beg sb for sthg.

qu'en-dira-t-on [kɑ̃diratɔ̃] *nm inv fam* tittle-tattle.

quenelle [kənɛl] *nf* very finely chopped mixture of fish or chicken cooked in stock.

querelle [kərɛl] *nf* quarrel.

quereller [4] [kərele] ➧ **se quereller** *vp* : **se ~ (avec)** to quarrel (with).

querelleur, euse [kərɛlœr, øz] *adj* quarrelsome.

qu'est-ce que [kɛskə] ➩ **que**.

qu'est-ce qui [kɛski] ➩ **que**.

question [kɛstjɔ̃] *nf* question ; **poser une ~ à qqn** to ask sb a question ; **il est ~ de faire qqch** it's a question ou matter of doing sthg ; **il n'en est pas ~** there is no question of it ; **remettre qqn/qqch en ~** to question sb/sthg, to challenge sb/sthg ; ~ **subsidiaire** tiebreaker.

questionnaire [kɛstjɔnɛr] *nm* questionnaire.

questionner [3] [kɛstjɔne] *vt* to question.

quête [kɛt] *nf* - **1.** *sout* [d'objet, de personne] quest ; **se mettre en ~ de** to go in search of - **2.** [d'aumône] : **faire la ~** to take a collection.

quêter [4] [kete] ◇ *vi* to collect. ◇ *vt fig* to seek, to look for.

queue [kø] *nf* - **1.** [d'animal] tail ; **faire une ~ de poisson à qqn** *fig & AUTOM* to cut sb up - **2.** [de fruit] stalk - **3.** [de poêle] handle - **4.** [de liste, de classe] bottom ; [de file, peloton] rear - **5.** [file] queue *Br*, line *Am* ; **faire la ~** to queue *Br*, to stand in line *Am* ; **à la ~ leu leu** in single file.

queue-de-cheval [kødʃəval] (*pl* **queues-de-cheval**) *nf* ponytail.

queue-de-pie [kødpi] (*pl* **queues-de-pie**) *nf fam* tails (*pl*).

qui [ki] ◇ *pron rel* - **1.** (sujet) [personne] who ; [chose] which, that ; **l'homme ~ parle** the man who's talking ; **je l'ai vu ~ passait** I saw him pass ; **le chien ~ aboie** the barking dog, the dog which ou that is barking ; ~ **plus est** (and) what's more ; ~ **mieux est** even better, better still - **2.** (complément d'objet direct) who ; **tu vois ~ je veux dire** you see who I mean ; **invite ~ tu veux** invite whoever ou anyone you like - **3.** (après une préposition) who, whom ; **la personne à ~ je parle** the person I'm talking to, the person to whom I'm talking - **4.** (indéfini) : ~ **que tu sois** whoever you are ; ~ **que ce soit** whoever it may be. ◇ *pron interr* - **1.** (sujet) who ; ~ **es-tu?** who are you? ; **je voudrais savoir ~ est là** I would like to know who's there - **2.** (complément d'objet, après une préposition) who, whom ; ~ **demandez-vous?** who do you want to see? ; **dites-moi ~ vous demandez** tell me who you want to see ; **à ~ vas-tu le donner?** who are you going to give it to?, to whom are you going to give it? ➧ **qui est-ce qui** *pron interr* who ➧ **qui est-ce que** *pron interr* who, whom.

quiche [kiʃ] *nf* quiche.

quiconque [kikɔ̃k] ◇ *pron indéf* anyone, anybody. ◇ *pron rel indéf sout* anyone who, whoever.

quidam [kidam] *nm fam* chap *Br*, guy *Am*.

quiétude [kjetyd] *nf* tranquillity *Br*, tranquility *Am*.

quignon [kiɲɔ̃] *nm fam* hunk.

quille [kij] *nf* [de bateau] keel. ➧ **quilles** *nfpl* [jeu] : **(jeu de) ~s** skittles (*U*).

quincaillerie [kɛ̃kajri] *nf* - **1.** [magasin] ironmonger's (shop) *Br*, hardware shop - **2.** *fam fig* [bijoux] jewellery.

quinconce [kɛ̃kɔ̃s] *nm* : **en ~** in a staggered arrangement.

quinine [kinin] *nf* quinine.

quinquagénaire [kɛ̃kaʒenɛr] *nmf* fifty year old.

quinquennal, e, aux [kɛ̃kenal, o] *adj* [plan] five-year *(avant n)* ; [élection] five-yearly.

quintal, aux [kɛ̃tal, o] *nm* quintal.

quinte [kɛ̃t] *nf* MUS fifth. ◆ **quinte de toux** *nf* coughing fit.

quintuple [kɛ̃typl] *nm & adj* quintuple.

quinzaine [kɛ̃zɛn] *nf* - **1.** [nombre] fifteen (or so) ; **une ~ de** about fifteen - **2.** [deux semaines] fortnight *Br*, two weeks *(pl)*.

quinze [kɛ̃z] ◇ *adj num* fifteen ; **dans ~ jours** in a fortnight *Br*, in two weeks. ◇ *nm* [chiffre] fifteen ; *voir aussi* **six**.

quinzième [kɛ̃zjɛm] *adj num*, *nm* OU *nmf* fifteenth ; *voir aussi* **sixième**.

quiproquo [kiprɔko] *nm* misunderstanding.

quittance [kitɑ̃s] *nf* receipt.

quitte [kit] *adj* quits ; **en être ~ pour qqch/pour faire qqch** to get off with sthg/doing sthg ; **~ à faire qqch** even if it means doing sthg.

quitter [3] [kite] *vt* - **1.** [gén] to leave ; **ne quittez pas!** [au téléphone] hold the line, please! - **2.** [fonctions] to give up. ◆ **se quitter** *vp* to part.

qui-vive [kiviv] *nm inv* : **être sur le ~** to be on the alert.

quoi [kwa] ◇ *pron rel (après prép)* : **ce à ~ je me suis intéressé** what I was interested in ; **c'est en ~ vous avez tort** that's where you're wrong ; **après ~** after which ; **avoir de ~ vivre** to have enough to live on ; **avez-vous de ~ écrire?** have you got something to write with? ; **merci — il n'y a pas de ~** thank you — don't mention it. ◇ *pron interr* what ; **à ~ penses-tu?** what are you thinking about? ; **je ne sais pas ~ dire** I don't know what to say ; **à ~ bon?** what's the point OU use? ; **~ de neuf?** what's new? ; **décide-toi, ~!** *fam* make your mind up, will you? ; **tu viens ou ~?** *fam* are you coming or what? ◆ **quoi que** *loc conj (+ subjonctif)* whatever ; **~ qu'il arrive** whatever happens ; **~ qu'il dise** whatever he says ; **~ qu'il en soit** be that as it may.

quoique [kwakə] *conj* although, though.

quolibet [kɔlibɛ] *nm sout* jeer, taunt.

quota [k(w)ɔta] *nm* quota.

quotidien, enne [kɔtidjɛ̃, ɛn] *adj* daily. ◆ **quotidien** *nm* - **1.** [routine] daily life ; **au ~** on a day-to-day basis - **2.** [journal] daily (newspaper).

quotient [kɔsjɑ̃] *nm* quotient ; **~ intellectuel** intelligence quotient.

r¹, R [ɛr] *nm inv* [lettre] r, R.

r² *abr de* **rue**.

rabâcher [3] [rabaʃe] ◇ *vi fam* to harp on. ◇ *vt* to go over (and over).

rabais [rabɛ] *nm* reduction, discount ; **au ~** *péj* [artiste] third-rate ; [travailler] for a pittance.

rabaisser [4] [rabese] *vt* - **1.** [réduire] to reduce ; [orgueil] to humble - **2.** [personne] to belittle. ◆ **se rabaisser** *vp* - **1.** [se déprécier] to belittle o.s. - **2.** [s'humilier] : **se ~ à faire qqch** to demean o.s. by doing sthg.

rabat [raba] *nm* [partie rabattue] flap.

rabat-joie [rabaʒwa] ◇ *nm inv* killjoy. ◇ *adj inv* : **être ~** to be a killjoy.

rabattre [83] [rabatr] *vt* - **1.** [col] to turn down - **2.** [siège] to tilt back ; [couvercle] to shut - **3.** [gibier] to drive. ◆ **se rabattre** *vp* - **1.** [siège] to tilt back ; [couvercle] to shut - **2.** [voiture, coureur] to cut in - **3.** [se contenter] : **se ~ sur** to fall back on.

rabattu, e [rabaty] *pp* ⊳ **rabattre**.

rabbin [rabɛ̃] *nm* rabbi.

râble [rabl] *nm* [de lapin] back ; CULIN saddle.

râblé, e [rable] *adj* stocky.

rabot [rabo] *nm* plane.

raboter [3] [rabɔte] *vt* to plane.

rabougri, e [rabugri] *adj* - **1.** [plante] stunted - **2.** [personne] shrivelled, wizened.

rabrouer [3] [rabrue] *vt* to snub.

raccommodage [rakɔmɔdaʒ] *nm* mending.

raccommoder [3] [rakɔmɔde] *vt* - **1.** [vêtement] to mend - **2.** *fam fig* [personnes] to reconcile, to get back together.

raccompagner [3] [rakɔ̃paɲe] *vt* to see home, to take home.

raccord [rakɔr] *nm* - **1.** [liaison] join - **2.** [pièce] connector, coupling - **3.** CIN link.

raccordement [rakɔrdəmɑ̃] *nm* connection, linking.

raccorder [3] [rakɔrde] *vt* : **~ qqch (à)** to connect sthg (to), to join sthg (to). ◆ **se raccorder** *vp* : **se ~ à** to be connected to ; *fig* [faits] to tie in with.

raccourci [rakursi] *nm* shortcut.

raccourcir [32] [rakursir] ⬦ vt to shorten. ⬦ vi to grow shorter.

raccrocher [3] [rakrɔʃe] ⬦ vt to hang back up. ⬦ vi [au téléphone] : ~ **(au nez de qqn)** to hang up (on sb), to put the phone down (on sb). ➡ **se raccrocher** vp : se ~ à to cling to, to hang on to.

race [ras] nf [humaine] race ; [animale] breed ; **de ~** pedigree ; [cheval] thoroughbred.

racé, e [rase] adj - **1.** [animal] purebred - **2.** [voiture] of distinction.

rachat [raʃa] nm - **1.** [transaction] repurchase - **2.** fig [de péchés] atonement.

racheter [28] [raʃte] vt - **1.** [acheter en plus - gén] to buy another ; [- pain, lait] to buy some more - **2.** [acheter d'occasion] to buy - **3.** [acheter après avoir vendu] to buy back - **4.** fig [péché, faute] to atone for ; [défaut, lapsus] to make up for - **5.** [prisonnier] to ransom - **6.** [honneur] to redeem - **7.** COMM [société] to buy out. ➡ **se racheter** vp fig to redeem o.s.

rachitique [raʃitik] adj suffering from rickets.

racial, e, aux [rasjal, o] adj racial.

racine [rasin] nf root ; [de nez] base ; **~ carrée/cubique** MATHS square/cube root.

racisme [rasism] nm racism.

raciste [rasist] nmf & adj racist.

racketter [4] [rakɛte] vt : ~ **qqn** to subject sb to a protection racket.

raclée [rakle] nf fam hiding, thrashing.

racler [3] [rakle] vt to scrape. ➡ **se racler** vp : se ~ **la gorge** to clear one's throat.

raclette [raklɛt] nf CULIN melted Swiss cheese served with jacket potatoes.

racoler [3] [rakɔle] vt fam péj [suj : commerçant] to tout for ; [suj : prostituée] to solicit.

racoleur, euse [rakɔlœr, øz] adj fam péj [air, sourire] come-hither ; [publicité] strident.

racontar [rakɔ̃tar] nm fam péj piece of gossip. ➡ **racontars** nmpl fam péj tittle-tattle (U).

raconter [3] [rakɔ̃te] vt - **1.** [histoire] to tell, to relate ; [événement] to relate, to tell about ; ~ **qqch à qqn** to tell sb sthg, to relate sthg to sb - **2.** [ragot, mensonge] to tell ; **qu'est-ce que tu racontes?** what are you on about?

radar [radar] nm radar.

rade [rad] nf (natural) harbour Br ou harbor Am.

radeau, x [rado] nm [embarcation] raft.

radiateur [radjatœr] nm radiator.

radiation [radjasjɔ̃] nf - **1.** PHYS radiation - **2.** [de liste, du barreau] striking off.

radical, e, aux [radikal, o] adj radical. ➡ **radical** nm - **1.** [gén] radical - **2.** LING stem.

radier [9] [radje] vt to strike off.

radieux, euse [radjø, øz] adj radiant ; [soleil] dazzling.

radin, e [radɛ̃, in] fam péj ⬦ adj stingy. ⬦ nm, f skinflint.

radio [radjo] ⬦ nf - **1.** [station, poste] radio ; **à la ~** on the radio - **2.** MÉD : **passer une ~** to have an X-ray, to be X-rayed. ⬦ nm radio operator.

radioactif, ive [radjoaktif, iv] adj radioactive.

radioactivité [radjoaktivite] nf radioactivity.

radiodiffuser [3] [radjodifyze] vt to broadcast.

radiographie [radjografi] nf - **1.** [technique] radiography - **2.** [image] X-ray.

radiologue [radjɔlɔg], **radiologiste** [radjɔlɔʒist] nmf radiologist.

radioréveil, radio réveil [radjorevɛj] nm radio alarm, clock radio.

radiotélévisé, e [radjotelevize] adj broadcast on both radio and television.

radis [radi] nm radish.

radium [radjɔm] nm radium.

radoter [3] [radɔte] vi to ramble.

radoucir [32] [radusir] vt to soften. ➡ **se radoucir** vp [temps] to become milder ; [personne] to calm down.

radoucissement [radusismɑ̃] nm - **1.** [d'attitude] softening - **2.** [de température] rise ; **un ~ du temps** a spell of milder weather.

rafale [rafal] nf - **1.** [de vent] gust ; **en ~s** in gusts ou bursts - **2.** [de coups de feu, d'applaudissements] burst.

raffermir [32] [rafermir] vt - **1.** [muscle] to firm up - **2.** fig [pouvoir] to strengthen.

raffinage [rafinaʒ] nm refining.

raffiné, e [rafine] adj refined.

raffinement [rafinmɑ̃] nm refinement.

raffiner [3] [rafine] vt to refine.

raffinerie [rafinri] nf refinery.

raffoler [3] [rafɔle] vi : ~ **de qqn/qqch** to adore sb/sthg.

raffut [rafy] nm fam row, racket.

rafistoler [3] [rafistɔle] vt fam to patch up.

rafle [rafl] nf raid.

rafler [3] [rafle] vt to swipe.

rafraîchir [32] [rafreʃir] vt - **1.** [nourriture, vin] to chill, to cool ; [air] to cool - **2.** [vêtement, appartement] to smarten up ; *fig* [mémoire, idées] to refresh ; [connaissances] to brush up. ◆ **se rafraîchir** *vp* - 1. [se refroidir] to cool (down) - 2. [en buvant] to have a drink.

rafraîchissant, e [rafreʃisɑ̃, ɑ̃t] *adj* refreshing.

rafraîchissement [rafreʃismɑ̃] *nm* - 1. [de climat] cooling - 2. [boisson] cold drink.

raft(ing) [raft(iŋ)] *nm* whitewater rafting.

ragaillardir [32] [ragajardir] *vt fam* to buck up, to perk up.

rage [raʒ] *nf* - 1. [fureur] rage ; **faire ~** [tempête] to rage - 2. [maladie] rabies *(U)*. ◆ **rage de dents** *nf* (raging) toothache.

rager [17] [raʒe] *vi fam* to fume.

rageur, euse [raʒœr, øz] *adj* bad-tempered.

raglan [raglɑ̃] *adj inv* raglan *(avant n)*.

ragot [rago] *nm (gén pl) fam* (malicious) rumour *Br* ou rumor *Am*, tittle-tattle *(U)*.

ragoût [ragu] *nm* stew.

rai [rɛ] *nm littéraire* [de soleil] ray.

raid [rɛd] *nm* AÉRON, BOURSE & MIL raid ; **~ aérien** air raid.

raide [rɛd] ◇ *adj* - 1. [cheveux] straight - 2. [tendu - corde] taut ; [- membre, cou] stiff - 3. [pente] steep - 4. [personne - attitude physique] stiff, starchy ; [- caractère] inflexible - 5. *fam* [histoire] hard to swallow, far-fetched - 6. *fam* [chanson] rude, blue - 7. *fam* [sans le sou] broke. ◇ *adv* - 1. [abruptement] steeply - 2. *loc* : **tomber ~ mort** to fall down dead.

raideur [rɛdœr] *nf* - 1. [de membre] stiffness - 2. [de personne - attitude physique] stiffness, starchiness ; [- caractère] inflexibility.

raidir [32] [rɛdir] *vt* [muscle] to tense ; [corde] to tighten, to tauten. ◆ **se raidir** *vp* - 1. [se contracter] to grow stiff, to stiffen - 2. *fig* [résister] : **se ~ contre** to steel o.s. against.

raie [rɛ] *nf* - 1. [rayure] stripe - 2. [dans les cheveux] parting *Br*, part *Am* - 3. [des fesses] crack - 4. [poisson] skate.

rail [raj] *nm* rail.

raillerie [rajri] *nf sout* mockery *(U)*.

railleur, euse [rajœr, øz] *sout* ◇ *adj* mocking. ◇ *nm, f* scoffer.

rainure [renyr] *nf* [longue] groove, channel ; [courte] slot.

raisin [rezɛ̃] *nm* [fruit] grapes *(pl)*.

raison [rezɔ̃] *nf* - 1. [gén] reason ; **à plus forte ~** all the more (so) ; **se faire une ~** to

resign o.s. ; **~ de plus pour faire qqch** all the more reason to do sthg - 2. [justesse, équité] : **avoir ~** to be right ; **avoir ~ de faire qqch** to be right to do sthg ; **donner ~ à qqn** to prove sb right. ◆ **à raison de** *loc prép* at (the rate of). ◆ **en raison de** *loc prép* owing to, because of.

raisonnable [rezɔnabl] *adj* reasonable.

raisonnement [rezɔnmɑ̃] *nm* - 1. [faculté] reason, power of reasoning - 2. [argumentation] reasoning, argument.

raisonner [3] [rezɔne] ◇ *vt* [personne] to reason with. ◇ *vi* - 1. [penser] to reason - 2. [discuter] : **~ avec** to reason with.

rajeunir [32] [raʒœnir] ◇ *vt* - 1. [suj : couleur, vêtement] : **~ qqn** to make sb look younger - 2. [suj : personne] : **~ qqn de trois ans** to take three years off sb's age - 3. [vêtement, canapé] to renovate, to do up ; [meubles] to modernize - 4. *fig* [parti] to rejuvenate. ◇ *vi* [personne] to look younger ; [se sentir plus jeune] to feel younger ou rejuvenated.

rajouter [3] [raʒute] *vt* to add ; **en ~** *fam* to exaggerate.

rajuster [raʒyste], **réajuster** [3] [reaʒyste] *vt* to adjust ; [cravate] to straighten. ◆ **se rajuster** *vp* to straighten one's clothes.

râle [ral] *nm* moan ; [de mort] death rattle.

ralenti, e [ralɑ̃ti] *adj* slow. ◆ **ralenti** *nm* - 1. AUTOM idling speed ; **tourner au ~** AUTOM to idle ; *fig* to tick over *Br* - 2. CIN slow motion.

ralentir [32] [ralɑ̃tir] ◇ *vt* - 1. [allure, expansion] to slow (down) - 2. [rythme] to slacken. ◇ *vi* to slow down ou up.

ralentissement [ralɑ̃tismɑ̃] *nm* - 1. [d'allure, d'expansion] slowing (down) - 2. [de rythme] slackening - 3. [embouteillage] hold-up - 4. PHYS deceleration.

râler [3] [rale] *vi* - 1. [malade] to breathe with difficulty - 2. *fam* [grogner] to moan.

ralliement [ralimɑ̃] *nm* rallying.

rallier [9] [ralje] *vt* - 1. [poste, parti] to join - 2. [suffrages] to win - 3. [troupes] to rally. ◆ **se rallier** *vp* to rally ; **se ~ à** [parti] to join ; [cause] to rally to ; [avis] to come round to.

rallonge [ralɔ̃ʒ] *nf* - 1. [de table] leaf, extension - 2. [électrique] extension (lead).

rallonger [17] [ralɔ̃ʒe] ◇ *vt* to lengthen. ◇ *vi* to lengthen, to get longer.

rallumer [3] [ralyme] *vt* - 1. [feu, cigarette] to relight ; *fig* [querelle] to revive - 2. [appareil, lumière électrique] to switch (back) on again.

rallye [rali] *nm* rally.

ramadan [ramadã] *nm* Ramadan.

ramassage [ramasaʒ] *nm* collection ; ~ **scolaire** [action] pick-up (of school children) ; [service] school bus.

ramasser [3] [ramase] *vt* - **1.** [récolter, réunir] to gather, to collect ; *fig* [forces] to gather - **2.** [prendre] to pick up - **3.** *fam* [claque, rhume] to get. ◆ **se ramasser** *vp* - **1.** [se replier] to crouch - **2.** *fam* [tomber, échouer] to come a cropper.

rambarde [rɑ̃bard] *nf* (guard) rail.

rame [ram] *nf* - **1.** [aviron] oar - **2.** RAIL train - **3.** [de papier] ream.

rameau, x [ramo] *nm* branch.

ramener [19] [ramne] *vt* - **1.** [remmener] to take back - **2.** [rapporter, restaurer] to bring back - **3.** [réduire] : ~ **qqch à qqch** to reduce sthg to sthg, to bring sthg down to sthg.

ramer [3] [rame] *vi* [rameur] to row.

rameur, euse [ramœr, øz] *nm, f* rower.

ramification [ramifikasjɔ̃] *nf* [division] branch.

ramolli, e [ramɔli] *adj* soft ; *fig* soft (in the head).

ramollir [32] [ramɔlir] *vt* - **1.** [beurre] to soften - **2.** *fam fig* [ardeurs] to cool. ◆ **se ramollir** *vp* - **1.** [beurre] to go soft, to soften - **2.** *fam fig* [courage] to weaken.

ramoner [3] [ramone] *vt* to sweep.

ramoneur [ramɔnœr] *nm* (chimney) sweep.

rampant, e [rɑ̃pɑ̃, ɑ̃t] *adj* - **1.** [animal] crawling - **2.** [plante] creeping.

rampe [rɑ̃p] *nf* - **1.** [d'escalier] banister, handrail - **2.** [d'accès] ramp ; ~ **de lancement** launch pad - **3.** THÉÂTRE : **la ~** the footlights *(pl)*.

ramper [3] [rɑ̃pe] *vi* - **1.** [animal, soldat, enfant] to crawl - **2.** [plante] to creep.

rance [rɑ̃s] *adj* [beurre] rancid.

rancir [32] [rɑ̃sir] *vi* to go rancid.

rancœur [rɑ̃kœr] *nf* rancour *Br*, rancor *Am*, resentment.

rançon [rɑ̃sɔ̃] *nf* ransom ; *fig* price.

rancune [rɑ̃kyn] *nf* rancour *Br*, rancor *Am*, spite ; **garder** OU **tenir ~ à qqn de qqch** to hold a grudge against sb for sthg ; **sans ~!** no hard feelings!

rancunier, ère [rɑ̃kynje, ɛr] *adj* vindictive, spiteful.

randonnée [rɑ̃dɔne] *nf* - **1.** [promenade - à pied] walk ; [- à cheval, à bicyclette] ride ; [- en voiture] drive - **2.** [activité] : **la ~** [à pied] walking ; [à cheval] riding.

randonneur, euse [rɑ̃dɔnœr, øz] *nm, f* walker, rambler.

rang [rɑ̃] *nm* - **1.** [d'objets, de personnes] row ; **se mettre en ~ par deux** to line up in twos - **2.** MIL rank - **3.** [position sociale] station - **4.** *Can* [peuplement rural] rural district - **5.** *Can* [chemin] country road.

rangé, e [rɑ̃ʒe] *adj* [sérieux] well-ordered, well-behaved.

rangée [rɑ̃ʒe] *nf* row.

rangement [rɑ̃ʒmɑ̃] *nm* tidying up.

ranger [17] [rɑ̃ʒe] *vt* - **1.** [chambre] to tidy - **2.** [objets] to arrange - **3.** [voiture] to park - **4.** *fig* [livre, auteur] : ~ **parmi** to rank among. ◆ **se ranger** *vp* - **1.** [élèves, soldats] to line up - **2.** [voiture] to pull in - **3.** [piéton] to step aside - **4.** [s'assagir] to settle down - **5.** *fig* [se rallier] : **se ~ à** to go along with.

ranimer [3] [ranime] *vt* - **1.** [personne] to revive, to bring round - **2.** [feu] to rekindle - **3.** *fig* [sentiment] to reawaken.

rap [rap] *nm* rap (music).

rapace [rapas] ◇ *nm* bird of prey. ◇ *adj* [cupide] rapacious, grasping.

rapatrier [10] [rapatrije] *vt* to repatriate.

râpe [rɑp] *nf* - **1.** [de cuisine] grater - **2.** *Helv fam* [avare] miser, skinflint.

râpé, e [rape] *adj* - **1.** CULIN grated - **2.** [manteau] threadbare - **3.** *fam* [raté] : **c'est ~!** we've had it!

râper [3] [rape] *vt* CULIN to grate.

râpeux, euse [rapø, øz] *adj* - **1.** [tissu] rough - **2.** [vin] harsh.

rapide [rapid] ◇ *adj* - **1.** [gén] rapid - **2.** [train, coureur] fast - **3.** [musique, intelligence] lively, quick. ◇ *nm* - **1.** [train] express (train) - **2.** [de fleuve] rapid.

rapidement [rapidmɑ̃] *adv* rapidly.

rapidité [rapidite] *nf* rapidity.

rapiécer [20] [rapjese] *vt* to patch.

rappel [rapel] *nm* - **1.** [de réservistes, d'ambassadeur] recall - **2.** [souvenir] reminder ; ~ **à l'ordre** call to order - **3.** [de paiement] back pay - **4.** [de vaccination] booster - **5.** [au spectacle] curtain call, encore - **6.** SPORT abseiling ; **descendre en ~** to abseil (down).

rappeler [24] [raple] *vt* - **1.** [gén] to call back ; ~ **qqn à qqch** *fig* to bring sb back to sthg - **2.** [faire penser à] : ~ **qqch à qqn** to remind sb of sthg ; **ça me rappelle les vacances** it reminds me of my holidays. ◆ **se rappeler** *vp* to remember.

rapport [rapɔr] *nm* - **1.** [corrélation] link, connection - **2.** [compte-rendu] report - **3.** [profit] return, yield - **4.** MATHS ratio. ◆ **rapports** *nmpl* - **1.** [relations] relations - **2.** [sexuels] : ~**s (sexuels)** intercourse *(sg)*.

par rapport à *loc prép* in comparison to, compared with.

rapporter [3] [rapɔrte] *vt* to bring back.
➡ **se rapporter** *vp* : **se ~ à** to refer ou relate to.

rapporteur, euse [rapɔrtœr, øz] <> *adj* sneaky, telltale *(avant n)*. <> *nm, f* sneak, telltale. ➡ **rapporteur** *nm* - **1.** [de commission] rapporteur - **2.** GÉOM protractor.

rapprochement [raprɔʃmɑ̃] *nm* - **1.** [d'objets, de personnes] bringing together - **2.** *fig* [entre événements] link, connection - **3.** *fig* [de pays, de parti] rapprochement, coming together.

rapprocher [3] [raprɔʃe] *vt* - **1.** [mettre plus près] : **~ qqn/qqch de qqch** to bring sb/ sthg nearer to sthg, to bring sb/sthg closer to sthg - **2.** *fig* [personnes] to bring together - **3.** *fig* [idée, texte] : **~ qqch (de)** to compare sthg (with). ➡ **se rapprocher** *vp* - **1.** [approcher] : **se ~ (de qqn/qqch)** to approach (sb/sthg) - **2.** [se ressembler] : **se ~ de qqch** to be similar to sthg - **3.** [se réconcilier] : **se ~ de qqn** to become closer to sb.

rapt [rapt] *nm* abduction.

raquette [rakɛt] *nf* - **1.** [de tennis, de squash] racket ; [de ping-pong] bat - **2.** [à neige] snowshoe.

rare [rar] *adj* - **1.** [peu commun, peu fréquent] rare ; **ses ~s amis** his few friends - **2.** [peu dense] sparse - **3.** [surprenant] unusual, surprising.

raréfier [9] [rarefje] *vt* to rarefy. ➡ **se raréfier** *vp* to become rarefied.

rarement [rarmɑ̃] *adv* rarely.

rareté [rarte] *nf* - **1.** [de denrées, de nouvelles] scarcity - **2.** [de visites, de lettres] infrequency - **3.** [objet précieux] rarity.

ras, e [ra, raz] *adj* - **1.** [herbe, poil] short - **2.** [mesure] full. ➡ **ras** *adv* short ; **à ~ de** level with ; **en avoir ~ le bol** *fam* to be fed up.

rasade [razad] *nf* glassful.

rasage [razaʒ] *nm* shaving.

rasant, e [razɑ̃, ɑ̃t] *adj* - **1.** [lumière] low-angled - **2.** *fam* [film, discours] boring.

raser [3] [raze] *vt* - **1.** [barbe, cheveux] to shave off - **2.** [mur, sol] to hug - **3.** [village] to raze - **4.** *fam* [personne] to bore. ➡ **se raser** *vp* [avec rasoir] to shave.

ras-le-bol [ralbɔl] *nm inv fam* discontent.

rasoir [razwar] <> *nm* razor ; **~ électrique** electric shaver ; **~ mécanique** safety razor. <> *adj inv fam* boring.

rassasier [9] [rasazje] *vt* to satisfy.

rassemblement [rasɑ̃bləmɑ̃] *nm* - **1.** [d'objets] collecting, gathering - **2.** [foule] crowd, gathering - **3.** [union, parti] union - **4.** MIL parade ; **rassemblement!** fall in!

rassembler [3] [rasɑ̃ble] *vt* - **1.** [personnes, documents] to collect, to gather - **2.** [courage] to summon up ; [idées] to collect. ➡ **se rassembler** *vp* - **1.** [manifestants] to assemble - **2.** [famille] to get together.

rasseoir [65] [raswar] ➡ **se rasseoir** *vp* to sit down again.

rasséréner [18] [raserene] *vt sout* to calm down.

rassis, e [rasi, iz] *adj* [pain] stale.

rassurant, e [rasyrɑ̃, ɑ̃t] *adj* reassuring.

rassuré, e [rasyre] *adj* confident, at ease.

rassurer [3] [rasyre] *vt* to reassure.

rat [ra] <> *nm* rat ; **petit ~** *fig* young ballet pupil. <> *adj fam* [avare] mean, stingy.

ratatiné, e [ratatine] *adj* [fruit, personne] shrivelled.

rate [rat] *nf* - **1.** [animal] female rat - **2.** [organe] spleen.

raté, e [rate] *nm, f* [personne] failure. ➡ **raté** *nm* - **1.** *(gén pl)* AUTOM misfiring *(U)* ; **faire des ~s** to misfire - **2.** *fig* [difficulté] problem.

râteau, x [rato] *nm* rake.

rater [3] [rate] <> *vt* - **1.** [train, occasion] to miss - **2.** [plat, affaire] to make a mess of ; [examen] to fail. <> *vi* to go wrong.

ratification [ratifikasjɔ̃] *nf* ratification.

ratifier [9] [ratifje] *vt* to ratify.

ration [rasjɔ̃] *nf fig* share ; **~ alimentaire** food intake.

rationaliser [3] [rasjɔnalize] *vt* to rationalize.

rationnel, elle [rasjɔnɛl] *adj* rational.

rationnement [rasjɔnmɑ̃] *nm* rationing.

rationner [3] [rasjɔne] *vt* to ration.

ratissage [ratisaʒ] *nm* - **1.** [de jardin] raking - **2.** [de quartier] search.

ratisser [3] [ratise] *vt* - **1.** [jardin] to rake - **2.** [quartier] to search, to comb.

raton [ratɔ̃] *nm* ZOOL young rat. ➡ **raton laveur** *nm* racoon.

RATP *(abr de Régie autonome des transports parisiens) nf* Paris transport authority.

rattacher [3] [rataʃe] *vt* - **1.** [attacher de nouveau] to do up, to fasten again - **2.** [relier] : **~ qqch à** to join sthg to ; *fig* to link sthg with - **3.** [unir] : **~ qqn à** to bind sb to. ➡ **se rattacher** *vp* : **se ~ à** to be linked to.

rattrapage [ratrapaʒ] *nm* - **1.** SCOL : **cours de ~** remedial class - **2.** [de salaires, prix] adjustment.

rattraper [3] [ratrape] *vt* - **1.** [animal, prisonnier] to recapture - **2.** [temps] : **~ le**

temps perdu to make up for lost time - **3.** [rejoindre] to catch up with - **4.** [erreur] to correct - **5.** [personne qui tombe] to catch. ◆ **se rattraper** *vp* - **1.** [se retenir] : **se ~ à qqn/qqch** to catch hold of sb/sthg - **2.** [se faire pardonner] to make amends.

rature [ratyr] *nf* alteration.

rauque [rok] *adj* hoarse, husky.

ravager [17] [ravaʒe] *vt* [gén] to devastate, to ravage.

ravages [ravaʒ] *nmpl* [de troupes] ravages, devastation (*sg*) ; [d'inondation] devastation (*sg*) ; [du temps] ravages.

ravaler [3] [ravale] *vt* - **1.** [façade] to clean, to restore - **2.** [personne] : **~ qqn au rang de** to lower sb to the level of - **3.** *fig* [larmes, colère] to stifle, to hold back.

ravauder [3] [ravode] *vt* to mend, to repair.

ravi, e [ravi] *adj* : **~ (de)** delighted (with) ; **je suis ~ de l'avoir trouvé** I'm delighted that I found it, I'm delighted to have found it ; **~ de vous connaître** pleased to meet you.

ravin [ravɛ̃] *nm* ravine, gully.

raviolis [ravjɔli] *nmpl* ravioli (*U*).

ravir [32] [ravir] *vt* - **1.** [charmer] to delight ; **à ~** beautifully - **2.** *littéraire* [arracher] : **~ qqch à qqn** to rob sb of sthg.

raviser [3] [ravize] ◆ **se raviser** *vp* to change one's mind.

ravissant, e [ravisɑ̃, ɑ̃t] *adj* delightful, beautiful.

ravisseur, euse [raviscer, øz] *nm, f* abductor.

ravitaillement [ravitajmɑ̃] *nm* [en denrées] resupplying ; [en carburant] refuelling.

ravitailler [3] [ravitaje] *vt* [en denrées] to resupply ; [en carburant] to refuel.

raviver [3] [ravive] *vt* - **1.** [feu] to rekindle - **2.** [couleurs] to brighten up - **3.** *fig* [douleur] to revive - **4.** [plaie] to reopen.

rayé, e [reje] *adj* - **1.** [tissu] striped - **2.** [disque, vitre] scratched.

rayer [11] [reje] *vt* - **1.** [disque, vitre] to scratch - **2.** [nom, mot] to cross out.

rayon [rejɔ̃] *nm* - **1.** [de lumière] beam, ray ; *fig* [d'espoir] ray - **2.** (*gén pl*) [radiation] radiation (*U*) ; **~ laser** laser beam ; **~s X** X-rays - **3.** [de roue] spoke - **4.** GÉOM radius ; **dans un ~ de** *fig* within a radius of - **5.** [étagère] shelf - **6.** [dans un magasin] department.

rayonnant, e [rejɔnɑ̃, ɑ̃t] *adj litt & fig* radiant.

rayonnement [rejɔnmɑ̃] *nm* - **1.** [gén] ra-

diance ; [des arts] influence - **2.** PHYS radiation.

rayonner [3] [rejɔne] *vi* - **1.** [soleil] to shine ; **~ de joie** *fig* to radiate happiness - **2.** [culture] to be influential - **3.** [avenues, lignes, chaleur] to radiate - **4.** [touriste] to tour around *(from a base)*.

rayure [rejyr] *nf* - **1.** [sur étoffe] stripe - **2.** [sur disque, sur meuble] scratch.

raz [ra] ◆ **raz de marée** *nm* tidal wave ; POLIT & *fig* landslide.

razzia [razja] *nf fam* raid.

RDA (*abr de* **République démocratique allemande**) *nf* GDR.

RdC *abr de* **rez-de-chaussée**.

ré [re] *nm inv* MUS D ; [chanté] re.

réacteur [reaktœr] *nm* [d'avion] jet engine ; **~ nucléaire** nuclear reactor.

réaction [reaksjɔ̃] *nf* : **~ (à/contre)** reaction (to/against).

réactionnaire [reaksjɔner] *nmf & adj péj* reactionary.

réactiver [3] [reaktive] *vt* to reactivate.

réactualiser [3] [reaktɥalize] *vt* [moderniser] to update, to bring up to date.

réadapter [3] [readapte] *vt* to readapt ; [accidenté] to rehabilitate.

réagir [32] [reaʒir] *vi* : **~ (à/contre)** to react (to/against) ; **~ sur** to affect.

réajuster = **rajuster**.

réalisable [realizabl] *adj* - **1.** [projet] feasible - **2.** FIN realizable.

réalisateur, trice [realizatœr, tris] *nm, f* CIN & TÉLÉ director.

réaliser [3] [realize] *vt* - **1.** [projet] to carry out ; [ambitions, rêves] to achieve, to realize - **2.** CIN & TÉLÉ to produce - **3.** [s'apercevoir de] to realize. ◆ **se réaliser** *vp* - **1.** [ambition] to be realized ; [rêve] to come true - **2.** [personne] to fulfil o.s.

réaliste [realist] ◇ *nmf* realist. ◇ *adj* - **1.** [personne, objectif] realistic - **2.** ART & LITTÉRATURE realist.

réalité [realite] *nf* reality ; **en ~** in reality.

reality-show, reality show [realitiʃo] (*pl* reality(-)shows) *nm* talk show *focussing on real-life drama*.

réaménagement [reamenaʒmɑ̃] *nm* - **1.** [de projet] restructuring - **2.** [de taux d'intérêt] readjustment.

réamorcer [16] [reamɔrse] *vt* to start up again.

réanimation [reanimasjɔ̃] *nf* resuscitation ; **en ~** in intensive care.

réanimer [3] [reanime] *vt* to resuscitate.

réapparaître [91] [reaparetr] *vi* to reappear.

rébarbatif, ive [rebarbatif, iv] *adj* - **1.** [personne, visage] forbidding - **2.** [travail] daunting.

rebâtir [32] [rəbatir] *vt* to rebuild.

rebattu, e [rəbaty] *adj* overworked, hackneyed.

rebelle [rəbɛl] *adj* - **1.** [personne] rebellious ; [troupes] rebel *(avant n)* - **2.** [mèche, boucle] unruly.

rebeller [4] [rəbele] ➡ **se rebeller** *vp* : **se ~ (contre)** to rebel (against).

rébellion [rebeljɔ̃] *nf* rebellion.

rebiffer [3] [rəbife] ➡ **se rebiffer** *vp fam* : **se ~ (contre)** to rebel (against).

reboiser [3] [rəbwaze] *vt* to reafforest.

rebond [rəbɔ̃] *nm* bounce.

rebondir [32] [rəbɔ̃dir] *vi* - **1.** [objet] to bounce ; [contre mur] to rebound - **2.** *fig* [affaire] to come to life (again).

rebondissement [rəbɔ̃dismɑ̃] *nm* [d'affaire] new development.

rebord [rəbɔr] *nm* [de table] edge ; [de fenêtre] sill, ledge.

reboucher [3] [rəbuʃe] *vt* [bouteille] to put the cork back in, to recork ; [trou] to fill in.

rebours [rəbur] ➡ **à rebours** *loc adv* the wrong way ; *fig* the wrong way round, back to front.

reboutonner [3] [rəbutɔne] *vt* to rebutton.

rebrousse-poil [rəbruspwal] ➡ **à rebrousse-poil** *loc adv* the wrong way ; **prendre qqn à ~** *fig* to rub sb up the wrong way.

rebrousser [3] [rəbruse] *vt* to brush back ; **~ chemin** *fig* to retrace one's steps.

rébus [rebys] *nm* rebus.

rebut [rəby] *nm* scrap ; **mettre qqch au ~** to get rid of sthg, to scrap sthg.

rebuter [3] [rəbyte] *vt* [suj : travail] to dishearten.

récalcitrant, e [rekalsitrɑ̃, ɑ̃t] *adj* recalcitrant, stubborn.

recaler [3] [rəkale] *vt fam* to fail.

récapitulatif, ive [rekapitylatif, iv] *adj* summary *(avant n)*. ➡ **récapitulatif** *nm* summary.

récapituler [3] [rekapityle] *vt* to recapitulate, to recap.

recel [rəsɛl] *nm* [action] receiving ou handling stolen goods ; [délit] possession of stolen goods.

receleur, euse [rəsəlœr, øz] *nm, f* receiver *(of stolen goods)*.

récemment [resamɑ̃] *adv* recently.

recensement [rəsɑ̃smɑ̃] *nm* - **1.** [de population] census - **2.** [d'objets] inventory.

recenser [3] [rəsɑ̃se] *vt* - **1.** [population] to take a census of - **2.** [objets] to take an inventory of.

récent, e [resɑ̃, ɑ̃t] *adj* recent.

recentrer [3] [rəsɑ̃tre] *vt* to refocus.

récépissé [resepise] *nm* receipt.

récepteur, trice [reseptœr, tris] *adj* receiving. ➡ **récepteur** *nm* receiver.

réception [resɛpsjɔ̃] *nf* - **1.** [gén] reception ; **donner une ~** to hold a reception - **2.** [de marchandises] receipt - **3.** [bureau] reception (desk) - **4.** SPORT [de sauteur, skieur] landing ; [du ballon, avec la main] catch ; **bonne ~ de X** [avec le pied] X traps the ball.

réceptionner [3] [resɛpsjɔne] *vt* - **1.** [marchandises] to take delivery of - **2.** [SPORT - avec la main] to catch ; [- avec le pied] to control.

réceptionniste [resɛpsjɔnist] *nmf* receptionist.

récession [resesjɔ̃] *nf* recession.

recette [rəsɛt] *nf* - **1.** COMM takings *(pl)* - **2.** CULIN recipe ; *fig* [méthode] recipe, formula.

recevable [rəsəvabl] *adj* - **1.** [excuse, offre] acceptable - **2.** JUR admissible.

receveur, euse [rəsəvœr, øz] *nm, f* - **1.** ADMIN : **~ des impôts** tax collector ; **~ des postes** postmaster *(f* postmistress*)* - **2.** [de bus] conductor *(f* conductress*)* - **3.** [de greffe] recipient.

recevoir [52] [rəsəvwar] *vt* - **1.** [gén] to receive - **2.** [coup] to get, to receive - **3.** [invités] to entertain ; [client] to see - **4.** SCOL. & UNIV : **être reçu à un examen** to pass an exam. ➡ **se recevoir** *vp* SPORT to land.

rechange [rəʃɑ̃ʒ] ➡ **de rechange** *loc adj* spare ; *fig* alternative.

réchapper [3] [reʃape] *vi* : **~ de** to survive.

recharge [rəʃarʒ] *nf* [cartouche] refill.

rechargeable [rəʃarʒabl] *adj* [batterie] rechargeable ; [briquet] refillable.

réchaud [reʃo] *nm* (portable) stove.

réchauffé, e [reʃofe] *adj* [plat] reheated ; *fig* rehashed.

réchauffement [reʃofmɑ̃] *nm* warming (up).

réchauffer [3] [reʃofe] *vt* - **1.** [nourriture] to reheat - **2.** [personne] to warm up. ➡ **se réchauffer** *vp* to warm up.

rêche [rɛʃ] *adj* rough.

recherche [rəʃɛrʃ] *nf* - **1.** [quête & INFORM] search ; **être à la ~ de** to be in search of ; **faire** OU **effectuer des ~s** to make inquiries - **2.** SCIENCE research ; **faire de la ~** to do research - **3.** [raffinement] elegance.

recherché, e [rəʃɛrʃe] *adj* - **1.** [ouvrage] sought-after - **2.** [raffiné - vocabulaire] refined ; [- mets] exquisite.

rechercher [3] [rəʃɛrʃe] *vt* - **1.** [objet, personne] to search for, to hunt for - **2.** [compagnie] to seek out.

rechigner [3] [rəʃiɲe] *vi* : **~ à** to balk at.

rechute [rəʃyt] *nf* relapse.

récidive [residiv] *nf* - **1.** JUR repeat offence *Br* OU offense *Am* - **2.** MÉD recurrence.

récidiver [3] [residive] *vi* - **1.** JUR to commit another offence *Br* OU offense *Am* - **2.** MÉD to recur.

récidiviste [residivist] *nmf* repeat OU persistent offender.

récif [resif] *nm* reef.

récipient [resipjɑ̃] *nm* container.

réciproque [resiprɔk] <> *adj* reciprocal. <> *nf* : **la ~** the reverse.

réciproquement [resiprɔkmɑ̃] *adv* mutually ; **et ~** and vice versa.

récit [resi] *nm* story.

récital, als [resital] *nm* recital.

récitation [resitasjɔ̃] *nf* recitation.

réciter [3] [resite] *vt* to recite.

réclamation [reklamasjɔ̃] *nf* complaint ; **faire/déposer une ~** to make/lodge a complaint.

réclame [reklam] *nf* - **1.** [annonce] advert, advertisement - **2.** [publicité] : **la ~** advertising - **3.** [promotion] : **en ~** on special offer.

réclamer [3] [reklame] *vt* - **1.** [demander] to ask for, to request ; [avec insistance] to demand - **2.** [nécessiter] to require, to demand.

reclasser [3] [rəklase] *vt* - **1.** [dossiers] to refile - **2.** ADMIN to regrade.

réclusion [reklyzjɔ̃] *nf* imprisonment ; **~ à perpétuité** life imprisonment.

recoiffer [3] [rəkwafe] **➞ se recoiffer** *vp* to do one's hair again.

recoin [rəkwɛ̃] *nm* nook.

recoller [3] [rəkɔle] *vt* [objet brisé] to stick back together.

récolte [rekɔlt] *nf* - **1.** [AGRIC - action] harvesting *(U)*, gathering *(U)* ; [- produit] harvest, crop - **2.** *fig* collection.

récolter [3] [rekɔlte] *vt* to harvest ; *fig* to collect.

recommandable [rəkɔmɑ̃dabl] *adj* commendable ; **peu ~** undesirable.

recommandation [rəkɔmɑ̃dasjɔ̃] *nf* recommendation.

recommandé, e [rəkɔmɑ̃de] *adj* - **1.** [envoi] registered ; **envoyer qqch en ~** to send sthg by registered post *Br* OU mail *Am* - **2.** [conseillé] advisable.

recommander [3] [rəkɔmɑ̃de] *vt* to recommend ; **~ à qqn de faire qqch** to advise sb to do sthg ; **~ qqn à qqn** to recommend sb to sb.

recommencer [16] [rəkɔmɑ̃se] <> *vt* [travail] to start OU begin again ; [erreur] to make again ; **~ à faire qqch** to start OU begin doing sthg again. <> *vi* to start OU begin again ; **ne recommence pas!** don't do that again!

récompense [rekɔ̃pɑ̃s] *nf* reward.

récompenser [3] [rekɔ̃pɑ̃se] *vt* to reward.

recompter [3] [rəkɔ̃te] *vt* to recount.

réconciliation [rekɔ̃siljasjɔ̃] *nf* reconciliation.

réconcilier [9] [rekɔ̃silje] *vt* to reconcile.

reconduire [98] [rəkɔ̃dɥir] *vt* - **1.** [personne] to accompany, to take - **2.** [politique, bail] to renew.

reconduit, e [rəkɔ̃dɥi, it] *pp* ➞ **reconduire**.

réconfort [rekɔ̃fɔr] *nm* comfort.

réconfortant, e [rekɔ̃fɔrtɑ̃, ɑ̃t] *adj* comforting.

réconforter [3] [rekɔ̃fɔrte] *vt* to comfort.

reconnaissable [rəkɔnɛsabl] *adj* recognizable.

reconnaissance [rəkɔnɛsɑ̃s] *nf* - **1.** [gén] recognition - **2.** MIL reconnaissance ; **aller/partir en ~** to go out on reconnaissance - **3.** [gratitude] gratitude ; **exprimer sa ~ à qqn** to show OU express one's gratitude to sb.

reconnaissant, e [rəkɔnɛsɑ̃, ɑ̃t] *adj* grateful ; **je vous serais ~ de m'aider** I would be grateful if you would help me.

reconnaître [91] [rəkɔnɛtr] *vt* - **1.** [gén] to recognize - **2.** [erreur] to admit, to acknowledge - **3.** MIL to reconnoitre.

reconnu, e [rəkɔny] <> *pp* ➞ **reconnaître**. <> *adj* well-known.

reconquérir [39] [rəkɔ̃kerir] *vt* to reconquer.

reconquis, e [rəkɔ̃ki, iz] *pp* ➞ **reconquérir**.

reconsidérer [18] [rəkɔ̃sidere] *vt* to reconsider.

reconstituant, e [rəkɔ̃stitɥɑ̃, ɑ̃t] *adj* invigorating. **➞ reconstituant** *nm* tonic.

reconstituer [7] [rəkɔ̃stitɥe] *vt* - **1.** [puzzle] to put together - **2.** [crime, délit] to reconstruct.

reconstitution [rəkɔ̃stitysjɔ̃] *nf* - **1.** [de

puzzle] putting together - **2.** [de crime, délit] reconstruction.

reconstruction [rəkɔ̃stryksjɔ̃] *nf* reconstruction, rebuilding.

reconstruire [98] [rəkɔ̃strɥir] *vt* to reconstruct, to rebuild.

reconstruit, e [rəkɔ̃strɥi, it] *pp* ▷ reconstruire.

reconversion [rəkɔ̃vɛrsjɔ̃] *nf* - **1.** [d'employé] redeployment - **2.** [d'usine, de société] conversion ; ~ **économique/technique** economic/technical restructuring.

reconvertir [32] [rəkɔ̃vɛrtir] *vt* - **1.** [employé] to redeploy - **2.** [économie] to restructure. ◆ **se reconvertir** *vp* : **se ~ dans** to move into.

recopier [9] [rəkɔpje] *vt* to copy out.

record [rəkɔr] ◇ *nm* record ; **détenir/améliorer/battre un ~** to hold/improve/beat a record. ◇ *adj inv* record *(avant n)*.

recoucher [3] [rəkuʃe] *vt* to put back to bed. ◆ **se recoucher** *vp* to go back to bed.

recoudre [86] [rəkudr] *vt* to sew (up) again.

recoupement [rəkupmɑ̃] *nm* crosscheck ; **par ~** by cross-checking.

recouper [3] [rəkupe] *vt* - **1.** [pain] to cut again - **2.** COUTURE to recut - **3.** *fig* [témoignages] to compare, to cross-check. ◆ **se recouper** *vp* - **1.** [lignes] to intersect - **2.** [témoignages] to match up.

recourir [45] [rəkurir] *vi* : **~ à** [médecin, agence] to turn to ; [force, mensonge] to resort to.

recours [rəkur] *nm* - **1.** [emploi] : **avoir ~ à** [médecin, agence] to turn to ; [force, mensonge] to resort to, to have recourse to - **2.** [solution] solution, way out ; **en dernier ~** as a last resort - **3.** JUR action ; **~ en cassation** appeal.

recouvert, e [rəkuvɛr, ɛrt] *pp* ▷ recouvrir.

recouvrir [34] [rəkuvrir] *vt* - **1.** [gén] to cover ; [fauteuil] to re-cover - **2.** [personne] to cover (up). ◆ **se recouvrir** *vp* - **1.** [tuiles] to overlap - **2.** [surface] : **se ~ (de)** to be covered (with).

recracher [3] [rəkraʃe] *vt* to spit out.

récréatif, ive [rekreatif, iv] *adj* entertaining.

récréation [rekreasjɔ̃] *nf* - **1.** [détente] relaxation, recreation - **2.** SCOL break.

recréer [15] [rəkree] *vt* to recreate.

récrimination [rekriminasjɔ̃] *nf* complaint.

récrire [rekrir], **réécrire** [99] [reekrir] *vt* to rewrite.

recroqueviller [3] [rəkrɔkvije] ◆ **se recroqueviller** *vp* to curl up.

recru, e [rəkry] *adj* : **~ de fatigue** *littéraire* exhausted. ◆ **recrue** *nf* recruit.

recrudescence [rəkrydɛsɑ̃s] *nf* renewed outbreak.

recrutement [rəkrytmɑ̃] *nm* recruitment.

recruter [3] [rəkryte] *vt* to recruit.

rectal, e, aux [rɛktal, o] *adj* rectal.

rectangle [rɛktɑ̃gl] *nm* rectangle.

rectangulaire [rɛktɑ̃gylɛr] *adj* rectangular.

recteur [rɛktœr] *nm* SCOL *chief administrative officer of an education authority*, ≃ (Chief) Education Officer *Br*.

rectificatif, ive [rɛktifikatif, iv] *adj* correcting. ◆ **rectificatif** *nm* correction.

rectification [rɛktifikasjɔ̃] *nf* - **1.** [correction] correction - **2.** [de tir] adjustment.

rectifier [9] [rɛktifje] *vt* - **1.** [tir] to adjust - **2.** [erreur] to rectify, to correct ; [calcul] to correct.

rectiligne [rɛktiliɲ] *adj* rectilinear.

recto [rɛkto] *nm* right side ; **~ verso** on both sides.

rectorat [rɛktɔra] *nm* SCOL *offices of the education authority*, ≃ Education Offices *Br*.

reçu, e [rəsy] *pp* ▷ recevoir. ◆ **reçu** *nm* receipt.

recueil [rəkœj] *nm* collection.

recueillement [rəkœjmɑ̃] *nm* meditation.

recueillir [41] [rəkœjir] *vt* - **1.** [fonds] to collect - **2.** [suffrages] to win - **3.** [enfant] to take in. ◆ **se recueillir** *vp* to meditate.

recul [rəkyl] *nm* - **1.** [mouvement arrière] step backwards ; MIL retreat - **2.** [d'arme à feu] recoil - **3.** [de civilisation] decline ; [d'inflation, de chômage] : **~ (de)** downturn (in) - **4.** *fig* [retrait] : **avec du ~** with hindsight.

reculé, e [rəkyle] *adj* distant.

reculer [3] [rəkyle] ◇ *vt* - **1.** [voiture] to back up - **2.** [date] to put back, to postpone. ◇ *vi* - **1.** [aller en arrière] to move backwards ; [voiture] to reverse ; **ne ~ devant rien** *fig* to stop at nothing - **2.** [maladie, pauvreté] to be brought under control.

reculons [rəkylɔ̃] ◆ **à reculons** *adv* backwards.

récupération [rekyperasjɔ̃] *nf* [de déchets] salvage.

récupérer [18] [rekypere] ◇ *vt* - **1.** [objet] to get back - **2.** [déchets] to salvage

- **3.** [idée] to pick up - **4.** [journée] to make up. ◇ *vi* to recover, to recuperate.

récurer [3] [rekyre] *vt* to scour.

récuser [3] [rekyze] *vt* - **1.** JUR to challenge - **2.** *sout* [refuser] to reject.

recyclage [rəsiklaʒ] *nm* - **1.** [d'employé] retraining - **2.** [de déchets] recycling.

recycler [3] [rəsikle] *vt* - **1.** [employé] to retrain - **2.** [déchets] to recycle. ◆ **se recycler** *vp* [employé] to retrain.

rédacteur, trice [redaktœr, tris] *nm, f* [de journal] subeditor ; [d'ouvrage de référence] editor ; **~ en chef** editor-in-chief.

rédaction [redaksjɔ̃] *nf* - **1.** [de texte] editing - **2.** SCOL essay - **3.** [personnel] editorial staff.

redécouvrir [34] [rədekuvrir] *vt* to rediscover.

redéfinir [32] [rədefinir] *vt* to redefine.

redéfinition [rədefinisjɔ̃] *nf* redefinition.

redemander [3] [rədəmɑ̃de] *vt* to ask again for.

rédemption [redɑ̃psjɔ̃] *nf* redemption.

redescendre [73] [rədesɑ̃dr] ◇ *vt (aux : avoir)* - **1.** [escalier] to go/come down again - **2.** [objet - d'une étagère] to take down again. ◇ *vi (aux : être)* to go/come down again.

redevable [rədəvabl] *adj* : **être ~ de 20 euros à qqn** to owe sb 20 euros ; **être ~ à qqn de qqch** [service] to be indebted to sb for sthg.

redevance [rədəvɑ̃s] *nf* [de radio, télévision] licence fee ; [téléphonique] rental (fee).

rédhibitoire [redibitwar] *adj* [défaut] crippling ; [prix] prohibitive.

rediffusion [rədifyzjɔ̃] *nf* repeat.

rédiger [17] [rediʒe] *vt* to write.

redire [102] [rədir] *vt* to repeat ; **avoir** OU **trouver à ~ à qqch** *fig* to find fault with sthg.

redistribuer [7] [rədistribɥe] *vt* to redistribute.

redit, e [rədi, it] *pp* ⊳ redire.

redite [rədit] *nf* repetition.

redondance [rədɔ̃dɑ̃s] *nf* redundancy.

redonner [3] [rədɔne] *vt* to give back ; [confiance, forces] to restore.

redoublant, e [rədublɑ̃, ɑ̃t] *nm, f* pupil who is repeating a year.

redoubler [3] [rəduble] ◇ *vt* - **1.** [syllabe] to reduplicate - **2.** [efforts] to intensify - **3.** SCOL to repeat. ◇ *vi* to intensify.

redoutable [rədutabl] *adj* formidable.

redouter [3] [rədute] *vt* to fear.

redoux [rədu] *nm* thaw.

redressement [rədrɛsmɑ̃] *nm* - **1.** [de pays, d'économie] recovery - **2.** JUR : **~ fiscal** payment of back taxes.

redresser [4] [rədrɛse] ◇ *vt* - **1.** [poteau, arbre] to put OU set upright ; **~ la tête** to raise one's head ; *fig* to hold up one's head - **2.** [situation] to set right. ◇ *vi* AUTOM to straighten up. ◆ **se redresser** *vp* - **1.** [personne] to stand OU sit straight - **2.** [pays] to recover.

réducteur, trice [redyktœr, tris] *adj* [limitatif] simplistic.

réduction [redyksjɔ̃] *nf* - **1.** [gén] reduction - **2.** MÉD setting.

réduire [98] [redɥir] ◇ *vt* - **1.** [gén] to reduce ; **~ en** to reduce to - **2.** MÉD to set - **3.** *Helv* [ranger] to put away. ◇ *vi* CULIN to reduce.

réduit, e [redɥi, it] ◇ *pp* ⊳ réduire. ◇ *adj* reduced. ◆ **réduit** *nm* [local] small room.

rééchelonner [3] [reeʃlone] *vt* to reschedule.

réécrire = récrire.

réédition [reedisjɔ̃] *nf* new edition.

rééducation [reedykasjɔ̃] *nf* - **1.** [de membre] re-education - **2.** [de délinquant, malade] rehabilitation.

réel, elle [reɛl] *adj* real.

réélection [reelɛksjɔ̃] *nf* re-election.

réellement [reelmɑ̃] *adv* really.

rééquilibrer [3] [reekilibre] *vt* to balance (again).

réessayer [reeseje] [11] *vt* to try again.

réévaluer [7] [reevalɥe] *vt* to revalue.

réexaminer [3] [reɛgzamine] *vt* to re-examine.

réexpédier [9] [reɛkspedje] *vt* to send back.

réf. *(abr de* **référence)** ref.

refaire [109] [rəfɛr] *vt* - **1.** [faire de nouveau - travail, devoir] to do again ; [- voyage] to make again - **2.** [mur, toit] to repair.

refait, e [rəfɛ, ɛt] *pp* ⊳ refaire.

réfection [refɛksjɔ̃] *nf* repair.

réfectoire [refɛktwar] *nm* refectory.

référence [referɑ̃s] *nf* reference ; **faire ~ à** to refer to.

référendum [referɛ̃dɔm] *nm* referendum.

référer [18] [refere] *vi* : **en ~ à qqn** to refer the matter to sb.

refermer [3] [rəfɛrme] *vt* to close OU shut again.

réfléchi, e [refleʃi] *adj* - **1.** [action] considered ; **c'est tout ~** I've made up my mind, I've decided - **2.** [personne] thoughtful - **3.** GRAM reflexive.

réfléchir [32] [refleʃir] ◇ *vt* - **1.** [refléter] to reflect - **2.** [penser] : **~ que** to think OU to reflect that. ◇ *vi* to think, to reflect ; **~ à** OU **sur qqch** to think about sthg.

reflet [rəfle] *nm* - **1.** [image] reflection - **2.** [de lumière] glint.

refléter [18] [rəflete] *vt* to reflect. ◆ **se refléter** *vp* - **1.** [se réfléchir] to be reflected - **2.** [transparaître] to be mirrored.

refleurir [32] [rəflœrir] *vi* [fleurir à nouveau] to flower again.

réflexe [refleks] ◇ *nm* reflex. ◇ *adj* reflex (avant n).

réflexion [refleksjɔ̃] *nf* - **1.** [de lumière, d'ondes] reflection - **2.** [pensée] reflection, thought - **3.** [remarque] remark.

refluer [3] [rəflye] *vi* - **1.** [liquide] to flow back - **2.** [foule] to flow back ; [avec violence] to surge back.

reflux [rəfly] *nm* - **1.** [d'eau] ebb - **2.** [de personnes] backward surge.

refonte [rəfɔ̃t] *nf* - **1.** [de métal] remelting - **2.** [d'ouvrage] recasting - **3.** [d'institution, de système] overhaul, reshaping.

reforestation [rəfɔrɛstasjɔ̃] *nf* reforestation.

réformateur, trice [reformatœr, tris] ◇ *adj* reforming. ◇ *nm, f* - **1.** [personne] reformer - **2.** RELIG Reformer.

réforme [reform] *nf* reform.

réformé, e [reforme] *adj & nm, f* Protestant. ◆ **réformé** *nm* MIL *soldier who has been invalided out.*

reformer [3] [rəforme] *vt* to re-form.

réformer [3] [reforme] *vt* - **1.** [améliorer] to reform, to improve - **2.** MIL to invalid out - **3.** [matériel] to scrap.

réformiste [reformist] *adj & nmf* reformist.

refoulé, e [rəfule] ◇ *adj* repressed, frustrated. ◇ *nm, f* repressed person.

refouler [3] [rəfule] *vt* - **1.** [personnes] to repel, to repulse - **2.** PSYCHOL to repress.

réfractaire [refraktɛr] ◇ *adj* - **1.** [rebelle] insubordinate ; **~ à** resistant to - **2.** [matière] refractory. ◇ *nmf* insubordinate.

refrain [rəfrɛ̃] *nm* MUS refrain, chorus ; **c'est toujours le même ~** *fam fig* it's always the same old story.

refréner [18] [rəfrene] *vt* to check, to hold back.

réfrigérant, e [refriʒerɑ̃, ɑ̃t] *adj* - **1.** [liquide] refrigerating, refrigerant - **2.** *fam* [accueil] icy.

réfrigérateur [refriʒeratœr] *nm* refrigerator.

refroidir [32] [rəfrwadir] ◇ *vt* - **1.** [plat] to cool - **2.** [décourager] to discourage - **3.** *fam* [tuer] to rub out, to do in. ◇ *vi* to cool.

refroidissement [rəfrwadismɑ̃] *nm* - **1.** [de température] drop, cooling - **2.** [grippe] chill.

refuge [rəfyʒ] *nm* - **1.** [abri] refuge - **2.** [de montagne] hut.

réfugié, e [refyʒje] *nm, f* refugee.

réfugier [9] [refyʒje] ◆ **se réfugier** *vp* to take refuge.

refus [rəfy] *nm inv* refusal ; **ce n'est pas de ~** *fam* I wouldn't say no.

refuser [3] [rəfyze] *vt* - **1.** [repousser] to refuse ; **~ de faire qqch** to refuse to do sthg - **2.** [contester] : **~ qqch à qqn** to deny sb sthg - **3.** [clients, spectateurs] to turn away - **4.** [candidat] : **être refusé** to fail. ◆ **se refuser** *vp* : **se ~ à faire qqch** to refuse to do sthg.

réfuter [3] [refyte] *vt* to refute.

regagner [3] [rəgaɲe] *vt* - **1.** [reprendre] to regain, to win back - **2.** [revenir à] to get back to.

regain [rəgɛ̃] *nm* [retour] : **un ~ de** a revival of, a renewal of ; **un ~ de vie** a new lease of life.

régal, als [regal] *nm* treat, delight.

régaler [3] [regale] *vt* to treat ; **c'est moi qui régale!** it's my treat! ◆ **se régaler** *vp* : **je me régale** [nourriture] I'm thoroughly enjoying it ; [activité] I'm having the time of my life.

regard [rəgar] *nm* look.

regardant, e [rəgardɑ̃, ɑ̃t] *adj* - **1.** *fam* [économe] mean - **2.** [minutieux] : **être très/peu ~ sur qqch** to be very/not very particular about sthg.

regarder [3] [rəgarde] ◇ *vt* - **1.** [observer, examiner, consulter] to look at ; [télévision, spectacle] to watch ; **~ qqn faire qqch** to watch sb doing sthg ; **~ les trains passer** to watch the trains go by - **2.** [considérer] to consider, to regard ; **~ qqn/qqch comme** to regard sb/sthg as, to consider sb/sthg as - **3.** [concerner] to concern ; **cela ne te regarde pas** it's none of your business. ◇ *vi* - **1.** [observer, examiner] to look - **2.** [faire attention] : **sans ~** à la dépense regardless of the expense ; **y ~ à deux fois** to think twice about it.

régate [regat] *nf* (gén pl) regatta.

régénérer [18] [reʒenere] *vt* to regenerate. ◆ **se régénérer** *vp* to regenerate.

régent, e [reʒɑ̃, ɑ̃t] *nm, f* regent.

régenter [3] [reʒɑ̃te] vt : **vouloir tout ~** péj to want to be the boss.

reggae [rege] nm & adj inv reggae.

régie [reʒi] nf - **1.** [entreprise] state-controlled company - **2.** RADIO & TÉLÉ [pièce] control room ; CIN, THÉÂTRE & TÉLÉ [équipe] production team.

regimber [3] [rəʒɛ̃be] vi to balk.

régime [reʒim] nm - **1.** [politique] regime - **2.** [administratif] system ; **~ carcéral** prison regime - **3.** [alimentaire] diet ; **se mettre au/suivre un ~** to go on/to be on a diet - **4.** [de moteur] speed - **5.** [de fleuve, des pluies] cycle - **6.** [de bananes, dattes] bunch.

régiment [reʒimɑ̃] nm - **1.** MIL regiment - **2.** fam [grande quantité] : **un ~ de** masses of, loads of.

région [reʒjɔ̃] nf region.

régional, e, aux [reʒjɔnal, o] adj regional.

régir [32] [reʒir] vt to govern.

régisseur [reʒisœr] nm - **1.** [intendant] steward - **2.** [de théâtre] stage manager.

registre [rəʒistr] nm [gén] register ; **~ de comptabilité** ledger.

réglable [reglabl] adj - **1.** [adaptable] adjustable - **2.** [payable] payable.

réglage [reglaʒ] nm adjustment, setting.

règle [rɛgl] nf - **1.** [instrument] ruler - **2.** [principe, loi] rule ; **je suis en ~** my papers are in order. ◆ **en règle générale** loc adv as a general rule. ◆ **règles** nfpl [menstruation] period (sg).

réglé, e [regle] adj [organisé] regular, well-ordered.

règlement [rɛgləmɑ̃] nm - **1.** [résolution] settling ; **~ de comptes** fig settling of scores - **2.** [règle] regulation - **3.** [paiement] settlement.

réglementaire [rɛgləmɑ̃tɛr] adj - **1.** [régulier] statutory - **2.** [imposé] regulation (avant n).

réglementation [rɛgləmɑ̃tasjɔ̃] nf - **1.** [action] regulation - **2.** [ensemble de règles] regulations (pl), rules (pl).

régler [18] [regle] vt - **1.** [affaire, conflit] to settle, to sort out - **2.** [appareil] to adjust - **3.** [payer - note] to settle, to pay ; [- commerçant] to pay.

réglisse [reglis] nf liquorice.

règne [rɛɲ] nm - **1.** [de souverain] reign ; **sous le ~ de** in the reign of - **2.** [pouvoir] rule - **3.** BIOL kingdom.

régner [18] [reɲe] vi - **1.** [souverain] to rule, to reign - **2.** [silence] to reign.

regonfler [3] [rəgɔ̃fle] vt - **1.** [pneu, ballon] to blow up again, to reinflate - **2.** fam [personne] to cheer up.

regorger [17] [rəgɔrʒe] vi : **~ de** to be abundant in.

regresser [4] [regrese] vi - **1.** [sentiment, douleur] to diminish - **2.** [personne] to regress.

régression [regresjɔ̃] nf - **1.** [recul] decline - **2.** PSYCHOL regression.

regret [rəgrɛ] nm : **~ (de)** regret (for) ; **à ~** with regret ; **sans ~** with no regrets.

regrettable [rəgrɛtabl] adj regrettable.

regretter [4] [rəgrɛte] ◇ vt - **1.** [époque] to miss, to regret ; [personne] to miss - **2.** [faute] to regret ; **~ d'avoir fait qqch** to regret having done sthg - **3.** [déplorer] : **~ que** (+ subjonctif) to be sorry ou regret that. ◇ vi to be sorry.

regrouper [3] [rəgrupe] vt - **1.** [grouper à nouveau] to regroup, to reassemble - **2.** [réunir] to group together. ◆ **se regrouper** vp to gather, to assemble.

régulariser [3] [regylarize] vt - **1.** [documents] to sort out, to put in order ; [situation] to straighten out - **2.** [circulation, fonctionnement] to regulate.

régularité [regylarite] nf - **1.** [gén] regularity - **2.** [de travail, résultats] consistency.

régulateur, trice [regylatœr, tris] adj regulating.

régulation [regylasjɔ̃] nf [contrôle] control, regulation.

régulier, ère [regylje, ɛr] adj - **1.** [gén] regular - **2.** [uniforme, constant] steady, regular - **3.** [travail, résultats] consistent - **4.** [légal] legal ; **être en situation régulière** to have all the legally required documents.

régulièrement [regyljɛrmɑ̃] adv - **1.** [gén] regularly - **2.** [uniformément] steadily, regularly ; [étalé, façonné] evenly.

réhabilitation [reabilitasjɔ̃] nf rehabilitation.

réhabiliter [3] [reabilite] vt - **1.** [accusé] to rehabilitate, to clear ; fig [racheter] to restore to favour Br ou favor Am - **2.** [rénover] to restore.

rehausser [3] [rəose] vt - **1.** [surélever] to heighten - **2.** fig [mettre en valeur] to enhance.

rehausseur [rəosœr] nm booster seat.

rein [rɛ̃] nm kidney. ◆ **reins** nmpl small of the back (sg) ; **avoir mal aux ~s** to have backache.

réincarnation [reɛ̃karnasjɔ̃] nf reincarnation.

reine [rɛn] nf queen.

réinsertion [reɛ̃sɛrsjɔ̃] nf [de délinquant]

rehabilitation ; [dans la vie professionnelle] reintegration.

réintégrer [18] [reɛ̃tegre] *vt* - **1.** [rejoindre] to return to - **2.** JUR to reinstate.

rejaillir [32] [rəʒajir] *vi* to splash up ; **~ sur qqn** *fig* to rebound on sb.

rejet [rəʒɛ] *nm* - **1.** [gén] rejection - **2.** [pousse] shoot.

rejeter [27] [rəʒte] *vt* - **1.** [relancer] to throw back - **2.** [offre, personne] to reject - **3.** [partie du corps] : **~ la tête/les bras en arrière** to throw back one's head/one's arms - **4.** [imputer] : **~ la responsabilité de qqch sur qqn** to lay the responsibility for sthg at sb's door.

rejeton [rəʒtɔ̃] *nm* offspring *(U)*.

rejoindre [82] [rəʒwɛ̃dr] *vt* - **1.** [retrouver] to join - **2.** [regagner] to return to - **3.** [concorder avec] to agree with - **4.** [rattraper] to catch up with. ◆ **se rejoindre** *vp* - **1.** [personnes, routes] to meet - **2.** [opinions] to agree.

rejoint, e [rəʒwɛ̃, ɛ̃t] *pp* ▷ rejoindre.

réjoui, e [reʒwi] *adj* joyful.

réjouir [32] [reʒwir] *vt* to delight. ◆ **se réjouir** *vp* to be delighted ; **se ~ de qqch** to be delighted at ou about sthg.

réjouissance [reʒwisɑ̃s] *nf* rejoicing. ◆ **réjouissances** *nfpl* festivities.

relâche [rəlɑʃ] *nf* - **1.** [pause] : **sans ~** without respite ou a break - **2.** THÉÂTRE : **faire ~** to be closed.

relâchement [rəlɑʃmɑ̃] *nm* relaxation.

relâcher [3] [rəlɑʃe] *vt* - **1.** [étreinte, cordes] to loosen - **2.** [discipline, effort] to relax, to slacken - **3.** [prisonnier] to release. ◆ **se relâcher** *vp* - **1.** [se desserrer] to loosen - **2.** [faiblir - discipline] to become lax ; [- attention] to flag - **3.** [se laisser aller] to slacken off.

relais [rəlɛ] *nm* - **1.** [auberge] post house ; **~ routier** transport cafe - **2.** SPORT & TÉLÉ : **prendre/passer le ~** to take/hand over ; **(course de) ~** relay.

relance [rəlɑ̃s] *nf* [économique] revival, boost ; [de projet] relaunch.

relancer [16] [rəlɑ̃se] *vt* - **1.** [renvoyer] to throw back - **2.** [faire reprendre - économie] to boost ; [- projet] to relaunch ; [- moteur, machine] to restart.

relater [3] [rəlate] *vt littéraire* to relate.

relatif, ive [rəlatif, iv] *adj* relative ; **~ à** relating to ; **tout est ~** it's all relative. ◆ **relative** *nf* GRAM relative clause.

relation [rəlasjɔ̃] *nf* relationship ; **mettre qqn en ~ avec qqn** to put sb in touch with sb. ◆ **relations** *nfpl* - **1.** [rapport] rela-

tionship *(sg)* ; **~s sexuelles** sexual relations, intercourse *(U)* - **2.** [connaissance] acquaintance ; **avoir des ~s** to have connections.

relationnel, elle [rəlasjɔnɛl] *adj* [problèmes] relationship *(avant n)*.

relative ▷ relatif.

relativement [rəlativmɑ̃] *adv* relatively.

relativiser [3] [rəlativize] *vt* to relativize.

relativité [rəlativite] *nf* relativity.

relax, relaxe [rəlaks] *adj fam* relaxed.

relaxation [rəlaksasjɔ̃] *nf* relaxation.

relaxe = relax.

relaxer [3] [rəlakse] *vt* - **1.** [reposer] to relax - **2.** JUR to discharge. ◆ **se relaxer** *vp* to relax.

relayer [11] [rəleje] *vt* to relieve. ◆ **se relayer** *vp* to take over from one another.

relecture [rəlɛktyr] *nf* second reading, rereading.

reléguer [18] [rəlege] *vt* to relegate.

relent [rəlɑ̃] *nm* - **1.** [odeur] stink, stench - **2.** *fig* [trace] whiff.

relevé, e [rəlve] *adj* CULIN spicy. ◆ **relevé** *nm* reading ; **faire le ~ de qqch** to read sthg ; **~ de compte** bank statement ; **~ d'identité bancaire** bank account number.

relève [rəlɛv] *nf* relief ; **prendre la ~** to take over.

relever [19] [rəlve] ◇ *vt* - **1.** [redresser - personne] to help up ; [- pays, économie] to rebuild ; [- moral, niveau] to raise - **2.** [ramasser] to collect - **3.** [tête, col, store] to raise ; [manches] to push up - **4.** [CULIN - mettre en valeur] to bring out ; [- pimenter] to season - **5.** *fig* [récit] to liven up, to spice up - **6.** [noter] to note down ; [compteur] to read - **7.** [relayer] to take over from, to relieve - **8.** [erreur] to note. ◇ *vi* - **1.** [se rétablir] : **~ de** to recover from - **2.** [être du domaine] : **~ de** to come under. ◆ **se relever** *vp* [se mettre debout] to stand up ; [sortir du lit] to get up.

relief [rəljɛf] *nm* relief ; **en ~** in relief, raised ; **une carte en ~** relief map ; **mettre en ~** *fig* to enhance, to bring out.

relier [9] [rəlje] *vt* - **1.** [livre] to bind - **2.** [joindre] to connect - **3.** *fig* [associer] to link up.

religieux, euse [rəliʒjø, øz] *adj* - **1.** [vie, chant] religious ; [mariage] religious, church *(avant n)* - **2.** [respectueux] reverent. ◆ **religieux** *nm* monk. ◆ **religieuse** *nf* RELIG nun.

religion [rəliʒjɔ̃] *nf* - **1.** [culte] religion - **2.** [croyance] religion, faith.

relique [rəlik] *nf* relic.

relire [106] [rəlir] *vt* - **1.** [lire] to reread - **2.** [vérifier] to read over. ◆ **se relire** *vp* to read what one has written.

reliure [rəljyr] *nf* binding.

reloger [17] [rələʒe] *vt* to rehouse.

relu, e [rəly] *pp* ▷ relire.

reluire [97] [rəlɥir] *vi* to shine, to gleam.

reluisant, e [rəlɥizɑ̃, ɑ̃t] *adj* shining, gleaming ; **peu** ou **pas très ~** *fig* [avenir, situation] not all that brilliant ; [personne] shady.

remaniement [rəmanimɑ̃] *nm* restructuring ; **~ ministériel** cabinet reshuffle.

remarier [9] [rəmarje] ◆ **se remarier** *vp* to remarry.

remarquable [rəmarkabl] *adj* remarkable.

remarque [rəmark] *nf* - **1.** [observation] remark ; [critique] critical remark - **2.** [annotation] note.

remarquer [3] [rəmarke] ⬦ *vt* - **1.** [apercevoir] to notice ; **faire ~ qqch (à qqn)** to point sthg out (to sb) ; **se faire ~** *péj* to draw attention to o.s. - **2.** [noter] to remark, to comment. ⬦ *vi* : **ce n'est pas l'idéal, remarque!** it's not ideal, mind you! ◆ **se remarquer** *vp* to be noticeable.

rembarrer [3] [rɑ̃bare] *vt fam* to snub.

remblai [rɑ̃blɛ] *nm* embankment.

rembobiner [3] [rɑ̃bɔbine] *vt* to rewind.

rembourrer [3] [rɑ̃bure] *vt* to stuff, to pad.

remboursement [rɑ̃bursəmɑ̃] *nm* refund, repayment.

rembourser [3] [rɑ̃burse] *vt* - **1.** [dette] to pay back, to repay - **2.** [personne] to pay back ; **~ qqn de qqch** to reimburse sb for sthg.

rembrunir [32] [rɑ̃brynir] ◆ **se rembrunir** *vp* to cloud over, to become gloomy.

remède [rəmɛd] *nm litt & fig* remedy, cure.

remédier [9] [rəmedje] *vi* : **~ à qqch** to put sthg right, to remedy sthg.

remembrement [rəmɑ̃brəmɑ̃] *nm* land regrouping.

remerciement [rəmɛrsimɑ̃] *nm* thanks *(pl)* ; **une lettre de ~** a thank-you letter.

remercier [9] [rəmɛrsje] *vt* - **1.** [dire merci à] to thank ; **~ qqn de** ou **pour qqch** to thank sb for sthg ; **non, je vous remercie** no, thank you - **2.** [congédier] to dismiss.

remettre [84] [rəmɛtr] *vt* - **1.** [replacer] to put back ; **~ en question** to call into question ; **~ qqn à sa place** to put sb in his place

- **2.** [enfiler de nouveau] to put back on - **3.** [rétablir - lumière, son] to put back on ; **~ qqch en marche** to restart sthg ; **~ de l'ordre dans qqch** to tidy sthg up ; **~ une montre à l'heure** to put a watch right ; **~ qqch en état de marche** to put sthg back in working order - **4.** [donner] : **~ qqch à qqn** to hand sthg over to sb ; [médaille, prix] to present sthg to sb - **5.** [ajourner] : **~ qqch (à)** to put sthg off (until). ◆ **se remettre** *vp* - **1.** [recommencer] : **se ~ à qqch** to take up sthg again ; **se ~ à fumer** to start smoking again - **2.** [se rétablir] to get better ; **se ~ de qqch** to get over sthg - **3.** [redevenir] : **se ~ debout** to stand up again ; **le temps s'est remis au beau** the weather has cleared up.

réminiscence [reminisɑ̃s] *nf* reminiscence.

remis, e [rəmi, iz] *pp* ▷ remettre.

remise [rəmiz] *nf* - **1.** [action] : **~ en jeu** throw-in ; **~ en marche** restarting ; **~ en question** ou **cause** calling into question - **2.** [de message, colis] handing over ; [de médaille, prix] presentation - **3.** [réduction] discount ; **~ de peine** JUR remission - **4.** [hangar] shed.

rémission [remisjɔ̃] *nf* remission ; **sans ~** [punir, juger] without mercy.

remodeler [25] [rəmɔdle] *vt* - **1.** [forme] to remodel - **2.** [remanier] to restructure.

remontant, e [rəmɔ̃tɑ̃, ɑ̃t] *adj* [tonique] invigorating. ◆ **remontant** *nm* tonic.

remonte-pente [rəmɔ̃tpɑ̃t] *(pl* remonte-pentes*) nm* ski-tow.

remonter [3] [rəmɔ̃te] ⬦ *vt (aux : avoir)* - **1.** [escalier, pente] to go/come back up - **2.** [assembler] to put together again - **3.** [manches] to turn up - **4.** [horloge, montre] to wind up - **5.** [ragaillardir] to put new life into, to cheer up. ⬦ *vi (aux : être)* - **1.** [monter à nouveau - personne] to go/come back up ; [- baromètre] to rise again ; [- prix, température] to go up again, to rise ; [- sur vélo] to get back on ; **~ dans une voiture** to get back into a car - **2.** [dater] : **~ à** to date ou go back to.

remontoir [rəmɔ̃twar] *nm* winder.

remontrer [3] [rəmɔ̃tre] *vt* to show again ; **vouloir en ~ à qqn** to try to show sb up.

remords [rəmɔr] *nm* remorse.

remorque [rəmɔrk] *nf* trailer ; **être en ~ to** be on tow.

remorquer [3] [rəmɔrke] *vt* [voiture, bateau] to tow.

remorqueur [rəmɔrkœr] *nm* tug, tugboat.

remous [rəmu] ⬦ *nm* [de bateau] wash,

backwash ; [de rivière] eddy. ◇ *nmpl fig* stir, upheaval.

rempailler [3] [rɑ̃paje] *vt* to re-cane.

rempart [rɑ̃par] *nm* (*gén pl*) rampart.

rempiler [3] [rɑ̃pile] ◇ *vt* to pile up again. ◇ *vi fam* MIL to sign on again.

remplaçable [rɑ̃plasabl] *adj* replaceable.

remplaçant, e [rɑ̃plasɑ̃, ɑ̃t] *nm, f* [suppléant] stand-in ; SPORT substitute.

remplacement [rɑ̃plasmɑ̃] *nm* - **1.** [changement] replacing, replacement - **2.** [intérim] substitution ; **faire des ~s** to stand in ; [docteur] to act as a locum.

remplacer [16] [rɑ̃plase] *vt* - **1.** [gén] to replace - **2.** [prendre la place de] to stand in for ; SPORT to substitute.

remplir [32] [rɑ̃plir] *vt* - **1.** [gén] to fill ; **~ de** to fill with ; **~ qqn de joie/d'orgueil** to fill sb with happiness/pride - **2.** [questionnaire] to fill in OU out - **3.** [mission, fonction] to complete, to fulfil.

remplissage [rɑ̃plisaʒ] *nm* - **1.** [de récipient] filling up - **2.** *fig & péj* [de texte] padding out.

remporter [3] [rɑ̃pɔrte] *vt* - **1.** [repartir avec] to take away again - **2.** [gagner] to win.

remuant, e [rəmɥɑ̃, ɑ̃t] *adj* restless, overactive.

remue-ménage [rəmymenaʒ] *nm inv* commotion, confusion.

remuer [7] [rəmɥe] ◇ *vt* - **1.** [bouger, émouvoir] to move - **2.** [café, thé] to stir ; [salade] to toss. ◇ *vi* to move, to stir ; **arrête de ~ comme ça** stop being so restless. ◆ **se remuer** *vp* - **1.** [se mouvoir] to move - **2.** *fig* [réagir] to make an effort.

rémunération [remynerasjɔ̃] *nf* remuneration.

rémunérer [18] [remynere] *vt* - **1.** [personne] to remunerate, to pay - **2.** [activité] to pay for.

renâcler [3] [rənakle] *vi fam* to make a fuss ; **~ devant** OU **à qqch** to balk at sthg.

renaissance [rənɛsɑ̃s] *nf* rebirth.

renaître [92] [rənɛtr] *vi* - **1.** [ressusciter] to come back to life, to come to life again ; **faire ~** [passé, tradition] to revive - **2.** [revenir - sentiment, printemps] to return ; [- économie] to revive, to recover.

renard [rənar] *nm* fox.

renchérir [32] [rɑ̃ʃerir] *vi* - **1.** [augmenter] to become more expensive ; [prix] to go up - **2.** [surenchérir] : **~ sur** to add to.

rencontre [rɑ̃kɔ̃tr] *nf* [gén] meeting ; **faire une bonne ~** to meet somebody interesting ; **faire une mauvaise ~** to meet an un-

pleasant person ; **aller/venir à la ~ de qqn** to go/come to meet sb.

rencontrer [3] [rɑ̃kɔ̃tre] *vt* - **1.** [gén] to meet - **2.** [heurter] to strike. ◆ **se rencontrer** *vp* - **1.** [gén] to meet - **2.** [opinions] to agree.

rendement [rɑ̃dmɑ̃] *nm* [de machine, travailleur] output ; [de terre, placement] yield.

rendez-vous [rɑ̃devu] *nm inv* - **1.** [rencontre] appointment ; [amoureux] date ; **on a tous ~ au café** we're all meeting at the café ; **lors de notre dernier ~** at our last meeting ; **prendre ~ avec qqn** to make an appointment with sb ; **donner ~ à qqn** to arrange to meet sb - **2.** [lieu] meeting place.

rendormir [36] [rɑ̃dɔrmir] ◆ **se rendormir** *vp* to go back to sleep.

rendre [73] [rɑ̃dr] ◇ *vt* - **1.** [restituer] : **~ qqch à qqn** to give sthg back to sb, to return sthg to sb - **2.** [donner en retour - invitation, coup] to return - **3.** [JUR - jugement] to pronounce - **4.** [produire - effet] to produce - **5.** [vomir] to vomit, to cough up - **6.** MIL [céder] to surrender ; **~ les armes** to lay down one's arms - **7.** (+ *adj*) [faire devenir] to make ; **~ qqn fou** to drive sb mad - **8.** [exprimer] to render. ◇ *vi* - **1.** [produire - champ] to yield - **2.** [vomir] to vomit, to be sick. ◆ **se rendre** *vp* - **1.** [céder, capituler] to give in ; **j'ai dû me ~ à l'évidence** I had to face facts - **2.** [aller] : **se ~ à** to go to - **3.** (+ *adj*) [se faire tel] : **se ~ utile/malade** to make o.s. useful/ill.

rêne [rɛn] *nf* rein.

renégat, e [rənega, at] *nm, f sout* renegade.

renégocier [9] [rənegɔsje] *vt* to renegotiate.

renfermé, e [rɑ̃fɛrme] *adj* introverted, withdrawn. ◆ **renfermé** *nm* : **ça sent le ~** it smells stuffy in here.

renfermer [3] [rɑ̃fɛrme] *vt* [contenir] to contain. ◆ **se renfermer** *vp* to withdraw.

renflé, e [rɑ̃fle] *adj* bulging.

renflouer [3] [rɑ̃flue] *vt* - **1.** [bateau] to refloat - **2.** *fig* [entreprise, personne] to bail out.

renfoncement [rɑ̃fɔ̃smɑ̃] *nm* recess.

renforcer [16] [rɑ̃fɔrse] *vt* to reinforce, to strengthen ; **cela me renforce dans mon opinion** that confirms my opinion.

renfort [rɑ̃fɔr] *nm* reinforcement ; **venir en ~** to come as reinforcements.

renfrogné, e [rɑ̃frɔɲe] *adj* scowling.

renfrogner [3] [rɑ̃frɔɲe] ◆ **se renfrogner** *vp* to scowl, to pull a face.

rengaine [rɑ̃gɛn] *nf* - **1.** [formule répétée] (old) story - **2.** [chanson] (old) song.

rengorger [17] [rɑ̃gɔrʒe] ➭ **se rengorger** *vp fig* to puff o.s. up.

renier [9] [rənje] *vt* - **1.** [famille, ami] to disown - **2.** [foi, opinion] to renounce, to repudiate.

renifler [3] [rənifle] ◇ *vi* to sniff. ◇ *vt* to sniff ; **~ quelque chose de louche** to smell a rat.

renne [rɛn] *nm* reindeer *(inv)*.

renom [rənɔ̃] *nm* renown, fame.

renommé, e [rənɔme] *adj* renowned, famous. ➭ **renommée** *nf* renown, fame ; **de ~e internationale** world-famous, internationally renowned.

renoncement [rənɔ̃smɑ̃] *nm* : **~ (à)** renunciation (of).

renoncer [16] [rənɔ̃se] *vi* : **~ à** to give up ; **~ à comprendre qqch** to give up trying to understand sthg.

renouer [6] [rənwe] ◇ *vt* - **1.** [lacet, corde] to re-tie, to tie up again - **2.** [contact, conversation] to resume. ◇ *vi* : **~ avec qqn** to take up with sb again ; **~ avec sa famille** to make it up with one's family again.

renouveau, x [rənuvo] *nm* [transformation] revival.

renouvelable [rənuvlabl] *adj* renewable ; [expérience] repeatable.

renouveler [24] [rənuvle] *vt* [gén] to renew. ➭ **se renouveler** *vp* - **1.** [être remplacé] to be renewed - **2.** [changer, innover] to have new ideas - **3.** [se répéter] to be repeated, to recur.

renouvellement [rənuvɛlmɑ̃] *nm* renewal.

rénovation [renɔvasjɔ̃] *nf* renovation, restoration.

rénover [3] [renɔve] *vt* - **1.** [immeuble] to renovate, to restore - **2.** [système, méthodes] to reform.

renseignement [rɑ̃sɛɲəmɑ̃] *nm* information *(U)* ; **un ~** a piece of information ; **prendre des ~s (sur)** to make enquiries (about). ➭ **renseignements** *nmpl* [service d'information] enquiries, information.

renseigner [4] [rɑ̃seɲe] *vt* : **~ qqn (sur)** to give sb information (about), to inform sb (about). ➭ **se renseigner** *vp* - **1.** [s'enquérir] to make enquiries, to ask for information - **2.** [s'informer] to find out.

rentabiliser [3] [rɑ̃tabilize] *vt* to make profitable.

rentabilité [rɑ̃tabilite] *nf* profitability.

rentable [rɑ̃tabl] *adj* - **1.** COMM profitable - **2.** *fam* [qui en vaut la peine] worthwhile.

rente [rɑ̃t] *nf* - **1.** [d'un capital] revenue, income - **2.** [pension] pension, annuity.

rentier, ère [rɑ̃tje, ɛr] *nm, f* person of independent means.

rentrée [rɑ̃tre] *nf* - **1.** [fait de rentrer] return - **2.** [reprise des activités] : **la ~ parlementaire** the reopening of parliament ; **la ~ des classes** the start of the new school year - **3.** CIN & THÉÂTRE comeback - **4.** [recette] income ; **avoir une ~ d'argent** to come into some money.

rentrer [3] [rɑ̃tre] ◇ *vi (aux : être)* - **1.** [entrer de nouveau] to go/come back in ; **tout a fini par ~ dans l'ordre** everything returned to normal - **2.** [entrer] to go/come in - **3.** [revenir chez soi] to go/come back, to go/come home - **4.** [recouvrer, récupérer] : **~ dans** to recover, to get back ; **~ dans ses frais** to cover one's costs, to break even - **5.** [se jeter avec violence] : **~ dans** to crash into - **6.** [s'emboîter] to go in, to fit ; **~ les uns dans les autres** to fit together - **7.** [être perçu - fonds] to come in. ◇ *vt (aux : avoir)* - **1.** [mettre ou remettre à l'intérieur] to bring in ; [chemise] to tuck in - **2.** [ventre] to pull in ; [griffon] to retract, to draw in - **3.** *fig* [rage, larmes] to hold back.

renversant, e [rɑ̃vɛrsɑ̃, ɑ̃t] *adj* staggering, astounding.

renverse [rɑ̃vɛrs] *nf* : **tomber à la ~** to fall over backwards.

renversement [rɑ̃vɛrsəmɑ̃] *nm* - **1.** [inversion] turning upside down - **2.** [de situation] reversal.

renverser [3] [rɑ̃vɛrse] *vt* - **1.** [mettre à l'envers] to turn upside down - **2.** [faire tomber - objet] to knock over ; [- piéton] to run over ; [- liquide] to spill - **3.** *fig* [obstacle] to overcome ; [régime] to overthrow ; [ministre] to throw out of office - **4.** [tête, buste] to tilt back. ➭ **se renverser** *vp* - **1.** [incliner le corps en arrière] to lean back - **2.** [tomber] to overturn.

renvoi [rɑ̃vwa] *nm* - **1.** [licenciement] dismissal - **2.** [de colis, lettre] return, sending back - **3.** [ajournement] postponement - **4.** [référence] cross-reference - **5.** JUR referral - **6.** [éructation] belch.

renvoyer [30] [rɑ̃vwaje] *vt* - **1.** [faire retourner] to send back - **2.** [congédier] to dismiss - **3.** [colis, lettre] to send back, to return - **4.** [balle] to throw back - **5.** [réfléchir - lumière] to reflect ; [- son] to echo - **6.** [référer] : **~ qqn à** to refer sb to - **7.** [différer] to postpone, to put off.

réorganisation [reɔrganizasjɔ̃] *nf* reorganization.

réorganiser [3] [reɔrganize] *vt* to reorganize.

réorienter [3] [reɔrjɑ̃te] *vt* to reorient, to reorientate.

réouverture [reuvɛrtyr] *nf* reopening.

repaire [rəpɛr] *nm* den.

répandre [74] [repɑ̃dr] *vt* - 1. [verser, renverser] to spill ; [larmes] to shed - 2. [diffuser, dégager] to give off - 3. *fig* [bienfaits] to pour out ; [effroi, terreur, nouvelle] to spread.

répandu, e [repɑ̃dy] ◇ *pp* ▷ **répandre.** ◇ *adj* [opinion, maladie] widespread.

réparable [reparabl] *adj* - 1. [objet] repairable - 2. [erreur] that can be put right.

réparateur, trice [reparatœr, tris] ◇ *adj* [sommeil] refreshing. ◇ *nm, f* repairer.

réparation [reparasjɔ̃] *nf* - 1. [d'objet - action] repairing ; [- résultat] repair ; **en ~** under repair - 2. [de faute] : **~ (de)** atonement (for) - 3. [indemnité] reparation, compensation.

réparer [3] [repare] *vt* - 1. [objet] to repair - 2. [faute, oubli] to make up for ; **~ ses torts** to make amends.

reparler [3] [rəparle] *vi* : **~ de qqn/qqch** to talk about sb/sthg again.

repartie [rəparti] *nf* retort ; **avoir de la ~** to be good at repartee.

repartir [43] [rəpartir] ◇ *vt littéraire* to reply. ◇ *vi* - 1. [retourner] to go back, to return - 2. [partir de nouveau] to set off again - 3. [recommencer] to start again.

répartir [32] [repartir] *vt* - 1. [partager] to share out, to divide up - 2. [dans l'espace] to spread out, to distribute - 3. [classer] to divide ou split up. ◆ **se répartir** *vp* to divide up.

répartition [repartisjɔ̃] *nf* - 1. [partage] sharing out ; [de tâches] allocation - 2. [dans l'espace] distribution.

repas [rəpa] *nm* meal ; **prendre son ~** to eat.

repassage [rəpasaʒ] *nm* ironing.

repasser [3] [rəpase] ◇ *vi (aux : être)* [passer à nouveau] to go/come back ; [film] to be on again. ◇ *vt (aux : avoir)* - 1. [frontière, montagne] to cross again, to recross - 2. [examen] to resit - 3. [film] to show again - 4. [linge] to iron.

repêchage [rəpeʃaʒ] *nm* [de noyé, voiture] recovery.

repêcher [4] [rəpeʃe] *vt* - 1. [noyé, voiture] to fish out - 2. *fam* [candidat] to let through.

repeindre [81] [rəpɛ̃dr] *vt* to repaint.

repeint, e [rəpɛ̃, ɛ̃t] *pp* ▷ **repeindre.**

repenser [3] [rəpɑ̃se] *vt* to rethink.

repentir [37] [rəpɑ̃tir] *nm* repentance.

◆ **se repentir** *vp* to repent ; **se ~ de qqch/d'avoir fait qqch** to be sorry for sthg/for having done sthg.

répercussion [repɛrkysjɔ̃] *nf* repercussion.

répercuter [3] [repɛrkyte] *vt* - 1. [lumière] to reflect ; [son] to throw back - 2. [ordre, augmentation] to pass on. ◆ **se répercuter** *vp* - 1. [lumière] to be reflected ; [son] to echo - 2. [influer] : **se ~ sur** to have repercussions on.

repère [rəpɛr] *nm* [marque] mark ; [objet concret] landmark ; **point de ~** point of reference.

repérer [18] [rəpere] *vt* - 1. [situer] to locate, to pinpoint - 2. *fam* [remarquer] to spot ; **se faire ~** to be spotted.

répertoire [repɛrtwar] *nm* - 1. [agenda] thumb-indexed notebook - 2. [de théâtre, d'artiste] repertoire - 3. INFORM directory.

répertorier [9] [repɛrtɔrje] *vt* to make a list of.

répéter [18] [repete] ◇ *vt* - 1. [gén] to repeat - 2. [leçon] to go over, to learn ; [rôle] to rehearse. ◇ *vi* to rehearse. ◆ **se répéter** *vp* - 1. [radoter] to repeat o.s. - 2. [se reproduire] to be repeated ; **que cela ne se répète pas!** don't let it happen again!

répétitif, ive [repetitif, iv] *adj* repetitive.

répétition [repetisjɔ̃] *nf* - 1. [réitération] repetition - 2. MUS & THÉÂTRE rehearsal.

repeupler [5] [rəpœple] *vt* - 1. [région, ville] to repopulate - 2. [forêt] to replant ; [étang] to restock.

repiquer [3] [rəpike] *vt* - 1. [replanter] to plant out - 2. [disque, cassette] to tape.

répit [repi] *nm* respite ; **sans ~** without respite.

replacer [16] [rəplase] *vt* - 1. [remettre] to replace, to put back - 2. [situer] to place, to put. ◆ **se replacer** *vp* to find new employment.

replanter [3] [rəplɑ̃te] *vt* to replant.

replet, ète [rəplɛ, ɛt] *adj* chubby.

repli [rəpli] *nm* - 1. [de tissu] fold ; [de rivière] bend - 2. [de troupes] withdrawal.

replier [10] [rəplije] *vt* - 1. [plier de nouveau] to fold up again - 2. [ramener en pliant] to fold back - 3. [armée] to withdraw. ◆ **se replier** *vp* - 1. [armée] to withdraw - 2. [personne] : **se ~ sur soi-même** to withdraw into o.s. - 3. [journal, carte] to fold.

réplique [replik] *nf* - 1. [riposte] reply ; **sans ~** [argument] irrefutable - 2. [d'acteur] line ; **donner la ~ à qqn** to play opposite sb - 3. [copie] replica ; [sosie] double.

répliquer [3] [replike] <> *vt* : ~ à qqn que to reply to sb that. <> *vi* - **1.** [répondre] to reply ; [avec impertinence] to answer back - **2.** *fig* [riposter] to retaliate.

replonger [17] [rəplɔ̃ʒe] <> *vt* to plunge back. <> *vi* to dive back. ◆ **se replonger** *vp* : se ~ dans qqch to immerse o.s. in sthg again.

répondeur [repɔ̃dœr] *nm* : ~ (**téléphonique** ou **automatique** ou **-enregistreur**) answering machine.

répondre [75] [repɔ̃dr] <> *vi* : ~ à qqn [faire connaître sa pensée] to answer sb, to reply to sb ; [riposter] to answer sb back ; ~ à qqch [faire une réponse] to reply to sthg, to answer sthg ; [en se défendant] to respond to sthg ; ~ au téléphone to answer the telephone. <> *vt* to answer, to reply. ◆ **répondre à** *vt* - **1.** [correspondre à - besoin] to answer ; [- conditions] to meet - **2.** [ressembler à - description] to match. ◆ **répondre de** *vt* to answer for.

répondu, e [repɔ̃dy] *pp* ➪ **répondre**.

réponse [repɔ̃s] *nf* - **1.** [action de répondre] answer, reply ; **en ~ à votre lettre** ... in reply ou in answer ou in response to your letter ... - **2.** [solution] answer - **3.** [réaction] response.

report [rəpɔr] *nm* - **1.** [de réunion, rendezvous] postponement - **2.** COMM [d'écritures] carrying forward.

reportage [rəpɔrtaʒ] *nm* [article, enquête] report.

reporter¹ [rəpɔrtɛr] *nm* reporter.

reporter² [3] [rəpɔrte] *vt* - **1.** [rapporter] to take back - **2.** [différer] : ~ qqch à to postpone sthg off till - **3.** [somme] : ~ (**sur**) to carry forward (to) - **4.** [transférer] : ~ **sur** to transfer to. ◆ **se reporter** *vp* : se ~ à [se référer à] to refer to.

repos [rəpo] *nm* - **1.** [gén] rest ; **prendre un jour de ~** to take a day off - **2.** [tranquillité] peace and quiet.

reposé, e [rəpoze] *adj* rested ; **à tête ~e** with a clear head.

reposer [3] [rəpoze] <> *vt* - **1.** [poser à nouveau] to put down again, to put back down - **2.** [remettre] to put sthg off till - **3.** [poser de nouveau - question] to ask again - **4.** [appuyer] to rest - **5.** [délasser] to rest, to relax. <> *vi* - **1.** [pâte] to sit, to stand ; [vin] to stand - **2.** [théorie] : ~ **sur** to rest on. ◆ **se reposer** *vp* - **1.** [se délasser] to rest - **2.** [faire confiance] : **se ~ sur qqn** to rely on sb.

repoussant, e [rəpusã, ãt] *adj* repulsive.

repousser [3] [rəpuse] <> *vi* to grow again, to grow back. <> *vt* - **1.** [écarter] to push away, to push back ; [l'ennemi] to

repel, to drive back - **2.** [éconduire] to reject - **3.** [proposition] to reject, to turn down - **4.** [différer] to put back, to postpone.

répréhensible [repreãsibl] *adj* reprehensible.

reprendre [79] [rəprãdr] <> *vt* - **1.** [prendre de nouveau] to take again ; **je passe te ~ dans une heure** I'll come by and pick you up again in an hour ; ~ **la route** to take to the road again ; ~ **haleine** to get one's breath back - **2.** [récupérer - objet prêté] to take back ; [- prisonnier, ville] to recapture - **3.** COMM [entreprise, affaire] to take over - **4.** [se resservir] : ~ **un gâteau/de la viande** to take another cake/some more meat - **5.** [recommencer] to resume ; **'et ainsi' reprit-il ...** 'and so', he continued ... - **6.** [retoucher] to repair ; [jupe] to alter - **7.** [corriger] to correct. <> *vi* - **1.** [affaires, plante] to pick up - **2.** [recommencer] to start again.

représailles [rəprezaj] *nfpl* reprisals.

représentant, e [rəprezãtã, ãt] *nm, f* representative.

représentatif, ive [rəprezãtatif, iv] *adj* representative.

représentation [rəprezãtasjɔ̃] *nf* - **1.** [gén] representation - **2.** [spectacle] performance.

représentativité [rəprezãtativite] *nf* representativeness.

représenter [3] [rəprezãte] *vt* to represent. ◆ **se représenter** *vp* - **1.** [s'imaginer] : se ~ **qqch** to visualize sthg - **2.** [se présenter à nouveau] : **se ~ à** [aux élections] to stand again at ; [à un examen] to resit, to represent.

répression [represjɔ̃] *nf* - **1.** [de révolte] repression - **2.** [de criminalité, d'injustices] suppression.

réprimande [reprimãd] *nf* reprimand.

réprimander [3] [reprimãde] *vt* to reprimand.

réprimer [3] [reprime] *vt* - **1.** [émotion, rire] to repress, to check - **2.** [révolte, crimes] to put down, to suppress.

repris, e [rəpri, iz] *pp* ➪ **reprendre**. ◆ **repris** *nm* : ~ **de justice** habitual criminal.

reprise [rəpriz] *nf* - **1.** [recommencement - des hostilités] resumption, renewal ; [- des affaires] revival, recovery ; [- de pièce] revival ; **à plusieurs ~s** on several occasions, several times - **2.** BOXE round - **3.** [raccommodage] mending.

repriser [3] [rəprize] *vt* to mend.

réprobateur, trice [reprɔbatœr, tris] *adj* reproachful.

réprobation [reprɔbasjɔ̃] *nf* disapproval.

reproche [rəprɔʃ] *nm* reproach ; **faire des ~s à qqn** to reproach sb ; **avec ~** reproachfully ; **sans ~** blameless.

reprocher [3] [rəprɔʃe] *vt* : **~ qqch à qqn** to reproach sb for sthg. ◆ **se reprocher** *vp* : **se ~ (qqch)** to blame o.s. (for sthg).

reproducteur, trice [rəprɔdyktœr, tris] *adj* reproductive.

reproduction [rəprɔdyksjɔ̃] *nf* reproduction ; **~ interdite** all rights (of reproduction) reserved.

reproduire [98] [rəprɔdɥir] *vt* to reproduce. ◆ **se reproduire** *vp* - **1.** BIOL to reproduce, to breed - **2.** [se répéter] to recur.

reproduit, e [rəprɔdɥi, it] *pp* ⊳ **reproduire**.

réprouver [3] [repruve] *vt* [blâmer] to reprove.

reptile [rɛptil] *nm* reptile.

repu, e [rəpy] *adj* full, sated.

républicain, e [repyblikɛ̃, ɛn] *adj & nm, f* republican.

république [repyblik] *nf* republic ; **la République française** the French Republic ; **la République populaire de Chine** the People's Republic of China ; **la République tchèque** the Czech Republic.

répudier [9] [repydje] *vt* [femme] to repudiate.

répugnance [repyɲɑ̃s] *nf* - **1.** [horreur] repugnance - **2.** [réticence] reluctance ; **avoir** ou **éprouver de la ~ à faire qqch** to be reluctant to do sthg.

répugnant, e [repyɲɑ̃, ɑ̃t] *adj* repugnant.

répugner [3] [repyɲe] *vi* : **~ à qqn** to disgust sb, to fill sb with repugnance ; **~ à faire qqch** to be reluctant to do sthg, to be loath to do sthg.

répulsion [repylsjɔ̃] *nf* repulsion.

réputation [repytasjɔ̃] *nf* reputation ; **avoir une ~ de** to have a reputation for ; **avoir bonne/mauvaise ~** to have a good/bad reputation.

réputé, e [repyte] *adj* famous, well-known.

requérir [39] [rəkerir] *vt* - **1.** [nécessiter] to require, to call for - **2.** [solliciter] to solicit - **3.** JUR [réclamer au nom de la loi] to demand.

requête [rəkɛt] *nf* - **1.** [prière] petition - **2.** JUR appeal.

requiem [rekɥijɛm] *nm inv* requiem.

requin [rəkɛ̃] *nm* shark.

requis, e [rəki, iz] ◇ *pp* ⊳ **requérir**. ◇ *adj* required, requisite.

réquisition [rekizisjɔ̃] *nf* - **1.** MIL requisi-

tion - **2.** JUR closing speech for the prosecution.

réquisitionner [3] [rekizisjɔne] *vt* to requisition.

réquisitoire [rekizitwar] *nm* JUR closing speech for the prosecution ; **~ (contre)** *fig* indictment (of).

RER (*abr de* réseau express régional) *nm train service linking central Paris with its suburbs and airports.*

rescapé, e [rɛskape] *nm, f* survivor.

rescousse [rɛskus] ◆ **à la rescousse** *loc adv* : **venir à la ~ de qqn** to come to sb's rescue ; **appeler qqn à la ~** to call on sb for help.

réseau, x [rezo] *nm* network ; **~ ferroviaire/routier** rail/road network.

réservation [rezɛrvasjɔ̃] *nf* reservation.

réserve [rezɛrv] *nf* - **1.** [gén] reserve ; **en ~** in reserve ; **officier de ~** MIL reserve officer - **2.** [restriction] reservation ; **faire des ~s (sur)** to have reservations (about) ; **sous ~ de** subject to ; **sans ~** unreservedly - **3.** [d'animaux, de plantes] reserve ; [d'Indiens] reservation ; **~ faunique** *Can* wildlife reserve ; **~ naturelle** nature reserve - **4.** [local] storeroom.

réservé, e [rezɛrve] *adj* reserved.

réserver [3] [rezɛrve] *vt* - **1.** [destiner] : **~ qqch (à qqn)** [chambre, place] to reserve ou book sthg (for sb) ; *fig* [surprise, désagrément] to have sthg in store (for sb) - **2.** [mettre de côté, garder] : **~ qqch (pour)** to put sthg on one side (for), to keep sthg (for). ◆ **se réserver** *vp* - **1.** [s'accorder] : **se ~ qqch** to keep sthg for o.s. ; **se ~ le droit de faire qqch** to reserve the right to do sthg - **2.** [se ménager] to save o.s.

réservoir [rezɛrvwar] *nm* - **1.** [cuve] tank - **2.** [bassin] reservoir.

résidence [rezidɑ̃s] *nf* - **1.** [habitation] residence ; **~ principale** main residence ou home ; **~ secondaire** second home ; **~ universitaire** hall of residence - **2.** [immeuble] block of luxury flats *Br*, luxury apartment block *Am*. ◆ **résidence surveillée** *nf* : **en ~ surveillée** under house arrest.

résident, e [rezidɑ̃, ɑ̃t] *nm, f* - **1.** [de pays] : **les ~s français en Écosse** French nationals resident in Scotland - **2.** [habitant d'une résidence] resident.

résidentiel, elle [rezidɑ̃sjɛl] *adj* residential.

résider [3] [rezide] *vi* - **1.** [habiter] : **~ à/dans/en** to reside in - **2.** [consister] : **~ dans** to lie in.

résidu [rezidy] *nm* [reste] residue ; [déchet] waste.

résignation [rezinasjɔ̃] *nf* resignation.

résigné, e [rezine] *adj* resigned.

résigner [3] [rezine] ➤ **se résigner** *vp* : **se ~ (à)** to resign o.s. (to).

résilier [9] [rezilje] *vt* to cancel, to terminate.

résille [rezij] *nf* - **1.** [pour cheveux] hairnet - **2.** : **bas ~** fishnet stockings.

résine [rezin] *nf* resin.

résineux, euse [rezinø, øz] *adj* resinous. ➤ **résineux** *nm* conifer.

résistance [rezistɑ̃s] *nf* - **1.** [gén, ÉLECTR & PHYS] resistance ; **manquer de ~** to lack stamina ; **opposer une ~** to put up resistance - **2.** [de radiateur, chaudière] element. ➤ **Résistance** *nf* : **la Résistance** HIST the Resistance.

résistant, e [rezistɑ̃, ɑ̃t] ◇ *adj* [personne] tough ; [tissu] hard-wearing, tough ; **être ~ au froid/aux infections** to be resistant to the cold/to infection. ◇ *nm, f* [gén] resistance fighter ; [de la Résistance] member of the Resistance.

résister [3] [reziste] *vi* to resist ; **~ à** [attaque, désir] to resist ; [tempête, fatigue] to withstand ; [personne] to stand up to, to oppose.

résolu, e [rezɔly] ◇ *pp* ➤ **résoudre**. ◇ *adj* resolute ; **être bien ~ à faire qqch** to be determined to do sthg.

résolument [rezɔlymɑ̃] *adv* resolutely

résolution [rezɔlysjɔ̃] *nf* - **1.** [décision] resolution ; **prendre la ~ de faire qqch** to make a resolution to do sthg - **2.** [détermination] resolve, determination - **3.** [solution] solving.

résonance [rezɔnɑ̃s] *nf* - **1.** ÉLECTR & PHYS resonance - **2.** *fig* [écho] echo.

résonner [3] [rezɔne] *vi* [retentir] to resound ; [renvoyer le son] to echo.

résorber [3] [rezɔrbe] *vt* - **1.** [déficit] to absorb - **2.** MÉD to resorb. ➤ **se résorber** *vp* - **1.** [déficit] to be absorbed - **2.** MÉD to be resorbed.

résoudre [88] [rezudr] *vt* [problème] to solve, to resolve. ➤ **se résoudre** *vp* : **se ~ à faire qqch** to make up one's mind to do sthg, to decide ou resolve to do sthg.

respect [rɛspɛ] *nm* respect.

respectable [rɛspɛktabl] *adj* respectable.

respecter [4] [rɛspɛkte] *vt* to respect ; **faire ~ la loi** to enforce the law.

respectif, ive [rɛspɛktif, iv] *adj* respective.

respectivement [rɛspɛktivmɑ̃] *adv* respectively.

respectueux, euse [rɛspɛktɥø, øz] *adj* respectful ; **être ~ de** to have respect for.

respiration [rɛspirasjɔ̃] *nf* breathing *(U)* ; **retenir sa ~** to hold one's breath.

respiratoire [rɛspiratwar] *adj* respiratory.

respirer [3] [rɛspire] ◇ *vi* - **1.** [inspirer-expirer] to breathe - **2.** *fig* [se reposer] to get one's breath ; [être soulagé] to be able to breathe again. ◇ *vt* - **1.** [aspirer] to breathe in - **2.** *fig* [exprimer] to exude.

resplendissant, e [rɛsplɑ̃disɑ̃, ɑ̃t] *adj* radiant.

responsabiliser [3] [rɛspɔ̃sabilize] *vt* : **~ qqn** to make sb aware of his/her responsibilities.

responsabilité [rɛspɔ̃sabilite] *nf* - **1.** [morale] responsibility ; **avoir la ~ de** to be responsible for, to have the responsibility of - **2.** JUR liability.

responsable [rɛspɔ̃sabl] ◇ *adj* - **1.** [gén] : **~ (de)** responsible (for) ; [légalement] liable (for) ; [chargé de] in charge (of), responsible (for) - **2.** [sérieux] responsible. ◇ *nmf* - **1.** [auteur, coupable] person responsible - **2.** [dirigeant] official - **3.** [personne compétente] person in charge.

resquiller [3] [rɛskije] *vi* - **1.** [au théâtre etc] to sneak in without paying - **2.** [dans autobus etc] to dodge paying the fare.

resquilleur, euse [rɛskijœr, øz] *nm, f* - **1.** [au théâtre etc] person who sneaks in without paying - **2.** [dans autobus etc] fare-dodger.

ressac [rəsak] *nm* undertow.

ressaisir [32] [rəsezir] ➤ **se ressaisir** *vp* to pull o.s. together.

ressasser [3] [rəsase] *vt* - **1.** [répéter] to keep churning out - **2.** *fig* [mécontentement] to dwell on.

ressemblance [rəsɑ̃blɑ̃s] *nf* [gén] resemblance, likeness ; [trait] resemblance.

ressemblant, e [rəsɑ̃blɑ̃, ɑ̃t] *adj* life-like.

ressembler [3] [rəsɑ̃ble] *vi* : **~ à** [physiquement] to resemble, to look like ; [moralement] to be like, to resemble ; **cela ne lui ressemble pas** that's not like him. ➤ **se ressembler** *vp* to look alike, to resemble each other.

ressemeler [24] [rəsəmle] *vt* to resole.

ressentiment [rəsɑ̃timɑ̃] *nm* resentment.

ressentir [37] [rəsɑ̃tir] *vt* to feel.

resserrer [4] [rəsere] *vt* - **1.** [ceinture, boulon] to tighten - **2.** *fig* [lien] to strengthen. ➤ **se resserrer** *vp* - **1.** [route] to (become) narrow - **2.** [nœud, étreinte] to tighten

- **3.** *fig* [relations] to grow stronger, to strengthen.

resservir [38] [rəsɛrvir] ⬦ *vt* - **1.** [plat] to serve again ; *fig* [histoire] to trot out - **2.** [personne] to give another helping to. ⬦ *vi* to be used again. ➡ **se resservir** *vp* : **se ~ de qqch** [ustensile] to use sthg again ; [plat] to take another helping of sthg.

ressort [rəsɔr] *nm* - **1.** [mécanisme] spring - **2.** *fig* [énergie] spirit - **3.** *fig* [compétence] : **être du ~ de qqn** to be sb's area of responsibility, to come under sb's jurisdiction. ➡ **en dernier ressort** *loc adv* in the last resort, as a last resort.

ressortir [43] [rəsɔrtir] ⬦ *vi (aux : être)* - **1.** [personne] to go out again - **2.** *fig* [couleur] : **~ (sur)** to stand out (against) ; **faire ~** to highlight - **3.** *fig* [résulter de] : **~ de** to emerge from. ⬦ *vt (aux : avoir)* to take ou get ou bring out again.

ressortissant, e [rəsɔrtisɑ̃, ɑ̃t] *nm, f* national.

ressource [rəsurs] *nf* resort ; **votre seule ~ est de ...** the only course open to you is to ... ➡ **ressources** *nfpl* - **1.** [financières] means - **2.** [énergétiques, de langue] resources ; **~s naturelles** natural resources - **3.** [de personne] resourcefulness *(U)*.

ressurgir [32] [rəsyrʒir] *vi* to reappear.

ressusciter [3] [resysite] *vi* to rise (from the dead) ; *fig* to revive.

restant, e [rɛstɑ̃, ɑ̃t] *adj* remaining, left. ➡ **restant** *nm* rest, remainder.

restaurant [rɛstɔrɑ̃] *nm* restaurant ; **manger au ~** to eat out ; **~ d'entreprise** staff canteen.

restaurateur, trice [rɛstɔratœr, tris] *nm, f* - **1.** CULIN restaurant owner - **2.** ART restorer.

restauration [rɛstɔrasjɔ̃] *nf* - **1.** CULIN restaurant business ; **~ rapide** fast food - **2.** ART & POLIT restoration.

restaurer [3] [rɛstɔre] *vt* to restore. ➡ **se restaurer** *vp* to have something to eat.

reste [rɛst] *nm* - **1.** [de lait, temps] : **le ~ (de)** the rest (of) - **2.** MATHS remainder. ➡ **restes** *nmpl* - **1.** [de repas] leftovers - **2.** [de mort] remains. ➡ **au reste, du reste** *loc adv* besides.

rester [3] [rɛste] ⬦ *vi* - **1.** [dans lieu, état] to stay, to remain ; **restez calme!** stay ou keep calm! - **2.** [subsister] to remain, to be left ; **le seul bien qui me reste** the only thing I have left - **3.** [s'arrêter] : **en ~ à qqch** to stop at sthg ; **en ~ là** to finish there - **4.** *loc* : **y ~** *fam* [mourir] to pop one's clogs.

⬦ *v impers* : **il en reste un peu** there's still a little left ; **il te reste de l'argent?** do you still have some money left?

restituer [7] [rɛstitɥe] *vt* - **1.** [objet volé] to return, to restore ; [argent] to refund, to return - **2.** [énergie] to release - **3.** [son] to reproduce.

resto [rɛsto] *nm fam* restaurant ; **les ~s du cœur** *charity food distribution centres* ; **~-U** UNIV university refectory, cafeteria.

Restoroute® [rɛstorut] *nm* motorway cafe *Br*, highway restaurant *Am*.

restreindre [81] [rɛstrɛ̃dr] *vt* to restrict. ➡ **se restreindre** *vp* - **1.** [domaine, champ] to narrow - **2.** [personne] to cut back ; **se ~ dans qqch** to restrict sthg.

restreint, e [rɛstrɛ̃, ɛ̃t] *pp* ➡ **restreindre.**

restrictif, ive [rɛstriktif, iv] *adj* restrictive.

restriction [rɛstriksjɔ̃] *nf* - **1.** [condition] condition ; **sans ~** unconditionally - **2.** [limitation] restriction. ➡ **restrictions** *nfpl* [alimentaires] rationing *(U)*.

restructurer [3] [rəstryktyre] *vt* to restructure.

résultat [rezylta] *nm* result ; [d'action] outcome.

résulter [3] [rezylte] ⬦ *vi* : **~ de** to be the result of, to result from. ⬦ *v impers* : **il en résulte que ...** as a result, ...

résumé [rezyme] *nm* summary, résumé ; **en ~** [pour conclure] to sum up ; [en bref] in brief, summarized.

résumer [3] [rezyme] *vt* to summarize. ➡ **se résumer** *vp* [se réduire] : **se ~ à qqch/à faire qqch** to come down to sthg/to doing sthg.

résurgence [rezyrʒɑ̃s] *nf* resurgence.

résurrection [rezyrɛksjɔ̃] *nf* resurrection.

rétablir [32] [retablir] *vt* - **1.** [gén] to restore ; [malade] to restore (to health) - **2.** [communications, contact] to reestablish. ➡ **se rétablir** *vp* - **1.** [silence] to return, to be restored - **2.** [malade] to recover - **3.** GYM to pull o.s. up.

rétablissement [retablismɑ̃] *nm* - **1.** [d'ordre] restoration - **2.** [de communications] reestablishment - **3.** [de malade] recovery - **4.** GYM pull-up.

retard [rətar] *nm* - **1.** [délai] delay ; **être en ~** [sur heure] to be late ; [sur échéance] to be behind ; **avoir du ~** to be late ou delayed - **2.** [de pays, peuple, personne] backwardness.

retardataire [rətardatɛr] *nmf* [en retard] latecomer.

retardement [rətardəmɑ̃] *nm* : **à ~** belatedly ; *voir aussi* **bombe**.

retarder [3] [rətarde] <> *vt* **- 1.** [personne, train] to delay ; [sur échéance] to put back **- 2.** [ajourner - rendez-vous] to put back ou off ; [- départ] to put back ou off, to delay **- 3.** [montre] to put back. <> *vi* **- 1.** [horloge] to be slow **- 2.** *fam* [ne pas être au courant] to be behind the times **- 3.** [être en décalage] : **~ sur** to be out of step ou tune with.

retenir [40] [rətnir] *vt* **- 1.** [physiquement - objet, personne, cri] to hold back ; [- souffle] to hold ; **~ qqn de faire qqch** to stop ou restrain sb from doing sthg **- 2.** [retarder] to keep, to detain **- 3.** [montant, impôt] to keep back, to withhold **- 4.** [chambre] to reserve **- 5.** [leçon, cours] to remember **- 6.** [projet] to accept, to adopt **- 7.** [eau, chaleur] to retain **- 8.** MATHS to carry **- 9.** [intérêt, attention] to hold. ◆ **se retenir** *vp* **- 1.** [s'accrocher] : **se ~ à** to hold onto **- 2.** [se contenir] to hold on ; **se ~ de faire qqch** to refrain from doing sthg.

rétention [retɑ̃sjɔ̃] *nf* MÉD retention.

retentir [32] [rətɑ̃tir] *vi* **- 1.** [son] to ring (out) **- 2.** [pièce, rue] : **~ de** to resound with **- 3.** *fig* [fatigue, blessure] : **~ sur** to have an effect on.

retentissant, e [rətɑ̃tisɑ̃, ɑ̃t] *adj* resounding.

retentissement [rətɑ̃tismɑ̃] *nm* [de mesure] repercussions *(pl)*.

retenu, e [rətny] *pp* ⊳ **retenir**.

retenue [rətny] *nf* **- 1.** [prélèvement] deduction **2.** MATHS amount carried **- 3.** SCOL detention **- 4.** *fig* [de personne - dans relations] reticence ; [- dans comportement] restraint ; **sans ~** without restraint.

réticence [retisɑ̃s] *nf* [hésitation] hesitation, reluctance ; **avec ~** hesitantly

réticent, e [retisɑ̃, ɑ̃t] *adj* hesitant, reluctant.

rétine [retin] *nf* retina.

retiré, e [rətire] *adj* [lieu] remote, isolated ; [vie] quiet.

retirer [3] [rətire] *vt* **- 1.** [vêtement, emballage] to take off, to remove ; [permis, jouet] to take away ; **~ qqch à qqn** to take sthg away from sb **- 2.** [plainte] to withdraw, to take back **- 3.** [avantages, bénéfices] : **~ qqch de qqch** to get ou derive sthg from sthg **- 4.** [bagages, billet] to collect ; [argent] to withdraw. ◆ **se retirer** *vp* **- 1.** [s'isoler] to withdraw, to retreat **- 2.** [des affaires] : **se ~ (de)** to retire (from) **- 3.** [refluer] to recede.

retombées [rətɔ̃be] *nfpl* repercussions, fallout *(sg)*.

retomber [3] [rətɔ̃be] *vi* **- 1.** [gymnaste, chat] to land **- 2.** [redevenir] : **~ malade** to relapse **- 3.** *fig* [colère] to die away **- 4.** [cheveux] to hang down **- 5.** *fig* [responsabilité] : **~ sur** to fall on.

rétorquer [3] [retɔrke] *vt* to retort ; **~ à qqn que ...** to retort to sb that ...

retors, e [rətɔr, ɔrs] *adj* wily.

rétorsion [retɔrsjɔ̃] *nf* retaliation ; **mesures de ~** reprisals.

retouche [rətuʃ] *nf* **- 1.** [de texte, vêtement] alteration **- 2.** ART & PHOT touching up.

retoucher [3] [rətuʃe] *vt* **- 1.** [texte, vêtement] to alter **- 2.** ART & PHOT to touch up.

retour [rətur] *nm* **- 1.** [gén] return ; **à mon/ton ~** when I/you get back, on my/your return ; **être de ~ (de)** to be back (from) ; **~ en arrière** flashback ; **en ~** in return **- 2.** [trajet] journey back, return journey.

retourner [3] [rəturne] <> *vt* (aux : avoir) **- 1.** [carte, matelas] to turn over ; [terre] to turn (over) **- 2.** [compliment, objet prêté] : **~ qqch (à qqn)** to return sthg (to sb) **- 3.** [lettre, colis] to send back, to return **- 4.** *fam fig* [personne] to shake up. <> *vi* (aux : être) to come/go back, **~ en arrière** ou **sur ses pas** to retrace one's steps. ◆ **se retourner** *vp* **- 1.** [basculer] to turn over **- 2.** [pivoter] to turn round **- 3.** *fam fig* [s'adapter] to sort o.s. out **- 4.** [rentrer] : **s'en ~** to go back (home) **- 5.** *fig* [s'opposer] : **se ~ contre** to turn against.

retracer [16] [rətrase] *vt* **- 1.** [ligne] to redraw **- 2.** [événement] to relate.

rétracter [3] [retrakte] *vt* to retract. ◆ **se rétracter** *vp* **- 1.** [se contracter] to retract **- 2.** [se dédire] to back down.

retrait [rətrɛ] *nm* **- 1.** [gén] withdrawal ; **~ du permis** disqualification from driving **- 2.** [de bagages] collection **- 3.** [des eaux] ebbing. ◆ **en retrait** *loc adj* & *loc adv* **- 1.** [maison] set back from the road ; **rester en ~** *fig* to hang back **- 2.** [texte] indented.

retraite [rətrɛt] *nf* **- 1.** [gén] retreat **- 2.** [cessation d'activité] retirement ; **être à la ~** to be retired **- 3.** [revenu] (retirement) pension.

retraité, e [rətrete] <> *adj* **- 1.** [personne] retired **- 2.** TECHNOL reprocessed. <> *nm, f* retired person, pensioner.

retrancher [3] [rətrɑ̃ʃe] *vt* **- 1.** [passage] : **~ qqch (de)** to cut sthg out (from) **- 2.** [montant] : **~ qqch (de)** to take sthg away (from), to deduct sthg (from). ◆ **se retrancher** *vp* to entrench o.s. ; **se ~ derrière/dans** *fig* to take refuge behind/in.

retransmettre [84] [rətrɑ̃smɛtr] *vt* to broadcast.

retransmis, e [rətrãsmi, iz] *pp* ▷ retransmettre.

retransmission [rətrãsmisjɔ̃] *nf* broadcast.

retravailler [3] [rətravaje] ◇ *vt* : ~ qqch to work on sthg again. ◇ *vi* to start work again.

rétrécir [32] [retresir] *vi* [tissu] to shrink.

rétrécissement [retresismã] *nm* - 1. [de vêtement] shrinkage - 2. MÉD stricture.

rétribution [retribysjɔ̃] *nf* remuneration.

rétro [retro] ◇ *nm* - 1. [style] old style ou fashion - 2. *fam* [rétroviseur] rear-view mirror. ◇ *adj inv* old-style.

rétroactif, ive [retroaktif, iv] *adj* retrospective.

rétrograde [retrograd] *adj péj* reactionary.

rétrograder [3] [retrograde] ◇ *vt* to demote. ◇ *vi* AUTOM to change down.

rétroprojecteur [retroprɔʒɛktœr] *nm* overhead projector.

rétrospectif, ive [retrospɛktif, iv] *adj* retrospective. ◆ **rétrospective** *nf* retrospective.

rétrospectivement [retrospɛktivmã] *adv* retrospectively.

retrousser [3] [rətruse] *vt* - 1. [manches, pantalon] to roll up - 2. [lèvres] to curl.

retrouvailles [rətruvaj] *nfpl* reunion *(sg)*.

retrouver [8] [rətruve] *vt* - 1. [gén] to find ; [appétit] to recover, to regain - 2. [reconnaître] to recognize - 3. [ami] to meet, to see. ◆ **se retrouver** *vp* - 1. [entre amis] to meet (up) again ; **on se retrouve au café?** shall we meet up ou see each other at the café? - 2. [être de nouveau] to find o.s. again - 3. [s'orienter] to find one's way ; **ne pas s'y ~** [dans ses papiers] to be completely lost - 4. [erreur, style] to be found, to crop up - 5. [financièrement] : **s'y ~** *fam* to break even.

rétroviseur [retrovizœr] *nm* rear-view mirror.

réunification [reynifikasjɔ̃] *nf* reunification.

réunifier [9] [reynifje] *vt* to reunify.

réunion [reynjɔ̃] *nf* - 1. [séance] meeting - 2. [jonction] union, merging - 3. [d'amis, de famille] reunion.

Réunion [reynjɔ̃] *nf* : **(l'île de) la ~** Réunion.

réunir [32] [reynir] *vt* - 1. [fonds] to collect - 2. [extrémités] to put together, to bring together - 3. [qualités] to combine - 4. [personnes] to bring together ; [après séparation] to reunite. ◆ **se réunir** *vp* - 1. [per-

sonnes] to meet - 2. [entreprises] to combine ; [états] to unite - 3. [fleuves, rues] to converge.

réussi, e [reysi] *adj* successful ; **c'est ~!** *fig & iron* congratulations!, well done!.

réussir [32] [reysir] ◇ *vi* - 1. [personne, affaire] to succeed, to be a success ; ~ **à faire qqch** to succeed in doing sthg - 2. [climat] : ~ **à** to agree with. ◇ *vt* - 1. [portrait, plat] to make a success of - 2. [examen] to pass.

réussite [reysit] *nf* - 1. [succès] success - 2. [jeu de cartes] patience *Br*, solitaire *Am*.

réutiliser [3] [reytilize] *vt* to reuse.

revaloriser [3] [rəvalɔrize] *vt* [monnaie] to revalue ; [salaires] to raise ; *fig* [idée, doctrine] to rehabilitate.

revanche [rəvãʃ] *nf* - 1. [vengeance] revenge ; **prendre sa ~** to take one's revenge - 2. SPORT return (match). ◆ **en revanche** *loc adv* [par contre] on the other hand.

rêvasser [3] [revase] *vi* to daydream.

rêve [rɛv] *nm* dream.

rêvé, e [reve] *adj* ideal.

revêche [rəvɛʃ] *adj* surly.

réveil [revɛj] *nm* - 1. [de personne] waking (up) ; *fig* awakening - 2. [pendule] alarm clock.

réveiller [4] [reveje] *vt* - 1. [personne] to wake up - 2. [courage] to revive. ◆ **se réveiller** *vp* - 1. [personne] to wake (up) - 2. [ambitions] to reawaken.

réveillon [revɛjɔ̃] *nm* [jour - de Noël] Christmas Eve ; [- de nouvel an] New Year's Eve.

réveillonner [3] [revɛjɔne] *vi* to have a Christmas Eve/New Year's Eve meal.

révélateur, trice [revelatœr, tris] *adj* revealing. ◆ **révélateur** *nm* PHOT developer ; *fig* [ce qui révèle] indication.

révélation [revelasjɔ̃] *nf* - 1. [gén] revelation - 2. [artiste] discovery.

révéler [18] [revele] *vt* - 1. [gén] to reveal - 2. [artiste] to discover. ◆ **se révéler** *vp* - 1. [apparaître] to be revealed - 2. [s'avérer] to prove to be.

revenant [rəvnã] *nm* - 1. [fantôme] spirit, ghost - 2. *fam* [personne] stranger.

revendeur, euse [rəvãdœr, øz] *nm, f* retailer.

revendication [rəvãdikasjɔ̃] *nf* claim, demand.

revendiquer [3] [rəvãdike] *vt* [dû, responsabilité] to claim ; [avec force] to demand.

revendre [73] [rəvãdr] *vt* - 1. [après utilisation] to resell - 2. [vendre plus de] to sell more of.

revendu, e [rəvãdy] *pp* ▷ revendre.

revenir [40] [rəvnir] *vi* - **1.** [gén] to come back, to return ; **~ de** to come back from, to return from ; **~ à** to come back to, to return to ; **~ sur** [sujet] to go over again ; [décision] to go back on ; **~ à soi** to come to - **2.** [mot, sujet] to crop up - **3.** [à l'esprit] : **~ à** to come back to - **4.** [impliquer] : **cela revient au même/à dire que ...** it amounts to the same thing/to saying (that) ... - **5.** [coûter] : **~ à** to come to, to amount to ; **~ cher** to be expensive - **6.** [honneur, tâche] : **~ à** to fall to ; **c'est à lui qu'il revient de ...** it is up to him to ... - **7.** CULIN : **faire ~** to brown - **8.** *loc* : **sa tête ne me revient pas** I don't like the look of him/her ; **il n'en revenait pas** he couldn't get over it.

revente [rəvãt] *nf* resale.

revenu, e [rəvny] *pp* ⌐⟩ revenir.
◆ **revenu** *nm* [de pays] revenue ; [de personne] income.

rêver [4] [reve] ⟨⟩ *vi* to dream ; [rêvasser] to daydream ; **~ de/à** to dream of/about. ⟨⟩ *vt* to dream ; **~ que** to dream (that).

réverbération [reverberasjɔ̃] *nf* reverberation.

réverbère [reverber] *nm* street lamp *ou* light.

révérence [reverãs] *nf* - **1.** [salut] bow - **2.** *littéraire* [déférence] reverence.

révérend, e [reverã, ãd] *adj* reverend.
◆ **révérend** *nm* reverend.

révérer [18] [revere] *vt* to revere.

rêverie [revri] *nf* reverie.

revers [rəver] *nm* - **1.** [de main] back ; [de pièce] reverse - **2.** [de veste] lapel ; [de pantalon] turn-up *Br*, cuff *Am* - **3.** TENNIS backhand - **4.** *fig* [de fortune] reversal.

reverser [3] [rəverse] *vt* - **1.** [liquide] to pour out more of - **2.** FIN : **~ qqch sur** to pay sthg into.

réversible [reversibl] *adj* reversible.

revêtement [rəvɛtmã] *nm* surface.

revêtir [44] [rəvetir] *vt* - **1.** [mur, surface] : **~ (de)** to cover (with) - **2.** [aspect] to take on, to assume - **3.** [vêtement] to put on ; [personne] to dress.

revêtu, e [rəvety] *pp* ⌐⟩ revêtir.

rêveur, euse [rɛvœr, øz] ⟨⟩ *adj* dreamy. ⟨⟩ *nm, f* dreamer.

revient [rəvjɛ̃] ⌐⟩ prix.

revigorer [3] [rəvigɔre] *vt* to invigorate.

revirement [rəvirmã] *nm* change.

réviser [3] [revize] *vt* - **1.** [réexaminer, modifier] to revise, to review - **2.** SCOL to revise - **3.** [machine] to check.

révision [revizjɔ̃] *nf* - **1.** [réexamen, modi-

fication] revision, review - **2.** SCOL revision - **3.** [de machine] checkup.

revisser [3] [rəvise] *vt* to screw back again.

revivre [90] [rəvivr] ⟨⟩ *vi* [personne] to come back to life, to revive ; *fig* [espoir] to be revived, to revive ; **faire ~** to revive. ⟨⟩ *vt* to relive ; **faire ~ qqch à qqn** to bring sthg back to sb.

revoici [rəvwasi] *prép* : **me ~!** it's me again!, I'm back!

revoir [62] [rəvwar] *vt* - **1.** [renouer avec] to see again - **2.** [corriger, étudier] to revise *Br*, to review *Am*. ◆ **se revoir** *vp* [amis] to see each other again ; [professionnellement] to meet again. ◆ **au revoir** *interj & nm* goodbye.

révoltant, e [revɔltã, ãt] *adj* revolting.

révolte [revɔlt] *nf* revolt.

révolter [3] [revɔlte] *vt* to disgust. ◆ **se révolter** *vp* : **se ~ (contre)** to revolt (against).

révolu, e [revɔly] *adj* past ; **avoir 15 ans ~s** ADMIN to be over 15.

révolution [revɔlysjɔ̃] *nf* - **1.** [gén] revolution ; **la Révolution française** the French Revolution - **2.** *fam* [effervescence] uproar.

révolutionnaire [revɔlysjɔner] *nmf & adj* revolutionary.

révolutionner [3] [revɔlysjɔne] *vt* - **1.** [transformer] to revolutionize - **2.** [mettre en émoi] to stir up.

revolver [revɔlver] *nm* revolver.

révoquer [3] [revɔke] *vt* - **1.** [fonctionnaire] to dismiss - **2.** [loi] to revoke.

revue [rəvy] *nf* - **1.** [gén] review ; **~ de presse** press review ; **passer en ~** *fig* to review - **2.** [défilé] march-past - **3.** [magazine] magazine - **4.** [spectacle] revue.

rez-de-chaussée [redʃose] *nm inv* ground floor *Br*, first floor *Am*.

RFA (*abr de* **République fédérale d'Allemagne**) *nf* FRG.

rhabiller [3] [rabije] *vt* to dress again. ◆ **se rhabiller** *vp* to get dressed again.

rhésus [rezys] *nm* rhesus (factor) ; **~ positif/négatif** rhesus positive/negative.

rhétorique [retɔrik] *nf* rhetoric.

Rhin [rɛ̃] *nm* : **le ~** the Rhine.

rhinocéros [rinɔserɔs] *nm* rhinoceros.

rhino-pharyngite [rinɔfarɛ̃ʒit] (*pl* **rhinopharyngites**) *nf* throat infection.

rhododendron [rɔdɔdɛ̃drɔ̃] *nm* rhododendron.

Rhône [ron] *nm* : **le ~** the (River) Rhone.

rhubarbe [rybarb] *nf* rhubarb.

rhum [rɔm] *nm* rum.

rhumatisme [rymatism] *nm* rheumatism.

rhume [rym] *nm* cold ; **attraper un ~** to catch a cold ; **~ des foins** hay fever.

ri [ri] *pp inv* ⊳ **rire**.

riant, e [rijã, ãt] *adj* smiling ; *fig* cheerful.

RIB, Rib [rib] (*abr de* **relevé d'identité bancaire**) *nm bank account identification slip.*

ribambelle [ribãbɛl] *nf* : **~ de** string of.

ricaner [3] [rikane] *vi* to snigger.

riche [riʃ] ◇ *adj* - **1.** [gén] rich ; [personne, pays] rich, wealthy ; **~ en** ou **de** rich in - **2.** [idée] great. ◇ *nmf* rich person ; **les ~s** the rich.

richesse [riʃɛs] *nf* - **1.** [de personne, pays] wealth *(U)* - **2.** [de faune, flore] abundance. ◆ **richesses** *nfpl* [gén] wealth *(U).*

ricochet [rikɔʃɛ] *nm litt & fig* rebound ; [de balle d'arme] ricochet ; **par ~** in an indirect way.

rictus [riktys] *nm* rictus.

ride [rid] *nf* wrinkle ; [de surface d'eau] ripple.

rideau, x [rido] *nm* curtain ; **~ de fer** [frontière] Iron Curtain.

rider [3] [ride] *vt* - **1.** [peau] to wrinkle - **2.** [surface] to ruffle. ◆ **se rider** *vp* to become wrinkled.

ridicule [ridikyl] ◇ *adj* ridiculous. ◇ *nm* : **se couvrir de ~** to make o.s. look ridiculous ; **tourner qqn/qqch en ~** to ridicule sb/sthg.

ridiculiser [3] [ridikylize] *vt* to ridicule. ◆ **se ridiculiser** *vp* to make o.s. look ridiculous.

rien [rjɛ̃] ◇ *pron indéf* - **1.** [en contexte négatif] : **ne ... rien** nothing, not ... anything ; **je n'ai ~ fait** I've done nothing, I haven't done anything ; **je n'en sais ~** I don't know (anything about it), I know nothing about it ; **~ ne m'intéresse** nothing interests me ; **il n'y a plus ~ dans le réfrigérateur** there's nothing left in the fridge - **2.** [aucune chose] nothing ; **que fais-tu?** — **~** what are you doing? — nothing ; **~ de nouveau** nothing new ; **~ d'autre** nothing else ; **~ du tout** nothing at all ; **~ à faire** it's no good ; **de ~!** don't mention it!, not at all! ; **pour ~** for nothing - **3.** [quelque chose] anything ; **sans ~ dire** without saying anything. ◇ *nm* : **pour un ~** [se fâcher, pleurer] for nothing, at the slightest thing ; **perdre son temps à des ~s** to waste one's time with trivia ; **en un ~ de temps** in no time at all. ◆ **rien que** *loc adv* only, just ; **la vérité, ~ que la vérité** the truth and nothing but the truth ; **~ que l'idée des vacances la comblait** just

thinking about the holiday filled her with joy.

rieur, rieuse [rijœr, rijøz] *adj* cheerful.

rigide [riʒid] *adj* rigid ; [muscle] tense.

rigidité [riʒidite] *nf* rigidity ; [de muscle] tenseness ; [de principes, mœurs] strictness.

rigole [rigɔl] *nf* channel.

rigoler [3] [rigɔle] *vi fam* - **1.** [rire] to laugh - **2.** [plaisanter] : **~ (de)** to joke (about).

rigolo, ote [rigɔlo, ɔt] *fam* ◇ *adj* funny. ◇ *nm, f péj* phoney *Br*, phony *Am.*

rigoureux, euse [rigurø, øz] *adj* - **1.** [discipline, hiver] harsh - **2.** [analyse] rigorous.

rigueur [rigœr] *nf* - **1.** [de punition] severity, harshness - **2.** [de climat] harshness - **3.** [d'analyse] rigour *Br*, rigor *Am*, exactness. ◆ **à la rigueur** *loc adv* if necessary, if need be.

rime [rim] *nf* rhyme.

rimer [3] [rime] *vi* : **~ (avec)** to rhyme (with).

rinçage [rɛ̃saʒ] *nm* rinsing.

rincer [16] [rɛ̃se] *vt* [bouteille] to rinse out ; [cheveux, linge] to rinse.

ring [riŋ] *nm* - **1.** BOXE ring - **2.** *Belg* [route] bypass.

riposte [ripɔst] *nf* - **1.** [réponse] retort, riposte - **2.** [contre-attaque] counterattack.

riposter [3] [ripɔste] ◇ *vt* : **~ que** to retort ou riposte that. ◇ *vi* - **1.** [répondre] to riposte - **2.** [contre-attaquer] to counter, to retaliate.

rire [95] [rir] ◇ *nm* laugh ; **éclater de ~** to burst out laughing. ◇ *vi* - **1.** [gén] to laugh - **2.** [plaisanter] : **pour ~** *fam* as a joke, for a laugh.

risée [rize] *nf* ridicule ; **être la ~ de** to be the laughing stock of.

risible [rizibl] *adj* [ridicule] ridiculous.

risque [risk] *nm* risk ; **prendre des ~s** to take risks ; **à tes/vos ~s et périls** at your own risk.

risqué, e [riske] *adj* - **1.** [entreprise] risky, dangerous - **2.** [plaisanterie] risqué, daring.

risquer [3] [riske] *vt* - **1.** [vie, prison] to risk ; **~ de faire qqch** to be likely to do sthg ; **je risque de perdre tout ce que j'ai** I'm running the risk of losing everything I have ; **cela ne risque rien** it will be all right - **2.** [tenter] to venture. ◆ **se risquer** *vp* to venture ; **se ~ à faire qqch** to dare to do sthg.

rissoler [3] [risɔle] *vi* to brown.

rite [rit] *nm* - **1.** RELIG rite - **2.** [cérémonial] *fig* ritual.

rituel, elle [rituɛl] *adj* ritual. ◆ **rituel** *nm* ritual.

rivage [rivaʒ] *nm* shore.

rival, e, aux [rival, o] ◇ *adj* rival *(avant n)*. ◇ *nm, f* rival.

rivaliser [3] [rivalize] *vi* : ~ avec to compete with.

rivalité [rivalite] *nf* rivalry.

rive [riv] *nf* [de rivière] bank ; **la ~ droite** [à Paris] the north bank of the Seine *(generally considered more affluent than the south bank)* ; **la ~ gauche** [à Paris] the south bank of the Seine *(generally associated with students and artists)*.

river [3] [rive] *vt* - **1.** [fixer] : ~ qqch à qqch to rivet sthg to sthg - **2.** [clou] to clinch ; **être rivé à** *fig* to be riveted ou glued to.

riverain, e [rivrɛ̃, ɛn] *nm, f* resident.

rivet [rivɛ] *nm* rivet.

rivière [rivjɛr] *nf* river.

rixe [riks] *nf* fight, brawl.

riz [ri] *nm* rice.

rizière [rizjɛr] *nf* paddy (field).

RMI *(abr de* revenu minimum d'insertion) *nm* minimum guaranteed income *(for people with no other source of income)*.

robe [rɔb] *nf* - **1.** [de femme] dress ; **~ de mariée** wedding dress - **2.** [peignoir] : **~ de chambre** dressing gown - **3.** [de cheval] coat - **4.** [de vin] colour *Br*, color *Am*.

robinet [rɔbinɛ] *nm* tap *Br*, faucet *Am*.

robinetterie [rɔbinɛtri] *nf* [installations] taps *(pl)* *Br*, faucets *(pl)* *Am*.

robot [rɔbo] *nm* - **1.** [gén] robot - **2.** [ménager] food processor.

robotique [rɔbɔtik] *nf* robotics *(U)*.

robotisation [rɔbɔtizasjɔ̃] *nf* automation.

robuste [rɔbyst] *adj* - **1.** [personne, santé] robust - **2.** [plante] hardy - **3.** [voiture] sturdy.

roc [rɔk] *nm* rock.

rocade [rɔkad] *nf* bypass.

rocaille [rɔkaj] *nf* - **1.** [cailloux] loose stones *(pl)* - **2.** [dans un jardin] rockery.

rocailleux, euse [rɔkajø, øz] *adj* - **1.** [terrain] rocky - **2.** *fig* [voix] harsh.

rocambolesque [rɔkãbɔlɛsk] *adj* fantastic.

roche [rɔʃ] *nf* rock.

rocher [rɔʃe] *nm* rock.

rocheux, euse [rɔʃø, øz] *adj* rocky. ◆ **Rocheuses** *nfpl* : **les Rocheuses** the Rockies.

rock [rɔk] *nm* rock ('n' roll).

rodage [rɔdaʒ] *nm* - **1.** [de véhicule] running-in ; **'en ~'** 'running in' - **2.** *fig* [de méthode] running-in ou debugging period.

rodéo [rɔdeo] *nm* rodeo ; *fig & iron* free-for-all.

roder [3] [rɔde] *vt* - **1.** [véhicule] to run in - **2.** *fam* [méthode] to run in, to debug ; [personne] to break in.

rôdeur, euse [rodœr, øz] *nm, f* prowler.

rogne [rɔɲ] *nf fam* bad temper ; **être/se mettre en ~** to be in/to get into a bad mood, to be in/to get into a temper.

rogner [3] [rɔɲe] ◇ *vt* - **1.** [ongles] to trim - **2.** [revenus] to eat into. ◇ *vi* : ~ sur qqch to cut down on sthg.

roi [rwa] *nm* king ; **tirer les ~s** to celebrate Epiphany.

rôle [rol] *nm* role, part.

roller [rɔl·lœr] *nm* [sport] rollerblading ; **les ~s** [patins] Rollerblades® ; **faire du ~** to go rollerblading, to go rollerblade.

romain, e [rɔmɛ̃, ɛn] *adj* Roman. ◆ **Romain, e** *nm, f* Roman.

roman, e [rɔmã, an] *adj* - **1.** [langue] Romance - **2.** ARCHIT Romanesque. ◆ **roman** *nm* LITTÉRATURE novel.

romance [rɔmãs] *nf* [chanson] love song.

romancier, ère [rɔmãsje, ɛr] *nm, f* novelist.

romanesque [rɔmanɛsk] *adj* - **1.** LITTÉRATURE novelistic - **2.** [aventure] fabulous, storybook *(avant n)*.

roman-feuilleton [rɔmãfœjtɔ̃] *nm* serial ; *fig* soap opera.

roman-photo [rɔmãfɔto] *nm* story told in photographs.

romantique [rɔmãtik] *nmf & adj* romantic.

romantisme [rɔmãtism] *nm* - **1.** ART Romantic movement - **2.** [sensibilité] romanticism.

romarin [rɔmarɛ̃] *nm* rosemary.

rompre [78] [rɔ̃pr] ◇ *vt* - **1.** *sout* [objet] to break - **2.** [charme, marché] to break ; [fiançailles, relations] to break off. ◇ *vi* to break ; ~ avec qqn *fig* to break up with sb. ◆ **se rompre** *vp* to break ; **se ~ le cou/les reins** to break one's neck/back.

ronce [rɔ̃s] *nf* [arbuste] bramble.

ronchonner [3] [rɔ̃ʃɔne] *vi fam* : ~ (après) to grumble (at).

rond, e [rɔ̃, rɔ̃d] *adj* - **1.** [forme, chiffre] round - **2.** [joue, ventre] chubby, plump - **3.** *fam* [ivre] tight. ◆ **rond** *nm* - **1.** [cercle] circle ; **en ~** in a circle ou ring ; **tourner en ~** *fig* to go round in circles - **2.** [anneau] ring - **3.** *fam* [argent] : **je n'ai pas un ~** I haven't got a penny ou bean.

ronde [rɔ̃d] *nf* - **1.** [de surveillance] rounds *(pl)* ; [de policier] beat - **2.** [danse] round - **3.** MUS semibreve *Br*, whole note *Am*. ◆ **à la ronde** *loc adv* : **à des kilomètres à la ~** for miles around.

rondelle [rɔ̃dɛl] *nf* - **1.** [de saucisson] slice - **2.** [de métal] washer.

rondement [rɔ̃dmɑ̃] *adv* [efficacement] efficiently, briskly.

rondeur [rɔ̃dœr] *nf* - **1.** [forme] roundness - **2.** [partie charnue] curve.

rond-point [rɔ̃pwɛ̃] *nm* roundabout *Br*, traffic circle *Am*.

ronflant, e [rɔ̃flɑ̃, ɑ̃t] *adj péj* grandiose.

ronflement [rɔ̃fləmɑ̃] *nm* - **1.** [de dormeur] snore - **2.** [de poêle, moteur] hum, purr.

ronfler [3] [rɔ̃fle] *vi* - **1.** [dormeur] to snore - **2.** [poêle, moteur] to hum, to purr.

ronger [17] [rɔ̃ʒe] *vt* [bois, os] to gnaw ; [métal, falaise] to eat away at ; *fig* to gnaw at, to eat away at. ◆ **se ronger** *vp* - **1.** [grignoter] : **se ~ les ongles** to bite one's nails - **2.** *fig* [se tourmenter] to worry, to torture o.s.

rongeur, euse [rɔ̃ʒœr, øz] *adj* gnawing, rodent *(avant n)*. ◆ **rongeur** *nm* rodent.

ronronner [3] [rɔ̃rɔne] *vi* [chat] to purr ; [moteur] to purr, to hum.

rosace [rozas] *nf* - **1.** [ornement] rose - **2.** [vitrail] rose window - **3.** [figure géométrique] rosette.

rosbif [rɔsbif] *nm* [viande] roast beef.

rose [roz] ◇ *nf* rose. ◇ *nm* pink. ◇ *adj* pink.

rosé, e [roze] *adj* [teinte] rosy. ◆ **rosé** *nm* rosé. ◆ **rosée** *nf* dew.

roseau, x [rozo] *nm* reed.

rosier [rozje] *nm* rose bush.

rosir [32] [rozir] *vt & vi* to turn pink.

rosser [3] [rɔse] *vt* to thrash.

rossignol [rɔsiɲɔl] *nm* [oiseau] nightingale.

rot [ro] *nm* burp.

rotatif, ive [rɔtatif, iv] *adj* rotary.

rotation [rɔtasjɔ̃] *nf* rotation.

roter [3] [rɔte] *vi fam* to burp.

rôti, e [roti] *adj* roast. ◆ **rôti** *nm* roast, joint.

rotin [rɔtɛ̃] *nm* rattan.

rôtir [32] [rotir] ◇ *vt* to roast. ◇ *vi* CULIN to roast.

rôtisserie [rotisri] *nf* - **1.** [restaurant] ≃ steakhouse - **2.** [magasin] *shop selling roast meat*.

rotonde [rɔtɔ̃d] *nf* [bâtiment] rotunda.

rotule [rɔtyl] *nf* kneecap.

rouage [rwaʒ] *nm* cog, gearwheel ; **les ~s de l'État** *fig* the wheels of State.

rouble [rubl] *nm* rouble.

roucouler [3] [rukule] ◇ *vt* to warble ; *fig* to coo. ◇ *vi* to coo ; *fig* to bill and coo.

roue [ru] *nf* - **1.** [gén] wheel ; **~ de secours** spare wheel ; **un deux ~s** a two-wheeled vehicle - **2.** [de paon] : **faire la ~** to display - **3.** GYM cartwheel.

rouer [6] [rwe] *vt* : **~ qqn de coups** to thrash sb, to beat sb.

rouge [ruʒ] ◇ *nm* - **1.** [couleur] red - **2.** *fam* [vin] red (wine) - **3.** [fard] rouge, blusher ; **~ à lèvres** lipstick - **4.** AUTOM : **passer au ~** to turn red ; [conducteur] to go through a red light. ◇ *nmf* POLIT & *péj* Red. ◇ *adj* - **1.** [gén] red - **2.** [fer, tison] red-hot - **3.** POLIT & *péj* Red.

rouge-gorge [ruʒgɔrʒ] *nm* robin.

rougeole [ruʒɔl] *nf* measles *(sg)*.

rougeoyer [13] [ruʒwaje] *vi* to turn red.

rougeur [ruʒœr] *nf* - **1.** [de visage, de chaleur, d'effort] flush ; [de gêne] blush - **2.** [sur peau] red spot ou blotch.

rougir [32] [ruʒir] ◇ *vt* - **1.** [colorer] to turn red - **2.** [chauffer] to make red-hot. ◇ *vi* - **1.** [devenir rouge] to turn red - **2.** [d'émotion] : **~ (de)** [de plaisir, colère] to flush (with) ; [de gêne] to blush (with) - **3.** *fig* [avoir honte] : **~ de qqch** to be ashamed of sthg.

rougissant, e [ruʒisɑ̃, ɑ̃t] *adj* [ciel] reddening ; [jeune fille] blushing.

rouille [ruj] ◇ *nf* - **1.** [oxyde] rust - **2.** CULIN *spicy garlic sauce for fish soup*. ◇ *adj inv* rust.

rouiller [3] [ruje] ◇ *vt* to rust, to make rusty. ◇ *vi* to rust.

roulade [rulad] *nf* [galipette] roll.

rouleau, x [rulo] *nm* - **1.** [gén & TECHNOL] roller ; **~ compresseur** steamroller - **2.** [de papier] roll - **3.** [à pâtisserie] rolling pin - **4.** CULIN : **~ de printemps** spring roll.

roulement [rulmɑ̃] *nm* - **1.** [gén] rolling - **2.** [de personnel] rotation ; **travailler par ~** to work to a rota - **3.** [de tambour, tonnerre] roll - **4.** TECHNOL rolling bearing - **5.** FIN circulation.

rouler [3] [rule] ◇ *vt* - **1.** [déplacer] to wheel - **2.** [enrouler - tapis] to roll up ; [- cigarette] to roll - **3.** *fam* [balancer] to sway - **4.** LING to roll - **5.** *fam fig* [duper] to swindle, to do. ◇ *vi* - **1.** [ballon, bateau] to roll - **2.** [véhicule] to go, to run ; [suj : personne] to drive. ◆ **se rouler** *vp* to roll about ; **se ~ par terre** to roll on the ground ; **se ~ en boule** to roll o.s. into a ball.

roulette [rulɛt] *nf* - **1.** [petite roue] castor - **2.** [de dentiste] drill - **3.** JEU roulette.

roulis [ruli] *nm* roll.

roulotte [rulɔt] *nf* [de gitan] caravan ; [de tourisme] caravan *Br*, trailer *Am*.

roumain, e [rumɛ̃, ɛn] *adj* Romanian.
➡ **roumain** *nm* [langue] Romanian.
➡ **Roumain, e** *nm, f* Romanian.

Roumanie [rumani] *nf* : la ~ Romania.

rouquin, e [rukɛ̃, in] *fam* ⬦ *adj* red-headed. ⬦ *nm, f* redhead.

rouspéter [18] [ruspete] *vi fam* to grumble, to moan.

rousse ➡ roux.

rousseur [rusœr] *nf* redness. ➡ **taches de rousseur** *nfpl* freckles.

roussir [32] [rusir] ⬦ *vt* - **1.** [rendre roux] to turn brown ; CULIN to brown - **2.** [brûler légèrement] to singe. ⬦ *vi* to turn brown ; CULIN to brown.

route [rut] *nf* - **1.** [gén] road ; **en ~** on the way ; **en ~!** let's go! ; **mettre en ~** [démarrer] to start up ; *fig* to get under way - **2.** [itinéraire] route.

routier, ère [rutje, ɛr] *adj* road *(avant n)*.
➡ **routier** *nm* - **1.** [chauffeur] long-distance lorry driver *Br* ou trucker *Am* - **2.** [restaurant] ≃ transport cafe *Br*, ≃ truck stop *Am*.

routine [rutin] *nf* routine.

routinier, ère [rutinje, ɛr] *adj* routine.

rouvert, e [ruver, ɛrt] *pp* ➡ rouvrir.

rouvrir [34] [ruvrir] *vt* to reopen, to open again. ➡ **se rouvrir** *vp* to reopen, to open again.

roux, rousse [ru, rus] ⬦ *adj* - **1.** [cheveux] red - **2.** [sucre] brown. ⬦ *nm, f* [personne] redhead. ➡ **roux** *nm* [couleur] red, russet.

royal, e, aux [rwajal, o] *adj* - **1.** [de roi] royal - **2.** [magnifique] princely.

royaliste [rwajalist] *nmf & adj* royalist.

royaume [rwajom] *nm* kingdom.

Royaume-Uni [rwajomyni] *nm* : **le ~** the United Kingdom.

royauté [rwajote] *nf* - **1.** [fonction] kingship - **2.** [régime] monarchy.

RPR *(abr de* **Rassemblement pour la République***) nm* French political party to the right of the political spectrum.

rte *abr de* **route**.

RTT *(abr de* **réduction du temps de travail***)* ⬦ *nf* French government employment scheme to reduce working hours to 35 hours per week. ⬦ *adj* : **jours ~** paid holiday *Br*, paid vacation *Am*.

ruade [ryad] *nf* kick.

ruban [rybɑ̃] *nm* ribbon ; **~ adhésif** adhesive tape.

rubéole [rybeɔl] *nf* German measles *(sg)*, rubella.

rubis [rybi] *nm* [pierre précieuse] ruby.

rubrique [rybrik] *nf* - **1.** [chronique] column - **2.** [dans classement] heading.

ruche [ryʃ] *nf* [abri] hive, beehive ; *fig* hive of activity.

rude [ryd] *adj* - **1.** [surface] rough - **2.** [voix] harsh - **3.** [personne, manières] rough, uncouth - **4.** [hiver, épreuve] harsh, severe ; [tâche, adversaire] tough.

rudement [rydmɑ̃] *adv* - **1.** [brutalement - tomber] hard ; [- répondre] harshly - **2.** *fam* [très] damn.

rudesse [rydɛs] *nf* harshness, severity.

rudimentaire [rydimɑ̃tɛr] *adj* rudimentary.

rudoyer [13] [rydwaje] *vt* to treat harshly.

rue [ry] *nf* street.

ruée [rɥe] *nf* rush.

ruelle [rɥɛl] *nf* [rue] alley, lane.

ruer [7] [rɥe] *vi* to kick. ➡ **se ruer** *vp* : **se ~ sur** to pounce on.

rugby [rygbi] *nm* rugby.

rugir [32] [ryʒir] *vi* to roar ; [vent] to howl.

rugissement [ryʒismɑ̃] *nm* roar, roaring *(U)* ; [de vent] howling.

rugosité [rygozite] *nf* - **1.** [de surface] roughness - **2.** [aspérité] rough patch.

rugueux, euse [rygø, øz] *adj* rough.

ruine [rɥin] *nf* - **1.** [gén] ruin - **2.** [effondrement] ruin, downfall - **3.** [humaine] wreck.

ruiner [3] [rɥine] *vt* to ruin. ➡ **se ruiner** *vp* to ruin o.s., to bankrupt o.s.

ruineux, euse [rɥinø, øz] *adj* ruinous.

ruisseau, x [rɥiso] *nm* - **1.** [cours d'eau] stream - **2.** *fig & péj* [caniveau] gutter.

ruisseler [24] [rɥisle] *vi* : **~ (de)** to stream (with).

rumeur [rymœr] *nf* - **1.** [bruit] murmur - **2.** [nouvelle] rumour *Br*, rumor *Am*.

ruminer [3] [rymine] *vt* to ruminate ; *fig* to mull over.

rupture [ryptyr] *nf* - **1.** [cassure] breaking - **2.** *fig* [changement] abrupt change - **3.** [dénégociations, fiançailles] breaking off ; [de contrat] breach - **4.** [amoureuse] breakup, split.

rural, e, aux [ryral, o] *adj* country *(avant n)*, rural.

ruse [ryz] *nf* - **1.** [habileté] cunning, craftiness - **2.** [subterfuge] ruse.

rusé, e [ryze] *adj* cunning, crafty.

russe [rys] ⬦ *adj* Russian. ⬦ *nm* [langue] Russian. ➡ **Russe** *nmf* Russian.

Russie [rysi] *nf* : **la ~** Russia.

rustine [rystin] *nf* small rubber patch for repairing bicycle tyres.

rustique [rystik] *adj* rustic.

rustre [rystr] *péj* ⬦ *nmf* lout. ⬦ *adj* loutish.

rutilant, e [rytilɑ̃, ɑ̃t] *adj* [brillant] gleaming.

rythme [ritm] *nm* - **1.** MUS rhythm ; **en ~ in** rhythm - **2.** [de travail, production] pace, rate.

rythmique [ritmik] *adj* rhythmical.

s, S [ɛs] *nm inv* - **1.** [lettre] s, S - **2.** [forme] zigzag. ◆ **S** (*abr de* **Sud**) S.

s' ⊳ se, si.

s/ *abr de* sur.

sa ⊳ son².

SA (*abr de* société anonyme) *nf* ≃ Ltd *Br*, ≃ Inc. *Am*.

sabbatique [sabatik] *adj* - **1.** RELIG Sabbath (*avant n*) - **2.** [congé] sabbatical.

sable [sabl] *nm* sand ; **~s mouvants** quicksand (*sg*), quicksands.

sablé, e [sable] *adj* [route] sandy. ◆ **sablé** *nm* ≃ shortbread (*U*).

sabler [3] [sable] *vt* - **1.** [route] to sand - **2.** [boire] : **~ le champagne** to crack a bottle of champagne.

sablier [sablije] *nm* hourglass.

sablonneux, euse [sablɔnø, øz] *adj* sandy.

saborder [3] [sabɔrde] *vt* [navire] to scuttle ; *fig* [entreprise] to wind up ; *fig* [projet] to scupper.

sabot [sabo] *nm* - **1.** [chaussure] clog - **2.** [de cheval] hoof - **3.** AUTOM : **~ de Denver** wheel clamp, Denver boot.

sabotage [sabɔtaʒ] *nm* - **1.** [volontaire] sabotage - **2.** [bâclage] bungling.

saboter [3] [sabɔte] *vt* - **1.** [volontairement] to sabotage - **2.** [bâcler] to bungle.

saboteur, euse [sabɔtœr, øz] *nm, f* MIL & POLIT saboteur.

sabre [sabr] *nm* sabre *Br*, saber *Am*.

sac [sak] *nm* - **1.** [gén] bag ; [pour grains] sack ; [contenu] bag, bagful, sack, sackful ; **~ de couchage** sleeping bag ; **~ à dos** rucksack ; **~ à main** handbag - **2.** *fam* [10 francs] 10 francs - **3.** *littéraire* [pillage] sack.

saccade [sakad] *nf* jerk.

saccadé, e [sakade] *adj* jerky.

saccage [sakaʒ] *nm* havoc.

saccager [17] [sakaʒe] *vt* - **1.** [piller] to sack - **2.** [dévaster] to destroy.

sacerdoce [saserdɔs] *nm* priesthood ; *fig* vocation.

sachant *ppr* ⊳ savoir.

sache, saches *etc* ⊳ savoir.

sachet [saʃɛ] *nm* [de bonbons] bag ; [de shampooing] sachet ; **~ de thé** teabag.

sacoche [sakɔʃ] *nf* - **1.** [de médecin, d'écolier] bag - **2.** [de cycliste] pannier.

sac-poubelle [sakpubɛl] (*pl* **sacs-poubelle**) *nm* [petit] dustbin liner ; [grand] rubbish bag *Br*, garbage bag *Am*.

sacre [sakr] *nm* [de roi] coronation ; [d'évêque] consecration.

sacré, e [sakre] *adj* - **1.** [gén] sacred - **2.** RELIG [ordres, écritures] holy - **3.** (*avant n*) *fam* [maudit] bloody *Br* (*avant n*), goddam *Am* (*avant n*).

sacrement [sakrəmɑ̃] *nm* sacrament.

sacrément [sakremɑ̃] *adv* *fam vieilli* dashed.

sacrer [3] [sakre] *vt* - **1.** [roi] to crown ; [évêque] to consecrate - **2.** *fig* [déclarer] to hail.

sacrifice [sakrifis] *nm* sacrifice.

sacrifié, e [sakrifje] *adj* - **1.** [personne] sacrificed - **2.** [prix] giveaway (*avant n*).

sacrifier [9] [sakrifje] *vt* [gén] to sacrifice ; **~ qqn/qqch à** to sacrifice sb/sthg to. ◆ **se sacrifier** *vp* : **se ~ à/pour** to sacrifice o.s. to/for.

sacrilège [sakrilɛʒ] ⬦ *nm* sacrilege. ⬦ *adj* sacrilegious.

sacristain [sakristɛ̃] *nm* sacristan.

sacristie [sakristi] *nf* sacristy.

sadique [sadik] ⬦ *nmf* sadist. ⬦ *adj* sadistic.

sadisme [sadism] *nm* sadism.

safari [safari] *nm* safari.

safran [safrɑ̃] *nm* [épice] saffron.

saga [saga] *nf* saga.

sage [saʒ] ⬦ *adj* - **1.** [personne, conseil] wise, sensible - **2.** [enfant, chien] good - **3.** [goûts] modest ; [propos, vêtement] sober. ⬦ *nm* wise man, sage.

sage-femme [saʒfam] *nf* midwife.

sagement [saʒmɑ̃] *adv* - **1.** [avec bon sens] wisely, sensibly - **2.** [docilement] like a good girl/boy.

sagesse [saʒɛs] *nf* - **1.** [bon sens] wisdom, good sense - **2.** [docilité] good behaviour *Br* ou behavior *Am*.

Sagittaire [saʒitɛr] *nm* ASTROL Sagittarius.

Sahara [saara] *nm* : **le ~** the Sahara.

saignant, e [sɛɲɑ̃, ɑ̃t] *adj* - **1.** [blessure] bleeding - **2.** [viande] rare, underdone.

saignement [sɛɲmɑ̃] *nm* bleeding.

saigner [4] [seɲe] <> *vt* - **1.** [malade, animal] to bleed - **2.** [financièrement] : **~ qqn (à blanc)** to bleed sb (white). <> *vi* to bleed ; **je saigne du nez** my nose is bleeding, I've got a nosebleed.

saillant, e [sajɑ̃, ɑ̃t] *adj* [proéminent] projecting, protruding ; [muscles] bulging ; [pommettes] prominent.

saillie [saji] *nf* [avancée] projection ; **en ~** projecting.

saillir [50] [sajir] *vi* [balcon] to project, to protrude ; [muscles] to bulge.

sain, e [sɛ̃, sɛn] *adj* - **1.** [gén] healthy ; **~ et sauf** safe and sound - **2.** [lecture] wholesome - **3.** [fruit] fit to eat ; [mur, gestion] sound.

saint, e [sɛ̃, sɛ̃t] <> *adj* - **1.** [sacré] holy - **2.** [pieux] saintly - **3.** [extrême] : **avoir une ~e horreur de qqch** to detest sthg. <> *nm, f* saint.

saint-bernard [sɛ̃bɛrnar] *nm inv* - **1.** [chien] St Bernard - **2.** *fig* [personne] good Samaritan.

saintement [sɛ̃tmɑ̃] *adv* : **vivre ~** to lead a saintly life.

sainte-nitouche [sɛ̃tnituʃ] *nf pej* : **c'est une ~** butter wouldn't melt in her mouth.

sainteté [sɛ̃te] *nf* holiness.

saint-glinglin [sɛ̃glɛ̃glɛ̃] ◆ **à la saint-glinglin** *loc adv fam* till Doomsday.

Saint-Père [sɛ̃pɛr] *nm* Holy Father.

sais, sait *etc* ⊳ **savoir**.

saisie [sezi] *nf* - **1.** HIST & JUR distraint, seizure - **2.** INFORM input ; **~ de données** data capture.

saisir [32] [sezir] *vt* - **1.** [empoigner] to take hold of ; [avec force] to seize - **2.** FIN & JUR to seize, to distrain - **3.** INFORM to capture - **4.** [comprendre] to grasp - **5.** [suj : sensation, émotion] to grip, to seize - **6.** [surprendre] : **être saisi par** to be struck by - **7.** CULIN to seal. ◆ **se saisir** *vp* : **se ~ de qqn/qqch** to seize sb/sthg, to grab sb/sthg.

saisissant, e [sezisɑ̃, ɑ̃t] *adj* - **1.** [spectacle] gripping ; [ressemblance] striking - **2.** [froid] biting.

saison [sɛzɔ̃] *nf* season ; **en/hors ~** in/out of season ; **la haute/basse/morte ~** the high/low/off season.

saisonnier, ère [sɛzɔnje, ɛr] <> *adj* seasonal. <> *nm, f* seasonal worker.

salace [salas] *adj* salacious.

salade [salad] *nf* - **1.** [plante] lettuce - **2.** [plat] (green) salad ; **~ de fruits** fruit salad.

saladier [saladje] *nm* salad bowl.

salaire [salɛr] *nm* - **1.** [rémunération] salary, wage ; **~ brut/net/de base** gross/net/basic salary, gross/net/basic wage - **2.** *fig* [récompense] reward.

salant [salɑ̃] ⊳ **marais**.

salarial, e, aux [salarjal, o] *adj* wage *(avant n)*.

salarié, e [salarje] <> *adj* - **1.** [personne] wage-earning - **2.** [travail] paid. <> *nm, f* salaried employee.

salaud [salo] *vulg* <> *nm* bastard. <> *adj m* shitty.

sale [sal] *adj* - **1.** [linge, mains] dirty ; [couleur] dirty, dingy - **2.** *(avant n)* [type, gueule, coup] nasty ; [tour, histoire] dirty ; [bête, temps] filthy.

salé, e [sale] *adj* - **1.** [eau, saveur] salty ; [beurre] salted ; [viande, poisson] salt *(avant n)*, salted - **2.** *fig* [histoire] spicy - **3.** *fam fig* [addition, facture] steep.

saler [3] [sale] *vt* - **1.** [gén] to salt - **2.** *fam fig* [note] to bump up.

saleté [salte] *nf* - **1.** [malpropreté] dirtiness, filthiness - **2.** [crasse] dirt *(U)*, filth *(U)* ; **faire des ~s** to make a mess - **3.** *fam* [maladie] bug - **4.** [obscénité] dirty thing, obscenity ; **il m'a dit des ~s** he used obscenities to me - **5.** [action] disgusting thing ; **faire une ~ à qqn** to play a dirty trick on sb - **6.** *fam pej* [personne] nasty piece of work.

salière [saljɛr] *nf* saltcellar.

salir [32] [salir] *vt* - **1.** [linge, mains] to (make) dirty, to soil - **2.** *fig* [réputation, personne] to sully.

salissant, e [salisɑ̃, ɑ̃t] *adj* - **1.** [tissu] easily soiled - **2.** [travail] dirty, messy.

salive [saliv] *nf* saliva.

saliver [3] [salive] *vi* to salivate.

salle [sal] *nf* - **1.** [pièce] room ; **en ~** inside ; [dans un café] inside ; **~ d'attente** waiting room ; **~ de bains** bathroom ; **~ de cinéma** cinema ; **~ de classe** classroom ; **~ d'eau, ~ de douches** shower room ; **~ d'embarquement** gate lounge ; **~ à manger** dining room ; **~ d'opération** operating theatre *Br* ou room *Am* ; **~ de séjour** living room ; **~ de spectacle** theatre *Br*, theater *Am* ; **~ des ventes** saleroom *Br*, salesroom *Am* - **2.** [de spectacle] auditorium - **3.** [public] audience, house ; **faire ~ comble** to have a full house.

salon [salɔ̃] *nm* - **1.** [de maison] lounge *Br*, living room - **2.** [commerce] : **~ de coiffure**

hairdressing salon, hairdresser's ; ~ de thé tearoom - **3.** [foire-exposition] show.

salope [salɔp] *nf vulg* bitch.

saloperie [salɔpri] *nf fam* - **1.** [pacotille] rubbish *(U)* - **2.** [maladie] bug - **3.** [saleté] junk *(U)*, rubbish *(U)* ; **faire des ~s** to make a mess - **4.** [action] dirty trick ; **faire des ~s à qqn** to play dirty tricks on sb - **5.** [propos] dirty comment.

salopette [salɔpɛt] *nf* [d'ouvrier] overalls *(pl)* ; [à bretelles] dungarees *(pl)* Br, overalls Am.

saltimbanque [saltɛ̃bɑ̃k] *nmf* acrobat.

salubrité [salybrite] *nf* healthiness.

saluer [7] [salɥe] *vt* - **1.** [accueillir] to greet - **2.** [dire au revoir à] to take one's leave of - **3.** MIL & *fig* to salute. ◆ **se saluer** *vp* to say hello/goodbye (to one another).

salut [saly] ◇ *nm* - **1.** [de la main] wave ; [de la tête] nod ; [propos] greeting - **2.** MIL salute - **3.** [sauvegarde] safety - **4.** RELIG salvation. ◇ *interj fam* [bonjour] hi! ; [au revoir] bye!, see you!

salutaire [salytɛr] *adj* - **1.** [conseil, expérience] salutary - **2.** [remède, repos] beneficial.

salutation [salytasjɔ̃] *nf littéraire* salutation, greeting. ◆ **salutations** *nfpl* : **veuillez agréer, Monsieur, mes ~s distinguées** ou **mes sincères ~s** *sout* yours faithfully, yours sincerely.

salve [salv] *nf* salvo.

samedi [samdi] *nm* Saturday ; **nous sommes partis ~** we left on Saturday ; **~ 13 septembre** Saturday 13th September ; **~ dernier/prochain** last/next Saturday ; **le ~** on Saturdays.

SAMU, Samu [samy] (*abr de* **Service d'aide médicale d'urgence**) *nm French ambulance and emergency service*, ≃ Ambulance Brigade Br, ≃ Paramedics Am.

sanatorium [sanatɔrjɔm] *nm* sanatorium.

sanctifier [9] [sɑ̃ktifje] *vt* - **1.** [rendre saint] to sanctify - **2.** [révérer] to hallow.

sanction [sɑ̃ksjɔ̃] *nf* sanction ; *fig* [conséquence] penalty, price ; **prendre des ~s contre** to impose sanctions on.

sanctionner [3] [sɑ̃ksjɔne] *vt* to sanction.

sanctuaire [sɑ̃ktɥer] *nm* - **1.** [d'église] sanctuary - **2.** [lieu saint] shrine.

sandale [sɑ̃dal] *nf* sandal.

sandalette [sɑ̃dalɛt] *nf* sandal.

sandwich [sɑ̃dwitʃ] (*pl* **sandwiches** ou **sandwichs**) *nm* sandwich.

sang [sɑ̃] *nm* blood.

sang-froid [sɑ̃frwa] *nm inv* calm ; **de ~** in cold blood ; **perdre/garder son ~** to lose/to keep one's head.

sanglant, e [sɑ̃glɑ̃, ɑ̃t] *adj* bloody ; *fig* cruel.

sangle [sɑ̃gl] *nf* strap ; [de selle] girth.

sangler [3] [sɑ̃gle] *vt* [attacher] to strap ; [cheval] to girth.

sanglier [sɑ̃glije] *nm* boar.

sanglot [sɑ̃glo] *nm* sob ; **éclater en ~s** to burst into sobs.

sangloter [3] [sɑ̃glɔte] *vi* to sob.

sangsue [sɑ̃sy] *nf* leech ; *fig* [personne] bloodsucker.

sanguin, e [sɑ̃gɛ̃, in] *adj* - **1.** ANAT blood *(avant n)* - **2.** [rouge - visage] ruddy ; [- orange] blood *(avant n)* - **3.** [emporté] quick-tempered.

sanguinaire [sɑ̃giner] *adj* - **1.** [tyran] bloodthirsty - **2.** [lutte] bloody.

Sanisette® [sanizɛt] *nf automatic public toilet.*

sanitaire [saniter] *adj* - **1.** [service, mesure] health *(avant n)* - **2.** [installation, appareil] bathroom *(avant n)*. ◆ **sanitaires** *nmpl* toilets and showers.

sans [sɑ̃] ◇ *prép* without ; **~ argent** without any money ; **~ faire un effort** without making an effort. ◇ *adv* : **passe-moi mon manteau, je ne veux pas sortir ~** pass me my coat, I don't want to go out without it. ◆ **sans que** *loc conj* : **~ que vous le sachiez** without your knowing.

sans-abri [sɑ̃zabri] *nmf inv* homeless person.

sans-emploi [sɑ̃zɑ̃plwa] *nmf inv* unemployed person.

sans-gêne [sɑ̃ʒɛn] ◇ *nm inv* [qualité] rudeness, lack of consideration. ◇ *nmf inv* [personne] rude ou inconsiderate person. ◇ *adj inv* rude, inconsiderate.

sans-plomb [sɑ̃plɔ̃] *nm inv* unleaded (petrol Br ou gas Am), lead-free petrol Br ou gas Am.

santé [sɑ̃te] *nf* health ; **à ta/votre ~!** cheers!, good health!

santon [sɑ̃tɔ̃] *nm figure placed in Christmas crib.*

saoul = **soûl.**

saouler = **soûler.**

sapeur-pompier [sapœrpɔ̃pje] (*pl* **sapeurs-pompiers**) *nm* fireman, fire fighter.

saphir [safir] *nm* sapphire.

sapin [sapɛ̃] *nm* - **1.** [arbre] fir, firtree ; **~ de Noël** Christmas tree - **2.** [bois] fir, deal Br.

sarcasme [sarkasm] *nm* sarcasm.

sarcastique [sarkastik] *adj* sarcastic.

sarcler [3] [sarkle] *vt* to weed.
sarcophage [sarkɔfaʒ] *nm* sarcophagus.
Sardaigne [sardɛɲ] *nf* : **la ~** Sardinia.
sardine [sardin] *nf* sardine.
SARL, Sarl (*abr de* **société à responsabilité limitée**) *nf* limited liability company ; **Leduc, ~** ≃ Leduc Ltd.
sarment [sarmɑ̃] *nm* [de vigne] shoot.
sas [sas] *nm* - **1.** AÉRON & NAVIG airlock - **2.** [d'écluse] lock - **3.** [tamis] sieve.
satanique [satanik] *adj* satanic.
satelliser [3] [satelize] *vt* - **1.** [fusée] to put into orbit - **2.** [pays] to make a satellite.
satellite [satelit] *nm* satellite.
satiété [sasjete] *nf* : **à ~** [boire, manger] one's fill ; [répéter] ad nauseam.
satin [satɛ̃] *nm* satin.
satiné, e [satine] *adj* satin (*avant n*) ; [peau] satiny-smooth. ◆ **satiné** *nm* satin-like quality.
satire [satir] *nf* satire.
satirique [satirik] *adj* satirical.
satisfaction [satisfaksjɔ̃] *nf* satisfaction.
satisfaire [109] [satisfɛr] *vt* to satisfy. ◆ **se satisfaire** *vp* : **se ~ de** to be satisfied with.
satisfaisant, e [satisfəzɑ̃, ɑ̃t] *adj* - **1.** [travail] satisfactory - **2.** [expérience] satisfying.
satisfait, e [satisfɛ, ɛt] ◇ *pp* ⇨ **satisfaire**. ◇ *adj* satisfied ; **être ~ de** to be satisfied with.
saturation [satyrasjɔ̃] *nf* saturation.
saturé, e [satyre] *adj* : **~ (de)** saturated (with).
saturne [satyrn] *nm vieilli* lead. ◆ **Saturne** *nf* ASTRON Saturn.
satyre [satir] *nm* satyr ; *fig* sex maniac.
sauce [sos] *nf* CULIN sauce.
saucière [sosjɛr] *nf* sauceboat.
saucisse [sosis] *nf* CULIN sausage.
saucisson [sosisɔ̃] *nm* slicing sausage.
sauf¹, sauve [sof, sov] *adj* [personne] safe, unharmed ; *fig* [honneur] saved, intact.
sauf² [sof] *prép* - **1.** [à l'exclusion de] except, apart from - **2.** [sous réserve de] barring ; **~ que** except (that).
sauf-conduit [sofkɔ̃dɥi] (*pl* **sauf-conduits**) *nm* safe-conduct.
sauge [soʒ] *nf* CULIN sage.
saugrenu, e [sogrəny] *adj* ridiculous, nonsensical.
saule [sol] *nm* willow ; **~ pleureur** weeping willow.
saumon [somɔ̃] *nm* salmon.

saumoné, e [somɔne] *adj* salmon (*avant n*).
saumure [somyr] *nf* brine.
sauna [sona] *nm* sauna.
saupoudrer [3] [sopudre] *vt* : **~ qqch de** to sprinkle sthg with.
saurai, sauras *etc* ⇨ **savoir**.
saut [so] *nm* - **1.** [bond] leap, jump - **2.** SPORT : **~ en hauteur** high jump ; **~ en longueur** long jump, broad jump *Am* ; **~ à l'élastique** bungee-jumping ; **faire du ~ à l'élastique** to go bungee-jumping - **3.** [visite] : **faire un ~ chez qqn** *fig* to pop in and see sb - **4.** INFORM : **~ de page** page break.
sauté, e [sote] *adj* sautéed.
saute-mouton [sotmutɔ̃] *nm inv* : **jouer à ~** to play leapfrog.
sauter [3] [sote] ◇ *vi* - **1.** [bondir] to jump, to leap ; **~ à la corde** to skip ; **~ d'un sujet à l'autre** *fig* to jump from one subject to another ; **~ de joie** *fig* to jump for joy ; **~ au cou de qqn** *fig* to throw one's arms around sb - **2.** [exploser] to blow up ; [fusible] to blow - **3.** [être projeté - bouchon] to fly out ; [- serrure] to burst off ; [- bouton] to fly off, [- chaîne de vélo] to come off - **4.** *fam* [employé] to get the sack. ◇ *vt* - **1.** [fossé, obstacle] to jump ou leap over - **2.** *fig* [page, repas] to skip.
sauterelle [sotrɛl] *nf* ZOOL grasshopper.
sauteur, euse [sotœr, øz] ◇ *adj* [insecte] jumping (*avant n*). ◇ *nm, f* [athlète] jumper.
sautiller [3] [sotije] *vi* to hop.
sautoir [sotwar] *nm* [bijou] chain.
sauvage [sovaʒ] ◇ *adj* - **1.** [plante, animal] wild - **2.** [farouche - animal familier] shy, timid ; [- personne] unsociable - **3.** [conduite, haine] savage. ◇ *nmf* - **1.** [solitaire] recluse - **2.** *péj* [brute, indigène] savage.
sauvagerie [sovaʒri] *nf* - **1.** [férocité] brutality, savagery - **2.** [insociabilité] unsociableness.
sauve ⇨ **sauf¹**.
sauvegarde [sovgard] *nf* - **1.** [protection] safeguard - **2.** INFORM saving ; [copie] backup.
sauvegarder [3] [sovgarde] *vt* - **1.** [protéger] to safeguard - **2.** INFORM to save ; [copier] to back up.
sauve-qui-peut [sovkipø] ◇ *nm inv* [débandade] stampede. ◇ *interj* every man for himself!
sauver [3] [sove] *vt* - **1.** [gén] to save ; **~ qqn/qqch de** to save sb/sthg from, to rescue sb/sthg from - **2.** [navire, biens] to sal-

vage. ◆ **se sauver** *vp* : se ~ (de) to run away (from) ; [prisonnier] to escape (from).

sauvetage [sovtaʒ] *nm* - **1.** [de personne] rescue - **2.** [de navire, biens] salvage.

sauveteur [sovtœr] *nm* rescuer.

sauvette [sovɛt] ◆ **à la sauvette** *loc adv* hurriedly, at great speed.

savamment [savamɑ̃] *adv* - **1.** [avec érudition] learnedly - **2.** [avec habileté] skilfully, cleverly.

savane [savan] *nf* savanna.

savant, e [savɑ̃, ɑ̃t] *adj* - **1.** [érudit] scholarly - **2.** [habile] skilful, clever - **3.** [animal] performing *(avant n).* ◆ **savant** *nm* scientist.

saveur [savœr] *nf* flavour *Br*, flavor *Am* ; *fig* savour *Br*, savor *Am*.

savoir [59] [savwar] ◇ *vt* - **1.** [gén] to know ; **faire ~ qqch à qqn** to tell sb sthg, to inform sb of sthg ; **si j'avais su** ... had I but known ..., if I had only known ... ; **sans le ~** unconsciously, without being aware of it ; **tu (ne) peux pas ~** *fam* you have no idea ; **pas que je sache** not as far as I know - **2.** [être capable de] to know how to ; **sais-tu conduire?** can you drive? ◇ *nm* learning. ◆ **à savoir** *loc conj* namely, that is.

savoir-faire [savwarfɛr] *nm inv* know-how, expertise.

savoir-vivre [savwarvivr] *nm inv* good manners *(pl).*

savon [savɔ̃] *nm* - **1.** [matière] soap ; [pain] cake OU bar of soap - **2.** *fam* [réprimande] telling-off.

savonner [3] [savɔne] *vt* [linge] to soap. ◆ **se savonner** *vp* to soap o.s.

savonnette [savɔnɛt] *nf* guest soap.

savourer [3] [savure] *vt* to savour *Br*, to savor *Am*.

savoureux, euse [savurø, øz] *adj* - **1.** [mets] tasty - **2.** *fig* [anecdote] juicy.

saxophone [saksɔfɔn] *nm* saxophone.

s/c *(abr de* sous couvert de*)* c/o.

scabreux, euse [skabrø, øz] *adj* - **1.** [propos] shocking, indecent - **2.** [entreprise] risky.

scalpel [skalpɛl] *nm* scalpel.

scalper [3] [skalpe] *vt* to scalp.

scandale [skɑ̃dal] *nm* - **1.** [fait choquant] scandal - **2.** [indignation] uproar - **3.** [tapage] scene ; **faire du** OU **un ~** to make a scene.

scandaleux, euse [skɑ̃dalø, øz] *adj* scandalous, outrageous.

scandaliser [3] [skɑ̃dalize] *vt* to shock, to scandalize.

scander [3] [skɑ̃de] *vt* - **1.** [vers] to scan - **2.** [slogan] to chant.

scandinave [skɑ̃dinav] *adj* Scandinavian. ◆ **Scandinave** *nmf* Scandinavian.

Scandinavie [skɑ̃dinavi] *nf* : la ~ Scandinavia.

scanner¹ [4] [skane] *vt* to scan.

scanner² [skanɛr] *nm* scanner.

scaphandre [skafɑ̃dr] *nm* - **1.** [de plongeur] diving suit - **2.** [d'astronaute] spacesuit.

scarabée [skarabe] *nm* beetle, scarab.

scatologique [skatɔlɔʒik] *adj* scatological.

sceau, x [so] *nm* seal ; *fig* stamp, hallmark.

scélérat, e [selera, at] *littéraire* ◇ *adj* wicked. ◇ *nm, f* villain ; *péj* rogue, rascal.

sceller [4] [sele] *vt* - **1.** [gén] to seal - **2.** CONSTR [fixer] to embed.

scénario [senarjo] *nm* - **1.** CIN, LITTÉRA-TURE & THÉÂTRE [canevas] scenario - **2.** CIN & TÉLÉ [découpage, synopsis] screenplay, script - **3.** *fig* [rituel] pattern.

scénariste [senarist] *nmf* scriptwriter.

scène [sɛn] *nf* - **1.** [gén] scene - **2.** [estrade] stage ; **entrée en ~** THÉÂTRE entrance ; *fig* appearance ; **mettre en ~** THÉÂTRE to stage ; CIN to direct.

scepticisme [sɛptisism] *nm* scepticism *Br*, skepticism *Am*.

sceptique [sɛptik] ◇ *nmf* sceptic *Br*, skeptic *Am*. ◇ *adj* - **1.** [incrédule] sceptical *Br*, skeptical *Am* - **2.** PHILO sceptic *Br*, skeptic *Am*.

sceptre [sɛptr] *nm* sceptre *Br*, scepter *Am*.

schéma [ʃema] *nm* [diagramme] diagram.

schématique [ʃematik] *adj* - **1.** [dessin] diagrammatic - **2.** [interprétation, exposé] simplified.

schématiser [3] [ʃematize] *vt* *péj* [généraliser] to oversimplify.

schisme [ʃism] *nm* - **1.** RELIG schism - **2.** [d'opinion] split.

schizophrène [skizɔfrɛn] *nmf & adj* schizophrenic.

schizophrénie [skizɔfreni] *nf* schizophrenia.

sciatique [sjatik] ◇ *nf* sciatica. ◇ *adj* sciatic.

scie [si] *nf* [outil] saw.

sciemment [sjamɑ̃] *adv* knowingly.

science [sjɑ̃s] *nf* - **1.** [connaissances scientifiques] science ; **~s humaines** OU **sociales** UNIV social sciences - **2.** [érudition] knowledge - **3.** [art] art.

science-fiction [sjɑ̃sfiksjɔ̃] *nf* science fiction.

sciences-po [sjɑ̃spo] *nfpl* UNIV political

science *(sg).* ◆ **Sciences-Po** *n* grande école for political science.

scientifique [sjɑ̃tifik] ◇ *nmf* scientist. ◇ *adj* scientific.

scier [9] [sje] *vt* [branche] to saw.

scierie [siri] *nf* sawmill.

scinder [3] [sɛ̃de] *vt* : **~ (en)** to split (into), to divide (into). ◆ **se scinder** *vp* : **se ~ (en)** to split (into), to divide (into).

scintiller [3] [sɛ̃tije] *vi* to sparkle.

scission [sisjɔ̃] *nf* split.

sciure [sjyr] *nf* sawdust.

sclérose [skleroz] *nf* sclerosis ; *fig* ossification ; **~ en plaques** multiple sclerosis.

sclérosé, e [skleroze] *adj* sclerotic ; *fig* ossified.

scolaire [skɔlɛr] *adj* school *(avant n)* ; *péj* bookish.

scolarisable [skɔlarizabl] *adj* of school age.

scolarité [skɔlarite] *nf* schooling ; **frais de ~** SCOL school fees ; UNIV tuition fees.

scooter [skutœr] *nm* scooter.

scorbut [skɔrbyt] *nm* scurvy.

score [skɔr] *nm* SPORT score.

scorpion [skɔrpjɔ̃] *nm* scorpion. ◆ **Scorpion** *nm* ASTROL Scorpio.

scotch [skɔtʃ] *nm* [alcool] whisky, Scotch.

Scotch® [skɔtʃ] *nm* [adhésif] ≃ Sellotape® *Br*, ≃ Scotch tape® *Am*.

scotcher [3] [skɔtʃe] *vt* to sellotape *Br*, to scotch-tape *Am*.

scout, e [skut] *adj* scout *(avant n)*. ◆ **scout** *nm* scout.

scribe [skrib] *nm* HIST scribe.

script [skript] *nm* CIN & TÉLÉ script.

scripte [skript] *nmf* CIN & TÉLÉ continuity person.

scrupule [skrypyl] *nm* scruple ; **avec ~** scrupulously ; **sans ~s** [être] unscrupulous ; [agir] unscrupulously.

scrupuleux, euse [skrypylø, øz] *adj* scrupulous.

scrutateur, trice [skrytatœr, tris] *adj* searching.

scruter [3] [skryte] *vt* to scrutinize.

scrutin [skrytɛ̃] *nm* - **1.** [vote] ballot - **2.** [système] voting system ; **~ majoritaire** first-past-the-post system ; **~ proportionnel** proportional representation system.

sculpter [3] [skylte] *vt* to sculpt.

sculpteur [skyltœr] *nm* sculptor.

sculpture [skyltyr] *nf* sculpture.

SDF *(abr de* **sans domicile fixe)** *nmf* : **les ~** the homeless.

se [sə], **s'** *(devant voyelle ou h muet) pron pers* - **1.** *(réfléchi)* [personne] oneself, himself *(f* herself*), (pl)* themselves ; [chose, animal] itself, *(pl)* themselves ; **elle ~ regarde dans le miroir** she looks at herself in the mirror - **2.** *(réciproque)* each other, one another ; **ils ~ sont rencontrés hier** they met yesterday - **3.** *(passif)* : **ce produit ~ vend bien/partout** this product is selling well/is sold everywhere - **4.** [remplace l'adjectif possessif] : **~ laver les mains** to wash one's hands ; **~ couper le doigt** to cut one's finger.

séance [seɑ̃s] *nf* - **1.** [réunion] meeting, sitting, session - **2.** [période] session ; [de pose] sitting - **3.** CIN & THÉÂTRE performance - **4.** *loc* : **~ tenante** right away, forthwith.

seau, x [so] *nm* - **1.** [récipient] bucket - **2.** [contenu] bucketful.

sec, sèche [sɛk, sɛʃ] *adj* - **1.** [gén] dry - **2.** [fruits] dried - **3.** [personne - maigre] lean ; [- austère] austere - **4.** *fig* [cœur] hard ; [voix, ton] sharp - **5.** [sans autre prestation] : **vol ~** flight only. ◆ **sec** ◇ *adv* - **1.** [beaucoup] : **boire ~** to drink heavily - **2.** [démarrer] sharply. ◇ *nm* : **tenir au ~** to keep in a dry place.

sécable [sekabl] *adj* divisible.

sécateur [sekatœr] *nm* secateurs *(pl)*.

sécession [sesesjɔ̃] *nf* secession ; **faire ~ (de)** to secede (from).

sèche-cheveux [sɛʃʃəvø] *nm inv* hairdryer.

sèche-linge [sɛʃlɛ̃ʒ] *nm inv* tumble-dryer.

sécher [18] [seʃe] ◇ *vt* - **1.** [linge] to dry - **2.** *arg scol* [cours] to skip, to skive off *Br*. ◇ *vi* - **1.** [linge] to dry - **2.** [peau] to dry out ; [rivière] to dry up - **3.** *arg scol* [ne pas savoir répondre] to dry up.

sécheresse [seʃrɛs] *nf* - **1.** [de terre, climat, style] dryness - **2.** [absence de pluie] drought - **3.** [de réponse] curtness.

séchoir [seʃwar] *nm* - **1.** [tringle] airer, clotheshorse - **2.** [électrique] dryer ; **~ à cheveux** hairdryer.

second, e [səgɔ̃, ɔd] ◇ *adj num* second ; **dans un état ~** dazed. ◇ *nm, f* second ; *voir aussi* **sixième.** ◆ **seconde** *nf* - **1.** [unité de temps & MUS] second - **2.** SCOL ≃ fifth year *ou* form *Br*, ≃ tenth grade *Am* - **3.** TRANSPORT second class.

secondaire [səgɔ̃dɛr] ◇ *nm* : **le ~** GÉOL the Mesozoic ; SCOL secondary education ; ÉCON the secondary sector. ◇ *adj* - **1.** [gén & SCOL] secondary ; **effets ~s** MÉD side effects - **2.** GÉOL Mesozoic.

seconder [3] [səgɔ̃de] *vt* to assist.

secouer [6] [səkwe] *vt* [gén] to shake. ◆ **se secouer** *vp fam* to snap out of it.

secourable [səkurabl] *adj* helpful ; **main ~** helping hand.

secourir [45] [səkurir] *vt* [blessé, miséreux] to help ; [personne en danger] to rescue.

secouriste [səkurist] *nmf* first-aid worker.

secours [səkur] *nm* - **1.** [aide] help ; **appeler au ~** to call for help ; **les ~** emergency services ; **au ~!** help! - **2.** [dons] aid, relief - **3.** [renfort] relief, reinforcements *(pl)* - **4.** [soins] aid ; **les premiers ~** first aid *(U)*. ➭ **de secours** *loc adj* - **1.** [trousse, poste] first-aid *(avant n)* - **2.** [éclairage, issue] emergency *(avant n)* - **3.** [roue] spare.

secouru, e [səkury] *pp* ➭ **secourir**.

secousse [səkus] *nf* - **1.** [mouvement] jerk, jolt - **2.** *fig* [bouleversement] upheaval ; [psychologique] shock - **3.** [tremblement de terre] tremor.

secret, ète [səkrɛ, ɛt] *adj* - **1.** [gén] secret - **2.** [personne] reticent. ➭ **secret** *nm* - **1.** [gén] secret - **2.** [discrétion] secrecy ; **dans le plus grand ~** in the utmost secrecy.

secrétaire [səkretɛr] <> *nmf* [personne] secretary ; **~ de direction** executive secretary. <> *nm* [meuble] writing desk, secretaire.

secrétariat [səkretarja] *nm* - **1.** [bureau] secretary's office ; [d'organisation internationale] secretariat - **2.** [personnel] secretarial staff - **3.** [métier] secretarial work.

sécréter [18] [sekrete] *vt* to secrete ; *fig* to exude.

sécrétion [sekresjɔ̃] *nf* secretion.

sectaire [sɛktɛr] *nmf & adj* sectarian.

secte [sɛkt] *nf* sect.

secteur [sɛktœr] *nm* - **1.** [zone] area ; **se trouver dans le ~** *fam* to be somewhere *Br* ou someplace *Am* around - **2.** ADMIN district - **3.** ÉCON, GÉOM & MIL sector ; **~ privé/ public** private/public sector ; **~ primaire/ secondaire/tertiaire** primary/secondary/ tertiary sector - **4.** ÉLECTR mains ; **sur ~** off ou from the mains.

section [sɛksjɔ̃] *nf* - **1.** [gén] section ; [de parti] branch - **2.** MIL platoon.

sectionner [3] [sɛksjɔne] *vt* - **1.** *fig* [diviser] to divide into sections - **2.** [trancher] to sever.

Sécu [seky] *fam abr de* **Sécurité sociale**.

séculaire [sekylɛr] *adj* [ancien] age-old.

sécurisant, e [sekyrizɑ̃, ɑ̃t] *adj* [milieu] secure ; [attitude] reassuring.

sécurité [sekyrite] *nf* - **1.** [d'esprit] security - **2.** [absence de danger] safety ; **la ~ routière** road safety ; **en toute ~** safe and sound - **3.** [dispositif] safety catch - **4.** [orga-**

nisme**] : **la Sécurité sociale** ≃ the DSS *Br*, ≃ the Social Security *Am*.

sédatif, ive [sedatif, iv] *adj* sedative. ➭ **sédatif** *nm* sedative.

sédentaire [sedɑ̃tɛr] *adj* [personne, métier] sedentary ; [casanier] stay-at-home.

sédentariser [3] [sedɑ̃tarize] ➭ **se sédentariser** *vp* [tribu] to settle, to become settled.

sédiment [sedimɑ̃] *nm* sediment.

sédition [sedisjɔ̃] *nf* sedition.

séducteur, trice [sedyktœr, tris] <> *adj* seductive. <> *nm, f* seducer (*f* seductress).

séduire [98] [seɥir] *vt* - **1.** [plaire à] to attract, to appeal to - **2.** [abuser de] to seduce.

séduisant, e [seɥizɑ̃, ɑ̃t] *adj* attractive.

séduit, e [seɥi, it] *pp* ➭ **séduire**.

segment [sɛgmɑ̃] *nm* GÉOM segment.

segmenter [3] [sɛgmɑ̃te] *vt* to segment.

ségrégation [segregasjɔ̃] *nf* segregation.

seigle [sɛgl] *nm* rye.

seigneur [sɛɲœr] *nm* lord. ➭ **Seigneur** *nm* : **le Seigneur** the Lord.

sein [sɛ̃] *nm* breast ; *fig* bosom ; **donner le ~ (à un bébé)** to breast-feed (a baby). ➭ **au sein de** *loc prép* within.

Seine [sɛn] *nf* : **la ~** the (River) Seine.

séisme [seism] *nm* earthquake.

seize [sɛz] *adj num & nm* sixteen ; *voir aussi* **six**.

seizième [sɛzjɛm] *adj num, nm* ou *nmf* sixteenth ; *voir aussi* **sixième**.

séjour [seʒur] *nm* - **1.** [durée] stay ; **interdit de ~** ≃ banned ; **~ linguistique** stay abroad *(to develop language skills)* - **2.** [pièce] living room.

séjourner [3] [seʒurne] *vi* to stay.

sel [sɛl] *nm* salt ; *fig* piquancy.

sélection [selɛksjɔ̃] *nf* selection.

sélectionner [3] [selɛksjɔne] *vt* to select, to pick.

self-service [sɛlfsɛrvis] *(pl* **self-services)** *nm* self-service cafeteria.

selle [sɛl] *nf* [gén] saddle.

seller [4] [sele] *vt* to saddle.

selon [səlɔ̃] *prép* - **1.** [conformément à] in accordance with - **2.** [d'après] according to. ➭ **selon que** *loc conj* depending on whether.

semaine [səmɛn] *nf* [période] week ; **à la ~** [être payé] by the week.

sémantique [semɑ̃tik] *adj* semantic.

semblable [sɑ̃blabl] <> *nm* [prochain] fellow man ; **il n'a pas son ~** there's nobody like him. <> *adj* - **1.** [analogue] similar ; **~ à** like, similar to - **2.** *(avant n)* [tel] such.

semblant [sãblã] *nm* : un ~ de a semblance of ; faire ~ (de faire qqch) to pretend (to do sthg).

sembler [3] [sãble] <> *vi* to seem. <> *v impers* : il (me/te) semble que it seems (to me/you) that.

semelle [səmɛl] *nf* [de chaussure - dessous] sole ; [- à l'intérieur] insole.

semence [səmãs] *nf* - **1.** [graine] seed - **2.** [sperme] semen *(U)*.

semer [19] [səme] *vt* - **1.** [planter] *fig* to sow - **2.** [répandre] to scatter ; ~ qqch de to scatter sthg with, to strew sthg with - **3.** *fam* [se débarrasser de] to shake off - **4.** *fam* [perdre] to lose.

semestre [səmɛstr] *nm* half year, six-month period ; SCOL semester.

semestriel, elle [səmɛstrijɛl] *adj* - **1.** [qui a lieu tous les six mois] half-yearly, six-monthly - **2.** [qui dure six mois] six months', six-month.

séminaire [seminɛr] *nm* - **1.** RELIG seminary - **2.** UNIV [colloque] seminar.

séminariste [seminarist] *nm* seminarist.

semi-remorque [səmirəmɔrk] *(pl* semi-remorques) *nm* articulated lorry *Br*, semi trailer *Am*.

semis [səmi] *nm* - **1.** [méthode] sowing broadcast - **2.** [plant] seedling.

semoule [səmul] *nf* semolina.

sempiternel, elle [sãpitɛrnɛl] *adj* eternal.

sénat [sena] *nm* senate ; le Sénat upper house of the French parliament.

sénateur [senatœr] *nm* senator.

Sénégal [senegal] *nm* : le ~ Senegal.

sénile [senil] *adj* senile.

sénilité [senilite] *nf* senility.

sens [sãs] *nm* - **1.** [fonction, instinct, raison] sense ; avoir le ~ de l'humour to have a sense of humour *Br* ou humor *Am* ; bon ~ good sense - **2.** [direction] direction ; dans le ~ de la longueur lengthways ; dans le ~ des aiguilles d'une montre clockwise ; dans le ~ contraire des aiguilles d'une montre anticlockwise *Br*, counterclockwise *Am* ; ~ dessus dessous upside down ; ~ interdit ou unique one-way street - **3.** [signification] meaning ; cela n'a pas de ~! it's nonsensical! ; dans ou en un ~ in one sense ; ~ propre/figuré literal/figurative sense.

sensation [sãsasjɔ̃] *nf* - **1.** [perception] sensation, feeling - **2.** [impression] feeling.

sensationnel, elle [sãsasjɔnɛl] *adj* sensational.

sensé, e [sãse] *adj* sensible.

sensibiliser [3] [sãsibilize] *vt* - **1.** MÉD & PHOT to sensitize - **2.** *fig* [public] : ~ (à) to make aware (of).

sensibilité [sãsibilite] *nf* : ~ (à) sensitivity (to).

sensible [sãsibl] *adj* - **1.** [gén] : ~ (à) sensitive (to) - **2.** [notable] considerable, appreciable.

sensiblement [sãsibləmã] *adv* - **1.** [à peu près] more or less - **2.** [notablement] appreciably, considerably.

sensoriel, elle [sãsɔrjɛl] *adj* sensory.

sensualité [sãsɥalite] *nf* [lascivité] sensuousness ; [charnelle] sensuality.

sensuel, elle [sãsɥɛl] *adj* - **1.** [charnel] sensual - **2.** [lascif] sensuous.

sentence [sãtãs] *nf* - **1.** [jugement] sentence - **2.** [maxime] adage.

sentencieux, euse [sãtãsjø, øz] *adj péj* sententious.

senteur [sãtœr] *nf littéraire* perfume.

senti, e [sãti] <> *pp* ▷ sentir. <> *adj* : bien ~ [mots] well-chosen.

sentier [sãtje] *nm* path.

sentiment [sãtimã] *nm* feeling ; veuillez agréer, Monsieur, l'expression de mes ~s distingués/cordiaux/les meilleurs yours faithfully/sincerely/truly.

sentimental, e, aux [sãtimãtal, o] <> *adj* - **1.** [amoureux] love *(avant n)* - **2.** [sensible, romanesque] sentimental. <> *nm, f* sentimentalist.

sentinelle [sãtinɛl] *nf* sentry.

sentir [37] [sãtir] <> *vt* - **1.** [percevoir - par l'odorat] to smell ; [- par le goût] to taste ; [- par le toucher] to feel - **2.** [exhaler - odeur] to smell of - **3.** [colère, tendresse] to feel - **4.** [affectation, plagiat] to smack of - **5.** [danger] to sense, to be aware of ; ~ que to feel (that) - **6.** [beauté] to feel, to appreciate. <> *vi* : ~ bon/mauvais to smell good/bad. ◆ se sentir <> *v attr* : se ~ bien/fatigué to feel well/tired. <> *vp* [être perceptible] : ça se sent! you can really tell!

séparation [separasjɔ̃] *nf* separation.

séparatiste [separatist] *nmf* separatist.

séparé, e [separe] *adj* - **1.** [intérêts] separate - **2.** [couple] separated.

séparer [3] [separe] *vt* - **1.** [gén] : ~ (de) to separate (from) - **2.** [suj : divergence] to divide. ◆ se séparer *vp* - **1.** [se défaire] : se ~ de to part with - **2.** [conjoints] to separate, to split up ; se ~ de to separate from, to split up with - **3.** [participants] to disperse - **4.** [route] : se ~ (en) to split (into), to divide (into).

sept [sɛt] adj num & nm seven ; voir aussi six.

septembre [sɛptɑ̃br] nm September ; en ~, au mois de ~ in September ; début ~, au début du mois de ~ at the beginning of September ; fin ~, à la fin du mois de ~ at the end of September ; d'ici ~ by September ; (à la) mi-~ (in) mid-September ; le premier/deux/dix ~ the first/second/tenth of September.

septennat [sɛptena] nm seven-year term (of office).

septicémie [sɛptisemi] nf septicaemia Br, septicemia Am, blood poisoning.

septième [sɛtjɛm] adj num, nm OU nmf seventh ; voir aussi sixième.

sépulcre [sepylkr] nm sepulchre Br, sepulcher Am.

sépulture [sepyltyr] nf - 1. [lieu] burial place - 2. [inhumation] burial.

séquelle [sekɛl] nf (gén pl) aftermath ; MÉD aftereffect.

séquence [sekɑ̃s] nf sequence ; CARTES run, sequence.

séquestrer [3] [sekɛstre] vt - 1. [personne] to confine - 2. [biens] to impound.

serai, seras etc ▷ être.

serbe [sɛrb] adj Serbian. ◆ Serbe nmf Serb.

Serbie [sɛrbi] nf : la ~ Serbia.

serein, e [sərɛ̃, ɛn] adj - 1. [calme] serene - 2. [impartial] calm, dispassionate.

sérénade [serenad] nf MUS serenade.

sérénité [serenite] nf serenity.

serf, serve [sɛrf, sɛrv] nm, f serf.

sergent [sɛrʒɑ̃] nm sergeant.

série [seri] nf - 1. [gén] series (sg) - 2. SPORT rank ; [au tennis] seeding - 3. COMM & IND : produire qqch en ~ to mass-produce sthg ; hors ~ custom-made ; fig outstanding, extraordinary.

sérieusement [serjøzmɑ̃] adv seriously.

sérieux, euse [serjø, øz] adj - 1. [grave] serious - 2. [digne de confiance] reliable ; [client, offre] genuine - 3. [consciencieux] responsible ; ce n'est pas ~ it's irresponsible - 4. [considérable] considerable. ◆ sérieux nm - 1. [application] sense of responsibility - 2. [gravité] seriousness ; garder son ~ to keep a straight face ; prendre qqn/qqch au ~ to take sb/sthg seriously.

serin, e [sərɛ̃, in] nm, f [oiseau] canary.

seringue [sərɛ̃g] nf syringe.

serment [sɛrmɑ̃] nm - 1. [affirmation solennelle] oath ; sous ~ on OU under oath - 2. [promesse] vow, pledge.

sermon [sɛrmɔ̃] nm litt & fig sermon.

séronégatif, ive [serɔnegatif, iv] adj HIV-negative.

séropositif, ive [serɔpozitif, iv] adj HIV-positive.

séropositivité [serɔpozitivite] nf HIV infection.

serpe [sɛrp] nf billhook.

serpent [sɛrpɑ̃] nm ZOOL snake.

serpenter [3] [sɛrpɑ̃te] vi to wind.

serpillière [sɛrpijɛr] nf floor cloth.

serre [sɛr] nf [bâtiment] greenhouse, glasshouse. ◆ serres nfpl ZOOL talons, claws.

serré, e [sere] adj - 1. [écriture] cramped ; [tissu] closely-woven ; [rangs] serried - 2. [vêtement, chaussure] tight - 3. [discussion] closely argued ; [match] close-fought - 4. [poing, dents] clenched ; la gorge ~e with a lump in one's throat ; j'en avais le cœur ~ fig it was heartbreaking - 5. [café] strong.

serrer [4] [sere] ◇ vt - 1. [saisir] to grip, to hold tight ; ~ la main à qqn to shake sb's hand ; ~ qqn dans ses bras to hug sb - 2. fig [rapprocher] to bring together ; ~ les rangs to close ranks - 3. [poing, dents] to clench ; [lèvres] to purse ; fig [cœur] to wring - 4. [suj : vêtement, chaussure] to be too tight for - 5. [vis, ceinture] to tighten - 6. [trottoir, bordure] to hug. ◇ vi AUTOM : ~ à droite/gauche to keep right/left. ◆ se serrer vp - 1. [se blottir] : se ~ contre to huddle up to OU against - 2. [se rapprocher] to squeeze up.

serre-tête [sɛrtɛt] nm inv headband.

serrure [seryr] nf lock.

serrurier [seryrje] nm locksmith.

sertir [32] [sertir] vt - 1. [pierre précieuse] to set - 2. TECHNOL [assujettir] to crimp.

sérum [serɔm] nm serum.

servage [sɛrvaʒ] nm serfdom ; fig bondage.

servante [sɛrvɑ̃t] nf [domestique] maidservant.

serveur, euse [sɛrvœr, øz] nm, f [de restaurant] waiter (f waitress) ; [de bar] barman (f barmaid). ◆ serveur nm INFORM server.

servi, e [sɛrvi] pp ▷ servir.

serviable [sɛrvjabl] adj helpful, obliging.

service [sɛrvis] nm - 1. [gén] service ; être en ~ to be in use, to be set up ; hors ~ out of order - 2. [travail] duty ; pendant le ~ while on duty - 3. [département] department ; ~ d'ordre police and stewards (at a demonstration) - 4. MIL : ~ (militaire) military OU national service - 5. [aide, assistance] favour Br, favor Am ; rendre un ~ à qqn to do sb a favour *Br* ou favor *Am* ; **rendre ~** to be helpful ; **~ après-vente** after-sales service - **6.** [à table] : **premier/deuxième ~** first/second sitting - **7.** [pourboire] service (charge) ; **~ compris/non compris** service included/not included - **8.** [assortiment - de porcelaine] service, set ; [- de linge] set.

serviette [sɛrvjɛt] *nf* - **1.** [de table] serviette, napkin - **2.** [de toilette] towel - **3.** [porte-documents] briefcase. ◆ **serviette hygiénique** *nf* sanitary towel *Br* ou napkin *Am*.

serviette-éponge [sɛrvjɛtepɔ̃ʒ] *nf* terry towel.

servile [sɛrvil] *adj* - **1.** [gén] servile - **2.** [traduction, imitation] slavish.

servir [38] [sɛrvir] ⬦ *vt* - **1.** [gén] to serve ; **~ qqch à qqn** to serve sb sthg, to help sb to sthg - **2.** [avantager] to serve (well), to help. ⬦ *vi* - **1.** [avoir un usage] to be useful ou of use ; **ça peut toujours/encore ~** it may/may still come in useful - **2.** [être utile] : **~ à qqch/à faire qqch** to be used for sthg/for doing sthg ; **ça ne sert à rien** it's pointless - **3.** [tenir lieu] : **~ de** [personne] to act as ; [chose] to serve as - **4.** [domestique] to be in service - **5.** MIL & SPORT to serve - **6.** CARTES to deal. ◆ **se servir** *vp* - **1.** [prendre] : **se ~ (de)** to help o.s. (to) ; **servez-vous!** help yourself! - **2.** [utiliser] : **se ~ de qqn/qqch** to use sb/sthg.

serviteur [sɛrvitœr] *nm* servant.

servitude [sɛrvityd] *nf* - **1.** [esclavage] servitude - **2.** *(gén pl)* [contrainte] constraint.

ses ⬦ **son²**.

session [sɛsjɔ̃] *nf* - **1.** [d'assemblée] session, sitting - **2.** UNIV exam session - **3.** INFORM : **ouvrir une ~** to log in ou on ; **fermer** ou **clore une ~** to log out ou off.

set [sɛt] *nm* - **1.** TENNIS set - **2.** [napperon] : **~ (de table)** set of table ou place mats.

seuil [sœj] *nm litt* & *fig* threshold.

seul, e [sœl] ⬦ *adj* - **1.** [isolé] alone ; **~ à ~** alone (together), privately - **2.** [sans compagnie] alone, by o.s. ; **parler tout ~** to talk to o.s. - **3.** [sans aide] on one's own, by o.s. - **4.** [unique] : **le ~ ...** the only ... ; **un ~ ...** a single ... ; **pas un ~ ...** not one ..., not a single ... - **5.** [esseulé] lonely. ⬦ *nm, f* : **le ~** the only one ; **un ~** a single one, only one.

seulement [sœlmɑ̃] *adv* - **1.** [gén] only ; [exclusivement] only, solely - **2.** [même] even. ◆ **non seulement ... mais (encore)** *loc corrélative* not only ... but (also).

sève [sɛv] *nf* BOT sap.

sévère [sever] *adj* severe.

sévérité [severite] *nf* severity.

sévices [sevis] *nmpl sout* ill treatment *(U)*.

sévir [32] [sevir] *vi* - **1.** [épidémie, guerre] to rage - **2.** [punir] to give out a punishment.

sevrer [19] [səvre] *vt* to wean.

sexe [sɛks] *nm* - **1.** [gén] sex - **2.** [organe] genitals *(pl)*.

sexiste [sɛksist] *nmf* & *adj* sexist.

sexologue [sɛksɔlɔg] *nmf* sexologist.

sex-shop [sɛksʃɔp] *(pl* **sex-shops)** *nm* sex shop.

sextant [sɛkstɑ̃] *nm* sextant.

sexualité [sɛksɥalite] *nf* sexuality.

sexuel, elle [sɛksɥɛl] *adj* sexual.

sexy [sɛksi] *adj inv fam* sexy.

seyant, e [sɛjɑ̃, ɑ̃t] *adj* becoming.

shampooing [ʃɑ̃pwɛ̃] *nm* shampoo.

shérif [ʃerif] *nm* sheriff.

shopping [ʃɔpiŋ] *nm* shopping ; **faire du ~** to go (out) shopping.

short [ʃɔrt] *nm* shorts *(pl)*, pair of shorts.

show-business [ʃobiznɛs] *nm inv* show business.

si¹ [si] *nm inv* MUS B ; [chanté] ti.

si² [si] ⬦ *adv* - **1.** [tellement] so ; **elle est ~ belle** she is so beautiful ; **il roulait ~ vite qu'il a eu un accident** he was driving so fast (that) he had an accident ; **ce n'est pas ~ facile que ça** it's not as easy as that ; **~ vieux qu'il soit** however old he may be, old as he is - **2.** [oui] yes ; **tu n'aimes pas le café? — ~** don't you like coffee? — yes, I do. ⬦ *conj* - **1.** [gén] if ; **tu veux, on y va** we'll go if you want ; **tu faisais cela, je te détesterais** I would hate you if you did that ; **~ seulement** if only - **2.** [dans une question indirecte] if, whether ; **dites-moi ~ vous venez** tell me if ou whether you're coming. ◆ **si bien que** *loc conj* so that, with the result that.

SI *nm* *(abr de* **syndicat d'initiative)** tourist office.

siamois, e [sjamwa, az] *adj* : **frères ~, sœurs ~es** MÉD Siamese twins.

Sibérie [siberi] *nf* : **la ~** Siberia.

sibyllin, e [sibilɛ̃, in] *adj* enigmatic.

SICAV, Sicav [sikav] *(abr de* **société d'investissement à capital variable)** *nf* - **1.** [société] unit trust, mutual fund - **2.** [action] share in a unit trust.

Sicile [sisil] *nf* : **la ~** Sicily.

SIDA, Sida [sida] *(abr de* **syndrome immunodéficitaire acquis)** *nm* AIDS.

side-car [sidkar] *(pl* **side-cars)** *nm* sidecar.

sidéen, enne [sideɛ̃, ɛn] *nm, f* person with AIDS.

sidérer [18] [sidere] *vt fam* to stagger.

sidérurgie [sideryrʒi] *nf* [industrie] iron and steel industry.

siècle [sjɛkl] *nm* - **1.** [cent ans] century - **2.** [époque, âge] age - **3.** *(gén pl) fam* [longue durée] ages *(pl)*.

siège [sjɛʒ] *nm* - **1.** [meuble & POLIT] seat - **2.** MIL siege - **3.** [d'organisme] headquarters, head office ; ~ **social** registered office - **4.** MÉD **: se présenter par le ~** to be in the breech position.

siéger [22] [sjeʒe] *vi* - **1.** [juge, assemblée] to sit - **2.** *littéraire* [mal] to have its seat ; [maladie] to be located.

sien [sjɛ̃] ◆ **le sien** (*f* **la sienne** [lasjɛn], *mpl* **les siens** [lesjɛ̃], *fpl* **les siennes** [lesjɛn]) *pron poss* [d'homme] his ; [de femme] hers ; [de chose, d'animal] its ; **les ~s** his/her family ; **faire des siennes** to be up to one's usual tricks.

sieste [sjɛst] *nf* siesta.

sifflement [sifləmɑ̃] *nm* [son] whistling ; [de serpent] hissing.

siffler [3] [sifle] ◇ *vi* to whistle ; [serpent] to hiss. ◇ *vt* - **1.** [air de musique] to whistle - **2.** [femme] to whistle at - **3.** [chien] to whistle (for) - **4.** [acteur] to boo, to hiss - **5.** *fam* [verre] to knock back.

sifflet [siflɛ] *nm* whistle. ◆ **sifflets** *nmpl* hissing (*U*), boos.

siffloter [3] [siflɔte] *vi & vt* to whistle.

sigle [sigl] *nm* acronym, (set of) initials.

signal, aux [siɲal, o] *nm* - **1.** [geste, son] signal ; ~ **d'alarme** alarm (signal) ; **donner le ~ (de)** to give the signal (for) - **2.** [panneau] sign.

signalement [siɲalmɑ̃] *nm* description.

signaler [3] [siɲale] *vt* - **1.** [fait] to point out ; **rien à ~** nothing to report - **2.** [à la police] to denounce.

signalétique [siɲaletik] *adj* identifying.

signalisation [siɲalizasjɔ̃] *nf* [panneaux] signs *(pl)* ; [au sol] (road) markings *(pl)* ; NAVIG signals *(pl)*.

signataire [siɲatɛr] *nmf* signatory.

signature [siɲatyr] *nf* - **1.** [nom, marque] signature - **2.** [acte] signing.

signe [siɲ] *nm* - **1.** [gén] sign ; **être ~ de** to be a sign of ; **être né sous le ~ de** ASTROL to be born under the sign of ; ~ **avant-coureur** advance indication - **2.** [trait] mark ; ~ **particulier** distinguishing mark.

signer [3] [siɲe] *vt* to sign. ◆ **se signer** *vp* to cross o.s.

signet [siɲɛ] *nm* bookmark *(attached to spine of book)*.

significatif, ive [siɲifikatif, iv] *adj* significant.

signification [siɲifikasjɔ̃] *nf* [sens] meaning.

signifier [9] [siɲifje] *vt* - **1.** [vouloir dire] to mean - **2.** [faire connaître] to make known - **3.** JUR to serve notice of.

silence [silɑ̃s] *nm* - **1.** [gén] silence ; **garder le ~ (sur)** to remain silent (about) - **2.** MUS rest.

silencieux, euse [silɑ̃sjø, øz] *adj* - **1.** [lieu, appareil] quiet - **2.** [personne - taciturne] quiet ; [- muet] silent. ◆ **silencieux** *nm* silencer.

silex [silɛks] *nm* flint.

silhouette [silwɛt] *nf* - **1.** [de personne] silhouette ; [de femme] figure ; [d'objet] outline - **2.** ART silhouette.

silicium [silisjɔm] *nm* silicon.

silicone [silikon] *nf* silicone.

sillage [sijaʒ] *nm* wake.

sillon [sijɔ̃] *nm* - **1.** [tranchée, ride] furrow - **2.** [de disque] groove.

sillonner [3] [sijɔne] *vt* - **1.** [champ] to furrow - **2.** [ciel] to crisscross.

silo [silo] *nm* silo.

simagrées [simagre] *nfpl péj* **: faire des ~** to make a fuss.

similaire [similɛr] *adj* similar.

similicuir [similikɥir] *nm* imitation leather.

similitude [similityd] *nf* similarity.

simple [sɛ̃pl] ◇ *adj* - **1.** [gén] simple - **2.** [ordinaire] ordinary - **3.** [billet] **: un aller ~** a single ticket. ◇ *nm* TENNIS singles *(sg)*.

simplicité [sɛ̃plisite] *nf* simplicity.

simplifier [9] [sɛ̃plifje] *vt* to simplify.

simpliste [sɛ̃plist] *adj péj* simplistic.

simulacre [simylakr] *nm* - **1.** [semblant] **: un ~ de** a pretence of, a sham - **2.** [action simulée] enactment.

simulateur, trice [simylatœr, tris] *nm, f* pretender ; [de maladie] malingerer. ◆ **simulateur** *nm* TECHNOL simulator.

simulation [simylasjɔ̃] *nf* - **1.** [gén] simulation - **2.** [comédie] shamming, feigning ; [de maladie] malingering.

simuler [3] [simyle] *vt* - **1.** [gén] to simulate - **2.** [feindre] to feign, to sham.

simultané, e [simyltane] *adj* simultaneous.

sincère [sɛ̃sɛr] *adj* sincere.

sincèrement [sɛ̃sɛrmɑ̃] *adv* - **1.** [franchement] honestly, sincerely - **2.** [vraiment] really, truly.

sincérité [sɛ̃serite] *nf* sincerity.

sine qua non [sinekwanɔn] *adj* **: condition ~** prerequisite.

Singapour [sɛ̃gapur] *n* Singapore.

singe [sɛ̃ʒ] *nm* ZOOL monkey ; [de grande taille] ape.

singer [17] [sɛ̃ʒe] *vt* - **1.** [personne] to mimic, to ape - **2.** [sentiment] to feign.

singerie [sɛ̃ʒri] *nf* - **1.** [grimace] face - **2.** [manières] fuss *(U)*.

singulariser [3] [sɛ̃gylarize] *vt* to draw OU call attention to. ◆ **se singulariser** *vp* to draw OU call attention to o.s.

singularité [sɛ̃gylarite] *nf* - **1.** littéraire [bizarrerie] strangeness - **2.** [particularité] peculiarity.

singulier, ère [sɛ̃gylje, ɛr] *adj* - **1.** sout [bizarre] strange ; [spécial] uncommon - **2.** GRAM singular - **3.** [d'homme à homme] : **combat ~** single combat. ◆ **singulier** *nm* GRAM singular.

singulièrement [sɛ̃gyljɛrmɑ̃] *adv* - **1.** littéraire [bizarrement] strangely - **2.** [beaucoup, très] particularly.

sinistre [sinistr] ◇ *nm* - **1.** [catastrophe] disaster - **2.** JUR damage *(U)*. ◇ *adj* - **1.** [personne, regard] sinister - **2.** [maison, ambiance] gloomy - **2.** (avant n) péj [crétin, imbécile] dreadful, terrible.

sinistré, e [sinistre] ◇ *adj* [région] disaster (avant n), disaster-stricken ; [famille] disaster-stricken. ◇ *nm, f* disaster victim.

sinon [sinɔ̃] *conj* - **1.** [autrement] or else, otherwise - **2.** [sauf] except, apart from - **3.** [si ce n'est] if not.

sinueux, euse [sinɥø, øz] *adj* winding ; fig tortuous.

sinuosité [sinɥozite] *nf* bend, twist.

sinus [sinys] *nm* - **1.** ANAT sinus - **2.** MATHS sine.

sinusite [sinyzit] *nf* sinusitis *(U)*.

sionisme [sjɔnism] *nm* Zionism.

siphon [sifɔ̃] *nm* - **1.** [tube] siphon - **2.** [bouteille] soda siphon.

siphonner [3] [sifɔne] *vt* to siphon.

sirène [sirɛn] *nf* siren.

sirop [siro] *nm* syrup ; **~ d'érable** maple syrup ; **~ de grenadine** (syrup of) grenadine ; **~ de menthe** mint cordial.

siroter [3] [sirɔte] *vt* fam to sip.

sis, e [si, siz] *adj* JUR located.

sismique [sismik] *adj* seismic.

site [sit] *nm* - **1.** [emplacement] site ; **~ archéologique/historique** archaeological/historic site - **2.** [paysage] beauty spot - **3.** INFORM : **~ Web** website, Web site.

sitôt [sito] *adv* : **~ après** immediately after ; **pas de ~** not for some time, not for a while ; **~ arrivé, ...** as soon as I/he etc ar-

rived, ... ; **~ dit, ~ fait** no sooner said than done. ◆ **sitôt que** loc conj as soon as.

situation [sitɥasjɔ̃] *nf* - **1.** [position, emplacement] position, location - **2.** [contexte, circonstance] situation ; **~ de famille** marital status - **3.** [emploi] job, position - **4.** FIN financial statement.

situer [7] [sitɥe] *vt* - **1.** [maison] to site, to situate ; **bien/mal situé** well/badly situated - **2.** [sur carte] to locate. ◆ **se situer** *vp* [scène] to be set ; [dans classement] to be.

six [sis en fin de phrase, si devant consonne ou h aspiré, siz devant voyelle ou h muet] ◇ *adj num* six ; **il a ~ ans** he is six (years old) ; **il est ~ heures** it's six (o'clock) ; **le ~ janvier** (on) the sixth of January ; **daté du ~ septembre** dated the sixth of September ; **Charles Six** Charles the Sixth ; **page ~** page six. ◇ *nm inv* - **1.** [gén] six ; **~ de pique** six of spades - **2.** [adresse] (number) six. ◇ *pron* six ; **ils étaient ~** there were six of them ; **~ par ~** six at a time.

sixième [sizjɛm] ◇ *adj num* sixth. ◇ *nmf* sixth ; **arriver/se classer ~** to come (in)/to be placed sixth. ◇ *nf* SCOL ≃ first year OU form Br, ≃ sixth grade Am ; **être en ~** to be in the first year OU form Br, to be in sixth grade Am ; **entrer en ~** to go to secondary school. ◇ *nm* - **1.** [part] : **le/un ~ de** one/a sixth of ; **cinq ~s** five sixths - **2.** [arrondissement] sixth arrondissement - **3.** [étage] sixth floor Br, seventh floor Am.

skateboard [skɛtbɔrd] *nm* skateboard.

sketch [skɛtʃ] *(pl* **sketches)** *nm* sketch (in a revue etc).

ski [ski] *nm* - **1.** [objet] ski - **2.** [sport] skiing ; **faire du ~** to ski ; **~ acrobatique/alpin/de fond** freestyle/alpine/cross-country skiing ; **~ nautique** water-skiing.

skier [10] [skje] *vi* to ski.

skieur, euse [skjœr, øz] *nm, f* skier.

skipper [skipœr] *nm* - **1.** [capitaine] skipper - **2.** [barreur] helmsman.

slalom [slalɔm] *nm* - **1.** SKI slalom - **2.** [zigzags] : **faire du ~** to zigzag.

slave [slav] *adj* Slavonic. ◆ **Slave** *nmf* Slav.

slip [slip] *nm* briefs *(pl)* ; **~ de bain** [d'homme] swimming trunks *(pl)* ; [de femme] bikini bottoms *(pl)*.

slogan [slɔgɑ̃] *nm* slogan.

Slovaquie [slɔvaki] *nf* : **la ~** Slovakia.

Slovénie [slɔveni] *nf* : **la ~** Slovenia.

slow [slo] *nm* slow dance.

smasher [3] [sma(t)ʃe] *vi* TENNIS to smash (the ball).

SME (*abr de* **Système monétaire européen**) *nm* EMS.

SMIC, Smic [smik] (*abr de* **salaire minimum interprofessionnel de croissance**) *nm* *index-linked guaranteed minimum wage*.

smiley [smaɪlɪ] *nm* smiley.

smoking [smɔkiŋ] *nm* dinner jacket, tuxedo *Am*.

SNCF (*abr de* **Société nationale des chemins de fer français**) *nf* French railways board, ≃ BR *Br*.

snob [snɔb] ⬦ *nmf* snob. ⬦ *adj* snobbish.

snober [3] [snɔbe] *vt* to snub, to cold-shoulder.

snobisme [snɔbism] *nm* snobbery, snobbishness.

soap opera [sopɔpera] (*pl* **soap operas**), **soap** [sop] (*pl* **soaps**) *nm* soap (opera).

sobre [sɔbr] *adj* - **1.** [personne] temperate - **2.** [style] sober ; [décor, repas] simple.

sobriété [sɔbrijete] *nf* sobriety.

sobriquet [sɔbrikɛ] *nm* nickname.

soc [sɔk] *nm* ploughshare *Br*, plowshare *Am*.

sociable [sɔsjabl] *adj* sociable.

social, e, aux [sɔsjal, o] *adj* - **1.** [rapports, classe, service] social - **2.** COMM : **capital ~** share capital ; **raison ~e** company name. ➔ **social** *nm* : **le ~** social affairs (*pl*).

socialisme [sɔsjalism] *nm* socialism.

socialiste [sɔsjalist] *nmf & adj* socialist.

sociétaire [sɔsjetɛr] *nmf* member.

société [sɔsjete] *nf* - **1.** [communauté, classe sociale, groupe] society ; **en ~** in society - **2.** [présence] company, society - **3.** COMM company, firm.

sociologie [sɔsjɔlɔʒi] *nf* sociology.

sociologue [sɔsjɔlɔg] *nmf* sociologist.

socioprofessionnel, elle [sɔsjɔprɔfɛsjɔnɛl] *adj* socioprofessional.

socle [sɔkl] *nm* - **1.** [de statue] plinth, pedestal - **2.** [de lampe] base.

socquette [sɔkɛt] *nf* ankle ou short sock.

soda [sɔda] *nm* fizzy drink.

sodium [sɔdjɔm] *nm* sodium.

sodomiser [3] [sɔdɔmize] *vt* to sodomize.

sœur [sœr] *nf* - **1.** [gén] sister ; **grande/petite ~** big/little sister - **2.** RELIG nun, sister.

sofa [sɔfa] *nm* sofa.

Sofia [sɔfja] *n* Sofia.

software [sɔftwɛr] *nm* software.

soi [swa] *pron pers* oneself ; **chacun pour ~** every man for himself ; **cela va de ~ que** that goes without saying. ➔ **soi-même** *pron pers* oneself.

soi-disant [swadizɑ̃] ⬦ *adj inv* (*avant n*) so-called. ⬦ *adv fam* supposedly.

soie [swa] *nf* - **1.** [textile] silk - **2.** [poil] bristle.

soierie [swari] *nf* (*gén pl*) [textile] silk.

soif [swaf] *nf* thirst ; **~ (de)** *fig* thirst (for), craving (for) ; **avoir ~** to be thirsty.

soigné, e [swaɲe] *adj* - **1.** [travail] meticulous - **2.** [personne] well-groomed ; [jardin, mains] well-cared-for.

soigner [3] [swaɲe] *vt* - **1.** [suj : médecin] to treat ; [suj : infirmière, parent] to nurse - **2.** [invités, jardin, mains] to look after - **3.** [travail, présentation] to take care over. ➔ **se soigner** *vp* to take care of o.s., to look after o.s.

soigneusement [swaɲøzmɑ̃] *adv* carefully.

soigneux, euse [swaɲø, øz] *adj* - **1.** [personne] tidy, neat - **2.** [travail] careful.

soin [swɛ̃] *nm* - **1.** [attention] care ; **avoir** ou **prendre ~ de faire qqch** to be sure to do sthg ; **avec ~** carefully ; **sans ~** [procéder] carelessly ; [travail] careless ; **être aux petits ~s pour qqn** *fig* to wait on sb hand and foot - **2.** [souci] concern. ➔ **soins** *nmpl* care (*U*) ; **les premiers ~s** first aid (*sg*).

soir [swar] *nm* evening ; **demain ~** tomorrow evening ou night ; **le ~** in the evening ; **à ce ~!** see you tonight!

soirée [sware] *nf* - **1.** [soir] evening - **2.** [réception] party.

sois ▷ être.

soit¹ [swat] *adv* so be it.

soit² [swa] ⬦ *vb* ▷ être. ⬦ *conj* - **1.** [c'est-à-dire] in other words, that is to say - **2.** MATHS [étant donné] : **une droite AB** given a straight line AB. ➔ **soit ... soit** *loc corrélative* either ... or. ➔ **soit que ... soit que** *loc corrélative* (+ *subjonctif*) whether ... or (whether).

soixante [swasɑ̃t] ⬦ *adj num* sixty ; **les années ~** the Sixties. ⬦ *nm* sixty ; *voir aussi* **six**.

soixante-dix [swasɑ̃tdis] ⬦ *adj num* seventy ; **les années ~** the Seventies. ⬦ *nm* seventy ; *voir aussi* **six**.

soixante-dixième [swasɑ̃tdizjɛm] *adj num, nm, nm* OU *nmf* seventieth ; *voir aussi* **sixième**.

soixantième [swasɑ̃tjɛm] *adj num, nm* OU *nmf* sixtieth ; *voir aussi* **sixième**.

soja [sɔʒa] *nm* soya.

sol [sɔl] *nm* - **1.** [terre] ground - **2.** [de maison] floor - **3.** [territoire] soil - **4.** MUS G ; [chanté] so.

solaire [sɔlɛr] *adj* - **1.** [énergie, four] solar - **2.** [crème] sun *(avant n)*.

solarium [sɔlarjɔm] *nm* solarium.

soldat [sɔlda] *nm* - **1.** MIL soldier ; [grade] private ; **le ~ inconnu** the Unknown Soldier - **2.** [jouet] (toy) soldier.

solde [sɔld] <> *nm* - **1.** [de compte, facture] balance ; **~ créditeur/débiteur** credit/debit balance - **2.** [rabais] : **en ~** [acheter] in a sale. <> *nf* MIL pay. ◆ **soldes** *nmpl* sales.

solder [3] [sɔlde] *vt* - **1.** [compte] to close - **2.** [marchandises] to sell off. ◆ **se solder** *vp* : **se ~ par** FIN to show ; *fig* [aboutir] to end in.

sole [sɔl] *nf* sole.

soleil [sɔlɛj] *nm* - **1.** [astre, motif] sun ; **~ couchant/levant** setting/rising sun - **2.** [lumière, chaleur] sun, sunlight ; **au ~** in the sun ; **en plein ~** right in the sun ; **il fait (du) ~** it's sunny ; **prendre le ~** to sunbathe.

solennel, elle [sɔlanɛl] *adj* - **1.** [cérémonieux] ceremonial - **2.** [grave] solemn - **3.** *péj* [pompeux] pompous.

solennité [sɔlanite] *nf* - **1.** [gravité] solemnity - **2.** [raideur] stiffness, formality - **3.** [fête] special occasion.

solfège [sɔlfɛʒ] *nm* : **apprendre le ~** to learn the rudiments of music.

solidaire [sɔlidɛr] *adj* - **1.** [lié] : **être ~ de qqn** to be behind sb, to show solidarity with sb - **2.** [relié] interdependent, integral.

solidarité [sɔlidarite] *nf* [entraide] solidarity ; **par ~** [se mettre en grève] in sympathy.

solide [sɔlid] <> *adj* - **1.** [état, corps] solid - **2.** [construction] solid, sturdy - **3.** [personne] sturdy, robust - **4.** [argument] solid, sound - **5.** [relation] stable, strong. <> *nm* solid ; **il nous faut du ~** *fig* we need something solid ou concrete.

solidifier [9] [sɔlidifje] *vt* - **1.** [ciment, eau] to solidify - **2.** [structure] to reinforce. ◆ **se solidifier** *vp* to solidify.

solidité [sɔlidite] *nf* - **1.** [de matière, construction] solidity - **2.** [de mariage] stability, strength - **3.** [de raisonnement, d'argument] soundness.

soliloque [sɔlilɔk] *nm sout* soliloquy.

soliste [sɔlist] *nmf* soloist.

solitaire [sɔlitɛr] <> *adj* - **1.** [de caractère] solitary - **2.** [esseulé, retiré] lonely. <> *nmf* [personne] loner, recluse. <> *nm* [jeu, diamant] solitaire.

solitude [sɔlityd] *nf* - **1.** [isolement] loneliness - **2.** [retraite] solitude.

sollicitation [sɔlisitasjɔ̃] *nf* *(gén pl)* entreaty.

solliciter [3] [sɔlisite] *vt* - **1.** [demander - entretien, audience] to request ; [- attention, intérêt] to seek - **2.** [s'intéresser à] : **être sollicité** to be in demand - **3.** [faire appel à] : **~ qqn pour faire qqch** to appeal to sb to do sthg.

sollicitude [sɔlisityd] *nf* solicitude, concern.

solo [sɔlo] *nm* solo ; **en ~** solo.

solstice [sɔlstis] *nm* : **~ d'été/d'hiver** summer/winter solstice.

soluble [sɔlybl] *adj* - **1.** [matière] soluble ; [café] instant - **2.** *fig* [problème] solvable.

solution [sɔlysjɔ̃] *nf* - **1.** [résolution] solution, answer - **2.** [liquide] solution.

solvable [sɔlvabl] *adj* solvent, creditworthy.

solvant [sɔlvɑ̃] *nm* solvent.

Somalie [sɔmali] *nf* : **la ~** Somalia.

sombre [sɔ̃br] *adj* - **1.** [couleur, costume, pièce] dark - **2.** *fig* [pensées, avenir] dark, gloomy - **3.** *(avant n) fam* [profond] : **c'est un ~ crétin** he's a prize idiot.

sombrer [3] [sɔ̃bre] *vi* to sink ; **~ dans** *fig* to sink into.

sommaire [sɔmɛr] <> *adj* - **1.** [explication] brief - **2.** [exécution] summary - **3.** [installation] basic. <> *nm* summary.

sommation [sɔmasjɔ̃] *nf* - **1.** [assignation] summons *(sg)* - **2.** [ordre - de payer] demand ; [- de se rendre] warning.

somme [sɔm] <> *nf* - **1.** [addition] total, sum - **2.** [d'argent] sum, amount - **3.** [ouvrage] overview. <> *nm* nap. ◆ **en somme** *loc adv* in short. ◆ **somme toute** *loc adv* when all's said and done.

sommeil [sɔmɛj] *nm* sleep ; **avoir ~** to be sleepy.

sommeiller [4] [sɔmeje] *vi* - **1.** [personne] to doze - **2.** *fig* [qualité] to be dormant.

sommelier, ère [sɔmalje, ɛr] *nm, f* wine waiter (*f* wine waitress).

sommes ⇨ **être**.

sommet [sɔmɛ] *nm* - **1.** [de montagne] summit, top - **2.** *fig* [de hiérarchie] top ; [de perfection] height - **3.** GÉOM apex.

sommier [sɔmje] *nm* base, bed base.

sommité [sɔmite] *nf* [personne] leading light.

somnambule [sɔmnɑ̃byl] <> *nmf* sleepwalker. <> *adj* : **être ~** to be a sleepwalker.

somnifère [sɔmnifɛr] *nm* sleeping pill.

somnolent, e [sɔmnɔlɑ̃, ɑ̃t] *adj* [personne] sleepy, drowsy ; *fig* [vie] dull ; *fig* [économie] sluggish.

somnoler [3] [sɔmnɔle] *vi* to doze.

somptueux, euse [sɔ̃ptɥø, øz] *adj* sumptuous, lavish.

somptuosité [sɔ̃ptɥozite] *nf* lavishness *(U)*.

son¹ [sɔ̃] *nm* - **1.** [bruit] sound ; **au ~ de** to the sound of ; **~ et lumière** son et lumière - **2.** [céréale] bran.

son² [sɔ̃] (*f* **sa** [sa], *pl* **ses** [se]) *adj poss* - **1.** [possesseur défini - homme] his ; [- femme] her ; [- chose, animal] its ; **il aime ~ père** he loves his father ; **elle aime ses parents** she loves her parents ; **la ville a perdu ~ charme** the town has lost its charm - **2.** [possesseur indéfini] one's ; [après «chacun», «tout le monde» etc] his/her, their.

sonate [sɔnat] *nf* sonata.

sondage [sɔ̃daʒ] *nm* - **1.** [enquête] poll, survey ; **~ d'opinion** opinion poll - **2.** TECH-NOL drilling - **3.** MÉD probing.

sonde [sɔ̃d] *nf* - **1.** MÉTÉOR sonde ; [spatiale] probe - **2.** MÉD probe - **3.** NAVIG sounding line - **4.** TECHNOL drill.

sonder [3] [sɔ̃de] *vt* - **1.** MÉD & NAVIG to sound - **2.** [terrain] to drill - **3.** *fig* [opinion, personne] to sound out.

songe [sɔ̃ʒ] *nm littéraire* dream.

songer [17] [sɔ̃ʒe] ◇ *vt* : **~ que** to consider that. ◇ *vi* : **~ à** to think about.

songeur, euse [sɔ̃ʒœr, øz] *adj* pensive, thoughtful.

sonnant, e [sɔnɑ̃, ɑ̃t] *adj* : **à six heures ~es** at six o'clock sharp.

sonné, e [sɔne] *adj* - **1.** [passé] : **il est trois heures ~es** it's gone three o'clock ; **il a quarante ans bien ~s** *fam fig* he's the wrong side of forty - **2.** *fig* [étourdi] groggy.

sonner [3] [sɔne] ◇ *vt* - **1.** [cloche] to ring - **2.** [retraite, alarme] to sound - **3.** [domestique] to ring for - **4.** *fam fig* [siffler] : **je ne t'ai pas sonné!** who asked you! ◇ *vi* [gén] to ring ; **~ chez qqn** to ring sb's bell.

sonnerie [sɔnri] *nf* - **1.** [bruit] ringing - **2.** [mécanisme] striking mechanism - **3.** [signal] call.

sonnet [sɔnɛ] *nm* sonnet.

sonnette [sɔnɛt] *nf* bell.

sono [sɔno] *nf fam* [de salle] P.A. (system) ; [de discothèque] sound system.

sonore [sɔnɔr] *adj* - **1.** CIN & PHYS sound (*avant n*) - **2.** [voix, rire] ringing, resonant - **3.** [salle] resonant.

sonorisation [sɔnɔrizasjɔ̃] *nf* - **1.** [action - de film] addition of the soundtrack ; [- de salle] wiring for sound - **2.** [matériel - de salle] public address system, P.A. (system) ; [- de discothèque] sound system.

sonoriser [3] [sɔnɔrize] *vt* - **1.** [film] to add

the soundtrack to - **2.** [salle] to wire for sound.

sonorité [sɔnɔrite] *nf* - **1.** [de piano, voix] tone - **2.** [de salle] acoustics *(pl)*.

sont ➩ **être**.

sophistiqué, e [sɔfistike] *adj* sophisticated.

soporifique [sɔpɔrifik] ◇ *adj* soporific. ◇ *nm* sleeping drug, soporific.

soprano [sɔprano] (*pl* **sopranos** *ou* **soprani** [sɔprani]) *nm* OU *nmf* soprano.

sorbet [sɔrbɛ] *nm* sorbet.

Sorbonne [sɔrbɔn] *nf* : **la ~** the Sorbonne *(highly respected Paris university)*.

sorcellerie [sɔrsɛlri] *nf* witchcraft, sorcery.

sorcier, ère [sɔrsje, ɛr] *nm, f* sorcerer (*f* witch).

sordide [sɔrdid] *adj* squalid ; *fig* sordid.

sornettes [sɔrnɛt] *nfpl* nonsense *(U)*.

sort [sɔr] *nm* - **1.** [maléfice] spell ; **jeter un ~ (à qqn)** to cast a spell (on sb) - **2.** [destinée] fate - **3.** [condition] lot - **4.** [hasard] : **le ~** fate ; **tirer au ~** to draw lots.

sortant, e [sɔrtɑ̃, ɑ̃t] *adj* - **1.** [numéro] winning - **2.** [président, directeur] outgoing *(avant n)*.

sorte [sɔrt] *nf* sort, kind ; **une ~ de** a sort of, a kind of ; **toutes ~s de** all kinds of, all sorts of.

sortie [sɔrti] *nf* - **1.** [issue] exit, way out ; [d'eau, d'air] outlet ; **d'autoroute** motorway junction *ou* exit ; **~ de secours** emergency exit - **2.** [départ] : **c'est la ~ de l'école** it's home-time ; **à la ~ du travail** when work finishes, after work - **3.** [de produit] launch, launching ; [de disque] release ; [de livre] publication - **4.** (*gén pl*) [dépense] outgoings *(pl)*, expenditure *(U)* - **5.** [excursion] outing ; [au cinéma, au restaurant] evening *ou* night out ; **faire une ~** to go out - **6.** MIL sortie - **7.** INFORM : **imprimante** printout.

sortilège [sɔrtileʒ] *nm* spell.

sortir [43] [sɔrtir] ◇ *vi* (*aux* : **être**) - **1.** [de la maison, du bureau etc] to leave, to go/come out ; **~ de** to go/come out of, to leave - **2.** [pour se distraire] to go out - **3.** *fig* [quitter] : **~ de** [réserve, préjugés] to shed - **4.** *fig* [de maladie] : **~ de** to get over, to recover from ; [coma] to come out of - **5.** [film, livre, produit] to come out ; [disque] to be released - **6.** [au jeu - carte, numéro] to come up - **7.** [s'écarter de] : **~ de** [sujet] to get away from ; [légalité, compétence] to be outside - **8.** *loc* : **~ de l'ordinaire** to be out of the ordinary ; **d'où il sort, celui-là?** where did HE spring from? ◇ *vt* (*aux* : **avoir**) - **1.** [gén] : **~ qqch (de)** to take sthg out (of) - **2.** [de si-

tuation difficile] to get out, to extract
- **3.** [produit] to launch ; [disque] to bring
out, to release ; [livre] to bring out, to publish. ◆ **se sortir** *vp fig* [de pétrin] to get
out ; **s'en ~** [en réchapper] to come out of it ;
[y arriver] to get through it.

SOS *nm* SOS ; **lancer un ~** to send out an
SOS.

sosie [sɔzi] *nm* double.

sot, sotte [so, sɔt] ◇ *adj* silly, foolish.
◇ *nm, f* fool.

sottise [sɔtiz] *nf* stupidity *(U)*, foolishness
(U) ; **dire/faire une ~** to say/do something
stupid.

sou [su] *nm* : **être sans le ~** to be penniless.
◆ **sous** *nmpl fam* money *(U)*.

soubassement [subasmɑ̃] *nm* base.

soubresaut [subrəso] *nm* - **1.** [de voiture]
jolt - **2.** [de personne] start.

souche [suʃ] *nf* - **1.** [d'arbre] stump - **2.** [de
carnet] counterfoil, stub.

souci [susi] *nm* - **1.** [tracas] worry ; **se faire
du ~** to worry - **2.** [préoccupation] concern
3. [fleur] marigold.

soucier [9] [susje] ◆ **se soucier** *vp* : se
~ de to care about.

soucieux, euse [susjø, øz] *adj* - **1.** [préoc-
cupé] worried, concerned - **2.** [concerné] :
être ~ de qqch/de faire qqch to be concerned about sthg/about doing sthg.

soucoupe [sukup] *nf* - **1.** [assiette] saucer
- **2.** [vaisseau] : **~ volante** flying saucer.

soudain, e [sudɛ̃, ɛn] *adj* sudden.
◆ **soudain** *adv* suddenly, all of a sudden.

Soudan [sudɑ̃] *nm* : **le ~** the Sudan.

soude [sud] *nf* soda.

souder [3] [sude] *vt* - **1.** TECHNOL to weld,
to solder - **2.** MÉD to knit - **3.** *fig* [unir] to
bind together.

soudoyer [13] [sudwaje] *vt* to bribe.

soudure [sudyr] *nf* TECHNOL welding ; [ré-
sultat] weld.

souffert, e [sufɛr, ɛrt] *pp* ▷ **souffrir**.

souffle [sufl] *nm* - **1.** [respiration] breathing ; [expiration] puff, breath ; **un ~ d'air** *fig*
a breath of air, a puff of wind - **2.** *fig* [inspi-
ration] inspiration - **3.** [d'explosion] blast
- **4.** MÉD : **~ au cœur** heart murmur - **5.** *loc* :
avoir le ~ coupé to have one's breath taken
away.

souffler [3] [sufle] ◇ *vt* - **1.** [bougie] to
blow out - **2.** [vitre] to blow out, to shatter
- **3.** [chuchoter] : **~ qqch à qqn** to whisper
sthg to sb - **4.** *fam* [prendre] : **~ qqch à qqn** to
pinch sthg from sb. ◇ *vi* - **1.** [gén] to blow
- **2.** [respirer] to puff, to pant.

soufflet [suflɛ] *nm* - **1.** [instrument] bellows *(sg)* - **2.** [de train] connecting corridor,
concertina vestibule - **3.** COUTURE gusset.

souffleur, euse [suflœr, øz] *nm, f* THÉÂ-
TRE prompt. ◆ **souffleur** *nm* [de verre]
blower.

souffrance [sufrɑ̃s] *nf* suffering.

souffrant, e [sufrɑ̃, ɑ̃t] *adj* poorly.

souffre-douleur [sufrədulœr] *nm inv*
whipping boy.

souffrir [34] [sufrir] ◇ *vi* to suffer ; **~ de**
to suffer from ; **~ du dos/cœur** to have
back/heart problems. ◇ *vt* - **1.** [ressentir]
to suffer - **2.** *littéraire* [supporter] to stand, to
bear.

soufre [sufr] *nm* sulphur *Br*, sulfur *Am*.

souhait [swɛ] *nm* wish ; **à tes/vos ~s!**
bless you!

souhaiter [4] [swete] *vt* : **~ qqch** to wish
for sthg ; **~ faire qqch** to hope to do sthg ;
~ qqch à qqn to wish sb sthg ; **~ à qqn de
faire qqch** to hope that sb does sthg ; **souhaiter que ...** (*+ subjonctif*) to hope that ...

souiller [3] [suje] *vt littéraire* [salir] to soil ;
fig & sout to sully.

souillon [sujɔ̃] *nf péj* slut.

soûl, e, saoul, e [su, sul] *adj* drunk.

soulagement [sulaʒmɑ̃] *nm* relief.

soulager [17] [sulaʒe] *vt* [gén] to relieve.

soûler, saouler [3] [sule] *vt* - **1.** *fam* [eni-
vrer] : **~ qqn** to get sb drunk ; *fig* to intoxicate sb - **2.** *fig & péj* [de plaintes] : **~ qqn** to
bore sb silly. ◆ **se soûler** *vp fam* to get
drunk.

soulèvement [sulɛvmɑ̃] *nm* uprising.

soulever [19] [sulve] *vt* - **1.** [fardeau, poids]
to lift ; [rideau] to raise - **2.** *fig* [question] to
raise, to bring up - **3.** *fig* [enthousiasme] to
generate, to arouse ; [foule] to stir up ;
~ qqn contre to stir sb against. ◆ **se
soulever** *vp* - **1.** [s'élever] to raise o.s., to lift
o.s. - **2.** [se révolter] to rise up.

soulier [sulje] *nm* shoe.

souligner [3] [suliɲe] *vt* - **1.** [par un trait] to
underline - **2.** *fig* [insister sur] to underline,
to emphasize - **3.** [mettre en valeur] to emphasize.

soumettre [84] [sumɛtr] *vt* - **1.** [astrein-
dre] : **~ qqn à** to subject sb to - **2.** [ennemi,
peuple] to subjugate - **3.** [projet, problème] :
~ qqch (à) to submit sthg (to). ◆ **se soumettre** *vp* : **se ~ (à)** to submit (to).

soumis, e [sumi, iz] ◇ *pp* ▷ **soumettre**. ◇ *adj* submissive.

soumission [sumisjɔ̃] *nf* submission.

soupape [supap] *nf* valve.

soupçon [supsɔ̃] *nm* [suspicion, intuition] suspicion.

soupçonner [3] [supsɔne] *vt* [suspecter] to suspect ; **~ qqn de qqch/de faire qqch** to suspect sb of sthg/of doing sthg.

soupçonneux, euse [supsɔnø, øz] *adj* suspicious.

soupe [sup] *nf* CULIN soup ; **~ populaire** soup kitchen.

souper [3] [supe] <> *nm* supper. <> *vi* to have supper.

soupeser [19] [supəze] *vt* **- 1.** [poids] to feel the weight of **- 2.** *fig* [évaluer] to weigh up.

soupière [supjɛr] *nf* tureen.

soupir [supir] *nm* **- 1.** [souffle] sigh ; **pousser un ~** to let out OU give a sigh **- 2.** MUS crotchet rest *Br*, quarter-note rest *Am*.

soupirail, aux [supiraj, o] *nm* barred basement window *(for ventilation purposes).*

soupirant [supirɑ̃] *nm* suitor.

soupirer [3] [supire] *vi* [souffler] to sigh.

souple [supl] *adj* **- 1.** [gymnaste] supple **- 2.** [pas] lithe **- 3.** [paquet, col] soft **- 4.** [tissu, cheveux] flowing **- 5.** [tuyau, horaire, caractère] flexible.

souplesse [suplɛs] *nf* **- 1.** [de gymnaste] suppleness **- 2.** [flexibilité - de tuyau] pliability, flexibility ; [- de matière] suppleness **- 3.** [de personne] flexibility.

source [surs] *nf* **- 1.** [gén] source **- 2.** [d'eau] spring ; **prendre sa ~ à** to rise in.

sourcil [sursi] *nm* eyebrow ; **froncer les ~s** to frown.

sourcilière [sursiljɛr] ⊏> arcade.

sourciller [3] [sursije] *vi* : **sans ~** without batting an eyelid.

sourcilleux, euse [sursijø, øz] *adj* fussy, finicky.

sourd, e [sur, surd] <> *adj* **- 1.** [personne] deaf **- 2.** [bruit, voix] muffled **- 3.** [douleur] dull **- 4.** [lutte, hostilité] silent. <> *nm, f* deaf person.

sourdement [surdəmɑ̃] *adv* **- 1.** [avec un bruit sourd] dully **- 2.** *fig* [secrètement] silently.

sourdine [surdin] *nf* mute ; **en ~** [sans bruit] softly ; [secrètement] in secret.

sourd-muet, sourde-muette [surmɥe, surdmɥet] *nm, f* deaf-mute, deaf and dumb person.

sourdre [73] [surdr] *vi* to well up.

souriant, e [surjɑ̃, ɑ̃t] *adj* smiling, cheerful.

souricière [surisjɛr] *nf* mousetrap ; *fig* trap.

sourire [95] [surir] <> *vi* to smile ; **~ à qqn** to smile at sb. <> *nm* smile.

souris [suri] *nf* INFORM & ZOOL mouse.

sournois, e [surnwa, az] *adj* **- 1.** [personne] underhand **- 2.** *fig* [maladie, phénomène] unpredictable.

sous [su] *prép* **- 1.** [gén] under ; **nager ~ l'eau** to swim underwater ; **~ la pluie** in the rain ; **~ cet aspect** OU **angle** from that point of view **- 2.** [dans un délai de] within ; **~ huit jours** within a week.

sous-alimenté, e [suzalimɑ̃te] *adj* malnourished, underfed.

sous-bois [subwa] *nm inv* undergrowth.

souscription [suskripsjɔ̃] *nf* subscription.

souscrire [99] [suskrir] *vi* : **~ à** to subscribe to.

sous-développé, e [sudevlɔpe] *adj* ÉCON underdeveloped ; *fig* & *péj* backward.

sous-directeur, trice [sudirɛktœr, tris] *nm, f* assistant manager (*f* assistant manageress).

sous-ensemble [suzɑ̃sɑ̃bl] *nm* subset.

sous-entendu [suzɑ̃tɑ̃dy] *nm* insinuation.

sous-estimer [3] [suzɛstime] *vt* to underestimate, to underrate.

sous-évaluer [7] [suzevalɥe] *vt* to underestimate.

sous-jacent, e [suʒasɑ̃, ɑ̃t] *adj* underlying.

sous-louer [6] [sulwe] *vt* to sublet.

sous-marin, e [sumarɛ̃, in] *adj* underwater *(avant n).* ◆ **sous-marin** *nm* submarine.

sous-officier [suzɔfisje] *nm* non-commissioned officer.

sous-préfecture [suprefɛktyr] *nf* subprefecture.

sous-préfet [suprefɛ] *nm* sub-prefect.

sous-produit [suprɔdɥi] *nm* **- 1.** [objet] by-product **- 2.** *fig* [imitation] pale imitation.

soussigné, e [susiɲe] <> *adj* : **je ~** I the undersigned. <> *nm, f* undersigned.

sous-sol [susɔl] *nm* **- 1.** [de bâtiment] basement **- 2.** [naturel] subsoil.

sous-tasse [sutas] *nf* saucer.

sous-titre [sutitr] *nm* subtitle.

soustraction [sustraksjɔ̃] *nf* MATHS subtraction.

soustraire [112] [sustrer] *vt* **- 1.** [retrancher] : **~ qqch de** to subtract sthg from **- 2.** *sout* [voler] : **~ qqch à qqn** to take sthg away from sb. ◆ **se soustraire** *vp* : se ~ à to escape from.

sous-traitant, e [sutrɛtɑ̃, ɑ̃t] *adj* sub-contracting. ◆ **sous-traitant** *nm* subcontractor.

sous-verre [suvɛr] *nm inv picture or document framed between a sheet of glass and a rigid backing.*

sous-vêtement [suvɛtmɑ̃] *nm* undergarment ; ~s underwear *(U)*, underclothes.

soutane [sutan] *nf* cassock.

soute [sut] *nf* hold.

soutenance [sutnɑ̃s] *nf* viva.

souteneur [sutnœr] *nm* procurer.

soutenir [40] [sutnir] *vt* - **1.** [immeuble, personne] to support, to hold up - **2.** [effort, intérêt] to sustain - **3.** [encourager] to support ; POLIT to back, to support - **4.** [affirmer] : ~ que to maintain (that) - **5.** [résister à] to withstand ; [regard, comparaison] to bear.

soutenu, e [sutny] *adj* - **1.** [style, langage] elevated - **2.** [attention, rythme] sustained - **3.** [couleur] vivid.

souterrain, e [sutɛrɛ̃, ɛn] *adj* underground. ◆ **souterrain** *nm* underground passage.

soutien [sutjɛ̃] *nm* support ; apporter son ~ à to give one's support to.

soutien-gorge [sutjɛ̃gɔrʒ] *(pl* soutiens-gorge) *nm* bra.

soutirer [3] [sutire] *vt fig* [tirer] : ~ qqch à qqn to extract sthg from sb.

souvenir [40] [suvnir] *nm* - **1.** [réminiscence, mémoire] memory - **2.** [objet] souvenir. ◆ **se souvenir** *vp* [ne pas oublier] : se ~ de qqch/de qqn to remember sthg/sb ; se ~ que to remember (that).

souvent [suvɑ̃] *adv* often.

souvenu, e [suvny] *pp* ▷ souvenir.

souverain, e [suvrɛ̃, ɛn] ◇ *adj* - **1.** [remède, état] sovereign - **2.** [indifférence] supreme. ◇ *nm, f* [monarque] sovereign, monarch.

souveraineté [suvrɛnte] *nf* sovereignty.

soviétique [sɔvjetik] *adj* Soviet ◆ **Soviétique** *nmf* Soviet (citizen).

soyeux, euse [swajø, øz] *adj* silky.

soyez ▷ être.

SPA *(abr de* **Société protectrice des animaux)** *nf French society for the protection of animals,* ≃ RSPCA *Br,* ≃ SPCA *Am.*

spacieux, euse [spasjø, øz] *adj* spacious.

spaghettis [spageti] *nmpl* spaghetti *(U).*

sparadrap [sparadra] *nm* sticking plaster *Br,* Band-Aid® *Am.*

spartiate [sparsjat] *adj* [austère] Spartan.

spasme [spasm] *nm* spasm.

spasmodique [spasmɔdik] *adj* spasmodic.

spatial, e, aux [spasjal, o] *adj* space *(avant n).*

spatule [spatyl] *nf* - **1.** [ustensile] spatula - **2.** [de ski] tip.

speaker, speakerine [spikœr, spikrin] *nm, f* announcer.

spécial, e, aux [spesjal, o] *adj* - **1.** [particulier] special - **2.** *fam* [bizarre] peculiar.

spécialiser [3] [spesjalize] *vt* to specialize. ◆ **se spécialiser** *vp* : se ~ (dans) to specialize (in).

spécialiste [spesjalist] *nmf* specialist.

spécialité [spesjalite] *nf* speciality.

spécifier [9] [spesifje] *vt* to specify.

spécifique [spesifik] *adj* specific.

spécimen [spesimɛn] *nm* - **1.** [représentant] specimen - **2.** [exemplaire] sample.

spectacle [spɛktakl] *nm* - **1.** [représentation] show - **2.** [domaine] show business, entertainment - **3.** [tableau] spectacle, sight.

spectaculaire [spɛktakylɛr] *adj* spectacular.

spectateur, trice [spɛktatœr, tris] *nm, f* - **1.** [témoin] witness - **2.** [de spectacle] spectator.

spectre [spɛktr] *nm* - **1.** [fantôme] spectre *Br,* specter *Am* - **2.** PHYS spectrum.

spéculateur, trice [spekylatœr, tris] *nm, f* speculator.

spéculation [spekylasjɔ̃] *nf* speculation.

spéculer [3] [spekyle] *vi* : ~ sur FIN to speculate in ; *fig* [miser] to count on.

speech [spitʃ] *(pl* speeches) *nm* speech.

speed [spid] *adj* hyper ; il est très ~ he's really hyper.

speeder [spide] *vi fam* to hurry.

spéléologie [speleɔlɔʒi] *nf* [exploration] potholing ; [science] speleology.

spermatozoïde [spɛrmatozɔid] *nm* sperm, spermatozoon.

sperme [spɛrm] *nm* sperm, semen.

sphère [sfɛr] *nf* sphere.

sphérique [sferik] *adj* spherical.

spirale [spiral] *nf* spiral.

spirituel, elle [spirityɛl] *adj* - **1.** [de l'âme, moral] spiritual - **2.** [vivant, drôle] witty.

spiritueux [spirityø] *nm* spirit.

splendeur [splɑ̃dœr] *nf* - **1.** [beauté, prospérité] splendour *Br,* splendor *Am* - **2.** [merveille] : c'est une ~! it's magnificent!

splendide [splɑ̃did] *adj* magnificent, splendid.

spongieux, euse [spɔ̃ʒjø, øz] *adj* spongy.

sponsor [spɔ̃sɔr] *nm* sponsor.

sponsoriser [3] [spɔ̃sɔrize] *vt* to sponsor.

spontané, e [spɔ̃tane] *adj* spontaneous.

spontanéité [spɔ̃taneite] *nf* spontaneity.

sporadique [spɔradik] *adj* sporadic.

sport [spɔr] ◇ *nm* sport ; **~s d'hiver** winter sports. ◇ *adj inv* - **1.** [vêtement] sports *(avant n)* - **2.** [fair play] sporting.

sportif, ive [spɔrtif, iv] ◇ *adj* - **1.** [association, résultats] sports *(avant n)* - **2.** [personne, physique] sporty, athletic - **3.** [fair play] sportsmanlike, sporting. ◇ *nm, f* sportsman (*f* sportswoman).

spot [spɔt] *nm* - **1.** [lampe] spot, spotlight - **2.** [publicité] : **~ (publicitaire)** commercial, advert.

sprint [sprint] *nm* [SPORT - accélération] spurt ; [- course] sprint.

square [skwar] *nm* small public garden.

squash [skwaʃ] *nm* squash.

squelette [skəlɛt] *nm* skeleton.

squelettique [skəletik] *adj* [corps] emaciated.

St *(abr de* saint) St.

stabiliser [3] [stabilize] *vt* - **1.** [gén] to stabilize ; [meuble] to steady - **2.** [terrain] to make firm. ◆ **se stabiliser** *vp* - **1.** [véhicule, prix, situation] to stabilize - **2.** [personne] to settle down.

stabilité [stabilite] *nf* stability.

stable [stabl] *adj* - **1.** [gén] stable - **2.** [meuble] steady, stable.

stade [stad] *nm* - **1.** [terrain] stadium - **2.** [étape & MÉD] stage ; **en être au ~ de/où** to reach the stage of/at which.

Stade de France *nm* Stade de France, *stadium built for the 1998 World Cup in the north of Paris.*

stage [staʒ] *nm* SCOL work placement ; [sur le temps de travail] in-service training ; **faire un ~** [cours] to go on a training course ; [expérience professionnelle] to go on a work placement.

stagiaire [staʒjɛr] ◇ *nmf* trainee. ◇ *adj* trainee *(avant n)*.

stagnant, e [stagnɑ̃, ɑ̃t] *adj* stagnant.

stagner [3] [stagne] *vi* to stagnate.

stalactite [stalaktit] *nf* stalactite.

stalagmite [stalagmit] *nf* stalagmite.

stand [stɑ̃d] *nm* - **1.** [d'exposition] stand - **2.** [de fête] stall.

standard [stɑ̃dar] ◇ *adj inv* standard. ◇ *nm* - **1.** [norme] standard - **2.** [téléphonique] switchboard.

standardiste [stɑ̃dardist] *nmf* switchboard operator.

standing [stɑ̃diŋ] *nm* standing ; **quartier de grand ~** select district.

star [star] *nf* CIN star.

starter [starter] *nm* AUTOM choke ; **mettre le ~** to pull the choke out.

starting-block [startiŋblɔk] *(pl* **starting-blocks)** *nm* starting-block.

start up [startɔp] *nf* start up.

station [stasjɔ̃] *nf* - **1.** [arrêt - de bus] stop ; [- de métro] station ; **à quelle ~ dois-je descendre?** which stop do I get off at? ; **~ de taxis** taxi stand - **2.** [installations] station ; **~ d'épuration** sewage treatment plant - **3.** [ville] resort ; **~ balnéaire** seaside resort ; **~ de ski/de sports d'hiver** ski/winter sports resort ; **~ thermale** spa (town) - **4.** [position] position - **5.** INFORM : **~ de travail** work station.

stationnaire [stasjɔnɛr] *adj* stationary.

stationnement [stasjɔnmɑ̃] *nm* parking ; **'~ interdit'** 'no parking'.

stationner [3] [stasjɔne] *vi* to park.

station-service [stasjɔ̃sɛrvis] *(pl* **stations-service)** *nf* service station, petrol station *Br*, gas station *Am*.

statique [statik] *adj* static.

statisticien, enne [statistisjɛ̃, ɛn] *nm, f* statistician.

statistique [statistik] ◇ *adj* statistical. ◇ *nf* [donnée] statistic.

statue [staty] *nf* statue.

statuer [7] [statɥe] *vi* : **~ sur** to give a decision on.

statuette [statɥɛt] *nf* statuette.

statu quo [statykwo] *nm inv* status quo.

stature [statyr] *nf* stature.

statut [staty] *nm* status. ◆ **statuts** *nmpl* statutes.

statutaire [statytɛr] *adj* statutory.

Ste *(abr de* sainte) St.

Sté *(abr de* société) Co.

steak [stɛk] *nm* steak ; **~ haché** mince.

stèle [stɛl] *nf* stele.

sténo [steno] ◇ *nmf* stenographer. ◇ *nf* shorthand.

sténodactylo [stenodaktilo] *nmf* shorthand typist.

sténodactylographie [stenodaktilografi] *nf* shorthand typing.

stentor [stɑ̃tɔr] ▷ **voix.**

steppe [stɛp] *nf* steppe.

stéréo [stereo] ◇ *adj inv* stereo. ◇ *nf* stereo ; **en ~** in stereo.

stéréotype [stereotip] *nm* stereotype.

stérile [steril] *adj* - **1.** [personne] sterile, infertile ; [terre] barren - **2.** *fig* [inutile - discussion] sterile ; [- efforts] futile - **3.** MÉD sterile.

stérilet [sterilɛ] *nm* IUD, intra-uterine device.

stériliser [3] [sterilize] *vt* to sterilize.

stérilité [sterilite] *nf litt & fig* sterility ; [d'efforts] futility.

sterling [stɛrliŋ] *adj inv & nm inv* sterling.

sternum [stɛrnɔm] *nm* breastbone, sternum.

stéthoscope [stetɔskɔp] *nm* stethoscope.

steward [stiwart] *nm* steward.

stigmate [stigmat] *nm* (*gén pl*) mark, scar.

stimulant, e [stimylɑ̃, ɑ̃t] *adj* stimulating. ◆ **stimulant** *nm* - **1.** [remontant] stimulant - **2.** [motivation] incentive, stimulus.

stimulation [stimylasjɔ̃] *nf* stimulation.

stimuler [3] [stimyle] *vt* to stimulate.

stipuler [3] [stipyle] *vt* : ~ que to stipulate (that).

stock [stɔk] *nm* stock ; **en ~** in stock.

stocker [3] [stɔke] *vt* - **1.** [marchandises] to stock - **2.** INFORM to store.

Stockholm [stɔkɔlm] *n* Stockholm.

stoïque [stɔik] *adj* stoical.

stop [stɔp] ◇ *interj* stop! ◇ *nm* - **1.** [panneau] stop sign - **2.** [auto-stop] hitch-hiking, hitching.

stopper [3] [stɔpe] ◇ *vt* [arrêter] to stop, to halt. ◇ *vi* to stop.

store [stɔr] *nm* - **1.** [de fenêtre] blind - **2.** [de magasin] awning.

strabisme [strabism] *nm* squint.

strangulation [strɑ̃gylasjɔ̃] *nf* strangulation.

strapontin [strapɔ̃tɛ̃] *nm* [siège] pulldown seat.

strass [stras] *nm* paste.

stratagème [strataʒɛm] *nm* stratagem.

stratégie [strateʒi] *nf* strategy.

stratégique [strateʒik] *adj* strategic.

stress [strɛs] *nm* stress.

stressant, e [strɛsɑ̃, ɑ̃t] *adj* stressful.

strict, e [strikt] *adj* - **1.** [personne, règlement] strict - **2.** [sobre] plain - **3.** [absolu - minimum] bare, absolute ; [- vérité] absolute ; **dans la plus ~e intimité** strictly in private ; **au sens ~ du terme** in the strict sense of the word.

strident, e [stridɑ̃, ɑ̃t] *adj* strident, shrill.

strié, e [strije] *adj* [rayé] striped.

strier [10] [strije] *vt* to streak.

strip-tease [striptiz] (*pl* **strip-teases**) *nm* striptease.

strophe [strɔf] *nf* verse.

structure [stryktyr] *nf* structure.

structurer [3] [stryktyre] *vt* to structure.

studieux, euse [stydjø, øz] *adj* - **1.** [personne] studious - **2.** [vacances] study *(avant n)*.

studio [stydjo] *nm* - **1.** CIN, PHOT & TÉLÉ studio - **2.** [appartement] studio flat *Br*, studio apartment *Am*.

stupéfaction [stypefaksjɔ̃] *nf* astonishment, stupefaction.

stupéfait, e [stypefɛ, ɛt] *adj* astounded, stupefied.

stupéfiant, e [stypefjɑ̃, ɑ̃t] *adj* astounding, stunning. ◆ **stupéfiant** *nm* narcotic, drug.

stupeur [stypœr] *nf* - **1.** [stupéfaction] astonishment - **2.** MÉD stupor.

stupide [stypid] *adj* - **1.** *péj* [abruti] stupid - **2.** [insensé mort] senseless ; [- accident] stupid.

stupidité [stypidite] *nf* stupidity.

style [stil] *nm* - **1.** [gén] style - **2.** GRAM : ~ **direct/indirect** direct/indirect speech.

styliste [stilist] *nmf* COUTURE designer.

stylo [stilo] *nm* pen ; ~ **plume** fountain pen.

stylo-feutre [stiloføtr] *nm* felt-tip pen.

su, e [sy] *pp* ⮕ **savoir**.

suave [sɥav] *adj* [voix] smooth ; [parfum] sweet.

subalterne [sybaltɛrn] ◇ *nmf* subordinate, junior. ◇ *adj* [rôle] subordinate ; [employé] junior.

subconscient, e [sybkɔsjɑ̃, ɑ̃t] *adj* subconscious. ◆ **subconscient** *nm* subconscious.

subdiviser [3] [sybdivize] *vt* to subdivide.

subir [32] [sybir] *vt* - **1.** [conséquences, colère] to suffer ; [personne] to put up with - **2.** [opération, épreuve, examen] to undergo - **3.** [dommages, pertes] to sustain, to suffer ; ~ **une hausse** to be increased.

subit, e [sybi, it] *adj* sudden.

subitement [sybitmɑ̃] *adv* suddenly.

subjectif, ive [sybʒɛktif, iv] *adj* [personnel, partial] subjective.

subjonctif [sybʒɔ̃ktif] *nm* subjunctive.

subjuguer [3] [sybʒyge] *vt* to captivate.

sublime [syblim] *adj* sublime.

submerger [17] [sybmɛrʒe] *vt* - **1.** [inonder] to flood - **2.** [envahir] to overcome, to overwhelm - **3.** [déborder] to overwhelm ;

être submergé de travail to be swamped with work.

subordination [sybɔrdinasjɔ̃] *nf* subordination.

subordonné, e [sybɔrdɔne] <> *adj* GRAM subordinate, dependent. <> *nm, f* subordinate.

subornation [sybɔrnasjɔ̃] *nf* bribing, subornation.

subrepticement [sybrɛptismɑ̃] *adv* surreptitiously.

subsidiaire [sybzidjɛr] *adj* subsidiary.

subsistance [sybzistɑ̃s] *nf* subsistence.

subsister [3] [sybziste] *vi* - 1. [chose] to remain - 2. [personne] to live, to subsist.

substance [sypstɑ̃s] *nf* - 1. [matière] substance - 2. [essence] gist.

substantiel, elle [sypstɑ̃sjɛl] *adj* substantial.

substantif [sypstɑ̃tif] *nm* noun.

substituer [7] [sypstitɥe] *vt* : ~ **qqch à qqch** to substitute sthg for sthg. ◆ **se substituer** *vp* : **se ~ à** [personne] to stand in for, to substitute for ; [chose] to take the place of.

substitut [sypstity] *nm* - 1. [remplacement] substitute - 2. JUR deputy public prosecutor.

substitution [sypstitysjɔ̃] *nf* substitution.

subterfuge [sybtɛrfyʒ] *nm* subterfuge.

subtil, e [syptil] *adj* subtle.

subtiliser [3] [syptilize] *vt* to steal.

subtilité [syptilite] *nf* subtlety.

subvenir [40] [sybvənir] *vi* : ~ **à** to meet, to cover.

subvention [sybvɑ̃sjɔ̃] *nf* grant, subsidy.

subventionner [3] [sybvɑ̃sjɔne] *vt* to give a grant to, to subsidize.

subversif, ive [sybvɛrsif, iv] *adj* subversive.

succédané [syksedane] *nm* substitute.

succéder [18] [syksede] *vt* : ~ **à** [suivre] to follow ; [remplacer] to succeed, to take over from. ◆ **se succéder** *vp* to follow one another.

succès [syksɛ] *nm* - 1. [gén] success ; **avoir du ~** to be very successful ; **sans ~** [essai] unsuccessful ; [essayer] unsuccessfully - 2. [chanson, pièce] hit.

successeur [syksesœr] *nm* - 1. [gén] successor - 2. JUR successor, heir.

successif, ive [syksesif, iv] *adj* successive.

succession [syksesjɔ̃] *nf* - 1. [gén] succession ; **une ~ de** a succession of ; **prendre la**

~ **de qqn** to take over from sb, to succeed sb - 2. JUR succession, inheritance ; **droits de ~** death duties.

succinct, e [syksɛ̃, ɛ̃t] *adj* - 1. [résumé] succinct - 2. [repas] frugal.

succion [syksjɔ̃, sysjɔ̃] *nf* suction, sucking.

succomber [3] [sykɔ̃be] *vi* : ~ **(à)** to succumb (to).

succulent, e [sykylɑ̃, ɑ̃t] *adj* delicious.

succursale [sykyrsal] *nf* branch.

sucer [16] [syse] *vt* to suck.

sucette [sysɛt] *nf* [friandise] lolly *Br*, lollipop.

sucre [sykr] *nm* sugar ; ~ **en morceaux** lump sugar ; ~ **en poudre**, ~ **semoule** caster sugar.

sucré, e [sykre] *adj* [goût] sweet.

sucrer [3] [sykre] *vt* - 1. [café, thé] to sweeten, to sugar - 2. *fam* [permission] to withdraw ; [passage, réplique] to cut ; ~ **qqch à qqn** to take sthg away from sb.

sucrerie [sykrəri] *nf* - 1. [usine] sugar refinery - 2. [friandise] sweet *Br*, candy *Am*.

sucrette [sykrɛt] *nf* sweetener.

sucrier [sykrije] *nm* sugar bowl.

sud [syd] <> *nm* south ; **un vent du ~** a southerly wind ; **au ~** in the south ; **au ~ (de)** to the south (of). <> *adj inv* [gén] south ; [province, région] southern.

sud-africain, e [sydafrikɛ̃, ɛn] (*mpl* **sud-africains**, *fpl* **sud-africaines**) *adj* South African. ◆ **Sud-Africain, e** *nm, f* South African.

sud-américain, e [sydamerikɛ̃, ɛn] (*mpl* **sud-américains**, *fpl* **sud-américaines**) *adj* South American. ◆ **Sud-Américain, e** *nm, f* South American.

sudation [sydasjɔ̃] *nf* sweating.

sud-est [sydɛst] *nm* & *adj inv* southeast.

sud-ouest [sydwɛst] *nm* & *adj inv* southwest.

Suède [sɥɛd] *nf* : **la ~** Sweden.

suédois, e [sɥedwa, az] *adj* Swedish. ◆ **suédois** *nm* [langue] Swedish. ◆ **Suédois, e** *nm, f* Swede.

suer [7] [sɥe] <> *vi* [personne] to sweat. <> *vt* to exude.

sueur [sɥœr] *nf* sweat ; **avoir des ~s froides** *fig* to be in a cold sweat.

Suez [sɥɛz] *n* : **le canal de ~** the Suez Canal.

suffi [syfi] *pp inv* ▷ **suffire**.

suffire [100] [syfir] <> *vi* - 1. [être assez] : ~ **pour qqch/pour faire qqch** to be enough for sthg/to do sthg, to be sufficient for

sthg/to do sthg ; **ça suffit!** that's enough!
- 2. [satisfaire] : **~ à** to be enough for. ◇ *v
impers* : **il suffit de ...** all that is necessary is
..., all that you have to do is ... ; **il suffit
d'un moment d'inattention pour que ...** it
only takes a moment of carelessness for
... ; **il suffit que vous lui écriviez** all (that) you need do is
write to him. ◆ **se suffire** *vp* : **se ~ à soi-
même** to be self-sufficient.

suffisamment [syfizamɑ̃] *adv* sufficiently.

suffisant, e [syfizɑ̃, ɑ̃t] *adj* **- 1.** [satisfai-
sant] sufficient **- 2.** [vaniteux] self-
important.

suffixe [syfiks] *nm* suffix.

suffocation [syfɔkasjɔ̃] *nf* suffocation.

suffoquer [3] [syfɔke] ◇ *vt* **- 1.** [suj : chaleur, fumée] to suffocate **- 2.** *fig* [suj : colère]
to choke ; [suj : nouvelle, révélation] to astonish, to stun. ◇ *vi* to choke.

suffrage [syfraʒ] *nm* vote.

suggérer [18] [sygʒere] *vt* **- 1.** [proposer]
to suggest ; **~ qqch à qqn** to suggest sthg to
sb ; **~ à qqn de faire qqch** to suggest that sb
(should) do sthg **- 2.** [faire penser à] to
evoke.

suggestif, ive [sygʒɛstif, iv] *adj* **- 1.** [mu-
sique] evocative **- 2.** [pose, photo] suggestive.

suggestion [sygʒɛstjɔ̃] *nf* suggestion.

suicidaire [sɥisidɛr] *adj* suicidal.

suicide [sɥisid] *nm* suicide.

suicider [3] [sɥiside] ◆ **se suicider** *vp*
to commit suicide, to kill o.s.

suie [sɥi] *nf* soot.

suinter [3] [sɥɛ̃te] *vi* **- 1.** [eau, sang] to
ooze, to seep **- 2.** [surface, mur] to sweat ;
[plaie] to weep.

suis ⊳ être.

suisse [sɥis] ◇ *adj* Swiss. ◇ *nm* RELIG
verger. ◆ **Suisse** ◇ *nf* [pays] : **la ~** Switzerland ; **la ~ allemande/italienne/romande**
German-/Italian-/French- speaking Switzerland. ◇ *nmf* [personne] Swiss (person) ; **les Suisses** the Swiss.

suite [sɥit] *nf* **- 1.** [de liste, feuilleton] continuation **- 2.** [série - de maisons, de succès]
series ; [- d'événements] sequence **- 3.** [suc-
cession] : **prendre la ~ de** [personne] to succeed, to take over from ; [affaire] to take
over ; **à la ~** one after the other ; **à la ~ de** *fig*
following **- 4.** [escorte] retinue **- 5.** MUS suite
- 6. [appartement] suite. ◆ **suites** *nfpl*
consequences. ◆ **par la suite** *loc adv*
afterwards. ◆ **par suite de** *loc prép* owing to, because of.

suivant, e [sɥivɑ̃, ɑ̃t] ◇ *adj* next, fol-

lowing. ◇ *nm, f* next ou following one ;
au ~! next!

suivi, e [sɥivi] ◇ *pp* ⊳ suivre. ◇ *adj*
[visites] regular ; [travail] sustained ; [qua-
lité] consistent. ◆ **suivi** *nm* follow-up.

suivre [89] [sɥivr] ◇ *vt* **- 1.** [gén] to follow ; **'faire ~'** 'please forward' ; **à ~** to be
continued **- 2.** [suj : médecin] to treat. ◇ *vi*
- 1. SCOL to keep up **- 2.** [venir après] to follow. ◆ **se suivre** *vp* to follow one another.

sujet, ette [syʒɛ, ɛt] ◇ *adj* : **être ~ à
qqch** to be subject ou prone to sthg. ◇ *nm,
f* [de souverain] subject. ◆ **sujet** *nm* [gén]
subject ; **c'est à quel ~?** what is it about? ;
~ de conversation topic of conversation ;
au ~ de about, concerning.

sulfate [sylfat] *nm* sulphate *Br*, sulfate
Am.

sulfurique [sylfyrik] *adj* sulphuric *Br*, sul-
furic *Am*.

super [sypɛr] *fam* ◇ *adj inv* super, great.
◇ *nm* four star (petrol) *Br*, premium *Am*.

superbe [sypɛrb] *adj* superb ; [enfant,
femme] beautiful.

supercherie [sypɛrʃəri] *nf* deception,
trickery.

superficie [sypɛrfisi] *nf* **- 1.** [surface] area
- 2. *fig* [aspect superficiel] surface.

superficiel, elle [sypɛrfisjɛl] *adj* superficial.

superflu, e [sypɛrfly] *adj* superfluous.
◆ **superflu** *nm* superfluity.

supérieur, e [sypɛrjœr] ◇ *adj* **- 1.** [étage]
upper **- 2.** [intelligence, qualité] superior ;
~ à superior to ; [température] higher than,
above **- 3.** [dominant - équipe] superior ;
[- cadre] senior **- 4.** [SCOL - classe] upper, senior ; [- enseignement] higher **- 5.** *péj* [air]
superior. ◇ *nm, f* superior.

supériorité [sypɛrjɔrite] *nf* superiority.

superlatif [sypɛrlatif] *nm* superlative.

supermarché [sypɛrmarʃe] *nm* supermarket.

superposer [3] [sypɛrpoze] *vt* to stack.
◆ **se superposer** *vp* to be stacked.

superproduction [sypɛrprɔdyksjɔ̃] *nf*
spectacular.

superpuissance [sypɛrpɥisɑ̃s] *nf* superpower.

supersonique [sypɛrsɔnik] *adj* supersonic.

superstitieux, euse [sypɛrstisjø, øz] *adj*
superstitious.

superstition [sypɛrstisjɔ̃] *nf* [croyance]
superstition.

superviser [3] [sypɛrvize] *vt* to supervise.

supplanter [3] [syplɑ̃te] *vt* to supplant.

suppléant, e [sypleɑ̃, ɑ̃t] ⇔ *adj* acting *(avant n)*, temporary. ⇔ *nm, f* substitute, deputy.

suppléer [15] [syplee] *vt* - 1. *littéraire* [carence] to compensate for - 2. [personne] to stand in for.

supplément [syplemɑ̃] *nm* - 1. [surplus] : un ~ de détails additional details, extra details - 2. PRESSE supplement - 3. [de billet] extra charge.

supplémentaire [syplemɑ̃tɛr] *adj* extra, additional.

supplication [syplikasjɔ̃] *nf* plea.

supplice [syplis] *nm* torture ; *fig* [souffrance] torture, agony.

supplier [10] [syplije] *vt* : ~ qqn de faire qqch ou implore sb to do sthg ; je t'en ou vous en supplie I beg ou implore you.

support [sypɔr] *nm* - 1. [socle] support, base - 2. *fig* [de communication] medium ; ~ pédagogique teaching aid ; ~ publicitaire advertising medium.

supportable [sypɔrtabl] *adj* - 1. [douleur] bearable - 2. [conduite] tolerable, acceptable.

supporter¹ [3] [sypɔrte] *vt* - 1. [soutenir, encourager] to support - 2. [endurer] to bear, to stand ; ~ que (+ *subjonctif*) : il ne supporte pas qu'on le contredise he cannot bear being contradicted - 3. [résister à] to withstand. ◆ se supporter *vp* [se tolérer] to bear ou stand each other.

supporter² [sypɔrtɛr] *nm* supporter.

supposer [3] [sypoze] *vt* - 1. [imaginer] to suppose, to assure ; en supposant que (+ *subjonctif*), à ~ que (+ *subjonctif*) supposing (that) - 2. [impliquer] to imply, to presuppose.

supposition [sypozisjɔ̃] *nf* supposition, assumption.

suppositoire [sypozitwar] *nm* suppository.

suppression [sypresjɔ̃] *nf* - 1. [de permis de conduire] withdrawal ; [de document] suppression - 2. [de mot, passage] deletion - 3. [de loi, poste] abolition.

supprimer [3] [syprime] *vt* - 1. [document] to suppress ; [obstacle, difficulté] to remove - 2. [mot, passage] to delete - 3. [loi, poste] to abolish - 4. [témoin] to do away with, to eliminate - 5. [permis de conduire, revenus] : ~ qqch à qqn to take sthg away from sb - 6. [douleur] to take away, to suppress.

suprématie [sypremasi] *nf* supremacy.

suprême [syprɛm] *adj* [gén] supreme.

sur [syr] *prép* - 1. [position - dessus] on ; [- au-dessus de] above, over ; ~ la table on the table - 2. [direction] towards *Br*, toward *Am* ; ~ la droite/gauche on the right/left, to the right/left - 3. [distance] : travaux ~ 10 kilomètres roadworks for 10 kilometres *Br* ou kilometers *Am* - 4. [d'après] : juger qqn ~ sa mine to judge sb by his/her appearance - 5. [grâce à] on ; il vit ~ les revenus de ses parents he lives on ou off his parents' income - 6. [au sujet de] on, about - 7. [proportion] out of ; [mesure] by ; 9 ~ 10 9 out of 10 ; un mètre ~ deux one metre *Br* ou meter *Am* by two ; un jour ~ deux every other day ; une fois ~ deux every other time. ◆ sur ce *loc adv* whereupon.

sûr, e [syr] *adj* - 1. [sans danger] safe - 2. [digne de confiance - personne] reliable, trustworthy ; [- goût] reliable, sound ; [- investissement] sound - 3. [certain] sure, certain ; ~ de sure of ; ~ et certain absolutely certain ; ~ de soi self-confident.

surabondance [syrabɔ̃dɑ̃s] *nf* overabundance.

suraigu, ë [syregy] *adj* high-pitched, shrill.

suranné, e [syrane] *adj* *littéraire* old-fashioned, outdated.

surcharge [syrʃarʒ] *nf* - 1. [de poids] excess load ; [de bagages] excess weight - 2. *fig* [surcroît] : une ~ de travail extra work - 3. [surabondance] surfeit - 4. [de document] alteration.

surcharger [17] [syrʃarʒe] *vt* - 1. [véhicule, personne] : ~ (de) to overload (with) - 2. [texte] to alter extensively.

surchauffer [3] [syrʃofe] *vt* to overheat.

surcroît [syrkrwa] *nm* : un ~ de travail/ d'inquiétude additional work/anxiety.

surdimensionné, e [syrdimɑ̃sjɔne] *adj* oversize(d).

surdité [syrdite] *nf* deafness.

surdoué, e [syrdwe] *adj* exceptionally ou highly gifted.

sureffectif [syrefɛktif] *nm* overmanning, overstaffing.

surélever [19] [syrɛlve] *vt* to raise, to heighten.

sûrement [syrmɑ̃] *adv* - 1. [certainement] certainly ; ~ pas! *fam* no way!, definitely not! - 2. [sans doute] certainly, surely - 3. [sans risque] surely, safely.

surenchère [syrɑ̃ʃɛr] *nf* higher bid ; *fig* overstatement, exaggeration.

surenchérir [32] [syrɑ̃ʃerir] *vi* to bid higher ; *fig* to try to go one better.

surendetté, e [syrɑ̃dete] *adj* overindebted.

surendettement [syrɑ̃dɛtmɑ̃] *nm* over-indebtedness.

surestimer [3] [syrɛstime] *vt* - **1.** [exagérer] to overestimate - **2.** [surévaluer] to overvalue. ◆ **se surestimer** *vp* to overestimate o.s.

sûreté [syrte] *nf* - **1.** [sécurité] safety ; **en ~ safe ; de ~ safety** *(avant n)* - **2.** [fiabilité] reliability - **3.** JUR surety.

surexposer [3] [syrɛkspoze] *vt* to overexpose.

surf [sœrf] *nm* surfing ; **~ des neiges** snowboarding.

surface [syrfas] *nf* - **1.** [extérieur, apparence] surface - **2.** [superficie] surface area. ◆ **grande surface** *nf* hypermarket.

surfait, e [syrfɛ, ɛt] *adj* overrated.

surfer [3] [sœrfe] *vi* - **1.** SPORT to go surfing - **2.** INFORM to surf.

surgelé, e [syrʒəle] *adj* frozen. ◆ **surgelé** *nm* frozen food.

surgir [32] [syrʒir] *vi* to appear suddenly ; *fig* [difficulté] to arise, to come up.

surhumain, e [syrymɛ̃, ɛn] *adj* superhuman.

surimpression [syrɛ̃presjɔ̃] *nf* double exposure.

sur-le-champ [syrləʃɑ̃] *loc adv* immediately, straightaway.

surlendemain [syrlɑ̃dmɛ̃] *nm* : **le ~** two days later ; **le ~ de mon départ** two days after I left.

surligner [3] [syrliɲe] *vt* to highlight.

surligneur [syrliɲœr] *nm* highlighter (pen).

surmenage [syrmənaʒ] *nm* overwork.

surmener [19] [syrməne] *vt* to overwork. ◆ **se surmener** *vp* to overwork.

surmonter [3] [syrmɔ̃te] *vt* - **1.** [obstacle, peur] to overcome, to surmount - **2.** [suj : statue, croix] to surmount, to top.

surnager [17] [syrnaʒe] *vi* - **1.** [flotter] to float (on the surface) - **2.** *fig* [subsister] to remain, to survive.

surnaturel, elle [syrnatyrɛl] *adj* supernatural. ◆ **surnaturel** *nm* : **le ~** the supernatural.

surnom [syrnɔ̃] *nm* nickname.

surpasser [3] [syrpase] *vt* to surpass, to outdo. ◆ **se surpasser** *vp* to surpass OU excel o.s.

surpeuplé, e [syrpœple] *adj* overpopulated.

surplomb [syrplɔ̃] ◆ **en surplomb** *loc adj* overhanging.

surplomber [3] [syrplɔ̃be] ◇ *vt* to overhang. ◇ *vi* to be out of plumb.

surplus [syrply] *nm* [excédent] surplus.

surprenant, e [syrprənɑ̃, ɑ̃t] *adj* surprising, amazing.

surprendre [79] [syrprɑ̃dr] *vt* - **1.** [voleur] to catch (in the act) - **2.** [secret] to overhear - **3.** [prendre à l'improviste] to surprise, to catch unawares - **4.** [étonner] to surprise, to amaze.

surpris, e [syrpri, iz] *pp* ⊳ **surprendre**.

surprise [syrpriz] ◇ *nf* surprise ; **par ~** by surprise ; **faire une ~ à qqn** to give sb a surprise. ◇ *adj* [inattendu] surprise *(avant n)* ; **grève ~** lightning strike.

surproduction [syrprodyksjɔ̃] *nf* overproduction.

surréalisme [syrrealism] *nm* surrealism.

sursaut [syrso] *nm* - **1.** [de personne] jump, start ; **en ~** with a start - **2.** [d'énergie] burst, surge.

sursauter [3] [syrsote] *vi* to start, to give a start.

sursis [syrsi] *nm* JUR & *fig* reprieve ; **six mois avec ~** six months' suspended sentence.

sursitaire [syrsitɛr] *nmf* MIL *person whose call-up has been deferred.*

surtaxe [syrtaks] *nf* surcharge.

surtout [syrtu] *adv* - **1.** [avant tout] above all - **2.** [spécialement] especially, particularly ; **~ pas** certainly not. ◆ **surtout que** *loc conj fam* especially as.

survécu [syrveky] *pp* ⊳ **survivre**.

surveillance [syrvejɑ̃s] *nf* supervision ; [de la police, de militaire] surveillance.

surveillant, e [syrvɛjɑ, ɑt] *nm, f* supervisor ; [de prison] guard, warder Br.

surveiller [4] [syrvɛje] *vt* - **1.** [enfant] to watch, to keep an eye on ; [suspect] to keep a watch on - **2.** [travaux] to supervise ; [examen] to invigilate - **3.** [ligne, langage] to watch. ◆ **se surveiller** *vp* to watch o.s.

survenir [40] [syrvənir] *vi* [incident] to occur.

survenu, e [syrvəny] *pp* ⊳ **survenir**.

survêtement [syrvɛtmɑ̃] *nm* tracksuit.

survie [syrvi] *nf* [de personne] survival.

survivant, e [syrvivɑ̃, ɑ̃t] ◇ *nm, f* survivor. ◇ *adj* surviving.

survivre [90] [syrvivr] *vi* to survive ; **~ à** [personne] to outlive, to survive ; [accident, malheur] to survive.

survoler [3] [syrvole] *vt* - **1.** [territoire] to fly over - **2.** [texte] to skim (through).

sus [sy(s)] *interj* : **~ à l'ennemi!** at the

enemy! **◆ en sus** *loc adv* moreover, in addition ; **en ~ de** over and above, in addition to.

susceptibilité [syseptibilite] *nf* touchiness, sensitivity.

susceptible [syseptibl] *adj* - **1.** [ombrageux] touchy, sensitive - **2.** [en mesure de] : **~ de faire qqch** liable OU likely to do sthg ; **~ d'amélioration, ~ d'être amélioré** open to improvement.

susciter [3] [sysite] *vt* - **1.** [admiration, curiosité] to arouse - **2.** [ennuis, problèmes] to create.

suspect, e [syspɛ, ɛkt] <> *adj* - **1.** [personne] suspicious - **2.** [douteux] suspect. <> *nm, f* suspect.

suspecter [4] [syspɛkte] *vt* to suspect, to have one's suspicions about ; **~ qqn de qqch/de faire qqch** to suspect sb of sthg/of doing sthg.

suspendre [73] [syspɑ̃dr] *vt* - **1.** [lustre, tableau] to hang (up) - **2.** [pourparlers] to suspend ; [séance] to adjourn ; [journal] to suspend publication of - **3.** [fonctionnaire, constitution] to suspend - **4.** [jugement] to postpone, to defer.

suspendu, e [syspɑ̃dy] <> *pp* ▷ **suspendre.** <> *adj* - **1.** [fonctionnaire] suspended - **2.** [séance] adjourned - **3.** [lustre, tableau] : **au plafond/au mur** hanging from the ceiling/on the wall.

suspens [syspɑ̃] **◆ en suspens** *loc adv* in abeyance.

suspense [syspɛns] *nm* suspense.

suspension [syspɑ̃sjɔ̃] *nf* - **1.** [gén] suspension ; **en ~** in suspension, suspended - **2.** [de combat] halt ; [d'audience] adjournment - **3.** [lustre] light fitting.

suspicieux, euse [syspisjø, øz] *adj* suspicious.

suspicion [syspisjɔ̃] *nf* suspicion.

susurrer [3] [sysyre] *vt & vi* to murmur.

suture [sytyr] *nf* suture.

svelte [zvɛlt] *adj* slender.

SVP *abr de* **s'il vous plaît.**

sweat-shirt [switʃœrt] (*pl* **sweat-shirts**) *nm* sweatshirt.

syllabe [silab] *nf* syllable.

symbole [sɛ̃bɔl] *nm* symbol.

symbolique [sɛ̃bɔlik] *adj* - **1.** [figure] symbolic - **2.** [geste, contribution] token (*avant n*) - **3.** [rémunération] nominal.

symboliser [3] [sɛ̃bɔlize] *vt* to symbolize.

symétrie [simetri] *nf* symmetry.

symétrique [simetrik] *adj* symmetrical.

sympa [sɛ̃pa] *adj fam* [personne] likeable, nice ; [soirée, maison] pleasant, nice ; [ambiance] friendly.

sympathie [sɛ̃pati] *nf* - **1.** [pour personne, projet] liking ; **accueillir un projet avec ~** to look sympathetically OU favourably on a project - **2.** [condoléances] sympathy.

sympathique [sɛ̃patik] *adj* - **1.** [personne] likeable, nice ; [soirée, maison] pleasant, nice ; [ambiance] friendly - **2.** ANAT & MÉD sympathetic.

sympathiser [3] [sɛ̃patize] *vi* to get on well ; **~ avec qqn** to get on well with sb.

symphonie [sɛ̃fɔni] *nf* symphony.

symphonique [sɛ̃fɔnik] *adj* [musique] symphonic ; [concert, orchestre] symphony (*avant n*).

symptomatique [sɛ̃ptɔmatik] *adj* symptomatic.

symptôme [sɛ̃ptom] *nm* symptom.

synagogue [sinagɔg] *nf* synagogue.

synchroniser [3] [sɛ̃krɔnize] *vt* to synchronize.

syncope [sɛ̃kɔp] *nf* - **1.** [évanouissement] blackout - **2.** MUS syncopation.

syndic [sɛ̃dik] *nm* [de copropriété] representative.

syndicaliste [sɛ̃dikalist] <> *nmf* trade unionist. <> *adj* (trade) union (*avant n*).

syndicat [sɛ̃dika] *nm* [d'employés, d'agriculteurs] (trade) union ; [d'employeurs, de propriétaires] association. **◆ syndicat d'initiative** *nm* tourist office.

syndiqué, e [sɛ̃dike] *adj* unionized.

syndrome [sɛ̃drom] *nm* syndrome.

synergie [sinɛrʒi] *nf* synergy, synergism.

synonyme [sinɔnim] <> *nm* synonym. <> *adj* synonymous.

syntaxe [sɛ̃taks] *nf* syntax.

synthé [sɛ̃te] *nm fam* synth.

synthèse [sɛ̃tɛz] *nf* - **1.** [opération & CHIM] synthesis - **2.** [exposé] overview.

synthétique [sɛ̃tetik] *adj* - **1.** [vue] overall - **2.** [produit] synthetic.

synthétiseur [sɛ̃tetizœr] *nm* synthesizer.

syphilis [sifilis] *nf* syphilis.

Syrie [siri] *nf* : **la ~** Syria.

syrien, enne [sirjɛ̃, ɛn] *adj* Syrian. **◆ Syrien, enne** *nm, f* Syrian.

systématique [sistematik] *adj* systematic.

systématiser [3] [sistematize] *vt* to systematize.

système [sistɛm] *nm* system ; **~ expert** INFORM expert system ; **~ d'exploitation** INFORM operating system ; **~ nerveux** nervous system ; **~ solaire** solar system.

t, T [te] *nm inv* t, T.

t' ⊳ te.

ta ⊳ ton².

tabac [taba] *nm* - **1.** [plante, produit] tobacco ; ~ **blond** mild *ou* Virginia tobacco ; ~ **brun** dark tobacco ; ~ **à priser** snuff - **2.** [magasin] tobacconist's.

tabagisme [tabaʒism] *nm* - **1.** [intoxication] nicotine addiction - **2.** [habitude] smoking.

tabernacle [tabɛrnakl] *nm* tabernacle.

table [tabl] *nf* [meuble] table ; **à ~!** lunch/dinner *etc* is ready! ; **être à ~** to be at table, to be having a meal ; **se mettre à ~** to sit down to eat ; *fig* to come clean ; **dresser** *ou* **mettre la ~** to lay the table ; ~ **de chevet** *ou* **de nuit** bedside table. ➡ **table des matières** *nf* contents (*pl*), table of contents. ➡ **table de multiplication** *nf* (multiplication) table.

tableau, x [tablo] *nm* - **1.** [peinture] painting, picture ; *fig* [description] picture - **2.** THÉÂTRE scene - **3.** [panneau] board ; ~ **d'affichage** notice board *Br*, bulletin board *Am* ; ~ **de bord** AÉRON instrument panel ; AUTOM dashboard ; ~ **noir** black board - **4.** [de données] table.

tabler [3] [table] *vi* : ~ **sur** to count *ou* bank on.

tablette [tablɛt] *nf* - **1.** [planchette] shelf - **2.** [de chewing-gum] stick ; [de chocolat] bar.

tableur [tablœr] *nm* INFORM spreadsheet.

tablier [tablije] *nm* - **1.** [de cuisinière] apron ; [d'écolier] smock - **2.** [de pont] roadway, deck.

tabloïd(e) [tabloid] *nm* tabloid.

tabou, e [tabu] *adj* taboo. ➡ **tabou** *nm* taboo.

tabouret [taburɛ] *nm* stool.

tabulateur [tabylatœr] *nm* tabulator, tab.

tac [tak] *nm* : **du ~ au ~** tit for tat.

tache [taʃ] *nf* - **1.** [de pelage] marking ; [de peau] mark ; ~ **de rousseur** *ou* **de son** freckle - **2.** [de couleur, lumière] spot, patch - **3.** [sur nappe, vêtement] stain.

tâche [taʃ] *nf* task.

tacher [3] [taʃe] *vt* - **1.** [nappe, vêtement] to stain, to mark - **2.** *fig* [réputation] to tarnish.

tâcher [3] [taʃe] *vi* : ~ **de faire qqch** to try to do sthg.

tacheter [27] [taʃte] *vt* to spot, to speckle.

tacite [tasit] *adj* tacit.

taciturne [tasityrn] *adj* taciturn.

tact [takt] *nm* [délicatesse] tact ; **avoir du ~** to be tactful ; **manquer de ~** to be tactless.

tactique [taktik] ◇ *adj* tactical. ◇ *nf* tactics (*pl*).

taffe [taf] *nf fam* drag, puff.

tag [tag] *nm identifying name written with a spray can on walls, the sides of trains etc.*

tagueur, euse [tagœr, øz] *nm, f person who sprays their 'tag' on walls, the sides of trains etc.*

taie [tɛ] *nf* [enveloppe] : ~ **(d'oreiller)** pillowcase, pillow slip.

taille [taj] *nf* - **1.** [action - de pierre, diamant] cutting ; [- d'arbre, de haie] pruning - **2.** [stature] height - **3.** [mesure, dimensions] size ; **vous faites quelle ~?** what size are you?, what size do you take? ; **ce n'est pas à ma ~** it doesn't fit me ; **de ~** sizeable, considerable - **4.** [milieu du corps] waist.

taille-crayon [tajkrɛjɔ̃] (*pl* **taille-crayons**) *nm* pencil sharpener.

tailler [3] [taje] *vt* - **1.** [couper - chair, pierre, diamant] to cut ; [- arbre, haie] to prune ; [- crayon] to sharpen ; [- bois] to carve - **2.** [vêtement] to cut out.

tailleur [tajœr] *nm* - **1.** [couturier] tailor - **2.** [vêtement] (lady's) suit - **3.** [de diamants, pierre] cutter.

taillis [taji] *nm* coppice, copse.

tain [tɛ̃] *nm* silvering ; **miroir sans ~** two-way mirror.

taire [111] [tɛr] *vt* to conceal. ➡ **se taire** *vp* - **1.** [rester silencieux] to be silent *ou* quiet - **2.** [cesser de s'exprimer] to fall silent ; **tais-toi!** shut up!

Taiwan [tajwan] *n* Taiwan.

talc [talk] *nm* talcum powder.

talent [talɑ̃] *nm* talent ; **avoir du ~** to be talented, to have talent ; **les jeunes ~s** young talent (*U*).

talentueux, euse [talɑ̃tɥø, øz] *adj* talented.

talisman [talismɑ̃] *nm* talisman.

talkie-walkie [tɔkiwɔki] *nm* walkie-talkie.

talon [talɔ̃] *nm* - **1.** [gén] heel ; ~**s aiguilles/hauts** stiletto/high heels ; ~**s plats** low *ou* flat heels - **2.** [de chèque] counterfoil, stub - **3.** CARTES stock.

talonner [3] [talɔne] *vt* - **1.** [suj : poursuivant] to be hard on the heels of - **2.** [suj : créancier] to harry, to hound.

talonnette [talɔnɛt] *nf* [de chaussure] heel cushion, heel-pad.

talquer [3] [talke] *vt* to put talcum powder on.

talus [taly] *nm* embankment.

tambour [tābur] *nm* - **1.** [instrument, cylindre] drum - **2.** [musicien] drummer - **3.** [porte à tourniquet] revolving door.

tambourin [tāburē] *nm* - **1.** [à grelots] tambourine - **2.** [tambour] tambourin.

tambouriner [3] [tāburine] *vi* : ~ **sur** ou **à** to drum on ; ~ **contre** to drum against.

tamis [tami] *nm* [crible] sieve.

Tamise [tamiz] *nf* : **la ~ the** Thames.

tamisé, e [tamize] *adj* [éclairage] subdued.

tamiser [3] [tamize] *vt* - **1.** [farine] to sieve - **2.** [lumière] to filter.

tampon [tāpɔ̃] *nm* - **1.** [bouchon] stopper, plug - **2.** [éponge] pad ; ~ **à récurer** scourer - **3.** [de coton, d'ouate] pad ; ~ **hygiénique** ou **périodique** tampon - **4.** [cachet] stamp - **5.** *litt & fig* [amortisseur] buffer.

tamponner [3] [tāpɔne] *vt* - **1.** [document] to stamp - **2.** [plaie] to dab.

tam-tam [tamtam] (*pl* **tam-tams**) *nm* tom-tom.

tandem [tādɛm] *nm* - **1.** [vélo] tandem - **2.** [duo] pair ; **en ~** together, in tandem.

tandis [tādi] ➡ **tandis que** *loc conj* - **1.** [pendant que] while - **2.** [alors que] while, whereas.

tangage [tāgaʒ] *nm* pitching, pitch.

tangent, e [tāʒā, āt] *adj* : **c'était ~** *fig* it was close, it was touch and go. ➡ **tangente** *nf* tangent.

tangible [tāʒibl] *adj* tangible.

tango [tāgo] *nm* tango.

tanguer [3] [tāge] *vi* to pitch.

tanière [tanjɛr] *nf* den, lair.

tank [tāk] *nm* tank.

tanner [3] [tane] *vt* - **1.** [peau] to tan - **2.** *fam* [personne] to pester, to annoy.

tant [tā] *adv* - **1.** [quantité] : ~ **de** so much ; ~ **de travail** so much work - **2.** [nombre] : ~ **de** so many ; ~ **de livres/d'élèves** so many books/pupils - **3.** [tellement] such a lot, so much ; **il l'aime ~** he loves her so much - **4.** [quantité indéfinie] so much ; **ça coûte ~** it costs so much - **5.** [un jour indéfini] : **votre lettre du ~** your letter of such-and-such a date - **6.** [comparatif] : ~ **que** as much as - **7.** [valeur temporelle] : ~ **que** [aussi longtemps que] as long as ; [pendant que] while. ➡ **en tant que** *loc conj* as. ➡ **tant bien que mal** *loc adv* after a fashion, somehow or other. ➡ **tant mieux**

loc adv so much the better ; ~ **mieux pour lui** good for him. ➡ **tant pis** *loc adv* too bad ; ~ **pis pour lui** too bad for him.

tante [tāt] *nf* [parente] aunt.

tantinet [tātinɛ] *nm* : **un ~ exagéré/trop long** a bit exaggerated/too long.

tantôt [tāto] *adv* - **1.** [parfois] sometimes - **2.** *vieilli* [après-midi] this afternoon.

tapage [tapaʒ] *nm* - **1.** [bruit] row - **2.** *fig* [battage] fuss (*U*).

tapageur, euse [tapaʒœr, øz] *adj* - **1.** [hôte, enfant] rowdy - **2.** [style] flashy - **3.** [liaison, publicité] blatant.

tape [tap] *nf* slap.

tape-à-l'œil [tapalœj] *adj inv* flashy.

taper [3] [tape] ⬦ *vt* - **1.** [personne, cuisse] to slap ; ~ **(un coup) à la porte** to knock at the door - **2.** [à la machine] to type. ⬦ *vi* - **1.** [frapper] to hit ; ~ **du poing sur** to bang one's fist on ; ~ **dans ses mains** to clap - **2.** [à la machine] to type - **3.** *fam* [soleil] to beat down - **4.** *fig* [critiquer] : ~ **sur qqn** to knock sb.

tapis [tapi] *nm* [gén] carpet ; [de gymnase] mat ; ~ **roulant** [pour bagages] conveyor belt ; [pour personnes] travolator ; **dérouler le ~ rouge** *fig* to roll out the red carpet.

tapisser [3] [tapise] *vt* : ~ **(de)** to cover (with).

tapisserie [tapisri] *nf* [de laine] tapestry ; [papier peint] wallpaper.

tapissier, ère [tapisje, ɛr] *nm, f* - **1.** [artisan] tapestry maker - **2.** [décorateur] (interior) decorator - **3.** [commerçant] upholsterer.

tapoter [3] [tapɔte] ⬦ *vt* to tap ; [joue] to pat. ⬦ *vi* : ~ **sur** to tap on.

taquin, e [takē, in] *adj* teasing.

taquiner [3] [takine] *vt* - **1.** [suj : personne] to tease - **2.** [suj : douleur] to worry.

tarabuster [3] [tarabyste] *vt* - **1.** [suj : personne] to badger - **2.** [suj : idée] to niggle at.

tard [tar] *adv* late ; **plus ~** later ; **au plus ~** at the latest.

tarder [3] [tarde] ⬦ *vi* : ~ **à faire qqch** [attendre pour] to delay ou put off doing sthg ; [être lent à] to take a long time to do sthg ; **le feu ne va pas ~ à s'éteindre** it won't be long before the fire goes out ; **elle ne devrait plus ~ maintenant** she should be here any time now. ⬦ *v impers* : **il me tarde de te revoir/qu'il vienne** I am longing to see you again/for him to come.

tardif, ive [tardif, iv] *adj* [heure] late.

tare [tar] *nf* - **1.** [défaut] defect - **2.** [de balance] tare.

tarif [tarif] *nm* - **1.** [prix - de restaurant, café] price ; [- de service] rate, price ; [douanier] tariff ; **demi-~** half rate ou price ; **~ réduit** reduced price ; [au cinéma, théâtre] concession - **2.** [tableau] price list.

tarir [32] [tariʀ] *vi* to dry up ; **elle ne tarit pas d'éloges sur son professeur** she never stops praising her teacher. ➤ **se tarir** *vp* to dry up.

tarot [taʀo] *nm* tarot. ➤ **tarots** *nmpl* tarot cards.

tartare [taʀtaʀ] *adj* Tartar ; **steak ~** steak tartare.

tarte [taʀt] <> *nf* - **1.** [gâteau] tart - **2.** *fam fig* [gifle] slap. <> *adj* (*avec ou sans accord*) *fam* [idiot] stupid.

tartine [taʀtin] *nf* [de pain] piece of bread and butter.

tartiner [3] [taʀtine] *vt* - **1.** [pain] to spread ; **chocolat/fromage à ~** chocolate/cheese spread - **2.** *fam fig* [pages] to cover.

tartre [taʀtʀ] *nm* - **1.** [de dents, vin] tartar - **2.** [de chaudière] fur, scale.

tas [ta] *nm* heap ; **un ~ de** a lot of.

tasse [tɑs] *nf* cup ; **~ à café/à thé** coffee/ tea cup ; **~ de café/de thé** cup of coffee/tea.

tasser [3] [tɑse] *vt* - **1.** [neige] to compress, to pack down - **2.** [vêtements, personnes] : **~ qqn/qqch dans** to stuff sb/sthg into. ➤ **se tasser** *vp* - **1.** [fondations] to settle - **2.** *fig* [vieillard] to shrink - **3.** [personnes] to squeeze up - **4.** *fam fig* [situation] to settle down.

tâter [3] [tate] *vt* to feel ; *fig* to sound out. ➤ **se tâter** *vp fam fig* [hésiter] to be in two minds.

tatillon, onne [tatijɔ̃, ɔn] *adj* finicky.

tâtonnement [tatɔnmɑ̃] *nm* (*gén pl*) [tentative] trial and error (*U*).

tâtonner [3] [tatɔne] *vi* to grope around.

tâtons [tatɔ̃] ➤ **à tâtons** *loc adv* : **marcher/procéder à ~** to feel one's way.

tatouage [tatwaʒ] *nm* [dessin] tattoo.

tatouer [6] [tatwe] *vt* to tattoo.

taudis [todi] *nm* slum.

taupe [top] *nf litt & fig* mole.

taureau, x [tɔʀo] *nm* [animal] bull. ➤ **Taureau** *nm* ASTROL Taurus.

tauromachie [tɔʀɔmaʃi] *nf* bullfighting.

taux [to] *nm* rate ; [de cholestérol, d'alcool] level ; **~ de change** exchange rate ; **~ d'Intérêt** interest rate ; **~ de natalité** birth rate.

taverne [tavɛʀn] *nf* tavern.

taxe [taks] *nf* tax ; **hors ~** COMM exclusive of tax, before tax ; [boutique, achat] dutyfree ; **toutes ~s comprises** inclusive of tax ; **~ sur la valeur ajoutée** value added tax.

taxer [3] [takse] *vt* [imposer] to tax.

taxi [taksi] *nm* - **1.** [voiture] taxi - **2.** [chauffeur] taxi driver.

TB, tb (*abr de* très bien) VG.

Tchad [tʃad] *nm* : **le ~** Chad.

tchatche [tʃatʃ] *nf fam* : **avoir la ~** to have the gift of the gab.

tchatcher [tʃatʃe] *vi fam* to chat (away).

tchécoslovaque [tʃekɔslɔvak] *adj* Czechoslovakian. ➤ **Tchécoslovaque** *nmf* Czechoslovak.

Tchécoslovaquie [tʃekɔslɔvaki] *nf* : **la ~** Czechoslovakia.

tchèque [tʃɛk] <> *adj* Czech. <> *nm* [langue] Czech. ➤ **Tchèque** *nmf* Czech.

TD (*abr de* travaux dirigés) *nmpl* supervised practical work.

te [tə], **t'** *pron pers* - **1.** [complément d'objet direct] you - **2.** [complément d'objet indirect] (to) you - **3.** [réfléchi] yourself - **4.** [avec un présentatif] : **~ voici!** here you are!

technicien, enne [tɛknisjɛ̃, ɛn] *nm, f* - **1.** [professionnel] technician - **2.** [spécialiste] : **~ (de)** expert (in).

technico-commercial, e [tɛknikokɔmɛʀsjal] (*mpl* technico-commerciaux, *fpl* technico-commerciales) *nm, f* sales engineer.

technique [tɛknik] <> *adj* technical. <> *nf* technique.

techno [tɛkno] *adj & nf* techno.

technocrate [tɛknɔkʀat] *nmf* technocrat.

technologie [tɛknɔlɔʒi] *nf* technology.

technologique [tɛknɔlɔʒik] *adj* technological.

teckel [tekɛl] *nm* dachshund.

tee-shirt (*pl* tee-shirts), **T-shirt** (*pl* T-shirts) [tiʃœʀt] *nm* T-shirt.

teigne [tɛɲ] *nf* - **1.** [mite] moth - **2.** MÉD ringworm - **3.** *fam fig & péj* [femme] cow ; [homme] bastard.

teindre [81] [tɛ̃dʀ] *vt* to dye.

teint, e [tɛ̃, tɛ̃t] <> *pp* ⊳ teindre. <> *adj* dyed. ➤ **teint** *nm* [carnation] complexion. ➤ **teinte** *nf* colour *Br*, color *Am*.

teinté, e [tɛ̃te] *adj* tinted ; **~ de** *fig* tinged with.

teinter [3] [tɛ̃te] *vt* to stain.

teinture [tɛ̃tyʀ] *nf* - **1.** [action] dyeing - **2.** [produit] dye. ➤ **teinture d'iode** *nf* tincture of iodine.

teinturerie [tɛ̃tyʀʀi] *nf* - **1.** [pressing] dry cleaner's - **2.** [métier] dyeing.

teinturier, ère [tɛ̃tyʀje, ɛʀ] *nm, f* [de pressing] dry cleaner.

tel [tɛl] (*f* telle, *mpl* tels, *fpl* telles) *adj* - **1.** [valeur indéterminée] such-and-such a ; **~ et ~** such-and-such a - **2.** [semblable] such ; **un ~ homme** such a man ; **de telles gens** such people ; **je n'ai rien dit de ~** I never said anything of the sort - **3.** [valeur emphatique ou intensive] such ; **un ~ génie** such a genius ; **un ~ bonheur** such happiness - **4.** [introduit un exemple ou une énumération] : **~ (que)** such as, like - **5.** [introduit une comparaison] like ; **il est ~ que je l'avais toujours rêvé** he's just like I always dreamt he would be ; **~ quel** as it is/was etc. ➠ **à tel point que** *loc conj* to such an extent that. ➠ **de telle manière que** *loc conj* in such a way that. ➠ **de telle sorte que** *loc conj* with the result that, so that.

tél. (*abr de* **téléphone**) tel.

télé [tele] *nf fam* TV, telly *Br*.

téléachat [teleaʃa] *nm* teleshopping.

téléacteur, trice [teleaktɛr, tris] *nm, f* telesalesperson.

télébenne [teleben], **télécabine** [telekabin] *nf* cable car.

télécharger [17] [teleʃarʒe] *vt* to download.

télécommande [telekɔmɑ̃d] *nf* remote control.

télécommunication [telekɔmynikasjɔ̃] *nf* telecommunications (*pl*).

télécopie [telekɔpi] *nf* fax.

télécopieur [telekɔpjœr] *nm* fax (machine).

téléfilm [telefilm] *nm* film made for television.

télégramme [telegram] *nm* telegram.

télégraphe [telegraf] *nm* telegraph.

télégraphier [9] [telegrafje] *vt* to telegraph.

téléguider [3] [telegide] *vt* to operate by remote control ; *fig* to mastermind.

télématique [telematik] *nf* telematics (*U*).

téléobjectif [teleɔbʒɛktif] *nm* telephoto lens (*sg*).

télépathie [telepati] *nf* telepathy.

téléphérique [teleferik] *nm* cableway.

téléphone [telefɔn] *nm* telephone ; **~ à carte** cardphone ; **~ sans fil** cordless telephone ; **~ portable** mobile phone.

téléphoner [3] [telefɔne] *vi* to telephone, to phone ; **~ à qqn** to telephone sb, to phone sb (up).

téléphonique [telefɔnik] *adj* telephone (*avant n*), phone (*avant n*).

téléprospection [teleprɔspɛksjɔ̃] *nf* telemarketing.

télescope [teleskɔp] *nm* telescope.

télescoper [3] [teleskɔpe] *vt* [véhicule] to

crash into. ➠ **se télescoper** *vp* [véhicules] to concertina.

télescopique [teleskɔpik] *adj* [antenne] telescopic.

téléscripteur [teleskriptœr] *nm* teleprinter *Br*, teletypewriter *Am*.

télésiège [telesjɛʒ] *nm* chairlift.

téléski [teleski] *nm* ski tow.

téléspectateur, trice [telespɛktatœr, tris] *nm, f* (television) viewer.

télétravail, aux [teletravaj, o] *nm* teleworking.

télétravailleur, euse [teletravajœr,øz] *nm, f* teleworker.

téléviseur [televizœr] *nm* television (set).

télévision [televizjɔ̃] *nf* television ; **à la ~** on television ; **~ numérique** digital television.

télex [telɛks] *nm inv* telex.

tellement [tɛlmɑ̃] *adv* - **1.** [si, à ce point] so ; (*+ comparatif*) so much ; **~ plus jeune que** so much younger than ; **pas ~** not especially, not particularly - **2.** [autant] : **~ de** [personnes, objets] so many ; [gentillesse, travail] so much - **3.** [tant] so much ; **elle a ~ changé** she's changed so much ; **je ne comprends rien ~ il parle vite** he talks so quickly that I can't understand a word.

téméraire [temerɛr] ◇ *adj* - **1.** [audacieux] bold - **2.** [imprudent] rash. ◇ *nmf* hothead.

témérité [temerite] *nf* - **1.** [audace] boldness - **2.** [imprudence] rashness.

témoignage [temwaɲaʒ] *nm* - **1.** JUR testimony, evidence (*U*) ; **faux ~** perjury - **2.** [gage] token, expression ; **en ~ de** as a token of - **3.** [récit] account.

témoigner [3] [temwaɲe] ◇ *vt* - **1.** [manifester] to show, to display - **2.** JUR : **~ que** to testify that. ◇ *vi* JUR to testify ; **~ contre** to testify against.

témoin [temwɛ̃] ◇ *nm* - **1.** [gén] witness ; **être ~ de qqch** to be a witness to sthg, to witness sthg ; **~ oculaire** eyewitness - **2.** *littéraire* [marque] : **~ de** evidence (*U*) of - **3.** SPORT baton. ◇ *adj* [appartement] show (*avant n*).

tempe [tɑ̃p] *nf* temple.

tempérament [tɑ̃peramɑ̃] *nm* temperament ; **avoir du ~** to be hot-blooded.

température [tɑ̃peratyr] *nf* temperature ; **avoir de la ~** to have a temperature.

tempéré, e [tɑ̃pere] *adj* [climat] temperate.

tempérer [18] [tɑ̃pere] *vt* [adoucir] to temper ; *fig* [enthousiasme, ardeur] to moderate.

tempête [tɑ̃pɛt] *nf* storm.
tempêter [4] [tɑ̃pete] *vi* to rage.
temple [tɑ̃pl] *nm* **- 1.** HIST temple **- 2.** [protestant] church.
tempo [tɛmpo] *nm* tempo.
temporaire [tɑ̃pɔrɛr] *adj* temporary.
temporairement [tɑ̃pɔrɛrmɑ̃] *adv* temporarily.
temporel, elle [tɑ̃pɔrɛl] *adj* **- 1.** [défini dans le temps] time *(avant n)* **- 2.** [terrestre] temporal.
temps [tɑ̃] *nm* **- 1.** [gén] time ; **à plein ~** full-time ; **à mi-~** half-time ; **à ~ partiel** part-time ; **en un ~ record** in record time ; **au** ou **du ~ où** (in the days) when ; **de mon ~** in my day ; **ça prend un certain ~** it takes some time ; **ces ~-ci, ces derniers ~** these days ; **pendant ce ~** meanwhile ; **en ~ utile** in due course ; **en ~ de guerre/paix** in wartime/peacetime ; **il était ~!** *iron* and about time too! ; **avoir le ~ de faire qqch** to have time to do sthg ; **~ libre** free time ; **à ~ in time** ; **de ~ à autre** now and then ou again ; **de ~ en ~** from time to time ; **en même ~** at the same time ; **tout le ~** all the time, the whole time , **avoir tout son ~** to have all the time in the world **- 2.** MUS beat **- 3.** GRAM tense **- 4.** MÉTÉOR weather.
tenable [tənabl] *adj* bearable.
tenace [tənas] *adj* **- 1.** [gén] stubborn **- 2.** *fig* [odeur, rhume] lingering.
ténacité [tenasite] *nf* **1.** [d'odeur] lingering nature **- 2.** [de préjugé, personne] stubbornness.
tenailler [3] [tənaje] *vt* to torment.
tenailles [tənaj] *nfpl* pincers.
tenancier, ère [tənɑ̃sje, ɛr] *nm, f* manager (*f* manageress).
tendance [tɑ̃dɑ̃s] *nf* **- 1.** [disposition] tendency ; **avoir ~ à qqch/à faire qqch** to have a tendency to sthg/to do sthg, to be inclined to sthg/to do sthg **- 2.** [économique, de mode] trend.
tendancieux, euse [tɑ̃dɑ̃sjø, øz] *adj* tendentious.
tendeur [tɑ̃dœr] *nm* [sangle] elastic strap *(for fastening luggage etc)*.
tendinite [tɑ̃dinit] *nf* tendinitis.
tendon [tɑ̃dɔ̃] *nm* tendon.
tendre¹ [tɑ̃dr] <> *adj* **- 1.** [gén] tender **- 2.** [matériau] soft **- 3.** [couleur] delicate. <> *nmf* tender-hearted person.
tendre² [73] [tɑ̃dr] *vt* **- 1.** [corde] to tighten **- 2.** [muscle] to tense **- 3.** [objet, main] : **~ qqch à qqn** to hold out sthg to sb **- 4.** [bâche] to hang **- 5.** [piège] to set (up). ◆ **se tendre** *vp* to tighten ; *fig* [relations] to become strained.

tendresse [tɑ̃drɛs] *nf* **- 1.** [affection] tenderness **- 2.** [indulgence] sympathy.
tendu, e [tɑ̃dy] <> *pp* ▷ **tendre²**. <> *adj* **- 1.** [fil, corde] taut **- 2.** [personne] tense **- 3.** [atmosphère, rapports] strained **- 4.** [main] outstretched.
ténèbres [tenɛbr] *nfpl* darkness *(sg)*, shadows ; *fig* depths.
ténébreux, euse [tenebrø, øz] *adj* **- 1.** *fig* [dessein, affaire] mysterious **- 2.** [personne] serious, solemn.
teneur [tənœr] *nf* content ; [de traité] terms *(pl)* ; **~ en alcool/cuivre** alcohol/copper content.
tenir [40] [tənir] <> *vt* **- 1.** [objet, personne, solution] to hold **- 2.** [garder, conserver, respecter] to keep **- 3.** [gérer - boutique] to keep, to run **- 4.** [apprendre] : **~ qqch de qqn** to have sthg from sb **- 5.** [considérer] : **~ qqn pour** to regard sb as. <> *vi* **- 1.** [être solide] to stay up, to hold together **- 2.** [durer] to last **- 3.** [pouvoir être contenu] to fit **- 4.** [être attaché] : **~ à** [personne] to care about ; [privilèges] to value **- 5.** [vouloir absolument] : **~ à faire qqch** to insist on doing sthg **- 6.** [ressembler] : **~ de** to take after **- 7.** [relever de] : **~ de** to have something of **- 8.** [dépendre de] : **il ne tient qu'à toi de ...** it's entirely up to you to ... **- 9.** *loc* : **~ bon** to stand firm ; **tiens!** [en donnant] here! ; [surprise] well, well! ; [pour attirer attention] look! ◆ **se tenir** *vp* **- 1.** [réunion] to be held **- 2.** [personnes] to hold one another ; **se ~ par la main** to hold hands **- 3.** [être présent] to be **- 4.** [être cohérent] to make sense **- 5.** [se conduire] to behave (o.s.) **- 6.** [se retenir] : **se ~ (à)** to hold on (to) **- 7.** [se borner] : **s'en ~ à** to stick to.
tennis [tenis] <> *nm* [sport] tennis. <> *nmpl* tennis shoes.
ténor [tenɔr] *nm* **- 1.** [chanteur] tenor **- 2.** *fig* [vedette] : **un ~ de la politique** a political star performer.
tension [tɑ̃sjɔ̃] *nf* **- 1.** [contraction, désaccord] tension **- 2.** MÉD pressure , **avoir de la ~** to have high blood pressure **- 3.** ÉLECTR voltage ; **haute/basse ~** high/low voltage.
tentaculaire [tɑ̃takylɛr] *adj* *fig* sprawling.
tentant, e [tɑ̃tɑ̃, ɑ̃t] *adj* tempting.
tentation [tɑ̃tasjɔ̃] *nf* temptation.
tentative [tɑ̃tativ] *nf* attempt ; **~ de suicide** suicide attempt.
tente [tɑ̃t] *nf* tent.
tenter [3] [tɑ̃te] *vt* **- 1.** [entreprendre] : **~ qqch/de faire qqch** to attempt sthg/to do sthg **- 2.** [plaire] to tempt ; **être tenté par**

qqch/de faire qqch to be tempted by sthg/ to do sthg.

tenture [tɑ̃tyr] *nf* hanging.

tenu, e [təny] ◇ *pp* ⊳ **tenir**. ◇ *adj* - **1.** [obligé] : **être ~ de faire qqch** to be required OU obliged to do sthg - **2.** [en ordre] : **bien/mal ~** [maison] well/badly kept.

ténu, e [teny] *adj* - **1.** [fil] fine ; *fig* [distinction] tenuous - **2.** [voix] thin.

tenue [təny] *nf* - **1.** [entretien] running - **2.** [manières] good manners *(pl)* - **3.** [maintien du corps] posture - **4.** [costume] dress ; **être en petite ~** to be scantily dressed. ➧ **tenue de route** *nf* roadholding.

ter [tɛr] ◇ *adv* MUS three times. ◇ *adj* : 12 ~ 12B.

Tergal® [tɛrgal] *nm* ≃ Terylene®.

tergiverser [3] [tɛrʒivɛrse] *vi* to shilly-shally.

terme [tɛrm] *nm* - **1.** [fin] end ; **mettre un ~ à** to put an end OU a stop to - **2.** [de grossesse] term ; **avant ~** prematurely - **3.** [échéance] time limit ; [de loyer] rent day ; **à court/moyen/long ~** [calculer] in the short/medium/long term ; [projet] short-/medium-/long-term - **4.** [mot, élément] term. ➧ **termes** *nmpl* - **1.** [expressions] words - **2.** [de contrat] terms.

terminaison [tɛrminɛzɔ̃] *nf* GRAM ending.

terminal, e, aux [tɛrminal, o] *adj* - **1.** [au bout] final - **2.** MÉD [phase] terminal. ➧ **terminal, aux** *nm* terminal. ➧ **terminale** *nf* SCOL ≃ upper sixth year OU form *Br*, ≃ twelfth grade *Am*.

terminer [3] [tɛrmine] *vt* to end, to finish ; [travail, repas] to finish. ➧ **se terminer** *vp* to end, to finish.

terminologie [tɛrminɔlɔʒi] *nf* terminology.

terminus [tɛrminys] *nm* terminus.

termite [tɛrmit] *nm* termite.

terne [tɛrn] *adj* dull.

ternir [32] [tɛrnir] *vt* to dirty ; [métal, réputation] to tarnish.

terrain [tɛrɛ̃] *nm* - **1.** [sol] soil ; **vélo tout ~** mountain bike - **2.** [surface] piece of land - **3.** [emplacement] [de football, rugby] pitch ; [- de golf] course ; **~ d'aviation** airfield ; **~ de camping** campsite - **4.** *fig* [domaine] ground.

terrasse [tɛras] *nf* terrace.

terrassement [tɛrasmɑ̃] *nm* [action] excavation.

terrasser [3] [tɛrase] *vt* [suj : personne] to bring down ; [suj : émotion] to overwhelm ; [suj : maladie] to conquer.

terre [tɛr] *nf* - **1.** [monde] world - **2.** [sol] ground ; **par ~** on the ground ; **~ à ~** *fig* down-to-earth - **3.** [matière] earth, soil - **4.** [propriété] land *(U)* - **5.** [territoire, continent] land - **6.** ÉLECTR earth *Br*, ground *Am*. ➧ **Terre** *nf* : **la Terre** Earth.

terreau [tɛro] *nm* compost.

terre-plein [tɛrplɛ̃] (*pl* **terre-pleins**) *nm* platform.

terrer [4] [tɛre] ➧ **se terrer** *vp* to go to earth.

terrestre [tɛrɛstr] *adj* - **1.** [croûte, atmosphère] of the earth - **2.** [animal, transport] land *(avant n)* - **3.** [plaisir, paradis] earthly - **4.** [considérations] worldly.

terreur [tɛrœr] *nf* terror.

terrible [tɛribl] *adj* - **1.** [gén] terrible - **2.** [appétit, soif] terrific, enormous - **3.** *fam* [excellent] brilliant.

terriblement [tɛribləmɑ̃] *adv* terribly.

terrien, enne [tɛrjɛ̃, ɛn] ◇ *adj* [foncier] : **propriétaire ~** landowner. ◇ *nm, f* [habitant de la Terre] earthling.

terrier [tɛrje] *nm* - **1.** [tanière] burrow - **2.** [chien] terrier.

terrifier [9] [tɛrifje] *vt* to terrify.

terrine [tɛrin] *nf* terrine.

territoire [tɛritwar] *nm* - **1.** [pays, zone] territory - **2.** ADMIN area. ➧ **territoire d'outre-mer** *nm* (French) overseas territory.

territorial, e, aux [tɛritɔrjal, o] *adj* territorial.

terroir [tɛrwar] *nm* - **1.** [sol] soil - **2.** [région rurale] country.

terroriser [3] [tɛrɔrize] *vt* to terrorize.

terrorisme [tɛrɔrism] *nm* terrorism.

terroriste [tɛrɔrist] *nmf* terrorist.

tertiaire [tɛrsjɛr] ◇ *nm* tertiary sector. ◇ *adj* tertiary.

tes ⊳ **ton²**.

tesson [tɛsɔ̃] *nm* piece of broken glass.

test [tɛst] *nm* test ; **~ de grossesse** pregnancy test.

testament [tɛstamɑ̃] *nm* will ; *fig* legacy.

tester [3] [tɛste] *vt* to test.

testicule [tɛstikyl] *nm* testicle.

tétaniser [3] [tetanize] *vt* to cause to go into spasm ; *fig* to paralyse *Br*, to paralyze *Am*.

tétanos [tetanos] *nm* tetanus.

têtard [tɛtar] *nm* tadpole.

tête [tɛt] *nf* - **1.** [gén] head ; **de la ~ aux pieds** from head to foot OU toe ; **la ~ en bas** head down ; **la ~ la première** head first ; **calculer qqch de ~** to calculate sthg in one's head ; **~ chercheuse** homing head ; **~ de lecture** INFORM read head ; **~ de liste** POLIT main candidate ; **être ~ en l'air** to have one's head in the clouds ; **faire la ~** to sulk ; **tenir ~ à qqn** to stand up to sb - **2.** [visage] face - **3.** [devant - de cortège, peloton] head, front ; **en ~** [- SPORT] in the lead.

tête-à-queue [tɛtakø] *nm inv* spin.

tête-à-tête [tɛtatɛt] *nm inv* tête-à-tête.

tête-bêche [tɛtbɛʃ] *loc adv* head to tail.

tétée [tete] *nf* feed.

tétine [tetin] *nf* - **1.** [de biberon, mamelle] nipple, teat - **2.** [sucette] dummy *Br*, pacifier *Am*.

Tétrabrick® [tetrabrik] *nm* carton.

têtu, e [tety] *adj* stubborn.

tex mex [tɛksmɛks] ◇ *adj* Tex Mex. ◇ *nm* Tex Mex food.

texte [tɛkst] *nm* - **1.** [écrit] wording - **2.** [imprimé] text - **3.** [extrait] passage.

textile [tɛkstil] ◇ *adj* textile *(avant n)*. ◇ *nm* - **1.** [matière] textile - **2.** [industrie] : **le ~ textiles** *(pl)*, the textile industry.

Texto® [tɛksto] *nm fam* TEL SMS message word for word.

textuel, elle [tɛkstɥɛl] *adj* - **1.** [analyse] textual ; [citation] exact ; **il a dit ça, ~ those were his very ou exact words** - **2.** [traduction] literal.

texture [tɛkstyr] *nf* texture.

TF1 *(abr de* Télévision Française 1*) nf* French independent television company.

TGV *(abr de* train à grande vitesse*) nm* French high-speed train.

thaïlandais, e [tajlɑ̃dɛ, ɛz] *adj* Thai. ➤ **Thaïlandais, e** *nm, f* Thai.

Thaïlande [tajlɑ̃d] *nf* : **la ~** Thailand.

thalasso(thérapie) [talaso(terapi)] *nf* seawater therapy.

thé [te] *nm* tea.

théâtral, e, aux [teatral, o] *adj* [ton] theatrical.

théâtre [teatr] *nm* - **1.** [bâtiment, représentation] theatre - **2.** [art] : **faire du ~** to be on the stage ; **adapté pour le ~** adapted for the stage - **3.** [œuvre] plays *(pl)* - **4.** [lieu] scene ; **~ d'opérations** MIL theatre of operations.

théière [tejɛr] *nf* teapot.

thématique [tematik] ◇ *adj* thematic. ◇ *nf* themes *(pl)*.

thème [tɛm] *nm* - **1.** [sujet & MUS] theme - **2.** SCOL prose.

théologie [teɔlɔʒi] *nf* theology.

théorème [teɔrɛm] *nm* theorem.

théoricien, enne [teɔrisjɛ̃, ɛn] *nm, f* theoretician.

théorie [teɔri] *nf* theory ; **en ~** in theory.

théorique [teɔrik] *adj* theoretical.

thérapeute [terapøt] *nmf* therapist.

thérapie [terapi] *nf* therapy.

thermal, e, aux [tɛrmal, o] *adj* thermal.

thermes [tɛrm] *nmpl* thermal baths.

thermique [tɛrmik] *adj* thermal.

thermomètre [tɛrmɔmɛtr] *nm* [instrument] thermometer.

Thermos® [tɛrmos] *nm* OU *nf* Thermos® (flask).

thermostat [tɛrmɔsta] *nm* thermostat.

thèse [tɛz] *nf* - **1.** [opinion] argument - **2.** PHILO & UNIV thesis ; **~ de doctorat** doctorate - **3.** [théorie] theory.

thon [tɔ̃] *nm* tuna.

thorax [tɔraks] *nm* thorax.

thym [tɛ̃] *nm* thyme.

thyroïde [tirɔid] *nf* thyroid (gland).

Tibet [tibɛ] *nm* : **le ~** Tibet.

tibia [tibja] *nm* tibia.

tic [tik] *nm* tic.

ticket [tikɛ] *nm* ticket ; **~ de caisse** (till) receipt ; **~-repas** ≃ luncheon voucher.

tic-tac [tiktak] *nm inv* tick-tock.

tiède [tjɛd] *adj* - **1.** [boisson, eau] tepid, lukewarm - **2.** [vent] mild - **3.** *fig* [accueil] lukewarm.

tiédir [tjedir] ◇ *vt* to warm. ◇ *vi* to become warm ; **faire ~ qqch** to warm sthg.

tien [tjɛ̃] ➤ **le tien** *(f* **la tienne** [latjɛn], *mpl* **les tiens** [letjɛ], *fpl* **les tiennes** [letjɛn]) *pron poss* yours ; **à la tienne!** cheers!

tierce [tjɛrs] ◇ *nf* - **1.** MUS third - **2.** CARTES & ESCRIME tierce. ◇ *adj* ➤ **tiers**.

tiercé [tjɛrse] *nm* system of betting involving the first three horses in a race.

tiers, tierce [tjɛr, tjɛrs] *adj* : **une tierce personne** a third party, ➤ **tiers** *nm* - **1.** [étranger] outsider, stranger - **2.** [tierce personne] third party - **3.** [de fraction] : **le ~ de** one-third of.

tiers-monde [tjɛrmɔ̃d] *nm* : **le ~** the Third World.

tiers-mondisation [tjɛrmɔ̃dizasjɔ̃] *nf* : **la ~ de ce pays** this country's economic degeneration to Third World levels.

tige [tiʒ] *nf* - **1.** [de plante] stem, stalk - **2.** [de bois, métal] rod.

tignasse [tiɲas] *nf fam* mop (of hair).

tigre [tigr] *nm* tiger.

tigresse [tigrɛs] *nf* tigress.

tilleul [tijœl] *nm* lime (tree).

timbale [tɛ̃bal] *nf* - **1.** [gobelet] (metal) cup - **2.** MUS kettledrum.

timbre [tɛ̃br] *nm* - **1.** [gén] stamp - **2.** [de voix] timbre - **3.** [de bicyclette] bell.

timbrer [ʒ] [tɛ̃bre] *vt* to stamp.

timide [timid] ◇ *adj* - **1.** [personne] shy

- **2.** [protestation, essai] timid - **3.** [soleil] uncertain. ◇ *nmf* shy person.

timing [tajmiŋ] *nm* - **1.** [emploi du temps] schedule - **2.** [organisation] timing.

timoré, e [timɔre] *adj* fearful, timorous.

tintamarre [tɛ̃tamar] *nm fam* racket.

tintement [tɛ̃tmɑ̃] *nm* [de cloche, d'horloge] chiming ; [de pièces] jingling.

tinter [3] [tɛ̃te] *vi* - **1.** [cloche, horloge] to chime - **2.** [pièces] to jingle.

tir [tir] *nm* - **1.** [SPORT - activité] shooting ; [- lieu] : **(centre de) ~** shooting range ; **~ au but** penalty shoot-out - **2.** [trajectoire] shot - **3.** [salve] fire *(U)* - **4.** [manière, action de tirer] firing.

tirage [tiraʒ] *nm* - **1.** [de journal] circulation ; [de livre] print run ; **à grand ~** mass circulation - **2.** [du loto] draw ; **~ au sort** drawing lots - **3.** [de cheminée] draught *Br*, draft *Am*.

tiraillement [tirajmɑ̃] *nm (gén pl)* - **1.** [crampe] cramp - **2.** *fig* [conflit] conflict.

tirailler [3] [tiraje] ◇ *vt* - **1.** [tirer sur] to tug (at) - **2.** *fig* [écarteler] : **être tiraillé par/entre qqch** to be torn by/between sthg. ◇ *vi* to fire wildly.

tiré, e [tire] *adj* [fatigué] : **avoir les traits ~s** ou **le visage ~** to look drawn.

tire-bouchon [tirbuʃɔ̃] *(pl tire-bouchons)* *nm* corkscrew. ◆ **en tire-bouchon** *loc adv* corkscrew *(avant n)*.

tirelire [tirlir] *nf* moneybox.

tirer [3] [tire] ◇ *vt* - **1.** [gén] to pull ; [rideaux] to draw ; [tiroir] to pull open - **2.** [tracer - trait] to draw - **3.** [revue, livre] to print - **4.** [avec arme] to fire - **5.** [faire sortir - vin] to draw off ; **~ qqn de** *litt* & *fig* to help ou get sb out of ; **~ un revolver/un mouchoir de sa poche** to pull a gun/a handkerchief out of one's pocket ; **~ la langue** to stick out one's tongue - **6.** [aux cartes, au loto] to draw - **7.** [plaisir, profit] to derive - **8.** [déduire - conclusion] to draw ; [- leçon] to learn. ◇ *vi* - **1.** [tendre] : **~ sur** to pull on ou at - **2.** [aspirer] : **~ sur** [pipe] to draw ou pull on - **3.** [couleur] : **bleu tirant sur le vert** greenish blue - **4.** [cheminée] to draw - **5.** [avec arme] to fire, to shoot - **6.** SPORT to shoot. ◆ **se tirer** *vp* - **1.** *fam* [s'en aller] to push off - **2.** [se sortir] : **se ~ de** to get o.s. out of ; **s'en ~** *fam* to escape.

tiret [tire] *nm* dash.

tireur, euse [tirœr, øz] *nm, f* [avec arme] gunman ; **~ d'élite** marksman (*f* markswoman).

tiroir [tirwar] *nm* drawer.

tiroir-caisse [tirwarkɛs] *nm* till.

tisane [tizan] *nf* herb tea.

tisonnier [tizɔnje] *nm* poker.

tissage [tisaʒ] *nm* weaving.

tisser [3] [tise] *vt litt* & *fig* to weave ; [suj : araignée] to spin.

tissu [tisy] *nm* - **1.** [étoffe] cloth, material - **2.** BIOL tissue.

titiller [3] [titije] *vt* to titillate.

titre [titr] *nm* - **1.** [gén] title - **2.** [de presse] headline ; **gros ~** headline - **3.** [universitaire] diploma, qualification - **4.** JUR title ; **~ de propriété** title deed - **5.** FIN security. ◆ **titre de transport** *nm* ticket. ◆ **à titre de** *loc prép* : **à ~ d'exemple** by way of example ; **à ~ d'information** for information.

tituber [3] [titybe] *vi* to totter.

titulaire [titylɛr] ◇ *adj* [employé] permanent ; UNIV with tenure. ◇ *nmf* [de passeport, permis] holder ; [de poste, chaire] occupant.

titulariser [3] [titylarize] *vt* to give tenure to.

TNP (*abr de* traité de non-prolifération) *nm* NPT.

toast [tost] *nm* - **1.** [pain grillé] toast *(U)* - **2.** [discours] toast ; **porter un ~ à** to drink a toast to.

toboggan [tɔbɔgɑ̃] *nm* - **1.** [traîneau] toboggan - **2.** [de terrain de jeu] slide ; [de piscine] chute.

toc [tɔk] ◇ *interj* : **et ~!** so there! ◇ *nm fam* : **c'est du ~** it's fake ; **en ~** fake *(avant n)*.

Togo [tɔgo] *nm* : **le ~** Togo.

toi [twa] *pron pers* you. ◆ **toi-même** *pron pers* yourself.

toile [twal] *nf* - **1.** [étoffe] cloth ; [de lin] linen ; **~ cirée** oilcloth - **2.** [tableau] canvas, picture. ◆ **toile d'araignée** *nf* spider's web. ◆ **Toile** *nf* : **la Toile** INFORM the Web, the web.

toilette [twalɛt] *nf* - **1.** [de personne, d'animal] washing ; **faire sa ~** to (have a) wash - **2.** [parure, vêtements] outfit, clothes *(pl)*. ◆ **toilettes** *nfpl* toilet *(sg)*, toilets.

toise [twaz] *nf* height gauge.

toison [twazɔ̃] *nf* - **1.** [pelage] fleece - **2.** [chevelure] mop (of hair).

toit [twa] *nm* roof ; **~ ouvrant** sunroof.

toiture [twatyr] *nf* roof, roofing.

tôle [tol] *nf* [de métal] sheet metal ; **~ ondulée** corrugated iron.

tolérance [tɔlerɑ̃s] *nf* - **1.** [gén] tolerance - **2.** [liberté] concession.

tolérant, e [tɔlerɑ̃, ɑ̃t] *adj* - **1.** [large d'esprit] tolerant - **2.** [indulgent] liberal.

tolérer [18] [tɔlere] *vt* to tolerate. ◆ **se tolérer** *vp* to put up with ou tolerate each other.

tollé [tɔle] *nm* protest.

tomate [tɔmat] *nf* tomato.

tombal, e, aux [tɔ̃bal, o] *adj* : pierre ~e gravestone.

tombant, e [tɔ̃bɑ̃, ɑ̃t] *adj* [moustaches] drooping ; [épaules] sloping.

tombe [tɔ̃b] *nf* [fosse] grave, tomb.

tombeau, x [tɔ̃bo] *nm* tomb.

tombée [tɔ̃be] *nf* fall ; **à la ~ du jour** OU **de la nuit** at nightfall.

tomber [3] [tɔ̃be] *vi (aux : être)* - **1.** [gén] to fall ; **faire ~ qqn** to knock sb over OU down ; **~ raide mort** to drop down dead ; **~ bien** [robe] to hang well ; *fig* [visite, personne] to come at a good time - **2.** [cheveux] to fall out - **3.** [nouvelle] to break - **4.** [diminuer - prix] to drop, to fall ; [- fièvre, vent] to drop ; [- jour] to come to an end ; [- colère] to die down - **5.** [devenir brusquement] : **~ malade** to fall ill ; **~ amoureux** to fall in love ; **être bien/mal tombé** to be lucky/unlucky - **6.** [trouver] : **~ sur** to come across - **7.** [attaquer] : **~ sur** to set about - **8.** [date, événement] to fall on.

tombola [tɔ̃bɔla] *nf* raffle.

tome [tɔm] *nm* volume.

ton¹ [tɔ̃] *nm* - **1.** [de voix] tone ; **hausser/ baisser le ~** to raise/lower one's voice - **2.** MUS key ; **donner le ~** to give the chord ; *fig* to set the tone.

ton² [tɔ̃] (*f* **ta** [ta], *pl* **tes** [te]) *adj poss* your.

tonalité [tɔnalite] *nf* - **1.** MUS tonality - **2.** [au téléphone] dialling tone.

tondeuse [tɔ̃døz] *nf* [à cheveux] clippers (*pl*) ; **~ (à gazon)** mower, lawnmower.

tondre [75] [tɔ̃dr] *vt* [gazon] to mow ; [mouton] to shear ; [caniche, cheveux] to clip.

tondu, e [tɔ̃dy] *adj* [caniche, cheveux] clipped ; [pelouse] mown.

tonicité [tɔnisite] *nf* [des muscles] tone.

tonifier [9] [tɔnifje] *vt* [peau] to tone ; [esprit] to stimulate.

tonique [tɔnik] *adj* - **1.** [boisson] tonic (*avant n*) ; [froid] bracing ; [lotion] toning - **2.** LING & MUS tonic.

tonitruant, e [tɔnitryɑ̃, ɑ̃t] *adj* booming.

tonnage [tɔnaʒ] *nm* tonnage.

tonnant, e [tɔnɑ̃, ɑ̃t] *adj* thundering, thunderous.

tonne [tɔn] *nf* [1000 kg] tonne.

tonneau, x [tɔno] *nm* - **1.** [baril] barrel, cask - **2.** [de voiture] roll - **3.** NAVIG ton.

tonnelle [tɔnɛl] *nf* bower, arbour.

tonner [3] [tɔne] *vi* to thunder.

tonnerre [tɔnɛr] *nm* thunder ; **coup de ~** thunderclap ; *fig* bombshell.

tonte [tɔ̃t] *nf* [de mouton] shearing ; [de gazon] mowing ; [de caniche, cheveux] clipping.

tonus [tɔnys] *nm* - **1.** [dynamisme] energy - **2.** [de muscle] tone.

top [tɔp] *nm* [signal] beep.

toper [3] [tɔpe] *vi* : **tope-là!** right, you're on!

topographie [tɔpɔgrafi] *nf* topography.

toque [tɔk] *nf* [de juge, de jockey] cap ; [de cuisinier] hat.

torche [tɔrʃ] *nf* torch.

torcher [3] [tɔrʃe] *vt fam* - **1.** [assiette, fesses] to wipe - **2.** [travail] to dash off.

torchon [tɔrʃɔ̃] *nm* - **1.** [serviette] cloth - **2.** *fam* [travail] mess.

tordre [76] [tɔrdr] *vt* [gén] to twist. ◆ **se tordre** *vp* : **se ~ la cheville** to twist one's ankle ; **se ~ de rire** *fam fig* to double up with laughter.

tordu, e [tɔrdy] ◇ *pp* ▷ **tordre**. ◇ *adj fam* [bizarre, fou] crazy ; [esprit] warped.

tornade [tɔrnad] *nf* tornado.

torpeur [tɔrpœr] *nf* torpor.

torpille [tɔrpij] *nf* MIL torpedo.

torpiller [3] [tɔrpije] *vt* to torpedo.

torréfaction [tɔrefaksjɔ̃] *nf* roasting.

torrent [tɔrɑ̃] *nm* torrent ; **un ~ de** *fig* [injures] a stream of ; [lumière, larmes] a flood of.

torrentiel, elle [tɔrɑ̃sjɛl] *adj* torrential.

torride [tɔrid] *adj* torrid.

torse [tɔrs] *nm* chest.

torsade [tɔrsad] *nf* - **1.** [de cheveux] twist, coil - **2.** [de pull] cable.

torsader [3] [tɔrsade] *vt* to twist.

torsion [tɔrsjɔ̃] *nf* twisting ; PHYS torsion.

tort [tɔr] *nm* - **1.** [erreur] fault ; **avoir ~** to be wrong ; **être dans son** OU **en ~** to be in the wrong ; **à ~** wrongly - **2.** [préjudice] wrong.

torticolis [tɔrtikɔli] *nm* stiff neck.

tortiller [3] [tɔrtije] *vt* [enrouler] to twist ; [moustache] to twirl. ◆ **se tortiller** *vp* to writhe, to wriggle.

tortionnaire [tɔrsjɔnɛr] *nmf* torturer.

tortue [tɔrty] *nf* tortoise ; *fig* slowcoach *Br*, slowpoke *Am*.

tortueux, euse [tɔrtɥø, øz] *adj* winding, twisting ; *fig* tortuous.

torture [tɔrtyr] *nf* torture.

torturer [3] [tɔrtyre] *vt* to torture.

tôt [to] *adv* - **1.** [de bonne heure] early - **2.** [vite] soon, early. ◆ **au plus tôt** *loc adv* at the earliest.

total, e, aux [tɔtal, o] *adj* total. ◆ **total** *nm* total.

totalement [tɔtalmã] *adv* totally.

totaliser [3] [tɔtalize] *vt* - **1.** [additionner] to add up, to total - **2.** [réunir] to have a total of.

totalitaire [tɔtalitɛr] *adj* totalitarian.

totalitarisme [tɔtalitarism] *nm* totalitarianism.

totalité [tɔtalite] *nf* whole ; **en ~** entirely.

totem [tɔtɛm] *nm* totem.

toubib [tubib] *nmf fam* doc.

touchant, e [tuʃã, ãt] *adj* touching.

touche [tuʃ] *nf* - **1.** [de clavier] key ; **~ de fonction** function key - **2.** [de peinture] stroke - **3.** *fig* [note] : **une ~ de** a touch of - **4.** PÊCHE bite - **5.** [FOOTBALL - ligne] touch line ; [- remise en jeu] throw-in ; [RUGBY - ligne] touch (line) ; [- remise en jeu] line-out - **6.** ESCRIME hit.

toucher [3] [tuʃe] ◇ *nm* : **le ~** the (sense of) touch ; **au ~** to the touch. ◇ *vt* - **1.** [palper, émouvoir] to touch - **2.** [rivage, correspondant] to reach ; [cible] to hit - **3.** [salaire] to get, to be paid ; [chèque] to cash ; [gros lot] to win - **4.** [concerner] to affect, to concern. ◇ *vi* : **~ à** to touch ; [problème] to touch on ; **~ à sa fin** to draw to a close. ◆ **se toucher** *vp* [maisons] to be adjacent (to each other), to adjoin (each other).

touffe [tuf] *nf* tuft.

touffu, e [tufy] *adj* [forêt] dense ; [barbe] bushy.

toujours [tuʒur] *adv* - **1.** [continuité, répétition] always ; **ils s'aimeront ~** they will always love one another, they will love one another forever ; **~ plus** more and more ; **~ moins** less and less - **2.** [encore] still - **3.** [de toute façon] anyway, anyhow. ◆ **de toujours** *loc adj* : **ce sont des amis de ~** they are lifelong friends. ◆ **pour toujours** *loc adv* forever, for good. ◆ **toujours est-il que** *loc conj* the fact remains that.

toupet [tupɛ] *nm* - **1.** [de cheveux] quiff *Br*, tuft of hair - **2.** *fam fig* [aplomb] cheek ; **avoir du ~, ne pas manquer de ~** *fam* to have a cheek.

toupie [tupi] *nf* (spinning) top.

tour [tur] ◇ *nm* - **1.** [périmètre] circumference ; **faire le ~ de** to go round ; **faire un ~** to go for a walk/drive *etc* ; **~ d'horizon** survey ; **~ de piste** SPORT lap ; **~ de taille** waist measurement - **2.** [rotation] turn ; **fermer à double** ~ to double-lock - **3.** [plaisanterie] trick - **4.** [succession] turn ; **c'est à mon ~** it's my turn ; **à ~ de rôle** in turn ; **~ à ~** alternately, in turn - **5.** [d'événements] turn - **6.** [de potier] wheel. ◇ *nf* - **1.** [monument, de château] tower ; [immeuble] tower-

block *Br*, high-rise *Am* - **2.** ÉCHECS rook, castle. ◆ **tour de contrôle** *nf* control tower.

tourbe [turb] *nf* peat.

tourbillon [turbijɔ̃] *nm* - **1.** [de vent] whirlwind - **2.** [de poussière, fumée] swirl - **3.** [d'eau] whirlpool - **4.** *fig* [agitation] hurly-burly.

tourbillonner [3] [turbijɔne] *vi* to whirl, to swirl ; *fig* to whirl (round).

tourelle [turɛl] *nf* turret.

tourisme [turism] *nm* tourism.

touriste [turist] *nmf* tourist.

touristique [turistik] *adj* tourist *(avant n)*.

tourment [turmã] *nm* *sout* torment.

tourmente [turmãt] *nf* - **1.** *littéraire* [tempête] storm, tempest - **2.** *fig* turmoil.

tourmenter [3] [turmãte] *vt* to torment. ◆ **se tourmenter** *vp* to worry o.s., to fret.

tournage [turnaʒ] *nm* CIN shooting.

tournant, e [turnã, ãt] *adj* [porte] revolving ; [fauteuil] swivel *(avant n)* ; [pont] swing *(avant n)*. ◆ **tournant** *nm* bend ; *fig* turning point.

tourné, e [turne] *adj* [lait] sour, off.

tourne-disque [turnədisk] *(pl* **tourne-disques)** *nm* record player.

tournée [turne] *nf* - **1.** [voyage] tour - **2.** *fam* [consommations] round.

tourner [3] [turne] ◇ *vt* - **1.** [gén] to turn - **2.** [pas, pensées] to turn, to direct - **3.** [obstacle, loi] to get round - **4.** CIN to shoot. ◇ *vi* - **1.** [gén] to turn ; [moteur] to turn over ; [planète] to revolve ; **~ autour de qqn** *fig* to hang around sb ; **~ autour du pot** OU **du sujet** *fig* to beat about the bush - **2.** *fam* [entreprise] to tick over - **3.** [lait] to go off. ◆ **se tourner** *vp* to turn (right) round ; **se ~ vers** to turn towards *Br* OU toward *Am*.

tournesol [turnəsɔl] *nm* [plante] sunflower.

tournevis [turnəvis] *nm* screwdriver.

tourniquet [turnikɛ] *nm* - **1.** [entrée] turnstile - **2.** MÉD tourniquet.

tournis [turni] *nm fam* : **avoir le ~** to feel dizzy OU giddy.

tournoi [turnwa] *nm* tournament.

tournoyer [13] [turnwaje] *vi* to wheel, to whirl.

tournure [turnyr] *nf* - **1.** [apparence] turn - **2.** [formulation] form ; **~ de phrase** turn of phrase.

tourteau, x [turto] *nm* [crabe] crab.

tourterelle [turtərɛl] *nf* turtledove.

tous ▷ tout.

Toussaint [tusɛ̃] *nf* : **la ~** All Saints' Day.

tousser [3] [tuse] *vi* to cough.

toussotement [tusɔtmã] *nm* coughing.

toussoter [3] [tusɔte] *vi* to cough.

tout [tu] (*f* **toute** [tut], *mpl* **tous** [tus], *fpl* **toutes** [tut]) <> *adj qualificatif* **- 1.** *(avec substantif singulier déterminé)* all ; **~ le vin** all the wine ; **~ un gâteau** a whole cake ; **toute la journée/la nuit** all day/night, the whole day/night ; **toute sa famille** all his family, his whole family **- 2.** *(avec pronom démonstratif)* : **~ ceci/cela** all this/that ; **~ ce que je sais** all I know. <> *adj indéf* **- 1.** [exprime la totalité] all ; **tous les gâteaux** all the cakes ; **tous les deux** both of us/them etc ; **tous les trois** all three of us/them etc **- 2.** [chaque] every ; **tous les jours** every day ; **tous les deux ans** every two years ; **tous les combien?** how often? **- 3.** [n'importe quel] any ; **à toute heure** at any time. <> *pron indéf* everything, all ; **je t'ai ~ dit** I've told you everything ; **ils voulaient tous la voir** they all wanted to see her ; **ce sera ~?** will that be all ; **c'est ~** that's all. ◆ **tout** <> *adv* **- 1.** [entièrement, tout à fait] very, quite ; **jeune/près** very young/near ; **ils étaient ~ seuls** they were all alone ; **~ en haut** right at the top **- 2.** (avec un gérondif) : **~ en marchant** while walking. <> *nm* : **un ~** a whole ; **le ~ est de ...** the main thing is to ... ◆ **du tout au tout** *loc adv* completely, entirely. ◆ **pas du tout** *loc adv* not at all. ◆ **tout à fait** *loc adv* **1.** [complètement] quite, entirely **- 2.** [exactement] exactly. ◆ **tout à l'heure** *loc adv* **- 1.** [futur] in a little while, shortly ; **à ~ à l'heure!** see you later! **- 2.** [passé] a little while ago. ◆ **tout de suite** *loc adv* immediately, at once.

tout-à-l'égout [tutalegu] *nm inv* mains drainage.

toutefois [tutfwa] *adv* however.

tout-petit [tup(ə)ti] (*pl* **tout-petits**) *nm* toddler.

tout-puissant, toute-puissante [tupɥisã, tutpɥisãt] (*mpl* **tout-puissants**, *fpl* **toutes-puissantes**) *adj* omnipotent, all-powerful.

toux [tu] *nf* cough.

toxicomane [tɔksikɔman] *nmf* drug addict.

toxine [tɔksin] *nf* toxin.

toxique [tɔksik] *adj* toxic.

trac [trak] *nm* nerves (*pl*) ; THÉÂTRE stage fright ; **avoir le ~** to get nervous ; THÉÂTRE to get stage fright.

tracas [traka] *nm* worry.

tracasser [3] [trakase] *vt* to worry, to bother. ◆ **se tracasser** *vp* to worry.

tracasserie [trakasri] *nf* annoyance.

trace [tras] *nf* **- 1.** [d'animal] track **- 2.** [de brûlure, fatigue] mark **- 3.** *(gén pl)* [vestige] trace **- 4.** [très petite quantité] : **une ~ de** a trace of.

tracé [trase] *nm* [lignes] plan, drawing ; [de parcours] line.

tracer [16] [trase] *vt* **- 1.** [dessiner, dépeindre] to draw **- 2.** [route, piste] to mark out.

trachéite [trakeit] *nf* throat infection.

tract [trakt] *nm* leaflet.

tractations [traktasjɔ̃] *nfpl* negotiations, dealings.

tracter [3] [trakte] *vt* to tow.

tracteur [traktœr] *nm* tractor.

traction [traksjɔ̃] *nf* **- 1.** [action de tirer] towing, pulling ; **~ avant/arrière** front-/rear-wheel drive **- 2.** TECHNOL tensile stress **- 3.** [SPORT - au sol] press-up *Br*, push-up *Am* ; [- à la barre] pull-up.

tradition [tradisjɔ̃] *nf* tradition.

traditionnel, elle [tradisjɔnɛl] *adj* **- 1.** [de tradition] traditional **- 2.** [habituel] usual.

traducteur, trice [tradyktœr, tris] *nm, f* translator.

traduction [tradyksjɔ̃] *nf* [gén] translation.

traduire [98] [tradɥir] *vt* **- 1.** [texte] to translate ; **~ qqch en français/anglais** to translate sthg into French/English **- 2.** [révéler - crise] to reveal, to betray ; [- sentiments, pensée] to render, to express **- 3.** JUR : **~ qqn en justice** to bring sb before the courts.

trafic [trafik] *nm* **- 1.** [de marchandises] traffic, trafficking **- 2.** [circulation] traffic.

trafiquant, e [trafikã, ãt] *nm, f* trafficker, dealer.

trafiquer [3] [trafike] <> *vt* **- 1.** [falsifier] to tamper with **- 2.** *fam* [manigancer] : **qu'est-ce que tu trafiques?** what are you up to? <> *vi* to be involved in trafficking.

tragédie [traʒedi] *nf* tragedy.

tragi-comédie [traʒikɔmedi] (*pl* **tragi-comédies**) *nf* tragicomedy.

tragique [traʒik] *adj* tragic.

tragiquement [traʒikmã] *adv* tragically.

trahir [32] [trair] *vt* **- 1.** [gén] to betray **- 2.** [suj : moteur] to let down ; [suj : forces] to fail. ◆ **se trahir** *vp* to give o.s. away.

trahison [traizɔ̃] *nf* **- 1.** [gén] betrayal **- 2.** JUR treason.

train [trɛ̃] *nm* **- 1.** TRANSPORT train **- 2.** [allure] pace **- 3.** *loc* : **être en ~** *fig* to be on form. ◆ **train de vie** *nm* lifestyle. ◆ **en train**

de *loc prép* : **être en ~ de lire/travailler** to be reading/working.

traînant, e [trɛnɑ̃, ɑ̃t] *adj* [voix] drawling ; [démarche] dragging.

traîne [trɛn] *nf* - **1.** [de robe] train - **2.** *loc* : **être à la ~** to lag behind.

traîneau, x [trɛno] *nm* sleigh, sledge.

traînée [trene] *nf* - **1.** [trace] trail - **2.** *tfam péj* [prostituée] tart, whore.

traîner [4] [trene] ◇ *vt* - **1.** [tirer, emmener] to drag - **2.** [trimbaler] to lug around, to cart around - **3.** [maladie] to be unable to shake off. ◇ *vi* - **1.** [personne] to dawdle - **2.** [maladie, affaire] to drag on ; **~ en longueur** to drag - **3.** [vêtements, livres] to lie around ou about. ◆ **se traîner** *vp* - **1.** [personne] to drag o.s. along - **2.** [jour, semaine] to drag.

train-train [trɛ̃trɛ̃] *nm fam* routine, daily grind.

traire [112] [trɛr] *vt* [vache] to milk.

trait [trɛ] *nm* - **1.** [ligne] line, stroke ; **~ d'union** hyphen - **2.** *(gén pl)* [de visage] feature - **3.** [caractéristique] trait, feature - **4.** *loc* : **avoir ~ à** to be to do with, to concern. ◆ **d'un trait** *loc adv* [boire, lire] in one go.

traitant, e [trɛtɑ̃, ɑ̃t] *adj* [shampooing, crème] medicated ▷ **médecin**.

traite [trɛt] *nf* - **1.** [de vache] milking - **2.** COMM bill, draft - **3.** [d'esclaves] : **la ~ des noirs** the slave trade ; **la ~ des blanches** the white slave trade. ◆ **d'une seule traite** *loc adv* without stopping, in one go.

traité [trete] *nm* - **1.** [ouvrage] treatise - **2.** POLIT treaty ; **~ de non-prolifération** non-proliferation treaty.

traitement [trɛtmɑ̃] *nm* - **1.** [gén & MÉD] treatment ; **mauvais ~** ill-treatment - **2.** [rémunération] wage - **3.** IND & INFORM processing ; **~ de texte** word processing - **4.** [de problème] handling.

traiter [4] [trete] ◇ *vt* - **1.** [gén & MÉD] to treat ; **bien/mal ~ qqn** to treat sb well/badly - **2.** [qualifier] : **~ qqn d'imbécile/de lâche** *etc* to call sb an imbecile/a coward *etc* - **3.** [question, thème] to deal with - **4.** IND & INFORM to process. ◇ *vi* - **1.** [négocier] to negotiate - **2.** [livre] : **~ de** to deal with.

traiteur [trɛtœr] *nm* caterer.

traître, esse [trɛtr, ɛs] ◇ *adj* treacherous. ◇ *nm, f* traitor.

traîtrise [trɛtriz] *nf* - **1.** [déloyauté] treachery - **2.** [acte] act of treachery.

trajectoire [traʒɛktwar] *nf* trajectory, path ; *fig* path.

trajet [traʒɛ] *nm* - **1.** [distance] distance - **2.** [itinéraire] route - **3.** [voyage] journey.

trame [tram] *nf* weft ; *fig* framework.

tramer [3] [trame] *vt sout* to plot. ◆ **se tramer** ◇ *vp* to be plotted. ◇ *v impers* : **il se trame quelque chose** there's something afoot.

tramontane [tramɔ̃tan] *nf* strong cold wind that blows through Languedoc-Roussillon in southwest France.

trampoline [trɑ̃pɔlin] *nm* trampoline.

tram(way) [tram(wɛ)] *nm* tram *Br*, streetcar *Am*.

tranchant, e [trɑ̃ʃɑ̃, ɑ̃t] *adj* - **1.** [instrument] sharp - **2.** [personne] assertive - **3.** [ton] curt. ◆ **tranchant** *nm* edge.

tranche [trɑ̃ʃ] *nf* - **1.** [de gâteau, jambon] slice ; **~ d'âge** *fig* age bracket - **2.** [de livre, pièce] edge - **3.** [période] part, section - **4.** [de revenus] portion ; [de paiement] instalment *Br*, installment *Am* ; [fiscale] bracket.

trancher [3] [trɑ̃ʃe] ◇ *vt* [couper] to cut ; [pain, jambon] to slice ; **la question** *fig* to settle the question. ◇ *vi* - **1.** *fig* [décider] to decide - **2.** [contraster] : **~ avec** ou **sur** to contrast with.

tranquille [trɑ̃kil] *adj* - **1.** [endroit, vie] quiet ; **laisser qqn/qqch ~** to leave sb/sthg alone ; **se tenir/rester ~** to keep/remain quiet - **2.** [rassuré] at ease, easy ; **soyez ~** don't worry.

tranquillement [trɑ̃kilmɑ̃] *adv* - **1.** [sans s'agiter] quietly - **2.** [sans s'inquiéter] calmly.

tranquillisant, e [trɑ̃kilizɑ̃, ɑ̃t] *adj* - **1.** [nouvelle] reassuring - **2.** [médicament] tranquillizing. ◆ **tranquillisant** *nm* tranquillizer *Br*, tranquilizer *Am*.

tranquilliser [3] [trɑ̃kilize] *vt* to reassure. ◆ **se tranquilliser** *vp* to set one's mind at rest.

tranquillité [trɑ̃kilite] *nf* - **1.** [calme] peacefulness, quietness - **2.** [sérénité] peace, tranquillity *Br*, tranquility *Am*.

transaction [trɑ̃zaksjɔ̃] *nf* transaction.

transat [trɑ̃zat] ◇ *nm* deckchair. ◇ *nf* transatlantic race.

transatlantique [trɑ̃zatlɑ̃tik] ◇ *adj* transatlantic. ◇ *nm* transatlantic liner. ◇ *nf* transatlantic race.

transcription [trɑ̃skripsjɔ̃] *nf* [de document & MUS] transcription ; [dans un autre alphabet] transliteration ; **~ phonétique** phonetic transcription.

transcrire [99] [trɑ̃skrir] *vt* [document & MUS] to transcribe ; [dans un autre alphabet] to transliterate.

transcrit, e [trɑ̃skri, it] *pp* ▷ **transcrire**.

transe [trɑ̃s] *nf* : être en ~ *fig* to be beside o.s.

transférer [18] [trɑ̃sfere] *vt* to transfer.

transfert [trɑ̃sfɛr] *nm* transfer.

transfigurer [3] [trɑ̃sfigyre] *vt* to transfigure.

transformateur, trice [trɑ̃sfɔrmatœr, tris] *adj* IND processing *(avant n)*. ➡ **transformateur** *nm* transformer.

transformation [trɑ̃sfɔrmasjɔ̃] *nf* - **1.** [de pays, personne] transformation - **2.** IND processing - **3.** RUGBY conversion.

transformer [3] [trɑ̃sfɔrme] *vt* - **1.** [gén] to transform ; [magasin] to convert ; ~ **qqch en** to turn sthg into - **2.** IND & RUGBY to convert. ➡ **se transformer** *vp* : se ~ en monstre/papillon to turn into a monster/butterfly.

transfuge [trɑ̃sfyʒ] *nmf* renegade.

transfuser [3] [trɑ̃sfyze] *vt* [sang] to transfuse.

transfusion [trɑ̃sfyzjɔ̃] *nf* : ~ (sanguine) (blood) transfusion.

transgénique [trɑ̃sʒenik] *adj* transgenic.

transgresser [4] [trɑ̃sgrese] *vt* [loi] to infringe ; [ordre] to disobey.

transhumance [trɑ̃zymɑ̃s] *nf* transhumance.

transi, e [trɑ̃zi] *adj* : être ~ de to be paralysed *Br* ou paralyzed *Am*, to be transfixed with ; être ~ de froid to be chilled to the bone.

transiger [17] [trɑ̃ziʒe] *vi* : ~ (sur) to compromise (on).

transistor [3] [trɑ̃zistɔr] *nm* transistor.

transit [trɑ̃zit] *nm* transit.

transiter [3] [trɑ̃zite] *vi* to pass in transit.

transitif, ive [trɑ̃zitif, iv] *adj* transitive.

transition [trɑ̃zisjɔ̃] *nf* transition ; sans ~ with no transition, abruptly.

transitivité [trɑ̃zitivite] *nf* transitivity.

transitoire [trɑ̃zitwar] *adj* [passager] transitory.

translucide [trɑ̃slysid] *adj* translucent.

transmettre [84] [trɑ̃smɛtr] *vt* - **1.** [message, salutations] : ~ **qqch (à)** to pass sthg on (to) - **2.** [tradition, propriété] : ~ **qqch (à)** to hand sthg down (to) - **3.** [fonction, pouvoir] : ~ **qqch (à)** to hand sthg over (to) - **4.** [maladie] : ~ **qqch (à)** to transmit sthg (to), to pass sthg on (to) - **5.** [concert, émission] to broadcast. ➡ **se transmettre** *vp* - **1.** [maladie] to be passed on, to be transmitted - **2.** [nouvelle] to be passed on - **3.** [courant, onde] to be transmitted - **4.** [tradition] to be handed down.

transmis, e [trɑ̃smi, iz] *pp* ➡ transmettre.

transmissible [trɑ̃smisibl] *adj* - **1.** [patrimoine] transferable - **2.** [maladie] transmissible.

transmission [trɑ̃smisjɔ̃] *nf* - **1.** [de biens] transfer - **2.** [de maladie] transmission - **3.** [de message] passing on - **4.** [de tradition] handing down.

transparaître [91] [trɑ̃sparɛtr] *vi* to show.

transparence [trɑ̃sparɑ̃s] *nf* transparency.

transparent, e [trɑ̃sparɑ̃, ɑ̃t] *adj* transparent. ➡ **transparent** *nm* transparency.

transpercer [16] [trɑ̃sperse] *vt* to pierce ; *fig* [suj : froid, pluie] to go right through.

transpiration [trɑ̃spirasjɔ̃] *nf* [sueur] perspiration.

transpirer [3] [trɑ̃spire] *vi* [suer] to perspire.

transplanter [3] [trɑ̃splɑ̃te] *vt* to transplant.

transport [trɑ̃spɔr] *nm* transport *(U)* ; ~s **en commun** public transport *(sg)*.

transportable [trɑ̃spɔrtabl] *adj* [marchandise] transportable ; [blessé] fit to be moved.

transporter [3] [trɑ̃spɔrte] *vt* [marchandises, personnes] to transport.

transporteur [trɑ̃spɔrtœr] *nm* [personne] carrier ; ~ **routier** road haulier *Br* ou hauler *Am*.

transposer [3] [trɑ̃spoze] *vt* - **1.** [déplacer] to transpose - **2.** [adapter] : ~ **qqch (à)** to adapt sthg (for).

transposition [trɑ̃spozisjɔ̃] *nf* - **1.** [déplacement] transposition - **2.** [adaptation] : ~ **(à)** adaptation (for).

transsexuel, elle [trɑ̃sseksɥɛl] *adj* & *nm, f* transsexual.

transvaser [3] [trɑ̃svaze] *vt* to decant.

transversal, e, aux [trɑ̃sversal, o] *adj* - **1.** [coupe] cross *(avant n)* - **2.** [chemin] running at right angles, cross *(avant n)* *Am* - **3.** [vallée] transverse.

trapèze [trapɛz] *nm* - **1.** GÉOM trapezium - **2.** GYM trapeze.

trapéziste [trapezist] *nmf* trapeze artist.

trappe [trap] *nf* - **1.** [ouverture] trapdoor - **2.** [piège] trap.

trapu, e [trapy] *adj* - **1.** [personne] stocky, solidly built - **2.** [édifice] squat.

traquenard [traknar] *nm* trap ; *fig* trap, pitfall.

traquer [3] [trake] vt [animal] to track ; [personne, faute] to track ou hunt down.

traumatiser [3] [tromatize] vt to traumatize.

traumatisme [tromatism] nm traumatism.

travail [travaj] nm - 1. [gén] work (U) ; **se mettre au ~** to get down to work ; **demander du ~** [projet] to require some work - 2. [tâche, emploi] job ; **~ intérimaire** temporary work - 3. [du métal, du bois] working - 4. [phénomène - du bois] warping ; [- du temps, fermentation] action - 5. MÉD : **être en ~** to be in labour Br ou labor Am ; **entrer en ~** to go into labour Br ou labor Am. ◆ **travaux** nmpl - 1. [d'aménagement] work (U) ; [routiers] roadworks ; **travaux publics** civil engineering (sg) - 2. SCOL : **travaux dirigés** class work ; **travaux manuels** arts and crafts ; **travaux pratiques** practical work (U).

travaillé, e [travaje] adj - 1. [matériau] wrought, worked - 2. [style] laboured Br, labored Am - 3. [tourmenté] : **être ~ par** to be tormented by.

travailler [3] [travaje] ◇ vi - 1. [gén] to work ; **~ chez/dans** to work at/in ; **~ à qqch** to work on sthg ; **~ à temps partiel** to work part-time - 2. [métal, bois] to warp. ◇ vt - 1. [étudier] to work at ou on ; [piano] to practise - 2. [essayer de convaincre] to work on - 3. [suj : idée, remords] to torment - 4. [matière] to work, to fashion.

travailleur, euse [travajœr, øz] ◇ adj hard-working. ◇ nm, f worker.

travelling [travliŋ] nm [mouvement] travelling Br ou traveling Am shot.

travers [travɛr] nm failing, fault. ◆ **à travers** loc adv & loc prép through. ◆ **au travers** loc adv through. ◆ **au travers de** loc prép through. ◆ **de travers** loc adv - 1. [irrégulièrement - écrire] unevenly ; **marcher de ~** to stagger - 2. [nez, escalier] crooked - 3. [obliquement] sideways - 4. [mal] wrong ; **aller de ~** to go wrong ; **comprendre qqch de ~** to misunderstand sthg. ◆ **en travers** loc adv crosswise. ◆ **en travers de** loc prép across.

traverse [travɛrs] nf - 1. [de chemin de fer] sleeper, tie Am - 2. [chemin] short cut.

traversée [travɛrse] nf crossing.

traverser [3] [travɛrse] vt - 1. [rue, mer, montagne] to cross ; [ville] to go through - 2. [peau, mur] to go through, to pierce - 3. [crise, période] to go through.

traversin [travɛrsɛ̃] nm bolster.

travestir [32] [travɛstir] vt - 1. [déguiser] to dress up - 2. fig [vérité, idée] to distort.

◆ **se travestir** vp - 1. [pour bal] to wear fancy dress - 2. [en femme] to put on drag.

trébucher [3] [trebyʃe] vi : **~ (sur/contre)** to stumble (over/against).

trèfle [trɛfl] nm - 1. [plante] clover - 2. [carte] club ; [famille] clubs (pl).

treille [trɛj] nf - 1. [vigne] climbing vine - 2. [tonnelle] trellised vines (pl), vine arbour.

treillis [treji] nm - 1. [clôture] trellis (fencing) - 2. [toile] canvas - 3. MIL combat uniform.

treize [trɛz] adj num & nm thirteen ; voir aussi **six**.

treizième [trɛzjɛm] adj num, nm ou nmf thirteenth ; **~ mois** bonus corresponding to an extra month's salary which is paid annually ; voir aussi **sixième**.

trekking [trɛkiŋ] nm trek.

tréma [trema] nm diaeresis Br, dieresis Am.

tremblant, e [trɑ̃blɑ̃, ɑ̃t] adj - 1. [personne - de froid] shivering ; [- d'émotion] trembling, shaking - 2. [voix] quavering - 3. [lumière] flickering.

tremblement [trɑ̃bləmɑ̃] nm - 1. [de corps] trembling - 2. [de voix] quavering - 3. [de feuilles] fluttering. ◆ **tremblement de terre** nm earthquake.

trembler [3] [trɑ̃ble] vi - 1. [personne - de froid] to shiver ; [- d'émotion] to tremble, to shake - 2. [voix] to quaver - 3. [lumière] to flicker - 4. [terre] to shake.

trembloter [3] [trɑ̃blɔte] vi - 1. [personne] to tremble - 2. [voix] to quaver - 3. [lumière] to flicker.

trémousser [3] [tremuse] ◆ **se trémousser** vp to jig up and down.

trempe [trɑ̃p] nf - 1. [envergure] calibre ; **de sa ~** of his/her calibre - 2. fam [coups] thrashing.

tremper [3] [trɑ̃pe] ◇ vt - 1. [mouiller] to soak - 2. [plonger] : **~ qqch dans** to dip sthg into - 3. [métal] to harden, to quench. ◇ vi [linge] to soak.

tremplin [trɑ̃plɛ̃] nm litt & fig springboard ; SKI ski jump.

trentaine [trɑ̃tɛn] nf - 1. [nombre] : **une ~ de** about thirty - 2. [âge] : **avoir la ~** to be in one's thirties.

trente [trɑ̃t] ◇ adj num thirty. ◇ nm thirty ; voir aussi **six**.

trentième [trɑ̃tjɛm] adj num, nm ou nmf thirtieth ; voir aussi **sixième**.

trépasser [3] [trepase] vi littéraire to pass away.

trépidant, e [trepidɑ̃, ɑ̃t] adj [vie] hectic.

trépied [trepje] *nm* [support] tripod.

trépigner [3] [trepiɲe] *vi* to stamp one's feet.

très [trɛ] *adv* very ; ~ **bien** very well ; **être** ~ **aimé** to be much ou greatly liked ; **j'ai** ~ **envie de ...** I'd very much like to ...

trésor [trezɔr] *nm* treasure. ◆ **Trésor** *nm* : **le Trésor public** the public revenue department.

trésorerie [trezɔrri] *nf* **- 1.** [service] accounts department **- 2.** [gestion] accounts *(pl)* **- 3.** [fonds] finances *(pl)*, funds *(pl)*.

trésorier, ère [trezɔrje, ɛr] *nm, f* treasurer.

tressaillement [tresajmā] *nm* [de joie] thrill ; [de douleur] wince.

tressaillir [47] [tresajir] *vi* **- 1.** [de joie] to thrill ; [de douleur] to wince **- 2.** [sursauter] to start, to jump.

tressauter [3] [tresote] *vi* [sursauter] to jump, to start ; [dans véhicule] to be tossed about.

tresse [trɛs] *nf* **- 1.** [de cheveux] plait **- 2.** [de rubans] braid.

tresser [4] [trese] *vt* **- 1.** [cheveux] to plait **- 2.** [osier] to braid **- 3.** [panier, guirlande] to weave.

tréteau, x [treto] *nm* trestle.

treuil [trœj] *nm* winch, windlass.

trêve [trɛv] *nf* **- 1.** [cessez-le-feu] truce **- 2.** *fig* [répit] rest, respite ; ~ **de plaisanteries/de sottises** that's enough joking/nonsense. ◆ **sans trêve** *loc adv* relentlessly, unceasingly.

tri [tri] *nm* [de lettres] sorting ; [de candidats] selection ; **faire le** ~ **dans qqch** *fig* to sort sthg out.

triage [trijaʒ] *nm* [de lettres] sorting ; [de candidats] selection.

triangle [trijɑ̃gl] *nm* triangle.

triangulaire [trijɑ̃gylɛr] *adj* triangular.

triathlon [trijatlɔ̃] *nm* triathlon.

tribal, e, aux [tribal, o] *adj* tribal.

tribord [tribɔr] *nm* starboard ; **à** ~ on the starboard side, to starboard.

tribu [triby] *nf* tribe.

tribulations [tribylasjɔ̃] *nfpl* tribulations, trials.

tribunal, aux [tribynal, o] *nm* JUR court ; ~ **correctionnel** ≃ Magistrates' Court *Br*, ≃ County Court *Am* ; ~ **de grande instance** ≃ Crown Court *Br*, ≃ Circuit Court *Am*.

tribune [tribyn] *nf* **- 1.** [d'orateur] platform **- 2.** *(gén pl)* [de stade] stand.

tribut [triby] *nm littéraire* tribute.

tributaire [tribytɛr] *adj* : **être** ~ **de** to depend ou be dependent on.

tricher [3] [trife] *vi* **- 1.** [au jeu, à un examen] to cheat **- 2.** [mentir] : ~ **sur** to lie about.

tricherie [trifri] *nf* cheating.

tricheur, euse [trifœr, øz] *nm, f* cheat.

tricolore [trikɔlɔr] *adj* **- 1.** [à trois couleurs] three-coloured *Br*, three-colored *Am* **- 2.** [français] French.

tricot [triko] *nm* **- 1.** [vêtement] jumper *Br*, sweater **- 2.** [ouvrage] knitting ; **faire du** ~ to knit **- 3.** [étoffe] knitted fabric, jersey.

tricoter [3] [trikote] *vi & vt* to knit.

tricycle [trisikl] *nm* tricycle.

trier [10] [trije] *vt* **- 1.** [classer] to sort out **- 2.** [sélectionner] to select.

trilingue [trilɛ̃g] *adj* trilingual.

trimestre [trimɛstr] *nm* [période] term.

trimestriel, elle [trimɛstrijɛl] *adj* [loyer, magazine] quarterly ; SCOL end-of-term *(avant n)*.

tringle [trɛ̃gl] *nf* rod ; ~ **à rideaux** curtain rod.

trinité [trinite] *nf littéraire* trinity. ◆ **Trinité** *nf* : **la Trinité** the Trinity.

trinquer [3] [trɛ̃ke] *vi* [boire] to toast, to clink glasses ; ~ **à** to drink to.

trio [trijo] *nm* trio.

triomphal, e, aux [trijɔ̃fal, o] *adj* [succès] triumphal ; [accueil] triumphant.

triomphant, e [trijɔ̃fɑ̃, ɑ̃t] *adj* [équipe] winning ; [air] triumphant.

triomphe [trijɔ̃f] *nm* triumph.

triompher [3] [trijɔ̃fe] *vi* [gén] to triumph ; ~ **de** to triumph over.

tripes [trip] *nfpl* **- 1.** [d'animal, de personne] guts **- 2.** CULIN tripe *(sg)*.

triple [tripl] ◇ *adj* triple. ◇ *nm* : **le** ~ **(de)** three times as much (as).

triplé, ées [triple] *nm* **- 1.** [au turf] *bet on three horses winning in three different races* **- 2.** SPORT [trois victoires] hat-trick of victories. ◆ **triplés, ées** *nm, f pl* triplets.

triste [trist] *adj* **- 1.** [personne, nouvelle] sad ; **être** ~ **de qqch/de faire qqch** to be sad about sthg/about doing sthg **- 2.** [paysage, temps] gloomy ; [couleur] dull **- 3.** *(avant n)* [lamentable] sorry.

tristesse [tristɛs] *nf* **- 1.** [de personne, nouvelle] sadness **- 2.** [de paysage, temps] gloominess.

triturer [3] [trityre] *vt fam* [mouchoir] to knead. ◆ **se triturer** *vp fam* : **se** ~ **l'esprit** ou **les méninges** to rack one's brains.

trivial, e, aux [trivjal, o] *adj* **- 1.** [banal] trivial **- 2.** *péj* [vulgaire] crude, coarse.

troc [trɔk] *nm* - **1.** [échange] exchange - **2.** [système économique] barter.

trois [trwa] ◇ *nm* three. ◇ *adj num* three ; *voir aussi* **six**.

troisième [trwazjɛm] ◇ *adj num & nmf* third. ◇ *nm* third ; [étage] third floor *Br*, fourth floor *Am*. ◇ *nf* - **1.** SCOL ≃ fourth year *ou* form *Br*, ≃ ninth grade *Am* - **2.** [vitesse] third (gear) ; *voir aussi* **sixième**.

trombe [trɔ̃b] *nf* water spout.

trombone [trɔ̃bɔn] *nm* - **1.** [agrafe] paper clip - **2.** [instrument] trombone.

trompe [trɔ̃p] *nf* - **1.** [instrument] trumpet - **2.** [d'éléphant] trunk - **3.** [d'insecte] proboscis - **4.** ANAT tube.

trompe-l'œil [trɔ̃plœj] *nm inv* - **1.** [peinture] trompe-l'oeil ; **en ~** done in trompe-l'oeil - **2.** [apparence] deception.

tromper [3] [trɔ̃pe] *vt* - **1.** [personne] to deceive ; [époux] to be unfaithful to, to deceive - **2.** [vigilance] to elude. ◆ **se tromper** *vp* to make a mistake, to be mistaken ; **se ~ de jour/maison** to get the wrong day/house.

tromperie [trɔ̃pri] *nf* deception.

trompette [trɔ̃pɛt] *nf* trumpet.

trompettiste [trɔ̃petist] *nmf* trumpeter.

trompeur, euse [trɔ̃pœr, øz] *adj* - **1.** [personne] deceitful - **2.** [calme, apparence] deceptive.

tronc [trɔ̃] *nm* - **1.** [d'arbre, de personne] trunk - **2.** [d'église] collection box. ◆ **tronc commun** *nm* [de programmes] common element *ou* feature ; SCOL core syllabus.

tronçon [trɔ̃sɔ̃] *nm* - **1.** [morceau] piece, length - **2.** [de route, de chemin de fer] section.

tronçonneuse [trɔ̃sɔnøz] *nf* chain saw.

trône [tron] *nm* throne.

trôner [3] [trone] *vi* - **1.** [personne] to sit enthroned ; [objet] to have pride of place - **2.** *hum* [faire l'important] to lord it.

trop [tro] *adv* - **1.** (*devant adj, adv*) too ; **~ vieux/loin** too old/far ; **nous étions ~ nombreux** there were too many of us ; **avoir ~ chaud/froid/peur** to be too hot/cold/frightened - **2.** (*avec verbe*) too much ; **nous étions ~** there were too many of us ; **je n'aime pas ~ le chocolat** I don't like chocolate very much ; **sans ~ savoir pourquoi** without really knowing why - **3.** (*avec complément*) : **~ de** [quantité] too much ; [nombre] too many. ◆ **en trop, de trop** *loc adv* too much/many ; **2 euros de** *ou* **en ~** 2 euros too much ; **une personne de** *ou* **en ~** one person too many ; **être de ~** [personne] to be in the way, to be unwelcome.

trophée [trɔfe] *nm* trophy.

tropical, e, aux [trɔpikal, o] *adj* tropical.

tropique [trɔpik] *nm* tropic. ◆ **tropiques** *nmpl* tropics.

trop-plein [trɔplɛ̃] (*pl* **trop-pleins**) *nm* [excès] excess ; *fig* excess, surplus.

troquer [3] [trɔke] *vt* : **~ qqch (contre)** to barter sthg (for) ; *fig* to swap sthg (for).

trot [tro] *nm* trot ; **au ~** at a trot.

trotter [3] [trɔte] *vi* - **1.** [cheval] to trot - **2.** [personne] to run around.

trotteur, euse [trɔtœr, øz] *nm, f* trotter. ◆ **trotteuse** *nf* second hand.

trottiner [3] [trɔtine] *vi* to trot.

trottoir [trɔtwar] *nm* pavement *Br*, sidewalk *Am*.

trou [tru] *nm* - **1.** [gén] hole ; **~ d'air** air pocket - **2.** [manque, espace vide] gap ; **~ de mémoire** memory lapse.

troublant, e [trublɑ̃, ɑ̃t] *adj* disturbing.

trouble [trubl] ◇ *adj* - **1.** [eau] cloudy - **2.** [image, vue] blurred - **3.** [affaire] shady. ◇ *nm* - **1.** [désordre] trouble, discord - **2.** [gêne] confusion ; [émoi] agitation - **3.** (*gén pl*) [dérèglement] disorder. ◆ **troubles** *nmpl* [sociaux] unrest (*U*).

trouble-fête [trublɔfɛt] *nmf inv* spoilsport.

troubler [3] [truble] *vt* - **1.** [eau] to cloud, to make cloudy - **2.** [image, vue] to blur - **3.** [sommeil, événement] to disrupt, to disturb - **4.** [esprit, raison] to cloud - **5.** [inquiéter, émouvoir] to disturb - **6.** [rendre perplexe] to trouble. ◆ **se troubler** *vp* - **1.** [eau] to become cloudy - **2.** [personne] to become flustered.

trouée [true] *nf* gap ; MIL breach.

trouer [3] [true] *vt* - **1.** [chaussette] to make a hole in - **2.** *fig* [silence] to disturb.

trouille [truj] *nf fam* fear, terror.

troupe [trup] *nf* - **1.** MIL troop - **2.** [d'amis] group, band ; [de singes] troop - **3.** THÉÂTRE theatre troupe.

troupeau, x [trupo] *nm* [de vaches, d'éléphants] herd ; [de moutons, d'oies] flock ; *péj* [de personnes] herd.

trousse [trus] *nf* case, bag ; **~ de secours** first-aid kit ; **~ de toilette** toilet bag.

trousseau, x [truso] *nm* - **1.** [de mariée] trousseau - **2.** [de clefs] bunch.

trouvaille [truvaj] *nf* - **1.** [découverte] find, discovery - **2.** [invention] new idea.

trouver [3] [truve] ◇ *vt* to find ; **~ que** to feel (that) ; **~ bon/mauvais que ...** to think (that) it is right/wrong that ... ; **~ qqch à faire/à dire** *etc* to find sthg to do/say *etc*. ◇ *v impers* : **il se trouve que ...** the fact is that ... ➧ **se trouver** *vp* - **1.** [dans un endroit] to be - **2.** [dans un état] to find o.s. - **3.** [se sentir] to feel ; **se ~ mal** [s'évanouir] to faint.

truand [tryɑ̃] *nm* crook.

truc [tryk] *nm* - **1.** [combine] trick - **2.** *fam* [chose] thing, thingamajig ; **ce n'est pas son ~** it's not his thing.

trucage = truquage.

truculent, e [trykylɑ̃, ɑ̃t] *adj* colourful *Br*, colorful *Am*.

truelle [tryɛl] *nf* trowel.

truffe [tryf] *nf* - **1.** [champignon] truffle - **2.** [museau] muzzle.

truffer [3] [tryfe] *vt* - **1.** [volaille] to garnish with truffles - **2.** *fig* [discours] : **~ de** to stuff with.

truie [tryi] *nf* sow.

truite [tryit] *nf* trout.

truquage, trucage [trykaʒ] *nm* CIN (special) effect.

truquer [3] [tryke] *vt* - **1.** [élections] to rig - **2.** CIN to use special effects in.

trust [trœst] *nm* - **1.** [groupement] trust - **2.** [entreprise] corporation.

ts *abr de* **tous**

tsar [tsar], **tzar** [dzar] *nm* tsar.

tsigane = tzigane.

TSVP (*abr de* **tournez s'il vous plaît**) PTO.

tt *abr de* **tout**.

tt conf. *abr de* **tout confort**.

ttes *abr de* **toutes**.

TTX (*abr de* **traitement de texte**) WP.

tu[1], **e** [ty] *pp* ➤ **taire**.

tu[2] [ty] *pron pers* you.

tuba [tyba] *nm* - **1.** MUS tuba - **2.** [de plongée] snorkel.

tube [tyb] *nm* - **1.** [gén] tube ; **~ cathodique** cathode ray tube - **2.** *fam* [chanson] hit. ➧ **tube digestif** *nm* digestive tract.

tubercule [tyberkyl] *nm* BOT tuber.

tuberculose [tyberkyloz] *nf* tuberculosis.

tuer [7] [tɥe] *vt* to kill. ➧ **se tuer** *vp* - **1.** [se suicider] to kill o.s. - **2.** [par accident] to die.

tuerie [tyri] *nf* slaughter.

tue-tête [tytɛt] ➧ **à tue-tête** *loc adv* at the top of one's voice.

tueur, euse [tɥœr, øz] *nm, f* [meurtrier] killer ; **~ en série** serial killer.

tuile [tɥil] *nf* - **1.** [de toit] tile - **2.** *fam* [désagrément] blow.

tulipe [tylip] *nf* tulip.

tulle [tyl] *nm* tulle.

tuméfié, e [tymefje] *adj* swollen.

tumeur [tymœr] *nf* tumour *Br*, tumor *Am*.

tumulte [tymylt] *nm* - **1.** [désordre] hubbub - **2.** *littéraire* [trouble] tumult.

tunique [tynik] *nf* tunic.

Tunisie [tynizi] *nf* : **la ~** Tunisia.

tunisien, enne [tynizjɛ̃, ɛn] *adj* Tunisian. ➧ **Tunisien, enne** *nm, f* Tunisian.

tunnel [tynɛl] *nm* tunnel.

turban [tyrbɑ̃] *nm* turban.

turbine [tyrbin] *nf* turbine.

turbo [tyrbo] *nm* OU *nf* turbo.

turbulence [tyrbylɑ̃s] *nf* MÉTÉOR turbulence.

turbulent, e [tyrbylɑ̃, ɑ̃t] *adj* boisterous.

turc, turque [tyrk] *adj* Turkish. ➧ **turc** *nm* [langue] Turkish. ➧ **Turc, Turque** *nm, f* Turk.

turf [tœrf] *nm* [activité] : **le ~** racing.

turnover [tœrnɔvœr] *nm* turnover.

turque ➤ **turc**.

Turquie [tyrki] *nf* : **la ~** Turkey.

turquoise [tyrkwaz] *nf* & *adj inv* turquoise.

tutelle [tytɛl] *nf* - **1.** JUR guardianship - **2.** [dépendance] supervision.

tuteur, trice [tytœr, tris] *nm, f* guardian. ➧ **tuteur** *nm* [pour plante] stake.

tutoyer [13] [tytwaje] *vt* : **~ qqn** to use the 'tu' form to sb.

tuyau, x [tɥijo] *nm* - **1.** [conduit] pipe ; **~ d'arrosage** hosepipe - **2.** *fam* [renseignement] tip.

tuyauterie [tɥijotri] *nf* piping (*U*), pipes (*pl*).

TV (*abr de* **télévision**) *nf* TV.

TVA (*abr de* **taxe à la valeur ajoutée**) *nf* ~ VAT.

tweed [twid] *nm* tweed.

tympan [tɛ̃pɑ̃] *nm* ANAT eardrum.

type [tip] ◇ *nm* - **1.** [exemple caractéristique] perfect example - **2.** [genre] type - **3.** *fam* [individu] guy, bloke. ◇ *adj inv* [caractéristique] typical.

typhoïde [tifɔid] *nf* typhoid.

typhon [tifɔ̃] *nm* typhoon.

typhus [tifys] *nm* typhus.

typique [tipik] *adj* typical.

typographie [tipɔgrafi] *nf* typography.

tyran [tirɑ̃] *nm* tyrant.

tyrannique [tiranik] *adj* tyrannical.

tyranniser [3] [tiranize] *vt* to tyrannize.

tzar = tsar.

tzigane [dzigan], **tsigane** [tsigan] *nmf* gipsy.

U

u, U [y] *nm inv* u, U.

UDF (*abr de* **Union pour la démocratie française**) *nf French political party to the right of the political spectrum.*

UE (*abr de* **Union européenne**) *nf* EU.

UFR (*abr. de* **unité de formation et de recherche**) *nf* university department.

Ukraine [ykrɛn] *nf* : **l'~** the Ukraine.

ulcère [ylsɛr] *nm* ulcer.

ulcérer [18] [ylsere] *vt* - **1.** MÉD to ulcerate - **2.** *sout* [mettre en colère] to enrage.

ULM (*abr de* **ultra léger motorisé**) *nm* microlight.

ultérieur, e [ylterjœr] *adj* later, subsequent.

ultimatum [yltimatɔm] *nm* ultimatum.

ultime [yltim] *adj* ultimate, final.

ultramoderne [yltramɔdɛrn] *adj* ultra-modern.

ultrasensible [yltrasɑ̃sibl] *adj* [personne] ultra-sensitive ; [pellicule] high-speed.

ultrason [yltrasɔ̃] *nm* ultrasound (*U*).

ultraviolet, ette [yltravjɔlɛ, ɛt] *adj* ultraviolet. ◆ **ultraviolet** *nm* ultraviolet.

un [œ̃] (*f* **une** [yn]) ◇ *art indéf* a, an (*devant voyelle*) ; **~ homme** a man ; **~ livre** a book ; **une femme** a woman ; **une pomme** an apple. ◇ *pron indéf* one ; **l'~ de mes amis** one of my friends ; **l'~ l'autre** each other ; **les ~s les autres** one another ; **l'~ ..., l'autre** one ..., the other ; **les ~s ..., les autres** some ..., others ; **l'~ et l'autre** both (of them) ; **l'~ ou l'autre** either (of them) ; **ni l'~ ni l'autre** neither one nor the other, neither (of them). ◇ *adj num* one ; **une personne à la fois** one person at a time. ◇ *nm* one ; *voir aussi* **six**. ◆ **une** *nf* : **faire la/être à la une** PRESSE to make the/to be on the front page.

unanime [ynanim] *adj* unanimous.

unanimité [ynanimite] *nf* unanimity ; **faire l'~** to be unanimously approved ; **à l'~** unanimously.

UNESCO, Unesco [ynɛsko] (*abr de* **United Nations Educational, Scientific and Cultural Organization**) *nf* UNESCO.

uni, e [yni] *adj* - **1.** [joint, réuni] united - **2.** [famille, couple] close - **3.** [surface, mer] smooth ; [route] even - **4.** [étoffe, robe] plain, self-coloured *Br*, self-colored *Am*.

UNICEF, Unicef [ynisɛf] (*abr de* **United Nations International Children's Emergency Fund**) *nm* UNICEF.

unifier [9] [ynifje] *vt* - **1.** [régions, parti] to unify - **2.** [programmes] to standardize.

uniforme [yniform] ◇ *adj* uniform ; [régulier] regular. ◇ *nm* uniform.

uniformiser [3] [yniformize] *vt* - **1.** [couleur] to make uniform - **2.** [programmes, lois] to standardize.

unijambiste [yniʒɑ̃bist] ◇ *adj* one-legged. ◇ *nmf* one-legged person.

unilatéral, e, aux [ynilateral, o] *adj* unilateral ; **stationnement ~** parking on only one side of the street.

union [ynjɔ̃] *nf* - **1.** [de couleurs] blending - **2.** [mariage] union ; **~ libre** cohabitation - **3.** [de pays] union ; [de syndicats] confederation - **4.** [entente] unity. ◆ **Union européenne** *nf* European Union. ◆ **Union soviétique** *nf* : **l'(ex-)Union soviétique** the (former) Soviet Union.

unique [ynik] *adj* - **1.** [seul - enfant, veston] only ; [- préoccupation] sole - **2.** [principe, prix] single - **3.** [exceptionnel] unique.

uniquement [ynikmɑ̃] *adv* - **1.** [exclusivement] only, solely - **2.** [seulement] only, just.

unir [32] [ynir] *vt* - **1.** [assembler - mots, qualités] to put together, to combine ; [- pays] to unite ; **~ qqch à** [pays] to unite sthg with ; [mot, qualité] to combine sthg with - **2.** [réunir - partis, familles] to unite - **3.** [marier] to unite, to join in marriage. ◆ **s'unir** *vp* - **1.** [s'associer] to unite, to join together - **2.** [se marier] to be joined in marriage.

unitaire [yniter] *adj* [à l'unité] : **prix ~** unit price.

unité [ynite] *nf* - **1.** [cohésion] unity - **2.** COMM, MATHS & MIL unit. ◆ **unité centrale** *nf* INFORM central processing unit.

univers [yniver] *nm* universe ; *fig* world.

universel, elle [yniversɛl] *adj* universal.

universitaire [yniversiter] ◇ *adj* university (*avant n*). ◇ *nmf* academic.

université [yniversite] *nf* university.

uranium [yranjɔm] *nm* uranium.

urbain, e [yrbɛ̃, ɛn] *adj* - **1.** [de la ville] urban - **2.** *littéraire* [affable] urbane.

urbaniser [3] [yrbanize] *vt* to urbanize.

urbanisme [yrbanism] *nm* town planning.

urgence [yrʒɑ̃s] *nf* - **1.** [de mission] urgency - **2.** MÉD emergency ; **les ~s** the casualty department (*sg*). ◆ **d'urgence** *loc adv* immediately.

urgent, e [yrʒɑ̃, ɑ̃t] *adj* urgent.

urine [yrin] *nf* urine.

uriner [3] [yrine] *vi* to urinate.

urinoir [yrinwar] *nm* urinal.

urne [yrn] *nf* - **1.** [vase] urn - **2.** [de vote] ballot box.

URSS (*abr de* **Union des républiques socialistes soviétiques**) *nf* : l'(ex-)~ the (former) USSR.

urticaire [yrtikɛr] *nf* urticaria, hives *(pl)*.

Uruguay [yrygwɛ] *nm* : l'~ Uruguay.

USA (*abr de* **United States of America**) *nmpl* USA.

usage [yzaʒ] *nm* - **1.** [gén] use ; à ~ externe/interne for external/internal use ; hors d'~ out of action - **2.** [coutume] custom - **3.** LING usage.

usagé, e [yzaʒe] *adj* worn, old.

usager [yzaʒe] *nm* user.

usé, e [yze] *adj* - **1.** [détérioré] worn ; eaux ~es waste water *(sg)* - **2.** [personne] worn-out - **3.** [plaisanterie] hackneyed, well worn.

user [3] [yze] <> *vt* - **1.** [consommer] to use - **2.** [vêtement] to wear out - **3.** [forces] to use up ; [santé] to ruin ; [personne] to wear out. <> *vi* [se servir] : ~ de [charme] to use ; [droit, privilège] to exercise. ◆ **s'user** *vp* - **1.** [chaussure] to wear out - **2.** [amour] to burn itself out.

usine [yzin] *nf* factory.

usiner [3] [yzine] *vt* - **1.** [façonner] to machine - **2.** [fabriquer] to manufacture.

usité, e [yzite] *adj* in common use ; très/peu ~ commonly/rarely used.

ustensile [ystɑ̃sil] *nm* implement, tool.

usuel, elle [yzɥɛl] *adj* common, usual.

usufruit [yzyfrɥi] *nm* usufruct.

usure [yzyr] *nf* - **1.** [de vêtement, meuble] wear ; [de forces] wearing down ; avoir qqn à l'~ *fam* to wear sb down - **2.** [intérêt] usury.

usurier, ère [yzyrje, ɛr] *nm, f* usurer.

usurpateur, trice [yzyrpatœr, tris] *nm, f* usurper.

usurper [3] [yzyrpe] *vt* to usurp.

ut [yt] *nm inv* C.

utérus [yterys] *nm* uterus, womb.

utile [ytil] *adj* useful ; être ~ à qqn to be useful ou of help to sb, to help sb.

utilisateur, trice [ytilizatœr, tris] *nm, f* user.

utiliser [3] [ytilize] *vt* to use.

utilitaire [ytilitɛr] <> *adj* [pratique] utilitarian ; [véhicule] commercial. <> *nm* INFORM utility (program).

utilité [ytilite] *nf* - **1.** [usage] usefulness - **2.** JUR : entreprise d'~ publique public utility ; organisme d'~ publique registered charity.

utopie [ytɔpi] *nf* - **1.** [idéal] utopia - **2.** [projet irréalisable] unrealistic idea.

utopiste [ytɔpist] *nmf* utopian.

UV <> *nf* (*abr de* **unité de valeur**) *university course unit*, ≃ credit. <> (*abr de* **ultraviolet**) UV.

v, V [ve] *nm inv* v, V.

v. - 1. (*abr de* **vers**) LITTÉRATURE v. - **2.** (*abr de* **verset**) v. - **3.** (*abr de* **vers**) [environ] approx.

va [va] <> *interj* : courage, ~! come on, cheer up! ; ~ donc! come on! ; ~ pour 10 euros/demain OK, let's say 10 euros/tomorrow.

vacance [vakɑ̃s] *nf* vacancy. ◆ **vacances** *nfpl* holiday *Br (sg)*, vacation *Am (sg)* ; être/partir en ~s to be/go on holiday ; les grandes ~s the summer holidays.

vacancier, ère [vakɑ̃sje, ɛr] *nm, f* holiday-maker *Br*, vacationer *Am*.

vacant, e [vakɑ̃, ɑ̃t] *adj* [poste] vacant ; [logement] vacant, unoccupied.

vacarme [vakarm] *nm* racket, din.

vacataire [vakatɛr] <> *adj* [employé] temporary. <> *nmf* temporary worker.

vacation [vakasjɔ̃] *nf* [d'expert] session.

vaccin [vaksɛ̃] *nm* vaccine.

vaccination [vaksinasjɔ̃] *nf* vaccination.

vacciner [3] [vaksine] *vt* : ~ qqn (contre) MÉD to vaccinate sb (against) ; *fam fig* to make sb immune (to).

vache [vaʃ] <> *nf* - **1.** ZOOL cow - **2.** [cuir] cowhide - **3.** *fam péj* [femme] cow ; [homme] pig. <> *adj fam* rotten.

vachement [vaʃmɑ̃] *adv fam* bloody *Br*, dead *Br*, real *Am*.

vaciller [3] [vasije] *vi* - **1.** [jambes, fondations] to shake ; [lumière] to flicker ; ~ sur ses jambes to be unsteady on one's legs - **2.** [mémoire, santé] to fail.

va-et-vient [vaevjɛ̃] *nm inv* - **1.** [de personnes] comings and goings *(pl)*, toing and froing - **2.** [de balancier] to-and-fro movement - **3.** ÉLECTR two-way switch.

vagabond, e [vagabɔ̃, ɔ̃d] ◇ adj - **1.** [chien] stray ; [vie] vagabond *(avant n)* - **2.** [humeur] restless. ◇ nm, f [rôdeur] vagrant, tramp ; *littéraire* [voyageur] wanderer.

vagabondage [vagabɔ̃daʒ] nm [délit] vagrancy ; [errance] wandering, roaming.

vagin [vaʒɛ̃] nm vagina.

vagissement [vaʒismɑ̃] nm cry, wail.

vague [vag] ◇ adj - **1.** [idée, promesse] vague - **2.** [vêtement] loose-fitting - **3.** *(avant n)* [quelconque] : **il a un ~ travail dans un bureau** he has some job or other in an office - **4.** *(avant n)* [cousin] distant. ◇ nf wave ; **une ~ de froid** a cold spell ; **~ de chaleur** heatwave.

vaguement [vagmɑ̃] adv vaguely.

vaillant, e [vajɑ̃, ɑ̃t] adj - **1.** [enfant, vieillard] hale and hearty - **2.** *littéraire* [héros] valiant.

vain, e [vɛ̃, vɛn] adj - **1.** [inutile] vain, useless ; **en ~** in vain, to no avail - **2.** *littéraire* [vaniteux] vain.

vaincre [114] [vɛ̃kr] vt - **1.** [ennemi] to defeat - **2.** [obstacle, peur] to overcome.

vaincu, e [vɛ̃ky] ◇ pp ⊳ **vaincre**. ◇ adj defeated. ◇ nm, f defeated person.

vainement [vɛnmɑ̃] adv vainly.

vainqueur [vɛ̃kœr] ◇ nm - **1.** [de combat] conqueror, victor - **2.** SPORT winner. ◇ adj m victorious, conquering.

vais ⊳ **aller**.

vaisseau, x [vɛso] nm - **1.** NAVIG vessel, ship ; **~ spatial** AÉRON spaceship - **2.** ANAT vessel - **3.** ARCHIT nave.

vaisselle [vɛsɛl] nf crockery ; **faire** OU **laver la ~** to do the dishes, to wash up.

val [val] *(pl* **vals** OU **vaux** [vo]*)* nm valley.

valable [valabl] adj - **1.** [passeport] valid - **2.** [raison, excuse] valid, legitimate - **3.** [œuvre] good, worthwhile.

valet [valɛ] nm - **1.** [serviteur] servant - **2.** CARTES jack, knave.

valeur [valœr] nf - **1.** [gén & MUS] value ; **avoir de la ~** to be valuable ; **mettre en ~** [talents] to bring out ; **~ ajoutée** ÉCON added value ; **de (grande) ~** [chose] (very) valuable - **2.** *(gén pl)* BOURSE stocks and shares *(pl)*, securities *(pl)* - **3.** [mérite] worth, merit - **4.** *fig* [importance] value, importance - **5.** [équivalent] : **la ~ de** the equivalent of.

valide [valid] adj - **1.** [personne] spry - **2.** [contrat] valid.

valider [3] [valide] vt to validate, to authenticate.

validité [validite] nf validity.

valise [valiz] nf case, suitcase ; **faire sa ~/ses ~s** to pack one's case/cases ; *fam fig* [partir] to pack one's bags.

vallée [vale] nf valley.

vallon [valɔ̃] nm small valley.

vallonné, e [valɔne] adj undulating.

valoir [60] [valwar] ◇ vi - **1.** [gén] to be worth ; **ça vaut combien?** how much is it? ; **que vaut ce film?** is this film any good? ; **ne rien ~** not to be any good, to be worthless ; **ça vaut mieux** *fam* that's best ; **ça ne vaut pas la peine** it's not worth it ; **faire ~** [vues] to assert ; [talent] to show - **2.** [règle] : **~ pour** to apply to, to hold good for. ◇ vt [médaille, gloire] to bring, to earn. ◇ v impers : **il vaudrait mieux que nous partions** it would be better if we left, we'd better leave. ◆ **se valoir** vp to be equally good/bad.

valoriser [3] [valɔrize] vt [immeuble, région] to develop ; [individu, société] to improve the image of.

valse [vals] nf waltz.

valser [3] [valse] vi to waltz ; **envoyer ~ qqch** *fam fig* to send sthg flying.

valu [valy] pp inv ⊳ **valoir**.

valve [valv] nf valve.

vampire [vɑ̃pir] nm - **1.** [fantôme] vampire - **2.** ZOOL vampire bat.

vandalisme [vɑ̃dalism] nm vandalism.

vanille [vanij] nf vanilla.

vanité [vanite] nf vanity.

vaniteux, euse [vanitø, øz] adj vain, conceited.

vanne [van] nf - **1.** [d'écluse] lockgate - **2.** *fam* [remarque] gibe.

vannerie [vanri] nf basketwork, wickerwork.

vantard, e [vɑ̃tar, ard] ◇ adj bragging, boastful. ◇ nm, f boaster.

vanter [3] [vɑ̃te] vt to vaunt. ◆ **se vanter** vp to boast, to brag ; **se ~ de faire qqch** to boast OU brag about doing sthg.

va-nu-pieds [vanypje] nmf inv *fam* beggar.

vapeur [vapœr] nf - **1.** [d'eau] steam ; **à la ~** steamed ; **bateau à ~** steamboat, steamer ; **locomotive à ~** steam engine - **2.** [émanation] vapour *Br*, vapor *Am*. ◆ **vapeurs** nfpl - **1.** [émanations] fumes - **2.** *loc vieilli* : **avoir ses ~s** to have the vapours *Br* OU vapors *Am*.

vapocuiseur [vapɔkɥizœr] nm pressure cooker.

vaporisateur [vapɔrizatœr] nm - **1.** [atomiseur] spray, atomizer - **2.** IND vaporizer.

vaporiser [3] [vapɔrize] vt - **1.** [parfum, déodorant] to spray - **2.** PHYS to vaporize.

vaquer [3] [vake] vi : ~ **à** to see to, to attend to.

varappe [varap] nf rock climbing.

variable [varjabl] ◇ adj - **1.** [temps] changeable - **2.** [distance, résultats] varied, varying - **3.** [température] variable. ◇ nf variable.

variante [varjɑ̃t] nf variant.

variateur [varjatœr] nm ÉLECTR dimmer switch.

variation [varjasjɔ̃] nf variation.

varice [varis] nf varicose vein.

varicelle [varisɛl] nf chickenpox.

varié, e [varje] adj - **1.** [divers] various - **2.** [non monotone] varied, varying.

varier [9] [varje] vt & vi to vary.

variété [varjete] nf variety. ➡ **variétés** nfpl variety show (sg).

variole [varjɔl] nf smallpox.

Varsovie [varsɔvi] n Warsaw ; **le pacte de ~** the Warsaw Pact.

vas ▷ aller.

vase [vaz] ◇ nm vase. ◇ nf mud, silt.

vaseline [vazlin] nf Vaseline®, petroleum jelly.

vaste [vast] adj vast, immense.

Vatican [vatikɑ̃] nm : **le ~** the Vatican.

vaudrait ▷ valoir.

vaut ▷ valoir.

vautour [votur] nm vulture.

vd abr de vend.

veau, x [vo] nm - **1.** [animal] calf - **2.** [viande] veal - **3.** [peau] calfskin.

vecteur [vɛktœr] nm - **1.** GÉOM vector - **2.** [intermédiaire] vehicle ; MÉD carrier.

vécu, e [veky] ◇ pp ▷ vivre. ◇ adj real.

vedette [vədɛt] nf - **1.** NAVIG patrol boat - **2.** [star] star.

végétal, e, aux [veʒetal, o] adj [huile] vegetable (avant n) ; [cellule, fibre] plant (avant n).

végétalien, enne [veʒetaljɛ̃, ɛn] adj & nm, f vegan.

végétarien, enne [veʒetarjɛ̃, ɛn] adj & nm, f vegetarian.

végétation [veʒetasjɔ̃] nf vegetation. ➡ **végétations** nfpl adenoids.

végéter [18] [veʒete] vi to vegetate.

véhémence [veemɑ̃s] nf vehemence.

véhicule [veikyl] nm vehicle.

veille [vɛj] nf - **1.** [jour précédent] day before, eve ; **la ~ de mon anniversaire** the day before my birthday ; **la ~ de Noël** Christ-mas Eve - **2.** [éveil] wakefulness ; [privation de sommeil] sleeplessness.

veillée [veje] nf - **1.** [soirée] evening - **2.** [de mort] watch.

veiller [4] [veje] ◇ vi - **1.** [rester éveillé] to stay up - **2.** [rester vigilant] : **~ à qqch** to look after sthg ; **~ à faire qqch** to see that sthg is done ; **~ sur** to watch over. ◇ vt to sit up with.

veilleur [vejœr] nm : **~ de nuit** night watchman.

veilleuse [vejøz] nf - **1.** [lampe] nightlight - **2.** AUTOM sidelight - **3.** [de chauffe-eau] pilot light.

veinard, e [vɛnar, ard] fam ◇ adj lucky. ◇ nm, f lucky devil.

veine [vɛn] nf - **1.** [gén] vein - **2.** [de marbre] vein ; [de bois] grain - **3.** [filon] seam, vein - **4.** fam [chance] luck.

veineux, euse [vɛnø, øz] adj - **1.** ANAT venous - **2.** [marbre] veined ; [bois] grainy.

véliplanchiste [veliplɑ̃ʃist] nmf windsurfer.

velléité [veleite] nf whim.

vélo [velo] nm fam bike ; **faire du ~** to go cycling.

vélocité [velɔsite] nf swiftness, speed.

vélodrome [velɔdrom] nm velodrome.

vélomoteur [velɔmɔtœr] nm light motor cycle.

velours [vəlur] nm velvet.

velouté, e [vəlute] adj velvety. ➡ **velouté** nm - **1.** [de peau] velvetiness - **2.** [potage] cream soup.

velu, e [vəly] adj hairy.

vénal, e, aux [venal, o] adj venal.

vendange [vɑ̃dɑ̃ʒ] nf - **1.** [récolte] grape harvest, wine harvest - **2.** [période] : **les ~s** (grape) harvest time (sg).

vendanger [17] [vɑ̃dɑ̃ʒe] vi to harvest the grapes.

vendeur, euse [vɑ̃dœr, øz] nm, f salesman (f saleswoman).

vendre [73] [vɑ̃dr] vt to sell ; **'à ~'** 'for sale'.

vendredi [vɑ̃drədi] nm Friday ; **Vendredi Saint** Good Friday ; voir aussi **samedi**.

vendu, e [vɑ̃dy] ◇ pp ▷ vendre. ◇ adj - **1.** [cédé] sold - **2.** [corrompu] corrupt. ◇ nm, f traitor.

vénéneux, euse [venenø, øz] adj poisonous.

vénérable [venerabl] adj venerable.

vénération [venerasjɔ̃] nf veneration, reverence.

vénérer [18] [venere] vt to venerate, to revere.

vénérien, enne [venerjɛ̃, ɛn] *adj* venereal.

Venezuela [venezɥela] *nm* : **le ~** Venezuela.

vengeance [vɑ̃ʒɑ̃s] *nf* vengeance.

venger [17] [vɑ̃ʒe] *vt* to avenge. **se venger** *vp* to get one's revenge ; **se ~ de qqn** to take revenge on sb ; **se ~ de qqch** to take revenge for sthg ; **se ~ sur** to take it out on.

vengeur, vengeresse [vɑ̃ʒœr, vɑ̃ʒrɛs] *adj* vengeful. *nm, f* avenger.

venimeux, euse [vənimø, øz] *adj* venomous.

venin [vənɛ̃] *nm* venom.

venir [40] [vənir] *vi* to come ; [plante, arbre] to come on ; **~ de** [personne, mot] to come from ; [échec] to be due to ; **~ de faire qqch** to have just done sthg ; **je viens de la voir** I've just seen her ; **s'il venait à mourir ...** if he was to die ... ; **où veux-tu en ~?** what are you getting at?

vent [vɑ̃] *nm* wind ; **il fait** OU **il y a du ~** headwind.

vente [vɑ̃t] *nf* - **1.** [cession, transaction] sale ; **en ~** on sale ; **en ~ libre** available over the counter ; **~ par correspondance** mail order - **2.** [technique] selling.

venteux, euse [vɑ̃tø, øz] *adj* windy.

ventilateur [vɑ̃tilatœr] *nm* fan.

ventilation [vɑ̃tilasjɔ̃] *nf* - **1.** [de pièce] ventilation - **2.** FIN breakdown.

ventouse [vɑ̃tuz] *nf* - **1.** [de caoutchouc] suction pad ; [d'animal] sucker - **2.** MÉD cupping glass - **3.** TECHNOL air vent.

ventre [vɑ̃tr] *nm* [de personne] stomach ; **avoir/prendre du ~** to have/be getting (a bit of) a paunch ; **à plat ~** flat on one's stomach.

ventriloque [vɑ̃trilɔk] *nmf* ventriloquist.

venu, e [vəny] *pp* venir. *adj* : **bien ~** welcome ; **mal ~** unwelcome ; **il serait mal ~ de faire cela** it would be improper to do that. *nm, f* : **nouveau ~** newcomer. **venue** *nf* coming, arrival.

vêpres [vɛpr] *nfpl* vespers.

ver [vɛr] *nm* worm.

véracité [verasite] *nf* truthfulness.

véranda [verɑ̃da] *nf* veranda.

verbal, e, aux [vɛrbal, o] *adj* - **1.** [promesse, violence] verbal - **2.** GRAM verb *(avant n)*.

verbaliser [3] [vɛrbalize] *vt* to verbalize. *vi* to make out a report.

verbe [vɛrb] *nm* GRAM verb.

verdeur [vɛrdœr] *nf* - **1.** [de personne] vig-

our *Br*, vigor *Am*, vitality - **2.** [de langage] crudeness.

verdict [vɛrdikt] *nm* verdict.

verdir [32] [vɛrdir] *vt* & *vi* to turn green.

verdoyant, e [vɛrdwajɑ̃, ɑ̃t] *adj* green.

verdure [vɛrdyr] *nf* [végétation] greenery.

véreux, euse [verø, øz] *adj* worm-eaten, maggoty ; *fig* shady.

verge [vɛrʒ] *nf* - **1.** ANAT penis - **2.** *littéraire* [baguette] rod, stick.

verger [vɛrʒe] *nm* orchard.

vergeture [vɛrʒətyr] *nf* stretchmark.

verglas [vɛrgla] *nm* (black) ice.

véridique [veridik] *adj* truthful.

vérification [verifikasjɔ̃] *nf* [contrôle] check, checking.

vérifier [9] [verifje] *vt* - **1.** [contrôler] to check - **2.** [confirmer] to prove, to confirm.

véritable [veritabl] *adj* real ; [ami] true.

vérité [verite] *nf* - **1.** [chose vraie, réalité, principe] truth *(U)* - **2.** [sincérité] sincerity. **en vérité** *loc adv* actually, really.

vermeil, eille [vɛrmɛj] *adj* scarlet. **vermeil** *nm* silver-gilt.

vermicelle [vɛrmisɛl] *nm* vermicelli *(U)*.

vermine [vɛrmin] *nf* [parasites] vermin.

vermoulu, e [vɛrmuly] *adj* riddled with woodworm ; *fig* moth-eaten.

verni, e [vɛrni] *adj* - **1.** [bois] varnished - **2.** [souliers] : **chaussures ~es** patent-leather shoes - **3.** *fam* [chanceux] lucky.

vernir [32] [vɛrnir] *vt* to varnish.

vernis [vɛrni] *nm* varnish ; *fig* veneer ; **~ à ongles** nail polish OU varnish.

vernissage [vɛrnisaʒ] *nm* - **1.** [de meuble] varnishing - **2.** [d'exposition] private viewing.

verre [vɛr] *nm* - **1.** [matière, récipient] glass ; [quantité] glassful, glass ; **~ dépoli** frosted glass - **2.** [optique] lens ; **~s de contact** contact lenses ; **~s progressifs** progressive lenses, progressives - **3.** [boisson] drink ; **boire un ~** to have a drink.

verrière [vɛrjɛr] *nf* [toit] glass roof.

verrou [vɛru] *nm* bolt.

verrouillage [vɛruijaʒ] *nm* AUTOM : **~ central** central locking.

verrouiller [3] [vɛruije] *vt* - **1.** [porte] to bolt - **2.** [personne] to lock up.

verrue [vɛry] *nf* wart ; **~ plantaire** verruca.

vers¹ [vɛr] *nm* line. *nmpl* : **en ~** in verse ; **faire des ~** to write poetry.

vers² [vɛr] *prép* - **1.** [dans la direction de] towards *Br*, toward *Am* - **2.** [aux environs de - temporel] around, about ; [- spatial] near ; ~ **la fin du mois** towards *Br* ou toward *Am* the end of the month.

versant [vɛrsɑ̃] *nm* side.

versatile [vɛrsatil] *adj* changeable, fickle.

verse [vɛrs] ➤ **à verse** *loc adv* : **pleuvoir à ~** to pour down.

Verseau [vɛrso] *nm* ASTROL Aquarius.

versement [vɛrsəmɑ̃] *nm* payment.

verser [3] [vɛrse] ◇ *vt* - **1.** [eau] to pour ; [larmes, sang] to shed - **2.** [argent] to pay. ◇ *vi* to overturn, to tip over.

verset [vɛrse] *nm* verse.

version [vɛrsjɔ̃] *nf* - **1.** [gén] version ; ~ **française/originale** French/original version - **2.** [traduction] translation *(into mother tongue)*.

verso [vɛrso] *nm* back.

vert, e [vɛr, vɛrt] *adj* - **1.** [couleur, fruit, légume, bois] green - **2.** *fig* [vieillard] spry, sprightly - **3.** [réprimande] sharp - **4.** [à la campagne] : **le tourisme ~** country holidays *(pl)*. ➤ **vert** *nm* [couleur] green. ➤ **Verts** *nmpl* : **les Verts** POLIT the Greens.

vertébral, e, aux [vɛrtebral, o] *adj* vertebral.

vertèbre [vɛrtɛbr] *nf* vertebra.

vertébré, e [vɛrtebre] *adj* vertebrate. ➤ **vertébré** *nm* vertebrate.

vertement [vɛrtəmɑ̃] *adv* sharply.

vertical, e, aux [vɛrtikal, o] *adj* vertical. ➤ **verticale** *nf* vertical ; **à la ~e** [descente] vertical ; [descendre] vertically.

vertige [vɛrtiʒ] *nm* - **1.** [peur du vide] vertigo - **2.** [étourdissement] dizziness ; *fig* intoxication ; **avoir des ~s** to suffer from ou have dizzy spells.

vertigineux, euse [vɛrtiʒinø, øz] *adj* - **1.** *fig* [vue, vitesse] breathtaking - **2.** [hauteur] dizzy.

vertu [vɛrty] *nf* - **1.** [morale, chasteté] virtue - **2.** [pouvoir] properties *(pl)*, power.

vertueux, euse [vɛrtɥø, øz] *adj* virtuous.

verve [vɛrv] *nf* eloquence.

vésicule [vezikyl] *nf* vesicle.

vessie [vesi] *nf* bladder.

veste [vɛst] *nf* [vêtement] jacket ; ~ **croisée/droite** double-/single-breasted jacket.

vestiaire [vɛstjɛr] *nm* - **1.** [au théâtre] cloakroom - **2.** *(gén pl)* SPORT changing-room, locker-room.

vestibule [vɛstibyl] *nm* [pièce] hall, vestibule.

vestige [vɛstiʒ] *nm* *(gén pl)* [de ville] re-

mains *(pl)* ; *fig* [de civilisation, grandeur] vestiges *(pl)*, relic.

vestimentaire [vɛstimɑ̃tɛr] *adj* [industrie] clothing *(avant n)* ; [dépense] on clothes ; **détail ~** accessory.

veston [vɛstɔ̃] *nm* jacket.

vêtement [vɛtmɑ̃] *nm* garment, article of clothing ; **~s** clothing *(U)*, clothes.

vétéran [veterɑ̃] *nm* veteran.

vétérinaire [veterinɛr] *nmf* vet, veterinary surgeon.

vêtir [44] [vetir] *vt* to dress. ➤ **se vêtir** *vp* to dress, to get dressed.

veto [veto] *nm inv* veto ; **mettre son ~ à qqch** to veto sthg.

véto [veto] *nmf fam* vet.

vêtu, e [vety] ◇ *pp* ➤ **vêtir**. ◇ *adj* : ~ **(de)** dressed (in).

vétuste [vetyst] *adj* dilapidated.

veuf, veuve [vœf, vœv] *nm, f* widower (*f* widow).

veuille *etc* ➤ **vouloir**.

veut ➤ **vouloir**.

veuvage [vœvaʒ] *nm* [de femme] widowhood ; [d'homme] widowerhood.

veuve ➤ **veuf**.

veux ➤ **vouloir**.

vexation [vɛksasjɔ̃] *nf* [humiliation] insult.

vexer [4] [vɛkse] *vt* to offend. ➤ **se vexer** *vp* to take offence *Br* ou offense *Am*.

VF *(abr de* **version française)** *nf* indicates that a film has been dubbed into French.

via [vja] *prép* via.

viabiliser [3] [vjabilize] *vt* to service.

viable [vjabl] *adj* viable.

viaduc [vjadyk] *nm* viaduct.

viager, ère [vjaʒe, ɛr] *adj* life *(avant n)*. ➤ **viager** *nm* life annuity.

viande [vjɑ̃d] *nf* meat.

vibration [vibrasjɔ̃] *nf* vibration.

vibrer [3] [vibre] *vi* - **1.** [trembler] to vibrate - **2.** *fig* [être ému] : ~ **(de)** to be stirred (with).

vice [vis] *nm* - **1.** [de personne] vice - **2.** [d'objet] fault, defect.

vice-président, e [visprezidɑ̃, ɑ̃t] *(mpl* **vice-présidents,** *fpl* **vice-présidentes)** *nm, f* POLIT vice-president ; [de société] vice-chairman (*f* vice-chairwoman).

vice versa [vis(e)vɛrsa] *loc adv* vice versa.

vicié, e [visje] *adj* [air] polluted, tainted.

vicieux, euse [visjø, øz] *adj* - **1.** [personne, conduite] perverted, depraved - **2.** [animal] restive - **3.** [attaque] underhand.

victime [viktim] *nf* victim ; [blessé] casualty.

victoire [viktwar] *nf* MIL victory ; POLIT & SPORT win, victory.

victorieux, euse [viktɔrjø, øz] *adj* - **1.** MIL victorious ; POLIT & SPORT winning *(avant n)*, victorious - **2.** [air] triumphant.

victuailles [viktɥaj] *nfpl* provisions.

vidange [vidãʒ] *nf* - **1.** [action] emptying, draining - **2.** AUTOM oil change - **3.** [mécanisme] waste outlet. ◆ **vidanges** *nfpl* sewage *(U)*.

vidanger [17] [vidãʒe] *vt* to empty, to drain.

vide [vid] ◇ *nm* - **1.** [espace] void ; *fig* [néant, manque] emptiness - **2.** [absence d'air] vacuum ; **conditionné sous ~** vacuum-packed - **3.** [ouverture] gap, space. ◇ *adj* empty.

vidéo [video] ◇ *nf* video. ◇ *adj inv* video *(avant n)*.

vidéocassette [videokasɛt] *nf* video cassette.

vidéoconférence [videokɔ̃ferɑ̃s] = **visioconférence**.

vidéodisque [videodisk] *nm* videodisc.

vide-ordures [vidɔrdyr] *nm inv* rubbish chute.

vidéothèque [videotɛk] *nf* video library.

vidéotransmission [videotrɑ̃smisjɔ̃] *nf* video transmission.

vide-poches [vidpɔʃ] *nm inv* [de voiture] glove compartment.

vider [3] [vide] *vt* - **1.** [rendre vide] to empty - **2.** [évacuer] : **~ les lieux** to vacate the premises - **3.** [poulet] to clean - **4.** *fam* [personne - épuiser] to drain ; [- expulser] to chuck out. ◆ **se vider** *vp* - **1.** [eaux] : **se ~ dans** to empty into, to drain into - **2.** [baignoire, salle] to empty.

videur [vidœr] *nm* bouncer.

vie [vi] *nf* - **1.** [gén] life ; **sauver la ~ à qqn** to save sb's life ; **être en ~** to be alive ; **à ~** for life - **2.** [subsistance] cost of living ; **gagner sa ~** to earn one's living.

vieil ▷ **vieux**.

vieillard [vjɛjar] *nm* old man.

vieille ▷ **vieux**.

vieillerie [vjɛjri] *nf* [objet] old thing.

vieillesse [vjɛjɛs] *nf* [fin de la vie] old age.

vieillir [32] [vjejir] ◇ *vi* - **1.** [personne] to grow old, to age - **2.** CULIN to mature, to age - **3.** [tradition, idée] to become dated ou outdated. ◇ *vt* - **1.** [suj : coiffure, vêtement] : **~ qqn** to make sb look older - **2.** [suj : personne] : **ils m'ont vieilli de cinq ans** they said I was five years older than I actually am.

vieillissement [vjejismã] *nm* [de personne] ageing.

Vienne [vjɛn] *n* [en Autriche] Vienna.

vierge [vjɛrʒ] ◇ *nf* virgin ; **la (Sainte) Vierge** the Virgin (Mary). ◇ *adj* - **1.** [personne] virgin - **2.** [terre] virgin ; [page] blank ; [casier judiciaire] clean. ◆ **Vierge** *nf* ASTROL Virgo.

Viêt Nam [vjɛtnam] *nm* : **le ~** Vietnam.

vieux, vieille [vjø, vjɛj] ◇ *adj (vieil devant voyelle ou h muet)* old ; **~ jeu** old-fashioned. ◇ *nm, f* - **1.** [personne âgée] old man *(f woman)* ; **les ~** the old - **2.** *fam* [ami] : **mon ~** old chap ou boy *Br*, old buddy *Am* ; **ma vieille** old girl.

vif, vive [vif, viv] *adj* - **1.** [preste - enfant] lively ; [- imagination] vivid - **2.** [couleur, œil] bright ; **rouge/jaune ~** bright red/yellow - **3.** [reproche] sharp ; [discussion] bitter - **4.** *sout* [vivant] alive - **5.** [douleur, déception] acute ; [intérêt] keen ; [amour, haine] intense, deep. ◆ **à vif** *loc adj* [plaie] open ; **j'ai les nerfs à ~** *fig* my nerves are frayed.

vigie [viʒi] *nf* [NAVIG - personne] look-out ; [- poste] crow's nest.

vigilant, e [viʒilɑ̃, ɑ̃t] *adj* vigilant, watchful.

vigile [viʒil] *nm* watchman.

vigne [viɲ] *nf* - **1.** [plante] vine, grapevine - **2.** [plantation] vineyard. ◆ **vigne vierge** *nf* Virginia creeper.

vigneron, onne [viɲərɔ̃, ɔn] *nm, f* wine grower.

vignette [viɲɛt] *nf* - **1.** [timbre] label ; [de médicament] price sticker *(for reimbursement by the social security services)* ; AUTOM tax disc *Br*, license sticker *Am* - **2.** [motif] vignette.

vignoble [viɲɔbl] *nm* - **1.** [plantation] vineyard - **2.** [vignes] vineyards *(pl)*.

vigoureux, euse [vigurø, øz] *adj* [corps, personne] vigorous ; [bras, sentiment] strong.

vigueur [vigœr] *nf* vigour *Br*, vigor *Am*. ◆ **en vigueur** *loc adj* in force.

vilain, e [vilɛ̃, ɛn] *adj* - **1.** [gén] nasty - **2.** [laid] ugly.

vilebrequin [vilbrəkɛ̃] *nm* - **1.** [outil] brace and bit - **2.** AUTOM crankshaft.

villa [vila] *nf* villa.

village [vilaʒ] *nm* village.

villageois, e [vilaʒwa, az] *nm, f* villager.

ville [vil] *nf* [petite, moyenne] town ; [importante] city ; **aller en ~** to go into town ; **habiter en ~** to live in town ; **~ d'eau** spa (town).

villégiature [vileʒjatyr] *nf* holiday.

vin [vɛ̃] *nm* wine ; ~ blanc/rosé/rouge white/rosé/red wine. ➡ **vin d'honneur** *nm* reception.

vinaigre [vinegr] *nm* vinegar.

vinaigrette [vinegret] *nf* oil and vinegar dressing.

vindicatif, ive [vɛ̃dikatif, iv] *adj* vindictive.

vingt [vɛ̃] *adj num & nm* twenty ; *voir aussi* six.

vingtaine [vɛ̃tɛn] *nf* : une ~ de about twenty.

vingtième [vɛ̃tjɛm] *adj num, nm* OU *nmf* twentieth ; *voir aussi* sixième.

vinicole [vinikɔl] *adj* wine-growing, wine-producing.

viol [vjɔl] *nm* - 1. [de femme] rape - 2. [de sépulture] desecration ; [de sanctuaire] violation.

violation [vjɔlasjɔ̃] *nf* violation, breach.

violence [vjɔlɑ̃s] *nf* violence ; se faire ~ to force o.s.

violent, e [vjɔlɑ̃, ɑ̃t] *adj* - 1. [personne, tempête] violent - 2. *fig* [douleur, angoisse, chagrin] acute ; [haine, passion] violent.

violer [3] [vjɔle] *vt* - 1. [femme] to rape - 2. [loi, traité] to break - 3. [sépulture] to desecrate ; [sanctuaire] to violate.

violet, ette [vjɔle, ɛt] *adj* purple ; [pâle] violet. ➡ **violet** *nm* purple ; [pâle] violet.

violette [vjɔlɛt] *nf* violet.

violeur [vjɔlœr] *nm* rapist.

violon [vjɔlɔ̃] *nm* [instrument] violin.

violoncelle [vjɔlɔ̃sɛl] *nm* [instrument] cello.

violoniste [vjɔlɔnist] *nmf* violinist.

vipère [viper] *nf* viper.

virage [viraʒ] *nm* - 1. [sur route] bend - 2. [changement] turn.

viral, e, aux [viral, o] *adj* viral.

virement [virmɑ̃] *nm* FIN transfer ; ~ bancaire/postal bank/giro transfer ; ~ automatique automatic transfer.

virer [3] [vire] <> *vi* - 1. [tourner] : ~ à droite/à gauche to turn right/left - 2. [étoffe] to change colour *Br* ou color *Am* ; ~ au blanc/jaune to go white/yellow - 3. MÉD to react positively. <> *vt* - 1. FIN to transfer - 2. *fam* [renvoyer] to kick out.

virevolter [3] [virvɔlte] *vi* [tourner] to twirl ou spin round.

virginité [virʒinite] *nf* - 1. [de personne] virginity - 2. [de sentiment] purity.

virgule [virgyl] *nf* [entre mots] comma ; [entre chiffres] (decimal) point.

viril, e [viril] *adj* virile.

virilité [virilite] *nf* virility.

virtuel, elle [virtɥɛl] *adj* potential.

virtuose [virtɥoz] *nmf* virtuoso.

virulence [virylɑ̃s] *nf* virulence.

virulent, e [virylɑ̃, ɑ̃t] *adj* virulent.

virus [virys] *nm* INFORM & MÉD virus.

vis [vis] *nf* screw.

visa [viza] *nm* visa.

visage [vizaʒ] *nm* face.

vis-à-vis [vizavi] *nm* - 1. [personne] person sitting opposite - 2. [immeuble] : avoir un ~ to have a building opposite. ➡ **vis-à-vis de** *loc prép* - 1. [en face de] opposite - 2. [en comparaison de] beside, compared with - 3. [à l'égard de] towards *Br*, toward *Am*.

viscéral, e, aux [viseral, o] *adj* - 1. ANAT visceral - 2. *fam* [réaction] gut *(avant n)* ; [haine, peur] deep-seated.

viscère [viser] *nm (gén pl)* innards *(pl)*.

viscose [viskoz] *nf* viscose.

visé, e [vize] *adj* - 1. [concerné] concerned - 2. [vérifié] stamped.

visée [vize] *nf* - 1. [avec arme] aiming - 2. *(gén pl) fig* [intention, dessein] aim.

viser [3] [vize] <> *vt* - 1. [cible] to aim at - 2. *fig* [poste] to aspire to, to aim for ; [personne] to be directed ou aimed at - 3. [document] to check, to stamp. <> *vi* to aim, to take aim ; ~ à to aim at ; ~ à faire qqch to aim to do sthg, to be intended to do sthg ; ~ haut *fig* to aim high.

viseur [vizœr] *nm* - 1. [d'arme] sights *(pl)* - 2. PHOT viewfinder.

visibilité [vizibilite] *nf* visibility.

visible [vizibl] *adj* - 1. [gén] visible - 2. [personne] : il n'est pas ~ he's not seeing visitors.

visiblement [vizibləmɑ̃] *adv* visibly.

visière [vizjer] *nf* - 1. [de casque] visor - 2. [de casquette] peak - 3. [de protection] eyeshade.

visioconférence [vizjokɔ̃ferɑ̃s], **vidéoconférence** [videokɔ̃ferɑ̃s] *nf* videoconference.

vision [vizjɔ̃] *nf* - 1. [faculté] eyesight, vision - 2. [représentation] view, vision - 3. [mirage] vision.

visionnaire [vizjɔner] *nmf & adj* visionary.

visionner [3] [vizjɔne] *vt* to view.

visite [vizit] *nf* - 1. [chez un ami, officielle] visit ; rendre ~ à qqn to pay sb a visit - 2. [MÉD - à l'extérieur] call, visit ; [- à l'hôpital] rounds *(pl)* ; passer une ~ médicale to have a medical - 3. [de monument] tour - 4. [d'expert] inspection.

visiter [3] [vizite] *vt* - 1. [en touriste] to tour - 2. [malade, prisonnier] to visit.

visiteur, euse [vizitœr, øz] *nm, f* visitor.

vison [vizɔ̃] *nm* mink.

visqueux, euse [viskø, øz] *adj* - **1.** [liquide] viscous - **2.** [surface] sticky.

visser [3] [vise] *vt* - **1.** [planches] to screw together - **2.** [couvercle] to screw down - **3.** [bouchon] to screw in ; [écrou] to screw on.

visualiser [3] [vizɥalize] *vt* - **1.** [gén] to visualize - **2.** INFORM to display ; TECHNOL to make visible.

visuel, elle [vizɥɛl] *adj* visual. ◆ **visuel** *nm* INFORM visual display unit ; **~ graphique** graphical display unit.

vital, e, aux [vital, o] *adj* vital.

vitalité [vitalite] *nf* vitality.

vitamine [vitamin] *nf* vitamin.

vitaminé, e [vitamine] *adj* with added vitamins, vitamin-enriched.

vite [vit] *adv* - **1.** [rapidement] quickly, fast ; **fais ~!** hurry up! - **2.** [tôt] soon.

vitesse [vitɛs] *nf* - **1.** [gén] speed ; **à toute ~** at top speed - **2.** AUTOM gear.

viticole [vitikɔl] *adj* wine-growing.

viticulteur, trice [vitikyltœr, tris] *nm, f* wine-grower.

vitrail, aux [vitraj, o] *nm* stained-glass window.

vitre [vitr] *nf* - **1.** [de fenêtre] pane of glass, windowpane - **2.** [de voiture, train] window.

vitré, e [vitre] *adj* glass *(avant n)*.

vitreux, euse [vitrø, øz] *adj* - **1.** [roche] vitreous - **2.** [œil, regard] glassy, glazed.

vitrifier [9] [vitrifje] *vt* - **1.** [parquet] to seal and varnish - **2.** [émail] to vitrify.

vitrine [vitrin] *nf* - **1.** [de boutique] (shop) window ; *fig* showcase - **2.** [meuble] display cabinet.

vivable [vivabl] *adj* [appartement] livable-in ; [situation] bearable, tolerable ; [personne] : **il n'est pas ~** he's impossible to live with.

vivace [vivas] *adj* - **1.** [plante] perennial ; [arbre] hardy - **2.** *fig* [haine, ressentiment] deep-rooted, entrenched ; [souvenir] enduring.

vivacité [vivasite] *nf* - **1.** [promptitude - de personne] liveliness, vivacity ; **~ d'esprit** quick-wittedness - **2.** [de coloris, teint] intensity, brightness - **3.** [de propos] sharpness.

vivant, e [vivɑ̃, ɑ̃t] *adj* - **1.** [en vie] alive, living - **2.** [enfant, quartier] lively - **3.** [souvenir] still fresh. ◆ **vivant** *nm* [personne] : **les ~s** the living.

vive¹ [viv] *nf* [poisson] weever.

vive² [viv] *interj* three cheers for ; **~ le roi!** long live the King!

vivement [vivmɑ̃] ◇ *adv* - **1.** [agir] quickly - **2.** [répondre] sharply - **3.** [affecter] deeply. ◇ *interj* : **~ les vacances!** roll on the holidays! ; **~ que l'été arrive** I'll be glad when summer comes, summer can't come quick enough.

vivifiant, e [vivifjɑ̃, ɑ̃t] *adj* invigorating, bracing.

vivisection [viviseksjɔ̃] *nf* vivisection.

vivre [90] [vivr] ◇ *vi* to live ; [être en vie] to be alive ; **~ de** to live on ; **faire ~ sa famille** to support one's family ; **être difficile/facile à ~** to be hard/easy to get on with ; **avoir vécu** to have seen life. ◇ *vt* - **1.** [passer] to spend - **2.** [éprouver] to experience. ◆ **vivres** *nmpl* provisions.

vizir [vizir] *nm* vizier.

VO (*abr de* version originale) *nf indicates that a film has not been dubbed*.

vocable [vɔkabl] *nm* term.

vocabulaire [vɔkabylɛr] *nm* - **1.** [gén] vocabulary - **2.** [livre] lexicon, glossary.

vocal, e, aux [vɔkal, o] *adj* : **ensemble ~** choir ; ⊳ **corde**.

vocation [vɔkasjɔ̃] *nf* - **1.** [gén] vocation - **2.** [d'organisation] mission.

vocifération [vɔsiferasjɔ̃] *nf* shout, scream.

vociférer [18] [vɔsifere] *vt* to shout, to scream.

vodka [vɔdka] *nf* vodka.

vœu, x [vø] *nm* - **1.** RELIG [résolution] vow ; **faire ~ de silence** to take a vow of silence - **2.** [souhait, requête] wish. ◆ **vœux** *nmpl* greetings.

vogue [vɔg] *nf* vogue, fashion ; **en ~** fashionable, in vogue.

voguer [3] [vɔge] *vi littéraire* to sail.

voici [vwasi] *prép* - **1.** [pour désigner, introduire] here is/are ; **le ~** here he/it is ; **les ~** here they are ; **vous cherchiez des allumettes? — en ~** were you looking for matches? — there are some here ; **~ ce qui s'est passé** this is what happened - **2.** [il y a] : **~ trois mois** three months ago ; **~ quelques années que je ne l'ai pas vu** I haven't seen him for some years (now), it's been some years since I last saw him.

voie [vwa] *nf* - **1.** [route] road ; **route à deux ~s** two-lane road ; **la ~ publique** the public highway ; **~ sans issue** no through road ; **~ privée** private road - **2.** [rails] track, line ; [quai] platform ; **~ ferrée** railway line *Br*, railroad line *Am* ; **~ de garage** siding ; *fig* dead-end job - **3.** [mode de transport] route - **4.** ANAT passage, tract ; **par ~ buccale**

ou **orale** orally, by mouth ; **par ~ rectale** by rectum ; **~ respiratoire** respiratory tract - **5.** *fig* [chemin] way - **6.** [filière, moyen] means *(pl)*. ◆ **Voie lactée** *nf* : la Voie lactée the Milky Way. ◆ **en voie de** *loc prép* on the way ou road to ; **en ~ de développement** developing.

voilà [vwala] *prép* - **1.** [pour désigner] there is/are ; **le ~** there he/it is ; **les ~** there they are ; **me ~** that's me, there I am ; **vous cherchiez de l'encre? — en ~** you were looking for ink? — there is some (over) there ; **nous ~ arrivés** we've arrived - **2.** [reprend ce dont on a parlé] that is ; [introduit ce dont on va parler] this is ; **~ ce que j'en pense** this is/ that is what I think ; **~ tout** that's all ; **et ~!** there we are! - **3.** [il y a] : **~ dix jours** ten days ago ; **~ dix ans que je le connais** I've known him for ten years (now).

voile [vwal] ◇ *nf* - **1.** [de bateau] sail - **2.** [activité] sailing. ◇ *nm* - **1.** [textile] voile - **2.** [coiffure] veil - **3.** [de brume] mist.

voilé, e [vwale] *adj* - **1.** [visage, allusion] veiled - **2.** [ciel, regard] dull - **3.** [roue] buckled - **4.** [son, voix] muffled.

voiler [3] [vwale] *vt* - **1.** [visage] to veil - **2.** [vérité, sentiment] to hide - **3.** [suj : brouillard, nuages] to cover. ◆ **se voiler** *vp* - **1.** [femme] to wear a veil - **2.** [ciel] to cloud over ; [yeux] to mist over - **3.** [roue] to buckle.

voilier [vwalje] *nm* [bateau] sailing boat, sailboat *Am*.

voilure [vwalyr] *nf* [de bateau] sails *(pl)*.

voir [62] [vwar] ◇ *vt* [gén] to see ; **je l'ai vu tomber** I saw him fall ; **faire ~ qqch à qqn** to show sb sthg ; **ne rien avoir à ~ avec** *fig* to have nothing to do with ; **voyons, ...** [en réfléchissant] let's see, ... ◇ *vi* to see. ◆ **se voir** *vp* - **1.** [se regarder] to see o.s., to watch o.s. - **2.** [se rencontrer] to see one another ou each other - **3.** [se remarquer] to be obvious, to show ; **ça se voit!** you can tell!

voire [vwar] *adv* even.

voirie [vwari] *nf* ADMIN ≈ Department of Transport.

voisin, e [vwazɛ̃, in] ◇ *adj* - **1.** [pays, ville] neighbouring *Br*, neighboring *Am* ; [maison] next-door - **2.** [idée] similar. ◇ *nm, f* neighbour *Br*, neighbor *Am* ; **~ de palier** next-door neighbour ou neighbor *Am* (in a flat).

voisinage [vwazinaʒ] *nm* - **1.** [quartier] neighbourhood *Br*, neighborhood *Am* - **2.** [environs] vicinity - **3.** [relations] : **rapports de bon ~** (good) neighbourliness *Br* ou neighborliness *Am*.

voiture [vwatyr] *nf* - **1.** [automobile] car ;

~ de fonction company car ; **~ de location** hire car ; **~ d'occasion/de sport** second-hand/sports car - **2.** [de train] carriage.

voix [vwa] *nf* - **1.** [gén] voice ; **~ de stentor** stentorian voice ; **à mi-~** in an undertone ; **à ~ basse** in a low voice, quietly ; **à ~ haute** [parler] in a loud voice ; [lire] aloud ; **de vive ~** in person - **2.** [suffrage] vote.

vol [vɔl] *nm* - **1.** [d'oiseau, avion] flight ; **à ~ d'oiseau** as the crow flies ; **en plein ~** in flight - **2.** [groupe d'oiseaux] flight, flock - **3.** [délit] theft.

vol. (*abr de* **volume**) vol.

volage [vɔlaʒ] *adj littéraire* fickle.

volaille [vɔlaj] *nf* : **la ~** poultry, (domestic) fowl.

volant, e [vɔlɑ̃, ɑ̃t] *adj* - **1.** [qui vole] flying - **2.** [mobile] : **feuille ~e** loose sheet. ◆ **volant** *nm* - **1.** [de voiture] steering wheel - **2.** [de robe] flounce - **3.** [de badminton] shuttlecock.

volatiliser [3] [vɔlatilize] ◆ **se volatiliser** *vp* to volatilize ; *fig* to vanish into thin air.

volcan [vɔlkɑ̃] *nm* volcano ; *fig* spitfire.

volcanique [vɔlkanik] *adj* volcanic ; *fig* [tempérament] fiery.

volée [vɔle] *nf* - **1.** [de flèches] volley ; **une ~ de coups** a hail of blows - **2.** FOOTBALL & TENNIS volley.

voler [3] [vɔle] ◇ *vi* to fly. ◇ *vt* [personne] to rob ; [chose] to steal.

volet [vɔlɛ] *nm* - **1.** [de maison] shutter - **2.** [de dépliant] leaf ; [d'émission] part.

voleur, euse [vɔlœr, øz] *nm, f* thief.

volière [vɔljɛr] *nf* aviary.

volley-ball [vɔlɛbol] (*pl* **volley-balls**) *nm* volleyball.

volontaire [vɔlɔ̃tɛr] ◇ *nmf* volunteer. ◇ *adj* - **1.** [omission] deliberate ; [activité] voluntary - **2.** [enfant] strong-willed.

volonté [vɔlɔ̃te] *nf* - **1.** [vouloir] will ; **à ~** unlimited, as much as you like - **2.** [disposition] : **bonne ~** willingness, good will ; **mauvaise ~** unwillingness - **3.** [détermination] willpower.

volontiers [vɔlɔ̃tje] *adv* - **1.** [avec plaisir] with pleasure, gladly, willingly - **2.** [affable, bavard] naturally.

volt [vɔlt] *nm* volt.

voltage [vɔltaʒ] *nm* voltage.

volte-face [vɔltafas] *nf inv* about-turn *Br*, about-face *Am* ; *fig* U-turn, about-turn *Br*, about-face *Am*.

voltige [vɔltiʒ] *nf* - **1.** [au trapèze] trapeze work ; **haute ~** flying trapeze act ; *fam fig* mental gymnastics *(U)* - **2.** [à cheval] circus riding - **3.** [en avion] aerobatics *(U)*.

voltiger [17] [vɔltiʒe] *vi* - **1.** [insecte, oiseau] to flit OU flutter about - **2.** [feuilles] to flutter about.

volubile [vɔlybil] *adj* voluble.

volume [vɔlym] *nm* volume.

volumineux, euse [vɔlyminø, øz] *adj* voluminous, bulky.

volupté [vɔlypte] *nf* [sensuelle] sensual OU voluptuous pleasure ; [morale, esthétique] delight.

voluptueux, euse [vɔlyptɥø, øz] *adj* voluptuous.

volute [vɔlyt] *nf* - **1.** [de fumée] wreath - **2.** ARCHIT volute, helix.

vomi [vɔmi] *nm fam* vomit.

vomir [32] [vɔmir] *vt* - **1.** [aliments] to bring up - **2.** [fumées] to belch, to spew (out) ; [injures] to spit out.

vont ▷ aller.

vorace [vɔras] *adj* voracious.

voracité [vɔrasite] *nf* voracity.

vos ▷ votre.

vote [vɔt] *nm* vote.

voter [3] [vɔte] ◇ *vi* to vote. ◇ *vt* POLIT to vote for ; [crédits] to vote ; [loi] to pass.

votre [vɔtr] (*pl* vos [vo]) *adj poss* your.

vôtre [votr] ◆ **le vôtre** (*f* la vôtre, *pl* les vôtres) *pron poss* yours ; **les ~s** your family ; **vous et les ~s** people like you ; **à la ~!** your good health!

vouer [6] [vwe] *vt* - **1.** [promettre, jurer] : **~ qqch à qqn** to swear OU vow sthg to sb - **2.** [consacrer] to devote - **3.** [condamner] : **être voué à** to be doomed to.

vouloir [57] [vulwar] ◇ *vt* - **1.** [gén] to want ; **voulez-vous boire quelque chose?** would you like something to drink? ; **veux-tu te taire!** will you be quiet! ; **je voudrais savoir** I would like to know ; **~ que** (+ *subjonctif*) : **je veux qu'il parte** I want him to leave ; **~ qqch de qqn/qqch** to want sthg from sb/sthg ; **combien voulez-vous de votre maison?** how much do you want for your house? ; **ne pas ~ de qqn/qqch** not to want sb/sthg ; **je veux bien** I don't mind ; **si tu veux** if you like, if you want ; **veuillez vous asseoir** please take a seat ; **sans le ~** without meaning OU wishing to, unintentionally - **2.** [suj : coutume] to demand - **3.** [s'attendre à] to expect ; **que voulez-vous que j'y fasse?** what do you want me to do about it? - **4.** *loc* : **~ dire** to mean ; **si on veut** more or less, if you like ; **en ~ à qqn** to have a grudge against sb. ◆ *nm* : **le bon ~ de qqn** sb's good will. ◆ **se vouloir** *vp* : **elle se veut différente** she thinks she's

different ; **s'en ~ de faire qqch** to be cross with o.s. for doing sthg.

voulu, e [vuly] ◇ *pp* ▷ vouloir. ◇ *adj* - **1.** [requis] requisite - **2.** [délibéré] intentional.

vous [vu] *pron pers* - **1.** [sujet, objet direct] you - **2.** [objet indirect] (to) you - **3.** [après préposition, comparatif] you - **4.** [réfléchi] yourself, (*pl*) yourselves. ◆ **vous-même** *pron pers* yourself. ◆ **vous-mêmes** *pron pers* yourselves.

voûte [vut] *nf* - **1.** ARCHIT vault ; *fig* arch - **2.** ANAT : **~ du palais** roof of the mouth ; **~ plantaire** arch (of the foot).

voûter [3] [vute] *vt* to arch over, to vault. ◆ **se voûter** *vp* to be OU become stooped.

vouvoyer [13] [vuvwaje] *vt* : **~ qqn** to use the 'vous' form to sb.

voyage [vwajaʒ] *nm* journey, trip ; **les ~s** travel *(sg)*, travelling *(U)* *Br*, traveling *(U)* *Am* ; **partir en ~** to go away, to go on a trip ; **~ d'affaires** business trip ; **~ organisé** package tour ; **~ de noces** honeymoon.

voyager [17] [vwajaʒe] *vi* to travel.

voyageur, euse [vwajaʒœr, øz] *nm, f* traveller *Br*, traveler *Am*.

voyance [vwajɑ̃s] *nf* clairvoyance.

voyant, e [vwajɑ̃, ɑ̃t] ◇ *adj* loud, gaudy. ◇ *nm, f* [devin] seer. ◆ **voyant** *nm* [lampe] light ; AUTOM indicator (light) ; **~ d'essence/d'huile** petrol/oil warning light.

voyelle [vwajɛl] *nf* vowel.

voyeur, euse [vwajœr, øz] *nm, f* voyeur, Peeping Tom.

voyou [vwaju] *nm* - **1.** [garnement] urchin - **2.** [loubard] lout.

vrac [vrak] ◆ **en vrac** *loc adv* - **1.** [sans emballage] loose - **2.** [en désordre] higgledy-piggledy - **3.** [au poids] in bulk.

vrai, e [vrɛ] *adj* - **1.** [histoire] true ; **c'est** OU **il est ~ que ...** it's true that ... - **2.** [or, perle, nom] real - **3.** [personne] natural - **4.** [ami, raison] real, true. ◆ **vrai** *nm* : **à ~ dire, à dire ~** to tell the truth.

vraiment [vrɛmɑ̃] *adv* really.

vraisemblable [vrɛsɑ̃blabl] *adj* likely, probable ; [excuse] plausible.

vraisemblance [vrɛsɑ̃blɑ̃s] *nf* likelihood, probability ; [d'excuse] plausibility.

V/Réf (*abr de* Votre référence) your ref.

vrille [vrij] *nf* - **1.** BOT tendril - **2.** [outil] gimlet - **3.** [spirale] spiral.

vrombir [32] [vrɔ̃bir] *vi* to hum.

vrombissement [vrɔ̃bismɑ̃] *nm* humming *(U)*.

VTT (*abr de* **vélo tout terrain**) *nm* mountain bike.

vu, e [vy] ◇ *pp* ▷ **voir.** ◇ *adj* - **1.** [perçu] : **être bien/mal ~** to be acceptable/unacceptable - **2.** [compris] clear. ◆ **vu** *prép* given, in view of. ◆ **vue** *nf* - **1.** [sens, vision] sight, eyesight - **2.** [regard] gaze ; **à première ~e** at first sight ; **de ~e** by sight ; **en ~e** [vedette] in the public eye ; **perdre qqn de ~e** to lose touch with sb - **3.** [panorama, idée] view - **4.** CIN ▷ **prise.** ◆ **en vue de** *loc prép* with a view to. ◆ **vu que** *loc conj* given that, seeing that.

vulgaire [vylgɛr] *adj* - **1.** [grossier] vulgar, coarse - **2.** (*avant n*) *péj* [quelconque] common.

vulgarisation [vylgarizasjɔ̃] *nf* popularization.

vulgariser [3] [vylgarize] *vt* to popularize.

vulgarité [vylgarite] *nf* vulgarity, coarseness.

vulnérable [vylnerabl] *adj* vulnerable.

vulve [vylv] *nf* vulva.

x, X [iks] *nm inv* x, X ; **l'X** *prestigious engineering college in Paris.*

xénophobie [gzenɔfɔbi] *nf* xenophobia.

xérès [gzerɛs, xeres] *nm* sherry.

xylophone [ksilɔfɔn] *nm* xylophone.

webmestre [wɛbmɛstr], **webmaster** [wɛbmastər] *nm* webmaster.

week-end [wikɛnd] (*pl* **week-ends**) *nm* weekend.

western [wɛstɛrn] *nm* western.

whisky [wiski] (*pl* **whiskies**) *nm* whisky.

white-spirit [wajtspirit] (*pl* **white-spirits**) *nm* white spirit.

WWW (*abr de* **World Wide Web**) *nf* WWW.

w, W [dublave] *nm inv* w, W.

wagon [vagɔ̃] *nm* carriage ; **~ de première/seconde classe** first-class/second-class carriage.

wagon-lit [vagɔ̃li] *nm* sleeping car, sleeper.

wagon-restaurant [vagɔ̃rɛstɔrɑ̃] *nm* restaurant *ou* dining car.

Walkman® [wɔkman] *nm* personal stereo, Walkman®.

wallon, onne [walɔ̃, ɔn] *adj* Walloon. ◆ **wallon** *nm* [langue] Walloon. ◆ **Wallon, onne** *nm, f* Walloon.

Washington [waʃintɔn] *n* - **1.** [ville] Washington DC - **2.** [État] Washington State.

water-polo [waterpolo] *nm* water polo.

waterproof [waterpruːf] *adj inv* waterproof.

watt [wat] *nm* watt.

W.-C. [vese] (*abr de* **water closet**) *nmpl* WC (*sg*), toilets.

Web [wɛb] *nm* : **le ~** the Web, the web.

y¹, Y [igrɛk] *nm inv* y, Y.

y² [i] ◇ *adv* [lieu] there ; **j'y vais demain** I'm going there tomorrow ; **mets-y du sel** put some salt in it ; **va voir sur la table si les clefs y sont** go and see if the keys are on the table ; **ils ont ramené des vases anciens et y ont fait pousser des fleurs exotiques** they brought back some antique vases and grew exotic flowers in them. ◇ *pron (la traduction varie selon la préposition utilisée avec le verbe)* : **pensez-y** think about it ; **n'y comptez pas** don't count on it ; **j'y suis!** I've got it! ; *voir aussi* **aller** ; *voir aussi* **avoir** *etc.*

yacht [jot] *nm* yacht.

yaourt [jaurt], **yogourt, yoghourt** [jɔgurt] *nm* yoghurt.

Yémen [jemɛn] *nm* : **le ~** Yemen.

yen [jɛn] *nm* yen.

yeux ▷ **œil.**

yiddish [jidiʃ] *nm inv & adj inv* Yiddish.

yoga [jɔga] *nm* yoga.

yoghourt = yaourt.

yogourt = yaourt.

yougoslave [jugɔslav] *adj* Yugoslav, Yugoslavian. ➤ **Yougoslave** *nmf* Yugoslav, Yugoslavian.

Yougoslavie [jugɔslavi] *nf* : la ~ Yugoslavia ; l'ex-~ the former Yugoslavia.

z, Z [zɛd] *nm inv* z, Z.

Zaïre [zair] *nm* : le ~ Zaïre.

zapper [3] [zape] *vi* to zap, to channel-hop.

zapping [zapiŋ] *nm* zapping, channel-hopping.

zèbre [zɛbr] *nm* zebra ; **un drôle de** ~ *fam fig* an oddball.

zébrure [zebryr] *nf* - **1.** [de pelage] stripe - **2.** [marque] weal.

zébu [zeby] *nm* zebu.

zèle [zɛl] *nm* zeal ; **faire du** ~ *péj* to be overzealous.

zélé, e [zele] *adj* zealous.

zénith [zenit] *nm* zenith.

zéro [zero] ◇ *nm* - **1.** [chiffre] zero, nought ; [énoncé dans un numéro de téléphone] O *Br*, zero *Am* - **2.** [nombre] nought, nothing - **3.** [de graduation] freezing point, zero ; **au-dessus/au-dessous de** ~ above/below (zero) ; **avoir le moral à** ~ *fig* to be ou feel down. ◇ *adj* : ~ **faute** no mistakes.

zeste [zɛst] *nm* peel, zest.

zézayer [11] [zezeje] *vi* to lisp.

zigzag [zigzag] *nm* zigzag ; **en** ~ winding.

zigzaguer [3] [zigzage] *vi* to zigzag (along).

zinc [zɛ̃g] *nm* - **1.** [matière] zinc - **2.** *fam* [comptoir] bar - **3.** *fam* [avion] crate.

zizi [zizi] *nm fam* willy *Br*, peter *Am*.

zodiaque [zɔdjak] *nm* zodiac.

zone [zon] *nf* - **1.** [région] zone, area ; ~ **bleue** restricted parking zone ; ~ **industrielle** industrial estate *Br* ou park *Am* ; ~ **piétonne** ou **piétonnière** pedestrian precinct *Br* ou zone *Am* - **2.** *fam* [faubourg] : **la** ~ the slum belt.

zoner [3] [zone] *vi* to hang about, to hang around.

zoo [zo(o)] *nm* zoo.

zoologie [zɔɔlɔʒi] *nf* zoology.

zoom [zum] *nm* - **1.** [objectif] zoom (lens) - **2.** [gros plan] zoom.

zut [zyt] *interj fam* damn!

a¹ (*pl* as OR a's), **A** (*pl* As OR A's) [eɪ] *n* [letter] a *m inv*, A *m inv* ; **to get from A to B** aller d'un point à un autre. ◆ **A** *n* - **1.** MUS la *m inv* - **2.** SCH [mark] A *m inv*.

a² [stressed eɪ, unstressed ə] (before vowel or silent 'h' **an** [stressed æn, unstressed ən]) *indef art* - **1.** [gen] un (une) ; **a boy** un garçon ; **a table** une table ; **an orange** une orange - **2.** [referring to occupation] : **to be a doctor/lawyer/plumber** être médecin/avocat/plombier - **3.** [instead of the number one] un (une) ; **a hundred/thousand pounds** cent/mille livres - **4.** [to express prices, ratios etc] : **20p a kilo** 20p le kilo ; **£10 a person** 10 livres par personne ; **twice a week/month** deux fois par semaine/mois ; **50 km an hour** 50 km à l'heure.

AA *n* - **1.** (*abbr of* **Automobile Association**) *automobile club britannique,* ≃ ACF *m,* ≃ TCF *m* - **2.** (*abbr of* **Alcoholics Anonymous**) Alcooliques Anonymes *mpl.*

AAA *n* (*abbr of* **American Automobile Association**) *automobile club américain,* ≃ ACF *m,* ≃ TCF *m.*

AB *n Am abbr of* **Bachelor of Arts.**

aback [ə'bæk] *adv* : **to be taken** ~ être décontenancé(e).

abandon [ə'bændən] ◇ *vt* abandonner. ◇ *n* : **with** ~ avec abandon.

abashed [ə'bæʃt] *adj* confus(e).

abate [ə'beɪt] *vi* [storm, fear] se calmer ; [noise] faiblir.

abattoir ['æbətwɑː'] *n* abattoir *m.*

abbey ['æbɪ] *n* abbaye *f.*

abbot ['æbət] *n* abbé *m.*

abbreviate [ə'briːvɪeɪt] *vt* abréger.

abbreviation [ə,briːvɪ'eɪʃn] *n* abréviation *f.*

ABC *n* - **1.** [alphabet] alphabet *m* - **2.** *fig* [basics] B.A.-Ba *m,* abc *m.*

abdicate ['æbdɪkeɪt] *vt & vi* abdiquer.

abdomen ['æbdəmən] *n* abdomen *m.*

abduct [əb'dʌkt] *vt* enlever.

aberration [,æbə'reɪʃn] *n* aberration *f.*

abet [ə'bet] *vt* ⊳ **aid.**

abeyance [ə'beɪəns] *n* : **in** ~ en attente.

abhor [əb'hɔː'] *vt* exécrer, abhorrer.

abide [ə'baɪd] *vt* supporter, souffrir. ◆ **abide by** *vt fus* respecter, se soumettre à.

ability [ə'bɪlətɪ] *n* - **1.** [capacity, capability] aptitude *f* - **2.** [skill] talent *m.*

abject ['æbdʒekt] *adj* - **1.** [poverty] noir(e) - **2.** [person] pitoyable ; [apology] servile.

ablaze [ə'bleɪz] *adj* [on fire] en feu.

able ['eɪbl] *adj* - **1.** [capable] : **to be** ~ **to do sthg** pouvoir faire qqch - **2.** [accomplished] compétent(e).

ably ['eɪblɪ] *adv* avec compétence, habilement.

abnormal [æb'nɔːml] *adj* anormal(e).

aboard [ə'bɔːd] ◇ *adv* à bord. ◇ *prep* [ship, plane] à bord ; [bus, train] dans.

abode [ə'bəʊd] *n fml* : **of no fixed** ~ sans domicile fixe.

abolish [ə'bɒlɪʃ] *vt* abolir.

abolition [,æbə'lɪʃn] *n* abolition *f.*

abominable [ə'bɒmɪnəbl] *adj* abominable.

aborigine [,æbə'rɪdʒənɪ] *n* aborigène *mf* d'Australie.

abort [ə'bɔːt] *vt* - **1.** [pregnancy] interrompre - **2.** *fig* [plan, project] abandonner, faire avorter - **3.** COMPUT abandonner.

abortion [ə'bɔːʃn] *n* avortement *m,* interruption *f* (volontaire) de grossesse ; **to have an** ~ se faire avorter.

abortive [ə'bɔːtɪv] *adj* manqué(e).

abound [ə'baʊnd] *vi* - **1.** [be plentiful] abonder - **2.** [be full] : **to** ~ **with** OR **in** abonder en.

about [ə'baʊt] ◇ *adv* - **1.** [approximately]

environ, à peu pr : ; **~ fifty/a hundred/a thousand** enviror cinquante/cent/mille ; **at ~ five o'clock** v s cinq heures ; **I'm just ~ ready** je suis pr que prêt - **2.** [referring to place] : **to run ~** ourir çà et là ; **to leave things lying ~** laisser traîner des affaires ; **to walk ~** aller et enir, se promener - **3.** [on the point of] : **to be ~ to do sthg** être sur le point de faire quch. ◇ *prep* - **1.** [relating to, concerning] au ujet de ; **a film ~ Paris** un film sur Paris ; **what is it ~?** de quoi s'agit-il? ; **to talk ~ sthg** parler de qqch - **2.** [referring to place] : **his belongings were scattered ~ the room** ses affaires étaient éparpillées dans toute la pièce ; **to wander ~ the streets** errer de par les rues.

about-turn *Br*, **about-face** *Am n* MIL demi-tour *m* ; *fig* volte-face *f inv*.

above [ə'bʌv] ◇ *adv* - **1.** [on top, higher up] au-dessus - **2.** [in text] ci-dessus, plus haut - **3.** [more, over] plus ; **children aged 5 and ~** les enfants âgés de 5 ans et plus OR de plus de 5 ans. ◇ *prep* - **1.** [on top of, higher up than] au-dessus de - **2.** [more than] plus de. ◆ **above all** *adv* avant tout.

aboveboard [ə bʌv'bɔːd] *adj* honnête.

abrasive [ə'breɪsɪv] *adj* [substance] abrasif(ive) ; *fig* caustique, acerbe.

abreast [ə'brest] *adv* de front. ◆ **abreast of** *prep* : **to keep ~ of** se tenir au courant de.

abridged [ə'brɪdʒd] *adj* abrégé(e).

abroad [ə'brɔːd] *adv* à l'étranger.

abrupt [ə'brʌpt] *adj* - **1.** [sudden] soudain(e), brusque - **2.** [brusque] abrupt(e).

abscess ['æbsɪs] *n* abcès *m*.

abscond [əb'skɒnd] *vi* s'enfuir.

abseil ['æbseɪl] *vi* descendre en rappel.

absence ['æbsəns] *n* absence *f*.

absent ['æbsənt] *adj* : **~ (from)** absent(e) (de).

absentee [,æbsən'tiː] *n* absent *m*, -e *f*.

absent-minded [-'maɪndɪd] *adj* distrait(e).

absolute ['æbsəluːt] *adj* - **1.** [complete - fool, disgrace] complet(ète) - **2.** [total-itarian - ruler, power] absolu(e).

absolutely ['æbsəluːtlɪ] *adv* absolument.

absolve [əb'zɒlv] *vt* : **to ~ sb (from)** absoudre qqn (de).

absorb [əb'zɔːb] *vt* absorber ; [information] retenir, assimiler ; **to be ~ed in sthg** être absorbé(e) dans qqch.

absorbent [əb'zɔːbənt] *adj* absorbant(e).

absorption [əb'zɔːpʃn] *n* absorption *f*.

abstain [əb'steɪn] *vi* : **to ~ (from)** s'abstenir (de).

abstemious [æb'stiːmjəs] *adj fml* frugal(e), sobre.

abstention [əb'stenʃn] *n* abstention *f*.

abstract ['æbstrækt] ◇ *adj* abstrait(e). ◇ *n* [summary] résumé *m*, abrégé *m*.

absurd [əb'sɜːd] *adj* absurde.

ABTA ['æbtə] (*abbr of* **Association of British Travel Agents**) *n* association des agences de voyage britanniques.

abundant [ə'bʌndənt] *adj* abondant(e).

abundantly [ə'bʌndəntlɪ] *adv* - **1.** [clear, obvious] parfaitement, tout à fait - **2.** [exist, grow] en abondance.

abuse [*n* ə'bjuːs, *vb* ə'bjuːz] ◇ *n (U)* - **1.** [offensive remarks] insultes *fpl*, injures *fpl* - **2.** [maltreatment] mauvais traitement *m* ; **child ~** mauvais traitements infligés aux enfants - **3.** [of power, drugs etc] abus *m*. ◇ *vt* - **1.** [insult] insulter, injurier - **2.** [maltreat] maltraiter - **3.** [power, drugs etc] abuser de.

abusive [ə'bjuːsɪv] *adj* grossier(ère), injurieux(euse).

abysmal [ə'bɪzml] *adj* épouvantable, abominable.

abyss [ə'bɪs] *n* abîme *m*, gouffre *m*.

a/c (*abbr of* **account (current)**) cc.

AC *n* (*abbr of* **alternating current**) courant *m* alternatif.

academic [,ækə'demɪk] ◇ *adj* - **1.** [of college, university] universitaire - **2.** [person] intellectuel(elle) - **3.** [question, discussion] théorique. ◇ *n* universitaire *mf*.

academy [ə'kædəmɪ] *n* - **1.** [school, college] école *f* ; **~ of music** conservatoire *m* - **2.** [institution, society] académie *f*.

ACAS ['eɪkæs] (*abbr of* **Advisory Conciliation and Arbitration Service**) *n organisme britannique de conciliation des conflits du travail*.

accede [æk'siːd] *vi* - **1.** [agree] : **to ~ to** agréer, donner suite à - **2.** [monarch] : **to ~ to the throne** monter sur le trône.

accelerate [ək'seləreɪt] *vi* - **1.** [car, driver] accélérer - **2.** [inflation, growth] s'accélérer.

acceleration [ək,selə'reɪʃn] *n* accélération *f*.

accelerator [ək'seləreɪtə[r]] *n* accélérateur *m*.

accent ['æksent] *n* accent *m*.

accept [ək'sept] *vt* - **1.** [gen] accepter ; [for job, as member of club] recevoir, admettre - **2.** [agree] : **to ~ that ...** admettre que ...

acceptable [ək'septəbl] *adj* acceptable.

acceptance [ək'septəns] n - 1. [gen] acceptation f - 2. [for job, as member of club] admission f.

access ['ækses] n - 1. [entry, way in] accès m - 2. [opportunity to use, see] : **to have ~ to sthg** avoir qqch à sa disposition, disposer de qqch.

accessible [ək'sesəbl] adj - 1. [reachable - place] accessible - 2. [available] disponible.

accessory [ək'sesərɪ] n - 1. [of car, vacuum cleaner] accessoire m - 2. JUR complice mf.

accident ['æksɪdənt] n accident m ; **~ and emergency department** Br (service m des) urgences fpl ; **by ~** par hasard, par accident.

accidental [ˌæksɪ'dentl] adj accidentel(elle).

accidentally [ˌæksɪ'dentəlɪ] adv - 1. [drop, break] par mégarde - 2. [meet] par hasard.

accident-prone adj prédisposé(e) aux accidents.

acclaim [ə'kleɪm] <> n (U) éloges mpl. <> vt louer.

acclimatize, -ise [ə'klaɪmətaɪz], **acclimate** Am ['ækləmeɪt] vi : **to ~ (to)** s'acclimater (à).

accommodate [ə'kɒmədeɪt] vt - 1. [provide room for] loger - 2. [oblige - person, wishes] satisfaire.

accommodating [ə'kɒmədeɪtɪŋ] adj obligeant(e).

accommodation Br [əˌkɒmə'deɪʃn] n, **accommodations** Am [əˌkɒmə'deɪʃnz] npl logement m.

accompany [ə'kʌmpənɪ] vt [gen] accompagner.

accomplice [ə'kʌmplɪs] n complice mf.

accomplish [ə'kʌmplɪʃ] vt accomplir.

accomplishment [ə'kʌmplɪʃmənt] n - 1. [action] accomplissement m - 2. [achievement] réussite f. ◆ **accomplishments** npl talents mpl.

accord [ə'kɔːd] n : **to do sthg of one's own ~** faire qqch de son propre chef OR de soi-même.

accordance [ə'kɔːdəns] n : **in ~ with** conformément à.

according [ə'kɔːdɪŋ] ◆ **according to** prep - 1. [as stated or shown by] d'après ; **to go ~ to plan** se passer comme prévu - 2. [with regard to] suivant, en fonction de.

accordingly [ə'kɔːdɪŋlɪ] adv - 1. [appropriately] en conséquence - 2. [consequently] par conséquent.

accordion [ə'kɔːdjən] n accordéon m.

accost [ə'kɒst] vt accoster.

account [ə'kaʊnt] n - 1. [with bank, shop, company] compte m - 2. [report] compterendu m - 3. phr : **to take ~ of sthg, to take sthg into ~** prendre qqch en compte ; **to be of no ~** n'avoir aucune importance ; **on no ~** sous aucun prétexte, en aucun cas. ◆ **accounts** npl [of business] comptabilité f, comptes mpl. ◆ **by all accounts** adv d'après ce que l'on dit, au dire de tous. ◆ **on account of** prep à cause de. ◆ **account for** vt fus - 1. [explain] justifier, expliquer - 2. [represent] représenter.

accountable [ə'kaʊntəbl] adj [responsible] : **~ (for)** responsable (de).

accountancy [ə'kaʊntənsɪ] n comptabilité f.

accountant [ə'kaʊntənt] n comptable mf.

accrue [ə'kruː] vi [money] fructifier ; [interest] courir.

accumulate [ə'kjuːmjʊleɪt] <> vt accumuler, amasser. <> vi s'accumuler.

accuracy ['ækjʊrəsɪ] n - 1. [of description, report] exactitude f - 2. [of weapon, typist, figures] précision f.

accurate ['ækjʊrət] adj - 1. [description, report] exact(e) - 2. [weapon, typist, figures] précis(e).

accurately ['ækjʊrətlɪ] adv - 1. [truthfully - describe, report] fidèlement - 2. [precisely - aim] avec précision ; [- type] sans faute.

accusation [ˌækjuː'zeɪʃn] n accusation f.

accuse [ə'kjuːz] vt : **to ~ sb of sthg/of doing sthg** accuser qqn de qqch/de faire qqch.

accused [ə'kjuːzd] (pl inv) n JUR : **the ~** l'accusé m, -e f.

accustomed [ə'kʌstəmd] adj : **to be ~ to sthg/to doing sthg** avoir l'habitude de qqch/de faire qqch.

ace [eɪs] n as m.

ache [eɪk] <> n douleur f. <> vi - 1. [back, limb] faire mal ; **my head ~s** j'ai mal à la tête - 2. fig [want] : **to be aching for sthg/to do sthg** mourir d'envie de qqch/de faire qqch.

achieve [ə'tʃiːv] vt [success, victory] obtenir, remporter ; [goal] atteindre ; [ambition] réaliser ; [fame] parvenir à.

achievement [ə'tʃiːvmənt] n [success] réussite f.

Achilles' tendon n tendon m d'Achille.

acid ['æsɪd] <> adj lit & fig acide. <> n acide m.

acid house n MUS house f (music).

acid rain (U) n pluies fpl acides.

acknowledge [ək'nɒlɪdʒ] vt - **1.** [fact, situation, person] reconnaître - **2.** [letter] : **to ~ (receipt of)** accuser réception de - **3.** [greet] saluer.

acknowledg(e)ment [ək'nɒlɪdʒmənt] n - **1.** [gen] reconnaissance f - **2.** [letter] accusé m de réception. ◆ **acknowledg(e)ments** npl [in book] remerciements mpl.

acne ['ækni] n acné f.

acorn ['eɪkɔːn] n gland m.

acoustic [ə'kuːstɪk] adj acoustique. ◆ **acoustics** npl [of room] acoustique f.

acquaint [ə'kweɪnt] vt : **to ~ sb with sthg** mettre qqn au courant de qqch ; **to be ~ed with sb** connaître qqn.

acquaintance [ə'kweɪntəns] n [person] connaissance f.

acquire [ə'kwaɪəʳ] vt acquérir.

acquisitive [ə'kwɪzɪtɪv] adj avide de possessions.

acquit [ə'kwɪt] vt - **1.** JUR acquitter - **2.** [perform] : **to ~ o.s. well/badly** bien/mal se comporter.

acquittal [ə'kwɪtl] n acquittement m.

acre ['eɪkəʳ] n ≃ demi-hectare m (= 4046,9 m²).

acrid ['ækrɪd] adj [taste, smell] âcre ; fig acerbe.

acrimonious [ˌækrɪ'məʊnjəs] adj acrimonieux(euse).

acrobat ['ækrəbæt] n acrobate mf.

across [ə'krɒs] ◇ adv - **1.** [from one side to the other] en travers - **2.** [in measurements] : **the river is 2 km ~** la rivière mesure 2 km de large - **3.** [in crossword] : **21 ~** 21 horizontalement. ◇ prep - **1.** [from one side to the other] d'un côté à l'autre de, en travers de ; **to walk ~ the road** traverser la route ; **to run ~ the road** traverser la route en courant - **2.** [on the other side of] de l'autre côté de ; **the house ~ the road** la maison d'en face. ◆ **across from** prep en face de.

acrylic [ə'krɪlɪk] ◇ adj acrylique. ◇ n acrylique m.

act [ækt] ◇ n - **1.** [action, deed] acte m ; **to catch sb in the ~ of doing sthg** surprendre qqn en train de faire qqch - **2.** JUR loi f - **3.** [of play, opera] acte m ; [in cabaret etc] numéro m ; fig [pretence] : **to put on an ~** jouer la comédie - **4.** phr : **to get one's ~ together** se reprendre en main. ◇ vi - **1.** [gen] agir - **2.** [behave] se comporter ; **to ~ as if** se conduire comme si, se comporter comme si ; **to ~ like** se conduire comme, se comporter comme - **3.** [in play, film] jouer ; fig [pretend]

jouer la comédie - **4.** [function] : **to ~ as** [person] être ; [object] servir de. ◇ vt [part] jouer.

ACT (abbr of **American College Test**) n examen américain de fin d'études secondaires.

acting ['æktɪŋ] ◇ adj par intérim, provisoire. ◇ n [in play, film] interprétation f.

action ['ækʃn] n - **1.** [gen] action f ; **to take ~** agir, prendre des mesures ; **to put sthg into ~** mettre qqch à exécution ; **in ~** [person] en action ; [machine] en marche ; **out of ~** [person] hors de combat ; [machine] hors service, hors d'usage - **2.** JUR procès m, action f.

action movie n film m d'action.

action replay n répétition f immédiate (au ralenti).

activate ['æktɪveɪt] vt mettre en marche.

active ['æktɪv] adj - **1.** [gen] actif(ive) ; [encouragement] vif (vive) - **2.** [volcano] en activité.

actively ['æktɪvlɪ] adv activement.

activity [æk'tɪvətɪ] n activité f.

actor ['æktəʳ] n acteur m.

actress ['æktrɪs] n actrice f.

actual ['æktʃʊəl] adj réel(elle).

actually ['æktʃʊəlɪ] adv - **1.** [really, in truth] vraiment - **2.** [by the way] au fait.

acumen ['ækjʊmen] n flair m.

acupuncture ['ækjʊpʌŋktʃəʳ] n acupuncture f, acuponcture f.

acute [ə'kjuːt] adj - **1.** [severe - pain, illness] aigu(ë) ; [- danger] sérieux(euse), grave - **2.** [perceptive - person, mind] perspicace - **3.** [keen - eyesight] perçant(e) ; [- hearing] fin(e) ; [- sense of smell] développé(e) - **4.** MATH : **~ angle** angle m aigu - **5.** LING : **e ~** e accent aigu.

ad [æd] (abbr of **advertisement**) n inf [in newspaper] annonce f ; [on TV] pub f.

AD (abbr of **Anno Domini**) ap. J.-C.

adamant ['ædəmənt] adj : **to be ~** être inflexible.

Adam's apple ['ædəmz-] n pomme f d'Adam.

adapt [ə'dæpt] ◇ vt adapter. ◇ vi : **to ~ (to)** s'adapter (à).

adaptable [ə'dæptəbl] adj [person] souple.

adapter, adaptor [ə'dæptəʳ] n [ELEC - for several devices] prise f multiple ; [- for foreign plug] adaptateur m.

add [æd] vt - **1.** [gen] : **to ~ sthg (to)** ajouter qqch (à) - **2.** [numbers] additionner. ◆ **add on** vt sep : **to ~ sthg on (to)** ajouter

qqch (à) ; [charge, tax] rajouter qqch (à).
◆ **add to** *vt fus* ajouter à, augmenter.
◆ **add up** *vt sep* additionner. ◆ **add up to** *vt fus* se monter à.

adder ['ædə'] *n* vipère *f*.

addict ['ædɪkt] *n lit & fig* drogué *m*, -e *f* ; **drug** - drogué.

addicted [ə'dɪktɪd] *adj* : ~ (to) drogué(e)(à) ; *fig* passionné(e)(de).

addiction [ə'dɪkʃn] *n* : ~ (to) dépendance *f* (à) ; *fig* penchant *m* (pour).

addictive [ə'dɪktɪv] *adj* qui rend dépendant(e).

addition [ə'dɪʃn] *n* addition *f* ; **in** ~ (to) en plus (de).

additional [ə'dɪʃənl] *adj* supplémentaire.

additive ['ædɪtɪv] *n* additif *m*.

address [ə'dres] ◇ *n* - **1**. [place] adresse *f* - **2**. [speech] discours *m*. ◇ *vt* - **1**. [gen] adresser - **2**. [meeting, conference] prendre la parole à - **3**. [problem, issue] aborder, examiner.

address book *n* carnet *m* d'adresses.

adenoids ['ædɪnɔɪdz] *npl* végétations *fpl*.

adept ['ædept] *adj* : ~ (at) doué(e)(pour).

adequate ['ædɪkwət] *adj* adéquat(e).

adhere [əd'hɪə'] *vi* - **1**. [stick] : **to** ~ (to) adhérer (à) - **2**. [observe] : **to** ~ **to** obéir à - **3**. [keep] : **to** ~ **to** adhérer à.

adhesive [əd'hiːsɪv] ◇ *adj* adhésif(ive). ◇ *n* adhésif *m*.

adhesive tape *n* ruban *m* adhésif.

adjacent [ə'dʒeɪsənt] *adj* : ~ (to) adjacent(e)(à), contigu(ë)(à).

adjective ['ædʒɪktɪv] *n* adjectif *m*.

adjoining [ə'dʒɔɪnɪŋ] ◇ *adj* voisin(e). ◇ *prep* attenant à

adjourn [ə'dʒɜːn] ◇ *vt* ajourner. ◇ *vi* suspendre la séance.

adjudicate [ə'dʒuːdɪkeɪt] *vi* : **to** ~ (on OR upon) se prononcer (sur).

adjust [ə'dʒʌst] ◇ *vt* ajuster, régler. ◇ *vi* : **to** ~ (to) s'adapter (à).

adjustable [ə'dʒʌstəbl] *adj* réglable.

adjustment [ə'dʒʌstmənt] *n* - **1**. [modification] ajustement *m* ; TECH réglage *m* - **2**. [change in attitude] : ~ (to) adaptation *f* (à).

ad lib [ˌæd'lɪb] ◇ *adj* improvisé(e). ◇ *adv* à volonté. ◇ *n* improvisation *f*. ◆ **ad-lib** *vi* improviser.

administer [əd'mɪnɪstə'] *vt* - **1**. [company, business] administrer, gérer - **2**. [justice, punishment] dispenser - **3**. [drug, medication] administrer.

administration [əd,mɪnɪ'streɪʃn] *n* administration *f*.

administrative [əd'mɪnɪstrətɪv] *adj* administratif(ive).

admirable ['ædmərəbl] *adj* admirable.

admiral ['ædmərəl] *n* amiral *m*.

admiration [ˌædmə'reɪʃn] *n* admiration *f*.

admire [əd'maɪə'] *vt* admirer.

admirer [əd'maɪərə'] *n* admirateur *m*, -trice *f*.

admission [əd'mɪʃn] *n* - **1**. [permission to enter] admission *f* - **2**. [to museum etc] entrée *f* - **3**. [confession] confession *f*, aveu *m*.

admit [əd'mɪt] ◇ *vt* - **1**. [confess] reconnaître ; **to** ~ (that) ... reconnaître que ... ; **to** ~ **doing sthg** reconnaître avoir fait qqch ; **to** ~ **defeat** *fig* s'avouer vaincu(e) - **2**. [allow to enter, join] admettre ; **to be** ~**ted to hospital** *Br* OR **to the hospital** *Am* être admis(e) à l'hôpital. ◇ *vi* : **to** ~ **to** admettre, reconnaître.

admittance [əd'mɪtəns] *n* admission *f* ; **'no** ~**'** 'entrée interdite'.

admittedly [əd'mɪtɪdlɪ] *adv* de l'aveu général.

admonish [əd'mɒnɪʃ] *vt* réprimander.

ad nauseam [ˌæd'nɔːzɪæm] *adv* [talk] à n'en plus finir.

ado [ə'duː] *n* : **without further** OR **more** ~ sans plus de cérémonie.

adolescence [ˌædə'lesns] *n* adolescence *f*.

adolescent [ˌædə'lesnt] ◇ *adj* adolescent(e) ; *pej* puéril(e). ◇ *n* adolescent *m*, -e *f*.

adopt [ə'dɒpt] *vt* adopter.

adoption [ə'dɒpʃn] *n* adoption *f*.

adore [ə'dɔː'] *vt* adorer.

adorn [ə'dɔːn] *vt* orner.

adrenalin [ə'drenəlɪn] *n* adrénaline *f*.

Adriatic [ˌeɪdrɪ'ætɪk] *n* : **the** ~ (Sea) l'Adriatique *f*, la mer Adriatique.

adrift [ə'drɪft] ◇ *adj* à la dérive. ◇ *adv* : **to go** ~ *fig* aller à la dérive.

adult ['ædʌlt, ə'dʌlt] ◇ *adj* - **1**. [gen] adulte - **2**. [films, literature] pour adultes. ◇ *n* adulte *mf*.

adultery [ə'dʌltərɪ] *n* adultère *m*.

advance [əd'vɑːns] ◇ *n* - **1**. [gen] avance *f* - **2**. [progress] progrès *m*. ◇ *comp* à l'avance. ◇ *vt* - **1**. [gen] avancer - **2**. [improve] faire progresser OR avancer. ◇ *vi* - **1**. [gen] avancer - **2**. [improve] progresser. ◆ **advances** *npl* : **to make** ~**s to sb** [sexual] faire des avances à qqn ; [business] faire des propositions à qqn. ◆ **in advance** *adv* à l'avance.

advanced [əd'va:nst] *adj* avancé(e).

advantage [əd'va:ntɪdʒ] *n* : ~ (**over**) avantage *m* (sur) ; **to be to one's ~** être à son avantage ; **to take ~ of sthg** profiter de qqch ; **to take ~ of sb** exploiter qqn.

advent ['ædvənt] *n* avènement *m*. ◆ **Advent** *n* RELIG Avent *m*.

adventure [əd'ventʃəʳ] *n* aventure *f*.

adventure playground *n* terrain *m* d'aventures.

adventurous [əd'ventʃərəs] *adj* aventureux(euse).

adverb ['ædvɜ:b] *n* adverbe *m*.

adverse ['ædvɜ:s] *adj* défavorable.

advert ['ædvɜ:t] *Br* = advertisement.

advertise ['ædvətaɪz] <> *vt* COMM faire de la publicité pour ; [event] annoncer. <> *vi* faire de la publicité ; **to ~ for sb/sthg** chercher qqn/qqch par voie d'annonce.

advertisement [əd'vɜ:tɪsmənt] *n* [in newspaper] annonce *f* ; COMM & *fig* publicité *f*.

advertiser ['ædvətaɪzəʳ] *n* annonceur *m*.

advertising ['ædvətaɪzɪŋ] *n* (U) publicité *f*.

advice [əd'vaɪs] *n* (U) conseils *mpl* ; **a piece of ~** un conseil ; **to give sb ~** donner des conseils à qqn ; **to take sb's ~** suivre les conseils de qqn.

advisable [əd'vaɪzəbl] *adj* conseillé(e), recommandé(e).

advise [əd'vaɪz] <> *vt* - **1.** [give advice to] : **to ~ sb to do sthg** conseiller à qqn de faire qqch ; **to ~ sb against sthg** déconseiller qqch à qqn ; **to ~ sb against doing sthg** déconseiller à qqn de faire qqch - **2.** [professionally] : **to ~ sb on sthg** conseiller qqn sur qqch - **3.** [inform] : **to ~ sb (of sthg)** aviser qqn (de qqch). <> *vi* - **1.** [give advice] : **to ~ against sthg/against doing sthg** déconseiller qqch/de faire qqch - **2.** [professionally] : **to ~ on sthg** conseiller sur qqch.

advisedly [əd'vaɪzɪdlɪ] *adv* en connaissance de cause, délibérément.

adviser *Br*, **advisor** *Am* [əd'vaɪzəʳ] *n* conseiller *m*, -ère *f*.

advisory [əd'vaɪzərɪ] *adj* consultatif(ive).

advocate [*n* 'ædvəkət, *vb* 'ædvəkeɪt] <> *n* - **1.** JUR avocat *m*, -e *f* - **2.** [supporter] partisan *m*. <> *vt* préconiser, recommander.

Aegean [i:'dʒi:ən] *n* : **the ~ (Sea)** la mer Égée.

aerial ['eərɪəl] <> *adj* aérien(enne). <> *n Br* antenne *f*.

aerobics [eə'rəubɪks] *n* (U) aérobic *m*.

aerodynamic [,eərəudaɪ'næmɪk] *adj* aérodynamique. ◆ **aerodynamics** <> *n* (U) aérodynamique *f*. <> *npl* [aerodynamic qualities] aérodynamisme *m*.

aeroplane ['eərəpleɪn] *n Br* avion *m*.

aerosol ['eərəsɒl] *n* aérosol *m*.

aesthetic, esthetic *Am* [i:s'θetɪk] *adj* esthétique.

afar [ə'fa:ʳ] *adv* : **from ~** de loin.

affable ['æfəbl] *adj* affable.

affair [ə'feəʳ] *n* - **1.** [gen] affaire *f* - **2.** [extramarital relationship] liaison *f*.

affect [ə'fekt] *vt* - **1.** [influence] avoir un effet OR des conséquences sur - **2.** [emotionally] affecter, émouvoir - **3.** [put on] affecter.

affection [ə'fekʃn] *n* affection *f*.

affectionate [ə'fekʃnət] *adj* affectueux(euse).

affirm [ə'fɜ:m] *vt* - **1.** [declare] affirmer - **2.** [confirm] confirmer.

affix [ə'fɪks] *vt* [stamp] coller.

afflict [ə'flɪkt] *vt* affliger ; **to be ~ed with** souffrir de.

affluence ['æfluəns] *n* prospérité *f*.

affluent ['æfluənt] *adj* riche.

afford [ə'fɔ:d] *vt* - **1.** [buy, pay for] : **to be able to ~ sthg** avoir les moyens d'acheter qqch - **2.** [spare] : **to be able to ~ the time (to do sthg)** avoir le temps (de faire qqch) - **3.** [harmful, embarrassing thing] : **to be able to ~ sthg** pouvoir se permettre qqch - **4.** [provide, give] procurer.

affront [ə'frʌnt] <> *n* affront *m*, insulte *f*. <> *vt* insulter, faire un affront à.

Afghanistan [æf'gænɪstæn] *n* Afghanistan *m*.

afield [ə'fɪəld] *adv* : **far ~** loin.

afloat [ə'fləut] *adj lit & fig* à flot.

afoot [ə'fut] *adj* en préparation.

afraid [ə'freɪd] *adj* - **1.** [frightened] : **to be ~ (of)** avoir peur (de) ; **to be ~ of doing** OR **to do sthg** avoir peur de faire qqch - **2.** [reluctant, apprehensive] : **to be ~ of** craindre - **3.** [in apologies] : **to be ~ (that)** ... regretter que ... ; **I'm ~ so/not** j'ai bien peur que oui/non.

afresh [ə'freʃ] *adv* de nouveau.

Africa ['æfrɪkə] *n* Afrique *f*.

African ['æfrɪkən] <> *adj* africain(e). <> *n* Africain *m*, -e *f*.

aft [a:ft] *adv* sur OR à l'arrière.

after ['a:ftəʳ] <> *prep* - **1.** [gen] après ; **~ you!** après vous! ; **to be ~ sb/sthg** *inf* [in

search of] chercher qqn/qqch ; **to name sb ~ sb** *Br* donner à qqn le nom de qqn - **2.** *Am* [telling the time] **: it's twenty ~ three** il est trois heures vingt. ⬦ *adv* après. ⬦ *conj* après que. ➡ **afters** *npl Br inf* dessert *m*.
➡ **after all** *adv* après tout.

aftereffects ['ɑːftərɪˌfekts] *npl* suites *fpl*, répercussions *fpl*.

afterlife ['ɑːftəlaɪf] (*pl* **-lives** [-laɪvz]) *n* vie *f* future.

aftermath ['ɑːftəmæθ] *n* conséquences *fpl*, suites *fpl*.

afternoon [ˌɑːftə'nuːn] *n* après-midi *m inv* ; **in the ~** l'après-midi ; **good ~** bonjour.

aftershave ['ɑːftəʃeɪv] *n* après-rasage *m*.

aftertaste ['ɑːftəteɪst] *n lit & fig* arrière-goût *m*.

afterthought ['ɑːftəθɔːt] *n* pensée *f* OR réflexion *f* après coup.

afterward(s) ['ɑːftəwəd(z)] *adv* après.

again [ə'gen] *adv* encore une fois, de nouveau ; **to do ~** refaire ; **to say ~** répéter ; **to start ~** recommencer ; **~ and ~** à plusieurs reprises , **all over ~** une fois de plus ; **time and ~** maintes et maintes fois ; **half as much ~** à moitié autant ; **(twice) as much ~** deux fois autant ; **come ~?** *inf* comment?, pardon? ; **then** OR **there ~** d'autre part.

against [ə'genst] *prep & adv* contre ; **(as) ~** contre.

age [eɪdʒ] (*cont* **ageing** OR **aging**) ⬦ *n* - **1.** [gen] âge *m* ; **she's 20 years of ~** elle a 20 ans ; **what ~ are you?** quel âge avez vous? ; **to be under ~** être mineur(e) ; **to come of ~** atteindre sa majorité - **2.** [old age] vieillesse *f* - **3.** [in history] époque *f*. ⬦ *vt & vi* vieillir. ➡ **ages** *npl* : **~s ago** il y a une éternité ; **I haven't seen him for ~s** je ne l'ai pas vu depuis une éternité.

aged [*adj sense 1* eɪdʒd, *adj sense 2 & npl* 'eɪdʒɪd] ⬦ *adj* - **1.** [of stated age] **: ~ 15** âgé(e) de 15 ans - **2.** [very old] âgé(e), vieux (vieille). ⬦ *npl* : **the ~** les personnes *fpl* âgées.

age group *n* tranche *f* d'âge.

agency ['eɪdʒənsɪ] *n* - **1.** [business] agence *f* - **2.** [organization] organisme *m*.

agenda [ə'dʒendə] (*pl* **-s**) *n* ordre *m* du jour.

agent ['eɪdʒənt] *n* agent *m*.

aggravate ['ægrəveɪt] *vt* - **1.** [make worse] aggraver - **2.** [annoy] agacer.

aggregate ['ægrɪgət] ⬦ *adj* total(e). ⬦ *n* [total] total *m*.

aggressive [ə'gresɪv] *adj* agressif(ive).

aggrieved [ə'griːvd] *adj* blessé(e), froissé(e).

aghast [ə'gɑːst] *adj* : **~ (at sthg)** atterré(e) (par qqch).

agile ['ædʒaɪl, *Am* 'ædʒəl] *adj* agile.

agitate ['ædʒɪteɪt] ⬦ *vt* - **1.** [disturb] inquiéter - **2.** [shake] agiter. ⬦ *vi* : **to ~ for/ against** faire campagne pour/contre.

AGM (*abbr of* **annual general meeting**) *n Br* AGA *f*.

agnostic [æg'nɒstɪk] ⬦ *adj* agnostique. ⬦ *n* agnostique *mf*.

ago [ə'gəʊ] *adv* : **a long time ~** il y a long-temps ; **three days ~** il y a trois jours.

agog [ə'gɒg] *adj* : **to be ~ (with)** être en ébullition (à propos de).

agonizing ['ægənaɪzɪŋ] *adj* déchirant(e).

agony ['ægənɪ] *n* - **1.** [physical pain] douleur *f* atroce ; **to be in ~** souffrir le martyre - **2.** [mental pain] angoisse *f* ; **to be in ~** être angoissé(e).

agony aunt *n Br inf* personne qui tient la rubrique du courrier du cœur.

agree [ə'griː] ⬦ *vi* - **1.** [concur] : **to ~ (with/about)** être d'accord (avec/au sujet de) ; **to ~ on** [price, terms] convenir de - **2.** [consent] : **to ~ (to sthg)** donner son consentement (à qqch) - **3.** [be consistent] concorder - **4.** [food] : **to ~ with** réussir à - **5.** GRAMM : **to ~ (with)** s'accorder (avec). ⬦ *vt* - **1.** [price, conditions] accepter, convenir de - **2.** [concur, concede] : **to ~ (that)** ... admettre que ... - **3.** [arrange] : **to ~ to do sthg** se mettre d'accord pour faire qqch.

agreeable [ə'grɪəbl] *adj* - **1.** [pleasant] agréable - **2.** [willing] : **to be ~ to** consentir à.

agreed [ə'griːd] *adj* : **to be ~ (on sthg)** être d'accord (à propos de qqch).

agreement [ə'griːmənt] *n* - **1.** [gen] accord *m* ; **to be in ~ (with)** être d'accord (avec) - **2.** [consistency] concordance *f*.

agricultural [ˌægrɪ'kʌltʃərəl] *adj* agricole.

agriculture ['ægrɪkʌltʃə'] *n* agriculture *f*.

aground [ə'graʊnd] *adv* : **to run ~** s'échouer.

ahead [ə'hed] *adv* - **1.** [in front] devant, en avant ; **right ~, straight ~** droit devant - **2.** [in better position] en avance ; **Scotland are ~ by two goals to one** l'Écosse mène par deux à un ; **to get ~** [be successful] réussir - **3.** [in time] à l'avance ; **the months ~** les mois à venir. ➡ **ahead of** *prep* - **1.** [in front of] devant - **2.** [in time] avant ; **~ of schedule** [work] en avance sur le planning.

aid [eɪd] ◇ n aide f ; **with the ~ of** [person] avec l'aide de ; [thing] à l'aide de ; **in ~ of** au profit de. ◇ vt - **1.** [help] aider - **2.** JUR : **to ~ and abet** être complice de.

AIDS, Aids [eɪdz] (abbr of **acquired immune deficiency syndrome**) ◇ n SIDA m, sida m. ◇ comp : **~ patient** sidéen m, -enne f.

ailing ['eɪlɪŋ] adj - **1.** [ill] souffrant(e) - **2.** fig [economy, industry] dans une mauvaise passe.

ailment ['eɪlmənt] n maladie f.

aim [eɪm] ◇ n - **1.** [objective] but m, objectif m - **2.** [in firing gun, arrow] : **to take ~** at viser. ◇ vt - **1.** [gun, camera] : **to ~ sthg at** braquer qqch sur - **2.** fig : **to be ~ed at** [plan, campaign etc] être destiné(e) à, viser ; [criticism] être dirigé(e) contre. ◇ vi : **to ~ (at)** viser ; **to ~ at** OR **for** fig viser ; **to ~ to do sthg** viser à faire qqch.

aimless ['eɪmlɪs] adj [person] désœuvré(e) ; [life] sans but.

ain't [eɪnt] v inf = **am not, are not, is not, have not, has not.**

air [eər] ◇ n - **1.** [gen] air m ; **to throw sthg into the ~** jeter qqch en l'air ; **by ~** [travel] par avion ; **to be (up) in the ~** fig [plans] être vague - **2.** RADIO & TV : **on the ~** à l'antenne. ◇ comp [transport] aérien(enne). ◇ vt - **1.** [gen] aérer - **2.** [make publicly known] faire connaître OR communiquer - **3.** [broadcast] diffuser. ◇ vi sécher.

airbag ['eabæg] n AUT Airbag® m.

airbase ['eəbeɪs] n base f aérienne.

airbed ['eəbed] n Br matelas m pneumatique.

airborne ['eəbɔːn] adj - **1.** [troops etc] aéroporté(e) ; [seeds] emporté(e) par le vent - **2.** [plane] qui a décollé.

air-conditioned [-kən'dɪʃnd] adj climatisé(e), à air conditionné.

air-conditioning [-kən'dɪʃnɪŋ] n climatisation f.

aircraft ['eəkrɑːft] (pl inv) n avion m.

aircraft carrier n porte-avions m inv.

airfield ['eəfiːld] n terrain m d'aviation.

airforce ['eəfɔːs] n armée f de l'air.

airgun ['eəgʌn] n carabine f OR fusil m à air comprimé.

airhostess ['eə,həʊstɪs] n hôtesse f de l'air.

airlift ['eəlɪft] ◇ n pont m aérien. ◇ vt transporter par pont aérien.

airline ['eəlaɪn] n compagnie f aérienne.

airliner ['eəlaɪnər] n [short-distance] (avion m) moyen-courrier m ; [long-distance] (avion) long-courrier m.

airlock ['eəlɒk] n - **1.** [in tube, pipe] poche f d'air - **2.** [airtight chamber] sas m.

airmail ['eəmeɪl] n poste f aérienne ; **by ~** par avion.

airplane ['eəpleɪn] n Am avion m.

airport ['eəpɔːt] n aéroport m.

air raid n raid m aérien, attaque f aérienne.

air rifle n carabine f à air comprimé.

airsick ['eəsɪk] adj : **to be ~** avoir le mal de l'air.

airspace ['eəspeɪs] n espace m aérien.

air steward n steward m.

airstrip ['eəstrɪp] n piste f (d'atterrissage).

air terminal n aérogare f.

airtight ['eətaɪt] adj hermétique.

air-traffic controller n aiguilleur m (du ciel).

airy ['eərɪ] adj - **1.** [room] aéré(e) - **2.** [notions, promises] chimérique, vain(e) - **3.** [nonchalant] nonchalant(e).

aisle [aɪl] n allée f ; [in plane] couloir m.

ajar [ə'dʒɑːr] adj entrouvert(e).

aka (abbr of **also known as**) alias.

akin [ə'kɪn] adj : **to be ~ to** être semblable à.

alacrity [ə'lækrətɪ] n empressement m.

alarm [ə'lɑːm] ◇ n - **1.** [fear] alarme f, inquiétude f - **2.** [device] alarme f ; **to raise** OR **sound the ~** donner OR sonner l'alarme. ◇ vt alarmer, alerter.

alarm clock n réveil m, réveille-matin m inv.

alarming [ə'lɑːmɪŋ] adj alarmant(e), inquiétant(e).

alas [ə'læs] excl hélas!

Albania [æl'beɪnjə] n Albanie f.

Albanian [æl'beɪnjən] ◇ adj albanais(e). ◇ n - **1.** [person] Albanais m, -e f - **2.** [language] albanais m.

albeit [ɔːl'biːɪt] conj bien que (+ subjunctive).

albino [æl'biːnəʊ] (pl -s) n albinos mf.

album ['ælbəm] n album m.

alcohol ['ælkəhɒl] n alcool m.

alcoholic [,ælkə'hɒlɪk] ◇ adj [person] alcoolique ; [drink] alcoolisé(e). ◇ n alcoolique mf.

alcopop ['ælkəʊpɒp] n boisson gazeuse faiblement alcoolisée.

alcove ['ælkəʊv] n alcôve f.

alderman ['ɔːldəmən] (*pl* **-men** [-mən]) *n* conseiller *m* municipal.

ale [eɪl] *n* bière *f*.

alert [ə'lɜːt] ◇ *adj* **- 1.** [vigilant] vigilant(e) **- 2.** [perceptive] vif (vive), éveillé(e) **- 3.** [aware] : **to be ~ to** être conscient(e) de. ◇ *n* [warning] alerte *f* ; **on the ~** [watchful] sur le qui-vive ; MIL en état d'alerte. ◇ *vt* alerter ; **to ~ sb to sthg** avertir qqn de qqch.

A level (*abbr of* **Advanced level**) *n* Br ≃ baccalauréat *m*.

alfresco [æl'freskəʊ] *adj & adv* en plein air.

algae ['ældʒiː] *npl* algues *fpl*.

algebra ['ældʒɪbrə] *n* algèbre *f*.

Algeria [æl'dʒɪərɪə] *n* Algérie *f*.

alias ['eɪlɪəs] (*pl* **-es** [-iːz]) ◇ *adv* alias. ◇ *n* faux nom *m*, nom *m* d'emprunt.

alibi ['ælɪbaɪ] *n* alibi *m*.

alien ['eɪljən] ◇ *adj* **- 1.** [gen] étranger(ère) **- 2.** [from outer space] extraterrestre. ◇ *n* **- 1.** [from outer space] extraterrestre *mf* **- 2.** JUR [foreigner] étranger *m*, -ère *f*.

alienate ['eɪljəneɪt] *vt* aliéner.

alight [ə'laɪt] ◇ *adj* allumé(e), en feu. ◇ *vi* **- 1.** [bird etc] se poser **- 2.** [from bus, train] : **to ~ from** descendre de.

align [ə'laɪn] *vt* [line up] aligner.

alike [ə'laɪk] ◇ *adj* semblable. ◇ *adv* de la même façon ; **to look ~** se ressembler.

alimony ['ælɪmənɪ] *n* pension *f* alimentaire.

alive [ə'laɪv] *adj* **- 1.** [living] vivant(e), en vie **- 2.** [practice, tradition] vivace ; **to keep ~** préserver **- 3.** [lively] plein(e) de vitalité ; **to come ~** [story, description] prendre vie ; [person, place] s'animer.

alkali ['ælkəlaɪ] (*pl* **-s** OR **-es**) *n* alcali *m*.

all [ɔːl] ◇ *adj* **- 1.** (*with sg noun*) tout (toute) ; **~ day/night/evening** toute la journée/la nuit/la soirée ; **~ the drink** toute la boisson ; **~ the time** tout le temps **- 2.** (*with pl noun*) tous (toutes) ; **~ the boxes** toutes les boîtes ; **~ men** tous les hommes ; **~ three died** ils sont morts tous les trois, tous les trois sont morts. ◇ *pron* **- 1.** (*sg*) [the whole amount] tout *m* ; **she drank it ~**, she drank **~ of it** elle a tout bu **- 2.** (*pl*) [everybody, everything] tous (toutes) ; **~ of them came, they ~ came** ils sont tous venus **- 3.** (*with superl*) : **... of ~** ... de tous (toutes) ; **I like this one best of ~** je préfère celui-ci entre tous **- 4. :** **above ~** ▷ **above ; after ~** ▷ **after ; at ~** ▷ **at**. ◇ *adv* **- 1.** [entirely] complètement ; **I'd forgotten ~ about that** j'avais complètement oublié cela ; **~ alone** tout seul (toute seule) **- 2.** [in sport, competitions] : **the score is five ~** le score est cinq partout **- 3.** (*with compar*) : **to run ~ the faster** courir d'autant plus vite ; **~ the better** d'autant mieux. ◆ **all but** *adv* presque, pratiquement. ◆ **all in all** *adv* dans l'ensemble. ◆ **in all** *adv* en tout.

Allah ['ælə] *n* Allah *m*.

all-around *Am* = **all-round**.

allay [ə'leɪ] *vt* [fears, anger] apaiser, calmer ; [doubts] dissiper.

all clear *n* signal *m* de fin d'alerte ; *fig* feu *m* vert.

allegation [ˌælɪ'geɪʃn] *n* allégation *f*.

allege [ə'ledʒ] *vt* prétendre, alléguer ; **she is ~d to have done it** on prétend qu'elle l'a fait.

allegedly [ə'ledʒɪdlɪ] *adv* prétendument.

allegiance [ə'liːdʒəns] *n* allégeance *f*.

allergic [ə'lɜːdʒɪk] *adj* : **~ (to)** allergique (à).

allergy ['ælədʒɪ] *n* allergie *f* ; **to have an ~ to sthg** être allergique à qqch.

alleviate [ə'liːvɪeɪt] *vt* apaiser, soulager.

alley(way) ['ælɪ(weɪ)] *n* [street] ruelle *f* ; [in garden] allée *f*.

alliance [ə'laɪəns] *n* alliance *f*.

allied ['ælaɪd] *adj* **- 1.** MIL allié(e) **- 2.** [related] connexe.

alligator ['ælɪgeɪtə*r*] (*pl inv* OR **-s**) *n* alligator *m*.

all-important *adj* capital(e), crucial(e).

all-in *adj* Br [price] global(e). ◆ **all in** ◇ *adv* [inclusive] tout compris. ◇ *adj inf* [tired] crevé(e).

all-night *adj* [party etc] qui dure toute la nuit ; [bar etc] ouvert(e) toute la nuit.

allocate ['æləkeɪt] *vt* [money, resources] : **to ~ sthg (to sb)** attribuer qqch (à qqn).

allot [ə'lɒt] *vt* [job] assigner ; [money, resources] attribuer ; [time] allouer.

allotment [ə'lɒtmənt] *n* **- 1.** Br [garden] jardin *m* ouvrier (*loué par la commune*) **- 2.** [sharing out] attribution *f* **- 3.** [share] part *f*.

all-out *adj* [effort] maximum (*inv*) ; [war] total(e).

allow [ə'laʊ] *vt* **- 1.** [permit - activity, behaviour] autoriser, permettre ; **to ~ sb to do sthg** permettre à qqn de faire qqch, autoriser qqn à faire qqch **- 2.** [set aside - money, time] prévoir **- 3.** [officially accept] accepter **- 4.** [concede] : **to ~ that ...** admettre que ... ◆ **allow for** *vt fus* tenir compte de.

allowance [ə'laʊəns] *n* **- 1.** [money received] indemnité *f* **- 2.** *Am* [pocket money] argent *m* de poche **- 3.** [excuse] **: to make ~s for sb** faire preuve d'indulgence envers qqn **; to make ~s for sthg** prendre qqch en considération.

alloy ['ælɔɪ] *n* alliage *m*.

all right <> *adv* bien **;** [in answer - yes] d'accord. <> *adj* **- 1.** [healthy] en bonne santé **;** [unharmed] sain et sauf (saine et sauve) **- 2.** *inf* [acceptable, satisfactory] **: it was ~** c'était pas mal **; that's ~** [never mind] ce n'est pas grave.

all-round *Br*, **all-around** *Am adj* [multi-skilled] doué(e) dans tous les domaines.

all-time *adj* [record] sans précédent.

allude [ə'luːd] *vi* **: to ~ to** faire allusion à.

alluring [ə'ljʊərɪŋ] *adj* séduisant(e).

allusion [ə'luːʒn] *n* allusion *f*.

ally [*n* 'ælaɪ, *vb* ə'laɪ] <> *n* allié *m*, -e *f*. <> *vt* **: to ~ o.s. with** s'allier à.

almighty [ɔːl'maɪtɪ] *adj inf* [noise] terrible.

almond ['aːmənd] *n* [nut] amande *f*.

almost ['ɔːlməʊst] *adv* presque **;** I **~ missed the bus** j'ai failli rater le bus.

alms [aːmz] *npl dated* aumône *f*.

aloft [ə'lɒft] *adv* [in the air] en l'air.

alone [ə'ləʊn] <> *adj* seul(e). <> *adv* seul **; to leave sthg ~** ne pas toucher à qqch **; leave me ~!** laisse-moi tranquille!

along [ə'lɒŋ] <> *adv* **: to walk ~** se promener **; to move ~** avancer **; can I come ~ (with you)?** est-ce que je peux venir (avec vous)? <> *prep* le long de **; to run/walk ~ the street** courir/marcher le long de la rue.
➤ **all along** *adv* depuis le début.
➤ **along with** *prep* ainsi que.

alongside [ə,lɒŋ'saɪd] <> *prep* le long de, à côté de **;** [person] à côté de. <> *adv* bord à bord.

aloof [ə'luːf] <> *adj* distant(e). <> *adv* **: to remain ~ (from)** garder ses distances (vis-à-vis de).

aloud [ə'laʊd] *adv* à voix haute, tout haut.

alphabet ['ælfəbet] *n* alphabet *m*.

alphabetical [,ælfə'betɪkl] *adj* alphabétique.

Alps [ælps] *npl* **: the ~** les Alpes *fpl*.

already [ɔːl'redɪ] *adv* déjà.

alright [,ɔːl'raɪt] = **all right.**

Alsace [æl'sæs] *n* Alsace *f*.

Alsatian [æl'seɪʃn] *n* [dog] berger *m* allemand.

also ['ɔːlsəʊ] *adv* aussi.

altar ['ɔːltəʳ] *n* autel *m*.

alter ['ɔːltəʳ] <> *vt* changer, modifier. <> *vi* changer.

alteration [,ɔːltə'reɪʃn] *n* modification *f*, changement *m*.

alternate [*adj Br* ɔːl'tɜːnət, *Am* 'ɔːltərnət, *vb* 'ɔːltərneɪt] <> *adj* alterné(e), alternatif(ive) **; ~ days** tous les deux jours, un jour sur deux. <> *vt* faire alterner. <> *vi* **: to ~ (with)** alterner (avec) **; to ~ between sthg and sthg** passer de qqch à qqch.

alternately [*Br* ɔːl'tɜːnətlɪ, *Am* 'ɔːl-] *adv* alternativement.

alternating current ['ɔːltəneɪtɪŋ-] *n* courant *m* alternatif.

alternative [ɔːl'tɜːnətɪv] <> *adj* **- 1.** [different] autre **- 2.** [non-traditional - society] parallèle **;** [- art, energy] alternatif(ive). <> *n* **- 1.** [between two solutions] alternative *f* **- 2.** [other possibility] **: ~ (to)** solution *f* de remplacement (à) **; to have no ~ but to do sthg** ne pas avoir d'autre choix que de faire qqch.

alternatively [ɔːl'tɜːnətɪvlɪ] *adv* ou bien.

alternative medicine *n* médecine *f* parallèle OR douce.

alternator ['ɔːltəneɪtəʳ] *n* ELEC alternateur *m*.

although [ɔːl'ðəʊ] *conj* bien que (+ *subjunctive*).

altitude ['æltɪtjuːd] *n* altitude *f*.

alto ['æltəʊ] (*pl* -s) *n* **- 1.** [male voice] haute-contre *f* **- 2.** [female voice] contralto *m*.

altogether [,ɔːltə'geðəʳ] *adv* **- 1.** [completely] entièrement, tout à fait **- 2.** [considering all things] tout compte fait **- 3.** [in all] en tout.

aluminium *Br* [,æljʊ'mɪnɪəm], **aluminum** *Am* [ə'luːmɪnəm] <> *n* aluminium *m*. <> *comp* en aluminium.

always ['ɔːlweɪz] *adv* toujours.

Alzheimer's disease ['ælts,haɪməz-] *n* maladie *f* d'Alzheimer.

am [æm] ⊏⊐ **be.**

a.m. (*abbr of* ante meridiem) **: at 3 ~** à 3h (du matin).

AM (*abbr of* amplitude modulation) *n* AM *f*.

amalgamate [ə'mælgəmeɪt] *vt* & *vi* [unite] fusionner.

amass [ə'mæs] *vt* amasser.

amateur ['æmətəʳ] <> *adj* amateur *(inv)* **;** *pej* d'amateur. <> *n* amateur *m*.

amateurish [,æmə'tərɪʃ] *adj* d'amateur.

amaze [ə'meɪz] *vt* étonner, stupéfier.

amazed [ə'meɪzd] *adj* stupéfait(e).

amazement [ə'meɪzmənt] *n* stupéfaction *f.*

amazing [ə'meɪzɪŋ] *adj* - **1.** [surprising] étonnant(e), ahurissant(e) - **2.** [wonderful] excellent(e).

Amazon ['æməzn] *n* - **1.** [river] : **the ~** l'Amazone *f* - **2.** [region] : **the ~ (Basin)** l'Amazonie *f* ; **the ~ rainforest** la forêt amazonienne.

ambassador [æm'bæsədə'] *n* ambassadeur *m*, -drice *f.*

amber ['æmbə'] *n* [substance] ambre *m.*

ambiguous [æm'bɪgjʊəs] *adj* ambigu(ë).

ambition [æm'bɪʃn] *n* ambition *f.*

ambitious [æm'bɪʃəs] *adj* ambitieux(euse).

amble ['æmbl] *vi* déambuler.

ambulance ['æmbjʊləns] *n* ambulance *f.*

ambush ['æmbʊʃ] ⟨> *n* embuscade *f.* ⟨> *vt* tendre une embuscade à.

amenable [ə'mi:nəbl] *adj* : **~ (to)** ouvert(e)(à).

amend [ə'mend] *vt* modifier ; [law] amender. ◆ **amends** *npl* : **to make ~s (for)** se racheter (pour).

amendment [ə'mendmənt] *n* modification *f* ; [to law] amendement *m.*

amenities [ə'mi:nətɪz] *npl* aménagements *mpl*, équipements *mpl.*

America [ə'merɪkə] *n* Amérique *f* ; **in ~** en Amérique.

American [ə'merɪkn] ⟨> *adj* américain(e). ⟨> *n* Américain *m*, -e *f.*

American Indian *n* Indien *m*, -enne *f* d'Amérique, Amérindien *m*, -enne *f.*

amiable ['eɪmjəbl] *adj* aimable.

amicable ['æmɪkəbl] *adj* amical(e).

amid(st) [ə'mɪd(st)] *prep* au milieu de, parmi.

amiss [ə'mɪs] ⟨> *adj* : **is there anything ~?** y a-t-il quelque chose qui ne va pas? ⟨> *adv* : **to take sthg ~** prendre qqch de travers.

ammonia [ə'məʊnjə] *n* [liquid] ammoniaque *f.*

ammunition [ˌæmjʊ'nɪʃn] *(U) n* - **1.** MIL munitions *fpl* - **2.** *fig* [argument] argument *m.*

amnesia [æm'ni:zjə] *n* amnésie *f.*

amnesty ['æmnəstɪ] *n* amnistie *f.*

amok [ə'mɒk] *adv* : **to run ~** être pris(e) d'une crise de folie furieuse.

among(st) [ə'mʌŋ(st)] *prep* parmi, entre ; **~ other things** entre autres (choses).

amoral [ˌeɪ'mɒrəl] *adj* amoral(e).

amorous ['æmərəs] *adj* amoureux(euse).

amount [ə'maʊnt] *n* - **1.** [quantity] quantité *f* ; **a great ~ of** beaucoup de - **2.** [sum of money] somme *f*, montant *m.* ◆ **amount to** *vt fus* - **1.** [total] s'élever à - **2.** [be equivalent to] revenir à, équivaloir à.

amp [æmp] *n abbr of* ampere.

ampere ['æmpeə'] *n* ampère *m.*

amphibious [æm'fɪbɪəs] *adj* amphibie.

ample ['æmpl] *adj* - **1.** [enough] suffisamment de, assez de - **2.** [large] ample.

amplifier ['æmplɪfaɪə'] *n* amplificateur *m.*

amputate ['æmpjʊteɪt] *vt & vi* amputer.

Amsterdam [ˌæmstə'dæm] *n* Amsterdam.

Amtrak ['æmtræk] *n* société nationale de chemins de fer aux États-Unis.

amuck [ə'mʌk] = **amok.**

amuse [ə'mju:z] *vt* - **1.** [make laugh] amuser, faire rire - **2.** [entertain] divertir, distraire ; **to ~ o.s. (by doing sthg)** s'occuper (à faire qqch).

amused [ə'mju:zd] *adj* - **1.** [laughing] amusé(e) ; **to be ~ at OR by sthg** trouver qqch amusant - **2.** [entertained] : **to keep o.s. ~** s'occuper.

amusement [ə'mju:zmənt] *n* - **1.** [laughter] amusement *m* - **2.** [diversion, game] distraction *f.*

amusement arcade *n* galerie *f* de jeux.

amusement park *n* parc *m* d'attractions.

amusing [ə'mju:zɪŋ] *adj* amusant(e).

an [stressed æn, unstressed ən] ⟨> **a.**

anabolic steroid [ˌænə'bɒlɪk-] *n* (stéroïde *m*) anabolisant *m.*

anaemic *Br*, **anemic** *Am* [ə'ni:mɪk] *adj* anémique ; *fig & pej* fade, plat(e).

anaesthetic *Br*, **anesthetic** *Am* [ˌænɪs'θetɪk] *n* anesthésique *m* ; **under ~** sous anesthésie ; **local/general ~** anesthésie *f* locale/générale.

analogue *Br*, **analog** *Am* ['ænəlɒg] *adj* [watch, clock] analogique.

analogy [ə'nælədʒɪ] *n* analogie *f* ; **by ~** par analogie.

analyse *Br*, **-yze** *Am* ['ænəlaɪz] *vt* analyser.

analysis [ə'næləsɪs] *(pl* **-ses** [-si:z]) *n* analyse *f.*

analyst ['ænəlɪst] *n* analyste *mf.*

analytic(al) [ˌænə'lɪtɪk(l)] *adj* analytique.

analyze *Am* = **analyse.**

anarchist ['ænəkɪst] *n* anarchiste *mf.*

anarchy ['ænəkɪ] *n* anarchie *f.*

anathema [ə'næθəmə] *n* anathème *m*.

anatomy [ə'nætəmɪ] *n* anatomie *f*.

ANC (*abbr of* **African National Congress**) *n* ANC *m*.

ancestor ['ænsestə'] *n lit & fig* ancêtre *m*.

anchor ['æŋkə'] ◇ *n* ancre *f*; **to drop/ weigh ~** jeter/lever l'ancre. ◇ *vt* - **1.** [secure] ancrer - **2.** TV présenter. ◇ *vi* NAUT jeter l'ancre.

anchovy ['æntʃəvɪ] (*pl inv* OR **-ies**) *n* anchois *m*.

ancient ['eɪnʃənt] *adj* - **1.** [monument etc] historique ; [custom] ancien(enne) - **2.** *hum* [car etc] antique ; [person] vieux (vieille).

ancillary [æn'sɪlərɪ, *Am* 'æn-] *adj* auxiliaire.

and [*stressed* ænd, *unstressed* ənd, ən] *conj* - **1.** [as well as, plus] et - **2.** [in numbers] : **one hundred ~ eighty** cent quatre-vingts ; **six ~ a half** six et demi - **3.** [to] : **come ~ see!** venez voir! ; **try ~ come** essayez de venir ; **wait ~ see** vous verrez bien. ➤ **and so on, and so forth** *adv* et ainsi de suite.

Andes ['ændiːz] *npl* : **the ~** les Andes *fpl*.

Andorra [æn'dɔːrə] *n* Andorre *f*.

anecdote ['ænɪkdəʊt] *n* anecdote *f*.

anemic *Am* = **anaemic**.

anesthetic *etc Am* = **anaesthetic** *etc*.

anew [ə'njuː] *adv* : **to start ~** recommencer (à zéro).

angel ['eɪndʒəl] *n* ange *m*.

anger ['æŋgə'] ◇ *n* colère *f*. ◇ *vt* fâcher, irriter.

angina [æn'dʒaɪnə] *n* angine *f* de poitrine.

angle ['æŋgl] *n* - **1.** [gen] angle *m* ; **at an ~** de travers, en biais - **2.** [point of view] point *m* de vue, angle *m*.

angler ['æŋglə'] *n* pêcheur *m* (à la ligne).

Anglican ['æŋglɪkən] ◇ *adj* anglican(e). ◇ *n* anglican *m*, -e *f*.

angling ['æŋglɪŋ] *n* pêche *f* à la ligne.

angry ['æŋgrɪ] *adj* [person] en colère, fâché(e) ; [words, quarrel] violent(e) ; **to be ~ with** OR **at sb** être en colère OR fâché contre qqn ; **to get ~** se mettre en colère, se fâcher.

anguish ['æŋgwɪʃ] *n* angoisse *f*.

angular ['æŋgjʊlə'] *adj* anguleux(euse).

animal ['ænɪml] ◇ *n* animal *m* ; *pej* brute *f*. ◇ *adj* animal(e).

animate ['ænɪmət] *adj* animé(e), vivant(e).

animated ['ænɪmeɪtɪd] *adj* animé(e).

aniseed ['ænɪsiːd] *n* anis *m*.

ankle ['æŋkl] ◇ *n* cheville *f*. ◇ *comp* : **~ socks** socquettes *fpl* ; **~ boots** bottines *fpl*.

annex(e) ['æneks] ◇ *n* [building] annexe *f*. ◇ *vt* annexer.

annihilate [ə'naɪəleɪt] *vt* anéantir, annihiler.

anniversary [,ænɪ'vɜːsərɪ] *n* anniversaire *m*.

announce [ə'naʊns] *vt* annoncer.

announcement [ə'naʊnsmənt] *n* - **1.** [statement] déclaration *f*; [in newspaper] avis *m* - **2.** (*U*) [act of stating] annonce *f*.

announcer [ə'naʊnsə'] *n* RADIO & TV speaker *m*, speakerine *f*.

annoy [ə'nɔɪ] *vt* agacer, contrarier.

annoyance [ə'nɔɪəns] *n* contrariété *f*.

annoyed [ə'nɔɪd] *adj* mécontent(e), agacé(e) ; **to get ~** se fâcher ; **to be ~ at sthg** être contrarié(e) par qqch ; **to be ~ with sb** être fâché(e) contre qqn.

annoying [ə'nɔɪɪŋ] *adj* agaçant(e).

annual ['ænjʊəl] ◇ *adj* annuel(elle). ◇ *n* - **1.** [plant] plante *f* annuelle - **2.** [book - gen] publication *f* annuelle ; [- for children] album *m*.

annual general meeting *n* assemblée *f* générale annuelle.

annul [ə'nʌl] *vt* annuler ; [law] abroger.

annum ['ænəm] *n* : **per ~** par an.

anomaly [ə'nɒməlɪ] *n* anomalie *f*.

anonymous [ə'nɒnɪməs] *adj* anonyme.

anorak ['ænəræk] *n* anorak *m*.

anorexia (nervosa) [,ænə'reksɪə (nɜː'vəʊsə)] *n* anorexie *f* mentale.

anorexic [,ænə'reksɪk] ◇ *adj* anorexique. ◇ *n* anorexique *mf*.

another [ə'nʌðə'] ◇ *adj* - **1.** [additional] : **~ apple** encore une pomme, une pomme de plus, une autre pomme ; **in ~ few minutes** dans quelques minutes ; **(would you like) ~ drink?** (voulez-vous) encore un verre? - **2.** [different] : **~ job** un autre travail. ◇ *pron* - **1.** [additional one] un autre (une autre), encore un (encore une) ; **one after ~** l'un après l'autre (l'une après l'autre) - **2.** [different one] un autre (une autre) ; **one ~** l'un l'autre (l'une l'autre).

answer ['ɑːnsə'] ◇ *n* - **1.** [gen] réponse *f* ; **in ~ to** en réponse à - **2.** [to problem] solution *f*. ◇ *vt* répondre à ; **to ~ the door** aller ouvrir la porte ; **to ~ the phone** répondre au téléphone. ◇ *vi* [reply] répondre. ➤ **answer back** ◇ *vt sep* répondre à. ◇ *vi* répondre. ➤ **answer for** *vt fus* être responsable de, répondre de.

answerable ['ɑ:nsərəbl] *adj* : ~ **to sb/for sthg** responsable devant qqn/de qqch.

answering machine ['ɑ:nsərɪŋ-] *n* répondeur *m*.

ant [ænt] *n* fourmi *f*.

antagonism [æn'tægənɪzm] *n* antagonisme *m*, hostilité *f*.

antagonize, -ise [æn'tægənaɪz] *vt* éveiller l'hostilité de.

Antarctic [æn'tɑ:ktɪk] <> *n* : **the ~** l'Antarctique *m*. <> *adj* antarctique.

antelope ['æntɪləʊp] (*pl inv* OR **-s**) *n* antilope *f*.

antenatal [ˌæntɪ'neɪtl] *adj* prénatal(e).

antenatal clinic *n* service *m* de consultation prénatale.

antenna [æn'tenə] (*pl sense 1* **-nae** [-niː], *pl sense 2* **-s**) *n* - **1.** [of insect] antenne *f* - **2.** *Am* [for TV, radio] antenne *f*.

anthem ['ænθəm] *n* hymne *m*.

anthology [æn'θɒlədʒɪ] *n* anthologie *f*.

antibiotic [ˌæntɪbaɪ'ɒtɪk] *n* antibiotique *m*.

antibody ['æntɪˌbɒdɪ] *n* anticorps *m*.

anticipate [æn'tɪsɪpeɪt] *vt* - **1.** [expect] s'attendre à, prévoir - **2.** [request, movement] anticiper ; [competitor] prendre de l'avance sur - **3.** [look forward to] savourer à l'avance.

anticipation [æn.tɪsɪ'peɪʃn] *n* [expectation] attente *f* ; [eagerness] impatience *f* ; **in ~ of** en prévision de.

anticlimax [æntɪ'klaɪmæks] *n* déception *f*.

anticlockwise [ˌæntɪ'klɒkwaɪz] *adj* & *adv Br* dans le sens inverse des aiguilles d'une montre.

antics ['æntɪks] *npl* - **1.** [of children, animals] gambades *fpl* - **2.** *pej* [of politicians etc] bouffonneries *fpl*.

anticyclone [ˌæntɪ'saɪkləʊn] *n* anticyclone *m*.

antidepressant [ˌæntɪdɪ'presnt] *n* antidépresseur *m*.

antidote ['æntɪdəʊt] *n lit & fig* : ~ **(to)** antidote *m* (contre).

antifreeze ['æntɪfriːz] *n* antigel *m*.

antihistamine [ˌæntɪ'hɪstəmɪn] *n* antihistaminique *m*.

antiperspirant [ˌæntɪ'pɜːspərənt] *n* déodorant *m*, antiperspirant *m*.

antiquated ['æntɪkweɪtɪd] *adj* dépassé(e).

antique [æn'tiːk] <> *adj* ancien(enne).

<> *n* [object] objet *m* ancien ; [piece of furniture] meuble *m* ancien.

antique shop *n* magasin *m* d'antiquités.

anti-Semitism [-semɪtɪzəm] *n* antisémitisme *m*.

antiseptic [ˌæntɪ'septɪk] <> *adj* antiseptique. <> *n* désinfectant *m*.

antisocial [ˌæntɪ'səʊʃl] *adj* - **1.** [against society] antisocial(e) - **2.** [unsociable] peu sociable, sauvage.

antlers [ˌæntləz] *npl* bois *mpl* (*de cervidés*).

anus ['eɪnəs] *n* anus *m*.

anvil ['ænvɪl] *n* enclume *f*.

anxiety [æŋ'zaɪətɪ] *n* - **1.** [worry] anxiété *f* - **2.** [cause of worry] souci *m* - **3.** [keenness] désir *m* farouche.

anxious ['æŋkʃəs] *adj* - **1.** [worried] anxieux(euse), très inquiet(ète) ; **to be ~ about** se faire du souci au sujet de - **2.** [keen] : **to be ~ to do sthg** tenir à faire qqch ; **to be ~ that** tenir à ce que (*+ subjunctive*).

any ['enɪ] <> *adj* - **1.** (*with negative*) de, d' ; **I haven't got ~ money/tickets** je n'ai pas d'argent/de billets ; **he never does ~ work** il ne travaille jamais - **2.** [some with sg noun] du, de l', de la ; [- with pl noun] des ; **have you got ~ money/milk/cousins?** est-ce que vous avez de l'argent/du lait/des cousins? - **3.** [no matter which] n'importe quel (n'importe quelle) ; **~ box will do** n'importe quelle boîte fera l'affaire ; *see also* **case, day, moment, rate.** <> *pron* - **1.** (*with negative*) en ; **I didn't buy ~ (of them)** je n'en ai pas acheté ; **I didn't know ~ of the guests** je ne connaissais aucun des invités - **2.** [some] en ; **do you have ~?** est-ce que vous en avez? - **3.** [no matter which one or ones] n'importe lequel (n'importe laquelle) ; **take ~ you like** prenez n'importe lequel/laquelle, prenez celui/celle que vous voulez. <> *adv* - **1.** (*with negative*) : **I can't see it ~ more** je ne le vois plus ; **I can't stand it ~ longer** je ne peux plus le supporter - **2.** [some, a little] un peu ; **do you want ~ more potatoes?** voulez-vous encore des pommes de terre? ; **is that ~ better/different?** est-ce que c'est mieux/différent comme ça?

anybody ['enɪˌbɒdɪ] = **anyone.**

anyhow ['enɪhaʊ] *adv* - **1.** [in spite of that] quand même, néanmoins - **2.** [carelessly] n'importe comment - **3.** [in any case] de toute façon.

anyone ['enɪwʌn] *pron* - **1.** (*in negative sentences*) : **I didn't see ~** je n'ai vu personne - **2.** (*in questions*) quelqu'un - **3.** [any person] n'importe qui.

anyplace ['enɪpleɪs] *Am* = anywhere.

anything ['enɪθɪŋ] *pron* - **1.** *(in negative sentences)* **: I didn't see ~** je n'ai rien vu - **2.** *(in questions)* quelque chose ; **~ else?** [in shop] et avec ceci? - **3.** [any object, event] n'importe quoi ; **if ~ happens ...** s'il arrive quoi que ce soit ...

anyway ['enɪweɪ] *adv* [in any case] de toute façon.

anywhere ['enɪweəʳ], **anyplace** *Am* ['enɪpleɪs] *adv* - **1.** *(in negative sentences)* **: I haven't seen him ~** je ne l'ai vu nulle part - **2.** *(in questions)* quelque part - **3.** [any place] n'importe où.

apart [ə'paːt] *adv* - **1.** [separated] séparé(e), éloigné(e) ; **we're living ~** nous sommes séparés - **2.** [to one side] à l'écart - **3.** [aside] **:** joking ~ sans plaisanter, plaisanterie à part. ◆ **apart from** *prep* - **1.** [except for] à part, sauf - **2.** [as well as] en plus de, outre.

apartheid [ə'paːtheɪt] *n* apartheid *m*.

apartment [ə'paːtmənt] *n* appartement *m*.

apartment building *n Am* immeuble *m* (d'habitation).

apathy ['æpəθɪ] *n* apathie *f*.

ape [eɪp] *n* singe *m*. ◇ *vt* singer.

aperitif [əperə'tiːf] *n* apéritif *m*.

aperture ['æpə‚tjʊəʳ] *n* - **1.** [hole, opening] orifice *m*, ouverture *f* - **2.** PHOT ouverture *f*.

apex ['eɪpeks] (*pl* -es [-iːz], apices ['eɪpɪsiːz]) *n* sommet *m*.

APEX ['eɪpeks] (*abbr of* advance purchase excursion) *n* **: ~ ticket** billet *m* APEX.

apices ['eɪpɪsiːz] *pl* ⌦ apex.

apiece [ə'piːs] *adv* [for each person] chacun(e), par personne ; [for each thing] chacun(e), pièce (*inv*).

apocalypse [ə'pɒkəlɪps] *n* apocalypse *f*.

apologetic [ə‚pɒlə'dʒetɪk] *adj* [letter etc] d'excuse ; **to be ~ about sthg** s'excuser de qqch.

apologize, -ise [ə'pɒlədʒaɪz] *vi* s'excuser ; **to ~ to sb (for sthg)** faire des excuses à qqn (pour qqch).

apology [ə'pɒlədʒɪ] *n* excuses *fpl*.

apostle [ə'pɒsl] *n* RELIG apôtre *m*.

apostrophe [ə'pɒstrəfɪ] *n* apostrophe *f*.

appal *Br*, **appall** *Am* [ə'pɔːl] *vt* horrifier.

appalling [ə'pɔːlɪŋ] *adj* épouvantable.

apparatus [‚æpə'reɪtəs] (*pl inv* OR **-es** [-iːz]) *n* - **1.** [device] appareil *m*, dispositif *m* - **2.** (*U*) [in gym] agrès *mpl* - **3.** [system, organization] appareil *m*.

apparel [ə'pærəl] *n Am* habillement *m*.

apparent [ə'pærənt] *adj* - **1.** [evident] évident(e) - **2.** [seeming] apparent(e).

apparently [ə'pærəntlɪ] *adv* - **1.** [it seems] à ce qu'il paraît - **2.** [seemingly] apparemment, en apparence.

appeal [ə'piːl] *vi* - **1.** [request] **: to ~ (to sb for sthg)** lancer un appel (à qqn pour obtenir qqch) - **2.** [make a plea] **: to ~ to** faire appel à - **3.** JUR **: to ~ (against)** faire appel (de) - **4.** [attract, interest] **: to ~ to sb** plaire à qqn ; **it ~s to me** ça me plaît. ◇ *n* - **1.** [request] appel *m* - **2.** JUR appel *m* - **3.** [charm, interest] intérêt *m*, attrait *m*.

appealing [ə'piːlɪŋ] *adj* [attractive] attirant(e), sympathique.

appear [ə'pɪəʳ] *vi* - **1.** [gen] apparaître ; [book] sortir, paraître - **2.** [seem] sembler, paraître ; **to ~ to be/do** sembler être/faire ; **it would ~ (that) ...** il semblerait que ... - **3.** [in play, film etc] jouer - **4.** JUR comparaître.

appearance [ə'pɪərəns] *n* - **1.** [gen] apparition *f* ; **to make an ~** se montrer - **2.** [look] apparence *f*, aspect *m*.

appease [ə'piːz] *vt* apaiser.

append [ə'pend] *vt* ajouter ; [signature] apposer.

appendices [ə'pendɪsiːz] *pl* ⌦ appendix.

appendicitis [ə‚pendɪ'saɪtɪs] *n* (*U*) appendicite *f*.

appendix [ə'pendɪks] (*pl* **-dixes** [-dɪksiːz], **-dices** [-dɪsiːz]) *n* appendice *m* ; **to have one's ~ out** OR **removed** se faire opérer de l'appendicite.

appetite ['æpɪtaɪt] *n* - **1.** [for food] **: ~ (for)** appétit *m* (pour) - **2.** *fig* [enthusiasm] **: ~ (for)** goût *m* (de OR pour).

appetizer, -iser ['æpɪtaɪzəʳ] *n* [food] amuse-gueule *m inv* ; [drink] apéritif *m*.

appetizing, -ising ['æpɪtaɪzɪŋ] *adj* [food] appétissant(e).

applaud [ə'plɔːd] ◇ *vt* - **1.** [clap] applaudir - **2.** [approve] approuver, applaudir à. ◇ *vi* applaudir.

applause [ə'plɔːz] *n* (*U*) applaudissements *mpl*.

apple ['æpl] *n* pomme *f*.

apple tree *n* pommier *m*.

appliance [ə'plaɪəns] *n* [device] appareil *m*.

applicable [ə'plɪkəbl, 'æplɪkəbl] *adj* **: ~ (to)** applicable (à).

applicant ['æplɪkənt] *n* **: ~ (for)** [job] candidat *m*, -e *f* (à) ; [state benefit] demandeur *m*, -euse *f* (de).

application [ˌæplɪˈkeɪʃn] n - 1. [gen] application f - 2. [for job etc] : ~ **(for)** demande f (de).

application form n [for post] dossier m de candidature, UNIV dossier m d'inscription.

applications program [ˌæplɪˈkeɪʃns-] n COMPUT programme m d'application.

applied [əˈplaɪd] adj [science] appliqué(e).

apply [əˈplaɪ] ⬦ vt appliquer ; **to ~ the brakes** freiner. ⬦ vi - 1. [for work, grant] : **to ~ (for)** faire une demande (de) ; **to ~ for a job** faire une demande d'emploi ; **to ~ to sb (for sthg)** s'adresser à qqn (pour obtenir qqch) - 2. [be relevant] : **to ~ (to)** s'appliquer (à), concerner.

appoint [əˈpɔɪnt] vt - 1. [to job, position] : **to ~ sb (as sthg)** nommer qqn (qqch) ; **to ~ sb to sthg** nommer qqn à qqch - 2. [time, place] fixer.

appointment [əˈpɔɪntmənt] n - 1. [to job, position] nomination f, désignation f - 2. [job, position] poste m, emploi m - 3. [arrangement to meet] rendez-vous m ; **to make an ~** prendre un rendez-vous.

apportion [əˈpɔːʃn] vt répartir.

appraisal [əˈpreɪzl] n évaluation f.

appreciable [əˈpriːʃəbl] adj [difference] sensible ; [amount] appréciable.

appreciate [əˈpriːʃɪeɪt] ⬦ vt - 1. [value, like] apprécier, aimer - 2. [recognize, understand] comprendre, se rendre compte de - 3. [be grateful for] être reconnaissant(e) de. ⬦ vi FIN prendre de la valeur.

appreciation [əˌpriːʃɪˈeɪʃn] n - 1. [liking] contentement m - 2. [understanding] compréhension f - 3. [gratitude] reconnaissance f.

appreciative [əˈpriːʃjətɪv] adj [person] reconnaissant(e) ; [remark] élogieux(euse).

apprehensive [ˌæprɪˈhensɪv] adj inquiet(ète) ; **to be ~ about sthg** appréhender OR craindre qqch.

apprentice [əˈprentɪs] n apprenti m, -e f.

apprenticeship [əˈprentɪsʃɪp] n apprentissage m.

approach [əˈprəʊtʃ] ⬦ n - 1. [gen] approche f - 2. [method] démarche f, approche f - 3. [to person] : **to make an ~ to sb** faire une proposition à qqn. ⬦ vt - 1. [come near to - place, person, thing] s'approcher de - 2. [ask] : **to ~ sb about sthg** aborder qqch avec qqn ; COMM entrer en contact avec qqn au sujet de qqch - 3. [tackle - problem] aborder. ⬦ vi s'approcher.

approachable [əˈprəʊtʃəbl] adj accessible.

appropriate [adj əˈprəʊprɪət, vb əˈprəʊprɪeɪt] ⬦ adj [clothing] convenable ; [action] approprié(e) ; [moment] opportun(e). ⬦ vt - 1. JUR s'approprier - 2. [allocate] affecter.

approval [əˈpruːvl] n approbation f ; **on ~** COMM à condition, à l'essai.

approve [əˈpruːv] ⬦ vi : **to ~ (of sthg)** approuver (qqch). ⬦ vt [ratify] approuver, ratifier.

approx. [əˈprɒks] (abbr of **approximately**) approx., env.

approximate [əˈprɒksɪmət] adj approximatif(ive).

approximately [əˈprɒksɪmətlɪ] adv à peu près, environ.

apricot [ˈeɪprɪkɒt] n abricot m.

April [ˈeɪprəl] n avril m ; see also September.

April Fools' Day n le 1er avril.

apron [ˈeɪprən] n [clothing] tablier m.

apt [æpt] adj - 1. [pertinent] pertinent(e), approprié(e) - 2. [likely] : **to be ~ to do sthg** avoir tendance à faire qqch.

aptitude [ˈæptɪtjuːd] n aptitude f, disposition f ; **to have an ~ for** avoir des dispositions pour.

aptly [ˈæptlɪ] adv avec justesse, à propos.

aqualung [ˈækwəlʌŋ] n scaphandre m autonome.

aquarium [əˈkweərɪəm] (pl -riums OR -ria [-rɪə]) n aquarium m.

Aquarius [əˈkweərɪəs] n Verseau m.

aquarobics [ˌækwəˈrəʊbɪks] n aquagym® f.

aquatic [əˈkwætɪk] adj - 1. [animal, plant] aquatique - 2. [sport] nautique.

aqueduct [ˈækwɪdʌkt] n aqueduc m.

Arab [ˈærəb] ⬦ adj arabe. ⬦ n [person] Arabe mf.

Arabian [əˈreɪbjən] adj d'Arabie, arabe.

Arabic [ˈærəbɪk] ⬦ adj arabe. ⬦ n arabe m.

Arabic numeral n chiffre m arabe.

arable [ˈærəbl] adj arable.

arbitrary [ˈɑːbɪtrərɪ] adj arbitraire.

arbitration [ˌɑːbɪˈtreɪʃn] n arbitrage m ; **to go to ~** recourir à l'arbitrage.

arcade [ɑːˈkeɪd] n - 1. [for shopping] galerie f marchande - 2. [covered passage] arcades fpl.

arch [ɑːtʃ] ⬦ adj malicieux(euse), espiègle. ⬦ n - 1. ARCHIT arc m, voûte f - 2. [of foot] voûte f plantaire, cambrure f. ⬦ vt cambrer, arquer. ⬦ vi former une voûte.

archaeologist [ˌɑːkɪˈɒlədʒɪst] *n* archéologue *mf*.

archaeology [ˌɑːkɪˈɒlədʒɪ] *n* archéologie *f*.

archaic [ɑːˈkeɪɪk] *adj* archaïque.

archbishop [ˌɑːtʃˈbɪʃəp] *n* archevêque *m*.

archenemy [ˌɑːtʃˈenɪmɪ] *n* ennemi *m* numéro un.

archeology *etc* [ˌɑːkɪˈɒlədʒɪ] = **archaeology** *etc*.

archer [ˈɑːtʃəʳ] *n* archer *m*.

archery [ˈɑːtʃərɪ] *n* tir *m* à l'arc.

archetypal [ˌɑːkɪˈtaɪpl] *adj* typique.

architect [ˈɑːkɪtekt] *n lit & fig* architecte *mf*.

architecture [ˈɑːkɪtektʃəʳ] *n* [gen & COMPUT] architecture *f*.

archives [ˈɑːkaɪvz] *npl* archives *fpl*.

archway [ˈɑːtʃweɪ] *n* passage *m* voûté.

Arctic [ˈɑːktɪk] <> *adj* - **1.** GEOGR arctique - **2.** *inf* [very cold] glacial(e). <> *n* : **the ~** l'Arctique *m*.

ardent [ˈɑːdənt] *adj* fervent(e), passionné(e).

arduous [ˈɑːdjʊəs] *adj* ardu(e).

are [weak form əʳ, strong form ɑːʳ] ⊳ **be**.

area [ˈeərɪə] *n* - **1.** [region] région *f* ; **parking ~** aire *f* de stationnement ; **in the ~ of** [approximately] environ, à peu près - **2.** [surface size] aire *f*, superficie *f* - **3.** [of knowledge, interest etc] domaine *m*.

area code *n* indicatif *m* de zone.

arena [əˈriːnə] *n lit & fig* arène *f*.

aren't [ɑːnt] = are not.

Argentina [ˌɑːdʒənˈtiːnə] *n* Argentine *f*.

Argentine [ˈɑːdʒəntaɪn], **Argentinian** [ˌɑːdʒənˈtɪnɪən] <> *adj* argentin(e). <> *n* Argentin *m*, -e *f*.

arguably [ˈɑːgjʊəblɪ] *adv* : **she's ~ the best** on peut soutenir qu'elle est la meilleure.

argue [ˈɑːgjuː] <> *vi* - **1.** [quarrel] : **to ~ (with sb about sthg)** se disputer (avec qqn à propos de qqch) - **2.** [reason] : **to ~ (for/against)** argumenter (pour/contre). <> *vt* débattre de, discuter de ; **to ~ that** soutenir OR maintenir que.

argument [ˈɑːgjʊmənt] *n* - **1.** [quarrel] dispute *f* ; **to have an ~ (with sb)** se disputer (avec qqn) - **2.** [reason] argument *m* - **3.** *(U)* [reasoning] discussion *f*, débat *m*.

argumentative [ˌɑːgjʊˈmentətɪv] *adj* querelleur(euse), batailleur(euse).

arid [ˈærɪd] *adj lit & fig* aride.

Aries [ˈeəriːz] *n* Bélier *m*.

arise [əˈraɪz] (*pt* arose, *pp* arisen [əˈrɪzn]) *vi* [appear] surgir, survenir ; **to ~ from** résulter de, provenir de ; **if the need ~s** si le besoin se fait sentir.

aristocrat [*Br* ˈærɪstəkræt, *Am* əˈrɪstəkræt] *n* aristocrate *mf*.

arithmetic [əˈrɪθmətɪk] *n* arithmétique *f*.

ark [ɑːk] *n* arche *f*.

arm [ɑːm] <> *n* - **1.** [of person, chair] bras *m* ; **~ in ~** bras dessus bras dessous ; **to keep sb at ~'s length** *fig* tenir qqn à distance ; **to twist sb's ~** *fig* forcer la main à qqn - **2.** [of garment] manche *f*. <> *vt* armer. ◆ **arms** *npl* armes *fpl* ; **to take up ~s** prendre les armes ; **to be up in ~s about sthg** s'élever contre qqch.

armaments [ˈɑːməmənts] *npl* [weapons] matériel *m* de guerre, armements *mpl*.

armchair [ˈɑːmtʃeəʳ] *n* fauteuil *m*.

armed [ɑːmd] *adj lit & fig* : **~ (with)** armé(e) (de).

armed forces *npl* forces *fpl* armées.

armhole [ˈɑːmhəʊl] *n* emmanchure *f*.

armour *Br*, **armor** *Am* [ˈɑːməʳ] *n* - **1.** [for person] armure *f* - **2.** [for military vehicle] blindage *m*.

armoured car [ˌɑːməd-] *n* voiture *f* blindée.

armoury *Br*, **armory** *Am* [ˈɑːmərɪ] *n* arsenal *m*.

armpit [ˈɑːmpɪt] *n* aisselle *f*.

armrest [ˈɑːmrest] *n* accoudoir *m*.

arms control [ˈɑːmz-] *n* contrôle *m* des armements.

army [ˈɑːmɪ] *n lit & fig* armée *f*.

A road *n Br* route *f* nationale.

aroma [əˈrəʊmə] *n* arôme *m*.

arose [əˈrəʊz] *pt* ⊳ **arise**.

around [əˈraʊnd] <> *adv* - **1.** [about, round] : **to walk ~** se promener ; **to lie ~** [clothes etc] traîner - **2.** [on all sides] (tout) autour - **3.** [near] dans les parages - **4.** [in circular movement] : **to turn ~** se retourner - **5.** *phr* : **he has been ~** *inf* il n'est pas né d'hier, il a de l'expérience. <> *prep* - **1.** [gen] autour de ; **to walk ~ a garden/town** faire le tour d'un jardin/d'une ville ; **all ~ the country** dans tout le pays - **2.** [near] : **here** par ici - **3.** [approximately] environ, à peu près.

arouse [əˈraʊz] *vt* - **1.** [excite - feeling] éveiller, susciter ; [- person] exciter - **2.** [wake] réveiller.

arrange [əˈreɪndʒ] *vt* - **1.** [flowers, books,

furniture] arranger, disposer - 2. [event, meeting etc] organiser, fixer ; **to ~ to do sthg** convenir de faire qqch - 3. MUS arranger.

arrangement [ə'reɪndʒmənt] *n* - 1. [agreement] accord *m*, arrangement *m* ; **to come to an ~** s'entendre, s'arranger - 2. [of furniture, books] arrangement *m* - 3. MUS arrangement *m*. ◆ **arrangements** *npl* dispositions *fpl*, préparatifs *mpl*.

array [ə'reɪ] ◇ *n* [of objects] étalage *m*. ◇ *vt* [ornaments etc] disposer.

arrears [ə'rɪəz] *npl* [money owed] arriéré *m* ; **to be in ~** [late] être en retard ; [owing money] avoir des arriérés.

arrest [ə'rest] ◇ *n* [by police] arrestation *f* ; **under ~** en état d'arrestation. ◇ *vt* - 1. [gen] arrêter - 2. *fml* [sb's attention] attirer, retenir.

arrival [ə'raɪvl] *n* - 1. [gen] arrivée *f* ; **late ~** [of train etc] retard *m* - 2. [person - at airport, hotel] arrivant *m*, -e *f* ; **new ~** [person] nouveau venu *m*, nouvelle venue *f* ; [baby] nouveau-né *m*, nouveau-née *f*.

arrive [ə'raɪv] *vi* arriver ; [baby] être né(e) ; **to ~ at** [conclusion, decision] arriver à.

arrogant ['ærəgənt] *adj* arrogant(e).

arrow ['ærəʊ] *n* flèche *f*.

arse *Br* [ɑːs], **ass** *Am* [æs] *n vulg* cul *m*.

arsenic ['ɑːsnɪk] *n* arsenic *m*

arsenal ['ɑːsənl] *n* arsenal *m*.

arson ['ɑːsn] *n* incendie *m* criminel OR volontaire.

art [ɑːt] ◇ *n* art *m*. ◇ *comp* [exhibition] d'art ; [college] des beaux-arts ; **~ student** étudiant *m*, -e *f* d'une école des beaux-arts. ◆ **arts** *npl* - 1. SCH & UNIV lettres *fpl* - 2. [fine arts] : **the ~s** les arts *mpl*.

artefact ['ɑːtɪfækt] = artifact.

artery ['ɑːtərɪ] *n* artère *f*.

art gallery *n* [public] musée *m* d'art ; [for selling paintings] galerie *f* d'art.

art house *n* cinéma *m* d'art et d'essai.

art-house *adj* [cinema, film] d'art et d'essai.

arthritis [ɑː'θraɪtɪs] *n* arthrite *f*.

artichoke ['ɑːtɪtʃəʊk] *n* artichaut *m*.

article ['ɑːtɪkl] *n* article *m* ; **~ of clothing** vêtement *m*.

articulate [*adj* ɑː'tɪkjʊlət, *vb* ɑː'tɪkjʊleɪt] ◇ *adj* [person] qui sait s'exprimer ; [speech] net (nette), distinct(e). ◇ *vt* [thought, wish] formuler.

articulated lorry [ɑː'tɪkjʊleɪtɪd-] *n Br* semi-remorque *m*.

artifact ['ɑːtɪfækt] *n* objet *m* fabriqué.

artificial [ˌɑːtɪ'fɪʃl] *adj* - 1. [not natural] artificiel(elle) - 2. [insincere] affecté(e).

artillery [ɑː'tɪlərɪ] *n* artillerie *f*.

artist ['ɑːtɪst] *n* artiste *mf*.

artiste [ɑː'tiːst] *n* artiste *mf*.

artistic [ɑː'tɪstɪk] *adj* [person] artiste ; [style etc] artistique.

e-mail address *n* adresse *f* électronique, adresse *f* e-mail.

artistry ['ɑːtɪstrɪ] *n* art *m*, talent *m* artistique.

artless ['ɑːtlɪs] *adj* naturel(elle), ingénu(e).

as [*unstressed* əz, *stressed* æz] ◇ *conj* - 1. [referring to time] comme, alors que ; **she rang (just) ~ I was leaving** elle m'a téléphoné au moment même où OR juste comme je partais ; **~ time goes by** à mesure que le temps passe, avec le temps - 2. [referring to manner, way] comme ; **do ~ I say** fais ce que je (te) dis - 3. [introducing a statement] comme ; **~ you know, ...** comme tu le sais, ... - 4. [because] comme. ◇ *prep* - 1. [referring to function, characteristic] en, comme, en tant que ; **I'm speaking ~ your friend** je te parle en ami ; **she works ~ a nurse** elle est infirmière - 2. [referring to attitude, reaction] : **it came ~ a shock** cela nous a fait un choc. ◇ *adv* (*in comparisons*) : **~ rich ~** aussi riche que ; **~ red ~ a tomato** rouge comme une tomate ; **he's ~ tall ~ I am** il est aussi grand que moi, **twice ~ big ~** deux fois plus gros que ; **~ much/many ~** autant que ; **~ much wine/many chocolates ~** autant de vin/de chocolats que. ◆ **as for** *prep* quant à. ◆ **as from, as of** *prep* dès, à partir de. ◆ **as if, as though** *conj* comme si ; **it looks ~ if** OR **~ though it will rain** on dirait qu'il va pleuvoir. ◆ **as to** *prep* - 1. [concerning] en ce qui concerne, au sujet de - 2. = as for.

a.s.a.p. (*abbr of* **as soon as possible**) d'urgence, dans les meilleurs délais.

asbestos [æs'bestəs] *n* asbeste *m*, amiante *m*.

ascend [ə'send] *vt* & *vi* monter.

ascendant [ə'sendənt] *n* : **to be in the ~** avoir le dessus.

ascent [ə'sent] *n lit* & *fig* ascension *f*.

ascertain [ˌæsə'teɪn] *vt* établir.

ascribe [ə'skraɪb] *vt* : **to ~ sthg to** attribuer qqch à ; [blame] imputer qqch à.

ash [æʃ] *n* - 1. [from cigarette, fire] cendre *f* - 2. [tree] frêne *m*.

ashamed [əˈʃeɪmd] *adj* honteux(euse), confus(e) ; **to be ~ of** avoir honte de ; **to be ~ to do sthg** avoir honte de faire qqch.

ashen-faced [ˈæʃnˌfeɪst] *adj* blême.

ashore [əˈʃɔːʳ] *adv* à terre.

ashtray [ˈæʃtreɪ] *n* cendrier *m*.

Ash Wednesday *n* le mercredi des Cendres.

Asia [*Br* ˈeɪʃə, *Am* ˈeɪʒə] *n* Asie *f*.

Asian [*Br* ˈeɪʃn, *Am* ˈeɪʒn] <> *adj* asiatique. <> *n* [person] Asiatique *mf*.

aside [əˈsaɪd] <> *adv* **- 1.** [to one side] de côté ; **to move ~** s'écarter ; **to take sb ~** prendre qqn à part **- 2.** [apart] à part ; **~ from** à l'exception de. <> *n* **- 1.** [in play] aparté *m* **- 2.** [remark] réflexion *f*, commentaire *m*.

ask [aːsk] <> *vt* **- 1.** [gen] demander ; **to ~ sb sthg** demander qqch à qqn ; **he ~ed me my name** il m'a demandé mon nom ; **to ~ sb for sthg** demander qqch à qqn ; **to ~ sb to do sthg** demander à qqn de faire qqch **- 2.** [put - question] poser **- 3.** [invite] inviter. <> *vi* demander. ◆ **ask after** *vt fus* demander des nouvelles de. ◆ **ask for** *vt fus* **- 1.** [person] demander à voir **- 2.** [thing] demander.

askance [əˈskæns] *adv* : **to look ~ at sb** regarder qqn d'un air désapprobateur.

askew [əˈskjuː] *adj* [not straight] de travers.

asking price [ˈaːskɪŋ-] *n* prix *m* demandé.

asleep [əˈsliːp] *adj* endormi(e) ; **to fall ~** s'endormir.

asparagus [əˈspærəgəs] *n (U)* asperges *fpl.*

aspect [ˈæspekt] *n* **- 1.** [gen] aspect *m* **- 2.** [of building] orientation *f.*

aspersions [əˈspɜːʃnz] *npl* : **to cast ~ on** jeter le discrédit sur.

asphalt [ˈæsfælt] *n* asphalte *m*.

asphyxiate [əsˈfɪksɪeɪt] *vt* asphyxier.

aspiration [ˌæspəˈreɪʃn] *n* aspiration *f.*

aspire [əˈspaɪəʳ] *vi* : **to ~ to sthg/to do sthg** aspirer à qqch/à faire qqch.

aspirin [ˈæsprɪn] *n* aspirine *f.*

ass [æs] *n* **- 1.** [donkey] âne *m* **- 2.** *Br inf* [idiot] imbécile *mf*, idiot *m*, -e *f* **- 3.** *Am vulg* = arse.

assailant [əˈseɪlənt] *n* assaillant *m*, -e *f*.

assassin [əˈsæsɪn] *n* assassin *m*.

assassinate [əˈsæsɪneɪt] *vt* assassiner.

assassination [əˌsæsɪˈneɪʃn] *n* assassinat *m*.

assault [əˈsɔːlt] <> *n* **- 1.** MIL : **~ (on)** assaut *m* (de), attaque *f* (de) **- 2.** [physical at-

tack] : **~ (on sb)** agression *f* (contre qqn). <> *vt* [attack - physically] agresser ; [- sexually] violenter.

assemble [əˈsembl] <> *vt* **- 1.** [gather] réunir **- 2.** [fit together] assembler, monter. <> *vi* se réunir, s'assembler.

assembly [əˈsemblɪ] *n* **- 1.** [gen] assemblée *f* **- 2.** [fitting together] assemblage *m*.

assembly line *n* chaîne *f* de montage.

assent [əˈsent] <> *n* consentement *m*, assentiment *m*. <> *vi* : **to ~ (to)** donner son consentement OR assentiment (à).

assert [əˈsɜːt] *vt* **- 1.** [fact, belief] affirmer, soutenir **- 2.** [authority] imposer.

assertive [əˈsɜːtɪv] *adj* assuré(e).

assess [əˈses] *vt* évaluer, estimer.

assessment [əˈsesmənt] *n* **- 1.** [opinion] opinion *f* **- 2.** [calculation] évaluation *f*, estimation *f*.

assessor [əˈsesəʳ] *n* [of tax] contrôleur *m* (des impôts).

asset [ˈæset] *n* avantage *m*, atout *m*. ◆ **assets** *npl* COMM actif *m*.

assign [əˈsaɪn] *vt* **- 1.** [allot] : **to ~ sthg (to)** assigner qqch (à) **- 2.** [give task to] : **to ~ sb (to sthg/to do sthg)** nommer qqn (à qqch/pour faire qqch).

assignment [əˈsaɪnmənt] *n* **- 1.** [task] mission *f* ; SCH devoir *m* **- 2.** [act of assigning] attribution *f*.

assimilate [əˈsɪmɪleɪt] *vt* assimiler.

assist [əˈsɪst] *vt* : **to ~ sb (with sthg/in doing sthg)** aider qqn (dans qqch/à faire qqch) ; [professionally] assister qqn (dans qqch/pour faire qqch).

assistance [əˈsɪstəns] *n* aide *f* ; **to be of ~ (to)** être utile (à).

assistant [əˈsɪstənt] <> *n* assistant *m*, -e *f* ; (shop) ~ vendeur *m*, -euse *f*. <> *comp* : **~ editor** rédacteur en chef adjoint *m*, rédactrice en chef adjointe *f* ; **~ manager** sous-directeur *m*, -trice *f*.

associate [*adj & n* əˈsəʊʃɪət, *vb* əˈsəʊʃɪeɪt] <> *adj* associé(e). <> *n* associé *m*, -e *f.* <> *vt* : **to ~ sb/sthg (with)** associer qqn/qqch (à) ; **to be ~d with** être associé(e) à. <> *vi* : **to ~ with sb** fréquenter qqn.

association [əˌsəʊsɪˈeɪʃn] *n* association *f* ; **in ~ with** avec la collaboration de.

assorted [əˈsɔːtɪd] *adj* varié(e).

assortment [əˈsɔːtmənt] *n* mélange *m*.

assume [əˈsjuːm] *vt* **- 1.** [suppose] supposer, présumer **- 2.** [power, responsibility] assumer **- 3.** [appearance, attitude] adopter.

assumed name [əˈsjuːmd-] *n* nom *m* d'emprunt.

assuming [ə'sjuːmɪŋ] *conj* en supposant que.

assumption [ə'sʌmpʃn] *n* [supposition] supposition *f*.

assurance [ə'ʃʊərəns] *n* - **1**. [gen] assurance *f* - **2**. [promise] garantie *f*, promesse *f*.

assure [ə'ʃʊəʳ] *vt* : **to ~ sb (of)** assurer qqn (de).

assured [ə'ʃʊəd] *adj* assuré(e).

asterisk ['æstərɪsk] *n* astérisque *m*.

astern [ə'stɜːn] *adv* NAUT en poupe.

asthma ['æsmə] *n* asthme *m*.

astonish [ə'stɒnɪʃ] *vt* étonner.

astonishment [ə'stɒnɪʃmənt] *n* étonnement *m*.

astound [ə'staʊnd] *vt* stupéfier.

astray [ə'streɪ] *adv* : **to go ~** [become lost] s'égarer ; **to lead sb ~** détourner qqn du droit chemin.

astride [ə'straɪd] <> *adv* à cheval, à califourchon. <> *prep* à cheval OR califourchon sur.

astrology [ə'strɒlədʒɪ] *n* astrologie *f*.

astronaut ['æstrənɔːt] *n* astronaute *mf*.

astronomical [ˌæstrə'nɒmɪkl] *adj* astronomique.

astronomy [ə'strɒnəmɪ] *n* astronomie *f*.

astute [ə'stjuːt] *adj* malin(igne).

asylum [ə'saɪləm] *n* asile *m*.

at [unstressed ət, stressed æt] *prep* - **1**. [indicating place, position] à ; **~ my father's** chez mon père ; **~ home** à la maison, chez soi ; **~ school** à l'école ; **~ work** au travail - **2**. [indicating direction] vers ; **to look ~ sb** regarder qqn ; **to smile ~ sb** sourire à qqn ; **to shoot ~ sb** tirer sur qqn - **3**. [indicating a particular time] à ; **~ midnight/noon/eleven o'clock** à minuit/midi/onze heures ; **~ night** la nuit ; **~ Christmas/Easter** à Noël/Pâques - **4**. [indicating age, speed, rate] à ; **~ 52 (years of age)** à 52 ans ; **~ 100 mph** à 160 km/h - **5**. [indicating price] : **~ £50 a pair** 50 livres la paire - **6**. [indicating particular state, condition] en ; **~ peace/war** en paix/guerre ; **to be ~ lunch/dinner** être en train de déjeuner/dîner - **7**. (after adjectives) : **amused/appalled/puzzled ~ sthg** diverti(e)/effaré(e)/intrigué(e) par qqch ; **delighted ~ sthg** ravi(e) de qqch ; **to be bad/good ~ sthg** être mauvais(e)/bon (bonne) en qqch. ◆ **at all** *adv* - **1**. (with negative) : **not ~ all** [when thanked] je vous en prie ; [when answering a question] pas du tout ; **she's not ~ all happy** elle n'est pas du tout contente - **2**. [in the slightest] : **anything ~ all will do** n'importe quoi fera l'affaire ; **do**

you know her ~ all? est-ce que vous la connaissez?

ate [Br et, Am eɪt] *pt* ▷ **eat**.

atheist ['eɪθɪɪst] *n* athée *mf*.

Athens ['æθɪnz] *n* Athènes *f*.

athlete ['æθliːt] *n* athlète *mf*.

athletic [æθ'letɪk] *adj* athlétique. ◆ **athletics** *npl* athlétisme *m*.

Atlantic [ət'læntɪk] <> *adj* atlantique. <> *n* : **the ~ (Ocean)** l'océan *m* Atlantique, l'Atlantique *m*.

atlas ['ætləs] *n* atlas *m*.

ATM (abbr of **automatic teller machine**) *n* DAB *m*.

atmosphere ['ætmə,sfɪəʳ] *n* atmosphère *f*.

atmospheric [ˌætməs'ferɪk] *adj* - **1**. [pressure, pollution etc] atmosphérique - **2**. [film, music etc] d'ambiance.

atom ['ætəm] *n* - **1**. TECH atome *m* - **2**. *fig* [tiny amount] grain *m*, parcelle *f*.

atom bomb *n* bombe *f* atomique.

atomic [ə'tɒmɪk] *adj* atomique.

atomic bomb = **atom bomb**.

atomizer, -iser ['ætəmaɪzəʳ] *n* atomiseur *m*, vaporisateur *m*.

atone [ə'təʊn] *vi* : **to ~ for** racheter.

A to Z *n* plan *m* de ville.

atrocious [ə'trəʊʃəs] *adj* [very bad] atroce, affreux(euse).

atrocity [ə'trɒsətɪ] *n* [terrible act] atrocité *f*.

attach [ə'tætʃ] *vt* - **1**. [gen] : **to ~ sthg (to)** attacher qqch (à) - **2**. [letter etc] joindre.

attaché case *n* attaché-case *m*.

attached [ə'tætʃt] *adj* [fond] : **~ to** attaché(e) à.

attachment [ə'tætʃmənt] *n* - **1**. [device] accessoire *m* - **2**. [fondness] : **~ (to)** attachement *m* (à).

attack [ə'tæk] <> *n* - **1**. [physical, verbal] : **~ (on)** attaque *f* (contre) - **2**. [of illness] crise *f*. <> *vt* - **1**. [gen] attaquer - **2**. [job, problem] s'attaquer à. <> *vi* attaquer.

attacker [ə'tækəʳ] *n* - **1**. [assailant] agresseur *m* - **2**. SPORT attaquant *m*, -e *f*.

attain [ə'teɪn] *vt* atteindre, parvenir à.

attainment [ə'teɪnmənt] *n* - **1**. [of success, aims etc] réalisation *f* - **2**. [skill] talent *m*.

attempt [ə'tempt] <> *n* - **(at)** tentative *f* (de) ; **~ on sb's life** tentative d'assassinat. <> *vt* tenter, essayer ; **to ~ to do sthg** essayer OR tenter de faire qqch.

attend [ə'tend] <> *vt* - **1**. [meeting, party] assister à - **2**. [school, church] aller à. <> *vi* - **1**. [be present] être présent(e) - **2**. [pay at-

tention] : **to ~ (to)** prêter attention (à).
➤ **attend to** vt fus - **1.** [deal with] s'occuper de, régler - **2.** [look after - customer] s'occuper de ; [- patient] soigner.

attendance [ə'tendəns] n - **1.** [number present] assistance f, public m - **2.** [presence] présence f.

attendant [ə'tendənt] ◇ adj [problems] qui en découle. ◇ n [at museum, car park] gardien m, -enne f ; [at petrol station] pompiste mf.

attention [ə'tenʃn] ◇ n (U) - **1.** [gen] attention f ; **to bring sthg to sb's ~**, **to draw sb's ~ to sthg** attirer l'attention de qqn sur qqch ; **to attract** OR **catch sb's ~** attirer l'attention de qqn ; **to pay ~ to** prêter attention à ; **for the ~ of** COMM à l'attention de - **2.** [care] soins mpl, attentions fpl. ◇ excl MIL garde-à-vous!

attentive [ə'tentɪv] adj attentif(ive).

attic ['ætɪk] n grenier m.

attitude ['ætɪtjuːd] n - **1.** [gen] : **~ (to** OR **towards)** attitude f (envers) - **2.** [posture] pose f.

attn. (abbr of **for the attention of**) à l'attention de.

attorney [ə'tɜːnɪ] n Am avocat m, -e f.

attorney general (pl attorneys general) n ministre m de la Justice.

attract [ə'trækt] vt attirer.

attraction [ə'trækʃn] n - **1.** [gen] attraction f ; **~ to sb** attirance f envers qqn - **2.** [of thing] attrait m.

attractive [ə'træktɪv] adj [person] attirant(e), séduisant(e) ; [thing, idea] attrayant(e), séduisant(e) ; [investment] intéressant(e).

attribute [vb ə'trɪbjuːt, n 'ætrɪbjuːt] ◇ vt : **to ~ sthg to** attribuer qqch à. ◇ n attribut m.

attrition [ə'trɪʃn] n usure f.

aubergine ['əʊbəʒiːn] n Br aubergine f.

auburn ['ɔːbən] adj auburn (inv).

auction ['ɔːkʃn] ◇ n vente f aux enchères ; **at** OR **by ~** aux enchères ; **to put sthg up for ~** mettre qqch (dans une vente) aux enchères. ◇ vt vendre aux enchères. ➤ **auction off** vt sep vendre aux enchères.

auctioneer [ˌɔːkʃə'nɪəʳ] n commissaire-priseur m.

audacious [ɔː'deɪʃəs] adj audacieux (euse).

audible ['ɔːdəbl] adj audible.

audience ['ɔːdjəns] n - **1.** [of play, film] public m, spectateurs mpl ; [of TV programme] téléspectateurs mpl - **2.** [formal meeting] audience f.

audiovisual [ˌɔːdɪəʊvɪzjʊəl] adj audio-visuel(elle).

audit ['ɔːdɪt] ◇ n audit m, vérification f des comptes. ◇ vt vérifier, apurer.

audition [ɔː'dɪʃn] n THEATRE audition f ; CINEMA bout m d'essai.

auditor ['ɔːdɪtəʳ] n auditeur m, -trice f.

auditorium [ˌɔːdɪ'tɔːrɪəm] (pl -riums OR -ria [-rɪə]) n salle f.

augur ['ɔːgəʳ] vi : **to ~ well/badly** être de bon/mauvais augure.

August ['ɔːgəst] n août m ; see also **September**.

Auld Lang Syne [ˌɔːldlæŋ'saɪn] n chant traditionnel britannique correspondant à « ce n'est qu'un au revoir, mes frères ».

aunt [aːnt] n tante f.

auntie, aunty ['aːntɪ] n inf tata f, tantine f.

au pair [ˌəʊ'peəʳ] n jeune fille f au pair.

aura ['ɔːrə] n atmosphère f.

aural ['ɔːrəl] adj auditif(ive).

auspices ['ɔːspɪsɪz] npl : **under the ~ of** sous les auspices de.

auspicious [ɔː'spɪʃəs] adj prometteur (euse).

Aussie ['ɒzɪ] inf ◇ adj australien(enne). ◇ n Australien m, -enne f.

austere [ɒ'stɪəʳ] adj austère.

austerity [ɒ'sterətɪ] n austérité f.

Australia [ɒ'streɪljə] n Australie f.

Australian [ɒ'streɪljən] ◇ adj australien(enne). ◇ n Australien m, -enne f.

Austria ['ɒstrɪə] n Autriche f.

Austrian ['ɒstrɪən] ◇ adj autrichien (enne). ◇ n Autrichien m, -enne f.

authentic [ɔː'θentɪk] adj authentique.

author ['ɔːθəʳ] n auteur m.

authoritarian [ɔːˌθɒrɪ'teərɪən] adj autoritaire.

authoritative [ɔː'θɒrɪtətɪv] adj - **1.** [person, voice] autoritaire - **2.** [study] qui fait autorité.

authority [ɔː'θɒrətɪ] n - **1.** [organization, power] autorité f ; **to be in ~** être le/la responsable - **2.** [permission] autorisation f - **3.** [expert] : **~ (on sthg)** expert m, -e f (en qqch). ➤ **authorities** npl : **the authorities** les autorités fpl.

authorize, -ise ['ɔːθəraɪz] vt : **to ~ sb (to do sthg)** autoriser qqn (à faire qqch).

autistic [ɔː'tɪstɪk] *adj* [child] autiste ; [behaviour] autistique.

auto ['ɔːtəʊ] (*pl* -s) *n Am* auto *f*, voiture *f*.

autobiography [ˌɔːtəbaɪ'ɒɡrəfɪ] *n* autobiographie *f*.

autocratic [ˌɔːtə'krætɪk] *adj* autocratique.

autograph ['ɔːtəɡrɑːf] ◇ *n* autographe *m*. ◇ *vt* signer.

automate ['ɔːtəmeɪt] *vt* automatiser.

automatic [ˌɔːtə'mætɪk] ◇ *adj* [gen] automatique. ◇ *n* - 1. [car] voiture *f* à transmission automatique - 2. [gun] automatique *m* - 3. [washing machine] lave-linge *m* automatique.

automatically [ˌɔːtə'mætɪklɪ] *adv* [gen] automatiquement.

automation [ˌɔːtə'meɪʃn] *n* automatisation *f*, automation *f*.

automobile ['ɔːtəməbiːl] *n Am* automobile *f*.

autonomy [ɔː'tɒnəmɪ] *n* autonomie *f*.

autopsy ['ɔːtɒpsɪ] *n* autopsie *f*.

autumn ['ɔːtəm] *n* automne *m*.

auxiliary [ɔːɡ'zɪljərɪ] ◇ *adj* auxiliaire. ◇ *n* auxiliaire *mf*.

Av. (*abbr of* avenue) av.

avail [ə'veɪl] ◇ *n* : to no ~ en vain, sans résultat. ◇ *vt* : to ~ o.s. of profiter de.

available [ə'veɪləbl] *adj* disponible.

avalanche ['ævəlɑːnʃ] *n lit & fig* avalanche *f*.

avarice ['ævərɪs] *n* avarice *f*.

Ave. (*abbr of* avenue) av.

avenge [ə'vendʒ] *vt* venger.

avenue ['ævənjuː] *n* avenue *f*.

average ['ævərɪdʒ] ◇ *adj* moyen(enne). ◇ *n* moyenne *f* ; **on ~** en moyenne. ◇ *vt* : the cars were averaging 90 mph les voitures roulaient en moyenne à 150 km/h.
➧ **average out** *vi* : to ~ out at donner la moyenne de.

aversion [ə'vɜːʃn] *n* : ~ (to) aversion *f* (pour).

avert [ə'vɜːt] *vt* - 1. [avoid] écarter ; [accident] empêcher - 2. [eyes, glance] détourner.

aviary ['eɪvjərɪ] *n* volière *f*.

avid ['ævɪd] *adj* : ~ (for) avide (de).

avocado [ˌævə'kɑːdəʊ] (*pl* -s OR -es) *n* : ~ (pear) avocat *m*.

avoid [ə'vɔɪd] *vt* éviter ; to ~ doing sthg éviter de faire qqch.

avoidance [ə'vɔɪdəns] *n* ➪ **tax avoidance**.

await [ə'weɪt] *vt* attendre.

awake [ə'weɪk] (*pt* awoke OR awaked, *pp* awoken) ◇ *adj* [not sleeping] réveillé(e) ; are you ~? tu dors? ◇ *vt* - 1. [wake up] réveiller - 2. *fig* [feeling] éveiller. ◇ *vi* - 1. [wake up] se réveiller - 2. *fig* [feeling] s'éveiller.

awakening [ə'weɪknɪŋ] *n* - 1. [from sleep] réveil *m* - 2. *fig* [of feeling] éveil *m*.

award [ə'wɔːd] ◇ *n* [prize] prix *m*. ◇ *vt* : to ~ sb sthg, to ~ sthg to sb [prize] décerner qqch à qqn ; [compensation, free kick] accorder qqch à qqn.

aware [ə'weər] *adj* : to be ~ of sthg se rendre compte de qqch, être conscient(e) de qqch ; to be ~ that se rendre compte que, être conscient que.

awareness [ə'weənɪs] *n* (U) conscience *f*.

awash [ə'wɒʃ] *adj lit & fig* : ~ (with) inondé(e) (de).

away [ə'weɪ] ◇ *adv* - 1. [in opposite direction] : to move OR walk ~ (from) s'éloigner (de) ; to look ~ détourner le regard ; to turn ~ se détourner - 2. [in distance] : we live 4 miles ~ (from here) nous habitons à 6 kilomètres (d'ici) - 3. [in time] : the elections are a month ~ les élections se dérouleront dans un mois - 4. [absent] absent(e) ; she's ~ on holiday elle est partie en vacances - 5. [in safe place] : to put sthg ~ ranger qqch - 6. [so as to be gone or used up] : to fade ~ disparaître ; to give sthg ~ donner qqch, faire don de qqch ; to take sthg ~ emporter qqch - 7. [continuously] : to be working ~ travailler sans arrêt. ◇ *adj* SPORT [team, fans] de l'équipe des visiteurs ; ~ game match *m* à l'extérieur.

awe [ɔː] *n* respect *m* mêlé de crainte ; to be in ~ of sb être impressionné(e) par qqn.

awesome ['ɔːsəm] *adj* impressionnant(e).

awful ['ɔːfʊl] *adj* - 1. [terrible] affreux (euse) - 2. *inf* [very great] : an ~ lot (of) énormément (de).

awfully ['ɔːflɪ] *adv inf* [bad, difficult] affreusement ; [nice, good] extrêmement.

awhile [ə'waɪl] *adv* un moment.

awkward ['ɔːkwəd] *adj* - 1. [clumsy] gauche, maladroit(e) - 2. [embarrassed] mal à l'aise, gêné(e) - 3. [difficult - person, problem, task] difficile - 4. [inconvenient] incommode - 5. [embarrassing] embarrassant(e), gênant(e).

awning ['ɔːnɪŋ] *n* - 1. [of tent] auvent *m* - 2. [of shop] banne *f*.

awoke [ə'wəʊk] *pt* ⊳ awake.

awoken [ə'wəʊkn] *pp* ⊳ awake.

awry [ə'raɪ] ⟨⟩ *adj* de travers. ⟨⟩ *adv* : **to go ~** aller de travers, mal tourner.

axe *Br*, **ax** *Am* [æks] ⟨⟩ *n* hache *f.* ⟨⟩ *vt* [project] abandonner ; [jobs] supprimer.

axes ['æksiːz] *pl* ⊳ axis.

axis ['æksɪs] (*pl* axes ['æksiːz]) *n* axe *m.*

axle ['æksl] *n* essieu *m.*

aye [aɪ] ⟨⟩ *adv* oui. ⟨⟩ *n* oui *m* ; [in voting] voix *f* pour.

azalea [ə'zeɪljə] *n* azalée *f.*

Azores [ə'zɔːz] *npl* : **the ~** les Açores *fpl.*

b (*pl* b's OR bs), **B** (*pl* B's OR Bs) [biː] *n* [letter] b *m inv*, B *m inv*. ◆ **B** *n* - 1. MUS si *m* - 2. SCH [mark] B *m inv.*

BA *n abbr of* Bachelor of Arts.

babble ['bæbl] ⟨⟩ *n* [of voices] murmure *m*, rumeur *f.* ⟨⟩ *vi* [person] babiller.

baboon [bə'buːn] *n* babouin *m.*

baby ['beɪbɪ] *n* - 1. [child] bébé *m* - 2. *inf* [darling] chéri *m*, -e *f.*

baby buggy *n* - 1. *Br* [foldable pushchair] poussette *f* - 2. *Am* = baby carriage.

baby carriage *n Am* landau *m.*

baby-sit *vi* faire du baby-sitting.

baby-sitter [-,sɪtə'] *n* baby-sitter *mf.*

bachelor ['bætʃələ'] *n* célibataire *m.*

Bachelor of Arts *n* [degree] ≃ licence *f* en OR ès lettres ; [person] ≃ licencié *m*, -e *f* en OR ès lettres.

Bachelor of Science *n* [degree] ≃ licence *f* en OR ès sciences ; [person] ≃ licencié *m*, -e *f* en OR ès science.

back [bæk] ⟨⟩ *adv* - 1. [backwards] en arrière ; **to step/move ~** reculer ; **to push ~** repousser - 2. [to former position or state] : **I'll be ~ at five** je rentrerai OR serai de retour à dix-sept heures ; **I'd like my money ~** [in shop] je voudrais me faire rembourser ; **to go ~** retourner ; **to come ~** revenir, rentrer ; **to drive ~** rentrer en voiture ; **to go ~ to sleep** se rendormir ; **to go ~ and forth** [person] faire des allées et venues ; **to be ~ (in fashion)** revenir à la mode - 3. [in time] : **to think ~ (to)** se souvenir (de) - 4. [in return] : **to phone** OR **call ~** rappeler. ⟨⟩ *n* - 1. [of person, animal] dos *m* ; **behind sb's ~** *fig* derrière le dos de qqn - 2. [of door, book, hand] dos *m* ; [of head] derrière *m* ; [of envelope, cheque] revers *m* ; [of page] verso *m* ; [of chair] dossier *m* - 3. [of room, fridge] fond *m* ; [of car] arrière *m* - 4. SPORT arrière *m.* ⟨⟩ *adj (in compounds)* - 1. [at the back] de derrière ; [seat, wheel] arrière *(inv)* ; [page] dernier(ère) - 2. [overdue] : **~ rent** arriéré *m* de loyer. ⟨⟩ *vt* - 1. [reverse] reculer - 2. [support] appuyer, soutenir - 3. [bet on] parier sur, miser sur. ⟨⟩ *vi* reculer. ◆ **back to back** *adv* - 1. [stand] dos à dos - 2. [happen] l'un après l'autre. ◆ **back to front** *adv* à l'envers. ◆ **back down** *vi* céder. ◆ **back out** *vi* [of promise etc] se dédire. ◆ **back up** ⟨⟩ *vt sep* - 1. [support - claim] appuyer, soutenir ; [- person] épauler, soutenir - 2. [reverse] reculer - 3. COMPUT sauvegarder, faire une copie de sauvegarde de. ⟨⟩ *vi* [reverse] reculer.

backache ['bækeɪk] *n* : **to have** *Br*, **to have a ~** *Am* avoir mal aux reins OR au dos.

backbencher [,bæk'bentʃə'] *n Br* POL *député qui n'a aucune position officielle au gouvernement ni dans aucun parti.*

backbone ['bækbəʊn] *n* épine *f* dorsale, colonne *f* vertébrale ; *fig* [main support] pivot *m.*

backcloth ['bækklɒθ] *Br* = backdrop.

backdate [,bæk'deɪt] *vt* antidater.

back door *n* porte *f* de derrière.

backdrop ['bækdrɒp] *n lit & fig* toile *f* de fond.

backfire [,bæk'faɪə'] *vi* - 1. AUT pétarader - 2. [plan] : **to ~ (on sb)** se retourner (contre qqn).

backgammon ['bæk,gæmən] *n* backgammon *m*, ≃ jacquet *m.*

background ['bækgraʊnd] *n* - 1. [in picture, view] arrière-plan *m* ; **in the ~** dans le fond, à l'arrière-plan ; *fig* au second plan - 2. [of event, situation] contexte *m* - 3. [upbringing] milieu *m.*

backhand ['bækhænd] *n* TENNIS revers *m.*

backhanded ['bækhændɪd] *adj fig* ambigu(ë), équivoque.

backhander ['bækhændə'] *n Br inf* pot-de-vin *m.*

backing ['bækɪŋ] *n* - 1. [support] soutien *m* - 2. [lining] doublage *m.*

backlash ['bæklæʃ] *n* contrecoup *m*, choc *m* en retour.

backlog ['bæklɒg] *n* : **~ (of work)** arriéré *m* de travail, travail *m* en retard.

back number *n* vieux numéro *m*.

backpack ['bækpæk] *n* sac *m* à dos.

back pay *n* rappel *m* de salaire.

back seat *n* [in car] siège *m* OR banquette *f* arrière ; **to take a ~** *fig* jouer un rôle secondaire.

backside [ˌbæk'saɪd] *n inf* postérieur *m*, derrière *m*.

backstage [ˌbæk'steɪdʒ] *adv* dans les coulisses.

back street *n* petite rue *f*.

backstroke ['bækstrəʊk] *n* dos *m* crawlé.

backup ['bækʌp] ◇ *adj* [plan, team] de secours, de remplacement. ◇ *n* - **1.** [gen] aide *f*, soutien *m* - **2.** COMPUT (copie *f* de) sauvegarde *f*.

backward ['bækwəd] ◇ *adj* - **1.** [movement, look] en arrière - **2.** [country] arriéré(e) ; [person] arriéré, attardé(e). ◇ *adv Am* = **backwards**.

backwards ['bækwədz], **backward** *Am* ['bækwəd] *adv* [move, go] en arrière, à reculons ; [read list] à rebours, à l'envers ; **~ and forwards** [movement] de va-et-vient, d'avant en arrière et d'arrière en avant ; **to walk ~ and forwards** aller et venir.

backwater ['bækˌwɔːtər] *n fig* désert *m*.

backyard [ˌbæk'jɑːd] *n* - **1.** *Br* [yard] arrière-cour *f* - **2.** *Am* [garden] jardin *m* de derrière.

bacon ['beɪkən] *n* bacon *m*.

bacteria [bæk'tɪərɪə] *npl* bactéries *fpl*.

bad [bæd] (*compar* **worse**, *superl* **worst**) ◇ *adj* - **1.** [not good] mauvais(e) ; **to be ~ at sthg** être mauvais en qqch ; **too ~!** dommage! , *not* ~ pas mal - **2.** [unhealthy] malade ; **smoking is ~ for you** fumer est mauvais pour la santé ; **I'm feeling ~** je ne suis pas dans mon assiette - **3.** [serious] : **a ~ cold** un gros rhume - **4.** [rotten] pourri(e), gâté(e) ; **to go ~** se gâter, s'avarier - **5.** [guilty] : **to feel ~ about sthg** se sentir coupable de qqch - **6.** [naughty] méchant(e). ◇ *adv Am* = **badly**.

badge [bædʒ] *n* - **1.** [metal, plastic] badge *m* - **2.** [sewn-on] écusson *m*.

badger ['bædʒər] ◇ *n* blaireau *m*. ◇ *vt* : **to ~ sb (to do sthg)** harceler qqn (pour qu'il fasse qqch).

badly ['bædlɪ] (*compar* **worse**, *superl* **worst**) *adv* - **1.** [not well] mal - **2.** [seriously - wounded] grièvement ; [- affected] gravement, sérieusement ; **to be ~ in need of sthg** avoir vraiment OR absolument besoin de qqch.

badly-off *adj* [poor] pauvre, dans le besoin.

bad-mannered [-'mænəd] *adj* [child] mal élevé(e) ; [shop assistant] impoli(e).

badminton ['bædmɪntən] *n* badminton *m*.

bad-tempered [-'tempəd] *adj* - **1.** [by nature] qui a mauvais caractère - **2.** [in a bad mood] de mauvaise humeur.

baffle ['bæfl] *vt* déconcerter, confondre.

bag [bæg] ◇ *n* - **1.** [gen] sac *m* ; **to pack one's ~s** *fig* plier bagage - **2.** [handbag] sac *m* à main. ◇ *vt Br inf* [reserve] garder. ⬥ **bags** *npl* - **1.** [under eyes] poches *fpl* - **2.** *inf* [lots] : **~s of** plein OR beaucoup de.

bagel ['beɪgəl] *n* petit pain en couronne.

baggage ['bægɪdʒ] *n (U)* bagages *mpl*.

baggage reclaim *n* retrait *m* des bagages.

baggy ['bægɪ] *adj* ample.

bagpipes ['bægpaɪps] *npl* cornemuse *f*.

Bahamas [bə'hɑːməz] *npl* : **the ~** les Bahamas *fpl*.

bail [beɪl] *n (U)* caution *f* ; **on ~** sous caution. ⬥ **bail out** ◇ *vt sep* - **1.** [pay bail for] se porter garant(e) de - **2.** *fig* [rescue] tirer d'affaire. ◇ *vi* [from plane] sauter (en parachute).

bailiff ['beɪlɪf] *n* huissier *m*.

bait [beɪt] ◇ *n* appât *m*. ◇ *vt* - **1.** [put bait on] appâter - **2.** [tease] tourmenter.

bake [beɪk] ◇ *vt* - **1.** CULIN faire cuire au four - **2.** [clay, bricks] cuire. ◇ *vi* [food] cuire au four.

baked beans [beɪkt-] *npl* haricots *mpl* blancs à la tomate.

baked potato [beɪkt-] *n* pomme *f* de terre en robe des champs OR de chambre.

baker ['beɪkər] *n* boulanger *m*, ère *f* ; **~'s (shop)** boulangerie *f*.

bakery ['beɪkərɪ] *n* boulangerie *f*.

baking ['beɪkɪŋ] *n* cuisson *f*.

balaclava (helmet) [ˌbælə'klɑːvə-] *n Br* passe-montagne *m*.

balance ['bæləns] ◇ *n* - **1.** [equilibrium] équilibre *m* ; **to keep/lose one's ~** garder/perdre l'équilibre ; **off ~** déséquilibré(e) - **2.** *fig* [counterweight] contrepoids *m* ; [of evidence] poids *m*, force *f* - **3.** [scales] balance *f* - **4.** FIN solde *m*. ◇ *vt* - **1.** [keep in balance] maintenir en équilibre - **2.** [compare] : **to ~ sthg against sthg** mettre qqch et qqch en balance - **3.** [in accounting] : **to ~ a budget** équilibrer un budget ; **to ~ the books** clôturer les comptes, dresser le bilan. ◇ *vi* - **1.** [maintain equilibrium] se tenir en équilibre - **2.** [budget, accounts] s'équilibrer. ➡ **on balance** *adv* tout bien considéré.

balanced diet [ˌbælənst-] *n* alimentation *f* équilibrée.

balance of payments *n* balance *f* des paiements.

balance of trade *n* balance *f* commerciale.

balance sheet *n* bilan *m*.

balcony ['bælkənɪ] *n* balcon *m*.

bald [bɔːld] *adj* - **1.** [head, man] chauve - **2.** [tyre] lisse - **3.** *fig* [blunt] direct(e).

bale [beɪl] *n* balle *f*. ➡ **bale out** *Br* <> *vt sep* [boat] écoper, vider. <> *vi* [from plane] sauter en parachute.

Balearic Islands [ˌbælɪˈærɪk-], **Balearics** [ˌbælɪˈærɪks] *npl* : **the ~** les Baléares *fpl*.

baleful ['beɪlful] *adj* sinistre.

balk [bɔːk] *vi* : **to ~ (at)** hésiter OR reculer (devant).

Balkans ['bɔːlkənz], **Balkan States** ['bɔːlkən-] *npl* : **the ~** les Balkans *mpl*, les États-*m* balkaniques.

ball [bɔːl] *n* - **1.** [round shape] boule *f* ; [in game] balle *f* ; [football] ballon *m* ; **to be on the ~** *fig* connaître son affaire, s'y connaître - **2.** [of foot] plante *f* - **3.** [dance] bal *m*. ➡ **balls** *vulg* <> *npl* [testicles] couilles *fpl*. <> *n* (U) [nonsense] conneries *fpl*.

ballad ['bæləd] *n* ballade *f*.

ballast ['bæləst] *n* lest *m*.

ball bearing *n* roulement *m* à billes.

ball boy *n* ramasseur *m* de balles.

ballerina [ˌbæləˈriːnə] *n* ballerine *f*.

ballet ['bæleɪ] *n* - **1.** (U) [art of dance] danse *f* - **2.** [work] ballet *m*.

ballet dancer *n* danseur *m*, -euse *f* de ballet.

ball game *n* - **1.** *Am* [baseball match] match *m* de base-ball - **2.** *inf* [situation] : **it's a whole new ~** c'est une autre paire de manches.

balloon [bəˈluːn] *n* - **1.** [gen] ballon *m* - **2.** [in cartoon] bulle *f*.

ballot ['bælət] <> *n* - **1.** [voting paper] bulletin *m* de vote - **2.** [voting process] scrutin *m*. <> *vt* appeler à voter.

ballot box *n* - **1.** [container] urne *f* - **2.** [voting process] scrutin *m*.

ballot paper *n* bulletin *m* de vote.

ball park *n* *Am* terrain *m* de base-ball.

ballpoint (pen) ['bɔːlpɔɪnt-] *n* stylo *m* à bille.

ballroom ['bɔːlrum] *n* salle *f* de bal.

ballroom dancing *n* (U) danse *f* de salon.

balm [baːm] *n* baume *m*.

balmy ['baːmɪ] *adj* doux (douce).

balsa(wood) ['bɒlsə(wud)] *n* balsa *m*.

balti ['bɔːltɪ] *n* [pan] *récipient métallique utilisé dans la cuisine indienne* ; [food] *plat épicé préparé dans un 'balti'*.

Baltic ['bɔːltɪk] <> *adj* [port, coast] de la Baltique. <> *n* : **the ~ (Sea)** la Baltique.

Baltic Republic *n* : **the ~s** les républiques *fpl* baltes.

bamboo [bæmˈbuː] *n* bambou *m*.

bamboozle [bæmˈbuːzl] *vt* *inf* embobiner.

ban [bæn] <> *n* interdiction *f* ; **there is a ~ on smoking** il est interdit de fumer. <> *vt* interdire ; **to ~ sb from doing sthg** interdire à qqn de faire qqch.

banal [bəˈnaːl] *adj* *pej* banal(e), ordinaire.

banana [bəˈnaːnə] *n* banane *f*.

band [bænd] *n* - **1.** [MUS - rock] groupe *m* ; [- military] fanfare *f* ; [- jazz] orchestre *m* - **2.** [group, strip] bande *f* - **3.** [stripe] rayure *f* - **4.** [range] tranche *f*. ➡ **band together** *vi* s'unir.

bandage ['bændɪdʒ] <> *n* bandage *m*, bande *f*. <> *vt* mettre un pansement OR un bandage sur.

Band-Aid® *n* pansement *m* adhésif.

b and b, B and B *n* *abbr of* **bed and breakfast**.

bandit ['bændɪt] *n* bandit *m*.

bandstand ['bændstænd] *n* kiosque *m* à musique.

bandwagon ['bændwægən] *n* : **to jump on the ~** suivre le mouvement.

bandy ['bændɪ] *adj* qui a les jambes arquées. ➡ **bandy about, bandy around** *vt sep* répandre, faire circuler.

bandy-legged [-ˌlegd] *adj* = **bandy**.

bang [bæŋ] <> *adv* [exactly] : **~ in the middle** en plein milieu ; **to be ~ on time** être pile à l'heure. <> *n* - **1.** [blow] coup *m* violent - **2.** [of gun etc] détonation *f* ; [of door] claquement *m*. <> *vt* frapper violemment ; [door] claquer ; **to ~ one's head/knee** se cogner la tête/le genou. <> *vi* - **1.** [knock] : **to ~ on** frapper à - **2.** [make a loud noise - gun etc] détoner ; [- door] claquer - **3.** [crash] : **to ~ into** se cogner contre. <> *excl* boum ! ➡ **bangs** *npl* *Am* frange *f*.

banger ['bæŋəʳ] *n* *Br* - **1.** *inf* [sausage] saucisse *f* - **2.** *inf* [old car] vieille guimbarde *f* - **3.** [firework] pétard *m*.

bangle ['bæŋgl] *n* bracelet *m*.

banish ['bænɪʃ] *vt* bannir.

banister ['bænɪstəʳ] *n*, **banisters** ['bænɪstəz] *npl* rampe *f*.

bank [bæŋk] ◇ *n* - 1. FIN & *fig* banque *f* - 2. [of river, lake] rive *f*, bord *m* - 3. [of earth] talus *m* - 4. [of clouds] masse *f* ; [of fog] nappe *f*. ◇ *vt* FIN mettre OR déposer à la banque. ◇ *vi* - 1. FIN : **to ~ with** avoir un compte à - 2. [plane] tourner. ◆ **bank on** *vt fus* compter sur.

bank account *n* compte *m* en banque.

bank balance *n* solde *m* bancaire.

bank card = banker's card.

bank charges *npl* frais *mpl* bancaires.

bank draft *n* traite *f* bancaire.

banker ['bæŋkəʳ] *n* banquier *m*.

banker's card *n* Br carte *f* d'identité bancaire.

bank holiday *n* Br jour *m* férié.

banking ['bæŋkɪŋ] *n* : **to go into ~** travailler dans la banque.

bank manager *n* directeur *m*, -trice *f* de banque.

bank note *n* billet *m* de banque.

bank rate *n* taux *m* d'escompte.

bankrupt ['bæŋkrʌpt] *adj* failli(e) ; **to go ~** faire faillite.

bankruptcy ['bæŋkrəptsɪ] *n* [gen] faillite *f*.

bank statement *n* relevé *m* de compte.

banner ['bænəʳ] *n* banderole *f*.

bannister(s) ['bænɪstə(z)] = banister(s).

banquet ['bæŋkwɪt] *n* banquet *m*.

banter ['bæntəʳ] *n* (U) plaisanterie *f*, badinage *m*.

bap [bæp] *n* Br petit pain *m*.

baptism ['bæptɪzm] *n* baptême *m*.

Baptist ['bæptɪst] *n* baptiste *mf*.

baptize, -ise [Br bæp'taɪz, Am 'bæptaɪz] *vt* baptiser.

bar [baːʳ] ◇ *n* - 1. [piece - of gold] lingot *m* ; [- of chocolate] tablette *f* ; **a ~ of soap** une savonnette - 2. [length of wood, metal] barre *f* ; **to be behind ~s** être derrière les barreaux OR sous les verrous - 3. *fig* [obstacle] obstacle *m* - 4. [pub] bar *m* - 5. [counter of pub] comptoir *m*, zinc *m* - 6. MUS mesure *f*. ◇ *vt* - 1. [door, road] barrer ; [window] mettre des barreaux à ; **to ~ sb's way** barrer la route OR le passage à qqn - 2. [ban] interdire, défendre ; **to ~ sb (from)** interdire à qqn (de). ◇ *prep* sauf, excepté ; **~ none** sans exception. ◆ **Bar** *n* JUR : **the Bar** Br le barreau ; Am les avocats *mpl*.

barbaric [baː'bærɪk] *adj* barbare.

barbecue ['baːbɪkjuː] *n* barbecue *m*.

barbed wire [baːbd-] *n* (U) fil *m* de fer barbelé.

barber ['baːbəʳ] *n* coiffeur *m* (pour hommes) ; **~'s (shop)** salon *m* de coiffure (pour hommes) ; **to go to the ~'s** aller chez le coiffeur.

barbiturate [baː'bɪtjʊrət] *n* barbiturique *m*.

bar code *n* code *m* à barres, code-barres *m*.

bare [beəʳ] ◇ *adj* - 1. [feet, arms etc] nu(e) ; [trees, hills etc] dénudé(e) - 2. [absolute, minimum] : **the ~ facts** les simples faits ; **the ~ minimum** le strict minimum - 3. [empty] vide. ◇ *vt* découvrir ; **to ~ one's teeth** montrer les dents.

bareback ['beəbæk] *adv* à cru, à nu.

barefaced ['beəfeɪst] *adj* éhonté(e).

barefoot(ed) [ˌbeə'fʊt(ɪd)] ◇ *adj* aux pieds nus. ◇ *adv* nu-pieds, pieds nus.

barely ['beəlɪ] *adv* [scarcely] à peine, tout juste.

bargain ['baːgɪn] ◇ *n* - 1. [agreement] marché *m* ; **into the ~** en plus, par-dessus le marché - 2. [good buy] affaire *f*, occasion *f*. ◇ *vi* négocier ; **to ~ with sb for sthg** négocier qqch avec qqn. ◆ **bargain for, bargain on** *vt fus* compter sur, prévoir.

barge [baːdʒ] ◇ *n* péniche *f*. ◇ *vi inf* : **to ~ past sb** bousculer qqn. ◆ **barge in** *vi inf* : **to ~ in (on)** interrompre.

baritone ['bærɪtəʊn] *n* baryton *m*.

bark [baːk] ◇ *n* - 1. [of dog] aboiement *m* - 2. [on tree] écorce *f*. ◇ *vi* [dog] : **to ~ (at)** aboyer (après).

barley ['baːlɪ] *n* orge *f*.

barley sugar *n* Br sucre *m* d'orge.

barley water *n* Br orgeat *m*.

barmaid ['baːmeɪd] *n* barmaid *f*, serveuse *f* de bar.

barman ['baːmən] (*pl* -men [-mən]) *n* barman *m*, serveur *m* de bar.

barn [baːn] *n* grange *f*.

barometer [bə'rɒmɪtəʳ] *n* *lit* & *fig* baromètre *m*.

baron ['bærən] *n* baron *m*.

baroness ['bærənɪs] *n* baronne *f*.

barrack ['bærək] *vt* Br huer, conspuer. ◆ **barracks** *npl* caserne *f*.

barrage [Br 'bæraːʒ, Am bæ'raːz] *n* - 1. [of firing] barrage *m* - 2. [of questions etc] avalanche *f*, déluge *m* - 3. Br [dam] barrage *m*.

barrel ['bærəl] *n* - 1. [for beer, wine] tonneau *m*, fût *m* - **2.** [for oil] baril *m* - **3.** [of gun] canon *m*.

barren ['bærən] *adj* stérile.

barricade [ˌbærɪ'keɪd] *n* barricade *f*.

barrier ['bærɪəʳ] *n lit & fig* barrière *f*.

barring ['bɑːrɪŋ] *prep* sauf.

barrister ['bærɪstəʳ] *n Br* avocat *m*, -e *f*.

barrow ['bærəʊ] *n* brouette *f*.

bartender ['bɑːtendəʳ] *n Am* barman *m*.

barter ['bɑːtəʳ] ⋄ *n* troc *m*. ⋄ *vt* : **to ~ sthg (for)** troquer OR échanger qqch (contre). ⋄ *vi* faire du troc.

base [beɪs] ⋄ *n* base *f*. ⋄ *vt* baser ; **to ~ sthg on** OR **upon** baser OR fonder qqch sur. ⋄ *adj* indigne, ignoble.

baseball ['beɪsbɔːl] *n* base-ball *m*.

baseball cap *n* casquette *f* de base-ball.

Basel ['bɑːzl] *n* Bâle *f*.

basement ['beɪsmənt] *n* sous-sol *m*.

base rate *n* taux *m* de base.

bases ['beɪsiːz] *pl* ⋈ **basis**.

bash [bæʃ] *inf* ⋄ *n* - **1.** [painful blow] coup *m* - **2.** [attempt] : **to have a ~** tenter le coup. ⋄ *vt* [hit - gen] frapper, cogner ; [- car] percuter.

bashful ['bæʃfʊl] *adj* timide.

basic ['beɪsɪk] *adj* fondamental(e) ; [vocabulary, salary] de base. ◆ **basics** *npl* [rudiments] éléments *mpl*, bases *fpl*.

BASIC ['beɪsɪk] (*abbr of* **Beginner's All-purpose Symbolic Instruction Code**) *n* basic *m*.

basically ['beɪsɪklɪ] *adv* - **1.** [essentially] au fond, fondamentalement - **2.** [really] en fait.

basil ['bæzl] *n* basilic *m*.

basin ['beɪsn] *n* - **1.** *Br* [bowl - for cooking] terrine *f* ; [- for washing] cuvette *f* - **2.** [in bathroom] lavabo *m* - **3.** GEOGR bassin *m*.

basis ['beɪsɪs] (*pl* **-ses** [-siːz]) *n* base *f* ; **on the ~ of** sur la base de ; **on a regular ~** de façon régulière ; **to be paid on a weekly/monthly ~** toucher un salaire hebdomadaire/mensuel.

bask [bɑːsk] *vi* : **to ~ in the sun** se chauffer au soleil.

basket ['bɑːskɪt] *n* corbeille *f* ; [with handle] panier *m*.

basketball ['bɑːskɪtbɔːl] *n* basket-ball *m*, basket *m*.

bass [beɪs] ⋄ *adj* bas (basse). ⋄ *n* - **1.** [singer] basse *f* - **2.** [double bass] contrebasse *f* - **3.** = **bass guitar**.

bass drum [beɪs-] *n* grosse caisse *f*.

bass guitar [beɪs-] *n* basse *f*.

bassoon [bə'suːn] *n* basson *m*.

bastard ['bɑːstəd] *n* - **1.** [illegitimate child] bâtard *m*, -e *f*, enfant naturel *m*, enfant naturelle *f* - **2.** *v inf* [unpleasant person] salaud *m*, saligaud *m*.

bastion ['bæstɪən] *n* bastion *m*.

bat [bæt] *n* - **1.** [animal] chauve-souris *f* - **2.** [for cricket, baseball] batte *f* ; [for table-tennis] raquette *f* - **3.** *phr Br fam* : **to do sthg off one's own ~** faire qqch de son propre chef.

batch [bætʃ] *n* - **1.** [of papers] tas *m*, liasse *f* ; [of letters, applicants] série *f* - **2.** [of products] lot *m*.

bated ['beɪtɪd] *adj* : **with ~ breath** en retenant son souffle.

bath [bɑːθ] ⋄ *n* - **1.** [bathtub] baignoire *f* - **2.** [act of washing] bain *m* ; **to have** OR **take a bath** prendre un bain. ⋄ *vt* baigner, donner un bain à. ◆ **baths** *npl Br* piscine *f*.

bathe [beɪð] ⋄ *vt* - **1.** [wound] laver - **2.** [subj : light, sunshine] : **to be ~d in** OR **with** être baigné(e) de. ⋄ *vi* - **1.** [swim] se baigner - **2.** *Am* [take a bath] prendre un bain.

bathing ['beɪðɪŋ] *n (U)* baignade *f*.

bathing cap *n* bonnet *m* de bain.

bathing costume, bathing suit *n* maillot *m* de bain.

bathrobe ['bɑːθrəʊb] *n* [made of towelling] sortie *f* de bain ; [dressing gown] peignoir *m*.

bathroom ['bɑːθrʊm] *n* - **1.** *Br* [room with bath] salle *f* de bains - **2.** *Am* [toilet] toilettes *fpl*.

bath towel *n* serviette *f* de bain.

bathtub ['bɑːθtʌb] *n* baignoire *f*.

baton ['bætən] *n* - **1.** [of conductor] baguette *f* - **2.** [in relay race] témoin *m* - **3.** *Br* [of policeman] bâton *m*, matraque *f*.

batsman ['bætsmən] (*pl* **-men** [-mən]) *n* batteur *m*.

battalion [bə'tæljən] *n* bataillon *m*.

batten ['bætn] *n* planche *f*, latte *f*.

batter ['bætəʳ] ⋄ *n (U)* pâte *f*. ⋄ *vt* battre.

battered ['bætəd] *adj* - **1.** [child, woman] battu(e) - **2.** [car, hat] cabossé(e).

battery ['bætərɪ] *n* batterie *f* ; [of calculator, toy] pile *f*.

battle ['bætl] ⋄ *n* - **1.** [in war] bataille *f* - **2.** [struggle] : **~ (for/against/with)** lutte *f* (pour/contre/avec), combat *m* (pour/contre/avec). ⋄ *vi* : **to ~ (for/against/**

with) se battre (pour/contre/avec), lutter (pour/contre/avec).

battlefield ['bætlfiːld], **battleground** ['bætlgraʊnd] n MIL champ m de bataille.

battlements ['bætlmənts] npl remparts mpl.

battleship ['bætlʃɪp] n cuirassé m.

bauble ['bɔːbl] n babiole f, colifichet m.

baulk [bɔːk] = **balk**.

bawdy ['bɔːdɪ] adj grivois(e), salé(e).

bawl [bɔːl] vt & vi brailler.

bay [beɪ] n - 1. GEOGR baie f - 2. [for loading] aire f (de chargement) - 3. [for parking] place f (de stationnement) - 4. phr : **to keep sb/ sthg at ~** tenir qqn/qqch à distance, tenir qqn/qqch en échec.

bay leaf n feuille f de laurier.

bay window n fenêtre f en saillie.

bazaar [bə'zɑːʳ] n - 1. [market] bazar m - 2. Br [charity sale] vente f de charité.

B & B n abbr of **bed and breakfast**.

BBC (abbr of **British Broadcasting Corporation**) n office national britannique de radiodiffusion.

BC (abbr of **before Christ**) av. J.-C.

be [biː] (pt was OR were, pp been) <> aux vb - 1. (in combination with ppr : to form cont tense) : **what is he doing?** qu'est-ce qu'il fait? ; **it's snowing** il neige ; **they've been promising reform for years** ça fait des années qu'ils nous promettent des réformes - 2. (in combination with pp : to form passive) être ; **to ~ loved** être aimé(e) ; **there was no one to ~ seen** il n'y avait personne - 3. (in question tags) : **she's pretty, isn't she?** elle est jolie, n'est-ce pas? ; **the meal was delicious, wasn't it?** le repas était délicieux, non? OR vous n'avez pas trouvé? - 4. (followed by 'to' + infin). **I'm to ~ promoted** je vais avoir de l'avancement ; **you're not to tell anyone** ne le dis à personne. <> copulative vb - 1. (with adj, n) être ; **to ~ a doctor/ lawyer/plumber** être médecin/avocat/ plombier ; **she's intelligent/attractive** elle est intelligente/jolie ; **I'm hot/cold** j'ai chaud/froid ; **1 and 1 are 2** 1 et 1 font 2 - 2. [referring to health] aller, se porter ; **to ~ seriously ill** être gravement malade ; **she's better now** elle va mieux maintenant ; **how are you?** comment allez-vous? - 3. [referring to age] : **how old are you?** quel âge avez-vous? ; **I'm 20 (years old)** j'ai 20 ans - 4. [cost] coûter, faire ; **how much was it?** combien cela a-t-il coûté?, combien ça faisait? ; **that will ~ £10, please** cela fait 10 livres, s'il vous plaît. <> vi - 1. [exist] être, exister ; **~ that as it may** quoi qu'il en soit

- 2. [referring to place] être ; **Toulouse is in France** Toulouse se trouve OR est en France ; **he will ~ here tomorrow** il sera là demain - 3. [referring to movement] aller, être ; **I've been to the cinema** j'ai été OR je suis allé au cinéma. <> v impers - 1. [referring to time, dates, distance] être ; **it's two o'clock** il est deux heures ; **it's 3 km to the next town** la ville voisine est à 3 km - 2. [referring to the weather] faire ; **it's hot/cold** il fait chaud/froid ; **it's windy** il y a du vent - 3. [for emphasis] : **it's me/Paul/the milkman** c'est moi/Paul/le laitier.

beach [biːtʃ] <> n plage f. <> vt échouer.

beacon ['biːkən] n - 1. [warning fire] feu m, fanal m - 2. [lighthouse] phare m - 3. [radio beacon] radiophare m.

bead [biːd] n - 1. [of wood, glass] perle f - 2. [of sweat] goutte f.

beagle ['biːgl] n beagle m.

beak [biːk] n bec m.

beaker ['biːkəʳ] n gobelet m.

beam [biːm] n - 1. [of wood, concrete] poutre f - 2. [of light] rayon m. <> vt [signal, news] transmettre. <> vi [smile] faire un sourire radieux.

bean [biːn] n [gen] haricot m ; [of coffee] grain m ; **to be full of ~s** inf péter le feu ; **to spill the ~s** inf manger le morceau.

beanbag ['biːnbæg] n [chair] sacco m.

beanshoot ['biːnʃuːt], **beansprout** ['biːnspraʊt] n germe m OR pousse f de soja.

bear [beəʳ] (pt bore, pp borne) <> n [animal] ours m. <> vt - 1. [carry] porter - 2. [support, tolerate] supporter ; **to ~ responsibility (for)** assumer OR prendre la responsabilité (de) - 3. [feeling] : **to ~ sb a grudge** garder rancune à qqn. <> vi : **to ~ left/right** se diriger vers la gauche/la droite ; **to bring pressure/influence to ~ on sb** exercer une pression/une influence sur qqn. ◆ **bear out** vt sep confirmer, corroborer. ◆ **bear up** vi tenir le coup. ◆ **bear with** vt fus être patient(e) avec.

beard [bɪəd] n barbe f.

bearer ['beərəʳ] n - 1. [gen] porteur m, -euse f - 2. [of passport] titulaire mf.

bearing ['beərɪŋ] n - 1. [connection] : **~ (on)** rapport m (avec) - 2. [deportment] allure f, maintien m - 3. TECH [for shaft] palier m - 4. [on compass] orientation f ; **to get one's ~s** s'orienter, se repérer.

beast [biːst] n - 1. [animal] bête f - 2. inf pej [person] brute f.

beastly ['biːstlɪ] adj dated [person] malveillant(e), cruel(elle) ; [headache, weather] épouvantable.

beat [biːt] (*pt* beat, *pp* beaten) ◇ *n* - **1.** [of heart, drum, wings] battement *m* - **2.** MUS [rhythm] mesure *f*, temps *m* - **3.** [of policeman] ronde *f*. ◇ *vt* - **1.** [gen] battre ; **it ~s me** *inf* ça me dépasse - **2.** [be better than] être bien mieux que, valoir mieux que - **3.** *phr* : ~ **it!** *inf* décampe!, fiche le camp! ◇ *vi* battre. ◆ **beat off** *vt sep* [resist] repousser. ◆ **beat up** *vt sep inf* tabasser.

beating ['biːtɪŋ] *n* - **1.** [blows] raclée *f*, rossée *f* - **2.** [defeat] défaite *f*.

beautiful ['bjuːtɪfʊl] *adj* - **1.** [gen] beau (belle) - **2.** *inf* [very good] joli(e).

beautifully ['bjuːtəflɪ] *adv* - **1.** [attractively - dressed] élégamment ; [- decorated] avec goût - **2.** *inf* [very well] parfaitement, à la perfection.

beauty ['bjuːtɪ] *n* [gen] beauté *f*.

beauty parlour *n* institut *m* de beauté.

beauty salon = beauty parlour.

beauty spot *n* - **1.** [picturesque place] site *m* pittoresque - **2.** [on skin] grain *m* de beauté.

beaver ['biːvəʳ] *n* castor *m*.

became [bɪ'keɪm] *pt* ▷ become.

because [bɪ'kɒz] *conj* parce que. ◆ **because of** *prep* à cause de.

beck [bek] *n* : **to be at sb's ~ and call** être aux ordres OR à la disposition de qqn.

beckon ['bekən] ◇ *vt* [signal to] faire signe à. ◇ *vi* [signal] : **to ~ to sb** faire signe à qqn.

become [bɪ'kʌm] (*pt* became, *pp* become) *vi* devenir ; **to ~ quieter** se calmer ; **to ~ irritated** s'énerver.

becoming [bɪ'kʌmɪŋ] *adj* - **1.** [attractive] seyant(e), qui va bien - **2.** [appropriate] convenable.

bed [bed] *n* - **1.** [to sleep on] lit *m* ; **to go to ~** se coucher ; **to go to ~ with sb** *euphemism* coucher avec qqn - **2.** [flowerbed] parterre *m* - **3.** [of sea, river] lit *m*, fond *m*.

bed and breakfast *n* ≃ chambre *f* d'hôte.

bedclothes ['bedkləʊðz] *npl* draps *mpl* et couvertures *fpl*.

bedlam ['bedləm] *n* pagaille *f*.

bed linen *n* (U) draps *mpl* et taies *fpl*.

bedraggled [bɪ'drægld] *adj* [person] débraillé(e) ; [hair] embroussaillé(e).

bedridden ['bed,rɪdn] *adj* grabataire.

bedroom ['bedrʊm] *n* chambre *f* (à coucher).

bedside ['bedsaɪd] *n* chevet *m*.

bed-sit(ter) *n Br* chambre *f* meublée.

bedsore ['bedsɔːʳ] *n* escarre *f*.

bedspread ['bedspred] *n* couvre-lit *m*, dessus-de-lit *m inv*.

bedtime ['bedtaɪm] *n* heure *f* du coucher.

bee [biː] *n* abeille *f*.

beech [biːtʃ] *n* hêtre *m*.

beef [biːf] *n* bœuf *m*.

beefburger ['biːf,bɜːgəʳ] *n* hamburger *m*.

Beefeater ['biːf,iːtəʳ] *n* hallebardier *m* (de la Tour de Londres).

beefsteak ['biːf,steɪk] *n* bifteck *m*.

beehive ['biːhaɪv] *n* [for bees] ruche *f*.

beeline ['biːlaɪn] *n* : **to make a ~ for** *inf* aller tout droit OR directement vers.

been [biːn] *pp* ▷ be.

beer [bɪəʳ] *n* bière *f*.

beet [biːt] *n* betterave *f*.

beetle ['biːtl] *n* scarabée *m*.

beetroot ['biːtruːt] *n* betterave *f*.

before [bɪ'fɔːʳ] ◇ *adv* auparavant, avant ; **I've never been there** ~ je n'y suis jamais allé(e) ; **I've seen it** ~ je l'ai déjà vu ; **the year** ~ l'année d'avant OR précédente. ◇ *prep* - **1.** [in time] avant - **2.** [in space] devant. ◇ *conj* avant de (+ *infin*), avant que (+ *subjunctive*) ; ~ **leaving** avant de partir ; ~ **you leave** avant que vous ne partiez.

beforehand [bɪ'fɔːhænd] *adv* à l'avance.

befriend [bɪ'frend] *vt* prendre en amitié.

beg [beg] ◇ *vt* - **1.** [money, food] mendier - **2.** [favour] solliciter, quémander ; [forgiveness] demander ; **to ~ sb to do sthg** prier OR supplier qqn de faire qqch. ◇ *vi* - **1.** [for money, food] : **to ~ (for sthg)** mendier (qqch) - **2.** [plead] supplier ; **to ~ for** [forgiveness etc] demander.

began [bɪ'gæn] *pt* ▷ begin.

beggar ['begəʳ] *n* mendiant *m*, -e *f*.

begin [bɪ'gɪn] (*pt* began, *pp* begun) ◇ *vt* commencer ; **to ~ doing** OR **to do sthg** commencer OR se mettre à faire qqch. ◇ *vi* commencer ; **to ~ with** pour commencer, premièrement.

beginner [bɪ'gɪnəʳ] *n* débutant *m*, -e *f*.

beginning [bɪ'gɪnɪŋ] *n* début *m*, commencement *m*.

begrudge [bɪ'grʌdʒ] *vt* - **1.** [envy] : **to ~ sb sthg** envier qqch à qqn - **2.** [do unwillingly] : **to ~ doing sthg** rechigner à faire qqch.

begun [bɪ'gʌn] *pp* ▷ begin.

behalf [bɪ'hɑːf] *n* : **on ~ of** *Br*, **in ~ of** *Am* de la part de, au nom de.

behave [bɪ'heɪv] ◇ *vt* : **to ~ o.s.** bien se conduire OR se comporter. ◇ *vi* - **1.** [in a

particular way] se conduire, se comporter
- **2.** [acceptably] bien se tenir.

behaviour *Br*, **behavior** *Am* [bɪ'heɪvjəʳ]
n conduite *f*, comportement *m*.

behead [bɪ'hed] *vt* décapiter.

beheld [bɪ'held] *pt & pp* ⊳ **behold**.

behind [bɪ'haɪnd] ⟨⟩ *prep* - **1.** [gen] derrière - **2.** [in time] en retard sur. ⟨⟩ *adv*
- **1.** [gen] derrière - **2.** [in time] en retard ; **to
leave sthg ~** oublier qqch ; **to stay ~** rester ;
to be ~ with sthg être en retard dans qqch.
⟨⟩ *n inf* derrière *m*, postérieur *m*.

behold [bɪ'həʊld] (*pt & pp* **beheld**) *vt literary* voir, regarder.

beige [beɪʒ] ⟨⟩ *adj* beige. ⟨⟩ *n* beige *m*.

being ['biːɪŋ] *n* - **1.** [creature] être *m* - **2.** [ex-
istence] : **in ~** existant(e) ; **to come into ~**
voir le jour, prendre naissance.

Beirut [ˌbeɪ'ruːt] *n* Beyrouth.

belated [bɪ'leɪtɪd] *adj* tardif(ive).

belch [beltʃ] ⟨⟩ *n* renvoi *m*, rot *m*. ⟨⟩ *vt*
[smoke, fire] vomir, cracher. ⟨⟩ *vi* [person]
éructer, roter.

beleaguered [bɪ'liːgəd] *adj* assiégé(e) ;
fig harcelé(e), tracassé(e).

Belgian ['beldʒən] ⟨⟩ *adj* belge. ⟨⟩ *n* Belge
mf.

Belgium ['beldʒəm] *n* Belgique *f* ; **in ~** en
Belgique.

Belgrade [ˌbel'greɪd] *n* Belgrade.

belie [bɪ'laɪ] (*cont* **belying**) *vt* - **1.** [disprove]
démentir - **2.** [give false idea of] donner une
fausse idée de.

belief [bɪ'liːf] *n* - **1.** [faith, certainty] : **~ (in)**
croyance *f* (en) - **2.** [principle, opinion] opinion *f*, conviction *f*.

believe [bɪ'liːv] ⟨⟩ *vt* croire ; **~ it or not** tu
ne me croiras peut-être pas. ⟨⟩ *vi* croire ;
to ~ in sb croire en qqn ; **to ~ in sthg** croire
à qqch.

believer [bɪ'liːvəʳ] *n* - **1.** RELIG croyant *m*,
-e *f* - **2.** [in idea, action] : **~ in** partisan *m*, -e *f*
de.

belittle [bɪ'lɪtl] *vt* dénigrer, rabaisser.

bell [bel] *n* [of church] cloche *f* ; [handbell]
clochette *f* ; [on door] sonnette *f* ; [on bike]
timbre *m*.

belligerent [bɪ'lɪdʒərənt] *adj* - **1.** [at war]
belligérant(e) - **2.** [aggressive] belli-
queux(euse).

bellow ['beləʊ] *vi* - **1.** [person] brailler,
beugler - **2.** [bull] beugler.

bellows ['beləʊz] *npl* soufflet *m*.

belly ['belɪ] *n* [of person] ventre *m* ; [of ani-
mal] panse *f*.

bellyache ['belɪeɪk] *n* mal *m* de ventre.

belly button *n inf* nombril *m*.

belong [bɪ'lɒŋ] *vi* - **1.** [be property] : **to ~ to
sb** appartenir OR être à qqn - **2.** [be mem-
ber] : **to ~ to sthg** être membre de qqch
- **3.** [be in right place] être à sa place ; **that
chair ~s here** ce fauteuil va là.

belongings [bɪ'lɒŋɪŋz] *npl* affaires *fpl*.

beloved [bɪ'lʌvd] *adj* bien-aimé(e).

below [bɪ'ləʊ] ⟨⟩ *adv* - **1.** [lower] en dessous, en bas - **2.** [in text] ci-dessous - **3.** NAUT
en bas. ⟨⟩ *prep* sous, au-dessous de.

belt [belt] ⟨⟩ *n* - **1.** [for clothing] ceinture *f*
- **2.** TECH courroie *f*. ⟨⟩ *vt inf* flanquer une
raclée à.

beltway ['belt,weɪ] *n Am* route *f* périphérique.

bemused [bɪ'mjuːzd] *adj* perplexe.

bench [bentʃ] *n* - **1.** [gen & POL] banc *m*
- **2.** [in lab, workshop] établi *m*.

bend [bend] (*pt & pp* **bent**) ⟨⟩ *n* - **1.** [in
road] courbe *f*, virage *m* - **2.** [in pipe, river]
coude *m* - **3.** *phr* : **round the ~** *inf* dingue, fou
(folle). ⟨⟩ *vt* - **1.** [arm, leg] plier - **2.** [wire,
fork etc] tordre, courber. ⟨⟩ *vi* [person] se
baisser, se courber ; [tree, rod] plier ; **to
~ over backwards for sb** se mettre en quatre pour qqn.

beneath [bɪ'niːθ] ⟨⟩ *adv* dessous, en bas.
⟨⟩ *prep* - **1.** [under] sous - **2.** [unworthy of]
indigne de.

benefactor ['benɪfæktəʳ] *n* bienfaiteur *m*.

beneficial [ˌbenɪ'fɪʃl] *adj* : **~ (to sb)** salutaire (à qqn) ; **~ (to sthg)** utile (à qqch).

beneficiary [ˌbenɪ'fɪʃərɪ] *n* bénéficiaire
mf.

benefit ['benɪfɪt] ⟨⟩ *n* - **1.** [advantage]
avantage *m* ; **for the ~ of** dans l'intérêt de ;
to be to sb's ~, **to be of ~ to sb** être dans
l'intérêt de qqn - **2.** ADMIN [allowance of
money] allocation *f*, prestation *f*. ⟨⟩ *vt* profiter à. ⟨⟩ *vi* : **to ~ from** tirer avantage de,
profiter de.

Benelux ['benɪlʌks] *n* Bénélux *m*.

benevolent [bɪ'nevələnt] *adj* bienveil-
lant(e).

benign [bɪ'naɪn] *adj* - **1.** [person] gentil
(ille), bienveillant(e) - **2.** MED bénin(igne).

bent [bent] ⟨⟩ *pt & pp* ⊳ **bend**. ⟨⟩ *adj*
- **1.** [wire, bar] tordu(e) - **2.** [person, body]
courbé(e), voûté(e) - **3.** *Br inf* [dishonest] vé-
reux(euse) - **4.** [determined] : **to be ~ on doing sthg** vouloir absolument faire qqch,
être décidé(e) à faire qqch. ⟨⟩ *n* : **~ (for)**
penchant *m* (pour).

bequeath [bɪ'kwiːð] *vt lit & fig* léguer.

bequest [bɪ'kwest] *n* legs *m*.

berate [bɪ'reɪt] *vt* réprimander.

bereaved [bɪ'riːvd] (*pl inv*) ◇ *adj* endeuillé(e), affligé(e). ◇ *n* : **the ~** la famille du défunt.

beret ['bereɪ] *n* béret *m*.

berk [bɜːk] *n Br inf* idiot *m*, -e *f*, andouille *f*.

Berlin [bɜː'lɪn] *n* Berlin.

berm [bɜːm] *n Am* bas-côté *m*.

Bermuda [bə'mjuːdə] *n* Bermudes *fpl*.

Bern [bɜːn] *n* Berne.

berry ['berɪ] *n* baie *f*.

berserk [bə'zɜːk] *adj* : **to go ~** devenir fou furieux (folle furieuse).

berth [bɜːθ] ◇ *n* - **1.** [in harbour] poste *m* d'amarrage, mouillage *m* - **2.** [in ship, train] couchette *f*. ◇ *vi* [ship] accoster, se ranger à quai.

beseech [bɪ'siːtʃ] (*pt & pp* **besought** OR **beseeched**) *vt literary* : **to ~ sb (to do sthg)** implorer OR supplier qqn (de faire qqch).

beset [bɪ'set] (*pt & pp* **beset**) ◇ *adj* : **~ with** OR **by** [doubts etc] assailli(e) de. ◇ *vt* assaillir.

beside [bɪ'saɪd] *prep* - **1.** [next to] à côté de, auprès de - **2.** [compared with] comparé(e) à, à côté de - **3.** *phr* : **to be ~ o.s. with anger** être hors de soi ; **to be ~ o.s. with joy** être fou (folle) de joie.

besides [bɪ'saɪdz] ◇ *adv* en outre, en plus. ◇ *prep* en plus de.

besiege [bɪ'siːdʒ] *vt* - **1.** [town, fortress] assiéger - **2.** *fig* [trouble, annoy] assaillir, harceler.

besotted [bɪ'sɒtɪd] *adj* : **~ (with sb)** entiché(e) (de qqn).

besought [bɪ'sɔːt] *pt & pp* ▷ **beseech**.

best [best] ◇ *adj* le meilleur (la meilleure). ◇ *adv* le mieux. ◇ *n* le mieux ; **to do one's ~** faire de son mieux ; **all the ~!** meilleurs souhaits! ; **to be for the ~** être pour le mieux ; **to make the ~ of sthg** s'accommoder de qqch, prendre son parti de qqch. ➧ **at best** *adv* au mieux.

best man *n* garçon *m* d'honneur.

bestow [bɪ'stəʊ] *vt fml* : **to ~ sthg on sb** conférer qqch à qqn.

best-seller *n* [book] best-seller *m*.

bet [bet] (*pt & pp* **bet** OR **-ted**) ◇ *n* pari *m*. ◇ *vt* parier. ◇ *vi* parier ; **I wouldn't ~ on it** *fig* je n'en suis pas sûr(e).

betray [bɪ'treɪ] *vt* trahir.

betrayal [bɪ'treɪəl] *n* [of person] trahison *f*.

better ['betər] ◇ *adj (compar of good)* meilleur(e) ; **to get ~** s'améliorer ; [after illness] se remettre, se rétablir. ◇ *adv (compar of well)* mieux ; **I'd ~ leave** il faut que je parte, je dois partir. ◇ *n* meilleur *m*, -e *f* ; **to get the ~ of sb** avoir raison de qqn. ◇ *vt* améliorer ; **to ~ o.s.** s'élever.

better off *adj* - **1.** [financially] plus à son aise - **2.** [in better situation] mieux.

betting ['betɪŋ] *n (U)* paris *mpl*.

betting shop *n Br* ≃ bureau *m* de P.M.U.

between [bɪ'twiːn] ◇ *prep* entre. ◇ *adv* : **(in) ~** [in space] au milieu ; [in time] dans l'intervalle.

beverage ['bevərɪdʒ] *n fml* boisson *f*.

beware [bɪ'weər] *vi* : **to ~ (of)** prendre garde (à), se méfier (de) ; **~ of ...** attention à ...

bewildered [bɪ'wɪldəd] *adj* déconcerté(e), perplexe.

bewitching [bɪ'wɪtʃɪŋ] *adj* charmeur (euse), ensorcelant(e).

beyond [bɪ'jɒnd] ◇ *prep* - **1.** [in space] au-delà de - **2.** [in time] après, plus tard que - **3.** [exceeding] au-dessus de ; **it's ~ my control** je n'y peux rien ; **it's ~ my responsibility** cela n'entre pas dans le cadre de mes responsabilités. ◇ *adv* au-delà.

bias ['baɪəs] *n* - **1.** [prejudice] préjugé *m*, parti *m* pris - **2.** [tendency] tendance *f*.

biased ['baɪəst] *adj* partial(e) ; **to be ~ towards sb/sthg** favoriser qqn/qqch ; **to be ~ against sb/sthg** défavoriser qqn/qqch.

bib [bɪb] *n* [for baby] bavoir *m*, bavette *f*.

Bible ['baɪbl] *n* : **the ~** la Bible.

bicarbonate of soda [baɪ'kɑːbənət-] *n* bicarbonate *m* de soude.

biceps ['baɪseps] (*pl inv*) *n* biceps *m*.

bicker ['bɪkər] *vi* se chamailler.

bicycle ['baɪsɪkl] ◇ *n* bicyclette *f*, vélo *m*. ◇ *vi* aller à bicyclette OR vélo.

bicycle path *n* piste *f* cyclable.

bicycle pump *n* pompe *f* à vélo.

bid [bɪd] (*pt & pp* **bid**) ◇ *n* - **1.** [attempt] tentative *f* - **2.** [at auction] enchère *f* - **3.** COMM offre *f*. ◇ *vt* [at auction] faire une enchère de. ◇ *vi* - **1.** [at auction] : **to ~ (for)** faire une enchère (pour) - **2.** [attempt] : **to ~ for sthg** briguer qqch.

bidder ['bɪdər] *n* enchérisseur *m*, -euse *f*.

bidding ['bɪdɪŋ] *n (U)* enchères *fpl*.

bide [baɪd] *vt* : **to ~ one's time** attendre son heure OR le bon moment.

bifocals [ˌbaɪ'fəʊklz] *npl* lunettes *fpl* bifocales.

big [bɪg] *adj* - **1.** [gen] grand(e) - **2.** [in

amount, bulk - box, problem, book] **gros** (grosse).

bigamy ['bɪɡəmɪ] *n* bigamie *f*.

big deal *inf* ◇ *n* : it's no ~ ce n'est pas dramatique ; what's the ~? où est le problème? ◇ *excl* tu parles!, et alors?

Big Dipper [-'dɪpəʳ] *n* - **1.** *Br* [rollercoaster] montagnes *fpl* russes - **2.** *Am* ASTRON : the ~ la Grande Ourse.

bigheaded [ˌbɪɡ'hedɪd] *adj inf* crâneur(euse).

bigot ['bɪɡət] *n* sectaire *mf*.

bigoted ['bɪɡətɪd] *adj* sectaire.

bigotry ['bɪɡətrɪ] *n* sectarisme *m*.

big time *n inf* : to make the ~ réussir, arriver en haut de l'échelle.

big toe *n* gros orteil *m*.

big top *n* chapiteau *m*.

big wheel *n Br* [at fairground] grande roue *f*.

bike [baɪk] *n inf* - **1.** [bicycle] vélo *m* - **2.** [motorcycle] bécane *f*, moto *f*.

bikeway ['baɪkweɪ] *n Am* piste *f* cyclable.

bikini [bɪ'kiːnɪ] *n* Bikini® *m*.

bile [baɪl] *n* - **1.** [fluid] bile *f* - **2.** [anger] mauvaise humeur *f*.

bilingual [baɪ'lɪŋɡwəl] *adj* bilingue.

bill [bɪl] ◇ *n* - **1.** [statement of cost] : ~ **(for)** note *f* OR facture *f* (de) ; [in restaurant] addition *f* (de) - **2.** [in parliament] projet *m* de loi - **3.** [of show, concert] programme *m* - **4.** *Am* [banknote] billet *m* de banque - **5.** [poster] : '**post** OR **stick no ~s**' 'défense d'afficher' - **6.** [beak] bec *m*. ◇ *vt* [invoice] : **to ~ sb (for)** envoyer une facture à qqn (pour).

billboard ['bɪlbɔːd] *n* panneau *m* d'affichage.

billet ['bɪlɪt] *n* logement *m* (chez l'habitant).

billfold ['bɪlfəʊld] *n Am* portefeuille *m*.

billiards ['bɪljədz] *n* billard *m*.

billion ['bɪljən] *num* - **1.** *Am* [thousand million] milliard *m* - **2.** *Br* [million million] billion *m*.

Bill of Rights *n* : the ~ les *dix premiers amendements à la Constitution américaine*.

bimbo ['bɪmbəʊ] *(pl* -s OR -es) *n inf pej* : she's a bit of a ~ c'est le genre 'pin-up'.

bin [bɪn] *n* - **1.** *Br* [for rubbish] poubelle *f* - **2.** [for grain, coal] coffre *m*.

bind [baɪnd] *(pt & pp* bound) *vt* - **1.** [tie up] attacher, lier - **2.** [unite - people] lier - **3.** [bandage] panser - **4.** [book] relier - **5.** [constrain] contraindre, forcer.

binder ['baɪndəʳ] *n* [cover] classeur *m*.

binding ['baɪndɪŋ] ◇ *adj* qui lie OR engage ; [agreement] irrévocable. ◇ *n* [on book] reliure *f*.

binge [bɪndʒ] *inf* ◇ *n* : to go on a ~ prendre une cuite. ◇ *vi* : to ~ on sthg se gaver OR se bourrer de qqch.

bingo ['bɪŋɡəʊ] *n* bingo *m*, ≃ loto *m*.

binoculars [bɪ'nɒkjʊləz] *npl* jumelles *fpl*.

biochemistry [ˌbaɪəʊ'kemɪstrɪ] *n* biochimie *f*.

biodegradable [ˌbaɪəʊdɪ'ɡreɪdəbl] *adj* biodégradable.

biography [baɪ'ɒɡrəfɪ] *n* biographie *f*.

biological [ˌbaɪə'lɒdʒɪkl] *adj* biologique ; [washing powder] aux enzymes.

biology [baɪ'ɒlədʒɪ] *n* biologie *f*.

biotechnology [ˌbaɪəʊtek'nɒlədʒɪ] *n* biotechnologie *f*.

birch [bɜːtʃ] *n* [tree] bouleau *m*.

bird [bɜːd] *n* - **1.** [creature] oiseau *m* - **2.** *inf* [woman] gonzesse *f*.

birdie ['bɜːdɪ] *n* - **1.** [bird] petit oiseau *m* - **2.** GOLF birdie *m*.

bird's-eye view *n* vue *f* aérienne.

bird-watcher [ˌwɒtʃəʳ] *n* observateur *m*, -trice *f* d'oiseaux.

Biro® ['baɪərəʊ] *n Br* stylo *m* à bille.

birth [bɜːθ] *n lit & fig* naissance *f* ; to give ~ (to) donner naissance (à).

birth certificate *n* acte *m* OR extrait *m* de naissance.

birth control *n* (U) régulation *f* OR contrôle *m* des naissances.

birthday ['bɜːθdeɪ] *n* anniversaire *m*.

birthmark ['bɜːθmɑːk] *n* tache *f* de vin.

birthrate ['bɜːθreɪt] *n* (taux *m* de) natalité *f*.

Biscay ['bɪskeɪ] *n* : the Bay of ~ le golfe de Gascogne.

biscuit ['bɪskɪt] *n Br* gâteau *m* sec, biscuit *m* ; *Am* scone *m*.

bisect [baɪ'sekt] *vt* couper OR diviser en deux.

bishop ['bɪʃəp] *n* - **1.** RELIG évêque *m* - **2.** [in chess] fou *m*.

bison ['baɪsn] *(pl inv* OR -s) *n* bison *m*.

bit [bɪt] ◇ *pt* ▷ **bite.** ◇ *n* - **1.** [small piece - of paper, cheese etc] morceau *m*, bout *m* ; [- of book, film] passage *m* ; **~s and pieces** *Br* petites affaires *fpl* OR choses *fpl* ; **to take sthg to ~s** démonter qqch - **2.** [amount] : **a ~ of** un peu de ; **it's a ~ of shopping** quelques courses ; **it's a ~ of a nuisance** c'est un peu embêtant ; **a ~ of trouble** un petit problème ; **quite a ~ of** pas mal de, beaucoup de - **3.** [short time] : **for a ~** pendant quelque temps - **4.** [of drill] mèche *f* - **5.** [of bridle] mors *m* - **6.** COMPUT bit *m*. ◆ **a bit** *adv* un peu ; **I'm a ~ tired** je suis un peu fatigué(e). ◆ **bit by bit** *adv* petit à petit.

bitch [bɪtʃ] *n* - **1.** [female dog] chienne *f* - **2.** *v inf pej* [woman] salope *f*, garce *f*.

bitchy [bɪtʃɪ] *adj inf* vache, rosse.

bite [baɪt] (*pt* bit, *pp* bitten) ◇ *n* - **1.** [act of biting] morsure *f*, coup *m* de dent - **2.** *inf* [food] : **to have a ~ (to eat)** manger un morceau - **3.** [wound] piqûre *f*. ◇ *vt* - **1.** [subj : person, animal] mordre - **2.** [subj : insect, snake] piquer, mordre. ◇ *vi* - **1.** [animal, person] : **to ~ (into)** mordre (dans) ; **to ~ off sthg** arracher qqch d'un coup de dents - **2.** [insect, snake] mordre, piquer - **3.** [grip] adhérer, mordre - **4.** *fig* [take effect] se faire sentir.

biting [baɪtɪŋ] *adj* - **1.** [very cold] cinglant(e), piquant(e) - **2.** [humour, comment] mordant(e), caustique.

bitten [bɪtn] *pp* ⊳ bite.

bitter [bɪtəʳ] ◇ *adj* - **1.** [gen] amer(ère) - **2.** [icy] glacial(e) - **3.** [argument] violent(e). ◇ *n Br* bière relativement amère, à forte teneur en houblon.

bitter lemon *n* Schweppes® *m* au citron.

bitterness [bɪtənɪs] *n* - **1.** [gen] amertume *f* - **2.** [of wind, weather] âpreté *f*.

bizarre [bɪˈzɑːʳ] *adj* bizarre.

blab [blæb] *vi inf* lâcher le morceau.

black [blæk] ◇ *adj* noir(e). ◇ *n* - **1.** [colour] noir *m* - **2.** [person] noir *m*, -e *f* - **3.** *phr* : **in ~ and white** [in writing] noir sur blanc, par écrit ; **in the ~** [financially solvent] solvable, sans dettes. ◇ *vt Br* [boycott] boycotter. ◆ **black out** *vi* [faint] s'évanouir.

blackberry [blækbərɪ] *n* mûre *f*.

blackbird [blækbɜːd] *n* merle *m*.

blackboard [blækbɔːd] *n* tableau *m* (noir).

blackcurrant [ˌblækˈkʌrənt] *n* cassis *m*.

blacken [blækn] ◇ *vt* [make dark] noircir. ◇ *vi* s'assombrir.

black eye *n* œil *m* poché OR au beurre noir.

blackhead [blækhed] *n* point *m* noir.

black ice *n* verglas *m*.

blackleg [blækleg] *n Br pej* jaune *m*.

blacklist [blæklɪst] ◇ *n* liste *f* noire. ◇ *vt* mettre sur la liste noire.

blackmail [blækmeɪl] ◇ *n lit & fig* chantage *m*. ◇ *vt* - **1.** [for money] faire chanter - **2.** *fig* [emotionally] faire du chantage à.

black market *n* marché *m* noir.

blackout [blækaut] *n* - **1.** MIL & PRESS black-out *m* - **2.** [power cut] panne *f* d'électricité - **3.** [fainting fit] évanouissement *m*.

black pudding *n Br* boudin *m*.

Black Sea *n* : **the ~** la mer Noire.

black sheep *n* brebis *f* galeuse.

blacksmith [blæksmɪθ] *n* forgeron *m* ; [for horses] maréchal-ferrant *m*.

black spot *n* AUT point *m* noir.

bladder [blædəʳ] *n* vessie *f*.

blade [bleɪd] *n* - **1.** [of knife, saw] lame *f* - **2.** [of propeller] pale *f* - **3.** [of grass] brin *m*.

blame [bleɪm] ◇ *n* responsabilité *f*, faute *f* ; **to take the ~ for sthg** endosser la responsabilité de qqch. ◇ *vt* blâmer, condamner ; **to ~ sthg on** rejeter la responsabilité de qqch sur, imputer qqch à ; **to ~ sb/sthg for sthg** reprocher qqch à qqn/qqch ; **to be to ~ for sthg** être responsable de qqch.

bland [blænd] *adj* - **1.** [person] terne - **2.** [food] fade, insipide - **3.** [music, style] insipide.

blank [blæŋk] ◇ *adj* - **1.** [sheet of paper] blanc (blanche) ; [wall] nu(e) - **2.** *fig* [look] vide, sans expression. ◇ *n* - **1.** [empty space] blanc *m* - **2.** [cartridge] cartouche *f* à blanc.

blank cheque *n* chèque *m* en blanc ; *fig* carte *f* blanche.

blanket [blæŋkɪt] *n* - **1.** [for bed] couverture *f* - **2.** [of snow] couche *f*, manteau *m* ; [of fog] nappe *f*.

blare [bleəʳ] *vi* hurler ; [radio] beugler.

blasphemy [blæsfəmɪ] *n* blasphème *m*.

blast [blɑːst] ◇ *n* - **1.** [explosion] explosion *f* - **2.** [of air, from bomb] souffle *m*. ◇ *vt* [hole, tunnel] creuser à la dynamite. ◇ *excl Br inf* zut!, mince! ◆ **(at) full blast** *adv* [play music etc] à pleins gaz OR tubes ; [work] d'arrache-pied.

blasted [blɑːstɪd] *adj inf* fichu(e), maudit(e).

blast-off *n* SPACE lancement *m*.

blatant [bleɪtənt] *adj* criant(e), flagrant(e).

blaze [bleɪz] ◇ *n* - **1.** [fire] incendie *m* - **2.** *fig* [of colour, light] éclat *m*, flamboiement *m*. ◇ *vi* - **1.** [fire] flamber - **2.** *fig* [with colour] flamboyer.

blazer [bleɪzəʳ] *n* blazer *m*.

bleach [bliːtʃ] ◇ *n* eau *f* de Javel. ◇ *vt* [hair] décolorer ; [clothes] blanchir.

bleached [bliːtʃt] *adj* décoloré(e).

bleachers ['bli:tʃəz] *npl Am* SPORT gradins *mpl*.

bleak [bli:k] *adj* - **1.** [future] sombre - **2.** [place, weather, face] lugubre, triste.

bleary-eyed [ˌblɪərɪˈaɪd] *adj* aux yeux troubles.

bleat [bli:t] ⇔ *n* bêlement *m*. ⇔ *vi* bêler ; *fig* [person] se plaindre, geindre.

bleed [bli:d] (*pt* & *pp* **bled** [bled]) ⇔ *vi* saigner. ⇔ *vt* [radiator etc] purger.

bleeper ['bli:pəʳ] *n* bip *m*, biper *m*.

blemish ['blemɪʃ] *n lit* & *fig* défaut *m*.

blend [blend] ⇔ *n* mélange *m*. ⇔ *vt* : **to ~ sthg (with)** mélanger qqch (avec OR à). ⇔ *vi* : **to ~ (with)** se mêler (à OR avec).

blender ['blendəʳ] *n* mixer *m*.

bless [bles] (*pt* & *pp* **-ed** OR **blest**) *vt* bénir ; **~ you!** [after sneezing] à vos souhaits! ; [thank you] merci mille fois!

blessing ['blesɪŋ] *n lit* & *fig* bénédiction *f*.

blest [blest] *pt* & *pp* ⊏▷ **bless**.

blew [blu:] *pt* ⊏▷ **blow**.

blight [blaɪt] *vt* gâcher, briser.

blimey ['blaɪmɪ] *excl Br inf* zut alors!, mince alors!

blind [blaɪnd] ⇔ *adj lit* & *fig* aveugle ; **to be ~ to sthg** ne pas voir qqch. ⇔ *n* [for window] store *m*. ⇔ *npl* : **the ~** les aveugles *mpl*. ⇔ *vt* aveugler ; **to ~ sb to sthg** *fig* cacher qqch à qqn.

blind alley *n lit* & *fig* impasse *f*.

blind corner *n* virage *m* sans visibilité.

blind date *n* rendez-vous avec quelqu'un qu'on ne connaît pas.

blinders ['blaɪndəz] *npl Am* œillères *fpl*.

blindfold ['blaɪndfəʊld] ⇔ *adv* les yeux bandés. ⇔ *n* bandeau *m*. ⇔ *vt* bander les yeux à.

blindly ['blaɪndlɪ] *adv* [unseeingly] à l'aveuglette, [without thinking] aveuglément.

blindness ['blaɪndnɪs] *n* cécité *f* ; **~ (to sthg)** *fig* aveuglement *m* (devant qqch).

blind spot *n* - **1.** AUT angle *m* mort - **2.** *fig* [inability to understand] blocage *m*.

blink [blɪŋk] ⇔ *n phr* : **on the ~** [machine] détraqué(e). ⇔ *vt* [eyes] cligner. ⇔ *vi* - **1.** [person] cligner des yeux - **2.** [light] clignoter.

blinkered ['blɪŋkəd] *adj* : **to be ~** *lit* & *fig* avoir des œillères.

blinkers ['blɪŋkəz] *npl Br* œillères *fpl*.

bliss [blɪs] *n* bonheur *m* suprême, félicité *f*.

blissful ['blɪsfʊl] *adj* [day, silence] merveilleux(euse) ; [ignorance] total(e).

blister ['blɪstəʳ] ⇔ *n* [on skin] ampoule *f*, cloque *f*. ⇔ *vi* - **1.** [skin] se couvrir d'ampoules - **2.** [paint] cloquer, se boursoufler.

blithely ['blaɪðlɪ] *adv* gaiement, joyeusement.

blitz [blɪts] *n* MIL bombardement *m* aérien.

blizzard ['blɪzəd] *n* tempête *f* de neige.

bloated ['bləʊtɪd] *adj* - **1.** [face] bouffi(e) - **2.** [with food] ballonné(e).

blob [blɒb] *n* - **1.** [drop] goutte *f* - **2.** [indistinct shape] forme *f* ; **a ~ of colour** une tache de couleur.

block [blɒk] ⇔ *n* - **1.** [building] : **office ~** immeuble *m* de bureaux ; **~ of flats** *Br* immeuble *m* - **2.** *Am* [of buildings] pâté *m* de maisons - **3.** [of stone, ice] bloc *m* - **4.** [obstruction] blocage *m*. ⇔ *vt* - **1.** [road, pipe, view] boucher - **2.** [prevent] bloquer, empêcher.

blockade [blɒˈkeɪd] ⇔ *n* blocus *m*. ⇔ *vt* faire le blocus de.

blockage ['blɒkɪdʒ] *n* obstruction *f*.

blockbuster ['blɒkbʌstəʳ] *n inf* [book, film] film *m* à succès.

block capitals *npl* majuscules *fpl* d'imprimerie.

block letters *npl* majuscules *fpl* d'imprimerie.

bloke [bləʊk] *n Br inf* type *m*.

blond [blɒnd] *adj* blond(e).

blonde [blɒnd] ⇔ *adj* blond(e). ⇔ *n* [woman] blonde *f*.

blood [blʌd] *n* sang *m* ; **in cold ~** de sang-froid.

bloodbath ['blʌdbɑːθ, *pl* -bɑːðz] *n* bain *m* de sang, massacre *m*.

blood cell *n* globule *m*.

blood donor *n* donneur *m*, -euse *f* de sang.

blood group *n* groupe *m* sanguin.

bloodhound ['blʌdhaʊnd] *n* limier *m*.

blood poisoning *n* septicémie *f*.

blood pressure *n* tension *f* artérielle ; **to have high ~** faire de l'hypertension.

bloodshed ['blʌdʃed] *n* carnage *m*.

bloodshot ['blʌdʃɒt] *adj* [eyes] injecté(e) de sang.

bloodstream ['blʌdstri:m] *n* sang *m*.

blood test *n* prise *f* de sang.

bloodthirsty ['blʌdˌθɜːstɪ] *adj* sanguinaire.

blood transfusion *n* transfusion *f* sanguine.

bloody ['blʌdɪ] ⟨⟩ *adj* - **1.** [gen] sanglant(e) - **2.** *Br v inf* foutu(e) ; **you ~ idiot!** espèce de con! ⟨⟩ *adv Br v inf* vachement.

bloody-minded [-'maɪndɪd] *adj Br inf* contrariant(e).

bloom [bluːm] ⟨⟩ *n* fleur *f.* ⟨⟩ *vi* fleurir.

blooming ['bluːmɪŋ] ⟨⟩ *adj Br inf* [to show annoyance] sacré(e), fichu(e). ⟨⟩ *adv Br inf* sacrément.

blossom ['blɒsəm] ⟨⟩ *n* [of tree] fleurs *fpl*; **in ~** en fleur(s). ⟨⟩ *vi* - **1.** [tree] fleurir - **2.** *fig* [person] s'épanouir.

blot [blɒt] ⟨⟩ *n lit & fig* tache *f.* ⟨⟩ *vt* - **1.** [paper] faire des pâtés sur - **2.** [ink] sécher. ⬥ **blot out** *vt sep* voiler, cacher ; [memories] effacer.

blotchy ['blɒtʃɪ] *adj* couvert(e) de marbrures OR taches.

blotting paper ['blɒtɪŋ-] *n (U)* (papier *m*) buvard *m*.

blouse [blaʊz] *n* chemisier *m*.

blow [bləʊ] (*pt* **blew**, *pp* **blown**) ⟨⟩ *vi* - **1.** [gen] souffler - **2.** [in wind] : **to ~ off** s'envoler - **3.** [fuse] sauter. ⟨⟩ *vt* - **1.** [subj : wind] faire voler, chasser - **2.** [clear] : **to ~ one's nose** se moucher - **3.** [trumpet] jouer de, souffler dans ; **to ~ a whistle** donner un coup de sifflet, siffler. ⟨⟩ *n* [hit] coup *m*. ⬥ **blow out** ⟨⟩ *vt sep* souffler. ⟨⟩ *vi* - **1.** [candle] s'éteindre - **2.** [tyre] éclater. ⬥ **blow over** *vi* se calmer. ⬥ **blow up** ⟨⟩ *vt sep* - **1.** [inflate] gonfler - **2.** [with bomb] faire sauter - **3.** [photograph] agrandir. ⟨⟩ *vi* exploser.

blow-dry ⟨⟩ *n* Brushing® *m*. ⟨⟩ *vt* faire un Brushing® à.

blowlamp *Br* ['bləʊlæmp], **blowtorch** ['bləʊtɔːtʃ] *n* chalumeau *m*, lampe *f* à souder.

blown [bləʊn] *pp* ⟾ **blow**.

blowout ['bləʊaʊt] *n* [of tyre] éclatement *m*.

blowtorch = blowlamp.

blubber ['blʌbəʳ] ⟨⟩ *n* graisse *f* de baleine. ⟨⟩ *vi pej* chialer.

bludgeon ['blʌdʒən] *vt* matraquer.

blue [bluː] ⟨⟩ *adj* - **1.** [colour] bleu(e) - **2.** *inf* [sad] triste, cafardeux(euse) - **3.** [pornographic] porno *(inv)*. ⟨⟩ *n* bleu *m* ; **out of the ~** [happen] subitement ; [arrive] à l'improviste. ⬥ **blues** *npl* : **the ~s** MUS le blues ; *inf* [sad feeling] le blues, le cafard.

bluebell ['bluːbel] *n* jacinthe *f* des bois.

blueberry ['bluːbərɪ] *n* myrtille *f*.

bluebottle ['bluːˌbɒtl] *n* mouche *f* bleue, mouche de la viande.

blue cheese *n* (fromage *m*) bleu *m*.

blue-collar *adj* manuel(elle).

blue jeans *npl Am* blue-jean *m*, jean *m*.

blueprint ['bluːprɪnt] *n* photocalque *m* ; *fig* plan *m*, projet *m*.

bluff [blʌf] ⟨⟩ *adj* franc (franche). ⟨⟩ *n* - **1.** [deception] bluff *m* ; **to call sb's ~** prendre qqn au mot - **2.** [cliff] falaise *f* à pic. ⟨⟩ *vt* bluffer, donner le change à. ⟨⟩ *vi* faire du bluff, bluffer.

blunder ['blʌndəʳ] ⟨⟩ *n* gaffe *f*, bévue *f.* ⟨⟩ *vi* [make mistake] faire une gaffe, commettre une bévue.

blunt [blʌnt] ⟨⟩ *adj* - **1.** [knife] émoussé(e) ; [pencil] épointé(e) ; [object, instrument] contondant(e) - **2.** [person, manner] direct(e), carré(e). ⟨⟩ *vt lit & fig* émousser.

blur [blɜːʳ] ⟨⟩ *n* forme *f* confuse, tache *f* floue. ⟨⟩ *vt* [vision] troubler, brouiller.

blurb [blɜːb] *n* texte *m* publicitaire.

blurt [blɜːt] ⬥ **blurt out** *vt sep* laisser échapper.

blush [blʌʃ] ⟨⟩ *n* rougeur *f.* ⟨⟩ *vi* rougir.

blusher ['blʌʃəʳ] *n* fard *m* à joues, blush *m*.

blustery ['blʌstərɪ] *adj* venteux(euse).

BMX (*abbr of* **bicycle motorcross**) *n* bicross *m*.

BO *abbr of* **body odour**.

boar [bɔːʳ] *n* - **1.** [male pig] verrat *m* - **2.** [wild pig] sanglier *m*.

board [bɔːd] ⟨⟩ *n* - **1.** [plank] planche *f* - **2.** [for notices] panneau *m* d'affichage - **3.** [for games - gen] tableau *m* ; [- for chess] échiquier *m* - **4.** [blackboard] tableau *m* (noir) - **5.** [of company] : **~ (of directors)** conseil *m* d'administration - **6.** [committee] comité *m*, conseil *m* - **7.** *Br* [at hotel, guesthouse] pension *f* ; **~ and lodging** pension ; **full ~** pension complète ; **half ~** demi-pension *f* - **8.** : **on ~** [on ship, plane, bus, train] à bord - **9.** *phr* : **above ~** régulier(ère), dans les règles. ⟨⟩ *vt* [ship, aeroplane] monter à bord de ; [train, bus] monter dans.

boarder ['bɔːdəʳ] *n* - **1.** [lodger] pensionnaire *mf* - **2.** [at school] interne *mf*, pensionnaire *mf*.

boarding card ['bɔːdɪŋ-] *n* carte *f* d'embarquement.

boardinghouse ['bɔːdɪŋhaʊs, *pl* -haʊzɪz] *n* pension *f* de famille.

boarding school ['bɔːdɪŋ-] *n* pensionnat *m*, internat *m*.

Board of Trade *n Br* : the ~ ≃ le minis-tère *m* du Commerce.

boardroom ['bɔ:drʊm] *n* salle *f* du con-seil (d'administration).

boast [bəʊst] ◇ *n* vantardise *f*, fanfaron-nade *f*. ◇ *vi* : **to ~ (about)** se vanter (de).

boastful ['bəʊstfʊl] *adj* vantard(e), fanfa-ron(onne).

boat [bəʊt] *n* [large] bateau *m* ; [small] ca-not *m*, embarcation *f* ; **by ~** en bateau.

boater ['bəʊtə'] *n* [hat] canotier *m*.

boatswain ['bəʊsn] *n* maître *m* d'équi-page.

bob [bɒb] ◇ *n* - **1.** [hairstyle] coupe *f* au carré - **2.** *Br inf dated* [shilling] shilling *m* - **3.** = bobsleigh. ◇ *vi* [boat, ship] tanguer.

bobbin ['bɒbɪn] *n* bobine *f*.

bobby ['bɒbɪ] *n Br inf* agent *m* de police.

bobsleigh ['bɒbsleɪ] *n* bobsleigh *m*.

bode [bəʊd] *vi literary* : **to ~ ill/well (for)** être de mauvais/bon augure (pour).

bodily ['bɒdɪlɪ] ◇ *adj* [needs] matériel (elle) ; [pain] physique ◇ *adv* [lift, move] à bras-le-corps.

body ['bɒdɪ] *n* - **1.** [of person] corps *m* - **2.** [corpse] corps *m*, cadavre *m* - **3.** [organiz-ation] organisme *m*, organisation *f* - **4.** [of car] carrosserie *f* ; [of plane] fuselage *m* - **5.** *(U)* [of wine] corps *m* - **6.** *(U)* [of hair] vo-lume *m* - **7.** [garment] body *m*.

body building *n* culturisme *m*.

bodyguard ['bɒdɪgɑ:d] *n* garde *m* du corps.

body odour *n* odeur *f* corporelle.

body piercing *n* piercing *m*.

bodywork ['bɒdɪwɜ:k] *n* carrosserie *f*.

bog [bɒg] *n* - **1.** [marsh] marécage *m* - **2.** *Br v inf* [toilet] chiottes *fpl*.

bogged down [bɒgd-] *adj* - **1.** *fig* [in work] : **~ (in)** submergé(e) (de) - **2.** [car etc] : **~ (in)** enlisé(e) (dans).

boggle ['bɒgl] *vi* : **the mind ~s!** ce n'est pas croyable!, on croit rêver!

bogus ['bəʊgəs] *adj* faux (fausse), bidon *(inv)*.

boil [bɔɪl] ◇ *n* - **1.** MED furoncle *m* - **2.** [boiling point] : **to bring sthg to the ~** porter qqch à ébullition ; **to come to the ~** venir à ébullition. ◇ *vt* - **1.** [water, food] faire bouillir - **2.** [kettle] mettre sur le feu. ◇ *vi* [water] bouillir. ◆ **boil down to** *vt fus fig* revenir à, se résumer à. ◆ **boil over** *vi* - **1.** [liquid] déborder - **2.** *fig* [feelings] exploser.

boiled ['bɔɪld] *adj* : **~ egg** œuf *m* à la co-que ; **~ sweet** *Br* bonbon *m* (à sucer).

boiler ['bɔɪlə'] *n* chaudière *f*.

boiler suit *n Br* bleu *m* de travail.

boiling ['bɔɪlɪŋ] *adj* - **1.** [liquid] bouil-lant(e) - **2.** *inf* [weather] très chaud(e), tor-ride ; [person] : **I'm ~ (hot)!** je crève de cha-leur!

boiling point *n* point *m* d'ébullition.

boisterous ['bɔɪstərəs] *adj* turbulent(e), remuant(e).

bold [bəʊld] *adj* - **1.** [confident] hardi(e), audacieux(euse) - **2.** [lines, design] har-di(e) ; [colour] vif (vive), éclatant(e) - **3.** TYPO : **~ type** OR **print** caractères *mpl* gras.

bollard ['bɒlɑ:d] *n* [on road] borne *f*.

bollocks ['bɒləks] *Br v inf* ◇ *npl* couilles *fpl*. ◇ *excl* quelles conneries!

bolster ['bəʊlstə'] ◇ *n* [pillow] traversin *m*. ◇ *vt* renforcer, affirmer. ◆ **bolster up** *vt sep* soutenir, appuyer.

bolt [bəʊlt] ◇ *n* - **1.** [on door, window] verrou *m* - **2.** [type of screw] boulon *m*. ◇ *adv* : **~ upright** droit(e) comme un pi-quet. ◇ *vt* - **1.** [fasten together] boulonner - **2.** [close - door, window] verrouiller - **3.** [food] engouffrer, engloutir. ◇ *vi* [run] détaler.

bomb [bɒm] ◇ *n* bombe *f*. ◇ *vt* bom-barder.

bombard [bɒm'bɑ:d] *vt* MIL & *fig* : **to ~ (with)** bombarder (de).

bombastic [bɒm'bæstɪk] *adj* pom-peux(euse).

bomb disposal squad *n* équipe *f* de dé-minage.

bomber ['bɒmə'] *n* - **1.** [plane] bombardier *m* - **2.** [person] plastiqueur *m*.

bombing ['bɒmɪŋ] *n* bombardement *m*.

bombshell ['bɒmʃel] *n fig* bombe *f*.

bona fide [bəʊnə'faɪdɪ] *adj* véritable, au-thentique ; [offer] sérieux(euse).

bond [bɒnd] ◇ *n* - **1.** [between people] lien *m* - **2.** [promise] engagement *m* - **3.** FIN bon *m*, titre *m*. ◇ *vt* - **1.** [glue] : **to ~ sthg to sthg** coller qqch sur qqch - **2.** *fig* [people] unir.

bondage ['bɒndɪdʒ] *n* servitude *f*, escla-vage *m*.

bone [bəʊn] ◇ *n* os *m* ; [of fish] arête *f*. ◇ *vt* [meat] désosser ; [fish] enlever les arêtes de.

bone-dry *adj* tout à fait sec (sèche).

bone-idle *adj* paresseux(euse) comme une couleuvre OR un lézard.

bonfire ['bɒnˌfaɪəʳ] *n* [for fun] feu *m* de joie ; [to burn rubbish] feu.

bonfire night *n Br* le 5 novembre (*commémoration de la tentative de Guy Fawkes de faire sauter le Parlement en 1605*).

Bonn [bɒn] *n* Bonn.

bonnet ['bɒnɪt] *n* **- 1.** *Br* [of car] capot *m* **- 2.** [hat] bonnet *m*.

bonny ['bɒnɪ] *adj Scot* beau (belle), joli(e).

bonus ['bəʊnəs] (*pl* **-es** [-iːz]) *n* **- 1.** [extra money] prime *f*, gratification *f* **- 2.** *fig* [added advantage] plus *m*.

bony ['bəʊnɪ] *adj* **- 1.** [person, hand, face] maigre, osseux(euse) **- 2.** [meat] plein(e) d'os ; [fish] plein(e) d'arêtes.

boo [buː] (*pl* **-s**) ⬦ *excl* hou! ⬦ *n* huée *f*. ⬦ *vt* & *vi* huer.

boob [buːb] *n inf* [mistake] gaffe *f*, bourde *f*. ⬦ **boobs** *npl Br vi* [inf] nichons *mpl*.

booby trap ['buːbɪ-] *n* **- 1.** [bomb] objet *m* piégé **- 2.** [practical joke] farce *f*.

book [bʊk] ⬦ *n* **- 1.** [for reading] livre *m* **- 2.** [of stamps, tickets, cheques] carnet *m* ; [of matches] pochette *f*. ⬦ *vt* **- 1.** [reserve - gen] réserver ; [- performer] engager ; **to be fully ~ed** être complet(ète) **- 2.** *inf* [subj : police] coller un PV à **- 3.** *Br* FTBL prendre le nom de. ⬦ *vi* réserver. ⬦ **books** *npl* COMM livres *mpl* de comptes. ⬦ **book up** *vt sep* réserver, retenir.

bookcase ['bʊkkeɪs] *n* bibliothèque *f*.

Booker Prize ['bʊkə-] *n* : **the ~** *prix littéraire britannique*.

bookie ['bʊkɪ] *n inf* bookmaker *m*.

booking ['bʊkɪŋ] *n* **- 1.** [reservation] réservation *f* **- 2.** *Br* FTBL : **to get a ~** recevoir un carton jaune.

booking office *n* bureau *m* de réservation OR location.

bookkeeping ['bʊkˌkiːpɪŋ] *n* comptabilité *f*.

booklet ['bʊklɪt] *n* brochure *f*.

bookmaker ['bʊkˌmeɪkəʳ] *n* bookmaker *m*.

bookmark ['bʊkmaːk] *n* signet *m*.

bookseller ['bʊkˌseləʳ] *n* libraire *mf*.

bookshelf ['bʊkʃelf] (*pl* **-shelves** [-ˌʃelvz]) *n* rayon *m* OR étagère *f* à livres.

bookshop *Br* ['bʊkʃɒp], **bookstore** *Am* ['bʊkstɔːʳ] *n* librairie *f*.

book token *n* chèque-livre *m*.

boom [buːm] ⬦ *n* **- 1.** [loud noise] grondement *m* **- 2.** [in business, trade] boom *m* **- 3.** NAUT bôme *f* **- 4.** [for TV camera, microphone] girafe *f*, perche *f*. ⬦ *vi* **- 1.** [make

noise] gronder **- 2.** [business, trade] être en plein essor OR en hausse.

boon [buːn] *n* avantage *m*, bénédiction *f*.

boost [buːst] ⬦ *n* [to production, sales] augmentation *f* ; [to economy] croissance *f*. ⬦ *vt* **- 1.** [production, sales] stimuler **- 2.** [popularity] accroître, renforcer.

booster ['buːstəʳ] *n* MED rappel *m*.

boot [buːt] ⬦ *n* **- 1.** [for walking, sport] chaussure *f* **- 2.** [fashion item] botte *f* **- 3.** *Br* [of car] coffre *m*. ⬦ *vt inf* flanquer des coups de pied à. ⬦ **to boot** *adv* par-dessus le marché, en plus.

booth [buːð] *n* **- 1.** [at fair] baraque *f* foraine **- 2.** [telephone booth] cabine *f* **- 3.** [voting booth] isoloir *m*.

booty ['buːtɪ] *n* butin *m*.

booze [buːz] *inf* ⬦ *n (U)* alcool *m*, boisson *f* alcoolisée. ⬦ *vi* picoler.

bop [bɒp] *inf* ⬦ *n* **- 1.** [hit] coup *m* **- 2.** [disco, dance] boum *f*. ⬦ *vi* [dance] danser.

border ['bɔːdəʳ] ⬦ *n* **- 1.** [between countries] frontière *f* **- 2.** [edge] bord *m* **- 3.** [in garden] bordure *f*. ⬦ *vt* **- 1.** [country] être limitrophe de **- 2.** [edge] border. ⬦ **border on** *vt fus* friser, être voisin(e) de.

borderline ['bɔːdəlaɪn] ⬦ *adj* : **~ case** cas *m* limite. ⬦ *n fig* limite *f*, ligne *f* de démarcation.

bore [bɔːʳ] ⬦ *pt* ⊳ **bear**. ⬦ *n* **- 1.** [person] raseur *m*, -euse *f* ; [situation, event] corvée *f* **- 2.** [of gun] calibre *m*. ⬦ *vt* **- 1.** [not interest] ennuyer, raser ; **to ~ sb stiff** OR **to tears** OR **to death** ennuyer qqn à mourir **- 2.** [drill] forer, percer.

bored [bɔːd] *adj* [person] qui s'ennuie ; [look] d'ennui ; **to be ~ with** en avoir assez de.

boredom ['bɔːdəm] *n (U)* ennui *m*.

boring ['bɔːrɪŋ] *adj* ennuyeux(euse).

born [bɔːn] *adj* né(e) ; **to be ~** naître ; **I was ~ in 1965** je suis né(e) en 1965 ; **when were you ~?** quelle est ta date de naissance?

borne [bɔːn] *pp* ⊳ **bear**.

borough ['bʌrə] *n* municipalité *f*.

borrow ['bɒrəʊ] *vt* emprunter ; **to ~ sthg (from sb)** emprunter qqch (à qqn).

Bosnia ['bɒznɪə] *n* Bosnie *f*.

Bosnia-Herzegovina [-ˌhɜːtsəgəˈviːnə] *n* Bosnie-Herzégovine *f*.

Bosnian ['bɒznɪən] ⬦ *adj* bosniaque. ⬦ *n* Bosniaque *mf*.

bosom ['bʊzəm] *n* poitrine *f*, seins *mpl* ; *fig* sein *m* ; **~ friend** ami *m* intime.

boss [bɒs] ⬦ *n* patron *m*, -onne *f*, chef *m*.

◇ *vt pej* donner des ordres à, régenter.
➡ **boss about, boss around** *vt sep pej* donner des ordres à, régenter.

bossy ['bɒsɪ] *adj* autoritaire.

bosun ['bəʊsn] = **boatswain**.

botany ['bɒtənɪ] *n* botanique *f*.

botch [bɒtʃ] ➡ **botch up** *vt sep inf* bousiller, saboter.

both [bəʊθ] ◇ *adj* les deux. ◇ *pron* : ~ (of them) (tous) les deux (les deux) ; ~ of us are coming on vient tous les deux. ◇ *adv* : she is ~ intelligent and amusing elle est à la fois intelligente et drôle.

bother ['bɒðə'] ◇ *vt* - **1.** [worry] ennuyer, inquiéter ; **to ~ o.s. (about)** se tracasser (au sujet de) ; **I can't be ~ed to do it** je n'ai vraiment pas envie de le faire - **2.** [pester, annoy] embêter ; **I'm sorry to ~ you** excusez-moi de vous déranger. ◇ *vi* : **to ~ about sthg** s'inquiéter de qqch ; **don't ~ (to do it)** ce n'est pas la peine (de le faire). ◇ *n (U)* embêtement *m* ; **it's no ~ at all** cela ne me dérange OR m'ennuie pas du tout.

bothered ['bɒðəd] *adj* inquiet(ète).

bottle ['bɒtl] ◇ *n* - **1.** [gen] bouteille *f* ; [for medicine, perfume] flacon *m* ; [for baby] biberon *m* - **2.** *(U) Br inf* [courage] cran *m*, culot *m*. ◇ *vt* [wine etc] mettre en bouteilles ; [fruit] mettre en bocal. ➡ **bottle up** *vt sep* [feelings] refouler, contenir.

bottle bank *n* container *m* pour verre usagé.

bottleneck ['bɒtlnek] *n* - **1.** [in traffic] bouchon *m*, embouteillage *m* - **2.** [in production] goulet *m* d'étranglement.

bottle-opener *n* ouvre-bouteilles *m inv*, décapsuleur *m*.

bottom ['bɒtəm] ◇ *adj* - **1.** [lowest] du bas - **2.** [in class] dernier(ère). ◇ *n* - **1.** [of bottle, lake, garden] fond *m* ; [of page, ladder, street] bas *m* ; [of hill] pied *m* - **2.** [of scale] bas *m* ; [of class] dernier *m*, -ère *f* - **3.** [buttocks] derrière *m* - **4.** [cause] : **to get to the ~ of sthg** aller au fond de qqch, découvrir la cause de qqch. ➡ **bottom out** *vi* atteindre son niveau le plus bas.

bottom line *n fig* : **the ~** l'essentiel *m*.

bough [baʊ] *n* branche *f*.

bought [bɔːt] *pt & pp* ▷ **buy**.

boulder ['bəʊldə'] *n* rocher *m*.

bounce [baʊns] ◇ *vi* - **1.** [ball] rebondir ; [person] sauter - **2.** *inf* [cheque] être sans provision. ◇ *vt* [ball] faire rebondir. ◇ *n* rebond *m*.

bouncer ['baʊnsə'] *n inf* videur *m*.

bound [baʊnd] ◇ *pt & pp* ▷ **bind**.

◇ *adj* - **1.** [certain] : **he's ~ to win** il va sûrement gagner ; **she's ~ to see it** elle ne peut pas manquer de le voir - **2.** [obliged] : **to be ~ to do sthg** être obligé(e) OR tenu(e) de faire qqch ; **I'm ~ to say/admit** je dois dire/reconnaître - **3.** [for place] : **to be ~ for** [subj : person] être en route pour ; [subj : plane, train] être à destination de. ◇ *n* [leap] bond *m*, saut *m*. ◇ *vt* : **to be ~ed by** [subj : field] être limité(e) OR délimité(e) par ; [subj : country] être limitrophe de. ➡ **bounds** *npl* limites *fpl* ; **out of ~s** interdit, défendu.

boundary ['baʊndərɪ] *n* [gen] frontière *f* ; [of property] limite *f*, borne *f*.

bourbon ['bɜːbən] *n* bourbon *m*.

bout [baʊt] *n* - **1.** [of illness] accès *m* ; **a ~ of flu** une grippe - **2.** [session] période *f* - **3.** [boxing match] combat *m*.

bow¹ [baʊ] ◇ *n* - **1.** [in greeting] révérence *f* - **2.** [of ship] proue *f*, avant *m*. ◇ *vt* [head] baisser, incliner. ◇ *vi* - **1.** [make a bow] saluer - **2.** [defer] : **to ~ to** s'incliner devant.

bow² [bəʊ] *n* - **1.** [weapon] arc *m* - **2.** MUS archet *m* - **3.** [knot] nœud *m*.

bowels ['baʊəlz] *npl* intestins *mpl* ; *fig* entrailles *fpl*.

bowl [bəʊl] ◇ *n* - **1.** [container, gen] jatte *f*, saladier *m* ; [small] bol *m* ; [- for washing up] cuvette *f* - **2.** [of toilet, sink] cuvette *f* ; [of pipe] fourneau *m*. ◇ *vi* CRICKET lancer la balle. ➡ **bowls** *n (U)* boules *fpl (sur herbe)*.
➡ **bowl over** *vt sep lit & fig* renverser.

bow-legged [,bəʊ'legɪd] *adj* aux jambes arquées.

bowler ['bəʊlə'] *n* - **1.** CRICKET lanceur *m* - **2.** : **~ (hat)** chapeau *m* melon.

bowling ['bəʊlɪŋ] *n (U)* bowling *m*.

bowling alley *n* [building] bowling *m* ; [alley] piste *f* de bowling.

bowling green *n* terrain *m* de boules *(sur herbe)*.

bow tie [bəʊ-] *n* nœud *m* papillon.

box [bɒks] ◇ *n* - **1.** [gen] boîte *f* - **2.** THEATRE loge *f* - **3.** *Br inf* [television] : **the ~** la télé. ◇ *vi* boxer, faire de la boxe.

boxer ['bɒksə'] *n* - **1.** [fighter] boxeur *m* - **2.** [dog] boxer *m*.

boxer shorts *npl* boxer-short *m*.

boxing ['bɒksɪŋ] *n* boxe *f*.

Boxing Day *n* jour des étrennes en Grande-Bretagne (le 26 décembre).

boxing glove *n* gant *m* de boxe.

box office *n* bureau *m* de location.

boxroom ['bɒksrʊm] *n Br* débarras *m*.

boy [bɔɪ] ◇ *n* [male child] garçon *m*.

◇ *excl inf* : **(oh)** ~! ben, mon vieux!, ben, dis-donc!

boycott ['bɔɪkɒt] ◇ *n* boycott *m*, boy-cottage *m*. ◇ *vt* boycotter.

boyfriend ['bɔɪfrend] *n* copain *m*, petit ami *m*.

boyish ['bɔɪɪʃ] *adj* **- 1.** [appearance - of man] gamin(e) ; [- of woman] de garçon **- 2.** [behaviour] garçonnier(ère).

BR (*abbr of* **British Rail**) *n* ≃ SNCF *f*.

bra [brɑː] *n* soutien-gorge *m*.

brace [breɪs] ◇ *n* **- 1.** [on teeth] appareil *m* (dentaire) **- 2.** [on leg] appareil *m* orthopédique. ◇ *vt* **- 1.** [steady] soutenir, consolider ; **to ~ o.s.** s'accrocher, se cramponner **- 2.** *fig* [prepare] : **to ~ o.s. (for sthg)** se préparer (à qqch). ◆ **braces** *npl Br* bretelles *fpl*.

bracelet ['breɪslɪt] *n* bracelet *m*.

bracing ['breɪsɪŋ] *adj* vivifiant(e).

bracken ['brækn] *n* fougère *f*.

bracket ['brækɪt] ◇ *n* **- 1.** [support] support *m* **- 2.** [parenthesis - round] parenthèse *f* ; [- square] crochet *m* ; **in ~s** entre parenthèses/crochets **- 3.** [group] : **age/income ~** tranche *f* d'âge/de revenus. ◇ *vt* [enclose in brackets] mettre entre parenthèses/crochets.

brag [bræg] *vi* se vanter.

braid [breɪd] ◇ *n* **- 1.** [on uniform] galon *m* **- 2.** [of hair] tresse *f*, natte *f*. ◇ *vt* [hair] tresser, natter.

brain [breɪn] *n* cerveau *m*. ◆ **brains** *npl* [intelligence] intelligence *f*.

brainchild ['breɪntʃaɪld] *n inf* idée *f* personnelle, invention *f* personnelle.

brainwash ['breɪnwɒʃ] *vt* faire un lavage de cerveau à.

brainwave ['breɪnweɪv] *n* idée *f* géniale OR de génie.

brainy ['breɪnɪ] *adj inf* intelligent(e).

brake [breɪk] ◇ *n lit* & *fig* frein *m*. ◇ *vi* freiner.

brake light *n* stop *m*, feu *m* arrière.

bramble ['bræmbl] *n* [bush] ronce *f* ; [fruit] mûre *f*.

bran [bræn] *n* son *m*.

branch [brɑːntʃ] ◇ *n* **- 1.** [of tree, subject] branche *f* **- 2.** [of railway] bifurcation *f*, embranchement *m* **- 3.** [of company] filiale *f*, succursale *f* ; [of bank] agence *f*. ◇ *vi* bifurquer. ◆ **branch out** *vi* [person, company] étendre ses activités, se diversifier.

brand [brænd] ◇ *n* **- 1.** COMM marque *f* **- 2.** *fig* [type, style] type *m*, genre *m*. ◇ *vt* **- 1.** [cattle] marquer au fer rouge **- 2.** *fig* [clas-

sify] : **to ~ sb (as) sthg** étiqueter qqn comme qqch, coller à qqn l'étiquette de qqch.

brandish ['brændɪʃ] *vt* brandir.

brand name *n* marque *f*.

brand-new *adj* flambant neuf (flambant neuve), tout neuf (toute neuve).

brandy ['brændɪ] *n* cognac *m*.

brash [bræʃ] *adj* effronté(e).

brass [brɑːs] *n* **- 1.** [metal] laiton *m*, cuivre *m* jaune **- 2.** MUS : **the ~** les cuivres *mpl*.

brass band *n* fanfare *f*.

brassiere [*Br* 'bræsɪəʳ, *Am* brə'zɪr] *n* soutien-gorge *m*.

brat [bræt] *n inf pej* sale gosse *m*.

bravado [brə'vɑːdəʊ] *n* bravade *f*.

brave [breɪv] ◇ *adj* courageux(euse), brave. ◇ *n* guerrier *m* indien, brave *m*. ◇ *vt* braver, affronter.

bravery ['breɪvərɪ] *n* courage *m*, bravoure *f*.

brawl [brɔːl] *n* bagarre *f*, rixe *f*.

brawn [brɔːn] *n* (U) **- 1.** [muscle] muscle *m* **- 2.** *Br* [meat] fromage *m* de tête.

bray [breɪ] *vi* [donkey] braire.

brazen ['breɪzn] *adj* [person] effronté(e), impudent(e) ; [lie] éhonté(e). ◆ **brazen out** *vt sep* : **to ~ it out** crâner.

brazier ['breɪzjəʳ] *n* brasero *m*.

Brazil [brə'zɪl] *n* Brésil *m*.

Brazilian [brə'zɪljən] ◇ *adj* brésilien (enne). ◇ *n* Brésilien *m*, -enne *f*.

brazil nut *n* noix *f* du Brésil.

breach [briːtʃ] ◇ *n* **- 1.** [of law, agreement] infraction *f*, violation *f* ; [of promise] rupture *f* ; **to be in ~ of sthg** enfreindre OR violer qqch ; **~ of contract** rupture *f* de contrat **- 2.** [opening, gap] trou *m*, brèche *f*. ◇ *vt* **- 1.** [agreement, contract] rompre **- 2.** [make hole in] faire une brèche dans.

breach of the peace *n* atteinte *f* à l'ordre public.

bread [bred] *n* pain *m* ; **~ and butter** tartine *f* beurrée, pain beurré *m* ; *fig* gagne-pain *m*.

bread bin *Br*, **bread box** *Am n* boîte *f* à pain.

breadcrumbs ['bredkrʌmz] *npl* chapelure *f*.

breadline ['bredlaɪn] *n* : **to be on the ~** être sans ressources OR sans le sou.

breadth [bretθ] *n* **- 1.** [width] largeur *f* **- 2.** *fig* [scope] ampleur *f*, étendue *f*.

breadwinner ['bred,wɪnəʳ] *n* soutien *m* de famille.

break [breɪk] (*pt* **broke**, *pp* **broken**) ⬦ *n* - **1.** [gap] : **~ (in)** trouée *f* (dans) - **2.** [fracture] fracture *f* - **3.** [pause - gen] pause *f* ; [- at school] récréation *f* ; **to take a ~** [short] faire une pause ; [longer] prendre des jours de congé ; **without a ~** sans interruption ; **to have a ~ from doing sthg** arrêter de faire qqch - **4.** *inf* [luck] : **(lucky) ~** chance *f*, veine *f*. ⬦ *vt* - **1.** [gen] casser, briser ; **to ~ one's arm/leg** se casser le bras/la jambe ; **to ~ a record** battre un record - **2.** [interrupt - journey] interrompre ; [- contact, silence] rompre - **3.** [not keep - law, rule] enfreindre, violer ; [- promise] manquer à - **4.** [tell] : **to ~ the news (of sthg to sb)** annoncer la nouvelle (de qqch à qqn). ⬦ *vi* - **1.** [gen] se casser, se briser ; **to ~ loose** OR **free** se dégager, s'échapper - **2.** [pause] s'arrêter, faire une pause - **3.** [weather] se gâter - **4.** [voice - with emotion] se briser ; [- at puberty] muer - **5.** [news] se répandre, éclater - **6.** *phr* : **to ~ even** rentrer dans ses frais. ◆ **break away** *vi* [escape] s'échapper. ◆ **break down** ⬦ *vt sep* - **1.** [destroy - barrier] démolir ; [- door] enfoncer - **2.** [analyse] analyser ⬦ *vi* - **1.** [car, machine] tomber en panne ; [resistance] céder ; [negotiations] échouer - **2.** [emotionally] fondre en larmes, éclater en sanglots. ◆ **break in** ⬦ *vi* - **1.** [burglar] entrer par effraction - **2.** [interrupt] : **to ~ in (on sb/sthg)** interrompre (qqn/qqch). ⬦ *vt sep* [horse] dresser ; [person] rompre, accoutumer. ◆ **break into** *vt fus* - **1.** [subj : burglar] entrer par effraction dans - **2.** [begin] : **to ~ into song/applause** se mettre à chanter/applaudir. ◆ **break off** ⬦ *vt sep* - **1.** [detach] détacher - **2.** [talks, relationship] rompre ; [holiday] interrompre. ⬦ *vi* - **1.** [become detached] se casser, se détacher - **2.** [stop talking] s'interrompre, se taire. ◆ **break out** *vi* - **1.** [begin - fire] se déclarer ; [- fighting] éclater - **2.** [escape] : **to ~ out (of)** s'échapper (de), s'évader (de). ◆ **break up** ⬦ *vt sep* - **1.** [into smaller pieces] mettre en morceaux - **2.** [end - marriage, relationship] détruire ; [- fight, party] mettre fin à. ⬦ *vi* - **1.** [into smaller pieces - gen] se casser en morceaux ; [- ship] se briser - **2.** [end - marriage, relationship] se briser ; [- talks, party] prendre fin ; [- school] finir, fermer ; **to ~ up (with sb)** rompre (avec qqn) - **3.** [crowd] se disperser.

breakage ['breɪkɪdʒ] *n* bris *m*.

breakdown ['breɪkdaʊn] *n* - **1.** [of vehicle, machine] panne *f* ; [of negotiations] échec *m* ; [in communications] rupture *f* - **2.** [analysis] détail *m*.

breakfast ['brekfəst] *n* petit déjeuner *m*.

breakfast television *n Br* télévision *f* du matin.

break-in *n* cambriolage *m*.

breaking ['breɪkɪŋ] *n* : **~ and entering** JUR entrée *f* par effraction.

breakneck ['breɪknek] *adj* : **at ~ speed** à fond de train.

breakthrough ['breɪkθruː] *n* percée *f*.

breakup ['breɪkʌp] *n* [of marriage, relationship] rupture *f*.

breast [brest] *n* - **1.** [of woman] sein *m* ; [of man] poitrine *f* - **2.** [meat of bird] blanc *m*.

breast-feed *vt* & *vi* allaiter.

breaststroke ['breststrəʊk] *n* brasse *f*.

breath [breθ] *n* souffle *m*, haleine *f* ; **to take a deep ~** inspirer profondément ; **out of ~** hors d'haleine, à bout de souffle ; **to get one's ~ back** reprendre haleine OR son souffle.

breathalyse *Br*, **-yze** *Am* ['breθəlaɪz] *vt* ≃ faire subir l'Alcootest® à.

breathe [briːð] ⬦ *vi* respirer. ⬦ *vt* - **1.** [inhale] respirer - **2.** [exhale - smell] souffler des relents de. ◆ **breathe in** ⬦ *vi* inspirer. ⬦ *vt sep* aspirer. ◆ **breathe out** *vi* expirer.

breather ['briːðəʳ] *n inf* moment *m* de repos OR répit.

breathing ['briːðɪŋ] *n* respiration *f*.

breathless ['breθlɪs] *adj* - **1.** [out of breath] hors d'haleine, essoufflé(e) - **2.** [with excitement] fébrile, fiévreux(euse).

breathtaking ['breθˌteɪkɪŋ] *adj* à vous couper le souffle.

breed [briːd] (*pt* & *pp* **bred** [bred]) ⬦ *n lit* & *fig* race *f*, espèce *f*. ⬦ *vt* - **1.** [animals, plants] élever - **2.** *fig* [suspicion, contempt] faire naître, engendrer. ⬦ *vi* se reproduire.

breeding ['briːdɪŋ] *n (U)* - **1.** [of animals, plants] élevage *m* - **2.** [manners] bonnes manières *fpl*, savoir-vivre *m*.

breeze [briːz] *n* brise *f*.

breezy ['briːzɪ] *adj* - **1.** [windy] venteux(euse) - **2.** [cheerful] jovial(e), enjoué(e).

brevity ['brevɪtɪ] *n* brièveté *f*.

brew [bruː] ⬦ *vt* [beer] brasser ; [tea] faire infuser ; [coffee] préparer, faire. ⬦ *vi* - **1.** [tea] infuser ; [coffee] se faire - **2.** *fig* [trouble, storm] se préparer, couver.

brewer ['bruːəʳ] *n* brasseur *m*.

brewery ['brʊərɪ] *n* brasserie *f*.

bribe [braɪb] ⬦ *n* pot-de-vin *m*. ⬦ *vt* : **to**

~ **sb (to do sthg)** soudoyer qqn (pour qu'il fasse qqch).

bribery ['braɪbərɪ] *n* corruption *f*.

brick [brɪk] *n* brique *f*.

bricklayer ['brɪkˌleɪəʳ] *n* maçon *m*.

bridal ['braɪdl] *adj* [dress] de mariée ; [suite etc] nuptial(e).

bride [braɪd] *n* mariée *f*.

bridegroom ['braɪdgrʊm] *n* marié *m*.

bridesmaid ['braɪdzmeɪd] *n* demoiselle *f* d'honneur.

bridge [brɪdʒ] ⬦ *n* - **1.** [gen] pont *m* - **2.** [on ship] passerelle *f* - **3.** [of nose] arête *f* - **4.** [card game, for teeth] bridge *m*. ⬦ *vt fig* [gap] réduire.

bridle ['braɪdl] *n* bride *f*.

bridle path *n* piste *f* cavalière.

brief [briːf] ⬦ *adj* - **1.** [short] bref (brève), court(e) ; **in ~** en bref, en deux mots - **2.** [revealing] très court(e). ⬦ *n* - **1.** JUR affaire *f*, dossier *m* - **2.** *Br* [instructions] instructions *fpl*. ⬦ *vt* : **to ~ sb (on)** [bring up to date] mettre qqn au courant (de) ; [instruct] briefer qqn (sur). ⬥ **briefs** *npl* slip *m*.

briefcase ['briːfkeɪs] *n* serviette *f*.

briefing ['briːfɪŋ] *n* instructions *fpl*, briefing *m*.

briefly ['briːflɪ] *adv* - **1.** [for a short time] un instant - **2.** [concisely] brièvement.

brigade [brɪ'geɪd] *n* brigade *f*.

brigadier [ˌbrɪgə'dɪəʳ] *n* général *m* de brigade.

bright [braɪt] *adj* - **1.** [room] clair(e) ; [light, colour] vif (vive) ; [sunlight] éclatant(e) ; [eyes, future] brillant(e) - **2.** [intelligent] intelligent(e).

brighten ['braɪtn] *vi* - **1.** [become lighter] s'éclaircir - **2.** [face, mood] s'éclairer. ⬥ **brighten up** ⬦ *vt sep* égayer. ⬦ *vi* - **1.** [person] s'égayer, s'animer - **2.** [weather] se dégager, s'éclaircir.

brilliance ['brɪljəns] *n* - **1.** [cleverness] intelligence *f* - **2.** [of colour, light] éclat *m*.

brilliant ['brɪljənt] *adj* - **1.** [gen] brillant(e) - **2.** [colour] éclatant(e) - **3.** *inf* [wonderful] super *(inv)*, génial(e).

Brillo pad® ['brɪləʊ-] *n* ≃ tampon *m* Jex®.

brim [brɪm] ⬦ *n* bord *m*. ⬦ *vi* : **to ~ with** *lit & fig* être plein(e) de.

brine [braɪn] *n* saumure *f*.

bring [brɪŋ] *(pt & pp* **brought)** *vt* - **1.** [person] amener ; [object] apporter - **2.** [cause - happiness, shame] entraîner, causer ; **to ~ sthg to an end** mettre fin à qqch. ⬥ **bring about** *vt sep* causer, provoquer. ⬥ **bring around** *vt sep* [make conscious] ranimer. ⬥ **bring back** *vt sep* - **1.** [object] rapporter ; [person] ramener - **2.** [memories] rappeler - **3.** [reinstate] rétablir. ⬥ **bring down** *vt sep* - **1.** [plane] abattre ; [government] renverser - **2.** [prices] faire baisser. ⬥ **bring forward** *vt sep* - **1.** [gen] avancer - **2.** [in bookkeeping] reporter. ⬥ **bring in** *vt sep* - **1.** [law] introduire - **2.** [money - subj : person] gagner ; [- subj : deal] rapporter. ⬥ **bring off** *vt sep* [plan] réaliser, réussir ; [deal] conclure, mener à bien. ⬥ **bring out** *vt sep* - **1.** [product] lancer ; [book] publier, faire paraître - **2.** [cause to appear] faire ressortir. ⬥ **bring round, bring to** = bring around. ⬥ **bring up** *vt sep* - **1.** [raise - children] élever - **2.** [mention] mentionner - **3.** [vomit] rendre, vomir.

brink [brɪŋk] *n* : **on the ~ of** au bord de, à la veille de.

brisk [brɪsk] *adj* - **1.** [quick] vif (vive), rapide - **2.** [manner, tone] déterminé(e).

bristle ['brɪsl] ⬦ *n* poil *m*. ⬦ *vi lit & fig* se hérisser.

Britain ['brɪtn] *n* Grande-Bretagne *f* ; **in ~** en Grande-Bretagne.

British ['brɪtɪʃ] *adj* britannique.

British Isles *npl* : **the ~** les îles *fpl* Britanniques.

British Rail *n* société des chemins de fer britanniques, ≃ SNCF *f*.

British Telecom [-'telɪkɒm] *n* société britannique de télécommunications.

Briton ['brɪtn] *n* Britannique *mf*.

Brittany ['brɪtənɪ] *n* Bretagne *f*.

brittle ['brɪtl] *adj* fragile.

broach [brəʊtʃ] *vt* [subject] aborder.

broad [brɔːd] *adj* - **1.** [wide - gen] large ; [- range, interests] divers(e), varié(e) - **2.** [description] général(e) - **3.** [hint] transparent(e) ; [accent] prononcé(e). ⬥ **in broad daylight** *adv* en plein jour.

Broad *n Br* route *f* départementale.

broad bean *n* fève *f*.

broadcast ['brɔːdkɑːst] *(pt & pp* **broadcast)** ⬦ *n* RADIO & TV émission *f*. ⬦ *vt* RADIO radiodiffuser ; TV téléviser.

broaden ['brɔːdn] ⬦ *vt* élargir. ⬦ *vi* s'élargir.

broadly ['brɔːdlɪ] *adv* [generally] généralement.

broadminded [ˌbrɔːd'maɪndɪd] *adj* large d'esprit.

broccoli ['brɒkəlɪ] *n* brocoli *m*.

brochure ['brəʊʃəʳ] *n* brochure *f*, prospectus *m*.

broil [brɔɪl] *vt Am* griller.

broke [brəʊk] ⟨⟩ *pt* ▷ **break**. ⟨⟩ *adj inf* fauché(e).

broken ['brəʊkn] ⟨⟩ *pp* ▷ **break**. ⟨⟩ *adj* - **1**. [gen] cassé(e) ; **to have a ~ leg** avoir la jambe cassée - **2**. [interrupted - journey, sleep] interrompu(e) ; [- line] brisé(e) - **3**. [marriage] brisé(e), détruit(e) ; [home] désuni(e) - **4**. [hesitant] : **to speak in ~ English** parler un anglais hésitant.

broker ['brəʊkəʳ] *n* courtier *m* ; (insurance) ~ assureur *m*, courtier *m* d'assurances.

brolly ['brɒlɪ] *n Br inf* pépin *m*.

bronchitis [brɒŋ'kaɪtɪs] *n* (U) bronchite *f*.

bronze [brɒnz] ⟨⟩ *adj* [colour] (couleur) bronze *(inv)*. ⟨⟩ *n* [gen] bronze *m*.

brooch [brəʊtʃ] *n* broche *f*.

brood [bruːd] ⟨⟩ *n* [of animals] couvée *f*. ⟨⟩ *vi* : **to ~ (over OR about sthg)** ressasser (qqch), remâcher (qqch).

brook [brʊk] *n* ruisseau *m*.

broom [bruːm] *n* balai *m*.

broomstick ['bruːmstɪk] *n* manche *m* à balai.

Bros, bros *(abbr of* **brothers)** Frères.

broth [brɒθ] *n* bouillon *m*.

brothel ['brɒθl] *n* bordel *m*.

brother ['brʌðəʳ] *n* frère *m*.

brother-in-law *(pl* **brothers-in-law)** *n* beau-frère *m*.

brought [brɔːt] *pt & pp* ▷ **bring**.

brow [braʊ] *n* - **1**. [forehead] front *m* - **2**. [eyebrow] sourcil *m* - **3**. [of hill] sommet *m*.

brown [braʊn] ⟨⟩ *adj* **1**. [colour] brun(e), marron *(inv)* ; **~ bread** pain *m* bis - **2**. [tanned] bronzé(e), hâlé(e). ⟨⟩ *n* [colour] marron *m*, brun *m*. ⟨⟩ *vt* [food] faire dorer.

Brownie (Guide) ['braʊnɪ-] *n* ≃ jeannette *f*.

Brownie point ['braʊnɪ-] *n* bon point *m*.

brown paper *n* papier *m* d'emballage, papier kraft.

brown rice *n* riz *m* complet.

brown sugar *n* sucre *m* roux.

browse [braʊz] ⟨⟩ *vi* - **1**. [look] : **I'm just browsing** [in shop] je ne fais que regarder ; **to ~ through** [magazines etc] feuilleter - **2**. [animal] brouter - **3**. COMPUT naviguer. ⟨⟩ *vt* [file, document] parcourir ; **to ~ a site** COMPUT naviguer sur un site.

browser ['braʊzəʳ] *n* navigateur *m*, browser *m*.

bruise [bruːz] ⟨⟩ *n* bleu *m*. ⟨⟩ *vt* - **1**. [skin, arm] se faire un bleu à ; [fruit] taler - **2**. *fig* [pride] meurtrir, blesser.

brunch [brʌntʃ] *n* brunch *m*.

brunette [bruː'net] *n* brunette *f*.

brunt [brʌnt] *n* : **to bear OR take the ~ of** subir le plus gros de.

brush [brʌʃ] ⟨⟩ *n* - **1**. [gen] brosse *f* ; [of painter] pinceau *m* - **2**. [encounter] : **to have a ~ with the police** avoir des ennuis avec la police. ⟨⟩ *vt* - **1**. [clean with brush] brosser - **2**. [touch lightly] effleurer. ◆ **brush aside** *vt sep* [fig] écarter, repousser. ◆ **brush off** *vt sep* [dismiss] envoyer promener. ◆ **brush up** ⟨⟩ *vt sep* [revise] réviser. ⟨⟩ *vi* : **to ~ up on sthg** réviser qqch.

brush-off *n inf* : **to give sb the ~** envoyer promener qqn.

brushwood ['brʌʃwʊd] *n* (U) brindilles *fpl*.

brusque [bruːsk] *adj* brusque.

Brussels ['brʌslz] *n* Bruxelles.

brussels sprout *n* chou *m* de Bruxelles.

brutal ['bruːtl] *adj* brutal(e).

brute [bruːt] ⟨⟩ *adj* [force] brutal(e). ⟨⟩ *n* brute *f*.

BSc *(abbr of* **Bachelor of Science)** *n* *(titulaire d'une)* licence de sciences.

BT *(abbr of* **British Telecom)** *n* société britannique de télécommunications.

bubble ['bʌbl] ⟨⟩ *n* bulle *f*. ⟨⟩ *vi* - **1**. [liquid] faire des bulles, bouillonner - **2**. *fig* [person] : **to ~ with** déborder de.

bubble bath *n* bain *m* moussant.

bubble gum *n* bubble-gum *m*.

bubblejet printer ['bʌbldʒet-] *n* imprimante *f* à jet d'encre.

Bucharest [ˌbjuːkə'rest] *n* Bucarest.

buck [bʌk] ⟨⟩ *n* - **1**. [male animal] mâle *m* - **2**. *inf* [dollar] dollar *m* - **3**. *inf* [responsibility] : **to pass the ~** refiler la responsabilité. ⟨⟩ *vi* [horse] ruer. ◆ **buck up** *inf vi* - **1**. [hurry up] se remuer, se dépêcher - **2**. [cheer up] ne pas se laisser abattre.

bucket ['bʌkɪt] *n* [gen] seau *m*.

Buckingham Palace ['bʌkɪŋəm-] *n* le palais de Buckingham *(résidence officielle du souverain britannique)*.

buckle ['bʌkl] ⟨⟩ *n* boucle *f*. ⟨⟩ *vt* - **1**. [fasten] boucler - **2**. [bend] voiler. ⟨⟩ *vi* [wheel] se voiler ; [knees, legs] se plier.

bud [bʌd] ⟨⟩ *n* bourgeon *m*. ⟨⟩ *vi* bourgeonner.

Budapest [ˌbjuːdəˈpest] *n* Budapest.

Buddha [ˈbʊdə] *n* Bouddha *m*.

Buddhism [ˈbʊdɪzm] *n* bouddhisme *m*.

budding [ˈbʌdɪŋ] *adj* [writer, artist] en herbe.

buddy [ˈbʌdɪ] *n inf* pote *m*.

budge [bʌdʒ] ◇ *vt* faire bouger. ◇ *vi* bouger.

budgerigar [ˈbʌdʒərɪgaːʳ] *n* perruche *f*.

budget [ˈbʌdʒɪt] ◇ *adj* [holiday, price] pour petits budgets. ◇ *n* budget *m*.
◆ **budget for** *vt fus* prévoir.

budgie [ˈbʌdʒɪ] *n inf* perruche *f*.

buff [bʌf] ◇ *adj* [brown] chamois *(inv)*.
◇ *n inf* [expert] mordu *m*, -e *f*.

buffalo [ˈbʌfələʊ] *(pl inv OR* -es *OR* -s*)* *n* buffle *m*.

buffer [ˈbʌfəʳ] *n* - 1. [gen] tampon *m*
- 2. COMPUT mémoire *f* tampon.

buffet[1] [*Br* ˈbʊfeɪ, *Am* bəˈfeɪ] *n* [food, cafeteria] buffet *m*.

buffet[2] [ˈbʌfɪt] *vt* [physically] frapper.

buffet car [ˈbʊfeɪ-] *n* wagon-restaurant *m*.

bug [bʌg] ◇ *n* - 1. [insect] punaise *f* - 2. *inf* [germ] microbe *m* - 3. *inf* [listening device] micro *m* - 4. COMPUT bogue *m*, bug *m*. ◇ *vt*
- 1. *inf* [telephone] mettre sur table d'écoute ; [room] cacher des micros dans - 2. *inf* [annoy] embêter.

bugger [ˈbʌgəʳ] *Br v inf* ◇ *n* [person] con *m*, conne *f*. ◇ *excl* merde! ◆ **bugger off** *vi* : ~ off! fous le camp!

buggy [ˈbʌgɪ] *n* - 1. [carriage] boghei *m*
- 2. [pushchair] poussette *f* ; *Am* [pram] landau *m*.

bugle [ˈbjuːgl] *n* clairon *m*.

build [bɪld] *(pt & pp* built*)* ◇ *vt lit & fig* construire, bâtir. ◇ *n* carrure *f*. ◆ **build on, build upon** ◇ *vt fus* [success] tirer avantage de. ◇ *vt sep* [base on] baser sur.
◆ **build up** ◇ *vt sep* [business] développer ; [reputation] bâtir. ◇ *vi* [clouds] s'amonceler ; [traffic] augmenter.

builder [ˈbɪldəʳ] *n* entrepreneur *m*.

building [ˈbɪldɪŋ] *n* bâtiment *m*.

building and loan association *n Am* société d'épargne et de financement immobilier.

building site *n* chantier *m*.

building society *n Br* ≃ société *f* d'épargne et de financement immobilier.

buildup [ˈbɪldʌp] *n* [increase] accroissement *m*.

built [bɪlt] *pt & pp* ▷ **build**.

built-in *adj* - 1. CONSTR encastré(e) - 2. [inherent] inné(e).

built-up *adj* : ~ area agglomération *f*.

bulb [bʌlb] *n* - 1. ELEC ampoule *f* - 2. BOT oignon *m*.

Bulgaria [bʌlˈgeərɪə] *n* Bulgarie *f*.

Bulgarian [bʌlˈgeərɪən] ◇ *adj* bulgare.
◇ *n* - 1. [person] Bulgare *mf* - 2. [language] bulgare *m*.

bulge [bʌldʒ] ◇ *n* [lump] bosse *f*. ◇ *vi* : to ~ (with) être gonflé (de).

bulk [bʌlk] ◇ *n* - 1. [mass] volume *m*
- 2. [of person] corpulence *f* - 3. COMM : in ~ en gros - 4. [majority] : the ~ of le plus gros de. ◇ *adj* en gros.

bulky [ˈbʌlkɪ] *adj* volumineux(euse).

bull [bʊl] *n* [male cow] taureau *m* ; [male elephant, seal] mâle *m*.

bulldog [ˈbʊldɒg] *n* bouledogue *m*.

bulldozer [ˈbʊldəʊzəʳ] *n* bulldozer *m*.

bullet [ˈbʊlɪt] *n* [for gun] balle *f*.

bulletin [ˈbʊlətɪn] *n* bulletin *m*.

bullet-proof *adj* pare-balles *(inv)*.

bullfight [ˈbʊlfaɪt] *n* corrida *f*.

bullfighter [ˈbʊlˌfaɪtəʳ] *n* toréador *m*.

bullfighting [ˈbʊlˌfaɪtɪŋ] *n (U)* courses *fpl* de taureaux ; [art] tauromachie *f*.

bullion [ˈbʊljən] *n (U)* : gold ~ *m* or en barres.

bullock [ˈbʊlək] *n* bœuf *m*.

bullring [ˈbʊlrɪŋ] *n* arène *f*.

bull's-eye *n* centre *m*.

bully [ˈbʊlɪ] ◇ *n* tyran *m*. ◇ *vt* tyranniser, brutaliser.

bum [bʌm] *n* - 1. *inf* [bottom] derrière *m*
- 2. *inf pej* [tramp] clochard *m*.

bumblebee [ˈbʌmblbiː] *n* bourdon *m*.

bump [bʌmp] ◇ *n* - 1. [lump] bosse *f*
- 2. [knock, blow] choc *m* - 3. [noise] bruit *m* sourd. ◇ *vt* [head etc] cogner ; [car] heurter. ◆ **bump into** *vt fus* [meet by chance] rencontrer par hasard.

bumper [ˈbʌmpəʳ] ◇ *adj* [harvest, edition] exceptionnel(elle). ◇ *n* - 1. AUT pare-chocs *m inv* - 2. *Am* RAIL tampon *m*.

bumptious [ˈbʌmpʃəs] *adj* suffisant(e).

bumpy [ˈbʌmpɪ] *adj* - 1. [surface] défoncé(e) - 2. [ride] cahoteux(euse) ; [sea crossing] agité(e).

bun [bʌn] *n* - 1. [cake] petit pain *m* aux raisins ; [bread roll] petit pain *m* au lait - 2. [hairstyle] chignon *m*.

bunch [bʌntʃ] ◇ *n* [of people] groupe *m* ; [of flowers] bouquet *m* ; [of grapes] grappe *f* ; [of bananas] régime *m* ; [of keys] trousseau *m*. ◇ *vi* se grouper. ◆ **bunches** *npl* [hairstyle] couettes *fpl*.

bundle ['bʌndl] ◇ *n* [of clothes] paquet *m* ; [of notes, newspapers] liasse *f* ; [of wood] fagot *m*. ◇ *vt* [put roughly - person] entasser ; [- clothes] fourrer, entasser.

bung [bʌŋ] ◇ *n* bonde *f*. ◇ *vt* *Br inf* envoyer.

bungalow ['bʌŋgələʊ] *n* bungalow *m*.

bungle ['bʌŋgl] *vt* gâcher, bâcler.

bunion ['bʌnjən] *n* oignon *m*.

bunk [bʌŋk] *n* [bed] couchette *f*.

bunk bed *n* lit *m* superposé.

bunker ['bʌŋkəʳ] *n* - **1.** GOLF & MIL bunker *m* - **2.** [for coal] coffre *m*.

bunny ['bʌnɪ] *n* : ~ **(rabbit)** lapin *m*.

bunting ['bʌntɪŋ] *n* (*U*) guirlandes *fpl* (de drapeaux).

buoy [*Br* bɔɪ, *Am* 'buːɪ] *n* bouée *f*. ◆ **buoy up** *vt sep* [encourage] soutenir.

buoyant ['bɔɪənt] *adj* - **1.** [able to float] qui flotte - **2.** *fig* [person] enjoué(e) ; [economy] florissant(e) ; [market] ferme.

burden ['bɜːdn] ◇ *n* lit & fig : (on) charge *f* (pour), fardeau *m* (pour). ◇ *vt* : **to ~ sb with** [responsibilities, worries] accabler qqn de.

bureau ['bjʊərəʊ] (*pl* -**x** [-z]) *n* - **1.** *Br* [desk] bureau *m* ; *Am* [chest of drawers] commode *f* - **2.** [office] bureau *m*.

bureaucracy [bjʊə'rɒkrəsɪ] *n* bureaucratie *f*.

bureaux ['bjʊərəʊz] *pl* ⊏ ➢ **bureau**.

burger ['bɜːgəʳ] *n* hamburger *m*.

burglar ['bɜːgləʳ] *n* cambrioleur *m*, euse *f*.

burglar alarm *n* système *m* d'alarme.

burglarize *Am* = **burgle**.

burglary ['bɜːglərɪ] *n* cambriolage *m*.

burgle ['bɜːgl], **burglarize** *Am* ['bɜːgləraɪz] *vt* cambrioler.

Burgundy ['bɜːgəndɪ] *n* Bourgogne *f*.

burial ['berɪəl] *n* enterrement *m*.

burly ['bɜːlɪ] *adj* bien charpenté(e).

Burma ['bɜːmə] *n* Birmanie *f*.

burn [bɜːn] (*pt* & *pp* burnt OR -ed) ◇ *vt* brûler ; **I've -ed my hand** je me suis brûlé la main. ◇ *vi* brûler. ◇ *n* brûlure *f*. ◆ **burn down** ◇ *vt sep* [building, town] incendier. ◇ *vi* [building] brûler complètement.

burner ['bɜːnəʳ] *n* brûleur *m*.

Burns' Night [bɜːnz-] *n* fête célébrée en l'honneur du poète écossais Robert Burns, le 25 janvier.

burnt [bɜːnt] *pt* & *pp* ⊏➢ **burn**.

burp [bɜːp] *inf* ◇ *n* rot *m*. ◇ *vi* roter.

burrow ['bʌrəʊ] ◇ *n* terrier *m*. ◇ *vi* - **1.** [dig] creuser un terrier - **2.** *fig* [search] fouiller.

bursar ['bɜːsəʳ] *n* intendant *m*, -e *f*.

bursary ['bɜːsərɪ] *n* *Br* [scholarship, grant] bourse *f*.

burst [bɜːst] (*pt* & *pp* burst) ◇ *vi* [gen] éclater. ◇ *vt* faire éclater. ◇ *n* [of gunfire] rafale *f* ; [of enthusiasm] élan *m* ; **a ~ of applause** un tonnerre d'applaudissements. ◆ **burst into** *vt fus* - **1.** [room] faire irruption dans - **2.** [begin suddenly] : **to ~ into tears** fondre en larmes ; **to ~ into flames** prendre feu. ◆ **burst out** *vt fus* [say suddenly] s'exclamer ; **to ~ out laughing** éclater de rire.

bursting ['bɜːstɪŋ] *adj* - **1.** [full] plein(e), bourré(e) - **2.** [with emotion] : ~ **with** débordé(e) de - **3.** [eager] : **to be ~ to do sthg** mourir d'envie de faire qqch.

bury ['berɪ] *vt* - **1.** [in ground] enterrer - **2.** [hide] cacher, enfouir.

bus [bʌs] *n* autobus *m*, bus *m* ; [long-distance] car *m* ; **by ~** en autobus/car.

bush [bʊʃ] *n* - **1.** [plant] buisson *m* - **2.** [open country] : **the ~** la brousse - **3.** *phr* : **she doesn't beat about the ~** elle n'y va pas par quatre chemins.

bushy ['bʊʃɪ] *adj* touffu(e).

business ['bɪznɪs] *n* - **1.** (*U*) [commerce] affaires *fpl* ; **we do a lot of ~ with them** nous travaillons beaucoup avec eux ; **on ~** pour affaires ; **to mean ~** *inf* ne pas plaisanter ; **to go out of ~** fermer, faire faillite - **2.** [company, duty] affaire *f* ; **mind your own ~!** *inf* occupe-toi de tes oignons! - **3.** [affair, matter] histoire *f*, affaire *f*.

business class *n* classe *f* affaires.

businesslike ['bɪznɪslaɪk] *adj* efficace.

businessman ['bɪznɪsmæn] (*pl* -**men** [-men]) *n* homme *m* d'affaires.

business trip *n* voyage *m* d'affaires.

businesswoman ['bɪznɪsˌwʊmən] (*pl* -**women** [-ˌwɪmɪn]) *n* femme *f* d'affaires.

busker ['bʌskəʳ] *n* *Br* chanteur *m*, -euse *f* des rues.

bus shelter *n* Abribus® *m*.

bus station *n* gare *f* routière.

bus stop *n* arrêt *m* de bus.

bust [bʌst] (*pt* & *pp* bust OR -ed) ◇ *adj inf* - **1.** [broken] foutu(e) - **2.** [bankrupt] : **to go ~**

faire faillite. ◇ n - 1. [bosom] poitrine f - 2. [statue] buste m. ◇ vt inf [break] péter.

bustle ['bʌsl] ◇ n (U) [activity] remue-ménage m. ◇ vi s'affairer.

busy ['bɪzɪ] ◇ adj - 1. [gen] occupé(e) ; **to be ~ doing sthg** être occupé à faire qqch - 2. [life, week] chargé(e) ; [town, office] animé(e). ◇ vt : **to ~ o.s. (doing sthg)** s'occuper (à faire qqch).

busybody ['bɪzɪ,bɒdɪ] n pej mouche f du coche.

busy signal n Am TELEC tonalité f « occupé ».

but [bʌt] ◇ conj mais ; **I'm sorry, ~ I don't agree** je suis désolé, mais je ne suis pas d'accord. ◇ prep sauf, excepté ; **everyone was at the party ~ Jane** tout le monde était à la soirée sauf Jane ; **he has no one ~ himself to blame** il ne peut s'en prendre qu'à lui-même. ◇ adv fml seulement, ne ... que ; **had I ~ known!** si j'avais su! ; **we can ~ try** on peut toujours essayer. ◆ **but for** prep sans.

butcher ['bʊtʃə'] ◇ n boucher m ; **~'s (shop)** boucherie f. ◇ vt - 1. [animal] abattre - 2. fig [massacre] massacrer.

butler ['bʌtlə'] n maître m d'hôtel (chez un particulier).

butt [bʌt] ◇ n - 1. [of cigarette, cigar] mégot m - 2. [of rifle] crosse f - 3. [for water] tonneau m - 4. [of joke, criticism] cible f. ◇ vt donner un coup de tête à. ◆ **butt in** vi [interrupt] : **to ~ in on sb** interrompre qqn ; **to ~ in on sthg** s'immiscer OR s'imposer dans qqch.

butter ['bʌtə'] ◇ n beurre m. ◇ vt beurrer.

buttercup ['bʌtəkʌp] n bouton m d'or.

butter dish n beurrier m.

butterfly ['bʌtəflaɪ] n SWIMMING & ZOOL papillon m.

buttocks ['bʌtəks] npl fesses fpl.

button ['bʌtn] ◇ n - 1. [gen] bouton m - 2. Am [badge] badge m. ◇ vt = button up. ◆ **button up** vt sep boutonner.

button mushroom n champignon m de Paris.

buttress ['bʌtrɪs] n contrefort m.

buxom ['bʌksəm] adj bien en chair.

buy [baɪ] (pt & pp **bought**) ◇ vt acheter ; **to ~ sthg from sb** acheter qqch à qqn. ◇ n : **a good ~** une bonne affaire. ◆ **buy up** vt sep acheter en masse.

buyer ['baɪə'] n acheteur m, -euse f.

buyout ['baɪaʊt] n rachat m.

buzz [bʌz] ◇ n - 1. [of insect] bourdonne-ment m - 2. inf [telephone call] : **to give sb a ~** passer un coup de fil à qqn. ◇ vi : **to ~ (with)** bourdonner (de). ◇ vt [on intercom] appeler.

buzzer ['bʌzə'] n sonnerie f.

buzzword ['bʌzwɜːd] n inf mot m à la mode.

by [baɪ] ◇ prep - 1. [indicating cause, agent] par ; **caused/written/killed ~** causé/écrit/tué par - 2. [indicating means, method, manner] : **to pay ~ cheque** payer par chèque ; **to travel ~ bus/train/plane/ship** voyager en bus/par le train/en avion/en bateau ; **he's a lawyer ~ profession** il est avocat de son métier ; **~ doing sthg** en faisant qqch ; **~ nature** de nature, de tempérament - 3. [beside, close to] près de ; **~ the sea** au bord de la mer ; **I sat ~ her bed** j'étais assis à son chevet - 4. [past] : **to pass ~ sb/ sthg** passer devant qqn/qqch ; **to drive ~ sb/sthg** passer en voiture devant qqn/ qqch - 5. [via, through] par ; **come in ~ the back door** entrez par la porte de derrière - 6. [at or before a particular time] avant, pas plus tard que ; **I'll be there ~ eight** j'y serai avant huit heures ; **~ now** déjà - 7. [during] : **~ day** le OR de jour ; **~ night** la OR de nuit - 8. [according to] selon, suivant ; **~ law** conformément à la loi - 9. [in arithmetic] par ; **divide/multiply 20 ~ 2** divisez/ multipliez 20 par 2 - 10. [in measurements] : **2 metres ~ 4** 2 mètres sur 4 - 11. [in quantities, amounts] à ; **~ the yard** au mètre ; **~ the thousands** par milliers ; **paid ~ the day/week/month** payé à la journée/à la semaine/au mois ; **to cut prices ~ 50%** réduire les prix de 50% - 12. [indicating gradual change] : **day ~ day** jour après jour, de jour en jour ; **one ~ one** un à un, un par un - 13. phr : **(all) ~ oneself** (tout) seul (seule) ; **I'm all ~ myself today** je suis tout seul aujourd'hui. ◇ adv ⊏➣ **go, pass** etc.

bye(-bye) [baɪ(baɪ)] excl inf au revoir!, salut!

bye-election = by-election.

byelaw ['baɪlɔː] = bylaw.

by-election n élection f partielle.

bygone ['baɪgɒn] adj d'autrefois. ◆ **bygones** npl : **to let ~s be ~s** oublier le passé.

bylaw ['baɪlɔː] n arrête m.

bypass ['baɪpɑːs] ◇ n - 1. [road] route f de contournement - 2. MED : **~ (operation)** pontage m. ◇ vt [town, difficulty] contourner ; [subject] éviter.

by-product n - 1. [product] dérivé m - 2. fig [consequence] conséquence f.

bystander ['baɪ,stændə'] n spectateur m, -trice f.

byte [baɪt] *n* COMPUT octet *m*.

byword ['baɪwɜːd] *n* [symbol] : **to be a ~ for** être synonyme de.

c (*pl* **c's** OR **cs**), **C** (*pl* **C's** OR **Cs**) [siː] *n* [letter] c *m inv*, C *m inv*. ◆ **C** *n* - **1.** MUS do *m* - **2.** SCH [mark] C *m inv* - **3.** (*abbr of* **Celsius, centigrade**) C.

c., ca. *abbr of* **circa**.

cab [kæb] *n* - **1.** [taxi] taxi *m* - **2.** [of lorry] cabine *f*.

cabaret ['kæbəreɪ] *n* cabaret *m*.

cabbage ['kæbɪdʒ] *n* [vegetable] chou *m*.

cabin ['kæbɪn] *n* - **1.** [on ship, plane] cabine *f* - **2.** [house] cabane *f*.

cabin class *n* seconde classe *f*.

cabinet ['kæbɪnɪt] *n* - **1.** [cupboard] meuble *m* - **2.** POL cabinet *m*.

cable ['keɪbl] ◇ *n* câble *m*. ◇ *vt* [news] câbler ; [person] câbler à.

cable car *n* téléphérique *m*.

cable television, cable TV *n* télévision *f* par câble.

cache [kæʃ] *n* - **1.** [store] cache *f* - **2.** COMPUT mémoire-cache *f*, antémémoire *f*.

cackle ['kækl] *vi* - **1.** [hen] caqueter - **2.** [person] jacasser.

cactus ['kæktəs] (*pl* -**tuses** [-təsiːz], -**ti** [-taɪ]) *n* cactus *m*.

cadet [kə'det] *n* élève *m* officier.

cadge [kædʒ] *Br inf* ◇ *vt* : **to ~ sthg off** OR **from sb** taper qqn de qqch. ◇ *vi* : **to ~ off** OR **from sb** taper qqn.

caesarean (section) [sɪ'zeərɪən-] *Br*, **cesarean (section)** *Am n* césarienne *f*.

cafe, café ['kæfeɪ] *n* café *m*.

cafeteria [,kæfɪ'tɪərɪə] *n* cafétéria *f*.

caffeine ['kæfiːn] *n* caféine *f*.

cage [keɪdʒ] *n* [for animal] cage *f*.

cagey ['keɪdʒɪ] (*compar* -**ier**, *superl* -**iest**) *adj inf* discret(ète).

cagoule [kə'guːl] *n Br* K-way® *m inv*.

cajole [kə'dʒəʊl] *vt* : **to ~ sb (into doing sthg)** enjôler qqn (pour qu'il fasse qqch).

cake [keɪk] *n* - **1.** CULIN gâteau *m* ; [of fish, potato] croquette *f* ; **it's a piece of ~** *inf fig* c'est du gâteau - **2.** [of soap] pain *m*.

caked [keɪkt] *adj* : **~ with mud** recouvert(e) de boue séchée.

calcium ['kælsɪəm] *n* calcium *m*.

calculate ['kælkjʊleɪt] *vt* - **1.** [result, number] calculer ; [consequences] évaluer - **2.** [plan] : **to be ~d to do sthg** être calculé(e) pour faire qqch.

calculating ['kælkjʊleɪtɪŋ] *adj pej* calculateur(trice).

calculation [,kælkjʊ'leɪʃn] *n* calcul *m*.

calculator ['kælkjʊleɪtə'] *n* calculatrice *f*.

calendar ['kælɪndə'] *n* calendrier *m*.

calendar year *n* année *f* civile.

calf [kɑːf] (*pl* **calves** [kɑːvz]) *n* - **1.** [of cow, leather] veau *m* ; [of elephant] éléphanteau *m* ; [of seal] bébé *m* phoque - **2.** ANAT mollet *m*.

calibre, caliber *Am* ['kælɪbə'] *n* calibre *m*.

California [,kælɪ'fɔːnjə] *n* Californie *f*.

calipers *Am* = **callipers**.

call [kɔːl] ◇ *n* - **1.** [cry] appel *m*, cri *m* - **2.** TELEC appel *m* (téléphonique) - **3.** [summons, invitation] appel *m* ; **to be on ~** [doctor etc] être de garde - **4.** [visit] visite *f* ; **to pay a ~ on sb** rendre visite à qqn - **5.** [demand] : **~ (for)** demande *f* (de). ◇ *vt* - **1.** [name, summon, phone] appeler ; **what's this thing ~ed?** comment ça s'appelle ce truc? ; **she's ~ed Joan** elle s'appelle Joan ; **let's ~ it £10** disons 10 livres - **2.** [label] : **he ~ed me a liar** il m'a traité de menteur - **3.** [shout] appeler, crier - **4.** [announce - meeting] convoquer ; [- strike] lancer ; [- flight] appeler ; [- election] annoncer. ◇ *vi* - **1.** [shout - person] crier ; [- animal, bird] pousser un cri/des cris - **2.** TELEC appeler ; **who's ~ing?** qui est à l'appareil? - **3.** [visit] passer. ◆ **call back** ◇ *vt sep* rappeler. ◇ *vi* - **1.** TELEC rappeler - **2.** [visit again] repasser. ◆ **call for** *vt fus* - **1.** [collect - person] passer prendre ; [- package, goods] passer chercher - **2.** [demand] demander. ◆ **call in** ◇ *vt sep* - **1.** [expert, police etc] faire venir - **2.** COMM [goods] rappeler ; FIN [loan] exiger le remboursement de. ◇ *vi* passer. ◆ **call off** *vt sep* - **1.** [cancel] annuler - **2.** [dog] rappeler. ◆ **call on** *vt fus* - **1.** [visit] passer voir - **2.** [ask] : **to ~ on sb to do sthg** demander à qqn de faire qqch. ◆ **call out** ◇ *vt sep* - **1.** [police, doctor] appeler - **2.** [cry out] crier. ◇ *vi* [cry out] crier. ◆ **call round** *vi Br* passer. ◆ **call up** *vt sep* - **1.** MIL & TELEC appeler - **2.** COMPUT rappeler.

call box *n Br* cabine *f* (téléphonique).

caller ['kɔ:lə'] *n* - **1.** [visitor] visiteur *m*, -euse *f* - **2.** TELEC demandeur *m*.

call-in *n Am* RADIO & TV programme *m* à ligne ouverte.

calling ['kɔ:lɪŋ] *n* - **1.** [profession] métier *m* - **2.** [vocation] vocation *f*.

calling card *n Am* carte *f* de visite.

callipers *Br*, **calipers** *Am* ['kælɪpəz] *npl* - **1.** MATH compas *m* - **2.** MED appareil *m* orthopédique.

callous ['kæləs] *adj* dur(e).

callus ['kæləs] (*pl* -es [-i:z]) *n* cal *m*, durillon *m*.

calm [ka:m] ◇ *adj* calme. ◇ *n* calme *m*. ◇ *vt* calmer. ◆ **calm down** ◇ *vt sep* calmer. ◇ *vi* se calmer.

Calor gas® ['kælə'-] *n Br* butane *m*.

calorie ['kælərɪ] *n* calorie *f*.

calves [ka:vz] *pl* ▷ **calf**.

camber ['kæmbə'] *n* [of road] bombement *m*.

Cambodia [kæm'bəʊdjə] *n* Cambodge *m*.

camcorder ['kæm,kɔ:də'] *n* Caméscope® *m*.

came [keɪm] *pt* ▷ **come**.

camel ['kæml] *n* chameau *m*.

cameo ['kæmɪəʊ] (*pl* -s) *n* - **1.** [jewellery] camée *m* - **2.** CINEMA & THEATRE courte apparition *f* (d'une grande vedette).

camera ['kæmərə] *n* PHOT appareil-photo *m* ; CINEMA & TV caméra *f*. ◆ **in camera** *adv* à huis clos.

cameraman ['kæmərəmæn] (*pl* -men [-men]) *n* cameraman *m*.

Cameroon [,kæmə'ru:n] *n* Cameroun *m*.

camouflage ['kæməfla:ʒ] ◇ *n* camouflage *m*. ◇ *vt* camoufler.

camp [kæmp] ◇ *n* camp *m*. ◇ *vi* camper. ◆ **camp out** *vi* camper.

campaign [kæm'peɪn] ◇ *n* campagne *f*. ◇ *vi* : **to ~ (for/against)** mener une campagne (pour/contre).

camp bed *n* lit *m* de camp.

camper ['kæmpə'] *n* - **1.** [person] campeur *m*, -euse *f* - **2.** [vehicle] : **~ (van)** camping-car *m*.

campground ['kæmpgraʊnd] *n Am* terrain *m* de camping.

camping ['kæmpɪŋ] *n* camping *m* ; **to go ~** faire du camping.

camping site, campsite ['kæmpsaɪt] *n* (terrain *m* de) camping *m*.

campus ['kæmpəs] (*pl* -es [-i:z]) *n* campus *m*.

can¹ [kæn] (*pt & pp* -ned, *cont* -ning) ◇ *n* [of drink, food] boîte *f* ; [of oil] bidon *m* ; [of paint] pot *m*. ◇ *vt* mettre en boîte.

can² [*weak form* kən, *strong form* kæn] (*pt & conditional* could, *negative* cannot OR can't) *modal vb* - **1.** [be able to] pouvoir ; **you come to lunch?** tu peux venir déjeuner? ; **~ you see/hear/smell something?** tu vois/entends/sens quelque chose? - **2.** [know how to] savoir ; **~ you drive/cook?** tu sais conduire/cuisiner? ; **I ~ speak French** je parle le français - **3.** [indicating permission, in polite requests] pouvoir ; **you ~ use my car if you like** tu peux prendre ma voiture si tu veux ; **~ I speak to John, please?** est-ce que je pourrais parler à John, s'il vous plaît? - **4.** [indicating disbelief, puzzlement] pouvoir ; **what ~ she have done with it?** qu'est-ce qu'elle a bien pu en faire? ; **you ~'t be serious!** tu ne parles pas sérieusement! - **5.** [indicating possibility] : **I could see you tomorrow** je pourrais vous voir demain ; **the train could have been cancelled** peut-être que le train a été annulé.

Canada ['kænədə] *n* Canada *m* ; **in ~** au Canada.

Canadian [kə'neɪdjən] ◇ *adj* canadien(enne). ◇ *n* Canadien *m*, -enne *f*.

canal [kə'næl] *n* canal *m*.

Canaries [kə'neərɪz] *npl* : **the ~** les Canaries *fpl*.

canary [kə'neərɪ] *n* canari *m*.

cancel ['kænsl] *vt* - **1.** [gen] annuler ; [appointment, delivery] décommander - **2.** [stamp] oblitérer ; [cheque] faire opposition à. ◆ **cancel out** *vt sep* annuler ; **to ~ each other out** s'annuler.

cancellation [,kænsə'leɪʃn] *n* annulation *f*.

cancer ['kænsə'] *n* cancer *m*. ◆ **Cancer** *n* Cancer *m*.

candelabra [,kændɪ'la:brə] *n* candélabre *m*.

candid ['kændɪd] *adj* franc (franche).

candidate ['kændɪdət] *n* : **~ (for)** candidat *m*, -e *f* (pour).

candle ['kændl] *n* bougie *f*, chandelle *f*.

candlelight ['kændllaɪt] *n* lueur *f* d'une bougie OR d'une chandelle.

candlelit ['kændllɪt] *adj* aux chandelles.

candlestick ['kændlstɪk] *n* bougeoir *m*.

candour *Br*, **candor** *Am* ['kændə'] *n* franchise *f*.

candy ['kændɪ] *n* - **1.** (*U*) [confectionery] confiserie *f* - **2.** [sweet] bonbon *m*.

candyfloss ['kændɪflɒs] *n Br* barbe *f* à papa.

cane [keɪn] ⬦ *n* - **1.** *(U)* [for furniture] rotin *m* - **2.** [walking stick] canne *f* - **3.** [for punishment] : **the ~** la verge - **4.** [for supporting plant] tuteur *m*. ⬦ *vt* fouetter.

canine ['keɪnaɪn] ⬦ *adj* canin(e). ⬦ *n* : **~ (tooth)** canine *f*.

canister ['kænɪstəʳ] *n* [for film, tea] boîte *f*; [for gas, smoke] bombe *f*.

cannabis ['kænəbɪs] *n* cannabis *m*.

canned [kænd] *adj* [food, drink] en boîte.

cannibal ['kænɪbl] *n* cannibale *mf*.

cannon ['kænən] (*pl inv* OR **-s**) *n* canon *m*.

cannonball ['kænənbɔːl] *n* boulet *m* de canon.

cannot ['kænɒt] *fml* ⬅ **can²**.

canny ['kænɪ] *adj* [shrewd] adroit(e).

canoe [kə'nuː] *n* canoë *m*, kayak *m*.

canoeing [kə'nuːɪŋ] *n (U)* canoë-kayak *m*.

canon ['kænən] *n* canon *m*.

can opener *n* ouvre-boîtes *m inv*.

canopy ['kænəpɪ] *n* - **1.** [over bed] baldaquin *m*, [over seat] dais *m* - **2.** [of trees, branches] voûte *f*.

can't [kɑːnt] = **cannot**.

cantankerous [kæn'tæŋkərəs] *adj* hargneux(euse).

canteen [kæn'tiːn] *n* - **1.** [restaurant] cantine *f* - **2.** [box of cutlery] ménagère *f*.

canter ['kæntəʳ] ⬦ *n* petit galop *m*. ⬦ *vi* aller au petit galop.

cantilever ['kæntɪliːvəʳ] *n* cantilever *m*.

canvas ['kænvəs] *n* toile *f*.

canvass ['kænvəs] *vt* - **1.** POL [person] solliciter la voix de - **2.** [opinion] sonder.

canyon ['kænjən] *n* canyon *m*, cañon *m*.

cap [kæp] ⬦ *n* - **1.** [hat - gen] casquette *f* - **2.** [of pen] capuchon *m* ; [of bottle] capsule *f* ; [of lipstick] bouchon *m*. ⬦ *vt* - **1.** [top] : **to be ~ ped with** être coiffé(e) de - **2.** [outdo] : **to ~ it all** pour couronner le tout.

capability [ˌkeɪpə'bɪlətɪ] *n* capacité *f*.

capable ['keɪpəbl] *adj* : **~ (of)** capable (de).

capacity [kə'pæsɪtɪ] *n* - **1.** *(U)* [limit] capacité *f*, contenance *f* - **2.** [ability] : **~ (for)** aptitude *f* (à) - **3.** [role] qualité *f* ; **in an advisory ~** en tant que conseiller.

cape [keɪp] *n* - **1.** GEOGR cap *m* - **2.** [cloak] cape *f*.

caper ['keɪpəʳ] *n* - **1.** CULIN câpre *f* - **2.** *inf* [dishonest activity] coup *m*, combine *f*.

capita ⬅ **per capita.**

capital ['kæpɪtl] ⬦ *adj* - **1.** [letter] majuscule - **2.** [offence] capital(e). ⬦ *n* - **1.** [of country] : **~ (city)** capitale *f* - **2.** TYPO : **~ (letter)** majuscule *f* - **3.** *(U)* [money] capital *m* ; **to make ~ (out) of** *fig* tirer profit de.

capital expenditure *n (U)* dépenses *fpl* d'investissement.

capital gains tax *n* impôt *m* sur les plus-values.

capital goods *npl* biens *mpl* d'équipement.

capitalism ['kæpɪtəlɪzm] *n* capitalisme *m*.

capitalist ['kæpɪtəlɪst] ⬦ *adj* capitaliste. ⬦ *n* capitaliste *mf*.

capitalize, -ise ['kæpɪtəlaɪz] *vi* : **to ~ on** tirer parti de.

capital punishment *n* peine *f* capitale OR de mort.

Capitol Hill ['kæpɪtl-] *n* siège du Congrès à Washington.

capitulate [kə'pɪtjuleɪt] *vi* capituler.

Capricorn ['kæprɪkɔːn] *n* Capricorne *m*.

capsize [kæp'saɪz] ⬦ *vt* faire chavirer. ⬦ *vi* chavirer.

capsule ['kæpsjuːl] *n* - **1.** [gen] capsule *f* - **2.** MED gélule *f*.

captain ['kæptɪn] *n* capitaine *m*.

caption ['kæpʃn] *n* légende *f*.

captivate ['kæptɪveɪt] *vt* captiver.

captive ['kæptɪv] ⬦ *adj* captif(ive). ⬦ *n* captif *m*, -ive *f*.

captor ['kæptəʳ] *n* ravisseur *m*, -euse *f*.

capture ['kæptʃəʳ] ⬦ *vt* - **1.** [person, animal] capturer ; [city] prendre ; [market] conquérir - **2.** [attention, imagination] captiver - **3.** COMPUT saisir. ⬦ *n* [of person, animal] capture *f* ; [of city] prise *f*.

car [kɑːʳ] ⬦ *n* - **1.** AUT voiture *f* - **2.** RAIL wagon *m*, voiture *f*. ⬦ *comp* [door, accident] de voiture ; [industry] automobile.

carafe [kə'ræf] *n* carafe *f*.

caramel ['kærəmel] *n* caramel *m*.

carat ['kærət] *n Br* carat *m* ; **24-~ gold** or à 24 carats.

caravan ['kærəvæn] *n* [gen] caravane *f* ; [towed by horse] roulotte *f*.

caravan site *n Br* camping *m* pour caravanes.

carbohydrate [ˌkɑːbəʊ'haɪdreɪt] *n* CHEM hydrate *m* de carbone. ➡ **carbohydrates** *npl* [in food] glucides *mpl*.

carbon ['kɑːbən] *n* [element] carbone *m*.

carbonated ['kɑːbəneɪtɪd] *adj* [mineral water] gazeux(euse).

carbon copy n - 1. [document] carbone m - 2. fig [exact copy] réplique f.

carbon dioxide [-daɪˈɒksaɪd] n gaz m carbonique.

carbon monoxide n oxyde m de carbone.

carbon paper n (U) (papier m) carbone m.

car-boot sale n Br brocante en plein air où les coffres des voitures servent d'étal.

carburettor Br, **carburetor** Am [ˌkɑːbəˈretər] n carburateur m.

carcass [ˈkɑːkəs] n [of animal] carcasse f.

card [kɑːd] n - 1. [gen] carte f - 2. (U) [cardboard] carton m. ◆ **cards** npl : to play ~s jouer aux cartes. ◆ **on the cards** Br, **in the cards** Am adv inf : it's on the ~s that ... il y a de grandes chances pour que ...

cardboard [ˈkɑːdbɔːd] ◇ n (U) carton m. ◇ comp en carton.

cardboard box n boîte f en carton.

cardiac [ˈkɑːdɪæk] adj cardiaque.

cardigan [ˈkɑːdɪgən] n cardigan m.

cardinal [ˈkɑːdɪnl] ◇ adj cardinal(e). ◇ n RELIG cardinal m.

card index n Br fichier m.

cardphone [ˈkɑːdfəʊn] n Br téléphone m à carte.

card table n table f de jeu.

care [keər] ◇ n - 1. (U) [protection, attention] soin m, attention f ; **to be in** ~ Br être à l'Assistance publique ; **to take** ~ **of** [look after] s'occuper de ; **to take** ~ **(to do sthg)** prendre soin (de faire qqch) ; **take** ~! faites bien attention à vous! - 2. [cause of worry] souci m. ◇ vi - 1. [be concerned] : **to** ~ **about** se soucier de - 2. [mind] : **I don't** ~ ça m'est égal ; **who** ~s? qu'est-ce que ça peut faire? ◆ **care of** prep chez. ◆ **care for** vt fus dated [like] aimer.

career [kəˈrɪər] ◇ n carrière f. ◇ vi aller à toute vitesse.

careers adviser n conseiller m, -ère f d'orientation.

carefree [ˈkeəfriː] adj insouciant(e).

careful [ˈkeəfʊl] adj - 1. [cautious] prudent(e) ; **to be** ~ **to do sthg** prendre soin de faire qqch, faire attention à faire qqch ; **be** ~! fais attention! ; **to be** ~ **with one's money** regarder à la dépense - 2. [work] soigné(e) ; [worker] consciencieux(euse).

carefully [ˈkeəflɪ] adv - 1. [cautiously] prudemment - 2. [thoroughly] soigneusement.

careless [ˈkeəlɪs] adj - 1. [work] peu soigné(e) ; [driver] négligent(e) - 2. [unconcerned] insouciant(e).

caress [kəˈres] ◇ n caresse f. ◇ vt caresser.

caretaker [ˈkeəˌteɪkər] n Br gardien m, -enne f.

car ferry n ferry m.

cargo [ˈkɑːgəʊ] (pl -es or -s) n cargaison f.

car hire n Br location f de voitures.

Caribbean [Br kærɪˈbiːən, Am kəˈrɪbɪən] n : **the** ~ **(Sea)** la mer des Caraïbes OR des Antilles.

caring [ˈkeərɪŋ] adj bienveillant(e).

carnage [ˈkɑːnɪdʒ] n carnage m.

carnal [ˈkɑːnl] adj literary charnel(elle).

carnation [kɑːˈneɪʃn] n œillet m.

carnival [ˈkɑːnɪvl] n carnaval m.

carnivorous [kɑːˈnɪvərəs] adj carnivore.

carol [ˈkærəl] n : **(Christmas)** ~ chant m de Noël.

carousel [ˌkærəˈsel] n - 1. [at fair] manège m - 2. [at airport] carrousel m.

carp [kɑːp] (pl inv or -s) ◇ n carpe f. ◇ vi : **to** ~ **(about sthg)** critiquer (qqch).

car park n Br parking m.

carpenter [ˈkɑːpəntər] n [on building site, in shipyard] charpentier m ; [furniture-maker] menuisier m.

carpentry [ˈkɑːpəntrɪ] n [on building site, in shipyard] charpenterie f ; [furniture-making] menuiserie f.

carpet [ˈkɑːpɪt] ◇ n lit & fig tapis m ; **(fitted)** ~ moquette f. ◇ vt [floor] recouvrir d'un tapis ; [with fitted carpet] recouvrir de moquette, moquetter.

carpet slipper n pantoufle f.

carpet sweeper [-ˌswiːpər] n balai m mécanique.

car phone n téléphone m pour automobile.

car rental n Am location f de voitures.

carriage [ˈkærɪdʒ] n - 1. [of train, horse-drawn] voiture f - 2. (U) [transport of goods] transport m ; ~ **paid** OR **free** Br franco de port.

carriage return n retour m chariot.

carriageway [ˈkærɪdʒweɪ] n Br chaussée f.

carrier [ˈkærɪər] n - 1. COMM transporteur m - 2. [of disease] porteur m, -euse f - 3. = **carrier bag**.

carrier bag n sac m (en plastique).

carrot [ˈkærət] n carotte f.

carry [ˈkærɪ] ◇ vt - 1. [subj : person, wind, water] **porter** ; [subj : vehicle] **transporter** - 2. [disease] **transmettre** - 3. [responsibility] impliquer ; [consequences] entraîner - **4.** [motion, proposal] voter - **5.** [baby] attendre - **6.** MATH retenir. <> *vi* [sound] porter. ➧ **carry away** *vt fus* : **to get carried away** s'enthousiasmer. ➧ **carry forward** *vt sep* FIN reporter. ➧ **carry off** *vt sep* - **1.** [plan] mener à bien - **2.** [prize] remporter. ➧ **carry on** <> *vt fus* continuer ; **to ~ on doing sthg** continuer à OR de faire qqch. <> *vi* - **1.** [continue] continuer ; **to ~ on with sthg** continuer qqch - **2.** *inf* [make a fuss] faire des histoires. ➧ **carry out** *vt fus* [task] remplir ; [plan, order] exécuter ; [experiment] effectuer ; [investigation] mener. ➧ **carry through** *vt sep* [accomplish] réaliser.

carryall ['kærɪɔːl] *n Am* fourre-tout *m inv*.

carrycot ['kærɪkɒt] *n* couffin *m*.

carry-out *n* plat *m* à emporter.

carsick ['kaːˌsɪk] *adj* : **to be ~** être malade en voiture.

cart [kaːt] <> *n* charrette *f*. <> *vt inf* traîner.

carton ['kaːtn] *n* - **1.** [box] boîte *f* en carton - **2.** [of cream, yoghurt] pot *m* ; [of milk] carton *m*.

cartoon [kaː'tuːn] *n* - **1.** [satirical drawing] dessin *m* humoristique - **2.** [comic strip] bande *f* dessinée - **3.** [film] dessin *m* animé.

cartridge ['kaːtrɪdʒ] *n* - **1.** [for gun, pen] cartouche *f* - **2.** [for camera] chargeur *m*.

cartwheel ['kaːtwiːl] *n* [movement] roue *f*.

carve [kaːv] <> *vt* - **1.** [wood, stone] sculpter ; [design, name] graver - **2.** [slice - meat] découper. <> *vi* découper. ➧ **carve out** *vt sep fig* se tailler. ➧ **carve up** *vt sep fig* diviser.

carving ['kaːvɪŋ] *n* [of wood] sculpture *f* ; [of stone] ciselure *f*.

carving knife *n* couteau *m* à découper.

car wash *n* [process] lavage *m* de voitures ; [place] station *f* de lavage de voitures.

case [keɪs] *n* - **1.** [gen] cas *m* ; **to be the ~** être le cas ; **in ~ of** en cas de ; **in that ~** dans ce cas ; **in which ~** auquel cas ; **as or whatever the ~ may be** selon le cas - **2.** [argument] : **~ (for/against)** arguments *mpl* (pour/contre) - **3.** JUR affaire *f*, procès *m* - **4.** [container - gen] caisse *f* ; [- for glasses etc] étui *m* - **5.** *Br* [suitcase] valise *f*. ➧ **in any case** *adv* quoi qu'il en soit, de toute façon. ➧ **in case** <> *conj* au cas où. <> *adv* : **(just) in ~** à tout hasard.

cash [kæʃ] <> *n* (*U*) - **1.** [notes and coins] liquide *m* ; **to pay (in) ~** payer comptant OR en espèces - **2.** *inf* [money] sous *mpl*, fric *m*

- **3.** [payment] : **~ in advance** paiement *m* à l'avance ; **~ on delivery** paiement *m* à la livraison. <> *vt* encaisser.

cash and carry *n* libre-service *m* de gros, cash-and-carry *m*.

cashbook ['kæʃbʊk] *n* livre *m* de caisse.

cash box *n* caisse *f*.

cash card *n* carte *f* de retrait.

cash desk *n Br* caisse *f*.

cash dispenser [-dɪˌspensəʳ] *n* distributeur *m* automatique de billets.

cashew (nut) ['kæʃuː-] *n* noix *f* de cajou.

cashier [kæ'ʃɪəʳ] *n* caissier *m*, -ère *f*.

cash machine *n* distributeur *m* de billets.

cashmere [kæʃ'mɪəʳ] *n* cachemire *m*.

cash register *n* caisse *f* enregistreuse.

casing ['keɪsɪŋ] *n* revêtement *m* ; TECH boîtier *m*.

casino [kə'siːnəʊ] (*pl* -s) *n* casino *m*.

cask [kaːsk] *n* tonneau *m*.

casket ['kaːskɪt] *n* - **1.** [for jewels] coffret *m* - **2.** *Am* [coffin] cercueil *m*.

casserole ['kæsərəʊl] *n* - **1.** [stew] ragoût *m* - **2.** [pan] cocotte *f*.

cassette [kæ'set] *n* [of magnetic tape] cassette *f* ; PHOT recharge *f*.

cassette player *n* lecteur *m* de cassettes.

cassette recorder *n* magnétophone *m* à cassettes.

cast [kaːst] (*pt & pp* cast) <> *n* [CINEMA & THEATRE - actors] acteurs *mpl* ; [- list of actors] distribution *f*. <> *vt* - **1.** [throw] jeter ; **to ~ doubt on sthg** jeter le doute sur qqch - **2.** CINEMA & THEATRE donner un rôle à - **3.** [vote] : **to ~ one's vote** voter - **4.** [metal] couler ; [statue] mouler. ➧ **cast aside** *vt sep fig* écarter, rejeter. ➧ **cast off** *vi* NAUT larguer les amarres.

castaway ['kaːstəweɪ] *n* naufragé *m*, -e *f*.

caster ['kaːstəʳ] *n* [wheel] roulette *f*.

caster sugar *n Br* sucre *m* en poudre.

casting vote *n* voix *f* prépondérante.

cast iron *n* fonte *f*.

castle ['kaːsl] *n* - **1.** [building] château *m* - **2.** CHESS tour *f*.

castor ['kaːstəʳ] = **caster**.

castor oil *n* huile *f* de ricin.

castor sugar = **caster sugar**.

castrate [kæ'streɪt] *vt* châtrer.

casual ['kæʒʊəl] *adj* - **1.** [relaxed, indifferent] désinvolte - **2.** [offhand] sans-gêne - **3.** [chance] fortuit(e) - **4.** [clothes] décontracté(e), sport (*inv*) - **5.** [work, worker] temporaire.

casually ['kæʒʊəlɪ] *adv* [in a relaxed manner] avec désinvolture ; ~ **dressed** habillé simplement.

casualty ['kæʒjʊəltɪ] *n* - 1. [dead person] mort *m*, -e *f*, victime *f* ; [injured person] blessé *m*, -e *f* ; [of road accident] accidenté *m*, -e *f* - 2. = casualty department.

casualty department *n Br* service *m* des urgences.

cat [kæt] *n* - 1. [domestic] chat *m* - 2. [wild] fauve *m*.

catalogue *Br*, **catalog** *Am* ['kætəlɒg] <> *n* [gen] catalogue *m* ; [in library] fichier *m*. <> *vt* cataloguer.

catalyst ['kætəlɪst] *n lit & fig* catalyseur *m*.

catalytic convertor [ˌkætə'lɪtɪkkən'-vɜːtəʳ] *n* pot *m* catalytique.

catapult ['kætəpʌlt] *Br* <> *n* [hand-held] lance-pierres *m inv*. <> *vt lit & fig* catapulter.

cataract ['kætərækt] *n* cataracte *f*.

catarrh [kə'tɑːʳ] *n* catarrhe *m*.

catastrophe [kə'tæstrəfɪ] *n* catastrophe *f*.

catch [kætʃ] (*pt & pp* caught) <> *vt* - 1. [gen] attraper ; **to ~ sight** OR **a glimpse of** apercevoir ; **to ~ sb's attention** attirer l'attention de qqn ; **to ~ sb's imagination** séduire qqn ; **to ~ the post** *Br* arriver à temps pour la levée - 2. [discover, surprise] prendre, surprendre ; **to ~ sb doing sthg** surprendre qqn à faire qqch - 3. [hear clearly] saisir, comprendre - 4. [trap] : **I caught my finger in the door** je me suis pris le doigt dans la porte - 5. [strike] frapper. <> *vi* - 1. [become hooked, get stuck] se prendre - 2. [fire] prendre, partir. <> *n* - 1. [of ball, thing caught] prise *f* - 2. [fastener - of box] fermoir *m* ; [- of window] loqueteau *m* ; [- of door] loquet *m* - 3. [snag] hic *m*, entourloupette *f*. ◆ **catch on** *vi* - 1. [become popular] prendre - 2. *inf* [understand] : **to ~ on (to sthg)** piger (qqch). ◆ **catch out** *vt sep* [trick] prendre en défaut, coincer. ◆ **catch up** <> *vt sep* rattraper. <> *vi* : **to ~ up on sthg** rattraper qqch. ◆ **catch up with** *vt fus* rattraper.

catching ['kætʃɪŋ] *adj* contagieux(euse).

catchment area ['kætʃmənt-] *n Br* [of school] secteur *m* de recrutement scolaire ; [of hospital] circonscription *f* hospitalière.

catchphrase ['kætʃfreɪz] *n* rengaine *f*.

catchy ['kætʃɪ] *adj* facile à retenir, entraînant(e).

categorically [ˌkætɪ'gɒrɪklɪ] *adv* catégoriquement.

category ['kætəgərɪ] *n* catégorie *f*.

cater ['keɪtəʳ] *vi* [provide food] s'occuper de la nourriture, prévoir les repas. ◆ **cater for** *vt fus Br* - 1. [tastes, needs] pourvoir à, satisfaire ; [customers] s'adresser à - 2. [anticipate] prévoir. ◆ **cater to** *vt fus* satisfaire.

caterer ['keɪtərəʳ] *n* traiteur *m*.

catering ['keɪtərɪŋ] *n* [trade] restauration *f*.

caterpillar ['kætəpɪləʳ] *n* chenille *f*.

caterpillar tracks *npl* chenille *f*.

cathedral [kə'θiːdrəl] *n* cathédrale *f*.

Catholic ['kæθlɪk] <> *adj* catholique. <> *n* catholique *mf*. ◆ **catholic** *adj* [tastes] éclectique.

Catseyes® ['kætsaɪz] *npl Br* catadioptres *mpl*.

cattle ['kætl] *npl* bétail *m*.

catty ['kætɪ] *adj inf pej* [spiteful] rosse, vache.

catwalk ['kætwɔːk] *n* passerelle *f*.

caucus ['kɔːkəs] *n* - 1. *Am* POL comité *m* électoral *(d'un parti)* - 2. *Br* POL comité *m* *(d'un parti)*.

caught [kɔːt] *pt & pp* ⊳ **catch**.

cauliflower ['kɒlɪˌflaʊəʳ] *n* chou-fleur *m*.

cause [kɔːz] <> *n* cause *f* ; **I have no ~ for complaint** je n'ai pas à me plaindre, je n'ai pas lieu de me plaindre ; **to have ~ to do sthg** avoir lieu OR des raisons de faire qqch. <> *vt* causer ; **to ~ sb to do sthg** faire faire qqch à qqn ; **to ~ sthg to be done** faire faire qqch.

caustic ['kɔːstɪk] *adj* caustique.

caution ['kɔːʃn] <> *n* - 1. (U) [care] précaution *f*, prudence *f* - 2. [warning] avertissement *m* - 3. *Br* JUR réprimande *f*. <> *vt* - 1. [warn] : **to ~ sb against doing sthg** déconseiller à qqn de faire qqch - 2. *Br* [subj : policeman] : **to ~ sb for sthg** réprimander qqn pour qqch.

cautious ['kɔːʃəs] *adj* prudent(e).

cavalry ['kævlrɪ] *n* cavalerie *f*.

cave [keɪv] *n* caverne *f*, grotte *f*. ◆ **cave in** *vi* [roof, ceiling] s'affaisser.

caveman ['keɪvmæn] (*pl* -men [-men]) *n* homme *m* des cavernes.

cavernous ['kævənəs] *adj* [room, building] immense.

caviar(e) ['kævɪɑːʳ] *n* caviar *m*.

cavity ['kævətɪ] *n* cavité *f*.

cavort [kə'vɔːt] *vi* gambader.

CB *n* (*abbr of* citizens' band) CB *f*.

CBI *n abbr of* **Confederation of British Industry.**

cc ⬥ *n* (*abbr of* **cubic centimetre**) cm³. ⬥ (*abbr of* **carbon copy**) pcc.

CD *n* (*abbr of* **compact disc**) CD *m*.

CD player *n* lecteur *m* de CD.

CD-ROM [ˌsiːdiːˈrɒm] (*abbr of* **compact disc read only memory**) *n* CD-ROM *m*, CD-Rom *m*.

cease [siːs] *fml* ⬥ *vt* cesser ; **to ~ doing** OR **to do sthg** cesser de faire qqch. ⬥ *vi* cesser.

cease-fire *n* cessez-le-feu *m inv*.

ceaseless ['siːslɪs] *adj fml* incessant(e), continuel(elle).

cedar (tree) ['siːdər-] *n* cèdre *m*.

cedilla [sɪˈdɪlə] *n* cédille *f*.

ceiling ['siːlɪŋ] *n lit & fig* plafond *m*.

celebrate ['selɪbreɪt] ⬥ *vt* [gen] célébrer, fêter. ⬥ *vi* faire la fête.

celebrated ['selɪbreɪtɪd] *adj* célèbre.

celebration [ˌselɪˈbreɪʃn] *n* - 1. (U) [activity, feeling] fête *f*, festivités *fpl* - 2. [event] festivités *fpl*.

celebrity [sɪˈlebrətɪ] *n* célébrité *f*.

celery ['selərɪ] *n* céleri *m* (en branches).

celibate ['selɪbət] *adj* célibataire.

cell [sel] *n* [gen & COMPUT] cellule *f*.

cellar ['selər] *n* cave *f*.

cello ['tʃeləʊ] (*pl* -s) *n* violoncelle *m*.

Cellophane® ['seləfeɪn] *n* Cellophane® *f*.

Celsius ['selsɪəs] *adj* Celsius (*inv*).

Celt [kelt] *n* Celte *mf*.

Celtic ['keltɪk] ⬥ *adj* celte. ⬥ *n* [language] celte *m*.

cement [sɪˈment] ⬥ *n* ciment *m*. ⬥ *vt lit & fig* cimenter.

cement mixer *n* bétonnière *f*.

cemetery ['semɪtrɪ] *n* cimetière *m*.

censor ['sensər] ⬥ *n* censeur *m*. ⬥ *vt* censurer.

censorship ['sensəʃɪp] *n* censure *f*.

censure ['senʃər] ⬥ *n* blâme *m*, critique *f*. ⬥ *vt* blâmer, critiquer.

census ['sensəs] (*pl* -es [-iːz]) *n* recensement *m*.

cent [sent] *n* cent *m*.

centenary Br [sen'tiːnərɪ], **centennial** Am [sen'tenjəl] *n* centenaire *m*.

center Am = centre.

centigrade ['sentɪgreɪd] *adj* centigrade.

centilitre Br, **centiliter** Am ['sentɪˌliːtər] *n* centilitre *m*.

centimetre Br, **centimeter** Am ['sentɪˌmiːtər] *n* centimètre *m*.

centipede ['sentɪpiːd] *n* mille-pattes *m inv*.

central ['sentrəl] *adj* central(e).

Central America *n* Amérique *f* centrale.

central heating *n* chauffage *m* central.

centralize, **-ise** ['sentrəlaɪz] *vt* centraliser.

central locking [-ˈlɒkɪŋ] *n* AUT verrouillage *m* centralisé.

central reservation *n* Br AUT terre-plein *m* central.

centre Br, **center** Am ['sentər] ⬥ *n* centre *m* ; **~ of attention** centre d'attraction, point *m* de mire ; **~ of gravity** centre de gravité. ⬥ *adj* - 1. [middle] central(e) ; **a ~ parting** une raie au milieu - 2. POL du centre, centriste. ⬥ *vt* centrer.

centre back *n* FTBL arrière *m* central.

centre forward *n* FTBL avant-centre *m inv*.

centre half *n* FTBL arrière *m* central.

century ['sentʃʊrɪ] *n* siècle *m*.

CEO (*abbr of* **chief executive officer**) *n* Am président-directeur général *m*.

ceramic [sɪˈræmɪk] *adj* en céramique. ◆ **ceramics** *npl* [objects] objets *mpl* en céramique.

cereal ['sɪərɪəl] *n* céréale *f*.

ceremonial [ˌserɪˈməʊnjəl] ⬥ *adj* [dress] de cérémonie ; [duties] honorifique. ⬥ *n* cérémonial *m*.

ceremony ['serɪmənɪ] *n* - 1. [event] cérémonie *f* - 2. (U) [pomp, formality] cérémonies *fpl* ; **to stand on ~** faire des cérémonies.

certain ['sɜːtn] *adj* [gen] certain(e) ; **he is ~ to be late** il est certain qu'il sera en retard, il sera certainement en retard ; **to be ~ of sthg/of doing sthg** être assuré de qqch/de faire qqch, être sûr de qqch/de faire qqch ; **to make ~** vérifier ; **to make ~ of** s'assurer de ; **I know for ~ that ...** je suis sûr OR certain que ... ; **to a ~ extent** jusqu'à un certain point, dans une certaine mesure.

certainly ['sɜːtnlɪ] *adv* certainement.

certainty ['sɜːtntɪ] *n* certitude *f*.

certificate [səˈtɪfɪkət] *n* certificat *m*.

certified ['sɜːtɪfaɪd] *adj* [teacher] diplômé(e) ; [document] certifié(e).

certified mail *n* Am envoi *m* recommandé.

certified public accountant *n* Am expert-comptable *m*.

certify ['sɜːtɪfaɪ] *vt* - 1. [declare true] : **to**

~ **(that)** certifier OR attester que - **2.** [declare insane] déclarer mentalement aliéné(e).

cervical [sə'vaɪkl] *adj* [cancer] du col de l'utérus.

cervical smear *n* frottis *m* vaginal.

cervix ['sɜːvɪks] (*pl* -**ices** [-ɪsiːz]) *n* col *m* de l'utérus.

cesarean (section) [sɪ'zeərɪən-] = **caesarean (section)**.

cesspit ['sespɪt], **cesspool** ['sespuːl] *n* fosse *f* d'aisance.

cf. (*abbr of* confer) cf.

CFC (*abbr of* chlorofluorocarbon) *n* CFC *m*.

ch. (*abbr of* chapter) chap.

chafe [tʃeɪf] *vt* [rub] irriter.

chaffinch ['tʃæfɪntʃ] *n* pinson *m*.

chain [tʃeɪn] ◇ *n* chaîne *f* ; ~ **of events** suite *f* OR série *f* d'événements. ◇ *vt* [person, animal] enchaîner ; [object] attacher avec une chaîne.

chain reaction *n* réaction *f* en chaîne.

chain saw *n* tronçonneuse *f*.

chain-smoke *vi* fumer cigarette sur cigarette.

chain store *n* grand magasin *m* (*à succursales multiples*).

chair [tʃeəʳ] ◇ *n* - **1.** [gen] chaise *f* ; [armchair] fauteuil *m* - **2.** [university post] chaire *f* - **3.** [of meeting] présidence *f*. ◇ *vt* [meeting] présider ; [discussion] diriger.

chair lift *n* télésiège *m*.

chairman ['tʃeəmən] (*pl* -**men** [-mən]) *n* président *m*.

chairperson ['tʃeə,pɜːsn] (*pl* -**s**) *n* président *m*, -e *f*.

chalet ['ʃæleɪ] *n* chalet *m*.

chalk [tʃɔːk] *n* craie *f*.

chalkboard ['tʃɔːkbɔːd] *n Am* tableau *m* (noir).

challenge ['tʃælɪndʒ] ◇ *n* défi *m*. ◇ *vt* - **1.** [to fight, competition] : **she ~d me to a race/a game of chess** elle m'a défié à la course/aux échecs ; **to ~ sb to do sthg** défier qqn de faire qqch - **2.** [question] mettre en question OR en doute.

challenging ['tʃælɪndʒɪŋ] *adj* - **1.** [task, job] stimulant(e) - **2.** [look, tone of voice] provocateur(trice).

chamber ['tʃeɪmbəʳ] *n* [gen] chambre *f*.

chambermaid ['tʃeɪmbəmeɪd] *n* femme *f* de chambre.

chamber music *n* musique *f* de chambre.

chamber of commerce *n* chambre *f* de commerce.

chameleon [kə'miːljən] *n* caméléon *m*.

champagne [,ʃæm'peɪn] *n* champagne *m*.

champion ['tʃæmpjən] *n* champion *m*, -onne *f*.

championship ['tʃæmpjənʃɪp] *n* championnat *m*.

chance [tʃɑːns] ◇ *n* - **1.** (U) [luck] hasard *m* ; **by ~** par hasard ; **if by any ~** si par hasard - **2.** [likelihood] chance *f* ; **she didn't stand a ~ (of doing sthg)** elle n'avait aucune chance (de faire qqch) ; **on the off ~** à tout hasard - **3.** [opportunity] occasion *f* - **4.** [risk] risque *m* ; **to take a ~** risquer le coup ; **to take a ~ on doing sthg** se risquer à faire qqch. ◇ *adj* fortuit(e), accidentel(elle). ◇ *vt* [risk] risquer ; **to ~ it** tenter sa chance.

chancellor ['tʃɑːnsələʳ] *n* - **1.** [chief minister] chancelier *m* - **2.** UNIV président *m*, -e *f* honoraire.

Chancellor of the Exchequer *n Br* Chancelier *m* de l'Échiquier, ≃ ministre *m* des Finances.

chandelier [,ʃændə'lɪəʳ] *n* lustre *m*.

change [tʃeɪndʒ] ◇ *n* - **1.** [gen] : ~ **(in sb/in sthg)** changement *m* (en qqn/de qqch) ; ~ **of clothes** vêtements *mpl* de rechange ; **for a ~** pour changer (un peu) - **2.** [money] monnaie *f*. ◇ *vt* - **1.** [gen] changer ; **to ~ sthg into sthg** changer OR transformer qqch en qqch ; **to ~ one's mind** changer d'avis - **2.** [jobs, trains, sides] changer de - **3.** [money - into smaller units] faire la monnaie de ; [- into different currency] changer. ◇ *vi* - **1.** [gen] changer - **2.** [change clothes] se changer - **3.** [be transformed] : **to ~ into** se changer en. ◆ **change over** *vi* [convert] : **to ~ over from/to** passer de/à.

changeable ['tʃeɪndʒəbl] *adj* [mood] changeable ; [weather] variable.

change machine *n* distributeur *m* de monnaie.

changeover ['tʃeɪndʒ,əʊvəʳ] *n* : ~ **(to)** passage *m* (à), changement *m* (pour).

changing ['tʃeɪndʒɪŋ] *adj* changeant(e).

changing room *n* SPORT vestiaire *m* ; [in shop] cabine *f* d'essayage.

channel ['tʃænl] ◇ *n* - **1.** TV chaîne *f* ; RADIO station *f* - **2.** [for irrigation] canal *m* ; [duct] conduit *m* - **3.** [on river, sea] chenal *m*. ◇ *vt lit & fig* canaliser. ◆ **Channel** *n* : **the (English) Channel** la Manche. ◆ **channels** *npl* : **to go through the proper ~s** suivre OR passer la filière.

Channel Islands *npl* : **the ~** les îles *fpl* Anglo-Normandes.

Channel tunnel *n* : **the ~** le tunnel sous la Manche.
chant [tʃɑ:nt] ◇ *n* chant *m*. ◇ *vt* - 1. RELIG chanter - 2. [words, slogan] scander.
chaos ['keɪɒs] *n* chaos *m*.
chaotic [keɪˈɒtɪk] *adj* chaotique.
chap [tʃæp] *n Br inf* [man] type *m*.
chapel ['tʃæpl] *n* chapelle *f*.
chaplain ['tʃæplɪn] *n* aumônier *m*.
chapped [tʃæpt] *adj* [skin, lips] gercé(e).
chapter ['tʃæptəʳ] *n* chapitre *m*.
char [tʃɑːʳ] *vt* [burn] calciner.
character ['kærəktəʳ] *n* - 1. [gen] caractère *m* - 2. [in film, book, play] personnage *m* - 3. *inf* [eccentric] phénomène *m*, original *m*.
characteristic [ˌkærəktəˈrɪstɪk] ◇ *adj* caractéristique. ◇ *n* caractéristique *f*.
characterize, ise ['kærəktəraɪz] *vt* caractériser.
charade [ʃəˈrɑːd] *n* farce *f*. ◆ **charades** *n* (U) charades *fpl*.
charcoal ['tʃɑːkəʊl] *n* [for drawing] charbon *m* ; [for burning] charbon de bois.
charge [tʃɑːdʒ] ◇ *n* - 1. [cost] prix *m* ; **free of ~** gratuit - 2. JUR accusation *f*, inculpation *f* - 3. [responsibility] : **to take ~ of** se charger de ; **to be in ~ of, to have ~ of** être responsable de, s'occuper de ; **in ~** responsable - 4. ELEC & MIL charge *f*. ◇ *vt* - 1. [customer, sum] faire payer ; **how much do you ~?** vous prenez combien? ; **to ~ sthg to sb** mettre qqch sur le compte de qqn - 2. [suspect, criminal] : **to ~ sb (with)** accuser qqn (de) - 3. ELEC & MIL charger. ◇ *vi* [rush] se précipiter, foncer.
charge card *n* carte *f* de compte crédit (auprès d'un magasin).
charger ['tʃɑːdʒəʳ] *n* [for batteries] chargeur *m*.
chariot ['tʃærɪət] *n* char *m*.
charisma [kəˈrɪzmə] *n* charisme *m*.
charity ['tʃærətɪ] *n* charité *f*.
charm [tʃɑːm] ◇ *n* charme *m*. ◇ *vt* charmer.
charming ['tʃɑːmɪŋ] *adj* charmant(e).
chart [tʃɑːt] ◇ *n* - 1. [diagram] graphique *m*, diagramme *m* - 2. [map] carte *f*. ◇ *vt* - 1. [plot, map] porter sur une carte - 2. *fig* [record] retracer. ◆ **charts** *npl* : **the ~s** le hit-parade.
charter ['tʃɑːtəʳ] ◇ *n* [document] charte *f*. ◇ *vt* [plane, boat] affréter.
chartered accountant [ˌtʃɑːtəd-] *n Br* expert-comptable *m*.
charter flight *n* vol *m* charter.

chase [tʃeɪs] ◇ *n* [pursuit] poursuite *f*, chasse *f*. ◇ *vt* - 1. [pursue] poursuivre - 2. [drive away] chasser. ◇ *vi* : **to ~ after sb/sthg** courir après qqn/qqch.
chasm ['kæzm] *n lit & fig* abîme *m*.
chassis ['ʃæsɪ] (*pl inv*) *n* châssis *m*.
chat [tʃæt] ◇ *n* causerie *f*, bavardage *m* ; **to have a ~** causer, bavarder. ◇ *vi* causer, bavarder. ◆ **chat up** *vt sep Br inf* baratiner.
chatline ['tʃætlaɪn] *n* [gen] réseau *m* téléphonique (payant) ; [for sexual encounters] téléphone *m* rose.
chat room *n* COMPUT forum *m* de discussion.
chat show *n Br* talk-show *m*.
chatter ['tʃætəʳ] ◇ *n* - 1. [of person] bavardage *m* - 2. [of animal, bird] caquetage *m*. ◇ *vi* - 1. [person] bavarder - 2. [animal, bird] jacasser, caqueter - 3. [teeth] : **his teeth were ~ing** il claquait des dents.
chatterbox ['tʃætəbɒks] *n inf* moulin *m* à paroles.
chatty ['tʃætɪ] *adj* [person] bavard(e) ; [letter] plein(e) de bavardages.
chauffeur ['ʃəʊfəʳ] *n* chauffeur *m*.
chauvinist ['ʃəʊvɪnɪst] *n* - 1. [sexist] mâcho *m* - 2. [nationalist] chauvin *m*, -e *f*.
cheap [tʃiːp] ◇ *adj* - 1. [inexpensive] pas cher (chère), bon marché (inv) - 2. [at a reduced price - fare, rate] réduit(e) ; [- ticket] à prix réduit - 3. [low-quality] de mauvaise qualité - 4. [joke, comment] facile. ◇ *adv* (à) bon marché.
cheapen ['tʃiːpn] *vt* [degrade] rabaisser.
cheaply ['tʃiːplɪ] *adv* à bon marché, pour pas cher.
cheat [tʃiːt] ◇ *n* tricheur *m*, -euse *f*. ◇ *vt* tromper ; **to ~ sb out of sthg** escroquer qqch à qqn. ◇ *vi* - 1. [in game, exam] tricher - 2. *inf* [be unfaithful] : **to ~ on sb** tromper qqn.
Chechnya ['tʃetʃnɪə] *n* Tchétchénie *f*.
check [tʃek] ◇ *n* - 1. [inspection, test] : **~ (on)** contrôle *m* (de) - 2. [restraint] : **~ (on)** frein *m* (à), restriction *f* (sur) - 3. *Am* [bill] note *f* - 4. [pattern] carreaux *mpl* - 5. *Am* = **cheque**. ◇ *vt* - 1. [test, verify] vérifier ; [passport, ticket] contrôler - 2. [restrain, stop] enrayer, arrêter. ◇ *vi* : **to ~ (for sthg)** vérifier (qqch) ; **to ~ on sthg** vérifier OR contrôler qqch. ◆ **check in** ◇ *vt sep* [luggage, coat] enregistrer. ◇ *vi* - 1. [at hotel] signer le registre - 2. [at airport] se présenter à l'enregistrement. ◆ **check out** ◇ *vt sep* - 1. [luggage, coat] retirer - 2. [investigate] vérifier. ◇ *vi* [from hotel] régler sa

note. ➣ **check up** *vi* : to ~ up on sb prendre des renseignements sur qqn ; **to ~ up (on sthg)** vérifier (qqch).

checkbook *Am* = chequebook.

checked [tʃekt] *adj* à carreaux.

checkered *Am* = chequered.

checkers ['tʃekəz] *n (U) Am* jeu *m* de dames.

check-in *n* enregistrement *m*.

checking account ['tʃekɪŋ-] *n Am* compte *m* courant.

checkmate ['tʃekmeɪt] *n* échec et mat *m*.

checkout ['tʃekaʊt] *n* [in supermarket] caisse *f*.

checkpoint ['tʃekpɔɪnt] *n* [place] (poste *m* de) contrôle *m*.

checkup ['tʃekʌp] *n* MED bilan *m* de santé, check-up *m*.

Cheddar (cheese) ['tʃedəʳ-] *n* (fromage *m* de) cheddar *m*.

cheek [tʃiːk] *n* - 1. [of face] joue *f* - 2. *inf* [impudence] culot *m*.

cheekbone ['tʃiːkbəʊn] *n* pommette *f*.

cheeky ['tʃiːkɪ] *adj* insolent(e), effronté(e).

cheer [tʃɪəʳ] <> *n* [shout] acclamation *f*. <> *vt* - 1. [shout for] acclamer - 2. [gladden] réjouir. <> *vi* applaudir. ➣ **cheers** *excl* - 1. [said before drinking] santé! - 2. *inf* [goodbye] salut!, ciao!, tchao! - 3. *inf* [thank you] merci. ➣ **cheer up** <> *vt sep* remonter le moral à. <> *vi* s'égayer.

cheerful ['tʃɪəfʊl] *adj* joyeux(euse), gai(e).

cheerio [ˌtʃɪərɪ'əʊ] *excl inf* au revoir!, salut!

cheese [tʃiːz] *n* fromage *m*.

cheeseboard ['tʃiːzbɔːd] *n* plateau *m* à fromage.

cheeseburger ['tʃiːzˌbɜːgəʳ] *n* cheeseburger *m*, hamburger *m* au fromage.

cheesecake ['tʃiːzkeɪk] *n* CULIN gâteau *m* au fromage blanc, cheesecake *m*.

cheetah ['tʃiːtə] *n* guépard *m*.

chef [ʃef] *n* chef *m*.

chemical ['kemɪkl] <> *adj* chimique. <> *n* produit *m* chimique.

chemist ['kemɪst] *n* - 1. *Br* [pharmacist] pharmacien *m*, -enne *f* ; **~'s (shop)** pharmacie *f* - 2. [scientist] chimiste *m/f*.

chemistry ['kemɪstrɪ] *n* chimie *f*.

cheque *Br*, **check** *Am* [tʃek] *n* chèque *m*.

chequebook *Br*, **checkbook** *Am* ['tʃekbʊk] *n* chéquier *m*, carnet *m* de chèques.

cheque card *n Br* carte *f* bancaire.

chequered *Br* ['tʃekəd], **checkered** *Am* ['tʃekerd] *adj fig* [career, life] mouvementé(e).

cherish ['tʃerɪʃ] *vt* chérir ; [hope] nourrir, caresser.

cherry ['tʃerɪ] *n* [fruit] cerise *f* ; **~ (tree)** cerisier *m*.

chess [tʃes] *n* échecs *mpl*.

chessboard ['tʃesbɔːd] *n* échiquier *m*.

chessman ['tʃesmæn] (*pl* **-men** [-men]) *n* pièce *f*.

chest [tʃest] *n* - 1. ANAT poitrine *f* - 2. [box] coffre *m*.

chestnut ['tʃesnʌt] <> *adj* [colour] châtain *(inv)*. <> *n* [nut] châtaigne *f* ; **~ (tree)** châtaignier *m*.

chest of drawers (*pl* **chests of drawers**) *n* commode *f*.

chew [tʃuː] <> *n* [sweet] bonbon *m* (à mâcher). <> *vt* mâcher. ➣ **chew up** *vt sep* mâchouiller.

chewing gum ['tʃuːɪŋ-] *n* chewing-gum *m*.

chic [ʃiːk] *adj* chic *(inv)*.

chick [tʃɪk] *n* [baby bird] oisillon *m*.

chicken ['tʃɪkɪn] *n* - 1. [bird, food] poulet *m* - 2. *inf* [coward] froussard *m*, -e *f*. ➣ **chicken out** *vi inf* se dégonfler.

chickenpox ['tʃɪkɪnpɒks] *n (U)* varicelle *f*.

chickpea ['tʃɪkpiː] *n* pois *m* chiche.

chicory ['tʃɪkərɪ] *n* [vegetable] endive *f*.

chief [tʃiːf] <> *adj* - 1. [main - aim, problem] principal(e) - 2. [head] en chef. <> *n* chef *m*.

chief executive *n* directeur général *m*, directrice générale *f*.

chiefly ['tʃiːflɪ] *adv* - 1. [mainly] principalement - 2. [above all] surtout.

chiffon ['ʃɪfɒn] *n* mousseline *f*.

chilblain ['tʃɪlbleɪn] *n* engelure *f*.

child [tʃaɪld] (*pl* **children** ['tʃɪldrən]) *n* enfant *mf*.

child benefit *n (U) Br* ≃ allocations *fpl* familiales.

childbirth ['tʃaɪldbɜːθ] *n (U)* accouchement *m*.

childhood ['tʃaɪldhʊd] *n* enfance *f*.

childish ['tʃaɪldɪʃ] *adj pej* puéril(e), enfantin(e).

childlike ['tʃaɪldlaɪk] *adj* enfantin(e), d'enfant.

childminder ['tʃaɪldˌmaɪndəʳ] *n Br* gardienne *f* d'enfants, nourrice *f*.

childproof ['tʃaɪldpruːf] *adj* [container] *qui ne peut pas être ouvert par les enfants* ; **~ lock** verrouillage *m* de sécurité pour enfants.

children ['tʃɪldrən] *pl* ⊏ child.

children's home *n* maison *f* d'enfants.

Chile ['tʃɪlɪ] *n* Chili *m*.

Chilean ['tʃɪlɪən] ◇ *adj* chilien(enne). ◇ *n* Chilien *m*, -enne *f*.

chili ['tʃɪlɪ] = chilli.

chill [tʃɪl] ◇ *adj* frais (fraîche). ◇ *n* - **1.** [illness] coup *m* de froid - **2.** [in temperature] : **there's a ~ in the air** le fond de l'air est frais - **3.** [feeling of fear] frisson *m*. ◇ *vt* - **1.** [drink, food] mettre au frais - **2.** [person] faire frissonner. ◇ *vi* [drink, food] rafraîchir.

chilli ['tʃɪlɪ] (*pl* **-es**) *n* [vegetable] piment *m*.

chilling ['tʃɪlɪŋ] *adj* - **1.** [very cold] glacial(e) - **2.** [frightening] qui glace le sang.

chilly ['tʃɪlɪ] *adj* froid(e) ; **to feel ~** avoir froid ; **it's ~** il fait froid.

chime [tʃaɪm] ◇ *n* [of bell, clock] carillon *m*. ◇ *vt* [time] sonner. ◇ *vi* [bell, clock] carillonner.

chimney ['tʃɪmnɪ] *n* cheminée *f*.

chimneypot ['tʃɪmnɪpɒt] *n* mitre *f* de cheminée.

chimneysweep ['tʃɪmnɪswiːp] *n* ramoneur *m*.

chimp(anzee) [tʃɪmp(ən'ziː)] *n* chimpanzé *m*.

chin [tʃɪn] *n* menton *m*.

china ['tʃaɪnə] *n* porcelaine *f*.

China ['tʃaɪnə] *n* Chine *f*.

Chinese [ˌtʃaɪ'niːz] ◇ *adj* chinois(e). ◇ *n* [language] chinois *m*. ◇ *npl* : **the ~ les** Chinois *mpl*.

Chinese cabbage *n* chou *m* chinois.

Chinese leaves *npl Br* = Chinese cabbage.

chink [tʃɪŋk] *n* - **1.** [narrow opening] fente *f* - **2.** [sound] tintement *m*.

chip [tʃɪp] ◇ *n* - **1.** *Br* [fried potato] frite *f* ; *Am* [potato crisp] chip *m* - **2.** [of glass, metal] éclat *m* ; [of wood] copeau *m* - **3.** [flaw] ébréchure *f* - **4.** [microchip] puce *f* - **5.** [for gambling] jeton *m*. ◇ *vt* [cup, glass] ébrécher. ◆ **chip in** *inf vi* - **1.** [contribute] contribuer - **2.** [interrupt] mettre son grain de sel. ◆ **chip off** *vt sep* enlever petit morceau par petit morceau.

chipboard ['tʃɪpbɔːd] *n* aggloméré *m*.

chip shop *n Br* friterie *f*.

chiropodist [kɪ'rɒpədɪst] *n* pédicure *mf*.

chirp [tʃɜːp] *vi* [bird] pépier ; [cricket] chanter.

chirpy ['tʃɜːpɪ] *adj* gai(e).

chisel ['tʃɪzl] ◇ *n* [for wood] ciseau *m* ; [for metal, rock] burin *m*. ◇ *vt* ciseler.

chit [tʃɪt] *n* [note] note *f*, reçu *m*.

chitchat ['tʃɪttʃæt] *n* (U) *inf* bavardage *m*.

chivalry ['ʃɪvlrɪ] *n* (U) - **1.** *literary* [of knights] chevalerie *f* - **2.** [good manners] galanterie *f*.

chives [tʃaɪvz] *npl* ciboulette *f*.

chlorine ['klɔːriːn] *n* chlore *m*.

choc-ice ['tʃɒkaɪs] *n Br* Esquimau® *m*.

chock [tʃɒk] *n* cale *f*.

chock-a-block, chock-full *adj inf* : **~ (with)** plein(e) à craquer (de).

chocolate ['tʃɒkələt] ◇ *n* chocolat *m* ◇ *comp* au chocolat.

choice [tʃɔɪs] ◇ *n* choix *m*. ◇ *adj* de choix.

choir ['kwaɪər] *n* chœur *m*.

choirboy ['kwaɪbɔɪ] *n* jeune choriste *m*.

choke [tʃəʊk] ◇ *n* AUT starter *m*. ◇ *vt* - **1.** [strangle] étrangler, étouffer - **2.** [block] obstruer, boucher. ◇ *vi* s'étrangler.

cholera ['kɒlərə] *n* choléra *m*.

choose [tʃuːz] (*pt* chose, *pp* chosen) ◇ *vt* - **1.** [select] choisir - **2.** [decide] : **to ~ to do sthg** décider OR choisir de faire qqch. ◇ *vi* [select] : **to ~ (from)** choisir (parmi OR entre).

choos(e)y ['tʃuːzɪ] (*compar* **-ier**, *superl* **-iest**) *adj* difficile.

chop [tʃɒp] ◇ *n* CULIN côtelette *f*. ◇ *vt* - **1.** [wood] couper ; [vegetables] hacher - **2.** *inf fig* [funding, budget] réduire - **3.** *phr* : **to ~ and change** changer sans cesse d'avis. ◆ **chops** *npl inf* babines *fpl*. ◆ **chop down** *vt sep* [tree] abattre. ◆ **chop up** *vt sep* couper en morceaux.

chopper ['tʃɒpər] *n* - **1.** [axe] couperet *m* - **2.** *inf* [helicopter] hélico *m*.

choppy ['tʃɒpɪ] *adj* [sea] agité(e).

chopsticks ['tʃɒpstɪks] *npl* baguettes *fpl*.

chord [kɔːd] *n* MUS accord *m*.

chore [tʃɔːr] *n* corvée *f* ; **household ~s** travaux *mpl* ménagers.

chortle ['tʃɔːtl] *vi* glousser.

chorus ['kɔːrəs] *n* - **1.** [part of song] refrain *m* - **2.** [singers] chœur *m* - **3.** *fig* [of praise, complaints] concert *m*.

chose [tʃəʊz] *pt* ⊏ choose.

chosen ['tʃəʊzn] *pp* ⊏ choose.

Christ [kraɪst] ◇ *n* Christ *m*. ◇ *excl* Seigneur!, bon Dieu!

christen ['krɪsn] *vt* - **1.** [baby] baptiser - **2.** [name] nommer.

christening ['krɪsnɪŋ] *n* baptême *m.*

Christian ['krɪstʃən] <> *adj* RELIG chrétien(enne). <> *n* chrétien *m*, -enne *f.*

Christianity [ˌkrɪstɪ'ænətɪ] *n* christianisme *m.*

Christian name *n* prénom *m.*

Christmas ['krɪsməs] *n* Noël *m* ; **happy** OR **merry ~!** joyeux Noël!

Christmas card *n* carte *f* de Noël.

Christmas Day *n* jour *m* de Noël.

Christmas Eve *n* veille *f* de Noël.

Christmas pudding *n Br* pudding *m* (de Noël).

Christmas tree *n* arbre *m* de Noël.

chrome [krəʊm], **chromium** ['krəʊmɪəm] <> *n* chrome *m.* <> *comp* chromé(e).

chronic ['krɒnɪk] *adj* [illness, unemployment] chronique ; [liar, alcoholic] invétéré(e).

chronicle ['krɒnɪkl] *n* chronique *f.*

chronological [ˌkrɒnə'lɒdʒɪkl] *adj* chronologique.

chrysanthemum [krɪ'sænθəməm] (*pl* -s) *n* chrysanthème *m.*

chubby ['tʃʌbɪ] *adj* [cheeks, face] joufflu(e) ; [hands, hands] potelé(e).

chuck [tʃʌk] *vt inf* - **1.** [throw] lancer, envoyer - **2.** [job, boyfriend] laisser tomber. ◆ **chuck away, chuck out** *vt sep inf* jeter, balancer.

chuckle ['tʃʌkl] *vi* glousser.

chug [tʃʌg] *vi* [train] faire teuf-teuf.

chum [tʃʌm] *n inf* copain *m*, copine *f.*

chunk [tʃʌŋk] *n* gros morceau *m.*

church [tʃɜːtʃ] *n* [building] église *f* ; **to go to ~** aller à l'église ; [Catholics] aller à la messe.

Church of England *n* : **the ~** l'Église d'Angleterre.

churchyard ['tʃɜːtʃjɑːd] *n* cimetière *m.*

churlish ['tʃɜːlɪʃ] *adj* grossier(ère).

churn [tʃɜːn] <> *n* - **1.** [for making butter] baratte *f* - **2.** [for milk] bidon *m.* <> *vt* [stir up] battre. ◆ **churn out** *vt sep inf* produire en série.

chute [ʃuːt] *n* glissière *f* ; **rubbish ~** vide-ordures *m inv.*

chutney ['tʃʌtnɪ] *n* chutney *m.*

CIA (*abbr of* **Central Intelligence Agency**) *n* CIA *f.*

CID (*abbr of* **Criminal Investigation Department**) *n la police judiciaire britannique.*

cider ['saɪdər] *n* cidre *m.*

cigar [sɪ'gɑːr] *n* cigare *m.*

cigarette [ˌsɪgə'ret] *n* cigarette *f.*

cinder ['sɪndər] *n* cendre *f.*

Cinderella [ˌsɪndə'relə] *n* Cendrillon *f.*

cine-camera ['sɪnɪ-] *n* caméra *f.*

cine-film ['sɪnɪ-] *n* film *m.*

cinema ['sɪnəmə] *n* cinéma *m.*

cinnamon ['sɪnəmən] *n* cannelle *f.*

cipher ['saɪfər] *n* [secret writing] code *m.*

circa ['sɜːkə] *prep* environ.

circle ['sɜːkl] <> *n* - **1.** [gen] cercle *m* ; **to go round in ~s** *fig* tourner en rond - **2.** [in theatre, cinema] balcon *m.* <> *vt* - **1.** [draw a circle round] entourer (d'un cercle) - **2.** [move round] faire le tour de. <> *vi* [plane] tourner en rond.

circuit ['sɜːkɪt] *n* - **1.** [gen & ELEC] circuit *m* - **2.** [lap] tour *m* ; [movement round] révolution *f.*

circuitous [sə'kjuːɪtəs] *adj* indirect(e).

circular ['sɜːkjʊlər] <> *adj* [gen] circulaire. <> *n* [letter] circulaire *f* ; [advertisement] prospectus *m.*

circulate ['sɜːkjʊleɪt] <> *vi* - **1.** [gen] circuler - **2.** [socialize] se mêler aux invités. <> *vt* [rumour] propager ; [document] faire circuler.

circulation [ˌsɜːkjʊ'leɪʃn] *n* - **1.** [gen] circulation *f* - **2.** PRESS tirage *m.*

circumcision [ˌsɜːkəm'sɪʒn] *n* circoncision *f.*

circumference [sə'kʌmfərəns] *n* circonférence *f.*

circumflex ['sɜːkəmfleks] *n* : **~ (accent)** accent *m* circonflexe.

circumspect ['sɜːkəmspekt] *adj* circonspect(e).

circumstances ['sɜːkəmstənsɪz] *npl* circonstances *fpl* ; **under** OR **in no ~** en aucun cas ; **under** OR **in the ~** en de telles circonstances.

circumvent [ˌsɜːkəm'vent] *vt fml* [law, rule] tourner.

circus ['sɜːkəs] *n* cirque *m.*

CIS (*abbr of* **Commonwealth of Independent States**) *n* CEI *f.*

cistern ['sɪstən] *n* - **1.** *Br* [inside roof] réservoir *m* d'eau - **2.** [in toilet] réservoir *m* de chasse d'eau.

cite [saɪt] *vt* citer.

citizen ['sıtızn] *n* - **1.** [of country] citoyen *m*, -enne *f* - **2.** [of town] habitant *m*, -e *f*.

Citizens' Advice Bureau *n service britannique d'information et d'aide au consommateur.*

Citizens' Band *n fréquence radio réservée au public*, citizen band *f*.

citizenship ['sıtıznʃıp] *n* citoyenneté *f*.

citrus fruit ['sıtrəs-] *n* agrume *m*.

city ['sıtı] *n* ville *f*, cité *f*. ◆ **City** *n Br* : **the City** la City *(quartier financier de Londres).*

city centre *n* centre-ville *m*.

city hall *n Am* ≃ mairie *f*, ≃ hôtel *m* de ville.

city technology college *n Br établissement d'enseignement technique du secondaire subventionné par les entreprises.*

civic ['sıvık] *adj* [leader, event] municipal(e) ; [duty, pride] civique.

civic centre *n Br* centre *m* administratif municipal.

civil ['sıvl] *adj* - **1.** [public] civil(e) - **2.** [polite] courtois(e), poli(e).

civil engineering *n* génie *m* civil.

civilian [sı'vıljən] ◇ *n* civil *m*, -e *f* ◇ *comp* civil(e).

civilization [ˌsıvəlaı'zeıʃn] *n* civilisation *f*.

civilized ['sıvəlaızd] *adj* civilisé(e).

civil law *n* droit *m* civil.

civil liberties *npl* libertés *fpl* civiques.

civil rights *npl* droits *mpl* civils.

civil servant *n* fonctionnaire *mf*.

civil service *n* fonction *f* publique.

civil war *n* guerre *f* civile.

cl *(abbr of* **centilitre***)* cl.

clad [klæd] *adj literary* [dressed] : **~ in** vêtu(e) de.

claim [kleım] ◇ *n* - **1.** [for pay etc] revendication *f* ; [for expenses, insurance] demande *f* - **2.** [right] droit *m* ; **to lay ~ to sthg** revendiquer qqch - **3.** [assertion] affirmation *f*. ◇ *vt* - **1.** [ask for] réclamer - **2.** [responsibility, credit] revendiquer - **3.** [maintain] prétendre. ◇ *vi* : **to ~ for sthg** faire une demande d'indemnité pour qqch ; **to ~ (on one's insurance)** faire une déclaration de sinistre.

claimant ['kleımənt] *n* [to throne] prétendant *m*, -e *f* ; [of state benefit] demandeur *m*, -eresse *f*, requérant *m*, -e *f*.

clairvoyant [kleə'vɔıənt] *n* voyant *m*, -e *f*.

clam [klæm] *n* palourde *f*.

clamber ['klæmbər] *vi* grimper.

clammy ['klæmı] *adj* [skin] moite ; [weather] lourd et humide.

clamour *Br*, **clamor** *Am* ['klæmər] ◇ *n (U)* [noise] cris *mpl*. ◇ *vi* : **to ~ for sthg** demander qqch à cor et à cri.

clamp [klæmp] ◇ *n* [gen] pince *f*, agrafe *f* ; [for carpentry] serre-joint *m* ; MED clamp *m*. ◇ *vt* - **1.** [gen] serrer - **2.** AUT poser un sabot de Denver à. ◆ **clamp down** *vi* : **to ~ down (on)** sévir (contre).

clan [klæn] *n* clan *m*.

clandestine [klæn'destın] *adj* clandestin(e).

clang [klæŋ] *n* bruit *m* métallique.

clap [klæp] ◇ *vt* [hands] : **to ~ one's hands** applaudir, taper des mains. ◇ *vi* applaudir, taper des mains.

clapping ['klæpıŋ] *n (U)* applaudissements *mpl*.

claret ['klærət] *n* - **1.** [wine] bordeaux *m* rouge - **2.** [colour] bordeaux *m inv*.

clarify ['klærıfaı] *vt* [explain] éclaircir, clarifier.

clarinet [ˌklærə'net] *n* clarinette *f*.

clarity ['klærətı] *n* clarté *f*.

clash [klæʃ] ◇ *n* - **1.** [of interests, personalities] conflit *m* - **2.** [fight, disagreement] heurt *m*, affrontement *m* - **3.** [noise] fracas *m*. ◇ *vi* - **1.** [fight, disagree] se heurter - **2.** [differ, conflict] entrer en conflit - **3.** [coincide] : **to ~ (with sthg)** tomber en même temps (que qqch) - **4.** [colours] jurer.

clasp [klɑ:sp] ◇ *n* [on necklace etc] fermoir *m* ; [on belt] boucle *f*. ◇ *vt* [hold tight] serrer.

class [klɑ:s] ◇ *n* - **1.** [gen] classe *f* - **2.** [lesson] cours *m*, classe *f* - **3.** [category] catégorie *f* ◇ *vt* classer.

classic ['klæsık] ◇ *adj* classique ◇ *n* classique *m*.

classical ['klæsıkl] *adj* classique.

classified ['klæsıfaıd] *adj* [information, document] classé secret (classée secrète).

classified ad *n* petite annonce *f*.

classify ['klæsıfaı] *vt* classifier, classer.

classmate ['klɑ:smeıt] *n* camarade *mf* de classe.

classroom ['klɑ:srom] *n* (salle *f* de) classe *f*.

classy ['klɑ:sı] *adj inf* chic *(inv)*.

clatter ['klætər] *n* cliquetis *m* ; [louder] fracas *m*.

clause [klɔ:z] *n* - **1.** [in document] clause *f* - **2.** GRAMM proposition *f*.

claw [klɔ:] ◇ *n* - **1.** [of cat, bird] griffe *f*

- 2. [of crab, lobster] pince *f.* ◇ *vt* griffer. ◇ *vi* [person] : **to ~ at** s'agripper à.

clay [kleɪ] *n* argile *f.*

clean [kliːn] ◇ *adj* **- 1.** [not dirty] propre **- 2.** [sheet of paper, driving licence] vierge ; [reputation] sans tache **- 3.** [joke] de bon goût **- 4.** [smooth] net (nette). ◇ *vt* nettoyer ; **to ~ one's teeth** se brosser OR laver les dents. ◇ *vi* faire le ménage. ◆ **clean out** *vt sep* [room, drawer] nettoyer à fond. ◆ **clean up** *vt sep* [clear up] nettoyer.

cleaner [ˈkliːnəʳ] *n* **- 1.** [person] personne *f* qui fait le ménage **- 2.** [substance] produit *m* d'entretien.

cleaning [ˈkliːnɪŋ] *n* nettoyage *m.*

cleanliness [ˈklenlɪnɪs] *n* propreté *f.*

cleanse [klenz] *vt* **- 1.** [skin, wound] nettoyer **- 2.** *fig* [make pure] purifier.

cleanser [ˈklenzəʳ] *n* [detergent] détergent *m* ; [for skin] démaquillant *m.*

clean-shaven [-ˈʃeɪvn] *adj* rasé(e) de près.

clear [klɪəʳ] ◇ *adj* **- 1.** [gen] clair(e) ; [glass, plastic] transparent(e) ; [difference] net (nette) ; **to make sthg ~ (to sb)** expliquer qqch clairement (à qqn) ; **to make it ~ that** préciser que ; **to make o.s. ~** bien se faire comprendre **- 2.** [voice, sound] qui s'entend nettement **- 3.** [road, space] libre, dégagé(e). ◇ *adv* : **to stand ~** s'écarter ; **to stay ~ of sb/sthg, to steer ~ of sb/sthg** éviter qqn/qqch. ◇ *vt* **- 1.** [road, path] dégager ; [table] débarrasser **- 2.** [obstacle, fallen tree] enlever **- 3.** [jump] sauter, franchir **- 4.** [debt] s'acquitter de **- 5.** [authorize] donner le feu vert à **- 6.** JUR innocenter. ◇ *vi* [fog, smoke] se dissiper ; [weather, sky] s'éclaircir. ◆ **clear away** *vt sep* [plates] débarrasser ; [books] enlever. ◆ **clear off** *vi Br inf* dégager. ◆ **clear out** ◇ *vt sep* [cupboard] vider ; [room] ranger. ◇ *vi inf* [leave] dégager. ◆ **clear up** ◇ *vt sep* **- 1.** [tidy] ranger **- 2.** [mystery, misunderstanding] éclaircir. ◇ *vi* **- 1.** [weather] s'éclaircir **- 2.** [tidy up] tout ranger.

clearance [ˈklɪərəns] *n* **- 1.** [of rubbish] enlèvement *m* ; [of land] déblaiement *m* **- 2.** [permission] autorisation *f.*

clear-cut *adj* net (nette).

clearing [ˈklɪərɪŋ] *n* [in wood] clairière *f.*

clearing bank *n Br* banque *f* de clearing.

clearly [ˈklɪəlɪ] *adv* **- 1.** [distinctly, lucidly] clairement **- 2.** [obviously] manifestement.

clearway [ˈklɪəweɪ] *n Br* route où le stationnement n'est autorisé qu'en cas d'urgence.

cleavage [ˈkliːvɪdʒ] *n* [between breasts] décolleté *m.*

cleaver [ˈkliːvəʳ] *n* couperet *m.*

clef [klef] *n* clef *f.*

cleft [kleft] *n* fente *f.*

clench [klentʃ] *vt* serrer.

clergy [ˈklɜːdʒɪ] *npl* : **the ~** le clergé.

clergyman [ˈklɜːdʒɪmən] (*pl* **-men** [-mən]) *n* membre *m* du clergé.

clerical [ˈklerɪkl] *adj* **- 1.** ADMIN de bureau **- 2.** RELIG clérical(e).

clerk [*Br* klɑːk, *Am* klɜːrk] *n* **- 1.** [in office] employé *m*, -e *f* de bureau **- 2.** JUR clerc *m* **- 3.** *Am* [shop assistant] vendeur *m*, -euse *f.*

clever [ˈklevəʳ] *adj* **- 1.** [intelligent - person] intelligent(e) ; [- idea] ingénieux(euse) **- 2.** [skilful] habile, adroit(e).

click [klɪk] ◇ *n* [of lock] déclic *m* ; [of tongue, heels] claquement *m.* ◇ *vt* faire claquer. ◇ *vi* [heels] claquer ; [camera] faire un déclic.

client [ˈklaɪənt] *n* client *m*, -e *f.*

cliff [klɪf] *n* falaise *f.*

climate [ˈklaɪmɪt] *n* climat *m.*

climax [ˈklaɪmæks] *n* [culmination] apogée *m.*

climb [klaɪm] ◇ *n* ascension *f*, montée *f.* ◇ *vt* [tree, rope] monter à ; [stairs] monter ; [wall, hill] escalader. ◇ *vi* **- 1.** [person] monter, grimper **- 2.** [plant] grimper ; [road] monter ; [plane] prendre de l'altitude **- 3.** [increase] augmenter.

climb-down *n* reculade *f.*

climber [ˈklaɪməʳ] *n* [person] alpiniste *mf*, grimpeur *m*, -euse *f.*

climbing [ˈklaɪmɪŋ] *n* [rock climbing] escalade *f* ; [mountain climbing] alpinisme *m.*

clinch [klɪntʃ] *vt* [deal] conclure.

cling [klɪŋ] (*pt & pp* clung) *vi* **- 1.** [hold tightly] : **to ~ (to)** s'accrocher (à), se cramponner (à) **- 2.** [clothes] : **to ~ (to)** coller (à).

clingfilm [ˈklɪŋfɪlm] *n Br* film *m* alimentaire transparent.

clinic [ˈklɪnɪk] *n* [building] centre *m* médical, clinique *f.*

clinical [ˈklɪnɪkl] *adj* **- 1.** MED clinique **- 2.** *fig* [attitude] froid(e).

clink [klɪŋk] *vi* tinter.

clip [klɪp] ◇ *n* **- 1.** [for paper] trombone *m* ; [for hair] pince *f* ; [of earring] clip *m* **- 2.** [excerpt] extrait *m.* ◇ *vt* **- 1.** [fasten] attacher **- 2.** [nails] couper ; [hedge] tailler ; [newspaper cutting] découper.

clipboard [ˈklɪpbɔːd] *n* écritoire *f* à pince, clipboard *m.*

clippers [ˈklɪpəz] *npl* [for hair] tondeuse *f* ;

[for nails] pince *f* à ongles ; [for hedge] cisaille *f* à haie ; [for pruning] sécateur *m*.

clipping ['klɪpɪŋ] *n* [from newspaper] coupure *f*.

cloak [kləʊk] *n* [garment] cape *f*.

cloakroom ['kləʊkrʊm] *n* - 1. [for clothes] vestiaire *m* - 2. Br [toilets] toilettes *fpl*.

clock [klɒk] *n* - 1. [large] horloge *f* ; [small] pendule *f* ; **round the ~** [work, be open] 24 heures sur 24 - 2. AUT [mileometer] compteur *m*. ◆ **clock in, clock on** *vi* Br [at work] pointer *(à l'arrivée)*. ◆ **clock off, clock out** *vi* Br [at work] pointer *(à la sortie)*.

clockwise ['klɒkwaɪz] *adj & adv* dans le sens des aiguilles d'une montre.

clockwork ['klɒkwɜːk] ⬦ *n* : **to go like ~** *fig* aller OR marcher comme sur des roulettes. ⬦ *comp* [toy] mécanique.

clog [klɒg] *vt* boucher. ◆ **clogs** *npl* sabots *mpl*. ◆ **clog up** ⬦ *vt sep* boucher. ⬦ *vi* se boucher.

close[1] [kləʊs] ⬦ *adj* - 1. [near] : **~ (to)** proche (de), près (de) ; **a ~ friend** un ami intime (une amie intime) ; **~ up, ~ to** de près ; **~ by, ~ at hand** tout près ; **that was a ~ shave** OR **thing** OR **call** on l'a échappé belle - 2. [link, resemblance] fort(e) ; [cooperation, connection] étroit(e) - 3. [questioning] serré(e) ; [examination] minutieux(euse) ; **to keep a ~ watch on sb/sthg** surveiller qqn/qqch de près ; **to pay ~ attention** faire très attention - 4. [weather] lourd(e) ; [air in room] renfermé(e) - 5. [result, contest, race] serré(e). ⬦ *adv* : **~ (to)** près (de) ; **to come ~r (together)** se rapprocher. ◆ **close on, close to** *prep* [almost] près de.

close[2] [kləʊz] ⬦ *vt* - 1. [gen] fermer - 2. [end] clore. ⬦ *vi* - 1. [shop, bank] fermer ; [door, lid] (se) fermer - 2. [end] se terminer, finir. ⬦ *n* fin *f*. ◆ **close down** *vt sep & vi* fermer.

closed [kləʊzd] *adj* fermé(e).

close-knit [,kləʊs-] *adj* (très) uni(e).

closely ['kləʊslɪ] *adv* [listen, examine, watch] de près ; [resemble] beaucoup ; **to be ~ related to** OR **with** être proche parent de.

closet ['klɒzɪt] ⬦ *n* Am [cupboard] placard *m*. ⬦ *adj inf* non avoué(e).

close-up ['kləʊs-] *n* gros plan *m*.

closing time ['kləʊzɪŋ-] *n* heure *f* de fermeture.

closure ['kləʊʒə'] *n* fermeture *f*.

clot [klɒt] ⬦ *n* - 1. [of blood, milk] caillot *m* - 2. Br inf [fool] empoté *m*, -e *f*. ⬦ *vi* [blood] coaguler.

cloth [klɒθ] *n* - 1. (U) [fabric] tissu *m*

- 2. [duster] chiffon *m* ; [for drying] torchon *m*.

clothe [kləʊð] *vt fml* [dress] habiller.

clothes [kləʊðz] *npl* vêtements *mpl*, habits *mpl* ; **to put one's ~ on** s'habiller ; **to take one's ~ off** se déshabiller.

clothes brush *n* brosse *f* à habits.

clothesline ['kləʊðzlaɪn] *n* corde *f* à linge.

clothes peg Br, **clothespin** Am ['kləʊðzpɪn] *n* pince *f* à linge.

clothing ['kləʊðɪŋ] *n* (U) vêtements *mpl*, habits *mpl*.

cloud [klaʊd] *n* nuage *m*. ◆ **cloud over** *vi* [sky] se couvrir.

cloudy ['klaʊdɪ] *adj* - 1. [sky, day] nuageux(euse) - 2. [liquid] trouble.

clout [klaʊt] *inf* ⬦ *n* (U) [influence] poids *m*, influence *f*. ⬦ *vt* donner un coup à.

clove [kləʊv] *n* : **a ~ of garlic** une gousse d'ail. ◆ **cloves** *npl* [spice] clous *mpl* de girofle.

clover ['kləʊvə'] *n* trèfle *m*.

clown [klaʊn] ⬦ *n* - 1. [performer] clown *m* - 2. [fool] pitre *m*. ⬦ *vi* faire le pitre.

cloying ['klɔɪɪŋ] *adj* - 1. [smell] écœurant(e) - 2. [sentiment] à l'eau de rose.

club [klʌb] ⬦ *n* - 1. [organization, place] club *m* - 2. [weapon] massue *f* - 3. : **(golf) ~ club** *m*. ⬦ *vt* matraquer. ◆ **clubs** *npl* CARDS trèfle *m*. ◆ **club together** *vi* se cotiser.

club car *n* Am RAIL wagon-restaurant *m*.

club class *n* classe *f* club.

clubhouse ['klʌbhaʊs, *pl* -haʊzɪz] *n* club *m*, pavillon *m*.

cluck [klʌk] *vi* glousser.

clue [kluː] *n* - 1. [in crime] indice *m* ; **I haven't (got) a ~ (about)** je n'ai aucune idée (sur) - 2. [in crossword] définition *f*.

clued-up [kluːd] *adj* Br inf calé(e).

clump [klʌmp] *n* [of trees, bushes] massif *m*, bouquet *m*.

clumsy ['klʌmzɪ] *adj* - 1. [ungraceful] gauche, maladroit(e) - 2. [tactless] sans tact.

clung [klʌŋ] *pt & pp* ⊳ **cling**.

cluster ['klʌstə'] ⬦ *n* [group] groupe *m*. ⬦ *vi* [people] se rassembler ; [buildings etc] être regroupé(e).

clutch [klʌtʃ] ⬦ *n* AUT embrayage *m*. ⬦ *vt* agripper. ⬦ *vi* : **to ~ at** s'agripper à.

clutter ['klʌtə'] ⬦ *n* désordre *m*. ⬦ *vt* mettre en désordre.

cm *(abbr of centimetre)* *n* cm.

CND *(abbr of Campaign for Nuclear Dis-*

armament) *n mouvement pour le désarmement nucléaire.*

c/o (*abbr of* **care of**) a/s.

Co. - **1.** (*abbr of* **Company**) Cie - **2.** *abbr of* **County.**

coach [kəʊtʃ] ◇ *n* - **1.** [bus] car *m*, autocar *m* - **2.** RAIL voiture *f* - **3.** [horsedrawn] carrosse *m* - **4.** SPORT entraîneur *m* - **5.** [tutor] répétiteur *m*, -trice *f.* ◇ *vt* - **1.** SPORT entraîner - **2.** [tutor] donner des leçons (particulières) à.

coal [kəʊl] *n* charbon *m.*

coalfield ['kəʊlfiːld] *n* bassin *m* houiller.

coalition [ˌkəʊə'lɪʃn] *n* coalition *f.*

coalman ['kəʊlmæn] (*pl* **-men** [-men]) *n* Br charbonnier *m.*

coalmine ['kəʊlmaɪn] *n* mine *f* de charbon.

coarse [kɔːs] *adj* - **1.** [rough - cloth] grossier(ère) ; [- hair] épais(aisse) ; [- skin] granuleux(euse) - **2.** [vulgar] grossier(ère).

coast [kəʊst] ◇ *n* côte *f.* ◇ *vi* [in car, on bike] avancer en roue libre.

coastal ['kəʊstl] *adj* côtier(ère).

coaster ['kəʊstə'] *n* [small mat] dessous *m* de verre.

coastguard ['kəʊstgɑːd] *n* - **1.** [person] garde-côte *m* - **2.** [organization] : **the ~** la gendarmerie maritime.

coastline ['kəʊstlaɪn] *n* côte *f.*

coat [kəʊt] ◇ *n* - **1.** [garment] manteau *m* - **2.** [of animal] pelage *m* - **3.** [layer] couche *f.* ◇ *vt* : **to ~ sthg (with)** recouvrir qqch (de) ; [with paint etc] enduire qqch (de).

coat hanger *n* cintre *m.*

coating ['kəʊtɪŋ] *n* couche *f* ; CULIN glaçage *m.*

coat of arms (*pl* **coats of arms**) *n* blason *m.*

coax [kəʊks] *vt* : **to ~ sb (to do** OR **into doing sthg)** persuader qqn (de faire qqch) à force de cajoleries.

cob [kɒb] *n* ⊏➤ **corn.**

cobbled ['kɒbld] *adj* pavé(e).

cobbler ['kɒblə'] *n* cordonnier *m.*

cobbles ['kɒblz], **cobblestones** ['kɒblstəʊnz] *npl* pavés *mpl.*

cobweb ['kɒbweb] *n* toile *f* d'araignée.

Coca-Cola® [ˌkəʊkə'kəʊlə] *n* Coca-Cola® *m inv.*

cocaine [kəʊ'keɪn] *n* cocaïne *f.*

cock [kɒk] ◇ *n* - **1.** [male chicken] coq *m* - **2.** [male bird] mâle *m.* ◇ *vt* - **1.** [gun] armer - **2.** [head] incliner. ➠ **cock up** *vt sep* Br v *inf* faire merder.

cockerel ['kɒkrəl] *n* jeune coq *m.*

cockeyed ['kɒkaɪd] *adj inf* - **1.** [lopsided] de travers - **2.** [foolish] complètement fou (folle).

cockle ['kɒkl] *n* [shellfish] coque *f.*

Cockney ['kɒknɪ] (*pl* **Cockneys**) *n* [person] Cockney *mf* (*personne issue des quartiers populaires de l'est de Londres).*

cockpit ['kɒkpɪt] *n* [in plane] cockpit *m.*

cockroach ['kɒkrəʊtʃ] *n* cafard *m.*

cocksure [ˌkɒk'ʃɔː'] *adj* trop sûr(e) de soi.

cocktail ['kɒkteɪl] *n* cocktail *m.*

cock-up *n Br v inf* : **to make a ~** se planter.

cocky ['kɒkɪ] *adj inf* suffisant(e).

cocoa ['kəʊkəʊ] *n* cacao *m.*

coconut ['kəʊkənʌt] *n* noix *f* de coco.

cod [kɒd] (*pl inv*) *n* morue *f.*

COD *abbr of* **cash on delivery.**

code [kəʊd] ◇ *n* code *m.* ◇ *vt* coder.

cod-liver oil *n* huile *f* de foie de morue.

coerce [kəʊ'ɜːs] *vt* : **to ~ sb (into doing sthg)** contraindre qqn (à faire qqch).

C of E *abbr of* **Church of England.**

coffee ['kɒfɪ] *n* café *m.*

coffee bar *n Br* café *m.*

coffee break *n* pause-café *f.*

coffee morning *n Br réunion matinale pour prendre le café.*

coffeepot ['kɒfɪpɒt] *n* cafetière *f.*

coffee shop *n* - **1.** *Br* [shop] café *m* - **2.** *Am* [restaurant] ≃ café-restaurant *m.*

coffee table *n* table *f* basse.

coffin ['kɒfɪn] *n* cercueil *m.*

cog [kɒg] *n* [tooth on wheel] dent *f* ; [wheel] roue *f* dentée.

coherent [kəʊ'hɪərənt] *adj* cohérent(e).

cohesive [kəʊ'hiːsɪv] *adj* cohésif(ive).

coil [kɔɪl] ◇ *n* - **1.** [of rope etc] rouleau *m* ; [one loop] boucle *f* - **2.** ELEC bobine *f* - **3.** *Br* [contraceptive device] stérilet *m.* ◇ *vt* enrouler. ◇ *vi* s'enrouler. ➠ **coil up** *vt sep* enrouler.

coin [kɔɪn] ◇ *n* pièce *f* (de monnaie). ◇ *vt* [word] inventer.

coinage ['kɔɪnɪdʒ] *n* (U) [currency] monnaie *f.*

coin-box *n Br* cabine *f* (publique) à pièces.

coincide [ˌkəʊɪn'saɪd] *vi* coïncider.

coincidence [kəʊ'ɪnsɪdəns] *n* coïncidence *f.*

coincidental [kəʊˌɪnsɪ'dentl] *adj* de coïncidence.

coke [kəʊk] n - 1. [fuel] coke m - 2. drugs sl coco f, coke f.

Coke® [kəʊk] n Coca® m.

cola ['kəʊlə] n cola m.

colander ['kʌləndəʳ] n passoire f.

cold [kəʊld] ◇ adj froid(e) ; it's ~ il fait froid ; to be ~ avoir froid ; to get ~ [person] avoir froid ; [hot food] refroidir. ◇ n - 1. [illness] rhume m ; to catch (a) ~ attraper un rhume, s'enrhumer - 2. [low temperature] froid m.

cold-blooded [-'blʌdɪd] adj fig [killer] sans pitié ; [murder] de sang-froid.

cold sore n bouton m de fièvre.

cold war n : the ~ la guerre froide.

coleslaw ['kəʊlslɔː] n chou m cru mayonnaise.

colic ['kɒlɪk] n colique f.

collaborate [kə'læbəreɪt] vi collaborer.

collapse [kə'læps] ◇ n [gen] écroulement m, effondrement m ; [of marriage] échec m. ◇ vi - 1. [building, person] s'effondrer, s'écrouler ; [marriage] échouer - 2. [fold up] être pliant(e)

collapsible [kə'læpsəbl] adj pliant(e).

collar ['kɒləʳ] ◇ n - 1. [on clothes] col m - 2. [for dog] collier m - 3. TECH collier m, bague f. ◇ vt inf [detain] coincer.

collarbone ['kɒləbəʊn] n clavicule f.

collate [kə'leɪt] vt collationner.

collateral [kɒ'lætərəl] n (U) nantissement m.

colleague ['kɒliːg] n collègue mf.

collect [kə'lekt] ◇ vt - 1. [gather together - gen] rassembler, recueillir ; [- wood etc] ramasser ; to ~ o.s. se reprendre - 2. [as a hobby] collectionner - 3. [go to get] aller chercher, passer prendre - 4. [money] recueillir ; [taxes] percevoir. ◇ vi - 1. [crowd, people] se rassembler - 2. [dust, leaves, dirt] s'amasser, s'accumuler - 3. [for charity, gift] faire la quête. ◇ adv Am TELEC : to call (sb) ~ téléphoner (à qqn) en PCV.

collection [kə'lekʃn] n - 1. [of objects] collection f - 2. LITERATURE recueil m - 3. [of money] quête f - 4. [of mail] levée f.

collective [kə'lektɪv] ◇ adj collectif(ive). ◇ n coopérative f.

collector [kə'lektəʳ] n - 1. [as a hobby] collectionneur m, -euse f - 2. [of debts, rent] encaisseur m ; ~ of taxes percepteur m.

college ['kɒlɪdʒ] n - 1. [gen] ≈ école f d'enseignement (technique) supérieur - 2. [of university] maison communautaire d'étudiants sur un campus universitaire.

college of education n ≈ institut m de formation de maîtres.

collide [kə'laɪd] vi : to ~ (with) entrer en collision (avec).

collie ['kɒlɪ] n colley m.

colliery ['kɒljərɪ] n mine f.

collision [kə'lɪʒn] n [crash] : ~ (with/between) collision f (avec/entre) ; to be on a ~ course (with) fig aller au-devant de l'affrontement (avec).

colloquial [kə'ləʊkwɪəl] adj familier(ère).

collude [kə'luːd] vi : to ~ with sb comploter avec qqn.

Colombia [kə'lɒmbɪə] n Colombie f.

colon ['kəʊlən] n - 1. ANAT côlon m - 2. [punctuation mark] deux-points m inv.

colonel ['kɜːnl] n colonel m.

colonial [kə'ləʊnjəl] adj colonial(e).

colonize, -ise ['kɒlənaɪz] vt coloniser.

colony ['kɒlənɪ] n colonie f.

color etc Am = colour etc.

colossal [kə'lɒsl] adj colossal(e).

colour Br, **color** Am ['kʌləʳ] ◇ n couleur f ; in ~ en couleur. ◇ adj en couleur. ◇ vt - 1. [food, liquid etc] colorer ; [with pen, crayon] colorier - 2. [dye] teindre - 3. fig [judgment] fausser. ◇ vi rougir.

colour bar n discrimination f raciale.

colour-blind adj daltonien(enne).

coloured Br, **colored** Am ['kʌləd] adj de couleur ; brightly ~ de couleur vive.

colourful Br, **colorful** Am ['kʌləfʊl] adj - 1. [gen] coloré(e) - 2. [person, area] haut(e) en couleur.

colouring Br, **coloring** Am ['kʌlərɪŋ] n - 1. [dye] colorant m - 2. (U) [complexion] teint m.

colour scheme n combinaison f de couleurs.

colt [kəʊlt] n [young horse] poulain m.

column ['kɒləm] n - 1. [gen] colonne f - 2. PRESS [article] rubrique f.

columnist ['kɒləmnɪst] n chroniqueur m.

coma ['kəʊmə] n coma m.

comb [kəʊm] ◇ n [for hair] peigne m. ◇ vt - 1. [hair] peigner - 2. [search] ratisser.

combat ['kɒmbæt] ◇ n combat m. ◇ vt combattre.

combination [ˌkɒmbɪ'neɪʃn] n combinaison f.

combine [vb kəm'baɪn, n 'kɒmbaɪn] ◇ vt [gen] rassembler ; [pieces] combiner ; to ~ sthg with sthg [two substances] mélanger qqch avec OR à qqch ; fig allier qqch à qqch.

◇ *vi* COMM & POL : **to ~ (with)** fusionner (avec). ◇ *n* **- 1.** [group] cartel *m* **- 2.** = **combine harvester**.

combine harvester [-'ha:vɪstəʳ] *n* moissonneuse-batteuse *f*.

come [kʌm] (*pt* **came**, *pp* **come**) *vi* **- 1.** [move] venir ; [arrive] arriver, venir ; **the news came as a shock** la nouvelle m'a/lui a *etc.* fait un choc ; **coming!** j'arrive! **- 2.** [reach] : **to ~ up to** arriver à, monter jusqu'à ; **to ~ down to** descendre OR tomber jusqu'à **- 3.** [happen] arriver, se produire ; **~ what may** quoi qu'il arrive **- 4.** [become] : **to ~ true** se réaliser ; **to ~ undone** se défaire ; **to ~ unstuck** se décoller **- 5.** [begin gradually] : **to ~ to do sthg** en arriver à OR en venir à faire qqch **- 6.** [be placed in order] venir, être placé(e) ; **P ~s before Q** P vient avant Q, P précède Q ; **she came second in the exam** elle était deuxième à l'examen **- 7.** *phr* : **to think of it** maintenant que j'y pense, réflexion faite. ◆ **to come** *adv* à venir ; **in (the) days/years to ~** dans les jours/années à venir. ◆ **come about** *vi* [happen] arriver, se produire. ◆ **come across** *vt fus* tomber sur, trouver par hasard. ◆ **come along** *vi* **- 1.** [arrive by chance] arriver **- 2.** [improve - work] avancer ; [- student] faire des progrès. ◆ **come apart** *vi* **- 1.** [fall to pieces] tomber en morceaux **- 2.** [come off] se détacher. ◆ **come at** *vt fus* [attack] attaquer. ◆ **come back** *vi* **- 1.** [in talk, writing] : **to ~ back to sthg** revenir à qqch **- 2.** [memory] : **to ~ back (to sb)** revenir (à qqn). ◆ **come by** *vt fus* [get, obtain] trouver, dénicher. ◆ **come down** *vi* **- 1.** [decrease] baisser **- 2.** [descend] descendre. ◆ **come down to** *vt fus* se résumer à, se réduire à. ◆ **come down with** *vt fus* [cold, flu] attraper. ◆ **come forward** *vi* se présenter. ◆ **come from** *vt fus* venir de. ◆ **come in** *vi* [enter] entrer. ◆ **come in for** *vt fus* [criticism] être l'objet de. ◆ **come into** *vt fus* **- 1.** [inherit] hériter de **- 2.** [begin to be] : **to ~ into being** prendre naissance, voir le jour. ◆ **come off** *vi* **- 1.** [button, label] se détacher ; [stain] s'enlever **- 2.** [joke, attempt] réussir **- 3.** *phr* : **~ off it!** *inf* et puis quoi encore!, non mais sans blague! ◆ **come on** *vi* **- 1.** [start] commencer, apparaître **- 2.** [start working - light, heating] s'allumer **- 3.** [progress, improve] avancer, faire des progrès **- on!** [expressing encouragement] allez! ; [hurry up] allez, dépêche-toi! ; [expressing disbelief] allons donc! ◆ **come out** *vi* **- 1.** [become known] être découvert(e) **- 2.** [appear - product, book, film] sortir, paraître ; [- sun, moon, stars] paraître **- 3.** [go on

strike] faire grève **- 4.** [declare publicly] : **to ~ out for/against sthg** se déclarer pour/contre qqch. ◆ **come round** *vi* [regain consciousness] reprendre connaissance, revenir à soi. ◆ **come through** *vt fus* survivre à. ◆ **come to** ◇ *vt fus* **- 1.** [reach] : **to ~ to an end** se terminer, prendre fin ; **to ~ to a decision** arriver à OR prendre une décision **- 2.** [amount to] s'élever à. ◇ *vi* [regain consciousness] revenir à soi, reprendre connaissance. ◆ **come under** *vt fus* **- 1.** [be governed by] être soumis(e) à **- 2.** [suffer] : **to ~ under attack (from)** être en butte aux attaques (de). ◆ **come up** *vi* **- 1.** [be mentioned] survenir **- 2.** [be imminent] approcher **- 3.** [happen unexpectedly] se présenter **- 4.** [sun] se lever. ◆ **come up against** *vt fus* se heurter à. ◆ **come up to** *vt fus* **- 1.** [approach - in space] s'approcher de **- 2.** [equal] répondre à. ◆ **come up with** *vt fus* [answer, idea] proposer.

comeback ['kʌmbæk] *n* come-back *m* ; **to make a ~** [fashion] revenir à la mode ; [actor etc] revenir à la scène.

comedian [kə'miːdjən] *n* [comic] comique *m* ; THEATRE comédien *m*.

comedown ['kʌmdaʊn] *n inf* : **it was a ~ for her** elle est tombée bien bas pour faire ça.

comedy ['kɒmədɪ] *n* comédie *f*.

comet ['kɒmɪt] *n* comète *f*.

come-uppance [ˌkʌm'ʌpəns] *n* : **to get one's ~** *inf* recevoir ce qu'on mérite.

comfort ['kʌmfət] ◇ *n* **- 1.** (U) [ease] confort *m* **- 2.** [luxury] commodité *f* **- 3.** [solace] réconfort *m*, consolation *f*. ◇ *vt* réconforter, consoler.

comfortable ['kʌmftəbl] *adj* **- 1.** [gen] confortable **- 2.** *fig* [person - at ease, financially] à l'aise **- 3.** [after operation, accident] : **he's ~** son état est stationnaire.

comfortably ['kʌmftəblɪ] *adv* **- 1.** [sit, sleep] confortablement **- 2.** [without financial difficulty] à l'aise **- 3.** [win] aisément.

comfort station *n Am* toilettes *fpl* publiques.

comic ['kɒmɪk] ◇ *adj* comique, amusant(e). ◇ *n* **- 1.** [comedian] comique *m*, actrice *f* comique **- 2.** [magazine] bande *f* dessinée.

comical ['kɒmɪkl] *adj* comique, drôle.

comic strip *n* bande *f* dessinée.

coming ['kʌmɪŋ] ◇ *adj* [future] à venir, futur(e). ◇ *n* : **~s and goings** allées et venues *fpl*.

comma ['kɒmə] *n* virgule *f*.

command [kə'mɑ:nd] ◇ n - **1.** [order] ordre m - **2.** (U) [control] commandement m - **3.** [of language, subject] maîtrise f ; **to have at one's ~** [language] maîtriser ; [resources] avoir à sa disposition - **4.** COMPUT commande f. ◇ vt - **1.** [order] : **to ~ sb to do sthg** ordonner OR commander à qqn de faire qqch - **2.** MIL [control] commander - **3.** [deserve - respect] inspirer ; [- attention, high price] mériter.

commandeer [ˌkɒmən'dɪəʳ] vt réquisitionner.

commander [kə'mɑ:ndəʳ] n - **1.** [in army] commandant m - **2.** [in navy] capitaine m de frégate.

commando [kə'mɑ:ndəʊ] (pl -s OR -es) n commando m.

commemorate [kə'meməreɪt] vt commémorer.

commemoration [kəˌmemə'reɪʃn] n commémoration f.

commence [kə'mens] fml ◇ vt commencer, entamer ; **to ~ doing sthg** commencer à faire qqch. ◇ vi commencer.

commend [kə'mend] vt - **1.** [praise] : **to ~ sb (on OR for)** féliciter qqn (de) - **2.** [recommend] : **to ~ sthg (to sb)** recommander qqch (à qqn).

commensurate [kə'menʃərət] adj fml : **~ with** correspondant(e) à.

comment ['kɒment] ◇ n commentaire m, remarque f ; **no ~!** sans commentaire! ◇ vt : **to ~ that** remarquer que. ◇ vi : **to ~ (on)** faire des commentaires OR remarques (sur).

commentary ['kɒməntrɪ] n commentaire m.

commentator ['kɒmənteɪtəʳ] n commentateur m, -trice f.

commerce ['kɒmɜːs] n (U) commerce m, affaires fpl.

commercial [kə'mɜːʃl] ◇ adj commercial(e). ◇ n publicité f, spot m publicitaire.

commercial break n publicités fpl.

commiserate [kə'mɪzəreɪt] vi : **to ~ with sb** témoigner de la compassion pour qqn.

commission [kə'mɪʃn] ◇ n - **1.** [money, investigative body] commission f - **2.** [order for work] commande f. ◇ vt [work] commander ; **to ~ sb to do sthg** charger qqn de faire qqch.

commissionaire [kəˌmɪʃə'neəʳ] n Br chasseur m.

commissioner [kə'mɪʃnəʳ] n [in police] commissaire m.

commit [kə'mɪt] vt - **1.** [crime, sin etc]

commettre ; **to ~ suicide** se suicider - **2.** [promise - money, resources] allouer ; **to ~ o.s. (to sthg/to doing sthg)** s'engager (à qqch/à faire qqch) - **3.** [consign] : **to ~ sb to prison** faire incarcérer qqn ; **to ~ sthg to memory** apprendre qqch par cœur.

commitment [kə'mɪtmənt] n - **1.** (U) [dedication] engagement m - **2.** [responsibility] obligation f.

committee [kə'mɪtɪ] n commission f, comité m.

commodity [kə'mɒdətɪ] n marchandise f.

common ['kɒmən] ◇ adj - **1.** [frequent] courant(e) - **2.** [shared] : **~ (to)** commun(e) (à) - **3.** [ordinary] banal(e) - **4.** Br pej [vulgar] vulgaire. ◇ n [land] terrain m communal.
◆ **in common** adv en commun.

common law n droit m coutumier.
◆ **common-law** adj : **common-law wife** concubine f.

commonly ['kɒmənlɪ] adv [generally] d'une manière générale, généralement.

Common Market n : **the ~** le Marché commun.

commonplace ['kɒmənpleɪs] adj banal(e), ordinaire.

common room n [staffroom] salle f des professeurs ; [for students] salle commune.

Commons ['kɒmənz] npl Br : **the ~** les Communes fpl, la Chambre des Communes.

common sense n (U) bon sens m.

Commonwealth ['kɒmənwelθ] n : **the ~** le Commonwealth.

Commonwealth of Independent States n : **the ~** la Communauté des États Indépendants.

commotion [kə'məʊʃn] n remue-ménage m.

communal ['kɒmjʊnl] adj [kitchen, garden] commun(e) ; [life etc] communautaire, collectif(ive).

commune [n 'kɒmjuːn vb kə'mjuːn] ◇ n communauté f. ◇ vi : **to ~ with** communier avec.

communicate [kə'mjuːnɪkeɪt] vt & vi communiquer.

communication [kəˌmjuːnɪ'keɪʃn] n contact m ; TELEC communication f.

communication cord n Br sonnette f d'alarme.

communion [kə'mjuːnjən] n communion f. ◆ **Communion** n (U) RELIG communion f.

Communism ['kɒmjʊnɪzm] n communisme m.

Communist ['kɒmjʊnɪst] <> *adj* communiste. <> *n* communiste *mf*.

community [kə'mju:nɪtɪ] *n* communauté *f*.

community centre *n* foyer *m* municipal.

community charge *n Br* ≃ impôts *mpl* locaux.

commutation ticket [ˌkɒmju:'teɪʃn] *n Am* carte *f* de transport.

commute [kə'mju:t] <> *vt* JUR commuer. <> *vi* [to work] *faire la navette pour se rendre à son travail.*

commuter [kə'mju:tər] *n personne qui fait tous les jours la navette de banlieue en ville pour se rendre à son travail.*

compact [*adj & vb* kəm'pækt, *n* 'kɒmpækt] <> *adj* compact(e). <> *n* - 1. [for face powder] poudrier *m* - 2. *Am* AUT : ~ (car) petite voiture *f*.

compact disc *n* compact *m* (disc *m*), disque *m* compact.

compact disc player *n* lecteur *m* de disques compacts.

companion [kəm'pænjən] *n* [person] camarade *mf*.

companionship [kəm'pænjənʃɪp] *n* compagnie *f*.

company ['kʌmpənɪ] *n* - 1. [COMM - gen] société *f* ; [- insurance, airline, shipping company] compagnie *f* - 2. [companionship] compagnie *f* ; **to keep sb** ~ tenir compagnie à qqn - 3. [of actors] troupe *f*.

company secretary *n* secrétaire général *m*, secrétaire générale *f*.

comparable ['kɒmprəbl] *adj* : ~ (to OR with) comparable (à).

comparative [kəm'pærətɪv] *adj* - 1. [relative] relatif(ive) - 2. [study, in grammar] comparatif(ive).

comparatively [kəm'pærətɪvlɪ] *adv* [relatively] relativement.

compare [kəm'peər] <> *vt* : **to** ~ **sb/sthg (with), to** ~ **sb/sthg (to)** comparer qqn/qqch (avec), comparer qqn/qqch (à) ; ~**d with** OR **to** par rapport à. <> *vi* : **to** ~ **(with)** être comparable (à).

comparison [kəm'pærɪsn] *n* comparaison *f* ; **in** ~ **with** OR **to** en comparaison de, par rapport à.

compartment [kəm'pa:tmənt] *n* compartiment *m*.

compass ['kʌmpəs] *n* [magnetic] boussole *f*. ➠ **compasses** *npl* : **(a pair of)** ~**es** un compas.

compassion [kəm'pæʃn] *n* compassion *f*.

compassionate [kəm'pæʃənət] *adj* compatissant(e).

compatible [kəm'pætəbl] *adj* [gen & COMPUT] : ~ **(with)** compatible (avec).

compel [kəm'pel] *vt* [force] : **to** ~ **sb (to do sthg)** contraindre OR obliger qqn (à faire qqch).

compelling [kəm'pelɪŋ] *adj* [forceful] irrésistible.

compensate ['kɒmpenseɪt] <> *vt* : **to** ~ **sb for sthg** [financially] dédommager OR indemniser qqn de qqch. <> *vi* : **to** ~ **for sthg** compenser qqch.

compensation [ˌkɒmpen'seɪʃn] *n* - 1. [money] : ~ **(for)** dédommagement *m* (pour) - 2. [way of compensating] : ~ **(for)** compensation *f* (pour).

compete [kəm'pi:t] *vi* - 1. [vie - people] : **to** ~ **with sb for sthg** disputer qqch à qqn ; **to** ~ **for sthg** se disputer qqch - 2. COMM : **to** ~ **(with)** être en concurrence (avec) ; **to** ~ **for sthg** se faire concurrence pour qqch - 3. [take part] être en compétition.

competence ['kɒmpɪtəns] *n* (U) [proficiency] compétence *f*, capacité *f*.

competent ['kɒmpɪtənt] *adj* compétent(e).

competition [ˌkɒmpɪ'tɪʃn] *n* - 1. (U) [rivalry] rivalité *f*, concurrence *f* - 2. (U) COMM concurrence *f* - 3. [race, contest] concours *m*, compétition *f*.

competitive [kəm'petətɪv] *adj* - 1. [person] qui a l'esprit de compétition ; [match, sport] de compétition - 2. [COMM - goods] compétitif(ive) ; [- manufacturer] concurrentiel(elle).

competitor [kəm'petɪtər] *n* concurrent *m*, -e *f*.

compile [kəm'paɪl] *vt* rédiger.

complacency [kəm'pleɪsnsɪ] *n* autosatisfaction *f*.

complain [kəm'pleɪn] *vi* - 1. [moan] : **to** ~ **(about)** se plaindre (de) - 2. MED : **to** ~ **of** se plaindre de.

complaint [kəm'pleɪnt] *n* - 1. [gen] plainte *f* ; [in shop] réclamation *f* - 2. MED affection *f*, maladie *f*.

complement [*n* 'kɒmplɪmənt, *vb* 'kɒmplɪˌment] <> *n* - 1. [accompaniment] accompagnement *m* - 2. [number] effectif *m* - 3. GRAMM complément *m*. <> *vt* aller bien avec.

complementary [ˌkɒmplɪ'mentərɪ] *adj* complémentaire.

complete [kəm'pli:t] <> *adj* - 1. [gen] complet(ète) ; ~ **with** doté(e) de, muni(e) de - 2. [finished] achevé(e). <> *vt* - 1. [make whole] compléter - **2.** [finish] achever, terminer - **3.** [questionnaire, form] remplir.

completely [kəm'pliːtlɪ] adv complètement.

completion [kəm'pliːʃn] n achèvement m.

complex ['kɒmpleks] <> adj complexe. <> n [mental, of buildings] complexe m.

complexion [kəm'plekʃn] n teint m.

compliance [kəm'plaɪəns] n : ~ (with) conformité f (à).

complicate ['kɒmplɪkeɪt] vt compliquer.

complicated ['kɒmplɪkeɪtɪd] adj compliqué(e).

complication [ˌkɒmplɪ'keɪʃn] n complication f.

compliment [n 'kɒmplɪmənt, vb 'kɒmplɪ ment] <> n compliment m. <> vt : to ~ sb (on) féliciter qqn (de). ◆ **compliments** npl fml compliments mpl.

complimentary [ˌkɒmplɪ'mentərɪ] adj - **1.** [admiring] flatteur(euse) - **2.** [free] gratuit(e).

complimentary ticket n billet m de faveur.

comply [kəm'plaɪ] vi : to ~ with se conformer à.

component [kəm'pəʊnənt] n composant m.

compose [kəm'pəʊz] vt - **1.** [gen] composer ; to be ~d of se composer de, être composé de - **2.** [calm] : to ~ o.s. se calmer.

composed [kəm'pəʊzd] adj [calm] calme.

composer [kəm'pəʊzər] n compositeur m, -trice f.

composition [ˌkɒmpə'zɪʃn] n composition f.

compost [Br 'kɒmpɒst, Am 'kɒmpəʊst] n compost m.

composure [kəm'pəʊʒər] n sang-froid m, calme m.

compound ['kɒmpaʊnd] n - **1.** CHEM & LING composé m - **2.** [enclosed area] enceinte f.

compound fracture n fracture f multiple.

comprehend [ˌkɒmprɪ'hend] vt [understand] comprendre.

comprehension [ˌkɒmprɪ'henʃn] n compréhension f.

comprehensive [ˌkɒmprɪ'hensɪv] <> adj - **1.** [account, report] exhaustif(ive), détaillé(e) - **2.** [insurance] tous-risques (inv). <> n = comprehensive school.

comprehensive school n établissement secondaire britannique d'enseignement général.

compress [kəm'pres] vt - **1.** [squeeze, press] comprimer - **2.** [shorten - text] condenser.

comprise [kəm'praɪz] vt comprendre ; to be ~d of consister en, comprendre.

compromise ['kɒmprəmaɪz] <> n compromis m. <> vt compromettre. <> vi transiger.

compulsion [kəm'pʌlʃn] n - **1.** [strong desire] : to have a ~ to do sthg ne pas pouvoir s'empêcher de faire qqch - **2.** (U) [obligation] obligation f.

compulsive [kəm'pʌlsɪv] adj - **1.** [smoker, liar etc] invétéré(e) - **2.** [book, TV programme] captivant(e).

compulsory [kəm'pʌlsərɪ] adj obligatoire.

computer [kəm'pjuːtər] <> n ordinateur m. <> comp : ~ **graphics** Infographie® f ; ~ **program** programme m informatique ; ~ **scientist** programme m informatique.

computer game n jeu m électronique.

computerized [kəm'pjuːtəraɪzd] adj informatisé(e).

computer science n informatique f.

computer scientist n informaticien m, -enne f.

computing [kəm'pjuːtɪŋ] n informatique f.

comrade ['kɒmreɪd] n camarade mf.

con [kɒn] inf <> n [trick] escroquerie f. <> vt [trick] : to ~ sb (out of) escroquer qqn (de) ; to ~ sb into doing sthg persuader qqn de faire qqch (en lui mentant).

concave [ˌkɒn'keɪv] adj concave.

conceal [kən'siːl] vt cacher, dissimuler ; to ~ sthg from sb cacher qqch à qqn.

concede [kən'siːd] <> vt concéder. <> vi céder.

conceit [kən'siːt] n [arrogance] vanité f.

conceited [kən'siːtɪd] adj vaniteux(euse).

conceive [kən'siːv] <> vt concevoir. <> vi - **1.** MED concevoir - **2.** [imagine] : to ~ of concevoir.

concentrate ['kɒnsəntreɪt] <> vt concentrer. <> vi : to ~ (on) se concentrer (sur).

concentration [ˌkɒnsən'treɪʃn] n concentration f.

concentration camp n camp m de concentration.

concept ['kɒnsept] n concept m.

concern [kən'sɜːn] <> n - **1.** [worry, anxiety] souci *m*, inquiétude *f* - **2.** COMM [company] affaire *f*. ◇ *vt* - **1.** [worry] inquiéter ; **to be ~ed (about)** s'inquiéter (de) - **2.** [involve] concerner, intéresser ; **as far as I'm ~ed** en ce qui me concerne ; **to be ~ed with** [subj : person] s'intéresser à ; **to ~ o.s. with sthg** s'intéresser à, s'occuper de - **3.** [subj : book, film] traiter de.

concerning [kən'sɜːnɪŋ] *prep* en ce qui concerne.

concert ['kɒnsət] *n* concert *m*.

concerted [kən'sɜːtɪd] *adj* [effort] concerté(e).

concert hall *n* salle *f* de concert.

concertina [ˌkɒnsə'tiːnə] *n* concertina *m*.

concerto [kən'tʃɜːtəʊ] (*pl* -s) *n* concerto *m*.

concession [kən'seʃn] *n* - **1.** [gen] concession *f* - **2.** [special price] réduction *f*.

conciliatory [kən'sɪlɪətrɪ] *adj* conciliant(e).

concise [kən'saɪs] *adj* concis(e).

conclude [kən'kluːd] ◇ *vt* conclure. ◇ *vi* [meeting] prendre fin ; [speaker] conclure.

conclusion [kən'kluːʒn] *n* conclusion *f*.

conclusive [kən'kluːsɪv] *adj* concluant(e).

concoct [kən'kɒkt] *vt* préparer ; *fig* concocter.

concoction [kən'kɒkʃn] *n* préparation *f*.

concourse ['kɒŋkɔːs] *n* [hall] hall *m*.

concrete ['kɒŋkriːt] ◇ *adj* [definite] concret(ète). ◇ *n* (*U*) béton *m*. ◇ *comp* [made of concrete] en béton.

concubine ['kɒŋkjʊbaɪn] *n* maîtresse *f*.

concur [kən'kɜːʳ] *vi* [agree] : **to ~ (with)** être d'accord (avec).

concurrently [kən'kʌrəntlɪ] *adv* simultanément.

concussion [kən'kʌʃn] *n* commotion *f*.

condemn [kən'dem] *vt* condamner.

condensation [ˌkɒnden'seɪʃn] *n* condensation *f*.

condense [kən'dens] ◇ *vt* condenser. ◇ *vi* se condenser.

condensed milk [kən'denst-] *n* lait *m* concentré.

condescending [ˌkɒndɪ'sendɪŋ] *adj* condescendant(e).

condition [kən'dɪʃn] ◇ *n* - **1.** [gen] condition *f* ; **in (a) good/bad ~** en bon/mauvais état ; **out of ~** pas en forme - **2.** MED maladie *f*. ◇ *vt* [gen] conditionner.

conditional [kən'dɪʃənl] *adj* conditionnel(elle).

conditioner [kən'dɪʃnəʳ] *n* - **1.** [for hair] après-shampooing *m* - **2.** [for clothes] assouplissant *m*.

condo ['kɒndəʊ] *n inf abbr of* **condominium**.

condolences [kən'dəʊlənsɪz] *npl* condoléances *fpl*.

condom ['kɒndəm] *n* préservatif *m*.

condominium [ˌkɒndə'mɪnɪəm] *n Am* - **1.** [apartment] appartement *m* dans un immeuble en copropriété - **2.** [apartment block] immeuble *m* en copropriété.

condone [kən'dəʊn] *vt* excuser.

conducive [kən'djuːsɪv] *adj* : **to be ~ to sthg/to doing sthg** inciter à qqch/à faire qqch.

conduct [*n* 'kɒndʌkt, *vb* kən'dʌkt] ◇ *n* conduite *f*. ◇ *vt* - **1.** [carry out, transmit] conduire - **2.** [behave] : **to ~ o.s. well/badly** se conduire bien/mal - **3.** MUS diriger.

conducted tour [kən'dʌktɪd-] *n* visite *f* guidée.

conductor [kən'dʌktəʳ] *n* - **1.** MUS chef *m* d'orchestre - **2.** [on bus] receveur *m* - **3.** *Am* [on train] chef *m* de train.

conductress [kən'dʌktrɪs] *n* [on bus] receveuse *f*.

cone [kəʊn] *n* - **1.** [shape] cône *m* - **2.** [for ice cream] cornet *m* - **3.** [from tree] pomme *f* de pin.

confectioner [kən'fekʃnəʳ] *n* confiseur *m* ; **~'s (shop)** confiserie *f*.

confectionery [kən'fekʃnərɪ] *n* confiserie *f*.

confederation [kənˌfedə'reɪʃn] *n* confédération *f*.

Confederation of British Industry *n* : **the ~** ≃ le conseil du patronat.

confer [kən'fɜːʳ] ◇ *vt* : **to ~ sthg (on sb)** conférer qqch (à qqn). ◇ *vi* : **to ~ (with sb on** OR **about sthg)** s'entretenir (avec qqn de qqch).

conference ['kɒnfərəns] *n* conférence *f*.

confess [kən'fes] ◇ *vt* - **1.** [admit] avouer, confesser - **2.** RELIG confesser. ◇ *vi* : **to ~ (to sthg)** avouer (qqch).

confession [kən'feʃn] *n* confession *f*.

confetti [kən'fetɪ] *n* (*U*) confettis *mpl*.

confide [kən'faɪd] *vi* : **to ~ in sb** se confier à qqn.

confidence ['kɒnfɪdəns] *n* - **1.** [self-assurance] confiance *f* en soi, assurance *f* - **2.** [trust] confiance *f* ; **to have ~ in** avoir confiance en - **3.** [secrecy] : **in ~** en confidence - **4.** [secret] confidence *f*.

confidence trick *n* abus *m* de confiance.

confident ['kɒnfɪdənt] *adj* - **1.** [self-assured] : **to be ~** avoir confiance en soi - **2.** [sure] sûr(e).

confidential [ˌkɒnfɪ'denʃl] *adj* confidentiel(elle).

confine [kən'faɪn] *vt* - **1.** [limit] limiter ; **to ~ o.s. to** se limiter à - **2.** [shut up] enfermer, confiner.

confined [kən'faɪnd] *adj* [space, area] restreint(e).

confinement [kən'faɪnmənt] *n* [imprisonment] emprisonnement *m*.

confines ['kɒnfaɪnz] *npl* confins *mpl*.

confirm [kən'fɜːm] *vt* confirmer.

confirmation [ˌkɒnfə'meɪʃn] *n* confirmation *f*.

confirmed [kən'fɜːmd] *adj* [habitual] invétéré(e) ; [bachelor, spinster] endurci(e).

confiscate ['kɒnfɪskeɪt] *vt* confisquer.

conflict [*n* 'kɒnflɪkt, *vb* kən'flɪkt] <> *n* conflit *m*. <> *vi* : **to ~ (with)** s'opposer (à), être en conflit (avec).

conflicting [kən'flɪktɪŋ] *adj* contradictoire.

conform [kən'fɔːm] *vi* : **to ~ (to** OR **with)** se conformer (à).

confound [kən'faʊnd] *vt* [confuse, defeat] déconcerter.

confront [kən'frʌnt] *vt* - **1.** [problem, enemy] affronter - **2.** [challenge] : **to ~ sb (with)** confronter qqn (avec).

confrontation [ˌkɒnfrʌn'teɪʃn] *n* affrontement *m*.

confuse [kən'fjuːz] *vt* - **1.** [disconcert] troubler ; **to ~ the issue** brouiller les cartes - **2.** [mix up] confondre.

confused [kən'fjuːzd] *adj* - **1.** [not clear] compliqué(e) - **2.** [disconcerted] troublé(e), désorienté(e) ; **I'm ~** je n'y comprends rien.

confusing [kən'fjuːzɪŋ] *adj* pas clair(e).

confusion [kən'fjuːʒn] *n* confusion *f*.

congeal [kən'dʒiːl] *vi* [blood] se coaguler.

congenial [kən'dʒiːnjəl] *adj* sympathique, agréable.

congested [kən'dʒestɪd] *adj* - **1.** [street, area] encombré(e) - **2.** MED congestionné(e).

congestion [kən'dʒestʃn] *n* - **1.** [of traffic] encombrement *m* - **2.** MED congestion *f*.

conglomerate [ˌkən'glɒmərət] *n* COMM conglomérat *m*.

congratulate [kən'grætʃʊleɪt] *vt* : **to ~ sb (on sthg/on doing sthg)** féliciter qqn (de qqch/d'avoir fait qqch).

congratulations [kənˌgrætʃʊ'leɪʃənz] *npl* félicitations *fpl*.

congregate ['kɒngrɪgeɪt] *vi* se rassembler.

congregation [ˌkɒngrɪ'geɪʃn] *n* assemblée *f* des fidèles.

congress ['kɒngres] *n* [meeting] congrès *m*. **Congress** *n Am* POL le Congrès.

congressman ['kɒngresmən] (*pl* -men [-mən]) *n Am* POL membre *m* du Congrès.

conifer ['kɒnɪfə'] *n* conifère *m*.

conjugation [ˌkɒndʒʊ'geɪʃn] *n* GRAMM conjugaison *f*.

conjunction [kən'dʒʌŋkʃn] *n* GRAMM conjonction *f*.

conjunctivitis [kənˌdʒʌŋktɪ'vaɪtɪs] *n* conjonctivite *f*.

conjure ['kʌndʒə'] *vi* [by magic] faire des tours de prestidigitation. **conjure up** *vt sep* évoquer.

conjurer ['kʌndʒərə'] *n* prestidigitateur *m*, -trice *f*.

conjuror ['kʌndʒərə'] = **conjurer**.

conk [kɒŋk] *n Br inf* pif *m*. **conk out** *vi inf* tomber en panne.

conker ['kɒŋkə'] *n Br inf* marron *m*.

conman ['kɒnmæn] (*pl* -men [-mən]) *n* escroc *m*.

connect [kə'nekt] <> *vt* - **1.** [join] : **to ~ sthg (to)** relier qqch (à) - **2.** [on telephone] mettre en communication - **3.** [associate] associer ; **to ~ sb/sthg to, to ~ sb/sthg with** associer qqn/qqch à - **4.** ELEC [to power supply] : **to ~ sthg to** brancher qqch à. <> *vi* [train, plane, bus] : **to ~ (with)** assurer la correspondance (avec).

connected [kə'nektɪd] *adj* [related] : **to be ~ with** avoir un rapport avec.

connection [kə'nekʃn] *n* - **1.** [relationship] : **~ (between/with)** rapport *m* (entre/avec) ; **in ~ with** à propos de - **2.** ELEC branchement *m*, connexion *f* - **3.** [on telephone] communication *f* - **4.** [plane, train, bus] correspondance *f* - **5.** [professional acquaintance] relation *f*.

connive [kə'naɪv] *vi* - **1.** [plot] comploter - **2.** [allow to happen] : **to ~ at sthg** fermer les yeux sur qqch.

connoisseur [ˌkɒnə'sɜː'] *n* connaisseur *m*, -euse *f*.

conquer ['kɒŋkə'] *vt* - **1.** [country etc] conquérir - **2.** [fears, inflation etc] vaincre.

conqueror ['kɒŋkərə'] *n* conquérant *m*, -e *f*.

conquest ['kɒŋkwest] *n* conquête *f*.

cons [kɒnz] *npl* - **1.** *Br inf* : **all mod** ~ tout confort - **2.** ⊳ **pro.**

conscience ['kɒnʃəns] *n* conscience *f.*

conscientious [ˌkɒnʃɪ'enʃəs] *adj* consciencieux(euse).

conscious ['kɒnʃəs] *adj* - **1.** [not unconscious] conscient(e) - **2.** [aware] : ~ **of sthg** conscient(e) de qqch - **3.** [intentional - insult] délibéré(e), intentionnel(elle) ; [- effort] conscient(e).

consciousness ['kɒnʃəsnɪs] *n* conscience *f.*

conscript [kən'skrɪpt] MIL *n* conscrit *m.*

conscription [kən'skrɪpʃn] *n* conscription *f.*

consecutive [kən'sekjʊtɪv] *adj* consécutif(ive).

consent [kən'sent] ◇ *n* (*U*) - **1.** [permission] consentement *m* - **2.** [agreement] accord *m.* ◇ *vi* : **to** ~ **(to)** consentir (à).

consequence ['kɒnsɪkwəns] *n* - **1.** [result] conséquence *f* ; **in** ~ par conséquent - **2.** [importance] importance *f.*

consequently ['kɒnsɪkwəntlɪ] *adv* par conséquent.

conservation [ˌkɒnsə'veɪʃn] *n* [of nature] protection *f* ; [of buildings] conservation *f* ; [of energy, water] économie *f.*

conservative [kən'sɜːvətɪv] ◇ *adj* - **1.** [not modern] traditionnel(elle) - **2.** [cautious] prudent(e). ◇ *n* traditionaliste *mf.*
◆ **Conservative** POL ◇ *adj* conservateur(trice). ◇ *n* conservateur *m*, -trice *f.*

Conservative Party *n* : **the** ~ le parti conservateur.

conservatory [kən'sɜːvətrɪ] *n* [of house] véranda *f.*

conserve [*n* 'kɒnsɜːv, *vb* kən'sɜːv] ◇ *n* confiture *f.* ◇ *vt* [energy, supplies] économiser ; [nature, wildlife] protéger.

consider [kən'sɪdər] *vt* - **1.** [think about] examiner - **2.** [take into account] prendre en compte ; **all things ~ed** tout compte fait - **3.** [judge] considérer.

considerable [kən'sɪdrəbl] *adj* considérable.

considerably [kən'sɪdrəblɪ] *adv* considérablement.

considerate [kən'sɪdərət] *adj* prévenant(e).

consideration [kənˌsɪdə'reɪʃn] *n* - **1.** (*U*) [careful thought] réflexion *f* ; **to take sthg into** ~ tenir compte de qqch, prendre qqch en considération ; **under** ~ à l'étude - **2.** (*U*) [care] attention *f* - **3.** [factor] facteur *m.*

considering [kən'sɪdərɪŋ] ◇ *prep* étant donné. ◇ *conj* étant donné que.

consign [kən'saɪn] *vt* : **to** ~ **sb/sthg to** reléguer qqn/qqch à.

consignment [kən'saɪnmənt] *n* [load] expédition *f.*

consist [kən'sɪst] ◆ **consist in** *vt fus* : **to** ~ **in sthg** consister dans qqch ; **to** ~ **in doing sthg** consister à faire qqch. ◆ **consist of** *vt fus* consister en.

consistency [kən'sɪstənsɪ] *n* - **1.** [coherence] cohérence *f* - **2.** [texture] consistance *f.*

consistent [kən'sɪstənt] *adj* - **1.** [regular - behaviour] conséquent(e) ; [- improvement] régulier(ère) ; [- supporter] constant(e) - **2.** [coherent] cohérent(e) ; **to be** ~ **with** [with one's position] être compatible avec ; [with the facts] correspondre avec.

consolation [ˌkɒnsə'leɪʃn] *n* réconfort *m.*

console [*n* 'kɒnsəʊl, *vt* kən'səʊl] ◇ *n* tableau *m* de commande ; COMPUT & MUS console *f.* ◇ *vt* consoler.

consonant ['kɒnsənənt] *n* consonne *f.*

consortium [kən'sɔːtjəm] (*pl* -**tiums** OR -**tia** [-tjə]) *n* consortium *m.*

conspicuous [kən'spɪkjʊəs] *adj* voyant(e), qui se remarque.

conspiracy [kən'spɪrəsɪ] *n* conspiration *f*, complot *m.*

conspire [kən'spaɪər] *vt* : **to** ~ **to do sthg** comploter de faire qqch ; [subj : events] contribuer à faire qqch.

constable ['kʌnstəbl] *n* *Br* [policeman] agent *m* de police.

constabulary [kən'stæbjʊlərɪ] *n* police *f.*

constant ['kɒnstənt] *adj* - **1.** [unvarying] constant(e) - **2.** [recurring] continuel(elle).

constantly ['kɒnstəntlɪ] *adv* constamment.

consternation [ˌkɒnstə'neɪʃn] *n* consternation *f.*

constipated ['kɒnstɪpeɪtɪd] *adj* constipé(e).

constipation [ˌkɒnstɪ'peɪʃn] *n* constipation *f.*

constituency [kən'stɪtjʊənsɪ] *n* [area] circonscription *f* électorale.

constituent [kən'stɪtjʊənt] *n* - **1.** [voter] électeur *m*, -trice *f* - **2.** [element] composant *m.*

constitute ['kɒnstɪtjuːt] *vt* - **1.** [form, represent] représenter, constituer - **2.** [establish, set up] constituer.

constitution [ˌkɒnstɪˈtjuːʃn] *n* constitution *f.*

constraint [kənˈstreɪnt] *n* - **1.** [restriction] : ~ **(on)** limitation *f* (à) - **2.** *(U)* [self-control] retenue *f*, réserve *f* - **3.** [coercion] contrainte *f.*

construct [kənˈstrʌkt] *vt* construire.

construction [kənˈstrʌkʃn] *n* construction *f.*

constructive [kənˈstrʌktɪv] *adj* constructif(ive).

construe [kənˈstruː] *vt fml* [interpret] : **to ~ sthg as** interpréter qqch comme.

consul [ˈkɒnsəl] *n* consul *m.*

consulate [ˈkɒnsjʊlət] *n* consulat *m.*

consult [kənˈsʌlt] <> *vt* consulter. <> *vi* : **to ~ with sb** s'entretenir avec qqn.

consultant [kənˈsʌltənt] *n* - **1.** [expert] expert-conseil *m* - **2.** *Br* [hospital doctor] spécialiste *mf.*

consultation [ˌkɒnsəlˈteɪʃn] *n* [meeting, discussion] entretien *m.*

consulting room [kənˈsʌltɪŋ-] *n* cabinet *m* de consultation.

consume [kənˈsjuːm] *vt* [food, fuel etc] consommer.

consumer [kənˈsjuːməʳ] *n* consommateur *m*, -trice *f.*

consumer goods *npl* biens *mpl* de consommation.

consumer society *n* société *f* de consommation.

consummate [ˈkɒnsəmeɪt] *vt* consommer.

consumption [kənˈsʌmpʃn] *n* [use] consommation *f*

cont. *abbr of* continued.

contact [ˈkɒntækt] <> *n* - **1.** *(U)* [touch, communication] contact *m* ; **in ~ (with sb)** en rapport OR contact (avec qqn) ; **to lose ~ with sb** perdre le contact avec qqn - **2.** [person] relation *f*, contact *m.* <> *vt* contacter, prendre contact avec ; [by phone] joindre, contacter.

contact lens *n* verre *m* de contact, lentille *f* (cornéenne).

contagious [kənˈteɪdʒəs] *adj* contagieux(euse).

contain [kənˈteɪn] *vt* - **1.** [hold, include] contenir, renfermer - **2.** *fml* [control] contenir ; [epidemic] circonscrire.

container [kənˈteɪnəʳ] *n* - **1.** [box, bottle etc] récipient *m* - **2.** [for transporting goods] conteneur *m*, container *m.*

contaminate [kənˈtæmɪneɪt] *vt* contaminer.

cont'd *abbr of* continued.

contemplate [ˈkɒntempleɪt] <> *vt* - **1.** [consider] envisager - **2.** *fml* [look at] contempler. <> *vi* [consider] méditer.

contemporary [kənˈtempərərɪ] <> *adj* contemporain(e). <> *n* contemporain *m*, -e *f.*

contempt [kənˈtempt] *n* - **1.** [scorn] : ~ **(for)** mépris *m* (pour) - **2.** JUR : ~ **(of court)** outrage *m* à la cour.

contemptuous [kənˈtemptʃʊəs] *adj* méprisant(e) ; ~ **of sthg** dédaigneux(euse) de qqch.

contend [kənˈtend] <> *vi* - **1.** [deal] : **to ~ with sthg** faire face à qqch - **2.** [compete] : **to ~ for** [subj : several people] se disputer ; [subj : one person] lutter pour ; **to ~ against** lutter contre. <> *vt fml* [claim] : **to ~ that ...** soutenir OR prétendre que ...

contender [kənˈtendəʳ] *n* [in election] candidat *m*, -e *f* ; [in competition] concurrent *m*, -e *f* ; [in boxing etc] prétendant *m*, -e *f.*

content [*n* ˈkɒntent, *adj & vb* kənˈtent] <> *adj* : ~ **(with)** satisfait(e) (de), content(e) (de) ; **to be ~ to do sthg** ne pas demander mieux que de faire qqch. <> *n* - **1.** [amount] teneur *f* - **2.** [subject matter] contenu *m.* <> *vt* : **to ~ o.s. with sthg/with doing sthg** se contenter de qqch/de faire qqch.
➡ **contents** *npl* - **1.** [of container, document] contenu *m* - **2.** [at front of book] table *f* des matières.

contented [kənˈtentɪd] *adj* satisfait(e).

contention [kənˈtenʃn] *n fml* - **1.** [argument, assertion] assertion *f*, affirmation *f* - **2.** *(U)* [disagreement] dispute *f*, contestation *f.*

contest [*n* ˈkɒntest, *vb* kənˈtest] <> *n* - **1.** [competition] concours *m* - **2.** [for power, control] combat *m*, lutte *f.* <> *vt* - **1.** [compete for] disputer - **2.** [dispute] contester.

contestant [kənˈtestənt] *n* concurrent *m*, -e *f.*

context [ˈkɒntekst] *n* contexte *m.*

continent [ˈkɒntɪnənt] *n* continent *m.*
➡ **Continent** *n Br* : **the Continent** l'Europe *f* continentale.

continental [ˌkɒntɪˈnentl] *adj* GEOGR continental(e).

continental breakfast *n* petit déjeuner *m* (par opposition à 'English breakfast').

continental quilt *n Br* couette *f.*

contingency [kənˈtɪndʒənsɪ] *n* éventualité *f.*

contingency plan *n* plan *m* d'urgence.

continual [kən'tɪnjʊəl] *adj* continuel (elle).

continually [kən'tɪnjʊəlɪ] *adv* continuellement.

continuation [kənˌtɪnjʊ'eɪʃn] *n* - **1.** *(U)* [act] continuation *f* - **2.** [sequel] suite *f*.

continue [kən'tɪnjuː] ⬦ *vt* - **1.** [carry on] continuer, poursuivre ; **to ~ doing** OR **to do sthg** continuer à OR de faire qqch - **2.** [after an interruption] reprendre. ⬦ *vi* - **1.** [carry on] continuer ; **to ~ with sthg** poursuivre qqch, continuer qqch - **2.** [after an interruption] reprendre, se poursuivre.

continuous [kən'tɪnjʊəs] *adj* continu(e).

continuously [kən'tɪnjʊəslɪ] *adv* sans arrêt, continuellement.

contort [kən'tɔːt] *vt* tordre.

contortion [kən'tɔːʃn] *n* - **1.** *(U)* [twisting] torsion *f* - **2.** [position] contorsion *f*.

contour ['kɒnˌtʊəʳ] *n* - **1.** [outline] contour *m* - **2.** [on map] courbe *f* de niveau.

contraband ['kɒntrəbænd] ⬦ *adj* de contrebande. ⬦ *n* contrebande *f*.

contraception [ˌkɒntrə'sepʃn] *n* contraception *f*.

contraceptive [ˌkɒntrə'septɪv] ⬦ *adj* [method, device] anticonceptionnel(elle), contraceptif(ive) ; [advice] sur la contraception. ⬦ *n* contraceptif *m*.

contract [*n* 'kɒntrækt, *vb* kən'trækt] ⬦ *n* contrat *m*. ⬦ *vt* - **1.** [gen] contracter - **2.** COMM : **to ~ sb (to do sthg)** passer un contrat avec qqn (pour faire qqch) ; **to ~ to do sthg** s'engager par contrat à faire qqch. ⬦ *vi* [decrease in size, length] se contracter.

contraction [kən'trækʃn] *n* contraction *f*.

contractor [kən'træktəʳ] *n* entrepreneur *m*.

contradict [ˌkɒntrə'dɪkt] *vt* contredire.

contradiction [ˌkɒntrə'dɪkʃn] *n* contradiction *f*.

contraflow ['kɒntrəfləʊ] *n* circulation *f* à contre-sens.

contraption [kən'træpʃn] *n* machin *m*, truc *m*.

contrary ['kɒntrərɪ, *adj sense 2* kən'treərɪ] ⬦ *adj* - **1.** [opposite] : **~ (to)** contraire (à), opposé(e) (à) - **2.** [awkward] contrariant(e). ⬦ *n* contraire *m* ; **on the ~** au contraire. ➧ **contrary to** *prep* contrairement à.

contrast [*n* 'kɒntrɑːst, *vb* kən'trɑːst] ⬦ *n* contraste *m* ; **by** OR **in ~** par contraste ; **in ~ with** OR **to sthg** par contraste avec qqch.

⬦ *vt* contraster. ⬦ *vi* : **to ~ (with)** faire contraste (avec).

contravene [ˌkɒntrə'viːn] *vt* enfreindre, transgresser.

contribute [kən'trɪbjuːt] ⬦ *vt* [money] apporter ; [help, advice, ideas] donner, apporter. ⬦ *vi* - **1.** [gen] : **to ~ (to)** contribuer (à) - **2.** [write material] : **to ~ to** collaborer à.

contribution [ˌkɒntrɪ'bjuːʃn] *n* - **1.** [of money] : **~ (to)** cotisation *f* (à), contribution *f* (à) - **2.** [article] article *m*.

contributor [kən'trɪbjʊtəʳ] *n* - **1.** [of money] donateur *m*, -trice *f* - **2.** [to magazine, newspaper] collaborateur *m*, -trice *f*.

contrive [kən'traɪv] *vt* *fml* - **1.** [engineer] combiner - **2.** [manage] : **to ~ to do sthg** se débrouiller pour faire qqch, trouver moyen de faire qqch.

contrived [kən'traɪvd] *adj* tiré(e) par les cheveux.

control [kən'trəʊl] ⬦ *n* [gen] contrôle *m* ; [of traffic] régulation *f* ; **to get sb/sthg under ~** maîtriser qqn/qqch ; **to be in ~ of sthg** [subj : boss, government] diriger qqch ; [subj : army] avoir le contrôle de qqch ; [of emotions, situation] maîtriser qqch ; **to lose ~** [of emotions] perdre le contrôle. ⬦ *vt* - **1.** [company, country] être à la tête de, diriger - **2.** [operate] commander, faire fonctionner - **3.** [restrict, restrain - disease] enrayer, juguler ; [- inflation] mettre un frein à, contenir ; [- children] tenir ; [- crowd] contenir ; [- emotions] maîtriser, contenir ; **to ~ o.s.** se maîtriser, se contrôler. ➧ **controls** *npl* [of machine, vehicle] commandes *fpl*.

controller [kən'trəʊləʳ] *n* [person] contrôleur *m*.

control panel *n* tableau *m* de bord.

control tower *n* tour *f* de contrôle.

controversial [ˌkɒntrə'vɜːʃl] *adj* [writer, theory etc] controversé(e) ; **to be ~** donner matière à controverse.

controversy ['kɒntrəvɜːsɪ, *Br* kən'trɒvəsɪ] *n* controverse *f*, polémique *f*.

convalesce [ˌkɒnvə'les] *vi* se remettre d'une maladie, relever de maladie.

convene [kən'viːn] ⬦ *vt* convoquer, réunir. ⬦ *vi* se réunir, s'assembler.

convenience [kən'viːnjəns] *n* - **1.** [usefulness] commodité *f* - **2.** [personal comfort, advantage] agrément *m*, confort *m* ; **at your earliest ~** *fml* dès que possible.

convenience store *n* *Am* petit supermarché de quartier.

convenient [kən'viːnjənt] *adj* - **1.** [suitable] qui convient - **2.** [handy] pratique, commode.

convent ['kɒnvənt] *n* couvent *m*.

convention [kən'venʃn] *n* - **1.** [agreement, assembly] convention *f* - **2.** [practice] usage *m*, convention *f*.

conventional [kən'venʃənl] *adj* conventionnel(elle).

converge [kən'vɜːdʒ] *vi* : **to ~ (on)** converger (sur).

conversant [kən'vɜːsənt] *adj fml* : **~ with** sthg familiarisé(e) avec qqch, qui connaît bien qqch.

conversation [ˌkɒnvə'seɪʃn] *n* conversation *f*.

converse [*n & adj* 'kɒnvɜːs, *vb* kən'vɜːs] ◇ *n* [opposite] : **the ~** le contraire, l'inverse *m*. ◇ *vi fml* converser.

conversely [kən'vɜːslɪ] *adv fml* inversement.

conversion [kən'vɜːʃn] *n* - **1.** [changing, in religious beliefs] conversion *f* - **2.** [in building] aménagement *m*, transformation *f* - **3.** RUGBY transformation *f*.

convert [*vb* kən'vɜːt, *n* 'kɒnvɜːt] ◇ *vt* - **1.** [change] : **to ~ sthg to** OR **into** convertir qqch en ; **to ~ sb (to)** RELIG convertir qqn (à) - **2.** [building, ship] : **to ~ sthg to** OR **into** transformer qqch en, aménager qqch en. ◇ *vi* : **to ~ from sthg to sthg** passer de qqch à qqch. ◇ *n* converti *m*, -e *f*.

convertible [kən'vɜːtəbl] *n* (voiture *f*) décapotable *f*.

convex [kɒn'veks] *adj* convexe.

convey [kən'veɪ] *vt* - **1.** *fml* [transport] transporter - **2.** [express] : **to ~ sthg (to sb)** communiquer qqch (à qqn).

conveyer belt [kən'veɪə'-] *n* convoyeur *m*, tapis *m* roulant.

convict [*n* 'kɒnvɪkt, *vb* kən'vɪkt] ◇ *n* détenu *m*. ◇ *vt* : **to ~ sb of sthg** reconnaître qqn coupable de qqch.

conviction [kən'vɪkʃn] *n* - **1.** [belief, fervour] conviction *f* - **2.** JUR [of criminal] condamnation *f*.

convince [kən'vɪns] *vt* convaincre, persuader ; **to ~ sb of sthg/to do sthg** convaincre qqn de qqch/de faire qqch, persuader qqn de qqch/de faire qqch.

convincing [kən'vɪnsɪŋ] *adj* - **1.** [persuasive] convaincant(e) - **2.** [resounding - victory] retentissant(e), éclatant(e).

convoluted ['kɒnvəluːtɪd] *adj* [tortuous] compliqué(e).

convoy ['kɒnvɔɪ] *n* convoi *m*.

convulse [kən'vʌls] *vt* [person] : **to be ~d with** se tordre de.

convulsion [kən'vʌlʃn] *n* MED convulsion *f*.

coo [kuː] *vi* roucouler.

cook [kʊk] ◇ *n* cuisinier *m*, -ère *f*. ◇ *vt* [food] faire cuire ; [meal] préparer. ◇ *vi* [person] cuisiner, faire la cuisine ; [food] cuire.

cookbook ['kʊkbʊk] = **cookery book**.

cooker ['kʊkə'] *n Br* [stove] cuisinière *f*.

cookery ['kʊkərɪ] *n* cuisine *f*.

cookery book *n* livre *m* de cuisine.

cookie ['kʊkɪ] *n Am* [biscuit] biscuit *m*, gâteau *m* sec.

cooking ['kʊkɪŋ] *n* cuisine *f*.

cool [kuːl] ◇ *adj* - **1.** [not warm] frais (fraîche) ; [dress] léger(ère) - **2.** [calm] calme - **3.** [unfriendly] froid(e) - **4.** *inf* [excellent] génial(e) ; [trendy] branché(e). ◇ *vt* faire refroidir. ◇ *vi* [become less warm] refroidir. ◇ *n* [calm] : **to keep/lose one's ~** garder/ perdre son sang-froid, garder/perdre son calme. ◆ **cool down** *vi* [become less warm - food, engine] refroidir ; [- person] se rafraîchir.

cool box *n Br* glacière *f*.

coop [kuːp] *n* poulailler *m*. ◆ **coop up** *vt sep inf* confiner.

Co-op ['kəʊˌɒp] (*abbr of* **co-operative society**) *n* Coop *f*.

cooperate [kəʊ'ɒpəreɪt] *vi* : **to ~ (with sb/ sthg)** coopérer (avec qqn/à qqch), collaborer (avec qqn/à qqch).

cooperation [kəʊˌɒpə'reɪʃn] *n* (*U*) - **1.** [collaboration] coopération *f*, collaboration *f* - **2.** [assistance] aide *f*, concours *m*.

cooperative [kəʊ'ɒpərətɪv] ◇ *adj* coopératif(ive). ◇ *n* coopérative *f*.

coordinate [*n* kəʊ'ɔːdɪnət, *vt* kəʊ'ɔːdɪneɪt] ◇ *n* [on map, graph] coordonnée *f*. ◇ *vt* coordonner. ◆ **coordinates** *npl* [clothes] coordonnés *mpl*.

coordination [kəʊˌɔːdɪ'neɪʃn] *n* coordination *f*.

cop [kɒp] *n inf* flic *m*.

cope [kəʊp] *vi* se débrouiller ; **to ~ with** faire face à.

Copenhagen [ˌkəʊpən'heɪgən] *n* Copenhague.

copier ['kɒpɪə'] *n* copieur *m*, photocopieur *m*.

cop-out *n inf* dérobade *f*, échappatoire *f*.

copper ['kɒpə'] *n* - **1.** [metal] cuivre *m* - **2.** *Br inf* [policeman] flic *m*.

coppice ['kɒpɪs], **copse** [kɒps] n taillis m.

copy ['kɒpɪ] ◇ n - 1. [imitation] copie f, reproduction f - 2. [duplicate] copie f - 3. [of book] exemplaire m ; [of magazine] numéro m. ◇ vt - 1. [imitate] copier, imiter - 2. [photocopy] photocopier.

copyright ['kɒpɪraɪt] n copyright m, droit m d'auteur.

coral ['kɒrəl] n corail m.

cord [kɔːd] n - 1. [string] ficelle f ; [rope] corde f - 2. [electric] fil m, cordon m - 3. [fabric] velours m côtelé. ◆ **cords** npl pantalon m en velours côtelé.

cordial ['kɔːdjəl] ◇ adj cordial(e), chaleureux(euse). ◇ n cordial m.

cordon ['kɔːdn] n cordon m. ◆ **cordon off** vt sep barrer (par un cordon de police).

corduroy ['kɔːdərɔɪ] n velours m côtelé.

core [kɔːʳ] ◇ n - 1. [of apple etc] trognon m, cœur m - 2. [of cable, Earth] noyau m ; [of nuclear reactor] cœur m - 3. fig [of people] noyau m ; [of problem, policy] essentiel m. ◇ vt enlever le cœur de.

Corfu [kɔː'fuː] n Corfou.

corgi ['kɔːgɪ] (pl -s) n corgi m.

coriander [ˌkɒrɪ'ændəʳ] n coriandre f.

cork [kɔːk] n - 1. [material] liège m - 2. [stopper] bouchon m.

corkscrew ['kɔːkskruː] n tire-bouchon m.

corn [kɔːn] n - 1. Br [wheat] grain m ; Am [maize] maïs m ; ~ **on the cob** épi m de maïs cuit - 2. [on foot] cor m.

cornea ['kɔːnɪə] (pl -s) n cornée f.

corned beef [kɔːnd-] n corned-beef m inv.

corner ['kɔːnəʳ] ◇ n - 1. [angle] coin m, angle m ; **to cut ~s** fig brûler les étapes - 2. [bend in road] virage m, tournant m - 3. FTBL corner m. ◇ vt - 1. [person, animal] acculer - 2. [market] accaparer.

corner shop n magasin m du coin OR du quartier.

cornerstone ['kɔːnəstəʊn] n fig pierre f angulaire.

cornet ['kɔːnɪt] n - 1. [instrument] cornet m à pistons - 2. Br [ice-cream cone] cornet m de glace.

cornflakes ['kɔːnfleɪks] npl corn-flakes mpl.

cornflour Br ['kɔːnflaʊəʳ], **cornstarch** Am ['kɔːnstɑːtʃ] n ≃ Maïzena® f fécule f de maïs.

Cornwall ['kɔːnwɔːl] n Cornouailles f.

corny ['kɔːnɪ] adj inf [joke] peu original(e) ; [story, film] à l'eau de rose.

coronary ['kɒrənrɪ], **coronary thrombosis** [-θrɒm'bəʊsɪs] (pl -ses [-siːz]) n infarctus m du myocarde.

coronation [ˌkɒrə'neɪʃn] n couronnement m.

coroner ['kɒrənəʳ] n coroner m.

corporal ['kɔːpərəl] n [gen] caporal m ; [in artillery] brigadier m.

corporal punishment n châtiment m corporel.

corporate ['kɔːpərət] adj - 1. [business] corporatif(ive), de société - 2. [collective] collectif(ive).

corporation [ˌkɔːpə'reɪʃn] n - 1. Br [town council] conseil m municipal - 2. [large company] compagnie f, société f enregistrée.

corps [kɔːʳ] (pl inv) n corps m.

corpse [kɔːps] n cadavre m.

correct [kə'rekt] ◇ adj - 1. [accurate] correct(e), exact(e) ; **you're quite ~** tu as parfaitement raison - 2. [proper, socially acceptable] correct(e), convenable. ◇ vt corriger.

correction [kə'rekʃn] n correction f.

correlation [ˌkɒrə'leɪʃn] n corrélation f.

correspond [ˌkɒrɪ'spɒnd] vi - 1. [gen] : **to ~ (with to)** correspondre (à) - 2. [write letters] : **to ~ (with sb)** correspondre (avec qqn).

correspondence [ˌkɒrɪ'spɒndəns] n : **~ (with)** correspondance f (avec).

correspondence course n cours m par correspondance.

correspondent [ˌkɒrɪ'spɒndənt] n correspondant m, -e f.

corridor ['kɒrɪdɔːʳ] n [in building] couloir m, corridor m.

corroborate [kə'rɒbəreɪt] vt corroborer.

corrode [kə'rəʊd] ◇ vt corroder, attaquer. ◇ vi se corroder.

corrosion [kə'rəʊʒn] n corrosion f.

corrugated ['kɒrəgeɪtɪd] adj ondulé(e).

corrugated iron n tôle f ondulée.

corrupt [kə'rʌpt] ◇ adj [gen & COMPUT] corrompu(e). ◇ vt corrompre, dépraver.

corruption [kə'rʌpʃn] n corruption f.

corset ['kɔːsɪt] n corset m.

Corsica ['kɔːsɪkə] n Corse f.

cosh [kɒʃ] Br ◇ n matraque f, gourdin m. ◇ vt frapper, matraquer.

cosmetic [kɒz'metɪk] ◇ n cosmétique m, produit m de beauté. ◇ adj fig superficiel(elle).

cosmopolitan [ˌkɒzmə'pɒlɪtn] adj cosmopolite.

cosset ['kɒsɪt] vt dorloter, choyer.

cost [kɒst] (pt & pp **cost** OR **-ed**) ⋄ n lit & fig coût m ; **at all ~s** à tout prix, coûte que coûte. ⋄ vt - **1.** lit & fig coûter ; **it ~ me £10** ça m'a coûté 10 livres - **2.** COMM [estimate] évaluer le coût de. ⋄ vi coûter ; **how much does it ~?** combien ça coûte?, combien cela coûte-t-il? ➦ **costs** npl JUR dépens mpl.

co-star ['kəʊ-] n partenaire mf.

Costa Rica [ˌkɒstə'riːkə] n Costa Rica m.

cost-effective adj rentable.

costing ['kɒstɪŋ] n évaluation f du coût.

costly ['kɒstlɪ] adj lit & fig coûteux(euse).

cost of living n : **the ~** le coût de la vie.

cost price n prix m coûtant.

costume ['kɒstjuːm] n - **1.** [gen] costume m - **2.** [swimming costume] maillot m (de bain).

costume jewellery Br, **costume jewelery**, Am n (U) bijoux mpl fantaisie.

cosy Br, **cozy** Am ['kəʊzɪ] adj [house, room] douillet(ette) ; [atmosphere] chaleureux(euse), **to feel ~** se sentir bien au chaud

cot [kɒt] n - **1.** Br [for child] lit m d'enfant, petit lit - **2.** Am [folding bed] lit m de camp.

cottage ['kɒtɪdʒ] n cottage m, petite maison f (de campagne).

cottage cheese n fromage m blanc.

cottage pie n Br ≃ hachis m Parmentier.

cotton ['kɒtn] ⋄ n [gen] coton m. ⋄ comp de coton. ➦ **cotton on** vi inf : **to ~ on (to sthg)** piger (qqch), comprendre (qqch).

cotton candy n Am barbe f à papa.

cotton wool Br n ouate f, coton m hydrophile.

couch [kaʊtʃ] n - **1.** [sofa] canapé m - **2.** [in doctor's surgery] lit m.

cough [kɒf] ⋄ n toux f. ⋄ vi tousser.

cough mixture n Br sirop m pour la toux.

cough sweet n Br pastille f pour la toux.

cough syrup = cough mixture.

could [kʊd] pt ⊏ can².

couldn't ['kʊdnt] = could not.

could've ['kʊdəv] = could have.

council ['kaʊnsl] n conseil m municipal.

council estate Br n quartier m de logements sociaux.

council house n Br maison f qui appartient à la municipalité, ≃ H.L.M. m OR f.

councillor ['kaʊnsələr] n conseiller municipal m, conseillère municipale f.

council tax n Br ≃ impôts mpl locaux.

counsel ['kaʊnsəl] n - **1.** (U) fml [advice] conseil m - **2.** [lawyer] avocat m, -e f.

counsellor Br, **counselor** Am ['kaʊnsələr] n - **1.** [gen] conseiller m, -ère f - **2.** Am [lawyer] avocat m.

count [kaʊnt] ⋄ n - **1.** [total] total m ; **to keep ~ of** tenir le compte de ; **to lose ~ of sthg** ne plus savoir qqch, ne pas se rappeler qqch - **2.** [aristocrat] comte m. ⋄ vt - **1.** [gen] compter - **2.** [consider] : **to ~ sb as sthg** considérer qqn comme qqch. ⋄ vi [gen] compter ; **to ~ (up) to** compter jusqu'à. ➦ **count against** vt fus jouer contre. ➦ **count (up)on** vt fus - **1.** [rely on] compter sur - **2.** [expect] s'attendre à, prévoir. ➦ **count up** vt fus compter.

countdown ['kaʊntdaʊn] n compte m à rebours.

counter ['kaʊntər] ⋄ n - **1.** [in shop, bank] comptoir m - **2.** [in board game] pion m. ⋄ vt : **to ~ sthg (with)** contrer qqch (par). ⋄ vi : **to ~ with sthg/by doing sthg** riposter par qqch/en faisant qqch. ➦ **counter to** adv contrairement à ; **to run ~ to** aller à l'encontre de.

counteract [ˌkaʊntə'rækt] vt contrebalancer, compenser.

counterattack ['kaʊntərəˌtæk] vt & vi contre-attaquer.

counterclockwise [ˌkaʊntə'klɒkwaɪz] adj & adv Am dans le sens inverse des aiguilles d'une montre.

counterfeit ['kaʊntəfɪt] ⋄ adj faux (fausse). ⋄ vt contrefaire.

counterfoil ['kaʊntəfɔɪl] n talon m, souche f.

countermand [ˌkaʊntə'maːnd] vt annuler.

counterpart ['kaʊntəpaːt] n [person] homologue mf ; [thing] équivalent m, -e f.

counterproductive [ˌkaʊntəprə'dʌktɪv] adj qui a l'effet inverse.

countess ['kaʊntɪs] n comtesse f.

countless ['kaʊntlɪs] adj innombrable.

country ['kʌntrɪ] n - **1.** [nation] pays m - **2.** [countryside] : **the ~** la campagne ; **in the ~** à la campagne - **3.** [region] région f ; [terrain] terrain m.

country dancing n (U) danse f folklorique.

country house n manoir m.

countryman ['kʌntrɪmən] (pl **-men** [-mən]) n [from same country] compatriote m.

country park n Br parc m naturel.

countryside ['kʌntrɪsaɪd] *n* campagne *f.*

county ['kaʊntɪ] *n* comté *m.*

county council *n Br* conseil *m* général.

coup [kuː] *n* - 1. [rebellion] : ~ (d'état) coup *m* d'État - 2. [success] coup *m* (de maître), beau coup *m.*

couple ['kʌpl] ◇ *n* - 1. [in relationship] couple *m* - 2. [small number] : a ~ (of) [two] deux ; [a few] quelques, deux ou trois. ◇ *vt* [join] : to ~ sthg (to) atteler qqch (à).

coupon ['kuːpɒn] *n* - 1. [voucher] bon *m* - 2. [form] coupon *m.*

courage ['kʌrɪdʒ] *n* courage *m* ; to take ~ (from sthg) être encouragé (par qqch).

courgette [kɔːˈʒet] *n Br* courgette *f.*

courier ['kʊrɪəʳ] *n* - 1. [on holiday] guide *m*, accompagnateur *m*, -trice *f* - 2. [to deliver letters, packages] courrier *m*, messager *m.*

course [kɔːs] *n* - 1. [gen & SCH] cours *m* ; ~ of action ligne *f* de conduite ; in the ~ of au cours de - 2. MED [of injections] série *f* ; ~ of treatment traitement *m* - 3. [of ship, plane] route *f* ; to be on ~ suivre le cap fixé ; *fig* [on target] être dans la bonne voie ; to be off ~ faire fausse route - 4. [of meal] plat *m* - 5. SPORT terrain *m.* ◆ **of course** *adv* - 1. [inevitably, not surprisingly] évidemment, naturellement - 2. [certainly] bien sûr ; of ~ not bien sûr que non.

coursebook ['kɔːsbʊk] *n* livre *m* de cours.

coursework ['kɔːswɜːk] *n* (U) travail *m* personnel.

court [kɔːt] ◇ *n* - 1. [JUR - building, room] cour *f*, tribunal *m* ; [- judge, jury etc] : the ~ la justice ; to take sb to ~ suivre un procès à qqn - 2. [SPORT - gen] court *m* ; [- for basketball, volleyball] terrain *m* - 3. [courtyard, of monarch] cour *f.* ◇ *vi dated* sortir ensemble, se fréquenter.

courteous ['kɜːtjəs] *adj* courtois(e), poli(e).

courtesy ['kɜːtɪsɪ] *n* courtoisie *f*, politesse *f.* ◆ **(by) courtesy of** *prep* avec la permission de.

courthouse ['kɔːthaʊs, *pl* -haʊzɪz] *n Am* palais *m* de justice, tribunal *m.*

courtier ['kɔːtjəʳ] *n* courtisan *m.*

court-martial (*pl* **court-martials** OR **courts-martial**) *n* cour *f* martiale.

courtroom ['kɔːtrʊm] *n* salle *f* de tribunal.

courtyard ['kɔːtjaːd] *n* cour *f.*

cousin ['kʌzn] *n* cousin *m*, -e *f.*

cove [kəʊv] *n* [bay] crique *f.*

covenant ['kʌvənənt] *n* [of money] engagement *m* contractuel.

Covent Garden [ˌkɒvənt] *n* ancien marché de Londres, aujourd'hui importante galerie marchande.

cover ['kʌvəʳ] ◇ *n* - 1. [covering - of furniture] housse *f* ; [- of pan] couvercle *m* ; [- of book, magazine] couverture *f* - 2. [blanket] couverture *f* - 3. [protection, shelter] abri *m* ; to take ~ s'abriter, se mettre à l'abri ; under ~ à l'abri, à couvert ; under ~ of darkness à la faveur de la nuit - 4. [concealment] couverture *f* - 5. [insurance] couverture *f*, garantie *f.* ◇ *vt* - 1. [gen] : to ~ sthg (with) couvrir qqch (de) - 2. [insure] : to ~ sb against couvrir qqn en cas de - 3. [include] englober, comprendre. ◆ **cover up** *vt sep fig* [scandal etc] dissimuler, cacher.

coverage ['kʌvərɪdʒ] *n* [of news] reportage *m.*

cover charge *n* couvert *m.*

covering ['kʌvərɪŋ] *n* [of floor etc] revêtement *m* ; [of snow, dust] couche *f.*

covering letter *Br*, **cover letter** *Am n* lettre *f* explicative OR d'accompagnement.

cover note *n Br* lettre *f* de couverture, attestation *f* provisoire d'assurance.

covert ['kʌvət] *adj* [activity] clandestin(e) ; [look, glance] furtif(ive).

cover-up *n* étouffement *m.*

covet ['kʌvɪt] *vt* convoiter.

cow [kaʊ] ◇ *n* - 1. [female type of cattle] vache *f* - 2. [female elephant etc] femelle *f.* ◇ *vt* intimider, effrayer.

coward ['kaʊəd] *n* lâche *mf.*

cowardly ['kaʊədlɪ] *adj* lâche.

cowboy ['kaʊbɔɪ] *n* [cattlehand] cow-boy *m.*

cower ['kaʊəʳ] *vi* se recroqueviller.

cox [kɒks], **coxswain** ['kɒksən] *n* barreur *m.*

coy [kɔɪ] *adj* qui fait le/la timide.

cozy *Am* = cosy.

CPA *n abbr of* certified public accountant.

CPS (*abbr of* Crown Prosecution Service) *n Br* ≃ ministère *m* public.

crab [kræb] *n* crabe *m.*

crab apple *n* pomme *f* sauvage.

crack [kræk] ◇ *n* - 1. [in glass, pottery] fêlure *f* ; [in wall, wood, ground] fissure *f* ; [in skin] gerçure *f* - 2. [gap - in door] entrebâillement *m* ; [- in curtains] interstice *m* - 3. [noise - of whip] claquement *m* ; [- of twigs] craquement *m* - 4. *inf* [attempt] : to have a ~ at sthg tenter qqch, essayer de faire qqch - 5. *drugs sl* crack *m.* ◇ *adj* [troops etc] de première classe. ◇ *vt* - 1. [glass, plate] fêler ; [wood, wall] fissurer - 2. [egg, nut] casser **- 3.** [whip] faire claquer **- 4.** [bang, hit sharply] **: to ~ one's head** se cogner la tête **- 5.** [solve - problem] résoudre ; [- code] déchiffrer **- 6.** *inf* [make - joke] faire. ◇ *vi* **- 1.** [glass, pottery] se fêler ; [ground, wood, wall] se fissurer ; [skin] se crevasser, se gercer **- 2.** [break down - person] craquer, s'effondrer ; [- resistance] se briser. ◆ **crack down** *vi* **: to ~ down (on)** sévir (contre). ◆ **crack up** *vi* craquer.

cracker ['krækəʳ] *n* **- 1.** [biscuit] cracker *m*, craquelin *m* **- 2.** *Br* [for Christmas] diablotin *m*.

crackers ['krækəz] *adj Br inf* dingue, cinglé(e).

crackle ['krækl] *vi* [frying food] grésiller ; [fire] crépiter ; [radio etc] crachoter.

cradle ['kreɪdl] ◇ *n* berceau *m* ; TECH nacelle *f* ◇ *vt* [baby] bercer ; [object] tenir délicatement.

craft [krɑːft] (*pl sense 2 inv*) *n* **- 1.** [trade, skill] métier *m* **- 2.** [boat] embarcation *f*.

craftsman ['krɑːftsmən] (*pl* **-men** [-mən]) *n* artisan *m*, homme *m* de métier.

craftsmanship ['krɑːftsmənʃɪp] *n* (*U*) **- 1.** [skill] dextérité *f*, art *m* **- 2.** [skilled work] travail *m*, exécution *f*.

craftsmen *pl* ⊳ craftsman.

crafty ['krɑːftɪ] *adj* rusé(e).

crag [kræg] *n* rocher *m* escarpé.

cram [kræm] ◇ *vt* **- 1.** [stuff] fourrer **- 2.** [overfill] **: to ~ sthg with** bourrer qqch de. ◇ *vi* bachoter.

cramp [kræmp] ◇ *n* crampe *f*. ◇ *vt* gêner, entraver.

cranberry ['krænbərɪ] *n* canneberge *f*.

crane [kreɪn] *n* grue *f*.

crank [kræŋk] ◇ *n* **- 1.** TECH manivelle *f* **- 2.** *inf* [person] excentrique *mf*. ◇ *vt* [wind - handle] tourner ; [- mechanism] remonter (à la manivelle).

crankshaft ['kræŋkʃɑːft] *n* vilebrequin *m*.

cranny ['krænɪ] *n* ⊳ nook.

crap [kræp] *n* (*U*) *v inf* merde *f* ; **it's a load of ~** tout ça, c'est des conneries.

crash [kræʃ] ◇ *n* **- 1.** [accident] accident *m* **- 2.** [noise] fracas *m*. ◇ *vt* **: I ~ed the car** j'ai eu un accident avec la voiture. ◇ *vi* **- 1.** [cars, trains] se percuter, se rentrer dedans ; [car, train] avoir un accident ; [plane] s'écraser ; **to ~ into** [wall] rentrer dans, emboutir **- 2.** [FIN - business, company] faire faillite ; [- stock market] s'effondrer.

crash course *n* cours *m* intensif.

crash helmet *n* casque *m* de protection.

crash-land *vi* atterrir en catastrophe.

crass [kræs] *adj* grossier(ère).

crate [kreɪt] *n* cageot *m*, caisse *f*.

crater ['kreɪtəʳ] *n* cratère *m*.

cravat [krə'væt] *n* cravate *f*.

crave [kreɪv] ◇ *vt* [affection, luxury] avoir soif de ; [cigarette, chocolate] avoir un besoin fou OR maladif de. ◇ *vi* **: to ~ for** [affection, luxury] avoir soif de ; [cigarette, chocolate] avoir un besoin fou OR maladif de.

crawl [krɔːl] ◇ *vi* **- 1.** [baby] marcher à quatre pattes ; [person] se traîner **- 2.** [insect] ramper **- 3.** [vehicle, traffic] avancer au pas **- 4.** *inf* [place, floor] **: to be ~ing with** grouiller de. ◇ *n* [swimming stroke] **: the ~** le crawl.

crayfish ['kreɪfɪʃ] (*pl inv* OR **-es**) *n* écrevisse *f*.

crayon ['kreɪɒn] *n* crayon *m* de couleur.

craze [kreɪz] *n* engouement *m*.

crazy ['kreɪzɪ] *adj inf* **- 1.** [mad] fou (folle) **- 2.** [enthusiastic] **: to be ~ about sb/sthg** être fou (folle) de qqn/qqch.

creak [kriːk] *vi* [door, handle] craquer ; [floorboard, bed] grincer.

cream [kriːm] ◇ *adj* [in colour] crème (*inv*). ◇ *n* [gen] crème *f*.

cream cake *n Br* gâteau *m* à la crème.

cream cheese *n* fromage *m* frais.

cream cracker *n Br* biscuit *m* salé (*souvent mangé avec du fromage*).

cream tea *n Br* goûter se composant de thé et de scones servis avec de la crème et de la confiture.

crease [kriːs] ◇ *n* [in fabric - deliberate] pli *m* ; [- accidental] (faux) pli. ◇ *vt* froisser. ◇ *vi* [fabric] se froisser.

create [kriː'eɪt] *vt* créer.

creation [kriː'eɪʃn] *n* création *f*.

creative [kriː'eɪtɪv] *adj* créatif(ive).

creature ['kriːtʃəʳ] *n* créature *f*.

crèche [kreʃ] *n Br* crèche *f*.

credence ['kriːdns] *n* **: to give** OR **lend ~ to sthg** ajouter foi à qqch.

credentials [krɪ'denʃlz] *npl* **- 1.** [papers] pièce *f* d'identité ; *fig* [qualifications] capacités *fpl* **- 2.** [references] références *fpl*.

credibility [,kredə'bɪlətɪ] *n* crédibilité *f*.

credit ['kredɪt] ◇ *n* **- 1.** FIN crédit *m* ; **to be in ~** [person] avoir un compte approvisionné ; [account] être approvisionné ; **on ~** à crédit **- 2.** (*U*) [praise] honneur *m*, mérite *m* ; **to give sb ~ for sthg** reconnaître que qqn a fait qqch **- 3.** UNIV unité *f* de valeur. ◇ *vt* **- 1.** FIN **: to ~ £10 to an account, to ~ an ac-**

count with £10 créditer un compte de 10 livres - **2.** *inf* [believe] croire - **3.** [give the credit to] : **to ~ sb with sthg** accorder OR attribuer qqch à qqn. ◆ **credits** *npl* CINEMA générique *m*.

credit card *n* carte *f* de crédit.

credit note *n* avoir *m* ; FIN note *f* de crédit.

creditor ['kredɪtəʳ] *n* créancier *m*, -ère *f*.

creed [kriːd] *n* - **1.** [belief] principes *mpl* - **2.** RELIG croyance *f*.

creek [kriːk] *n* - **1.** [inlet] crique *f* - **2.** *Am* [stream] ruisseau *m*.

creep [kriːp] (*pt* & *pp* **crept**) <> *vi* - **1.** [insect] ramper ; [traffic] avancer au pas - **2.** [move stealthily] se glisser. <> *n inf* [nasty person] sale type *m*. ◆ **creeps** *npl* : **to give sb the ~s** *inf* donner la chair de poule à qqn.

creeper ['kriːpəʳ] *n* [plant] plante *f* grimpante.

creepy ['kriːpɪ] *adj inf* qui donne la chair de poule.

creepy-crawly [-'krɔːlɪ] (*pl* **creepy-crawlies**) *n inf* bestiole *f* qui rampe.

cremate [krɪ'meɪt] *vt* incinérer.

cremation [krɪ'meɪʃn] *n* incinération *f*.

crematorium *Br* [ˌkreməˈtɔːrɪəm] (*pl* **-riums** OR **-ria** [-rɪə]), **crematory** *Am* ['kremətrɪ] *n* crématorium *m*.

crepe [kreɪp] *n* - **1.** [cloth, rubber] crêpe *m* - **2.** [pancake] crêpe *f*.

crepe bandage *n Br* bande *f* Velpeau®.

crepe paper *n* (*U*) papier *m* crépon.

crept [krept] *pt* & *pp* ▷ creep.

crescent ['kresnt] *n* - **1.** [shape] croissant - **2.** [street] rue *f* en demi-cercle.

cress [kres] *n* cresson *m*.

crest [krest] *n* - **1.** [of bird, hill] crête *f* - **2.** [on coat of arms] timbre *m*.

crestfallen ['krest,fɔːln] *adj* découragé(e).

Crete [kriːt] *n* Crète *f*.

cretin ['kretɪn] *n inf* [idiot] crétin *m*, -e *f*.

Creutzfeldt-Jakob disease [ˌkrɔɪtsfelt'jækɒb-] *n* maladie *f* de Creutzfeldt-Jakob.

crevice ['krevɪs] *n* fissure *f*.

crew [kruː] *n* - **1.** [of ship, plane] équipage *m* - **2.** [team] équipe *f*.

crew cut *n* coupe *f* en brosse.

crew-neck(ed) [-nek(t)] *adj* ras du cou.

crib [krɪb] <> *n* [cot] lit *m* d'enfant. <> *vt inf* [copy] : **to ~ sthg off** OR **from sb** copier qqch sur qqn.

crick [krɪk] *n* [in neck] torticolis *m*.

cricket ['krɪkɪt] *n* - **1.** [game] cricket *m* - **2.** [insect] grillon *m*.

crime [kraɪm] *n* crime *m* ; **~s against humanity** crimes *mpl* contre l'humanité.

criminal ['krɪmɪnl] <> *adj* criminel(elle). <> *n* criminel *m*, -elle *f*.

crimson ['krɪmzn] <> *adj* [in colour] rouge foncé (*inv*) ; [with embarrassment] cramoisi(e). <> *n* cramoisi *m*.

cringe [krɪndʒ] *vi* - **1.** [in fear] avoir un mouvement de recul (par peur) - **2.** *inf* [with embarrassment] : **to ~ (at sthg)** ne plus savoir où se mettre (devant qqch).

crinkle ['krɪŋkl] *vt* [clothes] froisser.

cripple ['krɪpl] <> *n dated* & *offensive* infirme *mf*. <> *vt* - **1.** MED [disable] estropier - **2.** [country] paralyser ; [ship, plane] endommager.

crisis ['kraɪsɪs] (*pl* **crises** ['kraɪsiːz]) *n* crise *f*.

crisp [krɪsp] *adj* - **1.** [pastry] croustillant(e) ; [apple, vegetables] croquant(e) ; [snow] craquant(e) - **2.** [weather, manner] vif (vive). ◆ **crisps** *npl Br* chips *fpl*.

crisscross ['krɪskrɒs] <> *adj* entrecroisé(e). <> *vt* entrecroiser.

criterion [kraɪ'tɪərɪən] (*pl* **-rions** OR **-ria** [-rɪə]) *n* critère *m*.

critic ['krɪtɪk] *n* - **1.** [reviewer] critique *m* - **2.** [detractor] détracteur *m*, -trice *f*.

critical ['krɪtɪkl] *adj* critique ; **to be ~ of sb/sthg** critiquer qqn/qqch.

critically ['krɪtɪklɪ] *adv* - **1.** [ill] gravement ; **~ important** d'une importance capitale - **2.** [analytically] de façon critique.

criticism ['krɪtɪsɪzm] *n* critique *f*.

criticize, -ise ['krɪtɪsaɪz] *vt* & *vi* critiquer.

croak [krəʊk] *vi* - **1.** [frog] coasser ; [raven] croasser - **2.** [person] parler d'une voix rauque.

Croat ['krəʊæt], **Croatian** [krəʊ'eɪʃn] <> *adj* croate. <> *n* - **1.** [person] Croate *mf* - **2.** [language] croate *m*.

Croatia [krəʊ'eɪʃə] *n* Croatie *f*.

Croatian = Croat.

crochet ['krəʊʃeɪ] *n* crochet *m*.

crockery ['krɒkərɪ] *n* vaisselle *f*.

crocodile ['krɒkədaɪl] (*pl inv* OR **-s**) *n* crocodile *m*.

crocus ['krəʊkəs] (*pl* **-es** [-iːz]) *n* crocus *m*.

croft [krɒft] *n Br* petite ferme *f* (*particulièrement en Écosse*).

crony ['krəʊnɪ] *n inf* copain *m*, copine *f*.

crook [krʊk] *n* - **1.** [criminal] escroc *m*

- **2.** [of arm, elbow] pliure *f* - **3.** [shepherd's staff] houlette *f*.

crooked ['krʊkɪd] *adj* - **1.** [bent] courbé(e) - **2.** [teeth, tie] de travers - **3.** *inf* [dishonest] malhonnête.

crop [krɒp] *n* - **1.** [kind of plant] culture *f* - **2.** [harvested produce] récolte *f* - **3.** [whip] cravache *f*. ◆ **crop up** *vi* survenir.

croquette [krɒ'ket] *n* croquette *f*.

cross [krɒs] ◇ *adj* [person] fâché(e) ; [look] méchant(e) ; **to get ~ (with sb)** se fâcher (contre qqn). ◇ *n* - **1.** [gen] croix *f* - **2.** [hybrid] croisement *m*. ◇ *vt* - **1.** [gen] traverser - **2.** [arms, legs] croiser - **3.** *Br* [cheque] barrer. ◇ *vi* [intersect] se croiser. ◆ **cross off, cross out** *vt sep* rayer.

crossbar ['krɒsbɑːʳ] *n* - **1.** SPORT barre *f* transversale - **2.** [on bicycle] barre *f*.

cross-Channel *adj* transmanche.

cross-country ◇ *adj* : **~ running** cross *m* ; **~ skiing** ski *m* de fond. ◇ *n* cross-country *m*, cross *m*.

cross-examine *vt* JUR faire subir un contre-interrogatoire à ; *fig* questionner de près.

cross-eyed [-aɪd] *adj* qui louche.

crossfire ['krɒs,faɪəʳ] *n* (U) feu *m* croisé.

crossing ['krɒsɪŋ] *n* - **1.** [on road] passage *m* clouté ; [on railway line] passage à niveau - **2.** [sea journey] traversée *f*.

cross-legged [-legd] *adv* en tailleur.

cross-purposes *npl* : **to talk at ~** ne pas parler de la même chose ; **to be at ~** ne pas être sur la même longueur d'ondes.

cross-reference *n* renvoi *m*.

crossroads ['krɒsrəʊdz] (*pl inv*) *n* croisement *m*.

cross-section *n* - **1.** [drawing] coupe *f* transversale - **2.** [sample] échantillon *m*.

crosswalk ['krɒswɔːk] *n Am* passage *m* clouté, passage pour piétons.

crossways ['krɒsweɪz] = **crosswise**.

crosswind ['krɒswɪnd] *n* vent *m* de travers.

crosswise ['krɒswaɪz] *adv* en travers.

crossword (puzzle) ['krɒswɜːd-] *n* mots croisés *mpl*.

crotch [krɒtʃ] *n* entrejambe *m*.

crotchety ['krɒtʃɪtɪ] *adj Br inf* grognon(onne).

crouch [kraʊtʃ] *vi* s'accroupir.

crow [krəʊ] ◇ *n* corbeau *m* ; **as the ~ flies** à vol d'oiseau. ◇ *vi* - **1.** [cock] chanter - **2.** *inf* [person] frimer.

crowbar ['krəʊbɑːʳ] *n* pied-de-biche *m*.

crowd [kraʊd] ◇ *n* [mass of people] foule *f*. ◇ *vi* s'amasser. ◇ *vt* - **1.** [streets, town] remplir - **2.** [force into small space] entasser.

crowded ['kraʊdɪd] *adj* : **~ (with)** bondé(e) (de), plein(e) (de).

crown [kraʊn] ◇ *n* - **1.** [of king, on tooth] couronne *f* - **2.** [of head, hill] sommet *m* ; [of hat] fond *m*. ◇ *vt* couronner. ◆ **Crown** *n* : **the Crown** [monarchy] la Couronne.

crown jewels *npl* joyaux *mpl* de la Couronne.

crown prince *n* prince *m* héritier.

crow's feet *npl* pattes *fpl* d'oie.

crucial ['kruːʃl] *adj* crucial(e).

crucifix ['kruːsɪfɪks] *n* crucifix *m*.

Crucifixion [ˌkruːsɪ'fɪkʃn] *n* : **the ~** la Crucifixion.

crude [kruːd] *adj* - **1.** [material] brut(e) - **2.** [joke, drawing] grossier(ère).

crude oil *n* (U) brut *m*.

cruel [krʊəl] *adj* cruel(elle).

cruelty ['krʊəltɪ] *n* (U) cruauté *f*.

cruet ['kruːɪt] *n* service *m* à condiments.

cruise [kruːz] ◇ *n* croisière *f*. ◇ *vi* - **1.** [sail] croiser - **2.** [car] rouler ; [plane] voler.

cruiser ['kruːzəʳ] *n* - **1.** [warship] croiseur *m* - **2.** [cabin cruiser] yacht *m* de croisière.

crumb [krʌm] *n* [of food] miette *f*.

crumble ['krʌmbl] ◇ *n* crumble *m* (aux fruits). ◇ *vt* émietter. ◇ *vi* - **1.** [bread, cheese] s'émietter ; [building, wall] s'écrouler ; [cliff] s'ébouler ; [plaster] s'effriter - **2.** *fig* [society, relationship] s'effondrer.

crumbly ['krʌmblɪ] *adj* friable.

crumpet ['krʌmpɪt] *n* CULIN petite crêpe *f* épaisse.

crumple ['krʌmpl] *vt* [crease] froisser.

crunch [krʌntʃ] ◇ *n* crissement *m* ; **when it comes to the ~** *inf* au moment crucial OR décisif ; **if it comes to the ~** *inf* s'il le faut. ◇ *vt* - **1.** [with teeth] croquer - **2.** [underfoot] crisser.

crunchy ['krʌntʃɪ] *adj* [food] croquant(e).

crusade [kruː'seɪd] *n lit & fig* croisade *f*.

crush [krʌʃ] ◇ *n* - **1.** [crowd] foule *f* - **2.** *inf* [infatuation] : **to have a ~ on sb** avoir le béguin pour qqn. ◇ *vt* - **1.** [gen] écraser ; [seeds, grain] broyer ; [ice] piler - **2.** *fig* [hopes] anéantir.

crust [krʌst] *n* croûte *f*.

crutch [krʌtʃ] *n* [stick] béquille *f* ; *fig* soutien *m*.

crux [krʌks] *n* nœud *m*.

cry [kraɪ] <> n [of person, bird] cri m. <> vi - **1.** [weep] pleurer - **2.** [shout] crier. ◆ **cry off** vi se dédire. ◆ **cry out** <> vt crier. <> vi crier ; [in pain, dismay] pousser un cri.

cryptic ['krɪptɪk] adj mystérieux(euse), énigmatique.

crystal ['krɪstl] n cristal m.

crystal clear adj [obvious] clair(e) comme de l'eau de roche.

CSE (abbr of **Certificate of Secondary Education**) n ancien brevet de l'enseignement secondaire en Grande-Bretagne.

CTC abbr of **city technology college**.

cub [kʌb] n - **1.** [young animal] petit m - **2.** [boy scout] louveteau m.

Cuba ['kjuːbə] n Cuba.

Cuban ['kjuːbən] <> adj cubain(e). <> n Cubain m, -e f.

cubbyhole ['kʌbɪhəʊl] n cagibi m.

cube [kjuːb] <> n cube m. <> vt MATH élever au cube.

cubic ['kjuːbɪk] adj cubique.

cubicle ['kjuːbɪkl] n cabine f.

Cub Scout n louveteau m.

cuckoo ['kʊkuː] n coucou m.

cuckoo clock n coucou m.

cucumber ['kjuːkʌmbəʳ] n concombre m.

cuddle ['kʌdl] <> n caresse f, câlin m. <> vt caresser, câliner. <> vi s'enlacer.

cuddly toy n jouet m en peluche.

cue [kjuː] n - **1.** RADIO, THEATRE & TV signal m ; **on ~** au bon moment - **2.** [in snooker, pool] queue f (de billard).

cuff [kʌf] n - **1.** [of sleeve] poignet m ; **off the ~** au pied levé - **2.** Am [of trouser] revers m inv - **3.** [blow] gifle f.

cuff link n bouton m de manchette.

cul-de-sac ['kʌldəsæk] n cul-de-sac m.

cull [kʌl] <> n massacre m. <> vt - **1.** [kill] massacrer - **2.** [gather] recueillir.

culminate ['kʌlmɪneɪt] vi : **to ~ in sthg** se terminer par qqch, aboutir à qqch.

culmination [ˌkʌlmɪ'neɪʃn] n apogée m.

culottes [kjuː'lɒts] npl jupe-culotte f.

culpable ['kʌlpəbl] adj coupable.

culprit ['kʌlprɪt] n coupable mf.

cult [kʌlt] <> n culte m. <> comp culte.

cultivate ['kʌltɪveɪt] vt cultiver.

cultivation [ˌkʌltɪ'veɪʃn] n (U) [farming] culture f.

cultural ['kʌltʃərəl] adj culturel(elle).

culture ['kʌltʃəʳ] n culture f.

cultured ['kʌltʃəd] adj [educated] cultivé(e).

cumbersome ['kʌmbəsəm] adj [object] encombrant(e).

cunning ['kʌnɪŋ] <> adj [person] rusé(e) ; [plan, method, device] astucieux(euse). <> n (U) [of person] ruse f ; [of plan, method, device] astuce f.

cup [kʌp] n - **1.** [container, unit of measurement] tasse f - **2.** [prize, competition] coupe f - **3.** [of bra] bonnet m.

cupboard ['kʌbəd] n placard m.

Cup Final n : **the ~** la finale de la coupe.

cup tie n Br match m de coupe.

curate ['kjʊərət] n vicaire m.

curator [ˌkjʊə'reɪtəʳ] n conservateur m.

curb [kɜːb] <> n - **1.** [control] : **~ (on)** frein m (à) - **2.** Am [of road] bord m du trottoir. <> vt mettre un frein à.

curdle ['kɜːdl] vi cailler.

cure [kjʊəʳ] <> n : **~ (for)** MED remède m (contre) ; fig remède (à). <> vt - **1.** MED guérir - **2.** [solve - problem] éliminer - **3.** [rid] : **to ~ sb of sthg** guérir qqn de qqch, faire perdre l'habitude de qqch à qqn - **4.** [preserve - by smoking] fumer ; [- by salting] saler ; [- tobacco, hide] sécher.

cure-all n panacée f.

curfew ['kɜːfjuː] n couvre-feu m.

curio ['kjʊərɪəʊ] (pl -s) n bibelot m.

curiosity [ˌkjʊərɪ'ɒsətɪ] n curiosité f.

curious ['kjʊərɪəs] adj : **~ (about)** curieux(euse) (à propos de).

curl [kɜːl] <> n [of hair] boucle f. <> vt - **1.** [hair] boucler - **2.** [roll up] enrouler. <> vi - **1.** [hair] boucler - **2.** [roll up] s'enrouler. ◆ **curl up** vi [person, animal] se mettre en boule, se pelotonner.

curler ['kɜːləʳ] n bigoudi m.

curling tongs npl fer m à friser.

curly ['kɜːlɪ] adj [hair] bouclé(e).

currant ['kʌrənt] n [dried grape] raisin m de Corinthe, raisin sec.

currency ['kʌrənsɪ] n - **1.** [type of money] monnaie f - **2.** (U) [money] devise f - **3.** fml [acceptability] : **to gain ~** s'accréditer.

current ['kʌrənt] <> adj [price, method] actuel(elle) ; [year, week] en cours ; [boyfriend, girlfriend] du moment ; **~ issue** dernier numéro. <> n [of water, air, electricity] courant m.

current account n Br compte m courant.

current affairs npl actualité f, questions fpl d'actualité.

currently ['kʌrəntlɪ] adv actuellement.

curriculum [kə'rɪkjələm] (*pl* **-lums** OR **-la** [-lə]) *n* programme *m* d'études.

curriculum vitae [-'viːtaɪ] (*pl* **curricula vitae**) *n* curriculum vitae *m inv*.

curry ['kʌrɪ] *n* curry *m*.

curse [kɜːs] ◇ *n* **- 1.** [evil spell] malédiction *f*; *fig* fléau *m* **- 2.** [swearword] juron *m*. ◇ *vt* maudire. ◇ *vi* jurer.

cursor ['kɜːsəʳ] *n* COMPUT curseur *m*.

cursory ['kɜːsərɪ] *adj* superficiel(elle).

curt [kɜːt] *adj* brusque.

curtail [kɜː'teɪl] *vt* [visit] écourter.

curtain ['kɜːtn] *n* rideau *m*.

curts(e)y ['kɜːtsɪ] (*pt* & *pp* **curtsied**) ◇ *n* révérence *f*. ◇ *vi* faire une révérence.

curve [kɜːv] ◇ *n* courbe *f*. ◇ *vi* faire une courbe.

cushion ['kʊʃn] ◇ *n* coussin *m*. ◇ *vt* [fall, blow, effects] amortir.

cushy ['kʊʃɪ] *adj inf* pépère, peinard(e).

custard ['kʌstəd] *n* crème *f* anglaise.

custodian [kʌ'stəʊdjən] *n* [of building] gardien *m*, -enne *f*; [of museum] conservateur *m*.

custody ['kʌstədɪ] *n* **- 1.** [of child] garde *f* **- 2.** JUR : **in ~** en garde à vue.

custom ['kʌstəm] *n* **- 1.** [tradition, habit] coutume *f* **- 2.** COMM clientèle *f* ◆ **customs** *n* [place] douane *f*.

customary ['kʌstəmrɪ] *adj* [behaviour] coutumier(ère); [way, time] habituel(elle).

customer ['kʌstəməʳ] *n* **- 1.** [client] client *m*, -e *f* **- 2.** *inf* [person] type *m*.

customize, -ise ['kʌstəmaɪz] *vt* [make] fabriquer OR assembler sur commande; [modify] modifier sur commande.

Customs and Excise *n Br* ≃ service *m* des contributions indirectes.

customs duty *n* droit *m* de douane.

customs officer *n* douanier *m*, -ère *f*.

cut [kʌt] (*pt* & *pp* **cut**) ◇ *n* **- 1.** [in wood etc] entaille *f*; [in skin] coupure *f* **- 2.** [of meat] morceau *m* **- 3.** [reduction] : **~ (in)** [taxes, salary, personnel] réduction *f* (de); [film, article] coupure *f* (dans) **- 4.** [of suit, hair] coupe *f*. ◇ *vt* **- 1.** [gen] couper; [taxes, costs, workforce] réduire; **to ~ one's finger** se couper le doigt **- 2.** *inf* [lecture, class] sécher. ◇ *vi* **- 1.** [gen] couper **- 2.** [intersect] se couper. ◆ **cut back** ◇ *vt sep* **- 1.** [prune] tailler **- 2.** [reduce] réduire. ◇ *vi* : **to ~ back on** réduire, diminuer. ◆ **cut down** ◇ *vt sep* **- 1.** [chop down] couper **- 2.** [reduce] réduire, diminuer. ◇ *vi* : **to ~ down on** smoking/eating/spending fumer/manger/

dépenser moins. ◆ **cut in** *vi* **- 1.** [interrupt] : **to ~ in (on sb)** interrompre (qqn) **- 2.** AUT & SPORT se rabattre. ◆ **cut off** *vt sep* **- 1.** [piece, crust] couper **- 2.** [finger, leg - subj : surgeon] amputer **- 3.** [power, telephone, funding] couper **- 4.** [separate] : **to be ~ off (from)** [person] être coupé(e) (de); [village] être isolé(e) (de). ◆ **cut out** *vt sep* **- 1.** [photo, article] découper; [sewing pattern] couper; [dress] tailler **- 2.** [stop] : **to ~ out smoking/chocolates** arrêter de fumer/de manger des chocolats; **~ it out!** *inf* ça suffit! **- 3.** [exclude] exclure. ◆ **cut up** *vt sep* [chop up] couper, hacher.

cutback ['kʌtbæk] *n* : **~ (in)** réduction *f* (de).

cute [kjuːt] *adj* [appealing] mignon(onne).

cuticle ['kjuːtɪkl] *n* envie *f*.

cutlery ['kʌtlərɪ] *n (U)* couverts *mpl*.

cutlet ['kʌtlɪt] *n* côtelette *f*.

cutout ['kʌtaʊt] *n* **- 1.** [on machine] disjoncteur *m* **- 2.** [shape] découpage *m*.

cut-price, cut-rate *Am adj* à prix réduit.

cutthroat ['kʌtθrəʊt] *adj* [ruthless] acharné(e).

cutting ['kʌtɪŋ] ◇ *adj* [sarcastic - remark] cinglant(e); [- wit] acerbe. ◇ *n* **- 1.** [of plant] bouture *f* **- 2.** *Br* [from newspaper] coupure *f* **- 3.** *Br* [for road, railway] tranchée *f*.

CV (*abbr of* **curriculum vitae**) *n* CV *m*.

cwt. *abbr of* **hundredweight**.

cyanide ['saɪənaɪd] *n* cyanure *m*.

cybercafe ['saɪbə,kæfeɪ] *n* cybercafé *m*.

cybernaut ['saɪbə,nɔːt] *n* cybernaute *mf*.

cyberpet ['saɪbə,pet] *n* animal *m* virtuel.

cyberspace ['saɪbəspeɪs] *n* cyberespace *m*.

cybersurfer ['saɪbə,sɜːfəʳ] *n* cybernaute *mf*.

cycle ['saɪkl] ◇ *n* **- 1.** [of events, songs] cycle *m* **- 2.** [bicycle] bicyclette *f*. ◇ *comp* [path, track] cyclable; [race] cycliste; [shop] de cycles. ◇ *vi* faire de la bicyclette.

cycling ['saɪklɪŋ] *n* cyclisme *m*.

cyclist ['saɪklɪst] *n* cycliste *mf*.

cygnet ['sɪgnɪt] *n* jeune cygne *m*.

cylinder ['sɪlɪndəʳ] *n* cylindre *m*.

cymbals ['sɪmblz] *npl* cymbales *fpl*.

cynic ['sɪnɪk] *n* cynique *mf*.

cynical ['sɪnɪkl] *adj* cynique.

cynicism ['sɪnɪsɪzm] *n* cynisme *m*.

cypress ['saɪprəs] *n* cyprès *m*.

Cypriot ['sɪprɪət] ◇ *adj* chypriote. ◇ *n* Chypriote *mf*.

Cyprus ['saɪprəs] *n* Chypre *f*.

cyst [sɪst] *n* kyste *m*.

cystitis [sɪs'taɪtɪs] *n* cystite *f*.

czar [zaːʳ] *n* tsar *m*.

Czech [tʃek] ◇ *adj* tchèque. ◇ *n* - **1.** [person] Tchèque *mf* - **2.** [language] tchèque *m*.

Czechoslovak [ˌtʃekə'sləʊvæk] = **Czechoslovakian**.

Czechoslovakia [ˌtʃekəslə'vækɪə] *n* Tchécoslovaquie *f*.

Czechoslovakian [ˌtʃekəslə'vækɪən] ◇ *adj* tchécoslovaque. ◇ *n* Tchécoslovaque *mf*.

Czech Republic *n* République *f* tchèque.

d (*pl* d's OR ds), **D** (*pl* D's OR Ds) [diː] *n* [letter] d *m inv*, D *m inv*. ➡ **D** *n* - **1.** MUS ré *m* - **2.** SCH [mark] D *m inv*.

DA *abbr of* **district attorney**.

dab [dæb] ◇ *n* [of cream, powder, ointment] petit peu *m* ; [of paint] touche *f*. ◇ *vt* - **1.** [skin, wound] tamponner - **2.** [apply - cream, ointment] : **to ~ sthg on** OR **onto** appliquer qqch sur.

dabble ['dæbl] *vi* : **to ~ in** toucher un peu à.

dachshund ['dækshʊnd] *n* teckel *m*.

dad [dæd], **daddy** ['dædɪ] *n inf* papa *m*.

daddy longlegs [-'lɒŋlegz] (*pl inv*) *n* faucheur *m*.

daffodil ['dæfədɪl] *n* jonquille *f*.

daft [daːft] *adj Br inf* stupide, idiot(e).

dagger ['dægəʳ] *n* poignard *m*.

daily ['deɪlɪ] ◇ *adj* - **1.** [newspaper, occurrence] quotidien(enne) - **2.** [rate, output] journalier(ère). ◇ *adv* [happen, write] quotidiennement ; **twice ~** deux fois par jour. ◇ *n* [newspaper] quotidien *m*.

dainty ['deɪntɪ] *adj* délicat(e).

dairy ['deərɪ] *n* - **1.** [on farm] laiterie *f* - **2.** [shop] crémerie *f*.

dairy products *npl* produits *mpl* laitiers.

dais ['deɪɪs] *n* estrade *f*.

daisy ['deɪzɪ] *n* [weed] pâquerette *f* ; [cultivated] marguerite *f*.

daisy-wheel printer *n* imprimante *f* à marguerite.

dale [deɪl] *n* vallée *f*.

dam [dæm] ◇ *n* [across river] barrage *m*. ◇ *vt* construire un barrage sur.

damage ['dæmɪdʒ] ◇ *n* - **1.** [physical harm] dommage *m*, dégât *m* - **2.** [harmful effect] tort *m*. ◇ *vt* - **1.** [harm physically] endommager, abîmer - **2.** [have harmful effect on] nuire à. ➡ **damages** *npl* JUR dommages et intérêts *mpl*.

damn [dæm] ◇ *adj inf* fichu(e), sacré(e). ◇ *adv inf* sacrément. ◇ *n* : **not to give** OR **care a ~ (about sthg)** se ficher pas mal (de qqch). ◇ *vt* RELIG [condemn] damner. ◇ *excl inf* zut!

damned [dæmd] *inf* ◇ *adj* fichu(e), sacré(e) ; **well I'll be** OR **I'm ~!** c'est trop fort!, elle est bien bonne celle-là! ◇ *adv* sacrément.

damning ['dæmɪŋ] *adj* accablant(e).

damp [dæmp] ◇ *adj* humide. ◇ *n* humidité *f*. ◇ *vt* [make wet] humecter.

dampen ['dæmpən] *vt* - **1.** [make wet] humecter - **2.** *fig* [emotion] abattre.

damson ['dæmzn] *n* prune *f* de Damas.

dance [daːns] ◇ *n* - **1.** [gen] danse *f* - **2.** [social event] bal *m*. ◇ *vi* danser.

dancer ['daːnsəʳ] *n* danseur *m*, -euse *f*.

dancing ['daːnsɪŋ] *n* (U) danse *f*.

dandelion ['dændɪlaɪən] *n* pissenlit *m*.

dandruff ['dændrʌf] *n* (U) pellicules *fpl*.

Dane [deɪn] *n* Danois *m*, -e *f*.

danger ['deɪndʒəʳ] *n* - **1.** (U) [possibility of harm] danger *m* ; **in ~** en danger ; **out of ~** hors de danger - **2.** [hazard, risk] : **~ (to)** risque *m* (pour) ; **to be in ~ of doing sthg** risquer de faire qqch.

dangerous ['deɪndʒərəs] *adj* dangereux(euse).

dangle ['dæŋgl] ◇ *vt* laisser pendre. ◇ *vi* pendre.

Danish ['deɪnɪʃ] ◇ *adj* danois(e). ◇ *n* - **1.** [language] danois *m* - **2.** *Am* = **Danish pastry**. ◇ *npl* : **the ~** les Danois *mpl*.

Danish pastry *n* gâteau feuilleté fourré aux fruits.

dank [dæŋk] *adj* humide et froid(e).

dapper ['dæpəʳ] *adj* pimpant(e).

dappled ['dæpld] *adj* - **1.** [light] tacheté(e) - **2.** [horse] pommelé(e).

dare [deəʳ] ◇ *vt* - **1.** [be brave enough] : **to ~ to do sthg** oser faire qqch - **2.** [challenge] :

to ~ sb to do sthg défier qqn de faire qqch - 3. *phr* : **I ~ say** je suppose, sans doute. ◇ *vi* oser ; **how ~ you!** comment osez-vous! ◇ *n* défi *m*.

daredevil ['deə,devl] *n* casse-cou *m inv*.

daring ['deərɪŋ] ◇ *adj* audacieux(euse). ◇ *n* audace *f*.

dark [dɑːk] ◇ *adj* - **1.** [room, night] sombre ; **it's getting ~** il commence à faire nuit - **2.** [in colour] foncé(e) - **3.** [dark-haired] brun(e) ; [dark-skinned] basané(e). ◇ *n* - **1.** [darkness] : **the ~** l'obscurité *f* ; **to be in the ~ about sthg** ignorer tout de qqch - **2.** [night] : **before/after ~** avant/après la tombée de la nuit.

darken ['dɑːkn] ◇ *vt* assombrir. ◇ *vi* s'assombrir.

dark glasses *npl* lunettes *fpl* noires.

darkness ['dɑːknɪs] *n* obscurité *f*.

darkroom ['dɑːkrʊm] *n* chambre *f* noire.

darling ['dɑːlɪŋ] ◇ *adj* [dear] chéri(e). ◇ *n* - **1.** [loved person, term of address] chéri *m*, -e *f* - **2.** [idol] chouchou *m*, idole *f*.

darn [dɑːn] ◇ *vt* repriser. ◇ *adj inf* sacré(e), satané(e). ◇ *adv inf* sacrément.

dart [dɑːt] ◇ *n* [arrow] fléchette *f*. ◇ *vi* se précipiter. ➤ **darts** *n* [game] jeu *m* de fléchettes.

dartboard ['dɑːtbɔːd] *n* cible *f* de jeu de fléchettes.

dash [dæʃ] ◇ *n* - **1.** [of milk, wine] goutte *f* ; [of cream] soupçon *m* ; [of salt] pincée *f* ; [of colour, paint] touche *f* - **2.** [in punctuation] tiret *m* - **3.** [rush] : **to make a ~ for** se ruer vers. ◇ *vt* - **1.** [throw] jeter avec violence - **2.** [hopes] anéantir. ◇ *vi* se précipiter.

dashboard ['dæʃbɔːd] *n* tableau *m* de bord.

dashing ['dæʃɪŋ] *adj* fringant(e).

data ['deɪtə] *n* (U) données *fpl*.

database ['deɪtəbeɪs] *n* base *f* de données.

data processing *n* traitement *m* de données.

date [deɪt] ◇ *n* - **1.** [in time] date *f* ; **to ~** à ce jour - **2.** [appointment] rendez-vous *m* - **3.** [person] petit ami *m*, petite amie *f* - **4.** [fruit] datte *f*. ◇ *vt* - **1.** [gen] dater - **2.** [go out with] sortir avec. ◇ *vi* [go out of fashion] dater.

dated ['deɪtɪd] *adj* qui date.

date of birth *n* date *f* de naissance.

daub [dɔːb] *vt* : **to ~ sthg with sthg** barbouiller qqch de qqch.

daughter ['dɔːtə'] *n* fille *f*.

daughter-in-law (*pl* daughters-in-law) *n* belle-fille *f*.

daunting ['dɔːntɪŋ] *adj* intimidant(e).

dawdle ['dɔːdl] *vi* flâner.

dawn [dɔːn] ◇ *n lit & fig* aube *f*. ◇ *vi* - **1.** [day] poindre - **2.** [era, period] naître. ➤ **dawn (up)on** *vt fus* venir à l'esprit de.

day [deɪ] *n* jour *m* ; [duration] journée *f* ; **the ~ before** la veille ; **the ~ after** le lendemain ; **the ~ before yesterday** avant-hier ; **the ~ after tomorrow** après-demain ; **any ~ now** d'un jour à l'autre ; **one ~, some ~, one of these ~s** un jour (ou l'autre), un de ces jours ; **in my ~** de mon temps ; **to make sb's ~** réchauffer le cœur de qqn. ➤ **days** *adv* le jour.

daybreak ['deɪbreɪk] *n* aube *f* ; **at ~** à l'aube.

daycentre ['deɪsentə'] *n* Br [for children] garderie *f* ; [for elderly people] *centre de jour pour les personnes du troisième âge*.

daydream ['deɪdriːm] *vi* rêvasser.

daylight ['deɪlaɪt] *n* - **1.** [light] lumière *f* du jour - **2.** [dawn] aube *f*.

day off (*pl* days off) *n* jour *m* de congé.

day return *n* Br billet aller et retour valable *pour une journée*.

daytime ['deɪtaɪm] ◇ *n* jour *m*, journée *f*. ◇ *comp* [television] pendant la journée ; [job, flight] de jour.

day-to-day *adj* [routine, life] journalier(ère) ; **on a ~ basis** au jour le jour.

day trip *n* excursion *f* d'une journée.

daze [deɪz] ◇ *n* : **in a ~** hébété(e), ahuri(e). ◇ *vt* - **1.** [subj : blow] étourdir - **2.** *fig* [subj : shock, event] abasourdir, sidérer.

dazzle ['dæzl] *vt* éblouir.

DC *n* (*abbr of* **direct current**) courant *m* continu.

D-day ['diːdeɪ] *n* le jour J.

DEA (*abbr of* **Drug Enforcement Administration**) *n agence américaine de lutte contre la drogue*.

deacon ['diːkn] *n* diacre *m*.

deactivate [,diː'æktɪveɪt] *vt* désamorcer.

dead [ded] ◇ *adj* - **1.** [not alive, not lively] mort(e) ; **to shoot sb ~** abattre qqn - **2.** [numb] engourdi(e) - **3.** [not operating - battery] à plat - **4.** [complete - silence] de mort. ◇ *adv* - **1.** [directly, precisely] : **~ ahead** droit devant soi ; **~ on time** pile à l'heure - **2.** *inf* [completely] tout à fait - **3.** [suddenly] : **to stop ~** s'arrêter net. ◇ *npl* : **the ~** les morts *mpl*.

deaden ['dedn] *vt* [sound] assourdir ; [pain] calmer.

dead end *n* impasse *f*.

dead heat *n* arrivée *f* ex-aequo.

deadline ['dedlaɪn] *n* dernière limite *f*.

deadlock ['dedlɒk] *n* impasse *f*.

dead loss *n inf* : **to be a ~** [person] être bon (bonne) à rien ; [object] ne rien valoir.

deadly ['dedlɪ] ◇ *adj* - **1.** [poison, enemy] mortel(elle) - **2.** [accuracy] imparable. ◇ *adv* [boring, serious] tout à fait.

deadpan ['dedpæn] ◇ *adj* pince-sans-rire *(inv)*. ◇ *adv* impassiblement.

deaf [def] ◇ *adj* sourd(e) ; **to be ~ to sthg** être sourd à qqch. ◇ *npl* : **the ~** les sourds *mpl*.

deaf-aid *n Br* appareil *m* acoustique.

deaf-and-dumb *adj* sourd-muet (sourde-muette).

deafen ['defn] *vt* assourdir.

deaf-mute ◇ *adj* sourd-muet (sourde-muette). ◇ *n* sourd-muet *m*, sourde-muette *f*.

deafness ['defnɪs] *n* surdité *f*.

deal [diːl] *(pt & pp dealt)* ◇ *n* - **1.** [quantity] : **a good** OR **great ~** beaucoup ; **a good** OR **great ~ of** beaucoup, de bien de/des - **2.** [business agreement] marché *m*, affaire *f* ; **to do** OR **strike a ~ with sb** conclure un marché avec qqn - **3.** *inf* [treatment] : **to get a bad ~** ne pas faire une affaire. ◇ *vt* - **1.** [strike] : **to ~ sb/sthg a blow, to ~ a blow to sb/sthg** porter un coup à qqn/qqch - **2.** [cards] donner, distribuer. ◇ *vi* - **1.** [at cards] donner, distribuer - **2.** [in drugs] faire le trafic (de drogues). ◆ **deal in** *vt fus* COMM faire le commerce de. ◆ **deal out** *vt sep* distribuer. ◆ **deal with** *vt fus* - **1.** [handle] s'occuper de - **2.** [be about] traiter de - **3.** [be faced with] avoir affaire à.

dealer ['diːlər] *n* - **1.** [trader] négociant *m* ; [in drugs] trafiquant *m* - **2.** [cards] donneur *m*.

dealing ['diːlɪŋ] *n* commerce *m*. ◆ **dealings** *npl* relations *fpl*, rapports *mpl*.

dealt [delt] *pt & pp* ▷ **deal**.

dean [diːn] *n* doyen *m*.

dear [dɪər] ◇ *adj* : **~ (to)** cher (chère) (à) ; **Dear Sir** [in letter] Cher Monsieur ; **Dear Madam** Chère Madame. ◇ *n* chéri *m*, -e *f*. ◇ *excl* : **oh ~!** mon Dieu!

dearly ['dɪəlɪ] *adv* [love, wish] de tout son cœur.

death [deθ] *n* mort *f* ; **to frighten sb to ~** faire une peur bleue à qqn ; **to be sick to ~ of sthg/of doing sthg** en avoir marre de qqch/de faire qqch.

death certificate *n* acte *m* de décès.

death duty *Br*, **death tax** *Am n* droits *mpl* de succession.

deathly ['deθlɪ] *adj* de mort.

death penalty *n* peine *f* de mort.

death rate *n* taux *m* de mortalité.

death tax *Am* = death duty.

death trap *n inf* véhicule *m*/bâtiment *m* dangereux.

debar [diːˈbɑːr] *vt* : **to ~ sb (from)** [place] exclure qqn (de) ; **to ~ sb from doing sthg** interdire à qqn de faire qqch.

debase [dɪˈbeɪs] *vt* dégrader ; **to ~ o.s.** s'avilir.

debate [dɪˈbeɪt] ◇ *n* débat *m* ; **open to ~** discutable. ◇ *vt* débattre, discuter ; **to ~ whether** s'interroger pour savoir si. ◇ *vi* débattre.

debating society [dɪˈbeɪtɪŋ-] *n* club *m* de débats.

debauchery [dɪˈbɔːtʃərɪ] *n* débauche *f*.

debit ['debɪt] ◇ *n* débit *m*. ◇ *vt* débiter.

debit card *n* carte *f* de paiement à débit immédiat.

debit note *n* note *f* de débit.

debris ['deɪbriː] *n (U)* débris *mpl*.

debt [det] *n* dette *f* ; **to be in ~** avoir des dettes, être endetté(e) ; **to be in sb's ~** être redevable à qqn.

debt collector *n* agent *m* de recouvrements.

debtor ['detər] *n* débiteur *m*, -trice *f*.

debug [ˌdiːˈbʌg] *vt* COMPUT [program] mettre au point, déboguer.

debunk [ˌdiːˈbʌŋk] *vt* démentir.

debut ['deɪbjuː] *n* débuts *mpl*.

decade ['dekeɪd] *n* décennie *f*.

decadence ['dekədəns] *n* décadence *f*.

decadent ['dekədənt] *adj* décadent(e).

decaffeinated [dɪˈkæfɪneɪtɪd] *adj* décaféiné(e).

decanter [dɪˈkæntər] *n* carafe *f*.

decathlon [dɪˈkæθlɒn] *n* décathlon *m*.

decay [dɪˈkeɪ] ◇ *n* - **1.** [of body, plant] pourriture *f*, putréfaction *f* ; [of tooth] carie *f* - **2.** *fig* [of building] délabrement *m* ; [of society] décadence *f*. ◇ *vi* - **1.** [rot] pourrir ; [tooth] se carier - **2.** *fig* [building] se délabrer, tomber en ruines ; [society] tomber en décadence.

deceased [dɪˈsiːst] *(pl inv)* ◇ *adj* décédé(e). ◇ *n* : **the ~** le défunt, la défunte.

deceit [dɪˈsiːt] *n* tromperie *f*, supercherie *f*.

deceitful [dɪˈsiːtfʊl] *adj* trompeur(euse).

deceive [dɪ'siːv] *vt* [person] tromper, duper ; [subj : memory, eyes] jouer des tours à ; **to ~ o.s.** se leurrer, s'abuser.

December [dɪ'sembəʳ] *n* décembre *m* ; *see also* **September**.

decency ['diːsnsɪ] *n* décence *f*, bienséance *f* ; **to have the ~ to do sthg** avoir la décence de faire qqch.

decent ['diːsnt] *adj* - **1.** [behaviour, dress] décent(e) - **2.** [wage, meal] correct(e), décent(e) - **3.** [person] gentil(ille), brave.

deception [dɪ'sepʃn] *n* - **1.** [lie, pretence] tromperie *f*, duperie *f* - **2.** *(U)* [act of lying] supercherie *f*.

deceptive [dɪ'septɪv] *adj* trompeur(euse).

decide [dɪ'saɪd] <> *vt* décider ; **to ~ to do sthg** décider de faire qqch. <> *vi* se décider. ◆ **decide (up)on** *vt fus* se décider pour, choisir.

decided [dɪ'saɪdɪd] *adj* - **1.** [definite] certain(e), incontestable - **2.** [resolute] décidé(e), résolu(e).

decidedly [dɪ'saɪdɪdlɪ] *adv* - **1.** [clearly] manifestement, incontestablement - **2.** [resolutely] résolument.

deciduous [dɪ'sɪdjʊəs] *adj* à feuilles caduques.

decimal ['desɪml] <> *adj* décimal(e). <> *n* décimale *f*.

decimal point *n* virgule *f*.

decimate ['desɪmeɪt] *vt* décimer.

decipher [dɪ'saɪfəʳ] *vt* déchiffrer.

decision [dɪ'sɪʒn] *n* décision *f*.

decisive [dɪ'saɪsɪv] *adj* - **1.** [person] déterminé(e), résolu(e) - **2.** [factor, event] décisif(ive).

deck [dek] *n* - **1.** [of ship] pont *m* - **2.** [of bus] impériale *f* - **3.** [of cards] jeu *m* - **4.** *Am* [of house] véranda *f*.

deckchair ['dektʃeəʳ] *n* chaise longue *f*, transat *m*.

declaration [,deklə'reɪʃn] *n* déclaration *f*.

Declaration of Independence *n* : **the ~** la Déclaration d'Indépendance des États-Unis d'Amérique (1776).

declare [dɪ'kleəʳ] *vt* déclarer.

decline [dɪ'klaɪn] <> *n* déclin *m* ; **to be in ~** être en déclin ; **on the ~** en baisse. <> *vt* décliner ; **to ~ to do sthg** refuser de faire qqch. <> *vi* - **1.** [deteriorate] décliner - **2.** [refuse] refuser.

decode [,diː'kəʊd] *vt* décoder.

decompose [,diːkəm'pəʊz] *vi* se décomposer.

decongestant [,diːkən'dʒestənt] *n* décongestionnant *m*.

decorate ['dekəreɪt] *vt* décorer.

decoration [,dekə'reɪʃn] *n* décoration *f*.

decorator ['dekəreɪtəʳ] *n* décorateur *m*, -trice *f*.

decoy [*n* 'diːkɔɪ, *vt* dɪ'kɔɪ] <> *n* [for hunting] appât *m*, leurre *m* ; [person] compère *m*. <> *vt* attirer dans un piège.

decrease [*n* 'diːkriːs, *vb* dɪ'kriːs] <> *n* : **~ (in)** diminution *f* (de), baisse *f* (de). <> *vt* diminuer, réduire. <> *vi* diminuer, décroître.

decree [dɪ'kriː] <> *n* - **1.** [order, decision] décret *m* - **2.** *Am* JUR arrêt *m*, jugement *m*. <> *vt* décréter, ordonner.

decree nisi [-'naɪsaɪ] (*pl* **decrees nisi**) *n Br* jugement *m* provisoire.

decrepit [dɪ'krepɪt] *adj* [person] décrépit(e) ; [house] délabré(e).

dedicate ['dedɪkeɪt] *vt* - **1.** [book etc] dédier - **2.** [life, career] consacrer.

dedication [,dedɪ'keɪʃn] *n* - **1.** [commitment] dévouement *m* - **2.** [in book] dédicace *f*.

deduce [dɪ'djuːs] *vt* déduire, conclure.

deduct [dɪ'dʌkt] *vt* déduire, retrancher.

deduction [dɪ'dʌkʃn] *n* déduction *f*.

deed [diːd] *n* - **1.** [action] action *f*, acte *m* - **2.** JUR acte *m* notarié

deem [diːm] *vt* juger, considérer ; **to ~ it wise to do sthg** juger prudent de faire qqch.

deep [diːp] <> *adj* profond(e). <> *adv* profondément ; **~ down** [fundamentally] au fond.

deepen ['diːpn] *vi* - **1.** [river, sea] devenir profond(e) - **2.** [crisis, recession, feeling] s'aggraver.

deep freeze *n* congélateur *m*.

deep-fry *vt* faire frire.

deeply ['diːplɪ] *adv* profondément.

deep-sea *adj* : **~ diving** plongée *f* sous-marine ; **~ fishing** pêche *f* hauturière.

deer [dɪəʳ] (*pl inv*) *n* cerf *m*.

deface [dɪ'feɪs] *vt* barbouiller.

defamatory [dɪ'fæmətrɪ] *adj* diffamatoire, diffamant(e).

default [dɪ'fɔːlt] <> *n* - **1.** [failure] défaillance *f* ; **by ~** par défaut - **2.** COMPUT valeur *f* par défaut. <> *vi* manquer à ses engagements.

defeat [dɪ'fiːt] <> *n* défaite *f* ; **to admit ~** s'avouer battu(e) OR vaincu(e). <> *vt*

- **1.** [team, opponent] vaincre, battre - **2.** [motion, proposal] rejeter.

defeatist [dɪˈfiːtɪst] ◇ *adj* défaitiste. ◇ *n* défaitiste *mf*.

defect [*n* ˈdiːfekt, *vi* dɪˈfekt] ◇ *n* défaut *m*. ◇ *vi* : **to ~ to** passer à.

defective [dɪˈfektɪv] *adj* défectueux (euse).

defence *Br*, **defense** *Am* [dɪˈfens] *n* - **1.** [gen] défense *f* - **2.** [protective device, system] protection *f* - **3.** JUR : **the ~** la défense.

defenceless *Br*, **defenseless** *Am* [dɪˈfenslɪs] *adj* sans défense.

defend [dɪˈfend] *vt* défendre.

defendant [dɪˈfendənt] *n* défendeur *m*, -eresse *f* ; [in trial] accusé *m*, -e *f*.

defender [dɪˈfendəʳ] *n* défenseur *m*.

defense *Am* = **defence**.

defenseless *Am* = **defenceless**.

defensive [dɪˈfensɪv] ◇ *adj* défensif (ive). ◇ *n* : **on the ~** sur la défensive.

defer [dɪˈfɜːʳ] ◇ *vt* différer. ◇ *vi* : **to ~ to sb** s'en remettre à (l'opinion de) qqn.

deferential [ˌdefəˈrenʃl] *adj* respectueux(euse).

defiance [dɪˈfaɪəns] *n* défi *m* ; **in ~ of** au mépris de.

defiant [dɪˈfaɪənt] *adj* [person] intraitable, intransigeant(e) ; [action] de défi.

deficiency [dɪˈfɪʃnsɪ] *n* - **1.** [lack] manque *m* ; [of vitamins etc] carence *f* - **2.** [inadequacy] imperfection *f*.

deficient [dɪˈfɪʃnt] *adj* - **1.** [lacking] : **to be ~ in** manquer de - **2.** [inadequate] insuffisant(e), médiocre.

deficit [ˈdefɪsɪt] *n* déficit *m*.

defile [dɪˈfaɪl] *vt* souiller, salir.

define [dɪˈfaɪn] *vt* définir.

definite [ˈdefɪnɪt] *adj* - **1.** [plan] bien déterminé(e) ; [date] certain(e) - **2.** [improvement, difference] net (nette), marqué(e) - **3.** [answer] précis(e), catégorique - **4.** [confident - person] assuré(e).

definitely [ˈdefɪnɪtlɪ] *adv* - **1.** [without doubt] sans aucun doute, certainement - **2.** [for emphasis] catégoriquement.

definition [ˌdefɪˈnɪʃn] *n* - **1.** [gen] définition *f* - **2.** [clarity] clarté *f*, précision *f*.

deflate [dɪˈfleɪt] ◇ *vt* [balloon, tyre] dégonfler. ◇ *vi* [balloon, tyre] se dégonfler.

deflation [dɪˈfleɪʃn] *n* ECON déflation *f*.

deflect [dɪˈflekt] *vt* [ball, bullet] dévier ; [stream] détourner, dériver ; [criticism] détourner.

defogger [ˌdiːˈfɒgəʳ] *n* *Am* AUT dispositif *m* antibuée.

deformed [dɪˈfɔːmd] *adj* difforme.

defraud [dɪˈfrɔːd] *vt* [person] escroquer ; [Inland Revenue etc] frauder.

defrost [ˌdiːˈfrɒst] ◇ *vt* - **1.** [fridge] dégivrer ; [frozen food] décongeler - **2.** *Am* [AUT - de-ice] dégivrer ; [- demist] désembuer. ◇ *vi* [fridge] dégivrer ; [frozen food] se décongeler.

deft [deft] *adj* adroit(e).

defunct [dɪˈfʌŋkt] *adj* qui n'existe plus ; [person] défunt(e).

defuse [ˌdiːˈfjuːz] *vt* désamorcer.

defy [dɪˈfaɪ] *vt* - **1.** [gen] défier ; **to ~ sb to do sthg** mettre qqn au défi de faire qqch - **2.** [efforts] résister à, faire échouer.

degenerate [*adj & n* dɪˈdʒenərət, *vb* dɪˈdʒenəreɪt] ◇ *adj* dégénéré(e). ◇ *vi* : **to ~ (into)** dégénérer (en).

degrading [dɪˈgreɪdɪŋ] *adj* dégradant(e), avilissant(e).

degree [dɪˈgriː] *n* - **1.** [measurement] degré *m* - **2.** UNIV diplôme *m* universitaire ; **to have/take a ~ (in)** avoir/faire une licence (de) - **3.** [amount] : **to a certain ~** jusqu'à un certain point, dans une certaine mesure ; **a ~ of risk** un certain risque ; **a ~ of truth** une certaine part de vérité ; **by ~s** progressivement, petit à petit.

dehydrated [ˌdiːhaɪˈdreɪtɪd] *adj* déshydraté(e).

de-ice [diːˈaɪs] *vt* dégivrer.

deign [deɪn] *vt* : **to ~ to do sthg** daigner faire qqch.

deity [ˈdiːɪtɪ] *n* dieu *m*, déesse *f*, divinité *f*.

dejected [dɪˈdʒektɪd] *adj* abattu(e), découragé(e).

delay [dɪˈleɪ] ◇ *n* retard *m*, délai *m*. ◇ *vt* - **1.** [cause to be late] retarder - **2.** [defer] différer ; **to ~ doing sthg** tarder à faire qqch. ◇ *vi* : **to ~ (in doing sthg)** tarder (à faire qqch).

delayed [dɪˈleɪd] *adj* : **to be ~** [person, train] être retardé(e).

delectable [dɪˈlektəbl] *adj* délicieux (euse).

delegate [*n* ˈdelɪgət, *vb* ˈdelɪgeɪt] ◇ *n* délégué *m*, -e *f*. ◇ *vt* déléguer ; **to ~ sb to do sthg** déléguer qqn pour faire qqch ; **to ~ sthg to sb** déléguer qqch à qqn.

delegation [ˌdelɪˈgeɪʃn] *n* délégation *f*.

delete [dɪˈliːt] *vt* supprimer, effacer.

deli [ˈdelɪ] *n* *inf abbr of* **delicatessen**.

deliberate [*adj* dɪˈlɪbərət, *vb* dɪˈlɪbəreɪt]

◇ *adj* - **1.** [intentional] voulu(e), délibéré(e) - **2.** [slow] lent(e), sans hâte. ◇ *vi* délibérer.

deliberately [dɪ'lɪbərətlɪ] *adv* [on purpose] exprès, à dessein.

delicacy ['delɪkəsɪ] *n* - **1.** [gen] délicatesse *f* - **2.** [food] mets *m* délicat.

delicate ['delɪkət] *adj* délicat(e) ; [movement] gracieux(euse).

delicatessen [,delɪkə'tesn] *n* épicerie *f* fine.

delicious [dɪ'lɪʃəs] *adj* délicieux(euse).

delight [dɪ'laɪt] ◇ *n* [great pleasure] délice *m* ; to take ~ in doing sthg prendre grand plaisir à faire qqch. ◇ *vt* enchanter, charmer. ◇ *vi* : to ~ in sthg/in doing sthg prendre grand plaisir à qqch/à faire qqch.

delighted [dɪ'laɪtɪd] *adj* : ~ (by OR with) enchanté(e) (de), ravi(e) (de) ; to be ~ to do sthg être enchanté de faire qqch.

delightful [dɪ'laɪtful] *adj* ravissant(e), charmant(e) ; [meal] délicieux(euse).

delinquent [dɪ'lɪŋkwənt] ◇ *adj* délinquant(e). ◇ *n* délinquant *m*, -e *f*.

delirious [dɪ'lɪrɪəs] *adj* lit & fig délirant(e).

deliver [dɪ'lɪvər] *vt* - **1.** [distribute] : to ~ sthg (to sb) [mail, newspaper] distribuer qqch (à qqn) ; COMM livrer qqch (à qqn) - **2.** [speech] faire ; [warning] donner ; [message] remettre ; [blow, kick] donner, porter - **3.** [baby] mettre au monde - **4.** [free] délivrer - **5.** *Am* POL [votes] obtenir.

delivery [dɪ'lɪvərɪ] *n* - **1.** COMM livraison *f* - **2.** [way of speaking] élocution *f* - **3.** [birth] accouchement *m*.

delude [dɪ'luːd] *vt* tromper, induire en erreur ; to ~ o.s. se faire des illusions.

delusion [dɪ'luːʒn] *n* illusion *f*.

delve [delv] *vi* : to ~ into [past] fouiller ; [bag etc] fouiller dans.

demand [dɪ'mɑːnd] ◇ *n* - **1.** [claim, firm request] revendication *f*, exigence *f* ; on ~ sur demande - **2.** [need] : ~ (for) demande *f* (de) ; in ~ demandé(e), recherché(e). ◇ *vt* - **1.** [ask for - justice, money] réclamer ; [- explanation, apology] exiger ; to ~ to do sthg exiger de faire qqch - **2.** [require] demander, exiger.

demanding [dɪ'mɑːndɪŋ] *adj* - **1.** [exhausting] astreignant(e) - **2.** [not easily satisfied] exigeant(e).

demean [dɪ'miːn] *vt* : to ~ o.s. s'abaisser.

demeaning [dɪ'miːnɪŋ] *adj* avilissant(e), dégradant(e).

demeanour *Br*, **demeanor** *Am* [dɪ'miːnər] *n* (U) *fml* comportement *m*.

demented [dɪ'mentɪd] *adj* fou (folle), dément(e).

demise [dɪ'maɪz] *n* (U) décès *m* ; fig mort *f*, fin *f*.

demister [,diː'mɪstər] *n* Br dispositif *m* antibuée.

demo ['deməʊ] (*abbr of* **demonstration**) *n* Br inf manif *f*.

democracy [dɪ'mɒkrəsɪ] *n* démocratie *f*.

democrat ['deməkræt] *n* démocrate *mf*.
➡ **Democrat** *n* Am démocrate *mf*.

democratic [,demə'krætɪk] *adj* démocratique. ➡ **Democratic** *adj* Am démocrate.

Democratic Party *n* Am : the ~ le Parti démocrate.

demolish [dɪ'mɒlɪʃ] *vt* [destroy] démolir.

demonstrate ['demənstreɪt] ◇ *vt* - **1.** [prove] démontrer, prouver - **2.** [machine, computer] faire une démonstration de. ◇ *vi* : to ~ (for/against) manifester (pour/contre)

demonstration [,demən'streɪʃn] *n* - **1.** [of machine, emotions] démonstration *f* - **2.** [public meeting] manifestation *f*.

demonstrator ['demənstreɪtər] *n* - **1.** [in march] manifestant *m*, -e *f* - **2.** [of machine, product] démonstrateur *m*, -trice *f*.

demoralized [dɪ'mɒrəlaɪzd] *adj* démoralisé(e).

demote [,diː'məʊt] *vt* rétrograder.

demure [dɪ'mjʊər] *adj* modeste, réservé(e).

den [den] *n* [of animal] antre *m*, tanière *f*.

denial [dɪ'naɪəl] *n* [of rights, facts, truth] dénégation *f* ; [of accusation] démenti *m*.

denier ['denɪər] *n* denier *m*.

denigrate ['denɪgreɪt] *vt* dénigrer.

denim ['denɪm] *n* jean *m*. ➡ **denims** *npl* : a pair of ~s un jean.

denim jacket *n* veste *f* en jean.

Denmark ['denmɑːk] *n* Danemark *m*.

denomination [dɪ,nɒmɪ'neɪʃn] *n* - **1.** RELIG confession *f* - **2.** [money] valeur *f*.

denounce [dɪ'naʊns] *vt* dénoncer.

dense [dens] *adj* - **1.** [crowd, forest] dense ; [fog] dense, épais(aisse) - **2.** inf [stupid] bouché(e).

density ['densətɪ] *n* densité *f*.

dent [dent] ◇ *n* bosse *f*. ◇ *vt* cabosser.

dental ['dentl] *adj* dentaire ; ~ appointment rendez-vous *m* chez le dentiste.

dental floss *n* fil *m* dentaire.

dental surgeon *n* chirurgien-dentiste *m*.

dentist ['dentɪst] *n* dentiste *mf*.

dentures ['dentʃəz] *npl* dentier *m*.

deny [dɪ'naɪ] *vt* - **1.** [refute] nier - **2.** *fml* [refuse] nier, refuser ; **to ~ sb sthg** refuser qqch à qqn.

deodorant [di:'əʊdərənt] *n* déodorant *m*.

depart [dɪ'pɑːt] *vi fml* - **1.** [leave] : **to ~ (from)** partir de - **2.** [differ] : **to ~ from sthg** s'écarter de qqch.

department [dɪ'pɑːtmənt] *n* - **1.** [in organization] service *m* - **2.** [in shop] rayon *m* - **3.** SCH & UNIV département *m* - **4.** [in government] département *m*, ministère *m*.

department store *n* grand magasin *m*.

departure [dɪ'pɑːtʃə] *n* - **1.** [leaving] départ *m* - **2.** [change] nouveau départ *m* ; **a ~ from tradition** un écart par rapport à la tradition.

departure lounge *n* salle *f* d'embarquement.

depend [dɪ'pend] *vi* : **to ~ on** [be dependent on] dépendre de ; [rely on] compter sur ; [emotionally] se reposer sur ; **it ~s** cela dépend ; **~ing on** selon.

dependable [dɪ'pendəbl] *adj* [person] sur qui on peut compter ; [source of income] sûr(e) ; [car] fiable.

dependant [dɪ'pendənt] *n* personne *f* à charge.

dependent [dɪ'pendənt] *adj* - **1.** [reliant] : **~ (on)** dépendant(e) (de) ; **to be ~ on sb/ sthg** dépendre de qqn/qqch - **2.** [addicted] dépendant(e), accro - **3.** [contingent] : **to be ~ on** dépendre de.

depict [dɪ'pɪkt] *vt* - **1.** [show in picture] représenter - **2.** [describe] : **to ~ sb/sthg as** dépeindre qqn/qqch comme.

deplete [dɪ'pliːt] *vt* épuiser.

deplorable [dɪ'plɔːrəbl] *adj* déplorable.

deplore [dɪ'plɔː] *vt* déplorer.

deploy [dɪ'plɔɪ] *vt* déployer.

depopulation [di:ˌpɒpjʊ'leɪʃn] *n* dépeuplement *m*.

deport [dɪ'pɔːt] *vt* expulser.

depose [dɪ'pəʊz] *vt* déposer.

deposit [dɪ'pɒzɪt] <> *n* - **1.** [gen] dépôt *m* ; **to make a ~** [into bank account] déposer de l'argent - **2.** [payment - as guarantee] caution *f* ; [- as instalment] acompte *m* ; [- on bottle] consigne *f*. <> *vt* déposer.

deposit account *n Br* compte *m* sur livret.

depot ['depəʊ] *n* - **1.** [gen] dépôt *m* - **2.** *Am* [station] gare *f*.

depreciate [dɪ'priːʃɪeɪt] *vi* se déprécier.

depress [dɪ'pres] *vt* - **1.** [sadden, discourage] déprimer - **2.** [weaken - economy] affaiblir ; [- prices] faire baisser.

depressed [dɪ'prest] *adj* - **1.** [sad] déprimé(e) - **2.** [run-down - area] en déclin.

depressing [dɪ'presɪŋ] *adj* déprimant(e).

depression [dɪ'preʃn] *n* - **1.** [gen] dépression *f* - **2.** [sadness] tristesse *f*.

deprivation [ˌdeprɪ'veɪʃn] *n* privation *f*.

deprive [dɪ'praɪv] *vt* : **to ~ sb of sthg** priver qqn de qqch.

depth [depθ] *n* profondeur *f* ; **in ~** [study, analyse] en profondeur ; **to be out of one's ~** [in water] ne pas avoir pied ; *fig* avoir perdu pied, être dépassé. ◆ **depths** *npl* : **the ~s** [of seas] les profondeurs *fpl* ; [of memory, archives] le fin fond ; **in the ~s of winter** au cœur de l'hiver ; **to be in the ~s of despair** toucher le fond du désespoir.

deputation [ˌdepjʊ'teɪʃn] *n* délégation *f*.

deputize, -ise ['depjʊtaɪz] *vi* : **to ~ for sb** assurer les fonctions de qqn, remplacer qqn.

deputy ['depjʊtɪ] <> *adj* adjoint(e) ; **~ chairman** vice-président *m* ; **~ head** SCH directeur *m* adjoint ; **~ leader** POL vice-président *m*. <> *n* - **1.** [second-in-command] adjoint *m*, -e *f* - **2.** *Am* [deputy sheriff] shérif *m* adjoint.

derail [dɪ'reɪl] *vt* [train] faire dérailler.

deranged [dɪ'reɪndʒd] *adj* dérangé(e).

derby [*Br* 'dɑːbɪ, *Am* 'dɜːbɪ] *n* - **1.** SPORT derby *m* - **2.** *Am* [hat] chapeau *m* melon.

derelict ['derəlɪkt] *adj* en ruines.

deride [dɪ'raɪd] *vt* railler.

derisory [də'raɪzərɪ] *adj* - **1.** [puny, trivial] dérisoire - **2.** [derisive] moqueur(euse).

derivative [dɪ'rɪvətɪv] <> *adj pej* pas original(e). <> *n* dérivé *m*.

derive [dɪ'raɪv] <> *vt* - **1.** [draw, gain] : **to ~ sthg from sthg** tirer qqch de qqch - **2.** [originate] : **to be ~d from** venir de. <> *vi* : **to ~ from** venir de.

derogatory [dɪ'rɒgətrɪ] *adj* désobligeant(e).

derv [dɜːv] *n Br* gas-oil *m*.

descend [dɪ'send] <> *vt fml* [go down] descendre. <> *vi* - **1.** *fml* [go down] descendre - **2.** [fall] : **to ~ (on)** [enemy] s'abattre (sur) - **3.** [stoop] : **to ~ to sthg/to doing sthg** s'abaisser à qqch/à faire qqch.

descendant [dɪ'sendənt] *n* descendant *m*, -e *f*.

descended [dɪ'sendɪd] *adj* : to be ~ from sb descendre de qqn.

descent [dɪ'sent] *n* - **1.** [downward movement] descente *f* - **2.** *(U)* [origin] origine *f*.

describe [dɪ'skraɪb] *vt* décrire.

description [dɪ'skrɪpʃn] *n* - **1.** [account] description *f* - **2.** [type] sorte *f*, genre *m*.

desecrate ['desɪkreɪt] *vt* profaner.

desert [*n* 'dezət, *vb & npl* dɪ'zɜːt] ⬦ *n* désert *m*. ⬦ *vt* - **1.** [place] déserter - **2.** [person, group] déserter, abandonner. ⬦ *vi* MIL déserter. ◆ **deserts** *npl* : to get one's just ~s recevoir ce que l'on mérite.

deserted [dɪ'zɜːtɪd] *adj* désert(e).

deserter [dɪ'zɜːtəʳ] *n* déserteur *m*.

desert island ['dezət-] *n* île *f* déserte.

deserve [dɪ'zɜːv] *vt* mériter ; to ~ to do sthg mériter de faire qqch.

deserving [dɪ'zɜːvɪŋ] *adj* [person] méritant(e) ; [cause, charity] méritoire.

design [dɪ'zaɪn] ⬦ *n* - **1.** [plan, drawing] plan *m*, étude *f* - **2.** *(U)* [art] design *m* - **3.** [pattern] motif *m*, dessin *m* - **4.** [shape] ligne *f* ; [of dress] style *m* - **5.** *fml* [intention] dessein *m*, by ~ à dessein ; to have ~s on sb/sthg avoir des desseins sur qqn/qqch. ⬦ *vt* - **1.** [draw plans for building, car] faire les plans de, dessiner ; [dress] créer - **2.** [plan] concevoir, mettre au point ; to be ~ed for sthg/to do sthg être conçu pour qqch/pour faire qqch.

designate [*adj* 'dezɪgnət, *vb* 'dezɪgneɪt] ⬦ *adj* désigné(e). ⬦ *vt* désigner.

designer [dɪ'zaɪnəʳ] ⬦ *adj* de marque. ⬦ *n* INDUSTRY concepteur *m*, -trice *f* ; ARCHIT dessinateur *m*, -trice *f* ; [of dresses etc] styliste *mf* ; THEATRE décorateur *m*, -trice *f*.

desirable [dɪ'zaɪərəbl] *adj* - **1.** [enviable, attractive] désirable - **2.** *fml* [appropriate] désirable, souhaitable.

desire [dɪ'zaɪəʳ] ⬦ *n* désir *m* ; ~ for sthg/to do sthg désir de qqch/de faire qqch. ⬦ *vt* désirer.

desist [dɪ'zɪst] *vi fml* : to ~ (from doing sthg) cesser (de faire qqch).

desk [desk] *n* bureau *m* ; reception ~ réception *f* ; information ~ bureau *m* de renseignements.

desktop publishing *n* publication *f* assistée par ordinateur, PAO *f*.

desolate ['desələt] *adj* - **1.** [place] abandonné(e) - **2.** [person] désespéré(e), désolé(e).

despair [dɪ'speəʳ] ⬦ *n* *(U)* désespoir *m*. ⬦ *vi* désespérer ; to ~ of désespérer de ; to ~ of doing sthg désespérer de faire qqch.

despairing [dɪ'speərɪŋ] *adj* de désespoir.

despatch [dɪ'spætʃ] = dispatch.

desperate ['desprət] *adj* désespéré(e) ; to be ~ for sthg avoir absolument besoin de qqch.

desperately ['desprətlɪ] *adv* désespérément ; ~ ill gravement malade.

desperation [,despə'reɪʃn] *n* désespoir *m* ; in ~ de désespoir.

despicable [dɪ'spɪkəbl] *adj* ignoble.

despise [dɪ'spaɪz] *vt* [person] mépriser ; [racism] exécrer.

despite [dɪ'spaɪt] *prep* malgré.

despondent [dɪ'spɒndənt] *adj* découragé(e).

dessert [dɪ'zɜːt] *n* dessert *m*.

dessertspoon [dɪ'zɜːtspuːn] *n* [spoon] cuillère *f* à dessert.

destination [,destɪ'neɪʃn] *n* destination *f*.

destined ['destɪnd] *adj* - **1.** [intended] : ~ for destiné(e) à ; ~ to do sthg destiné à faire qqch - **2.** [bound] : ~ for à destination de.

destiny ['destɪnɪ] *n* destinée *f*.

destitute ['destɪtjuːt] *adj* indigent(e).

destroy [dɪ'strɔɪ] *vt* [ruin] détruire.

destruction [dɪ'strʌkʃn] *n* destruction *f*.

detach [dɪ'tætʃ] *vt* - **1.** [pull off] détacher ; to ~ sthg from sthg détacher qqch de qqch - **2.** [dissociate] : to ~ o.s. from sthg [from reality] se détacher de qqch ; [from proceedings, discussions] s'écarter de qqch.

detached [dɪ'tætʃt] *adj* [unemotional] détaché(e).

detached house *n* *Br* maison *f* individuelle.

detachment [dɪ'tætʃmənt] *n* détachement *m*.

detail ['diːteɪl] ⬦ *n* - **1.** [small point] détail *m* ; to go into ~ entrer dans les détails ; in ~ en détail - **2.** MIL détachement *m*. ⬦ *vt* [list] détailler. ◆ **details** *npl* [personal information] coordonnées *fpl*.

detailed ['diːteɪld] *adj* détaillé(e).

detain [dɪ'teɪn] *vt* - **1.** [in police station] détenir ; [in hospital] garder - **2.** [delay] retenir.

detect [dɪ'tekt] *vt* - **1.** [subj : person] déceler - **2.** [subj : machine] détecter.

detection [dɪ'tekʃn] *n* *(U)* - **1.** [of crime, disease] dépistage *m* - **2.** [of aircraft, submarine] détection *f*.

detective [dɪ'tektɪv] *n* détective *m*.

detective novel *n* roman *m* policier.

detention [dɪ'tenʃn] *n* - **1.** [of suspect, criminal] détention *f* - **2.** SCH retenue *f*.

deter [dɪ'tɜ:'] *vt* dissuader ; **to ~ sb from doing sthg** dissuader qqn de faire qqch.

detergent [dɪ'tɜ:dʒənt] *n* détergent *m*.

deteriorate [dɪ'tɪərɪəreɪt] *vi* se détériorer.

determination [dɪ,tɜ:mɪ'neɪʃn] *n* détermination *f*.

determine [dɪ'tɜ:mɪn] *vt* - **1.** [establish, control] déterminer - **2.** *fml* [decide] : **to ~ to do sthg** décider de faire qqch.

determined [dɪ'tɜ:mɪnd] *adj* - **1.** [person] déterminé(e) ; **~ to do sthg** déterminé à faire qqch - **2.** [effort] obstiné(e).

deterrent [dɪ'terənt] *n* moyen *m* de dissuasion.

detest [dɪ'test] *vt* détester.

detonate ['detəneɪt] <> *vt* faire détoner. <> *vi* détoner.

detour ['di:tʊə'] *n* détour *m*.

detract [dɪ'trækt] *vi* : **to ~ from** diminuer.

detriment ['detrɪmənt] *n* : **to the ~ of** au détriment de.

detrimental [,detrɪ'mentl] *adj* préjudiciable.

deuce [dju:s] *n* TENNIS égalité *f*.

devaluation [,di:væljʊ'eɪʃn] *n* dévaluation *f*.

devastated ['devəsteɪtd] *adj* - **1.** [area, city] dévasté(e) - **2.** *fig* [person] anéanti(e).

devastating ['devəsteɪtɪŋ] *adj* - **1.** [hurricane, remark] dévastateur(trice) - **2.** [upsetting] accablant(e) - **3.** [attractive] irrésistible.

develop [dɪ'veləp] <> *vt* - **1.** [gen] développer - **2.** [land, area] aménager, développer - **3.** [illness, fault, habit] contracter - **4.** [resources] développer, exploiter. <> *vi* - **1.** [grow, advance] se développer - **2.** [appear - problem, trouble] se déclarer.

developing country [dɪ'veləpɪŋ-] *n* pays *m* en voie de développement.

development [dɪ'veləpmənt] *n* - **1.** [gen] développement *m* - **2.** (U) [of land, area] exploitation *f* - **3.** [land being developed] zone *f* d'aménagement ; [developed area] zone aménagée - **4.** (U) [of illness, fault] évolution *f*.

deviate ['di:vɪeɪt] *vi* : **to ~ (from)** dévier (de), s'écarter (de).

device [dɪ'vaɪs] *n* - **1.** [apparatus] appareil *m*, dispositif *m* - **2.** [plan, method] moyen *m*.

devil ['devl] *n* - **1.** [evil spirit] diable *m* - **2.** *inf* [person] type *m* ; **poor ~!** pauvre diable! - **3.** [for emphasis] : **who/where/why the ~ ...?** qui/où/pourquoi diable ...? ➤ **Devil** *n* [Satan] : **the Devil** le Diable.

devious ['di:vjəs] *adj* - **1.** [dishonest - person] retors(e), à l'esprit tortueux ; [- scheme, means] détourné(e) - **2.** [tortuous] tortueux(euse).

devise [dɪ'vaɪz] *vt* concevoir.

devoid [dɪ'vɔɪd] *adj fml* : **~ of** dépourvu(e) de, dénué(e) de.

devolution [,di:və'lu:ʃn] *n* POL décentralisation *f*.

devote [dɪ'vəʊt] *vt* : **to ~ sthg to sthg** consacrer qqch à qqch.

devoted [dɪ'vəʊtɪd] *adj* dévoué(e) ; **a ~ mother** une mère dévouée à ses enfants.

devotee [,devə'ti:] *n* [fan] passionné *m*, -e *f*.

devotion [dɪ'vəʊʃn] *n* - **1.** [commitment] : **~ (to)** dévouement *m* (à) - **2.** RELIG dévotion *f*.

devour [dɪ'vaʊə'] *vt lit & fig* dévorer.

devout [dɪ'vaʊt] *adj* dévot(e).

dew [dju:] *n* rosée *f*.

diabetes [,daɪə'bi:ti:z] *n* diabète *m*.

diabetic [,daɪə'betɪk] <> *adj* [person] diabétique. <> *n* diabétique *mf*.

diabolic(al) [,daɪə'bɒlɪk(l)] *adj* - **1.** [evil] diabolique - **2.** *inf* [very bad] atroce.

diagnose ['daɪəgnəʊz] *vt* diagnostiquer.

diagnosis [,daɪəg'nəʊsɪs] (*pl* **-ses** [-si:z]) *n* diagnostic *m*.

diagonal [daɪ'ægənl] <> *adj* [line] diagonal(e). <> *n* diagonale *f*.

diagram ['daɪəgræm] *n* diagramme *m*.

dial ['daɪəl] <> *n* cadran *m* ; [of radio] cadran de fréquences. <> *vt* [number] composer.

dialect ['daɪəlekt] *n* dialecte *m*.

dialling code ['daɪəlɪŋ-] *n Br* indicatif *m*.

dialling tone *Br* ['daɪəlɪŋ-], **dial tone** *Am n* tonalité *f*.

dialogue *Br*, **dialog** *Am* ['daɪəlɒg] *n* dialogue *m*.

dial tone *Am* = **dialling tone**.

dialysis [daɪ'ælɪsɪs] *n* dialyse *f*.

diameter [daɪ'æmɪtə'] *n* diamètre *m*.

diamond ['daɪəmənd] *n* - **1.** [gem] diamant *m* - **2.** [shape] losange *m*. ➤ **diamonds** *npl* carreau *m*.

diaper ['daɪəpə'] *n Am* couche *f*.

diaphragm ['daɪəfræm] *n* diaphragme *m*.

diarrh(o)ea [,daɪə'rɪə] *n* diarrhée *f*.

diary ['daɪərɪ] *n* - **1.** [appointment book] agenda *m* - **2.** [journal] journal *m*.

dice [daɪs] (*pl inv*) <> *n* [for games] dé *m*. <> *vt* couper en dés.

dictate [*vb* dɪk'teɪt, *n* 'dɪkteɪt] <> *vt* dicter. <> *n* ordre *m*.

dictation [dɪk'teɪʃn] *n* dictée *f*.

dictator [*Br* dɪk'teɪtə', *Am* 'dɪk-] *n* dictateur *m*.

dictatorship [dɪk'teɪtəʃɪp] *n* dictature *f*.

dictionary ['dɪkʃənrɪ] *n* dictionnaire *m*.

did [dɪd] *pt* ⊳ **do**.

diddle ['dɪdl] *vt inf* escroquer, rouler.

didn't ['dɪdnt] = **did not**.

die [daɪ] (*pl* **dice** [daɪs], *pt & pp* **died**, *cont* **dying**) <> *vi* mourir ; **to be dying** se mourir ; **to be dying to do sthg** mourir d'envie de faire qqch ; **to be dying for a drink/cigarette** mourir d'envie de boire un verre/de fumer une cigarette. <> *n* [dice] dé *m*. ◆ **die away** *vi* [sound] s'éteindre ; [wind] tomber. ◆ **die down** *vi* [sound] s'affaiblir ; [wind] tomber ; [fire] baisser. ◆ **die out** *vi* s'éteindre, disparaître.

diehard ['daɪhɑːd] *n* : **to be a ~** être coriace ; [reactionary] être réactionnaire.

diesel ['diːzl] *n* diesel *m*.

diesel engine *n* AUT moteur *m* diesel ; RAIL locomotive *f* diesel.

diesel fuel, diesel oil *n* diesel *m*.

diet ['daɪət] <> *n* - **1.** [eating pattern] alimentation *f* - **2.** [to lose weight] régime *m* ; **to be on a ~** être au régime, faire un régime. <> *comp* [low-calorie] de régime. <> *vi* suivre un régime.

differ ['dɪfə'] *vi* - **1.** [be different] être différent(e), différer ; [people] être différent ; **to ~ from** être différent de - **2.** [disagree] : **to ~ with sb (about sthg)** ne pas être d'accord avec qqn (à propos de qqch).

difference ['dɪfrəns] *n* différence *f* ; **it doesn't make any ~** cela ne change rien.

different ['dɪfrənt] *adj* : **~ (from)** différent(e) (de).

differentiate [ˌdɪfə'renʃɪeɪt] <> *vt* : **to ~ sthg from sthg** différencier qqch de qqch, faire la différence entre qqch et qqch. <> *vi* : **to ~ (between)** faire la différence (entre).

difficult ['dɪfɪkəlt] *adj* difficile.

difficulty ['dɪfɪkəltɪ] *n* difficulté *f* ; **to have ~ in doing sthg** avoir de la difficulté OR du mal à faire qqch.

diffident ['dɪfɪdənt] *adj* [person] qui manque d'assurance ; [manner, voice, approach] hésitant(e).

diffuse [dɪ'fjuːz] *vt* diffuser, répandre.

dig [dɪg] (*pt & pp* **dug**) <> *vi* - **1.** [in ground] creuser - **2.** [subj : belt, strap] : **to ~ into sb** couper qqn. <> *n* - **1.** *fig* [unkind remark] pique *f* - **2.** ARCHEOL fouilles *fpl*. <> *vt* - **1.** [hole] creuser - **2.** [garden] bêcher. ◆ **dig out** *vt sep inf* [find] dénicher. ◆ **dig up** *vt sep* - **1.** [from ground] déterrer ; [potatoes] arracher - **2.** *inf* [information] dénicher.

digest [*n* 'daɪdʒest, *vb* dɪ'dʒest] <> *n* résumé *m*, digest *m*. <> *vt lit & fig* digérer.

digestion [dɪ'dʒestʃn] *n* digestion *f*.

digestive biscuit [daɪ'dʒestɪv-] *n Br* ≃ sablé *m* (à la farine complète).

digit ['dɪdʒɪt] *n* - **1.** [figure] chiffre *m* - **2.** [finger] doigt *m* ; [toe] orteil *m*.

digital ['dɪdʒɪtl] *adj* numérique, digital(e).

digital camera *n* appareil photo *m* numérique.

digital television *n* télévision *f* numérique.

dignified ['dɪgnɪfaɪd] *adj* digne, plein(e) de dignité.

dignity ['dɪgnətɪ] *n* dignité *f*.

digress [daɪ'gres] *vi* : **to ~ (from)** s'écarter (de).

digs [dɪgz] *npl Br inf* piaule *f*.

dike [daɪk] *n* - **1.** [wall, bank] digue *f* - **2.** *inf pej* [lesbian] gouine *f*.

dilapidated [dɪ'læpɪdeɪtɪd] *adj* délabré(e).

dilate [daɪ'leɪt] <> *vt* dilater. <> *vi* se dilater.

dilemma [dɪ'lemə] *n* dilemme *m*.

diligent ['dɪlɪdʒənt] *adj* appliqué(e).

dilute [daɪ'luːt] <> *adj* dilué(e). <> *vt* : **to ~ sthg (with)** diluer qqch (avec).

dim [dɪm] <> *adj* - **1.** [dark - light] faible ; [- room] sombre - **2.** [indistinct - memory, outline] vague - **3.** [weak - eyesight] faible - **4.** *inf* [stupid] borné(e). <> *vt & vi* baisser.

dime [daɪm] *n Am* (pièce *f* de) dix cents *mpl*.

dimension [dɪ'menʃn] *n* dimension *f*.

diminish [dɪ'mɪnɪʃ] *vt & vi* diminuer.

diminutive [dɪ'mɪnjʊtɪv] *fml* <> *adj* minuscule. <> *n* GRAMM diminutif *m*.

dimmers ['dɪmərz] *npl Am* [dipped headlights] phares *mpl* code (*inv*) ; [parking lights] feux *mpl* de position.

dimmer (switch) ['dɪmə'-] *n* variateur *m* de lumière.

dimple ['dɪmpl] *n* fossette *f*.

din [dɪn] *n inf* barouf *m*.

dine [daɪn] *vi fml* dîner. ◆ **dine out** *vi* dîner dehors.

diner ['daɪnər] *n* **- 1.** [person] dîneur *m*, -euse *f* **- 2.** *Am* [café] ≃ resto *m* routier.

dinghy ['dɪŋgɪ] *n* [for sailing] dériveur *m* ; [for rowing] (petit) canot *m*.

dingy ['dɪndʒɪ] *adj* miteux(euse), crasseux(euse).

dining car ['daɪnɪŋ-] *n* wagon-restaurant *m*.

dining room ['daɪnɪŋ-] *n* **- 1.** [in house] salle *f* à manger **- 2.** [in hotel] restaurant *m*.

dinner ['dɪnər] *n* dîner *m*.

dinner jacket *n* smoking *m*.

dinner party *n* dîner *m (sur invitation)*.

dinnertime ['dɪnətaɪm] *n* heure *f* du dîner.

dinosaur ['daɪnəsɔːr] *n* dinosaure *m*.

dint [dɪnt] *n fml* : **by ~ of** à force de.

dip [dɪp] ◇ *n* **- 1.** [in road, ground] déclivité *f* **- 2.** [sauce] sauce *f* **- 3.** [swim] baignade *f* (rapide) ; **to go for a ~** aller se baigner en vitesse, aller faire trempette. ◇ *vt* **- 1.** [into liquid] : **to ~ sthg in** OR **into** tremper OR plonger qqch dans **- 2.** *Br* AUT : **to ~ one's headlights** se mettre en code. ◇ *vi* **- 1.** [sun] baisser, descendre à l'horizon ; [wing] plonger **- 2.** [road, ground] descendre.

diploma [dɪ'pləʊmə] (*pl* -s) *n* diplôme *m*.

diplomacy [dɪ'pləʊməsɪ] *n* diplomatie *f*.

diplomat ['dɪpləmæt] *n* diplomate *m*.

diplomatic [ˌdɪplə'mætɪk] *adj* **- 1.** [service, corps] diplomatique **- 2.** [tactful] diplomate.

dipstick ['dɪpstɪk] *n* AUT jauge *f (de niveau d'huile)*.

dire ['daɪər] *adj* [need, consequences] extrême ; [warning] funeste.

direct [dɪ'rekt] ◇ *adj* direct(e) ; [challenge] manifeste. ◇ *vt* **- 1.** [gen] diriger **- 2.** [aim] : **to ~ sthg at sb** [question, remark] adresser qqch à qqn ; **the campaign is ~ed at teenagers** cette campagne vise les adolescents **- 3.** [order] : **to ~ sb to do sthg** ordonner à qqn de faire qqch. ◇ *adv* directement.

direct current *n* courant *m* continu.

direct debit *n Br* prélèvement *m* automatique.

direction [dɪ'rekʃn] *n* direction *f*. ◆ **directions** *npl* **- 1.** [to find a place] indications *fpl* **- 2.** [for use] instructions *fpl*.

directly [dɪ'rektlɪ] *adv* **- 1.** [in straight line] directement **- 2.** [honestly, clearly] sans détours **- 3.** [exactly - behind, above] exacte-

ment **- 4.** [immediately] immédiatement **- 5.** [very soon] tout de suite.

director [dɪ'rektər] *n* **- 1.** [of company] directeur *m*, -trice *f* **- 2.** THEATRE metteur *m* en scène ; CINEMA & TV réalisateur *m*, -trice *f*.

directory [dɪ'rektərɪ] *n* **- 1.** [annual publication] annuaire *m* **- 2.** COMPUT répertoire *m*.

directory enquiries *n Br* renseignements *mpl* (téléphoniques).

dire straits *npl* : **in ~** dans une situation désespérée.

dirt [dɜːt] *n* (*U*) **- 1.** [mud, dust] saleté *f* **- 2.** [earth] terre *f*.

dirt cheap *inf* ◇ *adj* très bon marché, donné(e). ◇ *adv* pour trois fois rien.

dirty ['dɜːtɪ] ◇ *adj* **- 1.** [not clean, not fair] sale **- 2.** [smutty - language, person] grossier(ère) ; [- book, joke] cochon(onne). ◇ *vt* salir.

disability [ˌdɪsə'bɪlətɪ] *n* infirmité *f*.

disabled [dɪs'eɪbld] ◇ *adj* [person] handicapé(e), infirme. ◇ *npl* : **the ~** les handicapés, les infirmes.

disadvantage [ˌdɪsəd'vɑːntɪdʒ] *n* désavantage *m*, inconvénient *m* ; **to be at a ~** être désavantagé.

disadvantaged [ˌdɪsəd'vɑːntɪdʒd] *adj* défavorisé(e).

disagree [ˌdɪsə'griː] *vi* **- 1.** [have different opinions] : **to ~ (with)** ne pas être d'accord (avec) **- 2.** [differ] ne pas concorder **- 3.** [subj : food, drink] : **to ~ with sb** ne pas réussir à qqn.

disagreeable [ˌdɪsə'griːəbl] *adj* désagréable.

disagreement [ˌdɪsə'griːmənt] *n* **- 1.** [in opinion] désaccord *m* **- 2.** [argument] différend *m*.

disallow [ˌdɪsə'laʊ] *vt* **- 1.** *fml* [appeal, claim] rejeter **- 2.** [goal] refuser.

disappear [ˌdɪsə'pɪər] *vi* disparaître.

disappearance [ˌdɪsə'pɪərəns] *n* disparition *f*.

disappoint [ˌdɪsə'pɔɪnt] *vt* décevoir.

disappointed [ˌdɪsə'pɔɪntɪd] *adj* : **~ (in** OR **with)** déçu(e) (par).

disappointing [ˌdɪsə'pɔɪntɪŋ] *adj* décevant(e).

disappointment [ˌdɪsə'pɔɪntmənt] *n* déception *f*.

disapproval [ˌdɪsə'pruːvl] *n* désapprobation *f*.

disapprove [ˌdɪsə'pruːv] *vi* : **to ~ of sb/ sthg** désapprouver qqn/qqch.

disarm [dɪs'ɑːm] vt & vi lit & fig désarmer.

disarmament [dɪs'ɑːməmənt] n désarmement m.

disarray [ˌdɪsə'reɪ] n : **in ~** en désordre ; [government] en pleine confusion.

disaster [dɪ'zɑːstər] n - 1. [damaging event] catastrophe f - 2. (U) [misfortune] échec m, désastre m - 3. inf [failure] désastre m.

disastrous [dɪ'zɑːstrəs] adj désastreux(euse).

disband [dɪs'bænd] <> vt dissoudre. <> vi se dissoudre.

disbelief [ˌdɪsbɪ'liːf] n : **in** OR **with ~** avec incrédulité.

disc Br, **disk** Am [dɪsk] n disque m.

discard [dɪ'skɑːd] vt mettre au rebut.

discern [dɪ'sɜːn] vt discerner, distinguer.

discerning [dɪ'sɜːnɪŋ] adj judicieux (euse).

discharge [n 'dɪstʃɑːdʒ, vt dɪs'tʃɑːdʒ] <> n - 1. [of patient] autorisation f de sortie, décharge f , JUR relaxe f ; **to get one's ~** MIL être rendu à la vie civile - 2. [emission - of smoke] émission f ; [- of sewage] déversement m ; [- MED] écoulement m. <> vt - 1. [allow to leave - patient] signer la décharge de ; [- prisoner, defendant] relaxer ; [- soldier] rendre à la vie civile - 2. fml [fulfil] assumer - 3. [emit - smoke] émettre ; [- sewage, chemicals] déverser.

disciple [dɪ'saɪpl] n disciple m.

discipline ['dɪsɪplɪn] <> n discipline f. <> vt - 1. [control] discipliner - 2. [punish] punir.

disc jockey n disc-jockey m.

disclaim [dɪs'kleɪm] vt fml nier.

disclose [dɪs'kləʊz] vt révéler, divulguer.

disclosure [dɪs'kləʊʒər] n révélation f, divulgation f.

disco ['dɪskəʊ] (pl -s) (abbr of **discotheque**) n discothèque f.

discomfort [dɪs'kʌmfət] n - 1. (U) [physical pain] douleur f - 2. (U) [anxiety, embarrassment] malaise m.

disconcert [ˌdɪskən'sɜːt] vt déconcerter.

disconnect [ˌdɪskə'nekt] vt - 1. [detach] détacher - 2. [from gas, electricity - appliance] débrancher ; [- house] couper - 3. TELEC couper.

disconsolate [dɪs'kɒnsələt] adj inconsolable.

discontent [ˌdɪskən'tent] n : **~ (with)** mécontentement m (à propos de).

discontented [ˌdɪskən'tentɪd] adj mécontent(e).

discontinue [ˌdɪskən'tɪnjuː] vt cesser, interrompre.

discord ['dɪskɔːd] n - 1. (U) [disagreement] discorde f, désaccord m - 2. MUS dissonance f.

discotheque ['dɪskəʊtek] n discothèque f.

discount [n 'dɪskaʊnt, vb, Br dɪs'kaʊnt, Am 'dɪskaʊnt] <> n remise f. <> vt [report, claim] ne pas tenir compte de.

discourage [dɪs'kʌrɪdʒ] vt décourager ; **to ~ sb from doing sthg** dissuader qqn de faire qqch.

discover [dɪ'skʌvər] vt découvrir.

discovery [dɪ'skʌvərɪ] n découverte f.

discredit [dɪs'kredɪt] <> n discrédit m. <> vt discréditer.

discreet [dɪ'skriːt] adj discret(ète).

discrepancy [dɪ'skrepənsɪ] n : **~ (in/between)** divergence f (entre).

discretion [dɪ'skreʃn] n (U) - 1. [tact] discrétion f - 2. [judgment] jugement m, discernement m ; **at the ~ of** avec l'autorisation de.

discriminate [dɪ'skrɪmɪneɪt] vi - 1. [distinguish] différencier, distinguer ; **to ~ between** faire la distinction entre - 2. [be prejudiced] : **to ~ against sb** faire de la discrimination envers qqn.

discriminating [dɪ'skrɪmɪneɪtɪŋ] adj avisé(e).

discrimination [dɪˌskrɪmɪ'neɪʃn] n - 1. [prejudice] discrimination f - 2. [judgment] discernement m, jugement m.

discus ['dɪskəs] (pl -es [-iːz]) n disque m.

discuss [dɪ'skʌs] vt discuter (de) ; **to ~ sthg with sb** discuter de qqch avec qqn.

discussion [dɪ'skʌʃn] n discussion f ; **under ~** en discussion.

disdain [dɪs'deɪn] n : **~ (for)** dédain m (pour).

disease [dɪ'ziːz] n [illness] maladie f.

disembark [ˌdɪsɪm'bɑːk] vi débarquer.

disenchanted [ˌdɪsɪn'tʃɑːntɪd] adj : **~ (with)** désenchanté(e) (de).

disengage [ˌdɪsɪn'geɪdʒ] vt - 1. [release] : **to ~ sthg (from)** libérer OR dégager qqch (de) - 2. TECH déclencher ; **to ~ the gears** débrayer.

disfavour Br, **disfavor** Am [dɪs'feɪvər] n [dislike, disapproval] désapprobation f.

disfigure [dɪs'fɪɡər] vt défigurer.

disgrace [dɪs'ɡreɪs] <> n - 1. [shame] honte

f ; **to bring ~ on sb** jeter la honte sur qqn ; **in ~ en défaveur - 2.** [cause of shame - thing] honte *f*, scandale *m* ; [- person] honte *f*. ◇ *vt* faire honte à ; **to ~ o.s.** se couvrir de honte.

disgraceful [dɪs'greɪsfʊl] *adj* honteux(euse), scandaleux(euse).

disgruntled [dɪs'grʌntld] *adj* mécontent(e).

disguise [dɪs'gaɪz] ◇ *n* déguisement *m* ; **in ~** déguisé(e). ◇ *vt* - **1.** [person, voice] déguiser - **2.** [hide - fact, feelings] dissimuler.

disgust [dɪs'gʌst] ◇ *n* : **~ (at)** [behaviour, violence etc] dégoût *m* (pour) ; [decision] dégoût (devant). ◇ *vt* dégoûter, écœurer.

disgusting [dɪs'gʌstɪŋ] *adj* dégoûtant(e).

dish [dɪʃ] *n* plat *m* ; *Am* [plate] assiette *f*. ◆ **dishes** *npl* vaisselle *f* ; **to do** OR **wash the ~es** faire la vaisselle. ◆ **dish out** *vt sep inf* distribuer. ◆ **dish up** *vt sep inf* servir.

dish aerial *Br*, **dish antenna** *Am n* antenne *f* parabolique.

dishcloth ['dɪʃklɒθ] *n* lavette *f*.

disheartened [dɪs'hɑːtnd] *adj* découragé(e).

dishevelled *Br*, **disheveled** *Am* [dɪ'ʃevəld] *adj* [person] échevelé(e) ; [hair] en désordre.

dishonest [dɪs'ɒnɪst] *adj* malhonnête.

dishonor *etc Am* = **dishonour** *etc*.

dishonour *Br*, **dishonor** *Am* [dɪs'ɒnər] ◇ *n* déshonneur *m*. ◇ *vt* déshonorer.

dishonourable *Br*, **dishonorable** *Am* [dɪs'ɒnərəbl] *adj* [person] peu honorable ; [behaviour] déshonorant(e).

dish soap *n Am* liquide *m* pour la vaisselle.

dish towel *n Am* torchon *m*.

dishwasher ['dɪʃ,wɒʃər] *n* [machine] lave-vaisselle *m inv*.

disillusioned [,dɪsɪ'luːʒnd] *adj* désillusionné(e), désenchanté(e) ; **to be ~ with** ne plus avoir d'illusions sur.

disincentive [,dɪsɪn'sentɪv] *n* : **to be a ~** avoir un effet dissuasif ; [in work context] être démotivant(e).

disinclined [,dɪsɪn'klaɪnd] *adj* : **to be ~ to do sthg** être peu disposé(e) à faire qqch.

disinfect [,dɪsɪn'fekt] *vt* désinfecter.

disinfectant [,dɪsɪn'fektənt] *n* désinfectant *m*.

disintegrate [dɪs'ɪntɪgreɪt] *vi* [object] se désintégrer, se désagréger.

disinterested [,dɪs'ɪntrəstɪd] *adj* - **1.** [objective] désintéressé(e) - **2.** *inf* [uninterested] : **~ (in)** indifférent(e) (à).

disjointed [dɪs'dʒɔɪntɪd] *adj* décousu(e).

disk [dɪsk] *n* - **1.** COMPUT disque *m*, disquette *f* - **2.** *Am* = **disc.**

disk drive *Br*, **diskette drive** *Am n* COMPUT lecteur *m* de disques OR de disquettes.

diskette [dɪs'ket] *n* COMPUT disquette *f*.

diskette drive *n Am* = **disk drive.**

dislike [dɪs'laɪk] ◇ *n* : **~ (of)** aversion *f* (pour) ; **to take a ~ to sb/sthg** prendre qqn/ qqch en grippe. ◇ *vt* ne pas aimer.

dislocate ['dɪsləkeɪt] *vt* - **1.** MED se démettre - **2.** [disrupt] désorganiser.

dislodge [dɪs'lɒdʒ] *vt* : **to ~ sthg (from)** déplacer qqch (de) ; [free] décoincer qqch (de).

disloyal [,dɪs'lɔɪəl] *adj* : **~ (to)** déloyal(e) (envers).

dismal ['dɪzml] *adj* - **1.** [gloomy, depressing] lugubre - **2.** [unsuccessful - attempt] infructueux(euse) ; [- failure] lamentable.

dismantle [dɪs'mæntl] *vt* démanteler.

dismay [dɪs'meɪ] ◇ *n* consternation *f*. ◇ *vt* consterner.

dismiss [dɪs'mɪs] *vt* - **1.** [from job] : **to ~ sb (from)** congédier qqn (de) - **2.** [refuse to take seriously - idea, person] écarter ; [- plan, challenge] rejeter - **3.** [allow to leave - class] laisser sortir ; [- troops] faire rompre les rangs à.

dismissal [dɪs'mɪsl] *n* - **1.** [from job] licenciement *m*, renvoi *m* - **2.** [refusal to take seriously] rejet *m*.

dismount [,dɪs'maʊnt] *vi* : **to ~ (from)** descendre (de).

disobedience [,dɪsə'biːdjəns] *n* désobéissance *f*.

disobedient [,dɪsə'biːdjənt] *adj* désobéissant(e).

disobey [,dɪsə'beɪ] *vt* désobéir à.

disorder [dɪs'ɔːdər] *n* - **1.** [disarray] : **in ~** en désordre - **2.** (*U*) [rioting] troubles *mpl* - **3.** MED trouble *m*.

disorderly [dɪs'ɔːdəlɪ] *adj* - **1.** [untidy - room] en désordre ; [- appearance] désordonné(e) - **2.** [unruly] indiscipliné(e).

disorganized, -ised [dɪs'ɔːgənaɪzd] *adj* [person] désordonné(e), brouillon(onne) ; [system] mal conçu(e).

disorientated *Br* [dɪs'ɔːrɪənteɪtɪd], **disoriented** *Am* [dɪs'ɔːrɪəntɪd] *adj* désorienté(e).

disown [dɪs'əʊn] *vt* désavouer.

disparaging [dɪ'spærɪdʒɪŋ] *adj* désobligeant(e).

dispassionate [dɪ'spæʃnət] *adj* impartial(e).

dispatch [dɪ'spætʃ] ◇ *n* [message] dépêche *f*. ◇ *vt* [send] envoyer, expédier.

dispel [dɪ'spel] *vt* [feeling] dissiper, chasser.

dispensary [dɪ'spensərɪ] *n* officine *f*.

dispense [dɪ'spens] *vt* [justice, medicine] administrer. ◆ **dispense with** *vt fus* - **1.** [do without] se passer de - **2.** [make unnecessary] rendre superflu(e) ; **to ~ with the need for sthg** rendre qqch superflu.

dispensing chemist *Br*, **dispensing pharmacist** *Am* [dɪ'spensɪŋ-] *n* pharmacien *m*, -enne *f*.

disperse [dɪ'spɜːs] ◇ *vt* - **1.** [crowd] disperser - **2.** [knowledge, news] répandre, propager. ◇ *vi* se disperser.

dispirited [dɪ'spɪrɪtɪd] *adj* découragé(e), abattu(e).

displace [dɪs'pleɪs] *vt* - **1.** [cause to move] déplacer - **2.** [supplant] supplanter.

display [dɪ'spleɪ] ◇ *n* - **1.** [arrangement] exposition *f* - **2.** [demonstration] manifestation *f* - **3.** [public event] spectacle *m* - **4.** [COMPUT - device] écran *m* ; [- information displayed] affichage *m*, visualisation *f*. ◇ *vt* - **1.** [arrange] exposer - **2.** [show] faire preuve de, montrer.

displease [dɪs'pliːz] *vt* déplaire à, mécontenter ; **to be ~d with** être mécontent(e) de.

displeasure [dɪs'pleʒə'] *n* mécontentement *m*.

disposable [dɪ'spəʊzəbl] *adj* - **1.** [throw away] jetable - **2.** [income] disponible.

disposal [dɪ'spəʊzl] *n* - **1.** [removal] enlèvement *m* - **2.** [availability] : **at sb's ~** à la disposition de qqn.

dispose [dɪ'spəʊz] ◆ **dispose of** *vt fus* [get rid of] se débarrasser de ; [problem] résoudre.

disposed [dɪ'spəʊzd] *adj* - **1.** [willing] : **to be ~ to do sthg** être disposé(e) à faire qqch - **2.** [friendly] : **to be well ~ to** OR **towards sb** être bien disposé(e) envers qqn.

disposition [ˌdɪspə'zɪʃn] *n* - **1.** [temperament] caractère *m*, tempérament *m* - **2.** [tendency] : **~ to do sthg** tendance *f* à faire qqch.

disprove [ˌdɪs'pruːv] *vt* réfuter.

dispute [dɪ'spjuːt] ◇ *n* - **1.** [quarrel] dispute *f* - **2.** (*U*) [disagreement] désaccord *m* - **3.** INDUSTRY conflit *m*. ◇ *vt* contester.

disqualify [ˌdɪs'kwɒlɪfaɪ] *vt* - **1.** [subj : authority] : **to ~ sb (from doing sthg)** interdire à qqn (de faire qqch) ; **to ~ sb from driving** *Br* retirer le permis de conduire à qqn - **2.** SPORT disqualifier.

disquiet [dɪs'kwaɪət] *n* inquiétude *f*.

disregard [ˌdɪsrɪ'gɑːd] ◇ *n* (*U*) : **~ (for)** [money, danger] mépris *m* (pour) ; [feelings] indifférence *f* (à). ◇ *vt* [fact] ignorer ; [danger] mépriser ; [warning] ne pas tenir compte de.

disrepair [ˌdɪsrɪ'peə'] *n* délabrement *m* ; **to fall into ~** tomber en ruines.

disreputable [dɪs'repjʊtəbl] *adj* peu respectable.

disrepute [ˌdɪsrɪ'pjuːt] *n* : **to bring sthg into ~** discréditer qqch ; **to fall into ~** acquérir une mauvaise réputation.

disrupt [dɪs'rʌpt] *vt* perturber.

dissatisfaction ['dɪsˌsætɪs'fækʃn] *n* mécontentement *m*.

dissatisfied [ˌdɪs'sætɪsfaɪd] *adj* : **~ (with)** mécontent(e) (de), pas satisfait(e) (de).

dissect [dɪ'sekt] *vt lit & fig* disséquer.

dissent [dɪ'sent] ◇ *n* dissentiment *m*. ◇ *vi* : **to ~ (from)** être en désaccord (avec).

dissertation [ˌdɪsə'teɪʃn] *n* dissertation *f*.

disservice [ˌdɪs'sɜːvɪs] *n* : **to do sb a ~** rendre un mauvais service à qqn.

dissimilar [ˌdɪ'sɪmɪlə'] *adj* : **~ (to)** différent(e) (de).

dissipate ['dɪsɪpeɪt] *vt* - **1.** [heat] dissiper - **2.** [efforts, money] gaspiller.

dissociate [dɪ'səʊʃɪeɪt] *vt* dissocier ; **to ~ o.s. from** se désolidariser de.

dissolute ['dɪsəluːt] *adj* dissolu(e).

dissolve [dɪ'zɒlv] ◇ *vt* dissoudre. ◇ *vi* - **1.** [substance] se dissoudre - **2.** *fig* [disappear] disparaître.

dissuade [dɪ'sweɪd] *vt* : **to ~ sb (from)** dissuader qqn (de).

distance ['dɪstəns] *n* distance *f* ; **at a ~** assez loin ; **from a ~** de loin ; **in the ~** au loin.

distant ['dɪstənt] *adj* - **1.** [gen] : **~ (from)** éloigné(e) (de) - **2.** [reserved - person, manner] distant(e).

distaste [dɪs'teɪst] *n* : **~ (for)** dégoût *m* (pour).

distasteful [dɪs'teɪstfʊl] *adj* répugnant(e), déplaisant(e).

distended [dɪ'stendɪd] *adj* [stomach] distendu(e).

distil *Br*, **distill** *Am* [dɪ'stɪl] *vt* - **1.** [liquid] distiller - **2.** *fig* [information] tirer.

distillery [dɪ'stɪlərɪ] *n* distillerie *f*.

distinct [dɪ'stɪŋkt] *adj* - 1. [different] : ~ (from) distinct(e) (de), différent(e) (de) ; as ~ from par opposition à - 2. [definite - improvement] net (nette).

distinction [dɪ'stɪŋkʃn] *n* - 1. [difference] distinction *f*, différence *f* ; to draw OR make a ~ between faire une distinction entre - 2. (U) [excellence] distinction *f* - 3. [exam result] mention *f* très bien.

distinctive [dɪ'stɪŋktɪv] *adj* caractéristique.

distinguish [dɪ'stɪŋgwɪʃ] *vt* - 1. [tell apart] : to ~ sthg from sthg distinguer qqch de qqch, faire la différence entre qqch et qqch - 2. [perceive] distinguer - 3. [characterize] caractériser.

distinguished [dɪ'stɪŋgwɪʃt] *adj* distingué(e).

distinguishing [dɪ'stɪŋgwɪʃɪŋ] *adj* [feature, mark] caractéristique.

distort [dɪ'stɔːt] *vt* déformer.

distract [dɪ'strækt] *vt* : to ~ sb (from) distraire qqn (de).

distracted [dɪ'stræktɪd] *adj* [preoccupied] soucieux(euse).

distraction [dɪ'strækʃn] *n* [interruption, diversion] distraction *f*.

distraught [dɪ'strɔːt] *adj* éperdu(e).

distress [dɪ'stres] <> *n* [anxiety] détresse *f* ; [pain] douleur *f*, souffrance *f*. <> *vt* affliger.

distressing [dɪ'stresɪŋ] *adj* [news, image] pénible.

distribute [dɪ'strɪbjuːt] *vt* - 1. [gen] distribuer - 2. [spread out] répartir.

distribution [ˌdɪstrɪ'bjuːʃn] *n* - 1. [gen] distribution *f* - 2. [spreading out] répartition *f*.

distributor [dɪ'strɪbjʊtəʳ] *n* AUT & COMM distributeur *m*.

district ['dɪstrɪkt] *n* - 1. [area - of country] région *f* ; [- of town] quartier *m* - 2. ADMIN district *m*.

district attorney *n* Am ≃ procureur *m* de la République.

district council *n* Br ≃ conseil *m* général.

district nurse *n* Br infirmière *f* visiteuse OR à domicile.

distrust [dɪs'trʌst] <> *n* méfiance *f*. <> *vt* se méfier de.

disturb [dɪ'stɜːb] *vt* - 1. [interrupt] déranger - 2. [upset, worry] inquiéter - 3. [sleep, surface] troubler.

disturbance [dɪ'stɜːbəns] *n* - 1. POL troubles *mpl* ; [fight] tapage *m* - 2. [interruption]

dérangement *m* - 3. [of mind, emotions] trouble *m*.

disturbed [dɪ'stɜːbd] *adj* - 1. [emotionally, mentally] perturbé(e) - 2. [worried] inquiet(ète).

disturbing [dɪ'stɜːbɪŋ] *adj* [image] bouleversant(e) ; [news] inquiétant(e).

disuse [ˌdɪs'juːs] *n* : to fall into ~ [factory] être à l'abandon ; [regulation] tomber en désuétude.

disused [ˌdɪs'juːzd] *adj* désaffecté(e).

ditch [dɪtʃ] <> *n* fossé *m*. <> *vt* inf [boyfriend, girlfriend] plaquer ; [old car, clothes] se débarrasser de ; [plan] abandonner.

dither ['dɪðəʳ] *vi* hésiter.

ditto ['dɪtəʊ] *adv* idem.

dive [daɪv] (Br pt & pp -d, Am pt & pp -d OR dove) <> *vi* plonger ; [bird, plane] piquer. <> *n* - 1. [gen] plongeon *m* - 2. [of plane] piqué *m* - 3. inf pej [bar, restaurant] bouge *m*.

diver ['daɪvəʳ] *n* plongeur *m*, -euse *f*.

diverge [daɪ'vɜːdʒ] *vi* : to ~ (from) diverger (de).

diversify [daɪ'vɜːsɪfaɪ] <> *vt* diversifier. <> *vi* se diversifier.

diversion [daɪ'vɜːʃn] *n* - 1. [amusement] distraction *f* ; [tactical] diversion *f* - 2. Br [of traffic] déviation *f* - 3. [of river, funds] détournement *m*.

diversity [daɪ'vɜːsətɪ] *n* diversité *f*.

divert [daɪ'vɜːt] *vt* - 1. [traffic] dévier - 2. [river, funds] détourner - 3. [person - amuse] distraire ; [- tactically] détourner.

divide [dɪ'vaɪd] <> *vt* - 1. [separate] séparer - 2. [share out] diviser, partager - 3. [split up] : to ~ sthg (into) diviser qqch (en) - 4. MATH : 89 ~d by 3 89 divisé par 3 - 5. [people - in disagreement] diviser. <> *vi* se diviser.

dividend ['dɪvɪdend] *n* dividende *m*.

divine [dɪ'vaɪn] *adj* divin(e).

diving ['daɪvɪŋ] *n* (U) plongeon *m* ; [with breathing apparatus] plongée *f* (sous-marine).

divingboard ['daɪvɪŋbɔːd] *n* plongeoir *m*.

divinity [dɪ'vɪnətɪ] *n* - 1. [godliness, god] divinité *f* - 2. [study] théologie *f*.

division [dɪ'vɪʒn] *n* - 1. [gen] division *f* - 2. [separation] séparation *f*.

divorce [dɪ'vɔːs] <> *n* divorce *m*. <> *vt* [husband, wife] divorcer.

divorced [dɪ'vɔːst] *adj* divorcé(e).

divorcee [dɪvɔː'siː] *n* divorcé *m*, -e *f*.

divulge [daɪ'vʌldʒ] *vt* divulguer.

DIY (*abbr of* **do-it-yourself**) *n Br* bricolage *m*.

dizzy ['dɪzɪ] *adj* [giddy] : **to feel ~** avoir la tête qui tourne.

DJ *n* (*abbr of* **disc jockey**) disc-jockey *m*.

DNA (*abbr of* **deoxyribonucleic acid**) *n* ADN *m*.

do [duː] (*pt* **did**, *pp* **done**, *pl* **dos** OR **do's**) ◇ *aux vb* - **1.** (*in negatives*) : **don't leave it there** ne le laisse pas là - **2.** (*in questions*) : **what did he want?** qu'est-ce qu'il voulait? ; **~ you think she'll come?** tu crois qu'elle viendra? - **3.** (*referring back to previous verb*) : **she reads more than I ~** elle lit plus que moi ; **I like reading — so ~ I** j'aime lire — moi aussi - **4.** (*in question tags*) : **so you think you can dance, ~ you?** alors tu t'imagines que tu sais danser, c'est ça? - **5.** [for emphasis] : **I did tell you but you've forgotten** je te l'avais bien dit, mais tu l'as oublié ; **~ come in** entrez donc. ◇ *vt* - **1.** [perform an activity, a service] faire ; **to ~ aerobics/gymnastics** faire de l'aérobic/de la gymnastique ; **to ~ the cooking/housework** faire la cuisine/le ménage ; **to ~ one's hair** se coiffer ; **to ~ one's teeth** se laver OR se brosser les dents - **2.** [take action] faire ; **to ~ something about sthg** trouver une solution pour qqch - **3.** (*referring to job*) : **what do you ~?** qu'est-ce que vous faites dans la vie? - **4.** [study] faire ; **I did physics at school** j'ai fait de la physique à l'école - **5.** [travel at a particular speed] faire, rouler ; **the car can ~ 110 mph** — la voiture peut faire du 180 à l'heure. ◇ *vi* - **1.** [act] faire ; **~ as I tell you** fais comme je te dis - **2.** [perform in a particular way] : **they're ~ing really well** leurs affaires marchent bien ; **he could ~ better** il pourrait mieux faire ; **how did you ~ in the exam?** comment ça a marché à l'examen? - **3.** [be good enough, be sufficient] suffire, aller ; **will £6 ~?** est-ce que 6 livres suffiront?, 6 livres, ça ira? ; **that will ~** ça suffit. ◇ *n* [party] fête *f*, soirée *f*. ◆ **dos** *npl* : **~s and don'ts** ce qu'il faut faire et ne pas faire. ◆ **do away with** *vt fus* supprimer. ◆ **do out of** *vt sep inf* : **to ~ sb out of sthg** escroquer OR carotter qqch à qqn. ◆ **do up** *vt sep* - **1.** [fasten - shoelaces, shoes] attacher ; [- buttons, coat] boutonner - **2.** [decorate - room, house] refaire - **3.** [wrap up] emballer. ◆ **do with** *vt fus* - **1.** [need] avoir besoin de - **2.** [have connection with] : **that has nothing to ~ with it** ça n'a rien à voir, ça n'a aucun rapport ; **I had nothing to ~ with it** je n'y étais pour rien. ◆ **do without** ◇ *vt fus* se passer de. ◇ *vi* s'en passer.

Doberman ['dəʊbəmən] (*pl* **-s**) *n* : **~ (pinscher)** doberman *m*.

docile [*Br* 'dəʊsaɪl, *Am* 'dɒsəl] *adj* docile.

dock [dɒk] ◇ *n* - **1.** [in harbour] docks *mpl* - **2.** JUR banc *m* des accusés. ◇ *vi* [ship] arriver à quai.

docker ['dɒkə'] *n* docker *m*.

docklands ['dɒkləndz] *npl Br* docks *mpl*.

dockworker ['dɒkwɜːkə'] *n* docker *m*.

dockyard ['dɒkjɑːd] *n* chantier *m* naval.

doctor ['dɒktə'] ◇ *n* - **1.** MED docteur *m*, médecin *m* ; **to go to the ~'s** aller chez le docteur - **2.** UNIV docteur *m*. ◇ *vt* [results, report] falsifier ; [text, food] altérer.

doctorate ['dɒktərət], **doctor's degree** *n* doctorat *m*.

doctrine ['dɒktrɪn] *n* doctrine *f*.

document ['dɒkjʊmənt] *n* document *m*.

documentary [ˌdɒkjʊ'mentərɪ] ◇ *adj* documentaire. ◇ *n* documentaire *m*.

dodge [dɒdʒ] ◇ *n inf* combine *f*. ◇ *vt* éviter, esquiver. ◇ *vi* s'esquiver.

dodgy ['dɒdʒɪ] *adj Br inf* [plan, deal] douteux(euse).

doe [dəʊ] *n* - **1.** [deer] biche *f* - **2.** [rabbit] lapine *f*.

does [*weak form* dəz, *strong form* dʌz] ▷ **do**.

doesn't ['dʌznt] = **does not**.

dog [dɒg] ◇ *n* [animal] chien *m*, chienne *f*. ◇ *vt* - **1.** [subj : person - follow] suivre de près - **2.** [subj : problems, bad luck] poursuivre.

dog collar *n* - **1.** [of dog] collier *m* de chien - **2.** [of priest] col *m* d'ecclésiastique.

dog-eared [-ɪəd] *adj* écorné(e).

dog food *n* nourriture *f* pour chiens.

dogged ['dɒgɪd] *adj* opiniâtre.

doggy bag *n* sac *en plastique pour emporter les restes d'un repas*, doggy bag *m*.

dogsbody ['dɒgzˌbɒdɪ] *n Br inf* [woman] bonne *f* à tout faire ; [man] factotum *m*.

doing ['duːɪŋ] *n* : **is this your ~?** c'est toi qui est cause de tout cela? ◆ **doings** *npl* actions *fpl*.

do-it-yourself *n* (*U*) bricolage *m*.

doldrums ['dɒldrəmz] *npl* : **to be in the ~** *fig* être dans le marasme.

dole [dəʊl] *n Br* [unemployment benefit] allocation *f* de chômage ; **to be on the ~** être au chômage. ◆ **dole out** *vt sep* [food, money] distribuer au compte-gouttes.

doleful ['dəʊlfʊl] *adj* morne.

doll [dɒl] *n* poupée *f*.

dollar ['dɒlə'] *n* dollar *m*.

dollop ['dɒləp] *n inf* bonne cuillerée *f*.

dolphin ['dɒlfɪn] *n* dauphin *m*.

domain [də'meɪn] *n lit & fig* domaine *m*.

dome [dəʊm] *n* dôme *m*.

domestic [də'mestɪk] ◇ *adj* - **1.** [policy,

politics, flight] intérieur(e) - **2.** [chores, animal] domestique - **3.** [home-loving] casanier(ère). ⋄ n domestique mf.

domestic appliance n appareil m ménager.

dominant ['dɒmɪnənt] adj dominant(e) ; [personality, group] dominateur(trice).

dominate ['dɒmɪneɪt] vt dominer.

domineering [,dɒmɪ'nɪərɪŋ] adj autoritaire.

dominion [də'mɪnjən] n - **1.** (U) [power] domination f - **2.** [land] territoire m.

domino ['dɒmɪnəʊ] (pl -es) n domino m.
➡ **dominoes** npl dominos mpl.

don [dɒn] n Br UNIV professeur m d'université.

donate [də'neɪt] vt faire don de.

done [dʌn] ⋄ pp ⊳ do. ⋄ adj - **1.** [job, work] achevé(e) ; **I'm nearly ~** j'ai presque fini - **2.** [cooked] cuit(e). ⋄ excl [to conclude deal] tope!

donkey ['dɒŋkɪ] (pl -s) n âne m, ânesse f.

donor ['dəʊnə'] n - **1.** MED donneur m, -euse f - **2.** [to charity] donateur m, -trice f.

donor card n carte f de donneur.

don't [dəʊnt] = do not.

doodle ['du:dl] ⋄ n griffonnage m. ⋄ vi griffonner.

doom [du:m] n [fate] destin m.

doomed [du:md] adj condamné(e) ; **the plan was ~ to failure** le plan était voué à l'échec.

door [dɔ:'] n porte f ; [of vehicle] portière f.

doorbell ['dɔ:bel] n sonnette f.

doorknob ['dɔ:nɒb] n bouton m de porte.

doorman ['dɔ:mən] (pl -men [-mən]) n portier m.

doormat ['dɔ:mæt] n lit & fig paillasson m.

doorstep ['dɔ:step] n pas m de la porte.

doorway ['dɔ:weɪ] n embrasure f de la porte.

dope [dəʊp] ⋄ n inf - **1.** drugs sl dope f, came f - **2.** [for athlete, horse] dopant m - **3.** inf [fool] imbécile mf. ⋄ vt [horse] doper.

dopey ['dəʊpɪ] (compar -ier, superl -iest) adj inf abruti(e).

dormant ['dɔ:mənt] adj - **1.** [volcano] endormi(e) - **2.** [law] inappliqué(e).

dormitory ['dɔ:mətrɪ] n - **1.** [gen] dortoir m - **2.** Am [in university] ≃ cité f universitaire.

Dormobile® ['dɔ:mə,bi:l] n Br camping-car m.

DOS [dɒs] (abbr of disk operating system) n DOS m.

dose [dəʊs] n - **1.** MED dose f - **2.** fig [amount] : **a ~ of the measles** la rougeole.

dosser ['dɒsə'] n Br inf clochard m, -e f.

dosshouse ['dɒshaʊs, pl -haʊzɪz] n Br inf asile m de nuit.

dot [dɒt] ⋄ n point m ; **on the ~** à l'heure pile. ⋄ vt : **dotted with** parsemé(e) de.

dote [dəʊt] ➡ **dote (up)on** vt fus adorer.

dot-matrix printer n imprimante f matricielle.

dotted line ['dɒtɪd-] n ligne f pointillée.

double ['dʌbl] ⋄ adj double ; **~ doors** porte f à deux battants. ⋄ adv - **1.** [twice] : **~ the amount** deux fois plus ; **to see ~** voir double - **2.** [in two] en deux ; **to bend ~** se plier en deux. ⋄ n - **1.** [twice as much] : **I earn ~ what I used to** je gagne le double de ce que je gagnais auparavant - **2.** [drink, look-alike] double m - **3.** CINEMA doublure f. ⋄ vt doubler. ⋄ vi [increase twofold] doubler. ➡ **doubles** npl TENNIS double m.

double-barrelled Br, **double-barreled** Am [-'bærəld] adj - **1.** [shotgun] à deux coups - **2.** [name] à rallonge.

double bass [-beɪs] n contrebasse f.

double bed n lit m pour deux personnes, grand lit.

double-breasted [-'brestɪd] adj [jacket] croisé(e).

double-check vt & vi revérifier.

double chin n double menton m.

double cream n Br crème f fraîche épaisse.

double-cross vt trahir.

double-decker [-'dekə'] n [bus] autobus m à impériale.

double-dutch n Br charabia m.

double-glazing [-'gleɪzɪŋ] n double vitrage m.

double room n chambre f pour deux personnes.

double vision n vue f double.

doubly ['dʌblɪ] adv doublement.

doubt [daʊt] ⋄ n doute m ; **there is no ~ that** il n'y a aucun doute que ; **without (a) ~** sans aucun doute ; **to be in ~** [person] ne pas être sûr(e) ; [outcome] être incertain(e) ; **to cast ~ on sthg** mettre qqch en doute ; **no ~** sans aucun doute. ⋄ vt douter ; **to ~ whether** OR **if** douter que.

doubtful ['daʊtfʊl] adj - **1.** [decision, future] incertain(e) - **2.** [person, value] douteux(euse).

doubtless ['daʊtlɪs] *adv* sans aucun doute.

dough [dəʊ] *n (U)* - **1.** CULIN pâte *f* - **2.** *v inf* [money] fric *m*.

doughnut ['dəʊnʌt] *n* beignet *m*.

douse [daʊs] *vt* - **1.** [fire, flames] éteindre - **2.** [drench] tremper.

dove[1] [dʌv] *n* [bird] colombe *f*.

dove[2] [dəʊv] *Am pt* ⊳ **dive**.

Dover ['dəʊvə'] *n* Douvres.

dovetail ['dʌvteɪl] *fig vi* coïncider.

dowdy ['daʊdɪ] *adj* sans chic.

down [daʊn] ◇ *adv* - **1.** [downwards] en bas, vers le bas ; **to bend ~** se pencher ; **to climb ~** descendre ; **to fall ~** tomber (par terre) ; **to pull ~** tirer vers le bas - **2.** [along] : **we went ~** to have a look on est allé jeter un coup d'œil ; **I'm going ~ to the shop** je vais au magasin - **3.** [southwards] : **we travelled ~ to London** on est descendu à Londres - **4.** [lower in amount] : **prices are coming ~** les prix baissent ; **~ to the last detail** jusqu'au moindre détail. ◇ *prep* - **1.** [downwards] : **they ran ~ the hill/stairs** ils ont descendu la colline/l'escalier en courant - **2.** [along] : **to walk ~ the street** descendre la rue. ◇ *adj* - **1.** *inf* [depressed] : **to feel ~** avoir le cafard - **2.** [computer, telephone] **en panne.** ◇ *n (U)* duvet *m*. ◇ *vt* - **1.** [knock over] abattre - **2.** [drink] avaler d'un trait. ◆ **downs** *npl Br* collines *fpl*.

down-and-out ◇ *adj* indigent(e). ◇ *n* personne *f* dans le besoin.

down-at-heel *adj* déguenillé(e).

downbeat ['daʊnbiːt] *adj inf* pessimiste.

downcast ['daʊnkɑːst] *adj* [sad] démoralisé(e).

downfall ['daʊnfɔːl] *n (U)* ruine *f*.

downhearted [,daʊn'hɑːtɪd] *adj* découragé(e).

downhill [,daʊn'hɪl] ◇ *adj* [downward] en pente. ◇ *n* SKIING [race] descente *f*. ◇ *adv* : **to walk ~** descendre la côte ; **her career is going ~** *fig* sa carrière est sur le déclin.

Downing Street ['daʊnɪŋ-] *n rue du centre de Londres où réside le premier ministre.*

down payment *n* acompte *m*.

downpour ['daʊnpɔː'] *n* pluie *f* torrentielle.

downright ['daʊnraɪt] ◇ *adj* franc (franche) ; [lie] effronté(e). ◇ *adv* franchement.

downstairs [,daʊn'steəz] ◇ *adj* du bas ; [on floor below] à l'étage en-dessous.

◇ *adv* en bas ; [on floor below] à l'étage en-dessous ; **to come** OR **go ~** descendre.

downstream [,daʊn'striːm] *adv* en aval.

down-to-earth *adj* pragmatique, terre-à-terre *(inv)*.

downtown [,daʊn'taʊn] *esp Am* ◇ *adj* : **~ New York** le centre de New York. ◇ *adv* en ville.

downturn ['daʊntɜːn] *n* : **~ (in)** baisse *f* (de).

down under *adv* en Australie/Nouvelle-Zélande.

downward ['daʊnwəd] ◇ *adj* - **1.** [towards ground] vers le bas - **2.** [trend] à la baisse. ◇ *adv Am* = **downwards**.

downwards ['daʊnwədz] *adv* [look, move] vers le bas.

dowry ['daʊərɪ] *n* dot *f*.

doz. (*abbr of* **dozen**) douz.

doze [dəʊz] ◇ *n* somme *m*. ◇ *vi* sommeiller. ◆ **doze off** *vi* s'assoupir.

dozen ['dʌzn] ◇ *num adj* : **a ~ eggs** une douzaine d'œufs. ◇ *n* douzaine *f* ; **50p a ~** 50p la douzaine ; **~s** *of inf* des centaines de.

dozy ['dəʊzɪ] *adj* - **1.** [sleepy] somnolent(e) - **2.** *Br inf* [stupid] lent(e).

Dr. - **1.** (*abbr of* **Drive**) av - **2.** (*abbr of* **Doctor**) Dr.

drab [dræb] *adj* terne.

draft [drɑːft] ◇ *n* - **1.** [early version] premier jet *m*, ébauche *f* ; [of letter] brouillon *m* - **2.** [money order] traite *f* - **3.** *Am* MIL : **the ~** la conscription *f* - **4.** *Am* = **draught**. ◇ *vt* - **1.** [speech] ébaucher, faire le plan de ; [letter] faire le brouillon de - **2.** *Am* MIL appeler - **3.** [staff] muter.

draftsman *Am* = **draughtsman**.

drafty *Am* = **draughty**.

drag [dræg] ◇ *vt* - **1.** [gen] traîner - **2.** [lake, river] draguer. ◇ *vi* - **1.** [dress, coat] traîner - **2.** *fig* [time, action] traîner en longueur. ◇ *n* - **1.** *inf* [bore] plaie *f* - **2.** *inf* [on cigarette] bouffée *f* - **3.** [cross-dressing] : **in ~** en travesti. ◆ **drag on** *vi* [meeting, time] s'éterniser, traîner en longueur.

dragon ['drægən] *n lit & fig* dragon *m*.

dragonfly ['drægnflaɪ] *n* libellule *f*.

drain [dreɪn] ◇ *n* - **1.** [pipe] égout *m* - **2.** [depletion - of resources, funds] : **~ on** épuisement *m* de. ◇ *vt* - **1.** [vegetables] égoutter ; [land] assécher, drainer - **2.** [strength, resources] épuiser - **3.** [drink, glass] boire. ◇ *vi* [dishes] égoutter.

drainage ['dreɪnɪdʒ] *n* - **1.** [pipes, ditches] (système *m* du) tout-à-l'égout *m inv* - **2.** [draining - of land] drainage *m*.

draining board *Br* ['dreɪnɪŋ-], **drain-board** *Am* ['dreɪnbɔːrd] *n* égouttoir *m*.

drainpipe ['dreɪnpaɪp] *n* tuyau *m* d'écoulement.

dram [dræm] *n* goutte *f* (de whisky).

drama ['drɑːmə] *n* - 1. [play, excitement] drame *m* - 2. *(U)* [art] théâtre *m*.

dramatic [drə'mætɪk] *adj* - 1. [gen] dramatique - 2. [sudden, noticeable] spectaculaire.

dramatist ['dræmətɪst] *n* dramaturge *mf*.

dramatize, -ise ['dræmətaɪz] *vt* - 1. [rewrite as play, film] adapter pour la télévision/la scène/l'écran - 2. *pej* [make exciting] dramatiser.

drank [dræŋk] *pt* ⊳ drink.

drape [dreɪp] *vt* draper ; **to be ~d with** OR **in** être drapé(e) de. ◆ **drapes** *npl Am* rideaux *mpl*.

drastic ['dræstɪk] *adj* - 1. [measures] drastique, radical(e) - 2. [improvement, decline] spectaculaire.

draught *Br*, **draft** *Am* [drɑːft] *n* - 1. [air current] courant *m* d'air - 2. [from barrel] : **on ~** [beer] à la pression. ◆ **draughts** *n Br* jeu *m* de dames.

draught beer *n Br* bière *f* à la pression.

draughtboard ['drɑːftbɔːd] *n Br* damier *m*.

draughtsman *Br*, **draftsman** *Am* (*pl* -men [-mən]) ['drɑːftsmən] *n* dessinateur *m*, -trice *f*.

draughty *Br*, **drafty** *Am*, **ier, iest** ['drɑːftɪ] *adj* plein(e) de courants d'air.

draw [drɔː] (*pt* drew, *pp* drawn) ⇔ *vt* - 1. [gen] tirer - 2. [sketch] dessiner - 3. [comparison, distinction] établir, faire - 4. [attract] attirer, entraîner ; **to ~ sb's attention to** attirer l'attention de qqn sur. ⇔ *vi* - 1. [sketch] dessiner - 2. [move] : **to ~ near** [person] s'approcher ; [time] approcher ; **to ~ away** reculer - 3. SPORT faire match nul ; **to be ~ing** être à égalité. ⇔ *n* - 1. SPORT [result] match *m* nul - 2. [lottery] tirage *m* - 3. [attraction] attraction *f*. ◆ **draw out** *vt sep* - 1. [encourage - person] faire sortir de sa coquille - 2. [prolong] prolonger - 3. [money] faire un retrait de, retirer. ◆ **draw up** ⇔ *vt sep* [contract, plan] établir, dresser. ⇔ *vi* [vehicle] s'arrêter.

drawback ['drɔːbæk] *n* inconvénient *m*, désavantage *m*.

drawbridge ['drɔːbrɪdʒ] *n* pont-levis *m*.

drawer [drɔːr] *n* [in desk, chest] tiroir *m*.

drawing ['drɔːɪŋ] *n* dessin *m*.

drawing board *n* planche *f* à dessin.

drawing pin *n Br* punaise *f*.

drawing room *n* salon *m*.

drawl [drɔːl] *n* voix *f* traînante.

drawn [drɔːn] *pp* ⊳ draw.

dread [dred] ⇔ *n (U)* épouvante *f*. ⇔ *vt* appréhender ; **to ~ doing sthg** appréhender de faire qqch.

dreadful ['dredfʊl] *adj* affreux(euse), épouvantable.

dreadfully ['dredfʊlɪ] *adv* - 1. [badly] terriblement - 2. [extremely] extrêmement ; **I'm ~ sorry** je regrette infiniment.

dream [driːm] (*pt* & *pp* -ed OR dreamt) ⇔ *n* rêve *m*. ⇔ *adj* de rêve. ⇔ *vt* : **to ~ (that)** ... rêver que ... ⇔ *vi* : **to ~ (of** OR **about)** rêver (de) ; **I wouldn't ~ of it** cela ne me viendrait même pas à l'idée. ◆ **dream up** *vt sep* inventer.

dreamt [dremt] *pt* & *pp* ⊳ dream.

dreamy ['driːmɪ] *adj* - 1. [distracted] rêveur(euse) - 2. [dreamlike] de rêve.

dreary ['drɪərɪ] *adj* - 1. [weather] morne - 2. [dull, boring] ennuyeux(euse).

dredge [dredʒ] *vt* draguer. ◆ **dredge up** *vt sep* - 1. [with dredger] draguer - 2. *fig* [from past] déterrer.

dregs [dregz] *npl lit* & *fig* lie *f*.

drench [drentʃ] *vt* tremper ; **to be ~ed in** OR **with** sthg être inondé(e) de.

dress [dres] ⇔ *n* - 1. [woman's garment] robe *f* - 2. *(U)* [clothing] costume *m*, tenue *f*. ⇔ *vt* - 1. [clothe] habiller ; **to be ~ed** être habillé(e) ; **to be ~ed in** être vêtu(e) de ; **to get ~ed** s'habiller - 2. [bandage] panser - 3. CULIN [salad] assaisonner. ⇔ *vi* s'habiller. ◆ **dress up** *vi* - 1. [in costume] se déguiser - 2. [in best clothes] s'habiller (élégamment).

dress circle *n* premier balcon *m*.

dresser ['dresər] *n* - 1. [for dishes] vaisselier *m* - 2. *Am* [chest of drawers] commode *f*.

dressing ['dresɪŋ] *n* - 1. [bandage] pansement *m* - 2. [for salad] assaisonnement *m* - 3. *Am* [for turkey etc] farce *f*.

dressing gown *n* robe *f* de chambre.

dressing room *n* - 1. THEATRE loge *f* - 2. SPORT vestiaire *m*.

dressing table *n* coiffeuse *f*.

dressmaker ['dres,meɪkər] *n* couturier *m*, -ère *f*.

dressmaking ['dres,meɪkɪŋ] *n* couture *f*.

dress rehearsal *n* générale *f*.

dressy ['dresɪ] *adj* habillé(e).

drew [druː] *pt* ⊳ draw.

dribble ['drɪbl] ⇔ *n* - 1. [saliva] bave *f* - 2. [trickle] traînée *f*. ⇔ *vt* SPORT dribbler.

◇ *vi* - **1.** [drool] baver - **2.** [liquid] tomber goutte à goutte, couler.

dried [draɪd] *adj* [milk, eggs] en poudre ; [fruit] sec (sèche) ; [flowers] séché(e).

drier ['draɪə^r] = dryer.

drift [drɪft] ◇ *n* - **1.** [movement] mouvement *m* ; [direction] direction *f*, sens *m* - **2.** [meaning] sens *m* général - **3.** [of snow] congère *f* ; [of sand, leaves] amoncellement *m*, entassement *m*. ◇ *vi* - **1.** [boat] dériver - **2.** [snow, sand, leaves] s'amasser, s'amonceler.

driftwood ['drɪftwʊd] *n* bois *m* flottant.

drill [drɪl] ◇ *n* - **1.** [tool] perceuse *f* ; [dentist's] fraise *f* ; [in mine etc] perforatrice *f* - **2.** [exercise, training] exercice *m*. ◇ *vt* - **1.** [wood, hole] percer ; [tooth] fraiser ; [well] forer - **2.** [soldiers] entraîner. ◇ *vi* [excavate] : **to ~ for oil** forer à la recherche de pétrole.

drink [drɪŋk] (*pt* drank, *pp* drunk) ◇ *n* - **1.** [gen] boisson *f* ; **to have a ~** boire un verre - **2.** (*U*) [alcohol] alcool *m*. ◇ *vt* boire. ◇ *vi* boire.

drink-driving *Br*, **drunk-driving** *Am n* conduite *f* en état d'ivresse.

drinker ['drɪŋkə^r] *n* buveur *m*, -euse *f*.

drinking water *n* eau *f* potable.

drip [drɪp] ◇ *n* - **1.** [drop] goutte *f* - **2.** MED goutte-à-goutte *m inv*. ◇ *vi* [gen] goutter, tomber goutte à goutte.

drip-dry *adj* qui ne se repasse pas.

drive [draɪv] (*pt* drove, *pp* driven) ◇ *n* - **1.** [in car] trajet *m* (en voiture) ; **to go for a ~** faire une promenade (en voiture) - **2.** [urge] désir *m*, besoin *m* - **3.** [campaign] campagne *f* - **4.** (*U*) [energy] dynamisme *m*, énergie *f* - **5.** [road to house] allée *f* - **6.** SPORT drive *m*. ◇ *vt* - **1.** [vehicle, passenger] conduire - **2.** TECH entraîner, actionner - **3.** [animals, people] pousser - **4.** [motivate] pousser - **5.** [force] : **to ~ sb to sthg/to do sthg** pousser qqn à qqch/à faire qqch, conduire qqn à qqch/à faire qqch ; **to ~ sb mad** OR **crazy** rendre qqn fou - **6.** [nail, stake] enfoncer. ◇ *vi* [driver] conduire ; [travel by car] aller en voiture.

drivel ['drɪvl] *n* (*U*) *inf* foutaises *fpl*, idioties *fpl*.

driven ['drɪvn] *pp* ▷ drive.

driver ['draɪvə^r] *n* [of vehicle - gen] conducteur *m*, -trice *f* ; [- of taxi] chauffeur *m*.

driver's license *Am* = driving licence.

drive shaft *n* arbre *m* de transmission.

driveway ['draɪvweɪ] *n* allée *f*.

driving ['draɪvɪŋ] ◇ *adj* [rain] battant(e) ; [wind] cinglant(e). ◇ *n* (*U*) conduite *f*.

driving instructor *n* moniteur *m*, -trice *f* d'auto-école.

driving lesson *n* leçon *f* de conduite.

driving licence *Br*, **driver's license** *Am n* permis *m* de conduire.

driving mirror *n* rétroviseur *m*.

driving school *n* auto-école *f*.

driving test *n* (examen *m* du) permis *m* de conduire.

drizzle ['drɪzl] ◇ *n* bruine *f*. ◇ *v impers* bruiner.

droll [drəʊl] *adj* drôle.

drone [drəʊn] *n* - **1.** [of traffic, voices] ronronnement *m* ; [of insect] bourdonnement *m* - **2.** [male bee] abeille *f* mâle, faux-bourdon *m*.

drool [druːl] *vi* baver ; **to ~ over** *fig* baver (d'admiration) devant.

droop [druːp] *vi* [head] pencher ; [shoulders, eyelids] tomber.

drop [drɒp] ◇ *n* - **1.** [of liquid] goutte *f* - **2.** [sweet] pastille *f* - **3.** [decrease] : **~ (in)** baisse *f* (de) - **4.** [distance down] dénivellation *f* ; **sheer ~** à-pic *m inv*. ◇ *vt* - **1.** [let fall] laisser tomber - **2.** [voice, speed, price] baisser - **3.** [abandon] abandonner ; [player] exclure - **4.** [let out of car] déposer - **5.** [utter] : **to ~ a hint that** laisser entendre que - **6.** [write] : **to ~ sb a note** OR **line** écrire un petit mot à qqn. ◇ *vi* - **1.** [fall] tomber - **2.** [temperature, demand] baisser ; [voice, wind] tomber. ◆ **drops** *npl* MED gouttes *fpl*. ◆ **drop in** *vi inf* : **to ~ in (on sb)** passer (chez qqn). ◆ **drop off** ◇ *vt sep* déposer. ◇ *vi* - **1.** [fall asleep] s'endormir - **2.** [interest, sales] baisser. ◆ **drop out** *vi* : **to ~ out (of** OR **from sthg)** abandonner (qqch) ; **to ~ out of society** vivre en marge de la société.

dropout ['drɒpaʊt] *n* [from society] marginal *m*, -e *f* ; [from college] étudiant *m*, -e *f* qui abandonne ses études.

droppings ['drɒpɪŋz] *npl* [of bird] fiente *f* ; [of animal] crottes *fpl*.

drought [draʊt] *n* sécheresse *f*.

drove [drəʊv] *pt* ▷ drive.

drown [draʊn] ◇ *vt* [in water] noyer. ◇ *vi* se noyer.

drowsy ['draʊzɪ] *adj* assoupi(e), somnolent(e).

drudgery ['drʌdʒərɪ] *n* (*U*) corvée *f*.

drug [drʌg] ◇ *n* - **1.** [medicine] médicament *m* - **2.** [narcotic] drogue *f*. ◇ *vt* droguer.

drug abuse n usage m de stupéfiants.

drug addict n drogué m, -e f.

druggist ['drʌgɪst] n Am pharmacien m, -enne f.

drug test n [of athlete, horse] contrôle m antidopage.

drum [drʌm] ◇ n - 1. MUS tambour m - 2. [container] bidon m. ◇ vt & vi tambouriner. ◆ **drums** npl batterie f. ◆ **drum up** vt sep [support, business] rechercheɪ, solliciter.

drummer ['drʌmə'] n [gen] (joueur m, -euse f de) tambour m ; [in pop group] batteur m, -euse f.

drumstick ['drʌmstɪk] n - 1. [for drum] baguette f de tambour - 2. [of chicken] pilon m.

drunk [drʌŋk] ◇ pp ▷ drink. ◇ adj [on alcohol] ivre, soûl(e) ; **to get ~** se soûler, s'enivrer. ◇ n soûlard m, -e f.

drunkard ['drʌŋkəd] n alcoolique mf, ivrogne mf.

drunk-driving Am = drink-driving.

drunken ['drʌŋkn] adj [person] ivre ; [quarrel] d'ivrognes.

drunken driving = drink-driving.

dry [draɪ] ◇ adj - 1. [gen] sec (sèche) ; [day] sans pluie - 2. [river, earth] asséché(e) - 3. [wry] pince-sans-rire (inv). ◇ vt [gen] sécher ; [with cloth] essuyer. ◇ vi sécher. ◆ **dry up** vt sep [dishes] essuyer. ◇ vi - 1. [river, lake] s'assécher - 2. [supply] se tarir - 3. [actor, speaker] avoir un trou, sécher - 4. [dry dishes] essuyer.

dry cleaner n : ~'s pressing m.

dryer ['draɪə'] n [for clothes] séchoir m.

dry land n terre f ferme.

dry rot n pourriture f sèche.

dry ski slope n piste f de ski artificielle.

DSS (abbr of Department of Social Security) n ministère britannique de la sécurité sociale.

DTI (abbr of Department of Trade and Industry) n ministère britannique du commerce et de l'industrie.

DTP (abbr of desktop publishing) n PAO f.

dual ['djuːəl] adj double.

dual carriageway n Br route f à quatre voies.

dubbed [dʌbd] adj - 1. CINEMA doublé(e) - 2. [nicknamed] surnommé(e).

dubious ['djuːbjəs] adj - 1. [suspect] douteux(euse) - 2. [uncertain] hésitant(e), incertain(e) ; **to be ~ about doing sthg** hésiter à faire qqch.

Dublin ['dʌblɪn] n Dublin.

duchess ['dʌtʃɪs] n duchesse f.

duck [dʌk] ◇ n canard m. ◇ vt - 1. [head] baisser - 2. [responsibility] esquiver, se dérober à. ◇ vi [lower head] se baisser.

duckling ['dʌklɪŋ] n caneton m.

duct [dʌkt] n - 1. [pipe] canalisation f - 2. ANAT canal m.

dud [dʌd] ◇ adj [bomb] non éclaté(e) ; [cheque] sans provision, en bois. ◇ n obus m non éclaté.

dude [djuːd] n Am inf [man] gars m, type m.

due [djuː] ◇ adj - 1. [expected] : **the book is ~ out in May** le livre doit sortir en mai ; **she's ~ back shortly** elle devrait rentrer sous peu ; **when is the train ~?** à quelle heure le train doit-il arriver? - 2. [appropriate] dû (due), qui convient ; **in ~ course** [at the appropriate time] en temps voulu ; [eventually] à la longue - 3. [owed, owing] dû (due). ◇ adv : ~ **west** droit vers l'ouest. ◇ n dû m. ◆ **dues** npl cotisation f. ◆ **due to** prep [owing to] dû à ; [because of] provoqué par, à cause de.

duel ['djuːəl] ◇ n duel m. ◇ vi se battre en duel.

duet [djuː'et] n duo m.

duffel bag ['dʌfl-] n sac m marin.

duffel coat ['dʌfl-] n duffel-coat m.

duffle bag ['dʌfl-] = duffel bag.

duffle coat ['dʌfl-] = duffel coat.

dug [dʌg] pt & pp ▷ dig.

duke [djuːk] n duc m.

dull [dʌl] ◇ adj - 1. [boring - book, conversation] ennuyeux(euse) ; [- person] terne - 2. [colour, light] terne - 3. [weather] maussade - 4. [sound, ache] sourd(e). ◇ vt - 1. [pain] atténuer ; [senses] émousser - 2. [make less bright] ternir.

duly ['djuːlɪ] adv - 1. [properly] dûment - 2. [as expected] comme prévu.

dumb [dʌm] adj - 1. [unable to speak] muet(ette) - 2. inf [stupid] idiot(e).

dumbfound [dʌm'faʊnd] vt stupéfier, abasourdir ; **to be ~ed** ne pas en revenir.

dummy ['dʌmɪ] ◇ adj faux (fausse). ◇ n - 1. [of tailor] mannequin m - 2. [copy] maquette f - 3. Br [for baby] sucette f, tétine f - 4. SPORT feinte f.

dump [dʌmp] ◇ n - 1. [for rubbish] décharge f - 2. MIL dépôt m. ◇ vt - 1. [put down] déposer - 2. [dispose of] jeter - 3. inf [boyfriend, girlfriend] laisser tomber, plaquer.

dumper (truck) ['dʌmpə'-] Br, **dump truck** Am n tombereau m, dumper m.

dumping ['dʌmpɪŋ] n décharge f ; '**no ~**' 'décharge interdite'.

dumpling ['dʌmplɪŋ] *n* boulette *f* de pâte.

dump truck *Am* = dumper (truck).

dumpy ['dʌmpɪ] *adj inf* boulot(otte).

dunce [dʌns] *n* cancre *m*.

dune [dju:n] *n* dune *f*.

dung [dʌŋ] *n* fumier *m*.

dungarees [ˌdʌŋɡə'ri:z] *npl Br* [for work] bleu *m* de travail ; [fashion garment] salopette *f*.

dungeon ['dʌndʒən] *n* cachot *m*.

Dunkirk [dʌn'kɜːk] *n* Dunkerque *f*.

duo ['dju:əʊ] *n* duo *m*.

duplex ['dju:pleks] *n Am* - **1.** [apartment] duplex *m* - **2.** [house] maison *f* jumelée.

duplicate [*adj & n* 'dju:plɪkət, *vb* 'dju:plɪkeɪt] ◇ *adj* [key, document] en double. ◇ *n* double *m* ; **in ~** en double. ◇ *vt* [copy - gen] faire un double de ; [on photocopier] photocopier.

durable ['djʊərəbl] *adj* solide, résistant(e).

duration [djʊ'reɪʃn] *n* durée *f* ; **for the ~ of** jusqu'à la fin de.

duress [djʊ'res] *n* . **under ~** sous la contrainte.

Durex® ['djʊəreks] *n* préservatif *m*.

during ['djʊərɪŋ] *prep* pendant, au cours de.

dusk [dʌsk] *n* crépuscule *m*.

dust [dʌst] ◇ *n* (U) poussière *f*. ◇ *vt* - **1.** [clean] épousseter - **2.** [cover with powder] : **to ~ sthg (with)** saupoudrer qqch (de).

dustbin ['dʌstbɪn] *n Br* poubelle *f*.

dustcart ['dʌstkɑːt] *n Br* camion *m* des boueux.

duster ['dʌstər] *n* [cloth] chiffon *m* (à poussière).

dust jacket *n* [on book] jaquette *f*.

dustman ['dʌstmən] (*pl* -**men** [-mən]) *n Br* éboueur *m*.

dustpan ['dʌstpæn] *n* pelle *f* à poussière.

dusty ['dʌstɪ] *adj* poussiéreux(euse).

Dutch [dʌtʃ] ◇ *adj* néerlandais(e), hollandais(e). ◇ *n* [language] néerlandais *m*, hollandais *m*. ◇ *npl* : **the ~** les Néerlandais, les Hollandais. ◇ *adv* : **to go ~** partager les frais.

dutiful ['dju:tɪfʊl] *adj* obéissant(e).

duty ['dju:tɪ] *n* - **1.** (U) [responsibility] devoir *m* ; **to do one's ~** faire son devoir - **2.** [work] : **to be on/off ~** être/ne pas être de service - **3.** [tax] droit *m*. ◆ **duties** *npl* fonctions *fpl*.

duty-free *adj* hors taxe.

duvet ['du:veɪ] *n Br* couette *f*.

duvet cover *n Br* housse *f* de couette.

DVD (*abbr of* Digital Video *or* Versatile Disc) *n* DVD *m*.

DVD-ROM (*abbr of* Digital Video *or* Versatile Disc read only memory) *n* DVD-ROM *m*.

dwarf [dwɔːf] (*pl* -**s** *or* **dwarves** [dwɔːvz]) ◇ *n* nain *m*, -e *f*. ◇ *vt* [tower over] écraser.

dwell [dwel] (*pt & pp* **dwelt** *or* -**ed**) *vi literary* habiter. ◆ **dwell on** *vt fus* s'étendre sur.

dwelling ['dwelɪŋ] *n literary* habitation *f*.

dwelt [dwelt] *pt & pp* ⊳ **dwell**.

dwindle ['dwɪndl] *vi* diminuer.

dye [daɪ] ◇ *n* teinture *f*. ◇ *vt* teindre.

dying ['daɪɪŋ] ◇ *cont* ⊳ **die**. ◇ *adj* [person] mourant(e), moribond(e) ; [plant, language, industry] moribond.

dyke [daɪk] = dike.

dynamic [daɪ'næmɪk] *adj* dynamique.

dynamite ['daɪnəmaɪt] *n* (U) *lit & fig* dynamite *f*.

dynamo ['daɪnəməʊ] (*pl* -**s**) *n* dynamo *f*.

dynasty [*Br* 'dɪnəstɪ, *Am* 'daɪnəstɪ] *n* dynastie *f*.

dyslexia [dɪs'leksɪə] *n* dyslexie *f*.

dyslexic [dɪs'leksɪk] *adj* dyslexique.

e (*pl* **e's** *or* **es**), **E** (*pl* **E's** *or* **Es**) [iː] *n* [letter] e *m inv*, E *m inv*. ◆ **E** *n* - **1.** MUS mi *m* - **2.** (*abbr of* **east**) E.

each [iːtʃ] ◇ *adj* chaque. ◇ *pron* chacun(e) ; **the books cost £10.99 ~** les livres coûtent 10,99 livres (la) pièce ; **~ other** l'un l'autre (l'une l'autre), les uns les autres (les unes les autres) ; **they love ~ other** ils s'aiment ; **we've known ~ other for years** nous nous connaissons depuis des années.

eager ['iːɡər] *adj* passionné(e), avide ; **to be ~ for** être avide de ; **to be ~ to do sthg** être impatient de faire qqch.

eagle ['iːɡl] *n* [bird] aigle *m*.

ear [ɪər] *n* - **1.** [gen] oreille *f* - **2.** [of corn] épi *m*.

earache ['ɪəreɪk] n : **to have ~** Br, **to have an ~** Am avoir mal à l'oreille.

eardrum ['ɪədrʌm] n tympan m.

earl [ɜːl] n comte m.

earlier ['ɜːlɪəʳ] ◇ adj [previous] précédent(e) ; [more early] plus tôt. ◇ adv plus tôt ; **~ on** plus tôt.

earliest ['ɜːlɪəst] ◇ adj [first] premier(ère) ; [most early] le plus tôt. ◇ n : **at the ~** au plus tôt.

earlobe ['ɪələʊb] n lobe m de l'oreille.

early ['ɜːlɪ] ◇ adj - 1. [before expected time] en avance - 2. [in day] de bonne heure ; **the ~ train** le premier train ; **to make an ~ start** partir de bonne heure - 3. [at beginning] : **in the ~ sixties** au début des années soixante. ◇ adv - 1. [before expected time] en avance ; **I was ten minutes ~** j'étais en avance de dix minutes - 2. [in day] de bonne heure ; **as ~ as** dès ; **~ on** tôt - 3. [at beginning] : **~ in her life** dans sa jeunesse.

early retirement n retraite f anticipée.

earmark ['ɪəmaːk] vt : **to be ~ed for** être réservé(e) à.

earn [ɜːn] vt - 1. [as salary] gagner - 2. COMM rapporter - 3. fig [respect, praise] gagner, mériter.

earnest ['ɜːnɪst] adj sérieux(euse). ◆ **in earnest** ◇ adj sérieux(euse). ◇ adv pour de bon, sérieusement.

earnings ['ɜːnɪŋz] npl [of person] salaire m, gains mpl ; [of company] bénéfices mpl.

earphones ['ɪəfəʊnz] npl casque m.

earplugs ['ɪəplʌgz] npl boules fpl Quiès®.

earring ['ɪərɪŋ] n boucle f d'oreille.

earshot ['ɪəʃɒt] n : **within ~** à portée de voix ; **out of ~** hors de portée de voix.

earth [ɜːθ] ◇ n [gen & ELEC] terre f ; **how/what/where/why on ~** ...? mais comment/que/où/pourquoi donc ...? ; **to cost the ~** Br coûter les yeux de la tête. ◇ vt Br : **to be ~ed** être à la masse.

earthenware ['ɜːθnweəʳ] n (U) poteries fpl.

earthquake ['ɜːθkweɪk] n tremblement m de terre.

earthworm ['ɜːθwɜːm] n ver m de terre.

earthy ['ɜːθɪ] adj - 1. fig [humour, person] truculent(e) - 2. [taste, smell] de terre, terreux(euse).

earwig ['ɪəwɪg] n perce-oreille m.

ease [iːz] ◇ n (U) - 1. [lack of difficulty] facilité f ; **to do sthg with ~** faire qqch sans difficulté OR facilement - 2. [comfort] : **at ~** à l'aise ; **ill at ~** mal à l'aise. ◇ vt - 1. [pain] calmer ; [restrictions] modérer - 2. [move

carefully] : **to ~ sthg in/out** faire entrer/ sortir qqch délicatement. ◇ vi [problem] s'arranger ; [pain] s'atténuer ; [rain] diminuer. ◆ **ease off** vi [pain] s'atténuer ; [rain] diminuer. ◆ **ease up** vi - 1. [rain] diminuer - 2. [relax] se détendre.

easel ['iːzl] n chevalet m.

easily ['iːzɪlɪ] adv - 1. [without difficulty] facilement - 2. [without doubt] de loin - 3. [in a relaxed manner] tranquillement.

east [iːst] ◇ n - 1. [direction] est m - 2. [region] : **the ~** l'est m. ◇ adj est (inv) ; [wind] d'est. ◇ adv à l'est, vers l'est ; **~ of** à l'est de. ◆ **East** n : **the East** [gen & POL] l'Est m ; [Asia] l'Orient m.

East End n : **the ~** les quartiers est de Londres.

Easter ['iːstəʳ] n Pâques m.

Easter egg n œuf m de Pâques.

easterly ['iːstəlɪ] adj à l'est, de l'est ; [wind] de l'est.

eastern ['iːstən] adj de l'est. ◆ **Eastern** adj [gen & POL] de l'Est ; [from Asia] oriental(e).

East German ◇ adj d'Allemagne de l'Est. ◇ n Allemand m, -e f de l'Est.

East Germany n : (former) **~** (l'ex-) Allemagne f de l'Est.

eastward ['iːstwəd] ◇ adj à l'est, vers l'est. ◇ adv = **eastwards**.

eastwards ['iːstwədz] adv vers l'est.

easy ['iːzɪ] ◇ adj - 1. [not difficult, comfortable] facile - 2. [relaxed - manner] naturel(elle). ◇ adv : **to take it** OR **things ~** inf ne pas se fatiguer.

easy chair n fauteuil m.

easygoing [ˌiːzɪ'gəʊɪŋ] adj [person] facile à vivre ; [manner] complaisant(e).

eat [iːt] (pt ate, pp eaten) vt & vi manger. ◆ **eat away, eat into** vt fus - 1. [subj : acid, rust] ronger - 2. [deplete] grignoter.

eaten ['iːtn] pp ▷ **eat**.

eaves ['iːvz] npl avant-toit m.

eavesdrop ['iːvzdrɒp] vi : **to ~ (on sb)** écouter (qqn) de façon indiscrète.

ebb [eb] ◇ n reflux m. ◇ vi [tide, sea] se retirer, refluer.

ebony ['ebənɪ] ◇ adj [colour] noir(e) d'ébène. ◇ n ébène f.

e-business n - 1. [company] cyberentreprise f - 2. (U) [trade] cybercommerce m, commerce m électronique.

EC (abbr of **European Community**) n CE f.

e-cash n argent m virtuel OR électronique.

ECB (abbr of **European Central bank**) n BCE f.

eccentric [ɪk'sentrɪk] ◇ adj [odd] excentrique, bizarre. ◇ n [person] excentrique mf.

echo ['ekəʊ] (pl **-es**) ◇ n lit & fig écho m. ◇ vt [words] répéter ; [opinion] faire écho à. ◇ vi retentir, résonner.

éclair [eɪ'kleə] n éclair m.

eclipse [ɪ'klɪps] ◇ n lit & fig éclipse f. ◇ vt fig éclipser.

eco-friendly adj qui respecte l'environnement.

ecological [,iːkə'lɒdʒɪkl] adj écologique.

ecology [ɪ'kɒlədʒɪ] n écologie f.

e-commerce n (U) commerce m électronique, cybercommerce m.

economic [,iːkə'nɒmɪk] adj - 1. ECON économique - 2. [profitable] rentable.

economical [,iːkə'nɒmɪkl] adj - 1. [cheap] économique - 2. [person] économe.

Economic and Monetary Union n Union f économique européenne.

economics [,iːkə'nɒmɪks] ◇ n (U) économie f (politique), sciences fpl économiques. ◇ npl [of plan, business] aspect m financier.

economize, -ise [ɪ'kɒnəmaɪz] vi économiser.

economy [ɪ'kɒnəmɪ] n économie f ; economies of scale économies d'échelle.

economy class n classe f touriste.

ecotourism ['iːkəʊ,tʊərɪzm] n écotourisme m.

ecstasy ['ekstəsɪ] n - 1. [pleasure] extase f, ravissement m - 2. [drug] ecstasy m OR f.

ecstatic [ek'stætɪk] adj [person] en extase ; [feeling] extatique.

ECU, Ecu ['ekjuː] (abbr of **European Currency Unit**) n ECU m, écu m.

eczema ['eksɪmə] n eczéma m.

Eden ['iːdn] n : **(the Garden of) ~** le jardin m d'Éden, l'Éden m.

edge [edʒ] ◇ n - 1. [gen] bord m ; [of coin, book] tranche f ; [of knife] tranchant m ; **to be on the ~ of** fig être à deux doigts de - 2. [advantage] : **to have an ~ over** OR **the ~ on** avoir un léger avantage sur. ◇ vi : **to ~ forward** avancer tout doucement. ➤ **on edge** adj contracté(e), tendu(e).

edgeways ['edʒweɪz], **edgewise** ['edʒwaɪz] adv latéralement, de côté.

edgy ['edʒɪ] adj contracté(e), tendu(e).

edible ['edɪbl] adj [safe to eat] comestible.

edict ['iːdɪkt] n décret m.

Edinburgh ['edɪnbrə] n Édimbourg.

edit ['edɪt] vt - 1. [correct - text] corriger

- **2.** CINEMA monter ; RADIO & TV réaliser - **3.** [magazine] diriger ; [newspaper] être le rédacteur en chef de.

edition [ɪ'dɪʃn] n édition f.

editor ['edɪtə] n - **1.** [of magazine] directeur m, -trice f ; [of newspaper] rédacteur m, -trice f en chef - **2.** [of text] correcteur m, -trice f - **3.** CINEMA monteur m, -euse f ; RADIO & TV réalisateur m, -trice f.

editorial [,edɪ'tɔːrɪəl] ◇ adj [department, staff] de la rédaction ; [style, policy] éditorial(e). ◇ n éditorial m.

educate ['edʒʊkeɪt] vt - **1.** SCH & UNIV instruire - **2.** [inform] informer, éduquer.

education [,edʒʊ'keɪʃn] n - **1.** [gen] éducation f - **2.** [teaching] enseignement m, instruction f.

educational [,edʒʊ'keɪʃənl] adj - **1.** [establishment, policy] pédagogique - **2.** [toy, experience] éducatif(ive).

EEC (abbr of **European Economic Community**) n ancien nom de la Communauté Européenne.

eel [iːl] n anguille f.

eerie ['ɪərɪ] adj inquiétant(e), sinistre.

efface [ɪ'feɪs] vt effacer.

effect [ɪ'fekt] ◇ n [gen] effet m ; **to have an ~ on** avoir OR produire un effet sur ; **for ~** pour attirer l'attention, pour se faire remarquer ; **to take ~** [law] prendre effet, entrer en vigueur ; **to put sthg into ~** [policy, law] mettre qqch en application. ◇ vt [repairs, change] effectuer ; [reconciliation] amener. ➤ **effects** npl · **(special) ~s** effets mpl spéciaux.

effective [ɪ'fektɪv] adj - **1.** [successful] efficace - **2.** [actual, real] effectif(ive).

effectively [ɪ'fektɪvlɪ] adv - **1.** [successfully] efficacement - **2.** [in fact] effectivement.

effectiveness [ɪ'fektɪvnɪs] n efficacité f.

effeminate [ɪ'femɪnət] adj efféminé(e).

effervescent [,efə'vesənt] adj [liquid] effervescent(e) ; [drink] gazeux(euse).

efficiency [ɪ'fɪʃənsɪ] n [of person, method] efficacité f ; [of factory, system] rendement m.

efficient [ɪ'fɪʃənt] adj efficace.

effluent ['efluənt] n effluent m.

effort ['efət] n effort m ; **to be worth the ~** valoir la peine ; **with ~** avec peine ; **to make the ~ to do sthg** s'efforcer de faire qqch ; **to make an/no ~ to do sthg** faire un effort/ne faire aucun effort pour faire qqch.

effortless ['efətlɪs] adj [easy] facile ; [natural] aisé(e).

effusive [ɪ'fjuːsɪv] *adj* [person] démonstratif(ive) ; [welcome] plein(e) d'effusions.

EFTPOS ['eftpɒs] (*abbr of* **electronic funds transfer at point of sale**) *n* transfert électronique de fonds au point de vente.

e.g. (*abbr of* **exempli gratia**) *adv* par exemple.

egg [eg] *n* œuf *m*. ◆ **egg on** *vt sep* pousser, inciter.

eggcup ['egkʌp] *n* coquetier *m*.

eggplant ['egplɑːnt] *n Am* aubergine *f*.

eggshell ['egʃel] *n* coquille *f* d'œuf.

egg white *n* blanc *m* d'œuf.

egg yolk *n* jaune *m* d'œuf.

ego ['iːgəʊ] (*pl* -s) *n* moi *m*.

egoism ['iːgəʊɪzm] *n* égoïsme *m*.

egoistic [ˌiːgəʊ'ɪstɪk] *adj* égoïste.

egotistic(al) [ˌiːgə'tɪstɪk(l)] *adj* égotiste.

Egypt ['iːdʒɪpt] *n* Égypte *f*.

Egyptian [ɪ'dʒɪpʃn] ◇ *adj* égyptien (enne). ◇ *n* Égyptien *m*, -enne *f*.

eiderdown ['aɪdədaʊn] *n esp Br* [bed cover] édredon *m*.

eight [eɪt] *num* huit ; *see also* **six**.

eighteen [ˌeɪ'tiːn] *num* dix-huit ; *see also* **six**.

eighth [eɪtθ] *num* huitième ; *see also* **sixth**.

eighty ['eɪtɪ] *num* quatre-vingts ; *see also* **sixty**.

Eire ['eərə] *n* République *f* d'Irlande.

either ['aɪðəʳ, 'iːðəʳ] ◇ *adj* - **1.** [one or the other] l'un ou l'autre (l'une ou l'autre) (des deux) ; **she couldn't find ~ jumper** elle ne trouva ni l'un ni l'autre des pulls ; **~ way** de toute façon - **2.** [each] chaque ; **on ~ side** de chaque côté. ◇ *pron* : **~ (of them)** l'un ou l'autre *m*, l'une ou l'autre *f* ; **I don't like ~ (of them)** je n'aime aucun des deux, je n'aime ni l'un ni l'autre. ◇ *adv (in negatives)* non plus ; **I don't ~** moi non plus. ◇ *conj* : **~ ... or** soit ... soit, ou ... ou ; **I'm not fond of ~ him or his wife** je ne les aime ni lui ni sa femme.

eject [ɪ'dʒekt] *vt* - **1.** [object] éjecter, émettre - **2.** [person] éjecter, expulser.

eke [iːk] ◆ **eke out** *vt sep* [money, food] économiser, faire durer.

elaborate [*adj* ɪ'læbrət, *vb* ɪ'læbəreɪt] ◇ *adj* [ceremony, procedure] complexe ; [explanation, plan] détaillé(e), minutieux(euse). ◇ *vi* : **to ~ (on)** donner des précisions (sur).

elapse [ɪ'læps] *vi* s'écouler.

elastic [ɪ'læstɪk] ◇ *adj lit & fig* élastique. ◇ *n (U)* élastique *m*.

elasticated [ɪ'læstɪkeɪtɪd] *adj* élastique.

elastic band *n Br* élastique *m*, caoutchouc *m*.

elated [ɪ'leɪtɪd] *adj* transporté(e) (de joie).

elbow ['elbəʊ] *n* coude *m*.

elder ['eldəʳ] ◇ *adj* aîné(e). ◇ *n* - **1.** [older person] aîné *m*, -e *f* - **2.** [of tribe, church] ancien *m* - **3.** : **~ (tree)** sureau *m*.

elderly ['eldəlɪ] ◇ *adj* âgé(e). ◇ *npl* : **the ~** les personnes *fpl* âgées.

eldest ['eldɪst] *adj* aîné(e).

elect [ɪ'lekt] ◇ *adj* élu(e). ◇ *vt* - **1.** [by voting] élire - **2.** *fml* [choose] : **to ~ to do sthg** choisir de faire qqch.

election [ɪ'lekʃn] *n* élection *f* ; **to have** OR **hold an ~** procéder à une élection.

electioneering [ɪˌlekʃə'nɪərɪŋ] *n (U) usu pej* propagande *f* électorale.

elector [ɪ'lektəʳ] *n* électeur *m*, -trice *f*.

electorate [ɪ'lektərət] *n* : **the ~** l'électorat *m*.

electric [ɪ'lektrɪk] *adj lit & fig* électrique. ◆ **electrics** *npl Br inf* [in car, machine] installation *f* électrique.

electrical [ɪ'lektrɪkl] *adj* électrique.

electrical shock *Am* = **electric shock**.

electric blanket *n* couverture *f* chauffante.

electric cooker *n* cuisinière *f* électrique.

electric fire *n* radiateur *m* électrique.

electrician [ˌɪlek'trɪʃn] *n* électricien *m*, -enne *f*.

electricity [ˌɪlek'trɪsətɪ] *n* électricité *f*.

electric shock *Br*, **electrical shock** *Am* *n* décharge *f* électrique.

electrify [ɪ'lektrɪfaɪ] *vt* - **1.** TECH électrifier - **2.** *fig* [excite] galvaniser, électriser.

electrocute [ɪ'lektrəkjuːt] *vt* électrocuter.

electrolysis [ˌɪlek'trɒləsɪs] *n* électrolyse *f*.

electron [ɪ'lektrɒn] *n* électron *m*.

electronic [ˌɪlek'trɒnɪk] *adj* électronique. ◆ **electronics** ◇ *n (U)* [technology, science] électronique *f*. ◇ *npl* [equipment] (équipement *m*) électronique *f*.

electronic data processing *n* traitement *m* électronique de données.

electronic mail *n* courrier *m* électronique.

e-mail address *n* adresse *f* électronique, adresse *f* e-mail.

elegant ['elɪgənt] *adj* élégant(e).

element ['elɪmənt] *n* - **1.** [gen] élément *m* ;

an ~ of truth une part de vérité - 2. [in heater, kettle] résistance f. ◆ **elements** *npl* - 1. [basics] rudiments *mpl* - 2. [weather]: the ~s les éléments *mpl*.

elementary [ˌelɪ'mentərɪ] *adj* élémentaire.

elementary school *n* Am école f primaire.

elephant ['elɪfənt] (*pl inv* OR **-s**) *n* éléphant *m*.

elevate ['elɪveɪt] *vt* - 1. [give importance to]: to ~ sb/sthg (to) élever qqn/qqch (à) - 2. [raise] soulever.

elevator ['elɪveɪtər] *n* Am ascenseur *m*.

eleven [ɪ'levn] *num* onze ; *see also* **six**.

elevenses [ɪ'levnzɪz] *n* (U) Br ≃ pause-café f.

eleventh [ɪ'levnθ] *num* onzième ; *see also* **sixth**.

elicit [ɪ'lɪsɪt] *vt fml* : to ~ sthg (from sb) arracher qqch (à qqn).

eligible ['elɪdʒəbl] *adj* [suitable, qualified] admissible ; to be ~ for sthg avoir droit à qqch ; to be ~ to do sthg avoir le droit de faire qqch.

eliminate [ɪ'lɪmɪneɪt] *vt* : to ~ sb/sthg (from) éliminer qqn/qqch (de).

elite [ɪ'liːt] ◇ *adj* d'élite. ◇ *n* élite f.

elitist [ɪ'liːtɪst] ◇ *adj* élitiste. ◇ *n* élitiste *mf*.

elk [elk] (*pl inv* OR **-s**) *n* élan *m*.

elm [elm] *n* : ~ (tree) orme *m*.

elocution [ˌelə'kjuːʃn] *n* élocution f, diction f.

elongated ['iːlɒŋgeɪtɪd] *adj* allongé(e) ; [fingers] long (longue).

elope [ɪ'ləʊp] *vi* : to ~ (with) s'enfuir (avec).

eloquent ['eləkwənt] *adj* éloquent(e).

El Salvador [ˌel'sælvədɔːr] *n* Salvador *m*.

else [els] *adv* : anything ~ n'importe quoi d'autre ; anything ~? [in shop] et avec ça?, ce sera tout? ; he doesn't need anything ~ il n'a besoin de rien d'autre ; everyone ~ tous les autres ; nothing ~ rien d'autre ; someone ~ quelqu'un d'autre ; something ~ quelque chose d'autre ; somewhere ~ autre part ; who/what ~? qui/quoi d'autre? ; where ~? (à) quel autre endroit? ◆ **or else** *conj* [or if not] sinon, sans quoi.

elsewhere [els'weər] *adv* ailleurs, autre part.

elude [ɪ'luːd] *vt* échapper à.

elusive [ɪ'luːsɪv] *adj* insaisissable ; [success] qui échappe.

emaciated [ɪ'meɪʃɪeɪtɪd] *adj* [face] émacié(e) ; [person, limb] décharné(e).

e-mail, email (*abbr of* **electronic mail**) *n* e-mail *m*, courrier *m* électronique.

emanate ['eməneɪt] *fml vi* : to ~ from émaner de.

emancipate [ɪ'mænsɪpeɪt] *vt* : to ~ sb (from) affranchir OR émanciper qqn (de).

embankment [ɪm'bæŋkmənt] *n* [of river] berge f ; [of railway] remblai *m* ; [of road] banquette f.

embark [ɪm'baːk] *vi* - 1. [board ship] : to ~ (on) embarquer (sur) - 2. [start] : to ~ on OR upon sthg s'embarquer dans qqch.

embarkation [ˌembaː'keɪʃn] *n* embarquement *m*.

embarrass [ɪm'bærəs] *vt* embarrasser.

embarrassed [ɪm'bærəst] *adj* embarrassé(e).

embarrassing [ɪm'bærəsɪŋ] *adj* embarrassant(e).

embarrassment [ɪm'bærəsmənt] *n* embarras *m* ; to be an ~ [person] causer de l'embarras ; [thing] être une source d'embarrassant.

embassy ['embəsɪ] *n* ambassade f.

embedded [ɪm'bedɪd] *adj* - 1. [buried] : ~ in [in rock, wood] incrusté(e) dans ; [in mud] noyé(e) dans - 2. [ingrained] enraciné(e).

embellish [ɪm'belɪʃ] *vt* - 1. [decorate] : to ~ sthg (with) [room, house] décorer qqch (de) ; [dress] orner qqch (de) - 2. [story] enjoliver.

embers ['embəz] *npl* braises *fpl*.

embezzle [ɪm'bezl] *vt* détourner.

embittered [ɪm'bɪtəd] *adj* aigri(e).

emblem ['embləm] *n* emblème *m*.

embody [ɪm'bɒdɪ] *vt* incarner ; to be embodied in sthg être exprimé dans qqch.

embossed [ɪm'bɒst] *adj* - 1. [heading, design] : ~ (on) inscrit(e) (sur), gravé(e) en relief (sur) - 2. [wallpaper] gaufré(e) ; [leather] frappé(e).

embrace [ɪm'breɪs] ◇ *n* étreinte f. ◇ *vt* embrasser. ◇ *vi* s'embrasser, s'étreindre.

embroider [ɪm'brɔɪdər] ◇ *vt* - 1. SEWING broder - 2. *pej* [embellish] enjoliver. ◇ *vi* SEWING broder.

embroidery [ɪm'brɔɪdərɪ] *n* (U) broderie f.

embroil [ɪm'brɔɪl] *vt* : to be ~ed (in) être mêlé(e) (à).

embryo ['embrɪəʊ] (*pl* **-s**) *n* embryon *m*.

emerald ['emərəld] ◇ *adj* [colour] émeraude *(inv)*. ◇ *n* [stone] émeraude f.

emerge [ɪ'mɜːdʒ] ◇ *vi* - **1.** [come out] : **to ~ (from)** émerger (de) - **2.** [from experience, situation] : **to ~ from** sortir de - **3.** [become known] apparaître - **4.** [come into existence - poet, artist] percer ; [- movement, organization] émerger. ◇ *vt* : **it ~s that ...** il ressort OR il apparaît que ...

emergence [ɪ'mɜːdʒəns] *n* émergence *f*.

emergency [ɪ'mɜːdʒənsɪ] ◇ *adj* d'urgence. ◇ *n* urgence *f* ; **in an ~, in emergencies** en cas d'urgence.

emergency exit *n* sortie *f* de secours.

emergency landing *n* atterrissage *m* forcé.

emergency services *npl* ≃ police-secours *f*.

emery board ['eməri-] *n* lime *f* à ongles.

emigrant ['emɪgrənt] *n* émigré *m*, -e *f*.

emigrate ['emɪgreɪt] *vi* : **to ~ (to)** émigrer (en/à).

eminent ['emɪnənt] *adj* éminent(e).

emission [ɪ'mɪʃn] *n* émission *f*.

emit [ɪ'mɪt] *vt* émettre.

emotion [ɪ'məʊʃn] *n* - **1.** *(U)* [strength of feeling] émotion *f* - **2.** [particular feeling] sentiment *m*.

emotional [ɪ'məʊʃənl] *adj* - **1.** [sensitive, demonstrative] émotif(ive) - **2.** [moving] émouvant(e) - **3.** [psychological] émotionnel(elle).

emperor ['empərəʳ] *n* empereur *m*.

emphasis ['emfəsɪs] (*pl* -ses [-siːz]) *n* : **~ (on)** accent *m* (sur) ; **to lay** OR **place ~ on sthg** insister sur OR souligner qqch.

emphasize, -ise ['emfəsaɪz] *vt* insister sur.

emphatic [ɪm'fætɪk] *adj* [forceful] catégorique.

emphatically [ɪm'fætɪklɪ] *adv* - **1.** [with emphasis] catégoriquement - **2.** [certainly] absolument.

empire ['empaɪəʳ] *n* empire *m*.

employ [ɪm'plɔɪ] *vt* employer ; **to be ~ed as** être employé comme ; **to ~ sthg as sthg/ to do sthg** employer qqch comme qqch/ pour faire qqch.

employee [ɪm'plɔiːː] *n* employé *m*, -e *f*.

employer [ɪm'plɔɪəʳ] *n* employeur *m*, -euse *f*.

employment [ɪm'plɔɪmənt] *n* emploi *m*, travail *m*.

employment agency *n* bureau *m* OR agence *f* de placement.

empower [ɪm'paʊəʳ] *vt fml* : **to be ~ed to do sthg** être habilité(e) à faire qqch.

empress ['emprɪs] *n* impératrice *f*.

empty ['emptɪ] ◇ *adj* - **1.** [containing nothing] vide - **2.** *pej* [meaningless] vain(e). ◇ *vt* vider ; **to ~ sthg into/out of** vider qqch dans/de. ◇ *vi* se vider. ◇ *n inf* bouteille *f* vide.

empty-handed [-'hændɪd] *adj* les mains vides.

EMS (*abbr of* European Monetary System) *n* SME *m*.

EMU (*abbr of* Economic and Monetary Union) *n* UEM *f*.

emulate ['emjʊleɪt] *vt* imiter.

emulsion [ɪ'mʌlʃn] *n* : **~ (paint)** peinture *f* mate OR à émulsion.

enable [ɪ'neɪbl] *vt* : **to ~ sb to do sthg** permettre à qqn de faire qqch.

enact [ɪ'nækt] *vt* - **1.** JUR promulguer - **2.** THEATRE jouer.

enamel [ɪ'næml] *n* - **1.** [material] émail *m* - **2.** [paint] peinture *f* laquée.

encampment [ɪn'kæmpmənt] *n* campement *m*.

encapsulate [ɪn'kæpsjʊleɪt] *vt* : **to ~ sthg (in)** résumer qqch (en).

encase [ɪn'keɪs] *vt* : **to be ~d in** [armour] être enfermé(e) dans ; [leather] être bardé(e) de.

enchanted [ɪn'tʃɑːntɪd] *adj* : **~ (by/with)** enchanté(e) (par/de).

enchanting [ɪn'tʃɑːntɪŋ] *adj* enchanteur(eresse).

encircle [ɪn'sɜːkl] *vt* entourer ; [subj : troops] encercler.

enclose [ɪn'kləʊz] *vt* - **1.** [surround, contain] entourer - **2.** [put in envelope] joindre ; **please find ~d ...** veuillez trouver ci-joint ...

enclosure [ɪn'kləʊʒəʳ] *n* - **1.** [place] enceinte *f* - **2.** [in letter] pièce *f* jointe.

encompass [ɪn'kʌmpəs] *vt fml* - **1.** [include] contenir - **2.** [surround] entourer ; [subj : troops] encercler.

encore ['ɒŋkɔːʳ] ◇ *n* rappel *m*. ◇ *excl* bis!

encounter [ɪn'kaʊntəʳ] ◇ *n* rencontre *f*. ◇ *vt fml* rencontrer.

encourage [ɪn'kʌrɪdʒ] *vt* - **1.** [give confidence to] : **to ~ sb (to do sthg)** encourager qqn (à faire qqch) - **2.** [promote] encourager, favoriser.

encouragement [ɪn'kʌrɪdʒmənt] *n* encouragement *m*.

encroach [ɪn'krəʊtʃ] *vi* : **to ~ on** OR **upon** empiéter sur.

encryption [en'krɪpʃn] *n (U)* - **1.** COMPUT cryptage *m* - **2.** TV codage *m*, encodage *m*.

encyclop(a)edia [ɪn,saɪklə'piːdjə] *n* encyclopédie *f*.

end [end] ◇ *n* - **1.** [gen] fin *f* ; **at an ~** terminé, fini ; **to come to an ~** se terminer, s'arrêter ; **to put an ~ to sthg** mettre fin à qqch ; **at the ~ of the day** *fig* en fin de compte ; **in the ~** [finally] finalement - **2.** [of rope, path, garden, table etc] bout *m*, extrémité *f* ; [of box] côté *m* - **3.** [leftover part - of cigarette] mégot *m* ; [- of pencil] bout *m*. ◇ *vt* mettre fin à ; [day] finir ; **to ~ sthg with** terminer OR finir qqch par. ◇ *vi* se terminer ; **to ~ in** se terminer par ; **to ~ with** se terminer par OR avec. **◆ on end** *adv* - **1.** [upright] debout - **2.** [continuously] d'affilée. **◆ end up** *vi* finir ; **to ~ up doing sthg** finir par faire qqch.

endanger [ɪn'deɪndʒər] *vt* mettre en danger.

endearing [ɪn'dɪərɪŋ] *adj* engageant(e).

endeavour *Br*, **endeavor** *Am* [ɪn'devər] *fml* ◇ *n* effort *m*, tentative *f*. ◇ *vi* **: to ~ to do sthg** s'efforcer OR tenter de faire qqch.

ending ['endɪŋ] *n* fin *f*, dénouement *m*.

endive ['endaɪv] *n* - **1.** [salad vegetable] endive *f* - **2.** [chicory] chicorée *f*.

endless ['endlɪs] *adj* - **1.** [unending] interminable ; [patience, possibilities] infini(e) ; [resources] inépuisable - **2.** [vast] infini(e).

endorse [ɪn'dɔːs] *vt* - **1.** [approve] approuver - **2.** [cheque] endosser.

endorsement [ɪn'dɔːsmənt] *n* - **1.** [approval] approbation *f* - **2.** *Br* [on driving licence] *contravention portée au permis de conduire*.

endow [ɪn'dau] *vt* - **1.** [equip] **: to be ~ed with sthg** être doté(e) de qqch - **2.** [donate money to] faire des dons à.

endurance [ɪn'djuərəns] *n* endurance *f*.

endure [ɪn'djuər] ◇ *vt* supporter, endurer. ◇ *vi* perdurer.

endways *Br* ['endweɪz], **endwise** *Am* ['endwaɪz] *adv* - **1.** [not sideways] en long - **2.** [with ends touching] bout à bout.

enemy ['enɪmɪ] ◇ *n* ennemi *m*, -e *f*. ◇ *comp* ennemi(e).

energetic [,enə'dʒetɪk] *adj* énergique ; [person] plein(e) d'entrain.

energy ['enədʒɪ] *n* énergie *f*.

enforce [ɪn'fɔːs] *vt* appliquer, faire respecter.

enforced [ɪn'fɔːst] *adj* forcé(e).

engage [ɪn'geɪdʒ] ◇ *vt* - **1.** [attention, interest] susciter, éveiller - **2.** TECH engager - **3.** *fml* [employ] engager ; **to be ~d in** OR **on**

sthg prendre part à qqch. ◇ *vi* [be involved] **: to ~ in** s'occuper de.

engaged [ɪn'geɪdʒd] *adj* - **1.** [to be married] **: ~ (to sb)** fiancé(e) (à qqn) ; **to get ~** se fiancer - **2.** [busy] occupé(e) ; **~ in sthg** engagé dans qqch - **3.** [telephone, toilet] occupé(e).

engaged tone *n Br* tonalité *f* « occupé ».

engagement [ɪn'geɪdʒmənt] *n* - **1.** [to be married] fiançailles *fpl* - **2.** [appointment] rendez-vous *m inv*.

engagement ring *n* bague *f* de fiançailles.

engaging [ɪn'geɪdʒɪŋ] *adj* engageant(e) ; [personality] attirant(e).

engender [ɪn'dʒendər] *vt fml* engendrer, susciter.

engine ['endʒɪn] *n* - **1.** [of vehicle] moteur *m* - **2.** RAIL locomotive *f*.

engine driver *n Br* mécanicien *m*.

engineer [,endʒɪ'nɪər] *n* - **1.** [of roads] ingénieur *m* ; [of machinery, on ship] mécanicien *m* ; [of electrical equipment] technicien *m* - **2.** *Am* [engine driver] mécanicien *m*.

engineering [,endʒɪ'nɪərɪŋ] *n* ingénierie *f*.

England ['ɪŋglənd] *n* Angleterre *f* ; **in ~** en Angleterre.

English ['ɪŋglɪʃ] ◇ *adj* anglais(e). ◇ *n* [language] anglais *m*. ◇ *npl* **: the ~** les Anglais.

English breakfast *n* petit déjeuner *m* anglais traditionnel.

English Channel *n* **: the ~** la Manche.

Englishman ['ɪŋglɪʃmən] (*pl* -men [-mən]) *n* Anglais *m*.

Englishwoman ['ɪŋglɪʃ,wumən] (*pl* -women [-wɪmɪn]) *n* Anglaise *f*.

engrave [ɪn'greɪv] *vt* **: to ~ sthg (on stone/in one's memory)** graver qqch (sur la pierre/dans sa mémoire).

engraving [ɪn'greɪvɪŋ] *n* gravure *f*.

engrossed [ɪn'grəust] *adj* **: to be ~ (in sthg)** être absorbé(e) (par qqch).

engulf [ɪn'gʌlf] *vt* engloutir.

enhance [ɪn'hɑːns] *vt* accroître.

enjoy [ɪn'dʒɔɪ] *vt* - **1.** [like] aimer ; **to ~ doing sthg** avoir plaisir à OR aimer faire qqch ; **to ~ o.s.** s'amuser - **2.** *fml* [possess] jouir de.

enjoyable [ɪn'dʒɔɪəbl] *adj* agréable.

enjoyment [ɪn'dʒɔɪmənt] *n* [gen] plaisir *m*.

enlarge [ɪn'lɑːdʒ] *vt* agrandir. **◆ enlarge (up)on** *vt fus* développer.

enlargement [ɪn'lɑːdʒmənt] *n* - **1.** [expansion] extension f - **2.** PHOT agrandissement m.

enlighten [ɪn'laɪtn] vt éclairer.

enlightened [ɪn'laɪtnd] adj éclairé(e).

enlightenment [ɪn'laɪtnmənt] n (U) éclaircissement m.

enlist [ɪn'lɪst] ⬦ vt - **1.** MIL enrôler - **2.** [recruit] recruter - **3.** [obtain] s'assurer. ⬦ vi MIL : **to ~ (in)** s'enrôler (dans).

enmity ['enmətɪ] n hostilité f.

enormity [ɪ'nɔːmətɪ] n [extent] étendue f.

enormous [ɪ'nɔːməs] adj énorme ; [patience, success] immense.

enough [ɪ'nʌf] ⬦ adj assez de ; **~ money/time** assez d'argent/de temps. ⬦ pron assez ; **more than ~** largement, bien assez ; **to have had ~ (of sthg)** en avoir assez (de qqch). ⬦ adv - **1.** [sufficiently] assez ; **big ~ for sthg/to do sthg** assez grand pour qqch/pour faire qqch ; **to be good ~ to do sthg** fml être assez gentil pour OR de faire qqch, être assez aimable pour OR de faire qqch - **2.** [rather] plutôt ; **strangely ~** bizarrement, c'est bizarre.

enquire [ɪn'kwaɪə'] ⬦ vt : **to ~ when/whether/how ...** demander quand/si/comment ... ⬦ vi : **to ~ (about)** se renseigner (sur).

enquiry [ɪn'kwaɪərɪ] n - **1.** [question] demande f de renseignements ; **'Enquiries'** 'renseignements' - **2.** [investigation] enquête f.

enraged [ɪn'reɪdʒd] adj déchaîné(e) ; [animal] enragé(e).

enrol, enroll Am [ɪn'rəʊl] ⬦ vt inscrire. ⬦ vi : **to ~ (in)** s'inscrire (à).

ensign ['ensaɪn] n [flag] pavillon m.

ensue [ɪn'sjuː] vi s'ensuivre.

ensure [ɪn'ʃʊə'] vt assurer ; **to ~ (that) ...** s'assurer que ...

ENT (abbr of Ear, Nose & Throat) n ORL f.

entail [ɪn'teɪl] vt entraîner ; **what does the work ~?** en quoi consiste le travail ?

enter ['entə'] ⬦ vt - **1.** [room, vehicle] entrer dans - **2.** [university, army] entrer à ; [school] s'inscrire à, s'inscrire dans - **3.** [competition, race] s'inscrire à ; [politics] se lancer dans - **4.** [register] : **to ~ sb/sthg for sthg** inscrire qqn/qqch à qqch - **5.** [write down] inscrire - **6.** COMPUT entrer. ⬦ vi - **1.** [come or go in] entrer - **2.** [register] : **to ~ (for)** s'inscrire (à). ⬥ **enter into** vt fus [negotiations, correspondence] entamer.

enter key n COMPUT (touche f) entrée f.

enterprise ['entəpraɪz] n entreprise f.

enterprise zone n Br zone dans une région défavorisée qui bénéficie de subsides de l'État.

enterprising ['entəpraɪzɪŋ] adj qui fait preuve d'initiative.

entertain [ˌentə'teɪn] vt - **1.** [amuse] divertir - **2.** [invite - guests] recevoir - **3.** fml [thought, proposal] considérer.

entertainer [ˌentə'teɪnə'] n fantaisiste mf.

entertaining [ˌentə'teɪnɪŋ] adj divertissant(e).

entertainment [ˌentə'teɪnmənt] n - **1.** (U) [amusement] divertissement m - **2.** [show] spectacle m.

enthral, enthrall Am [ɪn'θrɔːl] vt captiver.

enthrone [ɪn'θrəʊn] vt introniser.

enthusiasm [ɪn'θjuːzɪæzm] n - **1.** [passion, eagerness] : **~ (for)** enthousiasme m (pour) - **2.** [interest] passion f.

enthusiast [ɪn'θjuːzɪæst] n amateur m, -trice f.

enthusiastic [ɪnˌθjuːzɪ'æstɪk] adj enthousiaste.

entice [ɪn'taɪs] vt entraîner.

entire [ɪn'taɪə'] adj entier(ère).

entirely [ɪn'taɪəlɪ] adv totalement.

entirety [ɪn'taɪrətɪ] n : **in its ~** en entier.

entitle [ɪn'taɪtl] vt [allow] : **to ~ sb to sthg** donner droit à qqch à qqn ; **to ~ sb to do sthg** autoriser qqn à faire qqch.

entitled [ɪn'taɪtld] adj - **1.** [allowed] autorisé(e) ; **to be ~ to sthg** avoir droit à qqch ; **to be ~ to do sthg** avoir le droit de faire qqch - **2.** [called] intitulé(e).

entitlement [ɪn'taɪtlmənt] n droit m.

entrance [n 'entrəns, vt ɪn'trɑːns] ⬦ n - **1.** [way in] : **~ (to)** entrée f (de) - **2.** [arrival] entrée f - **3.** [entry] : **to gain ~ to** [building] obtenir l'accès à ; [society, university] être admis(e) dans. ⬦ vt ravir, enivrer.

entrance examination n examen m d'entrée.

entrance fee n - **1.** [to cinema, museum] droit m d'entrée - **2.** [for club] droit m d'inscription.

entrant ['entrənt] n [in race, competition] concurrent m, -e f.

entreat [ɪn'triːt] vt : **to ~ sb (to do sthg)** supplier qqn (de faire qqch).

entrenched [ɪn'trentʃt] adj ancré(e).

entrepreneur [ˌɒntrəprə'nɜː'] n entrepreneur m.

entrust [ɪn'trʌst] vt : **to ~ sthg to sb, to ~ sb with sthg** confier qqch à qqn.

entry ['entrɪ] *n* - **1.** [gen] entrée *f* ; **to gain ~ to** avoir accès à ; **'no ~'** 'défense d'entrer' ; AUT 'sens interdit' - **2.** [in competition] inscription *f* - **3.** [in dictionary] entrée *f* ; [in diary, ledger] inscription *f*.

entry form *n* formulaire *m* OR feuille *f* d'inscription.

entry phone *n* portier *m* électronique.

envelop [ɪn'veləp] *vt* envelopper.

envelope ['envələup] *n* enveloppe *f*.

envious ['envɪəs] *adj* envieux(euse).

environment [ɪn'vaɪərənmənt] *n* - **1.** [surroundings] milieu *m*, cadre *m* - **2.** [natural world] : **the ~** l'environnement *m*.

environmental [ɪn,vaɪərən'mentl] *adj* [pollution, awareness] de l'environnement ; [impact] sur l'environnement.

environmentally [ɪn,vaɪərən'mentəlɪ] *adv* [damaging] pour l'environnement ; **to be ~ aware** être sensible aux problèmes de l'environnement ; **~ friendly** qui préserve l'environnement.

envisage [ɪn'vɪzɪdʒ], **envision** *Am* [ɪn'vɪʒn] *vt* envisager.

envoy ['envɔɪ] *n* émissaire *m*.

envy ['envɪ] *n* envie *f*, jalousie *f*. ◇ *vt* envier ; **to ~ sb sthg** envier qqch a qqn.

epic ['epɪk] ◇ *adj* épique. ◇ *n* épopée *f*.

epidemic [,epɪ'demɪk] *n* épidémie *f*.

epileptic [,epɪ'leptɪk] ◇ *adj* épileptique. ◇ *n* épileptique *mf*.

episode ['epɪsəud] *n* épisode *m*.

epistle [ɪ'pɪsl] *n* épître *f*.

epitaph ['epɪtɑːf] *n* épitaphe *f*.

epitome [ɪ'pɪtəmɪ] *n* : **the ~ of** le modèle de.

epitomize, -ise [ɪ'pɪtəmaɪz] *vt* incarner.

epoch ['iːpɒk] *n* époque *f*.

equable ['ekwəbl] *adj* égal(e), constant(e).

equal ['iːkwəl] ◇ *adj* - **1.** [gen] : **~ (to)** égal(e) (à) ; **on ~ terms** d'égal à égal - **2.** [capable] : **~ to sthg** à la hauteur de qqch. ◇ *n* égal *m*, -e *f*. ◇ *vt* égaler.

equality [iː'kwɒlətɪ] *n* égalité *f*.

equalize, -ise ['iːkwəlaɪz] ◇ *vt* niveler. ◇ *vi* SPORT égaliser.

equalizer ['iːkwəlaɪzə'] *n* SPORT but *m* égalisateur.

equally ['iːkwəlɪ] *adv* - **1.** [important, stupid etc] tout aussi - **2.** [in amount] en parts égales - **3.** [also] en même temps.

equal opportunities *npl* égalité *f* des chances.

equanimity [,ekwə'nɪmətɪ] *n* sérénité *f*, égalité *f* d'âme.

equate [ɪ'kweɪt] *vt* : **to ~ sthg with** assimiler qqch à.

equation [ɪ'kweɪʒn] *n* équation *f*.

equator [ɪ'kweɪtə'] *n* : **the ~** l'équateur *m*.

equilibrium [,iːkwɪ'lɪbrɪəm] *n* équilibre *m*.

equip [ɪ'kwɪp] *vt* équiper ; **to ~ sb/sthg with** équiper qqn/qqch de, munir qqn/qqch de ; **he's well equipped for the job** il est bien préparé pour ce travail.

equipment [ɪ'kwɪpmənt] *n* (U) équipement *m*, matériel *m*.

equities ['ekwətɪz] *npl* ST EX actions *fpl* ordinaires.

equivalent [ɪ'kwɪvələnt] ◇ *adj* équivalent(e) ; **to be ~ to** être équivalent à, équivaloir à. ◇ *n* équivalent *m*.

equivocal [ɪ'kwɪvəkl] *adj* équivoque.

er [ɜː'] *excl* euh!

era ['ɪərə] (*pl* -**s**) *n* ère *f*, période *f*.

eradicate [ɪ'rædɪkeɪt] *vt* éradiquer.

erase [ɪ'reɪz] *vt* - **1.** [rub out] gommer - **2.** *fig* [memory] effacer ; [hunger, poverty] éliminer.

eraser [ɪ'reɪzə'] *n* gomme *f*.

erect [ɪ'rekt] ◇ *adj* - **1.** [person, posture] droit(e) - **2.** [penis] en érection. ◇ *vt* - **1.** [statue] ériger ; [building] construire - **2.** [tent] dresser.

erection [ɪ'rekʃn] *n* - **1.** (U) [of statue] érection *f* ; [of building] construction *f* - **2.** [erect penis] érection *f*.

ERM (*abbr of* **Exchange Rate Mechanism**) *n* mécanisme *m* des changes (du SME).

ermine ['ɜːmɪn] *n* [fur] hermine *f*.

erode [ɪ'rəud] ◇ *vt* - **1.** [rock, soil] éroder - **2.** *fig* [confidence, rights] réduire. ◇ *vi* - **1.** [rock, soil] s'éroder - **2.** *fig* [confidence] diminuer ; [rights] se réduire.

erosion [ɪ'rəuʒn] *n* - **1.** [of rock, soil] érosion *f* - **2.** *fig* [of confidence] baisse *f* ; [of rights] diminution *f*.

erotic [ɪ'rɒtɪk] *adj* érotique.

err [ɜː'] *vi* se tromper.

errand ['erənd] *n* course *f*, commission *f* ; **to go on** OR **run an ~** faire une course.

erratic [ɪ'rætɪk] *adj* irrégulier(ère).

error ['erə'] *n* erreur *f* ; **a spelling/typing ~** une faute d'orthographe/de frappe ; **an ~ of judgment** une erreur de jugement ; **in ~** par erreur.

erupt [ɪ'rʌpt] *vi* - **1.** [volcano] entrer en éruption - **2.** *fig* [violence, war] éclater.

eruption [ɪ'rʌpʃn] *n* - 1. [of volcano] éruption *f* - 2. [of violence] explosion *f* ; [of war] déclenchement *m*.

escalate ['eskəleɪt] *vi* - 1. [conflict] s'intensifier - 2. [costs] monter en flèche.

escalator ['eskəleɪtə'] *n* escalier *m* roulant.

escapade [,eskə'peɪd] *n* aventure *f*, exploit *m*.

escape [ɪ'skeɪp] ◇ *n* - 1. [gen] fuite *f*, évasion *f* ; **to make one's ~** s'échapper ; **to have a lucky ~** l'échapper belle - 2. [leakage - of gas, water] fuite *f*. ◇ *vt* échapper à. ◇ *vi* - 1. [gen] s'échapper, fuir ; [from prison] s'évader ; **to ~ from** [place] s'échapper de ; [danger, person] échapper à - 2. [survive] s'en tirer.

escapism [ɪ'skeɪpɪzm] *n (U)* évasion *f* (de la réalité).

escort [*n* 'eskɔːt, *vb* ɪ'skɔːt] ◇ *n* - 1. [guard] escorte *f* ; **under ~** sous escorte - 2. [companion - male] cavalier *m* ; [- female] hôtesse *f*. ◇ *vt* escorter, accompagner.

Eskimo ['eskɪməʊ] *(pl -s)* *n* [person] Esquimau *m*, -aude *f (attention : le terme 'Eskimo', comme son équivalent français, est souvent considéré comme injurieux en Amérique du Nord. On préférera le terme 'Inuit').*

espadrille [,espə'drɪl] *n* espadrille *f*.

especially [ɪ'speʃəlɪ] *adv* - 1. [in particular] surtout - 2. [more than usually] particulièrement - 3. [specifically] spécialement.

espionage ['espɪə,nɑːʒ] *n* espionnage *m*.

esplanade [,esplə'neɪd] *n* esplanade *f*.

Esquire [ɪ'skwaɪə'] *n* : **G. Curry ~** Monsieur G. Curry.

essay ['eseɪ] *n* - 1. SCH & UNIV dissertation *f* - 2. LITERATURE essai *m*.

essence ['esns] *n* - 1. [nature] essence *f*, nature *f* ; **in ~** par essence - 2. CULIN extrait *m*.

essential [ɪ'senʃl] *adj* - 1. [absolutely necessary] : **~ (to OR for)** indispensable (à) - 2. [basic] essentiel(elle), de base. ➤ **essentials** *npl* - 1. [basic commodities] produits *mpl* de première nécessité - 2. [most important elements] essentiel *m*.

essentially [ɪ'senʃəlɪ] *adv* fondamentalement, avant tout.

establish [ɪ'stæblɪʃ] *vt* - 1. [gen] établir ; **to ~ contact with** établir le contact avec - 2. [organization, business] fonder, créer.

establishment [ɪ'stæblɪʃmənt] *n* - 1. [gen] établissement *m* - 2. [of organization, business] fondation *f*, création *f*. ➤ **Establishment** *n* [status quo] : **the Es-**tablishment l'ordre *m* établi, l'Establishment *m*.

estate [ɪ'steɪt] *n* - 1. [land, property] propriété *f*, domaine *m* - 2. Br : **(housing) ~** lotissement *m* - 3. Br : **(industrial) ~** zone *f* industrielle - 4. JUR [inheritance] biens *mpl*.

estate agency *n Br* agence *f* immobilière.

estate agent *n Br* agent *m* immobilier.

estate car *n Br* break *m*.

esteem [ɪ'stiːm] ◇ *n* estime *f*. ◇ *vt* estimer.

esthetic *etc Am* = aesthetic *etc*.

estimate [*n* 'estɪmət, *vb* 'estɪmeɪt] ◇ *n* - 1. [calculation, judgment] estimation *f*, évaluation *f* - 2. COMM devis *m*. ◇ *vt* estimer, évaluer.

estimation [,estɪ'meɪʃn] *n* - 1. [opinion] opinion *f* - 2. [calculation] estimation *f*, évaluation *f*.

Estonia [e'stəʊnɪə] *n* Estonie *f*.

estranged [ɪ'streɪndʒd] *adj* [couple] séparé(e) ; [husband, wife] dont on s'est séparé.

estuary ['estjʊərɪ] *n* estuaire *m*.

etc. *(abbr of et cetera)* etc.

etching ['etʃɪŋ] *n* gravure *f* à l'eau forte.

eternal [ɪ'tɜːnl] *adj* - 1. [life] éternel(elle) - 2. *fig* [complaints, whining] sempiternel(elle) - 3. [truth, value] immuable.

eternity [ɪ'tɜːnətɪ] *n* éternité *f*.

ethic ['eθɪk] *n* éthique *f*, morale *f*. ➤ **ethics** ◇ *n (U)* [study] éthique *f*, morale *f*. ◇ *npl* [morals] morale *f*.

ethical ['eθɪkl] *adj* moral(e).

Ethiopia [,iːθɪ'əʊpɪə] *n* Éthiopie *f*.

ethnic ['eθnɪk] *adj* - 1. [traditions, groups] ethnique - 2. [clothes] folklorique.

ethos ['iːθɒs] *n* génie *m* (d'un peuple/ d'une civilisation).

etiquette ['etɪket] *n* convenances *fpl*, étiquette *f*.

e-trade *n (U)* cybercommerce *m*, commerce *m* électronique.

EU *(abbr of European Union)* *n* UE *f* ; **~ policy** la politique de l'Union Européenne, la politique communautaire.

eulogy ['juːlədʒɪ] *n* panégyrique *m*.

euphemism ['juːfəmɪzm] *n* euphémisme *m*.

euphoria [juː'fɔːrɪə] *n* euphorie *f*.

euro ['jʊərəʊ] *n* euro *m*.

Eurocheque ['jʊərəʊ,tʃek] *n* eurochèque *m*.

Euro MP *n Br* député *m* européen.

Europe ['jʊərəp] *n* Europe *f*.

European [ˌjʊərə'piːən] ◇ *adj* européen(enne). ◇ *n* Européen *m*, -enne *f*.

European Central Bank *n* Banque *f* centrale européenne.

European Commission *n* Commission *f* des communautés européennes.

European Community *n* : the ~ la Communauté européenne.

European Monetary System *n* : the ~ le Système monétaire européen.

European Parliament *n* : the ~ le Parlement européen.

European Union *n* Union *f* européenne.

Eurostar® ['jʊərəʊstɑːʳ] *n* Eurostar® *m*.

euro zone *n* zone *f* euro.

euthanasia [ˌjuːθə'neɪzjə] *n* euthanasie *f*.

evacuate [ɪ'vækjʊeɪt] *vt* évacuer.

evade [ɪ'veɪd] *vt* **- 1.** [gen] échapper à **- 2.** [issue, question] esquiver, éluder.

evaluate [ɪ'væljʊeɪt] *vt* évaluer.

evaporate [ɪ'væpəreɪt] *vi* **- 1.** [liquid] s'évaporer **- 2.** *fig* [hopes, fears] s'envoler ; [confidence] disparaître.

evaporated milk [ɪ'væpəreɪtɪd-] *n* lait *m* condensé (non sucré).

evasion [ɪ'veɪʒn] *n* **- 1.** [of responsibility] dérobade *f* **- 2.** [lie] faux-fuyant *m*.

evasive [ɪ'veɪsɪv] *adj* évasif(ive).

eve [iːv] *n* veille *f*.

even ['iːvn] ◇ *adj* **- 1.** [speed, rate] régulier(ère) ; [temperature, temperament] égal(e) **- 2.** [flat, level] plat(e), régulier(ère) **- 3.** [equal - contest] équilibré(e) ; [- teams, players] de la même force ; [- scores] à égalité ; **to get ~ with sb** se venger de qqn **- 4.** [not odd - number] pair(e). ◇ *adv* **- 1.** [gen] même ; **~ now** encore maintenant ; **~ then** même alors **- 2.** [in comparisons] : **~ bigger/better/more stupid** encore plus grand/mieux/plus bête. ◆ **even if** *conj* même si. ◆ **even so** *adv* quand même. ◆ **even though** *conj* bien que (+ subjunctive). ◆ **even out** ◇ *vt sep* égaliser. ◇ *vi* s'égaliser.

evening ['iːvnɪŋ] *n* soir *m* ; [duration, entertainment] soirée *f* ; **in the ~** le soir. ◆ **evenings** *adv Am* le soir.

evening class *n* cours *m* du soir.

evening dress *n* [worn by man] habit *m* de soirée ; [worn by woman] robe *f* du soir.

event [ɪ'vent] *n* **- 1.** [happening] événement *m* **- 2.** SPORT épreuve *f* **- 3.** [case] : **in the ~ of** en cas de ; **in the ~ that** au cas où. ◆ **in any event** *adv* en tout cas, de toute façon. ◆ **in the event** *adv Br* en l'occurrence, en réalité.

eventful [ɪ'ventfʊl] *adj* mouvementé(e).

eventual [ɪ'ventʃʊəl] *adj* final(e).

eventuality [ɪˌventʃʊ'ælətɪ] *n* éventualité *f*.

eventually [ɪ'ventʃʊəlɪ] *adv* finalement, en fin de compte.

ever ['evəʳ] *adv* **- 1.** [at any time] jamais ; **have you ~ been to Paris?** êtes-vous déjà allé à Paris? ; **I hardly ~ see him** je ne le vois presque jamais **- 2.** [all the time] toujours ; **as ~** comme toujours ; **for ~** pour toujours **- 3.** [for emphasis] : **~ so** tellement ; **~ such** vraiment ; **why/how ~?** pourquoi/comment donc? ◆ **ever since** ◇ *adv* depuis (ce moment-là). ◇ *conj* depuis que. ◇ *prep* depuis.

evergreen ['evəgriːn] ◇ *adj* à feuilles persistantes. ◇ *n* arbre *m* à feuilles persistantes.

everlasting [ˌevə'lɑːstɪŋ] *adj* éternel(elle).

every ['evrɪ] *adj* chaque ; **~ morning** chaque matin, tous les matins. ◆ **every now and then, every so often** *adv* de temps en temps, de temps à autre. ◆ **every other** *adj* : **~ other day** tous les deux jours, un jour sur deux ; **~ other street** une rue sur deux. ◆ **every which way** *adv Am* partout, de tous côtés.

everybody ['evrɪˌbɒdɪ] = **everyone**.

everyday ['evrɪdeɪ] *adj* quotidien(enne).

everyone ['evrɪwʌn] *pron* chacun, tout le monde.

everyplace *Am* = **everywhere**.

everything ['evrɪθɪŋ] *pron* tout.

everywhere ['evrɪweəʳ], **everyplace** *Am* ['evrɪˌpleɪs] *adv* partout.

evict [ɪ'vɪkt] *vt* expulser.

evidence ['evɪdəns] *n (U)* **- 1.** [proof] preuve *f* **- 2.** JUR [of witness] témoignage *m* ; **to give ~** témoigner.

evident ['evɪdənt] *adj* évident(e), manifeste.

evidently ['evɪdəntlɪ] *adv* **- 1.** [seemingly] apparemment **- 2.** [obviously] de toute évidence, manifestement.

evil ['iːvl] ◇ *adj* [person] mauvais(e), malveillant(e). ◇ *n* mal *m*.

evoke [ɪ'vəʊk] *vt* [memory] évoquer ; [emotion, response] susciter.

evolution [ˌiːvə'luːʃn] *n* évolution *f*.

evolve [ɪ'vɒlv] ◇ *vt* développer. ◇ *vi* : **to ~ (into/from)** se développer (en/à partir de).

ewe [juː] *n* brebis *f*.

ex- [eks] *prefix* ex-.

exacerbate [ɪɡ'zæsəbeɪt] *vt* [feeling] exacerber ; [problems] aggraver.

exact [ɪɡ'zækt] ◇ *adj* exact(e), précis(e) ; **to be ~** pour être exact OR précis, exactement. ◇ *vt* : **to ~ sthg (from)** exiger qqch (de).

exacting [ɪɡ'zæktɪŋ] *adj* [job, standards] astreignant(e) ; [person] exigeant(e).

exactly [ɪɡ'zæktlɪ] ◇ *adv* exactement. ◇ *excl* exactement!, parfaitement!

exaggerate [ɪɡ'zædʒəreɪt] *vt & vi* exagérer.

exaggeration [ɪɡˌzædʒə'reɪʃn] *n* exagération *f*.

exalted [ɪɡ'zɔːltɪd] *adj* haut placé(e).

exam [ɪɡ'zæm] *n* examen *m* ; **to take** OR **sit an ~** passer un examen.

examination [ɪɡˌzæmɪ'neɪʃn] *n* examen *m*.

examine [ɪɡ'zæmɪn] *vt* - **1.** [gen] examiner ; [passport] contrôler - **2.** JUR, SCH & UNIV interroger.

examiner [ɪɡ'zæmɪnə'] *n* examinateur *m*, -trice *f*.

example [ɪɡ'zɑːmpl] *n* exemple *m* ; **for ~** par exemple.

exasperate [ɪɡ'zæspəreɪt] *vt* exaspérer.

exasperation [ɪɡˌzæspə'reɪʃn] *n* exaspération *f*.

excavate ['ekskəveɪt] *vt* - **1.** [land] creuser - **2.** [object] déterrer.

exceed [ɪk'siːd] *vt* - **1.** [amount, number] excéder - **2.** [limit, expectations] dépasser.

exceedingly [ɪk'siːdɪŋlɪ] *adv* extrêmement.

excel [ɪk'sel] *vi* : **to ~ (in** OR **at)** exceller (dans) ; **to ~ o.s.** *Br* se surpasser.

excellence ['eksələns] *n* excellence *f*, supériorité *f*.

excellent ['eksələnt] *adj* excellent(e).

except [ɪk'sept] ◇ *prep & conj* : **~ (for)** à part, sauf. ◇ *vt* : **to ~ sb (from)** exclure qqn (de).

excepting [ɪk'septɪŋ] *prep & conj* = **except.**

exception [ɪk'sepʃn] *n* - **1.** [exclusion] : **~ (to)** exception *f* (à) ; **with the ~ of** à l'exception de - **2.** [offence] : **to take ~ to** s'offenser de, se froisser de.

exceptional [ɪk'sepʃənl] *adj* exceptionnel(elle).

excerpt ['eksɜːpt] *n* : **~ (from)** extrait *m* (de), passage *m* (de).

excess [ɪk'ses, *before nouns* 'ekses] ◇ *adj* excédentaire. ◇ *n* excès *m*.

excess baggage *n* excédent *m* de bagages.

excess fare *n Br* supplément *m*.

excessive [ɪk'sesɪv] *adj* excessif(ive).

exchange [ɪks'tʃeɪndʒ] ◇ *n* - **1.** [gen] échange *m* ; **in ~ (for)** en échange (de) - **2.** TELEC : (telephone) ~ central *m* (téléphonique). ◇ *vt* [swap] échanger ; **to ~ sthg for sthg** échanger qqch contre qqch ; **to ~ sthg with sb** échanger qqch avec qqn.

exchange rate *n* FIN taux *m* de change.

Exchequer [ɪks'tʃekə'] *n Br* : **the ~** ≃ le ministère des Finances.

excise ['eksaɪz] *n (U)* contributions *fpl* indirectes.

excite [ɪk'saɪt] *vt* exciter.

excited [ɪk'saɪtɪd] *adj* excité(e).

excitement [ɪk'saɪtmənt] *n* [state] excitation *f*.

exciting [ɪk'saɪtɪŋ] *adj* passionnant(e) ; [prospect] excitant(e).

exclaim [ɪk'skleɪm] ◇ *vt* s'écrier. ◇ *vi* s'exclamer.

exclamation [ˌeksklə'meɪʃn] *n* exclamation *f*.

exclamation mark *Br*, **exclamation point** *Am n* point *m* d'exclamation.

exclude [ɪk'skluːd] *vt* : **to ~ sb/sthg (from)** exclure qqn/qqch (de).

excluding [ɪk'skluːdɪŋ] *prep* sans compter, à l'exclusion de.

exclusive [ɪk'skluːsɪv] ◇ *adj* - **1.** [high-class] fermé(e) - **2.** [unique - use, news story] exclusif(ive). ◇ *n* PRESS exclusivité *f*.
➡ **exclusive of** *prep* : **~ of interest** intérêts non compris.

excrement ['ekskrɪmənt] *n* excrément *m*.

excruciating [ɪk'skruːʃɪeɪtɪŋ] *adj* atroce.

excursion [ɪk'skɜːʃn] *n* [trip] excursion *f*.

excuse [*n* ɪk'skjuːs, *vb* ɪk'skjuːz] ◇ *n* excuse *f*. ◇ *vt* - **1.** [gen] excuser ; **to ~ sb for sthg/for doing sthg** excuser qqn de qqch/de faire qqch ; **~ me** [to attract attention] excusez-moi ; [forgive me] pardon, excusez-moi ; *Am* [sorry] pardon - **2.** [let off] : **to ~ sb (from)** dispenser qqn (de).

ex-directory *adj Br* qui est sur la liste rouge.

execute ['eksɪkjuːt] *vt* exécuter.

execution [ˌeksɪ'kjuːʃn] *n* exécution *f*.

executioner [ˌeksɪ'kjuːʃnə'] *n* bourreau *m*.

executive [ɪɡ'zekjʊtɪv] ◇ *adj* [power,

board] exécutif(ive). <> *n* - **1.** COMM cadre *m* - **2.** [of government] exécutif *m* ; [of political party] comité *m* central, bureau *m*.

executive director *n* cadre *m* supérieur.

executor [ɪɡ'zekjʊtəʳ] *n* exécuteur *m* testamentaire.

exemplify [ɪɡ'zemplɪfaɪ] *vt* - **1.** [typify] exemplifier - **2.** [give example of] exemplifier, illustrer.

exempt [ɪɡ'zempt] <> *adj* : ~ **(from)** exempt(e) (de). <> *vt* : **to ~ sb (from)** exempter qqn (de).

exercise ['eksəsaɪz] <> *n* exercice *m*. <> *vt* [gen] exercer. <> *vi* prendre de l'exercice.

exercise book *n* [notebook] cahier *m* d'exercices ; [published book] livre *m* d'exercices.

exert [ɪɡ'zɜːt] *vt* exercer ; [strength] employer ; **to ~ o.s.** se donner du mal.

exertion [ɪɡ'zɜːʃn] *n* effort *m*.

exhale [eks'heɪl] <> *vt* exhaler. <> *vi* expirer.

exhaust [ɪɡ'zɔːst] <> *n* - **1.** *(U)* [fumes] gaz *mpl* d'échappement - **2.** : ~ **(pipe)** pot *m* d'échappement. <> *vt* épuiser.

exhausted [ɪɡ'zɔːstɪd] *adj* épuisé(e).

exhausting [ɪɡ'zɔːstɪŋ] *adj* épuisant(e).

exhaustion [ɪɡ'zɔːstʃn] *n* épuisement *m*.

exhaustive [ɪɡ'zɔːstɪv] *adj* complet(ète), exhaustif(ive).

exhibit [ɪɡ'zɪbɪt] <> *n* - **1.** ART objet *m* exposé - **2.** JUR pièce *f* à conviction. <> *vt* - **1.** [demonstrate - feeling] montrer ; [- skill] faire preuve de - **2.** ART exposer.

exhibition [ˌeksɪ'bɪʃn] *n* - **1.** ART exposition *f* - **2.** [of feeling] démonstration *f* - **3.** *phr* : **to make an ~ of o.s.** *Br* se donner en spectacle.

exhilarating [ɪɡ'zɪləreɪtɪŋ] *adj* [experience] grisant(e) ; [walk] vivifiant(e).

exile ['eksaɪl] <> *n* - **1.** [condition] exil *m* ; **in ~** en exil - **2.** [person] exilé *m*, -e *f*. <> *vt* : **to ~ sb (from/to)** exiler qqn (de/vers).

exist [ɪɡ'zɪst] *vi* exister.

existence [ɪɡ'zɪstəns] *n* existence *f* ; **in ~** qui existe, existant(e) ; **to come into ~** naître.

existing [ɪɡ'zɪstɪŋ] *adj* existant(e).

exit ['eksɪt] <> *n* sortie *f*. <> *vi* sortir.

exodus ['eksədəs] *n* exode *m*.

exonerate [ɪɡ'zɒnəreɪt] *vt* : **to ~ sb (from)** disculper qqn (de).

exorbitant [ɪɡ'zɔːbɪtənt] *adj* exorbitant(e).

exotic [ɪɡ'zɒtɪk] *adj* exotique.

expand [ɪk'spænd] <> *vt* [production, influence] accroître ; [business, department, area] développer. <> *vi* [population, influence] s'accroître ; [business, department, market] se développer ; [metal] se dilater.
◆ **expand (up)on** *vt fus* développer.

expanse [ɪk'spæns] *n* étendue *f*.

expansion [ɪk'spænʃn] *n* [of production, population] accroissement *m* ; [of business, department, area] développement *m* ; [of metal] dilatation *f*.

expect [ɪk'spekt] <> *vt* - **1.** [anticipate] s'attendre à ; [event, letter, baby] attendre ; **when do you ~ it to be ready?** quand pensez-vous que cela sera prêt? ; **to ~ sb to do sthg** s'attendre à ce que qqn fasse qqch - **2.** [count on] compter sur - **3.** [demand] exiger, demander ; **to ~ sb to do sthg** attendre de qqn qu'il fasse qqch ; **to ~ sthg from sb** exiger qqch de qqn - **4.** [suppose] supposer ; **I ~ so** je crois que oui. <> *vi* - **1.** [anticipate] : **to ~ to do sthg** compter faire qqch - **2.** [be pregnant] : **to be ~ing** être enceinte, attendre un bébé.

expectancy ⊳ **life expectancy**.

expectant [ɪk'spektənt] *adj* qui est dans l'expectative.

expectant mother *n* femme *f* enceinte.

expectation [ˌekspek'teɪʃn] *n* - **1.** [hope] espoir *m*, attente *f* - **2.** [belief] : **it's my ~ that ...** à mon avis, ... ; **against all ~** OR **~s, contrary to all ~** OR **~s** contre toute attente.

expedient [ɪk'spiːdjənt] *fml* <> *adj* indiqué(e). <> *n* expédient *m*.

expedition [ˌekspɪ'dɪʃn] *n* expédition *f*.

expel [ɪk'spel] *vt* - **1.** [gen] expulser - **2.** SCH renvoyer.

expend [ɪk'spend] *vt* : **to ~ time/money (on)** consacrer du temps/de l'argent (à).

expendable [ɪk'spendəbl] *adj* dont on peut se passer, qui n'est pas indispensable.

expenditure [ɪk'spendɪtʃəʳ] *n (U)* dépense *f*.

expense [ɪk'spens] *n* - **1.** [amount spent] dépense *f* - **2.** *(U)* [cost] frais *mpl* ; **at the ~ of** au prix de ; **at sb's ~** [financial] aux frais de qqn ; *fig* aux dépens de qqn. ◆ **expenses** *npl* COMM frais *mpl*.

expense account *n* frais *mpl* de représentation.

expensive [ɪk'spensɪv] *adj* - **1.** [financially] - gen] cher (chère), coûteux(euse) ; [- tastes] dispendieux(euse) - **2.** [mistake] qui coûte cher.

experience [ɪk'spɪərɪəns] <> *n* expérience *f*. <> *vt* [difficulty] connaître ; [disappointment] éprouver, ressentir ; [loss, change] subir.

experienced [ɪk'spɪərɪənst] *adj* expérimenté(e) ; **to be ~ at** OR **in sthg** avoir de l'expérience en OR en matière de qqch.

experiment [ɪk'sperɪmənt] <> *n* expérience *f* ; **to carry out an ~** faire une expérience. <> *vi* : **to ~ (with sthg)** expérimenter (qqch).

expert ['ekspɜːt] <> *adj* expert(e) ; [advice] d'expert. <> *n* expert *m*, -e *f*.

expertise [ˌekspɜː'tiːz] *n (U)* compétence *f*.

expire [ɪk'spaɪər] *vi* expirer.

expiry [ɪk'spaɪərɪ] *n* expiration *f*.

explain [ɪk'spleɪn] <> *vt* expliquer ; **to ~ sthg to sb** expliquer qqch à qqn. <> *vi* s'expliquer ; **to ~ to sb (about sthg)** expliquer (qqch) à qqn.

explanation [ˌekspləˈneɪʃn] *n* : **~ (for)** explication *f* (de).

explicit [ɪk'splɪsɪt] *adj* explicite.

explode [ɪk'spləʊd] <> *vt* [bomb] faire exploser. <> *vi lit & fig* exploser.

exploit [*n* 'eksplɔɪt, *vb* ɪk'splɔɪt] <> *n* exploit *m*. <> *vt* exploiter.

exploitation [ˌeksplɔɪ'teɪʃn] *n (U)* exploitation *f*.

exploration [ˌeksplə'reɪʃn] *n* exploration *f*.

explore [ɪk'splɔːr] *vt & vi* explorer.

explorer [ɪk'splɔːrər] *n* explorateur *m*, -trice *f*.

explosion [ɪk'spləʊʒn] *n* explosion *f* ; [of interest] débordement *m*.

explosive [ɪk'spləʊsɪv] <> *adj lit & fig* explosif(ive). <> *n* explosif *m*.

exponent [ɪk'spəʊnənt] *n* [of theory] défenseur *m*.

export [*n & comp* 'ekspɔːt, *vb* ɪk'spɔːt] <> *n* exportation *f*. <> *comp* d'exportation. <> *vt* exporter.

exporter [ek'spɔːtər] *n* exportateur *m*, -trice *f*.

expose [ɪk'spəʊz] *vt* - **1.** [uncover] exposer, découvrir ; **to be ~d to sthg** être exposé à qqch - **2.** [unmask - corruption] révéler ; [- person] démasquer.

exposed [ɪk'spəʊzd] *adj* [land, house, position] exposé(e).

exposure [ɪk'spəʊʒər] *n* - **1.** [to light, radiation] exposition *f* - **2.** MED : **to die of ~** mourir de froid - **3.** [PHOT - time] temps *m* de pose ; [- photograph] pose *f* - **4.** *(U)* [publicity] publicité *f* ; [coverage] couverture *f*.

exposure meter *n* posemètre *m*.

expound [ɪk'spaʊnd] *fml* <> *vt* exposer. <> *vi* : **to ~ on** faire un exposé sur.

express [ɪk'spres] <> *adj* - **1.** *Br* [letter, delivery] exprès *(inv)* - **2.** [train, coach] express *(inv)* - **3.** *fml* [specific] exprès(esse). <> *adv* exprès. <> *n* [train] rapide *m*, express *m*. <> *vt* exprimer.

expression [ɪk'spreʃn] *n* expression *f*.

expressive [ɪk'spresɪv] *adj* expressif(ive).

expressly [ɪk'spreslɪ] *adv* expressément.

expressway [ɪk'spresweɪ] *n Am* voie *f* express.

exquisite [ɪk'skwɪzɪt] *adj* exquis(e).

ext., extn. *(abbr of* **extension***)* : **~ 4174** p. 4174.

extend [ɪk'stend] <> *vt* - **1.** [enlarge - building] agrandir - **2.** [make longer - gen] prolonger ; [- visa] proroger ; [- deadline] repousser - **3.** [expand - rules, law] étendre ; [- power] accroître - **4.** [stretch out - arm, hand] étendre - **5.** [offer - help] apporter, offrir ; [- credit] accorder. <> *vi* [stretch - in space] s'étendre ; [- in time] continuer.

extension [ɪk'stenʃn] *n* - **1.** [to building] agrandissement *m* - **2.** [lengthening - gen] prolongement *m* ; [- of visit] prolongation *f* ; [- of visa] prorogation *f* ; [- of deadline] report *m* - **3.** [of power] accroissement *m* ; [of law] élargissement *m* - **4.** TELEC poste *m* - **5.** ELEC prolongateur *m*.

extension cable *n* rallonge *f*.

extensive [ɪk'stensɪv] *adj* - **1.** [in amount] considérable - **2.** [in area] vaste - **3.** [in range - discussions] approfondi(e) ; [- changes, use] considérable.

extensively [ɪk'stensɪvlɪ] *adv* - **1.** [in amount] considérablement - **2.** [in range] abondamment, largement.

extent [ɪk'stent] *n* - **1.** [of land, area] étendue *f*, superficie *f* ; [of problem, damage] étendue - **2.** [degree] : **to what ~ ...?** dans quelle mesure ...? ; **to the ~ that** [in so far as] dans la mesure où ; [to the point where] au point que ; **to a certain ~** jusqu'à un certain point ; **to a large** OR **great ~** en grande partie ; **to some ~** en partie.

extenuating circumstances [ɪk'stenjʊeɪtɪŋ-] *npl* circonstances *fpl* atténuantes.

exterior [ɪk'stɪərɪər] <> *adj* extérieur(e). <> *n* - **1.** [of house, car] extérieur *m* - **2.** [of person] dehors *m*, extérieur *m*.

exterminate [ɪk'stɜːmɪneɪt] *vt* exterminer.

external [ɪk'stɜːnl] *adj* externe.

115   **face**

extinct [ɪk'stɪŋkt] *adj* - **1.** [species] dispa-
ru(e) - **2.** [volcano] éteint(e).

extinguish [ɪk'stɪŋgwɪʃ] *vt* [fire, cigarette]
éteindre.

extinguisher [ɪk'stɪŋgwɪʃəʳ] *n* extincteur
m.

extn. = ext.

extol, extoll *Am* [ɪk'stəʊl] *vt* louer.

extort [ɪk'stɔːt] *vt* : **to ~ sthg from sb** extorquer qqch à qqn.

extortionate [ɪk'stɔːʃnət] *adj* exorbi-
tant(e).

extra ['ekstrə] ◇ *adj* supplémentaire.
◇ *n* - **1.** [addition] supplément *m* ; optional ~ option *f* - **2.** CINEMA & THEATRE figurant
m, -e *f*. ◇ *adv* [hard, big etc] extra ; [pay,
charge etc] en plus.

extra- ['ekstrə] *prefix* extra-.

extract [*n* 'ekstrækt, *vb* ɪk'strækt] ◇ *n*
extrait *m*. ◇ *vt* - **1.** [take out - tooth] arracher ; **to ~ sthg from** tirer qqch de - **2.** [con-
fession, information] : **to ~ sthg (from sb)**
arracher qqch (à qqn), tirer qqch (de qqn)
- **3.** [coal, oil] extraire.

extradite ['ekstrədaɪt] *vt* : **to ~ sb (from/
to)** extrader qqn (de/vers).

extramarital [ˌekstrə'mærɪtl] *adj* extra-
conjugal(e).

extramural [ˌekstrə'mjʊərəl] *adj* UNIV
hors faculté.

extraordinary [ɪk'strɔːdnrɪ] *adj* extraordinaire.

extraordinary general meeting *n* assemblée *f* générale extraordinaire.

extravagance [ɪk'strævəgəns] *n* - **1.** *(U)*
[excessive spending] gaspillage *m*, prodiga-
lités *fpl* - **2.** [luxury] extravagance *f*, folie *f*.

extravagant [ɪk'strævəgənt] *adj*
- **1.** [wasteful - person] dépensier(ère) ;
[- use, tastes] dispendieux(euse) - **2.** [elab-
orate, exaggerated] extravagant(e).

extreme [ɪk'striːm] ◇ *adj* extrême. ◇ *n*
extrême *m*.

extremely [ɪk'striːmlɪ] *adv* extrêmement.

extremist [ɪk'striːmɪst] ◇ *adj* extrémiste. ◇ *n* extrémiste *mf*.

extricate ['ekstrɪkeɪt] *vt* : **to ~ sthg (from)**
dégager qqch (de) ; **to ~ o.s. (from)** [from
seat belt etc] s'extirper (de) ; [from difficult
situation] se tirer (de).

extrovert ['ekstrəvɜːt] ◇ *adj* extraver-
ti(e). ◇ *n* extraverti *m*, -e *f*.

exuberance [ɪg'zjuːbərəns] *n* exubé-
rance *f*.

exultant [ɪg'zʌltənt] *adj* triomphant(e).

eye [aɪ] *(cont* eyeing *OR* eying) ◇ *n*
- **1.** [gen] œil *m* ; **to cast** *OR* **run one's ~ over**
sthg jeter un coup d'œil sur qqch ; **to catch
sb's ~** attirer l'attention de qqn ; **to have
one's ~ on sb** avoir qqn à l'œil ; **to have
one's ~ on sthg** avoir repéré qqch ; **to keep
one's ~s open for sthg** [try to find] essayer
de repérer qqch ; **to keep an ~ on sthg** surveiller qqch, garder l'œil sur qqch - **2.** [of
needle] chas *m*. ◇ *vt* regarder, reluquer.

eyeball ['aɪbɔːl] *n* globe *m* oculaire.

eyebath ['aɪbɑːθ] *n* œillère *f* *(pour bains
d'œil)*.

eyebrow ['aɪbraʊ] *n* sourcil *m*.

eyebrow pencil *n* crayon *m* à sourcils.

eyedrops ['aɪdrɒps] *npl* gouttes *fpl* pour
les yeux.

eyelash ['aɪlæʃ] *n* cil *m*.

eyelid ['aɪlɪd] *n* paupière *f*.

eyeliner ['aɪˌlaɪnəʳ] *n* eye-liner *m*.

eye-opener *n inf* révélation *f*.

eye shadow *n* fard *m* à paupières.

eyesight ['aɪsaɪt] *n* vue *f*.

eyesore ['aɪsɔːʳ] *n* horreur *f*.

eyestrain ['aɪstreɪn] *n* fatigue *f* des yeux.

eyewitness [ˌaɪ'wɪtnɪs] *n* témoin *m* oculaire.

f (*pl* **f's** *OR* **fs**), **F** (*pl* **F's** *OR* **Fs**) [ef] *n* [letter] f *m*
inv, F *m inv*. ◆ **F** *n* - **1.** MUS fa *m* - **2.** (*abbr of*
Fahrenheit) F.

fable ['feɪbl] *n* fable *f*.

fabric ['fæbrɪk] *n* - **1.** [cloth] tissu *m* - **2.** [of
building, society] structure *f*.

fabrication [ˌfæbrɪ'keɪʃn] *n* - **1.** [lie, lying]
fabrication *f*, invention *f* - **2.** [manufacture]
fabrication *f*.

fabulous ['fæbjʊləs] *adj* - **1.** [gen] fabu-
leux(euse) - **2.** *inf* [excellent] sensation-
nel(elle), fabuleux(euse).

facade [fə'sɑːd] *n* façade *f*.

face [feɪs] ◇ *n* - **1.** [of person] visage *m*, figure *f* ; **~ to ~** face à face ; **to say sthg to sb's
~** dire qqch à qqn en face - **2.** [expression]
visage *m*, mine *f* ; **to make** *OR* **pull a ~** faire la
grimace - **3.** [of cliff, mountain] face *f*, paroi

f ; [of building] façade *f* ; [of clock, watch] cadran *m* ; [of coin, shape] face - **4.** [surface - of planet] surface *f* ; **on the ~ of it** à première vue - **5.** [respect] : **to save/lose ~** sauver/perdre la face. ◇ *vt* - **1.** [look towards - subj : person] faire face à ; **the house ~s the sea/south** la maison donne sur la mer/est orientée vers le sud - **2.** [decision, crisis] être confronté(e) à ; [problem, danger] faire face à - **3.** [facts, truth] faire face à, admettre - **4.** *inf* [cope with] affronter.
➤ **face down** *adv* [person] face contre terre ; [object] à l'envers ; [card] face en dessous. ➤ **face up** *adv* [person] sur le dos ; [object] à l'endroit ; [card] face en dessus. ➤ **in the face of** *prep* devant. ➤ **face up to** *vt fus* faire face à.

facecloth ['feɪsklɒθ] *n* Br gant *m* de toilette.

face cream *n* crème *f* pour le visage.

face-lift *n* lifting *m* ; *fig* restauration *f*, rénovation *f*.

face powder *n* poudre *f* de riz, poudre pour le visage.

face-saving [-ˌseɪvɪŋ] *adj* qui sauve la face.

facet ['fæsɪt] *n* facette *f*.

facetious [fə'siːʃəs] *adj* facétieux(euse).

face value *n* [of coin, stamp] valeur *f* nominale ; **to take sthg at ~** prendre qqch au pied de la lettre.

facility [fə'sɪlətɪ] *n* [feature] fonction *f*.
➤ **facilities** *npl* [amenities] équipement *m*, aménagement *m*.

facing ['feɪsɪŋ] *adj* d'en face ; [sides] opposé(e).

facsimile [fæk'sɪmɪlɪ] *n* - **1.** [fax] télécopie *f*, fax *m* - **2.** [copy] fac-similé *m*.

fact [fækt] *n* - **1.** [true piece of information] fait *m* ; **to know sthg for a ~** savoir pertinemment qqch - (U) [truth] réalité *mpl*, réalité *f*. ➤ **in fact** ◇ *adv* de fait, effectivement. ◇ *conj* en fait.

fact of life *n* fait *m*, réalité *f* ; **the facts of life** *euphemism* les choses *fpl* de la vie.

factor ['fæktə'] *n* facteur *m*.

factory ['fæktərɪ] *n* fabrique *f*, usine *f*.

fact sheet *n* Br résumé *m*, brochure *f*.

factual ['fæktʃʊəl] *adj* factuel(elle), basé(e) sur les faits.

faculty ['fækltɪ] *n* - **1.** [gen] faculté *f* - **2.** Am [in college] : **the ~** le corps enseignant.

FA Cup *n en Angleterre, championnat de football dont la finale se joue à Wembley.*

fad [fæd] *n* engouement *m*, mode *f* ; [personal] marotte *f*.

fade [feɪd] ◇ *vt* [jeans, curtains, paint] décolorer. ◇ *vi* - **1.** [jeans, curtains, paint] se décolorer ; [colour] passer ; [flower] se flétrir - **2.** [light] baisser, diminuer - **3.** [sound] diminuer, s'affaiblir - **4.** [memory] s'effacer ; [feeling, interest] diminuer.

faeces Br, **feces** Am ['fiːsiːz] *npl* fèces *fpl*.

fag [fæg] *n inf* - **1.** Br [cigarette] clope *m* - **2.** Am *pej* [homosexual] pédé *m*.

Fahrenheit ['færənhaɪt] *adj* Fahrenheit *(inv)*.

fail [feɪl] ◇ *vt* - **1.** [exam, test] rater, échouer à - **2.** [not succeed] : **to ~ to do sthg** ne pas arriver à faire qqch - **3.** [neglect] : **to ~ to do sthg** manquer OR omettre de faire qqch - **4.** [candidate] refuser. ◇ *vi* - **1.** [not succeed] ne pas réussir OR y arriver - **2.** [not pass exam] échouer - **3.** [stop functioning] lâcher - **4.** [weaken - health, daylight] décliner ; [- eyesight] baisser.

failing ['feɪlɪŋ] ◇ *n* [weakness] défaut *m*, point *m* faible. ◇ *prep* à moins de ; **~ that** à défaut.

failure ['feɪljə'] *n* - **1.** [lack of success, unsuccessful thing] échec *m* - **2.** [person] raté *m*, -e *f* - **3.** [of engine, brake etc] défaillance *f* ; [of crop] perte *f*.

faint [feɪnt] ◇ *adj* - **1.** [smell] léger(ère) ; [memory] vague ; [sound, hope] faible - **2.** [slight - chance] petit(e), faible - **3.** [dizzy] : **I'm feeling a bit ~** je ne me sens pas bien. ◇ *vi* s'évanouir.

fair [feə'] ◇ *adj* - **1.** [just] juste, équitable ; **it's not ~!** ce n'est pas juste! - **2.** [quite large] grand(e), important(e) - **3.** [quite good] assez bon (assez bonne) - **4.** [hair] blond(e) - **5.** [skin, complexion] clair(e) - **6.** [weather] beau (belle). ◇ *n* - **1.** Br [funfair] fête *f* foraine - **2.** [trade fair] foire *f*. ◇ *adv* [fairly] loyalement. ➤ **fair enough** *adv* Br *inf* OK, d'accord.

fair-haired [-'heəd] *adj* [person] blond(e).

fairly ['feəlɪ] *adv* - **1.** [rather] assez ; **~ certain** presque sûr - **2.** [justly] équitablement ; [describe] avec impartialité ; [fight, play] loyalement.

fairness ['feənɪs] *n* [justness] équité *f*.

fairy ['feərɪ] *n* [imaginary creature] fée *f*.

fairy tale *n* conte *m* de fées.

faith [feɪθ] *n* - **1.** [belief] foi *f*, confiance *f* - **2.** RELIG foi *f*.

faithful ['feɪθfʊl] *adj* fidèle.

faithfully ['feɪθfʊlɪ] *adv* [loyally] fidèlement ; **Yours ~** Br [in letter] je vous prie d'agréer mes salutations distinguées.

fake [feɪk] ⇔ *adj* faux (fausse). ⇔ *n* - **1.** [object, painting] faux *m* - **2.** [person] imposteur *m*. ⇔ *vt* - **1.** [results] falsifier ; [signature] imiter - **2.** [illness, emotions] simuler. ⇔ *vi* [pretend] simuler, faire semblant.

falcon ['fɔ:lkən] *n* faucon *m*.

Falkland Islands ['fɔ:klənd-], **Falklands** ['fɔ:kləndz] *npl* : **the ~** les îles *fpl* Falkland, les Malouines *fpl*.

fall [fɔ:l] (*pt* fell, *pp* fallen) ⇔ *vi* - **1.** [gen] tomber ; **to ~ flat** [joke] tomber à plat - **2.** [decrease] baisser - **3.** [become] : **to ~ asleep** s'endormir ; **to ~ ill** tomber malade ; **to ~ in love** tomber amoureux(euse). ⇔ *n* - **1.** [gen] : **~ (in)** chute (de) - **2.** *Am* [autumn] automne *m*. ◆ **falls** *npl* chutes *fpl*. ◆ **fall apart** *vi* - **1.** [disintegrate - book, chair] tomber en morceaux - **2.** *fig* [country] tomber en ruine ; [person] s'effondrer. ◆ **fall back** *vi* [person, crowd] reculer. ◆ **fall back on** *vt fus* [resort to] se rabattre sur. ◆ **fall behind** *vi* - **1.** [in race] se faire distancer - **2.** [with rent] être en retard ; **to ~ behind with one's work** avoir du retard dans son travail. ◆ **fall for** *vt fus* - **1.** *inf* [fall in love with] tomber amoureux(euse) de - **2.** [trick, lie] se laisser prendre à. ◆ **fall in** *vi* - **1.** [roof, ceiling] s'écrouler, s'affaisser - **2.** MIL former les rangs. ◆ **fall off** *vi* - **1.** [branch, handle] se détacher, tomber - **2.** [demand, numbers] baisser, diminuer. ◆ **fall out** *vi* - **1.** [hair, tooth] tomber - **2.** [friends] se brouiller - **3.** MIL rompre les rangs. ◆ **fall over** ⇔ *vt fus* : **to ~ over sthg** trébucher sur qqch et tomber. ⇔ *vi* [person, chair etc] tomber. ◆ **fall through** *vi* [plan, deal] échouer.

fallacy ['fæləsɪ] *n* erreur *f*, idée *f* fausse.

fallen ['fɔ:ln] *pp* ▷ **fall**.

fallible ['fæləbl] *adj* faillible.

fallout ['fɔ:laʊt] *n* (U) [radiation] retombées *fpl*.

fallout shelter *n* abri *m* antiatomique.

fallow ['fæləʊ] *adj* : **to lie ~** être en jachère.

false [fɔ:ls] *adj* faux (fausse).

false alarm *n* fausse alerte *f*.

falsely ['fɔ:lslɪ] *adv* à tort ; [smile, laugh] faussement.

false teeth *npl* dentier *m*.

falsify ['fɔ:lsɪfaɪ] *vt* falsifier.

falter ['fɔ:ltər] *vi* - **1.** [move unsteadily] chanceler - **2.** [steps, voice] devenir hésitant(e) - **3.** [hesitate, lose confidence] hésiter.

fame [feɪm] *n* gloire *f*, renommée *f*.

familiar [fə'mɪljər] *adj* familier(ère) ; **~ with sthg** familiarisé(e) avec qqch.

familiarity [fə,mɪlɪ'ærətɪ] *n* (U) [knowledge] : **~ with sthg** connaissance *f* de qqch, familiarité *f* avec qqch.

familiarize, **-ise** [fə'mɪljəraɪz] *vt* : **to ~ o.s. with sthg** se familiariser avec qqch ; **to ~ sb with sthg** familiariser qqn avec qqch.

family ['fæmlɪ] *n* famille *f*.

family credit *n* (U) *Br* ≃ complément *m* familial.

family doctor *n* médecin *m* de famille.

family planning *n* planning *m* familial ; **~ clinic** centre *m* de planning familial.

famine ['fæmɪn] *n* famine *f*.

famished ['fæmɪʃt] *adj inf* [very hungry] affamé(e) ; **I'm ~!** je meurs de faim!

famous ['feɪməs] *adj* : **~ (for)** célèbre (pour).

famously ['feɪməslɪ] *adv dated* : **to get on** OR **along ~** s'entendre comme larrons en foire.

fan [fæn] ⇔ *n* - **1.** [of paper, silk] éventail *m* - **2.** [electric or mechanical] ventilateur *m* - **3.** [enthusiast] fan *mf*. ⇔ *vt* - **1.** [face] éventer - **2.** [fire, feelings] attiser. ◆ **fan out** *vi* se déployer.

fanatic [fə'nætɪk] *n* fanatique *mf*.

fan belt *n* courroie *f* de ventilateur.

fanciful ['fænsɪfʊl] *adj* - **1.** [odd] bizarre, fantasque - **2.** [elaborate] extravagant(e).

fancy ['fænsɪ] ⇔ *adj* - **1.** [elaborate - hat, clothes] extravagant(e) ; [- food, cakes] raffiné(e) - **2.** [expensive - restaurant, hotel] de luxe ; [- prices] fantaisiste. ⇔ *n* [desire, liking] envie *f*, lubie *f* ; **to take a ~ to sb** se prendre d'affection pour qqn ; **to take a ~ to sthg** se mettre à aimer qqch ; **to take sb's ~** faire envie à qqn, plaire à qqn. ⇔ *vt* - **1.** *inf* [want] avoir envie de ; **to ~ doing sthg** avoir envie de faire qqch - **2.** *inf* [like] : **I ~ her** elle me plaît - **3.** [imagine] : **~ that!** ça alors!

fancy dress *n* (U) déguisement *m*.

fancy-dress party *n* bal *m* costumé.

fanfare ['fænfeər] *n* fanfare *f*.

fang [fæŋ] *n* [of wolf] croc *m* ; [of snake] crochet *m*.

fan heater *n* radiateur *m* soufflant.

fanny ['fænɪ] *n Am inf* [buttocks] fesses *fpl*.

fantasize, **-ise** ['fæntəsaɪz] *vi* : **to ~ (about sthg/about doing sthg)** fantasmer (sur qqch/sur le fait de faire qqch).

fantastic [fæn'tæstɪk] *adj* - **1.** *inf* [wonderful] fantastique, formidable - **2.** [incredible] extraordinaire, incroyable.

fantasy ['fæntəsɪ] *n* - **1.** [dream, imaginary event] rêve *m*, fantasme *m* - **2.** *(U)* [fiction] fiction *f* - **3.** [imagination] fantaisie *f*.

fantasy football *n jeu où chaque participant se constitue une équipe virtuelle avec les noms de footballeurs réels, chaque but marqué par ceux-ci dans la réalité valant un point dans le jeu.*

fao *(abbr of* **for the attention of)** à l'attention de.

FAQ [fak, ɛfeɪ'kjuː] *(abbr of* **frequently asked questions)** *n* COMPUT foire *f* aux questions, FAQ *f*.

far [faːʳ] *(compar* **farther** OR **further**, *superl* **farthest** OR **furthest)** ⬦ *adv* - **1.** [in distance] loin ; **how ~ is it?** c'est à quelle distance?, (est-ce que) c'est loin? ; **have you come ~?** vous venez de loin? ; **~ away** OR **off** loin ; **~ and wide** partout ; **as ~ as** jusqu'à - **2.** [in time] : **~ away** OR **off** loin ; **so ~** jusqu'à maintenant, jusqu'ici - **3.** [in degree or extent] bien ; **as ~ as** autant que ; **as ~ as I'm concerned** en ce qui me concerne ; **as ~ as possible** autant que possible, dans la mesure du possible ; **~ and away, by ~** de loin ; **~ from it** loin de là, au contraire. ⬦ *adj* [extreme] : **the ~ end of the street** l'autre bout de la rue ; **the ~ right of the party** l'extrême droite du parti ; **the door on the ~ left** la porte la plus à gauche.

faraway ['faːrəweɪ] *adj* lointain(e).

farce [faːs] *n* - **1.** THEATRE farce *f* - **2.** *fig* [disaster] pagaille *f*, vaste rigolade *f*.

farcical ['faːsɪkl] *adj* grotesque.

fare [feəʳ] *n* - **1.** [payment] prix *m*, tarif *m* - **2.** *dated* [food] nourriture *f*.

Far East *n* : **the ~** l'Extrême-Orient *m*.

farewell [ˌfeə'wel] ⬦ *n* adieu *m*. ⬦ *excl literary* adieu!

farm [faːm] ⬦ *n* ferme *f*. ⬦ *vt* cultiver.

farmer ['faːməʳ] *n* fermier *m*.

farmhand ['faːmhænd] *n* ouvrier *m*, -ère *f* agricole.

farmhouse ['faːmhaʊs, *pl* -haʊzɪz] *n* ferme *f*.

farming ['faːmɪŋ] *n (U)* agriculture *f* ; [of animals] élevage *m*.

farm labourer = **farmhand**.

farmland ['faːmlænd] *n (U)* terres *fpl* cultivées OR arables.

farmstead ['faːmsted] *n Am* ferme *f*.

farm worker = **farmhand**.

farmyard ['faːmjaːd] *n* cour *f* de ferme.

far-reaching [ˌ-'riːtʃɪŋ] *adj* d'une grande portée.

farsighted [ˌfaː'saɪtɪd] *adj* - **1.** [person] prévoyant(e) ; [plan] élaboré(e) avec clairvoyance - **2.** *Am* [longsighted] hypermétrope.

fart [faːt] *v inf* ⬦ *n* [air] pet *m*. ⬦ *vi* péter.

farther ['faːðəʳ] *compar* ⬫ **far**.

farthest ['faːðəst] *superl* ⬫ **far**.

fascinate ['fæsɪneɪt] *vt* fasciner.

fascinating ['fæsɪneɪtɪŋ] *adj* [person, country] fascinant(e) ; [job] passionnant(e) ; [idea, thought] très intéressant(e).

fascination [ˌfæsɪ'neɪʃn] *n* fascination *f*.

fascism ['fæʃɪzm] *n* fascisme *m*.

fashion ['fæʃn] ⬦ *n* - **1.** [clothing, style] mode *f* ; **to be in/out of ~** être/ne plus être à la mode - **2.** [manner] manière *f*. ⬦ *vt fml* façonner, fabriquer.

fashionable ['fæʃnəbl] *adj* à la mode.

fashion show *n* défilé *m* de mode.

fast [faːst] ⬦ *adj* - **1.** [rapid] rapide - **2.** [clock, watch] qui avance. ⬦ *adv* - **1.** [rapidly] vite - **2.** [firmly] solidement ; **to hold ~ to sthg** *lit & fig* s'accrocher à qqch ; **~ asleep** profondément endormi. ⬦ *n* jeûne *m*. ⬦ *vi* jeûner.

fasten ['faːsn] ⬦ *vt* [jacket, bag] fermer ; [seat belt] attacher ; **to ~ sthg to sthg** attacher qqch à qqch. ⬦ *vi* : **to ~ on to sb/sthg** se cramponner à qqn/qqch.

fastener ['faːsnəʳ] *n* [of bag, necklace] fermoir *m* ; [of dress] fermeture *f*.

fastening ['faːsnɪŋ] *n* fermeture *f*.

fast food *n* fast food *m*.

fastidious [fə'stɪdɪəs] *adj* [fussy] méticuleux(euse).

fat [fæt] ⬦ *adj* - **1.** [overweight] gros (grosse), gras (grasse) ; **to get ~** grossir - **2.** [not lean - meat] gras (grasse) - **3.** [thick - file, wallet] gros (grosse), épais(aisse). ⬦ *n* - **1.** [flesh, on meat, in food] graisse *f* - **2.** *(U)* [for cooking] matière *f* grasse.

fatal ['feɪtl] *adj* - **1.** [serious - mistake] fatal(e) ; [- decision, words] fatidique - **2.** [accident, illness] mortel(elle).

fatality [fə'tælətɪ] *n* [accident victim] mort *m*.

fate [feɪt] *n* - **1.** [destiny] destin *m* ; **to tempt ~** tenter le diable - **2.** [result, end] sort *m*.

fateful ['feɪtfʊl] *adj* fatidique.

fat-free *adj* sans matières grasses.

father ['faːðəʳ] *n* père *m*.

Father Christmas *n Br* le Père Noël.

father-in-law (*pl* **fathers-in-law**) *n* beau-père *m*.

fatherly ['fɑːðəlɪ] *adj* paternel(elle).

fathom ['fæðəm] ◇ *n* brasse *f*. ◇ *vt* : **to ~ sb/sthg (out)** comprendre qqn/qqch.

fatigue [fə'tiːg] *n* - **1.** [exhaustion] épuise-ment *m* - **2.** [in metal] fatigue *f*.

fatten ['fætn] *vt* engraisser.

fattening ['fætnɪŋ] *adj* qui fait grossir.

fatty ['fætɪ] ◇ *adj* gras (grasse). ◇ *n inf pej* gros *m*, grosse *f*.

fatuous ['fætjuəs] *adj* stupide, niais(e).

faucet ['fɔːsɪt] *n Am* robinet *m*.

fault ['fɔːlt] ◇ *n* - **1.** [responsibility, in ten-nis] faute *f* ; **it's my ~** c'est de ma faute - **2.** [mistake, imperfection] défaut *m* ; **to find ~ with sb/sthg** critiquer qqn/qqch ; **at ~** fautif(ive) - **3.** GEOL faille *f*. ◇ *vt* : **to ~ sb (on sthg)** prendre qqn en défaut (sur qqch).

faultless ['fɔːltlɪs] *adj* impeccable.

faulty ['fɔːltɪ] *adj* défectueux(euse).

fauna ['fɔːnə] *n* faune *f*.

favour *Br*, **favor** *Am* ['feɪvə'] ◇ *n* - **1.** [approval] faveur *f*, approbation *f* ; **in sb's ~** en faveur de qqn ; **to be in/out of ~ with sb** avoir/ne pas avoir les faveurs de qqn, avoir/ne pas avoir la cote avec qqn ; **to curry ~ with sb** chercher à gagner la fa-veur de qqn - **2.** [kind act] service *m* ; **to do sb a ~** rendre (un) service à qqn - **3.** [favour-itism] favoritisme *m*. ◇ *vt* - **1.** [prefer] préfé-rer, privilégier - **2.** [treat better, help] favori-ser. ◆ **in favour** *adv* [in agreement] pour, d'accord. ◆ **in favour of** *prep* - **1.** [in preference to] au profit de - **2.** [in agreement with] : **to be in ~ of sthg/of doing sthg** être partisan(e) de qqch/de faire qqch.

favourable *Br*, **favorable** *Am* ['feɪvrəbl] *adj* [positive] favorable.

favourite *Br*, **favorite** *Am* ['feɪvrɪt] ◇ *adj* favori(ite). ◇ *n* favori *m*, -ite *f*.

favouritism *Br*, **favoritism** *Am* ['feɪvrɪtɪzm] *n* favoritisme *m*.

fawn [fɔːn] ◇ *adj* fauve (*inv*). ◇ *n* [ani-mal] faon *m*. ◇ *vi* : **to ~ on sb** flatter qqn servilement.

fax [fæks] ◇ *n* fax *m*, télécopie *f*. ◇ *vt* - **1.** [person] envoyer un fax à - **2.** [docu-ment] envoyer en fax.

fax machine *n* fax *m*, télécopieur *m*.

fax modem *n* modem *m* fax.

FBI (*abbr of* **Federal Bureau of Investiga-tion**) *n* FBI *m*.

fear [fɪə'] ◇ *n* - **1.** *(U)* [feeling] peur *f*

- **2.** [object of fear] crainte *f* - **3.** [risk] risque *m* ; **for ~ of** de peur de (*+ infin*), de peur que (*+ subjunctive*). ◇ *vt* - **1.** [be afraid of] crain-dre, avoir peur de - **2.** [anticipate] craindre ; **to ~ (that)** ... craindre que ..., avoir peur que ...

fearful ['fɪəful] *adj* - **1.** *fml* [frightened] peureux(euse) ; **to be ~ of sthg** avoir peur de qqch - **2.** [frightening] effrayant(e).

fearless ['fɪəlɪs] *adj* intrépide.

feasible ['fiːzəbl] *adj* faisable, possible.

feast [fiːst] ◇ *n* [meal] festin *m*, banquet *m*. ◇ *vi* : **to ~ on** OR **off sthg** se régaler de qqch.

feat [fiːt] *n* exploit *m*, prouesse *f*.

feather ['feðə'] *n* plume *f*.

feature ['fiːtʃə'] ◇ *n* - **1.** [characteristic] caractéristique *f* - **2.** GEOGR particularité *f* - **3.** [article] article *m* de fond - **4.** RADIO & TV émission *f* spéciale, spécial *m* - **5.** CINEMA long métrage *m*. ◇ *vt* - **1.** [subj : film, exhib-ition] mettre en vedette - **2.** [comprise] pré-senter, comporter. ◇ *vi* : **to ~ (in)** figurer en vedette (dans). ◆ **features** *npl* [of face] traits *mpl*.

feature film *n* long métrage *m*.

February ['februərɪ] *n* février *m* ; *see also* September.

feces *Am* = faeces.

fed [fed] *pt & pp* ⟶ feed.

federal ['fedrəl] *adj* fédéral(e).

federation [fedə'reɪʃn] *n* fédération *f*.

fed up *adj* : **to be ~ (with)** en avoir marre (de).

fee [fiː] *n* [of school] frais *mpl* ; [of doctor] honoraires *mpl* ; [for membership] coti-sation *f* ; [for entrance] tarif *m*, prix *m*.

feeble ['fiːbl] *adj* faible.

feed [fiːd] (*pt & pp* **fed**) ◇ *vt* - **1.** [give food to] nourrir - **2.** [fire, fears etc] alimenter - **3.** [put, insert] : **to ~ sthg into sthg** mettre OR insérer qqch dans qqch. ◇ *vi* [take food] : **to ~ (on** OR **off)** se nourrir (de). ◇ *n* - **1.** [for baby] repas *m* - **2.** [animal food] nourriture *f*.

feedback ['fiːdbæk] *n* *(U)* - **1.** [reaction] réactions *fpl* - **2.** ELEC réaction *f*, rétroaction *f*.

feeding bottle ['fiːdɪŋ-] *n Br* biberon *m*.

feel [fiːl] (*pt & pp* **felt**) ◇ *vt* - **1.** [touch] toucher - **2.** [sense, experience, notice] sen-tir ; [emotion] ressentir ; **to ~ o.s. doing sthg** se sentir faire qqch - **3.** [believe] : **to ~ (that)** ... croire que ..., penser que ... - **4.** *phr* : **I'm not ~ing myself today** je ne suis pas dans mon assiette aujourd'hui.

◇ *vi* - **1.** [have sensation] **: to ~ cold/hot/sleepy** avoir froid/chaud/sommeil **; to ~ like sthg/like doing sthg** [be in mood for] avoir envie de qqch/de faire qqch - **2.** [have emotion] se sentir **; to ~ angry** être en colère - **3.** [seem] sembler **; it ~s strange** ça fait drôle - **4.** [by touch] **: to ~ for sthg** chercher qqch. ◇ *n* - **1.** [sensation, touch] toucher *m*, sensation *f* - **2.** [atmosphere] atmosphère *f*.

feeler ['fi:lə'] *n* antenne *f*.

feeling ['fi:lɪŋ] *n* - **1.** [emotion] sentiment *m* - **2.** [physical sensation] sensation *f* - **3.** [intuition, sense] sentiment *m*, impression *f* - **4.** [understanding] sensibilité *f*. ◆ **feelings** *npl* sentiments *mpl* **; to hurt sb's ~s** blesser (la sensibilité de) qqn.

feet [fi:t] *pl* ▷ **foot**.

feign [feɪn] *vt fml* feindre.

fell [fel] ◇ *pt* ▷ **fall**. ◇ *vt* [tree, person] abattre. ◆ **fells** *npl Br* GEOGR lande *f*.

fellow ['feləʊ] ◇ *n* - **1.** *dated* [man] homme *m* - **2.** [comrade, peer] camarade *m*, compagnon *m* - **3.** [of society, college] membre *m*, associé *m*. ◇ *adj* **: one's ~ men** ses semblables **; ~ passenger** compagnon *m*, compagne *f* (de voyage) **; ~ student** camarade *mf* (d'études).

fellowship ['feləʊʃɪp] *n* - **1.** [comradeship] amitié *f*, camaraderie *f* - **2.** [society] association *f*, corporation *f* - **3.** [of society, college] titre *m* de membre OR d'associé.

felony ['felənɪ] *n* JUR crime *m*, forfait *m*.

felt [felt] ◇ *pt & pp* ▷ **feel**. ◇ *n* (*U*) feutre *m*.

felt-tip pen *n* stylo-feutre *m*.

female ['fi:meɪl] ◇ *adj* [person] de sexe féminin ; [animal, plant] femelle ; [sex, figure] féminin(e) **; ~ student** étudiante *f*. ◇ *n* femelle *f*.

feminine ['femɪnɪn] ◇ *adj* féminin(e). ◇ *n* GRAMM féminin *m*.

feminist ['femɪnɪst] *n* féministe *mf*.

fence [fens] ◇ *n* [barrier] clôture *f* **; to sit on the ~** *fig* ménager la chèvre et le chou. ◇ *vt* clôturer, entourer d'une clôture.

fencing ['fensɪŋ] *n* SPORT escrime *f*.

fend [fend] *vi* **: to ~ for o.s.** se débrouiller tout seul. ◆ **fend off** *vt sep* [blows] parer ; [questions, reporters] écarter.

fender ['fendə'] *n* - **1.** [round fireplace] pare-feu *m inv* - **2.** [on boat] défense *f* - **3.** *Am* [on car] aile *f*.

ferment [*n* 'fɜ:ment, *vb* fə'ment] ◇ *n* (*U*) [unrest] agitation *f*, effervescence *f*. ◇ *vi* [wine, beer] fermenter.

fern [fɜ:n] *n* fougère *f*.

ferocious [fə'rəʊʃəs] *adj* féroce.

ferret ['ferɪt] *n* furet *m*. ◆ **ferret about, ferret around** *vi inf* fureter un peu partout.

ferris wheel ['ferɪs-] *n esp Am* grande roue *f*.

ferry ['ferɪ] ◇ *n* ferry *m*, ferry-boat *m* ; [smaller] bac *m*. ◇ *vt* transporter.

ferryboat ['ferɪbəʊt] *n* = **ferry**.

fertile ['fɜ:taɪl] *adj* - **1.** [land, imagination] fertile, fécond(e) - **2.** [woman] féconde.

fertilizer ['fɜ:tɪlaɪzə'] *n* engrais *m*.

fervent ['fɜ:vənt] *adj* fervent(e).

fester ['festə'] *vi* [wound, sore] suppurer.

festival ['festəvl] *n* - **1.** [event, celebration] festival *m* - **2.** [holiday] fête *f*.

festive ['festɪv] *adj* de fête.

festive season *n* **: the ~** la période des fêtes.

festivities [fes'tɪvətɪz] *npl* réjouissances *fpl*.

festoon [fe'stu:n] *vt* décorer de guirlandes ; **to be ~ed with** être décoré de.

fetch [fetʃ] *vt* - **1.** [go and get] aller chercher - **2.** [raise - money] rapporter.

fetching ['fetʃɪŋ] *adj* séduisant(e).

fete, fête [feɪt] *n* fête *f*, kermesse *f*.

fetish ['fetɪʃ] *n* - **1.** [sexual obsession] objet *m* de fétichisme - **2.** [mania] manie *f*, obsession *f*.

fetus ['fi:təs] *n* = **foetus**.

feud [fju:d] ◇ *n* querelle *f*. ◇ *vi* se quereller.

feudal ['fju:dl] *adj* féodal(e).

fever ['fi:və'] *n* fièvre *f*.

feverish ['fi:vərɪʃ] *adj* fiévreux(euse).

few [fju:] ◇ *adj* peu de ; **the first ~ pages** les toutes premières pages ; **quite a ~, a good ~** pas mal de, un bon nombre de ; **~ and far between** rares. ◇ *pron* peu ; **a ~** quelques-uns *mpl*, quelques-unes *fpl*.

fewer ['fju:ə'] ◇ *adj* moins (de). ◇ *pron* moins.

fewest ['fju:əst] *adj* le moins (de).

fiancé [fɪ'ɒnseɪ] *n* fiancé *m*.

fiancée [fɪ'ɒnseɪ] *n* fiancée *f*.

fiasco [fɪ'æskəʊ] (*Br pl* -s, *Am pl* -es) *n* fiasco *m*.

fib [fɪb] *inf* ◇ *n* bobard *m*, blague *f*. ◇ *vi* raconter des bobards OR des blagues.

fibre *Br*, **fiber** *Am* ['faɪbə'] *n* fibre *f*.

fibreglass *Br*, **fiberglass** *Am* ['faɪbəglɑːs] *n* (*U*) fibre *f* de verre.

fickle ['fɪkl] *adj* versatile.

fiction ['fɪkʃn] *n* fiction *f*.

fictional ['fɪkʃənl] *adj* fictif(ive).

fictitious ['fɪk'tɪʃəs] *adj* [false] fictif(ive).

fiddle ['fɪdl] ⬦ *vi* [play around] : **to ~ with** sthg tripoter qqch. ⬦ *vt Br inf* truquer. ⬦ *n* - **1.** [violin] violon *m* - **2.** *Br inf* [fraud] combine *f*, escroquerie *f*.

fiddly ['fɪdlɪ] *adj Br inf* délicat(e).

fidget ['fɪdʒɪt] *vi* remuer.

field [fi:ld] *n* - **1.** [gen & COMPUT] champ *m* - **2.** [for sports] terrain *m* - **3.** [of knowledge] domaine *m*.

field day *n* : **to have a ~** s'en donner à cœur joie.

field glasses *npl* jumelles *fpl*.

field marshal *n* ≃ maréchal *m* (de France).

field trip *n* voyage *m* d'étude.

fieldwork ['fi:ldwɜ:k] *n (U)* recherches *fpl* sur le terrain.

fiend [fi:nd] *n* - **1.** [cruel person] monstre *m* - **2.** *inf* [fanatic] fou *m*, folle *f*, mordu *m*, -e *f*.

fiendish ['fi:ndɪʃ] *adj* - **1.** [evil] abominable - **2.** *inf* [very difficult, complex] compliqué(e), complexe.

fierce [fɪəs] *adj* féroce ; [heat] torride ; [storm, temper] violent(e).

fiery ['faɪərɪ] *adj* - **1.** [burning] ardent(e) - **2.** [volatile - speech] enflammé(e) ; [- temper, person] fougueux(euse).

fifteen [fɪf'ti:n] *num* quinze ; *see also* **six**.

fifth [fɪfθ] *num* cinquième ; *see also* **sixth**.

fifty ['fɪftɪ] *num* cinquante ; *see also* **sixty**.

fifty-fifty ⬦ *adj* moitié-moitié, fifty-fifty ; **to have a ~ chance** avoir cinquante pour cent de chances. ⬦ *adv* moitié-moitié, fifty-fifty.

fig [fɪg] *n* figue *f*.

fight [faɪt] (*pt & pp* **fought**) ⬦ *n* - **1.** [physical] bagarre *f* ; **to have a ~ (with sb)** se battre (avec qqn), se bagarrer (avec qqn) ; **to put up a ~** se battre, se défendre - **2.** *fig* [battle, struggle] lutte *f*, combat *m* - **3.** [argument] dispute *f* ; **to have a ~ (with sb)** se disputer (avec qqn). ⬦ *vt* - **1.** [physically] se battre contre OR avec - **2.** [conduct - war] mener - **3.** [enemy, racism] combattre. ⬦ *vi* - **1.** [in war, punch-up] se battre - **2.** *fig* [struggle] : **to ~ for/against sthg** lutter pour/contre qqch - **3.** [argue] : **to ~ (about OR over)** se battre OR se disputer (à propos de). ⬦ **fight back** ⬦ *vt fus* refouler. ⬦ *vi* riposter.

fighter ['faɪtər] *n* - **1.** [plane] avion *m* de chasse, chasseur *m* - **2.** [soldier] combattant *m* - **3.** [combative person] battant *m*, -e *f*.

fighting ['faɪtɪŋ] *n (U)* [punch-up] bagarres *fpl* ; [in war] conflits *mpl*.

figment ['fɪgmənt] *n* : **a ~ of sb's imagination** le fruit de l'imagination de qqn.

figurative ['fɪgərətɪv] *adj* [meaning] figuré(e).

figure [*Br* 'fɪgər, *Am* 'fɪgjər] ⬦ *n* - **1.** [statistic, number] chiffre *m* - **2.** [human shape, outline] silhouette *f*, forme *f* - **3.** [personality, diagram] figure *f* - **4.** [shape of body] ligne *f*. ⬦ *vt esp Am* [suppose] penser, supposer. ⬦ *vi* [feature] figurer, apparaître. ⬦ **figure out** *vt sep* [understand] comprendre ; [find] trouver.

figurehead ['fɪgəhed] *n* - **1.** [on ship] figure *f* de proue - **2.** *fig & pej* [leader] homme *m* de paille.

figure of speech *n* figure *f* de rhétorique.

Fiji ['fi:dʒi:] *n* Fidji *fpl*.

file [faɪl] ⬦ *n* - **1.** [folder, report] dossier *m* ; **on ~, on the ~s** répertorié dans les dossiers - **2.** COMPUT fichier *m* - **3.** [tool] lime *f* - **4.** [line] : **in single ~** en file indienne. ⬦ *vt* - **1.** [document] classer - **2.** JUR - accusation, complaint] porter, déposer ; [- lawsuit] intenter - **3.** [fingernails, wood] limer. ⬦ *vi* - **1.** [walk in single file] marcher en file indienne - **2.** JUR : **to ~ for divorce** demander le divorce.

filing cabinet ['faɪlɪŋ-] *n* classeur *m*, fichier *m*.

Filipino [ˌfɪlɪ'pi:nəʊ] (*pl* -s) ⬦ *adj* philippin(e). ⬦ *n* Philippin *m*, -e *f*.

fill [fɪl] ⬦ *vt* - **1.** [gen] remplir ; **to ~ sthg with sthg** remplir qqch de qqch - **2.** [gap, hole] boucher - **3.** [vacancy - subj : employer] pourvoir à ; [- subj : employee] prendre. ⬦ *n* : **to eat one's ~** manger à sa faim. ⬦ **fill in** ⬦ *vt sep* - **1.** [form] remplir - **2.** [inform] : **to ~ sb in (on)** mettre qqn au courant (de). ⬦ *vi* [substitute] : **to ~ in for sb** remplacer qqn. ⬦ **fill out** *vt sep* [form] remplir. ⬦ **fill up** ⬦ *vt sep* remplir. ⬦ *vi* se remplir.

fillet *Br*, **filet** *Am* ['fɪlɪt] *n* filet *m*.

fillet steak *n* filet *m* de bœuf.

filling ['fɪlɪŋ] ⬦ *adj* très nourrissant(e). ⬦ *n* - **1.** [in tooth] plombage *m* - **2.** [in cake, sandwich] garniture *f*.

filling station *n* station-service *f*.

film [fɪlm] ⬦ *n* - **1.** [movie] film *m* - **2.** [layer, for camera] pellicule *f* - **3.** [footage] images *fpl*. ⬦ *vt & vi* filmer.

film star *n* vedette *f* de cinéma.

Filofax® ['faɪləʊfæks] *n* Filofax® *m*.

filter ['fɪltər] ◇ *n* filtre *m*. ◇ *vt* [coffee] passer ; [water, oil, air] filtrer.

filter coffee *n* café *m* filtre.

filter lane *n Br* ≃ voie *f* de droite.

filter-tipped [-'tɪpt] *adj* à bout filtre.

filth [fɪlθ] *n (U)* - **1.** [dirt] saleté *f*, crasse *f* - **2.** [obscenity] obscénités *fpl*.

filthy ['fɪlθɪ] *adj* - **1.** [very dirty] dégoûtant(e), répugnant(e) - **2.** [obscene] obscène.

fin [fɪn] *n* [of fish] nageoire *f*.

final ['faɪnl] ◇ *adj* - **1.** [last] dernier(ère) - **2.** [at end] final(e) - **3.** [definitive] définitif(ive). ◇ *n* finale *f*. ◆ **finals** *npl* UNIV examens *mpl* de dernière année.

finale [fɪ'nɑːlɪ] *n* finale *m*.

finalize, -ise ['faɪnəlaɪz] *vt* mettre au point.

finally ['faɪnəlɪ] *adv* enfin.

finance [*n* 'faɪnæns, *vb* faɪ'næns] ◇ *n (U)* finance *f*. ◇ *vt* financer. ◆ **finances** *npl* finances *fpl*.

financial [fɪ'nænʃl] *adj* financier(ère).

find [faɪnd] (*pt & pp* found) ◇ *vt* - **1.** [gen] trouver - **2.** [realize] : **to ~ (that)** ... s'apercevoir que ... - **3.** JUR : **to be found guilty/not guilty (of)** être déclaré(e) coupable/non coupable (de). ◇ *n* trouvaille *f*. ◆ **find out** ◇ *vi* se renseigner. ◇ *vt fus* - **1.** [information] se renseigner sur - **2.** [truth] découvrir, apprendre. ◇ *vt sep* démasquer.

findings ['faɪndɪŋz] *npl* conclusions *fpl*.

fine [faɪn] ◇ *adj* - **1.** [good - work] excellent(e) ; [- building, weather] beau (belle) - **2.** [perfectly satisfactory] très bien ; **I'm ~** ça va bien - **3.** [thin, smooth] fin(e) - **4.** [minute - detail, distinction] subtil(e) ; [- adjustment, tuning] délicat(e). ◇ *adv* [very well] très bien. ◇ *n* amende *f*. ◇ *vt* condamner à une amende.

fine arts *npl* beaux-arts *mpl*.

finely ['faɪnlɪ] *adv* - **1.** [chopped, ground] fin - **2.** [tuned, balanced] délicatement.

finery ['faɪnərɪ] *n (U)* parure *f*.

fine-tune *vt* [mechanism] régler au quart de tour ; *fig* régler minutieusement.

finger ['fɪŋgər] ◇ *n* doigt *m*. ◇ *vt* [feel] palper.

fingernail ['fɪŋgəneɪl] *n* ongle *m* (*de la main*).

fingerprint ['fɪŋgəprɪnt] *n* empreinte *f* (digitale).

fingertip ['fɪŋgətɪp] *n* bout *m* du doigt ; **at one's ~s** sur le bout des doigts.

finicky ['fɪnɪkɪ] *adj pej* [eater, task] difficile ; [person] tatillon(onne).

finish ['fɪnɪʃ] ◇ *n* - **1.** [end] fin *f* ; [of race] arrivée *f* - **2.** [texture] finition *f*. ◇ *vt* finir, terminer ; **to ~ doing sthg** finir OR terminer de faire qqch. ◇ *vi* finir, terminer ; [school, film] se terminer. ◆ **finish off** *vt sep* finir, terminer. ◆ **finish up** *vi* finir.

finishing line ['fɪnɪʃɪŋ-] *n* ligne *f* d'arrivée.

finishing school ['fɪnɪʃɪŋ-] *n* école privée *pour jeunes filles surtout axée sur l'enseignement des bonnes manières.*

finite ['faɪnaɪt] *adj* fini(e).

Finland ['fɪnlənd] *n* Finlande *f*.

Finn [fɪn] *n* Finlandais *m*, -e *f*.

Finnish ['fɪnɪʃ] ◇ *adj* finlandais(e), finnois(e). ◇ *n* [language] finnois *m*.

fir [fɜːr] *n* sapin *m*.

fire ['faɪər] ◇ *n* - **1.** [gen] feu *m* ; **on ~** en feu ; **to catch ~** prendre feu ; **to set ~ to sthg** mettre le feu à qqch - **2.** [out of control] incendie *m* - **3.** *Br* [heater] appareil *m* de chauffage - **4.** *(U)* [shooting] coups *mpl* de feu ; **to open ~ (on)** ouvrir le feu (sur). ◇ *vt* - **1.** [shoot] tirer - **2.** *esp Am* [dismiss] renvoyer. ◇ *vi* : **to ~ (on OR at)** faire feu (sur), tirer (sur).

fire alarm *n* avertisseur *m* d'incendie.

firearm ['faɪərɑːm] *n* arme *f* à feu.

firebomb ['faɪəbɒm] ◇ *n* bombe *f* incendiaire. ◇ *vt* lancer des bombes incendiaires à.

fire brigade *Br*, **fire department** *Am n* sapeurs-pompiers *mpl*.

fire door *n* porte *f* coupe-feu.

fire engine *n* voiture *f* de pompiers.

fire escape *n* escalier *m* de secours.

fire extinguisher *n* extincteur *m* d'incendie.

fireguard ['faɪəgɑːd] *n* garde-feu *m inv*.

firelighter ['faɪəlaɪtər] *n* allume-feu *m inv*.

fireman ['faɪəmən] (*pl* -men [-mən]) *n* pompier *m*.

fireplace ['faɪəpleɪs] *n* cheminée *f*.

fireproof ['faɪəpruːf] *adj* ignifugé(e).

fireside ['faɪəsaɪd] *n* : **by the ~** au coin du feu.

fire station *n* caserne *f* des pompiers.

firewood ['faɪəwʊd] *n* bois *m* de chauffage.

firework ['faɪəwɜːk] *n* fusée *f* de feu d'artifice. ◆ **fireworks** *npl* [outburst of anger] étincelles *fpl*.

firing ['faɪərɪŋ] *n (U)* MIL tir *m*, fusillade *f*.

firing squad *n* peloton *m* d'exécution.

firm [fɜːm] ◇ *adj* - **1.** [gen] ferme ; **to stand ~** tenir bon - **2.** [support, structure] solide - **3.** [evidence, news] certain(e). ◇ *n* firme *f*, société *f*.

first [fɜːst] ◇ *adj* premier(ère) ; **for the ~ time** pour la première fois ; **~ thing in the morning** tôt le matin. ◇ *adv* - **1.** [before anyone else] en premier - **2.** [before anything else] d'abord ; **~ of all** tout d'abord - **3.** [for the first time] (pour) la première fois. ◇ *n* - **1.** [person] premier *m*, -ère *f* - **2.** [unprecedented event] première *f* - **3.** Br UNIV diplôme universitaire avec mention très bien. ◆ **at first** *adv* d'abord. ◆ **at first hand** *adv* de première main.

first aid *n (U)* premiers secours *mpl*.

first-aid kit *n* trousse *f* de premiers secours.

first-class *adj* - **1.** [excellent] excellent(e) - **2.** [ticket, compartment] de première classe ; [stamp, letter] tarif normal.

first floor *n* Br premier étage *m* ; Am rez-de-chaussée *m inv*.

firsthand [fɜːst'hænd] *adj & adv* de première main.

first lady *n* première dame *f* du pays.

firstly ['fɜːstlɪ] *adv* premièrement.

First Minister *n* [in Scottish Parliament] président *m* du Parlement écossais.

first name *n* prénom *m*.

first rate *adj* excellent(e).

First Secretary *n* [in Welsh Assembly] président *m* de l'Assemblée galloise.

firtree ['fɜːtriː] = **fir**.

fish [fɪʃ] *(pl inv)* ◇ *n* poisson *m*. ◇ *vt* [river, sea] pêcher dans. ◇ *vi* [fisherman] : **to ~ (for sthg)** pêcher (qqch).

fish and chips *npl* Br poisson *m* frit avec frites.

fish and chip shop *n* Br endroit où l'on vend du poisson frit et des frites.

fishbowl ['fɪʃbəʊl] *n* bocal *m* (à poissons).

fishcake ['fɪʃkeɪk] *n* croquette *f* de poisson.

fisherman ['fɪʃəmən] *(pl -men [-mən])* *n* pêcheur *m*.

fish farm *n* centre *m* de pisciculture.

fish fingers Br, **fish sticks** Am *npl* bâtonnets *mpl* de poisson panés.

fishing ['fɪʃɪŋ] *n* pêche *f* ; **to go ~** aller à la pêche.

fishing boat *n* bateau *m* de pêche.

fishing line *n* ligne *f*.

fishing rod *n* canne *f* à pêche.

fishmonger ['fɪʃˌmʌŋgə'] *n* Br poissonnier *m*, -ère *f* ; **~'s (shop)** poissonnerie *f*.

fish sticks Am = **fish fingers**.

fishy ['fɪʃɪ] *adj* - **1.** [smell, taste] de poisson - **2.** [suspicious] louche.

fist [fɪst] *n* poing *m*.

fit [fɪt] ◇ *adj* - **1.** [suitable] convenable ; **to be ~ for sthg** être bon (bonne) à qqch ; **to be ~ to do sthg** être apte à faire qqch - **2.** [healthy] en forme ; **to keep ~** se maintenir en forme. ◇ *n* - **1.** [of clothes, shoes etc] ajustement *m* ; **it's a tight ~** c'est un peu juste ; **it's a good ~** c'est la bonne taille - **2.** [epileptic seizure] crise *f* ; **to have a ~** avoir une crise ; *fig* piquer une crise - **3.** [bout - of crying] crise *f* ; [- of rage] accès *m* ; [- of sneezing] suite *f* ; **in ~s and starts** par à-coups. ◇ *vt* - **1.** [be correct size for] aller à - **2.** [place] : **to ~ sthg into sthg** insérer qqch dans qqch - **3.** [provide] : **to ~ sthg with sthg** équiper *or* munir qqch de qqch - **4.** [be suitable for] correspondre à. ◇ *vi* [be correct size, go] aller ; [into container] entrer, ◆ **fit in** ◇ *vt sep* [accommodate] prendre. ◇ *vi* s'intégrer ; **to ~ in with sthg** correspondre à qqch ; **to ~ in with sb** s'accorder à qqn.

fitful ['fɪtfʊl] *adj* [sleep] agité(e) ; [wind, showers] intermittent(e).

fitment ['fɪtmənt] *n* Br meuble *m* encastré.

fitness ['fɪtnɪs] *n (U)* - **1.** [health] forme *f* - **2.** [suitability] : **~ (for)** aptitude *f* (pour).

fitted carpet [ˌfɪtəd-] *n* moquette *f*.

fitted kitchen [ˌfɪtəd-] *n* Br cuisine *f* intégrée *or* équipée.

fitter ['fɪtə'] *n* [mechanic] monteur *m*.

fitting ['fɪtɪŋ] ◇ *adj fml* approprié(e). ◇ *n* - **1.** [part] appareil *m* - **2.** [for clothing] essayage *m*. ◆ **fittings** *npl* installations *fpl*.

fitting room *n* cabine *f* d'essayage.

five [faɪv] *num* cinq ; *see also* **six**.

fiver ['faɪvə'] *n inf* - **1.** Br [amount] cinq livres *fpl* ; [note] billet *m* de cinq livres - **2.** Am [amount] cinq dollars *mpl* ; [note] billet *m* de cinq dollars.

fix [fɪks] ◇ *vt* - **1.** [gen] fixer ; **to ~ sthg to sthg** fixer qqch à qqch - **2.** [in memory] graver - **3.** [repair] réparer - **4.** *inf* [rig] truquer - **5.** [food, drink] préparer. ◇ *n* - **1.** *inf* [difficult situation] : **to be in a ~** être dans le pétrin - **2.** *drugs sl* piqûre *f*. ◆ **fix up** *vt sep* - **1.** [provide] : **to ~ sb up with sthg** obtenir qqch pour qqn - **2.** [arrange] arranger.

fixation [fɪk'seɪʃn] *n* : **~ (on** *or* **about)** obsession *f* (de).

fixed [fɪkst] *adj* - **1.** [attached] fixé(e) - **2.** [set, unchanging] fixe ; [smile] figé(e).

fixture ['fɪkstʃəʳ] *n* - **1.** [furniture] installation *f* - **2.** [permanent feature] tradition *f* bien établie - **3.** *Br* SPORT rencontre *f* (sportive).

fizz [fɪz] *vi* [lemonade, champagne] pétiller ; [fireworks] crépiter.

fizzle ['fɪzl] ◆ **fizzle out** *vi* [fire] s'éteindre ; [firework] se terminer ; [interest, enthusiasm] se dissiper.

fizzy ['fɪzɪ] *adj* pétillant(e).

flabbergasted ['flæbəgɑːstɪd] *adj* sidéré(e).

flabby ['flæbɪ] *adj* mou (molle).

flag [flæg] ◇ *n* drapeau *m*. ◇ *vi* [person, enthusiasm, energy] faiblir ; [conversation] traîner. ◆ **flag down** *vt sep* [taxi] héler ; to ~ sb down faire signe à qqn de s'arrêter.

flagpole ['flægpəʊl] *n* mât *m*.

flagrant ['fleɪɡrənt] *adj* flagrant(e).

flagstone ['flægstəʊn] *n* dalle *f*.

flair [fleəʳ] *n* - **1.** [talent] don *m* - **2.** (U) [stylishness] style *m*.

flak [flæk] *n* (U) - **1.** [gunfire] tir *m* antiaérien - **2.** *inf* [criticism] critiques *fpl* sévères.

flake [fleɪk] ◇ *n* [of paint, plaster] écaille *f* ; [of snow] flocon *m* ; [of skin] petit lambeau *m*. ◇ *vi* [paint, plaster] s'écailler ; [skin] peler.

flamboyant [flæm'bɔɪənt] *adj* - **1.** [showy, confident] extravagant(e) - **2.** [brightly coloured] flamboyant(e).

flame [fleɪm] *n* flamme *f* ; in ~s en flammes ; to burst into ~s s'enflammer.

flamingo [flə'mɪŋgəʊ] (*pl* -s OR -es) *n* flamant *m* rose.

flammable ['flæməbl] *adj* inflammable.

flan [flæn] *n* tarte *f*.

flank [flæŋk] ◇ *n* flanc *m*. ◇ *vt* : to be ~ed by être flanqué(e) de.

flannel ['flænl] *n* - **1.** [fabric] flanelle *f* - **2.** *Br* [facecloth] gant *m* de toilette.

flap [flæp] ◇ *n* - **1.** [of envelope, pocket] rabat *m* - **2.** *inf* [panic] : in a ~ paniqué(e). ◇ *vt & vi* battre.

flapjack ['flæpdʒæk] *n* - **1.** *Br* [biscuit] biscuit *m* à l'avoine - **2.** *Am* [pancake] crêpe *f* épaisse.

flare [fleəʳ] ◇ *n* [distress signal] fusée *f* éclairante. ◇ *vi* - **1.** [burn brightly] : to ~ (up) s'embraser - **2.** [intensify] : to ~ (up) [war, revolution] s'intensifier soudainement ; [person] s'emporter - **3.** [widen - trousers, skirt] s'évaser ; [- nostrils] se dila-

ter. ◆ **flares** *npl Br* pantalon *m* à pattes d'éléphant.

flash [flæʃ] ◇ *n* - **1.** [of light, colour] éclat *m* ; ~ of lightning éclair *m* - **2.** PHOT flash *m* - **3.** [sudden moment] éclair *m* ; in a ~ en un rien de temps. ◇ *vt* - **1.** [shine] projeter ; to ~ one's headlights faire un appel de phares - **2.** [send out - signal, smile] envoyer ; [- look] jeter - **3.** [show] montrer. ◇ *vi* - **1.** [torch] briller - **2.** [light - on and off] clignoter ; [eyes] jeter des éclairs - **3.** [rush] : to ~ by OR past passer comme un éclair.

flashback ['flæʃbæk] *n* flash-back *m*, retour *m* en arrière.

flashbulb ['flæʃbʌlb] *n* ampoule *f* de flash.

flashgun ['flæʃgʌn] *n* flash *m*.

flashlight ['flæʃlaɪt] *n* [torch] lampe *f* électrique.

flashy ['flæʃɪ] *adj inf* tape-à-l'œil *(inv)*.

flask [flɑːsk] *n* - **1.** [thermos flask] Thermos® *m or f* - **2.** CHEM ballon *m* - **3.** [hip flask] flasque *f*.

flat [flæt] ◇ *adj* - **1.** [gen] plat(e) - **2.** [tyre] crevé(e) - **3.** [refusal, denial] catégorique - **4.** [business, trade] calme - **5.** [dull - voice, tone] monotone ; [- performance, writing] terne - **6.** [MUS - person] qui chante trop grave ; [- note] bémol - **7.** [fare, price] fixe - **8.** [beer, lemonade] éventé(e) - **9.** [battery] à plat. ◇ *adv* - **1.** [level] à plat - **2.** [exactly] : two hours ~ deux heures pile. ◇ *n* - **1.** *Br* [apartment] appartement *m* - **2.** MUS bémol *m*. ◆ **flat out** *adv* [work] d'arrache-pied ; [travel - subj : vehicle] le plus vite possible.

flatly ['flætlɪ] *adv* - **1.** [absolutely] catégoriquement - **2.** [dully - say] avec monotonie ; [- perform] de façon terne.

flatmate ['flætmeɪt] *n Br* personne avec laquelle on partage un appartement.

flat rate *n* tarif *m* forfaitaire.

flatten ['flætn] *vt* - **1.** [make flat - steel, paper] aplatir ; [- wrinkles, bumps] aplanir - **2.** [destroy] raser. ◆ **flatten out** ◇ *vi* s'aplanir. ◇ *vt sep* aplanir.

flatter ['flætəʳ] *vt* flatter.

flattering ['flætərɪŋ] *adj* - **1.** [complimentary] flatteur(euse) - **2.** [clothes] seyant(e).

flattery ['flætərɪ] *n* flatterie *f*.

flaunt [flɔːnt] *vt* faire étalage de.

flavour *Br*, **flavor** *Am* ['fleɪvəʳ] ◇ *n* - **1.** [of food] goût *m* ; [of ice cream, yoghurt] parfum *m* - **2.** *fig* [atmosphere] atmosphère *f*. ◇ *vt* parfumer.

flavouring *Br*, **flavoring** *Am* ['fleɪvərɪŋ] *n* (U) parfum *m*.

flaw [flɔ:] n [in material, character] défaut m ; [in plan, argument] faille f.

flawless ['flɔ:lɪs] adj parfait(e).

flax [flæks] n lin m.

flea [fli:] n puce f.

flea market n marché m aux puces.

fleck [flek] <> n moucheture f, petite tache f. <> vt : ~ed with moucheté(e) de.

fled [fled] pt & pp ▷ flee.

flee [fli:] (pt & pp fled) vt & vi fuir.

fleece [fli:s] <> n toison f. <> vt inf escroquer.

fleet [fli:t] n - 1. [of ships] flotte f - 2. [of cars, buses] parc m.

fleeting ['fli:tɪŋ] adj [moment] bref (brève) ; [look] fugitif(ive) ; [visit] éclair (inv).

Fleet Street n rue de Londres dont le nom est utilisé pour désigner la presse britannique.

Flemish ['flemɪʃ] <> adj flamand(e). <> n [language] flamand m. <> npl : the ~ les Flamands mpl.

flesh [fleʃ] n chair f ; his/her ~ and blood [family] les siens.

flesh wound n blessure f superficielle.

flew [flu:] pt ▷ fly.

flex [fleks] <> n ELEC fil m. <> vt [bend] fléchir.

flexible ['fleksəbl] adj flexible.

flexitime ['fleksɪtaɪm] n (U) horaire m à la carte OR flexible.

flick [flɪk] <> n - 1. [of whip, towel] petit coup m - 2. [with finger] chiquenaude f. <> vt [switch] appuyer sur. ◆ **flick through** vt fus feuilleter.

flicker ['flɪkə'] vi - 1. [candle, light] vaciller - 2. [shadow] trembler ; [eyelids] ciller.

flick knife n Br couteau m à cran d'arrêt.

flight [flaɪt] n - 1. [gen] vol m - 2. [of steps, stairs] volée f - 3. [escape] fuite f.

flight attendant n steward m, hôtesse f de l'air.

flight crew n équipage m.

flight deck n - 1. [of aircraft carrier] pont m d'envol - 2. [of plane] cabine f de pilotage.

flight recorder n enregistreur m de vol.

flimsy ['flɪmzɪ] adj [dress, material] léger(ère) ; [building, bookcase] peu solide ; [excuse] piètre.

flinch [flɪntʃ] vi tressaillir ; to ~ from sthg/from doing sthg reculer devant qqch/à l'idée de faire qqch.

fling [flɪŋ] (pt & pp flung) <> n [affair] aventure f, affaire f. <> vt lancer.

flint [flɪnt] n - 1. [rock] silex m - 2. [in lighter] pierre f.

flip [flɪp] <> vt - 1. [turn - pancake] faire sauter ; [- record] tourner - 2. [switch] appuyer sur. <> n - 1. [flick] chiquenaude f - 2. [somersault] saut m périlleux. ◆ **flip through** vt fus feuilleter.

flip-flop n [shoe] tong f.

flippant ['flɪpənt] adj désinvolte.

flipper ['flɪpə'] n - 1. [of animal] nageoire f - 2. [for swimmer, diver] palme f.

flirt [flɜ:t] <> n flirt m. <> vi [with person] : to ~ (with sb) flirter (avec qqn).

flirtatious [flɜ:'teɪʃəs] adj flirteur(euse).

flit [flɪt] vi [bird] voleter.

float [fləʊt] <> n - 1. [for buoyancy] flotteur m - 2. [in procession] char m - 3. [money] petite caisse f. <> vt [on water] faire flotter. <> vi [on water] flotter ; [through air] glisser.

flock [flɒk] n - 1. [of birds] vol m ; [of sheep] troupeau m - 2. fig [of people] foule f.

flog [flɒg] vt - 1. [whip] flageller - 2. Br inf [sell] refiler.

flood [flʌd] <> n - 1. [of water] inondation f - 2. [great amount] déluge m, avalanche f. <> vt - 1. [with water, light] inonder - 2. [overwhelm] : to ~ sthg (with) inonder qqch (de).

flooding ['flʌdɪŋ] n (U) inondations fpl.

floodlight ['flʌdlaɪt] n projecteur m.

floor [flɔ:'] <> n - 1. [of room] sol m ; [of club, disco] piste f - 2. [of valley, sea, forest] fond m - 3. [storey] étage m - 4. [at meeting, debate] auditoire m. <> vt - 1. [knock down] terrasser - 2. [baffle] dérouter.

floorboard ['flɔ:bɔ:d] n plancher m.

floor show n spectacle m de cabaret.

flop [flɒp] inf n [failure] fiasco m.

floppy ['flɒpɪ] adj [flower] flasque ; [collar] lâche.

floppy (disk) n disquette f, disque m souple.

flora ['flɔ:rə] n flore f.

florid ['flɒrɪd] adj - 1. [red] rougeaud(e) - 2. [extravagant] fleuri(e).

florist ['flɒrɪst] n fleuriste mf ; ~'s (shop) magasin m de fleuriste.

flotsam ['flɒtsəm] n (U) : ~ and jetsam débris mpl ; fig épaves fpl.

flounder ['flaʊndə'] vi - 1. [in water, mud, snow] patauger - 2. [in conversation] bredouiller.

flour ['flaʊə'] n farine f.

flourish ['flʌrɪʃ] <> vi [plant, flower] bien

pousser ; [children] être en pleine santé ; [company, business] prospérer ; [arts] s'épanouir. ◇ *vt* brandir. ◇ *n* grand geste *m*.

flout [flaʊt] *vt* bafouer.

flow [fləʊ] ◇ *n* - **1.** [movement - of water, information] circulation *f* ; [- of funds] mouvement *m* ; [- of words] flot *m* - **2.** [of tide] flux *m*. ◇ *vi* - **1.** [gen] couler - **2.** [traffic, days, weeks] s'écouler - **3.** [hair, clothes] flotter.

flow chart, flow diagram *n* organigramme *m*.

flower ['flaʊə'] ◇ *n* fleur *f*. ◇ *vi* [bloom] fleurir.

flowerbed ['flaʊəbed] *n* parterre *m*.

flowerpot ['flaʊəpɒt] *n* pot *m* de fleurs.

flowery ['flaʊərɪ] *adj* - **1.** [dress, material] à fleurs - **2.** *pej* [style] fleuri(e).

flown [fləʊn] *pp* ⊳ fly.

flu [fluː] *n (U)* grippe *f*.

fluctuate ['flʌktʃʊeɪt] *vi* fluctuer.

fluency ['fluːənsɪ] *n* aisance *f*.

fluent ['fluːənt] *adj* - **1.** [in foreign language] : to speak ~ French parler couramment le français - **2.** [writing, style] coulant(e), aisé(e).

fluff [flʌf] *n (U)* - **1.** [down] duvet *m* - **2.** [dust] moutons *mpl*.

fluffy ['flʌfɪ] *adj* duveteux(euse) ; [toy] en peluche.

fluid ['fluːɪd] ◇ *n* fluide *m* ; [in diet, for cleaning] liquide *m*. ◇ *adj* - **1.** [flowing] fluide - **2.** [unfixed] changeant(e).

fluid ounce *n* = 0,03 litre.

fluke [fluːk] *n inf* [chance] coup *m* de bol.

flummox ['flʌməks] *vt inf* désarçonner.

flung [flʌŋ] *pt & pp* ⊳ fling.

flunk [flʌŋk] *esp Am inf vt* - **1.** [exam, test] rater - **2.** [student] recaler.

fluorescent [flʊə'resənt] *adj* fluorescent(e).

fluoride ['flʊəraɪd] *n* fluorure *m*.

flurry ['flʌrɪ] *n* - **1.** [of snow] rafale *f* - **2.** *fig* [of objections] concert *m* ; [of activity, excitement] débordement *m*.

flush [flʌʃ] ◇ *adj* [level] : ~ with de niveau avec. ◇ *n* - **1.** [in lavatory] chasse *f* d'eau - **2.** [blush] rougeur *f* - **3.** [sudden feeling] accès *m*. ◇ *vt* [toilet] : to ~ the toilet tirer la chasse d'eau. ◇ *vi* [blush] rougir.

flushed [flʌʃt] *adj* - **1.** [red-faced] rouge - **2.** [excited] : ~ with exalté(e) par.

flustered ['flʌstəd] *adj* troublé(e).

flute [fluːt] *n* MUS flûte *f*.

flutter ['flʌtə'] ◇ *n* - **1.** [of wings] battement *m* - **2.** *inf* [of excitement] émoi *m*. ◇ *vi* - **1.** [bird, insect] voleter ; [wings] battre - **2.** [flag, dress] flotter.

flux [flʌks] *n* [change] : to be in a state of ~ être en proie à des changements permanents.

fly [flaɪ] (*pt* flew, *pp* flown) ◇ *n* - **1.** [insect] mouche *f* - **2.** [of trousers] braguette *f*. ◇ *vt* - **1.** [kite, plane] faire voler - **2.** [passengers, supplies] transporter par avion - **3.** [flag] faire flotter. ◇ *vi* - **1.** [bird, insect, plane] voler - **2.** [pilot] faire voler un avion - **3.** [passenger] voyager en avion - **4.** [move fast, pass quickly] filer - **5.** [flag] flotter.
◆ **fly away** *vi* s'envoler.

fly-fishing *n* pêche *f* à la mouche.

flying ['flaɪɪŋ] ◇ *adj* volant(e). ◇ *n* aviation *f* ; to like ~ aimer prendre l'avion.

flying colours *npl* : to pass (sthg) with ~ réussir (qqch) haut la main.

flying picket *n* piquet *m* de grève volant.

flying saucer *n* soucoupe *f* volante.

flying squad *n Br* force d'intervention rapide de la police.

flying start *n* : to get off to a ~ prendre un départ sur les chapeaux de roue.

flying visit *n* visite *f* éclair.

flyover ['flaɪ,əʊvə'] *n Br* autopont *m*.

flysheet ['flaɪʃiːt] *n* auvent *m*.

fly spray *n* insecticide *m*.

FM *n* (*abbr of* frequency modulation) FM *f*.

foal [fəʊl] *n* poulain *m*.

foam [fəʊm] ◇ *n (U)* - **1.** [bubbles] mousse *f* - **2.** : ~ (rubber) caoutchouc *m* Mousse®. ◇ *vi* [water, champagne] mousser.

fob [fɒb] ◆ **fob off** *vt sep* repousser ; to ~ sthg off on sb refiler qqch à qqn ; to ~ sb off with sthg se débarrasser de qqn à l'aide de qqch.

focal point *n* foyer *m* ; *fig* point *m* central.

focus ['fəʊkəs] (*pl* -cuses [-kəsiːz], -ci [-kaɪ]) ◇ *n* - **1.** PHOT mise *f* au point ; in ~ net ; out of ~ flou - **2.** [centre - of rays] foyer *m* ; [- of earthquake] centre *m*. ◇ *vt* [lens, camera] mettre au point. ◇ *vi* - **1.** [with camera, lens] se fixer ; [eyes] accommoder ; to ~ on sthg [with camera, lens] se fixer sur qqch ; [with eyes] fixer qqch - **2.** [attention] : to ~ on sthg se concentrer sur qqch.

fodder ['fɒdə'] *n (U)* fourrage *m*.

foe [fəʊ] *n literary* ennemi *m*.

foetus ['fiːtəs] *n* fœtus *m*.

fog [fɒg] *n (U)* brouillard *m*.

foggy ['fɒgɪ] *adj* [misty] brumeux(euse).

foghorn ['fɒghɔːn] n sirène f de brume.

fog lamp n feu m de brouillard.

foible ['fɔɪbl] n marotte f.

foil [fɔɪl] ◇ n (U) [metal sheet - of tin, silver] feuille f ; [- CULIN] papier m d'aluminium. ◇ vt déjouer.

fold [fəʊld] ◇ vt - 1. [bend, close up] plier ; **to ~ one's arms** croiser les bras - 2. [wrap] envelopper. ◇ vi - 1. [close up - table, chair] se plier ; [- petals, leaves] se refermer - 2. inf [company, project] échouer ; THEATRE quitter l'affiche. ◇ n - 1. [in material, paper] pli m - 2. [for animals] parc m - 3. fig [spiritual home] : **the ~ le bercail.** ◆ **fold up** ◇ vt sep plier. ◇ vi - 1. [close up - table, map] se plier ; [- petals, leaves] se refermer - 2. [company, project] échouer.

folder ['fəʊldəʳ] n [for papers - wallet] chemise f ; [- binder] classeur m.

folding ['fəʊldɪŋ] adj [table, umbrella] pliant(e) ; [doors] en accordéon.

foliage ['fəʊlɪɪdʒ] n feuillage m.

folk [fəʊk] ◇ adj [art, dancing] folklorique ; [medicine] populaire. ◇ npl [people] gens mpl. ◆ **folks** npl inf [relatives] famille f.

folklore ['fəʊklɔːʳ] n folklore m.

folk music n musique f folk.

folk song n chanson f folk.

follow ['fɒləʊ] ◇ vt suivre. ◇ vi - 1. [gen] suivre - 2. [be logical] tenir debout ; **it ~s that ...** il s'ensuit que ... ◆ **follow up** vt sep - 1. [pursue - idea, suggestion] prendre en considération ; [- advertisement] donner suite à - 2. [complete] : **to ~ sthg up with** faire suivre qqch de.

follower ['fɒləʊəʳ] n [believer] disciple mf.

following ['fɒləʊɪŋ] ◇ adj suivant(e). ◇ n groupe m d'admirateurs. ◇ prep après.

folly ['fɒlɪ] n (U) [foolishness] folie f.

fond [fɒnd] adj [affectionate] affectueux(euse) ; **to be ~ of** aimer beaucoup.

fondle ['fɒndl] vt caresser.

font [fɒnt] n - 1. [in church] fonts mpl baptismaux - 2. COMPUT & TYPO police f (de caractères).

food [fuːd] n nourriture f.

food mixer n mixer m.

food poisoning [-ˌpɔɪznɪŋ] n intoxication f alimentaire.

food processor [-ˌprəʊsesəʳ] n robot m ménager.

foodstuffs ['fuːdstʌfs] npl denrées fpl alimentaires.

fool [fuːl] ◇ n - 1. [idiot] idiot m, -e f - 2. Br [dessert] ≃ mousse f. ◇ vt duper ; **to ~ sb into doing sthg** amener qqn à faire qqch en le dupant. ◇ vi faire l'imbécile. ◆ **fool about, fool around** vi - 1. [behave foolishly] faire l'imbécile - 2. [be unfaithful] être infidèle.

foolhardy ['fuːlˌhɑːdɪ] adj téméraire.

foolish ['fuːlɪʃ] adj idiot(e), stupide.

foolproof ['fuːlpruːf] adj infaillible.

foot [fʊt] (pl sense 1 **feet** [fiːt], pl sense 2 inv or **feet**) ◇ n - 1. [gen] pied m ; [of animal] patte f ; [of page, stairs] bas m ; **to be on one's feet** être debout ; **to get to one's feet** se mettre debout, se lever ; **on ~** à pied ; **to put one's ~ in it** mettre les pieds dans le plat ; **to put one's feet up** se reposer - 2. [unit of measurement] = 30,48 cm, ≃ pied m. ◇ vt inf : **to ~ the bill** payer la note.

footage ['fʊtɪdʒ] n (U) séquences fpl.

football ['fʊtbɔːl] n - 1. [game - soccer] football m, foot m ; [- American football] football américain - 2. [ball] ballon m de football or foot.

footballer ['fʊtbɔːləʳ] n Br joueur m, -euse f de football, footballeur m, -euse f.

football ground n Br terrain m de football.

football player = footballer.

footbrake ['fʊtbreɪk] n frein m (à pied).

footbridge ['fʊtbrɪdʒ] n passerelle f.

foothills ['fʊthɪlz] npl contreforts mpl.

foothold ['fʊthəʊld] n prise f (de pied).

footing ['fʊtɪŋ] n - 1. [foothold] prise f ; **to lose one's ~** trébucher - 2. fig [basis] position f.

footlights ['fʊtlaɪts] npl rampe f.

footnote ['fʊtnəʊt] n note f de bas de page.

footpath ['fʊtpɑːθ, pl -pɑːðz] n sentier m.

footprint ['fʊtprɪnt] n empreinte f (de pied), trace f (de pas).

footstep ['fʊtstep] n - 1. [sound] bruit m de pas - 2. [footprint] empreinte f (de pied).

footwear ['fʊtweəʳ] n (U) chaussures fpl.

for [fɔːʳ] ◇ prep - 1. [referring to intention, destination, purpose] pour ; **this is ~ you** c'est pour vous ; **the plane ~ Paris** l'avion à destination de Paris ; **let's meet ~ a drink** retrouvons-nous pour prendre un verre ; **we did it ~ a laugh** or **~ fun** on l'a fait pour rire ; **what's it ~?** ça sert à quoi? - 2. [representing, on behalf of] pour ; **the MP ~ Barnsley** le député de Barnsley ; **let me do that**

~ **you** laissez-moi faire, je vais vous le faire - **3.** [because of] pour, en raison de ; ~ **various reasons** pour plusieurs raisons ; **a prize** ~ **swimming** un prix de natation ; ~ **fear of being ridiculed** - **4.** [with regard to] pour ; **to be ready** ~ **sthg** être prêt à OR pour qqch ; **it's not** ~ **me to say** ce n'est pas à moi à le dire ; **to be young** ~ **one's age** être jeune pour son âge ; **to feel sorry** ~ **sb** plaindre qqn - **5.** [indicating amount of time, space] : **there's no time** ~ **that** now on n'a pas le temps de faire cela OR de s'occuper de cela maintenant ; **there's room** ~ **another person** il y a de la place pour encore une personne - **6.** [indicating period of time] : **she'll be away** ~ **a month** elle sera absente (pendant) un mois ; **we talked** ~ **hours** on a parlé pendant des heures ; **I've lived here** ~ **3 years** j'habite ici depuis 3 ans, cela fait 3 ans que j'habite ici ; **I can do it for you** ~ **tomorrow** je peux vous le faire pour demain - **7.** [indicating distance] pendant, sur ; ~ **50 kilometres** pendant OR sur 50 kilomètres ; **I walked** ~ **miles** j'ai marché (pendant) des kilomètres - **8.** [indicating particular occasion] pour ; ~ **Christmas** pour Noël - **9.** [indicating amount of money, price] : **they're 50p** ~ **ten** cela coûte 50p les dix ; **I bought/sold it** ~ **£10** je l'ai acheté/vendu 10 livres - **10.** [in favour of, in support of] pour ; **to vote** ~ **sthg** voter pour qqch ; **to be all** ~ **sthg** être tout à fait pour OR en faveur de qqch - **11.** [in ratios] pour - **12.** [indicating meaning] : **P** ~ **Peter** P comme Peter ; **what's the Greek** ~ **'mother'?** comment dit-on 'mère' en grec ? ◇ *conj fml* [as, since] car. ◆ **for all** ◇ *prep* malgré ; ~ **all his money** ... malgré tout son argent ... ◇ *conj* : ~ **all I know** pour autant que je sache.

forage ['fɒrɪdʒ] *vi* : **to** ~ **(for)** fouiller (pour trouver).

foray ['fɒreɪ] *n* : ~ **(into)** *lit & fig* incursion *f* (dans).

forbad [fə'bæd], **forbade** [fə'beɪd] *pt* ⊳ **forbid**.

forbid [fə'bɪd] (*pt* -**bade** OR -**bad**, *pp* **forbid** OR -**bidden**) *vt* interdire, défendre ; **to** ~ **sb to do sthg** interdire OR défendre à qqn de faire qqch.

forbidden [fə'bɪdn] ◇ *pp* ⊳ **forbid**. ◇ *adj* interdit(e), défendu(e).

forbidding [fə'bɪdɪŋ] *adj* [severe, unfriendly] austère ; [threatening] sinistre.

force [fɔːs] ◇ *n* - **1.** [gen] force *f* ; **by** ~ de force - **2.** [effect] : **to be in/to come into** ~ être/entrer en vigueur. ◇ *vt* - **1.** [gen] forcer ; **to** ~ **sb to do sthg** forcer qqn à faire qqch - **2.** [press] : **to** ~ **sthg on sb** imposer qqch à qqn. ◆ **forces** *npl* : **the** ~**s** les forces *fpl* armées ; **to join** ~**s** joindre ses efforts.

force-feed *vt* nourrir de force.

forceful ['fɔːsfʊl] *adj* [person] énergique ; [speech] vigoureux(euse).

forceps ['fɔːseps] *npl* forceps *m*.

forcibly ['fɔːsəblɪ] *adv* - **1.** [using physical force] de force - **2.** [powerfully] avec vigueur.

ford [fɔːd] *n* gué *m*.

fore [fɔːʳ] ◇ *adj* NAUT à l'avant. ◇ *n* : **to come to the** ~ s'imposer.

forearm ['fɔːrɑːm] *n* avant-bras *m inv*.

foreboding [fɔː'bəʊdɪŋ] *n* pressentiment *m*.

forecast ['fɔːkɑːst] (*pt & pp* **forecast** OR -**ed**) ◇ *n* prévision *f* ; (weather) ~ prévisions météorologiques. ◇ *vt* prévoir.

foreclose [fɔː'kləʊz] ◇ *vt* saisir. ◇ *vi* : **to** ~ **on sb** saisir qqn.

forecourt ['fɔːkɔːt] *n* [of petrol station] devant *m* ; [of building] avant-cour *f*.

forefinger ['fɔːˌfɪŋgəʳ] *n* index *m*.

forefront ['fɔːfrʌnt] *n* : **in** OR **at the** ~ **of** au premier plan de.

forego [fɔː'gəʊ] = **forgo**.

foregone conclusion ['fɔːgɒn-] *n* : **it's a** ~ c'est couru.

foreground ['fɔːgraʊnd] *n* premier plan *m*.

forehand ['fɔːhænd] *n* TENNIS coup *m* droit.

forehead ['fɔːhed] *n* front *m*.

foreign ['fɒrən] *adj* - **1.** [gen] étranger(ère) ; [correspondent] à l'étranger - **2.** [policy, trade] extérieur(e).

foreign affairs *npl* affaires *fpl* étrangères.

foreign currency *n* (U) devises *fpl* étrangères.

foreigner ['fɒrənəʳ] *n* étranger *m*, -ère *f*.

foreign minister *n* ministre *m* des Affaires étrangères.

Foreign Office *n Br* : **the** ~ ≃ le ministère des Affaires étrangères.

Foreign Secretary *n Br* ≃ ministre *m* des Affaires étrangères.

foreleg ['fɔːleg] *n* [of horse] membre *m* antérieur ; [of other animals] patte *f* de devant.

foreman ['fɔːmən] (*pl* -**men** [-mən]) *n* - **1.** [of workers] contremaître *m* - **2.** JUR président *m* du jury.

foremost ['fɔ:məʊst] ⇔ *adj* principal(e). ⇔ *adv* : **first and ~ tout d'abord.**

forensic [fə'rensɪk] *adj* [department, investigation] médico-légal(e).

forensic medicine, forensic science *n* médecine *f* légale.

forerunner ['fɔ:ˌrʌnəʳ] *n* précurseur *m*.

foresee [fɔ:'si:] (*pt* -saw [-'sɔ:], *pp* -seen) *vt* prévoir.

foreseeable [fɔ:'si:əbl] *adj* prévisible ; **for the ~ future** pour tous les jours/mois *etc* à venir.

foreseen [fɔ:'si:n] *pp* ▭ foresee.

foreshadow [fɔ:'ʃædəʊ] *vt* présager.

foresight ['fɔ:saɪt] *n* (U) prévoyance *f*.

forest ['fɒrɪst] *n* forêt *f*.

forestall [fɔ:'stɔ:l] *vt* [attempt, discussion] prévenir ; [person] devancer.

forestry ['fɒrɪstrɪ] *n* sylviculture *f*.

foretaste ['fɔ:teɪst] *n* avant-goût *m*.

foretell [fɔ:'tel] (*pt* & *pp* -told) *vt* prédire.

foretold [fɔ:'təʊld] *pt* & *pp* ▭ foretell.

forever [fə'revəʳ] *adv* [eternally] (pour) toujours.

forewarn [fɔ:'wɔ:n] *vt* avertir.

foreword ['fɔ:wɜ:d] *n* avant-propos *m inv*.

forfeit ['fɔ:fɪt] ⇔ *n* amende *f* ; [in game] gage *m*. ⇔ *vt* perdre.

forgave [fə'geɪv] *pt* ▭ forgive.

forge [fɔ:dʒ] ⇔ *n* forge *f*. ⇔ *vt* - **1.** INDUSTRY & *fig* forger - **2.** [signature, money] contrefaire ; [passport] falsifier. ◆ **forge ahead** *vi* prendre de l'avance.

forger ['fɔ:dʒəʳ] *n* faussaire *mf*.

forgery ['fɔ:dʒərɪ] *n* - **1.** (U) [crime] contrefaçon *f* - **2.** [forged article] faux *m*.

forget [fə'get] (*pt* -got, *pp* -gotten) ⇔ *vt* oublier ; **to ~ to do sthg** oublier de faire qqch ; **~ it!** laisse tomber! ⇔ *vi* : **to ~ (about sthg)** oublier (qqch).

forgetful [fə'getfʊl] *adj* distrait(e), étourdi(e).

forget-me-not *n* myosotis *m*.

forgive [fə'gɪv] (*pt* -gave, *pp* -given [-'gɪvən]) *vt* pardonner ; **to ~ sb for sthg/for doing sthg** pardonner qqch à qqn/à qqn d'avoir fait qqch.

forgiveness [fə'gɪvnɪs] *n* (U) pardon *m*.

forgo [fɔ:'gəʊ] (*pt* -went, *pp* -gone [-'gɒn]) *vt* renoncer à.

forgot [fə'gɒt] *pt* ▭ forget.

forgotten [fə'gɒtn] *pp* ▭ forget.

fork [fɔ:k] ⇔ *n* - **1.** [for eating] fourchette

f - **2.** [for gardening] fourche *f* - **3.** [in road] bifurcation *f* ; [of river] embranchement *m*. ⇔ *vi* bifurquer. ◆ **fork out** *inf* ⇔ *vt fus* allonger, débourser. ⇔ *vi* : **to ~ out (for)** casquer (pour).

forklift truck ['fɔ:klɪft-] *n* chariot *m* élévateur.

forlorn [fə'lɔ:n] *adj* - **1.** [person, face] malheureux(euse), triste - **2.** [place, landscape] désolé(e) - **3.** [hope, attempt] désespéré(e).

form [fɔ:m] ⇔ *n* - **1.** [shape, fitness, type] forme *f* ; **on ~** *Br*, **in ~** *Am* en forme ; **off ~** pas en forme ; **in the ~ of** sous forme de - **2.** [questionnaire] formulaire *m* - **3.** *Br* SCH classe *f*. ⇔ *vt* former. ⇔ *vi* se former.

formal ['fɔ:ml] *adj* - **1.** [person] formaliste ; [language] soutenu(e) - **2.** [dinner party, announcement] officiel(elle) ; [dress] de cérémonie.

formality [fɔ:'mælətɪ] *n* formalité *f*.

format ['fɔ:mæt] ⇔ *n* [gen & COMPUT] format *m*. ⇔ *vt* COMPUT formater.

formation [fɔ:'meɪʃn] *n* - **1.** [gen] formation *f* - **2.** [of idea, plan] élaboration *f*.

formative ['fɔ:mətɪv] *adj* formateur (trice).

former ['fɔ:məʳ] ⇔ *adj* - **1.** [previous] ancien(enne) ; **~ husband** ex-mari *m* ; **~ pupil** ancien élève *m*, ancienne élève *f* - **2.** [first of two] premier(ère). ⇔ *n* : **the ~ le premier** (la première), celui-là (celle-là).

formerly ['fɔ:məlɪ] *adv* autrefois.

formidable ['fɔ:mɪdəbl] *adj* impressionnant(e).

formula ['fɔ:mjʊlə] (*pl* -as OR -ae [-i:]) *n* formule *f*.

formulate ['fɔ:mjʊleɪt] *vt* formuler.

forsake [fə'seɪk] (*pt* forsook, *pp* forsaken) *vt literary* [person] abandonner ; [habit] renoncer à.

forsaken [fə'seɪkn] *adj* abandonné(e).

forsook [fə'sʊk] *pt* ▭ forsake.

fort [fɔ:t] *n* fort *m*.

forte ['fɔ:tɪ] *n* point *m* fort.

forth [fɔ:θ] *adv literary* en avant.

forthcoming [fɔ:θ'kʌmɪŋ] *adj* - **1.** [imminent] à venir - **2.** [helpful] communicatif(ive).

forthright ['fɔ:θraɪt] *adj* franc (franche), direct(e).

forthwith [ˌfɔ:θ'wɪθ] *adv fml* aussitôt.

fortified wine ['fɔ:tɪfaɪd-] *n* vin *m* de liqueur.

fortify ['fɔ:tɪfaɪ] *vt* - **1.** MIL fortifier - **2.** *fig* [resolve etc] renforcer.

fortnight ['fɔːtnaɪt] n quinze jours mpl, quinzaine f.

fortnightly ['fɔːt,naɪtlɪ] <> adj bimensuel(elle). <> adv tous les quinze jours.

fortress ['fɔːtrɪs] n forteresse f.

fortunate ['fɔːtʃnət] adj heureux(euse) ; **to be ~** avoir de la chance.

fortunately ['fɔːtʃnətlɪ] adv heureusement.

fortune ['fɔːtʃuːn] n - **1.** [wealth] fortune f - **2.** [luck] fortune f, chance f - **3.** [future] : **to tell sb's ~** dire la bonne aventure à qqn.

fortune-teller [-,telə'] n diseuse f de bonne aventure.

forty ['fɔːtɪ] num quarante ; see also **sixty**.

forward ['fɔːwəd] <> adj - **1.** [movement] en avant - **2.** [planning] à long terme - **3.** [impudent] effronté(e). <> adv - **1.** [ahead] en avant ; **to go** OR **move ~** avancer - **2.** [in time] : **to bring a meeting ~** avancer la date d'une réunion. <> n SPORT avant m. <> vt [letter] faire suivre ; [goods] expédier.

forwarding address ['fɔːwədɪŋ-] n adresse f où faire suivre le courrier.

forwards ['fɔːwədz] adv = forward.

forwent [fɔː'went] pt ▷ forgo.

fossil ['fɒsl] n fossile m.

foster ['fɒstə'] <> adj [family] d'accueil. <> vt - **1.** [child] accueillir - **2.** fig [nurture] nourrir, entretenir.

foster child n enfant m placé en famille d'accueil.

foster parent n parent m nourricier.

fought [fɔːt] pt & pp ▷ fight.

foul [faʊl] <> adj - **1.** [gen] infect(e) ; [water] croupi(e) - **2.** [language] ordurier(ère). <> n SPORT faute f. <> vt - **1.** [make dirty] souiller, salir - **2.** SPORT commettre une faute contre.

found [faʊnd] <> pt & pp ▷ find. <> vt - **1.** [hospital, town] fonder - **2.** [base] : **to ~ sthg on** fonder OR baser qqch sur.

foundation [faʊn'deɪʃn] n - **1.** [creation, organization] fondation f - **2.** [basis] fondement m, base f - **3.** : **~ (cream)** fond m de teint. ◆ **foundations** npl CONSTR fondations fpl.

founder ['faʊndə'] <> n fondateur m, -trice f. <> vi [ship] sombrer.

foundry ['faʊndrɪ] n fonderie f.

fountain ['faʊntɪn] n fontaine f.

fountain pen n stylo m à encre.

four [fɔː'] num quatre ; **on all ~s** à quatre pattes ; see also **six**.

four-letter word n mot m grossier.

four-poster (bed) n lit m à baldaquin.

foursome ['fɔːsəm] n groupe m de quatre.

fourteen [,fɔː'tiːn] num quatorze ; see also **six**.

fourth [fɔːθ] num quatrième ; see also **sixth**.

Fourth of July n : **the ~** Fête f de l'Indépendance américaine, célébrée le 4 juillet.

four-wheel drive n : **with ~** à quatre roues motrices.

fowl [faʊl] (pl inv OR **-s**) n volaille f.

fox [fɒks] <> n renard m. <> vt laisser perplexe.

foxglove ['fɒksglʌv] n digitale f.

foyer ['fɔɪeɪ] n - **1.** [of hotel, theatre] foyer m - **2.** Am [of house] hall m d'entrée.

fracas ['frækaː, Am 'freɪkəs] (Br pl inv, Am pl **-ses** [-siːz]) n bagarre f.

fraction ['frækʃn] n fraction f ; **a ~ too big** légèrement OR un petit peu trop grand.

fractionally ['frækʃnəlɪ] adv un tout petit peu.

fracture ['fræktʃə'] <> n fracture f. <> vt fracturer.

fragile ['frædʒaɪl] adj fragile.

fragment ['frægmənt] n fragment m.

fragrance ['freɪgrəns] n parfum m.

fragrant ['freɪgrənt] adj parfumé(e).

frail [freɪl] adj fragile.

frame [freɪm] <> n - **1.** [gen] cadre m ; [of glasses] monture f ; [of door, window] encadrement m ; [of boat] carcasse f - **2.** [physique] charpente f. <> vt - **1.** [gen] encadrer - **2.** [express] formuler - **3.** inf [set up] monter un coup contre.

frame of mind n état m d'esprit.

framework ['freɪmwɜːk] n - **1.** [structure] armature f, carcasse f - **2.** fig [basis] structure f, cadre m.

France [frɑːns] n France f ; **in ~** en France.

franchise ['fræntʃaɪz] n - **1.** POL droit m de vote - **2.** COMM franchise f.

frank [fræŋk] <> adj franc (franche). <> vt affranchir.

frankly ['fræŋklɪ] adv franchement.

frantic ['fræntɪk] adj frénétique.

fraternity [frə'tɜːnətɪ] n - **1.** [community] confrérie f - **2.** (U) [friendship] fraternité f - **3.** Am [of students] club m d'étudiants.

fraternize, -ise ['frætənaɪz] vi fraterniser.

fraud [frɔːd] n - **1.** (U) [crime] fraude f - **2.** pej [impostor] imposteur m.

fraught [frɔːt] *adj* - **1.** [full] : ~ **with** plein(e) de - **2.** *Br* [person] tendu(e) ; [time, situation] difficile.

fray [freɪ] <> *vt fig* : my nerves were ~ed j'étais extrêmement tendu(e), j'étais à bout de nerfs. <> *vi* [material, sleeves] s'user ; **tempers ~ed** *fig* l'atmosphère était tendue OR électrique. <> *n literary* bagarre *f*.

frayed [freɪd] *adj* [jeans, collar] élimé(e).

freak [friːk] <> *adj* bizarre, insolite. <> *n* - **1.** [strange creature] monstre *m*, phénomène *m* - **2.** [unusual event] accident *m* bizarre - **3.** *inf* [fanatic] fana *mf*. ◆ **freak out** *inf* *vi* [get angry] exploser (de colère) ; [panic] paniquer.

freckle ['frekl] *n* tache *f* de rousseur.

free [friː] (*compar* **freer**, *superl* **freest**, *pt* & *pp* **freed**) <> *adj* - **1.** [gen] libre ; **to be ~ to do sthg** être libre de faire qqch ; **feel ~!** je t'en prie! ; **to set ~** libérer - **2.** [not paid for] gratuit(e) ; ~ **of charge** gratuitement. <> *adv* - **1.** [without payment] gratuitement ; **for ~** gratuitement - **2.** [run, live] librement. <> *vt* - **1.** [gen] libérer - **2.** [trapped person, object] dégager.

freedom ['friːdəm] *n* - **1.** [gen] liberté *f* ; ~ **of speech** liberté d'expression - **2.** [exception] : ~ **(from)** exemption *f* (de).

Freefone® ['friːfəʊn] *n Br* (U) ≃ numéro *m* vert.

free-for-all *n* mêlée *f* générale.

free gift *n* prime *f*.

freehand ['friːhænd] *adj* & *adv* à main levée.

freehold ['friːhəʊld] *n* propriété *f* foncière inaliénable.

free house *n* pub *m* en gérance libre.

free kick *n* coup *m* franc.

freelance ['friːlɑːns] <> *adj* indépendant(e), free-lance (*inv*). <> *n* indépendant *m*, -e *f*, free-lance *mf*.

freely ['friːlɪ] *adv* - **1.** [gen] librement - **2.** [generously] sans compter.

Freemason ['friːˌmeɪsn] *n* franc-maçon *m*.

Freephone® ['friːfəʊn] = **Freefone®**.

Freepost® ['friːpəʊst] *n* port *m* payé.

free-range *adj* de ferme.

freestyle ['friːstaɪl] *n* SWIMMING nage *f* libre.

free trade *n* (U) libre-échange *m*.

freeway ['friːweɪ] *n Am* autoroute *f*.

freewheel [ˌfriːˈwiːl] *vi* [on bicycle] rouler en roue libre ; [in car] rouler au point mort.

free will *n* (U) libre arbitre *m* ; **to do sthg**

of one's own ~ faire qqch de son propre gré.

freeze [friːz] (*pt* **froze**, *pp* **frozen**) <> *vt* - **1.** [gen] geler ; [food] congeler - **2.** [wages, prices] bloquer. <> *vi* - **1.** [gen] geler - **2.** [stop moving] s'arrêter. <> *n* - **1.** [cold weather] gel *m* - **2.** [of wages, prices] blocage *m*.

freeze-dried [-'draɪd] *adj* lyophilisé(e).

freezer ['friːzər] *n* congélateur *m*.

freezing ['friːzɪŋ] <> *adj* glacé(e) ; **I'm ~** je gèle. <> *n* = **freezing point**.

freezing point *n* point *m* de congélation.

freight [freɪt] *n* [goods] fret *m*.

freight train *n* train *m* de marchandises.

French [frentʃ] <> *adj* français(e). <> *n* [language] français *m*. <> *npl* : **the ~** les Français *mpl*.

French bean *n* haricot *m* vert.

French bread *n* (U) baguette *f*.

French Canadian <> *adj* canadien français (canadienne française). <> *n* Canadien français *m*, Canadienne française *f*.

French doors = **French windows**.

French dressing *n* [in UK] vinaigrette *f* ; [in US] sauce-salade à base de mayonnaise et de ketchup.

French fries *npl* frites *fpl*.

Frenchman ['frentʃmən] (*pl* -**men** [-mən]) *n* Français *m*.

French stick *n Br* baguette *f*.

French windows *npl* porte-fenêtre *f*.

Frenchwoman ['frentʃˌwʊmən] (*pl* -**women** [-ˌwɪmɪn]) *n* Française *f*.

frenetic [frə'netɪk] *adj* frénétique.

frenzy ['frenzɪ] *n* frénésie *f*.

frequency ['friːkwənsɪ] *n* fréquence *f*.

frequent [*adj* 'friːkwənt, *vb* frɪ'kwent] <> *adj* fréquent(e). <> *vt* fréquenter.

frequently ['friːkwəntlɪ] *adv* fréquemment.

fresh [freʃ] *adj* - **1.** [gen] frais (fraîche) - **2.** [not salty] doux (douce) - **3.** [new - drink, piece of paper] autre ; [- look, approach] nouveau(elle) - **4.** *inf dated* [cheeky] familier(ère).

freshen ['freʃn] <> *vt* rafraîchir. <> *vi* [wind] devenir plus fort. ◆ **freshen up** *vi* faire un brin de toilette.

fresher ['freʃər] *n Br inf* bleu *m*, -e *f*.

freshly ['freʃlɪ] *adv* [squeezed, ironed] fraîchement.

freshman ['freʃmən] (*pl* -**men** [-mən]) *n* étudiant *m*, -e *f* de première année.

freshness ['freʃnɪs] *n (U)* - **1.** [gen] fraîcheur *f* - **2.** [originality] nouveauté *f*.

freshwater ['freʃ‚wɔːtər] *adj* d'eau douce.

fret [fret] *vi* [worry] s'inquiéter.

friar ['fraɪər] *n* frère *m*.

friction ['frɪkʃn] *n (U)* friction *f*.

Friday ['fraɪdɪ] *n* vendredi *m* ; *see also* **Saturday**.

fridge [frɪdʒ] *n esp Br inf* frigo *m*.

fridge-freezer *n Br* réfrigérateur-congélateur *m*.

fried [fraɪd] *adj* frit(e) ; **~ egg** œuf *m* au plat.

friend [frend] *n* ami *m*, -e *f* ; **to be ~s with sb** être ami avec qqn ; **to make ~s (with sb)** se lier d'amitié (avec qqn).

friendly ['frendlɪ] *adj* [person, manner, match] amical(e) ; [nation] ami(e) ; [argument] sans conséquence ; **to be ~ with sb** être ami avec qqn.

friendship ['frendʃɪp] *n* amitié *f*.

fries [fraɪz] = **French fries**.

frieze [friːz] *n* frise *f*.

fright [fraɪt] *n* peur *f* ; **to give sb a ~** faire peur à qqn ; **to take ~** prendre peur.

frighten ['fraɪtn] *vt* faire peur à, effrayer.

frightened ['fraɪtnd] *adj* apeuré(e) ; **to be ~ of sth/of doing sth** avoir peur de qqch/de faire qqch.

frightening ['fraɪtnɪŋ] *adj* effrayant(e).

frightful ['fraɪtfʊl] *adj dated* effroyable.

frigid ['frɪdʒɪd] *adj* [sexually] frigide.

frill [frɪl] *n* - **1.** [decoration] volant *m* - **2.** *inf* [extra] supplément *m*.

fringe [frɪndʒ] *n* - **1.** [gen] frange *f* - **2.** [edge - of village] bordure *f* ; [- of wood, forest] lisière *f*.

fringe benefit *n* avantage *m* extrasalarial.

frisk [frɪsk] *vt* fouiller.

frisky ['frɪskɪ] *adj inf* vif (vive).

fritter ['frɪtər] *n* beignet *m*. ◆ **fritter away** *vt sep* gaspiller.

frivolous ['frɪvələs] *adj* frivole.

frizzy ['frɪzɪ] *adj* crépu(e).

fro [frəʊ] ⟿ **to**.

frock [frɒk] *n dated* robe *f*.

frog [frɒg] *n* [animal] grenouille *f* ; **to have a ~ in one's throat** avoir un chat dans la gorge.

frogman ['frɒgmən] (*pl* **-men** [-mən]) *n* homme-grenouille *m*.

frogmen ['frɒgmən] *pl* ⟿ **frogman**.

frolic ['frɒlɪk] (*pt & pp* **-ked**, *cont* **-king**) *vi* folâtrer.

from [*weak form* frəm, *strong form* frɒm] *prep* - **1.** [indicating source, origin, removal] de ; **where are you ~?** d'où venez-vous?, d'où êtes-vous? ; **I got a letter ~ her today** j'ai reçu une lettre d'elle aujourd'hui ; **a flight ~ Paris** un vol en provenance de Paris ; **to translate ~ Spanish into English** traduire d'espagnol en anglais ; **to drink ~ a glass** boire dans un verre ; **to take sth (away) ~ sb** prendre qqch à qqn - **2.** [indicating a deduction] de ; **to deduct sth ~ sth** retrancher qqch de qqch - **3.** [indicating escape, separation] de ; **he ran away ~ home** il a fait une fugue, il s'est sauvé de chez lui - **4.** [indicating position] de ; **seen ~ above/below** vu d'en haut/d'en bas - **5.** [indicating distance] de ; **it's 60 km ~ here** c'est à 60 km d'ici - **6.** [indicating material object is made out of] en ; **it's made ~ wood/plastic** c'est en bois/plastique - **7.** [starting at a particular time] de ; **~ 2 pm to** OR **till 6 pm** de 14 h à 18 h ; **~ the moment I saw him** dès que OR dès l'instant où je l'ai vu - **8.** [indicating difference] de ; **to be different ~ sb/sth** être différent de qqn/qqch - **9.** [indicating change] : **~ ... to** de ... à ; **the price went up ~ £100 to £150** le prix est passé OR monté de 100 livres à 150 livres - **10.** [because of, as a result of] de ; **to suffer ~ cold/hunger** souffrir du froid/de la faim - **11.** [on the evidence of] d'après, à - **12.** [indicating lowest amount] depuis, à partir de ; **prices start ~ £50** le premier prix est de 50 livres.

front [frʌnt] ⬦ *n* - **1.** [most forward part - gen] avant *m* ; [- of dress, envelope, house] devant *m* ; [- of class] premier rang *m* - **2.** METEOR & MIL front *m* - **3.** : **(sea) front** *m* de mer - **4.** [outward appearance - of person] contenance *f* ; [- of business] *pej* façade *f*. ⬦ *adj* [tooth, garden] de devant ; [row, page] premier(ère). ◆ **in front** *adv* - **1.** [further forward - walk, push] devant ; [- people] à l'avant - **2.** [winning] : **to be in ~** mener. ◆ **in front of** *prep* devant.

frontbench [‚frʌnt'bentʃ] *n à la chambre des Communes, bancs occupés respectivement par les ministres du gouvernement en exercice et ceux du gouvernement fantôme.*

front door *n* porte *f* d'entrée.

frontier ['frʌn‚tɪər, *Am* frʌn'tɪər] *n* [border] frontière *f* ; *fig* limite *f*.

front man *n* - **1.** [of company, organization] porte-parole *m inv* - **2.** TV présentateur *m*.

front room *n* salon *m*.

front-runner *n* favori *m*, -ite *f*.

front-wheel drive *n* traction *f* avant.

frost [frɒst] *n* gel *m*.

frostbite ['frɒstbaɪt] *n (U)* gelure *f*.

frosted ['frɒstɪd] *adj* - **1.** [glass] dépoli(e) - **2.** *Am* CULIN glacé(e).

frosty ['frɒstɪ] *adj* - **1.** [weather, welcome] glacial(e) - **2.** [field, window] gelé(e).

froth [frɒθ] *n* [on beer] mousse *f* ; [on sea] écume *f*.

frown [fraʊn] *vi* froncer les sourcils.
➡ **frown (up)on** *vt fus* désapprouver.

froze [frəʊz] *pt* ▷ **freeze**.

frozen [frəʊzn] ◇ *pp* ▷ **freeze**. ◇ *adj* gelé(e) ; [food] congelé(e).

frugal ['fru:gl] *adj* - **1.** [meal] frugal(e) - **2.** [person, life] économe.

fruit [fru:t] (*pl inv* OR **-s**) *n* fruit *m*.

fruitcake ['fru:tkeɪk] *n* cake *m*.

fruiterer ['fru:tərəʳ] *n Br* fruitier *m*.

fruitful ['fru:tfʊl] *adj* [successful] fructueux(euse).

fruition [fru:'ɪʃn] *n* : **to come to ~** se réaliser.

fruit juice *n* jus *m* de fruits.

fruitless ['fru:tlɪs] *adj* vain(e).

fruit machine *n Br* machine *f* à sous.

fruit salad *n* salade *f* de fruits.

frumpy ['frʌmpɪ] *adj* mal attifée(e), mal fagoté(e).

frustrate [frʌ'streɪt] *vt* - **1.** [annoy, disappoint] frustrer - **2.** [prevent] faire échouer.

frustrated [frʌ'streɪtɪd] *adj* - **1.** [person, artist] frustré(e) - **2.** [effort, love] vain(e).

frustration [frʌ'streɪʃn] *n* frustration *f*.

fry [fraɪ] (*pt* & *pp* **fried**) *vt* & *vi* frire.

frying pan ['fraɪɪŋ-] *n* poêle *f* à frire.

ft. *abbr of* **foot**, **feet**.

fuck [fʌk] *vulg vt* & *vi* baiser. ➡ **fuck off** *vi vulg* : **~ off!** fous le camp !

fudge [fʌdʒ] *n (U)* [sweet] caramel *m* (mou).

fuel [fjʊəl] ◇ *n* combustible *m* ; [for engine] carburant *m*. ◇ *vt* - **1.** [supply with fuel] alimenter (en combustible/carburant) - **2.** *fig* [speculation] nourrir.

fuel pump *n* pompe *f* d'alimentation.

fuel tank *n* réservoir *m* à carburant.

fugitive ['fju:dʒətɪv] *n* fugitif *m*, -ive *f*.

fulfil, fulfill *Am* [fʊl'fɪl] *vt* - **1.** [duty, role] remplir ; [hope] répondre à ; [ambition, prophecy] réaliser - **2.** [satisfy - need] satisfaire.

fulfilment, fulfillment *Am* [fʊl'fɪl-ment] *n (U)* - **1.** [satisfaction] grande satisfaction *f* - **2.** [of ambition, dream] réalisation *f* ; [of role, promise] exécution *f* ; [of need] satisfaction *f*.

full [fʊl] ◇ *adj* - **1.** [gen] plein(e) ; [bus, car park] complet(ète) ; [with food] gavé(e), repu(e) - **2.** [complete - recovery, control] total(e) ; [- explanation, day] entier(ère) ; [- volume] maximum - **3.** [busy - life] rempli(e) ; [- timetable, day] chargé(e) - **4.** [flavour] riche - **5.** [plump - figure] rondelet(ette) ; [- mouth] charnu(e) - **6.** [skirt, sleeve] ample. ◇ *adv* [very] : **you know ~ well that ...** tu sais très bien que ... ◇ *n* : **in ~** complètement, entièrement.

full-blown [-'bləʊn] *adj* général(e) ; **to have ~ AIDS** avoir le Sida avancé.

full board *n* pension *f* complète.

full-fledged *Am* = **fully-fledged**.

full moon *n* pleine lune *f*.

full-scale *adj* - **1.** [life-size] grandeur nature *(inv)* - **2.** [complete] de grande envergure.

full stop *n Br* point *m*.

full time *n Br* SPORT fin *f* de match.
➡ **full-time** *adj* & *adv* [work, worker] à temps plein.

full up *adj* [bus, train] complet(ète) ; [with food] gavé(e), repu(e).

fully ['fʊlɪ] *adv* [understand, satisfy] tout à fait ; [trained, describe] entièrement.

fully-fledged *Br*, **full-fledged** *Am* [-'fledʒd] *adj* diplômé(e).

fulsome ['fʊlsəm] *adj* excessif(ive).

fumble ['fʌmbl] *vi* fouiller, tâtonner ; **to ~ for** fouiller pour trouver.

fume [fju:m] *vi* [with anger] rager.
➡ **fumes** *npl* [from paint] émanations *fpl* ; [from smoke] fumées *fpl* ; [from car] gaz *mpl* d'échappement.

fumigate ['fju:mɪgeɪt] *vt* fumiger.

fun [fʌn] *n (U)* - **1.** [pleasure, amusement] : **to have ~** s'amuser ; **for ~, for the ~ of it** pour s'amuser - **2.** [playfulness] : **to be full of ~** être plein(e) d'entrain - **3.** [ridicule] : **to make ~ of** OR **poke ~ at sb** se moquer de qqn.

function ['fʌŋkʃn] ◇ *n* - **1.** [gen] fonction *f* - **2.** [formal social event] réception *f* officielle. ◇ *vi* fonctionner ; **to ~ as** servir de.

functional ['fʌŋkʃnəl] *adj* - **1.** [practical] fonctionnel(elle) - **2.** [operational] en état de marche.

fund [fʌnd] ◇ *n* fonds *m* ; *fig* [of knowledge] puits *m*. ◇ *vt* financer. ➡ **funds** *npl* fonds *mpl*.

fundamental [ˌfʌndə'mentl] *adj* : ~ **(to)** fondamental(e) (à).

fundamentalist [ˌfʌndə'mentəlɪst] ◇ *adj* RELIG fondamentaliste ; [Muslim] intégriste. ◇ *n* [Muslim] intégriste *mf*.

funding ['fʌndɪŋ] *n (U)* financement *m*.

funeral ['fju:nərəl] *n* obsèques *fpl*.

funeral parlour *n* entreprise *f* de pompes funèbres.

funfair ['fʌnfeəʳ] *n* Br fête *f* foraine.

fungus ['fʌŋgəs] (*pl* -gi [-gaɪ], -guses [-gəsi:z]) *n* champignon *m*.

funnel ['fʌnl] *n* - **1.** [tube] entonnoir *m* - **2.** [of ship] cheminée *f*.

funny ['fʌnɪ] *adj* - **1.** [amusing, odd] drôle - **2.** [ill] tout drôle (toute drôle).

fur [fɜːʳ] *n* fourrure *f*.

fur coat *n* (manteau *m* de) fourrure *f*.

furious ['fjʊərɪəs] *adj* - **1.** [very angry] furieux(euse) - **2.** [wild - effort, battle] acharné(e) ; [- temper] déchaîné(e).

furlong ['fɜːlɒŋ] *n* = 201,17 mètres.

furnace ['fɜːnɪs] *n* [fire] fournaise *f*.

furnish ['fɜːnɪʃ] *vt* - **1.** [fit out] meubler - **2.** *fml* [provide] fournir ; **to ~ sb with sthg** fournir qqch à qqn.

furnished ['fɜːnɪʃt] *adj* meublé(e).

furnishings ['fɜːnɪʃɪŋz] *npl* mobilier *m*.

furniture ['fɜːnɪtʃəʳ] *n (U)* meubles *mpl* ; **a piece of ~** un meuble.

furrow ['fʌrəʊ] *n* - **1.** [in field] sillon *m* - **2.** [on forehead] ride *f*.

furry ['fɜːrɪ] *adj* - **1.** [animal] à fourrure - **2.** [material] recouvert(e) de fourrure.

further ['fɜːðəʳ] ◇ *compar* ⊳ **far**. ◇ *adv* - **1.** [gen] plus loin ; **how much ~ is it?** combien de kilomètres y a-t-il? ; **~ on** plus loin - **2.** [more - complicate, develop] davantage ; [- enquire] plus avant - **3.** [in addition] de plus. ◇ *adj* nouveau(elle), supplémentaire ; **until ~ notice** jusqu'à nouvel ordre. ◇ *vt* [career, aims] faire avancer ; [cause] encourager.

further education *n* Br éducation *f* postscolaire.

furthermore [ˌfɜːðə'mɔːʳ] *adv* de plus.

furthest ['fɜːðɪst] ◇ *superl* ⊳ **far**. ◇ *adj* le plus éloigné (la plus éloignée). ◇ *adv* le plus loin.

furtive ['fɜːtɪv] *adj* [person] sournois(e) ; [glance] furtif(ive).

fury ['fjʊərɪ] *n* fureur *f*.

fuse, fuze *Am* [fju:z] ◇ *n* - **1.** ELEC fusible *m*, plomb *m* - **2.** [of bomb] détonateur *m* ; [of firework] amorce *f*. ◇ *vt* - **1.** [join by heat] réunir par la fusion - **2.** [combine] fusion-

ner. ◇ *vi* - **1.** ELEC : **the lights have ~d** les plombs ont sauté - **2.** [join by heat] fondre - **3.** [combine] fusionner.

fuse-box *n* boîte *f* à fusibles.

fused [fju:zd] *adj* [plug] avec fusible incorporé.

fuselage ['fju:zəlɑːʒ] *n* fuselage *m*.

fuss [fʌs] ◇ *n* - **1.** [excitement, anxiety] agitation *f* ; **to make a ~** faire des histoires - **2.** *(U)* [complaints] protestations *fpl*. ◇ *vi* faire des histoires.

fussy ['fʌsɪ] *adj* - **1.** [fastidious - person] tatillon(onne) ; [- eater] difficile - **2.** [overdecorated] tarabiscoté(e).

futile ['fju:taɪl] *adj* vain(e).

futon ['fu:tɒn] *n* futon *m*.

future ['fju:tʃəʳ] ◇ *n* - **1.** [gen] avenir *m* ; **in ~** à l'avenir ; **in the ~** dans le futur, à l'avenir - **2.** GRAMM : **~ (tense)** futur *m*. ◇ *adj* futur(e).

fuze *Am* = **fuse**.

fuzzy ['fʌzɪ] *adj* - **1.** [hair] crépu(e) - **2.** [photo, image] flou(e) - **3.** [thoughts, mind] confus(e).

g[1] (*pl* **g's** OR **gs**), **G** (*pl* **G's** OR **Gs**) [dʒi:] *n* [letter] g *m inv*, G *m inv*. ◆ **G** ◇ *n* MUS sol *m*. ◇ (*abbr of* **good**) B.

g[2] (*abbr of* **gram**) g.

gab [gæb] ⊳ **gift**.

gabble ['gæbl] ◇ *vt & vi* baragouiner. ◇ *n* charabia *m*.

gable ['geɪbl] *n* pignon *m*.

gadget ['gædʒɪt] *n* gadget *m*.

Gaelic ['geɪlɪk] ◇ *adj* gaélique. ◇ *n* gaélique *m*.

gag [gæg] ◇ *n* - **1.** [for mouth] bâillon *m* - **2.** *inf* [joke] blague *f*, gag *m*. ◇ *vt* [put gag on] bâillonner.

gage *Am* = **gauge**.

gaiety ['geɪətɪ] *n* gaieté *f*.

gaily ['geɪlɪ] *adv* - **1.** [cheerfully] gaiement - **2.** [thoughtlessly] allègrement.

gain [geɪn] ◇ *n* - **1.** [gen] profit *m* - **2.** [improvement] augmentation *f*. ◇ *vt* - **1.** [acquire] gagner - **2.** [increase in - speed, weight] prendre ; [- confidence] gagner en.

◇ *vi* - **1.** [advance] **: to ~ in sthg** gagner en qqch - **2.** [benefit] **: to ~ from** OR **by sthg** tirer un avantage de qqch - **3.** [watch, clock] avancer. ◆ **gain on** *vt fus* rattraper.

gait [geɪt] *n* démarche *f*.

gal. *abbr of* **gallon.**

gala ['ɡɑːlə] *n* [celebration] gala *m*.

galaxy ['ɡæləksɪ] *n* galaxie *f*.

gale [ɡeɪl] *n* [wind] grand vent *m*.

gall [ɡɔːl] *n* [nerve] **: to have the ~ to do sthg** avoir le toupet de faire qqch.

gallant [*sense 1* 'ɡælənt, *sense 2* ɡə'lænt, 'ɡælənt] *adj* - **1.** [courageous] courageux(euse) - **2.** [polite to women] galant.

gall bladder *n* vésicule *f* biliaire.

gallery ['ɡælərɪ] *n* - **1.** [gen] galerie *f* - **2.** [for displaying art] musée *m* - **3.** [in theatre] paradis *m*.

galley ['ɡælɪ] (*pl* **-s**) *n* - **1.** [ship] galère *f* - **2.** [kitchen] coquerie *f*.

Gallic ['ɡælɪk] *adj* français(e).

galling ['ɡɔːlɪŋ] *adj* humiliant(e).

gallivant [ˌɡælɪ'vænt] *vi inf* mener une vie de patachon.

gallon ['ɡælən] *n* = 4,546 litres, gallon *m*.

gallop ['ɡæləp] ◇ *n* galop *m*. ◇ *vi* galoper.

gallows ['ɡæləʊz] (*pl inv*) *n* gibet *m*.

gallstone ['ɡɔːlstəʊn] *n* calcul *m* biliaire.

galore [ɡə'lɔːʳ] *adj* en abondance.

galvanize, -ise ['ɡælvənaɪz] *vt* - **1.** TECH galvaniser - **2.** [impel] **: to ~ sb into action** pousser qqn à agir.

gambit ['ɡæmbɪt] *n* entrée *f* en matière.

gamble ['ɡæmbl] ◇ *n* [calculated risk] risque *m*. ◇ *vi* - **1.** [bet] jouer **; to ~ on** jouer de l'argent sur - **2.** [take risk] **: to ~ on** miser sur.

gambler ['ɡæmbləʳ] *n* joueur *m*, -euse *f*.

gambling ['ɡæmblɪŋ] *n* (*U*) jeu *m*.

game [ɡeɪm] ◇ *n* - **1.** [gen] jeu *m* - **2.** [match] match *m* - **3.** (*U*) [hunted animals] gibier *m*. ◇ *adj* - **1.** [brave] courageux(euse) - **2.** [willing] **: ~ (for sthg/to do sthg)** partant(e) (pour qqch/pour faire qqch). ◆ **games** ◇ *n* SCH éducation *f* physique. ◇ *npl* [sporting contest] jeux *mpl*.

gamekeeper ['ɡeɪmˌkiːpəʳ] *n* garde-chasse *m*.

game reserve *n* réserve *f* (de chasse).

games console [ɡeɪmz-] *n* COMPUT console *f* de jeux.

game show *n* jeu *m* télévisé.

gammon ['ɡæmən] *n Br* jambon *m* fumé.

gamut ['ɡæmət] *n* gamme *f*.

gang [ɡæŋ] *n* - **1.** [of criminals] gang *m* - **2.** [of young people] bande *f*. ◆ **gang up** *vi inf* **: to ~ up (on)** se liguer (contre).

gangland ['ɡæŋlænd] *n* (*U*) milieu *m*.

gangrene ['ɡæŋɡriːn] *n* gangrène *f*.

gangster ['ɡæŋstəʳ] *n* gangster *m*.

gangway ['ɡæŋweɪ] *n* - **1.** *Br* [aisle] allée *f* - **2.** [gangplank] passerelle *f*.

gantry ['ɡæntrɪ] *n* portique *m*.

gaol [dʒeɪl] *Br* = **jail.**

gap [ɡæp] *n* - **1.** [empty space] trou *m* ; [in text] blanc *m* ; *fig* [in knowledge, report] lacune *f* - **2.** [interval of time] période *f* - **3.** *fig* [great difference] fossé *m*.

gape [ɡeɪp] *vi* - **1.** [person] rester bouche bée - **2.** [hole, shirt] bâiller.

gaping ['ɡeɪpɪŋ] *adj* - **1.** [open-mouthed] bouche bée (*inv*) - **2.** [wide open] béant(e) ; [shirt] grand ouvert (grande ouverte).

garage [*Br* 'ɡærɑːʒ, 'ɡærɪdʒ , *Am* ɡə'rɑːʒ] *n* - **1.** [gen] garage *m* - **2.** *Br* [for fuel] station-service *f*.

garbage ['ɡɑːbɪdʒ] *n* (*U*) - **1.** [refuse] détritus *mpl* - **2.** *inf* [nonsense] idioties *fpl*.

garbage can *n Am* poubelle *f*.

garbage truck *n Am* camion-poubelle *m*.

garbled ['ɡɑːbld] *adj* confus(e).

garden ['ɡɑːdn] ◇ *n* jardin *m*. ◇ *vi* jardiner.

garden centre *n* jardinerie *f*, garden centre *m*.

gardener ['ɡɑːdnəʳ] *n* [professional] jardinier *m*, -ère *f*, [amateur] personne *f* qui aime jardiner, amateur *m* de jardinage.

gardening ['ɡɑːdnɪŋ] *n* jardinage *m*.

garden shed *n* abri *m* de jardin.

gargle ['ɡɑːɡl] *vi* se gargariser.

gargoyle ['ɡɑːɡɔɪl] *n* gargouille *f*.

garish ['ɡeərɪʃ] *adj* criard(e).

garland ['ɡɑːlənd] *n* guirlande *f* de fleurs.

garlic ['ɡɑːlɪk] *n* ail *m*.

garlic bread *n* pain *m* à l'ail.

garment ['ɡɑːmənt] *n* vêtement *m*.

garnish ['ɡɑːnɪʃ] ◇ *n* garniture *f*. ◇ *vt* garnir.

garrison ['ɡærɪsn] *n* [soldiers] garnison *f*.

garrulous ['ɡærələs] *adj* volubile.

garter ['ɡɑːtəʳ] *n* - **1.** [for socks] support-chaussette *m* ; [for stockings] jarretière *f* - **2.** *Am* [suspender] jarretelle *f*.

gas [ɡæs] (*pl* **gases** OR **gasses** [ɡæsiːz]) ◇ *n*

- **1.** [gen] gaz *m inv* - **2.** *Am* [for vehicle] essence *f.* ◇ *vt* gazer.

gas cooker *n Br* cuisinière *f* à gaz.

gas cylinder *n* bouteille *f* de gaz.

gas fire *n Br* appareil *m* de chauffage à gaz.

gas gauge *n Am* jauge *f* d'essence.

gash [gæʃ] ◇ *n* entaille *f.* ◇ *vt* entailler.

gasket ['gæskɪt] *n* joint *m* d'étanchéité.

gasman ['gæsmæn] (*pl* -**men** [-men]) *n* [who reads meter] employé *m* du gaz ; [for repairs] installateur *m* de gaz.

gas mask *n* masque *m* à gaz.

gas meter *n* compteur *m* à gaz.

gasoline ['gæsəliːn] *n Am* essence *f.*

gasp [gɑːsp] ◇ *n* halètement *m.* ◇ *vi* - **1.** [breathe quickly] haleter - **2.** [in shock, surprise] avoir le souffle coupé.

gas pedal *n Am* accélérateur *m.*

gas station *n Am* station-service *f.*

gas stove = gas cooker.

gas tank *n Am* réservoir *m.*

gas tap *n* [for mains supply] robinet *m* de gaz ; [on gas fire] prise *f* de gaz.

gastroenteritis ['gæstrəʊˌentə'raɪtɪs] *n* gastro-entérite *f.*

gastronomy [gæs'trɒnəmɪ] *n* gastronomie *f.*

gasworks ['gæswɜːks] (*pl inv*) *n* usine *f* à gaz.

gate [geɪt] *n* [of garden, farm] barrière *f* ; [of town, at airport] porte *f* ; [of park] grille *f.*

gatecrash ['geɪtkræʃ] *inf vt & vi prendre part à une réunion, une réception sans y avoir été convié.*

gateway ['geɪtweɪ] *n* - **1.** [entrance] entrée *f* - **2.** [means of access] : ~ **to** porte *f* de ; *fig* clé *f* de.

gather ['gæðə'] ◇ *vt* - **1.** [collect] ramasser ; [flowers] cueillir ; [information] recueillir ; [courage, strength] rassembler ; **to** ~ **together** rassembler - **2.** [increase - speed, force] prendre - **3.** [understand] : **to** ~ **(that)** ... croire comprendre que ... - **4.** [cloth - into folds] plisser. ◇ *vi* [come together] se rassembler ; [clouds] s'amonceler.

gathering ['gæðərɪŋ] *n* [meeting] rassemblement *m.*

gaudy ['gɔːdɪ] *adj* voyant(e).

gauge, gage *Am* [geɪdʒ] ◇ *n* - **1.** [for rain] pluviomètre *m* ; [for fuel] jauge *f* (d'essence) ; [for tyre pressure] manomètre *m* - **2.** [of gun, wire] calibre *m* - **3.** RAIL écartement *m.* ◇ *vt* - **1.** [measure] mesurer - **2.** [evaluate] jauger.

Gaul [gɔːl] *n* - **1.** [country] Gaule *f* - **2.** [person] Gaulois *m*, -e *f.*

gaunt [gɔːnt] *adj* - **1.** [thin] hâve - **2.** [bare, grim] désolé(e).

gauntlet ['gɔːntlɪt] *n* gant *m* (de protection) ; **to run the** ~ **of sthg** endurer qqch ; **to throw down the** ~ **(to sb)** jeter le gant (à qqn).

gauze [gɔːz] *n* gaze *f.*

gave [geɪv] *pt* ⊏ give.

gawky ['gɔːkɪ] *adj* [person] dégingandé(e) ; [movement] désordonné(e).

gawp [gɔːp] *vi* : **to** ~ **(at)** rester bouche bée (devant).

gay [geɪ] ◇ *adj* - **1.** [gen] gai(e) - **2.** [homosexual] homo *(inv)*, gay *(inv).* ◇ *n* homo *mf*, gay *mf.*

gaze [geɪz] ◇ *n* regard *m* (fixe). ◇ *vi* : **to** ~ **at sb/sthg** regarder qqn/qqch (fixement).

gazelle [gə'zel] (*pl inv* OR -**s**) *n* gazelle *f.*

gazetteer [ˌgæzɪ'tɪə'] *n* index *m* géographique.

gazump [gə'zʌmp] *vt Br inf* : **to be** ~**ed** être victime d'une suroffre.

GB (*abbr of* **Great Britain**) *n* G-B *f.*

GCE (*abbr of* **General Certificate of Education**) *n certificat de fin d'études secondaires en Grande-Bretagne.*

GCSE (*abbr of* **General Certificate of Secondary Education**) *n examen de fin d'études secondaires en Grande-Bretagne.*

GDP (*abbr of* **gross domestic product**) *n* PIB *m.*

gear [gɪə'] ◇ *n* - **1.** TECH [mechanism] embrayage *m* - **2.** [speed - of car, bicycle] vitesse *f* ; **to be in/out of** ~ être en prise/au point mort - **3.** *(U)* [equipment, clothes] équipement *m.* ◇ *vt* : **to** ~ **sthg to sb/sthg** destiner qqch à qqn/qqch. ◆ **gear up** *vi* : **to** ~ **up for sthg/to do sthg** se préparer pour qqch/à faire qqch.

gearbox ['gɪəbɒks] *n* boîte *f* de vitesses.

gear lever, gear stick *Br*, **gear shift** *Am n* levier *m* de changement de vitesse.

gear wheel *n* pignon *m*, roue *f* d'engrenage.

geek ['giːk] *n inf* débile *mf* ; **a movie/computer** ~ un dingue de cinéma/d'informatique.

geese [giːs] *pl* ⊏ goose.

gel [dʒel] ◇ *n* [for hair] gel *m.* ◇ *vi* - **1.** [thicken] prendre - **2.** *fig* [take shape] prendre tournure.

gelatin ['dʒelətɪn], **gelatine** [ˌdʒelə'tiːn] *n* gélatine *f.*

gelignite ['dʒelɪgnaɪt] *n* gélignite *f*.

gem [dʒem] *n* - **1.** [jewel] pierre *f* précieuse, gemme *f* - **2.** *fig* [person, thing] perle *f*.

Gemini ['dʒemɪnaɪ] *n* Gémeaux *mpl*.

gender ['dʒendə'] *n* - **1.** [sex] sexe *m* - **2.** GRAMM genre *m*.

gene [dʒiːn] *n* gène *m*.

general ['dʒenərəl] <> *adj* général(e). <> *n* général *m*. ➟ **in general** *adv* en général.

general anaesthetic *n* anesthésie *f* générale.

general delivery *n* *Am* poste *f* restante.

general election *n* élection *f* générale.

generalization [,dʒenərəlaɪ'zeɪʃn] *n* généralisation *f*.

general knowledge *n* culture *f* générale.

generally ['dʒenərəlɪ] *adv* - **1.** [usually, in most cases] généralement - **2.** [unspecifically] en général ; [describe] en gros.

general practitioner *n* (médecin *m*) généraliste *m*.

general public *n* : the ~ le grand public.

general strike *n* grève *f* générale.

generate ['dʒenəreɪt] *vt* [energy, jobs] générer ; [electricity, heat] produire ; [interest, excitement] susciter.

generation [,dʒenə'reɪʃn] *n* - **1.** [gen] génération *f* - **2.** [creation - of jobs] création *f* ; [- of interest, excitement] induction *f* ; [- of electricity] production *f*.

generator ['dʒenəreɪtə'] *n* générateur *m* ; ELEC génératrice *f*, générateur *m*.

generosity [,dʒenə'rɒsətɪ] *n* générosité *f*.

generous ['dʒenərəs] *adj* généreux(euse).

genetic [dʒɪ'netɪk] *adj* génétique. ➟ **genetics** *n* (*U*) génétique *f*.

genetically [dʒɪ'netɪklɪ] *adv* génétiquement ; ~ **modified** génétiquement modifié(e) ; ~ **modified organism** organisme *m* génétiquement modifié.

genetic code *n* code *m* génétique.

Geneva [dʒɪ'niːvə] *n* Genève.

genial ['dʒiːnjəl] *adj* affable.

genitals ['dʒenɪtlz] *npl* organes *mpl* génitaux.

genius ['dʒiːnjəs] (*pl* -es [-iːz]) *n* génie *m*.

gent [dʒent] *n* *Br* *inf* gentleman *m*. ➟ **gents** *n* *Br* [toilets] toilettes *fpl* pour hommes ; [sign on door] messieurs.

genteel [dʒen'tiːl] *adj* raffiné(e).

gentle ['dʒentl] *adj* doux (douce) ; [hint] discret(ète) ; [telling-off] léger(ère).

gentleman ['dʒentlmən] (*pl* -**men** [-mən]) *n* - **1.** [well-behaved man] gentleman *m* - **2.** [man] monsieur *m*.

gently ['dʒentlɪ] *adv* [gen] doucement ; [speak, smile] avec douceur.

gentry ['dʒentrɪ] *n* petite noblesse *f*.

genuine ['dʒenjuɪn] *adj* authentique ; [interest, customer] sérieux(euse) ; [person, concern] sincère.

geography [dʒɪ'ɒgrəfɪ] *n* géographie *f*.

geology [dʒɪ'ɒlədʒɪ] *n* géologie *f*.

geometric(al) [,dʒɪə'metrɪk(l)] *adj* géométrique.

geometry [dʒɪ'ɒmətrɪ] *n* géométrie *f*.

geranium [dʒɪ'reɪnjəm] (*pl* -s) *n* géranium *m*.

gerbil ['dʒɜːbɪl] *n* gerbille *f*.

geriatric [,dʒerɪ'ætrɪk] *adj* - **1.** MED gériatrique - **2.** *pej* [person] décrépit(e) ; [object] vétuste.

germ [dʒɜːm] *n* - **1.** [bacterium] germe *m* - **2.** *fig* [of idea, plan] embryon *m*.

German ['dʒɜːmən] <> *adj* allemand(e). <> *n* - **1.** [person] Allemand *m*, -e *f* - **2.** [language] allemand *m*.

German measles *n* (*U*) rubéole *f*.

Germany ['dʒɜːmənɪ] *n* Allemagne *f*.

germinate ['dʒɜːmɪneɪt] *vi* *lit* & *fig* germer.

gerund ['dʒerənd] *n* gérondif *m*.

gesticulate [dʒes'tɪkjʊleɪt] *vi* gesticuler.

gesture ['dʒestʃə'] <> *n* geste *m*. <> *vi* : **to** ~ **to** *OR* **towards sb** faire signe à qqn.

get [get] (*Br* *pt* & *pp* **got**, *Am* *pt* **got**, *pp* **gotten**) <> *vt* - **1.** [cause to do] : **to** ~ **sb to do sthg** faire faire qqch à qqn ; **I'll** ~ **my sister to help** je vais demander à ma sœur de nous aider - **2.** [cause to be done] : **to** ~ **sthg done** faire faire qqch ; **I got the car fixed** j'ai fait réparer la voiture - **3.** [cause to become] : **to** ~ **sb pregnant** rendre qqn enceinte ; **I can't** ~ **the car started** je n'arrive pas à mettre la voiture en marche - **4.** [cause to move] : **to** ~ **sb/sthg through sthg** faire passer qqn/qqch par qqch ; **to** ~ **sb/sthg out of sthg** faire sortir qqn/qqch de qqch - **5.** [bring, fetch] aller chercher ; **can I** ~ **you something to eat/drink?** est-ce que je peux vous offrir quelque chose à manger/boire? - **6.** [obtain - gen] obtenir ; [- job, house] trouver - **7.** [receive] recevoir, avoir ; **what did you** ~ **for your birthday?** qu'est-ce que tu as eu pour ton anniversaire? ; **she** ~**s a good salary** elle touche un bon traitement - **8.** [experience a sensation] avoir ; **do you** ~ **the feeling he doesn't like**

us? tu n'as pas l'impression qu'il ne nous aime pas ? - **9.** [be infected with, suffer from] avoir, attraper ; **to ~ a cold** attraper un rhume - **10.** [understand] comprendre, saisir ; **I don't ~ it** *inf* je ne comprends pas, je ne saisis pas - **11.** [catch - bus, train, plane] prendre - **12.** [capture] prendre, attraper - **13.** [find] : **you ~ a lot of artists here on** trouve OR il y a beaucoup d'artistes ici ; *see also* **have.** ◇ *vi* - **1.** [become] devenir ; **to ~ suspicious** devenir méfiant ; **I'm getting cold/bored** je commence à avoir froid/à m'ennuyer ; **it's getting late** il se fait tard - **2.** [arrive] arriver ; **I only got back yesterday** je suis rentré hier seulement - **3.** [eventually succeed in] : **to ~ to do sthg** parvenir à OR finir par faire qqch ; **did you ~ to see him?** est-ce que tu as réussi à le voir? - **4.** [progress] : **how far have you got?** où en es-tu? ; **we're getting nowhere** on n'arrive à rien. ◇ *aux vb* : **to ~ excited** s'exciter ; **to ~ hurt** se faire mal ; **to ~ beaten up** se faire tabasser ; **let's ~ going** OR **moving** allons-y ; *see also* **have.** ◆ **get about, get around** *vi* - **1.** [move from place to place] se déplacer - **2.** [circulate - news, rumour] circuler, se répandre ; *see also* **get around** ; *see also* **get round.** ◆ **get along** *vi* - **1.** [manage] se débrouiller - **2.** [progress] avancer, faire des progrès - **3.** [have a good relationship] s'entendre. ◆ **get around, get round** ◇ *vt fus* [overcome] venir à bout de, surmonter. ◇ *vi* - **1.** [circulate] circuler, se répandre - **2.** [eventually do] : **to ~ around to (doing) sthg** trouver le temps de faire qqch ; *see also* **get about.** ◆ **get at** *vt fus* - **1.** [reach] parvenir à - **2.** [imply] vouloir dire ; **what are you getting at?** où veux-tu en venir? - **3.** *inf* [criticize] critiquer, dénigrer. ◆ **get away** *vi* - **1.** [leave] partir, s'en aller - **2.** [go on holiday] partir en vacances - **3.** [escape] s'échapper, s'évader. ◆ **get away with** *vt fus* : **to let sb ~ away with sthg** passer qqch à qqn. ◆ **get back** ◇ *vt sep* [recover, regain] retrouver, récupérer. ◇ *vi* [move away] s'écarter. ◆ **get back to** *vt fus* - **1.** [return to previous state, activity] revenir à ; **to ~ back to sleep** se rendormir ; **to ~ back to work** [after pause] se remettre au travail ; [after illness] reprendre son travail - **2.** *inf* [phone back] rappeler ; **I'll ~ back to you on that** je te reparlerai de ça plus tard. ◆ **get by** *vi* se débrouiller, s'en sortir. ◆ **get down** *vt sep* - **1.** [depress] déprimer - **2.** [fetch from higher level] descendre. ◆ **get down to** *vt fus* : **to ~ down to doing sthg** se mettre à faire qqch. ◆ **get in** *vi* - **1.** [enter - gen] entrer ; [- referring to vehicle] monter - **2.** [arrive] arriver ; [arrive home] rentrer. ◆ **get into** *vt*

fus - **1.** [car] monter dans - **2.** [become involved in] se lancer dans ; **to ~ into an argument with sb** se disputer avec qqn - **3.** [enter into a particular situation, state] : **to ~ into a panic** s'affoler ; **to ~ into trouble** s'attirer des ennuis ; **to ~ into the habit of doing sthg** prendre l'habitude de faire qqch. ◆ **get off** ◇ *vt sep* [remove] enlever. ◇ *vt fus* - **1.** [go away from] partir de - **2.** [train, bus etc] descendre de. ◇ *vi* - **1.** [leave bus, train] descendre - **2.** [escape punishment] s'en tirer - **3.** [depart] partir. ◆ **get on** ◇ *vt fus* - **1.** [bus, train, plane] monter dans - **2.** [horse] monter sur. ◇ *vi* - **1.** [enter bus, train] monter - **2.** [have good relationship] s'entendre, s'accorder - **3.** [progress] avancer, progresser ; **how are you getting on?** comment ça va? - **4.** [proceed] : **to ~ on (with sthg)** continuer (qqch), poursuivre (qqch) - **5.** [be successful professionally] réussir. ◆ **get out** ◇ *vt sep* - **1.** [take out] sortir - **2.** [remove] enlever. ◇ *vi* - **1.** [from car, bus, train] descendre - **2.** [news] s'ébruiter. ◆ **get out of** *vt fus* - **1.** [car etc] descendre de, sortir de - **2.** [escape from prison] s'évader de, s'échapper de - **3.** [avoid] éviter, se dérober à ; **to ~ out of doing sthg** se dispenser de faire qqch. ◆ **get over** *vt fus* - **1.** [recover from] se remettre de - **2.** [overcome] surmonter, venir à bout de - **3.** [communicate] communiquer. ◆ **get round** = **get around.** ◆ **get through** ◇ *vt fus* - **1.** [job, task] arriver au bout de - **2.** [exam] réussir à - **3.** [food, drink] consommer - **4.** [unpleasant situation] endurer, supporter. ◇ *vi* - **1.** [make o.s. understood] : **to ~ through (to sb)** se faire comprendre (de qqn) - **2.** TELEC obtenir la communication. ◆ **get to** *vt fus* *inf* [annoy] taper sur les nerfs à. ◆ **get together** ◇ *vt sep* [organize - team, belongings] rassembler ; [- project, report] préparer. ◇ *vi* se réunir. ◆ **get up** ◇ *vi* se lever. ◇ *vt fus* [petition, demonstration] organiser. ◆ **get up to** *vt fus* *inf* faire.

getaway ['getəweɪ] *n* fuite *f.*

get-together *n inf* réunion *f.*

geyser ['giːzəʳ] *n* - **1.** [hot spring] geyser *m* - **2.** *Br* [water heater] chauffe-eau *m inv.*

Ghana ['gɑːnə] *n* Ghana *m.*

ghastly ['gɑːstlɪ] *adj* - **1.** *inf* [very bad, unpleasant] épouvantable - **2.** [horrifying, macabre] effroyable.

gherkin ['gɜːkɪn] *n* cornichon *m.*

ghetto ['getəʊ] (*pl* -s OR -es) *n* ghetto *m.*

ghetto blaster [-ˌblɑːstəʳ] *n inf* grand radiocassette *m* portatif.

ghost [gəʊst] *n* [spirit] spectre *m.*

giant ['dʒaɪənt] <> *adj* géant(e). <> *n* géant *m*.

gibberish ['dʒɪbərɪʃ] *n (U)* charabia *m*, inepties *fpl*.

gibe [dʒaɪb] *n* insulte *f*.

giblets ['dʒɪblɪts] *npl* abats *mpl*.

Gibraltar [dʒɪ'brɔːltər] *n* Gibraltar *m*.

giddy ['gɪdɪ] *adj* [dizzy] : **to feel ~** avoir la tête qui tourne.

gift [gɪft] *n* - **1.** [present] cadeau *m* - **2.** [talent] don *m* ; **to have a ~ for sthg/for doing sthg** avoir un don pour qqch/pour faire qqch ; **the ~ of the gab** le bagou.

gift certificate *Am* = **gift token**.

gifted ['gɪftɪd] *adj* doué(e).

gift token, gift voucher *n Br* chèque-cadeau *m*.

gig [gɪg] *n inf* [concert] concert *m*.

gigabyte ['gaɪgəbaɪt] *n* COMPUT giga-octet *m*.

gigantic [dʒaɪ'gæntɪk] *adj* énorme, gigantesque.

giggle ['gɪgl] <> *n* - **1.** [laugh] glousse-ment *m* - **2.** *Br inf* [fun] : **to be a ~** être marrant(e) OR tordant(e) ; **to have a ~** bien s'amuser. <> *vi* [laugh] glousser.

gilded ['gɪldɪd] *adj* = **gilt**.

gill [dʒɪl] *n* [unit of measurement] = 0,142 litre, quart *m* de pinte.

gills [gɪlz] *npl* [of fish] branchies *fpl*.

gilt [gɪlt] <> *adj* [covered in gold] doré(e). <> *n (U)* [gold layer] dorure *f*.

gimmick ['gɪmɪk] *n pej* artifice *m*.

gin [dʒɪn] *n* gin *m* ; **~ and tonic** gin tonic.

ginger ['dʒɪndʒər] <> *n* - **1.** [root] gingem-bre *m* - **2.** [powder] gingembre *m* en poudre. <> *adj Br* [colour] roux (rousse).

ginger ale *n* boisson gazeuse au gingembre.

ginger beer *n* boisson non-alcoolisée au gingembre.

gingerbread ['dʒɪndʒəbred] *n* pain *m* d'épice.

ginger-haired [-'heəd] *adj* roux (rousse).

gingerly ['dʒɪndʒəlɪ] *adv* avec précaution.

gipsy ['dʒɪpsɪ] <> *adj* gitan(e). <> *n* gitan *m*, -e *f* ; *Br pej* bohémien *m*, -enne *f*.

giraffe [dʒɪ'rɑːf] *(pl inv* OR *-s) n* girafe *f*.

girder ['gɜːdər] *n* poutrelle *f*.

girdle ['gɜːdl] *n* [corset] gaine *f*.

girl [gɜːl] *n* - **1.** [gen] fille *f* - **2.** [girlfriend] petite amie *f*.

girlfriend ['gɜːlfrend] *n* - **1.** [female lover] petite amie *f* - **2.** [female friend] amie *f*.

girl guide *Br*, **girl scout** *Am n* éclaireuse *f*, guide *f*.

giro ['dʒaɪrəʊ] *(pl -s) n Br* - **1.** *(U)* [system] virement *m* postal - **2.** : **~ (cheque)** chèque *m* d'indemnisation *f* (chômage OR maladie).

girth [gɜːθ] *n* - **1.** [circumference - of tree] circonférence *f* ; [- of person] tour *m* de taille - **2.** [of horse] sangle *f*.

gist [dʒɪst] *n* substance *f* ; **to get the ~ of sthg** comprendre OR saisir l'essentiel de qqch.

give [gɪv] *(pt* **gave**, *pp* **given)** <> *vt* - **1.** [gen] donner ; [message] transmettre ; [attention, time] consacrer ; **to ~ sb/sthg sthg** donner qqch à qqn/qqch ; **to ~ sb pleasure/a fright/a smile** faire plaisir/peur/un sourire à qqn ; **to ~ a sigh** pousser un soupir ; **to ~ a speech** faire un discours - **2.** [as present] : **to ~ sb sthg, to ~ sthg to sb** donner qqch à qqn, offrir qqch à qqn. <> *vi* [collapse, break] céder, s'affaisser. <> *n* [elasticity] élasticité *f*, souplesse *f*.

◆ **give or take** *prep* : **~ or take a day/£10** à un jour/10 livres près. ◆ **give away** *vt sep* - **1.** [get rid of] donner - **2.** [reveal] révéler. ◆ **give back** *vt sep* [return] rendre. ◆ **give in** *vi* - **1.** [admit defeat] abandonner, se rendre - **2.** [agree unwillingly] : **to ~ in to sthg** céder à qqch. ◆ **give off** *vt fus* [smell] exhaler ; [smoke] faire ; [heat] produire. ◆ **give out** <> *vt sep* [distribute] distribuer. <> *vi* [supplies] s'épuiser ; [car] lâcher. ◆ **give up** <> *vt sep* - **1.** [stop] renoncer à ; **to ~ up drinking/smoking** arrêter de boire/de fumer - **2.** [surrender] : **to ~ o.s. up (to sb)** se rendre (à qqn). <> *vi* abandonner, se rendre.

given ['gɪvn] <> *adj* - **1.** [set, fixed] conve-nu(e), fixé(e) - **2.** [prone] : **to be ~ to sthg/to doing sthg** être enclin(e) à qqch/à faire qqch. <> *prep* étant donné ; **~ that** étant donné que.

given name *n Am* prénom *m*.

glacier ['glæsjər] *n* glacier *m*.

glad [glæd] *adj* - **1.** [happy, pleased] content(e) ; **to be ~ about sthg** être content de qqch - **2.** [willing] : **to be ~ to do sthg** faire qqch volontiers OR avec plaisir - **3.** [grateful] : **to be ~ of sthg** être content(e) de qqch.

gladly ['glædlɪ] *adv* - **1.** [happily, eagerly] avec joie - **2.** [willingly] avec plaisir.

glamor *Am* = **glamour**.

glamorous ['glæmərəs] *adj* [person] sé-duisant(e) ; [appearance] élégant(e) ; [job, place] prestigieux(euse).

glamour *Br*, **glamor** *Am* ['glæmər] *n* [of

person] charme *m* ; [of appearance] élégance *f*, chic *m* ; [of job, place] prestige *m*.

glance [glaːns] ⬦ *n* [quick look] regard *m*, coup d'œil *m* ; **at a ~** d'un coup d'œil ; **at first ~** au premier coup d'œil. ⬦ *vi* [look quickly] : **to ~ at sb/sthg** jeter un coup d'œil à qqn/qqch. ◆ **glance off** *vt fus* [subj : ball, bullet] ricocher sur.

glancing ['glaːnsɪŋ] *adj* de côté, oblique.

gland [glænd] *n* glande *f*.

glandular fever [ˌglændjʊləʳ-] *n* mononucléose *f* infectieuse.

glare [gleəʳ] ⬦ *n* - 1. [scowl] regard *m* mauvais - 2. *(U)* [of headlights, publicity] lumière *f* aveuglante. ⬦ *vi* - 1. [scowl] : **to ~ at sb/sthg** regarder qqn/qqch d'un œil mauvais - 2. [sun, lamp] briller d'une lumière éblouissante.

glaring ['gleərɪŋ] *adj* - 1. [very obvious] flagrant(e) - 2. [blazing, dazzling] aveuglant(e).

glasnost ['glæznɒst] *n* glasnost *f*, transparence *f*.

glass [glaːs] ⬦ *n* - 1. [gen] verre *m* - 2. *(U)* [glassware] verrerie *f*. ⬦ *comp* [bottle, jar] en OR de verre ; [door, partition] vitré(e). ◆ **glasses** *npl* [spectacles] lunettes *fpl*.

glassware ['glaːsweəʳ] *n (U)* verrerie *f*.

glassy ['glaːsɪ] *adj* - 1. [smooth, shiny] lisse comme un miroir - 2. [blank, lifeless] vitreux(euse).

glaze [gleɪz] ⬦ *n* [on pottery] vernis *m* ; [on pastry, flan] glaçage *m*. ⬦ *vt* [pottery, tiles, bricks] vernisser ; [pastry, flan] glacer.

glazier ['gleɪzjəʳ] *n* vitrier *m*.

gleam [gliːm] ⬦ *n* [of gold] reflet *m* ; [of fire, sunset, disapproval] lueur *f*. ⬦ *vi* - 1. [surface, object] luire - 2. [light, eyes] briller.

gleaming ['gliːmɪŋ] *adj* brillant(e).

glean [gliːn] *vt* [gather] glaner.

glee [gliː] *n (U)* [joy] joie *f*, jubilation *f*.

glen [glen] *n Scot* vallée *f*.

glib [glɪb] *adj pej* [salesman, politician] qui a du bagout ; [promise, excuse] facile.

glide [glaɪd] *vi* - 1. [move smoothly - dancer, boat] glisser sans effort ; [- person] se mouvoir sans effort - 2. [fly] planer.

glider ['glaɪdəʳ] *n* [plane] planeur *m*.

gliding ['glaɪdɪŋ] *n* [sport] vol *m* à voile.

glimmer ['glɪməʳ] *n* [faint light] faible lueur *f* ; *fig* signe *m*, lueur.

glimpse [glɪmps] ⬦ *n* - 1. [look, sight] aperçu *m* - 2. [idea, perception] idée *f*. ⬦ *vt* - 1. [catch sight of] apercevoir, entrevoir - 2. [perceive] pressentir.

glint [glɪnt] ⬦ *n* - 1. [flash] reflet *m* - 2. [in eyes] éclair *m*. ⬦ *vi* étinceler.

glisten ['glɪsn] *vi* briller.

glitter ['glɪtəʳ] ⬦ *n (U)* scintillement *m*. ⬦ *vi* - 1. [object, light] scintiller - 2. [eyes] briller.

gloat [gləʊt] *vi* : **to ~ (over sthg)** se réjouir (de qqch).

global ['gləʊbl] *adj* [worldwide] mondial(e).

globalization [ˌgləʊbəlaɪ'zeɪʃn] *n* mondialisation *f*.

global warming [-'wɔːmɪŋ] *n* réchauffement *m* de la planète.

globe [gləʊb] *n* - 1. [Earth] : **the ~** la terre - 2. [spherical map] globe *m* terrestre - 3. [spherical object] globe *m*.

gloom [gluːm] *n (U)* - 1. [darkness] obscurité *f* - 2. [unhappiness] tristesse *f*.

gloomy ['gluːmɪ] *adj* - 1. [room, sky, prospects] sombre - 2. [person, atmosphere, mood] triste, lugubre.

glorious ['glɔːrɪəs] *adj* - 1. [beautiful, splendid] splendide - 2. [very enjoyable] formidable - 3. [successful, impressive] magnifique.

glory ['glɔːrɪ] *n* - 1. *(U)* [fame, admiration] gloire *f* - 2. *(U)* [beauty] splendeur *f*. ◆ **glory in** *vt fus* [relish] savourer.

gloss [glɒs] *n* - 1. *(U)* [shine] brillant *m*, lustre *m* - 2. : **~ (paint)** peinture *f* brillante. ◆ **gloss over** *vt fus* passer sur.

glossary ['glɒsərɪ] *n* glossaire *m*.

glossy ['glɒsɪ] *adj* - 1. [hair, surface] brillant(e) - 2. [book, photo] sur papier glacé.

glove [glʌv] *n* gant *m*.

glove compartment *n* boîte *f* à gants.

glow [gləʊ] ⬦ *n (U)* [of fire, light, sunset] lueur *f*. ⬦ *vi* - 1. [shine out - fire] rougeoyer ; [light, stars, eyes] flamboyer - 2. [shine in light] briller.

glower ['glaʊəʳ] *vi* : **to ~ (at)** lancer des regards noirs (à).

glucose ['gluːkəʊs] *n* glucose *m*.

glue [gluː] *(cont* glueing OR gluing*)* ⬦ *n (U)* colle *f*. ⬦ *vt* [stick with glue] coller ; **to ~ sthg to sthg** coller qqch à OR avec qqch.

glum [glʌm] *adj* [unhappy] morne.

glut [glʌt] *n* surplus *m*.

glutton ['glʌtn] *n* [greedy person] glouton *m*, -onne *f* ; **to be a ~ for punishment** être maso, être masochiste.

GM *(abbr of* **genetically modified***) adj* génétiquement modifié(e).

gnarled [naːld] *adj* [tree, hands] noueux(euse).

gnash [næʃ] *vt* : **to ~ one's teeth** grincer des dents.

gnat [næt] *n* moucheron *m*.

gnaw [nɔː] ⟷ *vt* [chew] ronger. ⟷ *vi* [worry] : **to ~ (away) at sb** ronger qqn.

gnome [nəʊm] *n* gnome *m*, lutin *m*.

GNP (*abbr of* **gross national product**) *n* PNB *m*.

GNVQ *Br* (*abbr of* **general national vocational qualification**) *n diplôme sanctionnant deux années d'études professionnelles à la fin du secondaire*, ≃ baccalauréat *m* professionnel.

go [gəʊ] (*pt* **went**, *pp* **gone**, *pl* **goes**) ⟷ *vi* - **1.** [move, travel] aller ; **where are you ~ing?** où vas-tu ? ; **he's gone to Portugal** il est allé au Portugal ; **we went by bus/train** nous sommes allés en bus/par le train ; **where does this path ~?** où mène ce chemin ? ; **to ~ and do sthg** aller faire qqch ; **to ~ swimming/shopping/jogging** aller nager/faire les courses/faire du jogging ; **to ~ for a walk** aller se promener, faire une promenade ; **to ~ to work** aller travailler OR à son travail - **2.** [depart] partir, s'en aller ; **I must ~, I have to ~** il faut que je m'en aille ; **what time does the bus ~?** à quelle heure part le bus ? ; **let's ~!** allons-y! - **3.** [become] devenir ; **to ~ grey** grisonner, devenir gris ; **to ~ mad** devenir fou - **4.** [pass - time] passer - **5.** [progress] marcher, se dérouler ; **the conference went very smoothly** la conférence s'est déroulée sans problème OR s'est très bien passée ; **to ~ well/badly** aller bien/mal ; **how's it ~ing?** *inf* comment ça va ? - **6.** [function, work] marcher ; **the car won't ~** la voiture ne veut pas démarrer - **7.** [indicating intention, expectation] : **to be ~ing to do sthg** aller faire qqch ; **he said he was ~ing to be late** il a prévenu qu'il allait arriver en retard ; **we're ~ing (to ~) to America in June** on va (aller) en Amérique en juin ; **she's ~ing to have a baby** elle attend un bébé - **8.** [bell, alarm] sonner - **9.** [stop working, break - light bulb, fuse] sauter - **10.** [deteriorate - hearing, sight etc] baisser - **11.** [match, be compatible] : **to ~ (with)** aller (avec) ; **those colours don't really ~** ces couleurs ne vont pas bien ensemble - **12.** [fit] aller - **13.** [belong] aller, se mettre ; **the plates ~ in the cupboard** les assiettes vont OR se mettent dans le placard - **14.** [in division] : **three into two won't ~** deux divisé par trois n'y va pas - **15.** *inf* [expressing irritation, anger] : **now what's he gone and done?** qu'est-ce qu'il a fait encore ? ⟷ *n* - **1.** [turn] tour *m* ; **it's my ~** c'est à moi (de jouer) - **2.** *inf* [attempt] : **to have a ~ (at sthg)** essayer (de faire qqch) - **3.** *phr* :

to have a ~ at sb *inf* s'en prendre à qqn, engueuler qqn ; **to be on the ~** *inf* être sur la brèche. ◆ **to go** *adv* [remaining] : **there are only three days to ~** il ne reste que trois jours. ◆ **go about** ⟷ *vt fus* [perform] : **to ~ about one's business** vaquer à ses occupations. ⟷ *vi* = **go around**. ◆ **go ahead** *vi* - **1.** [proceed] : **to ~ ahead with sthg** mettre qqch à exécution ; **~ ahead!** allez-y! - **2.** [take place] avoir lieu. ◆ **go along** *vi* [proceed] avancer ; **as you ~ along** au fur et à mesure. ◆ **go along with** *vt fus* [suggestion, idea] appuyer, soutenir ; [person] suivre. ◆ **go around** *vi* - **1.** [frequent] : **to ~ around with sb** fréquenter qqn - **2.** [spread] circuler, courir. ◆ **go back on** *vt fus* [one's word, promise] revenir sur. ◆ **go back to** *vt fus* - **1.** [return to activity] reprendre, se remettre à ; **to ~ back to sleep** se rendormir - **2.** [date from] remonter à, dater de. ◆ **go by** ⟷ *vi* [time] s'écouler, passer. ⟷ *vt fus* - **1.** [be guided by] suivre - **2.** [judge from] juger d'après. ◆ **go down** ⟷ *vi* - **1.** [get lower - prices etc] baisser - **2.** [be accepted] : **to ~ down well/badly** être bien/mal accueilli - **3.** [sun] se coucher - **4.** [tyre, balloon] se dégonfler. ⟷ *vt fus* descendre. ◆ **go for** *vt fus* - **1.** [choose] choisir - **2.** [be attracted to] être attiré(e) par - **3.** [attack] tomber sur, attaquer - **4.** [try to obtain - job, record] essayer d'obtenir. ◆ **go in** *vi* entrer. ◆ **go in for** *vt fus* - **1.** [competition] prendre part à ; [exam] se présenter à - **2.** [activity - enjoy] aimer ; [- participate in] faire, s'adonner à. ◆ **go into** *vt fus* - **1.** [investigate] étudier, examiner - **2.** [take up as a profession] entrer dans. ◆ **go off** ⟷ *vi* - **1.** [explode] exploser - **2.** [alarm] sonner - **3.** [go bad - food] se gâter - **4.** [lights, heating] s'éteindre. ⟷ *vt fus* [lose interest in] ne plus aimer. ◆ **go on** ⟷ *vi* - **1.** [take place, happen] se passer - **2.** [heating etc] se mettre en marche - **3.** [continue] : **to ~ on (doing)** continuer (à faire) - **4.** [proceed to further activity] : **to ~ on to sthg** passer à qqch ; **to ~ on to do sthg** faire qqch après - **5.** [talk for too long] parler à n'en plus finir ; **to ~ on about sthg** ne pas arrêter de parler de qqch. ⟷ *vt fus* [be guided by] se fonder sur. ◆ **go on at** *vt fus* [nag] harceler. ◆ **go out** *vi* - **1.** [leave] sortir - **2.** [for amusement] : **to ~ out (with sb)** sortir (avec qqn) - **3.** [light, fire, cigarette] s'éteindre. ◆ **go over** *vt fus* - **1.** [examine] examiner, vérifier - **2.** [repeat, review] repasser. ◆ **go round** *vi* [revolve] tourner ; *see also* **go around**. ◆ **go through** *vt fus* - **1.** [experience] subir, souffrir - **2.** [study, search through] examiner ; **she went through his pockets** elle lui a fait les poches, elle a fouillé dans ses poches. ◆ **go through with** vt fus [action, threat] aller jusqu'au bout de. ◆ **go towards** vt fus contribuer à. ◆ **go under** vi lit & fig couler. ◆ **go up** ⬦ vi - **1.** [gen] monter - **2.** [prices] augmenter. ⬦ vt fus monter. ◆ **go without** ⬦ vt fus se passer de. ⬦ vi s'en passer.

goad [gəʊd] vt [provoke] talonner.

go-ahead ⬦ adj [dynamic] dynamique. ⬦ n (U) [permission] feu m vert.

goal [gəʊl] n but m.

goalkeeper ['gəʊlˌkiːpəʳ] n gardien m de but.

goalmouth ['gəʊlmaʊθ, pl -maʊðz] n but m.

goalpost ['gəʊlpəʊst] n poteau m de but.

goat [gəʊt] n chèvre f.

gob [gɒb] ⬦ v inf ⬦ n Br [mouth] gueule f. ⬦ vi [spit] mollarder.

gobble ['gɒbl] vt engloutir. ◆ **gobble down, gobble up** vt sep engloutir.

go-between n intermédiaire mf.

gobsmacked ['gɒbsmækt] adj Br inf bouche bée (inv).

go-cart = go-kart.

god [gɒd] n dieu m, divinité f. ◆ **God** ⬦ n Dieu m ; **God knows** Dieu seul le sait ; **for God's sake** pour l'amour de Dieu ; **thank God** Dieu merci. ⬦ excl : **(my) God!** mon Dieu!

godchild ['gɒdtʃaɪld] (pl -children [-ˌtʃɪldrən]) n filleul m, -e f.

goddaughter ['gɒdˌdɔːtəʳ] n filleule f.

goddess ['gɒdɪs] n déesse f.

godfather ['gɒdˌfɑːðəʳ] n parrain m.

godforsaken ['gɒdfəˌseɪkn] adj morne, désolé(e).

godmother ['gɒdˌmʌðəʳ] n marraine f.

godsend ['gɒdsend] n aubaine f.

godson ['gɒdsʌn] n filleul m.

goes [gəʊz] ⬦ go.

goggles ['gɒglz] npl lunettes fpl.

going ['gəʊɪŋ] ⬦ n (U) - **1.** [rate of advance] allure f - **2.** [travel conditions] conditions fpl. ⬦ adj - **1.** Br [available] disponible - **2.** [rate, salary] en vigueur.

go-kart [-kɑːt] n kart m.

gold [gəʊld] ⬦ n (U) [metal, jewellery] or m. ⬦ comp [made of gold] en or. ⬦ adj [gold-coloured] doré(e).

golden ['gəʊldən] adj - **1.** [made of gold] en or - **2.** [gold-coloured] doré(e).

goldfish ['gəʊldfɪʃ] (pl inv) n poisson m rouge.

gold leaf n (U) feuille f d'or.

gold medal n médaille f d'or.

goldmine ['gəʊldmaɪn] n lit & fig mine f d'or.

gold-plated [-'pleɪtɪd] adj plaqué(e) or.

goldsmith ['gəʊldsmɪθ] n orfèvre m.

golf [gɒlf] n golf m.

golf ball n - **1.** [for golf] balle f de golf - **2.** [for typewriter] boule f.

golf club n [stick, place] club m de golf.

golf course n terrain m de golf.

golfer ['gɒlfəʳ] n golfeur m, -euse f.

gone [gɒn] ⬦ pp ⬦ go. ⬦ adj [no longer here] parti(e). ⬦ prep : **it's ~ ten (o'clock)** il est dix heures passées.

gong [gɒŋ] n gong m.

good [gʊd] (compar **better**, superl **best**) ⬦ adj - **1.** [gen] bon (bonne) ; **it's ~ to see you again** ça fait plaisir de te revoir ; **to be ~ at sthg** être bon en qqch ; **to be ~ with** [animals, children] savoir y faire avec ; [one's hands] être habile de ; **it's ~ for you** c'est bon pour toi OR pour la santé ; **to feel ~** [person] se sentir bien ; **it's ~ that ...** c'est bien que ... ; **good!** très bien! - **2.** [kind - person] gentil(ille) ; **to be ~ to sb** être très attentionné envers qqn ; **to be ~ enough to do sthg** avoir l'amabilité de faire qqch - **3.** [well-behaved - child] sage ; [- behaviour] correct(e) ; **be ~!** sois sage!, tiens-toi tranquille! ⬦ n - **1.** (U) [benefit] bien m ; **it will do him ~** ça lui fera du bien - **2.** [use] utilité f ; **what's the ~ of doing that?** à quoi bon faire ça? ; **it's no ~** ça ne sert à rien ; **it's no ~ crying/worrying** ça ne sert à rien de pleurer/de s'en faire - **3.** (U) [morally correct behaviour] bien m ; **to be up to no ~** préparer un sale coup. ◆ **goods** npl [merchandise] marchandises fpl, articles mpl. ◆ **as good as** adv pratiquement, pour ainsi dire. ◆ **for good** adv [forever] pour de bon, définitivement. ◆ **good afternoon** excl bonjour! ◆ **good evening** excl bonsoir! ◆ **good morning** excl bonjour! ◆ **good night** excl bonsoir! ; [at bedtime] bonne nuit!

goodbye [ˌgʊd'baɪ] ⬦ excl au revoir! ⬦ n au revoir m.

Good Friday n Vendredi m saint.

good-humoured [-'hjuːməd] adj [person] de bonne humeur ; [smile, remark, rivalry] bon enfant.

good-looking [-'lʊkɪŋ] adj [person] beau (belle).

good-natured [-'neɪtʃəd] adj [person]

d'un naturel aimable ; [rivalry, argument] bon enfant.

goodness ['gʊdnɪs] ⬦ *n (U)* - **1.** [kindness] bonté *f* - **2.** [nutritive quality] valeur *f* nutritive. ⬦ *excl* : (my) ~! mon Dieu!, Seigneur! ; **for ~' sake!** par pitié!, pour l'amour de Dieu! ; **thank ~!** grâce à Dieu!

goods train *n Br* train *m* de marchandises.

goodwill [,gʊd'wɪl] *n* bienveillance *f*.

goody ['gʊdɪ] *inf* ⬦ *n* [person] bon *m*. ⬦ *excl* chouette! ➡ **goodies** *npl inf* - **1.** [delicious food] friandises *fpl* - **2.** [desirable objects] merveilles *fpl*, trésors *mpl*.

goose [gu:s] (*pl* **geese** [gi:z]) *n* [bird] oie *f*.

gooseberry ['gʊzbərɪ] *n* - **1.** [fruit] groseille *f* à maquereau - **2.** *Br inf* [third person] : **to play ~** tenir la chandelle.

gooseflesh ['gu:sfleʃ], **goose pimples** *Br n*, **goosebumps** *Am* ['gu:sbʌmps] *npl* chair *f* de poule.

gore [gɔ:ʳ] ⬦ *n (U) literary* [blood] sang *m*. ⬦ *vt* encorner.

gorge [gɔ:dʒ] ⬦ *n* gorge *f*, défilé *m*. ⬦ *vt* : **to ~ o.s. on** OR **with sthg** se bourrer OR se goinfrer de qqch.

gorgeous ['gɔ:dʒəs] *adj* divin(e) ; *inf* [good-looking] magnifique, splendide.

gorilla [gə'rɪlə] *n* gorille *m*.

gormless ['gɔ:mlɪs] *adj Br inf* bêta (bêtasse).

gorse [gɔ:s] *n (U)* ajonc *m*.

gory ['gɔ:rɪ] *adj* sanglant(e).

gosh [gɒʃ] *excl inf* ça alors!

go-slow *n Br* grève *f* du zèle.

gospel ['gɒspl] *n* [doctrine] évangile *m*. ➡ **Gospel** *n* Évangile *m*.

gossip ['gɒsɪp] ⬦ *n* - **1.** [conversation] bavardage *m* ; *pej* commérage *m* - **2.** [person] commère *f*. ⬦ *vi* [talk] bavarder, papoter ; *pej* cancaner.

gossip column *n* échos *mpl*.

got [gɒt] *pt & pp* ▷ **get**.

gotten ['gɒtn] *Am pp* ▷ **get**.

goulash ['gu:læʃ] *n* goulache *m*.

gourmet ['gʊəmeɪ] ⬦ *n* gourmet *m*. ⬦ *comp* [food, restaurant] gastronomique ; [cook] gastronome.

gout [gaʊt] *n (U)* goutte *f*.

govern ['gʌvn] ⬦ *vt* - **1.** [gen] gouverner - **2.** [control] régir. ⬦ *vi* POL gouverner.

governess ['gʌvənɪs] *n* gouvernante *f*.

government ['gʌvnmənt] *n* gouvernement *m*.

governor ['gʌvənəʳ] *n* - **1.** POL gouverneur *m* - **2.** *Br* [of school] ≃ membre *m* du conseil d'établissement ; [of bank] gouverneur *m* - **3.** *Br* [of prison] directeur *m*.

gown [gaʊn] *n* - **1.** [for woman] robe *f* - **2.** [for surgeon] blouse *f* ; [for judge, academic] robe *f*, toge *f*.

GP *n abbr of* **general practitioner**.

grab [græb] ⬦ *vt* - **1.** [seize] saisir - **2.** *inf* [sandwich] avaler en vitesse ; **to ~ a few hours' sleep** dormir quelques heures - **3.** *inf* [appeal to] emballer. ⬦ *vi* : **to ~ at sthg** faire un geste pour attraper qqch.

grace [greɪs] ⬦ *n* - **1.** [elegance] grâce *f* - **2.** *(U)* [extra time] répit *m* - **3.** [prayer] grâces *fpl*. ⬦ *vt fml* - **1.** [honour] honorer de sa présence - **2.** [decorate] orner, décorer.

graceful ['greɪsfʊl] *adj* gracieux(euse), élégant(e).

gracious ['greɪʃəs] ⬦ *adj* [polite] courtois(e). ⬦ *excl* : **(good) ~!** juste ciel!

grade [greɪd] ⬦ *n* - **1.** [quality - of worker] catégorie *f* ; [- of wool, paper] qualité *f* ; [- of petrol] type *m* ; [- of eggs] calibre *m* - **2.** *Am* [class] classe *f* - **3.** [mark] note *f*. ⬦ *vt* - **1.** [classify] classer - **2.** [mark, assess] noter.

grade crossing *n Am* passage *m* à niveau.

grade school *n Am* école *f* primaire.

gradient ['greɪdjənt] *n* pente *f*, inclinaison *f*.

gradual ['grædʒʊəl] *adj* graduel(elle), progressif(ive).

gradually ['grædʒʊəlɪ] *adv* graduellement, petit à petit.

graduate [*n* 'grædʒʊət, *vb* 'grædʒʊeɪt] ⬦ *n* - **1.** [from university] diplômé *m*, -e *f* - **2.** *Am* [of high school] ≃ titulaire *mf* du baccalauréat. ⬦ *vi* - **1.** [from university] : **to ~ (from)** ≃ obtenir son diplôme (à) - **2.** *Am* [from high school] : **to ~ (from)** ≃ obtenir son baccalauréat (à).

graduation [,grædʒʊ'eɪʃn] *n (U)* [ceremony] remise *f* des diplômes.

graffiti [grə'fi:tɪ] *n (U)* graffiti *mpl*.

graft [grɑ:ft] ⬦ *n* - **1.** [from plant] greffe *f*, greffon *m* - **2.** MED greffe *f* - **3.** *Br* [hard work] boulot *m* - **4.** *Am inf* [corruption] graissage *m* de patte. ⬦ *vt* [plant, skin] greffer.

grain [greɪn] *n* - **1.** [gen] grain *m* - **2.** *(U)* [crops] céréales *fpl* - **3.** *(U)* [pattern - in wood] fil *m* ; [- in material] grain *m* ; [- in stone, marble] veines *fpl*.

gram [græm] *n* gramme *m*.

grammar ['græməʳ] *n* grammaire *f*.

grammar school *n* [in UK] ≃ lycée *m* ; [in US] école *f* primaire.

grammatical [grə'mætɪkl] *adj* grammatical(e).

gramme [græm] *Br* = gram.

gramophone ['græməfəʊn] *n dated* gramophone *m*, phonographe *m*.

gran [græn] *n Br inf* mamie *f*, mémé *f*.

grand [grænd] ⟷ *adj* - **1.** [impressive] grandiose, imposant(e) - **2.** [ambitious] grand(e) - **3.** [important] important(e) ; [socially] distingué(e) - **4.** *inf dated* [excellent] sensationnel(elle), formidable. ⟷ *n inf* [thousand pounds] mille livres *fpl* ; [thousand dollars] mille dollars *mpl*.

grand(d)ad ['grændæd] *n inf* papi *m*, pépé *m*.

grandchild ['græntʃaɪld] (*pl* **-children** [-ˌtʃɪldrən]) *n* [boy] petit-fils *m* ; [girl] petite-fille *f*. ⟷ **grandchildren** *npl* petits-enfants *mpl*.

granddaughter ['grænˌdɔːtə'] *n* petite-fille *f*.

grandeur ['grændʒə'] *n* [splendour] splendeur *f*, magnificence *f*.

grandfather ['grændˌfɑːðə'] *n* grand-père *m*.

grandma ['grænmɑː] *n inf* mamie *f*, mémé *f*.

grandmother ['grænˌmʌðə'] *n* grand-mère *f*.

grandpa ['grænpɑː] *n inf* papi *m*, pépé *m*.

grandparents ['grænˌpeərənts] *npl* grands-parents *mpl*.

grand piano *n* piano *m* à queue.

grand slam *n* SPORT grand chelem *m*.

grandson ['grænsʌn] *n* petit-fils *m*.

grandstand ['grændstænd] *n* tribune *f*.

grand total *n* somme *f* globale, total *m* général.

granulated sugar ['grænjʊleɪtɪd-] *n* sucre *m* cristallisé.

granule ['grænjuːl] *n* granule *m* ; [of sugar] grain *m*.

grape [greɪp] *n* (grain *m* de) raisin *m* ; **a bunch of ~s** une grappe de raisin.

grapefruit ['greɪpfruːt] (*pl inv* OR **-s**) *n* pamplemousse *m*.

grapevine ['greɪpvaɪn] *n* vigne *f* ; **on the ~** *fig* par le téléphone arabe.

graph [grɑːf] *n* graphique *m*.

graphic ['græfɪk] *adj* - **1.** [vivid] vivant(e) - **2.** ART graphique. ⟷ **graphics** *npl* graphique *f*.

graphite ['græfaɪt] *n* (*U*) graphite *m*, mine *f* de plomb.

graph paper *n* (*U*) papier *m* millimétré.

grapple ['græpl] ⟷ **grapple with** *vt fus* - **1.** [person, animal] lutter avec - **2.** [problem] se débattre avec, se colleter avec.

grasp [grɑːsp] ⟷ *n* - **1.** [grip] prise *f* - **2.** [understanding] compréhension *f* ; **to have a good ~ of sthg** avoir une bonne connaissance de qqch. ⟷ *vt* - **1.** [grip, seize] saisir, empoigner - **2.** [understand] saisir, comprendre - **3.** [opportunity] saisir.

grasping ['grɑːspɪŋ] *adj pej* avide, cupide.

grass [grɑːs] ⟷ *n* BOT & *drugs sl* herbe *f*. ⟷ *vi Br crime sl* moucharder ; **to ~ on sb** dénoncer qqn.

grasshopper ['grɑːsˌhɒpə'] *n* sauterelle *f*.

grass roots ⟷ *npl fig* base *f*. ⟷ *comp* du peuple.

grass snake *n* couleuvre *f*.

grate [greɪt] ⟷ *n* grille *f* de foyer. ⟷ *vt* râper. ⟷ *vi* grincer, crisser.

grateful ['greɪtfʊl] *adj* : **to be ~ to sb (for sthg)** être reconnaissant(e) à qqn (de qqch).

grater ['greɪtə'] *n* râpe *f*.

gratify ['grætɪfaɪ] *vt* - **1.** [please - person] : **to be gratified** être content(e), être satisfait(e) - **2.** [satisfy - wish] satisfaire, assouvir.

grating ['greɪtɪŋ] ⟷ *adj* grinçant(e) ; [voix] de crécelle. ⟷ *n* [grille] grille *f*.

gratitude ['grætɪtjuːd] *n* (*U*) : **~ (to sb for sthg)** gratitude *f* OR reconnaissance *f* (envers qqn de qqch).

gratuitous [grə'tjuːɪtəs] *adj fml* gratuit(e).

grave[1] [greɪv] ⟷ *adj* grave ; [concern] sérieux(euse). ⟷ *n* tombe *f*.

grave[2] [grɑːv] *adj* LING : **e ~ e** *m* accent grave.

gravel ['grævl] *n* (*U*) gravier *m*.

gravestone ['greɪvstəʊn] *n* pierre *f* tombale.

graveyard ['greɪvjɑːd] *n* cimetière *m*.

gravity ['grævətɪ] *n* - **1.** [force] gravité *f*, pesanteur *f* - **2.** [seriousness] gravité *f*.

gravy ['greɪvɪ] *n (U)* [meat juice] jus *m* de viande.

gray *Am* = **grey**.

graze [greɪz] ◇ *vt* - **1.** [subj : cows, sheep] brouter, paître - **2.** [subj : farmer] faire paître - **3.** [skin] écorcher, égratigner - **4.** [touch lightly] frôler, effleurer. ◇ *vi* brouter, paître. ◇ *n* écorchure *f*, égratignure *f*.

grease [gri:s] ◇ *n* graisse *f*. ◇ *vt* graisser.

greaseproof paper [ˌgri:spru:f-] *n (U) Br* papier *m* sulfurisé.

greasy ['gri:zɪ] *adj* - **1.** [covered in grease] graisseux(euse) ; [clothes] taché(e) de graisse - **2.** [food, skin, hair] gras (grasse).

great [greɪt] *adj* - **1.** [gen] grand(e) ; ~ **big** énorme - **2.** *inf* [splendid] génial(e), formidable ; **to feel** ~ se sentir en pleine forme ; **great!** super!, génial!

Great Britain *n* Grande-Bretagne *f* ; **in** ~ en Grande-Bretagne.

greatcoat ['greɪtkəʊt] *n* pardessus *m*.

Great Dane *n* danois *m*.

great-grandchild *n* [boy] arrière-petit-fils *m*, [girl] arrière-petite-fille *f*. ◆ **great-grandchildren** *npl* arrière-petits-enfants *mpl*.

great-grandfather *n* arrière-grand-père *m*.

great-grandmother *n* arrière-grand-mère *f*.

greatly ['greɪtlɪ] *adv* beaucoup ; [different] très.

greatness ['greɪtnɪs] *n* grandeur *f*.

Greece [gri:s] *n* Grèce *f*.

greed [gri:d] *n (U)* - **1.** [for food] gloutonnerie *f* - **2.** *fig* [for money, power] : ~ **(for)** avidité *f* (de).

greedy ['gri:dɪ] *adj* - **1.** [for food] glouton(onne) - **2.** [for money, power] : ~ **for sthg** avide de qqch.

Greek [gri:k] ◇ *adj* grec (grecque). ◇ *n* - **1.** [person] Grec *m*, Grecque *f* - **2.** [language] grec *m*.

green [gri:n] ◇ *adj* - **1.** [in colour, unripe] vert(e) - **2.** [ecological - issue, politics] écologique ; [- person] vert(e) - **3.** *inf* [inexperienced] inexpérimenté(e), jeune. ◇ *n* - **1.** [colour] vert *m* - **2.** GOLF green *m* - **3.** : **village** ~ pelouse *f* communale. ◆ **Green** *n* POL membre *m*, -e *f* écologiste *mf* ; **the Greens** les Verts, les Écologistes. ◆ **greens** *npl* [vegetables] légumes *mpl* verts.

greenback ['gri:nbæk] *n Am inf* billet *m* vert.

green belt *n Br* ceinture *f* verte.

green card *n* - **1.** *Br* [for vehicle] carte *f* verte - **2.** *Am* [residence permit] carte *f* de séjour.

greenery ['gri:nərɪ] *n* verdure *f*.

greenfly ['gri:nflaɪ] (*pl inv* OR **-ies**) *n* puceron *m*.

greengage ['gri:ngeɪdʒ] *n* reine-claude *f*.

greengrocer ['gri:nˌgrəʊsəʳ] *n Br* marchand *m*, -e *f* de légumes ; **~'s (shop)** magasin *m* de fruits et légumes.

greenhouse ['gri:nhaʊs, *pl* -haʊzɪz] *n* serre *f*.

greenhouse effect *n* : **the** ~ l'effet *m* de serre.

Greenland ['gri:nlənd] *n* Groenland *m*.

green salad *n* salade *f* verte.

greet [gri:t] *vt* - **1.** [say hello to] saluer - **2.** [receive] accueillir.

greeting ['gri:tɪŋ] *n* salutation *f*, salut *m*. ◆ **greetings** *npl* : **Christmas/birthday ~s** vœux *mpl* de Noël/d'anniversaire.

greetings card *Br*, **greeting card** *Am* *n* carte *f* de vœux.

grenade [grəˈneɪd] *n* : **(hand)** ~ grenade *f* (à main).

grew [gru:] *pt* ⟶ **grow**.

grey *Br*, **gray** *Am* [greɪ] ◇ *adj* - **1.** [in colour] gris(e) - **2.** [grey-haired] : **to go** ~ grisonner - **3.** [dull, gloomy] morne, triste. ◇ *n* gris *m*.

grey-haired [-ˈheəd] *adj* aux cheveux gris.

greyhound ['greɪhaʊnd] *n* lévrier *m*.

grid [grɪd] *n* - **1.** [grating] grille *f* - **2.** [system of squares] quadrillage *m*.

griddle ['grɪdl] *n* plaque *f* à cuire.

gridlock ['grɪdlɒk] *n Am* embouteillage *m*.

grief [gri:f] *n (U)* - **1.** [sorrow] chagrin *m*, peine *f* - **2.** *inf* [trouble] ennuis *mpl* - **3.** *phr* : **to come to** ~ [person] avoir de gros problèmes ; [project] échouer, tomber à l'eau ; **good** ~! Dieu du ciel!, mon Dieu!

grievance ['gri:vns] *n* grief *m*, doléance *f*.

grieve [gri:v] *vi* [at death] être en deuil ; **to** ~ **for sb/sthg** pleurer qqn/qqch.

grievous ['gri:vəs] *adj fml* grave ; [shock] cruel(elle).

grievous bodily harm *n (U)* coups *mpl* et blessures *fpl*.

grill [grɪl] ◇ *n* [on cooker, fire] gril *m*. ◇ *vt* - **1.** [cook on grill] griller, faire griller - **2.** *inf* [interrogate] cuisiner.

grille [grɪl] *n* grille *f*.

grim [grɪm] *adj* - **1.** [stern - face, expression] sévère ; [- determination] inflexible

- 2. [cheerless - truth, news] sinistre ; [- room, walls] lugubre ; [- day] morne, triste.

grimace [grɪ'meɪs] ⬦ *n* grimace *f.* ⬦ *vi* grimacer, faire la grimace.

grime [graɪm] *n (U)* crasse *f*, saleté *f.*

grimy ['graɪmɪ] *adj* sale, encrassé(e).

grin [grɪn] ⬦ *n* (large) sourire *m.* ⬦ *vi* : **to ~ (at sb/sthg)** adresser un large sourire (à qqn/qqch).

grind [graɪnd] (*pt* & *pp* ground) ⬦ *vt* [crush] moudre. ⬦ *vi* [scrape] grincer. ⬦ *n* [hard, boring work] corvée *f.* ◆ **grind down** *vt sep* [oppress] opprimer. ◆ **grind up** *vt sep* pulvériser.

grinder ['graɪndə'] *n* moulin *m.*

grip [grɪp] ⬦ *n* **- 1.** [grasp, hold] prise *f* **- 2.** [control] contrôle *m* ; **he's got a good ~ on the situation** il a la situation bien en main ; **to get to ~s with sthg** s'attaquer à qqch ; **to get a ~ on o.s.** se ressaisir **- 3.** [adhesion] adhérence *f* **- 4.** [handle] poignée *f* **- 5.** [bag] sac *m* (de voyage). ⬦ *vt* **- 1.** [grasp] saisir ; [subj : tyres] adhérer à **- 2.** *fig* [imagination, country] captiver.

gripe [graɪp] *inf* ⬦ *n* [complaint] plainte *f.* ⬦ *vi* : **to ~ (about sthg)** râler OR rouspéter (contre qqch).

gripping ['grɪpɪŋ] *adj* passionnant(e).

grisly ['grɪzlɪ] *adj* [horrible, macabre] macabre.

gristle ['grɪsl] *n (U)* nerfs *mpl.*

grit [grɪt] ⬦ *n* **- 1.** [stones] gravillon *m* ; [in eye] poussière *f* **- 2.** *inf* [courage] cran *m.* ⬦ *vt* sabler.

gritty ['grɪtɪ] *adj* **- 1.** [stony] couvert(e) de gravillon **- 2.** *inf* [brave - person] qui a du cran ; [- performance, determination] courageux(euse).

groan [grəʊn] ⬦ *n* gémissement *m.* ⬦ *vi* **- 1.** [moan] gémir **- 2.** [creak] grincer, gémir.

grocer ['grəʊsə'] *n* épicier *m*, -ère *f* ; **~'s (shop)** épicerie *f.*

groceries ['grəʊsərɪz] *npl* [foods] provisions *fpl.*

grocery ['grəʊsərɪ] *n* [shop] épicerie *f.*

groggy ['grɒgɪ] *adj* groggy *(inv).*

groin [grɔɪn] *n* aine *f.*

groom [gruːm] ⬦ *n* **- 1.** [of horses] palefrenier *m*, garçon *m* d'écurie **- 2.** [bridegroom] marié *m.* ⬦ *vt* **- 1.** [brush] panser **- 2.** *fig* [prepare] : **to ~ sb (for sthg)** préparer OR former qqn (pour qqch).

groove [gruːv] *n* [in metal, wood] rainure *f* ; [in record] sillon *m.*

groovy ['gruːvɪ] *adj inf* **- 1.** [excellent] super, génial(e) **- 2.** [fashionable] branché(e).

grope [grəʊp] *vi* : **to ~ (about) for sthg** chercher qqch à tâtons.

gross [grəʊs] (*pl inv* OR **-es** [-iːz]) ⬦ *adj* **- 1.** [total] brut(e) **- 2.** *fml* [serious - negligence] coupable ; [- misconduct] choquant(e) ; [- inequality] flagrant(e) **- 3.** [coarse, vulgar] grossier(ère) **- 4.** *inf* [obese] obèse, énorme. ⬦ *n* grosse *f*, douze douzaines *fpl.*

grossly ['grəʊslɪ] *adv* [seriously] extrêmement, énormément.

grotesque [grəʊ'tesk] *adj* grotesque.

grotto ['grɒtəʊ] (*pl* **-es** OR **-s**) *n* grotte *f.*

grotty ['grɒtɪ] *adj Br inf* minable.

ground [graʊnd] ⬦ *pt* & *pp* ⬡ grind. ⬦ *n* **- 1.** *(U)* [surface of earth] sol *m*, terre *f* ; **above ~** en surface ; **below ~** sous terre ; **on the ~** par terre, au sol **- 2.** *(U)* [area of land] terrain *m* **- 3.** [for sport etc] terrain *m* **- 4.** [advantage] : **to gain/lose ~** gagner/perdre du terrain. ⬦ *vt* **- 1.** [base] : **to be ~ed on** OR **in sthg** être fondé(e) sur qqch **- 2.** [aircraft, pilot] interdire de vol **- 3.** *esp Am inf* [child] priver de sortie **- 4.** *Am* ELEC : **to be ~ed** être à la masse. ◆ **grounds** *npl* **- 1.** [reason] motif *m*, raison *f* ; **~s for sthg** motifs de qqch ; **~s for doing sthg** raisons de faire qqch **- 2.** [land round building] parc *m* **- 3.** [of coffee] marc *m.*

ground crew *n* personnel *m* au sol.

ground floor *n* rez-de-chaussée *m inv.*

grounding ['graʊndɪŋ] *n* : **~ (in)** connaissances *fpl* de base (en).

groundless ['graʊndlɪs] *adj* sans fondement.

groundsheet ['graʊndʃiːt] *n* tapis *m* de sol.

ground staff *n* **- 1.** [at sports ground] personnel *m* d'entretien *(d'un terrain de sport)* **- 2.** *Br* = ground crew.

groundswell ['graʊndswel] *n* vague *f* de fond.

groundwork ['graʊndwɜːk] *n (U)* travail *m* préparatoire.

group [gruːp] ⬦ *n* groupe *m.* ⬦ *vt* grouper, réunir. ⬦ *vi* : **to ~ (together)** se grouper.

groupie ['gruːpɪ] *n inf* groupie *f.*

grouse [graʊs] (*pl inv* OR **-s**) ⬦ *n* [bird] grouse *f*, coq *m* de bruyère. ⬦ *vi inf* râler, rouspéter.

grove [grəʊv] *n* [group of trees] bosquet *m.*

grovel ['grɒvl] *vi* : **to ~ (to sb)** ramper (devant qqn).

grow [grəʊ] (*pt* **grew**, *pp* **grown**) ◇ *vi* - **1.** [gen] pousser ; [person, animal] grandir ; [company, city] s'agrandir ; [fears, influence, traffic] augmenter, s'accroître ; [problem, idea, plan] prendre de l'ampleur ; [economy] se développer - **2.** [become] devenir ; **to ~ old** vieillir ; **to ~ tired of sthg** se fatiguer de qqch. ◇ *vt* - **1.** [plants] faire pousser - **2.** [hair, beard] laisser pousser.
➡ **grow on** *vt fus inf* plaire de plus en plus à ; **it'll ~ on you** cela finira par te plaire.
➡ **grow out of** *vt fus* - **1.** [clothes, shoes] devenir trop grand pour - **2.** [habit] perdre.
➡ **grow up** *vi* - **1.** [become adult] grandir, devenir adulte ; **~ up!** ne fais pas l'enfant! - **2.** [develop] se développer.

grower ['grəʊəʳ] *n* cultivateur *m*, -trice *f*.

growl [graʊl] *vi* [animal] grogner, gronder ; [engine] vrombir, gronder ; [person] grogner.

grown [grəʊn] ◇ *pp* ➡ **grow**. ◇ *adj* adulte.

grown-up ◇ *adj* - **1.** [fully grown] adulte, grand(e) - **2.** [mature] mûr(e). ◇ *n* adulte *mf*, grande personne *f*.

growth [grəʊθ] *n* - **1.** [increase - gen] croissance *f* ; [- of opposition, company] développement *m* ; [- of population] augmentation *f*, accroissement *m* - **2.** MED [lump] tumeur *f*, excroissance *f*.

grub [grʌb] *n* - **1.** [insect] larve *f* - **2.** *inf* [food] bouffe *f*.

grubby ['grʌbɪ] *adj* sale, malpropre.

grudge [grʌdʒ] ◇ *n* rancune *f* ; **to bear sb a ~**, **to bear a ~ against sb** garder rancune à qqn. ◇ *vi* **to ~ sb sthg** donner qqch à qqn à contrecœur ; [success] en vouloir à qqn à cause de qqch.

gruelling *Br*, **grueling** *Am* ['grʊəlɪŋ] *adj* épuisant(e), exténuant(e).

gruesome ['gruːsəm] *adj* horrible.

gruff [grʌf] *adj* - **1.** [hoarse] gros (grosse) - **2.** [rough, unfriendly] brusque, bourru(e).

grumble ['grʌmbl] *vi* - **1.** [complain] : **to ~ about sthg** rouspéter OR grommeler contre qqch - **2.** [rumble - thunder, train] gronder ; [- stomach] gargouiller.

grumpy ['grʌmpɪ] *adj inf* renfrogné(e).

grunge [grʌndʒ] *n* - **1.** *inf* [dirt] crasse *f* - **2.** [music, fashion] grunge *m*.

grunt [grʌnt] ◇ *n* grognement *m*. ◇ *vi* grogner.

G-string *n* cache-sexe *m inv*.

guarantee [ˌgærən'tiː] ◇ *n* garantie *f*. ◇ *vt* garantir.

guard [gaːd] ◇ *n* - **1.** [person] garde *m* ; [in prison] gardien *m* - **2.** [group of guards] garde *f* - **3.** [defensive operation] garde *f* ; **to be on ~** être de garde OR de faction ; **to catch sb off ~** prendre qqn au dépourvu - **4.** *Br* RAIL chef *m* de train - **5.** [protective device - for body] protection *f* ; [- for fire] garde feu *m inv*. ◇ *vt* - **1.** [protect - building] protéger, garder ; [- person] protéger - **2.** [prisoner] garder, surveiller - **3.** [hide - secret] garder.

guard dog *n* chien *m* de garde.

guarded ['gaːdɪd] *adj* prudent(e).

guardian ['gaːdjən] *n* - **1.** [of child] tuteur *m*, -trice *f* - **2.** [protector] gardien *m*, -enne *f*, protecteur *m*, -trice *f*.

guardrail ['gaːdreɪl] *n Am* [on road] barrière *f* de sécurité.

guard's van *n Br* wagon *m* du chef de train.

guerilla [gə'rɪlə] = **guerrilla**.

Guernsey ['gɜːnzɪ] *n* [place] Guernesey *f*.

guerrilla [gə'rɪlə] *n* guérillero *m* ; **urban ~** guérillero *m* des villes.

guerrilla warfare *n* (U) guérilla *f*.

guess [ges] ◇ *n* conjecture *f*. ◇ *vt* deviner ; **~ what?** tu sais quoi? ◇ *vi* - **1.** [conjecture] deviner ; **to ~ at sthg** deviner qqch - **2.** [suppose] : **I ~ (so)** je suppose (que oui).

guesswork ['geswɜːk] *n* (U) conjectures *fpl*, hypothèses *fpl*.

guest [gest] *n* - **1.** [gen] invité *m*, -e *f* - **2.** [at hotel] client *m*, -e *f*.

guesthouse ['gesthaʊs, *pl* -haʊzɪz] *n* pension *f* de famille.

guestroom ['gestrʊm] *n* chambre *f* d'amis.

guffaw [gʌ'fɔː] ◇ *n* gros rire *m*. ◇ *vi* rire bruyamment.

guidance ['gaɪdəns] *n* (U) - **1.** [help] conseils *mpl* - **2.** [leadership] direction *f*.

guide [gaɪd] ◇ *n* - **1.** [person, book] guide *m* - **2.** [indication] indication *f*. ◇ *vt* - **1.** [show by leading] guider - **2.** [control] diriger - **3.** [influence] : **to be ~d by sb/sthg** se laisser guider par qqn/qqch. ➡ **Guide** *n* = **Girl Guide**.

guide book *n* guide *m*.

guide dog *n* chien *m* d'aveugle.

guidelines ['gaɪdlaɪnz] *npl* directives *fpl*, lignes *fpl* directrices.

guild [gɪld] *n* - **1.** HISTORY corporation *f*, guilde *f* - **2.** [association] association *f*.

guile [gaɪl] *n* (U) *literary* ruse *f*, astuce *f*.

guillotine ['gɪlətiːn] ◇ *n* - **1.** [for executions] guillotine *f* - **2.** [for paper] massicot *m*. ◇ *vt* [execute] guillotiner.

guilt [gɪlt] *n* culpabilité *f*.

guilty ['gɪltɪ] *adj* coupable ; **to be ~ of**

sthg être coupable de qqch ; **to be found ~/not ~** JUR être reconnu coupable/non coupable.

guinea pig ['gɪnɪ-] n cobaye m.

guise [gaɪz] n fml apparence f.

guitar [gɪ'tɑːʳ] n guitare f.

guitarist [gɪ'tɑːrɪst] n guitariste mf.

gulf [gʌlf] n - 1. [sea] golfe m - 2. [breach, chasm] : ~ **(between)** abîme m (entre). **◆ Gulf** n : **the Gulf** le Golfe.

gull [gʌl] n mouette f.

gullet ['gʌlɪt] n œsophage m ; [of bird] gosier m.

gullible ['gʌləbl] adj crédule.

gully ['gʌlɪ] n - 1. [valley] ravine f - 2. [ditch] rigole f.

gulp [gʌlp] <> n [of drink] grande gorgée f ; [of food] grosse bouchée f. <> vt avaler. <> vi avoir la gorge nouée. **◆ gulp down** vt sep avaler.

gum [gʌm] <> n - 1. [chewing gum] chewing-gum m - 2. [adhesive] colle f, gomme f - 3. ANAT gencive f. <> vt coller.

gumboots ['gʌmbuːts] npl Br bottes fpl de caoutchouc.

gun [gʌn] n - 1. [weapon - small] revolver m ; [- rifle] fusil m ; [- large] canon m - 2. [starting pistol] pistolet m - 3. [tool] pistolet m ; [for staples] agrafeuse f. **◆ gun down** vt sep abattre.

gunboat ['gʌnbəʊt] n canonnière f.

gunfire ['gʌnfaɪəʳ] n (U) coups mpl de feu.

gunman ['gʌnmən] (pl -men [-mən]) n personne f armée.

gunpoint ['gʌnpɔɪnt] n : **at ~** sous la menace d'un fusil OR pistolet.

gunpowder ['gʌn,paʊdəʳ] n poudre f à canon.

gunshot ['gʌnʃɒt] n [firing of gun] coup m de feu.

gunsmith ['gʌnsmɪθ] n armurier m.

gurgle ['gɜːgl] vi - 1. [water] glouglouter - 2. [baby] gazouiller.

guru ['gʊruː] n gourou m, guru m.

gush [gʌʃ] <> n jaillissement m. <> vi - 1. [flow out] jaillir - 2. pej [enthuse] s'exprimer de façon exubérante.

gusset ['gʌsɪt] n gousset m.

gust [gʌst] n rafale f, coup m de vent.

gusto ['gʌstəʊ] n : **with ~** avec enthousiasme.

gut [gʌt] <> n MED intestin m. <> vt - 1. [remove organs from] vider - 2. [destroy] éventrer. **◆ guts** npl inf - 1. [intestines] intestins mpl ; **to hate sb's ~s** ne pas pouvoir

piffer qqn, ne pas pouvoir voir qqn en peinture - 2. [courage] cran m.

gutter ['gʌtəʳ] n - 1. [ditch] rigole f - 2. [on roof] gouttière f.

gutter press n presse f à sensation.

guy [gaɪ] n - 1. inf [man] type m - 2. [person] copain m, copine f - 3. Br [dummy] effigie de Guy Fawkes.

Guy Fawkes' Night [-'fɔːks-] n fête célébrée le 5 novembre en Grande-Bretagne.

guy rope n corde f de tente.

guzzle ['gʌzl] <> vt bâfrer ; [drink] lamper. <> vi s'empiffrer.

gym [dʒɪm] n inf - 1. [gymnasium] gymnase m - 2. [exercises] gym f.

gymnasium [dʒɪm'neɪzjəm] (pl -iums OR -ia [-jə]) n gymnase m.

gymnast ['dʒɪmnæst] n gymnaste mf.

gymnastics [dʒɪm'næstɪks] n (U) gymnastique f.

gym shoes npl (chaussures fpl de) tennis mpl.

gymslip ['dʒɪm,slɪp] n Br tunique f.

gynaecologist Br, **gynecologist** Am [,gaɪnə'kɒlədʒɪst] n gynécologue mf.

gynaecology Br, **gynecology** Am [,gaɪnə'kɒlədʒɪ] n gynécologie f.

gypsy ['dʒɪpsɪ] = gipsy.

gyrate [dʒaɪ'reɪt] vi tournoyer.

h (pl h's OR hs), **H** (pl H's OR Hs) [eɪtʃ] n [letter] h m inv, H m inv.

haberdashery ['hæbədæʃərɪ] n mercerie f.

habit ['hæbɪt] n - 1. [customary practice] habitude f ; **out of ~** par habitude ; **to make a ~ of doing sthg** avoir l'habitude de faire qqch - 2. [garment] habit m.

habitat ['hæbɪtæt] n habitat m.

habitual [hə'bɪtjʊəl] adj - 1. [usual, characteristic] habituel(elle) - 2. [regular] invétéré(e).

hack [hæk] <> n [writer] écrivailleur m, -euse f. <> vt [cut] tailler. **◆ hack into** vt fus COMPUT pirater.

hacker ['hækəʳ] *n* : (computer) ~ pirate *m* informatique.

hackneyed ['hæknɪd] *adj* rebattu(e).

hacksaw ['hæksɔ:] *n* scie *f* à métaux.

had [*weak form* həd, *strong form* hæd] *pt & pp* ⊳ have.

haddock ['hædək] (*pl inv*) *n* églefin *m*, aiglefin *m*.

hadn't ['hædnt] = had not.

haemophiliac [ˌhi:məˈfɪlɪæk] = hemophiliac.

haemorrhage ['hemərɪdʒ] = hemorrhage.

haemorrhoids ['hemərɔɪdz] = hemorrhoids.

haggard ['hægəd] *adj* [face] défait(e) ; [person] abattu(e).

haggis ['hægɪs] *n* plat typique écossais fait d'une panse de brebis farcie, le plus souvent servie avec des navets et des pommes de terre.

haggle ['hægl] *vi* marchander ; **to ~ over** OR **about sthg** marchander qqch.

Hague [heɪg] *n* : **The ~** La Haye.

hall [heɪl] <> *n* grêle *f* ; *fig* pluie *f*. <> *vt* - **1.** [call] héler - **2.** [acclaim] : **to ~ sb/sthg as sthg** acclamer qqn/qqch comme qqch. <> *v impers* grêler.

hailstone ['heɪlstəʊn] *n* grêlon *m*.

hair [heəʳ] *n* - **1.** (U) [on human head] cheveux *mpl* ; **to do one's ~** se coiffer - **2.** (U) [on animal, human skin] poils *mpl* - **3.** [individual hair - on head] cheveu *m* ; [- on skin] poil *m*.

hairbrush ['heəbrʌʃ] *n* brosse *f* à cheveux.

haircut ['heəkʌt] *n* coupe *f* de cheveux.

hairdo ['heədu:] (*pl -s*) *n inf* coiffure *f*.

hairdresser ['heəˌdresəʳ] *n* coiffeur *m*, -euse *f* ; **~'s (salon)** salon *m* de coiffure.

hairdryer ['heəˌdraɪəʳ] *n* [handheld] sèche-cheveux *m inv* ; [with hood] casque *m*.

hair gel *n* gel *m* coiffant.

hairgrip ['heəgrɪp] *n Br* pince *f* à cheveux.

hairpin ['heəpɪn] *n* épingle *f* à cheveux.

hairpin bend *n* virage *m* en épingle à cheveux.

hair-raising [-ˌreɪzɪŋ] *adj* à faire dresser les cheveux sur la tête ; [journey] effrayant(e).

hair remover [-rɪˌmu:vəʳ] *n* (crème *f*) dépilatoire *m*.

hair slide *n Br* barrette *f*.

hairspray ['heəspreɪ] *n* laque *f*.

hairstyle ['heəstaɪl] *n* coiffure *f*.

hairy ['heərɪ] *adj* - **1.** [covered in hair] velu(e), poilu(e) - **2.** *inf* [frightening] à faire dresser les cheveux sur la tête.

Haiti ['heɪtɪ] *n* Haïti.

hake [heɪk] (*pl inv* OR **-s**) *n* colin *m*, merluche *f*.

half [*Br* ha:f, *Am* hæf] (*pl senses 1 and 2* **halves** [*Br* ha:vz, *Am* hævz], *pl senses 3, 4 and 5* **halves** OR **halfs**) <> *adj* demi(e) ; **~ a dozen** une demi-douzaine ; **~ an hour** une demi-heure ; **~ a pound** une demi-livre ; **~ English** à moitié anglais. <> *adv* - **1.** [gen] à moitié ; **~-and-~** moitié-moitié - **2.** [by half] de moitié - **3.** [in telling the time] : **~ past ten** *Br*, **~ after ten** *Am* dix heures et demie ; **it's ~ past** il est la demie. <> *n* - **1.** [gen] moitié *f* ; **in ~** en deux ; **to go halves (with sb)** partager (avec qqn) - **2.** SPORT [of match] mi-temps *f* - **3.** SPORT [halfback] demi *m* - **4.** [of beer] demi *m* - **5.** [child's ticket] demi-tarif *m*, tarif *m* enfant. <> *pron* la moitié ; **~ of them** la moitié d'entre eux.

halfback ['ha:fbæk] *n* demi *m*.

half board *n esp Br* demi-pension *f*.

half-breed <> *adj* métis(isse). <> *n* métis *m*, -isse *f* (attention : le terme 'half-breed' est considéré comme raciste).

half-caste [ˈka:st] <> *adj* métis(isse). <> *n* métis *m*, -isse *f* (attention : le terme 'half-caste' est considéré raciste).

half-hearted [-ˈha:tɪd] *adj* sans enthousiasme.

half hour *n* demi-heure *f*.

half-mast *n* : **at ~** [flag] en berne.

half moon *n* demi lune *f*.

half note *n Am* MUS blanche *f*.

halfpenny ['heɪpnɪ] (*pl* **-pennies** OR **-pence** [-pens]) *n* demi-penny *m*.

half-price *adj* à moitié prix.

half term *n Br* congé *m* de mi-trimestre.

half time *n* (U) mi-temps *f*.

halfway [ha:fˈweɪ] <> *adj* à mi-chemin. <> *adv* - **1.** [in space] à mi-chemin - **2.** [in time] à la moitié.

halibut ['hælɪbət] (*pl inv* OR **-s**) *n* flétan *m*.

hall [hɔ:l] *n* - **1.** [in house] vestibule *m*, entrée *f* - **2.** [meeting room, building] salle *f* - **3.** [country house] manoir *m*.

hallmark ['hɔ:lma:k] *n* - **1.** [typical feature] marque *f* - **2.** [on metal] poinçon *m*.

hallo [həˈləʊ] = hello.

hall of residence (*pl* **halls of residence**) *n Br* UNIV résidence *f* universitaire.

Hallowe'en [ˌhæləʊ'iːn] *n* Halloween *f* *(fête des sorcières et des fantômes).*

hallucinate [hə'luːsɪneɪt] *vi* avoir des hallucinations.

hallway ['hɔːlweɪ] *n* vestibule *m*.

halo ['heɪləʊ] *(pl* **-es** OR **-s)** *n* nimbe *m* ; AS-TRON halo *m*.

halt [hɔːlt] ◇ *n* [stop] **: to come to a ~** [vehicle] s'arrêter, s'immobiliser ; [activity] s'interrompre ; **to call a ~ to** sthg mettre fin à qqch. ◇ *vt* arrêter. ◇ *vi* s'arrêter.

halterneck ['hɔːltənek] *adj* dos nu *(inv)*.

halve [*Br* haːv, *Am* hæv] *vt* **- 1.** [reduce by half] réduire de moitié **- 2.** [divide] couper en deux.

halves [*Br* haːvz, *Am* hævz] *pl* ▷ **half**.

ham [hæm] ◇ *n* [meat] jambon *m*. ◇ *comp* au jambon.

hamburger ['hæmbɜːgə'] *n* **- 1.** [burger] hamburger *m* **- 2.** *(U) Am* [mince] viande *f* hachée.

hamlet ['hæmlɪt] *n* hameau *m*.

hammer ['hæmə'] ◇ *n* marteau *m*. ◇ *vt* **- 1.** [with tool] marteler ; [nail] enfoncer à coups de marteau **- 2.** [with fist] marteler du poing **- 3.** *fig* **: to ~ sthg into sb** faire entrer qqch dans la tête de qqn **- 4.** *inf* [defeat] battre à plates coutures. ◇ *vi* [with fist] **: to ~ (on)** cogner du poing (à). ◆ **hammer out** *vt fus* [agreement, solution] finalement à.

hammock ['hæmək] *n* hamac *m*.

hamper ['hæmpə'] ◇ *n* **- 1.** [for food] panier *m* d'osier **- 2.** *Am* [for laundry] coffre *m* à linge. ◇ *vt* gêner.

hamster ['hæmstə'] *n* hamster *m*.

hamstring ['hæmstrɪŋ] *n* tendon *m* du jarret.

hand [hænd] ◇ *n* **- 1.** [part of body] main *f* ; **to hold ~s** se tenir la main ; **by ~** à la main ; **to get** OR **lay one's ~s on** mettre la main sur ; **to get out of ~** échapper à tout contrôle ; **to have a situation in ~** avoir une situation en main ; **to have one's ~s full** avoir du pain sur la planche ; **to try one's ~ at** sthg s'essayer à qqch **- 2.** [help] coup *m* de main ; **to give** OR **lend sb a ~ (with** sthg) donner un coup de main à qqn (pour faire qqch) **- 3.** [worker] ouvrier *m*, -ère *f* **- 4.** [of clock, watch] aiguille *f* **- 5.** [handwriting] écriture *f* **- 6.** [of cards] jeu *m*, main *f*. ◇ *vt* **: to ~ sthg to sb**, **to ~ sb sthg** passer qqch à qqn. ◆ **(close) at hand** *adv* proche. ◆ **on hand** *adv* disponible. ◆ **on the other hand** *conj* d'autre part. ◆ **out of hand** *adv* [completely] d'emblée. ◆ **to hand** *adv* à portée de la main, sous la main.

◆ **hand down** *vt sep* transmettre. ◆ **hand in** *vt sep* remettre. ◆ **hand out** *vt sep* distribuer. ◆ **hand over** ◇ *vt sep* **- 1.** [baton, money] remettre **- 2.** [responsibility, power] transmettre. ◇ *vi* **: to ~ over (to)** passer le relais (à).

handbag ['hændbæg] *n* sac *m* à main.

handball ['hændbɔːl] *n* [game] handball *m*.

handbook ['hændbʊk] *n* manuel *m* ; [for tourist] guide *m*.

handbrake ['hændbreɪk] *n* frein *m* à main.

handcuffs ['hændkʌfs] *npl* menottes *fpl*.

handful ['hændfʊl] *n* [of sand, grass, people] poignée *f*.

handgun ['hændgʌn] *n* revolver *m*, pistolet *m*.

handicap ['hændɪkæp] ◇ *n* handicap *m*. ◇ *vt* handicaper ; [progress, work] entraver.

handicapped ['hændɪkæpt] ◇ *adj* handicapé(e). ◇ *npl* **: the ~** les handicapés *mpl*.

handicraft ['hændɪkrɑːft] *n* activité *f* artisanale.

handiwork ['hændɪwɜːk] *n* *(U)* ouvrage *m*.

handkerchief ['hæŋkətʃɪf] *(pl* **-chiefs** OR **-chieves** [-tʃiːvz]*) n* mouchoir *m*.

handle ['hændl] ◇ *n* poignée *f* ; [of jug, cup] anse *f* ; [of knife, pan] manche *m*. ◇ *vt* **- 1.** [with hands] manipuler ; [without permission] toucher à **- 2.** [deal with, be responsible for] s'occuper de ; [difficult situation] faire face à **- 3.** [treat] traiter, s'y prendre avec.

handlebars ['hændlbɑːz] *npl* guidon *m*.

handler ['hændlə'] *n* **- 1.** [of dog] maître-chien *m* **- 2.** [at airport] **: (baggage) ~** bagagiste *m*.

hand luggage *n* *(U) Br* bagages *mpl* à main.

handmade [ˌhænd'meɪd] *adj* fait(e) (à la main).

handout ['hændaʊt] *n* **- 1.** [gift] don *m* **- 2.** [leaflet] prospectus *m*.

handrail ['hændreɪl] *n* rampe *f*.

handset ['hændset] *n* combiné *m*.

handshake ['hændʃeɪk] *n* serrement *m* OR poignée *f* de main.

handsome ['hænsəm] *adj* **- 1.** [good-looking] beau (belle) **- 2.** [reward, profit] beau (belle) ; [gift] généreux(euse).

handstand ['hændstænd] *n* équilibre *m* (*sur les mains*).

handwriting ['hænd‚raɪtɪŋ] *n* écriture *f*.

handy ['hændɪ] *adj inf* - **1.** [useful] pratique ; **to come in ~** être utile - **2.** [skilful] adroit(e) - **3.** [near] tout près, à deux pas.

handyman ['hændɪmæn] (*pl* -**men** [-men]) *n* bricoleur *m*.

hang [hæŋ] (*pt & pp sense 1* hung, *pt & pp sense 2* hung OR hanged) <> *vt* - **1.** [fasten] suspendre - **2.** [execute] pendre. <> *vi* - **1.** [be fastened] pendre, être accroché(e) - **2.** [be executed] être pendu(e). <> *n* : **to get the ~ of sthg** *inf* saisir le truc OR attraper le coup pour faire qqch. ◆ **hang about, hang around** *vi* traîner. ◆ **hang on** *vi* - **1.** [keep hold] : **to ~ on (to)** s'accrocher OR se cramponner (à) - **2.** *inf* [continue waiting] attendre - **3.** [persevere] tenir bon. ◆ **hang out** *vi inf* [spend time] traîner. ◆ **hang round** = **hang about**. ◆ **hang up** <> *vt sep* pendre. <> *vi* [on telephone] raccrocher. ◆ **hang up on** *vt fus* TELEC raccrocher au nez de.

hangar ['hæŋə'] *n* hangar *m*.

hanger ['hæŋə'] *n* cintre *m*.

hanger-on (*pl* hangers-on) *n* parasite *m*.

hang gliding *n* deltaplane *m*, vol *m* libre.

hangover ['hæŋ‚əʊvə'] *n* [from drinking] gueule *f* de bois.

hang-up *n inf* complexe *m*.

hanker ['hæŋkə'] ◆ **hanker after, hanker for** *vt fus* convoiter.

hankie, hanky ['hæŋkɪ] (*abbr of* handkerchief) *n inf* mouchoir *m*.

haphazard [‚hæp'hæzəd] *adj* fait(e) au hasard.

hapless ['hæplɪs] *adj literary* infortuné(e).

happen ['hæpən] *vi* - **1.** [occur] arriver, se passer ; **to ~ to sb** arriver à qqn - **2.** [chance] : **I just ~ed to meet him** je l'ai rencontré par hasard ; **as it ~s** en fait.

happening ['hæpənɪŋ] *n* événement *m*.

happily ['hæpɪlɪ] *adv* - **1.** [with pleasure] de bon cœur - **2.** [contentedly] : **to be ~ doing sthg** être bien tranquillement en train de faire qqch - **3.** [fortunately] heureusement.

happiness ['hæpɪnɪs] *n* bonheur *m*.

happy ['hæpɪ] *adj* - **1.** [gen] heureux(euse) ; **to be ~ to do sthg** être heureux de faire qqch ; **~ Christmas/birthday!** joyeux Noël/ anniversaire ! ; **~ New Year!** bonne année ! - **2.** [satisfied] heureux(euse), content(e) ; **to be ~ with** OR **about sthg** être heureux de qqch.

happy-go-lucky *adj* décontracté(e).

happy medium *n* juste milieu *m*.

harangue [hə'ræŋ] <> *n* harangue *f.* <> *vt* haranguer.

harass ['hærəs] *vt* harceler.

harbour *Br*, **harbor** *Am* ['hɑːbə'] <> *n* port *m*. <> *vt* - **1.** [feeling] entretenir ; [doubt, grudge] garder - **2.** [person] héberger.

hard [hɑːd] <> *adj* - **1.** [gen] dur(e) ; **to be ~ on sb/sthg** être dur avec qqn/pour qqch - **2.** [winter, frost] rude - **3.** [water] calcaire - **4.** [fact] concret(ète) ; [news] sûr(e), vérifié(e) - **5.** *Br* POL : **~ left/right** extrême gauche/droite. <> *adv* - **1.** [strenuously - work] dur ; [- listen, concentrate] avec effort ; **to try ~ (to do sthg)** faire de son mieux (pour faire qqch) - **2.** [forcefully] fort - **3.** [heavily - rain] à verse ; [- snow] dru - **4.** *phr* : **to be ~ pushed** OR **put** OR **pressed to do sthg** avoir bien de la peine à faire qqch ; **to feel ~ done by** avoir l'impression d'avoir été traité injustement.

hardback ['hɑːdbæk] <> *adj* relié(e). <> *n* livre *m* relié.

hardboard ['hɑːdbɔːd] *n* panneau *m* de fibres.

hard-boiled *adj* CULIN : **~ egg** œuf *m* dur.

hard cash *n* (*U*) espèces *fpl.*

hard copy *n* COMPUT sortie *f* papier.

hard disk *n* COMPUT disque *m* dur.

harden ['hɑːdn] <> *vt* durcir ; [steel] tremper. <> *vi* - **1.** [glue, concrete] durcir - **2.** [attitude, opposition] se durcir.

hard-headed [-'hedɪd] *adj* [decision] pragmatique ; **to be ~** [person] avoir la tête froide.

hard-hearted [-'hɑːtɪd] *adj* insensible, impitoyable.

hard labour *n* (*U*) travaux *mpl* forcés.

hard-liner *n* partisan *m* de la manière forte.

hardly ['hɑːdlɪ] *adv* - **1.** [scarcely] à peine, ne ... guère ; **~ ever/anything** presque jamais/rien ; **I can ~ move/wait** je peux à peine bouger/attendre - **2.** [only just] à peine.

hardness ['hɑːdnɪs] *n* - **1.** [firmness] dureté *f* - **2.** [difficulty] difficulté *f.*

hardship ['hɑːdʃɪp] *n* - **1.** (*U*) [difficult conditions] épreuves *fpl* - **2.** [difficult circumstance] épreuve *f.*

hard shoulder *n Br* AUT bande *f* d'arrêt d'urgence.

hard up *adj inf* fauché(e) ; **~ for sthg** à court de qqch.

hardware ['hɑːdweə'] *n* (*U*) - **1.** [tools,

equipment] quincaillerie *f* - **2.** COMPUT hardware *m*, matériel *m*.

hardware shop *n* quincaillerie *f*.

hardwearing [ˌhaːdˈweərɪŋ] *adj* Br résistant(e).

hardworking [ˌhaːdˈwɜːkɪŋ] *adj* travailleur(euse).

hardy [ˈhaːdɪ] *adj* - **1.** [person, animal] vigoureux(euse), robuste - **2.** [plant] résistant(e), vivace.

hare [heəʳ] *n* lièvre *m*.

harebrained [ˈheəˌbreɪnd] *adj inf* [person] écervelé(e) ; [scheme, idea] insensé(e).

harelip [ˌheəˈlɪp] *n* bec-de-lièvre *m*.

haricot (bean) [ˈhærɪkəʊ-] *n* haricot *m* blanc.

harm [haːm] ◇ *n* - **1.** [injury] mal *m* - **2.** [damage - to clothes, plant] dommage *m* ; [- to reputation] tort *m* ; **to do ~ to sb, to do sb ~** faire du tort à qqn ; **to do ~ to sthg, to do sthg ~** endommager qqch ; **to be out of ~'s way** [person] être en sûreté OR lieu sûr ; [thing] être en lieu sûr. ◇ *vt* - **1.** [injure] faire du mal à - **2.** [damage - clothes, plant] endommager ; [- reputation] faire du tort à.

harmful [ˈhaːmfʊl] *adj* nuisible, nocif(ive).

harmless [ˈhaːmlɪs] *adj* - **1.** [not dangerous] inoffensif(ive) - **2.** [inoffensive] innocent(e).

harmonica [haːˈmɒnɪkə] *n* harmonica *m*.

harmonize, -ise [ˈhaːmənaɪz] ◇ *vt* harmoniser. ◇ *vi* s'harmoniser.

harmony [ˈhaːmənɪ] *n* harmonie *f*.

harness [ˈhaːnɪs] ◇ *n* [for horse, child] harnais *m*. ◇ *vt* - **1.** [horse] harnacher - **2.** [energy, resources] exploiter.

harp [haːp] *n* harpe *f*. ◆ **harp on** *vi* : **to ~ on (about sthg)** rabâcher (qqch).

harpoon [haːˈpuːn] ◇ *n* harpon *m*. ◇ *vt* harponner.

harpsichord [ˈhaːpsɪkɔːd] *n* clavecin *m*.

harrowing [ˈhærəʊɪŋ] *adj* [experience] éprouvant(e) ; [report, film] déchirant(e).

harsh [haːʃ] *adj* - **1.** [life, conditions] rude ; [criticism, treatment] sévère - **2.** [to senses - sound] discordant(e) ; [- light, voice] criard(e) ; [- surface] rugueux(euse), rêche ; [- taste] âpre.

harvest [ˈhaːvɪst] ◇ *n* [of cereal crops] moisson *f* ; [of fruit] récolte *f* ; [of grapes] vendange *f*, vendanges *fpl*. ◇ *vt* [cereals] moissonner ; [fruit] récolter ; [grapes] vendanger.

has [*weak form* həz, *strong form* hæz] ▷ have.

has-been *n inf pej* ringard *m*, -e *f*.

hash [hæʃ] *n* - **1.** [meat] hachis *m* - **2.** *inf* [mess] : **to make a ~ of sthg** faire un beau gâchis de qqch.

hashish [ˈhæʃiːʃ] *n* haschich *m*.

hasn't [ˈhæznt] = has not.

hassle [ˈhæsl] *inf* ◇ *n* [annoyance] tracas *m*, embêtement *m*. ◇ *vt* tracasser.

haste [heɪst] *n* hâte *f* ; **to do sthg in ~** faire qqch à la hâte ; **to make ~** *dated* se hâter.

hasten [ˈheɪsn] *fml* ◇ *vt* hâter, accélérer. ◇ *vi* se hâter, se dépêcher ; **to ~ to do sthg** s'empresser de faire qqch.

hastily [ˈheɪstɪlɪ] *adv* - **1.** [quickly] à la hâte - **2.** [rashly] sans réfléchir.

hasty [ˈheɪstɪ] *adj* - **1.** [quick] hâtif(ive) - **2.** [rash] irréfléchi(e).

hat [hæt] *n* chapeau *m*.

hatch [hætʃ] ◇ *vt* - **1.** [chick] faire éclore ; [egg] couver - **2.** *fig* [scheme, plot] tramer. ◇ *vi* [chick, egg] éclore. ◇ *n* [for serving food] passe-plats *m inv*.

hatchback [ˈhætʃˌbæk] *n* voiture *f* avec hayon.

hatchet [ˈhætʃɪt] *n* hachette *f*.

hatchway [ˈhætʃˌweɪ] *n* passe-plats *m inv*, guichet *m*.

hate [heɪt] ◇ *n* (U) haine *f*. ◇ *vt* - **1.** [detest] haïr - **2.** [dislike] détester ; **to ~ doing sthg** avoir horreur de faire qqch.

hateful [ˈheɪtfʊl] *adj* odieux(euse).

hatred [ˈheɪtrɪd] *n* (U) haine *f*.

hat trick *n* SPORT : **to score a ~** marquer trois buts.

haughty [ˈhɔːtɪ] *adj* hautain(e).

haul [hɔːl] ◇ *n* - **1.** [of drugs, stolen goods] prise *f*, butin *m* - **2.** [distance] : **long ~** long voyage *m* OR trajet *m*. ◇ *vt* [pull] traîner, tirer.

haulage [ˈhɔːlɪdʒ] *n* transport *m* routier, camionnage *m*.

haulier Br [ˈhɔːlɪəʳ], **hauler** Am [ˈhɔːlər] *n* entrepreneur *m* de transports routiers.

haunch [hɔːntʃ] *n* [of person] hanche *f* ; [of animal] derrière *m*, arrière-train *m*.

haunt [hɔːnt] ◇ *n* repaire *m*. ◇ *vt* hanter.

have [hæv] (*pt & pp* had) ◇ *aux vb* (to form perfect tenses - gen) avoir ; (- with many intransitive verbs) être ; **to ~ eaten** avoir mangé ; **to ~ left** être parti(e) ; **she hasn't gone yet, has she?** elle n'est pas encore partie, si? ; **I was out of breath, having run**

all the way j'étais essoufflé d'avoir couru tout le long du chemin. ⬦ *vt* - **1.** [possess, receive] : **to ~ (got)** avoir ; **I ~ no money, I haven't got any money** je n'ai pas d'argent ; **I've got things to do** j'ai (des choses) à faire - **2.** [experience illness] avoir ; **to ~ flu** *Br* **to ~ the flu** *Am* avoir la grippe - **3.** *(referring to an action, instead of another verb)* : **to ~ a read** lire ; **to ~ a swim** nager ; **to ~ a bath/shower** prendre un bain/une douche ; **to ~ a cigarette** fumer une cigarette ; **to ~ a meeting** tenir une réunion - **4.** [give birth to] : **to ~ a baby** avoir un bébé - **5.** [cause to be done] : **to ~ sb do sthg** faire faire qqch à qqn ; **to ~ sthg done** faire faire qqch ; **to ~ one's hair cut** se faire couper les cheveux - **6.** [be treated in a certain way] : **I had my car stolen** je me suis fait voler ma voiture, on m'a volé ma voiture - **7.** *inf* [cheat] : **to be had** se faire avoir - **8.** *phr* : **to ~ it in for sb** en avoir après qqn, en vouloir à qqn ; **to ~ had it** [car, machine, clothes] avoir fait son temps. ⬦ *modal vb* [be obliged] : **to ~ (got) to do sthg** devoir faire qqch, être obligé(e) de faire qqch ; **do you ~ to go?, ~ you got to go?** est-ce que tu dois partir?, est-ce que tu es obligé de partir? ; **I've got to go to work** il faut que j'aille travailler. ➜ **have on** *vt sep Br* - **1.** [be wearing] porter - **2.** [tease] faire marcher. ➜ **have out** *vt sep* - **1.** [have removed] : **to ~ one's appendix/tonsils out** se faire opérer de l'appendicite/des amygdales - **2.** [discuss frankly] : **to ~ it out with sb** s'expliquer avec qqn.

haven ['heɪvn] *n* havre *m*.

haven't ['hævnt] = **have not.**

haversack ['hævəsæk] *n* sac *m* à dos.

havoc ['hævək] *n* (U) dégâts *mpl* ; **to play ~ with** [gen] abîmer.

Hawaii [hə'waɪiː] *n* Hawaii *m*.

hawk [hɔːk] *n* faucon *m*.

hawker ['hɔːkə'] *n* colporteur *m*.

hay [heɪ] *n* foin *m*.

hay fever *n* (U) rhume *m* des foins.

haystack ['heɪˌstæk] *n* meule *f* de foin.

haywire ['heɪˌwaɪə'] *adj inf* : **to go ~** [person] perdre la tête ; [machine] se détraquer.

hazard ['hæzəd] ⬦ *n* hasard *m*. ⬦ *vt* hasarder.

hazardous ['hæzədəs] *adj* hasardeux(euse).

hazard warning lights *npl Br* AUT feux *mpl* de détresse.

haze [heɪz] *n* brume *f*.

hazel ['heɪzl] *adj* noisette *(inv)*.

hazelnut ['heɪzlˌnʌt] *n* noisette *f*.

hazy ['heɪzɪ] *adj* - **1.** [misty] brumeux(euse) - **2.** [memory, ideas] flou(e), vague.

he [hiː] *pers pron* - **1.** *(unstressed)* il ; **~'s tall** il est grand ; **there ~ is** le voilà - **2.** *(stressed)* lui ; **HE can't do it** lui ne peut pas le faire.

head [hed] ⬦ *n* - **1.** [of person, animal] tête *f* ; **a** OR **per ~** par tête, par personne ; **to laugh one's ~ off** rire à gorge déployée ; **to be off one's ~** *Br*, **to be out of one's ~** *Am* être dingue ; **to be soft in the ~** être débile ; **to go to one's ~** [alcohol, praise] monter à la tête ; **to keep one's ~** garder son sang-froid ; **to lose one's ~** perdre la tête - **2.** [of table, bed, hammer] tête *f* ; [of stairs, page] haut *m* - **3.** [of flower] tête *f* ; [of cabbage] pomme *f* - **4.** [leader] chef *m* ; **~ of state** chef *m* d'État - **5.** [head teacher] directeur *m*, -trice *f*. ⬦ *vt* - **1.** [procession, list] être en tête de - **2.** [be in charge of] être à la tête de - **3.** FTBL : **to ~ the ball** faire une tête. ⬦ *vi* : **where are you ~ing?** où allez-vous? ➜ **heads** *npl* [on coin] face *f* ; **~s or tails?** pile ou face? ➜ **head for** *vt fus* - **1.** [place] se diriger vers - **2.** *fig* [trouble, disaster] aller au devant de.

headache ['hedeɪk] *n* mal *m* de tête ; **to have a ~** avoir mal à la tête.

headband ['hedbænd] *n* bandeau *m*.

head boy *n Br* élève chargé de la discipline et qui siège aux conseils de son école.

headdress ['hedˌdres] *n* coiffe *f*.

header ['hedə'] *n* FTBL tête *f*.

headfirst [ˌhed'fɜːst] *adv* (la) tête la première.

head girl *n Br* élève chargée de la discipline et qui siège aux conseils de son école.

heading ['hedɪŋ] *n* titre *m*, intitulé *m*.

headlamp ['hedlæmp] *n Br* phare *m*.

headland ['hedlənd] *n* cap *m*.

headlight ['hedlaɪt] *n* phare *m*.

headline ['hedlaɪn] *n* [in newspaper] gros titre *m* ; TV & RADIO grand titre *m*.

headlong ['hedlɒŋ] *adv* - **1.** [quickly] à toute allure - **2.** [unthinkingly] tête baissée - **3.** [headfirst] (la) tête la première.

headmaster [ˌhed'mɑːstə'] *n* directeur *m* (d'une école).

headmistress [ˌhed'mɪstrɪs] *n* directrice *f* (d'une école).

head office *n* siège *m* social.

head-on ⬦ *adj* [collision] de plein fouet ; [confrontation] de front. ⬦ *adv* de plein fouet.

headphones ['hedfəʊnz] *npl* casque *m*.

headquarters [ˌhed'kwɔːtəz] *npl* [of

business, organization] siège m ; [of armed forces] quartier m général.

headrest ['hedrest] n appui-tête m.

headroom ['hedrʊm] n (U) hauteur f.

headscarf ['hedskɑːf] (pl -scarves [-skɑːvz], -scarfs) n foulard m.

headset ['hedset] n casque m.

head start n avantage m au départ ; ~ on OR over avantage sur.

headstrong ['hedstrɒŋ] adj volontaire, têtu(e).

head waiter n maître m d'hôtel.

headway ['hedweɪ] n : to make ~ faire des progrès.

headwind ['hedwɪnd] n vent m contraire.

headword ['hedwɜːd] n entrée f, adresse f.

heady ['hedɪ] adj - 1. [exciting] grisant(e) - 2. [causing giddiness] capiteux(euse).

heal [hiːl] ⟨⟩ vt - 1. [cure] guérir - 2. fig [troubles, discord] apaiser. ⟨⟩ vi se guérir.

healing ['hiːlɪŋ] ⟨⟩ adj curatif(ive). ⟨⟩ n (U) guérison f.

health [helθ] n santé f.

health centre n ≃ centre m médico-social.

health food n produits mpl diététiques OR naturels.

health food shop n magasin m de produits diététiques.

health service n ≃ sécurité f sociale.

healthy ['helθɪ] adj - 1. [gen] sain(e) - 2. [well] en bonne santé, bien portant(e) - 3. fig [economy, company] qui se porte bien - 4. [profit] bon (bonne).

heap [hiːp] ⟨⟩ n tas m. ⟨⟩ vt [pile up] entasser. ➡ **heaps** npl inf : ~s of [people, objects] des tas de ; [time, money] énormément de.

hear [hɪəʳ] (pt & pp heard [hɜːd]) ⟨⟩ vt - 1. [gen & JUR] entendre - 2. [learn of] apprendre ; to ~ (that) ... apprendre que ... ⟨⟩ vi - 1. [perceive sound] entendre - 2. [know] : to ~ about entendre parler de - 3. [receive news] : to ~ about avoir des nouvelles de ; to ~ from sb recevoir des nouvelles de qqn - 4. phr : to have heard of avoir entendu parler de ; I won't ~ of it! je ne veux pas en entendre parler!

hearing ['hɪərɪŋ] n - 1. [sense] ouïe f ; hard of ~ dur(e) d'oreille - 2. [trial] audience f.

hearing aid n audiophone m.

hearsay ['hɪəseɪ] n ouï-dire m inv.

hearse [hɜːs] n corbillard m.

heart [hɑːt] n lit & fig cœur m ; from the ~ du fond du cœur ; to lose ~ perdre cou-

rage ; to break sb's ~ briser le cœur à qqn. ➡ **hearts** npl cœur m. ➡ **at heart** adv au fond (de soi). ➡ **by heart** adv par cœur.

heartache ['hɑːteɪk] n peine f de cœur.

heart attack n crise f cardiaque.

heartbeat ['hɑːtbiːt] n battement m de cœur.

heartbroken ['hɑːtˌbrəʊkn] adj qui a le cœur brisé.

heartburn ['hɑːtbɜːn] n (U) brûlures fpl d'estomac.

heart failure n arrêt m cardiaque.

heartfelt ['hɑːtfelt] adj sincère.

hearth [hɑːθ] n foyer m.

heartless ['hɑːtlɪs] adj sans cœur.

heartwarming ['hɑːtˌwɔːmɪŋ] adj réconfortant(e).

hearty ['hɑːtɪ] adj - 1. [greeting, person] cordial(e) - 2. [substantial - meal] copieux(euse) ; [- appetite] gros (grosse).

heat [hiːt] ⟨⟩ n - 1. (U) [warmth] chaleur f - 2. (U) fig [pressure] pression f - 3. [eliminating round] éliminatoire f - 4. ZOOL : on Br OR in ~ en chaleur. ⟨⟩ vt chauffer. ➡ **heat up** ⟨⟩ vt sep réchauffer. ⟨⟩ vi chauffer.

heated ['hiːtɪd] adj [argument, discussion, person] animé(e) ; [issue] chaud(e).

heater ['hiːtəʳ] n appareil m de chauffage.

heath [hiːθ] n lande f.

heathen ['hiːðn] ⟨⟩ adj païen(enne). ⟨⟩ n païen m, -enne f.

heather ['heðəʳ] n bruyère f.

heating ['hiːtɪŋ] n chauffage m.

heatstroke ['hiːtstrəʊk] n (U) coup m de chaleur.

heat wave n canicule f, vague f de chaleur.

heave [hiːv] ⟨⟩ vt - 1. [pull] tirer (avec effort) ; [push] pousser (avec effort) - 2. inf [throw] lancer. ⟨⟩ vi - 1. [pull] tirer - 2. [rise and fall] se soulever - 3. [retch] avoir des haut-le-cœur.

heaven ['hevn] n paradis m. ➡ **heavens** ⟨⟩ npl : the ~s literary les cieux mpl. ⟨⟩ excl : (good) ~s! juste ciel !

heavenly ['hevnlɪ] adj inf [delightful] délicieux(euse), merveilleux(euse).

heavily ['hevɪlɪ] adv - 1. [booked, in debt] lourdement ; [rain, smoke, drink] énormément - 2. [solidly - built] solidement - 3. [breathe, sigh] péniblement, bruyamment - 4. [fall, sit] lourdement.

heavy ['hevɪ] adj - 1. [gen] lourd(e) ; how ~ is it? ça pèse combien ? - 2. [traffic] dense ; [rain] battant(e) ; [fighting] acharné(e) ;

[casualties, corrections] **nombreux(euses)** ; [smoker, drinker] **gros (grosse)** - **3.** [noisy - breathing] **bruyant(e)** - **4.** [schedule] **chargé(e)** - **5.** [physically exacting - work, job] **pénible**.

heavy cream n Am crème f fraîche épaisse.

heavy goods vehicle n Br poids lourd m.

heavyweight ['heviweit] SPORT <> adj poids lourd. <> n poids lourd m.

Hebrew ['hi:bru:] <> adj hébreu, hébraïque. <> n - **1.** [person] Hébreu m, Israélite mf - **2.** [language] hébreu m.

Hebrides ['hebridi:z] npl : **the ~** les (îles fpl) Hébrides.

heck [hek] excl inf : **what/where/why the ~ ...?** que/où/pourquoi diable ...? ; **a ~ of a nice guy** un type vachement sympa ; **a ~ of a lot of people** un tas de gens.

heckle ['hekl] <> vt interpeller. <> vi interrompre bruyamment.

hectic ['hektik] adj [meeting, day] agité(e), mouvementé(e).

he'd [hi:d] = he had, he would.

hedge [hedʒ] <> n haie f. <> vi [prevaricate] répondre de façon détournée.

hedgehog ['hedʒhɒg] n hérisson m.

heed [hi:d] <> n : **to take ~ of sthg** tenir compte de qqch. <> vt fml tenir compte de.

heedless ['hi:dlis] adj : **~ of sthg** qui ne tient pas compte de qqch.

heel [hi:l] n talon m.

hefty ['hefti] adj - **1.** [well-built] costaud(e) - **2.** [large] gros (grosse).

heifer ['hefəʳ] n génisse f.

height [hait] n - **1.** [of building, mountain] hauteur f ; [of person] taille f ; **5 metres in ~** 5 mètres de haut ; **what ~ is it?** ça fait quelle hauteur? ; **what ~ are you?** combien mesurez-vous? - **2.** [above ground - of aircraft] altitude f - **3.** [zenith] : **at the ~ of the summer/season** au cœur de l'été/de la saison ; **at the ~ of his fame** au sommet de sa gloire.

heighten ['haitn] vt & vi augmenter.

heir [eəʳ] n héritier m.

heiress ['eəris] n héritière f.

heirloom ['eəlu:m] n meuble m/bijou m de famille.

heist [haist] n inf casse m.

held [held] pt & pp ⊳ hold.

helicopter ['helikɒptəʳ] n hélicoptère m.

helium ['hi:liəm] n hélium m.

hell [hel] <> n - **1.** lit & fig enfer m - **2.** inf [for emphasis] : **he's a ~ of a nice guy** c'est

un type vachement sympa ; **what/where/why the ~ ...?** que/où/pourquoi ..., bon sang? - **3.** phr : **to do sthg for the ~ of it** inf faire qqch pour le plaisir, faire qqch juste comme ça ; **to give sb ~** inf [verbally] engueuler qqn ; **go to ~!** v inf va te faire foutre! <> excl inf merde!, zut!

he'll [hi:l] = he will.

hellish ['helɪʃ] adj inf infernal(e).

hello [hə'ləʊ] excl - **1.** [as greeting] bonjour! ; [on phone] allô! - **2.** [to attract attention] hé!

helm [helm] n lit & fig barre f.

helmet ['helmit] n casque m.

help [help] <> n - **1.** (U) [assistance] aide f ; **he gave me a lot of ~** il m'a beaucoup aidé ; **with the ~ of sthg** à l'aide de qqch ; **with sb's ~** avec l'aide de qqn ; **to be of ~** rendre service - **2.** (U) [emergency aid] secours m - **3.** [useful person or object] : **to be a ~** aider, rendre service. <> vi aider. <> vt - **1.** [assist] aider ; **to ~ sb (to) do sthg** aider qqn à faire qqch ; **to ~ sb with sthg** aider qqn à faire qqch - **2.** [avoid] : **I can't ~ it** je n'y peux rien ; **I couldn't ~ laughing** je ne pouvais pas m'empêcher de rire - **3.** phr : **to ~ o.s. (to sthg)** se servir (de qqch) <> excl au secours!, à l'aide! ◆ **help out** vt sep & vi aider.

help desk n assistance f technique, support m technique.

helper ['helpəʳ] n - **1.** [gen] aide mf - **2.** Am [to do housework] femme f de ménage.

helpful ['helpful] adj - **1.** [person] serviable - **2.** [advice, suggestion] utile.

helping ['helpɪŋ] n portion f ; [of cake, tart] part f.

helpless ['helplis] adj impuissant(e) ; [look, gesture] d'impuissance.

helpline ['helplain] n ligne f d'assistance téléphonique.

Helsinki [hel'siŋki] n Helsinki.

hem [hem] <> n ourlet m. <> vt ourler. ◆ **hem in** vt sep encercler.

hemisphere ['hemɪˌsfɪəʳ] n hémisphère m.

hemline ['hemlain] n ourlet m.

hemophiliac [ˌhi:mə'filiæk] n hémophile mf.

hemorrhage ['heməridʒ] n hémorragie f.

hemorrhoids ['hemərɔidz] npl hémorroïdes fpl.

hen [hen] n - **1.** [female chicken] poule f - **2.** [female bird] femelle f.

hence [hens] adv fml - **1.** [therefore] d'où - **2.** [from now] d'ici.

henceforth [ˌhens'fɔːθ] *adv fml* dorénavant.

henchman ['hentʃmən] (*pl* -**men** [-mən]) *n pej* acolyte *m*.

henna ['henə] ◇ *n* henné *m*. ◇ *vt* [hair] appliquer du henné sur.

henpecked ['henpekt] *adj pej* dominé par sa femme.

her [hɜːʳ] ◇ *pers pron* - **1.** *(direct - unstressed)* la, l' (+ *vowel or silent 'h'*) ; *(- stressed)* elle ; **I know/like ~** je la connais/l'aime ; **it's ~** c'est elle - **2.** *(referring to animal, car, ship etc) follow the gender of your translation* - **3.** *(indirect)* lui ; **we spoke to ~** nous lui avons parlé ; **he sent ~ a letter** il lui a envoyé une lettre - **4.** *(after prep, in comparisons etc)* elle ; **I'm shorter than ~** je suis plus petit qu'elle. ◇ *poss adj* son (sa), ses *(pl)* ; **~ coat** son manteau ; **~ bedroom** sa chambre ; **~ children** ses enfants ; **it was HER fault** c'était de sa faute à elle.

herald ['herəld] ◇ *vt fml* annoncer. ◇ *n* [messenger] héraut *m*.

herb [hɜːb] *n* herbe *f*.

herd [hɜːd] ◇ *n* troupeau *m*. ◇ *vt* - **1.** [cattle, sheep] mener - **2.** *fig* [people] conduire, mener ; [into confined space] parquer.

here [hɪəʳ] *adv* - **1.** [in this place] ici ; **~ he is/ they are** le/les voici ; **~ it is** le/la voici ; **~ is/ are** voici ; **~ and there** çà et là - **2.** [present] là.

hereabouts *Br* [ˌhɪərə'bauts], **hereabout** *Am* [ˌhɪərə'baut] *adv* par ici.

hereafter [ˌhɪər'aːftəʳ] ◇ *adv fml* ci-après. ◇ *n* : **the ~** l'au-delà *m*.

hereby [ˌhɪə'baɪ] *adv fml* par la présente.

hereditary [hɪ'redɪtrɪ] *adj* héréditaire.

heresy ['herəsɪ] *n* hérésie *f*.

herewith [ˌhɪə'wɪð] *adv fml* [with letter] ci-joint, ci-inclus.

heritage ['herɪtɪdʒ] *n* héritage *m*, patrimoine *m*.

hermetically [hɜː'metɪklɪ] *adv* : **~ sealed** fermé(e) hermétiquement.

hermit ['hɜːmɪt] *n* ermite *m*.

hernia ['hɜːnjə] *n* hernie *f*.

hero ['hɪərəu] (*pl* -**es**) *n* héros *m*.

heroic [hɪ'rəuɪk] *adj* héroïque.

heroin ['herəuɪn] *n* héroïne *f*.

heroine ['herəuɪn] *n* héroïne *f*.

heron ['herən] (*pl inv* OR -**s**) *n* héron *m*.

herring ['herɪŋ] (*pl inv* OR -**s**) *n* hareng *m*.

hers [hɜːz] *poss pron* le sien (la sienne), les siens (les siennes) *(pl)* ; **that money is ~** cet argent est à elle OR est le sien ; **a friend of ~** un ami à elle, un de ses amis.

herself [hɜː'self] *pron* - **1.** *(reflexive)* se ; *(after prep)* elle - **2.** *(for emphasis)* elle-même.

he's [hiːz] = **he is**, **he has**.

hesitant ['hezɪtənt] *adj* hésitant(e).

hesitate ['hezɪteɪt] *vi* hésiter ; **to ~ to do sthg** hésiter à faire qqch.

hesitation [ˌhezɪ'teɪʃn] *n* hésitation *f*.

heterogeneous [ˌhetərə'dʒiːnjəs] *adj fml* hétérogène.

heterosexual [ˌhetərəu'sekʃuəl] ◇ *adj* hétérosexuel(elle). ◇ *n* hétérosexuel *m*, -elle *f*.

het up [het-] *adj Br inf* excité(e), énervé(e).

hexagon ['heksəgən] *n* hexagone *m*.

hey [heɪ] *excl* hé !

heyday ['heɪdeɪ] *n* âge *m* d'or.

HGV *(abbr of* **heavy goods vehicle**) *n Br* PL *m*.

hi [haɪ] *excl inf* salut !

hiatus [haɪ'eɪtəs] (*pl* -**es** [-iːz]) *n fml* pause *f*.

hibernate ['haɪbəneɪt] *vi* hiberner.

hiccough, hiccup ['hɪkʌp] ◇ *n* hoquet *m* ; *fig* [difficulty] accroc *m* ; **to have ~s** avoir le hoquet. ◇ *vi* hoqueter.

hid [hɪd] *pt* ▷ **hide**.

hidden ['hɪdn] ◇ *pp* ▷ **hide**. ◇ *adj* caché(e).

hide [haɪd] (*pt* **hid**, *pp* **hidden**) ◇ *vt* : **to ~ sthg (from sb)** cacher qqch (à qqn) ; [information] taire qqch (à qqn). ◇ *vi* se cacher. ◇ *n* - **1.** [animal skin] peau *f* - **2.** [for watching birds, animals] cachette *f*.

hide-and-seek *n* cache-cache *m inv*.

hideaway ['haɪdəweɪ] *n* cachette *f*.

hideous ['hɪdɪəs] *adj* hideux(euse) ; [error, conditions] abominable.

hiding ['haɪdɪŋ] *n* - **1.** [concealment] : **to be in ~** se tenir caché(e) - **2.** *inf* [beating] : **to give sb a (good) ~** donner une (bonne) raclée OR correction à qqn.

hiding place *n* cachette *f*.

hierarchy ['haɪərɑːkɪ] *n* hiérarchie *f*.

hi-fi ['haɪfaɪ] *n* hi-fi *f inv*.

high [haɪ] ◇ *adj* - **1.** [gen] haut(e) ; **it's 3 feet/6 metres ~** cela fait 3 pieds/6 mètres de haut ; **how ~ is it?** cela fait combien de haut ? - **2.** [speed, figure, altitude, office] élevé(e) - **3.** [high-pitched] aigu(uë) - **4.** *drugs sl* qui plane, défoncé(e) - **5.** *inf* [drunk] bourré(e). ◇ *adv* haut. ◇ *n* [highest point] maximum *m*.

highbrow ['haɪbraʊ] *adj* intellectuel (elle).

high chair *n* chaise *f* haute *(d'enfant)*.

high-class *adj* de premier ordre ; [hotel, restaurant] de grande classe.

High Court *n Br* JUR Cour *f* suprême.

higher ['haɪəʳ] *adj* [exam, qualification] supérieur(e). ➨ **Higher (Grade)** *n* : Higher (Grade) SCH *examen de fin d'études secondaires en Écosse.*

higher education *n (U)* études *fpl* supérieures.

high-handed [-'hændɪd] *adj* despotique.

high jump *n* saut *m* en hauteur.

Highland Games ['haɪlənd-] *npl* jeux *mpl* écossais.

Highlands ['haɪləndz] *npl* : the ~ les Highlands *fpl* *(région montagneuse du nord de l'Écosse).*

highlight ['haɪlaɪt] ◇ *n* [of event, occasion] moment *m* OR point *m* fort. ◇ *vt* souligner ; [with highlighter] surligner. ➨ **highlights** *npl* [in hair] reflets *mpl*, mèches *fpl*.

highlighter (pen) ['haɪlaɪtəʳ-] *n* surligneur *m*.

highly ['haɪlɪ] *adv* - 1. [very] extrêmement, très - 2. [in important position] : ~ placed haut placé(e) - 3. [favourably] : to think ~ of sb/sthg penser du bien de qqn/qqch.

highly-strung *adj* nerveux(euse).

Highness ['haɪnɪs] *n* : His/Her/Your (Royal) ~ Son/Votre Altesse (Royale) ; their (Royal) ~es leurs Altesses (Royales).

high-pitched [-'pɪtʃt] *adj* aigu(ue).

high point *n* [of occasion] point *m* fort.

high-powered [-'paʊəd] *adj* - 1. [powerful] de forte puissance - 2. [prestigious - activity, place] de haut niveau ; [- job, person] très important(e).

high-ranking [-'ræŋkɪŋ] *adj* de haut rang.

high-rise *adj* : ~ block of flats tour *f*.

high school *n Br* lycée *m* ; *Am* établissement *m* d'enseignement supérieur.

high season *n* haute saison *f*.

high spot *n* point *m* fort.

high street *n Br* rue *f* principale.

high-tech [-'tek] *adj* [method, industry] de pointe.

high tide *n* marée *f* haute.

highway ['haɪweɪ] *n* - 1. *Am* [motorway] autoroute *f* - 2. [main road] grande route *f*.

Highway Code *n Br* : the ~ le code de la route.

hijack ['haɪdʒæk] ◇ *n* détournement *m*. ◇ *vt* détourner.

hijacker ['haɪdʒækəʳ] *n* [of aircraft] pirate *m* de l'air ; [of vehicle] pirate *m* de la route.

hike [haɪk] ◇ *n* [long walk] randonnée *f*. ◇ *vi* faire une randonnée.

hiker ['haɪkəʳ] *n* randonneur *m*, -euse *f*.

hiking ['haɪkɪŋ] *n* marche *f*.

hilarious [hɪ'leərɪəs] *adj* hilarant(e).

hill [hɪl] *n* - 1. [mound] colline *f* - 2. [slope] côte *f*.

hillside ['hɪlsaɪd] *n* coteau *m*.

hilly ['hɪlɪ] *adj* vallonné(e).

hilt [hɪlt] *n* garde *f* ; to support/defend sb to the ~ soutenir/défendre qqn à fond.

him [hɪm] *pers pron* - 1. *(direct - unstressed)* le, l' (+ vowel or silent 'h') ; *(- stressed)* lui ; I know/like ~ je le connais/l'aime ; it's ~ c'est lui - 2. *(indirect)* lui ; we spoke to ~ nous lui avons parlé ; she sent ~ a letter elle lui a envoyé une lettre - 3. *(after prep, in comparisons etc)* lui ; I'm shorter than ~ je suis plus petit que lui.

Himalayas [ˌhɪmə'leɪəz] *npl* : the ~ l'Himalaya *m*.

himself [hɪm'self] *pron* - 1. *(reflexive)* se ; *(after prep)* lui - 2. *(for emphasis)* lui-même.

hind [haɪnd] *(pl inv* OR *-s)* ◇ *adj* de derrière. ◇ *n* biche *f*.

hinder ['hɪndəʳ] *vt* gêner, entraver.

Hindi ['hɪndɪ] *n* hindi *m*.

hindrance ['hɪndrəns] *n* obstacle *m*.

hindsight ['haɪndsaɪt] *n* : with the benefit of ~ avec du recul.

Hindu ['hɪnduː] *(pl -s)* ◇ *adj* hindou(e). ◇ *n* Hindou *m*, -e *f*.

hinge [hɪndʒ] *n* [whole fitting] charnière *f* ; [pin] gond *m*. ➨ **hinge (up)on** *vt fus* [depend on] dépendre de.

hint [hɪnt] ◇ *n* - 1. [indication] allusion *f* ; to drop a ~ faire une allusion - 2. [piece of advice] conseil *m*, indication *f* - 3. [small amount] soupçon *m*. ◇ *vi* : to ~ at sthg faire allusion à qqch. ◇ *vt* : to ~ that ... insinuer que ...

hip [hɪp] *n* hanche *f*.

hippie ['hɪpɪ] = hippy.

hippo ['hɪpəʊ] *(pl -s)* *n* hippopotame *m*.

hippopotamus [ˌhɪpə'pɒtəməs] *(pl -muses* [-məsɪːz], *-mi* [-maɪ]) *n* hippopotame *m*.

hippy ['hɪpɪ] *n* hippie *mf*.

hire ['haɪəʳ] ◇ *n (U) Br* [of car, equipment] location *f* ; for ~ [bicycles etc] à louer ; [taxi] libre. ◇ *vt* - 1. *Br* [rent] louer - 2. [employ]

employer les services de. ◆ **hire out** vt sep Br louer.

hire car n Br voiture f de location.

hire purchase n (U) Br achat m à crédit OR à tempérament.

his [hɪz] ◇ poss adj son (sa), ses (pl) ; ~ **house** sa maison ; ~ **money** son argent ; ~ **children** ses enfants ; ~ **name is Joe** il s'appelle Joe. ◇ poss pron le sien (la sienne), les siens (les siennes) (pl) ; **that money is** ~ cet argent est à lui OR est le sien ; **it wasn't her fault, it was** HIS ce n'était pas de sa faute à elle, c'était de sa faute à lui ; **a friend of** ~ un ami à lui, un de ses amis.

hiss [hɪs] ◇ n [of animal, gas etc] sifflement m ; [of crowd] sifflet m. ◇ vi [animal, gas etc] siffler.

historic [hɪ'stɒrɪk] adj historique.

historical [hɪ'stɒrɪkəl] adj historique.

history ['hɪstərɪ] n - **1.** [gen] histoire f - **2.** [past record] antécédents mpl ; **medical** ~ passé m médical.

hit [hɪt] (pt & pp hit) ◇ n - **1.** [blow] coup m - **2.** [successful strike] coup m OR tir m réussi ; [in fencing] touche f - **3.** [success] succès m ; **to be a** ~ **with** plaire à - **4.** COMPUT visite f (d'un site Internet). ◇ comp à succès. ◇ vt - **1.** [strike] frapper ; [nail] taper sur - **2.** [crash into] heurter, percuter - **3.** [reach] atteindre - **4.** [affect badly] toucher, affecter - **5.** phr : **to** ~ **it off (with sb)** bien s'entendre (avec qqn).

hit-and-miss = hit-or-miss.

hit-and-run adj [accident] avec délit de fuite ; ~ **driver** chauffard m (qui a commis un délit de fuite).

hitch [hɪtʃ] ◇ n [problem, snag] ennui m. ◇ vt - **1.** [catch] : **to** ~ **a lift** faire du stop - **2.** [fasten] : **to** ~ **sthg on** OR **onto** accrocher OR attacher qqch à. ◇ vi [hitchhike] faire du stop. ◆ **hitch up** vt sep [pull up] remonter.

hitchhike ['hɪtʃhaɪk] vi faire de l'autostop.

hitchhiker ['hɪtʃhaɪkər] n auto-stoppeur m, -euse f.

hi-tech [ˌhaɪ'tek] = high-tech.

hitherto [ˌhɪðə'tuː] adv fml jusqu'ici.

hit-or-miss adj aléatoire.

HIV (abbr of human immunodeficiency virus) n VIH m, HIV m ; **to be** ~**-positive** être séropositif.

hive [haɪv] n ruche f ; **a** ~ **of activity** une véritable ruche. ◆ **hive off** vt sep [assets] séparer.

HNC (abbr of **Higher National Certificate**) n brevet de technicien en Grande-Bretagne.

HND (abbr of **Higher National Diploma**) n brevet de technicien supérieur en Grande-Bretagne.

hoard [hɔːd] ◇ n [store] réserves fpl ; [of useless items] tas m. ◇ vt amasser ; [food, petrol] faire des provisions de.

hoarding ['hɔːdɪŋ] n Br [for advertisements] panneau m d'affichage publicitaire.

hoarfrost ['hɔːfrɒst] n gelée f blanche.

hoarse [hɔːs] adj [person, voice] enroué(e) ; [shout, whisper] rauque.

hoax [həʊks] n canular m.

hob [hɒb] n Br [on cooker] rond m, plaque f.

hobble ['hɒbl] vi [limp] boitiller.

hobby ['hɒbɪ] n passe-temps m inv, hobby m.

hobbyhorse ['hɒbɪhɔːs] n - **1.** [toy] cheval m à bascule - **2.** fig [favourite topic] dada m.

hobo ['həʊbəʊ] (pl -es OR -s) n Am clochard m, -e f.

hockey ['hɒkɪ] n - **1.** [on grass] hockey m - **2.** Am [ice hockey] hockey m sur glace.

hoe [həʊ] ◇ n houe f. ◇ vt biner.

hog [hɒg] ◇ n - **1.** Am [pig] cochon m - **2.** inf [greedy person] goinfre m - **3.** phr : **to go the whole** ~ aller jusqu'au bout. ◇ vt inf [monopolize] accaparer, monopoliser.

Hogmanay ['hɒgməneɪ] n la Saint-Sylvestre en Écosse.

hoist [hɔɪst] ◇ n [device] treuil m. ◇ vt hisser.

hold [həʊld] (pt & pp held) ◇ vt - **1.** [gen] tenir - **2.** [keep in position] maintenir - **3.** [as prisoner] détenir ; **to** ~ **sb prisoner/hostage** détenir qqn prisonnier/comme otage - **4.** [have, possess] avoir - **5.** fml [consider] considérer, estimer ; **to** ~ **sb responsible for sthg** rendre qqn responsable de qqch, tenir qqn pour responsable de qqch - **6.** [on telephone] : **please** ~ **the line** ne quittez pas, je vous prie - **7.** [keep, maintain] retenir - **8.** [sustain, support] supporter - **9.** [contain] contenir - **10.** phr : ~ **it!**, ~ **everything!** attendez!, arrêtez! ; **to** ~ **one's own** se défendre. ◇ vi - **1.** [remain unchanged - gen] tenir ; [- luck] persister ; [- weather] se maintenir ; **to** ~ **still** OR **steady** ne pas bouger, rester tranquille - **2.** [on phone] attendre. ◇ n - **1.** [grasp, grip] prise f, étreinte f ; **to take** OR **lay** ~ **of sthg** saisir qqch ; **to get** ~ **of sthg** [obtain] se procurer qqch ; **to get** ~ **of sb** [find] joindre qqn - **2.** [of ship, aircraft] cale f - **3.** [control, influence] prise f. ◆ **hold back** vt sep - **1.** [restrain, prevent] retenir ; [anger] réprimer - **2.** [keep secret] cacher. ◆ **hold down** *vt sep* [job] garder. ◆ **hold off** *vt sep* [fend off] tenir à distance. ◆ **hold on** *vi* - **1.** [wait] attendre ; [on phone] ne pas quitter - **2.** [grip] : **to ~ on (to sthg)** se tenir (à qqch). ◆ **hold out** ◇ *vt sep* [hand, arms] tendre. ◇ *vi* - **1.** [last] durer - **2.** [resist] : **to ~ out (against sb/sthg)** résister (à qqn/qqch). ◆ **hold up** *vt sep* - **1.** [raise] lever - **2.** [delay] retarder.

holdall ['həʊldɔ:l] *n Br* fourre-tout *m inv*.

holder ['həʊldə'] *n* - **1.** [for cigarette] porte-cigarettes *m inv* - **2.** [owner] détenteur *m*, -trice *f* ; [of position, title] titulaire *mf*.

holding ['həʊldɪŋ] *n* - **1.** [investment] effets *mpl* en portefeuille - **2.** [farm] ferme *f*.

holdup ['həʊldʌp] *n* - **1.** [robbery] hold-up *m* - **2.** [delay] retard *m*.

hole [həʊl] *n* - **1.** [gen] trou *m* - **2.** *inf* [predicament] pétrin *m*.

holiday ['hɒlɪdeɪ] *n* - **1.** *Br* [vacation] vacances *fpl* ; **to be/go on ~** être/partir en vacances - **2.** [public holiday] jour *m* férié.

holiday camp *n Br* camp *m* de vacances.

holidaymaker ['hɒlɪdɪˌmeɪkə'] *n Br* vacancier *m*, -ère *f*.

holiday pay *n Br* salaire payé pendant les vacances.

holiday resort *n Br* lieu *m* de vacances.

holistic [həʊˈlɪstɪk] *adj* holistique.

Holland ['hɒlənd] *n* Hollande *f*.

holler ['hɒlə'] *vi & vt inf* gueuler, brailler.

hollow ['hɒləʊ] ◇ *adj* creux (creuse) ; [eyes] cave ; [promise, victory] faux (fausse) ; [laugh] qui sonne faux. ◇ *n* creux *m*. ◆ **hollow out** *vt sep* creuser, évider.

holly ['hɒlɪ] *n* houx *m*.

holocaust ['hɒləkɔːst] *n* [destruction] destruction *f*, holocauste *m*. ◆ **Holocaust** *n* : **the Holocaust** l'holocauste *m*.

holster ['həʊlstə'] *n* étui *m*.

holy ['həʊlɪ] *adj* saint(e) ; [ground] sacré(e).

Holy Ghost *n* : **the ~** le Saint-Esprit.

Holy Land *n* : **the ~** la Terre sainte.

Holy Spirit *n* : **the ~** le Saint-Esprit.

home [həʊm] ◇ *n* - **1.** [house, institution] maison *f* ; **to make one's ~** s'établir, s'installer - **2.** [own country] patrie *f* ; [city] ville *f* natale - **3.** [one's family] foyer *m* ; **to leave ~** quitter la maison - **4.** *fig* [place of origin] berceau *m*. ◇ *adj* - **1.** [not foreign - gen] intérieur(e) ; [- product] national(e) - **2.** [in one's own home - cooking] familial(e) ; [- life] de famille ; [- improvements] domestique - **3.** [SPORT - game] sur son propre terrain ; [- team] qui reçoit. ◇ *adv* [to or at one's

house] chez soi, à la maison. ◆ **at home** *adv* - **1.** [in one's house, flat] chez soi, à la maison - **2.** [comfortable] à l'aise ; **at ~ with sthg** à l'aise dans qqch ; **to make o.s. at ~** faire comme chez soi - **3.** [in one's own country] chez nous.

home address *n* adresse *f* du domicile.

home brew *n (U)* [beer] bière *f* faite à la maison.

home computer *n* ordinateur *m* domestique.

Home Counties *npl* : **the ~** les comtés entourant Londres.

home economics *n (U)* économie *f* domestique.

home help *n Br* aide *f* ménagère.

homeland ['həʊmlænd] *n* - **1.** [country of birth] patrie *f* - **2.** [in South Africa] homeland *m*, bantoustan *m*.

homeless ['həʊmlɪs] ◇ *adj* sans abri. ◇ *npl* : **the ~** les sans-abri *mpl*.

homely ['həʊmlɪ] *adj* - **1.** [simple] simple - **2.** [unattractive] ordinaire.

homemade [ˌhəʊmˈmeɪd] *adj* fait(e) (à la) maison.

Home Office *n Br* : **the ~** ≃ le ministère de l'Intérieur.

homeopathy [ˌhəʊmɪˈɒpəθɪ] *n* homéopathie *f*.

home page *n* COMPUT page *f* d'accueil.

Home Secretary *n Br* ≃ ministre *m* de l'Intérieur.

homesick ['həʊmsɪk] *adj* qui a le mal du pays.

hometown ['həʊmtaʊn] *n* ville *f* natale.

homeward ['həʊmwəd] ◇ *adj* de retour. ◇ *adv* = **homewards**.

homewards ['həʊmwədz] *adv* vers la maison.

homework ['həʊmwɜːk] *n (U)* - **1.** SCH devoirs *mpl* - **2.** *inf* [preparation] boulot *m*.

homey, homy ['həʊmɪ] *adj Am* confortable, agréable.

homicide ['hɒmɪsaɪd] *n* homicide *m*.

homoeopathy *etc* [ˌhəʊmɪˈɒpəθɪ] = **homeopathy** *etc*.

homogeneous [ˌhɒməˈdʒiːnjəs] *adj* homogène.

homosexual [ˌhɒməˈsekʃʊəl] ◇ *adj* homosexuel(elle). ◇ *n* homosexuel *m*, -elle *f*.

homy = **homey**.

hone [həʊn] *vt* aiguiser.

honest ['ɒnɪst] ◇ *adj* - **1.** [trustworthy] honnête, probe - **2.** [frank] franc (franche),

honestly

sincère ; **to be ~** ... pour dire la vérité ..., à dire vrai ... - **3.** [legal] légitime. ◇ *adv inf* = **honestly** 2.

honestly ['ɒnɪstlɪ] ◇ *adv* - **1.** [truthfully] honnêtement - **2.** [expressing sincerity] je vous assure. ◇ *excl* [expressing impatience, disapproval] franchement!

honesty ['ɒnɪstɪ] *n* honnêteté *f*, probité *f*.

honey ['hʌnɪ] *n* - **1.** [food] miel *m* - **2.** [dear] chéri *m*, -e *f*.

honeycomb ['hʌnɪkəʊm] *n* gâteau *m* de miel.

honeymoon ['hʌnɪmuːn] ◇ *n lit & fig* lune *f* de miel. ◇ *vi* aller en voyage de noces, passer sa lune de miel.

honeysuckle ['hʌnɪˌsʌkl] *n* chèvrefeuille *m*.

Hong Kong [ˌhɒŋ'kɒŋ] *n* Hong Kong, Hongkong.

honk [hɒŋk] ◇ *vi* - **1.** [motorist] klaxonner - **2.** [goose] cacarder. ◇ *vt* : **to ~ the horn** klaxonner.

honor *etc Am* = **honour** *etc.*

honorary [*Br* 'ɒnərərɪ, *Am* ɒnə'reərɪ] *adj* honoraire.

honour *Br*, **honor** *Am* ['ɒnəʳ] ◇ *n* honneur *m* ; **in ~ of sb/sthg** en l'honneur de qqn/qqch. ◇ *vt* honorer. ◆ **honours** *npl* - **1.** [tokens of respect] honneurs *mpl* - **2.** [of university degree] ≃ licence *f*.

honourable *Br*, **honorable** *Am* ['ɒnrəbl] *adj* honorable.

hood [hʊd] *n* - **1.** [on cloak, jacket] capuchon *m* - **2.** [of cooker] hotte *f* - **3.** [of pram, convertible car] capote *f* - **4.** *Am* [car bonnet] capot *m*.

hoodlum ['huːdləm] *n Am inf* gangster *m*, truand *m*.

hoof [huːf, hʊf] (*pl* **-s** OR **hooves** [huːvz]) *n* sabot *m*.

hook [hʊk] ◇ *n* - **1.** [for hanging things on] crochet *m* - **2.** [for catching fish] hameçon *m* - **3.** [fastener] agrafe *f* - **4.** [of telephone] : **off the ~** décroché. ◇ *vt* - **1.** [attach with hook] accrocher - **2.** [catch with hook] prendre. ◆ **hook up** *vt sep* : **to ~ sthg up to sthg** connecter qqch à qqch.

hooked [hʊkt] *adj* - **1.** [shaped like a hook] crochu(e) - **2.** *inf* [addicted] : **to be ~ (on)** être accro (à) ; [music, art] être mordu(e) (de).

hook(e)y ['hʊkɪ] *n Am inf* : **to play ~** faire l'école buissonnière.

hooligan ['huːlɪgən] *n* hooligan *m*, vandale *m*.

hoop [huːp] *n* - **1.** [circular band] cercle *m* - **2.** [toy] cerceau *m*.

hooray [hʊ'reɪ] = **hurray.**

hoot [huːt] ◇ *n* - **1.** [of owl] hululement *m* - **2.** [of horn] coup *m* de Klaxon® - **3.** *Br inf* [something amusing] : **to be a ~** être tordant(e). ◇ *vi* - **1.** [owl] hululer - **2.** [horn] klaxonner. ◇ *vt* : **to ~ the horn** klaxonner.

hooter ['huːtəʳ] *n Br* [horn] Klaxon® *m*.

Hoover® *Br* ['huːvəʳ] *n* aspirateur *m*. ◆ **hoover** *vt* [room] passer l'aspirateur dans ; [carpet] passer à l'aspirateur.

hooves [huːvz] *pl* ⊳ **hoof.**

hop [hɒp] ◇ *n* saut *m* ; [on one leg] saut à cloche-pied. ◇ *vi* sauter ; [on one leg] sauter à cloche-pied ; [bird] sautiller. ◆ **hops** *npl* houblon *m*.

hope [həʊp] ◇ *vi* espérer ; **to ~ for sthg** espérer qqch ; **I ~ so** j'espère bien ; **I ~ not** j'espère bien que non. ◇ *vt* : **to ~ (that)** espérer que ; **to ~ to do sthg** espérer faire qqch. ◇ *n* espoir *m* ; **in the ~ of** dans l'espoir de.

hopeful ['həʊpfʊl] *adj* - **1.** [optimistic] plein(e) d'espoir ; **to be ~ of doing sthg** avoir l'espoir de faire qqch ; **to be ~ of sthg** espérer qqch - **2.** [promising] encourageant(e), qui promet.

hopefully ['həʊpfəlɪ] *adv* - **1.** [in a hopeful way] avec bon espoir, avec optimisme - **2.** [with luck] : **~ ...** espérons que ...

hopeless ['həʊplɪs] *adj* - **1.** [gen] désespéré(e) ; [tears] de désespoir - **2.** *inf* [useless] nul (nulle).

hopelessly ['həʊplɪslɪ] *adv* - **1.** [despairingly] avec désespoir - **2.** [completely] complètement.

horizon [hə'raɪzn] *n* horizon *m* ; **on the ~** *lit & fig* à l'horizon.

horizontal [ˌhɒrɪ'zɒntl] ◇ *adj* horizontal(e). ◇ *n* : **the ~** l'horizontale *f*.

hormone ['hɔːməʊn] *n* hormone *f*.

horn [hɔːn] *n* - **1.** [of animal] corne *f* - **2.** MUS [instrument] cor *m* - **3.** [on car] Klaxon® *m* ; [on ship] sirène *f*.

hornet ['hɔːnɪt] *n* frelon *m*.

horny ['hɔːnɪ] *adj* - **1.** [hard] corné(e) ; [hand] calleux(euse) - **2.** *v inf* [sexually excited] excité(e) (sexuellement).

horoscope ['hɒrəskəʊp] *n* horoscope *m*.

horrendous [hɒ'rendəs] *adj* horrible.

horrible ['hɒrəbl] *adj* horrible.

horrid ['hɒrɪd] *adj* [unpleasant] horrible.

horrific [hɒ'rɪfɪk] *adj* horrible.

horrify ['hɒrɪfaɪ] *vt* horrifier.

horror ['hɒrəʳ] *n* horreur *f*.

horror film *n* film *m* d'épouvante.

horse [hɔːs] *n* [animal] cheval *m*.

horseback ['hɔːsbæk] <> *adj* à cheval ; ~ **riding** *Am* équitation *f*. <> *n* : **on** ~ à cheval.

horse chestnut *n* [nut] marron *m* d'Inde ; ~ **(tree)** marronnier *m* d'Inde.

horseman ['hɔːsmən] (*pl* -men [-mən]) *n* cavalier *m*.

horsepower ['hɔːs,paʊəʳ] *n* puissance *f* en chevaux.

horse racing *n* (U) courses *fpl* de chevaux.

horseradish ['hɔːs,rædɪʃ] *n* [plant] raifort *m*.

horse riding *n* équitation *f*.

horseshoe ['hɔːsʃuː] *n* fer *m* à cheval.

horsewoman ['hɔːs,wʊmən] (*pl* -women [-,wɪmɪn]) *n* cavalière *f*.

horticulture ['hɔːtɪkʌltʃəʳ] *n* horticulture *f*.

hose [həʊz] <> *n* [hosepipe] tuyau *m*. <> *vt* arroser au jet.

hosepipe ['həʊzpaɪp] *n* = hose.

hosiery ['həʊzɪərɪ] *n* bonneterie *f*.

hospitable [hɒ'spɪtəbl] *adj* hospitalier(ère), accueillant(e).

hospital ['hɒspɪtl] *n* hôpital *m*.

hospitality [,hɒspɪ'tælətɪ] *n* hospitalité *f*.

host [həʊst] <> *n* - 1. [gen] hôte *m* - 2. [compere] animateur *m*, -trice *f* - 3. [large number] : **a ~ of** une foule de... <> *vt* présenter, animer.

hostage ['hɒstɪdʒ] *n* otage *m*.

hostel ['hɒstl] *n* - 1. [basic accommodation] foyer *m* - 2. [youth hostel] auberge *f* de jeunesse.

hostess ['həʊstes] *n* hôtesse *f*.

host family *n* famille *f* d'accueil.

hostile [*Br* 'hɒstaɪl, *Am* 'hɒstl] *adj* : ~ **(to)** hostile (à).

hostility [hɒ'stɪlətɪ] *n* [antagonism, unfriendliness] hostilité *f*. ◆ **hostilities** *npl* hostilités *fpl*.

hot [hɒt] *adj* - 1. [gen] chaud(e) ; **I'm ~** j'ai chaud ; **it's ~** il fait chaud - 2. [spicy] épicé(e) - 3. *Br inf* [expert] fort(e), calé(e) ; **to be ~ on** OR **at sthg** être fort OR calé en qqch - 4. [recent] de dernière heure OR minute - 5. [temper] colérique.

hot-air balloon *n* montgolfière *f*.

hotbed ['hɒtbed] *n* foyer *m*.

hot-cross bun *n* petit pain sucré que l'on mange le vendredi saint.

hot dog *n* hot dog *m*.

hotel [həʊ'tel] *n* hôtel *m*.

hot flush *Br*, **hot flash** *Am* *n* bouffée *f* de chaleur.

hotfoot ['hɒt,fʊt] *adv* à toute vitesse.

hotheaded [,hɒt'hedɪd] *adj* impulsif(ive).

hothouse ['hɒthaʊs, *pl* -haʊzɪz] *n* [greenhouse] serre *f*.

hot line *n* - 1. [between government heads] téléphone *m* rouge - 2. [special line] hot line *f*.

hotly ['hɒtlɪ] *adv* - 1. [passionately] avec véhémence - 2. [closely] de près.

hotplate ['hɒtpleɪt] *n* plaque *f* chauffante.

hot-tempered [-'tempəd] *adj* colérique.

hot-water bottle *n* bouillotte *f*.

hound [haʊnd] <> *n* [dog] chien *m*. <> *vt* - 1. [persecute] poursuivre, pourchasser - 2. [drive] : **to ~ sb out (of)** chasser qqn (de).

hour ['aʊəʳ] *n* heure *f* ; **half an ~** une demi-heure ; **70 miles per** OR **an ~** 110 km à l'heure ; **on the ~** à l'heure juste. ◆ **hours** *npl* [of business] heures *fpl* d'ouverture.

hourly ['aʊəlɪ] <> *adj* - 1. [happening every hour] toutes les heures - 2. [per hour] à l'heure. <> *adv* - 1. [every hour] toutes les heures - 2. [per hour] à l'heure.

house [*n* & *adj* haʊs, *pl* 'haʊzɪz, *vb* haʊz] <> *n* - 1. [gen] maison *f* ; **on the ~** aux frais de la maison - 2. POL chambre *f* - 3. [in debates] assistance *f* - 4. THEATRE [audience] auditoire *m*, salle *f* ; **to bring the ~ down** *inf* faire crouler la salle sous les applaudissements - 5. MUS = house music. <> *vt* [accommodate] loger, héberger ; [department, store] abriter. <> *adj* - 1. [within business] d'entreprise ; [style] de la maison - 2. [wine] maison (*inv*).

house arrest *n* : **under ~** en résidence surveillée.

houseboat ['haʊsbəʊt] *n* péniche *f* aménagée.

housebreaking ['haʊs,breɪkɪŋ] *n* (U) cambriolage *m*.

housecoat ['haʊskəʊt] *n* peignoir *m*.

household ['haʊshəʊld] <> *adj* - 1. [domestic] ménager(ère) - 2. [word, name] connu(e) de tous. <> *n* maison *f*, ménage *m*.

housekeeper ['haʊs,kiːpəʳ] *n* gouvernante *f*.

housekeeping ['haʊs,kiːpɪŋ] *n* (U)

- 1. [work] ménage *m* **- 2. :** ~ **(money)** argent *m* du ménage.

house music, house *n* house music *f*.

House of Commons *n* Br : the ~ la Chambre des communes.

House of Lords *n* Br : the ~ la Chambre des lords.

House of Representatives *n* Am : the ~ la Chambre des représentants.

houseplant ['haʊspla:nt] *n* plante *f* d'appartement.

Houses of Parliament *npl* : the ~ le Parlement britannique *(où se réunissent la Chambre des communes et la Chambre des lords)*.

housewarming (party) ['haʊs‚wɔ:mɪŋ] *n* pendaison *f* de crémaillère.

housewife ['haʊswaɪf] *(pl* -wives [-waɪvz]*)* *n* femme *f* au foyer.

housework ['haʊswɜ:k] *n (U)* ménage *m*.

housing ['haʊzɪŋ] *n (U)* [accommodation] logement *m*.

housing association *n* Br association *f* d'aide au logement.

housing benefit *n (U)* Br allocation *f* logement.

housing estate Br, **housing project** Am *n* cité *f*.

hovel ['hɒvl] *n* masure *f*, taudis *m*.

hover ['hɒvə'] *vi* [fly] planer.

hovercraft ['hɒvəkra:ft] *(pl inv* OR -s*)* *n* aéroglisseur *m*, hovercraft *m*.

how [haʊ] *adv* **- 1.** [gen] comment ; ~ **do you do it?** comment fait-on ? ; ~ **are you?** comment allez-vous ? ; ~ **do you do?** enchanté(e) (de faire votre connaissance) **- 2.** [referring to degree, amount] : ~ **high is it?** combien cela fait-il de haut?, quelle en est la hauteur? ; ~ **long have you been waiting?** cela fait combien de temps que vous attendez? ; ~ **many people came?** combien de personnes sont venues? ; ~ **old are you?** quel âge as-tu? **- 3.** [in exclamations] : ~ **nice!** que c'est bien! ; ~ **awful!** quelle horreur! ➡ **how about** *adv* : ~ **about a drink?** si on prenait un verre? ; ~ **about you?** et toi? ➡ **how much** ◇ *pron* combien ; ~ **much does it cost?** combien ça coûte? ◇ *adj* combien de ; ~ **much bread?** combien de pain?

however [haʊ'evə'] ◇ *adv* **- 1.** [nevertheless] cependant, toutefois **- 2.** [no matter how] quelque ... que (+ *subjunctive)*, si ... que (+ *subjunctive)* ; ~ **many/much** peu importe la quantité de **- 3.** [how] comment.

conj [in whatever way] de quelque manière que (+ *subjunctive)*.

howl [haʊl] ◇ *n* hurlement *m* ; [of laughter] éclat *m*. ◇ *vi* hurler ; [with laughter] rire aux éclats.

hp *(abbr of* horsepower) *n* CV *m*.

HP *n* **- 1.** Br *(abbr of* hire purchase) : to buy sthg on ~ acheter qqch à crédit **- 2. = hp.**

HQ *(abbr of* headquarters) *n* QG *m*.

hr *(abbr of* hour) h.

hub [hʌb] *n* **- 1.** [of wheel] moyeu *m* **- 2.** [of activity] centre *m*.

hubbub ['hʌbʌb] *n* vacarme *m*, brouhaha *m*.

hubcap ['hʌbkæp] *n* enjoliveur *m*.

huddle ['hʌdl] ◇ *vi* se blottir. ◇ *n* petit groupe *m*.

hue [hju:] *n* [colour] teinte *f*, nuance *f*.

huff [hʌf] *n* : in a ~ froissé(e).

hug [hʌg] ◇ *n* étreinte *f* ; to give sb a ~ serrer qqn dans ses bras. ◇ *vt* **- 1.** [embrace] étreindre, serrer dans ses bras **- 2.** [hold] tenir **- 3.** [stay close to] serrer.

huge [hju:dʒ] *adj* énorme ; [subject] vaste ; [success] fou (folle).

hulk [hʌlk] *n* **- 1.** [of ship] carcasse *f* **- 2.** [person] malabar *m*, mastodonte *m*.

hull [hʌl] *n* coque *f*.

hullo [hə'ləʊ] *excl* = hello.

hum [hʌm] ◇ *vi* **- 1.** [buzz] bourdonner ; [machine] vrombir, ronfler **- 2.** [sing] fredonner, chantonner **- 3.** [be busy] être en pleine activité. ◇ *vt* fredonner, chantonner.

human ['hju:mən] ◇ *adj* humain(e). ◇ *n* : ~ **(being)** être *m* humain.

humane [hju:'meɪn] *adj* humain(e).

humanitarian [hju:‚mænɪ'teərɪən] *adj* humanitaire.

humanity [hju:'mænətɪ] *n* humanité *f*. ➡ **humanities** *npl* : the humanities les humanités *fpl*, les sciences *fpl* humaines.

human race *n* : the ~ la race humaine.

human rights *npl* droits *mpl* de l'homme.

humble ['hʌmbl] ◇ *adj* humble ; [origins, employee] modeste. ◇ *vt* humilier.

humbug ['hʌmbʌg] *n* **- 1.** dated [hypocrisy] hypocrisie *f* **- 2.** Br [sweet] type de bonbon dur.

humdrum ['hʌmdrʌm] *adj* monotone.

humid ['hju:mɪd] *adj* humide.

humidity [hju:'mɪdətɪ] *n* humidité *f*.

humiliate [hju:'mɪlɪeɪt] *vt* humilier.

humiliation [hju:‚mɪlɪ'eɪʃn] *n* humiliation *f*.

humility [hjuːˈmɪlətɪ] *n* humilité *f*.

humor *Am* = humour.

humorous [ˈhjuːmərəs] *adj* humoristique ; [person] plein(e) d'humour.

humour *Br*, **humor** *Am* [ˈhjuːməʳ] ◇ *n* - **1.** [sense of fun] humour *m* - **2.** [of situation, remark] côté *m* comique - **3.** *dated* [mood] humeur *f*. ◇ *vt* se montrer conciliant(e) envers.

hump [hʌmp] *n* bosse *f*.

humpbacked bridge [ˈhʌmpbækt-] *n* pont *m* en dos d'âne.

hunch [hʌntʃ] *n inf* pressentiment *m*, intuition *f*.

hunchback [ˈhʌntʃbæk] *n* bossu *m*, -e *f*.

hunched [hʌntʃt] *adj* voûté(e).

hundred [ˈhʌndrəd] *num* cent ; **a** OR **one** ~ cent ; *see also* **six**. ◆ **hundreds** *npl* des centaines.

hundredth [ˈhʌndrətθ] *num* centième ; *see also* **sixth**.

hundredweight [ˈhʌndrədweɪt] *n* [in UK] poids *m* de 112 livres, = 50,8 kg ; [in US] poids *m* de 100 livres, = 45,3 kg.

hung [hʌŋ] *pt & pp* ⟶ **hang**.

Hungarian [hʌŋˈɡeərɪən] ◇ *adj* hongrois(e). ◇ *n* - **1.** [person] Hongrois *m*, -e *f* - **2.** [language] hongrois *m*.

Hungary [ˈhʌŋɡərɪ] *n* Hongrie *f*.

hunger [ˈhʌŋɡəʳ] *n* - **1.** [gen] faim *f* - **2.** [strong desire] soif *f*. ◆ **hunger after**, **hunger for** *vt fus* avoir faim de, avoir soif de.

hunger strike *n* grève *f* de la faim.

hung over *adj inf* : **to be** ~ avoir la gueule de bois.

hungry [ˈhʌŋɡrɪ] *adj* - **1.** [for food] : **to be** ~ avoir faim ; [starving] être affamé(e) - **2.** [eager] : **to be** ~ **for** être avide de.

hung up *adj inf* : **to be** ~ **(on** OR **about)** être obsédé(e) (par).

hunk [hʌŋk] *n* - **1.** [large piece] gros morceau *m* - **2.** *inf* [man] beau mec *m*.

hunt [hʌnt] ◇ *n* chasse *f* ; [for missing person] recherches *fpl*. ◇ *vi* - **1.** [chase animals, birds] chasser - **2.** *Br* [chase foxes] chasser le renard - **3.** [search] : **to** ~ **(for sthg)** chercher partout (qqch). ◇ *vt* - **1.** [animals, birds] chasser - **2.** [person] poursuivre, pourchasser.

hunter [ˈhʌntəʳ] *n* [of animals, birds] chasseur *m*.

hunting [ˈhʌntɪŋ] *n* - **1.** [of animals] chasse *f* - **2.** *Br* [of foxes] chasse *f* au renard.

hurdle [ˈhɜːdl] ◇ *n* - **1.** [in race] haie *f*

- **2.** [obstacle] obstacle *m*. ◇ *vt* [jump over] sauter.

hurl [hɜːl] *vt* - **1.** [throw] lancer avec violence - **2.** [shout] lancer.

hurray [hʊˈreɪ] *excl* hourra !

hurricane [ˈhʌrɪkən] *n* ouragan *m*.

hurried [ˈhʌrɪd] *adj* [hasty] précipité(e).

hurriedly [ˈhʌrɪdlɪ] *adv* précipitamment ; [eat, write] vite, en toute hâte.

hurry [ˈhʌrɪ] ◇ *vt* [person] faire se dépêcher ; [process] hâter ; **to** ~ **to do sthg** se dépêcher OR se presser de faire qqch. ◇ *vi* se dépêcher, se presser. ◇ *n* hâte *f*, précipitation *f* ; **to be in a** ~ être pressé ; **to do sthg in a** ~ faire qqch à la hâte. ◆ **hurry up** *vi* se dépêcher.

hurt [hɜːt] (*pt & pp* **hurt**) ◇ *vt* - **1.** [physically, emotionally] blesser ; [one's leg, arm] se faire mal à ; **to** ~ **o.s.** se faire mal - **2.** *fig* [harm] faire du mal à. ◇ *vi* - **1.** [gen] faire mal ; **my leg** ~**s** ma jambe me fait mal - **2.** *fig* [do harm] faire du mal. ◇ *adj* blessé(e) ; [voice] offensé(e).

hurtful [ˈhɜːtfʊl] *adj* blessant(e).

hurtle [ˈhɜːtl] *vi* aller à toute allure.

husband [ˈhʌzbənd] *n* mari *m*.

hush [hʌʃ] ◇ *n* silence *m*. ◇ *excl* silence !, chut !

husk [hʌsk] *n* [of seed, grain] enveloppe *f*.

husky [ˈhʌskɪ] ◇ *adj* [hoarse] rauque. ◇ *n* husky *m*.

hustle [ˈhʌsl] ◇ *vt* [hurry] pousser, bousculer. ◇ *n* agitation *f*.

hut [hʌt] *n* - **1.** [rough house] hutte *f* - **2.** [shed] cabane *f*.

hutch [hʌtʃ] *n* clapier *m*.

hyacinth [ˈhaɪəsɪnθ] *n* jacinthe *f*.

hydrant [ˈhaɪdrənt] *n* bouche *f* d'incendie.

hydraulic [haɪˈdrɔːlɪk] *adj* hydraulique.

hydroelectric [ˌhaɪdrəʊɪˈlektrɪk] *adj* hydro-électrique.

hydrofoil [ˈhaɪdrəfɔɪl] *n* hydrofoil *m*.

hydrogen [ˈhaɪdrədʒən] *n* hydrogène *m*.

hyena [haɪˈiːnə] *n* hyène *f*.

hygiene [ˈhaɪdʒiːn] *n* hygiène *f*.

hygienic [haɪˈdʒiːnɪk] *adj* hygiénique.

hymn [hɪm] *n* hymne *m*, cantique *m*.

hype [haɪp] *inf* ◇ *n* (*U*) battage *m* publicitaire. ◇ *vt* faire un battage publicitaire autour de.

hyperactive [ˌhaɪpərˈæktɪv] *adj* hyperactif(ive).

hypermarket [ˈhaɪpəˌmɑːkɪt] n hyper-marché m.

hyphen [ˈhaɪfn] n trait m d'union.

hypnosis [hɪpˈnəʊsɪs] n hypnose f.

hypnotic [hɪpˈnɒtɪk] adj hypnotique.

hypnotize, -ise [ˈhɪpnətaɪz] vt hypnotiser.

hypocrisy [hɪˈpɒkrəsɪ] n hypocrisie f.

hypocrite [ˈhɪpəkrɪt] n hypocrite mf.

hypocritical [ˌhɪpəˈkrɪtɪkl] adj hypocrite.

hypothesis [haɪˈpɒθɪsɪs] (pl -theses [-θɪsiːz]) n hypothèse f.

hypothetical [ˌhaɪpəˈθetɪkl] adj hypothétique.

hysteria [hɪsˈtɪərɪə] n hystérie f.

hysterical [hɪsˈterɪkl] adj - 1. [gen] hystérique - 2. inf [very funny] désopilant(e).

hysterics [hɪsˈterɪks] npl - 1. [panic, excitement] crise f de nerfs - 2. inf [laughter] fou rire m.

i (pl i's or is), **I** (pl I's or Is) [aɪ] n [letter] i m inv, I m inv.

I [aɪ] pers pron - 1. (unstressed) je, j' (before vowel or silent 'h') ; **he and I are leaving for Paris** lui et moi (nous) partons pour Paris - 2. (stressed) moi ; **I can't do it** moi je ne peux pas le faire.

IBA (abbr of **Independent Broadcasting Authority**) n organisme d'agrément et de coordination des stations de radio et chaînes de télévision du secteur privé en Grande-Bretagne.

ice [aɪs] ◇ n - 1. [frozen water, ice cream] glace f - 2. (U) [on road] verglas m - 3. (U) [ice cubes] glaçons mpl. ◇ vt Br glacer. ◆ **ice over, ice up** vi [lake, pond] geler ; [window, windscreen] givrer ; [road] se couvrir de verglas.

iceberg [ˈaɪsbɜːg] n iceberg m.

iceberg lettuce n laitue f iceberg.

icebox [ˈaɪsbɒks] n - 1. Br [in refrigerator] freezer m - 2. Am [refrigerator] réfrigérateur m.

ice cream n glace f.

ice cube n glaçon m.

ice hockey n hockey m sur glace.

Iceland [ˈaɪslənd] n Islande f.

Icelandic [aɪsˈlændɪk] ◇ adj islandais(e). ◇ n [language] islandais m.

ice lolly n Br sucette f glacée.

ice pick n pic m à glace.

ice rink n patinoire f.

ice skate n patin m à glace. ◆ **ice-skate** vi faire du patin (à glace).

ice-skating n patinage m (sur glace).

icicle [ˈaɪsɪkl] n glaçon m (naturel).

icing [ˈaɪsɪŋ] n (U) glaçage m, glace f.

icing sugar n Br sucre m glace.

icon [ˈaɪkɒn] n [gen & COMPUT] icône f.

icy [ˈaɪsɪ] adj - 1. [weather, manner] glacial(e) - 2. [covered in ice] verglacé(e).

I'd [aɪd] = I would, I had.

ID n (U) (abbr of **identification**) papiers mpl.

idea [aɪˈdɪə] n idée f ; [intention] intention f ; **to have an ~ (that)** ... avoir idée que ... ; **to have no ~** n'avoir aucune idée ; **to get the ~** inf piger.

ideal [aɪˈdɪəl] ◇ adj idéal(e). ◇ n idéal m.

ideally [aɪˈdɪəlɪ] adv idéalement ; [suited] parfaitement.

identical [aɪˈdentɪkl] adj identique.

identification [aɪˌdentɪfɪˈkeɪʃn] n (U) - 1. [gen] : **~ (with)** identification f (à) - 2. [documentation] pièce f d'identité.

identify [aɪˈdentɪfaɪ] ◇ vt - 1. [recognize] identifier - 2. [subj : document, card] permettre de reconnaître - 3. [associate] : **to ~ sb with sthg** associer qqn à qqch. ◇ vi [empathize] : **to ~ with** s'identifier à.

Identikit picture® [aɪˈdentɪkɪt-] n portrait-robot m.

identity [aɪˈdentətɪ] n identité f.

identity card n carte f d'identité.

identity parade n séance d'identification d'un suspect dans un échantillon de plusieurs personnes.

ideology [ˌaɪdɪˈɒlədʒɪ] n idéologie f.

idiom [ˈɪdɪəm] n - 1. [phrase] expression f idiomatique - 2. fml [style] langue f.

idiomatic [ˌɪdɪəˈmætɪk] adj idiomatique.

idiosyncrasy [ˌɪdɪəˈsɪŋkrəsɪ] n particularité f, caractéristique f.

idiot [ˈɪdɪət] n idiot m, -e f, imbécile mf.

idiotic [ˌɪdɪˈɒtɪk] adj idiot(e).

idle [ˈaɪdl] ◇ adj - 1. [lazy] oisif(ive), désœuvré(e) - 2. [not working - machine, factory] arrêté(e) ; [- worker] qui chôme, en chômage - 3. [threat] vain(e) - 4. [curiosity] simple, pur(e). ◇ vi tourner au ralenti. ◆ **idle away** vt sep [time] perdre à ne rien faire.

idol [ˈaɪdl] n idole f.

idolize, -ise ['aɪdəlaɪz] *vt* idolâtrer, adorer.

idyllic [ɪ'dɪlɪk] *adj* idyllique.

i.e. (*abbr of* **id est**) c-à-d.

if [ɪf] *conj* - **1.** [gen] si ; ~ **I were you** à ta place, si j'étais toi - **2.** [though] bien que - **3.** [that] que. ➡ **if not** *conj* sinon. ➡ **if only** ⬦ *conj* - **1.** [naming a reason] ne serait-ce que - **2.** [expressing regret] si seulement. ⬦ *excl* si seulement!

igloo ['ɪgluː] (*pl* -s) *n* igloo *m*, iglou *m*.

ignite [ɪg'naɪt] ⬦ *vt* mettre le feu à, enflammer ; [firework] tirer. ⬦ *vi* prendre feu, s'enflammer.

ignition [ɪg'nɪʃn] *n* - **1.** [act of igniting] ignition *f* - **2.** AUT allumage *m* ; **to switch on the** ~ mettre le contact.

ignition key *n* clef *f* de contact.

ignorance ['ɪgnərəns] *n* ignorance *f*.

ignorant ['ɪgnərənt] *adj* - **1.** [uneducated, unaware] ignorant(e) ; **to be ~ of sthg** être ignorant de qqch - **2.** [rude] mal élevé(e).

Ignore [ɪg'nɔːʳ] *vt* [advice, facts] ne pas tenir compte de ; [person] faire semblant de ne pas voir.

ilk [ɪlk] *n* : **of that** ~ [of that sort] de cet acabit, de ce genre.

ill [ɪl] ⬦ *adj* - **1.** [unwell] malade ; **to feel** ~ se sentir malade OR souffrant ; **to be taken** ~, **to fall** ~ tomber malade - **2.** [bad] mauvais(e) ; ~ **luck** malchance *f*. ⬦ *adv* mal ; **to speak/think** ~ **of sb** dire/penser du mal de qqn.

I'll [aɪl] = **I will, I shall.**

ill-advised [-əd'vaɪzd] *adj* [remark, action] peu judicieux(euse) ; [person] malavisé(e).

ill at ease *adj* mal à l'aise

illegal [ɪ'liːgl] *adj* illégal(e) ; [immigrant] en situation irrégulière.

illegible [ɪ'ledʒəbl] *adj* illisible.

illegitimate [ˌɪlɪ'dʒɪtɪmət] *adj* illégitime.

ill-equipped [-ɪ'kwɪpt] *adj* : **to be ~ to do sthg** être mal placé(e) pour faire qqch.

ill-fated [-'feɪtɪd] *adj* fatal(e), funeste.

ill feeling *n* animosité *f*.

ill health *n* mauvaise santé *f*.

illicit [ɪ'lɪsɪt] *adj* illicite.

illiteracy [ɪ'lɪtərəsɪ] *n* analphabétisme *m*, illettrisme *m*.

illiterate [ɪ'lɪtərət] ⬦ *adj* analphabète, illettré(e). ⬦ *n* analphabète *mf*, illettré *m*, -e *f*.

illness ['ɪlnɪs] *n* maladie *f*.

illogical [ɪ'lɒdʒɪkl] *adj* illogique.

ill-suited *adj* mal assorti(e) ; **to be ~ for sthg** être inapte à qqch.

ill-timed [-'taɪmd] *adj* déplacé(e), mal à propos.

ill-treat *vt* maltraiter.

illuminate [ɪ'luːmɪneɪt] *vt* éclairer.

illumination [ɪˌluːmɪ'neɪʃn] *n* [lighting] éclairage *m*. ➡ **illuminations** *npl Br* illuminations *fpl*.

illusion [ɪ'luːʒn] *n* illusion *f* ; **to have no ~s about** ne se faire OR n'avoir aucune illusion sur ; **to be under the ~ that** croire OR s'imaginer que, avoir l'illusion que.

illustrate ['ɪləstreɪt] *vt* illustrer.

illustration [ˌɪlə'streɪʃn] *n* illustration *f*.

illustrious [ɪ'lʌstrɪəs] *adj* illustre, célèbre.

ill will *n* animosité *f*.

I'm [aɪm] = **I am.**

image ['ɪmɪdʒ] *n* - **1.** [gen] image *f* - **2.** [of company, politician] image *f* de marque.

imagery ['ɪmɪdʒrɪ] *n* (*U*) images *fpl*.

imaginary [ɪ'mædʒɪnrɪ] *adj* imaginaire.

imagination [ɪˌmædʒɪ'neɪʃn] *n* - **1.** [ability] imagination *f* - **2.** [fantasy] invention *f*.

imaginative [ɪ'mædʒɪnətɪv] *adj* imaginatif(ive) ; [solution] plein(e) d'imagination.

imagine [ɪ'mædʒɪn] *vt* imaginer ; **to ~ doing sthg** s'imaginer OR se voir faisant qqch ; ~ **(that)!** tu t'imagines!

imbalance [ˌɪm'bæləns] *n* déséquilibre *m*.

Imbecile ['ɪmbɪsiːl] *n* imbécile *mf*, idiot *m*, -e *f*.

IMF (*abbr of* **International Monetary Fund**) *n* FMI *m*.

imitate ['ɪmɪteɪt] *vt* imiter.

imitation [ˌɪmɪ'teɪʃn] ⬦ *n* imitation *f*. ⬦ *adj* [leather] imitation (*before n*) ; [jewellery] en toc.

immaculate [ɪ'mækjʊlət] *adj* impeccable.

immaterial [ˌɪmə'tɪərɪəl] *adj* [unimportant] sans importance.

immature [ˌɪmə'tjʊəʳ] *adj* - **1.** [lacking judgment] qui manque de maturité - **2.** [not fully grown] jeune, immature.

immediate [ɪ'miːdjət] *adj* - **1.** [urgent] immédiat(e) ; [problem, meeting] urgent(e) - **2.** [very near] immédiat(e) ; [family] le plus proche.

immediately [ɪ'miːdjətlɪ] ⬦ *adv* - **1.** [at once] immédiatement - **2.** [directly] directement. ⬦ *conj* dès que.

immense [ɪ'mens] *adj* immense ; [improvement, change] énorme.

immerse [ɪ'mɜːs] *vt* : **to ~ sthg in sthg** immerger OR plonger qqch dans qqch ; **to ~ o.s. in sthg** *fig* se plonger dans qqch.

immersion heater [ɪ'mɜːʃn-] *n* chauffe-eau *m inv* électrique.

immigrant ['ɪmɪgrənt] *n* immigré *m*, -e *f*.

immigration [ˌɪmɪ'greɪʃn] *n* immigration *f*.

imminent ['ɪmɪnənt] *adj* imminent(e).

immobilize, -ise [ɪ'məʊbɪlaɪz] *vt* immobiliser.

immobilizer [ɪ'məʊbɪlaɪzəʳ] *n* AUT système *m* antidémarrage.

immoral [ɪ'mɒrəl] *adj* immoral(e).

immortal [ɪ'mɔːtl] <> *adj* immortel(elle). <> *n* immortel *m*, -elle *f*.

immortalize, -ise [ɪ'mɔːtəlaɪz] *vt* immortaliser.

immovable [ɪ'muːvəbl] *adj* **- 1.** [fixed] fixe **- 2.** [determined] inébranlable.

immune [ɪ'mjuːn] *adj* **- 1.** MED : **~ (to)** immunisé(e) (contre) **- 2.** *fig* [protected] : **to be ~ to** OR **from** être à l'abri de.

immunity [ɪ'mjuːnətɪ] *n* **- 1.** MED : **~ (to)** immunité *f* (contre) **- 2.** *fig* [protection] : **~ to** OR **from** immunité *f* contre.

immunize, -ise ['ɪmjuːnaɪz] *vt* : **to ~ sb (against)** immuniser qqn (contre).

imp [ɪmp] *n* **- 1.** [creature] lutin *m* **- 2.** [naughty child] petit diable *m*, coquin *m*, -e *f*.

impact [*n* 'ɪmpækt, *vb* ɪm'pækt] <> *n* impact *m* ; **to make an ~ on** OR **upon sb** faire une forte impression sur qqn ; **to make an ~ on** OR **upon sthg** avoir un impact sur qqch. <> *vt* **- 1.** [collide with] entrer en collision avec **- 2.** [influence] avoir un impact sur.

impair [ɪm'peəʳ] *vt* affaiblir, abîmer ; [efficiency] réduire.

impart [ɪm'pɑːt] *vt fml* **- 1.** [information] : **to ~ sthg (to sb)** communiquer OR transmettre qqch (à qqn) **- 2.** [feeling, quality] : **to ~ sthg (to)** donner qqch (à).

impartial [ɪm'pɑːʃl] *adj* impartial(e).

impassable [ɪm'pɑːsəbl] *adj* impraticable.

impassive [ɪm'pæsɪv] *adj* impassible.

impatience [ɪm'peɪʃns] *n* **- 1.** [gen] impatience *f* **- 2.** [irritability] irritation *f*.

impatient [ɪm'peɪʃnt] *adj* **- 1.** [gen] impatient(e) ; **to be ~ to do sthg** être impatient de faire qqch ; **to be ~ for sthg** attendre qqch avec impatience **- 2.** [irritable] : **to become** OR **get ~** s'impatienter.

impeccable [ɪm'pekəbl] *adj* impeccable.

impede [ɪm'piːd] *vt* entraver, empêcher ; [person] gêner.

impediment [ɪm'pedɪmənt] *n* **- 1.** [obstacle] obstacle *m* **- 2.** [disability] défaut *m*.

impel [ɪm'pel] *vt* : **to ~ sb to do sthg** inciter qqn à faire qqch.

impending [ɪm'pendɪŋ] *adj* imminent(e).

imperative [ɪm'perətɪv] <> *adj* [essential] impératif(ive), essentiel(elle). <> *n* impératif *m*.

imperfect [ɪm'pɜːfɪkt] <> *adj* imparfait(e). <> *n* GRAMM : **~ (tense)** imparfait *m*.

imperial [ɪm'pɪərɪəl] *adj* **- 1.** [of empire] impérial(e) **- 2.** [system of measurement] *qui a cours légal dans le Royaume-Uni*.

imperil [ɪm'perɪl] *vt* mettre en péril OR en danger ; [project] compromettre.

impersonal [ɪm'pɜːsnl] *adj* impersonnel(elle).

impersonate [ɪm'pɜːsəneɪt] *vt* se faire passer pour.

impersonation [ɪmˌpɜːsə'neɪʃn] *n* usurpation *f* d'identité ; [by mimic] imitation *f*.

impertinent [ɪm'pɜːtɪnənt] *adj* impertinent(e).

impervious [ɪm'pɜːvjəs] *adj* [not influenced] : **~ to** indifférent(e) à.

impetuous [ɪm'petʃʊəs] *adj* impétueux(euse).

impetus ['ɪmpɪtəs] *n (U)* **- 1.** [momentum] élan *m* **- 2.** [stimulus] impulsion *f*.

impinge [ɪm'pɪndʒ] *vi* : **to ~ on sb/sthg** affecter qqn/qqch.

implant [*n* 'ɪmplɑːnt, *vb* ɪm'plɑːnt] <> *n* implant *m*. <> *vt* : **to ~ sthg in** OR **into sb** implanter qqch dans qqn.

implausible [ɪm'plɔːzəbl] *adj* peu plausible.

implement [*n* 'ɪmplɪmənt, *vb* 'ɪmplɪment] <> *n* outil *m*, instrument *m*. <> *vt* exécuter, appliquer.

implication [ˌɪmplɪ'keɪʃn] *n* implication *f* ; **by ~** par voie de conséquence.

implicit [ɪm'plɪsɪt] *adj* **- 1.** [inferred] implicite **- 2.** [belief, faith] absolu(e).

implore [ɪm'plɔːʳ] *vt* : **to ~ sb (to do sthg)** implorer qqn (de faire qqch).

imply [ɪm'plaɪ] *vt* **- 1.** [suggest] sous-entendre, laisser supposer OR entendre **- 2.** [involve] impliquer.

impolite [ˌɪmpə'laɪt] *adj* impoli(e).

import [*n* 'ɪmpɔːt, *vb* ɪm'pɔːt] <> *n* [product, action] importation *f*. <> *vt* [gen & COMPUT] importer.

importance [ɪmˈpɔːtns] *n* importance *f*.

important [ɪmˈpɔːtnt] *adj* important(e) ; **to be ~ to sb** importer à qqn.

importer [ɪmˈpɔːtəʳ] *n* importateur *m*, -trice *f*.

impose [ɪmˈpəʊz] <> *vt* [force] : **to ~ sthg (on)** imposer qqch (à). <> *vi* [cause trouble] : **to ~ (on sb)** abuser (de la gentillesse de qqn).

imposing [ɪmˈpəʊzɪŋ] *adj* imposant(e).

imposition [ˌɪmpəˈzɪʃn] *n* - **1.** [of tax, limitations etc] imposition *f* - **2.** [cause of trouble] : **it's an ~** c'est abuser de ma/notre gentillesse.

impossible [ɪmˈpɒsəbl] *adj* impossible.

impostor, imposter *Am* [ɪmˈpɒstəʳ] *n* imposteur *m*.

impotent [ˈɪmpətənt] *adj* impuissant(e).

impound [ɪmˈpaʊnd] *vt* confisquer.

impoverished [ɪmˈpɒvərɪʃt] *adj* appauvri(e).

impractical [ɪmˈpræktɪkl] *adj* pas pratique.

impregnable [ɪmˈpregnəbl] *adj* - **1.** [fortress, defences] imprenable - **2.** *fig* [person] inattaquable.

impregnate [ˈɪmpregneɪt] *vt* - **1.** [introduce substance into] : **to ~ sthg with** imprégner qqch de - **2.** *fml* [fertilize] féconder.

impress [ɪmˈpres] *vt* - **1.** [person] impressionner - **2.** [stress] : **to ~ sthg on sb** faire bien comprendre qqch à qqn.

impression [ɪmˈpreʃn] *n* - **1.** [gen] impression *f* ; **to be under the ~ (that)** ... avoir l'impression que ... ; **to make an ~** faire impression - **2.** [by mimic] imitation *f* - **3.** [of stamp, book] impression *f*, empreinte *f*.

impressive [ɪmˈpresɪv] *adj* impressionnant(e).

imprint [ˈɪmprɪnt] *n* - **1.** [mark] empreinte *f* - **2.** [publisher's name] nom *m* de l'éditeur.

imprison [ɪmˈprɪzn] *vt* emprisonner.

improbable [ɪmˈprɒbəbl] *adj* [story, excuse] improbable.

impromptu [ɪmˈprɒmptjuː] *adj* impromptu(e).

improper [ɪmˈprɒpəʳ] *adj* - **1.** [unsuitable] impropre - **2.** [incorrect, illegal] incorrect(e) - **3.** [rude] indécent(e).

improve [ɪmˈpruːv] <> *vi* s'améliorer ; [patient] aller mieux ; **to ~ on** OR **upon sthg** améliorer qqch. <> *vt* améliorer.

improvement [ɪmˈpruːvmənt] *n* : **~ (in/on)** amélioration *f* (de/par rapport à).

improvise [ˈɪmprəvaɪz] *vt* & *vi* improviser.

impudent [ˈɪmpjʊdənt] *adj* impudent(e).

impulse [ˈɪmpʌls] *n* impulsion *f* ; **on ~** par impulsion.

impulsive [ɪmˈpʌlsɪv] *adj* impulsif(ive).

impunity [ɪmˈpjuːnətɪ] *n* : **with ~** avec impunité.

impurity [ɪmˈpjʊərətɪ] *n* impureté *f*.

in [ɪn] <> *prep* - **1.** [indicating place, position] dans ; **~ a box/bag/drawer** dans une boîte/un sac/un tiroir ; **~ Paris** à Paris ; **~ Belgium** en Belgique ; **~ Canada** au Canada ; **~ the United States** aux États-Unis ; **~ the country** à la campagne ; **to be ~ hospital/prison** être à l'hôpital/en prison ; **~ here** ici ; **~ there** là - **2.** [wearing] en ; **dressed ~ a suit** vêtu d'un costume - **3.** [at a particular time, season] : **~ 1994** en 1994 ; **~ April** en avril ; **~ (the) spring** au printemps ; **~ (the) winter** en hiver ; **at two o'clock ~ the afternoon** à deux heures de l'après-midi - **4.** [period of time - within] en ; [- after] dans ; **he learned to type ~ two weeks** il a appris à taper à la machine en deux semaines ; **I'll be ready ~ five minutes** je serai prêt dans 5 minutes ; **it's my first decent meal ~ weeks** c'est mon premier repas correct depuis des semaines - **6.** [indicating situation, circumstances] : **~ the sun** au soleil ; **~ the rain** sous la pluie ; **to live/die ~ poverty** vivre/mourir dans la misère ; **~ danger/difficulty** en danger/ difficulté - **7.** [indicating manner, condition] : **~ a loud/soft voice** d'une voix forte/ douce ; **to write ~ pencil/ink** écrire au crayon/à l'encre ; **to speak ~ English/ French** parler (en) anglais/français - **8.** [indicating emotional state] : **~ anger** sous le coup de la colère ; **~ joy/delight** avec joie/ plaisir - **9.** [specifying area of activity] dans : **he's ~ computers** il est dans l'informatique - **10.** [referring to quantity, numbers, age] : **~ large/small quantities** en grande/petite quantité ; **~ (their) thousands** par milliers ; **she's ~ her sixties** elle a la soixantaine - **11.** [describing arrangement] : **~ twos** par deux ; **~ a line/row/circle** en ligne/rang/ cercle - **12.** [as regards] : **to be three metres ~ length/width** faire trois mètres de long/ large ; **a change ~ direction** un changement de direction - **13.** [in ratios] : **5 pence ~ the pound** 5 pence par livre sterling ; **one ~ ten** un sur dix - **14.** *(after superl)* de ; **the longest river ~ the world** le fleuve le plus long du monde - **15.** *(+ present participle)* : **~ doing sthg** en faisant qqch. <> *adv* - **1.** [inside] dedans, à l'intérieur - **2.** [at home, work] là ; **I'm staying ~ tonight** je reste à la maison OR chez moi ce soir ; **is Judith ~?** est-ce que Judith est là ? - **3**. [of train, boat, plane] : **to be ~** être arrivé(e) - **4**. [of tide] : **the tide's ~** c'est la marée haute - **5**. *phr* : **we're ~ for some bad weather** nous allons avoir du mauvais temps ; **you're ~ for a shock** tu vas avoir un choc. ⟡ *adj inf* à la mode. ➡ **ins** *npl* : **the ~s and outs** les tenants et les aboutissants *mpl.*

in. *abbr of* **inch**.

inability [,ɪnə'bɪlətɪ] *n* : **~ (to do sthg)** incapacité *f* (à faire qqch).

inaccessible [,ɪnək'sesəbl] *adj* inaccessible.

inaccurate [ɪn'ækjʊrət] *adj* inexact(e).

inadequate [ɪn'ædɪkwət] *adj* insuffisant(e).

inadvertently [,ɪnəd'vɜːtəntlɪ] *adv* par inadvertance.

inadvisable [,ɪnəd'vaɪzəbl] *adj* déconseillé(e).

inane [ɪ'neɪn] *adj* inepte ; [person] stupide.

inanimate [ɪn'ænɪmət] *adj* inanimé(e).

inappropriate [ɪnə'prəʊprɪət] *adj* inopportun(e) ; [expression, word] impropre ; [clothing] peu approprié(e).

inarticulate [,ɪnɑː'tɪkjʊlət] *adj* inarticulé(e), indistinct(e) ; [person] qui s'exprime avec difficulté ; [explanation] mal exprimé(e).

inasmuch [,ɪnəz'mʌtʃ] ➡ **inasmuch as** *conj fml* attendu que.

inaudible [ɪ'nɔːdɪbl] *adj* inaudible.

inaugural [ɪ'nɔːgjʊrəl] *adj* inaugural(e).

inauguration [ɪ,nɔːgjʊ'reɪʃn] *n* [of leader, president] investiture *f* ; [of building, system] inauguration *f*.

in-between *adj* intermédiaire.

inborn [,ɪn'bɔːn] *adj* inné(e).

inbound ['ɪnbaʊnd] *adj Am* qui arrive.

inbred [,ɪn'bred] *adj* - **1**. [closely related] consanguin(e) ; [animal] croisé(e) - **2**. [inborn] inné(e).

inbuilt [,ɪn'bɪlt] *adj* [inborn] inné(e).

inc. (*abbr of* **inclusive**) : **12-15 April ~** du 12 au 15 avril inclus.

Inc. [ɪŋk] (*abbr of* **incorporated**) ≃ SARL.

incapable [ɪn'keɪpəbl] *adj* incapable ; **to be ~ of sthg/of doing sthg** être incapable de qqch/de faire qqch.

incapacitated [,ɪnkə'pæsɪteɪtɪd] *adj* inapte physiquement ; **~ for work** mis(e) dans l'incapacité de travailler.

incarcerate [ɪn'kɑːsəreɪt] *vt* incarcérer.

incendiary device [ɪn'sendjərɪ-] *n* dispositif *m* incendiaire.

incense [*n* 'ɪnsens, *vb* ɪn'sens] ⟡ *n* encens *m*. ⟡ *vt* [anger] mettre en colère.

incentive [ɪn'sentɪv] *n* - **1**. [encouragement] motivation *f* - **2**. COMM récompense *f*, prime *f*.

incentive scheme *n* programme *m* d'encouragement.

inception [ɪn'sepʃn] *n fml* commencement *m*.

incessant [ɪn'sesnt] *adj* incessant(e).

incessantly [ɪn'sesntlɪ] *adv* sans cesse.

incest ['ɪnsest] *n* inceste *m*.

inch [ɪntʃ] ⟡ *n* = 2,5 cm, ≃ pouce *m*. ⟡ *vi* : **to ~ forward** avancer petit à petit.

incidence ['ɪnsɪdəns] *n* [of disease, theft] fréquence *f*.

incident ['ɪnsɪdənt] *n* incident *m*.

incidental [,ɪnsɪ'dentl] *adj* accessoire.

incidentally [,ɪnsɪ'dentəlɪ] *adv* à propos.

incinerate [ɪn'sɪnəreɪt] *vt* incinérer.

incipient [ɪn'sɪpɪənt] *adj fml* naissant(e).

incisive [ɪn'saɪsɪv] *adj* incisif(ive).

incite [ɪn'saɪt] *vt* inciter ; **to ~ sb to do sthg** inciter qqn à faire qqch.

inclination [,ɪnklɪ'neɪʃn] *n* - **1**. *(U)* [liking, preference] inclination *f*, goût *m* - **2**. [tendency] : **~ to do sthg** inclination *f* à faire qqch.

incline [*n* 'ɪnklaɪn, *vb* ɪn'klaɪn] ⟡ *n* inclinaison *f*. ⟡ *vt* [head] incliner.

inclined [ɪn'klaɪnd] *adj* - **1**. [tending] : **to be ~ to sthg/to do sthg** avoir tendance à qqch/à faire qqch - **2**. [wanting] : **to be ~ to do sthg** être enclin(e) à faire qqch - **3**. [sloping] incliné(e).

include [ɪn'kluːd] *vt* inclure.

included [ɪn'kluːdɪd] *adj* inclus(e).

including [ɪn'kluːdɪŋ] *prep* y compris.

inclusive [ɪn'kluːsɪv] *adj* inclus(e) ; [including all costs] tout compris ; **~ of VAT** TVA incluse OR comprise.

incoherent [,ɪnkəʊ'hɪərənt] *adj* incohérent(e).

income ['ɪnkʌm] *n* revenu *m*.

income support *n Br* allocations supplémentaires accordées aux personnes ayant un faible revenu.

income tax *n* impôt *m* sur le revenu.

incompatible [,ɪnkəm'pætɪbl] *adj* : **~ (with)** incompatible (avec).

incompetent [ɪn'kɒmpɪtənt] *adj* incompétent(e).

incomplete [ˌɪnkəm'pliːt] *adj* incomplet(ète).

incomprehensible [ɪnˌkɒmprɪ'hensəbl] *adj* incompréhensible.

inconceivable [ˌɪnkən'siːvəbl] *adj* inconcevable.

inconclusive [ˌɪnkən'kluːsɪv] *adj* peu concluant(e).

incongruous [ɪn'kɒŋgruəs] *adj* incongru(e).

inconsequential [ˌɪnkɒnsɪ'kwenʃl] *adj* sans importance.

inconsiderable [ˌɪnkən'sɪdərəbl] *adj* : not ~ non négligeable.

inconsiderate [ˌɪnkən'sɪdərət] *adj* inconsidéré(e) ; [person] qui manque de considération.

inconsistency [ˌɪnkən'sɪstənsɪ] *n* inconsistance *f*.

inconsistent [ˌɪnkən'sɪstənt] *adj* - 1. [not agreeing, contradictory] contradictoire ; [person] inconséquent(e) ; ~ with sthg en contradiction avec qqch - 2. [erratic] inconsistant(e).

inconspicuous [ˌɪnkən'spɪkjuəs] *adj* qui passe inaperçu(e).

inconvenience [ˌɪnkən'viːnjəns] <> *n* désagrément *m*. <> *vt* déranger.

inconvenient [ˌɪnkən'viːnjənt] *adj* inopportun(e).

incorporate [ɪn'kɔːpəreɪt] *vt* - 1. [integrate] : to ~ sb/sthg (into) incorporer qqn/qqch (dans) - 2. [comprise] contenir, comprendre.

incorporated [ɪn'kɔːpəreɪtɪd] *adj* COMM constitué(e) en société commerciale.

incorrect [ˌɪnkə'rekt] *adj* incorrect(e).

incorrigible [ɪn'kɒrɪdʒəbl] *adj* incorrigible.

increase [*n* 'ɪnkriːs, *vb* ɪn'kriːs] <> *n* : ~ (in) augmentation *f* (de) ; to be on the ~ aller en augmentant. <> *vt & vi* augmenter.

increasing [ɪn'kriːsɪŋ] *adj* croissant(e).

increasingly [ɪn'kriːsɪŋlɪ] *adv* de plus en plus.

incredible [ɪn'kredəbl] *adj* incroyable.

incredulous [ɪn'kredjʊləs] *adj* incrédule.

increment ['ɪnkrɪmənt] *n* augmentation *f*.

incriminating [ɪn'krɪmɪneɪtɪŋ] *adj* compromettant(e).

incubator ['ɪnkjʊbeɪtəʳ] *n* [for baby] incubateur *m*, couveuse *f*.

incumbent [ɪn'kʌmbənt] *fml* <> *adj* : to be ~ on OR upon sb to do sthg incomber à qqn de faire qqch. <> *n* [of post] titulaire *m*.

incur [ɪn'kɜːʳ] *vt* encourir.

indebted [ɪn'detɪd] *adj* [grateful] : ~ to sb redevable à qqn.

indecent [ɪn'diːsnt] *adj* - 1. [improper] indécent(e) - 2. [unreasonable] malséant(e).

indecent assault *n* attentat *m* à la pudeur.

indecent exposure *n* outrage *m* public à la pudeur.

indecisive [ˌɪndɪ'saɪsɪv] *adj* indécis(e).

indeed [ɪn'diːd] *adv* - 1. [certainly, to express surprise] vraiment ; ~ I am, yes ~ certainement - 2. [in fact] en effet - 3. [for emphasis] : very big/bad ~ extrêmement grand/mauvais, vraiment grand/mauvais.

indefinite [ɪn'defɪnɪt] *adj* - 1. [not fixed] indéfini(e) - 2. [imprecise] vague.

indefinitely [ɪn'defɪnətlɪ] *adv* - 1. [for unfixed period] indéfiniment - 2. [imprecisely] vaguement.

indemnity [ɪn'demnətɪ] *n* indemnité *f*.

indent [ɪn'dent] *vt* - 1. [dent] entailler - 2. [text] mettre en retrait.

independence [ˌɪndɪ'pendəns] *n* indépendance *f*.

Independence Day *n* fête de l'indépendance américaine, le 4 juillet.

independent [ˌɪndɪ'pendənt] *adj* : ~ (of) indépendant(e) (de).

independent school *n* Br école *f* privée.

in-depth *adj* approfondi(e).

indescribable [ˌɪndɪ'skraɪbəbl] *adj* indescriptible.

indestructible [ˌɪndɪ'strʌktəbl] *adj* indestructible.

index ['ɪndeks] (*pl senses 1 and 2* -dexes [-deksiːz], *sense 3* -dices OR -dices [-dɪsiːz]) *n* - 1. [of book] index *m* - 2. [in library] répertoire *m*, fichier *m* - 3. ECON indice *m*.

index card *n* fiche *f*.

index finger *n* index *m*.

index-linked [-ˌlɪŋkt] *adj* indexé(e).

India ['ɪndjə] *n* Inde *f*.

Indian ['ɪndjən] <> *adj* indien(enne). <> *n* Indien *m*, -enne *f*.

Indian Ocean *n* : the ~ l'océan *m* Indien.

indicate ['ɪndɪkeɪt] <> *vt* indiquer. <> *vi* Br AUT mettre son clignotant.

indication [ˌɪndɪ'keɪʃn] n - 1. [suggestion] indication f - 2. [sign] signe m.

indicative [ɪn'dɪkətɪv] ◇ adj : ~ of indicatif(ive) de. ◇ n GRAMM indicatif m.

indicator ['ɪndɪkeɪtə'] n - 1. [sign] indicateur m - 2. Br AUT clignotant m.

indices ['ɪndɪsiːz] pl ⊏> **index**.

indict [ɪn'daɪt] vt : **to ~ sb (for)** accuser qqn (de), mettre qqn en examen (pour).

indictment [ɪn'daɪtmənt] n [JUR - bill] acte m d'accusation ; [- process] mise f en examen.

indifference [ɪn'dɪfrəns] n indifférence f.

indifferent [ɪn'dɪfrənt] adj - 1. [uninterested] : ~ (to) indifférent(e) (à) - 2. [mediocre] médiocre.

indigenous [ɪn'dɪdʒɪnəs] adj indigène.

indigestion [ˌɪndɪ'dʒestʃn] n (U) indigestion f.

indignant [ɪn'dɪgnənt] adj : ~ (at) indigné(e) (de).

indignity [ɪn'dɪgnətɪ] n indignité f.

indigo ['ɪndɪgəʊ] ◇ adj indigo (inv). ◇ n indigo m.

indirect [ˌɪndɪ'rekt] adj indirect(e).

indiscreet [ˌɪndɪ'skriːt] adj indiscret(ète).

indiscriminate [ˌɪndɪ'skrɪmɪnət] adj [person] qui manque de discernement ; [treatment] sans distinction ; [killing] commis au hasard.

indispensable [ˌɪndɪ'spensəbl] adj indispensable.

indisputable [ˌɪndɪ'spjuːtəbl] adj indiscutable.

indistinguishable [ˌɪndɪ'stɪŋgwɪʃəbl] adj : ~ (from) que l'on ne peut distinguer (de).

individual [ˌɪndɪ'vɪdʒʊəl] ◇ adj - 1. [separate, for one person] individuel(elle) - 2. [distinctive] personnel(elle). ◇ n individu m.

individually [ˌɪndɪ'vɪdʒʊəlɪ] adv individuellement.

indoctrination [ɪnˌdɒktrɪ'neɪʃn] n endoctrinement m.

Indonesia [ˌɪndə'niːzjə] n Indonésie f.

indoor ['ɪndɔː'] adj d'intérieur ; [swimming pool] couvert(e) ; [sports] en salle.

indoors [ˌɪn'dɔːz] adv à l'intérieur.

induce [ɪn'djuːs] vt - 1. [persuade] : **to ~ sb to do sthg** inciter OR pousser qqn à faire qqch - 2. [bring about] provoquer.

inducement [ɪn'djuːsmənt] n [incentive] incitation f, encouragement m.

induction [ɪn'dʌkʃn] n - 1. [into official pos-

ition] : ~ (into) installation f (à) - 2. [introduction to job] introduction f - 3. ELEC induction f.

induction course n stage m d'initiation.

indulge [ɪn'dʌldʒ] ◇ vt - 1. [whim, passion] céder à - 2. [child, person] gâter. ◇ vi : **to ~ in sthg** se permettre qqch.

indulgence [ɪn'dʌldʒəns] n - 1. [act of indulging] indulgence f - 2. [special treat] gâterie f.

indulgent [ɪn'dʌldʒənt] adj indulgent(e).

industrial [ɪn'dʌstrɪəl] adj industriel (elle).

industrial action n : **to take ~** se mettre en grève.

industrial estate Br, **industrial park** Am n zone f industrielle.

industrialist [ɪn'dʌstrɪəlɪst] n industriel m.

industrial park Am = **industrial estate**.

industrial relations npl relations fpl patronat-syndicats.

industrial revolution n révolution f industrielle.

industrious [ɪn'dʌstrɪəs] adj industrieux(euse).

industry ['ɪndəstrɪ] n - 1. [gen] industrie f - 2. (U) [hard work] assiduité f, application f.

inebriated [ɪ'niːbrɪeɪtɪd] adj fml ivre.

inedible [ɪn'edɪbl] adj - 1. [meal, food] immangeable - 2. [plant, mushroom] non comestible.

ineffective [ˌɪnɪ'fektɪv] adj inefficace.

ineffectual [ˌɪnɪ'fektʃʊəl] adj inefficace ; [person] incapable, incompétent(e).

inefficiency [ˌɪnɪ'fɪʃnsɪ] n inefficacité f ; [of person] incapacité f, incompétence f.

inefficient [ˌɪnɪ'fɪʃnt] adj inefficace ; [person] incapable, incompétent(e).

ineligible [ɪn'elɪdʒəbl] adj inéligible ; **to be ~ for sthg** ne pas avoir droit à qqch.

inept [ɪ'nept] adj inepte ; [person] stupide.

inequality [ˌɪnɪ'kwɒlətɪ] n inégalité f.

inert [ɪ'nɜːt] adj inerte.

inertia [ɪ'nɜːʃə] n inertie f.

inescapable [ˌɪnɪ'skeɪpəbl] adj inéluctable.

inevitable [ɪn'evɪtəbl] ◇ adj inévitable. ◇ n : **the ~** l'inévitable m.

inevitably [ɪn'evɪtəblɪ] adv inévitablement.

inexcusable [ˌɪnɪk'skjuːzəbl] adj inexcusable, impardonnable.

inexhaustible [ˌɪnɪg'zɔːstəbl] *adj* inépuisable.

inexpensive [ˌɪnɪk'spensɪv] *adj* bon marché *(inv)*, pas cher (chère).

inexperienced [ˌɪnɪk'spɪərɪənst] *adj* inexpérimenté(e), qui manque d'expérience.

inexplicable [ˌɪnɪk'splɪkəbl] *adj* inexplicable.

infallible [ɪn'fæləbl] *adj* infaillible.

infamous ['ɪnfəməs] *adj* infâme.

infancy ['ɪnfənsɪ] *n* petite enfance *f* ; **in its ~** *fig* à ses débuts.

infant ['ɪnfənt] *n* - **1.** [baby] nouveau-né *m*, nouveau-née *f*, nourrisson *m* - **2.** [young child] enfant *mf* en bas âge.

infantry ['ɪnfəntrɪ] *n* infanterie *f*.

infant school *n Br* école *f* maternelle *(de 5 à 7 ans)*.

infatuated [ɪn'fætjʊeɪtɪd] *adj* : **~ (with)** entiché(e) (de).

infatuation [ɪnˌfætjʊ'eɪʃn] *n* : **~ (with)** béguin *m* (pour).

infect [ɪn'fekt] *vt* - **1.** MED infecter - **2.** *fig* [subj : enthusiasm etc] se propager à.

infection [ɪn'fekʃn] *n* infection *f*.

infectious [ɪn'fekʃəs] *adj* - **1.** [disease] infectieux(euse) **2.** *fig* [feeling, laugh] contagieux(euse).

infer [ɪn'fɜː'] *vt* [deduce] : **to ~ sthg (from)** déduire qqch (de).

inferior [ɪn'fɪərɪə'] <> *adj* - **1.** [in status] inférieur(e) - **2.** [product] de qualité inférieure ; [work] médiocre. <> *n* [in status] subalterne *mf*.

inferiority [ɪnˌfɪərɪ'ɒrətɪ] *n* infériorité *f*.

inferiority complex *n* complexe *m* d'infériorité.

inferno [ɪn'fɜːnəʊ] *(pl* **s)** *n* brasier *m*

infertile [ɪn'fɜːtaɪl] *adj* - **1.** [woman] stérile - **2.** [soil] infertile.

infested [ɪn'festɪd] *adj* : **~ with** infesté(e) de.

infighting ['ɪnˌfaɪtɪŋ] *n (U)* querelles *fpl* intestines.

infiltrate ['ɪnfɪltreɪt] *vt* infiltrer.

infinite ['ɪnfɪnət] *adj* infini(e).

infinitive [ɪn'fɪnɪtɪv] *n* infinitif *m*.

infinity [ɪn'fɪnətɪ] *n* infini *m*.

infirm [ɪn'fɜːm] <> *adj* infirme. <> *npl* : **the ~** les infirmes *mpl*.

infirmary [ɪn'fɜːmərɪ] *n* [hospital] hôpital *m*.

infirmity [ɪn'fɜːmətɪ] *n* infirmité *f*.

inflamed [ɪn'fleɪmd] *adj* MED enflammé(e).

inflammable [ɪn'flæməbl] *adj* inflammable.

inflammation [ˌɪnflə'meɪʃn] *n* MED inflammation *f*.

inflatable [ɪn'fleɪtəbl] *adj* gonflable.

inflate [ɪn'fleɪt] *vt* - **1.** [tyre, life jacket etc] gonfler - **2.** ECON [prices, salaries] hausser, gonfler.

inflation [ɪn'fleɪʃn] *n* ECON inflation *f*.

inflationary [ɪn'fleɪʃnrɪ] *adj* ECON inflationniste.

inflict [ɪn'flɪkt] *vt* : **to ~ sthg on sb** infliger qqch à qqn.

influence ['ɪnflʊəns] <> *n* influence *f* ; **under the ~ of** [person, group] sous l'influence de ; [alcohol, drugs] sous l'effet OR l'empire de. <> *vt* influencer.

influential [ˌɪnflʊ'enʃl] *adj* influent(e).

influenza [ˌɪnflʊ'enzə] *n (U)* grippe *f*.

influx ['ɪnflʌks] *n* afflux *m*.

inform [ɪn'fɔːm] *vt* : **to ~ sb (of)** informer qqn (de) ; **to ~ sb about** renseigner qqn sur.
  inform on *vt fus* dénoncer.

informal [ɪn'fɔːml] *adj* - **1.** [party, person] simple ; [clothes] de tous les jours - **2.** [negotiations, visit] officieux(euse) ; [meeting] informel(elle).

informant [ɪn'fɔːmənt] *n* informateur *m*, -trice *f*.

information [ˌɪnfə'meɪʃn] *n (U)* : **~ (on OR about)** renseignements *mpl* OR informations *fpl* (sur) ; **a piece of ~** un renseignement ; **for your ~** *fml* à titre d'information.

information desk *n* bureau *m* de renseignements.

information highway, information superhighway *n* autoroute *f* de l'information.

information superhighway = **information highway**.

information technology *n* informatique *f*.

informative [ɪn'fɔːmətɪv] *adj* informatif(ive).

informer [ɪn'fɔːmə'] *n* indicateur *m*, -trice *f*.

infrared [ˌɪnfrə'red] *adj* infrarouge.

infrastructure ['ɪnfrəˌstrʌktʃə'] *n* infrastructure *f*.

infringe [ɪn'frɪndʒ] <> *vt* - **1.** [right] empiéter sur - **2.** [law, agreement] enfreindre. <> *vi* - **1.** [on right] : **to ~ on** empiéter sur - **2.** [on law, agreement] : **to ~ on** enfreindre.

infringement [ɪnˈfrɪndʒmənt] *n* - 1. [of right] : ~ (of) atteinte *f* (à) - 2. [of law, agreement] transgression *f*.

infuriating [ɪnˈfjʊərɪeɪtɪŋ] *adj* exaspérant(e).

ingenious [ɪnˈdʒiːnjəs] *adj* ingénieux (euse).

ingenuity [ˌɪndʒɪˈnjuːətɪ] *n* ingéniosité *f*.

ingenuous [ɪnˈdʒenjʊəs] *adj* ingénu(e), naïf (naïve).

ingot [ˈɪŋgət] *n* lingot *m*.

ingrained [ˌɪnˈgreɪnd] *adj* - 1. [dirt] incrusté(e) - 2. *fig* [belief, hatred] enraciné(e).

ingratiating [ɪnˈgreɪʃɪeɪtɪŋ] *adj* doucereux(euse), mielleux(euse).

ingredient [ɪnˈgriːdjənt] *n* ingrédient *m* ; *fig* élément *m*.

inhabit [ɪnˈhæbɪt] *vt* habiter.

inhabitant [ɪnˈhæbɪtənt] *n* habitant *m*, -e *f*.

inhale [ɪnˈheɪl] <> *vt* inhaler, respirer. <> *vi* [breathe in] respirer.

inhaler [ɪnˈheɪləʳ] *n* MED inhalateur *m*.

inherent [ɪnˈhɪərənt, ɪnˈherənt] *adj* : ~ (in) inhérent(e) (à).

inherently [ɪnˈhɪərəntlɪ, ɪnˈherəntlɪ] *adv* fondamentalement, en soi.

inherit [ɪnˈherɪt] <> *vt* : to ~ sthg (from sb) hériter qqch (de qqn). <> *vi* hériter.

inheritance [ɪnˈherɪtəns] *n* héritage *m*.

inhibit [ɪnˈhɪbɪt] *vt* - 1. [prevent] empêcher - 2. PSYCH inhiber.

inhibition [ˌɪnhɪˈbɪʃn] *n* inhibition *f*.

inhospitable [ˌɪnhɒˈspɪtəbl] *adj* inhospitalier(ère).

in-house <> *adj* interne ; [staff] de la maison. <> *adv* [produce, work] sur place.

inhuman [ɪnˈhjuːmən] *adj* inhumain(e).

initial [ɪˈnɪʃl] <> *adj* initial(e), premier(ère) ; ~ letter initiale *f*. <> *vt* parapher. ➡ **initials** *npl* initiales *fpl*.

initially [ɪˈnɪʃəlɪ] *adv* initialement, au début.

initiate [ɪˈnɪʃɪeɪt] *vt* - 1. [talks] engager ; [scheme] ébaucher, inaugurer - 2. [teach] : to ~ sb into sthg initier qqn à qqch.

initiative [ɪˈnɪʃətɪv] *n* - 1. [gen] initiative *f* - 2. [advantage] : to have the ~ avoir l'avantage *m*.

inject [ɪnˈdʒekt] *vt* - 1. MED : to ~ sb with sthg, to ~ sthg into sb injecter qqch à qqn - 2. *fig* [excitement] insuffler ; [money] injecter.

injection [ɪnˈdʒekʃn] *n lit & fig* injection *f*.

injure [ˈɪndʒəʳ] *vt* - 1. [limb, person] blesser ; to ~ one's arm se blesser au bras - 2. *fig* [reputation, chances] compromettre.

injured [ˈɪndʒəd] <> *adj* [limb, person] blessé(e). <> *npl* : the ~ les blessés *mpl*.

injury [ˈɪndʒərɪ] *n* - 1. [to limb, person] blessure *f* ; to do o.s. an ~ se blesser - 2. *fig* [to reputation] coup *m*, atteinte *f*.

injury time *n* (U) arrêts *mpl* de jeu.

injustice [ɪnˈdʒʌstɪs] *n* injustice *f* ; to do sb an ~ se montrer injuste envers qqn.

ink [ɪŋk] *n* encre *f*.

ink-jet printer *n* COMPUT imprimante *f* à jet d'encre.

inkling [ˈɪŋklɪŋ] *n* : to have an ~ of avoir une petite idée de.

inlaid [ˌɪnˈleɪd] *adj* : ~ (with) incrusté(e) (de).

inland [*adj* ˈɪnlənd, *adv* ɪnˈlænd] <> *adj* intérieur(e). <> *adv* à l'intérieur.

Inland Revenue *n Br* : the ~ ≃ le fisc.

in-laws *npl inf* [parents-in-law] beaux-parents *mpl* ; [others] belle-famille *f*.

inlet [ˈɪnlet] *n* - 1. [of lake, sea] avancée *f* - 2. TECH arrivée *f*.

inmate [ˈɪnmeɪt] *n* [of prison] détenu *m*, -e *f* ; [of mental hospital] interné *m*, -e *f*.

inn [ɪn] *n* auberge *f*.

innate [ɪˈneɪt] *adj* inné(e).

inner [ˈɪnəʳ] *adj* - 1. [on inside] interne, intérieur(e) - 2. [feelings] intime.

inner city *n* : the ~ les quartiers *mpl* pauvres.

inner tube *n* chambre *f* à air.

innings [ˈɪnɪŋz] (*pl inv*) *n Br* CRICKET tour *m* de batte.

innocence [ˈɪnəsəns] *n* innocence *f*.

innocent [ˈɪnəsənt] <> *adj* innocent(e) ; ~ of [crime] non coupable de. <> *n* innocent *m*, -e *f*.

innocuous [ɪˈnɒkjʊəs] *adj* inoffensif(ive).

innovation [ˌɪnəˈveɪʃn] *n* innovation *f*.

innovative [ˈɪnəvətɪv] *adj* - 1. [idea, design] innovateur(trice) - 2. [person, company] novateur(trice).

innuendo [ˌɪnjuːˈendəʊ] (*pl -es* OR *-s*) *n* insinuation *f*.

innumerable [ɪˈnjuːmərəbl] *adj* innombrable.

inoculate [ɪˈnɒkjʊleɪt] *vt* : to ~ sb (with sthg) inoculer (qqch à) qqn.

inordinately [ɪˈnɔːdɪnətlɪ] *adv* excessivement.

in-patient *n* malade hospitalisé *m*, malade hospitalisée *f*.

input ['ɪnput] (*pt* & *pp* input OR -ted) ◇ *n* - **1.** [contribution] contribution *f*, concours *m* - **2.** COMPUT & ELEC entrée *f*. ◇ *vt* COMPUT entrer.

inquest ['ɪnkwest] *n* enquête *f*.

inquire [ɪn'kwaɪə'] ◇ *vt* : **to ~ when/ whether/how** ... demander quand/si/ comment ... ◇ *vi* : **to ~ (about)** se renseigner (sur). **◆ inquire after** *vt fus* s'enquérir de. **◆ inquire into** *vt fus* enquêter sur.

inquiry [ɪn'kwaɪərɪ] *n* - **1.** [question] demande *f* de renseignements ; **'Inquiries'** 'renseignements' - **2.** [investigation] enquête *f*.

inquiry desk *n* bureau *m* de renseignements.

inquisitive [ɪn'kwɪzətɪv] *adj* inquisiteur(trice).

inroads ['ɪnrəʊdz] *npl* : **to make ~ into** [savings] entamer.

insane [ɪn'seɪn] *adj* fou (folle).

insanity [ɪn'sænətɪ] *n* folie *f*.

insatiable [ɪn'seɪʃəbl] *adj* insatiable.

inscription [ɪn'skrɪpʃn] *n* - **1.** [engraved] inscription *f* - **2.** [written] dédicace *f*.

inscrutable [ɪn'skruːtəbl] *adj* impénétrable.

insect ['ɪnsekt] *n* insecte *m*.

insecticide [ɪn'sektɪsaɪd] *n* insecticide *m*.

insect repellent *n* lotion *f* antimoustiques.

insecure [ˌɪnsɪ'kjʊə'] *adj* - **1.** [person] anxieux(euse) - **2.** [job, investment] incertain(e).

insensible [ɪn'sensəbl] *adj* - **1.** [unconscious] inconscient(e) - **2.** [unaware, not feeling] : **~ of/to** insensible à.

insensitive [ɪn'sensətɪv] *adj* : **~ (to)** insensible (à).

inseparable [ɪn'seprəbl] *adj* inséparable.

insert [*vb* ɪn'sɜːt, *n* 'ɪnsɜːt] ◇ *vt* : **to ~ sthg (in** OR **into)** insérer qqch (dans). ◇ *n* [in newspaper] encart *m*.

insertion [ɪn'sɜːʃn] *n* insertion *f*.

in-service training *n* Br formation *f* en cours d'emploi.

inshore [*adj* 'ɪnʃɔː', *adv* ɪn'ʃɔː'] ◇ *adj* côtier(ère). ◇ *adv* [be situated] près de la côte ; [move] vers la côte.

inside [ɪn'saɪd] ◇ *prep* - **1.** [building, object] à l'intérieur de, dans ; [group, organization] au sein de - **2.** [time] : **~ three weeks** en moins de trois semaines. ◇ *adv* - **1.** [gen] dedans, à l'intérieur ; **to go ~** entrer ; **come ~!** entrez! - **2.** *prison sl* en taule. ◇ *adj* intérieur(e). ◇ *n* - **1.** [interior] : **the ~** l'intérieur *m* ; **~ out** [clothes] à l'envers ; **to know sthg ~ out** connaître qqch à fond - **2.** AUT : **the ~** [in UK] la gauche ; [in Europe, US etc] la droite. **◆ insides** *npl inf* tripes *fpl*. **◆ inside of** *prep* Am [building, object] à l'intérieur de, dans.

inside lane *n* AUT [in UK] voie *f* de gauche ; [in Europe, US etc] voie de droite.

insight ['ɪnsaɪt] *n* - **1.** [wisdom] sagacité *f*, perspicacité *f* - **2.** [glimpse] : **~ (into)** aperçu *m* (de).

insignificant [ˌɪnsɪg'nɪfɪkənt] *adj* insignifiant(e).

insincere [ˌɪnsɪn'sɪə'] *adj* pas sincère.

insinuate [ɪn'sɪnjʊeɪt] *vt* insinuer, laisser entendre.

insipid [ɪn'sɪpɪd] *adj* insipide.

insist [ɪn'sɪst] ◇ *vt* - **1.** [claim] : **to ~ (that)** ... insister sur le fait que ... - **2.** [demand] : **to ~ (that)** ... insister pour que (+ *subjunctive*) ... ◇ *vi* : **to ~ (on sthg)** exiger (qqch) ; **to ~ on doing sthg** tenir à faire qqch, vouloir absolument faire qqch.

insistent [ɪn'sɪstənt] *adj* - **1.** [determined] insistant(e) ; **to be ~ on** insister sur - **2.** [continual] incessant(e).

insofar [ˌɪnsəʊ'faː'] **◆ insofar as** *conj* dans la mesure où.

insole ['ɪnsəʊl] *n* semelle *f* intérieure.

insolent ['ɪnsələnt] *adj* insolent(e).

insolvent [ɪn'sɒlvənt] *adj* insolvable.

insomnia [ɪn'sɒmnɪə] *n* insomnie *f*.

inspect [ɪn'spekt] *vt* - **1.** [letter, person] examiner - **2.** [factory, troops etc] inspecter.

inspection [ɪn'spekʃn] *n* - **1.** [investigation] examen *m* - **2.** [official check] inspection *f*.

inspector [ɪn'spektə'] *n* inspecteur *m*, trice *f*.

inspiration [ˌɪnspə'reɪʃn] *n* inspiration *f*.

inspire [ɪn'spaɪə'] *vt* : **to ~ sb to do sthg** pousser OR encourager qqn à faire qqch ; **to ~ sb with sthg, to ~ sthg in sb** inspirer qqch à qqn.

install, instal *Am* [ɪn'stɔːl] *vt* [fit] installer.

installation [ˌɪnstə'leɪʃn] *n* installation *f*.

instalment *Br*, **installment** *Am* [ɪn'stɔːlmənt] *n* - **1.** [payment] acompte *m* ; **in ~s** par acomptes - **2.** [episode] épisode *m*.

instance ['ɪnstəns] *n* exemple *m* ; **for ~** par exemple.

instant ['ɪnstənt] <> *adj* - **1.** [immediate] instantané(e), immédiat(e) - **2.** [coffee] soluble ; [food] à préparation rapide. <> *n* instant *m* ; **the ~ (that)** ... dès or aussitôt que ... ; **this ~** tout de suite, immédiatement.

instantly ['ɪnstəntlɪ] *adv* immédiatement.

instead [ɪn'sted] *adv* au lieu de cela. ➡ **instead of** *prep* au lieu de ; **~ of him** à sa place.

instep ['ɪnstep] *n* cou-de-pied *m*.

instigate ['ɪnstɪgeɪt] *vt* être à l'origine de, entreprendre.

instil *Br*, **instill** *Am* [ɪn'stɪl] *vt* : **to ~ sthg in** or **into sb** instiller qqch à qqn.

instinct ['ɪnstɪŋkt] *n* - **1.** [intuition] instinct *m* - **2.** [impulse] réaction *f*, mouvement *m*.

instinctive [ɪn'stɪŋktɪv] *adj* instinctif(ive).

institute ['ɪnstɪtjuːt] <> *n* institut *m*. <> *vt* instituer.

institution [ˌɪnstɪ'tjuːʃn] *n* institution *f*.

instruct [ɪn'strʌkt] *vt* - **1.** [tell, order] : **to ~ sb to do sthg** charger qqn de faire qqch - **2.** [teach] instruire ; **to ~ sb in sthg** enseigner qqch à qqn.

instruction [ɪn'strʌkʃn] *n* instruction *f*. ➡ **instructions** *npl* mode *m* d'emploi, instructions *fpl*.

instructor [ɪn'strʌktə'] *n* - **1.** [gen] instructeur *m*, -trice *f*, moniteur *m*, -trice *f* - **2.** *Am* SCH enseignant *m*, -e *f*.

instrument ['ɪnstrʊmənt] *n lit & fig* instrument *m*.

instrumental [ˌɪnstrʊ'mentl] *adj* [important, helpful] : **to be ~ in** contribuer à.

instrument panel *n* tableau *m* de bord.

insubordinate [ˌɪnsə'bɔːdɪnət] *adj* insubordonné(e).

insubstantial [ˌɪnsəb'stænʃl] *adj* [structure] peu solide ; [meal] peu substantiel (elle).

insufficient [ˌɪnsə'fɪʃnt] *adj fml* insuffisant(e).

insular ['ɪnsjʊlə'] *adj* [outlook] borné(e) ; [person] à l'esprit étroit.

insulate ['ɪnsjʊleɪt] *vt* - **1.** [loft, cable] isoler ; [hot water tank] calorifuger - **2.** [protect] : **to ~ sb against** or **from sthg** protéger qqn de qqch.

insulating tape ['ɪnsjʊleɪtɪŋ-] *n Br* chatterton *m*.

insulation [ˌɪnsjʊ'leɪʃn] *n* isolation *f*.

insulin ['ɪnsjʊlɪn] *n* insuline *f*.

insult [*vt* ɪn'sʌlt, *n* 'ɪnsʌlt] <> *vt* insulter, injurier. <> *n* insulte *f*, injure *f*.

insuperable [ɪn'suːprəbl] *adj fml* insurmontable.

insurance [ɪn'ʃʊərəns] *n* - **1.** [against fire, accident, theft] assurance *f* - **2.** *fig* [safeguard, protection] protection *f*, garantie *f*.

insurance policy *n* police *f* d'assurance.

insure [ɪn'ʃʊə'] <> *vt* - **1.** [against fire, accident, theft] : **to ~ sb/sthg against sthg** assurer qqn/qqch contre qqch - **2.** *Am* [make certain] s'assurer. <> *vi* [prevent] : **to ~ against** se protéger de.

insurer [ɪn'ʃʊərə'] *n* assureur *m*.

insurmountable [ˌɪnsə'maʊntəbl] *adj fml* insurmontable.

intact [ɪn'tækt] *adj* intact(e).

intake ['ɪnteɪk] *n* - **1.** [amount consumed] consommation *f* - **2.** [people recruited] admission *f* - **3.** [inlet] prise *f*, arrivée *f*.

integral ['ɪntɪgrəl] *adj* intégral(e) ; **to be ~ to sthg** faire partie intégrante de qqch.

integrate ['ɪntɪgreɪt] <> *vi* s'intégrer. <> *vt* intégrer.

integrity [ɪn'tegrətɪ] *n* - **1.** [honour] intégrité *f*, honnêteté *f* - **2.** *fml* [wholeness] intégrité *f*, totalité *f*.

intellect ['ɪntəlekt] *n* - **1.** [ability to think] intellect *m* - **2.** [cleverness] intelligence *f*.

intellectual [ˌɪntə'lektjʊəl] <> *adj* intellectuel(elle). <> *n* intellectuel *m*, -elle *f*.

intelligence [ɪn'telɪdʒəns] *n (U)* - **1.** [ability to think] intelligence *f* - **2.** [information service] service *m* de renseignements - **3.** [information] informations *fpl*, renseignements *mpl*.

intelligent [ɪn'telɪdʒənt] *adj* intelligent(e).

intelligent card *n* carte *f* à puce or à mémoire.

intend [ɪn'tend] *vt* [mean] avoir l'intention de ; **to be ~ed for** être destiné à ; **to be ~ed to do sthg** être destiné à faire qqch, viser à faire qqch ; **to ~ doing** or **to do sthg** avoir l'intention de faire qqch.

intended [ɪn'tendɪd] *adj* [result] voulu(e) ; [victim] visé(e).

intense [ɪn'tens] *adj* - **1.** [gen] intense - **2.** [serious - person] sérieux(euse).

intensely [ɪn'tenslɪ] *adv* - **1.** [irritating, boring] extrêmement ; [suffer] énormément - **2.** [look] intensément.

intensify [ɪn'tensɪfaɪ] <> *vt* intensifier, augmenter. <> *vi* s'intensifier.

intensity [ɪn'tensətɪ] *n* intensité *f*.

intensive [ɪn'tensɪv] *adj* intensif(ive).

intensive care *n* : to be in ~ être en réanimation.

intent [ɪn'tent] <> *adj* - **1.** [absorbed] absorbé(e) - **2.** [determined] : to be ~ on OR upon doing sthg être résolu(e) OR décidé(e) à faire qqch. <> *n fml* intention *f*, dessein *m* ; to all ~s and purposes pratiquement, virtuellement.

intention [ɪn'tenʃn] *n* intention *f*.

intentional [ɪn'tenʃənl] *adj* intentionnel(elle), voulu(e).

intently [ɪn'tentlɪ] *adv* avec attention, attentivement.

interact [ˌɪntər'ækt] *vi* - **1.** [communicate, work together] : to ~ (with sb) communiquer (avec qqn) - **2.** [react] : to ~ (with sthg) interagir (avec qqch).

intercede [ˌɪntə'siːd] *vi fml* : to ~ (with sb) intercéder (auprès de qqn).

intercept [ˌɪntə'sept] *vt* intercepter.

interchange [*n* 'ɪntətʃeɪndʒ, *vb* ˌɪntə'tʃeɪndʒ] <> *n* - **1.** [exchange] échange *m* - **2.** [road junction] échangeur *m*. <> *vt* échanger.

interchangeable [ˌɪntə'tʃeɪndʒəbl] *adj* : ~ (with) interchangeable (avec).

intercity [ˌɪntə'sɪtɪ] *n* système de trains rapides reliant les grandes villes en Grande-Bretagne ; **Intercity 125®** train rapide pouvant rouler à 125 miles (200 km) à l'heure.

intercom ['ɪntəkɒm] *n* Interphone® *m*.

intercourse ['ɪntəkɔːs] *n* (U) [sexual] rapports *mpl* (sexuels).

interest ['ɪntrəst] <> *n* - **1.** [gen] intérêt *m* ; to lose ~ se désintéresser - **2.** [hobby] centre *m* d'intérêt - **3.** (U) FIN intérêt *m*, intérêts *mpl*. <> *vt* intéresser.

interested ['ɪntrəstɪd] *adj* intéressé(e), to be ~ in s'intéresser à ; I'm not ~ in that cela ne m'intéresse pas ; to be ~ in doing sthg avoir envie de faire qqch.

interesting ['ɪntrəstɪŋ] *adj* intéressant(e).

interest rate *n* taux *m* d'intérêt.

interface ['ɪntəfeɪs] *n* - **1.** COMPUT interface *f* - **2.** *fig* [junction] rapports *mpl*, relations *fpl*.

interfere [ˌɪntə'fɪər] *vi* - **1.** [meddle] : to ~ in sthg s'immiscer dans qqch, se mêler de qqch - **2.** [damage] : to ~ with sthg gêner OR contrarier qqch ; [routine] déranger qqch.

interference [ˌɪntə'fɪərəns] *n* (U) - **1.** [meddling] : ~ (with OR in) ingérence *f*

(dans), intrusion *f* (dans) - **2.** TELEC parasites *mpl*.

interim ['ɪntərɪm] <> *adj* provisoire. <> *n* : in the ~ dans l'intérim, entre-temps.

interior [ɪn'tɪərɪər] <> *adj* - **1.** [inner] intérieur(e) - **2.** POL de l'Intérieur. <> *n* intérieur *m*.

interlock [ˌɪntə'lɒk] *vi* [gears] s'enclencher, s'engrener ; [fingers] s'entrelacer.

interloper ['ɪntələupə'] *n* intrus *m*, -e *f*.

interlude ['ɪntəluːd] *n* - **1.** [pause] intervalle *m* - **2.** [interval] interlude *m*.

intermediary [ˌɪntə'miːdjərɪ] *n* intermédiaire *mf*.

intermediate [ˌɪntə'miːdjət] *adj* - **1.** [transitional] intermédiaire - **2.** [post-beginner - level] moyen(enne) ; [- student, group] de niveau moyen.

interminable [ɪn'tɜːmɪnəbl] *adj* interminable, sans fin.

intermission [ˌɪntə'mɪʃn] *n* entracte *m*.

intermittent [ˌɪntə'mɪtənt] *adj* intermittent(e).

intern [*vb* ɪn'tɜːn, *n* 'ɪntɜːn] <> *vt* interner. <> *n Am* [gen] stagiaire *mf* ; MED interne *mf*.

internal [ɪn'tɜːnl] *adj* - **1.** [gen] interne - **2.** [within country] intérieur(e).

internally [ɪn'tɜːnəlɪ] *adv* - **1.** [within the body] : to bleed ~ faire une hémorragie interne - **2.** [within country] à l'intérieur - **3.** [within organization] intérieurement.

Internal Revenue *n Am* : the ~ ≃ le fisc.

international [ˌɪntə'næʃənl] <> *adj* international(e). <> *n Br* SPORT - **1.** [match] match *m* international - **2.** [player] international *m*, -e *f*.

internet, Internet ['ɪntənet] *n* : the ~ l'Internet *m* ; on the ~ sur l'Internet.

internet café, Internet café *n* cybercafé *m*.

Internet Service Provider *n* fournisseur *m* d'accès (à Internet).

interpret [ɪn'tɜːprɪt] <> *vt* : to ~ sthg (as) interpréter qqch (comme). <> *vi* [translate] faire l'interprète.

interpreter [ɪn'tɜːprɪtə'] *n* interprète *mf*.

interracial [ˌɪntə'reɪʃl] *adj* entre des races différentes, racial(e).

interrelate [ˌɪntərɪ'leɪt] <> *vt* mettre en corrélation. <> *vi* : to ~ (with) être lié(e) (à), être en corrélation (avec).

interrogate [ɪn'terəgeɪt] *vt* interroger.

interrogation [ɪn,terə'geɪʃn] *n* interrogatoire *m*.

interrogation mark *n Am* point *m* d'interrogation.

interrogative [ˌɪntəˈrɒgətɪv] GRAMM ◇ *adj* interrogatif(ive). ◇ *n* interrogatif *m*.

interrupt [ˌɪntəˈrʌpt] ◇ *vt* interrompre ; [calm] rompre. ◇ *vi* interrompre.

interruption [ˌɪntəˈrʌpʃn] *n* interruption *f*.

intersect [ˌɪntəˈsekt] ◇ *vi* s'entrecroiser, s'entrecouper. ◇ *vt* croiser, couper.

intersection [ˌɪntəˈsekʃn] *n* [in road] croisement *m*, carrefour *m*.

intersperse [ˌɪntəˈspɜːs] *vt* : **to be ~d with** être émaillé(e) de, être entremêlé(e) de.

interstate (highway) [ˈɪntəsteɪt-] *n Am* autoroute *f*.

interval [ˈɪntəvl] *n* - **1.** [gen] intervalle *m* ; **at ~s** par intervalles, **at monthly/yearly ~s** tous les mois/ans - **2.** *Br* [at play, concert] entracte *m*.

intervene [ˌɪntəˈviːn] *vi* - **1.** [person, police] : **to ~ (in)** intervenir (dans), s'interposer (dans) - **2.** [event, war, strike] survenir - **3.** [time] s'écouler.

intervention [ˌɪntəˈvenʃn] *n* intervention *f*.

interview [ˈɪntəvjuː] ◇ *n* - **1.** [for job] entrevue *f*, entretien *m* - **2.** PRESS interview *f*. ◇ *vt* - **1.** [for job] faire passer une entrevue OR un entretien à - **2.** PRESS interviewer.

interviewer [ˈɪntəvjuːəʳ] *n* - **1.** [for job] personne *f* qui fait passer une entrevue - **2.** PRESS interviewer *m*.

intestine [ɪnˈtestɪn] *n* intestin *m*.

intimacy [ˈɪntɪməsɪ] *n* - **1.** [closeness] : **~ (between/with)** intimité *f* (entre/avec) - **2.** [intimate remark] familiarité *f*.

intimate [*adj* ˈɪntɪmət, *vb* ˈɪntɪmeɪt] ◇ *adj* - **1.** [gen] intime - **2.** [detailed - knowledge] approfondi(e). ◇ *vt fml* faire savoir, faire connaître.

intimately [ˈɪntɪmətlɪ] *adv* - **1.** [very closely] étroitement - **2.** [as close friends] intimement - **3.** [in detail] à fond.

intimidate [ɪnˈtɪmɪdeɪt] *vt* intimider.

into [ˈɪntʊ] *prep* - **1.** [inside] dans - **2.** [against] : **to bump ~ sthg** se cogner contre qqch ; **to crash ~** rentrer dans - **3.** [referring to change in state] en ; **to translate sthg ~ Spanish** traduire qqch en espagnol - **4.** [concerning] : **research/ investigation ~** recherche/enquête sur - **5.** MATH : **3 ~ 2** 2 divisé par 3 - **6.** *inf* [interested in] : **to be ~ sthg** être passionné(e) par qqch.

intolerable [ɪnˈtɒlrəbl] *adj* intolérable, insupportable.

intolerance [ɪnˈtɒlərəns] *n* intolérance *f*.

intolerant [ɪnˈtɒlərənt] *adj* intolérant(e).

intoxicated [ɪnˈtɒksɪkeɪtɪd] *adj* - **1.** [drunk] ivre - **2.** *fig* [excited] : **to be ~ by** OR **with sthg** être grisé(e) OR enivré(e) par qqch.

intractable [ɪnˈtræktəbl] *adj* - **1.** [stubborn] intraitable - **2.** [insoluble] insoluble.

intranet, Intranet [ˈɪntrənet] *n* intranet *m*.

intransitive [ɪnˈtrænzətɪv] *adj* intransitif(ive).

intravenous [ˌɪntrəˈviːnəs] *adj* intraveineux(euse).

in-tray *n* casier *m* des affaires à traiter.

intricate [ˈɪntrɪkət] *adj* compliqué(e).

intrigue [ɪnˈtriːg] ◇ *n* intrigue *f*. ◇ *vt* intriguer, exciter la curiosité de.

intriguing [ɪnˈtriːgɪŋ] *adj* fascinant(e).

intrinsic [ɪnˈtrɪnsɪk] *adj* intrinsèque.

introduce [ˌɪntrəˈdjuːs] *vt* - **1.** [present] présenter ; **to ~ sb to sb** présenter qqn à qqn - **2.** [bring in] : **to ~ sthg (to** OR **into)** introduire qqch (dans) - **3.** [allow to experience] : **to ~ sb to sthg** initier qqn à qqch, faire découvrir qqch à qqn - **4.** [signal beginning of] annoncer.

introduction [ˌɪntrəˈdʌkʃn] *n* - **1.** [in book, of new method etc] introduction *f* - **2.** [of people] : **~ (to sb)** présentation *f* (à qqn).

introductory [ˌɪntrəˈdʌktrɪ] *adj* d'introduction, préliminaire.

introvert [ˈɪntrəvɜːt] *n* introverti *m*, -e *f*.

introverted [ˈɪntrəvɜːtɪd] *adj* introverti(e).

intrude [ɪnˈtruːd] *vi* faire intrusion ; **to ~ on sb** déranger qqn.

intruder [ɪnˈtruːdəʳ] *n* intrus *m*, -e *f*.

intrusive [ɪnˈtruːsɪv] *adj* gênant(e), importun(e).

intuition [ˌɪntjuːˈɪʃn] *n* intuition *f*.

inundate [ˈɪnʌndeɪt] *vt* - **1.** *fml* [flood] inonder - **2.** [overwhelm] : **to be ~d with** être submergé(e) de.

invade [ɪnˈveɪd] *vt* - **1.** MIL & *fig* envahir - **2.** [disturb - privacy etc] violer.

invalid [*adj* ɪnˈvælɪd, *n* ˈɪnvəlɪd] ◇ *adj* - **1.** [illegal, unacceptable] non valide, non valable - **2.** [not reasonable] non valable. ◇ *n* invalide *mf*.

invaluable [ɪnˈvæljʊəbl] *adj* : **~ (to)** [help,

advice, person] précieux(euse) (pour) ; [experience, information] inestimable (pour).

invariably [ɪnˈveərɪəblɪ] *adv* invariablement, toujours.

invasion [ɪnˈveɪʒn] *n lit & fig* invasion *f*.

invent [ɪnˈvent] *vt* inventer.

invention [ɪnˈvenʃn] *n* invention *f*.

inventive [ɪnˈventɪv] *adj* inventif(ive).

inventor [ɪnˈventəʳ] *n* inventeur *m*, -trice *f*.

inventory [ˈɪnvəntrɪ] *n* - **1.** [list] inventaire *m* - **2.** *Am* [goods] stock *m*.

invert [ɪnˈvɜːt] *vt* retourner.

inverted commas [ɪnˌvɜːtɪd-] *npl Br* guillemets *mpl*.

invest [ɪnˈvest] <> *vt* - **1.** [money] : to ~ sthg (in) investir qqch (dans) - **2.** [time, energy] : to ~ sthg in sthg/in doing sthg consacrer qqch à qqch/à faire qqch, employer qqch à qqch/à faire qqch. <> *vi* - **1.** FIN : to ~ (in sthg) investir (dans qqch) - **2.** *fig* [buy] : to ~ in sthg se payer qqch, s'acheter qqch.

Investigate [ɪnˈvestɪgeɪt] *vt* enquêter sur, faire une enquête sur ; [subj: scientist] faire des recherches sur.

investigation [ɪnˌvestɪˈgeɪʃn] *n* - **1.** [enquiry] : ~ (into) enquête *f* (sur) ; [scientific] recherches *fpl* (sur) - **2.** (*U*) [investigating] investigation *f*.

investment [ɪnˈvestmənt] *n* - **1.** FIN investissement *m*, placement *m* - **2.** [of energy] dépense *f*.

investor [ɪnˈvestəʳ] *n* investisseur *m*.

inveterate [ɪnˈvetərət] *adj* invétéré(e).

invidious [ɪnˈvɪdɪəs] *adj* [task] ingrat(e) ; [comparison] injuste.

invigilate [ɪnˈvɪdʒɪleɪt] *Br* <> *vi* surveiller les candidats (à un examen). <> *vt* surveiller.

invigorating [ɪnˈvɪgəreɪtɪŋ] *adj* tonifiant(e), vivifiant(e).

invincible [ɪnˈvɪnsɪbl] *adj* [army, champion] invincible ; [record] imbattable.

invisible [ɪnˈvɪzɪbl] *adj* invisible.

invitation [ˌɪnvɪˈteɪʃn] *n* [request] invitation *f*.

invite [ɪnˈvaɪt] *vt* - **1.** [ask to come] : to ~ sb (to) inviter qqn (à) - **2.** [ask politely] : to ~ sb to do sthg inviter qqn à faire qqch - **3.** [encourage] : to ~ trouble aller au devant des ennuis ; to ~ gossip faire causer.

inviting [ɪnˈvaɪtɪŋ] *adj* attrayant(e), agréable ; [food] appétissant(e).

invoice [ˈɪnvɔɪs] <> *n* facture *f*. <> *vt*

- **1.** [client] envoyer la facture à - **2.** [goods] facturer.

invoke [ɪnˈvəʊk] *vt* - **1.** *fml* [law, act] invoquer - **2.** [feelings] susciter, faire naître ; [help] demander, implorer.

involuntary [ɪnˈvɒləntrɪ] *adj* involontaire.

involve [ɪnˈvɒlv] *vt* - **1.** [entail] nécessiter ; what's ~d? de quoi s'agit-il? ; to ~ doing sthg nécessiter de faire qqch - **2.** [concern, affect] toucher - **3.** [person] : to ~ sb in sthg impliquer qqn dans qqch.

involved [ɪnˈvɒlvd] *adj* - **1.** [complex] complexe, compliqué(e) - **2.** [participating] : to be ~ in sthg participer prendre part à qqch - **3.** [in relationship] : to be ~ with sb avoir des relations intimes avec qqn.

involvement [ɪnˈvɒlvmənt] *n* - **1.** [participation] : ~ (in) participation *f* (à) - **2.** [concern, enthusiasm] : ~ (in) engagement *m* (dans).

inward [ˈɪnwəd] <> *adj* - **1.** [inner] intérieur(e) - **2.** [towards the inside] vers l'intérieur. <> *adv Am* = **inwards**.

inwards [ˈɪnwədz] *adv* vers l'intérieur.

iodine [*Br* ˈaɪədiːn, *Am* ˈaɪədaɪn] *n* iode *m*.

iota [aɪˈəʊtə] *n* brin *m*, grain *m*,

IOU (*abbr of* **I owe you**) *n* reconnaissance *f* de dette.

IQ (*abbr of* **intelligence quotient**) *n* QI *m*.

IRA *n* (*abbr of* **Irish Republican Army**) IRA *f*.

Iran [ɪˈrɑːn] *n* Iran *m*.

Iranian [ɪˈreɪnjən] <> *adj* iranien(enne). <> *n* Iranien *m*, -enne *f*.

Iraq [ɪˈrɑːk] *n* Iraq *m*, Irak *m*.

Iraqi [ɪˈrɑːkɪ] <> *adj* iraquien(enne), irakien(enne). <> *n* Iraquien *m*, -enne *f*, Irakien *m*, -enne *f*.

irate [aɪˈreɪt] *adj* furieux(euse).

Ireland [ˈaɪələnd] *n* Irlande *f*.

iris [ˈaɪərɪs] (*pl* -es [-iːz]) *n* iris *m*.

Irish [ˈaɪrɪʃ] <> *adj* irlandais(e). <> *n* [language] irlandais *m*. <> *npl* : the ~ les Irlandais.

Irishman [ˈaɪrɪʃmən] (*pl* -men [-mən]) *n* Irlandais *m*.

Irish Sea *n* : the ~ la mer d'Irlande.

Irishwoman [ˈaɪrɪʃˌwʊmən] (*pl* -women [-ˌwɪmɪn]) *n* Irlandaise *f*.

irksome [ˈɜːksəm] *adj* ennuyeux(euse), assommant(e).

iron [ˈaɪən] <> *adj* - **1.** [made of iron] de OR en fer - **2.** *fig* [very strict] de fer. <> *n* - **1.** [metal, golf club] fer *m* - **2.** [for clothes] fer *m* à repasser. <> *vt* repasser. ◆ **iron**

out *vt sep fig* [difficulties] aplanir ; [problems] résoudre.

Iron Curtain *n* : **the ~** le rideau de fer.

ironic(al) [aɪˈrɒnɪk(l)] *adj* ironique.

ironing [ˈaɪənɪŋ] *n* repassage *m*.

ironing board *n* planche *f* OR table *f* à repasser.

ironmonger [ˈaɪənˌmʌŋgəʳ] *n Br* quincaillier *m* ; **~'s (shop)** quincaillerie *f*.

irony [ˈaɪrənɪ] *n* ironie *f*.

irrational [ɪˈræʃənl] *adj* irrationnel(elle), déraisonnable ; [person] non rationnel (elle).

irreconcilable [ɪˌrekənˈsaɪləbl] *adj* inconciliable.

irregular [ɪˈregjʊləʳ] *adj* irrégulier(ère).

irrelevant [ɪˈreləvənt] *adj* sans rapport.

irreparable [ɪˈrepərəbl] *adj* irréparable.

irreplaceable [ˌɪrɪˈpleɪsəbl] *adj* irremplaçable.

irrepressible [ˌɪrɪˈpresəbl] *adj* [enthusiasm] que rien ne peut entamer ; **he's ~** il est d'une bonne humeur à toute épreuve.

irresistible [ˌɪrɪˈzɪstəbl] *adj* irrésistible.

irrespective [ˌɪrɪˈspektɪv] ➡ **irrespective of** *prep* sans tenir compte de.

irresponsible [ˌɪrɪˈspɒnsəbl] *adj* irresponsable.

irrigate [ˈɪrɪgeɪt] *vt* irriguer.

irrigation [ˌɪrɪˈgeɪʃn] <> *n* irrigation *f.* <> *comp* d'irrigation.

irritable [ˈɪrɪtəbl] *adj* irritable.

irritate [ˈɪrɪteɪt] *vt* irriter.

irritating [ˈɪrɪteɪtɪŋ] *adj* irritant(e).

irritation [ɪrɪˈteɪʃn] *n* - **1.** [anger, soreness] irritation *f* - **2.** [cause of anger] source *f* d'irritation.

IRS (*abbr of* **Internal Revenue Service**) *n Am* : **the ~** ≃ le fisc.

is [ɪz] ➡ be.

Islam [ˈɪzlɑːm] *n* islam *m*.

island [ˈaɪlənd] *n* - **1.** [isle] île *f* - **2.** AUT refuge *m* pour piétons.

islander [ˈaɪləndəʳ] *n* habitant *m*, -e *f* d'une île.

isle [aɪl] *n* île *f*.

Isle of Man *n* : **the ~** l'île *f* de Man.

Isle of Wight [-waɪt] *n* : **the ~** l'île *f* de Wight.

isn't [ˈɪznt] = is not.

isobar [ˈaɪsəbɑːʳ] *n* isobare *f*.

isolate [ˈaɪsəleɪt] *vt* : **to ~ sb/sthg (from)** isoler qqn/qqch (de).

isolated [ˈaɪsəleɪtɪd] *adj* isolé(e).

ISP (*abbr of* **Internet Service Provider**) *n* F.A.I. *m*.

Israel [ˈɪzreɪəl] *n* Israël *m*.

Israeli [ɪzˈreɪlɪ] <> *adj* israélien(enne). <> *n* Israélien *m*, -enne *f*.

issue [ˈɪʃuː] <> *n* - **1.** [important subject] question *f*, problème *m* ; **to make an ~ of sthg** faire toute une affaire de qqch ; **at ~** en question, en cause - **2.** [edition] numéro *m* - **3.** [bringing out - of banknotes, shares] émission *f.* <> *vt* - **1.** [make public - decree, statement] faire ; [- warning] lancer - **2.** [bring out - banknotes, shares] émettre ; [- book] publier - **3.** [passport etc] délivrer.

isthmus [ˈɪsməs] *n* isthme *m*.

it [ɪt] *pron* - **1.** [referring to specific person or thing - subj] il (elle) ; [- direct object] le (la), l' *(+ vowel or silent 'h')* ; [- indirect object] lui ; **did you find ~?** tu l'as trouvé(e)? ; **give ~ to me at once** donne-moi ça tout de suite - **2.** [with prepositions] : **in/to/at ~** y ; **put the vegetables in ~** mettez-y les légumes ; **on ~** dessus ; **about ~** en ; **under ~** dessous ; **beside ~** à côté ; **from/of ~** en ; **he's very proud of ~** il en est très fier - **3.** [impersonal use] il, ce ; **~ is cold today** il fait froid aujourd'hui ; **~'s two o'clock** il est deux heures ; **who is ~?** — **~'s Mary/me** qui est-ce? — c'est Mary/moi.

IT *n abbr of* **information technology**.

Italian [ɪˈtæljən] <> *adj* italien(enne). <> *n* - **1.** [person] Italien *m*, -enne *f* - **2.** [language] italien *m*.

italic [ɪˈtælɪk] *adj* italique. ➡ **italics** *npl* italiques *fpl*.

Italy [ˈɪtəlɪ] *n* Italie *f*.

itch [ɪtʃ] <> *n* démangeaison *f.* <> *vi* - **1.** [be itchy] : **my arm ~es** mon bras me démange - **2.** *fig* [be impatient] : **to be ~ing to do sthg** mourir d'envie de faire qqch.

itchy [ˈɪtʃɪ] *adj* qui démange.

it'd [ˈɪtəd] = it would, it had.

item [ˈaɪtəm] *n* - **1.** [gen] chose *f*, article *m* ; [on agenda] question *f*, point *m* - **2.** PRESS article *m*.

itemize, -ise [ˈaɪtəmaɪz] *vt* détailler.

itinerary [aɪˈtɪnərərɪ] *n* itinéraire *m*.

it'll [ɪtl] = it will.

its [ɪts] *poss adj* son (sa), ses *(pl)*.

it's [ɪts] = it is, it has.

itself [ɪtˈself] *pron* - **1.** *(reflexive)* se ; *(after prep)* soi - **2.** *(for emphasis)* lui-même (elle-même) ; **in ~** en soi.

ITV (*abbr of* **Independent Television**) *n* sigle

désignant les programmes diffusés par les chaînes relevant de l'IBA.

I've [aɪv] = I have.

ivory ['aɪvərɪ] *n* ivoire *m*.

ivy ['aɪvɪ] *n* lierre *m*.

Ivy League *n Am* les huit grandes universités de l'est des États-Unis.

j (*pl* j's OR js), **J** (*pl* J's OR Js) [dʒeɪ] *n* [letter] j *m inv*, J *m inv*.

jab [dʒæb] ◇ *n* - **1.** *Br inf* [injection] piqûre *f* - **2.** BOXING direct *m*. ◇ *vt* : **to ~ sthg into** planter OR enfoncer qqch dans.

jabber ['dʒæbə'] *vt & vi* baragouiner.

jack [dʒæk] *n* - **1.** [device] cric *m* - **2.** [playing card] valet *m*. ◆ **jack up** *vt sep* - **1.** [car] soulever avec un cric - **2.** *fig* [prices] faire grimper.

jackal ['dʒækəl] *n* chacal *m*.

jackdaw ['dʒækdɔː] *n* choucas *m*.

jacket ['dʒækɪt] *n* - **1.** [garment] veste *f* - **2.** [of potato] peau *f*, pelure *f* - **3.** [of book] jaquette *f* - **4.** *Am* [of record] pochette *f*.

jacket potato *n* pomme de terre *f* en robe de chambre.

jackhammer ['dʒæk,hæmə'] *n Am* marteau-piqueur *m*.

jack knife *n* canif *m*. ◆ **jack-knife** *vi* [lorry] se mettre en travers de la route.

jack plug *n* jack *m*.

jackpot ['dʒækpɒt] *n* gros lot *m*.

jaded ['dʒeɪdɪd] *adj* blasé(e).

jagged ['dʒægɪd] *adj* déchiqueté(e), dentelé(e).

jail [dʒeɪl] ◇ *n* prison *f*. ◇ *vt* emprisonner, mettre en prison.

jailer ['dʒeɪlə'] *n* geôlier *m*, -ère *f*.

jam [dʒæm] ◇ *n* - **1.** [preserve] confiture *f* - **2.** [of traffic] embouteillage *m*, bouchon *m* - **3.** *inf* [difficult situation] : **to get into/be in a ~** se mettre/être dans le pétrin. ◇ *vt* - **1.** [mechanism, door] bloquer, coincer - **2.** [push tightly] : **to ~ sthg into** entasser OR tasser qqch dans ; **to ~ sthg onto** enfoncer qqch sur - **3.** [block - streets] emboutiller ; [- switchboard] surcharger - **4.** RADIO

brouiller. ◇ *vi* [lever, door] se coincer ; [brakes] se bloquer.

Jamaica [dʒə'meɪkə] *n* la Jamaïque.

jam-packed [-'pækt] *adj inf* plein(e) à craquer.

jangle ['dʒæŋgl] ◇ *vt* [keys] faire cliqueter ; [bells] faire retentir. ◇ *vi* [keys] cliqueter ; [bells] retentir.

janitor ['dʒænɪtə'] *n Am & Scot* concierge *mf*.

January ['dʒænjʊərɪ] *n* janvier *m* ; *see also* September.

Japan [dʒə'pæn] *n* Japon *m*.

Japanese [,dʒæpə'niːz] (*pl inv*) ◇ *adj* japonais(e). ◇ *n* [language] japonais *m*. ◇ *npl* [people] : **the ~** les Japonais *mpl*.

jar [dʒɑː'] ◇ *n* pot *m*. ◇ *vt* [shake] secouer. ◇ *vi* - **1.** [noise, voice] : **to ~ (on sb)** irriter (qqn), agacer (qqn) - **2.** [colours] jurer.

jargon ['dʒɑːgən] *n* jargon *m*.

jaundice ['dʒɔːndɪs] *n* jaunisse *f*.

jaundiced ['dʒɔːndɪst] *adj fig* [attitude, view] aigri(e).

jaunt [dʒɔːnt] *n* balade *f*.

jaunty ['dʒɔːntɪ] *adj* désinvolte, insouciant(e).

javelin ['dʒævlɪn] *n* javelot *m*.

jaw [dʒɔː] *n* mâchoire *f*.

jawbone ['dʒɔːbəʊn] *n* (os *m*) maxillaire *m*.

jay [dʒeɪ] *n* geai *m*.

jaywalker ['dʒeɪwɔːkə'] *n* piéton *m* qui traverse en dehors des clous.

jazz [dʒæz] *n* MUS jazz *m*. ◆ **jazz up** *vt sep inf* égayer.

jazzy ['dʒæzɪ] *adj* [bright] voyant(e).

jealous ['dʒeləs] *adj* jaloux(ouse).

jealousy ['dʒeləsɪ] *n* jalousie *f*.

jeans [dʒiːnz] *npl* jean *m*, blue-jean *m*.

Jeep® [dʒiːp] *n* Jeep® *f*.

jeer [dʒɪə'] ◇ *vt* huer, conspuer. ◇ *vi* : **to ~ (at sb)** huer (qqn), conspuer (qqn).

Jehovah's Witness [dʒɪ,həʊvəz-] *n* témoin *m* de Jéhovah.

Jello® ['dʒeləʊ] *n Am* gelée *f*.

jelly ['dʒelɪ] *n* gelée *f*.

jellyfish ['dʒelɪfɪʃ] (*pl inv* OR **-es** [-iːz]) *n* méduse *f*.

jeopardize, -ise ['dʒepədaɪz] *vt* compromettre, mettre en danger.

jerk [dʒɜːk] ◇ *n* - **1.** [movement] secousse *f*, saccade *f* - **2.** *v inf* [fool] abruti *m*, -e *f*. ◇ *vi* [person] sursauter ; [vehicle] cahoter.

jersey ['dʒɜːzɪ] (pl -s) n - 1. [sweater] pull m - 2. [cloth] jersey m.

Jersey ['dʒɜːzɪ] n Jersey f.

jest [dʒest] n plaisanterie f ; **in ~** pour rire.

Jesus (Christ) ['dʒiːzəs-] n Jésus m, Jésus-Christ m.

jet [dʒet] n - 1. [plane] jet m, avion m à réaction - 2. [of fluid] jet m - 3. [nozzle, outlet] ajutage m.

jet-black adj noir(e) comme (du) jais.

jet engine n moteur m à réaction.

jetfoil ['dʒetfɔɪl] n hydroglisseur m.

jet lag n fatigue f due au décalage horaire.

jetsam ['dʒetsəm] ⊏▷ **flotsam**.

jettison ['dʒetɪsən] vt - 1. [cargo] jeter, larguer - 2. fig [ideas] abandonner, renoncer à.

jetty ['dʒetɪ] n jetée f.

Jew [dʒuː] n Juif m, -ive f.

jewel ['dʒuːəl] n bijou m ; [in watch] rubis m.

jeweller Br, **jeweler** Am ['dʒuːələʳ] n bijoutier m ; **~'s (shop)** bijouterie f.

jewellery Br, **jewelry** Am ['dʒuːəlrɪ] n (U) bijoux mpl.

Jewess ['dʒuːɪs] n juive f.

Jewish ['dʒuːɪʃ] adj juif(ive).

jib [dʒɪb] n - 1. [of crane] flèche f - 2. [sail] foc m.

jibe [dʒaɪb] n inf : **in a ~** en un clin d'œil.

jiffy ['dʒɪfɪ] n inf : **in a ~** en un clin d'œil.

Jiffy bag® n enveloppe f matelassée.

jig [dʒɪg] n gigue f.

jigsaw (puzzle) ['dʒɪgsɔː-] n puzzle m.

jilt [dʒɪlt] vt laisser tomber.

jingle ['dʒɪŋgl] ⟨▷ n - 1. [sound] cliquetis m - 2. [song] jingle m, indicatif m. ⟨▷ vi [bell] tinter ; [coins, bracelets] cliqueter.

jinx [dʒɪŋks] n poisse f.

jitters ['dʒɪtəz] npl inf : **the ~** le trac.

job [dʒɒb] n - 1. [employment] emploi m - 2. [task] travail m, tâche f - 3. [difficult task] : **to have a ~ doing sthg** avoir du mal à faire qqch - 4. phr : **that's just the ~** Br inf c'est exactement OR tout à fait ce qu'il faut.

job centre n Br agence f pour l'emploi.

jobless ['dʒɒblɪs] adj au chômage.

jobsharing ['dʒɒbʃeərɪŋ] n partage m de l'emploi.

jockey ['dʒɒkɪ] (pl -s) ⟨▷ n jockey m. ⟨▷ vi : **to ~ for position** manœuvrer pour devancer ses concurrents.

jocular ['dʒɒkjʊləʳ] adj - 1. [cheerful] enjoué(e), jovial(e) - 2. [funny] amusant(e).

jodhpurs ['dʒɒdpəz] npl jodhpurs mpl, culotte f de cheval.

jog [dʒɒg] ⟨▷ n : **to go for a ~** faire du jogging. ⟨▷ vt pousser ; **to ~ sb's memory** rafraîchir la mémoire de qqn. ⟨▷ vi faire du jogging, jogger.

jogging ['dʒɒgɪŋ] n jogging m.

john [dʒɒn] n Am inf petit coin m, cabinets mpl.

join [dʒɔɪn] ⟨▷ n raccord m, joint m. ⟨▷ vt - 1. [connect - gen] unir, joindre ; [- towns etc] relier - 2. [get together with] rejoindre, retrouver - 3. [political party] devenir membre de ; [club] s'inscrire à ; [army] s'engager dans ; **to ~ a queue** Br, **to ~ a line** Am prendre la queue. ⟨▷ vi - 1. [connect] se joindre - 2. [become a member - gen] devenir membre ; [- of club] s'inscrire. ◆ **join in** ⟨▷ vt fus prendre part à, participer à. ⟨▷ vi participer. ◆ **join up** vi MIL s'engager dans l'armée.

joiner ['dʒɔɪnəʳ] n Br menuisier m.

joinery ['dʒɔɪnərɪ] n Br menuiserie f.

joint [dʒɔɪnt] ⟨▷ adj [effort] conjugué(e) ; [responsibility] collectif(ive). ⟨▷ n - 1. [gen & TECH] joint m - 2. ANAT articulation f - 3. Br [of meat] rôti m - 4. inf [place] bouge m - 5. drugs sl joint m.

joint account n compte m joint.

jointly ['dʒɔɪntlɪ] adv conjointement.

joke [dʒəʊk] ⟨▷ n blague f, plaisanterie f ; **to play a ~ on sb** faire une blague à qqn, jouer un tour à qqn ; **it's no ~** [not easy] ce n'est pas de la tarte. ⟨▷ vi plaisanter, blaguer ; **to ~ about sthg** plaisanter sur qqch, se moquer de qqch.

joker ['dʒəʊkəʳ] n - 1. [person] blagueur m, -euse f - 2. [playing card] joker m.

jolly ['dʒɒlɪ] ⟨▷ adj [person] jovial(e), enjoué(e) ; [time, party] agréable. ⟨▷ adv Br inf drôlement, rudement.

jolt [dʒəʊlt] ⟨▷ n - 1. [jerk] secousse f, soubresaut m - 2. [shock] choc m. ⟨▷ vt secouer.

Jordan ['dʒɔːdn] n Jordanie f.

jostle ['dʒɒsl] ⟨▷ vt bousculer. ⟨▷ vi se bousculer.

jot [dʒɒt] n [of truth] grain m, brin m. ◆ **jot down** vt sep noter, prendre note de.

jotter ['dʒɒtəʳ] n Br [notepad] bloc-notes m.

journal ['dʒɜːnl] n - 1. [magazine] revue f - 2. [diary] journal m.

journalism ['dʒɜːnəlɪzm] n journalisme m.

journalist ['dʒɜːnəlɪst] n journaliste mf.

journey ['dʒɜːnɪ] (*pl* -s) *n* voyage *m*.

jovial ['dʒəʊvjəl] *adj* jovial(e).

jowls [dʒaʊlz] *npl* bajoues *fpl*.

joy [dʒɔɪ] *n* joie *f*.

joyful ['dʒɔɪfʊl] *adj* joyeux(euse).

joyride ['dʒɔɪraɪd] (*pt* -rode, *pp* -ridden) *vi* faire une virée dans une voiture volée.

joyrode ['dʒɔɪrəʊd] *pt* ⊏▷ **joyride**.

joystick ['dʒɔɪstɪk] *n* AERON manche *m* (à balai) ; COMPUT manette *f*.

JP *n abbr of* **Justice of the Peace**.

Jr. (*abbr of* **Junior**) Jr.

jubilant ['dʒuːbɪlənt] *adj* [person] débordant(e) de joie, qui jubile ; [shout] de joie.

jubilee ['dʒuːbɪliː] *n* jubilé *m*.

judge [dʒʌdʒ] ◇ *n* juge *m*. ◇ *vt* **- 1.** [gen] juger **- 2.** [estimate] évaluer, juger. ◇ *vi* juger ; **to ~ from** OR **by, judging from** OR **by à** en juger par.

judg(e)ment ['dʒʌdʒmənt] *n* jugement *m*.

judicial [dʒuː'dɪʃl] *adj* judiciaire.

judiciary [dʒuː'dɪʃərɪ] *n* : **the ~** la magistrature.

judicious [dʒuː'dɪʃəs] *adj* judicieux(euse).

judo ['dʒuːdəʊ] *n* judo *m*.

jug [dʒʌg] *n* pot *m*, pichet *m*.

juggernaut ['dʒʌgənɔːt] *n* poids *m* lourd.

juggle ['dʒʌgl] ◇ *vt lit & fig* jongler avec. ◇ *vi* jongler.

juggler ['dʒʌglə'] *n* jongleur *m*, -euse *f*.

jugular (vein) ['dʒʌgjʊlə'-] *n* (veine *f*) jugulaire *f*.

juice [dʒuːs] *n* jus *m*.

juicy ['dʒuːsɪ] *adj* [fruit] juteux(euse).

jukebox ['dʒuːkbɒks] *n* juke-box *m*.

July [dʒuː'laɪ] *n* juillet *m* ; *see also* **September**.

jumble ['dʒʌmbl] ◇ *n* [mixture] mélange *m*, fatras *m*. ◇ *vt* : **to ~ (up)** mélanger, embrouiller.

jumble sale *n Br* vente *f* de charité (où sont vendus des articles d'occasion).

jumbo jet ['dʒʌmbəʊ-] *n* jumbo-jet *m*.

jumbo-sized [-saɪzd] *adj* géant(e), énorme.

jump [dʒʌmp] ◇ *n* **- 1.** [leap] saut *m*, bond *m* **- 2.** [fence] obstacle *m* **- 3.** [rapid increase] flambée *f*, hausse *f* brutale. ◇ *vt* **- 1.** [fence, stream etc] franchir d'un bond **- 2.** *inf* [attack] sauter sur, tomber sur. ◇ *vi* **- 1.** [gen] sauter, bondir ; [in surprise] sursauter **- 2.** [increase rapidly] grimper en flè-

che, faire un bond. ◆ **jump at** *vt fus fig* sauter sur.

jumper ['dʒʌmpə'] *n* **- 1.** *Br* [pullover] pull *m* **- 2.** *Am* [dress] robe *f* chasuble.

jump leads *npl* câbles *mpl* de démarrage.

jump-start *vt* : **to ~ a car** faire démarrer une voiture en la poussant.

jumpsuit ['dʒʌmpsuːt] *n* combinaison-pantalon *f*.

jumpy ['dʒʌmpɪ] *adj* nerveux(euse).

Jun. = **Junr**.

junction ['dʒʌŋkʃn] *n* [of roads] carrefour *m* ; RAIL embranchement *m*.

June [dʒuːn] *n* juin *m* ; *see also* **September**.

jungle ['dʒʌŋgl] *n lit & fig* jungle *f*.

junior ['dʒuːnjə'] ◇ *adj* **- 1.** [gen] jeune **- 2.** *Am* [after name] junior. ◇ *n* **- 1.** [in rank] subalterne *mf* **- 2.** [in age] cadet *m*, -ette *f* **- 3.** *Am* SCH ≃ élève *mf* de première ; UNIV ≃ étudiant *m*, -e *f* de troisième année.

junior high school *n Am* ≃ collège *m* d'enseignement secondaire.

junior school *n Br* école *f* primaire.

junk [dʒʌŋk] *n* [unwanted objects] bric-à-brac *m inv*.

junk food *n* (U) *pej* : **to eat ~** manger des cochonneries.

junkie ['dʒʌŋkɪ] *n drugs sl* drogué *m*, -e *f*.

junk mail *n* (U) *pej* prospectus *mpl* publicitaires envoyés par la poste.

junk shop *n* boutique *f* de brocanteur.

Junr (*abbr of* **Junior**) Jr.

Jupiter ['dʒuːpɪtə'] *n* [planet] Jupiter *f*.

Jurisdiction [ˌdʒʊərɪs'dɪkʃn] *n* juridiction *f*.

juror ['dʒʊərə'] *n* juré *m*, -e *f*.

jury ['dʒʊərɪ] *n* jury *m*.

just [dʒʌst] ◇ *adv* **- 1.** [recently] : **he's ~ left** il vient de partir **- 2.** [at that moment] : **I was ~ about to go** j'allais juste partir, j'étais sur le point de partir ; **I'm ~ going to do it now** je vais le faire tout de suite OR à l'instant ; **she arrived ~ as I was leaving** elle est arrivée au moment même où je partais OR juste comme je partais **- 3.** [only, simply] : **it's ~ a rumour** ce n'est qu'une rumeur ; **~ add water** vous n'avez plus qu'à ajouter de l'eau ; **~ a minute** OR **moment** OR **second!** un (petit) instant! **- 4.** [almost not] tout juste, à peine ; **I only ~ missed the train** j'ai manqué le train de peu ; **we have ~ enough time** on a juste assez de temps **- 5.** [for emphasis] : **the coast is ~ marvellous** la côte est vraiment magnifique ; **~ look at this mess!** non, mais regarde un peu ce désordre! - **6.** [exactly, precisely] tout à fait, exactement ; **it's ~ what I need** c'est tout à fait ce qu'il me faut - **7.** [in requests] : **could you ~ move over please?** pourriez-vous vous pousser un peu s'il vous plaît? <> *adj* juste, équitable. **just about** *adv* à peu près, plus ou moins. **just as** *adv* [in comparison] tout aussi ; **you're ~ as clever as he is** tu es tout aussi intelligent que lui. **just now** *adv* - **1.** [a short time ago] il y a un moment, tout à l'heure - **2.** [at this moment] en ce moment.

justice ['dʒʌstɪs] *n* - **1.** [gen] justice *f* - **2.** [of claim, cause] bien-fondé *m*.

Justice of the Peace (*pl* **Justices of the Peace**) *n* juge *m* de paix.

justify ['dʒʌstɪfaɪ] *vt* [give reasons for] justifier.

jut [dʒʌt] *vi* : **to ~ (out)** faire saillie, avancer.

juvenile ['dʒuːvənaɪl] <> *adj* - **1.** JUR mineur(e), juvénile - **2.** [childish] puéril(e). <> *n* JUR mineur *m*, -e *f*.

juxtapose [,dʒʌkstə'pəʊz] *vt* juxtaposer.

K

k (*pl* **k's** OR **ks**), **K** (*pl* **K's** OR **Ks**) [keɪ] *n* [letter] k *m inv*, K *m inv.* **K** - **1.** (*abbr of* **kilobyte**) Ko - **2.** (*abbr of* **thousand**) K.

kaleidoscope [kə'laɪdəskəʊp] *n* kaléidoscope *m*.

kangaroo [,kæŋgə'ruː] *n* kangourou *m*.

kaput [kə'pʊt] *adj inf* fichu(e), foutu(e).

karat ['kærət] *n Am* carat *m*.

karate [kə'rɑːtɪ] *n* karaté *m*.

kayak ['kaɪæk] *n* kayak *m*.

KB (*abbr of* **kilobyte(s)**) *n* COMPUT Ko *m*.

kcal (*abbr of* **kilocalorie**) Kcal.

kebab [kɪ'bæb] *n* brochette *f*.

keel [kiːl] *n* quille *f* ; **on an even ~** stable. **keel over** *vi* [ship] chavirer ; [person] tomber dans les pommes.

keen [kiːn] *adj* - **1.** [enthusiastic] enthousiaste, passionné(e) ; **to be ~ on sthg** avoir la passion de qqch ; **he's ~ on her** elle lui plaît ; **to be ~ to do** OR **on doing sthg** tenir à faire qqch - **2.** [interest, desire, mind] vif (vive) ; [competition] âpre, acharné(e)

- **3.** [sense of smell] fin(e) ; [eyesight] perçant(e).

keep [kiːp] (*pt & pp* **kept**) <> *vt* - **1.** [retain, store] garder ; **~ the change!** gardez la monnaie! ; **to ~ sthg warm** garder OR tenir qqch au chaud - **2.** [prevent] : **to keep sb/ sthg from doing sthg** empêcher qqn/qqch de faire qqch - **3.** [detain] retenir ; [prisoner] détenir ; **to ~ sb waiting** faire attendre qqn - **4.** [promise] tenir ; [appointment] aller à ; [vow] être fidèle à - **5.** [not disclose] : **to ~ sthg from sb** cacher qqch à qqn ; **to ~ sthg to o.s.** garder qqch pour soi - **6.** [diary, record, notes] tenir - **7.** [own - sheep, pigs etc] élever ; [- shop] tenir ; [- car] avoir, posséder - **8.** *phr* : **they ~ themselves to themselves** ils restent entre eux, ils se tiennent à l'écart. <> *vi* - **1.** [remain] : **to ~ warm** se tenir au chaud ; **to ~ quiet** garder le silence ; **~ quiet!** taisez-vous! - **2.** [continue] : **he ~s interrupting me** il n'arrête pas de m'interrompre ; **to ~ talking/walking** continuer à parler/à marcher - **3.** [continue moving] : **to ~ left/ right** garder sa gauche/sa droite ; **to ~ north/south** continuer vers le nord/le sud - **4.** [food] se conserver - **5.** *Br* [in health] : **how are you ~ing?** comment allez-vous? <> *n* : **to earn one's ~** gagner sa vie. **keeps** *n* : **for ~s** pour toujours.

 keep back *vt sep* [information] cacher, ne pas divulguer ; [money] retenir.

 keep off *vt fus* '**~ off the grass**' '(il est) interdit de marcher sur la pelouse'.

 keep on *vi* - **1.** [continue] : **to ~ on (doing sthg)** [without stopping] continuer (de OR à faire qqch) ; [repeatedly] ne pas arrêter (de faire qqch) - **2.** [talk incessantly] : **to ~ on (about sthg)** ne pas arrêter de parler (de qqch). **keep out** <> *vt sep* empêcher d'entrer. <> *vi* : '**~ out**' 'défense d'entrer'.

 keep to *vt fus* [rules, deadline] respecter, observer. **keep up** <> *vt sep* [continue to do] continuer ; [maintain] maintenir. <> *vi* [maintain pace, level etc] : **to ~ up (with sb)** aller aussi vite (que qqn).

keeper ['kiːpər] *n* gardien *m*, -enne *f*.

keep-fit *n* (U) *Br* gymnastique *f*.

keeping ['kiːpɪŋ] *n* - **1.** [care] garde *f* - **2.** [conformity, harmony] : **to be in/out of ~ with** [rules etc] être/ne pas être conforme à ; [subj : clothes, furniture] aller/ne pas aller avec.

keepsake ['kiːpseɪk] *n* souvenir *m*.

keg [keg] *n* tonnelet *m*, baril *m*.

kennel ['kenl] *n* - **1.** *Br* [shelter for dog] niche *f* - **2.** *Am* = **kennels**. **kennels** *npl Br* chenil *m*.

Kenya ['kenjə] *n* Kenya *m*.

Kenyan ['kenjən] ◇ *adj* kenyan(e). ◇ *n* Kenyan *m*, -e *f*.

kept [kept] *pt & pp* ⊏> **keep.**

kerb [kɜ:b] *n Br* bordure *f* du trottoir.

kernel ['kɜ:nl] *n* amande *f*.

kerosene ['kerəsi:n] *n* kérosène *m*.

ketchup ['ketʃəp] *n* ketchup *m*.

kettle ['ketl] *n* bouilloire *f*.

key [ki:] ◇ *n* - **1.** [gen & MUS] clef *f*, clé *f* ; **the ~ (to sthg)** *fig* la clé (de qqch) - **2.** [of typewriter, computer, piano] touche *f* - **3.** [of map] légende *f*. ◇ *adj* clé *(after n).* ◆ **key in** *vt sep* [text, data] saisir ; [code] composer.

keyboard ['ki:bɔ:d] *n* [gen & COMPUT] clavier *m*.

keyed up [ˌki:d-] *adj* tendu(e), énervé(e).

keyhole ['ki:həʊl] *n* trou *m* de serrure.

keynote ['ki:nəʊt] ◇ *n* note *f* dominante. ◇ *comp* : ~ **speech** discours-programme *m*.

keypad ['ki:pæd] *n* COMPUT pavé *m* numérique.

key ring *n* porte-clés *m inv.*

kg *(abbr of* **kilogram)** kg.

khaki ['ka:kɪ] ◇ *adj* kaki *(inv).* ◇ *n* [colour] kaki *m*.

kick [kɪk] ◇ *n* - **1.** [with foot] coup *m* de pied - **2.** *inf* [excitement] : **to get a ~ from sthg** trouver qqch excitant ; **to do sthg for ~s** faire qqch pour le plaisir. ◇ *vt* - **1.** [with foot] donner un coup de pied à ; **to ~ o.s.** *fig* se donner des gifles OR des claques - **2.** *inf* [give up] : **to ~ the habit** arrêter. ◇ *vi* - **1.** [person - repeatedly] donner des coups de pied ; [- once] donner un coup de pied - **2.** [baby] gigoter - **3.** [animal] ruer. ◆ **kick about, kick around** *vi Br inf* traîner. ◆ **kick off** *vi* - **1.** FTBL donner le coup d'envoi - **2.** *inf fig* [start] démarrer. ◆ **kick out** *vt sep inf* vider, jeter dehors.

kid [kɪd] ◇ *n* - **1.** *inf* [child] gosse *mf*, gamin *m*, -e *f* - **2.** *inf* [young person] petit jeune *m*, petite jeune *f* - **3.** [goat, leather] chevreau *m*. ◇ *comp inf* [brother, sister] petit(e). ◇ *vt inf* - **1.** [tease] faire marcher - **2.** [delude] : **to ~ o.s.** se faire des illusions. ◇ *vi inf* : **to be kidding** plaisanter.

kidnap ['kɪdnæp] *vt* kidnapper, enlever.

kidnapper, kidnaper *Am* ['kɪdnæpəʳ] *n* kidnappeur *m*, -euse *f*, ravisseur *m*, -euse *f*.

kidnapping, kidnaping *Am* ['kɪdnæpɪŋ] *n* enlèvement *m*.

kidney ['kɪdnɪ] *(pl -s) n* - **1.** ANAT rein *m* - **2.** CULIN rognon *m*.

kidney bean *n* haricot *m* rouge.

kill [kɪl] ◇ *vt* - **1.** [cause death of] tuer - **2.** *fig* [hope, chances] mettre fin à ; [pain] supprimer. ◇ *vi* tuer. ◇ *n* mise *f* à mort.

killer ['kɪləʳ] *n* [person] meurtrier *m*, -ère *f* ; [animal] tueur *m*, -euse *f*.

killing ['kɪlɪŋ] *n* meurtre *m*.

killjoy ['kɪldʒɔɪ] *n* rabat-joie *m inv.*

kiln [kɪln] *n* four *m*.

kilo ['ki:ləʊ] *(pl -s) (abbr of* **kilogram)** *n* kilo *m*.

kilobyte ['kɪləbaɪt] *n* COMPUT kilo-octet *m*.

kilogram(me) ['kɪləgræm] *n* kilogramme *m*.

kilohertz ['kɪləhɜ:tz] *(pl inv) n* kilohertz *m*.

kilometre *Br* ['kɪləˌmi:təʳ], **kilometer** *Am* [kɪ'lɒmɪtəʳ] *n* kilomètre *m*.

kilowatt ['kɪləwɒt] *n* kilowatt *m*.

kilt [kɪlt] *n* kilt *m*.

kin [kɪn] *n* ⊏> **kith.**

kind [kaɪnd] ◇ *adj* gentil(ille), aimable. ◇ *n* genre *m*, sorte *f* ; **they're two of a ~** ils se ressemblent ; **in ~** [payment] en nature ; **a ~ of** une espèce de, une sorte de ; **~ of** *Am inf* un peu.

kindergarten ['kɪndəˌgɑ:tn] *n* jardin *m* d'enfants.

kind-hearted [-'hɑ:tɪd] *adj* qui a un bon cœur, bon (bonne).

kindle ['kɪndl] *vt* - **1.** [fire] allumer - **2.** *fig* [feeling] susciter.

kindly ['kaɪndlɪ] ◇ *adj* - **1.** [person] plein(e) de bonté, bienveillant(e) - **2.** [gesture] plein(e) de gentillesse. ◇ *adv* - **1.** [speak, smile etc] avec gentillesse - **2.** [please] : ~ **leave the room!** veuillez sortir, s'il vous plaît! ; **will you ~ ...?** veuillez ..., je vous prie de ...

kindness ['kaɪndnɪs] *n* gentillesse *f*.

kindred ['kɪndrɪd] *adj* [similar] semblable, similaire ; ~ **spirit** âme *f* sœur.

king [kɪŋ] *n* roi *m*.

kingdom ['kɪŋdəm] *n* - **1.** [country] royaume *m* - **2.** [of animals, plants] règne *m*.

kingfisher ['kɪŋˌfɪʃəʳ] *n* martin-pêcheur *m*.

king-size(d) [-saɪz(d)] *adj* [cigarette] long (longue) ; [pack] géant(e) ; **a ~ bed** un grand lit *(de 195 cm).*

kinky ['kɪŋkɪ] *adj inf* vicieux(euse).

kiosk ['ki:ɒsk] *n* - **1.** [small shop] kiosque *m* - **2.** *Br* [telephone box] cabine *f* (téléphonique).

kip [kɪp] *Br inf* ◇ *n* somme *m*, roupillon *m*. ◇ *vi* faire OR piquer un petit somme.

kipper ['kɪpə'] *n* hareng *m* fumé OR saur.

kiss [kɪs] ◇ *n* baiser *m* ; **to give sb a ~** embrasser qqn, donner un baiser à qqn. ◇ *vt* embrasser. ◇ *vi* s'embrasser.

kiss of life *n* : **the ~** le bouche-à-bouche.

kit [kɪt] *n* - 1. [set] trousse *f* - 2. *(U)* SPORT affaires *fpl*, équipement *m* - 3. [to be assembled] kit *m*.

kit bag *n* sac *m* de marin.

kitchen ['kɪtʃɪn] *n* cuisine *f*.

kitchen sink *n* évier *m*.

kitchen unit *n* élément *m* de cuisine.

kite [kaɪt] *n* [toy] cerf-volant *m*.

kith [kɪθ] *n* : **~ and kin** parents et amis *mpl*.

kitten ['kɪtn] *n* chaton *m*.

kitty ['kɪtɪ] *n* [shared fund] cagnotte *f*.

kiwi ['kiːwiː] *n* - 1. [bird] kiwi *m*, aptéryx *m* - 2. *inf* [New Zealander] Néo-Zélandais *m*, -e *f*.

kiwi fruit *n* kiwi *m*.

km *(abbr of* **kilometre)** km.

km/h *(abbr of* **kilometres per hour)** km/h.

knack [næk] *n* : **to have a** OR **the ~ (for doing sthg)** avoir le coup (pour faire qqch).

knackered ['nækəd] *adj Br v inf* crevé(e), claqué(e).

knapsack ['næpsæk] *n* sac *m* à dos.

knead [niːd] *vt* pétrir.

knee [niː] *n* genou *m*.

kneecap ['niːkæp] *n* rotule *f*.

kneel [niːl] *(Br pt & pp* knelt, *Am pt & pp* knelt OR **-ed)** *vi* se mettre à genoux, s'agenouiller. ◆ **kneel down** *vi* se mettre à genoux, s'agenouiller.

knelt [nelt] *pt & pp* ▷ **kneel.**

knew [njuː] *pt* ▷ **know.**

knickers ['nɪkəz] *npl* - 1. *Br* [underwear] culotte *f* - 2. *Am* [knickerbockers] pantalon *m* de golf.

knick-knack ['nɪknæk] *n* babiole *f*, bibelot *m*.

knife [naɪf] *(pl* knives [naɪvz]) ◇ *n* couteau *m*. ◇ *vt* donner un coup de couteau à, poignarder.

knight [naɪt] ◇ *n* - 1. [in history, member of nobility] chevalier *m* - 2. [in chess] cavalier *m*. ◇ *vt* faire chevalier.

knighthood ['naɪthʊd] *n* titre *m* de chevalier.

knit [nɪt] *(pt & pp* knit OR **-ted)** ◇ *adj* : **closely** OR **tightly ~** *fig* très uni(e). ◇ *vt* tricoter. ◇ *vi* - 1. [with wool] tricoter - 2. [broken bones] se souder.

knitting ['nɪtɪŋ] *n (U)* tricot *m*.

knitting needle *n* aiguille *f* à tricoter.

knitwear ['nɪtweə'] *n (U)* tricots *mpl*.

knives [naɪvz] *pl* ▷ **knife.**

knob [nɒb] *n* - 1. [on door] poignée *f*, bouton *m* ; [on drawer] poignée ; [on bedstead] pomme *f* - 2. [on TV, radio etc] bouton *m*.

knock [nɒk] ◇ *n* - 1. [hit] coup *m* - 2. *inf* [piece of bad luck] coup *m* dur. ◇ *vt* - 1. [hit] frapper, cogner ; **to ~ sb/sthg over** renverser qqn/qqch - 2. *inf* [criticize] critiquer, dire du mal de. ◇ *vi* - 1. [on door] : **to ~ (at** OR **on)** frapper (à) - 2. [car engine] cogner, avoir des ratés. ◆ **knock down** *vt sep* - 1. [subj : car, driver] renverser - 2. [building] démolir. ◆ **knock off** *vi inf* [stop working] finir son travail OR sa journée. ◆ **knock out** *vt sep* - 1. [make unconscious] assommer - 2. [from competition] éliminer.

knocker ['nɒkə'] *n* [on door] heurtoir *m*.

knock-kneed [-'niːd] *adj* cagneux(euse), qui a les genoux cagneux.

knock-on effect *n Br* réaction *f* en chaîne.

knockout ['nɒkaʊt] *n* knock-out *m inv*, K.-O. *m*.

knot [nɒt] ◇ *n* - 1. [gen] nœud *m* ; **to tie/untie a ~** faire/défaire un nœud - 2. [of people] petit attroupement *m*. ◇ *vt* nouer, faire un nœud à.

knotty ['nɒtɪ] *adj fig* épineux(euse).

know [nəʊ] *(pt* knew, *pp* known) ◇ *vt* - 1. [gen] savoir ; [language] savoir parler ; **to ~ (that) ...** savoir que ... ; **to let sb ~ (about sthg)** faire savoir (qqch) à qqn, informer qqn (de qqch) ; **to ~ how to do sthg** savoir faire qqch ; **to get to ~ sthg** apprendre qqch - 2. [person, place] connaître ; **to get to ~ sb** apprendre à mieux connaître qqn. ◇ *vi* savoir ; **to ~ of sthg** connaître qqch ; **to ~ about** [be aware of] être au courant de ; [be expert in] s'y connaître en. ◇ *n* : **to be in the ~** être au courant.

know-all *n Br* (monsieur) je-sais-tout *m*, je-sais-tout *f*.

know-how *n* savoir-faire *m inv*, technique *f*.

knowing ['nəʊɪŋ] *adj* [smile, look] entendu(e).

knowingly ['nəʊɪŋlɪ] *adv* - 1. [smile, look] d'un air entendu - 2. [intentionally] sciemment.

know-it-all = **know-all.**

knowledge ['nɒlɪdʒ] *n (U)* - 1. [gen] connaissance *f* ; **without my ~** à mon insu ; **to the best of my ~** à ma connaissance, autant que je sache - **2.** [learning, understanding] savoir *m*, connaissances *fpl*.

knowledgeable ['nɒlɪdʒəbl] *adj* bien informé(e).

known [nəʊn] *pp* ⊏> **know.**

knuckle ['nʌkl] *n* - **1.** ANAT articulation *f* OR jointure *f* du doigt - **2.** [of meat] jarret *m*.

knuckle-duster *n* coup-de-poing *m* américain.

koala (bear) [kəʊ'ɑːlə-] *n* koala *m*.

Koran [kɒ'rɑːn] *n* : **the ~** le Coran.

Korea [kə'rɪə] *n* Corée *f*.

Korean [kə'rɪən] <> *adj* coréen(enne). <> *n* - **1.** [person] Coréen *m*, -enne *f* - **2.** [language] coréen *m*.

kosher ['kəʊʃə'] *adj* - **1.** [meat] kasher *(inv)* - **2.** *inf* [reputable] O.K. *(inv)*, réglo *(inv)*.

Kosovar [kɒsəvɑː'] *n* kosovar *mf*.

Kosovo [kɒsəvə] *n* Kosovo *m*.

Koweit = **Kuwait.**

kung fu [,kʌŋ'fuː] *n* kung-fu *m inv*.

Kurd [kɜːd] *n* Kurde *mf*.

Kuwait [kʊ'weɪt], **Koweit** [kəʊ'weɪt] *n* - **1.** [country] Koweït *m* - **2.** [city] Koweït City.

l[1] (*pl* **l's** OR **ls**), **L** (*pl* **L's** OR **Ls**) [el] *n* [letter] l *m inv*, L *m inv*.

l[2] (*abbr of* **litre**) l.

lab [læb] *n inf* labo *m*.

label ['leɪbl] <> *n* - **1.** [identification] étiquette *f* - **2.** [of record] label *m*, maison *f* de disques. <> *vt* - **1.** [fix label to] étiqueter - **2.** [describe] : **to ~ sb (as)** cataloguer OR étiqueter qqn (comme).

labor *etc Am* = **labour** *etc.*

laboratory [*Br* lə'bɒrətrɪ, *Am* 'læbrə,tɔːrɪ] *n* laboratoire *m*.

laborious [lə'bɔːrɪəs] *adj* laborieux(euse).

labor union *n Am* syndicat *m*.

labour *Br*, **labor** *Am* ['leɪbə'] <> *n* - **1.** [gen & MED] travail *m* - **2.** [workers, work carried out] main d'œuvre *f*. <> *vi* travailler dur ; **to ~ at** OR **over** peiner sur.

◆ **Labour** POL <> *adj* travailliste. <> *n* (U) *Br* les travaillistes *mpl*.

laboured *Br*, **labored** *Am* ['leɪbəd] *adj* [breathing] pénible ; [style] lourd(e), laborieux(euse).

labourer *Br*, **laborer** *Am* ['leɪbərə'] *n* travailleur manuel *m*, travailleuse manuelle *f* ; [agricultural] ouvrier agricole *m*, ouvrière agricole *f*.

Labour Party *n Br* : **the ~** le parti travailliste.

Labrador ['læbrədɔː'] *n* [dog] labrador *m*.

labyrinth ['læbərɪnθ] *n* labyrinthe *m*.

lace [leɪs] <> *n* - **1.** [fabric] dentelle *f* - **2.** [of shoe etc] lacet *m*. <> *vt* - **1.** [shoe etc] lacer - **2.** [drink] verser de l'alcool dans. ◆ **lace up** *vt sep* lacer.

lace-up *n Br* chaussure *f* à lacets.

lack [læk] <> *n* manque *m* ; **for** OR **through ~ of** par manque de ; **no ~ of** bien assez de. <> *vt* manquer de. <> *vi* : **to be ~ing in sthg** manquer de qqch ; **to be ~ing** manquer, faire défaut.

lackadaisical [,lækə'deɪzɪkl] *adj pej* nonchalant(e).

lacklustre *Br*, **lackluster** *Am* ['læk,lʌstə'] *adj* terne.

laconic [lə'kɒnɪk] *adj* laconique.

lacquer ['lækə'] <> *n* [for wood] vernis *m*, laque *f* ; [for hair] laque *f*. <> *vt* laquer.

lacrosse [lə'krɒs] *n* crosse *f*.

lad [læd] *n inf* [boy] garçon *m*, gars *m*.

ladder ['lædə'] <> *n* - **1.** [for climbing] échelle *f* - **2.** *Br* [in tights] maille *f* filée, estafilade *f*. <> *vt & vi Br* [tights] filer.

laden ['leɪdn] *adj* : **~ (with)** chargé(e) (de).

ladies *Br* ['leɪdɪz], **ladies' room** *Am n* toilettes *fpl* (pour dames).

ladle ['leɪdl] <> *n* louche *f*. <> *vt* servir (à la louche).

lady ['leɪdɪ] <> *n* [gen] dame *f*. <> *comp* : **a ~ doctor** une femme docteur. ◆ **Lady** *n* Lady *f*.

ladybird *Br* ['leɪdɪbɜːd], **ladybug** *Am* ['leɪdɪbʌg] *n* coccinelle *f*.

lady-in-waiting [-'weɪtɪŋ] (*pl* **ladies-in-waiting**) *n* dame *f* d'honneur.

ladylike ['leɪdɪlaɪk] *adj* distingué(e).

Ladyship ['leɪdɪʃɪp] *n* : **her/your ~** Madame la baronne/la duchesse *etc*.

lag [læg] <> *vi* : **to ~ (behind)** [person, runner] traîner ; [economy, development] être en retard, avoir du retard. <> *vt* [roof, pipe] calorifuger. <> *n* [timelag] décalage *m*.

lager ['lɑːgə'] *n* (bière *f*) blonde *f*.

lagoon [lə'guːn] *n* lagune *f*.
laid [leɪd] *pt & pp* ⊳ **lay**.
laid-back *adj inf* relaxe, décontracté(e).
lain [leɪn] *pp* ⊳ **lie**.
lair [leəʳ] *n* repaire *m*, antre *m*.
laity ['leɪətɪ] *n* RELIG : **the ~** les laïcs *mpl*.
lake [leɪk] *n* lac *m*.
Lake District *n* : **the ~** la région des lacs *(au nord-ouest de l'Angleterre)*.
Lake Geneva *n* le lac Léman OR de Genève.
lamb [læm] *n* agneau *m*.
lambswool ['læmzwʊl] ⋄ *n* lambswool *m*. ⋄ *comp* en lambswool, en laine d'agneau.
lame [leɪm] *adj lit & fig* boiteux(euse).
lament [lə'ment] ⋄ *n* lamentation *f*. ⋄ *vt* se lamenter sur.
lamentable ['læməntəbl] *adj* lamentable.
laminated ['læmɪneɪtɪd] *adj* [wood] stratifié(e) ; [glass] feuilleté(e) ; [steel] laminé(e).
lamp [læmp] *n* lampe *f*.
lampoon [læm'puːn] ⋄ *n* satire *f*. ⋄ *vt* faire la satire de.
lamppost ['læmppəʊst] *n* réverbère *m*.
lampshade ['læmpʃeɪd] *n* abat-jour *m inv*.
lance [lɑːns] ⋄ *n* lance *f*. ⋄ *vt* [boil] percer.
lance corporal *n* caporal *m*.
land [lænd] ⋄ *n* **- 1.** [solid ground] terre *f* (ferme) ; [farming ground] terre, terrain *m* **- 2.** [property] terres *fpl*, propriété *f* **- 3.** [nation] pays *m*. ⋄ *vt* **- 1.** [from ship, plane] débarquer **- 2.** [catch - fish] prendre **- 3.** [plane] atterrir **- 4.** *inf* [obtain] décrocher **- 5.** *inf* [place] : **to ~ sb in trouble** attirer des ennuis à qqn ; **to be ~ed with sthg** se coltiner qqch. ⋄ *vi* **- 1.** [plane] atterrir **- 2.** [fall] tomber. ➡ **land up** *vi inf* atterrir.
landing ['lændɪŋ] *n* **- 1.** [of stairs] palier *m* **- 2.** AERON atterrissage *m* **- 3.** [of goods from ship] débarquement *m*.
landing card *n* carte *f* de débarquement.
landing gear *n* (U) train *m* d'atterrissage.
landing stage *n* débarcadère *m*.
landing strip *n* piste *f* d'atterrissage.
landlady ['lænd,leɪdɪ] *n* [living in] logeuse *f* ; [owner] propriétaire *f*.
landlord ['lændlɔːd] *n* **- 1.** [of rented property] propriétaire *m* **- 2.** *Br* [of pub] patron *m*.
landmark ['lændmɑːk] *n* point *m* de repère ; *fig* événement *m* marquant.

landowner ['lænd,əʊnəʳ] *n* propriétaire foncier *m*, propriétaire foncière *f*.
landscape ['lændskeɪp] *n* paysage *m*.
landslide ['lændslaɪd] *n* **- 1.** [of earth] glissement *m* de terrain ; [of rocks] éboulement *m* **- 2.** *fig* [election victory] victoire *f* écrasante.
lane [leɪn] *n* **- 1.** [in country] petite route *f*, chemin *m* **- 2.** [in town] ruelle *f* **- 3.** [for traffic] voie *f* ; **'keep in ~'** 'ne changez pas de file' **- 4.** AERON & SPORT couloir *m*.
language ['læŋgwɪdʒ] *n* **- 1.** [of people, country] langue *f* **- 2.** [terminology, ability to speak] langage *m*.
language laboratory *n* laboratoire *m* de langues.
languid ['læŋgwɪd] *adj* indolent(e).
languish ['læŋgwɪʃ] *vi* languir.
lank [læŋk] *adj* terne.
lanky ['læŋkɪ] *adj* dégingandé(e).
lantern ['læntən] *n* lanterne *f*.
lap [læp] ⋄ *n* **- 1.** [of person] : **on sb's ~** sur les genoux de qqn **- 2.** [of race] tour *m* de piste. ⋄ *vt* **- 1.** [subj : animal] laper **- 2.** [in race] prendre un tour d'avance sur. ⋄ *vi* [water, waves] clapoter.
lapel [lə'pel] *n* revers *m*.
Lapland ['læplænd] *n* Laponie *f*.
lapse [læps] ⋄ *n* **- 1.** [failing] défaillance *f* **- 2.** [in behaviour] écart *m* de conduite **- 3.** [of time] intervalle *m*, laps *m* de temps. ⋄ *vi* **- 1.** [passport] être périmé(e) ; [membership] prendre fin ; [tradition] se perdre **- 2.** [person] : **to ~ into bad habits** prendre de mauvaises habitudes.
laptop computer *n* (ordinateur *m*) portable *m*.
larceny ['lɑːsənɪ] *n* (U) vol *m* (simple).
lard [lɑːd] *n* saindoux *m*.
larder ['lɑːdəʳ] *n* garde-manger *m inv*.
large [lɑːdʒ] *adj* grand(e) ; [person, animal, book] gros (grosse). ➡ **at large** *adv* **- 1.** [as a whole] dans son ensemble **- 2.** [prisoner, animal] en liberté. ➡ **by and large** *adv* dans l'ensemble.
largely ['lɑːdʒlɪ] *adv* en grande partie.
lark [lɑːk] *n* **- 1.** [bird] alouette *f* **- 2.** *inf* [joke] blague *f*. ➡ **lark about** *vi* s'amuser.
laryngitis [,lærɪn'dʒaɪtɪs] *n* (U) laryngite *f*.
larynx ['lærɪŋks] *n* larynx *m*.
lasagna, lasagne [lə'zænjə] *n* (U) lasagnes *fpl*.
laser ['leɪzəʳ] *n* laser *m*.
laser printer *n* imprimante *f* (à) laser.

lash [læʃ] ◇ n - **1.** [eyelash] cil m - **2.** [with whip] coup m de fouet. ◇ vt - **1.** [gen] fouetter - **2.** [tie] attacher. ◆ **lash out** vi - **1.** [physically] : **to ~ out (at** OR **against)** envoyer un coup (à) - **2.** Br inf [spend money] : **to ~ out (on sthg)** faire une folie (en s'achetant qqch).

lass [læs] n jeune fille f.

lasso [læ'su:] (pl -s) ◇ n lasso m. ◇ vt attraper au lasso.

last [lɑ:st] ◇ adj dernier(ère) ; **~ week/year** la semaine/l'année dernière, la semaine/l'année passée ; **~ night** hier soir ; **~ but one** avant-dernier (avant-dernière) ; **down to the ~ detail/penny** jusqu'au moindre détail/dernier sou. ◇ adv - **1.** [most recently] la dernière fois - **2.** [finally] en dernier, le dernier (la dernière). ◇ pron : **the Saturday before ~** pas samedi dernier, mais le samedi d'avant ; **the year before ~** il y a deux ans ; **the ~ but one** l'avant-dernier m, l'avant-dernière f ; **to leave sthg till ~** faire qqch en dernier. ◇ n : **the ~ I saw of him** la dernière fois que je l'ai vu. ◇ vi durer ; [food] se garder, se conserver ; [feeling] persister. ◆ **at (long) last** adv enfin.

last-ditch adj ultime, désespéré(e).

lasting ['lɑ:stɪŋ] adj durable.

lastly ['lɑ:stlɪ] adv pour terminer, finalement.

last-minute adj de dernière minute.

last name n nom m de famille.

latch [lætʃ] n loquet m. ◆ **latch onto** vt fus inf s'accrocher à.

late [leɪt] ◇ adj - **1.** [not on time] : **to be ~ (for sthg)** être en retard (pour qqch) - **2.** [near end of] : **in ~ December** vers la fin décembre - **3.** [later than normal] tardif(ive) - **4.** [former] ancien(enne) - **5.** [dead] feu(e). ◇ adv - **1.** [not on time] en retard ; **to arrive 20 minutes ~** arriver avec 20 minutes de retard - **2.** [later than normal] tard ; **to work/go to bed ~** travailler/se coucher tard. ◆ **of late** adv récemment, dernièrement.

latecomer ['leɪt,kʌmər] n retardataire mf.

lately ['leɪtlɪ] adv ces derniers temps, dernièrement.

latent ['leɪtənt] adj latent(e).

later ['leɪtər] ◇ adj [date] ultérieur(e) ; [edition] postérieur(e). ◇ adv : **~ (on)** plus tard.

lateral ['lætərəl] adj latéral(e).

latest ['leɪtɪst] ◇ adj dernier(ère). ◇ n : **at the ~** au plus tard.

lathe [leɪð] n tour m.

lather ['lɑ:ðər] ◇ n mousse f (de savon). ◇ vt savonner.

Latin ['lætɪn] ◇ adj latin(e). ◇ n [language] latin m.

Latin America n Amérique f latine.

Latin American ◇ adj latino-américain(e). ◇ n [person] Latino-Américain m, -e f.

latitude ['lætɪtjuːd] n latitude f.

latter ['lætər] ◇ adj - **1.** [later] dernier(ère) - **2.** [second] deuxième. ◇ n : **the ~** celui-ci (celle-ci), ce dernier (cette dernière).

latterly ['lætəlɪ] adv récemment.

lattice ['lætɪs] n treillis m, treillage m.

Latvia ['lætvɪə] n Lettonie f.

laudable ['lɔ:dəbl] adj louable.

laugh [lɑ:f] ◇ n rire m ; **we had a good ~** inf on a bien rigolé, on s'est bien amusé ; **to do sthg for ~s** OR **a ~** inf faire qqch pour rire OR rigoler. ◇ vi rire. ◆ **laugh at** vt fus [mock] se moquer de, rire de. ◆ **laugh off** vt sep tourner en plaisanterie.

laughable ['lɑ:fəbl] adj ridicule, risible.

laughingstock ['lɑ:fɪŋstɒk] n risée f.

laughter ['lɑ:ftər] n (U) rire m, rires mpl.

launch [lɔ:ntʃ] ◇ n - **1.** [gen] lancement m - **2.** [boat] chaloupe f. ◇ vt lancer.

launch(ing) pad ['lɔ:ntʃ(ɪŋ)-] n pas m de tir.

launder ['lɔ:ndər] vt lit & fig blanchir.

laund(e)rette, Laundromat® Am ['lɔ:ndrəmæt] n laverie f automatique.

laundry ['lɔ:ndrɪ] n - **1.** (U) [clothes] lessive f - **2.** [business] blanchisserie f.

laurel ['lɒrəl] n laurier m.

lava ['lɑ:və] n lave f.

lavatory ['lævətrɪ] n toilettes fpl.

lavender ['lævəndər] n [plant] lavande f.

lavish ['lævɪʃ] ◇ adj - **1.** [generous] généreux(euse) ; **to be ~ with** être prodigue de - **2.** [sumptuous] somptueux(euse). ◇ vt : **to ~ sthg on sb** prodiguer qqch à qqn.

law [lɔ:] n - **1.** [gen] loi f ; **against the ~** contraire à la loi, illégal(e) ; **to break the ~** enfreindre OR transgresser la loi ; **~ and order** ordre m public - **2.** JUR droit m.

law-abiding [-ə,baɪdɪŋ] adj respectueux(euse) des lois.

law court n tribunal m, cour f de justice.

lawful ['lɔ:fʊl] adj légal(e), licite.

lawn [lɔ:n] n pelouse f, gazon m.

lawnmower ['lɔːn‚məʊəʳ] *n* tondeuse *f* à gazon.

lawn tennis *n* tennis *m*.

law school *n* faculté *f* de droit.

lawsuit ['lɔːsuːt] *n* procès *m*.

lawyer ['lɔːjəʳ] *n* [in court] avocat *m* ; [of company] conseiller *m* juridique ; [for wills, sales] notaire *m*.

lax [læks] *adj* relâché(e).

laxative ['læksətɪv] *n* laxatif *m*.

lay [leɪ] (*pt* & *pp* laid) ◇ *pt* ⊳ **lie**. ◇ *vt* - **1.** [gen] poser, mettre ; *fig* : **to ~ the blame for sthg on sb** rejeter la responsabilité de qqch sur qqn - **2.** [trap, snare] tendre, dresser ; [plans] faire ; **to ~ the table** mettre la table OR le couvert - **3.** [egg] pondre. ◇ *adj* - **1.** RELIG laïque - **2.** [untrained] profane.
◆ **lay aside** *vt sep* mettre de côté.
◆ **lay down** *vt sep* - **1.** [guidelines, rules] imposer, stipuler - **2.** [put down] déposer.
◆ **lay off** ◇ *vt sep* [make redundant] licencier. ◇ *vt fus inf* - **1.** [leave alone] ficher la paix à - **2.** [give up] arrêter. ◆ **lay on** *vt sep Br* [provide, supply] organiser. ◆ **lay out** *vt sep* - **1.** [arrange] arranger, disposer - **2.** [design] concevoir.

layabout ['leɪəbaʊt] *n Br inf* fainéant *m*, -e *f*.

lay-by (*pl* lay-bys) *n Br* aire *f* de stationnement.

layer ['leɪəʳ] *n* couche *f* ; *fig* [level] niveau *m*.

layman ['leɪmən] (*pl* -men [-mən]) *n* - **1.** [untrained person] profane *m* - **2.** RELIG laïc *m*.

layout ['leɪaʊt] *n* [of office, building] agencement *m* ; [of garden] plan *m* ; [of page] mise *f* en page.

laze [leɪz] *vi* : **to ~ (about** OR **around)** paresser.

lazy ['leɪzɪ] *adj* [person] paresseux(euse), fainéant(e) ; [action] nonchalant(e).

lazybones ['leɪzɪbəʊnz] (*pl inv*) *n* paresseux *m*, -euse *f*, fainéant *m*, -e *f*.

lb (*abbr of* pound) livre (*unité de poids*).

LCD (*abbr of* liquid crystal display) *n* affichage à cristaux liquides.

lead¹ [liːd] (*pt* & *pp* led) ◇ *n* - **1.** [winning position] : **to be in** OR **have the ~** mener, être en tête - **2.** [amount ahead] : **to have a ~ of ...** devancer de ... - **3.** [initiative, example] initiative *f*, exemple *m* ; **to take the ~** montrer l'exemple - **4.** THEATRE : **the ~** le rôle principal - **5.** [clue] indice *m* - **6.** *Br* [for dog] laisse *f* - **7.** [wire, cable] câble *m*, fil *m*. ◇ *adj* [role etc] principal(e). ◇ *vt* - **1.** [be at front of]

mener, être à la tête de - **2.** [guide] guider, conduire - **3.** [be in charge of] être à la tête de, diriger - **4.** [organize - protest etc] mener, organiser - **5.** [life] mener - **6.** [cause] : **to ~ sb to do sthg** inciter OR pousser qqn à faire qqch. ◇ *vi* - **1.** [path, cable etc] mener, conduire - **2.** [give access] : **to ~ to/into** donner sur, donner accès à - **3.** [in race, match] mener - **4.** [result in] : **to ~ to sthg** aboutir à qqch, causer qqch. ◆ **lead up to** *vt fus* - **1.** [precede] conduire à, aboutir à - **2.** [build up to] amener.

lead² [led] ◇ *n* plomb *m* ; [in pencil] mine *f*. ◇ *comp* en OR de plomb.

leaded ['ledɪd] *adj* [petrol] au plomb ; [window] à petits carreaux.

leader ['liːdəʳ] *n* - **1.** [head, chief] chef *m* ; POL leader *m* - **2.** [in race, competition] premier *m*, -ère *f* - **3.** *Br* PRESS éditorial *m*.

leadership ['liːdəʃɪp] *n* - **1.** [people in charge] : **the ~** les dirigeants *mpl* - **2.** [position of leader] direction *f* - **3.** [qualities of leader] qualités *fpl* de chef.

lead-free [led-] *adj* sans plomb.

leading ['liːdɪŋ] *adj* - **1.** [most important] principal(e) - **2.** [at front] de tête.

leading light *n* personnage *m* très important OR influent.

leaf [liːf] (*pl* leaves [liːvz]) *n* - **1.** [of tree, plant] feuille *f* - **2.** [of table, book] abattant *m* ; [- pull-out] rallonge *f* - **3.** [of book] feuille *f*, page *f*. ◆ **leaf through** *vt fus* [magazine etc] parcourir, feuilleter.

leaflet ['liːflɪt] *n* prospectus *m*.

league [liːg] *n* ligue *f* ; SPORT championnat *m* ; **to be in ~ with** être de connivence avec.

leak [liːk] ◇ *n lit* & *fig* fuite *f*. ◇ *vt fig* [secret, information] divulguer. ◇ *vi* fuir.
◆ **leak out** *vi* - **1.** [liquid] fuir - **2.** *fig* [secret, information] transpirer, être divulgué(e).

leakage ['liːkɪdʒ] *n* fuite *f*.

lean [liːn] (*pt* & *pp* leant OR -ed) ◇ *adj* - **1.** [slim] mince - **2.** [meat] maigre - **3.** *fig* [month, time] mauvais(e). ◇ *vt* [rest] : **to ~ sthg against** appuyer qqch contre, adosser qqch à. ◇ *vi* - **1.** [bend, slope] se pencher - **2.** [rest] : **to ~ on/against** s'appuyer sur/contre.

leaning ['liːnɪŋ] *n* : **~ (towards)** penchant *m* (pour).

leant [lent] *pt* & *pp* ⊳ **lean**.

lean-to (*pl* lean-tos) *n* appentis *m*.

leap [liːp] (*pt* & *pp* leapt OR -ed) ◇ *n lit* & *fig* bond *m*. ◇ *vi* - **1.** [gen] bondir - **2.** *fig* [increase] faire un bond.

leapfrog ['li:pfrɒg] ◇ n saute-mouton m inv. ◇ vt dépasser (d'un bond). ◇ vi : **to ~ over** sauter par-dessus.

leapt [lept] pt & pp ⮕ leap.

leap year n année f bissextile.

learn [lɜ:n] (pt & pp **-ed** OR **learnt**) ◇ vt : **to ~ (that)** ... apprendre que ... ; **to ~ (how) to do sthg** apprendre à faire qqch. ◇ vi : **to ~ (of** OR **about sthg)** apprendre (qqch).

learned ['lɜ:nɪd] adj savant(e).

learner ['lɜ:nər] n débutant m, -e f.

learner (driver) n Br conducteur débutant m, conductrice débutante f (qui n'a pas encore son permis).

learning ['lɜ:nɪŋ] n savoir m, érudition f.

learnt [lɜ:nt] pt & pp ⮕ learn.

lease [li:s] ◇ n bail m. ◇ vt louer ; **to ~ sthg from sb** louer qqch à qqn ; **to ~ sthg to sb** louer qqch à qqn.

leasehold ['li:shəʊld] ◇ adj loué(e) à bail, tenu(e) à bail. ◇ adv à bail.

leash [li:ʃ] n laisse f.

least [li:st] (superl of little) ◇ adj : **the ~** le moindre (la moindre), le plus petit (la plus petite). ◇ pron [smallest amount] : **the ~** le moins ; **it's the ~ (that) he can do** c'est la moindre des choses qu'il puisse faire ; **not in the ~** pas du tout, pas le moins du monde ; **to say the ~** c'est le moins qu'on puisse dire. ◇ adv : **(the) ~** le moins (la moins). ◆ **at least** adv au moins ; [to correct] du moins. ◆ **least of all** adv surtout pas, encore moins. ◆ **not least** adv fml notamment.

leather ['leðər] ◇ n cuir m. ◇ comp en cuir.

leave [li:v] (pt & pp **left**) ◇ vt - **1.** [gen] laisser ; **to ~ sb alone** laisser qqn tranquille - **2.** [go away from] quitter - **3.** [bequeath] : **to ~ sb sthg, to ~ sthg to sb** léguer OR laisser qqch à qqn ; see also **left**. ◇ vi partir. ◇ n congé m ; **to be on ~** [from work] être en congé ; [from army] être en permission. ◆ **leave behind** vt sep - **1.** [abandon] abandonner, laisser - **2.** [forget] oublier, laisser. ◆ **leave out** vt sep omettre, exclure.

leave of absence n congé m.

leaves [li:vz] pl ⮕ leaf.

Lebanon ['lebənən] n Liban m.

lecherous ['letʃərəs] adj lubrique, libidineux(euse).

lecture ['lektʃər] ◇ n - **1.** [talk - gen] conférence f ; [- UNIV] cours m magistral - **2.** [scolding] : **to give sb a ~** réprimander qqn, sermonner qqn. ◇ vt [scold] réprimander, sermonner. ◇ vi : **to ~ on sthg** faire un cours sur qqch ; **to ~ in sthg** être professeur de qqch.

lecturer ['lektʃərər] n [speaker] conférencier m, -ère f ; UNIV maître assistant m.

led [led] pt & pp ⮕ lead[1].

ledge [ledʒ] n - **1.** [of window] rebord m - **2.** [of mountain] corniche f.

ledger ['ledʒər] n grand livre m.

leech [li:tʃ] n lit & fig sangsue f.

leek [li:k] n poireau m.

leer [lɪər] ◇ n regard m libidineux. ◇ vi : **to ~ at** reluquer.

leeway ['li:weɪ] n [room to manoeuvre] marge f de manœuvre.

left [left] ◇ pt & pp ⮕ leave. ◇ adj - **1.** [remaining] : **to be ~** rester ; **have you any money ~?** il te reste de l'argent? - **2.** [not right] gauche. ◇ adv à gauche. ◇ n : **on** OR **to the ~** à gauche. ◆ **Left** POL : **the Left** la Gauche.

left-hand adj de gauche ; **~ side** gauche f, côté m gauche.

left-hand drive adj [car] avec la conduite à gauche.

left-handed [-'hændɪd] adj - **1.** [person] gaucher(ère) - **2.** [implement] pour gaucher.

left luggage (office) n Br consigne f.

leftover ['leftəʊvər] adj qui reste, en surplus. ◆ **leftovers** npl restes mpl.

left wing n POL gauche f. ◆ **left-wing** adj POL de gauche.

leg [leg] n - **1.** [of person, trousers] jambe f ; [of animal] patte f ; **to pull sb's ~** faire marcher qqn - **2.** CULIN [of lamb] gigot m ; [of pork, chicken] cuisse f - **3.** [of furniture] pied m - **4.** [of journey, match] étape f.

legacy ['legəsɪ] n lit & fig legs m, héritage m.

legal ['li:gl] adj - **1.** [concerning the law] juridique - **2.** [lawful] légal(e).

legalize, -ise ['li:gəlaɪz] vt légaliser, rendre légal.

legal tender n monnaie f légale.

legend ['ledʒənd] n lit & fig légende f.

leggings ['legɪŋz] npl jambières fpl, leggings mpl OR fpl.

legible ['ledʒəbl] adj lisible.

legislation [ˌledʒɪs'leɪʃn] n législation f.

legislature ['ledʒɪsleɪtʃər] n corps m législatif.

legitimate [lɪ'dʒɪtɪmət] adj légitime.

legless ['legləs] adj Br inf [drunk] bourré(e), rond(e).

legroom ['legrʊm] *n (U)* place *f* pour les jambes.

leg-warmers [-ˌwɔːməz] *npl* jambières *fpl*.

leisure [*Br* 'leʒə', *Am* 'liːʒər] *n* loisir *m*, temps *m* libre ; **at (one's) ~** à loisir, tout à loisir.

leisure centre *Br,* **center** *Am n* centre *m* de loisirs.

leisurely [*Br* 'leʒəlı, *Am* 'liːʒərlı] ◇ *adj* [pace] lent(e), tranquille. ◇ *adv* [walk] sans se presser.

leisure time *n (U)* temps *m* libre, loisirs *mpl*.

lemon ['lemən] *n* [fruit] citron *m*.

lemonade [ˌlemə'neɪd] *n* - **1.** *Br* [fizzy] limonade *f* - **2.** [still] citronnade *f*.

lemon juice *n* jus *m* de citron.

lemon sole *n* limande-sole *f*.

lemon squash *n Br* citronnade *f*.

lemon squeezer [-'skwiːzər] *n* presse-citron *m inv*.

lemon tea *n* thé *m* (au) citron.

lend [lend] (*pt & pp* lent) *vt* - **1.** [loan] prêter ; **to ~ sb sthg, to ~ sthg to sb** prêter qqch à qqn - **2.** [offer] : **to ~ support (to sb)** offrir son soutien (à qqn) ; **to ~ assistance (to sb)** prêter assistance (à qqn) - **3.** [add] : **to ~ sthg to sthg** [quality etc] ajouter qqch à qqch.

lending rate ['lendɪŋ-] *n* taux *m* de crédit.

length [leŋθ] *n* - **1.** [gen] longueur *f* ; **what ~ is it?** ça fait quelle longueur? ; **it's five metres in ~** cela fait cinq mètres de long - **2.** [piece - of string, wood] morceau *m*, bout *m* ; [- of cloth] coupon *m* - **3.** [duration] durée *f* - **4.** *phr* : **to go to great ~s to do sthg** tout faire pour faire qqch. ◆ **at length** *adv* - **1.** [eventually] enfin - **2.** [in detail] à fond.

lengthen ['leŋθən] ◇ *vt* [dress etc] rallonger ; [life] prolonger. ◇ *vi* allonger.

lengthways ['leŋθweɪz] *adv* dans le sens de la longueur.

lengthy ['leŋθı] *adj* très long (longue).

lenient ['liːnjənt] *adj* [person] indulgent(e) ; [laws] clément(e).

lens [lenz] *n* - **1.** [of camera] objectif *m* ; [of glasses] verre *m* - **2.** [contact lens] verre *m* de contact, lentille *f* (cornéenne).

lent [lent] *pt & pp* ▷ **lend**.

Lent [lent] *n* Carême *m*.

lentil ['lentıl] *n* lentille *f*.

Leo ['liːəʊ] *n* Lion *m*.

leopard ['lepəd] *n* léopard *m*.

leotard ['liːətaːd] *n* collant *m*.

leper ['lepər] *n* lépreux *m*, -euse *f*.

leprosy ['leprəsı] *n* lèpre *f*.

lesbian ['lezbıən] *n* lesbienne *f*.

less [les] *(compar of little)* ◇ *adj* moins de ; **~ money/time than me** moins d'argent/de temps que moi. ◇ *pron* moins ; **it costs ~ than you think** ça coûte moins cher que tu ne le crois ; **no ~ than £50** pas moins de 50 livres ; **the ~ ... the ~ ...** moins ... moins ... ◇ *adv* moins ; **~ than five** moins de cinq ; **~ and ~** de moins en moins. ◇ *prep* [minus] moins.

lessen ['lesn] ◇ *vt* [risk, chance] diminuer, réduire ; [pain] atténuer. ◇ *vi* [gen] diminuer ; [pain] s'atténuer.

lesser ['lesər] *adj* moindre ; **to a ~ extent** OR **degree** à un degré moindre.

lesson ['lesn] *n* leçon *f*, cours *m* ; **to teach sb a ~** *fig* donner une (bonne) leçon à qqn.

let [let] (*pt & pp* let) *vt* - **1.** [allow] : **to ~ sb do sthg** laisser qqn faire qqch ; **to ~ sb know sthg** dire qqch à qqn ; **to ~ go of sb/ sthg** lâcher qqn/qqch ; **to ~ sb go** [gen] laisser (partir) qqn ; [prisoner] libérer qqn - **2.** [in verb forms] : **~ them wait** qu'ils attendent ; **~'s go!** allons-y! ; **~'s see** voyons - **3.** [rent out] louer ; **'to ~'** 'à louer'. ◆ **let alone** *conj* encore moins, sans parler de.
◆ **let down** *vt sep* - **1.** [deflate] dégonfler - **2.** [disappoint] décevoir. ◆ **let in** *vt sep* [admit] laisser OR faire entrer. ◆ **let off** *vt sep* - **1.** [excuse] : **to ~ sb off sthg** dispenser qqn de qqch - **2.** [not punish] ne pas punir - **3.** [bomb] faire éclater ; [gun, firework] faire partir. ◆ **let on** *vi* : **don't ~ on!** ne dis rien (à personne)!. ◆ **let out** *vt sep* - **1.** [allow to go out] laisser sortir ; **to ~ air out of sthg** dégonfler qqch - **2.** [laugh, scream] laisser échapper. ◆ **let up** *vi* - **1.** [rain] diminuer - **2.** [person] s'arrêter.

letdown ['letdaʊn] *n inf* déception *f*.

lethal ['liːθl] *adj* mortel(elle), fatal(e).

lethargic [lə'θaːdʒɪk] *adj* léthargique.

let's [lets] = let us.

letter ['letər] *n* lettre *f*.

letter bomb *n* lettre *f* piégée.

letterbox ['letəbɒks] *n Br* boîte *f* aux OR à lettres.

letter of credit *n* lettre *f* de crédit.

lettuce ['letıs] *n* laitue *f*, salade *f*.

letup ['letʌp] *n* [in fighting] répit *m* ; [in work] relâchement *m*.

leuk(a)emia [luː'kiːmıə] *n* leucémie *f*.

level ['levl] ◇ *adj* - **1.** [equal in height] à la même hauteur ; [horizontal] horizontal(e) ; **to be ~ with** être au niveau de - **2.** [equal in standard] à égalité - **3.** [flat] plat(e), plan(e). ⬦ *n* - **1.** [gen] niveau *m* ; **to be on the ~** *inf* être réglo - **2.** *Am* [spirit level] niveau *m* à bulle. ⬦ *vt* - **1.** [make flat] niveler, aplanir - **2.** [demolish] raser. ➠ **level off, level out** *vi* - **1.** [inflation etc] se stabiliser - **2.** [aeroplane] se mettre en palier. ➠ **level with** *vt fus inf* être franc (franche) OR honnête avec.

level crossing *n Br* passage *m* à niveau.

level-headed [-'hedɪd] *adj* raisonnable.

lever [*Br* 'liːvəᶜ, *Am* 'levəᶜ] *n* levier *m*.

leverage [*Br* 'liːvərɪdʒ, *Am* 'levərɪdʒ] *n (U)* - **1.** [force] : **to get ~ on sthg** avoir une prise sur qqch - **2.** *fig* [influence] influence *f*.

levy ['levɪ] ⬦ *n* prélèvement *m*, impôt *m*. ⬦ *vt* prélever, percevoir.

lewd [ljuːd] *adj* obscène.

liability [ˌlaɪə'bɪlətɪ] *n* responsabilité *f* ; *fig* [person] danger *m* public. ➠ **liabilities** *npl* FIN dettes *fpl*, passif *m*.

liable ['laɪəbl] *adj* - **1.** [likely] : **to be ~ to do sthg** risquer de faire qqch, être susceptible de faire qqch - **2.** [prone] : **to be ~ to sthg** être sujet(ette) à qqch - **3.** JUR : **to be ~ (for)** être responsable (de) ; **to be ~ to** être passible de.

liaise [lɪ'eɪz] *vi* : **to ~ with** assurer la liaison avec.

liar ['laɪəᶜ] *n* menteur *m*, -euse *f*.

libel ['laɪbl] ⬦ *n* diffamation *f*. ⬦ *vt* diffamer.

liberal ['lɪbərəl] ⬦ *adj* - **1.** [tolerant] libéral(e) - **2.** [generous] généreux(euse). ⬦ *n* libéral *m*, -e *f*. ➠ **Liberal** POL ⬦ *adj* libéral(e). ⬦ *n* libéral *m*, -e *f*.

Liberal Democrat *n* adhérent du principal parti centriste britannique.

liberate ['lɪbəreɪt] *vt* libérer.

liberation [ˌlɪbə'reɪʃn] *n* libération *f*.

liberty ['lɪbətɪ] *n* liberté *f* ; **at ~** en liberté ; **to be at ~ to do sthg** être libre de faire qqch ; **to take liberties (with sb)** prendre des libertés (avec qqn).

Libra ['liːbrə] *n* Balance *f*.

librarian [laɪ'breərɪən] *n* bibliothécaire *mf*.

library ['laɪbrərɪ] *n* bibliothèque *f*.

library book *n* livre *m* de bibliothèque.

libretto [lɪ'bretəʊ] (*pl* **-s**) *n* livret *m*.

Libya ['lɪbɪə] *n* Libye *f*.

lice [laɪs] *pl* ⬦ **louse**.

licence ['laɪsəns] ⬦ *n* - **1.** [gen] permis *m*, autorisation *f* ; **driving** *Br* OR **driver's** *Am* **~**

permis *m* de conduire ; TV **~** redevance *f* télé - **2.** COMM licence *f*. ⬦ *vt Am* = **license**.

license ['laɪsəns] ⬦ *vt* autoriser. ⬦ *n Am* = **licence**.

licensed ['laɪsənst] *adj* - **1.** [person] : **to be ~ to do sthg** avoir un permis pour OR l'autorisation de faire qqch - **2.** *Br* [premises] qui détient une licence de débit de boissons.

license plate *n Am* plaque *f* d'immatriculation.

lick [lɪk] *vt* - **1.** [gen] lécher - **2.** *inf* [defeat] écraser.

licorice ['lɪkərɪs] = **liquorice**.

lid [lɪd] *n* - **1.** [cover] couvercle *m* - **2.** [eyelid] paupière *f*.

lie [laɪ] (*pt sense 1* **lied**, *pt senses 2-6* **lay**, *pp sense 1* **lied**, *pp senses 2-6* **lain**, *cont all senses* **lying**) ⬦ *n* mensonge *m* ; **to tell ~s** mentir, dire des mensonges. ⬦ *vi* - **1.** [tell lie] : **to ~ (to sb)** mentir (à qqn) - **2.** [be horizontal] être allongé(e), être couché(e) - **3.** [lie down] s'allonger, se coucher - **4.** [be situated] se trouver, être - **5.** [difficulty, solution etc] résider - **6.** *phr* : **to ~ low** se planquer, se tapir. ➠ **lie about, lie around** *vi* traîner. ➠ **lie down** *vi* s'allonger, se coucher. ➠ **lie in** *vi Br* rester au lit, faire la grasse matinée.

Liechtenstein ['lɪktənstaɪn] *n* Liechtenstein *m*.

lie-down *n Br* : **to have a ~** faire une sieste OR un (petit) somme.

lie-in *n Br* : **to have a ~** faire la grasse matinée.

lieutenant [*Br* lef'tenənt, *Am* luː'tenənt] *n* lieutenant *m*.

life [laɪf] (*pl* **lives** [laɪvz]) *n* - **1.** [gen] vie *f* ; **that's ~!** c'est la vie! ; **for ~** à vie ; **to come to ~** s'éveiller, s'animer ; **to scare the ~ out of sb** faire une peur bleue à qqn - **2.** *(U) inf* [life imprisonment] emprisonnement *m* à perpétuité.

life assurance = **life insurance**.

life belt *n* bouée *f* de sauvetage.

lifeboat ['laɪfbəʊt] *n* canot *m* de sauvetage.

life buoy *n* bouée *f* de sauvetage.

life expectancy [-ɪk'spektənsɪ] *n* espérance *f* de vie.

lifeguard ['laɪfgɑːd] *n* [at swimming pool] maître-nageur sauveteur *m* ; [at beach] gardien *m* de plage.

life imprisonment [-ɪm'prɪznmənt] *n* emprisonnement *m* à perpétuité.

life insurance *n* assurance-vie *f*.

life jacket *n* gilet *m* de sauvetage.

lifeless ['laɪflɪs] *adj* - **1.** [dead] sans vie, inanimé(e) - **2.** [listless - performance] qui manque de vie ; [- voice] monotone.

lifelike ['laɪflaɪk] *adj* - **1.** [statue, doll] qui semble vivant(e) - **2.** [portrait] ressemblant(e).

lifeline ['laɪflaɪn] *n* corde *f* (de sauvetage) ; *fig* lien *m* vital (avec l'extérieur).

lifelong ['laɪflɒŋ] *adj* de toujours.

life preserver [-prɪˌzɜːvəʳ] *n Am* [life belt] bouée *f* de sauvetage ; [life jacket] gilet *m* de sauvetage.

life raft *n* canot *m* pneumatique (de sauvetage).

lifesaver ['laɪfˌseɪvəʳ] *n* [person] maître-nageur sauveteur *m*.

life sentence *n* condamnation *f* à perpétuité.

life-size(d) [-saɪz(d)] *adj* grandeur nature *(inv)*.

lifespan ['laɪfspæn] *n* - **1.** [of person, animal] espérance *f* de vie - **2.** [of product, machine] durée *f* de vie.

lifestyle ['laɪfstaɪl] *n* style *m* de vie.

life-support system *n* respirateur *m* artificiel.

lifetime ['laɪftaɪm] *n* vie *f* ; **in my ~** de mon vivant.

lift [lɪft] ◇ *n* - **1.** [in car] : **to give sb a ~** emmener OR prendre qqn en voiture - **2.** *Br* [elevator] ascenseur *m*. ◇ *vt* - **1.** [gen] lever ; [weight] soulever - **2.** [plagiarize] plagier - **3.** *inf* [steal] voler. ◇ *vi* - **1.** [lid etc] s'ouvrir - **2.** [fog etc] se lever.

lift-off *n* décollage *m*.

light [laɪt] (*pt & pp* lit OR **-ed**) ◇ *adj* - **1.** [not dark] clair(e) - **2.** [not heavy] léger(ère) - **3.** [traffic] fluide ; [corrections] peu nombreux(euses) - **4.** [work] facile. ◇ *n* - **1.** *(U)* [brightness] lumière *f* - **2.** [device] lampe *f* - **3.** AUT - gen] feu *m* ; [- headlamp] phare *m* - **4.** [for cigarette etc] feu *m* ; **have you got a ~?** vous avez du feu? ; **to set ~ to sthg** mettre le feu à qqch - **5.** [perspective] : **in the ~ of** *Br*, **in ~ of** *Am* à la lumière de - **6.** *phr* : **to come to ~** être découvert(e) OR dévoilé(e). ◇ *vt* - **1.** [fire, cigarette] allumer - **2.** [room, stage] éclairer. ◇ *adv* : **to travel ~** voyager léger. ◆ **light up** ◇ *vt sep* - **1.** [illuminate] éclairer - **2.** [cigarette etc] allumer. ◇ *vi* - **1.** [face] s'éclairer - **2.** *inf* [start smoking] allumer une cigarette.

light bulb *n* ampoule *f*.

lighten ['laɪtn] ◇ *vt* - **1.** [give light to] éclairer ; [make less dark] éclaircir - **2.** [make less heavy] alléger. ◇ *vi* [brighten] s'éclaircir.

lighter ['laɪtəʳ] *n* [cigarette lighter] briquet *m*.

light-headed [-'hedɪd] *adj* : **to feel ~** avoir la tête qui tourne.

light-hearted [-'hɑːtɪd] *adj* - **1.** [cheerful] joyeux(euse), gai(e) - **2.** [amusing] amusant(e).

lighthouse ['laɪthaʊs, *pl* -haʊzɪz] *n* phare *m*.

lighting ['laɪtɪŋ] *n* éclairage *m*.

light meter *n* posemètre *m*, cellule *f* photoélectrique.

lightning ['laɪtnɪŋ] *n (U)* éclair *m*, foudre *f*.

lightweight ['laɪtweɪt] ◇ *adj* [object] léger(ère). ◇ *n* [boxer] poids *m* léger.

likable ['laɪkəbl] *adj* sympathique.

like [laɪk] ◇ *prep* - **1.** [gen] comme ; **to look ~ sb/sthg** ressembler à qqn/qqch ; **to taste ~ sthg** avoir un goût de qqch ; **~ this/that** comme ci/ça - **2.** [such as] tel que, comme. ◇ *vt* - **1.** [gen] aimer ; **I ~ her** elle me plaît ; **to ~ doing** OR **to do sthg** aimer faire qqch - **2.** [expressing a wish] : **would you ~ some more cake?** vous prendrez encore du gâteau? ; **I'd ~ to go** je voudrais bien OR j'aimerais y aller ; **I'd ~ you to come** je voudrais bien OR j'aimerais que vous veniez ; **if you ~** si vous voulez. ◇ *n* : **the ~** une chose pareille. ◆ **likes** *npl* : **~s and dislikes** goûts *mpl*.

likeable ['laɪkəbl] = likable.

likelihood ['laɪklɪhʊd] *n (U)* chances *fpl*, probabilité *f*.

likely ['laɪklɪ] *adj* - **1.** [probable] probable ; **he's ~ to get angry** il risque de se fâcher ; **a ~ story!** *iro* à d'autres! - **2.** [candidate] prometteur(euse).

liken ['laɪkn] *vt* : **to ~ sb/sthg to** assimiler qqn/qqch à.

likeness ['laɪknɪs] *n* - **1.** [resemblance] : **~ (to)** ressemblance *f* (avec) - **2.** [portrait] portrait *m*.

likewise ['laɪkwaɪz] *adv* [similarly] de même ; **to do ~** faire pareil OR de même.

liking ['laɪkɪŋ] *n* [for person] affection *f*, sympathie *f* ; [for food, music] goût *m*, penchant *m* ; **to have a ~ for sthg** avoir le goût de qqch ; **to be to sb's ~** être du goût de qqn, plaire à qqn.

lilac ['laɪlək] ◇ *adj* [colour] lilas *(inv)*. ◇ *n* lilas *m*.

Lilo® ['laɪləʊ] (*pl* **-s**) *n Br* matelas *m* pneumatique.

lily ['lɪlɪ] *n* lis *m*.

lily of the valley (*pl* lilies of the valley) *n* muguet *m*.

limb [lɪm] *n* - **1.** [of body] membre *m* - **2.** [of tree] branche *f*.

limber ['lɪmbəʳ] ➡ **limber up** *vi* s'échauffer.

limbo ['lɪmbəʊ] (*pl* -s) *n* (U) [uncertain state] : **to be in** ~ être dans les limbes.

lime [laɪm] *n* - **1.** [fruit] citron *m* vert - **2.** [drink] : ~ **(juice)** jus *m* de citron vert - **3.** [linden tree] tilleul *m* - **4.** [substance] chaux *f*.

limelight ['laɪmlaɪt] *n* : **to be in the** ~ être au premier plan.

limerick ['lɪmərɪk] *n* poème humoristique en cinq vers.

limestone ['laɪmstəʊn] *n* (U) pierre *f* à chaux, calcaire *m*.

limey ['laɪmɪ] (*pl* -s) *n* Am inf terme péjoratif désignant un Anglais.

limit ['lɪmɪt] ◇ *n* limite *f* ; **off** ~**s** *esp Am* d'accès interdit ; **within** ~**s** [to an extent] dans une certaine mesure. ◇ *vt* limiter, restreindre.

limitation [ˌlɪmɪ'teɪʃn] *n* limitation *f*, restriction *f*.

limited ['lɪmɪtɪd] *adj* limité(e), restreint(e).

limited (liability) company *n* société *f* anonyme.

limo ['lɪməʊ] *n* inf abbr of **limousine**.

limousine ['lɪməzi:n] *n* limousine *f*.

limp [lɪmp] ◇ *adj* mou (molle). ◇ *n* : **to have a** ~ boiter. ◇ *vi* boiter.

limpet ['lɪmpɪt] *n* patelle *f*, bernique *f*.

line [laɪn] ◇ *n* - **1.** [gen] ligne *f* - **2.** [row] rangée *f* - **3.** [queue] file *f*, queue *f* ; **to stand** **on wait in** ~ faire la queue - **4.** [RAIL - track] voie *f* ; [- route] ligne *f* - **5.** [of poem, song] vers *m* - **6.** [wrinkle] ride *f* - **7.** [string, wire etc] corde *f* ; **a fishing** ~ une ligne - **8.** TELEC ligne *f* ; **hold the** ~! ne quittez pas! - **9.** *inf* [short letter] : **to drop sb a** ~ écrire un (petit) mot à qqn - **10.** *inf* [work] : ~ **of business** branche *f* - **11.** [borderline] frontière *f* - **12.** COMM gamme *f* - **13.** *phr* : **to draw the** ~ **at sthg** refuser de faire OR d'aller jusqu'à faire qqch ; **to step out of** ~ faire cavalier seul. ◇ *vt* [drawer, box] tapisser ; [clothes] doubler. ➡ **out of line** *adj* [remark, behaviour] déplacé(e). ➡ **line up** ◇ *vt sep* - **1.** [in rows] aligner - **2.** [organize] prévoir. ◇ *vi* [in row] s'aligner ; [in queue] faire la queue.

lined [laɪnd] *adj* - **1.** [paper] réglé(e) - **2.** [wrinkled] ridé(e).

linen ['lɪnɪn] *n* (U) - **1.** [cloth] lin *m* - **2.** [tablecloths, sheets] linge *m* (de maison).

liner ['laɪnəʳ] *n* [ship] paquebot *m*.

linesman ['laɪnzmən] (*pl* -men [-mən]) *n* TENNIS juge *m* de ligne ; FTBL juge de touche.

lineup ['laɪnʌp] *n* - **1.** SPORT équipe *f* - **2.** *Am* [identification parade] rangée *f* de suspects (pour identification par un témoin).

linger ['lɪŋgəʳ] *vi* - **1.** [person] s'attarder - **2.** [doubt, pain] persister.

lingo ['lɪŋgəʊ] (*pl* -es) *n* inf jargon *m*.

linguist ['lɪŋgwɪst] *n* linguiste *mf*.

linguistics [lɪŋ'gwɪstɪks] *n* (U) linguistique *f*.

lining ['laɪnɪŋ] *n* - **1.** [of coat, curtains, box] doublure *f* - **2.** [of stomach] muqueuse *f* - **3.** AUT [of brakes] garniture *f*.

link [lɪŋk] ◇ *n* - **1.** [of chain] maillon *m* - **2.** [connection] : ~ **(between/with)** lien *m* (entre/avec). ◇ *vt* [cities, parts] relier ; [events etc] lier ; **to** ~ **arms** se donner le bras. ➡ **link up** *vt sep* relier ; **to** ~ **sthg up** **with sthg** relier qqch avec OR à qqch.

links [lɪŋks] (*pl inv*) *n* terrain *m* de golf (au bord de la mer).

lino ['laɪnəʊ], **linoleum** [lɪ'nəʊlɪəm] *n* lino *m*, linoléum *m*.

lintel ['lɪntl] *n* linteau *m*.

lion ['laɪən] *n* lion *m*.

lioness ['laɪənes] *n* lionne *f*.

lip [lɪp] *n* - **1.** [of mouth] lèvre *f* - **2.** [of container] bord *m*.

lip-read *vi* lire sur les lèvres.

lip salve [-sælv] *n* Br pommade *f* pour les lèvres.

lip service *n* : **to pay** ~ **to sthg** approuver qqch pour la forme.

lipstick ['lɪpstɪk] *n* rouge *m* à lèvres.

liqueur [lɪ'kjʊəʳ] *n* liqueur *f*.

liquid ['lɪkwɪd] ◇ *adj* liquide. ◇ *n* liquide *m*.

liquidation [ˌlɪkwɪ'deɪʃn] *n* liquidation *f*.

liquidize, -ise ['lɪkwɪdaɪz] *vt* Br CULIN passer au mixer.

liquidizer ['lɪkwɪdaɪzəʳ] *n* Br mixer *m*.

liquor ['lɪkəʳ] *n* (U) alcool *m*, spiritueux *mpl*.

liquorice ['lɪkərɪs] *n* réglisse *f*.

liquor store *n* Am magasin *m* de vins et d'alcools.

Lisbon ['lɪzbən] *n* Lisbonne.

lisp [lɪsp] ◇ *n* zézaiement *m*. ◇ *vi* zézayer.

list [lɪst] ◇ *n* liste *f*. ◇ *vt* [in writing] faire la liste de ; [in speech] énumérer.

listed building [ˌlɪstɪd-] n Br monument m classé.

listen ['lɪsn] vi : **to ~ to** (sb/sthg) écouter (qqn/qqch) ; **to ~ for sthg** guetter qqch.

listener ['lɪsnəʳ] n auditeur m, -trice f.

listless ['lɪstlɪs] adj apathique, mou (molle).

lit [lɪt] pt & pp ⊳ **light**.

liter Am = litre.

literacy ['lɪtərəsɪ] n fait m de savoir lire et écrire.

literal ['lɪtərəl] adj littéral(e).

literally ['lɪtərəlɪ] adv littéralement ; **to take sthg ~** prendre qqch au pied de la lettre.

literary ['lɪtərərɪ] adj littéraire.

literate ['lɪtərət] adj - 1. [able to read and write] qui sait lire et écrire - 2. [well-read] cultivé(e).

literature ['lɪtrətʃəʳ] n littérature f ; [printed information] documentation f.

lithe [laɪð] adj souple, agile.

Lithuania [ˌlɪθjʊ'eɪnɪjə] n Lituanie f.

litigation [ˌlɪtɪ'geɪʃn] n litige m ; **to go to ~** aller en justice.

litre Br, **liter** Am ['liːtəʳ] n litre m.

litter ['lɪtəʳ] ⟨⟩ n - 1. (U) [rubbish] ordures fpl, détritus mpl - 2. [of animals] portée f. ⟨⟩ vt : **to be ~ed with** être couvert(e) de.

litterbin ['lɪtəˌbɪn] n Br boîte f à ordures.

little ['lɪtl] (compar sense 2 **less**, superl sense 2 **least**) ⟨⟩ adj - 1. [not big] petit(e) ; **a ~ while** un petit moment - 2. [not much] peu de ; **~ money** peu d'argent ; **a ~ money** un peu d'argent. ⟨⟩ pron : **~ of the money was left** il ne restait pas beaucoup d'argent, il restait peu d'argent ; **a ~** un peu. ⟨⟩ adv peu, pas beaucoup ; **~ by ~** peu à peu.

little finger n petit doigt m, auriculaire m.

live¹ [lɪv] ⟨⟩ vi - 1. [gen] vivre - 2. [have one's home] habiter, vivre ; **to ~ in Paris** habiter (à) Paris. ⟨⟩ vt : **to ~ a quiet life** mener une vie tranquille ; **to ~ it up** inf faire la noce. ⬥ **live down** vt sep faire oublier. ⬥ **live off** vt fus [savings, the land] vivre de ; [family] vivre aux dépens de. ⬥ **live on** ⟨⟩ vt fus vivre de. ⟨⟩ vi [memory, feeling] rester, survivre. ⬥ **live together** vi vivre ensemble. ⬥ **live up to** vt fus : **to ~ up to sb's expectations** répondre à l'attente de qqn ; **to ~ up to one's reputation** faire honneur à sa réputation. ⬥ **live with** vt fus - 1. [cohabit with] vivre avec - 2. inf [accept] se faire à, accepter.

live² [laɪv] adj - 1. [living] vivant(e)

- 2. [coal] ardent(e) - 3. [bullet, bomb] non explosé(e) - 4. ELEC sous tension - 5. RADIO & TV en direct ; [performance] en public.

livelihood ['laɪvlɪhʊd] n gagne-pain m inv.

lively ['laɪvlɪ] adj - 1. [person] plein(e) d'entrain - 2. [debate, meeting] animé(e) - 3. [mind] vif (vive).

liven ['laɪvn] ⬥ **liven up** ⟨⟩ vt sep [person] égayer ; [place] animer. ⟨⟩ vi s'animer.

liver ['lɪvəʳ] n foie m.

livery ['lɪvərɪ] n livrée f.

lives [laɪvz] pl ⊳ **life**.

livestock ['laɪvstɒk] n (U) bétail m.

livid ['lɪvɪd] adj - 1. [angry] furieux(euse) - 2. [bruise] violacé(e).

living ['lɪvɪŋ] ⟨⟩ adj vivant(e), en vie. ⟨⟩ n : **to earn** OR **make a ~** gagner sa vie ; **what do you do for a ~?** qu'est-ce que vous faites dans la vie ?

living conditions npl conditions fpl de vie.

living room n salle f de séjour, living m.

living standards npl niveau m de vie.

living wage n minimum m vital.

lizard ['lɪzəd] n lézard m.

llama ['lɑːmə] (pl inv OR **-s**) n lama m.

load [ləʊd] ⟨⟩ n - 1. [something carried] chargement m, charge f - 2. [large amount] : **~s of**, **a ~ of** inf des tas de, plein de ; **a ~ of rubbish** inf de la foutaise. ⟨⟩ vt [gen & COMPUT] charger ; [video recorder] mettre une vidéo-cassette dans ; **to ~ sb/sthg with** charger qqn/qqch de ; **to ~ a gun/camera (with)** charger un fusil/un appareil (avec). ⬥ **load up** vt sep & vi charger.

loaded ['ləʊdɪd] adj - 1. [question] insidieux(euse) - 2. inf [rich] plein(e) aux as.

loading bay ['ləʊdɪŋ-] n aire f de chargement.

loaf [ləʊf] (pl **loaves** [ləʊvz]) n : **a ~ (of bread)** un pain.

loafer ['ləʊfəʳ] n [shoe] mocassin m.

loan [ləʊn] ⟨⟩ n prêt m ; **on ~** prêté(e). ⟨⟩ vt prêter ; **to ~ sthg to sb**, **to ~ sb sthg** prêter qqch à qqn.

loath [ləʊθ] adj : **to be ~ to do sthg** ne pas vouloir faire qqch, hésiter à faire qqch.

loathe [ləʊð] vt détester ; **to ~ doing sthg** avoir horreur de OR détester faire qqch.

loathsome ['ləʊðsəm] adj dégoûtant(e), répugnant(e).

loaves [ləʊvz] pl ⊳ **loaf**.

lob [lɒb] ⟨⟩ n TENNIS lob m. ⟨⟩ vt

- 1. [throw] lancer **- 2.** TENNIS **: to ~ a ball** lober, faire un lob.

lobby ['lɒbɪ] ⬦ *n* **- 1.** [of hotel] hall *m* **- 2.** [pressure group] lobby *m*, groupe *m* de pression. ⬦ *vt* faire pression sur.

lobe [ləʊb] *n* lobe *m*.

lobster ['lɒbstəʳ] *n* homard *m*.

local ['ləʊkl] ⬦ *adj* local(e). ⬦ *n* **- 1.** [person] **: the ~s** les gens *mpl* du coin OR du pays **- 2.** Br [pub] café *m* OR bistro *m* du coin.

local authority *n* Br autorités *fpl* locales.

local call *n* communication *f* urbaine.

local government *n* administration *f* municipale.

locality [ləʊ'kælətɪ] *n* endroit *m*.

localized, -ised ['ləʊkəlaɪzd] *adj* localisé(e).

locally ['ləʊkəlɪ] *adv* **- 1.** [on local basis] localement **- 2.** [nearby] dans les environs, à proximité.

locate [Br ləʊ'keɪt, Am 'ləʊkeɪt] *vt* **- 1.** [find - position] trouver, repérer ; [- source, problem] localiser **- 2.** [situate - business, factory] implanter, établir ; **to be ~d** être situé.

location [ləʊ'keɪʃn] *n* **- 1.** [place] emplacement *m* **- 2.** CINEMA **: on ~** en extérieur.

loch [lɒk, lɒx] *n* Scot loch *m*, lac *m*.

lock [lɒk] ⬦ *n* **- 1.** [of door etc] serrure *f* **- 2.** [on canal] écluse *f* **- 3.** AUT [steering lock] angle *m* de braquage **- 4.** [of hair] mèche *f*. ⬦ *vt* **- 1.** [door, car, drawer] fermer à clef ; [bicycle] cadenasser **- 2.** [immobilize] bloquer. ⬦ *vi* **- 1.** [door, suitcase] fermer à clef **- 2.** [become immobilized] se bloquer. ◆ **lock in** *vt sep* enfermer (à clef). ◆ **lock out** *vt sep* **- 1.** [accidentally] enfermer dehors, laisser dehors ; **to lock o.s. out** s'enfermer dehors **- 2.** [deliberately] empêcher d'entrer, mettre à la porte. ◆ **lock up** *vt sep* **- 1.** [person - in prison] mettre en prison OR sous les verrous ; [- in asylum] enfermer **- 2.** [house] fermer à clef **- 3.** [valuables] enfermer, mettre sous clef.

locker ['lɒkəʳ] *n* casier *m*.

locker room *n* Am vestiaire *m*.

locket ['lɒkɪt] *n* médaillon *m*.

locksmith ['lɒksmɪθ] *n* serrurier *m*.

locomotive ['ləʊkə,məʊtɪv] *n* locomotive *f*.

locum ['ləʊkəm] (*pl* **-s**) *n* Br remplaçant *m*, -e *f*.

locust ['ləʊkəst] *n* sauterelle *f*, locuste *f*.

lodge [lɒdʒ] ⬦ *n* **- 1.** [of caretaker, freemasons] loge *f* **- 2.** [of manor house] pavillon *m* (de gardien) **- 3.** [for hunting] pavillon *m* de chasse. ⬦ *vi* **- 1.** [stay] **: to ~ with sb** loger chez qqn **- 2.** [become stuck] se loger, se coincer **- 3.** *fig* [in mind] s'enraciner, s'ancrer. ⬦ *vt* [complaint] déposer ; **to ~ an appeal** interjeter OR faire appel.

lodger ['lɒdʒəʳ] *n* locataire *mf*.

lodging ['lɒdʒɪŋ] *n* ▷ **board**. ◆ **lodgings** *npl* chambre *f* meublée.

loft [lɒft] *n* grenier *m*.

lofty ['lɒftɪ] *adj* **- 1.** [noble] noble **- 2.** *pej* [haughty] hautain(e), arrogant(e) **- 3.** *literary* [high] haut(e), élevé(e).

log [lɒg] ⬦ *n* **- 1.** [of wood] bûche *f* **- 2.** [of ship] journal *m* de bord ; [of plane] carnet *m* de vol. ⬦ *vt* consigner, enregistrer. ◆ **log in** *vi* COMPUT ouvrir une session. ◆ **log on** *vi* COMPUT ouvrir une session. ◆ **log off** *vi* COMPUT fermer une session. ◆ **log out** *vi* COMPUT fermer une session.

logbook ['lɒgbʊk] *n* **- 1.** [of ship] journal *m* de bord ; [of plane] carnet *m* de vol **- 2.** Br [of car] ≃ carte *f* grise.

loggerheads ['lɒgəhedz] *n* **: at ~** en désaccord.

logic ['lɒdʒɪk] *n* logique *f*.

logical ['lɒdʒɪkl] *adj* logique.

logistics [lə'dʒɪstɪks] ⬦ *n* (U) MIL logistique *f*. ⬦ *npl* *fig* organisation *f*.

logo ['ləʊgəʊ] (*pl* **-s**) *n* logo *m*.

loin [lɔɪn] *n* filet *m*.

loiter ['lɔɪtəʳ] *vi* traîner.

loll [lɒl] *vi* **- 1.** [sit, lie about] se prélasser **- 2.** [hang down - head, tongue] pendre.

lollipop ['lɒlɪpɒp] *n* sucette *f*.

lollipop lady *n* Br dame qui fait traverser la rue aux enfants à la sortie des écoles.

lollipop man *n* Br monsieur qui fait traverser la rue aux enfants à la sortie des écoles.

lolly ['lɒlɪ] *n* Br *inf* **- 1.** [lollipop] sucette *f* **- 2.** Br [ice lolly] sucette *f* glacée.

London ['lʌndən] *n* Londres.

Londoner ['lʌndənəʳ] *n* Londonien *m*, -enne *f*.

lone [ləʊn] *adj* solitaire.

loneliness ['ləʊnlɪnɪs] *n* [of person] solitude *f* ; [of place] isolement *m*.

lonely ['ləʊnlɪ] *adj* **- 1.** [person] solitaire, seul(e) **- 2.** [childhood] solitaire **- 3.** [place] isolé(e).

loner ['ləʊnəʳ] *n* solitaire *mf*.

lonesome ['ləʊnsəm] *adj* Am *inf* **- 1.** [person] solitaire, seul(e) **- 2.** [place] isolé(e).

long [lɒŋ] ⬦ *adj* long (longue) ; **two days/years ~** de deux jours/ans, qui dure deux jours/ans ; **10 metres/miles** ~ long de 10 mètres/miles, de 10 mètres/miles (de long). <> *adv* longtemps ; **how ~ will it take?** combien de temps cela va-t-il prendre? ; **how ~ will you be?** tu en as pour combien de temps? ; **how ~ is the book?** le livre fait combien de pages? ; **I no ~er like him** je ne l'aime plus ; **I can't wait any ~er** je ne peux pas attendre plus longtemps ; **so ~!** *inf* au revoir!, salut! ; **before ~** sous peu. <> *vt* : **to ~ to do sthg** avoir très envie de faire qqch. ◆ **as long as, so long as** *conj* tant que. ◆ **long for** *vt fus* [peace and quiet] désirer ardemment ; [holidays] attendre avec impatience.

long-distance *adj* [runner, race] de fond ; ~ **lorry driver** routier *m*.

long-distance call *n* communication *f* interurbaine.

longhand ['lɒŋhænd] *n* écriture *f* normale.

long-haul *adj* long-courrier.

longing ['lɒŋɪŋ] <> *adj* plein(e) de convoitise. <> *n* - **1.** [desire] envie *f*, convoitise *f* ; **a ~ for** un grand désir OR une grande envie de - **2.** [nostalgia] nostalgie *f*, regret *m*.

longitude ['lɒndʒɪtjuːd] *n* longitude *f*.

long jump *n* saut *m* en longueur.

long-life *adj* [milk] longue conservation *(inv)* ; [battery] longue durée *(inv)*.

long-playing record [-'pleɪɪŋ-] *n* 33 tours *m*.

long-range *adj* - **1.** [missile, bomber] à longue portée - **2.** [plan, forecast] à long terme.

long shot *n* [guess] coup *m* à tenter *(sans grand espoir de succès)*.

longsighted [,lɒŋ'saɪtɪd] *adj* presbyte.

long-standing *adj* de longue date.

longsuffering [,lɒŋ'sʌfərɪŋ] *adj* [person] à la patience infinie.

long term *n* : **in the ~** à long terme.

long wave *n (U)* grandes ondes *fpl*.

longwinded [,lɒŋ'wɪndɪd] *adj* [person] prolixe, verbeux(euse) ; [speech] interminable, qui n'en finit pas.

loo [luː] *(pl* **-s)** *n Br inf* cabinets *mpl*, petit coin *m*.

look [lʊk] <> *n* - **1.** [with eyes] regard *m* ; **to take** OR **have a ~ (at sthg)** regarder (qqch), jeter un coup d'œil (à qqch) ; **to give sb a ~** jeter un regard à qqn, regarder qqn de travers - **2.** [search] : **to have a ~ (for sthg)** chercher (qqch) - **3.** [appearance] aspect *m*, air *m* ; **by the ~** OR **~s of it, by the ~** OR **~s of things** vraisemblablement, selon toute

probabilité. <> *vi* - **1.** [with eyes] regarder - **2.** [search] chercher - **3.** [building, window] : **to ~ (out) onto** donner sur - **4.** [seem] avoir l'air, sembler ; **it ~s like rain** OR **as if it will rain** on dirait qu'il va pleuvoir ; **she ~s like her mother** elle ressemble à sa mère. ◆ **looks** *npl* [attractiveness] beauté *f*. ◆ **look after** *vt fus* s'occuper de. ◆ **look at** *vt fus* - **1.** [see, glance at] regarder ; [examine] examiner - **2.** [judge] considérer. ◆ **look down on** *vt fus* [condescend to] mépriser. ◆ **look for** *vt fus* chercher. ◆ **look forward to** *vt fus* attendre avec impatience. ◆ **look into** *vt fus* examiner, étudier. ◆ **look on** *vi* regarder. ◆ **look out** *vi* prendre garde, faire attention ; ~ **out!** attention! ◆ **look out for** *vt fus* [person] guetter ; [new book] être à l'affût de, essayer de repérer. ◆ **look round** <> *vt fus* [house, shop, town] faire le tour de. <> *vi* - **1.** [turn] se retourner - **2.** [browse] regarder. ◆ **look to** *vt fus* - **1.** [depend on] compter sur - **2.** [future] songer à. ◆ **look up** <> *vt sep* - **1.** [in book] chercher - **2.** [visit - person] aller OR passer voir. <> *vi* [improve - business] reprendre ; **things are ~ing up** ça va mieux, la situation s'améliore. ◆ **look up to** *vt fus* admirer.

lookout ['lʊkaʊt] *n* - **1.** [place] poste *m* de guet - **2.** [person] guetteur *m* - **3.** [search] : **to be on the ~ for** être à la recherche de.

loom [luːm] <> *n* métier *m* à tisser. <> *vi* [building, person] se dresser ; *fig* [date, threat] être imminent(e). ◆ **loom up** *vi* surgir.

loony ['luːnɪ] *inf* <> *adj* cinglé(e), timbré(e). <> *n* cinglé *m*, -e *f*, fou *m*, folle *f*.

loop [luːp] *n* - **1.** [gen & COMPUT] boucle *f* - **2.** [contraceptive] stérilet *m*.

loophole ['luːphəʊl] *n* faille *f*, échappatoire *f*.

loose [luːs] *adj* - **1.** [not firm - joint] desserré(e) ; [- handle, post] branlant(e) ; [- tooth] qui bouge OR branle ; [- knot] défait(e) - **2.** [unpackaged - sweets, nails] en vrac, au poids - **3.** [clothes] ample, large - **4.** [not restrained - hair] dénoué(e) ; [- animal] en liberté, détaché(e) - **5.** *pej & dated* [woman] facile ; [living] dissolu(e) - **6.** [inexact - translation] approximatif(ive).

loose change *n* petite OR menue monnaie *f*.

loose end *n* : **to be at a ~** *Br*, **to be at ~s** *Am* être désœuvré, n'avoir rien à faire.

loosely ['luːslɪ] *adv* - **1.** [not firmly] sans serrer - **2.** [inexactly] approximativement.

loosen ['luːsn] *vt* desserrer, défaire.

◆ **loosen up** vi - **1.** [before game, race] s'échauffer - **2.** inf [relax] se détendre.

loot [luːt] ◇ n butin m. ◇ vt piller.

looting ['luːtɪŋ] n pillage m.

lop [lɒp] n Br élaguer, émonder. ◆ **lop off** vt sep couper.

lop-sided [-'saɪdɪd] adj [table] bancal(e), boiteux(euse) ; [picture] de travers.

lord [lɔːd] n Br seigneur m. ◆ **Lord** n - **1.** RELIG : **the Lord** [God] le Seigneur ; **good Lord!** Seigneur!, mon Dieu! - **2.** [in titles] Lord m ; [as form of address] : **my Lord** Monsieur le duc/comte etc. ◆ **Lords** npl Br POL : **the (House of) Lords** la Chambre des lords.

Lordship ['lɔːdʃɪp] n : **your/his ~** Monsieur le duc/comte etc.

lore [lɔːʳ] n (U) traditions fpl.

lorry ['lɒrɪ] n Br camion m.

lorry driver n Br camionneur m, conducteur m de poids lourd.

lose [luːz] (pt & pp lost) ◇ vt - **1.** [gen] perdre ; **to ~ sight of** lit & fig perdre de vue ; **to ~ one's way** se perdre, perdre son chemin ; fig être un peu perdu - **2.** [subj : clock, watch] retarder de ; **to ~ time** retarder - **3.** [pursuers] semer. ◇ vi perdre. ◆ **lose out** vi être perdant(e).

loser ['luːzəʳ] n - **1.** [gen] perdant m, -e f - **2.** inf pej [unsuccessful person] raté m, -e f.

loss [lɒs] n - **1.** [gen] perte f - **2.** phr : **to be at a ~** être perplexe, être embarrassé(e).

lost [lɒst] ◇ pt & pp ▷ **lose**. ◇ adj [gen] perdu(e) ; **to get ~** se perdre ; **get ~!** inf fous/foutez le camp!

lost-and-found office n Am bureau m des objets trouvés.

lost property office n Br bureau m des objets trouvés.

lot [lɒt] n - **1.** [large amount] : **a (lot), ~ (of)** beaucoup (de) ; [entire amount] : **the ~** le tout - **2.** [at auction] lot m - **3.** [destiny] sort m - **4.** Am [of land] terrain m ; [car park] parking m - **5.** phr : **to draw ~s** tirer au sort. ◆ **a lot** adv beaucoup.

lotion ['ləʊʃn] n lotion f.

lottery ['lɒtərɪ] n lit & fig loterie f.

lottery ticket n billet m de loterie.

loud [laʊd] ◇ adj - **1.** [not quiet, noisy - gen] fort(e) ; [- person] bruyant(e) - **2.** [colour, clothes] voyant(e). ◇ adv fort ; **out ~** tout haut.

loudhailer [,laʊd'heɪləʳ] n Br mégaphone m, porte-voix m inv.

loudly ['laʊdlɪ] adv - **1.** [noisily] fort - **2.** [gaudily] de façon voyante.

loudspeaker [,laʊd'spiːkəʳ] n haut-parleur m.

lounge [laʊndʒ] ◇ n - **1.** [in house] salon m - **2.** [in airport] hall m, salle f - **3.** Br = **lounge bar.** ◇ vi se prélasser.

lounge bar n Br l'une des deux salles d'un bar, la plus confortable.

louse [laʊs] (pl sense 1 **lice** [laɪs], pl sense 2 **-s**) n - **1.** [insect] pou m - **2.** inf pej [person] salaud m.

lousy ['laʊzɪ] adj inf minable, nul(le) ; [weather] pourri(e).

lout [laʊt] n rustre m.

louvre Br, **louver** Am ['luːvəʳ] n persienne f.

lovable ['lʌvəbl] adj adorable.

love [lʌv] ◇ n - **1.** [gen] amour m ; **to be in ~** être amoureux(euse) ; **to fall in ~** tomber amoureux(euse) ; **to make ~** faire l'amour ; **give her my ~** embrasse-la pour moi ; **~ from** [at end of letter] affectueusement, grosses bises - **2.** inf [form of address] mon chéri (ma chérie) - **3.** TENNIS zéro m. ◇ vt aimer ; **to ~ to do sthg** OR **doing sthg** aimer OR adorer faire qqch.

love affair n liaison f.

love life n vie f amoureuse.

lovely ['lʌvlɪ] adj - **1.** [beautiful] très joli(e) - **2.** [pleasant] très agréable, excellent(e).

lover ['lʌvəʳ] n - **1.** [sexual partner] amant m, -e f - **2.** [enthusiast] passionné m, -e f, amoureux m, -euse f.

loving ['lʌvɪŋ] adj [person, relationship] affectueux(euse) ; [care] tendre.

low [ləʊ] ◇ adj - **1.** [not high - gen] bas (basse) ; [- wall, building] peu élevé(e) ; [- standard, quality] mauvais(e) ; [- intelligence] faible ; [- neckline] décolleté(e) - **2.** [little remaining] presque épuisé(e) - **3.** [not loud - voice] bas (basse) ; [- whisper, moan] faible - **4.** [depressed] déprimé(e) - **5.** [not respectable] bas (basse). ◇ adv - **1.** [not high] bas - **2.** [not loudly - speak] à voix basse ; [- whisper] faiblement. ◇ n - **1.** [low point] niveau m OR point m bas - **2.** METEOR dépression f.

low-calorie adj à basses calories.

low-cut adj décolleté(e).

lower ['ləʊəʳ] ◇ adj inférieur(e). ◇ vt - **1.** [gen] baisser ; [flag] abaisser - **2.** [reduce - price, level] baisser ; [- age of consent] abaisser ; [- resistance] diminuer.

low-fat adj [yoghurt, crisps] allégé(e) ; [milk] demi-écrémé(e).

low-key adj discret(ète).

lowly ['ləʊlɪ] adj modeste, humble.

low-lying *adj* bas (basse).

loyal ['lɔɪəl] *adj* loyal(e).

loyalty ['lɔɪəltɪ] *n* loyauté *f*.

lozenge ['lɒzɪndʒ] *n* - **1.** [tablet] pastille *f* - **2.** [shape] losange *m*.

LP (*abbr of* **long-playing record**) *n* 33 tours *m*.

L-plate *n Br* plaque *f* signalant que le conducteur du véhicule est en conduite accompagnée.

Ltd, ltd (*abbr of* **limited**) ≃ SARL ; **Smith and Sons,** ~ ≃ Smith & Fils, SARL.

lubricant ['luːbrɪkənt] *n* lubrifiant *m*.

lubricate ['luːbrɪkeɪt] *vt* lubrifier.

lucid ['luːsɪd] *adj* lucide.

luck [lʌk] *n* chance *f* ; **good** ~ chance ; **good** ~**!** bonne chance! ; **bad** ~ malchance *f* ; **bad** OR **hard** ~**!** pas de chance! ; **to be in** ~ avoir de la chance ; **with (any)** ~ avec un peu de chance.

luckily ['lʌkɪlɪ] *adv* heureusement.

lucky ['lʌkɪ] *adj* - **1.** [fortunate - person] qui a de la chance ; [- event] heureux(euse) - **2.** [bringing good luck] porte-bonheur (*inv*).

lucrative ['luːkrətɪv] *adj* lucratif(ive).

ludicrous ['luːdɪkrəs] *adj* ridicule.

lug [lʌg] *vt inf* traîner.

luggage ['lʌgɪdʒ] *n* (*U*) bagages *mpl*.

luggage rack *n Br* porte-bagages *m inv*.

lukewarm ['luːkwɔːm] *adj lit & fig* tiède.

lull [lʌl] ◇ *n* : ~ **(in)** [storm] accalmie *f* (de) ; [fighting, conversation] arrêt *m* (de). ◇ *vt* : **to** ~ **sb to sleep** endormir qqn en le berçant ; **to** ~ **sb into a false sense of security** endormir les soupçons de qqn.

lullaby ['lʌləbaɪ] *n* berceuse *f*.

lumber ['lʌmbəʳ] *n* (*U*) - **1.** *Am* [timber] bois *m* de charpente - **2.** *Br* [bric-a-brac] bric-à-brac *m inv*. ◆ **lumber with** *vt sep Br inf* : **to** ~ **sb with sthg** coller qqch à qqn.

lumberjack ['lʌmbədʒæk] *n* bûcheron *m*, -onne *f*.

luminous ['luːmɪnəs] *adj* [dial] lumineux(euse) ; [paint, armband] phosphorescent(e).

lump [lʌmp] ◇ *n* - **1.** [gen] morceau *m* ; [of earth, clay] motte *f* ; [in sauce] grumeau *m* - **2.** [on body] grosseur *f*. ◇ *vt* : **to** ~ **sthg together** réunir qqch ; **to** ~ **it** *inf* faire avec, s'en accommoder.

lump sum *n* somme *f* globale.

lunacy ['luːnəsɪ] *n* folie *f*.

lunar ['luːnəʳ] *adj* lunaire.

lunatic ['luːnətɪk] ◇ *adj pej* dément(e),

démentiel(elle). ◇ *n* - **1.** *pej* [fool] fou *m*, folle *f* - **2.** [insane person] fou *m*, folle *f*, aliéné *m*, -e *f*.

lunch [lʌntʃ] ◇ *n* déjeuner *m*. ◇ *vi* déjeuner.

luncheon ['lʌntʃən] *n fml* déjeuner *m*.

luncheon meat *n* sorte de saucisson.

luncheon voucher *n Br* ticket-restaurant *m*.

lunch hour *n* pause *f* de midi.

lunchtime ['lʌntʃtaɪm] *n* heure *f* du déjeuner.

lung [lʌŋ] *n* poumon *m*.

lunge [lʌndʒ] *vi* faire un brusque mouvement (du bras) en avant ; **to** ~ **at sb** s'élancer sur qqn.

lurch [lɜːtʃ] ◇ *n* [of person] écart *m* brusque ; [of car] embardée *f* ; **to leave sb in the** ~ laisser qqn dans le pétrin. ◇ *vi* [person] tituber ; [car] faire une embardée.

lure [ljʊəʳ] ◇ *n* charme *m* trompeur. ◇ *vt* attirer OR persuader par la ruse.

lurid ['ljʊərɪd] *adj* - **1.** [outfit] aux couleurs criardes - **2.** [story, details] affreux(euse).

lurk [lɜːk] *vi* - **1.** [person] se cacher, se dissimuler - **2.** [memory, danger, fear] subsister.

luscious ['lʌʃəs] *adj* - **1.** [delicious] succulent(e) - **2.** *fig* [woman] appétissant(e).

lush [lʌʃ] *adj* - **1.** [luxuriant] luxuriant(e) - **2.** [rich] luxueux(euse).

lust [lʌst] *n* - **1.** [sexual desire] désir *m* - **2.** *fig* : ~ **for sthg** soif de qqch. ◆ **lust after, lust for** *vt fus* - **1.** [wealth, power etc] être assoiffé(e) de - **2.** [person] désirer.

lusty ['lʌstɪ] *adj* vigoureux(euse).

Luxembourg ['lʌksəmbɜːg] *n* - **1.** [country] Luxembourg *m* - **2.** [city] Luxembourg.

luxurious [lʌg'ʒʊərɪəs] *adj* - **1.** [expensive] luxueux(euse) - **2.** [pleasurable] voluptueux(euse).

luxury ['lʌkʃərɪ] ◇ *n* luxe *m*. ◇ *comp* de luxe.

LW (*abbr of* **long wave**) GO.

Lycra® ['laɪkrə] ◇ *n* Lycra® *m*. ◇ *comp* en Lycra®.

lying ['laɪɪŋ] ◇ *adj* [person] menteur(euse). ◇ *n* (*U*) mensonges *mpl*.

lynch [lɪntʃ] *vt* lyncher.

lyric ['lɪrɪk] *adj* lyrique.

lyrical ['lɪrɪkl] *adj* lyrique.

lyrics ['lɪrɪks] *npl* paroles *fpl*.

M

m¹ (*pl* m's or ms), **M** (*pl* M's or Ms) [em] *n* [letter] m *m inv*, M *m inv*. ➤ **M** *Br abbr of* motorway.

m² - **1.** (*abbr of* metre) m - **2.** (*abbr of* million) M - **3.** *abbr of* mile.

MA *n abbr of* Master of Arts.

mac [mæk] (*abbr of* mackintosh) *n Br inf* [coat] imper *m*.

macaroni [,mækə'rəʊnɪ] *n* (U) macaronis *mpl*.

mace [meɪs] *n* - **1.** [ornamental rod] masse *f* - **2.** [spice] macis *m*.

machine [mə'ʃiːn] <> *n lit & fig* machine *f*. <> *vt* - **1.** SEWING coudre à la machine - **2.** TECH usiner.

machinegun [mə'ʃiːngʌn] *n* mitrailleuse *f*.

machine language *n* COMPUT langage *m* machine.

machinery [mə'ʃiːnərɪ] *n* (U) machines *fpl* ; *fig* mécanisme *m*.

macho ['mætʃəʊ] *adj* macho (*inv*).

mackerel ['mækrəl] (*pl inv* or -s) *n* maquereau *m*.

mackintosh ['mækɪntɒʃ] *n Br* imperméable *m*.

mad [mæd] *adj* - **1.** [insane] fou (folle) ; **to go ~** devenir fou - **2.** [foolish] insensé(e) - **3.** [furious] furieux(euse) - **4.** [hectic - rush, pace] fou (folle) - **5.** [very enthusiastic] : **to be ~ about sb/sthg** être fou (folle) de qqn/qqch.

Madagascar [,mædə'gæskə'] *n* Madagascar *m*.

madam ['mædəm] *n* madame *f*.

madcap ['mædkæp] *adj* risqué(e), insensé(e).

mad cow disease *n inf* maladie *f* de la vache folle.

madden ['mædn] *vt* exaspérer.

made [meɪd] *pt & pp* ➤ make.

Madeira [mə'dɪərə] *n* - **1.** [wine] madère *m* - **2.** GEOGR Madère *f*.

made-to-measure *adj* fait(e) sur mesure.

made-up *adj* - **1.** [with make-up] maquillé(e) - **2.** [invented] fabriqué(e).

madly ['mædlɪ] *adv* [frantically] comme un fou ; **~ in love** follement amoureux.

madman ['mædmən] (*pl* -men [-mən]) *n* fou *m*.

madness ['mædnɪs] *n lit & fig* folie *f*, démence *f*.

Madrid [mə'drɪd] *n* Madrid.

Mafia ['mæfɪə] *n* : **the ~** la Mafia.

magazine [,mægə'ziːn] *n* - **1.** PRESS revue *f*, magazine *m* ; RADIO & TV magazine - **2.** [of gun] magasin *m*.

maggot ['mægət] *n* ver *m*, asticot *m*.

magic ['mædʒɪk] <> *adj* magique. <> *n* magie *f*.

magical ['mædʒɪkl] *adj* magique.

magician [mə'dʒɪʃn] *n* magicien *m*.

magistrate ['mædʒɪstreɪt] *n* magistrat *m*, juge *m*.

magistrates' court *n Br* ≃ tribunal *m* d'instance.

magnanimous [mæg'nænɪməs] *adj* magnanime.

magnate ['mægneɪt] *n* magnat *m*.

magnesium [mæg'niːzɪəm] *n* magnésium *m*.

magnet ['mægnɪt] *n* aimant *m*.

magnetic [mæg'netɪk] *adj lit & fig* magnétique.

magnetic tape *n* bande *f* magnétique.

magnificent [mæg'nɪfɪsənt] *adj* magnifique, superbe.

magnify ['mægnɪfaɪ] *vt* [in vision] grossir ; [sound] amplifier ; *fig* exagérer.

magnifying glass ['mægnɪfaɪɪŋ-] *n* loupe *f*.

magnitude ['mægnɪtjuːd] *n* envergure *f*, ampleur *f*.

magpie ['mægpaɪ] *n* pie *f*.

mahogany [mə'hɒgənɪ] *n* acajou *m*.

maid [meɪd] *n* [servant] domestique *f*.

maiden ['meɪdn] <> *adj* [flight, voyage] premier(ère). <> *n literary* jeune fille *f*.

maiden aunt *n* tante *f* célibataire.

maiden name *n* nom *m* de jeune fille.

mail [meɪl] <> *n* - **1.** [letters, parcels] courrier *m* - **2.** [system] poste *f*. <> *vt esp Am* poster.

mailbox ['meɪlbɒks] *n Am* boîte *f* à or aux lettres.

mailing list ['meɪlɪŋ-] *n* liste *f* d'adresses.

mailman ['meɪlmən] (*pl* -men [-mən]) *n Am* facteur *m*.

mail order *n* vente *f* par correspondance.

mailshot ['meɪlʃɒt] *n* publipostage *m*.

maim [meɪm] *vt* estropier.

main [meɪn] ◇ *adj* principal(e). ◇ *n* [pipe] conduite *f*. ◆ **mains** *npl* : **the ~s** le secteur. ◆ **in the main** *adv* dans l'ensemble.

main course *n* plat *m* principal.

mainframe (computer) ['meɪnfreɪm-] *n* ordinateur *m* central.

mainland ['meɪnlənd] ◇ *adj* continental(e). ◇ *n* : **the ~** le continent.

main line *n* RAIL grande ligne *f*.

mainly ['meɪnlɪ] *adv* principalement.

main road *n* route *f* à grande circulation.

mainstay ['meɪnsteɪ] *n* pilier *m*, élément *m* principal.

mainstream ['meɪnstri:m] ◇ *adj* dominant(e). ◇ *n* : **the ~** la tendance générale.

maintain [meɪn'teɪn] *vt* - **1.** [preserve, keep constant] maintenir - **2.** [provide for, look after] entretenir - **3.** [assert] : **to ~ (that)** ... maintenir que ..., soutenir que ...

maintenance ['meɪntənəns] *n* - **1.** [of public order] maintien *m* - **2.** [care] entretien *m*, maintenance *f* - **3.** JUR pension *f* alimentaire.

maize [meɪz] *n* maïs *m*.

majestic [mə'dʒestɪk] *adj* majestueux (euse).

majesty ['mædʒəstɪ] *n* [grandeur] majesté *f*. ◆ **Majesty** *n* : **His/Her Majesty** Sa Majesté le roi/la reine.

major ['meɪdʒər] ◇ *adj* - **1.** [important] majeur(e) - **2.** [main] principal(e) - **3.** MUS majeur(e). ◇ *n* - **1.** [in army] ≃ chef *m* de bataillon ; [in air force] commandant *m* - **2.** UNIV [subject] matière *f*.

Majorca [mə'dʒɔːkə, mə'jɔːkə] *n* Majorque *f*.

majority [mə'dʒɒrətɪ] *n* majorité *f* ; **in a** OR **the ~** dans la majorité.

make [meɪk] (*pt* & *pp* **made**) ◇ *vt* - **1.** [gen - produce] faire ; [- manufacture] faire, fabriquer ; **to ~ a meal** préparer un repas ; **to ~ a film** tourner OR réaliser un film - **2.** [perform an action] faire ; **to ~ a decision** prendre une décision ; **to ~ a mistake** faire une erreur, se tromper - **3.** [cause to be] rendre ; **to ~ sb happy/sad** rendre qqn heureux/triste - **4.** [force, cause to do] : **to ~ sb do sthg** faire faire qqch à qqn, obliger qqn à faire qqch ; **to ~ sb laugh** faire rire qqn - **5.** [be constructed] : **to be made of** être en ; **what's it made of?** c'est en quoi? - **6.** [add up to] faire ; **2 and 2 ~ 4** 2 et 2 font 4 - **7.** [calculate] : **I ~ it 50** d'après moi il y en

a 50, j'en ai compté 50 ; **what time do you ~ it?** quelle heure as-tu ? ; **I ~ it 6 o'clock** il est 6 heures (à ma montre) - **8.** [earn] gagner, se faire ; **to ~ a profit** faire des bénéfices ; **to ~ a loss** essuyer des pertes - **9.** [reach] arriver à - **10.** [gain - friend, enemy] se faire ; **to ~ friends (with sb)** se lier d'amitié (avec qqn) - **11.** *phr* : **to ~ it** [reach in time] arriver à temps ; [be a success] réussir, arriver ; [be able to attend] se libérer, pouvoir venir ; **to ~ do with** se contenter de. ◇ *n* [brand] marque *f*. ◆ **make for** *vt fus* - **1.** [move towards] se diriger vers - **2.** [contribute to, be conducive to] rendre probable, favoriser. ◆ **make of** *vt sep* - **1.** [understand] comprendre - **2.** [have opinion of] penser de. ◆ **make off** *vi* filer. ◆ **make out** ◇ *vt sep* - **1.** [see, hear] discerner ; [understand] comprendre - **2.** [fill out - cheque] libeller ; [- bill, receipt] faire ; [- form] remplir. ◇ *vt fus* [pretend, claim] : **to ~ out (that) ...** prétendre que ... ◆ **make up** ◇ *vt sep* - **1.** [compose, constitute] composer, constituer - **2.** [story, excuse] inventer - **3.** [apply cosmetics to] maquiller - **4.** [prepare - gen] faire ; [- prescription] préparer, exécuter - **5.** [make complete] compléter. ◇ *vi* [become friends again] se réconcilier. ◆ **make up for** *vt fus* compenser. ◆ **make up to** *vt sep* : **to ~ it up to sb (for sthg)** se racheter auprès de qqn (pour qqch).

make-believe *n* : **it's all ~** c'est (de la) pure fantaisie.

maker ['meɪkər] *n* [of product] fabricant *m*, -e *f* ; [of film] réalisateur *m*, -trice *f*.

makeshift ['meɪkʃɪft] *adj* de fortune.

make-up *n* - **1.** [cosmetics] maquillage *m* ; **~ remover** démaquillant *m* - **2.** [person's character] caractère *m* - **3.** [of team, group, object] constitution *f*.

making ['meɪkɪŋ] *n* fabrication *f* ; **his problems are of his own ~** ses problèmes sont de sa faute ; **in the ~** en formation ; **to have the ~s of** avoir l'étoffe de.

malaise [mə'leɪz] *n fml* malaise *m*.

malaria [mə'leərɪə] *n* malaria *f*.

Malaya [mə'leɪə] *n* Malaisie *f*, Malaysia *f* occidentale.

Malaysia [mə'leɪzɪə] *n* Malaysia *f*.

male [meɪl] ◇ *adj* [gen] mâle ; [sex] masculin(e). ◇ *n* mâle *m*.

male nurse *n* infirmier *m*.

malevolent [mə'levələnt] *adj* malveillant(e).

malfunction [mæl'fʌŋkʃn] *vi* mal fonctionner.

malice ['mælɪs] *n* méchanceté *f*.

malicious [mə'lɪʃəs] *adj* malveillant(e).

malign [mə'laɪn] ⟨⟩ *adj* pernicieux(euse). ⟨⟩ *vt* calomnier.

malignant [mə'lɪgnənt] *adj* MED malin(igne).

mall [mɔːl] *n esp Am* : **(shopping) ~** centre *m* commercial.

mallet ['mælɪt] *n* maillet *m*.

malnutrition [ˌmælnjuːˈtrɪʃn] *n* malnutrition *f*.

malpractice [ˌmælˈpræktɪs] *n (U)* JUR faute *f* professionnelle.

malt [mɔːlt] *n* malt *m*.

Malta ['mɔːltə] *n* Malte *f*.

mammal ['mæml] *n* mammifère *m*.

mammoth ['mæməθ] ⟨⟩ *adj* gigantesque. ⟨⟩ *n* mammouth *m*.

man [mæn] (*pl* **men** [men]) ⟨⟩ *n* - 1. homme *m* ; **the ~ in the street** l'homme de la rue - 2. [as form of address] mon vieux. ⟨⟩ *vt* [ship, spaceship] fournir du personnel pour ; [telephone] répondre au ; [switchboard] assurer le service de.

manage ['mænɪdʒ] ⟨⟩ *vi* - 1. [cope] se débrouiller, y arriver - 2. [survive, get by] s'en sortir. ⟨⟩ *vt* - 1. [succeed] : **to ~ to do sthg** arriver à faire qqch - 2. [be responsible for, control] gérer.

manageable ['mænɪdʒəbl] *adj* maniable.

management ['mænɪdʒmənt] *n* - 1. [control, running] gestion *f* - 2. [people in control] direction *f*.

manager ['mænɪdʒə'] *n* [of organization] directeur *m*, -trice *f* ; [of shop, restaurant, hotel] gérant *m*, -e *f* ; [of football team, pop star] manager *m*.

manageress [ˌmænɪdʒə'res] *n Br* [of organization] directrice *f* ; [of shop, restaurant, hotel] gérante *f*.

managerial [ˌmænɪ'dʒɪərɪəl] *adj* directorial(e).

managing director ['mænɪdʒɪŋ-] *n* directeur général *m*, directrice générale *f*.

mandarin ['mændərɪn] *n* [fruit] mandarine *f*.

mandate ['mændeɪt] *n* mandat *m*.

mandatory ['mændətrɪ] *adj* obligatoire.

mane [meɪn] *n* crinière *f*.

maneuver *Am* = manoeuvre.

manfully ['mænfʊlɪ] *adv* courageusement, vaillamment.

mangle ['mæŋgl] *vt* mutiler, déchirer.

mango ['mæŋgəʊ] (*pl* -**es** *or* -**s**) *n* mangue *f*.

mangy ['meɪndʒɪ] *adj* galeux(euse).

manhandle ['mæn,hændl] *vt* malmener.

manhole ['mænhəʊl] *n* regard *m*, trou *m* d'homme.

manhood ['mænhʊd] *n* : **to reach ~** devenir un homme.

manhour ['mæn,aʊə'] *n* heure-homme *f*.

mania ['meɪnjə] *n* : **~ (for)** manie *f* (de).

maniac ['meɪnɪæk] *n* fou *m*, folle *f* ; **a sex ~** un obsédé sexuel (une obsédée sexuelle).

manic ['mænɪk] *adj fig* [person] surexcité(e) ; [behaviour] de fou.

manicure ['mænɪ,kjʊə'] *n* manucure *f*.

manifest ['mænɪfest] *fml* ⟨⟩ *adj* manifeste, évident(e). ⟨⟩ *vt* manifester.

manifesto [ˌmænɪ'festəʊ] (*pl* -**s** *or* -**es**) *n* manifeste *m*.

manipulate [mə'nɪpjʊleɪt] *vt lit & fig* manipuler.

manipulative [mə'nɪpjʊlətɪv] *adj* [person] rusé(e) ; [behaviour] habile, subtil(e).

mankind [mæn'kaɪnd] *n* humanité *f*, genre *m* humain.

manly ['mænlɪ] *adj* viril(e).

man-made *adj* [fabric, fibre] synthétique ; [environment] artificiel(elle) ; [problem] causé(e) par l'homme.

manner ['mænə'] *n* - 1. [method] manière *f*, façon *f* - 2. [attitude] attitude *f*, comportement *m*. ◆ **manners** *npl* manières *fpl*.

mannerism ['mænərɪzm] *n* tic *m*, manie *f*.

mannish ['mænɪʃ] *adj* masculin(e).

manoeuvre *Br*, **maneuver** *Am* [mə'nuːvə'] ⟨⟩ *n* manœuvre *f*. ⟨⟩ *vt & vi* manœuvrer.

manor ['mænə'] *n* manoir *m*.

manpower ['mæn,paʊə'] *n* main-d'œuvre *f*.

mansion ['mænʃn] *n* château *m*.

manslaughter ['mæn,slɔːtə'] *n* homicide *m* involontaire.

mantelpiece ['mæntlpiːs] *n* (dessus *m* de) cheminée *f*.

manual ['mænjʊəl] ⟨⟩ *adj* manuel(elle). ⟨⟩ *n* manuel *m*.

manual worker *n* travailleur manuel *m*, travailleuse manuelle *f*.

manufacture [ˌmænjuˈfæktʃə'] ⟨⟩ *n* fabrication *f* ; [of cars] construction *f*. ⟨⟩ *vt* fabriquer ; [cars] construire.

manufacturer [ˌmænjʊˈfæktʃərəʳ] *n* fabricant *m* ; [of cars] constructeur *m*.

manure [məˈnjʊəʳ] *n* fumier *m*.

manuscript [ˈmænjʊskrɪpt] *n* manuscrit *m*.

many [ˈmenɪ] (*compar* more, *superl* most) ⟨⟩ *adj* beaucoup de ; **how ~ ...?** combien de ...? ; **too ~** trop de ; **as ~ ... as** autant de ... que ; **so ~** autant de ; **a good** OR **great ~** un grand nombre de. ⟨⟩ *pron* (a lot, plenty) beaucoup.

map [mæp] *n* carte *f*. ◆ **map out** *vt sep* [plan] élaborer ; [timetable] établir ; [task] définir.

maple [ˈmeɪpl] *n* érable *m*.

mar [maːʳ] *vt* gâter, gâcher.

marathon [ˈmærəθn] ⟨⟩ *adj* marathon *(inv)*. ⟨⟩ *n* marathon *m*.

marauder [məˈrɔːdəʳ] *n* maraudeur *m*, -euse *f*.

marble [ˈmaːbl] *n* **- 1.** [stone] marbre *m* **- 2.** [for game] bille *f*.

march [maːtʃ] ⟨⟩ *n* marche *f*. ⟨⟩ *vi* **- 1.** [soldiers etc] marcher au pas **- 2.** [demonstrators] manifester, faire une marche de protestation **- 3.** [quickly] : **to ~ up to sb** s'approcher de qqn d'un pas décidé.

March [maːtʃ] *n* mars *m* ; *see also* **September**.

marcher [ˈmaːtʃəʳ] *n* [protester] marcheur *m*, -euse *f*.

mare [meəʳ] *n* jument *f*.

margarine [ˌmaːdʒəˈriːn, ˌmaːgəˈriːn] *n* margarine *f*.

marge [maːdʒ] *n inf* margarine *f*.

margin [ˈmaːdʒɪn] *n* **- 1.** [gen] marge *f* ; **to win by a narrow ~** gagner de peu OR de justesse **- 2.** [edge - of an area] bord *m*.

marginal [ˈmaːdʒɪnl] *adj* **- 1.** [unimportant] marginal(e), secondaire **- 2.** *Br* POL : **~ seat** circonscription électorale où la majorité passe facilement d'un parti à un autre.

marginally [ˈmaːdʒɪnəlɪ] *adv* très peu.

marigold [ˈmærɪgəʊld] *n* souci *m*.

marihuana, marijuana [ˌmærɪˈwaːnə] *n* marihuana *f*.

marine [məˈriːn] ⟨⟩ *adj* marin(e). ⟨⟩ *n* marine *m*.

marital [ˈmærɪtl] *adj* [sex, happiness] conjugal(e) ; [problems] matrimonial(e).

marital status *n* situation *f* de famille.

maritime [ˈmærɪtaɪm] *adj* maritime.

mark [maːk] ⟨⟩ *n* **- 1.** [stain] tache *f*, marque *f* **- 2.** [sign, written symbol] marque *f* **- 3.** [in exam] note *f*, point *m* **- 4.** [stage, level]

barre *f*. **5.** [currency] mark *m*. ⟨⟩ *vt* **- 1.** [gen] marquer **- 2.** [stain] marquer, tacher **- 3.** [exam, essay] noter, corriger. ◆ **mark off** *vt sep* [cross off] cocher.

marked [maːkt] *adj* [change, difference] marqué(e) ; [improvement, deterioration] sensible.

marker [ˈmaːkəʳ] *n* [sign] repère *m*.

marker pen *n* marqueur *m*.

market [ˈmaːkɪt] ⟨⟩ *n* marché *m*. ⟨⟩ *vt* commercialiser.

market garden *n esp Br* jardin *m* maraîcher.

marketing [ˈmaːkɪtɪŋ] *n* marketing *m*.

marketplace [ˈmaːkɪtpleɪs] *n* **- 1.** [in a town] place *f* du marché **- 2.** COMM marché *m*.

market research *n* étude *f* de marché.

market value *n* valeur *f* marchande.

marking [ˈmaːkɪŋ] *n* SCH correction *f*. ◆ **markings** *npl* [on animal, flower] taches *fpl*, marques *fpl* ; [on road] signalisation *f* horizontale.

marksman [ˈmaːksmən] (*pl* -men [-mən]) *n* tireur *m* d'élite.

marmalade [ˈmaːməleɪd] *n* confiture *f* d'oranges amères.

maroon [məˈruːn] *adj* bordeaux *(inv)*.

marooned [məˈruːnd] *adj* abandonné(e).

marquee [maːˈkiː] *n* grande tente *f*.

marriage [ˈmærɪdʒ] *n* mariage *m*.

marriage bureau *n Br* agence *f* matrimoniale.

marriage certificate *n* acte *m* de mariage.

marriage guidance *n* conseil *m* conjugal.

married [ˈmærɪd] *adj* **- 1.** [person] marié(e) ; **to get ~** se marier **- 2.** [life] conjugal(e).

marrow [ˈmærəʊ] *n* **- 1.** *Br* [vegetable] courge *f* **- 2.** [in bones] moelle *f*.

marry [ˈmærɪ] ⟨⟩ *vt* **- 1.** [become spouse of] épouser, se marier avec **- 2.** [subj : priest, registrar] marier. ⟨⟩ *vi* se marier.

Mars [maːz] *n* [planet] Mars *f*.

marsh [maːʃ] *n* marais *m*, marécage *m*.

marshal [ˈmaːʃl] ⟨⟩ *n* **- 1.** MIL maréchal *m* **- 2.** [steward] membre *m* du service d'ordre **- 3.** *Am* [law officer] officier *m* de police fédérale. ⟨⟩ *vt lit & fig* rassembler.

martial arts *npl* arts *mpl* martiaux.

martial law *n* loi *f* martiale.

martyr [ˈmaːtəʳ] *n* martyr *m*, -e *f*.

martyrdom ['mɑːtədəm] *n* martyre *m*.

marvel ['mɑːvl] ◇ *n* merveille *f*. ◇ *vi* : **to ~ (at)** s'émerveiller (de), s'étonner (de).

marvellous *Br*, **marvelous** *Am* ['mɑːvələs] *adj* merveilleux(euse).

Marxism ['mɑːksɪzm] *n* marxisme *m*.

Marxist ['mɑːksɪst] ◇ *adj* marxiste. ◇ *n* marxiste *mf*.

marzipan ['mɑːzɪpæn] *n* *(U)* pâte *f* d'amandes.

mascara [mæs'kɑːrə] *n* mascara *m*.

masculine ['mæskjʊlɪn] *adj* masculin(e).

mash [mæʃ] *vt* faire une purée de.

mashed potatoes [mæʃt-] *npl* purée *f* de pommes de terre.

mask [mɑːsk] *lit & fig* ◇ *n* masque *m*. ◇ *vt* masquer.

masochist ['mæsəkɪst] *n* masochiste *mf*.

mason ['meɪsn] *n* - **1.** [stonemason] maçon *m* - **2.** [freemason] franc-maçon *m*.

masonry ['meɪsnrɪ] *n* [stones] maçonnerie *f*.

masquerade [ˌmæskə'reɪd] *vi* : **to ~ as** se faire passer pour.

mass [mæs] ◇ *n* [gen & PHYSICS] masse *f*. ◇ *adj* [protest, meeting] en masse, en nombre ; [unemployment, support] massif(ive). ◇ *vi* se masser. **◆ Mass** *n* RELIG messe *f*. **◆ masses** *npl* - **1.** *inf* [lots] : **~es (of)** des masses (de) ; [food] des tonnes (de) - **2.** [workers] : **the ~es** les masses *fpl*.

massacre ['mæsəkər] ◇ *n* massacre *m*. ◇ *vt* massacrer.

massage [*Br* 'mæsɑːʒ, *Am* mə'sɑːʒ] ◇ *n* massage *m*. ◇ *vt* masser.

massive ['mæsɪv] *adj* massif(ive), énorme.

mass media *n & npl* : **the ~** les (mass) media *mpl*.

mass production *n* fabrication *f* OR production *f* en série.

mast [mɑːst] *n* - **1.** [on boat] mât *m* - **2.** RADIO & TV pylône *m*.

master ['mɑːstər] ◇ *n* - **1.** [gen] maître *m* - **2.** *Br* [SCH - in primary school] instituteur *m*, maître *m* ; [- in secondary school] professeur *m*. ◇ *adj* maître. ◇ *vt* maîtriser ; [difficulty] surmonter, vaincre ; [situation] se rendre maître de.

master key *n* passe *m*, passe-partout *m* *inv*.

masterly ['mɑːstəlɪ] *adj* magistral(e).

mastermind ['mɑːstəmaɪnd] ◇ *n* cerveau *m*. ◇ *vt* organiser, diriger.

Master of Arts (*pl* **Masters of Arts**) *n*

\- **1.** [degree] maîtrise *f* ès lettres - **2.** [person] titulaire *mf* d'une maîtrise ès lettres.

Master of Science (*pl* **Masters of Science**) *n* - **1.** [degree] maîtrise *f* ès sciences - **2.** [person] titulaire *mf* d'une maîtrise ès sciences.

masterpiece ['mɑːstəpiːs] *n* chef-d'œuvre *m*.

master's degree *n* ≃ maîtrise *f*.

mastery ['mɑːstərɪ] *n* maîtrise *f*.

mat [mæt] *n* - **1.** [on floor] petit tapis *m* ; [at door] paillasson *m* - **2.** [on table] set *m* de table ; [coaster] dessous *m* de verre.

match [mætʃ] ◇ *n* - **1.** [game] match *m* - **2.** [for lighting] allumette *f* - **3.** [equal] : **to be no ~ for sb** ne pas être de taille à lutter contre qqn. ◇ *vt* - **1.** [be the same as] correspondre à, s'accorder avec - **2.** [pair off] faire correspondre - **3.** [be equal with] égaler, rivaliser avec. ◇ *vi* - **1.** [be the same] correspondre - **2.** [go together well] être assorti(e).

matchbox ['mætʃbɒks] *n* boîte *f* à allumettes.

matching ['mætʃɪŋ] *adj* assorti(e).

mate [meɪt] ◇ *n* - **1.** *inf* [friend] copain *m*, copine *f*, pote *m* - **2.** *Br inf* [term of address] mon vieux - **3.** [of female animal] mâle *m* ; [of male animal] femelle *f* - **4.** NAUT : **(first) ~** second *m*. ◇ *vi* s'accoupler.

material [mə'tɪərɪəl] ◇ *adj* - **1.** [goods, benefits, world] matériel(elle) - **2.** [important] important(e), essentiel(elle). ◇ *n* - **1.** [substance] matière *f*, substance *f* ; [type of substance] matériau *m*, matière - **2.** [fabric] tissu *m*, étoffe *f* ; [type of fabric] tissu - **3.** *(U)* [information - for book, article etc] matériaux *mpl*. **◆ materials** *npl* matériaux *mpl*.

materialistic [məˌtɪərɪə'lɪstɪk] *adj* matérialiste.

materialize, -ise [mə'tɪərɪəlaɪz] *vi* - **1.** [offer, threat] se concrétiser, se réaliser - **2.** [person, object] apparaître.

maternal [mə'tɜːnl] *adj* maternel(elle).

maternity [mə'tɜːnətɪ] *n* maternité *f*.

maternity dress *n* robe *f* de grossesse.

maternity hospital *n* maternité *f*.

math *Am* = **maths**.

mathematical [ˌmæθə'mætɪkl] *adj* mathématique.

mathematics [ˌmæθə'mætɪks] *n* *(U)* mathématiques *fpl*.

maths *Br* [mæθs], **math** *Am* [mæθ] (*abbr of* **mathematics**) *inf n* *(U)* maths *fpl*.

matinée ['mætɪneɪ] *n* matinée *f*.

mating season ['meɪtɪŋ-] *n* saison *f* des amours.

matrices ['meɪtrɪsiːz] *pl* ⊏▷ **matrix**.

matriculation [məˌtrɪkjʊ'leɪʃn] *n* inscription *f*.

matrimonial [ˌmætrɪ'məʊnjəl] *adj* matrimonial(e), conjugal(e).

matrimony ['mætrɪmənɪ] *n (U)* mariage *m*.

matrix ['meɪtrɪks] *(pl* matrices ['meɪtrɪsiːz], **-es** [-iːz]) *n* - **1.** [context, framework] contexte *m*, structure *f* - **2.** MATH & TECH matrice *f*.

matron ['meɪtrən] *n* - **1.** *Br* [in hospital] infirmière *f* en chef - **2.** [in school] infirmière *f*.

matronly ['meɪtrənlɪ] *adj euphemism* [woman] qui a l'allure d'une matrone ; [figure] de matrone.

matt *Br*, **matte** *Am* [mæt] *adj* mat(e).

matted ['mætɪd] *adj* emmêlé(e).

matter ['mætə'] ◇ *n* - **1.** [question, situation] question *f*, affaire *f* ; **that's another** OR **a different** ~ c'est tout autre chose, c'est une autre histoire ; **as a ~ of course** automatiquement ; **to make ~s better** arranger la situation ; **and to make ~s worse** ... pour tout arranger ... ; **that's a ~ of opinion** c'est (une) affaire OR question d'opinion - **2.** [trouble, cause of pain] : **there's something the ~ with my radio** il y a quelque chose qui cloche OR ne va pas dans ma radio ; **what's the ~?** qu'est-ce qu'il y a? ; **what's the ~ with him?** qu'est-ce qu'il a? - **3.** PHYSICS matière *f* - **4.** *(U)* [material] matière *f* ; **reading ~** choses *fpl* à lire. ◇ *vi* [be important] importer, avoir de l'importance ; **it doesn't ~** cela n'a pas d'importance. ◆ **as a matter of fact** *adv* en fait, à vrai dire. ◆ **for that matter** *adv* d'ailleurs. ◆ **no matter** *adv* : **no ~ what** coûte que coûte, à tout prix ; **no ~ how hard I try to explain** ... j'ai beau essayer de lui expliquer ...

Matterhorn ['mætəhɔːn] *n* : **the ~** le mont Cervin.

matter-of-fact *adj* terre-à-terre, neutre.

mattress ['mætrɪs] *n* matelas *m*.

mature [mə'tjʊə'] ◇ *adj* - **1.** [person, attitude] mûr(e) - **2.** [cheese] fait(e) ; [wine] arrivé(e) à maturité. ◇ *vi* - **1.** [person] mûrir - **2.** [cheese, wine] se faire.

mature student *n Br* UNIV *étudiant qui a commencé ses études sur le tard.*

maul [mɔːl] *vt* mutiler.

mauve [məʊv] ◇ *adj* mauve. ◇ *n* mauve *m*.

max. [mæks] *(abbr of* maximum) max.

maxim ['mæksɪm] *(pl* **-s**) *n* maxime *f*.

maxima ['mæksɪmə] *pl* ⊏▷ **maximum**.

maximum ['mæksɪməm] *(pl* **maxima** ['mæksɪmə], **-s**) ◇ *adj* maximum *(inv)*. ◇ *n* maximum *m*.

may [meɪ] *modal vb* - **1.** [expressing possibility] : **it ~ rain** il se peut qu'il pleuve, il va peut-être pleuvoir ; **be that as it ~** quoi qu'il en soit - **2.** [can] pouvoir ; **on a clear day the coast ~ be seen** on peut voir la côte par temps clair - **3.** [asking permission] : **~ I come in?** puis-je entrer? - **4.** [as contrast] : **it ~ be expensive but ...** c'est peut-être cher, mais ... - **5.** *fml* [expressing wish, hope] : **~ they be happy!** qu'ils soient heureux! ; *see also* **might**.

May [meɪ] *n* mai *m* ; *see also* **September**.

maybe ['meɪbiː] *adv* peut-être ; **~ I'll come** je viendrai peut-être.

May Day *n* le Premier mai.

mayhem ['meɪhem] *n* pagaille *f*.

mayonnaise [ˌmeɪə'neɪz] *n* mayonnaise *f*.

mayor [meə'] *n* maire *m*.

mayoress ['meərɪs] *n* - **1.** [female mayor] femme *f* maire - **2.** [mayor's wife] femme *f* du maire.

maze [meɪz] *n lit & fig* labyrinthe *m*, dédale *m*.

MB *(abbr of* megabyte) Mo.

MD *n abbr of* managing director, Doctor of Medicine.

me [miː] *pers pron* - **1.** [direct, indirect] me, m' *(+ vowel or silent 'h')* ; **can you see/hear ~?** tu me vois/m'entends? ; **it's ~** c'est moi ; **they spoke to ~** ils m'ont parlé ; **she gave it to ~** elle me l'a donné - **2.** [stressed, after prep, in comparisons etc] moi ; **you can't expect ME to do it** tu ne peux pas exiger que ce soit moi qui le fasse ; **she's shorter than ~** elle est plus petite que moi.

meadow ['medəʊ] *n* prairie *f*, pré *m*.

meagre *Br*, **meager** *Am* ['miːgə'] *adj* maigre.

meal [miːl] *n* repas *m*.

mealtime ['miːltaɪm] *n* heure *f* du repas.

mean [miːn] *(pt & pp* meant) ◇ *vt* - **1.** [signify] signifier, vouloir dire ; **money ~s nothing to him** l'argent ne compte pas pour lui - **2.** [intend] : **to ~ to do sthg** vouloir faire qqch, avoir l'intention de faire qqch ; **I didn't ~ to drop it** je n'ai pas fait exprès de le laisser tomber ; **to be meant for sb/sthg** être destiné(e) à qqn/qqch ; **to be meant to do sthg** être censé(e) faire qqch ; **to ~ well**

agir dans une bonne intention - **3.** [be serious about] **: I ~ it** je suis sérieux(euse) - **4.** [entail] occasionner, entraîner - **5.** phr **: I ~** [as explanation] c'est vrai ; [as correction] je veux dire. <> adj - **1.** [miserly] radin(e), chiche **; to be ~ with sthg** être avare de qqch - **2.** [unkind] mesquin(e), méchant(e) **; to be ~ to sb** être mesquin envers qqn - **3.** [average] moyen(enne). <> n [average] moyenne f ; see also **means**.

meander ['mɪ'ændə'] vi [river, road] serpenter ; [person] errer.

meaning ['miːnɪŋ] n sens m, signification f.

meaningful ['miːnɪŋfʊl] adj [look] significatif(ive) ; [relationship, discussion] important(e).

meaningless ['miːnɪŋlɪs] adj [gesture, word] dénué(e) OR vide de sens ; [proposal, discussion] sans importance.

means [miːnz] <> n [method, way] moyen m **; by ~ of** au moyen de. <> npl [money] moyens mpl, ressources fpl. ◆ **by all means** adv mais certainement, bien sûr. ◆ **by no means** adv fml nullement, en aucune façon.

meant [ment] pt & pp ⊳ **mean**.

meantime ['miːn,taɪm] n **: in the ~** en attendant.

meanwhile ['miːn,waɪl] adv - **1.** [at the same time] pendant ce temps - **2.** [between two events] en attendant.

measles ['miːzlz] n **: (the) ~** la rougeole.

measly ['miːzlɪ] adj inf misérable, minable.

measure ['meʒə'] <> n - **1.** [gen] mesure f - **2.** [indication] **: it is a ~ of her success that** ... la preuve de son succès, c'est que ... <> vt & vi mesurer.

measurement ['meʒəmənt] n mesure f.

meat [miːt] n viande f.

meatball ['miːtbɔːl] n boulette f de viande.

meat pie n Br tourte f à la viande.

meaty ['miːtɪ] adj fig important(e).

Mecca ['mekə] n La Mecque.

mechanic [mɪ'kænɪk] n mécanicien m, -enne f. ◆ **mechanics** <> n (U) [study] mécanique f. <> npl fig mécanisme m.

mechanical [mɪ'kænɪkl] adj - **1.** [device] mécanique - **2.** [person, mind] fort(e) en mécanique - **3.** [routine, automatic] machinal(e).

mechanism ['mekənɪzm] n lit & fig mécanisme m.

medal ['medl] n médaille f.

medallion [mɪ'dæljən] n médaillon m.

meddle ['medl] vi **: to ~ in** se mêler de.

media ['miːdjə] <> pl ⊳ **medium**. <> n & npl **: the ~** les médias mpl.

mediaeval [,medɪ'iːvl] = **medieval**.

median ['miːdjən] n Am [of road] bande f médiane (qui sépare les deux côtés d'une grande route).

mediate ['miːdɪeɪt] <> vt négocier. <> vi **: to ~ (for/between)** servir de médiateur (pour/entre).

mediator ['miːdɪeɪtə'] n médiateur m, -trice f.

Medicaid ['medɪkeɪd] n Am assistance médicale aux personnes sans ressources.

medical ['medɪkl] <> adj médical(e). <> n examen m médical.

medical officer n [in factory etc] médecin m du travail ; MIL médecin militaire.

Medicare ['medɪkeə'] n Am programme fédéral d'assistance médicale pour personnes âgées.

medicated ['medɪkeɪtɪd] adj traitant(e).

medicine ['medsɪn] n - **1.** [subject, treatment] médecine f **; Doctor of Medicine** UNIV docteur m en médecine - **2.** [substance] médicament m.

medieval [,medɪ'iːvl] adj médiéval(e).

mediocre [,miːdɪ'əʊkə'] adj médiocre.

meditate ['medɪteɪt] vi **: to ~ (on OR upon)** méditer (sur).

Mediterranean [,medɪtə'reɪnjən] <> n [sea] **: the ~ (Sea)** la (mer) Méditerranée. <> adj méditerranéen(enne).

medium ['miːdjəm] (pl sense 1 media ['miːdjə], pl sense 2 mediums) <> adj moyen(enne). <> n - **1.** [way of communicating] moyen m - **2.** [spiritualist] médium m.

medium-size(d) [-saɪz(d)] adj de taille moyenne.

medium wave n onde f moyenne.

medley ['medlɪ] (pl -s) n - **1.** [mixture] mélange m - **2.** MUS pot-pourri m.

meek [miːk] adj docile.

meet [miːt] (pt & pp met) <> vt - **1.** [gen] rencontrer ; [by arrangement] retrouver - **2.** [go to meet - person] aller/venir attendre, aller/venir chercher ; [- train, plane] aller attendre - **3.** [need, requirement] satisfaire, répondre à - **4.** [problem] résoudre ; [challenge] répondre à - **5.** [costs] payer - **6.** [join] rejoindre. <> vi - **1.** [gen] se rencontrer ; [by arrangement] se retrouver ;

[for a purpose] se réunir - **2.** [join] se joindre. ◇ *n Am* [meeting] meeting *m*. ◆ **meet up** *vi* se retrouver ; **to ~ up with sb** rencontrer qqn, retrouver qqn. ◆ **meet with** *vt fus* - **1.** [encounter - disapproval] être accueilli(e) par ; [- success] remporter ; [- failure] essuyer - **2.** *Am* [by arrangement] retrouver.

meeting ['miːtɪŋ] *n* - **1.** [for discussions, business] réunion *f* - **2.** [by chance] rencontre *f* ; [by arrangement] entrevue *f*.

megabyte ['megəbaɪt] *n* COMPUT mégaoctet *m*.

megaphone ['megəfəʊn] *n* mégaphone *m*, porte-voix *m inv*.

melancholy ['melənkəlɪ] ◇ *adj* [person] mélancolique ; [news, facts] triste. ◇ *n* mélancolie *f*.

mellow ['meləʊ] ◇ *adj* [light, voice] doux (douce) ; [taste, wine] moelleux(euse). ◇ *vi* s'adoucir.

melody ['melədɪ] *n* mélodie *f*.

melon ['melən] *n* melon *m*.

melt [melt] ◇ *vt* faire fondre. ◇ *vi* - **1.** [become liquid] fondre - **2.** *fig* : **his heart ~ed at the sight** il fut tout attendri devant ce spectacle - **3.** [disappear] : **to ~ (away)** fondre. ◆ **melt down** *vt sep* fondre.

meltdown ['meltdaʊn] *n* fusion *f* du cœur (du réacteur).

melting pot ['meltɪŋ-] *n fig* creuset *m*.

member ['membəʳ] *n* membre *m* ; [of club] adhérent *m*, -e *f*.

Member of Congress (*pl* **Members of Congress**) *n Am* membre *m* du Congrès.

Member of Parliament (*pl* **Members of Parliament**) *n Br* ≃ député *m*.

Member of the Scottish Parliament *n* membre *m* du Parlement écossais.

membership ['membəʃɪp] *n* - **1.** [of organization] adhésion *f* - **2.** [number of members] nombre *m* d'adhérents - **3.** [members] : **the ~** les membres *mpl*.

membership card *n* carte *f* d'adhésion.

memento [mɪ'mentəʊ] (*pl* **-s**) *n* souvenir *m*.

memo ['meməʊ] (*pl* **-s**) *n* note *f* de service.

memoirs ['memwɑːz] *npl* mémoires *mpl*.

memorandum [,memə'rændəm] (*pl* **-da** [-də], **-dums**) *n* note *f* de service.

memorial [mɪ'mɔːrɪəl] ◇ *adj* commémoratif(ive). ◇ *n* monument *m*.

memorize, -ise ['meməraɪz] *vt* [phone number, list] retenir ; [poem] apprendre par cœur.

memory ['memərɪ] *n* - **1.** [gen & COMPUT] mémoire *f* ; **from ~** de mémoire - **2.** [event, experience] souvenir *m*.

men [men] *pl* ▷ **man**.

menace ['menəs] ◇ *n* - **1.** [gen] menace *f* - **2.** *inf* [nuisance] plaie *f*. ◇ *vt* menacer.

menacing ['menəsɪŋ] *adj* menaçant(e).

mend [mend] ◇ *n inf* : **to be on the ~** aller mieux. ◇ *vt* réparer ; [clothes] raccommoder ; [sock, pullover] repriser.

menial ['miːnjəl] *adj* avilissant(e).

meningitis [,menɪn'dʒaɪtɪs] *n* (*U*) méningite *f*.

menopause ['menəpɔːz] *n* : **the ~** la ménopause.

men's room *n Am* : **the ~** les toilettes *fpl* pour hommes.

menstruation [,menstrʊ'eɪʃn] *n* menstruation *f*.

menswear ['menzweəʳ] *n* (*U*) vêtements *mpl* pour hommes.

mental ['mentl] *adj* mental(e) ; [image, picture] dans la tête.

mental hospital *n* hôpital *m* psychiatrique.

mentality [men'tælətɪ] *n* mentalité *f*.

mentally handicapped *npl* : **the ~** les handicapés *mpl* mentaux.

mention ['menʃn] ◇ *vt* mentionner, signaler ; **not to ~** sans parler de ; **don't ~ it!** je vous en prie! ◇ *n* mention *f*.

menu ['menjuː] *n* [gen & COMPUT] menu *m*.

meow *Am* = **miaow**.

MEP (*abbr of* **Member of the European Parliament**) *n* parlementaire *m* européen.

mercenary ['mɜːsɪnrɪ] ◇ *adj* mercenaire. ◇ *n* mercenaire *m*.

merchandise ['mɜːtʃəndaɪz] *n* (*U*) marchandises *fpl*.

merchant ['mɜːtʃənt] *n* marchand *m*, -e *f*, commerçant *m*, -e *f*.

merchant bank *n Br* banque *f* d'affaires.

merchant navy *Br*, **merchant marine** *Am n* marine *f* marchande.

merciful ['mɜːsɪfʊl] *adj* - **1.** [person] clément(e) - **2.** [death, release] qui est une délivrance.

merciless ['mɜːsɪlɪs] *adj* impitoyable.

mercury ['mɜːkjʊrɪ] *n* mercure *m*.

Mercury ['mɜːkjʊrɪ] *n* [planet] Mercure *f*.

mercy ['mɜːsɪ] *n* - **1.** [kindness, pity] pitié *f* ; **at the ~ of** *fig* à la merci de - **2.** [blessing] : **what a ~ that ...** quelle chance que ...

mere [mɪəʳ] *adj* seul(e) ; **she's a ~ child** ce n'est qu'une enfant ; **it cost a ~ £10** cela n'a coûté que 10 livres.

merely ['mɪəlɪ] *adv* seulement, simplement.

merge [mɜːdʒ] <> *vt* COMM & COMPUT fusionner. <> *vi* - 1. COMM : **to ~ (with)** fusionner (avec) - 2. [roads, lines] : **to ~ (with)** se joindre (à) - 3. [colours] se fondre. <> *n* COMPUT fusion *f*.

merger ['mɜːdʒəʳ] *n* fusion *f*.

meringue [mə'ræŋ] *n* meringue *f*.

merit ['merɪt] <> *n* [value] mérite *m*, valeur *f*. <> *vt* mériter. ◆ **merits** *npl* [advantages] qualités *fpl*.

mermaid ['mɜːmeɪd] *n* sirène *f*.

merry ['merɪ] *adj* - 1. *literary* [happy] joyeux(euse) ; **Merry Christmas!** joyeux Noël! - 2. *inf* [tipsy] gai(e), éméché(e).

merry-go-round *n* manège *m*.

mesh [meʃ] <> *n* maille *f* (du filet) ; **wire ~** grillage *m*. <> *vi* [gears] s'engrener.

mesmerize, -ise ['mezməraɪz] *vt* : **to be ~d by** être fasciné(e) par.

mess [mes] *n* - 1. [untidy state] désordre *m* ; *fig* gâchis *m* - 2. MIL mess *m*. ◆ **mess about, mess around** *inf* <> *vt sep* : **to ~ sb about** traiter qqn par-dessus OR par-dessous la jambe. <> *vi* - 1. [fool around] perdre OR gaspiller son temps - 2. [interfere] : **to ~ about with sthg** s'immiscer dans qqch. ◆ **mess up** *vt sep inf* - 1. [room] mettre en désordre ; [clothes] salir - 2. *fig* [spoil] gâcher.

message ['mesɪdʒ] *n* message *m*.

messenger ['mesɪndʒəʳ] *n* messager *m*, -ère *f*.

Messrs, Messrs. ['mesəz] (*abbr of messieurs*) MM.

messy ['mesɪ] *adj* - 1. [dirty] sale ; [untidy] désordonné(e) ; **a ~ job** un travail salissant - 2. *inf* [divorce] difficile ; [situation] embrouillé(e).

met [met] *pt* & *pp* ▷ **meet**.

metal ['metl] <> *n* métal *m*. <> *comp* en OR de métal.

metallic [mɪ'tælɪk] *adj* - 1. [sound, ore] métallique - 2. [paint, finish] métallisé(e).

metalwork ['metlwɜːk] *n* [craft] ferronnerie *f*.

metaphor ['metəfəʳ] *n* métaphore *f*.

mete [miːt] ◆ **mete out** *vt sep* [punishment] infliger.

meteor ['miːtɪəʳ] *n* météore *m*.

meteorology [miːtjə'rɒlədʒɪ] *n* météorologie *f*.

meter ['miːtəʳ] <> *n* - 1. [device] compteur *m* - 2. *Am* = **metre**. <> *vt* [gas, electricity] établir la consommation de.

method ['meθəd] *n* méthode *f*.

methodical [mɪ'θɒdɪkl] *adj* méthodique.

Methodist ['meθədɪst] <> *adj* méthodiste. <> *n* méthodiste *mf*.

meths [meθs] *n Br inf* alcool *m* à brûler.

methylated spirits ['meθɪleɪtɪd-] *n* alcool *m* à brûler.

meticulous [mɪ'tɪkjʊləs] *adj* méticuleux(euse).

metre *Br*, **meter** *Am* ['miːtəʳ] *n* mètre *m*.

metric ['metrɪk] *adj* métrique.

metronome ['metrənəʊm] *n* métronome *m*.

metropolitan [ˌmetrə'pɒlɪtn] *adj* métropolitain(e).

Metropolitan Police *npl* : **the ~** la police de Londres.

mettle ['metl] *n* : **to be on one's ~** être d'attaque ; **to show** OR **prove one's ~** montrer ce dont on est capable.

mew [mjuː] = **miaow**.

mews [mjuːz] (*pl inv*) *n Br* ruelle *f*.

Mexican ['meksɪkn] <> *adj* mexicain(e). <> *n* Mexicain *m*, -e *f*.

Mexico ['meksɪkəʊ] *n* Mexique *m*.

MI5 (*abbr of Military Intelligence 5*) *n service de contre-espionnage britannique.*

MI6 (*abbr of Military Intelligence 6*) *n service de renseignements britannique.*

miaow *Br* [miːˈaʊ], **meow** *Am* [mɪˈaʊ] <> *n* miaulement *m*, miaou *m*. <> *vi* miauler.

mice [maɪs] *pl* ▷ **mouse**.

mickey ['mɪkɪ] *n* : **to take the ~ out of sb** *Br inf* se payer la tête de qqn, faire marcher qqn.

microchip ['maɪkrəʊtʃɪp] *n* COMPUT puce *f*.

microcomputer [ˌmaɪkrəʊkəm'pjuːtəʳ] *n* micro-ordinateur *m*.

microfilm ['maɪkrəʊfɪlm] *n* microfilm *m*.

microphone ['maɪkrəfəʊn] *n* microphone *m*, micro *m*.

microscope ['maɪkrəskəʊp] *n* microscope *m*.

microscopic [ˌmaɪkrə'skɒpɪk] *adj* microscopique.

microwave (oven) ['maɪkrəweɪv-] *n* (four *m* à) micro-ondes *m*.

mid- [mɪd] *prefix* : **~height** mi-hauteur ; **~morning** milieu de la matinée ; **~winter** plein hiver.

midair [mɪd'eəʳ] ◇ *adj* en plein ciel. ◇ *n* : **in ~** en plein ciel.

midday [mɪd'deɪ] *n* midi *m*.

middle ['mɪdl] ◇ *adj* [centre] du milieu, du centre. ◇ *n* - **1.** [centre] milieu *m*, centre *m* ; **in the ~ (of)** au milieu (de) - **2.** [in time] milieu *m* ; **to be in the ~ of doing sthg** être en train de faire qqch ; **to be in the ~ of a meeting** être en pleine réunion ; **in the ~ of the night** au milieu de la nuit, en pleine nuit - **3.** [waist] taille *f*.

middle-aged *adj* d'une cinquantaine d'années.

Middle Ages *npl* : **the ~** le Moyen Âge.

middle-class *adj* bourgeois(e).

middle classes *npl* : **the ~** la bourgeoisie.

Middle East *n* : **the ~** le Moyen-Orient.

middleman ['mɪdlmæn] (*pl* **-men** [-men]) *n* intermédiaire *m*.

middle name *n* second prénom *m*.

middleweight ['mɪdlweɪt] *n* poids *m* moyen.

middling ['mɪdlɪŋ] *adj* moyen(enne).

Mideast [ˌmɪd'iːst] *n Am* : **the ~** le Moyen-Orient.

midfield [ˌmɪd'fiːld] *n* FTBL milieu *m* de terrain.

midge [mɪdʒ] *n* moucheron *m*.

midget ['mɪdʒɪt] *n* nain *m*, -e *f*.

midi system ['mɪdɪ-] *n* chaîne *f* midi.

Midlands ['mɪdləndz] *npl* : **the ~** *les comtés du centre de l'Angleterre.*

midnight ['mɪdnaɪt] *n* minuit *m*.

midriff ['mɪdrɪf] *n* diaphragme *m*.

midst [mɪdst] *n* - **1.** [in space] : **in the ~ of** au milieu de - **2.** [in time] : **to be in the ~ of doing sthg** être en train de faire qqch.

midsummer ['mɪdˌsʌməʳ] *n* cœur *m* de l'été.

Midsummer Day *n* la Saint-Jean.

midway [ˌmɪd'weɪ] *adv* - **1.** [in space] : **~ (between)** à mi-chemin (entre) - **2.** [in time] : **~ through the meeting** en pleine réunion.

midweek [*adj* 'mɪdwiːk, *adv* mɪd'wiːk] ◇ *adj* du milieu de la semaine. ◇ *adv* en milieu de semaine.

midwife ['mɪdwaɪf] (*pl* **-wives** [-waɪvz]) *n* sage-femme *f*.

midwifery ['mɪdˌwɪfərɪ] *n* obstétrique *f*.

might [maɪt] ◇ *modal vb* - **1.** [expressing possibility] : **the criminal ~ be armed** il est possible que le criminel soit armé - **2.** [expressing suggestion] : **it ~ be better to wait** il vaut peut-être mieux attendre - **3.** *fml* [asking permission] : **he asked if he ~ leave the room** il demanda s'il pouvait sortir de la pièce - **4.** [expressing concession] : **you ~ well be right** vous avez peut-être raison - **5.** *phr* : **I ~ have known** OR **guessed** j'aurais dû m'en douter. ◇ *n* (U) force *f*.

mighty ['maɪtɪ] ◇ *adj* [powerful] puissant(e). ◇ *adv Am inf* drôlement, vachement.

migraine ['miːgreɪn, 'maɪgreɪn] *n* migraine *f*.

migrant ['maɪgrənt] ◇ *adj* - **1.** [bird, animal] migrateur(trice) - **2.** [workers] émigré(e). ◇ *n* - **1.** [bird, animal] migrateur *m* - **2.** [person] émigré *m*, -e *f*.

migrate [*Br* maɪ'greɪt, *Am* 'maɪgreɪt] *vi* - **1.** [bird, animal] migrer - **2.** [person] émigrer.

mike [maɪk] (*abbr of* **microphone**) *n inf* micro *m*.

mild [maɪld] *adj* - **1.** [disinfectant, reproach] léger(ère) - **2.** [tone, weather] doux (douce) - **3.** [illness] bénin(igne).

mildew ['mɪldjuː] *n* (U) moisissure *f*.

mildly ['maɪldlɪ] *adv* - **1.** [gently] doucement ; **that's putting it ~** c'est le moins qu'on puisse dire - **2.** [not strongly] légèrement - **3.** [slightly] un peu.

mile [maɪl] *n* mile *m* ; NAUT mille *m* ; **to be ~s away** *fig* être très loin.

mileage ['maɪlɪdʒ] *n* distance *f* en miles, ≃ kilométrage *m*.

mileometer [maɪ'lɒmɪtəʳ] *n* compteur *m* de miles, ≃ compteur kilométrique.

milestone ['maɪlstəʊn] *n* [marker stone] borne *f* ; *fig* événement *m* marquant OR important.

militant ['mɪlɪtənt] ◇ *adj* militant(e). ◇ *n* militant *m*, -e *f*.

military ['mɪlɪtrɪ] ◇ *adj* militaire. ◇ *n* : **the ~** les militaires *mpl*, l'armée *f*.

militia [mɪ'lɪʃə] *n* milice *f*.

milk [mɪlk] ◇ *n* lait *m*. ◇ *vt* - **1.** [cow] traire - **2.** *fig* [use to own ends] exploiter.

milk chocolate *n* chocolat *m* au lait.

milkman ['mɪlkmən] (*pl* **-men** [-mən]) *n* laitier *m*.

milk shake *n* milk-shake *m*.

milky ['mɪlkɪ] *adj* - **1.** *Br* [coffee] avec beaucoup de lait - **2.** [pale white] laiteux(euse).

Milky Way *n* : **the ~** la Voie lactée.

mill [mɪl] ⬦ n - **1.** [flour-mill, grinder] moulin m - **2.** [factory] usine f. ⬦ vt moudre. ◆ **mill about**, **mill around** vi grouiller.

millennium [mɪ'lenɪəm] (pl **millennia** [mɪ'lenɪə]) n - **1.** [thousand years] millénaire m - **2.** RELIG & fig : **the** ~ le millénium.

miller ['mɪləʳ] n meunier m.

millet ['mɪlɪt] n millet m.

milligram(me) ['mɪlɪgræm] n milligramme m.

millimetre Br, **millimeter** Am ['mɪlɪˌmiːtəʳ] n millimètre m.

millinery ['mɪlɪnrɪ] n chapellerie f féminine.

million ['mɪljən] n million m ; **a ~, ~s of** fig des milliers de, un million de.

millionaire [ˌmɪljə'neəʳ] n millionnaire mf.

millstone ['mɪlstəʊn] n meule f.

milometer [maɪ'lɒmɪtəʳ] = mileometer.

mime [maɪm] ⬦ n mime m. ⬦ vt & vi mimer.

mimic ['mɪmɪk] (pt & pp **-ked**, cont **-king**) ⬦ n imitateur m, -trice f. ⬦ vt imiter.

mimicry ['mɪmɪkrɪ] n imitation f.

min. [mɪn] - **1.** (abbr of **minute**) mn, min - **2.** (abbr of **minimum**) min.

mince [mɪns] ⬦ n Br viande f hachée. ⬦ vt [meat] hacher. ⬦ vi marcher à petits pas maniérés.

mincemeat ['mɪnsmiːt] n - **1.** [fruit] mélange de pommes, raisins secs et épices utilisé en pâtisserie - **2.** Am [meat] viande f hachée.

mince pie n tartelette f de Noël.

mincer ['mɪnsəʳ] n hachoir m.

mind [maɪnd] ⬦ n - **1.** [gen] esprit m ; **state of** ~ état d'esprit ; **to bear sthg in** ~ ne pas oublier qqch ; **to come into/cross sb's** ~ venir à/traverser l'esprit de qqn ; **to keep an open** ~ réserver son jugement ; **to have a ~ to do sthg** avoir bien envie de faire qqch ; **to have sthg in** ~ avoir qqch dans l'idée ; **to make one's** ~ **up** se décider - **2.** [attention] : **to put one's** ~ **to sthg** s'appliquer à qqch ; **to keep one's** ~ **on sthg** se concentrer sur qqch - **3.** [opinion] : **to change one's** ~ changer d'avis ; **to my** ~ à mon avis ; **to speak one's** ~ parler franchement ; **to be in two ~s (about sthg)** se tâter OR être indécis (à propos de qqch) - **4.** [person] cerveau m. ⬦ vi [be bothered] : **I don't** ~ ça m'est égal ; **I hope you don't** ~ j'espère que vous n'y voyez pas d'inconvénient ; **never** ~ [don't worry] ne t'en fais pas ; [it's not important] ça ne fait rien. ⬦ vt - **1.** [be bothered about, dislike] : **I don't** ~ **waiting** ça ne me gêne OR dérange pas d'attendre ; **do you** ~ **if ...?** cela ne vous ennuie pas si ...? ; **I wouldn't** ~ **a beer** je prendrais bien une bière - **2.** [pay attention to] faire attention à, prendre garde à - **3.** [take care of - luggage] garder, surveiller ; [- shop] tenir. ◆ **mind you** adv remarquez.

minder ['maɪndəʳ] n Br inf [bodyguard] ange m gardien.

mindful ['maɪndfʊl] adj : ~ **of** [risks] attentif(ive) à ; [responsibility] soucieux(euse) de.

mindless ['maɪndlɪs] adj stupide, idiot(e).

mine[1] [maɪn] poss pron le mien (la mienne), les miens (les miennes) (pl) ; **that money is** ~ cet argent est à moi ; **it wasn't your fault, it was** MINE ce n'était pas de votre faute, c'était de la mienne OR de ma faute à moi ; **a friend of** ~ un ami à moi, un de mes amis.

mine[2] [maɪn] ⬦ n mine f. ⬦ vt - **1.** [coal, gold] extraire - **2.** [road, beach, sea] miner.

minefield ['maɪnfiːld] n champ m de mines ; fig situation f explosive.

miner ['maɪnəʳ] n mineur m.

mineral ['mɪnərəl] ⬦ adj minéral(e). ⬦ n minéral m.

mineral water n eau f minérale.

minesweeper ['maɪnˌswiːpəʳ] n dragueur m de mines.

mingle ['mɪŋgl] vi : **to ~ (with)** [sounds, fragrances] se mélanger (à) ; [people] se mêler (à).

miniature ['mɪnətʃəʳ] ⬦ adj miniature. ⬦ n - **1.** [painting] miniature f - **2.** [of alcohol] bouteille f miniature. **3.** [small scale] : **in** ~ en miniature.

minibus ['mɪnɪbʌs] (pl **-es**) n minibus m.

minicab ['mɪnɪkæb] n Br radiotaxi m.

minima ['mɪnɪmə] pl ⮑ **minimum**.

minimal ['mɪnɪml] adj [cost] insignifiant(e) ; [damage] minime.

minimum ['mɪnɪməm] (pl **minima** ['mɪnɪmə], **-s**) ⬦ adj minimum (inv). ⬦ n minimum m.

mining ['maɪnɪŋ] ⬦ n exploitation f minière. ⬦ adj minier(ère).

miniskirt ['mɪnɪskɜːt] n minijupe f.

minister ['mɪnɪstəʳ] n - **1.** POL ministre m - **2.** RELIG pasteur m. ◆ **minister to** vt fus [person] donner OR prodiguer ses soins à ; [needs] pourvoir à.

ministerial [ˌmɪnɪˈstɪərɪəl] *adj* ministériel(elle).

minister of state *n* secrétaire *mf* d'État.

ministry [ˈmɪnɪstrɪ] *n* - 1. POL ministère *m* - 2. RELIG : **the ~** le saint ministère.

mink [mɪŋk] (*pl inv*) *n* vison *m*.

minnow [ˈmɪnəʊ] *n* vairon *m*.

minor [ˈmaɪnəʳ] ◇ *adj* [gen & MUS] mineur(e) ; [detail] petit(e) ; [role] secondaire. ◇ *n* mineur *m*, -e *f*.

minority [maɪˈnɒrətɪ] *n* minorité *f*.

mint [mɪnt] ◇ *n* - 1. [herb] menthe *f* - 2. [sweet] bonbon *m* à la menthe - 3. [for coins] : **the Mint** l'hôtel de la Monnaie ; **in ~ condition** en parfait état. ◇ *vt* [coins] battre.

minus [ˈmaɪnəs] (*pl* -es [-iːz]) ◇ *prep* moins. ◇ *adj* [answer, quantity] négatif(ive). ◇ *n* - 1. MATH signe *m* moins - 2. [disadvantage] handicap *m*.

minus sign *n* signe *m* moins.

minute¹ [ˈmɪnɪt] *n* minute *f* ; **at any ~** à tout moment, d'une minute à l'autre ; **stop that this ~!** arrête tout de suite OR immédiatement! ◆ **minutes** *npl* procès-verbal *m*, compte rendu *m*.

minute² [maɪˈnjuːt] *adj* minuscule.

miracle [ˈmɪrəkl] *n* miracle *m*.

miraculous [mɪˈrækjʊləs] *adj* miraculeux(euse).

mirage [mɪˈrɑːʒ] *n lit & fig* mirage *m*.

mire [maɪəʳ] *n* fange *f*, boue *f*.

mirror [ˈmɪrəʳ] ◇ *n* miroir *m*, glace *f*. ◇ *vt* refléter.

mirth [mɜːθ] *n* hilarité *f*, gaieté *f*.

misadventure [ˌmɪsədˈventʃəʳ] *n* : **death by ~** JUR mort *f* accidentelle.

misapprehension [ˈmɪsˌæprɪˈhenʃn] *n* idée *f* fausse.

misappropriation [ˈmɪsəˌprəʊprɪˈeɪʃn] *n* détournement *m*.

misbehave [ˌmɪsbɪˈheɪv] *vi* se conduire mal.

miscalculate [ˌmɪsˈkælkjʊleɪt] ◇ *vt* mal calculer. ◇ *vi* se tromper.

miscarriage [ˌmɪsˈkærɪdʒ] *n* MED fausse couche *f* ; **to have a ~** faire une fausse couche.

miscarriage of justice *n* erreur *f* judiciaire.

miscellaneous [ˌmɪsəˈleɪnjəs] *adj* varié(e), divers(e).

mischief [ˈmɪstʃɪf] *n* (U) - 1. [playfulness] malice *f*, espièglerie *f* - 2. [naughty behav-

iour] sottises *fpl*, bêtises *fpl* - 3. [harm] dégât *m*.

mischievous [ˈmɪstʃɪvəs] *adj* - 1. [playful] malicieux(euse) - 2. [naughty] espiègle, coquin(e).

misconception [ˌmɪskənˈsepʃn] *n* idée *f* fausse.

misconduct [ˌmɪsˈkɒndʌkt] *n* inconduite *f*.

misconstrue [ˌmɪskənˈstruː] *vt fml* mal interpréter.

miscount [ˌmɪsˈkaʊnt] *vt & vi* mal compter.

misdeed [ˌmɪsˈdiːd] *n* méfait *m*.

misdemeanour *Br*, **misdemeanor** *Am* [ˌmɪsdɪˈmiːnəʳ] *n* JUR délit *m*.

miser [ˈmaɪzəʳ] *n* avare *mf*.

miserable [ˈmɪzrəbl] *adj* - 1. [person] malheureux(euse), triste - 2. [conditions, life] misérable ; [pay] dérisoire ; [weather] maussade - 3. [failure] pitoyable, lamentable.

miserly [ˈmaɪzəlɪ] *adj* avare.

misery [ˈmɪzərɪ] *n* - 1. [of person] tristesse *f* - 2. [of conditions, life] misère *f*.

misfire [ˌmɪsˈfaɪəʳ] *vi* - 1. [gun, plan] rater - 2. [car engine] avoir des ratés.

misfit [ˈmɪsfɪt] *n* inadapté *m*, -e *f*.

misfortune [mɪsˈfɔːtʃuːn] *n* - 1. [bad luck] malchance *f* - 2. [piece of bad luck] malheur *m*.

misgivings [mɪsˈgɪvɪŋz] *npl* craintes *fpl*, doutes *mpl*.

misguided [ˌmɪsˈgaɪdɪd] *adj* [person] malavisé(e) ; [attempt] malencontreux(euse) ; [opinion] peu judicieux(euse).

mishandle [ˌmɪsˈhændl] *vt* - 1. [person, animal] manier sans précaution - 2. [negotiations] mal mener ; [business] mal gérer.

mishap [ˈmɪshæp] *n* mésaventure *f*.

misinterpret [ˌmɪsɪnˈtɜːprɪt] *vt* mal interpréter.

misjudge [ˌmɪsˈdʒʌdʒ] *vt* - 1. [distance, time] mal évaluer - 2. [person, mood] méjuger, se méprendre sur.

mislay [ˌmɪsˈleɪ] (*pt & pp* -**laid** [-ˈleɪd]) *vt* égarer.

mislead [ˌmɪsˈliːd] (*pt & pp* -**led**) *vt* induire en erreur.

misleading [ˌmɪsˈliːdɪŋ] *adj* trompeur(euse).

misled [ˌmɪsˈled] *pt & pp* ▷ **mislead**.

misnomer [ˌmɪsˈnəʊməʳ] *n* nom *m* mal approprié.

misplace [ˌmɪsˈpleɪs] *vt* égarer.

misprint [ˈmɪsprɪnt] *n* faute *f* d'impression.

miss [mɪs] ⇔ *vt* - **1.** [gen] rater, manquer - **2.** [home, person] : **I ~ my family/her** ma famille/elle me manque - **3.** [avoid, escape] échapper à ; **I just ~ed being run over** j'ai failli me faire écraser. ⇔ *vi* rater. ⇔ *n* : **to give sthg a ~** *inf* ne pas aller à qqch. ◆ **miss out** ⇔ *vt sep* [omit - by accident] oublier ; [- deliberately] omettre. ⇔ *vi* : **to ~ out on sthg** ne pas pouvoir profiter de qqch.

Miss [mɪs] *n* Mademoiselle *f*.

misshapen [ˌmɪsˈʃeɪpn] *adj* difforme.

missile [*Br* ˈmɪsaɪl, *Am* ˈmɪsəl] *n* - **1.** [weapon] missile *m* - **2.** [thrown object] projectile *m*.

missing [ˈmɪsɪŋ] *adj* - **1.** [lost] perdu(e), égaré(e) - **2.** [not present] manquant(e), qui manque.

mission [ˈmɪʃn] *n* mission *f*.

missionary [ˈmɪʃənrɪ] *n* missionnaire *mf*.

misspend [ˌmɪsˈspend] (*pt & pp* -**spent** [-ˈspent]) *vt* gaspiller.

mist [mɪst] *n* brume *f*. ◆ **mist over, mist up** *vi* s'embuer.

mistake [mɪˈsteɪk] (*pt* -**took**, *pp* -**taken**) ⇔ *n* erreur *f* ; **by ~** par erreur ; **to make a ~** faire une erreur, se tromper. ⇔ *vt* - **1.** [misunderstand - meaning] mal comprendre ; [- intention] se méprendre sur - **2.** [fail to recognize] : **to ~ sb/sthg for** prendre qqn/qqch pour, confondre qqn/qqch avec.

mistaken [mɪˈsteɪkn] ⇔ *pp* ▷ **mistake**. ⇔ *adj* - **1.** [person] : **to be ~ (about)** se tromper (en ce qui concerne *or* sur) - **2.** [belief, idea] erroné(e), faux (fausse).

mister [ˈmɪstər] *n* *inf* monsieur *m*. ◆ **Mister** *n* Monsieur *m*.

mistletoe [ˈmɪsltəʊ] *n* gui *m*.

mistook [mɪˈstʊk] *pt* ▷ **mistake**.

mistreat [ˌmɪsˈtriːt] *vt* maltraiter.

mistress [ˈmɪstrɪs] *n* maîtresse *f*.

mistrust [ˌmɪsˈtrʌst] ⇔ *n* méfiance *f*. ⇔ *vt* se méfier de.

misty [ˈmɪstɪ] *adj* brumeux(euse).

misunderstand [ˌmɪsʌndəˈstænd] (*pt & pp* -**stood**) *vt & vi* mal comprendre.

misunderstanding [ˌmɪsʌndəˈstændɪŋ] *n* malentendu *m*.

misunderstood [ˌmɪsʌndəˈstʊd] *pt & pp* ▷ **misunderstand**.

misuse [*n* ˌmɪsˈjuːs, *vb* ˌmɪsˈjuːz] ⇔ *n* - **1.** [of one's time, resources] mauvais emploi *m* - **2.** [of power] abus *m* ; [of funds] dé-

tournement *m*. ⇔ *vt* - **1.** [one's time, resources] mal employer - **2.** [power] abuser de ; [funds] détourner.

miter *Am* = **mitre**.

mitigate [ˈmɪtɪgeɪt] *vt* atténuer, mitiger.

mitre *Br*, **miter** *Am* [ˈmaɪtər] *n* - **1.** [hat] mitre *f* - **2.** [joint] onglet *m*.

mitt [mɪt] *n* - **1.** = **mitten** - **2.** [in baseball] gant *m*.

mitten [ˈmɪtn] *n* moufle *f*.

mix [mɪks] ⇔ *vt* - **1.** [gen] mélanger - **2.** [activities] : **to ~ sthg with sthg** combiner *or* associer qqch et qqch - **3.** [drink] préparer ; [cement] malaxer. ⇔ *vi* - **1.** [gen] se mélanger - **2.** [socially] : **to ~ with** fréquenter. ⇔ *n* - **1.** [gen] mélange *m* - **2.** MUS mixage *m*. ◆ **mix up** *vt sep* - **1.** [confuse] confondre - **2.** [disorganize] mélanger.

mixed [mɪkst] *adj* - **1.** [assorted] assortis(ies) - **2.** [education] mixte.

mixed-ability *adj Br* [class] tous niveaux confondus.

mixed grill *n* assortiment *m* de grillades.

mixed up *adj* - **1.** [confused - person] qui ne sait plus où il en est, paumé(e) ; [- mind] embrouillé(e) - **2.** [involved] : **to be ~ in sthg** être mêlé(e) à qqch.

mixer [ˈmɪksər] *n* [for food] mixer *m*.

mixture [ˈmɪkstʃər] *n* - **1.** [gen] mélange *m* - **2.** MED préparation *f*.

mix-up *n* *inf* confusion *f*.

mm (*abbr of* **millimetre**) mm.

moan [məʊn] ⇔ *n* [of pain, sadness] gémissement *m*. ⇔ *vi* - **1.** [in pain, sadness] gémir - **2.** *inf* [complain] : **to ~ (about)** rouspéter *or* râler (à propos de).

moat [məʊt] *n* douves *fpl*.

mob [mɒb] ⇔ *n* foule *f*. ⇔ *vt* assaillir.

mobile [ˈməʊbaɪl] ⇔ *adj* - **1.** [gen] mobile - **2.** [able to travel] motorisé(e). ⇔ *n* mobile *m*.

mobile home *n* auto-caravane *f*.

mobile phone *n* téléphone *m* portatif, portable *m*.

mobilize, -ise [ˈməʊbɪlaɪz] *vt & vi* mobiliser.

mock [mɒk] ⇔ *adj* faux (fausse) ; **~ exam** examen blanc. ⇔ *vt* se moquer de. ⇔ *vi* se moquer.

mockery [ˈmɒkərɪ] *n* moquerie *f*.

mod cons [ˌmɒd-] (*abbr of* **modern con-**

veniences) *npl Br inf* : **all** ~ tout confort, tt. conf.

mode [məʊd] *n* mode *m*.

model ['mɒdl] <> *n* - **1.** [gen] modèle *m* - **2.** [fashion model] mannequin *m*. <> *adj* - **1.** [perfect] modèle - **2.** [reduced-scale] (en) modèle réduit. <> *vt* - **1.** [clay] modeler - **2.** [clothes] : **to** ~ **a dress** présenter un modèle de robe - **3.** [copy] : **to** ~ **o.s. on sb** prendre modèle OR exemple sur qqn, se modeler sur qqn. <> *vi* être mannequin.

modem ['məʊdem] *n* COMPUT modem *m*.

moderate [*adj & n* 'mɒdərət, *vb* 'mɒdəreɪt] <> *adj* modéré(e). <> *n* POL modéré *m*, -e *f*. <> *vt* modérer. <> *vi* se modérer.

moderation [ˌmɒdə'reɪʃn] *n* modération *f* ; **in** ~ avec modération.

modern ['mɒdən] *adj* moderne.

modernize, -ise ['mɒdənaɪz] <> *vt* moderniser. <> *vi* se moderniser.

modern languages *npl* langues *fpl* vivantes.

modest ['mɒdɪst] *adj* modeste.

modesty ['mɒdɪstɪ] *n* modestie *f*.

modicum ['mɒdɪkəm] *n* minimum *m*.

modify ['mɒdɪfaɪ] *vt* modifier.

module ['mɒdjuːl] *n* module *m*.

mogul ['məʊgl] *n fig* magnat *m*.

mohair ['məʊheə'] *n* mohair *m*.

moist [mɔɪst] *adj* [soil, climate] humide ; [cake] moelleux(euse).

moisten ['mɔɪsn] *vt* humecter.

moisture ['mɔɪstʃə'] *n* humidité *f*.

moisturizer ['mɔɪstʃəraɪzə'] *n* crème *f* hydratante, lait *m* hydratant.

molar ['məʊlə'] *n* molaire *f*.

molasses [mə'læsɪz] *n* (U) mélasse *f*.

mold *etc Am* = **mould**.

mole [məʊl] *n* - **1.** [animal, spy] taupe *f* - **2.** [on skin] grain *m* de beauté.

molecule ['mɒlɪkjuːl] *n* molécule *f*.

molest [mə'lest] *vt* - **1.** [attack sexually] attenter à la pudeur de - **2.** [attack] molester.

mollusc, mollusk *Am* ['mɒləsk] *n* mollusque *m*.

mollycoddle ['mɒlɪˌkɒdl] *vt inf* chouchouter.

molt *Am* = **moult**.

molten ['məʊltn] *adj* en fusion.

mom [mɒm] *n Am inf* maman *f*.

moment ['məʊmənt] *n* moment *m*, instant *m* ; **at any** ~ d'un moment à l'autre ; **at**

the ~ en ce moment ; **for the** ~ pour le moment.

momentarily ['məʊməntərɪlɪ] *adv* - **1.** [for a short time] momentanément - **2.** *Am* [soon] très bientôt.

momentary ['məʊməntrɪ] *adj* momentané(e), passager(ère).

momentous [mə'mentəs] *adj* capital(e), très important(e).

momentum [mə'mentəm] *n* (U) - **1.** PHYSICS moment *m* - **2.** *fig* [speed, force] vitesse *f* ; **to gather** ~ prendre de la vitesse.

momma ['mɒmə], **mommy** ['mɒmɪ] *n Am inf* maman *f*.

Monaco ['mɒnəkəʊ] *n* Monaco.

monarch ['mɒnək] *n* monarque *m*.

monarchy ['mɒnəkɪ] *n* monarchie *f*.

monastery ['mɒnəstrɪ] *n* monastère *m*.

Monday ['mʌndɪ] *n* lundi *m* ; *see also* **Saturday**.

monetary ['mʌnɪtrɪ] *adj* monétaire.

money ['mʌnɪ] *n* argent *m* ; **to make** ~ gagner de l'argent ; **to get one's ~'s worth** en avoir pour son argent.

moneybox ['mʌnɪbɒks] *n Br* tirelire *f*.

moneylender ['mʌnɪˌlendə'] *n* prêteur *m*, -euse *f* sur gages.

money order *n* mandat *m* postal.

money-spinner [-ˌspɪnə'] *n esp Br inf* mine *f* d'or.

mongol ['mɒŋgəl] *dated & offensive n* mongolien *m*, -ienne *f*.

Mongolia [mɒŋ'gəʊliə] *n* Mongolie *f*.

mongrel ['mʌŋgrəl] *n* [dog] bâtard *m*.

monitor ['mɒnɪtə'] <> *n* COMPUT, MED & TV moniteur *m*. <> *vt* - **1.** [check] contrôler, suivre de près - **2.** [broadcasts, messages] être à l'écoute de.

monk [mʌŋk] *n* moine *m*.

monkey ['mʌŋkɪ] (*pl* -**s**) *n* singe *m*.

monkey nut *n Br* cacahuète *f*.

monkey wrench *n* clef *f* à molette.

mono ['mɒnəʊ] <> *adj* mono (*inv*). <> *n* [sound] monophonie *f*.

monochrome ['mɒnəkrəʊm] *adj* monochrome.

monocle ['mɒnəkl] *n* monocle *m*.

monologue, monolog *Am* ['mɒnəlɒg] *n* monologue *m*.

monopolize, -ise [mə'nɒpəlaɪz] *vt* monopoliser.

monopoly [mə'nɒpəlɪ] *n* : ~ **(on** OR **of)** monopole *m* (de).

monotone ['mɒnətəʊn] *n* ton *m* monocorde.

monotonous [mə'nɒtənəs] *adj* monotone.

monotony [mə'nɒtənɪ] *n* monotonie *f*.

monsoon [mɒn'suːn] *n* mousson *f*.

monster ['mɒnstər] *n* - **1.** [creature, cruel person] monstre *m* - **2.** [huge thing, person] colosse *m*.

monstrosity [mɒn'strɒsətɪ] *n* monstruosité *f*.

monstrous ['mɒnstrəs] *adj* monstrueux(euse).

Mont Blanc [ˌmɔ̃'blɑ̃] *n* le mont Blanc.

month [mʌnθ] *n* mois *m*.

monthly ['mʌnθlɪ] <> *adj* mensuel(elle). <> *adv* mensuellement. <> *n* [publication] mensuel *m*

Montreal [ˌmɒntrɪ'ɔːl] *n* Montréal.

monument ['mɒnjʊmənt] *n* monument *m*.

monumental [ˌmɒnjʊ'mentl] *adj* monumental(e).

moo [muː] (*pl* **-s**) <> *n* meuglement *m*, beuglement *m*. <> *vi* meugler, beugler

mood [muːd] *n* humeur *f* ; **in a (bad)** ~ de mauvaise humeur ; **in a good** ~ de bonne humeur.

moody ['muːdɪ] *adj pej* - **1.** [changeable] lunatique - **2.** [bad-tempered] de mauvaise humeur, mal luné(e).

moon [muːn] *n* lune *f*.

moonlight ['muːnlaɪt] (*pt & pp* **-ed**) <> *n* clair *m* de lune <> *vi* travailler au noir.

moonlighting ['muːnlaɪtɪŋ] *n* (U) travail *m* au noir.

moonlit ['muːnlɪt] *adj* [countryside] éclairé(e) par la lune ; [night] de lune.

moor [mɔːr] <> *n esp Br* lande *f*. <> *vt* amarrer. <> *vi* mouiller.

moorland ['mɔːlənd] *n esp Br* lande *f*.

moose [muːs] (*pl inv*) *n* [North American] orignal *m*.

mop [mɒp] <> *n* - **1.** [for cleaning] balai *m* à laver - **2.** *inf* [hair] tignasse *f*. <> *vt* - **1.** [floor] laver - **2.** [sweat] essuyer ; **to** ~ **one's face** s'essuyer le visage. ◆ **mop up** *vt sep* [clean up] éponger.

mope [məʊp] *vi* broyer du noir.

moped ['məʊped] *n* vélomoteur *m*.

moral ['mɒrəl] <> *adj* moral(e). <> *n* [lesson] morale *f*. ◆ **morals** *npl* moralité *f*.

morale [mə'rɑːl] *n* (U) moral *m*.

morality [mə'rælətɪ] *n* moralité *f*.

morass [mə'ræs] *n fig* [of detail, paperwork] fatras *m*.

morbid ['mɔːbɪd] *adj* morbide.

more [mɔːr] <> *adv* - **1.** (*with adjectives and adverbs*) plus ; ~ **important (than)** plus important (que) ; ~ **often/quickly (than)** plus souvent/rapidement (que) - **2.** [to a greater degree] plus, davantage - **3.** [another time] : **once/twice** ~ une fois/deux fois de plus, encore une fois/deux fois. <> *adj* - **1.** [larger number, amount of] plus de, davantage de ; **there are** ~ **trains in the morning** il y a plus de trains le matin ; ~ **than 70 people died** plus de 70 personnes ont péri - **2.** [an extra amount of] encore (de) ; **have some** ~ **tea** prends encore du thé ; **I finished two** ~ **chapters today** j'ai fini deux autres or encore deux chapitres aujourd'hui ; **we need** ~ **money/time** il nous faut plus d'argent/de temps, il nous faut davantage d'argent/de temps. <> *pron* plus, davantage ; ~ **than five** plus de cinq ; **he's got** ~ **than I have** il en a plus que moi ; **there's no** ~ **(left)** il n'y en a plus, il n'y a plus ; **(and) what's** ~ de plus, qui plus est. ◆ **any more** *adv* : **not ... any** ~ ne ... plus. ◆ **more and more** <> *adv & pron* de plus en plus ; ~ **and** ~ **depressed** de plus en plus déprimé. <> *adj* de plus en plus de ; **there are** ~ **and** ~ **cars on the roads** il y a de plus en plus de voitures sur les routes. ◆ **more or less** *adv* - **1.** [almost] plus ou moins - **2.** [approximately] environ, à peu près.

moreover [mɔː'rəʊvər] *adv* de plus.

morgue [mɔːg] *n* morgue *f*.

Mormon ['mɔːmən] *n* mormon *m*, -e *f*.

morning ['mɔːnɪŋ] *n* matin *m* ; [duration] matinée *f* ; **I work in the** ~ je travaille le matin ; **I'll do it tomorrow** ~ or **in the** ~ je le ferai demain. ◆ **mornings** *adv Am* le matin.

Moroccan [mə'rɒkən] <> *adj* marocain(e). <> *n* Marocain *m*, -e *f*.

Morocco [mə'rɒkəʊ] *n* Maroc *m*.

moron ['mɔːrɒn] *n inf* idiot *m*, -e *f*, crétin *m*, -e *f*.

morose [mə'rəʊs] *adj* morose.

morphine ['mɔːfiːn] *n* morphine *f*.

Morse (code) [mɔːs-] *n* morse *m*.

morsel ['mɔːsl] *n* bout *m*, morceau *m*.

mortal ['mɔːtl] <> *adj* mortel(elle). <> *n* mortel *m*, -elle *f*.

mortality [mɔː'tælətɪ] *n* mortalité *f*.

mortar ['mɔːtər] *n* mortier *m*.

mortgage ['mɔːgɪdʒ] <> *n* emprunt-logement *m*. <> *vt* hypothéquer.

mortified ['mɔːtɪfaɪd] *adj* mortifié(e).

mortuary ['mɔːtʃʊərɪ] *n* morgue *f*.

mosaic [mə'zeɪɪk] *n* mosaïque *f*.

Moscow ['mɒskəʊ] *n* Moscou.

Moslem ['mɒzləm] = **Muslim**.

mosque [mɒsk] *n* mosquée *f*.

mosquito [mə'skiːtəʊ] (*pl* **-es** OR **-s**) *n* moustique *m*.

moss [mɒs] *n* mousse *f*.

most [məʊst] (*superl of* **many**) ◇ *adj* - **1.** [the majority of] la plupart de ; ~ **tourists here are German** la plupart des touristes ici sont allemands - **2.** [largest amount of] : **(the)** ~ le plus de ; **she's got (the) ~ money/sweets** c'est elle qui a le plus d'argent/de bonbons. ◇ *pron* - **1.** [the majority] la plupart ; ~ **of the tourists here are German** la plupart des touristes ici sont allemands ; ~ **of them** la plupart d'entre eux - **2.** [largest amount] : **(the)** ~ le plus ; **at** ~ au maximum, tout au plus - **3.** *phr* : **to make the** ~ **of sthg** profiter de qqch au maximum. ◇ *adv* - **1.** [to greatest extent] : **(the)** ~ le plus - **2.** *fml* [very] très, fort - **3.** *Am* [almost] presque.

mostly ['məʊstlɪ] *adv* principalement, surtout.

MOT *n* (*abbr of* **Ministry of Transport (test)**) *Br contrôle technique annuel obligatoire pour les véhicules de plus de trois ans.*

motel [məʊ'tel] *n* motel *m*.

moth [mɒθ] *n* papillon *m* de nuit ; [in clothes] mite *f*.

mothball ['mɒθbɔːl] *n* boule *f* de naphtaline.

mother ['mʌðər] ◇ *n* mère *f*. ◇ *vt* [child] materner, dorloter.

motherhood ['mʌðəhʊd] *n* maternité *f*.

mother-in-law (*pl* **mothers-in-law**) *n* belle-mère *f*.

motherly ['mʌðəlɪ] *adj* maternel(elle).

mother-of-pearl *n* nacre *f*.

mother-to-be (*pl* **mothers-to-be**) *n* future maman *f*.

mother tongue *n* langue *f* maternelle.

motif [məʊ'tiːf] *n* motif *m*.

motion ['məʊʃn] ◇ *n* - **1.** [gen] mouvement *m* ; **to set sthg in** ~ mettre qqch en branle - **2.** [in debate] motion *f*. ◇ *vt* : **to** ~ **sb to do sthg** faire signe à qqn de faire qqch. ◇ *vi* : **to** ~ **to sb** faire signe à qqn.

motionless ['məʊʃənlɪs] *adj* immobile.

motion picture *n Am* film *m*.

motivated ['məʊtɪveɪtɪd] *adj* motivé(e).

motivation [,məʊtɪ'veɪʃn] *n* motivation *f*.

motive ['məʊtɪv] *n* motif *m*.

motley ['mɒtlɪ] *adj pej* hétéroclite.

motor ['məʊtər] ◇ *adj Br* automobile. ◇ *n* [engine] moteur *m*.

motorbike ['məʊtəbaɪk] *n inf* moto *f*.

motorboat ['məʊtəbəʊt] *n* canot *m* automobile.

motorcar ['məʊtəkɑːr] *n Br* automobile *f*, voiture *f*.

motorcycle ['məʊtə,saɪkl] *n* moto *f*.

motorcyclist ['məʊtə,saɪklɪst] *n* motocycliste *mf*.

motoring ['məʊtərɪŋ] *Br* ◇ *adj* [magazine, correspondent] automobile. ◇ *n* tourisme *m* automobile.

motorist ['məʊtərɪst] *n* automobiliste *mf*.

motor racing *n* (*U*) course *f* automobile.

motor scooter *n* scooter *m*.

motor vehicle *n* véhicule *m* automobile.

motorway ['məʊtəweɪ] *Br n* autoroute *f*.

mottled ['mɒtld] *adj* [leaf] tacheté(e) ; [skin] marbré(e).

motto ['mɒtəʊ] (*pl* **-s** OR **-es**) *n* devise *f*.

mould, mold *Am* [məʊld] ◇ *n* - **1.** [growth] moisissure *f* - **2.** [shape] moule *m*. ◇ *vt* - **1.** [shape] mouler, modeler - **2.** *fig* [influence] former, façonner.

moulding, molding *Am* ['məʊldɪŋ] *n* [decoration] moulure *f*.

mouldy, moldy *Am* ['məʊldɪ] *adj* moisi(e).

moult, molt *Am* [məʊlt] *vi* muer.

mound [maʊnd] *n* - **1.** [small hill] tertre *m*, butte *f* - **2.** [pile] tas *m*, monceau *m*.

mount [maʊnt] ◇ *n* - **1.** [support - for jewel] monture *f* ; [- for photograph] carton *m* de montage ; [- for machine] support *m* - **2.** [horse] monture *f* - **3.** [mountain] mont *m*. ◇ *vt* monter ; **to** ~ **a horse** monter sur un cheval ; **to** ~ **a bike** monter sur OR enfourcher un vélo. ◇ *vi* - **1.** [increase] monter, augmenter - **2.** [climb on horse] se mettre en selle.

mountain ['maʊntɪn] *n lit & fig* montagne *f*.

mountain bike *n* VTT *m*.

mountaineer [,maʊntɪ'nɪər] *n* alpiniste *mf*.

mountaineering [,maʊntɪ'nɪərɪŋ] *n* alpinisme *m*.

mountainous ['maʊntɪnəs] *adj* [region] montagneux(euse).

mounted police *n* : the ~ la police montée.

mourn [mɔːn] <> *vt* pleurer. <> *vi* : to ~ (for sb) pleurer (qqn).

mourner ['mɔːnə'] *n* [related] parent *m* du défunt ; [unrelated] ami *m*, -e *f* du défunt.

mournful ['mɔːnfʊl] *adj* [face] triste ; [sound] lugubre.

mourning ['mɔːnɪŋ] *n* deuil *m* ; in ~ en deuil.

mouse [maʊs] (*pl* **mice** [maɪs]) *n* COMPUT & ZOOL souris *f*.

mousetrap ['maʊstræp] *n* souricière *f*.

mousse [muːs] *n* mousse *f*.

moustache *Br* [mə'staːʃ], **mustache** *Am* ['mʌstæʃ] *n* moustache *f*.

mouth [maʊθ] *n* - **1.** [of person, animal] bouche *f* ; [of dog, cat, lion] gueule *f* - **2.** [of cave] entrée *f* ; [of river] embouchure *f*.

mouthful ['maʊθfʊl] *n* [of food] bouchée *f* ; [of drink] gorgée *f*.

mouthorgan ['maʊθ,ɔːgən] *n* harmonica *m*.

mouthpiece ['maʊθpiːs] *n* - **1.** [of telephone] microphone *m* ; [of musical instrument] bec *m* - **2.** [spokesperson] porte-parole *m inv*.

mouthwash ['maʊθwɒʃ] *n* eau *f* dentifrice.

mouth-watering [ˌwɔːtərɪŋ] *adj* alléchant(e).

movable ['muːvəbl] *adj* mobile.

move [muːv] <> *n* - **1.** [movement] mouvement *m* ; to get a ~ on *inf* se remuer, se grouiller - **2.** [change - of house] déménagement *m* ; [- of job] changement *m* d'emploi - **3.** [in game - action] coup *m* ; [- turn to play] tour *m* ; *fig* démarche *f*. <> *vt* - **1.** [shift] déplacer, bouger - **2.** [change - job, office] changer de ; to ~ house *Br* déménager - **3.** [cause] : to ~ sb to do sthg inciter qqn à faire qqch - **4.** [emotionally] émouvoir - **5.** [propose] : to ~ sthg/that ... proposer qqch/que ... <> *vi* - **1.** [shift] bouger - **2.** [act] agir - **3.** [to new house] déménager ; [to new job] changer d'emploi. ◆ **move about** *vi* - **1.** [fidget] remuer - **2.** [travel] voyager. ◆ **move along** <> *vt sep* faire avancer. <> *vi* se déplacer ; the police asked him to ~ along la police lui a demandé de circuler. ◆ **move around** = **move about**. ◆ **move away** *vi* [leave] partir. ◆ **move in** *vi* [to house] emménager. ◆ **move on** *vi* - **1.** [after stopping] se remettre en route - **2.** [in discussion] changer de sujet. ◆ **move out** *vi* [from house] déménager. ◆ **move over** *vi* s'écarter, se pousser. ◆ **move up** *vi* [on bench etc] se déplacer.

moveable ['muːvəbl] = movable.

movement ['muːvmənt] *n* mouvement *m*.

movie ['muːvɪ] *n esp Am* film *m*.

movie camera *n* caméra *f*.

moving ['muːvɪŋ] *adj* - **1.** [emotionally] émouvant(e), touchant(e) - **2.** [not fixed] mobile.

mow [məʊ] (*pt* -ed, *pp* -ed OR mown) *vt* faucher ; [lawn] tondre. ◆ **mow down** *vt sep* faucher.

mower ['məʊə'] *n* tondeuse *f* à gazon.

mown [məʊn] *pp* ▷ mow.

MP *n* - **1.** (*abbr of* **Military Police**) PM - **2.** *Br* (*abbr of* **Member of Parliament**) ≃ député *m*.

mpg (*abbr of* **miles per gallon**) *n* miles *au* gallon.

mph (*abbr of* **miles per hour**) *n* miles à l'heure.

Mr ['mɪstə'] *n* Monsieur *m* ; [on letter] M.

Mrs ['mɪsɪz] *n* Madame *f* ; [on letter] Mme.

Ms [mɪz] *n titre que les femmes peuvent utiliser au lieu de madame ou mademoiselle pour éviter la distinction entre les femmes mariées et les célibataires.*

MS *n* (*abbr of* **multiple sclerosis**) SEP *f*.

MSc (*abbr of* **Master of Science**) *n* (*titulaire d'une*) maîtrise de sciences.

MSP *n abbr of* **Member of the Scottish Parliament**.

much [mʌtʃ] (*compar* **more**, *superl* **most**) <> *adj* beaucoup de ; there isn't ~ rice left il ne reste pas beaucoup de riz ; as ~ money as ... autant d'argent que ... ; too ~ trop de ; how ~ ...? combien de ...? ; how much money do you earn? tu gagnes combien? <> *pron* beaucoup ; I don't think ~ of his new house sa nouvelle maison ne me plaît pas trop ; as ~ as autant que ; too ~ trop ; how ~? combien? ; I'm not ~ of a cook je suis un piètre cuisinier ; so ~ for all my hard work tout ce travail pour rien ; I thought as ~ c'est bien ce que je pensais. <> *adv* beaucoup ; I don't go out ~ je ne sors pas beaucoup OR souvent ; as ~ as autant que ; thank you very ~ merci beaucoup ; without so ~ as ... sans même ... ◆ **much as** *conj* bien que (+ subjunctive).

muck [mʌk] *inf n* (U) - **1.** [dirt] saletés *fpl* - **2.** [manure] fumier *m*. ◆ **muck about, muck around** *Br inf* <> *vt sep* : to ~ sb about traiter qqn par-dessus OR par-dessous la jambe. ◇ *vi* traîner. ◆ **muck up** *vt sep Br inf* gâcher.

mucky ['mʌkɪ] *adj* sale.

mucus ['mju:kəs] *n* mucus *m*.

mud [mʌd] *n* boue *f*.

muddle ['mʌdl] ◇ *n* désordre *m*, fouillis *m*. ◇ *vt* - 1. [papers] mélanger - 2. [person] embrouiller. ◆ **muddle along** *vi* se débrouiller tant bien que mal. ◆ **muddle through** *vi* se tirer d'affaire, s'en sortir tant bien que mal. ◆ **muddle up** *vt sep* mélanger.

muddy ['mʌdɪ] ◇ *adj* boueux(euse). ◇ *vt fig* embrouiller.

mudguard ['mʌdgɑ:d] *n* garde-boue *m inv*.

mudslinging ['mʌd,slɪŋɪŋ] *n (U) fig* attaques *fpl*.

muesli ['mju:zlɪ] *n Br* muesli *m*.

muff [mʌf] ◇ *n* manchon *m*. ◇ *vt inf* louper.

muffin ['mʌfɪn] *n* muffin *m*.

muffle ['mʌfl] *vt* étouffer.

muffler ['mʌflər] *n Am* [for car] silencieux *m*.

mug [mʌg] ◇ *n* - 1. [cup] (grande) tasse *f* - 2. *inf* [fool] andouille *f*. ◇ *vt* [attack] agresser.

mugging ['mʌgɪŋ] *n* agression *f*.

muggy ['mʌgɪ] *adj* lourd(e), moite.

mule [mju:l] *n* mule *f*.

mull [mʌl] ◆ **mull over** *vt sep* ruminer, réfléchir à.

mulled [mʌld] *adj* : ~ wine vin *m* chaud.

multicoloured *Br*, **multicolored** *Am* ['mʌltɪ,kʌləd] *adj* multicolore.

multigym ['mʌltɪdʒɪm] *n* appareil *m* de musculation.

multilateral [,mʌltɪ'lætərəl] *adj* multilatéral(e).

multinational [,mʌltɪ'næʃənl] *n* multinationale *f*.

multiple ['mʌltɪpl] ◇ *adj* multiple. ◇ *n* multiple *m*.

multiple sclerosis [-sklɪ'rəʊsɪs] *n* sclérose *f* en plaques.

multiplex cinema ['mʌltɪpleks-] *n* complexe *m* multisalles.

multiplication [,mʌltɪplɪ'keɪʃn] *n* multiplication *f*.

multiply ['mʌltɪplaɪ] ◇ *vt* multiplier. ◇ *vi* se multiplier.

multistorey *Br*, **multistory** *Am* [,mʌltɪ'stɔ:rɪ] ◇ *adj* à étages. ◇ *n* [car park] parking *m* à étages.

multitude ['mʌltɪtju:d] *n* multitude *f*.

multivitamin [*Br* 'mʌltɪvɪtəmɪn, *Am* 'mʌltɪvaɪtəmɪn] *n* multivitamine *f*.

mum [mʌm] *Br inf* ◇ *n* maman *f*. ◇ *adj* : to keep ~ ne pas piper mot.

mumble ['mʌmbl] *vt & vi* marmotter.

mummy ['mʌmɪ] *n* - 1. *Br inf* [mother] maman *f* - 2. [preserved body] momie *f*.

mumps [mʌmps] *n (U)* oreillons *mpl*.

munch [mʌntʃ] *vt & vi* croquer.

mundane [mʌn'deɪn] *adj* banal(e), ordinaire.

municipal [mju:'nɪsɪpl] *adj* municipal(e).

municipality [mju:,nɪsɪ'pælətɪ] *n* municipalité *f*.

mural ['mjʊərəl] *n* peinture *f* murale.

murder ['mɜːdər] ◇ *n* meurtre *m*. ◇ *vt* assassiner.

murderer ['mɜːdərər] *n* meurtrier *m*, assassin *m*.

murderous ['mɜːdərəs] *adj* meurtrier(ère).

murky ['mɜːkɪ] *adj* - 1. [place] sombre - 2. [water, past] trouble.

murmur ['mɜːmər] ◇ *n* murmure *m* ; MED souffle *m* au cœur. ◇ *vt & vi* murmurer.

muscle ['mʌsl] *n* muscle *m* ; *fig* [power] poids *m*, impact *m*. ◆ **muscle in** *vi* intervenir, s'immiscer.

muscular ['mʌskjʊlər] *adj* - 1. [spasm, pain] musculaire - 2. [person] musclé(e).

muse [mju:z] ◇ *n* muse *f*. ◇ *vi* méditer, réfléchir.

museum [mju:'zi:əm] *n* musée *m*.

mushroom ['mʌʃrʊm] ◇ *n* champignon *m*. ◇ *vi* [organization, party] se développer, grandir ; [houses] proliférer.

music ['mju:zɪk] *n* musique *f*.

musical ['mju:zɪkl] ◇ *adj* - 1. [event, voice] musical(e) - 2. [child] doué(e) pour la musique, musicien(enne). ◇ *n* comédie *f* musicale.

musical instrument *n* instrument *m* de musique.

music centre *n Br* chaîne *f* compacte.

music hall *n Br* music-hall *m*.

musician [mju:'zɪʃn] *n* musicien *m*, -enne *f*.

Muslim ['mʊzlɪm] ◇ *adj* musulman(e). ◇ *n* Musulman *m*, -e *f*.

muslin ['mʌzlɪn] *n* mousseline *f*.

mussel ['mʌsl] *n* moule *f*.

must [mʌst] ◇ *modal vb* - **1.** [expressing obligation] devoir ; **I ~ go** il faut que je m'en aille, je dois partir ; **you ~ come and visit** il faut absolument que tu viennes nous voir - **2.** [expressing likelihood] : **they ~ have known** ils devaient le savoir. ◇ *n inf* : **a ~** un must, un impératif.

mustache *Am* = **moustache**.

mustard ['mʌstəd] *n* moutarde *f*.

muster ['mʌstər] ◇ *vt* rassembler. ◇ *vi* se réunir, se rassembler.

mustn't [mʌsnt] = **must not**.

must've ['mʌstəv] = **must have**.

musty ['mʌstɪ] *adj* [smell] de moisi ; [room] qui sent le renfermé OR le moisi.

mute [mju:t] ◇ *adj* muet(ette). ◇ *n* muet *m*, -ette *f*.

muted ['mju:tɪd] *adj* - **1.** [colour] sourd(e) - **2.** [reaction] peu marqué(e) ; [protest] voilé(e).

mutilate ['mju:tɪleɪt] *vt* mutiler.

mutiny ['mju:tɪnɪ] ◇ *n* mutinerie *f*. ◇ *vi* se mutiner.

mutter ['mʌtər] ◇ *vt* [threat, curse] marmonner. ◇ *vi* marmotter, marmonner.

mutton ['mʌtn] *n* mouton *m*.

mutual ['mju:tʃʊəl] *adj* - **1.** [feeling, help] réciproque, mutuel(elle) - **2.** [friend, interest] commun(e).

mutually ['mju:tʃʊəlɪ] *adv* mutuellement, réciproquement.

muzzle ['mʌzl] ◇ *n* - **1.** [of dog - mouth] museau *m* ; [- guard] muselière *f* - **2.** [of gun] gueule *f*. ◇ *vt lit & fig* museler.

MW (*abbr of* **medium wave**) PO.

my [maɪ] *poss adj* - **1.** [referring to oneself] mon (ma), mes (*pl*) ; **~ dog** mon chien ; **~ house** ma maison, **~ children** mes enfants ; **~ name is Joe/Sarah** je m'appelle Joe/Sarah ; **it wasn't MY fault** ce n'était pas de ma faute à moi - **2.** [in titles] : **yes, ~ Lord** oui, monsieur le comte/duc *etc*.

myriad ['mɪrɪəd] *literary* ◇ *adj* innombrable. ◇ *n* myriade *f*.

myself [maɪ'self] *pron* - **1.** (*reflexive*) me ; (*after prep*) moi - **2.** (*for emphasis*) moi-même ; **I did it ~** je l'ai fait tout seul.

mysterious [mɪ'stɪərɪəs] *adj* mystérieux(euse).

mystery ['mɪstərɪ] *n* mystère *m*.

mystical ['mɪstɪkl] *adj* mystique.

mystified ['mɪstɪfaɪd] *adj* perplexe.

mystifying ['mɪstɪfaɪɪŋ] *adj* inexplicable, déconcertant(e).

mystique [mɪ'sti:k] *n* mystique *f*.

myth [mɪθ] *n* mythe *m*.

mythical ['mɪθɪkl] *adj* mythique.

mythology [mɪ'θɒlədʒɪ] *n* mythologie *f*.

n (*pl* **n's** OR **ns**), **N** (*pl* **N's** OR **Ns**) [en] *n* [letter] n *m inv*, N *m inv*. ◆ **N** (*abbr of* **north**) N.

n/a, N/A (*abbr of* **not applicable**) s.o.

nab [næb] *vt inf* - **1.** [arrest] pincer - **2.** [get quickly] attraper, accaparer.

nag [næg] ◇ *vt* harceler. ◇ *n inf* [horse] canasson *m*.

nagging ['nægɪŋ] *adj* - **1.** [doubt] persistant(e), tenace - **2.** [husband, wife] enquiquineur(euse).

nail [neɪl] ◇ *n* - **1.** [for fastening] clou *m* - **2.** [of finger, toe] ongle *m*. ◇ *vt* clouer. ◆ **nail down** *vt sep* - **1.** [lid] clouer - **2.** *fig* [person] : **to ~ sb down to sthg** faire préciser qqch à qqn.

nailbrush ['neɪlbrʌʃ] *n* brosse *f* à ongles.

nail file *n* lime *f* à ongles.

nail polish *n* vernis *m* à ongles.

nail scissors *npl* ciseaux *mpl* à ongles.

nail varnish *n* vernis *m* à ongles.

nail varnish remover [-rɪ'mu:vər] *n* dissolvant *m*.

naive, naïve [naɪ'i:v] *adj* naïf(ïve).

naked ['neɪkɪd] *adj* - **1.** [body, flame] nu(r), **with the ~ eye** à l'œil nu - **2.** [emotions] manifeste, évident(e) ; [aggression] non déguisé(e).

name [neɪm] ◇ *n* - **1.** [identification] nom *m* ; **what's your ~?** comment vous appelez-vous? ; **to know sb by ~** connaître qqn de nom ; **in my/his ~** à mon/son nom ; **in the ~ of peace** au nom de la paix ; **to call sb ~s** traiter qqn de tous les noms, injurier qqn - **2.** [reputation] réputation *f* - **3.** [famous person] grand nom *m*, célébrité *f*. ◇ *vt* - **1.** [gen] nommer ; **to ~ sb/sthg after** *Br*, **to ~ sb/sthg for** *Am* donner à qqn/à qqch le nom de - **2.** [date, price] fixer.

nameless ['neɪmlɪs] *adj* inconnu(e), sans nom ; [author] anonyme.

namely ['neɪmlɪ] *adv* à savoir, c'est-à-dire.

namesake ['neɪmseɪk] *n* homonyme *m*.

nanny ['nænɪ] *n Br* nurse *f*, bonne *f* d'enfants.

nap [næp] ⟨> *n* : **to have** OR **take a ~** faire un petit somme. ⟨> *vi* faire un petit somme ; **to be caught napping** *inf fig* être pris au dépourvu.

nape [neɪp] *n* nuque *f*.

napkin ['næpkɪn] *n* serviette *f*.

nappy ['næpɪ] *n Br* couche *f*.

nappy liner *n Br* change *m* (jetable).

narcissi [nɑː'sɪsaɪ] *pl* ⟼ **narcissus**.

narcissus [nɑː'sɪsəs] (*pl* **-cissuses** OR **-cissi** [-sɪsaɪ]) *n* narcisse *m*.

narcotic [nɑː'kɒtɪk] *n* stupéfiant *m*.

narrative ['nærətɪv] ⟨> *adj* narratif(ive). ⟨> *n* - **1.** [story] récit *m*, narration *f* - **2.** [skill] art *m* de la narration.

narrator [*Br* nə'reɪtəʳ, *Am* 'næreɪtər] *n* narrateur *m*, -trice *f*.

narrow ['nærəʊ] ⟨> *adj* - **1.** [gen] étroit(e) ; **to have a ~ escape** l'échapper belle - **2.** [victory, majority] de justesse. ⟨> *vt* - **1.** [reduce] réduire, limiter - **2.** [eyes] fermer à demi, plisser. ⟨> *vi lit & fig* se rétrécir. ◆ **narrow down** *vt sep* réduire, limiter.

narrowly ['nærəʊlɪ] *adv* - **1.** [win, lose] de justesse - **2.** [miss] de peu.

narrow-minded ['-'maɪndɪd] *adj* [person] à l'esprit étroit, borné(e) ; [attitude] étroit(e), borné(e).

nasal ['neɪzl] *adj* nasal(e).

NASDAQ ['næzdæk] (*abbr of* **National Association of Securities Dealers Automated Quotation**) *n* [in US] NASDAQ *m*.

nasty ['nɑːstɪ] *adj* - **1.** [unpleasant - smell, feeling] mauvais(e) ; [- weather] vilain(e), mauvais(e) - **2.** [unkind] méchant(e) - **3.** [problem] difficile, délicat(e) - **4.** [injury] vilain(e) ; [accident] grave ; [fall] mauvais(e).

nation ['neɪʃn] *n* nation *f*.

national ['næʃənl] ⟨> *adj* national(e) ; [campaign, strike] à l'échelon national ; [custom] du pays, de la nation. ⟨> *n* ressortissant *m*, -e *f*.

national anthem *n* hymne *m* national.

national dress *n* costume *m* national.

National Health Service *n* : **the ~** *le service national de santé britannique*.

National Insurance *Br n* (U) - **1.** [system] *système de sécurité sociale (maladie, retraite) et d'assurance chômage* - **2.** [payment] ≃ contributions *fpl* à la Sécurité sociale.

National Lottery *n Br* : **the ~** la loterie nationale.

nationalism ['næʃnəlɪzm] *n* nationalisme *m*.

nationalist ['næʃnəlɪst] ⟨> *adj* nationaliste. ⟨> *n* nationaliste *mf*.

nationality [,næʃə'nælətɪ] *n* nationalité *f*.

nationalize, -ise ['næʃnəlaɪz] *vt* nationaliser.

national park *n* parc *m* national.

national service *n Br* MIL service *m* national OR militaire.

National Trust *n Br* : **the ~** *organisme non gouvernemental assurant la conservation de certains sites et monuments historiques.*

nationwide ['neɪʃənwaɪd] ⟨> *adj* dans tout le pays ; [campaign, strike] à l'échelon national. ⟨> *adv* à travers tout le pays.

native ['neɪtɪv] ⟨> *adj* - **1.** [country, area] natal(e) - **2.** [language] maternel(elle) ; **an English ~ speaker** une personne de langue maternelle anglaise - **3.** [plant, animal] indigène ; **~ to** originaire de. ⟨> *n* autochtone *mf* ; [of colony] indigène *mf*.

Native American *n* Indien *m*, -enne *f* d'Amérique, Amérindien *m*, -enne *f*.

Nativity [nə'tɪvətɪ] *n* : **the ~** la Nativité.

NATO ['neɪtəʊ] (*abbr of* **North Atlantic Treaty Organization**) *n* OTAN *f*.

natural ['nætʃrəl] *adj* - **1.** [gen] naturel (elle) - **2.** [instinct, talent] inné(e) - **3.** [footballer, musician] né(e).

natural gas *n* gaz *m* naturel.

natural history *n* histoire *f* naturelle.

naturalize, -ise ['nætʃrəlaɪz] *vt* naturaliser ; **to be ~d** se faire naturaliser.

naturally ['nætʃrəlɪ] *adv* - **1.** [gen] naturellement - **2.** [unaffectedly] sans affectation, avec naturel.

natural wastage *n* (U) départs *mpl* volontaires.

nature ['neɪtʃəʳ] *n* nature *f* ; **by ~** [basically] par essence ; [by disposition] de nature, naturellement.

nature reserve *n* réserve *f* naturelle.

naughty ['nɔːtɪ] *adj* - **1.** [badly behaved] vilain(e), méchant(e) - **2.** [rude] grivois(e).

nausea ['nɔːzjə] *n* nausée *f*.

nauseam ['nɔːzɪæm] ⟼ **ad nauseam**.

nauseating ['nɔːsɪeɪtɪŋ] *adj lit & fig* écœurant(e).

nautical ['nɔːtɪkl] *adj* nautique.

naval ['neɪvl] *adj* naval(e).

nave [neɪv] *n* nef *f*.

navel ['neɪvl] *n* nombril *m*.

navigate ['nævɪgeɪt] ⬦ *vt* - **1.** [plane] piloter ; [ship] gouverner - **2.** [seas, river] naviguer sur. ⬦ *vi* AERON & NAUT naviguer ; AUT lire la carte.

navigation [ˌnævɪ'geɪʃn] *n* navigation *f*.

navigator ['nævɪgeɪtə'] *n* navigateur *m*.

navvy ['nævɪ] *n* Br inf terrassier *m*.

navy ['neɪvɪ] ⬦ *n* marine *f*. ⬦ *adj* [in colour] bleu marine *(inv)*.

navy blue ⬦ *adj* bleu marine *(inv)*. ⬦ *n* bleu *m* marine.

Nazareth ['næzərɪθ] *n* Nazareth.

Nazi ['nɑːtsɪ] *(pl* -s*)* ⬦ *adj* nazi(e). ⬦ *n* Nazi *m*, -e *f*.

NB *(abbr of* nota bene*)* NB.

near [nɪə'] ⬦ *adj* proche ; **a ~ disaster** une catastrophe évitée de justesse OR de peu ; **in the ~ future** dans un proche avenir, dans un avenir prochain ; **it was a ~ thing** il a été moins cinq. ⬦ *adv* - **1.** [close] près - **2.** [almost] : **~ impossible** presque impossible ; **nowhere ~ ready/enough** loin d'être prêt/ assez. ⬦ *prep* : **~ (to)** [in space] près de ; [in time] près de, vers ; **~ to tears** au bord des larmes ; **~ (to) death** sur le point de mourir ; **~ (to) the truth** proche de la vérité. ⬦ *vt* approcher de. ⬦ *vi* approcher.

nearby [nɪə'baɪ] ⬦ *adj* proche. ⬦ *adv* tout près, à proximité.

nearly ['nɪəlɪ] *adv* presque ; **I ~ fell** j'ai failli tomber ; **not ~ enough/as good** loin d'être suffisant/aussi bon.

near miss *n* - **1.** SPORT coup *m* qui a raté de peu - **2.** [between planes, vehicles] quasi-collision *f*.

nearside ['nɪəsaɪd] *n* Br [right-hand drive] côté *m* droit ; [left-hand drive] côté gauche.

nearsighted [ˌnɪə'saɪtɪd] *adj* Am myope.

neat [niːt] *adj* - **1.** [room, house] bien tenu(e), en ordre ; [work] soigné(e) ; [handwriting] net (nette) ; [appearance] soigné(e), net (nette) - **2.** [solution, manoeuvre] habile, ingénieux(euse) - **3.** [alcohol] pur(e), sans eau - **4.** Am inf [very good] chouette, super *(inv)*.

neatly ['niːtlɪ] *adv* - **1.** [arrange] avec ordre, [write] soigneusement ; [dress] avec soin - **2.** [skilfully] habilement, adroitement.

nebulous ['nebjʊləs] *adj* nébuleux(euse).

necessarily [Br 'nesəsrəlɪ, ˌnesə'serɪlɪ] *adv* forcément, nécessairement.

necessary ['nesəsrɪ] *adj* - **1.** [required] nécessaire, indispensable ; **to make the ~ ar-** rangements faire le nécessaire - **2.** [inevitable] inévitable, inéluctable.

necessity [nɪ'sesətɪ] *n* nécessité *f*; **of ~** inévitablement, fatalement.

neck [nek] ⬦ *n* - **1.** ANAT cou *m* - **2.** [of shirt, dress] encolure *f* - **3.** [of bottle] col *m*, goulot *m*. ⬦ *vi inf* se bécoter.

necklace ['neklɪs] *n* collier *m*.

neckline ['neklaɪn] *n* encolure *f*.

necktie ['nektaɪ] *n* Am cravate *f*.

nectarine ['nektərɪn] *n* brugnon *m*, nectarine *f*.

need [niːd] ⬦ *n* besoin *m* ; **there's no ~ to get up** ce n'est pas la peine de te lever ; **there's no ~ for such language** tu n'as pas besoin d'être grossier ; **~ for sthg/to do sthg** besoin de qqch/de faire qqch ; **to be in** OR **have ~ of sthg** avoir besoin de qqch ; **if ~ be** si besoin est, si nécessaire ; **in ~** dans le besoin. ⬦ *vt* - **1.** [require] : **to ~ sthg/to do sthg** avoir besoin de qqch/de faire qqch ; **I ~ to go to the doctor** il faut que j'aille chez le médecin - **2.** [be obliged] : **to ~ to do sthg** être obligé(e) de faire qqch. ⬦ *modal vb* : **~ we go?** faut-il qu'on y aille ? ; **it ~ not happen** cela ne doit pas forcément se produire.

needle ['niːdl] ⬦ *n* - **1.** [gen] aiguille *f* - **2.** [stylus] saphir *m*. ⬦ *vt inf* [annoy] asticoter, lancer des piques à.

needless ['niːdlɪs] *adj* [risk, waste] inutile ; [remark] déplacé(e) ; **~ to say ...** bien entendu ...

needlework ['niːdlwɜːk] *n* - **1.** [embroidery] travail *m* d'aiguille - **2.** *(U)* [activity] couture *f*.

needn't ['niːdnt] = need not.

needy ['niːdɪ] *adj* nécessiteux(euse), indigent(e).

negative ['negətɪv] ⬦ *adj* négatif(ive). ⬦ *n* - **1.** PHOT négatif *m* - **2.** LING négation *f* ; **to answer in the ~** répondre négativement OR par la négative.

neglect [nɪ'glekt] ⬦ *n* [of garden] mauvais entretien *m* ; [of children] manque *m* de soins ; [of duty] manquement *m*. ⬦ *vt* négliger ; [garden] laisser à l'abandon ; **to ~ to do sthg** négliger OR omettre de faire qqch.

neglectful [nɪ'glektfʊl] *adj* négligent(e).

negligee ['neglɪʒeɪ] *n* déshabillé *m*, négligé *m*.

negligence ['neglɪdʒəns] *n* négligence *f*.

negligible ['neglɪdʒəbl] *adj* négligeable.

negotiate [nɪ'gəʊʃɪeɪt] ⬦ *vt* - **1.** COMM & POL négocier - **2.** [obstacle] franchir ; [bend] prendre, négocier. ⬦ *vi* négocier ; **to ~ with sb (for sthg)** engager des négociations avec qqn (pour obtenir qqch).

negotiation [nɪˌgəʊʃɪ'eɪʃn] *n* négociation *f*.

Negress ['niːgrɪs] *n* négresse *f* (attention : le terme 'Negress' est considéré raciste).

Negro ['niːgrəʊ] (*pl* **-es**) ⋄ *adj* noir(e). ⋄ *n* Noir *m* (attention : le terme 'Negro' est considéré raciste).

neigh [neɪ] *vi* [horse] hennir.

neighbour *Br*, **neighbor** *Am* ['neɪbə'] *n* voisin *m*, -e *f*.

neighbourhood *Br*, **neighborhood** *Am* ['neɪbəhʊd] *n* - **1.** [of town] voisinage *m*, quartier *m* - **2.** [approximate figure] : **in the ~ of £300** environ 300 livres, dans les 300 livres.

neighbouring *Br*, **neighboring** *Am* ['neɪbərɪŋ] *adj* avoisinant(e).

neighbourly *Br*, **neighborly** *Am* ['neɪbəlɪ] *adj* bon voisin (bonne voisine).

neither ['naɪðə', 'niːðə'] ⋄ *adv* : **~ good nor bad** ni bon ni mauvais ; **that's ~ here nor there** cela n'a rien à voir. ⋄ *pron & adj* ni l'un ni l'autre (ni l'une ni l'autre). ⋄ *conj* : **~ do I** moi non plus.

neon ['niːɒn] *n* néon *m*.

neon light *n* néon *m*, lumière *f* au néon.

nephew ['nefjuː] *n* neveu *m*.

Neptune ['neptjuːn] *n* [planet] Neptune *f*.

nerve [nɜːv] *n* - **1.** ANAT nerf *m* - **2.** [courage] courage *m*, sang-froid *m inv* ; **to lose one's ~** se dégonfler, flancher - **3.** [cheek] culot *m*, toupet *m*. ◆ **nerves** *npl* nerfs *mpl* ; **to get on sb's ~s** taper sur les nerfs OR le système de qqn.

nerve-racking [-ˌrækɪŋ] *adj* angoissant(e), éprouvant(e).

nervous ['nɜːvəs] *adj* - **1.** [gen] nerveux(euse) - **2.** [apprehensive - smile, person etc] inquiet(ète) ; [- performer] qui a le trac ; **to be ~ about sthg** appréhender qqch.

nervous breakdown *n* dépression *f* nerveuse.

nest [nest] ⋄ *n* nid *m* ; **~ of tables** table *f* gigogne. ⋄ *vi* [bird] faire son nid, nicher.

nest egg *n* pécule *m*, bas *m* de laine.

nestle ['nesl] *vi* se blottir.

net¹ [net] ⋄ *adj* net (nette) ; **~ result** résultat final. ⋄ *n* - **1.** [gen] filet *m* - **2.** [fabric] voile *m*, tulle *m*. ⋄ *vt* - **1.** [fish] prendre au filet - **2.** [money - subj : person] toucher net, gagner net ; [- subj : deal] rapporter net.

net², **Net** [net] *n* : **the ~** le Net ; **to surf the ~** surfer sur le Net.

netball ['netbɔːl] *n* netball *m*.

net curtains *npl* voilage *m*.

Netherlands ['neðələndz] *npl* : **the ~** les Pays-Bas *mpl*.

netiquette ['netiket] *n* nétiquette *f*.

net profit *n* bénéfice *m* net.

net revenue *n Am* chiffre *m* d'affaires.

net surfer *n* internaute *mf*.

nett [net] *adj* = **net¹**.

netting ['netɪŋ] *n* - **1.** [metal, plastic] grillage *m* - **2.** [fabric] voile *m*, tulle *m*.

nettle ['netl] *n* ortie *f*.

network ['netwɜːk] ⋄ *n* réseau *m*. ⋄ *vt* RADIO & TV diffuser.

neurosis [ˌnjʊə'rəʊsɪs] (*pl* **-ses** [-siːz]) *n* névrose *f*.

neurotic [ˌnjʊə'rɒtɪk] ⋄ *adj* névrosé(e). ⋄ *n* névrosé *m*, -e *f*.

neuter ['njuːtə'] ⋄ *adj* neutre. ⋄ *vt* [cat] châtrer.

neutral ['njuːtrəl] ⋄ *adj* [gen] neutre. ⋄ *n* AUT point *m* mort.

neutrality [njuː'trælətɪ] *n* neutralité *f*.

neutralize, -ise ['njuːtrəlaɪz] *vt* neutraliser.

never ['nevə'] *adv* jamais ... ne, ne ... jamais ; **~ ever** jamais, au grand jamais ; **well I ~!** ça par exemple!

never-ending *adj* interminable.

nevertheless [ˌnevəðə'les] *adv* néanmoins, pourtant.

new [*adj* njuː; *n* njuːz] *adj* - **1.** [gen] nouveau(elle) - **2.** [not used] neuf (neuve) ; **as good as ~** comme neuf. ◆ **news** *n* (*U*) - **1.** [information] nouvelle *f* ; **a piece of ~** une nouvelle ; **that's ~s to me** première nouvelle - **2.** RADIO informations *fpl* - **3.** TV journal *m* télévisé, actualités *fpl*.

New Age travel(l)er *n* voyageur *m* New Age.

newborn ['njuːbɔːn] *adj* nouveau-né(e).

newcomer ['njuːˌkʌmə'] *n* : **~ (to sthg)** nouveau-venu *m*, nouvelle-venue *f* (dans qqch).

newfangled [ˌnjuː'fæŋgld] *adj inf pej* ultramoderne, trop moderne.

new-found *adj* récent(e), de fraîche date.

newly ['njuːlɪ] *adv* récemment, fraîchement.

newlyweds ['njuːlɪwedz] *npl* nouveaux OR jeunes mariés *mpl*.

new moon *n* nouvelle lune *f*.

news agency *n* agence *f* de presse.

newsagent *Br* ['njuːzeɪdʒənt], **newsdealer** *Am* ['njuːzdiːlər] *n* marchand *m* de journaux.

newscaster ['njuːzkaːstər] *n* présentateur *m*, -trice *f*.

newsdealer *Am* = newsagent.

newsflash ['njuːzflæʃ] *n* flash *m* d'information.

newsletter ['njuːzˌletər] *n* bulletin *m*.

newspaper ['njuːzˌpeɪpər] *n* journal *m*.

newsprint ['njuːzprɪnt] *n* papier *m* journal.

newsreader ['njuːzˌriːdər] *n Br* présentateur *m*, -trice *f*.

newsreel ['njuːzriːl] *n* actualités *fpl* filmées.

newsstand ['njuːzstænd] *n* kiosque *m* à journaux.

newt [njuːt] *n* triton *m*.

new town *n Br* ville *f* nouvelle.

New Year *n* nouvel an *m*, nouvelle année *f*; **Happy ~!** bonne année!

New Year's Day *n* jour *m* de l'an, premier *m* de l'an.

New Year's Eve *n* la Saint-Sylvestre.

New York [-'jɔːk] *n* **- 1.** [city] : **~ (City)** New York **- 2.** [state] : **~ (State)** l'État *m* de New York.

New Zealand [-'ziːlənd] *n* Nouvelle-Zélande *f*.

New Zealander [-'ziːləndər] *n* Néo-Zélandais *m*, -e *f*.

next [nekst] <> *adj* prochain(e) ; [room] d'à côté ; [page] suivant(e) ; **~ Tuesday** mardi prochain ; **~ time** la prochaine fois ; **~ week** la semaine prochaine ; **the ~ week** la semaine suivante OR d'après ; **~ year** l'année prochaine ; **~, please!** au suivant! ; **the day after ~** le surlendemain ; **the week after ~** dans deux semaines. <> *adv* **- 1.** [afterwards] ensuite, après **- 2.** [again] la prochaine fois **- 3.** (*with superlatives*) : **he's the ~ biggest after Dan** c'est le plus grand après OR à part Dan. <> *prep Am* à côté de. ◆ **next to** *prep* à côté de ; **it cost ~ to nothing** cela a coûté une bagatelle OR trois fois rien ; **I know ~ to nothing** je ne sais presque OR pratiquement rien.

next door *adv* à côté. ◆ **next-door** *adj* : **next-door neighbour** voisin *m*, -e *f* d'à côté.

next of kin *n* plus proche parent *m*.

NF *n* (*abbr of* National Front) ≃ FN *m*.

NHS (*abbr of* National Health Service) *n* service national de santé en Grande-Bretagne, ≃ sécurité sociale *f*.

NI *n abbr of* National Insurance.

nib [nɪb] *n* plume *f*.

nibble ['nɪbl] *vt* grignoter, mordiller.

Nicaragua [ˌnɪkə'rægjʊə] *n* Nicaragua *m*.

nice [naɪs] *adj* **- 1.** [holiday, food] bon (bonne) ; [day, picture] beau (belle) ; [dress] joli(e) **- 2.** [person] gentil(ille), sympathique ; **to be ~ to sb** être gentil OR aimable avec qqn.

nice-looking [-'lʊkɪŋ] *adj* joli(e), beau (belle).

nicely ['naɪslɪ] *adv* **- 1.** [made, manage etc] bien ; [dressed] joliment ; **that will do ~** cela fera très bien l'affaire **- 2.** [politely - ask] poliment, gentiment ; [- behave] bien.

niche [niːʃ] *n* [in wall] niche *f* ; *fig* bonne situation *f*, voie *f*.

nick [nɪk] <> *n* **- 1.** [cut] entaille *f*, coupure *f* **- 2.** *Br* [condition] : **in good/bad ~** en bon/mauvais état **- 3.** *phr* : **in the ~ of time** juste à temps. <> *vt* **- 1.** [cut] couper, entailler **- 2.** *Br inf* [steal] piquer, faucher **- 3.** *Br inf* [arrest] pincer, choper.

nickel ['nɪkl] *n* **- 1.** [metal] nickel *m* **- 2.** *Am* [coin] pièce *f* de cinq cents.

nickname ['nɪkneɪm] <> *n* sobriquet *m*, surnom *m*. <> *vt* surnommer.

nicotine ['nɪkətiːn] *n* nicotine *f*.

niece [niːs] *n* nièce *f*.

Nigeria [naɪ'dʒɪərɪə] *n* Nigeria *m*.

Nigerian [naɪ'dʒɪərɪən] <> *adj* nigérian(e). <> *n* Nigérian *m*, -e *f*.

niggle ['nɪgl] *vt Br* **- 1.** [worry] tracasser **- 2.** [criticize] faire des réflexions à, critiquer.

night [naɪt] *n* **- 1.** [not day] nuit *f* ; **at ~** la nuit **- 2.** [evening] soir *m* ; **at ~** le soir **- 3.** *phr* : **to have an early ~** se coucher de bonne heure ; **to have a late ~** veiller, se coucher tard. ◆ **nights** *adv* **- 1.** *Am* [at night] la nuit **- 2.** *Br* [nightshift] : **to work ~s** travailler OR être de nuit.

nightcap ['naɪtkæp] *n* [drink] boisson alcoolisée prise avant de se coucher.

nightclub ['naɪtklʌb] *n* boîte *f* de nuit, night-club *m*.

nightdress ['naɪtdres] *n* chemise *f* de nuit.

nightfall ['naɪtfɔːl] *n* tombée *f* de la nuit OR du jour.

nightgown ['naɪtgaʊn] *n* chemise *f* de nuit.

nightie ['naɪtɪ] *n inf* chemise *f* de nuit.

nightingale ['naɪtɪŋgeɪl] *n* rossignol *m*.

nightlife ['naɪtlaɪf] *n* vie *f* nocturne, activités *fpl* nocturnes.

nightly ['naɪtlɪ] ◇ *adj* (de) toutes les nuits OR tous les soirs. ◇ *adv* toutes les nuits, tous les soirs.

nightmare ['naɪtmeə'] *n lit & fig* cauchemar *m*.

night porter *n* veilleur *m* de nuit.

night school *n (U)* cours *mpl* du soir.

night shift *n* [period] poste *m* de nuit.

nightshirt ['naɪtʃɜːt] *n* chemise *f* de nuit d'homme.

nighttime ['naɪttaɪm] *n* nuit *f*.

nil [nɪl] *n* néant *m* ; *Br* SPORT zéro *m*.

Nile [naɪl] *n* : **the ~** le Nil.

nimble ['nɪmbl] *adj* agile, leste ; *fig* [mind] vif (vive).

nine [naɪn] *num* neuf ; *see also* **six**.

nineteen [,naɪn'tiːn] *num* dix-neuf ; *see also* **six**.

ninety ['naɪntɪ] *num* quatre-vingt-dix ; *see also* **sixty**.

ninth [naɪnθ] *num* neuvième ; *see also* **sixth**.

nip [nɪp] ◇ *n* - **1.** [pinch] pinçon *m* ; [bite] morsure *f* - **2.** [of drink] goutte *f*, doigt *m*. ◇ *vt* [pinch] pincer ; [bite] mordre.

nipple ['nɪpl] *n* - **1.** ANAT bout *m* de sein, mamelon *m* - **2.** [of bottle] tétine *f*.

nit [nɪt] *n* - **1.** [in hair] lente *f* - **2.** *Br inf* [idiot] idiot *m*, -e *f*, crétin *m*, -e *f*.

nitpicking ['nɪtpɪkɪŋ] *n inf* ergotage *m*, pinaillage *m*.

nitrogen ['naɪtrədʒən] *n* azote *m*.

nitty-gritty [,nɪtɪ'grɪtɪ] *n inf* : **to get down to the ~** en venir à l'essentiel OR aux choses sérieuses.

no [nəʊ] *(pl* noes [nəʊz]*)* ◇ *adv* - **1.** [gen] non ; [expressing disagreement] mais non - **2.** [not any] : **~ bigger/smaller** pas plus grand/petit ; **~ better** pas mieux. ◇ *adj* aucun(e), pas de ; **there's ~ telling what will happen** impossible de dire ce qui va se passer ; **he's ~ friend of mine** je ne le compte pas parmi mes amis. ◇ *n* non *m* ; **she won't take ~ for an answer** elle n'accepte pas de refus OR qu'on lui dise non.

No., no. *(abbr of* number*)* No, no.

nobility [nə'bɪlətɪ] *n* noblesse *f*.

noble ['nəʊbl] ◇ *adj* noble. ◇ *n* noble *m*.

nobody ['nəʊbədɪ] ◇ *pron* personne, au-

cun(e). ◇ *n pej* rien-du-tout *mf*, moins que rien *mf*.

nocturnal [nɒk'tɜːnl] *adj* nocturne.

nod [nɒd] ◇ *vt* : **to ~ one's head** incliner la tête, faire un signe de tête. ◇ *vi* - **1.** [in agreement] faire un signe de tête affirmatif, faire signe que oui - **2.** [to indicate sthg] faire un signe de tête - **3.** [as greeting] : **to ~ to sb** saluer qqn d'un signe de tête. ◆ **nod off** *vi* somnoler, s'assoupir.

noise [nɔɪz] *n* bruit *m*.

noisy ['nɔɪzɪ] *adj* bruyant(e).

no-man's-land *n* no man's land *m*.

nominal ['nɒmɪnl] *adj* - **1.** [in name only] de nom seulement, nominal(e) - **2.** [very small] nominal(e), insignifiant(e).

nominate ['nɒmɪneɪt] *vt* - **1.** [propose] : **to ~ sb (for/as sthg)** proposer qqn (pour/comme qqch) - **2.** [appoint] : **to ~ sb (as sthg)** nommer qqn (qqch) ; **to ~ sb (to sthg)** nominer qqn (à qqch).

nominee [,nɒmɪ'niː] *n* personne *f* nommée OR désignée.

non- [nɒn] *prefix* non-.

nonalcoholic [,nɒnælkə'hɒlɪk] *adj* non-alcoolisé(e).

nonaligned [,nɒnə'laɪnd] *adj* non-aligné(e).

nonchalant [*Br* 'nɒnʃələnt, *Am* ,nɒnʃə'lɑːnt] *adj* nonchalant(e).

noncommittal [,nɒnkə'mɪtl] *adj* évasif(ive).

nonconformist [,nɒnkən'fɔːmɪst] ◇ *adj* non-conformiste. ◇ *n* non-conformiste *mf*.

nondescript [*Br* 'nɒndɪskrɪpt, *Am* ,nɒndɪ'skrɪpt] *adj* quelconque, terne.

none [nʌn] ◇ *pron* - **1.** [gen] aucun(e) ; **there was ~ left** il n'y en avait plus, il n'en restait plus ; **I'll have ~ of your nonsense** je ne tolérerai pas de bêtises de ta part - **2.** [nobody] personne, nul (nulle). ◇ *adv* : **~ the worse/wiser** pas plus mal/avancé ; **~ the better** pas mieux. ◆ **none too** *adv* pas tellement OR trop.

nonentity [nɒ'nentətɪ] *n* nullité *f*, zéro *m*.

nonetheless [,nʌnðə'les] *adv* néanmoins, pourtant.

non-event *n* événement *m* raté OR décevant.

nonexistent [,nɒnɪg'zɪstənt] *adj* inexistant(e).

nonfiction [,nɒn'fɪkʃn] *n (U)* ouvrages *mpl* généraux.

no-nonsense *adj* direct(e), sérieux(euse).

nonpayment [ˌnɒn'peɪmənt] *n* non-paiement *m*.

nonplussed, nonplused *Am* [ˌnɒn'plʌst] *adj* déconcerté(e), perplexe.

nonreturnable [ˌnɒnrɪ'tɜːnəbl] *adj* [bottle] non consigné(e).

nonsense ['nɒnsəns] ◇ *n (U)* - **1.** [meaningless words] charabia *m* - **2.** [foolish idea] : **it was ~ to suggest** ... il était absurde de suggérer ... - **3.** [foolish behaviour] bêtises *fpl*, idioties *fpl* ; **to make (a) ~ of sthg** gâcher OR saboter qqch. ◇ *excl* quelles bêtises OR foutaises!

nonsensical [nɒn'sensɪkl] *adj* absurde, qui n'a pas de sens.

nonsmoker [ˌnɒn'sməʊkəʳ] *n* non-fumeur *m*, -euse *f*, personne *f* qui ne fume pas.

nonstick [ˌnɒn'stɪk] *adj* qui n'attache pas, téflonisé(e).

nonstop [ˌnɒn'stɒp] ◇ *adj* [flight] direct(e), sans escale ; [activity] continu(e) ; [rain] continuel(elle). ◇ *adv* [talk, work] sans arrêt ; [rain] sans discontinuer.

noodles ['nuːdlz] *npl* nouilles *fpl*.

nook [nʊk] *n* [of room] coin *m*, recoin *m* ; **every ~ and cranny** tous les coins, les coins et les recoins.

noon [nuːn] *n* midi *m*.

no one *pron* = **nobody**.

noose [nuːs] *n* nœud *m* coulant.

no-place *Am* = **nowhere**.

nor [nɔːʳ] *conj* : **~ do I** moi non plus ⊳ **neither**.

norm [nɔːm] *n* norme *f*.

normal ['nɔːml] *adj* normal(e).

normality [nɔː'mælɪtɪ], **normalcy** *Am* ['nɔːmlsɪ] *n* normalité *f*.

normally ['nɔːməlɪ] *adv* normalement.

Normandy ['nɔːməndɪ] *n* Normandie *f*.

north [nɔːθ] ◇ *n* - **1.** [direction] nord *m* - **2.** [region] : **the ~** le nord. ◇ *adj* nord *(inv)* ; [wind] du nord. ◇ *adv* au nord, vers le nord ; **~ of** au nord de.

North Africa *n* Afrique *f* du Nord.

North America *n* Amérique *f* du Nord.

North American ◇ *adj* nord-américain(e). ◇ *n* Nord-Américain *m*, -e *f*.

northeast [ˌnɔːθ'iːst] ◇ *n* - **1.** [direction] nord-est *m* - **2.** [region] : **the ~** le nord-est. ◇ *adj* nord-est *(inv)* ; [wind] du nord-est. ◇ *adv* au nord-est, vers le nord-est ; **~ of** au nord-est de.

northerly ['nɔːðəlɪ] *adj* du nord ; **in a ~ direction** vers le nord, en direction du nord.

northern ['nɔːðən] *adj* du nord, nord *(inv)*.

Northern Ireland *n* Irlande *f* du Nord.

northernmost ['nɔːðənməʊst] *adj* le plus au nord (la plus au nord), à l'extrême nord.

North Korea *n* Corée *f* du Nord.

North Pole *n* : **the ~** le pôle Nord.

North Sea *n* : **the ~** la mer du Nord.

northward ['nɔːθwəd] ◇ *adj* au nord. ◇ *adv* = **northwards**.

northwards ['nɔːθwədz] *adv* au nord, vers le nord.

northwest [ˌnɔːθ'west] ◇ *n* - **1.** [direction] nord-ouest *m* - **2.** [region] : **the ~** le nord-ouest. ◇ *adj* nord-ouest *(inv)* ; [wind] du nord-ouest. ◇ *adv* au nord-ouest, vers le nord-ouest ; **~ of** au nord-ouest de.

Norway ['nɔːweɪ] *n* Norvège *f*.

Norwegian [nɔː'wiːdʒən] ◇ *adj* norvégien(enne). ◇ *n* - **1.** [person] Norvégien *m*, -enne *f* - **2.** [language] norvégien *m*.

nose [nəʊz] *n* nez *m* ; **keep your ~ out of my business** occupe-toi OR mêle-toi de tes affaires, occupe-toi OR mêle-toi de tes oignons ; **to look down one's ~ at sb** *fig* traiter qqn de haut ; **to look down one's ~ at sthg** *fig* considérer qqch avec mépris ; **to poke** OR **stick one's ~ into sthg** mettre OR fourrer son nez dans qqch ; **to turn up one's ~ at sthg** dédaigner qqch. ◆ **nose about, nose around** *vi* fouiner, fureter.

nosebleed ['nəʊzbliːd] *n* : **to have a ~** saigner du nez.

nosedive ['nəʊzdaɪv] ◇ *n* [of plane] piqué *m*. ◇ *vi* - **1.** [plane] descendre en piqué, piquer du nez - **2.** *fig* [prices] dégringoler ; [hopes] s'écrouler.

nosey ['nəʊzɪ] = **nosy**.

nostalgia [nɒ'stældʒə] *n* : **~ (for sthg)** nostalgie *f* (de qqch).

nostril ['nɒstrəl] *n* narine *f*.

nosy ['nəʊzɪ] *adj* curieux(euse), fouinard(e).

not [nɒt] *adv* ne pas, pas ; **I think ~** je ne crois pas ; **I'm afraid ~** je crains que non ; **~ always** pas toujours ; **~ that** ... ce n'est pas que ..., non pas que ... ; **~ at all** [no] pas du tout ; [to acknowledge thanks] de rien, je vous en prie.

notable ['nəʊtəbl] *adj* notable, remarquable ; **to be ~ for sthg** être célèbre pour qqch.

notably ['nəʊtəblɪ] *adv* - **1.** [in particular] notamment, particulièrement - **2.** [noticeably] sensiblement, nettement.

notary ['nəʊtərɪ] n : ~ **(public)** notaire m.

notch [nɒtʃ] n - **1.** [cut] entaille f, encoche f - **2.** fig [on scale] cran m.

note [nəʊt] ◇ n - **1.** [gen & MUS] note f ; [short letter] mot m ; **to take ~ of sthg** prendre note de qqch - **2.** [money] billet m (de banque). ◇ vt - **1.** [notice] remarquer, constater - **2.** [mention] mentionner, signaler. ◆ **notes** npl [in book] notes fpl. ◆ **note down** vt sep noter, inscrire.

notebook ['nəʊtbʊk] n - **1.** [for notes] carnet m, calepin m - **2.** COMPUT ordinateur m portable compact.

noted ['nəʊtɪd] adj célèbre, éminent(e).

notepad ['nəʊtpæd] n bloc-notes m.

notepaper ['nəʊtpeɪpər] n papier m à lettres.

noteworthy ['nəʊt‚wɜːðɪ] adj remarquable, notable.

nothing ['nʌθɪŋ] ◇ pron rien ; **I've got ~ to do** je n'ai rien à faire ; **for ~** pour rien ; **~ if not** avant tout, surtout ; **~ but** ne ... que, rien que ; **there's ~ for it (but to do sthg)** Br il n'y a rien d'autre à faire (que de faire qqch). ◇ adv : **you're ~ like your brother** tu ne ressembles pas du tout OR en rien à ton frère ; **I'm ~ like finished** je suis loin d'avoir fini.

notice ['nəʊtɪs] ◇ n - **1.** [written announcement] affiche f, placard m - **2.** [attention] **to take ~ (of sb/sthg)** faire OR prêter attention (à qqn/qqch) ; **to take no ~ (of sb/sthg)** ne pas faire attention (à qqn/qqch) - **3.** [warning] avis m, avertissement m ; **at short ~** dans un bref délai ; **until further ~** jusqu'à nouvel ordre - **4.** [at work] : **to be given one's ~** recevoir son congé, être renvoyé(e) ; **to hand in one's ~** donner sa démission, demander son congé. ◇ vt remarquer, s'apercevoir de.

noticeable ['nəʊtɪsəbl] adj sensible, perceptible.

notice board n Br panneau m d'affichage.

notify ['nəʊtɪfaɪ] vt : **to ~ sb (of sthg)** avertir OR aviser qqn (de qqch).

notion ['nəʊʃn] n idée f, notion f. ◆ **notions** npl Am mercerie f.

notorious [nəʊ'tɔːrɪəs] adj [criminal] notoire ; [place] mal famé(e).

notwithstanding [‚nɒtwɪð'stændɪŋ] fml ◇ prep malgré, en dépit de. ◇ adv néanmoins, malgré tout.

nought [nɔːt] num Br zéro m ; **~s and crosses** morpion m.

noun [naʊn] n nom m.

nourish ['nʌrɪʃ] vt nourrir.

nourishing ['nʌrɪʃɪŋ] adj nourrissant(e).

nourishment ['nʌrɪʃmənt] n (U) nourriture f, aliments mpl.

novel ['nɒvl] ◇ adj nouveau (nouvelle), original(e). ◇ n roman m.

novelist ['nɒvəlɪst] n romancier m, -ère f.

novelty ['nɒvltɪ] n - **1.** [gen] nouveauté f - **2.** [cheap object] gadget m.

November [nə'vembər] n novembre m ; see also **September**.

novice ['nɒvɪs] n novice mf.

now [naʊ] ◇ adv - **1.** [at this time, at once] maintenant ; **any day/time ~** d'un jour/ moment à l'autre ; **~ and then** OR **again** de temps en temps, de temps à autre - **2.** [in past] à ce moment-là, alors - **3.** [to introduce statement] : **~ let's just calm down** bon, on se calme maintenant. ◇ conj : **~ (that)** maintenant que. ◇ n : **for ~** pour le présent ; **from ~ on** à partir de maintenant, désormais ; **up until ~** jusqu'à présent ; **by ~** déjà.

nowadays ['naʊədeɪz] adv actuellement, aujourd'hui.

nowhere ['nəʊweər], **no-place** Am adv nulle part ; **~ near** loin de ; **we're getting ~** on n'avance pas, on n'arrive à rien.

nozzle ['nɒzl] n ajutage m, buse f.

nuance ['njuːɒns] n nuance f.

nuclear ['njuːklɪər] adj nucléaire.

nuclear bomb n bombe f nucléaire.

nuclear disarmament n désarmement m nucléaire.

nuclear energy n énergie f nucléaire.

nuclear power n énergie f nucléaire.

nuclear reactor n réacteur m nucléaire.

nucleus ['njuːklɪəs] (pl -lei [-lɪaɪ]) n lit & fig noyau m.

nude [njuːd] ◇ adj nu(e). ◇ n nu m ; **in the ~** nu(e).

nudge [nʌdʒ] vt pousser du coude ; fig encourager, pousser.

nudist ['njuːdɪst] ◇ adj nudiste. ◇ n nudiste mf.

nugget ['nʌgɪt] n pépite f.

nuisance ['njuːsns] n ennui m, embêtement m ; **to make a ~ of o.s.** embêter le monde ; **what a ~!** quelle plaie !

nuke [njuːk] inf ◇ n bombe f nucléaire. ◇ vt atomiser.

null [nʌl] adj : **~ and void** nul et non avenu.

numb [nʌm] ◇ adj engourdi(e) ; **to be ~ with** [fear] être paralysé par ; [cold] être transi de. ◇ vt engourdir.

number ['nʌmbəʳ] ◇ n - **1.** [numeral] chiffre m - **2.** [of telephone, house, car] numéro m - **3.** [quantity] nombre m ; **a ~ of** un certain nombre de, plusieurs ; **any ~ of** un grand nombre de, bon nombre de - **4.** [song] chanson f. ◇ vt - **1.** [amount to, include] compter ; **to ~ among** compter parmi - **2.** [give number to] numéroter.

number one ◇ adj premier(ère), principal(e). ◇ n inf [oneself] soi, sa pomme.

numberplate ['nʌmbəpleɪt] n Br plaque f d'immatriculation.

Number Ten n la résidence officielle du premier ministre britannique.

numeral ['nju:mərəl] n chiffre m.

numerate ['nju:mərət] adj Br [person] qui sait compter.

numerical [nju:'merɪkl] adj numérique.

numerous ['nju:mərəs] adj nombreux(euse).

nun [nʌn] n religieuse f, sœur f.

nurse [nɜːs] ◇ n infirmière f ; **(male) ~** infirmier m. ◇ vt - **1.** [patient, cold] soigner - **2.** fig [desires, hopes] nourrir - **3.** [subj : mother] allaiter.

nursery ['nɜːsərɪ] n - **1.** [for children] garderie f - **2.** [for plants] pépinière f.

nursery rhyme n comptine f.

nursery school n (école f) maternelle f.

nursery slopes npl Br pistes fpl pour débutants.

nursing ['nɜːsɪŋ] n métier m d'infirmière.

nursing home n [for old people] maison f de retraite privée ; [for childbirth] maternité f privée.

nurture ['nɜːtʃəʳ] vt - **1.** [children] élever ; [plants] soigner - **2.** fig [hopes etc] nourrir.

nut [nʌt] n - **1.** [to eat] terme générique désignant les fruits tels que les noix, noisettes etc - **2.** [of metal] écrou m - **3.** inf [mad person] cinglé m, -e f. ◆ **nuts** ◇ adj inf : **to be ~s** être dingue. ◇ excl Am inf zut!

nutcrackers ['nʌt,krækəz] npl casse-noix m inv, casse-noisettes m inv.

nutmeg ['nʌtmeg] n noix f (de) muscade.

nutritious [nju:'trɪʃəs] adj nourrissant(e).

nutshell ['nʌtʃel] n : **in a ~** en un mot.

nuzzle ['nʌzl] ◇ vt frotter son nez contre. ◇ vi : **to ~ (up) against** se frotter contre, frotter son nez contre.

NVQ (abbr of National Vocational Qualification) n Br examen sanctionnant une formation professionnelle.

nylon ['naɪlɒn] ◇ n Nylon® m. ◇ comp en Nylon®.

o (pl **o's** OR **os**), **O** (pl **O's** OR **Os**) [əʊ] n - **1.** [letter] o m inv, O m inv - **2.** [zero] zéro m.

oak [əʊk] ◇ n chêne m. ◇ comp de OR en chêne.

OAP (abbr of old age pensioner) n Br retraité m, -e f.

oar [ɔːʳ] n rame f, aviron m.

oasis [əʊ'eɪsɪs] (pl **oases** [əʊ'eɪsiːz]) n oasis f.

oatcake ['əʊtkeɪk] n galette f d'avoine.

oath [əʊθ] n - **1.** [promise] serment m ; **on** OR **under ~** sous serment - **2.** [swearword] juron m.

oatmeal ['əʊtmiːl] n (U) flocons mpl d'avoine.

oats [əʊts] npl [grain] avoine f.

obedience [ə'biːdjəns] n obéissance f.

obedient [ə'biːdjənt] adj obéissant(e), docile.

obese [əʊ'biːs] adj fml obèse.

obey [ə'beɪ] vt obéir à. ◇ vi obéir.

obituary [ə'bɪtʃʊərɪ] n nécrologie f.

object [n 'ɒbdʒɪkt, vb əb'dʒekt] ◇ n - **1.** [gen] objet m - **2.** [aim] objectif m, but m - **3.** GRAMM complément m d'objet. ◇ vt objecter. ◇ vi protester ; **to ~ to sthg** faire objection à qqch, s'opposer à qqch ; **to ~ to doing sthg** se refuser à faire qqch.

objection [əb'dʒekʃn] n objection f ; **to have no ~ to sthg/to doing sthg** ne voir aucune objection à qqch/à faire qqch.

objectionable [əb'dʒekʃnəbl] adj [person, behaviour] désagréable ; [language] choquant(e).

objective [əb'dʒektɪv] ◇ adj objectif(ive). ◇ n objectif m.

obligation [,ɒblɪ'geɪʃn] n obligation f.

obligatory [ə'blɪgətrɪ] adj obligatoire.

oblige [ə'blaɪdʒ] vt - **1.** [force] : **to ~ sb to do sthg** forcer OR obliger qqn à faire qqch - **2.** fml [do a favour to] obliger.

obliging [ə'blaɪdʒɪŋ] adj obligeant(e).

oblique [ə'bliːk] ◇ adj oblique ; [refer-

ence, hint] indirect(e). <> *n* TYPO barre *f*
oblique.

obliterate [ə'blɪtəreɪt] *vt* [destroy] détruire, raser.

oblivion [ə'blɪvɪən] *n* oubli *m*.

oblivious [ə'blɪvɪəs] *adj* : **to be ~ to** OR **of**
être inconscient(e) de.

oblong ['ɒblɒŋ] <> *adj* rectangulaire.
<> *n* rectangle *m*.

obnoxious [əb'nɒkʃəs] *adj* [person]
odieux(euse) ; [smell] infect(e), fétide ;
[comment] désobligeant(e).

oboe ['əʊbəʊ] *n* hautbois *m*.

obscene [əb'siːn] *adj* obscène.

obscure [əb'skjʊəʳ] <> *adj* obscur(e).
<> *vt* - **1.** [gen] obscurcir - **2.** [view] mas-
quer.

observance [əb'zɜːvəns] *n* observation *f*.

observant [əb'zɜːvnt] *adj* observa-
teur(trice).

observation [ˌɒbzə'veɪʃn] *n* observation
f.

observatory [əb'zɜːvətrɪ] *n* observatoire
m.

observe [əb'zɜːv] *vt* - **1.** [gen] observer
- **2.** [remark] remarquer, faire observer.

observer [əb'zɜːvəʳ] *n* observateur *m*,
-trice *f*.

obsess [əb'ses] *vt* obséder ; **to be ~ed by**
OR **with sb/sthg** être obsédé par qqn/qqch.

obsessive [əb'sesɪv] *adj* [person] obses-
sionnel(elle) ; [need etc] qui est une obsession.

obsolescent [ˌɒbsə'lesnt] *adj* [system]
qui tombe en désuétude ; [machine] obso-
lescent(e).

obsolete ['ɒbsəliːt] *adj* obsolète.

obstacle ['ɒbstəkl] *n* obstacle *m*.

obstetrics [ɒb'stetrɪks] *n* obstétrique *f*.

obstinate ['ɒbstənət] *adj* - **1.** [stubborn]
obstiné(e) - **2.** [cough] persistant(e) ; [stain,
resistance] tenace.

obstruct [əb'strʌkt] *vt* - **1.** [block] obstruer
- **2.** [hinder] entraver, gêner.

obstruction [əb'strʌkʃn] *n* - **1.** [in road]
encombrement *m* ; [in pipe] engorgement
m - **2.** SPORT obstruction *f*.

obtain [əb'teɪn] *vt* obtenir.

obtainable [əb'teɪnəbl] *adj* que l'on peut
obtenir.

obtrusive [əb'truːsɪv] *adj* [behaviour] qui
attire l'attention ; [smell] fort(e).

obtuse [əb'tjuːs] *adj* obtus(e).

obvious ['ɒbvɪəs] *adj* évident(e).

obviously ['ɒbvɪəslɪ] *adv* - **1.** [of course]
bien sûr - **2.** [clearly] manifestement.

occasion [ə'keɪʒn] <> *n* - **1.** [gen] occasion *f* - **2.** [important event] événement *m* ;
to rise to the ~ se montrer à la hauteur de la
situation. <> *vt* [cause] provoquer, occasionner.

occasional [ə'keɪʒənl] *adj* [showers] pas-
sager(ère) ; [visit] occasionnel(elle) ; **I have
the ~ drink/cigarette** je bois un verre/je
fume une cigarette de temps à autre.

occasionally [ə'keɪʒnəlɪ] *adv* de temps
en temps, quelquefois.

occult [ɒ'kʌlt] *adj* occulte.

occupant ['ɒkjʊpənt] *n* occupant *m*, -e *f* ;
[of vehicle] passager *m*, -ère *f*.

occupation [ˌɒkjʊ'peɪʃn] *n* - **1.** [job] profession *f* - **2.** [pastime, by army] occupation
f.

occupational hazard *n* risque *m* du métier.

occupational therapy *n* thérapeutique
f occupationnelle, ergothérapie *f*.

occupier ['ɒkjʊpaɪəʳ] *n* occupant *m*, -e *f*.

occupy ['ɒkjʊpaɪ] *vt* occuper ; **to ~ o.s.**
s'occuper.

occur [ə'kɜːʳ] *vi* - **1.** [happen - gen] avoir
lieu, se produire ; [- difficulty] se présenter
- **2.** [be present] se trouver, être présent(e)
- **3.** [thought, idea] : **to ~ to sb** venir à l'esprit
de qqn.

occurrence [ə'kʌrəns] *n* [event] événement *m*, circonstance *f*.

ocean ['əʊʃn] *n* océan *m* ; *Am* [sea] mer *f*.

oceangoing ['əʊʃnˌgəʊɪŋ] *adj* au long
cours.

ochre *Br*, **ocher** *Am* ['əʊkəʳ] *adj* ocre *(inv)*.

o'clock [ə'klɒk] *adv* : **two ~** deux heures.

octave ['ɒktɪv] *n* octave *f*.

October [ɒk'təʊbəʳ] *n* octobre *m* ; *see also*
September.

octopus ['ɒktəpəs] *(pl* **-puses** OR **-pi** [-paɪ])
n pieuvre *f*.

OD - **1.** *abbr of* **overdose** - **2.** *abbr of* **overdrawn**.

odd [ɒd] *adj* - **1.** [strange] bizarre, étrange
- **2.** [leftover] qui reste - **3.** [occasional] : **I
play the ~ game of tennis** je joue au tennis
de temps en temps - **4.** [not part of pair] dé-
pareillé(e) - **5.** [number] impair(e) - **6.** *phr* :
twenty ~ years une vingtaine d'années.
◆ **odds** *npl* : **the ~s** les chances *fpl* ; **the ~s
are that ...** il y a des chances pour que ... (+
subjunctive), il est probable que ... ; **against
the ~s** envers et contre tout ; **~s and ends**

petites choses *fpl*, petits bouts *mpl* ; **to be at ~s** with sb être en désaccord avec qqn.
oddity ['ɒdɪtɪ] *n* - **1.** [person] personne *f* bizarre ; [thing] chose *f* bizarre - **2.** [strange-ness] étrangeté *f*.
odd jobs *npl* petits travaux *mpl*.
oddly ['ɒdlɪ] *adv* curieusement ; **~ enough** chose curieuse.
oddments ['ɒdmənts] *npl Br* fins *fpl* de série.
odds-on ['ɒdz-] *adj inf* : **~ favourite** grand favori.
odometer [əʊ'dɒmɪtə'] *n* odomètre *m*.
odour *Br*, **odor** *Am* ['əʊdə'] *n* odeur *f*.
of [*unstressed* əv, *stressed* ɒv] *prep* - **1.** [gen] de ; **the cover ~ a book** la couverture d'un livre ; **to die ~ cancer** mourir d'un cancer - **2.** [expressing quantity, amount, age etc] de ; **thousands ~ people** des milliers de gens ; **a piece ~ cake** un morceau de gâteau ; **a pound ~ tomatoes** une livre de tomates ; **a child ~ five** un enfant de cinq ans ; **a cup ~ coffee** une tasse de café - **3.** [made from] en - **4.** [with dates, periods of time] : **the 12th ~ February** le 12 février.
off [ɒf] <> *adv* - **1.** *Br* [at a distance, away] : **10 miles ~** à 16 kilomètres ; **two days ~** dans deux jours ; **far ~** au loin ; **to be ~** partir, s'en aller - **2.** [so as to remove] : **to take ~** enlever ; **to cut sthg ~** couper qqch - **3.** [so as to complete] : **to finish ~** terminer ; **to kill ~** achever - **4.** [not at work etc] : **a day/week ~** un jour/une semaine de congé - **5.** [discounted] : **£10 ~** 10 livres de remise OR réduction. <> *prep* - **1.** [at a distance from, away from] de , **to get ~ a bus** descendre d'un bus ; **to take a book ~ a shelf** prendre un livre sur une étagère ; **~ the coast** près de la côte - **2.** [not attending] : **to be ~ work** ne pas travailler ; **~ school** absent de l'école - **3.** [no longer liking] : **she's ~ her food** elle n'a pas d'appétit - **4.** [deducted from] sur - **5.** *inf Br* [from] : **to buy sthg ~ sb** acheter qqch à qqn. <> *adj* - **1.** [food] avarié(e), gâté(e) ; [milk] tourné(e) - **2.** [TV, light] éteint(e) ; [engine] coupé(e) - **3.** [cancelled] annulé(e) - **4.** [not at work etc] absent(e) - **5.** *inf* [offhand] : **he was a bit ~ with me** il n'a pas été sympa avec moi.
offal ['ɒfl] *n* (U) abats *mpl*.
off-chance *n* : **on the ~ that** ... au cas où ...
off colour *adj* [ill] *Br* patraque.
off duty *adj* qui n'est pas de service ; [doctor, nurse] qui n'est pas de garde.
offence *Br*, **offense** *Am* [ə'fens] *n* - **1.** [crime] délit *m* - **2.** [upset] : **to cause sb ~** vexer qqn ; **to take ~** se vexer.
offend [ə'fend] *vt* offenser.

offender [ə'fendə'] *n* - **1.** [criminal] criminel *m*, -elle *f* - **2.** [culprit] coupable *mf*.
offense [*sense 2* 'ɒfens] *n Am* - **1.** = **offence** - **2.** SPORT attaque *f*.
offensive [ə'fensɪv] <> *adj* - **1.** [behaviour, comment] blessant(e) - **2.** [weapon, action] offensif(ive). <> *n* offensive *f*.
offer ['ɒfə'] <> *n* - **1.** [gen] offre *f*, proposition *f* - **2.** [price, bid] offre *f* - **3.** [in shop] promotion *f* ; **on ~** [available] en vente ; [at a special price] en réclame, en promotion. <> *vt* - **1.** [gen] offrir ; **to ~ sthg to sb**, **to ~ sb sthg** offrir qqch à qqn ; **to ~ to do sthg** proposer OR offrir de faire qqch - **2.** [provide - services etc] proposer ; [- hope] donner. <> *vi* s'offrir.
offering ['ɒfərɪŋ] *n* RELIG offrande *f*.
off-guard *adv* au dépourvu.
offhand [ˌɒf'hænd] <> *adj* cavalier(ère). <> *adv* tout de suite.
office ['ɒfɪs] *n* - **1.** [place, staff] bureau *m* - **2.** [department] département *m*, service *m* - **3.** [position] fonction *f*, poste *m* ; **in ~** en fonction ; **to take ~** entrer en fonction.
office automation *n* bureautique *f*.
office block *n Br* immeuble *m* de bureaux.
office hours *npl* heures *fpl* de bureau.
officer ['ɒfɪsə'] *n* - **1.** [in armed forces] officier *m* - **2.** [in organization] agent *m*, fonctionnaire *mf* - **3.** [in police force] officier *m* (de police).
office worker *n* employé *m*, -e *f* de bureau.
official [ə'fɪʃl] <> *adj* officiel(elle). <> *n* fonctionnaire *mf*.
officialdom [ə'fɪʃəldəm] *n* bureaucratie *f*.
offing ['ɒfɪŋ] *n* : **in the ~** en vue, en perspective.
off-licence *n Br magasin autorisé à vendre des boissons alcoolisées à emporter*.
off-line *adj* COMPUT non connecté(e).
off-peak *adj* [electricity] utilisé(e) aux heures creuses ; [fare] réduit(e) aux heures creuses.
off-putting [ˌ-ˈpʊtɪŋ] *adj* désagréable, rébarbatif(ive).
off season *n* : **the ~** la morte-saison.
offset [ˌɒf'set] (*pt & pp* offset) *vt* [losses] compenser.
offshoot ['ɒfʃuːt] *n* : **to be an ~ of sthg** être né(e) OR provenir de qqch.
offshore ['ɒfʃɔː'] <> *adj* [oil rig] offshore (*inv*) ; [island] proche de la côte ; [fishing] côtier(ère). <> *adv* au large.

offside [*adj & adv* ˌɒf'saɪd, *n* 'ɒfsaɪd] ⋄ *adj* - **1.** *Br* [right-hand drive] de droite ; [left-hand drive] de gauche - **2.** SPORT hors-jeu *(inv)*. ⋄ *adv* SPORT hors-jeu. ⋄ *n Br* [right-hand drive] côté *m* droit ; [left-hand drive] côté gauche.

offspring ['ɒfsprɪŋ] *(pl inv)* *n* rejeton *m*.

offstage [ˌɒf'steɪdʒ] *adj & adv* dans les coulisses.

off-the-peg *adj Br* de prêt-à-porter.

off-the-record ⋄ *adj* officieux(euse). ⋄ *adv* confidentiellement.

off-white *adj* blanc cassé *(inv)*.

often ['ɒfn, 'ɒftn] *adv* souvent, fréquemment ; **how ~ do you visit her?** vous la voyez tous les combien? ; **as ~ as not** assez souvent ; **every so ~** de temps en temps ; **more ~ than not** le plus souvent, la plupart du temps.

ogle ['əʊgl] *vt* reluquer.

oh [əʊ] *excl* oh! ; [expressing hesitation] euh!

oil [ɔɪl] ⋄ *n* - **1.** [gen] huile *f* - **2.** [for heating] mazout *m* - **3.** [petroleum] pétrole *m*. ⋄ *vt* graisser, lubrifier.

oilcan ['ɔɪlkæn] *n* burette *f* d'huile.

oilfield ['ɔɪfiːld] *n* gisement *m* pétrolifère.

oil filter *n* filtre *m* à huile.

oil-fired [-ˌfaɪəd] *adj* au mazout.

oil painting *n* peinture *f* à l'huile.

oilrig ['ɔɪlrɪg] *n* [at sea] plate-forme *f* de forage OR pétrolière ; [on land] derrick *m*.

oilskins ['ɔɪlskɪnz] *npl* ciré *m*.

oil slick *n* marée *f* noire.

oil tanker *n* - **1.** [ship] pétrolier *m*, tanker *m* - **2.** [lorry] camion-citerne *m*.

oil well *n* puits *m* de pétrole.

oily ['ɔɪlɪ] *adj* [rag etc] graisseux(euse) ; [food] gras (grasse).

ointment ['ɔɪntmənt] *n* pommade *f*.

OK (*pt & pp* **OKed**, *cont* **OKing**), **okay** [ˌəʊ'keɪ] *inf* ⋄ *adj* : **is it ~ with** OR **by you?** ça vous va?, vous êtes d'accord? ; **are you ~?** ça va? ⋄ *excl* - **1.** [expressing agreement] d'accord, O.K. - **2.** [to introduce new topic] : **~, can we start now?** bon, on commence? ⋄ *vt* approuver, donner le feu vert à.

old [əʊld] ⋄ *adj* - **1.** [gen] vieux (vieille), âgé(e) ; **I'm 20 years ~** j'ai 20 ans ; **how ~ are you?** quel âge as-tu? - **2.** [former] ancien(enne) - **3.** *inf* [as intensifier] : **any ~** n'importe quel (n'importe quelle). ⋄ *npl* : **the ~** les personnes *fpl* âgées.

old age *n* vieillesse *f*.

old age pensioner *n Br* retraité *m*, -e *f*.

Old Bailey [-'beɪlɪ] *n* : **the ~** la Cour d'assises de Londres.

old-fashioned [-'fæʃnd] *adj* - **1.** [outmoded] démodé(e), passé(e) de mode - **2.** [traditional] vieux jeu *(inv)*.

old people's home *n* hospice *m* de vieillards.

O level *n Br* examen optionnel destiné, jusqu'en 1988, aux élèves de niveau seconde ayant obtenu de bons résultats.

olive ['ɒlɪv] ⋄ *adj* olive *(inv)*. ⋄ *n* olive *f*.

olive green *adj* vert olive *(inv)*.

olive oil *n* huile *f* d'olive.

Olympic [ə'lɪmpɪk] *adj* olympique. ➽ **Olympics** *npl* : **the ~s** les Jeux *mpl* Olympiques.

Olympic Games *npl* : **the ~** les Jeux *mpl* Olympiques.

ombudsman ['ɒmbʊdzmən] *(pl* -**men** [-mən]) *n* ombudsman *m*.

omelet(te) ['ɒmlɪt] *n* omelette *f* ; **mushroom ~** omelette aux champignons.

omen ['əʊmen] *n* augure *m*, présage *m*.

ominous ['ɒmɪnəs] *adj* [event, situation] de mauvais augure ; [sign] inquiétant(e) ; [look, silence] menaçant(e).

omission [ə'mɪʃn] *n* omission *f*.

omit [ə'mɪt] *vt* omettre ; **to ~ to do sthg** oublier de faire qqch.

omnibus ['ɒmnɪbəs] *n* - **1.** [book] recueil *m* - **2.** *Br* RADIO & TV diffusion groupée des épisodes de la semaine.

on [ɒn] ⋄ *prep* - **1.** [indicating position, location] sur ; **~ a chair/the wall** sur une chaise/le mur ; **~ the ceiling** au plafond ; **the information is ~ disk** l'information est sur disquette ; **~ the left/right** à gauche/droite - **2.** [indicating means] : **the car runs ~ petrol** la voiture marche à l'essence ; **to be shown ~ TV** passer à la télé ; **~ the radio** à la radio ; **~ the telephone** au téléphone ; **to live ~ fruit** vivre OR se nourrir de fruits ; **to hurt o.s. ~ sthg** se faire mal avec qqch - **3.** [indicating mode of transport] : **to travel ~ a bus/train/ship** voyager en bus/par le train/en bateau ; **I was ~ the bus** j'étais dans le bus ; **~ foot** à pied - **4.** [concerning] sur ; **a book ~ astronomy** un livre sur l'astronomie - **5.** [indicating time, activity] : **~ Thursday** jeudi ; **~ the 10th of February** le 10 février ; **~ my birthday** le jour de mon anniversaire ; **~ my return**, **~ returning** à mon retour ; **~ holiday** en vacances - **6.** [indicating influence] sur ; **the impact ~ the environment** l'impact sur l'environnement - **7.** [using, supported by] : **to be ~ social se-**

curity recevoir l'aide sociale ; **he's ~ tran-
quillizers** il prend des tranquillisants ; **to
be ~ drugs** se droguer **- 8.** [earning] : **to be
~ £25,000 a year** gagner 25 000 livres par
an ; **to be ~ a low income** avoir un faible revenu **- 9.** [referring to musical instrument] :
to play sthg ~ the violin/flute/guitar jouer
qqch au violon/à la flûte/à la guitare
- 10. inf [paid by] : **the drinks are ~ me** c'est
moi qui régale, c'est ma tournée. <> adv
- 1. [indicating covering, clothing] : **put the
lid ~** mettez le couvercle ; **to put a sweater
~** mettre un pull ; **what did she have ~?**
qu'est-ce qu'elle portait? ; **he had nothing
~** il était tout nu **- 2.** [being shown] : **what's
~ at the Ritz?** qu'est-ce qu'on joue OR donne
au Ritz? **- 3.** [working - radio, TV, light]
allumé(e) ; [- machine] en marche ; [- tap]
ouvert(e) ; **turn ~ the power** mets le courant **- 4.** [indicating continuing action] : **to
work ~** continuer à travailler ; **he kept
~ walking** il continua à marcher **- 5.** [for-
ward] : **send my mail ~ (to me)** faites suivre
mon courrier ; **later ~** plus tard ; **earlier ~**
plus tôt **- 6.** Br inf [referring to behaviour] :
it's just not ~! cela ne se fait pas! ◆ **from
... on** adv : **from now ~** dorénavant, désormais ; **from then ~** à partir de ce moment-
là. ◆ **on and off** adv de temps en temps.
◆ **on to, onto** prep (only written as onto for
senses 4 and 5) **- 1.** [to a position on top of]
sur ; **she jumped ~ to the chair** elle a sauté
sur la chaise **- 2.** [to a position on a vehicle]
dans ; **she got ~ to the bus** elle est montée
dans le bus ; **he jumped ~ to his bicycle** il a
sauté sur sa bicyclette **- 3.** [to a position attached to] : **stick the photo ~ to the page
with glue** colle la photo sur la page
- 4. [aware of wrongdoing] : **to be onto sb**
être sur la piste de qqn **- 5.** [into contact
with] : **get onto the factory** contactez l'usine.

once [wʌns] <> adv **- 1.** [on one occasion]
une fois ; **~ a day** une fois par jour ; **~ again**
OR **more** encore une fois ; **~ and for all** une
fois pour toutes ; **~ in a while** de temps en
temps ; **~ or twice** une ou deux fois ; **for ~**
pour une fois **- 2.** [previously] autrefois,
jadis ; **~ upon a time** il était une fois. <> conj
dès que. ◆ **at once** adv **- 1.** [immediately]
immédiatement **- 2.** [at the same time] en
même temps ; **all at ~** tout d'un coup.

oncoming ['ɒn,kʌmɪŋ] adj [traffic] venant
en sens inverse ; [danger] imminent(e).

one [wʌn] <> num [the number 1] un
(une) ; **page ~** page un ; **~ of my friends** l'un
de mes amis, un ami à moi ; **~ fifth** un cinquième. <> adj **- 1.** [only] seul(e), unique ;
it's her ~ ambition/love c'est son unique
ambition/son seul amour **- 2.** [indefinite] :

~ of these days un de ces jours. <> pron
- 1. [referring to a particular thing or person] :
which ~ do you want? lequel voulez-
vous? ; **this ~** celui-ci ; **that ~** celui-là ; **she's
the ~ I told you about** c'est celle dont je
vous ai parlé **- 2.** fml [you, anyone] on ; **to
do ~'s duty** faire son devoir. ◆ **for one**
adv : **I for ~ remain unconvinced** pour ma
part je ne suis pas convaincu.

one-armed bandit n machine f à sous.

one-man adj [business] dirigé(e) par un
seul homme.

one-man band n [musician] homme-
orchestre m.

one-off Br inf <> adj [offer, event, product]
unique. <> n : **a ~** [product] un exemplaire
unique ; [event] un événement unique.

one-on-one Am = one-to-one.

one-parent family n famille f monoparentale.

oneself [wʌn'self] pron **- 1.** (reflexive) se ;
(after prep) soi **- 2.** (emphatic) soi-même.

one-sided [-'saɪdɪd] adj **- 1.** [unequal] iné-
gal(e) **- 2.** [biased] partial(e).

one-to-one Br, **one-on-one** Am adj [dis-
cussion] en tête-à-tête ; **~ tuition** cours mpl
particuliers.

one-upmanship [,wʌn'ʌpmənʃɪp] n art
m de faire toujours mieux que les autres.

one-way adj **- 1.** [street] à sens unique
- 2. [ticket] simple.

ongoing ['ɒn,gəʊɪŋ] adj en cours, conti-
nu(e).

onion ['ʌnjən] n oignon m.

online ['ɒnlaɪn] adj & adv COMPUT en ligne, connecté(e).

onlooker ['ɒn,lʊkəʳ] n spectateur m, -trice
f.

only ['əʊnlɪ] <> adj seul(e), unique ; **~
child** un enfant unique. <> adv **- 1.** [gen]
ne ... que, seulement ; **he ~ reads science
fiction** il ne lit que de la science fiction ; **it's
~ a scratch** c'est juste une égratignure ; **he
left ~ a few minutes ago** il est parti il n'y a
pas deux minutes **- 2.** [for emphasis] : **I
~ wish I could** je voudrais bien ; **it's ~ natural (that)** ... c'est tout à fait normal que
... ; **I was ~ too willing to help** je ne deman-
dais qu'à aider ; **not ~ ... but also** non seulement ... mais encore ; **I ~ just caught the
train** j'ai eu le train de justesse. <> conj
seulement, mais.

onset ['ɒnset] n début m, commencement
m.

onshore ['ɒnʃɔːʳ] adj & adv [from sea] du
large ; [on land] à terre.

onslaught ['ɒnslɔːt] *n* attaque *f*.

onto ['ɒntʊ:] = **on to**.

onus ['əʊnəs] *n* responsabilité *f*, charge *f*.

onward ['ɒnwəd] *adj & adv* en avant.

onwards ['ɒnwədz] *adv* en avant ; **from now ~** dorénavant, désormais ; **from then ~** à partir de ce moment-là.

ooze [uːz] ◇ *vt fig* [charm, confidence] respirer. ◇ *vi* : **to ~ from** OR **out of sthg** suinter de qqch.

opaque [əʊ'peɪk] *adj* opaque ; *fig* obscur(e).

OPEC ['əʊpek] (*abbr of* **Organization of Petroleum Exporting Countries**) *n* OPEP *f*.

open ['əʊpn] ◇ *adj* - **1.** [gen] ouvert(e) - **2.** [receptive] : **to be ~ (to)** être réceptif(ive) (à) - **3.** [view, road, space] dégagé(e) - **4.** [uncovered - car] découvert(e) - **5.** [meeting] public(ique) ; [competition] ouvert(e) à tous - **6.** [disbelief, honesty] manifeste, évident(e) - **7.** [unresolved] non résolu(e). ◇ *n* : **in the ~** [sleep] à la belle étoile ; [eat] au grand air ; **to bring sthg out into the ~** divulguer qqch, exposer qqch au grand jour. ◇ *vt* - **1.** [gen] ouvrir - **2.** [inaugurate] inaugurer. ◇ *vi* - **1.** [door, flower] s'ouvrir - **2.** [shop, library etc] ouvrir - **3.** [meeting, play etc] commencer. ◆ **open on to** *vt fus* [subj : room, door] donner sur. ◆ **open up** ◇ *vt sep* [develop] exploiter, développer. ◇ *vi* - **1.** [possibilities etc] s'offrir, se présenter - **2.** [unlock door] ouvrir.

opener ['əʊpnə'] *n* [for cans] ouvre-boîtes *m inv* ; [for bottles] ouvre-bouteilles *m inv*, décapsuleur *m*.

opening ['əʊpnɪŋ] ◇ *adj* [first] premier(ère) ; [remarks] préliminaire. ◇ *n* - **1.** [beginning] commencement *m*, début *m* - **2.** [in fence] trou *m*, percée *f* ; [in clouds] trouée *f*, déchirure *f* - **3.** [opportunity - gen] occasion *f* ; [- COMM] débouché *m* - **4.** [job vacancy] poste *m*.

opening hours *npl* heures *fpl* d'ouverture.

openly ['əʊpənlɪ] *adv* ouvertement, franchement.

open-minded [-'maɪndɪd] *adj* [person] qui a l'esprit large ; [attitude] large.

open-plan *adj* non cloisonné(e).

Open University *n Br* : **the ~ ≃** centre *m* national d'enseignement à distance.

opera ['ɒpərə] *n* opéra *m*.

opera house *n* opéra *m*.

operate ['ɒpəreɪt] ◇ *vt* - **1.** [machine] faire marcher, faire fonctionner - **2.** COMM diriger. ◇ *vi* - **1.** [rule, law, system] jouer, être appliqué(e) ; [machine] fonctionner,

marcher - **2.** COMM opérer, travailler - **3.** MED opérer ; **to ~ on sb/sthg** opérer qqn/qqch.

operating theatre *Br*, **operating room** *Am* ['ɒpəreɪtɪŋ-] *n* salle *f* d'opération.

operation [,ɒpə'reɪʃn] *n* - **1.** [gen & MED] opération *f* ; **to have an ~ (for)** se faire opérer (de) - **2.** [of machine] marche *f*, fonctionnement *m* ; **to be in ~** [machine] être en marche OR en service ; [law, system] être en vigueur - **3.** [COMM - company] exploitation *f* ; [- management] administration *f*, gestion *f*.

operational [,ɒpə'reɪʃənl] *adj* [machine] en état de marche.

operative ['ɒprətɪv] ◇ *adj* en vigueur. ◇ *n* ouvrier *m*, -ère *f*.

operator ['ɒpəreɪtə'] *n* - **1.** TELEC standardiste *mf* - **2.** [of machine] opérateur *m*, -trice *f* - **3.** COMM directeur *m*, -trice *f*.

opinion [ə'pɪnjən] *n* opinion *f*, avis *m* ; **to be of the ~ that** être d'avis que, estimer que ; **in my ~** à mon avis.

opinionated [ə'pɪnjəneɪtɪd] *adj pej* dogmatique.

opinion poll *n* sondage *m* d'opinion.

opponent [ə'pəʊnənt] *n* adversaire *mf*.

opportune ['ɒpətjuːn] *adj* opportun(e).

opportunist [,ɒpə'tjuːnɪst] *n* opportuniste *mf*.

opportunity [,ɒpə'tjuːnətɪ] *n* occasion *f* ; **to take the ~ to do** OR **of doing sthg** profiter de l'occasion pour faire qqch.

oppose [ə'pəʊz] *vt* s'opposer à.

opposed [ə'pəʊzd] *adj* opposé(e) ; **to be ~ to** être contre, être opposé à ; **as ~ to** par opposition à.

opposing [ə'pəʊzɪŋ] *adj* opposé(e).

opposite ['ɒpəzɪt] ◇ *adj* opposé(e) ; [house] d'en face. ◇ *adv* en face. ◇ *prep* en face de. ◇ *n* contraire *m*.

opposite number *n* homologue *mf*.

opposition [,ɒpə'zɪʃn] *n* - **1.** [gen] opposition *f* - **2.** [opposing team] adversaire *mf*. ◆ **Opposition** *n Br* POL : **the Opposition** l'opposition.

oppress [ə'pres] *vt* - **1.** [persecute] opprimer - **2.** [depress] oppresser.

oppressive [ə'presɪv] *adj* - **1.** [unjust] oppressif(ive) - **2.** [weather, heat] étouffant(e), lourd(e) - **3.** [silence] oppressant(e).

opt [ɒpt] ◇ *vt* : **to ~ to do sthg** choisir de faire qqch. ◇ *vi* : **to ~ for** opter pour. ◆ **opt in** *vi* : **to ~ in (to)** choisir de participer (à). ◆ **opt out** *vi* : **to ~ out (of)** [gen] choisir de ne pas participer (à) ; [of responsibility] se dérober (à) ; [of NHS] ne plus faire partie (de).

optical ['ɒptɪkl] *adj* optique.

optician [ɒp'tɪʃn] *n* - **1.** [who sells glasses] opticien *m*, -enne *f* - **2.** [ophthalmologist] ophtalmologiste *mf*.

optimist ['ɒptɪmɪst] *n* optimiste *mf*.

optimistic [ˌɒptɪ'mɪstɪk] *adj* optimiste.

optimum ['ɒptɪməm] *adj* optimum.

option ['ɒpʃn] *n* option *f*, choix *m* ; **to have the ~ to** OR **of doing sthg** pouvoir faire qqch, avoir la possibilité de faire qqch.

optional ['ɒpʃənl] *adj* facultatif(ive) ; **an ~ extra** un accessoire.

or [ɔːr] *conj* - **1.** [gen] ou - **2.** [after negative] : **he can't read ~ write** il ne sait ni lire ni écrire - **3.** [otherwise] sinon - **4.** [as correction] ou plutôt.

oral ['ɔːrəl] <> *adj* - **1.** [spoken] oral(e) - **2.** MED - medicine] par voie orale, par la bouche ; [- hygiene] buccal(e). <> *n* oral *m*, épreuve *f* orale.

orally ['ɔːrəlɪ] *adv* - **1.** [in spoken form] oralement - **2.** MED par voie orale.

orange ['ɒrɪndʒ] <> *adj* orange (*inv*). <> *n* - **1.** [fruit] orange *f* - **2.** [colour] orange *m*.

orator ['ɒrətər] *n* orateur *m*, -trice *f*.

orbit ['ɔːbɪt] <> *n* orbite *f*. <> *vt* décrire une orbite autour de.

orchard ['ɔːtʃəd] *n* verger *m* ; **apple ~** champ *m* de pommiers, pommeraie *f*.

orchestra ['ɔːkɪstrə] *n* orchestre *m*.

orchestral [ɔː'kestrəl] *adj* orchestral(e).

orchid ['ɔːkɪd] *n* orchidée *f*.

ordain [ɔː'deɪn] *vt* - **1.** [decree] ordonner, décréter - **2.** RELIG : **to be ~ed** être ordonné prêtre.

ordeal [ɔː'diːl] *n* épreuve *f*.

order ['ɔːdər] <> *n* - **1.** [gen] ordre *m* ; **to be under ~s to do sthg** avoir (reçu) l'ordre de faire qqch - **2.** COMM commande *f* ; **to place an ~ with sb for sthg** passer une commande de qqch à qqn ; **to ~** sur commande - **3.** [sequence] ordre *m* ; **in ~** dans l'ordre ; **in ~ of importance** par ordre d'importance - **4.** [fitness for use] : **in working ~** en état de marche ; **out of ~** [machine] en panne ; [behaviour] déplacé(e) ; **in ~** [correct] en ordre - **5.** (*U*) [discipline - gen] ordre *m* ; [- in classroom] discipline *f* - **6.** *Am* [portion] part *f*. <> *vt* - **1.** [command] ordonner ; **to ~ sb to do sthg** ordonner à qqn de faire qqch ; **to ~ that** ordonner que - **2.** COMM commander. ◆ **in the order of** *Br*, **on the order**

of *Am adv* environ, de l'ordre de. ◆ **in order that** *conj* pour que, afin que (*+ subjunctive*). ◆ **in order to** *conj* pour, afin de. ◆ **order about, order around** *vt sep* commander.

order form *n* bulletin *m* de commande.

orderly ['ɔːdəlɪ] <> *adj* [person] ordonné(e) ; [crowd] discipliné(e) ; [office, room] en ordre. <> *n* [in hospital] garçon *m* de salle.

ordinarily ['ɔːdənrəlɪ] *adv* d'habitude, d'ordinaire.

ordinary ['ɔːdnrɪ] <> *adj* - **1.** [normal] ordinaire - **2.** *pej* [unexceptional] ordinaire, quelconque. <> *n* : **out of the ~** qui sort de l'ordinaire, exceptionnel(elle).

ordnance ['ɔːdnəns] *n* (*U*) - **1.** [supplies] matériel *m* militaire - **2.** [artillery] artillerie *f*.

ore [ɔːr] *n* minerai *m*.

oregano [ˌɒrɪ'gɑːnəʊ] *n* origan *m*.

organ ['ɔːgən] *n* - **1.** [gen] organe *m* - **2.** MUS orgue *m*.

organic [ɔː'gænɪk] *adj* - **1.** [of animals, plants] organique - **2.** [farming, food] biologique.

organization [ˌɔːgənaɪ'zeɪʃn] *n* organisation *f*.

organize, -ise ['ɔːgənaɪz] *vt* organiser.

organizer ['ɔːgənaɪzər] *n* - **1.** [person] organisateur *m*, -trice *f* - **2.** [diary] organiseur *m*.

orgasm ['ɔːgæzm] *n* orgasme *m*.

orgy ['ɔːdʒɪ] *n lit & fig* orgie *f*.

Orient ['ɔːrɪənt] *n* : **the ~** l'Orient *m*.

oriental [ˌɔːrɪ'entl] *adj* oriental(e).

orienteering [ˌɔːrɪən'tɪərɪŋ] *n* (*U*) course *f* d'orientation.

origami [ˌɒrɪ'gɑːmɪ] *n* origami *m*.

origin ['ɒrɪdʒɪn] *n* - **1.** [of river] source *f* ; [of word, conflict] origine *f* - **2.** [birth] : **country of ~** pays *m* d'origine. ◆ **origins** *npl* origines *fpl*.

original [ə'rɪdʒənl] <> *adj* original(e) ; [owner] premier(ère). <> *n* original *m*.

originally [ə'rɪdʒənəlɪ] *adv* à l'origine, au départ.

originate [ə'rɪdʒəneɪt] <> *vt* être l'auteur de, être à l'origine de. <> *vi* [belief, custom] : **to ~ in** prendre naissance (dans) ; **to ~ from** provenir de.

Orkney Islands ['ɔːknɪ-], **Orkneys** ['ɔːknɪz] *npl* : **the ~ les Orcades *fpl*.

ornament ['ɔːnəmənt] *n* - **1.** [object] bibelot *m* - **2.** (*U*) [decoration] ornement *m*.

ornamental [ˌɔːnə'mentl] *adj* [garden, pond] d'agrément ; [design] décoratif(ive).

ornate [ɔː'neɪt] *adj* orné(e).

ornithology [ˌɔːnɪ'θɒlədʒɪ] *n* ornithologie *f*.

orphan ['ɔːfn] <> *n* orphelin *m*, -e *f*. <> *vt* : **to be ~ed** devenir orphelin(e).

orphanage ['ɔːfənɪdʒ] *n* orphelinat *m*.

orthodox ['ɔːθədɒks] *adj* - **1.** [conventional] orthodoxe - **2.** RELIG [traditional] traditionaliste.

orthopaedic [ˌɔːθə'piːdɪk] *adj* orthopédique.

orthopedic *etc* [ˌɔːθə'piːdɪk] = **orthopaedic** *etc*.

oscillate ['ɒsɪleɪt] *vi lit & fig* osciller.

Oslo ['ɒzləʊ] *n* Oslo.

ostensible [ɒ'stensəbl] *adj* prétendu(e).

ostentatious [ˌɒstən'teɪʃəs] *adj* ostentatoire.

osteopath ['ɒstɪəpæθ] *n* ostéopathe *mf*.

ostracize, **-ise** ['ɒstrəsaɪz] *vt* frapper d'ostracisme, mettre au ban.

ostrich ['ɒstrɪtʃ] *n* autruche *f*.

other ['ʌðə'] <> *adj* autre ; **the ~ one** l'autre ; **the ~ day/week** l'autre jour/semaine. <> *adv* : **there was nothing to do ~ than confess** il ne pouvait faire autrement que d'avouer ; **~ than John** John à part. <> *pron* : **~s** d'autres ; **the ~** l'autre ; **the ~s** les autres ; **one after the ~** l'un après l'autre (l'une après l'autre) ; **one or ~ of you** l'un (l'une) de vous deux ; **none ~ than** nul (nulle) autre que. **something or other** *pron* quelque chose, je ne sais quoi. **somehow or other** *adv* d'une manière ou d'une autre.

otherwise ['ʌðəwaɪz] <> *adv* autrement ; **or ~** [or not] ou non. <> *conj* sinon.

otter ['ɒtə'] *n* loutre *f*.

ouch [aʊtʃ] *excl* aïe!, ouïe!

ought [ɔːt] *aux vb* - **1.** [sensibly] : **I really ~ to go** il faut absolument que je m'en aille ; **you ~ to see a doctor** tu devrais aller chez le docteur - **2.** [morally] : **you ~ not to have done that** tu n'aurais pas dû faire cela ; **you ~ to look after your children better** tu devrais t'occuper un peu mieux de tes enfants - **3.** [expressing probability] : **she ~ to pass her exam** elle devrait réussir à son examen.

ounce [aʊns] *n* = 28,35 g, once *f*.

our ['aʊə'] *poss adj* notre, nos *(pl)* ; **~ money/house** notre argent/maison ; **~ children** nos enfants ; **it wasn't our fault** ce n'était pas de notre faute à nous.

ours ['aʊəz] *poss pron* le nôtre (la nôtre), les nôtres *(pl)* ; **that money is ~** cet argent est à nous OR est le nôtre ; **it wasn't their fault, it was ours** ce n'était pas de leur faute, c'était de notre faute à nous OR de la nôtre ; **a friend of ~** un ami à nous, un de nos amis.

ourselves [aʊə'selvz] *pron pl* - **1.** (*reflexive*) nous - **2.** (*for emphasis*) nous-mêmes ; **we did it by ~** nous l'avons fait tout seuls.

oust [aʊst] *vt* : **to ~ sb (from)** évincer qqn (de).

out [aʊt] *adv* - **1.** [not inside, out of doors] dehors ; **I'm going ~ for a walk** je sors me promener ; **to run ~** sortir en courant ; **~ here** ici ; **~ there** là-bas - **2.** [away from home, office, published] sorti(e) ; **John's ~ at the moment** John est sorti, John n'est pas là en ce moment ; **an afternoon ~** une sortie l'après-midi - **3.** [extinguished] éteint(e) ; **the lights went ~** les lumières se sont éteintes - **4.** [of tides] : **the tide is ~** la marée est basse - **5.** [out of fashion] démodé(e), passé(e) de mode - **6.** [in flower] en fleur - **7.** *inf* [on strike] en grève - **8.** [determined] : **to be ~ to do sthg** être résolu(e) OR décidé(e) à faire qqch. **out of** *prep* - **1.** [outside] en dehors de ; **to go ~ of the room** sortir de la pièce ; **to be ~ of the country** être à l'étranger - **2.** [indicating cause] par ; **~ of spite/love/boredom** par dépit/amour/ennui - **3.** [indicating origin, source] de, dans ; **a page ~ of a book** une page d'un livre ; **it's made ~ of plastic** c'est en plastique - **4.** [without] sans ; **~ of petrol/money** à court d'essence/d'argent - **5.** [sheltered from] à l'abri de ; **we're ~ of the wind here** nous sommes à l'abri du vent ici - **6.** [to indicate proportion] sur ; **one ~ of ten people** une personne sur dix ; **ten ~ of ten** dix sur dix.

out-and-out *adj* [liar] fieffé(e) ; [disgrace] complet(ète).

outback ['aʊtbæk] *n* : **the ~** l'intérieur *m* du pays *(en Australie)*.

outboard (motor) ['aʊtbɔːd-] *n* (moteur *m*) hors-bord *m*.

outbreak ['aʊtbreɪk] *n* [of war, crime] début *m*, déclenchement *m* ; [of spots etc] éruption *f*.

outburst ['aʊtbɜːst] *n* explosion *f*.

outcast ['aʊtkɑːst] *n* paria *m*.

outcome ['aʊtkʌm] *n* issue *f*, résultat *m*.

outcrop ['aʊtkrɒp] *n* affleurement *m*.

outcry ['aʊtkraɪ] *n* tollé *m*.

outdated [ˌaʊt'deɪtɪd] *adj* démodé(e), vieilli(e).

outdid [ˌaʊt'dɪd] *pt* ⊳ outdo.

outdo [ˌaʊt'duː] (*pt* -did, *pp* -done [-'dʌn]) *vt* surpasser.

outdoor ['aʊtdɔːʳ] *adj* [life, swimming pool] en plein air ; [activities] de plein air.

outdoors [aʊt'dɔːz] *adv* dehors.

outer ['aʊtəʳ] *adj* extérieur(e).

outer space *n* cosmos *m*.

outfit ['aʊtfɪt] *n* - 1. [clothes] tenue *f* - 2. *inf* [organization] équipe *f*.

outfitters ['aʊtˌfɪtəz] *n* Br dated [for clothes] magasin *m* spécialisé de confection pour hommes.

outgoing ['aʊtˌgəʊɪŋ] *adj* - 1. [chairman etc] sortant(e) ; [mail] à expédier ; [train] en partance - 2. [friendly, sociable] ouvert(e).
 ◆ **outgoings** *npl* Br dépenses *fpl*.

outgrow [ˌaʊt'grəʊ] (*pt* -grew, *pp* -grown) *vt* - 1. [clothes] devenir trop grand(e) pour - 2. [habit] se défaire de.

outhouse ['aʊthaʊs, *pl* -haʊzɪz] *n* - 1. appentis *m* - 2. Am latrines *fpl* extérieures.

outing ['aʊtɪŋ] *n* [trip] sortie *f*.

outlandish [aʊt'lændɪʃ] *adj* bizarre.

outlaw ['aʊtlɔː] <> *n* hors-la-loi *m inv*. <> *vt* [practice] proscrire.

outlay ['aʊtleɪ] *n* dépenses *fpl*.

outlet ['aʊtlet] *n* - 1. [for emotion] exutoire *m* - 2. [hole, pipe] sortie *f* - 3. [shop] : **retail ~** point *m* de vente - 4. Am ELEC prise *f* (de courant).

outline ['aʊtlaɪn] <> *n* - 1. [brief description] grandes lignes *fpl* ; **in ~** en gros - 2. [silhouette] silhouette *f*. <> *vt* [describe briefly] exposer les grandes lignes de.

outlive [ˌaʊt'lɪv] *vt* [subj : person] survivre à.

outlook ['aʊtlʊk] *n* - 1. [disposition] attitude *f*, conception *f* - 2. [prospect] perspective *f*.

outlying ['aʊtˌlaɪɪŋ] *adj* [village] reculé(e) ; [suburbs] écarté(e).

outmoded [ˌaʊt'məʊdɪd] *adj* démodé(e).

outnumber [ˌaʊt'nʌmbəʳ] *vt* surpasser en nombre.

out-of-date *adj* [passport] périmé(e) ; [clothes] démodé(e) ; [belief] dépassé(e).

out of doors *adv* dehors.

out-of-the-way *adj* [village] perdu(e) ; [pub] peu fréquenté(e).

outpatient ['aʊtˌpeɪʃnt] *n* malade *mf* en consultation externe.

outpost ['aʊtpəʊst] *n* avant-poste *m*.

output ['aʊtpʊt] *n* - 1. [production] production *f* - 2. COMPUT sortie *f*.

outrage ['aʊtreɪdʒ] <> *n* - 1. [emotion] indignation *f* - 2. [act] atrocité *f*. <> *vt* outrager.

outrageous [aʊt'reɪdʒəs] *adj* - 1. [offensive, shocking] scandaleux(euse), monstrueux(euse) - 2. [very unusual] choquant(e).

outright [*adj* 'aʊtraɪt, *adv* ˌaʊt'raɪt] <> *adj* absolu(e), total(e). <> *adv* - 1. [deny] carrément, franchement - 2. [win, fail] complètement, totalement.

outset ['aʊtset] *n* : **at the ~** au commencement, au début ; **from the ~** depuis le commencement OR début.

outside [*adv* ˌaʊt'saɪd, *adj, prep & n* 'aʊtsaɪd] <> *adj* - 1. [gen] extérieur(e) ; **an ~ opinion** une opinion indépendante - 2. [unlikely - chance, possibility] faible. <> *adv* à l'extérieur ; **to go/run/look ~** aller/courir/regarder dehors. <> *prep* - 1. [not inside] à l'extérieur de, en dehors de - 2. [beyond] : **~ office hours** en dehors des heures de bureau. <> *n* extérieur *m*.
 ◆ **outside of** *prep* Am [apart from] à part.

outside lane *n* AUT [in UK] voie *f* de droite ; [in Europe, US] voie *f* de gauche.

outside line *n* TELEC ligne *f* extérieure.

outsider [ˌaʊt'saɪdəʳ] *n* - 1. [in race] outsider *m* - 2. [from society] étranger *m*, -ère *f*.

outsize ['aʊtsaɪz] *adj* - 1. [bigger than usual] énorme, colossal(e) - 2. [clothes] grande taille (*inv*).

outskirts ['aʊtskɜːts] *npl* : **the ~** la banlieue.

outspoken [ˌaʊt'spəʊkn] *adj* franc (franche).

outstanding [ˌaʊt'stændɪŋ] *adj* - 1. [excellent] exceptionnel(elle), remarquable - 2. [example] marquant(e) - 3. [not paid] impayé(e) - 4. [unfinished - work, problem] en suspens.

outstay [ˌaʊt'steɪ] *vt* : **I don't want to ~ my welcome** je ne veux pas abuser de votre hospitalité.

outstretched [ˌaʊt'stretʃt] *adj* [arms, hands] tendu(e) ; [wings] déployé(e).

outstrip [ˌaʊt'strɪp] *vt* devancer.

out-tray *n* corbeille *f* pour le courrier à expédier.

outward ['aʊtwəd] <> *adj* - 1. [going away] : **~ journey** aller *m* - 2. [apparent, visible] extérieur(e). <> *adv* Am = **outwards**.

outwardly ['aʊtwədlɪ] *adv* [apparently] en apparence.

outwards Br ['aʊtwədz], **outward** Am *adv* vers l'extérieur.

outweigh [,aʊt'weɪ] *vt fig* primer sur.

outwit [,aʊt'wɪt] *vt* se montrer plus malin(igne) que.

oval ['əʊvl] <> *adj* ovale. <> *n* ovale *m*.

Oval Office *n* : **the ~** bureau du président des États-Unis à la Maison-Blanche.

ovary ['əʊvərɪ] *n* ovaire *m*.

ovation [əʊ'veɪʃn] *n* ovation *f* ; **the audience gave her a standing ~** le public l'a ovationnée.

oven ['ʌvn] *n* [for cooking] four *m*.

ovenproof ['ʌvnpruːf] *adj* qui va au four.

over ['əʊvər] <> *prep* - **1.** [above] au-dessus de - **2.** [on top of] sur - **3.** [on other side of] de l'autre côté de ; **they live ~ the road** ils habitent en face - **4.** [to other side of] par-dessus ; **to go ~ the border** franchir la frontière - **5.** [more than] plus de ; **~ and above** en plus de - **6.** [concerning] à propos de, au sujet de - **7.** [during] pendant. <> *adv* - **1.** [distance away] : **~ here** ici ; **~ there** là-bas - **2.** [across] : **they flew ~ to America** ils se sont envolés pour les États-Unis ; **we invited them ~** nous les avons invités chez nous - **3.** [more] plus - **4.** [remaining] : **there's nothing (left) ~** il ne reste rien - **5.** RADIO : **~ and out!** à vous! - **6.** [involving repetitions] : **(all) ~ again** (tout) au début ; **~ and ~ again** à maintes reprises, maintes fois. <> *adj* [finished] fini(e), terminé(e).
• all over <> *prep* [throughout] partout, dans tout ; **all ~ the world** dans le monde entier. <> *adv* [everywhere] partout. <> *adj* [finished] fini(e).

overall [*adj & n* 'əʊvərɔːl, *adv* ,əʊvər'ɔːl] <> *adj* [general] d'ensemble. <> *adv* en général. <> *n* - **1.** [gen] tablier *m* - **2.** *Am* [for work] bleu *m* de travail. **• overalls** *npl* - **1.** [for work] bleu *m* de travail - **2.** *Am* [dungarees] salopette *f*.

overawe [,əʊvər'ɔː] *vt* impressionner.

overbalance [,əʊvə'bæləns] *vi* basculer.

overbearing [,əʊvə'beərɪŋ] *adj* autoritaire.

overboard ['əʊvəbɔːd] *adv* : **to fall ~** tomber par-dessus bord.

overbook [,əʊvə'bʊk] *vi* surréserver.

overcame [,əʊvə'keɪm] *pt* ▷ overcome.

overcast [,əʊvə'kɑːst] *adj* couvert(e).

overcharge [,əʊvə'tʃɑːdʒ] *vt* : **to ~ sb (for sthg)** faire payer (qqch) trop cher à qqn.

overcoat ['əʊvəkəʊt] *n* pardessus *m*.

overcome [,əʊvə'kʌm] (*pt* -came, *pp* -come) *vt* - **1.** [fears, difficulties] surmonter - **2.** [overwhelm] : **to be ~ (by** OR **with)** [emo-tion] être submergé(e) (de) ; [grief] être accablé(e) (de).

overcrowded [,əʊvə'kraʊdɪd] *adj* bondé(e).

overcrowding [,əʊvə'kraʊdɪŋ] *n* surpeuplement *m*.

overdo [,əʊvə'duː] (*pt* -**did** [-'dɪd], *pp* -**done**) *vt* - **1.** [exaggerate] exagérer - **2.** [do too much] trop faire ; **to ~ it** se surmener - **3.** [overcook] trop cuire.

overdone [,əʊvə'dʌn] <> *pp* ▷ overdo. <> *adj* [food] trop cuit(e).

overdose ['əʊvədəʊs] *n* overdose *f*.

overdraft ['əʊvədrɑːft] *n* découvert *m*.

overdrawn [,əʊvə'drɔːn] *adj* à découvert.

overdue [,əʊvə'djuː] *adj* - **1.** [late] : **~ (for)** en retard (pour) - **2.** [change, reform] : **(long) ~** attendu(e) (depuis longtemps) - **3.** [unpaid] arriéré(e), impayé(e).

overestimate [,əʊvər'estɪmeɪt] *vt* surestimer.

overflow [*vb* ,əʊvə'fləʊ, *n* 'əʊvəfləʊ] <> *vi* - **1.** [gen] déborder - **2.** [streets, box] : **to be ~ing (with)** regorger (de). <> *n* [pipe, hole] trop-plein *m*.

overgrown [,əʊvə'grəʊn] *adj* [garden] envahi(e) par les mauvaises herbes.

overhaul [*n* 'əʊvəhɔːl, *vb* ,əʊvə'hɔːl] <> *n* - **1.** [of car, machine] révision *f* - **2.** *fig* [of system] refonte *f*, remaniement *m*. <> *vt* - **1.** [car, machine] réviser - **2.** *fig* [system] refondre, remanier.

overhead [*adv* ,əʊvə'hed, *adj & n* 'əʊvəhed] <> *adj* aérien(enne). <> *adv* au-dessus. <> *n* (*U*) *Am* frais *mpl* généraux.
• overheads *npl* *Br* frais *mpl* généraux.

overhead projector *n* rétroprojecteur *m*.

overhear [,əʊvə'hɪər] (*pt & pp* -**heard** [-'hɜːd]) *vt* entendre par hasard.

overheat [,əʊvə'hiːt] <> *vt* surchauffer. <> *vi* [engine] chauffer.

overjoyed [,əʊvə'dʒɔɪd] *adj* : **~ (at)** transporté(e) de joie (à).

overkill ['əʊvəkɪl] *n* [excess] : **that would be ~** ce serait de trop.

overladen [,əʊvə'leɪdn] <> *pp* ▷ overload. <> *adj* surchargé(e).

overland ['əʊvəlænd] *adj & adv* par voie de terre.

overlap [,əʊvə'læp] *vi* *lit & fig* se chevaucher.

overleaf [,əʊvə'liːf] *adv* au verso, au dos.

overload [,əʊvə'ləʊd] (*pp* -**loaded** OR -**laden**) *vt* surcharger.

overlook [ˌəʊvə'lʊk] *vt* - **1.** [subj : building, room] donner sur - **2.** [disregard, miss] oublier, négliger - **3.** [excuse] passer sur, fermer les yeux sur.

overnight [*adj* 'əʊvənaɪt, *adv* ˌəʊvə'naɪt] ⬦ *adj* - **1.** [journey, parking] de nuit ; [stay] d'une nuit - **2.** *fig* [sudden] : ~ **success** succès *m* immédiat. ⬦ *adv* - **1.** [stay, leave] la nuit - **2.** [suddenly] du jour au lendemain.

overpass ['əʊvəpɑ:s] *n Am* ≃ Toboggan® *m*.

overpower [ˌəʊvə'paʊə'] *vt* - **1.** [in fight] vaincre - **2.** *fig* [overwhelm] accabler, terrasser.

overpowering [ˌəʊvə'paʊərɪŋ] *adj* [desire] irrésistible ; [smell] entêtant(e).

overran [ˌəʊvə'ræn] *pt* ⬅ overrun.

overrated [ˌəʊvə'reɪtɪd] *adj* surfait(e).

override [ˌəʊvə'raɪd] (*pt* -**rode**, *pp* -**ridden**) *vt* - **1.** [be more important than] l'emporter sur, prévaloir sur - **2.** [overrule - decision] annuler.

overriding [ˌəʊvə'raɪdɪŋ] *adj* [need, importance] primordial(e).

overrode [ˌəʊvə'rəʊd] *pt* ⬅ override.

overrule [ˌəʊvə'ru:l] *vt* [person] prévaloir contre ; [decision] annuler ; [objection] rejeter.

overrun [ˌəʊvə'rʌn] (*pt* -**ran**, *pp* -**run**) ⬦ *vt* - **1.** MIL [occupy] occuper - **2.** *fig* [cover, fill] : **to be ~ with** [weeds] être envahi(e) de ; [rats] être infesté(e) de. ⬦ *vi* dépasser (le temps alloué).

oversaw [ˌəʊvə'sɔ:] *pt* ⬅ oversee.

overseas [*adj* 'əʊvəsi:z, *adv* ˌəʊvə'si:z] ⬦ *adj* [sales, company] à l'étranger ; [market] extérieur(e) ; [visitor, student] étranger(ère) ; ~ **aid** aide *f* aux pays étrangers. ⬦ *adv* à l'étranger.

oversee [ˌəʊvə'si:] (*pt* -**saw**, *pp* -**seen** ['si:n]) *vt* surveiller.

overseer ['əʊvəˌsi:ə'] *n* contremaître *m*.

overshadow [ˌəʊvə'ʃædəʊ] *vt* [subj : building, tree] dominer ; *fig* éclipser.

overshoot [ˌəʊvə'ʃu:t] (*pt* & *pp* -**shot**) *vt* dépasser, rater.

oversight ['əʊvəsaɪt] *n* oubli *m* ; **through ~** par mégarde.

oversleep [ˌəʊvə'sli:p] (*pt* & *pp* -**slept** [-'slept]) *vi* ne pas se réveiller à temps.

overspill ['əʊvəspɪl] *n* [of population] excédent *m*.

overstep [ˌəʊvə'step] *vt* dépasser ; **to ~ the mark** dépasser la mesure.

overt ['əʊvɜ:t] *adj* déclaré(e), non déguisé(e).

overtake [ˌəʊvə'teɪk] (*pt* -**took**, *pp* -**taken** [-'teɪkn]) ⬦ *vt* - **1.** *Br* AUT doubler, dépasser - **2.** [subj : misfortune, emotion] frapper. ⬦ *vi Br* AUT doubler.

overthrow [*n* 'əʊvəθrəʊ, *vb* ˌəʊvə'θrəʊ] (*pt* -**threw** [-'θru:], *pp* -**thrown** [-'θrəʊn]) ⬦ *n* [of government] coup *m* d'État. ⬦ *vt* [government] renverser.

overtime ['əʊvətaɪm] ⬦ *n* (U) - **1.** [extra work] heures *fpl* supplémentaires - **2.** *Am* SPORT prolongations *fpl*. ⬦ *adv* : **to work ~** faire des heures supplémentaires.

overtones ['əʊvətəʊnz] *npl* notes *fpl*, accents *mpl*.

overtook [ˌəʊvə'tʊk] *pt* ⬅ overtake.

overture ['əʊvəˌtjʊə'] *n* MUS ouverture *f*.

overturn [ˌəʊvə'tɜ:n] ⬦ *vt* - **1.** [gen] renverser - **2.** [decision] annuler. ⬦ *vi* [vehicle] se renverser ; [boat] chavirer.

overweight [ˌəʊvə'weɪt] *adj* trop gros (grosse).

overwhelm [ˌəʊvə'welm] *vt* - **1.** [subj : grief, despair] accabler ; **to be ~ed with joy** être au comble de la joie - **2.** MIL [gain control of] écraser.

overwhelming [ˌəʊvə'welmɪŋ] *adj* - **1.** [overpowering] irrésistible, irrépressible - **2.** [defeat, majority] écrasant(e).

overwork [ˌəʊvə'wɜ:k] ⬦ *n* surmenage *m*. ⬦ *vt* [person, staff] surmener.

overwrought [ˌəʊvə'rɔ:t] *adj* excédé(e), à bout.

owe [əʊ] *vt* : **to ~ sthg to sb, to ~ sb sthg** devoir qqch à qqn.

owing ['əʊɪŋ] *adj* dû (due). ⬥ **owing to** *prep* à cause de, en raison de.

owl [aʊl] *n* hibou *m*.

own [əʊn] ⬦ *adj* propre ; **my ~ car** ma propre voiture ; **she has her ~ style** elle a son style à elle. ⬦ *pron* : **I've got my ~** j'ai le mien ; **he has a house of his ~** il a une maison a lui, il a sa propre maison ; **on one's ~** tout seul (toute seule) ; **to get one's ~ back** *inf* prendre sa revanche. ⬦ *vt* posséder. ⬥ **own up** *vi* : **to ~ up (to sthg)** avouer OR confesser (qqch).

owner ['əʊnə'] *n* propriétaire *mf*.

ownership ['əʊnəʃɪp] *n* propriété *f*.

ox [ɒks] (*pl* **oxen** ['ɒksn]) *n* bœuf *m*.

Oxbridge ['ɒksbrɪdʒ] *n* désignation collective des universités d'Oxford et de Cambridge.

oxen ['ɒksn] *pl* ⬅ ox.

oxtail soup ['ɒksteɪl-] *n* soupe *f* à la queue de bœuf.

oxygen ['ɒksɪdʒən] *n* oxygène *m*.

oxygen mask n masque m à oxygène.

oxygen tent n tente f à oxygène.

oyster ['ɔɪstə'] n huître f.

oz. abbr of **ounce**.

ozone ['əʊzəʊn] n ozone m.

ozone-friendly adj qui préserve la couche d'ozone.

ozone layer n couche f d'ozone.

P

p¹ (pl **p's** OR **ps**), **P** (pl **P's** OR **Ps**) [pi:] n [letter] p m inv, P m inv.

p² - 1. (abbr of **page**) p - 2. abbr of **penny, pence**.

pa [pɑː] n inf esp Am papa m.

p.a. (abbr of **per annum**) p.a.

PA n - 1. abbr of **personal assistant** - 2. (abbr of **public address system**) sono f.

pace [peɪs] <> n - 1. [speed, rate] vitesse f, allure f ; **to keep ~ (with sb)** marcher à la même allure (que qqn) ; **to keep ~ (with sthg)** se maintenir au même niveau (que qqch) - 2. [step] pas m. <> vi : **to ~ (up and down)** faire les cent pas.

pacemaker ['peɪsˌmeɪkə'] n - 1. MED stimulateur m cardiaque, pacemaker m - 2. SPORT meneur m, -euse f.

Pacific [pə'sɪfɪk] <> adj du Pacifique. <> n : **the ~ (Ocean)** l'océan m Pacifique, le Pacifique.

pacifier ['pæsɪfaɪə'] n Am [for child] tétine f, sucette f.

pacifist ['pæsɪfɪst] n pacifiste mf.

pacify ['pæsɪfaɪ] vt - 1. [person, baby] apaiser - 2. [country] pacifier.

pack [pæk] <> n - 1. [bag] sac m - 2. esp Am [packet] paquet m - 3. [of cards] jeu m - 4. [of dogs] meute f ; [of wolves, thieves] bande f. <> vt - 1. [clothes, belongings] emballer ; **to ~ one's bags** faire ses bagages - 2. [fill] remplir ; **to be ~ed into** être entassé dans. <> vi [for journey] faire ses bagages OR sa valise. ◆ **pack in** <> vt sep Br inf [stop] plaquer ; **~ it in!** [stop annoying me] arrête!, ça suffit maintenant! ; [shut up] la ferme! <> vi tomber en panne. ◆ **pack off** vt sep inf [send away] expédier.

package ['pækɪdʒ] <> n - 1. [of books, goods] paquet m - 2. fig [of proposals etc] ensemble m, série f - 3. COMPUT progiciel m. <> vt [wrap up] conditionner.

package deal n contrat m global.

package tour n vacances fpl organisées.

packaging ['pækɪdʒɪŋ] n conditionnement m.

packed [pækt] adj : **~ (with)** bourré(e) (de).

packed lunch n Br panier-repas m.

packet ['pækɪt] n [gen] paquet m.

packing ['pækɪŋ] n [material] emballage m.

packing case n caisse f d'emballage.

pact [pækt] n pacte m.

pad [pæd] <> n - 1. [of cotton wool etc] morceau m - 2. [of paper] bloc m - 3. SPACE : **(launch) ~** pas m de tir - 4. [of cat, dog] coussinet m - 5. inf [home] pénates mpl. <> vt [furniture, jacket] rembourrer ; [wound] tamponner. <> vi [walk softly] marcher à pas feutrés.

padding ['pædɪŋ] n - 1. [material] rembourrage m - 2. fig [in speech, letter] délayage m.

paddle ['pædl] <> n - 1. [for canoe etc] pagaie f - 2. [in sea] : **to have a ~** faire trempette. <> vi - 1. [in canoe etc] avancer en pagayant - 2. [in sea] faire trempette.

paddle boat, paddle steamer n bateau m à aubes.

paddling pool ['pædlɪŋ-] n Br - 1. [in park etc] pataugeoire f - 2. [inflatable] piscine f gonflable.

paddock ['pædək] n - 1. [small field] enclos m - 2. [at racecourse] paddock m.

paddy field ['pædɪ-] n rizière f.

padlock ['pædlɒk] <> n cadenas m. <> vt cadenasser.

paediatrics [ˌpiːdɪ'ætrɪks] = **pediatrics**.

pagan ['peɪgən] <> adj païen(enne). <> n païen m, -enne f.

page [peɪdʒ] <> n - 1. [of book] page f - 2. [sheet of paper] feuille f. <> vt [in airport] appeler au micro.

pageant ['pædʒənt] n [show] spectacle m historique.

pageantry ['pædʒəntrɪ] n apparat m.

paid [peɪd] <> pt & pp ▷ **pay**. <> adj [work, holiday, staff] rémunéré(e), payé(e).

pail [peɪl] n seau m.

pain [peɪn] n - 1. [hurt] douleur f ; **to be in ~** souffrir - 2. inf [annoyance] : **it's/he is such a ~** c'est/il est vraiment assommant. ◆ **pains** npl [effort, care] : **to be at ~s to**

do sthg vouloir absolument faire qqch ; **to take ~s to do sthg** se donner beaucoup de mal OR peine pour faire qqch.

pained [peɪnd] *adj* peiné(e).

painful ['peɪnfʊl] *adj* - **1.** [physically] douloureux(euse) - **2.** [emotionally] pénible.

painfully ['peɪnfʊlɪ] *adv* - **1.** [fall, hit] douloureusement - **2.** [remember, feel] péniblement.

painkiller ['peɪnˌkɪləʳ] *n* calmant *m*, analgésique *m*.

painless ['peɪnlɪs] *adj* - **1.** [without hurt] indolore, sans douleur - **2.** *fig* [changeover] sans heurt.

painstaking ['peɪnzˌteɪkɪŋ] *adj* [worker] assidu(e) ; [detail, work] soigné(e).

paint [peɪnt] <> *n* peinture *f.* <> *vt* [gen] peindre.

paintbrush ['peɪntbrʌʃ] *n* pinceau *m.*

painter ['peɪntəʳ] *n* peintre *m.*

painting ['peɪntɪŋ] *n* - **1.** (U) [gen] peinture *f* - **2.** [picture] toile *f*, tableau *m.*

paint stripper *n* décapant *m.*

paintwork ['peɪntwɜːk] *n* (U) surfaces *fpl* peintes.

pair [peəʳ] *n* - **1.** [of shoes, wings etc] paire *f* ; **a ~ of trousers** un pantalon - **2.** [couple] couple *m.*

pajamas [pəˈdʒɑːməz] *esp Am* = pyjamas.

Pakistan [*Br* ˌpɑːkɪˈstɑːn, *Am* ˌpækɪˈstæn] *n* Pakistan *m.*

Pakistani [*Br* ˌpɑːkɪˈstɑːnɪ, *Am* ˌpækɪˈstænɪ] <> *adj* pakistanais(e). <> *n* Pakistanais *m*, -e *f.*

pal [pæl] *n inf* - **1.** [friend] copain *m*, copine *f* - **2.** [as term of address] mon vieux *m.*

palace ['pælɪs] *n* palais *m.*

palatable ['pælətəbl] *adj* - **1.** [food] agréable au goût - **2.** *fig* [idea] acceptable, agréable.

palate ['pælət] *n* palais *m.*

palaver [pəˈlɑːvəʳ] *n* (U) *inf* - **1.** [talk] palabres *fpl* - **2.** [fuss] histoire *f*, affaire *f.*

pale [peɪl] *adj* pâle.

Palestine ['pæləˌstaɪn] *n* Palestine *f.*

Palestinian [ˌpæləˈstɪnɪən] <> *adj* palestinien(enne). <> *n* Palestinien *m*, -enne *f.*

palette ['pælət] *n* palette *f.*

palings ['peɪlɪŋz] *npl* palissade *f.*

pall [pɔːl] <> *n* - **1.** [of smoke] voile *m* - **2.** *Am* [coffin] cercueil *m.* <> *vi* perdre de son charme.

pallet ['pælɪt] *n* palette *f.*

pallor ['pæləʳ] *n literary* pâleur *f.*

palm [pɑːm] *n* - **1.** [tree] palmier *m* - **2.** [of hand] paume *f.* ◆ **palm off** *vt sep inf* : **~ sthg off on sb** refiler qqch à qqn ; **to ~ sb off with sthg** se débarrasser de qqn avec qqch.

Palm Sunday *n* dimanche *m* des Rameaux.

palmtop *n* COMPUT ordinateur *m* de poche.

palm tree *n* palmier *m.*

palpable ['pælpəbl] *adj* évident(e), manifeste.

paltry ['pɔːltrɪ] *adj* dérisoire.

pamper ['pæmpəʳ] *vt* choyer, dorloter.

pamphlet ['pæmflɪt] *n* brochure *f.*

pan [pæn] <> *n* - **1.** [gen] casserole *f* - **2.** *Am* [for bread, cakes etc] moule *m.* <> *vt inf* [criticize] démolir. <> *vi* CINEMA faire un panoramique.

panacea [ˌpænəˈsɪə] *n* panacée *f.*

panama [ˌpænəˈmɑː] *n* : **~ (hat)** panama *m.*

Panama ['pænəmɑː] *n* Panama *m.*

Panama Canal *n* : **the ~** le canal de Panama.

pancake ['pænkeɪk] *n* crêpe *f.*

Pancake Day *n Br* mardi gras *m.*

Pancake Tuesday *n Br* mardi gras *m.*

panda ['pændə] (*pl inv* OR **-s**) *n* panda *m.*

Panda car *n Br* voiture *f* de patrouille.

pandemonium [ˌpændɪˈməʊnjəm] *n* tohu-bohu *m inv.*

pander ['pændəʳ] *vi* : **to ~ to sb** se prêter aux exigences de qqn ; **to ~ to sthg** se plier à qqch.

pane [peɪn] *n* vitre *f*, carreau *m.*

panel ['pænl] *n* - **1.** TV & RADIO invités *mpl* ; [of experts] comité *m* - **2.** [of wood] panneau *m* - **3.** [of machine] tableau *m* de bord.

panelling *Br*, **paneling** *Am* ['pænəlɪŋ] *n* (U) lambris *m.*

pang [pæŋ] *n* tiraillement *m.*

panic ['pænɪk] (*pt & pp* **-ked**, *cont* **-king**) <> *n* panique *f* <> *vi* paniquer.

panicky ['pænɪkɪ] *adj* [person] paniqué(e) ; [feeling] de panique.

panic-stricken *adj* affolé(e), pris(e) de panique.

panorama [ˌpænəˈrɑːmə] *n* panorama *m.*

pansy ['pænzɪ] *n* [flower] pensée *f.*

pant [pænt] *vi* haleter.

panther ['pænθəʳ] (*pl inv* OR **-s**) *n* panthère *f.*

panties ['pæntɪz] *npl inf* culotte *f*.

pantihose ['pæntɪhəʊz] = **panty hose**.

pantomime ['pæntəmaɪm] *n Br* spectacle de Noël pour enfants, généralement inspiré de contes de fée.

pantry ['pæntrɪ] *n* garde-manger *m inv*.

pants [pænts] *npl* - **1.** *Br* [underpants - for men] slip *m* ; [- for women] culotte *f*, slip - **2.** *Am* [trousers] pantalon *m*.

panty hose ['pæntɪhəʊz] *npl Am* collant *m*.

papa [*Br* pə'pɑː, *Am* 'pæpə] *n* papa *m*.

paper ['peɪpə'] ◇ *n* - **1.** *(U)* [for writing on] papier *m* ; **a piece of ~** [sheet] une feuille de papier ; [scrap] un bout de papier ; **on ~** [written down] par écrit ; [in theory] sur le papier - **2.** [newspaper] journal *m* - **3.** [in exam - test] épreuve *f* ; [- answers] copie *f* - **4.** [essay] : **~ (on)** essai *m* (sur). ◇ *adj* [hat, bag etc] en papier ; *fig* [profits] théorique. ◇ *vt* tapisser. ➡ **papers** *npl* [official documents] papiers *mpl*.

paperback ['peɪpəbæk] *n* : **~ (book)** livre *m* de poche.

paper clip *n* trombone *m*.

paper handkerchief *n* mouchoir *m* en papier.

paper knife *n* coupe-papier *m inv*.

paper shop *n Br* marchand *m* de journaux.

paperweight ['peɪpəweɪt] *n* presse-papiers *m inv*.

paperwork ['peɪpəwɜːk] *n* paperasserie *f*.

paprika ['pæprɪkə] *n* paprika *m*.

par [pɑː'] *n* - **1.** [parity] : **on a ~ with** à égalité avec - **2.** GOLF par *m*, normale *f Can* - **3.** [good health] : **below** OR **under ~** pas en forme.

parable ['pærəbl] *n* parabole *f*.

paracetamol [,pærə'siːtəmɒl] *n* paracétamol *m*.

parachute ['pærəʃuːt] ◇ *n* parachute *m*. ◇ *vi* sauter en parachute.

parade [pə'reɪd] ◇ *n* - **1.** [celebratory] parade *f*, revue *f* - **2.** MIL défilé *m*. ◇ *vt* - **1.** [people] faire défiler - **2.** [object] montrer - **3.** *fig* [flaunt] afficher. ◇ *vi* défiler.

paradise ['pærədaɪs] *n* paradis *m*.

paradox ['pærədɒks] *n* paradoxe *m*.

paradoxically [,pærə'dɒksɪklɪ] *adv* paradoxalement.

paraffin ['pærəfɪn] *n* paraffine *f*.

paragliding ['pærə,glaɪdɪŋ] *n* parapente *m*.

paragon ['pærəgən] *n* modèle *m*, parangon *m*.

paragraph ['pærəgrɑːf] *n* paragraphe *m*.

Paraguay ['pærəgwaɪ] *n* Paraguay *m*.

parallel ['pærəlel] ◇ *adj lit & fig* : **~ (to** OR **with)** parallèle (à). ◇ *n* - **1.** GEOM parallèle *f* - **2.** [similarity & GEOGR] parallèle *m* - **3.** *fig* [similar person, object] équivalent *m*.

paralyse *Br*, **paralyze** *Am* ['pærəlaɪz] *vt lit & fig* paralyser.

paralysis [pə'rælɪsɪs] (*pl* **-lyses** [-lɪsiːz]) *n* paralysie *f*.

paramedic [,pærə'medɪk] *n esp Am* auxiliaire médical *m*, auxiliaire médicale *f*.

parameter [pə'ræmɪtə'] *n* paramètre *m*.

paramount ['pærəmaʊnt] *adj* primordial(e) ; **of ~ importance** d'une importance suprême.

paranoid ['pærənɔɪd] *adj* paranoïaque.

paraphernalia [,pærəfə'neɪljə] *n (U)* attirail *m*, bazar *m*.

parasite ['pærəsaɪt] *n lit & fig* parasite *m*.

parasol ['pærəsɒl] *n* [above table] parasol *m* ; [hand-held] ombrelle *f*.

paratrooper ['pærətruːpə'] *n* parachutiste *mf*.

parcel ['pɑːsl] *n* paquet *m*. ➡ **parcel up** *vt sep* empaqueter.

parched [pɑːtʃt] *adj* - **1.** [gen] desséché(e) - **2.** *inf* [very thirsty] assoiffé(e), mort(e) de soif.

parchment ['pɑːtʃmənt] *n* parchemin *m*.

pardon ['pɑːdn] ◇ *n* - **1.** JUR grâce *f* - **2.** *(U)* [forgiveness] pardon *m* ; **I beg your ~?** [showing surprise, asking for repetition] comment?, pardon? ; **I beg your ~!** [to apologize] je vous demande pardon! ◇ *vt* - **1.** [forgive] pardonner ; **to ~ sb for sthg** pardonner qqch à qqn ; **~ me!** pardon!, excusez-moi! - **2.** JUR gracier. ◇ *excl* comment?

parent ['peərənt] *n* père *m*, mère *f*. ➡ **parents** *npl* parents *mpl*.

parental [pə'rentl] *adj* parental(e).

parenthesis [pə'renθɪsɪs] (*pl* **-theses** [-θɪsiːz]) *n* parenthèse *f*.

Paris ['pærɪs] *n* Paris.

parish ['pærɪʃ] *n* - **1.** RELIG paroisse *f* - **2.** *Br* [area of local government] commune *f*.

Parisian [pə'rɪzjən] ◇ *adj* parisien(enne). ◇ *n* Parisien *m*, -enne *f*.

parity ['pærɪtɪ] *n* égalité *f*.

park [pɑːk] ◇ *n* parc *m*, jardin *m* public. ◇ *vt* garer. ◇ *vi* se garer, stationner.

parking ['pɑːkɪŋ] *n* stationnement *m* ; **'no**

~' 'défense de stationner' , 'stationnement interdit'.

parking lot *n Am* parking *m*.

parking meter *n* parcmètre *m*.

parking ticket *n* contravention *f*, PV *m*.

parlance ['pɑːləns] *n* : **in common/legal** *etc* ~ en langage courant/juridique *etc*.

parliament ['pɑːləmənt] *n* parlement *m*.

parliamentary [,pɑːlə'mentərɪ] *adj* parlementaire.

parlour *Br*, **parlor** *Am* ['pɑːləʳ] *n dated* salon *m*.

parochial [pə'rəʊkjəl] *adj pej* de clocher.

parody ['pærədɪ] ⟨⟩ *n* parodie *f*. ⟨⟩ *vt* parodier.

parole [pə'rəʊl] *n (U)* parole *f* ; **on ~** en liberté conditionnelle.

parrot ['pærət] *n* perroquet *m*.

parry ['pærɪ] *vt* - **1.** [blow] parer - **2.** [question] éluder.

parsley ['pɑːslɪ] *n* persil *m*.

parsnip ['pɑːsnɪp] *n* panais *m*.

parson ['pɑːsn] *n* pasteur *m*.

part [pɑːt] ⟨⟩ *n* - **1.** [gen] partie *f* ; **for the most ~** dans l'ensemble - **2.** [of TV serial etc] épisode *m* - **3.** [component] pièce *f* - **4.** [in proportions] mesure *f* - **5.** THEATRE rôle *m* - **6.** [involvement] : ~ **in** participation *f* à ; **to play an important ~ in** jouer un rôle important dans ; **to take ~ in** participer à ; **for my ~** en ce qui me concerne - **7.** *Am* [hair parting] raie *f*. ⟨⟩ *adv* en partie. ⟨⟩ *vt* : **to ~ one's hair** se faire une raie ⟨⟩ *vi* - **1.** [couple] se séparer - **2.** [curtains] s'écarter, s'ouvrir. ◆ **parts** *npl* : **in these ~s** dans cette région. ◆ **part with** *vt fus* [money] débourser ; [possession] se défaire de.

part exchange *n Br* reprise *f* ; **to take sthg in ~** reprendre qqch.

partial ['pɑːʃl] *adj* - **1.** [incomplete] partiel(elle) - **2.** [biased] partial(e) - **3.** [fond] : **to be ~ to** avoir un penchant pour.

participant [pɑː'tɪsɪpənt] *n* participant *m*, -e *f*.

participate [pɑː'tɪsɪpeɪt] *vi* : **to ~ (in)** participer (à).

participation [pɑː,tɪsɪ'peɪʃn] *n* participation *f*.

participle ['pɑːtɪsɪpl] *n* participe *m*.

particle ['pɑːtɪkl] *n* particule *f*.

parti-coloured ['pɑːtɪ-] *adj* bariolé(e).

particular [pə'tɪkjʊləʳ] *adj* - **1.** [gen] particulier(ère) - **2.** [fussy] pointilleux(euse) ; ~ **about** exigeant(e) à propos de. ◆ **par-**

ticulars *npl* renseignements *mpl*. ◆ **in particular** *adv* en particulier.

particularly [pə'tɪkjʊləlɪ] *adv* particulièrement.

parting ['pɑːtɪŋ] *n* - **1.** [separation] séparation *f* - **2.** *Br* [in hair] raie *f*.

partisan [,pɑːtɪ'zæn] ⟨⟩ *adj* partisan(e). ⟨⟩ *n* partisan *m*, -e *f*.

partition [pɑː'tɪʃn] ⟨⟩ *n* [wall, screen] cloison *f*. ⟨⟩ *vt* - **1.** [room] cloisonner - **2.** [country] partager.

partly ['pɑːtlɪ] *adv* partiellement, en partie.

partner ['pɑːtnəʳ] ⟨⟩ *n* - **1.** [in game dance] partenaire *mf* ; [spouse] conjoint *m*, -e *f* ; [not married] compagnon *m*, compagne *f* - **2.** [in a business, crime] associé *m*, -e *f*. ⟨⟩ *vt* être le partenaire de.

partnership ['pɑːtnəʃɪp] *n* association *f*.

partridge ['pɑːtrɪdʒ] *n* perdrix *f*.

part-time *adj & adv* à temps partiel.

party ['pɑːtɪ] ⟨⟩ *n* - **1.** POL parti *m* - **2.** [social gathering] fête *f*, réception *f* ; **to have** OR **throw a ~** donner une fête - **3.** [group] groupe *m* - **4.** JUR partie *f*. ⟨⟩ *vi inf* faire la fête.

party line *n* - **1.** POL ligne *f* du parti - **2.** TELEC ligne *f* commune à deux abonnés.

pass [pɑːs] ⟨⟩ *n* - **1.** SPORT passe *f* - **2.** [document - for security] laissez-passer *m inv* ; [- for travel] carte *f* d'abonnement - **3.** *Br* [in exam] mention *f* passable - **4.** [between mountains] col *m* - **5.** *phr* : **to make a ~ at sb** faire du plat à qqn. ⟨⟩ *vt* - **1.** [object, time] passer ; **to ~ sthg to sb**, **to ~ sb sthg** passer qqch à qqn - **2.** [person in street etc] croiser - **3.** [place] passer devant - **4.** AUT dépasser, doubler - **5.** [exceed] dépasser - **6.** [exam] réussir (à) ; [driving test] passer - **7.** [candidate] recevoir, admettre - **8.** [law, motion] voter - **9.** [opinion] émettre ; [judgment] rendre, prononcer. ⟨⟩ *vi* - **1.** [gen] passer - **2.** AUT doubler, dépasser - **3.** SPORT faire une passe - **4.** [in exam] réussir, être reçu(e). ◆ **pass as** *vt fus* passer pour. ◆ **pass away** *vi* s'éteindre. ◆ **pass by** ⟨⟩ *vt sep* : **the news ~ed him by** la nouvelle ne l'a pas affecté. ⟨⟩ *vi* passer à côté. ◆ **pass for** = **pass as.** ◆ **pass on** ⟨⟩ *vt sep* : **to ~ sthg on (to)** [object] faire passer qqch (à) ; [tradition, information] transmettre qqch (à). ⟨⟩ *vi* - **1.** [move on] continuer son chemin - **2.** = **pass away.** ◆ **pass out** *vi* - **1.** [faint] s'évanouir - **2.** *Br* MIL finir OR terminer les classes. ◆ **pass over** *vt fus* [problem, topic] passer sous silence. ◆ **pass up** *vt sep* [opportunity, invitation] laisser passer.

passable ['pɑːsəbl] *adj* - **1.** [satisfactory]

passable - **2.** [road] praticable ; [river] franchissable.

passage ['pæsɪdʒ] *n* - **1.** [gen] passage *m* - **2.** [between rooms] couloir *m* - **3.** [sea journey] traversée *f*.

passageway ['pæsɪdʒweɪ] *n* [between houses] passage *m* ; [between rooms] couloir *m*.

passbook ['pɑːsbʊk] *n* livret *m* (d'épargne).

passenger ['pæsɪndʒəʳ] *n* passager *m*, -ère *f*.

passerby [,pɑːsə'baɪ] (*pl* passersby [,pɑːsəz'baɪ]) *n* passant *m*, -e *f*.

passing ['pɑːsɪŋ] *adj* [remark] en passant ; [trend] passager(ère). ✦ **in passing** *adv* en passant.

passion ['pæʃn] *n* passion *f*.

passionate ['pæʃənət] *adj* passionné(e).

passive ['pæsɪv] *adj* passif(ive).

Passover ['pɑːs,əʊvəʳ] *n* : (the) ~ la Pâque juive.

passport ['pɑːspɔːt] *n* [document] passeport *m*.

passport control *n* contrôle *m* des passeports.

password ['pɑːswɜːd] *n* mot *m* de passe.

past [pɑːst] ◇ *adj* - **1.** [former] passé(e) ; **for the ~ five years** ces cinq dernières années ; **the ~ week** la semaine passée OR dernière - **2.** [finished] fini(e). ◇ *adv* - **1.** [in times] : **it's ten ~** il est dix - **2.** [in front] : **to drive ~** passer (devant) en voiture ; **to run ~** passer (devant) en courant. ◇ *n* passé *m* ; **in the ~** dans le temps. ◇ *prep* - **1.** [in times] : **it's half ~ eight** il est huit heures et demie ; **it's five ~ nine** il est neuf heures cinq - **2.** [in front of] devant ; **we drove ~ them** nous les avons dépassés en voiture - **3.** [beyond] après, au-delà de.

pasta ['pæstə] *n* (*U*) pâtes *fpl*.

paste [peɪst] ◇ *n* - **1.** [gen] pâte *f* - **2.** CULIN pâté *m* - **3.** (*U*) [glue] colle *f*. ◇ *vt* coller.

pastel ['pæstl] ◇ *adj* pastel (*inv*). ◇ *n* pastel *m*.

pasteurize, -ise ['pɑːstʃəraɪz] *vt* pasteuriser.

pastille ['pæstɪl] *n* pastille *f*.

pastime ['pɑːstaɪm] *n* passe-temps *m inv*.

pastor ['pɑːstəʳ] *n* pasteur *m*.

past participle *n* participe *m* passé.

pastry ['peɪstrɪ] *n* - **1.** [mixture] pâte *f* - **2.** [cake] pâtisserie *f*.

past tense *n* passé *m*.

pasture ['pɑːstʃəʳ] *n* pâturage *m*, pré *m*.

pasty¹ ['peɪstɪ] *adj* blafard(e), terreux (euse).

pasty² ['pæstɪ] *n Br* petit pâté *m*, friand *m*.

pat [pæt] ◇ *n* - **1.** [light stroke] petite tape *f* ; [to animal] caresse *f* - **2.** [of butter] noix *f*, noisette *f*. ◇ *vt* [person] tapoter, donner une tape à ; [animal] caresser.

patch [pætʃ] ◇ *n* - **1.** [piece of material] pièce *f* ; [to cover eye] bandeau *m* - **2.** [small area - of snow, ice] plaque *f* - **3.** [of land] parcelle *f*, lopin *m* ; **vegetable ~** carré *m* de légumes - **4.** MED patch *m* - **5.** [period of time] : **a difficult ~** une mauvaise passe. ◇ *vt* rapiécer. ✦ **patch up** *vt sep* - **1.** [mend] rafistoler, bricoler - **2.** *fig* [quarrel] régler, arranger ; **to ~ up a relationship** se raccommoder.

patchwork ['pætʃwɜːk] *n* patchwork *m*.

patchy ['pætʃɪ] *adj* [gen] inégal(e) ; [knowledge] insuffisant(e), imparfait(e).

pâté ['pæteɪ] *n* pâté *m*.

patent [*Br* 'peɪtənt, *Am* 'pætənt] ◇ *adj* [obvious] évident(e), manifeste. ◇ *n* brevet *m* (d'invention). ◇ *vt* faire breveter.

patent leather *n* cuir *m* verni.

paternal [pə'tɜːnl] *adj* paternel(elle).

path [pɑːθ, *pl* pɑːðz] *n* - **1.** [track] chemin *m*, sentier *m* - **2.** [way ahead, course of action] voie *f*, chemin *m* - **3.** [trajectory] trajectoire *f*.

pathetic [pə'θetɪk] *adj* - **1.** [causing pity] pitoyable, attendrissant(e) - **2.** [useless - efforts, person] pitoyable, minable.

pathological [,pæθə'lɒdʒɪkl] *adj* pathologique.

pathology [pə'θɒlədʒɪ] *n* pathologie *f*.

pathos ['peɪθɒs] *n* pathétique *m*.

pathway ['pɑːθweɪ] *n* chemin *m*, sentier *m*.

patience ['peɪʃns] *n* - **1.** [of person] patience *f* - **2.** *Br* [card game] réussite *f*.

patient ['peɪʃnt] ◇ *adj* patient(e). ◇ *n* [in hospital] patient *m*, -e *f*, malade *mf* ; [of doctor] patient.

patio ['pætɪəʊ] (*pl* -s) *n* patio *m*.

patriotic [*Br* ,pætrɪ'ɒtɪk, *Am* ,peɪtrɪ'ɒtɪk] *adj* [gen] patriotique ; [person] patriote.

patrol [pə'trəʊl] ◇ *n* patrouille *f*. ◇ *vt* patrouiller dans, faire une patrouille dans.

patrol car *n* voiture *f* de police.

patrolman [pə'trəʊlmən] (*pl* -men [-mən]) *n Am* agent *m* de police.

patron ['peɪtrən] *n* - **1.** [of arts] mécène *m*, protecteur *m*, -trice *f* - **2.** *Br* [of charity] patron *m*, -onne *f* - **3.** *fml* [customer] client *m*, -e *f*.

patronize, -ise ['pætrənaɪz] *vt* - **1.** [talk down to] traiter avec condescendance - **2.** *fml* [back financially] patronner, protéger.

patronizing ['pætrənaɪzɪŋ] *adj* condescendant(e).

patter ['pætə'] ⬦ *n* - **1.** [sound - of rain] crépitement *m* - **2.** [talk] baratin *m*, bavardage *m*. ⬦ *vi* [feet, paws] trottiner ; [rain] frapper, fouetter.

pattern ['pætən] *n* - **1.** [design] motif *m*, dessin *m* - **2.** [of distribution, population] schéma *m* ; [of life, behaviour] mode *m* - **3.** [diagram] : **(sewing)** ~ patron *m* - **4.** [model] modèle *m*.

paunch [pɔːntʃ] *n* bedaine *f*.

pauper ['pɔːpə'] *n* indigent *m*, -e *f*, nécessiteux *m*, -euse *f*.

pause [pɔːz] ⬦ *n* - **1.** [short silence] pause *f*, silence *m* - **2.** [break] pause *f*, arrêt *m*. ⬦ *vi* - **1.** [stop speaking] marquer un temps - **2.** [stop moving, doing] faire une pause, s'arrêter.

pave [peɪv] *vt* paver ; **to ~ the way for sb/ sthg** ouvrir la voie à qqn/qqch.

pavement ['peɪvmənt] *n* - **1.** *Br* [at side of road] trottoir *m* - **2.** *Am* [roadway] chaussée *f*.

pavilion [pə'vɪljən] *n* pavillon *m*.

paving ['peɪvɪŋ] *n* (*U*) pavé *m*.

paving stone *n* pavé *m*.

paw [pɔː] *n* patte *f*.

pawn [pɔːn] ⬦ *n lit & fig* pion *m*. ⬦ *vt* mettre en gage.

pawnbroker ['pɔːn,brəʊkə'] *n* prêteur *m*, -euse *f* sur gages.

pawnshop ['pɔːnʃɒp] *n* boutique *f* de prêteur sur gages.

pay [peɪ] (*pt & pp* **paid**) ⬦ *vt* - **1.** [gen] payer ; **to ~ sb for sthg** payer qqn pour qqch, payer qqch à qqn ; **I paid £20 for that shirt** j'ai payé cette chemise 20 livres ; **to ~ money into an account** *Br* verser de l'argent sur un compte ; **to a cheque into an account** déposer un chèque sur un compte - **2.** [be profitable to] rapporter à - **3.** [give, make] : **to ~ attention (to sb/sthg)** prêter attention (à qqn/qqch) ; **to ~ sb a compliment** faire un compliment à qqn ; **to ~ sb a visit** rendre visite à qqn. ⬦ *vi* payer ; **to ~ dearly for sthg** *fig* payer qqch cher. ⬦ *n* salaire *m*, traitement *m*. ➡ **pay back** *vt sep* - **1.** [return loan of money] rembourser - **2.** [revenge oneself on] revaloir ; **I'll ~ you back for that** tu me le paieras, je te le revaudrai. ➡ **pay off** ⬦ *vt sep* - **1.** [repay - debt] s'acquitter de, régler ; [- loan] rembourser - **2.** [dismiss] licencier, congédier - **3.** [bribe] soudoyer, acheter. ⬦ *vi* [course of action] être payant(e). ➡ **pay up** *vi* payer.

payable ['peɪəbl] *adj* - **1.** [gen] payable - **2.** [on cheque] : **~ to** à l'ordre de.

paycheck ['peɪtʃek] *n Am* paie *f*.

payday ['peɪdeɪ] *n* jour *m* de paie.

payee [peɪ'iː] *n* bénéficiaire *mf*.

pay envelope *n Am* salaire *m*.

payment ['peɪmənt] *n* paiement *m*.

pay packet *n Br* - **1.** [envelope] enveloppe *f* de paie - **2.** [wages] paie *f*.

pay phone, pay station *Am n* téléphone *m* public, cabine *f* téléphonique.

payroll ['peɪrəʊl] *n* registre *m* du personnel.

payslip ['peɪslɪp] *n Br* feuille *f* OR bulletin *m* de paie.

pay station *Am* = **pay phone**.

pc (*abbr of* **per cent**) p. cent.

PC *n* - **1.** (*abbr of* **personal computer**) PC *m*, micro *m* - **2.** *Br abbr of* **police constable**.

PE (*abbr of* **physical education**) *n* EPS *f*.

pea [piː] *n* pois *m*.

peace [piːs] *n* (*U*) paix *f* ; [quiet, calm] calme *m*, tranquillité *f* ; **to make (one's) ~ with sb** faire la paix avec qqn.

peaceable ['piːsəbl] *adj* paisible, pacifique.

peaceful ['piːsfʊl] *adj* - **1.** [quiet, calm] paisible, calme - **2.** [not aggressive - person] pacifique ; [- demonstration] non-violent(e).

peacetime ['piːstaɪm] *n* temps *m* de paix.

peach [piːtʃ] ⬦ *adj* couleur pêche (*inv*). ⬦ *n* pêche *f*.

peacock ['piːkɒk] *n* paon *m*.

peak [piːk] ⬦ *n* - **1.** [mountain top] sommet *m*, cime *f* - **2.** *fig* [of career, success] apogée *m*, sommet *m* - **3.** [of cap] visière *f*. ⬦ *adj* [condition] optimum. ⬦ *vi* atteindre un niveau maximum.

peaked [piːkt] *adj* [cap] à visière.

peak hours *npl* heures *fpl* d'affluence OR de pointe.

peak period *n* période *f* de pointe.

peak rate *n* tarif *m* normal.

peal [piːl] ⬦ *n* [of bells] carillonnement *m* ; [of laughter] éclat *m* ; [of thunder] coup *m*. ⬦ *vi* [bells] carillonner.

peanut ['piːnʌt] *n* cacahuète *f*.

peanut butter *n* beurre *m* de cacahuètes.

pear [peə^r] *n* poire *f*.

pearl [pɜːl] *n* perle *f*.

peasant ['peznt] *n* [in countryside] paysan *m*, -anne *f*.

peat [piːt] *n* tourbe *f*.

pebble ['pebl] *n* galet *m*, caillou *m*.

peck [pek] ◇ *n* - **1.** [with beak] coup *m* de bec - **2.** *inf* [kiss] bise *f*. ◇ *vt* - **1.** [with beak] picoter, becqueter - **2.** *inf* [kiss] : **to ~ sb on the cheek** faire une bise à qqn.

pecking order ['pekɪŋ-] *n* hiérarchie *f*.

peckish ['pekɪʃ] *adj Br inf*: **to feel ~** avoir un petit creux.

peculiar [pɪ'kjuːljə^r] *adj* - **1.** [odd] bizarre, curieux(euse) - **2.** [slightly ill] : **to feel ~** se sentir tout drôle (toute drôle) OR tout chose (toute chose) - **3.** [characteristic] : **~ to** propre à, particulier(ère) à.

peculiarity [pɪˌkjuːlɪ'ærətɪ] *n* - **1.** [oddness] bizarrerie *f*, singularité *f* - **2.** [characteristic] particularité *f*, caractéristique *f*.

pedal ['pedl] ◇ *n* pédale *f*. ◇ *vi* pédaler.

pedal bin *n Br* poubelle *f* à pédale.

pedantic [pɪ'dæntɪk] *adj pej* pédant(e).

peddle ['pedl] *vt* - **1.** [drugs] faire le trafic de - **2.** [gossip, rumour] colporter, répandre.

pedestal ['pedɪstl] *n* piédestal *m*.

pedestrian [pɪ'destrɪən] ◇ *adj pej* médiocre, dépourvu(e) d'intérêt. ◇ *n* piéton *m*.

pedestrian crossing *n Br* passage *m* pour piétons, passage clouté.

pedestrian precinct *Br*, **pedestrian zone** *Am n* zone *f* piétonne.

pediatrics [ˌpiːdɪ'ætrɪks] *n* pédiatrie *f*.

pedigree ['pedɪgriː] ◇ *adj* [animal] de race. ◇ *n* - **1.** [of animal] pedigree *m* - **2.** [of person] ascendance *f*, généalogie *f*.

pedlar *Br*, **peddler** *Am* ['pedlə^r] *n* colporteur *m*.

pee [piː] *inf* ◇ *n* pipi *m*, pisse *f*. ◇ *vi* faire pipi, pisser.

peek [piːk] *inf* ◇ *n* coup *m* d'œil furtif. ◇ *vi* jeter un coup d'œil furtif.

peel [piːl] ◇ *n* [of apple, potato] peau *f*; [of orange, lemon] écorce *f*. ◇ *vt* éplucher, peler. ◇ *vi* - **1.** [paint] s'écailler - **2.** [wallpaper] se décoller - **3.** [skin] peler.

peelings ['piːlɪŋz] *npl* épluchures *fpl*.

peep [piːp] ◇ *n* - **1.** [look] coup *m* d'œil OR regard *m* furtif - **2.** *inf* [sound] bruit *m*. ◇ *vi* jeter un coup d'œil furtif. ◆ **peep out** *vi* apparaître, se montrer.

peephole ['piːphəʊl] *n* judas *m*.

peer [pɪə^r] ◇ *n* pair *m*. ◇ *vi* scruter, regarder attentivement.

peerage ['pɪərɪdʒ] *n* [rank] pairie *f*; **the ~** les pairs *mpl*.

peer group *n* pairs *mpl*.

peeved [piːvd] *adj inf* fâché(e), irrité(e).

peevish ['piːvɪʃ] *adj* grincheux(euse).

peg [peg] ◇ *n* - **1.** [hook] cheville *f* - **2.** *Br* [for clothes] pince *f* à linge - **3.** [for tent] piquet *m*. ◇ *vt fig* [prices] bloquer.

pejorative [pɪ'dʒɒrətɪv] *adj* péjoratif(ive).

pekinese [ˌpiːkə'niːz], **pekingese** [ˌpiːkɪŋ'iːz] (*pl inv*) *n* [dog] pékinois *m*.

Peking [piː'kɪŋ] *n* Pékin.

pekingese = **pekinese**.

pelican ['pelɪkən] (*pl inv* OR **-s**) *n* pélican *m*.

pelican crossing *n Br* passage pour piétons avec feux de circulation.

pellet ['pelɪt] *n* - **1.** [small ball] boulette *f* - **2.** [for gun] plomb *m*.

pelmet ['pelmɪt] *n Br* lambrequin *m*.

pelt [pelt] ◇ *n* [animal skin] peau *f*, fourrure *f*. ◇ *vt*: **to ~ sb (with sthg)** bombarder qqn (de qqch). ◇ *vi* [run fast]: **to ~ along** courir ventre à terre ; **to ~ down the stairs** dévaler l'escalier. ◆ **pelt down** *v impers* [rain]: **it's ~ing down** il pleut à verse.

pelvis ['pelvɪs] (*pl* **-vises** OR **-ves** [-viːz]) *n* pelvis *m*, bassin *m*.

pen [pen] ◇ *n* - **1.** [for writing] stylo *m* - **2.** [enclosure] parc *m*, enclos *m*. ◇ *vt* [enclose] parquer.

penal ['piːnl] *adj* pénal(e).

penalize, **-ise** ['piːnəlaɪz] *vt* - **1.** [gen] pénaliser - **2.** [put at a disadvantage] désavantager.

penalty ['penltɪ] *n* - **1.** [punishment] pénalité *f*; **to pay the ~ (for sthg)** *fig* supporter OR subir les conséquences (de qqch) - **2.** [fine] amende *f* - **3.** HOCKEY pénalité *f*; **~ (kick)** FTBL penalty *m* ; RUGBY (coup *m* de pied de) pénalité *f*.

penance ['penəns] *n* - **1.** RELIG pénitence *f* - **2.** *fig* [punishment] corvée *f*, pensum *m*.

pence [pens] *Br pl* ▷ **penny**.

penchant [*Br* pɑ̃ʃɑ̃, *Am* 'pentʃənt] *n*: **to have a ~ for sthg** avoir un faible pour qqch ; **to have a ~ for doing sthg** avoir tendance à OR bien aimer faire qqch.

pencil ['pensl] ◇ *n* crayon *m* ; **in ~** au crayon. ◇ *vt* griffonner au crayon, crayonner.

pencil case *n* trousse *f* (d'écolier).

pencil sharpener *n* taille-crayon *m*.

pendant ['pendənt] *n* [jewel on chain] pendentif *m*.

pending ['pendɪŋ] *fml* ◇ *adj* - **1.** [imminent] imminent(e) - **2.** [court case] en instance. ◇ *prep* en attendant.

pendulum ['pendjʊləm] (*pl* -**s**) *n* balancier *m*.

penetrate ['penɪtreɪt] *vt* - **1.** [gen] pénétrer dans ; [subj : light] percer ; [subj : rain] s'infiltrer dans - **2.** [subj : spy] infiltrer.

pen friend *n Br* correspondant·m, -e *f*.

penguin ['peŋgwɪn] *n* manchot *m*.

penicillin [ˌpenɪ'sɪlɪn] *n* pénicilline *f*.

peninsula [pə'nɪnsjʊlə] (*pl* -**s**) *n* péninsule *f*.

penis ['piːnɪs] (*pl* penises [-ɪz]) *n* pénis *m*.

penitentiary [ˌpenɪ'tenʃərɪ] *n Am* prison *f*.

penknife ['pennaɪf] (*pl* -**knives** [-naɪvz]) *n* canif *m*.

pen name *n* pseudonyme *m*.

pennant ['penənt] *n* fanion *m*, flamme *f*.

penniless ['penɪlɪs] *adj* sans le sou.

penny ['penɪ] (*pl sense 1* -**ies**, *pl sense 2* **pence** [pens]) *n* - **1.** [coin] *Br* penny *m* ; *Am* cent *m* - **2.** [value] pence *m*.

pen pal *n inf* correspondant *m*, -e *f*.

pension ['penʃn] *n* - **1.** *Br* [on retirement] retraite *f* - **2.** [from disability] pension *f*.

pensioner ['penʃənə'] *n Br* : **(old-age)** ~ retraité *m*, -e *f*.

pensive ['pensɪv] *adj* songeur(euse).

pentagon ['pentəgən] *n* pentagone *m*.
◆ **Pentagon** *n Am* : **the Pentagon** le Pentagone *(siège du ministère américain de la Défense).*

Pentecost ['pentɪkɒst] *n* Pentecôte *f*

penthouse ['penthaʊs, *pl* -haʊzɪz] *n* appartement *m* de luxe (au dernier étage).

pent up ['pent-] *adj* [emotions] refoulé(e) ; [energy] contenu(e).

penultimate [pe'nʌltɪmət] *adj* avant-dernier(ère).

people ['piːpl] ◇ *n* [nation, race] nation *f*, peuple *m*. ◇ *npl* - **1.** [persons] personnes *fpl* ; few/a lot of ~ peu/beaucoup de monde, des beaucoup de gens ; **there were a lot of ~ present** il y avait beaucoup de monde - **2.** [in general] gens *mpl* ; ~ **say that** ... on dit que ... - **3.** [inhabitants] habitants *mpl* - **4.** POL : **the ~ le** peuple. ◇ *vt* : **to be ~d by** OR **with** être peuplé(e) de.

people carrier *n* monospace *m*.

pep [pep] *n inf (U)* entrain *m*, pep *m*.

◆ **pep up** *vt sep inf* - **1.** [person] remonter, requinquer - **2.** [party, event] animer.

pepper ['pepə'] *n* - **1.** [spice] poivre *m* - **2.** [vegetable] poivron *m*.

pepperbox *n Am* = pepper pot.

peppermint ['pepəmɪnt] *n* - **1.** [sweet] bonbon *m* à la menthe - **2.** [herb] menthe *f* poivrée.

pepper pot *Br*, **pepperbox** *Am* ['pepəbɒks] *n* poivrier *m*.

pep talk *n inf* paroles *fpl* OR discours *m* d'encouragement.

per [pɜːʳ] *prep* : ~ **person** par personne ; **to be paid £10 ~ hour** être payé 10 livres de l'heure ; ~ **kilo** le kilo ; **as ~ instructions** conformément aux instructions.

per annum *adv* par an.

per capita [pə'kæpɪtə] *adj & adv* par habitant OR tête.

perceive [pə'siːv] *vt* - **1.** [notice] percevoir - **2.** [understand, realize] remarquer, s'apercevoir de - **3.** [consider] : **to ~ sb/sthg as** considérer qqn/qqch comme.

percent *adv* pour cent.

percentage [pə'sentɪdʒ] *n* pourcentage *m*.

perception [pə'sepʃn] *n* - **1.** [aural, visual] perception *f* - **2.** [insight] perspicacité *f*, intuition *f*.

perceptive [pə'septɪv] *adj* perspicace.

perch [pɜːtʃ] (*pl sense 2 only, inv* OR -**es**) ◇ *n* - **1.** *lit & fig* [position] perchoir *m* - **2.** [fish] perche *f*. ◇ *vi* se percher.

percolator ['pɜːkəleɪtə'] *n* cafetière *f* à pression.

percussion [pə'kʌʃn] *n* MUS percussion *f*.

perennial [pə'renjəl] ◇ *adj* permanent(e), perpétuel(elle) ; BOT vivace. ◇ *n* BOT plante *f* vivace.

perfect [*adj & n* 'pɜːfɪkt, *vb* pə'fekt] ◇ *adj* parfait(e) ; **he's a ~ nuisance** il est absolument insupportable. ◇ *n* GRAMM : ~ **(tense)** parfait *m*. ◇ *vt* parfaire, mettre au point.

perfection [pə'fekʃn] *n* perfection *f* ; **to ~** parfaitement (bien).

perfectionist [pə'fekʃənɪst] *n* perfectionniste *mf*.

perfectly ['pɜːfɪktlɪ] *adv* parfaitement ; **you know ~ well** tu sais très bien.

perforate ['pɜːfəreɪt] *vt* perforer.

perforations [ˌpɜːfə'reɪʃnz] *npl* [in paper] pointillés *mpl*.

perform [pə'fɔːm] ◇ *vt* - **1.** [carry out - gen] exécuter ; [- function] remplir

- **2.** [play, concert] jouer. <> *vi* - **1.** [machine] marcher, fonctionner ; [team, person] : **to ~ well/badly** avoir de bons/mauvais résultats - **2.** [actor] jouer ; [singer] chanter.

performance [pə'fɔːməns] *n* - **1.** [carrying out] exécution *f* - **2.** [show] représentation *f* - **3.** [by actor, singer etc] interprétation *f* - **4.** [of car, engine] performance *f*.

performer [pə'fɔːməʳ] *n* artiste *mf*, interprète *mf*.

perfume ['pɜːfjuːm] *n* parfum *m*.

perfunctory [pə'fʌŋktərɪ] *adj* rapide, superficiel(elle).

perhaps [pə'hæps] *adv* peut-être ; **~ so/not** peut-être que oui/non.

peril ['perɪl] *n* danger *m*, péril *m*.

perimeter [pə'rɪmɪtəʳ] *n* périmètre *m* ; **~ fence** clôture *f* ; **~ wall** mur *m* d'enceinte.

period ['pɪərɪəd] <> *n* - **1.** [gen] période *f* - **2.** SCH ≃ heure *f* - **3.** [menstruation] règles *fpl* - **4.** *Am* [full stop] point *m*. <> *comp* [dress, house] d'époque.

periodic [ˌpɪərɪ'ɒdɪk] *adj* périodique.

periodical [ˌpɪərɪ'ɒdɪkl] <> *adj* = **periodic**. <> *n* [magazine] périodique *m*.

peripheral [pə'rɪfərəl] <> *adj* - **1.** [unimportant] secondaire - **2.** [at edge] périphérique. <> *n* COMPUT périphérique *m*.

perish ['perɪʃ] *vi* - **1.** [die] périr, mourir - **2.** [food] pourrir, se gâter ; [rubber] se détériorer.

perishable ['perɪʃəbl] *adj* périssable.
➡ **perishables** *npl* denrées *fpl* périssables.

perjury ['pɜːdʒərɪ] *n* (U) JUR parjure *m*, faux serment *m*.

perk [pɜːk] *n inf* à-côté *m*, avantage *m*.
➡ **perk up** *vi* se ragaillardir.

perky ['pɜːkɪ] *adj inf* [cheerful] guilleret (ette) ; [lively] plein(e) d'entrain.

perm [pɜːm] *n* permanente *f*.

permanent ['pɜːmənənt] <> *adj* permanent(e). <> *n Am* [perm] permanente *f*.

permeate ['pɜːmɪeɪt] *vt* - **1.** [subj : liquid, smell] s'infiltrer dans, pénétrer - **2.** [subj : feeling, idea] se répandre dans.

permissible [pə'mɪsəbl] *adj* acceptable, admissible.

permission [pə'mɪʃn] *n* permission *f*, autorisation *f*.

permissive [pə'mɪsɪv] *adj* permissif(ive).

permit [*vb* pə'mɪt, *n* 'pɜːmɪt] <> *vt* permettre ; **to ~ sb to do sthg** permettre à qqn de faire qqch, autoriser qqn à faire qqch ;

to ~ sb sthg permettre qqch à qqn. <> *n* permis *m*.

pernicious [pə'nɪʃəs] *adj fml* [harmful] pernicieux(euse).

pernickety [pə'nɪkətɪ] *adj inf* [fussy] tatillon(onne), pointilleux(euse).

perpendicular [ˌpɜːpən'dɪkjʊləʳ] <> *adj* perpendiculaire. <> *n* perpendiculaire *f*.

perpetrate ['pɜːpɪtreɪt] *vt* perpétrer, commettre.

perpetual [pə'petʃʊəl] *adj* - **1.** *pej* [continuous] continuel(elle), incessant(e) - **2.** [long-lasting] perpétuel(elle).

perplex [pə'pleks] *vt* rendre perplexe.

perplexing [pə'pleksɪŋ] *adj* déroutant(e), déconcertant(e).

persecute ['pɜːsɪkjuːt] *vt* persécuter, tourmenter.

perseverance [ˌpɜːsɪ'vɪərəns] *n* persévérance *f*, ténacité *f*.

persevere [ˌpɜːsɪ'vɪəʳ] *vi* - **1.** [with difficulty] persévérer, persister ; **to ~ with** persévérer OR persister dans - **2.** [with determination] : **to ~ in doing sthg** persister à faire qqch.

Persian ['pɜːʃn] *adj* persan(e) ; HIST perse.

persist [pə'sɪst] *vi* : **to ~ (in doing sthg)** persister OR s'obstiner (à faire qqch).

persistence [pə'sɪstəns] *n* persistance *f*.

persistent [pə'sɪstənt] *adj* - **1.** [noise, rain] continuel(elle) ; [problem] constant(e) - **2.** [determined] tenace, obstiné(e).

person ['pɜːsn] (*pl* **people** ['piːpl], **persons** *fml*) *n* - **1.** [man or woman] personne *f* ; **in ~** en personne - **2.** *fml* [body] : **about one's ~** sur soi.

personable ['pɜːsnəbl] *adj* sympathique, agréable.

personal ['pɜːsənl] *adj* - **1.** [gen] personnel(elle) - **2.** *pej* [rude] désobligeant(e).

personal assistant *n* secrétaire *mf* de direction.

personal column *n* petites annonces *fpl*.

personal computer *n* ordinateur *m* personnel OR individuel.

personality [ˌpɜːsə'nælətɪ] *n* personnalité *f*.

personally ['pɜːsnəlɪ] *adv* personnellement ; **to take sthg ~** se sentir visé par qqch.

personal organizer *n* organiseur *m*.

personal property *n* (U) JUR biens *mpl* personnels.

personal stereo *n* baladeur *m*, Walkman® *m*.

personify [pə'sɒnɪfaɪ] *vt* personnifier.

personnel [,pɜːsə'nel] ⬦ *n (U)* [department] service *m* du personnel. ⬦ *npl* [staff] personnel *m*.

perspective [pə'spektɪv] *n* - **1.** ART perspective *f* - **2.** [view, judgment] point *m* de vue, optique *f*.

Perspex® ['pɜːspeks] *n Br* ≃ Plexiglas® *m*.

perspiration [,pɜːspə'reɪʃn] *n* - **1.** [sweat] sueur *f* - **2.** [act of perspiring] transpiration *f*.

persuade [pə'sweɪd] *vt* **: to ~ sb to do sthg** persuader OR convaincre qqn de faire qqch ; **to ~ sb that** convaincre qqn que ; **to ~ sb of** convaincre qqn de.

persuasion [pə'sweɪʒn] *n* - **1.** [act of persuading] persuasion *f* - **2.** [belief - religious] confession *f* ; [- political] opinion *f*, conviction *f*.

persuasive [pə'sweɪsɪv] *adj* [person] persuasif(ive) ; [argument] convaincant(e).

pert [pɜːt] *adj* mutin(e), coquin(e).

pertain [pə'teɪn] *vi fml* **: ~ing to** concernant, relatif(ive) à.

pertinent ['pɜːtɪnənt] *adj* pertinent(e), approprié(e).

perturb [pə'tɜːb] *vt* inquiéter, troubler.

Peru [pə'ruː] *n* Pérou *m*.

peruse [pə'ruːz] *vt* lire attentivement.

pervade [pə'veɪd] *vt* [subj : smell] se répandre dans ; [subj : feeling, influence] envahir.

perverse [pə'vɜːs] *adj* [contrary - person] contrariant(e) ; [enjoyment] malin(igne).

perversion [*Br* pə'vɜːʃn, *Am* pə'vɜːrʒn] *n* - **1.** [sexual] perversion *f* - **2.** [of truth] travestissement *m*.

pervert [*n* 'pɜːvɜːt, *vb* pə'vɜːt] ⬦ *n* pervers *m*, -e *f*. ⬦ *vt* - **1.** [truth, meaning] travestir, déformer ; [course of justice] entraver - **2.** [sexually] pervertir.

pessimist ['pesɪmɪst] *n* pessimiste *mf*.

pessimistic [,pesɪ'mɪstɪk] *adj* pessimiste.

pest [pest] *n* - **1.** [insect] insecte *m* nuisible ; [animal] animal *m* nuisible - **2.** *inf* [nuisance] casse-pieds *mf inv*.

pester ['pestər] *vt* harceler, importuner.

pet [pet] ⬦ *adj* [favourite] **: ~ subject** dada *m* ; **~ hate** bête *f* noire. ⬦ *n* - **1.** [animal] animal *m* (familier) - **2.** [favourite person] chouchou *m*, -oute *f*. ⬦ *vt* caresser, câliner. ⬦ *vi* se peloter, se caresser.

petal ['petl] *n* pétale *m*.

peter ['piːtər] ➤ **peter out** *vi* [path] s'arrêter, se perdre ; [interest] diminuer, décliner.

petite [pə'tiːt] *adj* menu(e).

petition [pɪ'tɪʃn] ⬦ *n* pétition *f*. ⬦ *vt* adresser une pétition à.

petrified ['petrɪfaɪd] *adj* [terrified] paralysé(e) OR pétrifié(e) de peur.

petrol ['petrəl] *n Br* essence *f*.

petrol bomb *n Br* cocktail *m* Molotov.

petrol can *n Br* bidon *m* à essence.

petroleum [pɪ'trəʊljəm] *n* pétrole *m*.

petrol pump *n Br* pompe *f* à essence.

petrol station *n Br* station-service *f*.

petrol tank *n Br* réservoir *m* d'essence.

pet shop *n* animalerie *f*.

petticoat ['petɪkəʊt] *n* jupon *m*.

petty ['petɪ] *adj* - **1.** [small-minded] mesquin(e) - **2.** [trivial] insignifiant(e), sans importance.

petty cash *n (U)* caisse *f* des dépenses courantes.

petty officer *n* second maître *m*.

petulant ['petjʊlənt] *adj* irritable.

pew [pjuː] *n* banc *m* d'église.

pewter ['pjuːtər] *n* étain *m*.

phantom ['fæntəm] ⬦ *adj* fantomatique, spectral(e). ⬦ *n* [ghost] fantôme *m*.

pharmaceutical [,faːmə'sjuːtɪkl] *adj* pharmaceutique.

pharmacist ['faːməsɪst] *n* pharmacien *m*, -enne *f*.

pharmacy ['faːməsɪ] *n* pharmacie *f*.

phase [feɪz] *n* phase *f*. ➤ **phase in** *vt sep* introduire progressivement. ➤ **phase out** *vt sep* supprimer progressivement.

PhD (*abbr of* **Doctor of Philosophy**) *n* (*titulaire d'un*) doctorat de 3e cycle.

pheasant ['fezɪt] (*pl inv* OR **-s**) *n* faisan *m*.

phenomena [fɪ'nɒmɪnə] *pl* ⊏> **phenomenon**.

phenomenal [fɪ'nɒmɪnl] *adj* phénoménal(e), extraordinaire.

phenomenon [fɪ'nɒmɪnən] (*pl* **-mena** [-mɪnə]) *n* phénomène *m*.

phial ['faɪəl] *n* fiole *f*.

philanthropist [fɪ'lænθrəpɪst] *n* philanthrope *mf*.

philately [fɪ'lætəlɪ] *n* philatélie *f*.

Philippine ['fɪlɪpiːn] *adj* philippin(e). ➤ **Philippines** *npl* **: the ~s** les Philippines *fpl*.

philosopher [fɪ'lɒsəfər] *n* philosophe *mf*.

philosophical [,fɪlə'sɒfɪkl] *adj* - **1.** [gen] philosophique - **2.** [stoical] philosophe.

philosophy [fɪ'lɒsəfɪ] *n* philosophie *f*.

phlegm [flem] *n* flegme *m*.

phlegmatic [fleg'mætɪk] *adj* flegmatique.

phobia ['fəʊbjə] *n* phobie *f*.

phone [fəʊn] <> *n* téléphone *m* ; **to be on the ~** [speaking] être au téléphone ; *Br* [connected to network] avoir le téléphone. <> *comp* téléphonique. <> *vt* téléphoner à, appeler. <> *vi* téléphoner. ➤ **phone up** *vt sep & vi Br* téléphoner.

phone book *n* annuaire *m* (du téléphone).

phone booth *n* cabine *f* téléphonique.

phone box *n Br* cabine *f* téléphonique.

phone call *n* coup *m* de téléphone OR fil ; **to make a ~** passer OR donner un coup de fil.

phonecard ['fəʊnkɑːd] *n Br* ≃ Télécarte® *f*.

phone-in *n* RADIO & TV programme *m* à ligne ouverte.

phone number *n* numéro *m* de téléphone.

phonetics [fə'netɪks] *n* (U) phonétique *f*.

phoney *Br*, **phony** *Am* ['fəʊnɪ] *inf* <> *adj* **- 1.** [passport, address] bidon *(inv)* **- 2.** [person] hypocrite, pas franc (pas franche). <> *n* poseur *m*, -euse *f*.

phosphorus ['fɒsfərəs] *n* phosphore *m*.

photo ['fəʊtəʊ] *n* photo *f* ; **to take a ~ of sb/sthg** photographier qqn/qqch, prendre qqn/qqch en photo.

photocopier ['fəʊtəʊˌkɒpɪə'] *n* photocopieur *m*, copieur *m*.

photocopy ['fəʊtəʊˌkɒpɪ] <> *n* photocopie *f*. <> *vt* photocopier.

photograph ['fəʊtəgrɑːf] <> *n* photographie *f* ; **to take a ~ (of sb/sthg)** prendre (qqn/qqch) en photo, photographier (qqn/qqch). <> *vt* photographier, prendre en photo.

photographer [fə'tɒgrəfə'] *n* photographe *mf*.

photography [fə'tɒgrəfɪ] *n* photographie *f*.

phrasal verb ['freɪzl-] *n* verbe *m* à postposition.

phrase [freɪz] <> *n* expression *f*. <> *vt* exprimer, tourner.

phrasebook ['freɪzbʊk] *n* guide *m* de conversation *(pour touristes)*.

physical ['fɪzɪkl] <> *adj* **- 1.** [gen] physique **- 2.** [world, objects] matériel(elle). <> *n* [examination] visite *f* médicale.

physical education *n* éducation *f* physique.

physically ['fɪzɪklɪ] *adv* physiquement.

physically handicapped <> *adj* : **to be ~** être handicapé(e) physique. <> *npl* : **the ~** les handicapés *mpl* physiques.

physician [fɪ'zɪʃn] *n* médecin *m*.

physicist ['fɪzɪsɪst] *n* physicien *m*, -enne *f*.

physics ['fɪzɪks] *n* (U) physique *f*.

physiotherapy [ˌfɪzɪəʊ'θerəpɪ] *n* kinésithérapie *f*.

physique [fɪ'ziːk] *n* physique *m*.

pianist ['pɪənɪst] *n* pianiste *mf*.

piano [pɪ'ænəʊ] (*pl* -s) *n* piano *m*.

pick [pɪk] <> *n* **- 1.** [tool] pioche *f*, pic *m* **- 2.** [selection] : **to take one's ~** choisir, faire son choix **- 3.** [best] : **the ~ of** le meilleur (la meilleure) de. <> *vt* **- 1.** [select, choose] choisir, sélectionner **- 2.** [gather] cueillir **- 3.** [remove] enlever **- 4.** [nose] : **to ~ one's nose** se décrotter le nez ; **to ~ one's teeth** se curer les dents **- 5.** [fight, quarrel] chercher ; **to ~ a fight (with sb)** chercher la bagarre (à qqn) **- 6.** [lock] crocheter. ➤ **pick on** *vt fus* s'en prendre à, être sur le dos de. ➤ **pick out** *vt sep* **- 1.** [recognize] repérer, reconnaître **- 2.** [select, choose] choisir, désigner. ➤ **pick up** <> *vt sep* **- 1.** [lift up] ramasser **- 2.** [collect] aller chercher, passer prendre **- 3.** [collect in car] prendre, chercher **- 4.** [skill, language] apprendre ; [habit] prendre ; [bargain] découvrir ; **to ~ up speed** prendre de la vitesse **- 5.** *inf* [sexually - woman, man] draguer **- 6.** RADIO & TELEC [detect, receive] capter, recevoir **- 7.** [conversation, work] reprendre, continuer. <> *vi* [improve, start again] reprendre.

pickaxe *Br*, **pickax** *Am* ['pɪkæks] *n* pioche *f*, pic *m*.

picket ['pɪkɪt] <> *n* piquet *m* de grève. <> *vt* mettre un piquet de grève devant.

picket line *n* piquet *m* de grève.

pickle ['pɪkl] <> *n* pickles *mpl* ; **to be in a ~** *inf* être dans le pétrin. <> *vt* conserver dans du vinaigre, de la saumure *etc*.

pickpocket ['pɪkˌpɒkɪt] *n* pickpocket *m*, voleur *m* à la tire.

pick-up *n* **- 1.** [of record player] pick-up *m* **- 2.** [truck] camionnette *f*.

picnic ['pɪknɪk] (*pt & pp* -ked, *cont* -king) <> *n* pique-nique *m*. <> *vi* pique-niquer.

pictorial [pɪk'tɔːrɪəl] *adj* illustré(e).

picture ['pɪktʃə'] <> *n* **- 1.** [painting] tableau *m*, peinture *f* ; [drawing] dessin *m* **- 2.** [photograph] photo *f*, photographie *f* **- 3.** TV image *f* **- 4.** CINEMA film *m* **- 5.** [in mind] tableau *m*, image *f* **- 6.** *fig* [situation] tableau *m* **- 7.** *phr* : **to get the ~** *inf* piger ; **to put sb in the ~** mettre qqn au courant.

◇ *vt* - **1.** [in mind] imaginer, s'imaginer, se représenter - **2.** [in photo] photographier - **3.** [in painting] représenter, peindre. ◆ **pictures** *npl Br* : **the ~s** le cinéma.

picture book *n* livre *m* d'images.

picturesque [ˌpɪktʃə'resk] *adj* pittoresque.

pie [paɪ] *n* [savoury] tourte *f* ; [sweet] tarte *f*.

piece [piːs] *n* - **1.** [gen] morceau *m* ; [of string] bout *m* ; **a ~ of furniture** un meuble ; **a ~ of clothing** un vêtement ; **a ~ of advice** un conseil ; **a ~ of information** un renseignement ; **to fall to ~s** tomber en morceaux ; **to take sthg to ~s** démonter qqch ; **in ~s** en morceaux ; **in one ~** [intact] intact(e) ; [unharmed] sain et sauf (saine et sauve) - **2.** [coin, item, in chess] pièce *f* ; [in draughts] pion *m* - **3.** PRESS article *m*. ◆ **piece together** *vt sep* [facts] coordonner.

piecemeal ['piːsmiːl] ◇ *adj* fait(e) petit à petit. ◇ *adv* petit à petit, peu à peu.

piecework ['piːswɜːk] *n (U)* travail *m* à la pièce OR aux pièces.

pie chart *n* camembert *m*, graphique *m* rond.

pier [pɪə'] *n* [at seaside] jetée *f*.

pierce [pɪəs] *vt* percer, transpercer ; **to have one's ears ~d** se faire percer les oreilles.

piercing ['pɪəsɪŋ] *adj* - **1.** [sound, look] perçant(e) - **2.** [wind] pénétrant(e).

pig [pɪg] *n* - **1.** [animal] porc *m*, cochon *m* - **2.** *inf pej* [greedy eater] goinfre *m*, glouton *m* - **3.** *inf pej* [unkind person] sale type *m*.

pigeon ['pɪdʒɪn] *(pl inv* OR **-s)** *n* pigeon *m*.

pigeonhole ['pɪdʒɪnhəʊl] ◇ *n* [compartment] casier *m*. ◇ *vt* [classify] étiqueter, cataloguer.

piggybank ['pɪgɪbæŋk] *n* tirelire *f*.

pigheaded [ˌpɪg'hedɪd] *adj* têtu(e).

pigment ['pɪgmənt] *n* pigment *m*.

pigpen *Am* = **pigsty**.

pigskin ['pɪgskɪn] *n* (peau *f* de) porc *m*.

pigsty ['pɪgstaɪ], **pigpen** *Am* ['pɪgpen] *n lit & fig* porcherie *f*.

pigtail ['pɪgteɪl] *n* natte *f*.

pike [paɪk] *(pl sense 1 only, inv* OR **-s)** *n* - **1.** [fish] brochet *m* - **2.** [spear] pique *f*.

pilchard ['pɪltʃəd] *n* pilchard *m*.

pile [paɪl] ◇ *n* - **1.** [heap] tas *m* ; **a ~ of, ~s of** un tas OR des tas de - **2.** [neat stack] pile *f* - **3.** [of carpet] poil *m*. ◇ *vt* empiler. ◆ **piles** *npl* MED hémorroïdes *fpl*.

◆ **pile into** *vt fus inf* s'entasser dans, s'empiler dans. ◆ **pile up** ◇ *vt sep* empiler, entasser. ◇ *vi* - **1.** [form a heap] s'entasser - **2.** *fig* [work, debts] s'accumuler.

pileup ['paɪlʌp] *n* AUT carambolage *m*.

pilfer ['pɪlfə'] ◇ *vt* chaparder. ◇ *vi* : **to ~ (from)** faire du chapardage (dans).

pilgrim ['pɪlgrɪm] *n* pèlerin *m*.

pilgrimage ['pɪlgrɪmɪdʒ] *n* pèlerinage *m*.

pill [pɪl] *n* - **1.** [gen] pilule *f* - **2.** [contraceptive] : **the ~** la pilule ; **to be on the ~** prendre la pilule.

pillage ['pɪlɪdʒ] *vt* piller.

pillar ['pɪlə'] *n lit & fig* pilier *m*.

pillar box *n Br* boîte *f* aux lettres.

pillion ['pɪljən] *n* siège *m* arrière ; **to ride ~** monter derrière.

pillow ['pɪləʊ] *n* - **1.** [for bed] oreiller *m* - **2.** *Am* [on sofa, chair] coussin *m*.

pillowcase ['pɪləʊkeɪs], **pillowslip** ['pɪləʊslɪp] *n* taie *f* d'oreiller.

pilot ['paɪlət] ◇ *n* - **1.** AERON & NAUT pilote *m* - **2.** TV émission *f* pilote. ◇ *comp* pilote. ◇ *vt* piloter.

pilot burner, pilot light *n* veilleuse *f*.

pilot study *n* étude *f* pilote OR expérimentale.

pimp [pɪmp] *n inf* maquereau *m*, souteneur *m*.

pimple ['pɪmpl] *n* bouton *m*.

pin [pɪn] ◇ *n* - **1.** [for sewing] épingle *f* ; **to have ~s and needles** avoir des fourmis - **2.** [drawing pin] punaise *f* - **3.** [safety pin] épingle *f* de nourrice OR de sûreté - **4.** [of plug] fiche *f* - **5.** TECH goupille *f*, cheville *f*. ◇ *vt* : **to ~ sthg to/on sthg** épingler qqch à/sur qqch ; **to ~ sthg on** *OR* **to sb** [blame] mettre OR coller qqch sur le dos de qqn ; **to ~ one's hopes on sb/sthg** mettre tous ses espoirs en qqn/dans qqch. ◆ **pin down** *vt sep* - **1.** [identify] définir, identifier - **2.** [force to make a decision] : **to ~ sb down** obliger qqn à prendre une décision.

pinafore ['pɪnəfɔːr] *n* - **1.** [apron] tablier *m* - **2.** *Br* [dress] chasuble *f*.

pinball ['pɪnbɔːl] *n* flipper *m*.

pincers ['pɪnsəz] *npl* - **1.** [tool] tenailles *fpl* - **2.** [of crab] pinces *fpl*.

pinch [pɪntʃ] ◇ *n* - **1.** [nip] pincement *m* - **2.** [of salt] pincée *f*. ◇ *vt Br* - **1.** [nip] pincer - **2.** [subj : shoes] serrer - **3.** *inf* [steal] piquer, faucher. ◆ **at a pinch** *Br*, **in a pinch** *Am* *adv* à la rigueur.

pincushion ['pɪnˌkʊʃn] *n* pelote *f* à épingles.

pine [paɪn] ◇ *n* pin *m*. ◇ *vi* : **to ~ for** désirer ardemment. ➡ **pine away** *vi* languir.

pineapple ['paɪnæpl] *n* ananas *m*.

pinetree ['paɪntriː] *n* pin *m*.

ping [pɪŋ] *n* [of bell] tintement *m* ; [of metal] bruit *m* métallique.

Ping-Pong® [-pɒŋ] *n* ping-pong *m*.

pink [pɪŋk] ◇ *adj* rose ; **to go** OR **turn ~** rosir, rougir. ◇ *n* [colour] rose *m*.

pinnacle ['pɪnəkl] *n* - 1. [mountain peak, spire] pic *m*, cime *f* - 2. *fig* [high point] apogée *m*.

pinpoint ['pɪnpɔɪnt] *vt* - 1. [cause, problem] définir, mettre le doigt sur - 2. [position] localiser.

pin-striped [-ˌstraɪpt] *adj* à très fines rayures.

pint [paɪnt] *n* - 1. *Br* [unit of measurement] = 0,568 *litre*, ≃ demi-litre *m* - 2. *Am* [unit of measurement] = 0,473 *litre*, ≃ demi-litre *m* - 3. *Br* [beer] ≃ demi *m*.

pioneer [ˌpaɪə'nɪər] ◇ *n lit & fig* pionnier *m*. ◇ *vt* : **to ~ sthg** être un des premiers (une des premières) à faire qqch.

pious ['paɪəs] *adj* - 1. RELIG pieux (pieuse) - 2. *pej* [sanctimonious] moralisateur(trice).

pip [pɪp] *n* - 1. [seed] pépin *m* - 2. *Br* RADIO top *m*.

pipe [paɪp] ◇ *n* - 1. [for gas, water] tuyau *m* - 2. [for smoking] pipe *f*. ◇ *vt* acheminer par tuyau. ➡ **pipes** *npl* MUS cornemuse *f*. ➡ **pipe down** *vi inf* se taire, la fermer. ➡ **pipe up** *vi inf* se faire entendre.

pipe cleaner *n* cure-pipe *m*.

pipe dream *n* projet *m* chimérique.

pipeline ['paɪplaɪn] *n* [for gas] gazoduc *m* ; [for oil] oléoduc *m*, pipeline *m*.

piper ['paɪpər] *n* joueur *m*, -euse *f* de cornemuse.

piping hot ['paɪpɪŋ-] *adj* bouillant(e).

pique [piːk] *n* dépit *m*.

pirate ['paɪrət] ◇ *adj* [video, program] pirate. ◇ *n* pirate *m*. ◇ *vt* [video, program] pirater.

pirate radio *n Br* radio *f* pirate.

pirouette [ˌpɪru'et] ◇ *n* pirouette *f*. ◇ *vi* pirouetter.

Pisces ['paɪsiːz] *n* Poissons *mpl*.

piss [pɪs] *vulg* ◇ *n* [urine] pisse *f*. ◇ *vi* pisser.

pissed [pɪst] *adj vulg* - 1. *Br* [drunk] bourré(e) - 2. *Am* [annoyed] en boule.

pissed off *adj vulg* qui en a plein le cul.

pistol ['pɪstl] *n* pistolet *m*.

piston ['pɪstən] *n* piston *m*.

pit [pɪt] ◇ *n* - 1. [hole] trou *m* ; [in road] petit trou ; [on face] marque *f* - 2. [for orchestra] fosse *f* - 3. [mine] mine *f* - 4. *Am* [of fruit] noyau *m*. ◇ *vt* : **to ~ sb against sb** opposer qqn à qqn. ➡ **pits** *npl* [in motor racing] : **the ~s** les stands *mpl*.

pitch [pɪtʃ] ◇ *n* - 1. SPORT terrain *m* - 2. MUS ton *m* - 3. [level, degree] degré *m* - 4. [selling place] place *f* - 5. *inf* [sales talk] baratin *m*. ◇ *vt* - 1. [throw] lancer - 2. [set - price] fixer ; [- speech] adapter - 3. [tent] dresser ; [camp] établir. ◇ *vi* - 1. [ball] rebondir - 2. [fall] : **to ~ forward** être projeté(e) en avant - 3. AERON & NAUT tanguer.

pitch-black *adj* : **it's ~ in here** il fait noir comme dans un four.

pitched battle [ˌpɪtʃt-] *n* bataille *f* rangée.

pitcher ['pɪtʃər] *n Am* - 1. [jug] cruche *f* - 2. [in baseball] lanceur *m*.

pitchfork ['pɪtʃfɔːk] *n* fourche *f*.

piteous ['pɪtɪəs] *adj* pitoyable.

pitfall ['pɪtfɔːl] *n* piège *m*.

pith [pɪθ] *n* - 1. [in plant] moelle *f* - 2. [of fruit] peau *f* blanche.

pithy ['pɪθɪ] *adj* [brief] concis(e) ; [terse] piquant(e).

pitiful ['pɪtɪfʊl] *adj* [condition] pitoyable ; [excuse, effort] lamentable.

pitiless ['pɪtɪlɪs] *adj* sans pitié, impitoyable.

pit stop *n* [in motor racing] arrêt *m* aux stands.

pittance ['pɪtəns] *n* [wage] salaire *m* de misère.

pity ['pɪtɪ] ◇ *n* pitié *f* ; **what a ~!** quel dommage! ; **it's a ~** c'est dommage ; **to take** OR **have ~ on sb** prendre qqn en pitié, avoir pitié de qqn. ◇ *vt* plaindre.

pivot ['pɪvət] *n lit & fig* pivot *m*.

pizza ['piːtsə] *n* pizza *f*.

placard ['plækaːd] *n* placard *m*, affiche *f*.

placate [plə'keɪt] *vt* calmer, apaiser.

place [pleɪs] ◇ *n* - 1. [location] endroit *m*, lieu *m* ; **~ of birth** lieu de naissance - 2. [proper position, seat, vacancy, rank] place *f* - 3. [home] : **at/to my ~** chez moi - 4. [in book] : **to lose one's ~** perdre sa page - 5. MATH : **decimal ~** décimale *f* - 6. [instance] : **in the first ~** tout de suite ; **in the first ~ ... and in the second ~ ...** premièrement ... et deuxièmement ... - 7. *phr* : **to take ~** avoir lieu ; **to take the ~ of** prendre la place de, remplacer. ◇ *vt* - 1. [position, put] placer, mettre - **2.** [apportion] : **to ~ the responsibility for sthg on sb** tenir qqn pour responsable de qqch - **3.** [identify] remettre - **4.** [an order] passer ; **to ~ a bet** parier - **5.** [in race] : **to be ~d** être placé(e). ➠ **all over the place** adv [everywhere] partout. ➠ **in place** adv - **1.** [in proper position] à sa place - **2.** [established] mis en place. ➠ **in place of** prep à la place de. ➠ **out of place** adv pas à sa place ; fig déplacé(e).

place mat n set m (de table).

placement ['pleɪsmənt] n placement m.

placid ['plæsɪd] adj - **1.** [person] placide - **2.** [sea, place] calme.

plagiarize, -ise ['pleɪdʒəraɪz] vt plagier.

plague [pleɪg] <> n - **1.** MED peste f - **2.** fig [nuisance] fléau m. <> vt : **to be ~d by** [bad luck] être poursuivi(e) par ; [doubt] être rongé(e) par ; **to ~ sb with questions** harceler qqn de questions.

plaice [pleɪs] (pl inv) n carrelet m.

plaid [plæd] n plaid m.

Plaid Cymru [ˌplaɪd'kʌmrɪ] n parti nationaliste gallois.

plain [pleɪn] <> adj - **1.** [not patterned] uni(e) - **2.** [simple] simple - **3.** [clear] clair(e), évident(e) - **4.** [blunt] carré(e), franc (franche) - **5.** [absolute] pur(e) (et simple) - **6.** [not pretty] quelconque, ordinaire. <> adv inf complètement. <> n GEOGR plaine f.

plain chocolate n Br chocolat m à croquer.

plain-clothes adj en civil.

plain flour n Br farine f (sans levure).

plainly ['pleɪnlɪ] adv - **1.** [obviously] manifestement - **2.** [distinctly] clairement - **3.** [frankly] carrément, sans détours - **4.** [simply] simplement.

plaintiff ['pleɪntɪf] n demandeur m, -eresse f.

plait [plæt] <> n natte f. <> vt natter, tresser.

plan [plæn] <> n plan m, projet m ; **to go according to ~** se passer OR aller comme prévu. <> vt - **1.** [organize] préparer - **2.** [propose] : **to ~ to do sthg** projeter de faire qqch, avoir l'intention de faire qqch - **3.** [design] concevoir. <> vi : **to ~ (for sthg)** faire des projets (pour qqch). ➠ **plans** npl plans mpl, projets mpl ; **have you any ~s for tonight?** avez-vous prévu quelque chose pour ce soir ? ➠ **plan on** vt fus : **to ~ on doing sthg** prévoir de faire qqch.

plane [pleɪn] <> adj plan(e). <> n - **1.** [air-

craft] avion m - **2.** GEOM plan m - **3.** fig [level] niveau m - **4.** [tool] rabot m - **5.** [tree] platane m.

planet ['plænɪt] n planète f.

plank [plæŋk] n - **1.** [of wood] planche f - **2.** POL [policy] point m.

planning ['plænɪŋ] n - **1.** [designing] planification f - **2.** [preparation] préparation f, organisation f.

planning permission n permis m de construire.

plant [plɑːnt] <> n - **1.** BOT plante f - **2.** [factory] usine f - **3.** (U) [heavy machinery] matériel m. <> vt - **1.** [gen] planter - **2.** [bomb] poser.

plantation [plæn'teɪʃn] n plantation f.

plaque [plɑːk] n - **1.** [commemorative sign] plaque f - **2.** (U) [on teeth] plaque f dentaire.

plaster ['plɑːstər] <> n - **1.** [material] plâtre m - **2.** Br [bandage] pansement m adhésif. <> vt - **1.** [wall, ceiling] plâtrer - **2.** [cover] : **to ~ sthg (with)** couvrir qqch (de).

plaster cast n - **1.** [for broken bones] plâtre m - **2.** [model, statue] moule m.

plastered ['plɑːstəd] adj inf [drunk] bourré(e).

plasterer ['plɑːstərər] n plâtrier m.

plaster of Paris n plâtre m de moulage.

plastic ['plæstɪk] <> adj plastique. <> n plastique m.

Plasticine® Br ['plæstɪsiːn] n pâte f à modeler.

plastic surgery n chirurgie f esthétique OR plastique.

plate [pleɪt] <> n - **1.** [dish] assiette f - **2.** [sheet of metal, plaque] tôle f - **3.** (U) [metal covering] : **gold/silver ~** plaqué m or/ argent m - **4.** [in book] planche f - **5.** [in dentistry] dentier m. <> vt : **to be ~d (with)** être plaqué(e) (de).

plateau ['plætəʊ] (pl -s OR -x [-z]) n plateau m ; fig phase f OR période f de stabilité.

plate-glass adj vitré(e).

platform ['plætfɔːm] n - **1.** [stage] estrade f ; [for speaker] tribune f - **2.** [raised structure, of bus, of political party] plate-forme f - **3.** RAIL quai m.

platform ticket n Br ticket m de quai.

platinum ['plætɪnəm] n platine m.

platoon [plə'tuːn] n section f.

platter ['plætər] n [dish] plat m.

plausible ['plɔːzəbl] adj plausible.

play [pleɪ] <> n - **1.** (U) [amusement] jeu m, amusement m - **2.** THEATRE pièce f (de théâtre) ; **a radio ~** une pièce radiophonique

- 3. [game] : **~ on words** jeu *m* de mots **- 4.** TECH jeu *m*. ◇ *vt* **- 1.** [gen] jouer ; **to ~ a part** OR **role in** *fig* jouer un rôle dans **- 2.** [game, sport] jouer à **- 3.** [team, opponent] jouer contre **- 4.** MUS [instrument] jouer de **- 5.** *phr* : **to ~ it safe** ne pas prendre de risques. ◇ *vi* jouer. ➡ **play along** *vi* : **to ~ along (with sb)** entrer dans le jeu (de qqn). ➡ **play down** *vt sep* minimiser. ➡ **play up** ◇ *vt sep* [emphasize] insister sur. ◇ *vi* **- 1.** [machine] faire des siennes **- 2.** [child] ne pas être sage.

play-act *vi* jouer la comédie.

playboy ['pleɪbɔɪ] *n* playboy *m*.

play dough *Am* pâte *f* à modeler.

player ['pleɪəʳ] *n* **- 1.** [gen] joueur *m*, -euse *f* **- 2.** THEATRE acteur *m*, -trice *f*.

playful ['pleɪful] *adj* **- 1.** [person, mood] taquin(e) **- 2.** [kitten, puppy] joueur(euse).

playground ['pleɪgraʊnd] *n* cour *f* de récréation.

playgroup ['pleɪgruːp] *n Br* jardin *m* d'enfants.

playing card ['pleɪɪŋ-] *n* carte *f* à jouer.

playing field ['pleɪɪŋ-] *n* terrain *m* de sport.

playmate ['pleɪmeɪt] *n* camarade *mf*.

play-off *n* SPORT belle *f*.

playpen ['pleɪpen] *n* parc *m*.

playschool ['pleɪskuːl] *n* jardin *m* d'enfants.

plaything ['pleɪθɪŋ] *n lit & fig* jouet *m*.

playtime ['pleɪtaɪm] *n* récréation *f*.

playwright ['pleɪraɪt] *n* dramaturge *m*.

plc *abbr of* **public limited company.**

plea [pliː] *n* **- 1.** [for forgiveness, mercy] supplication *f* ; [for help, quiet] appel *m* **- 2.** JUR : **to enter a ~ of not guilty** plaider non coupable.

plead [pliːd] (*pt & pp* **-ed** OR **pled**) ◇ *vt* **- 1.** JUR plaider **- 2.** [give as excuse] invoquer. ◇ *vi* **- 1.** [beg] : **to ~ with sb (to do sthg)** supplier qqn (de faire qqch) ; **to ~ for sthg** implorer qqch **- 2.** JUR plaider.

pleasant ['pleznt] *adj* agréable.

pleasantry ['plezntrɪ] *n* : **to exchange pleasantries** échanger des propos aimables.

please [pliːz] ◇ *vt* plaire à, faire plaisir à ; **to ~ o.s.** faire comme on veut ; **~ yourself!** comme vous voulez! ◇ *vi* plaire, faire plaisir ; **to do as one ~s** faire comme on veut. ◇ *adv* s'il vous plaît.

pleased [pliːzd] *adj* **- 1.** [satisfied] : **to be ~ (with)** être content(e) (de) **- 2.** [happy] : **to be ~ (about)** être heureux(euse) (de) ; **~ to meet you!** enchanté(e)!

pleasing ['pliːzɪŋ] *adj* plaisant(e).

pleasure ['pleʒəʳ] *n* plaisir *m* ; **with ~** avec plaisir, volontiers ; **it's a ~, my ~** je vous en prie.

pleat [pliːt] ◇ *n* pli *m*. ◇ *vt* plisser.

pled [pled] *pt & pp* ⊳ **plead.**

pledge [pledʒ] ◇ *n* **- 1.** [promise] promesse *f* **- 2.** [token] gage *m*. ◇ *vt* **- 1.** [promise] promettre **- 2.** [make promise] : **to ~ o.s.** **to** s'engager à ; **to ~ sb to secrecy** faire promettre le secret à qqn **- 3.** [pawn] mettre en gage.

plentiful ['plentɪful] *adj* abondant(e).

plenty ['plentɪ] ◇ *n (U)* abondance *f*. ◇ *pron* : **~ of** beaucoup de ; **we've got ~ of time** nous avons largement le temps. ◇ *adv Am* [very] très.

pliable ['plaɪəbl], **pliant** ['plaɪənt] *adj* **- 1.** [material] pliable, souple **- 2.** *fig* [person] docile.

pliers ['plaɪəz] *npl* tenailles *fpl*, pinces *fpl*.

plight [plaɪt] *n* condition *f* critique.

plimsoll ['plɪmsəl] *n Br* tennis *m*.

plinth [plɪnθ] *n* socle *m*.

PLO (*abbr of* **Palestine Liberation Organization**) *n* OLP *f*.

plod [plɒd] *vi* **- 1.** [walk slowly] marcher lentement OR péniblement **- 2.** [work slowly] peiner.

plodder ['plɒdəʳ] *n pej* bûcheur *m*, -euse *f*.

plonk [plɒŋk] *n (U) Br inf* [wine] pinard *m*, vin *m* ordinaire. ➡ **plonk down** *vt sep inf* poser brutalement.

plot [plɒt] ◇ *n* **- 1.** [plan] complot *m*, conspiration *f* **- 2.** [story] intrigue *f* **- 3.** [of land] (parcelle *f* de) terrain *m*, lopin *m*. ◇ *vt* **- 1.** [plan] comploter ; **to ~ to do sthg** comploter de faire qqch **- 2.** [chart] déterminer, marquer **- 3.** MATH tracer, marquer. ◇ *vi* comploter.

plotter ['plɒtəʳ] *n* [schemer] conspirateur *m*, -trice *f*.

plough *Br*, **plow** *Am* [plaʊ] ◇ *n* charrue *f*. ◇ *vt* [field] labourer. ➡ **plough into** ◇ *vt sep* [money] investir. ◇ *vt fus* [subj : car] rentrer dans.

ploughman's ['plaʊmənz] (*pl inv*) *n Br* : **~ (lunch)** *repas de pain, fromage et pickles.*

plow *etc Am* = **plough** *etc.*

ploy [plɔɪ] *n* stratagème *m*, ruse *f*.

pluck [plʌk] ◇ *vt* **- 1.** [flower, fruit] cueillir **- 2.** [pull sharply] arracher **- 3.** [chicken, turkey] plumer **- 4.** [eyebrows] épiler **- 5.** MUS

pincer. ⬦ *n (U) dated* courage *m*, cran *m*.
➡ **pluck up** *vt fus* : **to ~ up the courage to do sthg** rassembler son courage pour faire qqch.

plucky ['plʌkɪ] *adj dated* qui a du cran, courageux(euse).

plug [plʌg] ⬦ *n* - **1.** ELEC prise *f* de courant - **2.** [for bath, sink] bonde *f*. ⬦ *vt* - **1.** [hole] boucher, obturer - **2.** *inf* [new book, film etc] faire de la publicité pour. ➡ **plug in** *vt sep* brancher.

plughole ['plʌghəʊl] *n* bonde *f*, trou *m* d'écoulement.

plum [plʌm] ⬦ *adj* - **1.** [colour] prune *(inv)* - **2.** [very good] : **a ~ job** un poste en or. ⬦ *n* [fruit] prune *f*.

plumb [plʌm] ⬦ *adv* - **1.** *Br* [exactly] exactement, en plein - **2.** *Am* [completely] complètement. ⬦ *vt* : **to ~ the depths of** toucher le fond de.

plumber ['plʌmə'] *n* plombier *m*.

plumbing ['plʌmɪŋ] *n (U)* - **1.** [fittings] plomberie *f*, tuyauterie *f* - **2.** [work] plomberie *f*.

plume [pluːm] *n* - **1.** [feather] plume *f* - **2.** [on hat] panache *m* - **3.** [column] : **a ~ of** smoke un panache de fumée.

plummet ['plʌmɪt] *vi* - **1.** [bird, plane] plonger - **2.** *fig* [decrease] dégringoler.

plump [plʌmp] *adj* bien en chair, grassouillet(ette). ➡ **plump for** *vt fus* opter pour, choisir. ➡ **plump up** *vt sep* [cushion] secouer.

plum pudding *n* pudding *m* de Noël.

plunder ['plʌndə'] ⬦ *n (U)* - **1.** [stealing, raiding] pillage *m* - **2.** [stolen goods] butin *m*. ⬦ *vt* piller.

plunge [plʌndʒ] ⬦ *n* - **1.** [dive] plongeon *m* ; **to take the ~** se jeter à l'eau - **2.** *fig* [decrease] dégringolade *f*, chute *f*. ⬦ *vt* : **to ~ sthg into** plonger qqch dans. ⬦ *vi* - **1.** [dive] plonger, tomber - **2.** *fig* [decrease] dégringoler.

plunger ['plʌndʒə'] *n* débouchoir *m* à ventouse.

pluperfect [ˌpluːˈpɜːfɪkt] *n* : **~ (tense)** plus-que-parfait *m*.

plural ['plʊərəl] ⬦ *adj* - **1.** GRAMM pluriel(elle) - **2.** [not individual] collectif(ive) - **3.** [multicultural] multiculturel(elle). ⬦ *n* pluriel *m*.

plus [plʌs] *(pl* pluses OR plusses [plʌsiːz]*)* ⬦ *adj* : **30 ~ 30 ou plus.** ⬦ *n* - **1.** MATH signe *m* plus - **2.** *inf* [bonus] plus *m*, atout *m*. ⬦ *prep* et. ⬦ *conj* [moreover] de plus.

plush [plʌʃ] *adj* luxueux(euse), somptueux(euse).

plus sign *n* signe *m* plus.

Pluto ['pluːtəʊ] *n* [planet] Pluton *f*.

plutonium [pluːˈtəʊnɪəm] *n* plutonium *m*.

ply [plaɪ] ⬦ *n* [of wool] fil *m* ; [of wood] pli *m*. ⬦ *vt* - **1.** [trade] exercer - **2.** [supply] : **to ~ sb with drink** ne pas arrêter de remplir le verre de qqn. ⬦ *vi* [ship etc] faire la navette.

plywood ['plaɪwʊd] *n* contreplaqué *m*.

p.m., pm *(abbr of* post meridiem*)* : **at 3 ~** à 15 h.

PM *abbr of* prime minister.

PMT *abbr of* premenstrual tension.

pneumatic [njuːˈmætɪk] *adj* pneumatique.

pneumatic drill *n* marteau piqueur *m*.

pneumonia [njuːˈməʊnjə] *n (U)* pneumonie *f*.

poach [pəʊtʃ] ⬦ *vt* - **1.** [fish] pêcher sans permis ; [deer etc] chasser sans permis - **2.** *fig* [idea] voler - **3.** CULIN pocher. ⬦ *vi* braconner.

poacher ['pəʊtʃə'] *n* braconnier *m*.

poaching ['pəʊtʃɪŋ] *n* braconnage *m*.

PO Box *(abbr of* Post Office Box*) n* BP *f*.

pocket ['pɒkɪt] ⬦ *n lit & fig* poche *f* ; **to be out of ~** *Br* en être de sa poche ; **to pick sb's ~** faire les poches à qqn. ⬦ *adj* de poche. ⬦ *vt* empocher.

pocketbook ['pɒkɪtbʊk] *n* - **1.** [notebook] carnet *m* - **2.** *Am* [handbag] sac *m* à main.

pocketknife ['pɒkɪtnaɪf] *(pl* -knives [-naɪvz]*) n* canif *m*.

pocket money *n* argent *m* de poche.

pockmark ['pɒkmɑːk] *n* marque *f* de la petite vérole.

pod [pɒd] *n* - **1.** [of plants] cosse *f* - **2.** [of spacecraft] nacelle *f*.

podgy ['pɒdʒɪ] *adj inf* boulot(otte), rondelet(ette).

podiatrist [pəˈdaɪətrɪst] *n Am* pédicure *mf*.

podium ['pəʊdɪəm] *(pl* -diums OR -dia [-dɪə]*) n* podium *m*.

poem ['pəʊɪm] *n* poème *m*.

poet ['pəʊɪt] *n* poète *m*.

poetic [pəʊˈetɪk] *adj* poétique.

poetry ['pəʊɪtrɪ] *n* poésie *f*.

poignant ['pɔɪnjənt] *adj* poignant(e).

point [pɔɪnt] ⬦ *n* - **1.** [tip] pointe *f* - **2.** [place] endroit *m*, point *m* - **3.** [time] stade *m*, moment *m* - **4.** [detail, argument] question *f*, détail *m* ; **you have a ~** il y a du vrai dans ce que vous dites ; **to make a ~** faire une remarque ; **to make one's ~** dire ce qu'on a à dire, dire son mot - **5.** [main idea] point *m* essentiel ; **to get** OR **come to the ~** en venir au fait ; **to miss the ~** ne pas comprendre ; **beside the ~** à côté de la question - **6.** [feature] : **good ~** qualité *f* ; **bad ~** défaut *m* - **7.** [purpose] : **what's the ~ in buying a new car?** à quoi bon acheter une nouvelle voiture? ; **there's no ~ in having a meeting** cela ne sert à rien d'avoir une réunion - **8.** [on scale, in scores] point *m* - **9.** MATH : **two ~ six** deux virgule six - **10.** [of compass] aire *f* du vent - **11.** *Br* ELEC prise *f* (de courant) - **12.** *Am* [full stop] point *m* (final) - **13.** *phr* : **to make a ~ of doing sthg** ne pas manquer de faire qqch. <> *vt* : **to ~ sthg (at)** [gun, camera] braquer qqch (sur) ; [finger, hose] pointer qqch (sur). <> *vi* - **1.** [indicate with finger] : **to ~ (at sb/ sthg), to ~ (to sb/sthg)** montrer (qqn/qqch) du doigt, indiquer (qqn/qqch) du doigt - **2.** *fig* [suggest] : **to ~ to sthg** suggérer qqch, laisser supposer qqch. ◆ **points** *npl Br* RAIL aiguillage *m*. ◆ **up to a point** *adv* jusqu'à un certain point, dans une certaine mesure. ◆ **on the point of** *prep* sur le point de. ◆ **point out** *vt sep* [person, place] montrer, indiquer ; [fact, mistake] signaler.

•**point-blank** *adv* - **1.** [refuse] catégoriquement ; [ask] de but en blanc - **2.** [shoot] à bout portant.

pointed ['pɔɪntɪd] *adj* - **1.** [sharp] pointu(e) - **2.** *fig* [remark] mordant(e), incisif(ive).

pointer ['pɔɪntə^r] *n* - **1.** [piece of advice] tuyau *m*, conseil *m* - **2.** [needle] aiguille *f* - **3.** [stick] baguette *f* - **4.** COMPUT pointeur *m*.

pointless ['pɔɪntlɪs] *adj* inutile, vain(e).

point of view (*pl* **points of view**) *n* point *m* de vue.

poise [pɔɪz] *n fig* calme *m*, sang-froid *m*.

poised [pɔɪzd] *adj* - **1.** [ready] : **~ (for)** prêt(e) (pour) ; **to be ~ to do sthg** se tenir prêt à faire qqch - **2.** *fig* [calm] calme, posé(e).

poison ['pɔɪzn] <> *n* poison *m*. <> *vt* - **1.** [gen] empoisonner - **2.** [pollute] polluer.

poisoning ['pɔɪznɪŋ] *n* empoisonnement *m* ; **food ~** intoxication *f* alimentaire.

poisonous ['pɔɪznəs] *adj* - **1.** [fumes] toxique ; [plant] vénéneux(euse) - **2.** [snake] venimeux(euse).

poke [pəʊk] <> *vt* - **1.** [prod] pousser, donner un coup de coude à - **2.** [put] fourrer - **3.** [fire] attiser, tisonner. <> *vi* [protrude]

sortir, dépasser. ◆ **poke about, poke around** *vi inf* fouiller, fourrager.

poker ['pəʊkə^r] *n* - **1.** [game] poker *m* - **2.** [for fire] tisonnier *m*.

poker-faced [-ˌfeɪst] *adj* au visage impassible.

poky ['pəʊkɪ] *adj pej* [room] exigu(ë), minuscule.

Poland ['pəʊlənd] *n* Pologne *f*.

polar ['pəʊlə^r] *adj* polaire.

Polaroid® ['pəʊlərɔɪd] *n* - **1.** [camera] Polaroïd® *m* - **2.** [photograph] photo *f* polaroïd.

pole [pəʊl] *n* - **1.** [rod, post] perche *f*, mât *m* - **2.** ELEC & GEOGR pôle *m*.

Pole [pəʊl] *n* Polonais *m*, -e *f*.

pole vault *n* : **the ~** le saut à la perche.

police [pə'liːs] <> *npl* - **1.** [police force] : **the ~** la police - **2.** [policemen] agents *mpl* de police. <> *vt* maintenir l'ordre dans.

police car *n* voiture *f* de police.

police constable *n Br* agent *m* de police.

police force *n* police *f*.

policeman [pə'liːsmən] (*pl* **-men** [-mən]) *n* agent *m* de police.

police officer *n* policier *m*.

police record *n* casier *m* judiciaire.

police station *n* commissariat *m* (de police).

policewoman [pə'liːsˌwʊmən] (*pl* **-women** [-ˌwɪmɪn]) *n* femme *f* agent de police.

policy ['pɒləsɪ] *n* - **1.** [plan] politique *f* - **2.** [document] police *f*.

polio ['pəʊlɪəʊ] *n* polio *f*.

polish ['pɒlɪʃ] <> *n* - **1.** [for shoes] cirage *m* ; [for floor] cire *f*, encaustique *f* - **2.** [shine] brillant *m*, lustre *m* - **3.** *fig* [refinement] raffinement *m*. <> *vt* [shoes, floor] cirer ; [car] astiquer ; [cutlery, glasses] faire briller. ◆ **polish off** *vt sep inf* expédier. ◆ **polish up** *vt sep* [maths, language] perfectionner ; [travail] peaufiner.

Polish ['pəʊlɪʃ] <> *adj* polonais(e). <> *n* [language] polonais *m*. <> *npl* : **the ~** les Polonais *mpl*.

polished ['pɒlɪʃt] *adj* - **1.** [refined] raffiné(e) - **2.** [accomplished] accompli(e), parfait(e).

polite [pə'laɪt] *adj* [courteous] poli(e).

politic ['pɒlɪtɪk] *adj* politique.

political [pə'lɪtɪkl] *adj* politique.

politically correct [pəˌlɪtɪklɪ-] *adj conforme au mouvement qui préconise le remplacement de termes jugés discriminants par d'autres 'politiquement corrects'.*

politician [ˌpɒlɪ'tɪʃn] n homme m politique, femme f politique.

politics ['pɒlətɪks] ⟨⟩ n (U) politique f. ⟨⟩ npl - **1.** [personal beliefs] : **what are his ~?** de quel bord est-il? - **2.** [of group, area] politique f.

polka ['pɒlkə] n polka f.

polka dot n pois m.

poll [pəʊl] ⟨⟩ n vote m, scrutin m. ⟨⟩ vt - **1.** [people] interroger, sonder - **2.** [votes] obtenir. ◆ **polls** npl : **to go to the ~s** aller aux urnes.

pollen ['pɒlən] n pollen m.

polling booth n isoloir m.

polling day n Br jour m du scrutin OR des élections.

polling station n bureau m de vote.

pollute [pə'luːt] vt polluer.

pollution [pə'luːʃn] n pollution f.

polo ['pəʊləʊ] n polo m.

polo neck n Br - **1.** [neck] col m roulé - **2.** [jumper] pull m à col roulé.

polyethylene Am = **polythene**.

Polynesia [ˌpɒlɪ'niːzjə] n Polynésie f.

polystyrene [ˌpɒlɪ'staɪriːn] n polystyrène m.

polytechnic [ˌpɒlɪ'teknɪk] n Br établissement d'enseignement supérieur ; en 1993, les 'polytechnics' ont été transformés en universités.

polythene Br ['pɒlɪθiːn], **polyethylene** Am [ˌpɒlɪ'eθɪliːn] n polyéthylène m.

polythene bag n Br sac m en plastique.

pomegranate ['pɒmɪˌɡrænɪt] n grenade f.

pomp [pɒmp] n pompe f, faste m.

pompom ['pɒmpɒm] n pompon m.

pompous ['pɒmpəs] adj - **1.** [person] fat, suffisant(e) - **2.** [style, speech] pompeux(euse).

pond [pɒnd] n étang m, mare f.

ponder ['pɒndə'] vt considérer, peser.

ponderous ['pɒndərəs] adj - **1.** [dull] lourd(e) - **2.** [large, heavy] pesant(e).

pong [pɒŋ] n Br inf puanteur f.

pontoon [pɒn'tuːn] n - **1.** [bridge] ponton m - **2.** Br [game] vingt-et-un m.

pony ['pəʊnɪ] n poney m.

ponytail ['pəʊnɪteɪl] n queue-de-cheval f.

pony-trekking [-ˌtrekɪŋ] n randonnée f à cheval OR en poney.

poodle ['puːdl] n caniche m.

pool [puːl] ⟨⟩ n - **1.** [pond, of blood] mare f ; [of rain, light] flaque f - **2.** [swimming pool] piscine f - **3.** SPORT billard m américain. ⟨⟩ vt [resources etc] mettre en commun. ◆ **pools** npl Br : **the ~s** ≃ le loto sportif.

poor [pɔː'] ⟨⟩ adj - **1.** [gen] pauvre - **2.** [not very good] médiocre, mauvais(e). ⟨⟩ npl : **the ~** les pauvres mpl.

poorly ['pɔːlɪ] ⟨⟩ adj Br souffrant(e). ⟨⟩ adv mal, médiocrement.

pop [pɒp] ⟨⟩ n - **1.** (U) [music] pop m - **2.** (U) inf [fizzy drink] boisson f gazeuse - **3.** esp Am inf [father] papa m - **4.** [sound] pan m. ⟨⟩ vt - **1.** [burst] faire éclater, crever - **2.** [put quickly] mettre, fourrer. ⟨⟩ vi - **1.** [balloon] éclater, crever ; [cork, button] sauter - **2.** [eyes] : **his eyes popped** il a écarquillé les yeux. ◆ **pop in** vi faire une petite visite. ◆ **pop up** vi surgir.

pop concert n concert m pop.

popcorn ['pɒpkɔːn] n pop-corn m.

pope [pəʊp] n pape m.

pop group n groupe m pop.

poplar ['pɒplə'] n peuplier m.

poppy ['pɒpɪ] n coquelicot m, pavot m.

Popsicle® ['pɒpsɪkl] n Am sucette f glacée.

populace ['pɒpjʊləs] n : **the ~** le peuple.

popular ['pɒpjʊlə'] adj - **1.** [gen] populaire - **2.** [name, holiday resort] à la mode.

popularize, -ise ['pɒpjʊləraɪz] vt - **1.** [make popular] populariser - **2.** [simplify] vulgariser.

population [ˌpɒpjʊ'leɪʃn] n population f.

porcelain ['pɔːsəlɪn] n porcelaine f.

porch [pɔːtʃ] n - **1.** [entrance] porche m - **2.** Am [verandah] véranda f.

porcupine ['pɔːkjʊpaɪn] n porc-épic m.

pore [pɔː'] n pore m. ◆ **pore over** vt fus examiner de près.

pork [pɔːk] n porc m.

pork pie n pâté m de porc en croûte.

pornography [pɔː'nɒɡrəfɪ] n pornographie f.

porous ['pɔːrəs] adj poreux(euse).

porridge ['pɒrɪdʒ] n porridge m.

port [pɔːt] n - **1.** [town, harbour] port m - **2.** NAUT [left-hand side] bâbord m - **3.** [drink] porto m - **4.** COMPUT port m.

portable ['pɔːtəbl] adj portatif(ive).

portent ['pɔːtənt] n présage m.

porter ['pɔːtə'] n - **1.** Br [doorman] concierge m, portier m - **2.** [for luggage] porteur m - **3.** Am [on train] employé m, -e f des wagons-lits.

portfolio [ˌpɔːt'fəʊljəʊ] (pl -s) n - **1.** [case]

serviette *f* - **2.** [sample of work] portfolio *m* - **3.** FIN portefeuille *m*.

porthole ['pɔːthəʊl] *n* hublot *m*.

portion ['pɔːʃn] *n* - **1.** [section] portion *f*, part *f* - **2.** [of food] portion *f*.

portly ['pɔːtlɪ] *adj* corpulent(e).

portrait ['pɔːtreɪt] *n* portrait *m*.

portray [pɔːˈtreɪ] *vt* - **1.** CINEMA & THEATRE jouer, interpréter - **2.** [describe] dépeindre - **3.** [paint] faire le portrait de.

Portugal ['pɔːtʃʊgl] *n* Portugal *m*.

Portuguese [ˌpɔːtʃʊˈgiːz] <> *adj* portugais(e). <> *n* [language] portugais *m*. <> *npl* : the ~ les Portugais *mpl*.

pose [pəʊz] <> *n* - **1.** [stance] pose *f* - **2.** *pej* [affectation] pose *f*, affectation *f*. <> *vt* - **1.** [danger] présenter - **2.** [problem, question] poser. <> *vi* - **1.** ART & *pej* poser - **2.** [pretend to be] : to ~ as se faire passer pour.

posh [pɒʃ] *adj inf* - **1.** [hotel, clothes etc] chic (*inv*) - **2.** *Br* [accent, person] de la haute.

position [pəˈzɪʃn] <> *n* - **1.** [gen] position *f* - **2.** [job] poste *m*, emploi *m* - **3.** [state] situation *f*. <> *vt* placer, mettre en position.

positive ['pɒzətɪv] *adj* - **1.** [gen] positif(ive) - **2.** [sure] sûr(e), certain(e) ; to be ~ about sthg être sûr de qqch - **3.** [optimistic] positif(ive), optimiste ; to be ~ about sthg avoir une attitude positive au sujet de qqch - **4.** [definite] formel(elle), précis(e) - **5.** [evidence] irréfutable, indéniable - **6.** [downright] véritable.

posse ['pɒsɪ] *n Am* détachement *m*, troupe *f*.

possess [pəˈzes] *vt* posséder.

possession [pəˈzeʃn] *n* possession *f*.
➡ **possessions** *npl* possessions *fpl*, biens *mpl*.

possessive [pəˈzesɪv] <> *adj* possessif(ive). <> *n* GRAMM possessif *m*.

possibility [ˌpɒsəˈbɪlətɪ] *n* - **1.** [chance, likelihood] possibilité *f*, chances *fpl* ; there is a ~ that ... il se peut que ... (+ *subjunctive*) - **2.** [option] possibilité *f*, option *f*.

possible ['pɒsəbl] <> *adj* possible ; as much as ~ autant que possible ; as soon as ~ dès que possible. <> *n* possible *m*.

possibly ['pɒsəblɪ] *adv* - **1.** [perhaps] peut-être - **2.** [expressing surprise] : how could he ~ have known? mais comment a-t-il pu le savoir? - **3.** [for emphasis] : I can't ~ accept your money je ne peux vraiment pas accepter cet argent.

post [pəʊst] <> *n* - **1.** *Br* [service] : the ~ la poste ; by ~ par la poste - **2.** *Br* [letters, deliv-

ery] courrier *m* - **3.** *Br* [collection] levée *f* - **4.** [pole] poteau *m* - **5.** [position, job] poste *m*, emploi *m* - **6.** MIL poste *m*. <> *vt* - **1.** *Br* [by mail] poster, mettre à la poste - **2.** [employee] muter - **3.** COMPUT [message, question, advertisement] envoyer sur Internet.

postage ['pəʊstɪdʒ] *n* affranchissement *m* ; ~ and packing frais *mpl* de port et d'emballage.

postal ['pəʊstl] *adj* postal(e).

postal order *n Br* mandat *m* postal.

postbox ['pəʊstbɒks] *n Br* boîte *f* aux lettres.

postcard ['pəʊstkɑːd] *n* carte *f* postale.

postcode ['pəʊstkəʊd] *n Br* code *m* postal.

postdate [ˌpəʊstˈdeɪt] *vt* postdater.

poster ['pəʊstəʳ] *n* [for advertising] affiche *f* ; [for decoration] poster *m*.

poste restante [ˌpəʊstˈrestɑːnt] *n* poste *f* restante.

posterior [pɒˈstɪərɪəʳ] <> *adj* postérieur(e). <> *n hum* postérieur *m*, derrière *m*.

postgraduate [ˌpəʊstˈgrædʒʊət] <> *adj* de troisième cycle. <> *n* étudiant *m*, -e *f* de troisième cycle.

posthumous ['pɒstjʊməs] *adj* posthume.

Post-it (note)® *n* Post-it® *m*.

postman ['pəʊstmən] (*pl* **-men** [-mən]) *n* facteur *m*.

postmark ['pəʊstmɑːk] <> *n* cachet *m* de la poste. <> *vt* timbrer, tamponner.

postmaster ['pəʊstˌmɑːstəʳ] *n* receveur *m* des postes.

postmortem [ˌpəʊstˈmɔːtəm] *n lit & fig* autopsie *f*.

post office *n* - **1.** [organization] : the Post Office les Postes et Télécommunications *fpl* - **2.** [building] (bureau *m* de) poste *f*.

post office box *n* boîte *f* postale.

postpone [ˌpəʊstˈpəʊn] *vt* reporter, remettre.

postscript ['pəʊstskrɪpt] *n* post-scriptum *m inv* ; *fig* supplément *m*, addenda *m inv*.

posture ['pɒstʃəʳ] *n* - **1.** (U) [pose] position *f*, posture *f* - **2.** *fig* [attitude] attitude *f*.

postwar [ˌpəʊstˈwɔːʳ] *adj* d'après-guerre.

posy ['pəʊzɪ] *n* petit bouquet *m* de fleurs.

pot [pɒt] <> *n* - **1.** [for cooking] marmite *f*, casserole *f* - **2.** [for tea] théière *f* ; [for coffee] cafetière *f* - **3.** [for paint, jam, plant] pot *m* - **4.** (U) *inf* [cannabis] herbe *f*. <> *vt* [plant] mettre en pot.

potassium [pəˈtæsɪəm] *n* potassium *m*.

potato [pə'teɪtəʊ] (*pl* **-es**) *n* pomme *f* de terre.

potato peeler [-ˌpiːləʳ] *n* (couteau *m*) éplucheur *m*, économiseur *m*.

potent ['pəʊtənt] *adj* - **1.** [powerful, influential] puissant(e) - **2.** [drink] fort(e) - **3.** [man] viril.

potential [pə'tenʃl] <> *adj* [energy, success] potentiel(elle) ; [uses, danger] possible ; [enemy] en puissance. <> *n (U)* [of person] capacités *fpl* latentes ; **to have ~** [person] promettre ; [company] avoir de l'avenir ; [scheme] offrir des possibilités.

potentially [pə'tenʃəlɪ] *adv* potentiellement.

pothole ['pɒthəʊl] *n* - **1.** [in road] nid-de-poule *m* - **2.** [underground] caverne *f*, grotte *f*.

potholing ['pɒtˌhəʊlɪŋ] *n Br* : **to go ~** faire de la spéléologie.

potion ['pəʊʃn] *n* [magic] breuvage *m* ; **love ~** philtre *m*.

potluck [ˌpɒt'lʌk] *n* : **to take ~** - [gen] choisir au hasard ; [at meal] manger à la fortune du pot.

potshot ['pɒtˌʃɒt] *n* : **to take a ~ (at sthg)** tirer (sur qqch) sans viser.

potted ['pɒtɪd] *adj* - **1.** [plant] : **~ plant** plante *f* d'appartement - **2.** [food] conservé(e) en pot.

potter ['pɒtəʳ] *n* potier *m*.   **potter about, potter around** *vi Br* bricoler.

pottery ['pɒtərɪ] *n* poterie *f*, **a piece of ~** une poterie.

potty ['pɒtɪ] *Br inf* <> *adj* : **~ (about)** toqué(e) (de). <> *n* pot *m* (de chambre).

pouch [paʊtʃ] *n* - **1.** [small bag] petit sac *m* ; **tobacco ~** blague *f* à tabac - **2.** [of kangaroo] poche *f* ventrale.

poultry ['pəʊltrɪ] <> *n (U)* [meat] volaille *f*. <> *npl* [birds] volailles *fpl*.

pounce [paʊns] *vi* : **to ~ (on)** [bird] fondre (sur) ; [person] se jeter (sur).

pound [paʊnd] <> *n* - **1.** *Br* [money] livre *f* - **2.** [weight] = 453,6 grammes, ≃ livre *f* - **3.** [for cars, dogs] fourrière *f*. <> *vt* - **1.** [strike loudly] marteler - **2.** [crush] piler, broyer. <> *vi* - **1.** [strike loudly] : **to ~ on** donner de grands coups à - **2.** [heart] battre fort ; **my head is ~ing** j'ai des élancements dans la tête.

pound sterling *n* livre *f* sterling.

pour [pɔːʳ] <> *vt* verser ; **shall I ~ you a drink?** je te sers quelque chose à boire? <> *vi* - **1.** [liquid] couler à flots - **2.** *fig* [rush] : **to ~ in/out** entrer/sortir en foule. <> *v im-*

pers [rain hard] pleuvoir à verse.   **pour in** *vi* [letters, news] affluer.   **pour out** *vt sep* - **1.** [empty] vider - **2.** [serve - drink] verser, servir.

pouring ['pɔːrɪŋ] *adj* [rain] torrentiel(elle).

pout [paʊt] *vi* faire la moue.

poverty ['pɒvətɪ] *n* pauvreté *f* ; *fig* [of ideas] indigence *f*, manque *m*.

poverty-stricken *adj* [person] dans la misère ; [area] misérable, très pauvre.

powder ['paʊdəʳ] <> *n* poudre *f*. <> *vt* [face, body] poudrer.

powder compact *n* poudrier *m*.

powdered ['paʊdəd] *adj* - **1.** [milk, eggs] en poudre - **2.** [face] poudré(e).

powder puff *n* houpette *f*.

powder room *n* toilettes *fpl* pour dames.

power ['paʊəʳ] <> *n* - **1.** *(U)* [authority, ability] pouvoir *m* ; **to take ~** prendre le pouvoir ; **to come to ~** parvenir au pouvoir ; **to be in ~** être au pouvoir ; **to be in OR within one's ~ to do sthg** être en son pouvoir de faire qqch - **2.** [strength, powerful person] puissance *f*, force *f* - **3.** *(U)* [energy] énergie *f* - **4.** [electricity] courant *m*, électricité *f*. <> *vt* faire marcher, actionner.

powerboat ['paʊəbəʊt] *n* hors-bord *m inv*.

power cut *n* coupure *f* de courant.

power failure *n* panne *f* de courant.

powerful ['paʊəful] *adj* - **1.** [gen] puissant(e) - **2.** [smell, voice] fort(e) - **3.** [speech, novel] émouvant(e).

powerless ['paʊəlɪs] *adj* impuissant(e) ; **to be ~ to do sthg** être dans l'impossibilité de faire qqch, ne pas pouvoir faire qqch.

power point *n Br* prise *f* de courant.

power station *n* centrale *f* électrique.

power steering *n* direction *f* assistée.

pp (*abbr of* per procurationem) pp.

p & p *abbr of* postage and packing.

PR *n* - **1.** *abbr of* proportional representation - **2.** *abbr of* public relations.

practicable ['præktɪkəbl] *adj* réalisable, faisable.

practical ['præktɪkl] <> *adj* - **1.** [gen] pratique - **2.** [plan, solution] réalisable. <> *n* épreuve *f* pratique.

practicality [ˌpræktɪ'kælətɪ] *n (U)* aspect *m* pratique.

practical joke *n* farce *f*.

practically ['præktɪklɪ] *adv* - **1.** [in a practical way] d'une manière pratique - **2.** [almost] presque, pratiquement.

practice, practise *Am* ['præktɪs] *n* - **1.** *(U)*

[at sport] entraînement *m* ; [at music etc] répétition *f* ; **to be out of ~** être rouillé(e) - **2.** [training session - at sport] séance *f* d'entraînement ; [- at music etc] répétition *f* - **3.** [act of doing] : **to put sthg into ~** mettre qqch en pratique ; **in ~** [in fact] en réalité, en fait - **4.** [habit] pratique *f*, coutume *f* - **5.** *(U)* [of profession] exercice *m* - **6.** [of doctor] cabinet *m* ; [of lawyer] étude *f*.

practicing *Am* = practising.

practise, practice *Am* ['præktɪs] ⟨⟩ *vt* - **1.** [sport] s'entraîner à ; [piano etc] s'exercer à - **2.** [custom] suivre, pratiquer ; [religion] pratiquer - **3.** [profession] exercer. ⟨⟩ *vi* - **1.** SPORT s'entraîner ; MUS s'exercer - **2.** [doctor, lawyer] exercer.

practising, practicing *Am* ['præktɪsɪŋ] *adj* [doctor, lawyer] en exercice ; [Christian etc] pratiquant(e) ; [homosexual] déclaré(e).

practitioner [præk'tɪʃnə'] *n* praticien *m*, -enne *f*.

Prague [prɑːg] *n* Prague.

prairie ['preərɪ] *n* prairie *f*.

praise [preɪz] ⟨⟩ *n (U)* louange *f*, louanges *fpl*, éloge *m*, éloges *mpl*. ⟨⟩ *vt* louer, faire l'éloge de.

praiseworthy ['preɪzˌwɜːðɪ] *adj* louable, méritoire.

pram [præm] *n Br* landau *m*.

prance [prɑːns] *vi* - **1.** [person] se pavaner - **2.** [horse] caracoler.

prank [præŋk] *n* tour *m*, niche *f*.

prawn [prɔːn] *n* crevette *f* rose.

pray [preɪ] *vi* : **to ~ (to sb)** prier (qqn).

prayer [preə'] *n lit & fig* prière *f*.

prayer book *n* livre *m* de messe.

preach [priːtʃ] ⟨⟩ *vt* [gen] prêcher ; [sermon] prononcer. ⟨⟩ *vi* - **1.** RELIG : **to ~ (to sb)** prêcher (qqn) - **2.** *pej* [pontificate] : **to ~ (at sb)** sermonner (qqn).

preacher ['priːtʃə'] *n* prédicateur *m*, pasteur *m*.

precarious [prɪ'keərɪəs] *adj* précaire.

precaution [prɪ'kɔːʃn] *n* précaution *f*.

precede [prɪ'siːd] *vt* précéder.

precedence ['presɪdəns] *n* : **to take ~ over sthg** avoir la priorité sur qqch ; **to have OR take ~ over sb** avoir la préséance sur qqn.

precedent ['presɪdənt] *n* précédent *m*.

precinct ['priːsɪŋkt] *n* - **1.** *Br* [area] : **pedestrian ~** zone *f* piétonne ; **shopping ~** centre *m* commercial - **2.** *Am* [district] circonscrip-

tion *f* (administrative). ⬦ **precincts** *npl* [of institution] enceinte *f*.

precious ['preʃəs] *adj* - **1.** [gen] précieux(euse) - **2.** *inf iro* [damned] sacré(e) - **3.** [affected] affecté(e).

precipice ['presɪpɪs] *n* précipice *m*, paroi *f* à pic.

precipitate [*adj* prɪ'sɪpɪtət, *vb* prɪ'sɪpɪteɪt] *fml* ⟨⟩ *adj* hâtif(ive). ⟨⟩ *vt* [hasten] hâter, précipiter.

precise [prɪ'saɪs] *adj* précis(e) ; [measurement, date] exact(e).

precisely [prɪ'saɪslɪ] *adv* précisément, exactement.

precision [prɪ'sɪʒn] *n* précision *f*, exactitude *f*.

preclude [prɪ'kluːd] *vt fml* empêcher ; [possibility] écarter ; **to ~ sb from doing sthg** empêcher qqn de faire qqch.

precocious [prɪ'kəuʃəs] *adj* précoce.

preconceived [ˌpriːkən'siːvd] *adj* préconçu(e).

precondition [ˌpriːkən'dɪʃn] *n fml* condition *f* sine qua non.

predator ['predətə'] *n* - **1.** [animal, bird] prédateur *m*, rapace *m* - **2.** *fig* [person] corbeau *m*.

predecessor ['priːdɪsesə'] *n* - **1.** [person] prédécesseur *m* - **2.** [thing] précédent *m*, -e *f*.

predicament [prɪ'dɪkəmənt] *n* situation *f* difficile ; **to be in a ~** être dans de beaux draps.

predict [prɪ'dɪkt] *vt* prédire.

predictable [prɪ'dɪktəbl] *adj* prévisible.

prediction [prɪ'dɪkʃn] *n* prédiction *f*.

predispose [ˌpriːdɪs'pəuz] *vt* : **to be ~d to sthg/to do sthg** être prédisposé(e) à qqch/à faire qqch.

predominant [prɪ'dɒmɪnənt] *adj* prédominant(e).

predominantly [prɪ'dɒmɪnəntlɪ] *adv* principalement, surtout.

preempt [ˌpriː'empt] *vt* [action, decision] devancer, prévenir.

preemptive [ˌpriː'emptɪv] *adj* préventif(ive).

preen [priːn] *vt* - **1.** [subj : bird] lisser, nettoyer - **2.** *fig* [subj : person] : **to ~ o.s.** se faire beau (belle).

prefab ['priːfæb] *n inf* maison *f* préfabriquée.

preface ['prefɪs] *n* : **~ (to)** préface *f* (de), préambule *m* (de).

prefect ['priːfekt] *n Br* [pupil] *élève de termi-*

nale qui aide les professeurs à maintenir la discipline.

prefer [prɪ'fɜːʳ] *vt* préférer ; **to ~ sthg** préférer qqch à qqch, aimer mieux qqch que qqch ; **to ~ to do sthg** préférer faire qqch, aimer mieux faire qqch.

preferable ['prefrəbl] *adj* : ~ **(to)** préférable (à).

preferably ['prefrəblɪ] *adv* de préférence.

preference ['prefərəns] *n* préférence *f*.

preferential [,prefə'renʃl] *adj* préférentiel(elle).

prefix ['priːfɪks] *n* préfixe *m*.

pregnancy ['pregnənsɪ] *n* grossesse *f*.

pregnant ['pregnənt] *adj* [woman] enceinte ; [animal] pleine, gravide.

prehistoric [,priːhɪ'stɒrɪk] *adj* préhistorique.

prejudice ['predʒʊdɪs] ⟨⟩ *n* - **1.** [biased view] : ~ **(in favour of/against)** préjugé *m* (en faveur de/contre), préjugés *mpl* (en faveur de/contre) - **2.** *(U)* [harm] préjudice *m*, tort *m*. ⟨⟩ *vt* - **1.** [bias] : **to ~ sb (in favour of/against)** prévenir qqn (en faveur de/contre), influencer qqn (en faveur de/contre) - **2.** [harm] porter préjudice à.

prejudiced ['predʒʊdɪst] *adj* [person] qui a des préjugés ; [opinion] préconçu(e) ; **to be ~ in favour of/against** avoir des préjugés en faveur de/contre.

prejudicial [,predʒʊ'dɪʃl] *adj* : ~ **(to)** préjudiciable (à), nuisible (à).

preliminary [prɪ'lɪmɪnərɪ] *adj* préliminaire.

prelude ['preljuːd] *n* [event] : ~ **to sthg** prélude *m* de qqch.

premarital [,priː'mærɪtl] *adj* avant le mariage.

premature ['premə,tjʊəʳ] *adj* prématuré(e).

premeditated [,priː'medɪteɪtɪd] *adj* prémédité(e).

premenstrual syndrome, premenstrual tension [priː'menstruəl-] *n* syndrome *m* prémenstruel.

premier ['premjəʳ] ⟨⟩ *adj* primordial(e), premier(ère). ⟨⟩ *n* premier ministre *m*.

premiere ['premɪeəʳ] *n* première *f*.

premise ['premɪs] *n* prémisse *f*. ➡ **premises** *npl* local *m*, locaux *mpl* ; **on the ~s** sur place, sur les lieux.

premium ['priːmjəm] *n* prime *f* ; **at a ~** [above usual value] à prix d'or ; [in great demand] très recherché OR demandé.

premium bond *n* Br ≃ billet *m* de loterie.

premonition [,premə'nɪʃn] *n* prémonition *f*, pressentiment *m*.

preoccupied [priː'ɒkjʊpaɪd] *adj* : ~ **(with)** préoccupé(e) (de).

prep [prep] *n* *(U)* Br *inf* devoirs *mpl*.

prepaid ['priːpeɪd] *adj* payé(e) d'avance ; [envelope] affranchi(e).

preparation [,prepə'reɪʃn] *n* préparation *f*. ➡ **preparations** *npl* préparatifs *mpl* ; **to make ~s for** faire des préparatifs pour, prendre ses dispositions pour.

preparatory [prɪ'pærətrɪ] *adj* [work, classes] préparatoire ; [actions, measures] préliminaire.

preparatory school *n* [in UK] école *f* primaire privée ; [in US] *école privée qui prépare à l'enseignement supérieur.*

prepare [prɪ'peəʳ] ⟨⟩ *vt* préparer. ⟨⟩ *vi* : **to ~ for sthg/to do sthg** se préparer à qqch/à faire qqch.

prepared [prɪ'peəd] *adj* - **1.** [done beforehand] préparé(e) d'avance - **2.** [willing] : **to be ~ to do sthg** être prêt(e) OR disposé(e) à faire qqch - **3.** [ready] : **to be ~ for sthg** être prêt(e) pour qqch.

preposition [,prepə'zɪʃn] *n* préposition *f*.

preposterous [prɪ'pɒstərəs] *adj* ridicule, absurde.

prep school *abbr of* preparatory school.

prerequisite [,priː'rekwɪzɪt] *n* condition *f* préalable.

prerogative [prɪ'rɒgətɪv] *n* prérogative *f*, privilège *m*.

Presbyterian [,prezbɪ'tɪərɪən] ⟨⟩ *adj* presbytérien(enne). ⟨⟩ *n* presbytérien *m*, -enne *f*.

preschool [,priː'skuːl] ⟨⟩ *adj* préscolaire. ⟨⟩ *n* Am école *f* maternelle.

prescribe [prɪ'skraɪb] *vt* - **1.** MED prescrire - **2.** [order] ordonner, imposer.

prescription [prɪ'skrɪpʃn] *n* [MED - written form] ordonnance *f* ; [- medicine] médicament *m*.

prescriptive [prɪ'skrɪptɪv] *adj* normatif(ive).

presence ['prezns] *n* présence *f* ; **to be in sb's ~** OR **in the ~ of sb** être en présence de qqn.

presence of mind *n* présence *f* d'esprit.

present [*adj & n* 'preznt, *vb* prɪ'zent] ⟨⟩ *adj* - **1.** [current] actuel(elle) - **2.** [in attendance] présent(e) ; **to be ~ at** assister à. ⟨⟩ *n* - **1.** [current time] : **the ~** le présent ; **at ~** actuellement, en ce moment - **2.** [gift] ca-

deau *m* - **3.** GRAMM : ~ **(tense)** présent *m*.
◇ *vt* - **1.** [gen] présenter ; [opportunity]
donner - **2.** [give] donner, remettre ; **to ~ sb
with sthg, to ~ sthg to sb** donner OR remettre qqch à qqn - **3.** [portray] représenter,
décrire - **4.** [arrive] : **to ~ o.s.** se présenter.

presentable [prɪ'zentəbl] *adj* présentable.

presentation [ˌprezn'teɪʃn] *n* - **1.** [gen]
présentation *f* - **2.** [ceremony] remise *f* (de
récompense/prix) - **3.** [talk] exposé *m* - **4.** [of
play] représentation *f*.

present day *n* : **the ~** aujourd'hui.
➡ **present-day** *adj* d'aujourd'hui, con-
temporain(e).

presenter [prɪ'zentə'] *n Br* présentateur
m, -trice *f*.

presently ['prezəntlɪ] *adv* - **1.** [soon] bientôt, tout à l'heure - **2.** [at present] actuellement, en ce moment.

preservation [ˌprezə'veɪʃn] *n* (U)
- **1.** [maintenance] maintien *m* - **2.** [protec-
tion] protection *f*, conservation *f*.

preservative [prɪ'zɜːvətɪv] *n* conservateur *m*.

preserve [prɪ'zɜːv] ◇ *vt* - **1.** [maintain]
maintenir - **2.** [protect] conserver - **3.** [food]
conserver, mettre en conserve. ◇ *n* [jam]
confiture *f*. ➡ **preserves** *npl* [jam] confiture *f* ; [vegetables] pickles *mpl*, condiments
mpl.

preset [ˌpriː'set] (*pt & pp* preset) *vt* préré-
gler.

president ['prezɪdənt] *n* - **1.** [gen] président *m* - **2.** *Am* [company chairman] P-DG *m*.

presidential [ˌprezɪ'denʃl] *adj* présiden-
tiel(elle).

press [pres] ◇ *n* - **1.** [push] pression *f*
- **2.** [journalism] : **the ~** [newspapers] la
presse, les journaux *mpl* ; [reporters] les
journalistes *mpl* - **3.** [printing machine]
presse *f* ; [for wine] pressoir *m*. ◇ *vt*
- **1.** [push] appuyer sur ; **to ~ sthg against
sthg** appuyer qqch sur qqch - **2.** [squeeze]
serrer - **3.** [iron] repasser, donner un coup
de fer à - **4.** [urge] : **to ~ sb (to do sthg** OR **into
doing sthg)** presser qqn (de faire qqch)
- **5.** [pursue - claim] insister sur. ◇ *vi*
- **1.** [push] : **to ~ (on sthg)** appuyer (sur
qqch) - **2.** [squeeze] : **to ~ (on sthg)** serrer
(qqch) - **3.** [crowd] se presser. ➡ **press
for** *vt fus* demander avec insistance.
➡ **press on** *vi* [continue] : **to ~ on (with
sthg)** continuer (qqch), ne pas abandonner
(qqch).

press agency *n* agence *f* de presse.

press conference *n* conférence *f* de
presse.

pressed [prest] *adj* : **to be ~ for time/
money** être à court de temps/d'argent.

pressing ['presɪŋ] *adj* urgent(e).

press officer *n* attaché *m* de presse.

press release *n* communiqué *m* de
presse.

press-stud *n Br* pression *f*.

press-up *n Br* pompe *f*, traction *f*.

pressure ['preʃə'] *n* (U) - **1.** [gen] pression
f ; **to put ~ on sb (to do sthg)** faire pression
sur qqn (pour qu'il fasse qqch) - **2.** [stress]
tension *f*.

pressure cooker *n* Cocotte-Minute® *f*,
autocuiseur *m*.

pressure gauge *n* manomètre *m*.

pressure group *n* groupe *m* de pression.

pressurize, -ise ['preʃəraɪz] *vt* - **1.** TECH
pressuriser - **2.** *Br* [force] : **to ~ sb to do** OR **into doing sthg** forcer qqn à faire qqch.

prestige [pre'stiːʒ] *n* prestige *m*.

presumably [prɪ'zjuːməblɪ] *adv* vraisemblablement.

presume [prɪ'zjuːm] *vt* présumer ; **to
~ (that)** ... supposer que ...

presumption [prɪ'zʌmpʃn] *n* - **1.** [as-
sumption] supposition *f*, présomption *f*
- **2.** (U) [audacity] présomption *f*.

presumptuous [prɪ'zʌmptʃʊəs] *adj* pré-
somptueux(euse).

pretence, pretense *Am* [prɪ'tens] *n* prétention *f* ; **to make a ~ of doing sthg** faire
semblant de faire qqch ; **under false ~s**
sous des prétextes fallacieux.

pretend [prɪ'tend] ◇ *vt* : **to ~ to do sthg**
faire semblant de faire qqch. ◇ *vi* faire
semblant.

pretense *Am* = pretence.

pretension [prɪ'tenʃn] *n* prétention *f*.

pretentious [prɪ'tenʃəs] *adj* préten-
tieux(euse).

pretext ['priːtekst] *n* prétexte *m* ; **on** OR
under the ~ that ... sous prétexte que ... ;
on OR **under the ~ of doing sthg** sous prétexte de faire qqch.

pretty ['prɪtɪ] ◇ *adj* joli(e). ◇ *adv* [quite]
plutôt ; **~ much** OR **well** pratiquement, presque.

prevail [prɪ'veɪl] *vi* - **1.** [be widespread]
avoir cours, régner - **2.** [triumph] : **to
~ (over)** prévaloir (sur), l'emporter (sur)
- **3.** [persuade] : **to ~ on** OR **upon sb to do
sthg** persuader qqn de faire qqch.

prevailing [prɪ'veɪlɪŋ] *adj* - **1.** [current] ac-
tuel(elle) - **2.** [wind] dominant(e).

prevalent ['prevələnt] *adj* courant(e), répandu(e).

prevent [prɪ'vent] *vt* : **to ~ sb/sthg (from doing sthg)** empêcher qqn/qqch (de faire qqch).

preventive [prɪ'ventɪv] *adj* préventif(ive).

preview ['priːvjuː] *n* avant-première *f*.

previous ['priːvjəs] *adj* - 1. [earlier] antérieur(e) - 2. [preceding] précédent(e).

previously ['priːvjəslɪ] *adv* avant, auparavant.

prewar [ˌpriː'wɔːʳ] *adj* d'avant-guerre.

prey [preɪ] *n* proie *f*. ◆ **prey on** *vt fus* - 1. [live off] faire sa proie de - 2. [trouble] : **to ~ on sb's mind** ronger qqn, tracasser qqn.

price [praɪs] ◇ *n* [cost] prix *m* ; **at any ~** à tout prix. ◇ *vt* fixer le prix de.

priceless ['praɪslɪs] *adj* sans prix, inestimable.

price list *n* tarif *m*.

price tag *n* [label] étiquette *f*.

pricey ['praɪsɪ] *adj inf* chérot.

prick [prɪk] ◇ *n* - 1. [scratch, wound] piqûre *f* - 2. *vulg* [stupid person] con *m*, conne *f*. ◇ *vt* piquer. ◆ **prick up** *vt fus* : **to ~ up one's ears** [animal] dresser les oreilles ; [person] dresser OR tendre l'oreille.

prickle ['prɪkl] ◇ *n* - 1. [thorn] épine *f* - 2. [sensation on skin] picotement *m*. ◇ *vi* picoter.

prickly ['prɪklɪ] *adj* - 1. [plant, bush] épineux(euse) - 2. *fig* [person] irritable.

prickly heat *n* (U) boutons *mpl* de chaleur.

pride [praɪd] ◇ *n* (U) - 1. [satisfaction] fierté *f* ; **to take ~ in sthg/in doing sthg** être fier de qqch/de faire qqch - 2. [self-esteem] orgueil *m*, amour-propre *m* - 3. *pej* [arrogance] orgueil *m*. ◇ *vt* : **to ~ o.s. on sthg** être fier (fière) de qqch.

priest [priːst] *n* prêtre *m*.

priestess ['priːstɪs] *n* prêtresse *f*.

priesthood ['priːsthʊd] *n* - 1. [position, office] : **the ~** le sacerdoce - 2. [priests] : **the ~** le clergé.

prig [prɪg] *n* petit saint *m*, petite sainte *f*.

prim [prɪm] *adj* guindé(e).

primarily ['praɪmərɪlɪ] *adv* principalement.

primary ['praɪmərɪ] ◇ *adj* - 1. [main] premier(ère), principal(e) - 2. SCH primaire. ◇ *n Am* POL primaire *f*.

primary school *n* école *f* primaire.

primate ['praɪmeɪt] *n* - 1. ZOOL primate *m* - 2. RELIG primat *m*.

prime [praɪm] ◇ *adj* - 1. [main] principal(e), primordial(e) - 2. [excellent] excellent(e) ; **~ quality** première qualité. ◇ *n* : **to be in one's ~** être dans la fleur de l'âge. ◇ *vt* - 1. [gun, pump] amorcer - 2. [paint] apprêter - 3. [inform] : **to ~ sb about sthg** mettre qqn au courant de qqch.

prime minister *n* premier ministre *m*.

primer ['praɪməʳ] *n* - 1. [paint] apprêt *m* - 2. [textbook] introduction *f*.

primeval [praɪ'miːvl] *adj* [ancient] primitif(ive).

primitive ['prɪmɪtɪv] *adj* primitif(ive).

primrose ['prɪmrəʊz] *n* primevère *f*.

Primus stove® ['praɪməs-] *n* réchaud *m* de camping.

prince [prɪns] *n* prince *m*.

princess [prɪn'ses] *n* princesse *f*.

principal ['prɪnsəpl] ◇ *adj* principal(e). ◇ *n* SCH directeur *m*, -trice *f* ; UNIV doyen *m*, -enne *f*.

principle ['prɪnsəpl] *n* principe *m* ; **on ~, as a matter of ~** par principe. ◆ **in principle** *adv* en principe.

print [prɪnt] ◇ *n* - 1. (U) [type] caractères *mpl* ; **to be in ~** être disponible ; **to be out of ~** être épuisé - 2. ART gravure *f* - 3. [photograph] épreuve *f* - 4. [fabric] imprimé *m* - 5. [mark] empreinte *f* ◇ *vt* - 1. [produce by printing] imprimer - 2. [publish] publier - 3. [write in block letters] écrire en caractères d'imprimerie. ◇ *vi* [printer] imprimer. ◆ **print out** *vt sep* COMPUT imprimer.

printed matter ['prɪntɪd-] *n* (U) imprimés *mpl*.

printer ['prɪntəʳ] *n* - 1. [person, firm] imprimeur *m* - 2. COMPUT imprimante *f*.

printing ['prɪntɪŋ] *n* (U) - 1. [act of printing] impression *f* - 2. [trade] imprimerie *f*.

printout ['prɪntaʊt] *n* COMPUT sortie *f* d'imprimante, listing *m*.

prior ['praɪəʳ] ◇ *adj* antérieur(e), précédent(e). ◇ *n* [monk] prieur *m*. ◆ **prior to** *prep* avant ; **~ to doing sthg** avant de faire qqch.

priority [praɪ'ɒrətɪ] *n* priorité *f* ; **to have OR take ~ (over)** avoir la priorité (sur).

prise [praɪz] *vt* : **to ~ sthg away from sb** arracher qqch à qqn ; **to ~ sthg open** forcer qqch.

prison ['prɪzn] *n* prison *f*.

prisoner ['prɪznəʳ] *n* prisonnier *m*, -ère *f*.

prisoner of war (*pl* prisoners of war) *n* prisonnier *m*, -ère *f* de guerre.

privacy [*Br* 'prɪvəsɪ, *Am* 'praɪvəsɪ] *n* intimité *f*.

private ['praɪvɪt] ◇ *adj* - **1.** [not public] privé(e) - **2.** [confidential] confidentiel(elle) - **3.** [personal] personnel(elle) - **4.** [unsociable - person] secret(ète). ◇ *n* - **1.** [soldier] (simple) soldat *m* - **2.** [secrecy] : **in ~** en privé.

private enterprise *n* (*U*) entreprise *f* privée.

private eye *n* détective *m* privé.

privately ['praɪvɪtlɪ] *adv* - **1.** [not by the state] : **~ owned** du secteur privé - **2.** [confidentially] en privé - **3.** [personally] intérieurement, dans son for intérieur.

private property *n* propriété *f* privée.

private school *n* école *f* privée.

privatize, -ise ['praɪvɪtaɪz] *vt* privatiser.

privet ['prɪvɪt] *n* troène *m*.

privilege ['prɪvɪlɪdʒ] *n* privilège *m*.

privy ['prɪvɪ] *adj* : **to be ~ to sthg** être dans le secret de qqch.

Privy Council *n Br* : **the ~** le Conseil privé.

prize [praɪz] ◇ *adj* [possession] très précieux(euse) ; [animal] primé(e) ; [idiot, example] parfait(e). ◇ *n* prix *m*. ◇ *vt* priser.

prize-giving [-ˌgɪvɪŋ] *n Br* distribution *f* des prix.

prizewinner ['praɪzˌwɪnəʳ] *n* gagnant *m*, -e *f*.

pro [prəʊ] (*pl* **-s**) *n* - **1.** *inf* [professional] pro *mf* - **2.** [advantage] : **the ~s and cons** le pour et le contre.

probability [ˌprɒbə'bɪlətɪ] *n* probabilité *f*.

probable ['prɒbəbl] *adj* probable.

probably ['prɒbəblɪ] *adv* probablement.

probation [prə'beɪʃn] *n* (*U*) - **1.** JUR mise *f* à l'épreuve ; **to put sb on ~** mettre qqn en sursis avec mise à l'épreuve - **2.** [trial period] essai *m* ; **to be on ~** être à l'essai.

probe [prəʊb] ◇ *n* - **1.** [investigation] : **~ (into)** enquête *f* (sur) - **2.** MED & TECH sonde *f*. ◇ *vt* sonder.

problem ['prɒbləm] ◇ *n* problème *m* ; **no ~!** *inf* pas de problème! ◇ *comp* difficile.

procedure [prə'siːdʒəʳ] *n* procédure *f*.

proceed [*vb* prə'siːd, *npl* 'prəʊsiːdz] ◇ *vt* [do subsequently] : **to ~ to do sthg** se mettre à faire qqch. ◇ *vi* - **1.** [continue] : **to ~ (with sthg)** continuer (qqch), poursuivre (qqch) - **2.** *fml* [advance] avancer. ◆ **proceeds** *npl* recette *f*.

proceedings [prə'siːdɪŋz] *npl* - **1.** [of meeting] débats *mpl* - **2.** JUR poursuites *fpl*.

process ['prəʊses] ◇ *n* - **1.** [series of actions] processus *m* ; **in the ~** ce faisant ; **to be in the ~ of doing sthg** être en train de faire qqch - **2.** [method] procédé *m*. ◇ *vt* [raw materials, food, data] traiter, transformer ; [application] s'occuper de.

processing ['prəʊsesɪŋ] *n* traitement *m*, transformation *f*.

procession [prə'seʃn] *n* cortège *m*, procession *f*.

proclaim [prə'kleɪm] *vt* [declare] proclamer.

procrastinate [prə'kræstɪneɪt] *vi* faire traîner les choses.

procure [prə'kjʊəʳ] *vt* [for oneself] se procurer ; [for someone else] procurer ; [release] obtenir.

prod [prɒd] *vt* [push, poke] pousser doucement.

prodigal ['prɒdɪgl] *adj* prodigue.

prodigy ['prɒdɪdʒɪ] *n* prodige *m*.

produce [*n* 'prɒdjuːs, *vb* prə'djuːs] ◇ *n* (*U*) produits *mpl*. ◇ *vt* - **1.** [gen] produire - **2.** [cause] provoquer, causer - **3.** [show] présenter - **4.** THEATRE mettre en scène.

producer [prə'djuːsəʳ] *n* - **1.** [of film, manufacturer] producteur *m*, -trice *f* - **2.** THEATRE metteur *m* en scène.

product ['prɒdʌkt] *n* produit *m*.

production [prə'dʌkʃn] *n* - **1.** (*U*) [manufacture, of film] production *f* - **2.** (*U*) [output] rendement *m* - **3.** (*U*) THEATRE [of play] mise *f* en scène - **4.** [show - gen] production *f* ; [- THEATRE] pièce *f*.

production line *n* chaîne *f* de fabrication.

productive [prə'dʌktɪv] *adj* - **1.** [land, business, workers] productif(ive) - **2.** [meeting, experience] fructueux(euse).

productivity [ˌprɒdʌk'tɪvətɪ] *n* productivité *f*.

profane [prə'feɪn] *adj* impie.

profession [prə'feʃn] *n* profession *f* ; **by ~** de son métier.

professional [prə'feʃənl] ◇ *adj* - **1.** [gen] professionnel(elle) - **2.** [of high standard] de (haute) qualité. ◇ *n* professionnel *m*, -elle *f*.

professor [prə'fesəʳ] *n* - **1.** *Br* UNIV professeur *m* (de faculté) - **2.** *Am & Can* [teacher] professeur *m*.

proficiency [prə'fɪʃənsɪ] *n* : **~ (in)** compétence *f* (en).

profile ['prəʊfaɪl] *n* profil *m*.

profit ['prɒfɪt] ◇ *n* - **1.** [financial] bénéfice *m*, profit *m* ; **to make a ~** faire un bénéfice - **2.** [advantage] profit *m.* <> *vi* [financially] être le bénéficiaire ; [gain advantage] tirer avantage OR profit.

profitability [ˌprɒfɪtə'bɪlətɪ] *n* rentabilité *f.*

profitable ['prɒfɪtəbl] *adj* - **1.** [financially] rentable, lucratif(ive) - **2.** [beneficial] fructueux(euse), profitable.

profiteering [ˌprɒfɪ'tɪərɪŋ] *n* affairisme *m*, mercantilisme *m.*

profound [prə'faʊnd] *adj* profond(e).

profusely [prə'fju:slɪ] *adv* [sweat, bleed] abondamment ; **to apologize ~** se confondre en excuses.

profusion [prə'fju:ʒn] *n* profusion *f.*

progeny ['prɒdʒənɪ] *n* progéniture *f.*

prognosis [prɒg'nəʊsɪs] (*pl* **-ses** [-si:z]) *n* pronostic *m.*

program ['prəʊgræm] (*pt & pp* **-med** OR **-ed**, *cont* **-ming** OR **-ing**) <> *n* - **1.** COMPUT programme *m* - **2.** *Am* = **programme.** <> *vt* - **1.** COMPUT programmer - **2.** *Am* = **programme.**

programer *Am* = **programmer.**

programme *Br*, **program** *Am* ['prəʊgræm] <> *n* - **1.** [schedule, booklet] programme *m* - **2.** RADIO & TV émission *f* <> *vt* programmer ; **to ~ sthg to do sthg** programmer qqch pour faire qqch.

programmer *Br*, **programer** *Am* ['prəʊgræmə'] *n* COMPUT programmeur *m*, -euse *f.*

programming ['prəʊgræmɪŋ] *n* programmation *f.*

progress [*n* 'prəʊgres, *vb* prə'gres] <> *n* progrès *m*, progression *f* ; [improvement] faire des progrès ; **to make ~ in sthg** avancer dans qqch ; **in ~** en cours. <> *vi* - **1.** [improve - gen] progresser, avancer ; [- person] faire des progrès - **2.** [continue] avancer.

progressive [prə'gresɪv] *adj* - **1.** [enlightened] progressiste - **2.** [gradual] progressif(ive).

prohibit [prə'hɪbɪt] *vt* prohiber ; **to ~ sb from doing sthg** interdire OR défendre à qqn de faire qqch.

project [*n* 'prɒdʒekt, *vb* prə'dʒekt] <> *n* - **1.** [plan, idea] projet *m*, plan *m* - **2.** SCH [study] : **~ (on)** dossier *m* (sur), projet *m* (sur). <> *vt* - **1.** [gen] projeter - **2.** [estimate] prévoir. <> *vi* [jut out] faire saillie.

projectile [prə'dʒektaɪl] *n* projectile *m.*

projection [prə'dʒekʃn] *n* - **1.** [estimate] prévision *f* - **2.** [protrusion] saillie *f* - **3.** (*U*) [display, showing] projection *f.*

projector [prə'dʒektə'] *n* projecteur *m.*

proletariat [ˌprəʊlɪ'teərɪət] *n* prolétariat *m.*

prolific [prə'lɪfɪk] *adj* prolifique.

prologue, prolog *Am* ['prəʊlɒg] *n lit & fig* prologue *m.*

prolong [prə'lɒŋ] *vt* prolonger.

prom [prɒm] *n* - **1.** *Br inf* (*abbr of* **promenade**) promenade *f*, front *m* de mer - **2.** *Am* [ball] bal *m* d'étudiants - **3.** *Br inf* (*abbr of* **promenade concert**) concert *m* promenade.

promenade [ˌprɒmə'nɑ:d] *n Br* [road by sea] promenade *f*, front *m* de mer.

promenade concert *n Br* concert *m* promenade.

prominent ['prɒmɪnənt] *adj* - **1.** [important] important(e) - **2.** [noticeable] proéminent(e).

promiscuous [prɒ'mɪskjʊəs] *adj* [person] aux mœurs légères ; [behaviour] immoral(e).

promise ['prɒmɪs] <> *n* promesse *f.* <> *vt* : **to ~ (sb) to do sthg** promettre (à qqn) de faire qqch ; **to ~ sb sthg** promettre qqch à qqn. <> *vi* promettre.

promising ['prɒmɪsɪŋ] *adj* prometteur(euse).

promontory ['prɒməntrɪ] *n* promontoire *m.*

promote [prə'məʊt] *vt* - **1.** [foster] promouvoir - **2.** [push, advertise] promouvoir, lancer - **3.** [in job] promouvoir.

promoter [prə'məʊtə'] *n* - **1.** [organizer] organisateur *m*, -trice *f* - **2.** [supporter] promoteur *m*, -trice *f.*

promotion [prə'məʊʃn] *n* promotion *f*, avancement *m.*

prompt [prɒmpt] <> *adj* rapide, prompt(e). <> *adv* : **at nine o'clock ~** à neuf heures précises OR tapantes. <> *vt* - **1.** [motivate, encourage] : **to ~ sb (to do sthg)** pousser OR inciter qqn (à faire qqch) - **2.** THEATRE souffler sa réplique à. <> *n* THEATRE réplique *f.*

promptly ['prɒmptlɪ] *adv* - **1.** [immediately] rapidement, promptement - **2.** [punctually] ponctuellement.

prone [prəʊn] *adj* - **1.** [susceptible] : **to be ~ to sthg** être sujet(ette) à qqch ; **to be ~ to do sthg** avoir tendance à faire qqch - **2.** [lying flat] étendu(e) face contre terre.

prong [prɒŋ] *n* [of fork] dent *f.*

pronoun ['prəʊnaʊn] *n* pronom *m.*

pronounce [prə'naʊns] <> *vt* prononcer. <> *vi* : **to ~ on** se prononcer sur.

pronounced [prə'naʊnst] *adj* prononcé(e).

pronouncement [prə'naʊnsmənt] *n* déclaration *f*.

pronunciation [prəˌnʌnsɪ'eɪʃn] *n* prononciation *f*.

proof [pruːf] *n* - **1.** [evidence] preuve *f* - **2.** [of book etc] épreuve *f* - **3.** [of alcohol] teneur *f* en alcool.

prop [prɒp] <> *n* - **1.** [physical support] support *m*, étai *m* - **2.** *fig* [supporting thing, person] soutien *m*. <> *vt* : **to ~ sthg against** appuyer qqch contre OR à. ◆ **props** *npl* accessoires *mpl*. ◆ **prop up** *vt sep* - **1.** [physically support] soutenir, étayer - **2.** *fig* [sustain] soutenir.

propaganda [ˌprɒpə'gændə] *n* propagande *f*.

propel [prə'pel] *vt* propulser ; *fig* pousser.

propeller [prə'pelər] *n* hélice *f*.

propelling pencil [prə'pelɪŋ-] *n Br* portemine *m inv*.

propensity [prə'pensətɪ] *n* : **~ (for OR to)** propension *f* (à).

proper ['prɒpər] *adj* - **1.** [real] vrai(e) - **2.** [correct] correct(e), bon (bonne) - **3.** [decent - behaviour etc] convenable.

properly ['prɒpəlɪ] *adv* - **1.** [satisfactorily, correctly] correctement, comme il faut - **2.** [decently] convenablement, comme il faut.

proper noun *n* nom *m* propre.

property ['prɒpətɪ] *n* - **1.** (U) [possessions] biens *mpl*, propriété *f* - **2.** [building] bien *m* immobilier ; [land] terres *fpl* - **3.** [quality] propriété *f*.

property owner *n* propriétaire *m* (foncier).

prophecy ['prɒfɪsɪ] *n* prophétie *f*.

prophesy ['prɒfɪsaɪ] *vt* prédire.

prophet ['prɒfɪt] *n* prophète *m*.

proportion [prə'pɔːʃn] *n* - **1.** [part] part *f*, partie *f* - **2.** [ratio] rapport *m*, proportion *f* - **3.** ART : **in ~** proportionné(e) ; **out of ~** mal proportionné ; **a sense of ~** *fig* le sens de la mesure.

proportional [prə'pɔːʃənl] *adj* proportionnel(elle).

proportional representation *n* représentation *f* proportionnelle.

proportionate [prə'pɔːʃnət] *adj* proportionnel(elle).

proposal [prə'pəʊzl] *n* - **1.** [suggestion] proposition *f*, offre *f* - **2.** [offer of marriage] demande *f* en mariage.

propose [prə'pəʊz] <> *vt* - **1.** [suggest] proposer - **2.** [intend] : **to ~ to do** OR **doing sthg** avoir l'intention de faire qqch, se proposer de faire qqch - **3.** [toast] porter. <> *vi* faire une demande en mariage ; **to ~ to sb** demander qqn en mariage.

proposition [ˌprɒpə'zɪʃn] *n* proposition *f*.

proprietor [prə'praɪətər] *n* propriétaire *mf*.

propriety [prə'praɪətɪ] *fml n* (U) [moral correctness] bienséance *f*.

pro rata [-'rɑːtə] <> *adj* proportionnel(elle). <> *adv* au prorata.

prose [prəʊz] *n* (U) prose *f*.

prosecute ['prɒsɪkjuːt] <> *vt* poursuivre (en justice). <> *vi* [police] engager des poursuites judiciaires ; [lawyer] représenter la partie plaignante.

prosecution [ˌprɒsɪ'kjuːʃn] *n* poursuites *fpl* judiciaires, accusation *f* ; **the ~** la partie plaignante ; [in Crown case] ≃ le ministère public.

prosecutor ['prɒsɪkjuːtər] *n esp Am* plaignant *m*, -e *f*.

prospect [*n* 'prɒspekt, *vb* prə'spekt] <> *n* - **1.** [hope] possibilité *f*, chances *fpl* - **2.** [probability] perspective *f*. <> *vi* : **to ~ (for sthg)** prospecter (pour chercher qqch). ◆ **prospects** *npl* : **~s (for)** chances *fpl* (de), perspectives *fpl* (de).

prospecting [prə'spektɪŋ] *n* prospection *f*.

prospective [prə'spektɪv] *adj* éventuel(elle).

prospector [prə'spektər] *n* prospecteur *m*, -trice *f*.

prospectus [prə'spektəs] (*pl* -es) *n* prospectus *m*.

prosper ['prɒspər] *vi* prospérer.

prosperity [prɒ'sperətɪ] *n* prospérité *f*.

prosperous ['prɒspərəs] *adj* prospère.

prostitute ['prɒstɪtjuːt] *n* prostituée *f*.

prostrate ['prɒstreɪt] *adj* - **1.** [lying down] à plat ventre - **2.** [with grief etc] prostré(e).

protagonist [prə'tægənɪst] *n* protagoniste *mf*.

protect [prə'tekt] *vt* : **to ~ sb/sthg (against), to ~ sb/sthg (from)** protéger qqn/qqch (contre), protéger qqn/qqch (de).

protection [prə'tekʃn] *n* : **~ (from** OR **against)** protection *f* (contre), défense *f* (contre).

protective [prə'tektɪv] *adj* - **1.** [layer,

clothing] de protection - **2.** [person, feelings] protecteur(trice).

protein ['prəʊtiːn] *n* protéine *f*.

protest [*n* 'prəʊtest, *vb* prə'test] ◇ *n* protestation *f*. ◇ *vt* - **1.** [state] protester de - **2.** *Am* [protest against] protester contre. ◇ *vi* : **to ~ (about/against)** protester (à propos de/contre).

Protestant ['prɒtɪstənt] ◇ *adj* protestant(e). ◇ *n* protestant *m*, -e *f*.

protester [prə'testə'] *n* [on march, at demonstration] manifestant *m*, -e *f*.

protest march *n* manifestation *f*, marche *f* de protestation.

protocol ['prəʊtəkɒl] *n* protocole *m*.

prototype ['prəʊtətaɪp] *n* prototype *m*.

protracted [prə'træktɪd] *adj* prolongé(e).

protrude [prə'truːd] *vi* avancer, dépasser.

protuberance [prə'tjuːbərəns] *n* protubérance *f*.

proud [praʊd] *adj* - **1.** [satisfied, dignified] fier (fière) - **2.** *pej* [arrogant] orgueilleux (euse), fier (fière).

prove [pruːv] (*pp* -d OR **proven**) *vt* - **1.** [show to be true] prouver - **2.** [turn out] : **to ~ (to be) false/useful** s'avérer faux/ utile , **to ~ o.s. to be sthg** se révéler être qqch.

proven ['pruːvn, 'prəʊvn] ◇ *pp* ▷ **prove.** ◇ *adj* [fact] avéré(e), établi(e) ; [liar] fieffé(e).

Provence [prɒ'vɑːns] *n* Provence *f*.

proverb ['prɒvɜːb] *n* proverbe *m*.

provide [prə'vaɪd] *vt* fournir ; **to ~ sb with sthg** fournir qqch à qqn ; **to ~ sthg for sb** fournir qqch à qqn. ◆ **provide for** *vt fus* - **1.** [support] subvenir aux besoins de - **2.** *fml* [make arrangements for] prévoir.

provided [prə'vaɪdɪd] ◆ **provided (that)** *conj* à condition que (+ *subjunctive*), pourvu que (+ *subjunctive*).

providing [prə'vaɪdɪŋ] ◆ **providing (that)** *conj* à condition que (+ *subjunctive*), pourvu que (+ *subjunctive*).

province ['prɒvɪns] *n* - **1.** [part of country] province *f* - **2.** [speciality] domaine *m*, compétence *f*.

provincial [prə'vɪnʃl] *adj* - **1.** [town, newspaper] de province - **2.** *pej* [narrow-minded] provincial(e).

provision [prə'vɪʒn] *n* - **1.** (U) [act of supplying] : **~ (of)** approvisionnement *m* (en), fourniture *f* (de) - **2.** [supply] provision *f*, réserve *f* - **3.** (U) [arrangements] : **to make ~ for** [the future] prendre des mesures pour - **4.** [in agreement, law] clause *f*, disposition

f. ◆ **provisions** *npl* [supplies] provisions *fpl*.

provisional [prə'vɪʒənl] *adj* provisoire.

proviso [prə'vaɪzəʊ] (*pl* **-s**) *n* condition *f*, stipulation *f* ; **with the ~ that** à (la) condition que (+ *subjunctive*).

provocative [prə'vɒkətɪv] *adj* provocant(e).

provoke [prə'vəʊk] *vt* - **1.** [annoy] agacer, contrarier - **2.** [cause - fight, argument] provoquer ; [- reaction] susciter.

prow [praʊ] *n* proue *f*.

prowess ['praʊɪs] *n* prouesse *f*.

prowl [praʊl] ◇ *n* : **to be on the ~** rôder. ◇ *vt* [streets etc] rôder dans. ◇ *vi* rôder.

prowler ['praʊlə'] *n* rôdeur *m*, -euse *f*.

proxy ['prɒksɪ] *n* : **by ~** par procuration.

prudent ['pruːdnt] *adj* prudent(e).

prudish ['pruːdɪʃ] *adj* prude, pudibond(e).

prune [pruːn] ◇ *n* [fruit] pruneau *m*. ◇ *vt* [tree, bush] tailler.

pry [praɪ] *vi* se mêler de ce qui ne vous regarde pas ; **to ~ into sthg** chercher à découvrir qqch.

PS (*abbr of* **postscript**) *n* PS *m*.

psalm [sɑːm] *n* psaume *m*.

pseudonym ['sjuːdənɪm] *n* pseudonyme *m*.

psyche ['saɪkɪ] *n* psyché *f*.

psychiatric [,saɪkɪ'ætrɪk] *adj* psychiatrique.

psychiatrist [saɪ'kaɪətrɪst] *n* psychiatre *mf*.

psychiatry [saɪ'kaɪətrɪ] *n* psychiatrie *f*.

psychic ['saɪkɪk] ◇ *adj* - **1.** [clairvoyant - person] doué(e) de seconde vue ; [- powers] parapsychique - **2.** MED psychique. ◇ *n* médium *m*.

psychoanalysis [,saɪkəʊə'næləsɪs] *n* psychanalyse *f*.

psychoanalyst [,saɪkəʊ'ænəlɪst] *n* psychanalyste *mf*.

psychological [,saɪkə'lɒdʒɪkl] *adj* psychologique.

psychologist [saɪ'kɒlədʒɪst] *n* psychologue *mf*.

psychology [saɪ'kɒlədʒɪ] *n* psychologie *f*.

psychopath ['saɪkəpæθ] *n* psychopathe *mf*.

psychotic [saɪ'kɒtɪk] ◇ *adj* psychotique. ◇ *n* psychotique *mf*.

pt - **1.** *abbr of* **pint** - **2.** *abbr of* **point.**

PT (*abbr of* **physical training**) *n* EPS *f*.

PTO (*abbr of* **please turn over**) TSVP.

pub [pʌb] *n* pub *m*.

puberty ['pju:bətɪ] *n* puberté *f*.

pubic ['pju:bɪk] *adj* du pubis.

public ['pʌblɪk] ◇ *adj* public(ique) ; [library] municipal(e). ◇ *n* : **the ~** le public ; **in ~** en public.

public-address system *n* système *m* de sonorisation.

publican ['pʌblɪkən] *n Br* gérant *m*, -e *f* d'un pub.

publication [ˌpʌblɪ'keɪʃn] *n* publication *f*.

public bar *n Br* bar *m*.

public company *n* société *f* anonyme (*cotée en Bourse*).

public convenience *n Br* toilettes *fpl* publiques.

public holiday *n Br* jour *m* férié.

public house *n Br* pub *m*.

publicity [pʌb'lɪsɪtɪ] *n* (*U*) publicité *f*.

publicize, -ise ['pʌblɪsaɪz] *vt* faire connaître au public.

public limited company *n* société *f* anonyme (*cotée en Bourse*).

public opinion *n* (*U*) opinion *f* publique.

public prosecutor *n* ≃ procureur *m* de la République.

public relations ◇ *n* (*U*) relations *fpl* publiques. ◇ *npl* relations *fpl* publiques.

public school *n* - **1.** *Br* [private school] école *f* privée - **2.** *Am* [state school] école *f* publique.

public-spirited *adj* qui fait preuve de civisme.

public transport *n* (*U*) transports *mpl* en commun.

publish ['pʌblɪʃ] *vt* publier.

publisher ['pʌblɪʃər] *n* éditeur *m*, -trice *f*.

publishing ['pʌblɪʃɪŋ] *n* (*U*) [industry] édition *f*.

pub lunch *n repas de midi servi dans un pub*.

pucker ['pʌkər] *vt* plisser.

pudding ['pudɪŋ] *n* - **1.** [food - sweet] entremets *m* ; [- savoury] pudding *m* - **2.** (*U*) *Br* [course] dessert *m*.

puddle ['pʌdl] *n* flaque *f*.

puff [pʌf] ◇ *n* - **1.** [of cigarette, smoke] bouffée *f* - **2.** [gasp] souffle *m*. ◇ *vt* [cigarette etc] tirer sur. ◇ *vi* - **1.** [smoke] : **to ~ at** OR **on sthg** fumer qqch - **2.** [pant] haleter. ◆ **puff out** *vt sep* [cheeks, chest] gonfler.

puffed [pʌft] *adj* [swollen] : **~ (up)** gonflé(e).

puffin ['pʌfɪn] *n* macareux *m*.

puff pastry, puff paste *Am n* (*U*) pâte *f* feuilletée.

puffy ['pʌfɪ] *adj* gonflé(e), bouffi(e).

pugnacious [pʌg'neɪʃəs] *adj fml* querelleur(euse), batailleur(euse).

Pulitzer Prize [pʊlɪtsə-] *n* [in US] prix *m* Pulitzer.

pull [pʊl] ◇ *vt* - **1.** [gen] tirer - **2.** [strain - muscle, hamstring] se froisser - **3.** [tooth] arracher - **4.** [attract] attirer - **5.** [gun] sortir. ◇ *vi* - **1.** [tug with hand] : **to give sthg a ~** tirer sur qqch - **2.** (*U*) [influence] influence *f*. ◆ **pull apart** *vt sep* [separate] séparer. ◆ **pull at** *vt fus* tirer sur. ◆ **pull away** *vi* - **1.** AUT démarrer - **2.** [in race] prendre de l'avance. ◆ **pull down** *vt sep* [building] démolir. ◆ **pull in** *vi* AUT se ranger. ◆ **pull off** *vt sep* - **1.** [take off] enlever, ôter - **2.** [succeed in] réussir. ◆ **pull out** ◇ *vt sep* [troops etc] retirer. ◇ *vi* - **1.** RAIL partir, démarrer - **2.** AUT déboîter - **3.** [withdraw] se retirer. ◆ **pull over** *vi* AUT se ranger. ◆ **pull through** *vi* s'en sortir, s'en tirer. ◆ **pull together** *vt sep* : **to ~ o.s. together** se ressaisir, se reprendre. ◆ **pull up** ◇ *vt sep* - **1.** [raise] remonter - **2.** [chair] avancer. ◇ *vi* s'arrêter.

pulley ['pʊlɪ] (*pl* -s) *n* poulie *f*.

pullover ['pʊlˌəʊvər] *n* pull *m*.

pulp [pʌlp] ◇ *adj* [fiction, novel] de quatre sous. ◇ *n* - **1.** [for paper] pâte *f* à papier - **2.** [of fruit] pulpe *f*.

pulpit ['pʊlpɪt] *n* chaire *f*.

pulsate [pʌl'seɪt] *vi* [heart] battre fort ; [air, music] vibrer.

pulse [pʌls] ◇ *n* - **1.** MED pouls *m* - **2.** TECH impulsion *f*. ◇ *vi* battre, palpiter. ◆ **pulses** *npl* [food] légumes *mpl* secs.

puma ['pju:mə] (*pl inv* OR -s) *n* puma *m*.

pumice (stone) ['pʌmɪs-] *n* pierre *f* ponce.

pummel ['pʌml] *vt* bourrer de coups.

pump [pʌmp] ◇ *n* pompe *f*. ◇ *vt* - **1.** [water, gas etc] pomper - **2.** *inf* [interrogate] essayer de tirer les vers du nez à. ◇ *vi* [heart] battre fort. ◆ **pumps** *npl* [shoes] escarpins *mpl*.

pumpkin ['pʌmpkɪn] *n* potiron *m*.

pun [pʌn] *n* jeu *m* de mots, calembour *m*.

punch [pʌntʃ] ◇ *n* - **1.** [blow] coup *m* de poing - **2.** [tool] poinçonneuse *f* - **3.** [drink] punch *m*. ◇ *vt* - **1.** [hit - once] donner un coup de poing à ; [- repeatedly] donner des coups de poing à - **2.** [ticket] poinçonner ; [paper] perforer.

Punch-and-Judy show [-'dʒuːdɪ-] *n* guignol *m*.

punch(ed) card [pʌntʃ(t)-] *n* carte *f* perforée.

punch line *n* chute *f*.

punch-up *n* Br inf bagarre *f*.

punchy ['pʌntʃɪ] *adj* inf [style] incisif(ive).

punctual ['pʌŋktʃʊəl] *adj* ponctuel(elle).

punctuation [ˌpʌŋktʃʊ'eɪʃn] *n* ponctuation *f*.

punctuation mark *n* signe *m* de ponctuation.

puncture ['pʌŋktʃə'] ◇ *n* crevaison *f*. ◇ *vt* [tyre, ball] crever ; [skin] piquer.

pundit ['pʌndɪt] *n* pontife *m*.

pungent ['pʌndʒənt] *adj* - 1. [smell] âcre ; [taste] piquant(e) - 2. *fig* [criticism] caustique, acerbe.

punish ['pʌnɪʃ] *vt* punir ; to ~ sb for sthg/for doing sthg punir qqn pour qqch/pour avoir fait qqch.

punishing ['pʌnɪʃɪŋ] *adj* [schedule, work] épuisant(e), éreintant(e) , [defeat] cuisant(e).

punishment ['pʌnɪʃmənt] *n* punition *f*, châtiment *m*.

punk [pʌŋk] ◇ *adj* punk *(inv)*. ◇ *n* - 1. *(U)* [music] : ~ (rock) punk *m* - 2. : ~ (rocker) punk *mf* - 3. Am inf [lout] loubard *m*.

punt [pʌnt] *n* [boat] bateau *m* à fond plat.

punter ['pʌntə'] *n* Br - 1. [gambler] parieur *m*, -euse *f* - 2. inf [customer] client *m*, -e *f*.

puny ['pjuːnɪ] *adj* chétif(ive).

pup [pʌp] *n* - 1. [young dog] chiot *m* - 2. [young seal] bébé phoque *m*.

pupil ['pjuːpɪl] *n* - 1. [student] élève *mf* - 2. [of eye] pupille *f*.

puppet ['pʌpɪt] *n* - 1. [toy] marionnette *f* - 2. *pej* [person, country] fantoche *m*, pantin *m*.

puppy ['pʌpɪ] *n* chiot *m*.

purchase ['pɜːtʃəs] ◇ *n* achat *m*. ◇ *vt* acheter.

purchaser ['pɜːtʃəsə'] *n* acheteur *m*, -euse *f*.

purchasing power ['pɜːtʃəsɪŋ-] *n* pouvoir *m* d'achat.

pure [pjʊə'] *adj* pur(e).

puree ['pjʊəreɪ] *n* purée *f*.

purely ['pjʊəlɪ] *adv* purement.

purge [pɜːdʒ] ◇ *n* POL purge *f*. ◇ *vt* - 1. POL purger - 2. [rid] débarrasser, purger.

purify ['pjʊərɪfaɪ] *vt* purifier, épurer.

purist ['pjʊərɪst] *n* puriste *mf*.

puritan ['pjʊərɪtən] ◇ *adj* puritain(e). ◇ *n* puritain *m*, -e *f*.

purity ['pjʊərətɪ] *n* pureté *f*.

purl [pɜːl] ◇ *n* maille *f* à l'envers. ◇ *vt* tricoter à l'envers.

purple ['pɜːpl] ◇ *adj* violet(ette). ◇ *n* violet *m*.

purport [pə'pɔːt] *vi fml* : to ~ to do/be sthg prétendre faire/être qqch.

purpose ['pɜːpəs] *n* - 1. [reason] raison *f*, motif *m* - 2. [aim] but *m*, objet *m* ; to no ~ en vain, pour rien - 3. [determination] détermination *f*. ◆ on purpose *adv* exprès.

purposeful ['pɜːpəsfʊl] *adj* résolu(e), déterminé(e).

purr [pɜː'] *vi* ronronner.

purse [pɜːs] ◇ *n* - 1. [for money] portemonnaie *m inv*, bourse *f* - 2. Am [handbag] sac *m* à main. ◇ *vt* [lips] pincer.

purser ['pɜːsə'] *n* commissaire *m* de bord.

pursue [pə'sjuː] *vt* - 1. [follow] poursuivre, pourchasser - 2. [policy, aim] poursuivre ; [question] continuer à débattre ; [matter] approfondir ; [project] donner suite à ; to ~ an interest in sthg se livrer à qqch.

pursuer [pə'sjuːə'] *n* poursuivant *m*, -e *f*.

pursuit [pə'sjuːt] *n* - 1. *(U)* *fml* [attempt to obtain] recherche *f*, poursuite *f* - 2. [chase, in sport] poursuite *f* - 3. [occupation] occupation *f*, activité *f*.

pus [pʌs] *n* pus *m*.

push [pʊʃ] ◇ *vt* - 1. [press, move - gen] pousser ; [- button] appuyer sur - 2. [encourage] : to ~ sb (to do sthg) inciter OR pousser qqn (à faire qqch) - 3. [force] : to ~ sb (into doing sthg) forcer OR obliger qqn (à faire qqch) - 4. inf [promote] faire de la réclame pour. ◇ *vi* - 1. [gen] pousser ; [on button] appuyer - 2. [campaign] : to ~ for sthg faire pression pour obtenir qqch. ◇ *n* - 1. [with hand] poussée *f* - 2. [forceful effort] effort *m*. ◆ push around *vt sep inf fig* marcher sur les pieds de. ◆ push in *vi* [in queue] resquiller. ◆ push off *vi inf* filer, se sauver. ◆ push on *vi* continuer. ◆ push through *vt sep* [law, reform] faire accepter.

pushchair ['pʊʃtʃeə'] *n* Br poussette *f*.

pushed [pʊʃt] *adj inf* : to be ~ for sthg être à court de qqch ; to be hard ~ to do sthg avoir du mal OR de la peine à faire qqch.

pusher ['pʊʃə'] *n* drugs sl dealer *m*.

pushover ['pʊʃˌəʊvə'] *n* inf : it's a ~ c'est un jeu d'enfant.

push-up *n* pompe *f*, traction *f*.

pushy ['puʃɪ] *adj pej* qui se met toujours en avant.

puss [pus], **pussy (cat)** ['pusɪ-] *n inf* minet *m*, minou *m*.

put [put] (*pt & pp* put) *vt* - **1.** [gen] mettre - **2.** [place] mettre, poser, placer ; **to ~ the children to bed** coucher les enfants - **3.** [express] dire, exprimer - **4.** [question] poser - **5.** [estimate] estimer, évaluer - **6.** [invest] : **to ~ money into** investir de l'argent dans. ➤ **put across** *vt sep* [ideas] faire comprendre. ➤ **put away** *vt sep* - **1.** [tidy away] ranger - **2.** *inf* [lock up] enfermer. ➤ **put back** *vt sep* - **1.** [replace] remettre (à sa place OR en place) - **2.** [postpone] remettre - **3.** [clock, watch] retarder. ➤ **put by** *vt sep* [money] mettre de côté. ➤ **put down** *vt sep* - **1.** [lay down] poser, déposer - **2.** [quell - rebellion] réprimer - **3.** [write down] inscrire, noter - **4.** *Br* [kill] : **to have a dog/cat ~ down** faire piquer un chien/chat. ➤ **put down to** *vt sep* attribuer à. ➤ **put forward** *vt sep* - **1.** [propose] proposer, avancer - **2.** [meeting, clock, watch] avancer. ➤ **put in** *vt sep* - **1.** [spend - time] passer - **2.** [submit] présenter. ➤ **put off** *vt sep* - **1.** [postpone] remettre (à plus tard) - **2.** [cause to wait] décommander - **3.** [discourage] dissuader - **4.** [disturb] déconcerter, troubler - **5.** [cause to dislike] dégoûter - **6.** [switch off - radio, TV] éteindre. ➤ **put on** *vt sep* - **1.** [clothes] mettre, enfiler - **2.** [arrange - exhibition etc] organiser ; [- play] monter - **3.** [gain] : **to ~ on weight** prendre du poids, grossir - **4.** [switch on - radio, TV] allumer, mettre ; **to ~ the light on** allumer (la lumière) ; **to ~ the brake on** freiner - **5.** [record, CD, tape] passer, mettre - **6.** [start cooking] mettre à cuire - **7.** [pretend - gen] feindre ; [- accent etc] prendre - **8.** [bet] parier, miser - **9.** [add] ajouter. ➤ **put out** *vt sep* - **1.** [place outside] mettre dehors - **2.** [book, statement] publier ; [record] sortir - **3.** [fire, cigarette] éteindre ; **to ~ the light out** éteindre (la lumière) - **4.** [extend - hand] tendre - **5.** [annoy, upset] : **to be ~ out** être contrarié(e) - **6.** [inconvenience] déranger. ➤ **put through** *vt sep* TELEC passer. ➤ **put up** *vt sep* - **1.** [build - gen] ériger ; [- tent] dresser - **2.** [umbrella] ouvrir ; [flag] hisser - **3.** [fix to wall] accrocher - **4.** [provide - money] fournir - **5.** [propose - candidate] proposer - **6.** [increase] augmenter - **7.** [provide accommodation for] loger, héberger. ➤ *vt fus* : **to ~ up a fight** se défendre. ➤ **put up with** *vt fus* supporter.

putrid ['pju:trɪd] *adj* putride.

putt [pʌt] ◇ *n* putt *m*. ◇ *vt & vi* putter.

putting green ['pʌtɪŋ-] *n* green *m*.

putty ['pʌtɪ] *n* mastic *m*.

puzzle ['pʌzl] ◇ *n* - **1.** [toy] puzzle *m* ; [mental] devinette *f* - **2.** [mystery] mystère *m*, énigme *f*. ◇ *vt* rendre perplexe. ◇ *vi* : **to ~ over sthg** essayer de comprendre qqch. ➤ **puzzle out** *vt sep* comprendre.

puzzling ['pʌzlɪŋ] *adj* curieux(euse).

pyjamas [pə'dʒɑ:məz] *npl* pyjama *m* ; **a pair of ~** un pyjama.

pylon ['paɪlən] *n* pylône *m*.

pyramid ['pɪrəmɪd] *n* pyramide *f*.

Pyrenees [ˌpɪrə'ni:z] *npl* : **the ~** les Pyrénées *fpl*.

Pyrex® ['paɪreks] *n* Pyrex® *m*.

python ['paɪθn] (*pl inv* OR **-s**) *n* python *m*.

q (*pl* **q's** OR **qs**), **Q** (*pl* **Q's** OR **Qs**) [kju:] *n* [letter] q *m inv*, Q *m inv*.

quack [kwæk] *n* - **1.** [noise] coin-coin *m inv* - **2.** *inf pej* [doctor] charlatan *m*.

quad [kwɒd] *abbr of* **quadrangle**.

quadrangle ['kwɒdræŋgl] *n* - **1.** [figure] quadrilatère *m* - **2.** [courtyard] cour *f*.

quadruple [kwɒ'dru:pl] ◇ *adj* quadruple. ◇ *vt & vi* quadrupler.

quadruplets ['kwɒdruplɪts] *npl* quadruplés *mpl*.

quads [kwɒdz] *npl inf* quadruplés *mpl*.

quagmire ['kwægmaɪə'] *n* bourbier *m*.

quail [kweɪl] (*pl inv* OR **-s**) ◇ *n* caille *f*. ◇ *vi literary* reculer.

quaint [kweɪnt] *adj* pittoresque.

quake [kweɪk] ◇ *n* (*abbr of* **earthquake**) *inf* tremblement *m* de terre. ◇ *vi* trembler.

Quaker ['kweɪkə'] *n* quaker *m*, -eresse *f*.

qualification [ˌkwɒlɪfɪ'keɪʃn] *n* - **1.** [certificate] diplôme *m* - **2.** [quality, skill] compétence *f* - **3.** [qualifying statement] réserve *f*.

qualified ['kwɒlɪfaɪd] *adj* - **1.** [trained] diplômé(e) - **2.** [able] : **to be ~ to do sthg** avoir la compétence nécessaire pour faire qqch - **3.** [limited] restreint(e), modéré(e).

qualify ['kwɒlɪfaɪ] ◇ *vt* - **1.** [modify] apporter des réserves à - **2.** [entitle] : **to ~ sb to**

do sthg qualifier qqn pour faire qqch.
◇ *vi* - **1.** [pass exams] obtenir un diplôme - **2.** [be entitled] : **to ~ (for sthg)** avoir droit (à qqch), remplir les conditions requises (pour qqch) - **3.** SPORT se qualifier.

quality ['kwɒlətɪ] ◇ *n* qualité *f.* ◇ *comp* de qualité.

qualms [kwa:mz] *npl* doutes *mpl.*

quandary ['kwɒndərɪ] *n* embarras *m* ; **to be in a ~ about** OR **over sthg** être bien embarrassé à propos de qqch.

quantify ['kwɒntɪfaɪ] *vt* quantifier.

quantity ['kwɒntətɪ] *n* quantité *f.*

quantity surveyor *n* métreur *m*, -euse *f.*

quarantine ['kwɒrəntiːn] ◇ *n* quarantaine *f.* ◇ *vt* mettre en quarantaine.

quark [kwa:k] *n* quark *m.*

quarrel ['kwɒrəl] ◇ *n* querelle *f*, dispute *f.* ◇ *vi* : **to ~ (with)** se quereller (avec), se disputer (avec).

quarrelsome ['kwɒrəlsəm] *adj* querelleur(euse).

quarry ['kwɒrɪ] *n* - **1.** [place] carrière *f* - **2.** [prey] proie *f.*

quart [kwɔːt] *n* = 1,136 litre *Br*, = 0,946 litre *Am*, ≈ litre *m.*

quarter ['kwɔːtəʳ] *n* - **1.** [fraction, weight] quart *m* ; **a ~ past two** *Br*, **a ~ after two** *Am* deux heures et quart ; **a ~ to two** *Br*, **a ~ of two** *Am* deux heures moins le quart - **2.** [of year] trimestre *m* - **3.** *Am* [coin] pièce *f* de 25 cents - **4.** [area in town] quartier *m* - **5.** [direction] : **from all ~s** de tous côtés. ➤ **quarters** *npl* [rooms] quartiers *mpl.* ➤ **at close quarters** *adv* de près.

quarterfinal [,kwɔːtə'faɪnl] *n* quart *m* de finale.

quarterly ['kwɔːtəlɪ] ◇ *adj* trimestriel(elle). ◇ *adv* trimestriellement. ◇ *n* publication *f* trimestrielle.

quartermaster ['kwɔːtə,mɑːstəʳ] *n* MIL intendant *m.*

quartet [kwɔː'tet] *n* quatuor *m.*

quartz [kwɔːts] *n* quartz *m.*

quartz watch *n* montre *f* à quartz.

quash [kwɒʃ] *vt* - **1.** [sentence] annuler, casser - **2.** [rebellion] réprimer.

quasi- ['kweɪzaɪ] *prefix* quasi-.

quaver ['kweɪvəʳ] ◇ *n* - **1.** MUS croche *f* - **2.** [in voice] tremblement *m*, chevrotement *m.* ◇ *vi* trembler, chevroter.

quay [kiː] *n* quai *m.*

quayside ['kiːsaɪd] *n* bord *m* du quai.

queasy ['kwiːzɪ] *adj* : **to feel ~** avoir mal au cœur.

Quebec [kwɪ'bek] *n* [province] Québec *m.*

queen [kwiːn] *n* - **1.** [gen] reine *f* - **2.** [playing card] dame *f.*

Queen Mother *n* : **the ~** la reine mère.

queer [kwɪəʳ] ◇ *adj* [odd] étrange, bizarre. ◇ *n inf pej* pédé *m*, homosexuel *m.*

quell [kwel] *vt* réprimer, étouffer.

quench [kwentʃ] *vt* : **to ~ one's thirst** se désaltérer.

querulous ['kwerʊləs] *adj* [child] ronchonneur(euse) ; [voice] plaintif(ive).

query ['kwɪərɪ] ◇ *n* question *f.* ◇ *vt* mettre en question, douter de.

quest [kwest] *n literary* : **~ (for)** quête *f* (de).

question ['kwestʃn] ◇ *n* - **1.** [gen] question *f* ; **to ask (sb) a ~** poser une question (à qqn) - **2.** [doubt] doute *m* ; **to call** OR **bring sthg into ~** mettre qqch en doute ; **without ~** incontestablement, sans aucun doute ; **beyond ~** [know] sans aucun doute - **3.** *phr* : **there's no ~ of ...** il n'est pas question de ... ◇ *vt* - **1.** [interrogate] questionner - **2.** [express doubt about] mettre en question OR doute. ➤ **In question** *adv* : **the ... in ~** le/la/les ... en question. ➤ **out of the question** *adv* hors de question.

questionable ['kwestʃənəbl] *adj* - **1.** [uncertain] discutable - **2.** [not right, not honest] douteux(euse).

question mark *n* point *m* d'interrogation.

questionnaire [,kwestʃə'neəʳ] *n* questionnaire *m.*

queue [kjuː] *Br* ◇ *n* queue *f*, file *f.* ◇ *vi* faire la queue.

quibble ['kwɪbl] *pej* ◇ *n* chicane *f.* ◇ *vi* : **to ~ (over** OR **about)** chicaner (à propos de).

quiche [kiːʃ] *n* quiche *f.*

quick [kwɪk] ◇ *adj* - **1.** [gen] rapide - **2.** [response, decision] prompt(e), rapide. ◇ *adv* vite, rapidement.

quicken ['kwɪkn] ◇ *vt* accélérer, presser. ◇ *vi* s'accélérer.

quickly ['kwɪklɪ] *adv* - **1.** [rapidly] vite, rapidement - **2.** [without delay] promptement, immédiatement.

quicksand ['kwɪksænd] *n* sables *mpl* mouvants.

quick-witted [-'wɪtɪd] *adj* [person] à l'esprit vif.

quid [kwɪd] (*pl inv*) *n Br inf* livre *f.*

quiet ['kwaɪət] ◇ *adj* - **1.** [not noisy] tranquille ; [voice] bas (basse) ; [engine] silencieux(euse) ; **be ~!** taisez-vous! - **2.** [not busy] calme - **3.** [silent] silencieux(euse) ; **to keep ~ about sthg** ne rien dire à propos de qqch, garder qqch secret - **4.** [intimate] intime - **5.** [colour] discret(ète), sobre. ◇ *n* tranquillité *f* ; **on the ~** *inf* en douce. ◇ *vt Am* calmer, apaiser. ◆ **quiet down** ◇ *vt sep* calmer, apaiser. ◇ *vi* se calmer.

quieten ['kwaɪətn] *vt* calmer, apaiser. ◆ **quieten down** ◇ *vt sep* calmer, apaiser. ◇ *vi* se calmer.

quietly ['kwaɪətlɪ] *adv* - **1.** [without noise] sans faire de bruit, silencieusement ; [say] doucement - **2.** [without excitement] tranquillement, calmement - **3.** [without fuss - leave] discrètement.

quilt [kwɪlt] *n* [padded] édredon *m* ; **(continental) ~** couette *f*.

quinine [kwɪ'niːn] *n* quinine *f*.

quins *Br* [kwɪnz], **quints** *Am* [kwɪnts] *npl inf* quintuplés *mpl*.

quintet [kwɪn'tet] *n* quintette *m*.

quints *Am* = **quins**.

quintuplets [kwɪn'tjuːplɪts] *npl* quintuplés *mpl*.

quip [kwɪp] ◇ *n* raillerie *f*. ◇ *vi* railler.

quirk [kwɜːk] *n* bizarrerie *f*.

quit [kwɪt] (*Br pt & pp* quit *or* -**ted**, *Am pt & pp* quit) ◇ *vt* - **1.** [resign from] quitter - **2.** [stop] : **to ~ smoking** arrêter de fumer. ◇ *vi* - **1.** [resign] démissionner - **2.** [give up] abandonner.

quite [kwaɪt] *adv* - **1.** [completely] tout à fait, complètement ; **I ~ agree** je suis entièrement d'accord ; **not ~** pas tout à fait ; **I don't ~ understand** je ne comprends pas bien - **2.** [fairly] assez, plutôt - **3.** [for emphasis] : **she's ~ a singer** c'est une chanteuse formidable - **4.** *Br* [to express agreement] : **~ (so)!** exactement !

quits [kwɪts] *adj inf* : **to be ~ (with sb)** être quitte (envers qqn) ; **to call it ~** en rester là.

quiver ['kwɪvə'] ◇ *n* - **1.** [shiver] frisson *m* - **2.** [for arrows] carquois *m*. ◇ *vi* frissonner.

quiz [kwɪz] (*pl* quizzes) ◇ *n* - **1.** [gen] quiz *m*, jeu-concours *m* - **2.** *Am* SCH interrogation *f*. ◇ *vt* : **to ~ sb (about sthg)** interroger qqn (au sujet de qqch).

quizzical ['kwɪzɪkl] *adj* narquois(e), moqueur(euse).

quota ['kwəʊtə] *n* quota *m*.

quotation [kwəʊ'teɪʃn] *n* - **1.** [citation] citation *f* - **2.** COMM devis *m*.

quotation marks *npl* guillemets *mpl* ; **in ~** entre guillemets.

quote [kwəʊt] ◇ *n* - **1.** [citation] citation *f* - **2.** COMM devis *m*. ◇ *vt* - **1.** [cite] citer - **2.** COMM indiquer, spécifier. ◇ *vi*

- **1.** [cite] : **to ~ (from sthg)** citer (qqch) - **2.** COMM : **to ~ for sthg** établir un devis pour qqch.

quotient ['kwəʊʃnt] *n* quotient *m*.

R

r (*pl* r's *or* rs), **R** (*pl* R's *or* Rs) [aːʳ] *n* [letter] r *m inv*, R *m inv*.

rabbi ['ræbaɪ] *n* rabbin *m*.

rabbit ['ræbɪt] *n* lapin *m*.

rabbit hutch *n* clapier *m*.

rabble ['ræbl] *n* cohue *f*.

rabies ['reɪbiːz] *n* rage *f*.

RAC (*abbr of* Royal Automobile Club) *n club automobile britannique*, ≃ TCF *m*, ≃ ACF *m*.

race [reɪs] ◇ *n* - **1.** [competition] course *f* - **2.** [people, ethnic background] race *f*. ◇ *vt* - **1.** [compete against] faire la course avec - **2.** [horse] faire courir. ◇ *vi* - **1.** [compete] courir ; **to ~ against sb** faire la course avec qqn - **2.** [rush] : **to ~ in/out** entrer/sortir à toute allure - **3.** [pulse] être très rapide - **4.** [engine] s'emballer.

race car *Am* = **racing car**.

racecourse ['reɪskɔːs] *n* champ *m* de courses.

race driver *Am* = **racing driver**.

racehorse ['reɪshɔːs] *n* cheval *m* de course.

racetrack ['reɪstræk] *n* piste *f*.

racial discrimination ['reɪʃl-] *n* discrimination *f* raciale.

racing ['reɪsɪŋ] *n (U)* : **(horse) ~** les courses *fpl*.

racing car *Br*, **race car** *Am n* voiture *f* de course.

racing driver *Br*, **race driver** *Am n* coureur *m* automobile, pilote *m* de course.

racism ['reɪsɪzm] *n* racisme *m*.

racist ['reɪsɪst] ◇ *adj* raciste. ◇ *n* raciste *mf*.

rack [ræk] *n* [for bottles] casier *m* ; [for luggage] porte-bagages *m inv* ; [for plates] égouttoir *m* ; **toast ~** porte-toasts *m inv*.

racket ['rækɪt] *n* - **1.** [noise] boucan *m* - **2.** [illegal activity] racket *m* - **3.** SPORT raquette *f*.

racquet ['rækɪt] *n* raquette *f*.

racy ['reɪsɪ] *adj* [novel, style] osé(e).

radar ['reɪdɑːʳ] *n* radar *m*.

radial (tyre) ['reɪdjəl-] *n* pneu *m* à carcasse radiale.

radiant ['reɪdjənt] *adj* [happy] radieux(euse).

radiate ['reɪdɪeɪt] ◇ *vt* - **1.** [heat, light] émettre, dégager - **2.** *fig* [confidence, health] respirer. ◇ *vi* - **1.** [heat, light] irradier - **2.** [roads, lines] rayonner.

radiation [ˌreɪdɪ'eɪʃn] *n* [radioactive] radiation *f*.

radiator ['reɪdɪeɪtəʳ] *n* radiateur *m*.

radical ['rædɪkl] ◇ *adj* radical(e). ◇ *n* POL radical *m*, -e *f*.

radically ['rædɪklɪ] *adv* radicalement.

radii ['reɪdɪaɪ] *pl* ⊏▷ radius.

radio ['reɪdɪəʊ] (*pl* -s) ◇ *n* radio *f* ; on the ~ à la radio. ◇ *comp* de radio. ◇ *vt* [person] appeler par radio ; [information] envoyer par radio.

radioactive [ˌreɪdɪəʊ'æktɪv] *adj* radioactif(ive).

radio alarm *n* radio-réveil *m*.

radio-controlled [-kən'trəʊld] *adj* téléguidé(e).

radiography [ˌreɪdɪ'ɒgrəfɪ] *n* radiographie *f*.

radiology [ˌreɪdɪ'ɒlədʒɪ] *n* radiologie *f*.

radiotherapy [ˌreɪdɪəʊ'θerəpɪ] *n* radiothérapie *f*.

radish ['rædɪʃ] *n* radis *m*.

radius ['reɪdɪəs] (*pl* **radii** ['reɪdɪaɪ]) *n* - **1.** MATH rayon *m* - **2.** ANAT radius *m*.

RAF [ɑːreɪ'ef, ræf] *n abbr of* Royal Air Force.

raffle ['ræfl] ◇ *n* tombola *f*. ◇ *vt* mettre en tombola.

raft [rɑːft] *n* [of wood] radeau *m*.

rafter ['rɑːftəʳ] *n* chevron *m*.

rag [ræg] *n* - **1.** [piece of cloth] chiffon *m* - **2.** *pej* [newspaper] torchon *m*. ➡ **rags** *npl* [clothes] guenilles *fpl*.

rag-and-bone man *n* Br chiffonnier *m*.

rag doll *n* poupée *f* de chiffon.

rage [reɪdʒ] ◇ *n* - **1.** [fury] rage *f*, fureur *f* - **2.** *inf* [fashion] : **to be (all) the ~** faire fureur. ◇ *vi* - **1.** [person] être furieux(euse) - **2.** [storm, argument] faire rage.

ragged ['rægɪd] *adj* - **1.** [person] en haillons ; [clothes] en lambeaux - **2.** [line, edge, performance] inégal(e).

rag week *n* Br semaine de carnaval organisée par des étudiants afin de collecter des fonds pour des œuvres charitables.

raid [reɪd] ◇ *n* - **1.** MIL raid *m* - **2.** [by criminals] hold-up *m inv* ; [by police] descente *f*. ◇ *vt* - **1.** MIL faire un raid sur - **2.** [subj : criminals] faire un hold-up dans ; [subj : police] faire une descente dans.

raider ['reɪdəʳ] *n* - **1.** [attacker] agresseur *m* - **2.** [thief] braqueur *m*.

rail [reɪl] ◇ *n* - **1.** [on ship] bastingage *m* ; [on staircase] rampe *f* ; [on walkway] garde-fou *m* - **2.** [bar] barre *f* - **3.** RAIL rail *m* ; **by ~** en train. ◇ *comp* [transport, travel] par le train ; [strike] des cheminots.

railcard ['reɪlkɑːd] *n Br* carte donnant droit à des tarifs préférentiels sur les chemins de fer.

railing ['reɪlɪŋ] *n* [fence] grille *f* ; [on ship] bastingage *m* ; [on staircase] rampe *f* ; [on walkway] garde-fou *m*.

railway *Br* ['reɪlweɪ], **railroad** *Am* ['reɪlrəʊd] *n* [system, company] chemin *m* de fer ; [track] voie *f* ferrée.

railway line *n* [route] ligne *f* de chemin de fer ; [track] voie *f* ferrée.

railwayman ['reɪlweɪmən] (*pl* -men [-mən]) *n Br* cheminot *m*.

railway station *n* gare *f*.

railway track *n* voie *f* ferrée.

rain [reɪn] ◇ *n* pluie *f*. ◇ *v impers* METEOR pleuvoir ; **it's ~ing** il pleut. ◇ *vi* [fall like rain] pleuvoir.

rainbow ['reɪnbəʊ] *n* arc-en-ciel *m*.

rain check *n Am* : **I'll take a ~ (on that)** une autre fois peut-être.

raincoat ['reɪnkəʊt] *n* imperméable *m*.

raindrop ['reɪndrɒp] *n* goutte *f* de pluie.

rainfall ['reɪnfɔːl] *n* [shower] chute *f* de pluie ; [amount] précipitations *fpl*.

rain forest *n* forêt *f* tropicale humide.

rainy ['reɪnɪ] *adj* pluvieux(euse).

raise [reɪz] ◇ *vt* - **1.** [lift up] lever ; **to ~ o.s.** se lever - **2.** [increase - gen] augmenter ; [- standards] élever ; **to ~ one's voice** élever la voix - **3.** [obtain] : **to ~ money** [from donations] collecter des fonds ; [by selling, borrowing] se procurer de l'argent - **4.** [subject, doubt] soulever ; [memories] évoquer - **5.** [children, cattle] élever - **6.** [crops] cultiver - **7.** [build] ériger, élever. ◇ *n Am* augmentation *f* (de salaire).

raisin ['reɪzn] *n* raisin *m* sec.

rake [reɪk] ◇ *n* - **1.** [implement] râteau *m* - **2.** *dated & literary* [immoral man] débauché *m*. ◇ *vt* [path, lawn] ratisser ; [leaves] râteler.

rally ['rælɪ] ◇ *n* - **1.** [meeting] rassemblement *m* - **2.** [car race] rallye *m* - **3.** SPORT [exchange of shots] échange m. ◇ *vt* rallier. ◇ *vi* - **1.** [supporters] se rallier - **2.** [patient] aller mieux ; [prices] remonter. ◆ **rally round** ◇ *vt fus* apporter son soutien à. ◇ *vi inf* venir en aide.

ram [ræm] ◇ *n* bélier m. ◇ *vt* - **1.** [crash into] percuter contre, emboutir - **2.** [force] tasser.

RAM [ræm] (*abbr of* **random access memory**) *n* RAM *f*.

ramble ['ræmbl] ◇ *n* randonnée *f*, promenade *f* à pied. ◇ *vi* - **1.** [walk] faire une promenade à pied - **2.** *pej* [talk] radoter. ◆ **ramble on** *vi pej* radoter.

rambler ['ræmblə'] *n* [walker] randonneur *m*, -euse *f*.

rambling ['ræmblɪŋ] *adj* - **1.** [house] plein(e) de coins et recoins - **2.** [speech] décousu(e).

ramp [ræmp] *n* - **1.** [slope] rampe *f* - **2.** AUT [to slow traffic down] ralentisseur *m*.

rampage [ræm'peɪdʒ] *n* : **to go on the ~** tout saccager.

rampant ['ræmpənt] *adj* qui sévit.

ramparts ['ræmpɑːts] *npl* rempart *m*.

ramshackle ['ræm ʃækl] *adj* branlant(e).

ran [ræn] *pt* ⊏▷ **run**.

ranch [rɑːntʃ] *n* ranch *m*.

rancher ['rɑːntʃə'] *n* propriétaire *mf* de ranch.

rancid ['rænsɪd] *adj* rance.

rancour Br, **rancor** Am ['ræŋkə'] *n* rancœur *f*.

random ['rændəm] ◇ *adj* fait(e) au hasard ; [number] aléatoire. ◇ *n* : **at ~** au hasard.

random access memory *n* COMPUT mémoire *f* vive.

R and R (*abbr of* **rest and recreation**) *n* Am permission *f*.

randy ['rændɪ] *adj inf* excité(e).

rang [ræŋ] *pt* ⊏▷ **ring**.

range [reɪndʒ] ◇ *n* - **1.** [of plane, telescope etc] portée *f* ; **at close ~** à bout portant - **2.** [of subjects, goods] gamme *f* ; **price ~** éventail *m* des prix - **3.** [of mountains] chaîne *f* - **4.** [shooting area] champ *m* de tir - **5.** MUS [of voice] tessiture *f*. ◇ *vt* [place in row] mettre en rang. ◇ *vi* - **1.** [vary] : **to ~ between ... and ...** varier entre ... et ... ; **to ~ from ... to ...** varier de ... à ... - **2.** [include] : **to ~ over sthg** couvrir qqch.

ranger ['reɪndʒə'] *n* garde *m* forestier.

rank [ræŋk] ◇ *adj* - **1.** [absolute - disgrace,

stupidity] complet(ète) ; [- injustice] flagrant(e) ; **he's a ~ outsider** il n'a aucune chance - **2.** [smell] fétide. ◇ *n* - **1.** [in army, police etc] grade *m* - **2.** [social class] rang *m* - **3.** [row] rangée *f* - **4.** *phr* : **the ~ and file** la masse ; [of union] la base. ◇ *vt* [classify] classer. ◇ *vi* : **to ~ among** compter parmi ; **to ~ as** être aux rangs de. ◆ **ranks** *npl* - **1.** MIL : **the ~s** le rang - **2.** *fig* [members] rangs *mpl*.

rankle ['ræŋkl] *vi* : **it ~d with him** ça lui est resté sur l'estomac OR le cœur.

ransack ['rænsæk] *vt* [search through] mettre tout sens dessus dessous dans ; [damage] saccager.

ransom ['rænsəm] *n* rançon *f* ; **to hold sb to ~** [keep prisoner] mettre qqn à rançon ; *fig* exercer un chantage sur qqn.

rant [rænt] *vi* déblatérer.

rap [ræp] ◇ *n* - **1.** [knock] coup *m* sec - **2.** MUS rap *m*. ◇ *vt* [table] frapper sur ; [knuckles] taper sur.

rape [reɪp] ◇ *n* - **1.** [crime, attack] viol *m* - **2.** *fig* [of countryside etc] destruction *f* - **3.** [plant] colza *m*. ◇ *vt* violer.

rapeseed ['reɪpsiːd] *n* graine *f* de colza.

rapid ['ræpɪd] *adj* rapide. ◆ **rapids** *npl* rapides *mpl*.

rapidly ['ræpɪdlɪ] *adv* rapidement.

rapist ['reɪpɪst] *n* violeur *m*.

rapport [ræ'pɔː'] *n* rapport *m*.

rapture ['ræptʃə'] *n* ravissement *m*.

rapturous ['ræptʃərəs] *adj* [applause, welcome] enthousiaste.

rare [reə'] *adj* - **1.** [gen] rare - **2.** [meat] saignant(e).

rarely ['reəlɪ] *adv* rarement.

raring ['reərɪŋ] *adj* : **to be ~ to go** être impatient(e) de commencer.

rarity ['reərətɪ] *n* rareté *f*.

rascal ['rɑːskl] *n* polisson *m*, -onne *f*.

rash [ræʃ] ◇ *adj* irréfléchi(e), imprudent(e). ◇ *n* - **1.** MED éruption *f* - **2.** [spate] succession *f*, série *f*.

rasher ['ræʃə'] *n* tranche *f*.

rasp [rɑːsp] *n* [harsh sound] grincement *m*.

raspberry ['rɑːzbərɪ] *n* - **1.** [fruit] framboise *f* - **2.** [rude sound] : **to blow a ~** faire pfft.

rat [ræt] *n* - **1.** [animal] rat *m* - **2.** *inf pej* [person] ordure *f*, salaud *m*.

rate [reɪt] ◇ *n* - **1.** [speed] vitesse *f* ; [of pulse] fréquence *f* ; **at this ~** à ce train-là - **2.** [ratio, proportion] taux *m* - **3.** [price] tarif *m*. ◇ *vt* - **1.** [consider] : **I ~ her very highly** je la tiens en haute estime ; **to ~ sb/sthg as**

considérer qqn/qqch comme ; **to ~ sb/sthg among** classer qqn/qqch parmi **- 2.** [deserve] mériter. **rates** *npl Br* impôts *mpl* locaux. **at any rate** *adv* en tout cas.

ratepayer ['reɪtˌpeɪəʳ] *n Br* contribuable *mf.*

rather ['rɑːðəʳ] *adv* **- 1.** [somewhat, more exactly] plutôt **- 2.** [to small extent] un peu **- 3.** [preferably] : **I'd ~ wait** je préférerais attendre ; **she'd ~ not go** elle préférerait ne pas y aller **- 4.** [on the contrary] : **(but) ~ ...** au contraire ... **rather than** *conj* plutôt que.

ratify ['rætɪfaɪ] *vt* ratifier, approuver.

rating ['reɪtɪŋ] *n* [of popularity etc] cote *f.*

ratio ['reɪʃɪəʊ] (*pl* -**s**) *n* rapport *m.*

ration ['ræʃn] ⟨⟩ *n* ration *f.* ⟨⟩ *vt* rationner. **rations** *npl* vivres *mpl.*

rational ['ræʃənl] *adj* rationnel(elle).

rationale [ˌræʃə'nɑːl] *n* logique *f.*

rationalize, ise ['ræʃənəlaɪz] *vt* rationaliser.

rat race *n* jungle *f.*

rattle ['rætl] ⟨⟩ *n* **- 1.** [of bottles, typewriter keys] cliquetis *m* ; [of engine] bruit *m* de ferraille **- 2.** [toy] hochet *m.* ⟨⟩ *vt* **- 1.** [bottles] faire s'entrechoquer ; [keys] faire cliqueter **- 2.** [unsettle] secouer. ⟨⟩ *vi* [bottles] s'entrechoquer ; [keys, machine] cliqueter ; [engine] faire un bruit de ferraille.

rattlesnake ['rætlsneɪk], **rattler** *Am* ['rætləʳ] *n* serpent *m* à sonnettes.

raucous ['rɔːkəs] *adj* [voice, laughter] rauque ; [behaviour] bruyant(e).

ravage ['rævɪdʒ] *vt* ravager. **ravages** *npl* ravages *mpl.*

rave [reɪv] ⟨⟩ *adj* [review] élogieux(euse). ⟨⟩ *n Br inf* [party] rave *f.* ⟨⟩ *vi* **- 1.** [talk angrily] : **to ~ at** OR **against** tempêter OR fulminer contre **- 2.** [talk enthusiastically] : **to ~ about** parler avec enthousiasme de.

raven ['reɪvn] *n* corbeau *m.*

ravenous ['rævənəs] *adj* [person] affamé(e) ; [animal, appetite] vorace.

ravine [rə'viːn] *n* ravin *m.*

raving ['reɪvɪŋ] *adj* : **~ lunatic** fou furieux (folle furieuse).

ravioli [ˌrævɪ'əʊlɪ] *n* (*U*) ravioli *mpl.*

ravishing ['rævɪʃɪŋ] *adj* ravissant(e), enchanteur(eresse).

raw [rɔː] *adj* **- 1.** [uncooked] cru(e) **- 2.** [untreated] brut(e) **- 3.** [painful] à vif **- 4.** [inexperienced] novice ; **~ recruit** bleu *m* **- 5.** [weather] froid(e) ; [wind] âpre.

raw deal *n* : **to get a ~** être défavorisé(e).

raw material *n* matière *f* première.

ray [reɪ] *n* [beam] rayon *m* ; *fig* [of hope] lueur *f.*

rayon ['reɪɒn] *n* rayonne *f.*

raze [reɪz] *vt* raser.

razor ['reɪzəʳ] *n* rasoir *m.*

razor blade *n* lame *f* de rasoir.

RC *abbr of* **Roman Catholic.**

Rd *abbr of* **Road.**

R & D (*abbr of* **research and development**) *n* R-D *f.*

re [riː] *prep* concernant.

RE *n* (*abbr of* **religious education**) instruction *f* religieuse.

reach [riːtʃ] ⟨⟩ *vt* **- 1.** [gen] atteindre ; [place, destination] arriver à ; [agreement, decision] parvenir à **- 2.** [contact] joindre, contacter. ⟨⟩ *vi* [land] s'étendre ; **to ~ out** tendre le bras ; **to ~ down to pick sthg up** se pencher pour ramasser qqch. ⟨⟩ *n* [of arm, boxer] allonge *f* ; **within ~** [object] à portée ; [place] à proximité ; **out of** OR **beyond sb's ~** [object] hors de portée ; [place] d'accès difficile, difficilement accessible.

react [rɪ'ækt] *vi* [gen] réagir.

reaction [rɪ'ækʃn] *n* réaction *f.*

reactionary [rɪ'ækʃənrɪ] ⟨⟩ *adj* réactionnaire. ⟨⟩ *n* réactionnaire *mf.*

reactor [rɪ'æktəʳ] *n* réacteur *m.*

read [riːd] (*pt & pp* **read** [red]) ⟨⟩ *vt* **- 1.** [gen] lire **- 2.** [subj : sign, letter] dire **- 3.** [interpret, judge] interpréter **- 4.** [subj : meter, thermometer etc] indiquer **- 5.** *Br* UNIV étudier. ⟨⟩ *vi* lire ; **the book ~s well** le livre se lit bien. **read out** *vt sep* lire à haute voix. **read up on** *vt fus* étudier.

readable ['riːdəbl] *adj* agréable à lire.

reader ['riːdəʳ] *n* [of book, newspaper] lecteur *m*, -trice *f.*

readership ['riːdəʃɪp] *n* [of newspaper] nombre *m* de lecteurs.

readily ['redɪlɪ] *adv* **- 1.** [willingly] volontiers **- 2.** [easily] facilement.

reading ['riːdɪŋ] *n* **- 1.** (*U*) [gen] lecture *f* **- 2.** [interpretation] interprétation *f* **- 3.** [on thermometer, meter etc] indications *fpl.*

readjust [ˌriːə'dʒʌst] ⟨⟩ *vt* [instrument] régler (de nouveau) ; [mirror] rajuster ; [policy] rectifier. ⟨⟩ *vi* [person] : **to ~ (to)** se réadapter (à).

readout ['riːdaʊt] *n* COMPUT affichage *m.*

ready ['redɪ] ⟨⟩ *adj* **- 1.** [prepared] prêt(e) ; **to be ~ to do sthg** être prêt à faire qqch ; **to get ~** se préparer ; **to get sthg ~** préparer qqch **- 2.** [willing] : **to be ~ to do sthg** être prêt(e) OR disposé(e) à faire qqch. ⬦ vt préparer.

ready cash n liquide m.

ready-made adj lit & fig tout fait (toute faite).

ready meal n plat m préparé.

ready money n liquide m.

ready-to-wear adj prêt-à-porter.

reafforestation [ˌriːəˌfɒrɪ'steɪʃn] n reboisement m.

real ['rɪəl] ⬦ adj - 1. [gen] vrai(e), véritable ; ~ life réalité f ; for ~ pour de vrai ; this is the ~ thing [object] c'est de l'authentique ; [situation] c'est pour de vrai OR de bon - 2. [actual] réel(elle) ; in ~ terms dans la pratique. ⬦ adv Am très.

real estate n (U) biens mpl immobiliers.

realign [ˌriːə'laɪn] vt POL regrouper.

realism ['rɪəlɪzm] n réalisme m.

realistic [ˌrɪə'lɪstɪk] adj réaliste.

reality [rɪ'ælətɪ] n réalité f.

realization [ˌrɪəlaɪ'zeɪʃn] n réalisation f.

realize, -ise ['rɪəlaɪz] vt - 1. [understand] se rendre compte de, réaliser - 2. [sum of money, idea, ambition] réaliser.

really ['rɪəlɪ] ⬦ adv - 1. [gen] vraiment - 2. [in fact] en réalité. ⬦ excl - 1. [expressing doubt] vraiment? - 2. [expressing surprise] pas possible! - 3. [expressing disapproval] franchement!, ça alors!

realm [relm] n - 1. fig [subject area] domaine m - 2. [kingdom] royaume m.

realtor ['rɪəltər] n Am agent m immobilier.

reap [riːp] vt - 1. [harvest] moissonner - 2. fig [obtain] récolter.

reappear [ˌriːə'pɪər] vi réapparaître, reparaître.

rear [rɪər] ⬦ adj arrière (inv), de derrière. ⬦ n - 1. [back] arrière m ; to bring up the ~ fermer la marche - 2. inf [bottom] derrière m. ⬦ vt [children, animals] élever. ⬦ vi [horse] : to ~ (up) se cabrer.

rearm [riː'ɑːm] vt & vi réarmer.

rearmost ['rɪəməʊst] adj dernier(ère).

rearrange [ˌriːə'reɪndʒ] vt - 1. [furniture, room] réarranger ; [plans] changer - 2. [meeting - to new time] changer l'heure de ; [- to new date] changer la date de.

rearview mirror ['rɪəvjuː-] n rétroviseur m.

reason ['riːzn] ⬦ n - 1. [cause] : ~ (for) raison f (de) ; for some ~ pour une raison ou pour une autre - 2. (U) [justification] : to have ~ to do sthg avoir de bonnes raisons de faire qqch - 3. [common sense] bon sens m ; he won't listen to ~ on ne peut pas lui faire entendre raison ; it stands to ~ c'est logique. ⬦ vt déduire. ⬦ vi raisonner.
➤ **reason with** vt fus raisonner (avec).

reasonable ['riːznəbl] adj raisonnable.

reasonably ['riːznəblɪ] adv - 1. [quite] assez - 2. [sensibly] raisonnablement.

reasoned ['riːznd] adj raisonné(e).

reasoning ['riːznɪŋ] n raisonnement m.

reassess [ˌriːə'ses] vt réexaminer.

reassurance [ˌriːə'ʃʊərəns] n - 1. [comfort] réconfort m - 2. [promise] assurance f.

reassure [ˌriːə'ʃʊər] vt rassurer.

reassuring [ˌriːə'ʃʊərɪŋ] adj rassurant(e).

rebate ['riːbeɪt] n [on product] rabais m ; tax ~ ≃ dégrèvement m fiscal.

rebel [n 'rebl, vb rɪ'bel] ⬦ n rebelle mf. ⬦ vi : to ~ (against) se rebeller (contre).

rebellion [rɪ'beljən] n rébellion f.

rebellious [rɪ'beljəs] adj rebelle.

rebound [n 'riːbaʊnd, vb rɪ'baʊnd] ⬦ n [of ball] rebond m. ⬦ vi [ball] rebondir.

rebuff [rɪ'bʌf] n rebuffade f.

rebuild [ˌriː'bɪld] (pt & pp **rebuilt** [ˌriː'bɪlt]) vt reconstruire.

rebuke [rɪ'bjuːk] ⬦ n réprimande f. ⬦ vt réprimander.

rebuttal [riː'bʌtl] n réfutation f.

recalcitrant [rɪ'kælsɪtrənt] adj récalcitrant(e).

recall [rɪ'kɔːl] ⬦ n [memory] rappel m. ⬦ vt - 1. [remember] se rappeler, se souvenir de - 2. [summon back] rappeler.

recant [rɪ'kænt] vi se rétracter ; RELIG abjurer.

recap ['riːkæp] ⬦ n récapitulation f. ⬦ vt [summarize] récapituler. ⬦ vi récapituler.

recapitulate [ˌriːkə'pɪtjʊleɪt] vt & vi récapituler.

recd, rec'd abbr of **received**.

recede [riː'siːd] vi [person, car etc] s'éloigner ; [hopes] s'envoler.

receding [rɪ'siːdɪŋ] adj [hairline] dégarni(e) ; [chin, forehead] fuyant(e).

receipt [rɪ'siːt] n - 1. [piece of paper] reçu m - 2. (U) [act of receiving] réception f. ➤ **receipts** npl recettes fpl.

receive [rɪ'siːv] vt - 1. [gen] recevoir ; [news] apprendre - 2. [welcome] accueillir, recevoir.

receiver [rɪ'siːvər] n - 1. [of telephone] récepteur m, combiné m - 2. [radio, TV set] récepteur m - 3. [criminal] receleur m, -euse f

- **4.** FIN [official] administrateur *m*, -trice *f* judiciaire.

recent ['riːsnt] *adj* récent(e).

recently ['riːsntlɪ] *adv* récemment ; **until ~** jusqu'à ces derniers temps.

receptacle [rɪ'septəkl] *n* récipient *m*.

reception [rɪ'sepʃn] *n* - **1.** [gen] réception *f* - **2.** [welcome] accueil *m*, réception *f*.

reception desk *n* réception *f*.

receptionist [rɪ'sepʃənɪst] *n* réceptionniste *mf*.

recess ['riːses, rɪ'ses] *n* - **1.** [alcove] niche *f* - **2.** [secret place] recoin *m* - **3.** POL : **to be in ~** être en vacances - **1.** *Am* SCH récréation *f*.

recession [rɪ'seʃn] *n* récession *f*.

recharge [ˌriː'tʃɑːdʒ] *vt* recharger.

recipe ['resɪpɪ] *n lit & fig* recette *f*.

recipient [rɪ'sɪpɪənt] *n* [of letter] destinataire *mf* ; [of cheque] bénéficiaire *mf* ; [of award] récipiendaire *mf*.

reciprocal [rɪ'sɪprəkl] *adj* réciproque.

recital [rɪ'saɪtl] *n* récital *m*

recite [rɪ'saɪt] *vt* - **1.** [say aloud] réciter - **2.** [list] énumérer.

reckless ['reklɪs] *adj* imprudent(e).

reckon ['rekn] *vt* - **1.** *inf* [think] penser - **2.** [consider, judge] considérer - **3.** [calculate] calculer. **◆ reckon on** *vt fus* compter sur. **◆ reckon with** *vt fus* [expect] s'attendre à.

reckoning ['rekənɪŋ] *n (U)* [calculation] calculs *mpl*.

reclaim [rɪ'kleɪm] *vt* - **1.** [claim back] réclamer - **2.** [land] assécher.

recline [rɪ'klaɪn] *vi* [person] être allongé(e).

reclining [rɪ'klaɪnɪŋ] *adj* [chair] à dossier réglable.

recluse [rɪ'kluːs] *n* reclus *m*, -e *f*.

recognition [ˌrekəg'nɪʃn] *n* reconnaissance *f* ; **in ~ of** en reconnaissance de ; **the town has changed beyond** OR **out of all ~** la ville est méconnaissable.

recognizable ['rekəgnaɪzəbl] *adj* reconnaissable.

recognize, -ise ['rekəgnaɪz] *vt* reconnaître.

recoil [*vb* rɪ'kɔɪl, *n* 'riːkɔɪl] *⟨⟩ vi* : **to ~ (from)** reculer (devant). *⟨⟩ n* [of gun] recul *m*.

recollect [ˌrekə'lekt] *vt* se rappeler.

recollection [ˌrekə'lekʃn] *n* souvenir *m*.

recommend [ˌrekə'mend] *vt* - **1.** [commend] : **to ~ sb/sthg (to sb)** recommander

qqn/qqch (à qqn) - **2.** [advise] conseiller, recommander.

recompense ['rekəmpens] *⟨⟩ n* dédommagement *m*. *⟨⟩ vt* dédommager.

reconcile ['rekənsaɪl] *vt* - **1.** [beliefs, ideas] concilier - **2.** [people] réconcilier - **3.** [accept] : **to ~ o.s. to sthg** se faire à l'idée de qqch.

reconditioned [ˌriːkən'dɪʃnd] *adj* remis(e) en état.

reconnaissance [rɪ'kɒnɪsəns] *n* reconnaissance *f*.

reconnoitre *Br*, **reconnoiter** *Am* [ˌrekə'nɔɪtəʳ] *⟨⟩ vt* reconnaître. *⟨⟩ vi* aller en reconnaissance.

reconsider [ˌriːkən'sɪdəʳ] *⟨⟩ vt* reconsidérer. *⟨⟩ vi* reconsidérer la question.

reconstruct [ˌriːkən'strʌkt] *vt* - **1.** [gen] reconstruire - **2.** [crime, event] reconstituer.

record [*n & adj* 'rekɔːd, *vb* rɪ'kɔːd] *⟨⟩ n* - **1.** [written account] rapport *m* ; [file] dossier *m* ; **to keep sthg on ~** archiver qqch ; **(police) ~** casier *m* judiciaire ; **off the ~** non officiel - **2.** [vinyl disc] disque *m* - **3.** [best achievement] record *m*. *⟨⟩ adj* record (*inv*). *⟨⟩ vt* - **1.** [write down] noter - **2.** [put on tape] enregistrer.

recorded delivery [rɪ'kɔːdɪd-] *n Br* : **to send sthg by ~** envoyer qqch en recommandé.

recorder [rɪ'kɔːdəʳ] *n* [musical instrument] flûte *f* à bec.

record holder *n* détenteur *m*, -trice *f* du record.

recording [rɪ'kɔːdɪŋ] *n* enregistrement *m*.

record player *n* tourne-disque *m*.

recount [*n* 'riːkaʊnt, *vt sense 1* rɪ'kaʊnt, *sense 2* ˌriː'kaʊnt] *⟨⟩ n* [of vote] deuxième dépouillement *m* du scrutin. *⟨⟩ vt* - **1.** [narrate] raconter - **2.** [count again] recompter.

recoup [rɪ'kuːp] *vt* récupérer.

recourse [rɪ'kɔːs] *n* : **to have ~ to** avoir recours à.

recover [rɪ'kʌvəʳ] *⟨⟩ vt* - **1.** [retrieve] récupérer ; **to ~ sthg from sb** reprendre qqch à qqn - **2.** [one's balance] retrouver ; [consciousness] reprendre. *⟨⟩ vi* - **1.** [from illness] se rétablir ; [from shock, divorce] se remettre - **2.** *fig* [economy] se redresser ; [trade] reprendre.

recovery [rɪ'kʌvərɪ] *n* - **1.** [from illness] guérison *f*, rétablissement *m* - **2.** *fig* [of economy] redressement *m*, reprise *f* - **3.** [retrieval] récupération *f*.

recreation [ˌrekrɪ'eɪʃn] *n (U)* [leisure] récréation *f*, loisirs *mpl*.

recrimination [rɪˌkrɪmɪ'neɪʃn] *n* récrimination *f*.

recruit [rɪ'kru:t] ◇ *n* recrue *f*. ◇ *vt* recruter ; **to ~ sb to do sthg** *fig* embaucher qqn pour faire qqch. ◇ *vi* recruter.

recruitment [rɪ'kru:tmənt] *n* recrutement *m*.

rectangle ['rek,tæŋgl] *n* rectangle *m*.

rectangular [rek'tæŋgjʊləʳ] *adj* rectangulaire.

rectify ['rektɪfaɪ] *vt* [mistake] rectifier.

rector ['rektəʳ] *n* - **1.** [priest] pasteur *m* - **2.** *Scot* [head - of school] directeur *m* ; [- of college, university] *président élu par les étudiants*.

rectory ['rektərɪ] *n* presbytère *m*.

recuperate [rɪ'ku:pəreɪt] *vi* se rétablir.

recur [rɪ'kɜːʳ] *vi* [error, problem] se reproduire ; [dream] revenir ; [pain] réapparaître.

recurrence [rɪ'kʌrəns] *n* répétition *f*.

recurrent [rɪ'kʌrənt] *adj* [error, problem] qui se reproduit souvent ; [dream] qui revient souvent.

recycle [ˌriː'saɪkl] *vt* recycler.

recycling [ˌriː'saɪklɪŋ] *n* recyclage *m*.

red [red] ◇ *adj* rouge ; [hair] roux (rousse). ◇ *n* rouge *m* ; **to be in the ~** *inf* être à découvert.

red card *n* FTBL : **to be shown the ~, to get a ~** recevoir un carton rouge.

red carpet *n* : **to roll out the ~ for sb** dérouler le tapis rouge pour qqn. ◆ **red-carpet** *adj* : **to give sb the red-carpet treatment** recevoir qqn en grande pompe.

Red Cross *n* : **the ~** la Croix-Rouge.

redcurrant ['red,kʌrənt] *n* [fruit] groseille *f* ; [bush] groseillier *m*.

redden ['redn] *vt & vi* rougir.

redecorate [ˌriː'dekəreɪt] ◇ *vt* repeindre et retapisser. ◇ *vi* refaire la peinture et les papiers peints.

redeem [rɪ'diːm] *vt* - **1.** [save, rescue] racheter - **2.** [from pawnbroker] dégager.

redeeming [rɪ'diːmɪŋ] *adj* qui rachète (les défauts).

redeploy [ˌriːdɪ'plɔɪ] *vt* MIL redéployer ; [staff] réorganiser, réaffecter.

red-faced [-'feɪst] *adj* rougeaud(e), rubicond(e) ; [with embarrassment] rouge de confusion.

red-haired [-'heəd] *adj* roux (rousse).

red-handed [-'hændɪd] *adj* : **to catch sb ~** prendre qqn en flagrant délit OR la main dans le sac.

redhead ['redhed] *n* roux *m*, rousse *f*.

red herring *n fig* fausse piste *f*.

red-hot *adj* - **1.** [extremely hot] brûlant(e) ; [metal] chauffé(e) au rouge - **2.** [very enthusiastic] ardent(e).

redid [ˌriː'dɪd] *pt* ⊏▷ redo.

redirect [ˌriːdɪ'rekt] *vt* - **1.** [energy, money] réorienter - **2.** [traffic] détourner - **3.** [letters] faire suivre.

rediscover [ˌriːdɪ'skʌvəʳ] *vt* redécouvrir.

red light *n* [traffic signal] feu *m* rouge.

red-light district *n* quartier *m* chaud.

redo [ˌriː'duː] (*pt* -did, *pp* -done) *vt* refaire.

redolent ['redələnt] *adj literary* - **1.** [reminiscent] : **~ of** qui rappelle, évocateur (trice) de - **2.** [smelling] : **~ of** qui sent.

redone [ˌriː'dʌn] *pp* ⊏▷ redo.

redouble [ˌriː'dʌbl] *vt* : **to ~ one's efforts (to do sthg)** redoubler d'efforts (pour faire qqch).

redraft [ˌriː'drɑːft] *vt* rédiger à nouveau.

redress [rɪ'dres] ◇ *n* (U) *fml* réparation *f*. ◇ *vt* : **to ~ the balance** rétablir l'équilibre.

Red Sea *n* : **the ~** la mer Rouge.

red tape *n fig* paperasserie *f* administrative.

reduce [rɪ'djuːs] ◇ *vt* réduire ; **to be ~d to doing sthg** en être réduit à faire qqch ; **to ~ sb to tears** faire pleurer qqn. ◇ *vi Am* [diet] suivre un régime amaigrissant.

reduction [rɪ'dʌkʃn] *n* - **1.** [decrease] : **~ (in)** réduction *f* (de), baisse *f* (de) - **2.** [discount] rabais *m*, réduction *f*.

redundancy [rɪ'dʌndənsɪ] *n Br* [dismissal] licenciement *m* ; [unemployment] chômage *m*.

redundant [rɪ'dʌndənt] *adj* - **1.** *Br* [jobless] : **to be made ~** être licencié(e) - **2.** [not required] superflu(e).

reed [riːd] *n* - **1.** [plant] roseau *m* - **2.** MUS anche *f*.

reef [riːf] *n* récif *m*, écueil *m*.

reek [riːk] ◇ *n* relent *m*. ◇ *vi* : **to ~ (of sthg)** puer (qqch), empester (qqch).

reel [riːl] ◇ *n* - **1.** [roll] bobine *f* - **2.** [on fishing rod] moulinet *m*. ◇ *vi* [stagger] chanceler. ◆ **reel in** *vt sep* remonter. ◆ **reel off** *vt sep* [list] débiter.

reenact [ˌriːɪ'nækt] *vt* [play] reproduire ; [event] reconstituer.

ref [ref] *n* - **1.** *inf* (*abbr of* referee) arbitre *m* - **2.** (*abbr of* reference) ADMIN réf. *f*.

refectory [rɪ'fektərɪ] *n* réfectoire *m*.

refer [rɪ'fɜːʳ] *vt* - **1.** [person] : **to ~ sb to** [hospital] envoyer qqn à ; [specialist] adresser qqn à ; ADMIN renvoyer qqn à - **2.** [report, case, decision] : **to ~ sthg to** soumettre qqch à. ◆ **refer to** *vt fus* **- 1.** [speak about] parler de, faire allusion à OR mention de **- 2.** [apply to] s'appliquer à, concerner **- 3.** [consult] se référer à, se reporter à.

referee [ˌrefə'riː] ◇ *n* **- 1.** SPORT arbitre *m* **- 2.** *Br* [for job application] répondant *m*, -e *f*. ◇ *vt* SPORT arbitrer. ◇ *vi* SPORT être arbitre.

reference ['refrəns] *n* **- 1.** [mention] : **~ (to)** allusion *f* (à), mention *f* (de) ; **with ~ to** comme suite à **- 2.** *(U)* [for advice, information] : **~ (to)** consultation *f* (de), référence *f* (à) **- 3.** COMM référence *f* **- 4.** [in book] renvoi *m* ; **map ~** coordonnées *fpl* **- 5.** [for job application - letter] référence *f* ; [- person] répondant *m*, -e *f*.

reference book *n* ouvrage *m* de référence.

reference number *n* numéro *m* de référence.

referendum [ˌrefə'rendəm] (*pl* **-s** OR **-da** [-də]) *n* référendum *m*.

refill [*n* 'riːfɪl, *vb* ˌriː'fɪl] ◇ *n* **- 1.** [for pen] recharge *f* **- 2.** *inf* [drink] : **would you like a ~?** vous voulez encore un verre? ◇ *vt* remplir à nouveau.

refine [rɪ'faɪn] *vt* raffiner ; *fig* peaufiner.

refined [rɪ'faɪnd] *adj* raffiné(e) ; [system, theory] perfectionné(e).

refinement [rɪ'faɪnmənt] *n* **- 1.** [improvement] perfectionnement *m* **- 2.** *(U)* [gentility] raffinement *m*.

reflect [rɪ'flekt] ◇ *vt* **- 1.** [be a sign of] refléter **- 2.** [light, image] réfléchir, refléter ; [heat] réverbérer **- 3.** [think] : **to ~ that ... se dire que ...** ◇ *vi* [think] : **to ~ (on** OR **upon)** réfléchir (sur), penser (à).

reflection [rɪ'flekʃn] *n* **- 1.** [sign] indication *f*, signe *m* **- 2.** [criticism] : **~ on** critique *f* de **- 3.** [image] reflet *m* **- 4.** *(U)* [of light, heat] réflexion *f* **- 5.** [thought] réflexion *f* ; **on ~** réflexion faite.

reflector [rɪ'flektəʳ] *n* réflecteur *m*.

reflex ['riːfleks] *n* : **~ (action)** réflexe *m*.

reflexive [rɪ'fleksɪv] *adj* GRAMM [pronoun] réfléchi(e) ; **~ verb** verbe *m* pronominal réfléchi.

reforestation [riːˌfɒrɪ'steɪʃn] = **reafforestation**.

reform [rɪ'fɔːm] ◇ *n* réforme *f*. ◇ *vt* [gen] réformer ; [person] corriger. ◇ *vi* [behave better] se corriger, s'amender.

Reformation [ˌrefə'meɪʃn] *n* : **the ~** la Réforme.

reformatory [rɪ'fɔːmətrɪ] *n Am* centre *m*

d'éducation surveillée (pour jeunes délinquants).

reformer [rɪ'fɔːməʳ] *n* réformateur *m*, -trice *f*.

refrain [rɪ'freɪn] ◇ *n* refrain *m*. ◇ *vi* : **to ~ from doing sthg** s'abstenir de faire qqch.

refresh [rɪ'freʃ] *vt* rafraîchir, revigorer.

refreshed [rɪ'freʃt] *adj* reposé(e).

refresher course [rɪ'freʃəʳ-] *n* cours *m* de recyclage OR remise *f* à niveau.

refreshing [rɪ'freʃɪŋ] *adj* **- 1.** [pleasantly different] agréable, réconfortant(e) **- 2.** [drink, swim] rafraîchissant(e).

refreshments [rɪ'freʃmənts] *npl* rafraîchissements *mpl*.

refrigerator [rɪ'frɪdʒəreɪtəʳ] *n* réfrigérateur *m*, Frigidaire® *m*.

refuel [ˌriː'fjʊəl] ◇ *vt* ravitailler. ◇ *vi* se ravitailler en carburant.

refuge ['refjuːdʒ] *n lit & fig* refuge *m*, abri *m* ; **to take ~ in** se réfugier dans.

refugee [ˌrefjʊ'dʒiː] *n* réfugié *m*, -e *f*.

refund [*n* 'riːfʌnd, *vb* rɪ'fʌnd] ◇ *n* remboursement *m*. ◇ *vt* : **to ~ sthg to sb, to ~ sb sthg** rembourser qqch à qqn.

refurbish [ˌriː'fɜːbɪʃ] *vt* remettre à neuf, rénover.

refusal [rɪ'fjuːzl] *n* : **~ (to do sthg)** refus *m* (de faire qqch).

refuse[1] [rɪ'fjuːz] ◇ *vt* refuser ; **to ~ to do sthg** refuser de faire qqch. ◇ *vi* refuser.

refuse[2] ['refjuːs] *n (U)* [rubbish] ordures *fpl*, détritus *mpl*.

refuse collection ['refjuːs] *n* enlèvement *m* des ordures ménagères.

refute [rɪ'fjuːt] *vt* réfuter.

regain [rɪ'geɪn] *vt* [composure, health] retrouver ; [leadership] reprendre.

regal ['riːgl] *adj* majestueux(euse), royal(e).

regalia [rɪ'geɪljə] *n (U)* insignes *mpl*.

regard [rɪ'gaːd] ◇ *n* **- 1.** *(U)* [respect] estime *f*, respect *m* **- 2.** [aspect] : **in this/that ~** à cet égard. ◇ *vt* considérer ; **to ~ o.s. as** se considérer comme ; **to be highly ~ed** être tenu(e) en haute estime. ◆ **regards** *npl* : **(with best) ~s** bien amicalement ; **give my ~s** faites-lui mes amitiés. ◆ **as regards** *prep* en ce qui concerne. ◆ **in regard to, with regard to** *prep* en ce qui concerne, relativement à.

regarding [rɪ'gaːdɪŋ] *prep* concernant, en ce qui concerne.

regardless [rɪ'gaːdlɪs] *adv* quand même.

regardless of *prep* sans tenir compte de, sans se soucier de.

regime [reɪˈʒiːm] *n* régime *m*.

regiment [ˈredʒɪmənt] *n* régiment *m*.

region [ˈriːdʒən] *n* région *f* ; **in the ~ of** environ.

regional [ˈriːdʒənl] *adj* régional(e).

register [ˈredʒɪstər] ⬦ *n* [record] registre *m*. ⬦ *vt* - **1.** [record officially] déclarer - **2.** [show, measure] indiquer, montrer - **3.** [express] exprimer. ⬦ *vi* - **1.** [on official list] s'inscrire, se faire inscrire - **2.** [at hotel] signer le registre - **3.** *inf* [advice, fact] : **it didn't ~** je n'ai pas compris.

registered [ˈredʒɪstəd] *adj* - **1.** [person] inscrit(e) ; [car] immatriculé(e) ; [charity] agréé(e) par le gouvernement - **2.** [letter, parcel] recommandé(e).

registered trademark *n* marque *f* déposée.

registrar [ˌredʒɪˈstrɑːr] *n* - **1.** [keeper of records] officier *m* de l'état civil - **2.** UNIV secrétaire *m* général - **3.** *Br* [doctor] chef *m* de clinique.

registration [ˌredʒɪˈstreɪʃn] *n* - **1.** [gen] enregistrement *m*, inscription *f* - **2.** AUT = **registration number**.

registration number *n* AUT numéro *m* d'immatriculation.

registry [ˈredʒɪstrɪ] *n* bureau *m* de l'enregistrement.

registry office *n* bureau *m* de l'état civil.

regret [rɪˈɡret] ⬦ *n* regret *m*. ⬦ *vt* [be sorry about] : **to ~ sthg/doing sthg** regretter qqch/d'avoir fait qqch.

regretfully [rɪˈɡretfʊlɪ] *adv* à regret.

regrettable [rɪˈɡretəbl] *adj* regrettable, fâcheux(euse).

regroup [ˌriːˈɡruːp] *vi* se regrouper.

regular [ˈreɡjʊlər] ⬦ *adj* - **1.** [gen] régulier(ère) ; [customer] fidèle - **2.** [usual] habituel(elle) - **3.** *Am* [normal - size] standard *(inv)* - **4.** *Am* [pleasant] sympa *(inv)*. ⬦ *n* [at pub] habitué *m*, -e *f* ; [at shop] client *m*, -e *f* fidèle.

regularly [ˈreɡjʊlərlɪ] *adv* régulièrement.

regulate [ˈreɡjʊleɪt] *vt* régler.

regulation [ˌreɡjʊˈleɪʃn] ⬦ *adj* [standard] réglementaire. ⬦ *n* - **1.** [rule] règlement *m* - **2.** *(U)* [control] réglementation *f*.

rehabilitate [ˌriːəˈbɪlɪteɪt] *vt* [criminal] réinsérer, réhabiliter ; [patient] rééduquer.

rehearsal [rɪˈhɜːsl] *n* répétition *f*.

rehearse [rɪˈhɜːs] *vt & vi* répéter.

reign [reɪn] ⬦ *n* règne *m*. ⬦ *vi* : **to ~ (over)** *lit & fig* régner (sur).

reimburse [ˌriːɪmˈbɜːs] *vt* : **to ~ sb (for)** rembourser qqn (de).

rein [reɪn] *n fig* : **to give (a) free ~ to sb, to give sb free ~** laisser la bride sur le cou à qqn. ⬦ **reins** *npl* [for horse] rênes *fpl*.

reindeer [ˈreɪnˌdɪər] *(pl inv)* *n* renne *m*.

reinforce [ˌriːɪnˈfɔːs] *vt* - **1.** [strengthen] renforcer - **2.** [back up, confirm] appuyer, étayer.

reinforced concrete [ˌriːɪnˈfɔːst-] *n* béton *m* armé.

reinforcement [ˌriːɪnˈfɔːsmənt] *n* - **1.** *(U)* [strengthening] renforcement *m* - **2.** [strengthener] renfort *m*. ⬦ **reinforcements** *npl* renforts *mpl*.

reinstate [ˌriːɪnˈsteɪt] *vt* [employee] rétablir dans ses fonctions, réintégrer ; [policy, method] rétablir.

reissue [riːˈɪʃuː] ⬦ *n* [of book] réédition *f*. ⬦ *vt* [book] rééditer ; [film, record] ressortir.

reiterate [riːˈɪtəreɪt] *vt* réitérer, répéter.

reject [*n* ˈriːdʒekt, *vb* rɪˈdʒekt] ⬦ *n* [product] article *m* de rebut. ⬦ *vt* - **1.** [not accept] rejeter - **2.** [candidate, coin] refuser.

rejection [rɪˈdʒekʃn] *n* - **1.** [non-acceptance] rejet *m* - **2.** [of candidate] refus *m*.

rejoice [rɪˈdʒɔɪs] *vi* : **to ~ (at** OR **in)** se réjouir (de).

rejuvenate [rɪˈdʒuːvəneɪt] *vt* rajeunir.

rekindle [ˌriːˈkɪndl] *vt fig* ranimer, raviver.

relapse [rɪˈlæps] ⬦ *n* rechute *f*. ⬦ *vi* : **to ~ into** retomber dans.

relate [rɪˈleɪt] ⬦ *vt* - **1.** [connect] : **to ~ sthg to sthg** établir un lien OR rapport entre qqch et qqch - **2.** [tell] raconter. ⬦ *vi* - **1.** [be connected] : **to ~ to** avoir un rapport avec - **2.** [concern] : **to ~ to** se rapporter à - **3.** [empathize] : **to ~ (to sb)** s'entendre (avec qqn). ⬦ **relating to** *prep* concernant.

related [rɪˈleɪtɪd] *adj* - **1.** [people] apparenté(e) - **2.** [issues, problems etc] lié(e).

relation [rɪˈleɪʃn] *n* - **1.** [connection] : **~ (to/between)** rapport *m* (avec/entre) - **2.** [person] parent *m*, -e *f*. ⬦ **relations** *npl* [relationship] relations *fpl*, rapports *mpl*.

relationship [rɪˈleɪʃnʃɪp] *n* - **1.** [between people, countries] relations *fpl*, rapports *mpl* ; [romantic] liaison *f* - **2.** [connection] rapport *m*, lien *m*.

relative [ˈrelətɪv] ⬦ *adj* relatif(ive). ⬦ *n* parent *m*, -e *f*. ⬦ **relative to** *prep* [compared with] relativement à ; [connected with] se rapportant à, relatif(ive) à.

relatively ['relətɪvlɪ] *adv* relativement.

relax [rɪ'læks] <> *vt* - **1.** [person] détendre, relaxer - **2.** [muscle, body] décontracter, relâcher ; [one's grip] desserrer - **3.** [rule] relâcher. <> *vi* - **1.** [person] se détendre, se décontracter - **2.** [muscle, body] se relâcher, se décontracter - **3.** [one's grip] se desserrer.

relaxation [ˌriːlæk'seɪʃn] *n* - **1.** [of person] relaxation *f*, détente *f* - **2.** [of rule] relâchement *m*.

relaxed [rɪ'lækst] *adj* détendu(e), décontracté(e).

relaxing [rɪ'læksɪŋ] *adj* relaxant(e), qui détend.

relay ['riːleɪ] <> *n* - **1.** SPORT : ~ **(race)** course *f* de relais - **2.** RADIO & TV [broadcast] retransmission *f*. <> *vt* - **1.** RADIO & TV [broadcast] relayer - **2.** [message, information] transmettre, communiquer.

release [rɪ'liːs] <> *n* - **1.** [from prison, cage] libération *f* - **2.** [from pain, misery] délivrance *f* - **3.** [statement] communiqué *m* - **4.** [of gas, heat] échappement *m* - **5.** *(U)* [of film, record] sortie *f* - **6.** [film] nouveau film *m* ; [record] nouveau disque *m*. <> *vt* - **1.** [set free] libérer - **2.** [lift restriction on] : **to ~ sb from** dégager qqn de - **3.** [make available - supplies] libérer ; [- funds] débloquer - **4.** [let go of] lâcher - **5.** [TECH - brake, handle] desserrer ; [- mechanism] déclencher - **6.** [gas, heat] : **to be ~d (from/into)** se dégager (de/dans), s'échapper (de/dans) - **7.** [film, record] sortir ; [statement, report] publier.

relegate ['relɪgeɪt] *vt* reléguer ; **to be ~d** *Br* SPORT être relégué à la division inférieure

relent [rɪ'lent] *vi* [person] se laisser fléchir ; [wind, storm] se calmer.

relentless [rɪ'lentlɪs] *adj* implacable.

relevant ['reləvənt] *adj* - **1.** [connected] : ~ **(to)** qui a un rapport (avec) - **2.** [significant] : ~ **(to)** important(e) (pour) - **3.** [appropriate - information] utile ; [- document] justificatif(ive).

reliable [rɪ'laɪəbl] *adj* [person] sur qui on peut compter, fiable ; [device] fiable ; [company, information] sérieux(euse).

reliably [rɪ'laɪəblɪ] *adv* de façon fiable ; **to be ~ informed (that)** ... savoir de source sûre que ...

reliant [rɪ'laɪənt] *adj* : **to be ~ on** être dépendant(e) de.

relic ['relɪk] *n* relique *f* ; [of past] vestige *m*.

relief [rɪ'liːf] *n* - **1.** [comfort] soulagement

m - **2.** [for poor, refugees] aide *f*, assistance *f* - **3.** *Am* [social security] aide *f* sociale.

relieve [rɪ'liːv] *vt* - **1.** [pain, anxiety] soulager ; **to ~ sb of sthg** [take away from] délivrer qqn de qqch - **2.** [take over from] relayer - **3.** [give help to] secourir, venir en aide à.

religion [rɪ'lɪdʒn] *n* religion *f*.

religious [rɪ'lɪdʒəs] *adj* religieux(euse) ; [book] de piété.

relinquish [rɪ'lɪŋkwɪʃ] *vt* [power] abandonner ; [claim, plan] renoncer à ; [post] quitter.

relish ['relɪʃ] <> *n* - **1.** [enjoyment] : **with (great) ~** avec délectation - **2.** [pickle] condiment *m*. <> *vt* [enjoy] prendre plaisir à ; **I don't ~ the thought** OR **idea** OR **prospect of seeing him** la perspective de le voir ne m'enchante OR ne me sourit guère.

relocate [ˌriːləʊ'keɪt] <> *vt* installer ailleurs, transférer. <> *vi* s'installer ailleurs, déménager.

reluctance [rɪ'lʌktəns] *n* répugnance *f*.

reluctant [rɪ'lʌktənt] *adj* peu enthousiaste ; **to be ~ to do sthg** rechigner à faire qqch, être peu disposé à faire qqch.

reluctantly [rɪ'lʌktəntlɪ] *adv* à contrecœur, avec répugnance.

rely [rɪ'laɪ] ◆ **rely on** *vt fus* - **1.** [count on] compter sur ; **to ~ on sb to do sthg** compter sur qqn OR faire confiance à qqn pour faire qqch - **2.** [be dependent on] dépendre de.

remain [rɪ'meɪn] <> *vt* rester ; **to ~ to be done** rester à faire. <> *vi* rester. ◆ **remains** *npl* - **1.** [remnants] restes *mpl* - **2.** [antiquities] ruines *fpl*, vestiges *mpl*.

remainder [rɪ'meɪndə^r] *n* reste *m*.

remaining [rɪ'meɪnɪŋ] *adj* qui reste.

remand [rɪ'mɑːnd] JUR <> *n* : **on ~** en détention préventive. <> *vt* : **to ~ sb (in custody)** placer qqn en détention préventive.

remark [rɪ'mɑːk] <> *n* [comment] remarque *f*, observation *f*. <> *vt* [comment] : **to ~ that** ... faire remarquer que ...

remarkable [rɪ'mɑːkəbl] *adj* remarquable.

remarry [ˌriː'mærɪ] *vi* se remarier.

remedial [rɪ'miːdjəl] *adj* - **1.** [pupil, class] de rattrapage - **2.** [exercise] correctif(ive) ; [action] de rectification.

remedy ['remədɪ] <> *n* : ~ **(for)** MED remède *m* (pour OR contre) ; *fig* remède (à OR contre). <> *vt* remédier à.

remember [rɪ'membə^r] <> *vt* [gen] se souvenir de, se rappeler ; **to ~ to do sthg** ne pas oublier de faire qqch, penser à faire qqch ; **to ~ doing sthg** se souvenir d'avoir fait qqch, se rappeler avoir fait qqch. <> *vi* se souvenir, se rappeler.

remembrance [rɪ'membrəns] *n* : **in ~ of** en souvenir OR mémoire de.

Remembrance Day *n Br* l'Armistice *m*.

remind [rɪ'maɪnd] *vt* : **to ~ sb of** OR **about sthg** rappeler qqch à qqn ; **to ~ sb to do sthg** rappeler à qqn de faire qqch, faire penser à qqn à faire qqch.

reminder [rɪ'maɪndə'] *n* - 1. [to jog memory] : **to give sb a ~ (to do sthg)** faire penser à qqn (à faire qqch) - 2. [letter, note] rappel *m*.

reminisce [,remɪ'nɪs] *vi* évoquer des souvenirs ; **to ~ about sthg** évoquer qqch.

reminiscent [,remɪ'nɪsnt] *adj* : **~ of** qui rappelle, qui fait penser à.

remiss [rɪ'mɪs] *adj* négligent(e).

remit[1] [rɪ'mɪt] *vt* [money] envoyer, verser.

remit[2] ['ri:mɪt] *n Br* [responsibility] attributions *fpl*.

remittance [rɪ'mɪtns] *n* - 1. [amount of money] versement *m* - 2. COMM règlement *m*, paiement *m*.

remnant ['remnənt] *n* - 1. [remaining part] reste *m*, restant *m* - 2. [of cloth] coupon *m*.

remold *Am* = remould.

remorse [rɪ'mɔ:s] *n (U)* remords *m*.

remorseful [rɪ'mɔ:sful] *adj* plein(e) de remords.

remorseless [rɪ'mɔ:slɪs] *adj* implacable.

remote [rɪ'məʊt] *adj* - 1. [far-off - place] éloigné(e) ; [- time] lointain(e) - 2. [person] distant(e) - 3. [possibility, chance] vague.

remote control *n* télécommande *f*.

remotely [rɪ'məʊtlɪ] *adv* - 1. [in the slightest] : **not ~** pas le moins du monde, absolument pas - 2. [far off] au loin.

remould *Br*, **remold** *Am* ['ri:məʊld] *n* pneu *m* rechapé.

removable [rɪ'mu:vəbl] *adj* [detachable] détachable, amovible.

removal [rɪ'mu:vl] *n* - 1. *(U)* [act of removing] enlèvement *m* - 2. *Br* [change of house] déménagement *m*.

removal van *n Br* camion *m* de déménagement.

remove [rɪ'mu:v] *vt* - 1. [take away - gen] enlever ; [- stain] faire partir, enlever ; [- problem] résoudre ; [- suspicion] dissiper - 2. [clothes] ôter, enlever - 3. [employee] renvoyer.

remuneration [rɪ,mju:nə'reɪʃn] *n* rémunération *f*.

Renaissance [rə'neɪsəns] *n* : **the ~** la Renaissance.

render ['rendə'] *vt* rendre ; [assistance] porter ; FIN [account] présenter.

rendering ['rendərɪŋ] *n* [of play, music etc] interprétation *f*.

rendezvous ['rɒndɪvu:] *(pl inv)* *n* rendez-vous *m inv*.

renegade ['renɪgeɪd] *n* renégat *m*, -e *f*.

renew [rɪ'nju:] *vt* - 1. [gen] renouveler ; [negotiations, strength] reprendre ; [interest] faire renaître ; **to ~ acquaintance with sb** renouer connaissance avec qqn - 2. [replace] remplacer.

renewable [rɪ'nju:əbl] *adj* renouvelable.

renewal [rɪ'nju:əl] *n* - 1. [of activity] reprise *f* - 2. [of contract, licence etc] renouvellement *m*.

renounce [rɪ'naʊns] *vt* [reject] renoncer à.

renovate ['renəveɪt] *vt* rénover.

renown [rɪ'naʊn] *n* renommée *f*, renom *m*.

renowned [rɪ'naʊnd] *adj* : **~ (for)** renommé(e) (pour).

rent [rent] <> *n* [for house] loyer *m*. <> *vt* louer.

rental ['rentl] <> *adj* de location. <> *n* [for car, television, video] prix *m* de location ; [for house] loyer *m*.

renunciation [rɪ,nʌnsɪ'eɪʃn] *n* renonciation *f*.

reorganize, -ise [,ri:'ɔ:gənaɪz] *vt* réorganiser.

rep [rep] *n* - 1. *(abbr of* **representative)** VRP *m* - 2. *abbr of* **repertory**.

repaid [ri:'peɪd] *(pt & pp* > **repay.**

repair [rɪ'peə'] <> *n* réparation *f* ; **in good/bad ~** en bon/mauvais état. <> *vt* réparer.

repair kit *n* trousse *f* à outils.

repartee [,repa:'ti:] *n* repartie *f*.

repatriate [,ri:'pætrɪeɪt] *vt* rapatrier.

repay [ri:'peɪ] *(pt & pp* **repaid)** *vt* - 1. [money] : **to ~ sb sthg, to ~ sthg to sb** rembourser qqch à qqn - 2. [favour] payer de retour, récompenser.

repayment [ri:'peɪmənt] *n* remboursement *m*.

repeal [rɪ'pi:l] <> *n* abrogation *f*. <> *vt* abroger.

repeat [rɪ'pi:t] <> *vt* - 1. [gen] répéter - 2. RADIO & TV rediffuser. <> *n* RADIO & TV reprise *f*, rediffusion *f*.

repeatedly [rɪ'pi:tɪdlɪ] *adv* à maintes reprises, très souvent.

repel [rɪ'pel] *vt* repousser.

repellent [rɪ'pelənt] $\Leftrightarrow$ *adj* répugnant(e), repoussant(e). $\Leftrightarrow$ *n* : insect ~ crème *f* antiinsecte.

repent [rɪ'pent] $\Leftrightarrow$ *vt* se repentir de. $\Leftrightarrow$ *vi* : to ~ (of) se repentir (de).

repentance [rɪ'pentəns] *n (U)* repentir *m*.

repercussions [ˌriːpəˈkʌʃnz] *npl* répercussions *fpl*.

repertoire ['repətwaːʳ] *n* répertoire *m*.

repertory ['repətrɪ] *n* répertoire *m*.

repetition [ˌrepɪ'tɪʃn] *n* répétition *f*.

repetitious [ˌrepɪ'tɪʃəs], **repetitive** [rɪ'petɪtɪv] *adj* [action, job] répétitif(ive) ; [article, speech] qui a des redites.

replace [rɪ'pleɪs] *vt* - **1.** [gen] remplacer - **2.** [put back] remettre (à sa place).

replacement [rɪ'pleɪsmənt] *n* - **1.** [substituting] remplacement *m* ; [putting back] replacement *m* - **2.** [new person] : ~ (for sb) remplaçant *m*, -e *f* (de qqn).

replay [*n* 'riːpleɪ, *vb* ˌriː'pleɪ] $\Leftrightarrow$ *n* match *m* rejoué. $\Leftrightarrow$ *vt* - **1.** [match, game] rejouer - **2.** [film, tape] repasser.

replenish [rɪ'plenɪʃ] *vt* : to ~ one's supply of sthg se réapprovisionner en qqch.

replica ['replɪkə] *n* copie *f* exacte, réplique *f*.

reply [rɪ'plaɪ] $\Leftrightarrow$ *n* : ~ (to) réponse *f* (à). $\Leftrightarrow$ *vt & vi* répondre.

reply coupon *n* coupon-réponse *m*.

report [rɪ'pɔːt] $\Leftrightarrow$ *n* - **1.** [account] rapport *m*, compte *m* rendu ; PRESS reportage *m* - **2.** *Br* SCH bulletin *m*. $\Leftrightarrow$ *vt* - **1.** [news, crime] rapporter, signaler - **2.** [make known] : to ~ that ... annoncer que ... - **3.** [complain about] : to ~ sb (to) dénoncer qqn (à). $\Leftrightarrow$ *vi* - **1.** [give account] : to ~ (on) faire un rapport (sur) ; PRESS faire un reportage (sur) - **2.** [present oneself] : to ~ (to sb/for sthg) se présenter (à qqn/pour qqch).

report card *n* bulletin *m* scolaire.

reportedly [rɪ'pɔːtɪdlɪ] *adv* à ce qu'il paraît.

reporter [rɪ'pɔːtəʳ] *n* reporter *m*.

repose [rɪ'pəʊz] *n literary* repos *m*.

repossess [ˌriːpə'zes] *vt* saisir.

reprehensible [ˌreprɪ'hensəbl] *adj* répréhensible.

represent [ˌreprɪ'zent] *vt* [gen] représenter.

representation [ˌreprɪzen'teɪʃn] *n* [gen] représentation *f*. ◆ **representations** *npl* : to make ~s to sb faire une démarche auprès de qqn.

representative [ˌreprɪ'zentətɪv] $\Leftrightarrow$ *adj* représentatif(ive). $\Leftrightarrow$ *n* représentant *m*, -e *f*.

repress [rɪ'pres] *vt* réprimer.

repression [rɪ'preʃn] *n* répression *f* ; [sexual] refoulement *m*.

reprieve [rɪ'priːv] $\Leftrightarrow$ *n* - **1.** *fig* [delay] sursis *m*, répit *m* - **2.** JUR sursis *m*. $\Leftrightarrow$ *vt* accorder un sursis à.

reprimand ['reprɪmaːnd] $\Leftrightarrow$ *n* réprimande *f*. $\Leftrightarrow$ *vt* réprimander.

reprisal [rɪ'praɪzl] *n* représailles *fpl*.

reproach [rɪ'prəʊtʃ] $\Leftrightarrow$ *n* reproche *m*. $\Leftrightarrow$ *vt* : to ~ sb for OR with sthg reprocher qqch à qqn.

reproachful [rɪ'prəʊtʃful] *adj* [look, words] de reproche.

reproduce [ˌriːprə'djuːs] $\Leftrightarrow$ *vt* reproduire. $\Leftrightarrow$ *vi* se reproduire.

reproduction [ˌriːprə'dʌkʃn] *n* reproduction *f*.

reproof [rɪ'pruːf] *n* reproche *m*, blâme *m*.

reprove [rɪ'pruːv] *vt* : to ~ sb (for) blâmer qqn (pour OR de), réprimander qqn (pour).

reptile ['reptaɪl] *n* reptile *m*.

republic [rɪ'pʌblɪk] *n* république *f*.

republican [rɪ'pʌblɪkən] $\Leftrightarrow$ *adj* républicain(e). $\Leftrightarrow$ *n* républicain *m*, -e *f*. ◆ **Republican** $\Leftrightarrow$ *adj* républicain(e) ; the Republican Party *Am* le parti républicain. $\Leftrightarrow$ *n* républicain *m*, -e *f*.

repudiate [rɪ'pjuːdɪeɪt] *vt fml* [offer, suggestion] rejeter ; [friend] renier.

repulse [rɪ'pʌls] *vt* repousser.

repulsive [rɪ'pʌlsɪv] *adj* repoussant(e).

reputable ['repjʊtəbl] *adj* de bonne réputation.

reputation [ˌrepjʊ'teɪʃn] *n* réputation *f*.

repute [rɪ'pjuːt] *n* : of good ~ de bonne réputation.

reputed [rɪ'pjuːtɪd] *adj* réputé(e) ; to be ~ to be sthg être réputé pour être qqch, avoir la réputation d'être qqch.

reputedly [rɪ'pjuːtɪdlɪ] *adv* à OR d'après ce qu'on dit.

request [rɪ'kwest] $\Leftrightarrow$ *n* : ~ (for) demande *f* (de) ; on ~ sur demande. $\Leftrightarrow$ *vt* demander ; to ~ sb to do sthg demander à qqn de faire qqch.

request stop *n Br* arrêt *m* facultatif.

require [rɪ'kwaɪəʳ] *vt* [subj : person] avoir besoin de ; [subj : situation] nécessiter ; to ~ sb to do sthg exiger de qqn qu'il fasse qqch.

requirement [rɪ'kwaɪəmənt] *n* besoin *m*.

requisition [ˌrekwɪ'zɪʃn] *vt* réquisition-ner.

reran [ˌriː'ræn] *pt* ⮡ **rerun**.

rerun [*n* 'riːrʌn, *vb* ˌriː'rʌn] (*pt* **-ran**, *pp* **-run**) ⬦ *n* [of TV programme] rediffusion *f*, reprise *f* ; *fig* répétition *f*. ⬦ *vt* **- 1.** [race] réorganiser **- 2.** [TV programme] rediffuser ; [tape] passer à nouveau, repasser.

resat [ˌriː'sæt] *pt* & *pp* ⮡ **resit**.

rescind [rɪ'sɪnd] *vt* [contract] annuler ; [law] abroger.

rescue ['reskjuː] ⬦ *n* **- 1.** (*U*) [help] secours *mpl* **- 2.** [successful attempt] sauvetage *m*. ⬦ *vt* sauver, secourir.

rescuer ['reskjʊəʳ] *n* sauveteur *m*.

research [rɪ'sɜːtʃ] ⬦ *n* (*U*) **: ~ (on** OR **into)** recherche *f* (sur), recherches *fpl* (sur) ; **~ and development** recherche et développement. ⬦ *vt* faire des recherches sur.

researcher [rɪ'sɜːtʃəʳ] *n* chercheur *m*, -euse *f*.

resemblance [rɪ'zembləns] *n* **: ~ (to)** ressemblance *f* (avec).

resemble [rɪ'zembl] *vt* ressembler à.

resent [rɪ'zent] *vt* être indigné(e) par.

resentful [rɪ'zentfʊl] *adj* plein(e) de ressentiment.

resentment [rɪ'zentmənt] *n* ressentiment *m*.

reservation [ˌrezə'veɪʃn] *n* **- 1.** [booking] réservation *f* **- 2.** [uncertainty] **: without ~** sans réserve **- 3.** *Am* [for Native Americans] réserve *f* indienne. ◆ **reservations** *npl* [doubts] réserves *fpl*.

reserve [rɪ'zɜːv] ⬦ *n* **- 1.** [gen] réserve *f* ; **in ~** en réserve **- 2.** SPORT remplaçant *m*, -e *f*. ⬦ *vt* **- 1.** [save] garder, réserver **- 2.** [book] réserver **- 3.** [retain] **: to ~ the right to do sthg** se réserver le droit de faire qqch.

reserved [rɪ'zɜːvd] *adj* réservé(e).

reservoir ['rezəvwɑːʳ] *n* réservoir *m*.

reset [ˌriː'set] (*pt* & *pp* **reset**) *vt* **- 1.** [clock, watch] remettre à l'heure ; [meter, controls] remettre à zéro **- 2.** COMPUT ré-initialiser.

reshape [ˌriː'ʃeɪp] *vt* [policy, thinking] réorganiser.

reshuffle [ˌriː'ʃʌfl] ⬦ *n* remaniement *m* ; **cabinet ~** remaniement ministériel. ⬦ *vt* remanier.

reside [rɪ'zaɪd] *vi fml* résider.

residence ['rezɪdəns] *n* résidence *f*.

residence permit *n* permis *m* de séjour.

resident ['rezɪdənt] ⬦ *adj* résidant(e) ; [chaplain, doctor] à demeure. ⬦ *n* résident *m*, -e *f*.

residential [ˌrezɪ'denʃl] *adj* **: ~ course** stage ou formation avec logement sur place ; **~ institution** internat *m*.

residential area *n* quartier *m* résidentiel.

residue ['rezɪdjuː] *n* reste *m* ; CHEM résidu *m*.

resign [rɪ'zaɪn] ⬦ *vt* **- 1.** [job] démissionner de **- 2.** [accept calmly] **: to ~ o.s. to** se résigner à. ⬦ *vi* **: to ~ (from)** démissionner (de).

resignation [ˌrezɪg'neɪʃn] *n* **- 1.** [from job] démission *f* **- 2.** [calm acceptance] résignation *f*.

resigned [rɪ'zaɪnd] *adj* **: ~ (to)** résigné(e) (à).

resilient [rɪ'zɪlɪənt] *adj* [material] élastique ; [person] qui a du ressort.

resin ['rezɪn] *n* résine *f*.

resist [rɪ'zɪst] *vt* résister à.

resistance [rɪ'zɪstəns] *n* résistance *f*.

resit [*n* 'riːsɪt, *vb* ˌriː'sɪt] (*pt* & *pp* **-sat**) *Br* ⬦ *n* deuxième session *f*. ⬦ *vt* repasser, se représenter à.

resolute ['rezəluːt] *adj* résolu(e).

resolution [ˌrezə'luːʃn] *n* résolution *f*.

resolve [rɪ'zɒlv] ⬦ *n* (*U*) [determination] résolution *f*. ⬦ *vt* **- 1.** [decide] **: to ~ (that)** ... décider que ... ; **to ~ to do sthg** résoudre OR décider de faire qqch **- 2.** [solve] résoudre.

resort [rɪ'zɔːt] *n* **- 1.** [for holidays] lieu *m* de vacances **- 2.** [recourse] recours *m* ; **as a last ~, in the last ~** en dernier ressort OR recours. ◆ **resort to** *vt fus* recourir à, avoir recours à.

resound [rɪ'zaʊnd] *vi* **- 1.** [noise] résonner **- 2.** [place] **: to ~ with** retentir de.

resounding [rɪ'zaʊndɪŋ] *adj* retentissant(e).

resource [rɪ'sɔːs] *n* ressource *f*.

resourceful [rɪ'sɔːsfʊl] *adj* plein(e) de ressources, débrouillard(e).

respect [rɪ'spekt] ⬦ *n* **- 1.** [gen] **: ~ (for)** respect *m* (pour) ; **with ~** avec respect ; **with ~, ...** sauf votre respect, ... **- 2.** [aspect] **: in this** OR **that ~** à cet égard ; **in some ~s** à certains égards. ⬦ *vt* respecter ; **to ~ sb for sthg** respecter qqn pour qqch. ◆ **respects** *npl* respects *mpl*, hommages *mpl*. ◆ **with respect to** *prep* en ce qui concerne, quant à.

respectable [rɪ'spektəbl] *adj* **- 1.** [morally correct] respectable **- 2.** [adequate] raisonnable, honorable.

respectful [rɪ'spektful] *adj* respectueux(euse).

respective [rɪ'spektɪv] *adj* respectif(ive).

respectively [rɪ'spektɪvlɪ] *adv* respectivement.

respite ['respaɪt] *n* répit *m*.

resplendent [rɪ'splendənt] *adj* resplendissant(e).

respond [rɪ'spɒnd] *vi* : **to ~ (to)** répondre (à).

response [rɪ'spɒns] *n* réponse *f*.

responsibility [rɪ‚spɒnsə'bɪlətɪ] *n* : **~ (for)** responsabilité *f* (de).

responsible [rɪ'spɒnsəbl] *adj* - **1.** [gen] : **~ (for sthg)** responsable (de qqch) ; **to be ~ to sb** être responsable devant qqn - **2.** [job, position] qui comporte des responsabilités.

responsibly [rɪ'spɒnsəblɪ] *adv* de façon responsable.

responsive [rɪ'spɒnsɪv] *adj* - **1.** [quick to react] qui réagit bien - **2.** [aware] : **~ (to)** attentif(ive) (à).

rest [rest] <> *n* - **1.** [remainder] : **the ~ (of)** le reste (de) ; **the ~ (of them)** les autres *mfpl* - **2.** [relaxation, break] repos *m* ; **to have a ~** se reposer - **3.** [support] support *m*, appui *m*. <> *vt* - **1.** [relax] faire OR laisser reposer - **2.** [support] : **to ~ sthg on/against** appuyer qqch sur/contre - **3.** *phr* : **~ assured soyez certain(e).** <> *vi* - **1.** [relax] se reposer - **2.** [be supported] : **to ~ on/against** s'appuyer sur/contre - **3.** *fig* [argument, result] : **to ~ on** reposer sur.

restaurant ['restərɒnt] *n* restaurant *m*.

restaurant car *n Br* wagon-restaurant *m*.

restful ['restful] *adj* reposant(e).

rest home *n* maison *f* de repos.

restive ['restɪv] *adj* agité(e).

restless ['restlɪs] *adj* agité(e).

restoration [‚restə'reɪʃn] *n* - **1.** [of law and order, monarchy] rétablissement *m* - **2.** [renovation] restauration *f*.

restore [rɪ'stɔːʳ] *vt* - **1.** [law and order, monarchy] rétablir ; [confidence] redonner - **2.** [renovate] restaurer - **3.** [give back] rendre, restituer.

restrain [rɪ'streɪn] *vt* [person, crowd] contenir, retenir ; [emotions] maîtriser, contenir ; **to ~ o.s. from doing sthg** se retenir de faire qqch.

restrained [rɪ'streɪnd] *adj* [tone] mesuré(e) ; [person] qui se domine.

restraint [rɪ'streɪnt] *n* - **1.** [restriction] res-

triction *f*, entrave *f* - **2.** (U) [self-control] mesure *f*, retenue *f*.

restrict [rɪ'strɪkt] *vt* restreindre, limiter.

restriction [rɪ'strɪkʃn] *n* restriction *f*, limitation *f*.

restrictive [rɪ'strɪktɪv] *adj* restrictif(ive).

rest room *n Am* toilettes *fpl*.

result [rɪ'zʌlt] <> *n* résultat *m* ; **as a ~** en conséquence ; **as a ~ of** [as a consequence of] à la suite de ; [because of] à cause de. <> *vi* - **1.** [cause] : **to ~ in** aboutir à - **2.** [be caused] : **to ~ (from)** résulter (de).

resume [rɪ'zjuːm] *vt & vi* reprendre.

résumé ['rezjuːmeɪ] *n* - **1.** [summary] résumé *m* - **2.** *Am* [curriculum vitae] curriculum vitae *m inv*, CV *m*.

resumption [rɪ'zʌmpʃn] *n* reprise *f*.

resurgence [rɪ'sɜːdʒəns] *n* réapparition *f*.

resurrection [‚rezə'rekʃn] *n fig* résurrection *f*.

resuscitation [rɪ‚sʌsɪ'teɪʃn] *n* réanimation *f*.

retail ['riːteɪl] <> *n* (U) détail *m*. <> *adv* au détail.

retailer ['riːteɪləʳ] *n* détaillant *m*, -e *f*.

retail price *n* prix *m* de détail.

retain [rɪ'teɪn] *vt* conserver.

retainer [rɪ'teɪnəʳ] *n* [fee] provision *f*.

retaliate [rɪ'tælieɪt] *vi* rendre la pareille, se venger.

retaliation [rɪ‚tæli'eɪʃn] *n* (U) vengeance *f*, représailles *fpl*.

retarded [rɪ'tɑːdɪd] *adj* retardé(e).

retch [retʃ] *vi* avoir des haut-le-cœur.

retentive [rɪ'tentɪv] *adj* [memory] fidèle.

reticent ['retɪsənt] *adj* peu communicatif(ive) ; **to be ~ about sthg** ne pas beaucoup parler de qqch.

retina ['retɪnə] (*pl* -nas OR -nae [-niː]) *n* rétine *f*.

retinue ['retɪnjuː] *n* suite *f*.

retire [rɪ'taɪəʳ] *vi* - **1.** [from work] prendre sa retraite - **2.** [withdraw] se retirer - **3.** [to bed] (aller) se coucher.

retired [rɪ'taɪəd] *adj* à la retraite, retraité(e).

retirement [rɪ'taɪəmənt] *n* retraite *f*.

retiring [rɪ'taɪərɪŋ] *adj* [shy] réservé(e).

retort [rɪ'tɔːt] <> *n* [sharp reply] riposte *f*. <> *vt* riposter.

retrace [rɪ'treɪs] *vt* : **to ~ one's steps** revenir sur ses pas.

retract [rɪ'trækt] <> *vt* - **1.** [statement] rétracter - 2. [undercarriage] rentrer, escamoter ; [claws] rentrer. ◇ *vi* [undercarriage] rentrer, s'escamoter.

retrain [ˌriː'treɪn] *vt* recycler.

retraining [ˌriː'treɪnɪŋ] *n* recyclage *m*.

retread ['riːtred] *n* pneu *m* rechapé.

retreat [rɪ'triːt] ◇ *n* retraite *f*. ◇ *vi* [move away] se retirer ; MIL battre en retraite.

retribution [ˌretrɪ'bjuːʃn] *n* châtiment *m*.

retrieval [rɪ'triːvl] *n* (U) COMPUT recherche *f* et extraction *f*.

retrieve [rɪ'triːv] *vt* - 1. [get back] récupérer - 2. COMPUT rechercher et extraire - 3. [situation] sauver.

retriever [rɪ'triːvə'] *n* [dog] retriever *m*.

retrograde ['retrəɡreɪd] *adj* rétrograde.

retrospect ['retrəspekt] *n* : in ~ après coup.

retrospective [ˌretrə'spektɪv] *adj* - 1. [mood, look] rétrospectif(ive) - 2. JUR [law, pay rise] rétroactif(ive).

return [rɪ'tɜːn] ◇ *n* - 1. (U) [arrival back, giving back] retour *m* - 2. TENNIS renvoi *m* - 3. Br [ticket] aller et retour *m* - 4. [profit] rapport *m*, rendement *m*. ◇ *vt* - 1. [gen] rendre ; [a loan] rembourser ; [library book] rapporter - 2. [send back] renvoyer - 3. [replace] remettre - 4. POL élire. ◇ *vi* [come back] revenir ; [go back] retourner. ◆ **returns** *npl* COMM recettes *fpl* ; **many happy ~s (of the day)!** bon anniversaire! ◆ **in return** *adv* en retour, en échange. ◆ **in return for** *prep* en échange de.

return ticket *n* Br aller et retour *m*.

reunification [ˌriːjuːnɪfɪ'keɪʃn] *n* réunification *f*.

reunion [ˌriː'juːnjən] *n* réunion *f*.

reunite [ˌriːjuː'naɪt] *vt* : **to be ~d with sb** retrouver qqn.

rev [rev] *inf* ◇ *n* (abbr of **revolution**) tour *m*. ◇ *vt* : **to ~ the engine (up)** emballer le moteur. ◇ *vi* : **to ~ (up)** s'emballer.

revamp [ˌriː'væmp] *vt* inf [system, department] réorganiser ; [house] retaper.

reveal [rɪ'viːl] *vt* révéler.

revealing [rɪ'viːlɪŋ] *adj* - 1. [clothes - low-cut] décolleté(e) ; [- transparent] qui laisse deviner le corps - 2. [comment] révélateur(trice).

reveille [Br rɪ'vælɪ, Am 'revəlɪ] *n* réveil *m*.

revel ['revl] *vi* : **to ~ in sthg** se délecter de qqch.

revelation [ˌrevə'leɪʃn] *n* révélation *f*.

revenge [rɪ'vendʒ] ◇ *n* vengeance *f* ; **to take ~ (on sb)** se venger (de qqn). ◇ *vt* venger ; **to ~ o.s. on sb** se venger de qqn.

revenue ['revənjuː] *n* revenu *m*.

reverberate [rɪ'vɜːbəreɪt] *vi* retentir, se répercuter ; fig avoir des répercussions.

reverberations [rɪˌvɜːbə'reɪʃnz] *npl* réverbérations *fpl* ; fig répercussions *fpl*.

revere [rɪ'vɪə'] *vt* révérer, vénérer.

reverence ['revərəns] *n* révérence *f*, vénération *f*.

Reverend ['revərənd] *n* révérend *m*.

reverie ['revərɪ] *n* rêverie *f*.

reversal [rɪ'vɜːsl] *n* - 1. [of policy, decision] revirement *m* - 2. [ill fortune] revers *m* de fortune.

reverse [rɪ'vɜːs] ◇ *adj* [order, process] inverse. ◇ *n* - 1. AUT : ~ **(gear)** marche *f* arrière - 2. [opposite] : **the ~ le contraire** - 3. [back] : **the ~** [of paper] le verso, le dos ; [of coin] le revers. ◇ *vt* - 1. [order, positions] inverser ; [decision, trend] renverser - 2. [turn over] retourner - 3. Br TELEC : **to ~ the charges** téléphoner en PCV. ◇ *vi* AUT faire marche arrière.

reverse-charge call *n* Br appel *m* en PCV.

reversing light [rɪ'vɜːsɪŋ-] *n* Br feu *m* de marche arrière.

revert [rɪ'vɜːt] *vi* : **to ~ to** retourner à.

review [rɪ'vjuː] ◇ *n* - 1. [of salary, spending] révision *f* ; [of situation] examen *m* - 2. [of book, play etc] critique *f*, compte rendu *m*. ◇ *vt* - 1. [salary] réviser ; [situation] examiner - 2. [book, play etc] faire la critique de - 3. [troops] passer en revue - 4. Am [study again] réviser.

reviewer [rɪ'vjuːə'] *n* critique *mf*.

revile [rɪ'vaɪl] *vt* injurier.

revise [rɪ'vaɪz] ◇ *vt* - 1. [reconsider] modifier - 2. [rewrite] corriger - 3. Br [study again] réviser. ◇ *vi* Br : **to ~ (for)** réviser (pour).

revision [rɪ'vɪʒn] *n* révision *f*.

revitalize, -ise [ˌriː'vaɪtəlaɪz] *vt* revitaliser.

revival [rɪ'vaɪvl] *n* [of economy, trade] reprise *f* ; [of interest] regain *m*.

revive [rɪ'vaɪv] ◇ *vt* - 1. [person] ranimer - 2. fig [economy] relancer ; [interest] faire renaître ; [tradition] rétablir ; [musical, play] reprendre ; [memories] ranimer, raviver. ◇ *vi* - 1. [person] reprendre connaissance - 2. fig [economy] repartir, reprendre ; [hopes] renaître.

revolt [rɪ'vəʊlt] ◇ *n* révolte *f.* ◇ *vt* révolter, dégoûter. ◇ *vi* se révolter.

revolting [rɪ'vəʊltɪŋ] *adj* dégoûtant(e) ; [smell] infect(e).

revolution [ˌrevə'lu:ʃn] *n* - **1.** [gen] révolution *f* - **2.** TECH tour *m*, révolution *f.*

revolutionary [ˌrevə'lu:ʃnərɪ] ◇ *adj* révolutionnaire. ◇ *n* révolutionnaire *mf.*

revolve [rɪ'vɒlv] *vi* : **to ~ (around)** tourner (autour de).

revolver [rɪ'vɒlvəʳ] *n* revolver *m.*

revolving [rɪ'vɒlvɪŋ] *adj* tournant(e) ; [chair] pivotant(e).

revolving door *n* tambour *m.*

revue [rɪ'vju:] *n* revue *f.*

revulsion [rɪ'vʌlʃn] *n* répugnance *f.*

reward [rɪ'wɔ:d] ◇ *n* récompense *f.* ◇ *vt* : **to ~ sb (for/with sthg)** récompenser qqn (de/par qqch).

rewarding [rɪ'wɔ:dɪŋ] *adj* [job] qui donne de grandes satisfactions ; [book] qui vaut la peine d'être lu(e).

rewind [ˌri:'waɪnd] (*pt & pp* **rewound**) *vt* [tape] rembobiner.

rewire [ˌri:'waɪəʳ] *vt* [house] refaire l'installation électrique de.

reword [ˌri:'wɔ:d] *vt* reformuler.

rewound [ˌri:'waʊnd] *pt & pp* ⊳ **rewind**.

rewrite [ˌri:'raɪt] (*pt* **rewrote** [ˌri:'rəʊt], *pp* **rewritten** [ˌri:'rɪtn]) *vt* récrire.

Reykjavik ['rekjəvɪk] *n* Reykjavik.

rhapsody ['ræpsədɪ] *n* rhapsodie *f* ; **to go into rhapsodies about sthg** s'extasier sur qqch.

rhetoric ['retərɪk] *n* rhétorique *f.*

rhetorical question [rɪ'tɒrɪkl-] *n* question *f* pour la forme.

rheumatism ['ru:mətɪzm] *n* (U) rhumatisme *m.*

Rhine [raɪn] *n* : **the ~** le Rhin.

rhino ['raɪnəʊ] (*pl inv* OR **-s**), **rhinoceros** [raɪ'nɒsərəs] (*pl inv* OR **-es**) *n* rhinocéros *m.*

rhododendron [ˌrəʊdə'dendrən] *n* rhododendron *m.*

Rhône [rəʊn] *n* : **the (River) ~** le Rhône.

rhubarb ['ru:ba:b] *n* rhubarbe *f.*

rhyme [raɪm] ◇ *n* - **1.** [word, technique] rime *f* - **2.** [poem] poème *m.* ◇ *vi* : **to ~ (with)** rimer (avec).

rhythm ['rɪðm] *n* rythme *m.*

rib [rɪb] *n* - **1.** ANAT côte *f* - **2.** [of umbrella] baleine *f* ; [of structure] membrure *f.*

ribbed [rɪbd] *adj* [jumper, fabric] à côtes.

ribbon ['rɪbən] *n* ruban *m.*

rice [raɪs] *n* riz *m.*

rice pudding *n* riz *m* au lait.

rich [rɪtʃ] ◇ *adj* riche ; [clothes, fabrics] somptueux(euse) ; **to be ~ in** être riche en. ◇ *npl* : **the ~** les riches *mpl.* ◆ **riches** *npl* richesses *fpl*, richesse *f.*

richly ['rɪtʃlɪ] *adv* - **1.** [rewarded] largement ; [provided] très bien - **2.** [sumptuously] richement.

richness ['rɪtʃnɪs] *n* (U) richesse *f.*

rickets ['rɪkɪts] *n* (U) rachitisme *m.*

rickety ['rɪkətɪ] *adj* branlant(e).

rickshaw ['rɪkʃɔ:] *n* pousse-pousse *m inv.*

ricochet ['rɪkəʃeɪ] (*pt & pp* **-ed** OR **-ted**, *cont* **-ing** OR **-ting**) ◇ *n* ricochet *m.* ◇ *vi* : **to ~ (off)** ricocher (sur).

rid [rɪd] (*pt* **rid** OR **-ded**, *pp* **rid**) *vt* : **to ~ sb/ sthg of** débarrasser qqn/qqch de ; **to get ~ of** se débarrasser de.

ridden ['rɪdn] *pp* ⊳ **ride**.

riddle ['rɪdl] *n* énigme *f.*

riddled ['rɪdld] *adj* : **to be ~ with** être criblé(e) de.

ride [raɪd] (*pt* **rode**, *pp* **ridden**) ◇ *n* promenade *f*, tour *m* ; **to go for a ~** [on horse] faire une promenade à cheval ; [on bike] faire une promenade à vélo ; [in car] faire un tour en voiture ; **to take sb for a ~** *inf fig* faire marcher qqn. ◇ *vt* - **1.** [travel on] : **to ~ a horse/a bicycle** monter à cheval/à bicyclette - **2.** *Am* [travel in - bus, train, elevator] prendre - **3.** [distance] parcourir, faire. ◇ *vi* [on horseback] monter à cheval, faire du cheval ; [on bicycle] faire de la bicyclette OR du vélo ; **to ~ in a car/bus** aller en voiture/bus.

rider ['raɪdəʳ] *n* [of horse] cavalier *m*, -ère *f* ; [of bicycle] cycliste *mf* ; [of motorbike] motocycliste *mf.*

ridge [rɪdʒ] *n* - **1.** [of mountain, roof] crête *f*, arête *f* - **2.** [on surface] strie *f.*

ridicule ['rɪdɪkju:l] ◇ *n* ridicule *m.* ◇ *vt* ridiculiser.

ridiculous [rɪ'dɪkjʊləs] *adj* ridicule.

riding ['raɪdɪŋ] *n* équitation *f.*

riding school *n* école *f* d'équitation.

rife [raɪf] *adj* répandu(e).

riffraff ['rɪfræf] *n* racaille *f.*

rifle ['raɪfl] ◇ *n* fusil *m.* ◇ *vt* [drawer, bag] vider.

rifle range *n* [indoor] stand *m* de tir ; [outdoor] champ *m* de tir.

rift [rɪft] n - 1. GEOL fissure f - 2. [quarrel] désaccord m.

rig [rɪg] ◇ n : (oil) ~ [on land] derrick m ; [at sea] plate-forme f de forage. ◇ vt [match, election] truquer. ◆ **rig up** vt sep installer avec les moyens du bord.

rigging ['rɪgɪŋ] n [of ship] gréement m.

right [raɪt] ◇ adj - 1. [correct · answer, time] juste, exact(e) ; [· decision, direction, idea] bon (bonne) ; **to be ~ (about)** avoir raison (au sujet de) - 2. [morally correct] bien (inv) ; **to be ~ to do sthg** avoir raison de faire qqch - 3. [appropriate] qui convient - 4. [not left] droit(e) - 5. Br inf [complete] véritable. ◇ n - 1. (U) [moral correctness] bien m ; **to be in the ~** avoir raison - 2. [entitlement, claim] droit m ; **by ~s** en toute justice - 3. [not left] droite f. ◇ adv - 1. [correctly] correctement - 2. [not left] à droite - 3. [emphatic use] : ~ **down/up** tout en bas/en haut ; ~ **here** ici (même) ; ~ **in the middle** en plein milieu ; ~ **to the end of the street** allez tout au bout de la rue ; ~ **now** tout de suite ; ~ **away** immédiatement. ◇ vt - 1. [injustice, wrong] réparer - 2. [ship] redresser. ◇ excl bon! ◆ **Right** n POL : **the Right** la droite.

right angle n angle m droit ; **to be at ~s (to)** faire un angle droit (avec).

righteous ['raɪtʃəs] adj [person] droit(e) ; [indignation] justifié(e).

rightful ['raɪtful] adj légitime.

right-hand adj de droite ; ~ **side** droite f, côté m droit.

right-hand drive adj avec conduite à droite.

right-handed [-'hændɪd] adj [person] droitier(ère).

right-hand man n bras m droit.

rightly ['raɪtlɪ] adv - 1. [answer, believe] correctement - 2. [behave] bien - 3. [angry, worried etc] à juste titre.

right of way n - 1. AUT priorité f - 2. [access] droit m de passage.

right-on adj inf branché(e).

right wing n : **the ~** la droite. ◆ **right-wing** adj de droite.

rigid ['rɪdʒɪd] adj - 1. [gen] rigide - 2. [harsh] strict(e).

rigmarole ['rɪgmərəʊl] n pej - 1. [process] comédie f - 2. [story] galimatias m.

rigor Am = rigour.

rigorous ['rɪgərəs] adj rigoureux(euse).

rigour Br, **rigor** Am ['rɪgə'] n rigueur f.

rile [raɪl] vt agacer.

rim [rɪm] n [of container] bord m ; [of wheel] jante f ; [of spectacles] monture f.

rind [raɪnd] n [of fruit] peau f ; [of cheese] croûte f ; [of bacon] couenne f.

ring [rɪŋ] (pt rang, pp vt senses 1 & 2 & vi rung, pt & pp vt sense 3 only ringed) ◇ n - 1. [telephone call] : **to give sb a ~** donner OR passer un coup de téléphone à qqn - 2. [sound of bell] sonnerie f - 3. [circular object] anneau m ; [on finger] bague f ; [for napkin] rond m - 4. [of people, trees etc] cercle m - 5. [for boxing] ring m - 6. [of criminals, spies] réseau m. ◇ vt - 1. Br [make phone call to] téléphoner à, appeler - 2. [bell] (faire) sonner ; **to ~ the doorbell** sonner à la porte - 3. [draw a circle round, surround] entourer. ◇ vi - 1. Br [make phone call] téléphoner - 2. [bell, telephone, person] sonner ; **to ~ for sb** sonner qqn - 3. [resound] : **to ~ with** résonner de. ◆ **ring back** vt sep & vi Br rappeler. ◆ **ring off** vi Br raccrocher. ◆ **ring up** vt sep Br téléphoner à, appeler.

ring binder n classeur m à anneaux.

ringing ['rɪŋɪŋ] n [of bell] sonnerie f ; [in ears] tintement m.

ringing tone n sonnerie f.

ringleader ['rɪŋ,liːdə'] n chef m.

ringlet ['rɪŋlɪt] n anglaise f.

ring road n Br (route f) périphérique m.

rink [rɪŋk] n [for ice skating] patinoire f ; [for roller-skating] skating m.

rinse [rɪns] vt rincer ; **to ~ one's mouth out** se rincer la bouche.

riot ['raɪət] ◇ n émeute f ; **to run ~** se déchaîner. ◇ vi participer à une émeute.

rioter ['raɪətə'] n émeutier m, -ère f.

riotous ['raɪətəs] adj [crowd] tapageur(euse) ; [behaviour] séditieux(euse) ; [party] bruyant(e).

riot police npl ≃ CRS mpl.

rip [rɪp] ◇ n déchirure f, accroc m. ◇ vt - 1. [tear] déchirer - 2. [remove violently] arracher. ◇ vi se déchirer.

RIP (abbr of rest in peace) qu' il/elle repose en paix.

ripe [raɪp] adj mûr(e).

ripen ['raɪpn] vt & vi mûrir.

rip-off n inf : **that's a ~!** c'est de l'escroquerie OR de l'arnaque!

ripple ['rɪpl] ◇ n ondulation f, ride f ; **a ~ of applause** des applaudissements discrets. ◇ vt rider.

rise [raɪz] (pt rose, pp risen ['rɪzn]) ◇ n - 1. [increase] augmentation f, hausse f ;

[in temperature] élévation *f*, hausse - **2.** *Br* [increase in salary] augmentation *f* (de salaire) - **3.** [to power, fame] ascension *f* - **4.** [slope] côte *f*, pente *f* - **5.** *phr* : **to give ~ to** donner lieu à. ◇ *vi* - **1.** [move upwards] s'élever, monter ; **to ~ to power** arriver au pouvoir ; **to ~ to fame** devenir célèbre ; **to ~ to a challenge/to the occasion** se montrer à la hauteur d'un défi/de la situation - **2.** [from chair, bed] se lever - **3.** [increase - gen] monter, augmenter ; [- voice, level] s'élever - **4.** [rebel] se soulever.

rising ['raɪzɪŋ] ◇ *adj* - **1.** [ground, tide] montant(e) - **2.** [prices, inflation, temperature] en hausse - **3.** [star, politician etc] à l'avenir prometteur. ◇ *n* [revolt] soulèvement *m*.

risk [rɪsk] ◇ *n* risque *m*, danger *m* ; **at one's own ~** à ses risques et périls ; **to run the ~ of doing sthg** courir le risque de faire qqch ; **to take a ~** prendre un risque ; **at ~** en danger. ◇ *vt* [health, life etc] risquer ; **to ~ doing sthg** courir le risque de faire qqch.

risky ['rɪskɪ] *adj* risqué(e).

risqué ['riːskeɪ] *adj* risqué(e), osé(e).

rissole ['rɪsəʊl] *n Br* rissole *f*.

rite [raɪt] *n* rite *m*.

ritual ['rɪtʃʊəl] ◇ *adj* rituel(elle). ◇ *n* rituel *m*.

rival ['raɪvl] ◇ *adj* rival(e), concurrent(e). ◇ *n* rival *m*, -e *f*. ◇ *vt* rivaliser avec.

rivalry ['raɪvlrɪ] *n* rivalité *f*.

river ['rɪvə'] *n* rivière *f*, fleuve *m*.

river bank *n* berge *f*, rive *f*.

riverbed ['rɪvəbed] *n* lit *m* (de rivière OR de fleuve).

riverside ['rɪvəsaɪd] *n* : **the ~** le bord de la rivière OR du fleuve.

rivet ['rɪvɪt] ◇ *n* rivet *m*. ◇ *vt* - **1.** [fasten with rivets] river, riveter - **2.** *fig* [fascinate] : **to be ~ed by** être fasciné(e) par.

Riviera [,rɪvɪ'eərə] *n* : **the French ~** la Côte d'Azur ; **the Italian ~** la Riviera italienne.

road [rəʊd] *n* route *f* ; [small] chemin *m* ; [in town] rue *f* ; **by ~** par la route ; **on the ~ to** *fig* sur le chemin de.

roadblock ['rəʊdblɒk] *n* barrage *m* routier.

road hog *n inf pej* chauffard *m*.

road map *n* carte *f* routière.

road rage *n* accès de colère de la part d'un automobiliste, se traduisant parfois par un acte de violence.

road safety *n* sécurité *f* routière.

roadside ['rəʊdsaɪd] *n* : **the ~** le bord de la route.

road sign *n* panneau *m* routier OR de signalisation.

road tax *n Br* ≃ vignette *f*.

roadway ['rəʊdweɪ] *n* chaussée *f*.

road works [-wɜːks] *npl* travaux *mpl* (de réfection des routes).

roadworthy ['rəʊd,wɜːðɪ] *adj* en bon état de marche.

roam [rəʊm] ◇ *vt* errer dans. ◇ *vi* errer.

roar [rɔː'] ◇ *vi* [person, lion] rugir ; [wind] hurler ; [car] gronder ; [plane] vrombir ; **to ~ with laughter** se tordre de rire. ◇ *vt* hurler. ◇ *n* [of person, lion] rugissement *m* ; [of traffic] grondement *m* ; [of plane, engine] vrombissement *m*.

roaring ['rɔːrɪŋ] *adj* : **a ~ fire** une belle flambée ; **~ drunk** complètement saoul(e) ; **to do a ~ trade** faire des affaires en or.

roast [rəʊst] ◇ *adj* rôti(e). ◇ *n* rôti *m*. ◇ *vt* - **1.** [meat, potatoes] rôtir - **2.** [coffee, nuts etc] griller.

roast beef *n* rôti *m* de bœuf, rosbif *m*.

rob [rɒb] *vt* [person] voler ; [bank] dévaliser ; **to ~ sb of sthg** [money, goods] voler OR dérober qqch à qqn ; [opportunity, glory] enlever qqch à qqn.

robber ['rɒbə'] *n* voleur *m*, -euse *f*.

robbery ['rɒbərɪ] *n* vol *m*.

robe [rəʊb] *n* - **1.** [gen] robe *f* - **2.** *Am* [dressing gown] peignoir *m*.

robin ['rɒbɪn] *n* rouge-gorge *m*.

robot ['rəʊbɒt] *n* robot *m*.

robust [rəʊ'bʌst] *adj* robuste.

rock [rɒk] ◇ *n* - **1.** (U) [substance] roche *f* - **2.** [boulder] rocher *m* - **3.** *Am* [pebble] caillou *m* - **4.** [music] rock *m* - **5.** *Br* [sweet] sucre *m* d'orge. ◇ *comp* [music, band] de rock. ◇ *vt* - **1.** [baby] bercer ; [cradle, boat] balancer - **2.** [shock] secouer. ◇ *vi* (se) balancer. ◆ **on the rocks** *adv* - **1.** [drink] avec de la glace OR des glaçons - **2.** [marriage, relationship] près de la rupture.

rock and roll *n* rock *m*, rock and roll *m*.

rock bottom *n* : **at ~** au plus bas ; **to hit ~** toucher le fond. ◆ **rock-bottom** *adj* [price] sacrifié(e).

rockery ['rɒkərɪ] *n* rocaille *f*.

rocket ['rɒkɪt] *n* - **1.** [gen] fusée *f* - **2.** MIL fusée *f*, roquette *f* - **3.** *vi* monter en flèche.

rocket launcher [-,lɔːntʃə'] *n* lance-fusées *m inv*, lance-roquettes *m inv*.

rocking chair ['rɒkɪŋ-] *n* fauteuil *m* à bascule, rocking-chair *m*.

rocking horse ['rɒkɪŋ-] *n* cheval *m* à bascule.

rock'n'roll [ˌrɒkən'rəʊl] = rock and roll.

rocky ['rɒkɪ] *adj* - **1.** [ground, road] rocailleux(euse), caillouteux(euse) - **2.** *fig* [economy, marriage] précaire.

Rocky Mountains *npl* : **the** ~ les montagnes *fpl* Rocheuses.

rod [rɒd] *n* [metal] tige *f* ; [wooden] baguette *f* ; **(fishing)** ~ canne *f* à pêche.

rode [rəʊd] *pt* ⊳ ride.

rodent ['rəʊdənt] *n* rongeur *m*.

roe [rəʊ] *n* (*U*) œufs *mpl* de poisson.

roe deer *n* chevreuil *m*.

rogue [rəʊg] *n* - **1.** [likeable rascal] coquin *m* - **2.** *dated* [dishonest person] filou *m*, crapule *f*.

role [rəʊl] *n* rôle *m*.

roll [rəʊl] ◇ *n* - **1.** [of material, paper etc] rouleau *m* - **2.** [of bread] petit pain *m* - **3.** [list] liste *f* - **4.** [of drums, thunder] roulement *m*. ◇ *vt* rouler ; [log, ball etc] faire rouler. ◇ *vi* rouler. ◆ **roll about, roll around** *vi* [person] se rouler ; [object] rouler çà et là. ◆ **roll over** *vi* se retourner. ◆ **roll up** ◇ *vt sep* - **1.** [carpet, paper etc] rouler - **2.** [sleeves] retrousser. ◇ *vi inf* [arrive] s'amener, se pointer.

roll call *n* appel *m*.

roller ['rəʊlə'] *n* rouleau *m*.

Rollerblades® ['rəʊləbleɪd] *n* rollers *mpl*, patins *mpl* en ligne.

rollerblading ['rəʊləbleɪdɪŋ] *n* roller *m* ; **to go** ~ faire du roller.

roller coaster *n* montagnes *fpl* russes.

roller skate *n* patin *m* à roulettes.

rolling ['rəʊlɪŋ] *adj* - **1.** [hills] onduleux(euse) - **2.** *phr* : **to be** ~ **in it** *inf* rouler sur l'or.

rolling pin *n* rouleau *m* à pâtisserie.

rolling stock *n* matériel *m* roulant.

roll-on *adj* [deodorant] à bille.

ROM [rɒm] (*abbr of* read only memory) *n* ROM *f*.

Roman ['rəʊmən] ◇ *adj* romain(e). ◇ *n* Romain *m*, -e *f*.

Roman Catholic ◇ *adj* catholique. ◇ *n* catholique *mf*.

romance [rəʊ'mæns] *n* - **1.** (*U*) [romantic quality] charme *m* - **2.** [love affair] idylle *f* - **3.** [book] roman *m* (d'amour).

Romania [ru:'meɪnjə] *n* Roumanie *f*.

Romanian [ru:'meɪnjən] ◇ *adj* rou-

main(e). ◇ *n* - **1.** [person] Roumain *m*, -e *f* - **2.** [language] roumain *m*.

Roman numerals *npl* chiffres *mpl* romains.

romantic [rəʊ'mæntɪk] *adj* romantique.

Rome [rəʊm] *n* Rome.

romp [rɒmp] ◇ *n* ébats *mpl*. ◇ *vi* s'ébattre.

rompers ['rɒmpəz] *npl*, **romper suit** ['rɒmpə'-] *n* barboteuse *f*.

roof [ru:f] *n* toit *m* ; [of cave, tunnel] plafond *m* ; **the** ~ **of the mouth** la voûte du palais ; **to go through** OR **hit the** ~ *fig* exploser.

roofing ['ru:fɪŋ] *n* toiture *f*.

roof rack *n* galerie *f*.

rooftop ['ru:ftɒp] *n* toit *m*.

rook [rʊk] *n* - **1.** [bird] freux *m* - **2.** [chess piece] tour *f*.

rookie ['rʊkɪ] *n* Am inf bleu *m*.

room [ru:m, rʊm] *n* - **1.** [in building] pièce *f* - **2.** [bedroom] chambre *f* - **3.** (*U*) [space] place *f*.

rooming house ['ru:mɪŋ-] *n* Am maison *f* de rapport.

roommate ['ru:mmeɪt] *n* camarade *mf* de chambre.

room service *n* service *m* dans les chambres.

roomy ['ru:mɪ] *adj* spacieux(euse).

roost [ru:st] ◇ *n* perchoir *m*, juchoir *m*. ◇ *vi* se percher, se jucher.

rooster ['ru:stə'] *n* coq *m*.

root [ru:t] ◇ *n* racine *f* ; *fig* [of problem] origine *f* ; **to take** ~ *lit & fig* prendre racine. ◇ *vi* : **to** ~ **through** fouiller dans. ◆ **roots** *npl* racines *fpl*. ◆ **root for** *vt fus* Am inf encourager. ◆ **root out** *vt sep* [eradicate] extirper.

rope [rəʊp] ◇ *n* corde *f* ; **to know the** ~**s** connaître son affaire, être au courant. ◇ *vt* corder ; [climbers] encorder. ◆ **rope in** *vt sep inf fig* enrôler.

rosary ['rəʊzərɪ] *n* rosaire *m*.

rose [rəʊz] ◇ *pt* ⊳ rise. ◇ *adj* [pink] rose. ◇ *n* [flower] rose *f*.

rosé ['rəʊzeɪ] *n* rosé *m*.

rosebud ['rəʊzbʌd] *n* bouton *m* de rose.

rose bush *n* rosier *m*.

rosemary ['rəʊzmərɪ] *n* romarin *m*.

rosette [rəʊ'zet] *n* rosette *f*.

roster ['rɒstə'] *n* liste *f*, tableau *m*.

rostrum ['rɒstrəm] (*pl* **-trums** OR **-tra** [-trə]) *n* tribune *f*.

rosy ['rəʊzı] *adj* rose.

rot [rɒt] ◇ *n (U)* **- 1.** [decay] pourriture *f*
- 2. *Br dated* [nonsense] bêtises *fpl*, balivernes *fpl*. ◇ *vt & vi* pourrir.

rota ['rəʊtə] *n Br* liste *f*, tableau *m*.

rotary ['rəʊtərı] ◇ *adj* rotatif(ive). ◇ *n
Am* [roundabout] rond-point *m*.

rotate [rəʊ'teɪt] ◇ *vt* [turn] faire tourner.
◇ *vi* [turn] tourner.

rotation [rəʊ'teɪʃn] *n* [turning movement]
rotation *f*.

rote [rəʊt] *n* : **by ~** de façon machinale, par
cœur.

rotten ['rɒtn] *adj* **- 1.** [decayed] pourri(e)
- 2. *inf* [bad] moche **- 3.** *inf* [unwell] : **to feel ~**
se sentir mal fichu(e).

rouge [ruːʒ] *n* rouge *m* à joues.

rough [rʌf] ◇ *adj* **- 1.** [not smooth - sur-
face] rugueux(euse), rêche ; [- road] acci-
denté(e) ; [- sea] agité(e), houleux(euse) ;
[- crossing] mauvais(e) **- 2.** [person, treat-
ment] brutal(e) ; [manners, conditions]
rude ; [area] mal fréquenté(e) **- 3.** [guess]
approximatif(ive) ; ~ **copy**, ~ **draft** brouillon *m* ; ~ **sketch** ébauche *f* **- 4.** [harsh - voice,
wine] âpre ; [- life] dur(e) ; **to have a ~ time**
en baver. ◇ *adv* Br : **to sleep ~** coucher à
la dure. ◇ *n* **- 1.** GOLF rough *m* **- 2.** [unde-
tailed form] : **in ~** au brouillon. ◇ *vt phr* : **to
~ it** vivre à la dure.

roughage ['rʌfɪdʒ] *n (U)* fibres *fpl* alimentaires.

rough and ready *adj* rudimentaire.

roughcast ['rʌfkɑːst] *n* crépi *m*.

roughen ['rʌfn] *vt* rendre rugueux(euse)
OR rêche.

roughly ['rʌflı] *adv* **- 1.** [approximately]
approximativement **- 2.** [handle, treat] brutalement **- 3.** [build, made] grossièrement.

roulette [ruː'let] *n* roulette *f*.

round [raʊnd] ◇ *adj* rond(e). ◇ *prep Br*
autour de ; ~ **here** par ici ; **all ~ the country**
dans tout le pays ; **just ~ the corner** au coin
de la rue ; *fig* tout près ; **to go ~ sthg** [obs-
tacle] contourner qqch ; **to go ~ a museum**
visiter un musée. ◇ *adv Br* **- 1.** [surround-
ing] : **all ~** tout autour **- 2.** [near] : ~ **about**
dans le coin **- 3.** [in measurements] : **10 metres ~** 10 mètres de diamètre **- 4.** [to other
side] : **to go ~** faire le tour ; **to turn ~** se retourner ; **to look ~** se retourner (pour regarder) **- 5.** [at or to nearby place] : **come
~ and see us** venez OR passez nous voir ;
he's ~ at her house il est chez elle **- 6.** [ap-
proximately] : ~ **(about)** vers, environ. ◇ *n*
- 1. [of talks etc] série *f* ; **a ~ of applause** une
salve d'applaudissements **- 2.** [of competi-

tion] manche *f* **- 3.** [of doctor] visites *fpl* ; [of
postman, milkman] tournée *f* **- 4.** [of ammu-
nition] cartouche *f* **- 5.** [of drinks] tournée *f*
- 6. BOXING reprise *f*, round *m* **- 7.** GOLF partie
f. ◇ *vt* [corner] tourner ; [bend] prendre.
➤ **rounds** *npl* [of doctor] visites *fpl* ; **to do**
OR **go the ~s** [story, joke] circuler ; [illness]
faire des ravages. ➤ **round off** *vt sep* terminer, conclure. ➤ **round up** *vt sep*
- 1. [gather together] rassembler **- 2.** MATH
arrondir.

roundabout ['raʊndəbaʊt] ◇ *adj* dé-
tourné(e). ◇ *n Br* **- 1.** [on road] rond-point
m **- 2.** [at fairground] manège *m*.

rounders ['raʊndəz] *n Br* sorte de baseball.

roundly ['raʊndlı] *adv* [beaten] complètement ; [condemned etc] franchement, carrément.

round-shouldered [-'ʃəʊldəd] *adj* voû-
té(e).

round trip *n* aller et retour *m*.

roundup ['raʊndʌp] *n* [summary] résumé
m.

rouse [raʊz] *vt* **- 1.** [wake up] réveiller
- 2. [impel] : **to ~ o.s. to do sthg** se forcer à
faire qqch ; **to ~ sb to action** pousser OR inciter qqn à agir **- 3.** [emotions] susciter, provoquer.

rousing ['raʊzɪŋ] *adj* [speech] vibrant(e),
passionné(e) ; [welcome] enthousiaste.

rout [raʊt] ◇ *n* déroute *f*. ◇ *vt* mettre en
déroute.

route [ruːt] ◇ *n* **- 1.** [gen] itinéraire *m*
- 2. *fig* [way] chemin *m*, voie *f*. ◇ *vt* [goods]
acheminer.

route map *n* [for journey] croquis *m* d'itinéraire ; [for buses, trains] carte *f* du réseau.

routine [ruː'tiːn] ◇ *adj* **- 1.** [normal] habi-
tuel(elle), de routine **- 2.** *pej* [uninteresting]
de routine. ◇ *n* routine *f*.

roving ['rəʊvɪŋ] *adj* itinérant(e).

row[1] [rəʊ] ◇ *n* **- 1.** [line] rangée *f* ; [of
seats] rang *m* **- 2.** *fig* [of defeats, victories] série *f* ; **in a ~** d'affilée, de suite. ◇ *vt* [boat]
faire aller à la rame ; [person] transporter
en canot OR bateau. ◇ *vi* ramer.

row[2] [raʊ] ◇ *n* **- 1.** [quarrel] dispute *f*, querelle *f* **- 2.** *inf* [noise] vacarme *m*, raffut *m*.
◇ *vi* [quarrel] se disputer, se quereller.

rowboat ['rəʊbəʊt] *n Am* canot *m*.

rowdy ['raʊdı] *adj* chahuteur(euse), tapa-
geur(euse).

row house [rəʊ-] *n Am* maison *attenante
aux maisons voisines*.

rowing ['rəʊɪŋ] *n* SPORT aviron *m*.

rowing boat *n Br* canot *m*.

royal ['rɔɪəl] ◇ *adj* royal(e). ◇ *n inf* membre *m* de la famille royale.

Royal Air Force *n* : **the ~** l'armée *f* de l'air britannique.

royal family *n* famille *f* royale.

Royal Mail *n Br* : **the ~** ≃ la Poste.

Royal Navy *n* : **the ~** la marine de guerre britannique.

royalty ['rɔɪəltɪ] *n* royauté *f*. ◆ **royalties** *npl* droits *mpl* d'auteur.

rpm *npl* (*abbr of* **revolutions per minute**) tours *mpl* par minute, tr/min.

RSPCA (*abbr of* **Royal Society for the Prevention of Cruelty to Animals**) *n* société britannique protectrice des animaux, ≃ SPA *f*.

RSVP (*abbr of* **répondez s'il vous plaît**) RSVP.

Rt Hon (*abbr of* **Right Honourable**) *expression utilisée pour des titres nobiliaires.*

rub [rʌb] ◇ *vt* frotter ; **to ~ sthg in** [cream etc] faire pénétrer qqch (en frottant) ; **to ~ one's eyes/hands** se frotter les yeux/les mains ; **to ~ sb up the wrong way** *Br*, **to ~ sb the wrong way** *Am fig* prendre qqn à rebrousse-poil. ◇ *vi* frotter. ◆ **rub off on** *vt fus* [subj : quality] déteindre sur. ◆ **rub out** *vt sep* [erase] effacer.

rubber ['rʌbər] ◇ *adj* en caoutchouc. ◇ *n* **- 1.** [substance] caoutchouc *m* **- 2.** *Br* [eraser] gomme *f* **- 3.** *Am inf* [condom] préservatif *m* **- 4.** [in bridge] robre *m*, rob *m*.

rubber band *n* élastique *m*.

rubber plant *n* caoutchouc *m*.

rubber stamp *n* tampon *m*. ◆ **rubber-stamp** *vt fig* approuver sans discussion.

rubbish ['rʌbɪʃ] ◇ *n* (*U*) **- 1.** [refuse] détritus *mpl*, ordures *fpl* **- 2.** *inf fig* [worthless objects] camelote *f* ; **the play was ~** la pièce était nulle **- 3.** *inf* [nonsense] bêtises *fpl*, inepties *fpl*. ◇ *vt inf* débiner.

rubbish bin *n Br* poubelle *f*.

rubbish dump *n Br* dépotoir *m*.

rubble ['rʌbl] *n* (*U*) décombres *mpl*.

ruby ['ru:bɪ] *n* rubis *m*.

rucksack ['rʌksæk] *n* sac *m* à dos.

ructions ['rʌkʃnz] *npl inf* grabuge *m*.

rudder ['rʌdər] *n* gouvernail *m*.

ruddy ['rʌdɪ] *adj* **- 1.** [complexion, face] coloré(e) **- 2.** *Br inf dated* [damned] sacré(e).

rude [ru:d] *adj* **- 1.** [impolite - gen] impoli(e) ; [- word] grossier(ère) ; [- noise] incongru(e) **- 2.** [sudden] : **it was a ~ awakening** le réveil fut pénible.

rudimentary [,ru:dɪ'mentərɪ] *adj* rudimentaire.

rueful ['ru:fʊl] *adj* triste.

ruffian ['rʌfjən] *n* voyou *m*.

ruffle ['rʌfl] *vt* **- 1.** [hair] ébouriffer ; [water] troubler ; [person] froisser ; [composure] faire perdre.

rug [rʌg] *n* **- 1.** [carpet] tapis *m* **- 2.** [blanket] couverture *f*.

rugby ['rʌgbɪ] *n* rugby *m*.

rugged ['rʌgɪd] *adj* **- 1.** [landscape] accidenté(e) ; [features] rude **- 2.** [vehicle etc] robuste.

rugger ['rʌgər] *n Br inf* rugby *m*.

ruin ['ru:ɪn] ◇ *n* ruine *f*. ◇ *vt* ruiner ; [clothes, shoes] abîmer. ◆ **in ruin(s)** *adv lit & fig* en ruine.

rule [ru:l] ◇ *n* **- 1.** [gen] règle *f* ; **as a ~** en règle générale **- 2.** [regulation] règlement *m* **- 3.** (*U*) [control] autorité *f*. ◇ *vt* **- 1.** [control] dominer **- 2.** [govern] gouverner **- 3.** [decide] : **to ~ (that) ...** décider que ... ◇ *vi* **- 1.** [give decision - gen] décider ; [- JUR] statuer **- 2.** *fml* [be paramount] prévaloir **- 3.** [king, queen] régner ; POL gouverner. ◆ **rule out** *vt sep* exclure, écarter.

ruled [ru:ld] *adj* [paper] réglé(e).

ruler ['ru:lər] *n* **- 1.** [for measurement] règle *f* **- 2.** [leader] chef *m* d'État.

ruling ['ru:lɪŋ] ◇ *adj* au pouvoir. ◇ *n* décision *f*.

rum [rʌm] *n* rhum *m*.

Rumania [ru:'meɪnjə] = **Romania**.

Rumanian [ru:'meɪnjən] = **Romanian**.

rumble ['rʌmbl] ◇ *n* [of thunder, traffic] grondement *m* ; [in stomach] gargouillement *m*. ◇ *vi* [thunder, traffic] gronder ; [stomach] gargouiller.

rummage ['rʌmɪdʒ] *vi* fouiller.

rumour *Br*, **rumor** *Am* ['ru:mər] *n* rumeur *f*.

rumoured *Br*, **rumored** *Am* ['ru:məd] *adj* : **he is ~ to be very wealthy** le bruit court OR on dit qu'il est très riche.

rump [rʌmp] *n* **- 1.** [of animal] croupe *f* **- 2.** *inf* [of person] derrière *m*.

rump steak *n* romsteck *m*.

rumpus ['rʌmpəs] *n inf* chahut *m*.

run [rʌn] (*pt* ran, *pp* run) ◇ *n* **- 1.** [on foot] course *f* ; **to go for a ~** faire un petit peu de course à pied ; **on the ~** en fuite, en cavale **- 2.** [in car - for pleasure] tour *m* ; [- journey] trajet *m* **- 3.** [series] suite *f*, série *f* ; **a ~ of bad luck** une période de déveine ; **in the short/long ~** à court/long terme **- 4.** THEATRE : **to have a long ~** tenir longtemps l'affiche **- 5.** [great demand] : **~ on** ruée *f* sur **- 6.** [in tights] échelle *f* - **7.** [in cricket, baseball] point *m* - **8.** [track - for skiing, bobsleigh] piste *f.* ⬦ *vt* - **1.** [race, distance] courir - **2.** [manage - business] diriger ; [- shop, hotel] tenir ; [- course] organiser - **3.** [operate] faire marcher - **4.** [car] avoir, entretenir - **5.** [water, bath] faire couler - **6.** [publish] publier - **7.** *inf* [drive] : **can you ~ me to the station?** tu peux m'amener OR me conduire à la gare? - **8.** [move] : **to ~ sthg along/over sthg** passer qqch le long de/sur qqch. ⬦ *vi* - **1.** [on foot] courir - **2.** [pass - road, river, pipe] passer ; **to ~ through sthg** traverser qqch - **3.** *Am* [in election] : **to ~ (for)** être candidat (à) - **4.** [operate - machine, factory] marcher ; [- engine] tourner ; **everything is running smoothly** tout va comme sur des roulettes, tout va bien ; **to ~ on sthg** marcher à qqch ; **to ~ off sthg** marcher sur qqch - **5.** [bus, train] faire le service ; **trains ~ every hour** il y a un train toutes les heures - **6.** [flow] couler ; **my nose is running** j'ai le nez qui coule - **7.** [colour] déteindre ; [ink] baver - **8.** [continue - contract, insurance policy] être valide ; [- THEATRE] se jouer. ◆ **run across** *vt fus* [meet] tomber sur. ◆ **run away** *vi* [flee] : **to ~ away (from)** s'enfuir (de) ; **to ~ away from home** faire une fugue. ◆ **run down** ⬦ *vt sep* - **1.** [in vehicle] renverser - **2.** [criticize] dénigrer - **3.** [production] restreindre ; [industry] réduire l'activité de. ⬦ *vi* [clock] s'arrêter ; [battery] se décharger. ◆ **run into** *vt fus* - **1.** [encounter - problem] se heurter à ; [- person] tomber sur - **2.** [in vehicle] rentrer dans. ◆ **run off** ⬦ *vt sep* [a copy] tirer. ⬦ *vi* : **to ~ off (with)** s'enfuir (avec). ◆ **run out** *vi* - **1.** [food, supplies] s'épuiser ; **time is running out** il ne reste plus beaucoup de temps - **2.** [licence, contract] expirer. ◆ **run out of** *vt fus* manquer de ; **to ~ out of petrol** tomber en panne d'essence, tomber en panne sèche. ◆ **run over** *vt sep* renverser. ◆ **run through** *vt fus* - **1.** [practise] répéter - **2.** [read through] parcourir. ◆ **run to** *vt fus* [amount to] monter à, s'élever à. ◆ **run up** *vt fus* [bill, debt] laisser accumuler. ◆ **run up against** *vt fus* se heurter à.

runaway ['rʌnəweɪ] ⬦ *adj* [train, lorry] fou (folle) ; [horse] emballé(e) ; [victory] haut la main ; [inflation] galopant(e). ⬦ *n* fuyard *m*, fugitif *m*, -ive *f.*

rundown ['rʌndaʊn] *n* - **1.** [report] bref résumé - **2.** [of industry] réduction *f* délibérée. ◆ **run-down** *adj* - **1.** [building] délabré(e) - **2.** [person] épuisé(e).

rung [rʌŋ] ⬦ *pp* ⊳ **ring.** ⬦ *n* échelon *m*, barreau *m.*

runner ['rʌnəʳ] *n* - **1.** [athlete] coureur *m*, -euse *f* - **2.** [of guns, drugs] contrebandier *m* - **3.** [of sledge] patin *m* ; [for car seat] glissière *f* ; [for drawer] coulisseau *m.*

runner bean *n Br* haricot *m* à rames.

runner-up (*pl* runners-up) *n* second *m*, -e *f.*

running ['rʌnɪŋ] ⬦ *adj* - **1.** [argument, battle] continu(e) - **2.** [consecutive] : **three weeks ~** trois semaines de suite - **3.** [water] courant(e). ⬦ *n* - **1.** (*U*) SPORT course *f* ; **to go ~** faire de la course - **2.** [management] direction *f*, administration *f* - **3.** [of machine] marche *f*, fonctionnement *m* - **4.** *phr* : **to be in the ~ (for)** avoir des chances de réussir (dans) ; **to be out of the ~ (for)** n'avoir aucune chance de réussir (dans).

runny ['rʌnɪ] *adj* - **1.** [food] liquide - **2.** [nose] qui coule.

run-of-the-mill *adj* banal(e), ordinaire.

runt [rʌnt] *n* avorton *m.*

run-up *n* - **1.** [preceding time] : **in the ~ to sthg** dans la période qui précède qqch - **2.** SPORT course *f* d'élan.

runway ['rʌnweɪ] *n* piste *f.*

rupture ['rʌptʃəʳ] *n* rupture *f.*

rural ['rʊərəl] *adj* rural(e).

ruse [ruːz] *n* ruse *f.*

rush [rʌʃ] ⬦ *n* - **1.** [hurry] hâte *f* - **2.** [surge] ruée *f*, bousculade *f* ; **to make a ~ for sthg** se ruer OR se précipiter vers qqch ; **a ~ of air** une bouffée d'air - **3.** [demand] : **~ (on OR for)** ruée *f* (sur). ⬦ *vt* - **1.** [hurry - work] faire à la hâte ; [- person] bousculer ; [- meal] expédier - **2.** [send quickly] transporter OR envoyer d'urgence - **3.** [attack suddenly] prendre d'assaut. ⬦ *vi* - **1.** [hurry] se dépêcher ; **to ~ into sthg** faire qqch sans réfléchir - **2.** [move quickly, suddenly] se précipiter, se ruer ; **the blood ~ed to her head** le sang lui monta à la tête. ◆ **rushes** *npl* BOT joncs *mpl.*

rush hour *n* heures *fpl* de pointe OR d'affluence.

rusk [rʌsk] *n* biscotte *f.*

Russia ['rʌʃə] *n* Russie *f.*

Russian ['rʌʃn] ⬦ *adj* russe. ⬦ *n* - **1.** [person] Russe *mf* - **2.** [language] russe *m.*

rust [rʌst] ⬦ *n* rouille *f.* ⬦ *vi* se rouiller.

rustic ['rʌstɪk] *adj* rustique.

rustle ['rʌsl] ⬦ *vt* - **1.** [paper] froisser - **2.** *Am* [cattle] voler. ⬦ *vi* [leaves] bruire ; [papers] produire un froissement.

rusty ['rʌstɪ] *adj lit* & *fig* rouillé(e).

rut [rʌt] *n* ornière *f* ; **to get into a ~** s'encroûter ; **to be in a ~** être prisonnier de la routine.

ruthless ['ru:θlɪs] *adj* impitoyable.

RV *n Am (abbr of* **recreational vehicle)** camping-car *m.*

rye [raɪ] *n* [grain] seigle *m.*

rye bread *n* pain *m* de seigle.

s *(pl* **ss** OR **s's), S** *(pl* **Ss** OR **S's)** [es] *n* [letter] s *m inv,* S *m inv.* ➤ **S** *(abbr of* **south)** S.

Sabbath ['sæbəθ] *n* : **the ~** le sabbat.

sabbatical [sə'bætɪkl] *n* année *f* sabbatique ; **to be on ~** faire une année sabbatique.

sabotage ['sæbətɑ:ʒ] ◇ *n* sabotage *m.* ◇ *vt* saboter.

saccharin(e) ['sækərɪn] *n* saccharine *f.*

sachet ['sæʃeɪ] *n* sachet *m.*

sack [sæk] ◇ *n* - **1.** [bag] sac *m* - **2.** *Br inf* [dismissal] : **to get** OR **be given the ~** être renvoyé(e), se faire virer. ◇ *vt Br inf* [dismiss] renvoyer, virer.

sacking ['sækɪŋ] *n* [fabric] toile *f* à sac.

sacred ['seɪkrɪd] *adj* sacré(e).

sacrifice ['sækrɪfaɪs] *lit & fig* ◇ *n* sacrifice *m.* ◇ *vt* sacrifier.

sacrilege ['sækrɪlɪdʒ] *n lit & fig* sacrilège *m.*

sacrosanct ['sækrəʊsæŋkt] *adj* sacrosaint(e).

sad [sæd] *adj* triste.

sadden ['sædn] *vt* attrister, affliger.

saddle ['sædl] ◇ *n* selle *f.* ◇ *vt* - **1.** [horse] seller - **2.** *fig* [burden] : **to ~ sb with sthg** coller qqch à qqn.

saddlebag ['sædlbæg] *n* sacoche *f (de selle ou de bicyclette).*

sadistic [sə'dɪstɪk] *adj* sadique.

sadly ['sædlɪ] *adv* - **1.** [unhappily] tristement - **2.** [unfortunately] malheureusement.

sadness ['sædnɪs] *n* tristesse *f.*

s.a.e., sae *abbr of* **stamped addressed envelope.**

safari [sə'fɑ:rɪ] *n* safari *m.*

safe [seɪf] ◇ *adj* - **1.** [not dangerous - gen] sans danger ; [- driver, play, guess] prudent(e) ; **it's ~ to say (that)** ... on peut dire à coup sûr que ... - **2.** [not in danger] hors de danger, en sécurité ; **~ and sound** sain et sauf (saine et sauve) - **3.** [not risky - bet, method] sans risque ; [- investment] sûr(e) ; **to be on the ~ side** par précaution. ◇ *n* coffre-fort *m.*

safe-conduct *n* sauf-conduit *m.*

safe-deposit box *n* coffre-fort *m.*

safeguard ['seɪfgɑ:d] ◇ *n* : **~ (against)** sauvegarde *f* (contre). ◇ *vt* : **to ~ sb/sthg (against)** sauvegarder qqn/qqch (contre), protéger qqn/qqch (contre).

safekeeping [ˌseɪf'ki:pɪŋ] *n* bonne garde *f.*

safely ['seɪflɪ] *adv* - **1.** [not dangerously] sans danger - **2.** [not in danger] en toute sécurité, à l'abri du danger - **3.** [arrive - person] à bon port, sain et sauf (saine et sauve) ; [- parcel] à bon port - **4.** [for certain] : **I can ~ say (that)** ... je peux dire à coup sûr que ...

safe sex *n* sexe *m* sans risques, S.S.R. *m.*

safety ['seɪftɪ] *n* sécurité *f.*

safety belt *n* ceinture *f* de sécurité.

safety pin *n* épingle *f* de sûreté OR de nourrice.

saffron ['sæfrən] *n* safran *m.*

sag [sæg] *vi* [sink downwards] s'affaisser, fléchir.

sage [seɪdʒ] ◇ *adj* sage. ◇ *n* - **1.** *(U)* [herb] sauge *f* - **2.** [wise man] sage *m.*

Sagittarius [ˌsædʒɪ'teərɪəs] *n* Sagittaire *m.*

Sahara [sə'hɑ:rə] *n* : **the ~ (Desert)** le (désert du) Sahara.

said [sed] *pt & pp* ▷ **say.**

sail [seɪl] ◇ *n* - **1.** [of boat] voile *f* ; **to set ~** faire voile, prendre la mer - **2.** [journey] tour *m* en bateau. ◇ *vt* - **1.** [boat] piloter, manœuvrer - **2.** [sea] parcourir. ◇ *vi* - **1.** [person - gen] aller en bateau ; [- SPORT] faire de la voile - **2.** [boat - move] naviguer ; [- leave] partir, prendre la mer - **3.** *fig* [through air] voler. ➤ **sail through** *vt fus fig* réussir les doigts dans le nez.

sailboat *Am* = **sailing boat.**

sailing ['seɪlɪŋ] *n* - **1.** *(U)* SPORT voile *f* ; **to go ~** faire de la voile - **2.** [departure] départ *m.*

sailing boat *Br,* **sailboat** *Am* ['seɪlbəʊt] *n* bateau *m* à voiles, voilier *m.*

sailing ship *n* voilier *m.*

sailor ['seɪlər] *n* marin *m,* matelot *m.*

saint [seɪnt] *n* saint *m,* -e *f.*

saintly ['seɪntlɪ] *adj* [person] saint(e) ; [life] de saint.

Saint Patrick's Day [-'pætrɪks-] *n* la Saint-Patrick.

sake [seɪk] *n* : **for the ~ of sb** par égard pour qqn, pour (l'amour de) qqn ; **for the children's ~** pour les enfants ; **for the ~ of argument** à titre d'exemple ; **for God's** OR **heaven's ~** pour l'amour de Dieu OR du ciel.

salad ['sæləd] *n* salade *f*.

salad bowl *n* saladier *m*.

salad cream *n Br* sorte de mayonnaise douce.

salad dressing *n* vinaigrette *f*.

salami [sə'lɑːmɪ] *n* salami *m*.

salary ['sælərɪ] *n* salaire *m*, traitement *m*.

sale [seɪl] *n* - **1.** [gen] vente *f* ; **on ~** en vente ; **(up) for ~** à vendre - **2.** [at reduced prices] soldes *mpl*. ◆ **sales** *npl* - **1.** [quantity sold] ventes *fpl* - **2.** [at reduced prices] : **the ~s** les soldes *mpl*.

saleroom *Br* ['seɪlrʊm], **salesroom** *Am* ['seɪlzrʊm] *n* salle *f* des ventes.

sales assistant ['seɪlz-], **salesclerk** ['seɪlzklɜːrk] *Am n* vendeur *m*, -euse *f*.

salesman ['seɪlzmən] (*pl* **-men** [-mən]) *n* [in shop] vendeur *m* ; [travelling] représentant *m* de commerce.

sales rep *n inf* représentant *m* de commerce.

salesroom *Am* = **saleroom**.

saleswoman ['seɪlz,wʊmən] (*pl* **-women** [-,wɪmɪn]) *n* [in shop] vendeuse *f* ; [travelling] représentante *f* de commerce.

salient ['seɪljənt] *adj fml* qui ressort.

saliva [sə'laɪvə] *n* salive *f*.

sallow ['sæləʊ] *adj* cireux(euse).

salmon ['sæmən] (*pl inv* OR **-s**) *n* saumon *m*.

salmonella [,sælmə'nelə] *n* salmonelle *f*.

salon ['sælɒn] *n* salon *m*.

saloon [sə'luːn] *n* - **1.** *Br* [car] berline *f* - **2.** *Am* [bar] saloon *m* - **3.** *Br* [in pub] : **~ (bar)** bar *m* - **4.** [in ship] salon *m*.

salt [sɔːlt, sɒlt] ◇ *n* sel *m*. ◇ *vt* [food] saler ; [roads] mettre du sel sur. ◆ **salt away** *vt sep* mettre de côté.

saltcellar *Br*, **salt shaker** *Am* [-,ʃeɪkər] *n* salière *f*.

saltwater ['sɔːlt,wɔːtər] ◇ *n* eau *f* de mer. ◇ *adj* de mer.

salty ['sɔːltɪ] *adj* [food] salé(e) ; [water] saumâtre.

salutary ['sæljʊtrɪ] *adj* salutaire.

salute [sə'luːt] ◇ *n* salut *m*. ◇ *vt* saluer. ◇ *vi* faire un salut.

salvage ['sælvɪdʒ] ◇ *n (U)* - **1.** [rescue of ship] sauvetage *m* - **2.** [property rescued] biens *mpl* sauvés. ◇ *vt* sauver.

salvation [sæl'veɪʃn] *n* salut *m*.

Salvation Army *n* : **the ~** l'Armée *f* du Salut.

same [seɪm] ◇ *adj* même ; **she was wearing the ~ jumper as I was** elle portait le même pull que moi ; **at the ~ time** en même temps ; **one and the ~** un seul et même (une seule et même). ◇ *pron* : **the ~** le même (la même), les mêmes *(pl)* ; **I'll have the ~ as you** je prendrai la même chose que toi ; **she earns the ~ as I do** elle gagne autant que moi ; **to do the ~** faire de même, en faire autant ; **all** OR **just the ~** [anyway] quand même, tout de même ; **it's all the ~ to me** ça m'est égal ; **it's not the ~** ce n'est pas pareil. ◇ *adv* : **the ~** [treat, spelled] de la même manière.

sample ['sɑːmpl] ◇ *n* échantillon *m*. ◇ *vt* [taste] goûter.

sanatorium, **sanitorium** *Am* [,sænə'tɔːrɪəm] (*pl* **-riums** OR **-ria** [-rɪə]) *n* sanatorium *m*.

sanctimonious [,sæŋktɪ'məʊnjəs] *adj* moralisateur(trice).

sanction ['sæŋkʃn] ◇ *n* sanction *f*. ◇ *vt* sanctionner.

sanctity ['sæŋktətɪ] *n* sainteté *f*.

sanctuary ['sæŋktʃʊərɪ] *n* - **1.** [for birds, wildlife] réserve *f* - **2.** [refuge] asile *m*.

sand [sænd] ◇ *n* sable *m*. ◇ *vt* [wood] poncer.

sandal ['sændl] *n* sandale *f*.

sandalwood ['sændlwʊd] *n* (bois *m* de) santal *m*.

sandbox *Am* = **sandpit**.

sandcastle ['sænd,kɑːsl] *n* château *m* de sable.

sand dune *n* dune *f*.

sandpaper ['sænd,peɪpər] ◇ *n (U)* papier *m* de verre. ◇ *vt* poncer (au papier de verre).

sandpit *Br* ['sændpɪt], **sandbox** *Am* ['sændbɒks] *n* bac *m* à sable.

sandstone ['sændstəʊn] *n* grès *m*.

sandwich ['sænwɪdʒ] ◇ *n* sandwich *m*. ◇ *vt fig* : **to be ~ed between** être (pris(e)) en sandwich entre.

sandwich board *n* panneau *m* publicitaire (d'homme sandwich ou posé comme un tréteau).

sandwich course *n Br* stage *m* de formation professionnelle.

sandy ['sændɪ] *adj* - **1.** [beach] de sable ;

[earth] sableux(euse) **- 2.** [sand-coloured] sable *(inv)*.

sane [seɪn] *adj* **- 1.** [not mad] sain(e) d'esprit **- 2.** [sensible] raisonnable, sensé(e).

sang [sæŋ] *pt* ⊳ sing.

sanitary ['sænɪtrɪ] *adj* **- 1.** [method, system] sanitaire **- 2.** [clean] hygiénique, salubre.

sanitary towel, sanitary napkin *Am n* serviette *f* hygiénique.

sanitation [ˌsænɪ'teɪʃn] *n (U)* [in house] installations *fpl* sanitaires.

sanitorium *Am* = sanatorium.

sanity ['sænətɪ] *n (U)* **- 1.** [saneness] santé *f* mentale, raison *f* **- 2.** [good sense] bon sens *m*.

sank [sæŋk] *pt* ⊳ sink.

Santa (Claus) ['sæntə(ˌklɔːz)] *n* le père Noël.

sap [sæp] ⇔ *n* [of plant] sève *f*. ⇔ *vt* [weaken] saper.

sapling ['sæplɪŋ] *n* jeune arbre *m*.

sapphire ['sæfaɪəʳ] *n* saphir *m*.

sarcastic [saːˈkæstɪk] *adj* sarcastique.

sardine [saːˈdiːn] *n* sardine *f*.

Sardinia [saːˈdɪnjə] *n* Sardaigne *f*.

sardonic [saːˈdɒnɪk] *adj* sardonique.

SAS *(abbr of* **Special Air Service)** *n commando d'intervention spéciale de l'armée britannique.*

SASE *abbr of* **self-addressed stamped envelope.**

sash [sæʃ] *n* [of cloth] écharpe *f*.

sat [sæt] *pt & pp* ⊳ sit.

SAT [sæt] *n* **- 1.** *(abbr of* **Standard Assessment Test)** *examen national en Grande-Bretagne pour les élèves de 7 ans, 11 ans et 14 ans* **- 2.** *(abbr of* **Scholastic Aptitude Test)** *examen d'entrée à l'université aux États-Unis.*

Satan ['seɪtn] *n* Satan *m*.

satchel ['sætʃəl] *n* cartable *m*.

satellite ['sætəlaɪt] ⇔ *n* satellite *m*. ⇔ *comp* **- 1.** [link] par satellite ; **~ dish** antenne *f* parabolique **- 2.** [country, company] satellite.

satellite TV *n* télévision *f* par satellite.

satin ['sætɪn] ⇔ *n* satin *m*. ⇔ *comp* [sheets, pyjamas] de OR en satin ; [wallpaper, finish] satiné(e).

satire ['sætaɪəʳ] *n* satire *f*.

satisfaction [ˌsætɪsˈfækʃn] *n* satisfaction *f*.

satisfactory [ˌsætɪsˈfæktərɪ] *adj* satisfaisant(e).

satisfied ['sætɪsfaɪd] *adj* [happy] : **~ (with)** satisfait(e) (de).

satisfy ['sætɪsfaɪ] *vt* **- 1.** [gen] satisfaire **- 2.** [convince] convaincre, persuader ; **to ~ sb that** convaincre qqn que.

satisfying ['sætɪsfaɪɪŋ] *adj* satisfaisant(e).

satsuma [ˌsætˈsuːmə] *n* satsuma *f*.

saturate ['sætʃəreɪt] *vt* : **to ~ sthg (with)** saturer qqch (de).

Saturday ['sætədɪ] ⇔ *n* samedi *m* ; **it's ~** on est samedi ; **on ~** samedi ; **on ~s** le samedi ; **last ~** samedi dernier ; **this ~** ce samedi ; **next ~** samedi prochain ; **every ~** tous les samedis ; **every other ~** un samedi sur deux ; **the ~ before** l'autre samedi ; **the ~ before last** pas samedi dernier, mais le samedi d'avant ; **the ~ after next, ~ week, a week on ~** samedi en huit. ⇔ *comp* [paper] du OR de samedi ; **~ morning/afternoon/evening** samedi matin/après-midi/soir.

sauce [sɔːs] *n* CULIN sauce *f*.

saucepan ['sɔːspən] *n* casserole *f*.

saucer ['sɔːsəʳ] *n* sous-tasse *f*, soucoupe *f*.

saucy ['sɔːsɪ] *adj inf* coquin(e).

Saudi Arabia ['saʊdɪ-] *n* Arabie *f* Saoudite.

Saudi (Arabian) ['saʊdɪ-] ⇔ *adj* saoudien(enne). ⇔ *n* [person] Saoudien *m*, -enne *f*.

sauna ['sɔːnə] *n* sauna *m*.

saunter ['sɔːntəʳ] *vi* flâner.

sausage ['sɒsɪdʒ] *n* saucisse *f*.

sausage roll *n Br* feuilleté *m* à la saucisse.

sauté [*Br* 'səʊteɪ, *Am* səʊ'teɪ] *(pt & pp* **sautéed** OR **sautéd)** ⇔ *adj* sauté(e). ⇔ *vt* [potatoes] faire sauter ; [onions] faire revenir.

savage ['sævɪdʒ] ⇔ *adj* [fierce] féroce. ⇔ *n* sauvage *mf*. ⇔ *vt* attaquer avec férocité.

save [seɪv] ⇔ *vt* **- 1.** [rescue] sauver ; **to ~ sb's life** sauver la vie à OR de qqn **- 2.** [money - set aside] mettre de côté ; [- spend less] économiser **- 3.** [time] gagner ; [strength] économiser ; [food] garder **- 4.** [avoid] éviter, épargner ; **to ~ sb sthg** épargner qqch à qqn ; **to ~ sb from doing sthg** éviter à qqn de faire qqch **- 5.** SPORT arrêter **- 6.** COMPUT sauvegarder. ⇔ *vi* [save money] mettre de l'argent de côté. ⇔ *n* SPORT arrêt *m*. ⇔ *prep fml* : **~ (for)** sauf, à l'exception de. ◆ **save up** *vi* mettre de l'argent de côté.

saving grace ['seɪvɪŋ-] *n* : **its ~ was ...** ce qui le rachetait, c'était ...

savings ['seɪvɪŋz] *npl* économies *fpl*.

savings account *n Am* compte *m* d'épargne.

savings and loan association *n Am* société *f* de crédit immobilier.

savings bank *n* caisse *f* d'épargne.

saviour *Br*, **savior** *Am* ['seɪvjəʳ] *n* sauveur *m*.

savour *Br*, **savor** *Am* ['seɪvəʳ] *vt lit & fig* savourer.

savoury *Br*, **savory** *Am* ['seɪvəri] <> *adj* - **1.** [food] salé(e) - **2.** [respectable] recommandable. <> *n Br* petit plat *m* salé.

saw [sɔː] (*Br pt* -ed, *pp* sawn, *Am pt & pp* -ed) <> *pt* ⊳ see. <> *n* scie *f*. <> *vt* scier.

sawdust ['sɔːdʌst] *n* sciure *f* (de bois).

sawed-off shotgun *Am* = sawn-off shotgun.

sawmill ['sɔːmɪl] *n* scierie *f*, moulin *m* à scie *Can*.

sawn [sɔːn] *Br pp* ⊳ saw.

sawn-off shotgun *Br*, **sawed-off shotgun** ['sɔːd-] *Am n* carabine *f* à canon scié.

saxophone ['sæksəfəʊn] *n* saxophone *m*.

say [seɪ] (*pt & pp* said) <> *vt* - **1.** [gen] dire ; **could you ~ that again?** vous pouvez répéter ce que vous venez de dire? ; **(let's) ~ you won a lottery ...** supposons que tu gagnes le gros lot ... ; **it ~s a lot about him** cela en dit long sur lui ; **she's said to be ...** on dit qu'elle est ... ; **that goes without ~ing** cela va sans dire ; **it has a lot to be said for it** cela a beaucoup d'avantages - **2.** [subj : clock, watch] indiquer. <> *n* : **to have a/no ~** avoir/ne pas avoir voix au chapitre ; **to have a ~ in sthg** avoir son mot à dire sur qqch ; **to have one's ~** dire ce que l'on a à dire, dire son mot. ◆ **that is to say** *adv* c'est-à-dire.

saying ['seɪɪŋ] *n* dicton *m*.

scab [skæb] *n* - **1.** [of wound] croûte *f* - **2.** *inf pej* [non-striker] jaune *m*.

scaffold ['skæfəʊld] *n* échafaud *m*.

scaffolding ['skæfəldɪŋ] *n* échafaudage *m*.

scald [skɔːld] <> *n* brûlure *f*. <> *vt* ébouillanter ; **to ~ one's arm** s'ébouillanter le bras.

scale [skeɪl] <> *n* - **1.** [gen] échelle *f* ; **to ~** [map, drawing] à l'échelle - **2.** [of ruler, thermometer] graduation *f* - **3.** MUS gamme *f* - **4.** [of fish, snake] écaille *f* - **5.** *Am* = scales. <> *vt* - **1.** [cliff, mountain, fence] escalader - **2.** [fish] écailler. ◆ **scales** *npl* balance *f*. ◆ **scale down** *vt fus* réduire.

scale model *n* modèle *m* réduit.

scallop ['skɒləp] <> *n* [shellfish] coquille *f* Saint-Jacques. <> *vt* [edge, garment] festonner.

scalp [skælp] <> *n* - **1.** ANAT cuir *m* chevelu - **2.** [trophy] scalp *m*. <> *vt* scalper.

scalpel ['skælpəl] *n* scalpel *m*.

scamper ['skæmpəʳ] *vi* trottiner.

scampi ['skæmpɪ] *n* (*U*) scampi *mpl*.

scan [skæn] <> *n* MED scanographie *f* ; [during pregnancy] échographie *f*. <> *vt* - **1.** [examine carefully] scruter - **2.** [glance at] parcourir - **3.** TECH balayer - **4.** COMPUT faire un scannage de.

scandal ['skændl] *n* - **1.** [gen] scandale *m* - **2.** [gossip] médisance *f*.

scandalize, -ise ['skændəlaɪz] *vt* scandaliser.

Scandinavia [ˌskændɪ'neɪvjə] *n* Scandinavie *f*.

Scandinavian [ˌskændɪ'neɪvjən] <> *adj* scandinave. <> *n* [person] Scandinave *mf*.

scant [skænt] *adj* insuffisant(e).

scanty ['skæntɪ] *adj* [amount, resources] insuffisant(e) ; [income] maigre ; [dress] minuscule.

scapegoat ['skeɪpgəʊt] *n* bouc *m* émissaire.

scar [skɑːʳ] *n* cicatrice *f*.

scarce ['skeəs] *adj* rare, peu abondant(e).

scarcely ['skeəslɪ] *adv* à peine ; **~ anyone** presque personne ; **I ~ ever go there now** je n'y vais presque OR pratiquement plus jamais.

scare [skeəʳ] <> *n* - **1.** [sudden fear] : **to give sb a ~** faire peur à qqn - **2.** [public fear] panique *f* ; **bomb ~** alerte *f* à la bombe. <> *vt* faire peur à, effrayer. ◆ **scare away, scare off** *vt sep* faire fuir.

scarecrow ['skeəkrəʊ] *n* épouvantail *m*.

scared ['skeəd] *adj* apeuré(e) ; **to be ~** avoir peur ; **to be ~ stiff** OR **to death** être mort de peur.

scarf [skɑːf] (*pl* -s OR **scarves** [skɑːvz]) *n* [wool] écharpe *f* ; [silk etc] foulard *m*.

scarlet ['skɑːlət] <> *adj* écarlate. <> *n* écarlate *f*.

scarlet fever *n* scarlatine *f*.

scarves [skɑːvz] *pl* ⊳ scarf.

scathing ['skeɪðɪŋ] *adj* [criticism] acerbe ; [reply] cinglant(e).

scatter ['skætəʳ] <> *vt* [clothes, paper etc] éparpiller ; [seeds] semer à la volée. <> *vi* se disperser.

scatterbrained ['skætəbreɪnd] *adj inf* écervelé(e).

scavenger ['skævɪndʒə'] *n* **- 1.** [animal] animal *m* nécrophage **- 2.** [person] personne *f* qui fait les poubelles.

scenario [sɪ'nɑːrɪəʊ] (*pl* **-s**) *n* **- 1.** [possible situation] hypothèse *f*, scénario *m* **- 2.** [of film, play] scénario *m*.

scene [siːn] *n* **- 1.** [in play, film, book] scène *f* ; **behind the ~s** dans les coulisses **- 2.** [sight] spectacle *m*, vue *f* ; [picture] tableau *m* **- 3.** [location] lieu *m*, endroit *m* **- 4.** [area of activity] : **the political ~** la scène politique ; **the music ~** le monde de la musique **- 5.** *phr* : **to set the ~ for sb** mettre qqn au courant de la situation ; **to set the ~ for sthg** préparer la voie à qqch.

scenery ['siːnərɪ] *n* (*U*) **- 1.** [of countryside] paysage *m* **- 2.** THEATRE décor *m*, décors *mpl*.

scenic ['siːnɪk] *adj* [tour] touristique ; **a ~ view** un beau panorama.

scent [sent] *n* **- 1.** [smell - of flowers] senteur *f*, parfum *m* ; [- of animal] odeur *f*, fumet *m* **- 2.** (*U*) [perfume] parfum *m*.

scepter *Am* = sceptre.

sceptic *Br*, **skeptic** *Am* ['skeptɪk] *n* sceptique *mf*.

sceptical *Br*, **skeptical** *Am* ['skeptɪkl] *adj* : **~ (about)** sceptique (sur).

sceptre *Br*, **scepter** *Am* ['septə'] *n* sceptre *m*.

schedule [*Br* 'ʃedjuːl, *Am* 'skedʒʊl] ⬦ *n* **- 1.** [plan] programme *m*, plan *m* ; **on ~** [at expected time] à l'heure (prévue) ; [on expected day] à la date prévue ; **ahead of/behind ~** en avance/en retard (sur le programme) **- 2.** [list - of times] horaire *m* ; [- of prices] tarif *m.* ⬦ *vt* : **to ~ sthg (for)** prévoir qqch (pour).

scheduled flight [*Br* 'ʃedjuːld-, *Am* 'skedʒʊld-] *n* vol *m* régulier.

scheme [skiːm] ⬦ *n* **- 1.** [plan] plan *m*, projet *m* **- 2.** *pej* [dishonest plan] combine *f* **- 3.** [arrangement] arrangement *m* ; **colour ~** combinaison *f* de couleurs. ⬦ *vi pej* conspirer.

scheming ['skiːmɪŋ] *adj* intrigant(e).

schism ['sɪzm, 'skɪzm] *n* schisme *m*.

schizophrenic [ˌskɪtsə'frenɪk] ⬦ *adj* schizophrène. ⬦ *n* schizophrène *mf*.

scholar ['skɒlə'] *n* **- 1.** [expert] érudit *m*, -e *f*, savant *m*, -e *f* **- 2.** *dated* [student] écolier *m*, -ère *f*, élève *mf* **- 3.** [holder of scholarship] boursier *m*, -ère *f*.

scholarship ['skɒləʃɪp] *n* **- 1.** [grant] bourse *f* (d'études) **- 2.** [learning] érudition *f*.

school [skuːl] *n* **- 1.** [gen] école *f* ; [secondary school] lycée *m*, collège *m* **- 2.** [university department] faculté *f* **- 3.** *Am* [university] université *f*.

school age *n* âge *m* scolaire.

schoolbook ['skuːlbʊk] *n* livre *m* scolaire OR de classe.

schoolboy ['skuːlbɔɪ] *n* écolier *m*, élève *m*.

schoolchild ['skuːltʃaɪld] (*pl* **-children** [-tʃɪldrən]) *n* écolier *m*, -ère *f*, élève *mf*.

schooldays ['skuːldeɪz] *npl* années *fpl* d'école.

schoolgirl ['skuːlgɜːl] *n* écolière *f*, élève *f*.

schooling ['skuːlɪŋ] *n* instruction *f*.

school-leaver [-ˌliːvə'] *n Br* élève *qui a fini ses études secondaires.*

schoolmaster ['skuːlˌmɑːstə'] *n* [primary] instituteur *m*, maître *m* d'école ; [secondary] professeur *m*.

schoolmistress ['skuːlˌmɪstrɪs] *n* [primary] institutrice *f*, maîtresse *f* d'école ; [secondary] professeur *m*.

school of thought *n* école *f* (de pensée).

schoolteacher ['skuːlˌtiːtʃə'] *n* [primary] instituteur *m*, -trice *f* ; [secondary] professeur *m*.

school year *n* année *f* scolaire.

schooner ['skuːnə'] *n* **- 1.** [ship] schooner *m*, goélette *f* **- 2.** *Br* [sherry glass] grand verre *m* à xérès.

sciatica [saɪ'ætɪkə] *n* sciatique *f*.

science ['saɪəns] *n* science *f*.

science fiction *n* science-fiction *f*.

scientific [ˌsaɪən'tɪfɪk] *adj* scientifique.

scientist ['saɪəntɪst] *n* scientifique *mf*.

scintillating ['sɪntɪleɪtɪŋ] *adj* brillant(e).

scissors ['sɪzəz] *npl* ciseaux *mpl* ; **a pair of ~** une paire de ciseaux.

sclerosis [sklɪ'rəʊsɪs] ▷ **multiple sclerosis**.

scoff [skɒf] ⬦ *vt Br inf* bouffer, boulotter. ⬦ *vi* : **to ~ (at)** se moquer (de).

scold [skəʊld] *vt* gronder, réprimander.

scone [skɒn] *n* scone *m*.

scoop [skuːp] ⬦ *n* **- 1.** [for sugar] pelle *f* à main ; [for ice cream] cuiller *f* à glace **- 2.** [of ice cream] boule *f* **- 3.** [news report] exclusivité *f*, scoop *m.* ⬦ *vt* [with hands] prendre avec les mains ; [with scoop] prendre avec une pelle à main. ◆ **scoop out** *vt sep* évider.

scooter ['skuːtə'] *n* **- 1.** [toy] trottinette *f* **- 2.** [motorcycle] scooter *m*.

scope [skəʊp] *n (U)* - **1.** [opportunity] occasion *f*, possibilité *f* - **2.** [of report, inquiry] étendue *f*, portée *f*.

scorch [skɔ:tʃ] *vt* [clothes] brûler légèrement, roussir ; [skin] brûler ; [land, grass] dessécher.

scorching ['skɔ:tʃɪŋ] *adj inf* [day] torride ; [sun] brûlant(e).

score [skɔ:ʳ] *n* - **1.** SPORT score *m* - **2.** [in test] note *f* - **3.** *dated* [twenty] vingt - **4.** MUS partition *f* - **5.** [subject] : **on that ~** à ce sujet, sur ce point. ◇ *vt* - **1.** [goal, point etc] marquer ; **to ~ 100%** avoir 100 sur 100 - **2.** [success, victory] remporter - **3.** [cut] entailler. ◇ *vi* SPORT marquer (un but/point *etc*). ◆ **score out** *vt sep Br* barrer, rayer.

scoreboard ['skɔ:bɔ:d] *n* tableau *m*.

scorer ['skɔ:rəʳ] *n* marqueur *m*.

scorn [skɔ:n] ◇ *n (U)* mépris *m*, dédain *m*. ◇ *vt* - **1.** [person, attitude] mépriser - **2.** [help, offer] rejeter, dédaigner.

scornful ['skɔ:nfʊl] *adj* méprisant(e) ; **to be ~ of sthg** mépriser qqch, dédaigner qqch.

Scorpio ['skɔ:pɪəʊ] (*pl* -**s**) *n* Scorpion *m*.

scorpion ['skɔ:pjən] *n* scorpion *m*.

Scot [skɒt] *n* Écossais *m*, -e *f*.

scotch [skɒtʃ] *vt* [rumour] étouffer ; [plan] faire échouer.

Scotch [skɒtʃ] ◇ *adj* écossais(e). ◇ *n* scotch *m*, whisky *m*.

Scotch (tape)® *n Am* Scotch® *m*.

scot-free *adj inf* : **to get off ~** s'en tirer sans être puni(e).

Scotland ['skɒtlənd] *n* Écosse *f*.

Scots [skɒts] ◇ *adj* écossais(e). ◇ *n* [dialect] écossais *m*.

Scotsman ['skɒtsmən] (*pl* -**men** [-mən]) *n* Écossais *m*.

Scotswoman ['skɒtswʊmən] (*pl* -**women** [-ˌwɪmɪn]) *n* Écossaise *f*.

Scottish ['skɒtɪʃ] *adj* écossais(e).

Scottish Parliament *n* Parlement *m* écossais.

scoundrel ['skaʊndrəl] *n dated* gredin *m*.

scour [skaʊəʳ] *vt* - **1.** [clean] récurer - **2.** [search - town etc] parcourir ; [- countryside] battre.

scourge [skɜ:dʒ] *n* fléau *m*.

scout [skaʊt] *n* MIL éclaireur *m*. ◆ **Scout** *n* [boy scout] Scout *m*. ◆ **scout around** *vi* : **to ~ around (for)** aller à la recherche (de).

scowl [skaʊl] ◇ *n* regard *m* noir. ◇ *vi* se renfrogner, froncer les sourcils ; **to ~ at sb** jeter des regards noirs à qqn.

scrabble ['skræbl] *vi* - **1.** [scrape] : **to ~ at sthg** gratter qqch - **2.** [feel around] : **to ~ around for sthg** tâtonner pour trouver qqch.

scraggy ['skrægɪ] *adj* décharné(e), maigre.

scramble ['skræmbl] ◇ *n* [rush] bousculade *f*, ruée *f*. ◇ *vi* - **1.** [climb] : **to ~ up a hill** grimper une colline en s'aidant des mains OR à quatre pattes - **2.** [compete] : **to ~ for sthg** se disputer qqch.

scrambled eggs ['skræmbld-] *npl* œufs *mpl* brouillés.

scrap [skræp] ◇ *n* - **1.** [of paper, material] bout *m* ; [of information] fragment *m* ; [of conversation] bribe *f* - **2.** [metal] ferraille *f* - **3.** *inf* [fight, quarrel] bagarre *f*. ◇ *vt* [car] mettre à la ferraille ; [plan, system] abandonner, laisser tomber. ◆ **scraps** *npl* [food] restes *mpl*.

scrapbook ['skræpbʊk] *n* album *m* (de coupures de journaux etc).

scrap dealer *n* ferrailleur *m*, marchand *m* de ferraille.

scrape [skreɪp] ◇ *n* - **1.** [scraping noise] raclement *m*, grattement *m* - **2.** *dated* [difficult situation] : **to get into a ~** se fourrer dans le pétrin. ◇ *vt* - **1.** [clean, rub] gratter, racler ; **to ~ sthg off sthg** enlever qqch de qqch en grattant OR raclant - **2.** [surface, car, skin] érafler. ◇ *vi* gratter. ◆ **scrape through** *vt fus* réussir de justesse.

scraper ['skreɪpəʳ] *n* grattoir *m*, racloir *m*.

scrap merchant *n Br* ferrailleur *m*, marchand *m* de ferraille.

scrap paper *Br*, **scratch paper** *Am n* (papier *m*) brouillon *m*.

scrapyard ['skræpjɑ:d] *n* parc *m* à ferraille.

scratch [skrætʃ] ◇ *n* - **1.** [wound] égratignure *f*, éraflure *f* - **2.** [on glass, paint etc] éraflure *f* - **3.** *phr* : **to be up to ~** être à la hauteur ; **to do sthg from ~** faire qqch à partir de rien. ◇ *vt* - **1.** [wound] écorcher, égratigner - **2.** [mark - paint, glass etc.] rayer, érafler - **3.** [rub] gratter. ◇ *vi* gratter ; [person] se gratter.

scratch card *n* carte *f* à gratter.

scratch paper *Am* = **scrap paper**.

scrawl [skrɔ:l] ◇ *n* griffonnage *m*, gribouillage *m*. ◇ *vt* griffonner, gribouiller.

scrawny ['skrɔ:nɪ] *adj* [person] efflanqué(e) ; [body, animal] décharné(e).

scream [skri:m] ◇ *n* [cry] cri *m* perçant,

hurlement *m* ; [of laughter] éclat *m*. ◇ *vt* hurler. ◇ *vi* [cry out] crier, hurler.

scree [skri:] *n* éboulis *m*.

screech [skri:tʃ] ◇ *n* - **1.** [cry] cri *m* perçant - **2.** [of tyres] crissement *m*. ◇ *vt* hurler. ◇ *vi* - **1.** [cry out] pousser des cris perçants - **2.** [tyres] crisser.

screen [skri:n] ◇ *n* - **1.** [gen] écran *m* - **2.** [panel] paravent *m*. ◇ *vt* - **1.** CINEMA projeter, passer ; TV téléviser, passer - **2.** [hide] cacher, masquer - **3.** [shield] protéger - **4.** [candidate, employee] passer au crible, filtrer.

screening ['skri:nɪŋ] *n* - **1.** CINEMA projection *f* ; TV passage *m* à la télévision - **2.** [for security] sélection *f*, tri *m* - **3.** MED dépistage *m*.

screenplay ['skri:npleɪ] *n* scénario *m*.

screw [skru:] ◇ *n* [for fastening] vis *f*. ◇ *vt* - **1.** [fix with screws] : **to ~ sthg to sthg** visser qqch à OR sur qqch - **2.** [twist] visser - **3.** *vulg* [woman] baiser. ◇ *vi* [bolt, lid] se visser. ◆ **screw up** *vt sep* - **1.** [crumple up] froisser, chiffonner - **2.** [eyes] plisser ; [face] tordre - **3.** *v inf* [ruin] gâcher, bousiller.

screwdriver ['skru:ˌdraɪvəʳ] *n* [tool] tournevis *m*.

scribble ['skrɪbl] ◇ *n* gribouillage *m*, griffonnage *m*. ◇ *vt* & *vi* gribouiller, griffonner.

script [skrɪpt] *n* - **1.** [of play, film etc] scénario *m*, script *m* - **2.** [writing system] écriture *f* - **3.** [handwriting] (écriture *f*) script *m*.

Scriptures ['skrɪptʃəz] *npl* : **the ~** les (saintes) Écritures *fpl*.

scriptwriter ['skrɪptˌraɪtəʳ] *n* scénariste *mf*.

scroll [skrəʊl] ◇ *n* rouleau *m*. ◇ *vt* COMPUT faire défiler.

scrounge [skraʊndʒ] *inf vt* : **to ~ money off sb** taper qqn ; **can I ~ a cigarette off you?** je peux te piquer une cigarette ?

scrounger ['skraʊndʒəʳ] *n inf* parasite *m*.

scrub [skrʌb] ◇ *n* - **1.** [rub] : **to give sthg a ~** nettoyer qqch à la brosse - **2.** (*U*) [undergrowth] broussailles *fpl*. ◇ *vt* [floor, clothes etc] laver OR nettoyer à la brosse ; [hands, back] frotter ; [saucepan] récurer.

scruff [skrʌf] *n* : **by the ~ of the neck** par la peau du cou.

scruffy ['skrʌfɪ] *adj* mal soigné(e), débraillé(e).

scrum(mage) ['skrʌm(ɪdʒ)] *n* RUGBY mêlée *f*.

scruples ['skru:plz] *npl* scrupules *mpl*.

scrutinize, -ise ['skru:tɪnaɪz] *vt* scruter, examiner attentivement.

scrutiny ['skru:tɪnɪ] *n (U)* examen *m* attentif.

scuba diving ['sku:bə-] *n* plongée *f* sousmarine *(avec bouteilles)*.

scuff [skʌf] *vt* - **1.** [damage] érafler - **2.** [drag] : **to ~ one's feet** traîner les pieds.

scuffle ['skʌfl] *n* bagarre *f*, échauffourée *f*.

scullery ['skʌlərɪ] *n* arrière-cuisine *f*.

sculptor ['skʌlptəʳ] *n* sculpteur *m*.

sculpture ['skʌlptʃəʳ] ◇ *n* sculpture *f*. ◇ *vt* sculpter.

scum [skʌm] *n* - **1.** (*U*) [froth] écume *f*, mousse *f* - **2.** *v inf pej* [person] salaud *m* - **3.** (*U*) *v inf pej* [people] déchets *mpl*.

scupper ['skʌpəʳ] *vt* - **1.** NAUT couler - **2.** *Br fig* [plan] saboter, faire tomber à l'eau.

scurrilous ['skʌrələs] *adj* calomnieux (euse).

scurry ['skʌrɪ] *vi* se précipiter ; **to ~ away** OR **off** se sauver, détaler.

scuttle ['skʌtl] ◇ *n* seau *m* à charbon. ◇ *vi* courir précipitamment OR à pas précipités.

scythe [saɪð] *n* faux *f*.

SDLP (*abbr of* **Social Democratic and Labour Party**) *n* parti travailliste d'Irlande du Nord.

sea [si:] ◇ *n* - **1.** [gen] mer *f* ; **at ~** en mer ; **by ~** par mer ; **by the ~** au bord de la mer ; **out to ~** au large - **2.** *phr* : **to be all at ~** nager complètement. ◇ *comp* [voyage] en mer ; [animal] marin(e), de mer.

seabed ['si:bed] *n* : **the ~** le fond de la mer.

seaboard ['si:bɔ:d] *n* littoral *m*, côte *f*.

sea breeze *n* brise *f* de mer.

seafood ['si:fu:d] *n* (*U*) fruits *mpl* de mer.

seafront ['si:frʌnt] *n* front *m* de mer.

seagull ['si:gʌl] *n* mouette *f*.

seal [si:l] (*pl inv* OR **-s**) ◇ *n* - **1.** [animal] phoque *m* - **2.** [official mark] cachet *m*, sceau *m* - **3.** [official fastening] cachet *m*. ◇ *vt* - **1.** [envelope] coller, fermer - **2.** [document, letter] sceller, cacheter - **3.** [block off] obturer, boucher. ◆ **seal off** *vt sep* [area, entrance] interdire l'accès de.

sea level *n* niveau *m* de la mer.

sea lion (*pl inv* OR **-s**) *n* otarie *f*.

seam [si:m] *n* - **1.** SEWING couture *f* - **2.** [of coal] couche *f*, veine *f*.

seaman ['si:mən] (*pl* **-men** [-mən]) *n* marin *m*.

seamy ['si:mɪ] *adj* sordide.

séance ['seɪɒns] *n* séance *f* de spiritisme.

seaplane ['si:pleɪn] *n* hydravion *m*.

seaport ['si:pɔ:t] *n* port *m* de mer.

search [sɜ:tʃ] <> *n* [of person, luggage, house] fouille *f* ; [for lost person, thing] recherche *f*, recherches *fpl* ; ~ **for** recherche de ; **in ~ of** à la recherche de. <> *vt* [house, area, person] fouiller ; [memory, mind, drawer] fouiller dans. <> *vi* : **to ~ (for sb/ sthg)** chercher (qqn/qqch).

search engine *n* COMPUT moteur *m* de recherche.

searching ['sɜ:tʃɪŋ] *adj* [question] poussé(e), approfondi(e) ; [look] pénétrant(e) ; [review, examination] minutieux(euse).

searchlight ['sɜ:tʃlaɪt] *n* projecteur *m*.

search party *n* équipe *f* de secours.

search warrant *n* mandat *m* de perquisition.

seashell ['si:ʃel] *n* coquillage *m*.

seashore ['si:ʃɔ:ʳ] *n* : **the ~** le rivage, la plage.

seasick ['si:sɪk] *adj* : **to be** OR **feel ~** avoir le mal de mer.

seaside ['si:saɪd] *n* : **the ~** le bord de la mer.

seaside resort *n* station *f* balnéaire.

season ['si:zn] <> *n* - **1.** [gen] saison *f* ; **in ~** [food] de saison ; **out of ~** [holiday] hors saison ; [food] hors de saison - **2.** [of films] cycle *m*. <> *vt* assaisonner, relever.

seasonal ['si:zənl] *adj* saisonnier(ère).

seasoned ['si:znd] *adj* [traveller, campaigner] chevronné(e), expérimenté(e) ; [soldier] aguerri(e).

seasoning ['si:znɪŋ] *n* assaisonnement *m*.

season ticket *n* carte *f* d'abonnement.

seat [si:t] <> *n* - **1.** [gen] siège *m* ; [in theatre] fauteuil *m* ; **take a ~!** asseyez-vous! - **2.** [place to sit - in bus, train] place *f* - **3.** [of trousers] fond *m*. <> *vt* [sit down] faire asseoir, placer ; **please be ~ed** veuillez vous asseoir.

seat belt *n* ceinture *f* de sécurité.

seating ['si:tɪŋ] *n* (U) [capacity] sièges *mpl*, places *fpl* (assises).

seawater ['si:,wɔ:təʳ] *n* eau *f* de mer.

seaweed ['si:wi:d] *n* (U) algue *f*.

seaworthy ['si:,wɜ:ðɪ] *adj* en bon état de navigabilité.

sec. *abbr of* **second**.

secede [sɪ'si:d] *vi fml* : **to ~ (from)** se séparer (de), faire sécession (de).

secluded [sɪ'klu:dɪd] *adj* retiré(e), écarté(e).

seclusion [sɪ'klu:ʒn] *n* solitude *f*, retraite *f*.

second ['sekənd] <> *n* - **1.** [gen] seconde *f* ; **wait a ~!** une seconde!, (attendez) un instant! ; ~ **(gear)** seconde *f* - **2.** *Br* UNIV ≃ licence *f* avec mention assez bien. <> *num* deuxième, second(e) ; **his score was ~ only to hers** il n'y a qu'elle qui ait fait mieux que lui OR qui l'ait surpassé ; *see also* **sixth**. <> *vt* [proposal, motion] appuyer. **◆ seconds** *npl* - **1.** COMM articles *mpl* de second choix - **2.** [of food] rabiot *m*.

secondary ['sekəndrɪ] *adj* secondaire ; **to be ~ to** être moins important(e) que.

secondary school *n* école *f* secondaire, lycée *m*.

second-class ['sekənd-] *adj* - **1.** *pej* [citizen] de deuxième zone ; [product] de second choix - **2.** [ticket] de seconde OR deuxième classe - **3.** [stamp] à tarif réduit - **4.** *Br* UNIV [degree] ≃ avec mention assez bien.

second-hand ['sekənd-] <> *adj* - **1.** [goods, shop] d'occasion - **2.** *fig* [information] de seconde main. <> *adv* [not new] d'occasion.

second hand ['sekənd-] *n* [of clock] trotteuse *f*.

secondly ['sekəndlɪ] *adv* deuxièmement, en second lieu.

secondment [sɪ'kɒndmənt] *n* *Br* affectation *f* temporaire.

second-rate ['sekənd-] *adj* *pej* de deuxième ordre, médiocre.

second thought ['sekənd-] *n* : **to have ~s about sthg** avoir des doutes sur qqch ; **on ~s** *Br*, **on ~** *Am* réflexion faite, tout bien réfléchi.

secrecy ['si:krəsɪ] *n* (U) secret *m*.

secret ['si:krɪt] <> *adj* secret(ète). <> *n* secret *m* ; **in ~** en secret.

secretarial [,sekrə'teərɪəl] *adj* [course, training] de secrétariat, de secrétaire ; ~ **staff** secrétaires *mpl*.

secretary [*Br* 'sekrətrɪ, *Am* 'sekrə,terɪ] *n* - **1.** [gen] secrétaire *mf* - **2.** POL [minister] ministre *m*.

Secretary of State *n* - **1.** *Br* : ~ **(for)** ministre *m* (de) - **2.** *Am* ≃ ministre *m* des Affaires étrangères.

secretive ['si:krətɪv] *adj* secret(ète), dissimulé(e).

secretly ['si:krɪtlɪ] *adv* secrètement.

sect [sekt] *n* secte *f*.

sectarian [sek'teərɪən] *adj* [killing, violence] d'ordre religieux.

section ['sekʃn] <> *n* - **1.** [portion - gen] section *f*, partie *f* ; [- of road, pipe] tronçon *m* ; [- of document, law] article *m* - **2.** GEOM coupe *f*, section *f*. <> *vt* sectionner.

sector ['sektə'] *n* secteur *m*.

secular ['sekjʊlə'] *adj* [life] séculier(ère) ; [education] laïque ; [music] profane.

secure [sɪ'kjʊə'] <> *adj* - **1.** [fixed - gen] fixe ; [- windows, building] bien fermé(e) - **2.** [safe - job, future] sûr(e) ; [- valuable object] en sécurité, en lieu sûr - **3.** [free of anxiety - childhood] sécurisant(e) ; [- marriage] solide. <> *vt* - **1.** [obtain] obtenir - **2.** [fasten - gen] attacher ; [- door, window] bien fermer - **3.** [make safe] assurer la sécurité de.

security [sɪ'kjʊərətɪ] *n* sécurité *f*. **securities** *npl* FIN titres *mpl*, valeurs *fpl*.

security guard *n* garde *m* de sécurité.

sedan [sɪ'dæn] *n Am* berline *f*.

sedate [sɪ'deɪt] <> *adj* posé(e), calme. <> *vt* donner un sédatif à.

sedation [sɪ'deɪʃn] *n (U)* sédation *f* ; **under ~** sous calmants.

sedative ['sedətɪv] *n* sédatif *m*, calmant *m*.

sediment ['sedɪmənt] *n* sédiment *m*, dépôt *m*.

seduce [sɪ'dju:s] *vt* séduire ; **to ~ sb into doing sthg** amener OR entraîner qqn à faire qqch.

seductive [sɪ'dʌktɪv] *adj* séduisant(e).

see [si:] (*pt* saw, *pp* seen) <> *vt* - **1.** [gen] voir ; **~ you!** au revoir! ; **~ you soon/later/tomorrow!** *etc* à bientôt/tout à l'heure/demain! *etc.* - **2.** [accompany] : **I saw her to the door** je l'ai accompagnée OR reconduite jusqu'à la porte ; **I saw her onto the train** je l'ai accompagnée au train - **3.** [make sure] : **to ~ (that) ...** s'assurer que ... <> *vi* voir ; **you ~,** ... voyez-vous, ... ; **I ~** je vois, je comprends ; **let's ~, let me ~** voyons, voyons voir. **seeing as, seeing that** *conj inf* vu que, étant donné que. **see about** *vt fus* [arrange] s'occuper de. **see off** *vt sep* - **1.** [say goodbye to] accompagner (pour dire au revoir) - **2.** *Br* [chase away] faire partir OR fuir. **see through** <> *vt fus* [scheme] voir clair dans ; **to ~ through sb** voir dans le jeu de qqn. <> *vt sep* [deal, project] mener à terme, mener à bien. **see to** *vt fus* s'occuper de, se charger de.

seed [si:d] *n* - **1.** [of plant] graine *f* - **2.** SPORT : **fifth ~** joueur classé cinquième *m*, joueuse classée cinquième *f*. **seeds** *npl fig* germes *mpl*, semences *fpl*.

seedling ['si:dlɪŋ] *n* jeune plant *m*, semis *m*.

seedy ['si:dɪ] *adj* miteux(euse).

seek [si:k] (*pt & pp* sought) *vt* - **1.** [gen] chercher ; [peace, happiness] rechercher ; **to ~ to do sthg** chercher à faire qqch - **2.** [advice, help] demander.

seem [si:m] <> *vi* sembler, paraître ; **to ~ bored** avoir l'air de s'ennuyer ; **to ~ sad/tired** avoir l'air triste/fatigué. <> *v impers* : **it ~s (that) ...** il semble OR paraît que ...

seemingly ['si:mɪŋlɪ] *adv* apparemment.

seen [si:n] *pp* > see.

seep [si:p] *vi* suinter.

seesaw ['si:sɔ:] *n* bascule *f*.

seethe [si:ð] *vi* - **1.** [person] bouillir, être furieux(euse) - **2.** [place] : **to be seething with** grouiller de.

see-through *adj* transparent(e).

segment ['segmənt] *n* - **1.** [section] partie *f*, section *f* - **2.** [of fruit] quartier *m*.

segregate ['segrɪgeɪt] *vt* séparer.

Seine [seɪn] *n* : **the (River) ~** la Seine.

seize [si:z] *vt* - **1.** [grab] saisir, attraper - **2.** [capture] s'emparer de, prendre - **3.** [arrest] arrêter - **4.** *fig* [opportunity, chance] saisir, sauter sur. **seize (up)on** *vt fus* saisir, sauter sur. **seize up** *vi* - **1.** [body] s'ankyloser - **2.** [engine, part] se gripper.

seizure ['si:ʒə'] *n* - **1.** MED crise *f*, attaque *f* - **2.** *(U)* [of town] capture *f* ; [of power] prise *f*.

seldom ['seldəm] *adv* peu souvent, rarement.

select [sɪ'lekt] <> *adj* - **1.** [carefully chosen] choisi(e) - **2.** [exclusive] de premier ordre, d'élite. <> *vt* sélectionner, choisir.

selection [sɪ'lekʃn] *n* sélection *f*, choix *m*.

selective [sɪ'lektɪv] *adj* sélectif(ive) ; [person] difficile.

self [self] (*pl* selves [selvz]) *n* moi *m* ; **she's her old ~ again** elle est redevenue elle-même.

self-addressed stamped envelope [-ə'drest-] *n Am* enveloppe *f* affranchie pour la réponse.

self-assured *adj* sûr(e) de soi, plein(e) d'assurance.

self-catering *adj Br* [holiday - in house] en maison louée ; [- in flat] en appartement loué.

self-centred *Br,* **self-centered** *Am* [-'sentəd] *adj* égocentrique.

self-confessed [-kən'fest] *adj* de son propre aveu.

self-confident *adj* sûr(e) de soi, plein(e) d'assurance.

self-conscious *adj* timide.

self-contained [-kən'teɪnd] *adj* [flat] indépendant(e), avec entrée particulière ; [person] qui se suffit à soi-même.

self-control *n* maîtrise *f* de soi.

self-defence *Br*, **-defense** *Am n* autodéfense *f*.

self-discipline *n* autodiscipline *f*.

self-employed [-ɪm'plɔɪd] *adj* qui travaille à son propre compte.

self-esteem *n* respect *m* de soi, estime *f* de soi.

self-evident *adj* qui va de soi, évident(e).

self-explanatory *adj* évident(e), qui ne nécessite pas d'explication.

self-government *n* autonomie *f*.

self-important *adj* suffisant(e).

self-indulgent *adj pej* [person] qui ne se refuse rien ; [film, book, writer] nombriliste.

self-interest *n (U) pej* intérêt *m* personnel.

selfish ['selfɪʃ] *adj* égoïste.

selfishness ['selfɪʃnɪs] *n* égoïsme *m*.

selfless ['selflɪs] *adj* désintéressé(e).

self-made *adj* : ~ **man** self-made-man *m*.

self-medication *n* automédication *f*.

self-opinionated *adj* opiniâtre.

self-pity *n* apitoiement *m* sur soi-même.

self-portrait *n* autoportrait *m*.

self-possessed *adj* maître (maîtresse) de soi.

self-raising flour *Br* [-ˌreɪzɪŋ-], **self-rising flour** *Am n* farine *f* avec levure incorporée.

self-reliant *adj* indépendant(e), qui ne compte que sur soi.

self-respect *n* respect *m* de soi.

self-respecting [-rɪs'pektɪŋ] *adj* qui se respecte.

self-restraint *n (U)* retenue *f*, mesure *f*.

self-righteous *adj* satisfait(e) de soi.

self-rising flour *Am* = **self-raising flour**.

self-sacrifice *n* abnégation *f*.

self-satisfied *adj* suffisant(e), content(e) de soi.

self-service *n* libre-service *m*, self-service *m*.

self-sufficient *adj* autosuffisant(e) ; **to be ~ in** satisfaire à ses besoins en.

self-taught *adj* autodidacte.

sell [sel] (*pt & pp* **sold**) <> *vt* - **1.** [gen] vendre ; **to ~ sthg for £100** vendre qqch 100 livres ; **to ~ sthg to sb, to ~ sb sthg** vendre qqch à qqn - **2.** *fig* [make acceptable] : **to ~ sthg to sb, to ~ sb sthg** faire accepter qqch à qqn. <> *vi* - **1.** [person] vendre - **2.** [product] se vendre ; **it ~s for** *OR* **at £10** il se vend 10 livres. ◆ **sell off** *vt sep* vendre, liquider. ◆ **sell out** <> *vt sep* : **the performance is sold out** il ne reste plus de places, tous les billets ont été vendus. <> *vi* - **1.** [shop] : **we've sold out** on n'en a plus - **2.** [betray one's principles] être infidèle à ses principes.

sell-by date *n Br* date *f* limite de vente.

seller ['selə'] *n* vendeur *m*, -euse *f*.

selling price *n* prix *m* de vente.

Sellotape® ['seləteɪp] *n Br* ≃ Scotch® *m* ruban *m* adhésif.

sell-out *n* : **the match was a ~** on a joué à guichets fermés.

selves [selvz] *pl* ⊳ **self**.

semaphore ['seməfɔ:'] *n (U)* signaux *mpl* à bras.

semblance ['sembləns] *n* semblant *m*.

semen ['si:men] *n (U)* sperme *m*, semence *f*.

semester [sɪ'mestə'] *n* semestre *m*.

semicircle ['semɪˌsɜ:kl] *n* demi-cercle *m*.

semicolon [ˌsemɪ'kəʊlən] *n* point-virgule *m*.

semidetached [ˌsemɪdɪ'tætʃt] <> *adj* jumelé(e). <> *n Br* maison *f* jumelée.

semifinal [ˌsemɪ'faɪnl] *n* demi-finale *f*.

seminar ['semɪnɑ:'] *n* séminaire *m*.

seminary ['semɪnərɪ] *n* RELIG séminaire *m*.

semiskilled [ˌsemɪ'skɪld] *adj* spécialisé(e).

semolina [ˌsemə'li:nə] *n* semoule *f*.

Senate ['senɪt] *n* POL : **the ~** le sénat ; **the United States ~** le Sénat américain.

senator ['senətə'] *n* sénateur *m*.

send [send] (*pt & pp* **sent**) *vt* [gen] envoyer ; [letter] expédier, envoyer ; **to ~ sb sthg, to ~ sthg to sb** envoyer qqch à qqn ; **~ her my love** embrasse-la pour moi ; **to ~ sb for sthg** envoyer qqn chercher qqch. ◆ **send for** *vt fus* - **1.** [person] appeler, faire venir - **2.** [by post] commander par correspondance. ◆ **send in** *vt sep* [report, application] envoyer, soumettre. ◆ **send off** *vt sep* - **1.** [by post] expédier - **2.** SPORT expulser. ◆ **send off for** *vt fus* commander par correspondance. ◆ **send up** *vt sep Br inf* [imitate] parodier, ridiculiser.

sender ['sendə'] *n* expéditeur *m*, -trice *f*.

send-off *n* fête *f* d'adieu.

senile ['si:naɪl] *adj* sénile.

senior ['si:njəʳ] <> *adj* - **1.** [highest-ranking] plus haut placé(e) - **2.** [higher-ranking] : **~ to sb** d'un rang plus élevé que qqn - **3.** SCH [pupils, classes] grand(e). <> *n* - **1.** [older person] aîné *m*, -e *f* - **2.** SCH grand *m*, -e *f*.

senior citizen *n* personne *f* âgée OR du troisième âge.

sensation [sen'seɪʃn] *n* sensation *f*.

sensational [sen'seɪʃənl] *adj* [gen] sensationnel(elle).

sensationalist [sen'seɪʃnəlɪst] *adj pej* à sensation.

sense [sens] <> *n* - **1.** [ability, meaning] sens *m* ; **to make ~** [have meaning] avoir un sens ; **~ of humour** sens de l'humour ; **~ of smell** odorat *m* - **2.** [feeling] sentiment *m* - **3.** [wisdom] bon sens *m*, intelligence *f* ; **to make ~** [be sensible] être logique - **4.** *phr* : **to come to one's ~s** [be sensible again] revenir à la raison ; [regain consciousness] reprendre connaissance. <> *vt* [feel] sentir. ◆ **in a sense** *adv* dans un sens.

senseless ['senslɪs] *adj* - **1.** [stupid] stupide - **2.** [unconscious] sans connaissance.

sensibilities [‚sensɪ'bɪlətɪz] *npl* susceptibilité *f*.

sensible ['sensəbl] *adj* [reasonable] raisonnable, judicieux(euse).

sensitive ['sensɪtɪv] *adj* - **1.** [gen] : **~ (to)** sensible (à) - **2.** [subject] délicat(e) - **3.** [easily offended] : **~ (about)** susceptible (en ce qui concerne).

sensual ['sensjʊəl] *adj* sensuel(elle).

sensuous ['sensjʊəs] *adj* qui affecte les sens.

sent [sent] *pt & pp* ▷ **send**.

sentence ['sentəns] <> *n* - **1.** GRAMM phrase *f* - **2.** JUR condamnation *f*, sentence *f*. <> *vt* : **to ~ sb (to)** condamner qqn (à).

sentiment ['sentɪmənt] *n* - **1.** [feeling] sentiment *m* - **2.** [opinion] opinion *f*, avis *m*.

sentimental [‚sentɪ'mentl] *adj* sentimental(e).

sentry ['sentrɪ] *n* sentinelle *f*.

separate [*adj & n* 'seprət, *vb* 'sepəreɪt] <> *adj* - **1.** [not joined] : **~ (from)** séparé(e) (de) - **2.** [individual, distinct] distinct(e). <> *vt* - **1.** [gen] : **to ~ sb/sthg (from)** séparer qqn/qqch (de) - **2.** [distinguish] : **to ~ sb/ sthg (from)** distinguer qqn/qqch (de). <> *vi* se séparer ; **to ~ into** se diviser OR se séparer en. ◆ **separates** *npl Br* coordonnés *mpl*.

separately ['seprətlɪ] *adv* séparément.

separation [‚sepə'reɪʃn] *n* séparation *f*.

September [sep'tembəʳ] *n* septembre *m* ; **in ~** en septembre ; **last ~** en septembre dernier ; **this ~** en septembre de cette année ; **next ~** en septembre prochain ; **by ~** en septembre, d'ici septembre ; **every ~** tous les ans en septembre ; **during ~** pendant le mois de septembre ; **at the beginning of ~** au début du mois de septembre, début septembre ; **at the end of ~** à la fin du mois de septembre, fin septembre ; **in the middle of ~** au milieu du mois de septembre, à la mi-septembre.

septic ['septɪk] *adj* infecté(e).

septic tank *n* fosse *f* septique.

sequel ['si:kwəl] *n* - **1.** [book, film] : **~ (to)** suite *f* (de) - **2.** [consequence] : **~ (to)** conséquence *f* (de).

sequence ['si:kwəns] *n* - **1.** [series] suite *f*, succession *f* - **2.** [order] ordre *m* - **3.** [of film] séquence *f*.

Serb = **Serbian**.

Serbia ['sɜ:bjə] *n* Serbie *f*.

Serbian ['sɜ:bjən], **Serb** [sɜ:b] <> *adj* serbe. <> *n* - **1.** [person] Serbe *mf* - **2.** [dialect] serbe *m*.

serene [sɪ'ri:n] *adj* [calm] serein(e), tranquille.

sergeant ['sɑ:dʒənt] *n* - **1.** MIL sergent *m* - **2.** [in police] brigadier *m*.

sergeant major *n* sergent-major *m*.

serial ['sɪərɪəl] *n* feuilleton *m*.

serial number *n* numéro *m* de série.

series ['sɪəri:z] *n* (*pl inv*) série *f*.

serious ['sɪərɪəs] *adj* sérieux(euse) ; [illness, accident, trouble] grave ; **to be ~ about doing sthg** songer sérieusement à faire qqch.

seriously ['sɪərɪəslɪ] *adv* sérieusement ; [ill] gravement ; [wounded] grièvement, gravement ; **to take sb/sthg ~** prendre qqn/qqch au sérieux.

seriousness ['sɪərɪəsnɪs] *n* - **1.** [of mistake, illness] gravité *f* - **2.** [of person, speech] sérieux *m*.

sermon ['sɜ:mən] *n* sermon *m*.

serrated [sɪ'reɪtɪd] *adj* en dents de scie.

servant ['sɜ:vənt] *n* domestique *mf*.

serve [sɜ:v] <> *vt* - **1.** [work for] servir - **2.** [have effect] : **to ~ to do sthg** servir à faire qqch ; **to ~ a purpose** [subj : device etc] servir à un usage - **3.** [provide for] desservir - **4.** [meal, drink, customer] servir ; **to ~ sthg to sb**, **to ~ sb sthg** servir qqch à qqn - **5.** JUR : **to ~ sb with a summons/writ**, **to ~ a summons/writ on sb** signifier une assignation/une citation à qqn - **6.** [prison sentence] purger, faire ; [apprenticeship] faire - **7.** SPORT servir - **8.** *phr* : **it ~s him/you right** c'est bien fait pour lui/toi. ◇ *vi* servir ; **to ~ as** servir de. ◇ *n* SPORT service *m*. ◆ **serve out, serve up** *vt sep* [food] servir.

service ['sɜːvɪs] ◇ *n* - **1.** [gen] service *m* ; **in/out of ~** en/hors service ; **to be of ~ (to sb)** être utile (à qqn), rendre service (à qqn) - **2.** [of car] révision *f* ; [of machine] entretien *m*. ◇ *vt* [car] réviser ; [machine] assurer l'entretien de. ◆ **services** *npl* - **1.** [on motorway] aire *f* de services - **2.** [armed forces] : **the ~s** les forces *fpl* armées - **3.** [help] service *m*.

serviceable ['sɜːvɪsəbl] *adj* pratique.

service area *n* aire *f* de services.

service charge *n* service *m*.

serviceman ['sɜːvɪsmən] (*pl* **-men** [-mən]) *n* soldat *m*, militaire *m*.

service provider *n* COMPUT fournisseur *m* d'accès, provider *m*.

service station *n* station-service *f*.

serviette [ˌsɜːvɪ'et] *n* serviette *f* (de table).

sesame ['sesəmɪ] *n* sésame *m*.

session ['seʃn] *n* - **1.** [gen] séance *f* - **2.** *Am* [school term] trimestre *m*.

set [set] (*pt & pp* set) ◇ *adj* - **1.** [fixed - gen] fixe ; [- phrase] figé(e) - **2.** *Br* SCH [book] au programme - **3.** [ready] : **- (for sthg/to do sthg)** prêt(e) (à qqch/à faire qqch) - **4.** [determined] : **to be ~ on sthg** vouloir absolument qqch ; **to be ~ on doing sthg être résolu(e) à faire qqch ; to be dead ~ against sthg** s'opposer formellement à qqch. ◇ *n* - **1.** [of keys, tools, golf clubs etc] jeu *m* ; [of stamps, books] collection *f* ; [of saucepans] série *f* ; [of tyres] train *m* ; **a ~ of teeth** [natural] une dentition, une denture ; [false] un dentier - **2.** [television, radio] poste *m* - **3.** CINEMA plateau *m* ; THEATRE scène *f* - **4.** TENNIS manche *f*, set *m*. ◇ *vt* - **1.** [place] placer, poser, mettre ; [jewel] sertir, monter - **2.** [cause to be] : **to ~ sb free** libérer qqn, mettre qqn en liberté ; **to ~ sthg in motion** mettre qqch en branle OR en route ; **to ~ sthg on fire** mettre le feu à qqch - **3.** [prepare - trap] tendre ; [- table] mettre - **4.** [adjust] régler - **5.** [fix - date, deadline, target] fixer - **6.** [establish - example] donner ; [- trend] lancer ; [- record] établir - **7.** [homework, task] donner ; [problem] poser - **8.** MED [bone, leg] remettre - **9.** [story] : **to be ~ se** passer, se dérouler. ◇ *vi* - **1.** [sun] se coucher - **2.** [jelly] prendre ; [glue, cement] durcir. ◆ **set about**

vt fus [start] entreprendre, se mettre à ; **to ~ about doing sthg** se mettre à faire qqch. ◆ **set aside** *vt sep* - **1.** [save] mettre de côté - **2.** [not consider] rejeter, écarter. ◆ **set back** *vt sep* [delay] retarder. ◆ **set off** ◇ *vt sep* - **1.** [cause] déclencher, provoquer - **2.** [bomb] faire exploser ; [firework] faire partir. ◇ *vi* se mettre en route, partir. ◆ **set out** ◇ *vt sep* - **1.** [arrange] disposer - **2.** [explain] présenter, exposer. ◇ *vt fus* [intend] : **to ~ out to do sthg** entreprendre OR tenter de faire qqch. ◇ *vi* [on journey] se mettre en route, partir. ◆ **set up** *vt sep* - **1.** [organization] créer, fonder ; [committee, procedure] constituer, mettre en place ; [meeting] arranger, organiser - **2.** [statue, monument] dresser, ériger ; [roadblock] placer, installer - **3.** [equipment] préparer, installer - **4.** *inf* [make appear guilty] monter un coup contre.

setback ['setbæk] *n* contretemps *m*, revers *m*.

set menu *n* menu *m* fixe.

settee [se'tiː] *n* canapé *m*.

setting ['setɪŋ] *n* - **1.** [surroundings] décor *m*, cadre *m* - **2.** [of dial, machine] réglage *m*.

settle ['setl] ◇ *vt* - **1.** [argument] régler ; **that's ~d then** (c'est) entendu - **2.** [bill, account] régler, payer - **3.** [calm - nerves] calmer ; **to ~ one's stomach** calmer les douleurs d'estomac - **4.** [make comfortable] installer. ◇ *vi* - **1.** [make one's home] s'installer, se fixer - **2.** [make oneself comfortable] s'installer - **3.** [dust] retomber ; [sediment] se déposer - **4.** [bird, insect] se poser. ◆ **settle down** *vi* - **1.** [give one's attention] : **to ~ down to sthg/to doing sthg** se mettre à qqch/à faire qqch - **2.** [make oneself comfortable] s'installer - **3.** [become respectable] se ranger - **4.** [become calm] se calmer. ◆ **settle for** *vt fus* accepter, se contenter de. ◆ **settle in** *vi* s'adapter. ◆ **settle on** *vt fus* [choose] fixer son choix sur, se décider pour. ◆ **settle up** *vi* : **to ~ up (with sb)** régler (qqn).

settlement ['setlmənt] *n* - **1.** [agreement] accord *m* - **2.** [colony] colonie *f* - **3.** [payment] règlement *m*.

settler ['setlə'] *n* colon *m*.

set-up *n* *inf* - **1.** [system] : **what's the ~?** comment est-ce que c'est organisé? - **2.** [deception to incriminate] coup *m* monté.

seven ['sevn] *num* sept ; *see also* **six**.

seventeen [ˌsevn'tiːn] *num* dix-sept ; *see also* **six**.

seventeenth [ˌsevn'tiːnθ] *num* dix-septième ; *see also* **sixth**.

seventh ['sevnθ] *num* septième ; *see also* **sixth**.

seventy ['sevntɪ] *num* soixante-dix ; *see also* **sixty**.

sever ['sevəʳ] *vt* - **1.** [cut through] couper - **2.** *fig* [relationship, ties] rompre.

several ['sevrəl] ◇ *adj* plusieurs. ◇ *pron* plusieurs *mfpl*.

severance ['sevrəns] *n* [of relations] rupture *f*.

severance pay *n* indemnité *f* de licenciement.

severe [sɪ'vɪəʳ] *adj* - **1.** [weather] rude, rigoureux(euse) ; [shock] gros (grosse), dur(e) ; [pain] violent(e) ; [illness, injury] grave - **2.** [person, criticism] sévère.

severity [sɪ'verətɪ] *n* - **1.** [of storm] violence *f* ; [of problem, illness] gravité *f* - **2.** [sternness] sévérité *f*.

sew [səʊ] (*Br pp* sewn, *Am pp* sewed OR sewn) *vt & vi* coudre. ➫ **sew up** *vt sep* [join] recoudre.

sewage ['suːɪdʒ] *n* (*U*) eaux *fpl* d'égout, eaux usées.

sewer ['suəʳ] *n* égout *m*.

sewing ['səʊɪŋ] *n* (*U*) - **1.** [activity] couture *f* - **2.** [work] ouvrage *m*.

sewing machine *n* machine *f* à coudre.

sewn [səʊn] *pp* ▷ **sew**.

sex [seks] *n* - **1.** [gender] sexe *m* - **2.** (*U*) [sexual intercourse] rapports *mpl* (sexuels) ; **to have ~ with** avoir des rapports (sexuels) avec.

sexist ['seksɪst] ◇ *adj* sexiste. ◇ *n* sexiste *mf*.

sexual ['sekʃʊəl] *adj* sexuel(elle).

sexual harassment *n* harcèlement *m* sexuel.

sexual intercourse *n* (*U*) rapports *mpl* (sexuels).

sexy ['seksɪ] *adj inf* sexy (*inv*).

shabby ['ʃæbɪ] *adj* - **1.** [clothes] élimé(e), râpé(e) ; [furniture] minable ; [person, street] miteux(euse) - **2.** [behaviour] moche, méprisable.

shack [ʃæk] *n* cabane *f*, hutte *f*.

shackle ['ʃækl] *vt* enchaîner ; *fig* entraver. ➫ **shackles** *npl* fers *mpl* ; *fig* entraves *fpl*.

shade [ʃeɪd] ◇ *n* - **1.** (*U*) [shadow] ombre *f* - **2.** [lampshade] abat-jour *m inv* - **3.** [colour] nuance *f*, ton *m* - **4.** [of meaning, opinion] nuance *f*. ◇ *vt* [from light] abriter. ➫ **shades** *npl inf* [sunglasses] lunettes *fpl* de soleil.

shadow ['ʃædəʊ] *n* ombre *f* ; **there's not a** OR **the ~ of a doubt** il n'y a pas l'ombre d'un doute.

shadow cabinet *n* cabinet *m* fantôme.

shadowy ['ʃædəʊɪ] *adj* - **1.** [dark] ombreux(euse) - **2.** [sinister] mystérieux(euse).

shady ['ʃeɪdɪ] *adj* - **1.** [garden, street etc] ombragé(e) ; [tree] qui donne de l'ombre - **2.** *inf* [dishonest] louche.

shaft [ʃaːft] *n* - **1.** [vertical passage] puits *m* ; [of lift] cage *f* - **2.** TECH arbre *m* - **3.** [of light] rayon *m* - **4.** [of tool, golf club] manche *m*.

shaggy ['ʃægɪ] *adj* hirsute.

shake [ʃeɪk] (*pt* shook, *pp* shaken) ◇ *vt* - **1.** [move vigorously - gen] secouer ; [- bottle] agiter ; **to ~ sb's hand** serrer la main de OR à qqn ; **to ~ hands** se serrer la main ; **to ~ one's head** secouer la tête ; [to say no] faire non de la tête - **2.** [shock] ébranler, secouer. ◇ *vi* trembler. ◇ *n* [tremble] tremblement *m* ; **to give sthg a ~** secouer qqch. ➫ **shake off** *vt sep* [police, pursuers] semer ; [illness] se débarrasser de.

shaken ['ʃeɪkn] *pp* ▷ **shake**.

shaky ['ʃeɪkɪ] *adj* [building, table] branlant(e) ; [hand] tremblant(e) ; [person] faible ; [argument, start] incertain(e).

shall [weak form ʃəl, strong form ʃæl] *aux vb* - **1.** (*1st person sg & 1st person pl*) (*to express future tense*) : **I ~ be ... je** serai ... - **2.** (*esp 1st person sg & 1st person pl*) (*in questions*) : **~ we have lunch now?** tu veux qu'on déjeune maintenant? ; **where ~ I put this?** où est-ce qu'il faut mettre ça? - **3.** (*in orders*) : **you ~ tell me!** tu vas OR dois me le dire!

shallow ['ʃæləʊ] *adj* - **1.** [water, dish, hole] peu profond(e) - **2.** *pej* [superficial] superficiel(elle).

sham [ʃæm] ◇ *adj* feint(e), simulé(e). ◇ *n* comédie *f*.

shambles ['ʃæmblz] *n* désordre *m*, pagaille *f*.

shame [ʃeɪm] ◇ *n* - **1.** (*U*) [remorse, humiliation] honte *f* ; **to bring ~ on** OR **upon sb** faire la honte de qqn - **2.** [pity] : **it's a ~ (that ...)** c'est dommage (que ... (+ *subjunctive*)) ; **what a ~!** quel dommage! ◇ *vt* faire honte à, mortifier ; **to ~ sb into doing sthg** obliger qqn à faire qqch en lui faisant honte.

shamefaced [ˌʃeɪm'feɪst] *adj* honteux(euse), penaud(e).

shameful ['ʃeɪmfʊl] *adj* honteux(euse), scandaleux(euse).

shameless ['ʃeɪmlɪs] *adj* effronté(e), éhonté(e).

shampoo [ʃæm'puː] (*pl* **-s**, *pt & pp* **-ed**,

cont **-ing)** ⬦ *n* shampooing *m*. ⬦ *vt* : **to ~ sb** OR **sb's hair** faire un shampooing à qqn.

shamrock ['ʃæmrɒk] *n* trèfle *m*.

shandy ['ʃændɪ] *n* panaché *m*.

shan't [ʃɑːnt] = shall not.

shantytown ['ʃæntɪtaʊn] *n* bidonville *m*.

shape [ʃeɪp] ⬦ *n* - **1.** [gen] forme *f* ; **to take ~** prendre forme OR tournure - **2.** [health] : **to be in good/bad ~** être en bonne/mauvaise forme. ⬦ *vt* - **1.** [pastry, clay etc] : **to ~ sthg (into)** façonner OR modeler qqch (en) - **2.** [ideas, project, character] former. ➤ **shape up** *vi* [person, plans] se développer, progresser ; [job, events] prendre tournure OR forme.

-shaped [ʃeɪpt] *suffix* : **egg~** en forme d'œuf ; **L~** en forme de L.

shapeless ['ʃeɪplɪs] *adj* informe.

shapely ['ʃeɪplɪ] *adj* bien fait(e).

share [ʃeəʳ] ⬦ *n* [portion, contribution] part *f*. ⬦ *vt* partager. ⬦ *vi* : **to ~ (in sthg)** partager (qqch). ➤ **shares** *npl* actions *fpl*. ➤ **share out** *vt sep* partager, répartir.

shareholder ['ʃeə,həʊldəʳ] *n* actionnaire *mf*.

shark [ʃɑːk] (*pl inv* OR **-s**) *n* [fish] requin *m*.

sharp [ʃɑːp] ⬦ *adj* - **1.** [knife, razor] tranchant(e), affilé(e) ; [needle, pencil, teeth] pointu(e) - **2.** [image, outline, contrast] net (nette) - **3.** [person, mind] vif (vive) ; [eyesight] perçant(e) - **4.** [sudden - change, rise] brusque, soudain(e) ; [- hit, rap] sec (sèche) - **5.** [words, order, voice] cinglant(e) - **6.** [cry, sound] perçant(e) ; [pain, cold] vif (vive) ; [taste] piquant(e) - **7.** MUS : **C/D ~** do/ré dièse. ⬦ *adv* - **1.** [punctually] : **at 8 o'clock ~** à 8 heures pile OR tapantes - **2.** [immediately] : **~ left/right** tout à fait à gauche/droite. ⬦ *n* MUS dièse *m*.

sharpen ['ʃɑːpn] *vt* [knife, tool] aiguiser ; [pencil] tailler.

sharpener ['ʃɑːpnəʳ] *n* [for pencil] taille-crayon *m* ; [for knife] aiguisoir *m* (pour couteaux).

sharp-eyed [-'aɪd] *adj* : **she's very ~** elle remarque tout, rien ne lui échappe.

sharply ['ʃɑːplɪ] *adv* - **1.** [distinctly] nettement - **2.** [suddenly] brusquement - **3.** [harshly] sévèrement, durement.

shat [ʃæt] *pt* & *pp vulg* ⊳ shit.

shatter ['ʃætəʳ] ⬦ *vt* - **1.** [window, glass] briser, fracasser - **2.** *fig* [hopes, dreams] détruire. ⬦ *vi* se fracasser, voler en éclats.

shattered ['ʃætəd] *adj* - **1.** [upset] bouleversé(e) - **2.** *Br inf* [very tired] flapi(e).

shave [ʃeɪv] ⬦ *n* : **to have a ~** se raser.

⬦ *vt* - **1.** [remove hair from] raser - **2.** [wood] planer, raboter. ⬦ *vi* se raser.

shaver ['ʃeɪvəʳ] *n* rasoir *m* électrique.

shaving brush ['ʃeɪvɪŋ-] *n* blaireau *m*.

shaving cream ['ʃeɪvɪŋ-] *n* crème *f* à raser.

shaving foam ['ʃeɪvɪŋ-] *n* mousse *f* à raser.

shavings ['ʃeɪvɪŋz] *npl* [of wood, metal] copeaux *mpl*.

shawl [ʃɔːl] *n* châle *m*.

she [ʃiː] ⬦ *pers pron* - **1.** [referring to woman, girl, animal] elle ; **~'s tall** elle est grande ; **SHE can't do it** elle, elle ne peut pas le faire ; **there ~ is** la voilà ; **if I were** OR **was ~** *fml* si j'étais elle, à sa place - **2.** [referring to boat, car, country] *follow the gender of your translation*. ⬦ *comp* : **~-elephant** éléphant *m* femelle ; **~-wolf** louve *f*.

sheaf [ʃiːf] (*pl* **sheaves** [ʃiːvz]) *n* - **1.** [of papers, letters] liasse *f* - **2.** [of corn, grain] gerbe *f*.

shear [ʃɪəʳ] (*pt* **-ed**, *pp* **-ed** OR **shorn**) *vt* [sheep] tondre. ➤ **shears** *npl* - **1.** [for garden] sécateur *m*, cisaille *f* - **2.** [for dressmaking] ciseaux *mpl*. ➤ **shear off** ⬦ *vt sep* [branch] couper ; [piece of metal] cisailler. ⬦ *vi* se détacher.

sheath [ʃiːθ] (*pl* **sheaths** [ʃiːðz]) *n* - **1.** [for knife, cable] gaine *f* - **2.** *Br* [condom] préservatif *m*.

sheaves [ʃiːvz] *pl* ⊳ sheaf.

shed [ʃed] (*pt* & *pp* **shed**) ⬦ *n* [small] remise *f*, cabane *f* ; [larger] hangar *m*. ⬦ *vt* - **1.** [hair, skin, leaves] perdre - **2.** [tears] verser, répandre - **3.** [employees] se défaire de, congédier.

she'd [weak form ʃɪd, strong form ʃiːd] = she had, she would.

sheen [ʃiːn] *n* lustre *m*, éclat *m*.

sheep [ʃiːp] (*pl inv*) *n* mouton *m*.

sheepdog ['ʃiːpdɒg] *n* chien *m* de berger.

sheepish ['ʃiːpɪʃ] *adj* penaud(e).

sheepskin ['ʃiːpskɪn] *n* peau *f* de mouton.

sheer [ʃɪəʳ] *adj* - **1.** [absolute] pur(e) - **2.** [very steep] à pic, abrupt(e) - **3.** [material] fin(e).

sheet [ʃiːt] *n* - **1.** [for bed] drap *m* - **2.** [of paper, glass, wood] feuille *f* ; [of metal] plaque *f*.

sheik(h) [ʃeɪk] *n* cheik *m*.

shelf [ʃelf] (*pl* **shelves** [ʃelvz]) *n* [for storage] rayon *m*, étagère *f*.

shell [ʃel] ⬦ *n* - **1.** [of egg, nut, snail] coquille *f* - **2.** [of tortoise, crab] carapace *f* - **3.** [on beach] coquillage *m* - **4.** [of building,

car] carcasse *f* - **5.** MIL obus *m.* ◇ *vt*
- **1.** [peas] écosser ; [nuts, prawns] décortiquer ; [eggs] enlever la coquille de, écaler
- **2.** MIL bombarder.

she'll [ʃiːl] = she will, she shall.

shellfish ['ʃelfɪʃ] (*pl inv*) *n* - **1.** [creature]
crustacé *m*, coquillage *m* - **2.** (U) [food]
fruits *mpl* de mer.

shell suit *n Br* survêtement *m (en)* Nylon®
imperméabilisé.

shelter ['ʃeltəʳ] ◇ *n* abri *m.* ◇ *vt*
- **1.** [protect] abriter, protéger - **2.** [refugee,
homeless person] offrir un asile à ; [criminal,
fugitive] cacher. ◇ *vi* s'abriter, se mettre à
l'abri.

sheltered ['ʃeltəd] *adj* - **1.** [from weather]
abrité(e) - **2.** [life, childhood] protégé(e),
sans soucis.

shelve [ʃelv] *vt fig* mettre au Frigidaire®,
mettre en sommeil.

shelves [ʃelvz] *pl* ⊳ shelf.

shepherd ['ʃepəd] ◇ *n* berger *m.* ◇ *vt*
fig conduire.

shepherd's pie ['ʃepədz-] *n* ≃ hachis *m*
Parmentier.

sheriff ['ʃerɪf] *n Am* shérif *m.*

sherry ['ʃerɪ] *n* xérès *m*, sherry *m.*

she's [ʃiːz] = she is, she has.

Shetland ['ʃetlənd] *n* : (the) ~ (Islands) les
(îles) Shetland *fpl.*

sh(h) [ʃ] *excl* chut !

shield [ʃiːld] ◇ *n* - **1.** [armour] bouclier *m*
- **2.** *Br* [sports trophy] plaque *f.* ◇ *vt* : to
~ sb (from) protéger qqn (de OR contre).

shift [ʃɪft] ◇ *n* - **1.** [change] changement
m, modification *f* - **2.** [period of work] poste
m ; [workers] équipe *f.* ◇ *vt* - **1.** [move] déplacer, changer de place - **2.** [change] changer, modifier. ◇ *vi* - **1.** [move - gen] changer de place ; [- wind] tourner, changer
- **2.** [change] changer, se modifier - **3.** *Am*
AUT changer de vitesse.

shiftless ['ʃɪftlɪs] *adj* fainéant(e), pares-
seux(euse).

shifty ['ʃɪftɪ] *adj inf* sournois(e), louche.

shilling ['ʃɪlɪŋ] *n* shilling *m.*

shilly-shally ['ʃɪlɪ,ʃælɪ] *vi* hésiter, être in-
décis(e).

shimmer ['ʃɪməʳ] ◇ *n* reflet *m*, miroite-
ment *m.* ◇ *vi* miroiter.

shin [ʃɪn] *n* tibia *m.*

shinbone ['ʃɪnbəʊn] *n* tibia *m.*

shine [ʃaɪn] (*pt & pp* shone) ◇ *n* brillant
m. ◇ *vt* - **1.** [direct] : to ~ a torch on sthg
éclairer qqch - **2.** [polish] faire briller, astiquer. ◇ *vi* briller.

shingle ['ʃɪŋgl] *n (U)* [on beach] galets *mpl.*
➤ **shingles** *n (U)* zona *m.*

shiny ['ʃaɪnɪ] *adj* brillant(e).

ship [ʃɪp] ◇ *n* bateau *m* ; [larger] navire *m.*
◇ *vt* [goods] expédier ; [troops, passen-
gers] transporter.

shipbuilding ['ʃɪp,bɪldɪŋ] *n* construction
f navale.

shipment ['ʃɪpmənt] *n* [cargo] cargaison *f*,
chargement *m.*

shipper ['ʃɪpəʳ] *n* affréteur *m*, chargeur *m.*

shipping ['ʃɪpɪŋ] *n (U)* - **1.** [transport]
transport *m* maritime - **2.** [ships] navires
mpl.

shipshape ['ʃɪpʃeɪp] *adj* bien rangé(e), en
ordre.

shipwreck ['ʃɪprek] ◇ *n* - **1.** [destruction
of ship] naufrage *m* - **2.** [wrecked ship]
épave *f.* ◇ *vt* : to be ~ed faire naufrage.

shipyard ['ʃɪpjaːd] *n* chantier *m* naval.

shire [ʃaɪəʳ] *n* [county] comté *m.*

shirk [ʃɜːk] *vt* se dérober à.

shirt [ʃɜːt] *n* chemise *f.*

shirtsleeves ['ʃɜːtsliːvz] *npl* : to be in
(one's) ~ être en manches OR en bras de
chemise.

shit [ʃɪt] (*pt & pp* -ted OR shat) *vulg* ◇ *n*
- **1.** [excrement] merde *f* - **2.** (U) [nonsense]
conneries *fpl.* ◇ *vi* chier. ◇ *excl* merde !

shiver ['ʃɪvəʳ] ◇ *n* frisson *m.* ◇ *vi* : to
~ (with) trembler (de), frissonner (de).

shoal [ʃəʊl] *n* [of fish] banc *m.*

shock [ʃɒk] ◇ *n* - **1.** [surprise] choc *m*,
coup *m* - **2.** (U) MED [state] : to be in a state of) ~,
to be in (a state of) ~ être en état de choc
- **3.** [impact] choc *m*, heurt *m* - **4.** ELEC décharge *f* électrique. ◇ *vt* - **1.** [upset] bouleverser - **2.** [offend] choquer, scandaliser.

shock absorber [-əb,zɔːbəʳ] *n* amortis-
seur *m.*

shocking ['ʃɒkɪŋ] *adj* - **1.** [very bad] épouvantable, terrible - **2.** [outrageous] scanda-
leux(euse).

shod [ʃɒd] ◇ *pt & pp* ⊳ shoe. ◇ *adj*
chaussé(e).

shoddy ['ʃɒdɪ] *adj* [goods, work] de mauvaise qualité ; [treatment] indigne, méprisable.

shoe [ʃuː] (*pt & pp* -ed OR shod) ◇ *n*
chaussure *f*, soulier *m.* ◇ *vt* [horse] ferrer.

shoebrush ['ʃuːbrʌʃ] *n* brosse *f* à chaussures.

shoehorn ['ʃuːhɔːn] *n* chausse-pied *m.*

shoelace ['ʃuːleɪs] *n* lacet *m* de soulier.

shoe polish *n* cirage *m.*

shoe shop *n* magasin *m* de chaussures.

shoestring ['ʃuːstrɪŋ] *n fig* : **on a ~** à peu de frais.

shone [ʃɒn] *pt & pp* ⊳ **shine**.

shoo [ʃuː] ⬦ *vt* chasser. ⬦ *excl* ouste!

shook [ʃʊk] *pt* ⊳ **shake**.

shoot [ʃuːt] (*pt & pp* **shot**) ⬦ *vt* - **1.** [kill with gun] tuer d'un coup de feu ; [wound with gun] blesser d'un coup de feu ; **to ~ o.s.** [kill o.s.] se tuer avec une arme à feu - **2.** *Br* [hunt] chasser - **3.** [arrow] décocher, tirer - **4.** CINEMA tourner. ⬦ *vi* - **1.** [fire gun] : **to ~ (at)** tirer (sur) - **2.** *Br* [hunt] chasser - **3.** [move quickly] : **to ~ in/out/past** entrer/sortir/passer en trombe, entrer/sortir/passer comme un bolide - **4.** CINEMA tourner - **5.** SPORT tirer, shooter. ⬦ *n* - **1.** *Br* [hunting expedition] partie *f* de chasse - **2.** [of plant] pousse *f*. ➤ **shoot down** *vt sep* - **1.** [aeroplane] descendre, abattre - **2.** [person] abattre. ➤ **shoot up** *vi* - **1.** [child, plant] pousser vite - **2.** [price, inflation] monter en flèche.

shooting ['ʃuːtɪŋ] *n* - **1.** [killing] meurtre *m* - **2.** *(U)* [hunting] chasse *f*.

shooting star *n* étoile *f* filante.

shop [ʃɒp] ⬦ *n* - **1.** [store] magasin *m*, boutique *f* - **2.** [workshop] atelier *m*. ⬦ *vi* faire ses courses ; **to go shopping** aller faire les courses OR commissions.

shop assistant *n Br* vendeur *m*, -euse *f*.

shop floor *n* : **the ~ floor** les ouvriers *mpl*.

shopkeeper ['ʃɒpˌkiːpə'] *n* commerçant *m*, -e *f*.

shoplifting ['ʃɒpˌlɪftɪŋ] *n (U)* vol *m* à l'étalage.

shopper ['ʃɒpə'] *n* personne *f* qui fait ses courses.

shopping ['ʃɒpɪŋ] *n (U)* [purchases] achats *mpl*.

shopping bag *n* sac *m* à provisions.

shopping centre *Br*, **shopping mall** *Am*, **shopping plaza** *Am* [-ˌplaːzə] *n* centre *m* commercial.

shopsoiled *Br* ['ʃɒpsɔɪld], **shopworn** *Am* ['ʃɒpwɔːn] *adj* qui a fait l'étalage, abîmé(e) (en magasin).

shop steward *n* délégué syndical *m*, déléguée syndicale *f*.

shopwindow [ˌʃɒp'wɪndəʊ] *n* vitrine *f*.

shopworn *Am* = shopsoiled.

shore [ʃɔː'] *n* rivage *m*, bord *m* ; **on ~** à terre. ➤ **shore up** *vt sep* étayer, étançonner ; *fig* consolider.

shorn [ʃɔːn] ⬦ *pp* ⊳ **shear**. ⬦ *adj* tondu(e).

short [ʃɔːt] ⬦ *adj* - **1.** [not long - in time] court(e), bref (brève) ; [- in space] court - **2.** [not tall] petit(e) - **3.** [curt] brusque, sec (sèche) - **4.** [lacking] : **time/money is ~** nous manquons de temps/d'argent ; **to be ~ of** manquer de - **5.** [abbreviated] : **to be ~ for** être le diminutif de. ⬦ *adv* : **to be running ~ of** [running out of] commencer à manquer de, commencer à être à court de ; **to cut sthg ~** [visit, speech] écourter qqch ; [discussion] couper court à qqch ; **to stop ~** s'arrêter net. ⬦ *n* - **1.** *Br* [alcoholic drink] alcool *m* fort - **2.** [film] court métrage *m*. ➤ **shorts** *npl* - **1.** [gen] short *m* - **2.** *Am* [underwear] caleçon *m*. ➤ **for short** *adv* : **he's called Bob for ~** Bob est son diminutif. ➤ **in short** *adv* (enfin) bref. ➤ **nothing short of** *prep* rien moins que, pratiquement. ➤ **short of** *prep* [unless, without] : **~ of doing sthg** à moins de faire qqch, à part faire qqch.

shortage ['ʃɔːtɪdʒ] *n* manque *m*, insuffisance *f*.

shortbread ['ʃɔːtbred] *n* sablé *m*.

short-change *vt* - **1.** [subj : shopkeeper] : **to ~ sb** ne pas rendre assez à qqn - **2.** *fig* [cheat] tromper, rouler.

short circuit *n* court-circuit *m*.

shortcomings ['ʃɔːtˌkʌmɪŋz] *npl* défauts *mpl*.

shortcrust pastry ['ʃɔːtkrʌst-] *n* pâte *f* brisée.

short cut *n* - **1.** [quick route] raccourci *m* - **2.** [quick method] solution *f* miracle.

shorten ['ʃɔːtn] ⬦ *vt* - **1.** [holiday, time] écourter - **2.** [skirt, rope etc] raccourcir. ⬦ *vi* [days] raccourcir.

shortfall ['ʃɔːtfɔːl] *n* déficit *m*.

shorthand ['ʃɔːthænd] *n (U)* [writing system] sténographie *f*.

shorthand typist *n Br* sténodactylo *f*.

short list *n Br* liste *f* des candidats sélectionnés.

shortly ['ʃɔːtlɪ] *adv* [soon] bientôt.

shortsighted [ˌʃɔːt'saɪtɪd] *adj* myope ; *fig* imprévoyant(e).

short staffed [-'stɑːft] *adj* : **to be ~** manquer de personnel.

short story *n* nouvelle *f*.

short-tempered [-'tempəd] *adj* emporté(e), irascible.

short-term *adj* [effects, solution] à court terme ; [problem] de courte durée.

short wave *n (U)* ondes *fpl* courtes.

shot [ʃɒt] ⬦ *pt & pp* ⊳ **shoot**. ⬦ *n* - **1.** [gunshot] coup *m* de feu ; **like a ~** sans

tarder, sans hésiter - **2.** [marksman] tireur *m*
- **3.** SPORT coup *m* - **4.** [photograph] photo *f* ;
CINEMA plan *m* - **5.** *inf* [attempt] : **to have a
~ at sthg** essayer de faire qqch - **6.** [injection] piqûre *f*.

shotgun ['ʃɒtgʌn] *n* fusil *m* de chasse.

should [ʃʊd] *aux vb* - **1.** [indicating duty] :
we ~ leave now il faudrait partir maintenant - **2.** [seeking advice, permission] : **~ I go
too?** est-ce que je devrais y aller aussi?
- **3.** [as suggestion] : **I ~ deny everything**
moi, je nierais tout - **4.** [indicating probability] : **she ~ be home soon** elle devrait être
de retour bientôt, elle va bientôt rentrer
- **5.** [was or were expected] : **they ~ have
won the match** ils auraient dû gagner le
match - **6.** [indicating intention, wish] : **I
~ like to come with you** j'aimerais bien venir avec vous - **7.** *(as conditional)* : **you ~ go if
you're invited** tu devrais y aller si tu es invité - **8.** *(in subordinate clauses)* : **we decided
that you ~ meet him** nous avons décidé
que ce serait toi qui irais le chercher
- **9.** [expressing uncertain opinion] : **I ~ think
he's about 50 (years old)** je pense qu'il doit
avoir dans les 50 ans.

shoulder ['ʃəʊldə^r] ◇ *n* épaule *f*. ◇ *vt*
- **1.** [carry] porter - **2.** [responsibility] endosser.

shoulder blade *n* omoplate *f*.

shoulder strap *n* - **1.** [on dress] bretelle *f*
- **2.** [on bag] bandoulière *f*.

shouldn't ['ʃʊdnt] = should not.

should've ['ʃʊdəv] = should have.

shout [ʃaʊt] ◇ *n* [cry] cri *m*. ◇ *vt & vi*
crier. ◆ **shout down** *vt sep* huer, conspuer.

shouting ['ʃaʊtɪŋ] *n* (U) cris *mpl*.

shove [ʃʌv] ◇ *n* : **to give sb/sthg a ~**
pousser qqn/qqch. ◇ *vt* pousser ; **to
~ clothes into a bag** fourrer des vêtements
dans un sac. ◆ **shove off** *vi* - **1.** [in boat]
pousser au large - **2.** *inf* [go away] ficher le
camp, filer.

shovel ['ʃʌvl] ◇ *n* [tool] pelle *f*. ◇ *vt* enlever à la pelle, pelleter.

show [ʃəʊ] (*pt* -ed, *pp* shown OR -ed) ◇ *n*
- **1.** [display] démonstration *f*, manifestation *f* - **2.** [at theatre] spectacle *m* ; [on radio, TV] émission *f* - **3.** CINEMA séance *f*
- **4.** [exhibition] exposition *f*. ◇ *vt* - **1.** [gen]
montrer ; [profit, loss] indiquer ; [respect]
témoigner ; [courage, mercy] faire preuve
de ; **to ~ sb sthg, to ~ sthg to sb** montrer
qqch à qqn - **2.** [escort] : **to ~ sb to his seat/
table** conduire qqn à sa place/sa table
- **3.** [film] projeter, passer ; [TV programme]
donner, passer. ◇ *vi* - **1.** [indicate] indi-

quer, montrer - **2.** [be visible] se voir, être
visible - **3.** CINEMA : **what's ~ing tonight?**
qu'est-ce qu'on joue comme film ce soir?
◆ **show off** ◇ *vt sep* exhiber. ◇ *vi*
faire l'intéressant(e). ◆ **show up** ◇ *vt
sep* [embarrass] embarrasser, faire honte à.
◇ *vi* - **1.** [stand out] se voir, ressortir
- **2.** [arrive] s'amener, rappliquer.

show business *n* (U) monde *m* du spectacle, show-business *m*.

showdown ['ʃəʊdaʊn] *n* : **to have a
~ with sb** s'expliquer avec qqn, mettre les
choses au point avec qqn.

shower ['ʃaʊə^r] ◇ *n* - **1.** [device, act] douche *f* ; **to have** OR **take a ~** prendre une douche, se doucher - **2.** [of rain] averse *f* - **3.** *fig*
[of questions, confetti] avalanche *f*, déluge
m. ◇ *vt* : **to ~ sb with** couvrir qqn de. ◇ *vi*
[wash] prendre une douche, se doucher.

shower cap *n* bonnet *m* de douche.

shower room *n* salle *f* d'eau.

showing ['ʃəʊɪŋ] *n* CINEMA projection *f*.

show jumping [-ˌdʒʌmpɪŋ] *n* jumping *m*.

shown [ʃəʊn] *pp* ▷ show.

show-off *n* *inf* m'as-tu-vu *m*, -e *f*.

showpiece ['ʃəʊpiːs] *n* [main attraction]
joyau *m*, trésor *m*.

showroom ['ʃəʊrʊm] *n* salle *f* OR magasin
m d'exposition ; [for cars] salle de démonstration.

shrank [ʃræŋk] *pt* ▷ shrink.

shrapnel ['ʃræpnl] *n* (U) éclats *mpl* d'obus.

shred [ʃred] ◇ *n* - **1.** [of material, paper]
lambeau *m*, brin *m* - **2.** *fig* [of evidence] parcelle *f* ; [of truth] once *f*, grain *m*. ◇ *vt*
[food] râper ; [paper] déchirer en lambeaux.

shredder ['ʃredə^r] *n* [machine] destructeur *m* de documents.

shrewd [ʃruːd] *adj* fin(e), astucieux(euse).

shriek [ʃriːk] ◇ *n* cri *m* perçant, hurlement *m* ; [of laughter] éclat *m*. ◇ *vi* pousser
un cri perçant.

shrill [ʃrɪl] *adj* [sound, voice] aigu(ë) ;
[whistle] strident(e).

shrimp [ʃrɪmp] *n* crevette *f*.

shrine [ʃraɪn] *n* [place of worship] lieu *m*
saint.

shrink [ʃrɪŋk] (*pt* shrank, *pp* shrunk) ◇ *vt*
rétrécir. ◇ *vi* - **1.** [cloth, garment] rétrécir ;
[person] rapetisser ; *fig* [income, popularity
etc] baisser, diminuer - **2.** [recoil] : **to
~ away from sthg** reculer devant qqch ; **to
~ from doing sthg** rechigner OR répugner à
faire qqch.

shrinkage ['ʃrɪŋkɪdʒ] *n* rétrécissement *m* ; *fig* diminution *f*, baisse *f*.

shrink-wrap *vt* emballer sous film plastique.

shrivel ['ʃrɪvl] ⋄ *vt* : **to ~ (up)** rider, flétrir. ⋄ *vi* : **to ~ (up)** se rider, se flétrir.

shroud [ʃraʊd] ⋄ *n* [cloth] linceul *m*. ⋄ *vt* : **to be ~ed in** [darkness, fog] être enseveli(e) sous ; [mystery] être enveloppé(e) de.

Shrove Tuesday ['ʃrəʊv-] *n* Mardi *m* gras.

shrub [ʃrʌb] *n* arbuste *m*.

shrubbery ['ʃrʌbərɪ] *n* massif *m* d'arbustes.

shrug [ʃrʌg] ⋄ *vt* : **to ~ one's shoulders** hausser les épaules. ⋄ *vi* hausser les épaules. ◆ **shrug off** *vt sep* ignorer.

shrunk [ʃrʌŋk] *pp* ⊳ **shrink**.

shudder ['ʃʌdə] *vi* - **1.** [tremble] : **to ~ (with)** frémir (de), frissonner (de) - **2.** [shake] vibrer, trembler.

shuffle ['ʃʌfl] *vt* - **1.** [drag] : **to ~ one's feet** traîner les pieds - **2.** [cards] mélanger, battre.

shun [ʃʌn] *vt* fuir, éviter.

shunt [ʃʌnt] *vt* RAIL aiguiller.

shut [ʃʌt] (*pt* & *pp* **shut**) ⋄ *adj* [closed] fermé(e). ⋄ *vt* fermer. ⋄ *vi* - **1.** [door, window] se fermer - **2.** [shop] fermer. ◆ **shut away** *vt sep* [valuables, papers] mettre sous clef. ◆ **shut down** *vt sep* & *vi* fermer. ◆ **shut out** *vt sep* [noise] supprimer ; [light] ne pas laisser entrer ; **to ~ sb out** laisser qqn à la porte. ◆ **shut up** *inf* ⋄ *vt sep* [silence] faire taire. ⋄ *vi* se taire.

shutter ['ʃʌtə] *n* - **1.** [on window] volet *m* - **2.** [in camera] obturateur *m*.

shuttle ['ʃʌtl] ⋄ *adj* : **~ service** (service *m* de) navette *f*. ⋄ *n* [train, bus, plane] navette *f*.

shuttlecock ['ʃʌtlkɒk] *n* volant *m*.

shy [ʃaɪ] ⋄ *adj* [timid] timide. ⋄ *vi* [horse] s'effaroucher.

Siberia [saɪ'bɪərɪə] *n* Sibérie *f*.

sibling ['sɪblɪŋ] *n* [brother] frère *m* ; [sister] sœur *f*.

Sicily ['sɪsɪlɪ] *n* Sicile *f*.

sick [sɪk] *adj* - **1.** [ill] malade - **2.** [nauseous] : **to feel ~** avoir envie de vomir, avoir mal au cœur ; **to be ~** *Br* [vomit] vomir - **3.** [fed up] : **to be ~ of** en avoir assez OR marre de - **4.** [joke, humour] macabre.

sickbay ['sɪkbeɪ] *n* infirmerie *f*.

sicken ['sɪkn] ⋄ *vt* écœurer, dégoûter. ⋄ *vi Br* : **to be ~ing for sthg** couver qqch.

sickening ['sɪknɪŋ] *adj* [disgusting] écœurant(e), dégoûtant(e).

sickle ['sɪkl] *n* faucille *f*.

sick leave *n* (U) congé *m* de maladie.

sickly ['sɪklɪ] *adj* - **1.** [unhealthy] maladif(ive), souffreteux(euse) - **2.** [smell, taste] écœurant(e).

sickness ['sɪknɪs] *n* - **1.** [illness] maladie *f* - **2.** *Br* (U) [nausea] nausée *f*, nausées *fpl* ; [vomiting] vomissement *m*, vomissements *mpl*.

sick pay *n* (U) indemnité *f* OR allocation *f* de maladie.

side [saɪd] ⋄ *n* - **1.** [gen] côté *m* ; **at** OR **by my/her** *etc* **~** à mes/ses *etc* côtés ; **on every ~, on all ~s** de tous côtés ; **from ~ to ~** d'un côté à l'autre ; **~ by ~** côte à côte - **2.** [of table, river] bord *m* - **3.** [of hill, valley] versant *m*, flanc *m* - **4.** [in war, debate] camp *m*, côté *m* ; SPORT équipe *f*, camp ; [of argument] point *m* de vue ; **to take sb's ~** prendre le parti de qqn - **5.** [aspect - gen] aspect *m* ; [- of character] facette *f* ; **to be on the safe ~** pour plus de sûreté, par précaution. ⋄ *adj* [situated on side] latéral(e). ◆ **side with** *vt fus* prendre le parti de, se ranger du côté de.

sideboard ['saɪdbɔːd] *n* [cupboard] buffet *m*.

sideboards *Br* ['saɪdbɔːdz], **sideburns** *Am* ['saɪdbɜːnz] *npl* favoris *mpl*, rouflaquettes *fpl*.

side effect *n* - **1.** MED effet *m* secondaire OR indésirable - **2.** [unplanned result] effet *m* secondaire, répercussion *f*.

sidelight ['saɪdlaɪt] *n* AUT feu *m* de position.

sideline ['saɪdlaɪn] *n* - **1.** [extra business] activité *f* secondaire - **2.** SPORT ligne *f* de touche.

sidelong ['saɪdlɒŋ] *adj* & *adv* de côté.

sidesaddle ['saɪdˌsædl] *adv* : **to ride ~** monter en amazone.

sideshow ['saɪdʃəʊ] *n* spectacle *m* forain.

sidestep ['saɪdstep] *vt* faire un pas de côté pour éviter OR esquiver ; *fig* éviter.

side street *n* [not main street] petite rue *f* ; [off main street] rue transversale.

sidetrack ['saɪdtræk] *vt* : **to be ~ed** se laisser distraire.

sidewalk ['saɪdwɔːk] *n Am* trottoir *m*.

sideways ['saɪdweɪz] *adj* & *adv* de côté.

siding ['saɪdɪŋ] *n* voie *f* de garage.

sidle ['saɪdl] ◆ **sidle up** *vi* : **to ~ up to sb** se glisser vers qqn.

siege [siːdʒ] *n* siège *m*.

sieve [sɪv] ⋄ *n* [for flour, sand etc] tamis

m ; [for liquids] **passoire** *f.* $\diamond$ *vt* [flour etc] tamiser ; [liquid] **passer.**

sift [sɪft] $\diamond$ *vt* - **1.** [flour, sand] tamiser - **2.** *fig* [evidence] passer au crible. $\diamond$ *vi* : **to ~ through** examiner, éplucher.

sigh [saɪ] $\diamond$ *n* soupir *m.* $\diamond$ *vi* [person] soupirer, pousser un soupir.

sight [saɪt] $\diamond$ *n* - **1.** [seeing] vue *f* ; **in ~** en vue ; **in/out of ~** en/hors de vue ; **at first ~** à première vue, au premier abord - **2.** [spectacle] spectacle *m* - **3.** [on gun] mire *f.* $\diamond$ *vt* apercevoir. $\blacklozenge$ **sights** *npl* [of city] attractions *fpl* touristiques.

sightseeing ['saɪt,siːɪŋ] *n* tourisme *m* ; **to go ~** faire du tourisme.

sightseer ['saɪt,siːəʳ] *n* touriste *mf.*

sign [saɪn] $\diamond$ *n* - **1.** [gen] signe *m* ; **no ~ of** aucune trace de - **2.** [notice] enseigne *f* ; AUT panneau *m.* $\diamond$ *vt* signer. $\blacklozenge$ **sign on** *vi* - **1.** [enrol - MIL] s'engager ; [- for course] s'inscrire - **2.** *Br* [register as unemployed] s'inscrire au chômage. $\blacklozenge$ **sign up** $\diamond$ *vt sep* [worker] embaucher ; [soldier] engager. $\diamond$ *vi* MIL s'engager ; [for course] s'inscrire.

signal ['sɪgnl] $\diamond$ *n* signal *m.* $\diamond$ *vt* - **1.** [indicate] indiquer - **2.** [gesture to] : **to ~ sb (to do sthg)** faire signe à qqn (de faire qqch). $\diamond$ *vi* - **1.** AUT clignoter, mettre son clignotant - **2.** [gesture] : **to ~ sb (to do sthg)** faire signe à qqn (de faire qqch).

signalman ['sɪgnlmən] (*pl* -men [-mən]) *n* RAIL aiguilleur *m.*

signature ['sɪgnətʃəʳ] *n* [name] signature *f.*

signature tune *n* indicatif *m.*

signet ring ['sɪgnɪt-] *n* chevalière *f.*

significance [sɪg'nɪfɪkəns] *n* - **1.** [importance] importance *f*, portée *f* - **2.** [meaning] signification *f.*

significant [sɪg'nɪfɪkənt] *adj* - **1.** [considerable] considérable - **2.** [important] important(e) - **3.** [meaningful] significatif(ive).

signify ['sɪgnɪfaɪ] *vt* signifier, indiquer.

signpost ['saɪnpəʊst] *n* poteau *m* indicateur.

Sikh [siːk] $\diamond$ *adj* sikh *(inv).* $\diamond$ *n* [person] Sikh *mf.*

silence ['saɪləns] $\diamond$ *n* silence *m.* $\diamond$ *vt* réduire au silence, faire taire.

silencer ['saɪlənsəʳ] *n* silencieux *m.*

silent ['saɪlənt] *adj* - **1.** [person, place] silencieux(euse) - **2.** CINEMA & LING muet (ette).

silhouette [,sɪluː'et] *n* silhouette *f.*

silicon chip [,sɪlɪkən-] *n* puce *f*, pastille *f* de silicium.

silk [sɪlk] $\diamond$ *n* soie *f.* $\diamond$ *comp* en OR de soie.

silky ['sɪlkɪ] *adj* soyeux(euse).

sill [sɪl] *n* [of window] rebord *m.*

silly ['sɪlɪ] *adj* stupide, bête.

silo ['saɪləʊ] (*pl* -s) *n* silo *m.*

silt [sɪlt] *n* vase *f*, limon *m.*

silver ['sɪlvəʳ] $\diamond$ *adj* [colour] argenté(e). $\diamond$ *n (U)* - **1.** [metal] argent *m* - **2.** [coins] pièces *fpl* d'argent - **3.** [silverware] argenterie *f.* $\diamond$ *comp* en argent, d'argent.

silver foil, silver paper *n (U)* papier *m* d'argent OR d'étain.

silver-plated [-'pleɪtɪd] *adj* plaqué(e) argent.

silversmith ['sɪlvəsmɪθ] *n* orfèvre *mf.*

silverware ['sɪlvəweəʳ] *n (U)* - **1.** [dishes, spoons, etc] argenterie *f* - **2.** *Am* [cutlery] couverts *mpl.*

similar ['sɪmɪləʳ] *adj* : **~ (to)** semblable (à), similaire (à).

similarly ['sɪmɪləlɪ] *adv* de la même manière, pareillement.

simmer ['sɪməʳ] *vt* faire cuire à feu doux, mijoter.

simpering ['sɪmpərɪŋ] *adj* affecté(e).

simple ['sɪmpl] *adj* - **1.** [gen] simple - **2.** *dated* [mentally retarded] simplet(ette), simple d'esprit.

simple-minded [-'maɪndɪd] *adj* simplet(ette), simple d'esprit.

simplicity [sɪm'plɪsətɪ] *n* simplicité *f.*

simplify ['sɪmplɪfaɪ] *vt* simplifier.

simply ['sɪmplɪ] *adv* - **1.** [gen] simplement - **2.** [for emphasis] absolument ; **quite ~** tout simplement.

simulate ['sɪmjʊleɪt] *vt* simuler.

simultaneous [*Br* ,sɪmʊl'teɪnjəs, *Am* ,saɪməl'teɪnjəs] *adj* simultané(e).

sin [sɪn] $\diamond$ *n* péché *m.* $\diamond$ *vi* : **to ~ (against)** pécher (contre).

since [sɪns] $\diamond$ *adv* depuis. $\diamond$ *prep* depuis. $\diamond$ *conj* - **1.** [in time] depuis que - **2.** [because] comme, puisque.

sincere [sɪn'sɪəʳ] *adj* sincère.

sincerely [sɪn'sɪəlɪ] *adv* sincèrement ; **Yours ~** [at end of letter] veuillez agréer, Monsieur/Madame, l'expression de mes sentiments les meilleurs.

sincerity [sɪn'serətɪ] *n* sincérité *f.*

sinew ['sɪnjuː] *n* tendon *m.*

sinful ['sɪnfʊl] *adj* [thought] mauvais(e) ; [desire, act] coupable ; **~ person** pécheur *m*, -eresse *f.*

sing [sɪŋ] (*pt* **sang**, *pp* **sung**) *vt & vi* chanter.

Singapore [ˌsɪŋə'pɔːʳ] *n* Singapour *m*.

singe [sɪndʒ] *vt* brûler légèrement ; [cloth] roussir.

singer ['sɪŋəʳ] *n* chanteur *m*, -euse *f*.

singing ['sɪŋɪŋ] *n (U)* chant *m*.

single ['sɪŋgl] ⬦ *adj* - **1.** [only one] seul(e), unique ; **every ~** chaque - **2.** [unmarried] célibataire - **3.** *Br* [ticket] simple. ⬦ *n* - **1.** *Br* [one-way ticket] billet *m* simple, aller *m* (simple) - **2.** MUS (disque *m*) 45 tours *m*. ➧ **singles** *npl* TENNIS simples *mpl*.
➧ **single out** *vt sep* : **to ~ sb out (for)** choisir qqn (pour).

single bed *n* lit *m* à une place.

single-breasted [-'brestɪd] *adj* [jacket] droit(e).

single cream *n Br* crème *f* liquide.

single currency *n* monnaie *f* unique.

single file *n* : **in ~** en file indienne, à la file.

single-handed [-'hændɪd] *adv* tout seul (toute seule).

single-minded [-'maɪndɪd] *adj* résolu(e).

single parent *n* père *m* OR mère *f* célibataire.

single-parent family *n* famille *f* monoparentale.

single room *n* chambre *f* pour une personne OR à un lit.

singlet ['sɪŋglɪt] *n Br* tricot *m* de peau ; SPORT maillot *m*.

singular ['sɪŋgjʊləʳ] ⬦ *adj* singulier(ère). ⬦ *n* singulier *m*.

sinister ['sɪnɪstəʳ] *adj* sinistre.

sink [sɪŋk] (*pt* **sank**, *pp* **sunk**) ⬦ *n* [in kitchen] évier *m* ; [in bathroom] lavabo *m*. ⬦ *vt* - **1.** [ship] couler - **2.** [teeth, claws] : **to ~ sthg into** enfoncer qqch dans. ⬦ *vi* - **1.** [in water - ship] couler, sombrer ; [- person, object] couler - **2.** [ground] s'affaisser ; [sun] baisser ; **to ~ into poverty/despair** sombrer dans la misère/le désespoir - **3.** [value, amount] baisser, diminuer ; [voice] faiblir. ➧ **sink in** *vi* : **it hasn't sunk in yet** je n'ai pas encore réalisé.

sink unit *n* bloc-évier *m*.

sinner ['sɪnəʳ] *n* pécheur *m*, -eresse *f*.

sinus ['saɪnəs] (*pl* **-es** [-iːz]) *n* sinus *m inv*.

sip [sɪp] ⬦ *n* petite gorgée *f*. ⬦ *vt* siroter, boire à petits coups.

siphon ['saɪfn] ⬦ *n* siphon *m*. ⬦ *vt* - **1.** [liquid] siphonner - **2.** *fig* [money] canaliser. ➧ **siphon off** *vt sep* - **1.** [liquid] siphonner - **2.** *fig* [money] canaliser.

sir [sɜːʳ] *n* - **1.** [form of address] monsieur *m* - **2.** [in titles] : **Sir Phillip Holden** sir Phillip Holden.

siren ['saɪərən] *n* sirène *f*.

sirloin (steak) ['sɜːlɔɪn-] *n* bifteck *m* dans l'aloyau OR d'aloyau.

sissy ['sɪsɪ] *n inf* poule *f* mouillée, dégonflé *m*, -e *f*.

sister ['sɪstəʳ] *n* - **1.** [sibling] sœur *f* - **2.** [nun] sœur *f*, religieuse *f* - **3.** *Br* [senior nurse] infirmière *f* chef.

sister-in-law (*pl* **sisters-in-law**) *n* belle-sœur *f*.

sit [sɪt] (*pt & pp* **sat**) ⬦ *vt Br* [exam] passer. ⬦ *vi* - **1.** [person] s'asseoir ; **to be sitting** être assis(e) ; **to ~ on a committee** faire partie OR être membre d'un comité - **2.** [court, parliament] siéger, être en séance.
➧ **sit about, sit around** *vi* rester assis(e) à ne rien faire. ➧ **sit down** *vi* s'asseoir.
➧ **sit in on** *vt fus* assister à. ➧ **sit through** *vt fus* rester jusqu'à la fin de.
➧ **sit up** *vi* - **1.** [sit upright] se redresser, s'asseoir - **2.** [stay up] veiller.

sitcom ['sɪtkɒm] *n inf* sitcom *f*.

site [saɪt] ⬦ *n* [of town, building] emplacement *m* ; [archaeological] site *m* ; CONSTR chantier *m*. ⬦ *vt* situer, placer.

sit-in *n* sit-in *m*, occupation *f* des locaux.

sitting ['sɪtɪŋ] *n* - **1.** [of meal] service *m* - **2.** [of court, parliament] séance *f*.

sitting room *n* salon *m*.

situated ['sɪtjʊeɪtɪd] *adj* : **to be ~** être situé(e), se trouver.

situation [ˌsɪtjʊ'eɪʃn] *n* - **1.** [gen] situation *f* - **2.** [job] situation *f*, emploi *m* ; **'~s vacant'** *Br* 'offres d'emploi'.

six [sɪks] ⬦ *num adj* six *(inv)* ; **she's ~ (years old)** elle a six ans. ⬦ *num pron* six *mfpl* ; **I want ~** j'en veux six ; **there were ~ of us** nous étions six. ⬦ *num n* - **1.** [gen] six *m inv* ; **two hundred and ~** deux cent six - **2.** [six o'clock] : **it's ~** il est six heures ; **we arrived at ~** nous sommes arrivés à six heures.

sixteen [sɪks'tiːn] *num* seize ; *see also* **six**.

sixteenth [sɪks'tiːnθ] *num* seizième ; *see also* **sixth**.

sixth [sɪksθ] ⬦ *num adj* sixième. ⬦ *num adv* - **1.** [in race, competition] sixième, en sixième place - **2.** [in list] sixièmement. ⬦ *num pron* sixième *mf*. ⬦ *n* - **1.** [fraction] sixième *m* - **2.** [in dates] : **the ~ (of September)** le six (septembre).

sixth form *n Br* SCH ≃ (classe *f*) terminale *f*.

sixth form college n Br établissement préparant aux A-levels.

sixty ['sɪkstɪ] num soixante ; see also **six**. ◆ **sixties** npl - **1.** [decade] : **the sixties** les années fpl soixante - **2.** [in ages] : **to be in one's sixties** être sexagénaire.

size [saɪz] n [of person, clothes, company] taille f ; [of building] grandeur f, dimensions fpl ; [of problem] ampleur f, taille ; [of shoes] pointure f. ◆ **size up** vt sep [person] jauger ; [situation] apprécier, peser.

sizeable ['saɪzəbl] adj assez important(e).

sizzle ['sɪzl] vi grésiller.

skate [skeɪt] (pl sense 2 only, inv OR -s) ◇ n - **1.** [ice skate, roller skate] patin m - **2.** [fish] raie f. ◇ vi [on ice skates] faire du patin à glace, patiner ; [on roller skates] faire du patin à roulettes.

skateboard ['skeɪtbɔːd] n planche f à roulettes, skateboard m, skate m.

skater ['skeɪtə'] n [on ice] patineur m, -euse f ; [on roller skates] patineur à roulettes.

skating ['skeɪtɪŋ] n [on ice] patinage m ; [on roller skates] patinage à roulettes.

skating rink n patinoire f.

skeleton ['skelɪtn] n squelette m.

skeleton key n passe m, passe-partout m inv.

skeleton staff n personnel m réduit.

skeptic etc Am = **sceptic** etc.

sketch [sketʃ] ◇ n - **1.** [drawing] croquis m, esquisse f - **2.** [description] aperçu m, résumé m - **3.** [by comedian] sketch m. ◇ vt - **1.** [draw] dessiner, faire un croquis de - **2.** [describe] donner un aperçu de, décrire à grands traits.

sketchbook ['sketʃbʊk] n carnet m à dessins.

sketchpad ['sketʃpæd] n bloc m à dessins.

sketchy ['sketʃɪ] adj incomplet(ète).

skewer ['skjʊə'] ◇ n brochette f, broche f. ◇ vt embrocher.

ski [skiː] ◇ n (pt & pp **skied**, cont **skiing**) ◇ n ski m. ◇ vi skier, faire du ski.

ski boots npl chaussures fpl de ski.

skid [skɪd] ◇ n dérapage m ; **to go into a ~** déraper. ◇ vi déraper.

skier ['skiːə'] n skieur m, -euse f.

skies [skaɪz] pl ▷ **sky**.

skiing ['skiːɪŋ] n (U) ski m ; **to go ~** faire du ski.

ski jump n [slope] tremplin m ; [event] saut m à OR en skis.

skilful, skillful Am ['skɪlfʊl] adj habile, adroit(e).

ski lift n remonte-pente m.

skill [skɪl] n - **1.** (U) [ability] habileté f, adresse f - **2.** [technique] technique f, art m.

skilled [skɪld] adj - **1.** [skilful] : **~ (in** OR **at doing sthg)** habile OR adroit(e) (pour faire qqch) - **2.** [trained] qualifié(e).

skillful etc Am = **skilful** etc.

skim [skɪm] ◇ vt - **1.** [cream] écrémer ; [soup] écumer - **2.** [move above] effleurer, raser. ◇ vi : **to ~ through sthg** [newspaper, book] parcourir qqch.

skim(med) milk [skɪm(d)-] n lait m écrémé.

skimp [skɪmp] ◇ vt lésiner sur. ◇ vi : **to ~ on** lésiner sur.

skimpy ['skɪmpɪ] adj [meal] maigre ; [clothes] étriqué(e) ; [facts] insuffisant(e).

skin [skɪn] ◇ n peau f. ◇ vt - **1.** [dead animal] écorcher, dépouiller ; [fruit] éplucher, peler - **2.** [graze] : **to ~ one's knee** s'érafler OR s'écorcher le genou.

skin-deep adj superficiel(elle).

skin diving n plongée f sous-marine.

skinny ['skɪnɪ] adj maigre.

skin-tight adj moulant(e), collant(e).

skip [skɪp] ◇ n - **1.** [jump] petit saut m - **2.** Br [container] benne f. ◇ vt [page, class, meal] sauter. ◇ vi - **1.** [gen] sauter, sautiller - **2.** Br [over rope] sauter à la corde.

ski pants npl fuseau m.

ski pole n bâton m de ski.

skipper ['skɪpə'] n NAUT & SPORT capitaine m.

skipping rope n Br corde f à sauter.

skirmish ['skɜːmɪʃ] n escarmouche f.

skirt [skɜːt] ◇ n [garment] jupe f. ◇ vt - **1.** [town, obstacle] contourner - **2.** [problem] éviter. ◆ **skirt round** vt fus - **1.** [town, obstacle] contourner - **2.** [problem] éviter.

skit [skɪt] n sketch m.

skittle ['skɪtl] n Br quille f. ◆ **skittles** n (U) [game] quilles fpl.

skive [skaɪv] vi Br inf : **to ~ (off)** s'esquiver, tirer au flanc.

skulk [skʌlk] vi [hide] se cacher ; [prowl] rôder.

skull [skʌl] n crâne m.

skunk [skʌŋk] n [animal] mouffette f.

sky [skaɪ] n ciel m.

skylight ['skaɪlaɪt] n lucarne f.

skyscraper ['skaɪˌskreɪpə'] n gratte-ciel m inv.

slab [slæb] n [of concrete] dalle f ; [of stone] bloc m ; [of cake] pavé m.

slack [slæk] ◇ *adj* - **1.** [not tight] lâche - **2.** [not busy] calme - **3.** [person] négligent(e), pas sérieux(euse). ◇ *n* [in rope] mou *m*.

slacken ['slækn] ◇ *vt* [speed, pace] ralentir ; [rope] relâcher. ◇ *vi* [speed, pace] ralentir.

slag [slæg] *n (U)* [waste material] scories *fpl*.

slagheap ['slæghi:p] *n* terril *m*.

slain [sleɪn] *pp* ⊏> slay.

slam [slæm] ◇ *vt* - **1.** [shut] claquer - **2.** [place with force] : **to ~ sthg on** OR **onto** jeter qqch brutalement sur, flanquer qqch sur. ◇ *vi* claquer.

slander ['slɑ:ndə'] ◇ *n* calomnie *f* ; JUR diffamation *f*. ◇ *vt* calomnier ; JUR diffamer.

slang [slæŋ] *n (U)* argot *m*.

slant [slɑ:nt] ◇ *n* - **1.** [angle] inclinaison *f* - **2.** [perspective] point *m* de vue, perspective *f*. ◇ *vt* [bias] présenter d'une manière tendancieuse. ◇ *vi* [slope] être incliné(e), pencher.

slanting ['slɑ:ntɪŋ] *adj* [roof] en pente.

slap [slæp] ◇ *n* claque *f*, tape *f* ; [on face] gifle *f*. ◇ *vt* - **1.** [person, face] gifler ; [back] donner une claque or une tape à - **2.** [place with force] : **to ~ sthg on** OR **onto** jeter qqch brutalement sur, flanquer qqch sur. ◇ *adv inf* [directly] en plein.

slapdash ['slæpdæʃ], **slaphappy** ['slæp,hæpɪ] *adj inf* [work] bâclé(e) ; [person, attitude] insouciant(e).

slapstick ['slæpstɪk] *n (U)* grosse farce *f*.

slap-up *adj Br inf* [meal] fameux(euse).

slash [slæʃ] ◇ *n* - **1.** [long cut] entaille *f* - **2.** *esp Am* [oblique stroke] barre *f* oblique. ◇ *vt* - **1.** [cut] entailler - **2.** *inf* [prices] casser ; [budget, unemployment] réduire considérablement.

slat [slæt] *n* lame *f* ; [wooden] latte *f*.

slate [sleɪt] ◇ *n* ardoise *f*. ◇ *vt Br inf* [criticize] descendre en flammes.

slaughter ['slɔ:tə'] ◇ *n* - **1.** [of animals] abattage *m* - **2.** [of people] massacre *m*, carnage *m*. ◇ *vt* - **1.** [animals] abattre - **2.** [people] massacrer.

slaughterhouse ['slɔ:təhaʊs, *pl* -haʊzɪz] *n* abattoir *m*.

slave [sleɪv] ◇ *n* esclave *mf*. ◇ *vi* travailler comme un nègre ; **to ~ over sthg** peiner sur qqch.

slavery ['sleɪvərɪ] *n* esclavage *m*.

slay [sleɪ] (*pt* **slew**, *pp* **slain**) *vt literary* tuer.

sleazy ['sli:zɪ] *adj* [disreputable] mal famé(e).

sledge [sledʒ], **sled** *Am* [sled] *n* luge *f* ; [larger] traîneau *m*.

sledgehammer ['sledʒ,hæmə'] *n* masse *f*.

sleek [sli:k] *adj* - **1.** [hair, fur] lisse, luisant(e) - **2.** [shape] aux lignes pures.

sleep [sli:p] (*pt & pp* **slept**) ◇ *n* sommeil *m* ; **to go to ~** s'endormir. ◇ *vi* - **1.** [be asleep] dormir - **2.** [spend night] coucher.
➡ **sleep in** *vi* faire la grasse matinée.
➡ **sleep with** *vt fus euphemism* coucher avec.

sleeper ['sli:pə'] *n* - **1.** [person] : **to be a heavy/light ~** avoir le sommeil lourd/léger - **2.** [RAIL - berth] couchette *f* ; [- carriage] wagon-lit *m* ; [- train] train-couchettes *m* - **3.** *Br* [on railway track] traverse *f*.

sleeping bag ['sli:pɪŋ-] *n* sac *m* de couchage.

sleeping car ['sli:pɪŋ-] *n* wagon-lit *m*.

sleeping pill ['sli:pɪŋ-] *n* somnifère *m*.

sleepless ['sli:plɪs] *adj* : **to have a ~ night** passer une nuit blanche.

sleepwalk ['sli:pwɔ:k] *vi* être somnambule.

sleepy ['sli:pɪ] *adj* [person] qui a envie de dormir.

sleet [sli:t] ◇ *n* neige *f* fondue. ◇ *v impers* : **it's ~ing** il tombe de la neige fondue.

sleeve [sli:v] *n* - **1.** [of garment] manche *f* - **2.** [for record] pochette *f*.

sleigh [sleɪ] *n* traîneau *m*.

sleight of hand [,slaɪt-] *n (U)* - **1.** [skill] habileté *f* - **2.** [trick] tour *m* de passe-passe.

slender ['slendə'] *adj* - **1.** [thin] mince - **2.** *fig* [resources, income] modeste, maigre ; [hope, chance] faible.

slept [slept] *pt & pp* ⊏> sleep.

slew [slu:] ◇ *pt* ⊏> slay. ◇ *vi* [car] déraper.

slice [slaɪs] ◇ *n* - **1.** [thin piece] tranche *f* - **2.** *fig* [of profits, glory] part *f* - **3.** SPORT slice *m*. ◇ *vt* - **1.** [cut into slices] couper en tranches - **2.** [cut cleanly] trancher - **3.** SPORT slicer.

slick [slɪk] ◇ *adj* - **1.** [skilful] bien mené(e), habile - **2.** *pej* [superficial - talk] facile ; [- person] rusé(e). ◇ *n* nappe *f* de pétrole, marée *f* noire.

slide [slaɪd] (*pt & pp* **slid** [slɪd]) ◇ *n* - **1.** [in playground] toboggan *m* - **2.** PHOT diapositive *f*, diapo *f* - **3.** *Br* [for hair] barrette *f* - **4.** [decline] déclin *m* ; [in prices] baisse *f*. ◇ *vt* faire glisser. ◇ *vi* glisser.

sliding door [ˌslaɪdɪŋ-] n porte f coulissante.

sliding scale [ˌslaɪdɪŋ-] n échelle f mobile.

slight [slaɪt] ◇ adj - 1. [minor] léger(ère) ; **the ~est** le moindre (la moindre) ; **not in the ~est** pas du tout - 2. [thin] mince. ◇ n affront m. ◇ vt offenser.

slightly ['slaɪtlɪ] adv [to small extent] légèrement.

slim [slɪm] ◇ adj - 1. [person, object] mince - 2. [chance, possibility] faible. ◇ vi maigrir ; [diet] suivre un régime amaigrissant.

slime [slaɪm] n (U) substance f visqueuse ; [of snail] bave f.

slimming ['slɪmɪŋ] ◇ n amaigrissement m. ◇ adj [product] amaigrissant(e).

sling [slɪŋ] (pt & pp slung) ◇ n - 1. [for arm] écharpe f - 2. NAUT [for loads] élingue f. ◇ vt - 1. [hammock etc] suspendre - 2. inf [throw] lancer.

slip [slɪp] ◇ n - 1. [mistake] erreur f ; **a ~ of the pen** un lapsus ; **a ~ of the tongue** un lapsus - 2. [of paper - gen] morceau m ; [- strip] bande f - 3. [underwear] combinaison f - 4. phr : **to give sb the ~** inf fausser compagnie à qqn. ◇ vi - 1. [slide] glisser ; **to ~ sthg on** enfiler qqch. ◇ vi - 1. [slide] glisser ; **to ~ into sthg** se glisser dans qqch - 2. [decline] décliner. ◆ **slip up** vi fig faire une erreur.

slipped disc [ˌslɪpt-] n hernie f discale.

slipper ['slɪpəʳ] n pantoufle f, chausson m.

slippery ['slɪpərɪ] adj glissant(e).

slip road n Br bretelle f.

slipshod ['slɪpʃɒd] adj peu soigné(e).

slip-up n inf gaffe f.

slipway ['slɪpweɪ] n cale f de lancement.

slit [slɪt] (pt & pp slit) ◇ n [opening] fente f ; [cut] incision f. ◇ vt [make opening in] faire une fente dans, fendre ; [cut] inciser.

slither ['slɪðəʳ] vi [person] glisser ; [snake] onduler.

sliver ['slɪvəʳ] n [of glass, wood] éclat m ; [of meat, cheese] lamelle f.

slob [slɒb] n inf [in habits] saligaud m ; [in appearance] gros lard m.

slog [slɒg] inf ◇ n [tiring work] corvée f. ◇ vi [work] travailler comme un bœuf OR un nègre.

slogan ['sləʊgən] n slogan m.

slop [slɒp] ◇ vt renverser. ◇ vi déborder.

slope [sləʊp] ◇ n pente f. ◇ vi [land] être en pente ; [handwriting, table] pencher.

sloping ['sləʊpɪŋ] adj [land, shelf] en pente ; [handwriting] penché(e).

sloppy ['slɒpɪ] adj [careless] peu soigné(e).

slot [slɒt] n - 1. [opening] fente f - 2. [groove] rainure f - 3. [in schedule] créneau m.

slot machine n - 1. Br [vending machine] distributeur m automatique - 2. [for gambling] machine f à sous.

slouch [slaʊtʃ] vi être avachi(e).

Slovakia [slə'vækɪə] n Slovaquie f.

slovenly ['slʌvnlɪ] adj négligé(e).

slow [sləʊ] ◇ adj - 1. [gen] lent(e) - 2. [clock, watch] : **to be ~** retarder. ◇ adv lentement ; **to go ~** [driver] aller lentement ; [workers] faire la grève perlée. ◇ vt & vi ralentir. ◆ **slow down, slow up** vt sep & vi ralentir.

slowdown ['sləʊdaʊn] n ralentissement m.

slowly ['sləʊlɪ] adv lentement.

slow motion n : **in ~** au ralenti m.

sludge [slʌdʒ] n boue f.

slug [slʌg] n - 1. [animal] limace f - 2. inf [of alcohol] rasade f - 3. Am inf [bullet] balle f.

sluggish ['slʌgɪʃ] adj [person] apathique ; [movement, growth] lent(e) ; [business] calme, stagnant(e).

sluice [sluːs] n écluse f.

slum [slʌm] n [area] quartier m pauvre.

slumber ['slʌmbəʳ] literary ◇ n sommeil m. ◇ vi dormir paisiblement.

slump [slʌmp] ◇ n - 1. [decline] : **~ (in)** baisse f (de) - 2. [period of poverty] crise f (économique). ◇ vi lit & fig s'effondrer.

slung [slʌŋ] pt & pp ▷ sling.

slur [slɜːʳ] ◇ n - 1. [slight] : **~ (on)** atteinte f (à) - 2. [insult] affront m, insulte f. ◇ vt mal articuler.

slush [slʌʃ] n [snow] neige f fondue.

slush fund, slush money Am n fonds mpl secrets, caisse f noire.

slut [slʌt] n - 1. inf [dirty, untidy] souillon f - 2. v inf [sexually immoral] salope f.

sly [slaɪ] (compar slyer OR slier, superl slyest OR sliest) adj - 1. [look, smile] entendu(e) - 2. [person] rusé(e), sournois(e).

smack [smæk] ◇ n - 1. [slap] claque f ; [on face] gifle f - 2. [impact] claquement m. ◇ vt - 1. [slap] donner une claque à ; [face] gifler - 2. [place violently] poser violemment.

small [smɔːl] adj - 1. [gen] petit(e) - 2. [trivial] petit, insignifiant(e).

small ads [-ædz] *npl Br* petites annonces *fpl.*

small change *n* petite monnaie *f.*

smallholder ['smɔːlˌhəʊldər] *n Br* petit cultivateur *m.*

small hours *npl* : **in the ~** au petit jour OR matin.

smallpox ['smɔːlpɒks] *n* variole *f*, petite vérole *f.*

small print *n* : **the ~** les clauses *fpl* écrites en petits caractères.

small talk *n (U)* papotage *m*, bavardage *m.*

smarmy ['smaːmɪ] *adj* mielleux(euse).

smart [smaːt] <> *adj* - **1.** [stylish - person, clothes, car] élégant(e) - **2.** *esp Am* [clever] intelligent(e) - **3.** [fashionable - club, society, hotel] à la mode, in *(inv)* - **4.** [quick - answer, tap] vif (vive), rapide. <> *vi* - **1.** [eyes, skin] brûler, piquer - **2.** [person] être blessé(e).

smarten ['smaːtn] **smarten up** *vt sep* [room] arranger ; **to ~ o.s. up** se faire beau (belle).

smash [smæʃ] <> *n* - **1.** [sound] fracas *m* - **2.** *inf* [car crash] collision *f*, accident *m* - **3.** SPORT smash *m.* <> *vt* - **1.** [glass, plate etc] casser, briser - **2.** *fig* [defeat] détruire. <> *vi* - **1.** [glass, plate etc] se briser - **2.** [crash] : **to ~ into sthg** s'écraser contre qqch.

smashing ['smæʃɪŋ] *adj inf* super *(inv).*

smattering ['smætərɪŋ] *n* : **to have a ~ of German** savoir quelques mots d'allemand.

smear [smɪər] <> *n* - **1.** [dirty mark] tache *f* - **2.** MED frottis *m* - **3.** [slander] diffamation *f.* <> *vt* - **1.** [smudge] barbouiller, maculer - **2.** [spread] : **to ~ sthg onto sthg** étaler qqch sur qqch ; **to ~ sthg with sthg** enduire qqch de qqch - **3.** [slander] calomnier.

smell [smel] *(pt & pp* **-ed** OR **smelt)** <> *n* - **1.** [odour] odeur *f* - **2.** [sense of smell] odorat *m.* <> *vt* sentir. <> *vi* - **1.** [gen] sentir ; **to ~ of sthg** sentir qqch ; **to ~ good/ bad** sentir bon/mauvais - **2.** [smell unpleasantly] sentir (mauvais), puer.

smelly ['smelɪ] *adj* qui sent mauvais, qui pue.

smelt [smelt] <> *pt & pp* ⊳ **smell.** <> *vt* [metal] extraire par fusion ; [ore] fondre.

smile [smaɪl] <> *n* sourire *m.* <> *vi* sourire.

smiley ['smaɪlɪ] *n* smiley.

smirk [smɜːk] *n* sourire *m* narquois.

smock [smɒk] *n* blouse *f.*

smog [smɒg] *n* smog *m.*

smoke [sməʊk] <> *n (U)* [from fire] fumée *f.* <> *vt & vi* fumer.

smoked [sməʊkt] *adj* [food] fumé(e).

smoker ['sməʊkər] *n* - **1.** [person] fumeur *m*, -euse *f* - **2.** RAIL compartiment *m* fumeurs.

smokescreen ['sməʊkskriːn] *n fig* couverture *f.*

smoke shop *n Am* bureau *m* de tabac.

smoking ['sməʊkɪŋ] *n* tabagisme *m* ; **'no ~'** 'défense de fumer'.

smoky ['sməʊkɪ] *adj* - **1.** [room, air] enfumé(e) - **2.** [taste] fumé(e).

smolder *Am* = smoulder.

smooth [smuːð] <> *adj* - **1.** [surface] lisse - **2.** [sauce] homogène, onctueux(euse) - **3.** [movement] régulier(ère) - **4.** [taste] moelleux(euse) - **5.** [flight, ride] confortable ; [landing, take-off] en douceur - **6.** *pej* [person, manner] doucereux(euse), mielleux(euse) - **7.** [operation, progress] sans problèmes. <> *vt* [hair] lisser ; [clothes, tablecloth] défroisser. **smooth out** *vt sep* défroisser.

smother ['smʌðər] *vt* - **1.** [cover thickly] : **to ~ sb/sthg with** couvrir qqn/qqch de - **2.** [person, fire] étouffer - **3.** *fig* [emotions] cacher, étouffer.

smoulder *Br*, **smolder** *Am* ['sməʊldər] *vi lit & fig* couver.

smudge [smʌdʒ] <> *n* tache *f* ; [of ink] bavure *f.* <> *vt* [drawing, painting] maculer ; [paper] faire une marque OR trace sur ; [face] salir.

smug [smʌg] *adj* suffisant(e).

smuggle ['smʌgl] *vt* [across frontiers] faire passer en contrebande.

smuggler ['smʌglər] *n* contrebandier *m*, -ère *f.*

smuggling ['smʌglɪŋ] *n (U)* contrebande *f.*

smutty ['smʌtɪ] *adj pej* [book, language] cochon(onne).

snack [snæk] *n* casse-croûte *m inv.*

snack bar *n* snack *m*, snack-bar *m.*

snag [snæg] <> *n* [problem] inconvénient *m*, écueil *m.* <> *vi* : **to ~ (on)** s'accrocher (à).

snail [sneɪl] *n* escargot *m.*

snake [sneɪk] *n* serpent *m.*

snap [snæp] <> *adj* [decision, election] subit(e) ; [judgment] irréfléchi(e). <> *n* - **1.** [of branch] craquement *m* ; [of fingers] claquement *m* - **2.** [photograph] photo *f* - **3.** [card game] ≃ bataille *f.* <> *vt* - **1.** [break] casser net - **2.** [speak sharply] dire d'un ton sec. <> *vi* - **1.** [break] se casser net - **2.** [dog] : **to**

~ **at** essayer de mordre - **3.** [speak sharply] : **to** ~ **(at sb)** parler (à qqn) d'un ton sec. ◆ **snap up** *vt sep* [bargain] sauter sur.

snap fastener *n esp Am* pression *f.*

snappy ['snæpɪ] *adj inf* - **1.** [stylish] chic - **2.** [quick] prompt(e) ; **make it ~!** dépêche-toi!, et que ça saute!

snapshot ['snæpʃɒt] *n* photo *f.*

snare [sneə^r] ⟨⟩ *n* piège *m*, collet *m.* ⟨⟩ *vt* prendre au piège, attraper.

snarl [snɑ:l] ⟨⟩ *n* grondement *m.* ⟨⟩ *vi* gronder.

snatch [snætʃ] ⟨⟩ *n* [of conversation] bribe *f* ; [of song] extrait *m.* ⟨⟩ *vt* [grab] saisir.

sneak [sni:k] (*Am pt* **snuck**) ⟨⟩ *n Br inf* rapporteur *m*, -euse *f.* ⟨⟩ *vt* : **to ~ a look at sb/ sthg** regarder qqn/qqch à la dérobée. ⟨⟩ *vi* [move quietly] se glisser.

sneakers ['sni:kəz] *npl Am* tennis *mpl*, baskets *fpl.*

sneaky ['sni:kɪ] *adj inf* sournois(e).

sneer [snɪə^r] ⟨⟩ *n* [smile] sourire *m* dédaigneux ; [laugh] ricanement *m.* ⟨⟩ *vi* [smile] sourire dédaigneusement.

sneeze [sni:z] ⟨⟩ *n* éternuement *m.* ⟨⟩ *vi* éternuer.

snide [snaɪd] *adj* sournois(e).

sniff [snɪf] ⟨⟩ *vt* [smell] renifler. ⟨⟩ *vi* [to clear nose] renifler.

snigger ['snɪgə^r] ⟨⟩ *n* rire *m* en dessous. ⟨⟩ *vi* ricaner.

snip [snɪp] ⟨⟩ *n Br inf* [bargain] bonne affaire *f.* ⟨⟩ *vt* couper.

sniper ['snaɪpə^r] *n* tireur *m* isolé.

snippet ['snɪpɪt] *n* fragment *m.*

snivel ['snɪvl] *vi* geindre.

snob [snɒb] *n* snob *mf.*

snobbish ['snɒbɪʃ], **snobby** ['snɒbɪ] *adj* snob *(inv).*

snooker ['snu:kə^r] *n* [game] ≃ jeu *m* de billard.

snoop [snu:p] *vi inf* fureter.

snooty ['snu:tɪ] *adj inf* prétentieux(euse).

snooze [snu:z] ⟨⟩ *n* petit somme *m.* ⟨⟩ *vi* faire un petit somme.

snore [snɔ:^r] ⟨⟩ *n* ronflement *m.* ⟨⟩ *vi* ronfler.

snoring ['snɔ:rɪŋ] *n (U)* ronflement *m*, ronflements *mpl.*

snorkel ['snɔ:kl] *n* tuba *m.*

snort [snɔ:t] ⟨⟩ *n* [of person] grognement *m* ; [of horse, bull] ébrouement *m.* ⟨⟩ *vi* [person] grogner ; [horse] s'ébrouer.

snout [snaʊt] *n* groin *m.*

snow [snəʊ] ⟨⟩ *n* neige *f.* ⟨⟩ *v impers* neiger.

snowball ['snəʊbɔ:l] ⟨⟩ *n* boule *f* de neige. ⟨⟩ *vi fig* faire boule de neige.

snowbank ['snəʊbæŋk] *n* congère *f*, banc *m* de neige *Can.*

snowboard ['snəʊˌbɔ:d] *n* surf *m* des neiges.

snowboarding ['snəʊˌbɔ:dɪŋ] *n* surf *m* (des neiges).

snowbound ['snəʊbaʊnd] *adj* bloqué(e) par la neige.

snowdrift ['snəʊdrɪft] *n* congère *f.*

snowdrop ['snəʊdrɒp] *n* perce-neige *m inv.*

snowfall ['snəʊfɔ:l] *n* chute *f* de neige.

snowflake ['snəʊfleɪk] *n* flocon *m* de neige.

snowman ['snəʊmæn] (*pl* **-men** [-men]) *n* bonhomme *m* de neige.

snowmobile ['snəʊməbi:l] *n* scooter *m* des neiges, motoneige *f Can.*

snowplough *Br*, **snowplow** *Am* ['snəʊplaʊ] *n* chasse-neige *m inv.*

snowshoe ['snəʊʃu:] *n* raquette *f.*

snowstorm ['snəʊstɔ:m] *n* tempête *f* de neige.

SNP (*abbr of* **Scottish National Party**) *n parti nationaliste écossais.*

Snr, snr *abbr of* **senior.**

snub [snʌb] ⟨⟩ *n* rebuffade *f.* ⟨⟩ *vt* snober, ignorer.

snuck [snʌk] *Am pt* ▷ **sneak.**

snuff [snʌf] *n* tabac *m* à priser.

snug [snʌg] *adj* - **1.** [person] à l'aise, confortable ; [in bed] bien au chaud - **2.** [place] douillet(ette) - **3.** [close-fitting] bien ajusté(e).

snuggle ['snʌgl] *vi* se blottir.

so [səʊ] ⟨⟩ *adv* - **1.** [to such a degree] si, tellement ; ~ **difficult (that)** ... si OR tellement difficile que ... ; **don't be ~ stupid!** ne sois pas si bête! ; **we had ~ much work!** nous avions tant de travail! ; **I've never seen ~ much money/many cars** je n'ai jamais vu autant d'argent/de voitures - **2.** [in referring back to previous statement, event etc] : ~ **what's the point then?** alors à quoi bon? ; ~ **you knew already?** alors tu le savais déjà? ; **I don't think ~** je ne crois pas ; **I'm afraid ~** je crains bien que oui ; **if ~** si oui ; **is that ~?** vraiment? - **3.** [also] aussi ; ~ **can/do/would** *etc* **I** moi aussi ; **she speaks French and ~ does her husband** elle parle français et son mari aussi - **4.** [in this way] : **(like)** ~ comme cela OR ça, de cette façon

- **5.** [in expressing agreement] : **~ there is** en effet, c'est vrai ; **~ I see** c'est ce que je vois - **6.** [unspecified amount, limit] : **they pay us ~ much a week** ils nous payent tant par semaine ; **or ~** environ, à peu près. <> *conj* alors ; **I'm away next week ~ I won't be there** je suis en voyage la semaine prochaine donc OR par conséquent je ne serai pas là ; **~ what have you been up to?** alors, qu'est-ce que vous devenez? ; **~ what?** *inf* et alors?, et après? ; **~ there!** *inf* là!, et voilà! ◆ **so as** *conj* afin de, pour ; **we didn't knock ~ as not to disturb them** nous n'avons pas frappé pour ne pas les déranger. ◆ **so that** *conj* [for the purpose that] pour que (+ *subjunctive*).

soak [səʊk] <> *vt* laisser OR faire tremper. <> *vi* - **1.** [become thoroughly wet] : **to leave sthg to ~, to let sthg ~** laisser OR faire tremper qqch - **2.** [spread] : **to ~ into sthg** tremper dans qqch ; **to ~ through (sthg)** traverser (qqch). ◆ **soak up** *vt sep* absorber.

soaking ['səʊkɪŋ] *adj* trempé(e).

so-and-so *n inf* - **1.** [to replace a name] : **Mr ~** Monsieur Untel - **2.** [annoying person] enquiquineur *m*, -euse *f*.

soap [səʊp] *n* - **1.** (U) [for washing] savon *m* - **2.** TV soap opera *m*.

soap flakes *npl* savon *m* en paillettes.

soap opera *n* soap opera *m*.

soap powder *n* lessive *f*.

soapy ['səʊpɪ] *adj* [water] savonneux(euse) ; [taste] de savon.

soar [sɔːʳ] *vi* - **1.** [bird] planer - **2.** [balloon, kite] monter - **3.** [prices, temperature] monter en flèche.

sob [sɒb] <> *n* sanglot *m*. <> *vi* sangloter.

sober ['səʊbəʳ] *adj* - **1.** [not drunk] qui n'est pas ivre - **2.** [serious] sérieux(euse) - **3.** [plain - clothes, colours] sobre. ◆ **sober up** *vi* dessoûler.

sobering ['səʊbərɪŋ] *adj* qui donne à réfléchir.

so-called [-kɔːld] *adj* - **1.** [misleadingly named] soi-disant *(inv)* - **2.** [widely known as] ainsi appelé(e).

soccer ['sɒkəʳ] *n* football *m*.

sociable ['səʊʃəbl] *adj* sociable.

social ['səʊʃl] *adj* social(e).

social club *n* club *m*.

socialism ['səʊʃəlɪzm] *n* socialisme *m*.

socialist ['səʊʃəlɪst] <> *adj* socialiste. <> *n* socialiste *mf*.

socialize, -ise ['səʊʃəlaɪz] *vi* fréquenter

des gens ; **to ~ with sb** fréquenter qqn, frayer avec qqn.

social security *n* aide *f* sociale.

social services *npl* services *mpl* sociaux.

social worker *n* assistant social *m*, assistante sociale *f*.

society [sə'saɪətɪ] *n* - **1.** [gen] société *f* - **2.** [club] association *f*, club *m*.

sociology [,səʊsɪ'ɒlədʒɪ] *n* sociologie *f*.

sock [sɒk] *n* chaussette *f*.

socket ['sɒkɪt] *n* - **1.** [for light bulb] douille *f* ; [for plug] prise *f* de courant - **2.** [of eye] orbite *f* ; [for bone] cavité *f* articulaire.

sod [sɒd] *n* - **1.** [of turf] motte *f* de gazon - **2.** *Br v inf* [person] con *m*.

soda ['səʊdə] *n* - **1.** CHEM soude *f* - **2.** [soda water] eau *f* de Seltz - **3.** *Am* [fizzy drink] soda *m*.

soda water *n* eau *f* de Seltz.

sodden ['sɒdn] *adj* trempé(e), détrempé(e).

sodium ['səʊdɪəm] *n* sodium *m*.

sofa ['səʊfə] *n* canapé *m*.

Sofia ['səʊfjə] *n* Sofia.

soft [sɒft] *adj* - **1.** [not hard] doux (douce), mou (molle) - **2.** [smooth, not loud, not bright] doux (douce) - **3.** [without force] léger(ère) - **4.** [caring] tendre - **5.** [lenient] faible, indulgent(e).

soft drink *n* boisson *f* non alcoolisée.

soften ['sɒfn] <> *vt* - **1.** [fabric] assouplir ; [substance] ramollir ; [skin] adoucir - **2.** [shock, blow] atténuer, adoucir - **3.** [attitude] modérer, adoucir. <> *vi* - **1.** [substance] se ramollir - **2.** [attitude, person] s'adoucir, se radoucir.

softhearted [,sɒft'hɑːtɪd] *adj* au cœur tendre.

softly ['sɒftlɪ] *adv* - **1.** [gently, quietly] doucement - **2.** [not brightly] faiblement - **3.** [leniently] avec indulgence.

soft-spoken *adj* à la voix douce.

software ['sɒftweəʳ] *n* (U) COMPUT logiciel *m*.

soggy ['sɒgɪ] *adj* trempé(e), détrempé(e).

soil [sɔɪl] <> *n* (U) - **1.** [earth] sol *m*, terre *f* - **2.** *fig* [territory] sol *m*, territoire *m*. <> *vt* souiller, salir.

soiled [sɔɪld] *adj* sale.

solace ['sɒləs] *n literary* consolation *f*, réconfort *m*.

solar ['səʊləʳ] *adj* solaire.

sold [səʊld] *pt & pp* ⊳ **sell**.

solder ['səʊldəʳ] <> *n* (U) soudure *f*. <> *vt* souder.

soldier ['səʊldʒəʳ] n soldat m.

sold-out adj [tickets] qui ont tous été vendus ; [play, concert] qui joue à guichets fermés.

sole [səʊl] (pl sense 2 only, inv OR -s) ◇ adj - 1. [only] seul(e), unique - 2. [exclusive] exclusif(ive). ◇ n - 1. [of foot] semelle f - 2. [fish] sole f.

solemn ['sɒləm] adj solennel(elle) ; [person] sérieux(euse).

solicit [sə'lɪsɪt] ◇ vt [request] solliciter. ◇ vi [prostitute] racoler.

solicitor [sə'lɪsɪtəʳ] n Br JUR notaire m.

solid ['sɒlɪd] ◇ adj - 1. [not fluid, sturdy, reliable] solide - 2. [not hollow - tyres] plein(e) ; [- wood, rock, gold] massif(ive) - 3. [without interruption] : **two hours ~** deux heures d'affilée. ◇ n solide m.

solidarity [ˌsɒlɪ'dærətɪ] n solidarité f.

solitaire [ˌsɒlɪ'teəʳ] n - 1. [jewel, board game] solitaire m - 2. Am [card game] réussite f, patience f.

solitary ['sɒlɪtrɪ] adj - 1. [lonely, alone] solitaire - 2. [just one] seul(e).

solitary confinement n isolement m cellulaire.

solitude ['sɒlɪtjuːd] n solitude f.

solo ['səʊləʊ] (pl -s) ◇ adj solo (inv). ◇ n solo m. ◇ adv en solo.

soloist ['səʊləʊɪst] n soliste mf.

soluble ['sɒljʊbl] adj soluble.

solution [sə'luːʃn] n - 1. [to problem] : **~ (to)** solution f (de) - 2. [liquid] solution f.

solve [sɒlv] vt résoudre.

solvent ['sɒlvənt] ◇ adj FIN solvable. ◇ n dissolvant m, solvant m.

Somalia [sə'mɑːlɪə] n Somalie f.

sombre Br, **somber** Am ['sɒmbəʳ] adj sombre.

some [sʌm] ◇ adj - 1. [a certain amount, number of] : **~ meat** de la viande ; **~ money** de l'argent ; **~ coffee** du café ; **~ sweets** des bonbons - 2. [fairly large number or quantity of] quelque ; **I had ~ difficulty getting here** j'ai eu quelque mal à venir ici ; **I've known him for ~ years** je le connais depuis plusieurs années OR pas mal d'années - 3. (contrastive use) [certain] : **~ jobs are better paid than others** certains boulots sont mieux rémunérés que d'autres ; **people like his music** il y en a qui aiment sa musique - 4. [in imprecise statements] quelque, quelconque ; **she married ~ writer or other** elle a épousé un écrivain quelconque OR quelque écrivain ; **there must be ~ mistake** il doit y avoir erreur - 5. inf [very good] : **that**

was ~ party! c'était une soirée formidable!, quelle soirée! ◇ pron - 1. [a certain amount] : **can I have ~?** [money, milk, coffee etc] est-ce que je peux en prendre? ; **~ of it is mine** une partie est à moi - 2. [a certain number] quelques-uns (quelques-unes), certains (certaines) ; **can I have ~?** [books, pens, potatoes etc] est-ce que je peux en prendre (quelques-uns)? ; **~ (of them) left early** quelques-uns d'entre eux sont partis tôt. ◇ adv quelque, environ ; **there were ~ 7,000 people there** il y avait quelque OR environ 7 000 personnes.

somebody ['sʌmbədɪ] pron quelqu'un.

someday ['sʌmdeɪ] adv un jour, un de ces jours.

somehow ['sʌmhaʊ], **someway** Am ['sʌmweɪ] adv - 1. [by some action] d'une manière ou d'une autre - 2. [for some reason] pour une raison ou pour une autre.

someone ['sʌmwʌn] pron quelqu'un.

someplace Am = somewhere.

somersault ['sʌməsɔːlt] ◇ n cabriole f, culbute f. ◇ vi faire une cabriole OR culbute.

something ['sʌmθɪŋ] ◇ pron [unknown thing] quelque chose ; **~ odd/interesting** quelque chose de bizarre/d'intéressant ; **or ~** inf ou quelque chose comme ça. ◇ adv : **~ like, ~ in the region of** environ, à peu près.

sometime ['sʌmtaɪm] ◇ adj ancien (enne). ◇ adv un de ces jours ; **~ last week** la semaine dernière.

sometimes ['sʌmtaɪmz] adv quelquefois, parfois.

someway Am = somehow.

somewhat ['sʌmwɒt] adv quelque peu.

somewhere Br ['sʌmweəʳ], **someplace** Am ['sʌmpleɪs] adv - 1. [unknown place] quelque part ; **~ else** ailleurs ; **~ near here** près d'ici - 2. [used in approximations] environ, à peu près.

son [sʌn] n fils m.

song [sɒŋ] n chanson f ; [of bird] chant m, ramage m.

sonic ['sɒnɪk] adj sonique.

son-in-law (pl sons-in-law) n gendre m, beau-fils m.

sonnet ['sɒnɪt] n sonnet m.

sonny ['sʌnɪ] n inf fiston m.

soon [suːn] adv - 1. [before long] bientôt ; **~ after** peu après - 2. [early] tôt ; **write back ~** réponds-moi vite ; **how ~ will it be ready?** ce sera prêt quand?, dans combien de temps est-ce que ce sera prêt? ; **as ~ as** dès que, aussitôt que.

sooner ['su:nər] adv - **1.** [in time] plus tôt ; no ~ ... than ... à peine ... que ... ; ~ **or later** tôt ou tard ; **the ~ the better** le plus tôt sera le mieux - **2.** [expressing preference] : **I would ~** ... je préférerais ..., j'aimerais mieux ...

soot [sʊt] n suie f.

soothe [su:ð] vt calmer, apaiser.

sophisticated [sə'fɪstɪkeɪtɪd] adj - **1.** [stylish] raffiné(e), sophistiqué(e) - **2.** [intelligent] averti(e) - **3.** [complicated] sophistiqué(e), très perfectionné(e).

sophomore ['sɒfəmɔːr] n Am étudiant m, -e f de seconde année.

soporific [ˌsɒpə'rɪfɪk] adj soporifique.

sopping ['sɒpɪŋ] adj : ~ (wet) tout trempé (toute trempée).

soppy ['sɒpɪ] adj inf - **1.** [sentimental - book, film] à l'eau de rose ; [- person] sentimental(e) - **2.** [silly] bêta(bêtasse), bête.

soprano [sə'prɑːnəʊ] (pl -s) n [person] soprano mf ; [voice] soprano m.

sorbet ['sɔːbeɪ] n sorbet m.

sorcerer ['sɔːsərər] n sorcier m.

sordid ['sɔːdɪd] adj sordide.

sore [sɔːr] <> adj - **1.** [painful] douloureux(euse) ; **to have a ~ throat** avoir mal à la gorge - **2.** Am [upset] fâché(e), contrarié(e). <> n plaie f.

sorely ['sɔːlɪ] adv literary [needed] grandement.

sorrow ['sɒrəʊ] n peine f, chagrin m.

sorry ['sɒrɪ] <> adj - **1.** [expressing apology, disappointment, sympathy] désolé(e) ; **to be ~ about sthg** s'excuser pour qqch ; **to be ~ for sthg** regretter qqch ; **to be ~ to do sthg** regretter OR être désolé de faire qqch ; **to be** OR **feel ~ for sb** plaindre qqn - **2.** [poor] : **in a ~ state** en piteux état, dans un triste état. <> excl - **1.** [expressing apology] pardon!, excusez-moi! ; ~, **we're sold out** désolé, on n'en a plus - **2.** [asking for repetition] pardon?, comment? - **3.** [to correct oneself] non, pardon OR je veux dire.

sort [sɔːt] <> n genre m, sorte f, espèce f ; ~ **of** [rather] plutôt, quelque peu ; **a ~ of** une espèce OR sorte de. <> vt trier, classer. ◆ **sort out** vt sep - **1.** [classify] ranger, classer - **2.** [solve] résoudre.

sorting office ['sɔːtɪŋ-] n centre m de tri.

SOS (abbr of save our souls) n SOS m.

so-so inf <> adj quelconque. <> adv comme ci comme ça.

sought [sɔːt] pt & pp ▷ seek.

soul [səʊl] n - **1.** [gen] âme f - **2.** [music] soul m.

soul-destroying [-dɪˌstrɔɪɪŋ] adj abrutissant(e).

soulful ['səʊlfʊl] adj [look] expressif(ive) ; [song etc] sentimental(e).

sound [saʊnd] <> adj - **1.** [healthy - body] sain(e), en bonne santé ; [- mind] sain - **2.** [sturdy] solide - **3.** [reliable - advice] judicieux(euse), sage ; [- investment] sûr(e). <> adv : **to be ~ asleep** dormir à poings fermés, dormir d'un sommeil profond. <> n son m ; [particular sound] bruit m, son m ; **by the ~ of it** ... d'après ce que j'ai compris ... <> vt [alarm, bell] sonner. <> vi - **1.** [make a noise] sonner, retentir ; **to ~ like sthg** ressembler à qqch - **2.** [seem] sembler, avoir l'air ; **to ~ like sthg** avoir l'air de qqch, sembler être qqch. ◆ **sound out** vt sep : **to ~ sb out (on** OR **about)** sonder qqn (sur).

sound barrier n mur m du son.

sound effects npl bruitage m, effets mpl sonores.

sounding ['saʊndɪŋ] n NAUT & fig sondage m.

soundly ['saʊndlɪ] adv - **1.** [beaten] à plates coutures - **2.** [sleep] profondément.

soundproof ['saʊndpruːf] adj insonorisé(e).

soundtrack ['saʊndtræk] n bande-son f.

soup [suːp] n soupe f, potage m.

soup plate n assiette f creuse OR à soupe.

soup spoon n cuiller f à soupe.

sour ['saʊər] <> adj - **1.** [taste, fruit] acide, aigre - **2.** [milk] aigre - **3.** [ill-tempered] aigre, acerbe. <> vt fig faire tourner au vinaigre, faire mal tourner.

source [sɔːs] n - **1.** [gen] source f - **2.** [cause] origine f, cause f.

sour grapes n (U) inf : **what he said was just ~** il a dit ça par dépit.

south [saʊθ] <> n - **1.** [direction] sud m - **2.** [region] : **the ~** le sud ; **the South of France** le Sud de la France, le Midi (de la France). <> adj sud (inv) ; [wind] du sud. <> adv au sud, vers le sud ; ~ **of** au sud de.

South Africa n Afrique f du Sud.

South African <> adj sud-africain(e). <> n [person] Sud-Africain m, -e f.

South America n Amérique f du Sud.

South American <> adj sud-américain(e). <> n [person] Sud-Américain m, -e f.

southeast [ˌsaʊθ'iːst] <> n - **1.** [direction] sud-est m - **2.** [region] : **the ~** le sud-est. <> adj au sud-est, du sud-est ; [wind] du sud-est. <> adv au sud-est, vers le sud-est ; ~ **of** au sud-est de.

southerly ['sʌðəlɪ] *adj* au sud, du sud ; [wind] du sud.

southern ['sʌðən] *adj* du sud ; [France] du Midi.

South Korea *n* Corée *f* du Sud.

South Pole *n* : **the ~** le pôle Sud.

southward ['saʊθwəd] ◇ *adj* au sud, du sud. ◇ *adv* = **southwards**.

southwards ['saʊθwədz] *adv* vers le sud.

southwest [ˌsaʊθ'west] ◇ *n* - **1.** [direction] sud-ouest *m* - **2.** [region] : **the ~** le sud-ouest. ◇ *adj* au sud-ouest, du sud-ouest ; [wind] du sud-ouest. ◇ *adv* au sud-ouest, vers le sud-ouest ; **~ of** au sud-ouest de.

souvenir [ˌsuːvə'nɪəʳ] *n* souvenir *m*.

sovereign ['sɒvrɪn] ◇ *adj* souverain(e). ◇ *n* - **1.** [ruler] souverain *m*, -e *f* - **2.** [coin] souverain *m*.

soviet ['səʊvɪət] *n* soviet *m*. ◆ **Soviet** ◇ *adj* soviétique. ◇ *n* [person] Soviétique *mf*.

Soviet Union *n* : **the (former) ~** l'(ex-) Union *f* soviétique.

sow¹ [səʊ] (*pt* -**ed**, *pp* **sown** OR -**ed**) *vt lit* & *fig* semer.

sow² [saʊ] *n* truie *f*.

sown [səʊn] *pp* ▷ **sow¹**.

soya ['sɔɪə] *n* soja *m*.

soy(a) bean ['sɔɪ(ə)-] *n* graine *f* de soja.

spa [spɑː] *n* station *f* thermale.

space [speɪs] ◇ *n* - **1.** [gap, roominess, outer space] espace *m* ; [on form] blanc *m*, espace - **2.** [room] place *f* - **3.** [of time] : **within** OR **in the ~ of** ten minutes en l'espace de dix minutes. ◇ *comp* spatial(e). ◇ *vt* espacer. ◆ **space out** *vt sep* espacer.

spacecraft ['speɪskrɑːft] (*pl inv*) *n* vaisseau *m* spatial.

spaceman ['speɪsmæn] (*pl* -**men** [-men]) *n* astronaute *m*, cosmonaute *m*.

spaceship ['speɪsʃɪp] *n* vaisseau *m* spatial.

space shuttle *n* navette *f* spatiale.

spacesuit ['speɪssuːt] *n* combinaison *f* spatiale.

spacing ['speɪsɪŋ] *n* TYPO espacement *m*.

spacious ['speɪʃəs] *adj* spacieux(euse).

spade [speɪd] *n* - **1.** [tool] pelle *f* - **2.** [playing card] pique *m*. ◆ **spades** *npl* pique *m*.

spaghetti [spə'getɪ] *n* (*U*) spaghettis *mpl*.

Spain [speɪn] *n* Espagne *f*.

span [spæn] ◇ *pt* ▷ **spin**. ◇ *n* - **1.** [in time] espace *m* de temps, durée *f* - **2.** [range] éventail *m*, gamme *f* - **3.** [of bird, plane] en-

vergure *f* - **4.** [of bridge] travée *f* ; [of arch] ouverture *f*. ◇ *vt* - **1.** [in time] embrasser, couvrir - **2.** [subj : bridge] franchir.

Spaniard ['spænjəd] *n* Espagnol *m*, -e *f*.

spaniel ['spænjəl] *n* épagneul *m*.

Spanish ['spænɪʃ] ◇ *adj* espagnol(e). ◇ *n* [language] espagnol *m*. ◇ *npl* : **the ~** les Espagnols.

spank [spæŋk] *vt* donner une fessée à, fesser.

spanner ['spænəʳ] *n* clé *f* à écrous.

spar [spɑːʳ] ◇ *n* espar *m*. ◇ *vi* BOXING s'entraîner à la boxe.

spare [speəʳ] ◇ *adj* - **1.** [surplus] de trop ; [component, clothing etc] de réserve, de rechange ; **~ bed** lit *m* d'appoint - **2.** [available - seat, time, tickets] disponible. ◇ *n* [part] pièce *f* détachée OR de rechange. ◇ *vt* - **1.** [make available - staff, money] se passer de ; [- time] disposer de ; **to have an hour to ~** avoir une heure de battement OR de libre ; **with a minute to ~** avec une minute d'avance - **2.** [not harm] épargner - **3.** [not use] épargner, ménager ; **to ~ no expense** ne pas regarder à la dépense - **4.** [save from] : **to ~ sb sthg** épargner qqch à qqn, éviter qqch à qqn.

spare part *n* pièce *f* détachée OR de rechange.

spare time *n* (*U*) temps *m* libre, loisirs *mpl*.

spare wheel *n* roue *f* de secours.

sparing ['speərɪŋ] *adj* : **to be ~ with** OR **of sthg** être économe de qqch, ménager qqch.

sparingly ['speərɪŋlɪ] *adv* [use] avec modération ; [spend] avec parcimonie.

spark [spɑːk] *n lit* & *fig* étincelle *f*.

sparking plug ['spɑːkɪŋ-] *Br* = **spark plug**.

sparkle ['spɑːkl] ◇ *n* (*U*) [of eyes, jewel] éclat *m* ; [of stars] scintillement *m*. ◇ *vi* étinceler, scintiller.

sparkling wine ['spɑːklɪŋ-] *n* vin *m* mousseux OR pétillant.

spark plug *n* bougie *f*.

sparrow ['spærəʊ] *n* moineau *m*.

sparse [spɑːs] *adj* clairsemé(e), épars(e).

spasm ['spæzm] *n* - **1.** MED spasme *m* ; [of coughing] quinte *f* - **2.** [of emotion] accès *m*.

spastic ['spæstɪk] MED *n* handicapé *m*, -e *f* moteur.

spat [spæt] *pt* & *pp* ▷ **spit**.

spate [speɪt] *n* [of attacks etc] série *f*.

spatter ['spætəʳ] *vt* éclabousser.

spawn [spɔːn] ◇ *n* (*U*) frai *m*, œufs *mpl*.

◇ *vt fig* donner naissance à, engendrer.
◇ *vi* [fish, frog] frayer.

speak [spi:k] (*pt* spoke, *pp* spoken) ◇ *vt*
- **1.** [say] dire - **2.** [language] parler. ◇ *vi*
parler ; **to ~ to** OR **with sb** parler à qqn ; **to
~ to sb about sthg** parler de qqch à qqn ; **to
~ about sb/sthg** parler de qqn/qqch.
➜ **so to speak** *adv* pour ainsi dire.
➜ **speak for** *vt fus* [represent] parler
pour, parler au nom de. ➜ **speak up** *vi*
- **1.** [support] : **to ~ up for sb/sthg** parler en
faveur de qqn/qqch, soutenir qqn/qqch
- **2.** [speak louder] parler plus fort.

speaker ['spi:kə'] *n* - **1.** [person talking]
personne *f* qui parle - **2.** [person making
speech] orateur *m* - **3.** [of language] : **a German ~** une personne qui parle allemand
un(e) germanophone - **4.** [loudspeaker]
haut-parleur *m*.

speaking ['spi:kıŋ] *adv* : **politically ~** politiquement parlant.

spear [spıə'] ◇ *n* lance *f*. ◇ *vt* transpercer d'un coup de lance.

spearhead ['spıəhed] ◇ *n* fer *m* de lance.
◇ *vt* [campaign] mener ; [attack] être le fer
de lance de.

spec [spek] *n Br inf* : **on ~** à tout hasard.

special ['speʃl] *adj* - **1.** [gen] spécial(e)
- **2.** [needs, effort, attention] particulier(ère).

special delivery *n* (*U*) [service] exprès *m*,
envoi *m* par exprès ; **by ~** en exprès.

specialist ['speʃəlıst] ◇ *adj* spécia-
lisé(e). ◇ *n* spécialiste *mf*.

speciality *Br* [,speʃı'ælətı], **specialty**
Am ['speʃltı] *n* spécialité *f*.

specialize, -ise ['speʃəlaız] *vi* : **to ~ (in)** se
spécialiser (dans).

specially ['speʃəlı] *adv* - **1.** [specifically]
spécialement ; [on purpose] exprès - **2.** [par-
ticularly] particulièrement.

specialty *n Am* = speciality.

species ['spi:ʃi:z] (*pl inv*) *n* espèce *f*.

specific [spə'sıfık] *adj* - **1.** [particular] par-
ticulier(ère), précis(e) - **2.** [precise] précis(e)
- **3.** [unique] : **~ to** propre à.

specifically [spə'sıfıklı] *adv* - **1.** [particu-
larly] particulièrement, spécialement
- **2.** [precisely] précisément.

specify ['spesıfaı] *vt* préciser, spécifier.

specimen ['spesımən] *n* - **1.** [example]
exemple *m*, spécimen *m* - **2.** [of blood] prélèvement *m* ; [of urine] échantillon *m*.

speck [spek] *n* - **1.** [small stain] toute petite
tache *f* - **2.** [of dust] grain *m*.

speckled ['spekld] *adj* : **~ (with)** tacheté(e)
de.

specs [speks] *npl inf* [glasses] lunettes *fpl*.

spectacle ['spektəkl] *n* spectacle *m*.
➜ **spectacles** *npl Br* [glasses] lunettes *fpl*.

spectacular [spek'tækjulə'] *adj* spectaculaire.

spectator [spek'teıtə'] *n* spectateur *m*,
-trice *f*.

spectre *Br*, **specter** *Am* ['spektə'] *n* spectre *m*.

spectrum ['spektrəm] (*pl* -tra [-trə]) *n*
- **1.** PHYSICS spectre *m* - **2.** *fig* [variety] gamme
f.

speculation [,spekjʊ'leıʃn] *n* - **1.** [gen]
spéculation *f* - **2.** [conjecture] conjectures
fpl.

sped [sped] *pt* & *pp* ⊳ speed.

speech [spi:tʃ] *n* - **1.** (*U*) [ability] parole *f*
- **2.** [formal talk] discours *m* - **3.** THEATRE
texte *m* - **4.** [manner of speaking] façon *f* de
parler - **5.** [dialect] parler *m*.

speechless ['spi:tʃlıs] *adj* : **~ (with)**
muet(ette) (de).

speed [spi:d] (*pt* & *pp* -ed OR sped) ◇ *n*
vitesse *f* ; [of reply, action] vitesse, rapidité
f. ◇ *vi* - **1.** [move fast] : **to ~ along** aller à
toute allure OR vitesse ; **to ~ away** démarrer
à toute allure - **2.** AUT [go too fast] rouler
trop vite, faire un excès de vitesse.
➜ **speed up** ◇ *vt sep* [person] faire aller
plus vite ; [work, production] accélérer.
◇ *vi* aller plus vite ; [car] accélérer.

speedboat ['spi:dbəʊt] *n* hors-bord *m inv*.

speed bump *n* dos-d'âne *m inv*.

speeding ['spi:dıŋ] *n* (*U*) excès *m* de
vitesse.

speed limit *n* limitation *f* de vitesse.

speedometer [spı'dɒmıtə'] *n* compteur
m (de vitesse).

speedway ['spi:dweı] *n* - **1.** (*U*) SPORT
piste *f* de motos - **2.** *Am* [road] voie *f* express.

speedy ['spi:dı] *adj* rapide.

spell [spel] (*Br pt* & *pp* spelt OR -ed, *Am pt*
& *pp* -ed) ◇ *n* - **1.** [period of time] période
f - **2.** [enchantment] charme *m* ; [words] formule *f* magique ; **to cast** OR **put a ~ on sb** jeter un sort à qqn, envoûter qqn. ◇ *vt*
- **1.** [word, name] écrire - **2.** *fig* [signify] signifier. ◇ *vi* épeler. ➜ **spell out** *vt sep*
- **1.** [read aloud] épeler - **2.** [explain] : **to
~ sthg out (for** OR **to sb)** expliquer qqch clairement (à qqn).

spellbound ['spelbaʊnd] *adj* subjugué(e).

spell-check ◇ *vt* [text, file, document]
vérifier l'orthographe de. ◇ *n* vérification
f orthographique.

spell-checker [-tʃekə^r] *n* correcteur *m* OR vérificateur *m* orthographique.

spelling ['spelɪŋ] *n* orthographe *f*.

spelt [spelt] *Br pt & pp* ▷ **spell**.

spend [spend] (*pt & pp* **spent**) *vt* **- 1.** [pay out] : **to ~ money (on)** dépenser de l'argent (pour) **- 2.** [time, life] passer ; [effort] consacrer.

spendthrift ['spendθrɪft] *n* dépensier *m*, -ère *f*.

spent [spent] ◇ *pt & pp* ▷ **spend**. ◇ *adj* [fuel, match, ammunition] utilisé(e) ; [patience, energy] épuisé(e).

sperm [spɜːm] (*pl inv* OR **-s**) *n* sperme *m*.

spew [spjuː] *vt & vi* vomir.

sphere [sfɪə^r] *n* sphère *f*.

spice [spaɪs] *n* **- 1.** CULIN épice *f* **- 2.** *(U) fig* [excitement] piment *m*.

spick-and-span [,spɪkən'spæn] *adj* impeccable, nickel *(inv)*.

spicy ['spaɪsɪ] *adj* **- 1.** CULIN épicé(e) **- 2.** *fig* [story] pimenté(e), piquant(e).

spider ['spaɪdə^r] *n* araignée *f*.

spike [spaɪk] *n* [metal] pointe *f*, lance *f* ; [of plant] piquant *m* ; [of hair] épi *m*.

spill [spɪl] (*Br pt & pp* **spilt** OR **-ed**, *Am pt & pp* **-ed**) ◇ *vt* renverser. ◇ *vi* [liquid] se répandre.

spilt [spɪlt] *Br pt & pp* ▷ **spill**.

spin [spɪn] (*pt* **span** OR **spun**, *pp* **spun**) ◇ *n* **- 1.** [turn] : **to give sthg a ~** faire tourner qqch **- 2.** AERON vrille *f* **- 3.** *inf* [in car] tour *m* **- 4.** SPORT effet *m*. ◇ *vt* **- 1.** [wheel] faire tourner ; **to ~ a coin** jouer à pile ou face **- 2.** [washing] essorer **- 3.** [thread, wool, cloth] filer **- 4.** SPORT [ball] donner de l'effet à. ◇ *vi* tourner, tournoyer. ◆ **spin out** *vt sep* [money, story] faire durer.

spinach ['spɪnɪdʒ] *n (U)* épinards *mpl*.

spinal column ['spaɪnl-] *n* colonne *f* vertébrale.

spinal cord ['spaɪnl-] *n* moelle *f* épinière.

spindly ['spɪndlɪ] *adj* grêle, chétif(ive).

spin-dryer *n Br* essoreuse *f*.

spine [spaɪn] *n* **- 1.** ANAT colonne *f* vertébrale **- 2.** [of book] dos *m* **- 3.** [of plant, hedgehog] piquant *m*.

spinning ['spɪnɪŋ] *n* [of thread] filage *m*.

spinning top *n* toupie *f*.

spin-off *n* [by-product] dérivé *m*.

spinster ['spɪnstə^r] *n* célibataire *f* ; *pej* vieille fille *f*.

spiral ['spaɪərəl] ◇ *adj* spiral(e). ◇ *n* spirale *f*. ◇ *vi* [staircase, smoke] monter en spirale.

spiral staircase *n* escalier *m* en colimaçon.

spire ['spaɪə^r] *n* flèche *f*.

spirit ['spɪrɪt] *n* **- 1.** [gen] esprit *m* **- 2.** *(U)* [determination] caractère *m*, courage *m*. ◆ **spirits** *npl* **- 1.** [mood] humeur *f* ; **to be in high ~s** être gai(e) ; **to be in low ~s** être déprimé(e) **- 2.** [alcohol] spiritueux *mpl*.

spirited ['spɪrɪtɪd] *adj* fougueux(euse) ; [performance] interprété(e) avec brio.

spirit level *n* niveau *m* à bulle d'air.

spiritual ['spɪrɪtʃʊəl] *adj* spirituel(elle).

spit [spɪt] (*Br pt & pp* **spat**, *Am pt & pp* **spit**) ◇ *n* **- 1.** *(U)* [spittle] crachat *m* ; [saliva] salive *f* **- 2.** [skewer] broche *f*. ◇ *vi* cracher. ◇ *v impers Br* : **it's spitting** il tombe quelques gouttes.

spite [spaɪt] ◇ *n* rancune *f*. ◇ *vt* contrarier. ◆ **in spite of** *prep* en dépit de, malgré.

spiteful ['spaɪtfʊl] *adj* malveillant(e).

spittle ['spɪtl] *n (U)* crachat *m*.

splash [splæʃ] ◇ *n* **- 1.** [sound] plouf *m* **- 2.** [of colour, light] tache *f*. ◇ *vt* éclabousser. ◇ *vi* **- 1.** [person] : **to ~ about** OR **around** barboter **- 2.** [liquid] jaillir. ◆ **splash out** *inf vi* : **to ~ out (on)** dépenser une fortune (pour).

spleen [spliːn] *n* **- 1.** ANAT rate *f* **- 2.** *(U) fig* [anger] mauvaise humeur *f*.

splendid ['splendɪd] *adj* splendide ; [work, holiday, idea] excellent(e).

splint [splɪnt] *n* attelle *f*.

splinter ['splɪntə^r] ◇ *n* éclat *m*. ◇ *vi* [wood] se fendre en éclats ; [glass] se briser en éclats.

split [splɪt] (*pt & pp* **split**, *cont* **-ting**) ◇ *n* **- 1.** [in wood] fente *f* **- 2.** [in garment - tear] déchirure *f* ; [- by design] échancrure *f* **- 3.** POL : **~ (in)** division *f* OR scission *f* (au sein de) **- 4.** [difference] : **~ between** écart *m* entre. ◇ *vt* **- 1.** [wood] fendre ; [clothes] déchirer **- 2.** POL diviser **- 3.** [share] partager ; **to ~ the difference** *fig* couper la poire en deux. ◇ *vi* **- 1.** [wood] se fendre ; [clothes] se déchirer **- 2.** POL se diviser ; [road, path] se séparer. ◆ **split up** *vi* [group, couple] se séparer.

split second *n* fraction *f* de seconde.

splutter ['splʌtə^r] *vi* [person] bredouiller, bafouiller ; [engine] tousser ; [fire] crépiter.

spoil [spɔɪl] (*pt & pp* **-ed** OR **spoilt**) *vt* **- 1.** [ruin - holiday] gâcher, gâter ; [- view] gâter ; [- food] gâter, abîmer **- 2.** [overindulge, treat well] gâter. ◆ **spoils** *npl* butin *m*.

spoiled [spɔɪld] *adj* = **spoilt**.

spoilsport ['spɔɪlspɔːt] *n* trouble-fête *mf inv*.

spoilt [spɔɪlt] <> *pt & pp* ⊳ **spoil**. <> *adj* [child] gâté(e).

spoke [spəʊk] <> *pt* ⊳ **speak**. <> *n* rayon *m*.

spoken ['spəʊkn] *pp* ⊳ **speak**.

spokesman ['spəʊksmən] (*pl* -men [-mən]) *n* porte-parole *m inv*.

spokeswoman ['spəʊks,wʊmən] (*pl* -women [-,wɪmɪn]) *n* porte-parole *m inv*.

sponge [spʌndʒ] (*Br cont* **spongeing**, *Am cont* **sponging**) <> *n* - **1**. [for cleaning, washing] éponge *f* - **2**. [cake] gâteau *m* OR biscuit *m* de Savoie. <> *vt* éponger. <> *vi inf*: **to ~ off sb** taper qqn.

sponge bag *n Br* trousse *f* de toilette.

sponge cake *n* gâteau *m* OR biscuit *m* de Savoie.

sponsor ['spɒnsəʳ] <> *n* sponsor *m*. <> *vt* - **1**. [finance, for charity] sponsoriser, parrainer - **2**. [support] soutenir.

sponsored walk [,spɒnsəd-] *n* marche organisée pour recueillir des fonds.

sponsorship ['spɒnsəʃɪp] *n* sponsoring *m*, parrainage *m*.

spontaneous [spɒn'teɪnjəs] *adj* spontané(e).

spooky ['spuːkɪ] *adj inf* qui donne la chair de poule.

spool [spuːl] *n* [gen & COMPUT] bobine *f*.

spoon [spuːn] *n* cuillère *f*, cuiller *f*.

spoon-feed *vt* nourrir à la cuillère ; **to ~ sb** *fig* mâcher le travail à qqn.

spoonful ['spuːnfʊl] (*pl* -s OR **spoonsful** ['spuːnsfʊl]) *n* cuillerée *f*.

sporadic [spə'rædɪk] *adj* sporadique.

sport [spɔːt] *n* - **1**. [game] sport *m* - **2**. *dated* [cheerful person] chic type *m*/fille *f*.

sporting ['spɔːtɪŋ] *adj* - **1**. [relating to sport] sportif(ive) - **2**. [generous, fair] chic (*inv*) ; **to have a ~ chance of doing sthg** avoir des chances de faire qqch.

sports car ['spɔːts-] *n* voiture *f* de sport.

sports jacket ['spɔːts-] *n* veste *f* sport.

sportsman ['spɔːtsmən] (*pl* -men [-mən]) *n* sportif *m*.

sportsmanship ['spɔːtsmənʃɪp] *n* sportivité *f*, esprit *m* sportif.

sportswear ['spɔːtsweəʳ] *n* (*U*) vêtements *mpl* de sport.

sportswoman ['spɔːts,wʊmən] (*pl* -women [-,wɪmɪn]) *n* sportive *f*.

sporty ['spɔːtɪ] *adj inf* [person] sportif(ive).

spot [spɒt] <> *n* - **1**. [mark, dot] tache *f* - **2**. [pimple] bouton *m* - **3**. [drop] goutte *f* - **4**. *Br inf* [small amount] : **to have a ~ of bother** avoir quelques ennuis - **5**. [place] endroit *m* ; **on the ~** sur place ; **to do sthg on the ~** faire qqch immédiatement OR sur-le-champ - **6**. RADIO & TV numéro *m*. <> *vt* [notice] apercevoir.

spot check *n* contrôle *m* au hasard OR intermittent.

spotless ['spɒtlɪs] *adj* [clean] impeccable.

spotlight ['spɒtlaɪt] *n* [in theatre] projecteur *m*, spot *m* ; [in home] spot *m* ; **to be in the ~** *fig* être en vedette.

spotted ['spɒtɪd] *adj* [pattern, material] à pois.

spotty ['spɒtɪ] *adj Br* [skin] boutonneux(euse).

spouse [spaʊs] *n* époux *m*, épouse *f*.

spout [spaʊt] <> *n* bec *m*. <> *vi*: **to ~ from** OR **out of** jaillir de.

sprain [spreɪn] <> *n* entorse *f*. <> *vt*: **to ~ one's ankle/wrist** se faire une entorse à la cheville/au poignet, se fouler la cheville/le poignet.

sprang [spræŋ] *pt* ⊳ **spring**.

sprawl [sprɔːl] *vi* - **1**. [person] être affalé(e) - **2**. [city] s'étaler.

spray [spreɪ] <> *n* - **1**. (*U*) [of water] gouttelettes *fpl* ; [from sea] embruns *mpl* - **2**. [container] bombe *f*, pulvérisateur *m* - **3**. [of flowers] gerbe *f*. <> *vt* [product] pulvériser ; [plants, crops] pulvériser de l'insecticide sur.

spread [spred] (*pt & pp* **spread**) <> *n* - **1**. (*U*) [food] pâte *f* à tartiner - **2**. [of fire, disease] propagation *f* - **3**. [of opinions] gamme *f*. <> *vt* - **1**. [map, rug] étaler, étendre ; [fingers, arms, legs] écarter - **2**. [butter, jam etc] : **to ~ sthg (over)** étaler qqch (sur) - **3**. [disease, rumour, germs] répandre, propager - **4**. [wealth, work] distribuer, répartir. <> *vi* - **1**. [disease, rumour] se propager, se répandre - **2**. [water, cloud] s'étaler.

➤ **spread out** *vi* se disperser.

spread-eagled [-,iːgld] *adj* affalé(e).

spreadsheet ['spredʃiːt] *n* COMPUT tableur *m*.

spree [spriː] *n* : **to go on a spending** OR **shopping ~** faire des folies.

sprightly ['spraɪtlɪ] *adj* alerte, fringant(e).

spring [sprɪŋ] (*pt* **sprang**, *pp* **sprung**) <> *n* - **1**. [season] printemps *m* ; **in ~** au printemps - **2**. [coil] ressort *m* - **3**. [water source] source *f*. <> *vi* - **1**. [jump] sauter, bondir - **2**. [originate] : **to ~ from** provenir de.

spring up *vi* [problem] surgir, se présenter ; [friendship] naître ; [wind] se lever.

springboard ['sprɪŋbɔːd] *n lit & fig* tremplin *m*.

spring-clean *vt* nettoyer de fond en comble.

spring onion *n Br* ciboule *f*.

springtime ['sprɪŋtaɪm] *n* : **in (the) ~** au printemps.

springy ['sprɪŋɪ] *adj* [carpet] moelleux (euse) ; [mattress, rubber] élastique.

sprinkle ['sprɪŋkl] *vt* : **to ~ water over** OR **on sthg, to ~ sthg with water** asperger qqch d'eau ; **to ~ salt** *etc* **over** OR **on sthg, to ~ sthg with salt** *etc* saupoudrer qqch de sel *etc*.

sprinkler ['sprɪŋkləʳ] *n* [for water] arroseur *m*.

sprint [sprɪnt] <> *n* sprint *m*. <> *vi* sprinter.

sprout [spraʊt] <> *n* **- 1.** [vegetable] : **(Brussels) ~s** choux *mpl* de Bruxelles **- 2.** [shoot] pousse *f*. <> *vt* [leaves] produire ; **to ~ shoots** germer. <> *vi* [grow] pousser.

spruce [spruːs] <> *adj* net (nette), pimpant(e). <> *n* épicéa *m*. **spruce up** *vt sep* astiquer, briquer.

sprung [sprʌŋ] *pp* spring.

spry [spraɪ] *adj* vif (vive).

spun [spʌn] *pt & pp* spin.

spur [spɜːʳ] <> *n* **- 1.** [incentive] incitation *f* **- 2.** [on rider's boot] éperon *m*. <> *vt* [encourage] : **to ~ sb to do sthg** encourager OR inciter qqn à faire qqch. **on the spur of the moment** *adv* sur un coup de tête, sous l'impulsion du moment. **spur on** *vt sep* encourager.

spurious ['spʊərɪəs] *adj* **- 1.** [affection, interest] feint(e) **- 2.** [argument, logic] faux (fausse).

spurn [spɜːn] *vt* repousser.

spurt [spɜːt] <> *n* **- 1.** [gush] jaillissement *m* **- 2.** [of activity, energy] sursaut *m* **- 3.** [burst of speed] accélération *f*. <> *vi* [gush] : **to ~ (out of** OR **from)** jaillir (de).

spy [spaɪ] <> *n* espion *m*. <> *vt inf* apercevoir. <> *vi* espionner, faire de l'espionnage ; **to ~ on sb** espionner qqn.

spying ['spaɪɪŋ] *n (U)* espionnage *m*.

Sq., sq. *abbr of* **square**.

squabble ['skwɒbl] <> *n* querelle *f*. <> *vi* : **to ~ (about** OR **over)** se quereller (à propos de).

squad [skwɒd] *n* **- 1.** [of police] brigade *f* **- 2.** MIL peloton *m* **- 3.** SPORT [group of play-

ers] équipe *f (parmi laquelle la sélection sera faite)*.

squadron ['skwɒdrən] *n* escadron *m*.

squalid ['skwɒlɪd] *adj* sordide, ignoble.

squall [skwɔːl] *n* [storm] bourrasque *f*.

squalor ['skwɒləʳ] *n (U)* conditions *fpl* sordides.

squander ['skwɒndəʳ] *vt* gaspiller.

square [skweəʳ] <> *adj* **- 1.** [in shape] carré(e) ; **one ~ metre** *Br* un mètre carré ; **three metres ~** trois mètres sur trois **- 2.** [not owing money] : **to be ~** être quitte. <> *n* **- 1.** [shape] carré *m* **- 2.** [in town] place *f* **- 3.** *inf* [unfashionable person] : **he's a ~** il est vieux jeu. <> *vt* **- 1.** MATH élever au carré **- 2.** [reconcile] accorder. **square up** *vi* [settle up] : **to ~ up with sb** régler ses comptes avec qqn.

squarely ['skweəlɪ] *adv* **- 1.** [directly] carrément **- 2.** [honestly] honnêtement.

square meal *n* bon repas *m*.

squash [skwɒʃ] <> *n* **- 1.** SPORT squash *m* **- 2.** *Br* [drink] : **orange ~** orangeade *f* **- 3.** *Am* [vegetable] courge *f*. <> *vt* écraser.

squat [skwɒt] <> *adj* courtaud(e), ramassé(e). <> *vi* [crouch] : **to ~ (down)** s'accroupir.

squatter ['skwɒtəʳ] *n* squatter *m*.

squawk [skwɔːk] *n* cri *m* strident OR perçant.

squeak [skwiːk] *n* **- 1.** [of animal] petit cri *m* aigu **- 2.** [of door, hinge] grincement *m*.

squeal [skwiːl] *vi* [person, animal] pousser des cris aigus.

squeamish ['skwiːmɪʃ] *adj* facilement dégoûté(e).

squeeze [skwiːz] <> *n* [pressure] pression *f*. <> *vt* **- 1.** [press firmly] presser **- 2.** [liquid, toothpaste] exprimer **- 3.** [cram] : **to ~ sthg into sthg** entasser qqch dans qqch.

squelch [skweltʃ] *vi* : **to ~ through mud** patauger dans la boue.

squid [skwɪd] *(pl inv* OR **-s)** *n* calmar *m*.

squiggle ['skwɪgl] *n* gribouillis *m*.

squint [skwɪnt] <> *n* : **to have a ~** loucher, être atteint(e) de strabisme. <> *vi* : **to ~ at sthg** regarder qqch en plissant les yeux.

squire ['skwaɪəʳ] *n* [landowner] propriétaire *m*.

squirm [skwɜːm] *vi* [wriggle] se tortiller.

squirrel [*Br* 'skwɪrəl, *Am* 'skwɜːrəl] *n* écureuil *m*.

squirt [skwɜːt] <> *vt* [water, oil] faire jaillir, faire gicler. <> *vi* : **to ~ (out of)** jaillir (de), gicler (de).

Sr *abbr of* senior.

Sri Lanka [ˌsriːˈlæŋkə] *n* Sri Lanka *m*.

St - 1. (*abbr of* **saint**) St, Ste **- 2.** *abbr of* Street.

stab [stæb] ◇ *n* **- 1.** [with knife] coup *m* de couteau **- 2.** *inf* [attempt] **: to have a ~ (at sthg)** essayer (qqch), tenter (qqch) **- 3.** [twinge] **: ~ of pain** élancement *m* **; ~ of guilt** remords *m*. ◇ *vt* **- 1.** [person] poignarder **- 2.** [food] piquer.

stable [ˈsteɪbl] ◇ *adj* stable. ◇ *n* écurie *f*.

stack [stæk] ◇ *n* [pile] pile *f*. ◇ *vt* [pile up] empiler.

stadium [ˈsteɪdjəm] (*pl* **-diums** OR **-dia** [-djə]) *n* stade *m*.

staff [stɑːf] ◇ *n* [employees] personnel *m* ; [of school] personnel enseignant, professeurs *mpl*. ◇ *vt* pourvoir en personnel.

stag [stæg] (*pl inv* OR **-s**) *n* cerf *m*.

stage [steɪdʒ] ◇ *n* **- 1.** [phase] étape *f*, phase *f*, stade *m* **- 2.** [platform] scène *f* **- 3.** [acting profession] **: the ~** le théâtre. ◇ *vt* **- 1.** THEATRE monter, mettre en scène **- 2.** [organize] organiser.

stagecoach [ˈsteɪdʒkəʊtʃ] *n* diligence *f*.

stage fright *n* trac *m*.

stage-manage *vt lit & fig* mettre en scène.

stagger [ˈstægər] ◇ *vt* **- 1.** [astound] stupéfier **- 2.** [working hours] échelonner ; [holidays] étaler. ◇ *vi* tituber.

stagnant [ˈstægnənt] *adj* stagnant(e).

stagnate [stægˈneɪt] *vi* stagner.

stag party *n* soirée *f* entre hommes ; [before wedding] soirée où un futur marié enterre sa vie de garçon avec ses amis.

staid [steɪd] *adj* guindé(e), collet monté.

stain [steɪn] ◇ *n* [mark] tache *f*. ◇ *vt* [discolour] tacher.

stained glass [ˌsteɪnd-] *n* (U) [windows] vitraux *mpl*.

stainless steel [ˈsteɪnlɪs-] *n* acier *m* inoxydable, Inox® *m*.

stain remover [-ˌrɪmuːvər] *n* détachant *m*.

stair [steər] *n* marche *f*. ◆ **stairs** *npl* escalier *m*.

staircase [ˈsteəkeɪs] *n* escalier *m*.

stairway [ˈsteəweɪ] *n* escalier *m*.

stairwell [ˈsteəwel] *n* cage *f* d'escalier.

stake [steɪk] ◇ *n* **- 1.** [share] **: to have a ~ in sthg** avoir des intérêts dans qqch **- 2.** [wooden post] poteau *m* **- 3.** [in gambling] enjeu *m*. ◇ *vt* **: to ~ money (on** OR

upon) jouer OR miser de l'argent (sur) ; **to ~ one's reputation (on)** jouer OR risquer sa réputation (sur). ◆ **at stake** *adv* en jeu.

stale [steɪl] *adj* [food, water] pas frais (fraîche) ; [bread] rassis(e) ; [air] qui sent le renfermé.

stalemate [ˈsteɪlmeɪt] *n* **- 1.** [deadlock] impasse *f* **- 2.** CHESS pat *m*.

stalk [stɔːk] ◇ *n* **- 1.** [of flower, plant] tige *f* **- 2.** [of leaf, fruit] queue *f*. ◇ *vt* [hunt] traquer. ◇ *vi* **: to ~ in/out** entrer/sortir d'un air hautain.

stall [stɔːl] ◇ *n* **- 1.** [in street, market] éventaire *m*, étal *m* ; [at exhibition] stand *m* **- 2.** [in stable] stalle *f*. ◇ *vt* AUT caler. ◇ *vi* **- 1.** AUT caler **- 2.** [delay] essayer de gagner du temps. ◆ **stalls** *npl Br* [in cinema, theatre] orchestre *m*.

stallion [ˈstæljən] *n* étalon *m*.

stalwart [ˈstɔːlwət] *n* pilier *m*.

stamina [ˈstæmɪnə] *n* (U) résistance *f*.

stammer [ˈstæmər] ◇ *n* bégaiement *m*. ◇ *vi* bégayer.

stamp [stæmp] ◇ *n* **- 1.** [for letter] timbre *m* **- 2.** [tool] tampon *m* **- 3.** *fig* [of authority etc] marque *f*. ◇ *vt* **- 1.** [mark by stamping] tamponner **- 2.** [stomp] **: to ~ one's foot** taper du pied. ◇ *vi* **- 1.** [stomp] taper du pied **- 2.** [tread heavily] **: to ~ on sthg** marcher sur qqch.

stamp album *n* album *m* de timbres.

stamp-collecting [-kəˌlektɪŋ] *n* philatélie *f*.

stamped addressed envelope [ˈstæmptəˌdrest-] *n Br* enveloppe *f* affranchie pour la réponse.

stampede [stæmˈpiːd] *n* débandade *f*.

stance [stæns] *n lit & fig* position *f*.

stand [stænd] (*pt & pp* **stood**) ◇ *n* **- 1.** [stall] stand *m* ; [selling newspapers] kiosque *m* **- 2.** [supporting object] **: umbrella ~** porte-parapluies *m inv* ; **hat ~** porte-chapeaux *m inv* **- 3.** SPORT tribune *f* **- 4.** MIL résistance *f* ; **to make a ~** résister **- 5.** [public position] position *f* **- 6.** *Am* JUR barre *f*. ◇ *vt* **- 1.** [place] mettre (debout), poser (debout) **- 2.** [withstand, tolerate] supporter. ◇ *vi* **- 1.** [be upright - person] être OR se tenir debout ; [- object] se trouver ; [- building] se dresser ; **~ still!** ne bouge pas!, reste tranquille! **- 2.** [stand up] se lever **- 3.** [liquid] reposer **- 4.** [offer] tenir toujours ; [decision] demeurer valable **- 5.** [be in particular state] **: as things ~ ...** vu l'état actuel des choses ... **- 6.** *Br* POL se présenter **- 7.** *Am* [park car] **: 'no ~ing'** 'stationnement interdit'. ◆ **stand back** *vi* reculer. ◆ **stand**

by ◇ *vt fus* - **1.** [person] soutenir - **2.** [statement, decision] s'en tenir à. ◇ *vi* - **1.** [in readiness] : **to ~ by (for sthg/to do sthg)** être prêt(e) (pour qqch/pour faire qqch) - **2.** [remain inactive] rester là. ◆ **stand down** *vi* [resign] démissionner. ◆ **stand for** *vt fus* - **1.** [signify] représenter - **2.** [tolerate] supporter, tolérer. ◆ **stand in** *vi* : **to ~ in for sb** remplacer qqn. ◆ **stand out** *vi* ressortir. ◆ **stand up** ◇ *vt sep inf* [boyfriend, girlfriend] poser un lapin à. ◇ *vi* [rise from seat] se lever ; **~ up!** debout! ◆ **stand up for** *vt fus* défendre. ◆ **stand up to** *vt fus* - **1.** [weather, heat etc] résister à - **2.** [person, boss] tenir tête à.

standard ['stændəd] ◇ *adj* - **1.** [normal - gen] normal(e) ; [- size] standard (*inv*) - **2.** [accepted] correct(e). ◇ *n* - **1.** [level] niveau *m* - **2.** [point of reference] critère *m* ; TECH norme *f* - **3.** [flag] étendard *m*. ◆ **standards** *npl* [principles] valeurs *fpl*.

standard lamp *n Br* lampadaire *m*.

standard of living (*pl* standards of living) *n* niveau *m* de vie.

standby ['stændbaɪ] (*pl* -s) ◇ *n* [person] remplaçant *m*, -e *f* ; **on ~** prêt à intervenir. ◇ *comp* [ticket, flight] stand-by (*inv*).

stand-in *n* remplaçant *m*, -e *f*.

standing ['stændɪŋ] ◇ *adj* [invitation, army] permanent(e) ; [joke] continuel(elle). ◇ *n* - **1.** [reputation] importance *f*, réputation *f* - **2.** [duration] : **of long ~** de longue date ; **we're friends of 20 years' ~** nous sommes amis depuis 20 ans.

standing order *n Br* prélèvement *m* automatique.

standing room *n* (*U*) places *fpl* debout.

standoffish [ˌstænd'ɒfɪʃ] *adj* distant(e).

standpoint ['stændpɔɪnt] *n* point *m* de vue.

standstill ['stændstɪl] *n* : **at a ~** [traffic, train] à l'arrêt ; [negotiations, work] paralysé(e) ; **to come to a ~** [traffic, train] s'immobiliser ; [negotiations, work] cesser.

stank [stæŋk] *pt* ▷ stink.

staple ['steɪpl] ◇ *adj* [principal] principal(e), de base. ◇ *n* - **1.** [for paper] agrafe *f* - **2.** [principal commodity] produit *m* de base. ◇ *vt* agrafer.

stapler ['steɪplər] *n* agrafeuse *f*.

star [stɑːr] ◇ *n* - **1.** [gen] étoile *f* - **2.** [celebrity] vedette *f*, star *f*. ◇ *comp* [quality] de star ; **~ performer** vedette *f*. ◇ *vi* : **to ~ (in)** être la vedette (de). ◆ **stars** *npl* horoscope *m*.

starboard ['stɑːbəd] ◇ *adj* de tribord. ◇ *n* : **to ~** à tribord.

starch [stɑːtʃ] *n* amidon *m*.

stardom ['stɑːdəm] *n* (*U*) célébrité *f*.

stare [steər] ◇ *n* regard *m* fixe. ◇ *vi* : **to ~ at sb/sthg** fixer qqn/qqch du regard.

stark [stɑːk] ◇ *adj* - **1.** [room, decoration] austère ; [landscape] désolé(e) - **2.** [reality, fact] à l'état brut ; [contrast] dur(e). ◇ *adv* : **~ naked** tout nu (toute nue), à poil.

starling ['stɑːlɪŋ] *n* étourneau *m*.

starry ['stɑːrɪ] *adj* étoilé(e).

starry-eyed [-'aɪd] *adj* innocent(e).

Stars and Stripes *n* : **the ~** le drapeau des États-Unis, la bannière étoilée.

start [stɑːt] ◇ *n* - **1.** [beginning] début *m* - **2.** [jump] sursaut *m* - **3.** [starting place] départ *m* - **4.** [time advantage] avance *f*. ◇ *vt* - **1.** [begin] commencer ; **to ~ doing** OR **to do sthg** commencer à faire qqch - **2.** [turn on - machine] mettre en marche ; [- engine, vehicle] démarrer, mettre en marche - **3.** [set up - business, band] créer. ◇ *vi* - **1.** [begin] commencer, débuter ; **to ~ with** pour commencer, d'abord - **2.** [function - machine] se mettre en marche ; [- car] démarrer - **3.** [begin journey] partir - **4.** [jump] sursauter. ◆ **start off** *vt sep* [meeting] ouvrir, commencer ; [rumour] faire naître ; [discussion] entamer, commencer. ◇ *vi* - **1.** [begin] commencer ; [begin job] débuter - **2.** [leave on journey] partir. ◆ **start out** *vi* - **1.** [in job] débuter - **2.** [leave on journey] partir. ◆ **start up** ◇ *vt sep* - **1.** [business] créer ; [shop] ouvrir - **2.** [car, engine] mettre en marche. ◇ *vi* - **1.** [begin] commencer - **2.** [machine] se mettre en route ; [car, engine] démarrer.

starter ['stɑːtər] *n* - **1.** *Br* [of meal] hors-d'œuvre *m inv* - **2.** AUT démarreur *m* - **3.** [to begin race] starter *m*.

starting point ['stɑːtɪŋ-] *n* point *m* de départ.

startle ['stɑːtl] *vt* faire sursauter.

startling ['stɑːtlɪŋ] *adj* surprenant(e).

start-up *n* (*U*) - **1.** [launch] création *f* (d'entreprise) ; **~ costs** frais *mpl* de création d'une entreprise - **2.** [new company] start-up *f*.

starvation [stɑː'veɪʃn] *n* faim *f*.

starve [stɑːv] ◇ *vt* [deprive of food] affamer. ◇ *vi* - **1.** [have no food] être affamé(e) ; **to ~ to death** mourir de faim - **2.** *inf* [be hungry] avoir très faim, crever OR mourir de faim.

state [steɪt] ◇ *n* état *m* ; **to be in a ~** être dans tous ses états. ◇ *comp* d'État. ◇ *vt* - **1.** [express - reason] donner ; [- name and address] décliner ; **to ~ that ...** déclarer que

... - **2.** [specify] préciser. ➧ **State** *n* : the State l'État *m*. ➧ **States** *npl inf* : the States les États-Unis *mpl*.

State Department *n Am* ≃ ministère *m* des Affaires étrangères.

stately ['steɪtlɪ] *adj* majestueux(euse).

statement ['steɪtmənt] *n* - **1.** [declaration] déclaration *f* - **2.** JUR déposition *f* - **3.** [from bank] relevé *m* de compte.

state of mind (*pl* states of mind) *n* humeur *f*.

statesman ['steɪtsmən] (*pl* -men [-mən]) *n* homme *m* d'État.

static ['stætɪk] ◇ *adj* statique. ◇ *n* (U) parasites *mpl*.

static electricity *n* électricité *f* statique.

station ['steɪʃn] ◇ *n* - **1.** RAIL gare *f* ; [for buses, coaches] gare routière - **2.** RADIO station *f* - **3.** [building] poste *m* - **4.** *fml* [rank] rang *m*. ◇ *vt* - **1.** [position] placer, poster - **2.** MIL poster.

stationary ['steɪʃnərɪ] *adj* immobile.

stationer ['steɪʃnər] *n* papetier *m*, -ère *f* ; **~'s (shop)** papeterie *f*.

stationery ['steɪʃnərɪ] *n* (U) [equipment] fournitures *fpl* de bureau ; [paper] papier *m* à lettres.

stationmaster ['steɪʃn,mɑːstər] *n* chef *m* de gare.

station wagon *n Am* break *m*.

statistic [stə'tɪstɪk] *n* statistique *f*. ➧ **statistics** *n* (U) [science] statistique *f*.

statistical [stə'tɪstɪkl] *adj* statistique ; [expert] en statistiques ; [report] de statistiques.

statue ['stætʃuː] *n* statue *f*.

stature ['stætʃər] *n* - **1.** [height, size] stature *f*, taille *f* - **2.** [importance] envergure *f*.

status ['steɪtəs] *n* (U) - **1.** [legal or social position] statut *m* - **2.** [prestige] prestige *m*.

status symbol *n* signe *m* extérieur de richesse.

statute ['stætjuːt] *n* loi *f*.

statutory ['stætjʊtrɪ] *adj* statutaire.

staunch [stɔːntʃ] ◇ *adj* loyal(e). ◇ *vt* [flow] arrêter ; [blood] étancher.

stave [steɪv] (*pt & pp* -d OR stove) *n* MUS portée *f*. ➧ **stave off** *vt sep* [disaster, defeat] éviter ; [hunger] tromper.

stay [steɪ] ◇ *vi* - **1.** [not move away] rester - **2.** [as visitor - with friends] passer quelques jours ; [- in town, country] séjourner ; **to ~ in a hotel** descendre à l'hôtel - **3.** [continue, remain] rester, demeurer ; **to ~ out of** sthg ne pas se mêler de qqch. ◇ *n* [visit] séjour *m*. ➧ **stay in** *vi* rester chez soi, ne

pas sortir. ➧ **stay on** *vi* rester (plus long-temps). ➧ **stay out** *vi* [from home] ne pas rentrer. ➧ **stay up** *vi* ne pas se coucher, veiller ; **to ~ up late** se coucher tard.

staying power ['steɪɪŋ-] *n* endurance *f*.

stead [sted] *n* : **to stand sb in good ~** être utile à qqn.

steadfast ['stedfɑːst] *adj* ferme, résolu(e) ; [supporter] loyal(e).

steadily ['stedɪlɪ] *adv* - **1.** [gradually] progressivement - **2.** [regularly - breathe] régulièrement ; [- move] sans arrêt - **3.** [calmly] de manière imperturbable.

steady ['stedɪ] ◇ *adj* - **1.** [gradual] progressif(ive) - **2.** [regular] régulier(ère) - **3.** [not shaking] ferme - **4.** [calm - voice] calme ; [- stare] imperturbable - **5.** [stable - job, relationship] stable - **6.** [sensible] sérieux(euse). ◇ *vt* - **1.** [stop from shaking] empêcher de bouger ; **to ~ o.s.** se remettre d'aplomb - **2.** [control - nerves] calmer.

steak [steɪk] *n* steak *m*, bifteck *m* ; [of fish] darne *f*.

steal [stiːl] (*pt* stole, *pp* stolen) ◇ *vt* voler, dérober. ◇ *vi* [move secretly] se glisser.

stealthy ['stelθɪ] *adj* furtif(ive).

steam [stiːm] ◇ *n* (U) vapeur *f*. ◇ *vt* CULIN cuire à la vapeur. ◇ *vi* [give off steam] fumer. ➧ **steam up** ◇ *vt sep* [mist up] embuer. ◇ *vi* se couvrir de buée.

steamboat ['stiːmbəʊt] *n* (bateau *m* à) vapeur *m*.

steam engine *n* locomotive *f* à vapeur.

steamer ['stiːmər] *n* [ship] (bateau *m* à) vapeur *m*.

steamroller ['stiːm,rəʊlər] *n* rouleau *m* compresseur.

steamy ['stiːmɪ] *adj* - **1.** [full of steam] embué(e) - **2.** *inf* [erotic] érotique.

steel [stiːl] ◇ *n* (U) acier *m*. ◇ *comp* en acier, d'acier.

steelworks ['stiːlwɜːks] (*pl inv*) *n* aciérie *f*.

steep [stiːp] *adj* - **1.** [hill, road] raide, abrupt(e) - **2.** [increase, decline] énorme - **3.** *inf* [expensive] excessif(ive).

steeple ['stiːpl] *n* clocher *m*, flèche *f*.

steeplechase ['stiːpltʃeɪs] *n* - **1.** [horse race] steeple-chase *m* - **2.** [athletics race] steeple *m*.

steer ['stɪər] ◇ *n* bœuf *m*. ◇ *vt* - **1.** [ship] gouverner ; [car, aeroplane] conduire, diriger - **2.** [person] diriger, guider. ◇ *vi* : **to ~ well** [ship] gouverner bien ; [car] être facile à manœuvrer ; **to ~ clear of sb/sthg** éviter qqn/qqch.

steering ['stɪərɪŋ] *n (U)* direction *f*.

steering wheel *n* volant *m*.

stem [stem] ◇ *n* - **1.** [of plant] tige *f* - **2.** [of glass] pied *m* - **3.** [of pipe] tuyau *m* - **4.** GRAMM radical *m*. ◇ *vt* [stop] arrêter.

◆ **stem from** *vt fus* provenir de.

stench [stentʃ] *n* puanteur *f*.

stencil ['stensl] ◇ *n* pochoir *m*. ◇ *vt* faire au pochoir.

stenographer [stə'nɒɡrəfər] *n Am* sténographe *mf*.

step [step] ◇ *n* - **1.** [pace] pas *m* ; **in/out of** ~ **with** *fig* en accord/désaccord avec - **2.** [action] mesure *f* - **3.** [stage] étape *f* ; ~ **by** ~ petit à petit, progressivement - **4.** [stair] marche *f* - **5.** [of ladder] barreau *m*, échelon *m*. ◇ *vi* - **1.** [move foot] : **to** ~ **forward** avancer ; **to** ~ **off** OR **down from sthg** descendre de qqch ; **to** ~ **back** reculer - **2.** [tread] : **to** ~ **on/in sthg** marcher sur/dans qqch.

◆ **steps** *npl* - **1.** [stairs] marches *fpl* - **2.** *Br* [stepladder] escabeau *m*. ◆ **step down** *vi* [leave job] démissionner. ◆ **step in** *vi* intervenir. ◆ **step up** *vt sep* intensifier.

stepbrother ['step,brʌðər] *n* demi-frère *m*.

stepdaughter ['step,dɔːtər] *n* belle-fille *f*.

stepfather ['step,fɑːðər] *n* beau-père *m*.

stepladder ['step,lædər] *n* escabeau *m*.

stepmother ['step,mʌðər] *n* belle-mère *f*.

stepping-stone ['stepɪŋ-] *n* pierre *f* de gué ; *fig* tremplin *m*.

stepsister ['step,sɪstər] *n* demi-sœur *f*.

stepson ['stepsʌn] *n* beau-fils *m*.

stereo ['steriəʊ] *(pl* -s) ◇ *adj* stéréo *(inv)*. ◇ *n* - **1.** [appliance] chaîne *f* stéréo - **2.** [sound] : **in** ~ en stéréo.

stereotype ['steriətaip] *n* stéréotype *m*.

sterile ['sterail] *adj* stérile.

sterilize, -ise ['sterəlaiz] *vt* stériliser.

sterling ['stɜːlɪŋ] ◇ *adj* - **1.** [of British money] sterling *(inv)* - **2.** [excellent] exceptionnel(elle). ◇ *n (U)* livre *f* sterling.

sterling silver *n* argent *m* fin.

stern [stɜːn] ◇ *adj* sévère. ◇ *n* NAUT arrière *m*.

steroid ['stɪərɔid] *n* stéroïde *m*.

stethoscope ['steθəskəʊp] *n* stéthoscope *m*.

stew [stjuː] ◇ *n* ragoût *m*. ◇ *vt* [meat] cuire en ragoût ; [fruit] faire cuire.

steward ['stjʊəd] *n* - **1.** [on plane, ship, train] steward *m* - **2.** *Br* [at demonstration, meeting] membre *m* du service d'ordre.

stewardess ['stjʊədɪs] *n* hôtesse *f*.

stick [stɪk] *(pt & pp* **stuck)** ◇ *n* - **1.** [of wood, dynamite, candy] bâton *m* - **2.** [walking stick] canne *f* - **3.** SPORT crosse *f*. ◇ *vt* - **1.** [push] : **to** ~ **sthg in** OR **into** planter qqch dans - **2.** [with glue, adhesive tape] : **to** ~ **sthg (on** OR **to)** coller qqch (sur) - **3.** *inf* [put] mettre - **4.** *Br inf* [tolerate] supporter. ◇ *vi* - **1.** [adhere] : **to** ~ **(to)** coller (à) - **2.** [jam] se coincer. ◆ **stick out** ◇ *vt sep* - **1.** [head] sortir ; [hand] tendre ; [tongue] tirer - **2.** *inf* [endure] : **to** ~ **it out** tenir le coup. ◇ *vi* - **1.** [protrude] dépasser - **2.** *inf* [be noticeable] se remarquer. ◆ **stick to** *vt fus* - **1.** [follow closely] suivre - **2.** [principles] rester fidèle à ; [decision] s'en tenir à ; [promise] tenir. ◆ **stick up** *vi* dépasser. ◆ **stick up for** *vt fus* défendre.

sticker ['stɪkər] *n* [label] autocollant *m*.

sticking plaster ['stɪkɪŋ-] *n Br* sparadrap *m*.

stickler ['stɪklər] *n* : **to be a** ~ **for** être à cheval sur.

stick shift *n Am* levier *m* de vitesses.

stick-up *n inf* vol *m* à main armée.

sticky ['stɪki] *adj* - **1.** [hands, sweets] poisseux(euse) ; [label, tape] adhésif(ive) - **2.** *inf* [awkward] délicat(e).

stiff [stɪf] ◇ *adj* - **1.** [rod, paper, material] rigide ; [shoes, brush] dur(e) ; [fabric] raide - **2.** [door, drawer, window] dur(e) (à ouvrir/fermer) ; [joint] ankylosé(e) ; **to have a** ~ **back** avoir des courbatures dans le dos ; **to have a** ~ **neck** avoir le torticolis - **3.** [formal] guindé(e) - **4.** [severe - penalty] sévère ; [- resistance] tenace ; [- competition] serré(e) - **5.** [difficult - task] difficile. ◇ *adv inf* : **to be bored** ~ s'ennuyer à mourir ; **to be frozen/scared** ~ mourir de froid/peur.

stiffen ['stɪfn] ◇ *vt* - **1.** [material] raidir ; [with starch] empeser - **2.** [resolve] renforcer. ◇ *vi* - **1.** [body] se raidir ; [joints] s'ankyloser - **2.** [competition, resistance] s'intensifier.

stifle ['staifl] *vt & vi* étouffer.

stifling ['staiflɪŋ] *adj* étouffant(e).

stigma ['stɪɡmə] *n* - **1.** [disgrace] honte *f*, stigmate *m* - **2.** BOT stigmate *m*.

stile [stail] *n* échalier *m*.

stiletto heel [stɪ'letəʊ-] *n Br* talon *m* aiguille.

still [stɪl] ◇ *adv* - **1.** [up to now, up to then] encore, toujours ; **I've** ~ **got £5 left** il me reste encore 5 livres - **2.** [even now] encore - **3.** [nevertheless] tout de même - **4.** *(with comparatives)* : ~ **bigger/more important** encore plus grand/plus important. ◇ *adj* - **1.** [not moving] immobile - **2.** [calm] calme, tranquille - **3.** [not windy] sans vent - **4.** [not fizzy - gen] non

gazeux(euse) ; [- mineral water] plat(e).
◇ n - 1. PHOT photo f - 2. [for making alcohol] alambic m.

stillborn ['stɪlbɔːn] adj mort-né(e).

still life (pl -s) n nature f morte.

stilted ['stɪltɪd] adj emprunté(e), qui manque de naturel.

stilts ['stɪlts] npl - 1. [for person] échasses fpl - 2. [for building] pilotis mpl.

stimulate ['stɪmjʊleɪt] vt stimuler.

stimulating ['stɪmjʊleɪtɪŋ] adj stimulant(e).

stimulus ['stɪmjʊləs] (pl -li [-laɪ]) n - 1. [encouragement] stimulant m - 2. BIOL & PSYCH stimulus m.

sting [stɪŋ] (pt & pp stung) ◇ n - 1. [by bee] piqûre f ; [of bee] dard m - 2. [sharp pain] brûlure f. ◇ vt [gen] piquer. ◇ vi piquer.

stingy ['stɪndʒɪ] adj inf radin(e).

stink [stɪŋk] (pt stank OR stunk, pp stunk) ◇ n puanteur f. ◇ vi [smell] puer, empester.

stinking ['stɪŋkɪŋ] inf adj [cold] gros (grosse) ; [weather] pourri(e) ; [place] infect(e).

stint [stɪnt] ◇ n [period of work] part f de travail. ◇ vi : to ~ on lésiner sur.

stipulate ['stɪpjʊleɪt] vt stipuler.

stir [stɜːʳ] ◇ n [public excitement] sensation f. ◇ vt - 1. [mix] remuer - 2. [move gently] agiter - 3. [move emotionally] émouvoir. ◇ vi bouger, remuer. ◆ **stir up** vt sep - 1. [dust] soulever - 2. [trouble] provoquer ; [resentment, dissatisfaction] susciter ; [rumour] faire naître.

stirrup ['stɪrəp] n étrier m.

stitch [stɪtʃ] ◇ n - 1. SEWING point m ; [in knitting] maille f - 2. MED point m de suture - 3. [stomach pain] : to have a ~ avoir un point de côté. ◇ vt - 1. SEWING coudre - 2. MED suturer.

stoat [stəʊt] n hermine f.

stock [stɒk] ◇ n - 1. [supply] réserve f - 2. (U) COMM stock m, réserve f ; in ~ en stock ; out of ~ épuisé(e) - 3. FIN valeurs fpl ; ~s and shares titres mpl - 4. [ancestry] souche f - 5. CULIN bouillon m - 6. [livestock] cheptel m - 7. phr : to take ~ (of) faire le point (de). ◇ adj classique. ◇ vt - 1. COMM vendre, avoir en stock - 2. [fill - shelves] garnir. ◆ **stock up** vi : to ~ up (with) faire des provisions (de).

stockbroker ['stɒk,brəʊkəʳ] n agent m de change.

stock cube n Br bouillon-cube m.

stock exchange n Bourse f.

stockholder ['stɒk,həʊldəʳ] n Am actionnaire mf.

Stockholm ['stɒkhəʊm] n Stockholm.

stocking ['stɒkɪŋ] n [for woman] bas m.

stockist ['stɒkɪst] n Br dépositaire m, stockiste m.

stock market n Bourse f.

stock phrase n cliché m.

stockpile ['stɒkpaɪl] ◇ n stock m. ◇ vt [weapons] amasser ; [food] stocker.

stocktaking ['stɒk,teɪkɪŋ] n (U) inventaire m.

stocky ['stɒkɪ] adj trapu(e).

stodgy ['stɒdʒɪ] adj [food] lourd(e) (à digérer).

stoical ['stəʊɪkl] adj stoïque.

stoke [stəʊk] vt [fire] entretenir.

stole [stəʊl] ◇ pt ⊳ **steal**. ◇ n étole f.

stolen ['stəʊln] pp ⊳ **steal**.

stolid ['stɒlɪd] adj impassible.

stomach ['stʌmək] ◇ n [organ] estomac m ; [abdomen] ventre m. ◇ vt [tolerate] encaisser, supporter.

stomachache ['stʌməkeɪk] n : to have ~ Br, to have a ~ Am avoir mal au ventre.

stomach upset n embarras m gastrique.

stone [stəʊn] (pl sense 3 only, inv OR -s) ◇ n - 1. [rock] pierre f ; [smaller] caillou m - 2. [seed] noyau m - 3. Br [unit of measurement] = 6,348 kg. ◇ comp de OR en pierre. ◇ vt [person, car etc] jeter des pierres sur.

stone-cold adj complètement froid(e) OR glacé(e).

stonewashed ['stəʊnwɒʃt] adj délavé(e).

stonework ['stəʊnwɜːk] n maçonnerie f.

stood [stʊd] pt & pp ⊳ **stand**.

stool [stuːl] n [seat] tabouret m.

stoop [stuːp] ◇ n [bent back] : to walk with a ~ marcher le dos voûté. ◇ vi - 1. [bend down] se pencher - 2. [hunch shoulders] être voûté(e).

stop [stɒp] ◇ n - 1. [gen] arrêt m ; to put a ~ to sthg mettre un terme à qqch - 2. [full stop] point m. ◇ vt - 1. [gen] arrêter ; [end] mettre fin à ; to ~ doing sthg arrêter de faire qqch ; to ~ work arrêter de travailler, cesser le travail - 2. Br [prevent] : to ~ sb/ sthg (from doing sthg) empêcher qqn/ qqch (de faire qqch) - 3. [block] boucher. ◇ vi s'arrêter, cesser. ◆ **stop off** vi s'arrêter, faire halte. ◆ **stop up** vt sep [block] boucher.

stopgap ['stɒpgæp] n bouche-trou m.

stopover ['stɒp,əʊvəʳ] n halte f.

stoppage ['stɒpɪdʒ] n - 1. [strike] grève f - 2. Br [deduction] retenue f.

stopper ['stɒpə^r] n bouchon m.

stop press n nouvelles fpl de dernière heure.

stopwatch ['stɒpwɒtʃ] n chronomètre m.

storage ['stɔːrɪdʒ] n - 1. [of goods] entreposage m, emmagasinage m ; [of household objects] rangement m - 2. COMPUT stockage m, mémorisation f.

storage heater n Br radiateur m à accumulation.

store [stɔː^r] ◇ n - 1. esp Am [shop] magasin m - 2. [supply] provision f - 3. [place of storage] réserve f. ◇ vt - 1. [save] mettre en réserve ; [goods] entreposer, emmagasiner - 2. COMPUT stocker, mémoriser. ◆ **store up** vt sep [provisions] mettre en réserve ; [goods] emmagasiner ; [information] mettre en mémoire, noter.

storekeeper ['stɔːˌkiːpə^r] n Am commerçant m, -e f.

storeroom ['stɔːrʊm] n magasin m.

storey Br (pl -s), **story** Am (pl -ies) ['stɔːrɪ] n étage m.

stork [stɔːk] n cigogne f.

storm [stɔːm] ◇ n - 1. [bad weather] orage m - 2. fig [of abuse] torrent m ; [of applause] tempête f. ◇ vt MIL prendre d'assaut. ◇ vi - 1. [go angrily] : **to ~ in/out** entrer/sortir comme un ouragan - 2. [speak angrily] fulminer.

stormy ['stɔːmɪ] adj lit & fig orageux (euse).

story ['stɔːrɪ] n - 1. [gen] histoire f - 2. PRESS article m ; RADIO & TV nouvelle f - 3. Am = storey.

storybook ['stɔːrɪbʊk] adj [romance etc] de conte de fées.

storyteller ['stɔːrɪˌtelə^r] n - 1. [narrator] conteur m, -euse f - 2. euphemism [liar] menteur m, -euse f.

stout [staʊt] ◇ adj - 1. [rather fat] corpulent(e) - 2. [strong] solide - 3. [resolute] ferme, résolu(e). ◇ n (U) stout m, bière f brune.

stove [stəʊv] ◇ pt & pp ▷ **stave**. ◇ n [for cooking] cuisinière f ; [for heating] poêle m, calorifère m Can.

stow [stəʊ] vt : **to ~ sthg (away)** ranger qqch.

stowaway ['stəʊəweɪ] n passager m clandestin.

straddle ['strædl] vt enjamber ; [chair] s'asseoir à califourchon sur.

straggle ['strægl] vi - 1. [buildings] s'étendre, s'étaler ; [hair] être en désordre - 2. [person] traîner, lambiner.

straggler ['stræglə^r] n traînard m, -e f.

straight [streɪt] ◇ adj - 1. [not bent] droit(e) ; [hair] raide - 2. [frank] franc (franche), honnête - 3. [tidy] en ordre - 4. [choice, exchange] simple - 5. [alcoholic drink] sec, sans eau - 6. phr : **let's get this ~** entendons-nous bien. ◇ adv - 1. [in a straight line] droit - 2. [directly, immediately] droit, tout de suite - 3. [frankly] carrément, franchement - 4. [undiluted] sec, sans eau. ◆ **straight off** adv tout de suite, sur-le-champ. ◆ **straight out** adv sans mâcher ses mots.

straightaway [ˌstreɪtə'weɪ] adv tout de suite, immédiatement.

straighten ['streɪtn] vt - 1. [tidy - hair, dress] arranger ; [- room] mettre de l'ordre dans - 2. [make straight - horizontally] rendre droit(e) ; [- vertically] redresser. ◆ **straighten out** vt sep [problem] résoudre.

straight face n : **to keep a ~** garder son sérieux.

straightforward [ˌstreɪt'fɔːwəd] adj - 1. [easy] simple - 2. [frank] honnête, franc (franche).

strain [streɪn] ◇ n - 1. [mental] tension f, stress m - 2. MED foulure f - 3. TECH contrainte f, effort m. ◇ vt - 1. [work hard - eyes] plisser fort ; **to ~ one's ears** tendre l'oreille - 2. [MED - muscle] se froisser ; [- eyes] se fatiguer ; **to ~ one's back** se faire un tour de reins - 3. [patience] mettre à rude épreuve ; [budget] grever - 4. [drain] passer - 5. TECH exercer une contrainte sur. ◇ vi [try very hard] : **to ~ to do sthg** faire un gros effort pour faire qqch, se donner du mal pour faire qqch. ◆ **strains** npl [of music] accords mpl, airs mpl.

strained [streɪnd] adj - 1. [worried] contracté(e), tendu(e) - 2. [relations, relationship] tendu(e) - 3. [unnatural] forcé(e).

strainer ['streɪnə^r] n passoire f.

strait [streɪt] n détroit m. ◆ **straits** npl : **in dire** OR **desperate ~s** dans une situation désespérée.

straitjacket ['streɪtˌdʒækɪt] n camisole f de force.

straitlaced [ˌstreɪt'leɪst] adj collet monté (inv).

strand [strænd] n - 1. [of cotton, wool] brin m, fil m ; [of hair] mèche f - 2. [theme] fil m.

stranded ['strændɪd] adj [boat] échoué(e) ; [people] abandonné(e), en rade.

strange [streɪndʒ] adj - 1. [odd] étrange, bizarre - 2. [unfamiliar] inconnu(e).

stranger ['streɪndʒə'] *n* - **1.** [unfamiliar person] inconnu *m*, -e *f* - **2.** [from another place] étranger *m*, -ère *f*.

strangle ['stræŋgl] *vt* étrangler ; *fig* étouffer.

stranglehold ['stræŋglhəʊld] *n* - **1.** [round neck] étranglement *m* - **2.** *fig* [control] : ~ **(on)** domination *f* (de).

strap [stræp] ◇ *n* [for fastening] sangle *f*, courroie *f* ; [of bag] bandoulière *f* ; [of rifle, dress, bra] bretelle *f* ; [of watch] bracelet *m*. ◇ *vt* [fasten] attacher.

strapping ['stræpɪŋ] *adj* bien bâti(e), robuste.

Strasbourg ['stræzbɜːg] *n* Strasbourg.

strategic [strə'tiːdʒɪk] *adj* stratégique.

strategy ['strætɪdʒɪ] *n* stratégie *f*.

straw [strɔː] *n* paille *f* ; **that's the last ~!** ça c'est le comble!

strawberry ['strɔːbərɪ] ◇ *n* [fruit] fraise *f*. ◇ *comp* [tart, yoghurt] aux fraises ; [jam] de fraises.

stray [streɪ] ◇ *adj* - **1.** [animal] errant(e), perdu(e) - **2.** [bullet] perdu(e) ; [example] isolé(e). ◇ *vi* - **1.** [person, animal] errer, s'égarer - **2.** [thoughts] vagabonder, errer.

streak [striːk] ◇ *n* - **1.** [line] bande *f*, marque *f* ; ~ **of lightning** éclair *m* - **2.** [in character] côté *m*. ◇ *vi* [move quickly] se déplacer comme un éclair.

stream [striːm] ◇ *n* **1.** [small river] ruisseau *m* - **2.** [of liquid, light] flot *m*, jet *m* - **3.** [of people, cars] flot *m* ; [of complaints, abuse] torrent *m* - **4.** *Br* SCH classe *f* de niveau. ◇ *vi* - **1.** [liquid] couler à flots, ruisseler ; [light] entrer à flots - **2.** [people, cars] affluer ; **to ~ past** passer à flots. ◇ *vt Br* SCH répartir par niveau.

streamer ['striːmə'] *n* [for party] serpentin *m*.

streamlined ['striːmlaɪnd] *adj* - **1.** [aerodynamic] au profil aérodynamique - **2.** [efficient] rationalisé(e).

street [striːt] *n* rue *f*.

streetcar ['striːtkaː'] *n Am* tramway *m*.

street lamp, street light *n* réverbère *m*.

street plan *n* plan *m*.

streetwise ['striːtwaɪz] *adj inf* averti(e), futé(e).

strength [streŋθ] *n* - **1.** [gen] force *f* - **2.** [power, influence] puissance *f* - **3.** [solidity, of currency] solidité *f*.

strengthen ['streŋθn] *vt* - **1.** [structure, team, argument] renforcer - **2.** [economy, currency, friendship] consolider - **3.** [re-

solve, dislike] fortifier, affermir - **4.** [person] enhardir.

strenuous ['strenjʊəs] *adj* [exercise, activity] fatigant(e), dur(e) ; [effort] vigoureux(euse), acharné(e).

stress [stres] ◇ *n* - **1.** [emphasis] : ~ **(on)** accent *m* (sur) - **2.** [mental] stress *m*, tension *f* - **3.** TECH : ~ **(on)** contrainte *f* (sur), effort *m* (sur) - **4.** LING accent *m*. ◇ *vt* - **1.** [emphasize] souligner, insister sur - **2.** LING accentuer.

stressful ['stresfʊl] *adj* stressant(e).

stretch [stretʃ] ◇ *n* - **1.** [of land, water] étendue *f* ; [of road, river] partie *f*, section *f* - **2.** [of time] période *f*. ◇ *vt* - **1.** [arms] allonger ; [legs] se dégourdir ; [muscles] distendre - **2.** [pull taut] tendre, étirer - **3.** [overwork - person] surmener ; [- resources, budget] grever - **4.** [challenge] : **to ~ sb** pousser qqn à la limite de ses capacités. ◇ *vi* - **1.** [area] : **to ~ over** s'étendre sur ; **to ~ from ... to** s'étendre de ... à - **2.** [person, animal] s'étirer - **3.** [material, elastic] se tendre, s'allonger. ◆ **stretch out** ◇ *vt sep* [arm, leg, hand] tendre. ◇ *vi* [lie down] s'étendre, s'allonger.

stretcher ['stretʃə'] *n* brancard *m*, civière *f*.

strew [struː] (*pt* -ed, *pp* strewn [struːn], -ed) *vt* : **to be strewn with** être jonché(e) de.

stricken ['strɪkn] *adj* : **to be ~ by** OR **with panic** être pris(e) de panique ; **to be ~ by an illness** souffrir OR être atteint(e) d'une maladie.

strict [strɪkt] *adj* [gen] strict(e).

strictly ['strɪktlɪ] *adv* - **1.** [gen] strictement ; ~ **speaking** à proprement parler - **2.** [severely] d'une manière stricte, sévèrement.

stride [straɪd] (*pt* strode, *pp* stridden ['strɪdn]) ◇ *n* [long step] grand pas *m*, enjambée *f*. ◇ *vi* marcher à grandes enjambées OR à grands pas.

strident ['straɪdnt] *adj* - **1.** [voice, sound] strident(e) - **2.** [demand, attack] véhément(e), bruyant(e).

strife [straɪf] *n (U)* conflit *m*, lutte *f*.

strike [straɪk] (*pt* & *pp* struck) ◇ *n* - **1.** [by workers] grève *f* ; **to be (out) on ~** être en grève ; **to go on ~** faire grève ; **to go on ~** se mettre en grève - **2.** MIL raid *m* - **3.** [of oil, gold] découverte *f*. ◇ *vt* - **1.** [hit - deliberately] frapper ; [- accidentally] heurter - **2.** [subj : thought] venir à l'esprit de - **3.** [conclude - deal, bargain] conclure - **4.** [light - match] frotter. ◇ *vi* - **1.** [workers] faire grève - **2.** [hit] frapper - **3.** [attack]

attaquer - **4.** [chime] sonner. ➡ **strike down** *vt sep* terrasser. ➡ **strike out** ◇ *vt sep* rayer, barrer. ◇ *vi* [head out] se mettre en route, partir. ➡ **strike up** *vt fus* - **1.** [conversation] commencer, engager ; **to ~ up a friendship (with)** se lier d'amitié (avec) - **2.** [music] commencer à jouer.

striker ['straɪkə'] *n* - **1.** [person on strike] gréviste *mf* - **2.** FTBL buteur *m*.

striking ['straɪkɪŋ] *adj* - **1.** [noticeable] frappant(e), saisissant(e) - **2.** [attractive] d'une beauté frappante.

string [strɪŋ] (*pt & pp* strung) *n* - **1.** (U) [thin rope] ficelle *f* - **2.** [piece of thin rope] bout *m* de ficelle ; **to pull ~s** faire jouer le piston - **3.** [of beads, pearls] rang *m* - **4.** [series] série *f*, suite *f* - **5.** [of musical instrument] corde *f*. ➡ **strings** *npl* MUS : **the ~s** les cordes *fpl*. ➡ **string out** *vt fus* échelonner. ➡ **string together** *vt sep fig* aligner.

string bean *n* haricot *m* vert.

stringed instrument [ˌstrɪŋd-] *n* instrument *m* à cordes.

stringent ['strɪndʒənt] *adj* strict(e), rigoureux(euse).

strip [strɪp] ◇ *n* - **1.** [narrow piece] bande *f* - **2.** *Br* SPORT tenue *f*. ◇ *vt* - **1.** [undress] déshabiller, dévêtir - **2.** [paint, wallpaper] enlever. ◇ *vi* [undress] se déshabiller, se dévêtir. ➡ **strip off** *vi* se déshabiller, se dévêtir.

strip cartoon *n Br* bande *f* dessinée.

stripe [straɪp] *n* - **1.** [band of colour] rayure *f* - **2.** [sign of rank] galon *m*.

striped [straɪpt] *adj* à rayures, rayé(e).

strip lighting *n Br* éclairage *m* au néon.

stripper ['strɪpə'] *n* - **1.** [performer of striptease] strip-teaseuse *f*, effeuilleuse *f* - **2.** [for paint] décapant *m*.

striptease ['stripti:z] *n* strip-tease *m*.

strive [straɪv] (*pt* strove, *pp* striven ['strɪvn]) *vi* : **to ~ for sthg** essayer d'obtenir qqch ; **to ~ to do sthg** s'efforcer de faire qqch.

strode [strəʊd] *pt* ▷ **stride**.

stroke [strəʊk] ◇ *n* - **1.** MED attaque *f* cérébrale - **2.** [of pen, brush] trait *m* - **3.** [in swimming - movement] mouvement *m* des bras ; [- style] nage *f* - **4.** [in rowing] coup *m* d'aviron - **5.** [in golf, tennis etc] coup *m* - **6.** [of clock] : **on the third ~** ≃ au quatrième top - **7.** *Br* TYPO [oblique] barre *f* - **8.** [piece] : **a ~ of genius** un trait de génie ; **a ~ of luck** un coup de chance OR de veine ; **at a ~** d'un seul coup. ◇ *vt* caresser.

stroll [strəʊl] ◇ *n* petite promenade *f*, petit tour *m*. ◇ *vi* se promener, flâner.

stroller ['strəʊlə'] *n Am* [for baby] poussette *f*.

strong [strɒŋ] *adj* - **1.** [gen] fort(e) ; **~ point** point *m* fort - **2.** [structure, argument, friendship] solide - **3.** [healthy] robuste, vigoureux(euse) - **4.** [policy, measures] énergique - **5.** [in numbers] : **the crowd was 2,000 ~** il y avait une foule de 2 000 personnes - **6.** [team, candidate] sérieux(euse), qui a des chances de gagner.

strongbox ['strɒŋbɒks] *n* coffre-fort *m*.

stronghold ['strɒŋhəʊld] *n fig* bastion *m*.

strongly ['strɒŋlɪ] *adv* - **1.** [gen] fortement - **2.** [solidly] solidement.

strong room *n* chambre *f* forte.

strove [strəʊv] *pt* ▷ **strive**.

struck [strʌk] *pt & pp* ▷ **strike**.

structure ['strʌktʃə'] *n* - **1.** [organization] structure *f* - **2.** [building] construction *f*.

struggle ['strʌgl] ◇ *n* - **1.** [great effort] : **~ (for sthg/to do sthg)** lutte *f* (pour qqch/ pour faire qqch) - **2.** [fight] bagarre *f*. ◇ *vi* - **1.** [make great effort] : **to ~ (for)** lutter (pour) ; **to ~ to do sthg** s'efforcer de faire qqch - **2.** [to free oneself] se débattre ; [fight] se battre.

strum [strʌm] *vt* [guitar] gratter de ; [tune] jouer.

strung [strʌŋ] *pt & pp* ▷ **string**.

strut [strʌt] ◇ *n* CONSTR étai *m*, support *m*. ◇ *vi* se pavaner.

stub [stʌb] ◇ *n* - **1.** [of cigarette] mégot *m* ; [of pencil] morceau *m* - **2.** [of ticket, cheque] talon *m*. ◇ *vt* : **to ~ one's toe** se cogner le doigt de pied. ➡ **stub out** *vt sep* écraser.

stubble ['stʌbl] *n* (U) - **1.** [in field] chaume *m* - **2.** [on chin] barbe *f* de plusieurs jours.

stubborn ['stʌbən] *adj* - **1.** [person] têtu(e), obstiné(e) - **2.** [stain] qui ne veut pas partir, rebelle.

stuck [stʌk] ◇ *pt & pp* ▷ **stick**. ◇ *adj* - **1.** [jammed, trapped] coincé(e) - **2.** [stumped] : **to be ~** sécher - **3.** [stranded] bloqué(e), en rade.

stuck-up *adj inf pej* bêcheur(euse).

stud [stʌd] *n* - **1.** [metal decoration] clou *m* décoratif - **2.** [earring] clou *m* d'oreille - **3.** [on boot, shoe] clou *m* ; [on sports boots] crampon *m* - **4.** [of horses] haras *m*.

studded ['stʌdɪd] *adj* : **~ (with)** parsemé(e) (de), constellé(e) (de).

student ['stju:dnt] ◇ *n* étudiant *m*, -e *f*. ◇ *comp* [life] estudiantin(e) ; [politics] des étudiants ; [disco] pour étudiants.

studio ['stju:dɪəʊ] (*pl* **-s**) *n* studio *m* ; [of artist] atelier *m*.

studio flat *Br*, **studio apartment** *Am n* studio *m*.

studious ['stju:dɪəs] *adj* studieux(euse).

studiously ['stju:dɪəslɪ] *adv* studieusement.

study ['stʌdɪ] ◇ *n* - **1.** [gen] étude *f* - **2.** [room] bureau *m*. ◇ *vt* - **1.** [learn] étudier, faire des études de - **2.** [examine] examiner, étudier. ◇ *vi* étudier, faire ses études.

stuff [stʌf] ◇ *n* (U) - **1.** *inf* [things] choses *fpl* - **2.** [substance] substance *f* - **3.** *inf* [belongings] affaires *fpl*. ◇ *vt* - **1.** [push] fourrer - **2.** [fill] : **to ~ sthg (with)** remplir OR bourrer qqch (de) - **3.** CULIN farcir.

stuffed [stʌft] *adj* - **1.** [filled] : **~ with** bourré(e) de - **2.** *inf* [with food] gavé(e) - **3.** CULIN farci(e) - **4.** [toy] en peluche ; **he loves ~ animals** il adore les peluches - **5.** [preserved - animal] empaillé(e).

stuffing ['stʌfɪŋ] *n* (U) - **1.** [filling] bourre *f*, rembourrage *m* - **2.** CULIN farce *f*.

stuffy ['stʌfɪ] *adj* - **1.** [room] mal aéré(e), qui manque d'air - **2.** [person, club] vieux jeu (*inv*).

stumble ['stʌmbl] *vi* trébucher.
➡ **stumble across**, **stumble on** *vt fus* tomber sur.

stumbling block ['stʌmblɪŋ-] *n* pierre *f* d'achoppement.

stump [stʌmp] ◇ *n* [of tree] souche *f* ; [of arm, leg] moignon *m*. ◇ *vt* [subj : question, problem] dérouter, rendre perplexe.

stun [stʌn] *vt* - **1.** [knock unconscious] étourdir, assommer - **2.** [surprise] stupéfier, renverser.

stung [stʌŋ] *pt & pp* ▷ **sting**.

stunk [stʌŋk] *pt & pp* ▷ **stink**.

stunning ['stʌnɪŋ] *adj* - **1.** [very beautiful] ravissant(e) ; [scenery] merveilleux(euse) - **2.** [surprising] stupéfiant(e), renversant(e).

stunt [stʌnt] ◇ *n* - **1.** [for publicity] coup *m* - **2.** CINEMA cascade *f*. ◇ *vt* retarder, arrêter.

stunted ['stʌntɪd] *adj* rabougri(e).

stunt man *n* cascadeur *m*.

stupefy ['stju:pɪfaɪ] *vt* - **1.** [tire] abrutir - **2.** [surprise] stupéfier, abasourdir.

stupendous [stju:'pendəs] *adj* extraordinaire, prodigieux(euse).

stupid ['stju:pɪd] *adj* - **1.** [foolish] stupide, bête - **2.** *inf* [annoying] fichu(e).

stupidity [stju:'pɪdətɪ] *n* (U) bêtise *f*, stupidité *f*.

sturdy ['stɜːdɪ] *adj* [person] robuste ; [furniture, structure] solide.

stutter ['stʌtəʳ] *vi* bégayer.

sty [staɪ] *n* [pigsty] porcherie *f*.

stye [staɪ] *n* orgelet *m*, compère-loriot *m*.

style [staɪl] ◇ *n* - **1.** [characteristic manner] style *m* - **2.** (U) [elegance] chic *m*, élégance *f* - **3.** [design] genre *m*, modèle *m*. ◇ *vt* [hair] coiffer.

stylish ['staɪlɪʃ] *adj* chic (*inv*), élégant(e).

stylist ['staɪlɪst] *n* [hairdresser] coiffeur *m*, -euse *f*.

stylus ['staɪləs] (*pl* **-es**) *n* [on record player] pointe *f* de lecture, saphir *m*.

suave [swɑːv] *adj* doucereux(euse).

sub [sʌb] *n inf* - **1.** SPORT (*abbr of* **substitute**) remplaçant *m*, -e *f* - **2.** (*abbr of* **submarine**) sous-marin *m* - **3.** *Br* (*abbr of* **subscription**) cotisation *f*.

subconscious [ˌsʌb'kɒnʃəs] ◇ *adj* inconscient(e). ◇ *n* : **the ~** l'inconscient *m*.

subcontract [ˌsʌbkən'trækt] *vt* sous-traiter.

subdivide [ˌsʌbdɪ'vaɪd] *vt* subdiviser.

subdue [səb'dju:] *vt* [control - rioters, enemy] soumettre, subjuguer ; [- temper, anger] maîtriser, réprimer.

subdued [səb'dju:d] *adj* - **1.** [person] abattu(e) - **2.** [anger, emotion] contenu(e) - **3.** [colour] doux (douce) ; [light] tamisé(e).

subject [*adj*, *n* & *prep* 'sʌbdʒekt, *vt* səb'dʒekt] ◇ *adj* soumis(e) ; **to be ~ to** [tax, law] être soumis à ; [disease, headaches] être sujet (sujette) à. ◇ *n* - **1.** [gen] sujet *m* - **2.** SCH & UNIV matière *f*. ◇ *vt* - **1.** [control] soumettre, assujettir - **2.** [force to experience] : **to ~ sb to sthg** exposer OR soumettre qqn à qqch. ➡ **subject to** *prep* sous réserve de.

subjective [səb'dʒektɪv] *adj* subjectif(ive).

subject matter *n* (U) sujet *m*.

subjunctive [səb'dʒʌŋktɪv] *n* GRAMM : **~ (mood)** (mode *m*) subjonctif *m*.

sublet [ˌsʌb'let] (*pt & pp* **sublet**) *vt* sous-louer.

sublime [sə'blaɪm] *adj* sublime.

submachine gun [ˌsʌbmə'ʃiːn-] *n* mitraillette *f*.

submarine [ˌsʌbmə'riːn] *n* sous-marin *m*.

submenu ['sʌbˌmenjuː] *n* COMPUT sous-menu *m*.

submerge [səb'mɜːdʒ] ◇ *vt* immerger, plonger. ◇ *vi* s'immerger, plonger.

submission [səb'mɪʃn] *n* - **1.** [obedience]

soumission *f* - **2.** [presentation] présentation *f*, soumission *f*.

submissive [səb'mɪsɪv] *adj* soumis(e), docile.

submit [səb'mɪt] ◇ *vt* soumettre. ◇ *vi* : **to ~ (to)** se soumettre (à).

subnormal [ˌsʌb'nɔːml] *adj* arriéré(e), attardé(e).

subordinate [sə'bɔːdɪnət] ◇ *adj fml* [less important] : **~ (to)** subordonné(e) (à), moins important(e) (que). ◇ *n* subordonné *m*, -e *f*.

subpoena [sə'piːnə] (*pt* & *pp* **-ed**) JUR ◇ *n* citation *f*, assignation *f*. ◇ *vt* citer OR assigner à comparaitre.

subscribe [səb'skraɪb] *vi* - **1.** [to magazine, newspaper] s'abonner, être abonné - **2.** [to view, belief] : **to ~ to** être d'accord avec, approuver.

subscriber [səb'skraɪbəʳ] *n* [to magazine, service] abonné *m*, -e *f*.

subscription [səb'skrɪpʃn] *n* - **1.** [to magazine] abonnement *m* - **2.** [to charity, campaign] souscription *f* - **3.** [to club] cotisation *f*.

subsequent ['sʌbsɪkwənt] *adj* ultérieur(e), suivant(e).

subsequently ['sʌbsɪkwəntlɪ] *adv* par la suite, plus tard.

subservient [səb'sɜːvjənt] *adj* [servile] : **~ (to)** servile (vis-à-vis de), obséquieux (euse) (envers).

subside [səb'saɪd] *vi* - **1.** [pain, anger] se calmer, s'atténuer ; [noise] diminuer - **2.** [CONSTR - building] s'affaisser ; [- ground] se tasser.

subsidence [səb'saɪdns, 'sʌbsɪdns] *n* [CONSTR - of building] affaissement *m* ; [- of ground] tassement *m*.

subsidiary [səb'sɪdjərɪ] ◇ *adj* subsidiaire. ◇ *n* : **~ (company)** filiale *f*.

subsidize, -ise ['sʌbsɪdaɪz] *vt* subventionner.

subsidy ['sʌbsɪdɪ] *n* subvention *f*, subside *m*.

substance ['sʌbstəns] *n* - **1.** [gen] substance *f* - **2.** [importance] importance *f*.

substantial [səb'stænʃl] *adj* - **1.** [considerable] considérable, important(e) ; [meal] substantiel(elle) - **2.** [solid, well-built] solide.

substantially [səb'stænʃəlɪ] *adv* - **1.** [considerably] considérablement - **2.** [mainly] en grande partie.

substantiate [səb'stænʃɪeɪt] *vt fml* prouver, établir.

substitute ['sʌbstɪtjuːt] ◇ *n* - **1.** [replacement] : **~ (for)** [person] remplaçant *m*, -e *f* (de) ; [thing] succédané *m* (de) - **2.** SPORT remplaçant *m*, -e *f*. ◇ *vt* : **to ~ A for B** substituer A à B, remplacer B par A.

subtitle ['sʌb,taɪtl] *n* sous-titre *m*.

subtle ['sʌtl] *adj* subtil(e).

subtlety ['sʌtltɪ] *n* subtilité *f*.

subtract [səb'trækt] *vt* : **to ~ sthg (from)** soustraire qqch (de).

subtraction [səb'trækʃn] *n* soustraction *f*.

suburb ['sʌbɜːb] *n* faubourg *m*. ◆ **suburbs** *npl* : **the ~s** la banlieue.

suburban [sə'bɜːbn] *adj* - **1.** [of suburbs] de banlieue - **2.** *pej* [life] étriqué(e) ; [person] à l'esprit étroit.

suburbia [sə'bɜːbɪə] *n (U)* la banlieue.

subversive [səb'vɜːsɪv] ◇ *adj* subversif(ive). ◇ *n* personne *f* qui agit de façon subversive.

subway ['sʌbweɪ] *n* - **1.** *Br* [underground walkway] passage *m* souterrain - **2.** *Am* [underground railway] métro *m*.

succeed [sək'siːd] ◇ *vt* succéder à. ◇ *vi* réussir ; **to ~ in doing sthg** réussir à faire qqch.

succeeding [sək'siːdɪŋ] *adj fml* [in future] à venir ; [in past] suivant(e).

success [sək'ses] *n* succès *m*, réussite *f*.

successful [sək'sesfʊl] *adj* - **1.** [attempt] couronné(e) de succès - **2.** [film, book etc] à succès ; [person] qui a du succès.

succession [sək'seʃn] *n* succession *f*.

successive [sək'sesɪv] *adj* successif(ive).

succinct [sək'sɪŋkt] *adj* succinct(e).

succumb [sə'kʌm] *vi* : **to ~ (to)** succomber (à).

such [sʌtʃ] ◇ *adj* tel (telle), pareil(eille) ; **~ nonsense** de telles inepties ; **do you have ~ a thing as a tin-opener?** est-ce que tu aurais un ouvre-boîtes par hasard? ; **~ money/books as I have** le peu d'argent/ de livres que j'ai ; **~ ... that** tel ... que. ◇ *adv* - **1.** [for emphasis] si, tellement ; **it's ~ a horrible day!** quelle journée épouvantable! ; **~ a lot of books** tellement de livres ; **~ a long time** si OR tellement longtemps - **2.** [in comparisons] aussi. ◇ *pron* : **and ~ (like)** et autres choses de ce genre. ◆ **as such** *adv* en tant que tel (telle), en soi. ◆ **such and such** *adj* tel et tel (telle et telle).

suck [sʌk] *vt* - **1.** [with mouth] sucer - **2.** [draw in] aspirer.

sucker ['sʌkəʳ] *n* - **1.** [suction pad] ventouse

f - **2.** *inf* [gullible person] poire *f*.

suction ['sʌkʃn] *n* succion *f*.

Sudan [su:'da:n] *n* Soudan *m*.

sudden ['sʌdn] *adj* soudain(e), brusque ; **all of a ~** tout d'un coup, soudain.

suddenly ['sʌdnlɪ] *adv* soudainement, tout d'un coup.

suds [sʌdz] *npl* mousse *f* de savon.

sue [su:] *vt* : **to ~ sb (for)** poursuivre qqn en justice (pour).

suede [sweɪd] *n* daim *m*.

suet ['soɪt] *n* graisse *f* de rognon.

suffer ['sʌfə'] *vt* - **1.** [pain, injury] souffrir de - **2.** [consequences, setback, loss] subir. ◇ *vi* souffrir ; **to ~ from** MED souffrir de.

sufferer ['sʌfrə'] *n* MED malade *mf*.

suffering ['sʌfrɪŋ] *n* souffrance *f*.

suffice [sə'faɪs] *vi fml* suffire.

sufficient [sə'fɪʃnt] *adj* suffisant(e).

sufficiently [sə'fɪʃntlɪ] *adv* suffisamment.

suffocate ['sʌfəkeɪt] *vt & vi* suffoquer.

suffrage ['sʌfrɪdʒ] *n* suffrage *m*.

suffuse [sə'fju:z] *vt* baigner.

sugar ['ʃʊgə'] ◇ *n* sucre *m*. ◇ *vt* sucrer.

sugar beet *n* betterave *f* à sucre.

sugarcane ['ʃʊgəkeɪn] *n* (U) canne *f* à sucre.

sugary ['ʃʊgərɪ] *adj* [food] sucré(e).

suggest [sə'dʒest] *vt* - **1.** [propose] proposer, suggérer - **2.** [imply] suggérer.

suggestion [sə'dʒestʃn] *n* - **1.** [proposal] proposition *f*, suggestion *f* - **2.** (U) [implication] suggestion *f*.

suggestive [sə'dʒestɪv] *adj* suggestif(ive) ; **to be ~ of sthg** suggérer qqch.

suicide ['suɪsaɪd] *n* suicide *m* ; **to commit ~** se suicider.

suit [su:t] ◇ *n* - **1.** [for man] costume *m*, complet *m* ; [for woman] tailleur *m* - **2.** [in cards] couleur *f* - **3.** JUR procès *m*, action *f*. ◇ *vt* - **1.** [subj : clothes, hairstyle] aller à - **2.** [be convenient, appropriate to] convenir a. ◇ *vi* convenir, aller.

suitable ['su:təbl] *adj* qui convient, qui va.

suitably ['su:təblɪ] *adv* convenablement.

suitcase ['su:tkeɪs] *n* valise *f*.

suite [swi:t] *n* - **1.** [of rooms] suite *f* - **2.** [of furniture] ensemble *m*.

suited ['su:tɪd] *adj* - **1.** [suitable] : **to be ~ to/for** convenir à/pour, aller à/pour - **2.** [couple] : **well ~** très bien assortis.

suitor ['su:tə'] *n dated* soupirant *m*.

sulfur *Am* = sulphur.

sulk [sʌlk] *vi* bouder.

sulky ['sʌlkɪ] *adj* boudeur(euse).

sullen ['sʌlən] *adj* maussade.

sulphur *Br*, **sulfur** *Am* ['sʌlfə'] *n* soufre *m*.

sultana [səl'ta:nə] *n Br* [dried grape] raisin *m* sec.

sultry ['sʌltrɪ] *adj* - **1.** [weather] lourd(e) - **2.** [sexual] sensuel(elle).

sum [sʌm] *n* - **1.** [amount of money] somme *f* - **2.** [calculation] calcul *m*. ◆ **sum up** ◇ *vt sep* [summarize] résumer. ◇ *vi* récapituler.

summarize, -ise ['sʌməraɪz] ◇ *vt* résumer. ◇ *vi* récapituler.

summary ['sʌmərɪ] *n* résumé *m*.

summer ['sʌmə'] ◇ *n* été *m* ; **in ~** en été. ◇ *comp* d'été ; **the ~ holidays** les grandes vacances *fpl*.

summerhouse ['sʌməhaʊs, *pl* -haʊzɪz] *n* pavillon *m* (de verdure).

summer school *n* université *f* d'été.

summertime ['sʌmətaɪm] *n* été *m*.

summit ['sʌmɪt] *n* sommet *m*.

summon ['sʌmən] *vt* appeler, convoquer. ◆ **summon up** *vt sep* rassembler.

summons ['sʌmənz] (*pl* -**es** [-i:z]) JUR ◇ *n* assignation *f*. ◇ *vt* assigner.

sump [sʌmp] *n* carter *m*.

sumptuous ['sʌmptʃʊəs] *adj* somptueux(euse).

sun [sʌn] *n* soleil *m* ; **in the ~** au soleil.

sunbathe ['sʌnbeɪð] *vi* prendre un bain de soleil.

sunbed ['sʌnbed] *n* lit *m* à ultra-violets.

sunburn ['sʌnbɜ:n] *n* (U) coup *m* de soleil.

sunburned ['sʌnbɜ:nd], **sunburnt** ['sʌnbɜ:nt] *adj* brûlé(e) par le soleil, qui a attrapé un coup de soleil.

Sunday ['sʌndɪ] *n* dimanche *m* ; **~ lunch** déjeuner *m* du dimanche OR dominical ; *see also* **Saturday.**

Sunday school *n* catéchisme *m*.

sundial ['sʌndaɪəl] *n* cadran *m* solaire.

sundown ['sʌndaʊn] *n* coucher *m* du soleil.

sundries ['sʌndrɪz] *npl fml* articles *mpl* divers, objets *mpl* divers.

sundry ['sʌndrɪ] *adj fml* divers ; **all and ~** tout le monde, n'importe qui.

sunflower ['sʌn,flaʊə'] *n* tournesol *m*.

sung [sʌŋ] *pp* ▷ sing.

sunglasses ['sʌn͵glɑːsɪz] *npl* lunettes *fpl* de soleil.

sunk [sʌŋk] *pp* ⊏ sink.

sunlight ['sʌnlaɪt] *n* lumière *f* du soleil.

sunny ['sʌnɪ] *adj* - **1.** [day, place] ensoleillé(e) ; **it's ~** il fait beau, il fait (du) soleil - **2.** [cheerful] radieux(euse), heureux(euse).

sunrise ['sʌnraɪz] *n* lever *m* du soleil.

sunroof ['sʌnruːf] *n* toit *m* ouvrant.

sunscreen ['sʌnskriːn] *n* écran *m* OR filtre *m* solaire.

sunset ['sʌnset] *n* coucher *m* du soleil.

sunshade ['sʌnʃeɪd] *n* parasol *m*.

sunshine ['sʌnʃaɪn] *n* lumière *f* du soleil.

sunstroke ['sʌnstrəʊk] *n* (U) insolation *f*.

suntan ['sʌntæn] ⋄ *n* bronzage *m*. ⋄ *comp* [lotion, cream] solaire.

suntrap ['sʌntræp] *n* endroit très ensoleillé.

super ['suːpəʳ] *adj inf* génial(e), super *(inv)*.

superannuation ['suːpə͵rænjʊ'eɪʃn] *n* (U) pension *f* de retraite.

superb [suː'pɜːb] *adj* superbe.

superbug ['suːpəbʌg] *n* germe résistant aux traitements antibiotiques.

supercilious [͵suːpə'sɪlɪəs] *adj* hautain(e).

superficial [͵suːpə'fɪʃl] *adj* superficiel (elle).

superfluous [suː'pɜːflʊəs] *adj* superflu(e).

superhighway ['suːpə͵haɪweɪ] *n* - **1.** *Am* autoroute *f* - **2.** = information highway.

superhuman [͵suːpə'hjuːmən] *adj* surhumain(e).

superimpose [͵suːpərɪm'pəʊz] *vt* : **to ~ sthg (on)** superposer qqch (à).

superintendent [͵suːpərɪn'tendənt] *n* - **1.** *Br* [of police] ≃ commissaire *m* - **2.** [of department] directeur *m*, -trice *f*.

superior [suː'pɪərɪəʳ] ⋄ *adj* - **1.** [gen] : **~ (to)** supérieur(e) (à) - **2.** [goods, craftsmanship] de qualité supérieure. ⋄ *n* supérieur *m*, -e *f*.

superlative [suː'pɜːlətɪv] ⋄ *adj* exceptionnel(elle), sans pareil(eille). ⋄ *n* GRAMM superlatif *m*.

supermarket ['suːpə͵mɑːkɪt] *n* supermarché *m*.

supernatural [͵suːpə'nætʃrəl] *adj* surnaturel(elle).

superpower ['suːpə͵paʊəʳ] *n* superpuissance *f*.

supersede [͵suːpə'siːd] *vt* remplacer.

supersonic [͵suːpə'sɒnɪk] *adj* supersonique.

superstitious [͵suːpə'stɪʃəs] *adj* superstitieux(euse).

superstore ['suːpəstɔːʳ] *n* hypermarché *m*.

supertanker ['suːpə͵tæŋkəʳ] *n* supertanker *m*.

supervise ['suːpəvaɪz] *vt* surveiller ; [work] superviser.

supervisor ['suːpəvaɪzəʳ] *n* surveillant *m*, -e *f*.

supper ['sʌpəʳ] *n* [evening meal] dîner *m*.

supple ['sʌpl] *adj* souple.

supplement [*n* 'sʌplɪmənt, *vb* 'sʌplɪment] ⋄ *n* supplément *m*. ⋄ *vt* compléter.

supplementary [͵sʌplɪ'mentərɪ] *adj* supplémentaire.

supplementary benefit *n Br* ancien nom *des allocations supplémentaires accordées aux personnes ayant un faible revenu.*

supplier [sə'plaɪəʳ] *n* fournisseur *m*.

supply [sə'plaɪ] ⋄ *n* - **1.** [store] réserve *f*, provision *f* - **2.** [system] alimentation *f* - **3.** (U) ECON offre *f*. ⋄ *vt* - **1.** [provide] : **to ~ sthg (to sb)** fournir qqch (à qqn) - **2.** [provide to] : **to ~ sb (with)** fournir qqn (en), approvisionner qqn (en) ; **to ~ sthg with sthg** alimenter qqch en qqch. ◆ **supplies** *npl* [food] vivres *mpl* ; MIL approvisionnements *mpl* ; **office supplies** fournitures *fpl* de bureau.

support [sə'pɔːt] ⋄ *n* - **1.** (U) [physical help] appui *m* - **2.** (U) [emotional, financial help] soutien *m* - **3.** [object] support *m*, appui *m*. ⋄ *vt* - **1.** [physically] soutenir, supporter ; [weight] supporter - **2.** [emotionally] soutenir - **3.** [financially] subvenir aux besoins de - **4.** [theory] être en faveur de, être partisan de ; [political party, candidate] appuyer ; SPORT être un supporter de.

supporter [sə'pɔːtəʳ] *n* - **1.** [of person, plan] partisan *m*, -e *f* - **2.** SPORT supporter *m*.

suppose [sə'pəʊz] ⋄ *vt* supposer. ⋄ *vi* supposer ; **I ~ (so)** je suppose que oui ; **I ~ not** je suppose que non.

supposed [sə'pəʊzd] *adj* - **1.** [doubtful] supposé(e) - **2.** [reputed, intended] : **to be ~ to be** être censé(e) être.

supposedly [sə'pəʊzɪdlɪ] *adv* soi-disant.

supposing [sə'pəʊzɪŋ] *conj* et si, à supposer que (+ *subjunctive*).

suppress [sə'pres] *vt* - **1.** [uprising] réprimer - **2.** [information] supprimer - **3.** [emotions] réprimer, étouffer.

supreme [soˈpriːm] *adj* suprême.
Supreme Court *n* [in US] : **the ~** la Cour suprême.

surcharge [ˈsɜːtʃɑːdʒ] *n* [extra payment] surcharge *f* ; [extra tax] surtaxe *f*.

sure [ʃʊəˈ] <> *adj* - **1.** [gen] sûr(e) ; **to be ~ of o.s.** être sûr de soi - **2.** [certain] : **to be ~ (of sthg/of doing sthg)** être sûr(e) (de qqch/de faire qqch), être certain(e) (de qqch/de faire qqch) ; **to make ~ (that)** ... s'assurer OR vérifier que ... - **3.** *phr* : **I am** OR **I'm ~ (that)** ... je suis bien certain que ..., je ne doute pas que ... <> *adv* - **1.** *inf* [yes] bien sûr - **2.** *Am* [really] vraiment. ◆ **for sure** *adv* sans aucun doute. ◆ **sure enough** *adv* en effet, effectivement.

surely [ˈʃʊəlɪ] *adv* sûrement.

surety [ˈʃʊərətɪ] *n (U)* caution *f*.

surf [sɜːf] *n* ressac *m*.

surface [ˈsɜːfɪs] <> *n* surface *f* ; **on the ~** *fig* à première vue, vu de l'extérieur. <> *vi* - **1.** [diver] remonter à la surface ; [submarine] faire surface - **2.** [problem, rumour] apparaître OR s'étaler au grand jour.

surface mail *n* courrier *m* par voie de terre/de mer.

surfboard [ˈsɜːfbɔːd] *n* planche *f* de surf.

surfeit [ˈsɜːfɪt] *n fml* excès *m*.

surfing [ˈsɜːfɪŋ] *n* surf *m*.

surge [sɜːdʒ] <> *n* - **1.** [of people, vehicles] déferlement *m* ; ELEC surtension *f* - **2.** [of emotion, interest] vague *f*, montée *f* ; [of anger] bouffée *f* ; [of sales, applications] afflux *m*. <> *vi* [people, vehicles] déferler.

surgeon [ˈsɜːdʒən] *n* chirurgien *m*.

surgery [ˈsɜːdʒərɪ] *n* - **1.** *(U)* MED [performing operations] chirurgie *f* - **2.** *Br* MED [place] cabinet *m* de consultation.

surgical [ˈsɜːdʒɪkl] *adj* chirurgical(e) ; **~ stocking** bas *m* orthopédique.

surgical spirit *n Br* alcool *m* à 90°.

surly [ˈsɜːlɪ] *adj* revêche, renfrogné(e).

surmount [sɜːˈmaʊnt] *vt* surmonter.

surname [ˈsɜːneɪm] *n* nom *m* de famille.

surpass [səˈpɑːs] *vt fml* dépasser.

surplus [ˈsɜːpləs] <> *adj* en surplus. <> *n* surplus *m*.

surprise [səˈpraɪz] <> *n* surprise *f*. <> *vt* surprendre.

surprised [səˈpraɪzd] *adj* surpris(e).

surprising [səˈpraɪzɪŋ] *adj* surprenant(e).

surprisingly [səˈpraɪzɪŋlɪ] *adv* étonnamment.

surrender [səˈrendəˈ] <> *n* reddition *f*, capitulation *f*. <> *vi* - **1.** [stop fighting] : **to ~ (to)** se rendre (à) - **2.** *fig* [give in] : **to ~ (to)** se laisser aller (à), se livrer (à).

surreptitious [ˌsʌrəpˈtɪʃəs] *adj* subreptice.

surrogate [ˈsʌrəgeɪt] <> *adj* de substitution. <> *n* substitut *m*.

surrogate mother *n* mère *f* porteuse.

surround [səˈraʊnd] *vt* entourer ; [subj : police, army] cerner.

surrounding [səˈraʊndɪŋ] *adj* environnant(e).

surroundings [səˈraʊndɪŋz] *npl* environnement *m*.

surveillance [sɜːˈveɪləns] *n* surveillance *f*.

survey [*n* ˈsɜːveɪ, *vb* səˈveɪ] <> *n* - **1.** [investigation] étude *f* ; [of public opinion] sondage *m* - **2.** [of land] levé *m* ; [of building] inspection *f*. <> *vt* - **1.** [contemplate] passer en revue - **2.** [investigate] faire une étude de, enquêter sur - **3.** [land] faire le levé de ; [building] inspecter.

surveyor [səˈveɪəˈ] *n* [of building] expert *m* ; [of land] géomètre *m*.

survival [səˈvaɪvl] *n* [continuing to live] survie *f*.

survive [səˈvaɪv] <> *vt* survivre à. <> *vi* survivre.

survivor [səˈvaɪvəˈ] *n* survivant *m*, -e *f* ; *fig* battant *m*, -e *f*.

susceptible [səˈseptəbl] *adj* : **~ (to)** sensible (à).

suspect [*adj & n* ˈsʌspekt, *vb* səˈspekt] <> *adj* suspect(e). <> *n* suspect *m*, -e *f*. <> *vt* - **1.** [distrust] douter de - **2.** [think likely, consider guilty] soupçonner ; **to ~ sb of sthg** soupçonner qqn de qqch.

suspend [səˈspend] *vt* - **1.** [gen] suspendre - **2.** [from school] renvoyer temporairement.

suspended sentence [səˈspendɪd-] *n* condamnation *f* avec sursis.

suspender belt [səˈspendəˈ-] *n Br* porte-jarretelles *m inv*.

suspenders [səˈspendəz] *npl* - **1.** *Br* [for stockings] jarretelles *fpl* - **2.** *Am* [for trousers] bretelles *fpl*.

suspense [səˈspens] *n* suspense *m*.

suspension [səˈspenʃn] *n* - **1.** [gen & AUT] suspension *f* - **2.** [from school] renvoi *m* temporaire.

suspension bridge *n* pont *m* suspendu.

suspicion [səˈspɪʃn] *n* soupçon *m*.

suspicious [səˈspɪʃəs] *adj* - **1.** [having suspicions] soupçonneux(euse) - **2.** [causing suspicion] suspect(e), louche.

sustain [sə'steɪn] vt - 1. [maintain] soutenir - 2. fml [suffer - damage] subir ; [- injury] recevoir - 3. fml [weight] supporter.

sustainable [sə'steɪnəbl] adj [growth, energy] durable.

sustenance ['sʌstɪnəns] n (U) fml nourriture f.

SW (abbr of **short wave**) OC.

swab [swɒb] n MED tampon m.

swagger ['swægə'] vi parader.

Swahili [swa:'hi:lɪ] n [language] swahili m.

swallow ['swɒləʊ] ◇ n [bird] hirondelle f. ◇ vt avaler ; fig [anger, tears] ravaler. ◇ vi avaler.

swam [swæm] pt ▷ swim.

swamp [swɒmp] ◇ n marais m. ◇ vt - 1. [flood] submerger - 2. [overwhelm] déborder, submerger.

swan [swɒn] n cygne m.

swap [swɒp] vt : **to ~ sthg (with sb/for sthg)** échanger qqch (avec qqn/contre qqch).

swarm [swɔ:m] ◇ n essaim m. ◇ vi fig [people] grouiller ; **to be ~ing (with)** [place] grouiller (de).

swarthy ['swɔ:ðɪ] adj basané(e).

swastika ['swɒstɪkə] n croix f gammée.

swat [swɒt] vt écraser.

sway [sweɪ] ◇ vt [influence] influencer. ◇ vi se balancer.

swear [sweə'] (pt **swore**, pp **sworn**) ◇ vt jurer ; **to ~ to do sthg** jurer de faire qqch. ◇ vi jurer.

swearword ['sweəwɜ:d] n juron m, gros mot m.

sweat [swet] ◇ n [perspiration] transpiration f, sueur f. ◇ vi - 1. [perspire] transpirer, suer - 2. inf [worry] se faire du mouron.

sweater ['swetə'] n pullover m.

sweatshirt ['swetʃɜ:t] n sweat-shirt m.

sweaty ['swetɪ] adj [skin, clothes] mouillé(e) de sueur.

swede [swi:d] n Br rutabaga m.

Swede [swi:d] n Suédois m, -e f.

Sweden ['swi:dn] n Suède f.

Swedish ['swi:dɪʃ] ◇ adj suédois(e). ◇ n [language] suédois m. ◇ npl : **the ~** les Suédois mpl.

sweep [swi:p] (pt & pp **swept**) ◇ n - 1. [sweeping movement] grand geste m - 2. [with brush] : **to give sthg a ~** donner un coup de balai à qqch, balayer qqch - 3. [chimney sweep] ramoneur m. ◇ vt - [gen] balayer ; [scan with eyes] parcourir des yeux. ➨ **sweep away** vt sep [destroy] emporter, entraîner. ➨ **sweep up** ◇ vt sep [with brush] balayer. ◇ vi balayer.

sweeping ['swi:pɪŋ] adj - 1. [effect, change] radical(e) - 2. [statement] hâtif(ive).

sweet [swi:t] ◇ adj - 1. [gen] doux (douce) ; [cake, flavour, pudding] sucré(e) - 2. [kind] gentil(ille) - 3. [attractive] adorable, mignon(onne). ◇ n Br - 1. [candy] bonbon m - 2. [dessert] dessert m.

sweet corn n maïs m.

sweeten ['swi:tn] vt sucrer.

sweetheart ['swi:tha:t] n - 1. [term of endearment] chéri m, -e f, mon cœur m - 2. [boyfriend, girlfriend] petit ami m, petite amie f.

sweetness ['swi:tnɪs] n - 1. [gen] douceur f ; [of taste] goût m sucré, douceur - 2. [attractiveness] charme m.

sweet pea n pois m de senteur.

swell [swel] (pt **-ed**, pp **swollen** OR **-ed**) ◇ vi - 1. [leg, face etc] enfler ; [lungs, balloon] se gonfler ; **to ~ with pride** se gonfler d'orgueil - 2. [crowd, population etc] grossir, augmenter ; [sound] grossir, s'enfler. ◇ vt grossir, augmenter. ◇ n [of sea] houle f. ◇ adj Am inf chouette, épatant(e).

swelling ['swelɪŋ] n enflure f.

sweltering ['sweltərɪŋ] adj étouffant(e), suffocant(e).

swept [swept] pt & pp ▷ sweep.

swerve [swɜ:v] vi faire une embardée.

swift [swɪft] ◇ adj - 1. [fast] rapide - 2. [prompt] prompt(e). ◇ n [bird] martinet m.

swig [swɪg] inf n lampée f.

swill [swɪl] ◇ n (U) [pig food] pâtée f. ◇ vt Br [wash] laver à grande eau.

swim [swɪm] (pt **swam**, pp **swum**) ◇ n : **to have a ~** nager ; **to go for a ~** aller se baigner, aller nager. ◇ vi - 1. [person, fish, animal] nager - 2. [room] tourner ; **my head was swimming** j'avais la tête qui tournait.

swimmer ['swɪmə'] n nageur m, -euse f.

swimming ['swɪmɪŋ] n natation f ; **to go ~** aller nager.

swimming cap n bonnet m de bain.

swimming costume n Br maillot m de bain.

swimming pool n piscine f.

swimming trunks npl maillot m OR slip m de bain.

swimsuit ['swɪmsu:t] n maillot m de bain.

swindle ['swɪndl] ◇ n escroquerie f. ◇ vt escroquer, rouler ; **to ~ sb out of sthg** escroquer qqch à qqn.

swine [swaɪn] n inf [person] salaud m.

swing [swɪŋ] (pt & pp **swung**) ◇ n - 1. [child's toy] balançoire f - 2. [change - of opinion] revirement *m* ; [- of mood] changement *m*, saute *f* - **3.** [sway] balancement *m* - **4.** *phr* : **to be in full ~** battre son plein. <> *vt* - **1.** [move back and forth] balancer - **2.** [move in a curve] faire virer. <> *vi* - **1.** [move back and forth] se balancer - **2.** [turn - vehicle] virer, tourner ; **to ~ round** [person] se retourner - **3.** [change] changer.

swing bridge *n* pont *m* tournant.

swing door *n* porte *f* battante.

swingeing ['swɪndʒɪŋ] *adj esp Br* très sévère.

swipe [swaɪp] <> *vt inf* [steal] faucher, piquer. <> *vi* : **to ~ at** envoyer OR donner un coup à.

swirl [swɜːl] <> *n* tourbillon *m*. <> *vi* tourbillonner, tournoyer.

swish [swɪʃ] *vt* [tail] battre l'air de.

Swiss [swɪs] <> *adj* suisse. <> *n* [person] Suisse *mf*. <> *npl* : **the ~** les Suisses *mpl*.

switch [swɪtʃ] <> *n* - **1.** [control device] interrupteur *m*, commutateur *m* ; [on radio, stereo etc] bouton *m* - **2.** [change] changement *m*. <> *vt* [swap] échanger ; [jobs] changer de. ◆ **switch off** *vt sep* éteindre. ◆ **switch on** *vt sep* allumer.

Switch® *n* système de paiement non différé par carte bancaire.

switchboard ['swɪtʃbɔːd] *n* standard *m*.

Switzerland ['swɪtsələnd] *n* Suisse *f* ; **in ~** en Suisse.

swivel ['swɪvl] <> *vt* [chair] faire pivoter ; [head, eyes] faire tourner. <> *vi* [chair] pivoter ; [head, eyes] tourner.

swivel chair *n* fauteuil *m* pivotant OR tournant.

swollen ['swəʊln] <> *pp* ▷ swell. <> *adj* [ankle, face] enflé(e) ; [river] en crue.

swoop [swuːp] <> *n* [raid] descente *f*. <> *vi* - **1.** [bird, plane] piquer - **2.** [police, army] faire une descente.

swop [swɒp] = **swap**.

sword [sɔːd] *n* épée *f*.

swordfish ['sɔːdfɪʃ] (*pl inv* OR **-es** [-iːz]) *n* espadon *m*

swore [swɔːr] *pt* ▷ swear.

sworn [swɔːn] <> *pp* ▷ swear. <> *adj* JUR sous serment.

swot [swɒt] *Br inf* <> *n pej* bûcheur *m*, -euse *f*. <> *vi* : **to ~ (for)** bûcher (pour).

swum [swʌm] *pp* ▷ swim.

swung [swʌŋ] *pt* & *pp* ▷ swing.

sycamore ['sɪkəmɔːr] *n* sycomore *m*.

syllable ['sɪləbl] *n* syllabe *f*.

syllabus ['sɪləbəs] (*pl* **-buses** [-bəsiːz], **-bi** [-baɪ]) *n* programme *m*.

symbol ['sɪmbl] *n* symbole *m*.

symbolize, -ise ['sɪmbəlaɪz] *vt* symboliser.

symmetry ['sɪmɪtrɪ] *n* symétrie *f*.

sympathetic [ˌsɪmpə'θetɪk] *adj* - **1.** [understanding] compatissant(e), compréhensif(ive) - **2.** [willing to support] : **~ (to)** bien disposé(e) (à l'égard de).

sympathize, -ise ['sɪmpəθaɪz] *vi* - **1.** [feel sorry] compatir ; **to ~ with sb** plaindre qqn ; [in grief] compatir à la douleur de qqn - **2.** [understand] : **to ~ with sthg** comprendre qqch - **3.** [support] : **to ~ with sthg** approuver qqch, soutenir qqch.

sympathizer, -iser ['sɪmpəθaɪzər] *n* sympathisant *m*, -e *f*.

sympathy ['sɪmpəθɪ] *n* (*U*) - **1.** [understanding] : **~ (for)** compassion *f* (pour), sympathie *f* (pour) - **2.** [agreement] approbation *f*, sympathie *f*. ◆ **sympathies** *npl* [to bereaved person] condoléances *fpl*.

symphony ['sɪmfənɪ] *n* symphonie *f*.

symposium [sɪm'pəʊzjəm] (*pl* **-siums** OR **-sia** [-zjə]) *n* symposium *m*.

symptom ['sɪmptəm] *n* symptôme *m*.

synagogue ['sɪnəgɒg] *n* synagogue *f*.

syndicate ['sɪndɪkət] *n* syndicat *m*, consortium *m*.

syndrome ['sɪndrəʊm] *n* syndrome *m*.

synonym ['sɪnənɪm] *n* : **~ (for** OR **of)** synonyme *m* (de).

synopsis [sɪ'nɒpsɪs] (*pl* **-ses** [-siːz]) *n* résumé *m* ; [film] synopsis *m*.

syntax ['sɪntæks] *n* syntaxe *f*.

synthesis ['sɪnθəsɪs] (*pl* **-ses** [-siːz]) *n* synthèse *f*.

synthetic [sɪn'θetɪk] *adj* - **1.** [man-made] synthétique - **2.** *pej* [insincere] artificiel(elle), forcé(e).

syphilis ['sɪfɪlɪs] *n* syphilis *f*.

syphon ['saɪfn] = **siphon**.

Syria ['sɪrɪə] *n* Syrie *f*.

syringe [sɪ'rɪndʒ] *n* seringue *f*.

syrup ['sɪrəp] *n* (*U*) - **1.** [sugar and water] sirop *m* - **2.** *Br* [golden syrup] mélasse *f* raffinée.

system ['sɪstəm] *n* - **1.** [gen] système *m* ; **road/railway ~** réseau *m* routier/de chemins de fer - **2.** [equipment - gen] installation *f* ; [- electric, electronic] appareil *m* - **3.** (*U*) [methodical approach] système *m*, méthode *f*.

systematic [ˌsɪstə'mætɪk] *adj* systématique.

system disk *n* COMPUT disque *m* système.

systems analyst ['sɪstəmz-] *n* COMPUT analyste fonctionnel *m*, analyste fonctionnelle *f*.

t (*pl* **t's** OR **ts**), **T** (*pl* **T's** OR **Ts**) [tiː] *n* [letter] t *m inv*, T *m inv*.

ta [taː] *excl Br inf* merci!

tab [tæb] *n* - **1.** [of cloth] étiquette *f* - **2.** [of metal] languette *f* - **3.** *Am* [bill] addition *f* - **4.** *phr* : **to keep ~s on sb** tenir OR avoir qqn à l'œil, surveiller qqn.

tabby ['tæbɪ] *n* : **~ (cat)** chat tigré *m*, chatte tigrée *f*.

table ['teɪbl] <> *n* table *f*. <> *vt Br* [propose] présenter, proposer.

tablecloth ['teɪblklɒθ] *n* nappe *f*.

table lamp *n* lampe *f*.

tablemat ['teɪblmæt] *n* dessous-de-plat *m inv*.

tablespoon ['teɪblspuːn] *n* - **1.** [spoon] cuiller *f* de service - **2.** [spoonful] cuillerée *f* à soupe.

tablet ['tæblɪt] *n* - **1.** [pill] comprimé *m*, cachet *m* - **2.** [of stone] plaque *f* commémorative - **3.** [of soap] savonnette *f*, pain *m* de savon.

table tennis *n* ping-pong *m*, tennis *m* de table.

table wine *n* vin *m* de table.

tabloid ['tæblɔɪd] *n* : **~ (newspaper)** tabloïd *m*, tabloïde *m* ; **the ~ press** la presse populaire.

tabulate ['tæbjʊleɪt] *vt* présenter sous forme de tableau.

tacit ['tæsɪt] *adj* tacite.

taciturn ['tæsɪtɜːn] *adj* taciturne.

tack [tæk] <> *n* - **1.** [nail] clou *m* - **2.** NAUT bord *m*, bordée *f* - **3.** *fig* [course of action] tactique *f*, méthode *f*. <> *vt* - **1.** [fasten with nail - gen] clouer ; [- notice] punaiser - **2.** SEWING faufiler. <> *vi* NAUT tirer une bordée.

tackle ['tækl] <> *n* - **1.** FTBL tacle *m* ; RUGBY plaquage *m* - **2.** [equipment] équipement *m*, matériel *m* - **3.** [for lifting] palan *m*, appareil *m* de levage. <> *vt* - **1.** [deal with] s'attaquer

à - **2.** FTBL tacler ; RUGBY plaquer - **3.** [attack] empoigner.

tacky ['tækɪ] *adj* - **1.** *inf* [film, remark] d'un goût douteux ; [jewellery] de pacotille - **2.** [sticky] collant(e), pas encore sec (sèche).

tact [tækt] *n (U)* tact *m*, délicatesse *f*.

tactful ['tæktfʊl] *adj* [remark] plein(e) de tact ; [person] qui a du tact OR de la délicatesse.

tactic ['tæktɪk] *n* tactique *f*. <> **tactics** *n (U)* MIL tactique *f*.

tactical ['tæktɪkl] *adj* tactique.

tactless ['tæktlɪs] *adj* qui manque de tact OR délicatesse.

tadpole ['tædpəʊl] *n* têtard *m*.

tag [tæg] *n* - **1.** [of cloth] marque *f* - **2.** [of paper] étiquette *f*. <> **tag along** *vi inf* suivre.

tail [teɪl] <> *n* - **1.** [gen] queue *f* - **2.** [of coat] basque *f*, pan *m* ; [of shirt] pan. <> *vt inf* [follow] filer. <> **tails** <> *n* [side of coin] pile *f*. <> *npl* [formal dress] queue-de-pie *f*, habit *m*. <> **tail off** *vi* [voice] s'affaiblir ; [noise] diminuer.

tailback ['teɪlbæk] *n Br* bouchon *m*.

tailcoat [ˌteɪl'kəʊt] *n* habit *m*, queue-de-pie *f*.

tail end *n* fin *f*.

tailgate ['teɪlgeɪt] *n* AUT hayon *m*.

tailor ['teɪlər] <> *n* tailleur *m*. <> *vt fig* adapter.

tailor-made *adj fig* sur mesure.

tailwind ['teɪlwɪnd] *n* vent *m* arrière.

tainted ['teɪntɪd] *adj* - **1.** [reputation] souillé(e), entaché(e) - **2.** *Am* [food] avarié(e) - **3.** [blood] contaminé.

Taiwan [ˌtaɪ'waːn] *n* Taiwan.

take [teɪk] (*pt* took, *pp* taken) <> *vt* - **1.** [gen] prendre ; **to ~ an exam** passer un examen ; **to ~ a walk** se promener, faire une promenade ; **to ~ a bath/photo** prendre un bain/une photo ; **to ~ offence** se vexer, s'offenser - **2.** [lead, drive] emmener - **3.** [accept] accepter - **4.** [contain] contenir, avoir une capacité de - **5.** [tolerate] supporter - **6.** [require] demander ; **how long will it ~?** combien de temps cela va-t-il prendre? - **7.** [wear] : **what size do you ~?** [clothes] quelle taille faites-vous? ; [shoes] vous chaussez du combien? - **8.** [assume] : **I ~ it (that)** ... je suppose que ..., je pense que ... - **9.** [rent] prendre, louer. <> *n* CINEMA prise *f* de vues. <> **take after** *vt fus* tenir de, ressembler à. <> **take apart** *vt sep* [dismantle] démonter. <> **take away** *vt sep*

- **1.** [remove] enlever - **2.** [deduct] retrancher, soustraire. ◆ **take back** vt sep - **1.** [return] rendre, rapporter - **2.** [accept] reprendre - **3.** [statement, accusation] retirer. ◆ **take down** vt sep - **1.** [dismantle] démonter - **2.** [write down] prendre - **3.** [lower] baisser. ◆ **take in** vt sep - **1.** [deceive] rouler, tromper - **2.** [understand] comprendre - **3.** [include] englober, couvrir - **4.** [provide accommodation for] recueillir. ◆ **take off** ◇ vt sep - **1.** [remove] enlever, ôter - **2.** [have as holiday] : **to ~ a week/day off** prendre une semaine/un jour de congé - **3.** Br [imitate] imiter. ◇ vi - **1.** [plane] décoller - **2.** [go away suddenly] partir. ◆ **take on** vt sep - **1.** [accept] accepter, prendre - **2.** [employ] embaucher, prendre - **3.** [confront] s'attaquer à ; [competitor] faire concurrence à ; SPORT jouer contre. ◆ **take out** vt sep - **1.** [from container] sortir ; [from pocket] prendre - **2.** [go out with] emmener, sortir avec. ◆ **take over** ◇ vt sep - **1.** [take control of] reprendre, prendre la direction de - **2.** [job] : **to ~ over sb's job** remplacer qqn, prendre la suite de qqn. ◇ vi - **1.** [take control] prendre le pouvoir - **2.** [in job] prendre la relève. ◆ **take to** vt fus - **1.** [person] éprouver de la sympathie pour, sympathiser avec ; [activity] prendre goût à - **2.** [begin] : **to ~ to doing sthg** se mettre à faire qqch. ◆ **take up** vt sep - **1.** [begin - job] prendre ; [- singing] se mettre au chant - **2.** [use up] prendre, occuper. ◆ **take up on** vt sep [accept] : **to ~ sb up on an offer** accepter l'offre de qqn.

takeaway Br ['teɪkəˌweɪ], **takeout** Am ['teɪkaʊt] n [food] plat m à emporter.

taken ['teɪkn] pp ▷ take.

takeoff ['teɪkɒf] n [of plane] décollage m.

takeout Am = takeaway.

takeover ['teɪkˌəʊvəʳ] n - **1.** [of company] prise f de contrôle, rachat m - **2.** [of government] prise f de pouvoir.

takings ['teɪkɪŋz] npl recette f.

talc [tælk], **talcum (powder)** ['tælkəm-] n talc m.

tale [teɪl] n - **1.** [fictional story] histoire f, conte m - **2.** [anecdote] récit m, histoire f.

talent ['tælənt] n : **~ (for)** talent m (pour).

talented ['tæləntɪd] adj qui a du talent, talentueux(euse).

talk [tɔːk] ◇ n - **1.** [conversation] discussion f, conversation f - **2.** (U) [gossip] bavardages mpl, racontars mpl - **3.** [lecture] conférence f, causerie f. ◇ vi - **1.** [speak] : **to ~ (to sb)** parler (à qqn) ; **to ~ about** parler de - **2.** [gossip] bavarder, jaser - **3.** [make a

speech] faire un discours, parler ; **to ~ on** OR **about** parler de. ◇ vt parler. ◆ **talks** npl entretiens mpl, pourparlers mpl. ◆ **talk into** vt sep : **to ~ sb into doing sthg** persuader qqn de faire qqch. ◆ **talk out of** vt sep : **to ~ sb out of doing sthg** dissuader qqn de faire qqch. ◆ **talk over** vt sep discuter de.

talkative ['tɔːkətɪv] adj bavard(e), loquace.

talk show n Am talk-show m, causerie f.

tall [tɔːl] adj grand(e) ; **how ~ are you?** combien mesurez-vous? ; **she's 5 feet ~** elle mesure 1,50 m.

tall story n histoire f à dormir debout.

tally ['tælɪ] ◇ n compte m. ◇ vi correspondre, concorder.

talon ['tælən] n serre f, griffe f.

tambourine [ˌtæmbəˈriːn] n tambourin m.

tame [teɪm] ◇ adj - **1.** [animal, bird] apprivoisé(e) - **2.** pej [person] docile ; [party, story, life] terne, morne. ◇ vt - **1.** [animal, bird] apprivoiser - **2.** [people] mater, dresser.

tamper ['tæmpəʳ] ◆ **tamper with** vt fus [machine] toucher à ; [records, file] altérer, falsifier ; [lock] essayer de crocheter.

tampon ['tæmpɒn] n tampon m.

tan [tæn] ◇ adj brun clair (inv). ◇ n bronzage m, hâle m. ◇ vi bronzer.

tang [tæŋ] n [taste] saveur f forte OR piquante ; [smell] odeur f forte OR piquante.

tangent ['tændʒənt] n GEOM tangente f ; **to go off at a ~** fig changer de sujet, faire une digression.

tangerine [ˌtændʒəˈriːn] n mandarine f.

tangible ['tændʒəbl] adj tangible.

Tangier [tænˈdʒɪəʳ] n Tanger.

tangle ['tæŋgl] n - **1.** [mass] enchevêtrement m, emmêlement m - **2.** fig [confusion] : **to get into a ~** s'empêtrer, s'embrouiller.

tank [tæŋk] n - **1.** [container] réservoir m ; **fish ~** aquarium m - **2.** MIL tank m, char m (d'assaut).

tanker ['tæŋkəʳ] n - **1.** [ship - for oil] pétrolier m - **2.** [truck] camion-citerne m - **3.** [train] wagon-citerne m.

tanned [tænd] adj bronzé(e), hâlé(e).

Tannoy® ['tænɔɪ] n système m de haut-parleurs.

tantalizing ['tæntəlaɪzɪŋ] adj [smell] très appétissant(e) ; [possibility, thought] très tentant(e).

tantamount ['tæntəmaʊnt] *adj* : ~ **to** équivalent(e) à.

tantrum ['tæntrəm] (*pl* **-s**) *n* crise *f* de colère ; **to have** OR **throw a ~** faire OR piquer une colère.

Tanzania [ˌtænzə'nɪə] *n* Tanzanie *f*.

tap [tæp] ◇ *n* - **1.** [device] robinet *m* - **2.** [light blow] petite tape *f*, petit coup *m*. ◇ *vt* - **1.** [hit] tapoter, taper - **2.** [resources, energy] exploiter, utiliser - **3.** [telephone, wire] mettre sur écoute.

tap dance *n* claquettes *fpl*.

tape [teɪp] ◇ *n* - **1.** [magnetic tape] bande *f* magnétique ; [cassette] cassette *f* - **2.** [strip of cloth, adhesive material] ruban *m*. ◇ *vt* - **1.** [record] enregistrer ; [on video] magnétoscoper, enregistrer au magnétoscope - **2.** [stick] scotcher.

tape measure *n* centimètre *m*, mètre *m*.

taper ['teɪpə'] *vi* s'effiler ; [trousers] se terminer en fuseau.

tape recorder *n* magnétophone *m*.

tapestry ['tæpɪstrɪ] *n* tapisserie *f*.

tar [tɑːʳ] *n* (U) goudron *m*.

target ['tɑːgɪt] ◇ *n* - **1.** [of missile, bomb] objectif *m* ; [for archery, shooting] cible *f* - **2.** *fig* [for criticism] cible *f* - **3.** *fig* [goal] objectif *m*. ◇ *vt* - **1.** [city, building] viser - **2.** *fig* [subj : policy] s'adresser à, viser ; [subj : advertising] cibler.

tariff ['tærɪf] *n* - **1.** [tax] tarif *m* douanier - **2.** [list] tableau *m* OR liste *f* des prix.

Tarmac® ['tɑːmæk] *n* [material] macadam *m*. ◆ **tarmac** *n* AERON : **the tarmac** la piste.

tarnish ['tɑːnɪʃ] *vt* *lit & fig* ternir.

tarpaulin [tɑː'pɔːlɪn] *n* [material] toile *f* goudronnée ; [sheet] bâche *f*.

tart [tɑːt] ◇ *adj* - **1.** [bitter] acide - **2.** [sarcastic] acide, acerbe. ◇ *n* - **1.** CULIN tarte *f* - **2.** *v inf* [prostitute] pute *f*. ◆ **tart up** *vt sep Br inf pej* [room] retaper, rénover ; **to ~ o.s. up** se faire beau (belle).

tartan ['tɑːtn] ◇ *n* tartan *m*. ◇ *comp* écossais(e).

tartar(e) sauce ['tɑːtəʳ-] *n* sauce *f* tartare.

task [tɑːsk] *n* tâche *f*, besogne *f*.

task force *n* MIL corps *m* expéditionnaire.

tassel ['tæsl] *n* pompon *m*, gland *m*.

taste [teɪst] ◇ *n* - **1.** [gen] goût *m* ; **have a ~! **goûte! ; **in good/bad ~** de bon/mauvais goût - **2.** *fig* [liking] : **~ (for)** penchant *m* (pour), goût *m* (pour) - **3.** *fig* [experience] aperçu *m*. ◇ *vt* - **1.** [sense - food] sentir - **2.** [test, try] déguster, goûter - **3.** *fig* [experience] tâter de, goûter de. ◇ *vi* : **to ~ of/like**

avoir le goût de ; **to ~ good/odd** *etc* avoir bon goût/un drôle de goût *etc*.

tasteful ['teɪstfʊl] *adj* de bon goût.

tasteless ['teɪstlɪs] *adj* - **1.** [object, decor, remark] de mauvais goût - **2.** [food] qui n'a aucun goût, fade.

tasty ['teɪstɪ] *adj* [delicious] délicieux (euse), succulent(e).

tatters ['tætəz] *npl* : **in ~** [clothes] en lambeaux ; [confidence] brisé(e) ; [reputation] ruiné(e).

tattoo [tə'tuː] (*pl* **-s**) ◇ *n* - **1.** [design] tatouage *m* - **2.** *Br* [military display] parade *f* OR défilé *m* militaire. ◇ *vt* tatouer.

tatty ['tætɪ] *adj Br inf pej* [clothes] défraîchi(e), usé(e) ; [flat, area] miteux(euse), minable.

taught [tɔːt] *pt & pp* ▷ **teach**.

taunt [tɔːnt] ◇ *vt* railler, se moquer de. ◇ *n* raillerie *f*, moquerie *f*.

Taurus ['tɔːrəs] *n* Taureau *m*.

taut [tɔːt] *adj* tendu(e).

tawdry ['tɔːdrɪ] *adj pej* [jewellery] clinquant(e) ; [clothes] voyant(e), criard(e).

tax [tæks] ◇ *n* taxe *f*, impôt *m*. ◇ *vt* - **1.** [goods] taxer - **2.** [profits, business, person] imposer - **3.** [strain] mettre à l'épreuve.

taxable ['tæksəbl] *adj* imposable.

tax allowance *n* abattement *m* fiscal.

taxation [tæk'seɪʃn] *n* (U) - **1.** [system] imposition *f* - **2.** [amount] impôts *mpl*.

tax avoidance [-ə'vɔɪdəns] *n* évasion *f* fiscale.

tax collector *n* percepteur *m*.

tax disc *n Br* vignette *f*.

tax evasion *n* fraude *f* fiscale.

tax-free *Br*, **tax-exempt** *Am adj* exonéré(e) (d'impôt).

taxi ['tæksɪ] ◇ *n* taxi *m*. ◇ *vi* [plane] rouler au sol.

taxi driver *n* chauffeur *m* de taxi.

tax inspector *n* inspecteur *m* des impôts.

taxi rank *Br*, **taxi stand** *n* station *f* de taxis.

taxpayer ['tæksˌpeɪəʳ] *n* contribuable *mf*.

tax relief *n* allègement *m* OR dégrèvement *m* fiscal.

tax return *n* déclaration *f* d'impôts.

TB *n abbr of* **tuberculosis**.

tea [tiː] *n* - **1.** [drink, leaves] thé *m* - **2.** *Br* [afternoon meal] goûter *m* ; [evening meal] dîner *m*.

teabag ['tiːbæg] *n* sachet *m* de thé.

tea break *n Br* pause pour prendre le thé, ≃ pause-café *f*.

teach [tiːtʃ] (*pt & pp* **taught**) ◇ *vt* - **1.** [instruct] apprendre ; **to ~ sb sthg, to ~ sthg to sb** apprendre qqch à qqn ; **to ~ sb to do sthg** apprendre à qqn à faire qqch - **2.** [subj : teacher] enseigner ; **to ~ sb sthg, to ~ sthg to sb** enseigner qqch à qqn. ◇ *vi* enseigner.

teacher ['tiːtʃər] *n* [in primary school] instituteur *m*, -trice *f*, maître *m*, maîtresse *f* ; [in secondary school] professeur *m*.

teacher training college *Br*, **teachers college** *Am n* ≃ institut *m* universitaire de formation des maîtres, ≃ IUFM *m*.

teaching ['tiːtʃɪŋ] *n* enseignement *m*.

teaching aid *n* support *m* pédagogique.

tea cloth *n Br* - **1.** [tablecloth] nappe *f* - **2.** [tea towel] torchon *m*.

tea cosy *Br*, **tea cozy** *Am n* couvre-théière *m inv*, cosy *m*.

teacup ['tiːkʌp] *n* tasse *f* à thé.

teak [tiːk] *n* teck *m*.

team [tiːm] *n* équipe *f*.

teammate ['tiːmmeɪt] *n* co-équipier *m*, -ère *f*.

teamwork ['tiːmwɜːk] *n (U)* travail *m* d'équipe, collaboration *f*.

teapot ['tiːpɒt] *n* théière *f*.

tear[1] [tɪər] *n* larme *f*.

tear[2] [teər] (*pt* **tore**, *pp* **torn**) ◇ *vt* - **1.** [rip] déchirer - **2.** [remove roughly] arracher. ◇ *vi* - **1.** [rip] se déchirer - **2.** [move quickly] foncer, aller à toute allure. ◇ *n* déchirure *f*, accroc *m*. ◆ **tear apart** *vt sep* - **1.** [rip up] déchirer, mettre en morceaux - **2.** *fig* [country, company] diviser ; [person] déchirer. ◆ **tear down** *vt sep* [building] démolir ; [poster] arracher. ◆ **tear up** *vt sep* déchirer.

teardrop ['tɪədrɒp] *n* larme *f*.

tearful ['tɪəfʊl] *adj* [person] en larmes.

tear gas [tɪər-] *n (U)* gaz *m* lacrymogène.

tearoom ['tiːrʊm] *n* salon *m* de thé.

tease [tiːz] ◇ *n* taquin *m*, -e *f* ◇ *vt* [mock] : **to ~ sb (about sthg)** taquiner qqn (à propos de qqch).

tea service, tea set *n* service *m* à thé.

teaspoon ['tiːspuːn] *n* - **1.** [utensil] petite cuillère *f*, cuillère à café - **2.** [amount] cuillerée *f* à café.

teat [tiːt] *n* tétine *f*.

teatime ['tiːtaɪm] *n Br* l'heure *f* du thé.

tea towel *n* torchon *m*.

technical ['teknɪkl] *adj* technique.

technical college *n Br* collège *m* technique.

technicality [ˌteknɪˈkælətɪ] *n* - **1.** [intricacy] technicité *f* - **2.** [detail] détail *m* technique.

technically ['teknɪklɪ] *adv* - **1.** [gen] techniquement - **2.** [theoretically] en théorie.

technician [tekˈnɪʃn] *n* technicien *m*, -enne *f*.

technique [tekˈniːk] *n* technique *f*.

techno ['teknəʊ] *n* MUS techno *f*.

technological [ˌteknəˈlɒdʒɪkl] *adj* technologique.

technology [tekˈnɒlədʒɪ] *n* technologie *f*.

teddy ['tedɪ] *n* : **~ (bear)** ours *m* en peluche, nounours *m*.

tedious ['tiːdjəs] *adj* ennuyeux(euse).

tee [tiː] *n* GOLF tee *m*.

teem [tiːm] *vi* - **1.** [rain] pleuvoir à verse - **2.** [place] : **to be ~ing with** grouiller de.

teenage ['tiːneɪdʒ] *adj* adolescent(e).

teenager ['tiːnˌeɪdʒər] *n* adolescent *m*, -e *f*.

teens [tiːnz] *npl* adolescence *f*.

tee shirt *n* tee-shirt *m*.

teeter ['tiːtər] *vi* vaciller ; **to ~ on the brink of** *fig* être au bord de.

teeth [tiːθ] *pl* ☞ **tooth**.

teethe [tiːð] *vi* [baby] percer ses dents.

teething troubles ['tiːðɪŋ-] *npl fig* difficultes *fpl* initiales.

teetotaller *Br*, **teetotaler** *Am* [tiːˈtəʊtlər] *n* personne *f* qui ne boit jamais d'alcool.

TEFL ['tefl] (*abbr of* teaching of English as a foreign language) *n* enseignement de l'anglais langue étrangère.

tel. (*abbr of* telephone) tél.

telecommunications ['telɪkəˌmjuːnɪˈkeɪʃnz] *npl* télécommunications *fpl*.

teleconference ['telɪˌkɒnfərəns] *n* téléconférence *f*.

telegram ['telɪgræm] *n* télégramme *m*.

telegraph ['telɪgrɑːf] ◇ *n* telegraphe *m*. ◇ *vt* télégraphier.

telegraph pole, telegraph post *Br n* poteau *m* télégraphique.

telepathy [tɪˈlepəθɪ] *n* télépathie *f*.

telephone ['telɪfəʊn] ◇ *n* téléphone *m* ; **to be on the ~** *Br* [connected] avoir le téléphone ; [speaking] être au téléphone. ◇ *vt* téléphoner à. ◇ *vi* téléphoner.

telephone book *n* annuaire *m*.

telephone booth *n* cabine *f* téléphonique.

telephone box *n Br* cabine *f* téléphonique.

telephone call *n* appel *m* téléphonique, coup *m* de téléphone.

telephone directory *n* annuaire *m*.

telephone number *n* numéro *m* de téléphone.

telephonist [tɪ'lefənɪst] *n Br* téléphoniste *mf*.

telephoto lens [ˌtelɪ'fəʊtəʊ-] *n* téléobjectif *m*.

telescope ['telɪskəʊp] *n* télescope *m*.

teletext ['telɪtekst] *n* télétexte *m*.

televise ['telɪvaɪz] *vt* téléviser.

television ['telɪˌvɪʒn] *n* - **1.** *(U)* [medium, industry] télévision *f* ; **on** ~ à la télévision - **2.** [apparatus] (poste *m* de) télévision *f*, téléviseur *m*.

television set *n* poste *m* de télévision, téléviseur *m*.

telex ['teleks] ◇ *n* télex *m*. ◇ *vt* [message] envoyer par télex, télexer ; [person] envoyer un télex à.

tell [tel] *(pt & pp* **told**) ◇ *vt* - **1.** [gen] dire ; [story] raconter ; **to** ~ **sb (that)** ... dire à qqn que ... ; **to** ~ **sb sth, to** ~ **sth to sb** dire qqch à qqn ; **to** ~ **sb to do sth** dire OR ordonner à qqn de faire qqch - **2.** [judge, recognize] savoir, voir ; **could you** ~ **me the time?** tu peux me dire l'heure (qu'il est)? ◇ *vi* - **1.** [speak] parler - **2.** [judge] savoir - **3.** [have effect] se faire sentir. ◆ **tell apart** *vt sep* distinguer. ◆ **tell off** *vt sep* gronder.

telling ['telɪŋ] *adj* [remark] révélateur (trice).

telltale ['telteɪl] ◇ *adj* révélateur(trice). ◇ *n* rapporteur *m*, -euse *f*, mouchard *m*, -e *f*.

telly ['telɪ] *(abbr of* **television**) *n Br inf* télé *f* ; **on** ~ à la télé.

temp [temp] *Br inf* ◇ *n (abbr of* **temporary (employee)**) intérimaire *mf*. ◇ *vi* travailler comme intérimaire.

temper ['tempə'] ◇ *n* - **1.** [angry state] : **to be in a** ~ être en colère ; **to lose one's** ~ se mettre en colère - **2.** [mood] humeur *f* - **3.** [temperament] tempérament *m*. ◇ *vt* [moderate] tempérer.

temperament ['tempramənt] *n* tempérament *m*.

temperamental [ˌtemprə'mentl] *adj* [volatile, unreliable] capricieux(euse).

temperate ['temprət] *adj* tempéré(e).

temperature ['temprətʃə'] *n* température *f* ; **to have a** ~ avoir de la température OR de la fièvre.

tempestuous [tem'pestjʊəs] *adj lit & fig* orageux(euse).

template ['templɪt] *n* gabarit *m*.

temple ['templ] *n* - **1.** RELIG temple *m* - **2.** ANAT tempe *f*.

temporarily [ˌtempə'rerəlɪ] *adv* temporairement, provisoirement.

temporary ['tempərərɪ] *adj* temporaire, provisoire.

tempt [tempt] *vt* tenter ; **to** ~ **sb to do sthg** donner à qqn l'envie de faire qqch.

temptation [temp'teɪʃn] *n* tentation *f*.

tempting ['temptɪŋ] *adj* tentant(e).

ten [ten] *num* dix ; *see also* **six**.

tenable ['tenəbl] *adj* [argument, position] défendable.

tenacious [tɪ'neɪʃəs] *adj* tenace.

tenancy ['tenənsɪ] *n* location *f*.

tenant ['tenənt] *n* locataire *mf*.

tend [tend] *vt* - **1.** [have tendency] : **to** ~ **to do sthg** avoir tendance à faire qqch - **2.** [look after] s'occuper de, garder.

tendency ['tendənsɪ] *n* : ~ **(to do sthg)** tendance *f* (à faire qqch).

tender ['tendə'] ◇ *adj* tendre ; [bruise, part of body] sensible, douloureux(euse). ◇ *n* COMM soumission *f*. ◇ *vt fml* [apology, money] offrir ; [resignation] donner.

tendon ['tendən] *n* tendon *m*.

tenement ['tenəmənt] *n* immeuble *m*.

Tenerife [ˌtenə'riːf] *n* Tenerife.

tenet ['tenɪt] *n fml* principe *m*.

tennis ['tenɪs] *n (U)* tennis *m*.

tennis ball *n* balle *f* de tennis.

tennis court *n* court *m* de tennis.

tennis racket *n* raquette *f* de tennis.

tenor ['tenə'] *n* [singer] ténor *m*.

tense [tens] ◇ *adj* tendu(e). ◇ *n* temps *m*. ◇ *vt* tendre.

tension ['tenʃn] *n* tension *f*.

tent [tent] *n* tente *f*.

tentacle ['tentəkl] *n* tentacule *m*.

tentative ['tentətɪv] *adj* - **1.** [hesitant] hésitant(e) - **2.** [not final] provisoire.

tenterhooks ['tentəhʊks] *npl* : **to be on** ~ être sur des charbons ardents.

tenth [tenθ] *num* dixième ; *see also* **sixth**.

tent peg *n* piquet *m* de tente.

tent pole *n* montant *m* OR mât *m* de tente.

tenuous ['tenjʊəs] *adj* ténu(e).

tenure ['tenjər] *n (U) fml* - **1.** [of property] bail *m* - **2.** [of job] : **to have ~** être titulaire.

tepid ['tepid] *adj* tiède.

term [tɜːm] ⬦ *n* - **1.** [word, expression] terme *m* - **2.** SCH & UNIV trimestre *m* - **3.** [period of time] durée *f*, période *f* ; **in the long/short ~** à long/court terme. ⬦ *vt* appeler. ➡ **terms** *npl* - **1.** [of contract, agreement] conditions *fpl* - **2.** [basis] : **in international/real ~s** en termes internationaux/réels ; **to be on good ~s (with sb)** être en bons termes (avec qqn) ; **to come to ~s with sthg** accepter qqch. ➡ **in terms of** *prep* sur le plan de, en termes de.

terminal ['tɜːmɪnl] ⬦ *adj* MED en phase terminale. ⬦ *n* - **1.** AERON, COMPUT & RAIL terminal *m* - **2.** ELEC borne *f*.

terminate ['tɜːmɪneɪt] ⬦ *vt* - **1.** *fml* [end - gen] terminer, mettre fin à ; [- contract] résilier - **2.** [pregnancy] interrompre. ⬦ *vi* - **1.** [bus, train] s'arrêter - **2.** [contract] se terminer.

termini ['tɜːmɪnaɪ] *pl* ⬅ **terminus**.

terminus ['tɜːmɪnəs] (*pl* -**ni** [-naɪ], -**nuses** [-nəsiːz]) *n* terminus *m*.

terrace ['terəs] *n* - **1.** [patio, on hillside] terrasse *f* - **2.** *Br* [of houses] rangée *f* de maisons. ➡ **terraces** *Br npl* FTBL : **the ~s** les gradins *mpl*.

terraced ['terəst] *adj* [hillside] en terrasses.

terraced house *n Br maison attenante aux maisons voisines.*

terrain [te'reɪn] *n* terrain *m*.

terrible ['terəbl] *adj* terrible ; [holiday, headache, weather] affreux(euse), épouvantable.

terribly ['terəbli] *adv* terriblement ; [sing, write, organized] affreusement mal ; [injured] affreusement.

terrier ['teriər] *n* terrier *m*.

terrific [tə'rɪfɪk] *adj* - **1.** [wonderful] fantastique, formidable - **2.** [enormous] énorme, fantastique.

terrified ['terɪfaɪd] *adj* terrifié(e) ; **to be ~ of** avoir une terreur folle OR peur folle de.

terrifying ['terɪfaɪɪŋ] *adj* terrifiant(e).

territory ['terətri] *n* territoire *m*.

terror ['terər] *n* terreur *f*.

terrorism ['terərɪzm] *n* terrorisme *m*.

terrorist ['terərɪst] *n* terroriste *mf*.

terrorize, -ise ['terəraɪz] *vt* terroriser.

terse [tɜːs] *adj* brusque.

Terylene® ['terəliːn] *n* Térylène® *m*.

test [test] ⬦ *n* - **1.** [trial] essai *m* ; [of friendship, courage] épreuve *f* - **2.** [examination - of aptitude, psychological] test *m* ; SCH & UNIV interrogation *f* écrite/orale ; [- of driving] (examen *m* du) permis *m* de conduire - **3.** [MED - of blood, urine] analyse *f* ; [- of eyes] examen *m*. ⬦ *vt* - **1.** [try] essayer ; [determination, friendship] mettre à l'épreuve - **2.** SCH & UNIV faire faire une interrogation écrite/orale à ; **to ~ sb on sthg** interroger qqn sur qqch - **3.** [MED - blood, urine] analyser ; [- eyes, reflexes] faire un examen de.

testament ['testəmənt] *n* [will] testament *m*.

test-drive *vt* essayer.

testicles ['testɪklz] *npl* testicules *mpl*.

testify ['testɪfaɪ] ⬦ *vt* : **to ~ that ...** témoigner que ... ⬦ *vi* - **1.** JUR témoigner - **2.** [be proof] : **to ~ to sthg** témoigner de qqch.

testimony [*Br* 'testɪmənɪ, *Am* 'testəməʊnɪ] *n* témoignage *m*.

testing ['testɪŋ] *adj* éprouvant(e).

test match *n Br* match *m* international.

test pilot *n* pilote *m* d'essai.

test tube *n* éprouvette *f*.

test-tube baby *n* bébé-éprouvette *m*.

tetanus ['tetənəs] *n* tétanos *m*.

tether ['teðər] ⬦ *vt* attacher. ⬦ *n* : **to be at the end of one's ~** être au bout du rouleau.

text [tekst] *n* texte *m*.

textbook ['tekstbʊk] *n* livre *m* OR manuel *m* scolaire.

textile ['tekstaɪl] *n* textile *m*.

texture ['tekstʃər] *n* texture *f* ; [of paper, wood] grain *m*.

Thai [taɪ] ⬦ *adj* thaïlandais(e). ⬦ *n* - **1.** [person] Thaïlandais *m*, -e *f* - **2.** [language] thaï *m*.

Thailand ['taɪlænd] *n* Thaïlande *f*.

Thames [temz] *n* : **the ~** la Tamise.

than [weak form ðən, strong form ðæn] *conj* que ; **Sarah is younger ~ her sister** Sarah est plus jeune que sa sœur ; **more ~ three days/50 people** plus de trois jours/50 personnes.

thank [θæŋk] *vt* : **to ~ sb (for)** remercier qqn (pour OR de) ; **~ God** OR **goodness** OR **heavens!** Dieu merci! ➡ **thanks** ⬦ *npl* remerciements *mpl*. ⬦ *excl* merci! ➡ **thanks to** *prep* grâce à.

thankful ['θæŋkfʊl] *adj* - **1.** [grateful] : **~ (for)** reconnaissant(e) (de) - **2.** [relieved] soulagé(e).

thankless ['θæŋklɪs] *adj* ingrat(e).

thanksgiving ['θæŋks,gɪvɪŋ] *n* action *f* de grâce. ◆ **Thanksgiving (Day)** *n* fête nationale américaine commémorant l'installation des premiers colons en Amérique.

thank you *excl* : ~ **(for)** merci (pour OR de).

that [ðæt, *weak form of pron sense 2 & conj* ðət] (*pl* those [ðəʊz]) ◇ *pron* - **1.** (demonstrative use : *pl* 'those') ce, cela, ça ; (as opposed to 'this') celui-là (celle-là) ; **who's ~?** qui est-ce? ; **is ~ Maureen?** c'est Maureen? ; **what's ~?** qu'est-ce que c'est que ça? ; **~'s a shame** c'est dommage ; **which shoes are you going to wear, these or those?** quelles chaussures vas-tu mettre, celles-ci ou celles-là? ; **those who** ceux (celles) qui - **2.** (to introduce relative clauses - subject) qui ; (- object) que ; (- with prep) lequel (laquelle), lesquels (lesquelles) (*pl*) ; **we came to a path ~ led into the woods** nous arrivâmes à un sentier qui menait dans les bois ; **show me the book ~ you bought** montre-moi le livre que tu as acheté ; **on the day ~ we left** le jour où nous sommes partis. ◇ *adj* (demonstrative : *pl* 'those') ce (cette), cet (before vowel or silent 'h'), ces (*pl*) ; (as opposed to 'this') ce (cette) ...-là, ces ...-là (*pl*) ; **those chocolates are delicious** ces chocolats sont délicieux ; **later ~ day** plus tard ce jour-là ; **I prefer ~ book** je préfère ce livre-là ; **I'll have ~ one** je prendrai celui-là. ◇ *adv* aussi, si ; **it wasn't ~ bad/good** ce n'était pas si mal/bien que ça. ◇ *conj* que ; **tell him ~ the children aren't coming** dites-lui que les enfants ne viennent pas ; **he recommended ~ I phone you** il m'a conseillé de vous appeler. ◆ **that is (to say)** *adv* c'est-à-dire.

thatched [θætʃt] *adj* de chaume.

that's [ðæts] = that is.

thaw [θɔː] ◇ *vt* [ice] faire fondre OR dégeler ; [frozen food] décongeler. ◇ *vi* - **1.** [ice] dégeler, fondre ; [frozen food] décongeler - **2.** *fig* [people, relations] se dégeler. ◇ *n* dégel *m*.

the [*weak form* ðə, *before vowel* ðɪ, *strong form* ðiː] *def art* - **1.** [gen] le (la), l' (+ vowel or silent 'h'), les (*pl*) ; **~ book** le livre ; **~ sea** la mer ; **~ man** l'homme ; **~ boys/girls** les garçons/filles ; **~ Joneses are coming to supper** les Jones viennent dîner ; **to play ~ piano** jouer du piano - **2.** (with an adjective to form a noun) - **~ British** les Britanniques ; **~ old/young** les vieux/jeunes ; **~ impossible** l'impossible - **3.** [in dates] : **~ twelfth of May** le douze mai ; **~ forties** les années quarante - **4.** [in comparisons] : **~ more ... ~ less** plus ... moins ; **~ sooner ~ better** le plus tôt sera le mieux - **5.** [in titles] : **Alexander ~ Great** Alexandre le Grand ; **George ~ First** Georges Premier.

theatre, theater *Am* ['θɪətə'] *n* - **1.** THEATRE théâtre *m* - **2.** *Br* MED salle *f* d'opération - **3.** *Am* [cinema] cinéma *m*.

theatregoer, theatergoer *Am* ['θɪətə,gəʊə'] *n* habitué *m*, -e *f* du théâtre.

theatrical [θɪ'ætrɪkl] *adj* théâtral(e) ; [company] de théâtre.

theft [θeft] *n* vol *m*.

their [ðeə'] *poss adj* leur, leurs (*pl*) ; **~ house** leur maison ; **~ children** leurs enfants ; **it wasn't THEIR fault** ce n'était pas de leur faute à eux.

theirs [ðeəz] *poss pron* le leur (la leur), les leurs (*pl*) ; **that house is ~** cette maison est la leur, cette maison est à eux/elles ; **it wasn't our fault, it was THEIRS** ce n'était pas de notre faute, c'était de la leur ; **a friend of ~** un de leurs amis, un ami à eux/elles.

them [*weak form* ðəm, *strong form* ðem] *pers pron pl* - **1.** (direct) les ; **I know ~** je les connais ; **if I were OR was ~** si j'étais eux/elles, à leur place - **2.** (indirect) leur ; **we spoke to ~** nous leur avons parlé ; **she sent ~ a letter** elle leur a envoyé une lettre ; **I gave it to ~** je le leur ai donné - **3.** (stressed, after prep, in comparisons etc) eux (elles) ; **you can't expect THEM to do it** tu ne peux pas exiger que ce soit eux qui le fassent ; **with ~** avec eux/elles ; **without ~** sans eux/elles ; **we're not as wealthy as ~** nous ne sommes pas aussi riches qu'eux/qu'elles.

theme [θiːm] *n* - **1.** [topic, motif] thème *m*, sujet *m* - **2.** MUS thème *m* ; [signature tune] indicatif *m*.

theme park *n* parc *m* à thème.

theme pub *n* *Br* pub *m* à décor thématique.

theme tune *n* chanson *f* principale.

themselves [ðem'selvz] *pron* - **1.** (reflexive) se ; (after prep) eux (elles) - **2.** (for emphasis) eux-mêmes *mpl*, elles-mêmes *fpl* ; **they did it ~** ils l'ont fait tout seuls.

then [ðen] *adv* - **1.** [not now] alors, à cette époque - **2.** [next] puis, ensuite - **3.** [in that case] alors, dans ce cas - **4.** [therefore] donc - **5.** [also] d'ailleurs, et puis.

theology [θɪ'ɒlədʒɪ] *n* théologie *f*.

theoretical [θɪə'retɪkl] *adj* théorique.

theorize, -ise ['θɪəraɪz] *vi* : **to ~ (about)** émettre une théorie (sur), théoriser (sur).

theory ['θɪərɪ] *n* théorie *f* ; **in ~** en théorie.

therapist ['θerəpɪst] *n* thérapeute *mf*, psychothérapeute *mf*.

therapy ['θerəpɪ] *n (U)* thérapie *f*.

there [ðeəʳ] ⟨⟩ pron [indicating existence of sthg] : ~ **is/are** il y a ; ~'s **someone at the door** il y a quelqu'un à la porte ; ~ **must be some mistake** il doit y avoir erreur. ⟨⟩ adv - **1.** [in existence, available] y, là ; **is anybody ~?** il y a quelqu'un? ; **is John ~,** please? [when telephoning] est-ce que John est là, s'il vous plaît? - **2.** [referring to place] y, là ; **I'm going ~ next week** j'y vais la semaine prochaine ; ~ **it is** c'est là ; ~ **he is!** le voilà! ; **over ~** là-bas ; **it's six kilometres ~ and back** cela fait six kilomètres aller-retour. ⟨⟩ excl : ~, **I knew he'd turn up** tiens OR voilà, je savais bien qu'il s'amènerait ; ~, ~ **allons, allons.** ◆ **there and then, then and there** adv immédiatement, sur-le-champ.

thereabouts [ˌðeərə'baʊts], **thereabout** Am [ˌðeərə'baʊt] adv : **or ~** [nearby] par là ; [approximately] environ.

thereafter [ˌðeər'ɑːftəʳ] adv fml après cela, par la suite.

thereby [ˌðeər'baɪ] adv fml ainsi, de cette façon.

therefore ['ðeəfɔːʳ] adv donc, par conséquent.

there's [ðeəz] = **there is.**

thermal ['θɜːml] adj thermique ; [clothes] en Thermolactyl®.

thermometer [θə'mɒmɪtəʳ] n thermomètre m.

Thermos (flask)® ['θɜːməs-] n (bouteille f) Thermos® m or f.

thermostat ['θɜːməstæt] n thermostat m.

thesaurus [θɪ'sɔːrəs] (pl -es [-iːz]) n dictionnaire m de synonymes.

these [ðiːz] pl ⟹ **this.**

thesis ['θiːsɪs] (pl **theses** ['θiːsiːz]) n thèse f.

they [ðeɪ] pers pron pl - **1.** [people, things, animals - unstressed] ils (elles) ; [- stressed] eux (elles) ; ~'**re pleased** ils sont contents (elles sont contentes) ; ~'**re pretty earrings** ce sont de jolies boucles d'oreille ; **THEY can't do it** eux (elles), ils (elles) ne peuvent pas le faire ; **there ~ are** les voilà - **2.** [unspecified people] on, ils ; ~ **say it's going to snow** on dit qu'il va neiger.

they'd [ðeɪd] = **they had, they would.**

they'll [ðeɪl] = **they shall, they will.**

they're [ðeəʳ] = **they are.**

they've [ðeɪv] = **they have.**

thick [θɪk] ⟨⟩ adj - **1.** [gen] épais (épaisse) ; [forest, hedge, fog] dense ; [voice] indistinct(e) ; **to be 6 inches ~** avoir 15 cm d'épaisseur - **2.** inf [stupid] bouché(e).

⟨⟩ n : **in the ~ of** au plus fort de, en plein OR au beau milieu de.

thicken ['θɪkn] ⟨⟩ vt épaissir. ⟨⟩ vi s'épaissir.

thicket ['θɪkɪt] n fourré m.

thickness ['θɪknɪs] n épaisseur f.

thickset [ˌθɪk'set] adj trapu(e).

thick-skinned [-'skɪnd] adj qui a la peau dure.

thief [θiːf] (pl **thieves** [θiːvz]) n voleur m, -euse f.

thieve [θiːv] vt & vi voler.

thieves [θiːvz] pl ⟹ **thief.**

thigh [θaɪ] n cuisse f.

thimble ['θɪmbl] n dé m (à coudre).

thin [θɪn] adj - **1.** [slice, layer, paper] mince ; [cloth] léger(ère) ; [person] maigre - **2.** [liquid, sauce] clair(e), peu épais (peu épaisse) - **3.** [sparse - crowd] épars(e) ; [- vegetation, hair] clairsemé(e). ◆ **thin down** vt sep [liquid, paint] délayer, diluer ; [sauce] éclaircir.

thing [θɪŋ] n - **1.** [gen] chose f ; **the (best) ~ to do would be** ... le mieux serait de ... ; **the ~ is** ... le problème, c'est que ... - **2.** [anything] : **I don't know a ~** je n'y connais absolument rien - **3.** [object] chose f, objet m - **4.** [person] : **you poor ~!** mon pauvre! ◆ **things** npl - **1.** [clothes, possessions] affaires fpl - **2.** inf [life] : **how are ~s?** comment ça va?

think [θɪŋk] (pt & pp **thought**) ⟨⟩ vt - **1.** [believe] : **to ~ (that)** croire que, penser que ; **I ~ so/not** je crois que oui/non, je pense que oui/non - **2.** [have in mind] penser à - **3.** [imagine] s'imaginer - **4.** [in polite requests] : **do you ~ you could help me?** tu pourrais m'aider? ⟨⟩ vi - **1.** [use mind] réfléchir, penser - **2.** [have stated opinion] : **what do you ~ of** OR **about his new film?** que pensez-vous de son dernier film? ; **to ~ a lot of sb/sthg** penser beaucoup de bien de qqn/qqch - **3.** phr : **to ~ twice** y réfléchir à deux fois. ◆ **think about** vt fus : **to ~ about sb/sthg** songer à OR penser à qqn/qqch ; **to ~ about doing sthg** songer à faire qqch ; **I'll ~ about it** je vais y réfléchir. ◆ **think of** vt fus - **1.** [consider] = **think about** - **2.** [remember] se rappeler - **3.** [conceive] penser à, avoir l'idée de ; **to ~ of doing sthg** avoir l'idée de faire qqch. ◆ **think over** vt sep réfléchir à. ◆ **think up** vt sep imaginer.

think tank n comité m d'experts.

third [θɜːd] ⟨⟩ num troisième ; see also **sixth.** ⟨⟩ n Br UNIV ≃ licence f mention passable.

thirdly ['θɜːdlɪ] *adv* troisièmement, tertio.

third party insurance *n* assurance *f* de responsabilité civile.

third-rate *adj pej* de dernier OR troisième ordre.

Third World *n* : the ~ le tiers-monde.

thirst [θɜːst] *n* soif *f* ; ~ **for** *fig* soif de.

thirsty ['θɜːstɪ] *adj* - 1. [person] : **to be** OR **feel** ~ avoir soif - 2. [work] qui donne soif.

thirteen [ˌθɜː'tiːn] *num* treize ; *see also* six.

thirty ['θɜːtɪ] *num* trente ; *see also* sixty.

this [ðɪs] (*pl* these [ðiːz]) <> *pron (demonstrative use)* ce, ceci ; *(as opposed to 'that')* celui-ci (celle-ci) ; ~ **is for you** c'est pour vous ; **who's** ~? qui est-ce? ; **what's** ~? qu'est-ce que c'est? ; **which sweets does she prefer, these or those?** quels bonbons préfère-t-elle, ceux-ci ou ceux-là? ; ~ **is Daphne Logan** [introducing another person] je vous présente Daphne Logan ; [introducing oneself on phone] ici Daphne Logan, Daphne Logan à l'appareil. <> *adj* - 1. *(demonstrative use)* ce (cette), cet *(before vowel or silent 'h')*, ces *(pl)* ; *(as opposed to 'that')* ce (cette) ...-ci, ces ...-ci *(pl)* ; **these chocolates are delicious** ces chocolats sont délicieux ; **I prefer** ~ **book** je préfère ce livre-ci ; **I'll have** ~ **one** je prendrai celui-ci ; ~ **afternoon** cet après-midi ; ~ **morning** ce matin ; ~ **week** cette semaine - 2. *inf* [a certain] un certain (une certaine). <> *adv* aussi ; **it was** ~ **big** c'était aussi grand que ça ; **you'll need about** ~ **much** il vous en faudra à peu près comme ceci.

thistle ['θɪsl] *n* chardon *m*.

thong [θɒŋ] *n* [of leather] lanière *f*.

thorn [θɔːn] *n* épine *f*.

thorny ['θɔːnɪ] *adj lit & fig* épineux(euse).

thorough ['θʌrə] *adj* - 1. [exhaustive - search, inspection] minutieux(euse) ; [- investigation, knowledge] approfondi(e) - 2. [meticulous] méticuleux(euse) - 3. [complete, utter] complet(ète), absolu(e).

thoroughbred ['θʌrəbred] *n* pur-sang *m inv*.

thoroughfare ['θʌrəfeəʳ] *n fml* rue *f*, voie *f* publique.

thoroughly ['θʌrəlɪ] *adv* - 1. [fully, in detail] à fond - 2. [completely, utterly] absolument, complètement.

those [ðəʊz] *pl* ▷ that.

though [ðəʊ] <> *conj* bien que (+ *subjunctive*), quoique (+ *subjunctive*). <> *adv* pourtant, cependant.

thought [θɔːt] <> *pt & pp* ▷ think. <> *n* - 1. [gen] pensée *f* ; [idea] idée *f*, pensée ; **after much** ~ après avoir mûrement réfléchi - 2. [intention] intention *f*. ◆ **thoughts** *npl* - 1. [reflections] pensées *fpl*, réflexions *fpl* - 2. [views] opinions *fpl*, idées *fpl*.

thoughtful ['θɔːtfʊl] *adj* - 1. [pensive] pensif(ive) - 2. [considerate - person] prévenant(e), attentionné(e) ; [- remark, act] plein(e) de gentillesse.

thoughtless ['θɔːtlɪs] *adj* [person] qui manque d'égards (envers les autres) ; [remark, behaviour] irréfléchi(e).

thousand ['θaʊznd] *num* mille ; **a** OR **one** ~ mille ; **~s of** des milliers de ; *see also* six.

thousandth ['θaʊzntθ] *num* millième ; *see also* sixth.

thrash [θræʃ] *vt* - 1. [hit] battre, rosser - 2. *inf* [defeat] écraser, battre à plates coutures. ◆ **thrash about, thrash around** *vi* s'agiter. ◆ **thrash out** *vt sep* [problem] débrouiller, démêler ; [idea] débattre, discuter.

thread [θred] <> *n* - 1. [gen] fil *m* - 2. [of screw] filet *m*, pas *m*. <> *vt* [needle] enfiler.

threadbare ['θredbeəʳ] *adj* usé(e) jusqu'à la corde.

threat [θret] *n* : ~ **(to)** menace *f* (pour).

threaten ['θretn] <> *vt* : **to** ~ **sb (with)** menacer qqn (de) ; **to** ~ **to do sthg** menacer de faire qqch. <> *vi* menacer.

three [θriː] *num* trois ; *see also* six.

three-dimensional [-dɪ'menʃənl] *adj* [film, picture] en relief ; [object] à trois dimensions.

threefold ['θriːfəʊld] <> *adj* triple. <> *adv* : **to increase** ~ tripler.

three-piece *adj* : ~ **suit** (costume *m*) trois pièces *m* ; ~ **suite** canapé *m* et deux fauteuils assortis.

three-ply *adj* [wool] à trois fils.

thresh [θreʃ] *vt* battre.

threshold ['θreʃhəʊld] *n* seuil *m*.

threw [θruː] *pt* ▷ throw.

thrifty ['θrɪftɪ] *adj* économe.

thrill [θrɪl] <> *n* - 1. [sudden feeling] frisson *m*, sensation *f* - 2. [enjoyable experience] plaisir *m*. <> *vt* transporter, exciter.

thrilled [θrɪld] *adj* : ~ **(with sthg/to do sthg)** ravi(e) (de qqch/de faire qqch), enchanté(e) (de qqch/de faire qqch).

thriller ['θrɪləʳ] *n* thriller *m*.

thrilling ['θrɪlɪŋ] *adj* saisissant(e), palpitant(e).

thrive [θraɪv] (*pt* -d OR **throve**, *pp* -d) *vi*

[person] bien se porter ; [plant] pousser bien ; [business] prospérer.

thriving ['θraɪvɪŋ] *adj* [person] bien portant(e) ; [plant] qui pousse bien ; [business] prospère.

throat [θrəʊt] *n* gorge *f*.

throb [θrɒb] *vi* [heart] palpiter, battre fort ; [engine] vibrer ; [music] taper ; **my head is throbbing** j'ai des élancements dans la tête.

throes [θrəʊz] *npl* : **to be in the ~ of** [war, disease] être en proie à ; **to be in the ~ of an argument** être en pleine dispute.

throne [θrəʊn] *n* trône *m*.

throng [θrɒŋ] ◇ *n* foule *f*, multitude *f*. ◇ *vt* remplir, encombrer.

throttle ['θrɒtl] ◇ *n* [valve] papillon *m* des gaz ; [lever] commande *f* des gaz. ◇ *vt* [strangle] étrangler.

through [θru:] ◇ *adj* [finished] : **are you ~?** tu as fini ? ; **to be ~ with sthg** avoir fini qqch. ◇ *adv* : **to let sb ~** laisser passer qqn ; **to read sthg ~** lire qqch jusqu'au bout ; **to sleep ~ till ten** dormir jusqu'à dix heures. ◇ *prep* - **1.** [relating to place, position] à travers ; **to travel ~ sthg** traverser qqch ; **to cut ~ sthg** couper qqch - **2.** [during] pendant - **3.** [because of] à cause de - **4.** [by means of] par l'intermédiaire de, par l'entremise de - **5.** *Am* [up till and including] : **Monday ~ Friday** du lundi au vendredi. ◆ **through and through** *adv* [completely] jusqu'au bout des ongles ; [thoroughly] par cœur, à fond.

throughout [θru:'aʊt] ◇ *prep* - **1.** [during] pendant, durant ; **~ the meeting** pendant toute la réunion - **2.** [everywhere in] partout dans. ◇ *adv* - **1.** [all the time] tout le temps - **2.** [everywhere] partout.

throve [θrəʊv] *pt* ⊏ thrive.

throw [θrəʊ] (*pt* threw, *pp* thrown) ◇ *vt* - **1.** [gen] jeter ; [ball, javelin] lancer - **2.** [rider] désarçonner - **3.** *fig* [confuse] déconcerter, décontenancer. ◇ *n* lancement *m*, jet *m*. ◆ **throw away** *vt sep* - **1.** [discard] jeter - **2.** *fig* [money] gaspiller ; [opportunity] perdre. ◆ **throw out** *vt sep* - **1.** [discard] jeter - **2.** *fig* [reject] rejeter - **3.** [from house] mettre à la porte ; [from army, school] expulser, renvoyer. ◆ **throw up** *vi inf* [vomit] dégobiller, vomir.

throwaway ['θrəʊəˌweɪ] *adj* - **1.** [disposable] jetable, à jeter - **2.** [remark] désinvolte.

throw-in *n Br* FTBL rentrée *f* en touche.

thrown [θrəʊn] *pp* ⊏ throw.

thru [θru:] *Am inf* = through.

thrush [θrʌʃ] *n* - **1.** [bird] grive *f* - **2.** MED muguet *m*.

thrust [θrʌst] ◇ *n* - **1.** [forward movement] poussée *f* ; [of knife] coup *m* - **2.** [main aspect] idée *f* principale, aspect *m* principal. ◇ *vt* [shove] enfoncer, fourrer.

thud [θʌd] ◇ *n* bruit *m* sourd. ◇ *vi* tomber en faisant un bruit sourd.

thug [θʌg] *n* brute *f*, voyou *m*.

thumb [θʌm] ◇ *n* pouce *m*. ◇ *vt inf* [hitch] : **to ~ a lift** faire du stop OR de l'autostop. ◆ **thumb through** *vt fus* feuilleter, parcourir.

thumbs down [ˌθʌmz-] *n* : **to get** OR **be given the ~** être rejeté(e).

thumbs up [ˌθʌmz-] *n* [go-ahead] : **to give sb the ~** donner le feu vert à qqn.

thumbtack ['θʌmtæk] *n Am* punaise *f*.

thump [θʌmp] ◇ *n* - **1.** [blow] grand coup *m* - **2.** [thud] bruit *m* sourd. ◇ *vt* [hit] cogner, taper sur. ◇ *vi* [heart] battre fort.

thunder ['θʌndə^r] ◇ *n* (U) - **1.** METEOR tonnerre *m* - **2.** *fig* [of traffic] vacarme *m* ; [of applause] tonnerre *m*. ◇ *v impers* METEOR tonner.

thunderbolt ['θʌndəbəʊlt] *n* coup *m* de foudre.

thunderclap ['θʌndəklæp] *n* coup *m* de tonnerre.

thunderstorm ['θʌndəstɔ:m] *n* orage *m*.

thundery ['θʌndərɪ] *adj* orageux(euse).

Thursday ['θɜːzdɪ] *n* jeudi *m* ; *see also* **Saturday**.

thus [ðʌs] *adv fml* - **1.** [therefore] par conséquent, donc, ainsi - **2.** [in this way] ainsi, de cette façon, comme ceci.

thwart [θwɔːt] *vt* contrecarrer, contrarier.

thyme [taɪm] *n* thym *m*.

thyroid ['θaɪrɔɪd] *n* thyroïde *f*.

tiara [tɪ'ɑːrə] *n* [worn by woman] diadème *m*.

Tibet [tɪ'bet] *n* Tibet *m*.

tic [tɪk] *n* tic *m*.

tick [tɪk] ◇ *n* - **1.** [written mark] coche *f* - **2.** [sound] tic tac *m* - **3.** [insect] tique *f*. ◇ *vt* cocher. ◇ *vi* faire tic-tac. ◆ **tick off** *vt sep* - **1.** [mark off] cocher - **2.** [tell off] enguirlander. ◆ **tick over** *vi* [engine, business] tourner au ralenti.

ticket ['tɪkɪt] *n* - **1.** [for access, train, plane] billet *m* ; [for bus] ticket *m* ; [for library] carte *f* ; [label on product] étiquette *f* - **2.** [for traffic offence] P.-V. *m*, papillon *m*.

ticket collector *n Br* contrôleur *m*, -euse *f*.

ticket inspector *n Br* contrôleur *m*, -euse *f*.

ticket machine *n* distributeur *m* de billets.

ticket office *n* bureau *m* de vente des billets.

tickle ['tɪkl] ◇ *vt* - **1.** [touch lightly] chatouiller - **2.** *fig* [amuse] amuser. ◇ *vi* chatouiller.

ticklish ['tɪklɪʃ] *adj* [person] qui craint les chatouilles, chatouilleux(euse).

tidal ['taɪdl] *adj* [force] de la marée ; [river] à marées ; [barrier] contre la marée.

tidal wave *n* raz-de-marée *m inv*.

tidbit *Am* = titbit.

tiddlywinks ['tɪdlɪwɪŋks], **tiddledywinks** *Am* ['tɪdldɪwɪŋks] *n* jeu *m* de puce.

tide [taɪd] *n* - **1.** [of sea] marée *f* - **2.** *fig* [of opinion, fashion] courant *m*, tendance *f* ; [of protest] vague *f*.

tidy ['taɪdɪ] ◇ *adj* - **1.** [room, desk] en ordre, bien rangé(e) ; [hair, dress] soigné(e) - **2.** [person - in habits] ordonné(e) ; [- in appearance] soigné(e). ◇ *vt* ranger, mettre de l'ordre dans. ◆ **tidy up** ◇ *vt sep* ranger, mettre de l'ordre dans. ◇ *vi* ranger.

tie [taɪ] (*pt & pp* **tied**, *cont* **tying**) ◇ *n* - **1.** [necktie] cravate *f* - **2.** [in game, competition] égalité *f* de points. ◇ *vt* - **1.** [fasten] attacher - **2.** [shoelaces] nouer, attacher ; **to ~ a knot** faire un nœud - **3.** *fig* [link] : **to be ~d to** être lié(e) à. ◇ *vi* [draw] être à égalité. ◆ **tie down** *vt sep fig* [restrict] restreindre la liberté de. ◆ **tie in with** *vt fus* concorder avec, coïncider avec. ◆ **tie up** *vt sep* - **1.** [with string, rope] attacher - **2.** [shoelaces] nouer, attacher - **3.** *fig* [money, resources] immobiliser - **4.** *fig* [link] : **to be ~d up with** être lié(e) à.

tiebreak(er) ['taɪbreɪk(əʳ)] *n* - **1.** TENNIS tie-break *m* - **2.** [in game, competition] question *f* subsidiaire.

tiepin ['taɪpɪn] *n* épingle *f* de cravate.

tier [tɪəʳ] *n* [of seats] gradin *m* ; [of cake] étage *m*.

tiff [tɪf] *n* bisbille *f*, petite querelle *f*.

tiger ['taɪgəʳ] *n* tigre *m*.

tight [taɪt] ◇ *adj* - **1.** [clothes, group, competition, knot] serré(e) - **2.** [taut] tendue(e) - **3.** [schedule] serré(e), minuté(e) - **4.** [strict] strict(e), sévère - **5.** [corner, bend] raide - **6.** *inf* [drunk] soûl(e), rond(e) - **7.** *inf* [miserly] radin(e), avare. ◇ *adv* - **1.** [firmly, securely] bien, fort ; **to hold ~** tenir bien ; **hold ~!** tiens bon! ; **to shut** OR **close sthg ~** bien fermer qqch - **2.** [tautly] à fond. ◆ **tights** *npl* collant *m*, collants *mpl*.

tighten ['taɪtn] ◇ *vt* - **1.** [belt, knot, screw] resserrer ; **to ~ one's hold** OR **grip on** resserrer sa prise sur - **2.** [pull tauter] tendre - **3.** [make stricter] renforcer. ◇ *vi* - **1.** [rope] se tendre - **2.** [grip, hold] se resserrer.

tightfisted [ˌtaɪt'fɪstɪd] *adj pej* radin(e), pingre.

tightly ['taɪtlɪ] *adv* [firmly] bien, fort.

tightrope ['taɪtrəʊp] *n* corde *f* raide.

tile [taɪl] *n* [on roof] tuile *f* ; [on floor, wall] carreau *m*.

tiled [taɪld] *adj* [floor, wall] carrelé(e) ; [roof] couvert de tuiles.

till [tɪl] ◇ *prep* jusqu'à ; **from six ~ ten o'clock** de six heures à dix heures. ◇ *conj* jusqu'à ce que (*+ subjunctive*) ; **wait - I come back** attends que je revienne ; *(after negative)* avant que (*+ subjunctive*) ; **it won't be ready ~ tomorrow** ça ne sera pas prêt avant demain. ◇ *n* tiroir-caisse *m*.

tiller ['tɪləʳ] *n* NAUT barre *f*.

tilt [tɪlt] ◇ *vt* incliner, pencher. ◇ *vi* s'incliner, pencher.

timber ['tɪmbəʳ] *n* - **1.** (*U*) [wood] bois *m* de charpente OR de construction - **2.** [beam] poutre *f*, madrier *m*.

time [taɪm] ◇ *n* - **1.** [gen] temps *m* ; **a long ~** longtemps ; **in a short ~** dans peu de temps, sous peu ; **to take ~** prendre du temps ; **to be ~ for sthg** être l'heure de qqch ; **to have a good ~** s'amuser bien ; **in good ~** de bonne heure ; **ahead of ~** en avance, avant l'heure ; **on ~** à l'heure ; **to have no ~ for sb/sthg** ne pas supporter qqn/qqch ; **to pass the ~** passer le temps ; **to play for ~** essayer de gagner du temps - **2.** [as measured by clock] heure *f* ; **what's the ~?** quelle heure est-il? ; **in a week's/year's ~** dans une semaine/un an - **3.** [point in time in past] époque *f* ; **before my ~** avant que j'arrive ici - **4.** [occasion] fois *f* ; **from ~ to ~** de temps en temps, de temps à autre ; **~ after ~, ~ and again** à maintes reprises, maintes et maintes fois - **5.** MUS mesure *f*. ◇ *vt* - **1.** [schedule] fixer, prévoir - **2.** [race, runner] chronométrer - **3.** [arrival, remark] choisir le moment de. ◆ **times** ◇ *npl* fois *fpl* ; **four ~s as much as me** quatre fois plus que moi. ◇ *prep* MATH fois. ◆ **at a time** *adv* d'affilée ; **one at a ~** un par un, un seul à la fois ; **months at a ~** des mois et des mois. ◆ **at times** *adv* quelquefois, parfois. ◆ **at the same time** *adv* en même temps. ◆ **about time** *adv* : **it's about ~ (that) ...** il est grand temps que ... ; **about ~ too!** ce n'est pas trop tôt! ◆ **for the time being** *adv* pour le moment. ◆ **in time** *adv* - **1.** [not late] : **in**

~ **(for)** à l'heure (pour) - **2.** [eventually] à la fin, à la longue ; [after a while] avec le temps, à la longue.

time bomb *n lit & fig* bombe *f* à retardement.

time lag *n* décalage *m*.

timeless ['taɪmlɪs] *adj* éternel(elle).

time limit *n* délai *m*.

timely ['taɪmlɪ] *adj* opportun(e).

time off *n* temps *m* libre.

time out *n* SPORT temps *m* mort.

timer ['taɪmə'] *n* minuteur *m*.

time scale *n* période *f* ; [of project] délai *m*.

time-share *n Br* logement *m* en multipropriété.

time switch *n* minuterie *f*.

timetable ['taɪm,teɪbl] *n* - **1.** SCH emploi *m* du temps - **2.** [of buses, trains] horaire *m* - **3.** [schedule] calendrier *m*.

time zone *n* fuseau *m* horaire.

timid ['tɪmɪd] *adj* timide.

timing ['taɪmɪŋ] *n* (*U*) - **1.** [of remark] à-propos *m* - **2.** [scheduling] : **the ~ of the election** le moment choisi pour l'élection - **3.** [measuring] chronométrage *m*.

timpani ['tɪmpənɪ] *npl* timbales *fpl*.

tin [tɪn] *n* - **1.** (*U*) [metal] étain *m* ; [in sheets] fer-blanc *m* - **2.** *Br* [can] boîte *f* de conserve - **3.** [small container] boîte *f*.

tin can *n* boîte *f* de conserve.

tinfoil ['tɪnfɔɪl] *n* (*U*) papier *m* (d')aluminium.

tinge [tɪndʒ] *n* - **1.** [of colour] teinte *f*, nuance *f* - **2.** [of feeling] nuance *f*.

tinged [tɪndʒd] *adj* : **~ with** teinté(e) de.

tingle ['tɪŋgl] *vi* picoter.

tinker ['tɪŋkə'] <> *n Br pej* [gypsy] romanichel *m*, -elle *f* <> *vi* : **to ~ (with sthg)** bricoler (qqch).

tinkle ['tɪŋkl] *vi* [ring] tinter.

tinned [tɪnd] *adj Br* en boîte.

tin opener *n Br* ouvre-boîtes *m inv*.

tinsel ['tɪnsl] *n* (*U*) guirlandes *fpl* de Noël.

tint [tɪnt] *n* teinte *f*, nuance *f* ; [in hair] rinçage *m*.

tinted ['tɪntɪd] *adj* [glasses, windows] teinté(e).

tiny ['taɪnɪ] *adj* minuscule.

tip [tɪp] <> *n* - **1.** [end] bout *m* - **2.** *Br* [dump] décharge *f* - **3.** [to waiter etc] pourboire *m* - **4.** [piece of advice] tuyau *m*. <> *vt* - **1.** [tilt] faire basculer - **2.** [spill] renverser - **3.** [waiter etc] donner un pourboire à.

<> *vi* - **1.** [tilt] basculer - **2.** [spill] se renverser. ◆ **tip over** <> *vt sep* renverser. <> *vi* se renverser.

tip-off *n* tuyau *m* ; [to police] dénonciation *f*.

tipped ['tɪpt] *adj* [cigarette] à bout filtre.

tipsy ['tɪpsɪ] *adj inf* gai(e).

tiptoe ['tɪptəʊ] <> *n* : **on ~** sur la pointe des pieds. <> *vi* marcher sur la pointe des pieds.

tip-top *adj inf dated* excellent(e).

tire ['taɪə'] <> *n Am* = tyre. <> *vt* fatiguer. <> *vi* - **1.** [get tired] se fatiguer - **2.** [get fed up] : **to ~ of** se lasser de.

tired ['taɪəd] *adj* - **1.** [sleepy] fatigué(e), las (lasse) - **2.** [fed up] : **to be ~ of sthg/of doing sthg** en avoir assez de qqch/de faire qqch.

tireless ['taɪəlɪs] *adj* infatigable.

tiresome ['taɪəsəm] *adj* ennuyeux(euse).

tiring ['taɪərɪŋ] *adj* fatigant(e).

tissue ['tɪʃuː] *n* - **1.** [paper handkerchief] mouchoir *m* en papier - **2.** (*U*) BIOL tissu *m*.

tissue paper *n* (*U*) papier *m* de soie.

tit [tɪt] *n* - **1.** [bird] mésange *f* - **2.** *vulg* [breast] nichon *m*, néné *m*.

titbit *Br* ['tɪtbɪt], **tidbit** *Am* ['tɪdbɪt] *n* - **1.** [of food] bon morceau *m* - **2.** *fig* [of news] petite nouvelle *f*.

tit for tat [-'tæt] *n* un prêté pour un rendu.

titillate ['tɪtɪleɪt] *vt* titiller.

title ['taɪtl] *n* titre *m*.

title deed *n* titre *m* de propriété.

title role *n* rôle *m* principal.

titter ['tɪtə'] *vi* rire bêtement.

TM *abbr of* **trademark**.

to [unstressed before consonant tə, unstressed before vowel tu, stressed tuː] <> *prep* - **1.** [indicating place, direction] à ; **to go ~ Liverpool/Spain/school** aller à Liverpool/en Espagne/à l'école ; **to go ~ the butcher's** aller chez le boucher ; **~ the left/right** à gauche/droite - **2.** (*to express indirect object*) à ; **to give sthg ~ sb** donner qqch à qqn ; **we were listening ~ the radio** nous écoutions la radio - **3.** [indicating reaction, effect] à ; **~ my delight/surprise** à ma grande joie/surprise - **4.** [in stating opinion] : **~ me, ...** à mon avis, ... ; **it seemed quite unnecessary ~ me/him** *etc* cela me/lui *etc* semblait tout à fait inutile - **5.** [indicating state, process] : **to drive sb ~ drink** pousser qqn à boire ; **it could lead ~ trouble** cela pourrait causer des ennuis - **6.** [as far as] à, jusqu'à ; **to count ~ 10** compter jusqu'à 10 ; **we work from 9 ~ 5** nous travaillons de 9 heures à 17 heures

- **7.** [in expressions of time] moins ; **it's ten ~ three/quarter ~ one** il est trois heures moins dix/une heure moins le quart - **8.** [per] à ; **40 miles ~ the gallon** ≃ 7 litres aux cent (km) - **9.** [of, for] de ; **the key ~ the car** la clef de la voiture ; **a letter ~ my daughter** une lettre à ma fille. ◇ *adv* [shut] : **push the door ~** fermez la porte. ◇ *with infinitive* - **1.** *(forming simple infinitive)* : **~ walk** marcher ; **~ laugh** rire - **2.** *(following another verb)* : **to begin ~ do sthg** commencer à faire qqch ; **to try ~ do sthg** essayer de faire qqch ; **to want ~ do sthg** vouloir faire qqch - **3.** *(following an adjective)* : **difficult ~ do** difficile à faire ; **ready ~ go** prêt à partir - **4.** *(indicating purpose)* pour ; **he worked hard ~ pass his exam** il a travaillé dur pour réussir son examen - **5.** *(substituting for a relative clause)* : **I have a lot ~ do** j'ai beaucoup à faire ; **he told me ~ leave** il m'a dit de partir - **6.** *(to avoid repetition of infinitive)* : **I meant to call him but I forgot ~** je voulais l'appeler, mais j'ai oublié - **7.** [in comments] : **~ be honest ...** en toute franchise ... ; **~ sum up, ...** en résumé, ..., pour récapituler, ...

toad [təʊd] *n* crapaud *m*.

toadstool ['təʊdstu:l] *n* champignon *m* vénéneux.

to and fro *adv* : **to go ~** aller et venir ; **to walk ~** marcher de long en large. ◆ **to-and-fro** *adj* de va-et-vient.

toast [təʊst] ◇ *n* - **1.** *(U)* [bread] pain *m* grillé, toast *m* - **2.** [drink] toast *m*. ◇ *vt* - **1.** [bread] (faire) griller - **2.** [person] porter un toast à.

toasted sandwich [ˌtəʊstɪd-] *n* sandwich *m* grillé.

toaster ['təʊstə[r]] *n* grille-pain *m inv*.

tobacco [tə'bækəʊ] *n* *(U)* tabac *m*.

tobacconist [tə'bækənɪst] *n* Br buraliste *mf* ; **~'s (shop)** bureau *m* de tabac.

toboggan [tə'bɒgən] *n* luge *f*, traîne *f* sauvage Can.

today [tə'deɪ] ◇ *n* aujourd'hui *m*. ◇ *adv* aujourd'hui.

toddler ['tɒdlə[r]] *n* tout-petit *m* *(qui commence à marcher)*.

toddy ['tɒdɪ] *n* grog *m*.

to-do *(pl -s)* *n inf dated* histoire *f*.

toe [təʊ] ◇ *n* [of foot] orteil *m*, doigt *m* de pied ; [of sock, shoe] bout *m*. ◇ *vt* : **to ~ the line** se plier.

TOEFL [tɒfl] *(abbr of* **Test of English as a Foreign Language)** *n* test d'anglais passé par les étudiants étrangers désirant faire des études dans une université américaine.

toenail ['təʊneɪl] *n* ongle *m* d'orteil.

toffee ['tɒfɪ] *n* caramel *m*.

toga ['təʊgə] *n* toge *f*.

together [tə'geðə[r]] *adv* - **1.** [gen] ensemble - **2.** [at the same time] en même temps. ◆ **together with** *prep* ainsi que.

toil [tɔɪl] *literary* ◇ *n* labeur *m*. ◇ *vi* travailler dur.

toilet ['tɔɪlɪt] *n* [lavatory] toilettes *fpl*, cabinets *mpl* ; **to go to the ~** aller aux toilettes OR aux cabinets.

toilet bag *n* trousse *f* de toilette.

toilet paper *n* *(U)* papier *m* hygiénique.

toiletries ['tɔɪlɪtrɪz] *npl* articles *mpl* de toilette.

toilet roll *n* rouleau *m* de papier hygiénique.

toilet water *n* eau *f* de toilette.

token ['təʊkn] ◇ *adj* symbolique. ◇ *n* - **1.** [voucher] bon *m* - **2.** [symbol] marque *f*. ◆ **by the same token** *adv* de même.

told [təʊld] *pt & pp* ▷ **tell**.

tolerable ['tɒlərəbl] *adj* passable.

tolerance ['tɒlərəns] *n* tolérance *f*.

tolerant ['tɒlərənt] *adj* tolérant(e).

tolerate ['tɒləreɪt] *vt* - **1.** [put up with] supporter - **2.** [permit] tolérer.

toll [təʊl] ◇ *n* - **1.** [number] nombre *m* - **2.** [fee] péage *m* - **3.** *phr* : **to take its ~** se faire sentir. ◇ *vt & vi* sonner.

toll-free *Am adv* : **to call ~** appeler un numéro vert.

tomato [*Br* tə'ma:təʊ, *Am* tə'meɪtəʊ] *(pl -es)* *n* tomate *f*.

tomb [tu:m] *n* tombe *f*.

tomboy ['tɒmbɔɪ] *n* garçon *m* manqué.

tombstone ['tu:mstəʊn] *n* pierre *f* tombale.

tomcat ['tɒmkæt] *n* matou *m*.

tomorrow [tə'mɒrəʊ] ◇ *n* demain *m*. ◇ *adv* demain.

ton [tʌn] *(pl inv* OR *-s)* *n* - **1.** [imperial] = 1016 kg *Br*, = 907,2 kg *Am*, ≃ tonne *f* - **2.** [metric] = 1000 kg, tonne *f*. ◆ **tons** *npl inf* : **~s (of)** des tas (de), plein (de).

tone [təʊn] *n* - **1.** [gen] ton *m* - **2.** [on phone] tonalité *f* ; [on answering machine] bip *m* sonore. ◆ **tone down** *vt sep* modérer. ◆ **tone up** *vt sep* tonifier.

tone-deaf *adj* qui n'a aucune oreille.

tongs [tɒŋz] *npl* pinces *fpl* ; [for hair] fer *m* à friser.

tongue [tʌŋ] *n* - **1.** [gen] langue *f* ; **to hold**

one's ~ *fig* tenir sa langue - **2.** [of shoe] languette *f*.

tongue-in-cheek *adj* ironique.

tongue-tied [-ˌtaɪd] *adj* muet(ette).

tongue twister [-ˌtwɪstə'] *n* phrase *f* difficile à dire.

tonic ['tɒnɪk] *n* - **1.** [tonic water] Schweppes® *m* - **2.** [medicine] tonique *m*.

tonic water *n* Schweppes® *m*.

tonight [tə'naɪt] ◇ *n* ce soir *m* ; [late] cette nuit *f*. ◇ *adv* ce soir ; [late] cette nuit.

tonnage ['tʌnɪdʒ] *n* tonnage *m*.

tonne [tʌn] (*pl inv* OR **-s**) *n* tonne *f*.

tonsil ['tɒnsl] *n* amygdale *f*.

tonsil(l)itis [ˌtɒnsɪ'laɪtɪs] *n* (*U*) amygdalite *f*.

too [tu:] *adv* - **1.** [also] aussi - **2.** [excessively] trop ; ~ **many people** trop de gens ; **it was over all ~ soon** ça s'était terminé bien trop tôt ; **I'd be only ~ happy to help** je serais trop heureux de vous aider ; **I wasn't ~ impressed** ça ne m'a pas impressionné outre mesure.

took [tʊk] *pt* ▷ **take**.

tool [tu:l] *n lit & fig* outil *m*.

tool box *n* boîte *f* à outils.

tool kit *n* trousse *f* à outils.

toot [tu:t] ◇ *n* coup *m* de Klaxon®. ◇ *vi* klaxonner.

tooth [tu:θ] (*pl* **teeth** [ti:θ]) *n* dent *f*.

toothache ['tu:θeɪk] *n* mal *m* OR rage *f* de dents ; **to have ~** *Br*, **to have a ~** *Am* avoir mal aux dents.

toothbrush ['tu:θbrʌʃ] *n* brosse *f* à dents.

toothpaste ['tu:θpeɪst] *n* (pâte *f*) dentifrice *m*.

toothpick ['tu:θpɪk] *n* cure-dents *m inv*.

top [tɒp] ◇ *adj* - **1.** [highest] du haut - **2.** [most important, successful - officials] important(e) ; [- executives] supérieur(e) ; [- pop singer] fameux(euse) ; [- sportsman, sportswoman] meilleur(e) ; [- in exam] premier(ère) - **3.** [maximum] maximum. ◇ *n* - **1.** [highest point - of hill] sommet *m* ; [- of page, pile] haut *m* ; [- of tree] cime *f* ; [- of list] début *m*, tête *f* ; **on ~** dessus ; **at the ~ of one's voice** à tue-tête - **2.** [lid - of bottle, tube] bouchon *m* ; [- of pen] capuchon *m* ; [- of jar] couvercle *m* - **3.** [of table, box] dessus *m* - **4.** [clothing] haut *m* - **5.** [toy] toupie *f* - **6.** [highest rank - in league] tête *f* ; [- in scale] haut *m* ; [- SCH] premier *m*, -ère *f*. ◇ *vt* - **1.** [be first in] être en tête de - **2.** [better] surpasser - **3.** [exceed] dépasser. ◆ **on top of** *prep* - **1.** [in space] sur - **2.** [in addition to] en plus de. ◆ **top up** *Br*, **top off** *Am vt sep* remplir.

top floor *n* dernier étage *m*.

top hat *n* haut-de-forme *m*.

top-heavy *adj* mal équilibré(e).

topic ['tɒpɪk] *n* sujet *m*.

topical ['tɒpɪkl] *adj* d'actualité.

topless ['tɒplɪs] *adj* [woman] aux seins nus.

top-level *adj* au plus haut niveau.

topmost ['tɒpməʊst] *adj* le plus haut (la plus haute).

topping ['tɒpɪŋ] *n* garniture *f*.

topple ['tɒpl] ◇ *vt* renverser. ◇ *vi* basculer.

top-secret *adj* top secret (top secrète).

topspin ['tɒpspɪn] *n* lift *m*.

topsy-turvy [ˌtɒpsɪ'tɜːvɪ] *adj* - **1.** [messy] sens dessus dessous - **2.** [confused] : **to be ~** ne pas tourner rond.

torch [tɔːtʃ] *n* - **1.** *Br* [electric] lampe *f* électrique - **2.** [burning] torche *f*.

tore [tɔː'] *pt* ▷ **tear²**.

torment [*n* 'tɔːment, *vb* tɔː'ment] ◇ *n* tourment *m*. ◇ *vt* tourmenter.

torn [tɔːn] *pp* ▷ **tear²**.

tornado [tɔː'neɪdəʊ] (*pl* **-es** OR **-s**) *n* tornade *f*.

torpedo [tɔː'piːdəʊ] (*pl* **-es**) *n* torpille *f*.

torrent ['tɒrənt] *n* torrent *m*.

torrid ['tɒrɪd] *adj* - **1.** [hot] torride - **2.** *fig* [passionate] ardent(e).

tortoise ['tɔːtəs] *n* tortue *f*.

tortoiseshell ['tɔːtəʃel] ◇ *adj* : ~ **cat** chat *m* roux tigré. ◇ *n* (*U*) [material] écaille *f*.

torture ['tɔːtʃə'] ◇ *n* torture *f*. ◇ *vt* torturer.

Tory ['tɔːrɪ] ◇ *adj* tory, conservateur (trice). ◇ *n* tory *mf*, conservateur *m*, -trice *f*.

toss [tɒs] ◇ *vt* - **1.** [throw] jeter ; **to ~ a coin** jouer à pile ou face ; **to ~ one's head** rejeter la tête en arrière - **2.** [salad] remuer ; [pancake] faire sauter - **3.** [throw about] ballotter. ◇ *vi* [move about] : **to ~ and turn** se tourner et se retourner. ◆ **toss up** *vi* jouer à pile ou face.

tot [tɒt] *n* - **1.** *inf* [small child] tout-petit *m* - **2.** [of drink] larme *f*, goutte *f*.

total ['təʊtl] ◇ *adj* total(e) ; [disgrace, failure] complet(ète). ◇ *n* total *m*. ◇ *vt* - **1.** [add up] additionner - **2.** [amount to] s'élever à.

totalitarian [ˌtəʊtælɪ'teərɪən] *adj* totalitaire.

totally ['təʊtəlɪ] *adv* totalement ; **I ~ agree** je suis entièrement d'accord.

totter ['tɒtəʳ] *vi lit & fig* chanceler.

touch [tʌtʃ] ◇ *n* **- 1.** *(U)* [sense] toucher *m* **- 2.** [detail] touche *f* **- 3.** *(U)* [skill] marque *f*, note *f* **- 4.** [contact] : **to keep in ~ (with sb)** rester en contact (avec qqn) ; **to get in ~ with sb** entrer en contact avec qqn ; **to lose ~ with sb** perdre qqn de vue ; **to be out of ~ with** ne plus être au courant de **- 5.** SPORT : **in ~** en touche **- 6.** [small amount] : **a ~** un petit peu. ◇ *vt* toucher. ◇ *vi* [be in contact] se toucher. ◆ **touch down** *vi* [plane] atterrir. ◆ **touch on** *vt fus* effleurer.

touch-and-go *adj* incertain(e).

touchdown ['tʌtʃdaʊn] *n* **- 1.** [of plane] atterrissage *m* **- 2.** [in American football] but *m*.

touched [tʌtʃt] *adj* **- 1.** [grateful] touché(e) **- 2.** *inf* [slightly mad] fêlé(e).

touching ['tʌtʃɪŋ] *adj* touchant(e).

touchline ['tʌtʃlaɪn] *n* ligne *f* de touche.

touchy ['tʌtʃɪ] *adj* **- 1.** [person] susceptible **- 2.** [subject, question] délicat(e).

tough [tʌf] *adj* **- 1.** [material, vehicle, person] solide ; [character, life] dur(e) **- 2.** [meat] dur(e) **- 3.** [decision, problem, task] difficile **- 4.** [rough - area of town] dangereux(euse) **- 5.** [strict] sévère.

toughen ['tʌfn] *vt* **- 1.** [character] endurcir **- 2.** [material] renforcer.

toupee ['tu:peɪ] *n* postiche *m*.

tour [tʊəʳ] ◇ *n* **- 1.** [journey] voyage *m* ; [by pop group etc] tournée *f* **- 2.** [of town, museum] visite *f*, tour *m*. ◇ *vt* visiter.

touring ['tʊərɪŋ] *n* tourisme *m*.

tourism ['tʊərɪzm] *n* tourisme *m*.

tourist ['tʊərɪst] *n* touriste *mf*.

tourist (information) office *n* office *m* de tourisme.

tournament ['tɔːnəmənt] *n* tournoi *m*.

tour operator *n* voyagiste *m*.

tousle ['taʊzl] *vt* ébouriffer.

tout [taʊt] ◇ *n Br* revendeur *m* de billets. ◇ *vt* [tickets] revendre ; [goods] vendre. ◇ *vi* : **to ~ for trade** racoler les clients.

tow [təʊ] ◇ *n* : **'on ~'** *Br* 'véhicule en remorque'. ◇ *vt* remorquer.

towards *Br* [tə'wɔːdz], **toward** *Am* [tə'wɔːd] *prep* **- 1.** [gen] vers ; [movement] vers, en direction de **- 2.** [in attitude] envers **- 3.** [for the purpose of] pour.

towel ['taʊəl] *n* serviette *f* ; [tea towel] torchon *m*.

towelling *Br*, **toweling** *Am* ['taʊəlɪŋ] *n* *(U)* tissu *m* éponge.

towel rail *n* porte-serviettes *m inv*.

tower ['taʊəʳ] ◇ *n* tour *f*. ◇ *vi* s'élever ; **to ~ over sb/sthg** dominer qqn/qqch.

tower block *n Br* tour *f*.

towering ['taʊərɪŋ] *adj* imposant(e).

town [taʊn] *n* ville *f* ; **to go out on the ~** faire la tournée des grands ducs ; **to go to ~ on sthg** *fig* ne pas lésiner sur qqch.

town centre *n Br* centre-ville *m*.

town council *n Br* conseil *m* municipal.

town hall *n* mairie *f*.

town plan *n* plan *m* de ville.

town planning *n* urbanisme *m*.

township ['taʊnʃɪp] *n* **- 1.** [in South Africa] township *f* **- 2.** [in US] ≃ canton *m*.

towpath ['təʊpɑːθ, *pl* -pɑːðz] *n* chemin *m* de halage.

towrope ['təʊrəʊp] *n* câble *m* de remorquage.

tow truck *n Am* dépanneuse *f*.

toxic ['tɒksɪk] *adj* toxique.

toy [tɔɪ] *n* jouet *m*. ◆ **toy with** *vt fus* **- 1.** [idea] caresser **- 2.** [coin etc] jouer avec ; **to ~ with one's food** manger du bout des dents.

toy shop *n* magasin *m* de jouets.

trace [treɪs] ◇ *n* trace *f*. ◇ *vt* **- 1.** [relatives, criminal] retrouver ; [development, progress] suivre ; [history, life] retracer **- 2.** [on paper] tracer.

tracing paper ['treɪsɪŋ-] *n* *(U)* papier-calque *m*.

track [træk] ◇ *n* **- 1.** [path] chemin *m* **- 2.** SPORT piste *f* **- 3.** RAIL voie *f* ferrée **- 4.** [of animal, person] trace *f* **- 5.** [on record, tape] piste *f* **- 6.** *phr* : **to keep ~ of sb** rester en contact avec qqn ; **to lose ~ of sb** perdre contact avec qqn ; **to be on the right ~** être sur la bonne voie ; **to be on the wrong ~** être sur la mauvaise piste. ◇ *vt* suivre la trace de. ◆ **track down** *vt sep* [criminal, animal] dépister ; [object, address etc] retrouver.

track record *n* palmarès *m*.

tracksuit ['træksuːt] *n* survêtement *m*.

tract [trækt] *n* **- 1.** [pamphlet] tract *m* **- 2.** [of land, forest] étendue *f*.

traction ['trækʃn] *n* *(U)* **- 1.** PHYSICS traction *f* **- 2.** MED : **in ~** en extension.

tractor ['træktəʳ] *n* tracteur *m*.

trade [treɪd] ◇ *n* **- 1.** *(U)* [commerce] commerce *m* **- 2.** [job] métier *m* ; **by ~ de son état.** ◇ *vt* [exchange] : **to ~ sthg (for)**

échanger qqch (contre). <> *vi* COMM : **to ~ (with sb)** commercer (avec qqn).
◆ **trade in** *vt sep* [exchange] échanger, faire reprendre.

trade fair *n* exposition *f* commerciale.

trade-in *n* reprise *f*.

trademark ['treidma:k] *n* - **1.** COMM marque *f* de fabrique - **2.** *fig* [characteristic] marque *f*.

trade name *n* nom *m* de marque.

trader ['treidə'] *n* marchand *m*, -e *f*, commerçant *m*, -e *f*.

tradesman ['treidzmən] (*pl* **-men** [-mən]) *n* commerçant *m*.

trade(s) union *n Br* syndicat *m*.

Trades Union Congress *n Br* : **the ~** la Confédération des syndicats britanniques.

trade(s) unionist [-'ju:njənɪst] *n Br* syndicaliste *mf*.

trading ['treidɪŋ] *n* (U) commerce *m*.

trading estate *n Br* zone *f* industrielle.

tradition [trə'dɪʃn] *n* tradition *f*.

traditional [trə'dɪʃənl] *adj* traditionnel(elle).

traffic ['træfɪk] (*pt* & *pp* **-ked**, *cont* **-king**) <> *n* (U) - **1.** [vehicles] circulation *f* - **2.** [illegal trade] : **~ (in)** trafic *m* (de). <> *vi* : **to ~ in** faire le trafic de.

traffic circle *n Am* rond-point *m*.

traffic jam *n* embouteillage *m*.

trafficker ['træfɪkə'] *n* : **~ (in)** trafiquant *m*, -e *f* (de).

traffic lights *npl* feux *mpl* de signalisation.

traffic warden *n Br* contractuel *m*, -elle *f*.

tragedy ['trædʒədɪ] *n* tragédie *f*.

tragic ['trædʒɪk] *adj* tragique.

trail [treil] <> *n* - **1.** [path] sentier *m* - **2.** [trace] piste *f*. <> *vt* - **1.** [drag] traîner - **2.** [follow] suivre. <> *vi* - **1.** [drag, move slowly] traîner - **2.** SPORT [lose] : **to be ~ing** être mené(e). ◆ **trail away, trail off** *vi* s'estomper.

trailer ['treilə'] *n* - **1.** [vehicle - for luggage] remorque *f* ; [- for living in] caravane *f* - **2.** CINEMA bande-annonce *f*.

train [trein] <> *n* - **1.** RAIL train *m* - **2.** [of dress] traîne *f*. <> *vt* - **1.** [teach] : **to ~ sb to do sthg** apprendre à qqn à faire qqch - **2.** [for job] former ; **to ~ sb as/in** former qqn comme/dans - **3.** SPORT : **to ~ sb (for)** entraîner qqn (pour) - **4.** [gun, camera] braquer. <> *vi* - **1.** [for job] : **to ~ (as)** recevoir OR faire une formation (de) - **2.** SPORT : **to ~ (for)** s'entraîner (pour).

trained [treind] *adj* formé(e).

trainee [trei'ni:] *n* stagiaire *mf*.

trainer ['treinə'] *n* - **1.** [of animals] dresseur *m*, -euse *f* - **2.** SPORT entraîneur *m*.
◆ **trainers** *npl Br* chaussures *fpl* de sport.

training ['treinɪŋ] *n* (U) - **1.** [for job] : **~ (in)** formation *f* (de) - **2.** SPORT entraînement *m*.

training college *n Br* école *f* professionnelle.

training shoes *npl Br* chaussures *fpl* de sport.

train of thought *n* : **my/his ~** le fil de mes/ses pensées.

traipse [treips] *vi* traîner.

trait [treit] *n* trait *m*.

traitor ['treitə'] *n* traître *m*, -esse *f*.

trajectory [trə'dʒektərɪ] *n* trajectoire *f*.

tram [træm], **tramcar** ['træmka:'] *n Br* tram *m*, tramway *m*.

tramp [træmp] <> *n* [homeless person] clochard *m*, -e *f*. <> *vi* marcher d'un pas lourd.

trample ['træmpl] *vt* piétiner.

trampoline ['træmpəli:n] *n* trampoline *m*.

trance [tra:ns] *n* transe *f*.

tranquil ['træŋkwɪl] *adj* tranquille.

tranquillizer *Br*, **tranquilizer** *Am* ['træŋkwɪlaɪzə'] *n* tranquillisant *m*, calmant *m*.

transaction [træn'zækʃn] *n* transaction *f*.

transcend [træn'send] *vt* transcender.

transcript ['trænskrɪpt] *n* transcription *f*.

transfer [*n* 'trænsfɜ:', *vb* træns'fɜ:'] <> *n* - **1.** [gen] transfert *m* ; [of power] passation *f* ; [of money] virement *m* - **2.** [design] décalcomanie *f*. <> *vt* - **1.** [gen] transférer ; [power, control] faire passer ; [money] virer - **2.** [employee] transférer, muter. <> *vi* être transféré.

transfix [træns'fɪks] *vt* : **to be ~ed with** fear être paralysé(e) par la peur.

transform [træns'fɔ:m] *vt* : **to ~ sb/sthg (into)** transformer qqn/qqch (en).

transfusion [træns'fju:ʒn] *n* transfusion *f*.

transient ['trænzɪənt] *adj* passager(ère).

transistor [træn'zɪstə'] *n* transistor *m*.

transistor radio *n* transistor *m*.

transit ['trænsɪt] *n* : **in ~** en transit.

transition [træn'zɪʃn] *n* transition *f*.

transitive ['trænzɪtɪv] *adj* GRAMM transitif(ive).

transitory ['trænzɪtrɪ] *adj* transitoire.

translate [træns'leɪt] vt traduire.

translation [træns'leɪʃn] n traduction f.

translator [træns'leɪtə'] n traducteur m, -trice f.

transmission [trænz'mɪʃn] n - 1. [gen] transmission f - 2. RADIO & TV [programme] émission f.

transmit [trænz'mɪt] vt transmettre.

transmitter [trænz'mɪtə'] n émetteur m.

transparency [trans'pærənsɪ] n PHOT diapositive f ; [for overhead projector] transparent m.

transparent [træns'pærənt] adj transparent(e).

transpire [træn'spaɪə'] fml <> vt : **it ~s that ...** on a appris que ... <> vi [happen] se passer, arriver.

transplant [n 'trænsplɑːnt, vb træns'plɑːnt] <> n MED greffe f, transplantation f. <> vt - 1. MED greffer, transplanter - 2. [seedlings] repiquer.

transport [n 'trænspɔːt, vb træn'spɔːt] <> n transport m. <> vt transporter.

transportation [,trænspɔː'teɪʃn] n esp Am transport m.

transport cafe n Br restaurant m de routiers, routier m.

transpose [træns'pəʊz] vt transposer.

trap [træp] <> n piège m. <> vt prendre au piège ; **to be trapped** être coincé.

trapdoor [,træp'dɔː'] n trappe f.

trapeze [trə'piːz] n trapèze m.

trappings ['træpɪŋz] npl signes mpl extérieurs.

trash [træʃ] n (U) - 1. Am [refuse] ordures fpl - 2. inf pej [poor-quality thing] camelote f.

trashcan ['træʃkæn] n Am poubelle f.

traumatic [trɔː'mætɪk] adj traumatisant(e).

travel ['trævl] <> n (U) voyage m, voyages mpl. <> vt parcourir. <> vi - 1. [make journey] voyager - 2. [move - current, signal] aller, passer ; [- news] se répandre, circuler.

travel agency n agence f de voyages.

travel agent n agent m de voyages ; **to/at the ~'s** à l'agence f de voyages.

traveller Br, **traveler** Am ['trævlə'] n - 1. [person on journey] voyageur m, -euse f - 2. [sales representative] représentant m.

traveller's cheque Br, **traveler's cheque** Am n chèque m de voyage.

travelling Br, **traveling** Am ['trævlɪŋ] adj - 1. [theatre, circus] ambulant(e)

- 2. [clock, bag etc] de voyage ; [allowance] de déplacement.

travelsick ['trævəlsɪk] adj : **to be ~** avoir le mal de la route/de l'air/de mer.

travesty ['trævəstɪ] n parodie f.

trawler ['trɔːlə'] n chalutier m.

tray [treɪ] n plateau m.

treacherous ['tretʃərəs] adj traître (traîtresse).

treachery ['tretʃərɪ] n traîtrise f.

treacle ['triːkl] n Br mélasse f.

tread [tred] (pt **trod**, pp **trodden**) <> n - 1. [on tyre] bande f de roulement ; [of shoe] semelle f - 2. [way of walking] pas m ; [sound] bruit m de pas. <> vi : **to ~ (on)** marcher (sur).

treason ['triːzn] n trahison f.

treasure ['treʒə'] <> n trésor m. <> vt [object] garder précieusement ; [memory] chérir.

treasurer ['treʒərə'] n trésorier m, -ère f.

treasury ['treʒərɪ] n [room] trésorerie f.
➤ **Treasury** n : **the Treasury** le ministère des Finances.

treat [triːt] <> vt - 1. [gen] traiter - 2. [on special occasion] : **to ~ sb to sthg** offrir OR payer qqch à qqn. <> n - 1. [gift] cadeau m - 2. [delight] plaisir m.

treatise ['triːtɪz] n : **~ (on)** traité m (de).

treatment ['triːtmənt] n traitement m.

treaty ['triːtɪ] n traité m.

treble ['trebl] <> adj - 1. [MUS - voice] de soprano ; [- recorder] aigu (aiguë) - 2. [triple] triple. <> n [on stereo control] aigu m ; [boy singer] soprano m. <> vt & vi tripler.

treble clef n clef f de sol.

tree [triː] n - 1. [gen] arbre m - 2. COMPUT arbre m, arborescence f.

treetop ['triːtɒp] n cime f.

tree-trunk n tronc m d'arbre.

trek [trek] n randonnée f.

trellis ['trelɪs] n treillis m.

tremble ['trembl] vi trembler.

tremendous [trɪ'mendəs] adj - 1. [size, success, difference] énorme ; [noise] terrible - 2. inf [really good] formidable.

tremor ['tremə'] n tremblement m.

trench [trentʃ] n tranchée f.

trench coat n trench-coat m.

trend [trend] n [tendency] tendance f.

trendy ['trendɪ] inf adj branché(e), à la mode.

trepidation [,trepɪ'deɪʃn] n fml : **in** OR **with ~** avec inquiétude.

trespass ['trespəs] *vi* [on land] entrer sans permission ; **'no ~ing'** 'défense d'entrer'.

trespasser ['trespəsəʳ] *n* intrus *m*, -e *f* ; **'~s will be prosecuted'** 'défense d'entrer sous peine de poursuites'.

trestle ['tresl] *n* tréteau *m*.

trestle table *n* table *f* à tréteaux.

trial ['traɪəl] *n* - **1.** JUR procès *m* ; **to be on ~ (for)** passer en justice (pour) - **2.** [test, experiment] essai *m* ; **on ~** à l'essai ; **by ~ and error** en tâtonnant - **3.** [unpleasant experience] épreuve *f*.

triangle ['traɪæŋgl] *n* [gen] triangle *m*.

tribe [traɪb] *n* tribu *f*.

tribunal [traɪ'bjuːnl] *n* tribunal *m*.

tributary ['trɪbjʊtrɪ] *n* affluent *m*.

tribute ['trɪbjuːt] *n* tribut *m*, hommage *m* ; **to pay ~** to payer tribut à, rendre hommage à ; **to be a ~ to sthg** témoigner de qqch.

trice [traɪs] *n* : **in a ~** en un clin d'œil.

trick [trɪk] ◇ *n* - **1.** [to deceive] tour *m*, farce *f* ; **to play a ~ on sb** jouer un tour à qqn - **2.** [to entertain] tour *m* - **3.** [knack] truc *m* ; **that will do the ~** *inf* ça fera l'affaire. ◇ *vt* attraper, rouler ; **to ~ sb into doing sthg** amener qqn à faire qqch (par la ruse).

trickery ['trɪkərɪ] *n* (U) ruse *f*.

trickle ['trɪkl] ◇ *n* [of liquid] filet *m*. ◇ *vi* [liquid] dégouliner ; **to ~ in/out** [people] entrer/sortir par petits groupes.

tricky ['trɪkɪ] *adj* [difficult] difficile.

tricycle ['traɪsɪkl] *n* tricycle *m*.

tried [traɪd] *adj* : **~ and tested** [method, system] qui a fait ses preuves.

trifle ['traɪfl] *n* - **1.** *Br* CULIN ~ diplomate *m* - **2.** [unimportant thing] bagatelle *f*. ◆ **a trifle** *adv* un peu, un tantinet.

trifling ['traɪflɪŋ] *adj* insignifiant(e).

trigger ['trɪgəʳ] *n* [on gun] détente *f*, gâchette *f*. ◆ **trigger off** *vt sep* déclencher, provoquer.

trill [trɪl] *n* trille *m*.

trim [trɪm] ◇ *adj* - **1.** [neat and tidy] net (nette) - **2.** [slim] svelte. ◇ *n* [of hair] coupe *f*. ◇ *vt* - **1.** [cut - gen] couper ; [- hedge] tailler - **2.** [decorate] : **to ~ sthg (with)** garnir OR orner qqch (de).

trimming ['trɪmɪŋ] *n* - **1.** [on clothing] parement *m* - **2.** CULIN garniture *f*.

trinket ['trɪŋkɪt] *n* bibelot *m*.

trio ['triːəʊ] (*pl* -s) *n* trio *m*.

trip [trɪp] ◇ *n* - **1.** [journey] voyage *m* - **2.** *drugs sl* trip *m*. ◇ *vt* [make stumble] faire un croche-pied à. ◇ *vi* [stumble] : **to ~ (over)** trébucher (sur). ◆ **trip up** *vt sep* [make stumble] faire un croche-pied à.

tripe [traɪp] *n* (U) - **1.** CULIN tripe *f* - **2.** *inf* [nonsense] bêtises *fpl*, idioties *fpl*.

triple ['trɪpl] ◇ *adj* triple. ◇ *vt & vi* tripler.

triple jump *n* : **the ~** le triple saut.

triplets ['trɪplɪts] *npl* triplés *mpl*, triplées *fpl*.

triplicate ['trɪplɪkət] *n* : **in ~** en trois exemplaires.

tripod ['traɪpɒd] *n* trépied *m*.

trite [traɪt] *adj pej* banal(e).

triumph ['traɪəmf] ◇ *n* triomphe *m*. ◇ *vi* : **to ~ (over)** triompher (de).

trivia ['trɪvɪə] *n* (U) [trifles] vétilles *fpl*, riens *mpl*.

trivial ['trɪvɪəl] *adj* insignifiant(e).

trod [trɒd] *pt* ▷ **tread**.

trodden ['trɒdn] *pp* ▷ **tread**.

trolley ['trɒlɪ] (*pl* -s) *n* - **1.** *Br* [for shopping, luggage] chariot *m*, caddie® *m* - **2.** *Br* [for food, drinks] chariot *m*, table *f* roulante - **3.** *Am* [tram] tramway *m*, tram *m*.

trombone [trɒm'bəʊn] *n* MUS trombone *m*.

troop [truːp] ◇ *n* bande *f*, troupe *f*. ◇ *vi* : **to ~ in/out/off** entrer/sortir/partir en groupe. ◆ **troops** *npl* troupes *fpl*.

trophy ['trəʊfɪ] *n* trophée *m*.

tropical ['trɒpɪkl] *adj* tropical(e).

tropics ['trɒpɪks] *npl* : **the ~** les tropiques *mpl*.

trot [trɒt] ◇ *n* [of horse] trot *m*. ◇ *vi* trotter. ◆ **on the trot** *adv inf* de suite, d'affilée.

trouble ['trʌbl] ◇ *n* (U) - **1.** [difficulty] problème *m*, difficulté *f* ; **to be in ~** avoir des ennuis - **2.** [bother] peine *f*, mal *m* ; **to take the ~ to do sthg** se donner la peine de faire qqch ; **it's no ~!** ça ne me dérange pas! - **3.** [pain, illness] mal *m*, ennui *m* - **4.** [fighting] bagarre *f* ; POL troubles *mpl*, conflits *mpl* ◇ *vt* - **1.** [worry, upset] peiner, troubler - **2.** [bother] déranger - **3.** [give pain to] faire mal à. ◆ **troubles** *npl* - **1.** [worries] ennuis *mpl* - **2.** POL troubles *mpl*, conflits *mpl*.

troubled ['trʌbld] *adj* - **1.** [worried] inquiet(ète) - **2.** [disturbed - period] de troubles, agité(e) ; [- country] qui connaît une période de troubles.

troublemaker ['trʌbl,meɪkəʳ] *n* fauteur *m*, -trice *f* de troubles.

troubleshooter ['trʌblˌʃuːtəʳ] *n* expert *m*, spécialiste *mf*.

troublesome ['trʌblsəm] *adj* [job] pénible ; [cold] gênant(e) ; [back, knee] qui fait souffrir.

trough [trɒf] *n* - 1. [for animals - with water] abreuvoir *m* ; [- with food] auge *f* - 2. [low point - of wave] creux *m* ; *fig* point *m* bas.

troupe [truːp] *n* troupe *f*.

trousers ['traʊzəz] *npl* pantalon *m*.

trout [traʊt] (*pl inv* OR **-s**) *n* truite *f*.

trowel ['traʊəl] *n* [for gardening] déplantoir *m* ; [for cement, plaster] truelle *f*.

truant ['truːənt] *n* [child] élève *mf* absentéiste ; **to play ~** faire l'école buissonnière.

truce [truːs] *n* trêve *f*.

truck [trʌk] *n* - 1. *esp Am* [lorry] camion *m* - 2. RAIL wagon *m* à plate-forme.

truck driver *n esp Am* routier *m*.

trucker ['trʌkəʳ] *n Am* routier *m*.

truck farm *n Am* jardin *m* maraîcher.

truculent ['trʌkjʊlənt] *adj* agressif(ive).

trudge [trʌdʒ] *vi* marcher péniblement.

true ['truː] *adj* - 1. [factual] vrai(e) ; **to come ~** se réaliser - 2. [genuine] vrai(e), authentique ; **~ love** le grand amour - 3. [exact] exact(e) - 4. [faithful] fidèle, loyal(e).

truffle ['trʌfl] *n* truffe *f*.

truly ['truːlɪ] *adv* - 1. [gen] vraiment - 2. [sincerely] vraiment, sincèrement - 3. *phr* : **yours ~** [at end of letter] je vous prie de croire à l'expression de mes sentiments distingués.

trump [trʌmp] *n* atout *m*.

trumped-up ['trʌmpt-] *adj pej* inventé(e) de toutes pièces.

trumpet ['trʌmpɪt] *n* trompette *f*.

truncheon ['trʌntʃən] *n* matraque *f*.

trundle ['trʌndl] *vi* aller lentement.

trunk [trʌŋk] *n* - 1. [of tree, person] tronc *m* - 2. [of elephant] trompe *f* - 3. [box] malle *f* - 4. *Am* [of car] coffre *m*. ◆ **trunks** *npl* maillot *m* de bain.

trunk call *n Br* communication *f* interurbaine.

trunk road *n Br* (route *f*) nationale *f*.

truss [trʌs] *n* MED bandage *m* herniaire.

trust [trʌst] ◇ *vt* - 1. [have confidence in] avoir confiance en, se fier à ; **to ~ sb to do sthg** compter sur qqn pour faire qqch - 2. [entrust] : **to ~ sb with sthg** confier qqch à qqn - 3. *fml* [hope] : **to ~ (that) ...** espérer que ... ◇ *n* - 1. *(U)* [faith] : **~ (in sb/sthg)**

confiance *f* (en qqn/dans qqch) - 2. *(U)* [responsibility] responsabilité *f* - 3. FIN : **in ~** en dépôt - 4. COMM trust *m*.

trusted ['trʌstɪd] *adj* [person] de confiance ; [method] qui a fait ses preuves.

trustee [trʌsˈtiː] *n* FIN & JUR fidéicommissaire *mf* ; [of institution] administrateur *m*, -trice *f*.

trust fund *n* fonds *m* en fidéicommis.

trusting ['trʌstɪŋ] *adj* confiant(e).

trustworthy ['trʌstˌwɜːðɪ] *adj* digne de confiance.

truth [truːθ] *n* vérité *f* ; **in (all) ~** à dire vrai, en vérité.

truthful ['truːθfʊl] *adj* [person, reply] honnête ; [story] véridique.

try [traɪ] ◇ *vt* - 1. [attempt, test] essayer ; [food, drink] goûter ; **to ~ to do sthg** essayer de faire qqch - 2. JUR juger - 3. [put to the test] éprouver, mettre à l'épreuve. ◇ *vi* essayer ; **to ~ for sthg** essayer d'obtenir qqch. ◇ *n* - 1. [attempt] essai *m*, tentative *f* ; **to give sthg a ~** essayer qqch - 2. RUGBY essai *m*. ◆ **try on** *vt sep* [clothes] essayer. ◆ **try out** *vt sep* essayer.

trying ['traɪɪŋ] *adj* pénible, éprouvant(e).

T-shirt *n* tee-shirt *m*.

T-square *n* té *m*.

tub [tʌb] *n* - 1. [of ice cream - large] boîte *f* ; [- small] petit pot *m* ; [of margarine] barquette *f* - 2. [bath] baignoire *f*.

tubby ['tʌbɪ] *adj inf* rondouillard(e), boulot(otte).

tube [tjuːb] *n* - 1. [cylinder, container] tube *m* - 2. *Br* [underground train] métro *m* ; **the ~** [system] le métro ; **by ~** en métro.

tuberculosis [tjuːˌbɜːkjʊˈləʊsɪs] *n* tuberculose *f*.

tubing ['tjuːbɪŋ] *n* *(U)* tubes *mpl*, tuyaux *mpl*.

tubular ['tjuːbjʊləʳ] *adj* tubulaire.

TUC *n abbr of* **Trades Union Congress**.

tuck [tʌk] *vt* [place neatly] ranger. ◆ **tuck away** *vt sep* [store] mettre de côté OR en lieu sûr. ◆ **tuck in** ◇ *vt* - 1. [child, patient] border - 2. [clothes] rentrer. ◇ *vi inf* boulotter. ◆ **tuck up** *vt sep* [child, patient] border.

tuck shop *n Br* [at school] *petite boutique qui vend des bonbons et des gâteaux*.

Tuesday ['tjuːzdɪ] *n* mardi *m* ; *see also* **Saturday**.

tuft [tʌft] *n* touffe *f*.

tug [tʌg] ◇ *n* - 1. [pull] : **to give sthg a ~**

tirer sur qqch - **2.** [boat] remorquer *m.*
◇ *vt* tirer. ◇ *vi* : **to ~ (at)** tirer (sur).

tug-of-war *n* lutte *f* de traction à la corde ; *fig* lutte acharnée.

tuition [tjuː'ɪʃn] *n (U)* cours *mpl.*

tulip ['tjuːlɪp] *n* tulipe *f.*

tumble ['tʌmbl] ◇ *vi* - **1.** [person] tomber, faire une chute ; [water] tomber en cascades - **2.** *fig* [prices] tomber, chuter. ◇ *n* chute *f*, culbute *f.* ◆ **tumble to** *vt fus Br inf* piger.

tumbledown ['tʌmbldaʊn] *adj* délabré(e), qui tombe en ruines.

tumble-dryer [-ˌdraɪər] *n* sèche-linge *m inv.*

tumbler ['tʌmblər] *n* [glass] verre *m* (droit).

tummy ['tʌmɪ] *n inf* ventre *m.*

tumour *Br*, **tumor** *Am* ['tjuːmər] *n* tumeur *f.*

tuna [*Br* 'tjuːnə, *Am* 'tuːnə] (*pl inv* OR **-s**) *n* thon *m.*

tune [tjuːn] ◇ *n* - **1.** [song, melody] air *m* - **2.** [harmony] : **in ~** [instrument] accordé(e), juste ; [play, sing] juste ; **out of ~** [instrument] mal accordé(e) ; [play, sing] faux ; **to be in/out of ~ (with)** *fig* être en accord/désaccord (avec). ◇ *vt* - **1.** MUS accorder - **2.** RADIO & TV régler - **3.** [engine] régler. ◆ **tune in** *vi* RADIO & TV être à l'écoute ; **to ~ in to** se mettre sur. ◆ **tune up** *vi* MUS accorder son instrument.

tuneful ['tjuːnfʊl] *adj* mélodieux(euse).

tuner ['tjuːnər] *n* - **1.** RADIO & TV syntoniseur *m*, tuner *m* - **2.** MUS [person] accordeur *m.*

tunic ['tjuːnɪk] *n* tunique *f.*

tuning fork ['tjuːnɪŋ-] *n* diapason *m.*

Tunisia [tjuː'nɪzɪə] *n* Tunisie *f.*

tunnel ['tʌnl] ◇ *n* tunnel *m.* ◇ *vi* faire OR creuser un tunnel.

turban ['tɜːbən] *n* turban *m.*

turbine ['tɜːbaɪn] *n* turbine *f.*

turbocharged ['tɜːbəʊtʃɑːdʒd] *adj* turbo (*inv*).

turbulence ['tɜːbjʊləns] *n (U)* - **1.** [in air, water] turbulence *f* - **2.** *fig* [unrest] agitation *f.*

turbulent ['tɜːbjʊlənt] *adj* - **1.** [air, water] agité(e) - **2.** *fig* [disorderly] tumultueux (euse), agité(e).

tureen [tə'riːn] *n* soupière *f.*

turf [tɜːf] (*pl* **-s** OR **turves** [tɜːvz]) ◇ *n* [grass surface] gazon *m* ; [clod] motte *f* de gazon. ◇ *vt* gazonner. ◆ **turf out** *vt sep*

Br inf [person] virer ; [old clothes] balancer, bazarder.

turgid ['tɜːdʒɪd] *adj fml* [style, writing] pompeux(euse), ampoulé(e).

Turk [tɜːk] *n* Turc *m*, Turque *f.*

turkey ['tɜːkɪ] (*pl* **-s**) *n* dinde *f.*

Turkey ['tɜːkɪ] *n* Turquie *f.*

Turkish ['tɜːkɪʃ] ◇ *adj* turc (turque). ◇ *n* [language] turc *m.* ◇ *npl* : **the ~** les Turcs *mpl.*

Turkish delight *n* loukoum *m.*

turmoil ['tɜːmɔɪl] *n* agitation *f*, trouble *m.*

turn [tɜːn] ◇ *n* - **1.** [in road] virage *m*, tournant *m* ; [in river] méandre *m* - **2.** [revolution, twist] tour *m* - **3.** [change] tournure *f*, tour *m* - **4.** [in game] tour *m* ; **it's my ~** c'est (à) mon tour ; **in ~** tour à tour, chacun à son tour - **5.** [performance] numéro *m* - **6.** MED crise *f*, attaque *f* - **7.** *phr* : **to do sb a good ~** rendre (un) service à qqn. ◇ *vt* - **1.** [gen] tourner ; [omelette, steak etc] retourner ; **to ~ sthg inside out** retourner qqch ; **to ~ one's thoughts/attention to sthg** tourner ses pensées/son attention vers qqch - **2.** [change] : **to ~ sthg into** changer qqch en - **3.** [become] : **to ~ red** rougir. ◇ *vi* - **1.** [gen] tourner ; [person] se tourner, se retourner - **2.** [in book] : **to ~ to a page** se reporter OR aller à une page - **3.** [for consolation] : **to ~ to sb/sthg** se tourner vers qqn/qqch - **4.** [change] : **to ~ into** se changer en, se transformer en. ◆ **turn around = turn round.** ◆ **turn away** ◇ *vt sep* [refuse entry to] refuser. ◇ *vi* se détourner. ◆ **turn back** ◇ *vt sep* [sheets] replier ; [person, vehicle] refouler. ◇ *vi* rebrousser chemin. ◆ **turn down** *vt sep* - **1.** [reject] rejeter, refuser - **2.** [radio, volume, gas] baisser. ◆ **turn in** *vi inf* [go to bed] se pieuter. ◆ **turn off** ◇ *vt fus* [road, path] quitter. ◇ *vt sep* [radio, TV, engine, gas] éteindre ; [tap] fermer. ◇ *vi* [leave path, road] tourner. ◆ **turn on** ◇ *vt sep* - **1.** [radio, TV, engine, gas] allumer ; [tap] ouvrir ; **to ~ the light on** allumer la lumière - **2.** *inf* [excite sexually] exciter. ◇ *vt fus* [attack] attaquer. ◆ **turn out** ◇ *vt sep* - **1.** [light, gas fire] éteindre - **2.** [empty - pocket, bag] retourner, vider. ◇ *vt fus* : **to ~ out to be** s'avérer ; **it ~s out that ...** il s'avère OR se trouve que ... ◇ *vi* - **1.** [end up] finir - **2.** [arrive - person] venir. ◆ **turn over** ◇ *vt sep* - **1.** [playing card, stone] retourner ; [page] tourner - **2.** [consider] retourner dans sa tête - **3.** [hand over] rendre, remettre. ◇ *vi* - **1.** [roll over] se retourner - **2.** *Br* TV changer de chaîne. ◆ **turn round** ◇ *vt sep Br* - **1.** [reverse] retourner - **2.** [wheel, words] tourner. ◇ *vi* [person] se retourner. ◆ **turn up** ◇ *vt sep* [TV, radio] mettre plus fort ; [gas] monter. ◇ *vi* **- 1.** [arrive - person] se pointer **- 2.** [be found - person, object] être retrouvé ; [- opportunity] se présenter.

turning ['tɜːnɪŋ] *n* [off road] route *f* latérale.

turning point *n* tournant *m*, moment *m* décisif.

turnip ['tɜːnɪp] *n* navet *m*.

turnout ['tɜːnaʊt] *n* [at election] taux *m* de participation ; [at meeting] assistance *f*.

turnover ['tɜːn‚əʊvər] *n* (U) **- 1.** [of personnel] renouvellement *m* **- 2.** FIN chiffre *m* d'affaires.

turnpike ['tɜːnpaɪk] *n* Am autoroute *f* à péage.

turnstile ['tɜːnstaɪl] *n* tourniquet *m*.

turntable ['tɜːn‚teɪbl] *n* platine *f*.

turn-up *n* Br [on trousers] revers *m* inv ; **a ~ for the books** inf une sacrée surprise.

turpentine ['tɜːpəntaɪn] *n* térébenthine *f*.

turquoise ['tɜːkwɔɪz] ◇ *adj* turquoise *(inv)*. ◇ *n* **- 1.** [mineral, gem] turquoise *f* **- 2.** [colour] turquoise *m*.

turret ['tʌrɪt] *n* tourelle *f*.

turtle ['tɜːtl] (*pl inv* OR **-s**) *n* tortue *f* de mer.

turtleneck ['tɜːtlnek] *n* [garment] pull *m* à col montant ; [neck] col *m* montant.

turves [tɜːvz] Br *pl* ▷ **turf**.

tusk [tʌsk] *n* défense *f*.

tussle ['tʌsl] ◇ *n* lutte *f*. ◇ *vi* se battre ; **to ~ over sthg** se disputer qqch.

tutor ['tjuːtər] *n* **- 1.** [private] professeur *m* particulier **- 2.** UNIV directeur *m*, -trice *f* d'études.

tutorial [tjuːˈtɔːrɪəl] *n* travaux *mpl* dirigés.

tuxedo [tʌkˈsiːdəʊ] (*pl* **-s**) *n* smoking *m*.

TV (*abbr of* **television**) *n* **- 1.** (U) [medium, industry] télé *f* **- 2.** [apparatus] (poste *m* de) télé *f*.

TV movie *n* téléfilm *m*.

twang [twæŋ] *n* **- 1.** [sound] bruit *m* de pincement **- 2.** [accent] nasillement *m*.

tweed [twiːd] *n* tweed *m*.

tweezers ['twiːzəz] *npl* pince *f* à épiler.

twelfth [twelfθ] *num* douzième ; *see also* **sixth**.

twelve [twelv] *num* douze ; *see also* **six**.

twentieth ['twentɪəθ] *num* vingtième ; *see also* **sixth**.

twenty ['twentɪ] *num* vingt ; *see also* **six**.

twice [twaɪs] *adv* deux fois ; **~ a day** deux

fois par jour ; **he earns ~ as much as me** il gagne deux fois plus que moi ; **~ as big** deux fois plus grand ; **~ my size/age** le double de ma taille/mon âge.

twiddle ['twɪdl] ◇ *vt* jouer avec. ◇ *vi* : **to ~ with sthg** jouer avec qqch.

twig [twɪg] *n* brindille *f*, petite branche *f*.

twilight ['twaɪlaɪt] *n* crépuscule *m*.

twin [twɪn] ◇ *adj* jumeau (jumelle) ; [town] jumelé(e) ; **~ beds** lits *mpl* jumeaux. ◇ *n* jumeau *m*, jumelle *f*.

twin-bedded [-'bedɪd] *adj* à deux lits.

twine [twaɪn] ◇ *n* (U) ficelle *f*. ◇ *vt* : **~ sthg round sthg** enrouler qqch autour de qqch.

twinge [twɪndʒ] *n* [of pain] élancement *m* ; **a ~ of guilt** un remords.

twinkle ['twɪŋkl] *vi* [star, lights] scintiller ; [eyes] briller, pétiller.

twin room *n* chambre *f* à deux lits.

twin town *n* Br ville *f* jumelée.

twirl [twɜːl] ◇ *vt* faire tourner. ◇ *vi* tournoyer.

twist [twɪst] ◇ *n* **- 1.** [in road] zigzag *m*, tournant *m* ; [in river] méandre *m*, coude *m* ; [in rope] entortillement *m* **- 2.** *fig* [in plot] tour *m*. ◇ *vt* **- 1.** [wind, curl] entortiller **- 2.** [contort] tordre **- 3.** [turn] tourner ; [lid - to open] dévisser ; [- to close] visser **- 4.** [sprain] : **to ~ one's ankle** se tordre OR se fouler la cheville **- 5.** [words, meaning] déformer. ◇ *vi* **- 1.** [river, path] zigzaguer **- 2.** [be contorted] se tordre **- 3.** [turn] : **to ~ round** se retourner.

twit [twɪt] *n* Br inf crétin *m*, -e *f*.

twitch [twɪtʃ] ◇ *n* tic *m*. ◇ *vi* [muscle, eye, face] se contracter.

two [tuː] *num* deux ; **in ~** en deux ; *see also* **six**.

two-door *adj* [car] à deux portes.

twofaced [‚tuːˈfeɪst] *adj* pej fourbe.

twofold ['tuːfəʊld] ◇ *adj* double. ◇ *adv* doublement ; **to increase ~** doubler.

two-piece *adj* : **~ swimsuit** deux-pièces *m inv* ; **~ suit** [for man] costume *m* (deux-pièces).

twosome ['tuːsəm] *n* inf couple *m*.

two-way *adj* [traffic, trade] dans les deux sens.

tycoon [taɪˈkuːn] *n* magnat *m*.

type [taɪp] ◇ *n* **- 1.** [sort, kind] genre *m*, sorte *f* ; [model] modèle *m* ; [in classification] type *m* **- 2.** (U) TYPO caractères *mpl*.

◇ *vt* [letter, reply] taper (à la machine).
◇ *vi* taper (à la machine).

typecast ['taɪpkɑːst] (*pt & pp* **typecast**) *vt* : **to be ~ as** être cantonné dans le rôle de ; **to be ~** être cantonné aux mêmes rôles.

typeface ['taɪpfeɪs] *n* TYPO œil *m* de caractère.

typescript ['taɪpskrɪpt] *n* texte *m* dactylographié.

typeset ['taɪpset] (*pt & pp* **typeset**) *vt* composer.

typewriter ['taɪpˌraɪtə'] *n* machine *f* à écrire.

typhoid (fever) ['taɪfɔɪd-] *n* typhoïde *f*.

typhoon [taɪ'fuːn] *n* typhon *m*.

typical ['tɪpɪkl] *adj* : **~ (of)** typique (de), caractéristique (de) ; **that's ~ (of him/her)!** c'est bien de lui/d'elle!

typing ['taɪpɪŋ] *n* dactylo *f*, dactylographie *f*.

typist ['taɪpɪst] *n* dactylo *mf*, dactylographe *mf*.

typography [taɪ'pɒɡrəfɪ] *n* typographie *f*.

tyranny ['tɪrənɪ] *n* tyrannie *f*.

tyrant ['taɪrənt] *n* tyran *m*.

tyre *Br*, **tire** *Am* ['taɪə'] *n* pneu *m*.

tyre pressure *Br*, **tire-** *Am* *n* pression *f* (de gonflage).

u (*pl* **u's** OR **us**), **U** (*pl* **U's** OR **Us**) [juː] *n* [letter] u *m inv*, U *m inv*.

U-bend *n* siphon *m*.

udder ['ʌdə'] *n* mamelle *f*.

UFO (*abbr of* **unidentified flying object**) *n* OVNI *m*, ovni *m*.

Uganda [juː'ɡændə] *n* Ouganda *m*.

ugh [ʌɡ] *excl* pouah!, beurk!

ugly ['ʌɡlɪ] *adj* - **1.** [unattractive] laid(e) - **2.** *fig* [unpleasant] pénible, désagréable.

UHF (*abbr of* **ultra-high frequency**) *n* UHF.

UK (*abbr of* **United Kingdom**) *n* Royaume-Uni *m*, R.U. *m*.

Ukraine [juː'kreɪn] *n* : **the ~** l'Ukraine *f*.

ulcer ['ʌlsə'] *n* ulcère *m*.

ulcerated ['ʌlsəreɪtɪd] *adj* ulcéré(e).

Ulster ['ʌlstə'] *n* Ulster *m*.

ulterior [ʌl'tɪərɪə'] *adj* : **~ motive** arrière-pensée *f*.

ultimata [ˌʌltɪ'meɪtə] *pl* ⟾ **ultimatum**.

ultimate ['ʌltɪmət] ◇ *adj* - **1.** [final] final(e), ultime - **2.** [most powerful] ultime, suprême. ◇ *n* : **the ~ in** le fin du fin dans.

ultimately ['ʌltɪmətlɪ] *adv* [finally] finalement.

ultimatum [ˌʌltɪ'meɪtəm] (*pl* **-tums** OR **-ta** [-tə]) *n* ultimatum *m*.

ultrasound ['ʌltrəsaʊnd] *n (U)* ultrasons *mpl*.

ultraviolet [ˌʌltrə'vaɪələt] *adj* ultraviolet(ette).

umbilical cord [ʌm'bɪlɪkl-] *n* cordon *m* ombilical.

umbrella [ʌm'brelə] ◇ *n* [portable] parapluie *m* ; [fixed] parasol *m*. ◇ *adj* [organization] qui en regroupe plusieurs autres.

umpire ['ʌmpaɪə'] ◇ *n* arbitre *m*. ◇ *vt* arbitrer.

umpteen [ˌʌmp'tiːn] *num adj inf* je ne sais combien de.

umpteenth [ˌʌmp'tiːnθ] *num adj inf* énième.

UN (*abbr of* **United Nations**) *n* : **the ~** l'ONU *f*, l'Onu *f*.

unabated [ˌʌnə'beɪtɪd] *adj* : **the rain continued ~** la pluie continua de tomber sans répit.

unable [ʌn'eɪbl] *adj* : **to be ~ to do sthg** ne pas pouvoir faire qqch, être incapable de faire qqch.

unacceptable [ˌʌnək'septəbl] *adj* inacceptable.

unaccompanied [ˌʌnə'kʌmpənɪd] *adj* - **1.** [child] non accompagné(e) ; [luggage] sans surveillance - **2.** [song] a capella, sans accompagnement.

unaccountably [ˌʌnə'kaʊntəblɪ] *adv* [inexplicably] de façon inexplicable, inexplicablement.

unaccounted [ˌʌnə'kaʊntɪd] *adj* : **to be ~ for** manquer.

unaccustomed [ˌʌnə'kʌstəmd] *adj* [unused] : **to be ~ to sthg/to doing sthg** ne pas être habitué(e) à qqch/à faire qqch.

unadulterated [ˌʌnə'dʌltəreɪtɪd] *adj* - **1.** [unspoilt - wine] non frelaté(e) ; [- food] naturel(elle) - **2.** [absolute - joy] sans mélange ; [- nonsense, truth] pur et simple (pure et simple).

unanimous [juː'nænɪməs] *adj* unanime.

unanimously [juː'nænɪməslɪ] *adv* à l'unanimité.

unanswered [ˌʌn'aːnsəd] *adj* qui reste sans réponse.

unappetizing, -ising [ˌʌn'æpɪtaɪzɪŋ] *adj* peu appétissant(e).

unarmed [ˌʌn'aːmd] *adj* non armé(e).

unarmed combat *n* combat *m* sans armes.

unashamed [ˌʌnə'ʃeɪmd] *adj* [luxury] insolent(e) ; [liar, lie] effronté(e), éhonté(e).

unassuming [ˌʌnə'sjuːmɪŋ] *adj* modeste, effacé(e).

unattached [ˌʌnə'tætʃt] *adj* - 1. [not fastened, linked] : **~ (to)** indépendant(e) (de) - 2. [without partner] libre, sans attaches.

unattended [ˌʌnə'tendɪd] *adj* [luggage, shop] sans surveillance ; [child] seul(e).

unattractive [ˌʌnə'træktɪv] *adj* - 1. [not beautiful] peu attrayant(e), peu séduisant(e) - 2. [not pleasant] déplaisant(e).

unauthorized, -ised [ˌʌn'ɔːθəraɪzd] *adj* non autorisé(e).

unavailable [ˌʌnə'veɪləbl] *adj* qui n'est pas disponible, indisponible.

unavoidable [ˌʌnə'vɔɪdəbl] *adj* inévitable.

unaware [ˌʌnə'weəʳ] *adj* ignorant(e), inconscient(e) ; **to be ~ of sthg** ne pas avoir conscience de qqch, ignorer qqch.

unawares [ˌʌnə'weəz] *adv* : **to catch** OR **take sb ~** prendre qqn au dépourvu.

unbalanced [ˌʌn'bælənst] *adj* - 1. [biased] tendancieux(euse), partial(e) - 2. [deranged] déséquilibré(e).

unbearable [ʌn'beərəbl] *adj* insupportable.

unbeatable [ˌʌn'biːtəbl] *adj* imbattable.

unbeknown(st) [ˌʌnbɪ'nəʊn(st)] *adv* : **~ to** à l'insu de.

unbelievable [ˌʌnbɪ'liːvəbl] *adj* incroyable.

unbending [ˌʌn'bendɪŋ] *adj* inflexible, intransigeant(e).

unbia(s)sed [ˌʌn'baɪəst] *adj* impartial(e).

unborn [ˌʌn'bɔːn] *adj* [child] qui n'est pas encore né(e).

unbreakable [ˌʌn'breɪkəbl] *adj* incassable.

unbridled [ˌʌn'braɪdld] *adj* effréné(e), débridé(e).

unbutton [ˌʌn'bʌtn] *vt* déboutonner.

uncalled-for [ˌʌn'kɔːld-] *adj* [remark] déplacé(e) ; [criticism] injustifié(e).

uncanny [ʌn'kænɪ] *adj* étrange, mystérieux(euse) ; [resemblance] troublant(e).

unceasing [ˌʌn'siːsɪŋ] *adj* *fml* incessant(e), continuel(elle).

unceremonious ['ʌnˌserɪ'məʊnjəs] *adj* brusque.

uncertain [ʌn'sɜːtn] *adj* incertain(e) ; **in no ~ terms** sans mâcher ses mots.

unchanged [ˌʌn'tʃeɪndʒd] *adj* inchangé(e).

unchecked [ˌʌn'tʃekt] *adj* non maîtrisé(e), sans frein.

uncivilized, -ised [ˌʌn'sɪvɪlaɪzd] *adj* non civilisé(e), barbare.

uncle ['ʌŋkl] *n* oncle *m*.

unclear [ˌʌn'klɪəʳ] *adj* - 1. [message, meaning, motive] qui n'est pas clair(e) - 2. [uncertain - person, future] incertain(e).

uncomfortable [ˌʌn'kʌmftəbl] *adj* - 1. [shoes, chair, clothes etc] inconfortable ; *fig* [fact, truth] désagréable - 2. [person - physically] qui n'est pas à l'aise ; [- ill at ease] mal à l'aise.

uncommon [ʌn'kɒmən] *adj* - 1. [rare] rare - 2. *fml* [extreme] extraordinaire.

uncompromising [ˌʌn'kɒmprəmaɪzɪŋ] *adj* intransigeant(e).

unconcerned [ˌʌnkən'sɜːnd] *adj* [not anxious] qui ne s'inquiète pas.

unconditional [ˌʌnkən'dɪʃənl] *adj* inconditionnel(elle).

unconscious [ʌn'kɒnʃəs] <> *adj* - 1. [having lost consciousness] sans connaissance - 2. *fig* [unaware] : **to be ~ of** ne pas avoir conscience de, ne pas se rendre compte de - 3. [unnoticed - desires, feelings] inconscient(e). <> *n* PSYCH inconscient *m*.

unconsciously [ʌn'kɒnʃəslɪ] *adv* inconsciemment.

uncontrollable [ˌʌnkən'trəʊləbl] *adj* - 1. [unrestrainable - emotion, urge] irrépressible, irrésistible ; [- increase, epidemic] qui ne peut être enrayé(e) - 2. [unmanageable - person] impossible, difficile.

unconventional [ˌʌnkən'venʃənl] *adj* peu conventionnel(elle), original(e).

unconvinced [ˌʌnkən'vɪnst] *adj* qui n'est pas convaincu(e), sceptique.

uncouth [ʌn'kuːθ] *adj* grossier(ère).

uncover [ʌn'kʌvəʳ] *vt* découvrir.

undecided [ˌʌndɪ'saɪdɪd] *adj* [person] indécis(e), irrésolu(e) ; [issue] indécis(e).

undeniable [ˌʌndɪ'naɪəbl] *adj* indéniable, incontestable.

under ['ʌndəʳ] <> *prep* - 1. [gen] sous

- **2.** [less than] moins de ; **children ~ five** les enfants de moins de cinq ans - **3.** [subject to - effect, influence] sous ; **~ the circumstances** dans ces circonstances, étant donné les circonstances ; **to be ~ the impression that ...** avoir l'impression que ... - **4.** [undergoing] : **~ discussion** en discussion ; **~ consideration** à l'étude, à l'examen - **5.** [according to] selon, conformément à. <> *adv* - **1.** [underneath] dessous ; [underwater] sous l'eau ; **to go ~** [company] couler, faire faillite - **2.** [less] au-dessous.

underage [ˌʌndərˈeɪdʒ] *adj* mineur(e).

undercarriage [ˈʌndəˌkærɪdʒ] *n* train *m* d'atterrissage.

undercharge [ˌʌndəˈtʃɑːdʒ] *vt* faire payer insuffisamment à.

underclothes [ˈʌndəkləʊðz] *npl* sous-vêtements *mpl*.

undercoat [ˈʌndəkəʊt] *n* [of paint] couche *f* de fond.

undercover [ˈʌndəˌkʌvəʳ] *adj* secret(ète).

undercurrent [ˈʌndəˌkʌrənt] *n* *fig* [tendency] courant *m* sous-jacent.

undercut [ˌʌndəˈkʌt] (*pt* & *pp* **undercut**) *vt* [in price] vendre moins cher que.

underdeveloped [ˌʌndədɪˈveləpt] *adj* [country] sous-développé(e) ; [person] qui n'est pas complètement développé(e) OR formé(e).

underdog [ˈʌndədɒg] *n* : **the ~ l'**opprimé *m* ; SPORT celui (celle) que l'on donne perdant(e).

underdone [ˌʌndəˈdʌn] *adj* [food] pas assez cuit(e) ; [steak] saignant(e).

underestimate [ˌʌndərˈestɪmeɪt] *vt* sous-estimer.

underexposed [ˌʌndərɪkˈspəʊzd] *adj* PHOT sous-exposé(e).

underfoot [ˌʌndəˈfʊt] *adv* sous les pieds.

undergo [ˌʌndəˈgəʊ] (*pt* **-went,** *pp* **-gone** [-ˈgɒn]) *vt* subir ; [pain, difficulties] éprouver.

undergraduate [ˌʌndəˈgrædjʊət] *n* étudiant *m*, -e *f* qui prépare la licence.

underground [*adj* & *n* ˈʌndəgraʊnd, *adv* ˌʌndəˈgraʊnd] <> *adj* - **1.** [below the ground] souterrain(e) - **2.** *fig* [secret] clandestin(e). <> *adv* : **to go/be forced ~** entrer dans la clandestinité. <> *n* - **1.** *Br* [subway] métro *m* - **2.** [activist movement] résistance *f*.

undergrowth [ˈʌndəgrəʊθ] *n* (U) sous-bois *m inv*.

underhand [ˌʌndəˈhænd] *adj* sournois(e), en dessous.

underline [ˌʌndəˈlaɪn] *vt* souligner.

underlying [ˌʌndəˈlaɪɪŋ] *adj* sous-jacent(e).

undermine [ˌʌndəˈmaɪn] *vt* *fig* [weaken] saper, ébranler.

underneath [ˌʌndəˈniːθ] <> *prep* - **1.** [beneath] sous, au-dessous de - **2.** [in movements] sous. <> *adv* - **1.** [beneath] en dessous, dessous - **2.** *fig* [fundamentally] au fond. <> *adj inf* d'en dessous. <> *n* [underside] : **the ~** le dessous.

underpaid [ˈʌndəpeɪd] *adj* sous-payé(e).

underpants [ˈʌndəpænts] *npl* slip *m*.

underpass [ˈʌndəpɑːs] *n* [for cars] passage *m* inférieur ; [for pedestrians] passage *m* souterrain.

underprivileged [ˌʌndəˈprɪvɪlɪdʒd] *adj* défavorisé(e), déshérité(e).

underrated [ˌʌndəˈreɪtɪd] *adj* sous-estimé(e).

undershirt [ˈʌndəʃɜːt] *n* *Am* maillot *m* de corps.

underside [ˈʌndəsaɪd] *n* : **the ~** le dessous.

underskirt [ˈʌndəskɜːt] *n* jupon *m*.

understand [ˌʌndəˈstænd] (*pt* & *pp* **-stood**) <> *vt* - **1.** [gen] comprendre - **2.** *fml* [be informed] : **I ~ (that) ...** je crois comprendre que ..., il paraît que ... <> *vi* comprendre.

understandable [ˌʌndəˈstændəbl] *adj* compréhensible.

understanding [ˌʌndəˈstændɪŋ] <> *n* - **1.** [knowledge, sympathy] compréhension *f* - **2.** [agreement] accord *m*, arrangement *m* <> *adj* [sympathetic] compréhensif(ive).

understatement [ˌʌndəˈsteɪtmənt] *n* - **1.** [inadequate statement] affirmation *f* en dessous de la vérité - **2.** (U) [quality of understating] euphémisme *m*.

understood [ˌʌndəˈstʊd] *pt* & *pp* ▷ understand.

understudy [ˈʌndəˌstʌdɪ] *n* doublure *f*.

undertake [ˌʌndəˈteɪk] (*pt* **-took,** *pp* **-taken** [-ˈteɪkn]) *vt* - **1.** [take on - gen] entreprendre ; [- responsibility] assumer - **2.** [promise] : **to ~ to do sthg** promettre de faire qqch, s'engager à faire qqch.

undertaker [ˈʌndəˌteɪkəʳ] *n* entrepreneur *m* des pompes funèbres.

undertaking [ˌʌndəˈteɪkɪŋ] *n* - **1.** [task] entreprise *f* - **2.** [promise] promesse *f*.

undertone [ˈʌndətəʊn] *n* - **1.** [quiet voice] voix *f* basse - **2.** [vague feeling] courant *m*.

undertook [ˌʌndə'tʊk] *pt* ▷ under-take.

underwater [ˌʌndə'wɔːtəʳ] ◇ *adj* sous-marin(e). ◇ *adv* sous l'eau.

underwear ['ʌndəweəʳ] *n* (U) sous-vêtements *mpl*.

underwent [ˌʌndə'went] *pt* ▷ under-go.

underworld ['ʌndəˌwɜːld] *n* [criminal society] : **the ~** le milieu, la pègre.

underwriter ['ʌndəˌraɪtəʳ] *n* assureur *m*.

undid [ˌʌn'dɪd] *pt* ▷ undo.

undies ['ʌndɪz] *npl inf* dessous *mpl*, lingerie *f*.

undisputed [ˌʌndɪ'spjuːtɪd] *adj* incontesté(e).

undistinguished [ˌʌndɪ'stɪŋgwɪʃt] *adj* médiocre, quelconque.

undo [ˌʌn'duː] (*pt* -did, *pp* -done) *vt* - 1. [unfasten] défaire - 2. [nullify] annuler, détruire.

undoing [ˌʌn'duːɪŋ] *n* (U) *fml* perte *f*, ruine *f*.

undone [ˌʌn'dʌn] ◇ *pp* ▷ undo. ◇ *adj* - 1. [unfastened] défait(e) - 2. [task] non accompli(e).

undoubted [ʌn'daʊtɪd] *adj* indubitable, certain(e).

undoubtedly [ʌn'daʊtɪdlɪ] *adv* sans aucun doute.

undress [ˌʌn'dres] ◇ *vt* déshabiller. ◇ *vi* se déshabiller.

undue [ˌʌn'djuː] *adj fml* excessif(ive).

undulate ['ʌndjʊleɪt] *vi* onduler.

unduly [ˌʌn'djuːlɪ] *adv fml* trop, excessivement.

unearth [ˌʌn'ɜːθ] *vt* - 1. [dig up] déterrer - 2. *fig* [discover] découvrir, dénicher.

unearthly [ʌn'ɜːθlɪ] *adj inf* [uncivilized - time of day] indu(e), impossible.

unease [ʌn'iːz] *n* (U) malaise *m*.

uneasy [ʌn'iːzɪ] *adj* [person, feeling] mal à l'aise, gêné(e) ; [peace] troublé(e), incertain(e) ; [silence] gêné(e).

uneconomic ['ʌnˌiːkə'nɒmɪk] *adj* peu économique, peu rentable.

uneducated [ˌʌn'edjʊkeɪtɪd] *adj* [person] sans instruction.

unemployed [ˌʌnɪm'plɔɪd] ◇ *adj* au chômage, sans travail. ◇ *npl* : **the ~** les chômeurs *mpl*.

unemployment [ˌʌnɪm'plɔɪmənt] *n* chômage *m*.

unemployment benefit *Br*, **unem-**

ployment compensation *Am n* allocation *f* de chômage.

unerring [ˌʌn'ɜːrɪŋ] *adj* sûr(e), infaillible.

uneven [ˌʌn'iːvn] *adj* - 1. [not flat - surface] inégal(e) ; [- ground] accidenté(e) - 2. [inconsistent] inégal(e) - 3. [unfair] injuste.

unexpected [ˌʌnɪk'spektɪd] *adj* inattendu(e), imprévu(e).

unexpectedly [ˌʌnɪk'spektɪdlɪ] *adv* subitement, d'une manière imprévue.

unfailing [ʌn'feɪlɪŋ] *adj* qui ne se dément pas, constant(e).

unfair [ˌʌn'feəʳ] *adj* injuste.

unfaithful [ˌʌn'feɪθfʊl] *adj* infidèle.

unfamiliar [ˌʌnfə'mɪljəʳ] *adj* - 1. [not well-known] peu familier(ère), peu connu(e) - 2. [not acquainted] : **to be ~ with sb/sthg** mal connaître qqn/qqch, ne pas connaître qqn/qqch.

unfashionable [ˌʌn'fæʃnəbl] *adj* démodé(e), passé(e) de mode ; [person] qui n'est plus à la mode.

unfasten [ˌʌn'fɑːsn] *vt* défaire.

unfavourable *Br*, **unfavorable** *Am* [ˌʌn'feɪvrəbl] *adj* défavorable.

unfeeling [ʌn'fiːlɪŋ] *adj* impitoyable, insensible.

unfinished [ˌʌn'fɪnɪʃt] *adj* inachevé(e).

unfit [ˌʌn'fɪt] *adj* - 1. [not in good health] qui n'est pas en forme - 2. [not suitable] : **~ (for)** impropre (à) ; [person] inapte (à).

unfold [ʌn'fəʊld] ◇ *vt* [map, newspaper] déplier. ◇ *vi* [become clear] se dérouler.

unforeseen [ˌʌnfɔː'siːn] *adj* imprévu(e).

unforgettable [ˌʌnfə'getəbl] *adj* inoubliable.

unforgivable [ˌʌnfə'gɪvəbl] *adj* impardonnable.

unfortunate [ʌn'fɔːtʃnət] *adj* - 1. [unlucky] malheureux(euse), malchanceux(euse) - 2. [regrettable] regrettable, fâcheux(euse).

unfortunately [ʌn'fɔːtʃnətlɪ] *adv* malheureusement.

unfounded [ˌʌn'faʊndɪd] *adj* sans fondement, dénué(e) de tout fondement.

unfriendly [ˌʌn'frendlɪ] *adj* hostile, malveillant(e).

unfurnished [ˌʌn'fɜːnɪʃt] *adj* non meublé(e).

ungainly [ʌn'geɪnlɪ] *adj* gauche.

ungodly [ˌʌn'gɒdlɪ] *adj inf* [unreasonable] indu(e), impossible.

ungrateful [ʌn'greɪtfʊl] *adj* ingrat(e), peu reconnaissant(e).

unhappy [ʌn'hæpɪ] *adj* - **1.** [sad] triste, malheureux(euse) - **2.** [uneasy] : **to be ~ (with** OR **about)** être inquiet(ète) (au sujet de) - **3.** [unfortunate] malheureux(euse), regrettable.

unharmed [ˌʌn'hɑːmd] *adj* indemne, sain et sauf (saine et sauve).

unhealthy [ʌn'helθɪ] *adj* - **1.** [person, skin] maladif(ive) ; [conditions, place] insalubre, malsain(e) ; [habit] malsain - **2.** *fig* [undesirable] malsain(e).

unheard-of [ʌn'hɜːdɒv] *adj* - **1.** [unknown] inconnu(e) - **2.** [unprecedented] sans précédent, inouï(e).

unhook [ˌʌn'hʊk] *vt* - **1.** [dress, bra] dégrafer - **2.** [coat, picture, trailer] décrocher.

unhurt [ˌʌn'hɜːt] *adj* indemne, sain et sauf (saine et sauve).

unhygienic [ˌʌnhaɪˈdʒiːnɪk] *adj* non hygiénique.

unidentified flying object [ˌʌnaɪ'dentɪfaɪd-] *n* objet *m* volant non identifié.

unification [ˌjuːnɪfɪ'keɪʃn] *n* unification *f*.

uniform ['juːnɪfɔːm] <> *adj* [rate, colour] uniforme ; [size] même. <> *n* uniforme *m*.

unify ['juːnɪfaɪ] *vt* unifier.

unilateral [ˌjuːnɪ'lætərəl] *adj* unilatéral(e).

unimportant [ˌʌnɪm'pɔːtənt] *adj* sans importance, peu important(e).

uninhabited [ˌʌnɪn'hæbɪtɪd] *adj* inhabité(e).

uninjured [ˌʌn'ɪndʒəd] *adj* qui n'est pas blessé(e), indemne.

unintelligent [ˌʌnɪn'telɪdʒənt] *adj* inintelligent(e).

unintentional [ˌʌnɪn'tenʃənl] *adj* involontaire, non intentionnel(elle).

union ['juːnjən] <> *n* - **1.** [trade union] syndicat *m* - **2.** [alliance] union *f*. <> *comp* syndical(e).

Union Jack *n* : **the ~** l'Union Jack *m*, le drapeau britannique.

unique [juː'niːk] *adj* - **1.** [exceptional] unique, exceptionnel(elle) - **2.** [exclusive] : **~ to** propre à - **3.** [very special] unique.

unison ['juːnɪzn] *n* unisson *m* ; **in ~** à l'unisson ; [say] en chœur, en même temps.

unit ['juːnɪt] *n* - **1.** [gen] unité *f* - **2.** [machine part] élément *m*, bloc *m* - **3.** [of furniture] élément *m* - **4.** [department] service *m*.

unite [juː'naɪt] <> *vt* unifier. <> *vi* s'unir.

united [juː'naɪtɪd] *adj* - **1.** [in harmony] uni(e) - **2.** [unified] unifié(e).

United Kingdom *n* : **the ~** le Royaume-Uni.

United Nations *n* : **the ~** les Nations *fpl* Unies.

United States *n* : **the ~ (of America)** les États-Unis *mpl* (d'Amérique) ; **in the ~** aux États-Unis.

unit trust *n Br* société *f* d'investissement à capital variable.

unity ['juːnətɪ] *n* (U) unité *f*.

universal [ˌjuːnɪ'vɜːsl] *adj* universel(elle).

universe ['juːnɪvɜːs] *n* univers *m*.

university [ˌjuːnɪ'vɜːsətɪ] <> *n* université *f*. <> *comp* universitaire ; [lecturer] d'université ; **~ student** étudiant *m*, -e *f* à l'université.

unjust [ˌʌn'dʒʌst] *adj* injuste.

unkempt [ˌʌn'kempt] *adj* [clothes, person] négligé(e), débraillé(e) ; [hair] mal peigné(e).

unkind [ʌn'kaɪnd] *adj* [uncharitable] méchant(e), pas gentil(ille).

unknown [ˌʌn'nəʊn] *adj* inconnu(e).

unlawful [ˌʌn'lɔːfʊl] *adj* illégal(e).

unleaded [ˌʌn'ledɪd] <> *adj* sans plomb. <> *n* essence *f* sans plomb.

unleash [ˌʌn'liːʃ] *vt literary* déchaîner.

unless [ən'les] *conj* à moins que (+ subjunctive) ; **~ I'm mistaken** à moins que je (ne) me trompe.

unlike [ˌʌn'laɪk] *prep* - **1.** [different from] différent(e) de - **2.** [in contrast to] contrairement à, à la différence de - **3.** [not typical of] : **it's ~ you to complain** cela ne te ressemble pas de te plaindre.

unlikely [ʌn'laɪklɪ] *adj* - **1.** [event, result] peu probable, improbable ; [story] invraisemblable - **2.** [bizarre - clothes etc] invraisemblable.

unlisted [ʌn'lɪstɪd] *adj Am* [phone number] qui est sur la liste rouge.

unload [ˌʌn'ləʊd] *vt* décharger.

unlock [ˌʌn'lɒk] *vt* ouvrir.

unlucky [ʌn'lʌkɪ] *adj* - **1.** [unfortunate - person] malchanceux(euse), qui n'a pas de chance ; [- experience, choice] malheureux(euse) - **2.** [object, number etc] qui porte malheur.

unmarried [ˌʌn'mærɪd] *adj* célibataire, qui n'est pas marié(e).

unmistakable [ˌʌnmɪ'steɪkəbl] *adj* facilement reconnaissable.

unmitigated [ʌnˈmɪtɪgeɪtɪd] *adj* [disaster] total(e) ; [evil] non mitigé(e).

unnatural [ʌnˈnætʃrəl] *adj* - **1.** [unusual] anormal(e), qui n'est pas naturel(elle) - **2.** [affected] peu naturel(elle) ; [smile] forcé(e).

unnecessary [ʌnˈnesəsərɪ] *adj* [remark, expense, delay] inutile.

unnerving [ˌʌnˈnɜːvɪŋ] *adj* troublant(e).

unnoticed [ˌʌnˈnəʊtɪst] *adj* inaperçu(e).

unobtainable [ˌʌnəbˈteɪnəbl] *adj* impossible à obtenir.

unobtrusive [ˌʌnəbˈtruːsɪv] *adj* [person] effacé(e) ; [object] discret(ète) ; [building] que l'on remarque à peine.

unofficial [ˌʌnəˈfɪʃl] *adj* non officiel(elle).

unorthodox [ˌʌnˈɔːθədɒks] *adj* peu orthodoxe.

unpack [ˌʌnˈpæk] <> *vt* [suitcase] défaire ; [box] vider ; [clothes] déballer. <> *vi* défaire ses bagages.

unpalatable [ʌnˈpælətəbl] *adj* d'un goût désagréable ; *fig* dur(e) à avaler.

unparalleled [ʌnˈpærəleld] *adj* [success, crisis] sans précédent ; [beauty] sans égal.

unpleasant [ʌnˈpleznt] *adj* désagréable.

unplug [ʌnˈplʌg] *vt* débrancher.

unpopular [ˌʌnˈpɒpjʊləʳ] *adj* impopulaire.

unprecedented [ʌnˈpresɪdəntɪd] *adj* sans précédent.

unpredictable [ˌʌnprɪˈdɪktəbl] *adj* imprévisible.

unprofessional [ˌʌnprəˈfeʃənl] *adj* [person, work] peu professionnel(elle) ; [attitude] contraire à l'éthique de la profession.

unqualified [ˌʌnˈkwɒlɪfaɪd] *adj* - **1.** [person] non qualifié(e) ; [teacher, doctor] non diplômé(e) - **2.** [success] formidable ; [support] inconditionnel(elle).

unquestionable [ʌnˈkwestʃənəbl] *adj* [fact] incontestable ; [honesty] certain(e).

unquestioning [ʌnˈkwestʃənɪŋ] *adj* aveugle, absolu(e).

unravel [ʌnˈrævl] *vt* - **1.** [undo - knitting] défaire ; [- fabric] effiler ; [- threads] démêler - **2.** *fig* [solve] éclaircir.

unreal [ˌʌnˈrɪəl] *adj* [strange] irréel(elle).

unrealistic [ˌʌnrɪəˈlɪstɪk] *adj* irréaliste.

unreasonable [ʌnˈriːznəbl] *adj* qui n'est pas raisonnable, déraisonnable.

unrelated [ˌʌnrɪˈleɪtɪd] *adj* : **to be ~ (to)** n'avoir aucun rapport (avec).

unrelenting [ˌʌnrɪˈlentɪŋ] *adj* implacable.

unreliable [ˌʌnrɪˈlaɪəbl] *adj* [machine, method] peu fiable ; [person] sur qui on ne peut pas compter.

unremitting [ˌʌnrɪˈmɪtɪŋ] *adj* inlassable.

unrequited [ˌʌnrɪˈkwaɪtɪd] *adj* non partagé(e).

unreserved [ˌʌnrɪˈzɜːvd] *adj* [support, admiration] sans réserve.

unresolved [ˌʌnrɪˈzɒlvd] *adj* non résolu(e).

unrest [ˌʌnˈrest] *n (U)* troubles *mpl*.

unrivalled *Br*, **unrivaled** *Am* [ʌnˈraɪvld] *adj* sans égal(e).

unroll [ˌʌnˈrəʊl] *vt* dérouler.

unruly [ʌnˈruːlɪ] *adj* [crowd, child] turbulent(e) ; [hair] indisciplinés.

unsafe [ˌʌnˈseɪf] *adj* - **1.** [dangerous] dangereux(euse) - **2.** [in danger] : **to feel ~** ne pas se sentir en sécurité.

unsaid [ˌʌnˈsed] *adj* : **to leave sthg ~** passer qqch sous silence.

unsatisfactory [ˈʌnˌsætɪsˈfæktərɪ] *adj* qui laisse à désirer, peu satisfaisant(e).

unsavoury *Br*, **unsavory** *Am* [ˌʌnˈseɪvərɪ] *adj* [person] peu recommandable ; [district] mal famé(e).

unscathed [ˌʌnˈskeɪðd] *adj* indemne.

unscrew [ˌʌnˈskruː] *vt* dévisser.

unscrupulous [ʌnˈskruːpjʊləs] *adj* sans scrupules.

unseemly [ʌnˈsiːmlɪ] *adj* inconvenant(e).

unselfish [ˌʌnˈselfɪʃ] *adj* désintéressé(e).

unsettled [ˌʌnˈsetld] *adj* - **1.** [person] perturbé(e), troublé(e) - **2.** [weather] variable, incertain(e) - **3.** [argument] qui n'a pas été résolu(e) ; [situation] incertain(e).

unshak(e)able [ʌnˈʃeɪkəbl] *adj* inébranlable.

unshaven [ˌʌnˈʃeɪvn] *adj* non rasé(e).

unsightly [ʌnˈsaɪtlɪ] *adj* laid(e).

unskilled [ˌʌnˈskɪld] *adj* non qualifié(e).

unsociable [ʌnˈsəʊʃəbl] *adj* sauvage.

unsocial [ˌʌnˈsəʊʃl] *adj Br* : **to work ~ hours** travailler en dehors des heures normales.

unsound [ˌʌnˈsaʊnd] *adj* - **1.** [theory] mal fondé(e) ; [decision] peu judicieux(euse) - **2.** [building, structure] en mauvais état.

unspeakable [ʌnˈspiːkəbl] *adj* indescriptible.

unstable [ˌʌnˈsteɪbl] *adj* instable.

unsteady [ˌʌnˈstedɪ] *adj* [hand] tremblant(e) ; [table, ladder] instable.

unstoppable [ˌʌnˈstɒpəbl] *adj* qu'on ne peut pas arrêter.

unstuck [ˌʌnˈstʌk] *adj* : **to come ~** [notice, stamp, label] se décoller ; *fig* [plan, system] s'effondrer ; *fig* [person] essuyer un échec.

unsuccessful [ˌʌnsəkˈsesfʊl] *adj* [attempt] vain(e) ; [meeting] infructueux (euse) ; [candidate] refusé(e).

unsuccessfully [ˌʌnsəkˈsesfʊlɪ] *adv* en vain, sans succès.

unsuitable [ˌʌnˈsuːtəbl] *adj* qui ne convient pas ; [clothes] peu approprié(e) ; **to be ~ for** ne pas convenir à.

unsure [ˌʌnˈʃɔːʳ] *adj* - **1.** [not certain] : **to be ~ (about/of)** ne pas être sûr(e) (de) - **2.** [not confident] : **to be ~ (of o.s.)** ne pas être sûr(e) de soi.

unsuspecting [ˌʌnsəˈspektɪŋ] *adj* qui ne se doute de rien.

unsympathetic [ˈʌnˌsɪmpəˈθetɪk] *adj* [unfeeling] indifférent(e).

untangle [ˌʌnˈtæŋgl] *vt* [string, hair] démêler.

untapped [ˌʌnˈtæpt] *adj* inexploité(e).

untenable [ˌʌnˈtenəbl] *adj* indéfendable.

unthinkable [ʌnˈθɪŋkəbl] *adj* impensable.

untidy [ʌnˈtaɪdɪ] *adj* [room, desk] en désordre ; [work, handwriting] brouillon *(inv)* ; [person, appearance] négligé(e).

untie [ˌʌnˈtaɪ] *(cont* **untying)** *vt* [knot, parcel, shoelaces] défaire ; [prisoner] détacher.

until [ʌnˈtɪl] *prep* - **1.** [gen] jusqu'à ; **~ now** jusqu'ici - **2.** *(after negative)* avant ; **not ~ tomorrow** pas avant demain. *conj* - **1.** [gen] jusqu'à ce que (+ *subjunctive)* - **2.** *(after negative)* avant que (+ *subjunctive)*.

untimely [ʌnˈtaɪmlɪ] *adj* [death] prématuré(e) ; [arrival] intempestif(ive) ; [remark] mal à propos ; [moment] mal choisi(e).

untold [ˌʌnˈtəʊld] *adj* [amount, wealth] incalculable ; [suffering, joy] indescriptible.

untoward [ˌʌntəˈwɔːd] *adj* malencontreux(euse).

untrue [ˌʌnˈtruː] *adj* [not accurate] faux (fausse), qui n'est pas vrai(e).

unused [*sense 1* ˌʌnˈjuːzd, *sense 2* ʌnˈjuːst] *adj* - **1.** [clothes] neuf (neuve) ; [machine] qui n'a jamais servi ; [land] qui n'est pas exploité - **2.** [unaccustomed] : **to be ~ to sthg/ to doing sthg** ne pas avoir l'habitude de qqch/de faire qqch.

unusual [ʌnˈjuːʒl] *adj* rare, inhabituel (elle).

unusually [ʌnˈjuːʒəlɪ] *adv* exceptionnellement.

unveil [ˌʌnˈveɪl] *vt lit & fig* dévoiler.

unwanted [ˌʌnˈwɒntɪd] *adj* [object] dont on ne se sert pas ; [child] non désiré(e) ; **to feel ~** se sentir mal-aimé(e).

unwavering [ʌnˈweɪvərɪŋ] *adj* [determination] inébranlable.

unwelcome [ʌnˈwelkəm] *adj* [news, situation] fâcheux(euse) ; [visitor] importun(e).

unwell [ˌʌnˈwel] *adj* : **to be/feel ~** ne pas être/se sentir bien.

unwieldy [ʌnˈwiːldɪ] *adj* - **1.** [cumbersome] peu maniable - **2.** *fig* [system] lourd(e) ; [method] trop complexe.

unwilling [ˌʌnˈwɪlɪŋ] *adj* : **to be ~ to do sthg** ne pas vouloir faire qqch.

unwind [ˌʌnˈwaɪnd] *(pt & pp* **-wound)** ⟨⟩ *vt* dérouler. ⟨⟩ *vi fig* [person] se détendre.

unwise [ˌʌnˈwaɪz] *adj* imprudent(e), peu sage.

unwitting [ʌnˈwɪtɪŋ] *adj fml* involontaire.

unworkable [ˌʌnˈwɜːkəbl] *adj* impraticable.

unworthy [ʌnˈwɜːðɪ] *adj* [undeserving] : **~ (of)** indigne (de).

unwound [ˌʌnˈwaʊnd] *pt & pp* ⟩ **unwind**.

unwrap [ˌʌnˈræp] *vt* défaire.

unwritten law [ˌʌnrɪtn-] *n* droit *m* coutumier

up [ʌp] ⟨⟩ *adv* - **1.** [towards or in a higher position] en haut ; **she's ~ in her bedroom** elle est en haut dans sa chambre ; **we walked ~ to the top** on est montés jusqu'en haut ; **prices are going ~** les prix augmentent ; **~ there** là-haut - **2.** [into an upright position] : **to stand ~** se lever ; **to sit ~** s'asseoir (bien droit) - **3.** [northwards] : **I'm coming ~ to York next week** je viens à York la semaine prochaine ; **~ north** dans le nord - **4.** [along a road, river] : **their house is a little further ~** leur maison est un peu plus loin. ⟨⟩ *prep* - **1.** [towards or in a higher position] en haut de ; **~ a hill/mountain** en haut d'une colline/d'une montagne ; **~ a ladder** sur une échelle ; **I went ~ the stairs** j'ai monté l'escalier - **2.** [at far end of] : **they live ~ the road from us** ils habitent un peu plus haut OR loin que nous (dans la même rue) - **3.** [against current of river] : **to sail ~ the Amazon** remonter l'Amazone en bateau. <> *adj* - **1.** [out of bed] levé(e) ; **I was ~ at six today** je me suis levé à six heures aujourd'hui - **2.** [at an end] : **time's ~** c'est l'heure - **3.** *inf* [wrong] : **is something ~?** il y a quelque chose qui ne va pas ? ; **what's ~?** qu'est-ce qui ne va pas?, qu'est-ce qu'il y a ? <> *n* : **~s and downs** hauts et bas *mpl*.

◆ **up and down** <> *adv* : **to jump ~ and down** sauter ; **to walk ~ and down** faire les cent pas. <> *prep* : **we walked ~ and down the avenue** nous avons arpenté l'avenue.

◆ **up to** *prep* - **1.** [as far as] jusqu'à - **2.** [indicating level] jusqu'à ; **it could take ~ to six weeks** cela peut prendre jusqu'à six semaines ; **it's not ~ standard** ce n'est pas de la qualité voulue, ceci n'a pas le niveau requis - **3.** [well or able enough for] : **to be ~ to doing sthg** [able to] être capable de faire qqch ; [well enough for] être en état de faire qqch ; **my French isn't ~ to much** mon français ne vaut pas grand-chose OR n'est pas fameux - **4.** *inf* [secretly doing something] : **what are you ~ to?** qu'est-ce que tu fabriques? ; **they're ~ to something** ils mijotent quelque chose, ils préparent un coup - **5.** [indicating responsibility] : **it's not ~ to me to decide** ce n'est pas moi qui décide, il ne m'appartient pas de décider ; **it's ~ to you** c'est à vous de voir. ◆ **up until** *prep* jusqu'à.

up-and-coming *adj* à l'avenir prometteur.

upbringing ['ʌpˌbrɪŋɪŋ] *n* éducation *f*.

update [ˌʌp'deɪt] *vt* mettre à jour.

upheaval [ʌp'hiːvl] *n* bouleversement *m*.

upheld [ʌp'held] *pt & pp* ⊏> **uphold**.

uphill [ˌʌp'hɪl] <> *adj* - **1.** [slope, path] qui monte - **2.** *fig* [task] ardu(e). <> *adv* : **to go ~** monter.

uphold [ʌp'həʊld] (*pt & pp* **-held**) *vt* [law] maintenir ; [decision, system] soutenir.

upholstery [ʌp'həʊlstərɪ] *n* rembourrage *m* ; [of car] garniture *f* intérieure.

upkeep ['ʌpkiːp] *n* entretien *m*.

uplifting [ʌp'lɪftɪŋ] *adj* édifiant(e).

up-market *adj* haut de gamme *(inv)*.

upon [ə'pɒn] *prep fml* sur ; **~ hearing the news** ... à ces nouvelles ... ; **summer/the weekend is ~ us** l'été/le week-end approche.

upper ['ʌpə'] <> *adj* supérieur(e). <> *n* [of shoe] empeigne *f*.

upper class *n* : **the ~** la haute société.
◆ **upper-class** *adj* [accent, person] aristocratique.

upper hand *n* : **to have the ~** avoir le dessus ; **to gain** OR **get the ~** prendre le dessus.

uppermost ['ʌpəməʊst] *adj* le plus haut (la plus haute) ; **it was ~ in his mind** c'était sa préoccupation majeure.

upright [*adj sense 1 & adv* ˌʌp'raɪt, *adj sense 2 & n* 'ʌpraɪt] <> *adj* - **1.** [person] droit(e) ; [structure] vertical(e) ; [chair] à dossier droit - **2.** *fig* [honest] droit(e). <> *adv* [stand, sit] droit. <> *n* montant *m*.

uprising ['ʌpˌraɪzɪŋ] *n* soulèvement *m*.

uproar ['ʌprɔːʳ] *n* - **1.** (*U*) [commotion] tumulte *m* - **2.** [protest] protestations *fpl*.

uproot [ʌp'ruːt] *vt lit & fig* déraciner.

upset [ʌp'set] (*pt & pp* **upset**) <> *adj* - **1.** [distressed] peiné(e), triste ; [offended] vexé(e) - **2.** MED : **to have an ~ stomach** avoir l'estomac dérangé. <> *n* : **to have a stomach ~** avoir l'estomac dérangé. <> *vt* - **1.** [distress] faire de la peine à - **2.** [plan, operation] déranger - **3.** [overturn] renverser.

upshot ['ʌpʃɒt] *n* résultat *m*.

upside down [ˌʌpsaɪd-] <> *adj* à l'envers. <> *adv* à l'envers ; **to turn sthg ~** *fig* mettre qqch sens dessus dessous.

upstairs [ˌʌp'steəz] <> *adj* d'en haut, du dessus. <> *adv* en haut. <> *n* étage *m*.

upstart ['ʌpstaːt] *n* parvenu *m*, -e *f*.

upstream [ˌʌp'striːm] <> *adj* d'amont ; **to be ~ (from)** être en amont (de). <> *adv* vers l'amont ; [swim] contre le courant.

upsurge ['ʌpsɜːdʒ] *n* : **~ (of/in)** recrudescence *f* (de).

uptake ['ʌpteɪk] *n* : **to be quick on the ~** saisir vite ; **to be slow on the ~** être lent(e) à comprendre.

uptight [ʌp'taɪt] *adj inf* tendu(e).

up-to-date *adj* - **1.** [modern] moderne - **2.** [most recent - news] tout dernier (toute dernière) - **3.** [informed] : **to keep ~ with** se tenir au courant de.

upturn ['ʌptɜːn] *n* : **~ (in)** reprise *f* (de).

upward ['ʌpwəd] <> *adj* [movement] ascendant(e) ; [look, rise] vers le haut. <> *adv Am* = **upwards**.

upwards ['ʌpwədz] *adv* vers le haut.
◆ **upwards of** *prep* plus de.

uranium [juˈreɪnjəm] *n* uranium *m*.

urban ['ɜːbən] *adj* urbain(e).

urbane [ɜːˈbeɪn] *adj* courtois(e).

urchin ['ɜːtʃɪn] *n dated* gamin *m*, -e *f*.

Urdu ['ʊəduː] *n* ourdou *m*.

urge [ɜːdʒ] <> *n* forte envie *f* ; **to have an ~ to do sthg** avoir une forte envie de faire qqch. <> *vt* - **1.** [try to persuade] : **to ~ sb to do sthg** pousser qqn à faire qqch, presser qqn de faire qqch - **2.** [advocate] conseiller.

urgency [ˈɜːdʒənsɪ] *n (U)* urgence *f*.

urgent [ˈɜːdʒənt] *adj* [letter, case, request] urgent(e) ; [plea, voice, need] pressant(e).

urinal [ˌjʊəˈraɪnl] *n* urinoir *m*.

urinate [ˈjʊərɪneɪt] *vi* uriner.

urine [ˈjʊərɪn] *n* urine *f*.

URL (*abbr of* **uniform resource locator**) *n* COMPUT URL *m* (*adresse électronique*).

urn [ɜːn] *n* **- 1.** [for ashes] urne *f* **- 2.** [for tea] : **tea ~** fontaine *f* à thé.

Uruguay [ˈjʊərəgwaɪ] *n* Uruguay *m*.

us [ʌs] *pers pron* nous ; **can you see/hear ~?** vous nous voyez/entendez? ; **it's ~** c'est nous ; **you can't expect us to do it** vous ne pouvez pas exiger que ce soit nous qui le fassions ; **she gave it to ~** elle nous l'a donné ; **with/without ~** avec/sans nous ; **they are more wealthy than ~** ils sont plus riches que nous ; **some of ~** quelques-uns d'entre nous.

US *n abbr of* **United States**.

USA *n abbr of* **United States of America**.

usage [ˈjuːzɪdʒ] *n* **- 1.** LING usage *m* **- 2.** (*U*) [handling, treatment] traitement *m*.

use [*n & vb* juːs, *vi* juːz] ⬦ *n* **- 1.** [act of using] utilisation *f*, emploi *m* ; **to be in ~** être utilisé ; **to be out of ~** être hors d'usage ; **to make ~ of sthg** utiliser qqch **- 2.** [ability to use] usage *m* **- 3.** [usefulness] : **to be of ~** être utile ; **it's no ~** ça ne sert à rien ; **what's the ~ (of doing sthg)?** à quoi bon (faire qqch)? ⬦ *aux vb* : **I ~d to live in London** avant j'habitais à Londres ; **he didn't ~ to be so fat** il n'était pas si gros avant ; **there ~d to be a tree here** (autrefois) il y avait un arbre ici. ⬦ *vt* **- 1.** [gen] utiliser, se servir de, employer **- 2.** *pej* [exploit] se servir de. ◆ **use up** *vt sep* [supply] épuiser ; [food] finir ; [money] dépenser.

used [*senses 1 and 2* juːzd, *sense 3* juːst] *adj* **- 1.** [handkerchief, towel] sale **- 2.** [car] d'occasion **- 3.** [accustomed] : **to be ~ to sthg/to doing sthg** avoir l'habitude de qqch/de faire qqch ; **to get ~ to sthg** s'habituer à qqch.

useful [ˈjuːsfʊl] *adj* utile.

useless [ˈjuːslɪs] *adj* **- 1.** [gen] inutile **- 2.** *inf* [person] incompétent(e), nul (nulle).

Usenet® [ˈjuːznet] *n* Usenet® *m*, forum *m* électronique.

user [ˈjuːzəʳ] *n* [of product, machine] utilisateur *m*, -trice *f* ; [of service] usager *m*.

user-friendly *adj* convivial(e), facile à utiliser.

usher [ˈʌʃəʳ] ⬦ *n* placeur *m*. ⬦ *vt* : **to ~ sb in/out** faire entrer/sortir qqn.

usherette [ˌʌʃəˈret] *n* ouvreuse *f*.

USSR (*abbr of* **Union of Soviet Socialist Republics**) *n* : **the (former) ~** l'(ex-)URSS *f*.

usual [ˈjuːʒəl] *adj* habituel(elle) ; **as ~** comme d'habitude.

usually [ˈjuːʒəlɪ] *adv* d'habitude, d'ordinaire.

usurp [juːˈzɜːp] *vt* usurper.

utensil [juːˈtensl] *n* ustensile *m*.

uterus [ˈjuːtərəs] (*pl* **-ri** [-raɪ], **-ruses** [-rəsiːz]) *n* utérus *m*.

utility [juːˈtɪlətɪ] *n* **- 1.** (*U*) [usefulness] utilité *f* **- 2.** [public service] service *m* public **- 3.** COMPUT utilitaire *m*.

utility room *n* buanderie *f*.

utilize, -ise [ˈjuːtəlaɪz] *vt* utiliser ; [resources] exploiter, utiliser.

utmost [ˈʌtməʊst] ⬦ *adj* le plus grand (la plus grande). ⬦ *n* : **to do one's ~** faire tout son possible, faire l'impossible ; **to the ~** au plus haut point.

utter [ˈʌtəʳ] ⬦ *adj* total(e), complet(ète). ⬦ *vt* prononcer, [cry] pousser.

utterly [ˈʌtəlɪ] *adv* complètement.

U-turn *n* demi-tour *m* ; *fig* revirement *m*.

v[1] (*pl* **v's** OR **vs**), **V** (*pl* **V's** OR **Vs**) [viː] *n* [letter] v *m inv*, V *m inv*.

v[2] **- 1.** (*abbr of* **verse**) v. **- 2.** (*abbr of* **vide**) [cross-reference] v. **- 3.** *abbr of* **versus** **- 4.** (*abbr of* **volt**) v.

vacancy [ˈveɪkənsɪ] *n* **- 1.** [job] poste *m* vacant **- 2.** [room available] chambre *f* à louer ; **'vacancies'** 'chambres à louer' ; **'no vacancies'** 'complet'.

vacant [ˈveɪkənt] *adj* **- 1.** [room] inoccupé(e) ; [chair, toilet] libre **- 2.** [job, post] vacant(e) **- 3.** [look, expression] distrait(e).

vacant lot *n* terrain *m* inoccupé ; [for sale] terrain *m* à vendre.

vacate [vəˈkeɪt] *vt* quitter.

vacation [vəˈkeɪʃn] *n* *Am* vacances *fpl*.

vacationer [vəˈkeɪʃənəʳ] *n* *Am* vacancier *m*, -ère *f*.

vaccinate [ˈvæksɪneɪt] *vt* vacciner.

vaccine [Br 'væksi:n, Am væk'si:n] n vaccin m.

vacuum ['vækjʊəm] ⟨⟩ n - **1.** TECH & fig vide m - **2.** [cleaner] aspirateur m. ⟨⟩ vt [room] passer l'aspirateur dans ; [carpet] passer à l'aspirateur.

vacuum cleaner n aspirateur m.

vacuum-packed adj emballé(e) sous vide.

vagina [və'dʒaɪnə] n vagin m.

vagrant ['veɪɡrənt] n vagabond m, -e f.

vague [veɪɡ] adj - **1.** [gen] vague, imprécis(e) - **2.** [absent-minded] distrait(e).

vaguely ['veɪɡlɪ] adv vaguement.

vain [veɪn] adj - **1.** [futile, worthless] vain(e) - **2.** pej [conceited] vaniteux(euse). ◆ **in vain** adv en vain, vainement.

valentine card ['væləntaɪn-] n carte f de la Saint-Valentin.

Valentine's Day ['væləntaɪnz-] n : (St) ~ la Saint-Valentin.

valet ['væleɪ, 'vælɪt] n valet m de chambre.

valiant ['væljənt] adj vaillant(e).

valid ['vælɪd] adj - **1.** [reasonable] valable - **2.** [legally usable] valide.

valley ['vælɪ] (pl **-s**) n vallée f.

valour Br, **valor** Am ['vælə'] n (U) fml & literary bravoure f.

valuable ['væljʊəbl] adj - **1.** [advice, time, information] précieux(euse) - **2.** [object, jewel] de valeur. ◆ **valuables** npl objets mpl de valeur.

valuation [,væljʊ'eɪʃn] n - **1.** (U) [pricing] estimation f, expertise f - **2.** [estimated price] valeur f estimée.

value ['vælju:] ⟨⟩ n valeur f ; **to be good ~** être d'un bon rapport qualité-prix ; **to get ~ for money** en avoir pour son argent. ⟨⟩ vt - **1.** [estimate price of] expertiser - **2.** [cherish] apprécier. ◆ **values** npl [morals] valeurs fpl.

value-added tax [-ædɪd-] n taxe f sur la valeur ajoutée.

valued ['vælju:d] adj précieux(euse).

valve [vælv] n [on tyre] valve f ; TECH soupape f.

van [væn] n - **1.** AUT camionnette f - **2.** Br RAIL fourgon m.

vandal ['vændl] n vandale mf.

vandalism ['vændəlɪzm] n vandalisme m.

vandalize, -ise ['vændəlaɪz] vt saccager.

vanguard ['vænɡɑ:d] n avant-garde f ; **in the ~ of** à l'avant-garde de.

vanilla [və'nɪlə] n vanille f.

vanish ['vænɪʃ] vi disparaître.

vanity ['vænətɪ] n (U) pej vanité f.

vantagepoint ['vɑ:ntɪdʒ,pɔɪnt] n [for view] bon endroit m ; fig position f avantageuse.

vapour Br, **vapor** Am ['veɪpə'] n (U) vapeur f ; [condensation] buée f.

variable ['veərɪəbl] adj variable ; [mood] changeant(e).

variance ['veərɪəns] n fml : **at ~ (with)** en désaccord (avec).

variation [,veərɪ'eɪʃn] n : **~ (in)** variation f (de).

varicose veins ['værɪkəʊs-] npl varices fpl.

varied ['veərɪd] adj varié(e).

variety [və'raɪətɪ] n - **1.** [gen] variété f - **2.** [type] variété f, sorte f.

variety show n spectacle m de variétés.

various ['veərɪəs] adj - **1.** [several] plusieurs - **2.** [different] divers.

varnish ['vɑ:nɪʃ] ⟨⟩ n vernis m. ⟨⟩ vt vernir.

vary ['veərɪ] ⟨⟩ vt varier. ⟨⟩ vi : **to ~ (in/ with)** varier (en/selon), changer (en/ selon).

vase [Br vɑ:z, Am veɪz] n vase m.

Vaseline® ['væsəli:n] n vaseline f.

vast [vɑ:st] adj vaste, immense.

vat [væt] n cuve f.

VAT [væt, vi:eɪ'ti:] (abbr of value added tax) n TVA f.

Vatican ['vætɪkən] n : **the ~** le Vatican.

vault [vɔ:lt] ⟨⟩ n - **1.** [in bank] chambre f forte - **2.** [roof] voûte f - **3.** [in church] caveau m. ⟨⟩ vt sauter. ⟨⟩ vi : **to ~ over sthg** sauter (par-dessus) qqch.

VCR (abbr of video cassette recorder) n magnétoscope m.

VD (abbr of venereal disease) n (U) MST f.

VDU (abbr of visual display unit) n moniteur m.

veal [vi:l] n (U) veau m.

veer [vɪə'] vi virer.

vegan ['vi:gən] ⟨⟩ adj végétalien(enne). ⟨⟩ n végétalien m, -enne f.

vegetable ['vedʒtəbl] ⟨⟩ n légume m. ⟨⟩ adj [matter, protein] végétal(e) ; [soup, casserole] de OR aux légumes.

vegetarian [,vedʒɪ'teərɪən] ⟨⟩ adj végétarien(enne). ⟨⟩ n végétarien m, -enne f.

vegetation [,vedʒɪ'teɪʃn] n (U) végétation f.

vehement ['vi:ɪmənt] adj véhément(e).

vehicle ['vi:ɪkl] n lit & fig véhicule m.

veil [veɪl] n lit & fig voile m.

vein [veɪn] *n* - **1.** ANAT veine *f* - **2.** [of leaf] nervure *f* - **3.** [of mineral] filon *m*.

velocity [vɪ'lɒsətɪ] *n* vélocité *f*.

velvet ['velvɪt] *n* velours *m*.

vendetta [ven'detə] *n* vendetta *f*.

vending machine ['vendɪŋ-] *n* distributeur *m* automatique.

vendor ['vendə'] *n* - **1.** *fml* [salesperson] marchand *m*, -e *f* - **2.** JUR vendeur *m*, -eresse *f*.

veneer [və'nɪə'] *n* placage *m* ; *fig* apparence *f*.

venereal disease [vɪ'nɪərɪəl-] *n* maladie *f* vénérienne.

venetian blind [vɪˌniːʃn-] *n* store *m* vénitien.

Venezuela [ˌvenɪz'weɪlə] *n* Venezuela *m*.

vengeance ['vendʒəns] *n* vengeance *f* ; **it began raining with a ~** il a commencé à pleuvoir très fort.

venison ['venɪzn] *n* venaison *f*.

venom ['venəm] *n lit & fig* venin *m*.

vent [vent] <> *n* [pipe] tuyau *m* ; [opening] orifice *m* ; **to give ~ to** donner libre cours à. <> *vt* [anger, feelings] donner libre cours à ; **to ~ sthg on sb** décharger qqch sur qqn.

ventilate ['ventɪleɪt] *vt* ventiler.

ventilator ['ventɪleɪtə'] *n* ventilateur *m*.

ventriloquist [ven'trɪləkwɪst] *n* ventriloque *mf*.

venture ['ventʃə'] <> *n* entreprise *f*. <> *vt* risquer ; **to ~ to do sthg** se permettre de faire qqch. <> *vi* s'aventurer.

venue ['venjuː] *n* lieu *m*.

veranda(h) [və'rændə] *n* véranda *f*.

verb [vɜːb] *n* verbe *m*.

verbal ['vɜːbl] *adj* verbal(e).

verbatim [vɜː'beɪtɪm] *adj & adv* mot pour mot.

verbose [vɜː'bəʊs] *adj* verbeux(euse).

verdict ['vɜːdɪkt] *n* - **1.** JUR verdict *m* - **2.** [opinion] : **~ (on)** avis *m* (sur).

verge [vɜːdʒ] *n* - **1.** [of lawn] bordure *f* ; [of road] bas-côté *m*, accotement *m* - **2.** [brink] : **on the ~ of sthg** au bord de qqch ; **on the ~ of doing sthg** sur le point de faire qqch.
➤ **verge (up)on** *vt fus* friser, approcher de.

verify ['verɪfaɪ] *vt* vérifier.

veritable ['verɪtəbl] *adj hum or fml* véritable.

vermin ['vɜːmɪn] *npl* vermine *f*.

vermouth ['vɜːməθ] *n* vermouth *m*.

versa ▷ vice versa.

versatile ['vɜːsətaɪl] *adj* [person, player] aux talents multiples ; [machine, tool, food] souple d'emploi.

verse [vɜːs] *n* - **1.** (*U*) [poetry] vers *mpl* - **2.** [stanza] strophe *f* - **3.** [in Bible] verset *m*.

versed [vɜːst] *adj* : **to be well ~ in sthg** être versé(e) dans qqch.

version ['vɜːʃn] *n* version *f*.

versus ['vɜːsəs] *prep* - **1.** SPORT contre - **2.** [as opposed to] par opposition à.

vertebra ['vɜːtɪbrə] (*pl* **-brae** [-briː]) *n* vertèbre *f*.

vertical ['vɜːtɪkl] *adj* vertical(e).

vertigo ['vɜːtɪgəʊ] *n* (*U*) vertige *m*.

verve [vɜːv] *n* verve *f*.

very ['verɪ] <> *adv* - **1.** [as intensifier] très ; **~ much beaucoup - 2.** [as euphemism] : **not ~** pas très. <> *adj* : **the ~ room/book** la pièce/le livre même ; **the ~ man/thing I've been looking for** juste l'homme/la chose que je cherchais ; **at the ~ least** tout au moins ; **~ last/first** tout dernier/premier ; **of one's ~ own** bien à soi. ➤ **very well** *adv* très bien ; **I can't ~ well tell him ...** je ne peux tout de même pas lui dire que ...

vessel ['vesl] *n fml* - **1.** [boat] vaisseau *m* - **2.** [container] récipient *m*.

vest [vest] *n* - **1.** *Br* [undershirt] maillot *m* de corps - **2.** *Am* [waistcoat] gilet *m*.

vested interest ['vestɪd-] *n* : **~ (in)** intérêt *m* particulier (à).

vestibule ['vestɪbjuːl] *n fml* [entrance hall] vestibule *m*.

vestige ['vestɪdʒ] *n* vestige *m*.

vestry ['vestrɪ] *n* sacristie *f*.

vet [vet] <> *n* (*abbr of* **veterinary surgeon**) vétérinaire *mf*. <> *vt* [candidates] examiner avec soin.

veteran ['vetrən] <> *adj* [experienced] chevronné(e). <> *n* - **1.** MIL ancien combattant *m*, vétéran *m* - **2.** [experienced person] vétéran *m*.

veterinarian [ˌvetərɪ'neərɪən] *n Am* vétérinaire *mf*.

veterinary surgeon ['vetərɪnrɪ-] *n Br fml* vétérinaire *mf*.

veto ['viːtəʊ] (*pl* **-es**, *pt & pp* **-ed**, *cont* **-ing**) <> *n* veto *m*. <> *vt* opposer son veto à.

vex [veks] *vt* contrarier.

vexed question [ˌvekst-] *n* question *f* controversée.

vg (*abbr of* **very good**) tb.

VHF (*abbr of* **very high frequency**) VHF.

VHS (*abbr of* **video home system**) *n* VHS *m*.

via ['vaɪə] *prep* - **1.** [travelling through] via, par - **2.** [by means of] au moyen de.

viable ['vaɪəbl] *adj* viable.

vibrate [vaɪ'breɪt] *vi* vibrer.

vicar ['vɪkə'] *n* [in Church of England] pasteur *m*.

vicarage ['vɪkərɪdʒ] *n* presbytère *m*.

vicarious [vɪ'keərɪəs] *adj* : **to take a ~ pleasure in sthg** retirer du plaisir indirectement de qqch.

vice [vaɪs] *n* - 1. [immorality, fault] vice *m* - 2. [tool] étau *m*.

vice-chairman *n* vice-président *m*, -e *f*.

vice-chancellor *n* UNIV président *m*, -e *f*.

vice-president *n* vice-président *m*, -e *f*.

vice versa [,vaɪsɪ'vɜːsə] *adv* vice versa.

vicinity [vɪ'sɪnətɪ] *n* : **in the ~ (of)** aux alentours (de), dans les environs (de).

vicious ['vɪʃəs] *adj* violent(e), brutal(e).

vicious circle *n* cercle *m* vicieux.

victim ['vɪktɪm] *n* victime *f*.

victimize, -ise ['vɪktɪmaɪz] *vt* faire une victime de.

victor ['vɪktə'] *n* vainqueur *m*.

victorious [vɪk'tɔːrɪəs] *adj* victorieux (euse).

victory ['vɪktərɪ] *n* : **~ (over)** victoire *f* (sur).

video ['vɪdɪəʊ] (*pl* -s, *pt* & *pp* -ed, *cont* -ing) ⬦ *n* - 1. [medium, recording] vidéo *f* - 2. [machine] magnétoscope *m* - 3. [cassette] vidéocassette *f*. ⬦ *comp* vidéo *(inv)*. ⬦ *vt* - 1. [using video recorder] enregistrer sur magnétoscope - 2. [using camera] faire une vidéo de, filmer.

video camera *n* caméra *f* vidéo.

video cassette *n* vidéocassette *f*.

videoconference ['vɪdɪəʊ'kɒnfərəns] *n* vidéoconférence *f*.

video game *n* jeu *m* vidéo.

videorecorder ['vɪdɪəʊrɪˌkɔːdə'] *n* magnétoscope *m*.

video shop *n* vidéoclub *m*.

videotape ['vɪdɪəʊteɪp] *n* - 1. [cassette] vidéocassette *f* - 2. (*U*) [ribbon] bande *f* vidéo.

vie [vaɪ] (*pt* & *pp* **vied**, *cont* **vying**) *vi* : **to ~ for sthg** lutter pour qqch ; **to ~ with sb (for sthg/to do sthg)** rivaliser avec qqn (pour qqch/pour faire qqch).

Vienna [vɪ'enə] *n* Vienne.

Vietnam [*Br* ,vjet'næm, *Am* ,vjet'naːm] *n* Viêt-nam *m*.

Vietnamese [,vjetnə'miːz] ⬦ *adj* vietnamien(enne). ⬦ *n* [language] vietnamien *m*. ⬦ *npl* : **the ~** les Vietnamiens.

view [vjuː] ⬦ *n* - 1. [opinion] opinion *f*, avis *m* ; **in my ~** à mon avis - 2. [scene, ability to see] vue *f* ; **to come into ~** apparaître.

⬦ *vt* - 1. [consider] considérer - 2. [examine - gen] examiner ; [- house] visiter.
➤ **in view of** *prep* vu, étant donné.
➤ **with a view to** *conj* dans l'intention de, avec l'idée de.

viewer ['vjuːə'] *n* - 1. TV téléspectateur *m*, -trice *f* - 2. [for slides] visionneuse *f*.

viewfinder ['vjuːˌfaɪndə'] *n* viseur *m*.

viewpoint ['vjuːpɔɪnt] *n* point *m* de vue.

vigil ['vɪdʒɪl] *n* veille *f* ; RELIG vigile *f*.

vigilante [,vɪdʒɪ'læntɪ] *n* membre *m* d'un groupe d'autodéfense.

vigorous ['vɪgərəs] *adj* vigoureux(euse).

vile [vaɪl] *adj* [mood] massacrant(e), exécrable ; [person, act] vil(e), ignoble ; [food] infect(e), exécrable.

villa ['vɪlə] *n* villa *f* ; [bungalow] pavillon *m*.

village ['vɪlɪdʒ] *n* village *m*.

villager ['vɪlɪdʒə'] *n* villageois *m*, -e *f*.

villain ['vɪlən] *n* - 1. [of film, book] méchant *m*, -e *f* ; [of play] traître *m* - 2. [criminal] bandit *m*.

vindicate ['vɪndɪkeɪt] *vt* justifier.

vindictive [vɪn'dɪktɪv] *adj* vindicatif(ive).

vine [vaɪn] *n* vigne *f*.

vinegar ['vɪnɪgə'] *n* vinaigre *m*.

vineyard ['vɪnjəd] *n* vignoble *m*.

vintage ['vɪntɪdʒ] ⬦ *adj* - 1. [wine] de grand cru - 2. [classic] typique. ⬦ *n* année *f*, millésime *m*.

vintage wine *n* vin *m* de grand cru.

vinyl ['vaɪnɪl] *n* vinyle *m*.

viola [vɪ'əʊlə] *n* alto *m*.

violate ['vaɪəleɪt] *vt* violer.

violence ['vaɪələns] *n* violence *f*.

violent ['vaɪələnt] *adj* [gen] violent(e).

violet ['vaɪələt] ⬦ *adj* violet(ette). ⬦ *n* - 1. [flower] violette *f* - 2. [colour] violet *m*.

violin [,vaɪə'lɪn] *n* violon *m*.

violinist [,vaɪə'lɪnɪst] *n* violoniste *mf*.

VIP (*abbr of* **very important person**) *n* VIP *mf*.

viper ['vaɪpə'] *n* vipère *f*.

virgin ['vɜːdʒɪn] ⬦ *adj literary* [land, forest, soil] vierge. ⬦ *n* [woman] vierge *f* ; [man] garçon *m*/homme *m* vierge.

Virgo ['vɜːgəʊ] (*pl* -s) *n* Vierge *f*.

virile ['vɪraɪl] *adj* viril(e).

virtually ['vɜːtʃʊəlɪ] *adv* virtuellement, pratiquement.

virtual reality *n* réalité *f* virtuelle.

virtue ['vɜːtjuː] *n* - 1. [good quality] vertu *f* - 2. [benefit] : **~ (in doing sthg)** mérite *m* (à faire qqch). **by virtue of** *prep fml* en vertu de.

virtuous ['vɜːtʃʊəs] *adj* vertueux(euse).

virus ['vaɪrəs] *n* COMPUT & MED virus *m*.

visa ['viːzə] *n* visa *m*.

vis-à-vis [ˌviːzaːˈviː] *prep fml* par rapport à.

viscose ['vɪskəʊs] *n* viscose *f*.

visibility [ˌvɪzɪˈbɪlətɪ] *n* visibilité *f*.

visible ['vɪzəbl] *adj* visible.

vision ['vɪʒn] *n* - 1. *(U)* [ability to see] vue *f* - 2. [foresight, dream] vision *f*.

visit ['vɪzɪt] ⇔ *n* visite *f* ; **on a ~** en visite. ⇔ *vt* [person] rendre visite à ; [place] visiter.

visiting hours ['vɪzɪtɪŋ-] *npl* heures *fpl* de visite.

visitor ['vɪzɪtər] *n* [to person] invité *m*, -e *f* ; [to place] visiteur *m*, -euse *f* ; [to hotel] client *m*, -e *f*.

visitors' book *n* livre *m* d'or ; [in hotel] registre *m*.

visitor's passport *n* Br passeport *m* temporaire.

visor ['vaɪzər] *n* visière *f*.

vista ['vɪstə] *n* [view] vue *f*.

visual ['vɪʒʊəl] *adj* visuel(elle).

visual aids *npl* supports *mpl* visuels.

visual display unit *n* écran *m* de visualisation.

visualize, -ise ['vɪʒʊəlaɪz] *vt* se représenter, s'imaginer.

vital ['vaɪtl] *adj* - 1. [essential] essentiel (elle) - 2. [full of life] plein(e) d'entrain.

vitally ['vaɪtəlɪ] *adv* absolument.

vital statistics *npl inf* [of woman] mensurations *fpl*.

vitamin [Br 'vɪtəmɪn, Am 'vaɪtəmɪn] *n* vitamine *f*.

vivacious [vɪˈveɪʃəs] *adj* enjoué(e).

vivid ['vɪvɪd] *adj* - 1. [bright] vif (vive) - 2. [clear - description] vivant(e) ; [- memory] net (nette), précis(e).

vividly ['vɪvɪdlɪ] *adv* [describe] d'une manière vivante ; [remember] clairement.

vixen ['vɪksn] *n* [fox] renarde *f*.

VLF (*abbr of* very low frequency) *n* très basse fréquence.

V-neck *n* [neck] décolleté *m* en V ; [sweater] pull *m* à décolleté en V.

vocabulary [vəˈkæbjʊlərɪ] *n* vocabulaire *m*.

vocal ['vəʊkl] *adj* - 1. [outspoken] qui se fait entendre - 2. [of the voice] vocal(e).

vocal cords *npl* cordes *fpl* vocales.

vocation [vəʊˈkeɪʃn] *n* vocation *f*.

vocational [vəʊˈkeɪʃənl] *adj* professionnel(elle).

vociferous [vəˈsɪfərəs] *adj* bruyant(e).

vodka ['vɒdkə] *n* vodka *f*.

vogue [vəʊg] *n* vogue *f*, mode *f* ; **in ~** en vogue, à la mode.

voice [vɔɪs] ⇔ *n* [gen] voix *f*. ⇔ *vt* [opinion, emotion] exprimer.

voice mail *n* COMPUT [device] boîte *f* vocale ; [system] messagerie *f* vocale ; **to send/receive ~** envoyer/recevoir un message sur une boîte vocale.

void [vɔɪd] ⇔ *adj* - 1. [invalid] nul (nulle) ▷ **null** - 2. *fml* [empty] : **~ of** dépourvu(e) de, dénué(e) de. ⇔ *n* vide *m*.

volatile [Br 'vɒlətaɪl, Am 'vɒlətl] *adj* [situation] explosif(ive) ; [person] lunatique, versatile ; [market] instable.

volcano [vɒlˈkeɪnəʊ] (*pl* **-es** OR **-s**) *n* volcan *m*.

volition [vəˈlɪʃn] *n fml* : **of one's own ~** de son propre gré.

volley ['vɒlɪ] (*pl* **-s**) ⇔ *n* - 1. [of gunfire] salve *f* - 2. *fig* [of questions, curses] torrent *m* ; [of blows] volée *f*, pluie *f* - 3. SPORT volée *f*. ⇔ *vt* frapper à la volée, reprendre de volée.

volleyball ['vɒlɪbɔːl] *n* volley-ball *m*.

volt [vəʊlt] *n* volt *m*.

voltage ['vəʊltɪdʒ] *n* voltage *m*, tension *f*.

voluble ['vɒljʊbl] *adj* volubile, loquace.

volume ['vɒljuːm] *n* - 1. [gen] volume *m* - 2. [of work, letters] quantité *f* ; [of traffic] densité *f*.

voluntarily [Br 'vɒləntrɪlɪ, Am ˌvɒlənˈterəlɪ] *adv* volontairement.

voluntary ['vɒləntrɪ] *adj* - 1. [not obligatory] volontaire - 2. [unpaid] bénévole.

volunteer [ˌvɒlənˈtɪər] ⇔ *n* - 1. [gen & MIL] volontaire *mf* - 2. [unpaid worker] bénévole *mf*. ⇔ *vt* - 1. [offer] : **to ~ to do sthg** se proposer OR se porter volontaire pour faire qqch - 2. [information, advice] donner spontanément. ⇔ *vi* - 1. [offer one's services] : **to ~ (for)** se porter volontaire (pour), proposer ses services (pour) - 2. MIL s'engager comme volontaire.

vomit ['vɒmɪt] ⇔ *n* vomi *m*. ⇔ *vi* vomir.

vote [vəʊt] ⇔ *n* - 1. [individual decision] : **~ (for/against)** vote *m* (pour/contre), voix *f* (pour/contre) - 2. [ballot] vote *m* - 3. [right to vote] droit *m* de vote. ⇔ *vt* - 1. [declare] élire - 2. [choose] : **to ~ to do sthg** voter OR se prononcer pour faire qqch ; **they ~d to return to work** ils ont voté le retour au travail.

◇ *vi* : **to ~ (for/against)** voter (pour/contre).

vote of thanks (*pl* votes of thanks) *n* discours *m* de remerciement.

voter ['vəʊtə^r] *n* électeur *m*, -trice *f*.

voting ['vəʊtɪŋ] *n* scrutin *m*.

vouch [vaʊtʃ] ◆ **vouch for** *vt fus* répondre de, se porter garant de.

voucher ['vaʊtʃə^r] *n* bon *m*, coupon *m*.

vow [vaʊ] ◇ *n* vœu *m*, serment *m*. ◇ *vt* : **to ~ to do sthg** jurer de faire qqch ; **to ~ (that) ...** jurer que ...

vowel ['vaʊəl] *n* voyelle *f*.

voyage ['vɔɪɪdʒ] *n* voyage *m* en mer ; [in space] vol *m*.

vs *abbr of* **versus**.

VSO (*abbr of* **Voluntary Service Overseas**) *n organisation britannique envoyant des travailleurs bénévoles dans des pays en voie de développement pour contribuer à leur développement technique.*

vulgar ['vʌlgə^r] *adj* - **1.** [in bad taste] vulgaire - **2.** [offensive] grossier(ère).

vulnerable ['vʌlnərəbl] *adj* vulnérable ; ↗ **to** [attack] exposé(e) à ; [colds] sensible à.

vulture ['vʌltʃə^r] *n lit & fig* vautour *m*.

w (*pl* w's OR ws), **W** (*pl* W's OR Ws) ['dʌblju:] *n* [letter] w *m inv*, W *m inv*. ◆ **W - 1.** (*abbr of* west) O, W - **2.** (*abbr of* watt) w.

wad [wɒd] *n* - **1.** [of cotton wool, paper] tampon *m* - **2.** [of banknotes, documents] liasse *f* - **3.** [of tobacco] chique *f* ; [of chewing-gum] boulette *f*.

waddle ['wɒdl] *vi* se dandiner.

wade [weɪd] *vi* patauger. ◆ **wade through** *vt fus fig* se taper.

wading pool ['weɪdɪŋ-] *n Am* pataugeoire *f*.

wafer ['weɪfə^r] *n* [thin biscuit] gaufrette *f*.

waffle ['wɒfl] ◇ *n* - **1.** CULIN gaufre *f* - **2.** *Br inf* [vague talk] verbiage *m*. ◇ *vi* parler pour ne rien dire.

waft [wɑːft, wɒft] *vi* flotter.

wag [wæg] ◇ *vt* remuer, agiter. ◇ *vi* [tail] remuer.

wage [weɪdʒ] ◇ *n* salaire *m*, paie *f*, paye *f*. ◇ *vt* : **to ~ war against** faire la guerre à. ◆ **wages** *npl* salaire *m*.

wage earner [-ˌɜːnə^r] *n* salarié *m*, -e *f*.

wage packet *n Br* - **1.** [envelope] enveloppe *f* de paye - **2.** *fig* [pay] paie *f*, paye *f*.

wager ['weɪdʒə^r] *n* pari *m*.

waggle ['wægl] *inf vt* agiter, remuer ; [ears] remuer.

waggon ['wægən] *Br* = **wagon**.

wagon ['wægən] *n* - **1.** [horse-drawn] chariot *m*, charrette *f* - **2.** *Br* RAIL wagon *m*.

wail [weɪl] ◇ *n* gémissement *m*. ◇ *vi* gémir.

waist [weɪst] *n* taille *f*.

waistcoat ['weɪskəʊt] *n esp Br* gilet *m*.

waistline ['weɪstlaɪn] *n* taille *f*.

wait [weɪt] ◇ *n* attente *f*. ◇ *vi* attendre ; **I can't ~ to see you** je brûle d'impatience de te voir ; **~ and see!** tu vas bien voir! ◆ **wait for** *vt fus* attendre ; **to ~ for sb to do sthg** attendre que qqn fasse qqch. ◆ **wait on** *vt fus* [serve food to] servir. ◆ **wait up** *vi* veiller, ne pas se coucher.

waiter ['weɪtə^r] *n* garçon *m*, serveur *m*.

waiting list ['weɪtɪŋ-] *n* liste *f* d'attente.

waiting room ['weɪtɪŋ-] *n* salle *f* d'attente.

waitress ['weɪtrɪs] *n* serveuse *f*.

waive [weɪv] *vt* [fee] renoncer à ; [rule] prévoir une dérogation à.

wake [weɪk] (*pt* woke OR -d, *pp* woken OR -d) ◇ *n* [of ship] sillage *m*. ◇ *vt* réveiller. ◇ *vi* se réveiller. ◆ **wake up** ◇ *vt sep* réveiller. ◇ *vi* [wake] se réveiller.

waken ['weɪkən] *fml* ◇ *vt* réveiller. ◇ *vi* se réveiller.

Wales [weɪlz] *n* pays *m* de Galles.

walk [wɔːk] ◇ *n* - **1.** [way of walking] démarche *f*, façon *f* de marcher - **2.** [journey - for pleasure] promenade *f* ; [- long distance] marche *f* ; **it's a long ~** c'est loin à pied ; **to go for a ~** aller se promener, aller faire une promenade. ◇ *vt* - **1.** [accompany - person] accompagner ; [- dog] promener - **2.** [distance] faire à pied. ◇ *vi* - **1.** [gen] marcher - **2.** [for pleasure] se promener. ◆ **walk out** *vi* - **1.** [leave suddenly] partir - **2.** [go on strike] se mettre en grève, faire grève. ◆ **walk out on** *vt fus* quitter.

walker ['wɔːkə^r] *n* [for pleasure] promeneur *m*, -euse *f* ; [long-distance] marcheur *m*, -euse *f*.

walkie-talkie [ˌwɔːkɪ'tɔːkɪ] *n* talkie-walkie *m*.

walking ['wɔ:kɪŋ] *n* (*U*) marche *f* (à pied), promenade *f*.

walking shoes *npl* chaussures *fpl* de marche.

walking stick *n* canne *f*.

Walkman® ['wɔ:kmən] *n* baladeur *m*, Walkman® *m*.

walk of life (*pl* walks of life) *n* milieu *m*.

walkout ['wɔ:kaʊt] *n* [strike] grève *f*, débrayage *m*.

walkover ['wɔ:k,əʊvəʳ] *n* victoire *f* facile.

walkway ['wɔ:kweɪ] *n* passage *m* ; [between buildings] passerelle *f*.

wall [wɔ:l] *n* - 1. [of room, building] mur *m* ; [of rock, cave] paroi *f* - 2. ANAT paroi *f*.

wallchart ['wɔ:ltʃɑ:t] *n* planche *f* murale.

walled [wɔ:ld] *adj* fortifié(e).

wallet ['wɒlɪt] *n* portefeuille *m*.

wallflower ['wɔ:l,flaʊəʳ] *n* - 1. [plant] giroflée *f* - 2. *inf fig* [person] : **to be a ~** faire tapisserie.

wallop ['wɒləp] *inf vt* [person] flanquer un coup à ; [ball] taper fort dans.

wallow ['wɒləʊ] *vi* [in liquid] se vautrer.

wallpaper ['wɔ:l,peɪpəʳ] <> *n* papier *m* peint. <> *vt* tapisser.

Wall Street *n* Wall Street *m* (*quartier financier de New York*).

wally ['wɒlɪ] *n Br inf* idiot *m*, -e *f*, andouille *f*.

walnut ['wɔ:lnʌt] *n* - 1. [nut] noix *f* - 2. [tree, wood] noyer *m*.

walrus ['wɔ:lrəs] (*pl inv* OR **-es** [-i:z]) *n* morse *m*.

waltz [wɔ:ls] <> *n* valse *f*. <> *vi* [dance] valser, danser la valse.

wan [wɒn] *adj* pâle, blême.

wand [wɒnd] *n* baguette *f*.

wander ['wɒndəʳ] *vi* - 1. [person] errer - 2. [mind] divaguer ; [thoughts] vagabonder.

wane [weɪn] *vi* - 1. [influence, interest] diminuer, faiblir - 2. [moon] décroître.

wangle ['wæŋgl] *vt inf* se débrouiller pour obtenir.

want [wɒnt] <> *n* - 1. [need] besoin *m* - 2. [lack] manque *m* ; **for ~ of** faute de, par manque de - 3. [deprivation] pauvreté *f*, besoin *m*. <> *vt* - 1. [desire] vouloir ; **to ~ to do sthg** vouloir faire qqch ; **to ~ sb to do sthg** vouloir que qqn fasse qqch - 2. *inf* [need] avoir besoin de.

wanted ['wɒntɪd] *adj* : **to be ~ (by the police)** être recherché(e) (par la police).

wanton ['wɒntən] *adj* [destruction, neglect] gratuit(e).

war [wɔ:ʳ] *n* guerre *f*.

ward [wɔ:d] *n* - 1. [in hospital] salle *f* - 2. *Br* POL circonscription *f* électorale - 3. JUR pupille *mf*. **ward off** *vt fus* [danger] écarter ; [disease, blow] éviter ; [evil spirits] éloigner.

warden ['wɔ:dn] *n* - 1. [of park etc] gardien *m*, -enne *f* - 2. *Br* [of youth hostel, hall of residence] directeur *m*, -trice *f* - 3. *Am* [of prison] directeur *m*, -trice *f*.

warder ['wɔ:dəʳ] *n Br* [in prison] gardien *m*, -enne *f*.

wardrobe ['wɔ:drəʊb] *n* garde-robe *f*.

warehouse ['weəhaʊs, *pl* -haʊzɪz] *n* entrepôt *m*, magasin *m*.

wares [weəz] *npl* marchandises *fpl*.

warfare ['wɔ:feəʳ] *n* (*U*) guerre *f*.

warhead ['wɔ:hed] *n* ogive *f*, tête *f*.

warily ['weərɪlɪ] *adv* avec précaution OR circonspection.

warm [wɔ:m] <> *adj* - 1. [gen] chaud(e) ; **it's ~ today** il fait chaud aujourd'hui - 2. [friendly] chaleureux(euse). <> *vt* chauffer. **warm to** *vt fus* [person] se prendre de sympathie pour ; [idea, place] se mettre à aimer. **warm up** <> *vt sep* réchauffer. <> *vi* - 1. [person, room] se réchauffer - 2. [machine, engine] chauffer - 3. SPORT s'échauffer.

warm-hearted [-'hɑ:tɪd] *adj* chaleureux(euse), affectueux(euse).

warmly ['wɔ:mlɪ] *adv* - 1. [in warm clothes] : **to dress ~** s'habiller chaudement - 2. [in a friendly way] chaleureusement.

warmth [wɔ:mθ] *n* chaleur *f*.

warn [wɔ:n] *vt* avertir, prévenir ; **to ~ sb of sthg** avertir qqn de qqch ; **to ~ sb not to do sthg** conseiller à qqn de ne pas faire qqch, déconseiller à qqn de faire qqch.

warning ['wɔ:nɪŋ] *n* avertissement *m*.

warning light *n* voyant *m*, avertisseur *m* lumineux.

warning triangle *n Br* triangle *m* de signalisation.

warp [wɔ:p] <> *vt* - 1. [wood] gauchir, voiler - 2. [personality] fausser, pervertir. <> *vi* [wood] gauchir, se voiler.

warrant ['wɒrənt] <> *n* JUR mandat *m*. <> *vt* - 1. [justify] justifier - 2. [guarantee] garantir.

warranty ['wɒrəntɪ] *n* garantie *f*.

warren ['wɒrən] *n* terrier *m*.

warrior ['wɒrɪəʳ] *n* guerrier *m*, -ère *f*.

Warsaw ['wɔːsɔː] n Varsovie ; **the ~ Pact** le pacte de Varsovie.

warship ['wɔːʃɪp] n navire m de guerre.

wart [wɔːt] n verrue f.

wartime ['wɔːtaɪm] n : **in ~** en temps de guerre.

war-torn adj déchiré(e) par la guerre.

wary ['weərɪ] adj prudent(e), circonspect(e) ; **to be ~ of** se méfier de ; **to be ~ of doing sthg** hésiter à faire qqch.

was [weak form wəz, strong form wɒz] pt ⊳ **be**.

wash [wɒʃ] <> n - **1.** [act] lavage m ; **to have a ~** se laver ; **to give sthg a ~** laver qqch - **2.** [clothes] lessive f - **3.** [from boat] remous m. <> vt [clean] laver ; **to ~ one's hands** se laver les mains. <> vi se laver.

◆ **wash away** vt sep emporter.

◆ **wash up** <> vt sep Br [dishes] : **to ~ the dishes up** faire OR laver la vaisselle. <> vi - **1.** Br [wash dishes] faire OR laver la vaisselle - **2.** Am [wash oneself] se laver.

washable ['wɒʃəbl] adj lavable.

washbasin Br ['wɒʃ,beɪsn], **washbowl** Am ['wɒʃbəʊl] n lavabo m.

washcloth ['wɒʃklɒθ] n Am gant m de toilette.

washer ['wɒʃər] n - **1.** TECH rondelle f - **2.** [washing machine] machine f à laver.

washing ['wɒʃɪŋ] n (U) - **1.** [action] lessive f - **2.** [clothes] linge m, lessive f.

washing line n corde f à linge.

washing machine n machine f à laver.

washing powder n Br lessive f, détergent m.

Washington ['wɒʃɪŋtən] n [city] : **~ D.C.** Washington.

washing-up n Br vaisselle f.

washing-up liquid n Br liquide m pour la vaisselle.

washout ['wɒʃaʊt] n inf fiasco m.

washroom ['wɒʃrʊm] n Am toilettes fpl.

wasn't [wɒznt] = was not.

wasp [wɒsp] n guêpe f.

wastage ['weɪstɪdʒ] n gaspillage m.

waste [weɪst] <> adj [material] de rebut ; [fuel] perdu(e) ; [area of land] en friche. <> n - **1.** [misuse] gaspillage m ; **it's a ~ of money** [extravagance] c'est du gaspillage ; [bad investment] c'est de l'argent perdu ; **a ~ of time** une perte de temps - **2.** (U) [refuse] déchets mpl, ordures fpl. <> vt [money, food, energy] gaspiller ; [time, opportunity] perdre. ◆ **wastes** npl literary étendues fpl désertes.

wastebasket Am = wastepaper basket.

waste disposal unit n broyeur m d'ordures.

wasteful ['weɪstfʊl] adj [person] gaspilleur(euse) ; [activity] peu économique.

waste ground n (U) terrain m vague.

wastepaper basket, wastepaper bin Br [,weɪst'peɪpər-], **wastebasket** Am ['weɪst,baːskɪt] n corbeille f à papier.

watch [wɒtʃ] <> n - **1.** [timepiece] montre f - **2.** [act of watching] : **to keep ~** faire le guet, monter la garde ; **to keep ~ on sb/ sthg** surveiller qqn/qqch - **3.** [guard] garde f ; NAUT [shift] quart m. <> vt - **1.** [look at] regarder - **2.** [spy on, guard] surveiller - **3.** [be careful about] faire attention à. <> vi regarder. ◆ **watch out** vi faire attention, prendre garde.

watchdog ['wɒtʃdɒg] n - **1.** [dog] chien m de garde - **2.** fig [organization] organisation f de contrôle.

watchful ['wɒtʃfʊl] adj vigilant(e).

watchmaker ['wɒtʃ,meɪkər] n horloger m.

watchman ['wɒtʃmən] (pl **-men** [-mən]) n gardien m.

water ['wɔːtər] <> n [liquid] eau f. <> vt arroser. <> vi - **1.** [eyes] pleurer, larmoyer - **2.** [mouth] : **my mouth was ~ing** j'en avais l'eau à la bouche. ◆ **waters** npl [sea] eaux fpl. ◆ **water down** vt sep - **1.** [dilute] diluer ; [alcohol] couper d'eau - **2.** usu pej [plan, demand] atténuer, modérer ; [play, novel] édulcorer.

water bottle n gourde f, bidon m (à eau).

water closet n dated toilettes fpl, waters mpl.

watercolour ['wɔːtə,kʌlər] n - **1.** [picture] aquarelle f - **2.** [paint] peinture f à l'eau, couleur f pour aquarelle.

watercress ['wɔːtəkres] n cresson m.

waterfall ['wɔːtəfɔːl] n chute f d'eau, cascade f.

water heater n chauffe-eau m inv.

waterhole ['wɔːtəhəʊl] n mare f, point m d'eau.

watering can ['wɔːtərɪŋ-] n arrosoir m.

water level n niveau m de l'eau.

water lily n nénuphar m.

waterline ['wɔːtəlaɪn] n NAUT ligne f de flottaison.

waterlogged ['wɔːtəlɒgd] adj - **1.** [land] détrempé(e) - **2.** [vessel] plein(e) d'eau.

water main n conduite f principale d'eau.

watermark ['wɔːtəmaːk] *n* - **1.** [in paper] filigrane *m* - **2.** [showing water level] laisse *f*.

watermelon ['wɔːtə,melən] *n* pastèque *f*.

water polo *n* water-polo *m*.

waterproof ['wɔːtəpruːf] <> *adj* imperméable. <> *n Br* imperméable *m*.

watershed ['wɔːtəʃed] *n fig* [turning point] tournant *m*, moment *m* critique.

water skiing *n* ski *m* nautique.

water tank *n* réservoir *m* d'eau, citerne *f*.

watertight ['wɔːtətaɪt] *adj* - **1.** [waterproof] étanche - **2.** *fig* [excuse, contract] parfait(e) ; [argument] irréfutable ; [plan] infaillible.

waterway ['wɔːtəweɪ] *n* voie *f* navigable.

waterworks ['wɔːtəwɜːks] (*pl inv*) *n* [building] installation *f* hydraulique, usine *f* de distribution d'eau.

watery ['wɔːtərɪ] *adj* - **1.** [food, drink] trop dilué(e) ; [tea, coffee] pas assez fort(e) - **2.** [pale] pâle.

watt [wɒt] *n* watt *m*.

wave [weɪv] <> *n* - **1.** [of hand] geste *m*, signe *m* - **2.** [of water, emotion, nausea] vague *f* - **3.** [of light, sound] onde *f* ; [of heat] bouffée *f* - **4.** [in hair] cran *m*, ondulation *f*. <> *vt* [arm, handkerchief] agiter ; [flag, stick] brandir. <> *vi* - **1.** [with hand] faire signe de la main ; **to ~ at** OR **to sb** faire signe à qqn, saluer qqn de la main - **2.** [flags, trees] flotter.

wavelength ['weɪvleŋθ] *n* longueur *f* d'ondes ; **to be on the same ~** *fig* être sur la même longueur d'ondes.

waver ['weɪvəʳ] *vi* - **1.** [falter] vaciller, chanceler - **2.** [hesitate] hésiter, vaciller - **3.** [fluctuate] fluctuer, varier.

wavy ['weɪvɪ] *adj* [hair] ondulé(e) ; [line] onduleux(euse).

wax [wæks] <> *n* (U) - **1.** [in candles, polish] cire *f* ; [for skis] fart *m* - **2.** [in ears] cérumen *m*. <> *vt* cirer ; [skis] farter. <> *vi* [moon] croître.

wax paper *n Am* papier *m* sulfurisé.

waxworks ['wækswɜːks] (*pl inv*) *n* [museum] musée *m* de cire.

way [weɪ] <> *n* - **1.** [means, method] façon *f* ; **to get** OR **have one's ~** obtenir ce qu'on veut - **2.** [manner, style] façon *f*, manière *f* ; **in the same ~** de la même manière OR façon ; **this/that ~** comme ça, de cette façon ; **in a ~** d'une certaine manière, en quelque sorte - **3.** [route, path] chemin *m* ; **~ in** entrée *f* ; **~ out** sortie *f* ; **to be out of one's ~** [place] ne pas être sur sa route ; **on the** OR **one's ~** sur le OR son chemin ; **to be under ~** [ship] faire route ; *fig* [meeting] être en cours ; **to get under ~** [ship] se mettre en route ; *fig* [meeting] démarrer ; **'give ~'** *Br* AUT 'vous n'avez pas la priorité' ; **to be in the ~** gêner ; **to go out of one's ~ to do sthg** se donner du mal pour faire qqch ; **to keep out of sb's ~** éviter qqn ; **keep out of the ~!** restez à l'écart ! ; **to make ~ for** faire place à - **4.** [direction] : **to go/look/come this ~** aller/regarder/venir par ici ; **the right/wrong ~ round** [in sequence] dans le bon/mauvais ordre ; **she had her hat on the wrong ~ round** elle avait mis son chapeau à l'envers ; **the right/wrong ~ up** dans le bon/mauvais sens - **5.** [distance] : **all the ~** tout le trajet ; *fig* [support etc] jusqu'au bout ; **a long ~** loin - **6.** *phr* : **to give ~** [under weight, pressure] céder ; **no ~!** pas question! <> *adv inf* [a lot] largement ; **~ better** bien mieux. **ways** *npl* [customs, habits] coutumes *fpl*. **by the way** *adv* au fait.

waylay [,weɪ'leɪ] (*pt & pp* **-laid** [-'leɪd]) *vt* arrêter (au passage).

wayward ['weɪwəd] *adj* qui n'en fait qu'à sa tête ; [behaviour] capricieux(euse).

WC (*abbr of* **water closet**) *n* W.-C. *mpl*.

we [wiː] *pers pron* nous ; **we can't do it** nous, nous ne pouvons pas le faire ; **as ~ say in France** comme on dit en France ; **~ British** nous autres Britanniques.

weak [wiːk] *adj* - **1.** [gen] faible - **2.** [delicate] fragile - **3.** [unconvincing] peu convaincant(e) - **4.** [drink] léger(ère).

weaken ['wiːkn] <> *vt* - **1.** [undermine] affaiblir - **2.** [reduce] diminuer - **3.** [physically - person] affaiblir ; [- structure] fragiliser. <> *vi* faiblir.

weakling ['wiːklɪŋ] *n pej* mauviette *f*.

weakness ['wiːknɪs] *n* - **1.** (U) [physical - of person] faiblesse *f* ; [- of structure] fragilité *f* - **2.** [imperfect point] point *m* faible, faiblesse *f*.

wealth [welθ] *n* - **1.** (U) [riches] richesse *f* - **2.** [abundance] : **a ~ of** une profusion de.

wealthy ['welθɪ] *adj* riche.

wean [wiːn] *vt* [baby, lamb] sevrer.

weapon ['wepən] *n* arme *f*.

weaponry ['wepənrɪ] *n* (U) armement *m*.

wear [weəʳ] (*pt* **wore**, *pp* **worn**) <> *n* (U) - **1.** [type of clothes] tenue *f* - **2.** [damage] usure *f* ; **~ and tear** usure - **3.** [use] : **these shoes have had a lot of ~** ces chaussures ont fait beaucoup d'usage. <> *vt* - **1.** [clothes, hair] porter - **2.** [damage] user. <> *vi* - **1.** [deteriorate] s'user - **2.** [last] : **to ~ well** durer longtemps, faire de l'usage ; **to ~ badly** ne pas durer longtemps. **wear away** <> *vt sep* [rock, wood] user ; [grass] abîmer. ◇ *vi* [rock, wood] s'user ; [grass] s'abîmer. ◆ **wear down** *vt sep* - **1.** [material] user - **2.** [person, resistance] épuiser. ◆ **wear off** *vi* disparaître. ◆ **wear out** ◇ *vt sep* - **1.** [shoes, clothes] user - **2.** [person] épuiser. ◇ *vi* s'user.

weary ['wɪərɪ] *adj* - **1.** [exhausted] las (lasse) ; [sigh] de lassitude - **2.** [fed up] : **to be ~ of sthg/of doing sthg** être las de qqch/de faire qqch.

weasel ['wi:zl] *n* belette *f*.

weather ['weðər] ◇ *n* temps *m* ; **to be under the ~** être patraque. ◇ *vt* [crisis, problem] surmonter.

weather-beaten [-ˌbi:tn] *adj* [face, skin] tanné(e).

weathercock ['weðəkɒk] *n* girouette *f*.

weather forecast *n* météo *f*, prévisions *fpl* météorologiques.

weatherman ['weðəmæn] (*pl* -men [-men]) *n* météorologue *m*.

weather vane [-veɪn] *n* girouette *f*.

weave [wi:v] (*pt* wove, *pp* woven) ◇ *vt* [using loom] tisser. ◇ *vi* [move] se faufiler.

weaver ['wi:vər] *n* tisserand *m*, -e *f*.

web, Web [web] *n* - **1.** [cobweb] toile *f* (d'araignée) - **2.** *fig* [of lies] tissu *m* ◆ **Web** COMPUT: **the ~** le Web.

webmaster ['webˌmɑːstər] *n* webmaster *m*, webmestre *m*.

web page, Web page *n* page *f* Web.

website, Web site *n* COMPUT site *m* Internet OR Web.

wed [wed] (*pt* & *pp* wed OR -ded) *literary* ◇ *vt* épouser. ◇ *vi* se marier.

we'd [wi:d] = we had, we would.

wedding ['wedɪŋ] *n* mariage *m*.

wedding anniversary *n* anniversaire *m* de mariage.

wedding cake *n* pièce *f* montée.

wedding dress *n* robe *f* de mariée.

wedding ring *n* alliance *f*.

wedge [wedʒ] ◇ *n* - **1.** [for steadying] cale *f* - **2.** [for splitting] coin *m* - **3.** [of cake, cheese] morceau *m*. ◇ *vt* caler.

Wednesday ['wenzdɪ] *n* mercredi *m* ; *see also* **Saturday**.

wee [wi:] ◇ *adj* Scot petit(e). ◇ *n inf* pipi *m*. ◇ *vi inf* faire pipi.

weed [wi:d] ◇ *n* - **1.** [plant] mauvaise herbe *f* - **2.** *Br inf* [feeble person] mauviette *f*. ◇ *vt* désherber.

weedkiller ['wi:dˌkɪlər] *n* désherbant *m*.

weedy ['wi:dɪ] *adj* Br inf [feeble] qui agit comme une mauviette.

week [wi:k] *n* semaine *f*.

weekday ['wi:kdeɪ] *n* jour *m* de semaine.

weekend [ˌwi:k'end] *n* week-end *m* ; **on** OR **at the ~** le week-end.

weekly ['wi:klɪ] ◇ *adj* hebdomadaire. ◇ *adv* chaque semaine. ◇ *n* hebdomadaire *m*.

weep [wi:p] (*pt* & *pp* wept) *vt* & *vi* pleurer.

weeping willow [ˌwi:pɪŋ-] *n* saule *m* pleureur.

weigh [weɪ] *vt* - **1.** [gen] peser - **2.** NAUT : **to ~ anchor** lever l'ancre. ◆ **weigh down** *vt sep* - **1.** [physically] : **to be ~ed down with sthg** plier sous le poids de qqch - **2.** [mentally] : **to be ~ed down by** OR **with sthg** être accablé par qqch. ◆ **weigh up** *vt sep* - **1.** [consider carefully] examiner - **2.** [size up] juger, évaluer.

weight [weɪt] *n lit* & *fig* poids *m* ; **to put on** OR **gain ~** prendre du poids, grossir ; **to lose ~** perdre du poids, maigrir ; **to pull one's ~** faire sa part du travail, participer à la tâche.

weighted ['weɪtɪd] *adj* : **to be ~ in favour of/against** être favorable/défavorable à.

weighting ['weɪtɪŋ] *n Br* indemnité *f*.

weightlifting ['weɪtˌlɪftɪŋ] *n* haltérophilie *f*.

weighty ['weɪtɪ] *adj* [serious] important(e), de poids.

weir [wɪər] *n* barrage *m*.

weird [wɪəd] *adj* bizarre.

welcome ['welkəm] ◇ *adj* - **1.** [guest, help etc] bienvenu(e) - **2.** [free] : **you're ~ to ...** n'hésitez pas à ... - **3.** [in reply to thanks] : **you're ~** il n'y a pas de quoi, de rien. ◇ *n* accueil *m*. ◇ *vt* - **1.** [receive] accueillir - **2.** [approve of] se réjouir de. ◇ *excl* bienvenue!

weld [weld] ◇ *n* soudure *f*. ◇ *vt* souder.

welfare ['welfeər] ◇ *adj* social(e). ◇ *n* - **1.** [well-being] bien-être *m* - **2.** *Am* [income support] assistance *f* publique.

welfare state *n* État-providence *m*.

well [wel] (*compar* **better**, *superl* **best**) ◇ *adj* bien ; **I'm very ~, thanks** je vais très bien, merci ; **all is ~** tout va bien ; **just as ~** aussi bien. ◇ *adv* bien ; **the team was ~ beaten** l'équipe a été battue à plates coutures ; **to go ~** aller bien ; **~ done!** bravo! ; **~ and truly** bel et bien. ◇ *n* [for water, oil] puits *m*. ◇ *excl* - **1.** [in hesitation] heu!, eh bien! - **2.** [to correct oneself] bon!, enfin! - **3.** [to express resignation] : **oh ~!** eh bien! - **4.** [in surprise] tiens! ◆ **as well** *adv* - **1.** [in addition] aussi, également - **2.** [with same result] : **I/you** *etc* **may** OR **might as ~** (**do sthg**) je/tu *etc.* ferais aussi bien (de faire qqch). ◆ **as well as** *conj* en plus de, aussi bien que. ◆ **well up** *vi* : tears ~ed up in her eyes les larmes ~ed montaient aux yeux.

we'll [wi:l] = we shall, we will.

well-advised [-əd'vaɪzd] *adj* sage ; **you would be ~ to do sthg** tu ferais bien de faire qqch.

well-behaved [-bɪ'heɪvd] *adj* sage.

wellbeing [ˌwel'bi:ɪŋ] *n* bien-être *m.*

well-built *adj* bien bâti(e).

well-done *adj* CULIN bien cuit(e).

well-dressed [-'drest] *adj* bien habillé(e).

well-earned [-ɜ:nd] *adj* bien mérité(e).

well-heeled [-'hi:ld] *adj inf* nanti(e).

wellington boots ['welɪŋtən-], **wellingtons** ['welɪŋtənz] *npl Br* bottes *fpl* de caoutchouc.

well-kept *adj* - 1. [building, garden] bien tenu(e) - 2. [secret] bien gardé(e).

well-known *adj* bien connu(e).

well-mannered [-'mænəd] *adj* bien élevé(e).

well-meaning *adj* bien intentionné(e).

well-nigh [naɪ] *adv* presque, pratiquement.

well-off *adj* - 1. [rich] riche - 2. [well-provided] : **to be ~ for sthg** être bien pourvu(e) en qqch.

well-read ['red] *adj* cultivé(e).

well-rounded [-'raʊndɪd] *adj* [education, background] complet(ète).

well-timed [-'taɪmd] *adj* bien calculé(e), qui vient à point nommé.

well-to-do *adj* riche.

well-wisher ['welˌwɪʃəʳ] *n* admirateur *m*, -trice *f.*

Welsh [welʃ] ◇ *adj* gallois(e). ◇ *n* [language] gallois *m.* ◇ *npl* : **the ~** les Gallois *mpl.*

Welsh Assembly *n* Assemblée *f* galloise.

Welshman ['welʃmən] (*pl* **-men** [-mən]) *n* Gallois *m.*

Welshwoman ['welʃˌwʊmən] (*pl* **-women** [-ˌwɪmɪn]) *n* Galloise *f.*

went [went] *pt* ▷ **go.**

wept [wept] *pt & pp* ▷ **weep.**

were [wɜ:ʳ] ▷ **be.**

we're [wɪəʳ] = we are.

weren't [wɜ:nt] = were not.

west [west] ◇ *n* - 1. [direction] ouest *m* - 2. [region] : **the ~** l'ouest *m.* ◇ *adj* ouest *(inv)* ; [wind] d'ouest. ◇ *adv* de l'ouest, vers l'ouest ; **~ of** à l'ouest de. ◆ **West** *n* POL : **the West** l'Occident *m.*

West Bank *n* : **the ~** la Cisjordanie.

West Country *n Br* : **the ~** le sud-ouest de l'Angleterre.

West End *n Br* : **the ~** le West-End *(quartier des grands magasins et des théâtres, à Londres).*

westerly ['westəlɪ] *adj* à l'ouest ; [wind] de l'ouest ; **in a ~ direction** vers l'ouest.

western ['westən] ◇ *adj* - 1. [gen] de l'ouest - 2. POL occidental(e). ◇ *n* [book, film] western *m.*

West German ◇ *adj* ouest-allemand(e). ◇ *n* Allemand *m*, -e *f* de l'Ouest.

West Germany *n* : (former) **~** (ex-) Allemagne *f* de l'Ouest.

West Indian ◇ *adj* antillais(e). ◇ *n* Antillais *m*, -e *f.*

West Indies [-'ɪndi:z] *npl* : **the ~** les Antilles *fpl.*

Westminster ['westmɪnstəʳ] *n* quartier de Londres où se situe le Parlement britannique.

westward ['westwəd] *adj & adv* vers l'ouest.

westwards ['westwədz] *adv* vers l'ouest.

wet [wet] (*pt & pp* **wet** OR **-ted**) ◇ *adj* - 1. [damp, soaked] mouillé(e) - 2. [rainy] pluvieux(euse) - 3. [not dry - paint, cement] frais (fraîche) - 4. *Br inf pej* [weak, feeble] ramolli(e). ◇ *n inf* POL modéré *m*, -e *f.* ◇ *vt* mouiller.

wet blanket *n inf pej* rabat-joie *m inv.*

wet suit *n* combinaison *f* de plongée.

we've [wi:v] = we have.

whack [wæk] *inf* ◇ *n* - 1. *Br* [share] part *f* - 2. [hit] grand coup *m.* ◇ *vt* donner un grand coup à, frapper fort

whale [weɪl] *n* baleine *f.*

wharf [wɔ:f] (*pl* **-s** OR **wharves** [wɔ:vz]) *n* quai *m.*

what [wɒt] ◇ *adj* - 1. (in direct, indirect questions) quel (quelle), quels (quelles) *(pl)* ; **~ colour is it?** c'est de quelle couleur? ; **he asked me ~ colour it was** il m'a demandé de quelle couleur c'était - 2. (in exclamations) quel (quelle), quels (quelles) *(pl)* ; **~ a surprise!** quelle surprise! ; **~ an idiot I am!** ce que je peux être bête! ◇ *pron* - 1. (interrogative - subject) qu'est-ce qui ; (- object) qu'est-ce que, que ; (- after prep) quoi ; **~ are they doing?** qu'est-ce qu'ils font? ; **~ are they talking about?** de quoi parlent-ils? ; **~ is going on?** qu'est-ce qui se passe? ; **~ are they talking about?** de quoi parlent-ils? ; **~ about another drink/going out for a meal?** et si on prenait un autre verre/allait manger au restaurant? ; **~ about the rest of us?** et nous alors? ; **~ if ...?** et si ...? - **2.** *(relative - subject)* ce qui ; *(- object)* ce que ; **I saw ~ happened/fell** j'ai vu ce qui s'était passé/était tombé ; **you can't have ~ you want** tu ne peux pas avoir ce que tu veux. <> *excl* [expressing disbelief] comment!, quoi!

whatever [wɒt'evə^r] <> *adj* quel (quelle) que soit ; **any book ~** n'importe quel livre ; **no chance ~** pas la moindre chance ; **nothing ~** rien du tout. <> *pron* quoi que *(+ subjunctive)* ; **I'll do ~ I can** je ferai tout ce que je peux ; **~ can this be?** qu'est-ce que cela peut-il bien être? ; **~ that may mean** quoi que cela puisse bien vouloir dire ; **or ~** ou n'importe quoi d'autre.

whatsoever [,wɒtsəʊ'evə^r] *adj* : **I had no interest ~** je n'éprouvais pas le moindre intérêt ; **nothing ~** rien du tout.

wheat [wiːt] *n* blé *m*.

wheedle ['wiːdl] *vt* : **to ~ sb into doing sthg** enjôler qqn pour qu'il fasse qqch ; **to ~ sthg out of sb** enjôler qqn pour obtenir qqch.

wheel [wiːl] <> *n* - **1.** [gen] roue *f* - **2.** [steering wheel] volant *m*. <> *vt* pousser. <> *vi* : **to ~ (round)** se retourner brusquement.

wheelbarrow ['wiːl,bærəʊ] *n* brouette *f*.

wheelchair ['wiːl,tʃeə^r] *n* fauteuil *m* roulant.

wheelclamp ['wiːl,klæmp] <> *n* sabot *m* de Denver. <> *vt* : **my car was ~ed** on a mis un sabot à ma voiture.

wheeze [wiːz] <> *n* [sound] respiration *f* sifflante. <> *vi* respirer avec un bruit sifflant.

whelk [welk] *n* bulot *m*, buccin *m*.

when [wen] <> *adv (in direct, indirect questions)* quand ; **~ does the plane arrive?** quand OR à quelle heure arrive l'avion? ; **he asked me ~ I would be in London** il m'a demandé quand je serais à Londres. <> *conj* - **1.** [referring to time] quand, lorsque ; **he came to see me ~ I was abroad** il est venu me voir quand j'étais à l'étranger ; **one day ~ I was on my own** un jour que OR où j'étais tout seul ; **on the day ~ it happened** le jour où cela s'est passé - **2.** [whereas, considering that] alors que.

whenever [wen'evə^r] <> *conj* quand ; [each time that] chaque fois que. <> *adv* n'importe quand.

where [weə^r] <> *adv (in direct, indirect questions)* où ; **~ do you live?** où habitez-vous? ; **do you know ~ he lives?** est-ce que vous savez où il habite? <> *conj* - **1.** [referring to

place, situation] où ; **this is ~ ...** c'est là que ... - **2.** [whereas] alors que.

whereabouts [adv ,weərə'baʊts, *n* 'weərəbaʊts] <> *adv* où. <> *npl* : **their ~ are still unknown** on ne sait toujours pas où ils se trouvent.

whereas [weər'æz] *conj* alors que.

whereby [weə'baɪ] *conj fml* par lequel (laquelle), au moyen duquel (de laquelle).

whereupon [,weərə'pɒn] *conj fml* après quoi, sur quoi.

wherever [weər'evə^r] <> *conj* où que *(+ subjunctive)*. <> *adv* - **1.** [no matter where] n'importe où - **2.** [where] où donc ; **~ did you hear that?** mais où donc as-tu entendu dire cela?

wherewithal ['weəwɪðɔːl] *n fml* : **to have the ~ to do sthg** avoir les moyens de faire qqch.

whet [wet] *vt* : **to ~ sb's appetite for sthg** donner à qqn envie de qqch.

whether ['weðə^r] *conj* - **1.** [indicating choice, doubt] si - **2.** [no matter if] : **~ I want to or not** que je le veuille ou non.

which [wɪtʃ] <> *adj* - **1.** *(in direct, indirect questions)* quel (quelle), quels (quelles) *(pl)* ; **~ house is yours?** quelle maison est la tienne? ; **~ one?** lequel (laquelle)? - **2.** [to refer back to sthg] : **in ~ case** auquel cas. <> *pron* - **1.** *(in direct, indirect questions)* lequel (laquelle), lesquels (lesquelles) *(pl)* ; **~ do you prefer?** lequel préférez-vous? ; **I can't decide ~ to have** je ne sais vraiment pas lequel prendre - **2.** *(in relative clauses - subject)* qui ; *(- object)* que ; *(- after prep)* lequel (laquelle), lesquels (lesquelles) *(pl)* ; **take the slice ~ is nearer to you** prends la tranche qui est le plus près de toi ; **the television ~ we bought** le téléviseur que nous avons acheté ; **the settee on ~ I am sitting** le canapé sur lequel je suis assis ; **the film of ~ you spoke** le film dont vous avez parlé - **3.** *(referring back - subject)* ce qui ; *(- object)* ce que ; **why did you say you were ill, ~ nobody believed?** pourquoi as-tu dit que tu étais malade, ce que personne n'a cru?

whichever [wɪtʃ'evə^r] <> *adj* quel (quelle) que soit ; **choose ~ colour you prefer** choisissez la couleur que vous préférez, n'importe laquelle. <> *pron* n'importe lequel (laquelle).

whiff [wɪf] *n* [of perfume, smoke] bouffée *f* ; [of food] odeur *f*.

while [waɪl] <> *n* moment *m* ; **let's stay here for a ~** restons ici un moment ; **for a long ~** longtemps ; **after a ~** après quelque temps. <> *conj* - **1.** [during the time that] pendant que - **2.** [as long as] tant que

- 3. [whereas] alors que. ◆ **while away** vt sep passer.

whilst [waɪlst] conj Br = while.

whim [wɪm] n lubie f.

whimper ['wɪmpəʳ] vt & vi gémir.

whimsical ['wɪmzɪkl] adj saugrenu(e).

whine [waɪn] vi [make sound] gémir.

whinge [wɪndʒ] vi Br : **to ~ (about)** se plaindre (de).

whip [wɪp] ◇ n - **1.** [for hitting] fouet m - **2.** Br POL chef m de file (d'un groupe parlementaire). ◇ vt - **1.** [gen] fouetter - **2.** [take quickly] : **to ~ sthg out** sortir qqch brusquement ; **to ~ sthg off** ôter OR enlever qqch brusquement.

whipped cream [wɪpt-] n crème f fouettée.

whip-round n Br inf : **to have a ~** faire une collecte.

whirl [wɜːl] ◇ n lit & fig tourbillon m. ◇ vt : **to ~ sb/sthg round** [spin round] faire tourbillonner qqn/qqch. ◇ vi tourbillonner ; fig [head, mind] tourner.

whirlpool ['wɜːlpuːl] n tourbillon m.

whirlwind ['wɜːlwɪnd] n tornade f.

whirr [wɜːʳ] vi [engine] ronronner.

whisk [wɪsk] ◇ n CULIN fouet m, batteur m (à œufs). ◇ vt - **1.** [move quickly] emmener OR emporter rapidement - **2.** CULIN battre.

whisker ['wɪskəʳ] n moustache f. ◆ **whiskers** npl favoris mpl.

whisky Br, **whiskey** Am & Irish (pl s) ['wɪskɪ] n whisky m.

whisper ['wɪspəʳ] ◇ vt murmurer, chuchoter. ◇ vi chuchoter.

whistle ['wɪsl] ◇ n - **1.** [sound] sifflement m - **2.** [device] sifflet m. ◇ vt & vi siffler.

white [waɪt] ◇ adj - **1.** [in colour] blanc (blanche) - **2.** Br [coffee, tea] au lait. ◇ n - **1.** [colour, of egg, eye] blanc m - **2.** [person] Blanc m, Blanche f.

white-collar adj de bureau.

white elephant n fig objet m coûteux et inutile.

Whitehall ['waɪthɔːl] n rue de Londres, centre administratif du gouvernement britannique.

white-hot adj chauffé(e) à blanc.

White House n : **the ~** la Maison-Blanche.

white lie n pieux mensonge m.

whiteness ['waɪtnɪs] n blancheur f.

white paper n POL livre m blanc.

white sauce n sauce f blanche.

white spirit n Br white-spirit m.

whitewash ['waɪtwɒʃ] ◇ n - **1.** (U) [paint] chaux f - **2.** pej [cover-up] : **a government ~** une combine du gouvernement pour étouffer l'affaire. ◇ vt [paint] blanchir à la chaux.

whiting ['waɪtɪŋ] (pl inv OR **-s**) n merlan m.

Whitsun ['wɪtsn] n Pentecôte f.

whittle ['wɪtl] vt [reduce] : **to ~ sthg away** OR **down** réduire qqch.

whiz, whizz [wɪz] vi [go fast] aller à toute allure.

whiz(z) kid n inf petit prodige m.

who [huː] pron - **1.** (in direct, indirect questions) qui ; **~ are you?** qui êtes-vous ? ; **I didn't know ~ she was** je ne savais pas qui c'était - **2.** (in relative clauses) qui ; **he's the doctor ~ treated me** c'est le médecin qui m'a soigné ; **I don't know the person ~ came to see you** je ne connais pas la personne qui est venue vous voir.

who'd [huːd] = who had, who would.

whodu(n)nit [ˌhuːˈdʌnɪt] n inf polar m.

whoever [huːˈevəʳ] pron - **1.** [unknown person] quiconque - **2.** [indicating surprise, astonishment] qui donc - **3.** [no matter who] qui que (+ subjunctive) ; **~ you are** qui que vous soyez ; **~ wins** qui que ce soit qui gagne.

whole [həʊl] ◇ adj - **1.** [entire, complete] entier(ère) - **2.** [for emphasis] : **a ~ lot bigger** bien plus gros ; **a ~ new idea** une idée tout à fait nouvelle. ◇ n - **1.** [all] : **the ~ of the school** toute l'école ; **the ~ of the summer** tout l'été - **2.** [unit, complete thing] tout m. ◆ **as a whole** adv dans son ensemble. ◆ **on the whole** adv dans l'ensemble.

wholefood ['həʊlfuːd] n Br aliments mpl complets.

whole-hearted [-ˈhɑːtɪd] adj sans réserve, total(e).

wholemeal ['həʊlmiːl] Br, **wholewheat** Am adj complet(ète).

wholesale ['həʊlseɪl] ◇ adj - **1.** [buying, selling] en gros ; [price] de gros - **2.** pej [excessive] en masse. ◇ adv - **1.** [in bulk] en gros - **2.** pej [excessively] en masse.

wholesaler ['həʊlˌseɪləʳ] n marchand m de gros, grossiste mf.

wholesome ['həʊlsəm] adj sain(e).

whole wheat Am = wholemeal.

who'll [huːl] = who will.

wholly ['həʊlɪ] adv totalement.

whom [huːm] pron fml - **1.** (in direct, indirect questions) qui ; **~ did you phone?** qui avez-vous appelé au téléphone? ; **for/of/to ~** pour/de/à qui - **2.** *(in relative clauses)* que ; **the girl ~ he married** la jeune fille qu'il a épousée ; **the man of ~ you speak** l'homme dont vous parlez ; **the man to ~ you were speaking** l'homme à qui vous parliez.

whooping cough ['huːpɪŋ-] *n* coqueluche *f*.

whopping ['wɒpɪŋ] *inf* ⬦ *adj* énorme. ⬦ *adv* : **a ~ great lorry/lie** un camion/mensonge absolument énorme.

whore [hɔːʳ] *n offensive* putain *f*.

who're ['huːəʳ] = who are.

whose [huːz] ⬦ *pron (in direct, indirect questions)* à qui ; **~ is this?** à qui est ceci? ⬦ *adj* - **1.** à qui ; **~ car is that?** à qui est cette voiture? ; **~ son is he?** de qui est-il le fils? - **2.** *(in relative clauses)* dont ; **that's the boy ~ father's an MP** c'est le garçon dont le père est député ; **the girl ~ mother you phoned yesterday** la fille à la mère de qui OR à laquelle tu as téléphoné hier.

who's who [huːz-] *n* [book] Bottin® *m* mondain.

who've [huːv] = who have.

why [waɪ] ⬦ *adv (in direct questions)* pourquoi ; **~ did you lie to me?** pourquoi m'as-tu menti? ; **~ don't you all come?** pourquoi ne pas tous venir?, pourquoi est-ce que vous ne viendriez pas tous? ; **~ not?** pourquoi pas? ⬦ *conj* pourquoi ; **I don't know ~ he said that** je ne sais pas pourquoi il a dit cela. ⬦ *pron* : **there are several reasons ~ he left** il est parti pour plusieurs raisons, les raisons pour lesquelles il est parti sont nombreuses ; **I don't know the reason ~** je ne sais pas pourquoi. ⬦ *excl* tiens! ➠ **why ever** *adv* pourquoi donc.

wick [wɪk] *n* [of candle, lighter] mèche *f*.

wicked ['wɪkɪd] *adj* - **1.** [evil] mauvais(e) - **2.** [mischievous, devilish] malicieux(euse).

wicker ['wɪkəʳ] *adj* en osier.

wickerwork ['wɪkəwɜːk] *n* vannerie *f*.

wicket ['wɪkɪt] *n* CRICKET - **1.** [stumps, dismissal] guichet *m* - **2.** [pitch] terrain *m* entre les guichets.

wide [waɪd] ⬦ *adj* - **1.** [gen] large ; **how ~ is the room?** quelle est la largeur de la pièce? ; **to be six metres ~** faire six mètres de large OR de largeur - **2.** [gap, difference] grand(e) - **3.** [experience, knowledge, issue] vaste. ⬦ *adv* - **1.** [broadly] largement ; **open ~!** ouvrez grand! - **2.** [off-target] : **the shot went ~** le coup est passé loin du but OR à côté.

wide-angle lens *n* PHOT objectif *m* grand angle.

wide-awake *adj* tout à fait réveillé(e).

widely ['waɪdlɪ] *adv* - **1.** [smile, vary] largement - **2.** [extensively] beaucoup ; **to be ~ read** avoir beaucoup lu ; **it is ~ believed that ...** beaucoup pensent que ..., nombreux sont ceux qui pensent que ...

widen ['waɪdn] *vt* - **1.** [make broader] élargir - **2.** [gap, difference] agrandir, élargir.

wide open *adj* grand ouvert (grande ouverte).

wide-ranging [-'reɪndʒɪŋ] *adj* varié(e) ; [consequences] de grande envergure.

widespread ['waɪdspred] *adj* très répandu(e).

widow ['wɪdəʊ] *n* veuve *f*.

widowed ['wɪdəʊd] *adj* veuf (veuve).

widower ['wɪdəʊəʳ] *n* veuf *m*.

width [wɪdθ] *n* largeur *f* ; **in ~** de large.

wield [wiːld] *vt* - **1.** [weapon] manier - **2.** [power] exercer.

wife [waɪf] *(pl* wives [waɪvz]*)* *n* femme *f*, épouse *f*.

wig [wɪg] *n* perruque *f*.

wiggle ['wɪgl] *inf vt* remuer.

wild [waɪld] *adj* - **1.** [animal, attack, scenery, flower] sauvage - **2.** [weather, sea] déchaîné(e) - **3.** [laughter, hope, plan] fou (folle) - **4.** [random - estimate] fantaisiste ; **I made a ~ guess** j'ai dit ça au hasard. ➠ **wilds** *npl* : **the ~s of** le fin fond de ; **to live in the ~s** habiter en pleine nature.

wilderness ['wɪldənɪs] *n* étendue *f* sauvage.

wild-goose chase *n inf* : **it turned out to be a ~** ça s'est révélé être inutile.

wildlife ['waɪldlaɪf] *n (U)* faune *f* et flore *f*.

wildly ['waɪldlɪ] *adv* - **1.** [enthusiastically, fanatically] frénétiquement - **2.** [guess, suggest] au hasard ; [shoot] dans tous les sens - **3.** [very - different, impractical] tout à fait.

wilful *Br*, **willful** *Am* ['wɪlfʊl] *adj* - **1.** [determined] obstiné(e) - **2.** [deliberate] délibéré(e).

will¹ [wɪl] ⬦ *n* - **1.** [mental] volonté *f* ; **against one's ~** contre son gré - **2.** [document] testament *m*. ⬦ *vt* : **to ~ sthg to happen** prier de toutes ses forces pour que qqch se passe ; **to ~ sb to do sthg** concentrer toute sa volonté sur qqn pour qu'il fasse qqch.

will² [wɪl] *modal vb* - **1.** *(to express future tense)* : **I ~ see you next week** je te verrai la semaine prochaine ; **when ~ you have finished it?** quand est-ce que vous l'aurez

fini? ; ~ **you be here next week? — yes I
~/no I won't** est-ce que tu seras là la semaine prochaine? — oui/non **- 2.** [indicating willingness] : ~ **you have some more tea?** voulez-vous encore du thé? ; **I won't do it** je refuse de le faire, je ne veux pas le faire **- 3.** [in commands, requests] : **you ~ leave this house at once** tu vas quitter cette maison tout de suite ; **close that window, ~ you?** ferme cette fenêtre, veux-tu? ; ~ **you be quiet!** veux-tu te taire!, tu vas te taire! **- 4.** [indicating possibility, what usually happens] : **the hall ~ hold up to 1000 people** la salle peut abriter jusqu'à 1000 personnes **- 5.** [expressing an assumption] : **that'll be your father** cela doit être ton père **- 6.** [indicating irritation] : **she ~ keep phoning me** elle n'arrête pas de me téléphoner.

willful _Am_ = wilful.

willing ['wɪlɪŋ] _adj_ **- 1.** [prepared] : **if you're ~** si vous voulez bien ; **to be ~ to do sthg** être disposé(e) OR prêt(e) à faire qqch **- 2.** [eager] enthousiaste.

willingly ['wɪlɪŋlɪ] _adv_ volontiers.

willow (tree) ['wɪləʊ-] _n_ saule _m_.

willpower ['wɪl,paʊə'] _n_ volonté _f_.

willy-nilly [,wɪlɪ'nɪlɪ] _adv_ **- 1.** [at random] n'importe comment **- 2.** [wanting to or not] bon gré mal gré.

wilt [wɪlt] _vi_ [plant] se faner ; _fig_ [person] dépérir.

wily ['waɪlɪ] _adj_ rusé(e).

wimp [wɪmp] _n pej inf_ mauviette _f_.

win [wɪn] (_pt_ & _pp_ **won**) ◇ _n_ victoire _f_. ◇ _vt_ **- 1.** [game, prize, competition] gagner **- 2.** [support, approval] obtenir ; [love, friendship] gagner. ◇ _vi_ gagner. ◆ **win over, win round** _vt sep_ convaincre, gagner à sa cause.

wince [wɪns] _vi_ : **to ~ (at/with)** [with body] tressaillir (à/de) ; [with face] grimacer (à/de).

winch [wɪntʃ] _n_ treuil _m_.

wind¹ [wɪnd] ◇ _n_ **- 1.** METEOR vent _m_ **- 2.** [breath] souffle _m_ **- 3.** (U) [in stomach] gaz _mpl_. ◇ _vt_ [knock breath out of] couper le souffle à.

wind² [waɪnd] (_pt_ & _pp_ **wound**) ◇ _vt_ **- 1.** [string, thread] enrouler **- 2.** [clock] remonter. ◇ _vi_ [river, road] serpenter. ◆ **wind down** ◇ _vt sep_ **- 1.** _Br_ [car window] baisser **- 2.** [business] cesser graduellement. ◇ _vi_ [relax] se détendre. ◆ **wind up** _vt sep_ **- 1.** [finish - meeting] clôturer ; [- business] liquider **- 2.** _Br_ [clock, car window] remonter **- 3.** _Br inf_ [deliberate-

ly annoy] faire marcher **- 4.** _inf_ [end up] : **to ~ up doing sthg** finir par faire qqch.

windfall ['wɪndfɔːl] _n_ [unexpected gift] aubaine _f_.

winding ['waɪndɪŋ] _adj_ sinueux(euse).

wind instrument [wɪnd-] _n_ instrument _m_ à vent.

windmill ['wɪndmɪl] _n_ moulin _m_ à vent.

window ['wɪndəʊ] _n_ **- 1.** [gen & COMPUT] fenêtre _f_ **- 2.** [pane of glass, in car] vitre _f_ **- 3.** [of shop] vitrine _f_.

window box _n_ jardinière _f_.

window cleaner _n_ laveur _m_, -euse _f_ de vitres.

window ledge _n_ rebord _m_ de fenêtre.

windowpane _n_ vitre _f_.

windowsill ['wɪndəʊsɪl] _n_ [outside] rebord _m_ de fenêtre ; [inside] appui _m_ de fenêtre.

windpipe ['wɪndpaɪp] _n_ trachée _f_.

windscreen _Br_ ['wɪndskriːn], **windshield** _Am_ ['wɪndʃiːld] _n_ pare-brise _m inv_.

windscreen washer _n Br_ lave-glace _m_.

windscreen wiper [-,waɪpə'] _n Br_ essuie-glace _m_.

windshield _Am_ = windscreen.

windsurfing ['wɪnd,sɜːfɪŋ] _n_ : **to go ~** faire de la planche à voile.

windswept ['wɪndswept] _adj_ [scenery] balayé(e) par les vents.

windy ['wɪndɪ] _adj_ venteux(euse) ; **it's ~** il fait OR il y a du vent.

wine [waɪn] _n_ vin _m_.

wine bar _n Br_ bar _m_ à vin.

wine cellar _n_ cave _f_ (à vin).

wineglass ['waɪnɡlɑːs] _n_ verre _m_ à vin.

wine list _n_ carte _f_ des vins.

wine merchant _n Br_ marchand _m_ de vins.

wine tasting [-,teɪstɪŋ] _n_ dégustation _f_ (de vins).

wine waiter _n_ sommelier _m_.

wing [wɪŋ] _n_ aile _f_. ◆ **wings** _npl_ THEATRE : **the ~s** les coulisses _fpl_.

winger ['wɪŋə'] _n_ SPORT ailier _m_.

wink [wɪŋk] ◇ _n_ clin _m_ d'œil. ◇ _vi_ [with eyes] : **to ~ (at sb)** faire un clin d'œil (à qqn).

winkle ['wɪŋkl] _n_ bigorneau _m_. ◆ **winkle out** _vt sep Br_ extirper ; **to ~ sthg out of sb** arracher qqch à qqn.

winner ['wɪnə'] _n_ [person] gagnant _m_, -e _f_.

winning ['wɪnɪŋ] _adj_ [victorious, successful] gagnant(e). ➠ **winnings** *npl* gains *mpl*.

winning post *n* poteau *m* d'arrivée.

winter ['wɪntə'] ⬦ *n* hiver *m* ; in ~ en hiver. ⬦ *comp* d'hiver.

winter sports *npl* sports *mpl* d'hiver.

wintertime ['wɪntətaɪm] *n* (*U*) hiver *m*.

wint(e)ry ['wɪntrɪ] *adj* d'hiver.

wipe [waɪp] ⬦ *n* - **1.** [action of wiping] : **to give sthg a ~** essuyer qqch, donner un coup de torchon à qqch - **2.** [cloth] lingette *f*. ⬦ *vt* essuyer. ➠ **wipe out** *vt sep* - **1.** [erase] effacer - **2.** [eradicate] anéantir. ➠ **wipe up** *vt sep* & *vi* essuyer.

wire ['waɪə'] ⬦ *n* - **1.** (*U*) [metal] fil *m* de fer - **2.** [cable etc] fil *m* - **3.** *esp Am* [telegram] télégramme *m*. ⬦ *vt* - **1.** [ELEC - plug] installer ; [- house] faire l'installation électrique de - **2.** *esp Am* [send telegram to] télégraphier à.

wireless ['waɪəlɪs] *n dated* T.S.F. *f*.

wiring ['waɪərɪŋ] *n* (*U*) installation *f* électrique.

wiry ['waɪərɪ] *adj* - **1.** [hair] crépu(e) - **2.** [body, man] noueux(euse).

wisdom ['wɪzdəm] *n* sagesse *f*.

wisdom tooth *n* dent *f* de sagesse.

wise [waɪz] *adj* sage.

wisecrack ['waɪzkræk] *n pej* vanne *f*.

wish [wɪʃ] ⬦ *n* - **1.** [desire] souhait *m*, désir *m* ; **to wish for/to do sthg** désir de qqch/ de faire qqch - **2.** [magic request] vœu *m*. ⬦ *vt* - **1.** [want] : **to ~ to do sthg** souhaiter faire qqch ; **I ~ (that) he'd come** j'aimerais bien qu'il vienne ; **I ~ I could** si seulement je pouvais - **2.** [expressing hope] : **to ~ sb sthg** souhaiter qqch à qqn. ⬦ *vi* [by magic] : **to ~ for sthg** souhaiter qqch. ➠ **wishes** *npl* : **best ~es** meilleurs vœux ; **(with) best ~es** [at end of letter] bien amicalement.

wishful thinking [,wɪʃful-] *n* : **that's just ~** c'est prendre mes/ses *etc* désirs pour des réalités.

wishy-washy ['wɪʃɪ,wɒʃɪ] *adj inf pej* [person] sans personnalité ; [ideas] vague.

wisp [wɪsp] *n* - **1.** [tuft] mèche *f* - **2.** [small cloud] mince filet *m* OR volute *f*.

wistful ['wɪstful] *adj* nostalgique.

wit [wɪt] *n* - **1.** [humour] esprit *m* - **2.** [intelligence] : **to have the ~ to do sthg** avoir l'intelligence de faire qqch. ➠ **wits** *npl* : **to have** OR **keep one's ~s about one** être attentif(ive) OR sur ses gardes.

witch [wɪtʃ] *n* sorcière *f*.

with [wɪð] *prep* - **1.** [in company of] avec ; **I play tennis ~ his wife** je joue au tennis avec sa femme ; **we stayed ~ them for a week** nous avons passé une semaine chez eux - **2.** [indicating opposition] avec ; **to argue ~ sb** discuter avec qqn ; **the war ~ Germany** la guerre avec OR contre l'Allemagne - **3.** [indicating means, manner, feelings] avec ; **I washed it ~ detergent** je l'ai lavé avec un détergent ; **she was trembling ~ fright** elle tremblait de peur - **4.** [having] avec ; **a man ~ a beard** un homme avec une barbe, un barbu ; **the man ~ the moustache** l'homme à la moustache - **5.** [regarding] : **he's very mean ~ money** il est très près de ses sous, il est très avare ; **the trouble ~ her is that ...** l'ennui avec elle OR ce qu'il y a avec elle c'est que ... - **6.** [indicating simultaneity] : **I can't do it ~ you watching me** je ne peux pas le faire quand OR pendant que tu me regardes - **7.** [because of] : **~ my luck, I'll probably lose** avec ma chance habituelle, je suis sûr de perdre - **8.** *phr* : **I'm ~ you** [I understand] je vous suis ; [I'm on your side] je suis des vôtres ; [I agree] je suis d'accord avec vous.

withdraw [wɪð'drɔ:] (*pt* -drew, *pp* -drawn) ⬦ *vt* - **1.** *fml* [remove] : **to ~ sthg (from)** enlever qqch (de) - **2.** [money, troops, remark] retirer. ⬦ *vi* - **1.** *fml* [leave] : **to ~ (from)** se retirer (de) - **2.** MIL se replier ; **to ~ from** évacuer - **3.** [quit, give up] : **to ~ (from)** se retirer (de).

withdrawal [wɪð'drɔːəl] *n* - **1.** [gen] : **~ (from)** retrait *m* (de) - **2.** MIL repli *m*.

withdrawal symptoms *npl* crise *f* de manque.

withdrawn [wɪð'drɔːn] ⬦ *pp* ➢ withdraw. ⬦ *adj* [shy, quiet] renfermé(e).

withdrew [wɪð'druː] *pt* ➢ withdraw.

wither ['wɪðə'] *vi* - **1.** [dry up] se flétrir - **2.** [weaken] mourir.

withhold [wɪð'həʊld] (*pt* & *pp* -held [-'held]) *vt* [services] refuser ; [information] cacher ; [salary] retenir.

within [wɪ'ðɪn] ⬦ *prep* - **1.** [inside] à l'intérieur de, dans ; **~ her** en elle, à l'intérieur d'elle-même - **2.** [budget, comprehension] dans les limites de ; [limits] dans - **3.** [less than - distance] à moins de ; [- time] d'ici, en moins de ; **~ the week** avant la fin de la semaine. ⬦ *adv* à l'intérieur.

without [wɪð'aʊt] ⬦ *prep* sans ; **~ a coat** sans manteau ; **I left ~ seeing him** je suis parti sans l'avoir vu ; **I left ~ him seeing me** je suis parti sans qu'il m'ait vu ; **to go ~ sthg** se passer de qqch. ⬦ *adv* : **to go** OR **do ~** s'en passer.

withstand [wɪð'stænd] (*pt* & *pp* **-stood** [-'stʊd]) *vt* résister à.

witness ['wɪtnɪs] <> *n* - **1.** [gen] témoin *m* - **2.** [testimony] : **to bear ~ to sthg** témoigner de qqch. <> *vt* - **1.** [accident, crime] être témoin de - **2.** *fig* [changes, rise in birth rate] assister à - **3.** [countersign] contresigner.

witness box *Br*, **witness stand** *Am n* barre *f* des témoins.

witticism ['wɪtɪsɪzm] *n* mot *m* d'esprit.

witty ['wɪtɪ] *adj* plein(e) d'esprit, spirituel(elle).

wives [waɪvz] *pl* ⊏> **wife**.

wizard ['wɪzəd] *n* magicien *m* ; *fig* as *m*, champion *m*, -onne *f*.

wobble ['wɒbl] *vi* [hand, wings] trembler ; [chair, table] branler.

woe [wəʊ] *n literary* malheur *m*.

woke [wəʊk] *pt* ⊏> **wake**.

woken ['wəʊkn] *pp* ⊏> **wake**.

wolf [wʊlf] (*pl* **wolves** ['wʊlvz]) *n* [animal] loup *m*.

woman ['wʊmən] (*pl* **women**) <> *n* femme *f*. <> *comp* : ~ **doctor** femme *f* médecin ; ~ **teacher** professeur *m* femme.

womanly ['wʊmənlɪ] *adj* féminin(e).

womb [wuːm] *n* utérus *m*.

women ['wɪmɪn] *pl* ⊏> **woman**.

women's lib *n* libération *f* de la femme.

women's liberation *n* libération *f* de la femme.

won [wʌn] *pt* & *pp* ⊏> **win**.

wonder ['wʌndə'] <> *n* - **1.** (*U*) [amazement] étonnement *m* - **2.** [cause for surprise] : **it's a ~ (that)** ... c'est un miracle que ... ; **it's no OR little OR small ~ (that)** ... il n'est pas étonnant que ... - **3.** [amazing thing, person] merveille *f*. <> *vt* - **1.** [speculate] : **to ~ (if OR whether)** se demander (si) - **2.** [in polite requests] : **I ~ whether you would mind shutting the window?** est-ce que cela ne vous ennuierait pas de fermer la fenêtre? <> *vi* - **1.** [speculate] se demander ; **to ~ about sthg** s'interroger sur qqch.

wonderful ['wʌndəfʊl] *adj* merveilleux(euse).

wonderfully ['wʌndəfʊlɪ] *adv* - **1.** [very well] merveilleusement, à merveille - **2.** [for emphasis] extrêmement.

won't [wəʊnt] = **will not**.

woo [wuː] *vt* - **1.** *literary* [court] courtiser - **2.** [try to win over] chercher à rallier (à soi OR à sa cause).

wood [wʊd] <> *n* bois *m*. <> *comp* en bois. ◆ **woods** *npl* bois *mpl*.

wooded ['wʊdɪd] *adj* boisé(e).

wooden ['wʊdn] *adj* - **1.** [of wood] en bois - **2.** *pej* [actor] gauche.

woodpecker ['wʊd,pekə'] *n* pivert *m*.

woodwind ['wʊdwɪnd] *n* : **the ~** les bois *mpl*.

woodwork ['wʊdwɜːk] *n* menuiserie *f*.

woodworm ['wʊdwɜːm] *n* ver *m* du bois.

wool [wʊl] *n* laine *f* ; **to pull the ~ over sb's eyes** *inf* rouler qqn (dans la farine).

woollen *Br*, **woolen** *Am* ['wʊlən] *adj* en laine, de laine. ◆ **woollens** *npl* lainages *mpl*.

woolly ['wʊlɪ] *adj* - **1.** [woollen] en laine, de laine - **2.** *inf* [idea, thinking] confus(e).

word [wɜːd] <> *n* - **1.** LING mot *m* ; **too stupid for ~s** vraiment trop bête ; **~ for ~** [repeat, copy] mot pour mot ; [translate] mot à mot ; **in other ~s** en d'autres mots OR termes ; **in a ~** en un mot ; **to have a ~ (with sb)** parler (à qqn) ; **she doesn't mince her ~s** elle ne mâche pas ses mots ; **I couldn't get a ~ in edgeways** je n'ai pas réussi à placer un seul mot - **2.** (*U*) [news] nouvelles *fpl* - **3.** [promise] parole *f* ; **to give sb one's ~** donner sa parole à qqn. <> *vt* [letter, reply] rédiger.

wording ['wɜːdɪŋ] *n* (*U*) termes *mpl*.

word processing *n* (*U*) COMPUT traitement *m* de texte.

word processor [-,prəʊsesə'] *n* COMPUT machine *f* à traitement de texte.

wore [wɔː'] *pt* ⊏> **wear**.

work [wɜːk] <> *n* - **1.** (*U*) [employment] travail *m*, emploi *m* ; **out of ~** sans emploi, au chômage ; **at ~** au travail - **2.** [activity, tasks] travail *m* - **3.** ART & LITERATURE œuvre *f*. <> *vt* - **1.** [person, staff] faire travailler - **2.** [machine] faire marcher - **3.** [wood, metal, land] travailler. <> *vi* - **1.** [do a job] travailler ; **to ~ on sthg** travailler à qqch - **2.** [function] fonctionner, marcher - **3.** [succeed] marcher - **4.** [become] : **to ~ loose** se desserrer. ◆ **works** <> *n* [factory] usine *f*. <> *npl* - **1.** [mechanism] mécanisme *m* - **2.** [digging, building] travaux *mpl*. ◆ **work on** *vt fus* - **1.** [pay attention to] travailler à - **2.** [take as basis] se baser sur. ◆ **work out** <> *vt sep* - **1.** [plan, schedule] mettre au point - **2.** [total, answer] trouver. <> *vi* - **1.** [figure, total] : **to ~ out at** se monter à - **2.** [turn out] se dérouler - **3.** [be successful] (bien) marcher - **4.** [train, exercise] s'entraîner. ◆ **work up** *vt sep* - **1.** [excite] : **to ~ o.s. up into** se mettre dans

- **2.** [generate] : **to ~ up an appetite** s'ouvrir l'appétit ; **to ~ up enthusiasm** s'enthousiasmer.

workable ['wɜːkəbl] *adj* [plan] réalisable ; [system] fonctionnel(elle).

workaholic [ˌwɜːkə'hɒlɪk] *n* bourreau *m* de travail.

workday ['wɜːkdeɪ] *n* [not weekend] jour *m* ouvrable.

worked up [ˌwɜːkt-] *adj* dans tous ses états.

worker ['wɜːkəʳ] *n* travailleur *m*, -euse *f*, ouvrier *m*, -ère *f*.

workforce ['wɜːkfɔːs] *n* main *f* d'œuvre.

working ['wɜːkɪŋ] *adj* - **1.** [in operation] qui marche - **2.** [having employment] qui travaille - **3.** [conditions, clothes, hours] de travail. ◆ **workings** *npl* [of system, machine] mécanisme *m*.

working class *n* : **the ~** la classe ouvrière. ◆ **working-class** *adj* ouvrier(ère).

working order *n* : **in ~** en état de marche.

workload ['wɜːkləʊd] *n* quantité *f* de travail.

workman ['wɜːkmən] (*pl* **-men** [-mən]) *n* ouvrier *m*.

workmanship ['wɜːkmənʃɪp] *n* (U) travail *m*.

workmate ['wɜːkmeɪt] *n* camarade *mf* OR collègue *mf* de travail.

work permit [-ˌpɜːmɪt] *n* permis *m* de travail.

workplace ['wɜːkpleɪs] *n* lieu *m* de travail.

workshop ['wɜːkʃɒp] *n* atelier *m*.

workstation ['wɜːkˌsteɪʃn] *n* COMPUT poste *m* de travail.

worktop ['wɜːktɒp] *n Br* plan *m* de travail.

work-to-rule *n Br* grève *f* du zèle.

world [wɜːld] *n* - **1.** [gen] monde *m* - **2.** *loc* : **to think the ~ of sb** admirer qqn énormément, ne jurer que par qqn ; **a ~ of difference** une énorme différence. ◆ *comp* [power] mondial(e) ; [language] universel(elle) ; [tour] du monde.

world-class *adj* de niveau international.

world-famous *adj* de renommée mondiale.

worldly ['wɜːldlɪ] *adj* de ce monde, matériel(elle).

World War I *n* la Première Guerre mondiale.

World War II *n* la Deuxième Guerre mondiale.

worldwide ['wɜːldwaɪd] ◇ *adj* mondial(e). ◇ *adv* dans le monde entier.

worm [wɜːm] *n* [animal] ver *m*.

worn [wɔːn] ◇ *pp* ➲ **wear**. ◇ *adj* - **1.** [threadbare] usé(e) - **2.** [tired] las (lasse).

worn-out *adj* - **1.** [old, threadbare] usé(e) - **2.** [tired] épuisé(e).

worried ['wʌrɪd] *adj* soucieux(euse), inquiet(ète).

worry ['wʌrɪ] ◇ *n* - **1.** [feeling] souci *m* - **2.** [problem] souci *m*, ennui *m*. ◇ *vt* inquiéter, tracasser. ◇ *vi* s'inquiéter ; **to ~ about** se faire du souci au sujet de ; **don't worry!, not to ~!** ne vous en faites pas !

worrying ['wʌrɪɪŋ] *adj* inquiétant(e).

worse [wɜːs] ◇ *adj* - **1.** [not as good] pire ; **to get ~** [situation] empirer - **2.** [more ill] : **he's ~ today** il va plus mal aujourd'hui. ◇ *adv* plus mal ; **they're ~ off** c'est encore pire pour eux ; **~ off** [financially] plus pauvre. ◇ *n* pire *m* ; **for the ~** pour le pire.

worsen ['wɜːsn] *vt* & *vi* empirer.

worship ['wɜːʃɪp] ◇ *vt* adorer. ◇ *n* - **1.** (U) RELIG culte *m* - **2.** [adoration] adoration *f*. ◆ **Worship** *n* : **Your/Her/His Worship** Votre/Son Honneur *m*.

worst [wɜːst] ◇ *adj* : **the ~** le pire (la pire), le plus mauvais (la plus mauvaise). ◇ *adv* le plus mal ; **the ~ affected area** la zone la plus touchée. ◇ *n* : **the ~** le pire ; **if the ~ comes to the ~** au pire. ◆ **at (the) worst** *adv* au pire.

worth [wɜːθ] ◇ *adj* - **1.** [in value] : **to be ~ sthg** valoir qqch ; **how much is it ~?** combien cela vaut-il? - **2.** [deserving of] : **it's ~ a visit** cela vaut une visite ; **to be ~ doing sthg** valoir la peine de faire qqch. ◇ *n* valeur *f* ; **a week's/£20 ~ of groceries** pour une semaine/20 livres d'épicerie.

worthless ['wɜːθlɪs] *adj* - **1.** [object] sans valeur, qui ne vaut rien - **2.** [person] qui n'est bon à rien.

worthwhile [ˌwɜːθ'waɪl] *adj* [job, visit] qui en vaut la peine ; [charity] louable.

worthy ['wɜːðɪ] *adj* - **1.** [deserving of respect] digne - **2.** [deserving] : **to be ~ of sthg** mériter qqch - **3.** *pej* [good but unexciting] méritant(e).

would [wʊd] *modal vb* - **1.** (in reported speech) : **she said she ~ come** elle a dit qu'elle viendrait - **2.** [indicating likelihood] : **what ~ you do?** que ferais-tu? ; **what ~ you have done?** qu'aurais-tu fait? ; **I ~ be most grateful** je vous en serais très reconnaissant - **3.** [indicating willingness] : **she ~n't go** elle ne voulait pas y aller ; **he ~ do any-**

thing for her il ferait n'importe quoi pour elle **- 4.** *(in polite questions)* **: ~ you like a drink?** voulez-vous OR voudriez-vous à boire ? ; **~ you mind closing the window?** cela vous ennuierait de fermer la fenêtre ? **- 5.** [indicating inevitability] **: he ~ say that** j'étais sûr qu'il allait dire ça, ça ne m'étonne pas de lui **- 6.** [giving advice] **: I ~ report it if I were you** si j'étais vous je préviendrais les autorités **- 7.** [expressing opinions] **: I ~ prefer** je préférerais ; **I ~ have thought (that)** ... j'aurais pensé que ... **- 8.** [indicating habit] **: he ~ smoke a cigar after dinner** il fumait un cigare après le dîner ; **she ~ often complain about the neighbours** elle se plaignait souvent des voisins.

would-be *adj* prétendu(e).

wouldn't ['wodnt] = would not.

would've ['wodəv] = would have.

wound[1] [wu:nd] ⬦ *n* blessure *f*. ⬦ *vt* blesser.

wound[2] [waond] *pt & pp* ⊏ **wind**[2].

wove [wəov] *pt* ⊏ **weave**.

woven ['wəovn] *pp* ⊏ **weave**.

WP *n* *(abbr of* **word processing, word processor***)* TTX *m*.

wrangle ['ræŋgl] ⬦ *n* dispute *f*. ⬦ *vi* **: to ~ (with sb over sthg)** se disputer (avec qqn à propos de qqch).

wrap [ræp] ⬦ *vt* [cover in paper, cloth] **: to ~ sthg (in)** envelopper OR emballer qqch (dans) ; **to ~ sthg around** OR **round sthg** enrouler qqch autour de qqch. ⬦ *n* [garment] châle *m*. ◆ **wrap up** ⬦ *vt sep* [cover in paper or cloth] envelopper, emballer. ⬦ *vi* [put warm clothes on] **: ~ up well** OR **warmly!** couvrez-vous bien !

wrapper ['ræpə'] *n* papier *m* ; *Br* [of book] jaquette *f*, couverture *f*.

wrapping ['ræpɪŋ] *n* emballage *m*.

wrapping paper *n (U)* papier *m* d'emballage.

wrath [rɒθ] *n (U)* *literary* courroux *m*.

wreak [ri:k] *vt* [destruction, havoc] entraîner.

wreath [ri:θ] *n* couronne *f*.

wreck [rek] ⬦ *n* **- 1.** [car, plane, ship] épave *f* **- 2.** *inf* [person] loque *f*. ⬦ *vt* **- 1.** [destroy] détruire **- 2.** NAUT provoquer le naufrage de ; **to be ~ed** s'échouer **- 3.** [spoil - holiday] gâcher ; [- health, hopes, plan] ruiner.

wreckage ['rekɪdʒ] *n (U)* débris *mpl*.

wren [ren] *n* roitelet *m*.

wrench [rentʃ] ⬦ *n* [tool] clef *f* anglaise. ⬦ *vt* **- 1.** [pull violently] tirer violemment ;

to ~ sthg off arracher qqch **- 2.** [arm, leg, knee] se tordre.

wrestle ['resl] *vi* **- 1.** [fight] **: to ~ (with sb)** lutter (contre qqn) **- 2.** *fig* [struggle] **: to ~ with sthg** se débattre OR lutter contre qqch.

wrestler ['reslə'] *n* lutteur *m*, -euse *f*.

wrestling ['reslɪŋ] *n* lutte *f*.

wretch [retʃ] *n* pauvre diable *m*.

wretched ['retʃɪd] *adj* **- 1.** [miserable] misérable **- 2.** *inf* [damned] fichu(e).

wriggle ['rɪgl] *vi* remuer, se tortiller.

wring [rɪŋ] *(pt & pp* **wrung***) vt* [washing] essorer, tordre.

wringing ['rɪŋɪŋ] *adj* **: ~ (wet)** [person] trempé(e) ; [clothes] mouillé(e), à tordre.

wrinkle ['rɪŋkl] ⬦ *n* **- 1.** [on skin] ride *f* **- 2.** [in cloth] pli *m*. ⬦ *vt* plisser. ⬦ *vi* se plisser, faire des plis.

wrist [rɪst] *n* poignet *m*.

wristwatch ['rɪstwɒtʃ] *n* montre-bracelet *f*.

writ [rɪt] *n* acte *m* judiciaire.

write [raɪt] *(pt* **wrote***, pp* **written***)* ⬦ *vt* **- 1.** [gen & COMPUT] écrire ; **to ~ to sb** *Am* [person] écrire à **- 3.** [cheque, prescription] faire. ⬦ *vi* [gen & COMPUT] écrire. ◆ **write back** *vi* répondre. ◆ **write down** *vt sep* écrire, noter. ◆ **write into** *vt sep* **: to ~ a clause into a contract** insérer une clause dans un contrat. ◆ **write off** *vt sep* **- 1.** [project] considérer comme fichu **- 2.** [debt, investment] passer aux profits et pertes **- 3.** [person] considérer comme fini **- 4.** *Br inf* [vehicle] bousiller. ◆ **write up** *vt sep* [notes] mettre au propre.

write-off *n* [vehicle] *Br* **: to be a ~** être complètement démoli(e).

writer ['raɪtə'] *n* **- 1.** [as profession] écrivain *m* **- 2.** [of letter, article, story] auteur *m*.

writhe [raɪð] *vi* se tordre.

writing ['raɪtɪŋ] *n (U)* **- 1.** [handwriting, activity] écriture *f* ; **in ~** par écrit **- 2.** [something written] écrit *m*.

writing paper *n (U)* papier *m* à lettres.

written ['rɪtn] ⬦ *pp* ⊏ **write**. ⬦ *adj* écrit(e).

wrong [rɒŋ] ⬦ *adj* **- 1.** [not normal, not satisfactory] qui ne va pas ; **is something ~?** y a-t-il quelque chose qui ne va pas ? ; **what's ~?** qu'est-ce qui ne va pas ? ; **there's something ~ with the switch** l'interrupteur ne marche pas bien **- 2.** [not suitable] qui ne convient pas **- 3.** [not correct - answer, address] faux (fausse), mauvais(e) ; [- decision] mauvais ; **to be ~** [person] avoir tort ;

to be ~ to do sthg avoir tort de faire qqch - **4.** [morally bad] **: it's ~ to ... c'est mal de ... ◇ adv** [incorrectly] mal ; **to get sthg ~** se tromper à propos de qqch ; **to go ~** [make a mistake] se tromper, faire une erreur ; [stop functioning] se détraquer. **◇ n** mal *m* ; **to be in the ~** être dans son tort. **◇ vt** faire du tort à.

wrongful ['rɒŋfʊl] *adj* [unfair] injuste ; [arrest, dismissal] injustifié(e).

wrongly ['rɒŋlɪ] *adv* - **1.** [unsuitably] mal - **2.** [mistakenly] à tort.

wrong number *n* faux numéro *m*.

wrote [rəʊt] *pt* ▷ **write**.

wrought iron [rɔːt-] *n* fer *m* forgé.

wrung [rʌŋ] *pt & pp* ▷ **wring**.

wry [raɪ] *adj* - **1.** [amused - smile, look] amusé(e) ; [- humour] ironique - **2.** [displeased] désabusé(e).

WWW (*abbr of* **World Wide Web**) *n* WWW *m*.

x (*pl* **x's** OR **xs**), **X** (*pl* **X's** OR **Xs**) [eks] *n* - **1.** [letter] x *m inv*, X *m inv* - **2.** [unknown thing] x *m inv* - **3.** [to mark place] croix *f* - **4.** [at end of letter] **: XXX** grosses bises.

xenophobia [ˌzenə'fəʊbjə] *n* xénophobie *f*.

Xmas ['eksməs, 'krɪsməs] *n* Noël *m*.

X-ray ◇ n - **1.** [ray] rayon *m* X - **2.** [picture] radiographie *f*, radio *f*. **◇ vt** radiographier.

xylophone ['zaɪləfəʊn] *n* xylophone *m*.

y (*pl* **y's** OR **ys**), **Y** (*pl* **Y's** OR **Ys**) [waɪ] *n* [letter] y *m inv*, Y *m inv*.

yacht [jɒt] *n* yacht *m*.

yachting ['jɒtɪŋ] *n* yachting *m*.

yachtsman ['jɒtsmən] (*pl* **-men** [-mən]) *n* yachtman *m*.

yam [jæm] *n* igname *f*.

Yank [jæŋk] *n Br inf* terme péjoratif désignant un Américain, Amerloque *mf*.

Yankee ['jæŋkɪ] *n Br inf* [American] terme péjoratif désignant un Américain, Amerloque *mf*.

yap [jæp] *vi* [dog] japper.

yard [jɑːd] *n* - **1.** [unit of measurement] = *91,44 cm*, yard *m* - **2.** [walled area] cour *f* - **3.** [area of work] chantier *m* - **4.** *Am* [attached to house] jardin *m*.

yardstick ['jɑːdstɪk] *n* mesure *f*.

yarn [jɑːn] *n* [thread] fil *m*.

yawn [jɔːn] ◇ *n* [when tired] bâillement *m*. ◇ *vi* [when tired] bâiller.

yd *abbr of* **yard**.

yeah [jeə] *adv inf* ouais.

year [jɪəˈ] *n* - **1.** [calendar year] année *f* ; **all (the) ~ round** toute l'année - **2.** [period of 12 months] année *f*, an *m* ; **to be 21 ~s old** avoir 21 ans - **3.** [financial year] année *f* ; **the ~ 1992-93** l'exercice 1992-93. ◆ **years** *npl* [long time] années *fpl*.

yearly ['jɪəlɪ] ◇ *adj* annuel(elle). ◇ *adv* - **1.** [once a year] annuellement - **2.** [every year] chaque année ; **twice ~** deux fois par an.

yearn [jɜːn] *vi* **: to ~ for sthg/to do sthg** aspirer à qqch/à faire qqch.

yearning ['jɜːnɪŋ] *n* **: ~ (for sb/sthg)** désir *m* ardent (pour qqn/de qqch).

yeast [jiːst] *n* levure *f*.

yell [jel] ◇ *n* hurlement *m*. ◇ *vi & vt* hurler.

yellow ['jeləʊ] ◇ *adj* [colour] jaune. ◇ *n* jaune *m*.

yellow card *n* FTBL carton *m* jaune.

yelp [jelp] *vi* japper.

yeoman of the guard ['jəʊmən-] (*pl* **yeomen of the guard** ['jəʊmən-]) *n* hallebardier *m* de la garde royale.

yes [jes] ◇ *adv* - **1.** [gen] oui ; **~, please** oui, s'il te/vous plaît - **2.** [expressing disagreement] si. ◇ *n* oui *m inv*.

yesterday ['jestədɪ] ◇ *n* hier *m* ; **the day before ~** avant-hier. ◇ *adv* hier.

yet [jet] ◇ *adv* - **1.** [gen] encore ; **~ faster** encore plus vite ; **not ~** pas encore ; **~ again** encore une fois ; **as ~** jusqu'ici - **2.** déjà ; **have they finished ~?** est-ce qu'ils ont déjà fini? ◇ *conj* et cependant, mais.

yew [juː] *n* if *m*.

yield [jiːld] ◇ *n* rendement *m*. ◇ *vt*

- 1. [produce] produire **- 2.** [give up] céder. ◇ *vi* **- 1.** [gen] **: to ~ (to)** céder (à) **- 2.** *Am* AUT [give way] **: '~'** 'cédez le passage'.

YMCA (*abbr of* **Young Men's Christian Association**) *n* union chrétienne de jeunes gens (*proposant notamment des services d'hébergement*).

yoga ['jəʊgə] *n* yoga *m*.

yoghourt, yoghurt, yogurt [*Br* 'jɒgət, *Am* 'jəʊgərt] *n* yaourt *m*.

yoke [jəʊk] *n lit & fig* joug *m*.

yolk [jəʊk] *n* jaune *m* (d'œuf).

you [ju:] *pers pron* **- 1.** (*subject - sg*) tu ; (*- polite form, pl*) vous ; **~'re a good cook** tu es/vous êtes bonne cuisinière ; **are ~ French?** tu es/vous êtes français ? ; **~ French** vous autres Français ; **~ idiot!** espèce d'idiot! ; **if I were** OR **was ~** si j'étais toi/vous, à ta/votre place ; **there ~ are** [you've appeared] te/vous voilà ; [have this] voilà, tiens/tenez ; **that jacket really isn't ~** cette veste n'est pas vraiment ton/votre style **- 2.** (*object - unstressed, sg*) te ; (*- polite form, pl*) vous ; **I can see ~** je te/vous vois ; **I gave it to ~** je te/vous l'ai donné **- 3.** (*object - stressed, sg*) toi ; (*- polite form, pl*) vous ; **I don't expect you to do it** je n'exige pas que ce soit toi qui le fasses/vous qui le fassiez **- 4.** (*after prep, in comparisons etc, sg*) toi ; (*- polite form, pl*) vous ; **we shall go without ~** nous irons sans toi/vous ; **I'm shorter than ~** je suis plus petit que toi/vous **- 5.** [anyone, one] on ; **~ have to be careful** on doit faire attention ; **exercise is good for ~** l'exercice est bon pour la santé.

you'd [ju:d] = you had, you would.

you'll [ju:l] = you will.

young [jʌŋ] ◇ *adj* jeune. ◇ *npl* **- 1.** [young people] **: the ~** les jeunes *mpl* **- 2.** [baby animals] les petits *mpl*.

younger ['jʌŋgə] *adj* plus jeune.

youngster ['jʌŋstə] *n* jeune *m*.

your [jɔː] *poss adj* **- 1.** (*referring to one person*) ton (ta), tes (*pl*) ; (*polite form, pl*) votre, vos (*pl*) ; **~ dog** ton/votre chien ; **~ house** ta/votre maison ; **~ children** tes/vos enfants ; **what's ~ name?** comment t'appelles-tu/vous appelez-vous? ; **it wasn't** YOUR **fault** ce n'était pas de ta faute à toi/de votre faute à vous **- 2.** (*impersonal - one's*) son (sa), ses (*pl*) ; **~ attitude changes as you get older** on change sa manière de voir en vieillissant ; **it's good for ~ teeth/ hair** c'est bon pour les dents/les cheveux ; **~ average Englishman** l'Anglais moyen.

you're [jɔː] = you are.

yours [jɔːz] *poss pron* (*referring to one person*) le tien (la tienne), les tiens (les tiennes) (*pl*) ; (*polite form, pl*) le vôtre (la vôtre), les vôtres (*pl*) ; **that desk is ~** ce bureau est à toi/à vous, ce bureau est le tien/le vôtre ; **it wasn't her fault, it was** YOURS ce n'était pas de sa faute, c'était de ta faute à toi/de votre faute à vous ; **a friend of ~** un ami à toi/ vous, un de tes/vos amis. ➡ **Yours** *adv* [in letter] ▷ **faithfully, sincerely** *etc*.

yourself [jɔː'self] (*pl* **-selves** [-'selvz]) *pron* **- 1.** (*reflexive - sg*) te ; (*- polite form, pl*) vous ; (*after preposition - sg*) toi ; (*- polite form, pl*) vous **- 2.** (*for emphasis - sg*) toi-même ; (*- polite form*) vous-même ; (*- pl*) vous-mêmes ; **did you do it ~?** tu l'as/vous l'avez fait tout seul?

youth [ju:θ] *n* **- 1.** (*U*) [period, quality] jeunesse *f* **- 2.** [young man] jeune homme *m* **- 3.** (*U*) [young people] jeunesse *f*, jeunes *mpl*.

youth club *n* centre *m* de jeunes.

youthful ['ju:θfʊl] *adj* **- 1.** [eager, innocent] de jeunesse, juvénile **- 2.** [young] jeune.

youth hostel *n* auberge *f* de jeunesse.

you've [ju:v] = you have.

YTS (*abbr of* **Youth Training Scheme**) *n* programme gouvernemental britannique d'insertion des jeunes dans la vie professionnelle.

Yugoslav = Yugoslavian.

Yugoslavia [ˌjuːgəˈslɑːvɪə] *n* Yougoslavie *f* ; **the former ~** l'ex-Yougoslavie.

Yugoslavian [ˌjuːgəˈslɑːvɪən], **Yugoslav** [ˌjuːgəˈslɑːv] ◇ *adj* yougoslave. ◇ *n* Yougoslave *mf*.

yuppie, yuppy ['jʌpɪ] *n inf* yuppie *mf*.

YWCA (*abbr of* **Young Women's Christian Association**) *n* union chrétienne de jeunes filles (*proposant notamment des services d'hébergement*).

z (*pl* **z's** OR **zs**), **Z** (*pl* **Z's** OR **Zs**) [*Br* zed, *Am* zi:] *n* [letter] z *m inv*, Z *m inv*.

Zambia ['zæmbɪə] *n* Zambie *f*.

zany ['zeɪnɪ] *adj inf* dingue.

zap [zæp] *vi inf* **: to ~ (off) somewhere** foncer quelque part.

zeal [ziːl] *n* zèle *m*.

zealous ['zeləs] *adj* zélé(e).

zebra [*Br* 'zebrə, *Am* 'ziːbrə] (*pl inv* OR **-s**) *n* zèbre *m*.

zebra crossing *n Br* passage *m* pour piétons.

zenith [*Br* 'zenɪθ, *Am* 'ziːnəθ] *n lit* & *fig* zénith *m*.

zero [*Br* 'zɪərəu, *Am* 'ziːrəu] (*pl inv* OR **-es**) ◇ *adj* zéro, aucun(e). ◇ *n* zéro *m*.

zest [zest] *n* (*U*) - **1.** [excitement] piquant *m* - **2.** [eagerness] entrain *m* - **3.** [of orange, lemon] zeste *m*.

zigzag ['zɪgzæg] *vi* zigzaguer.

Zimbabwe [zɪm'baːbwɪ] *n* Zimbabwe *m*.

zinc [zɪŋk] *n* zinc *m*.

zip [zɪp] *n Br* [fastener] fermeture *f* Éclair®.
◆ **zip up** *vt sep* [jacket] remonter la fermeture Éclair® de ; [bag] fermer la fermeture Éclair® de.

zip code *n Am* code *m* postal.

zip fastener *n Br* = **zip**.

zipper ['zɪpər] *n Am* = **zip**.

zodiac ['zəudɪæk] *n* : **the ~** le zodiaque.

zone [zəun] *n* zone *f*.

zoo [zuː] *n* zoo *m*.

zoology [zəu'ɒlədʒɪ] *n* zoologie *f*.

zoom [zuːm] ◇ *vi inf* [move quickly] aller en trombe. ◇ *n* PHOT zoom *m*.

zoom lens *n* zoom *m*.

zucchini [zuː'kiːnɪ] (*pl inv*) *n Am* courgette *f*.

Achevé d'imprimer par l'Imprimerie
Maury-Eurolivres à Manchecourt
N° de projet 10108797/10111677
Dépôt légal : février 2002 - N° d'imprimeur : 21999

Imprimé en France - (Printed in France)